GUIDE
TO THE
GODS

GUIDE TO THE GODS

Marjorie Leach

EDITED BY
Michael Owen Jones
Frances Cattermole-Tally

ABC·CLIO

Santa Barbara, California   Denver, Colorado   Oxford, England

Library of Congress Cataloging-in-Publication Data

Leach, Marjorie, 1911–
   Guide to the Gods / Marjorie Leach : edited by Michael Owen Jones, Frances Cattermole-Tally.
      p. cm.
   Includes bibliographical references and index.
   1. Gods. I. Jones, Michael Owen. II. Cattermole-Tally, Frances Maybell, 1924– . III. Title.
   BL473.L43 1992   291.2'11—dc20   91-35820

ISBN 0-87436-591-0

99 98 97 96 95 94 93 92   10 9 8 7 6 5 4 3 2 1

ABC-CLIO, Inc.
130 Cremona Drive, P.O. Box 1911
Santa Barbara, California 93116-1911

This book is printed on acid-free paper ∞ .
Manufactured in the United States of America

Contents

Contents

Preface

This reference dictionary presents a worldwide overview of deities. The approach is anthropological and endeavors to evaluate each in terms of function and attribute. Groupings under these categories bring together deities from different countries and different tribes so as to facilitate comparison and research. Similarities and differences vary greatly—thus Supreme Beings may be otiose and unapproachable, active and participatory, loved or feared, infallible or capricious.

Sources vary in their interpretation of the supernatural being, one calling him a god, another a spirit. Such distinctions are not germane to this work, which deals primarily with function, aspect, and the like. Among supernatural beings it is frequently the lesser deities who are more important to the people than the high gods. The determining factor for inclusion has been—are they or have they been worshipped, propitiated, or made offerings.

Numerous deities appear in several categories, as they have multiple functions, and at times it is difficult to determine their primary role. The separation into functional sections makes it possible to use a single section for comparative research.

Supreme Beings and Creator Deities were originally presented as individual categories. As there is a substantial duplication of functions between them, this separation has been abandoned and they have been merged. "Creator Deities" in this section primarily refer to those whose primary role can be so described.

When the term demiurge is used it is not always possible to determine the degree of subordination implied in the usage. Hence those with no clarification have been left in the major category. Creativity creeps into the classification of Primordial Beings when it refers to or is the principle or force of the creative. It belongs there preferably when not referring to physical creativity.

Lesser creators, of which there are many, appear in Section 38, Culture: Teachers/Givers of, Lesser Creator Gods. The culture hero frequently fulfills the role of creator where the indigenous religion is, or seems to be, less developed cosmogonically.

Some abstractions appear so frequently they are presented in specialized categories, e.g., Justice, Wisdom, Love. Under Justice have been included lesser classifications reflecting antitheses, e.g., order/disorder, which do not qualify for inclusion in the Gods of Evil as the epitome of depravity.

The deities included in the section Animal/Bird Gods either have the form of, or may assume or transform into, the animal or bird specified. Deities of masters of types or groups of animals are found under the category of Gods of Hunting, Wild Animals, and Domesticated Animals (Sections 27, 28, 30).

Phallic deities may appear in either or both of the sections on Fertility (21) and on Love (44) depending on the predominance in the usage of the term, whether natural fertility, strong sexuality, or conscious lewdity.

Soul also appears diversified due to application or usage in various cultures: some having spirits for the *soul in life* (19), some for the *soul in death* (23, 24), some in both sections.

The art of healing is universally present in some form, though its practice will vary from magical charms and incantations, shamanism, herbal and chemical infusions or poultices, to surgery. The practitioners, however divergent the fields, are usually subjected to rigorous and extensive training. Areas differ greatly in the emphasis given to the supernatural/spiritual and to the natural/practical application in healing. Some peoples rely almost totally on the first, others on the latter, some on both.

It will be noted that in China numerous parts of the body have specific deities. Their development of medicines led to a sophisticated pharmaceutical department in the Ministry of Medicine. The Asiatics, including India and Oceania, have innumerable deities protecting from or causing diseases and injuries, particularly those of an infectious or digestive nature, probably because these afflictions are so rampant.

Within the text annotations and in the bibliography the numerals following the year refer either to a volume number or indicate more than one publication by an author within a given year.

Variations in spellings will be noted due to usage by authors or to differences between tribes, e.g., Navaho, Navajo. Among authors this can occur because of language (French, German, etc.), or of ethnographical spellings where, when possible, a common simplified spelling is chosen, giving a cross-reference in the appropriate technical usage. These problems arise frequently among Amerindian names.

Titles, appellations, and explanatory words are frequently incorporated into names. Among Tibetan god-names such a mixture occurs that one must accept them as presented, though it is evident the initial units are frequently descriptive. Te, among the Polynesians, is another example. Here again, usage and authors have their influence. Therefore, names beginning with Te may be listed under Te or the next part of the name. At times, decisions were made on the basis of convenience.

With Japanese deities the terms *kami* and *Mikoto* may or may not be capitalized.

In ancient religions, primarily Hindu, there are marked diversities in roles and character due to different interpretations of a deity during varying periods of time as well as due to regional beliefs. Not presuming to be an authority on any of the religions, but purely a compiler, there is no attempt to interpret fine technicalities but only to present them as encountered through the numerous authors furnishing the materials cited within the bibliography.

Foreword

This guide is novel in several respects, from its breadth of coverage to the nature and arrangement of information. It serves a number of purposes not met by other works on gods and goddesses. How the book came into existence is unusual, too, and a story in its own right. In what follows we describe the book's unique features, remark on its origins, and mention some of its uses.

Guide to the Gods is an exceptionally well-organized compilation of deities throughout the world. Coverage is not limited to a single culture, country, or continent as in many other works; nor is it restricted to a particular time period. Information about the deities of Greek, Norse, and other people in the Western world as well as the spirtual beings of Asian, African, Polynesian, Meso-American, American Indian, and other populations is assembled together in a single volume. Some gods and goddesses populate only the ancient myths; others live today as vital elements in contemporary religions.

In most reference works deities are simply listed alphabetically. If more than one country is treated, then gods and goddesess are set forth in alphabetical order for each geographical area. This emphasizes cultural differences. As a consequence, readers might not be aware of similarities among the deities in regard to, say, functions and attributes.

The similarity in functional roles of gods and goddesses serves as an organizing principle in the present volume. Spiritual beings from all over the world are arranged alphabetically within functional categories. For example, Adronga is the creator of mankind according to stories told in the Congo, Sudan, and Uganda. His primary function is that of supreme being/creator. This is why he appears early in the dictionary under Cosmogonical Deities, and

why he is categorized as a Supreme/Creator Deity. He is in the same general grouping as, for example, Woden, Wotan, Odin (the Germanic All-Father), Buddha (the benevolent and hierarchically highest god of the Sinhalese in Ceylon), Obumo (the god of thunder, considered the principal deity of the Ibibio in Nigeria), and Michabo (The Great White Hare of Algonquin Indians in the U. S. and Canada who created the earth and also is the giver of culture). All of these gods, and scores of others, are described in their cultures as supreme beings and/or the First Cause.

Based on this logic of categorizing spirits according to their functions, the compiler has grouped gods and goddesses not only as various types of Cosmogonical Deities but also as Celestial Deities, Atmospheric Deities, and Terrestial Deities. Each major grouping has one or more subdivisions. The spirits' functions relate to particular domains, states of being, or activities. Hence, other categories in this dictionary that follow the section on Terrestial Deities are Life/Death Cycle Deities and gods associated with Economic Activities, Sociocultural Concepts (the Arts, Fortune, Justice, War, etc.), and Religion.

Each entry on a god or goddess contains several kinds of information. Of course one is the function of that deity—or, in some instances, the several functions. For example, according to information published by Ruth Benedict in 1916, Mamale is creator of the earth in myths known to the Bagobo in the Philippines. Contrast this single functional role with the multiple functions of Jupiter (Jove). Jupiter is the celestial god of the Roman pantheon and as such he controls the weather, wielding the thunder and lightning and providing omens through the latter. He is also a sovereign deity. In this second functional role he is the god of politics, law and order, justice, and oaths and contracts. He serves other functions as well.

Another type of information is the god or goddess's principal aspects, that is, the major characteristics, attributes, or associations. In Adronga's remote celestial aspect, this creator of human beings is beneficent and understanding. But in his immanent aspect he is feared by many people of the Congo, being considered evil and associated with death. Other supreme beings may be indolent and unapproachable; an example is Agwatana of the Bassa-komo of Nigeria, a remote creator who is approached "only in major disasters." They may be active and participatory such as Odin, the Scandinavian/Teutonic All-Father, a god of many functions, who was loved as well as feared. A god may be infallible and/or capricious as was Zeus, the supreme being of the ancient Greeks, who, like Odin, can also be found among the gods controlling weather.

When sources permit, entries include mention of related deities or alternative names. The entry on Odin also identifies him as Wotan (and both of these names appear in the listing on Woden). From the entry on Odin we learn that he was the son of Bor and Bestla and brother of Vili (Henir) and Ve (Lodr).

Descriptions in entries are usually minimal. This book is a finding list, not an encyclopedia. There is no unnecessary narrative. While there are quotes here and there, in general the description is short and sends the reader to fuller information elsewhere.

This volume differs from many in its inclusion of references and scrupulous attention to sources (with the complete citations given in a bibliography at the end of the book). Sometimes there are numerous works to refer to, as in the case of entries on Jupiter, Zeus, Odin, and other deities well known to the Western reader. For many, however, there are only a few ethnographical sources to consult. Such is the case for Jupka, a great god of the Yahi (southern Yana) of California. Were it not for the writings of anthropologist Alfred L. Kroeber, we might not know about this deity who shaped the world from the ocean's floor, instructed its people in the rules governing the wowi (the home), and taught them about death, before transforming himself into a many-colored butterfly.

Finally, the book has an index of deities' names. The index is especially useful because many gods and goddesses have several functions and, as a result, are included in more than one category.

By bringing together deities from different countries and tribes, the book facilitates comparison and research. The reader learns not only about similarities in functions, for example, but also how gods and goddesses having similar functions may differ in their attributes and aspects. Consider the listings in the category of "Love: Lust, Sexuality, Phallic, Lovers."

Baklum Chaam was a Mayan phallic god of the fertility of fields and animals. Bayugin, a god of the Tagalog in the Philippines, functioned to tempt women into lives of shame. Contrasting with both is Butu-Ulisiwa, a phallic god of the Ambon and Uliasa in Indonesia, who caused women to be fruitful and bestowed good fortune at sea and victory in battle. In ancient Egypt, Hator was the goddess of joy and the arts, and of women and childbirth; she was also said to be a goddess of the underworld and of the dead to whom she gave new life. The Aztec goddess Ixcuina was goddess of carnality, of prostitutes, and adulterers. To the Greeks, Aphrodite was goddess of love in its manifold nature, from human love both pure and lustful to the love of the world and the universe.

The juxtaposition of deities from disparate parts of the world may stimulate questions and hypotheses for future research. Why, for example, in the category on pleasures and related functions does happiness seem to be more prevalent in the entries for Asiatic gods and goddessess than in information reported about deities elsewhere? Is this merely coincidence, a relationship created by and among the data grouped together in the category? Does it result from what other authors found important to record and present? Or is there, for some reason, truly a greater emphasis on happiness in Japan, China, and Tibet than in many other countries? Further research is necessary to answer such questions; this dictionary can help.

Enhancing the book's usefulness is that it directs readers to works that are generally accessible, especially to the English-speaking reader. Primary sources in other languages, prized by dedicated academicians, tend to be inaccessible to most people because of language barriers or owing to a work's limited distribution and lack of availability. The compiler of this guide provides the titles of many secondary works rather than arcane tomes. Both the general public and scholars interested in information about deities with which they are not already familiar will find this volume an excellent starting point.

This book was compiled by a woman with a passion for learning who returned to the unversity after her husband died and her children were grown, earning a degree in anthropology. She continued to take courses and audit classes, travel, and visit museums and historical sites in search of information to include in her guide to gods and goddesses worldwide.

Marjorie Ryberg Leach was born in Minneapolis, Minnesota in 1911. Two years after graduating from Central High School, she moved to Los Angeles. She was married to Floyd C. Leach, an engineer, from 1936 until his death in 1954. They had three children: Marcia, Stephanie, and Richard. In 1946 her husband suggested she apply to Occidental College; she was accepted as a special student. Her studies were interrupted by her husband's heart condition, however, discovered the following year.

After her husband's death and with her own children in college, Marjorie Leach returned to school. She graduated from California State University, Northridge, at the same time as her daughter, Stephanie.

Between the years 1966 and 1970 Mrs. Leach traveled extensively in western Europe. She visited many types of sacred sites including ancient ones like Stonehenge and legendary ones such as the Giant's Causeway. She also visited cathedrals, museums, and bookstores furthering her studies in folklore, mythology, and anthropology. Her compelling interests centered on deities, mythology, and early religion. As she recalls, it was Stonehenge that stimulated her fascination with ancient religions. This monument to human ingenuity also strengthened her resolve to work in earnest on compiling information about gods and goddesses in many cultures.

From 1972 to 1980 Mrs. Leach travelled throughout the New World, especially Mexico, Central America, the Caribbean, and the Andes but also in the United States and Canada. She attended classes at UCLA taught by several outstanding professors. One is Johannes Wilbert, who specializes in the folklore and traditions of indigenous South American peoples. Another is Slavics professor Marija Gimbutas, whose interests are in pre-Indo-European religion. A third is C. Scott Littleton, a noted Indo-European mythologist from Occidental College, who at the time was a visiting professor at UCLA.

By 1975 Mrs. Leach had typed the first draft of a manuscript on the functions and aspects of deities. But she continued her research and travels throughout the 1970s and well into the 1980s. The book grew to astonishing proportions.

Despite the work's obvious value, none of the presses Mrs. Leach queried would publish the volume owing to its considerable length. Finally, she brought the material to us at the UCLA Center for the Study of Comparative Folklore and Mythology. She had heard about our several archives, including one containing nearly a million items on popular beliefs and superstitions. She asked if we would we be interested in having a copy of her manuscript for use in our own research.

The Center is in the process of preparing for publication a seven-volume work on American popular beliefs and superstitions, edited by Dr. Donald J. Ward and published by the University of California Press. Mrs. Leach's compilation of gods and goddesses is an adjunct to the encyclopedia archives. We are pleased that ABC-CLIO has chosen to publish it, making it available to the public. We are pleased also to have been able to help Mrs. Leach in some small measure find a publisher and ready her work for the compositor.

The Center has its own academically oriented publications and research projects. But it also seeks to bridge the gap between academe and the larger community. Cooperating with ABC-CLIO to assure the publication of Mrs. Leach's book is one of the ways we can accomplish this objective. Working with Mrs. Leach has been a great pleasure for us. We hope that others both enjoy and benefit from the intellectual passion of this woman who has compiled a unique volume of information about the functions and aspects of gods and goddesses throughout the world.

Michael Owen Jones, Director
UCLA Center for the Study of Comparative
Folklore and Mythology

Frances Cattermole-Tally, Executive Editor
*Encyclopedia of American Popular Beliefs
and Superstitions*

PART I

Cosmogonical Deities

1

Primordial Beings

Adi-Buddha The "Self-Existent . . . infinite, omniscient, . . . without beginning and without end." A deity known by numerous names: Aisvarika, Svabhava, Vairocana, Vajrapani, Vajradhara, Vajrasattva, Samantabhadra, Advaya, anghan burhan. About the 7th century A.D. "He becomes the primordial god and creator," the ultimate source from whom "evolves, by meditation," the five celestial Buddhas of Meditation (Dhyani Buddhas); they in turn, again through meditation, have lesser emanations of themselves, Bodhisattvas, who are the active, creative, and governing agents of the world, deriving their powers from the five Buddhas. Among the northern Buddhists Vairocana is considered the Adi-Buddha; the reformed sects of Lamas call him Vajradhara; "while the unreformed sects consider him to be Samantabhadra." Tibet. (Waddell, 1959: 130–131; Getty, 1962: 2, 3; Schlangintweit, 1969: 50, 51; Werner, 1932: 1)

Advaya The primordial principle from whom were "evolved the Buddhas, gods, and world of phenomena." Java. (Getty, 1962: 3)

Aelquntam The pre-existent "chief of all supernatural beings." The Bella Coola Indians, British Columbia. (Lissner, 1961: 91, 92)

Aireskouy Soutanditenr A primordial being, the source of all things, who is invoked for all need, in hunting, in war, etc. The Huron Indians, Eastern United States. (Gray, 1925, 6: 884)

Akaran *See* **Zervan**.

Ali A self-existent, all-powerful and invisible god whose "essence is the light." The Nusairis, Asia Minor. (Basset, 1925, 9: 418)

E Alom The "Conceiver of Children." With E Quaholom the primordial pair of deities. The Quiché, Guatemala. (Thompson, 1970: 201; Recinos, 1950: 78)

Amaunet, Ament With Amun (Amen), one of the initial primeval pairs representing the air, invisibility. Egypt. (Anthes, 1961: 67; Budge, 1969, 2: 1)

Amun, Amen With Amaunet (Ament), one of the initial primeval pairs representing the air. Egypt. (Anthes, 1961: 67; Budge, 1969, 2: 1)

anghan burhan The Adi-Buddha. Mongolia. (Getty, 1962: 2)

Anshar With Kishar the second primeval pair—"two aspects of 'the horizon'." Born of La(k)hmu and La(k)hamu and parents of Anu. Assyro/Babylonian. (Jastrow, 1898: 197; Jacobsen, 1946: 185; James, 1960: 209; Larousse, 1968: 49)

Anu Space, with Tangae the primeval pair of the evolutionary creation myth. The Marquesas, Polynesia. (Williamson, 1933, 1: 15)

Apna-Apha The primeval pair, a dual deity—Mother Earth, Apna, and Father Sky, Apha. Also called Uru-Wadu. Kisar Island, Indonesia. (Pettazzoni, 1956: 13, 335)

Apsu The "primal male Apsu, personifying the 'sweet waters' of the abyss, mingled with his consort Tiamat, the salt-water of the ocean, to produce a son Mummu, representing the mist and clouds arising from the watery chaos." Also parents of Lahmu and Lahamu. Akkadian/Babylonian. (James, 1960: 208–209; Jastrow, 1898: 410–411; Kramer, 1961: 120)

Arinna With her husband, Im or U, the primeval pair—she, the earth, the "queen of the lands," and he, the sky, the "god of storm." Hittite. (Eliade, 1976, 2: 364)

Atabei A mother goddess, the "First-in-Existence." The Taino, West Indies. (Alexander, 1920: 28)

3

Atavish The primordial female—"empty," sister of Kyuvish. She became successively Yamai, "not in existence;" Harurai Chatutai, "boring lowering;" Tamay-owut, "earth." The Luiseño Indians, California. (Kroeber, 1925: 677–678)

Atnatu The primordial god, self-existent, who lives in the sky. He had many sons and daughters, some of whom for disobedience he placed on earth where they are men. He provided them with all necessary things. The Kaitish, Central Australia. (Spencer, 1904: 498–499; Lang, 1905: 55)

Atungaki Twin/husband of Maimoa'alongona, the second primal pair, born of Touiafutuna, and parents of Vele-lahi. The Tongans, Polynesia. (Moulton, 1925, 12: 379; Collocott, 1921: 152; Williamson, 1933, 1: 10)

Awonawilona The self-created god of the beginning, the Sun Father, and Yaonan, the Moon Mother, a bisexual power and the "initiator of life. . . . created clouds and the great waters of the world." The Zuñi Indians, New Mexico. (Stevenson, 1898: 33; 1901/02: 22; Cushing, 1891/92: 379)

Bec diłxił xastin Black Metal Old Man, a pre-existent primordial being. He appears as one of the four creators of earth and sky in one myth. The San Carlos Apache, Arizona. (Goddard, 1918: 7, 27)

Biki "Sticky," twin/husband of Kele, the first primal twins born of Touiafutuna. Parents of Taufulifonua and Havea-lolo-fonua. The Tongans, Polynesia. (Moulton, 1925, 12: 379; Collocott, 1921: 152)

Bitol "Maker," with Tzacol, "Creator," the primeval pair of deities of the Maya Lowlands, Central America. (Thompson, 1970: 201; Recinos, 1950: 78)

Caligo "Dark," a primordial being, mother of Chaos. Greece. (Roscher, 1965, 1, 1: 846)

Chang-hko The "primeval mother" who demands pigs and cattle as sacrifice when there is trouble. The Kachins, Burma. (Temple, 1925: 26)

Chinun Way Shun A being "said to have existed before the formation of the world, and to have created all the Nats." The Kachins, Burma. (Temple, 1925: 22)

Dao The primordial mother, having first given birth to the first pairs, deities and humans—impregnated by the winds—"gave the earth being by her death." Batu Island, Indonesia. (Pettazzoni, 1956: 330)

Darukavaitere Male stone being whose wife was Uarahiulu. They were the parents of the sun and moon as well as the other celestial beings. The Paressi, Brazil. (Lowie, 1925, 4: 172)

Doying-Angong, Doying-Bote An omniscient primeval high god of the very beginning. By some considered remote and unconcerned. Others credit him with good harvests and fortune, the guardian of morals. The Adi, Northeastern India. (Chowdhury, 1971: 109–111)

Dua Nggae The omniscient, omnipresent, primeval supreme being who is a duality; usually Dua is male and Nggae female but this is sometimes reversed. Flores Island, Indonesia. (Pettazzoni, 1956: 7, 334)

Dyavaprthivi Sky (Dyaus) and Earth (Prthivi) as a combined deity, the primeval parents. India. (Keith, 1917: 16)

Edenkema The primeval supreme being who is invisible and eternal, the omnipotent and omniscient creator. Nyamenle is sometimes merged with him. The Nzema, Ghana. (Grottanelli, 1967: 33–41)

Eka Abassi The divine creatress, "the great First Cause." Some consider her as self-impregnated. The Ibibio, Nigeria. (Frazer, 1926: 128)

Enen A god given by some authorities as the fourth pair (with Enenet-hemset) of the primeval deities. Egypt. (Budge, 1969, 1: 289)

Ennit and Ni represent "the vast and inert watery mass" among the primeval gods. Egypt. (Budge, 1969, 1: 291)

Erlik Initially he existed with Kaira Kan (who created him) in the primordial water, and took part in the creation of the earth. He was rebellious and ambitious and was banished to the darkness as a god of evil, the god of hell. Siberia. (Casanowicz, 1924: 417–418)

Esaugetuh Emissee The pre-existent creator god who lived on Nunne Chaha, which had risen out of the primeval water. He caused the waters to recede, and created mankind. Those who have been good join him after death. He was considered the personification of the wind. The Choctaw, Mississippi. (Spence, 1925, 3: 568)

Geush Urvan The primeval ox "in which were contained the germs of the animal species and even of a certain number of useful plants." When killed by Mithra it "went to heaven to be the guardian of animals." Iran. (Carnoy, 1917: 286, 288)

Godiye Mirage—pre-existent—one of the four primordial beings. The San Carlos Apache, Arizona (Goddard, 1918: 7)

Gudatrigakwitl The pre-existent creator god of the Wiyot Indians. California. (Kroeber, 1925: 119)

Haapkemnas The creator of all things "existed in the dawn of time." The Takelma, Oregon. (Sapir, 1907: 34)

Hainuwele A primordial goddess, a creatress in the sense that through her ritual murder by the primordial beings her body was cut into pieces and planted from which grew new plants, particularly tubers. From her arms was made a doorway through which all primordial beings had to pass, remaining humans or becoming animals, birds, etc. Ceram, New Guinea. (Eliade, 1967: 19)

Han A primordial being—"the black of darkness." She was banished to "the regions under the world," then became the nighttime. The Lakota/Oglala, Plains Indians. (Walker, 1980: 51, 52)

Hauhet, Hehut With Huh one of the initial primeval pairs, "representing the infinity of space." Egypt. (Anthes, 1961: 67; Budge, 1969, 1: 285)

Hemoana Twin of Lube, the fourth primeval pair born of Touiafutuna. They are the only ones who did not mate. He is associated with the sea-snake; a god of the sea. The Tongans, Polynesia. (Collocott, 1921: 152–153; Moulton, 1925, 12: 376–379)

Hubur A primordial mother goddess by whom "a monstrous brood is spawned" to act as warriors for Tiamat. Babylonia. (Gray, 1930: 31)

Huh, Hehu, Heh With Hauhet (Hehut) one of the initial primeval pairs "representing the infinity of space." Other sources interpret them as fire, atmosphere. Egypt. (Anthes, 1961: 67; Budge, 1969, 1: 285)

Hutsipamamau ?u Ocean Woman forms a primal tetrad with Wolf and Coyote. Her role is predominant as the creatress of all things. The Chemehuevis, California, Arizona, and Nevada. (Laird, 1976: 45, 46, 148, 149, 213, 214)

Ihoiho The god of the beginning. Society Islands, Polynesia. (Williamson, 1933: 11)

Ilmatar The primordial mother who existed in the sea and was the creatress of the universe. Finland. (Leach, 1956: 239–243)

Im, U With his wife, Arinna, the primeval pair, the sky and earth deities. God of the storm. Hittite. (Eliade, 1976, 2: 364)

Inapirikuri The primordial god, but not a creator, who drew mankind from the ground and gave them their moral precepts. the Baniwa, Venezuela. (Zerries, 1968: 249)

Inyan The Rock, who existed before all else—"the primal source of all things." He was omniscient, omnipresent, omnipotent, yet "he was soft and shapeless like a cloud." He created Maka (Earth) from a part of himself and gave her a spirit. His powers were in his blood (blue) and in creating Maka he opened his veins and his blood flowed out from him and became the blue waters; and he "became hard and powerless." He created Wakinyan, the Winged One, "to be his active associate." Inyan had two sons: Ksa, the God of Wisdom, which power he abused, and was demoted to Imp of Mischief; and Iya who was "utterly evil and the chief of all evil beings." As the Spirit of Rocks Inyan was invoked more than any other god. The Lakota, Plains Indians. (Walker, 1980: 50–52, 118, 124, 140, 197; Jahner, 1977: 33–34; Vivian One Feather, 1982: 49)

Io The self- and always-existent supreme being, beneficent originator of all things. The Maori, New Zealand. (Long, 1963: 173; Pettazzoni, 1956: 344–345; Best, 1924: 235)

Ka A god identified with Kekui. Apparently variant names among the first eight gods. Egypt. (Budge, 1969, 1: 286)

Kaira Kan The high god who existed in the primordial waters, the benevolent creator. The Altaians, Siberia. (Casanowicz, 1924: 416–417)

Kait Female counterpart of Ka and identified with Kekuit of the group of the first eight gods. Egypt. (Budge, 1969, 1: 286)

Kayum-Polung-Sabbo A primeval spirit "who had the form of a great mithan [a form of cattle]," who dug a pit with his horns to let the waters drain away so there would be land. The people must sacrifice to him and to Sedi-Irping-Puing-Idum-Botte or "the Wiyus [spirits] get angry and try to turn the world again into water by shaking it." The Adi, the Minyong, Northeastern India. (Chowdhury, 1971: 70)

Kayum-Sedi-Nane-Wiyu A primeval spirit who had Kayum-Polung-Sabbo make a pit with his horns to drain away the water and make the land. All was water before. The Adi, the Minyong, Northeastern India. (Chowdhury, 1971: 70)

Kekui, Kuk With Kekuit the third of the four pairs of deities representing primeval matter, their aspect the "powers of darkness." He "represents that period of the night which immediately precedes the day." Sometimes identified with Ka. Egypt. (Budge, 1969, 1: 283, 285–286; Anthes, 1961: 67)

Kekuit, Kauket With Kekui the "powers of darkness." She represents "that period of the night which immediately follows the day." Sometimes identified with Kait. Egypt. (Budge, 1969, 1: 283, 285–286; Anthes, 1961: 67)

Kele With Biki (Piki) the first pair of primeval twins born of Touia-a-Futuna and parents of Taufulifonua and Havea-lolo-fonua. An earlier Kele is named as the mother of Touia-futuna who became the mother of the gods. Tonga, Polynesia. (Collocott, 1921: 152; Moulton, 1925, 12: 379; Williamson, 1933, 1: 9, 10)

Kerh With Kerhet the fourth pair of the primeval deities who are indefinite in nature. Sometimes the names of this pair are different. For Kerh: Ni, Amen, Enen. Egypt. (Budge, 1969, 1: 286–289)

Kerhet The female counterpart of Kerh, the fourth pair of primeval deities. She is sometimes named as Ennit, Ament, Enenet-hemset. Egypt. (Budge, 1969, 1: 286–289)

Ke-vish-a-tak-vish The first being of the beginning who lived in empty space; created Tuk-mit and To-mai-yo-vit. The San Luiseño, California. (Du Bois, 1906: 52)

Keyum "the hypothetical first cause, . . . also sometimes called the Great Mother, . . . " out of whom came Sedi-Melo. The Miris (Adi), Northeastern India. (Chowdhury, 1971: 115)

Khepera, Khepri The beetle god, the self-produced primordial deity who came into being before all else out of the Watery Abyss. Through self-conception he produced Shu and Tefnut. He is a form of solar god, the rising sun. Egypt. (Budge, 1969, 1: 294–295, 471; Eliade, 1967: 96–97; Casson, 1965: 50)

Konjini A self-created goddess who, with Mbasi, the snake god, produced an egg from which came the first human pair. Rossel Island, Indonesia. (MacKenzie, 1930: 148, 150)

Kuk *See* **Kekui**

Kumulipo The "Source-of-deep-darkness." The primordial male. With Po'ele the first pair, and "the parents of all hard-shelled things that came into being in the sea in the darkness and of all plant life." Hawaii. (Leach, 1956: 167)

Kyuvish The primordial male—"vacant"—the brother of Atavish. He became successively: Omai, "not alive"; Whaikut Piwkut, "white pale," the Milky Way; Tukomit, "night," with the implication of "Sky." The creators, through birth, of the things and features of the world, animate and inanimate. The Luiseño, California. (Kroeber, 1925: 677–678)

Lagatea With wife Papatea, the primordial pair. Father of Tagaloa. Rotuma Island (Fiji), Melanesia. (Gardiner, 1897: 467)

La(k)hmu (male) and **La(k)hamu** (female) The first primeval pair brought forth by Apsu and Tiamat. They represent silt formed in the primordial waters. Parents of Anshar, the male principle, and Kishar, the female principle. Assyro/Babylonia. (Jacobsen, 1946: 185; Hooke, 1963: 42; Jastrow, 1898: 197; Larousse, 1968: 49)

Lejman The "first living beings were two worms, Wulleb and Lejman, living together in a shell . . . [They] . . . raised the top shell to make the sky; the lower shell became the earth." The Marshall Islands (Radak chain), Micronesia. (Leach, 1956: 183)

Lube "Dove," twin of Hemoana, one of the primal pairs born of Touia-a-Futuna. She became the goddess of the forests and the land. Tonga, Polynesia. (Collocott, 1921: 152-153; Moulton, 1925, 12: 376, 379)

Maheo The pre-existent, powerful spirit who lived in the void, who created the water and its creatures, light and air. With the help of coot who brought up mud from the waters, made the land by placing the mud on the back of Grandmother Turtle (who became the earth) causing it to grow and spread out. The Cheyenne Indians, Western Plains. (Marriott and Rachlin, 1968: 22)

Maimoa-a-Longona The female twin of Atungake, the second pair of the primordial family born of Touia-a-Futuna. Parents of Vele-lahi. Tonga, Polynesia. (Collocott, 1921: 152; Moulton, 1925, 12: 379; Williamson, 1933, 1: 10)

Maisö The pre-existent mother goddess, mother of Darukavaitere and Uarahiulu. The Paressi, Brazil. (Lowie, 1925, 4: 172)

6

Makarom Manouwe The masculine of the primordial pair. Island of Keisar, Indonesia. (Eliade, 1958: 51)

Makarom Mawakhu The feminine of the primordial pair. Island of Keisar, Indonesia. (Eliade, 1958: 51)

Martummere A primordial supreme being and creator. The giver of tools and culture. Australia. Same as Nurrundere. (Eliade, 1964: 3)

Nainema Self-existent and always-existent "our father" who created the universe and all things out of a dream. Colombia. (Eliade, 1967: 85)

Naɬuletcu diɬxiɬn Black Big Spider, pre-existent. One of the four primordial beings of a creation myth. The San Carlos Apache, Arizona. (Goddard, 1918: 7)

Namakungwe "Originator, He from whom all things came." The Ila, Zambia. (Mbiti, 1970, 2: 331)

Nammu Sumerian goddess of the primeval sea. Mother of An, the heaven god, and Ki, the earth goddess. Asia Minor. (Kramer 1950: 57; 1967: 101; Jacobsen, 1946: 176; James, 1960: 80)

Narɪ̃wiinyapah The Immortal Water, Everlasting Water, upon which the primal tetrad floated in a basket. After the earth was created Tavutsi caused the waters to splash all over it forming streams, lakes, etc. The Chemehuevis, California, Nevada, and Arizona. (Laird, 1976: 148, 152)

Nau (with **Nen**) and **Ni** (with **Ennit**) Variants of the pair of primeval deities who represent the "watery abyss from which all things sprang." Egypt. (Budge, 1969, 1: 291; 1969, 2: 1)

Naunet With Nun the primeval pair of deities representing "the primeval unlimited ocean." Egypt. (Anthes, 1961: 67)

Nen The consort of Nau, the first pair of the primeval gods in the Pyramid Texts (Unas). Egypt. (Budge, 1969, 2: 1)

Nestis The name used by Empedocles for the personification of the humid element out of which all first materials came. Greece. (Roscher, 1965, 3, 1: 287)

Ni *See* **Nau**

Ningpang majan The primordial mother of the gods. The Katchins, Burma. (Gilhodes, 1908: 673)

Nourali The self-existent chief god and creator who was believed to have the form of a bird. The Murray River area, Australia. (Brinton, 1897: 159)

Numbakulla One (Eliade) or two (Poignant) self-existent primordial being(s) who created numerous things and mankind. the Aranda, Australia. (Eliade, 1973: 50-51; Poignant, 1967: 117)

Nun The primordial, celestial ocean out of which all things developed. His female counterpart is Nut, Naunet. The first of the primeval pairs of deities. Egypt. (Budge, 1969, 1: 283; Knight, 1915: 86-88; Ames, 1965: 27; Anthes, 1961: 67)

Nyamuzinda The "first cause, the principle of all things," and the creator. He is considered the source of disasters, of famine and epidemics. The Bashi, Zaire. (Williams, 1936: 107)

Orlog The "eternal law of the universe, an older and superior power, who apparently had neither beginning nor end." A deity of destiny or fate who controlled the Norns, whose decrees were inexorable. Scandinavia. (Guerber, 1895: 155, 186)

Ote Boram The self-created supreme god and creator. The Hos, India. (Majumdar, 1950: 251; Biswas, 1956: 102; Elwin, 1949: 18)

P'an-ku From the primordial unformed mass of the universe came P'an-ku, and the mass divided into the heavens and the earth. When P'an-ku died, from his body came the various features of the universe and the earth: the sun and moon and stars, the winds, the clouds and rain and thunder, the mountains and rivers, and vegetation. Others simply name him as the creator who gave form to the universe. China. (Bodde, 1961: 382–383; Werner, 1932: 355; Peeters, 1941: 27; Ferguson, 1937: 57-58)

Papa The earth, wife of Rangi, the sky. They were brought into existence by Io as the "primal parents" from whom all things originated. The Maori, New Zealand. (Best, 1924: 86; Grey, 1855: 1, 5; Long, 1963: 41)

Papa-Ao The "World-beneath"—the primary parents (with Papa-Uka or Papa-una, "the World-above") of the creation. Offspring: Atea, Aumia, Hakaoho, Kokioho, Mataoa, Mihi-toka, 'Ono-tapu, Pahi, Tane, Te Kopupu-aue, Tiki, Toka-i-venau, Tonofiti, Tu, Tupua-i-hakaava, Tuuhiti. The Marquesas, Polynesia. (Christian, 1895: 187; Buck, 1938: 149; Williamson, 1933, 1: 25–26)

Papatea   The primordial pair with Lagatea. Mother of Tagaloa. Rotuma (Fiji), Melanesia. (Gardiner, 1897: 467)

Pau-tere-fenua   A god of the chaotic period of the creation. Society Islands, Polynesia. (Henry, 1928: 341)

Po'ele   "Darkness"—the primordial female of the first pair of cosmogonic deities. With Kumulipo the "parents of all hard-shelled things that came into being in the sea in the darkness and of all plant life." Hawaii. (Leach, 1956: 167)

Po'el'ele   "Dark-night"—the male of the third pair of the primordial deities. With Pohaha the "parents of all tiny frail and flitting things which came into being in the ever-lessening night." Hawaii. (Leach, 1956: 168–169)

Pohaha   "Night-just-breaking-into-dawn" — With Po'el'ele the "parents of all tiny frail and flitting things which came into being in the ever-lessening night." Hawaii (Leach, 1956: 168–169)

Po-he'enalu-mamao   With Po-kinikini the eighth primordial pair, parents of mankind; the beginning of day. Hawaii. (Leach, 1956: 171)

Po-hiolo   "Night-falling-away." The male of the sixth pair of the primordial deities of the night period. With Po-ne'a-aku "the parents of Pilo'i, the rat child." Hawaii. (Leach, 1956: 170)

Po-kanokano   The "Nightdigger"—the male of the fifth pair of deities of the primordial night. With Po-lalo-uli the parents of the pig, Kamapua'a. Hawaii. (Leach, 1956: 170)

Po-kinikini   With Po-he'enalu-mamao the eighth primordial pair and parents of mankind. Hawaii. (Leach, 1956: 171)

Po-lalo-uli   The female of the fifth pair of primordial deities. With Po-kanokano the parents of "the pig child, Kamapua'a." Hawaii. (Leach, 1956: 170)

Polalowehi   Goddess of the night/dawn period. With Popanopano the fourth pair and the parents of turtles, geckos and other creatures of the mud/water element. Hawaii. (Leach, 1956: 169)

Po-ne'a-aku   "Night-creeping-away"—the female of the sixth pair of primordial deities. With Po-hiolo "the parents of Pilo'i, the rat child." Hawaii. (Leach, 1956: 170)

Po-ne'e-aku   "Night-receding"—With Po-neie-mai the seventh pair born in the primordial night. The parents of the dog and of the birth of light, of plant life. Hawaii. (Leach, 1956: 170)

Po-neie-mai   "Pregnant-night"—With Po-ne'e-aku the seventh pair of primordial deities and parents of the dog, of the birth of light, of plant life. Hawaii. (Leach, 1956: 170)

Popanopano   God of the night/dawn period of the primordial night period. With Polalowehi, the fourth pair, parents of turtles, geckos, and other creatures of the mud/water element. Hawaii. (Leach, 1956: 169)

Pouliuli   "Deep-profound-darkness"—the male of the second pair of primordial deities. With Powehiwehi the "parents of all the fish and creatures of the ocean." Hawaii. (Leach, 1956: 168)

Powehiwehi   "Darkness-streaked-with-glimmering light"— the female of the second pair of primordial deities. With Pouliuli the "parents of all the fish and creatures of the ocean." Hawaii. (Leach, 1956: 168)

Prah Prohm   The pre-existent and uncreated "being and non-being at one and the same time." Cambodia. (Marchal, 1963: 196)

Puntan   A pre-existent being from whose body, when he died, was formed the universe: "the sky and earth" from "his breast and back," the sun and moon from his eyes, the rainbow from his eyebrows. The Chamorro, Guan, the Marianas, Micronesia. (Beardsley, 1965: 93; Poignant, 1967: 71)

E Quaholom   The male of the primeval pair, the "Begetter of Children." The Quiche, Central America. (Thompson, 1970: 201; Recinos, 1950: 78)

Rajah Gantallah   The unformed original being "possessed of a soul with organs for hearing, speaking, and seeing" who "rested upon a *lumbu*" (which is interpreted as a serpent-dragon). Through his will he created two birds, male and female, who, again through his will, carried out the rest of the creation. The Dyaks of Sakarran, Borneo. (MacKenzie, 1930: 314)

Rangi   The personified sky, and Papa, the earth, formed the primordial pair who were brought into existence by Io. The Maori, New Zealand. (Best, 1924: 86; Long, 1963: 41; Pettazzoni, 1956: 344–345)

Samantabhadra   The primordial Buddha, "the Source of all Truth." Tibet. (Getty, 1962: 3; Evans-Wentz, 1960: 12, 13)

Samni   The primeval god, the male element, and father of the gods. When he died he became the clouds. The Katchins, Burma. (Gilhodes, 1908: 673, 675)

Shuzanghu   The pre-existent male whose wife was Jumiang-Nui. They were the parents of the earth and the sky. The Dhammai, Northeastern India. (Long, 1963: 105)

Sihai   The primordial being whose eyes are the sun and the moon. The father of the winds. Nias Island, Indonesia. (Pettazzoni, 1956: 7, 11)

Sing-bonga   Like Ote Borom a self-created supreme god and creator. Sometimes they are identified with each other, and again are two separate deities. India. (Majumdar, 1950: 251, 254; Basu, 1971: 62; Biswas, 1956: 102; Elwin, 1949: 4)

Sombov-Burkhan   A pre-existent god who singly (or with a triad made up of Esseghe-Burkhan, Maidari-Burkhan, and Shibegeni-Burkhan) caused the creation of the earth and then humans. The Buriats, Siberia, Mongolia. (Klementz, 1925, 3: 11)

Soutan   A variation of the creation myth makes "Soutan (soul)" the pre-existent deity, like Rajan Gantallah unformed, but with sight, hearing, and speech. Borneo. (MacKenzie, 1930: 315)

T'ai-Kih   "The 'Most Ultimate,' which produced the cosmic souls Yang and Yin, male and female, heaven and earth, warmth and cold, light and darkness." China. (MacCulloch, 1925, 8: 48)

Tangae   "Gasping," with Anu the primeval pair who produced the evolutionary deities of the creation myths. The Marquesas, Polynesia. (Williamson, 1933, 1: 15)

Tapuppa   The female of the primeval pair (stone deities) and mother of Totorro, Otaia, and Oru. Tahiti, Polynesia. (Williamson, 1933, 1: 17)

Targitaos   A Scythian primeval being, father of Kolaxais, Lipoxais, and Arpoxais. (Littleton, 1965: 11, 186)

Tatuma   The male primeval stone deity, with Tapuppa the parents of Totorro ("who was killed and divided into land"), Otaia and Oru. Tahiti, Polynesia. (Williamson, 1933, 1: 17)

Te-ake-ia-roe   "The root of all existence," the deity of the very beginning. Mangaia, Hervey Islands, Polynesia. (Westervelt, 1963, 1: 3; Long, 1963: 58)

Te Bo Ma   Darkness, of the abstract evolutionary process. With Te Maki—"Their descendants were Void, Night, Daylight, Thunder, and Lightning, as well as the Younger Nareau." Micronesia. (Poignant, 1967: 71)

Te Maki   *See* **Te Bo Ma**

Te Vaerua   "The breath, or The life." The second deity of the very beginning—after Te-ake-ia-roe. Hervey Islands, Polynesia. (Westervelt, 1963, 1: 3)

Tiamat   The sea, of the primeval watery chaos, and Abzu "the sweet waters," created the universe and the gods. Abzu was destroyed by Enki and Tiamat was overcome by Marduk. Babylonia. (Kramer, 1967: 107–108; Jastrow, 1898: 140, 409; Larousse, 1968: 49)

Tillili   A variant name of the primordial earth, the consort of Alala. Babylonia. (Sayce, 1898: 251)

Touia-a-Futuna, Tou'iafutuna   The primordial parent Rock which split apart giving birth to the primeval twins: Biki and Kele, Atungaki and Maimoa-a-Longona, Fonu-uta and Fonu-vai, Hemoana and Lube. Tonga, Polynesia. (Collocott, 1921: 152; Moulton, 1925, 12: 379; Williamson, 1933, 1: 9, 10)

Tumu-iti (female) and **Tumu-nui** (male)   The primal parents from whom the world developed. Paumotu, Society Islands, Polynesia. (Williamson, 1933, 1: 16; Henry, 1928: 338, 382)

Tzacol   "Creator," with Bitol, "Maker," the primeval pair of deities of the Maya Lowlands, Central America. (Thompson, 1970: 201; Recinos, 1950: 78)

Uarahiulu   A stone being, wife of Darukavaitere and mother of "the sun, the moon, and all the other celestial beings." The Paressi, Brazil. (Lowie, 1925, 4: 172)

Unvelingange   A pre-existent god, father of Unkulunkulu. The Kaffir, South Africa. (Larousse, 1973: 522)

Uwu Lowalangi   The "primordial Principle." North Nias Island, Indonesia. (Pettazzoni, 1956: 329)

Vari   A self-existent being of the beginning times. Mangaia, Polynesia. (Poignant, 1967: 33–34)

Vari-ma-te-takere   The primeval mother who lived in Avaiki, the coconut shell of the initial symbolism of the universe. Mangaia, Polynesia. (Williamson, 1933: 12; Long, 1963: 59)

Viraj Given sometimes as male, others as female—"perhaps symbolizes the cosmic waters. Like Brahman Viraj connotes vastness or all-pervasiveness." India. (Bhattacharji, 1970: 329–330)

Vula Ledza Moon-Sun. A variant name for Dua Nggae, the primeval being. Flores, Indonesia. (Pettazzoni, 1956: 334)

Wailan wangko Grandfather, who was alone in the beginning. He broke open a coconut tree which came ashore and from which a man emerged. Southern Minhassa, Northern Celebes, Indonesia. (MacKenzie, 1930: 331)

Wamutsini The original god "from whom the other supernaturals sprang." He and Atehle, the sun, were the chief creators. The Trumai, Brazil. (Murphy and Quain, 1955: 72–73)

Wulleb (male) "the first living beings were two worms, Wulleb and Lejman, living together in a shell. . . . They . . . raised the top shell to make the sky; the lower shell became the earth." The Marshall Islands, Micronesia. (Leach, 1956: 183)

Xchmel (male) and **Xtmana** (female) The self-existent divine pair, parents of Hunavan and Hunchevan. Guatemala. (Bancroft, 1886, 3: 74)

Yang dag rgyal po (pr. **Yangdak Gyelpo**) A primal Bon deity, an otiose god of the beginning prior to all creation. Tibet. (Tucci, 1980: 214)

Ye smon rgyal po, Ye rje A primal being of the beginning and a demiurge. As the God of Being he "ruled on the Mountain of Being." When he and Nyam rje, his enemy (who lived in his castle of darkness) were on friendly terms all was beautiful, but inevitably there was conflict, at which time he (Ye smon rgyal po) was victorious. His consort is Chu lcam. The Bon, Tibet. (Tucci, 1980: 221, 234–235)

Ymir The primeval frost giant who emerged from the frozen ocean and was nourished by Audhumla, the primeval cow. He was killed by Odin, Vili, and Ve and from his body they fashioned the earth. Scandinavia. (Guerber, 1895: 11–13; Grimm, 1883, 2: 559)

Yüan Shih T'ien Tsun The primordial first person of the Taoist triad (with Tao Chun and Lao Tzǔ) "who governed the world before turning it over to Yu-Huang." China. (Maspero, 1963: 263; Werner, 1932: 609; Ferguson, 1937: 109–111)

Zervan, Zurvan, Zrvan Akaran The pre-existent, primeval, hermaphorditic being—"Boundless Time"—from whom came Ormazd and Ahriman. Iran. (Seligmann, 1948: 40; Patai, 1967: 168; Schoeps, 1961: 88; Haydon, 1941: 75; Kramer, 1961: 355–356)

Zicum, Zikun, Zigara Assyro/Babylonian primeval goddess, at Eridu, the primordial abyss, from whom came the earth and the heavens, and the mother of the gods. (Rawlinson, 1885: 51; Sayce, 1898: 186, 374–375)

uZivelele "the Self-existent One." The Zulu, South Africa. (Mbiti, 1970, 2: 336)

Zumiang-Nui The pre-existent female whose husband was Shuzanghu. They were the parents of Subbu-Khai-Thung, the earth, and Jongsuli-Young-Jongbu, the sky. The Chammai, Northeastern India. (Long, 1963: 105)

2

Male/Female Principle, Androgynous

Abrao The planet Jupiter is a bisexual god. The Akan, Ghana. (Meyerowitz, 1958: 47)

Agdistis, Agditis A hermaphroditic creature born of the Agdos rock (Mother Earth), impregnated by the seed of Zeus. He was of evil and violent nature; was feared and castrated by the gods. From his blood on the ground grew a tree whose fruit impregnated the daughter of Sangarios. She became the mother of Attis. Among the Galli (priests) Agdistis was worshipped as a maternal figure, like Misa. Phrygia, Near East. (Kerenyi, 1951: 88, 89; James, 1960: 97; Delcourt, 1961: 31, 32; Eliade, 1979: 109)

Agni Agni became pregnant through "drinking Siva's seed . . . [considered perversion] (cool liquid semen placed in the fiery female, as the oblation is placed in fire); but then Agni places this seed in the Ganges (fiery semen placed in the cool liquid female)." Therefore "Skanda is said to be the child of Agni, [and Ganges] then the child of Siva and finally the child of Agni *and* Siva." Fire and water have androgynous natures functioning "in tandem, one changing in response to the other, adjusting in response to context in order to maintain an overall balance of qualities; "in his own right, Agni is an androgynous figure, a serial androgyne who varies according to the ritual context." India. (O'Flaherty, 1980: 49, 51, 55, 171, 220, 320)

Aku The planet Mercury is a bisexual god among the Akan. Ghana. (Meyerowitz, 1958: 47)

Amen The bisexual god of the planet Saturn who dispenses the "kra" to the abosom born on Saturday. Their character will be "experienced and seasoned." The Akan, Ghana. (Meyerowitz, 1958: 47)

Angamunggi The rainbow serpent who is described as the "primeval father of men, the giver of life . . .

[but] they suggested that he had a womb." Australia. (Eliade, 1973: 113–114)

'aǹl'tani Cornbeetle, "the symbols of female generative power, may be represented as male or female." The Navaho Indians, Arizona and New Mexico. (Reichard, 1950: 422)

Aphrodite, Aphroditos On Cyprus an androgynous Aphrodite was worshipped—"a bearded Aphrodite, called Aphroditos." She/he was also known in Pamphylia as a bisexual deity—body and clothes of a woman, but "beard and sexual organs of a man." (Delcourt, 1961: 15, 27)

Apsu The primordial male principle "personifying the 'sweet waters' of the abyss," whose consort is Tiamat. Akkadian/Babylonian. (James, 1960: 208; Jastrow, 1898: 410–411; Kramer, 1961: 120)

Ardhanarisvara An androgynous figure comprised of a combination of Siva and Parvati. Nepal. (Heeramaneck, 1966: 78, 83)

Armaiti An androgynous being but more female than male, the patron(ess) of the earth. Iran. (Littleton, 1965: 99)

Asgaya Gigagei A thunder god who is apparently androgynous "as in one of the formulae for rheumatism he is addressed both as 'Red Man' and as 'Red Woman,' his sex name to be applied . . . as the sex of the patient varies." If male, Red Woman, if female, Red Man. The Cherokee, Southeastern United States. (Spence, 1925, 3: 504)

Atea The male principle. With Hakahotu, the primary parents. Tongareva, Polynesia. (Buck, 1932, 2: 85)

Attr, Attar Venus, the morning star, is of an androgynous nature which "is shown by two personal names

(Atr'ab, 'Atr is father,' and Atr'um, 'Atr is mother.' . . . He has no wife, probably because of his androgynous nature." South Arabia. (Oldenburg, 1969: 41)

Atum Sometimes regarded as bisexual as the lone parent of Shu and Tefnut. Egypt. (Ames, 1965: 30, 45; Larousse, 1968: 11; Eliade, 1967: 25)

Awo The Moon is a bisexual deity among the Akan. Ghana. (Meyerowitz, 1958: 47)

Awonawilona The primordial being, a bisexual power, the He/She "initiator of life." The Zuñi, New Mexico. (Stevenson, 1901/02: 22; Cushing, 1891/1892: 379; Tyler, 1964: 81, 86)

Brahmā "In one cycle of myths, . . . Brahmā (the later form of Prajāpati) becomes an androgyne, divides himself into a man and a woman who separate and mate, and thus begets the race of mortals." India. (O'Flaherty, 1980: 312)

Burha-Burhi The androgynous earth deity. Bengal. (Crooke, 1925, 2: 487)

Chaos A neuter deity, the Void, from whom were born Erebus (also neuter) and Night (feminine). Greece. (Eliade, 1979: 108; Delcourt, 1961: 17)

Cybele The Great Mother "was sprung from the earth, originally a bisexual deity but then reduced to a female." Phrygia, Near East. (Morford and Lenardon, 1975: 103–104)

Da The rainbow serpent, "the symbol of flowing, sinuous movement" is of a dual nature, male and female. The Fon, Dahomey. (Mercier, 1954: 220–221)

Daksa As an androgyne Daksa divided himself into male and female, produced numerous daughters as wives for the gods. His daughter Rati was produced from his sweat. He is also the father of Sati, a wife of Siva. (O'Flaherty, 1980: 39, 132, 313)

Dan The Mahi bisexual deity, rainbow serpent, who symbolizes continuity, the vital force. Dahomey. (Verger, 1957: 233)

Deva The all-seeing supreme being is an androgynous figure who is associated with atmospheric phenomena. The Ngadha, Flores Island, Indonesia. (Pettazzoni, 1956: 333–334)

Devi The female principle which is identified with numerous goddesses, or numerous goddesses with her,

who are consorts of the deities in the pantheon. India. (Ghurye, 1962: 238; Brown, 1961: 312)

Dionysus A two-fold god—a man/woman. Archaically he was depicted with a beard, his virility unquestioned, yet he was always considered dressed in women's clothing. Later Hellenistic art made him effeminate—"the most bisexual of the gods"—androgynous both in appearance and function as well as being the child of the androgynous Zeus, born from his thigh. Greece. (O'Flaherty, 1980: 201, 277; Eliade, 1979: 109; Delcourt, 1961: 24–27)

Dudilaa, Upulera The sun god who is also the male principle and fertilizing agent. Timorlaut Island, Indonesia. (Frazer, 1926: 660)

Durgavva A goddess who represents the female creative principle. The village of Sivapur, state of Karnataka, India. (Ishwaran, 1974: 30)

Dyammavva A goddess who is considered a manifestation of the cosmic female creative energy. She "alleviates smallpox" and protects the fields. The village of Sivapur, state of Karnataka, India. (Ishwaran, 1974: 30, 34)

Dyāvā-Prthivī The earliest androgyne in India—Sky-Earth. The primeval parents. Their separation "reflects the need to dispel chaos (here regarded as noncreative) and establish order." India. (O'Flaherty, 1980: 310–311)

Eros In his early form particularly considered androgynous. Greece. (Delcourt, 1961: 17)

Gaea, Gaia A chthonic goddess, the Earth Mother, who of herself gave birth to Pontos and to Ouranos, the starry heaven. With the latter she had numerous progeny. Greece. (Eliade, 1976, 2: 358–359; Delcourt, 1961: 17)

Gynnis An androgynous being revered in Emesa. Asia Minor. (Roscher, 1965, 1, 2: 1778)

Hakahotu The female principle and earth mother. With Atea the primary parents. Tongareva, Polynesia. (Buck, 1932, 2: 85)

Hera She appears early as an androgyne, giving birth of herself to Hephaistos and Typhon. Greece. (Delcourt, 1961: 17; Eliade, 1979: 109)

Hermaphroditus Son of Aphrodite and Hermes who refused the love of the nymph Salmacis. Her frenzied desire never to be separated from him was taken pity on by the gods who merged them into one being—male/

female. Greece. (Morford and Lenardon, 1975: 99; Larousse, 1968: 132; Ovid, 1955: 102–104; Prentice Hall, 1965: 67; Delcourt, 1961: 50)

Indra He appears as an androgyne "when, as the result of a curse, he is marked with a thousand yonis." He also takes the form of "a man among men, and a woman among women." India. (O'Flaherty, 1980: 310)

Inyangba "Inyangba herself is Obatala. The two are one, or in other words, Obatala is an androgyne, representing the productive energy of nature, or the generative principle, as distinguished from the creative power of God." West Africa. (Jeffreys, 1972: 733)

Jok The omnipotent and omnipresent high god "is apparently a dual entity, male and female." The Lango, Uganda. (Driberg, 1923: 216–223)

Kahukura A "personification of the rainbow, . . . The upper and darker band, . . . is called Kahukura-pango, and the lower one Pou-te-aniwaniwa; the former . . . male, the latter . . . female." The Maori, New Zealand. (Best, 1924: 160–161)

Kariyavva A goddess who represents the female creative principle. The village of Sivapur, state of Karnataka, India. (Ishwaran, 1974: 30)

Khaṇḍobā As he "represents both sun [masc.] and moon [fem.]" their union in the cult represents "an interior androgynization within him." India. (O'Flaherty, 1980: 256–257)

Khem The personification of the male generative principle, of all productiveness, vegetable and animal. Egypt. (Budge, 1969, 2: 17; Rawlinson, 1885: 18; Bulfinch, 1898: 366)

Magna Mater Androgynous mother goddess who bore Agditis and Mise, both bisexual. Phrygia, Near East. (Eliade, 1979: 109)

Makarom Manouwe The masculine principle "lives in the sky and sometimes in the sun," a primordial pair with Makarom Mawakhu. Island of Keisar, Indonesia. (Eliade, 1958: 51)

Makarom Mawakhu The feminine principle is "present in the earth," and forms a primordial pair with Makarom Manouwe. Island of Keisar, Indonesia. (Eliade, 1958: 51)

Malimeihevao A bisexual god. Uoleva Island, Tonga, Polynesia. (Gifford, 1929: 294)

Guede Masaka An androgynous god, assistant of Guede Nibo. A grave-digger. Haiti. (Marcelin, 1950: 194)

Mawu, Mawu-Lisa It is sometimes suggested that this deity is androgynous. Mawu may be referred to as male or as female. In the Mawu-Lisa terminology Mawu is female and Lisa male, and as twins born of Nana-Buluku, herself an androgynous figure. Dahomey. (Herskovits, 1938, 2: 101, 249; Williams, 1936: 164; Mercier, 1954: 217)

Melo The male principle, the primeval sky, husband/brother of Sedi. The Adi, Northeastern India. Among the Minyong as a dual deity, Sedi-Melo is "credited with the creation of the earth." (Chowdhury, 1971: 75, 78, 105)

Mer Chor (mer tcor) The "Chorti guardian of the milpa . . . said to be dual sexed." Guatemala. (Thompson, 1970: 324; Wisdom, 1940: 401)

Misa, Mise Bisexual, but invoked as a goddess. She is named as a daughter of Isis, or of Magna Mater; companion of the Magna Mater of Phrygia. "Misa rejoices in good harvests." She is also associated with Dionysos, with Iachos. Near East. (Delcourt, 1961: 30–32; Eliade, 1979: 109)

Mwari The supreme being and creator "is both male and female. The terms Dziva, Mbuya (grandmother) and Zendere (the young woman who is regarded as Mwari's emanation) represent the female aspects of this ambivalent deity; the male is revealed in Sororezhou . . . Nyadenga . . . Wokumusoro . . . " The Southern Shona, Rhodesia. (Daneel, 1970: 15–17)

Nana-Buluku, Nanan-bouclou The androgynous creator deity, parent of Mawu-Lisa, or Mawu and Lisa, as twins. Dahomey. (Herskovits, 1938, 2: 101, 103; Deren, 1953: 55; Williams, 1936: 168)

nă thu pen do nă thu pĕ dŏ The omnipresent high god who rules over all the other spirits. A bisexual mother/father spirit who is appealed to in epidemics, rules over the animals of the forest and so is invoked by hunters. The Miao, China. (Bernatzik, 1947: 168–169)

Ndu The male principle (Yang). With Sse looked "upon as the creators of heaven and earth." The Na-khi, Yunnan Province, China. (Rock, 1936: 50)

Nenechen The Supreme Being and Creator is an androgynous deity called father/mother, young man/

woman, etc. The Mapuche-Huilliche (Araucanians), Chile. (Cooper, 1946, 6: 742, 747; Pettazzoni, 1956: 419)

Guede Nibo A hermaphroditic deity of the dead and of cemeteries who presides over tombs. The protector of the living and the dead and invoked for news of the living who are away. Plaisance, Haiti. (Marcelin, 1950: 146, 181, 183, 186)

Nous I In Gnosticism "the generator, . . . not a first couple, but one Principle, intelligible or above intelligence, . . . a male and female power, dividing itself into a syzygy which in its turn procreates." Nous created man as a bisexual; later divided the double beings into male and female. (Delcourt, 1961: 77)

Nyame The Great God is sometimes considered to be androgynous—as female represented by the moon, as male by the sun. The Ashanti, the Akan. Ghana. (Parrinder, 1949: 26; Danquah, 1952: 361)

Nyame Amowia The bisexual deity of the Akan of the Gold Coast "visible as the moon, gave birth to the Sun god . . . " (Meyerowitz, 1951: 24)

Nyingwan Mebege The moon goddess is "the female principle of the universe . . . the author of procreation and the guarantor of a prosperous life." The Fang, Gabon. (Fernandez, 1972: 241, 247)

Obasi The supreme sky god "used sometimes to be said . . . was of dual nature, Father God and Mother God . . . " The Ibibio, Nigeria. (Parrinder, 1949: 21)

Obatala *See* **Inyangba**

Olokun A hermaphroditic deity "who lives in the depths of the ocean with a great retinue of mermaids and tritons." Puerto Rico. (Gonzalez-Wippler, 1975: 26)

Ometecuhtli and **Omecíhuatl** Lord and Lady of Duality, The androgynous Ometéotl as the divine couple, yet combined in one being and embodying the cosmic principle of existence, expressing Ometéotl's qualities of the masculine/feminine. They dwell in Omeyocan, the topmost heaven. Aztec, Mexico. (Leon Portilla, 1982: 53, 83, 84, 90)

Ometéotl The God of Duality, the supreme being, omnipresent and omnipotent, has numerous aspects or manifestations, titles. As the self-existent, self-created his title is Moyocoyani. As an Androgyne he is the divine couple, Ometechuhtli and Omecíhuatl, Lord and Lady of Duality, embodying the creative energy, the concept of

generation and conception, the cosmic principle of existence. In his celestial manifestation he is again dual—Citlalinicue ("she of the starry skirt") and Citlallatonac ("celestial body which illumines things"), bringing starlight by night and sunlight by day. As the source of life he is the Lord and Lady of our flesh, Tonacatecuhtli and Tonacacíhuatl, deities of sustenance, and representing him in his relationship with man. Ometéotl, through them, has four sons, the four cosmic forces. (Because they were born "when darkness still rules," they were all called Tezcatlipocas, "smoking mirrors." They are: (1) Tlatlauhqui Tezcatlipoca, born red, the eldest; (2) Yayauhqui Tezcatlipoca, born black; (3) Quetzalcoatl, or Yoalli ehecatl, white; (4) Huitzilopochtli, or Omiteotl, or Maquizcoatl, the blue Tezcatlipoca. Ometéotl's omnipresence is an active principle of preservation, sustenance and maintained order as Master of the Universe. In ruling the heavens of the atmosphere and the clouds he was Tlallichcatl; "as the embodiment of wisdom and of the only truth on earth," he was personified as Quetzalcoatl. Xiuhtecuhtli was his name as "Lord of fire and of time." He was also called Huehueteotl, "the old god." Aztec, Mexico. (Reed, 1966: 69; Nicholson, 1967: 23; Leon-Portilla, 1961: 449; 1982: 30–34, 90–99, 122)

Onkoy "The supreme god . . . is a hybrid, both male and female, half-feline and half-reptile." Chavin, Peru. (Flornoy, 1958: 83)

Oyamakui A mountain god who is considered bisexual in nature and is protective of child-bearing. He is worshipped by industrialists and in some areas remains specifically a mountain god. Japan. (Herbert, 1967: 470–471)

Parjanya The rain god is androgynous—male and female. "Now he becomes sterile [F], now one who gives birth; he takes whatever body he wishes . . . [He is] . . . the bull and the cow; his rain is milk, seed, and his offspring, his calf. Thus he can give 'milk' (seed) to the mother, even as he can become pregnant though he is sterile." India. (O'Flaherty, 1980: 25, 26)

In P'en The Chorti deity of the soil is the "personification of the earth and patron of plant growth, fertility, family life, property, and other wealth . . . both male and female; as the passive spirit of maize, is male and the consort of Ix Kanan, the female spirit of the bean." Guatemala. (Thompson, 1970: 294)

Phanes An androgynous deity who emerged from the Orphic cosmogonical egg "is said to be 'woman and begetter and mighty god' . . . [who] created sun and moon, mountains and towns." Greece. (Barthell, 1971: 7; Kerenyi, 1951: 114–115; Delcourt, 1961: 69)

The Phoenix As the symbol of androgyny it "has both sexes, and receives the regenerating baptism of fire. Either one of these two traits would have been enough. The presence of both of them, with the symbolic beauty of the image—a bird flying out of the earthly pyre towards the Sun and the East—combined to make the Phoenix the symbol of the dogma of individual resurrection." Greece, Egypt, Near East. (Delcourt, 1961: 79)

Poreskoro A hermaphroditic demon who causes epidemics and parasitical diseases. Child of Ana. The Gypsies, Transsylvania. (Clebert, 1967: 186)

Prajāpati In the later Vedas he is androgynous. Known as a male god he "is suddenly endowed with a womb and breasts . . . [and also] . . . he is said to rub up milk and butter from himself and thus to propagate." In the Upanishads Prajāpati (Purusa) is an explicit androgyne, a very large being encompassing male and female. He caused himself to separate into two, copulated with his female self producing human beings. "She became a cow; he became a bull . . . and produced cattle. She became a mare; he a stallion. . . . Thus were born all pairs." India. (Keith, 1917: 74, 75; O'Flaherty, 1980: 26, 28, 311)

Prakrti In Puranic mythology she is the female principle, the immanent and active power which animates and stimulates the "latent powers" of the male principle, Purusa, though her powers are controlled and directed by the male (social force). India. (O'Flaherty, 1980: 81, 118)

Purusa He is the male principle, the inert and spiritual counterpart of Prakrti, the female principle who represents pure power. She animates and stimulates his "latent power." His authority controls "and shapes the life force that comes from her." *See also* **Prajāpati.** India. (O'Flaherty, 1980: 81, 82, 117, 118)

Rarang The invisible and remote benevolent high spirit, the male principle. The sun "is only the visible form of his power and activity." The Kaean, New Guinea. (Meiser, 1963: 905–906)

Rudra He was created by Brahmā as an androgyne; then divided himself into male and female as instructed by Brahmā. Daksa made the female half his daughter and then returned her to Rudra for his wife (to remove the implication of incest). India. (O'Flaherty, 1980: 313)

Sedi The female principle, the earth goddess, forms a primeval brother/sister pair with Melo. The Adi, Northeastern India. Among the Minyong as a dual deity, Sedi-Melo, they are "credited with the creation of the earth." (Chowdhury, 1971: 75, 78, 105)

Gran' Silibo, Silibo-Gweto One of "the ancient androgynous founders of the race." Haiti. (Deren, 1953: 146)

Siva As "the supreme Indian androgyne" Siva is both a Splitting Androgyne when he created "from his female half, the Goddess as a separate being" (as such she created a counterpart of herself for procreational purposes) and a Fusing Androgyne when she reentered Siva's body, he again becoming androgynous. "As usual, the androgyne itself is barren; Siva becomes the androgyne when he does *not* want to procreate sexually." India. (O'Flaherty, 1980: 310, 313–314)

Siwa "the source of all life, the synthesis of the creative and generative powers in nature; consequently in him are the two sexes in one—the Divine Hermaphrodite (*Windú*), symbol of completion, the ultimate perfection." Bali. (Covarrubias, 1937: 290)

So (1) The male principle, the personified sky, who controls the course of events. The Kalabari, Nigeria. (Horton, 1960: 16) **So, Sogbo** (2) An androgynous deity born of Mawu-Lisa and the parent of the gods of the thunder pantheon. Dahomey. (Herskovits, 1938, 2: 129; Williams, 1936: 168)

Sse The female principle (Yin). With Ndu looked "upon . . . as the creators of heaven and earth." The Nakhi, Yunnan Province, China. (Rock, 1936: 50)

Surasundari "The goddess is no longer a simple fertility symbol, but a Sakti, a manifestation of the divine itself as female energy." Khajuraho, India. (Heeramaneck, 1966: 52)

Sussistinako Thinking Woman, an asexual goddess of the beginning "seems to belong to the underworld, but her creative capacity for 'thinking outward into space,' brings everything into existence" relates her also to the heavenly world. Among the Keres, female, the Sia, male. New Mexico. (Tyler, 1964: 82)

Sx'nts The "hermaphrodite," guardian of the daughters of the supernaturals. He is supposedly responsible when a male or female assumes the role of the opposite sex. The Bella Coola Indians, British Columbia. (McIlwraith, 1948, 1: 45)

Tamayowut The female principle, the Earth. She evolved through transitions from Atavish. With her brother Tukomit the creators (through birth) of the things and features, animate and inanimate, of the world. The Luiseño, California. (Kroeber, 1925: 677–678)

Tano   A bisexual sky and fertility deity who receives powers from the planets and the fertile earth. The Akan, Ghana. (Meyerowitz, 1958: 48, 50)

Tata lat kola   "Grandfather Sun . . . the male principle" revered and invoked for help in numerous difficulties. Watubela Island, Indonesia. (Frazer, 1926: 667)

Teave   The primordial deity—"the Father-Mother and regent over the Kings of heaven and Tane was the Son." Hawaii. (Melville, 1969: 17–20)

Te Rongo   An androgynous deity—"besides being endowed with a most impressive phallus, he has, on his chest, three small figures, and above these figures, two small, but well-defined female breasts. . . . The three figures . . . represent his sons emerging from his breast, that is from himself." Polynesia. (Sierksma, 1960: 39)

Tloque Nahuaque   The remote and supreme bisexual deity who represents the creative principle. Also known as Ometeotl. Aztec, Mexico. (Nicholson, 1967: 114; Alexander, 1920: 88)

Turan   "The Etruscan Venus (Turan) wears the *tutulus,* the conical hat which not only is obviously the symbol of the phallus, but even seems to bear its name—that of Mutinus Tutunus, a priapic deity associated . . . with a prenuptial rite." Italy. (Delcourt, 1961: 29)

Tvastr   A complex androgyne—a god who impregnates women, yet is pregnant himself. "The bright bull of a thousand, rich in milk, bearing all forms in his bellies, . . . his seed is calf, afterbirth, fresh milk." India. (O'Flaherty, 1980: 26)

Upulero   The Sun, the male principle who impregnates Mother Earth. Leti, Moa, Lakor, the Moluccas. Indonesia. (Kern, 1925, 8: 347; Hartland, 1925, 9: 822)

Upunusa   Grandmother Earth, the female principle. In some areas fertilized by Upulero, in others by Dudilaa. Indonesia. (Hartland, 1925, 9: 822; Frazer, 1926: 660)

Venus   There was an "ancient cult of the bald Venus" wherein the statue "was bearded, had male and female organs," and was considered the protectress of births. Italy. (Delcourt, 1961: 29)

Voltumna   An Etruscan tutelary goddess/god was androgynous. Italy. (Campbell, 1964: 309; von Vacano, 1960: 39)

Yang   The male principle, which is positive, evident in the sun. Yang "came to mean Heaven, Light, Vigour, Male, Penetration, the Monad. It is symbolized by the Dragon and is associated with azure colour and oddness in numbers." [Quoted from the Encyclopedia Sinica.] China. (Graham, 1928: 37; Ferguson, 1937: 56–57; Day, 1940: 56; Schoeps, 1961: 195)

Yin   The female principle which is negative, recessive, evident in the moon. Yin "stands for Earth (the Antithesis of Heaven), Darkness, Quiescence, Female, Absorption, the Duad. It is symbolized by the Tiger and is associated with orange colour and even numbers. Valleys and streams possess the Yin Quality." [Quoted from the Encyclopaedia Sinica.] China. (Graham, 1928: 37; Ferguson, 1937: 56–57; Day, 1940: 56; Schoeps, 1961: 195)

Yurlunggur   The rainbow snake's sex is unclear and is probably bisexual as referred to as both he and she. Australia. (Eliade, 1973: 100–102; Poignant, 1967: 119, 125)

Zervan, Zurvan   The androgynous god of Time was the father/mother of Ohrmazd and Ahriman, the latter considered the first-born. Iran. (Patai, 1967: 168; Eliade, 1979: 83, 84, 110)

Zeus, Zeus Labrandeus   At Labranda in Caria he was seemingly worshipped as a bisexual deity—bearded and with six breasts. The androgyny of Zeus took the form of swallowing his pregnant wife, Metis, fearful that she would bear a son who would overthrow him, and subsequently himself gave birth to Athena from his forehead. Similarly, when Semele was consumed by the flames of Zeus' brilliance, he placed the unborn child in his thigh, from which Dionysus was born. Greece. (Delcourt, 1961: 18, 20; O'Flaherty, 1980: 201; Morford and Lenardon, 1975: 92, 93; Cox, 1870, 1: 360)

3

Deities of the Universe, Space

Aditi She "is the cosmic origin of space itself." She brings into being that which has been Unmanifest out of the immensity of the Vastness of Space. Aditi is the supreme creatress—that from which all is formed—the female principle which makes manifest Divine Truth. She is unlimited by time, is omnipresent, needing no vehicle as do the other gods. Yet she is a personal deity, approachable, and the mother of the sky gods. "In Sanskrit, *go* means at once the cow and the ray. This *double entendre* of the word led the Rishis to treat the physical cow as a symbol of light." (She is not the physical cow but the Cow of Light). India. (O'Flaherty, 1980: 79; Pandit, 1970: 4, 5, 10, 18, 20, 22)

Akasadhatvisvari "Lady of the Sphere of Space," one of the names of the goddess who is partner to Vairocana. Tibet. (Snellgrove, 1957: 82)

Akasagarbha A Dhyani-Bodhisttva—"(Essence of the Void Space above) . . . whose essence is ether." Buddhism. Also nam-mk'ahi snin-po (Tibet), oqtarghui-in jiruken (Mongolia), Hsuk'ung-tsang (China), Kokuzo (Japan). (Getty, 1962: 101)

Anu He represents Space. With Tangae the primeval pair of the evolutionary creation myth. The Marquesas, Polynesia. (Williamson, 1933, 1: 15)

Anu-mate A god of space, child of Rangi and Pokoharua-te-po. "Space of Cold Death" who was the source of death. Also named as the son of Anu-whaka-toro. The Maori, New Zealand. (Andersen, 1928: 375; White, 1887, 1: 29)

Anu-whakarere A god of space—"Space of Extreme Cold." Son of Rangi or of Anu-matao, and father of Anu-whaka-toro. The Maori, New Zealand. (Andersen, 1928: 375; White, 1887, 1: 29)

Anu-whaka-toro A god of space—"Cold Space creeping on." Son of Rangi or of Anu-whakarere, and father of Anu-mate. The Maori, New Zealand. (Andersen, 1928: 375; White, 1887, 1: 29)

A phyi gung rgyal (*pr*. Achhi Kunggyel) A variant name is gNam phyi gung rgyal. She is the Bon Goddess of Heavenly Space, the first born female being of Shangs po and Chu lcam Icam. She also as "Srid pa'i sman . . . resides on Ti se, Mt. Kailasa." Her consort is gNam gyi lha rgod thog pa, a god of heaven. Tibet. (Tucci, 1980: 216, 218)

Bhuvanesvari The benevolent "goddess-of-the-spheres" who nurtures the three worlds. She is the "consort of the Three-eyed Siva (Tryambaka)." India. (Danielou, 1964: 265, 279)

Chit Shakti The "all-permeating vital force of the universe." Among those invoked and propitiated at cremation ceremonies. Kashmir. (Biscoe, 1922: 157)

Coqui Xee, Coquixilla The god of infinity—"a supreme force or principle, . . . without 'beginning or end . . .' . . . . All deities were but aspects, attributes, or refractions" of Coqui Xee. He was also called Pije Xoo as "time" and as governing "the thirteen gods of the Zapotec sacred calendar." Also called Pijetao. Oaxaca, Mexico. (White-cotton, 1977: 165)

En-me-šar-ra The Sumerian Lord of the Universe—"the active principle of the world itself." Langdon calls this a title of Nergal, god of the underworld. (Jacobsen, 1970: 116; Langdon, 1931: 296)

Gwaza God of the universe of the Kagoro. Nigeria and Mali. (Mbiti, 1970, 2: 131)

Hauhet With Huh one of the initial primeval pairs "representing the infinity of space." Egypt. (Anthes, 1961: 67)

Hsu-k'ung-tsang A Dhyani-Bodhisattva, the "Essence of the Void Space above." Akasagarbha. China. (Getty, 1962: 101)

Huh With Hauhet one of the initial primeval pairs "representing the infinity of space." Egypt. (Anthes, 1961: 67)

Ilu Immensity—Father of Po (night) and Ao (day). Samoa, Polynesia. (Andersen, 1928: 385–386; Mackenzie, n.d.: 265–267)

Isivsanen The deity of the Universe, the World. The Karuk, California. (Eliade, 1979: 144)

Kilunge The Firmament to whom, with others, libations are offered for protection from "an unjust war by an enemy." The Wapare, Tanzania. (Frazer, 1926: 203)

Kokuzo A compassionate Dhyani-Bodhisattva, "Essence of the Void Space above." Akasagarbha. Japan. (Getty, 1962: 101; Eliseev, 1963: 435)

Kurn The god of the universe, and the universe itself, who is also the creator of all things. The Gilyak, Siberia. (Shternberg, 1933: 320; Czaplicka, 1969: 271)

Leta Aquichino "God of Infinity; and God of the Thirteen"—the gods of the sacred calendar. The southern Zapotec, Oaxaca, Mexico. (Whitecotton, 1977: 169)

Liwelelo A name or appellation of Lyuba, the High God, as meaning "the universe" and defining his omnipresence. The Sukuma, Tanzania. (Millroth, 1965: 96)

Mahalaya A Devi goddess, "the source of the universe." India. (Ghurye, 1962: 251)

Mamao Space—Mother of Po (night) and Ao (day). Samoa, Polynesia. (Andersen, 1928: 385–386; Mackenzie, n.d.: 265–267)

Maykapal "the lord of the universe who came down to earth to correct some mistakes in his works . . . he raised the sky." Then because of the heat of the sun he pierced one of its eyes, then seeded the barren earth to cover it with plants, and created the stars and moon for light. The Tagalog, Luzon, Philippines. (Jocano, 1969: 26–7)

nam-mk'ahi snin-po, Nam mkhahi-sning-po A Dhyani-Bodhisattva, the "Essence of the Void Space above." Akasagarbha. Tibet. (Getty, 1962: 101; Evans-Wentz, 1960: 111)

gNam phyi gung rgyal (pr. **Namcchi Kunggyel**) *See* **A phyi gung rgyal**

Neb-er-tcher A name of Ra as the "lord of the universe." Egypt. (Budge, 1969, 1: 294)

Nin-me-sar-ra Lady of the Universe. With En-me-sarra the first cause, in the genealogy of Anu. Sumer, Near East. (Jacobsen, 1970: 116)

Num He is considered to be the whole universe—the sea, the earth, the sky. Samoyeds, Siberia. (Eliade, 1958: 59)

Nyante A goddess, the "personification of the preexistent universe." Mother of Wamara. The Bantu, Africa. (Queval, 1968: 119; Larousse, 1973: 523)

opaochuse Universe or World Man is named as the begetter of Poseyemu, but sometimes identified with him. He is invoked for human fertility and increase. The Tewa, New Mexico. (Parsons, 1929: 267)

oqtarghui-in jiruken A Dhyani-Bodhisattva, the "Essence of the Void Space above." Akasagarbha. Mongolia. (Getty, 1962: 101)

Purusa The god of the universe, identical with it, "yet is above and more than it." From him all things exist. India. (Bhattacharji, 1970: 334–335; Elwin, 1949: 9)

Sam Hyam Vidi A "kind of Fatum presiding over the universe." Above both Siva and Buddha. Bali, Indonesia. (Levi, 1933: xiv)

Siûû "Elder Brother." With Tcuwut Makai lives in the east. They control the universe. The Pima, Arizona and Mexico. (Russell, 1904/05: 251)

Tcuwut Makai With Siûû he controls the universe. He rules over the winds and the weather. "Earth Magician." The Pima, Arizona and Mexico. (Russell, 1904/05: 251)

Thwasa An abstract god—"Space." Iran. (Gray, 1930: 162)

Tuhan, Pirman, Peng The god who presides over the universe and has the power of life and death. The Sakai, Malay Peninsula. (Skeat, 1906: 179)

Valevalenoa "Space," son of Tangaroa-the-explorer-of-lands. Samoa, Polynesia. (Williamson, 1933, 1: 4)

Vayah The god of space. Iran. (Gray, 1930: 169)

Wah-kon-tah This spirit is the "central force of the universe," is the all-encompassing power in all things, animate and/or inanimate. Man's consciousness and each individual are interrelated with all. He was praised and thanked for a bountiful harvest. The Quapaw, Arkansas and Oklahoma. (Baird, 1980: 17, 19)

Yaun-Goicoa The god of the universe who "created the three principles of life: Egia, the light of the spirit; Ekhia, the sun, the light of the world; Begia, the eye, the light of the body." The Basques, Spain/France. (Leach, 1949, 1: 117)

·Y·lyunda kotta The "mistress of the universe." The Selkups, (Ostyak-Samoyeds), Siberia. (Michael, 1963: 188)

4

Supreme Being, Great Spirit, High God

5

Creator Deities

Aba The beneficent Great Spirit of the Choctaw Indians created mankind and grasshoppers. Louisiana. (Bushnell, 1910: 527)

Abaangui A creator god and a transformer, brother of Zaguaguayu. The Guarayu, Bolivia. (Métraux, 1942: 108; Alexander, 1920: 297)

Ababinili The "supreme being . . . a composite force consisting of the Four Beloved Things Above, which were the Sun, Clouds, Clear Sky, and He that Lives in the Clear Sky." He created mankind; is manifest in the fire. The Chickasaw, northern Alabama and Mississippi to the Ohio River, and east of the Mississippi River. (Gibson, 1971: 9; Leach, 1949, 1: 1)

Aba-Inka The supreme god of the Appalachian Choctaw Indians. Mississippi/Alabama. (Schoolcraft, 1857, 5: 72)

Abassi The supreme deity, a sky god, was the creator of all things and ruler of all. The Ibibio, the Efik, Nigeria. (Mockler-Ferryman, 1925, 9: 280; Frazer, 1926: 127, 129–130; Jeffreys, 1939: 99)

Abi The jealous creator god of the Gio. Liberia. (Schwab, 1947: 315–316)

Abira The creator god of the Antioquians. Colombia. (Alexander, 1920: 197)

Abo The supreme being of the Kaffa whose name also means "sun," "father." Ethiopia. (Eliade, 1959: 121)

Abora The supreme being, a god of the heavens. Canary Islands, (La Palma). (Hooten, 1925, 7: 12)

Abradi The creator god of the Dilling who is invoked only in times of great trouble. Sudan. (Stevenson, 1950: 212; Mbiti, 1970, 2: 329)

Abwala The omniscient, omnipotent chief deity is beneficent and merciful, the creatress of all things. The Umundri, Nigeria. (Jeffreys, 1972: 723)

Acek A name by which Nialic, the supreme being and creator, is also known. Acek may, however, be his female counterpart as this deity is concerned with fertility, pregnancy, childbirth, and with agricultural sowing of seed. The Padang Dinka, Sudan. (Butt, 1952: 131)

Achaman The supreme being and a god of the heavens. Tenerife, Canary Islands. (Hooten, 1925, 7: 12)

A-chi A deity of the Lolos who created the sky. China. (Henry, 1903: 105)

Achidong The supreme god of the Jukun "controls the thunder and has charge of the souls of the dead." Nigeria. (Meek, 1925: 27–28; Williams, 1936: 215)

Ade Sakti The creative "primeval force" of the Madiga. India. (Elwin, 1949: 11)

ădŏ-dŭchŏ The god of heaven, a supreme being who "resides in and above the clouds" and rules over the other spirits. The Akha, China. (Bernatzik, 1947: 170)

Adosheba The supreme deity of the Gardulla, but he "has rather the characteristics of a bush spirit." Ethiopia. (Cerulli, 1956: 66)

Adro, Adroa, Adronga The omnipotent and omnipresent supreme being is the creator of mankind. In his remote, celestial aspect, considered beneficent and understanding, he is known as Adroa 'bua. In his immanent aspect he is evil, fearful, and associated with death, and known as Adro onzi. Adronga is, as well, a name applied to the spirits in general. Congo, Sudan, and Uganda. (Middleton, 1960: 27–28, 257; Baxter and Butt, 1953: 123; Gelfand, 1966: 118; Ramponi, 1937: 578, 584, 591)

Adung, Dung The supreme being, also the sun. The Kir, Nigeria. (Meek, 1931: 272)

Aelquntam *See* **Alquntam**

Afekan The creatress lived with men in the beginning to teach them "how to live in strength and dignity"; the secrets and rituals of men. She also created taro, pigs, cultural things. The Tifalmin, New Guinea. (Wheatcroft, 1973: 65)

agudar, agurur The principal god and creator whose functions are "concerned with hunting luck, protection from harm, and the reincarnation of souls." The Aleutian Eskimo, Alaska. (Marsh, 1967: 153)

Agugux' The benevolent supreme deity and creator god. The Aleuts, Alaska. (Jochelson, 1900/02: 236)

Agunowei The moon, the supreme being of a hinterland clan—the Bioloforn dialect. Nigeria. (Jeffreys, 1972: 730)

Agunua The supreme god and creator who has a serpent manifestation. San Cristoval, Melanesia. (MacCulloch, 1925, 11: 401; Leach, 1949, 1: 28)

Agwa pan The high god in Zaria Province. Nigeria. (Gunn, 1956: 86)

Agwatana The remote creator deity who is "the source of light and of all life, and who is approached only in major disasters." The Bassa-Komo, Nigeria. (Clifford, 1944: 115)

Ahnt ahs po-mee-kay The god "Who Rules Earth and Sky." The Seris, Sonora, Mexico. (Coolidge, 1939: 206)

Ahone The beneficent great god, the source of all good, is the creator of the sun, moon, and stars, and "governed the world." There is no need to propitiate him. The Huron, the Powhatan, Virginia. (McCary, 1979: 58; Lang, 1968: 232, 253; Swanton, 1946: 744)

Ahura-Mazda, Auramazda (old Persian), **Auharmazd** (Pahlavi), **Ohrmazd** The beneficent supreme one of the gods—an abstract concept—perfect light, truth, goodness—is also the omniscient creator god. The Ameša Spentas are personifications of his various aspects. He has nine wives: Īžā, Yaošti, Fərašti, Armaiti, Aši, Iš, Azūiti, Frasasti, and Pārəndi. Iran. (Gray, 1930: 20–22; Huart, 1963: 41; Littleton, 1965: 97; Gordon, 1961: 337; Campbell, 1964: 192; Pettazzoni, 1956: 132–133)

Aija Another name for the supreme god Ukko. Finland. (Eliade, 1964: 71)

Aijo, Aije The supreme god of the Lapps. It is also the name of the god of thunder. He is worshipped in the forms of nature—mountains, rocks, lakes. Northern Norway, Sweden, Finland, Kola Peninsula. (Eliade, 1965: 71; Collinder, 1949: 168)

Aiomun Kondi The supreme high god and creator. The Arawaks, Guiana. (Brett, 1880: 6, 7; Alexander, 1920: 273)

Ai Toyon The supreme being and creator god is represented by the eagle. The Yakut, Siberia. (Eliade, 1964: 69, 70)

Aiwamdzu A creator god and an ancestor deity. The Shavante, Brazil. (Maybury-Lewis, 1967: 284–285)

Ajok The omnipresent and omniscient supreme being and creator god was also the god of rain. Sacrifices were offered him at the harvest festival as well as for success in hunting and fishing. The Lotuko, Sudan. (Pettazzoni, 1956: 38; Huntingford, 1953: 90)

Ajy The creator god. Among his names are Yryn-Ajy "White Creator," Aihyt-Aga "Creator Father." The Yakut, Siberia. (MacCulloch, 1964: 398)

Akbatekdia The supreme being of the Crow Indians. Other names—Eehtreshbohedish and Bahkoore-Mahishtsedah. Montana. (Wildschut, 1960: 1)

Akongo The all-powerful, yet approachable, supreme being. The Ngombe, Congo. (Davidson, 1950: 163–164)

Akponanara The supreme being of a hinterland clan, of the Biloforn dialect. Nigeria. (Jeffreys, 1972: 730)

Akuj An omnipotent high god who, though remote, does sometimes punish by sending disaster, as well as benevolently controlling the rain, curing disease, and prophesying through diviners. Among the Karamojong, Jie, and Dodos he is more generally beneficent. The Turkana, the Karamojong, Kenya/Uganda. (Gulliver, 1952: 4; 1953: 26, 47; Blumenthal, 1973: 124)

Alata'ala, Hatalla The omnipotent and omniscient supreme being. The Maanjan (Dyaks), Borneo, Indonesia. (Pettazzoni, 1956: 332)

Alcoran, Acoran The supreme being, a god of the heavens. Gran Canaria, Canary Islands. (Hooten, 1925: 12)

Alhou   The omniscient, omnipotent, and omnipresent supreme deity and creator is usually, but not always beneficent, though otiose. The Sema Nagas, India. (Hutton, 1968: 191, 194; Pettazzoni, 1956: 289)

A-li   The creator of the earth. The Lolos, China. (Henry, 1903: 105)

Aliu-Lap   "The Creator or Supreme Being." His wife is Semiligoror. Father of Luke-e-lang and Olevat. Lamotrek, Caroline Islands, Micronesia. (Christian, 1897: 198)

Alla Tualla   The principal god of the tribes of Pasummah Lebar and Pasummah Ulu Manna. Sumatra, Indonesia. (Coleman, 1832: 361)

Alloloa   A creator god, but not worshipped. The Anyi, Ghana. (Grottanelli, 1967: 41)

Along, Phy-Ra-Ta-Ra   The creator god. The Ahom, Tai. (Gurdon, 1925, 1: 236)

Alow   The creator god of the Kachari. Assam/Burma. (Pettazzoni, 1956: 297)

Alquntam, Aelquntam   The supreme and chief god, though not all-powerful, inhabits the sky and sometimes the sun; controls the movements of the sun and moon. He was the creator of men and animals and of the "four supernatural Carpenters" who formed the world and populated it. One of his "principal functions is that of acting as leader of the *kusiut* dances of the supernatural beings." With his advisers he determines for the coming year "who shall be made a *kusiut,* who shall be born, who shall die." He is also called Senxälotła, Smaiaikila, Smaialotła, Snuselkäls, Menakais, Tätä, Ixilqotłam, Nonodjonostem, Sitlemsta, Nuxekmälsaix, O·tłok di Stältemx. The Bella Coola Indians, British Columbia. (McIlwaith, 1948, 1: 32–41; Lissner, 1961: 91, 92)

Altjerra   The benevolent supreme deity of the Arunndta. His name at Fowler's Bay—Nyege; among the Aluridja—Tukura. Australia. (Basedow, 1925: 279, 295)

Altjira iliinka   The beneficent supreme god of the Aranda. Among the Aranda Tjoritja he is malevolent. Australia. (Roheim, 1972: 65–66; Spencer, 1927: 593)

Aluberi   The remote supreme god of the Arawak. Among some also the creator, "their highest conception of a first cause." Guiana. (Brinton, 1868: 58; Tylor, 1891: 288; Alexander, 1920: 259)

Aluelap, Aluelob, Analap   The remote supreme sky-god and creator, father of Lugelung, to whom he leaves the affairs of the world. Ifaluk, the Carolines, Micronesia. (Spiro, 1951: 289; Pettazzoni, 1956: 342–343)

Alwani   Thunder, sometimes confused with Wan-Aisa. They are considered as the creators of the world and of mankind. The Mosquito, Nicaragua/Honduras. (Conzemius, 1932: 129)

Amabisa   The supreme deity of the Bakumu. Congo. (Williams, 1936: 82)

Amade Onhia, Amad'ongha   The supreme deity and god of thunder and of rain. His wife is Ale, the earth goddess. The Etche Ibo, Nigeria. (Talbot, 1967: 52, 61)

Amamikyu   A goddess who, with the god Shinerikyu, is credited with the creation. Okinawa, the Ryukyu Islands. (Lebra, 1966: 96)

Amma   The creator of the universe and their High God; "all the relatives on the father's side are *Amma* (God)"; on the mother's side—Nommo (the universe). The Dogon, the Mande, the Habe, Mali/Upper Volta/Nigeria. (Paulme, 1973: 92; Ottenburg, 1960: 366; Davidson, 1969: 170; Parrinder, 1969: 23; Griaule and Dieterlen, 1954: 85, 91; Meek, 1931: 191)

Ammon   The ram-god. Originally an oracular sky and fertility god who later became the great supreme god of the Berber. Libya. (Meyerowitz, 1958: 139–141; Bel, 1938: 73)

Amotken, Amotquen   The beneficent supreme god and creator of heaven, earth, and mankind. The Flathead, the Coeur d'Alene (Salishan tribes), Idaho and Washington. (Teit, 1927/28: 185–186, 383; Clark, 1966: 66–68; Schmidt, 1933: 114–115)

Ana   The Akkadian sky god, the chief deity and creator of the universe at Erech. He becomes the Semitic Anu. Near East. (Sayce, 1898: 186–187)

An Alai Chotoun   A goddess of the earth who is also the creator. Associated with Urun (urung) Ai (Toyon). The Yakut, Siberia. (Eliade, 1964: 187; Czaplicka, 1969: 278)

An'an', Etyny   The creator of the universe and of mankind. The Koryak, Siberia. (Antropova, 1964: 868)

Ananse   The Spider who created the sun, the moon, the stars, and mankind. But it was Nyame who gave man life. Ghana. (Queval, 1968: 16)

Añañ-vairgin The supreme being of the Chuckchee. Siberia. (Bogoras, 1928: 307)

Andin Bamban The wife of Ranying Pahatara in the creation myth. While he was away she agreed with Peres (Jata) that man should die and return again, and helped him with the creation of this kind of man, which Ranying Pahatara agreed with on his return. The Ngaju, Borneo. (Scharer, 1963: 22, 23)

Andriamanitra The creator of the universe and all therein to whom offerings of the first fruits are made. He instituted *Vintana* which is the power which is destiny. The Malagasy, Madagascar. (Ruud, 1960: 10, 20, 28)

Angana-Nzambi The supreme deity of certain Bantu peoples of Central Brazil. (Bastide, 1960: 560)

Angiki e Ha The wrathful supreme god. Rennell Island, Polynesia. (MacGregor, 1943: 33)

Anguta The supreme being who created "the earth, sea, and heavenly bodies" carries the dead to his daughter Sidne (Sedna) in Adlivun where they remain for a year before going to other afterworlds. The Nugumiut of Frobisher Bay, Canada. (Boas, 1884/85: 583; MacCulloch, 1925, 11: 825)

Anna The omniscient supreme being. The Kunama, Ethiopia. (Rossini, 1925, 6: 492; Pettazzoni, 1956: 42)

Antaboga "Through meditation, the world serpent Antaboga created the turtle Bedawang, on whom lie coiled two snakes as the foundation of the World." Bali, Indonesia. (Covarrubias, 1937: 7)

Antswa The chief deity of the Abkhasians. The name is in the plural as he is considered multiform—of many parts. Caucasus. (Janashia, 1937: 118–119)

Anu In one of the Akkadian creation myths he created the heavens while Enlil created the earth. Near East. (Kramer, 1961: 122)

Anuto A beneficent deity who created the sky, the earth, and mankind. The Tami Islanders, New Guinea. (Haddon, 1925, 9: 347)

Anyambi, Anyambia, Any-ambye The supreme being and the creator god who is not wholly benevolent as he is capricious. The Mpongwe, Gabon. (Mockler-Ferryman, 1925, 9: 277; Budge, 1973, 1: 365; Lang, 1968: 240; Williams, 1936: 122)

Anyangwu A god who forms a triad with Chuku and Agbala, sometimes inter-identified. Seems to mean the supreme being, the sun. The Umundri at Awka, Niger Basin. (Jeffreys, 1972: 724–726)

Anyara The supreme being of the Ndoro, associated with the sun. Nigeria. (Jeffreys, 1951: 104)

Apistotoke The creator god who was both beneficent and malignant. The Blackfeet, Plains Indians. (Maclean, 1876: 433)

Apna-Apha Mother Earth/Father Sky, a dual deity who was the supreme being and creator. Also called Uru-Wadu, "Moon-Sun." Kisar Island, Indonesia. (Pettazzoni, 1956: 13, 335)

A-p'u-gga-sa The creator god of the Lolos. China. (Graham, 1961: 83)

Ara Primeval creator god, in the form of a bird, who created the heavens, and with Irik, created mankind from clay. The Sea Dyaks of Sarawak, Borneo. (Nyuak, 1906: 16, 17; Sarawak Gazette, 1963: 21)

Aramazd The benevolent and most powerful supreme god is the creator of the heavens and the earth, the giver of abundance and prosperity. He is the father of all the gods and forms a triad with Anahit and Vahagn. Named Ahura Mazda in Iran. Armenia. (Ananikian, 1925, 1: 795; 1964: 17–21; Gray, 1930: 23)

Aramfe The god and creator of the heavens. He sent his sons Oduwa and Orisha "to create the world and to people it." In early days he was also the god of thunder. The Yoruba, Nigeria. (Wyndham, 1921: 13–15, 107–108)

Areop-Enap He existed in a mussel shell in the primordial sea. He "changed the little snail into the moon" and had the worm that was there separate the upper and lower shells of the mussel to make the sky and the earth. The worm died and made the salty sea. The large snail became the sun. The Nauru, Micronesia. (Leach, 1956: 184)

Arikuagnon The creator of the world whose wife was Pananmakoza, and whose son was Arikapua. The Amniapa and Guaratagaja, Bolivia and Brazil. (Métraux, 1942: 151; Levi-Strauss, 1948, 1: 378–379)

Arnam Kethe Their great god is a house god who lives in heaven. Offerings of a pig are made him every three years unless there is reason for more frequent sacrifice. The Mikirs, Assam and India. (Biswas, 1956: 102; Lyall, 1925, 8: 629; Barkataki, 1969: 58)

Asai, Isahi The supreme being of the Logoli. Kenya. (Wagner, 1949: 168)

Ashur The great god of the city of Ashur was the supreme deity and a god of war and of fertility. His wife was Ninlil. Assyria. (Jastrow, 1898: 82, 128, 189; Jacobsen, 1970: 37; Larousse, 1968: 57)

Asista The supreme being, who is also the sun, created man and beast, is the beneficent giver of all things. The Nandi, Kenya. (Hollis, 1909: 41; Budge, 1973, 1: 382; Pettazzoni, 1956: 8)

Asobëe The supreme deity of the Wabendu. Congo. (Williams, 1936: 82)

Assara Mazaas The creator god worshipped by Ashurbanipal. Assyria. (Larousse, 1968: 312)

Assiss The omnipotent and beneficent supreme being, associated with the sun. The Elgeyo, Kenya. (Massam, 1927: 188)

Ataguju The creator god—of the heavens, the earth, and all therein. The Quechua. Among the Huamachuco Indians the creator of everything as well as two servants known variously as Sagradzabra and Vaungrabad, Sugadcabra and Uciozgrabad, or as Uvigaicho and Vustiqui, who were considered as intercessors by the people. Peru. (Means, 1931: 429; Brinton, 1868: 152; Kubler, 1946: 406)

Atahocan The Great Spirit who created the heavens and the earth and all things. The Montagnais, Labrador/Quebec. (Alexander, 1964: 20; Emerson, 1884: 5; Janness, 1932: 170)

Atala The supreme deity who lives in the heavens. South Borneo. (Brinton, 1897: 77)

Atete Goddess of fertility of men and animals, and also of childbirth. According to some she also created the world giving to men and women their working tools. The Galla, Ethiopia. (Huntingford, 1955: 76; Bartels, 1969: 407; Rossini, 1925, 6: 491)

Atgezual The Great Spirit of the Puelche. Argentina. (Cooper, 1946, 5: 167)

Ati The highest goddess of the Ica of the Sierra Nevada of Santa Marta. She inhabits their heaven and dominates their life and death. Colombia. (Wilbert, 1974: 5, 14)

Atius Tirawa The beneficent omnipotent and omnipresent chief god created the features of the earth. He determines and controls man's good or bad fortune. The Pawnee, Nebraska. (Grinnell, 1893: 114, 121, 123; Lissner, 1893: 87)

Atua i Kafika The supreme god invoked to bring prosperity and to suppress winds and prevent storms. He is worshipped in the preparation of tumeric, "his perfume." Tikopia, Polynesia. (Firth, 1967, 2: 39, 282, 416, 436)

Aumia A god of the creation deities known only because he is mentioned in the sacred chants. The Marquesas, Polynesia. (Handy, 1923: 244)

Auramazda In the Achaemenian dynasty he was the variation of Ahura Mazda as the creator god. Persia. (Frazer, 1926: 33)

Awondo The sky and creator god who controlled "all natural phenomena . . . the author of good and evil." The Munshi, Nigeria. (Meek, 1925: 31)

Awundu, Aondo The omniscient supreme being, a sky god and creator, is manifest in and controls the natural forces. The Tiv, Nigeria. (East, 1939: 230–232; Temple, 1922: 301–302)

Ayeba The creator goddess was also the supreme deity. The Nembe, Niger Delta, Africa. (Alagoa, 1964: 2, 3)

Ayenanara The name of the supreme being among some of the Iduwini people. Nigeria. (Jeffreys, 1972: 730)

Ayibu The name of the supreme being of some of the Iduwini people. Nigeria. (Jeffreys, 1972: 730)

Ayi Toyon The supreme god of the Ayi who created the world and rules the universe, is the giver of children, and of vegetable and cattle fertility. The Yakut, Siberia. (Jochelson, 1900/02: 235)

Ayo-Caddi-Aymay Their only god who created all things. The Caddo, Plains Indians. (Swanton, 1942: 210–211)

Azmaz The chief deity of the Iberians. A local aspect of Aramazd. Caucasus. (Ananikian, 1964: 24, 382n.22)

Bagaios The Phrygian equivalent of Zeus. Asia Minor. (Fiske, 1900: 104)

Bahkoore-Mahishtsedah A variant name of Akbatekdia, the supreme being. The Crow, Montana. (Wildschut, 1960: 1)

Bahyra   The creator god of the heavens and the earth who "expressed his wrath by thunder and lightning." The Apiaca, Brazil. (Nimuendaju, 1948, 2: 319)

Baiamai   He is considered by some to be the creator. Others believe he created his son, Burambin, who then created the world. The Wellington tribes, Australia. (Tylor, 1891: 292)

Baiame   The omniscient intangible great spirit is self-created, lives in the sky, is the creator of all things. He is important in initiation rites; he "receives the souls of the innocent." His voice is the thunder, his will is manifest through the wind. The Kamilaroi, Wiradjuri, and Euahlayi. Australia. (Reed, 1965: 15, 21; Elaide, 1958: 41, 42; 1964: 136; 1973: 6, 134–135; Wales, 1957: 7; Howitt, 1904: 494; Poignant, 1967: 117)

Baira   The supreme being of the Amar Kokke. Ethiopia. (Cerulli, 1956: 66)

Bairo   The supreme being of the Banna. Ethiopia. (Cerulli, 1956: 66)

Bakuli   The supreme being of the Mbula. Nigeria. (Williams, 1936: 216)

Bali Penyalong   The beneficent supreme being who is only and always approached with a sacrificial pig as messenger to him. He is also god of war. The Kenyahs, Borneo. (Hose, 1912: 6; MacKenzie, 1930: 254)

Bali (Balli) Utong   The supreme being of the Klementans. Borneo. (Hose, 1912: 79; Pettazzoni, 1956: 332)

Balli Lutong   The supreme being of the Punans. Borneo. (Pettazzoni, 1956: 332)

Bamballe   The supreme being of the Konso. Also called Waq. Ethiopia. (Cerulli, 1956: 66)

Bartsing   With Dgagha, creators of "the sun, moon, and stars." The Amia, Formosa. (Campbell, 1925, 6: 87)

Bathala   Also called Abba. A bird god, the chief god and "creator of all things—the sea, the sky, the earth, and all the vegetation." He was just but, nevertheless, punitive of sinners. The Tagalog, Philippines. (Kroeber, 1918, 2: 40; Jocano, 1969: 8, 9)

Bathalang Meicapal   A vague concept of a supreme being/creator deity. The Tagalo-Bisaya, Philippines. (Best, 1892: 197)

Batto   The creator god who is believed to be dead. The Sidamo, Ethiopia. (Cerulli, 1956: 129)

Bayagaw, Banagaw   The god of wild animals and fish was also an omniscient, omnipotent supreme being and creator. The Negritos, Allakapan District, Philippines. (Pettazzoni, 1956: 319; Wales, 1957: 12)

Bec diłxił xastin   Black Metal Old Man, a pre-existent deity, one of the four primordial beings (in one creation myth). In another he appears as one of the four creators of earth and sky. The Apache Indians, Western United States. (Goddard, 1918: 7, 27)

Bel   A Palmyrene and Nabataean creator god who rules the universe and man's destiny. A later name of Enlil. Near East. (Vriezen, 1963: 67; Jastrow, 1898: 52, 53, 62)

Beru Pennu   The creator deity of the Khonds. India. (Roy, 1928: 20)

Bhagavan   The supreme deity among the Korwas is also the sun god. (Biswas, 1956: 102) Among the Raj Gonds he is "the giver of life and death." (Furer-Haimendorf, 1974: 250). Among the Baiga he is the creator who instituted the rules of conduct and whose present "functions are mainly concerned with life and death." India. (Elwin, 1939: 56)

Bhagwan   The otiose supreme deity is revered but not worshipped, is identified with the sun among the Kawar and Korwas. Also the Baiga, the Bhils, India. (Berreman, 1963: 83; Naik, 1956: 173; Crooke, 1894: 9; Russell, 1916, 3: 399; Briggs, 1920: 200)

Biheko   A beneficent but remote high god and the creator. Also known as Sebahanga, Kazoba. The Kiga, Uganda. (Taylor, 1962: 126)

Bilika   The supreme god who when angry sends bad weather and kills people. His wife is Mite. The Akarkede, Australia. (Roheim, 1972: 103)

Biral   "The greatest spirit" of the Kabi and Wakka tribes. Queensland, Australia. (Mathew, 1910: 170)

Black Hactcin   The most powerful of the Hactcin, the only beings of the beginning when nothing existed—yet they possessed all necessary for the creation of the universe and all pertaining to it. They lived in the underworld where Black Hactcin created the original animal and bird from whom all others derived, mankind, the sun and the moon. The Jicarilla Apache, New Mexico. (Campbell, 1974: 232–236; Leach, 1949, 1: 147)

Boa, Buga The omnipotent and omniscient supreme being and sky god who controls all life. The Tungus, Siberia. (Lissner, 1961: 161; Wallis, 1939: 90; Eliade, 1964: 9, 499; Pettazzoni, 1956: 263)

Boorala The benevolent creator god of the Cape River tribes. Southeast Australia. (Howitt, 1904: 504)

Boora (or **Bura** or **Bella**) **Pennu** The supreme being and god of light is among some also the creator. The Khonds, Orissa, India. (Robertson, 1911: 109; Biswas, 1956: 102; Eliade, 1959: 122; Crooke, 1925, 7: 651; Martin, 1914: 29)

Bope The self-existent, omnipresent creator god who is in all things, all things are him. Most animals, fish, and important plants are his food "and must be offered to him through an intermediary before consumption." He is identified with the jaguar and is believed to cause deaths. When one occurs the Bororo take revenge by killing a jaguar which is "surrounded with ritual." Brazil. (Levak, 1973: 180–183; Kozak, 1963: 42)

Boram The sun god and the creator who is invoked at the sowing season. The Bhuiyas, Bengal. (Frazer, 1926: 616)

Boro The supreme being of the Kharias. India. (Biswas, 1956: 102)

Brahmā The personified form of the universal and supreme Absolute is Brahmā as the creator of the universe and of all things. The Prajapatis "are called his spiritual sons, enumerated as Marici, Atri, Anginas, Pulastya, Pulaha, Kratu, and Vasistha." India. (Keith, 1917: 107–108; Martin, 1914: 82; Elwin, 1949: 4; Danielou, 1964: 232–233)

Bruku, Buku The omniscient supreme god, a sky god. Dahomey/Togo. (Parrinder, 1949: 19, 28; 1961: 19; Pettazzoni, 1956: 36; Frazer, 1926: 115)

Buddha The benevolent highest of the gods of the Sinhalese. Ceylon. (Ames, 1964: 35; Leach, 1958: 309–310; Obeyesekere, 1966: 5)

Budha Deo With Dhula Deo the benevolent yet punitive supreme deities. The Gonds of the Eastern Ghauts, India. (Rao, 1910: 796)

Buga The heaven god who caused the land and water to form and who also created humans. The Evenks, the Tungus, Siberia. (Michael, 1963: 64; Pettersson, 1957: 23; MacCulloch, 1964: 371; Eliade, 1964: 9, 499)

Bumba The self-existent primordial creator who vomited up his creations: the sun, moon, and stars, and "nine living creatures," Koy Bumba, Pongo Bumba, Ganda Bumba, Yo, Kono Bumba, Tsetse, Myanyi Bumba, Budi, and mankind. He had three sons: Nyonye Ngana, Chonganda., Chedi Bumba. The Bushongo, Zaire. (Eliade, 1967: 91–92; Larousse, 1968: 483)

Bumi Truko Sang-y-ang Dewato Bator The all-powerful god. Java, Indonesia. (Coleman, 1832: 357)

Bundjil, Bunjil The All-Father, the supreme being, who after creating the earth, the trees, men, and the animals withdrew and lives beyond the "dark heaven" manifesting his will through the rainbow. He is the father of Bimbeal and Karakarook. Among some he is the demiurge and the star Altair. The Kulin, the Kurnai, the Wotjobaluk, Australia. (Eliade, 1958: 41, 42; 1973: 134, 193; Wales, 1957: 7; Howitt, 1904: 492; Fallaize, 1925, 12: 63)

Burambin Some consider him the creator of the world rather than Baiamai, his father. The Wellington tribes, Australia. (Tylor, 1891: 292)

Bura Pen(nu) The supreme being and creator god. Also the god of light. His wife is Piteri. The Kandhs, Khonds, India. (Crooke, 1925, 7: 651; Biswas, 1956: 102; Eliade, 1959: 122; Rao, 1910: 796)

Buruku A supreme being and creator goddess identified with the moon. Among some a male deity. The Akan, Ghana. (Meyerowitz, 1958: 23, 24, 100)

Cabahuil, Qabauil The Supreme Being, Heart of Heaven, pre-existent to its creation of the cosmos, of heaven and earth, became essentially otiose (involved only with the universe), delegating the active roles and works to his "sons and Hypostases," who must meet and counsel on each creative act. They are: "Tzakol, Bitol, Tepeu, Gucumatz, Alom, and Cajolom, the formative aggregate of the Creator god or god-Seven." They are "no more than vital extrusions of It itself." The Quiché Maya, Guatemala. (Girard, 1979: 28, 31, 34, 35)

Cacoch, Kacoch A remote creator god of the Maya. Central America. (Thompson, 1970: 202)

Caddi Ayo The supreme being of the Caddoan Indians. Texas. (Chamberlain, 1900: 51; Waring, 1965: 33)

Cagn, Kaang The mantis god who was the creator or fashioner of all things. His wife was Coti. The Bushmen, Namibia/Lesotho. (Land, 1887: 175; Smith, 1950: 89; Larousse, 1968: 476)

C'ai A sky god "the same as Kai, who, not very long ago, was almost certainly the Supreme Being of all Gimira peoples." The Beneso, Ethiopia. (Cerulli, 1956: 94)

Calegede The supreme being who is identified with the sky. The Maji, Ethiopia. (Cerulli, 1956: 94)

Cao Dai The "Supreme Being symbolized by the eye above the altar." South Vietnam. (White and Garrett, 1971: 315)

Cara Among some Andamanese he was the first being, the ancestor, who created the earth, sun and moon, and caused the earth to be peopled. Andaman Islands, Bay of Bengal. (Radcliffe-Brown, 1967: 144, 193; Roheim, 1972: 29, 30)

car cajany The supreme god and creator. The Tatars of Minusinsk, Siberia. (Eliade, 1958: 61)

Caribou God The supreme deity of the Indians of the Labrador Peninsula who has five names: tepenamwesu (Chief Indian God); kanapenekastciwhiu; utnimatcisu, "Giver of Food"; pukwicemnimakin, "Giver of food to hunters"; tcamicuminu, "Grandfather of all." His home is in the far north. (Cooper, 1934: 35–36)

Caugh The raven god of the Tsimshians who created the world and all living things. British Columbia. (Deans, 1891: 34)

Chabatta Hatartstl One of the names of the supreme being to whom very little attention is paid. The Makah Indians, Washington. (Swanton, 1925, 12: 663)

Chaipakomat The sometimes used conjoined name of the two brother creator gods, Tuchaipa and Yokomatis. The Dieguen̄, California. (Du Bois, 1908: 233; Kroeber, 1925: 789)

Cha-kal-le The supreme being, a "negative being" with little active attributes. The Pomo, California. (Powers, 1877: 161)

Chanum With Woi-shun, parents of "all things in heaven and on earth." The Kachin, Burma. (Scott, 1964: 263)

Chareya The beneficent sky god who created the earth and all living beings. The Cahrocs, California. (Bancroft, 1886, 3: 90)

Chata The creator god of the Tonga of Malawi and Zambia. (Mbiti, 1970, 2: 335)

Chebbeniathan The supreme being and sky god to whom promises are made when hurricanes threaten or thunder is near. Algonquin Indians. (Eliade, 1958: 53, 55)

Cheptalil The benevolent supreme god who is invoked for help. Also called Asista. The Kipsigis, Kenya. (Orchardson, 1961: 20, 21)

Ches The supreme god of the Timote who was associated with the high mountains and with lakes. Venezuela. (Trimborn, 1968: 94, 95; Zerries, 1968: 251–252)

Chi The supreme being and creator conceived of as an earth god or goddess and a sky god as one being with the resulting confusion wherein Chi is sometimes male, sometimes female. The Ibo, the Ekoi, Nigeria. (Meek, 1931: 179; Talbot, 1967: 52; Williams, 1936: 199; Jeffreys, 1972: 728)

Chicociagat Associated with Tamagastat and Cipattonal in the creation. The Nicarao of Nicaragua. (Lothrop, 1926: 68)

Chicuna The supreme god and "the origin of all things." Darien, Panama. (Stout, 1947: 99; Alexander, 1920: 193)

Chido The supreme being and a sky god associated with celestial phenomena, the giver of rain. As the creator he is also known as Ama or Ma and associated with the earth. They are identified with each other yet are considered quite separately. The Jukun, Nigeria. (Meek, 1931: 178–179, 184–185; Williams, 1936: 217; Jeffreys, 1972: 731)

Chieng The supreme god and the sun. The Juo, Kenya. (Butt, 1952: 116; Budge, 1973, 1: 381)

Chikara The otiose creator of all animate and inanimate things. South Rhodesia. (Gelfand, 1962: 8; Mbiti, 1970, 2: 332)

Chilenga The creator god of the Ba-Ila, South Africa, and of the Ila, Zambia. (Junod, 1962: 375; Mbiti, 1970, 2: 330)

Chiminigagua, Chimigagua, Ciminagua The omnipotent supreme god and creator of the sun and moon, of all things in the universe. The Chibcha, the Muiscas, Colombia. (Alexander, 1920: 199; Loeb, 1931: 543; Kroeber, 1946: 908; Queval, 1968: 30; Trimborn, 1968: 90; Brinton, 1882: 222–223; Osborne, 1968: 110)

Chincha Camac The creator god and tutelary deity of the Chincha. Peru. (Alexander, 1925, 3: 740–745)

Chineke, Chi The beneficent chief deity and creatress. She protects from evil and punishes wrongdoers. The Ibo, Nigeria. (Williams, 1936: 203; Ezeanya, 1963: 1)

Chineke, Chukwu Abiama The name of Chukwu as the creator of all things. The Igbo, Nigeria. (Uchendu, 1965: 95)

Chiowotamahke The creator of the earth and of mankind. He flew over the world as a butterfly to find a desirable place for man. His son is Szeukha. The Pima Indians, Arizona. (Bancroft, 1886, 3: 78; Leach, 1949, 1: 176)

Chi-uku, Chi-ukwu, Chukwu The omnipotent, omnipresent, omniscient and all-seeing supreme god is the beneficent creator who provides the rain, gives mankind the power to create and his personal life-force. Agwù Nsî, Ubu, Ulaasi, Ekweñsu, Òsebùlùwà—all are Chukwu. The Ibo, the Ìgbo, Nigeria. (Meek, 1943: 112; Horton, 1956: 17–21; Ezeanya, 1967: 35; Parrinder, 1949: 21; Uchendu, 1965, 94–95; Williams, 1936: 210; Isichei, 1978: 178)

Chiuta The supreme being and the creator of all things; also associated with rain. The Tonga, the Tumbuka, Malawi and Rhodesia. (Frazer, 1926: 1983; Young, 1950: 50–52; Williams, 1936: 259)

Cholas The supreme being whose eyes are the stars lives in the sky. He is all-seeing and all-knowing; punitive measures are disease and death. The Alacaluf, Tierra del Fuego. (Pettazzoni, 1956: 6, 21, 423)

Chuen A creator god of the Maya. Central America. (Thompson, 1970: 322)

Chuewut Ma-cki The god who created the earth and all things. Apparently a variant spelling of Chiowotmahke. The Pima and Papago Indians, Arizona. (Neff, 1912: 51)

Chuku Oke Abiama The supreme god of the Oratta tribe. The Ibo, Nigeria. (Jeffreys, 1972: 730)

Chukwu *See* **Chi-uku**

Chum-dende The supreme deity of the Sherpas. Nepal. (Furer-Haimendorf, 1964: 195)

Chunchon The supreme god. Korea. (Clark, 1932: 195)

Chusor Phoenician god who "created the cosmic egg, which he then split into heaven and earth." He is also said to be a god of the sea with Asherat and a god ruling over the seasons. (Albright, 1968: 223; Herm, 1975: 111)

čičel siem The supreme god and creator of the world of the Upper Stalo Indians. British Columbia. (Duff, 1952: 119–120)

Cipattonal, Cipattoval Wife of Tamagostad (Tamagastat) and with him the supreme beings and creators of all things. The Nicarao, the Nahua, Nicaragua. (Lothrop, 1926: 66; Bancroft, 1886, 3: 490; Alexander, 1920: 120)

Cisumphi The creator god of the Matengo. Malawi. (Mbiti, 1970, 2: 333)

Cocijo The supreme god was a jaguar god, a god of water and of rains, and a god of the year. The Zapotecs, Monte Alban, Mexico. (Krickeberg, 1968: 55; Helfritz, 1971: 74; Peredo, 1974: 19)

Con, Coniraya A solar deity, the son of the Sun, who came as a creator god and introduced "agricultural terracing and irrigation," but was later dissatisfied and "converted the region to desert and disappeared." Among the Huarochiri he shared creative activities with Pariacaca. Coastal Peru. (Mishkin, 1940: 225–226; Osborne, 1968: 96, 107; Métraux, 1949: 560)

Coqui Xee, Coquixilla The self-existent god of the beginning, the "supreme force," of whom all deities "were but aspects, attributes, or refractions." He was also called Pijetao, or Pije Xoo, as Time, or its source, as he ruled over "the thirteen gods of the Zapotec sacred calendar." Oxaca, Mexico. (Whitecotton, 1977: 165; Alexander, 1920: 87)

Cotaá A beneficent sky deity who created the earth and "maintained the sun, moon and stars in their courses and made the earth fruitful." The Macobi of the Chaco tribes, Bolivia and Paraguay. (Osborne, 1968: 122)

Cotsipamapot An "old woman . . . made the whole country." The Southern Paiute Indians, Southwest United States. (Lowie, 1924: 157)

Coyocop-chill The supreme spirit and the "author of all things." The Natchez, Mississippi. (Swanton, 1911: 167; Waring, 1965: 33)

Coyote (1) The supreme being among the Coast Miwok, California. (Schmidt, 1933: 45) (2) The creator deity, sometimes working alone, sometimes collaborating with another, and among some the source of the imperfections found in man. He also has trickster characteristics among the Pomo and the Maidu. The Achomawi, Maidu, Miwok, Pomo, and Kuksu, of California; the Papago of Sonora, Mexico. (Kroeber, n.d.: 179, 187; 1912: 99; 1925: 270; Dixon, 1908: 159–160; Lissner, 1961: 90; Loeb, 1931: 520–525; 1932: 73–74, 101)

Cuaiguerry   The omniscient chief god of the Achagua. Venezuela and Colombia. (Hernandez de Alba, 1948, 2: 410; Pettazzoni, 1956: 417)

Cuerohperi, Cueravaperi   The mother goddess, the creatress, who gave birth to all the features of the earth, the animals, and mankind. She represented the female creative principle. She was a goddess of fertility who sometimes sent famine and drought, was offered human hearts in sacrifice. The Tarascans, Michoacans, Mexico. (Boyd, n.d.: 2, 3; Craine and Reindorp, 1970: 133, 197; Krickeberg, 1968: 59)

Cukun   The supreme being and the creative principle. The name for Pon in the Tundra dialect. The Yakaghir, Siberia. (Jochelson, 1900/02: 140, 234)

Cumbanama   The remote supreme god who is not worshipped. Also called Neche. The Jivaro, Peru/Ecuador. (Steward and Métraux, 1948, 1: 626; Stirling, 1938: 121)

Cuta   The creator god of the Ambo. Zambia. (Mbiti, 1970, 2: 327)

Dagda   The all-wise chief god of the Irish, the beneficent All-father "who arranges, provides, and superintends everything." He was a god of the sky, of the atmosphere, as well as a god of the earth symbolizing "fecundity and virility." An omnicompetent deity—the leader in times of war and the "lawgiver in times of peace." His wife or mistress was Boann (Boand), the river goddess. He was considered the father of Oengus, Brigit, Danu, and possibly Ogma. His attributes were a club and a cauldron. (MacBain, 1917: 121; MacCana, 1970: 33, 66; MacCulloch, 1911: 72, 77–78, 81; Ross, 1967: 166; Squire, 1906: 54–55, 78)

Dagubal   A demiurge, son of Wolaro. Kimberley, Australia. (Capell, 1939: 386)

Daksha   As one of the Prajapatis he is a god of the creation. He is also one of the Adityas, is regarded as a god of skillfulness, of intelligence. He is the father of Uma and of the twenty-seven Naksatras who are the wives of Soma. India. (Larousse, 1968: 335; Jayne, 1962: 166; MacCulloch, 1964: 18, 28, 136; Bhattacharji, 1970: 216)

uDali   The supreme being and creator god of the Xhosa. Also called uThixo, Qamata. He is "the rewarder of good and the punisher of evil." South Africa. (Schapera, 1937: 263; Williams, 1936: 293)

Daramulun   The supreme being and a primordial god whose voice is heard in the bull-roarer and in the thunder. He is important in initiation rites and gives medicine men their powers. The Yuin, Southeastern Australia. (Eliade, 1973: 4–7; Howitt, 1904: 431; Wales, 1957: 7)

Dasan   Among some of the northern Pomo he is the creator god rather than Kuksu. With his father, Makila, brought civilization to the Pomo. California. (Loeb, 1932: 4; Sykes, 1952: 57)

Dau   The supreme being who is identified with the sky. The Beru Adikas, Ethiopia. (Cerulli, 1956: 94)

Debata   Creator of the sun, the moon, and the stars. The Bataks, Sumatra. Indonesia. (Frazer, 1926: 656)

Debelmelek   A name of Ktahandowit, the Great Spirit. The Penobscot, Maine. (Muller, 1968: 159)

Debwenu   The remote creator god of all things, but who is not directly involved in or with human affairs—no altars or sacrifices. Father of Do. The Bwa, Mali. (Capron, 1962: 148)

Deivam   The supreme being is also the creator. The Pulaya (Cochin). India. (Thaliath, 1956: 1032)

oDel, oDevel   The high god of the Gypsies who is "the principle of Good" and who is constantly at war with oBengh, the god of evil. Europe. (Clebert, 1967: 171–172)

Delquen Sagan Burkan   "World White God, is the highest existence in the Universe. He is also called Esege Malan. In him are three spirits: Baronye Tabin Tabung Tengeri, Zum Dishin Dirlun Tengeri, and Sagade Ugugun. . . . From the first spirit came the fifty-five Tengeris; from the second the forty-four Tengeris; the third has seven sons and seven daughters." He is invoked "for cattle, for grass, and for health." The Mongol, Buriat, Siberia. (Curtin, 1909: 118)

Dendid   The omnipotent, all-seeing, and beneficent supreme being of the Dinkas. Upper Nile, Africa. (Lang, 1968: 230)

Deur   A name of the supreme being or creator. The Koyas, Orissa, India. (Elwin, 1954: 636)

Deva An androgynous supreme being, all-seeing, who is invoked in oaths. All celestial, atmospheric phenomena are representations of him, which he uses to punish misdeeds. The Ngadha, Flores Island, Indonesia. (Pettazzoni, 1956: 333–334)

Dgagha With Bartsing the creators of "the sun, moon, and stars." The Amia, Formosa. (Campbell, 1925, 6: 87)

Dharam Deota He emerged from the primordial muddy water and created male and female from the dirt on his body. They had a son whom the gods saw and caused to be killed, from whose body and blood the earth was formed. "His head became the sun, his chest the moon." The Bhuiya, India. (Elwin, 1949; 29)

Dharmes(h) The supreme god and creator is identified with the sun. He is also called Biri Bela. He controls and punishes the gods and mankind, and is invoked to avert sickness or calamity. As the one who gave mankind seed and taught him its cultivation he is propitiated at the planting season. The Oraons, India. (Crooke, 1925, 2: 484; 1894: 9, 10; Roy, 1928: 1, 15–23; Elwin, 1940: 135; 1949: 312; Biswas, 1956: 102)

Dharmo Deota The benevolent supreme being of many tribes of Orissa. India. (Elwin, 1954: 636)

Dhatr Creator of the universe. He is also a god of procreation invoked for offspring and for longevity. He is identified with Prajapati. India. (Macdonell, 1897: 115; Bhattacharji, 1970: 217; Jayne, 1962: 169–170)

Dhorom The creator god who is invoked in marriage ceremonies. The Santals, India. (Mukherjea, 1962: 33)

Dhula Deo He and Budha Deo are supreme deities, beneficent as well as punitive. "A warlike deity but he is reverenced as a household god." The Gonds, India. (Rao, 1910: 796)

Didigwari The sky god of the Ik (Icien) is also the remote creator god. Sudan, Kenya, and Uganda. (Turnbull, 1972: 184)

Dioslele The creator of all things who is "omnipotent and omniscient, stern and unforgiving and personally directs the punishment of sinners and admits the souls to heaven." His wife is Nana, or Olotililisop. This is another name of Papa. The San Blas Cuna Indians, Panama. (Stout, 1947: 40, 41)

Divata, Diwata A god of the Bagobos of Mindanao who created the sea, land, trees, then humans. Philippines. (Raats, 1969: 7; Keeler, 1960: 49)

Diwata-sa-langit The "god of heaven . . . the most powerful and the almighty lord of all!" The Subanun of Zambanga, Philippines. (Jocano, 1969: 24)

Djamar The supreme being and creator, the giver of the moral laws and of initiation rites. He was responsible for the first bull-roarer. The Bad of the West Kimberley, Australia. (Eliade, 1973: 35–37)

Doeadilah The supreme being. Timor-laut, Indonesia. (Forbes, 1884: 22)

Doing-angung The benevolent and all-seeing supreme sky god. The Minyong Abors, Assam. (Furer-Haimendorf, 1954: 593)

Dokibatt The creator god of all things and of man. In Twana and Nisqually, Washington. (Maclean, 1876: 439; Eells, 1886/87: 672, 680)

Dombe A god who, with the goddess Niwa, created the world and its creatures. The Tangsas (Khemsing tribe), Indo/Burmese. (Dutta, 1959: 3)

rDo-rje chang The Yellow-caps (reformed school) regarded him "as the Supreme Power and Creator of all things." Same as Vajradhara. Tibet. (Getty, 1962: 3)

Dra "Dra is interpreted variously as the name of the Supreme Being, a mountain, or a plant called *tse* with special curative properties. Dra is also believed to be a kind of avenging spirit which can point out a guilty person." The Lendu, Congo/Sudan. (Baxter and Butt, 1953: 127)

Duadleera-wulan, Duad-lerwuan, Duadlera The supreme god who dwells in the sun is also the creator and giver of fertility with the rain and the sunshine. He is the guardian of marriages, is consulted about the future, and invoked in oath-taking and to heal illness. His wife is Duanluteh. The Kei Archipelago, Indonesia. (Frazer, 1926: 663, 665; Pettazzoni, 1956: 335)

Dua Nggae A dual omniscient, omnipresent supreme and primeval being. "Generally Dua is male and lives in the sky, Nggae is female and lives in the earth," but sometimes this is reversed. Flores Island, Indonesia. (Pettazzoni, 1956: 7, 334)

Duata, Ruata The highest god in Siau. Indonesia. (Kruijt, 1925, 7: 248)

Dula Deb, Pharsi Pen The supreme being of the Gonds. India. (Biswas, 1956: 102)

Dushara   The principal god and sun god of the Nabataeans at Petra and Damascus. Also a god of fertility, and son of the virgin earth goddess Chaabou. Jordan and Syria. (Langdon, 1931: 16–18; Macler, 1925, 12: 166)

Dyuok, Djuok   The all-seeing supreme being is also a wind god. The Luo, Kenya and Utanda. (Pettazzoni, 1956: 10, 38)

Ea   Though not his major function, Ea appears in Chaldea, Assyria, and Akkadia as a creator of the world. (Jastrow, 1898: 230; Dragomanov, 1961: 31; Kramer, 1961: 122)

Ea-pe   The supreme being and creator of all things. The Red Karens, Burma. (Scott, 1964: 270)

Eç   The high god and the creator, as well as a sky god, watches over his creations. His wife is Khosadam. The Yenesei, Siberia. (Larousse, 1973: 433–434)

Edenkema   A primeval high god and creator, omnipotent and omniscient, created Nyamenle, a sky god, who though in second place is sometimes merged with him. He also created Azele, the earth goddess. The Nzema (Akan), Ghana. (Grottanelli, 1967: 33–41)

Eehtreshbohedish   An earlier name for the supreme being, Akbatekdia, meaning "Starter of All Things," "First Worker." This name is used in prayers only in very important ceremonies and in vision-quests. The Crow, Montana. (Wildschut, 1960: 1, 2)

Efile-mokulu   The supreme being of the Basonge and others of the Baluba family is also the creator of the world and all in it. He is invoked in oaths but not offered prayers or sacrifices. Zaire. (Frazer, 1926: 149–150; Pettazzoni, 1956: 19, 20)

Ehlaumel   Thunder is "the one great deity in the creation." The Coast Yuki, California. (Kroeber, 1925: 216; Leach, 1949, 1: 342)

Eiuga   The supreme being who takes the form of an enormous lizard, whose voice is the thunder and whose breath is the wind. He causes storms when angry. The Onges, Little Andaman Island, Bay of Bengal. (Cipriano, 1966: 43)

El   The supreme god of the pantheons of Phoenicia, Canaan, Syria who forms a triad with his wife Asherat and his son Baal. He was a remote and all-powerful god associated with the sky. (Herm, 1975: 108–109; Obermann, 1948: 1; Albright, 1968: 120; 1956: 72–73; Gray, 1964: 121; Ferm, 1950: 121)

El Elyon   In ancient Jerusalem a name of El considered as a creator god. Canaan. (Vriezen, 1963: 53)

Elkunirsa   A name of El as the creator of the earth. The Hittite, Asia Minor. (Guterbock, 1961: 155)

Elo   An otiose high god who sends the rain and is invoked for the fertility of cattle. The Nuba, Sudan. (Seligman, 1925, 9: 403)

Elob   A name of the supreme being. The Hottentot, Orange Free State, South Africa. (Williams, 1936: 304)

Eng-ai   The supreme being whose name also means "rain." The Masai, Kenya. (Williams, 1936: 199)

Enku, Bakawa, Badango   The "omniscient Supreme Being" and the maker of thunder and lightning. Among the Negritos of the Seran River he is thought of as a bear. Malaya. (Pettazzoni, 1956: 311)

Enore   The supreme being of the Paressi who "carved the first man and woman out of a piece of wood." Bolivia. (Métraux, 1942: 170)

Epa   The principal god of the Ora who is protective of their welfare. Nigeria. (Clarke, 1944: 91)

Eraoranzan   The supreme being, a god of the heavens, is worshipped by the men and invoked for rain. The Hierro, Canary Islands. (Hooten, 1925, 7: 12, 64)

Erob   The omniscient supreme being and sky god, the benevolent creator, is invoked for rain, for success in hunting, and in the curing of illness—when he is called Xu. The Western Kung, the Otjimpolo-Khun, South Africa. (Schapera, 1951: 184–185, 190; Pettazzoni, 1956: 32)

Eros, Phanes   In his early form as the principle of love he participated in the creation of the world out of chaos. Greece. (Barthell, 1971: 7, 8; Murray, 1935: 190; Kerenyi, 1951: 17, 114)

Es   The sun god of the Betoi as the creator. Colombia. (Hernandez de Alba, 1948, 1: 398)

Esaugetuh Emissee   "Master of Breath," the preexistent supreme god and creator to whom the deserving go after death. He "appears to be the personification of the wind." The Choctaw, the Creek, Georgia, Alabama, Mississippi. (Brinton, 1868: 50; Spence, 1925, 3: 568)

Eschetewuarha   The all-powerful mother goddess who rules over all and sees that mankind receives rain from the cloud-bird, Osasero. The Chamacoco, Grand Chaco, South America. (Métraux, 1946, 1: 350–351; Zerries, 1968: 238; Queval, 1968: 40)

Esege-Burkhan One of three creator gods, with Shibegeni-Burkhan and Maidari-Burkhan, who caused the creation of the earth and then mankind. The Buriats, Siberia. (Klementz, 1925, 3: 11; MacCulloch, 1964: 375)

Ess (*See also* **Eç**) The benevolent high god who lives in the seventh sky. The Yenisei Ostyaks, Siberia. (Czaplicka, 1925, 9: 578)

Etin Known as " 'master', a name for the Supreme Being." Siberia. (Czaplicka, 1969: 355)

Eugpamolak Manobo The supreme god, "the first cause and creator" who, though he is remote, is "invited to all important ceremonies." The Bagobo, Philippines. (Cole, 1945: 191)

Fakavelikele The most powerful and the chief god of Futuna who, with Songia and Fitu, was considered the source of all evils. Polynesia. (Smith, 1892: 44; Burrows, 1936: 106; Williamson, 1933, 2: 179)

Fidi Mukulu The supreme being and sky god of the Basonga. Africa. (Foucart, 1925, 11: 581)

Fogatza The supreme being of the Gumuz. Also called Robboqua. Ethiopia. (Cerulli, 1956: 32)

fo grong thing The god of the Lepchas who created the world is also a god of procreation. His wife is na zong nyu. Sikkim. (Siiger, 1967, 1: 91; 1967, 2: 141)

Fuyengeni The powerful and only god of the Kom. British Cameroons. (Reyher, 1952: 226)

Gainji The creator god of the Papuan Keraki people. New Guinea. (Leach, 1956: 175)

Gala The creator god of the Gbunde. Liberia. (Schwab, 1947: 315)

Gamab The supreme being and creator is omniscient, learning all as being manifest in the wind. He causes thunder and lightning and lives in the sky where he receives the souls of the dead. The Heikom, South Africa; the Damara, Namibia. (Larousse, 1973: 521; Smith, 1950: 92; Schapera, 1951: 169, 189; Pettazzoni, 1956: 12, 16, 33)

Gao!na The oldest name of the creator god. *See* Hishe. The !Kung Bushmen, Nyae Nyae Region, Namibia. (Marshall, 1962: 225, 233)

Gard The supreme being and creator of all things who also "gave them their language." The Yurok, California. (Powers, 1877: 64)

Gasani The chief god of the Bakene "who has power over the sky and water . . . is consulted more especially in cases of sickness and when an epidemic appears." Uganda. (Roscoe, 1915: 154)

!Gaunau The supreme being of the Bushmen. South Africa. (Pettersson, 1953: 146)

Gauteovan The mother of all things and the creatress of the world, the sun, even the evil spirits causing diseases. She is known also as Hava Sibalaneuman and Kalguasiza. The Kagaba, Colombia. (Trimborn, 1968: 86; Park, 1946, 2: 885; Preuss, 1926: 63–65)

Gǎvǔr li yalyal The beneficent supreme being and creator of the world and of the gods. Yap Island, Micronesia. (Muller, 1917: 306, 308)

Gawang The omniscient supreme god who represents "the unity of the universe arising from the duality of sky and earth." He punishes with poor hunting, with famine and disease. The Konyak Naga, Assam/Burma. (Pettazzoni, 1956: 13, 16, 21; Wales, 1957: 46)

Geunetchen, Gunechen A name of the supreme being. The Araucanians, Chile/Argentina. (Cooper, 1946, 6: 746)

Gicelemuhkaong, Gishelemuhkaong The Great Spirit and creator. The Unami (Lenape Delaware) Indians, Eastern United States. (Eliade, 1967: 12; Harrington, 1921: 18; Swanton, 1928: 212)

Gicholan A name of the supreme being—"The-One-on-High." The Koryak, Siberia. (Czaplicka, 1969: 262)

Gicholetinvilan Etin A name of the supreme being—"The-Master-on-High." The Koryak, Siberia. (Czaplicka, 1969: 262)

Gikimoi The supreme being at Halmahera. The Molucca Islands, Indonesia. (Kern, 1925, 8: 347; Pettazzoni, 1956: 336)

Gindri The supreme being and creator of all things, the giver of life and death, provided medicinal herbs for the use of the healers. Zaire. (Bosch, 1928: 988–993; Baxter and Butt, 1953: 127)

Girgol-vairgin The powerful "Upper Being" who is "just and benevolent." The Chukchee, Siberia. (Bogoras, 1904/09: 314)

Givi-uranga A deity whose name "means "the highest'." The Otomac, Venezuela. (Tylor, 1891: 288)

Giziulitolek A name of Ktahandowit as the creator. The Penobscot, Maine. (Muller, 1968: 159)

Gnabaia The Great Spirit. The women believe the bull-roarer is his voice, that he "swallows the novices and later disgorges them as initiates." The Anula, Australia. (Eliade, 1976, 1: 188)

go'á-mëe The "ultimate reality . . . supreme force." The Desana, Colombia. (Reichel-Dolmatoff, 1971: 48)

Gonaldjictco xastin An insect—one of the four creators of the earth and sky in one version of the creation myth. The San Carlos Apache, New Mexico and Arizona. (Goddard, 1918: 27)

Gongpoh The remote supreme god who controls all other deities both good and evil. The Kadengs of the Dafla tribes. Assam. (Stonor, 1957: 4)

Go-noeno-hodi The demiurge. The Caduveo, Brazil. (Levi-Strauss, 1973: 74n)

Gorakhnath By some considered the supreme god. Tibet. (Snellgrove, 1957: 151)

Gounia Tiquaa, Gounja Ticquoa The chief god of the Khoi-Khoi (Hottentots), South Africa. (Hahn, 1881: 41; Williams, 1936: 295)

Gran Gadu, Gran Gudu The great god and creator. Surinam. (Kahn, 1929: 482; Whiton, 1971: 15)

Guamaonocon A name of Iocauna, the supreme being. The Antilles, West Indies. (Alexander, 1920: 24)

Guanari The always existent supreme being who created the other deities and mankind. The Makiritare, Venezuela. (Zerries, 1968: 248)

Guayavacuni, Guayavacunnee The benevolent but remote supreme being and creator was also the god of the dead. The Puelche, the Tehuelcho, the Teheulhets. Patagonia and Tierra del Fuego. (Lissner, 1961: 99; Cooper, 1946, 1: 157; Grubb, 1925, 9: 597; Osborne, 1968: 117)

Gucumatz An hypostasis of Cabahuil as creator god-Seven. With him and Gucumatz "there arrived the Word"; now the earth could be created because the hypostases of god-Seven was complete. Gucumatz is a general name as well as particular. He is the sun at its setting. The Quiché, Guatemala. (Girard, 1979: 31–33)

Gudatrigakwitl The pre-existent supreme god and creator of the earth, man, animals, and material things. The Wiyot, the Wishosk, California. (Kroeber, 1905: 91; 1925: 119; Lissner, 1961: 88)

Gueggiahora The remote supreme being who is not worshipped. The Camacan of Bahia, Brazil. (Alexander, 1920: 297)

Gueno An omnipotent deity of the Peul. Mali. (Imperato, 1972: 79)

Gulu The supreme god of the Manyema to whom men go when they die. Uganda. (Budge, 1973, 1: 364)

Gwaza The beneficent supreme god helpful against evil spirits and invoked for rain during drought, for health and luck at the time of the new moon, and for children and wealth. The Kagoro (Katab), Nigeria. (Gunn, 1956: 79, 101; Meek, 1931, 2: 58, 61; Temple, 1922: 190)

Haap'k!emnas A creator of all things who existed "in the dawn of time." The Takelma, Oregon. (Sapir, 1907: 34)

Habuiri The remote principal god and creator is a sky god who causes the growth of food plants. The Arawak, West Indies. (Lovén, 1935: 563–564)

Hachacyum, Hachakyum, Nohochacyum The creator and principal deity of the Lacandon who added "lime and rock and sand" to the unfirm earth (produced by K'akoch) giving it strength and shape. He is believed to have created men "fair-skinned and curly-haired" but Kisin darkened them spoiling his work. Kisin was also one of his creations as well as people, animals, insects, snakes. Chiapas, Mexico. (Perera and Bruce, 1982: 90, 271–272; Thompson, 1970: 202)

Hahgwehdiyu The beneficent creator who fashioned the universe from the body of his mother Ataensic and populated the earth with animals and birds. Twin of the evil spirit, Hahgwehdaetgah, who was banished to the underworld for disrupting his work. The Iroquois, Eastern United States. (Leach, 1949, 1: 474)

Hainuwele A primordial creator goddess in the sense that through her ritual murder by the primordial beings her body was cut into pieces and planted from which grew new plants, particularly tubers. From her arms Satene made a doorway through which all primordial beings passed, remaining humans or becoming animals, birds, etc. Ceram, New Guinea. (Eliade, 1967: 19)

Haka A goddess who, with her husband Tetoo, created the sky and the earth. The Marquesas, Polynesia. (Williamson, 1933: 67)

Hakui A god of the creation group of deities known only through mention in the sacred chants. The Marquesas, Polynesia. (Handy, 1923: 244)

Hamendiju The Great Spirit, a sky god, who rules the world. The Wyandot (Huron), area of Lakes Huron and Erie. (Barbeau, 1914: 301–302; Hale, 1891: 289)

Ha'o The supreme being and a sky god "whose eye is the sun." The Northern Sidama, Ethiopia. (Pettazzoni, 1956: 41)

Harisu The benevolent and invisible great god who is the source of all good. The Elema tribe, Papuan Gulf, New Guinea. (Holmes, 1902: 429)

Debata Hasi Asi The supreme being and creator god. The Bataks of Silindung, Sumatra, Indonesia. (Coleman, 1832: 364)

Hatala The creator of the earth which he "poured out" upon the head of Naga Busai, the serpent in the primeval water. Borneo. (MacKenzie, 1930: 308)

Ha-tartstl Cha-batt-a The Great Spirit whose real name is never given, a secret among the initiated. The Makah (Nootka), Cape Flattery, Washington. (Swan, 1869: 61)

Hatuibwari (1) A dragon-god and the creator. San Cristoval, Solomon Islands, Melanesia. (MacKenzie, 1930: 177). (2) **Hasibwari** "The supreme being . . . represented as a winged serpent with a human head" who created "a woman from red clay and the heat of the sun." Then a man from her rib. (Claimed not attributable to Christianity.) Arosi, Melanesia. (Leach, 1949, 1: 485)

Havaki The high god of the Tungus who is anthropomorphic, but is also associated with the sun. Siberia. (Czaplicka, 1925, 12: 475–476)

Hawenniyu, Ha-wen-ne-yu The beneficent and just Great Spirit who is considered self-existent, a god of virtue and harmony, the creator of "man, and all useful animals, and products of the earth." The Iroquois, Eastern United States. (Morgan, 1901: 147; Barbeau, 1914: 302; Tooker, 1964: 80)

Heammawihio The beneficent chief god and creator lives in the sky. For a time he lived with the people teaching them to make arrowpoints, knives, bows and arrows, how to hunt, and to make fire. He is invoked for longevity, good health, and success. The Cheyenne, Plains Indians. (Grinnell, 1962: 88–91; 1907: 171; Wallis, 1939: 138)

Hecco, Deoc, Deotshe The invisible supreme deity of the Sidama (the Kaffa and the Ometi). Ethiopia. (Rossini, 1925, 6: 489)

Heqo, Yero The omniscient supreme being and sky god of the western Sidama. Ethiopia. (Pettazzoni, 1956: 42)

Hinegba, Ihinegba The beneficent supreme being and creator, the source of sunshine and rain, but also of illness as punishment for evil. The Igbira, Nigeria. (Brown, 1955: 70)

Hintubuet The supreme being is "our grandmother" and the creatress of the sky, earth, and humans. New Mecklenburg, the Bismarck Archipelago, Melanesia. (Pettazzoni, 1956: 434)

Hireroi'wa A creator god of the Sirentde'wa. Brazil. (Maybury-Lewis, 1967: 284)

Hisagita imisi The beneficent Great Spirit of the Creek Indians who was represented by the bush fire. Also called Ibofanga. Among the Seminole Indians of Florida he was His-a-kit-a-mis i. Southeastern United States. (Swanton, 1946: 773; Waring, 1965: 34; MacCauley, 1883/84: 520)

Hishe The great self-created god who then created the lesser god, the earth, mankind, wild animals and vegetation. His divine names—Hishe, Huwe, Kxo, Gara, Gani ga, Gaishi gai, Gauwa—he also gave to the lesser god, but retained his earthly name Gao!na for himself. His elder wife is Khwova!na. His younger wife is Gow who is also the wife of the lesser god. The Bushmen, Naron, Botswana, South Africa, Namibia. (Marshall, 1962: 223–225; Schapera, 1951: 182, 192; Smith, 1950: 91)

Hkun Hsang Long "The Creator Spirit" of the Wa. Burma. (Scott, 1964: 289)

Hlam Shua The highest deity of the Eskimo. Kodiak Island, Alaska. (Lantis, 1938: 139)

Hobatoke The otiose supreme god of the Sherbro, Bullom, and Krim lives in the sky. Sierra Leone. (McCulloch, 1950: 83)

Hodianokdoo Hediohe The omnipotent and incomprehensible creator deity was manifest in all things, was never beseeched, as were other deities, only thanked for his manifest blessings. The Iroquois, Eastern United States. (Keppler, 1941: 13)

Hoenir One of the Aesir gods, brother of Odin and Lodur. Together they slew Ymir, the great giant of the beginning. They created the earth from his flesh, the sea and fresh water from his blood, the mountains from his bones; then mankind from two trees, man from the ash and woman from the elm. Hoenir gave them their senses and understanding, intelligence and motion. The two lesser brothers are sometimes considered aspects of Odin, eventually disappearing, Hoenir as hostage to the Vanir at the end of the war with the Aesir. Scandinavia. (Grimm, 1883, 2: 559–561, 823; Anderson, 1891: 196; Branston, 1955: 144; Guerber, 1895: 19, 42)

Homanihiko, Humanihinku, Humenehinku The supreme god and the creator of the earth. (The latter is considered a possible later addition as the Cubeo believe the earth always existed.) He was unconcerned with human affairs. The Cubeo, the Tucano, Colombia. (Zerries, 1968: 254–255; Goldman, 1940: 243; 1948: 794)

Hubeane, Khutsoane A culture hero/ancestor god who created the world and the heavens which he then abandoned. Botswana. (Pettersson, 1953: 161–162; Werner, 1964: 213)

Hucanech The omnipotent supreme god who is "just and merciful." The Guanches, Canary Islands. (Basset, 1925, 2: 511)

Huecuvoe, Huecuvu The evil supreme being. The Moluches, Chile. (Grubb, 1925, 9: 598)

Huehuetéotl A name of Ometéotl as "the old god," the supreme being. Aztec, Mexico. (León-Portilla, 1982: 32, 35)

Huitzilopochtli One of the four sons of Ometéotl who as the primary forces were responsible for the formation of realities. With Quetzalcóatl created the heavens and earth, and the waters, fire, mankind and the time periods. Aztec, Mexico. (León-Portilla, 1982: 33, 35)

Humenehinku A variant of Homanihiko.

Hunab Ku The supreme and greatest of the gods of the Mayan of Yucatan, invisible and the source of all things. He was the creator of the world and of mankind (out of corn). His wife was Ixazaluoh, his son Itzamna. Mexico. (Tozzer, 1941: 146; Roys, 1965: xvii; Morley, 1946: 213–214; Bancroft, 1886, 3: 462; Thompson, 1970: 203; Hagar, 1913: 25)

Hunavan and **Hunchevan** Brother creators of the heavens and earth and all things including man. Sons of Xchmel and Xtmana. Guatemala. (Bancroft, 1886, 3: 74)

Huthas Coyote as the chief god of the Wappo Indians. California. (Driver, 1936: 217)

Hutsipamamau?u Ocean Woman, the primal creatress, created the earth by rubbing the dead skin from her body and forming small balls which she then "crumpled" and "sprinkled" on the Immortal Water, NariwiinYapah. When the area became large enough she lay down on it and stretched it with her hands and feet until its size was approved by Wolf and Coyote. She is the Great Mother, the creator of all things. At times she is a duality; usually presented as sisters, but sometimes as mother and daughter, as in the Coyote myth of Louse, the wise, mature mother and the seductive young female. The Chemehuevis, California/Nevada/Arizona. (Laird, 1976: 46, 148–149, 213–214)

Huwe The beneficent supreme being and creator of all things was invoked for food and for health. Among the northern Bushmen he is a deity of the forest. South Africa, Botswana, Angola. (Smith, 1950: 90–91; Schapera, 1951: 183)

Hyel, Hel The supreme deity of the Pabir and the Bura. Nigeria. (Williams, 1936: 216–217)

Iadalbaoth A Hebrew god who appears in Gnosticism below the High God as the creator of the world. (Seligmann, 1948: 106)

Iba The omnipotent and invisible supreme god and creator of the earth, sky, and mankind. Snakes and lizards, his servants, bring the rain when invoked by the shaman. The Shipibo (Chama), Western Brazil. (Zerries, 1968: 255)

Ibmel The supreme god and creator, a sky god. Some apply this name to various of the higher gods. The Lapps. Northern Norway, Sweden, Finland, Kola Peninsula. (Bosi, 1960: 129; Pettersson, 1957: 19, 20; Karsten, 1955: 30, 50)

Ibofanga The supreme deity, also called Hisagita-immisi, created the world and all things. The Creek, Alabama, Georgia. (Swanton, 1928: 207, 546)

Idioci The remote and indifferent sky and creator god who manifests himself in the thunder and sends the rain. The Macheyenga, Peru. (Farabee, 1922: 14, 15)

Ifilici W'acinaci A title of the supreme being and creator. The Arawaks, Guiana. (Brett, 1880: 6, 7; ImThurn, 1883: 366)

Iguanchi The benevolent and friendly chief spirit of the Jivaro who "takes account of all the important acts of life." Peru. (Farabee, 1922: 119)

Ikanam The creator of the universe, a beneficent god who perfected the creation of man inadequately started by Italapas. The Chinook, Oregon/Washington. (Bancroft, 1886, 3: 96, 155)

Ilai "The Torajas recognize two supreme powers: Ilai, 'the Man,' and Indara, 'the Maiden;' these formed men, but not animals or plants." The first represents the sun, the second, the earth. Celebes, Indonesia. (Kern, 1925, 8: 347; Kruijt, 1925, 7: 248; Raats, 1969: 8, 9)

Ilanzi The supreme god and creator whose name also means the sun. The Wafipa, Tanzania. (Frazer, 1926: 197)

Ilat The god of rain is believed by some to be the supreme deity and "lord of life and death." The Suk, Kenya. (Beech, 1911: 19; Mbiti, 1970, 2: 119)

Illalei The supreme being and creator and the "father of men." Also called Waq. The Burji-Konso tribes, Ethiopia. (Cerulli, 1956: 66)

Ilmatar The primordial mother, creatress of the universe, existed in the sea. Mother of Vainamoinen. Finland. (Leach, 1956: 239–243)

Ilyuba The supreme god, "identified with the sun," created the earth and brings life and prosperity. The Pimbwe, Tanzania. (Willis, 1966: 59)

Imana The beneficent supreme god and creator is all that is sacred—unapproachable; no sacrifices are made. He is also a god of fertility, protective of the cattle. Among the Warundi he governs life and death, good and bad fortune. Among the Banyaruanda he controls the weather, and with the Ha he is a remote and uninvolved deity. In Burundi he is manifest as a white lamb, in Ruanda as a calf. Ruanda, Burundi, Tanzania, Uganda. (Meyer, 1916: 60, 87, 184–185; Maquet, 1954: 166–169; Guillebaud, 1950: 181, 191–192; Pettazzoni, 1956: 35; Williams, 1936: 175; Scherer, 1959: 888; Frazer, 1926: 225–226)

Imberombera Creator goddess of the Northern Territory. Australia. Same as Waramurungundju. (Poignant, 1967: 114, 127)

Imra, Amra, Yamri The supreme god and creator. Kafiristan, Afghanistan. (Hackin, 1963, 1: 57–58; Dumézil, 1966, 1: 59; Robertson, 1925, 7: 635)

Inada Dao The goddess who created the world is the mother of Lowalani and Latura Dano. South Nias, Indonesia. (Suzuki, 1959: 4)

Inahitelan, Ginagitelan A name of the supreme being meaning "Supervisor." A celestial god and omniscient as to man's activities. The Koryaks, Siberia. (Pettazzoni, 1956: 263)

Indagarra The supreme being and god of judgment after death created a man and a woman. Under him is Ryangombe. The Wa-Twa, Burundi. (Haddon, 1925, 9: 272; MacCulloch, 1925, 11: 823)

Indara The Maiden, the earth. With Ilai, the sun, the supreme powers of the Torajas. They created mankind, but not plants and animals. Celebes, Indonesia. (Kern, 1925, 8: 347; Kruijt, 1925, 7: 248)

Indeesa, Indeza, Ileesa, Ilaansi The powerful and beneficent supreme being and the creator of the world. The Fipa, Tanzania. (Willis, 1966: 30; Williams, 1936: 205, 207)

Inkfwin-wetay The creator god and ruler of the universe. The Hare Indians (Dénés), British Columbia. (Morice, 1925, 4: 639; Pettazzoni, 1956: 396)

Inkosikasi A supreme being, a beneficent sky goddess. The Zulu, South Africa. (Pettersson, 1953: 180, 187)

In-Shushinak The supreme god of the Elamites. East of Babylonia. (Pinches, 1925, 5: 251; Larousse, 1968: 72)

Inû The sun god and the supreme being. The Kona, Nigeria. (Meek, 1931: 187, 270)

Inzak, Enzak The principal god of Dilman. Bahrain, Arabia. (Bibby, 1969: 43–44)

Io The self-existent and eternal beneficent supreme god whose name is very tapu. His cult is that primarily of the priests and higher classes, not public. He has numerous descriptive names, all beginning with Io-; as omniscient, Io-te-wananga; as all-seeing, Io-matanui; as the Vigilant, Io-mata-Kana. He created the universe, light and darkness, the gods and mankind. The Maori, New Zealand. (Best, 1924: 235; Andersen, 1928: 347–350, 353; Pettazzoni, 1956: 344–348; Poignant, 1967: 24, 40; Howells, 1948: 222)

Iocauna The supreme being and sky god. Variant names: Guamaonocon, Jocakuvague, Yocahu, Vague, Naorocon. His mother also had numerous names: Attabeira, Mamona, Guacarapita, Iella, Guimazoa. The Antilles, West Indies. (Alexander, 1920: 24–25)

Iopotari akuru An omnipresent beneficent and supreme power "whose name is not known even to the piaiyen. . . . He is called iopotari akuru ('boss spirit')." The Caribs, British Guiana. (Gillin, 1936: 156)

Ioskeha The benevolent chief god of the Huron/Iroquois. He was the twin of Tawiscaron (Tawiskara). They were considered by some as the sons of Aataentsic, by others as the grandsons. He was known also as Teharonhiawagon, Hamendiju, Hawenniyo. Eastern United States. (Hale, 1891: 293–294; Tooker, 1965: 146, 151; Voegelin, 1944: 374; Brinton, 1868: 171; Larousse, 1968: 431)

Ipalnemohuani A name of Ometeotl, Tloque Nahuaque, the supreme god as the "Giver of Life" and of movement to all things, and "regulates the motion of the moon and the stars." Aztec, Mexico. (Reed, 1966: 69; Caso, 1958: 8; Leon-Portilla, 1982: 7, 59, 93)

Ipu The supreme deity of the Milanows (Malanau). Borneo. (De Crespigny, 1875: 35; Roth, 1968: 219)

Irik A primeval creator spirit, in the form of a bird, who created the earth; with Ara, created mankind from clay. The Sea Dyaks of Sarawak, Borneo. (Sarawak Gazette, 1963: 21; Nyuak, 1906: 16, 17)

Irioba, Enokwe The sun, the sky, the only real god of the Kuria who "created the world and all that it contains." Kenya, Tanzania. (Ruel, 1965: 295–296)

Irma An early coastal name of the creator god. Peru. (Means, 1931: 423)

Isahi The supreme being of the Logoli. Kenya. (Wagner, 1949: 291)

Isakakate The supreme being of the Crow. Plains Indians. (Burland, 1965: 149)

Isewahanga The creator god of the Zinza. Tanzania. (Taylor, 1962: 147; Williams, 1936: 208)

Isha Hanga, Isha Wahanga, Ishwanga The supreme god of the Haya, the Bahaya, of the east coast of Lake Victoria. Tanzania. Also called Rugaba, Kazoba. (Williams, 1936: 208; Taylor, 1962: 142)

iso kamuy "Over and above all the deities in the Ainu pantheon, the bears, or iso kamuy (Ursus arctos collaris), occupy the throne of the supreme deities. Their power . . . is a generalized one, providing food and looking after the general welfare of the Ainu." Sakhalin. (Ohnuki-Tierney, 1974: 90)

Ithuwa The sun and the creator. Some consider him a separate deity. Others consider Kyumbi, Ithuwa and Mrungu as one god. The Wapare, Tanzania. (Frazer, 1926: 201)

Itpomu The mother goddess, creator of all things. Her husband is Débu. The Lepchas, Sikkim. (Gorer, 1938: 223–235)

Itukoviche The remote high god who accounted for "the existence of the world." The Terena, Brazil. (Altenfelder, 1946: 216)

Ixtcibenihehat The supreme being, the source of life and of all power is considered by some to be the creator of all things, though Earthmaker also plays a role. The Gros Ventres, Montana. (Cooper, 1957: 1–5)

Izanagi and **Izanami** Creator of the islands of Japan and some of the deities with his sister/wife Izanami. (Yasumaro, 1928: 3, 78; Holtom, 1938: 81, 109; Haydon, 1941: 202)

Izuwa The creator god among the Wasu. Tanzania. (Millroth, 1965: 28)

Jaboajne The high god and creator of mankind. Normanby Island, Australia. (Roheim, 1972: 121)

Jalang The all-powerful supreme being of the Bambara. Senegal to Niger. (Williams, 1936: 238)

Jessis A Slavic high god who is beneficent and protective. (Czaplicka, 1925, 11: 594)

Jin With Omel the creators of the world. Jin created all the good things, Omel the bad. Ziryen, Finno Ugrian, Russia. (Pettersson, 1957: 22)

Jok   An omnipotent and omnipresent high god and creator of the universe. He is a neutral power which can be activated by man for his benefit, is benevolent, but punishes neglect. The Lango and the Luo, Uganda. (Driberg, 1923: 216–225; Williams, 1936: 151; Thomas, 1950: 206; Hayley, 1947: 3)

Father Jose   He fashioned the earth and created the sun and moon and mankind. His wife is Maria Santissima, son is Jesus Cristo. They were the first Indians. The Chimalteco, Guatemala. (Wagley, 1949: 51)

Jubmel, Ibmel   The supreme sky god, an abstract deity. A term used also as "god" in general. The Lapps, Northern Norway, Sweden, Finland, Kola Peninsula. (Dioszegi, 1968: 30; MacCulloch, 1964: 217)

Jugumishanta   A goddess whose husband is Morufonu created the earth and the sky. They are the parents of all. She is "identified with the earth." The Kamano, Usurufa, Jate, and Fore, New Guinea. (Berndt, 1965: 80–81)

Jumala   A Finno-Ugric supreme being and sky god. (MacCulloch, 1964: 217; Queval, 1968: 63; Larousse, 1968: 304)

Jumo, Jume   The supreme deity and sky god of the Cheremis. Russia. (Bosi, 1960: 129; MacCulloch, 1964: 217, 266)

Juok   The supreme god and creator is omnipresent, omniscient, and omnipotent, is identified with the wind, with air in motion. He is usually approached through Nyakang. The Shilluk and the Anuak, Sudan, Ethiopia. (Seligman, 1931: 3, 4; Pettazzoni, 1956: 11, 12, 38; Queval, 1968: 64; Butt, 1952: 79; Gelfand, 1966: 121)

Jupiter, Jove   The celestial and sovereign god of the Roman pantheon. As the former he controlled the weather, wielding the thunder and lightning, and providing omens of the sky in the lightning and in the flight of birds. As a sovereign deity he was the god of politics, of law and order, of justice, and of oaths and contracts. His consort was Juno. As Jupiter Lucetius he was god of light; J. Elicius, god of rain; J. Fulgus, god of lightning; J. Fidius, god of oaths and treaties; J. Dapalis, god of the sowing; J. Terminus, god of boundary stones; J. Latiaris, god of state. (Dumézil, 1966, 1: 108, 178–180; Fairbanks, 1907: 98–99; Pettazzoni, 1956: 163; Jayne, 1962: 429–430; Larousse, 1968: 203; Morford and Lenardon, 1975: 399, 400)

Jupka   A great god who "fished up the uncreated world from the ocean floor." When it had been developed he created the people. He then taught them about the moons and the seasons and all the rites and activities pertaining to them; of the rules governing the wowi (the home, hearth) and the watgurwa (the men's house); about death and the land of the dead; of the Yahi way which was that of peace. When all was done he transformed himself into a many-colored butterfly. The Yahi (southern Yana), California. (Kroeber, 1964: 27–30, 32, 42)

Kabezya   The powerful and supreme sky god who controlled the elements. Zaire. (Kabezya-mpungu). (Williams, 1936: 82; Budge, 1973, 1: 374)

Kabunian   The supreme god of the universe who is the moral judge and the active force in important rites and ceremonies. The name is used as a term also denoting the sky as well as the deities collectively. The Nabaloi, the Kankanay, Luzon, Philippines. (De Raedt, 1964: 266, 269, 309; Moss, 1920: 280; Vanoverbergh, 1972: 74)

Kadabenjiget   The supreme being of the Ojibwa Indians. Great Lakes area. (Pettazzoni, 1956: 398)

Kadaklan   The supreme being, a sky god, created the universe. "The lightning is his dog, and the thunder his drum . . . " He is invoked for rain, and is punitive if offences are committed against customs. His wife is Agemem, a chthonic goddess, and their sons are Adam and Baliyen. The Tinguian of northern Luzon, Philippines. (De Raedt, 1964: 312, 315; Cole, 1922: 297, 343; Kroeber, 1918, 2: 43)

Kadavul   The omnipresent supreme being who is the source of all but is not worshipped. The Paraiya, Southern India. (Thurston, 1909, 6: 104)

Kaei   The supreme power who is over Tuhan and Ple created all things except the earth; is also the thunder god. The Kenta in Kedah, the Semang, Malaya. *See also* **Kari.** (Schebesta, 1957: 111; 1927: 221)

Kagaba   "A vague, distant, amoral creator." God of the Toro. Uganda. (Taylor, 1962: 63)

Kagingo   The creator god of the Ganda. Uganda. (Mbiti, 1970, 2: 330)

Kaila   The remote, supreme, and all-powerful god of the Ihalmiut Eskimo. He is also the creator and a sky and weather god. Keewatin District, Canada. (Mowat, 1968: 237)

Kaira Kan   The benevolent high god who created Erlik who helped him in the creation of the earth. However, Erlik's work was bad and he was banished into the darkness to become lord of the underworld. Kaira Kan is invoked by the shaman when he is to begin his ecstatic journey. The Altaians, Siberia. (Casanowicz, 1924: 416–417; Eliade, 1964: 88, 275)

K'akoch, Ka'k'och The "Prime Mover"—the remote supreme being "created the infirm earth and the first sun and moon, as well as the tuberose from which the primary gods emerged." He is invisible unless he "chooses to be seen." The Lacandon, Chiapas, Mexico. (Perera and Bruce, 1982: 271, 273, 307)

Kalesi A name of the supreme being, Kyala, as the omnipresent. The Konde, Tanzania. (MacKenzie, 1925: 179; Frazer, 1926: 188)

Kaleya Ngungu The supreme being of the Sunday Islanders. Australia. (Basedow, 1925: 295)

Kal-li-top-ti The "Chief Above" in the heavens—"a great ruling power. . . . But the coyote performed all the work of creation." The Gallinomero (Pomo Indians), California. (Powers, 1877: 182)

Kalo The sky god who is creator of all things, and is invoked in oaths. The Lafofa, Sudan. (Seligman, 1925, 9: 403)

Kaloaraik A supreme evil being "who created the world as miserable and full of suffering as it actually is in the mind of the Tobas." Argentina, Paraguay. (Karsten, 1932: 110)

Kals The highest god, "the Great Transformer" of the Coast Salish Indians. Pacific Northwestern North America. (Swanton, 1925, 11: 97)

Kalunga The supreme being among the Bakongo, Chokwe, Luena, some Luvale, Bakioko, Herero, and Aandonga Obambo peoples. Among the first four groups he is also associated with the sea. Among the latter three he is a god of natural phenomena, the weather, etc., and a god of death and the underworld, of fate, as well. Angola, Zaire, Rhodesia, and Namibia. (McCulloch, 1951: 72; White, 1961: 30–32; Pettersson, 1953: 144, 170, 174; Pettazzoni, 1956: 35; Williams, 1936: 90)

Kamantowit The great god of the Algonquin Indians and the creator of mankind. (Schoolcraft, 1857, 5: 71)

Kami-musubi Divine-Producing goddess, the third of the primeval creative deities to emerge. Mother of Suku-na-biko. Some name as male. Japan. (Anesaki, 1937: 222, 229; Herbert, 1967: 329; Yasumaro, 1928: 2; Yasumaro, 1965: 33; Holtom, 1938: 183; Hori, 1968: 4)

Kanaloa One of the gods, with Kane and Lono, who created the heavens and earth. He is better known as the ruler of Po, the Dark region, and leader of the rebellious spirits. He is the octopus god, the squid, and invoked by fishermen and sailors. Hawaii. (Beckwith, 1932: 174; 1940: 60, 62; Henry, 1928: 345)

kanapenekastciwhiu One of five names of the Caribou god, supreme deity of the Davis Inlet and Barren Ground bands. Labrador. (Cooper, 1934: 36)

Kande Yaka The greatest of the deities, "Lord of Beasts," and a god of hunters. The Veddas of Ceylon. (Wales, 1957: 15; Pettazzoni, 1956: 442)

Kando The supreme being and creator of all things, the giver and restorer of life. The Santal, India. (Biswas, 1956: 103, 135)

Kane The god of light and creator of the universe and mankind with Lono and Kanaloa. He has numerous aspects, many having to do with weather. He introduced much of their culture. A god of procreation. Hawaii. (Beckwith, 1932: 174; 1940: 42, 47–48, 61–63; Williamson, 1933: 23)

Kanitu The Great Spirit at Elema and at Perau. New Guinea. (Haddon, 1925, 9: 343; MacKenzie, 1930: 287)

Kanobo The benevolent supreme being and creator god who is propitiated at the time of the floods. The Warrau, Venezuela. (Zerries, 1968: 251)

Kanonatu, Kononatoo The creator god and supreme being who gives them rain to end drought, but also punishes with floods when they are sinful. The Warau, Guiana. (Brett, 1880: 62–63; Levi-Strauss, 1973: 192; ImThurn, 1883: 366)

Kanu The supreme god of the Safroko Limba. Also called Masala, Masaranka. Sierra Leone. (McCulloch, 1950: 71)

Kaptan The chief god who created the earth and plants lived in Kahilwayan, the sky, with his wife Maguayan. The Bisayan of Central Panay, Philippines. (Jocano, 1969: 19, 35)

Karai Kasang The omniscient, omnipotent, and omnipresent supreme being is invoked to testify to truth, is a god of destiny. The Katchins, Burma. (Pettazzoni, 1956: 19, 292–293; Gilhodes, 1908: 674)

Karei, Kari The supreme being is the creator of all but the earth and mankind. The latter were created by ple, but were given souls by Kari. He is the judge of the dead as well as being a god of thunder and storms which he sends as punishment. Among the Jehai his wife is Manoid with whom he communicates through lightning. Among the Menri his wife is Takel, his son Hanei. The Semang, Malay Peninsula. (Wales, 1957: 11; Roheim, 1972: 19, 20, 104; Eliade, 1964: 337; Evans, 1937: 151–152; Cole, 1945: 72; Schebesta, 1927: 170; 1954: 274; Skeat, 1906: 177–178; 1925, 8: 354)

Karmba A high god whom the Vais invoke "in moments of great distress and pain." Sudan. (Ellis, 1914: 86)

Karunga *See* **Kalunga**

Kashila, Kashiri The high god of the Igbiri, the Kitimi, the Anirago. Among the Bogana he is invoked at the planting season. Nigeria. (Gunn, 1956: 51, 54, 56, 60, 62; Mbiti, 1970, 2: 331)

Kasiwa An omniscient supreme being. Nukumanu, Micronesia. (Pettazzoni, 1956: 343)

Katema The name of the supreme being, also that of the sun. Ugala, East Africa. (Frazer, 1926: 197)

Katit The creator—the prairie falcon. The Patwin Indians, California. (Kroeber, 1932: 303)

Katkuyen The omnipresent and omniscient high god of the Didinga. Sudan. (Pettazzoni, 1956: 38–39)

Katonda The supreme being and creator god. The Baganda and the Basoga, Uganda. (Stam, 1908: 214; Roscoe, 1965: 312; Williams, 1936: 155; Millroth, 1965: 19)

Kaunzhe Pah-tum-owans The Great spirit, creator of the Indians. The Lenape/Delaware, Eastern United States. (Harrington, 1921: 22)

Kayai The supreme being, a sky god, and a god of thunder and storms. Also called Bayagaw. The Aeta (Negritos) of Luzon, Philippines. (Wales, 1957: 12; Pettazzoni, 1956: 318)

Kazoba The remote, yet benevolent, high god and creator. The Kiga, Uganda. (Taylor, 1962: 126)

Ke The supreme being who is identified with the sun. The northern Yungur, Nigeria. (Williams, 1936: 217)

Kea A god of the creation group of deities, known only because mentioned in the sacred chants. The Marquesas, Polynesia. (Handy, 1923: 244)

Kemush A shorter form of K'mukamtch, the creator god. The Modoc Indians, Oregon, California. (Gatschet, 1890: lxxix)

Kepenopfu The beneficent supreme being and creator whose sex is debatable, but who is generally considered female as the ancestress of mankind and the larger cats. The Angami Nagas, India. (Hutton, 1921: 180–181; Pettazzoni, 1956: 291)

Ketanitowet The Great Spirit, the same as Patumawas. The Minsi, Lenape Indians, Eastern United States. (Harrington, 1921: 19)

Ketchimanetowa The Great Spirit of the Fox Indians. Wisconsin. (Burland, 1965: 149; Cohane, 1969: 157)

Ketci Niweskwe The omnipresent Great Spirit and creator, the source of all power. The Penobscot, Maine. (Speck, 1935: 4)

Keto, Ketok The benevolent supreme god—"the light . . . whose eyes are the sun and moon." He controls the weather and the passage of night and day; observes the actions of mankind. Keto created Taogn and Tegn who are also creators. The Bateg, the Batek, Malaya. (Evans, 1937: 158–159, 183; Schebesta, 1927: 276; Pettazzoni, 1956: 7, 311)

Ketq Skwaye Grandmother Toad who is the creator. The Huron Indians, Eastern United States. (Burland, 1965: 149)

Khaldi, Khaldis The supreme god who forms a triad with Teisbas and Ardinis. Armenia. (Sayce, 1925, 1: 793–794; Ananikian, 1964: 11)

Khang, Kaang The high god of the Bushmen. South Africa. (Mutwa, 1966: 9; Pettazzoni, 1956: 32)

Khazang pa The supreme being and creator god was invoked for offspring, for prosperity, abundant crops and animals, good hunting. He was also a god of fate. The Lakher, India. (Wallis, 1939: 145; Pettazzoni, 1956: 293, 296; Elwin, 1949: 25, 26; Barkataki, 1969: 105–106)

Khepera, Kheprer, Khepri The beetle god, self-produced god of creation and resurrection, who created Shu and Tefnut, and represented the rising sun. Egypt. (Budge, 1969, 1: 294–295, 355, 471; Knight, 1915: 62; Casson, 1965: 50; Eliade, 1967: 96–97)

Khogein Pooteeang The supreme being of the Kookies, near Chittagong, India. (Coleman, 1832: 325)

Khonvoum, Khonvum The supreme god of the Pygmies is a sky god who "controls celestial phenomena" as well as a god of the forest, its game, and hunting. Equatorial Africa. (Queval, 1968: 65; Larousse, 1973: 520)

Khormusta-Tengri The supreme deity is the chief of the tengris. Another name for Ulghen. The Altaians, the Mongols, Siberia. (Klementz, 1925, 3: 2, 3; Grimm, 1883, 2: 716)

Khourrou The supreme being and creator god. The Khoi-Khoi (Hottentots), South Africa. (Pettersson, 1953: 145; Schapera, 1951: 380–381, 387)

Khovaki, Savaki The creator god. The Tungus, Siberia. (Larousse, 1973: 434)

Khri khug rgyal po (pr. Trhikhuk Gyelpo) The name of the creator in Bon religion. Also known as Kun snang khyab pa and sNang ba 'od ldan. His creation has "two aspects, the exterior world (phyi snod) and that contained within it (bcud)." Tibet. (Tucci, 1980: 215)

Khu, Khuva, Huve The omniscient supreme being whose punitive measure is the weather. The northwestern Bushmen, Africa. (Pettazzoni, 1956: 32)

Khudjana Believed to be the creator of the world. Son of Ribimbi. Transvaal. (Werner, 1964: 128)

Khuswane, Khuzwane, Khutsoane The creator god, of the world and mankind. The Lovedu, the BaVenda, Botswana, Transvaal. (Stayt, 1931: 236; Krige, 1954: 59; Smith, 1950: 123; Pettersson, 1953: 161–162, 203)

Kibumba The creator god of the Basoga and the Gwere. Uganda. (Mbiti, 1970, 2: 328, 330)

kice·manito The Great Spirit and omnipotent creator. The Cree, Plains Indians, Canada, United States. (Mandelbaum, 1940: 251)

Kickeron An earlier name of the Great Spirit of the Lenape Indians. Eastern United States. (Harrington, 1921: 20)

Kiehton The benevolent Great Spirit and creator of the other gods, of mankind, and of all things. The Algonquin, Massachusetts. Also known as Woonand and Cautantowit in Connecticut. (Lissner, 1961: 94; De Forest, 1853: 23; Alexander, 1964: 20)

Kihigilan A name for the supreme being in one of the myths of the Koryak. Siberia. (Jochelson, 1908: 24)

Kiho, Kio, Io The supreme god and creator of the universe, of all gods, of all things. Anaa Island, Tuamotua, Polynesia; Kio at Vahi-tahi. (Stimson, 1933: 9; Long, 1963: 149, 175–182)

Kinharingan With his wife Munsumundok the chief gods and creator deities. One myth states that "As there was no food, they killed their child, cut it up and planted it, from which came rice, coco-nut, betel-nut, vines, corn, sugar cane, etc." North Borneo. (MacKenzie, 1930: 336; Evans, 1923: 4, 5)

Kinnekasus Creator and chief god of the Wichita. Plains Indians, Kansas. (Dorsey, 1904, 1: 18, 25)

Kinohoingan, Kinoingan The supreme being who lives in the sky. He is invoked in oaths, punishes incest and immorality with "floods, epidemics and other disasters." His wife is Sinumundu and their son in Hinomodun. At Putatan his personal name is Sunumundu and his wife is Hinomodun. The Dusuns, Borneo. (Stall, 1925: 940–941; Pettazzoni, 1956: 331)

Kin-tash-i The otiose supreme being of the Kabinapek (Pomo Indians). California. (Powers, 1877: 208)

Kio The supreme primordial god and creator who gave "all his magical powers and inherent prestige to Oatea." Vahitahi Island, Tuamotua, Polynesia. (Stimson, 1933: 29–33)

Kitabumbuire The principal god of the Banabuddu. Uganda. (Budge, 1973, 1: 377)

Kitchemonedo, Kitche Manitou, Kitchi Manito, Kitci manitu The omnipresent and invisible Great Spirit and benevolent creator who brought into existence what he saw in a vision; "made the Great Laws of Nature for the well being and harmony of all things and all creatures." The Ojibway, the Potawatomi (Wisconsin). As identified with the sun the latter also called him Kisis. The Great Lakes area. (Skinner, 1913: 80; Schoolcraft, 1857, 1: 320; Coleman, 1937: 34, 35; Johnston, 1976: 12, 13, 149)

K'mukamtch The unapproachable and dreaded creator god is a sky god who represents the sun and its influence on the weather. He is associated with the pine-marten (Skel) in his wisdom and omniscience, but is also a trickster and deceiver. The Klamath, Modoc, and Lutuami Indians, Oregon and California. (Gatschet, 1890: lxxix-lxxxiv; Kroeber, n.d.: 183; Chamberlain, 1892: 253)

knaritja The immortal and otiose Great Father, "called also the Eternal Youth (altjira nditja)." An emu-footed being with an emu-footed family. Strehlow (authority quoted by Eliade) does not consider him a supernatural. However, Eliade feels he can be included with supreme beings because of "his immortality, his youth, and his beatific existence" and because he has been in the sky for so long, and anterior to the totemic heroes who were responsible for "all the creative and meaningful acts." The Aranda, Australia. (Eliade, 1976, 1: 28, 29)

Kobine A goddess who, with her father Naruau, created heaven and earth. Gilbert Island, Micronesia. (Larousse, 1968: 457)

Kohkomhthena "Our Grandmother"—the supreme deity and creatress. The Shawnee, East-central United States. (Voegelin, 1936: 3, 4)

Komba The supreme being of the Nkundo. Zaire. (Williams, 1936: 92)

Komwidapokuwia A creator goddess, patroness of shamans, and grandmother of Skatakaamcha. The Yava-pai, Arizona. (Gifford, 1936: 307–308; 1933: 353)

Konori A god who created the world. Geelvink Bay, New Guinea. (Larousse, 1968: 449)

Kors Torum The remote creator and highest god of the Vogul; father of the other gods. Siberia. (Czaplicka, 1969: 289)

Kosane, Kusane The benevolent but indifferent creator god of the Bawenda. South Africa. (Hartland, 1925, 2: 364; Wessman, 1908: 80; Willoughby, 1932: 41, 68)

Kot The omniscient supreme being is a sky and wind god who causes storms when angry; credited with the creation of the world. The Nuer, Sudan. (Pettazzoni, 1956: 10, 38; Huffman, 1931: viii)

Kotan kara Kamui Also called Moshiri Kara Kamui and Kando Koro Kamui. The supreme being and creator. The Ainu, Japan. (Czaplicka, 1968: 273; Chamberlain, 1887: 12)

Koulo-Tyolo The creator god of the Senufo. Central Guinea. (Tishman, 1968/69: museum)

Kpaya At Azu, among a sub-tribe of the Ewe, he is the high god and Mawu is his son. His wife is Kusoako. Ghana. (Jeffreys, 1972: 732)

Ktahandowit The Great Spirit. Also called Ketci Niweskwe. The Penobscot, Maine. (Müller, 1968: 159)

Ku A powerful and beneficent creator god. Liberia. (Schwab, 1947: 317)

Kuan-de The "supreme Architect of the Universe." Burma. (Scott, 1964: 305)

Kudai The benevolent supreme god who tried to instill in men a "pure soul" but was frustrated by Erlik. The Black Sea Tatars, Russia, Siberia. (Pettersson, 1957: 23; Chadwick, 1936: 89, 92)

Kugo-jumo The high god who lives in the sky and rules the lesser deities. The Cheremis, Russia. (Leach, 1949, 1: 214)

Kuksu With Marumda he created the world. The Pomo. Among the northern Pomo it was with Makila. California. (de Angulo and Freeland, 1928: 251; Loeb, 1931: 523; 1932: 3)

Kuma The moon goddess, creator of all things, assisted by her brothers Puana (the water snake) and Itciai (the jaguar). She is goddess of the afterworld of happiness where she receives the dead and where they receive all good things. Mother of Hatchawa. The Yaruro, Venezuela. (Métraux, 1946, 2: 115; Sierksma, 1960: 14; Kirchhoff, 1948, 2: 462; Petrullo, 1939: 241)

Kumokums Creator of the earth and all things in it. The Modoc, California, Oregon. (Marriott and Rachlin, 1968: 28)

Kunmanngur The rainbow-serpent as "the regenerative source of life, as the creator and source of fertility." The Murinbata tribe, Australia. (Robinson, 1966: 50, 67; Poignant, 1967: 126)

Kun snang khyab pa A name of the creator in Bon cosmogony. Other names: sNang ba 'od ldan and Khri khug rgyal po. Tibet. (Tucci, 1980: 215)

Kuñyan The demiurge of the Dené Hare of Northwest Canada. (Levi-Strauss, 1973: 379n)

Kurbystan The supreme god of the Altaian Turks. South Soviet Union. (Dragomanov, 1961: 41, 48)

Kurn The master of the universe (also the term applied to it) and creator of all things. The Gilyak, Siberia. (Shternberg, 1933: 320; Czaplicka, 1969: 271)

Kuru, Kurumasaba The all-powerful supreme god of the Temne who is associated with the sky. Sierra Leone. (McCulloch, 1950: 70; Goddard, 1925: 59; Thomas, 1916: 29)

Kutka, Kutkh, Kutku   The raven who was the creator of the world and the father of all creatures. His wife was Ilkxum. The Kamchadal, the Itelmen, Siberia. (Czaplicka, 1969: 269–270; Jochelson, 1908: 18; Antropova, 1964: 880; Brinton, 1897: 166)

Kutnahin   The supreme being of the Chitimacha also makes the thunder. Louisiana. (Swanton, 1946: 781)

Kwawar   The creator god of the Gabrielino Indians. California. (Kroeber, 1925: 622)

Kwikumat   Creator of the earth and of people. The Yuma Indians, Arizona. (Harrington, 1908: 324)

Kwoelecun   The creator deity of the Tolowa. Oregon. (Drucker, 1937: 267)

Kwoth (a nhial)   The omnipresent sky god, creator of the universe and of all things. Also a god of justice. (Evans-Pritchard, 1953: 201; 1956: 26–27; Gelfand, 1966: 127)

Kyala   The supreme god—"a first cause—the origin of death, and of social institutions." As the creator of life and of things he is also accused of their faults, their malfunctions. The Nyakyusa (Ngonde), Tanzania. Among the Konde he is manifested in many natural phenomena as well as in special things—e.g., animals, trees, etc.; has numerous names—Chata, Tenende, Nkurumuke, Kyaubiri, Kalesi, Mperi, Ndorombwike (used on solemn occasions). (Wilson, 1959: 158, 207; MacKenzie, 1925: 179, 181)

Kyoi, Nagaicho   The creator of earth and men. The Sinkyone, California. (Kroeber, 1925: 150)

Kyumbi   Beneficent creator of the world who gave mankind cattle and taught them to raise foods. Most of the people identify Kyumbi, Ithuwa (Izuwa), and Mrungu as one god. The Wapare or Wasu, Tanzania. (Frazer, 1926: 200–201; Millroth, 1965: 28)

La   The supreme being of the Mumuye who is identified with the sun. Nigeria. (Williams, 1936: 217)

Laha   A "supreme heaven-god . . . rules the destinies of mankind; . . . gave the religious laws and institutions." The Tsimshian Indians, British Columbia. (Swanton, 1925, 12: 465)

Lajok   A name of Naijok as "the creator, a formless being." The Lotuko, Sudan. (Huntingford, 1953: 90)

Laki Tengangang   The beneficent supreme being, omniscient and omnipotent, of the Kayans of Borneo.

His wife is Doh Tenangan. His name is also spelled Laki Tenangan. He is the same as Pa Silong of the Klemantans and Bali Penyalong of the Kenyahs. (Sarawak Gazette, 1963: 271; Hose, 1912: 5, 6; Kern, 1925, 8: 347; Roth, 1968: 219; Pettazzoni, 1956: 332)

LaKpa   A war god introduced from Nigeria who became the chief god and the source of all good among the Gā in Labadi and Teshi. Ghana. (Field, 1937: 34, 40, 62, 73)

Lambra   The creator deity who rules all things. The Kuki, Tibet, Burma. (Keane, 1925, 2: 122)

Larunaen   The creator of the earth and of all things who lives in the west, provides man with all his needs, but also causes earthquakes. His sister/wife is Hintabaran. New Ireland, Melanesia. (Cox, 1913: 195–196)

Lata, Rata   Creator of the earth and of all things. Reef Islands, Melanesia. (Williamson, 1933: 73)

Laxha   The supreme deity and sky god of the Tsimshian. British Columbia. (Swanton, 1904/05: 454; Alexander, 1964: 252)

Ledo no Bulan   A dual deity, Sun-Moon, and the supreme being. Roti Island, the Moluccas, Indonesia. (Pettazzoni, 1956: 336, 339)

Lera-Wulan   "Sun-Moon," the supreme being whose female counterpart is Tana Ekan, the earth. East Flores and Solor, Indonesia. (Pettazzoni, 1956: 334)

Leve   The supreme god and creator of the beginning times. Now referred to as Ngew. The Mende, Sierra Leone. (Little, 1951: 217)

Leza, Lesa   The supreme being and sky god who controls all atmospheric phenomena. He is omnipresent, the creator and master of all things, the ordainer of destiny. He provides mankind's needs, but also punishes evil-doing. Among some he is too remote to be concerned with human affairs. The Tonga, the Ila, the Lamba, Tabwa, Luba, Bemba, Iwa, Nyamwanga, Rhodesia, Zambia, Tanzania, and Zaire. (Smith, 1920: 197–211; Doke, 1931: 225–228; Ottenberg, 1960: 373, 374, 386; Parrinder, 1967: 29; Hopgood, 1950: 62, 63, 72; Williams, 1936: 83, 123; Gelfand, 1966: 124; Willis, 1966: 38, 52)

Liahan   The omnipotent and invisible creator of all. Buka Island, Melanesia. (Thomas, 1931/32: 228)

Libanza   The supreme being of the Bopoto. Among the Upotos, though he is the chief god, he was not the first being, but is eternal and has the power to bring back to life all divine beings on the point of death. He is the son of Lotenge and Ntsombobelle. While he lived on earth he was guilty of many misdeeds. Zaire. A creator god among the Bantu of the Upper Congo. (Frazer, 1926: 142, 146–149; Larousse, 1968: 482; Hartland, 1925, 2: 366)

Lichaba The greatest of the village and field spirits is considered to have created the world. The Ao Nagas, India. (Mills, 1926: 220)

Likube, Likuwe, Likuve, Lyuba The omnipresent and omniscient supreme being was also the creator of the world and the producer of the weather. He had numerous names—Limi, the sun, Limatunda, the creator, Liwelelo, as the universe, and also Mulungu. The Nyamwesi, Tanzania. (Abrahams, 1967: 78; Pettazzoni, 1956: 35; Millroth, 1965: 34–36)

Lingo Pen A great god of the Gond whose symbol is horses. Semurgaon, India. (Eliade, 1964: 468)

Linyabangwe The creator deity of the Sukuma-Nyamwezi. Tanzania. (Mbiti, 1970, 2: 335)

Liova The sun who was "the creator and first principle of all things." The Kumbi, Tanzania. (Millroth, 1965: 96)

Liowa The supreme god and creator was the sun. The Iramba, Tanzania. (Millroth, 1965: 22–23)

Liuba The supreme being of the Pimbwe. Also called Limlungu, Likatema, Liwawanga, Ikube, Limdimi, and Leza. Tanzania. (Williams, 1936: 201)

Liyele The omnipresent and incomprehensible supreme being, the giver of life. Upper Volta. (Hebert and Guilhem, 1967: 142–152)

Loak-Ishto-hoollo-Aba, Luak Ishto Holo Aba The supreme deity who seems to be associated with the sun, the source of warmth, light, and life. The Chickasaw, Mississippi. (Swanton, 1924/25: 482; Waring, 1965: 34)

Loba The high god and a god of light. The Bakwiri, Cameroon. (MacCulloch, 1925, 8: 49)

Lobanga The creator deity is remote though he does send the rain. The Labwor, Uganda. (Williams, 1936: 178)

Lodurr, Loder, Lodr Brother of Odin and Hoenir. Together they slew Ymir, the primordial giant, and from

his flesh they created the earth, from his blood the sea and fresh water, from his bones the mountains. From two trees they created mankind—man from the ash and woman from the elm. Lodurr gave them warm blood and "blooming complexions." The two lesser brothers are sometimes considered aspects of Odin, eventually disappearing. Scandinavia. (Guerber, 1895: 19, 42; Anderson, 1891: 196; Branston, 1955: 144, 146; Grimm, 1883, 2: 559–561, 823)

Lokpata The creator god of the Okpoto. Nigeria. (Armstrong, 1955: 152)

Lolo Zaho The high god and creator of mankind. Nias Island, Indonesia. (MacKenzie, 1930: 328)

Loma The "term used for the Supreme Being, can also . . . denote good or ill luck. Illness is attributed to *Loma*." The Bongo, Zaire and Sudan. (Baxter and Butt, 1953: 135)

Lono With Kane and Kanaloa the creators of the universe. Lono is a god associated with the atmosphere and the weather in all its forms as well as a god of agriculture and fertility. He is also a god of sound. Hawaii. (Beckwith, 1932: 174; 1940: 31–33, 350; Mackenzie, n.d.: 320–322; Poignant, 1967: 38)

Lowalangi (in north), **Lowalani** (in south) The omnipresent, omnipotent, and omniscient supreme being with power over man's destiny. He uses the weather punitively. In the north he is descended from Sirao, in the south from Inada Dao. Nias Island, Indonesia. (Kruijt, 1925, 7: 249; Suzuki, 1959: 6, 7; Pettazzoni, 1956: 11, 21, 329–330)

Lubanga The omniscient supreme being and creator god who sends the rain, was the teacher of all culture and civilization, is "responsible for birth and death." The Acholi, Sudan and Uganda. (Butt, 1952: 86–87; Pettazzoni, 1956: 38)

Lubare The creator deity of the Busoga. Kenya. (Frazer, 1926: 238)

Lubu-langi The chief god who is manifest in the wind, the beneficent source of all things, all good. A variant of Lowalangi. Nias Island, Indonesia. (Keane, 1925, 2: 238)

Lubumba Among the Baila the name of Leza as the creator. Zambia. (Werner, 1964: 126; Millroth, 1965: 55)

Lugaba The supreme sky god and creator of mankind and animals. He is the beneficent giver of life, but also sends illness and death if displeased. The Bahima, Uganda. (Roscoe, 1915: 131; Williams, 1936: 155; Frazer, 1961: iii, 190)

Lui The supreme being, identified with the sun. The Teme, Nigeria. (Williams, 1936: 217)

Lukelong The god or goddess who was the creator of the heavens and the earth. The Caroline Islands, Micronesia. (Larousse, 1968: 457; Poignant, 1967: 74)

Lulumoy The Great God who was represented "with three heads, six arms and six legs" was worshipped in the region of the Organos, to the west of the Neiva Valley. Colombia. (Hernandez de Alba, 1946: 959)

Lumauwig, Lumawig The supreme god and "the creator of all things and the preserver of life." His wife is Bugan and daughters are Bangan and Obban. Among the northern Kankanai he taught them healing and rituals. Krieger limits his creation to "the sky, the sea, and the kite." The Ifugao, the Kankanai, and the Bontok, Luzon, Philippines. (Krieger, 1942: 76; Jocano, 1969: 15; Vanoverbergh, 1972: 74–80; De Raedt, 1964: 320–321; Kroeber, 1918, 2: 44)

Lungkitsungba The omniscient supreme being is the creator of the celestial sphere and its orbs, and lives there. The Ao Nagas, Assam. (Pettazzoni, 1956: 289)

Lungwe The beneficent but remote and incorporeal creator god of the Bashi was imported from the Bazibaziba. Zaire. (Williams, 1936: 108)

lupi The sun whose wife is the moon. Some consider that he is "the supreme being . . . remote and unapproachable," others that he is malevolent and "the source of some diseases." The Aymara, Peru. (Tschopik, 1951: 196–197)

Ma "The Goddess of Creation," and mother of Mbali-yamswira. South Africa. (Mutwa, 1966: iii)

Madari-Burkhan, Maidari Burkan One of the three creator gods who with Shibegeni-Burkhan and Esege Burkhan created the earth and then made the first humans. The Buriats, Siberia. (MacCulloch, 1964: 375; Klementa, 1925, 3: 11)

Madumda The creator deity of the Pomo, frequently identified with Coyote. California. (Blackburn, 1975: 29)

Magano The supreme being of the Tambaro and the Sidamo, identified with the sky. Ethiopia. (Cerulli, 1956: 129)

Magbabaya The highest and most powerful divinity, the creator, who "lives in a house made of coins, high in the sky . . . " with no windows, as to see him causes all—men or objects—to "dissolve into water." As the creator he is usually known as Migloginsal or Agobinsal. The Bukidnon, Mindanao, Philippines. (Cole, 1956: 93; Jocano, 1969: 23)

Mahadara The supreme being and creator of all things. The Ot-danoms, Borneo and Indonesia. (MacKenzie, 1930: 353)

Mahadeva, Mahadewa An aspect of Siva as an all-powerful supreme god. Java, Bali, and India. (Goris, 1969: 92; Marchal, 1963: 231; Danielou, 1964: 206)

Mahaprabhu, Singi-Arke The supreme being and creator is generally benevolent but is known to cause fever and convulsions. His wife is Sita Mahalakshmi. The Bondo, India. (Elwin, 1950: 133–134, 140–144)

Mahapurub The creator god of the Raja Maria. Identified with Bhagavan. India. (Elwin, 1949: 64, 78)

Mahatala, Mahatara This name replaced the native names. The supreme being is a duality—Mahatala of the Upperworld, the Hornbill, and Jata of the Underworld, the Watersnake. Together they form a unity, represent the total divinity—"Upperworld and Underworld, man and woman, sun and moon, sacred spear and sacred cloth, good and evil, life and death, war and peace, security and disaster, etc." He was the creator, but called upon Jata to help with the second period of creation. The Ngaju, Borneo. (Scharer, 1963: 14–27; Wales, 1957: 78; Kern 1925, 8: 347; Kruijt, 1925, 7: 249)

Maheçwara One of the manifestations of the supreme god. Also called Batara Guru. Bali. (Swellengrebel, 1960: 62)

Maheo The pre-existent and omnipotent Great Spirit and creator lived in the void. He created the water, its creatures, light and air. With the help of coot, who brought up mud from the waters, he made the land by placing the mud on the back of Grandmother Turtle who became the earth, and caused it to grow and spread out. The Cheyenne, Minnesota to Montana and Colorado. (Marriott and Rachlin, 1968: 22; Powell, 1969: 433)

Maho Peneta The Great Spirit of the Mandan. North Dakota. (Burland, 1965: 149)

Mainatavasara The chief god of Somo Island. Fiji, Melanesia. (Pettazzoni, 1956: 342)

Maipe A supreme being among Pampean/Patagonian Indians. Among some "associated with the darkness of night, the violent wind of the desert" and other dangers. Argentina. (Cooper, 1946, 5: 158; Deniker, 1925, 9: 669)

Maiph A supreme being, considered beneficent. The Pampean/Patagonians. Argentina. (Cooper, 1946, 5: 158)

Mair The demiurge of the Urubu. Brazil. (Levi-Strauss, 1969: 269)

Maira-Monan, Maire-Monan Among the Tupinamba the creator god. Among the Tupi a culture hero. Brazil. (Zerries, 1968: 285; Wagley, 1964: 224; Larousse, 1968: 445)

Makawe The chief god of the Arawa, Ngatituwharetoa, and Whanganui tribes. New Zealand. (Gudgeon, 1892: 30)

Makila The thunder god who gave the people knowledge and taught them hunting and fishing and the arts. With Kuksu, the creators. The Northern Pomo, California. (Loeb, 1932: 3, 4; 1926, 2: 301)

Makonaima, Makunaima The supreme god and creator who sent his son Sigu to rule over the earth. Among the Makushi he created the sky and earth, vegetation, animals and men. Among the Ackawoi and Caribs he created birds, animals, and food plants, assisted by his son Sigu. British Guiana. (Brett, 1868: 378; 1880: 126–127; Métraux, 1946: 114; Alexander, 1920: 258, 269; ImTurn, 1883: 365)

Makumba A great god, the tribal god from whom the chief gets his authority. He gives, deprives, and kills, is invoked and made offerings. The Baushi, Rhodesia. (Philpot, 1936: 191–192)

Malayari The chief god of the pantheon of the Zambales, the creator of all things. He was the omnipotent ruler over life and death; "compassionate and loving"—sending rain, health, wealth, and abundance to the deserving, but punitive toward "those who ignored his commandments." Philippines. (Jocano, 1969: 13)

Maleiwa A culture hero/creator god who in some mythological versions is credited with creating the cosmos and vegetable and animal life, including humans. He was the giver of fire and rain, of moral laws, the punisher of incest. The Goajiro, Venezuela. (Wilbert, 1972, 1: 203–204; Zerries, 1968: 150)

Malengfung The otiose creator deity of the Kai. New Guinea. (Haddon, 1925, 9: 348)

Malunga, Waku The supreme being of the Galla who forms a triad with Oglie and Atetie. Ethiopia. (Budge, 1973, 1: 363)

Mama The Wakulwe "call the Creator god Mama or Mother, though they by no means regard him as feminine." Tanzania. (Meek, 1931: 178)

Mamaldi A goddess who "created the continent of Asia and the island of Sakhalin before she was killed by her husband," Khadau, but she "continued to quicken the souls of future shamans" whom he created. The Amur, Siberia. (Larousse, 1973: 433)

Mamale The creator of the earth. The Bagobo, Philippines. (Benedict, 1916: 29)

Manabozho God of the east, of light, and the creator god. *See* **Michabo**. The Winnebago and the Ojibwa, Wisconsin and Great Lakes area. (Emerson, 1884: 8, 337; Radin and Reagan, 1928: 70, 84; Fiske, 1900: 153)

Manama The chief god and creator who justly punishes and rewards. The Bagobo and the Ata, Philippines. (MacKenzie, 1930: 306–307; Benedict, 1916: 19)

Mangala The creator of the world and men. The Mande, Mali and Nigeria. (Dieterlen, 1957: 126; Long, 1963: 134)

Manibush The creator. The Menominee Indians, Wisconsin. (Maclean, 1876: 438)

Manitu The omniscient Great Spirit and creator of all things. The name is also used collectively to designate the lesser spirits as well as the mysterious power which pervades all of nature. The Algonquin Indians, eastern United States/Canada. (Cooper, 1934: 8, 9, 11, 12; Schmidt, 1933: 65–67; Larousse, 1968: 427)

Man'una The Earthmaker, the beneficent but remote creator god. The Winnebago, Wisconsin. (Radin, 1915/16: 285)

Mapu The creator of the earth. The Araucanians, Chile. (Lowie, 1925, 4: 173)

Marahtoo The supreme deity of the Pilamites invoked in times of danger. Formosa. (Campbell, 1925, 6: 86)

Marduk At one time in Akkadian and Assyro/Babylonian mythology he was the creator of heaven and earth from the body of Tiamat and of mankind from the blood of Kingu. Originally a solar god, his functions as god of war and politics, as a ruler and city-god of Babylon, took preeminence. Near East. (Jastrow, 1898: 55, 118–120; Kramer, 1961: 121)

Mareigua, Maleiwa The beneficent supreme being and creator god who taught mankind to make fire, and as a moral leader punishes incest. The Goajiro, Colombia. (Armstrong, 1948: 382; Pettazzoni, 1956: 21, 416)

Maretkhmakniam The chief spirit of the Botocudo who is responsible for rain and storms, and for the phases of the moon. Brazil. (Métraux, 1946, 3: 539–540; Pettazzoni, 1956: 21)

Marginen A "personification of the creative principle of the world." The Chukchee, Siberia. (Czaplicka, 1969: 256–257)

Martummere The supreme being, a primordial god, and the creator. He was the giver of tools and culture. The same as Nurrundere. Southeast Australia. (Eliade, 1964: 3; Howitt, 1904: 488)

Marumda, Marumbda A god who with Kuksu created the earth, animals and people. He created the details of the surface of the earth. The Eastern Pomo, California. (Loeb, 1926, 2: 300; de Angulo and Freeland, 1928: 251; de Angulo, 1935: 234; Lissner, 1961: 89)

Marunogere The creator god. The Papuan Kiwai, New Guinea. (Leach, 1956: 176)

Marure The creator god of the Shona. Rhodesia. (Mbiti, 1970, 2: 335)

Masala The supreme deity of the Sela Limba. Sierra Leone. (McCulloch, 1950: 71)

Masaranka The supreme god of the Tonko Limba. Sierra Leone. (McCulloch, 1950: 71)

Massim Biambe The omnipotent, incorporeal God and the creator. The Mundangs, Zaire. (Larousse, 1968: 483)

Matariki The creator of the heavens and the earth. Son of Tamaei. Danger Island, Polynesia. (Williamson, 1933, 1: 18)

Matc Hawatuk The beneficent but remote and little worshipped supreme god and the creator of the earth and "all its inhabitants." The Menomini, Wisconsin. (Skinner, 1913: 73, 88)

Matevil, Mathowelia The creator of heaven and earth, and the father of Mastamho. The Mojave Indians, Arizona and California. (Bancroft, 1886, 3: 175)

Math Hen An "old Welsh 'high god,' remembered for magic, which he taught to Gwydion; for the fact that the winds brought to him the least whisper of a conversation" for benevolence and justice. (MacCulloch, 1918: 98)

Mathunda The creator god of the Rimi and the Sandawe who was associated with the sun, either as himself or as his son. Tanzania. (Raa, 1969: 25)

Matunda The creator god of the Turu. Tanzania. (Mbiti, 1970, 2: 336). Kilya Matunda among the Sukuma. (Millroth, 1965: 97). Shida Matunda among the Nyamwezi. (Beier, 1966: 62)

Maunna Creator of the earth and of men, originally as wolves, then they became men. The Winnebago, Wisconsin. (Dorsey, 1889: 140; Maclean, 1876: 429, 438)

Mayandi The chief god to whom sacrifices are made. The Paliyans of the Palni Hills, India. (Dahmen, 1908: 28)

Maykapal Some of the Tagalogs believe that he is the god and creator of the universe "who came down to earth to correct some mistakes . . . raised the sky." Because of the heat of the sun he pierced one of its eyes. Then he seeded the barren earth to cover it with plants, and created the stars and moon for light. Luzon, Philippines. (Jocano, 1969: 26–27)

Mbamba, Kiara The supreme being and sky god of the Ngonde and the Konde. Invoked by the latter for health, fertility, and freedom from illness. Tanzania. (Eliade, 1976, 2: 356; Werner, 1964: 133; Wilson, 1939: 34)

Mbir The god of the Guarayu who created the world and was later known as Miracucha. Bolivia. (Métraux, 1948, 2: 437)

Mboli, Mbori The all-powerful supreme being is also the creator and owner of all, which he controls and is responsible for, including sickness and death, conception and birth. The Azande, Zaire and Sudan. (Williams, 1936: 119; Baxter and Butt, 1953: 94, 95; Pettazzoni, 1956: 38; Lagae, 1926: 66–68; Evans-Pritchard, 1932: 402; 1937: 441–442)

Më The supreme being and the sky. The Na-khi of Yunnan Province, China. (Pettazzoni, 1956: 283)

Meghnath   The omnipotent supreme god who is looked to for assistance when needed. The Gonds, India. (Kurup, 1970: 160)

Meke Meke, Make Make   The chief god and the creator of all things. Easter Island, Polynesia. (Gray, 1925, 5: 133; Williamson, 1933: 73)

Melo   The male of the dual creator Shedi-Melo. With sister Shedi the creators of earth and sky and parents of the human race. The Minyong Abors, Assam. (Furer-Haimendorf, 1954: 594)

Melu   The first being who sat at the head of the river flowing from the Upperworld to the Underworld. His constant washing formed silt which damned the river. When he opened it up and scattered the silt it formed the land. He was also the creator of the first two men. The Bilaan, Philippines. (Jocano, 1969: 32; MacKenzie, 1930: 307; Raats, 1969: 34)

Më-nyi-mo   The omniscient and supreme sky being. The Lolo, China. (Pettazzoni, 1956: 283)

Menzabac, Yum Canan Zabac   The creator is also the god of rain and the receiver of the souls of the good people. The Tzeltal, the Lacandon, Mexico. (Thompson, 1970: 265, 303)

Messon, Michabo, Manibojo   The Great White Hare, the creator of the earth and "elder brother to all beasts." The Montagnais, Quebec/Labrador. (Dragomanov, 1961: 19, 22; Alexander, 1964: 32)

Meu-nyi-mo   The omniscient sky god who created the earth and mankind. The Lo-lo-p'o, Yunnan, China. (Frazer, 1926: 81)

Meyuncame   The creator of all things. Durango, Mexico. (Bancroft, 1886, 3: 179)

Michabo   The Great White Hare was considered many things besides the creator of the earth—the god of light, the god of winds and weather, the giver of culture. Algonquin Indians, United States and Canada. (Spence, 1925, 4: 127; Fiske, 1900: 73, 153–154; Brinton, 1882: 44–47; Dragomanov, 1961: 19, 22)

Migloginsal, Agobinsal   The name of Diwata Magbabaya as the creator of the earth. The Bukidnon, Mindanao, Philippines. (Cole, 1956: 93)

Mikimatt, Nukimatt   The sun goddess and the creator of the world. The Klallam, Washington. (Maclean, 1876: 439; Eells, 1886/87: 680)

Milkom, Malkam   The supreme god of the Ammonites (east of the Jordan River). Near East. (Smith, 1969: 67; Moscati, 1960: 114)

Minjanní   The creator "who, with Sempulon, made men and animals out of stone." The Pari, Borneo. (MacKenzie, 1930: 337)

Miracucha   *See* **Mbir**

Mirirul   The creator among the Illawarra tribes and the judge of men "taking the good to the sky." Australia. (Tylor, 1891: 296)

Mirriki   A name of the supreme being as pure spirit, vital force, immaterial. Upper Volta. (Hebert and Guilhem, 1967: 149)

Mitipa   A god who rose out of the primeval water with the land, then created the sun and moon, and mankind. The Akwa'ala, Baja California. (Gifford and Lowie, 1928: 350–351)

Mkhulumqganti   The supreme being and creator of the world. The Zulu, South Africa. (Pettersson, 1953: 176–177)

Mlengi   A name of Mulungu as the Creator. The Tonga and the Nyanjas, Malawi and Zambia. (Hetherwick, 1925, 9: 420; Mbiti, 1970, 2: 335)

Mlimo   The supreme being of the amaNdebele tribe. Rhodesia. (Williams, 1936: 268)

Modimo   The otiose and little known supreme being and creator god. The Bavenda, the Bapedi, the Sotho, Tswana, Basuto, and Betshuana, South Africa/Botswana. (Schapera, 1937: 264; Willoughby, 1932: 12; Williams, 1936: 279–281, 293; Pettersson, 1953: 143)

(Po Yan) Moh, Amoh   The polymorphous creator god whose wife is Po Ino Nogar. The Chams, Annam and Cambodia. (Cabaton, 1925, 3: 342)

Moihernee   A star god and the creator who shaped the earth, the rivers, the islands, and created the first man and the gray kangaroo. Bruny Island, Tasmania. (Coon, 1971: 288–289)

Molemo   The name usually used for the god Njambe by the Marutse. Rhodesia. (Brinton, 1897: 97)

Moma   The creator god is a celestial deity in his identification with the moon, and also an underworld deity as god of the dead. He is also associated with food and fruits and through them is considered to have renewed life. The Witotoans, Colombia and Peru. (Zerries, 1968: 254)

Monaincherloo A self-existent god who created the sun, moon, and stars, mankind and other things. Adelaide, Australia. (Woods, 1879: 166)

Monan The god who created the earth and sky, and all living things. The Tupi, the Tupinamba, Brazil. (Wagley, 1940: 256n; 1964: 224; Larousse, 1968: 445; Brinton, 1868: 211)

Mooramoora The Good Spirit who created the sun and caused man and other beings to be created by the moon. The Dieyerie, South Australia. (Woods, 1879: 260)

Morigi, Morige The omnipotent supreme god and creator who lives in the seventh heaven. The Khevsurs and the P'shavs, Caucasus. (Gray, 1925, 12: 485; Marr, 1937: 164)

Mori Keraeng The "Highest Being" who created people from bamboo. The Manggarais, Western Flores, Indonesia. (Hatt, 1951: 887–888)

Motogon The omnipotent creator of the heavens and the earth. Western Australia. (Tylor, 1891: 290)

Mtanga Another name for Mulungu, the supreme being and creator, who sends the rain by Mpambe. The Wayao, Zaire. (Lang, 1968: 233–234)

Mu-bya-sei The supreme god, a sky deity, who is identified with the Jade Emperor. He protects the good from illness and disaster and provides for their needs. The Ch'iang of Szechwan, China. (Graham, 1958: 45–47)

Mudimo The creator god of the Sotho. Transvaal. (Krige, 1950: 59)

Mudzimu The supreme being between whom and man the ancestor gods act as intermediaries. The Ma-Lemba, South Africa. (Junod, 1962: 424)

Muhammad He "created the five 'incomparables,' who in their turn created the world and are the five planets." Muhammad was created by 'Ali, is identified with the sun, and forms a triad with 'Ali and Salman-al-Farisi. The Nusairis, Near East. (Basset, 1925, 9: 418)

Mukat With his brother Tumaiyowit (Tamaioit) the creators of the earth and all things in it. They were the sons of darkness (two nights, male and female). They "demonstrated the proper and improper uses of power,"

which Mukat used correctly, Tamaioit returning to the darkness causing earthquakes, storms, etc. Mukat gave life and creativity to the people but also sickness and death. This he alleviated by providing shamans with powers received through guardian intermediaries—an owl, bear, coyote, etc.—to help them, and Telmikish where the spirits of the dead could go. However, the instability and unpredictability which the people saw in all matter and things was reflected in Mukat himself who tricked the people and "violated basic moral principles" when he molested Man-el (Menily), the moon maiden. The rules he made, he broke, ruining the happiness and good will which had prevailed. When he taught useful things they also proved destructive (arrows to hunt but also to kill). With discontentment and disillusionment the people caused his death through bewitchment. The Cahuilla, the Cupeno, California. (Brumgardt and Bowles, 1981: 10–14, 16–19; Strong, 1929: 268; Kroeber, 1925: 692; Hooper, 1920: 317–320; Eliade, 1964: 103; Bean, 1974: 161, 163–164)

Mu-kulo Nzambi The Great God of the Lunda. Angola. (Williams, 1936: 123)

Mukuru The supreme being is the creator of the heavens and the earth, of animals and vegetation. "He made men and four-footed animals come forth from a tree; fowls and fishes . . . from a mountain." As the creator of the soul, *oruzo*, he is known as Ombepo. The north where he lives is closely associated with water and the netherworld—the area of birth, death, and rebirth—and like the netherworld he is the source of good as well as of evil. The Herero, the Bantu. Namibia. (Luttig, 1933: 13–23, 83; Pettersson, 1953: 166–167, 174, 177)

Mula djadi na bolon, Muladjadi The self-existent supreme god and creator of the universe is the father of Batara Guru, Soripada, and Mangalabulan. The Batak, Indonesia. (Wallis, 1939: 124; Eliade, 1964: 286)

Mulenga The creator god. The Lala, Zambia. (Mbiti, 1970, 2: 332)

Mulengi The creator god of the Tumbuka. Malawi. (Mbiti, 1970, 2: 336)

Mulenyi The creator, another name for Imana. Uganda. (Williams, 1936: 175)

Muluku The supreme being and creator of mankind. The Macouas and the Banyis, Mozambique. (Larousse, 1968: 475)

Mulungu, Murungu, Mluku, and many variants The supreme being of many tribes of Malawi, Rhodesia,

Zaire, Tanzania and Uganda. Mulungu is also looked upon as an impersonal power not associated with male or female. Among some he is the creator god, among others he is considered the cause of disasters. Among the Yao of Mozambique, though otiose, he does send the rain and receives the spirits of the dead. (Young, 1950: 50–52, 58; Williams, 1936: 129, 148–149, 212, 217–218, 262; Beidelman, 1963: 44; Hetherwick, 1925, 9: 420; Lang, 1968: 233–234; Stannus, 1922: 312–313)

Mulungu Mumbi The creator of all things. The Kamba, Kenya. (Millroth, 1965: 55)

Mumbi A name of Mulungu as the creator. The Akamba, Kenya and Uganda. (Frazer, 1926: 246; Mbiti, 1970, 2: 327)

Mungu The supreme being and creator god. Tanzania. (Near Stanley Falls). (Frazer, 1926: 143; Davidson, 1969: 272)

Munsumundok Wife of Kinharingan—the chief gods. They procured earth from Bisagit, mixed it with the rock to form the land. She made the sky and together they made the heavenly bodies. Their daughter they cut up, from her body came all food and animals. The Dusans of Tuaran and Tempassuk, North Borneo. (Evans, 1923: 5; MacKenzie, 1930: 336–337)

Muri-muri The creator god of the Efe. Zaire. (Wallis, 1939: 106)

Musa, Musa Gueza The supreme being of the Gumuz. Ethiopia. (Cerulli, 1956: 32)

Musiki One of the names for god as the creator. The Shona, the Korekore, Rhodesia. (Gelfand, 1962: 141; Mbiti, 1970, 2: 332)

Muyaataalemeetarkwau The name given for the supreme being in one myth of the Shawnee Indians. Oklahoma. (Voegelin, 1944: 372)

Mwari The supreme being and creator god is generally benevolent providing abundance and fertility, but in punishment of incest he sends pestilence or crop failure. Among the southern Shona this is an androgynous deity—male as Muali, god of fertility, Dzivaguru, god of rain, Soroezhou, Nyadenga, and Wokumusoro; female as Dziva, Mbuya (grandmother), and Zendere. "Whether god or goddess, the name Mwari conveys the idea of generation, not of creation from nothingness." The Shona and the Karanga, Rhodesia. (Daneel, 1970: 15–17; Gelfand, 1962: 141; 1966: 9, 33; Bullock, 1950: 144–145; Pettersson, 1953: 162–177, 195; Smith, 1950: 126–127)

Mwatuangi A name for God meaning "Cleaver," referring to his giving shape, details, distinctiveness to his creations. The Akamba, Kenya. (Mbiti, 1970, 1: 50)

Mw-ene Designates God—meaning "the Master, the Chief." The Sagala, East Africa. (Williams, 1936: 123)

Mwenenyaga The creator god who is involved in all life ceremonies. The Kikuyu, Kenya. (Gelfand, 1966: 122)

Mwetyi The supreme being who was also a god of oaths and punished perjury. The Shekuni, Guinea. (Lang, 1968: 240; Crawley, 1925, 9: 432)

Nabongo The supreme deity of the Abaluyia. Kenya. (Mbiti, 1970, 2: 327)

Nagaitco Great Traveler, the moon, who created the earth and all on it. He taught men the arts but also introduced dissension. He was subordinate to Tcenes. He was also called Kyoi. The Kato and the Sinkyone, California. (Loeb, 1931: 521; 1921: 23–25; Nomland, 1935: 167, 170; Kroeber, 1925: 150)

Nagi Tanka The powerful Great Spirit who was also called Taku Skanskan, the sky. The Oglala Dacotah. North and South Dakota. (Wallis, 1939: 7; Eliade, 1967: 12)

Naguset, Sa'gama The sun was the creator god and worshipped at sunrise and at sunset. The Micmac, Maritime Provinces, Canada. (Wallis, 1955: 97, 142)

Naicje'etcó dił̃xiłn In one creation version "large black spider" was one of the four who created the earth and sky. The San Carlos Apache, Arizona. (Goddard, 1918: 27)

Naijok The benevolent but sacrifice-demanding supreme being of the Lotuko. Also called Ajob, Lajob, Najok, referring to different aspects. Sudan. (Huntingford, 1953: 90)

Naimuena A great ancestral spirit worshipped as a supreme being, the creator, and a vegetation god. The Uitoto, Colombia and Ecuador. (Karsten, 1926: 301)

Nainema, Nainuema The self-existent, always existent god, who created the universe and all things out of a dream, a "phantasm." The Uitoto, Colombia. (Eliade, 1967: 85; Roheim, 1972: 2, 3)

Ñaiñinen The supreme being, known by numerous names, is sometimes identified with the sun. He "is particularly concerned in birth. He sends the souls of the new-born into the wombs of their mothers" and determines the length of life. He is the father of Yahal, Cloud Man, and Yahalñaut, Cloud Woman. The Koryak, Siberia. (Jochelson, 1908: 24–26)

Naiyenesgani A god who created "the world of the body of Yolgaiisdzan, his grandmother." The Jicarilla Apache. Among other tribes he is the grandson of Ests'unnadlehi. New Mexico. (Goddard, 1911: 206n; 1918: 8)

Najok A name or aspect of the supreme being (in feminine form) when "applied to sickness." The Lotuko, Sudan. (Huntingford, 1953: 90)

Nakwuge The supreme being of the Toposa (Central Nilo-Hamites) who lives in the sky and is indifferent to man though he is "believed to determine the length of a man's life." Sudan. (Gulliver, 1953: 92)

Nalban-Aiy A benevolent sky goddess who is also the creator. Also called Kubay-Khotun-La. The Yakut, Siberia. (Czaplicka, 1969: 277)

Ñamandu The chief deity and giver of life is invoked for game, for good health. He lives in the east. The Guarani, Paraguay/Brazil. (Métraux, 1948, 1: 90)

Namulenga, Namalenga A creator god of the Ila. Also of the Nyanja. Zambia/Malawi. (Mbiti, 1970, 2: 331, 334)

Nan The supreme god of the Yergum, the Anga, Pe, Montoil, Sura, Mumbeke. He is the giver of rain and is invoked for a good harvest. Among the Angas and the Bachama he "receives the souls of good men." Nigeria. (Meek, 1925, 2: 30; Wallis, 1939: 248; Williams, 1936: 215)

Nanabojou, Nanabozhu One of the names of the Great Hare. *See* **Michabo.**

Nana Buluku The primordial androgynous creator deity, parent of Mawu-Lisa. Dahomey. (Williams, 1936: 168; Herskovits, 1938, 2: 101; Parrinder, 1967: 21; Mercier, 1954: 217)

Guru Nanak The supreme god of the Banjara (Charan-Branch). India. (Crooke, 1925, 2: 347)

Ñanderuvucu "Our Great Father, who now resides in a dark region which he lights with the glimmer of his chest." It is believed that one day he will again destroy the world. The Apapocuva-Guarani, Paraguay/Brazil. (Métraux, 1948, 1: 90; 1949: 562)

sNang ba 'od ldan (pr. **Nangwa öden**), **Kun snang khyab pa Khri khug rgyal po**a The creator in Bon cosmogony wherein there are "two aspects, the exterior world (phyi snod) and that contained within it (bcud)." Tibet. (Tucci, 1980: 215)

Nanih Waiya The creator god. The Choctaw, Georgia/Alabama. (Cohane, 1969: 136; Burland, 1965: 150)

Narayana The cosmic supreme god associated with the primeval waters who manifests himself in Brahma, Vishnu, and Rudra. India. (Banerjea, 1953: 54; Long, 1963: 189–190, 197; Dowson, 1961: 220–221; Murray, 1935: 389)

Nasaye, Nasayi The supreme being and beneficent creator of the universe and all things in it; the giver of life and death. The Bahanga, the Kavirondo. Kenya. (Stam, 1910: 360; Williams, 1936: 186)

Nascakiyel, Nascakiyetl The "nearest approach to a supreme deity" that the Tlingit Indians have and from whom "Raven obtained the sun, moon, stars, and eulachon" (candlefish). He was also judge of the dead. Alaska. (Swanton, 1925, 12: 352; 1904/05: 454; Alexander, 1964: 160, 263)

Nawa The creator of all things is both beneficent and maleficent, providing good hunting, but also sending illness. The Bushmen, South Africa and Namibia. (Smith, 1950: 92; Lebzelter, 1934: 50, 56–57; Schapera, 1930: 195)

Naxokosse diłxiłn "black great dipper" (Ursus Major)—one of the four creators of earth and sky in one version of the creation myth. The San Carlos Apache, Arizona. (Goddard, 1918: 27)

Ncemi The creator—a triune god with Kofangana and Nyomi Ngana. The Bakuba, Zaire. (Jeffreys, 1972: 733)

Ndahoro The Great Spirit of the Batoro whose assistants are Wamala and Kyomya. Yganda. (Cunningham, 1905: 56)

Ndjambi, Ndjambi Karunga, Ndjambi Mpungu, Ndjambi Kalunga A beneficent and omnipresent supreme god of dual aspect: as Ndjambi, a heavenly god, as Karunga, a chthonic god with a wife Musisi, both of whom are considered a unity with Ndjambi—forming a bisexual deity. Ndjambi was the creator of the heavens and the earth, the source of rain and atmospheric phenomena; the giver of life as well as of death. The Herero, Namibia. Ndjambi is a name used "from the Congo tribes in the west to the Rotse people in the east, from the Ngala people in the north to the Herero in the south." (Pettersson, 1953: 167, 177, 195–196; Luttig, 1933: 7–9, 18; Smith, 1950: 132)

Ndo   The omniscient supreme being whose name also means the sky, the firmament, the weather. The Miao, China. (Pettazzoni, 1956: 282)

Ndorombwike   A name of the supreme being, Kyala, meaning the creative capacity of the god, the name which is "used on solemn occasions." No offerings are made to him, but rather to the spirits who intercede. The Konde, Tanzania. (MacKenzie, 1925: 179, 182)

Ndriananahary   The supreme being whose son is Ataokoloinona. Madagascar. (Larousse, 1968: 474)

Ndu   (1) The male principle who with Sse was considered creator of heaven and earth. The Na-khi, Yunnan Province, China. (Rock, 1936: 50) (2) A deity considered by the western Rengmas to have created the earth. India. (Mills, 1937: 165)

Nebele   The creatress of all things except mankind, created by her brother Naka. The Sonjo, Tanzania. (Gray, 1963: 98)

Nedamik   The creator god who "subjected the first humans to an ordeal by tickling. Those who laughed were changed into land or water animals. . . . Those humans who maintained self-control became jaguars or men who hunted jaguars." The Toba-Pilaga, Paraguay and Argentina. (Levi-Strauss, 1969: 120)

Nekilstlas   The raven who was the beneficent creator of all things was always-existent and could transform himself. He provided the Haida with light, water, fire, etc. British Columbia. (Niblack, 1888: 378; Maclean, 1876: 438)

Nemunemu   Two brothers who were the creators of the earth and the sky. The "elder made the mainland and gave his people the bow and stone club, the younger made the islands and the sea, and instructed his people in making spears and burning lime for betel-chewing." Papua, New Guinea. (Haddon, 1925, 9: 348)

Ne Nanatch   The supreme being who hears everything, everywhere. The Gros Ventres, Montana. (Pettazzoni, 1956: 15, 378)

Nenechen "Master of men" and **Nenemapun** "Master of the land"   Names of the supreme being and creator of all things. As Nenemapun he is invoked in rites for rain and fine weather, for fertility of land and animals, for longevity. This is an androgynous deity, called father/mother, young man/woman, etc. Also known as Pillan. The Mapuche-Huilliche (Araucanians), Chile. (Cooper, 1946, 6: 742, 747; Pettazzoni, 1956: 419; Faron, 1968: 63, 65, 66, 73, 100)

Nenekicex   A benevolent supreme deity and creator. The Kamchadal, Siberia. (Jochelson, 1900/02: 236)

Nenemapun   *See* **Nenechen**

Neo   The supreme god, "the Great Spirit of Life." The Iroquois, Eastern United States. (Schoolcraft, 1857, 1: 316; 1857, 6: 637)

Nesulk   The Great Spirit and creator. The Micmac Indians, Gulf of St. Lawrence, Canada. (Müller, 1968: 159)

Nexhequiriac   A god who created nine gods, sons (Shishec, Naac, Yahui, Cuhui, Cunma, Nanec, Yuhuec, Nima, Chunguy—all names preceded by "Naac") who helped him create all things on earth. The Trique Tribe, Oaxaca, Mexico. (Valantini, 1899: 38–39)

Ngai   The self-existent and omniscient high god and creator of all things lives in the sky and is manifest in the sun, the stars, the moon, the atmospheric phenomena. His attitude is governed by people's behavior. Animal sacrifices are made to him only in times of drought or epidemic, or severe troubles. Among the Masai the stars are his eyes at night, the sun by day. The Kikuyu, the Agekoyo, Kenya. (Kenyatta, 1937: 308, 312; Williams, 1936: 188, 190; Middleton, 1953: 66; Pettazzoni, 1956: 6, 39)

Ngala   The supreme god is a deity of the sky and of the atmosphere, of all its elements. He is identified with the Islamic Allah. The Bambara, Mali. (Tauxier, 1927: 169, 173). Among the Gbande he is the creator god. Liberia. (Schwab, 1947: 315)

Ngewo   The supreme god and creator of all including the spirits. He is otiose though he can be approached with prayers; sends the rain on his wife, Ndoi, the earth. The Mende, Sierra Leone. (Gelfand, 1966: 125; McCulloch, 1950: 39; Little, 1951: 217–218; 1954: 114)

Ngulaitait, Nguletet   Variant names of Uletet, the supreme being of the Kuku. Sudan. (Huntingford, 1953: 50)

Nguleso   The supreme being and sky god. The Kakwa, Sudan. (Huntingford, 1953: 55; Mbiti, 1970, 2: 131)

Nguluve   The remote "first cause" and creator of the world. The Hehe-Bena-Sangu peoples, Tanzania. (Mumford, 1934: 221)

Nguluvi "The supreme god of the Safwa . . . often identified with the sun." Tanzania. (Willis, 1966: 71)

Nguluwi The supreme being and creator god who bestows children, rain, good fortune, and health. The Wakulwe, Tanzania. (Frazer, 1926: 193–196)

Ngulwe The remote supreme god and creator of the world. The Kuulwe, Tanzania. (Willis, 1966: 66)

Ngun The beneficent creator god and one of duality: Ngun lo ki, the celestial aspect, associated with rain and lightning; Ngun lo kak, the chthonic aspect. The Bari, the Mondari, the Pojulu. Sudan. (Seligman, 1931: 7, 8; Huntingford, 1953: 42, 66, 70)

Nguruhi The all-powerful but remote supreme being and creator who controls the elements and human destiny, but leaves daily occurrences to the influence of the ancestor spirits. The Wahehe, East Africa. (Frazer, 1961: 188–189)

Nguruvi The supreme being and creator god who is sometimes manifest as the sun, sometimes "described as being like the wind and invisible." He punishes with epidemics. The Safwa, Tanzania. (Millroth, 1965: 19, 40)

Ninavanhu-Ma Mother goddess and creator. South Africa. (Mutwa, n.d.: vii)

Ninewu The creator and instructor "in behavior and work." The Tson, Formosa. (Er-wei, 1959: 536)

Ningkong wa The god who combined the three skies and earths which had appeared and placed them in position. Then with his brothers he formed the earth's surface. When the earth was habitable he formed man. The Katchins, Burma. (Gilhodes, 1908: 677, 679, 682)

Niottsi The name of Yeddariye, the supreme being, as the creator. The Chippewa Indians, Canada. (Cooper, 1934: 49)

Niparaja, Niparaya The omnipotent supreme god and creator of heaven and earth whose wife is Anajicojondi (Amayicoyondi). He was also called Añadian, and is a god of peace. The Pericues, Baja California. (Loeb, 1931: 549; Bancroft, 1886, 3: 169, 529; Larousse, 1968: 434)

Nirantali The creator goddess. The Konds, India. (Elwin, 1954: 639)

Nishkam A title of the Great Spirit. The Micmac Indians. Gulf of St. Lawrence, Canada. (Muller, 1968: 159)

Niwa A goddess who, with Dombe, created the world and its creatures. The Tangsas (Khemsing tribe), Indo/Burmese. (Dutta, 1959: 3)

Njakomba, Mbombianda The supreme being and creator god who rules over all is not worshipped. He is believed to make the procreation of children possible. The Nkundo, Zaire. (Hulstaert, 1938: 12, 439)

Njambe The high god of the Marutse whose common name is Molemo. Rhodesia. (Brinton, 1897: 97)

Nkir The supreme being among some Bantu tribes of Zaire. Also the creator god of the Badinga (Bantu). (Williams, 1936: 90)

Nkya A "vague, distant, amoral creator." The Toro, Uganda. (Taylor, 1962: 63)

Nobu The god who created the world. At Eromanga, Anaiteum, New Hebrides. (Codrington, 1881: 295; MacKenzie, 1930: 241; Larousse, 1968: 449)

Nocuma The omnipotent being who created the earth and all living things, including man, Ejoni, and woman, Ae, out of the earth. The coastal Acagchemem, California. (Bancroft, 1886, 3: 164–165; Boscana, 1933: 31)

Nodimo Nakaranga The supreme being of the Basuto. South Africa. (Williams, 1936: 309)

Noho Chac Yum, Nohotsakyum (*See also* **Hachakyum**) Great Father, the chief god of the Lacandon pantheon and the creator, the beneficent protector against Hapikern. Other names—Ara, Acakyum, Ac Bilam,'Umbrikam. He is one of four brothers—with Yanto, Sukukyum, and Uyitzin, sons of Chac Nicte. Mexico. (Tozzer, 1941: 138; Roys, 1949: 161; Thompson, 1970: 202; Cline, 1944: 112; Weyer, 1961: 84)

Notawinan "Our Father," a title of the supreme being of the Cree Indians. Ontario. (Cooper, 1934: 19)

Nourali The self-existent high god and creator who was envisioned as a bird, a crow or an eagle. Murray River, Australia. (Brinton, 1897: 159)

Nowutset With Utset the creators of the celestial bodies. She was the mother of men, other than Indians. The Sia, Pueblo Indians, New Mexico. (Fewkes, 1895, 1: 123; Alexander, 1964: 203)

Nphan Wa The supreme deity who formed the surface of the earth. The Kachin, Burma. (Scott, 1964: 263)

Ntse, Ntzi The supreme god who lives in the sky and is beneficent without need for ceremonies. He controls all. The Ch'uan Miano, Southwest China. (Graham, 1937: 61; 1961: 70)

Nua An omnipotent deity, creator of all. The Ngong, Nigeria. (Williams, 1936: 208)

Nukimatt, Mi-ki-matt A goddess, the incarnation of the sun, who was the creator of the world. Also called I-nach-tin-ak. The Klallam Indians, British Columbia. (Eells, 1886/87: 680)

Num The omniscient and omnipotent supreme god and creator is identified with the universe itself. The Nenets, the Samoyed, Siberia. (Prokof'yeva, 1964: 564; Struve, 1880: 794; Islavin, 1847: 57; Lissner, 1961: 165; Eliade, 1964: 9, 227; Michael, 1963: 167; Pettazzoni, 1956: 6, 443; Pettersson, 1957: 21; Wales, 1957: 66–67)

Numi-Tarem The omniscient and omnipotent sky god of the Voguls who created the earth and is "the Master of life and death." Considered a bear by some groups. Siberia. (MacCulloch, 1964: 330; Roheim, 1954: 26; 1972: 2)

Nun The creator god of the Bari tribe. Sudan. (Gelfand, 1966: 122)

Nunurao A goddess who was the creator of the universe. The Yami, Formosa. (Del Re, n.d.: 57)

Nurrendere, Nurunderi, Martummere The supreme being and sky god created all things on earth, the terrain along the Murray River and the fish which live in it. He has two wives who are sisters; gave man all culture; manifests his will through the rainbow. Australia. (Eliade, 1958: 42; 1964: 3; Mountford, 1969: 20; Howitt, 1904: 488; Poignant, 1967: 117)

Nustoo A goddess of the Yaros, Dravidians of North India, who created the world. (Brinton, 1897: 160)

Nwari The supreme being of the Nakaranga. Southern Rhodesia. (Williams, 1936: 268)

Nyadenga The remote supreme being and sky god, the creator. An otiose god, though he is credited at times as "knowing" (the truth, e.g.), as healing, as sending the rain. The Venda and the Shona, South Africa and Rhodesia. (Pettersson, 1953: 143–144, 194; Gelfand, 1962: 141; Williams, 1936: 264)

Nyalaka de "The Supreme Being . . . identified with the Sun . . . and regarded as the Creator of men and things." The Longuda, Nigeria. (Williams, 1936: 217)

Nyalic(h) The omniscient god of the firmament, the creator, and the establisher of order and giver of rain. The Dinka, Sudan. (Gelfand, 1966: 121; Butt, 1952: 131; Seligman, 1931: 3, 6; Pettazzoni, 1956: 15)

Nyama The supreme deity of the Mumbake, identified with the sun. Nigeria. (Meek, 1925, 2: 30)

Nyamahanga The creator god of the Konjo, the Toro. Uganda. (Taylor, 1962: 63, 94; Mbiti, 1970, 2: 331)

Nyamalenga The name of God as the creator. Other names—Lesa, Chiuta. The Ansenga, Rhodesia. (Williams, 1936: 259)

Nyambe (1) The supreme being and creator god, widespread over Western Equatorial Africa. Variants: Nzambi, Ndyambi, Dzambi, Tsambi, Yame, Sami, Zam, Monzam, Onayame. (Smith, 1950: 156, 159) (2) Nyambe, Nyambi–The creator of all things whose wife was Nasilele. They lived on earth for a time but left to avoid the evil actions of Kamunu. The Barotse, the Malozi, Zambia. (Feldman, 1963: 36–37; Beier, 1966: 7–14; Williams, 1936: 122; Smith, 1950: 156, 159) Among the Hambukushu of Botswana the creator god to whom their souls return at death. He permits people to be afflicted with *mandengure,* an illness and a form of madness, and the *mandengure* ceremony is performed to alleviate and cure it. (Larson, 1971: 57–60)

Nyame The supreme being is also usually named as the creator, is credited with omniscience and omnipresence, is presented as both male and female. Nyame is given as male (Pettazzoni, Clarke, Evans, Gelfand); as female (Meyerowitz—the mother goddess, "the one supreme deity without beginning or end. . . . The substance or body of Nyame, in her aspect of Moon- and Firmament-goddess, is envisaged as fire; the life-giving spirit or power that animated the fire, and caused the birth of the universe, is called the kra"); and as androgynous—(Parrinder—"Nyame of Ashanti is sometimes said to be both male and female; the female element is symbolized by the moon. . . . The male element is seen in the sun. . . . The female element created men with water, and the male sun shot its life-giving fire into human veins."). The Ashanti and the Akan, Ghana. (Parrinder, 1949: 26; Meyerowitz, 1958: 23–24; Clarke, 1930: 436, 438; Gelfand, 1966: 118; Pettazzoni, 1956: 6, 37; Evans, 1950: 244–245, 249–250; Queval, 1968: 16)

Nyamia The supreme god was associated with the sky, with atmospheric phenomena. The Guinea and Senegambia groups, West Africa. (Larousse, 1968: 483)

Nya-mpamvu-zentze The all-powerful god of the Tete. Upper Zambesi, Zaire. (Williams, 1936: 123)

Nyamuanga, Nyeruanga, Tsuba The supreme being of the Bakara of Lake Victoria Nyanza. East Africa. (Williams, 1936: 209)

Nyamuhanga, Ruhanga The beneficent creator god. The Bahima, the Ankore, Uganda. (Thomas, 1950: 204; Mbiti, 1970, 2: 327; Williams, 1936: 167)

Nyamuzinda The First Cause, the creator, the giver of life, but also the source of great disasters. The Bashi, Zaire. (Williams, 1936: 107)

Nyankopon A supreme being as one of a triad with Nyame and Odumankoma. He personifies the sun and represents the vital force. The Akan, the Ashanti, Ghana. (Danquah, 1952: 360–361; Meyerowitz, 1958: 37, 82–83; Parrinder, 1967: 67)

Nyasaye (of the south) or **Wele** (of the north) The creator god of the world and of mankind. The Abaluyia of Kavironda, Kenya. (Wagner, 1954: 28)

Nyasi The supreme being and creator god who controls birth and death but is not worshipped. The Luo, Kenya. (Butt, 1952: 115–116)

Nyege The supreme being at Fowler's Bay, Australia. (Basedow, 1925: 295)

Nyesoa The creator god of the French Ivory Coast. Africa. (Schwab, 1947: 315)

Nyimpo The remote supreme being and creator god. The Effutu, Ghana. (Wyllie, 1966: 477)

Nyongmo The supreme being and a sky and rain god. The Ga, Ghana. (Parrinder, 1950: 224–240; Field, 1937: 34; Pettazzoni, 1956: 36)

Nysaye The supreme being and creator god, the giver of life and death. The Nilotic Kavirondo. Same as Nasaye of the Bantu Kavirondo. Kenya. (Stam, 1910: 360)

Nzakomba The supreme being of the Lulanga. Upper Congo. (Frazer, 1926: 142)

Nzambi The supreme being and creator of all things punishes transgressions, is responsible for life and death, rains and fertility, is not approached directly, only through the ancestor spirits. The Chokwe, the Luchazi, the Lunda, the Bakongo, the Balari. Angola, Zaire, and Rhodesia. (McCulloch, 1951: 72–73; Williams, 1936: 94, 97; Feldman, 1963: 112; Werner, 1964: 125)

Nzambi Mpungu The supreme being and creator of all things who punishes wrong-doing. The Bantu, the Vili, the Bakongo, and the Fiorts, Angola, Gabon, and Zaire. (Williams, 1936: 90, 94, 122, 130; Lang, 1968: 249; Howells, 1948: 230; Werner, 1964: 125)

Nzame The sky god and creator of all things. The Fan of the Gabon forest. (Williams, 1936: 122; Lang, 1905: 54; Frazer, 1926: 135)

Obashi The supreme god who is also addressed in prayers as Ewerok-babi. The Ekoi, Cameroons. (Frazer, 1926: 135)

Obasi The supreme being and sky god was once considered of a dual nature—Father/Mother-god. The Ibibio, Nigeria. (Parrinder, 1949: 21, 38)

Obassi The supreme god of the Awhawzara and Ezza tribes of the Ibo, Nigeria. (Jeffreys, 1972: 730)

Obassi idi n'elu The supreme god of the Ututu tribe of the Ibo. Nigeria. (Jeffreys, 1972: 730)

Obatala A Yoruban sky god involved in the work of the creation. Nigeria, Brazil (Bahia). (Lucas, 1948: 89, 90; Courlander, 1973: 5, 6; Verger, 1954: 12; Bastide, 1960: 569)

Obumo The god of thunder was considered their principal deity, the First Cause, and the source of all things. His wife/mother is Eka Abassi. The Ibibio, Nigeria. (Williams, 1936: 203; Frazer, 1926: 127–128)

Odin, Wotan The Scandinavian/Teutonic All-Father, the chief of the gods of the Aesir pantheon, a god of many functions. He was the son of Bor and Bestla, brother of Vili (Hoenir) and Ve (Lodr). Together the brothers slew Ymir, the great giant of the beginning, and from his body formed the world, from his skull the heavens, from his blood the sea and fresh waters, from his bones the mountains. Then they created man from the ash tree and woman from the elm. Odin gave them soul and life, their spirit. He ruled the world organizing and arranging human affairs. He was always a god of war, controlling the battle and the victory, inspiring the berserks with their frenzy. As a god of death half of the fallen warriors came to him in Valhalla, the other half were claimed by Freya. He was an early god of the gallows, to whom humans were sacrificed by hanging. By his own voluntary sacrifice of hanging from the tree Yggdrasill and pierced by a sword, he gained the magic lore of the runes; by the sacrifice of one eye he gained the wisdom and foreknowledge found in Mimir's spring. His omniscience, however, was his only while seated on his throne in Valaskjalf where he lived, and from where he could see all worlds. As the personification of the sky, the heavens, he was associated with sunshine, the weather, the seasons, and was the spouse of the earth represented by his wives: Jord, "the primitive earth," mother of Thor; Frigga, "the fertile summer-earth," mother of Balder, Hermod, and Tyr; Rinda, "personification of the hard and frozen earth," mother of Vali. Odin was also versed in poetry and the arts (here associated with Saga); gained the draught of inspiration, the mead, by marrying Gunlod, the mother of Bragi. (Grimm, 1883, 1: 131–135; 2: 559–561; Guerber, 1895: 23–29, 36, 39, 43; Thorpe, 1851: 16, 167; Davidson, 1964: 27–29, 51, 66, 142, 144, 201; Frazer, 1960: 412; Branston, 1955: 41, 59, 79, 112; Stern, 1898: 8, 17; Anderson, 1891: 196, 215, 236; Murray, 1935: 358, 360–362; Schoeps, 1961: 105; Turville-Petre, 1964: 35–38, 43–65)

Odomankoma As a triad with Nyame and Nyankopon a ruler of the universe and continuously creative, representing "creative intelligence." He introduced the seven-day week, each day ruled by a planet, and also death. The Akan, Ghana. (Danquah, 1952: 360–361; Meyerowitz, 1958: 46, 55; Danquah, 1944: 30, 58)

Odudua, Oduduwa, Oduwa In some places a goddess and given variously as the wife of Orishala (with whom she was a creator) and Obatala. Also considered male and the creator of the world at the bidding of Olodumare. And again, as the brother of Orisha and sons of Aramfe, they were creators of the world and responsible for peopling it. The Yoruba, Nigeria. (Davidson, 1969: 51; Parrinder, 1950: 226; 1949: 27; Lucas, 1948: 93–95; Jeffreys, 1935: 352; Wyndham, 1919: 107–108; Courlander, 1973: 7)

Ogbora The supreme being, but his power was actually limited to the underworld. His wife was Odiong and son Osa. Nigeria. (Parrinder, 1950: 236; Jeffreys, 1972: 733)

Oghene The remote supreme being is associated with the sky and its atmospheric phenomena which he controls, and is the creator of all. He is also a god of rewards and retributions, receives no prayers or sacrifices directly. The Isoko tribe, Nigeria. (Welch, 1934: 163)

Ohe The omnipresent and supreme sky god. The Egede, Nigeria. (Armstrong, 1955: 146)

Oicok The supreme being of the Lokoya. Sudan. (Huntingford, 1953: 78)

Oiki, Oinoteki The omnipotent supreme being and creator. The Basabie and the Sabei, Uganda. (Williams, 1936: 177, 159; Mbiti, 1970, 2: 334)

Oke, Okeus The chief god, who takes the form of a great hare, created mankind, the land, the water, fish, and the "great deare" which became the source (through the magical scattering of its hair) of all deer. The Powhatan, the Potomac. Virginia. (Swanton, 1946: 743, 749)

Olelbis The chief god of the Wintun who lives in the heavens. Also called Nomhliestawa (Nomlestowa). California. (Curtin, 1903: xxix, xxx; Kroeber, n.d.: 176; Du Bois, 1935: 72)

Olodumare (the older name), **Olorun** The supreme god, omniscient, omnipresent, benevolent. The creator—himself and through others. He is the giver of laws, the impartial judge of all that occurs, the controller of destinies. The Yoruba, Nigeria. Also Brazil. (Idowu, 1962: 18, 39, 42–47; Davidson, 1962: 51; Parrinder, 1949: 19; 1950: 230; 1967: 20; Lucas, 1948: 34; Landes, 1940: 264)

Olokupilele The omniscient creator deity who punishes sin. The Cuna Indians, Panama. (Pettazzoni, 1956: 416)

Olorun, Oloron The omnipotent, omnipresent, omniscient supreme god who commissioned Orisha Nla to create the earth out of the watery space and to create man, to whom Olorun gave life. Men are accountable to him through his laws, with impartial judgement. The Yoruba, Nigeria. (Lucas, 1948: 34, 51; Parrinder, 1950: 226–230; 1967: 20; Williams, 1936: 211–212)

Omahank Numakchi The creator deity of the Mandan Indians. North Dakota. (Tylor, 1891: 287)

Omaua The supreme being and creator of the earth and of "most living things." He lives in the west and is considered also to be an enemy because he is associated with alien tribes and whites and "their pernicious influences, diseases." He is invoked "by shamans both for black and white magic" and is believed to send the rains. The Waika, Brazil and Venezuela. (Zerries, 1968: 248; Becher, 1960: 94)

Omecihuatl, Ome Ciuatl The female creative principle of Ometeotl. With Ometechutli the Lord and Lady of Duality, expressing the "powers of generation and conception" and expressing the masculine/feminine aspect of Ometeotl. Mexico. (Caso, 1958: 9, 10; Thompson, 1970: 200; Nicholson, 1967: 27; Leon-Portilla, 1982: 53, 83, 84)

Ometecuhtli A god representing the masculine creative principle of Ometeotl, Omecihuatl the femine creative principle, and together called the Lord and Lady of Duality. Also called Tonacatecuhtli. Mexico. (Reed, 1966: 69; Nicholson, 1967: 11, 23; Burland, 1967: 93, 130; Caso, 1958: 9, 10; Thompson, 1970: 200; Vaillant, 1962: 142; Leon-Portilla, 1982: 53, 83, 84)

Ometéotl The supreme deity, androgynous, the creative energy, and master of the universe maintaining and giving orders, is a god of duality in all things and qualities, representing "the equilibrium rather than the diversity with creation." As the god of duality he is reflected in all opposites, many manifestations of the one god—Ometecuhtli as the masculine principle of the creative energy, Omecíhuatl the feminine principle, Lord and Lady of Duality; Catlallatónac, the star "which illumines things" identified with the sun, and Citlalinicue "she of the starry skirt," making the stars shine at night; Tezcatlanextia (who illumines) and Tezcatlipoca (who obscures with smoke) as "the mirror of day and night;" Tonacatecuhtli and Tonacacíhuatl, Lord and Lady of our flesh, our sustenance (identifiable with the Lord and Lady of Duality), through whom Ometéotl is the parent of four sons, the cosmic powers or forces—(1) Tlatlauhqui Tezcatlipoca, born red, and identified with the east, Tlapallan; (2) Yayauhqui Tezcatlipoca, born black, associated with the night, the region of the dead, the north; (3) Quetzalcóatl, or Yoalli ehécatl, white, associated with the wind, the west, "region of fecundity and life" and as personifying Ometéotl "the embodiment of wisdom" and truth; (4) Omitéotl, or Maquizcóatl, or Huitzilopochtli, blue, associated with the south. Ometéotl is Xiuhtecuhtli as Lord of Fire, Time, and Huehuetéotl "the old god," mother/father. Among his titles are Moyocoyani as the self-existent, self-created, and Yohualliehecatl meaning "Invisible (like the night) and intangible (like the wind)." Ometeotl dwells in Omeyocan, the place of duality, above the highest heavens. The Aztec, the Nahua, Mexico. (Leon-Portilla, 1961: 449; 1982: 30–34, 53, 83, 84, 90–98; Reed, 1966: 69; Nicholson, 1967: 11, 23; Caso, 1958: 9, 10; Thompson, 1970: 200; Vaillant, 1962: 142; Burland, 1967: x, 93, 130)

Omeyacigoat, Omeyatecigoat With Omayateite, the supreme deities. Mother of Quiateot (the Nicarao), Tamagastad (the Pipil). Nicaragua. (Lothrop, 1926: 68; Krickeberg, 1968: 81)

Omeyateite, Omayateite With Omeyacigoat, the supreme deities. Father of Quiateot (the Nicarao), Tamagastad (the Pipil). Nicaragua. (Lothrop, 1926: 68; Krickeberg, 1968: 81)

Omitéotl, Maquizcóatl *See* **Huitzilopochtli**

Ompu mula jadi na bolan The high god and the great god of the creation under whom are Batara Guru, Soripada, and Mangala bulan. The Toba Battak, Malay Archipelago, Indonesia. (Kern, 1925, 8: 347)

Ompu Tuhan mula jadi The high god of the Battak whose daughter molded the earth and gave birth to mankind. He "transferred his power to three gods: Batara guru, Soripada, and Mañalabulan." The Battak, Indonesia. (Kruijt, 1925, 7: 249)

Omubumbi The creator deity of the Gisu. Uganda. (Mbiti, 1970, 2: 330)

Omuhangi The creator deity of the Ankore. Also given as Ruhanga and Nyamuhanga. Uganda. (Mbiti, 1907, 2: 327)

Omuqkatos The Great Spirit who is the sun. The Blackfeet, Northern Plains, Canada/United States. (Maclean, 1876: 439)

Onkoy The supreme god of the Chavin is "a hybrid, both male and female, half-feline and half-reptile." Peru. (Flornoy, 1958: 83)

Onulap The Great Spirit and highest god who lives in the region Letulap. He is the father of the gods and of human beings (though he has grandparents) and is the source of all things, both good and evil. Truk, Micronesia. (Bollig, 1927: 3, 6)

Onum The sun is the high god and the creator. The Kadara, Nigeria. (Gunn, 1956: 135; Mbiti, 1970, 2: 331)

Onyame, Onyankopon, Odomankoma The supreme god and creator—a god of light, of rain and sunshine, of growth. The Akan, the Ashanti, the Akim-Kotoku. Ghana. (Danquah, 1944: 30, 38–39, 46; Field, 1948: 158; Williams, 1936: 24; Busia, 1954: 192)

Opo geba snulat The omniscient high god and creator of mankind. His messenger is Nabiata. Buru Island (the Moluccas), Indonesia. (Kruijt, 1925, 7: 248; Pettazzoni, 1956: 334)

Orekajuvakai The demiurge who brought "men forth from the bowels of the earth." The Tereno, Brazil. (Levi-Strauss, 1969: 123)

Ori The all-seeing supreme being who controls the elements, but "takes little interest in human affairs." The Madi, Sudan, Zaire, and Uganda. (Baxter and Butt, 1953: 118; Budge, 1973, 1: 374)

Orisha-nla Creator of the earth at the behest of Olodumare (Olorun), and also of man to whom Olodumare gave life. The Yoruba, Nigeria. (Idowu, 1962: 19–21; Parrinder, 1949: 27; 1967: 20; Davidson, 1966: 124)

Ormuzd, Ohrmazd This name a later form of Ahura-Mazda, creator god of Iran. (Dresden, 1961: 337; Dragomanov, 1961: 24; Bulfinch, 1898: 392–393)

Osa, Osanobua The supreme sky god, ruler of the universe, and the creator. Son of Ogbora and Odiong. The Edo tribe of Benin, the Bini, Nigeria. (Jeffreys, 1972: 733; Parrinder, 1949: 21; Frazer, 1926: 126)

Osaw A sky god who together with Nsi created all things. The Ekoi, Nigeria and Cameroon. (Lowie, 1925: 46)

Oshala In Brazil a god of creation. (Verger, 1957: 440)

Osowo The supreme being, a sky god, who is also identified with or represented by the big tree which is worshipped. The Indem, Nigeria. (Mockler-Ferryman, 1925, 9: 277; Barns, 1925, 12: 449)

Oteborom, Ore Boram A self-created god, as was Sirma Thakoor, the sun. They created the earth and all things thereon. The Hos, India. (Elwin, 1949: 18; Majumdar, 1950: 251). Among the Mundas, with Singbonga "the self-existent primeval deities . . . created a boy and girl, taught them the art of love, and placed them in a cave to people the world." (Crooke, 1925, 5: 13)

Otshirvani The creator god, and with Chagan-Shukuty the creators of man. Central Siberia. (Long, 1963: 205; MacCulloch, 1964: 377)

Ove A god to whom the creation of the world is sometimes attributed, sometimes it is Ngendei. He is considered responsible for "all monsters and malformations." Fiji Islands, Melanesia. (MacKenzie, 1930: 147; Larousse, 1968: 449)

Owase The omniscient, omnipresent supreme being who bestows the rain. The Ba-Kwiri, Cameroons. (Pettazzoni, 1956: 36)

Owura The name of the supreme being of a hinterland clan of the Biloforn dialect. Niger Delta, West Africa. (Jeffreys, 1972: 730)

Oxala A remote supreme god who gave them their laws. Belem, Brazil. (Leacock, 1972: 156)

Oxomogo, Oxomoco A deity associated with Tamagastat and Cipattonal in the creation. The Nicarao of Nic-

aragua. Among the Aztec a goddess who is associated with Cipactonal as the creators of the calendar. Mexico. (Lothrop, 1926: 66–67; Krickeberg, 1968: 53)

Pabothkew, Paabothkew "Our Grandmother," Mother Earth, is considered omniscient—the Great Spirit and the Creator. The Shawnee, East-Central United States. (Harrington, 1921: 20; Pettazzoni, 1956: 13, 381)

Pachacamac The supreme god of the coastal Indians was the son of the Sun and the Moon and the brother of Con who had created people. He was more powerful and drove out Con, transforming the people into animals and birds, after which he created a new race as men presently are. He taught them the arts and crafts, and agriculture. Peru. (Osborne, 1968: 107; Larousse, 1968: 442–443; Brinton, 1882: 195–196; Mishkin, 1940: 225; Kubler, 1946, 2: 396)

Padma-sambhava T. kun-tu-bzang-po. Same as Samatabhadra. Universal Goodness; the supreme buddha. The Tibetan name "was a title of the supreme being and one of the earliest p'ön-po adaptions." The Tibetan Buddhists who based their traditions on Padma-sambhava adopted the Tibetan name, applying the same epithets to both; both are "the supreme buddha-body. Thus all the tranquil and fierce divinities emanate as much from him as from Samanta-bhadra." From the areas of the cosmic body emanate: the tranquil divinities, from the heart; the fierce divinities, from the head; Padma-Narteśvara (Lotus Lord of Dance) with his partner the Red Dākinî, from the throat; the Dākinî of Knowledge, from the navel; "the fierce divinity Vajra-kumāra (Adamantine Youth) with his partner. He is the defender of all the other divinities" from the groin. Tibet. (Snellgrove, 1957: 232)

pagé abé The omnipotent, omniscient, omnipresent god who created the universe, the animals, and the plants. His creating, fertilizing element is considered solar semen. He is the source of fertility, of heat, and of morals. The Desana, Colombia. (Reichel-Dolmatoff, 1971: 25, 41, 42, 48)

Pah-ah The Great Spirit of the Piute Indians. California (Lang, 1887: 132)

Pahatal and **Pahatara** Co-creators of all things except man. Pahatara created man and while doing so he left for materials. His wife Andin Bamban was convinced by Peres (a good-bad being) that man should be mortal and so joined him in finishing the creation. When Pahatara returned he agreed. The Ot Danum, Borneo. (Raats, 1969: 27)

Pahtumawas The Great Spirit of the Minsi, Lenape Indians, who taught them ceremonies and rituals. East Coast United States. (Harrington, 1921: 19, 127)

Pakbangha The supreme being of the Chawte clan of the Old Kuki. Indonesia. (Mackenzie, n.d.: 275)

Pakrokitat The "beneficent creator . . . from whose left shoulder Kukitat, the evil creator . . . was born . . . finally Pakrokitat left the earth to his evil brother and retired to a world of his own to which people go after death." The Serrano Indians, California. (Leach, 1950, 2: 841)

Pamulak Manobo The creator of the universe, of vegetation, and of man. The Bagobo, Philippines. (Benedict, 1916: 11, 19; Kroeber, 1918, 2: 43)

Papa The creator god, also called Dioslele, who created his own wife as well. The San Blas Cuna, Panama. (Stout, 1947: 40)

Para Brahma The supreme god of the monotheistic Siva Narayanis or Sio Naranis. Northwest India. (Grierson, 1925, 11: 579)

Paramesvar The supreme being of the Chamars. Among the Doms he is vaguely so, benevolent as well as malevolent and "stands for a number of deities"—among them Bhagwan, Narayana, Vishnu, Siva. India. (Lillingston, 1925, 3: 353; Briggs, 1953: 548–549)

Paramushela The beneficent and wise creator of the universe. The Konds, India. (Schulze, 1912: i, 1)

Pariacaca A falcon and the creator god, a god of wind and of waters. His four falcon brothers are the four winds. They were all hatched from "five eggs on the mountain Condorcoto." The Huarochiri Indians, Peru. (Brinton, 1882: 46; Osborne, 1968: 95–96; Alexander, 1920: 232)

Parikap and **Parikut** Brothers who were the creators of the world. The Arua, Bolivia. (Métraux, 1942: 151)

Pase-Kamui The beneficent supreme god and creator who is the source of "light and life, of health" and the judge of all after death. The Ainu, Japan. (Batchelor, 1925, 1: 240, 242, 252; Munro, 1963: 12)

Pa Silong The beneficent supreme being of the Klemantans. Same as Laki Tenangan. Borneo. (Kern, 1925, 8: 347; Hose, 1912: 6)

Pathel The supreme being and creator who is a sky god and is responsible for the weather. Same as Pathian. Bengal and Upper Burma. (Pettazzoni, 1956: 293)

Pathen, Patheng The supreme being and creator, the ruler of the universe, who uses the weather to vent his displeasure. The Thado and the Thadon Kuki, India, Bengal, and Upper Burma. (Elwin, 1949: 89; Pettazzoni, 1956: 293)

Pathian The supreme being and creator, beneficent, but little interested in human affairs. The Lushei, the Kukis, and the Mizos, India, Assam, and Burma. (Barkataki, 1969: 83; Hodson, 1925, 8: 197; Shakespear, 1912: 61; Biswas, 1956: 102)

Patol The chief god of the Tzental Indians whose wife is Alaghom Naom. Mexico. (Rhys, 1937: 7)

Pekujike The creator of the world is also an earthquake god, and a deity of the life after death "with whom the ghost must strive in combat." The Naga of Manipur, India. (Hodson, 1911: 127, 161)

Penkye Otu The beneficent chief god of the Effutu who protects their health and welfare, is also protective in war. Ghana. (Wyllie, 1966: 478)

Peritnalik In a later version of their mythology a supreme and benevolent deity "who created things good and useful and thenceforward took benevolent care of mankind" (in contrast to an earlier version with Kaloaraik). The Tobas, Argentina and Paraguay. (Karsten, 1932: 110)

Phanes In Orphic cosmogony he was the creator of the "sun and moon, mountains and towns." He was an androgynous deity born out of the cosmic egg produced by Aether and Chaos. Another name for Eros. Greece. (Delcourt, 1961: 69; Long, 1963: 121, 123; Kerenyi, 1951: 114; Barthell, 1971: 7n)

Piietzo The creator god of the Zaparo. Peru and Ecuador. (Métraux, 1948, 5: 649)

Pillan An omnipotent supreme being, "the author of all things," who is associated with "catastrophic natural phenomena," but also with crops and epidemics. The Mapuche-Huilliche and Araucanians, Chile. (Cooper, 1946. 6: 745, 747; Osborne, 1968: 166; Loeb, 1931: 545)

Pirman The creator of the world and of all visible things. The Benua, Malay Peninsula. (Skeat, 1906: 349)

Piyetao Piyexoo The "vague shape of a Supreme Being, bearing many titles," who was a creator and sustainer of all. The Mizteca and Zapoteca, Mexico. (Bancroft, 1886, 3: 449)

Ple Creator of the earth and of mankind. The Semang, Malay Peninsula. (Skeat, 1925, 8: 354; Schebesta, 1957: 121)

Poee-mpalaboeroe The Lord of the Sky who arranges the path of the sun is also the creator. The Toradja, Celebes, Indonesia. (Adriani and Kruyt, 1950: 372, 374)

Pokoh A deity who "made all things." The Pallawon-aps, California. (Bancroft, 1886, 3: 549)

Pon The supreme god is "a creative principle . . . of a most vague and indefinite character," who directs and controls natural phenomena. Reindeer are sacrificed to him though he does not interfere with mankind. The Yukaghir, Siberia. (Jochelson, 1900/02: 140, 235; Lissner, 1961: 169; Eliade, 1964: 246)

Ponomosor The supreme being and creator who destroyed mankind twice, by water and by fire, then let the survivors live and gave them grain. The Kharia, India. (Elwin, 1949: 24–25, 312)

Poon-Koo Wong "From a great mundane egg, which divided in two, came Poon-Koo Wong, who made the sky out of the upper and earth out of the lower half. He also made sun and moon." China. (MacCulloch, 1925, 8: 48)

Poré The Supreme Being of the Surara is also the god of the moon, just and benevolent, yet can be punitive. Brazil. (Becher, 1960: 91, 104)

Porona Minari A supreme being and ruler over all. He gave the animals their places on earth. The Bare, Colombia. (Zerries, 1968: 245)

Ppa hia The creator of all things whose wife is Mbache. The Yachi, Nigeria. (Armstrong, 1955: 150)

Praba "Breath"—the personification of creative power. India. (Sarma, 1953: 29; Keith, 1917: 93)

Prajapati In the Brahamanas the supreme god, a creator, a progenitor. At times he is considered an individual god. The favorite creation myth makes him born from the golden egg in the primeval waters, of an androgynous character, and thereafter through him the creation of all things. At other times the name or term is used as an epithet applied to numerous of the other gods. India. (Keith, 1917: 73–75; Kramer, 1961: 287; Sarma,

1953: 29, 30; Macdonell, 1897: 118; Bhattacharji, 1970: 322–329, 341; Long, 1963: 130–131)

Protogonos In Orphic Cosmogony the same as Phanes, the creator of the universe. Greece. (Kerenyi, 1951: 114–115)

Ptah The Egyptian creator of the universe through intelligence and will—the "architect of the universe." He was most prominently known as the god of artisans, of craftsmen. His wife is the lion goddess Sekhmet (Sekhet). (Budge, 1969, 1: 416, 500–502, 514; Casson, 1965: 72–74; Schoeps, 1961: 70; Knight, 1915: 98)

Pue di songi The supreme god of the Bare's Toradja who is invoked for the souls of sick people and for good rice crops. Celebes, Indonesia. (Eliade, 1964: 353; Downs, 1920: 12, 23)

Pue mpalaburu The supreme being whose eye is the sun. He sees all and is punitive, is invoked in the taking of oaths. He is the creator of heaven and earth, of mankind. His wife is Indo i Tuladidi. The Toradja, Celebes, Indonesia. (Kruijt, 1925, 7: 249; Downs, 1920: 10, 12, 23; Pettazzoni, 1956: 8, 20)

Puirše The beneficent creator who was a protective spirit. The Cheremis, Russia. (Leach, 1949, 1: 215)

Pukwicemnimakin "Giver of food to hunters." One of the five names of the Caribou God—supreme deity of the Davis Inlet and Barren Ground bands. Labrador. (Cooper, 1934: 36)

Pulang Gana With Raja Sua the creators of heaven and earth. A god of the soil and of agriculture as well as a god of the land of the dead, who must be propitiated on the arrival of a new corpse. The Sea Dyaks, Borneo. (Sarawak Gazette, 1963: 16, 133; Roth, 1891: 121; 1968: 177; Gomes, 1911: 196)

Puluga The self-existent supreme god who lives in the sky, whose voice is the thunder, who is omniscient only by day. Roheim states that he created the world and all things excepting evil, while Radcliffe-Brown says only that he created his wife Cana Aulola. He is also judge of the dead. Andaman Islands. (Roheim, 1972: 8, 44; Radcliffe-Brown, 1967: 158–159; Cipriani, 1966: 43; Moss, 1925: 116; Wales, 1957: 11)

Pulyallana A supreme being and sky god who manifests his will through the thunderbolt. Australia. (Eliade, 1958: 42)

Puntan A pre-existent being who, when dying, instructed his sister to make "the sky and the earth" from "his breast and back," the sun and moon from his eyes, the rainbow from his eyebrows. The Chamorro, Guam, the Marianas, Micronesia. (Beardsley, 1964: 93; Poignant, 1967: 71; Pettazzoni, 1956: 7)

Pura   The supreme being created people and animals, lives in the sky, controls all, and sends the rain. The Arikena (Carib), Guiana. (Zerries, 1968: 243–244)

Puru   The supreme being and creator is a god of destinies, primarily benevolent but can be punitive, sending to each according to his conduct. The other gods of the pantheon are emanations of him and act as intercessors between man and Puru. The Saliva, Colombia. (Walde-Waldegg, 1936: 40–41; Hernandez de Alba, 1948, 2: 410; Wallis 1939: 88–89)

Purukupale   The creator god, father of Jinini. Australia. (Mountford, 1969: 58)

Qamaits   The supreme goddess whose visits to earth cause sickness and death. "She is described as a great warrior." The Bella Coola, British Columbia. (Boas, 1898: 28–29)

Qawaneca   The deity who created the earth. The Athapascan Indians, Oregon. (Maclean, 1876: 426)

Qoluncotun   The supreme being and creator of the universe and animals. The Sinkaietk or southern Okanagan Indians, Washington. (Leach, 1950, 2: 914)

Quaoar   Their only god who "came down from heaven; and, after reducing chaos to order, put the world on the back of seven giants. He then created the lower animals," and then mankind. Los Angeles County Indians, California. (Bancroft, 1886, 3: 84)

Quawteaht   The creator of the earth and its features and also the animals. The Ahts, the Nootka, Vancouver Island, British Columbia. (Bancroft, 1886, 3: 152, 521; Lang, 1887: 188; Sproat, 1867: 253)

Quetzalcóatl   As a son of Ometéotl and one of the four cosmic forces, he, with Huitzilopochtli, was commissioned to give form and organization to the world. They created the sun and fire, the earth and the waters, mankind to people the earth, corn to feed them, the segments of time, and the land of the dead with the gods of hell, and the thirteen levels of heaven. The Aztec, Mexico. (Léon-Portilla, 1982: 33–35)

Ra   The Egyptian sun god was also considered the creator of the heavens and the earth, including the underworld, and of all visible things. (Knight, 1915: 102; Larousse, 1968: 13; Budge, 1969, 1: 322)

Radien Atzhie   The supreme god and ruler over all the gods, men, and things in the world. The first person in a trinity of Radien-Attje, Radien-Akka, Radien-Kiedde, who is his son. The Lapps, Northern Europe. (Bosi, 1960: 132; Pettersson, 1957: 18)

Radien-Kiedde   The creator of all things. Son of Radien Atzhie. He provides the soul or human spirit to Maddar-akko to care for until the body is formed when she turns it over to Sar-Akka to deliver to the mother. The Lapps, Northern Europe. (Pettersson, 1957: 18; Bosi, 1971: 133–134)

Raitubu   A son of Taaroa who at Taaroa's instigation, created the skies, the earth, and the seas. Windward Islands, Polynesia. (Mackenzie, n.d.: 282; Ellis, 1853: 324)

Rajah Gantallah   The unformed original being who through his will created two birds, male and female, who, again through his will, carried out the rest of the creation. The Dyaks of Sakarran, Borneo. (MacKenzie, 1930: 314)

Raja Pantha   The highest of the gods of the Bhils who improved conditions in the world and whose chief queen is Rani Pandhar. He is the son of Taria Baman. India. (Naik, 1956: 175–176)

Raja Sua   Among the Iban he is the creator of the heavens and earth with Pulang Gana, and also a god of the earth and giver of good crops. Borneo. (Sarawak Gazette, 1963: 133)

Raja Tontong Matanandau, Kanarohan Tambing Kabanteran Bulan   "prince of the sun, king of the moon." A name of the supreme being. The Ngaju, Borneo. (Scharer, 1963: 13)

Raluvhimba   The supreme being and creator, who is a god of the heavens and all its phenomena, brings the rains but also sends drought and floods. Sometimes identified with Mwari. The Venda, the Shona. South Africa and Rhodesia. (Smith, 1950: 124–125; Schapera, 1937: 264; Pettersson, 1953: 143, 165, 193–194)

Rañiñhuenu   The supreme being who, during the rites held at the winter solstice, was invoked "for general welfare during the year." The Araucanians, Argentina and Chile. (Cooper, 1946: 747)

Rarang   The invisible and remote benevolent high spirit, the male principle. The Kaean, New Guinea. (Meiser, 1963: 905–906)

Rarite A creator, founder of the E Wawe clan. The Shavante, Brazil. (Maybury-Lewis, 1967: 286)

Ribimbi The creator of heaven and earth and the giver of rain. The Tonga, Mozambique. (Pettersson, 1953: 179, 269)

Rimmon The "supreme god of the Syrians of Damascus," where he was identified with the sun-god Hadad. (Sayce, 1898: 203)

Rimpoche The creator of the world. The Lepchas, Sikkim. (Siiger, 1967: 172)

Rishi Salgong The high god who lives in the heavens. The Garos, India. (Biswas, 1956: 102)

Robboqua The supreme being of the Gumuz. Ethiopia. (Cerulli, 1956: 32; Mbiti, 1970, 2: 330)

Rog The benevolent creator god who required no propitiation but who "was invoked in case of hostile invasion." Senegal/Gambia. (Gamble, 1957: 103)

Rohita "originally an epithet of the sun, figures in the Atharvaveda as a separate deity in the capacity of a Creator." India. (Macdonell, 1897: 115)

Ru The supreme being who is identified with the sun. The Yendang, Nigeria. (Williams, 1936: 217)

Rua-hatu A supreme deity, with Tane. Mo'orea, Society Islands, Polynesia. (Henry, 1928: 128)

Rua-tupua-nui A creator god of the Society Islands. Ra'iatea. Son of Ra'a and Tu-papa. Wives: 'Ere'erefenua, Atea-ta'o-nui, and Hina-te-'iva'iva. Polynesia. (Henry, 1928: 96, 357–359)

Rubanga, Rubongo The supreme being of the Alurs who has the power to create, is little worshipped. Zaire and Uganda. (Frazer, 1926: 289; Williams, 1936: 96)

Rugaba The supreme being who had Irungu fashion the earth. He, himself, created men and cattle and is the source of all things, good and evil, can also take them away. Tanzania. (Frazer, 1926: 227, 426; Mbiti, 1970, 2: 331; Meyer, 1916: 185)

Ruhanga The remote creator and sky god is not worshipped, though among the Bahuma he is the arbiter of life, sickness, and death. The Bahuma, the Nyoro, the Bambwa, the Banyoro, the Ankore. Uganda. (Taylor, 1962: 38; Frazer, 1926: 230–231; Roscoe, 1915: 91; Thomas, 1950: 204; Mbiti, 1970, 2: 327)

Rumrok A name of the supreme being. The Didayis, Orissa, India. (Elwin, 1954: 640)

Rurema (1) The supreme being of the pygmies of Lake Kivu. Zaire. (Pettazzoni, 1956: 32) (2) The creator god of the Barundi. Burundi. (Mbiti, 1970, 2: 328)

Ruwa The supreme being of the Chagga is associated with the sun, determines destinies, but is merciful and tolerent. Tanzania. (Dundas, 1968: 107–108; Gelfand, 1962: 144; Williams, 1936: 125; Mbiti, 1970, 2: 133)

Sa "Death" who "created an immense sea of mud, by means of magic" but very dirty and uninhabitable, which Alatangana improved upon. Sa also provided the sun, moon, and stars for mankind. The Kono, Guinea. (Beier, 1966: 3–6)

Sabazius A Phrygian solar god who was "venerated as the supreme god in the Thracian Hellespont," and who was identified with Dionysus in Greece. (Larousse, 1968: 155, 160; Jayne, 1962: 346)

Sadasiwa One of the manifestations of the supreme god, associated with the shrine of origin. Bali, Indonesia. (Swellengrebel, 1960: 56, 62)

Saghalie Tyee The supreme god of the Chinook Indians. Washington. (Maclean, 1876: 439: Eells, 1886/1887: 679)

Sahale The creator. The Salishan Indians, Washington and British Columbia. (Alexander, 1964: 134)

Sakka The chief god, identified with Indra. Also considered the King of the nats, but benevolent. Burma. (Spiro, 1967: 52, 152, 248; Zimmer, 1955: 191; Basham, 1951: 86, 301)

Sakra The "King of the gods" in Buddhism and Jainism, the equivalent of Indra. India. (Larousse, 1973: 251; Ions, 1967: 135; Keith, 1917: 131)

Salgong The "chief deity, marries Apongma, a divine princess who descends on earth and gives birth to Kengra Barsa, father of fire and of all the heavenly bodies." The Garos, Tibet/Burma. (Keane, 1925, 2: 122)

Samanta-bhadra, kun-tu-bzang-po (Universal Goodness), the supreme buddha. *See also* **Padma-sambhava.** Tibet. (Snellgrove, 1957: 232)

Samba The high god whose wife is Qumba and their son Yero. All are considered high deities. The Fulani, Nigeria. (Webster, 1931: 241; Jeffreys, 1972: 732)

Sambulu The supreme being of the Ovimbundu. Zaire. (Williams, 1936: 98)

Sam-mor The supreme being of the Tembeh. He fought with and subdued Naing whom he imprisoned. He "rolled the fire with which he had fought into a ball, and this, as the sun, still revolves round the mountain to watch Naing." Malay Peninsula. (Skeat, 1906: 285; Fallaize, 1925, 12: 62)

Sanci Gai The creator, under Yere, who rules over life and is invoked during epidemics. The Mao and the Busasi, Ethiopia. (Cerulli, 1956: 32)

Sangyang Tunggal The supreme deity of the Kelantan. Malaya. (Hill, 1951: 64)

Sankara The creator god of the Bali-Hindu. He is associated with the North-West. Indonesia. (Hooykaas, 1964: 53)

Sanke The omniscient supreme being and sky god who bestows the power of shamanism. The Istyak, Siberia. (Eliade, 1964: 15, 220; Pettazzoni, 1956: 257; MacCulloch, 1964: 338)

Šara Xasar Tengeri A supreme being from whom some Buryats claim ancestry. The Sarat and Xangin clans. Siberia. (Krader, 1954: 339)

Saulal The creator of the universe who is half-man, half-lawud (a sea creature) is also god of the underworld. Ifalik, Micronesia. (Burrows, 1947/48: 2)

Sdach Nung The supreme god. The Samre, Cambodia. (Wales, 1957: 45)

Sebahanga A remote, yet benevolent, high god and creator. Known also as Kazoba, Biheko. The Kiga, Uganda. (Taylor, 1962: 126; Mbiti, 1970, 2: 331)

Sedi-Melo As a dual deity, Sedi, the earth, and Melo, the sky, the creator of the earth. The Minyong, Northeast India. *See also* **Shedi.** (Chowdhury, 1971: 78)

Sedna The supreme being and mistress of Adlivun, a part of the underworld, where she is also known as Idliragijenget. Among most, but not all, of the Eskimo she is the goddess of the sea and its creatures. (Boas, 1884/1885: 583–588; 1907: 119–121; Lantis, 1950: 323; Thompson, 1968: 3; Queval, 1968: 103)

Seh The supreme god who is represented by the leopard. Dahomey. (Williams, 1936: 121–122)

Selempata The god "who created matter." The Iban Dyaks of Sarawak, Borneo. (Sarawak Gazette, 1963: 133)

Semagid laxha The high god of the Tsimshian whose breath is the wind. He controls the weather which he uses to punish. The Tsimshian, British Columbia. (Pettazzoni, 1956: 11, 362)

Sri Sembu Mahadeo The supreme god of the Raj Gonds who provides the life substance for the embryo and when this leaves, death occurs. His shrine is essential to the ritual life of the village. India. (Furer-Haimendorf, 1974: 227, 243, 250)

Senga The high god of the Bavili. South Africa. (Willoughby, 1932: 277)

Sesom, Seso, Setebos Variant names of the supreme being of the Pampas. Patagonia. (Cooper, 1946, 5: 158; Lissner, 1961: 98–99)

Seveki, Kheveki The creator of the earth and people. Younger brother of Avasy. The Chumikan Evenks (Okhotsk Sea), Siberia. (Michael, 1963: 60)

Shang-ti (Tien) Believed to have been two separate gods combined very early into one. The supreme being, a god of moral order and of destiny, beneficent and just as a god of rewards and punishments. China. (Ferguson, 1937: 49–52; Haydon, 1941: 166, 168; Pettazzoni, 1956: 273, 277, 281; Werner, 1932: 410; Peeters, 1941: 7, 8)

Shanungetlagidas One of two supreme gods, the god who preferred light as against Hetgwaulana who preferred darkness. They created the lesser gods as their assistants and to protect the Haidas; are invoked when in deep trouble. Shanungetlagidas is the "possessor of the sun and moon . . . creator of the stars." He is worshipped and not feared though he punishes with pestilence. He and Hetgwaulana were once harmonious but then became antagonistic. British Columbia. (Harrison, 1891: 15–17)

Shan Wang Among some of the Ch'iang the mountain god is also the supreme deity. Szechwan, China. (Graham, 1958: 45)

Shedi, Shedi-Melo Shedi, the female of the dual Shedi-Melo personality, sister of Melo, the creators of the earth and sky and parents of the human race. The Minyong Abors, Assam. *See also* **Sedi-Melo.** (Furer-Haimendorf, 1954: 594)

Sheft-Hat A form of Khnemu wherein he absorbed the attributes of Ra, Shu, Qeb or Seb, and Osiris, and appears "with four rams' heads upon a human body . . . symbolizing fire, air, earth, and water" and representing "the great primeval creative force." Egypt. (Budge, 1969, 2: 51)

Sheli A mammoth god who created the earth for man to live on. The Evenks, Siberia. (Michael, 1963: 166)

Shenya The high god of the Angan. Zaria Province, Nigeria. (Gunn, 1956: 88)

Shi The sun, the proto-creator Shi (secret name Kumuñawana) "created Wanadi by blowing on some Wiriki" (small crystal quartz, shaman's power stone). He is not the same as the visible sun. The Makiritare, Venezuela. (Civrieux, 1980: 190)

Shibegeni-Burkhan One of the three creator gods, with Madari-Burkhan and Esege-Burkhan, who created the earth and mankind. Through deceit he won the right to give life to mankind who as a result are also deceivers. The Buriats, Siberia. (Klementz, 1925, 3: 11; MacCulloch, 1964: 375)

Shilup Chito Osh The Great Spirit of the Choctaw Indians. Mississippi. (Burland, 1965: 150)

Shimayet Lakkah The supreme being and a sky god who is aware of men's actions and punishes offenders. The Tsimshian, British Columbia. A variant of Semagid laxha. (Boas, 1909/10: 545)

Shinerikyu A god who, with the goddess Amamikyo, were the creators. Okinawa. Ryukyu Islands. (Lebra, 1966: 96)

Shingrawa The beneficent creator of the earth "which he shaped with a hammer" is little worshipped. The Kachins, Burma. (Temple, 1925, 3: 22; Leach, 1950, 2: 785)

Shippawn Ayawng A god of the Kachin of the stature of Zeus or Dyaus. Burma. (Scott, 1964: 340)

Shiwanni The god who created the heavens, and with Shiwanoka, his wife, created the Zuñi Indians. New Mexico. (Stevenson, 1898: 33; Alexander, 1964: 206; Tyler, 1964: 85, 94)

Shiwanoka, Shiwanokia A goddess who created Awitelintsita, the earth, and with Shiwanni, her husband, created the Zuñi Indians. New Mexico. (Stevenson, 1898: 33–34; Alexander, 1964: 206–207; Tyler, 1964: 85, 94)

Shoroyezhon The creator who forms a trinity with Runji, the son, and Bamarumbi, the mother. The Vazezuru, Rhodesia. (Jeffreys, 1972: 733)

Shuksiab The supreme god of the Nisqually Indians. Washington. (Maclean, 1876: 439; Eells, 1886/1887: 679)

Siang-tiei "Some Coreans believe that the name designates the Supreme Being, the creator and preserver of the world; others maintain . . . simply . . . the sky, to which they attribute a providential power of producing, preserving, and ripening the crops, banishing sickness." Korea. (Frazer, 1926: 82)

Sibu A beneficent omnipresent and omnipotent supreme deity and creator god. The Bribri, the Talamancan, Panama and Costa Rica. (Stone, 1962: 51; Pittier de Fabrega, 1903: 2; Alexander, 1920: 192)

Sichi The supreme creator and the earth mother. Same as Sedi. The Gallongs (Adi), Northeastern India. (Chowdhury, 1971: 115–116)

Si Dayang The rice-goddess who is "the maker of man, the creative and sustaining power of the universe, the All-life, the gracious mother of nature." The Karo Battas, Sumatra. (Keane, 1925, 2: 238)

Sikia The beneficent supreme being and creator of the world and of mankind. Known by various tribes as Pra, Rang Kau Hawa, Fra. The Tangsas, Indo/Burmese. (Dutta, 1959: 65)

Silewa A sky god created the earth, laying "at the foundations his mother's ring and coco-nut leaves." But she "changed her ring into a snake which still lies under the earth. When it turns, the earth shakes." Nias Island, Indonesia. (MacKenzie, 1930: 329)

Silewe Nazarata A goddess credited with the creation of the world and of mankind, giver of "wisdom and understanding" but also considered mischievous and the source of evil. Wife/sister of Lowalangi and also the goddess of the moon. She is associated with both the upper and the lower worlds. Nias Island, Indonesia. (Suzuki, 1959: 11–15, 24)

Silver Fox Creator of the world, and with Coyote the creator of people and animals, birds, etc. Shasta-Achomawi, California. (Dixon, 1905: 608; 1908: 159–160)

u sim shillong ramjah The "highest god of the Synteng." Assam. (Stegmiller, 1921: 410)

Sing-bonga A self-created god who alone, or with Oteborom, created the earth, animals, vegetation, and mankind and who among most was identified with the sun. Among some he is also the supreme god. The Mundas, Hos, Birhor, Santal, Barue, Asurs, Kols. India. (Majumdar, 1950: 251–256, 265; Basu, 1971: 62; Biswas, 1956: 102; Elwin, 1949: 4, 19, 50; 1950: 134–135; Crooke, 1925, 5: 13; 1894: 6; Russell, 1916, 3: 512)

Sins-sganagwai The supreme deity of the Haida who is omniscient even to thoughts. British Columbia/Alaska. (Swanton, 1904/05: 454; Pettazzoni, 1956: 19)

Sirao The high god of the north and central Nias Island. Indonesia. (Suzuki, 1959: 7)

Sirma Thakoor The sun, along with Ote Boram, self-created. Together they created the earth and all things. The Kol, India. (Elwin, 1949: 18)

Sitchtchenako The creator of all things. The Pueblo Indians, Arizona and New Mexico. (Stirling, 1942: 1)

Siva (**Mahadeva, Pasupati, Mahesvara,** and numerous variants) The supreme deity in Bali and Java. In Bali he is a god of the heavens, of light, the source of all life, the creative principle and is represented by the lingga as a fertility symbol. He has lost the destructive aspect of the Indian Siva. Of the cardinal points he occupies the center. (Grader, 1969, 2: 92, 183; Goris, 1960, 2: 123; Hooykaas, 1964: 53; Friederich, 1959: 39–43; Covarrubias, 1937: 290, 296; Marchal, 1963: 231)

Siwash The great god of the Saboba. San Jacinto area, California. (James, 1902: 36)

Skan The omnipotent, omnipresent Great Spirit, the sky, gave life and movement to all living things, the soul to man; established the time periods—day, night, moon, year; decreed that the four winds should establish the cardinal points; and is "the final and supreme judge of all things." He created Tate, the Wind, to be his companion; from his own essence he created Wohpe, his daughter, to be the Mediator; and "mankind to be servants of the Gods." His color is blue. The Lakota, Oglala, Teton, Plains Indians, United States. (Walker, 1980: 35, 50–54, 95, 115; Pettazzoni, 1956: 384; Eliade, 1967: 188; Jahner, 1977: 34)

Ski, Shki-Pas An omnipresent sky god and creator who is also associated with the weather. The Erzans (Mordvins), Russia. (Pettazzoni, 1956: 256; Leach, 1950, 2: 1007)

Sno-Nysoa The creator god. Liberia. (Bundy, 1919: 407)

Soko The remote supreme sky god and creator of the world is approached only through ritual. The Nupe, Nigeria. (Nadel, 1954: 10, 11; Forde, 1955: 17, 45; Parrinder, 1949: 21)

Sombov-Burkhan A pre-existent god (singly), or three—Esseghe-Burkhan, Maidari-Burkhan, and Shibegeni-Burkhan—who caused the creation of the earth, with the bird Anghir, and then humans. The Buriats, Siberia and Mongolia. (Klementz, 1925, 3: 11)

Sone-yah-tis-sa-ye The Great Spirit and the creator of the Indians. Iroquois, Eastern United States. (Beauchamp, 1892: 226)

Songinyu and **Song perinyu** A dual supreme deity "vaguely thought of as a divine pair who created all things and can bring good or evil upon men, but it is not known which is the male and which the female." The Rengma Nagas, Assam. (Mills, 1937: 165; Pettazzoni, 1956: 290)

Sosi The supreme god of the Male. Ethiopia. (Cerulli, 1956: 115; Mbiti, 1970, 2: 333)

Sotuknang A god created by Taiowa to create the universe, and life. In turn he created Kokyangwuti, Spider Woman, to help him. Hopi Indians, Arizona. (Waters, 1963: 3, 4)

Soulbiéche The supreme deity of the Alabama Indians. (Swanton, 1924/25: 482)

Soutan A variation of the creation myth makes "Soutan (soul)" the pre-existent deity, like Rajah Gantallah unformed, but with sight, hearing, and speech. He also created two birds who subsequently carried out the balance of the creation. Borneo. (MacKenzie, 1930: 315)

Soychu The benevolent supreme being among the Taluhets and Diuihets, Araucanians. Argentina and Patagonia. (Cooper, 1946, 5: 157; 1946, 6: 759; Lissner, 1962: 99; Grubb, 1925, 9: 597)

Sse The female principle who with Ndu was considered as "creators of heaven and earth." The Na-khi, Yunnan Province, China. (Rock, 1936: 50)

Suku The beneficent supreme god is the creator of the features of the earth as well as of humans whose needs he supplies. The Mbundu, Angola. (McCulloch, 1952: 35; White, 1961: 31; Hambly, 1934: 233, 262)

Sunawavi The primordial god who created the earth and man. The Southern Ute, Colorado. (Lowie, 1924: 1, 2)

Sussistinnako A spider, the first being, is given as male and/or female, but in either case is the creator in Sia cosmogony. She is Thinking Woman whose "creative capacity for "thinking outward into space,' brings everything into existence." The Keres, the Sia, New Mexico. (Tyler, 1964: 82, 358; Fewkes, 1895, 1: 123n; Alexander, 1964: 203; Parsons, 1939: 192; Stirling, 1942: 1n)

Ta'aroa Self-existent creator god of the other gods, of the earth and of all things. Tahiti, Ra'iatea, Polynesia. (Buck, 1938: 69, 70; Henry, 1928: 336, 341–344; Poignant, 1967: 34, 35; Williamson, 1933, 1: 31; Ellis, 1853: 323)

Tabui Kor (*also* **Ne Kidong**) The creator goddess, mother of Tilik and Tarai. New Britain, Melanesia. (MacKenzie, 1930: 150)

Tagaloa The creator and supreme god "became relegated to the sky." On Niue he is also a god of war. Samoa and Niue, Polynesia. Same as Tangaroa, Ta'aroa, Kanaloa. (Loeb, 1926, 1: 160; Smith, 1902: 195; Andersen, 1928: 18, 384; Henry, 1928: 346; Mead, 1930: 159)

Tahea A god of the creation group known only because he is mentioned in the sacred chants. The Marquesas, Polynesia. (Handy, 1923: 244)

T'ai I "The Great One. The Great Unity . . . is represented as the highest of the Heavenly Genii, the Ruler of the Five Celestial Sovereigns. . . . Hence he is of the same rank as Shang Ti, the Supreme Being." China. (Werner, 1932: 479)

Taikomol The supreme deity and creator god was identified with the moon and the sun. He introduced their ceremonies. The Yuki, northern California coast. (Kroeber, n.d.: 183; Loeb, 1931: 522)

Taio Aia The supreme god to whom human sacrifice was made. Austral Island, Polynesia. (Aitken, 1930: 115)

Takami-Musubi The second of the three creating deities to materialize—the others, Ame-no-Minaka-Nushi and Kammi-Musubi. Japan. (Yasumaro, 1928: 1; Hori, 1968: 4; Holtom, 1938: 25; Herbert, 1967: 242)

Tamagisanbach The chief god "who governs and inhabits the south." His wife is Taxankpada Agodales. Formosa. (Coleman, 1832: 342)

Tamagostad With his wife Cipattonal the supreme celestial pair and creators of all things, having culture hero attributes as well. Nicaragua. (Lothrop, 1926: 65–66; Bancroft, 1886: 490; Alexander, 1920: 120; Cohane, 1969: 208)

Tamaioit Twin brother of Mukat. They created the earth, and after it was stabilized, the plants and animals. Each worked individually to create people, but Mukat's proved the better as he was more careful. Disgruntled, Tamaioit returned to the darkness, taking all of *his* creations with him. The Cahuilla, California. (Brumgardt and Bowles, 1981: 10–13)

Tamakaia On some islands of the New Herbrides a god who with Maui-tikitiki created the world and all things. (Codrington, 1881: 295; Williamson, 1933, 1: 73; 1933, 2: 181)

Tamara The supreme being of a hinterland clan of the Biloforn dialect; "considered female in the Okita lineage." Niger Delta, West Africa. (Jeffreys, 1972: 730–731)

Tamayowut The Earth, the female principle. With Tukomit, her brother, the creators through birth, of the things and features of the world—animate and inanimate. The Luiseño Indians, California. Among the Cahuilla it is Tamaioit and her brother Mukat. (Kroeber, 1925: 677–678; Hooper, 1920: 317–320)

Tamosi The supreme being and creator who provides food in abundance. The Caribs, Guiana. (Brett, 1880: 104; ImThurn, 1883: 365)

Tamukujen The omnipresent and omniscient high god and creator who is associated with the rains. The Didinga, Sudan and Ethiopia. (Cerulli, 1956: 79; Pettazzoni, 1956: 38–39)

Tamuno The female creative principle who is both creatress of the world and also of the individual, joining his spirit to his body, determining his destiny, and seeing that the bond is maintained until the fate is fulfilled. The Kalabari of the Niger Delta. The Ijaw, Nigeria. (Horton, 1962: 204–206; 1960: 16; Williams, 1936: 199)

Tane The supreme being, the "creator of the heavens" and "the male generative force of creation." His sacred name was Eri Eri. He and Na' Vahine had three sons, Tanaroa, Rono, and Tu, and three daughters, Rata, Tapo, and Hina. Hawaii. In other areas of Polynesia Tane's functions varied. (Melville, 1969: 14–18, 25)

Tangaloa, Tangaroa A primordial creator god of Tonga, Samoa, Ellice Island, Wallis Island. Polynesia. In other areas he has numerous other functions. (Poignant, 1967: 29, 39; Williamson, 1933: 19; Burrows, 1937: 85; Mackenzie, n.d.: 280)

Tangaloa-fa'a-tutupu-nu'u   An emanation of Tangaloa as "Creator of lands." Samoa, Polynesia. (Mackenzie, n.d.: 267)

Tangar   The supreme deity of the Yakuts. Siberia. (Eliade, 1958: 60)

Tangaroa-Upao-Vahu   A sky god in their creation myth who "created the earth from rocks thrown into the void from the sky." Also created the other gods and mankind. Samoa. Elsewhere he was a god of the sea. Polynesia. (Larousse, 1973: 500)

Tano   A river god of the Ashanti who is credited with the creation. Ghana. (Parrinder, 1949: 30, 46)

Tanuva   The supreme spirit of the Yamana who is female. Tierra del Fuego. (Zerries, 1968: 306)

Ta Pedn, Tapern, Ta Ponn   The supreme being and creator is also a sky and weather god, and a god of the wind. He is considered beneficent and omniscient as to men's actions. His name and his relationships vary among the different tribes: wife—Jalang, Jamoi, Manoid; parents—Kukah and Yak Takel, Tang-ong and Yak Manoid; brothers—Bajiaig, Kari (Karei), Kalcegn. The Semang, Malay Peninsula. Among the Jehai he is the creator god. (Evans, 1923: 147, 149; 1937: 150–3; Skeat, 1906: 178, 182, 210, 309–310; Roheim, 1972: 104, 112; Eliade, 1964: 337–340; Pettazzoni, 1956: 310, 324; Cole, 1945: 72; Shryock, 1931: 337, 340)

Taras   The supreme god of the Tarascos. Michoacan, Mexico. (Brinton, 1882: 158; Bancroft, 1886, 3: 403)

Taronhiawagon, Tha-ron-hya-wa'-kon   The supreme god of the Onandaga Indians (Iroquois) who lives in the sky, is beneficent and "solicitous" of mankind. Eastern United States. (Brinton, 1882: 171; Hewitt, 1895: 111)

Tasheting   The "benevolent creator-god" who also formed their "ancestral parents . . . from the ice of its glaciers." The Lepchas, Sikkim. (Nebesky-Wojkowitz, 1956, 2: 29)

Tata Dios   The creator god of the Warihio Indians. Sonora and Chihuahua, Mexico. (Gentry, 1963: 133)

Tatara-Rabuga   The pre-existent creator god who sent Nostu-Nopantu, a goddess, to create the earth. He then placed the sun and moon in the sky, created the wind to dry the earth (with the sun), and then created animals, man, and all other things. The Garos, India. (Long, 1963: 211; MacCulloch, 1925, 8: 47; Playfair, 1909: 80–81)

Tatihi   A god of the creation group known only because mentioned in the sacred chants. The Marquesas, Polynesia. (Handy, 1923: 244)

Tat Opakwa, Tiolele   The old creator god of the Cuna Indians. San Blas, Panama. (Keeler, 1960: 46)

Tazitzete   The High God who created Caragabi, the creator/culture hero of the Chocó. Colombia. (Métraux, 1946, 2: 114–115)

tcamicuminu   "Grandfather of all"—one of five names of the supreme deity of the Davis Inlet and Barren Ground bands. Labrador. (Cooper, 1934: 36)

Tcementu   The creator god, without form, who is beneficent and controls the universe. No need for worship. The Naskapi, Labrador. (Speck, 1935: 37)

Te Atua   The beneficent supreme being of the Tokelau Islands. Polynesia. (Tutuila, 1892: 269)

Teave   The primordial, androgynous supreme being, parent of Tane and Marama. Also known as Mauriora, I'o. Hawaii. (Melville, 1969: 17–20, 93)

Te Hainggi-atua   The supreme and principal god and the god of thunder to whom first-fruit offerings are made of taro and yams. Rennell Island, Polynesia. (Birket-Smith, 1956: 22–23, 59)

Tekh   An early god who with others, among them Thoth, "planned the world." Egypt. (Budge, 1969, 1: 516)

Temauk(e)l   The beneficent and always-existent supreme being and creator of heaven and earth. He is the source of the moral code and punishes infractions with illness and death. The Selknam, the Ona. Tierra del Fuego. (Loeb, 1931: 528, 545; Osborn, 1968: 117; Lissner, 1961: 117–118; Lothrop, 1928: 96; Pettazzoni, 1956: 15, 19, 423; Gusinde, 1931: 499, 501)

Tenantomni, Tenantomwan   The creator deity "is often identified with the Big-Raven (Kuyqinnaqu) who represents the chief Deity." The Koryak, Siberia. (Bogoras, 1904/09: 315; Jochelson, 1908: 17)

Tenatiia   The god to whom the original creation is attributed. The Nahane Indians (Upper Liard Kaska), western Canada. (Honigmann, 1954: 100)

Tenga The earth goddess in upper Senegal is the powerful and supreme deity associated with Wends, the sky. She is a goddess of morality and justice who avenges wrong-doing. The Mossi, Upper Volta and Senegal. (Frazer, 1926: 403; Greenberg, 1946: 45)

Tengere Kaira Kan The supreme god of the Altaians, but not as popular as Bai Ulgan. Siberia. (Eliade, 1964: 198–199)

tepenamwesu One of the five names of the Caribou god, the supreme being of the Davis Inlet and Barren Ground bands. Labrador. (Cooper, 1934: 36)

Tepeu With Gucumatz the Mayan creator deities. The Quiché, Guatemala. (Recinos, 1950: 82; Long, 1963: 170–171)

Terhopfo, Kepenopfo The creator deity of the Angamis (Nagas). India. (Elwin, 1969: 505)

Tetoo The primary, among several, of the creator gods, who created the earth and sky. His wife is Haka. The Marquesas, Polynesia. (Williamson, 1933: 67)

Tezcatlipoca A Toltec god adopted by the Aztec and known also in Yucatan. A god with many functions he is "One of the gods of creation, associated with Huitzilopochtli, with the night sky . . . with darkness and destruction." Mexico. (Duran, 1971: 476; Brinton, 1882: 69–71; Caso, 1958: 27–31; Leonard, 1967: 54, 60, 104; Thompson, 1970: 328)

Thairgin "Dawn," a name of the supreme being. The Koryak, Siberia. (Czaplicka, 1969: 262)

Thakur, Thakur Jiu, Dhorom The supreme god and creator of the world, sometimes identified with Sing Bonga. The Santal, Bihar, India. (Mukherjea, 1962: 273–274; Kochar, 1966: 246–250; Biswas, 1956: 102; Elwin, 1949: 5)

Thangjing The chief god of the Moirang and the creator of mankind. Son of Nongshaba and Sarunglaima. Manipur, India. (Shakespear, 1913: 81, 84)

Tha-tha-puli The supreme being of the Wathi-wathi. Southeast Australia. (Howitt, 1904: 493–494)

Thi:-kong The supreme ruler of heaven, the Jade Emperor, who is protective of the community, and is superior to the various deities of Taoism and Buddhism. Taiwan (Formosa). (Diamond, 1969: 92)

Thora The Great Good Spirit of the Bushmen who supplies rain, abundant food, and good hunting. Botswana. (Smith, 1950: 90; Schapera, 1951: 185–186; Williams, 1936: 309; Lebzelter, 1934: 63, 64; Pettazzoni, 1956: 32)

Tien *See* **Shang-ti**

Tiggana Marrabona The "spirit of great creative power." Tasmania. (Worms, 1960: 5)

Tiguianes A goddess, "the creator of the world." The Gianges of Cotabato, Philippines. (Jocano, 1969: 24)

Tihmar The benevolent supreme deity and creator. The Tungus, Siberia. (Jochelson, 1900/02: 236)

Tiki Creator god and cultural teacher of the Marquesas. In Mangareva, the creator. As the creator on Easter Island "current accounts name Makemake, but in an old chant the feat is credited to Tiki." Polynesia. (Williamson, 1933, 2: 174; Burrows, 1938: 71)

Tikxo, Tixo The supreme being and creator of the world and of all things. The Xosa, South Africa. (Pettersson, 1953: 47, 148–149; Soga, 1931: 150)

Timei Tinggei The supreme being who is omniscient of men's misdeeds "which he punishes with bad crops . . . and other disasters." The Bahau of Mahakam, Borneo. (Pettazzoni, 1956: 332)

Timilhou The supreme being and creator, the equivalent of Alhou. The Sema Nagas, Assam. (Pettazzoni, 1956: 289)

Tinantumghi The Creator. The Chukchi, Siberia. (Bogoras, 1901: 98)

Tingang Also called Raja Tontong Matanandau, Kanarohan Tambing Kabanteran, "prince of the sun, king of the moon" with whom Mahatala is identified. The supreme deity, the hornbill, who is the Upperworld, and Tambon or Jata, the Underworld, form a duality; considered a unity and invoked together. The Ngaju (Dayak), Borneo. (Scharer, 1963: 13, 14, 33)

Tingwang The supreme god who rules the other gods and spirits. The Zemi Nagas, Assam. (Barkataki, 1969: 79)

Tinia, Tina The Etruscan equivalent of Jupiter, Zeus, the god of the heavens who presides over the north/north-eastern segments of the cosmos. He hurled thunderbolts from any part of the heavens, while other gods could hurl them from only certain directions. His wife was Uni. Italy. (Hamblin, 1975: 92, 93; von Vacano, 1960: 19, 21; Pallottino, 1975: 145; Rawlinson, 1885: 121)

Tiolele *See* **Tat Opakwa**

Tiox Dios (High God)—The equivalent of the "entire Christian pantheon of dioses. . . . [of] the standard trinity." He is invoked with Mundo and the Day Lords with offerings and prayers during the training of day-keepers. On pilgrimages to the mountains of the four directions he is invoked with other deities for "health, adequate rainfall, and protection from lightning, flood, hail, earthquakes, landslides, and fires." Momostenango, Guatemala. (Tedlock, 1982: 41, 60–61, 82)

Tipotani The chief god of the Chorotega in Matiari. Nicaragua. (Lothrop, 1926: 81; Bancroft, 1886, 3: 492)

Tirawa The Great Spirit, sky god, and creator of the universe and all things was omnipotent and beneficent. The other gods received their directives and powers from him. He revealed the hako ceremony to the priests at the beginning of time. His wife was Atira. The Pawnee, Plains Indians. (Dorsey, 1904: 3; 1906: 13; Fletcher, 1900/01: 27; 1902: 733; 1903: 10; Radin, 1914: 362; Eliade, 1976, 1: 133–134; 1976, 2: 355)

Tiw A sky god of the Anglo-Saxons and in England a creator god. (Branston, 1957: 68, 73; Larousse, 1968: 265)

uTixo, Tikxo Also called uDali and uQamata. The supreme god and creator of all things rewarded good and punished evil. The Xosa, South Africa. (Pettersson, 1953: 147–149; Soga, 1931: 150; Williams, 1936: 293, 310; Callaway, n.d.: 8)

Tloque Nahuaque The invisible, omnipresent supreme deity and creator of the world. An androgynous deity, the "principle of generation." Also known as Ometeotl, Ometecutli/Omeciuatl, Citlallatonac/Citlalicue, Tonacatecutli/Tonacaciutl. Aztec, Mexico. (Caso, 1958: 8; Nicholson, 1967: 114; Vaillant, 1962: 141; Alexander, 1920: 88)

togo mušun The chief deity, goddess of the fire and of the tent, protectress of the clan. The Evenki (Tunguso-Manchurian), Siberia. (Dioszegi, 1968: 468)

Tomingatoo The supreme being of the Wapiana. Guiana. (Im Thurn, 1883: 366)

Tonacacíhuatl and **Tonacatecuhtli** The primordial creative female and male principle, as manifestations of Ometéotl, are named as the parents of the four brothers— the cosmic powers or forces: Tlatlauhqui Tezcatlipoca, Yayauhqui Tezcatlipoca, Quetzalcóatl, or Yoalli ehecatl, and Omitéotl, or Maquizcóatl, or Huitzilopochtli. Known as Lord and Lady "of our flesh (of our sustenance)" it is to their house, Chichihuacuauhco, that children go when they die. Aztec, Mexico. (Spence, 1923: 131, 147, 148, 151; Brinton, 1882: 73; Vaillant, 1962: 142, 148; Leon-Portilla, 1982: 30, 34, 98, 127)

Tonige The moon, the supreme being among some Iduwini people of the Okun Ijaw dialect. Niger Delta, West Africa. (Jeffreys, 1972: 730)

Topoko The supreme being among les Toussians du Nord. Upper Volta. (Hébert and Guilhem, 1967: 142)

Toquichen The beneficent supreme being and creator is the protective governor of all things. The Araucanians of the Pampa, Argentina. (Cooper, 1946, 6: 746; Grubb, 1925, 9: 597)

Torai The Great Spirit of the Mru. India. (Brauns, 1973: 271)

Tore The supreme being of the Lego. Zaire and Sudan. (Baxter and Butt, 1953: 114)

Tororut The supreme being, the sky, created the earth and punishes sins by inflicting cattle diseases and other disasters. His wife is Seta, sons are Arawa and Ilat, daughter Topogh. The Suk, Kenya. (Beech, 1911: 19)

Tosa, Tuossa The supreme being of the Walamo and the Kullo. Ethiopia. (Cerulli, 1956: 113–114; Pettazzoni, 1956: 42)

Totilme'il A Mayan dual male/female creator deity of the Tzotzil of Chenalho. Mexico. (Thompson, 1970: 201)

Toyo-ke-o-dae-sin A god of the Dairis who is considered to have created the heaven and the earth. Japan. (Coleman, 1832: 332)

Triglav A three-headed god as ruler over heaven, earth, and the underworld. A black horse was dedicated to him and used in divination to determine the outcome of war expeditions. Slavic Prussia. (Machal, 1918: 284–285; Schoeps, 1961: 120; Queval, 1968: 114)

Tsiltsi The supreme god of the Klallam Indians. Washington. (Eells, 1886/87: 679; Maclean, 1876: 439)

Tsosa, Tsossa The supreme being of the Zala. Ethiopia. (Cerulli, 1956: 114; Pettazzoni, 1956: 42)

Tsuni Goam, Tsui-goab The beneficent supreme being, identified with the dawn. He was a god of storms, of thunder and lightning, and was lame, wounded in the knee by Gaunub. His wife was !Urisis, son !Urisib. The Khoi Khoi, South Africa. (Hahn, 1881: 37–38, 61, 127; Parrinder, 1967: 75; Brinton, 1897: 75)

Tsuossa The supreme being of the Gofa. Ethiopia. (Cerulli, 1956: 114; Pettazzoni, 1956: 42)

Tucapacha, Tucupacha The creator of the universe and of all things. The Michocans, the Tarascans. Among the latter he is also the giver of "life and death, good and evil fortune." Mexico. (Bancroft, 1886, 3: 445; Keeler, 1960: 50; Alexander, 1920: 85)

Tuchaipa With his brother Yokomatis, the creators of the world. Known jointly as Chaipakomat. The Die-gueño Indians, California. (Kroeber, 1925: 789; Du Bois, 1908: 233; 1901: 181)

Tuglay and **Tuglibong** Primeval beings who "made all things in the world." In the beginning the sky was so low it interfered with pounding the rice. Tuglibong (also called Mona) forced Tuglay to move higher by scolding and pounding with her pestle. He planted the seeds given him by Diwata. The Bagobo, Philippines. (Raats, 1969: 7, 8, 12)

Tuhan Allah The supreme god, creator of the universe, commanded Raja Brahil to create living things. The Mantra, Malay Peninsula. (Skeat, 1906: 322)

Tukma, Tokuma The creator of the world, the animal and vegetable kingdoms. The Juaneño Indians, California. (Kroeber, 1925: 637)

Tukmit, Tukomit The male principle. With his sister Tomaiyowit the creator gods, through birth, of the things and features of the world—animate and inanimate. The San Luiseño Indians, California. (Kroeber, 1925: 677–678; Du Bois, 1904: 52–53; Strong, 1929: 327)

Tukura The supreme being of the Aluridja. Australia. (Basedow, 1925: 295)

Tuli Sometimes female, sometimes male, but in any event involved in the creation of the earth and of man. Fiji, Samoa, Polynesia. (Williamson, 1933: 48, 49; Larousse, 1968: 449)

Tulong The supreme being of the Ta-tathi. Southeastern Australia. (Howitt, 1904: 493–494)

Tulugaak, Tulukauguk The raven god who created the earth. Bering Strait Eskimo, Alaska. (Nelson, 1896/1897: 425; Spencer, 1959: 257)

Tuma The supreme being of the Suri, associated with the sky. Ethiopia. (Cerulli, 1956: 49)

Tumayowit The Earth. With Mukat the creators of the earth and all things on it. She went to live in the underworld. The Cupeño Indians, California. (Kroeber, 1925: 692; Strong, 1929: 268)

Tuminikar, Tuminkar Benevolent creator god and giver of culture to the Wapisianas (Arawaks) and the Taruma. Twin of the evil Duid. Brazil and Guiana. (Farabee, 1918: 108; Métraux, 1946: 115; Queval, 1968: 115)

Tummu The supreme being of the Pibor Murle, identified with the sky and with the rain. Ethiopia. (Cerulli, 1956: 79). Also the Beirs. Sudan. (Logan, 1918: 244)

Tumo The supreme being of the Bodi, the Mekan, the Didinga. Southwest Ethiopia. (Cerulli, 1956: 115)

Tunpa, Iandapoha The creator god of the Chiriguano. Bolivia. (Métraux, 1948, 4: 482)

Tupa The chief deity, a god of storms, of thunder and lightning, and was considered an early culture hero who gave them fire and taught them agriculture. The Tupi, the Caingua, Brazil. (Brinton, 1868: 152; Spence, 1925, 2: 837; Karsten, 1926: 275)

Tupan The thunder god among the coastal Tupi appears as a creator god. Northeast Brazil. (Wagley and Galvao, 1948, 1: 145, 147; Bastide, 1960: 573)

Turpi The supreme being who lives in the sky and controls the weather, both good and bad. The Purek-amekran, Brazil. (Pettazzoni, 1956: 421)

Twanyirrika, Tuanjiraka The Great Spirit whose voice is the bull-roarer, and who participates in the circumcism ceremonies. The Arunta, Australia. (Eliade, 1976, 1: 188)

Tzacol Another name of the male of the original creator couple—Tzacol "Creator" and Bitol "Maker." Mayan, Guatemala. (Thompson, 1970: 201; Recinos, 1950: 78)

Ualare The creator god of the universe and of all living things except some "certain kinds of animals and foods." The Elema, Papuan Gulf, New Guinea. (Holmes, 1902: 430)

Uanari The creator of all things who is constantly at war with the malevolent Kahu. The Cunuana, Venezuela. (Zerries, 1968: 348)

Ubasi The creator deity of the Yako. Nigeria. (Mbiti, 1970, 2: 336)

U Blei Nong-thaw The creator god of the Khasis. Sometimes feminine as Ka'lei Nong-thaw. Assam. (Gurdon, 1914: 105; Bareh, 1967: 355; Pettazzoni, 1956: 291–292)

Uchtsiti, Ut'siti The creator of the universe and many things. The Acoma. Among the Keresan he also places Iyatiku and Nautsiti on the earth to complete it under the direction of Tsitstinako. Pueblo Indians, New Mexico. (Stirling, 1942: 3; Parsons, 1939: 243)

Ugatame The omniscient, omnipotent, omnipresent creator. Since he is the source of all things he is responsible for both good and evil, but is not punitive. He is a dual concept, considered of both sexes, "everything and nothing . . . manifested by the sun and the moon." The Kapauku Papuans, New Guinea. (Pospisil, 1958: 17, 18)

Ugelianged The supreme being is omniscient and identified with the sun. Pelew Island, Micronesia. (Pettazzoni, 1956: 170, 343)

Ugjo-Gosai The supreme deity of the Malers. India. (Roy, 1928: 20)

Uhubaput The sun god is supreme and the creator of all. The Sumu, Nicaragua and Honduras. (Conzemius, 1932: 129)

Ukko The high god is also the thunder god whose wife is known variously as Akka, Rauni, Maan-Eno. Finland and Estonia. (Larousse, 1968: 304, 307; de Kay, 1898: 13, 37; Krohn, 1925, 6: 24, Grimm, 1880: 176)

Uletet, Ngulaitait, Nguletet The supreme being is also the creator, "makes the thunder, and intervenes in human affairs." The Kuku, Sudan. (Huntingford, 1953: 50)

Ulgen, Ulghen The benevolent high god and creator to whom horses were sacrificed. The Altai, Siberia. (Potapov, 1964: 325; Klementz, 1925: 2; MacCulloch, 1964: 342, 377)

Ulgon The supreme god of the Vogul is considered to be the source of fire. Siberia. (Chadwick, 1936: 92–93; Roheim, 1954: 61)

Ulutuyer Ulu Toyon, Ulu-Toyon "The All-Powerful Lord of the Infinite" lives in the western sky and is closely associated with the activities of the earth. Though he is head of the dark spirits of the west he is not always harmful. He created the forest, birds and animals, gave

mankind fire, and is responsible for shamanism. He could appear on earth as a large animal. The Yakut, Siberia. (Czaplicka, 1925, 12: 828; Eliade, 1964: 187–188; Jochelson, 1933: 104; Tokarev and Gurvich, 1964: 279)

Umbu Walu Mendoku A sky god who is the creator but is not worshipped. Sumba Island, Indonesia. (Frazer, 1926: 659)

Umkhulumcandi The supreme god is an ancestor deity who gave them their culture. Also called Nkulunkuli. The Swazi, Swaziland. (Pettersson, 1953: 141, 155, 198; Smith, 1950: 111)

Umkulumqango, Umkulunqango, Umkurumqango The supreme being is the "creator of all things and the ultimate source of power, particularly of sending rain, success in war, and the deliverance from pestilence . . . giver of health and strength to mankind." The Ngoni, Malawi. (Frazer, 1926: 183; Read, 1956: 158)

Umlimo The creator deity of the Amantebele (Zulu). South Africa. (Callaway, n.d.: 14)

Umlungu The invisible supreme being of the Lake Nyasa region. East Africa. (Callaway, n.d.: 14)

Umubumbi The aspect of God as the creator, "the potter." The Gisu, Uganda. (Millroth, 1965: 54)

Umusemyi A creator god of the Barundi. Burundi. (Mbiti, 1970, 2: 328)

Umvelatanqi, Ukqamata The supreme being of the Amakxosa. South Africa. (Callaway, n.d.: 13)

Umvelinqangi The creator god. This name is used together with Unkulunkulu, but the latter is used more for the ancestor god aspect. The Zulu, South Africa. (Pettersson, 1953: 156–157)

uNkulunkulu A name of the supreme being and creator of all things, an ancestor deity. Also called Umvelinqangi, Villenangi, Umdali, Qamata, and other names. The Zulu, South Africa. (Pettersson, 1953: 141, 150, 152; Williams, 1936: 283, 287; Schapera, 1937: 263)

uQamata The older of two names for the supreme being. The newer one being uTixo. The amaPondo, South Africa. (Williams, 1936: 310; Callaway, n.d.: 8)

Urun Ajy (Aiy, Ayyy) Toyon A benevolent sky god, a god of light, and "the white lord and creator of the earth and man." The Yakut, Siberia. (Czaplicka, 1969: 277; Tokarev and Gurvich, 1964: 280; Jochelson, 1900/02: 207)

Usanisi The supreme being of the Amaswasi. South Africa. (Callaway, n.d.: 14)

Utabu An early name of the supreme being, later replaced by Utikxo. The Pondo, South Africa. (Callaway, n.d.: 15)

Utc'tsiti *See* **Uchtsiti** (Tyler, 1964: 117)

Uthlanga A creator god whose name "means a reed, and is metaphorically used for a source of being. Thus a father is described as the *Uthlanga* of his children." The Zulu, South Africa. (Hartland, 1925, 2: 364)

utnimatcisu One of five names of the Caribou God—supreme deity of the Davis Inlet and Barren Ground bands. The "Giver of Food." Labrador. (Cooper, 1934: 36)

Uwolowu, Uwoluwu The omniscient and beneficent supreme god, the personified sky, is the creator of all, the source of all good things. The Akposo, Togoland. Same as Buku of the Atakpames, and Mawu of the Ewe. (Frazer, 1926: 115; Eliade, 1958: 40; Pettazzoni, 1956: 36, 115)

Uyun-artoyen A variant name of the supreme being. Same as Ulghen. The Yakuts, Siberia. (Klementz, 1925, 3: 2)

Vahiynin " 'existence,' 'strength,' a name for the Supreme Being." The Koryak, Siberia. (Czaplicka, 1969: 364)

Vairgin The supreme being and creator. "But . . . is rather an appellative term for benevolent deities recalling the Yakut Ayi." The Chukchee, Siberia. (Jochelson, 1900/02: 234, 236)

Vairocana The "central and highest personage in the group," of the five Dhyani-Buddhas: Akshobhya, Amitabha, Amoghasiddhi, Ratnasambhava. The "Supreme and Eternal" Buddha. Japan, Java, Nepal, and Tibet. (Eliot, 1935: 100, 107; Marchal, 1963: 240; Getty, 1962: 31; Snellgrove, 1957: 96, 103)

Vajradhara (the Adi-Buddha), **Dorjechang, Dorjedzin** The "Yellow-caps" (reformed school sect) consider him the supreme being and creator of all things. Tibetan Buddhism. (Getty, 1962: 3)

Vang-vai A deity who created the heaven and the earth but who is not worshipped. The Heh Miao, Southwest China. (Clarke, 1911: 41, 63)

Varalden-olmai The supreme being and a god of the fertility of all things, guardian of the reindeer and the other animals. Called Radien among the Norwegian and Swedish Lapps. Lapland. (Karsten, 1955: 47–48; Dioszegi, 1968: 28; Bosi, 1960: 105, 132)

Varuna As an ancient Vedic deity he was a supreme god, sovereign, omnipresent and omniscient, creator of the universe and a god of cosmic and moral law and order. On the human level he was a god of righteousness, detesting falsehood, yet to the penitent forgiving. He was later relegated to individual functions, e.g. as a god of waters, a god of death, god of the dark night sky, god of the western quarter. India. (Keith, 1917: 22–26; Danielou, 1964: 118–121, 130; Bhattacharji, 1970: 25; Martin, 1914: 41, 44; Cox, 1870: 330; Ions, 1967: 14, 15)

Ve A Teutonic god, brother of Odin and Vili, who together created the world from the body of Ymir and also created man, to whom Ve contributed speech and the senses. (Grimm, 1883, 2: 560; Stern, 1898: 8; Guerber, 1895: 12, 13)

Vere-pas The supreme god, a sky deity. The Erza (Mordvins), Russia. (Paasonen, 1925, 8: 844)

Vili A Teutonic creator god with his brothers Odin and Ve. In the creation of man he gave intelligence and motion. (Stern, 1898: 8; Grimm, 1883, 2: 560; Guerber, 1895: 12, 13, 19)

Villenangi, Unkulukulu The supreme spirit, an ancestor god. The Zulu, South Africa. (Pettersson, 1953: 141, 157, 199)

Viracocha The greatest god who rose out of the depths of Lake Titicaca and created all things, giving light to the world which was before in darkness. The Aymara, the Inca, Peru. (Rowe, 1946: 281, 293, 315; Tschopik, 1946: 558, 570; Flornoy, 1958: 89, 90; Osborne, 1968: 31, 61–63; Brinton, 1882: 176; Means, 1931: 422)

Vochi Twin of Amalivaca, creator/culture heroes who created the earth and the Orinoco River. The Tamanak, Venezuela. (Métraux, 1946: 117; Zerries, 1968: 247)

Wa'a The omniscient supreme sky god whose eye is the sun. As the Black Wa'a he is the night or the cloud-covered sky; as the Red Wa'a, the day, the bright and sunny sky. The Hadya, Ethiopia. (Pettazzoni, 1956: 8, 41; Cerulli, 1956: 129)

Wa-cheaud "The Indians describe a fiery substance above the sun, which is ruler of all things, Wa-cheaud, the maker, or creative spirit." United States. (Emerson, 1884: 94)

Wa cinaci "Our father," the supreme being of the Arawak. Guiana. (Im Thurn, 1883: 366)

Wah-con-tun-ga The creator of all things. The Assiniboin of the Upper Missouri. (Denig, 1928/29: 486)

Wahhahnah The supreme spirit of the Winnebago Indians. Wisconsin. (Emerson, 1884: 525)

Wahkeeyan The Great Spirit of the Dacotah Indians who makes the thunder. The northern Plains. (Emerson, 1884: 3)

Wah'-Kon-Tah The Great Mystery and creator is identified with the sun—"Grandfather the Sun." He sent the Little Ones from the sky to live on the earth; is god of the day and the symbol of life. He taught them to make straight "arrow shafts from the dogwood and the ash tree" and about fire (firing the prairie grasses with lightning). He is also feared as he uses the lightning, thunder, and tornadoes to express his anger. *See also* **Wakanda**. The Osage, Plains Indians. (Mathews, 1982: 9, 11, 32, 271, 529, 744)

Wah-pec-wah-mow The ruler of the heavens who created the earth, gave it features, forests, animals. Omnipotent and omnipresent. The Yurok, California. (Thompson, 1916: 55, 60)

Wailan wangko "Grandfather," the chief god and first one of the beginning who broke open the coconut tree out of which came man. Southern Minahassa, Celebes, Indonesia. (MacKenzie, 1930: 331)

Wak, Waka, Waq, Waqa The "Father of the Universe," the omniscient sky god who is associated with the rains and the thunder. He is invoked for the prosperity of the crops and the stock, for good health. He is the creator and lord over numerous lesser spirits. The Galla, Somali, Afar, Saho, and the Boni (pygmies), Ethiopia, Somaliland, and Uganda. (Budge, 1973, 1: 362–363; Lewis, 1955: 172; Pettazzoni, 1956: 32; Foucart, 1925, 11: 581; Bartels, 1969: 406–407; Huntingford, 1955: 74; Barns, 1925, 12: 449; Rossini, 1925, 6: 491; Littmann, 1925, 1: 56)

Wakanda, Wakonda The Great Spirit and creator of all things. This is also a term applied to the supernatural quality inherent in all things. The Sioux, Osage, Omaha, Ponca, Assiniboin, Plains Indians. (Skinner, 1920: 189;

Eliade, 1967: 84–85; McGee, 1893/1894: 182; La-Flesche, 1917/18: 41–42; Alexander, 1964: 83; Howard, 1965: 99)

Wakantaka, Wakantanka, Wahkon-tun-kah The omnipotent and all-pervasive Great Spirit, the Great Mystery. He is the creator of the earth and all things, and of the white stones used by the medicine men who are taught the art of curing by the thunders who are Wakantaka's messengers. "Although singular in form, Wakantanka is collective in meaning . . . is not personified, but aspects of it are"—sun, moon, sky, winds, etc. There are sixteen aspects, good gods, but as each is *kan* they are "all only the same one." Wikan and Hanwikan; Taku Skanskan and Tatekan and Tobkin and Yumnikan; Makakan and Wohpe; Inyankan and Wakinyan; Tatankakan; Hunonpakan; Wanagi; Waniya; Nagila; and Wasicunpi. Tobtob Kin is the name used by the shamans. Among the Dakota of the Fort Snelling, Minnesota area he became remote and otiose, yet he was invoked when going to hunt or to war, and sometimes in oath-taking. He required no prayers or sacrifices. The Oglala, the Lakota, the Dakota of the northern Plains, United States and Canada. (Wallis, 1923: 36–37; 1947: 81–82; Skinner, 1902: 273; Powers, 1977: 45, 46, 54, 202; Jahner, 1977: 32, 33, 36; Lynd, 1889: 151–152, 172; Eastman, 1962: 71–73)

Wakea, Atea The creator of the universe with Papa (Rock). Hawaii. (Henry, 1928: 345; Andersen, 1928: 361)

Wal The omnipresent and omniscient supreme being of the Madin, a group of the Koma. Ethiopia. (Cerulli, 1956: 33)

Wala The benevolent and malevolent creator god who is propitiated for good fortune and sacrificed to before the planting in the hopes of a good harvest. The Mano, Liberia. (Schwab, 1947: 315–316; Zetterstrom, 1972: 174–177)

Wamara Among the Haya "the ruler of the universe, supreme spirit and sovereign of the souls of the dead." Tanzania. (Taylor, 1962: 142)

W'amurreti-kwonci A title of the supreme being and creator. The Arawaks, Guiana. (Im Thurn, 1883: 366; Brett, 1880: 6, 7)

Wanadi The benevolent supreme god who created all living things on earth—vegetation, animals, mankind. Son of the sun. The Makiritare, Venezuela. (Wilbert, 1972, 1: 136, 157)

Wan-Aisa, Dawan The Father god, the thunder, who is sometimes confused with Alwani. Both are considered the creator of the world and of mankind. The Mosquito, Nicaragua and Honduras. (Conzemius, 1932: 126, 129)

Wanin The supreme god. Korea. (Kato, 1926: 62)

Wantu Su The supreme god who sent his nephew, Wantu, to the earth with all living things. The Sara family of tribes, Chad. (Larousse, 1973: 530)

Waptokwa The sun god and the creator who was concerned in human affairs. The Sherenti, the Shavante, Brazil. (Maybury-Lewis, 1967: 286; Nimuendaju, 1942: 84)

Waq, Waqa *See* **Wak**

Waqaio The supreme being of the Masongo, identified with the sky. Ethiopia. (Cerulli, 1956: 50)

War The supreme being, omnipresent and omniscient. The Ciita (the Koma), Ethiopia. (Cerulli, 1956: 33)

Warongoe The remote, yet omnipresent, deity of the Sandawe. Tanzania. (Raa, 1969: 48)

Watauinewa The supreme omnipresent and beneficent god, the dispenser of life and death and of justice. The Yahgan, Tierra del Fuego. (Lothrop, 1928: 172; Cooper, 1946, 3: 103; Lissner, 1961: 110; Osborne, 1968: 117)

Waunthut Mennitoow The benevolent supreme being, "author of all things, in heaven and earth; the governor of all events." The Mahikan, New York. (Skinner, 1925: 103)

Wele, Wele omuwanga The supreme being and the creator of the world and of mankind is the beneficent source of all good. He is the giver of life and death and is concerned with man's welfare. Wele is also used as a noun applied to numerous deities. The Abaluyia, the Vugusu, Gishu, Wanga, Kakalelwa, Kabras, Bantu Kavirondo, Kenya. (Wagner, 1949: 168–169, 175; 1954: 28; Millroth, 1965: 30–33)

Wende, Ouende The omnipresent and omniscient supreme god who lives in the sun, and who punishes with lightning. He is the creator of the heavens and earth, and of all living things. The Mossi, Senegal and Upper Volta. (Hébert and Guilhem, 1967: 142; Frazer, 1926: 92; Pettazzoni, 1956: 8, 12, 37; Delobsom, 1933: 98)

Weni The omnipotent supreme being and creator of life has predetermined all things, is a god of destiny. He is

associated with the sky. The Builsa of the Gold Coast, West Africa. (Frazer, 1926: 95)

Wennam, Winnam The benevolent supreme god is associated with the sun, is venerated but not feared. He is also called Winde or Naba Zidiwinde and has various manifestations: Tenga Wende, Tido Wende, Siguiri Wende, Ki Wende, Saga Wende. The Mossi, Upper Volta. (Hammond, 1959: 246–247; Skinner, 1958: 1104)

Weri, Weri Kubumba The beneficent creator god of the Bagisu to whom offerings were made at the circumcision ceremonies. Uganda. (Williams, 1936: 175; Frazer, 1926: 241)

wesona-megetoL " 'world-maker.' fashioned the empyrean vault after the manner and pattern of a fish-net." The Yurok, California. (Waterman, 1920: 190)

Whanin, Chiso The creator god whose son was Whanung. Korea. (Clark, 1932: 138)

Wichaana A title of the supreme being as the "creator of men and fishes." The Mizteca, the Zapoteca, Mexico. (Bancroft, 1886, 3: 449)

Wigan A creator deity of the Kiangan. Philippines. (de Raedt, 1964: 293)

Wigan ad Angachal The chief god and creator of the earth and mankind, the giver of culture. The Mayawyaw, Luzon, Philippines. (Lambrecht, 1932: 14)

Wisagatcak, Wisaketcak The creator of the world and of the Indians is also a trickster. The Cree, United States and Canada. (Bjorklund, 1969: 136; Burland, 1965: 61; Maclean, 1876: 438)

Wisakaa The creator of the earth and of all things, including man. He lives in the north. The Fox Indians, Wisconsin. (Jones, 1911: 209; Leach, 1950, 2: 1179)

Wisakedjak, Wisekedjak The creator among the Nippissings. Among the Ojibwa he was a transformer who expanded the "mud retrieved by Muskrat" into the earth in their cosmography. (Maclean, 1876: 438; Hallowell, 1967: 223, 232)

Wisoulus, Wis-so-wul-us The supreme being of the Twana. Washington. (Maclean, 1876: 439; Eells, 1886/1887: 679)

Woden, Wotan, Odin The Germanic All-Father, the sovereign god who possessed all wisdom and was the master of magical powers. He was a god of battle who determined the victory, a god of death who determined man's destiny. Also England. (Guerber, 1895: 23; Davidson, 1965: 69; Larousse, 1968: 253–254; Branston, 1957: 87–88; Wagner, 1882: 5, 6)

Woi-shun With Chanum parents of "all things in heaven and on earth." The Kachin, Burma. (Scott, 1964: 263)

Wolaro The creator of heaven and earth and of all things "who, however, is not in any sense to be spoken of as a god." His creations were through demiurges, chiefly birds. Father of Bundulmiri and Dagubal. The Gwi: ni, Kimberley, Northwest Australia. (Capell, 1939: 385–386)

Wonajo Their chief god created the land and the stars. He lives on Mt. Rossel as a snake by day, a human by night, is armed with man-catchers, a form of weapon. Rossel Island, Melanesia. (Armstrong, 1923/24: 1, 2; MacKenzie, 1930: 148, 153)

Wonekau An omniscient and supreme celestial god whose means of punishment is usually the weather. He is also a god of animals who controls success or failure in hunting. New Guinea. (Pettazzoni, 1956: 9, 15, 21, 341, 443)

Wonomi The benevolent supreme being and creator of the world. Variant titles—Kodo-yapen, Kodo-yanpe, Kodo-yeponi. The Maidu, California. (Schmidt, 1933: 33; Loeb, 1932: 157)

Woot A god who initiated the creation which was carried out by his nine sons. The Bushong of Kasai District, Belgian Congo. (Vansina, 1955: 144–145)

Wuni The supreme being of the Nankanni was "the creator of life, and the moulder of destiny." He was associated with the sky. Gold Coast, Africa. (Frazer, 1926: 95)

Wuotan The Teutonic god of "the all-pervading creative and formative power"—the All-father, the one-eyed god, a god of war and battles, of victory. He inflicts with diseases but also heals. (Grimm, 1880: 131–137; 1883, 2: 703, 856; Keary, 1882: 234–236)

Wura Rera The dual deity of Sky-Earth or Sun-Moon as a supreme being. The Molucca Islands (Middle Flores), Indonesia. (Pettazzoni, 1956: 336)

Wuro The high god whose name also means firmament, rain. He is the total creator. The Bobo-Fing, Upper Volto. (Herbert and Guilhem, 1967: 142, 153)

Xamaba The benevolent supreme being and creator of all things including mankind provides the rain, is invoked for help on undertaking journeys, and in illness. The Heikum, South Africa. (Schapera, 1951: 184, 189; Lebzelter, 1934: 15)

Xixarama The principal god of the Anserma who is the father of the sun and the moon. Colombia. (Steward, 1948, 1: 17; Trimborn, 1968: 99)

Xmucané *See* **Xpiyacoc**

Xolas The supreme being and creator of the earth and of mankind upon whom he bestows the soul at birth and reabsorbs it at death. He is concerned with the activities of mankind and is beneficent or punitive accordingly. The Alacaluf, Tierra del Fuego. (Bird, 1946, 1: 79; Loeb, 1931: 532; Osborne, 1968: 117; Lissner, 1961: 115–116)

Xovalasi, Xowalaci, Xowaelece The creator god of the Joshua Indians, Oregon. (Farrand, 1915: 224; Drucker, 1937: 277; Pettazzoni, 1956: 371)

Xpiyacoc, Ixpiyacoc The great Father, with Ixmucané the supreme pair, the parents of the seven Ahpu. "As the Supreme Being, Ixpiyacoc has no life history." They are "the progenitors of 'divination with the seeds.'" The Quiché, Guatemala. (Girard, 1979: 52, 55, 87)

Xu The benevolent and all-powerful supreme being and sky god to whom the souls of the dead go. He "summons the magicians to their profession, and gives them super-natural powers." He provides the rain and is invoked in illness, before hunting and before travelling. The Bushmen, South Africa and Namibia. (Lebzelter, 1934: 54, 56; Schapera, 1930: 184; Marshall, 1962: 234)

Yagastaa "He who dwells on High." The Carrier Indians, Hagwilgate and Fort Fraser, British Columbia. (Jenness, 1934: 165)

Yakista The omnipresent supreme being, god of the universe. Athapascan Indians, Northwestern North America. (Müller, 1968: 159–160)

Yalafath, Yelafaz The supreme deity and creator of the universe is incarnate in the albatross. He is beneficent yet indifferent though he will overcome evil demons if invoked. It is the lesser spirits who are worshipped. It is to Falraman, Yalafath's home in the sky, to which go the souls of the dead. Yap Island, the Carolines, Micronesia. (Christian, 1899: 384; MacKenzie, 1930: 172; Furness, 1910: 147; Müller, 1917: 298; Eliade, 1958: 50; Walleser, n.d.: 8, 24)

Yamba, Yemba The supreme deity of the Kulu. Nigeria. (Meek, 1934: 260; Gelfand, 1966: 120)

Yaqhicnin The supreme being and creator. The Koryak, Siberia. (Jochelson, 1900/02: 234)

Yasi The moon and the creator of the earth and all things; the source of thunder and lightning. The Siriono, Bolivia. (Holmberg, 1969: 238)

Yataa, Yatala The supreme being of the Kono who does not communicate directly. Sierra Leone. (Parsons, 1950: 260, 262)

Yaun-Goicoa The "lord of the universe. He created the three principles of life: Egia, the light of the spirit; Ekhia, the sun, the light of the world; Begia, the eye, the light of the body." The Basques, France and Spain. (Leach, 1949, 1: 117)

Yaviza A name of the supreme being as someone who is unpredictable. Today gives the good, tomorrow the bad. Les Toussians, Upper Volta. (Hébert and Guilhem, 1967: 145)

Yayutsi The supreme creator who inhabits the fifth heaven, and who reveals the future to the shaman. The Altai, Siberia. (Czaplicka, 1969: 302; Eliade, 1964: 196)

Yeddariye The omniscient and omnipotent supreme god of the Chipewyan who ruled all, rewarding and punishing according to merit. As the creator known as Niottsi. Canada. (Cooper, 1934: 49; Pettazzoni, 1956: 16, 371)

Yəgzar The otiose high god of the Guarage. Ethiopia. (Shack, 1968: 460)

Yehl, Yetl The Raven, the beneficent creator of all things, was also a hero as well as a trickster. The Thlinkeets, Pacific Northwestern America. (Bancroft, 1886, 3: 98, 115; Knapp and Childe, 1896: 153; Burland, 1965: 148; Maclean, 1876: 438; Brinton, 1897: 159)

Yelafaz *See* **Yalafath**

Yenang, Yenong The supreme being who is closely associated with the sun. The Sakai, Malaysia. (Evans, 1923: 198; Cole, 1945: 107)

Yer The supreme being of the Gelaba (the delta of the Omo River). Ethiopia. (Cerulli, 1956: 84)

Yere, Yeretsi The supreme being of the northern Mao and the Anfillo Mao. Ethiopia. (Cerulli, 1956: 32; Mbiti, 1970, 2: 333)

Yere Siezi The omnipresent and omniscient supreme being of the Koma. Ethiopia. (Cerulli, 1956: 33; Grottanelli, 1947: 80)

Yi-na-yes-gon-i The supreme god of the Jicarilla Apache. New Mexico. (Russell, 1904/05: 255)

Yoalli Ehécatl The omnipotent, beneficent, invisible god and ruler of all things. The Chichimec, Mexico. (Alexander, 1920: 87)

Yocahu, Marcoti The beneficent Great Spirit. Puerto Rico. Variant names: Jocakuvague-Maorocon, Iocauna-Guamaonocon, Yocahu-Gagua-Maorocoti, Yacana-Gumanomocon, which tie him to the following deity, Yocahu Vagua Maorocoti. (Fewkes, 1903/04: 55)

Yocahu Vagua Maorocoti The remote, not-approached supreme god of the Taino. Haiti. (Lovén, 1935: 563–564)

Yokomatis, Kokomat With his brother Tuchaipa, the creator gods of the Diegueño Indians. Their names are sometimes conjoined as Chaipakomat. California. (Du Bois, 1908: 233; Kroeber, 1925: 789)

Youna An ancient supreme god of Northern Europe. "The largest tree is consecrated to Youna . . . one less large to his wife Youmon-Awa." (Bertrand, 1897: 90)

Ytsigy "The highest benevolent deity of the Gilyak . . . according to Schrenck. . . . But Sternberg says that they call the universe Kurn, and apply the same name to their highest anthropomorphic deity." Siberia. (Czaplicka, 1969: 271)

Yuba Paik "They allude to a Supreme Being whom they designate Yuba Paik, 'Our Father Above' . . . The term may be collective . . . and may include all the powers of the air." The Choctaw Indians, Georgia/Alabama. (Spence, 1925, 3: 567)

Yu Huang, Yu Huang Shang-ti The Jade Emperor, supreme ruler of heaven, earth, and hell. China. (Werner, 1932: 598; Maspero, 1963: 263; Day, 1940: 26, 123, 132)

Yulgen The high benevolent god of the Altaians who, when punishment is needed, sends Erlik to do it. Central Asia. (Czaplicka, 1925, 12: 482)

Yurugu He represents the creation of disorder because of his disruptive, premature breaking out of the original cosmic egg. The Dogon, Mali/Nigeria. (Griaule and Dieterlen, 1954: 86, 87, 89, 93)

Yusn A god of the beginning, the creator of all things. The Mescalero Apache, New Mexico. (Sonnichsen, 1958: 26)

Yu-ti *See* **Yu Huang Shang-ti**

Yuttoere The supreme god who governs the weather, hears all and punishes the wicked. The Dené, the Carrier Indians, British Columbia. (Morice, 1925, 4: 639; Alexander, 1964: 82; Pettazzoni, 1956: 15, 371)

Ywa The creator god of the Karen. Burma. (Marshall, 1922: 11–13)

Zabi The supreme being and creator god of the Sangama is remote, approachable only through the *godimi*. Also called Beri or Bericono. Ethiopia. (Cerulli, 1956: 115)

Zaguguayu A creator god of the Guarayu whose brother is Abaangui. Bolivia. (Métraux, 1948, 2: 437)

Zalmoxis, Salmoxis The supreme god who is also interpreted "as a Sky-god, a god of the dead, a Mystery-god," the Getae or Dacians. Thrace and Romania. (Eliade, 1974: 66)

Zamba A god of the Yaunde who created the earth. Cameroon and Zaire. (Larousse, 1968: 482)

Zambi, Nsambi A "Supreme Being, who, having no origin, is himself the origin of all things." He is a god of justice who punishes evil doing and judges the dead. The Bafioti in Loango, Gabon. (Frazer, 1926: 136–137; Larousse, 1968: 481) A sky god, the great god of the Bantus of Brazil. (Bastide, 1960: 82, 573)

Zanahary The all-powerful, yet just and benevolent, deity, creator and ruler of the world. The Ikongo, Madagascar. (Linton, 1933: 163)

Zayahung Yihe Zahasha The wise hedgehog god was the creator deity. The Buriat, Mongol, Siberia. (Curtin, 1909: 45)

Zena The creator god of the Ge. Liberia. (Schwab, 1947: 315)

Zeus The sovereign god of the Greek pantheon, son of Cronus and Rhea, was wise and just, concerned with the affairs of the universe and of mankind, with the sanctity of oaths. His power was in statesmanship, forming alliances in the battle against the Titans to provide additional strength, establishing a stable regime through wisdom and insight—attributes gained in his marriage to Metis (his first consort). His omnipotence and omniscience were reflected in his jurisdiction over justice, the moral order, the establishment of the potentialities of law as well as of the arts. His regime introduced the concepts of civilization and culture, in contrast to that of the brute force and strength of the earlier rules of Rhea and Cronus, of Gaea and Ouranus. His many other aspects included those of the sky and the atmosphere, of marriage and paternity, of vegetation. (Eliade, 1976, 2: 367; Barthell, 1971: 19; Kerenyi, 1951: 22; Keary, 1882: 160; Murray, 1935: 25; Schoeps, 1961: 126; Pettazzoni, 1956: 19, 145; Morford and Lenardon, 1975: 66, 70, 71; Hesiod-Brown, 1981: 20, 21, 30, 42)

Zume Topana The main god of the Omagua of the Amazon Basin. Brazil. (Métraux, 1948, 6: 702)

Zurvan, Zrvan The supreme god of the cult of Zervanism in which he is considered the parent (as an androgyne) of Ohrmazd and Ahriman. Generally considered the god of time and fate. Iran. (Kramer, 1961: 355–356; Patai, 1967: 168; Gray, 1930: 124–128)

PART II

Celestial Deities

6

Sky and Heaven Gods

Ababbawon A sky god who meets the earthly spirits coming to the sky. The Isneg, Luzon, Philippines. (Vanoverbergh, 1953: 90)

A-ba-ch'i The "Father in Heaven." The Ch'iang, China. (Graham, 1937: 62)

Abassi The sky god of the Ekoi. Among the Efiks also considered the creator and supreme god. Nigeria. (Jeffreys, 1939: 99; Frazer, 1926: 129–130)

Abyang A sky goddess of the Bisayan, sister of Suk-langmalayon. Philippines. (Jocano, 1969: 20)

Adro, Adroa 'bua As a god of the sky he is considered omnipotent, understanding, and good. In his earthly aspect, Adro (onzi), he is "bad" and in close association with mankind. The Lugbara, Zaire. (Middleton, 1960: 27–28, 253, 257; Mbiti, 1970, 2: 16; Gelfand, 1966: 118)

Ahul The sky god of the Hopi Indians. Arizona. (Fewkes, 1895, 1: 359)

Aizu A sky goddess, daughter of Mawu and Lisa, and with Akazu the guardian of the treasures. Dahomey. (Herskovits, 1938, 2: 108)

Akasagarbha T. Nam-k'ahi'ñin-po. A Celestial Bodhisat. "The matrix of the sky." Tibet. (Waddell, 1959: 358)

Ak Ayas "White Light," the sky or heaven god of the Tatars of the Altai, Siberia. (Eliade, 1964: 9)

Akazu A sky goddess, daughter of Mawu and Lisa, and with Aizu guardian of the treasures. Dahomey. (Herskovits, 1938, 2: 108)

Ake Antak The guardian of heaven. The Orang Lom in Banka, Indonesia. (Kruijt, 1925, 7: 245)

Akeb-ur "The god of the celestial waters, Akeb-ur, the fashioner of the gods and the guide of the Henmemet beings." Egypt. (Budge, 1973, 1: 131)

Alaliwot A god of the Skyworld who punishes infractions of enemy taboos with illness. The Ifugao, Philippines. (Barton, 1946: 53)

'Alapay Mishupashup, 'Alapayashup The Upper World, "supported by a giant eagle whose wing movements caused the phases of the moon, and perhaps also solar eclipses" is occupied by supernaturals—the Sun, Moon, etc. The Chumash, California. (Hudson and Underhay, 1978: 40)

Alaxpaca A sky god of the Aymara, Bolivia. (LaBarre, 1948: 169)

Alkuntam The great sky god, of equal importance to Senx, and with him associated in the creation of mankind. The Bella Coola, British Columbia. (Boas, 1900: 29, 30; Jenness, 1932: 170)

Altjira, Tukura The sky divinity of the Arunta and Loritja. Australia. (Eliade, 1976, 2: 356)

Alunsina The all-powerful goddess of Ibabawnon, the Upper World. The Sulod. Among the Bisayan, a sky goddess. Panay, Philippines. (Jocano, 1969: 19, 20)

Ambara The sky god—charioteer of Candra, the moon. Nepal. (Pal and Bhattacharyya, 1969: 23)

Ame-no-Minaka-Nushi-no Mikoto The "Deity-of-the-August-Centre-of-Heaven." One of the three creating deities—with Takami-Musubi-no-Mikoto and Kammi-Musubi-no-Mikoto. Japan. (Yasumaro, 1928: 1; Hori, 1968: 4; Kato, 1926: 15)

Ame-no-toko-tachi-no-kami A heavenly deity, the fifth deity formed, who is interpreted as "Eternal Law, which is formless, but acts upon existing matter." Japan (Herbert, 1967: 245; Hori, 1968: 4; Yasumaro, 1928: 2)

Ampual A god of the Skyworld from whom the Ifugaos received many things which he obtained from his brother Napuagan in the Underworld. Philippines. (Barton, 1946: 31–32; 1955: 173)

Amtalao A god of the Skyworld and a god of omens. The Ifugao, Philippines. (Barton, 1946: 32, 42)

An, Anu, Ana (Chaldean) Sumerian, Assyro/Babylonian god of the sky, the heavens, who ruled supreme in the universe. His wife was Ki, the earth. With Enlil (or Bel) he was the god of the first month Nisan (Semitic), Nisannu (Sumerian), and with Papsukal god of the tenth month. As a Hittite/Hurrian deity he was the second king of heaven, supplanting his father, Alalu, and in turn being supplanted by his son Kumarbi. (Jacobsen, 1970: 27; Kramer, 1967: 100; Ferm, 1950: 57; Hooke, 1963: 24; Guterbock, 1961: 156; Sayce, 1898: 186–191; Hommel, 1925, 3: 74; Littleton, 1970, 2: 94–95; Jastrow, 1898: 462–463)

An, Antum Wife of An. A sky goddess from whose breasts or udder, "since she was usually envisaged in cow shape," flowed the rain. Near East. (Jacobsen, 1976: 95)

Anenagi tayapiwa'ciga A celestial being, a manitou of the smoke-hole of the lodge, who represents the sky. The Fox Indians, Wisconsin. (Pettazzoni, 1956: 377)

'Ani-motua The Sky-father, a variant of Rangi-matua. Polynesia. (Buck, 1938: 152)

Aninito ad Angachal A god of the Skyworld. The Mayawyaw, Luzon, Philippines. (Lambrecht, 1932: 22)

Anuanima The ruler of a race of sky beings who have human form when there but otherwise have that of birds. The Arawak, Guiana. (Brett, 1880: 29)

Anulap The sky god whose wife or daughter is Ligoububfanu. Truk, the Carolines, Micronesia. (Leach, 1950, 2: 719; Poignant, 1967: 73–74)

Aondo The sky in all of its manifestations and power. The Tiv, Nigeria. (Downes, 1971: 17–18)

A-pa A sky god, the father of all men. The Bu-hoan, Formosa. (Campbell, 1925, 6: 85)

Ap'alani A sky spirit who knows more than any of the other spirits. The Aymara, Peru. (Tschopik, 1951: 196)

Apoyan Tachu The sky father. The Zuni Indians, New Mexico. (Cushing, 1891/1892: 379; Thompson, 1968: 17)

Aramfe The god of the heavens who sent his sons Oduwa and Orisha to "create the world and to people it." The Yoruba, Nigeria. (Wyndham, 1919: 107)

Arawotja A sky deity who while on the earth made the watercourses. The Dieri, Australia. (Lang, 1905: 55; Howitt, 1904: 432)

Arca-kercis A beneficent sky god. Southern Alacaluf, Tierra del Fuego. (Pettazzoni, 1956: 423)

Ariki-tu-te-rangi A god of the sky. Kapingamarangi, Polynesia. (Emory, 1965: 202)

Art Toyon Aga, Aar Toyon Chief of the sky gods, benevolent but remote, powerful yet inactive. His voice is the thunder. The Yakut, Siberia. (Czaplicka, 1969: 277; Eliade, 1964: 186–187; Tokarev and Gurvich, 1964: 280; MacCulloch, 1964: 354)

Asan, Asman An Iranian god who "represents the physical sky . . . bestowing all skill and wealth." Near East. (Gray, 1930: 138; Huart, 1963: 42)

Asi(ti) A Palestinian goddess of the heavens. Near East. (Cook, 1930: 109)

'Astar The Semitic sky god who forms a triad with Beher and Medr. Ethiopia. (Littmann, 1925, 1: 57; Moscati, 1960: 225)

Ataksak A sky god and god of joy who always responds to the invocation of the shaman. The Eskimo, Baffin Land. (Bilby, 1923: 209, 269)

Atira "Vault-of-the-Sky" is the wife of Tirawa. She is also Mother Corn and the leader of the Hako ceremony which is for children, longevity, abundance, and happiness. The Pawnee Indians, Nebraska. (Dorsey, 1904: 3; Fletcher, 1900/01: 26, 44–46; Grinnell, 1893: 114–115, 125)

Awondo The sky god and creator who controls "all natural phenomena . . . is the author of good and evil." The Munshi, Nigeria. (Meek, 1925: 31)

Azer-ava A Finno-Ugrian sky goddess and goddess of fruitfulness is the bringer of rain and corn. Oaths are taken in her name. The Mordvins, Russia. (Paasonen, 1925, 8: 844; MacCulloch, 1964: 258)

Baal Hamon The sky-fertility god represented the male principle, "the power that vitalized the matter" represented by Tanit. He was also a god of the weather. Libya. (Meyerowitz, 1958: 130–131; Larousse, 1968: 84)

Baal-shamem, Baal Shamin, Baal Shamayim The god of the heavens, of the sky in all its aspects, bright as well as weather. Phoenicia, Syria, and Arabia. (Langdon, 1931: 63; Pettazzoni, 1956: 91; Cook, 1930: 217; Vriezen, 1963: 66)

Ba-Chi, Iju The god of the sky sends the fertilizing rain. The Margi, Nigeria. (Meek, 1931: 180)

Bag-Mashtu, Bag-mazda A sky god with whom Khaldi was identified. Armenia. (Ananikian, 1964: 12)

Bagos Papaios A Phrygian sky god. Near East. (Ananikian, 1964: 12)

dBang po brgya byin Another name for sKyer rdzong snyanpo, the king of Heaven. Tibet. (Nebesky-Wojkowitz, 1956, 1: 287; Francke, 1923: 7)

Begjag, Begiag A sky god, a grandson of Manoid and younger brother of Kaei, "is the ruler of Ligoi, the place of the winds." His wife is Chemioi. The Kenta, the Kintak Bon, the Djahai. Malaya. (Schebesta, 1927: 217, 219; Evans, 1937: 186; Roheim, 1972: 23)

Bia-ka-pusud-an-langit "Lady of the navel of heaven," goddess of the sixth heaven. The Bagobo, Philippines. (Benedict, 1916: 17)

Biamban A sky god of Southeastern Australia. (Howitt, 1904: 489)

Bia-t'oden The goddess of the fifth heaven is the wife of Salamiawan. The Bagobo, Philippines. (Benedict, 1916: 16)

Bolatosa God of the sky of the Kullo. Ethiopia. (Cerulli, 1956: 114)

Bonga Sky god of the Tunguses. Siberia. *See also* **Buga.** (Foucart, 1925, 11: 581)

Bonsu A sky god "who dwells above the seven levels of the sky." Younger brother of Teng. The Semang, the Bateg, Malay Peninsula. (Evans, 1937: 146; Eliade, 1964: 339)

Buga The omnipotent, omniscient god of the sky was also the creator deity of the Tungus, the Evenks. Siberia.

(Eliade, 1964: 9, 499; MacCulloch, 1964: 371; Wallis, 1939: 90)

Buir Sagan Ugugun A heavenly spirit who, with his wife Qwir Sagan Qamagan, is worshipped at springs. The Buriat, Siberia. (Curtin, 1909: 119–120)

Buku The sky god and omniscient high god of the Atakpames. Togo/Dahomey. (Parrinder, 1949: 28; Pettazzoni, 1956: 36; Frazer, 1926: 115)

Buolla The god of the sky of the Gofa. Ethiopia. (Cerulli, 1956: 114)

Caddi Ayo The sky god of the Caddo is also the supreme being. Texas. (Waring, 1965: 33; Chamberlain, 1900: 51)

Caelus Roman god of heaven. (Roscher, 1965, 1, 1: 844)

Č'ai The sky god of the Beneso. Ethiopia. (Cerulli, 1956: 94)

Čar The god of the sky. The Gimira, Ethiopia. (Cerulli, 1956: 94)

Caragabi The god of the sky of the Uré, Cauca Valley, Colombia. Among the Choco he is a culture hero/creator deity. (Hernandez de Alba, 1948, 3: 324; Métraux, 1946, 2: 115)

Chambi The supreme sky god who controls the rains and the lightning, "whose voice is the thunder." Zaire. (Budge, 1973, 1: 374)

Chebbeniathan The supreme being and sky god to whom promises are made when hurricanes threaten or thunder seems near. Algonquin Indians. United States and Canada. (Eliade, 1958: 53, 55)

Ah Chembekur A Mayan god of "the highest of the seven heavens, . . . which is in complete darkness." The Lacandon, Mexico and Guatemala. (Thompson, 1970: 345)

Chemin A name of the sky god. The Carib, West Indies. (Alexander, 1920: 38)

Chemioi A heavenly goddess, wife of Begjag. The Kenta in Kedah, Malaya. (Schebesta, 1927: 219)

Chido The sky god and supreme being is the celestial aspect of a duality. As the creator and earth god he is known as Ama or Ma. They are identified with each

83

other yet considered quite separately. The Jukun, Nigeria. (Meek, 1931: 178–179, 184–185; Williams, 1936: 217; Jeffreys, 1972: 731)

Chipiropa   The sky god who controls all celestial and atmospheric phenomena. Panama. (Trimborn, 1968: 106)

Chiu T'ien Hou Mu   The "Empress Mother of Heaven." China. (Day, 1940: 27)

Cotokinunwu   The sky god is associated with the lightning as his symbol. The Hopi, Arizona. (Fewkes, 1899: 215; 1895, 1: 124; Keane, 1925, 1: 253)

Dame   A sky-fertility god of the Akan at Nkoranza. Ghana. (Meyerowitz, 1958: 73)

Dattas   The Luvian sky and storm god. Near East. (Eliade, 1958: 88)

Deban, Jar   The sky was the primary god of the Agao. Ethiopia. (Rossini, 1925, 6: 488)

Deus Coelestis   A name of Baal Hamon. Libya. (Meyerowitz, 1958: 130–131)

Didigwari   The sky god and remote creator of the Ik (Icien). Uganda, Sudan, and Kenya. (Turnbull, 1972: 184)

Dievas   The god of the sky, of heavenly light, stimulates the growth of the crops, and with Laima, controls human destiny. Lithuania. (Gimbutas, 1963: 189–190, 200)

Dievs, Debestevs   Baltic sky god and supreme deity. (Leach, 1950, 2: 607)

Diwata-sa-langit   The god of heaven is the most powerful of the deities. The Subanun of Zamboanga, Philippines. (Jocano, 1969: 24)

Diwya, Diwja   A goddess at Pylos to whom offerings were made. "She would appear to be a female counterpart to Zeus . . . perhaps a sky-goddess." Mycenean, Greece. (Chadwick, 1976: 95; Samuel, 1966: 89)

Djalai   A sky goddess of the Kenta (Negritos), Malaya. (Pettazzoni, 1956: 326)

rDo rje ne ne gnam sman sgron   A Tibetan sky goddess. (Nebesky-Wojkowitz, 1956, 1: 200)

Dumagwid   The god who "lives in the skyworld where the sun rises." The Ibaloy, Luzon, Philippines. (De Raedt, 1964: 319)

Duur ing Angkasa, Duwring Akasa   "Lord in the Sky," a deity of the firmament, is identified with Siwa. As a multiple term it indicates the ancestors as gods of the sky. Bali. (Grader, 1969: 143, 146; Covarrubias, 1937: 317)

Dyad shin   A Tibetan sky god. (Nebesky-Wojkowitz, 1956, 2: 183)

Dyaus   The omniscient Vedic sky god, the sky personified, is with Prithivi the primeval parents of the gods, and is the origin of all things. India. (Bhattacharji, 1970: 23; Martin, 1914: 25–26; Danielow, 1964: 92; Keith, 1917: 16; Pettazzoni, 1956: 6, 118; Cox, 1870, 1: 328; Keary, 1882: 117)

Dzakuta   A sky god—"the 'thrower of celestial stones.' " The Yoruba, Nigeria. (Foucart, 1925, 11: 581)

Ebore   The sky god of the Gbanya whose wife is Esesar. Gold Coast, Africa. (Rattray, 1932: 45; Williams, 1936: 43)

Ek Xib Chac   A Mayan sky god associated with the color black and with the west. Mexico and Guatemala. (Redfield and Rojas, 1962: 115; Tozzer, 1941: 137)

Engai, En-kai   The god of the sky is associated with the rain, and is invoked in taking oaths. The Masai, the En-jemusi. Kenya and Tanzania. (Beech, 1911: 19; Mbiti, 1970, 2: 131; Wallis, 1939: 191; Williams, 1936: 199)

Eñketa   The supreme sky god controls the elements. Zaire. (Budge, 1973, 1: 374)

Eri   A sky god from whom the royal family in Aguku claims ancestry. Nigeria. (Jeffreys, 1935: 346)

Erob   The god of the heavens sends the rain and is also invoked in illness. The Bushmen, South Africa and Namibia. (Lebzelter, 1934: 10, 11, 23)

Eruwa   God of the heavens. The Jagga (Chagga), Tanzania. (Budge, 1973, 1: 363)

Esege Malan   The god of the sky—"Grandfather Bald Head"—"the highest heaven itself." There are conflicting accounts about him from being the highest god to being a human who exchanged places with the gods. The Buriat, Siberia. (Curtin, 1909: 39, 46, 121; Klementz, 1925, 3: 3; Krader, 1954: 328, 338–339; Roheim, 1954: 18)

Ets   A sky god of the Yenisei-Ostyak, or Ket. (Roheim, 1954: 23)

Firie A supreme sky god who controls the elements. Zaire. (Budge, 1973, 1: 374)

Garang A sky deity associated with the sun and with "certain heated conditions of the human body"— illnesses. His emblems are giraffes and snakes. The Dinka, Sudan. (Lienhardt, 1961: 83–85, 160; Evans-Pritchard, 1956: 30)

Gasani The chief god of the Bakene, a god of the sky and of water, is invoked in illness. Uganda. (Roscoe, 1915: 154, 249)

Gbenebeka A goddess from the sky and mother of the Ogoni. Nigeria. (Jeffreys, 1970: 112)

Ghali matutsi The sky initiate. The Eastern Pomo, California. (Loeb, 1926, 2: 300)

Gileamberte The supreme being and sky god is as well the god of animals, particularly the reindeer. The Yurak-Samoyed. Siberia. (Pettazzoni, 1956: 443)

Gulambre The sky being from whom the novice medicine man receives his powers. Port Stephens area, Australia. (Eliade, 1973: 143)

Gulu The sky god of the Baganda. Father of Nambi and Walumbe. Uganda. (Feldman, 1963: 83–85)

Gwaza The sky god is associated also with the moon, and is invoked for children and wealth. The Katab, Nigeria. (Meek, 1931: 58, 61; Gunn, 1956: 79)

Ah Hadz'en Caan Chac The god of the sky and of rain also makes the thunder. Mayan, Guatemala and Mexico. (Redfield and Rojas, 1962: 115; Thompson, 1970: 254–255)

Haepuru A god of the heavens who with Roiho and Roake directed Tane where to find the female element from which to fashion a human female. The Maori, New Zealand. (Best, 1924: 115)

hailepi hawit, hawilai'ilam "Above Chief" of the "Four Chiefs" invoked in bathing rituals. The Nootkan tribes. Washington and Vancouver Island. (Drucker, 1951: 152)

Hala The sky god of the Kissi. Liberia and Guinea. (Mbiti, 1970, 2: 331)

Halakwulup A sky god whose "eyes" are the sun and the moon. The Fuegian, Tierra del Fuego. (Eliade, 1958: 41)

halsuis hawit, hawilsuisai "Horizon Chief" of the Nootkan tribes is invoked during bathing rituals. Washington and Vancouver Island. (Drucker, 1951: 152)

Hananim The ancient and omniscient god of the heavens is also supreme. Korea. (Clark, 1932: 139, 196; Pettazzoni, 1956: 287)

Ha'o The supreme being and sky god of the Giangero or northern Sidama. Ethiopia. (Pettazzoni, 1956: 41)

Haronga A sky god, who married Tongotongo, was the father of 'Ra, the sun, and Marama, the moon. The Maori, New Zealand. (Andersen, 1928: 376)

Hatan "The head anito, who made the laws of the sky world and rules it." His wife is Dinawagan. They are invoked for help particularly in illness. His fourth son is Ewagan to whom he passed on his powers; his daughter is Hinalingan. The Apayao, Philippines. (Wilson, 1947: 20)

Hathor The cow-goddess as a sky deity was associated with Horus, sometimes as his wife, sometimes his mother. She was a goddess of love and of merriment, the great protective mother, and a goddess of the underworld of benevolent aspect. Egypt. (Knight, 1915: 39; Ames, 1965: 76; Budge, 1969, 1: 428, 435; Jayne, 1962: 58; Larousse, 1968: 23)

Heart of Heaven Same as god-Seven, the seven Ahpú. *See also* **Cabahuil, Ixpiyacoc,** and **Ixcumané.** The Quiché, Guatemala. (Girard, 1979: 88)

Heqo, Yero The omniscient supreme being and sky god of the Kaffa or western Sidama. Ethiopia. (Pettazzoni, 1956: 42)

Heru-ur The personification of the Face of Heaven by day, while Set was that of night. He was depicted as a man or a lion with the head of a hawk. An aspect of Horus. Egypt. (Budge, 1969, 1: 78, 467; Knight, 1915: 48; Ames, 1965: 23, 68)

Hilo n di Bulan "Ray Floods of the Moon," a god of the sky-world. The Ifugao, Philippines. (Barton, 1946: 42)

Hiovaki A sky god who was also a creator and the god of war received in his home in the sky those warriors who die in battle. The Motumotu, Papuans, New Guinea. (MacKenzie, 1930: 291; Holmes, 1902: 428; Wallis, 1939: 241)

Horus the Elder *See* **Heru-ur**

Hunrakán Same as Cabahuil, Heart of Heaven. The God of Heaven, the one-footed god, "was the devil of the earlier cycle" (a demon of the Caribs). Regardless of the cycle he is god or demon of the elements—thunder and lightning, rain, storm, etc. Good or bad meaning depends exclusively upon "the cultural criterion." The Quiché, Guatemala. (Girard, 1979: 35, 110)

Ibantzu A sky god of the Bangala. Zaire. (Foucart, 1925, 11: 581)

Igwe The god of the bright sky was associated with oracles and with oath-taking. The Ibo, the Igbo, Nigeria. (Jeffreys, 1972: 730; Talbot, 1967: 52; Wallis, 1939: 189; Meek, 1943: 113; Uchendu, 1965: 97)

Iju The sky god of the Margi. Same as Ba-Chi. Nigeria. (Meek, 1931: 180)

I-lai The god of the heavens, with Indara, created mankind. The Toradja and Celebes, Indonesia. (Eliade, 1959: 121; Kruijt, 1925, 7: 248; Kern, 1925, 8: 347)

Ilem The heaven god of the Ostiaks. Siberia. (MacCulloch, 1964: 217)

Im, U Husband of Arinna, goddess of the lands. As a primeval pair they were the sky and earth deities. He was god of the storm. Hittite, Near East. (Eliade, 1976, 2: 364)

Inchin Temaga A goddess of the heavens, daughter of Singalang Buron. the Sea Dyaks of Sarawak, Borneo. (Sarawak Gazette, 1963: 96)

Ineb The sky deity of the Makooa. Mozambique. (Budge, 1973, 1: 363)

Ingalit A sky god invoked in healing ceremonies. Another name of Sagangan. The Tinguians, Philippines. (Cole, 1922: 334)

Inhu-Ankulu Sky god of the Kafir. South Africa. (Foucart, 1925, 11: 581)

Ini Anda A god of the heavens, son of Petara. The Sea Dyaks of Sarawak, Borneo. (Sarawak Gazette, 1963: 19)

Ini Andan A goddess of the heavens, a bringer of good luck. She is invoked particularly at the "Feast of the Whetstones" before the clearing of the land, is protective of all aspects of farming and blesses with abundance. The Dyaks of Sarawak, Borneo. (Sarawak Gazette, 1963: 77; Roth, 1968: 174–175)

Inkosatana A sky deity who is manifest in the rainbow and the lightning. The Bantu-Swazi, Namibia. (Smith, 1950: 112)

Inkosazana A goddess of the heavens manifest in the rainbow and the rain. She is also a goddess of agriculture and of women. The Zulu, South Africa. (Pettersson, 1953: 184–185; Schapera, 1937: 269)

Inkosi pezulu A sky god who is a god of weather and of all celestial phenomena. The Zulu, South Africa. (Pettersson, 1953: 180–184; Schapera, 1937: 263)

Inmar A god of the sky who is also a god of agriculture. The Votiaks, Siberia. (MacCulloch, 1964: 217, 219; Pettazzoni, 1956: 264)

Innen Nom A god of heaven of the Ostyaks, Siberia. (Bertrans, 1897: 87)

Itzamna The Mayan god of the heavens was the head of the pantheon, and god of civilization—of letters, of medicine. His wife was Ixchel. Mexico and Guatemala. (Morley, 1946: 223; Tozzer, 1941: 10, 146; Schellhas, 1904: 18; Nicholson, 1967: 119)

Izanagi-no-Mikoto He is the personification of the sky—with his sister/wife Izanami, created the Japanese islands and numerous deities. (Haydon, 1941: 202; Yasumaro, 1928: 3, 7; Holtom, 1938: 81, 109)

(Po) Jata The "god of the heavenly regions, who emanates from" Po Ovlah. The Chams, Annam and Cambodia. (Cabaton, 1925, 3: 342)

Jen Finno Ugric god of the heavens whose weapon is the lightning. The Ziryen, District of Perm. Russia. (Leach, 1950, 2: 1194)

Jewa-Jewa A sky god who intercedes with the creator for man and gives "medicine" to the magician. The Benua, Malay Peninsula. (Leach, 1950, 2: 550; Skeat, 1906: 353)

Jite-Jiro A compound deity—Heaven-Earth. The Gallongs (Adi), Northeastern India. (Chowdhury, 1971: 77)

Jocchu Vague Maorocon An "immortal invisible being . . . who lived in the heavens." The Arawak, West Indies. (Rouse, 1948, 1: 538)

Jomali God of the sky. Iceland. (Holmberg, 1964: 217)

Jongsuli-Young-Jongbu The sky, a deity of the Dhammai. Northeast India. (Long, 1963: 105)

Jubmel, Ibmel God of the sky. Also used as a general term for "god." The Lapps. (MacCulloch, 1964: 217)

Jumala Finno-Ugrian god of the sky. Eastern Europe. (MacCulloch, 1964: 217; Queval, 1968: 63)

Jumo, Jume The god of the heavens is the supreme god of the Cheremiss. Russia. (Bosi, 1960: 129; MacCulloch, 1964: 266)

Jupiter Roman god of the sky and of sovereignty. As god of the sky he ruled the upper atmosphere in all its aspects—as Jupiter Lucetius, the god of light; J. Elicius, god of rain; J. Fulgus, god of lightning. He wielded the thunder and lightning and provided omens for the priests in the lightning and in the flight of birds. (Fairbanks, 1907: 98–99; Jayne, 1962: 429–430; Dumézil, 1966, 1: 108, 178–179, 191; Larousse, 1968: 203)

Kabedya Mpungu A sky god of the Baholos and Balubas. Zaire. (Foucart, 1925, 11: 581)

Kabezya-mpungu The supreme sky god controlled the elements. Zaire. (Budge, 1973, 1: 374)

Kadeyuna The goddess of the seventh heaven is the younger sister of Tiun and the wife of Malaki Lunsud. The Bagobo, Philippines. (Benedict, 1916: 17)

Kaila The remote supreme god and creator is the god of the sky and of the weather. The Ihalmiut, Keewatin District, Canada. (Mowat, 1968: 237)

Kalaga A sky god of the Warega. Africa. (Foucart, 1925, 11: 581)

Kalangi The god of heaven is manifest in the west wind (the northwest monsoon) with which he fertilizes Lumimuut. The Alfures (Minahassa), Celebes, Indonesia. (Pettazzoni, 1956: 11)

Kali-matutsi "Sky-occupation," lived above, the zenith. The Pomo Indians, California. (Barrett, 1917: 424)

Kambel A sky god, father of the moon. Keraki-Papuans, New Guinea. (Poignant, 1967: 90)

Kando God of the sky. The Numba Mountains, Sudan. (Stevenson, 1950: 215; Mbiti, 1970, 2: 334)

Kane-hoa-lani God and ruler of the heavens. Hawaii. (Beckwith, 1940; 321; Alexander, 1968: 63)

Karakarook The daughter of Bunjil who gave her "power over the sky." Sister of Bimbeal. The Kulin tribes, Australia. (Eliade, 1958: 42)

Kashchar-Torum God and ruler of the highest of the three heavens. The Mansi, Siberia. (Michael, 1963: 209)

Kayai, Kadai The god of the sky whose voice is the thunder punishes with the elements. The Aeta, the Baluga, Luzon, Philippines. (Wales, 1957: 12; Pettazzoni, 1956: 318)

Khen-pa The master of the sky closes the doors of the sky when the proper ceremony is performed. He is "the grandfather of the three worlds" with white hair, white robes "and riding on the white dog of the sky, and in his hand he carries a crystal wand." Tibet. (Waddell, 1959: 487)

Khiou A celestial god, son of Lugeilang and Ilamamlul, half-brother of Iolofath. Ulithi, the Carolines, Micronesia. (Lessa, 1961: 20)

!Khuba, Hishe The sky, the heavens, is invoked for longevity and health. The Bushmen of the Kalahari, Botswana. (Smith, 1950: 91; Bleek, 1928: 25)

Kiara, Mbamba The beneficent sky, personified. The Konde, Tanzania. (Frazer, 1926: 187)

Kilima A sky god of the Bantu. South Africa. (Foucart, 1925, 11: 581)

Kimulani The sky is the husband of Sinekepapa and father of Naleau. Nukumanu and Ontong Java, Melanesia. (Lessa, 1961: 88)

Kinorohingan A god associated with the sky. Consort of Warunsasadun. The Dusun, Borneo. (Raats, 1969: 21)

Kongola A sky god. East Africa. (Foucart, 1925, 11: 581)

Koolukoolwani A "heavenly being of great power," created by Villenangi. The Zulu, South Africa. (Pettersson, 1953: 157)

Kuju A beneficent sky god who supplies men with good. The Yukaghir, Siberia. (Jochelson, 1900/02: 144)

Kwoth An omnipresent and invisible god who lives in the sky and is the creator of all—though "creation is more often explained in mythology by reference to ancestors." The Nuer, Sudan. (Gelfand, 1966: 127; Evans-Pritchard, 1953: 201; Howell, 1954: 204–205)

sKyer rdzong snyanpo The king of Heaven. Tibet. (Francke, 1925, 8: 75)

iLai *See also* **I-lai.** The god of the sky of the Toradjas of Celebes. Indonesia. (Wales, 1957: 78; Downs, 1920: 12; Pettersson, 1957: 27)

Lampra, Khabdi A deity "who rules sky and ocean." the Tiparas, Bengal. (Crooke, 1925, 2: 481)

Langi The heaven. Same as Rangi. Savage Island, Niue, Polynesia. (Williamson, 1933: 25)

Lanij A sky deity who causes the illness mijlan. The Marshall Islands, Micronesia. (Spoehr, 1949: 245)

La'n Koi Madai A great god of the sky to whom only princes may sacrifice. The Katchins, Burma. (Gilhodes, 1908: 678)

La'n La Sinlap A benevolent sky nat to whom sacrifices are made. The Katchins, Burma. (Gilhodes, 1908: 677)

La'n Yanng Sindu Madai A sky nat to whom sacrifices are made. The Katchins, Burma. (Gilhodes, 1908: 678)

Lare, Loro The sky god of the Samos. Senegal. (Frazer, 1926: 92)

Lelabalisela The sky chief of the Kwakiutl. Father of Sentlee. British Columbia. (Boas, 1935: 126)

Ah-lelem-caan-chaac A Mayan sky god is one of the Chacs, rain gods, and "produces the lightning." Mexico and Guatemala. (Redfield and Rojas, 1962: 115; Thompson, 1970: 255)

Lengdon A god of the heavens. Same as Indra. The Ahom, Tai. (Gurdon, 1925, 1: 236)

Leoij A sky deity who causes the illness mijlan. The Marshall Islands, Micronesia. (Spoehr, 1949: 245)

Li Ching "Prime Minister of Heaven. Guardian of the Gate of Heaven." China. (Werner, 1932: 245)

Lidum A god of the skyworld who was a god of divination taught them their customs and rituals. The Ifugao, Luzon, Philippines. (Barton, 1946: 28, 91; 1955: 140, 154)

Ling-pao T'ien-tsun A primordial god of the second heaven whose function was "to calculate time, and to divide it into periods." China. (Werner, 1932: 400)

Lokpata The sky god of the Effium Orri. The Okpoto also consider him the creator. Nigeria. (Armstrong, 1955: 152)

Lola The god of the heavens. The Bakusu, Zaire. (Williams, 1936: 82)

Loula A supreme sky god who controls the elements. Zaire. (Budge, 1973, 1: 374)

Lugaba A sky god and creator is the giver of life, but also of sickness and death if displeased. The Bahima, Uganda. (Roscie, 1915: 131; Williams, 1936: 155; Frazer, 1961: iii, 190)

Lugeilang A celestial god whose wife is Ilamamlul. Father of Iolofath and Khiou. Ulithi, the Carolines, Micronesia. (Lessa, 1961: 15–16, 30)

Lugeleng An omniscient sky god who rules the world punishes wrong-doing, or reports it to Aluelap, his father. Micronesia. (Pettazzoni, 1956: 342)

Lumabat God of the first heaven. The Bagoba, Philippines. (Benedict, 1916: 14–16; Raats, 1969: 25–26)

Lungkitsumba A sky god who is "like a man, but behaves like a wind." The Ao Naga, Assam. (Pettazzoni, 1956: 11)

Mahpiyato The Sky "is the source of all wisdom and power, and the great judge over all." He was directed by Inyan to create people inferior to the Pte people (servants of the spirits) to be "the subjects of Maka" (the earth), and the animals. The Lakota, Plains Indians, United States. (One Feather, 1982: 49)

Mai-waho A god of the heavens who taught the incantations to Ta-whaki. New Zealand. (White, 1877, 1: 59)

Makilehohoa A sky god, father of Kimulani. Nukumanu and Ontong Java, Melanesia. (Lessa, 1961: 88)

Makowasendo The sky god is the husband of Nangkwijo, the earth. The Tewa, Pueblo Indians, New Mexico. (Harrington, 1907/08: 45)

Malaki Lunsud, Malaki Lunson God of the eighth heaven whose wife is Kadeyuna. The Bagobo, Philippines. (Benedict, 1916: 17; Jocano, 1969: 21)

M'ba The sky god of the Ababua. Africa. (Foucart, 1925, 11: 581)

Mbamba   The sky god and supreme being of the Konde is invoked for health, fertility, and freedom from illness. Tanzania. (Eliade, 1976, 2: 356)

Medje   A sky god who is assistant to his older brother Loko. Son of Mawu and Lisa. Dahomey. (Herskovits, 1938, 2: 108)

Megit   A deity of the heavens invoked in the ceremony for children to make them strong, skillful, successful, brave, and to give them longevity. The Sea Dyaks, Borneo. (Roth, 1968: 171)

Melo   The primeval sky, the male principle, is the brother/husband of Sedi. The Adi, Northeastern India. (Chowdhury, 1971: 75)

Meu-nyi-mo   The omniscient sky father, creator of mankind. The Lo-lo p'o of Yunnan, China. (Frazer, 1926: 81)

Mfidi   The supreme sky god controls the elements. Zaire. (Budge, 1973, 1: 374)

Mhatzuu   The goddess of heaven. Taiwan, China. (Jordan, 1972: 109)

Miamakwa   The sky god of the Yavapai. Arizona. (Gifford, 1936: 308)

Milili   A great spirit of the sky is the source of obsidian, of the shaman's powers. The Yuki, California. (Kroeber, 1925: 196–197)

Minungara   Two unfriendly sky beings "who make doctors" but at the same time try to kill people who fall ill, but are prevented from harming them by Mumpani. The Mara, Australia. (Spencer, 1904: 501–502; Roheim, 1972: 68)

Mong-mu   A sky god of the Lolos. Southwest China. (Graham, 1961: 83)

Mphambi   A name of Mulungu as the heavens. The Nyanjas, Malawi. (Hetherwick, 1925, 9: 420)

Mu, Mushang   The "*nat* of the heavens." The Kachins, Burma. (Temple, 1925, 3: 22; Leach, 1950, 2: 785)

Mueraya   The god who rules the heavens is also helpful to the shamans. He controls the jaguars. The Conibo, Peru and Ecuador. (Steward and Métraux, 1948, 1: 592; Zerries, 1968: 255)

Mu Je   A sky goddess who came down to earth and married Ze-bi-ge-swa who was the only person, gave him children, and then returned to the sky. The Ch'iang at Ho-p'ing-chai. Szechwan, China. (Graham, 1958: 72)

Mukameiguru   A god who rules in the skies. The Ankore, Uganda. (Mbiti, 1970, 2: 327)

Mu Mi   The sky god whom some consider "rules the other gods and so is supreme." The Lolos, Southwest China. (Graham, 1961: 83)

Mumu Wunlang   The embryonic sky, of the second generation of deities, child of Kringkrong wa and Ynong majan. The Katchins, Burma. (Gilhodes, 1908: 675)

Mundagadji   Two sky spirits, ill-disposed towards man, whose depredations are thwarted by Ulurkura. The Binbinga, Australia. (Spencer, 1904: 50; Roheim, 1972: 68)

Mungangana   The sky god who originally lived on earth with men, then withdrew, manifests his will through the aurora borealis. Australia. (Eliade, 1976, 2: 356; 1958: 42)

Musoke   God of the sky who with Gulu controls the weather, makes rain from the water sent up to the clouds by the river divinity Mayanja. The Ganda, Uganda. (Mbiti, 1970, 2: 119, 138; Roscoe, 1965: 315)

Muyinwu-taka   A sky god of the Hopi Indians. Arizona and New Mexico. (Fewkes, 1895, 1: 350)

Mwali   A celestial deity who is invoked for rain and for relief from the rule of Europeans. The Kalanga, Rhodesia. (Werbner, 1964: 207)

Nab'Wen   The sky god whose wife is Teng. The Kusal, Ghana. (Rattray, 1932: 45)

naghe' nezghani   Monster Slayer, twin of tobadjictcini, child-of-the-water. A sky being and intermediary between man and the deities. The Navaho, Arizona and New Mexico. (Reichard, 1950: 417, 448–451; Haile, 1947: 9)

Namakon   A god of the sky. The Huanyam, Western Matto Grosso, South America. (Métraux, 1942: 95)

Nambajandi   God of "Cadija (heaven), the region of delight and abundant game." The Watchandi, Australia. (Tylor, 1891: 292)

Nambi A sky goddess who came to the earth and married Kintu, the first man. Daughter of Gulu. The Baganda, Uganda. (Feldman, 1963: 83–85)

gNam gyi lha rgod thog pa (pr. **Nam gyi lha Göthokpa**) God of heaven, of the sky, and consort of A phyi gung rgal (gNam phyi gung rgyal) goddess of heaven. The Bon, Tibet. (Tucci, 1980: 218)

Nam-k'ahi-ñiṅ-po, Ākāsagarbha (Sanskrit) A celestial Bodhisat, The "matrix of the sky." Tibet. (Waddell, 1959: 358)

gNam lha byang sman mthing gi go zu can A Bon goddess—probably a sky goddess. Tibet. (Nebesky-Wojkowitz, 1956, 1: 200)

gNam-lha dkar-mo The "White Goddess of Heaven." Vicinity of Mount Everest. Tibet. (Hoffman, 1956: 18)

Nam mkha' g·yu mdog snang srid mdzod A Bon sky goddess who causes the disturbances of the elements. Tibet. (Nebesky-Wojkowitz, 1956, 1: 468)

Nam mkha'i lha mo gsal byed ma A Tibetan sky goddess. (Nebesky-Wojkowitz, 1956, 1: 468)

Nam mkha'i lha mo Kun tu bzang mo A sky goddess invoked in pollution-eliminating ceremonies. Tibet. (Nebesky-Wojkowitz, 1956, 1: 388)

Nam mkha'i lha mo snyoms byed ma A Tibetan sky goddess residing in the northwest. (Nebesky-Wojkowitz, 1956, 1: 468)

Nam mkha'i lha mo sprin tshogs ma A sky goddess residing in the northeast. A goddess of weather. Tibet. (Nebesky-Wojkowitz, 1956, 1: 468)

Nam mkha'i lha mo tsha gsang snyoms A sky and weather goddess residing in the southwest. Tibet. (Nebesky-Wojkowitz, 1956, 1: 468)

Nam mkha'i lha mo tshod 'dzin ma A sky and weather goddess residing in the southeast. Tibet. (Nebesky-Wojkowitz, 1956, 1: 468)

Namwanga A supreme sky god who controls the elements. Zaire. (Budge, 1973, 1: 374)

Na-naki-me A heavenly goddess (pheasant) sent to the earth to check on the Heavenly Kamis sent to subdue the Earthly Kamis. Japan. (Herbert, 1967: 338)

Nanginath God as sky in Temein. Nuba Mountains, Sudan. (Stevenson, 1950: 215)

Na Nwen The sky god of the Loberu, whose wife is Teng. Ghana. (Rattray, 1932: 45)

Na Nwene The sky god of the Dagare, whose wife is Tenga. Ghana. (Rattray, 1932: 45)

Nawen The sky god of the Lobi. Gold Coast, Africa. (Williams, 1936: 46)

Ndjambi Karunga A god of dual aspect. Ndjambi is the heavenly god, the source of life, but also of death. Karunga is the earthly deity, "a god of the earth, water and netherworld." The Herero, Namibia. (Luttig, 1933: 7–9)

Ndri A sky deity of the Umundri. Nigeria. (Jeffreys, 1951: 93)

Nepelle The "ruler of the heavens and the father of all spirits." Australia. (Reed, 1965: 70)

Ne-u A spirit of the sky. Burma. (Temple, 1925, 3: 21)

Ngoc Hoang The sky god—"the Emperor of Jade . . . the supreme ruler of the universe." Annam. (Frazer, 1926: 86)

Nguleso The sky god and supreme being of the Kakwa. Sudan. (Huntingford, 1953: 55)

Ngun loki The benevolent sky god and creator is associated with rain and lightning. The Bari and the Pojulu, Sudan (Huntingford, 1953: 42, 70; Seligman, 1931: 8)

Ngunyari A sky god important in initiation ceremonies having made the bull-roarer and established the rules regarding it. The Ungarinyin, Australia. (Eliade, 1973: 74)

Nigsillik A sky god feared as dangerous, killing those who offend him. The Copper Eskimo, Canada. (Jenness, 1913/1918: 189)

Ningsang Woishun Youngest son of Ningsin and Ningthoi, a third generation deity and father of the fourth generation deities. He is the master of the sky. His wife was Phungkam Janun who died and became mistress of the earth. He sends her rain and she responds with the rainbow. The Katchins, Burma. (Gilhodes, 1908: 677–679)

Nogamain A self-existent celestial god of the Murinbata of Western Arnhem Land. Australia. (Eliade, 1973: 38–39)

Nomkubulwane A goddess of the heavens who must be propitiated because she sends illness. The Swazi, Swaziland. (Pettersson, 1953: 187)

Nuba The god of the sky who sent Su to bring "fruit-bearing seeds" to man. The Sara tribes, Chad. (Larousse, 1973: 530)

Num The sky, but *see* Supreme Beings.

The Numbakulla Two sky beings, brothers, saw the embryonic Inapatua who had only outlines of bodies. It was their duty to finish the creation of these creatures making them into the aboriginal men and women. The Aranda, Australia. (Mountford, 1965: 48)

Numi-Tarem, Numi-Torem The god of the sky, the upperworld, is also among some considered the creator, and the source of their civilization. The Vogul and the Ostyak, Siberia. (MacCulloch, 1964: 218, 330; Pettersson, 1957: 20; Roheim, 1954: 26; 1972: 2; Prokof'yeva, Chernetsov, and Prytkova, 1964: 536; Michael, 1963: 209; Eliade, 1958: 62)

Num-Senke The sky god of the Ostyak of the river Irtish whose name means luminous, light. Siberia. (Bosi, 1960: 131; Eliade, 1958: 60)

Nurrendere The sky god and supreme being manifests his will through the rainbow. Australia. (Eliade, 1958: 42)

Nut The cow goddess, the personification of the sky, was the daughter of Shu and Tefnut and the wife of Seb, the mother of Osiris and Isis, of Set and Nephthys. Also considered the female counterpart of Nu, a primeval goddess. Egypt. (Knight, 1915: 88; Budge, 1969, 1: 283–284; 1969, 2: 100; Ames, 1965: 53; Larousse, 1968: 16)

Nwende The sky god of the Mole whose wife is Tenga. Ghana. (Rattray, 1932: 45)

Nyadenga The great god of the sky from whom there is little intervention in human affairs though he is credited at times as "knowing" (the truth, for instance), as healing, and as sending rain. The Venda, South Africa; the Shona, Rhodesia. (Pettersson, 1953: 143–144; Gelfand, 1962: 141)

Nyame The sky god is sometimes considered as both male and female. The female aspect is identified with the moon and credited with the creation of humans. The male is identified with the sun infusing them with life. The Ashanti, Ghana. (Parrinder, 1949: 26; Queval, 1968: 16; Gelfand, 1966: 118; Clarke, 1930: 436)

Nyamenle A sky god created by, and sometimes merged with, Edenkema. He gave people the techniques of divination, and is, with Edenkema, "the master and

sender of death." His wife is Azele Yaba. The Nzema (Akan), Ghana. (Grottanelli, 1967: 33–41)

Obasi The sky god and supreme being was sometimes considered bisexual, both father and mother. However, "the earth goddess, Isong, is more prominent." The Ibibio, Nigeria. (Parrinder, 1949: 21, 38)

Obasi Osaw, Obassi The sky and sun god is believed to have created all things with Obassi Nsi, mother earth. He is considered harsh and cruel because of the hot sun and the wielding of the lightning and thunder. The Ekoi, Nigeria. (Meek, 1931: 180; Frazer, 1926: 131–132; Pettazzoni, 1956: 434)

Occopirmus Baltic god of the sky and the stars. Prussia, Latvia, and Lithuania. (Welsford, 1925, 9: 240, 488; Puhvel, 1974: 83)

Odin The Scandinavian All-father was a god of many aspects. As the personification of the sky he was the consort of the earth: Jord (Erda), the primitive earth, mother of Thor; Frigga, the fruitful earth, mother of Balder, Hermod, and Tyr; Rinda, the "hard and frozen earth," mother of Vali. (Guerber, 1895: 43; Stern, 1898: 17; Thorpe, 1851: 16, 167; Murray, 1935: 360–362; Pettazzoni, 1956: 220–221)

Ogwe The Sky. The Ibo, Nigeria. (Williams, 1936: 213)

Ohe A sky god of the Egede—"a supreme, all-pervasive being." Nigeria. (Armstrong, 1955: 146)

Oki, Okeus The omniscient sky god of some Iroquois Indians is a god of oaths and agreements. He punishes with storms and floods. Eastern United States. (Pettazzoni, 1956: 16, 20–21)

Olosiksikkalilel The foremost deity of the first layer of heaven. The Cuna, Panama. (Nordenskiold, 1938: 330)

Ombang God of the sky, the heavens. The Banen, Cameroon. (Mbiti, 1970, 2: 130)

Oshats A sky god and the sun. The Sia, Pueblo Indians. New Mexico. (Fewkes, 1895, 2: 124)

Otak God as sky in Katla. Nuba Mountains, Sudan. (Stevenson, 1950: 215)

Ouranos *See* **Uranus**

pan·a The goddess of heaven receives the souls of the dead, who are then reborn and returned to the earth by the moon to become other humans or animals. The Padler-miut Eskimo. Canada. (Rasmussen, 1930: 79)

Pangulili   God of the ninth heaven, son of Ubnuling. The Bagobo, Philippines. (Jocano, 1969: 21)

Papas   A Phrygian sky god. Asia Minor. (Kerenyi, 1951: 89)

Pautiwa   The sky god or sun. The Asa, Hopi Indians, Arizona. (Fewkes, 1902: 24)

Peddo-Dodum   The sky is the husband of Sitking-Kedding, the earth, and father of Doini and Pollo. The Bori (Adi), Northeastern India. (Chowdhury, 1971: 76)

Penardun   Daughter of Don and Beli and as such a sky goddess. Wife of Llyr and mother of Manawyddan. Britons. (Squire, 1906: 252, 269–270)

Perëndi   A god of the sky with close functional associations with the Slavic Perunu. Albania. (Leach, 1950, 2: 1026)

Perunŭ   A god of the heavens as well as a storm god. Russia. (Schrader, 1925: 38; Leach, 1950, 2: 1026)

Poalleritillik   A vengeful spirit who lives in the sky. The Copper Eskimo, Canada. (Jenness, 1913/1918: 189)

Poee-mpalaburu   The god of the sky, of the highest heaven, is the creator from whom "all souls originate." He arranges the path of the sun. The Toradja, Celebes, Indonesia. (Wales, 1957: 78, 89; Adriani and Kruyt, 1950: 372, 374)

Polo   God of the heavens. The Luo, Kenya. (Mbiti, 1970, 2: 332)

Ponphyoi   A sky god who concerns himself with human affairs. The Kachins, Burma. (Temple 1925, 3: 22)

Prah En   The sky god rules the celestial sphere, wields the thunderbolt, and is "regarded as the lord of the blessed." Identified with Indra. Cambodia. (Marchal, 1963: 202)

Pua, Pwa   The remote god of the sky of the Bachama. Northern Nigeria. (Meek, 1930: 323; Williams, 1936: 216; Frazer, 1926: 122)

Puges   A deity of the heavens invoked for children and for favorable childbirth. The Ostiaks, the Voguls, Siberia. (MacCulloch, 1964: 260)

Pulyallana   The sky god, a supreme being, who manifests his will through the thunderbolt. Australia. (Eliade, 1958: 42)

U Pyrthat   A sky god who wields the lightning. The Khasi, Assam and Burma. (Pettazzoni, 1956: 299)

Qamaits   A goddess of the heavens whose visits to the earth cause sickness and death. The Bella Coola Indians, British Columbia. (Boas, 1898: 28)

Raki   The sky god whose wife is Papa, the earth. New Zealand. (Mackenzie, n.d.: 209; Larousse, 1968: 465)

Raluvhimba   The god of the heavens and the creator is associated "with all astronomical and physical phenomena." He is invoked for rain, but punishes with drought, storm and insects. The Venda and the Shona, South Africa and Rhodesia. (Pettersson, 1953: 193–194, 273; Schapera, 1937: 264)

Rangi   The personified sky, husband of Papa, the earth—the primeval parents. Among their children—Tane-mahuta, Tangaroa, Tu-mata-nenga, Tawhiri Matea, Haumia-tikitiki, Rongo-ma-tane. The Maori, New Zealand. (Best, 1924: 86; Shand, 1894: 91; Pettazzoni, 1956: 344–345; Hongi, 1920: 25; Williamson, 1933: 24; Grey, 1855: 1)

Ranying Atala   A benevolent god of the sky descended to the earth, newly formed by Hatala, where he found seven eggs, two of which contained a man and a woman. He went back to the sky to get breath for them, meaning to give them immortality, eternal youth, and all good things, but was thwarted by Sangsang Angai. Burma. (MacKenzie, 1930: 309)

Ratu Champa   A sky god of the Sea Dyaks. Borneo. (MacKenzie, 1930: 349)

Ah Raxa Tzel   A god of the sky. The Quiché, Guatemala. (Recinos, 1950: 78)

Rehua   A benevolent god of the heavens who is also associated with the forests; with the star Antares, or with Sirius. New Zealand. (Best, 1924: 99, 102, 176, 129; Hongi, 1920: 25)

Rimassa   The sky deity of Minahassa. Northern Celebes, Indonesia. (MacKenzie, 1930: 322)

Ropi   A sky god of the Gold Coast. Ghana. (Foucart, 1925, 11: 581)

Sa   Also called Utakke. The sky god and a "god of righteousness who punishes violations of the moral code." The Carrier Indians, British Columbia. (Jenness, 1932: 171; 1934: 217)

Sagbata   As the son of Mawu and Lisa he is a god of the Sky Pantheon, but in descending to rule the earth is an earth god and ruler of that Pantheon. He is the giver of food as well as the punisher of evil with smallpox. Dahomey. (Herskovits, 1938, 2: 129, 131, 135–136)

Sago   The sky god of the Maji. Formerly called C'ai. Ethiopia. (Cerulli, 1956: 94)

Saku   The sky god of the Gimira. Ethiopia. (Cerulli, 1956: 94)

Salamiawan   God of the second heaven whose wife is Biat'odan. The Bagobo, Philippines. (Jocano, 1969: 21; Benedict, 1916: 16)

Salangayd   A god of the sky of the Bagobo. Philippines. (Benedict, 1916: 23)

Samantabhadra   Among the p'ön-pos "primarily the sky divinity." Nepal. (Snellgrove, 1961: 47)

Sangkoeroewira   The "god of the upperworld," whose son Batara Goeroe was the ancestor of the people. Brother of Goeroe ri Seleng. The Buginese, Indonesia. (Alkema and Bezemer, 1927: 189)

Sanke   The sky god of the Irtysh region who bestows his powers on the shaman. Siberia. (Eliade, 1964: 15; MacCulloch, 1964: 338)

Satta-kura-Djasagai-Aiy   In the pantheon of the sky gods they are "seven brothers, gods of light, war, etc." The Yakut, Siberia. (Czaplicka, 1969: 278)

Sebandal   A sky god of the Bagobo, Philippines. (Benedict, 1916: 23)

She-al-kaum   The "god of heaven or sky is called 'the good and rewarding god'. . . . and is also 'he who does not drink wine.' " Asia Minor. (Cook, 1930: 70)

Shimo-ra-po   A god of the second plane of the heavens associated with the goddess Shio-mi-ma. The Yami, Formosa. (Del Re, n.d.: 60)

Shi-nun-manuri   A goddess of the fourth plane of the heavens and chief of all on that plane who are all female. She and they control and supervise the birth of the sexes and determine longevity. The Yami, Formosa. (Del Re, n.d.: 64)

Shio-mi-ma   A goddess of the second plane of the heavens associated with Shimo-ra-po. The Yami, Formosa. (Del Re, n.d.: 60)

Shipariud   A god of the third plane of the heavens. The Yami, Formosa. (Del Re, n.d.: 63)

Shivairai   A god of the third plane of the heavens. The Yami, Formosa. (Del Re, n.d.: 63)

Shka-Bavas   The sky god is the chief god and is named first in all offerings and prayers. The Moksha-Mordvins, Russia. (Leach, 1950, 2: 1007)

Shljam Schoa   A great deity of the heavens who sent two others to create the features of the earth. The Koniagas, Pacific Northwestern America. (Bancroft, 1886, 3: 104)

Shnilemun   Sky Coyote always stays in the Upper World, is very benevolent toward mankind, and watches over them. He was considered their "father." He was active in the "creation of man after the great flood . . . was opposed to the institution of death," wanting to rejuvenate the old by throwing them into a lake. His suggested identification is with Polaris or Aldebaran. The Chumash, California. (Hudson and Underhay, 1978: 84, 101, 102)

Shotokunungwa   A god of the sky who is also a god of lightning and of fertility, of war and the hunt. The Hopi, Arizona. (Parsons, 1939: 178, 181, 184; Tyler, 1964: 81, 98, 101)

Sila   The sky god causes the sun to set. He is sometimes hostile, carrying men off, but also benevolent in curing "by imparting to him some of his own vitality." The Copper Eskimos, Canada. (Jenness, 1970: 189)

Singsing Lamu   The sky, child of Samni and Ningpang majan. the Katchins, Burma. (Gilhodes, 1908: 673)

Sinssganagwai   "Power of the Shining Heavens." The Haida, Washington. (Lissner, 1961: 92)

Skaj   The sky god and supreme being whose wife is Skabasava. The Moksha, Russia. (Paasonen, 1925: 844; Pettazzoni, 1956: 256)

Skan   The sky god and Great Spirit gave man his soul and judges the living and the dead. The Oglala. He is the blue dome of the sky, the omnipotent source of all energy, "superior to all because he is spirit." The Lakota. Jahner interprets him as "Movement." The northern Plains Indians. (Eliade, 1967: 188; Pettazzoni, 1956:

384; Jahner, 1977: 34; Powers, 1977: 54; Walker, 1980: 35, 50–54, 95)

Slo'w   The giant Golden Eagle whose great wings support the Upper World causes the phases of the moon and/or eclipses when he stretches. He was *wot* (chief) where he lived in the sky, where he was always thinking, and knew what was to be. In the game of peon he played on the side of the Sun against Sky Coyote and Morning Star. He, with buzzard and condor, removed "the foulness from the world." The Chumash, California. (Hudson and Underhay, 1978: 52, 81, 84, 85; Blackburn, 1957: 30, 92)

So   Earlier name of Xevioso. A sky god and a god of justice—benevolent in giving fertility to humans and their fields, malevolent in sending death and destruction. Dahomey. (Herskovits, 1938, 2: 129, 150–151; Horton, 1960: 16)

Sonole   The god of the heavens. The Daphla, Bengal and Assam. (Crooke, 1925, 4: 399)

Sorarel   The sky god of the Meitheis is identified with Indra. Manipur, Assam. (Hodson, 1908: 111)

Soumai   The "(master of the breadfruit) is the ruler of Eaur" located in the southern sky. Truk, Micronesia. (Bollig, 1927: 5)

Svarog   God of the heavens whose sons Dazhbog, the sun, and Svarogich, the fire, are the active deities. Slavic Russia. (Ralston, 1872: 75–76; Larousse, 1968: 283)

Tafaki-ngangi   The sky god of Rennell Island. Polynesia. Same as Rangi. (Birket-Smith, 1956: 199)

Ta-kok, Ta-kook, and **Ta-lyang**   Three deities born of Debu and Itpomu. They represent "the blue sky without ornament." The Lepchas, Sikkim. (Gorer, 1938: 223)

Taleng-Kode   A compound deity—Heaven-Earth. The Adi, Northeastern India. (Chowdhury, 1971: 77)

Ta-lyang   *See* **Ta-kok**

Tama-he-raki   A spirit of the heavens, son of Raki and Hekeheke-i-papa. New Zealand. (White, 1887, 1: 19)

Tama-i-a-raki   A spirit of the heavens, son of Raki and Hekeheke-i-papa. New Zealand. (White, 1887, 1: 19)

Tama-i-waho   The first son of Raki and Hekeheke-i-papa, a god of the highest heaven. New Zealand. (White, 1887, 1: 19, 31; Andersen, 1928: 375)

Tamapoulialamafoa   The King of the sky. Tonga, Polynesia. (Gifford, 1924: 16; Mackenzie, n.d.: 280)

Tama-rau-tu   A spirit of the heavens, son of Raki and Heke-heke-i-papa. New Zealand. (White, 1887, 1: 19)

Tamoussicabo   " 'the Ancient of Heaven' " The Carib, Guiana. (Alexander, 1920: 278)

Tane-nui-a-Atea   The sky god of Vahitahi Island. Tuamotua, Polynesia. (Stimson, 1933: 103)

Tangaloa   The god of the sky was the creator of all things, the god of thunder and lightning, and the god of craftsmen. Tonga, Polynesia. (Collocott, 1921: 152–153; Poignant, 1967: 29; Henry, 1928: 346)

Tangara   The great sky/heaven god of the Yakut and Dolgan. Siberia. (MacCulloch, 1964: 391; Eliade, 1964: 9)

Tangaroa-Upao-Vahu   A sky god and creator in the creation myth of the Samoans. Elsewhere he was a god of the sea. Polynesia. (Larousse, 1973: 500)

Tangere   Finno-Ugric god of the heavens. The Tatars, Siberia. (MacCulloch, 1964: 217, 391; Eliade, 1964: 9)

Yak Tanggoi   An ancestress who became a goddess in the sky. Wife of Tak Piagok. The Negritos, Malaya. (Evans, 1937: 140, 149)

Tao Chun   The second in the Taoist triad of "Three Purities," with Yuan Shih T'ien Tsun and Lao Tzu. He is "sovereign of the 'Superior Heaven' (Shang Ch'ing)." China. (Ferguson, 1937: 109–110)

Tarem   The sky god of the Vogul, the Ostyak. Western Siberia. (Roheim, 1954: 2)

Taru   The sky god of the Botocudo. Brazil. (Nimuendaju, 1946, 2: 110)

Tau   A sky deity of the Aka-Jeru. Child of Tarai and Kot. Andaman Islands, Bay of Bengal. (Radcliffe-Brown, 1967: 193)

Tecum   An Etruscan celestial god associated with the east in the divisions of the sky and whose name appears on the "bronze liver from Piacenza" used in divination. Italy. (Hamblin, 1975: 95; Pallottino, 1975: 145)

Tehitikaupeka   One of the three gods of the sky represented as a bird. The Marquesas, Polynesia. (Handy, 1923: 246)

Teng A sky god, brother of Bonsu. They look "after fruits and flowers." The Pahang, the Bateg. Malaya (Evans, 1937: 146; Eliade, 1964: 339)

Tengeri The god of the sky of the Buryats. Siberia. (Eliade, 1964: 9; MacCulloch, 1964: 391; Pettazzoni, 1956: 262)

Tengri The great god of the sky rules the universe and is a god of destiny, determining rewards and punishments. The Mongols, Asia. (Phillips, 1969: 34; Pettazzoni, 1956: 6,262; Eliade, 1964: 9; MacCulloch, 1964: 391–392)

Ten-no-kami-sama A deity of the heavens to whom offerings are made in healing rituals. Takashima, Japan. (Norbeck, 1954: 135)

Teuuhua and **Teuutoka** With Tehitikaupeka the three gods of the sky. The Marquesas, Polynesia. (Handy, 1923: 246)

Thares Upeme The "one-footed god . . . the Lame god" who parallels Hunrakán, the God of Heaven. The Tarascos, Mexico. (Girard, 1979: 111)

Thog gi bu yug A sky goddess who is the sakti of the mountain god Yar lha sham po. Tibet. (Nebesky-Wojkowitz, 1956, 1: 200, 204)

T'ien The great god of heaven of the Chou who was merged with Shang-ti of the Shang Dynasty. China. (Haydon, 1941: 168–169; Day, 1940: 74–75; Werner, 1932: 502; Pettazzoni, 1956: 273, 278–279)

T'ien Lao Yeh The Old god of the heavens. Szechwan, China. (Graham, 1928: 66)

Tijina papanguampa The sky god of the Milky Way aids hunters. The Yumu and Pindupi, Australia. (Roheim, 1972: 71)

Tilo The god of the heavens, though thought of more as an impersonal power than a deity, is nevertheless invoked. He is associated with atmospheric phenomena, with the birth of twins which is dreaded, and with maladies. Mozambique and South Africa. (Pettersson, 1953: 18, 189, 191; Junod, 1962: 429, 446; Schapera, 1937: 263; Smith, 1950: 113)

Tinami The god of the heavens, the zenith, whose color is slightly yellow. Sia, Pueblo Indians, New Mexico. (Fewkes, 1895, 2: 126)

Tingir The sky god of the Beltir. Siberia. (Eliade, 1964: 9)

ting nu kami A kami of the heavens. Okinawa. (Lebra, 1966: 223)

Tirawahut *See also* **Tirawa.** The sky god of the Skidi Pawnee, Plains Indians. (Wallis, 1939: 165)

Tiu, Tyr, Tiw, Tiwaz The great Germanic/Scandinavian sky god was a god of battle as well. Tiw or Tig in England. (Davidson, 1964: 57, 60; Schoeps, 1961: 105; Grimm, 1880: 196; Branston, 1957: 68)

Tiun Virgin goddess of the fourth heaven, elder sister of Kadeyuna. The Bagobo, Philippines. (Jocano, 1969: 21; Benedict, 1916: 16)

tlextlexagem A traveller in the upper world "visits the house of Red-Sky-Face . . . whose daughter is Dox-ewelkweilakw." An ancestor of the Koskimo (Kwakiutl), British Columbia. (Boas, 1935: 126, 144)

Tly-yz The beneficent god of the heavens who determines both life and death. The Nivkhi and the Gilyaks, Siberia. (Dioszegi, 1968: 410; Klementz, 1925, 6: 225)

To The "god of the heavens." The Meau, China. (Bernatzik, 1947: 156)

Toodlayoeetok A sky god who cannot walk but rides a sled, lassoes animals and "gives them to the Eskimo." Baffin Land. (Bilby, 1923: 270)

Torem, Torym, Torum, Turm A celestial god of the day sky is considered supreme, omniscient. The Voguls and the Ostiaks, Russia/Siberia. (Pettazzoni, 1956: 9, 16, 257; Queval, 1968: 114; Dioszegi, 1968: 29; Keane, 1925, 2: 121; Karsten, 1955: 26)

Tororut The god of the sky, "the universal father" and creator, punishes sins with disease and misfortunes. His wife is Seta, sons are Arawa and Ilat, daughter Topogh. The Suk, Kenya. (Beech, 1911: 19)

Tot-darugo "God of the Sky for Women." The Bagobo, Philippines. (Benedict, 1916: 26)

Totolu A "sky god who puts medicine, made by men, into coconuts, for the use of pregnant women." Ifalik, Micronesia. (Burrows, 1947/48: 12)

Tpereakl With the goddess Latmikaik the source of life. He became a god of the sky, she a goddess of the sea. Pelew Islands, Micronesia. (Larousse, 1973: 507–508)

Ts'ans-pa   Tibetan god of the Zenith. Same as Brahma. (Waddell, 1959: 367)

Tse-gu-dzih   The chief god of the sky "gave the boon of death to the world." The Lolos, Western China. (Henry, 1903: 105)

Tsikolkol   An anthropomorphic being who lived alone in the Upper World, was unconcerned with the world of humans. He was clothed from head to foot in a feather costume. Elder brother of Sky Coyote; same as Holhol of the Chumash. The Pomo, California. (Hudson and Underhay, 1978: 91)

Tubluck Lawi   The "lord and master of *Singgit*, highest realm of heaven." The Bisayan, Philippines. (Jocano, 1969: 30)

Tu-hakapuia   The god of the sky. Anaa Island, Tuamotua, Polynesia. (Stimson, 1933: 24)

Tui-hsien   A benevolent deity of the heavens who provides good things but is not worshipped. The Chung-chia, Southwest China. (Clarke, 1911: 103)

Tui Laga   The god of heaven of the Bure tribe. Fiji, Polynesia. (Lang, 1968: 272)

Tui Langi   The "Sky-King." Fiji, Polynesia. (Fison, 1904: 49)

Tuk-mit, Tukomit   The Sky, the male principle. With his sister Tamayowut the creators, through birth, of the things and features of the world—animate and inanimate. The Luiseño Indians, California. (Du Bois, 1904: 52–53; Kroeber, 1925: 677–678; Strong, 1929: 327)

Tukura, Altjira   The sky deity of the Arunta, the Loritja. Australia. (Eliade, 1976, 2: 356)

Tukutita tjinampara   The sky god of the Pitjentara. Australia. (Roheim, 1972: 71)

Tung Hkam   A heavenly god who sent down the first Shan kings. Burma. (Scott, 1964: 275)

Tururit   The god of the sky of the Dorobo. Kenya. (Mbiti, 1970, 2: 131)

Tuukumit   The sky personified. The brother/husband of Tamaayawut, parents of all things. The mountain Acagchemem, California. (Boscana, 1933: 115–116, 144)

Tuwale   A spirit associated with the sky "who eats bats, and whenever he eats one a man on earth dies." Husband of Rabie. The Wemale, Philippines. (Raats, 1969: 49)

Ubmuling   God of the third heaven, father of Pangulili. The Bagobo, Philippines. (Benedict, 1916: 16; Jocano, 1969: 21)

Uis Neno   A god of the heavens, not much concerned with human affairs. Timor, Indonesia. (Cunningham, 1958: 118; Middelkoop, 1960: 23)

Ulparalkirilkiri   A sky god, father of the *maliara* of the Milky Way whose stars are their girls. The Apata ngurara. Australia. (Roheim, 1972: 70)

Ululiarnaq   A vicious sky spirit who lives near the moon and who disembowels men whom she can persuade to smile or laugh at her "ludicrous and sensual gestures and movements." She must be avoided by shamans visiting the moon for success in hunting. The Eskimo, Canada. (Rasmussen, 1929: 76)

Umashi-Ashikabi-hikoji   "Pleasant-Reed-Shoot-Prince-Elder-Deity." The fourth deity formed from the developing earth. A heavenly deity. Japan. (Hori, 1968: 4; Yasumaro, 1928: 2; Herbert, 1967: 234, 245)

Umlenzengamuye   A god of the heavens who reveals himself to women only, and that rarely. He comes in the mist and causes fevers, is sacrificed to, propitiated. The Swazi, Swaziland. (Pettersson, 1953: 180, 188)

Undir Sagan Tengerin   The deity of "the lofty clear heaven." The Buriat and Mongol, Siberia. (Curtin, 1909: 45)

Upaka   A sky god who is concerned with mankind's activities. Burma. (Temple, 1925, 3: 22)

Upu Langi   A god of the sky who is associated with the sun and is invoked in taking oaths. Ceram, the Molucca Islands, Indonesia. (Pettazzoni, 1956: 20, 334)

Upu Lanito   A sky god who is associated with the elements and "sends the rain to fertilize Upu Ume." They are invoked jointly in taking oaths. Ambon Island, the Moluccas, Indonesia. (Pettazzoni, 1956: 334–335)

Uranus, Ouranos   Greek personification of the heavens. Son/husband of Gaea—parents of the Titans, the Cyclopes, the Hecatoncheires. When he was castrated by his son Cronus, the Furies were born of the spilled blood—to avenge all those shedding blood. (Barthell, 1971: 10–13; Murray, 1935: 25; Larousse, 1968: 88; Hesiod-Brown, 1981: 56–58)

Urtz, Ortz, Ost The personification of the sky, of the celestial light. The beneficent spring rains are attributed to her, as well as storms with thunder, lightning, hail, etc. The Basque, France and Spain. (Barandiaran, 1972: 195–196)

Utakke The sky god of the Carrier Indians, British Columbia. An eclipse was punishment for sin and "foreboded sickness." (Jenness, 1934: 118; 1943: 539)

Uwolowu The personified sky, the beneficent and omniscient supreme being and creator. The Akposo, Togoland. (Frazer, 1926: 115; Pettazzoni, 1956: 36)

Varuna A god whose characteristics varied with the different periods of Indian religion. As the god of the heavens he was omniscient, omnipresent, a sovereign god, the benevolent source of life and its blessings, a god of righteousness—punitive, yet to those who were penitent, forgiving. He was the guardian of all order, cosmic and moral. He gradually came to represent the sinister and dark aspects of the night sky, and became as well the god of waters. India. (Barth, 1921: 17; Bhattacharji, 1970: 25–33; Macdonell, 1897: 23–26; Keith, 1917: 22–26; Martin, 1914: 44; Danielou, 1964: 118–119)

Vere-pas Finno-Ugrian sky god. The Erza (Mordvins), Russia. (Paasonen, 1925, 8: 844)

Vilye Mukulu A sky god of the Baholos and Balubas. Zaire. (Foucart, 1925, 11: 581)

Wa'a The omniscient sky god whose eye is the sun: as the Black Wa'a, the night sky or the cloud-covered sky, as the Red Wa'a, the day sky, bright and sunny. The Hadya, Ethiopia. (Pettazzoni, 1956: 8, 41; Cerulli, 1956: 129)

Wa'banu The day sky, a supernatural personified force. The Naskapi, Labrador. (Speck, 1935: 62)

Waha The sky god of the Tambaro. Ethiopia. (Cerulli, 1956: 129)

Wak, Waq, Waka, Waqa The god of the heavens is among some also the omniscient and omnipresent supreme god. The Galla, Ethiopia. (Budge, 1973, 1: 362–363; Lewis, 1955: 172; Bartels, 1969: 406; Pettazzoni, 1956: 32; Littmann, 1925, 1: 56; Rossini, 1925, 6: 491; Huntingford, 1955: 74)

Walangala A celestial god and supreme being who gave them their "social and cultural institutions—and particularly the initiation rituals." The Ungarinyin, Australia. (Eliade, 1973: 72–73)

Wallanganda A sky god of the Unambal who with Ungud created all things. Australia. (Eliade, 1973: 72)

Wanadi The "celestial father of all Being" lives in the highest Sky, Kahuña, and gave light to the people. Through his damodedes (spirit messenger or double) Seruhe Ianadi, Nadeiumadi, Attawandi, order was established. He is "God, culture hero, and proto-shaman all in one." The Makiritari, Venezuela. (Civrieux, 1980: 6, 21, 178, 192)

We The sky god (not the sun) of the Kasene. His wife is Tega. Among the Kassunas-Buras sacrifices are offered him for many wives and children. Ghana. (Rattray, 1932: 45; Frazer, 1926: 92)

ya diɫxiɫ, Yadilyi, ya diɫhiɫ Sky and Earth (and/or Darkness and Dawn), the originators of all things, are considered the parents of Changing Woman. Sky as an important regulator of human life has strong winds, giving life and powers of communication. The Navaho, Arizona/New Mexico. (Reichard, 1950: 464; Matthews, 1902: 739; McNeley, 1981: 17, 22, 25, 28, 31)

Yamba The sky god of the Kamu, the Bolews, the Tangale, the Waja. Nigeria. (Williams, 1936: 215)

Yanolop The first being created by Gavur li yalyal. The "chief of the sky and is much older than the other high gods." Yap Island, Micronesia. (Muller, 1917: 307)

Yara-meng An old, white sky goddess, grandmother of Jamoi. When she is very old Jamoi rejuvenates her by sprinkling her with the sap of wild ginger leaves. Yara-meng accepts the blood sacrifices thrown upwards to placate the gods in thunderstorms. The Lanoh of Lenggong, Malaya. (Evans, 1937: 145–146, 174)

Yekaside The beneficent god of the sky. The Tahltan, British Columbia. (Jenness, 1937: 64)

Yero The sky god of the Nao and the Sidama. Among the Cara and the Kaffa he is also the omniscient supreme being. Ethiopia. (Cerulli, 1956: 94, 114; Pettazzoni, 1956: 6, 42)

Yes' The sky is the benevolent spirit whose wife is Khosedabam, the evil spirit, who was sent to earth. The Kets, Siberia. (Popov and Dolgikh, 1964: 617)

Yini Among the Nankanse the sky god and supreme being controls the rain and through it the harvests. His wife is Ten'gono, the earth goddess. Another name of Wene, the sky god of the Nankane. Ghana. (Rattray, 1932, 1: 45; 1932, 2: 307–308, 320, 335; Williams, 1936: 44)

Yuma, Yume, Yumo The sky god of the Cheremiss is god of the weather as well. Russia/Siberia. (Foucart, 1925, 11: 581; Pettazzoni, 1956: 264; Eliade, 1958: 60)

Yumala The sky god of the Lapps. Northern Europe. (Foucart, 1925, 11: 581)

Zac-xib-chaac A Mayan sky god is associated with a compass point and the color white. Guatemala/Mexico. (Redfield and Rojas, 1962: 115)

Zambi, Zumbi A god of the sky, the great god of the Bantus. Brazil. (Bastide, 1960: 82, 573)

Zalmoxis, Salmoxis "The scholars have interpreted Zalmoxis as a Sky-god, a god of the dead, a Mystery-god." The Getae or Dacians, Romania/Thrace. (Eliade, 1970: 66)

Zeus A god with many facets to his nature. As the great god of the sky he controlled all atmospheric phenomena, both for man's benefit and for his chastisement. Greece. (Fairbanks, 1907: 88; Larousse, 1968: 98; Frazer, 1926: 42–48; Pettazzoni, 1956: 145)

7

Solar Gods:
Dawn, Day, Light, Twilight, Eclipses

Â, Sirrida An Akkadian god "representing the solar disk." Among the Semites became a goddess. Near East. (Sayce, 1898: 177–179)

Abellio A solar god of Crete and of the Pyrenees. Known also in Gaul as Abelio, Abelionni. (Bertrand, 1897: 145–146; Renel, 1906: 391; Roscher, 1965, 1, 1: 3)

Abentrot A deity of light, brother of Ecke and Vasat (Fasolt). Teutonic. (Grimm, 1880: 232, n2)

Adaheli The sun. Now invoked as God. The Caribs, Surinam. (Alexander, 1920: 262)

Adaili The Sun. Haiti. Also the Arawaks of Guiana among whom, when he was on earth, his name was Arawidi. (Loven, 1935: 566; Brett, 1880: 27)

Adar As an Assyrian deity he was sometimes also called Nin-ip, and was "a form of the Sun-god, originally denoting the scorching sun of mid-day." In Babylonia he "was the sun who issues forth from the shades of night . . . a solar hero who belongs to the darkness and not to the light." Near East.(Sayce, 1898: 47, 152–154)

Adekagagwaa The Sun. The Iroquois Indians, Eastern United States. (Alexander, 1964: 25)

Aditya The sun, representing particularly the heat of the sun. As the Adityas, a group of the Asura, sons of Aditi, they represent the universal laws, the various aspects of the sun as well as "celestial" light beyond and behind the natural phenomenon of light, and the laws of social order. They are beneficent, yet punish sin. They are given sometimes as eight, sometimes as twelve: Mitra, Aryaman, Bhaga, Varuna, Daksa, Amsa, Tvastr,

Pusan, Savitr, Vivasvat, Sakra, and Vishnu. India. (Jayne, 1962: 161; Danielou, 1964: 112; Cox, 1870, 2: 190; Dowson, 1961: 3, 4; Brown, 1961: 282)

Adityak A solar deity—"the eclipse of the sun, is the homage rendered by Po Adityak to Po Jata." The Chams, Annam/Cambodia. (Cabaton, 1925, 3: 342)

Adota The sun is in one myth said to be the father of Bamballe who is the supreme being. The Konso, Ethiopia. (Cerulli, 1956: 66)

Adung, Dung The "Sun or Supreme Being" of the Kir. Nigeria. (Meek, 1931: 272)

Aed A name of the sun god. He "was not only the god of lightning and thunder; he was also the lord of the Other world, and the ancestor (or maker) of mankind." Other names Eochaid Ollathair, Goll, Balar, Dagda. Celtic Ireland. (O'Rahilly, 1946: 58–59, 527)

Aega Daughter of Perseis and Helios—a goddess of dazzling brightness. Mother of Aegipan by Zeus. Greece. (Barthell, 1971: 54)

Af, Afu The dead sun god, the sun of the night, travels through Tuat. Egypt. (Budge, 1969, 1: 206; Knight, 1915: 9)

!agash The sun god is the bestower of rain and fertility, and of health. The Sandawe, Tanzania. (Millroth, 1965: 42)

Agwatana A remote creator deity, "the source of light and of all life" is approached only in major disasters. The Bassa-Komo, Nigeria. (Clifford, 1944: 115)

Ahana The goddess of the dawn, daughter of Dyaus. Vedic India. (Cox, 1870, 2: 28, 343)

Ahula The sun god is also the sky god, as well as god of germs and of the afterworld. The Katcina clan, Hopi Indians, Arizona. (Fewkes, 1902: 16)

Aine A Celtic sun goddess whose name means "brightness, radiance." (O'Rahilly, 1946: 287, 290) Others variously give her associations as with water, fertility, love, the moon. Ireland. (Ross, 1967: 219; MacCulloch, 1911: 70; MacBain, 1917: 128)

Airyaman An early solar and healing god. Iran. (Gray, 1930: 132; Jayne, 1962: 188)

Aja A Babylonian goddess of light as well as of war with whom Ishtar was identified. Near East. (Mercer, 1925, 12: 700)

Akambep The sun taught the white men all their magic and prosperity before he ascended into the sky. The Sepik River area, Papua, New Guinea. (Kirk, 1973: 380)

Akhbath t-dia The sun god of the Crow Indians. Montana. (Lowie, 1922: 320)

Akou The priest consults the Sun to find out who will die. The Nabaloi of Northern Luzon, Philippines. (De Raedt, 1964: 267)

Akycha The sun. The Eskimo of Alaska. (Burland, 1965: 148)

Aleskoui The god of war is also a sun god. The Iroquois, Eastern United States. (Morgan, 1901: Appendix B)

Alinga, Ochirka The sun goddess. The Arunta, Central Australia. (Spencer, 1968: 561)

Alom One of the four regent gods of the quarters of the cosmos, of directions, with Tzakol, Bitol, Cajolom. Through their mediation they brought about "the birth of light"—material *and* spiritual. He is an hypostasis of Cabahuil as creator god-Seven. The Quiché, Guatemala. (Girard, 1979: 29, 32)

Alqol ti Manl t'aix "A sun-dog that appears westward from the sun . . . when it drops down to our earth, it causes epidemics." The Bella Coola Indians, British Columbia. (Boas, 1898, 2: 36)

Princesa d'Alva Goddess of the dawn, foster daughter of Averekete. Belem, Brazil. (Leacock, 1964: 129, 169)

Amadioha The spiritual aspect of the sun. "His voice is manifested in lightning and heard in thunder." The Igbo, Nigeria. (Uchendu, 1965: 96)

Amane The sun god. Abyssinia. (Meek, 1931: 192)

Amaterasu-Omikami The sun goddess, born of Izanagi's left eye, represents the beneficence of the sun. She taught man the cultivation of food and silkworms; is the ancestress of the Japanese Imperial Family. (Yasumaro, 1928: 21; Holtom, 1938: 123, 126; Herbert, 1967: 370)

Amen-ur Amen the elder, a god of light, with whom Heru-ur was identified. Egypt. (Budge, 1969, 1: 468)

Ammon The sun and the supreme god of the desert tribes—the setting sun. Among the Berber the ram-god. Libya. (Bel, 1938: 73; Meyerowitz, 1958: 139–141; Basset, 1925, 2: 508)

Amon Primarily a god of fertility, of generation, but at one period of time he was merged with Ra to be Sun-god at Thebes. Egypt. (Casson, 1965, 1: 73–74; 1965, 2: 89; Parrinder, 1950: 231; Bray, 1935: 121)

Amowia A deity of the Akan—"Giver of light or sun." Ghana. (Mbiti, 1970, 2: 327)

Amra The sun goddess was invoked for fertility—a part of Ayt'ar. The Abkhasians, Caucasus. (Janashia, 1937: 127–128)

Amsa A minor solar god, one of the Adityas. He is primarily a god of fate, of each individual's allotment in life. India. (Bhattacharji, 1970: 216; Littleton, 1965: 120; Danielou, 1964: 122)

Anatole "Sunrise," one of the Horae. Greece. (Roscher, 1965, 1, 1: 1209)

Anaγra Raocah A deity of light—"Light without Beginning." Iran. (Gray, 1930: 133)

Ancerika The sun god. The Tapirape, Brazil. (Wagley, 1940: 256)

Andaw The sun god is guardian of the earth. The Bagobo, Philippines. (Jocano, 1969: 31)

Ande The sun is invoked to make things grow. The Vandeke, the Deng glagu, New Guinea. (Aufenanger, 1962: 2, 3)

Anit A solar goddess, mother of Heru-Shu-p-khart (Harpo-crates). Egypt. (Knight, 1915: 17; Budge, 1969, 1: 469)

Anp   Skan, to appease Maka for not being a separate being but always attached to Inyan, "created *Anp*, who is not a thing for he is only the red of light," and placed him on the world providing light. Anp-etu, the daylight. The Lakota and Oglala, Plains Indians. (Walker, 1980: 52)

Anpao   The dawn. The Dakota, northern Plains Indians. (Burland, 1965: 149)

Anti   The sun, a deity—but "probably seasonal only." Chile. (Spence, 1925, 3: 549)

Antsnga   The sun god is invoked at the time of naming the newborn for its prosperity. New Guinea. (Aufenanger, 1962: 37–38)

antu fucha and **antu kushe**   "god and goddess of the sun." The Mapuche, Chile. (Faron, 1968: 65)

Anyangu, Anyanwu, Anyanu   The sun who is an intermediary with Chuku is invoked for good crops and good fortune. The Ibo, the Igbo, Nigeria. (Meek, 1943: 113; Parrinder, 1961: 22, 28; Horton, 1956: 18; Williams, 1936: 213; Uchendu, 1965: 96)

Anyara   The sun is associated with the supreme being under the same name. The Ndoro, Nigeria. (Jeffreys, 1951: 104)

Te Ao   The deity of light is the parent of Ao-marama, daylight. Samoa, New Zealand, Polynesia. (Poignant, 1967: 29; White, 1887, 1: 18; Mackenzie, n.d.: 183)

Ao-marama   Daylight, child of Te Ao, light. South Island, New Zealand. (Mackenzie, n.d.: 183; White, 1887, 1: 18)

Ao-tu-roa   "long-standing light," child of Ao-marama in the creation myth. Parent of Kore-te-whiwhia. South Island, New Zealand. (Mackenzie, n.d.: 183; White, 1887, 1: 18)

Apantrod   Teutonic god of the evening. (Grimm, 1883, 2: 884)

Apo   The Sun seems to correspond to the Great Spirit (who resides "in the sun, in the fire, and in the earth.") The people appeal to him through the shaman for vegetable and animal life for food. The Shoshoni, Wyoming, Utah, and Idaho. (Trenholm and Carley, 1981: 8, 15, 101)

Apolake   God of the sun and of warriors. Son of Anagolay and Dumakulem. His sister is Dian Masalanta. The Tagalog, Philippines. (Jocano, 1969: 10)

Apollo   The Greek/Roman sun god was equally well known as a god of prophecy and of music, of healing, but capable of sending disease and sudden death as well. He was the son of Zeus (Jupiter) and Leto (Latona) and twin of Artemis (Diana). An Oscan variant of his name is Apellu. (Kerenyi, 1951: 35, 142; Jayne, 1962: 223, 306; Fairbanks, 1907: 49; Barthell, 1971: 24–26; Conway, 1925, 8: 458; Bulfinch, 1898: 4, 8, 9)

Arakho   Demon of the eclipse of the sun and of the moon. Mongolia. (Grimm, 1883, 2: 707)

Arama   The god of light whose wife is the rainbow. The Moxos, South America. (Brinton, 1882: 150)

Arawidi   The name of the sun when on earth, when he battled with the alligator and gave him his indented head and notched tail. The Arawak, Guiana. (Brett, 1880: 27–28)

Ardinis   Vannic sun god who forms a triad with Khaldis and Teisbas. Armenia. (Sayce, 1925, 1: 793)

Artinis   The sun god of the Urartians forms a triad with Khaldi and Theispas. Armenia. (Ananikian, 1964: 11; Leach, 1950, 2: 576)

Art Toyon Aga   A god of light and life, a celestial god whose symbol is the sun and whose voice is the thunder. He is benevolent but passive, powerful yet inactive—remote. The Yakut, Siberia. (Czaplicka, 1925, 12: 828; 1969: 277; Eliade, 1964: 186–187)

Aruna   God of the dawn and charioteer of the sun. Son of Kasyapa. India. (Danielou, 1964: 95; Coleman, 1832: 374; Dowson, 1961: 24)

Arungquiltha   A malignant spirit who is believed to cause solar eclipses. The Arunta, Central Australia. (Spencer, 1968: 566)

Asis   The god of the sun of the Nandi, the Suk, the Dorobo, the Elgeyo is among some the younger brother of Tororut. The Kamsia believe the sun is female and the wife of Tororut, the sky. Kenya. (Huntingford, 1953: 131; Beech, 1911: 19; Mbiti, 1970, 2: 119, 133)

Asista   The sun (the Ndorobo) and the sky god (the bright sky) of the Nandi is the supreme being and creator of men and animals. Beneficent. Kenya. (Pettazzoni, 1956: 8, 39: Hollis, 1909: 41; Millroth, 1965: 44)

Assiss   Apparently a variant spelling of Asis—the supreme being and the sun, benevolent and omnipotent. The Elgeyo, Kenya. (Massam, 1927: 188)

The Asvins (Dasra and **Nasatya)** The twin gods of the dawn, of the morning, are the sons of Surya and Sanjna or of Vivaswat and Saranyu. They are the physicians of the gods and of men, bestowers of health and fecundity; the husbands of Suryā. India. (Bhattacharji, 1970: 236–248; Danielou, 1964: 128–129; Dowson, 1961: 278, 283; Macdonnell, 1952: 29; Jayne, 1962: 163–164; Martin, 1914: 36)

Ata The sun, the principal deity of the Kwakiutl, is also called Kanskiyi, Kansnola, Amiaeket, Gyikamae. His son is Kanikilak. British Columbia. (Swanton, 1925, 12: 662)

Ata-hiku-rangi The god of "full day" is the son of Rangi and Atutahi according to one genealogical legend. Polynesia. (Andersen, 1928: 376)

Te-ata-i-mahina The twilight is the child of Rangi and Wero-wero. New Zealand. (White, 1887, 1: 51)

Atanua Goddess of the dawn and wife of Atea. The Marquesas, Mangareva. Polynesia. (Buck, 1938: 150, 203; Andersen, 1928: 380; Handy, 1923: 245)

Atarapa Or "day-dawn," a child of Rangi and Atutahi. Polynesia. (Andersen, 1928: 376; White, 1887, 1: 51)

Atehle The sun, with Wamutsini, created people and gave them culture. The Trumai, Central Brazil. (Murphy and Quain, 1955: 72–74)

Aten A solar god, the disk itself, who became supreme deity during the 18th dynasty. Egypt. (Budge, 1969, 2: 68; Knight, 1915: 25; Ames, 1965: 27)

Aterat The sun goddess, mother of Attar by Il Il. South Arabia. (Gray, 1957: 123)

Atthar An Arabian sun goddess. (Larousse, 1968: 323)

Atum A solar god as the setting sun and represented as an eel-god with human head. He was also considered a bisexual god, creator of the gods as well as living things. Egypt. (Knight, 1915: 26; Eliade, 1967: 25; Ames, 1965: 30, 45)

Atymnos A Cretan solar god. Greece. (Willetts, 1962: 167)

Auf *See* **Afu**

Aurora The Roman goddess of the dawn, equivalent of Eos. (Bulfinch, 1898: 258; Murray, 1935: 186)

Auseklis The Latvian "morning star and goddess of the Dawn." (Gimbutas, 1963: 199)

Ausrine Goddess of the dawn and Venus as the morning star. Lithuania. (Gimbutas, 1963: 199; Gray, 1930: 109)

Auszra The dawn. Litu-Prussian. (Schraeder, 1925, 2: 34)

Avya The god of the sun as well as the moon. In the day he gives light and heat, at night less in quantity. He "causes women to menstruate." The Cubeo, Southeastern Colombia. (Goldman, 1940: 245)

Awonawilona The primordial god of the beginning is the great Sun-Father, the bisexual source of life. The Zuñi Indians, New Mexico. (Cushing, 1891/92: 22; Stevenson, 1901/02: 379; Kroeber, 1925, 12: 869)

Awusi, Ayisi The sun, a bisexual god and the patron deity of Sunday, dispenses the "kra" to the abosom born on Sunday, whose character "will be pure, immaculate and generous." The Akan, Ghana. (Meyerowitz, 1951: 25; 1958: 47)

Babbar Sumerian/Babylonian sun god. Same as Shamash, Utu. Near East. (Langdon, 1931: 4; Jastrow, 1898: 72, 75)

Baeldaeg, Baldag Teutonic god of the day, of light—the name used among the Saxons and Westphalians. (Grimm, 1880, 1: 222, 229)

Balanke The name of the sun god among the Kekchi (Mayan). Guatemala. (Thompson, 1970: 236)

Balder The Scandinavian god of light, of day, the beautiful and blameless god, was slain inadvertently by his brother Hodur. Son of Odin and Frigg. (Grimm, 1880: 222, 225; Frazer, 1960: 703–704; Turville-Petre, 1964: 106; Stern, 1898: 50–53)

Bamya The goddess who "guides the car of Mithra . . . and on the third night after death she shines before the righteous. . . . She is obviously the Dawn." Iran. (Gray, 1930: 139)

Beal, Beil, Beli *See* **Bel**

Behdety, Hor Behdetite Horus as defender of the king is "represented in the form of a winged sun-disk." Egypt. (Ames, 1965: 69; Larousse, 1968: 21)

Beive-Neida, Baei've The "sun maiden," daughter of the sun and its personification. The Lapps. (Holmberg, 1925, 7: 799; Karsten, 1955: 32; Bosi, 1960: 129)

Beiwe   The god of the sun. The Lapps, northern Europe. (Leach, 1950, 2: 604)

Bel, Belenus (variants—**Beal, Beil, Beli**)   The sun deity and god of light, identified with Apollo, is also considered a god of health, of medicine, and of curative springs. Celtic Ireland, Britain, Wales, Gaul. (Mac-Leish, 1970: 710; Renel, 1906: 309; MacCulloch, 1911: 26; MacBain, 1917: 66; Ross, 1967: 57; Grimm, 1883, 2: 613–614)

Bero   The sun god of the Kharias is worshipped also under the name of Giring Dubo. Bengal. (Crooke, 1894: 9; Frazer, 1926: 619; Choudhury, 1965: 146)

Bero Gosai, Ber Pitia, Ber Chichha   The sun god of the Malers, the Santal Parganas. India. (Roy, 1928: 20; Biswas, 1956: 102)

Bezlea   A solar god of Lithuania. (Gray, 1930: 152)

Bhagwan   The supreme deity who is identified with the sun is revered but not worshipped. The Korwas, India. (Crooke, 1894: 9; Russell, 1916, 3: 399)

Biri Bela   The sun god of the Oraons. The same as Dharmes. India. (Biswas, 1956: 102)

Bitol   One of the four regent gods of the quarters of the cosmos, of directions—with Tzakol, Alom, Cajolom. Through their mediation they brought about "the birth of light"—material *and* spiritual. He is an hypostasis of Cabahuil as creator god-Seven. The Quiché, Guatemala. (Girard, 1979: 29, 32)

ka Blai Sngi   The "sun-queen" of the Khasi. Assam. (Bareh, 1967: 375)

Bochica   The great culture hero of the Chibcha was identified with the sun. Colombia. (Kroeber, 1946: 906–909; Osborne, 1968: 112)

(Cana) Boda   "Lady Sun." Andaman Islands, Bay of Bengal. (Radcliffe-Brown, 1967: 45)

Bogdo-Gegen   Mongolian god of the dawn. (Klementz, 1925, 3: 5)

Boora Pennu, Bella Pennu   The god of light and the supreme deity of the Khonds of Orissa. He created his consort, Tari Pennu. India. (Robertson, 1911: 109; Martin, 1914: 29n)

Boram, Dharm devata   The sun god and the creator—the greatest of the gods of the Bhuiyas of Bengal.

He was invoked at the sowing season. Same as Bhagwan, Bero. (Crooke, 1894: 52; Frazer, 1926: 616)

Bozenos   A solar god of Asia Minor identified with Apollo. (Pettazzoni, 1956: 182)

Brond (Anglo Saxon), **Brono** (Scandinavian)   God of daylight, son of Balder (Baeldaeg). (Cox, 1870, 2: 93; Grimm, 1880: 222; Murray, 1935: 365)

Buga Nubrana   The sun. Tasmania. (Worms, 1960: 15)

Bunene   Charioteer of Shamash. Babylonian and Assyrian. Near East. (Zimmern, 1925, 2: 311)

bya Khyung dkrung nyima   The personification of the sun—in the "gLing Chos" (the Mythology of Tibetan Folklore). (Francke, 1925, 8: 78)

Byelobog   Slavonic god of light—the beneficent "white god." (Larousse, 1968: 283)

Cagjolom   One of four regent gods of the quarters of the cosmos, of directions, with Tzakol, Bitol, Alom. Through their mediation they brought about "the birth of light" material *and* spiritual. He is an hypostasis of Cabahuil as creator god-Seven. The Quiché, Guatemala. (Girard, 1979: 29, 32)

Camé   The god and culture hero of the Bacairis (Carib) represents the sun. Twin of Kéri, the moon. Brazil. (Girard, 1979: 111)

Catha   The Etruscan god of the sun is associated with the south and the southeast of the divisions of the sky, also with haruspicy. Italy. (Hamblin, 1975: 92; Pallottino, 1975: 145)

Chal-chal   The sun. The Igorot, Philippines. (Bray, 1935: 240)

oCham   The sun god was created by oDel. The Gypsies. (Clebert, 1967: 174)

Chando   The sun god and supreme deity of the Santal is invoked in oath-taking. India. (Frazer, 1926: 633; Wallis, 1939: 193)

Chasca   Venus, the morning star, is considered the god/goddess of the dawn. Peru. (Brinton, 1882: 170; Markham, 1969: 63; Larousse, 1968: 442)

Chebongolo   The sun. The Kipsigis, Kenya. (Mbiti, 1970, 2: 331)

Chenten The god of the day. China. (Du Bose, n.d.: 72)

Chepkeliensokol, Chepelienpokol A name of Asis, the god of the sun. This name implies something many-legged—referring "to the sun's rays." The Nandi, Kenya. (Mbiti, 1970, 2: 333; Huntingford, 1953: 134)

Chhatmata The sun goddess, female counterpart of the sun god and his consort. The Oraons, Bengal. (Crooke, 1925, 2: 484; Frazer, 1926: 610)

Chhaya "Shade." Sister of Sanjna (a wife of the sun), and a substitute wife; mother of Visti by Surya. India. (Bhattacharji, 1970: 85, 217; Dowson, 1961: 72)

Chieng The sun god and the supreme god of the Luo. Kenya and Uganda. (Butt, 1952: 116; Mbiti, 1970, 1: 68; Hobley, 1902: 35; Budge, 1973, 1: 381)

Chigo-na-ay The twelve suns of the Apache; also given in the singular form. Arizona and New Mexico. (Bourke, 1887/88: 502; 1890: 209)

Chih Jih The god of the day. China. (Werner, 1932: 70)

Chiuku The sun god among the Umundri. Nigeria. (Jeffreys, 1935: 346)

Chuh Kamuy The "Goddess of Sun and Moon . . . mediates between the Ainu and other deities. . . . The sun . . . (daytime moon), and the moon . . . (dark moon), are considered the same female deity, who is the most important of all sky deities." Sakhalin. (Ohnuki-Tierney, 1974: 103)

Chun-t'i The Buddhist goddess of light, of the dawn, is protective against wars. China. (Werner, 1932: 95; Day, 1940: 83)

Chup Kamui The sun god whose wife is the moon, though sometimes the name stands for both. He supplies the people with their subsistence. The Ainu, Japan. (Sternberg, 1906: 426; Munro, 1963: 13, 38)

Churiya The god of the sun is associated with the east. The Coorgs, India. (Srinivas, 1952: 79)

Ah Ciliz A Mayan god of the eclipses. The Chorti, Guatemala. (Thompson, 1970: 322)

Citlalinicue (female) and **Citlallatónac** (male) "she of the starry skirt" and "celestial body which illumines things" are a duality of Ometéotl, represented as causing the stars to shine at night and as "identified with the sun" by day—the source of light and life. Aztec, Mexico. (León-Portilla, 1982: 30, 90)

Colop-u-uich-kin God of the solar eclipse. Mayan, Mexico and Guatemala. (Roys, 1965: 145)

Coniraya A solar god, a creator, and a culture hero/deity in establishing "agricultural terracing and irrigation." Called Con on the coast. Peru. (Métraux, 1949: 560; Osborne, 1968: 96)

Copichja The sun god was associated with the macaw. The Zapotec, Oaxaca, Mexico. (Whitecotton, 1977: 158)

Coquihuani The god of light to whom in Tlalixtac sacrifices of "boys and men . . . quetzal feathers, dogs, and blood" were made. The Zapotec, Oaxaca, Mexico. (Whitecotton, 1977: 157)

Cuauhtemoc The name of Tonatiuh as the setting sun. Mexico. (Caso, 1958: 33)

Cuauhtlehuanitl The name of Tonatiuh as the rising sun. Mexico. (Caso, 1958: 33)

Cuhui God of light, son of Nexhiquiriac. The Trique tribe, Oaxaca, Mexico. (Valentini, 1899: 38)

Curicaveri, Curicaueri, Curicaneri A sun god who takes the form of a white eagle. Some consider he created the Sun (Huriata), that he was a god of the beginning. He was a god protective of the kings and warriors. The Tarascan, the Chichimec. Mexico. (Krickeberg, 1968: 58; Bancroft, 1886, 3: 445–446; Boyd, n.d.: iv, 2; Craine and Reindorp, 1970: 55)

Dag, Dagr Scandinavian god of the Day, son of Nott and Delling (r) (er). (Grimm, 1883, 2: 735; Guerber, 1895: 15; Anderson, 1891: 442)

Darawintha The sun god who dies and is resurrected. India. (Keeler, 1960: 122)

Dasra One of the Asvins, gods of the dawn, son of Vivaswat and Samjna. India. (Bhattacharji, 1970: 217)

Dat Ba'dan An Arabian solar goddess. (Fahd, 1968: 134)

Datu Patinggi Mata-ari The sun is invoked at the beginning of the rice-farming season. The Sea Dyaks, Borneo. (Roth, 1968: 174)

Daw-wa The "sun-chief." The Moquis, Arizona. (Stephen, 1888: 110)

Dazhbog, Dazbog, Daybog   Slavic god of the sun and the god of justice "punished the wicked and rewarded the virtuous." Son of Svarog. Russia and Poland. In Serbia he was the beneficent "personified sun and sunshine." (Wallis, 1939: 22; Queval, 1968: 32; Schoeps, 1961: 119; Larousse, 1968: 283–285; Ralston, 1872: 85)

Delling(r)   Scandinavian god of the dawn, third and last husband of Nott and father of Dagr. (Grimm, 1883, 2: 735; Anderson, 1891: 442; MacCulloch, 1964, 2: 200; Guerber, 1895: 15)

Dercetius   A solar god of the mountains. (Monte Castello). Spain. (Martinez, 1962: 88)

Derron   A Thracian deity—"probably a sun-god with whom Apollo had been identified." (Pettazzoni, 1956: 180)

Dharam Deota   The sun who is venerated but made no offerings. The Bhuiya, Central Provinces, India. (Russell, 1916, 2: 317) Elwin calls him a primordial being who created male and female from the dirt on his body. They had a son whom the gods saw and caused to be killed, from whose body and blood the earth was formed—"His head became the sun, his chest the moon." (Elwin, 1949: 29)

Dharih   A god of the extreme south seeming "to denote the rising Sun." Arabia. (Noldeke, 1925, 1: 660)

Dharma Thakar   A god "identified with Vishnu and the Sun," to whom offerings were made for the cure of leprosy. He was also a god of fertility and of prosperity. The Doms, Bengal. (Elwin, 1950: 135; Maity, 1971: 82–83)

Dharmer   God of the sun and head of the pantheon who is worshipped at the beginning of the harvest and to avert misfortune. The Mal, the Male Paharias. India. (Crooke, 1925, 5: 13; 1925, 8: 344)

Dharmes, Dharmesh   The supreme god with whom they identify the sun is also the creator god. The Oraons, India. (Crooke, 1925, 2: 484; Roy, 1928: 1, 15; Elwin, 1940: 135)

Dietyi   The sun goddess. Southeast Australia. (Howitt, 1904: 427)

Mimi Diu   The sun, wife of Maia Dula and mother of the stars. In the version where Dula is female, Diu is male and also called Torodiu. Andaman Islands, Bay of Bengal. (Radcliffe-Brown, 1967: 141)

Djua Mulungu   The sun god. The Mbugwe, Tanzania. (Millroth, 1965: 23)

Doini   The sun. Among the Bori, the daughter of Sitking-Kedding and Peddo-Dodum, and sister of Pollo. The Adi, Northeastern India. (Chowdhury, 1971: 175–176)

Doini-Polo, Donyi-Polo   The Sun-Moon duality. They hold a high place as the illuminators of the world and "are looked upon as the custodian of law and truth . . . are invoked in the beginning of kebands on disputes to reveal the truth and expose the false." The Adi. Among the Gallongs "Oaths taken in the name of Doini-Polo—Sun-Moon—are the most sacred and binding." Northeastern India. (Chowdhury, 1971: 92, 118)

Donyi   The benevolent sun goddess and second most powerful deity. The Kadengs, the Dafla tribes. Assam and India. (Stonor, 1957: 4, 5)

Duadleera-wulan   The "Sun-Moon" god who "lives in the sky and fertilizes the earth with rain . . . invoked in oaths." Kei Island, the Moluccas, Indonesia. (Pettazzoni, 1956: 335)

Dudilaa   The sun god, also known as Upulera, is the male principle fertilizing the earth, the female principle. Timorlaut Islands, Indonesia. (Frazer, 1926: 660)

Dumuzi   At Eridu the sun god of spring or of summer depending upon the area of worship climatically. He is the son of Ea and Dav-kina; consort of Istar. He is "slain by the cruel hand of night and winter." Festivals of lament and of joy are held celebrating his death and resurrection. Babylonia. Near East. (Sayce, 1898: 144, 221, 231)

Dushara   The principal god and sun god of the Nabataeans at Petra and Damascus. Also a god of fertility and son of the virgin earth goddess Chaabou. Near East. (Langdon, 1931: 16–17)

Dyabu lara   The sun who fertilizes the earth, Dyabu fafa, with the rains of the western monsoon. The Aru Islands (Moluccas), Indonesia. (Pettazzoni, 1956: 335)

Dyiowa, Jua   The beneficent sun god gives health and rain, is "also the master of life and death." The Issansu, Tanzania. (Millroth, 1965: 18, 22)

Dylacha   The benevolent sun god stores heat during the winter and distributes it to the people in the spring. The Evenks, Siberia. (Michael, 1963: 161)

Dysis   The sunset, one of the Horae. Greece. (Roscher, 1965, 1, 1: 1209)

Ear   A variant name of Zio, Teutonic god of light, of day. (Grimm, 1880: 193–194, 201)

Eguski, Euzki, Iguzki, Iuzki   The Sun. Euzki is the light of the sun or the day; Euzkibegi is the sun itself, the eye of the sun, the eye of God. Considered the daughter of the earth in some areas; occasionally considered masculine. The Basques, Spain/France. (Barandiaran, 1972: 75, 271)

Ekhia   The "sun, the light of the world;" created by Yaun-Goicoa. The Basques, Spain/France. (Leach, 1949, 1: 117)

Elagabal   The Syrian sun god is also a mountain god. (Frazer, 1926: 496–498; Roscher, 1965, 1, 1: 1229; Cook, 1930: 159)

Eluelap   The sun. The Caroline Islands (Elato), Micronesia. (Pettazzoni, 1956: 7, 8)

Emekori-mahse   The beneficent god of day, created by the sun to provide all the customs and laws. The Desana, Colombia. (Reichel-Dolmatoff, 1971: 27–28, 128)

Eos   Greek goddess of the dawn, daughter of Hyperion and Theia, sister of Helios and Selene, and wife of Astraeus by whom she was the mother of Astraea (daughter) and sons Zephyrus, Boreas, Notus, Eurus, Hesperus, and Eosphorus, the winds of the morning. She was also called Hemera or Tito. (Kerenyi, 1951: 22, 191–192, 199; Fairbanks, 1907: 59, 162–163; Barthell, 1971: 51–53; Hesiod-Brown, 1981: 63, 64)

Erioba   The sun god of the Gusii. Kenya. (Mbiti, 1970, 2: 330)

Eruwa, Iruwa   The High God and sun god. A variant of Ruwa. The Chagga, Tanzania. (Millroth, 1965: 18; Frazer, 1926: 286)

Es   The sun who is also the creator and the protector of the Betoi. Colombia. (Hernandez de Alba, 1948, 1: 398)

Esseneta'he   God of the southeast who "originates life and light." The Cheyenne Indians, the Plains, United States. (Powell, 1969: 436)

Estan   Hittite/Hattic sun god. Asia Minor. (Guterbock, 1961: 149)

Etsa   The sun contains "powerful tsarutama, which influences all that goes on on earth." The Jivaro, Ecuador. (Stirling, 1938: 116)

Euzkibegi   The physical sun, the eye of God. The Basques, France and Spain. (Barandiaran, 1972: 271)

Evua   The sun god of the Guinea and Senegambia groups. Africa. (Larousse, 1968: 483)

Eyo   The sun of the Ekoi. Nigeria. (Jeffreys, 1939: 99)

Eze Chite Okike   The sun and the supreme god forms a triad with Alo, the earth, his wife, and Igwe, the sky, his son. The Ibo (Abadja tribe). Nigeria. (Jeffreys, 1972: 730)

Feke   The "god of the sun, whose more mundane embodiment is the octopus" is invoked by the Torokinga and Ratia families in dart games. Tikopia, Melanesia. (Firth, 1930: 80)

Frey, Freyr, Fro   Scandinavian/Teutonic god of sunshine, of summer, of fertility and showers, and of plenty; a god of joy, of love and marriage, and of peace. He was the husband of Gerda, the son of Njord and Skadi (Nerthus), brother of Freya (Frowa). (Guerber, 1895: 112–120; Stern, 1898: 44, 50; Grimm, 1880: 212, 216; Wagner, 1882: 189)

Gaeto-Syrus   Scythian solar deity. (Tod, 1920: 659)

Gander-Prince   See Mir-susne-xum (Vogul), Ort-iki (Ostyak).

Gangaditya   The sun god as still worshipped in Murshidabad District. India. (Frazer, 1926: 609)

//Gaunub   A god of evil, the destroyer, who was associated with solar and lunar eclipses. The Khoi-Khoi (Hottentots), South Africa. (Smith, 1950: 93; Hahn, 1881: 40, 49)

The Gavite(s)   Twins, one solar, one lunar, whose father is the White Giant. In the Chorti drama he "assumes the role of redeemer of humanity, sacrificing himself only to save the rest, concentrating upon his own person the attention of the evil forces." Same as Hunahpú of the Quiché as a solar deity. Guatemala. (Girard, 1979: 100, 311–312)

Gbohulu   The sun of springtime. The Gā in Nungwa. Ghana. (Field, 1937: 27)

Gehyaguga The Sun. Cherokee Indians, North Carolina and Tennessee. (Mooney, 1900: 3)

Genneas, Gennaios A Syrian sun god shown on horseback. Near East. (Pettazzoni, 1956: 93, 192)

Gezis, Gizis (Ojibwa) The sun to whom the Algonquin "attribute life and light, vitality and intelligence," as they also do to Monedo. Northern United States. (Schoolcraft, 1857, 5: 402; Hallowell, 1967: 217)

Gickokwita The god of the sun, of light. The Lenape Indians, Eastern United States. (Harrington, 1921: 27)

Gickonikizho The sun god of the Unami (Lenape) Indians. eastern United States. (Harrington, 1921: 27)

Giring Dubo, Bero Names of the sun god of the Kharias of Chota Napur and Central Provinces, India. (Frazer, 1926: 619)

Gomaj The sun and the moon are both called Gomaj, which is also used as a general term of god. The sun, male, the moon, female, are the chief deities and are invoked at marriages. The Korku of Central Provinces and Berar, India. (Russell, 1916, 3: 559; Frazer, 1926: 616)

Grian A Celtic sun goddess who "dwelt in the side of Cnoc Grene, a hill near Pallas Green, . . . Elsewhere . . . Grian was another name of Macha, who is represented as wife of Cruind and daughter of Mider of Bri Leith." Ireland. (O'Rahilly, 1946: 289–290)

Grogoragally The beneficent sun god, son of the creator. He presents the soul of the dead to the supreme being. The Wiradjuri-Kamilaroi, southwest Australia. (Eliade, 1959: 120, 126)

Guaracy The sun god of the Tupi created the animals. Brazil. (Spence, 1925, 2: 837)

Gucumatz The sun at its setting. Gucumatz is a general name as well as particular. He is a counterpart of Quetzalcóatl. The Quiché, Guatemala. (Girard, 1979: 31–33)

Gwawl The son of Clud "was evidently a sun-god . . . for the meaning of 'Gwawl' is 'light'." Celtic (Britons). (Squire, 1906: 285)

Gwyrthur A Celtic solar deity who represents the sunshine and summer. He fought with Gwyn over Creurdilad. Britons. (Squire, 1906: 259)

Hadad Primarily known as a god of storms, of thunder and lightning, he was also worshipped as a sky and sun god, protective of the harvests. Syria. (Macler, 1925, 12: 165; Moscati, 1960: 175; Jastrow, 1898: 156; Goldziher, 1877: 94)

Halboredja The sun—"day wanderer." The northern forest Indians, North America. (Burland, 1965: 148)

Hanbwira The sun god known "ceremonially as hanboradjera, day-wanderer." The Winnebago, Wisconisn. (Radin, 1915/16: 286)

Hanoona wilapona The "Sun-father" of the Zuñi Indians. New Mexico. (Cushing, 1881/82: 13) See also Awonawilona.

Harakhte, Harakhtes The "sun on its daily course between the eastern and western horizon." Later absorbed by Ra. Egypt. (Ames, 1965: 68; Larousse, 1968: 22)

Hari A name of Vishnu as a solar deity. India. (Tod, 1920: 629; Choudhury, 1965: 116–117)

Haro The sun god whose wife is Taio, the moon. Also called Tauahili. The Lakalai of New Britain, Melanesia. (Valentine, 1965: 183)

Hastsehogan, haashch'éóghaan Calling God is the god of the sunset, the evening, the West, the inner form of San Francisco Peak. He is also the benevolent god of the house and the farm. He, with Talking God, "would assume the role of monitoring, guiding, and directing human life." The Navaho, Arizona and New Mexico. (Matthews, 1902: 10, 11; McNeley, 1981: 9, 10, 19–21, 66; Alexander, 1964: 156; Babington, 1950: 217)

Hastseyalti, haashch'eeIt'i, xa-ctce·Itihi, Yebitsai Talking God, god of the dawn and god of the east, is associated with Blanca Peak, the sacred mountain. Some consider him one of the gods of the corn. With Hastsehogan, later, "would assume the role of monitoring, guiding, and directing human life." The Navaho, Arizona and New Mexico. (Matthews, 1902: 9, 11; Babington, 1950: 218–219; McNeley, 1981: 9–12, 65; Alexander, 1964: 156; Pepper, 1908: 178)

hayooɫkaaɫ asdzą́ą́, xayoɫka·ɫ 'eszą́ Dawn Woman. One of the Holy People involved in the creation. She is in the North. She is one of those who causes people to think. Some say she "determines which Wind Soul shall enter the child to be born" and that it reports to her on its life. The Navaho, Arizona. (McNeley, 1981: 4, 22, 29, 81)

hayoołkáał hastiin, xayołka·ł xastxi·n Dawn Man. One of the Holy People involved in the creation of Earth, Sky, Sun, Moon, and various animals. He is in the cardinal position of the East; causes people to think. The Navajo. Arizona. (McNeley, 1981: 22, 29, 81)

Hebat The Hurrian sun goddess, wife of Teshub and mother of Sharruma. Asia Minor. (Albright, 1968: 143; Ferm, 1950: 90; James, 1960: 95; Gurney, 1952: 135)

Hekenjuk The Sun. The Ihalmiut Eskimo, Keewatin District, Canada. (Mowat, 1968: 237)

Helia A solar goddess, daughter of Helios and sister of Phaethon. Greece. (Kerenyi, 1951: 190)

Heliogabalus The god of the sun at Emesa. Syria. (Frazer, 1961: 35; Leach, 1949, 1: 488)

Helios Greek god of the sun, of light, who was omniscient, all-seeing, knowing all deeds. He was the son of Theia and Hyperion, and father of Phaethon, Lampetia, and Phaethousa by Nearia. (Kerenyi, 1951: 20, 22, 191–193; Jayne, 1962: 327; Pettazzoni, 1956: 5, 6)

Helliougmounis An Aquitainian goddess of a solar nature. Gaul. (Roscher, 1965, 1, 2: 2030)

Hemera Greek goddess of the day, who like Nyx, lives in the lower world. They pass each other at the gates on their daily rounds. Daughter of Nyx and Erebus. (Barthell, 1971: 8, 9; Kerenyi, 1951: 18; Larousse, 1968: 143)

Hepatu A variant name of Hebat.

Her-nub A name of Horus as god of the dawn, the morning. Egypt. (Frazer, 1926: 569)

Her-shef A ram-headed solar god and a god of strength and bravery. His female counterpart is Atet or Mersekhnet. Egypt. (Budge, 1969, 2: 58–61; Knight, 1915: 45)

Heru-Behutet An important form of Horus—the heat of the mid-day sun in which form he fought against Set. A god of light and of blacksmiths (at Edfu). Egypt. (Budge, 1969, 1: 473–476)

Heru-khuti "Horus of the two horizons" usually has the head of a hawk and represents the course of the sun from sunrise to sunset, across the skies. Egypt. (Budge, 1969, 1: 470–472) See also Harakhte.

Heru-pa-khart, Harpocrates God of the rising sun. Horus the Child, son of Isis and Osiris, originally a god of youth and vigor, later taking on the aspects of the Sun-god. At Mendes he was the son of Hat-mehit. Egypt. (Budge, 1969, 1: 114, 495; 1969, 2: 65)

Hillon A sun god and a god of music. Valley of Larboust, Gaul. (Bertrand, 1897: 146–147)

Hine-ahiahi The goddess of the evening, daughter of the sun, Tama-nui-te-ra, and sister of Hine-ata and Hine-aotea. Chatham Isles, Polynesia. (Best, 1924: 111, 131)

Hine-aotea Goddess of the day, daughter of Tama-nui-te-ra. Chatham Isles, Polynesia. (Best, 1924: 111, 131)

Hine-ata Goddess of the morning, daughter of Tama-nui-te-ra, the sun, and sister of Hine-aotea and Hine-ahiahi. Chatham Isles, Polynesia. (Best, 1924: 111, 131)

Hine-titama The "Dawn Maid," daughter of Tane and Hine-ahu-one. As the daughter/wife of Tane (Tane-matua) and mother of Hine-rau-wharangi, she fled to the underworld on learning their true relationship, where she became the goddess of the underworld as Hine-nui-te-po. The Maori, New Zealand. (Best, 1924: 116, 175, 314; Downes, 1920: 26, 32)

Hiruko The imperfect third child of Izanagi and Izanami. A sun god who was supplanted by the goddess Ohirumemuchi-no-Kami. Japan. (Kato, 1926: 13; Herbert, 1967: 260)

hod-zer-can-ma Tibetan goddess of the dawn. Same as Marici. (Getty, 1962: 132)

Hor-m-akhet God of the eastern horizon—the "personification of the rising sun and a symbol . . . of resurrection." Egypt. (Casson, 1965: 70)

Horus (Hor, Heru-ur) the Elder Son of Nut and Seb. A solar deity, or more a sky god whose eyes are the sun and the moon. He is symbolized by the falcon. Egypt. (Knight, 1915: 48; Ames, 1965: 23, 68; Budge, 1969, 1: 78)

Horus the Younger A solar deity, god of the rising sun, of light, son of Osiris and Isis. The latter taught him the arts of magic and healing through oracles. He absorbed and was identified with the other Horus gods—the Heru group. Egypt. (Knight, 1915: 46–50; Jayne, 1962: 60–61; Budge, 1969, 1: 493)

Hsi Ho An archaic sun goddess with whom Nü Kua is identified by some. China. (Schafer, 1980: 41)

Hsu Kai "The god of the star T'ai-yang (the sun)." China. (Werner, 1932: 175)

htotik The sun god and the creator, the source of all life. Son of the moon. The Chamula (Mayan), Central America. (Gossen, 1958: 136–138)

Hu Celtic sun god and a god of death and resurrection of vegetation, to whom human sacrifices were made "in honor of the victory of spring." (Bancroft, 1886, 3: 316, 320)

Huiracocha A variant of Viracocha.

Huisiniamui A solar deity and sky god, a god of vegetation, but also he is associated with headhunting and cannibalism. The Witotoans. Colombia and Peru. (Zerries, 1968: 253, 286)

Huitzilopochtli As the Blue Tezcatlipoca he was one of the four primary forces, the sons of Ometéotl, and identified with the sun, associated with the South. As a Sun God and also a War God human sacrifices were made to him. Mexico. (León-Portilla, 1982: 33, 35, 161–163; Caso, 1958: 13; Frazer, 1960: 66; Vaillant, 1962: 148)

Hunahpú A god of the Quiché Maya who with his twin Xbalamwqué overcame the powers of evil and of death of Xibalba, then rose to the heavens to become the sun (Hunahpú) and the moon. As a solar god he "personifies the aurora, light, the brightness that dissipates the shadows of ignorance . . . defends humanity against the forces of evil." Guatemala. (Recinos, 1950: 119, 124, 163; Brinton, 1868: 258; Thompson, 1970: 234, 237; Girard, 1979: 227)

Hunahpu-Vuch Goddess of the dawn—"a hunting-fox bitch." The Quiché Mayan, Guatemala. (Recinos, 1950: 78n.)

Hun Kak The name of the sun god among the Lacandon. Mexico. (Thompson, 1970: 236)

Huriata The sun god of the Tarascan to whom human sacrifices were made was created by Curicaueri, and in turn, created "the heavenly bodies." His wife was Cutzi, the moon, and daughter of Cuerohperi. Mexico. (Boyd, n.d.: xv, 2)

Hushtahli The sun god of the Choctaw Indians to whom is "ascribed the power of life and death . . . and . . . success in war." Mississippi and Alabama. (Swanton, 1928: 208)

Hvare The sun, a god of purification. Also known as Hvarekhshaeta, "as Ahura Mazda's eye." Iran. (Gray, 1930: 85; Huart, 1963: 42)

Hweve God of sunlight, younger brother of Gbosuzozo. Dahomey. (Herskovits, 1938, 2: 140)

Hyagnis A Phrygian god, a form of Vahagn, and as such he would be a sun god, a god of fire and of lightning. Father of Marsyas-Masses. Asia Minor. (Ananikian, 1964: 63)

Hyperion One of the Titans and an ancient Greek sun god. With his sister/wife Theia the parents of Selene, Eos, and Helio, by whom he was succeeded. (Kerenyi, 1951: 21–22; Barthell, 1971: 53–55; Bulfinch, 1898: 6, 7)

Ibmel A name for the sun, but it was also applied to the sky and to various phenomena, as well as the supreme god and creator. An abstract concept. The Lapps, Lapland. (Karsten, 1955: 30, 50; Pettersson, 1957: 20; Bosi, 1960: 129)

Ikhekhu " 'dusk,' is occasionally personified." Egypt. (Gardiner, 1925, 9: 791)

Ilai A god identified with the sun who with Indara made man. The Torajas, Celebes, Indonesia. (Kern, 1925, 8: 248)

Ilanze "God and sun"—an older name than Leza. The Fipa, Tanzania. (Millroth, 1965: 19, 40)

Ilat, Allat The sun goddess and mother goddess of South Arabia was invoked for success on journeys or in battle, and for good weather. (Langdon, 1931: 15; Bhattacharji, 1970: 225; Vriezen, 1963: 66)

Ilkwang The Sun Buddha. Korea. (Clark, 1932: 61)

Indra In India he was the mid-day sun, the god of heat and light and as such a vegetation/agricultural deity. However, he was primarily a god of the atmosphere and of weather, and as the bringer of rains a god of fertility. He was a god of war as well. In Mongolia he was the god of the sun and of light, associated with the east. (Bhattacharji, 1970: 267–270; Cox, 1870, 1: 338–343; Percheron, 1953: 62; Danielou, 1964: 106)

Inhungaraing The sun god of Aneiteum, New Hebrides. Melanesia. (Williamson, 1933, 2: 181)

Init-init The god of the sun of the Tinguian. Philippines. (Jocano, 1969: 65)

Innini The goddess of the planet Venus was an early goddess of light, a mother-and earth-goddess. Later she was considered a goddess of battle and identified with

Ishtar as a goddess of war. She was also a goddess of water and associated with serpents and vegetation. Sumero/Babylonian, Near East. (Mercer, 1925, 12: 700, 709; Langdon, 1931: 5, 14, 93)

Inti   The Incan sun god from whom they claim descent. He also was called Apu-Panchau or P'oncaw, the day-light. Tiahuanaco and Altiplano, Peru and Bolivia. The Aymara of Bolivia also call him wilka or lupi and do not worship him as highly as the Incas. His sister/wife is Mama Quilla, the moon. Also worshipped by the Quechua. (Kubler, 1946, 2: 294, 396; LaBarre, 1948: 169; Larousse, 1968: 442; Means, 1931: 390–391)

Inû   The sun god of the Jan Hwamba. At Kona he was also the supreme being. Nigeria. (Meek, 1931: 187, 270)

Irioba, Iriuba   The sun, the omniscient high god, the creator of the world and of all things, the source of all life. Also known as Enokwe. The Kuria, Kenya and Tanzania. (Ruel, 1965: 295–296; Millroth, 1965: 29)

Iruwa   The sun god of the Chaga. Kenya and Tanzania. (Frazer, 1926: 286)

Ishoye, Ishoko   The High God, the Sun, whose wife is Haine, the moon. He is invoked for successful hunting and "for protection from wild animals and diseases." The Hadzapi, Tanzania. (Millroth, 1965: 21, 40–41)

Istanu   A Hittite sun god who may be Protohattic. He was named in treaties as a god of justice. Asia Minor. (Ferm, 1950: 91; Hicks, 1974: 101; James, 1960: 95)

Ithuwa   The sun and the creator god. The Wapare or Wasu, the Pare Mountains, Tanzania. Some consider Kyumbi, Ithuwa, and Mrungu as one god. (Frazer, 1926: 201)

Itzeti Mara Edutzi   The sun god of the Araona. Bolivia. (Métraux, 1948, 3: 447)

Iusaaset   As the female counterpart of Tem (Tum) she must be a solar goddess. He represents the setting sun, but is also associated with the rising sun. Egypt. (Budge, 1969, 1: 349, 354; Knight, 1915: 59)

Iutri-bogh   Slavic god of the morning. (Grimm, 1888: 1520)

Izuwa, Izua, Izuva   The sun god and the High God is invoked "for children and increase of cattle . . . [and] to guard them against darkness and magic." The Pare, the Taveta. Among the Wasu he is the creator, identified with Kyumbi and Mrungu. Izua is the sun god among the Gogo. Tanzania. (Millroth, 1965: 18, 23, 28; Mbiti, 1970, 2: 334)

Jan   A beneficent nat of the Kachins—"the sun"—is invoked for protection of the village. Burma. (Temple, 1925, 3: 22; Leach, 1950, 2: 538)

Jangkarang Matanandau   The god of the sun. The Ngaju, Borneo. (Scharer, 1963: 205)

Janus   Originally a solar god associated with the day-break, and therefore with beginnings and initiative. An important deity in the Roman Pantheon. Later he was considered the god of doors and gateways, both public and private. His two faces allowed him to observe both sides at the same time. As God of Beginnings he was also a god of time and invoked before all gods in prayers. (Dumé-zil, 1966, 1: 173, 327–331; Fairbanks, 1907: 246–247; Pettazzoni, 1956: 167–169; Schoeps, 1961: 147)

Jan Wunlang   The god of the sun (the second generation of deities), son of Kringkrong wa and Ynong majan. The Katchins, Burma. (Gilhodes, 1908: 675)

Jarilo   God of light. Russia. (Schrader, 1925, 2: 38)

Jih Kuan T'ai Yang   A form of Jihn Kung T'ien Tsu as "Director of Sun's Orbit." China. (Day, 1940: 210)

Jih Kung T'ien Tsu, Jih Kuan T'ai Yang, Jih Kung T'ai, Yang Tsun T'ien   God of the day who "is composed of fire, symbolizing *yang* the great life-giving principle of light and warmth." China. (Day, 1940: 77–78)

jóhonaa'áí (McN), **Johanoai** (B), **djóxona'ai** (R), **Tsohanoai** (M)   The Sun is believed to regulate peoples' "activities and thoughts," to be omniscient regarding these and directing those which are good, constructive—influencing toward them. Considered by some to be an invisible solar god who guards and carries the sun. Husband of Estsanatlehi. The Navaho, Arizona and New Mexico. (McNeley, 1981: 22–24, 28, 97; Babington, 1950: 210; Reichard, 1950: 383; Matthews, 1902: 19, 30)

Jua, Dyiowa   The sun god. The Issansu, the Kiswahili, the Kogogo. Tanzania. (Millroth, 1965: 18)

Jupiter   Jupiter Lucetius as the god of light. His primary role was that of the sovereign of the skies, the god of the atmosphere and its phenomena. Italy. (Fairbanks, 1907: 98; Schoeps, 1961: 145; Larousse, 1968: 203; Dumézil, 1966, 1: 108, 163)

Jurupari   Among the Tupi a god associated with the sun. Brazil. (Bastide, 1960: 567)

Juti Mara Edutzi, Izeti Mara Edutzi   The sun god of the Araona. Bolivia. (Métraux, 1942: 41)

Ka'a djaj   God of the east who is "daylight man," whose wife is Ka'a mata. The Coast Central Pomo, California. (Loeb, 1926: 301)

Ka'a mata   Goddess of daylight, wife of Ka'a djaj. Pomo Indians, California. (Loeb, 1926: 301)

Tatik K'ak'al   Father Sun who burns the crops when angered. The Tzeltal, Mexico. (Nash, 1970: 42)

Kakunupmawa, Kaqunup?mawa   The Sun, an anthropomorphic supreme being, is a symbol of morality, of the male force. He is both benevolent and malevolent, providing "life, warmth, and light" and observing mankind's actions both good and evil, or receiving human lives in payment if he and Slo'w win at the nightly peon game which they play against Shnilemun and 'Alnahyit 'i 'akiwi, as he and his daughters are cannibalistic. His most important ceremonies are at the time of the winter solstice. The Chumash, California. (Hudson and Underhay, 1978: 41, 51, 52, 61; Blackburn, 1975: 36, 37, 97)

Kalliphos   One of the many names of the sun god, used with conjuring or magical invocation of spirits. Greece. (Roscher, 1965, 2, 1: 928)

Kanitika   Was "originally a god who controlled the sun" but was removed because his heat control was not liked. Some say he later went back to the sun "chastened," others that he changed to an "earthly god" named Te Atua Pule. Pukapuka, Polynesia. (Beaglehole, 1938: 311)

Kankin   The sun of the Mayas in the Corozal District invoked during the rain-making ceremonies. British Honduras. (Thompson, 1930: 64)

Ka-onohi-o-ka-la   The "eye-ball of the sun" who in some traditions escorted the souls of heroes to heaven. Hawaii. (Alexander, 1967: 103)

Karakwa   The sun. The Iroquois Indians, Eastern United States. (Emerson, 1884: 369)

Ka Singi   The sun, elder sister of the moon, who had incestuous intentions toward her. The Khasi, India. (Elwin, 1949: 55)

Kazoba, Kazooba   A god associated with the sun as well as the moon and the stars. The Haya, Tanzania. The Ankore, Uganda. (Taylor, 1962: 142; Mbiti, 1970, 1: 68)

Keesuckqu'and   The God of the Sun. The Narragansett Indians, Rhode Island. (Skinner, 1913: 91)

Keresani   A demon representing the burning sun. Iran. (Gray, 1930: 207)

Khalls   The sun god of the Okanagan Indians. Washington and British Columbia. (Keeler, 1960: 76)

Khambageu   A self-existent being, a culture hero type, who established customs and morals and had powers of healing. He died and rose again ascending to the sky to live in the sun. A sun god as identified with Riob. The Sonjo, Tanzania. (Gray, 1963: 97–107; Mbiti, 1970, 2: 126)

Khandobā   He "represents both sun [masc.] and moon [fem.] (who unite in an interior androgynization within him) . . . and his worship culminates on the day when sun and moon meet in a union that is by implication sexual." Mahārastra, India. (O'Flaherty, 1980: 255–257)

Khepera   The beetle god is a form of solar deity—the sun when about to rise. Egypt. (Budge, 1969, 1: 298) The creator god who raised things up out of Nu, a god of creation and resurrection. (Budge, 1969, 2: 294–295, 379; Knight, 1915: 62)

Khors, Khors Dazhbog   The sun "generated" by Svarog. Apparently identical with Dazhbog but sometimes separate deities. Slavic Russia. (Gimbutas, 1971: 162; Ralston, 1872: 85, 102)

Khotal-Ekva   The sun of the Mansi. Brother of Numi-Torum. Siberia. (Michael, 1963: 209)

Khu   Egyptian god of light. (Budge, 1969, 2: 407)

Kij   The "god of light and good principle." Guatemala, (Bancroft, 1886, 3: 482)

Kikaawei turide   The sun-father. The Pueblo Indians at Isleta, New Mexico. (Parsons, 1929/30: 341)

Ah Kilis   A deity of the Chorti who eats the sun causing eclipses. Guatemala. (Wisdom, 1940: 399–400)

Ah Kin, Qin   The sun god, a god of light and of knowledge, "rather dreaded," but not worshipped. The Chorti, Guatemala and Honduras. (Wisdom, 1940: 399; Thompson, 1930: 64; 1970: 235, 238)

Ah K'in   "He of the Sun . . . the god of ceremonies." The Lacandon, Chiapas, Mexico. (Perera and Bruce, 1982: 308)

Kinich Ahau, Kinich Kakmo The sun god, considered an aspect of Itzamna. He is a god of health and of medicine whose wife is Ix Azal Uoh. The Mayan, Yucatan, Mexico. (Hagar, 1913: 18, 20; Bancroft, 1886, 3: 464; Thompson, 1970: 207, 240, 312; Nicholson, 1967: 119)

Kisaludenos A sun god of Smyrna identified with Apollo and Helios. Turkey. (Pettazzoni, 1956: 182)

Kit, Kittum The sun god of the Kossaean. Near East. (Sayce, 1898: 175)

Kitix An Ixil name for the sun god. Mayan, Guatemala. (Thompson, 1970: 237)

Kizho, Kizhox The sun, the god of the day. The Minsi (Lenape Indians), Eastern United States. (Harrington, 1921: 27)

Kleseakarktl The sun is worshipped by the Makah and the Klallams on rising. He represents the supreme god. Washington. (Swanton, 1925, 12: 663; Eells, 1886/1887: 673)

K'paw ta thu The demon of the eclipses. The Karen, Burma. (Marshall, 1922: 316)

Kran, Kren The sun god of the Ona is invoked for fish. His wife is the moon, Kre. Tierra del Fuego. (Zerries, 1968: 264; Loeb, 1931: 528)

Krishna As an avatar (the eighth) of Vishnu, he is a solar deity. He represents love in all its forms from erotic to mystical. India. (Bhattacharji, 1970: 302–313; Brown, 1961: 297, 303; Ions, 1967: 61)

Krsanu A Vedic sun god who is manevolent or benevolent depending on the time of year. India. (Gray, 1930: 207–208)

Kuade The sun, who lived on earth, was killed by a Juruna, and then was replaced by his (Kuade's) youngest son. Xingu River area, Brazil. (Villas Boas, 1973: 94–97)

Kuaray The sun of the Guarani-Mbya. Paraguay. (Levi-Strauss, 1969: 74)

Kuat The beneficent sun god of the Kamaiura taught them how to fish and the arts of music and dancing. He is the brother of Iae, the moon. The Xingu River area, Brazil. (Villas Boas, 1973: 65–66, 93; Oberg, 1953: 53)

Kudai Among the South Yenesei Turks he is the "spirit of light." Siberia. (Klementz, 1925, 3: 5)

Ah K'ulel The Whirlwind. An assistant solar god who serves Hachäkyum, the creator; takes the ashes from the godpots (where the incense is burned) to him. He is also called "the Sweeper of Our Lord's House." The Lacandon, Mexico. (Perera and Bruce, 1982: 31)

Kun Goddess of the sun whose husband is Ai-ada, the moon. The Turks of Central Asia. (Czaplicka, 1925, 12: 482)

Kun-Toyon The sun god of the Yakut. Siberia. (Czaplicka, 1969: 277)

Kutnahin The sun, the supreme being, who also makes the thunder, was earlier considered female. He was represented as a traveller as well as a teacher of culture. The Chitimacha, Louisiana. (Swanton, 1928: 209; 1946: 781; Pettazzoni, 1956: 176)

La (1) The sun, son of Ilu and Mamao. The Malietoa of Samoa, Polynesia. (Williamson, 1933: 4) (2) The supreme being of the Mumuye with whom the sun is identified. Nigeria. (Williams, 1936: 217)

Lairbenos A solar god of Asia Minor identified with Apollo. (Pettazzoni, 1956: 182)

Laki Ramaoe The "monster that swallows sun and moon and thereby causes eclipses." The Toradja, Celebes, Indonesia. (Adriani and Kruyt, 1950: 378)

Lanipipili The aumakua in the sun and also the moon are "chiefly invoked as detectives in cases of petty thieving." Hawaii. (Emerson, 1967: 51)

Lem The "Young Sun Man" and the great hunter. The Yaghan, Tierra del Fuego. (Coon, 1971: 299)

Libtakan The god of the sunrise, of the sunset, and of good weather. The Manobo, Philippines. (Jocano, 1969: 23)

Limi The sun of the Sukuma-Nyamwezi. Tanzania. (Mbiti, 1970, 2: 335)

Liova The sun and the creator. The physical body is called limi. The Kumbi, Tanzania. (Millroth, 1965: 96)

Liowa The High God, the sun, and the creator. The Iramba, Tanzania. (Millroth, 1965: 22–23)

Lisa The sun in its strength and harshness, the god of the day, the male creative principle. He lives in the east. He is the twin/husband of Mawu, born of Nana-Buluku, and they are "parents of all the other gods." The Ewe,

Dahomey. (Herskovits, 1938, 2: 101–103; Parrinder, 1967: 21, 67; Queval, 1968: 73; Mercier, 1954: 219)

Liu-La The deity of "Twilight," a relative of Poli-ahu and Lili-no-e. Maui, Hawaii. (Ashdown, 1971: 68)

Lleu, Lleu Llaw Gyffes A sun god, representing its light, the son of Arianrhod and Gwydion. His wife, Blodeuwedd, arranged his death, at which he transformed himself into an eagle. After his restoration to human form, rather than kill her, he transformed her into an owl. Celtic Wales. (MacCana, 1970: 28; Ross, 1967: 227, 274; de Kay, 1898: 226)

Loa The sun goddess, whose husband is Netlang, is their chief deity. She also brings death. The Iraku, Tanzania. (Millroth, 1965: 23)

Loba A god of light. The high god of the Bakwiri. Cameroon. (MacCulloch, 1925, 8: 49)

Loko Atissou Beneficent god of sunlight. He is the chief escort of Legba and as such is also guardian of roads, paths, habitations, etc. He is a god of medicinal plants and of trees and forests. Identified with St. Joseph. Haiti. (Marcelin, 1950: 41, 43)

Lokomran "(Daymaker) in the east." The Marshall Islands, Micronesia. (Erdland, 1914: 308)

Louci Iuteri A Celtic solar god associated with the raven and equated with Lug of Ireland. Spain. (Martinez, 1962: 89)

Lougestericus A solar god. Spain. (Martinez, 1962: 90)

Lucoubus A solar god, the village of Sinoga. Spain. (Martinez, 1962: 90)

Lugoves A solar god named in Osma. Spain. (Martinez, 1962: 91)

Lupi The sun god among the Aymara whose wife is the moon. Some consider him the supreme being but remote and possibly malevolent. Peru. (Tschopik, 1951: 196–197)

Macaq The sun god of the Chugach Eskimos. Alaska. (Birket-Smith, 1953: 118–120)

Mahatara The sun, who with Jata, the earth, created the world. The Dayaks, Borneo. (Kruijt, 1925, 7: 249)

Mahui The "god who brings fertility and abundance, and is, according to Moerenhout, a personification of the sun." Believed to be present from October to May. The Marquesas, Polynesia. (Rivers, 1915: 433)

Jin Maktok The sun spirit of the Semang. Malay Peninsula. (Skeat, 1906: 182)

Malakbel A solar deity and god of fertility at Palmyra, Syria. (Vriezen, 1963: 67; Cook, 1930: 220; Langdon, 1931: 37)

Malamanganga'e "(Light eastwards)" married **Malamangangaifo** "(Light westwards)" Parents of Lupe, in the genealogy of the kings of Aana. Samoa, Polynesia. (Williamson, 1933, 1: 8)

Mallina The Sun, sister of Anningat, the Moon. Greenland. (Grimm, 1883, 2: 703)

Maluaga The sun, with Hintogolopi the moon, rules the heavens. New Ireland, Melanesia. (Cox, 1913: 198)

Manabozho God of the dawn, of light, is god of the east and of the east wind. *See also* **Michabo.** The Winnebago, Wisconsin. (Emerson, 1884: 8, 28, 337; Radin and Reagan, 1928: 70, 84)

Manggama The sun. Rennell Island, Polynesia. (Birket-Smith, 1956: 22)

Manito Wabos The Rabbit god, god of light and of the dawn lives in the east. The Cherokees, Carolina. Same as Michabo, Manabozho. (Spence, 1925, 3: 503–504)

Mapatal The sun god of the Mayawyaw. Northern Luzon, Philippines. (Lambrecht, 1932: 20)

Mapatal Bugan in Amalgo The sun goddess, wife of Mapatal. The Mayawyaw, Luzon, Philippines. (Lambrecht, 1932: 20)

Marapou The god of the sun. Yap Island, the Carolines, Micronesia. (Christian, 1899: 385)

Marduk Originally a solar and agricultural deity, the eldest son of Ea with whom he shared the creation of the heavens and earth from Tiamat's body, and mankind from Kingu's blood. Later with his power in war and politics he became predominant as ruler over all things, with power over life and death. He was a god of healing, second to Ea. As the planet Jupiter he was god of the month Marchesvan (Senitic), Arakh-samna (Sumerian). Assyro/Babylonian. (Jastrow, 1898: 118, 120, 463; Hommel, 1925, 3: 75; Jacobsen, 1970: 35–36; Kramer, 1961: 121; Larousse, 1968: 51, 56)

Marici, Marishi   Buddhist goddess of the dawn. She is given as the wife of Yama, and again as that of Hayagriva. Her Tibetan name is Od-zer-'c'an-ma. (Waddell, 1959: 361; Getty, 1962: 132; MacKenzie, 1930: 260)

Marikoriko   The god of the twilight whose wife is Tiki. The Maori, New Zealand. (Lang, 1887: 193)

Martanda   A solar god, the eighth son of Aditi whom she discards, then recalls. He seems "to stand for the setting sun with death inherent in him." India. (Bhattacharji, 1970: 3, 219; Macdonell, 1897: 43–44)

Masoandro   The sun is considered a deity or a power and is included in invocations. The Tanala. Madagascar. (Linton, 1933: 160–161)

Masomamakizahana   A "ceremonial name for the sun." Masoandro. The Tanala, Madagascar. (Linton, 1933: 163)

Mater Matuta   An early Roman goddess of the dawn who became a goddess of childbirth, of matrons and children. Her festival is the Matralia. (Dumézil, 1966, 1: 50–51; Jayne, 1962: 453; Fairbanks, 1907: 151; Altheim, 1937: 126)

Mayec   The sun, worshipped by the Guanches of Palma. Canary Islands. (Basset, 1925, 2: 508)

Menahka   The sun. The Mandan Indians, North Dakota. (Burland, 1965: 149)

Menthu   A form of the sun god—a personification of its destructive heat. Egypt. (Budge, 1969, 2: 23–24; Rhys, 1937: 116)

Meri   The sun god of the Bororo. Brazil. (Levi-Strauss, 1969: 51)

Merodach   *See* **Marduk**. (Sayce, 1898: 47, 94–98, 113–115)

Michabo   The Great White Hare, as a solar deity, was a god of light and of the dawn. He was, moreover, the creator of the earth, and god of the winds and weather. The Algonquin Indians, United States. (Brinton, 1868: 166; 1882: 46–47; Fiske, 1900: 25, 73, 153; Spence, 1925, 4: 127)

Mihr   The sun, the god of fire, is one of the seven chief deities from Iran. Son of Aramazd and brother of Anahit and Nane. He is identified with Vahagn who replaced him in importance. Armenia. (Ananikian, 1964: 17, 33–34; Gray, 1930: 23)

Mininga   An invisible, independent god sometimes identified with the sun. Others consider the sun as a torch which he carries. He is a creator god who controls life and death. The Kuma, New Guinea. (Aufenanger, 1962: 21–22)

Minokawa   An enormous bird who swallows the moon causing the eclipse. The Bagobo, Philippines. (Benedict, 1916: 40, 47)

Mir-Susne-Khum   (Gander Prince), also Mir-susne-xum—the sun god of the Vogul whose sister is Xoli-Kaltes, the Dawn-Woman. His function was to try to keep the peace among the gods and men. Siberia. (Roheim, 1954: 30–31; Czaplicka, 1969: 289)

Mithra   A solar deity, god of light, of truth, of good, of contracts, and of judgment—of all the beneficent aspects of duality. He was omniscient, sleepless, and constantly watchful of man's activities. Iran, also Rome, and known in Gaul. (Pettazzoni, 1956: 134–136; Jayne, 1962: 193; Gray, 1930: 97; Dresden, 1961: 347–348; Huart, 1963: 40–42)

Mitra   God of sunlight and of the day sky. He is a god of the moral order, of truth, of the sanctity of contracts. India. (Bhattacharji, 1970: 33, 221–222; Danielou, 1964: 116; Littleton, 1965: 8)

Mocio   A solar god with an altar found in Limia. Spain. (Martinez, 1962: 93)

Mont   A variant name of Menthu. Egypt.

Muhammad   A god identified with the sun. Created by 'Ali, he in turn "created the five 'incomparables,' who in their turn created the world and are the five planets." He forms a triad with 'Ali and Salman-al-Farisi. The Nusairis, Near East. (Basset, 1925, 9: 418)

Munamazuba   "He of the suns, the Everlasting One." The Ila, Zambia. (Mbiti, 1970, 2: 331)

Muntumuntu   God of the sun and the lawgiver. The Minahassa, Indonesia. (Kern, 1925, 8: 347)

Murupiangkala   Considered by some as a sun-woman, a daughter of Mudungkala. Melville Island, Australia. (Mountford, 1958: 24, 173)

Muš   A nocturnal demoness considered the cause of eclipses. Iran. (Gray, 1930: 210)

Naac   The sun god of the Trique tribe. Son of Nexhequiriac. Oaxaca, Mexico. (Valentini, 1899: 38)

naghe' nezghani (na·γe·' ne·zγani) Monster Slayer is a god of light associated with heat. He is an intermediary between man and the deities and "represents impulsive aggression . . . kills for the future benefit of mankind . . . the subjection of the minor evils." Twin of tobadjictcini. The Navaho, Arizona and New Mexico. (Reichard, 1950: 30, 417, 448–451, 482)

Naglfari Twilight, the first husband of Nott and father of Aud. Teutonic. (Branston, 1955: 203; Grimm, 1883, 2: 735; Guerber, 1895: 15)

Naguset, Sa'gama The sun, worshipped at its rising and setting, was also the creator. The Micmac, the Maritime Provinces, Canada. (Wallis, 1955: 97, 142)

Nahhunte The sun, god of light, and, as identified with Shamash, probably a god of justice and righteousness. The Elamites, Near East. (Pinces, 1925, 5: 251; Larousse, 1968: 72)

nahotsoi asdzą́ą́ (*see also* **naxo·coi 'eszá·**) Evening Twilight Woman. One of the Holy People involved in the creation of "Earth, Sky, Sun, Moon, and various animals." The Navaho, Arizona and New Mexico. (McNeley, 1981: 22, 78)

nahotsoi hastiin (*see also* **naxo·coi xast^Xi·n**) Evening Twilight Man. One of the Holy People of the creation of the "Earth, Sky, Sun, Moon, and various animals." He is in the West; is benevolent, guiding "people in coming together again." The Navaho, Arizona and New Mexico. (McNeley, 1981: 22, 28–29, 81)

Nairyaspa A god who "appear(s) to have been a deity of light; . . . would seem . . . to have been originally the god of the setting sun." Iran. (Gray, 1930: 152)

Nanahuatzin Modest and unafraid he cast himself as a sacrifice into the fire of the gods and was transformed into the sun. Mexico. (León-Portilla, 1961: 452)

Naolin The sun, Tonatiuh, is worshipped under this name "in his four motions." Mexico. (Bancroft, 1886, 3: 109)

Narayan Deo Among the Agaria in Mandla the sun is malevolent. Same as Suraj Deo. Among the Gond he is also a household deity. They and the Baiga offer a pig to him. India. (Elwin, 1942: 98; Russell, 1916, 2: 85; 3: 101)

Nasatya Twin of Dasra, the gods of the dawn. Together called the Asvins. They are, as well, gods of healing and of animal husbandry. (Bhattacharji, 1970: 217; Dumézil, 1966, 1: 171)

Natos The sun god, the principal deity of the Blackfoot. His wife is the moon. Plains Indians, Canada. (Wissler and Duvall, 1908: 10)

Natsutakatsuhi-no-Kami The deity of the high summer sun. Also called "Natsu-no-me-no-kami (Female Kami of summer)." Japan. (Yasumaro, 1965: 51; Herbert, 1967: 333)

Nawaye ayi The "Light Creator" appealed to by the shaman. The Yukaghir, Siberia. (Jochelson, 1900/02: 207)

naxatsoi God of the sunset. "Yellow-evening-light." The Navaho, Arizona and New Mexico. (Reichard, 1950: 505)

naxocoi'esza Goddess of the twilight, mother of Calling God. The Navaho, Arizona and New Mexico. *See also* **nahotsoi asdzą́ą́.** (Haile, 1947: 15)

naxo·coi xast^Xi·n God of the twilight, father of xašč'ê^γan (Calling God) and xá·da·č'i·ši (Destroyer or Whipping God). The Navaho, Arizona and New Mexico. *See also* **nahotsoi hastiin.** (Haile, 1947: 15)

Ndauthina The god of "light and fire" is also the god of seafarers and fishermen. Fiji, Melanesia. (MacCulloch, 1925, 8: 50; Thomson, 1925, 6: 15)

Nefer-Tem The lion-god who represents the rising sun is the son of Ptah and Sekhet. He is also one of the forty-two judges or assessors of the dead for the goddess Maat in the underworld. Egypt. (Budge, 1969, 1: 419, 514, 521; 1969, 2: 362; Knight, 1915: 74–75)

Nergal As a solar deity he represents the destructive powers of the sun. In marrying Ereshkigal he became god of the underworld, of evil, pestilence, and war. Sumer, Akkadia, Babylonia, Assyria, and Palestine. (Jastrow, 1898: 66–68; Cook, 1930: 121; Langdon, 1931: 93, 147; Seligmann, 1948: 30)

Niesehaman The sun god of the Cheyenne. Plains Indians, Colorado. (Powell, 1969: 437)

Nigi-haya-hi A solar god, "perhaps the morning sun," whose wife is Tomi-yama-bime. Japan. (Herbert, 1967: 334–335, 465)

Nikko, Nikko-bosatsu The Sun. Japanese Buddhism. (Eliot, 1935: 140; Eliseev, 1963: 428)

Ningirsu As identified with Nin-ib he is a solar god, as well as a god of war and of agriculture. He is also known as Ninurta. Sumerian/Assyro/Babylonian. (Jastrow, 1898: 56; Campbell, 1964: 117–119; Larousse, 1968: 60)

Ningthoi wa   A god of light, son of Kringkrong wa and Ynong majan. His wife is Ningsin majan. When he died he became Ningthoi u, a bird of the dawn. The Katchins, Burma. (Gilhodes, 1908: 676–677)

Ninib   A solar deity representing the morning sun. He was more notably a god of war as well as a god of hunting, of healing (in conjunction with his consort Gula), of agriculture, and of storms. He was identified with Ningirsu. Assyria and Babylonia, Near East. (Jayne, 1962: 126; Jastrow, 1898: 57, 67, 174, 217; Hommel, 1925, 3: 74; Mercer, 1925, 12: 700)

Nodons   A Celtic god of healing and also a god of the sun and of water in their therapeutic capacities. Britain. Identified with Nuada, Nudd. (Ross, 1967: 176, 201; MacCulloch, 1911: 85)

Nommo   The initial Nommo, the son of God, was a deity of the day, "associated with the sky, water, and fertility" and ruling the viable lands. There are numerous pairs of Nommo, avatars of the first, who express "the fundamental principle of twin-ness in creation," which is reflected in Dogon culture and organization. Mali and Nigeria. (Griaule and Dieterlen, 1954: 85–86)

Nongshaba   In the creation period he was the god who produced light. Manipur, India. (Shakespear, 1913: 85)

Nonorugami, onorugame   Also called Tata Dios. Father Sun guards people during the day in all their activities and, therefore, they do not transact business after sunset. The Tarahumara, Mexico. (Lumholtz, 1902: 295; Bennett and Zingg, 1935: 373; Pettazzoni, 1956: 405)

Nudd   *See* **Nodons**

Nuikukúi   A demon—"great sun, sun at midday." Also Master of the East. The Cagaba, the Kogi, Colombia. *See* **Surli.** (Preuss, 1926: 76; Reichel-Dolmatoff, 1949/50: 142)

NumKympoi   The chief god who as the Sun sees all. When displeased he sends the whirlwind. The Yurak Samoyeds, Siberia. (Pettazzoni, 1956: 260; Roheim, 1954: 48)

Nuñda   The common name for the sun and the moon. Priests call them Sutalidihi ("dwells in the day") and Geyaguga ("dwells in the night"). (Hagar, 1906: 357)

The common name of the sun as luminary of the day. Ritually known as Unelanuhi or Geyaguga. The Cherokee, North Carolina and Tennessee. (Mooney and Olbrechts, 1932: 20)

Nùqsɛlxwʻ   Eclipse, a supernatural being who blocks the way of the sun. The Bella Coola Indians, British Columbia. (McIlwraith, 1948, 2: 224)

Nuska, Nuzku   Originally a solar deity, but predominately the fire god in the beneficent aspect of destroying disease and as god of the sacred fire. Assyria and Babylonia. Near East. (Jastrow, 1898: 220; Jayne, 1962: 126; Larousse, 1968: 61; Sayce, 1898: 118–119)

Nyambe   In Mozambique he is the Sun-god. (Larousse, 1968: 475)

Nyankopon   The sun god who progressed from a clan god, through sky-fertility-god to the sun god. He is also considered a supreme deity. The Akan. Among the Ashanti he personifies the sun and is represented by the king. Ghana. (Meyerowitz, 1958: 82–83; Parrinder, 1967: 67)

Nzeanzo   An omniscient solar god to whom all is brought by the wind. Nigeria. (Pettazzoni, 1956: 37)

Ocatc   The sun god is worshipped but is not anthropomorphic, "merely a face with rays radiating" from it. The Acoma Indians, New Mexico. (White, 1929/30: 64)

Odur, Oder, Od   Guerber considers him the personification of the summer sun, while MacCulloch speaks of him as a man. Regardless he is the husband of Freya (Freyja) and the father of Hnoss and Gersemi. Teutonic. (Guerber, 1895: 125, 127; MacCulloch, 1964: 120, 125; Anderson, 1891: 364)

O-hirume, Ohirumemuchi-no-Kami   The sun goddess. Another name for Amaterasu Omikami. Japan. (Kato, 1926: 14; Hori, 1968: 166)

Olowaipippilele   The sun god, son/husband of Olokukurtilisop. They produced mankind, sacred plants, and animals. He was also the great judge. The Cuna Indians, Panama. (Keeler, 1960: 11, 46, 243)

Omuqkatos   The Great Spirit, the Sun. The Blackfeet, Plains Indians, Canada. (Maclean, 1876: 439)

O Ndo-i-ronda-eo   A deity "who lives at the sunrise" and is invoked at the planting season for favorable results. The Toradja, Celebes, Indonesia. (Adriani and Kruyt, 1950: 55)

Onum   The sun and creator god of the Kadara. Nigeria. (Gunn, 1956: 135; Mbiti, 1970, 2: 331)

Oramfe   A solar deity of the Ife. Nigeria. (Idowu, 1962: 94)

Ort-iki   An omniscient solar god, son of Torem, the sky god. "Gander-Chief." The Ostyak, Siberia. (Roheim, 1954: 48; Pettazzoni, 1956: 258)

Orun, Oroun   The sun god of the Yoruba. Nigeria/ Brazil. (Meek, 1925, 2: 29; Lucas, 1948: 98; Bastide, 1960: 570)

Orungan, Orunjan   The god of the noon-day sun. Son of Aganju and Yemaja. The Yoruba, Nigeria. (Meek, 1925, 2: 29; Lucas, 1948: 98)

Oshats   The Sun. The Sia and the Keresan, Pueblo Indians. New Mexico. (Fewkes, 1895, 2: 124; Tyler, 1964: 78)

Owia   The sun, son of the sky god and brother of Osrane (moon) and Esum (darkness). The Ashanti, Ghana. (Feldman, 1963: 125)

Oxlahun-oc   "god-Thirteen, formed of the solar deity in its zenithal position and its twelve stellar companions." The Quiché, Guatemala. (Girard, 1979: 53, 54)

Pagé abé   The physical sun is only the representative of the "Sun Father" who is the creative principle. The Desana, Colombia. (Reichel-Dolmatoff, 1971: 25, 41–42, 48)

Paive, Beive, Peive   The sun is thought of as a primeval being as well as a deity of light, of healing and warmth, of fertility. The Lapps, Northern Europe. (Dioszegi, 1968: 28; Karsten, 1955: 30, 32)

Paiyatemu, Paiyatuma   The "God of Dew and the Dawn." The son of the sun is a phallic god, who represents the fertility and sexuality of the sun. He is associated with the Corn Maidens in their seasonal disappearance and reappearance. The Zuñi Indians, New Mexico. (Cushing, 1891/92: 377; Tyler, 1964: 142–143, 145; Parsons, 1939: 179, 204)

Pa'ta   The sun. The Cayapa of Ecuador. (Barrett, 1925: 353)

Pautiwa   The sun god is chief of all the gods and appears at the solstice ceremonials. The Zuñi and Hopi Indians, New Mexico and Arizona. (Fewkes, 1901: 87; Tyler, 1964: 148–149; Stevenson, 1901/02: 33)

Pava   The sun, their primary god, provides light and warmth. The Campa, Peru. (Weiss, 1972: 164)

Phaenna   "light"—with Cleta the two Charities at Sparta. Greece. (Burns, 1925, 3: 373)

Phaethon   A young sun god given as the son of Helios or Apollo or Kephalos and Clymene or Eos. Greece. (Kerenyi, 1951: 194–195; Fairbanks, 1907: 161; Bulfinch, 1898: 51)

Pharoah   The reigning king as the living sun-god. Egypt. (Ames, 1965: 125)

Phol   Teutonic god of light (the Thuringians and Bavarians)—"If, as appears most likely, he is synonymous with Palter (Balder)." He is also associated with the whirlwind. (Grimm, 1880: 220–228; 1883, 2: 632; 1883, 3: xix)

Pi   The sun god of the Iowa. Plains Indians. (Dorsey, 1892: 300)

Pidrai   One of the daughters of Baal who symbolizes "light." Canaan. Near East. (Gordon, 1961: 196)

Pi hia yuan kiun   The goddess of the dawn, Princess of the colored clouds, is the daughter of T'ai Chan. China. (Chavannes, n.d.: 29)

Pii-moi   A sun god. Hawaii. (Westervelt, 1915: 170)

Piltzintecuhtli   A sun god identified with Tonatiuh. Father of Macuilxochitl. Mexico. (Alexander, 1920: 54; Spence, 1923: 187, 196; Vaillant, 1962: 150; Nicholson, 1967: 46)

Pioki   The sun, and a sky god. The Mayoruna, Brazil. (Pettazzoni, 1956: 8)

Po Aditjak   The sun god of the Cham. Indonesia. (Wales, 1957: 160)

Pori   The sun. The Mbula, Nigeria. (Williams, 1936: 216)

Prabha, Prabhata   Goddess of the dawn, of light, of health—particularly for that of cattle. India. (Danielou, 1964: 96; Briggs, 1953: 555)

Pratyusha   When he accompanies Surya in his chariot and "shooting arrows of light to dispel the darkness of the night" he symbolizes "pre-dawn." When he accompanies Candra he is "twilight." Nepal. (Pal and Bhattacharyya, 1969: 13, 23). In India he is the personification of light, an attendant upon Indra. (Dowson, 1961: 342)

Prsni "Ray-of-Light," wife of Savitr. India. (Danielou, 1964: 125)

Pudau Goddess and guardian of the place where the sun rises. The Lanoh, Malaya. (Evans, 1937: 163)

Pue mpalaburu The sun who is all-seeing and punishes wrong-doing is also the supreme being and creator. He is invoked in oath-taking and also for good rice crops. The Toradja, Celebes. (Downs, 1920: 10–14; Pettazzoni, 1956: 8, 20). In areas of Indonesia he is the chief servant of the creator. (Kruijt, 1925, 7: 249)

Pu'gu The sun is invoked and receives sacrifices in the making of peace. The Yukaghir, Siberia. (Jochelson, 1900/02: 218)

Pu'gud-emei The "Sun-mother" who is invoked for warmth and protection from evil. The Yukaghir, Siberia. (Jochelson, 1900/02: 218)

Puitcher The beneficent sun. Coconuco, Colombia. (Hernandez de Alba, 1946: 935)

Puksu The guardian of the day, the morning star god, and brother of Olowaipippilele. The Cuna Indians, Panama. (Keeler, 1960: 67, 84)

Pulekukwerek A god who procured the sun and the night for the Yurok. California. (Elmendorf, 1960: 536)

Punchau, Punchao Another name for Inti, the sun god. Peru. (Trimborn, 1968: 128; Kubler, 1946: 396)

Pushan A solar god who represents the beneficence of the sun. He is strongly involved in the prosperity and protection of man and his property in this world as well as guiding the souls of the dead in the next. India. (Bhattacharji, 1970: 186; Macdonell, 1897: 35–37; Danielou, 1964: 123–124; Gray, 1930: 101)

Put The sun is invoked for the protection of food plants and animals and for rain. The Timbira, Brazil. (Nimuendaju, 1946: 232)

Puto The sun whose wife is Puki. The A-Pucikwar tribe. Andaman Islands, Bay of Bengal. (Radcliffe-Brown, 1967: 142)

Qin The god of the sun protects against jaguars. His wife is Akna, the moon. The Lacandon Indians, Mexico. (Cline, 1944: 112)

Ra, Re The sun god, who is usually represented as hawk-headed, is considered the sun at the zenith. He has numerous manifestations and his female counterpart is Rat. In dynastic times he was considered the creator of all things. He is claimed as the father of the pharoahs. Egypt. (Knight, 1915: 102, 105; Ames, 1965: 27, 50; Budge, 1969, 1: 322)

Ra, 'Ra In Polynesia the sun god on the Hervey Islands. Among the Maori a shortened form of the sun's full name Tama-nui-te-ra. (Williamson, 1933: 97; Andersen, 1928: 199)

Rahu The demon of the eclipses. He was an Asura who drank of the amrita and gained immortality. He was discovered in this by the Sun and the Moon and, though decapitated by Vishnu, he swallows them in revenge. India/Cambodia. (Elwin, 1949: 68; Coreman, 1832: 134–135; Briggs, 1953: 544; Crooke, 1894: 10; Bray, 1935: 175)

Rahula God of the eclipse admitted to the Buddhist circles from the Hindu as a defender of the doctrine. Known here also as gZa-lha. Tibet. (Getty, 1962: 174; Snellgrove, 1957: 79, 242)

Ramiriqui The first two humans were the king of Ramiriqui and the king of Sogamoso who created mankind and then became the sun and the moon. The Muiscas, Colombia. (Trimborn, 1968: 90)

Rao Among some it is he who swallows the sun causing eclipses. He is also "the leader of the spirits of gluttony." The Toradja, Celebes, Indonesia. (Adriani and Kruyt, 1950: 378; Downs, 1920: 25)

Rarak The sun—invoked and worshipped on Solor Island. Indonesia. (Frazer, 1926: 660)

Rarang (1) The sun was the first human and the creator of mankind. The Alfuru, Northern Celebes, Indonesia. (Roheim, 1972: 31) (2) The sun represents the "power and activity" of Rarang, the remote high god. The Kaean, New Guinea, Melanexia. (Meiser, 1963: 905–906)

Rat The female counterpart of Ra and as such a goddess of the sun. Egypt. (Budge, 1969, 1: 446, 458; Knight, 1915: 106)

Reshuru The dawn, the Awakener, "gives the blessing of life." The Pawnee, Plains Indians, Nebraska. (Fletcher, 1900/01: 124–127)

Riob The sun god of the Sonjo with whom Khambageu became identified. Tanzania. (Gray, 1963: 107; Mbiti, 1970, 2: 133)

Rit   The sun, brother of Une, the moon. The Kuikuru of the Xingu River area. Brazil. (Villas Boas, 1973: 80)

Riuba   The omniscient sun god of the Kulia. Kenya and Tanzania. (Pettazzoni, 1956: 35)

Ro'onui   A "god of light and peace." Society Islands, Polynesia. (Henry, 1928: 314)

Sabazius, Sabazios   A Phrygian solar deity who became supreme god in Thrace. He was identified with Dionysus and Bacchus in Greece and Rome, sometimes with Zeus. He was also a god of fertility and of vegetation—of "corn . . . wine and beer." (Larousse, 1968: 155, 160; Jayne, 1962: 346; Ananikian, 1964: 12–13)

St. George   A protective solar god, a god of fertility and of healing, but also a storm god who sends hail as punishment. The Khevsurs, Caucasus. (Gray, 1925, 12: 485)

Sakaimoka   The god of the setting sun. The Huichol, Mexico. (Chamberlain, 1900: 305)

Sakidawaitsa   The sun who gives light and assists in the growth of everything. The Wichita, Plains Indians, Kansas. (Dorsey, 1904, 1: 18, 26)

Sakuru   The sun, a very powerful deity, lives in the east and gives light and warmth, vitality, and strength. The Pawnee, Nebraska. (Dorsey, 1904, 2: 3, 4; Fletcher, 1900/01: 30)

Sala   "She was . . . originally the goddess of the Sun . . . " and was linked as a wife to Tammuz, a sun-god at Eridu, to Merodach, a solar deity, and to Rimmon, who, as identified with Hadad at Damascus, was a solar as well as an atmospheric and weather god. Babylonia, Near East. (Sayce, 1898: 203, 209–212)

Sandhyā   Twilight—worshipped by Śiva, desired by Brahmā (who controlled his lust). She is the ghostly counterpart of Ushas, Dawn. India. (O'Flaherty, 1980: 39, 177, 314)

Sanihas   The goddess of daylight whose son is Sanihas Yupchi. The Wintu, California. (Curtin, 1903: 51, 57)

Sanihas Yupchi   The "archer of daylight." Son of Sanihas. The Wintu, California. (Curtin, 1903: 56)

Sapdu   A solar god "known as 'lord of the east and of the Asiatics' " in the area of Bubastis. Egypt. (Cook, 1930: 119)

Sarama   The goddess of the dawn, the twilight, Indra's watchdog who is sent to recover the celestial cattle. She is the mother of Sarameyas. India. (Oldenberg, 1896: 48)

Saranyu   She is spoken of as the Dawn and identified with Ushas, but is also called the cloud goddess. She is the wife of Vivasvat and the mother of the Asvins. India. (Ions, 1967: 32, 95; Danielou, 1964: 125; Choudhury, 1965: 183; Hahn, 1881: 125)

Sarpanitum   A solar deity and goddess of healing and of fertility. As identified with Erua, also a goddess of waters. She was the wife of Marduk. Assyro/Babylonian, Near East. (Jastrow, 1898: 121–122; Jayne, 1962: 127; Robertson, 1911: 221)

Sas   The sun (male) and the moon were originally one and were split in two by Tulchucherris, the larger portion being the sun, the smaller the moon. The Wintu Indians, California. (Curtin, 1903: 32, 157)

sa tsuk   The sun god to whom the Lepchas sacrifice a hog every third year. Sikkim. (Siiger, 1967, 1: 110)

Saule   The beneficent goddess of the sun is associated with all things feminine—spinning, weaving, laundering, music. Her clothes are of silk, embroidered in silver and gold, and her weaving is in silver, gold, copper. She provides the trees with foliage and strews riches on the earth. With Laima she protects women in childbirth, and orphans. Latvia and Lithuania. (Jonval, 1929: 11, 12; Gray, 1930: 75; Gimbutas, 1963: 198)

Saulele   The sun. Litu-Prussian. (Schraeder, 1925, 2: 34)

Savitri, Savitr, Savitar   One of the Adityas, a sun god representing its morning and evening aspects, but more of an abstraction than the other solar gods. He is a god of revivification, of healing, of longevity—the beneficent powers of the sun. Savitri is the inner aspect of the Vedic Sun, "the Sun of Spiritual Truth." This is the sun with whom the Rishis sought to attain union, to obtain his help to conquer the obstructions within their own being in order to achieve the realm of the spirit. India. (Campbell, 1968: 208; Macdonell, 1897: 32–34; Bhattacharji, 1970: 213–214; Danielou, 1964: 125; Ions, 1967: 20; Pandit, 1970: 29–45)

Sed   The sun god, "the Hunter," at Carthage and at Tyre—applied as a title of Melqart and also of Tanit. (Langdon, 1931: 53–54)

Semache   The sun god of the northeastern Yavapai. Arizona. (Gifford, 1932: 234)

Senlee   The sun, son of Lelabalisela, the sky chief. The Kwakiutl, British Columbia. (Boas, 1935: 126)

Senq, Senh, Senx   The sun—"our father"—the only deity worshipped by the Bella Coola. British Columbia. (Swanton, 1925, 11: 98; Boas, 1898: 29; Pettazzoni, 1956: 363)

Senxälotɬa   The name of Alquntam when he appears as the Sun, as the patron of the kusiut dance. The Bella Coola, British Columbia. (McIlwraith, 1948: 222)

Seqinek   The sun, sister of Aningap (Aningat). The Eskimo. Canada. (Rasmussen, 1929: 73, 81)

Shahar, Shachar   The god of the dawn, son of El. Canaan, Phoenicia. Near East. (Vriezen, 1963: 53; Ferm, 1950: 123; Driver, 1956: 22)

Shalem, Shalim, Shalmu   God of the sunset, of the evening. Son of El. Canaan, Phoenicia. Near East. (Vriezen, 1963: 53; Ferm, 1950: 123; Driver, 1956: 22; Albright, 1956: 33)

Shalimtum   The feminine counterpart of Shalim who is "Twilight" or "Dusk." Akkadia, Near East. (Roberts, 1972: 51)

Shamash   The beneficence of the sun as god of light, of justice, of divination, and giver of life and health. Assyria, Babylonia, and Canaan, Near East. (Langdon, 1931: 150; Jastrow, 1898: 71–72; Jayne, 1962: 127; Albright, 1956: 83; Dumézil, 1966, 2: 655)

Shams   Arabian sun goddess, also worshipped by the Sabaeans and Minaeans. In Kataban and Hadramaut—male. (Noldeke, 1925, 1: 660; Tritton, 1925, 10: 882; Moscati, 1960: 187)

Shamshu   The sun goddess of Southern Arabia. (Langdon, 1931: 4)

Shantash   The Hatti/Hurrian sun god at Yazilikaya. Asia Minor. (Van Buren, 1943: 82)

Shapash, Špš   The sun goddess is all-seeing. She is a goddess of fertility—"a great blessing for crops" when associated with Baal. But when "in the power of Mot . . . Špš can destroy the fields, burning the crops." Arabia, Canaan, Palestine, and Syria. Near East. (Vriezen, 1963: 52; Gordon, 1961: 213; Oldenburg, 1969: 20, 91, 94; Gray, 1957: 59; Obermann, 1948: 17; Pritchard, 1943: 3)

Shemesh   The sun and god of justice. Shapash is his female counterpart. Canaan and Phoenicia. Near East. (Ferm, 1950: 123; Jayne, 1962: 132)

gShen lha 'od dkar (pr. **Shenlha Ökar**)   Also referred to as Kun tu bzang po. "The White Light"—important as the principle of generation, "as a symbol of supreme reality, or as a visible perceptible manifestation of that reality." Bon Religion, Tibet. (Tucci, 1980: 64, 243)

Shi   The Sun, created by Attawanadi, the third damodede of Wanadi. The Makiritare, Venezuela. (Civrieux, 1980: 28)

Shimegi   A Hurrian/Hittite sun god. Asia Minor. (Ferm, 1950: 91)

Shu   A lion-headed god of light, of the atmosphere, whose twin and female counterpart is Tefnut. Egypt. (Budge, 1969, 2: 87–90; Knight, 1915: 122–123)

Shul-pa-uddu   A very early minor god of "solar character." Babylonia, Near East. (Jastrow, 1898: 99)

Si, Si-bavas   The sun god/goddess by whom they swear and who is invoked to punish perjury. The Moksha (Mordvins), Russia. (Paasonen, 1925, 8: 844; Pettazzoni, 1956: 257)

Siberu Dayang Mata-ni-ari   The goddess of rice is also considered "the light of the sky" and represents fertility. Sumatra, Indonesia. (Sierksma, 1960: 26–27)

Sikkut, Sakkut   A name of Ninurta as god of the sunrise and the opener of the gate for Shamash. Canaan, Near East. (Langdon, 1931: 34–35)

Simike   The Hurrian sun god who forms a triad with Tesup and Hepit. Near East. (Buren, 1943: 83; Moscati, 1962: 199)

Sing Bonga   The sun god and the creator, and among some considered the supreme god. The Santals, the Hos, the Kols. India. (Mukherjea, 1962: 174; Biswas, 1956: 102; Elwin, 1949: 50; Majumdar, 1950: 251–265)

Singi   The sun. The Bondo, Koraput District, India. (Elwin, 1949: 72)

Sin Kando   The sun. The Santal in Katikund, India. (Biswas, 1956: 103)

Sirma Thakoor   The sun who with Ote Boram created the earth and all things. The Kol, India. (Elwin, 1949: 18)

Siva   In Bali Siva is the sun, the supreme deity, highest of the gods with many names (Paramesvara, Mahesvara, Mahadeva, Srikanda, Sudasina, Givaka, Sangkara,

Garba, Soma, Vrekanda, Krittivasas, and many more). As a phallic god he is god of the fertility of all things, the source of all life, and is considered bisexual. Indonesia. (Friederich, 1959: 39–43; Covarrubias, 1937: 290; Swellengrebel, 1960: 63; Grader, 1960: 92, 123)

slukʷal   The sun is invoked for good fortune, and approves of good. The Twana, Washington. (Elmendorf, 1960: 530–531)

Soerja   The Sun. Bali, Indonesia. (Belo, 1953: 23)

Sol   (1) Roman god—the physical sun, the orb itself. (Altheim, 1937: 129; Madden, 1930: 80) (2) Teutonic goddess of the sun. The charioteer driving the horses. She is the daughter of Mundilfari, sister of Mani, and wife of Glaur. (Guerber, 1895: 14; MacCulloch, 1964: 183; Anderson, 1891: 458; Grimm, 1883, 2: 705)

Solboni   God of the dawn. The Buryat, Siberia. (Eliade, 1964: 75)

St. Soleil   The sun—in Mirebalais, Haiti. West Indies. (Herskovits, 1937: 281)

Sozon   A mounted solar god. Thrace and Asia Minor. (Pettazzoni, 1956: 182)

Spokani   The sun, son of Amotken. The Flathead Indians, Oregon and Idaho. (Clark, 1966: 67)

Sugu-n-sua   At Iraca a name of Bochica as the sun. The Chibcha Indians, Colombia. (Kroeber, 1946, 2: 909)

the Sun   The visible representation of Kitche Manitou, the supreme being, "giving light for guidance and heat for growth." The Ojibway, Great Lakes area. (Johnston, 1976: 149). The Potawatomi, Wisconsin. (Skinner, 1913: 80; Schoolcraft, 1857: 320; Larousse, 1968: 427))

Sunna   The sun goddess possessed magical charms for healing. Sister of Sinthgunt (Sindgund). Germany. (MacCulloch, 1964: 18; Grimm, 1880: 224; 1883, 2: 705)

Suraj Narayan   The name of Surya as he is worshipped among various tribes of the Doms. India. (Briggs, 1953: 542; Crooke, 1894: 5)

Surias   The sun god among the Kassites. Asia Minor. (Campbell, 1964: 122)

Surjahi   The sun spirit worshipped for health and abundance by the Oraon. Seems to be identified with Dharmes. India. (Roy, 1928: 80–81)

Surli, Nuikukui   The " 'Son of the Mother,' the one of the Sun or of the East" whose mask or dances appear with those of Heiséi as the " 'Masters of the East and of the West,' of life and death" in the annual fertility ceremonies. The Cagaba, the Kogi, Colombia. (Reichel-Dolmatoff, 1949/50: 137, 142)

Suruj Bhagwan, Biri, Suruj   The sun god, a name used when the sun itself is meant. The Oraon, India. (Roy, 1928: 21)

Sūryā   A minor solar goddess, daughter of Savitr, and intended as the bride of Soma but won by the Asvins. She was also loved by her brother Pusan. India. (Bhattacharji, 1970: 214, 224; Danielou, 1964: 124)

Surya   He is the outer aspect, the physical form, of the Vedic Sun representing its light and warmth and stimulating men to activity. He is particularly venerated as a god of healing and the bestower of longevity. He marks the days and in turn is controlled by Varuna. Surya is an all-seeing observer and judge of mankind. His wives are variously given as Sanjna, Suvarcala, and Ushas, who is also named as his daughter. He is the father also of the Asvins and Yama. India and Java. In Bali he is the chief god of the pantheon and is identified with Siva. (Elwin, 1949: 51; Macdonell, 1897: 30, 31; Basak, 1953: 51, 92; Martin, 1914: 35, 36; Bhattacharji, 1970: 211–212; Friederich, 1959: 51; Covarrubias, 1937: 316; Pandit, 1970: 29–45)

Suryan   The sun is worshipped by the Kaniyan who are astrologers. Southern India. (Thurston, 1909, 3: 193)

Sutalidihi, Unelanuhi   The name by which the sun is called by the priests. The common name used by the people is Nuñda. The Cherokee, North Carolina and Tennessee. (Hagar, 1906: 357; Burland, 1965: 150; Mooney and Olbrechts, 1932: 20)

su tsuk rum   The sun god of the Lepchas. Sikkim. (Siiger, 1967: 145)

Svarozits, Svarozic   Slavic god of the sun and of fire. Son of Svarog. (Queval, 1968: 107; Machal, 1918: 298)

Svasar, Svasara   Another name for the sun god Surya. India. (Bhattacharji, 1970: 163, 224)

Swayxtix, Suaixtis   Slavic god of light. Prussia. (Gimbutas, 1963: 202)

Iupiter Tabaliaenus   A solar god—from a church of San Vicente in Grases (Willaviciosa), Spain. (Martinez, 1962: 95)

Tabaminarro A goddess of twilight, "represented by a star." The Achaguas, West Indies. (Lovén, 1935: 590–591)

Tagarod Teutonic god of the morning. (Grimm, 1883, 2: 884)

Tahar In Atchin "a being who is usually supposed to have created man and to take an interest in his welfare." He "represents both sun and moon." New Hebrides, Melanesia. (Rivers, 1925, 9: 353)

T'ai Yang Chinese god of the sun. (Day, 1940: 165; Werner, 1934: 179)

Talatumsi Dawn Woman is "the mother of the novices" in initiatory ceremonies and "the owner 'of all the crops,' and the goddess of childbirth." The Hopi, Arizona. (Titiev, 1971: 131, 134, 137)

Tallaios, Talos Cretan sun god, whose form was that of a bull, was identified with Zeus. He was also considered the inventor "of such devices as the compasses and the potter's wheel" and was also invoked in oaths. Greece. (Willetts, 1962: 52; Fairbanks, 1907: 88; Roscher, 1965, 5: 21)

Tamagata An ancient sun god with whom Tamagastat is identified. Nicaragua. (Lothrop, 1926: 66)

Tama-nui-te-ra The beneficent sun, called 'Ra for short. The Maori, New Zealand. (Best, 1924: 109; Andersen, 1928: 200; Henry, 1928: 466)

Tamapah The Sun-Father, god of the day. The Shoshoni or Snake Indians, Idaho. (Brackett, 1879: 330)

Tama-uawhiti With Tane, Tama-nui-te-ra, personifies the sun. The Maori, New Zealand. (Best, 1924: 174)

Tami-ta-ra The sun god of the Moriori of the Chatham Islands, New Zealand. (Shand, 1894: 89)

Tane God of light and of the male generative power. The god of the forests and of all its life. His wife was Hinehaone. Their daughter Hineatauira later became his wife, but left for the underworld when she discovered their true relationship, where she became Hine-nui-te-po. The Maori, New Zealand. Known throughout Polynesia but not always as a god of light. (Best, 1924: 236; Wohlers, 1877: 343–344; Henry, 1928: 371; Benedict, 1916: 115; Howells, 1948: 222; Hongi, 1920: 26)

Tansendo The god who lives in the sun. The Tewa, Pueblo Indians, New Mexico. (Harrington, 1907/08: 45)

Tars The omnipotent sun whose invocations were made in the morning. The Pima, Arizona. (Russell, 1904/05: 250)

tät, táat The sun, brother of the moon. The Opata Sonora, Mexico. (Johnson, 1949: 33)

Tata lat kola "Grandfather Sun . . . the male principle" was revered and invoked for help in numerous difficulties. Watubela Island, Indonesia. (Frazer, 1926: 667)

Tautobitatmo A sky god who makes the daylight. North Andaman Islands, Bay of Bengal. (Radcliffe-Brown, 1967: 144)

Tavapitsi The Sun in ancient times was very hot. Tavutsi, Cottontail Rabbit, ambushed him and threw a stone which broke off huge chunks of the sun reducing its heat so that life became tolerable. The Chemehuevis, California, Nevada, and Arizona. (Laird, 1976: 152–154)

Ta-vi The sun god of the Ute Indians. Utah and Colorado. (Powell, 1879/80: 24; Emerson, 1884: 80)

Tawa The sun god of the Walpi Indians. Arizona. (Fewkes, 1896: 247; Burland, 1965: 14)

Tayau, Tayaupa "Father Sun . . . to whom belong the turkey, the rabbit, the tiger, the red-tailed hawk, the quail, the giant woodpecker, the swallow, and the cardinal-bird." The Huichol Indians of Jalisco, and the Cora Indians of Mesa del Nayar, Nayarit. Mexico. (Seler, 1925, 6: 829; Chamberlain, 1900: 305; Guillermo, 1971: 780; Furst, 1972: 140)

Te-ao *See* **Ao.** "Te Po (darkness) . . . begat Te-ao (light), who begat Ao-marama (daylight)." South Island, New Zealand. (Mackenzie, n.d.: 183)

Te-ata-tuhi Goddess of the early dawn, mother of the moon by Rangi. New Zealand. (MacKenzie, n.d.: 209)

Teendo The sun goddess who is malevolent. Adelaide, Australia. (Woods, 1879: 166)

Teikem-tilaen The "Sun-Man" whose wife in some tales is Yiñe'a-ñe'ut. The Koryak, Siberia. (Jochelson, 1908, 6: 31)

Tel The sun god of the Igassana who sends death. Ethiopia and Sudan. (Cerulli, 1956: 31; Mbiti, 1970, 2: 133)

Tem A solar god—"the personification of the setting sun." Identified with Ra as Ra-Tem. Egypt. (Budge, 1969, 1: 349, 351)

Temet   The all-seeing sun who watches during the day for wrong-doing. The Luiseño, California. (Du Bois, 1908: 97)

Tepeü   He is the rising sun and an hypostasis of Cabahuil as creator god-Seven. The Quiché, Guatemala. (Girard, 1979: 31–33)

Tesana, Thesan   Etruscan goddess of the dawn, equated with Aurora. Italy. (Herbig, 1925, 5: 534; Leland, 1963: 75; Rawlinson, 1885: 123)

Tezcatlanextía   The "mirror which illumines things"—an aspect of Ometéotl as lord of the day. Aztec, Mexico. (León-Portilla, 1982: 86)

Tezcatlipoca   A Toltec sun and war god adopted by the Aztec where he is, as well, a god of death and resurrection, of the "Smoking Mirror" used in divination. He is a god of the heavens—as the day the red Tezcatlipoca, as the night and black—and of the underworld. He is a versatile and variable god of duality, a god of darkness and light, of good qualities as well as evil, of strife but also of prosperity. Mexico. (Leonard, 1967: 54, 103; Alexander, 1920: 61–66; Caso, 1958: 27–31; Spence, 1923: 91, 103; Vaillant, 1962: 139, 142, 148)

Thairgin   The "Dawn," and a name of the supreme being. The Koryak, Siberia. (Czaplica, 1969: 262)

Theia   A Greek Titaness, daughter of Uranus and Gaea, and the sister/wife of Hyperion, and mother of Helios, Eos, and Selene, and so was "often considered as the principle of Light." (Barthell, 1971: 12, 53; Kerenyi, 1951: 21–22; Roscher, 1965, 5: 555; Hesiod-Brown, 1981: 56–57, 63)

Tiida-gami   The sun deity of Okinawa. Ryukyu Islands, Pacific. (Lebra, 1966: 223)

Tiknis, Tiklis   A demon who attacks the sun causing the eclipse. Lithuania. (Grimm, 1883, 2: 707)

Timet   The sun, born of Tuukumit and Tamaayawut. The mountain Acagchemem, San Juan Capistrano, California. (Boscana, 1933: 116)

Timondonar   The god of light whose brother is Ariconte, the night. The Tupi Indians, Brazil. (Rhys, 1937: 15)

Tlahuizcalpantecuhtli   The god of the dawn is Venus, the morning star. Aztec, Mexico. (Duran, 1971: 162n; Vaillant, 1962: 150)

Tlalchitonatiuh   A manifestation of Tonatiuh when near the earth—ergo, the rising or setting sun. Mexico. (Tozzer, 1957: 116; Thompson, 1970: 328)

Tñairgin, Tñahitnin   "Morning-Dawn"—he has "several divisions . . . the 'Top of the Dawn' (Tñesqan) and 'Right-hand Dawn' (Mratñairgin). 'Genuine Dawn' (Lietñairgin), and 'Left-hand Dawn' (Ñachi-tñairgin). The last-named is considered to be the brother of Darkness (Wusquus)." His wife is Tñe-ceivune. The Chukchee, the Koryak, Siberia. (Bogoras, 1904/09: 303, 312)

Tñe-ceivune   "Dawn-walking-Woman," wife of Tñairgin. The Chukchee, Siberia. (Bogoras, 1904/09: 303)

Tonatiuh   The sun god of the present age (Four Earthquake—which is expected to be destroyed by earthquakes). He gives light and heat, is god of time as well as a god of warriors, receiving human sacrifices from them. He is also called Piltzintecutli, Totec, and Xipilli. Aztec, Mexico. (Vaillant, 1962: 139; Spence, 1923: 300; Burland, 1967: x; Alexander, 1920: 54; Caso, 1958: 32; León-Portilla, 1982: 51)

Torodiu   God of the mid-day sun. Andaman Islands, Bay of Bengal. (Radcliffe-Brown, 1967: 144)

Tortali   The omniscient sun god. Pentecost Island, New Hebrides, Melanesia. (Pettazzoni, 1956: 342)

Toru-shom-pet   The "sun, stands for their principle of good." The Tupi, Brazil. (Spence, 1925, 2: 837)

Tou Mu   The goddess of light of Buddhism is also the goddess of the North Star and/or the goddess of the Northern Dipper. She is invoked to protect from disease and from war, and is also the patroness of fortunetellers. China. (Day, 1940: 27; Werner, 1932: 511; Graham, 1961: 180, 186)

Tsi-pas, Tsi   The sun god or goddess by whom they swear is invoked for punishment of perjury. The Erza (Mordvins), Russia. Same as Si-bavas of the Moksha. (Paasonen, 1925, 8: 844; Pettazzoni, 1956: 257)

Tso   The sun goddess/god of the Yuchi. South Carolina and Georgia. (Speck, 1909: 102, 106–107; Alexander, 1964: 56)

Tsohanoai   The invisible god, visible to man as the sun. He is the creator of game animals. Father of Nayenezgani, husband of Estsanatlehi. The Navaho, Arizona and New Mexico. *See* **jóhonaa'áí, Johanoai.** (Matthews, 1902: 19, 30; Alexander, 1964: 155, 157)

Tuina The sun of the Yanas. California. (Curtin, 1903: 281)

Tung Chün The "god of the sun rising in the East." China. (Ferguson, 1937: 90)

Tutu A solar god whose symbol is a lion. Also known as Ar-hes-nefer. Son of Net and a form of Shu. Egypt. (Budge, 1969, 1: 463–464) Among the Akkadians of Asia Minor he was the god of the setting sun, and a prophet-god. (Sayce, 1898: 117)

T'uub, T'uup "Little One"—The lord and keeper of the sun. Favorite son of Hachäkyum. The Lacandon, Chiapas, Mexico. (Perera and Bruce, 1972: 134, 310)

Tzaiic Mayan sun god of Jacalteca. Guatemala. (Thompson, 1970: 236)

Tzakol One of four regent gods of the quarters of the cosmos, of the directions, who with Bitol, Alom, and Cajolom, through mediation, brought about "the birth of light." The Quiché, Guatemala. (Girard, 1979: 29)

Udzal Babylonian god of the rising sun. Same as Ninib. Near East. (Jastrow, 1898: 166)

Ugelianged The omniscient supreme being is "identified with the Sun." The Pelew Islanders, Micronesia. (Pettazzoni, 1956: 170, 343)

Uha Soldong The god of the dawn is the creator of horses. The Buriat, Mongol, Siberia. (Curtin, 1909: 46)

Uhubaput The sun god and creator is their chief deity. The Sumu Indians, Nicaragua and Honduras. (Leach, 1950, 2: 1148; Conzemius, 1932: 129)

Uis Neno God of the sun, of the day. Timor, Indonesia. (Middelkoop, 1960: 23; Cunningham, 1958: 118)

Ulghen The Altaian god of light is invoked for protection from the evil spirit. Siberia. (Chadwick, 1936: 77)

Umu(m) "Day," a deity associated with Shamash. Near East. (Vriezen, 1963: 58; Roberts, 1972: 55)

Unelanuhi, Geyaguga The latter name shows feminine sex. The sun is the apportioner of time, "their most powerful spirit," sister of the moon. Unelanuhi is the ritualistic name invoked very humbly and propitiatingly in ritual and in medicine gathering. She may cause headache, fever, blisters, and is invoked for cures. Commonly called Nuñda, Nunta, and worshipped also by ballplayers. The Cherokee, North Carolina and Tennes-

see. (Mooney, 1885/86: 340–341; Mooney and Olbrechts, 1932: 20, 21; Spence, 1925, 3: 504; Maclean, 1876: 436)

Upulero The sun god is the male principle of impregnation, is invoked for fertility and abundance. The Moluccas, Babar Archipelago, Indonesia. (Hartland, 1925, 9: 822; Kern, 1925, 8: 347; Maity, 1971: 92; Eliade, 1959: 124)

!Urisib God of the day, of daylight. Son of Tsui/goab. The Khoi-Khoi (Hottentot), South Africa. (Hahn, 1881: 141)

!Urisis The sun is the wife of Tsui/goab. She is also called Soris. The Khoi-Khoi (Hottentot), South Africa. (Hahn, 1881: 127, 141)

Uru God of light. Canaan, Near East. (Paton, 1925, 3: 181)

Urun-Aiy-Toyon A benevolent god of light, a sky and creator god. The Yakut, Siberia. (Czaplicika, 1969: 277; Tokarev and Gurvich, 1964: 280; Jochelson, 1900/ 02: 207)

Uru-te-ngangana One of the seventy sons of Papa and Rangi. He is a god of light and is the father of the sun and the moon by Moe-ahuru, and of the stars by Hine-turama. The Maori, New Zealand. (Best, 1924: 95, 97)

Ushas Goddess of the dawn, daughter of Dyaus, the sky. She reawakens men and brings good and prosperity. She is also a dancer like Siva and Indra, but also, as a measurer of time, she implies the dance of death, and as a courtesan wears out and destroys men by aging them, gaining vital forces by draining them. India. (Bhattacharji, 1970: 223–224; Goldziher, 1877: 93; Ions, 1967: 21; O'Flaherty, 1980: 136–137, 211)

Usil Etruscan god of the sun. Italy. (Rawlinson, 1885: 123; Roscher, 1965, 6: 124)

Usi-Neno God of the sun whose wife is Usi-Afu. They are the source of all creation which provides fertility and growth. He is the personification of the sun itself and represents the male principle. Timor, Indonesia. (Eliade, 1959: 124; Frazer, 1926: 657)

Utaya Tampuran The god of the rising sun. The Pulayas, Southern India. (Thurston, 1909, 2: 87–88)

Utu Sumerian god of the sun and of order and justice. Son of Nanna and brother of Inanna. Near East. (Jacobsen, 1970: 8, 26; Kramer, 1967: 100, 107; Schoeps, 1961: 56)

Uwa shil   The sun is the abode of their highest object of worship. The Natchez, Mississippi. (Swanton, 1928: 482)

Uyungsum   The sun god of the Saora. Orissa, India. (Elwin, 1954: 641)

Vahagn   A god of the sun, of lightning, and of fire, as well as a god of war and of courage. One of the foremost of the gods of Armenia. (Ananikian, 1964: 34, 42; 1925, 1: 799; Jayne, 1962: 196)

Vali   A Teutonic god—"a personification of the lengthening days, . . . god of eternal light." Son of Odin and Rinda destined to survive the twilight of the gods and rule with Vidar. (Guerber, 1895: 152–153; Wagner, 1882: 12)

Varuna   As a god of the heavens he is a god of light whose eye is the sun by day and the moon by night with which he observes mankind. He controls all natural phenomena and is god of the celestial waters, is a god of truth and justice, punitive yet forgiving. India. (Barth, 1921: 17; Macdonell, 1897: 23–26; Martin, 1914: 41)

Vishnu   In his solar aspect Vishnu is a god of light, of the day, bestowing life and growth through the beneficence of the sun. India. In Nepal he is identified with the setting sun. (Bhattacharji, 1970: 15, 16; Crooke, 1894: 3)

Visucius   A native solar god identified with Mercury. The Rhine country, Gaul. (Renel, 1906: 406; Pettazzoni, 1956: 199; MacCulloch, 1911: 24)

Vivasvat, Vivasvant   He was originally mortal (as rejected by Aditi and not named as a god). His brothers fashioned him into the sun. As one of the Adityas and a solar god representing the rising sun and awakening men to consciousness he is the father of the Asvins by Saranyu, the light form of his wife; she abandoned Vivasvant substituting Chaya, her dark form, who bore him Manu, the ancestor of men. India. (Ions, 1967: 20; Danielou, 1964: 124–125; Macdonell, 1897: 42–43; Brown, 1961: 285; O'Flaherty, 1980: 175, 283)

Wah'-Kon-Tah, Wa-koⁿ-da hoⁿ-bado   in the Dhegiha tribe   "Grandfather." The sun is the god of the day and the creator. He is the symbol of life; is greatly feared as he sends lightning, thunder, and tornados when angry. The Osage Indians, Dakota/Nebraska. (La Flesche, 1928: 74; Mathews, 1982: 11, 32, 529, 744)

Wainako   The sun god is the son of Jugumishanta and Morufonu. His wife is Moa'ri and brother is Wajubu, the moon. He is also known as Pisiwa. The Kamano, Ururufa, Jate, and Fore, New Guinea. (Berndt, 1965: 80)

Wakahiru-Me   Goddess of the morning sun and sister of Amaterasu-Omikami. Japan. (Kato, 1926: 13)

Wakan Tanka Kin   The sun god of the Oglala (Dakota). Plains Indians. (Eliade, 1967: 12)

Wala   The dawn. The Fox Indians, Wisconsin. (Burland, 1965: 149)

Wan, Wanaka   The "sun-halo" is in constant association with Kumkamtch. The Klamath, Oregon. (Gatschet, 1890: lxxxii)

Waptokwa   The anthropomorphized sun, the creator and father of all Indians. The Savante and the Sherente, Brazil. (Nimuendaju, 1942: 84; Maybury-Lewis, 1967: 286)

Waqa   The Sun is also the omniscient supreme being and sky god—invoked in oaths. The Galla, Uganda. (Pettazzoni, 1956: 6, 20, 41)

Wazeparkwa   A goddess, the mother of the sun, who causes eclipses. The Sherente, Brazil. (Nimuendaju, 1942: 84)

Wi   The Sun is the fourth in existence of the superior gods, is omniscient, all-seeing, the "most powerful and august." Wi's *ton* (power) is in fire; his color is red. "This color is invoked by shamans, and it represents the coming and going of the Sun." He provides everything; appears in visions only to dancers of the Sun Dance. His wife is Hanwi, the moon, whom he lost because he allowed Ite to come between them. The Lakota/Oglala, northern Plains Indians. (Walker, 1980: 35, 50, 52, 53, 95, 108, 114; Powers, 1977: 54, 70; One Feather, 1982: 49)

Wungtena, Wne   The sun of the Nankanse whose wife is Namboa or Mwarega, the moon. Ghana. (Rattray, 1932: 335)

Wupamow   A sun god of the Hopi Indians. Arizona. (Fewkes, 1902: 26)

Wuriupranala   A daughter of Mudungkala who became the Sun Woman. The Tiwi of Melville Island, Australia. (Mountford, 1958: 24–25, 35; Lamb, 1973: May, 3)

Wurusemu   The Proto-Hattic/Hittite sun goddess was the principal deity and wife of the weather god, Taru. Asia Minor. (Ferm, 1950: 90, 92; Gurney, 1952: 136, 139; James, 1960: 95)

Wuwuyomo   A sun god of the Honani clan. Hopi Indians, Arizona. (Fewkes, 1902: 26)

xa·ctčé·'oγan (xashshe'oghan)   A companion of Talking God, and the god of the sunset. The Navaho, Arizona and New Mexico. *See also* **Hastsehogan.** (Reichard, 1950: 77–78, 502–503)

xašč'elͭxi'i (xashchelthi'i)   God of the dawn and of the east—Talking God. He is associated with Blanca Peak with the dawn, and with San Francisco Peak with the twilight. The Navaho, Arizona and New Mexico. *See also* **Hastseyalti.** (Haile, 1947: 3, 5, 6)

Xatel-Ekwa   The sun goddess. The Vogul, Siberia. (Roheim, 1954: 31)

xayolͭká·ɪ 'esͭzạ·   Dawn woman, mother of Talking God. The Navaho, Arizona and New Mexico. *See also* **hayoolͭkaaɪ asdzą́ą́.** (Haile, 1947: 15)

xayolͭka·ɪ xastxi·n   Dawn man, father of Talking God. The Navaho, Arizona and New Mexico. *See also* **hayoolͭkááɪ hastiin.** (Haile, 1947: 15)

Xungwid   The sun who initiates the shaman. The Kwakiutl of Knight Inlet, British Columbia. (Boas, 1966: 142)

Xursu Dazibogu   The son of Svarogu is the sun and the giver of wealth. Slavic Russia. (Leach, 1950, 2: 1027)

Xwarenah   Light—a beneficent and protective celestial god. Iran. (Gray, 1930: 120–122, 224)

Yani, Yanigelua   The sun, our Father, who is invoked against thieves. Sometimes sun and father are the same, sometimes the sun is his light. The Dom, New Guinea. (Aufenanger, 1962: 29, 30, 32)

Yar   The sun became the husband of Usi-diu who was carved out of a plum tree. Father of Makunaima and Pia.

The Warao, Guiana and Venezuela. (Levi-Strauss, 1973: 215, 217)

Yarihbol, Yarhibol   The sun god at Palmyra. Syria. (Cook, 1930: 220; Vriezen, 1963: 67)

Yatokia   The "(Sun Father) created two sons, Kowwituma and Watsusi." The Zuñi Indians, New Mexico. (Stevenson, 1901/02: 24)

Yeloje, Pugu   The beneficent sun god is "the guardian of justice and of morality." The Yukaghir, Siberia. (Jochelson, 1900/02: 141)

Yerpeyen   The name of Yeloje, the sun, in the Tundra dialect. The Yukaghir, Siberia. (Jochelson, 1900/02: 141)

Yhi   The goddess of the sun who caused things to grow and "brought out insects, water, fishes, birds and animals" from the caverns. Australia. (Reed, 1965: 15, 21)

Zeus   As a celestial deity he is a god of light who controls the atmospheric phenomena. Greece. (Murray, 1935: 36; Larousse, 1973: 114)

Zio, Ziu, Tyr, Tiw, and variants   The Teutonic sky god, god of light and of day, is also a god of storms and developed into a god of war. (Grimm, 1880: 133, 193–194; Pettazzoni, 1956: 221–222; Fiske, 1900: 108; Thorpe, 1851: 231)

Zorya   Dual Slavonic goddesses of the dawn, daughters of the sun—Zorya Utrennyaya "Aurora of the Morning" and Zorya Vechernyaya "Aurora of the Evening." They are charged with opening and closing the gates of the sun's palace. (Larousse, 1968: 285)

Zuhe, Xue   The sun. One of the names of Bochia. The Chibcha, Colombia. (Alexander, 1920: 202; Osborne, 1968: 110)

8

Lunar Gods: Eclipses

Àāh, Aah-Tehuti   The moon god, a manifestation of Thoth as the "measurer and regulator of times and seasons," the moon in all phases. Egypt. (Budge, 1969, 1: 409, 412; Knight, 1915: 9)

Acna, Akna   The goddess of the moon is the wife of Chi Chac Chob. Also given as the wife of Qin. She "carries loom to guard against jaguars of" the god Kisin. The Lacandon (Mayan), Mexico. (Thompson, 1970: 241; Tozzer, 1941: 10, 148; Cline, 1944: 112)

Adwo   The moon is patron deity of Monday. A child born on this day is under his protection and is given its *kra* (life-giving spirit or power) by him. The Akan, Ghana. (Meyerowitz, 1951: 25)

Aglibol   The god of the moon "who was originally a bull-god." Palmyra, Syria. (Vriezen, 1963: 67; Cook, 1930: 220)

Agunowei   The moon is also the supreme being of a hinterland clan—the Biloforn dialect. Niger Delta, Africa. (Jeffreys, 1972: 730)

Ai-ada   The moon is the husband of the sun, Kun. The Turks of Central Asia. (Czaplicka, 1925, 12: 482)

Akna'   *See* **Acna**

'Alaḫtin   The Moon Goddess provides light at night, is strongly associated with their calendar and is carefully observed by their astronomers. She has cleansing and purifying qualities, causes the movements of the sea, and affects things biological (including women's menses). She is invoked for health and good fortune. 'Alaḫtin keeps the score in the nightly peon game. The Chumash, California. (Hudson and Underhay, 1978: 75–77; Blackburn, 1975: 37)

Alignak   The god of the moon, their chief god, controls natural phenomena such as tides, weather, eclipses and earthquakes, as well as animals and their availability as game, which is dependent upon the behavior of men. The Alaskan Eskimo. (Larousse, 1973: 444)

Amavasya   Goddess of the new moon. India. (Gray, 1930: 133)

Ambolona   The moon—considered a deity or power and included in invocations. The Tanala, Madagascar. (Linton, 1933: 160–161)

Ambulan   The god of the moon. The Mayawyaw of Northern Luzon, Philippines. (Lambrecht, 1932: 21)

'Amm   Qatabanian god of the moon. South Arabia. (Pritchard, 1943: 64; Moscati, 1960: 187; Fahd, 1968: 44)

Amza   The god of the moon and "the god of men," a great part of Ayt'ar (the chief or head of a group of gods who constitute individual parts of him). The Abkhasians, Caucasus. (Janashia, 1937: 127)

Anchimallen, Anchimalen   The beneficent and protective goddess of the moon, wife of the sun. The Araucanian, Chile. (Chamberlain, 1900: 57; Eliade, 1964: 329; Larousse, 1968: 445)

Aningaa, Aningaaq, Aningait   The god of the moon of the Netsilik Eskimo, Canada. (Nungak and Arima, 1969: 114)

Aningarsuaq   The moon spirit—male. The Polar Eskimo, Canada. (Nungak and Arima, 1969: 114)

Aningat, Aningap   Beneficent male spirit of the moon who helps Takanakapsaluk in overseeing the conduct of mankind. Though he punishes, his intervention is more for guidance. He is a god of fertility and fruitfulness and controls the movements of the seal providing good hunting. The Iglulik Eskimo, Canada. (Rasmussen, 1929: 62–63, 73–75)

Anl'algila   The moon whose eclipse "is produced by several deities called Aiq oayosnem, which means 'painting the face black.'" The Bella Coola Indians, British Columbia. (Boas, 1900: 31)

Antare-mah   Deity of the new moon. Iran. (Gray, 1930: 133)

Antevorta   A Roman goddess who represents the waxing moon. She is a goddess of childbirth associated with favorable presentation at birth, and is a goddess of destiny, clairvoyant of the past. (Pettazzoni, 1956: 168; Dumézil, 1966, 1: 393; Roscher, 1965, 2, 1: 192)

Anumati   A goddess associated with the moon as "representing the day before full-moon." She is also a goddess of childbirth and invoked for offspring and for prosperity. India. (Macdonell, 1897: 119; Danielou, 1964: 319; Jayne, 1962: 160; Gray, 1930: 59)

Apām napāt   The "son of water." Originally the name of a vegetation spirit, it became used also to apply to the moon and to its nectar, soma. India. (Eliade, 1958: 159)

Aquit, Metza   Goddess of the moon whose brother is the sun. The Opata, Sonora, Mexico. (Johnson, 1949: 33)

Araua   The moon is considered the sister or the mother of Asis, the sun. The Ndorobo, Kenya and Tanzania. (Millroth, 1965: 44)

Arawa   God of the moon and first son of Tororut and Seta. The Suk of Kenya. Among the Nandi the moon is female and the wife of Asis, the sun. (Beech, 1911: 19; Huntingford, 1953: 134)

Arilpa   The moon. The Kaitish of Central Australia. (Spencer, 1904: 625)

Arke   The moon deity of the Bondo. Koraput District, India. (Elwin, 1949: 72)

Arma   The Hittite moon god. Asia Minor. (Ferm, 1950: 91)

Artemis   Among her numerous aspects is that of goddess of the night and of the moon and its influence on life. Greece. (Murray, 1935: 118; Larousse, 1968: 111; Schoeps, 1961: 131; Morford and Lenardon, 1975: 24)

Ash   The moon god with whom Set is sometimes identified. Libya. (Meyerowitz, 1958: 142)

Ashimbabbar   The name of Nanna, the moon, as "new light." Akkadian/Sumerian/Babylonian. Near East. (Jacobsen, 1970: 25, 26)

Ashtharthet, Ashtoreth   A lion-headed goddess introduced from Syria. A moon goddess, a goddess of war and of horses. Egypt. (Budge, 1969, 2: 178–179)

Aske   An earlier name for Mano, the moon. The Lapps. Northern Europe. (Bosi, 1960: 132; Dioszegi, 1968: 28)

Ataensic, Atahensic, and variants   Goddess of the moon and also of waters. She was the mother of twin sons, Good Mind and Evil Mind, and the grandmother of twins—Iouskeha and Tawiscara. She is also considered the creator of heaven and earth and of mankind. The Huron Indians, Ontario. (Schoolcraft, 1857: 317; Voegelin, 1944: 374; Brinton, 1868: 123, 170; Emerson, 1884: 75, 116, 119)

Atninja   The god of the moon is "associated with the opossum totem." The Arunta, Central Australia. (Spencer and Gillen, 1968: 564; Spencer, 1904: 625)

Atninja aluquirta   The Full Moon. The Arunta, Australia. (Spencer, 1927: 499)

Atninja kurka iwuminta   The Half Moon. **Atninja kurka utnamma**   The New Moon. **Atninja urteratera**   The Three-quarter Moon. The Arunta, Australia. (Spencer, 1927: 498, 499)

Avya   God of the sun and of the moon. He gives light and heat by day and less light and cold by night. He causes menstruation. The Cubeo Indians, Colombia. (Goldman, 1940: 245)

Awo   The bisexual planet moon is the dispenser of *kra* (life-giving spirit or power) to the abosom born on Monday, whose character will be "Calm, peaceful, cool and protective." The Akan, Ghana. (Meyerowitz, 1958: 47)

Bahloo   The moon god, husband of the Morning Star. Australia. (Reed, 1965: 18)

Barbij   The moon is revered by the Bhils, and by whom they swear. Gujarat area, India. (Naik, 1956: 172, 185)

Bast   As a cat-headed goddess she is a goddess of the moon and mother of Khensu; also a goddess of childbirth. As a lion-headed goddess she is a solar deity and associated with the heat and warmth of the sun. Egypt. (Budge, 1969, 1: 444–448; Knight, 1915: 30; Jayne, 1962: 84)

Bendis Phrygian/Thracian goddess of the moon as well as of fertility in nature. Wife of Sabazius. (Larousse, 1968: 111, 160; Fairbanks, 1907: 133; Grimm, 1888: 1398)

Bil A minor Norse goddess, sister of Hjuki, with whom she makes the spots on the moon—"two people carrying a basket on a pole." For some reason she is considered a goddess but she is not given the status of a deity. (MacCulloch, 1964: 183–184)

Bulan The moon is a guardian of the earth with the sun whose wife she became. The Bagobo, Philippines. (Jocano, 1969: 31)

byamo dkarmo The personification of the moon. Tibet. (Francke, 1925, 8: 78)

Caelestis Carthaginian goddess of the moon worshipped also in Rome. (Ferguson, 1970: 53, 215; Madden 1930: 83)

Cairé The "full moon." The Tupi, Brazil. (Spence, 1925, 2: 837)

Candra The moon, the god of the night, is associated with the lotus and is also called Kumudavandhava; as the full moon, called Purnacandra. He rides a chariot drawn by ten geese. His principal wives are Kanti and Sobha. Nepal. (Pal and Chattacharyya, 1969: 8, 22)

Carmentis The Roman goddess of women, of childbirth, and pregnancy was an early goddess of the moon. She was feted in the two Carmentalia in January which are related to the phases of the moon. (Pettazzoni, 1956: 168)

Mait' Carrefour As a power of darkness he is associated with the moon and midnight, "his noon." He is also a god of magicians. Haiti, West Indies. (Deren, 1953: 101–102)

Catití The new moon of the Tupi. Brazil. (Spence, 1925, 2: 837)

Chanahl The moon who was destined to "grow old quickly and die," then to come alive again, was the smaller portion formed when Sas, the sun, who was too strong and powerful, was split by Tulchuherris. The Wintu, California. (Curtin, 1903: 157–158)

Chandi Mata The moon. A deity whose tattooing symbol can only be worn after marriage when the hair is parted. "Chandi Mata will preserve and guard the parting of the hair . . . because the parting can only be worn so long as her husband is alive." The Gond, Central Provinces, India. (Russell, 1916, 3: 127)

Chando Omol, Chanala The goddess of the moon and wife of Singa-bonga. The Mundas, Bengal. (Crooke, 1925, 5: 3)

Chandra The moon, identified with Soma, though originally probably an individual god. India and Bali. (Crooke, 1894: 66; Ions, 1967: 20; Friederich, 1959: 51; Grader, 1969, 1: 143)

Chandran The moon is worshipped by the Kaniyan who are astrologers. Southern India. (Thurston, 1909, 3: 193)

Ch'ang-o, Heng-o The goddess of the moon and wife of Shen I, the Divine Archer. China. (Werner, 1932: 43, 418–419; Larousse, 1968: 379; Schafer, 1980: 51)

Ix Chel The goddess of the moon is also a goddess of childbirth and pregnancy and of weaving wherein she is benevolent. As a goddess of destructive waters she is malevolent. Mayan, Mexico and Guatemala. (Morley, 1946: 223, 230; Tozzer, 1941: 10, 154; Nicholson, 1967: 115; Thompson, 1970: 242)

Chiang, The Empress "The goddess of the star T'ai-yin (the moon)." China. (Werner, 1932: 58)

Chíchipáchu A demon of the night, half dog and half woman. An eclipse occurs when she starts eating the moon. The Cuna Indians, Panama. (Nordenskiold, 1930: 20, 21)

Chuh Kamuy "Goddess of Sun and Moon . . . mediates between the Ainu and other deities. The sun . . . (daytime moon) and the moon . . . (dark moon), are considered the same female deity, who is the most important of all sky deities." Sakhalin. (Ohnuku-Tierney, 1974: 103)

Maia Cirikli, Maia Dula The moon god of the Aka-Jeru tribe. He can transform himself into a pig. Andaman Islands, Bay of Bengal. (Radcliffe-Brown, 1967: 141)

Coyolxuahqui Goddess of the moon, daughter of Coatlicue and sister of Huitzilopochtli, Tezcatlipoca, Centzonhuitznauac. Aztec, Mexico. (Vaillant, 1962: 150; León-Portilla, 1961: 324, 461–462; Spence, 1923: 66, 324; Burland, 1967: ix)

Cutzi Tarascan goddess of the moon, created by Curicaueri. Wife of the Sun. Mexico. (Boyd, n.d.: 2)

Damhauja The "moon just before renewal." The Yana, California. (Curtin, 1903: 425)

Deak Pordjar The all-knowing deity who lives in the moon. The Toba Batak, Indonesia. (Pettazzoni, 1956: 339)

Diana A goddess of numerous aspects, many of which seem to be attributed to her through her identification with Artemis. She was considered a goddess of the moon, a goddess of women, of procreation and birth, as well as a goddess of the woods, of hunting. Italy. (Bulfinch, 1898: 9; Dumézil, 1966, 2: 407–411; Fairbanks, 1907: 140)

Dobeiba The moon, who is also goddess of the storm and punitively expresses her anger with thunder and lightning, the destruction of crops, is offered human sacrifices frequently to appease her and to restore her waning strength. The Río Sucío area, Colombia. (Trimborn, 1968: 102–103)

Duan-luteh The personification of the moon, consort of Duadlerwuan, the supreme god and the sun. The Kei Archipelago, Indonesia. (Frazer, 1926: 663)

Ensum The name of Nanna as the half moon. Akkadian/Summerian/Babylonian. Near East. (Jacobsen, 1970: 25, 26)

Etpos-Oyka The moon, brother of Numi-Torum. The Mansi, Siberia. (Michael, 1963: 209)

Etrah, Terah Phoenician moon god, father of Sib'ani. Near East. (Larousse, 1968: 79, 80)

Funan The goddess of the moon whose consort is the sun. Timor, Indonesia. (Frazer, 1926: 658)

Gakko The moon deity. Japan. (Eliot, 1935: 140)

Geyaguga The name by which the moon is called by the priests. The common people use "Nuñda that dwells in the night." The Cherokee, North Carolina and Tennessee. (Hagar, 1906: 357)

Gleti The goddess of the moon is the wife of Lissa, the sun. The Ewe, Dahomey. (Mockler-Ferryman, 1925, 9: 275; Ellis, 1890: 65)

Gomaj The goddess of the moon whose name is the same as that of the sun god. They are the principal deities of the Korku. Gomaj is also a general term for a god. The Central Provinces, India. (Russell, 1916, 3: 559; Frazer, 1926: 616)

Gwakko-Bosatsu The personification of the moon. Japanese Buddhism. Skt. Chandra-prabha. (Eliseev, 1963: 428)

Haiatiloq Called " 'The master of the moon,' the pestilence (Haiatiloq), appears as a powerful deity." The Tsimshian Indians, British Columbia. (Chamberlain, 1925, 4: 740)

Haine The goddess of the moon, wife of Ishoye, the sun, and grandmother of Shashaya, the morning star. Haine is sometimes given as male. The Hadzapi, Tanzania. (Millroth, 1965: 40–41)

Hana The daughter of Honabe and Timbu became the moon and an important deity. The Huli, New Guinea. (Glasse, 1965: 33–34)

Hanwi The moon was created by Wi, the sun, to be his companion. When assisting Mahpiyato in the creation of animals, they formed those having "horns and hooves." Hanwi was shamed when Wi let Ite come between them, and Skan judged Hanwi "free to go her own way . . . " giving her her own time, the Moon Time. She rules the night. The Oglala, Plains Indians. (Powers, 1977: 54, 70; Pettazzoni, 1956: 384; Walker, 1980: 50, 53; One Feather, 1982: 49)

Haubas "said to be the moon as the cause of ebb-tide." The Sabaeans, Yemen. (Tritton, 1925, 10: 882)

Hecate A goddess whose powers extended to all regions. In the heavenly sphere she was a goddess of the moon, of night and of darkness. Usually given as the daughter of Perses and Asteria. Greece. (Neumann, 1955: 170; Murrya, 1935: 76–77; Barthell, 1971: 51; Kerenyi, 1951: 35–37)

Helena Greek goddess of the moon in Sparta. (Schoeps, 1961: 131)

Heru-Aāh A name of Horus as a moon-god, in the Pyramid Texts. Egypt. (Budge, 1969, 1: 497)

Heru-merti A form of Horus—"a local form of the god Amsu, or Khem, or Min, as the Moon." Egypt. (Budge, 1969, 1: 469–470)

Hina Goddess of the moon in many areas of Polynesia. In the Society Islands she guards those travelling at night. Among the Maori she appears variously as sister/wife/mother of Maui. Same as Ina, Sina. (Gifford, 1924: 19,

181; Henry, 1928: 151, 462; Best, 1924: 131, 134; Williamson, 1933: 97, 105)

Hina-nui-te-a'ara The name of the goddess of the moon on Raiatea, Society Islands, Polynesia. (Henry, 1928: 214)

Hina-te-iwaiwa Goddess of the moon and of parturition. The Maori, New Zealand. (Hongi, 1920: 27)

Hina-uri Goddess of the dark phase of the moon and a goddess of childbirth. The Maori, New Zealand. (Best, 1924: 131; Hongi, 1920: 26; Andersen, 1928: 212, 237)

Hine-korako A deity who represents "the lunar halo or bow." The Maori, New Zealand. (Best, 1924: 238)

Hintogolopi The moon who with the sun, Maluaga, ruled the heavens. New Ireland, Melanesia. (Cox, 1913: 198)

hme?tik The moon who is the mother of the sun. They are the principal deities of the Mayan. Chamula, Mexico. (Gossen, 1958: 137–138)

Horsel A Germanic goddess of the moon. (Fiske, 1900: 28)

Hur-ki An Akkadīan/Babylonian lunar goddess. Near East. (Goldziher, 1877: 75)

Ix-huyne Mayan goddess of the moon. Mexico and Guatemala. (Nicholson, 1967: 127)

Huythaca Malevolent goddess of the moon. The Muyscas of Bogotá, Colombia. (Lang, 1887: 129)

Iaē The moon, brother of the sun. Together they forced the "urubutsin (king vulture), the bird's chief" to give them the day. The Kamaiura, Xingu River area, Brazil. (Villas Boas, 1973: 65, 89–93)

Igaluk The moon deity of the Alaskan Eskimo. (Burland, 1965: 148)

Il, Ilah One of the names of the moon god. South Arabia. (Gray, 1957: 123; Langdon, 1931: 5)

Ilazki The Moon—also called Illargi, Iratagi, Iretagi, Idetargi, Goiko. She is usually called Grandmother, and, like the sun, is considered a daughter of the earth. The Basques, France and Spain. (Barandiaran, 1972: 103, 271)

Ilogo A spirit "said to live in the moon" who was consulted near full moon regarding the "king's sufferings." East Africa. (Budge, 1973, 1: 392)

Ilumquh The moon god of the Sabaeans. South Arabia. Same as Wadd, Sin, Amm. (Moscati, 1960: 187)

Ilura The moon goddess of the Kadan (Cochin). India. She is the sister of Parama Shiva and identified with Parvathi. (Hermanns, 1955: 145)

Ina maram The goddess of the moon. Ponape, Caroline Islands, Micronesia. (Christian, 1899: 383)

Indo nTegolili The moon goddess reports to Pue-m-palaburu on the wrongs committed by people. The Celebes, Indonesia. (Downs, 1920: 13; Pettazzoni, 1956: 333)

Io A Palestinian moon goddess. Near East. (Andersen, 1928: 350; Cook, 1930: 182)

Iraca With Ramiquiri created men and women; transformed himself into the moon. The Chibcha, Colombia. (Osborne, 1968: 110)

Itzama The god of the moon and of fertility. The Cuna, Panama. (Keeler, 1960: 200)

Jacy God of the moon and creator of plants. The Tupi, Brazil. (Spence, 1925, 2: 837; Bastide, 1960: 567)

Ja Najek The all-knowing goddess of the moon who cannot be deceived. The Kerau, Indonesia. (Pettazzoni, 1956: 339)

Jangga The god of the moon who is also called Kajangga Bulan. The Ngaju, Borneo. (Scharer, 1963: 204, 215)

Japara The moon-man who eats so greedily of crab meat—to the bursting point (full moon)—that he dies, but is renewed each month, partly escaping the decree of Purukupali that there should be no resurrection of the dead, that death should be final. Australia. (Mountford, 1969: 58)

Jara-meng The moon goddess who has powers of rejuvenation—ages and becomes young again. The Semang of Lenggong in North Perak, Indonesia. (Pettazzoni, 1956: 339)

Juno Lucetia The great Italian goddess as a goddess of the moon. (Larousse, 1968: 204)

Jyolo Dubo The god of the moon of the Kharrias. Bengal. (Crooke, 1925, 2: 484)

Kappa The moon. North Queensland, Australia. (McConnel, 1957: 32)

Karkara The benevolent moon god. Adelaide, Australia. (Woods, 1879: 166)

Kashatskihakatidise The moon is also Mother Corn about which she taught the women. She was created by Kinnekasus as the woman for Kiarsidia. The Wichita, Plains Indians, Kansas. (Dorsey, 1904: 25–28)

Kashiri The moon god who introduced manioc and cultivation to the people. Father of the sun. The Campa, Peru. (Weiss, 1972: 163)

Kasku, Kashku Proto-Hattic god of the moon. Near East. (Ferm, 1950: 91; Patai, 1967: 166)

ka tu' Goddess of the moon and of childbirth, also of agricultural fertility. The Chorti, Guatemala. (Wisdom, 1940: 400)

Kayan The moon deity—"probably seasonal only." Chile (Spence, 1925, 3: 549)

Kazoba God of the sun and of the moon. Father of Hangi and son of Wamara. The Bahima, Uganda. Among the Haya of Tanzania he is also god of the stars. (Larousse, 1973: 523; Taylor, 1962: 142)

Keri A god associated with the moon. With Kame twin culture heroes of the Bacairi, and their ancestors. Upper Xingu, Brazil. (Zerries, 1968: 209; Girard, 1979: 112)

Ketanagai The moon. "Big Head," a cultural hero/ trickster character, is called by the same name. He is their main god and beneficent. The Wailaki, California. (Loeb, 1931: 523; 1932: 73)

Keyumka The moon god of the coastal Yuki. California. (Pettazzoni, 1956: 176)

Khab The moon, their Great Chief who "promises men immortality." The Hottentots, South Africa. (Hahn, 1881: 40–42; Schapera, 1951: 375)

Khaṇḍobā He represents the sun (male) as well as the moon (female) "(who unite in an interior androgynization within him). . . . his worship culminates on the day when sun and moon meet in a union that is by implication sexual." India. (O'Flaherty, 1980: 255–257)

Khensu, Khons A lunar god and a god of the fertility of vegetation, of women, and of cattle. He is given as the son of Bast or Mut and Amen. Egypt. (Budge, 1969, 1: 447–448; 1969, 2: 33–37; Knight, 1915: 30, 60; Rawlinson, 1885: 22; Ames, 1965: 27, 99)

Khyp The moon with whom Khosadam went to live when she left Ess. He was thrown down to the earth—his punishment to mark the time for man and foretell the weather. The Yenisei Ostyaks, Siberia. (Czaplicka, 1925, 9: 579)

Kikewei p'aide "our mother moon." The Pueblo Indians, Isleta, New Mexico. (Parsons, 1929/30: 341)

Kil·aq The one-eyed moon god. The Chugach Eskimo, Alaska. (Birket-Smith, 1953: 120)

Klego-na-ay Twelve moons, but also the name of the full moon. The Apache, Arizona and New Mexico. (Bourke, 1890: 209; 1892: 502)

Klehanoai The "Moon-Carrier" whose wife is Yolkai Estsan. As with the sun "the orb of night is only a shield that the god carries." The Navaho, Arizona and New Mexico. (Matthews, 1902: 30; Alexander, 1964: 157)

kov-ava The goddess of the moon. The Mordvins, Russia. (Leach, 1949, 1: 96)

Kov-bas, Kov-bavas The moon god of the Mordvins. Russia. (Paasonen, 1925, 8: 844)

Kre The moon goddess, wife of Kren, the sun. The Ona Indians, Tierra del Fuego. (Loeb, 1931: 528)

Kuhu Goddess of the days of the new moon. India. (Keith, 1917: 93; Macdonell, 1897: 125; Danielou, 1964: 319)

Kuksu The god of the south was also identified with the moon; with Marumda created the world. Among the northern Pomo it is with Makila. The Wappo, Pomo, California. (Loeb, 1931: 523, 525; 1932: 3; de Angulo and Freeland, 1928: 251)

Kuma The moon goddess, wife of the sun, is the creator of the world and of all things with the assistance of her brothers Puana, the water snake, and Itciai, the jaguar. She is powerful and beneficent and lives in the afterworld where she waits to receive the dead to live in happiness. The Yaruro, Venezuela. (Kirchhoff, 1948, 4: 462; Métraux, 1946, 2: 115; Sierksma, 1960: 14; Petrullo, 1939: 241)

Kundui The moon goddess, wife of Moyang Bertang. The Mantra, Malay Peninsula. (Skeat, 1906: 320)

Kushah Hittite god of the moon. Asia Minor. (Ferm, 1950: 91)

Kuu The moon. Finno-Ugric. (Larousse, 1968: 304)

küyen fucha and **küyen kushe** The "god and goddess of the moon." The Mapuche, Chile. (Faron, 1968: 65)

Lanipipili The aumakua in the sun and also the moon who are "chiefly invoked as detective(s) in cases of petty thieving." Hawaii. (Emerson, 1967: 51)

lham inga The moon god of the Alaskan Eskimo. (Marsh, 1967: 153)

Lingan Goddess of the moon. The Mayawyaw, the Ifugao. Luzon, Philippines. (Barton, 1946: 41)

Losna Etruscan goddess of the moon. Italy. (Rawlinson, 1885: 123; Leland, 1963: 90)

Luna Roman goddess of the moon who regulates the seasons and the months. (Dumézil, 1966, 1: 170; Murray, 1935: 118)

St. la Lune The deified moon. Mirebalais, Haiti. West Indies. (Herskovits, 1937, 1: 281)

Lusin Armenian goddess of the moon. Also called Ami(n)s. (Ananikian, 1964: 51)

Mah The moon is a deity of the fertility of cattle and of the growth of plants, as well as of time and of tides. Iran. (Huart, 1963: 42; Gray, 1930: 87; Larousse, 1973: 192)

Mahina The moon. Rennell Island, Polynesia. (Birket-Smith, 1956: 22)

Mama Quilla The goddess of the moon, of marriage and of love, is protective in childbirth. She is also a goddess of time and the festival calendar, and sometimes considered a "goddess of the sea and of the winds." She is the sister/wife of Inti, the sun, though sometimes regarded as without kinship. Inca, Peru. (Rowe, 1946, 2: 295; Brinton, 1868: 132; Means, 1931: 391)

Manchakori The first god who gave the Campa their food, taught the secrets of his powers to Mahonte's son, the first man, then ascended to the sky and became the moon. Peru. (Llosa Porras, 1977: 59, 61)

Mani Teutonic god of the moon who ruled its phases, brother of Sol, the sun, and son of the giant Mundilfare. (Grimm, 1883, 2: 705, 710; Anderson, 1891: 452)

Mano, Manno The god of the moon who was earlier called Aske. The Lapps, Northern Europe. (Bosi, 1960: 132; Holmberg, 1925, 7: 799; Karsten, 1955: 33)

Marama The goddess of the moon. Tahiti, the Marquesas. In Hawaii she is the wife of Tane and also called Uri Uri. Among the Maori the moon is the sister of Ra, the sun, with varying parentage given her. Polynesia. (Melville, 1969: 19, 25, 93; Henry, 1928: 400; Andersen, 1928: 376)

Mas An early moon god in the Rig Veda. India. (Schrader, 1925, 2: 34)

Masahkare Grandmother moon. The Crow Indians, Montana. (Lowie, 1922: 320)

Masina The moon god, son of Ilu and Mamao. Upolu, Samoa, Polynesia. (Williamson, 1933: 4)

Mata rica The all-seeing moon. The Ngadha of Central Flores, Indonesia. (Pettazzoni, 1956: 339)

Mawu, Mawu-Lisa The goddess of the sky, of the moon, of the night, lives in the west. She represents the female principle and is associated with rest, pleasure, love, relaxation. She is the mother of the gods and the creator of life. She is the twin and wife of Lisa, the sun, born of Nana-Buluku. They are frequently linked as a dual deity, the term designating the sky and the sky pantheon. Mawu is at times, or by some, considered to be male, and again androgynous. Dahomey. (Parrinder, 1967: 21; Mercier, 1954: 214, 217–219; Herskovits, 1938, 2: 101, 103, 292–293; Williams, 1936: 164)

Mayari The beautiful goddess of the moon is the sister of Hanan and Tala, daughters of Bathala, and a mortal. The Tagalog, Philippines. (Jocano, 1969: 10)

Men A Phrygian god of the moon as well as of the underworld. Asia Minor. (Bhattacharji, 1970: 106)

Mene A Greek goddess of the moon, similar to Selene. (Roscher, 1965, 2, 2: 2776)

Meness, Menesis Latvian god of the moon, son of Dievs, by whom he was given charge of the night and the stars. (Jonval, 1929: 12, 13; Gimbutas, 1963: 199)

Menuo Lithuanian god of the moon. He was closely associated with the sun, Saule, and "brought well-being, light and health . . . flowers must be planted either at new or full moon." (Gray, 1930: 89; Gimbutas, 1963: 199, 201)

Me?tik Čič?u "Our Grandmother the Moon." The Tzeltal, Mexico. (Nash, 1970: 198)

Metzli, Metztli, Meztli The goddess of the moon was also associated with marriage, procreation, and childbirth. However, she had a malignant side as "goddess of the night, the dampness, and the cold." Aztec, Mexico. (Caso, 1956: 36; Spence, 1923: 309; Brinton, 1868: 132; Bancroft, 1886, 3: 111)

Minokawa An enormous bird who swallows the moon causing the eclipse. The Bagobo, Philippines. (Benedict, 1916: 40, 47)

Mipa-ing The Crescent Moon, a god of the skyworld, descendent of Umbulan, the Moon. The Ifugao, Philippines. (Barton, 1946: 42)

MiYarogopitsi The moon god with whom crows are associated. His phases are known as: MiYarogopits kakarĭ—the new moon; MiYarogopits nanawa?aigYah—the waxing moon; MiYarogopits putcawa?aigYah—equivalent of the above; MiYarogopits togᵂᵃintĭ-rawaagantuᵂa—the full moon; MiYarogopits ya?a—the dark of the moon and/or an eclipse. The Chemehuevis, California, Nevada, and Arizona. (Laird, 1976: 154, 216, 305–306)

Moma The major god of the Witotoans is the creator who is identified with the moon. He is also associated with food and fruits which represent rebirth. Having died he is also god of the dead in the underworld in addition to his celestial role. Colombia and Peru. (Zerries, 1968: 254)

Moyang Bertang The malevolent moon whose wife is Kundui. The Mantra, Malay Peninsula. (Skeat, 1906: 319–320)

Moyla The moon observes men at night to catch wrongdoers. The Luiseño and Diegueño Indians, California. (Du Bois, 1908, 8: 97; 1908, 21: 233)

Muiyawu The moon deity of the Tusayan Hopi Indians. Arizona. (Fewkes, 1893/94: 291)

munya·k yekan "(Father Moon). . . . The great (*not* the waxing) moon." The Botocudo, Brazil. (Nimuendaju, 1946, 2: 110)

munya·k yopue Mother moon—the small moon. The Botocudo, Brazil. (Nimeundaju, 1946, 2: 110)

Munychia The name of Artemis as the moon goddess worshipped at the harbor of Athens. Greece. (Murray, 1935: 123)

Mweji, Mwezi The goddess of the moon who is the mother of mankind. The Wapare or Wasu, the Kumbi. Koko Mwezi, Grandmother Moon, of the Taveta. Tanzania. (Frazer, 1926: 202; Millroth, 1965: 28, 58–59)

Myesyats The Slavic moon deity, in some areas masculine (Serbia, Ukraine, Russia) and in some areas feminine and the wife of the Sun. (Larousse, 1968: 284–285; Cohane, 1969: 46)

Nagaitco, Nagaico Night Traveler, Big Head—the moon. He was subordinate to Tcenes. He was the source of the Kato's arts and customs, but also instigated "trickery and rivalry" among them. He was appealed to in sickness. California. (Loeb, 1931: 521; 1932: 23, 25; Pettazzoni, 1956: 176)

Namboa, Mwarega The goddess of the moon is the wife of Wuntenga, the sun, and mother of the stars. The Nankanse, Ghana. (Rattray, 1932, 2: 335)

Namshaya The moon who is the wife of the sun. The Kogi, Colombia. (Reichel-Dolmatoff, 1975: 45)

Nanepaushat The god of the moon of the Narragansett Indians. Rhode Island. (Skinner, 1913: 91)

Nanna, Nannar, Suen (later **Sin**) The Akkadian/Sumerian/Babylonian god of the moon, the regulator of the tides, the measurer of time, was also the city-god of Ur. He was Nanna as the full moon, Ensum as the half moon, Suen as the crescent, Ashimbabbar as "new light." He was also a deity of cowherders and boatmen of the marshes, as was his wife Ningal. His fertility aspect is that of the spring floods, which provide the "rise of the waters, growth of the reeds, increase of the herds, abundance of milk, cream, and cheese." First son of Enlil and Ninlil. Near East. (Jacobsen, 1970: 25, 26; 1976: 121–122, 125; Jastrow, 1898: 75, 76; Kramer, 1967: 102–103; Sayce, 1898: 156, 164)

Nantu The moon contains "powerful tsarutama, which influences all that goes on on earth." The Jivaro, Ecuador. (Stirling, 1938: 116)

Nasilele A goddess whose symbol is the moon; wife of Nyambe. On death women go to her, men to Nyambe. The Lozi, Zambia, and Northwest Rhodesia. (Turner, 1952: 31, 49)

Nenak Kebajan The all-knowing goddess of the moon. The Mantra Jakudn, Indonesia. (Pettazzoni, 1956: 339)

ni·bos·it The "night walker"—the moon. The Penobscot Indians, Maine. (Speck, 1935, 1: 20)

Nikkal, Nikkal-and-Eb The goddess of the moon was also goddess of fertility and vegetation. Wife of Yarih (Yarikh). Canaan, Near East. (Driver, 1956: 24; Gordon, 1961: 214)

Ninda Kando (Chando) Goddess of the moon, wife of Sing Chando, the sun, and mother of the stars. The Santal in Katikund. India. (Elwin, 1949: 55; Biswas, 1956: 103)

Nind-bong-a The moon. The Binjhias of Chota Nagpur, India. (Crooke, 1925, 5: 3)

Nokomis Grandmother Moon. A spirit woman who came to live on the earth, then returned again to the sky after the people were able to exist for themselves. She is remembered when the moon shines. The Ojibway, Lake Superior. (Johnston, 1976: 13–17)

Norfi, Narfi The "Dark Moon," a giant of Jotunheim, and father of Nott (Night). Teutonic. (Branston, 1955: 65, 203; MacCulloch, 1964: 200; Grimm, 1883, 2: 735)

Nuna The moon, who is evil and cannibalistic, was created by Attawanadi, the third damodede of Wanadi. When a ring around the moon indicates he is about to eat someone, the shaman must go to the rescue. The Makiritare, Venezuela. (Civrieux, 1980: 28, 47, 188)

Nuñda The luminary that lives in the nighttime. Brother of the Sun. The black spots on his face are the result of his love affair with her. He is considered to cause blindness. The Cherokee, North Carolina and Tennessee. (Mooney and Olbrechts, 1932: 20, 22)

Nyadeang The moon, daughter of Deng. The Nuer, Sudan. (Evans-Pritchard, 1956: 2)

Nyalindu The moon is the symbol of resurrection. Kuppapoingo tribe, Australia. (Robinson, 1966: 152)

Nyame Amowia The "bi-sexual deity of the cosmos Nyame Amowia, visible as the moon, gave birth to the Sun god" Nyankopon. The Akan of the Gold Coast, Ghana. (Meyerowitz, 1951: 24)

Nyami abe The god of the moon—the " 'nocturnal sun,' . . . two aspects of the same being . . . a negative, evil part." He is a seducer of women and a predator of graves. However, he has a positive side—as the dew which fertilizes nature and as the full moon beneficent in pregnancy. The Desana, Colombia. (Reichel-Dolmatoff, 1971: 72)

Nyingwan Mebege The moon is also goddess of procreation and of prosperity, and represents the female principle. The major deity of the Bwiti Cult of the Fang. Gabon. (Fernandez, 1972: 241, 247)

Obosom The planetary deities are considered "as bisexual, or as male and female deities . . . *he* represented the male principle in nature; *she*, as mother and wife, the female principle." In the Moon Cult, the Obosom is a clan goddess who is "the visible manifestation of the kra, or vital force, of the moon." The Akan, Ghana. (Meyerowitz, 1958: 24–25, 47; Danquah, 1944: 45)

Ochu "At one time goddess of the moon . . . no longer very popular." Puerto Rico, West Indies. (Gonzalez-Wippler, 1975: 26)

Maia Ogar The god of the moon. Aka-Bea, Andaman Islands, Bay of Bengal. (Radcliffe-Brown, 1967: 45)

Ol-apa The moon is the wife of Enk-ai. The Masai, Kenya. (Huntingford, 1953: 125)

Olonitalipipilele A god "identified with the moon." The father of Púgsu (Venus). The Cuna Indians, Panama. (Nordenskiold, 1938: 328)

Olotwalikippilele The Moon God is the brother/husband of Olomakriai, an earthmother. The sun and the stars are the result of their mating. The Cuna Indians, Panama. (Keeler, 1960: 46, 147)

Ongwa The moon was created by Chuku and is his messenger. The Northern Ibo, Nigeria. (Horton, 1956: 18)

Osiris-Aah Osiris as a moon god in which he symbolizes "stability, life, serenity, power, and dominion." Egypt. (Budge, 1973, 1: 59)

Osrane The moon is the son of the sky god and brother of Owia (sun) and Esum (darkness). The Ashanti, Ghana. (Feldman, 1963: 125)

Osu, Oshu The goddess of the moon. The Yoruba, Nigeria. (Lucas, 1948: 98; Meek, 1925, 2: 29)

Ouiot The crescent moon. The Diegueño Indians, California. (Du Bois, 1908, 21: 233)

Pacsa Mama "The name of the moon as a deity . . . as giving light by night, 'Quilla;' and there were names for its different phases." Peru. (Markham, 1969: 70)

Pah Goddess of the moon, giver of light at night, whose abode was in the west. She was the mother of the first boy (by the Sun) to be placed on the earth. The Skidi Pawnee, the Caddoan, Plains Indians, Nebraska. (Dorsey, 1904, 2: 3, 4; Larousse, 1968: 433)

Pajau (Paja) Yan A beneficent goddess identified with the moon, having been sent there by Po Jata "to prevent her from raising all the dead." She is a goddess of health and of healing, as well as of good fortune. A lunar eclipse is homage done by her to the sun. The Chams, Annam and Cambodia. (Cabaton, 1925, 3: 342; Wales, 1957: 160)

Pasiphae Daughter of Helios and Perseis, and a wife of Minos. She is interpreted as a goddess of light, as a moon goddess, identified with Selene, and associated with fertility. Cretan/Greek. (Willetts, 1962: 110, 177; Kerenyi, 1951: 110, 192; Roscher, 1965, 3, 2: 1666)

Paurnamasi Goddess of the full moon, from the Atharva. India. (Gray, 1930: 156)

Paxsi The moon, wife of Lupi, the sun, is a goddess whose phases govern agricultural and human activities. She is also consulted in divination. The Aymara, Peru. (Tschopik, 1951: 196–197)

Pe Goddess of the moon and of fecundity. The Pygmies, Zaire. (Eliade, 1959: 149)

Pereno-mah A lunar deity, of the full moon. Iran. (Gray, 1930: 156)

Periboriwa The "Spirit of the Moon" who used to come down and eat the souls of children. He was shot with an arrow by Suhirina, and the blood which dropped to the earth became men—the Yanomamo. Their origin from his blood is the source of their ferocity. Brazil and Venezuela. (Chagnon, 1968: 47)

Phoibe Goddess of the moon, daughter of Helios and Neaira. Same as Aigle. Greece. (Kerenyi, 1951: 193)

Piskewenikizho The moon, the giver of light at night. The Unami (Lenape Indians), Eastern United States. (Harrington, 1921: 28)

Po The moon goddess of the Kekchis (Mayans). British Honduras. (Thompson, 1930: 64)

Pollo The moon god, the son of Sitking-Kedding and Peddo-Dodum, and brother of Doini. The Adi, northeastern India. Among the Gallongs, oaths sworn by Doini-Polo, the sun/moon, are the most sacred. (Chowdhury, 1971: 75–76, 92)

Popata The deity of the moon of the Cayapa. Ecuador. (Barrett, 1925: 353)

Poré, Poré/Perimbó Perimbó, the moon; Poré, the "lord of the moon." They "constitute an inseparable unity that is regarded as eternal, just, and benevolent, but is

also able to punish, if necessary. To it is attributed the origin of the earth and all life." The supreme being of the Surára and the Pakidái. Brazil. (Becher, 1960: 91, 104; Zerries, 1968: 244–245)

Posendo The god who lives in the moon. The Tewa, Pueblo Indians, New Mexico. (Harrington, 1907/08: 45)

Postvorta A goddess who represents the waning moon. She is associated with breech presentation in childbirth and also with clairvoyance. Rome. (Pettazzoni, 1956: 168; Roscher, 1965, 2, 1: 216; Dumézil, 1966, 1: 393)

Puduvri The moon is invoked for the protection of the food plants and animals and for the prosperity of the crops. The Timbira, Brazil. (Nimuendaju, 1946, 1: 232)

Puhi, Puki The goddess of the moon, wife of Tomo. Some say the moon is a male whose wife is Puto. The A-Pucikwar, Andaman Islands, Bay of Bengal. (Roheim, 1972: 29; Radcliffe-Brown, 1967: 142)

Puil The moon is a malignant power. The Coconuco, Colombia. (Hernandez de Alba, 1946, 2: 935)

Purnacandra The full moon, a form of Candra. Nepal. (Pal and Bhattacharyya, 1969: 8)

Qaumavun The moon spirit—male. The East Baffin Eskimo, Canada. (Nungak and Arima, 1969: 114)

Qetesh A Syrian nature goddess of licentious worship introduced into Egypt. She was a goddess of "love and beauty" and as a moon goddess was considered a form of Hathor. (Knight, 1915: 101–102; Budge, 1969, 2: 279–280)

Quabso The moon is venerated but offered no prayers or sacrifices, is considered female but not a "being," is the emblem of fertility, of growth, of health, and is involved with rain-making. The Sandawe, Tanzania. (Raa, 1969: 24, 39, 41, 48)

Quilla The "roguish moon" whose sister/lover is Jilucu. Their mythic episodes influence ceramic designs. The Canelos Quichua, Ecuador. (Whitten, 1978: 91)

Rabia A divine maiden who was promised to Tuwale in marriage, but was denied him. He caused "her to sink into the earth among the roots of a tree." In response to her plea her mother caused a pig to be slaughtered, instituting the death feast. After three days Rabia rose in the sky as the moon. West Cerman, Indonesia. Perhaps the same as Rabie. (Campbell, 1974: 176)

Rabie A goddess associated with the earth and the moon, and considered identical with Mulua Satene and Hainuwele. Wife of Tuwale. The Wemale, Philippines. (Raats, 1969: 49)

Raka Goddess of the full moon. She is associated with birth and procreation and invoked for offspring. Daughter of Angiras and Sraddha. India. (Macdonell, 1897: 125; Danielou, 1964: 319; Crooke, 1894: 15; Barth, 1921: 25)

Ratih The moon, wife of Semara, to whom hymns are sung at weddings. Bali, Indonesia. (Covarrubias, 1937: 317; Hooykaas, 1964: 48)

Rona The goddess of the moon who controls the tides. The Maori, New Zealand. (Best, 1924: 97, 110)

Rongo In some areas the personification of the moon. He is primarily a god of agriculture—of fertility, harvest, and plenty—and also of peace. In Mangaia and Hervey Islands he is a god of war and of the underworld. Polynesia. (Best, 1924: 236; Howells, 1948: 222; Buck, 1934: 162; 1938, 2: 264–265; Hongi, 1930: 26; Andersen, 1928: 423–424)

Sahar, Sahr, Shahar Semitic god of the moon whose wife is Nikkal, son Nusk (Nusku). Syria and Arabia. (Macler, 1925, 12: 166; Langdon, 1931: 4; Vriezen, 1963: 57; Cook, 1930: 120)

Selardis Vannic god of the moon. Armenia. (Sayce, 1925, 1: 794)

Selene Greek goddess of the moon, daughter of Theia and Hyperion, sister of Helios. She was "mistress of the stars." (Fairbanks, 1907: 162; Kerenyi, 1951: 22, 192; Cox, 1870, 2: 30)

Shata Wunphrang The embryonic moon, of the second generation of deities, child of Kringkrong wa and Ynong majan. The Katchins, Burma. (Gilhodes, 1908: 675)

Shelartish The god of the moon of the Urartians. Armenia. (Ananikian, 1964: 11)

oShion The moon god was created by oDel. The Gypsies. Among the Kalderash a female deity and a goddess of time and of good fortune. (Clebert, 1967: 174, 176)

Shitta The moon, a beneficent nat, is invoked with Jan for the protection of the village. The Kachins, Burma. (Temple, 1925, 3: 22; Leach, 1950, 2: 538)

Si The primary deity of the Chimu was the moon who controlled the weather, causing storms, but also fostering the growth of crops. Sacrifices of children, animals and birds were made to her. Peru. (Alexander, 1920: 223; Markham, 1969: 122; Rowe, 1948: 50; Loeb, 1931: 545)

Sin The omniscient god of the moon, god of wisdom, is also the god of the month Sivan, Siwan, Simannu. He controlled the waters and is "the creator of the grasses." Sumer, Babylon, Canaan, and South Arabia, Near East. (Hommel, 1925, 3: 74; Pettazzoni, 1956: 78–79; Moscati, 1960: 187; Jastrow, 1898: 68, 78; Jayne, 1962: 128; Eliade, 1958: 159, 162)

Sin-galla The name of Sin, the moon god, at Tema, Northern Arabia. (Macler, 1925, 12: 166; Cook, 1930: 123)

Sinivali With Kuhu a goddess of the days of the new moon. She is associated with childbirth and procreation. India. (Keith, 1917: 93; Barth, 1921: 25; Jayne, 1962: 160)

So The Pangwe goddess of the moon. Nigeria. (Talbot, 1967: 118)

Sogamoso The moon. The King of Sogamoso and his nephew the King of Ramiriqui were the first two humans. They created mankind and to provide them with light Sogamoso became the moon and Ramiriqui the sun. Colombia. (Trimborn, 1968: 90–91)

Soma In later times the personification of the soma plant and its juice became identified with the moon. As such he "married the twenty-seven daughters of Daksha" who became jealous of Rohini, his favorite, and had Daksha curse Soma with "consumption and sterility," then repented and had the curse made periodic. Hence the waxing and waning of the moon. India. (Elwin, 1949: 51; Macdonell, 1897: 109–114; Basak, 1953: 93–94) In Mongolia the moon is also associated with the southeast. (Percheron, 1953: 63)

Songe The moon is mentioned by Schebesta as "the sky God of the archers." The Mbuti (Pygmies), Zaire. (Turnbull, 1965: 236)

Suen A Semitic moon god identified with Nanna as the crescent moon. Near East. (Jacobsen, 1976: 121; Roberts, 1972: 50)

Tahar In Atchin "a being who . . . represents both sun and moon . . . [and] . . . is usually supposed to have created man and to take an interest in his welfare." New Hebrides, Melanesia. (Rivers, 1925, 9: 353)

Taikomol   The supreme deity and the creatorgod of the Yuki was identified with the moon. California. (Kroeber, n.d.: 183; Loeb, 1931: 522)

Taio   The moon is the wife of Haro, the sun. The Lakalai, New Britain, Melanesia. (Valentine, 1965: 183)

T'ai Yin   Goddess of the moon. China. (Day, 1940: 165; Werner, 1934: 179)

Takaq   The moon gives them seals and deer. The Central Eskimo of Cumberland Sound. Canada. (Boas, 1884/85: 583)

Taktik   The moon of the Ihalmiut Eskimo. Keewatin District, Canada. (Mowat, 1968: 237)

Tamparawa   The moon was the wife of Anchopeteri, a culture hero of the Tapirape. Brazil. (Wagley, 1940: 256)

Tanit   The great goddess of the moon and of fecundity at Carthage. Among the Berbers she was bisexual and mother of the universe, represented by the moon. Also called Tanit Pene Baal. (Bel, 1938: 75, 78; Meyerowitz, 1958: 130–131; Ferguson, 1970: 215)

Tano, Twumpuduro   Among the Akan "Tano of Tuobodom, born on a Monday, is worshipped as a Moon-god or goddess." Ghana. (Meyerowitz, 1958: 48)

Tarqeq, Tarqiup   The moon spirit of the Iglulik Eskimo. Canada. *See* **Aningat.** (Rasmussen, 1929: 62)

Tatex   The moon deity of the Cora of the Sierra de Naharit. Mexico. (Pettazzoni, 1956: 404)

Tatqeq   The moon spirit is variously given as male or female, and is believed to bring success in hunting and "fertility to women." Also associated with the afterworld. The Netsilik and Mackenzie Eskimo. Canada. Same as Tarqeq, Aningat. (Balikci, 1970: 207; Nungak and Arima, 1969: 114; Rasmussen, 1931: 224)

Tawac   A sky god—the moon. The Sia, Pueblo Indians, New Mexico. (Fewkes, 1895, 2: 124)

Tebaran   A god associated with the moon. Invoked in the ceremony for children to make them strong, skillful, successful, brave, and to give them longevity. The Sea Dyaks, Borneo. (Roth, 1968: 171)

Tecciztecatl, Tecuciztecatl   "He from the Sea Snail" was equated with Metztli and subsequently became the moon god. Aztec, Mexico. (Vaillant, 1963: 150; León-Portilla, 1961: 451–452; Nicholson, 1967: 72)

Thoth   The ibis-headed god of the moon, of wisdom and of all learning, is the scribe of the gods and the recorder of judgments in the weighing and testing of the deceased in the afterworld. As a lunar god he is also called Åāh-Tehuti. Egypt. (Budge, 1969, 1: 401–402, 408, 412; Knight, 1915: 127–128; Jayne, 1962: 32; Ames, 1965: 82)

Tjapara   The seducer of Bima, the wife of Purukupali partially escaped the death decree of Purukupali by becoming the moon with its death and growth cycles. The Tiwi, Melville Island, Australia. (Mountford, 1958: 26, 29–30)

Tlazolteotl   Among the Huaxtec and the Cora the earth goddess was also the goddess of the moon. Mexico. (Thompson, 1970: 246; Tozzer, 1957: 113)

tł'éhonaa'ái, Tłe·xona'ái, Tlehanoai   The moon is an "important regulator(s) of human life, having strong Winds by which to lead people" and other winds with which to communicate. A deity who can be persuaded— "said to be the maternal uncle or father of the Sun." The Navaho, Arizona. (McNeley, 1981: 24, 28; Reichard, 1950: 451; Burland, 1965: 149)

Tonige   The moon is the supreme being among some Iduwini people of the Okun Ijaw dialect. Niger Delta, Nigeria. (Jeffreys, 1972: 730)

Toru-guenket   The goddess of the moon represents the principle of evil and causes thunder and floods, and other misfortunes. The Tupi, Brazil. (Spence, 1925, 2: 837)

Tripurasundari   A lunar goddess who is "considered as actually being *in* the moon." Tantrism, India. (Eliade, 1958: 176–177)

Tsukiyomi   The moon god, ruler of the realm of night, was born from the right eye of Izanagi. Japan. (Yasumaro, 1928: 22; 1965: 24–25; Kato, 1926: 14, 67)

Turu-meha   The waning moon, offspring of Raki and Hotu-papa. New Zealand. (White, 1887, 1: 20)

Tzontzose   The crescent moon. The Apache Indians, Arizona and New Mexico. (Bourke, 1892: 502)

U   The moon goddess at San Antonio. Same as Po of the Kekchis. Mayan, British Honduras. (Thompson, 1930: 64)

Udo   The moon god, companion of Uhubaput, is the Sumu Indian chief deity. "The planet Venus, when seen above the crescent moon, is called Udo's wife." Nicaragua and Honduras. (Leach, 1950, 2: 1148; Conzemius, 1932: 126)

Udsar A title of Sin as the new moon. Sumer, Near East. (Langdon, 1931: 152)

Ul God of the moon and of the night. New Hebrides, Melanesia. (Larousse, 1973: 503)

Umbulan The moon is a god of war as well as a god of justice, of divination, and of oaths. The Ifugao, Philippines. (Barton, 1946: 38–39)

Une The moon god, brother of Rit, the sun. The Kuikuru of the Xingu River, Brazil. (Villas Boas, 1973: 80)

Urur God of the moon on Yap Island. The Carolines, Micronesia. (Christian, 1899: 385)

Ix U Sihnal The Mayan moon goddess as "patroness of disease" is invoked to cure ulcers. She is also the patroness of procreation and childbirth, is associated with bodies of water. Mexico. (Thompson, 1970: 242–245)

Varuna A god with numerous associations. As a god of the heavens he is a god of light both by day (the sun) and by night (the moon), and came to symbolize "the night sky with its thousand stars as his eyes." India. (Macdonell, 1897: 23–26; Bhattacharji, 1970: 33; Ions, 1967: 15)

Verah The deity of the moon. Arabia. (Vriezen, 1963: 52)

Višaptatha A lunar deity, the "moon midway between waxing and waning." Iran. (Gray, 1930: 133, 224)

Volana The moon god among the Bara. Madagascar. (Ruud, 1960: 172)

Wadd Moon god of the Minaeans. Same as Ilumquh, Amm, Sin. Southern Arabia. (Moscati, 1960: 187; Pritchard, 1943: 63)

Wairie The moon deity of the Sherente, the Shavante. Brazil. (Maybury-Lewis, 1967: 286; Nimuendaju, 1942: 84)

Wajubu The moon god whose wife is Tagisomenaja, the Evening Star. The Kamano, Usurufa, Jate, and Fore, New Guinea. (Berndt, 1965: 80)

Wakara The god of the new moon. The Yana. Among the Yaki (southern Yana) the moon is female. California. (Curtin, 1903: 281, 389; Kroeber, 1964: 78)

Wa-koⁿ-da Hoⁿdoⁿ "Goddess of Night (the Moon), grandmother." The Dhegiha (Osage), Plains Indians. (La Flesche, 1928: 74)

Wulan The moon is invoked by the Solor Islanders. Indonesia. (Frazer, 1926: 660)

Wulkwang The Moon Buddha. Korea. (Clark, 1932: 61)

Xaratanga A Tarascan goddess of the earth and of agriculture is associated with the moon. She is also a goddess of birth and procreation. Mexico. (Krickeberg, 1968: 59)

Xbalamqué, Ixbalamqué (Some disagreement as to sex.) The lunar goddess, whose nahual is the jaguar, began her existence as the twin of Hunahpú. They are the civilizing deities born of Xquic, who was impregnated by the spittle of Hun-Hunahpu. Hunahpú and Xbalamqué are overcome by the dark powers of Xibalba and he is beheaded, symbolically the death of the maize god and his regeneration. Xbalamqué watches over his head to influence its germination, and "unaided defends humanity against the monsters of the night when the sun has disappeared." The Quiché, Guatemala. (Girard, 1979: 87, 134, 187, 193, 201–203; Thompson, 1970: 234; Recinos, 1950: 119, 124; Nicholson, 1967: 57; Brinton, 1868: 258)

Xmucané, Ixmucané The Great Mother is "the personification of the old Lunar-earth goddess." As Regent she heads the matriarchal-horticultural stage of the Quiché culture. She and Ixpiyacoc created the lunar calendar. Grandmother of Hunahpú and Xbalamqué. Guatemala. (Girard, 1979: 52, 55, 87, 240; Recinos, 1950: 79, 88, 107; Thompson, 1970: 335; Bancroft, 1886, 3: 462)

Yaeⁱlhimtilaⁱn The moon-man, but sometimes female. The Koryak, Siberia. (Jochelson, 1908: 31)

Naac Yahui The god of the moon, son of Nexhequiriac. The Trique tribe, Oaxaca, Mexico. (Valentini, 1899: 38)

Yai The moon who taught the Camayura to make fire. He also created their enemy tribes. The Mato Grosso, Brazil. (Oberg, 1953: 53)

Yaonan The Moon Mother existed above in the beginning with Awonawilona, the sun. The Zuñi Indians, New Mexico. (Stevenson, 1898: 33)

Yarikh, Yareah, Yarih, Yarakh The god of the moon whose wife is Nikkal. Canaan, Near East. (Paton, 1925,

3: 180; Gordon, 1961: 214; Ferm, 1950: 123; Albright, 1956: 83; Hooke, 1963: 93)

Yasi The moon is the only supernatural being of the Siriono. He created the world and everything in it, is the cause of thunder and lightning. Bolivia. (Holmberg, 1969: 238)

Yerah The moon god of the Ammonites, the Phoenicians. Near East. (Jayne, 1962: 132; Vriezen, 1963: 60)

Yerugami, Iyerugame Mother Moon, who watches over the Tarahumara by night, is the goddess of women

particularly. Mexico. (Lumholtz, 1902: 295; Bennett and Zingg, 1935: 373; Pettazzoni, 1956: 405)

Yin The female principle of the Chinese duad is associated with the moon, with darkness, as well as with passivity and other recessive qualities. (Day, 1940: 56; Graham, 1928: 37; Schopes, 1961: 195)

Yueh Fu T'ai Yin, Yueh Te Hsing Chun, Yueh Hu Hsing, Yueh Kung T'ai Yin Tsun T'ien The goddess of the moon who is "in charge of months, patroness of harvests, and ruler of the tides . . . symbolizes yin." China. (Day, 1940: 78)

9

Gods of Night, Darkness

Apep, Apepi The monstrous crocodile/serpent demon is the personification of darkness and night, of evil, of storms, and in daily conflict with Ra. Egypt. (Wallis, 1939: 17; Budge, 1969, 1: 11, 269; 2: 107)

Apophis The serpent demon of darkness and of evil "who might at any moment threaten the sun-god" was the antithesis of Re—together representing the eternal conflict of good and evil, or alternation of the powers of light and darkness. Egypt. (Larousse, 1973: 39)

Ariconte The god of the night, the dark, is in constant conflict with Timondonar, his brother, the day. The Tupi, Brazil. (Rhys, 1937: 15)

Astraios, Astraeus The god of the night sky and his wife Eos, the dawn, are the parents of Heosphoros, the morning star, and also of the gods of the winds. He is the son of Krios and Eurybia, brother of Pallas and Perses. Greece. (Kerenyi, 1951: 34, 204–205; Barthell, 1971: 51–53; Hesiod-Brown, 1981: 63, 64)

Atsu The god of the night is believed to be the son of Ama, the earth goddess. The Jukun, Nigeria. (Meek, 1931: 190)

Baau Phoenician goddess of the night, wife of the wind god, Kolpias, and mother of Aion and Protogonos. Near East. (Roscher, 1965, 1, 1: 744; Sayce, 1898: 375–376)

Babi The "Lord of Darkness." Egypt. (Budge, 1973, 1: 128)

Mimi Bat Goddess of the night. Andaman Islands, Bay of Bengal. (Radcliffe-Brown, 1967: 144)

Biri The darkness, a deity associated with Shango. The Yoruba, Nigeria. (MacCulloch, 1925, 8: 49; Budge, 1973, 1: 373)

Caligo The concept of "Dark," mother of Chaos. Greece. (Roscher, 1965, 1, 1: 846)

Mait' Carrefour As a power of darkness he is associated with the moon and midnight, "his noon." Haiti, West Indies. (Deren, 1953: 101–102)

chahałheeł *See* **Tcalyel**

Chaos The primordial void—space, matter, and darkness, one unity. Out of Chaos came Erebus and Nyx. Greece. (Roscher, 1965, 1, 1: 871–872; Kerenyi, 1951: 17–18)

Chaya "dark shadow"—the dark form of Saranyu. An identical substitute wife created by Saranyu to replace herself when she abandoned Vivasvant. Chaya became the mother of Manu (mortal), the ancestor of mankind. India. (O'Flaherty, 1980: 175–178)

Chernobog The Black God, the god of night filled with danger, evil spirits. He symbolizes evil and misfortune and is related to death. Baltic. (Machal, 1918: 288; Gimbutas, 1975: 10/16)

Dylan Son of Arianrod and Gwydion, twin of Lleu. He represented darkness and the sea, while Lleu represented light. Celtic. (Squire, 1906: 261)

Elathan A Celtic god of darkness, one of the Fomors. Ireland. (Squire, 1906: 49–50)

Erebus The "personification of the triple circles of darkness which surrounded the deep Tartarus." Son of Chaos. His sister/wife is Nyx; parents of Aether, Hemera, Charon. Greece. (Barthell, 1971: 9; Kerenyi, 1951: 18; Bulfinch, 1898: 19)

Esum "Darkness," Night. Son of the sky god and brother of Osrane (Moon) and Owia (Sun). The Ashanti, Gold Coast, Ghana. (Feldman, 1963: 125)

The Fomors The "demons of night, darkness, death, barrenness, and evil" who live under the sea. Celtic Ireland. (Squire, 1906: 47–48)

Gauargui A beneficent spirit of the night which takes the form of a nocturnal light or luminous point on the earth, in some tree or rock. Invoked to exorcise Inguma, a malignant spirit. The Basque, Spain and France. (Barandiaran, 1972: 93)

Gaueko The spirit of the night or the night personified. He punishes those who work at night or disturb the silence of his hours. But he is also considered gentle, appears sometimes as a cow, sometimes as a monster. The Basques, Spain and France. (Balandiaran, 1972: 92–93)

Grand Bois The "master of the night earth and night forests." A god of magicians. Plaisance, Haiti, West Indies. (Deren, 1953: 102)

Gronw Pebyr A Celtic god of darkness who killed Lleu (later revived) with a spear to take Blodeuwedd away from him. Britons. (Squire, 1906: 265)

Han A primordial female—"the black of darkness." Skan divided her: one half becoming the nighttime; from the other half he created light (Anp). They are "aspects of the same reality." The Lakota/Oglala, Plains Indians. (Walker, 1980: 51, 52; Jahner, 1977: 33, 34)

Hatu-atu-tupun A goddess of darkness who is very dangerous at twilight and at dawn to men sleeping without their wives. Kapingamarangi, Polynesia. (Emory, 1965: 203)

Hetgwaulana The god of darkness (a supreme deity) who lives in the lower regions called Hetgwauge where the wicked go. He is worshipped, not feared, and invoked for curses on enemies. The Haida, British Columbia. (Harrison, 1891: 16–18)

Hetu-ahin A goddess of darkness who is very dangerous at twilight and at dawn to men sleeping without their wives. Kapingamarangi, Polynesia. (Emory, 1965: 203)

Hine-nui-te-po The goddess of night is more completely the goddess of death and of the underworld. Polynesia. (Roheim, 1972: 32; Andersen, 1928: 212; Fallaize, 1925, 12: 63; Best, 1924: 116, 323)

Hotogov Mailgan The "goddess of the night heavens and creator of people." The Buriat, Siberia. (Curtin, 1909: 46)

Hsuan T'ien Shang Ti God of the dark heavens, of the North Pole, and also god of waters. He exorcizes evil spirits. China. (Day, 1940: 137–138; Werner, 1932: 177; Maspero, 1963: 339)

Hunahpu-Utiu A "hunting coyote . . . god of the night." The Quiché, Guatemala. (Recinos, 1950: 78)

Ikwaokinyapippilele Guardian of the night, a star deity, who causes headache and sickness. The Cuna Indians, Panama. (Keeler, 1960: 85)

Itzcoliuhqui A god represented by obsidian—"Deity of darkness, biting cold volcanic eruptions and destruction." Aztec, Mexico. (Burland, 1967: ix)

Joaltecutli A Mexican god of night. (Bancroft, 1886, 3: 112)

Kaku The male personification of darkness. Egypt. (Gardiner, 1925, 9: 791)

Kane-i-ka-wai-ola The god of the night era, after the darkness, when there was some light. He watered the plants and made the earth fruitful. Hawaii. (Leach, 1956: 168)

Karau The "Spirit of the Night," who can cause death. He is also the "Master of Peccary" and guardian of all animals. The Yupa, Venezuela. (Wilbert, 1974: 137)

Katoya The Black Snake god, guardian of the night and of the west. The Hopi Indians, Arizona. (Waters, 1963: 50)

Kauket With Kuk one of the initial primeval pairs "representing the darkness." Egypt. (Anthes, 1961: 67)

iKombengi The god of night and of the underworld who was invoked for good rice crops. Creator of man at the bidding of iLai. The Toradjas of Celebes, Indonesia. (Downs, 1920: 14, 16, 23, 45; Pettersson, 1957: 27)

Kuk *See* **Kauket**

Lilitu Aramaean demon of the night. Near East. (Vriezen, 1963: 58)

Lono God of the night, the thunder, lightning, and heavy rain. Society Islands, Polynesia. (Henry, 1928: 117)

Maiya Andhiyari The "goddess of the dark fortnight of the month." Also known as Rat Devi, Rat Mai. The Dhanwar, Central Provinces, India. (Russell, 1916, 2: 496–497)

Manuval The "evil spirit of night." Geelvink Bay, New Guinea. (Haddon, 1925, 9: 351)

Matangi The "Night-of-Delusion." A goddess who "establishes the rule of peace, of calm, of prosperity . . . fulfilling the wishes of her devotees. . . . The day is, however, a dream, a mirage that appears in the eternal night. As a form of night, [she] is therefore the Night of Delusion." India. (Danielou, 1964: 283–284)

Metzli, Metztli, Meztli The goddess of the moon had a malignant side as "goddess of the night, the dampness, and the cold." Aztec, Mexico. (Caso, 1956: 36; Spence, 1923: 309; Brinton, 1868: 132; Bancroft, 1886, 3: 111)

Mokwani A cultural hero/supernatural gave man night so he would not have to sleep in daylight. The Tenetehara, Maranhao, Brazil. (Wagley and Galvao, 1949: 101)

Muš A demoness of darkness of the night and considered "the eclipse-demon." Iran. (Gray, 1930: 210)

Nephthys A goddess of darkness and of "the death which is not eternal." Like her sister, Isis, she is possessed of magical powers which they used in resurrecting Osiris. Egypt. (Budge, 1969, 2: 255–256, 258; Knight, 1915: 83–84)

Ningsin majan Goddess of night, of darkness, of the second generation of gods, youngest daughter of Kringkrong wa and Ynong majan. With her brother Ningthoi wa, parents of the third generation of deities. When she died she became U Kaukon, a species of bird. The Katchins of Burma. (Gilhodes, 1908: 676–677)

Nott Teutonic goddess of night, daughter of the giant Norfi. Her marriage to Naglfari produced Aud(r) (space); to Anar (Annarr), Jord (Iord) (earth); to Dellingr, Dagr (day). (Branston, 1955: 65; Grimm, 1883, 2: 735; Guerber, 1895: 15)

Nyx, Nox Greek/Roman personification of night, daughter of Chaos. As the sister/wife of Erebus she was the mother of Aether and Hemera. She is described as "a bird with black wings" who "conceived of the Wind and laid her silver egg" from which was born Eros (Phanes). (Roscher, 1965, 3, 1: 569; Murray, 1935: 222; Kerenyi, 1951: 16–17)

Oroan The demon of darkness who causes eclipses. Guiana. (Brett, 1880: 189)

Piktis, Pikulas The frightening god of the night is a name of Velinas as the Angry God. Baltic. (Gimbutas, 1974: 88; 1975: 10, 16)

Po Night, the passive element in one of the creation stories; the active element, Ao (Day). They were the offspring of Ilu (Immensity) and Mamao (Space), and the parents of the sun. Polynesia. (Andersen, 1928: 385–386; Poignant, 1967: 29)

Po-tangotango A goddess—personification of the "gloomy night." Daughter of Hine-nui-te-po. The Maori, New Zealand. (Andersen, 1928: 411)

Po-uriuri Personification of "dark night," daughter of Hine-nui-te-po. The Maori, New Zealand. (Andersen, 1928: 411)

Qong The god of night caused the sun to set so that it was not continuously day, and taught Qat how to introduce night and sleep in the islands. Melanesia. (Codrington, 1881: 271; Fallaize, 1925, 12: 63)

Rat Devi Goddess of the night. A variant name of Maiya Andhiyari. Central Provinces, India. (Russell, 1916, 2: 497)

Rat Mai The "goddess of night, lives in the house, and makes children happy. . . . If she is angry, she may give you fever." The Baiga, India. (Elwin, 1939: 60)

Ratri Benevolent goddess of the night brings rest and is invoked for protection from wolves and thieves. India. (Macdonell, 1897: 124; Ions, 1967: 22)

Rukho The female "representative of darkness." Creates man but cannot give him a spirit. The Mandeans, Near East. (Dragomanov, 1961: 51)

Sakarabru The "demon of darkness" is a god of justice and of healing, but being just, is also punitive. The Guinea and Senegambia groups. West Africa. (Larousse, 1968: 484)

Saragnayan The god of darkness is an assistant to Sumpoy and Magyan in the underworld. The Bisayan, Philippines. (Jocano, 1969: 21)

Selem Canaanite god of darkness, known also in Arabia and Babylonia. Near East. (Paton, 1925, 3: 181)

Set God of the night sky, of darkness, of mist, of storms, and morally, of evil. Brother and slayer of Osiris, brother and husband of Nephthys, and father of Anubis. Egypt. (Budge, 1969, 2: 241–244; Knight, 1915: 48, 107, 119; Frazer, 1960: 421–422; Ames, 1965: 64–65)

Tanaoa, Tanaroa, Tangaroa Among his many aspects throughout Polynesia, in the Marquesas and in Hawaii he was considered a god of night, of darkness. Among the Maori as "controller of the tides" he was associated with the moon. (Melville, 1969: 35; Andersen, 1928: 380; Williamson, 1933, 1: 20–21; Mackenzie, n.d.: 301)

Tcalyel, tcaxalxe·l, tca·txe·l, chahalheel Darkness, female, is associated with the East, is not bad in itself. But "there is more of whatever is bad at this time than in the others" as Dark Wind is in association, promoting foolishness and illness. The Navajo, Arizona. (McNeley, 1981: 28, 29, 42: Matthews, 1889: 91)

Te Bo Ma In the abstract evolutionary process—Darkness. With Te Maki—"Their descendants were Void, Night, Daylight, Thunder, and Lightning, as well as the Younger Nareau." Micronesia. (Poignant, 1967: 71)

Teuri "Darkness," sister of 'Oro. Society Islands, Polynesia. (Henry, 1928: 231)

Tezcatlipoca As the great god of the Smoking Mirror he represents many dual aspects, e.g., day/night, life/death, good/evil. As god of the night and of darkness he is the powerful Black Tezcatlipoca associated with the region of the dead, with the north, with destruction. He is the patron of sorcerers. Aztec, Mexico. Alexander, 1920: 61–66; Caso, 1958: 14, 27–31; Brinton, 1882: 71–72; Duran, 1971: 476; León-Portilla, 1982: 33, 35)

Tlacatecolototl "Rational Owl," a god of the night and of evil. Toltec, Mexico. (Schoolcraft, 1857: 637; Bancroft, 1886, 3: 184)

tobadjictcini Child-of-the-Water is also a god of darkness, associated with moisture. He "represents reserve, caution, and thoughtful preparation." The Navaho, Arizona and New Mexico. (Reichard, 1950: 30, 417–418, 448)

Troian A "god of night with wax wings (like Icarus)"—a demoniacal creature. The Balkans and Russia. (Larousse, 1973: 407)

Tukomit, Tucomish, Tuukumit The personified night sky, darkness, the male principle who evolved through transitions from Kyuvish, the primordial male. With his sister Tamayowut, the creators, through birth, of the things and features of the world—animate and inanimate. The Luiseño, the Acagchemem. California. (Kroeber, 1925: 677–678; Du Bois, 1904: 185; Boscana, 1933: 115–116)

Ul God of the moon and of the night. New Hebrides, Melanesia. (Larousse, 1973: 503)

Varuna A god with numerous associations. As a god of the heavens he is a god of light both by day (the sun) and by night (the moon), and came to symbolize "the night sky with its thousand stars as his eyes." India. (Macdonell, 1897: 23–26; Bhattacharji, 1970: 33; Ions, 1967: 15)

Wus·quus The spirit of darkness and also of directions. The Chukchee, Siberia. (Bogoras, 1904/09: 303, 305)

Yaotl The god of darkness, a minor name of Tezcatlipoca meaning "Enemy." The Aztec, Mexico. (Burland, 1967: 98; Spence, 1923: 91; Vaillant, 1962: 151)

Yoaltecutli The god of night who is invoked to lull children to sleep. Mexico. (Bancroft, 1886, 2: 275)

Yohualticitl An aspect of Meztli as goddess of the night and guardian of babies. Aztec, Mexico. (Brinton, 1868: 132)

Yolokan Tamulu The son of Amana who was born at dusk and represents "the active but dark and hidden aspect of" his mother. He is "the source of darkness and mischief"—the counterpart of his twin Tamusi in the dual light/darkness concept. The Caliña (Carib) of Surinam. (Zerries, 1968: 246)

Yurugu The "dry, uncultivated, uninhabited earth belongs to Yurugu, a being of night." The Dogon of the French Sudan. (Griaule, 1954: 87)

10

Stellar Gods:
Constellations, Planets, Stars

Abrao Bisexual god of the planet Jupiter who dispenses the "kra" to the abosom born on Thursday—who "will become great heroes." The Akan, Ghana. (Meyerowitz, 1958: 47)

Achinoin A star believed "to be the cause of light rain and strong winds." The Callinago, Lesser Antilles, West Indies. (Rouse, 1948: 564)

Achitumetl A stellar god of Mexico. (Bancroft, 1886, 2: 113)

Adar The planet Saturn was a "god of hunting, was propitious to public affairs as well as to family life." However, he also had an evil influence. Near East. (Seligmann, 1948: 30)

Aelkap-anai The "nailed star"—the Polar Star. The Koryak, Siberia. (Bogoras, 1904/09: 312)

'agojo so'jo The morning star, a male deity of the Tewa. New Mexico. (Harrington, 1907/08: 49)

Ah Ahzah Cab Venus as the morning star. Yucatec and Lacandon Maya, Mexico. (Thompson, 1970: 250)

Ahishama One of the star people, transformed into the troupial bird, was the first to arrive in the black night sky. He became the planet Mars. The Makiritare, Venezuela. (Civrieux, 1980: 113, 114)

Aku The bisexual god of the planet Mercury, patron deity of Wednesday, is the one from whom those born this day receive their "kra," and will be wise. The Akan, Ghana. (Meyerowitz, 1958: 47)

Alcyone A Greek stellar goddess, one of the Pleiades, is the daughter of Pleione and Atlas and a wife of Poseidon, mother of Aethusa. (Barthell, 1971: 57, 129)

Allat A goddess of fate in her association with the planet Venus. As the "morning star she is goddess of War. . .and as evening star patroness of love and harlotry." Near East. (Langdon, 1931: 25)

'Alnahyit 'i 'akiwi The Morning Star (Venus, male) plays on the team with Shnilemun in the nightly peon game against Sun and Slo'w. From this it can be assumed he is benevolent, possibly brings rain. The Chumash, California. (Hudson and Underhay, 1978: 80, 81; Blackburn, 1975: 37, 96)

Amaduwakadi The Morning Star, one of the star people of the Makiritare. Venezuela. (Civrieux, 1980: 114)

Ama-no-Minakanushi-no-kami A god of the stars. Japan. (Larousse, 1968: 415)

Ambrosia A Greek stellar goddess, one of the Hyades, harbingers of rain and storm when rising with the sun. Daughter of Aethra and Atlas. (Barthell, 1971: 57)

Ame-no-kagase-wo A star god "identified with the . . . Pole-star, is believed to guard the land and to prevent disasters, and more particularly to cure eye-diseases." Japan. (Herbert, 1967: 467)

Ame-no-tanabata-hime-no-mikoto A star goddess also known as Shokujo. Japan. (Herbert, 1967: 467)

Anâ-heuheu-pô "Al Fard or Cor Hydra. . .a red star that flies in the open space south, is the lower pillar [of the sky], the pillar to debate by." Tahiti, Polynesia. (Henry, 1920: 102)

Anâ-iva A star deity—"Phaet in Columba . . . the pillar of exit." Tahiti, Polynesia. (Henry, 1920: 103)

Anâ-mua "Antares in Scorpio. . .is the entrance pillar of the dome of the sky." Tahiti, Polynesia. (Henry, 1920: 102)

Anâ-muri The "god of bonito and albicore fishers (Aldebaran in Taurus), is the pillar to blacken or tattoo by." Tahiti, Polynesia. (Henry, 1920: 102)

Anania God of the North Star, one of the "pillars of the sky. . .the pillar to fish by." Society Islands, Polynesia. (Henry, 1928: 362)

Anâ roto "Spica in Virgo. . .is the pillar of perfect purity." Tahiti, Polynesia. (Henry, 1920: 102)

Anâ-Tahu'a-Ta'ata-Metua "Arcturus in Bootis . . . is the pillar to stand by." Tahiti, Polynesia. (Henry, 1920: 103)

Anâ-tahu'a-vahine-o-toa-te-manava "Procyon in Canis minor. . .the pillar for elocution." Tahiti, Polynesia. (Henry, 1920: 103)

Anâ-tipû "(Deviating-aster, Dubbhe in Ursa major) is the upper side pillar, the pillar to guard by." Tahiti, Polynesia. (Henry, 1920: 102)

Anavaru A god identified with Betelgeuse, a "pillar of the sky. . .the pillar to sit by." Society Islands, Polynesia. (Henry, 1928: 361–362)

An Chiu Hsing Chün A malignant star god. China. (Day, 1940: 211)

Anchochinchay A star which was protective of the animals, other than tigers, lions, and bears. The Chimu, Peru. (Mishkin, 1940: 227)

Ao Ping God of the star Hua-kai. A son of Ao Kuang. China. (Werner, 1932: 9)

Ao-tahi "the first light," "the sacred star"—one of those who guided the priests and chiefs in their discussions and undertakings. New Zealand. (Mackenzie, n.d.: 210; White, 1887, 1: 15)

Apsetch An Egyptian star god. (Budge, 1969, 2: 310)

Apu-o-te-Ra'i A star goddess, wife of Maunu-'ura (Mars) and mother of Ta'urua (Fomalhaut). Tahiti, Polynesia. (Henry, 1920: 101)

Apuwenonu The planet Venus was formerly a cultural hero who taught the Tapirape agriculture and spinning. Brazil. (Wagley, 1940: 256)

Ara'a A star of great magnitude, child of Atu-tahi. Tahiti, Polynesia. (Henry, 1920: 101–102)

Ara'aara'a A star of great magnitude, child of Atu-tahi. Tahiti, Polynesia. (Henry, 1920: 101–102)

Arayriqui A star god who was the tutelary deity of the Mojo and Baure, Bolivia. (Métraux, 1942: 74)

Arcas The son of Jupiter (Zeus) and Callisto. Callisto was transformed into a bear by the jealous Juno, and to prevent their son Arcas from killing his mother unwittingly Zeus placed them in the sky as the constellations of the Great Bear and the Little Bear. Greece and Italy. (Ovid, 1955: 61–63)

Ariki A star goddess, daughter of Puaka and Taku-rua. New Zealand. (Mackenzie, n.d.: 210; White, 1887, 1: 52)

Aro A star of great magnitude, child of Atu-tahi. Tahiti, Polynesia. (Henry, 1920: 101–102)

Arsa, Arsu At Palmyra she is the goddess of Venus as the evening star, and a goddess of fate. Also considered as beneficent twins—Azizu and Arsu. Syria. (Langdon, 1931: 24; Gray, 1957: 12; Cook, 1930: 178)

Asare God of Kappa Orionis in the constellation of Orion, a god of thirst, of the arid season. His thirst caused his brothers to dig a well from which burst forth all the waters, eventually creating the sea. The Sherente, Brazil. (Nimuendaju, 1942: 85; Levi-Strauss, 1969: 200, 238)

Asase Yaa A goddess of the earth. She is also identified with the underworld and with the planet Jupiter. The Akan, Ghana. (Meyerowitz, 1958: 28; Parrinder, 1949: 27, 39; Queval, 1968: 16)

Ashira-o One of the Nijuhachi-bushu, a constellation deity. Japanese Buddhism. (Eliseev, 1963: 442)

Ashtar The Arabian god of the morning and evening stars is associated also with life and death. Possibly originally an androgynous deity. (Vriezen, 1963: 52; Albright, 1956: 83)

'Aska' Among the Chumash there are two supernatural Coyotes. 'Aska', Coyote of the Middle World, often visited the Upper World where he is possibly identified with Aldebaran, as he was among the Juaneño and Luiseño. Sky Coyote is Schnilemun, identified with Polaris. California. (Hudson and Underhay, 1978: 84, 102–103, 150–151)

Assanut-li-je An Apache god who created the Milky Way. Southwestern United States. (Bourke, 1892: 507)

Astarte A goddess of fate in her association with the planet Venus. "As the morning star she is goddess of war . . . and as the evening star patroness of love and harlotry." Near East. (Langdon, 1931: 25; Albright, 1956: 74–75, 77)

Asterope One of the Pleiades, a daughter of Atlas. Greece. (Roscher, 1965, 1, 1: 658)

Astraeus The Greek god of starlight, of the night sky, is the husband of Eos, father of Eosphorus, the morning star, Astraia, Virgo, and the winds. (Barthell, 1971: 51–53; Kerneyi, 1951: 104–105; Murray, 1935: 186)

Astraia A daughter of Eos and Astraeus. She lived during the golden period as Dike, a goddess of justice, of innocence, of purity; later retired to the skies as the constellation Virgo. Greece. (Roscher, 1965, 1, 1: 659; Barthell, 1971: 51, 63)

Astrik A goddess identified with the planet Venus, one of the seven chief deities in Armenia. (Ananikian, 1964: 17, 39)

Atar-samayin In Northern Arabia the morning star. Same as Athtar. (Albright, 1956: 228)

Atea-ta'o-nui A star goddess, wife of Rua-tupua-nui and mother of the heavenly bodies. Tahiti, Polynesia. (Henry, 1920: 101)

Athtar, Attar The god of the planet Venus is also associated with irrigation. Arabia and Canaan. (Albright, 1956: 228; Moscati, 1960: 187; Smith, 1969: 100; Fahd, 1968: 47; Gray, 1957: 12, 21)

Atutahi Given both as a god and as a goddess of the star Canopus. The Maori, New Zealand. In Tahiti a constellation god—"Single Bonito, Piscis Australis." Polynesia. Invoked with other deities for abundant harvests. Mother of the moon by Rangi. (Andersen, 1928: 376; Best, 1924: 183, 279; Henry, 1920: 101)

Auahi-turoa A personification of comets, son of Tamu-nui-te-ra. Also called Upoko-roa. The Maori, New Zealand. (Best, 1924: 175; Andersen, 1928: 217)

Auseklis Latvian goddess of the morning star, of the dawn. (Gimbutas, 1963: 199)

Ausrine, Auszrine Lithuanian goddess of Venus, the morning star, and of the dawn. (Gimbutas, 1963: 199; Welsford, 1925, 12: 102; Machal, 1918: 320)

awe'sus Ursa Major, an anthropomorphic supernatural being. The Penobscot Indians, Maine. (Speck, 1935: 19)

Awo The bisexual planet moon is the dispenser of "kra" to those born on Monday, represented as "Calm, peaceful, cool and protective." The Akan, Ghana. (Meyerowitz, 1958: 47)

Azizos, Azizu The Venus star considered as twins—Azizos and Monimos at Edessa, Azizu and Arsu at Palmyra. Near East. (Gray, 1957: 12; Cook, 1930: 178)

The Bagadjimbiri Two brothers, the namers of all things and establishers of culture and initiation ceremonies. They "transformed themselves into water snakes, while their spirits became the Magellanic Clouds." The Karadjeri, Australia. (Eliade, 1973: 53–54)

Basosennin A stellar deity, one of the Nijuhachi-bushu. Japanese Buddhism. (Eliseev, 1963: 442)

Batakagan The morning star, Venus, is invoked in prayers and at sacrifices. The Kankanay, Luzon, Philippines. (Vanoverbergh, 1972: 90)

Batalalan "Stars That Accompany the Moon" is a descendent of Umbulan, the moon. The Ifugao, Philippines. (Barton, 1946: 41)

Bintang Tunang The god of the evening star is the husband of the moon. The Mantra, Malay Peninsula. (Skeat, 1906: 338)

Budh, Budha The planet Mercury is an auspicious god who brings good fortune, is the god of merchants and their wares. His attribute is the bow and arrow. India and Nepal. (Coleman, 1832: 133; Martin, 1914: 296–297; Pal and Bhattacharyya, 1969: 30)

Budhan Mercury is worshipped by the Kaniyan who are astrologers. Southern India. (Thurston, 1909, 3: 193)

Bunjil "Our Father," a beneficent god and demiurge who bestows his powers on the novice medicine man, is identified with the star Altair. The Wurunjeri, Australia. (Eliade, 1973: 4, 139; Fallaize, 1925, 12: 63)

bya so mig dmar The personification of the morning star. Tibet. (Francke, 1925, 8: 78)

Callisto The constellation of the Great Bear was formerly a Greek nymph associated with Artemis. She was ravaged by Zeus and became the mother of Arcas. To protect Callisto Zeus transformed her into a bear; later, took mother and son to the skies forming the constellations of Ursa Major and Ursa Minor. (Prentice Hall, 1965: 30; Ovid, 1955: 61–63; Larousse, 1968: 101)

Canan Chul Chan The morning star as the guardian of the sky. The Tzeltal (Mayan), Mexico. (Thompson, 1970: 321)

gCer bu lag rdum A planetary god whose attribute is a snake-snare. Tibet. (Nebesky-Wojkowitz, 1956, 1: 260)

Ceyacatl A Mexican stellar god. (Bancroft, 1886, 3: 113)

Ah Chac Mitan Ch'oc The planet Venus, the morning star. Mayan, Mexico. (Thompson, 1970: 321; Roys, 1949: 176)

Chang Ch'i An evil god, the star Ti-yu. China. (Werner, 1932: 34, 496)

Chang Chih Hsiung God of the star T'ien-hui, of good omen. China. (Werner, 1932: 34, 506)

Chang-Fêng God of the star Tsuan-ku. China. (Werner, 1932: 34)

Ch'ang Hao God of the star Tao-chên. China. (Werner, 1932: 43)

Chang Hsien "The spirit of the star Chang is supposed to preside over the kitchen of Heaven and to arrange the banquets given by the gods." He is invoked to counteract the evil influence of the Dog Star, T'ien Kou Hsing. He is also invoked for children. China. (Werner, 1932: 34; 1934: 177–179; Day, 1940: 85, 93; Ferguson, 1937: 83–84)

Chang-Hsiung Tao-jen The "god of the constellation Lou. Alternatively with Liu Lung." China. (Werner, 1932: 36)

Chang Huan An evil god of the star Ti-ch'a. China. (Werner, 1932: 36, 496)

Chang K'uei God of the star Chi'i-sha. China. (Werner, 1932: 36)

Chang Kuei-Fang God of the star Sang-mên. China. (Werner, 1932: 36)

Chang Shan God of the star T'êng-shê. China. (Werner, 1932: 37)

Chan Hsiu A god of good omen, the star T'ien-ku. China. (Werner, 1932: 32, 506)

Chao Ch'i God of the star T'ien'shê. China. (Werner, 1932: 44)

Chao Pai-Kao The "god of the constellation Kuei. Alternatively with Wang Pa." China. (Werner, 1932: 44)

Chao Sheng God of the star Yang-jên. China. (Werner, 1932: 44)

Ch'ao T'ien God of the star Sui-p'o. China. (Werner, 1932: 45)

Chasca, Chaska Qoylyor The goddess of the dawn, the morning star, protectress of maidens. Inca, Peru. (Markham, 1969: 63; Brinton, 1882: 170; Rowe, 1946: 295; Larousse, 1968: 442; Means, 1931: 405)

Chekechani The morning star who lives in the east and is a wife of the moon whom she does not feed well so he fades away. The other wife, Puikani, feeds him well and causes him to grow. The Anyanja, Malawi. (Werner, 1964: 228)

Ch'ê K'un A god of evil influence, the star Ti-hui. China. (Werner, 1932: 45, 496)

Ch'ên Chi-Chêng God of the star Mieh-mo; of the star Ti-k'uei (an evil influence); and of the star Ssŭ-ch'i. China. (Werner, 1932: 47, 496)

Ch'ên Chün The "god of the constellation Pi. Alternatively with Chin Sheng-yang." China. (Werner, 1932: 47)

Chêng Ch'un God of the star Fou-ch'ên. China. (Werner, 1932: 48)

Ch'êng San-I God of the star T'ien'ch'iao, of good omen. China. (Werner, 1932: 51)

Chêng-Yüan Tao-Jên The "god of the constellation Nü. Alternatively with Ching Tan." China. (Werner, 1932: 48)

Ch'ên K'an   God of the star T'ien-kuei, of good omen. China. (Werner, 1932: 47, 506)

Ch'ên Kêng   God of the star Sui-sha who is associated with the Ministry of Epidemics and alleviates the plague. China. (Werner, 1932: 47, 560)

Ch'en Mêng-Kêng   An evil god of the star Ti-kou. China. (Werner, 1932: 47, 496)

Ch'ên T'ung   God of the star T'ien-lo. China. (Werner, 1932: 47)

Ch'ên Wu   God of the star Yüeh-hsing. China. (Werner, 1932: 47)

Ch'ên Yuan   An evil influence star god, of the star Ti-wei. China, (Werner, 1932: 47, 496)

Ch'ê-Ti Fu-Jen   Goddess of the star Yueh-k'uei. China. (Werner, 1932: 45)

Cheurfe   A supernatural being, a "comet or shooting star" who is also a cannibal. The Mapuche-Huilliche (Araucanians), Chile. (Cooper, 1946, 6: 753)

Chia Ch'êng   An evil god of the star Ti-yung. China. (Werner, 1932: 56, 496)

Chia Ch'ing   An evil god of the star Ti-yu. China. (Werner, 1932: 56, 496)

Chia Fu   The "god of the constellation Shih. Alternatively with Kao-ping Tao-jên." China. (Werner, 1932: 57)

Chiang   Goddess of the moon, T'ai-yin. China. (Werner, 1932: 58)

Chiang Chung   An evil god of the star Ti-chên. China. (Werner, 1932: 58, 496)

Chiang Huan-ch'u   God of the star Ti-ch'ê. China. (Werner, 1932: 58)

Chiao Ko   God of the star Tsou-shu. China. (Werner, 1932: 65)

Chiao Lung   An evil god of the star Ti-yin. China. (Werner, 1932: 65, 496)

Chia Shih   Goddess of the star Mao-tuan. China. (Werner, 1932: 58)

Chi Ch'ang   God of the star T'ien-chien, of good omen. China. (Werner, 1932: 52, 506)

Ch'i Ch'êng   God of the star T'ien-shou, of good omen. China. (Werner, 1932: 54, 506)

Chieh Shên Hsing Chün   A beneficent star—"Controller of God-given Calamities." China. (Day, 1940: 85)

Chieh Wei Hsiao Tsai   "Dispelling Peril (Dipper)," a sky power. China. (Day, 1940: 210)

Ch'ien Pao   God of the star T'ien-i. China. (Werner, 1932: 68)

Chien T'an   "The god of the constellation Wei. Alternatively with Hou T'ai-i." China. (Werner, 1932: 66)

Chih-nii   The "goddess of the star Alpha in the Lyre." Daughter of Yu-ti. China. (Larousse, 1968: 386)

Chih Nü   The goddess of weavers "is generally identified with the constellation. . .Lyra. . .or with Vega, its principal star." China. (Leach, 1949, 1: 216; Werner, 1932: 73)

Chi K'ang   God of the star T'ien-kou. China. (Werner, 1932: 52)

Ch'i Kung   An evil god, of the star Ti-ch'ang. China. (Werner, 1932: 55, 496)

Chin Ch'êng   God of the star Yin-ts'o. China. (Werner, 1932: 77)

Ching Tan   The "god of the constellation Nü. Alternatively with Chêng-yüan Tao-jên." China. (Werner, 1932: 82)

Ch'in Hsiang   An evil god of the star Ti-hsing. China. (Werner, 1932: 80, 496)

Chin Nan-tao   An evil god of the star Ti-shou. China. (Werner, 1932: 80, 496)

Chin Shêng-yang   The "god of the constellation Pi. Alternatively with Ch'ên Chün." China. (Werner, 1932: 80)

Chin Ta-shêng   God of the star T'ien-wên. China. (Werner, 1932: 80)

Ch'i Shen   "seven spirits of seven stars of the Big Dipper"—worshipped at Ting Hsien, North China. (Gamble, 1954: 418)

Chi Shu-Chi   God of the star Ti-kang. China. (Werner, 1932: 53)

Chi Shu-Ch'ien   God of the star T'ien-kuei. China. (Werner, 1932: 53)

Chi-Shu-I   God of the star Tu-huo. China. (Werner, 1932: 54)

Chi Shu K'un   God of the star Fei-lien. China. (Werner, 1932: 54)

Chi Shu-Li   God of the star T'ai-shên. China. (Werner, 1932: 54)

Chi Shu-tê   God of the star Tsê-lung. China. (Werner, 1932: 54)

Chi Tsun   The "god of the constellation Niu. Alternatively with Li Hung." China. (Werner, 1932: 54)

Chi Tu Hsing Chün   The "Star of Intelligence." China. (Day, 1940: 210)

Ch'iu Yin   God of the star Kuan-so. China. (Werner, 1932: 91)

Cho Kung   An evil god of the star Ti-man. China. (Werner, 1932: 91, 496)

Chou Hsin   God of the star Shih-ô and associated with the Ministry of Epidemics, those of the East. China. (Werner, 1932: 92, 560)

Chou Kêng   God of the star Ti-mo, an evil influence. China. (Werner, 1932: 92, 496)

Chou Pao   The "god of the constellation Hsü. Alternatively with Kai Yen." China. (Werner, 1932: 92)

Chovva   Mars is worshipped by the Kaniyan who are astrologers. Southern India. (Thurston, 1909, 3: 193)

Chuang-chou   The god of the planet Jupiter after Mao Meng. China. (Werner, 1932: 307)

Chu Chao   The "god of the constellation Wei. Alternatively with Ts'ên P'êng." China. (Werner, 1932: 92)

Chu I   God of the star T'ien-ying, of good omen. Seems to be the same as the beneficent god who protects those undergoing examinations. China. (Day, 1940: 113; Werner, 1932: 93, 506; Maspero, 1963: 314)

Chulavete   The morning star—a god among the Cora Indians of Mexico; a goddess among the Pima Indians of Mexico and Arizona. (Alexander, 1964: 176)

Ch'ung Hou-hu   God of the star Ta-hao. China. (Werner, 1932: 97)

Chuquichinchay   A star, the "guardian spirit of tigers, lions and bears." The Chimu, Peru. (Mishkin, 1940: 227)

Chu Shêng   God of the star Kua-hsü. China. (Werner, 1932: 93)

Chu Wei Hsing Ch'ên   "Chief Manager of Star Gods." China. (Day, 1940: 210)

Chu Yu   The "god of the constellation Tou. Alternatively with Yang Hsin." China. (Werner, 1932: 94)

Cista   The morning star, an Iranian goddess giving physical strength and keenness of vision. (Gray, 1930: 140, 221)

Citlalatonac   God of the Milky Way. Mexico. (Caso, 1958: 65)

Citlalcueitl   The "lady of the starry skirt," a stellar goddess invoked in cases of scorpion bites. Aztec, Mexico. (Caso, 1958: 85; Reed, 1966: 114)

Contemactli   A stellar god of Mexico. (Bancroft, 1886, 3: 113)

Coronis   One of the Hyades, harbingers of rain and storm when rising in conjunction with the sun. Daughter of Aethra and Atlas. Greece. (Barthell, 1971: 57)

Daibenzaiten   A constellation deity, one of the Nijuhachi-bushu. Japanese Buddhism. (Eliseev, 1963: 442)

Daibonten   A constellation deity, one of the Nijuhachi-bushu. Japanese Buddhism. (Eliseev, 1963: 442)

Dhruva   The personified Pole Star, a deity attendant upon Indra. India. (Dowson, 1961: 342)

Dhu-samawi   A variant name of Athtar and Atar-samayin, the morning star. Arabia. (Albright, 1968: 228)

Dione   One of the Hyades, harbingers of rain and storm when rising in conjunction with the sun. Daughter of Atlas and Aethra, wife of Tantalus. Greece. (Barthell, 1971: 57)

Djungun   A cultural hero of the primeval time who had the form of a small night bird became the star Beta Gemini. Australia. (Eliade, 1964: 74–75)

Don   A sky goddess associated with the constellation Cassiopeia. Wife of Beli and mother of Arianrod, Gwydion, Nudd. Wales. (Squire, 1906: 252)

Droemerdeener   The star god Canopus is also the creator of the burrowing animals. Bruny Island, Tasmania. (Coon, 1971: 288–289)

Dwyn   The planet Venus. Britain. (Rhys, 1937: 59)

Eosphorus   Greek god of the morning star, son of Eos and Astraeus. (Barthell, 1971: 51; Morford and Lenardon, 1975: 353)

Eshtar   A Semitic stellar goddess, Venus, and considered also a goddess of sex as well as of war. (Roberts, 1972: 39, 57, 60, 147)

Eudora   One of the Hyades, daughter of Atlas and Aethra. Greece. (Barthell, 1971: 57)

Fa'a-iti   The constellation Perseus, born of Rua-tupua-nui and Atea-ta'o-nui. Tahiti, Polynesia. (Henry, 1920: 101)

Fa'a-nui   The constellation Auriga; wife was Tahi-ari'i and son was Ta'urua, Venus. Tahiti, Polynesia. (Henry, 1920: 101)

Fa'a-tapotupotu   The constellation Gemeni, born of Ruatupua-nui and Atea-ta'o-nui. Tahiti, Polynesia. (Henry, 1920: 101)

Fang Chi   An evil god of the star Ti-ming. China. (Werner, 1932: 124, 496)

Fang Chi-ch'ing   The "god of the constellation Pi. Alternatively with Tsang Kuan." China. (Werner, 1932: 124)

Fang I'chên   God of the star Kuan-fu. China. (Werner, 1932: 124)

Fang Kuei   The "god of the constellation Tsui. Alternatively with Fu Chün." China. (Werner, 1932: 124)

Fang Pao   God of the star T'ien-man, of good omen. China. (Werner, 1932: 124)

Fan Huan   An evil god, of the star Ti-t'ui. China. (Werner, 1932: 122, 496)

Fanoui   The star Vega. Society Islands and Tuomotu, Polynesia. Same as Whanui (Maori). (Andersen, 1928: 398)

Fan Pin   An evil god, of the star Ti-lieh. China. (Werner, 1932: 123, 496)

Fei Chung   God of the star Kou-chiao. China. (Werner, 1932: 125)

Fêng I   The "god of the constellation Chi. Alternatively with Yang Chen." Also a god of waters. China. (Werner, 1932: 126; Ferguson, 1937: 90)

Fêng-lin   God of the star Tiao-k'o. China. (Werner, 1932: 126)

Fêng Po   The god of the wind is identified with the constellation of Sagittarius. He is considered also to be under the rule of the star Ch'i. China. (Ferguson, 1937: 73; Werner, 1932: 126)

Fetu-tea   The planet Saturn, father of many of the small stars. Tahiti, Polynesia. (Henry, 1920: 102)

Fu Chun   The "god of the constellation Tsui. Alternatively with Fang Kuei." China. (Werner, 1932: 142)

Fu-hsing   A stellar god and also one of the gods of happiness. China. (Day, 1940: 95; Maspero, 1963: 344)

Fur   The Pleiades is also a calendrical deity marking the beginning of the new year by its appearance. Guardian of agriculture and of crops. The Chimor, Peru. (Rowe, 1948: 50)

Gendenwitha   The morning star, a goddess beloved of Sosondowah. The Iroquois Indians, Eastern United States. (Alexander, 1964: 26)

Gobujô   A constellation deity, one of the Nijuhachi-bushu. Japanese Buddhism. (Eliseev, 1963: 442)

Gocihar   An Iranian demon "probably a shooting star or meteor." (Gray, 1930: 206)

Grahamatrka, Mahavidya   A star goddess described as having three faces or three heads and multi-armed. Nepal. (Pal and Bhattacharyya, 1969: 42)

Guih-teuct-li, Ix-coz-auh-qui   The god of the year and of the planets is also the god of fire. Mexico. (Schoolcraft, 1857, 6: 641)

Guyak   A god who dwells in the Pleiades and is invoked in the ceremony for children to make them strong, skillful, successful, brave, and to give longevity. The Sea Dyaks, Borneo. (Roth, 1968: 171)

Halaia The morning star spirit of the Yana Indians. California. (Curtin, 1903: 425)

Han Jung God of the star Lang-chi. China. (Werner, 1932: 154)

Hapto-iringa The Iranian god of the constellation Ursa Major is the guardian of the north, of the twelve signs of the zodiac, and is invoked to control witches and wizards. (Gray, 1930: 149; Jackson, 1925, 12: 86; Huart, 1963: 42)

Hatsikan The omniscient morning star. The Cora of Sierra de Naharit, Mexico. (Pettazzoni, 1956: 404)

Heng chan, Tch'ong Li God of the Peak of the South who presides over the stars and constellations, over fish and aquatic animals. China. (Chavannes, n.d.: 4, 419)

Heosphoros, Eosphoros The personified morning star, son of Eos and Astraios. Greece. (Roscher, 1965, 1, 2: 2036; Kerenyi, 1951: 204)

Hesamut A hippopotamus goddess identified with Draco as a star goddess. Egypt. (Budge, 1969, 2: 312)

Hesperus The evening star is associated with love, is the son of Eos and Astraeus. Greece. (Barthell, 1971: 51; Fairbanks, 1907: 167; Larousse, 1968: 144)

Hibakara-ô A constellation deity, one of the Nijuhachi-bushu. Japanese Buddhism. (Eliseev, 1963: 442)

Hikoboshi, Kengyu-seë God of the star Altair. Companion of Ame-no-tanabata-hime-no-mikoto. Japan. (Herbert, 1967: 467)

Hine-turama A wife of Uru-te-ngangana. Mother of the stars. The Maori, New Zealand. (Best, 1924: 97)

Hito-lap The planet Venus. As the morning star called Kêrgañalinin. The Chukchee, Siberia. (Bogoras, 1904/09: 314)

Ho Chih-yüan An evil god, of the star Ti-k'uang. China. (Werner, 1932: 158, 496)

Hoku kau opae, Newe The goddess Sirius "determined the best time for catching shrimp by her rising or setting." Hawaii. (Emerson, 1967: 51)

Hoku loa The planet Venus. Hawaii. (Emerson, 1967: 51)

Hokushin-ô-kami The constellation of Ursa Minor. Japan. (Herbert, 1967: 467)

Hokuʻula God of the star Aldebaran. With Ke Kao a navigational star. Maui, Hawaii. (Ashdown, 1971: 52)

Holhol The California Condor, who had powers of locating lost articles, persons, etc., was identified with Mars because he "traveled on a path across the Upper World, could be easily recognized, and was often sought out to locate Slo'w . . . . Mars at times moved quite rapidly against the backdrop of stars, which suggests the mythological ability of Huolhol to travel great distances in a short period of time . . . . Mars has a reddish color . . . a color parallel between the planet and the bird's reddish-orange colored head." The Chumash, California. (Hudson and Underhay, 1978: 84, 91, 93)

Ho-pi-ri-ku-tsu The morning star to whom human sacrifices were made. The Pawnee, Nebraska. (Fletcher, 1903: 12)

Horo A star goddess, wife of Ta'urua-nui-amo-'aha (Sirius), mother of Mahu-ni'a and Mahu-raro. Tahiti, Polynesia. (Henry, 1920: 103)

Hoseyasidaa The morning star who controls the stars and ushers in the day. The Wichita, Kansas. (Dorsey, 1904, 1: 18, 29)

Hou T'ai-i "The god of the constellation Wei. Alternatively with Chien Tan." China. (Werner, 1932: 160)

Hsia Chao God of the star Yüeh-tê. China. (Werner, 1932: 165)

Hsia Hsiang An evil god, of the star Ti-ch'iang. China. (Werner, 1932: 165, 496)

Hsiao Chên God of the star Chin-fu. China. (Werner, 1932: 165)

Hsiao Hao Hsing Chün A very malignant star god. China. (Day, 1940: 211)

Hsiao Tien An evil god, of the star Ti-k'ung. China. (Werner, 1932: 167, 496)

Hsieh T'ien-chun "The god of the planet Mars, . . . regulates the summer season." China. (Werner, 1932: 167)

Hsieh Ting "The god of the constellation Chang. Alternatively with Wan Hsiu." China. (Werner, 1932: 167)

Hsing Chu Ta Ti God of the stars. China. (Day, 1940: 210)

Hsing San-luan An evil god of the star Ti-su. China. (Werner, 1932: 173, 496)

Hsüan Wu Hsing The malignant Black Tortoise Star. China. (Day, 1940: 211)

Hsü Ch'êng An evil god, of the star Ti-wei. China. (Werner, 1932: 175, 496)

Hsü Chêng-tao God of the star T'ien-yu, of good omen. China. (Werner, 1932: 175, 506)

Hsü Chi An evil god, of the star Ti-chin. China. (Werner, 1932: 175–496)

Hsü Chung God of the star Hsien-ch'ih. China. (Werner, 1932: 175)

Hsü Fang God of the star Sui-hsing. China. (Werner, 1932: 175)

Hsü Kai God of the sun, T'ai-yang. China. (Werner, 1932: 175)

Hsü K'un God of the star Hsuan-wu. China. (Werner, 1932: 176)

Hsü Shan An evil god, of the star Ti-ch'ou. China. (Werner, 1932: 176–496)

Huang Goddess of the star Ti-hou. China. (Werner, 1932: 184)

Huang Ching-yüan An evil god, of the star Ti-sha. China. (Werner, 1932: 184, 496)

Huang Fei-pao God of the star T'ien-ssŭ. China. (Werner, 1932: 185)

Huang Ming God of the star Fu-lung. China. (Werner, 1932: 185)

Huang Ping-ch'ing An evil god, of the star Ti-tso. China. (Werner, 1932: 186, 496)

Huang Ts'ang The "god of the constellation Mao. Alternatively with Wang Liang." China. (Werner, 1932: 187)

Huang Wu An evil god, of the star Ti-sun. China. (Werner, 1932: 187, 496)

Huang Yüan-chi God of the star Ts'an-ch'u. China. (Werner, 1932: 187)

Hung Chin God of the star Lung'tê. China. (Werner, 1932: 193)

Hung Sha Hsing, Hung Sha Sha A malignant star who causes fires, miscarriages, deaths, if not propitiated. China. (Day, 1940: 85)

Huo-ling Shêng-mu Goddess of the star Huo-fu. China. (Werner, 1932: 194)

Hu Pai-yen An evil god, of the star Ti-chieh. China. (Werner, 1932: 179, 496)

Hu Tao-yüan The "god of the constellation Chên. Alternatively with Liu Chih." China. (Werner, 1932: 180)

Huu Win?nawa "Arrow's Flint. The cluster of stars that marks Orion's head." The Chemehuevis, California, Nevada, and Arizona. (Laird, 1976: 92)

Huu Wisi?Yah "Arrow's Feathers. These are the three stars in Orion's Sword." The Chemehuevis, California, Nevada, and Arizona. (Laird, 1976: 92)

The Hyades Daughters of Atlas and Aethra—named as: Ambrosia, Coronis, Dione, Eudora, Pedile, Phyto, and Polyxo. Their appearance foretells the rains. They are the sisters of the Pleiades. Greece. (Murray, 1935: 171; Barthell, 1971: 57; Larousse, 1968: 144; Roscher, 1965, 3, 2: 2492, 2745)

Icoquih Venus, the morning star. The Quiché, Guatemala. (Recinos, 1950: 71)

i'ge-reəxe God of the morning star who was invoked in war. The Crow Indians, Montana. (Lowie, 1922: 321)

Iguaoginyapiler, Iguaoginyalilel Another name for Venus—*see* **Pugsu.** Brother of Ibelele. The Cuna Indians, Panama. (Nordenskiold, 1938: 325)

Ihette One of the star people who became Orion's Belt. The Makiritare, Venezuela. (Civrieux, 1980: 114)

I'itoi The morning star who is invoked in maize ceremonies. The Pimans, the Papagos. Arizona and Mexico. (Underhill, 1948: 17, 23)

Te Ikaroa The personification of the Milky Way who is one of those who control the seasons. The Maori, New Zealand. (Best, 1924: 97, 105)

Ilukalin eñer The Pole Star whose house is in the zenith. The Chukchee, Siberia. (Bogoras, 1904/09: 307)

Inaiyuaiyud A constellation god. The Ifugao, Philippines. (Barton, 1946: 42)

Innini The Sumerian/Babylonian goddess of the planet Venus was also considered an earth goddess, a goddess of waters, as well as a goddess of battle. (Mercer, 1925, 12: 700, 709; Langdon, 1931: 5, 14, 93)

Intjinkinja Two hostile stellar gods, brothers, who cause death. Central Australia. (Roheim, 1972: 106)

Ipetiman The constellation Orion. The Carib Indians. Guiana. (Levi-Strauss, 1973: 241)

Ishtar The goddess of the planet Venus was of a dual character, the beneficent goddess of love, of childbirth, of healing, but also a goddess of war. She was goddess of the month Elul (Semitic), Ululu (Sumerian). Numerous goddesses were identified or merged with her—Anunit, Innini, Nana, Ninna, Inanna. Babylonia, Near East. (Hommel, 1925, 3: 74; Langdon, 1931: 25, 317; Jayne, 1962: 122; Jastrow, 1898: 82, 459; Seligmann, 1948: 30; Mercer, 1925, 12: 700)

Itzpapalotl "Obsidian Knife Butterfly" was originally a stellar goddess of the Chichimec who became an Aztec goddess of agriculture, of the cultivated fields. She was the goddess of the sixteenth day, Cozcaquauhtli. Mexico. (Vaillant, 1962: 150; Spence, 1923: 223–226; Nicholson, 1967: 109)

Ixquimilli A Mexican god known in the Mayan lowland as the god of the planet Venus. (Thompson, 1970: 328)

Janmagraha A planetary god of "terrifying nature" with ten arms. He rides a camel and "wears a garland of human heads." Nepal. (Pal and Bhattacharyya, 1969: 43)

Jên Kuang The "god of the constellation Liu. Alternatively with Wu K'un." China. (Werner, 1932: 209)

Jên Lai-p'in God of the star T'ien-sha, of good omen. China. (Werner, 1932: 209, 506)

Jilijoaibu The constellation of the Pleiades which is responsible for the rain. The Arecuna, Guiana. (Levi-Strauss, 1969: 244)

Kaimiki The god of the Milky Way. The Ifugao, Philippines. (Barton, 1946: 42)

Kai-waka A star god, one of those who guided the priests and chiefs in their discussions and undertakings. New Zealand. (White, 1887, 1: 15)

Kai Yen The "god of the constellation of Hsü. Alternatively with Chou Pao." China. (Werner, 1932: 212)

Kao Chên "The god of the constellation Shih. Alternatively with Kêng Shun." China. (Werner, 1932: 215)

Kao Chi-nêng God of the star Hei-sha. China. (Werner, 1932: 215)

K'ao Ko An evil god, of the star Ti-chêng. China. (Werner, 1932: 216, 496)

Kao K'o God of the star T'ien-t'ui, of good omen. China. (Werner, 1932: 215, 506)

Kao Lan-ying Goddess of the star T'ao-hua. China. (Werner, 1932: 215)

Ka-onohi-o-ka-la The "eye-ball of the sun" in some traditions "conducted the souls of heroes" to the Afterworld. Hawaii. (Alexander, 1967: 103)

Kao-ping Tao-jên The "god of the constellation Shih. Alternatively with Chia Fu." China. (Werner, 1932: 215)

Karariwari The Pole Star who lives in the north is the chief of all the heavenly gods. The Skidi Pawnee, Plains Indians, Nebraska. (Dorsey, 1904: 3, 4)

Karttikeya God of the planet Mars and god of war whose emblem is the spear. Nepal. (Pal and Bhattacharyya, 1969: 46)

Karura-ô A constellation deity, one of the Nijuhachi-bushu. Japanese Buddhism. (Eliseev, 1963: 442)

Kasasaniki The North Star, the guide at night and guardian of the medicine-men. The Wichita, Plains Indians, Kansas. (Dorsey, 1904, 1: 18, 69)

Kavya Usanas The "teacher of the Asuras, who is identified with the planet Venus." India. (Jacobi, 1925, 2: 806)

Ke Kao Taurus. With Hoku'ula a navigational star. Maui, Hawaii. (Ashdown, 1971: 52)

Kendatsuba A constellation deity, one of the Nijuhachibushu. Japanese Buddhism. (Eliseev, 1963: 442)

Kengra Barsa Son of Salgong and Apongma, "father of fire and of all the heavenly bodies." The Garos, Tibet and Burma. (Keane, 1925, 2: 122)

Kêng Shun   The "god of the constellation Shih. Alternatively with Kao Chên." China. (Werner, 1932: 217)

Kêng Yen   An evil god, of the star Ti-chieh. Also "god of the constellation Fang. Alternatively with Yao Kung-po." China. (Werner, 1932: 217, 218, 496)

Ketu   The demon of the descending node. The body of the demon Rahu whose head was cut off by Vishnu because he drank of the amrta of immortality. Rahu and Ketu cause eclipses by swallowing the sun and the moon periodically, Ketu usually associated with the moon. He is associated with falling stars and meteors. India. (Briggs, 1953: 544, 547; Martin, 1914: 295, 298)

Kewan   Assyrian god of the planet Saturn. (Roscher, 1965, 2, 1: 1179)

Khyab 'jug sgra can 'dzin   (Rahu) The chief of the planetary deities. Tibet. (Nebesky-Wojkowitz, 1956, 1: 387)

Kinamalig   The constellation Ursa Major, invoked at the *pakde* public sacrifice—before the sowing of rice, before the transplanting and before the harvest. The Kankanay, Luzon, Philippines. (Vanoverbergh, 1972: 91, 95)

Kinnara-ô   A constellation deity, one of the Nijuhachi-bushu. Japanese Buddhism. (Eliseev, 1963: 442)

Kirinte   God of the planet of the same name. He "has power over the spirits of men. Only the spirits of unconscious people come to Kirinte." They are given the choice of staying or returning. If they stay they die forever and cannot go to another planet. The Campa, Peru. (Llosa Porras, 1971: 61)

Kivana   The morning star. The Cora Indians, Mexico. (Roheim, 1972: 2)

Klu gza' nag mo   A planetary god. Tibet. (Nebesky-Wojko-witz, 1956, 1: 260)

Ko Fang   An evil god, of the star Ti-shu. China. (Werner, 1932: 220, 496)

Ko Kao   An evil god, of the star Ti-wên. China. (Werner, 1932: 220, 496)

Komeang   Goddess of the morning star who is involved with initiation signs and markings. The Western Mejbrat, New Guinea. (Elmberg, 1955: 42–44)

Konda-ô   A constellation deity, one of the Nijuhachi-bushu. Japanese Buddhism. (Eliseev, 1963: 442)

Konshiki-kujaku   A constellation deity, one of the Nijuhachi-bushu. Japanese Buddhism. (Eliseev, 1963: 442)

Kou Ch'ên T'ien Wang   A malignant, evil star deity. China. (Day, 1940: 210)

K'ou Hsün   The "god of the constellation Hsin. Alternatively with Su-yüan Tao-jên." China. (Werner, 1932: 222)

Krodo   The Teutonic planet Saturn. (Grimm, 1880: 248)

Kuamachi   The Evening Star. Not one of the star people, but he followed them into the sky. The Makiritare, Venezuela. (Civrieux, 1980: 103, 114)

K'uang Yü   An evil god, of the star Ti-ch'üan. China. (Werner, 1932: 231, 496)

Kuan Pin   An evil god, of the star Ti-ts'ang. China. (Werner, 1932: 224, 496)

Kukulcan   The plumed serpent of the Maya who was associated with Venus, the morning star. Mexico. (Nicholson, 1967: 23, 39; Tozzer, 1941: 18, 157; Thompson, 1970: 328)

K'ung Ch'êng   An evil god, of the star Ti-sui. China. (Werner, 1932: 235, 496)

Kung Ch'ien   An evil god, of the star Ti-yao. China. (Werner, 1932: 234, 496)

Kung Ch'ing   God of the star T'ien-wei, of good omen. China. (Werner, 1932: 234, 506)

Kung-sun To   God of the star Jên-sha. China. (Werner, 1932: 235)

K'ung Tao-ling   An evil god, of the star Ti-nu. China. (Werner, 1932: 236, 496)

K'ung T'ien-chao   An evil god, of the star Ti-chi. China. (Werner, 1932: 236, 496)

Kuo Chi   An evil god, of the star Ti-ling. China. (Werner, 1932: 236, 496)

Kuribu   A monster god—"the mythical being of Ea, serves in mythology as the fish-ram, symbol of the god of the Deep, and also as Capricorn." Sumer, Near East. (Langdon, 1931: 108)

Ku Tsung An evil god, of the star Ti-tsou. China. (Werner, 1932: 222, 496)

Kütto The second of the star people, transformed into a frog, to arrive in the black night sky. He became an unidentified constellation. The Makiritare, Venezuela. (Civrieux, 1980: 114, 185)

Ku-yu The Shooting Star, a malevolent god of the Mojave Indians, Arizona. (Bourke, 1889: 182, 186)

Kwakwastule The planet Saturn. The Cuna Indians, Panama. (Keeler, 1960: 85)

Ladon A Greek god who in one legend was made the constellation Draco by Hera. (Barthell, 1971: 11)

Lan Hu A god of evil influence, the star Ti-chio. China. (Werner, 1932: 238, 496)

Lan Kan Hsing Chün "Star-God of the Corral." China. (Day, 1940: 106)

Le-gerem A "female spirit-being" from whom Anagumang "had learned the seasonal movements of the stars." Yap Island, Micronesia. (Clerk, 1982: 370)

Lei K'ai God of the star I-ma. China. (Werner, 1932: 242)

Lei P'êng God of the star Kou-ch'ên. China. (Werner, 1932: 244)

Lemr'er The planet Venus. The Guanches of Teneriffe, Canary Islands. (Basset, 1925, 2: 509)

Li Ch'ang A god of evil influence, the star Ti-ch'iao. China. (Werner, 1932: 245, 496)

Li Chin God of the star Huang-ên. China. (Werner, 1932: 245)

Li Chung "The god of the constellation Hsing. Alternatively with Lü Nêng." China. (Werner, 1932: 246)

Li Hsien God of the star T'ien-fu, of good omen. China. (Werner, 1932: 246, 506)

Li Hsin An evil god, of the star T'i-o. China. (Werner, 1932: 246, 496)

Li Hsin God of the star T'ien-an, of good omen. China. (Werner, 1932: 246, 506)

Li Hsiung The "god of the constellation K'uei. Alternatively with Ma-wu." China. (Werner, 1932: 246)

Li Hung The "god of the constellation Niu. Alternatively with Chi Tsun." China. (Werner, 1932: 246)

Li Kung-jên God of the star T'ien-shang, of good omen. China. (Werner, 1932: 246, 506)

Li Liang God of the star Ta-huo. China. (Werner, 1932: 247)

Lin Shan God of the star P'i-ma. China. (Werner, 1932: 253)

Li Pao God of the star T'ien-wei, of good omen. China. (Werner, 1932: 249, 506)

Li Sui An evil god, of the star Ti-p'i. China. (Werner, 1932: 249, 496)

Li Tao-t'ung The "god of the constellation K'ang. Alternatively with Wu Han." China. (Werner, 1932: 249)

Liu Chih The "god of the constellation Chñ. Alternatively with Hu Tao-yüan." China. (Werner, 1932: 255)

Liu H'eng A god of evil influence, the star Ti-ho. China. (Werner, 1932: 257, 496)

Liu Lung The "god of the constellation Lou. Alternatively with Chang-hsiung Tao-jên." China. (Werner, 1932: 257)

Liu Ta God of the star T'ien-k'u, of good omen. China. (Werner, 1932: 258, 506)

Li Yo An evil god of the star Ti-mo. China. (Werner, 1932: 250, 496)

Lucero The morning star. The Zūi Indians, New Mexico. (Bourke, 1892: 508)

Lu Ch'ang God of the star T'ien-chi, of good omen. China. (Werner, 1932: 281, 506)

Lu Chih An evil god, of the star Ti-hui. China. (Werner, 1932: 281, 496)

Lucifer The Roman morning star and herald of the dawn, his mother. (Prentice Hall, 1965: 83; Leach, 1950, 2: 650)

Lu Hsiu-tê An evil god, of the star Ti-hsiung. China. (Werner, 1932: 281, 496)

Lü Nêng The "god of the constellation Hsing. Alternatively with Li Chung." China. (Werner, 1932: 298)

Lung An-chi God of the star Lan-kan. China. (Werner, 1932: 285)

Lung Ch'êng A god of evil influence, of the star Ti-p'ing. China. (Werner, 1932: 285, 496)

Lung-chi Kung-chu Goddess of the star Hung-luan. China. (Werner, 1932: 285)

Lung-Hsü Hu God of the star Chiu-ch'ou. China. (Werner, 1932: 285)

Lü Tzǔ-ch'êng God of the star T'ien-i, of good omen. China. (Werner, 1932: 298, 506)

Ma Ch'êng-lung God of the star Yan-ch'ai. China. (Werner, 1932: 299)

Ma Chung God of the star Hsieh-kuang. China. (Werner, 1932: 299)

Ma Fang God of the star Chu-ch'iao. China. (Werner, 1932: 299)

Magora-ô A constellation deity, one of the Nijuhachi-bushu. Japanese Buddhism. (Elizeev, 1963: 442)

Mahu-n'ia A stellar deity—"Upper-Magellan," son of Ta'urua-nui-amo-'aha and Horo. Tahiti, Polynesia. (Henry, 1920: 103)

Mahu-raro A stellar deity—"Lower-Magellan," son of Ta'urau-nui-amo-'aha (Sirius) and Horo. Tahiti, Polynesia. (Henry, 1920: 103)

The Makara The Pleiades are the Seven Sisters, the Ice Maidens. They are the beautiful "wives of the men of Orion," who disappear over the horizon enough ahead of them to make camp. In another tale they are the Emu sisters who are pursued by the Wanjin—becoming the Pleiades followed by Orion. Australia. (Mountford, 1965: 56; 1969: 38)

Makeshura, Mansen-ô, Manzenshao Constellation deities, three of the Nijuhachi-bushu. Japanese Buddhism. (Eliseev, 1963: 442)

Mao Meng God of the planet Jupiter who was replaced by Chuang Chou at the end of the Chou dynasty. China. (Werner, 1932: 307)

Ma Shih Goddess of the star Sao-chou. China. (Werner, 1932: 300)

Mata-ri'i The constellation of the Pleiades, child of Ta'urua-nui (Jupiter) and Te-'ura-taui-e-pâ. Tahiti, Polynesia. (Henry, 1920: 103)

Matariki The Pleiades are associated with the spring and the planting season. In New Zealand a star god, one of those who guided the priests and chiefs in their discussions and undertakings. (White, 1887, 1: 15; Andersen, 1928: 411)

Maunu-'ura Mars, son of Ta'urua (Venus) and Rua-o-mere. His wife is Apu-o-te-Ra'i. Father of Ta'urua (Fomalhaut). Tahiti, Polynesia. (Henry, 1920: 101)

Mawaraten A constellation deity, one of the Nijuhachi-bushu. Japanese Buddhism. (Eliseev, 1963: 442)

Ma Wu The "god of the constellation K'uei. Alternatively with Li Hsiung." China. (Werner, 1932: 301)

Megu God of the evening star who is invoked in the ceremony for children to make them strong, skillful, successful, brave, and to give longevity. The Sea Dyaks, Borneo. (Roth, 1968: 171)

Mei Po God of the star T'ien-tê. China. (Werner, 1932: 310)

Mei Tê God of the star Ti-i'ung. China. (Werner, 1932: 310)

Mei Wu God of the star T'ien K'ung. China. (Werner, 1932: 310)

Mên Tao-chêng An evil god, of the star Ti-fu. China. (Werner, 1932: 312)

Mere Orion's Belt—in the constellation. Child of Ta'urua-nui (Jupiter). Also called Ta'urua-o-Mere-ma-tû-tahi. Tahiti, Polynesia. (Henry, 1920: 103)

Merodach The Babylonian divine king, god of heaven, and solar deity was also associated with the planet Jupiter. Near East. (Sayce, 1898: 94, 113, 115; Rawlinson, 1885: 48)

Merope One of the Pleiades, daughter of Pleione and Atlas, and wife of Sisyphus. Greece. (Barthell, 1971: 57)

Meskheti An Egyptian star god—the Great Bear. (Budge, 1969, 2: 312)

Meto A personification of comets. The Maori, New Zealand. (Best, 1924: 175)

Metua-'ai-papa The constellation Corvus whose wife is Tera'i-tû-roroa. Father of Fetu-tea. Tahiti, Polynesia. (Henry, 1920: 102)

Mi-ka-k'e Hⁿn-baⁿdon The "Day-Star (Morning star), grandfather." The Dhegiha (Osage), Plains Indians, South Dakota and Nebraska. (La Flesche, 1928: 74)

Mi-ka-k'e Hⁿndoⁿ The "Night-star (Evening star), grandmother." The Dhegiha (Osage), South Dakota and Nebraska. (La Flesche, 1928: 74)

Mi-ka-k'eu-ki-thaç'iⁿ "Double-star, grandmother." The Dhegiha (Osage), South Dakota and Nebraska. (La Flesche, 1928: 74)

Mi-ka-k'e Zhu-dse "Red Star, the Pole Star, grandfather." A war god. The Dhegiha (Osage), South Dakota and Nebraska. (La Flesche, 1928: 74)

Ming Chiu Hsing Chün "Maximum Blessing Star." China. (Day, 1940: 210)

Ming K'uei T'ien Hsia A star god, the patron of scholars and of the professions. Also called K'uei Hsing. China. (Day, 1940: 112, 213)

Misshakukongô A constellation deity, one of the Nijuhachi-bushu. Japanese Buddhism. (Eliseev, 1963: 442)

Mixcoatl The Cloud Serpent, the god of the Pole Star, of the stars, and of hunting. The Chichimec, the Pipil, the Aztec, the Otomi. Mexico, Guatemala, and Nicaragua. (Caso, 1958: 31, 37; Vaillant, 1962: 140, 150; Krickeberg, 1968: 81)

Moana-'a'ano-huri-hara A stellar deity—"Wide-ocean-in-which-to-cast-crime, more sky," child of Atu-tahi and Tû-i-te-moana-'urifa. Tahiti, Polynesia. (Henry, 1920: 102)

Moana-'aere "Trackless Ocean, the clear sky under Hydra," child of Atu-tahi and Tû-i-te-moana-'urifa. Tahiti, Polynesia. (Henry, 1920: 102)

Moana-'ohu-noa-'ei-ha'a-moe-hara A constellation—"Vortex-Ocean-in-which-to-lose-crime, Crater." Tahiti, Polynesia. (Henry, 1920: 102)

mədawile The Pleiades. The Penobscot Indians, Maine. (Speck, 1935: 20)

Moihernee A star god and a creator who shaped the earth, the rivers, the islands, and the first man. Bruny Island, Tasmania. (Coon, 1971: 288–289)

Mönetta The scorpion, one of the star people, became the Big Dipper, Ursa Major. The Makiritare, Venezuela. (Civrieux, 1980: 114)

Monimos The Venus star considered as twins—Azizos and Monimos. Edessa, Near East. (Gray, 1957: 12)

Monkidikidim "Clusters of Small Stars," a god of the sky-world. The Ifugao, Philippines. (Barton, 1946: 42)

Monliwotan "Great Dipper," a god of the skyworld. The Ifugao, Philippines. (Barton, 1946: 42)

msa'tawe The north star, the guide of the Penobscot Indians. Maine. (Speck, 1935: 20)

Muhʷintɨ Aldebaran. The leader in the hunt for the Mountain Sheep. The Chemehuevis, California, Nevada, and Arizona. (Laird, 1976: 92)

Mungula A planetary god and a god of war. India. (Coleman, 1832: 132)

Myoken The Pole Star who is a guardian of the land and protective against disasters. Japan. (Herbert, 1967: 467; Kato, 1926: 15)

Nagawɨ "Mountain Sheep (plural). Orion's Belt." A shaman's helper. The Chemehuevis, California, Nevada, and Arizona. (Laird, 1976: 91, 112)

Na Hiku The Big Dipper, a navigational constellation. Maui, Hawaii. (Ashdown, 1971: 52)

Na huihui The constellation of the Pleiades. Hawaii. (Emerson, 1967: 51)

Na kao God of the constellation Orion. Hawaii. (Emerson, 1967: 52)

Nana A goddess of the planet Venus as the morning and evening stars. Babylonia, Near East. (Jastrow, 1898: 81)

Nandaryu-ô A constellation deity, one of the Nijuhachi-bushu. Japanese Buddhism. (Eliseev, 1963: 442)

Naraen A constellation deity, one of the Nijuhachi-bushu. Japanese Buddhism. (Eliseev, 1963: 442)

Na-u-kuzze The constellation of the Great Bear. The Apache Indians, Southwestern United States. (Bourke, 1892: 502)

Naxokosse diłxiłn The constellation Ursa Major, and in one version of the creation myth one of the four creators of earth and sky. The San Carlos Apache, Arizona. (Goddard, 1918: 27)

Nebo A god of wisdom and knowledge, of prophecy and literature, the recorder of men's deeds. He presided over the planet Mercury. He was the son of Merodach and Zarpanit, his wife was Tasmitu. Assyria and Babylonia. (Seligmann, 1948: 30; Ceram, 1968: 256; Jastrow, 1898: 124; Sayce, 1898: 42, 50, 95, 113–120; Rawlinson, 1885: 50)

Nergal The god identified with the planet Mars—a god of pestilence and death, of war and destruction, a god of the underworld in marrying Ereshkigal. Assyria and Babylonia. (Seligmann, 1948: 30; Jastrow, 1898: 172, 459; Ceram, 1968: 256; Schoeps, 1961: 58)

Nesru An Egyptian star god. (Budge, 1969, 2: 310)

Nesu A stellar god, Antares in Scorpio. Husband of Ninsikilla. Sumer and Akkadia, Near East. (Langdon, 1931: 110)

Newe, Hoku kau opae Sirius "determined the best time for catching shrimp by her rising or setting." Newe and Keoe are navigational stars. Hawaii. (Emerson, 1967: 51)

Ne-zil-la A stellar goddess, Coma Bereneces (Abundance). Babylonia, Near East. (Langdon, 1931: 317)

Nijuhachi Bushu The deities of the twenty-eight constellations, protective deities, associated with Kwanon. Japanese Buddhism. (Eliseev, 1963: 442; Larousse, 1968: 422)

Nin, Bar The god who presided over Saturn, a god of war and hunting. Assyria. (Rawlinson, 1885: 47)

Ningarope A stellar goddess, mother of Pungngane and Waijungngari. Encounter Bay, South Australia. (Woods, 1879: 201)

Ningishzida An early tree god and a god of the underworld who is also identified with the constellation Hydra. Babylonia, Near East. (Langdon, 1931: 90, 178; Jacobsen, 1970: 24)

Ning San'i A god of evil influence, of the star Ti-yin. China. (Werner, 1932: 327, 496)

Ninlil A Sumerian goddess identified with Ursa Major as well as with the planet Venus. (Langdon, 1931: 317; Campbell, 1962: 109)

Ninsubur A Babylonian god identified with the constellation of Orion. Near East. (Langdon, 1931: 177–178)

Nish-kan-ru Mat A stellar goddess of the Ainu. Japan. (Munro, 1963: 15)

Nochiu-e-ran-guru and **Nochiu-e-ran-mat** The god and goddess of the air whose duty was to "attend to the shining and well-being of the stars." The Ainu, Japan. (Batchelor, 1925, 1: 243)

Ntoa A state god/goddess whose planet is Venus. He-she "is expressed in the goat (sex, life), and the dog (death and resurrection)." In cult rituals a participant of death/rebirth ceremonies. The Akan, Ghana. (Meyerowitz, 1958: 49, 57)

Nurong The star Antares, brother of Bunjil. Australia. (Fallaize, 1925, 12: 63)

O Ch'ung'yü God of the star T'ien-ma. China. (Werner, 1932: 336)

Occopirmus An ancient god of the heavens and of the stars. Latvia, Lithuania, and Prussia. (Welsford, 1925, 9: 240, 488; Puhvel, 1974: 83)

Olotollalipippilele Shooting star, champion of Good Star people. The Cuna, Panama. (Keeler, 1960: 85)

Operikata The morning star who lives in the east and is also a warrior god. The Skidi Pawnee, Plains Indians, Nebraska. (Dorsey, 1904: 3, 4)

Opirikus The same as the above. (Grinnell, 1893: 115)

Opirit The god of the morning star, the herald of the dawn, represents "Life and strength and fruitfulness." The Pawnee, Plains Indians, Nebraska. (Fletcher, 1900/01: 128–129)

Opiritakata The Yellow-Star of the northwest who controls the north winds. The Skidi Pawnee, Plains Indians. Nebraska. (Dorsey, 1904: 4)

Oron God of the evening star who rules over the afterworld of the elderly dead. The Western Mejbrat, New Guinea. (Elmberg, 1955: 42)

Otava Finno-Ugric constellation of the Great Bear. (Larousse, 1968: 304)

Ou-yang Shun God of the star Wang-shên. China. (Werner, 1932: 339)

Ou-yang T'ien-lu   God of the star T'ien-hsing. China. (Werner, 1932: 339)

Ozza   The planet Venus as a god in Palmyra, a goddess in Mecca. Near East. (Vriezen, 1963: 68; Smith, 1969: 57)

Pai Hu Hsing   "White Tiger Star of the West, blighter of crops and curse of men sick unto death . . . (Specially Malignant)." China. (Day, 1940: 85, 210)

Paiowa   Goddess of the evening star, daughter of Wakara, sister of Halaia. The Yana Indians, California. (Curtin, 1903: 524)

Pai Yu-huan   A god of evil influence, of the star Ti'mêng. China. (Werner, 1932: 354)

Pakamu-sula-li   The constellation Corvus. The Caribs, Guiana. (Levi-Strauss, 1969: 230)

Pao Lung   An evil god, of the star Ti-fu. China. (Werner, 1932: 357, 496)

Patá   The constellation Orion's Belt—the center star a thief being escorted by "emissaries of the Moon, sent to feed him to the buzzards." The Chimor, Peru. (Rowe, 1948: 50)

Pedile   One of the Hyades, harbingers of rain and storm when rising in conjunction with the sun. Daughter of Atlas and Aethra. Greece. (Barthell, 1971: 57)

Pehittin   A constellation made up of Altair and Tarared—the god of the new year. The Chukchee, Siberia. (Borgoras, 1904/09: 307)

Peh-kih-kiun   The god of the North Pole. Confucist China. (De Groot, 1925, 4: 14)

Pei Tou Chiu Huang   The gods of the northern Dipper who control the length of life and record men's deeds. China. (Day, 1940: 84; Werner, 1932: 369)

P'ei T'ung   The "god of the constellation I. Alternatively with Wang Chiao." China. (Werner, 1932: 371)

P'êng Tsun   The "god of the star Lo-hou, the star of quarreling." China. (Werner, 1932: 372)

P'êng Tsu-shou   God of the star Sui-yen. China. (Werner, 1932: 372)

Pên Ming Hsing Chun   A star god, patron of men. China. (Day, 1940: 94)

Phosphorus   The morning star, harbinger of the day. Son of Eos and Astraeus or Cephalus. Greece. (Fairbanks, 1907: 166; Larousse, 1968: 144; Roscher, 1965, 3, 2: 2443)

Phyto   One of the Hyades, harbingers of rain and storm when rising in conjunction with the sun. Daughter of Atlas and Aethra. Greece. (Barthell, 1971: 57; Roscher, 1965, 3, 2: 2492)

Pien Chi   God of the star T'ien-sha. China. (Werner, 1932: 377)

Pien Chin-lung   God of the star Ssŭ-fu. China. (Werner, 1932: 377)

Pi Tê   God of the star T'ien-pao, of good omen. China. (Werner, 1932: 375, 506)

Po Hsien-chung   God of the star T'ien-pai. China. (Werner, 1932: 379)

Po I-k'ao   God of the star Tzŭ-wei. China. (Werner, 1932: 379)

Po-lin Tao-jên   The "god of the constellation Chio. Alternatively with Têng Yü." China. (Werner, 1932: 379)

Poloahilani   The "nebula of Andromeda," also known as Hoku makapaa. Hawaii. (Emerson, 1967: 52)

Polyxo   One of the Hyades, harbingers of rain and storm when rising in conjunction with the sun. Greece. (Barthell, 1971: 57; Roscher, 1965, 3, 2: 2745)

Ponochona   Sirius, the Dog Star, the protective star of the Ya Ya ceremony. Invoked to increase the animal kingdom. The Hopi, Arizona. (Waters, 1963: 299)

Ponuchona   A spirit identified with the Morning Star and invoked "for animals, game and domestic." The Hano Tewa, Pueblo Indians, New Mexico. (Parsons, 1939: 181)

Puaka   A star god, the direction of its flashing rays foretelling a good or bad year. Father of Ariki by Taku-rua. New Zealand. (Mackenzie, n.d.: 210)

Puanga   The star Rigel who, with Taku-rua, controls the planting and harvest seasons. New Zealand. (Mackenzie, n.d.: 226; Andersen, 1928: 411; White, 1887, 1: 52, 53, 149)

Pugsu, Puksu   The planet Venus "was left-handed. Those who are left-handed are the best harpooners." Also called Ekuakinyalilele. Brother of Olouaipipilele. The Cuna Indians, Panama. (Keeler, 1960: 67; Nordenskiold, 1938: 163, 331)

Puikani The evening star who lives in the west and is a wife of the moon, feeds him well and fattens him. The Anyanja, Malawi. (Werner, 1964: 228)

Pukasui Venus, the evening star. The Cuna, Panama. (Keeler, 1960: 85)

Pungngane A star god who is responsible for the abundance of the *ponde* fish. Brother of Waijungngari. Encounter Bay, South Australia. (Woods, 1879: 201–202)

Purupriki The "most famous singer and actor" of the early people was carried into the sky by the flying foxes, whom he had attacked and disturbed in the pre-dawn. There he became the star Antares and they the Milky Way. Australia. (Mountford, 1965: 42)

Pu T'ung God of the star T'ien-p'ing, of good omen. China. (Werner, 1932: 384, 506)

Queevet, Aharaigichi A god "identified with the constellation Pleiades" whom the Abipones believed was the source of "all their strength and courage." Paraguay. (Leach, 1950, 2: 915)

Quetzalcóatl One aspect of the Plumed Serpent was that of the god of the planet Venus, of the morning star, to whom warriors were sacrificed to insure his reappearance. Aztec, Mexico. (Nicholson, 1967: 45; Caso, 1958: 23–26; Vaillant, 1962: 143; Burland, 1967: x, 66)

Racumon A star god and a war god who takes the form of a human-headed snake. The Carib, Guiana. (Tyler, 1964: 102)

Radau A god of the Milky Way invoked in the ceremony for children to make them strong, skillful, successful, brave, and to give longevity. The Sea Dyaks, Borneo. (Roth, 1968: 171)

Rahu The eclipse demon and god of the ascending node. An Asura who drank of the amrita of the gods and gained immortality. Discovered by the sun and the moon, he was decapitated by Vishnu. In revenge he swallows the sun and moon causing the eclipses. He is worshipped to forestall evil spirits, disease, and catastrophes. India, Tibet, and Sikkim. (Elwin, 1949: 68; Coleman, 1832: 134–135; Briggs, 1953: 544, 547; Nebesky-Wojkowitz, 1956, 2: 106; 1956, 1: 94, 259; Martin, 1914: 298)

Rehua A god identified with the star Sirius or with Antares. He was one of those who guided the priests and chiefs in their discussions and undertakings. He was a benevolent deity having given them fire and instituted cooking; is invoked for protection and health. New Zealand. (Best, 1924: 129; White, 1887, 1: 15, 37, 40; Hongi, 1920: 25)

Rohanka-Tauihanda A supernatural who lives in the planet Venus and is protective of mankind. The Mandan, North Dakota. (Wied-Neuwied, 1843: 360)

Rohini The constellation Tauras is the favorite wife of Soma, the moon. Daughter of Daksha. India. (Wilman-Grabowska, 1963: 112; Elwin, 1949: 51)

Rongo-mai Among the Maori the god of comets, of meteors. He was also the god of the whale. New Zealand. (Best, 1924: 238; Hongi, 1920: 27; Andersen, 1928: 170)

Rowda, Ruda A goddess who is a "symbol of the evening star." Arabia and Syria. (Vriezen, 1963: 68; Larousse, 1968: 323; Cook, 1930: 178)

Rua-o-mere Capricornus—mother of Maunu-'ura (Mars). Tahiti, Polynesia. (Henry, 1920: 101)

Rua-tupua-nui A stellar goddess, wife of Atea-ta'o-nui. Parents of the heavenly bodies. Tahiti, Polynesia. (Henry, 1920: 101)

Rultennin Orion, the archer, whose wife is the constellation Vetca-ñeut (Leo). Variant names—Rulteyet, Rulteyelin, Yultayat, Wolviaki-r-imtilin, Ulveiyinitilaen. The Chukchee, Siberia. (Bogoras, 1904/09: 307–308, 313)

Ru-te-ragi God of the stars. Mangareva, Polynesia. (Buck, 1938, 1: 426)

Sa Ch'iang "One of the gods of the star San-shih. Brother of Sa Chien." China. (Werner, 1932: 397)

Sa Chien The brother of Sa Ch'iang with whom he is god of the star San Shih. China. (Werner, 1932: 397)

Sang Ch'êng-tao An evil god, of the star Ti-pao. China. (Werner, 1932: 405, 496)

Sani The planet Saturn, a god of evil influence and bad luck requiring propitiation. His mount is variously given as a tortoise, a crow, or a vulture, the latter two reflecting his sinister aspect. India and Nepal. (Pal and Bhattacharyya, 1969: 33, 47; Crooke, 1925, 2: 484; Martin, 1914: 298; Crooke, 1894: 287; Leach, 1950, 2: 971)

Sanshi-taishô A constellation deity, one of the Niju-hachibushu. Japanese Buddhism. (Eliseev, 1963: 442)

Satavaesa God of the southern heavens, possibly the star Fomalhaut. Or possibly identified with Aldebaran, Vega, or Antares, and associated with the rains. Iran. (Gray, 1930: 159–160; Jackson, 1925, 12: 86)

Sdai-kwasa A stellar god—the belt of Orion, who is associated with Waptokwa. The Sherente, Brazil. (Nimuendaju, 1942: 85)

Sebshes An Egyptian star god. (Budge, 1969, 2: 310)

Serisa A star god, a crocodile. Egypt. (Budge, 1969, 2: 312)

Set A god of adverse conditions representing darkness, of mist and storms as well as aridity and drought, of evil. He is identified with the planet Mercury. Egypt. (Budge, 1969, 2: 244, 303; Larousse, 1968: 20)

Seta Goddess of the Pleiades and wife of Tororut. The Suk, Kenya. (Beech, 1911: 19; Mbiti, 1970, 2: 119)

Shahar The morning star, who is associated with fertility, is the son of El. Canaan, Near East. (Oldenburg, 1969: 19, 94)

Shakara-ô A constellation deity, one of the Nijuhachi-bushu. Japanese Buddhism. (Eliseev, 1963: 442)

Shalem The evening star is associated with fertility. Son of El. Canaan, Near East. (Oldenburg, 1969: 19, 94)

Shang Ch'ing T'ien I Equivalent of T'ien I Chên Chün. China. (Day, 1940: 110–111)

Shang Jung God of the star Yü-t'ang. China. (Werner, 1932: 410)

Shashaya The morning star, grandchild of Haine, the moon. The Hadzapi, Tanzania. (Millroth, 1965: 41)

Sheba The Seven, the Pleiades. Canaan, Near East. Equivalent of the Babylonian Sibitti. (Paton, 1925, 3: 184)

Shên Kêng The "god of the constellation Ching. Alternatively with Yao Ch'i." China. (Werner, 1932: 419)

Shên Li God of the star T'ien-pai, of good omen. China. (Werner, 1932: 419, 506)

Shepet An Egyptian star god. (Budge, 1969, 2: 310)

Shih-chi Niang-niang Goddess of the star Yüeh-yu. China. (Werner, 1932: 422)

Shih Kuei God of the star T'ien-hsiung, of good omen. China. (Werner, 1932: 427, 506)

Shimmôten A constellation deity, one of the Nijuhachi-bushu. Japanese Buddhism. (Eliseev, 1963: 442)

Shnilemun Sky Coyote, benevolent and watchful over man, has a suggested identification with Polaris. Among some identified with Aldebaran. The Chumash, California. (Hudson and Underhay, 1978: 84, 101)

Shon-ge A-ga-k'e-e-gon "Dog Star, Sirius, grandfather." A war god. The Dhegiha (Osage), Lower Missouri Basin. (La Flesche, 1928: 74)

Shou-shên The god of the star Canopus is a god of longevity and determines the death of each individual. Also the "Ancient of the South Pole." China. (Maspero, 1963: 345)

Shuang Mên Hsing Chün A stellar god of bad luck. China. (Day, 1940: 85)

Shui Te Hsing Chun Mercury, a god of water, is invoked for rain as well as "for relief in time of floods." China. (Day, 1940: 72, 209)

Sibitti The Seven, the Pleiades, and god of the month Adar. Babylonia, Near East. (Paton, 1925, 3: 184; Hommel, 1925, 3: 75, 184)

Sirito The Pleiades. The Caribs, Guiana. (Levi-Strauss, 1973: 241)

Sitivrat Slavic god of the planet Saturn. Also called Kirt. (Grimm, 1880: 249)

Skiritiohuts A star god of the southeast called "Fool-Coyote" because he precedes the Morning Star and causes the coyote to begin howling. He created the wolf. The Skidi Pawnee, Plains Indians, Nebraska. (Dorsey, 1904: 17)

Sma'aiyi 'i 'akiwi The Evening Star (Venus) is associated with the West. Ritual name is Hutash, same as for Earth. Possibly the "wot" of the land of the dead, Shimilaqsha. The Chumash, California. (Hudson and Underhay, 1978: 80–83)

Solobung Yubun Beneficent god of the morning star to whom sacrifices are made for abundance of cattle. The Buriat, Mongol. Siberia. (Curtin, 1909: 306)

Songwuka The Milky Way. The Hopi, Oraibi, Arizona. (Titiev, 1971: 157)

Soniyawi The Pleiades. The Chemehuevis consider it six stars comprised of "Mythic Coyote's wife, his son, three daughters, and a shaman." California, Nevada and Arizona. (Laird, 1976: 92)

Sterope One of the Pleiades, wife of Oenomaus. Greece. (Barthell, 1971: 57)

Stonychia One of the Pleiades. Greece. (Roscher, 1965, 4: 1538)

Suaixtix A Baltic star god who rules over the stars. Litu-Prussian/Sudavian. (Welsford, 1925, 12: 103; Schrader, 1925, 2: 34)

Sukra God of the planet Venus—"a person born under this planet. . .will have the faculty of knowing the past, present, and future." India. (Martin, 1914: 297–298; Danielou, 1964: 325–326)

Sukran Venus is worshipped by the Kaniyan who are astrologers. Southern India. (Thurston, 1909, 3: 193)

Sumas Ho-o The morning star of the Pima Indians. Arizona. (Russell, 1904/05: 252)

Sung Kêng The "god of the constellation Wei. Alternatively with Wu Ch'êng." China. (Werner, 1932: 470)

Sung Lu An evil god, of the star Ti-ch'iu. China. (Werner, 1932: 470, 496)

Sun Ho God of the star Wu-ch'iung. China. (Werner, 1932: 461)

Sun Hsiang The "god of the constellation Ts'an. Alternatively with Tu Mao." As the god of the star Ti-ying, an evil influence. China. (Werner, 1932: 468, 496)

Sun I God of the star T'ien-mêng, of good omen. China. (Werner, 1932: 468, 506)

Suniblele A star or planet god, brother of Udule, Pugsu. The Cuna Indians, Panama. (Nordenskiold, 1938: 332)

Suni Kar A malevolent deity, the planet Saturn. The Hos. India. (Majumdar, 1950: 255)

Sun Yen-hung God of the star Hsieh-kuang. China. (Werner, 1932: 469)

Sururu A stellar deity, "the Seven Stars," associated with Wairie, the moon. The Sherente, Brazil. (Nimuendaju, 1942: 85)

Su Yüan Tao-jên The "god of the constellation Hsin. Alternatively with K'ou Hsün." China. (Werner, 1932: 460)

Sweigsdukks A "god of fixed stars." The Nadravians, Lithuania. (Welsford, 1925, 9: 240)

Sweigsdunka A Baltic star goddess, the female form of Szweigsdukks. She is considered the "bride of the sky" and the guide of the morning and evening stars. (Welsford, 1925, 12: 103)

Tabaminarro A goddess of the twilight, "represented by a star." The Achaguas, West Indies. (Lovén, 1935: 590–591)

Tabatzi God of the morning star as well as of the wind. The Cora, Jalisco, Mexico. (Seler, 1925, 6: 829)

Taeh ti God of the Pole Star. Finland. (Bray, 1935: 48)

Ta'ero "Bacchus or Mercury"—a stellar deity. Tahiti, Polynesia. (Henry, 1920: 101)

Tagisomenaja Goddess of the evening star, wife of Wajubu, the moon. The Kamano, Usurufa, Jate, and Fore, New Guinea. (Berndt, 1965: 80)

Tahadiidakotse "The Great-South-Star," guardian of warriors. The Wichita, Plains Indians, Kansas. (Dorsey, 1904: 47)

Ta Hao Hsing Chün A malignant star god, "Great Waster." China. (Day, 1940: 211)

Tahi-ari'i The star Capella in Auriga. Tahiti, Polynesia. (Henry, 1920: 101)

Tai Li God of the star Huang-wu. China. (Werner, 1932: 478)

T'ai Luan God of the star P'i-t'ou. China. (Werner, 1932: 481)

T'ai Po Chên Hsing, T'ai-po Chin-hsing The planet Venus. But Werner considers Tung-fan Shuo more popularly so. China. (Day, 1940: 209; Werner, 1932: 482)

T'ai Sui The god of the planet Jupiter is the god of time, of the year, and all-powerful in the destinies of men. China. (Day, 1940: 77; Werner, 1932: 483; Peeters, 1941: 16)

Taketake-hikuroa A personification of comets. The Maori, New Zealand. (Best, 1924: 175)

Taku-rua Goddess of the star Sirius is associated with the planting and harvest seasons. Mother of Ariki. New Zealand. (Mackenzie, n.d.: 210, 226; Andersen, 1928: 411; White, 1887, 1: 52, 149)

Takwish A fearful meteor god, son of Tukomit and Tamayowut. He is cannibalistic and "Sight of him portends disaster and death." The Luiseño Indians, California. (Kroeber, 1925: 678–680)

Tala Goddess of the stars, daughter of Bathala and a mortal, sister of Mayari and Hanan. The Tagalog, Philippines. (Jocano, 1969: 10)

Tamarau A deity who "represents meteors." The Maori, New Zealand. (Best, 1924: 238)

Tama-re-reti A star god placed in the sky by Tane to bedeck Raki. New Zealand. (White, 1887, 1: 53)

Tamusi A creator god who is associated with the constellation of the Pleiades. The Calina, Surinam. (Zerries, 1968: 246; Penard, 1917: 253)

T'ang T'ien-chêng God of the star T'ien-sun, of good omen. China. (Werner, 1932: 487, 506)

Tan Pai-chao God of the star T'ien-chiu, of good omen. China. (Werner, 1932: 485, 506)

Ta-pa "Deer-head, Pleiades, grandfather." The Dhegiha (Osage), Plains Indians, Lower Missouri Basin. (La Flesche, 1928: 74)

Tasupi A stellar god of the Hopi Indians. Arizona. (Parsons, 1939: 239)

Ta Tha-bthi[n] "Three-deer, the three great stars in Orion's belt, grandmother." The Dhegiha (Osage), Plains Indians, Lower Missouri Basin. (La Flesche, 1928: 74)

Tau-ha The Southern Cross. Tahiti, Polynesia. (Henry, 1920: 102)

Tauna An evil stellar god of destructive storms and lightning. Guiana. (Levi-Strauss, 1969: 231)

Ta'urua The "guiding star that rises in the evening," applied to several stars—Sirius, Venus, Fomalhaut. The Society Islands, Polynesia. (Henry, 1928: 362–363; 1920: 101, 104)

Ta'urua-i-te-ha'apâ-manu "Deneb in Cygnus." Tahiti, Polynesia. (Henry, 1920: 104)

Ta'urua-nui The planet Jupiter whose wife is Te-'ura-taui-e-pâ. Father of Mata-ri'i, Mere, Te-ura-meremere. Tahiti, Polynesia. (Henry, 1920: 103)

Ta'urua-nui-i-te-amoaha Sirius in Canis Major. He "created kings of the chiefs of earthly hosts on one side and of the chiefs in the skies on the other side." Tahiti, Polynesia. (Henry, 1920: 103–104)

Ta'urua-nui-o-te-hiti-apato'a "Canopus in Argo the ship." Tahiti, Polynesia. (Henry, 1920: 102)

oTchalai A star god of the Gypsies. Also called oNetchaphoro. (Clebert, 1967: 176–177)

Tcuperekata The goddess of the evening star is the mother/creatress of all things. The Skidi Pawnee, Plains Indians, Nebraska. (Dorsey, 1904, 2: 3, 4)

Teishakuten A constellation deity, one of the Nijuhachibushu. Japanese Buddhism. (Eliseev, 1963: 442)

Têng Ch'an-yü Goddess of the star Liu-ho. China. (Werner, 1932: 493)

Têng Chiu-kung God of the star Ch'ing-lung. China. (Werner, 1932: 493)

Têng Hsiu God of the star Wu-kuei. China. (Werner, 1932: 493)

Têng Hua God of the star Mu-fu. China. (Werner, 1932: 493)

Têng Yü The "god of the constellation Chio. Alternatively with Po-lin Tao-Jên." Also given as the god of the star T'ien-chieh, of good omen. China. (Werner, 1932: 493, 506)

Te-ra'i-tû-roroa A stellar goddess—"Long-extended-sky, between Leo and Hydra," wife of Metua-'ai-papa and mother of Fetu-tea (Saturn). Tahiti, Polynesia. (Henry, 1920: 102)

Tere The god of the constellation of the Southern Cross, also named as that of Orion. His mission was to bring animals and plants to the earth, in baskets, whose contents became scattered. Those regained became the domestic ones, those which escaped, the wild. The Bandas, Sudan. (Queval, 1968: 110; Larousse, 1973: 530)

Tere-e-fa'aari'i-mai-i-te-Ra'i "Errand-to-create-majesty-in-heaven, the sky there," wife of Anâ-heuheupo and mother of Ta'urua-nui, Jupiter. Tahiti, Polynesia. (Henry, 1920: 103)

Te'ura-taui-e-pâ Wife of Ta'urua-nui (Jupiter) and mother of Mata-ri'i, Mere, and Te-uru-meremere. Tahiti, Polynesia. (Henry, 1920: 103)

Te-uru-meremere The constellation of Orion except for the belt, which is Mere. Tahiti, Polynesia. (Henry, 1920: 103)

Thuraiya The Pleiades, associated with rain. Arabia. (Noldeke, 1925, 1: 660)

Tiao K'ê Hsing A stellar god "who mourns for those who die." China. (Day, 1940: 98)

Ti Chieh Hsing Chün A beneficent star, one of the "Solvers of Heaven's and Earth's Difficulties." China. (Day, 1940: 85)

Ti Ch'ung Hsing A malignant star god. China. (Day, 1940: 211)

T'ien Chieh Hsing Chün A beneficent star, one of the "Solvers of Heaven's and Earth's Difficulties." China. (Day, 1940: 85)

T'ien I Chên Chün A stellar god who is the patron of physicians. Also known as Shang Ch'ing T'ien I. China. (Day, 1940: 110–111)

T'ien K'o Hsing A very malignant star god. China. (Day, 1940: 211)

T'ien Kou Hsing The Dog Star, very malignant, and dangerous to pregnant women and children. Also considered the source of sterility. China. (Day, 1940: 85, 210)

T'ien K'u "Heavenly Weeping Star . . . (Specially Malignant)." China. (Day, 1940: 211)

T'ien Lo Hsing A malignant star, a source of misfortune. China. (Day, 1940: 85)

T'ien Sha Shên Chün A very malignant star deity. China. (Day, 1940: 211)

T'ien-ssŭ Fang A stellar god and also a god of silkworms. China. (Werner, 1932: 508)

T'ien Tê Hsing A star of virtue whose help is "sought in facing the issues of life." China. (Day, 1940: 84)

Tien T'ung God of the star T'ien-k'ung, of good omen. China. (Werner, 1932: 502, 506)

TihoWagantimi "Ambushers. Betelgeuse and Rigel. These were the ambushers in the great hunt for the Mountain Sheep." The Chemehuevis, California, Nevada, and Arizona. (Laird, 1976: 92)

Ti K'u "Earthly Weeping Star," a malignant deity. China. (Day, 1940: 211)

Ting Ts'ê God of the star Ti-lu. China. (Werner, 1932: 510)

Tir Iranian god of the planet Mercury, beneficent but also dangerous. (Gray, 1930: 110–114; Ananikian, 1964: 32)

Tirinapiganti Sirius. Follower. He "was the father of the Mountain Sheep who was shot." The Chemehuevis. California, Nevada, and Arizona. (Laird, 1976: 92)

Ti Sha A very malignant star god. China. (Day, 1940: 211)

Tishtrya, Tishtar The god of the star Sirius is associated with rain, with prosperity and fertility. Iran. (Gray, 1930: 115–116, 223; Ananikian, 1925, 1: 798; Jackson, 1925, 12: 86; Jayne, 1962: 195)

Ti Wang Hsing A malignant star who is the source of misfortune. China. (Day, 1940: 85)

Tjan-wangu-wangu A falling star god who with his father is considered an unfriendly deity. The Mara, Central Australia. (Spencer, 1904: 627–628)

Tlahuizcalpantecuhtli The god of Venus; Quetzalcóatl as the morning star. Aztec, Mexico. (Vaillant, 1962: 150; Duran, 1971: 162; Bancroft, 1886, 3: 113)

Tôhôten A constellation deity, one of the Nijuhachibushu. Japanese Buddhism. (Eliseev, 1963: 442)

Tom Hoscua Deity of the Southern Cross. Tarascan, Mexico. (Boyd, n.d.: 50)

Topogh Goddess of the evening star, daughter of Tororut and Seta. The Suk, Kenya. (Beech, 1911: 19; Mbiti, 1970, 2: 119)

Tou Mu Goddess of a constellation variously named as the Star-Bushel, the Southern Bushel, the North Star. She is invoked for protection from diseases, in traveling on water, from war. She controls the records of life and death, and so is worshipped for longevity. In Szechwan she is the goddess of the northern dipper and patroness of fortunetellers. China. (Day, 1940: 27, 110; Werner,

1932: 511; Maspero, 1963: 340; Graham, 1961: 180, 186)

Tsang Kuan The "god of the constellation Pi. Alternatively with Fang Chi-ch'ing." China. (Werner, 1932: 518)

Ts'an Hua Pên Ming Hsing Chün "Silkworm Life-Star" worshipped as the Life Star for each individual worm. China. (Day, 1940: 108, 213)

Ts'an Nü The goddess of the star T'ien Ssŭ is also a goddess of silkworms. China. (Werner, 1932: 517; 1934: 169)

Tsek'any'agojo Goddess of the evening star. The Tewa, Pueblo Indians, New Mexico. (Harrington, 1907/08: 49)

Ts'ên Pêng The "god of the constellation Wei. Alternatively with Chu Chao." China. (Werner, 1932: 522)

Tsu Lin A god of evil influence, the star Ti-p'i. China. (Werner, 1932: 523, 496)

Tudong A constellation of the Kankanay, comprised of stars from several other constellations, invoked at sacrifice for a sufferer from urine retention, and also before the transplantation of rice seedlings. Luzon, Philippines. (Vanoverbergh, 1972: 91)

T'u Hsing-sun God of the star T'u-fu. China. (Werner, 1932: 527)

Tu-i-te-moana-'urifa Hydra. Wife of Atu-tahi and mother of Metua-'ai-papa, Moana-'a'no-huri-hara, Moana-'ohu-noa-'ei-ha'a-moe-hara, and Moana-'aere. Tahiti, Polynesia. (Henry, 1920: 102)

Tu Mao The "god of the constellation Ts'an. Alternatively with Sun Hsiang." China. (Werner, 1932: 526)

T'ung Chêng An evil god, of the star Ti-li. China. (Werner, 1932: 496, 531)

Tung-fang Shuo God of the star Sui-hsing as well as the planet Venus is the patron of gold- and silver-smiths. China. (Werner, 1932: 528–529; Maspero, 1963: 332)

Tunui-a-te-ika A deity who is the personification of comets. The Maori, New Zealand. (Best, 1924: 238)

Tupa Deity of the planet Jupiter. The Marquesas, Polynesia. (Williamson, 1933, 2: 175)

Tuputuputu A stellar god, one of the Magellan Clouds, invoked with others for abundant food. The Maori, New Zealand. (Best, 1924: 279)

Tu Yüan-hsien God of the star P-shih. China. (Werner, 1932: 527)

Tzŭ Wei T'ien Chieh Hsing Chün The planet Venus. China. (Day, 1940: 96)

Uash-neter An Egyptian star god. (Budge, 1969, 2: 310)

Ukha-Solbon The god of the evening star, Venus, and the eldest son of Budurga-Sagan-Tengri, is the patron of horses. The Buriats, Siberia and Mongolia. (Klementz, 1925, 3: 4, 11)

Ungamilia Goddess of the evening star. The Arunta, Central Australia. (Spencer, 1968: 565)

Upoko-roa A personification of comets. The Maori, New Zealand. (Best, 1924: 175)

Uredecuauercara, Urendequa Vecara God of the morning star. The Tarascan, Mexico. (Craine and Reindorp, 1970: 21; Boyd, n.d.: 50; Krickeberg, 1968: 58)

Utule The planet Jupiter. The Cuna, Panama. (Keeler, 1960: 85)

al-Uzza Goddess of the planet Venus, of the morning and evening stars, upon whom oaths are sworn. Daughter of Allah. Arabia. (Noldeke, 1925, 1: 660; Abercrombie, 1972: 4)

Vakarine, Wakarine Goddess of the evening star, of the planet Venus. Lithuania. (Gimbutas, 1963: 199; Machal, 1918: 320; Welsford, 1925, 12: 102; Schrader, 1925, 2: 34)

Vanant A stellar god identified with Vega or with Fomalhaut, is guardian of the west, a god of strength, of victory, possessed of healing powers. Iran. (Huart, 1963: 42; Jackson, 1925, 12: 86; Gray, 1930: 166, 223)

Vechernyaya Zvezda Slavonic deity of the evening star. (Larousse, 1968: 285)

Venkiča The "knee of the god Venkiča became paralyzed in a bent position (which explains the hook shape) and became Orion." The Tucuna, Brazil. (Levi-Strauss, 1969: 223)

Vetca-ñeut The constellation Leo, wife of Orion. The Chukchee, Siberia. (Bogoras, 1904/09: 308)

Vrihaspati   A favorable Vedic deity, the planet Jupiter. Also Bhrishput or Vrihuspati. India. (Martin, 1914: 297; Coleman, 1832: 133)

Vyazham   Jupiter is worshipped by the Kaniyan who are astrologers. Southern India. (Thurston, 1909, 3: 193)

Wa-ba-ha   "Litter, the Dipper (Great Bear), grandfather." The Dhegiha (Osage), Plains Indians. Lower Missouri Basin. (La Flesche, 1928: 74)

Wabano   The morning star is invoked in the rain dance. The Menomini Indians, Wisconsin. (Skinner, 1915, 1: 207)

Wahie-roa   A personification of comets. The Maori, New Zealand. (Best, 1924: 175)

Waida Werris   The Polar Star. The Wintu, California. (Curtin, 1903: 177)

Waijungngari   A star god who is responsible for "the abundance of kangaroo." Encounter Bay, Australia. (Woods, 1879: 201–202)

Walusi   The "god of falling stars and red sky." The Baganda, Uganda. (Cunningham, 1905: 218; Budge, 1973, 1: 377n.3)

Wang Chiao   The "god of the constellation I. Alternatively with P'ei T'ung." China. (Werner, 1932: 545)

Wang Hsiang   An evil god, of the star Ti-lo. China. (Werner, 1932: 496, 546)

Wang Hu   God of the stars Yüeh-p'o and T'ien Chien, of good omen. China. (Werner, 1932: 506, 546)

Wang Liang   "The god of the constellation Mao. Alternatively with Huang Ts'ang." China. (Werner, 1932: 546)

Wang Lung-nao   God of the star T'ien-hsüan, of good omen. China. (Werner, 1932: 506, 547)

Wang Pao   God of the star Chi-tu. China. (Werner, 1932: 547)

Wang P'ing   A god of evil influence, of the star Ti-ch'i. China. (Werner, 1932: 496, 548)

Wang Tso   God of the star Ping-fu. China. (Werner, 1932: 549)

Wan Hsiu   "The god of the constellation Chang. Alternatively with Hsieh Ting." China. (Werner, 1932: 545)

Wapanananagwa   The morning star, a great manitu of the Fox. Wisconsin. (Leach, 1950, 2: 749)

Wasi-topre-pe   The planet Mars, associated with the moon, Wairie. The Sherente, Brazil. (Nimuendaju, 1942: 85)

Wasi-topre-ri'e   The planet Jupiter, associated with Waptokwa. The Sherente, Brazil. (Nimuendaju, 1942: 85)

Wasi-topre-zaure   The planet Venus, associated with Waptokwa. The Sherente, Brazil. (Nimuendaju, 1942: 85)

Wata-urdli   To punish his two sons who were unkind and disobedient he transformed them, their clubs, and the kangaroos they were hunting into stars. Then he himself became the Morning Star on the other side of the world so he would not have to associate with them. Australia. (Mountford, 1969: 48)

Wei Pi   God of the star Huang-fan. China. (Werner, 1932: 552)

Wen Ch'ang   The god of literature and of classical studies is a god who dwells in the constellation of the Great Bear. China. (De Groot, 1925, 4: 14; Ferguson, 1937: 112; Maspero, 1963: 310)

Wên Chieh   God of the star T'ien-lao, of good omen. China. (Werner, 1932: 506, 558)

Wero-i-takokoto, Wero-i-te-kokoto   A star who controls the winter. The Maori, New Zealand. (Andersen, 1928: 411; White, 1887, 1: 149)

Wero-i-te-ao-marie   A star who rules the summer. The Maori, New Zealand. (Andersen, 1928: 411; White, 1887, 1: 149)

Wero-i-te-ninihi   A star who rules the winter with Wero-i-takokoto. One of the personifications of cold. The Maori, New Zealand. (Anderson, 1928: 411; Best, 1924: 95; White, 1887, 1: 149)

Whanui   God of the star Vega who provided the sweet potato and whose rising signals the time for their harvest. The Maori, New Zealand. (Mackenzie, n.d.: 316–317; Best, 1924: 133; Andersen, 1928: 398)

Wikaler   The planet Mars. The Cuna, Panama. (Keeler, 1960: 85)

Wlaha   Chief of the star people, the Shiriche, with his six damodedes—the Pleiades. They symbolize "union, peace, and friendship." When they disappear in May the rains come; when they reappear in July it is the time of summer and dry weather. He is Master of the Akuaniye plant, the Peace Plant. The Makiritare, Venezuela. (Civrieux, 1980: 109–114)

Wodoi A cultural hero, in the form of a small night bird, of the primeval time who became the star Alpha. Australia. (Eliade, 1964: 74–75)

Wohpe The Falling Star, the Meteor. She is the daughter of Skan "created of his essence" (or the daughter of Skan and Hanwi) "to be the Mediator." She is the most beautiful—the "patron of harmony, beauty, and pleasure." She measured the time taken by the Four Winds to establish the seasons—the Wani-yetu. Her power (*ton*) "is in the smoke from the pipe and in the incense from sweetgrass." She is invoked when the ceremonial pipe is smoked, which she introduced and gave to men with its ceremonies and rituals. She chose to be Okaga's woman; taught Tate to wear hide clothing; and became the guardian of his unborn fifth son, Yum. The Lakota/ Oglala, Nebraska, Dakotas, and Montana. (Walker, 1980: 51, 54, 95, 99, 109–111, 125, 220–222; Powers, 1977: 54, 73, 77, 78)

Wu Ch'êng The "god of the constellation Wei. Alternatively with Sung Kêng." China. (Werner, 1932: 569)

Wu Ch'ien God of the star Pao-wei. China. (Werner, 1932: 569)

Wu Han "The god of the constellation K'ang. Alternatively with Li Tao-t'ung." China. (Werner, 1932: 571)

Wu Hsü God of the star T'ien-su, of good omen. China. (Werner, 1932: 506, 572)

Wu Jung God of the star Liu-hsia. China. (Werner, 1932: 572)

Wu Kuei Hsing A group of five stars—three of good omen, Fu, Lu, Shou, and two of evil, Ch'iang Tao and Tsei—leaving a favorable balance. China. (Day, 1940: 85)

Wu K'un "The god of the constellation Liu. Alternatively with Jên Kuang." China. (Werner, 1932: 572)

Wu Lung God of the star P'o-sui. China. (Werner, 1932: 573)

Wu Ssŭ-yü A god of evil influence, the star Ti-ku. China. (Werner, 1932: 496, 574)

Wu Wên-hua God of the star Li-shih. China. (Werner, 1932: 578)

Wu Yen-kung A god of evil influence, the star Ti-chuang. China. (Werner, 1932: 496, 578)

Xacupancalqui A stellar god of Mexico. (Bancroft, 1886, 3: 113)

Xaman Ek The god of the North Star, guardian of merchants and of travellers, is associated with the rain god. Mayan Mexico and Guatemala. (Morley, 1946: 227–228; Tozzer, 1941: 95)

Xolotl The god of the evening star, Venus, is the god of monsters, of twins, of abortions. Twin of Quetzalcóatl and his opposite. Mexico. (Reed, 1966: 95; Caso, 1958: 18, 24; Nicholson, 1956: 104; Vaillant, 1962: 151)

Xolxol *See* **Holhol**

Xulab The planet Venus is the "patron of hunting." The Kekchi, the Mopan, Guatemala. (Thompson, 1970: 250)

Xux Ek The morning star, "Wasp Star." Yucatan, Mexico. (Thompson, 1970: 250)

Yaalaut The star Vega, with Yanolaut and the Polar Star, gives the Chukchee their direction. Siberia. (Bogoras, 1904/09: 307)

Yang Chên The "god of the constellation Chi. Alternatively with Fêng I." China. (Werner, 1932: 583)

Yang Ch'eng The "Star of Happiness." China. (Maspero, 1963: 344)

Yang Ching "The Goat Spirit. The presiding deity of the star Fan-yin." China. (Werner, 1932: 583)

Yang Hsien The equivalent of Yang Ching. China. (Werner, 1932: 584)

Yang Hsin The "god of the constellation Tou. Alternatively with Chu Yu." China. (Werner, 1932: 584)

Yang Jên Hsing Chün A malignant star goddess. China. (Day, 1950: 211)

Yang Shih Goddess of the star Hung-yen. China. (Werner, 1932: 584)

Yanolaut The star Arcturus who is the leader of the three stars (Vega and the Pole Star) is consulted for direction at night. The Chukchee, Siberia. (Bogoras, 1904/09: 307)

Yao Ch'i The "god of the constellation Ching. Alternatively with Shên Kêng." China. (Werner, 1932: 585)

Yao Chin-hsiu A god of evil influence, the star Ti-chou. China. (Werner, 1932: 496, 585)

Yao Chung God of the star Yüeh-yen. China. (Werner, 1932: 586)

Yao Hua A god of evil influence, the star Ti-hao. China. (Werner, 1932: 496, 586)

Yao Kung God of the star T'ien-tsui, of good omen. China. (Werner, 1932: 506, 586)

Yao Kung-hsiao God of the star T'ien-yung, of good omen. China. (Werner, 1932: 506, 586)

Yao Kung-po The "god of the constellation Fang. Alternatively with Kêng Yen." China. (Werner, 1932: 586)

Yao Shu-liang God of the star Fu-yin. China. (Werner, 1932: 587)

Yeh Ching-ch'ang An evil god, the star Ti-chien. China. (Werner, 1932: 496, 589)

Yeh Chung A god of evil influence, the star Ti-fei. China. (Werner, 1932: 496, 589)

Yin-ch'êng-hsiu God of the star Pai-hu. China. (Werner, 1932: 594)

Yin Hung God of the star Wu-ku. China. (Werner, 1932: 594)

Yin P'o-pai God of the star Hsiao-hao. China. (Werner, 1932: 594)

Yüan Hung God of the star Ssu-fei. China. (Werner, 1932: 607)

Yüan Ting-hsiang An evil god, the star Ti-chün. China. (Werner, 1932: 496, 611)

Yü Chih A god of evil influence, the star Ti-i. China. (Werner, 1932: 496, 598)

Yü Chung God of the stars Ch'u-sha and Ti-an, the latter one of evil influence. China. (Werner, 1932: 496, 598)

Yü Hua God of the star Ku-ch'en. China. (Werner, 1932: 598)

Yü Hun God of the star Chuan-she. China. (Werner, 1932: 596)

Yü Yüan God of the star Shui-fu. China. (Werner, 1932: 604)

Yzacatecutli A stellar god of Mexico. (Bancroft, 1886, 3: 113)

gZa'chen rahu The "planetary god Rahu," an important protective deity. Tibet. (Nebesky-Wojkowitz, 1956, 1: 94)

Zamama The Babylonian god of war and of the city of Kish is identified with the constellation Aquila. Near East. (Langdon, 1931: 117, 119; Jastrow, 1898: 169)

Zôchôten A constellation deity, one of the Nijuhachi-bushu. Guardian of the south and a "Patron of Growth." Japan. (Eliseev, 1963: 442; Anesaki, 1937: 243)

Zvezda Dennitsa Slavonic goddess of the morning star, sometimes given as the wife of Myesyats. (Larousse, 1968: 285)

PART III

Atmospheric Deities

11

Weather Gods: Thunder, Lightning, Rain, Wind, Rainbow, Drought

Abassi Abumo The Thunderer, a sky god, Calabar, Nigeria. (Eliade, 1976, 2: 355)

Abedelam'sen The "warm wind" who with the other winds rules "human and animal destiny." The Penobscot Indians, Maine. (Speck, 1935: 21)

Abeguwo A female spirit who causes the rain; she "urinates down on the people." The Kapauku Papuans, New Guinea. (Pospisil, 1958: 19)

The Ačačila The underground spirits of mountains, rivers, and lakes "control meteorological phenomena, sending rain, hail, or frost" and use punitive measures to control society. The Aymara, Peru. (Tschopik, 1946: 559)

Achinoin A star believed "to be the cause of light rain and strong winds." The Callinago, Lesser Antilles, West Indies. (Rouse, 1948: 564)

Achu God of the storm, of the upper air, of rain; Achu Nyande, the lightning, and Achu Donde, the thunder, are manifestations of his wrath. The Jukun, Nigeria. (Meek, 1931: 199–200, 285)

Áchuprúakaletkíniti A wind demon who causes illness. The Cuna Indians, Panama. (Nordenskiold, 1930: 60–61)

Ac Net'bat Another name of Itzan Noh Ku, the Mayan god of hail. Mexico. (Thompson, 1970: 266)

Adad Akkadian/Babylonian storm and weather god who controlled the rain, thunder, and lightning. Near East. (Jacobsen, 1970: 34; James, 1960: 214; Schoeps, 1961: 57)

Adee, Idi The Thunderbird. Pacific Northwest Coastal Indians. (Burland, 1965: 148)

Aden A sky god, second child of Sogbo, was a god of "the fine rain" and protector of fruit trees. Dahomey. (Herskovits, 1938: 2: 152, 156)

Adjakata A sky god, fourth child of Sogbo, was god of the heavy shower, but not destructive. Dahomey. (Herskovits, 1938, 2: 152, 156)

Aello One of the Harpies, goddesses of the storm winds, who had the form of human-headed birds. Daughter of Thaumas and Elektra. Greece. (Barthell, 1971: 12; Kerenyi, 1951: 62; Murray, 1935: 218; Hesiod-Brown, 1981: 60)

Aeolus Greek/Roman god of the winds, their creator, who controlled them, though others also served in this function. (Fairbanks, 1907: 59; Roscher, 1965, 1, 1: 193; Ruskin, 1869: 23; Larousse, 1968: 144)

Aeryamoinen The personification of severe cold. Finland. (Grimm, 1888: 1573)

Afe The god of thunder of the Abkhasians. Caucasus. (Marr, 1937: 170)

Agaou The god of thunder, brother of Azaka Mede. Also called Missan and Poteau-colis. Plaisance, Haiti. West Indies. (Deren, 1953: 56; Marcelin, 1950: 101)

Agastya Muni A nature godling of rain who had the power to stop it. India. (Crooke, 1894: 46)

Agdy The benevolent god of thunder who causes the lightning and destroys the evil spirits. The Evenks, Siberia. (Michael, 1963: 161)

Agimaiyu "Sound of Coming Rain," a weather god and son of Kidul. The Ifugao, Philippines. (Barton, 1946: 31)

Agni The celestial god of fire is manifest in the atmosphere as the lightning. India. (Basak, 1953: 93; Keary, 1882: 101–102; Barth, 1921: 10; Ions, 1967: 18)

Agraulos, Aglauros A Greek goddess of the dew, sister of Herse and Pandrosos, is associated with the cult of Athena and human sacrifices. (Roscher, 1965, 1, 1: 106; Ruskin, 1869: 48; Bethe, 1925, 1: 226)

Agudumdum A weather god and son of Kidul, the thunder. The Ifugao, Philippines. (Barton, 1946: 31)

Ahmakiq A Mayan deity "who locks up the crop-destroying winds." Yucatan, Mexico. (Alexander, 1920: 141)

Aidegaxto The malignant spirit who forms and directs storms. The Basques, France and Spain. (Barandiaran, 1972: 18)

Aido Hwedo As the rainbow-serpent god, his celestial role, he wields the thunderbolts. In his chthonic role he supports the earth. Dahomey. (Herskovits, 1938, 2: 108, 158, 291; Williams, 1936: 165)

Aido Wedo The rainbow-serpent god in Porto-Alegre, Brazil. (Bastide, 1960: 289). In Haiti, the goddess of the rainbow and of fresh waters, symbolized by the snake; wife of Danballah-Wedo. (Verger, 1957: 235)

Aija, Aije Another name for the god of thunder, Tiermes. The Lapps, Northern Europe. (Karsten, 1955: 26; Collinder, 1949: 168)

Äijih The thunder god of the Lapps in Inari. Finland. (Minn, 1955: 72)

Aitupawa God of thunder and an attendant of Io. The Maori, New Zealand. (Best, 1924: 103, 238)

Aja Ekapad A god of the atmosphere and of storm. In his representation as a one-footed goat he indicates the point of the lightning's strike. India. (Keith, 1917: 36; Macdonell, 1897: 73–74)

Ajanutoe A god of the pantheon which controls the thunder, rain and waters. The Maranhão, Brazil. (Costa Eduardo, 1948: 78–79)

Ajauto A god of the pantheon which controls the thunder, rain and waters. The Maranhão Brazil. (Costa Eduardo, 1948: 78–79)

Ajishiki-takahikone A god of thunder, son of Okuninushi and brother of Shitateru-hime. Japan. (Herbert, 1967: 328, 488; Yasumaro, 1928: 67)

Aji-Suki-Taka-Hikone A god of rain, husband of Ama-tsu-haha-kami and father of Taki-Tsu-Hiko. Japan. (Herbert, 1967: 305; Larousse, 1968: 416)

Ajok The supreme being and creator of the Lotuko is also the god of rain. Sudan. (Pettazzoni, 1956: 38)

Akele A sky god, sixth child of Sogbo, is a thunder god who draws the water up out of the sea to form the rain. Dahomey. (Herskovits, 1938, 2: 152, 156)

Akolombe A sky god, third child of Sogbo. He "regulates the temperature of the world" so that when it hails he is responsible. He also causes floods. Dahomey. (Herskovits, 1938, 2: 152, 156)

Alefi The wind, messenger of Oya. Puerto Rico, West Indies. (Gonzalez-Wippler, 1975: 25)

Aleyan-Baal God of weather and of storms, the giver of the fertilizing rains. Canaan, Near East. (James, 1960: 87, 91)

Alibuyuhon A god of the winds. The Ifugao. Philippines. (Barton, 1946: 61)

Aloalo God of the weather, of the wind and rain, to whom offerings were made for good weather and fertility of vegetation. Tonga, Polynesia. (Moulton, 1925, 12: 377; Mariner, 1820: 385; Gifford, 1929: 304)

Amade-Awha The god of lightning of the Oratta tribe. The Ibo, Nigeria. (Jeffreys, 1972: 730)

Amade Onhia, Amado Oha The god of thunder who punishes evil-doers. He is beneficent as the god of rain and giver of fertility. The Ibo, Nigeria. (Talbot, 1967: 52, 61; Parrinder, 1949: 33; Williams, 1936: 213)

Amaunet With Amun one of the initial primeval pairs who represent the air. Also considered the north wind. Egypt. (Anthes, 1961: 67; Pettazzoni, 1956; 55)

Ambuyuwon A god of the winds—"Foreteller of Storm." The Ifugao, Philippines. (Barton, 1946: 62)

Ame-no-Mihashira A Shinto wind god. Japan. (Kato, 1926: 15; Herbert, 1967: 491)

Amitolane The rainbow. The Zuñi, New Mexico. (Burland, 1965: 150)

Amkidul   God of thunder, father of Maingit. The Ifugao, Philippines. (Barton, 1955: 224)

Amosu   A deity of the Akan—"Giver of rain." Ghana. (Mbiti, 1970, 2: 327)

Amun   With Amaunet one of the initial primeval pairs representing "air in motion." Considered a god of the weather, of storms and wind. Egypt. (Anthes, 1961: 67; Pettazzoni, 1956: 55–58)

Anak Raja   The rainbow in its entirety. A portion of it is called Manani. The Sea Dyaks, Borneo. (Roth, 1968: 171)

Angarmati Bhawani   Goddess of "the blazing charcoal . . . who rides through the sky in her chariot in the hot weather, causing sunstroke." India. (Briggs, 1953: 529–530)

Jin Angin   A harmless wind demon of the Sakai, the Jakun, and the Besisi. Malay Peninsula. (Skeat, 1906: 182, 301)

Ang-lah   A god who makes the thunder. The Kintak Bong, Malaya. (Evans, 1937: 143)

Angoro   A god of the rainbow (from Angola). Brazil. (Bastide, 1960: 560)

Angoromea   God of the rainbow (from Congo). Brazil. (Bastide, 1960: 560)

Anhel   The "rain deities of the Tzotzil." Mayan, Mexico. (Thompson, 1970: 267)

Anila   Personification of wind, a name of Vayu. An attendant upon Indra. India. (Dowson, 1961: 342, 344)

Animiki, Animkee   God of the thunder, the storm, who controls the west wind. The Winnebago, the Ojibway. Among the Anishnabeg the Thunder is the Spirit Grandfather who shot lightning at the villages; was joined by others, so the thunders and storms are called the Grandfathers; are offered tobacco. Ojibway. Wisconsin, Minnesota, and Manitoba. (Maclean, 1876: 437; Brinton, 1882: 50; Emerson, 1884: 8, 28; Johnston, 1976: 26, 27)

Aninnailaq   God of the bad weather which confines. The Copper Eskimo, Canada. (Nungak and Arima, 1969: 114)

Anit, Anitan   The "powerful guardian of the thunderbolt." The Manobo, Philippines. (Jocano; 1969: 23)

Aniton Tauo   Goddess of the rain and the wind. The Zambales, Philippines. (Jocano, 1969: 14)

Anitun Tabu   The goddess of the rain and the wind. Daughter of Dumangan and Idianale, sister of Dumakulem. The Tagalog, Philippines. (Jocano, 1969: 9)

Annawan   A "female spirit, who lives in a golden cave under water . . . where the sea flows under the ground. When the sea becomes angry and stops going under ground, a typhoon starts blowing . . ." whereon she must be propitiated to control the waters. The Isneg of Luzon, Philippines. (Vanoverbergh, 1953: 91)

Anore   God of the winds. The Iglulik Eskimo. Canada. (Nungak and Arima, 1969: 114)

Anu en marasi   God of the rainbow and also a god of navigation. Namoluk, the Carolines, Micronesia. (Lessa, 1961: 32)

Anuenue   The goddess of the rainbow, sister of Kane and Kanaloa. Hawaii. (Westervelt, 1915: 117)

Anu-matao   "Cold Space" and "personification of cold"—daughter of Rangi, and Pokoharau-te-po, a wife of Tangaroa and mother of the twins Pounamu and Poutini. New Zealand. (Andersen, 1928: 375; Mackenzie, n.d.: 301; White, 1887, 1: 34)

Anyi-ewo   The serpent-rainbow god of the Ewe. Dahomey. (Ellis, 1890: 47; Mockler-Ferryman, 1925, 9: 275)

Aoao-nui   A personification of clouds. The Maori, New Zealand. (Best, 1924: 175)

Ao Ch'in   One of the four major dragon kings who are rain gods and gods of the storm. China. (Werner, 1932: 285–286; Larousse, 1968: 384)

Ao-hore   A personified form of cloud. The Maori, New Zealand. (Best, 1924: 162)

Ao Jun   One of the four major dragon kings who bring the fertilizing rain as well as thunder and lightning. China. (Werner, 1932: 285–286; Larousse, 1968: 384)

Ao-kahiwahiwa   A storm god—of very black clouds. Child of Tawhiri-matea. The Maori, New Zealand. (Andersen, 1928: 369)

Ao-kanapanapa   "Clouds reflecting Glowing Red Light"—a storm god, child of Tawhiri-matea. The Maori, New Zealand. (Andersen, 1928: 369)

Ao Kuang One of the four major dragon kings who bring rain, invoked during drought. He is king of the Eastern Sea. China. (Werner, 1932: 292–293; Larousse, 1968: 384; Maspero, 1963: 277)

Ao-pakakina A storm god, of the wildly blowing clouds. Child of Tawhiri-matea. The Maori, New Zealand. (Andersen, 1928: 369)

Ao-pakarea A storm god—"Clouds of Thunderstorms." Child of Tawhiri-matea. The Maori, New Zealand. (Andersen, 1928: 369)

Ao-potango A storm god—"Gloomy Thick Clouds." The Maori, New Zealand. (Andersen, 1928: 369)

Ao-pouri "Dark Clouds"—a storm god. The Maori, New Zealand. (Andersen, 1928: 369)

Ao-roa "Massy Clouds"—a storm god of the Maori. New Zealand. (Andersen, 1928: 369)

Ao Shun One of the four major dragon kings who bring the fertilizing rains as well as thunder and lightning. King of the Northern Sea. China. (Werner, 1932: 285–286, 292; Maspero, 1963: 277; Larousse, 1968: 384)

Ao-takawe A storm god, of the scudding clouds. The Maori, New Zealand. (Andersen, 1928: 369)

Ao-tu A personified form of clouds. The Maori, New Zealand. (Best, 1924: 162)

Ao-whekere A storm god—"Clouds which precede Hurricanes." The Maori, New Zealand. (Andersen, 1928: 369)

Ao-whetuma A storm god—"Fiery Clouds." The Maori, New Zealand. (Andersen, 1928: 369)

Apah The god of the atmosphere. Bali, Indonesia. (Grader, 1969, 1: 143)

Apali A wind god—with heavy rains. The Ifugao, Philippines. (Barton, 1946: 62)

Apam Napat A god of lightning and of waters, an aspect of, or identified with, Agni. India and Iran. (Keith, 1917: 36–43; Macdonell, 1897: 70; Bhattacharji, 1970: 187)

Apaos(h)a The demon of drought, of the scorching heat, who endangers the waters. Iran. (Gray, 1930: 199; Dresden, 1961: 353–354; Hinnells, 1973: 31)

Ap(h)eliotes Given variously as the god of the east, the southeast, or the southwest wind, presumed son of Eos and Astraios. Greece. (Kerenyi, 1951: 205; Murray, 1895: 201; 1935: 184)

Apocatequil *See also* **Catequil.** Twin of Piguerao. Gods of thunder and lightning and considered as giving fertility to the fields. Peru. (Brinton, 1868: 153; Spence, 1925, 3: 504)

the Apoiaueue Benevolent spirit who "made the rain fall when it was needed." The Tupians. Brazil. (Larousse, 1968: 447)

Apu-hau A storm god of the Maori whose name means Fierce Squalls. New Zealand. (Andersen, 1928: 206, 369)

Apu-matangi A storm god—"Whirlwinds." The Maori, New Zealand. (Andersen,1928: 369)

Aputahi-a-Pawa A personification of thunder—"a single peal." The Maori, New Zealand. (Best, 1924: 175)

Aquilo An Italian wind god. The "Northeast-wind" who corresponds to the Greek Boreas. (Keane, 1925, 1: 256; Barthell, 1971: 51)

Ara The thunderclap, messenger of Shango. The Yoruba, Nigeria and Dahomey. (Budge, 1973, 1: 373)

Arabaize The west wind, a violent wind like Ernioaize, but colder. The Basques, France and Spain. (Barandiaran, 1972: 71)

Arges One of the Cyclopes, a storm demon—the lightning-or-thunderbolt. Son of Uranus and Gaea. Greece. (Fairbanks, 1907: 67; Larousse, 1968: 89, 129)

Ar^sharneq, Ar^shat The Aurora Borealis personified, helpful to the best shamans. The Copper Eskimo. Bathurst Inlet, Canada. (Rasmussen, 1932: 23)

Asalluhe An Assyro/Babylonian god of thunder and rainstorms. He and Marduk are sometimes identified. Near East. (Jacobsen, 1970: 35)

Asan-Sagan-Tengeri A mighty thunder god of the Buriats "who fights evil spirits with his fiery arrow." Siberia. (MacCulloch, 1964: 442)

Asgaya Gigagei A god of thunder who is also invoked in treatment for rheumatism and seems to be androgynous; when addressed for a male patient the term "Red Woman" is used, for a female, "Red Man." The Cherokee Indians, North Carolina and Tennessee. (Spence, 1925, 3: 504)

Asham A goddess of rain upon whose name oaths are taken. Arabia. (Fahd, 1968: 46)

Asiaq A female spirit who has some control over the weather and the atmosphere. She is approached by shamans "to obtain good weather." Also regarded as male. The Caribou Eskimo. Canada. (Larousse, 1973: 445)

Asias A maker of typhoons at Anu. Truk, Micronesia. (Krämer, 1932: 74)

Asibisidosi The spirit of the whirlwind or tornado who takes the form of a "brown insect" and brings misfortune if seen. The Ojibwa, Minnesota. (Coleman, 1937: 38)

Atam The god of thunder of the Moksha. Russia. (Pettazzoni, 1956: 256; MacCulloch, 1964: 228)

Athena As goddess of the air she had great power over its manifestation of calm or of storm. She represents its life- and health-giving qualities to animals and vegetation; "the air giving motion to the sea, and rendering navigation possible . . . the air nourishing artificial light . . . conveying vibration of sound." Greece. (Ruskin, 1869: 15–16, 40)

Atia The god of thunder of the Lapps. Northern Europe. (Grimm, 1883, 3: xxxi)

Atoja A powerful mountain goddess who controls the rain and whose shrine is used in rain-making ceremonies. The Aymara, Peru. (Tschopik, 1951: 195–197)

Atshe The god of thunder of the Samek. Lapland. (Karsten, 1955: 30)

Atswaqwa The vindictive and punitive god of the rainbow who punishes transgressions with illness and death. The Abkhasians, Caucasus. (Janashia, 1937: 151–152)

Aura Greek goddess of the morning wind. (Murray, 1895: 204)

Auster The Italian god of the south wind who brings rain. He corresponds to the Greek Notus. (Barthell, 1971: 51; Keane, 1925, 1: 256; Salkeld, 1844: 315)

Avaralaru The god of the northwest wind who must be propitiated before going to sea. The Elema, Papuan Gulf, New Guinea. (Holmes, 1902: 431)

Avuakuintana A thunder being—"the thunder of the mountains." The Kagaba, Colombia. (Preuss, 1926: 81)

Awhiowhio The god of the whirlwind. Child of Raka-maomao and parent of Te-pu-mara-kai. New Zealand. (White, 1887, 1: 18; Andersen, 1928: 375)

Awo The god of the wind. The Jukun, Nigeria. (Meek, 1931: 199)

Ayida Oueddo Variant spelling of Aido Wedo. Goddess of the rainbow, of atmospheric phenomenon, of sweet waters, and of fertility. Female counterpart of Damballah, but also the mistress of Agoue. She is represented by a serpent. Haiti, West Indies. (Marcelin, 1950: 69, 70, 88; Deren, 1953: 115)

Baal, Baalbek, Hadad, Baal-saphon A god of storms, of rain, lightning and thunder. As the god of rain he is a giver of fertility, but also in lack of rain a god of vegetal death and resurrection—a dying god when killed by Mot, the demon of drought, but rising again when Mot in turn is slain. In Canaan his female counterpart/sister/consort is Anath, but Astarte and Shera are also named as wives. In Syria he has three brides—Pidriya, Tilliya, and Arsiya, though they are also named as his daughters. Near East. (Albright, 1968: 127–128; 1956: 73–74; Driver, 1956: 3–5, 10, 20–21; Gordon, 1961: 814–815; Vriezen, 1963: 51; Obermann, 1948: 30–31; Crawford, 1957: 19, 23; Herm, 1975: 108–110; Oldenburg, 1969: 74–77)

Baba-buada The chief god of the Araona, the Takanan, was the god of the wind who controlled the seasons and "set the time for sowing or harvesting crops." Bolivia. (Métraux, 1942; 41)

Baba-farara The god of thunder of the Araona, Takanan. Bolivia. (Métraux, 1942: 41)

the Bacabs Four brothers who are gods of wind and rain, and also uphold the world, one at each cardinal point: Hobnil at the East, Can Tzicnal at the North, Zac Cimi at the West, and Hozanek at the South. They are also gods of bees and of divination. Mayan, Mexico. (Bancroft, 1886, 2: 699; Tozzer, 1941: 135; Thompson, 1970: 276–277)

Bade God of lightning in Dahomey, child of Mawu-Lisa. In Brazil and Haiti he is also associated with storms and thunder, and in the latter also identified with Badessy, the wind. (Deren, 1953: 116, 305; Bastide, 1960: 561; Costa Eduardo, 1948: 78–79; Marcelin, 1950: 118)

Badessy The wind god of Haiti. West Indies. (Deren, 1953: 116)

Badra Bae A deity invoked for rain. The Bheels, India. (Coleman, 1832: 375)

The Ba-Du'c-Chua The "Three Mothers . . . represent . . . the Spirit of the Forests, the Spirit of the Waters, and the Spirit of the Air and Sky." Annam. (Cabaton, 1925, 1: 539)

Bagilat The god of lightning and a messenger god. Son of Kidul. The Ifugao, Philippines. (Barton, 1946: 48, 60)

Bai Ulgan Beneficent god of the atmosphere and of the fertility of crops and animals. The Altaic, Siberia. (Eliade, 1964: 198; Casanowicz, 1924: 417; Wales, 1957: 71)

Baiyuhibi A god of rain and also of the winds. The Ifugao, Philippines. Son of Kidul. (Barton, 1946: 31, 62)

Sang Hyang Baju God of the winds, son of Batara Guru, and father of Radin Wrekudara and Hanoman. Java, Indonesia. (Anderson, 1965: 32)

Bakeela One of the names of the god of thunder. The Coast Central Pomo, California. (Loeb, 1926, 2: 301)

Bakiwa A god of winds of the Ifugao. Philippines. (Barton, 1946: 62)

Balaking A god who is responsible for the winds. His wife is Zagina-kugagt. The Itelmens, Siberia. (Michael, 1963: 211)

dBal gsas rngam pa khro rgyal 'gying kha A dark-blue Bon god from whom issues lightning, thunder, and the wind. Tibet. (Nebesky-Wojkowitz, 1956, 1: 316–317)

Baliknug "Clouds that Surround the Sun," and also the Moon; as the former, offspring of Umalgo, as the latter, of Umbulan. The Ifugao, Philippines. (Barton, 1946: 40–41)

Balikoko "Halo around the Sun," as well as the Moon—and again, as the former, offspring of Umalgo, as the latter, of Umbulan. The Ifugao, Philippines. (Barton, 1946: 40–41)

Balingo God of thunder of the Kenyah. Borneo, Indonesia. (Hose, 1912: 11)

Banghi-ilan A god of winds of the Ifugao. Philippines. (Barton, 1946: 62)

Bangputtis, Bangputys God of water and of storms, particularly the sea and waves. Lithuania. (Welsford, 1925, 9: 241; Gimbutas, 1963: 197)

dBang sdud kyi mkha' 'gro ma A goddess invoked for control of the weather. Tibet. (Nebesky-Wojkowitz, 1956, 1: 474)

Rainha Barba A virgin goddess "believed to have power over thunder and lightning." Belem, Brazil. (Leacock, 1972: 158)

basak^cwlaswak The lightning. The Penobscot Indians, Maine. (Speck, 1935: 20)

Basava A "bull god associated with Siva" worshipped on Mondays by the Lingayats and believed to relieve drought and bring rain. Karnataka, India. (Ishwaran, 1974: 30–34)

batl-et-tis The north wind. The Nootka, Washington and Vancouver Island. (Swan, 1869: 92)

Bayon God of the fresh breeze. The Tinguians, Philippines. (Cole, 1922: 300)

bedagiak The thunders. The Penobscot, Maine. (Speck, 1935: 20)

Be'elshamin God of the atmosphere, of clouds and thunder, of fertility. The Palmyrene and Nabataean, Near East. (Vriezen, 1963: 67)

Begjag God and "master of *Ligoi,* the place of the wind." The Kintak Bong, Malaya. (Evans, 1937: 186; Schebesta, 1927: 217, 219)

Begoe, Bigoe, Bigone, Bakchetis An Etruscan goddess of lightning and thunder. Italy. (Roscher, 1965, 1, 1: 755; Leland, 1963: 114)

behpo mahse God of thunder from whom the shaman must obtain the objects he uses. He sometimes appears as a jaguar. The Tukano, Colombia. (Reichel-Dolmatoff, 1975: 78)

Behyu Baji A deity invoked for rain. The Bheels, India. (Coleman, 1832: 375)

Bepkororoti God of storms of the Kayapo. Brazil. (Levi-Strauss, 1969: 248)

berkwi The rainbow. The Pueblo Indians at Isleta, New Mexico. (Parsons, 1929–30: 342)

Bha'a The storm god, the thunderbird, controlled the elements. The Gros Ventres, Montana. (Cooper, 1957: 4)

Po Bhauk God of storms as well as of boatmen and merchants. The Chams, Annam and Cambodia. (Cabaton, 1925, 3: 342)

Bhimai, Bhimsen, Bhimul God of rain and son of Vayu. A festival is celebrated for him before the sowing of seed. Among the Bondo he is associated "with the Sun or the Supreme Being." Among the Koyi he is given a festival in times of drought and an offering of a cow or a pig when rain comes. The Baiga, the Gond, the Muria, India. (Elwin, 1950: 141; 1939: 59; 1949: 99, 100; Crooke, 1894: 38; Kurup, 1970: 162; Russell, 1916, 2: 85; Thurston, 1909, 4: 61)

Biegg-Olmai, Biekagalles, Biekaolmai God of the wind and also of thunder. Among the Swedish Lapps he was the god of the summer wind who ruled "over weather and wind, water and sea." The Lapps, Northern Europe. (Karsten, 1955: 35, 36; Dioszegi, 1968: 28; Bosi, 1960: 132, 151; Collinder, 1949: 145)

Bijaldeo Kanya The lightning—daughter of Megh Raja and Megh Rani, and sister of the sun and moon. The Gond, India. (Elwin, 1949: 61–62)

Bijloki The lightning, one of the wives of Lakshman. The Rajnengi Pardhan, India. (Elwin, 1949: 67)

Biliku Whether male or female always associated with the Northeast monsoon, the parent of the winds which it controls except for the southwest wind. Considered to have created the earth, sun, and moon, and to be associated with the use of fire, of crafts, of high value foods. Andaman Islands and Malaysia. (Radcliffe-Brown, 1967: 147–150, 198–199; Roheim, 1972: 38, 43; Cole, 1945: 76; Pettazzoni, 1956: 302–303)

Bin Babylonian "god of the atmosphere, wind, rain, and thunder." Son of Anu. Near East. (Seligmann, 1948: 100)

Binabaan A god of thunder, son of Kidul. The Ifugao, Philippines. (Barton, 1946: 30, 48)

Binbeal, Bimbeal The rainbow. Son of Bunjil who gave him "power over the earth." Brother of Karakarook. The Kulin and the Warungerri, Australia. (Eliade, 1973: 5; 1958: 42)

Blizgulis Lithuanian god of snow. (Welsford, 1925, 9: 241)

Bobowissi God of thunder and lightning and of rain, all of which he controlled. He was the beneficent protector of travellers and was also invoked in war. His wife was Abu-mehsu. Gold Coast, Ghana. (Mockler-Ferryman, 1925, 9: 277; Ellis, 1887: 22, 31; Lang, 1968: 246)

Bohwaton A god of the wind. The Ifugao, Philippines. (Barton, 1946: 34)

Boinayol A stone idol invoked for rain. Haiti, West Indies (Arciniegas, 1971: 6, 7)

Bok Glaih Chief of the sky gods is "the god of lightning, whose voice is the thunder." He is also a god of war. Indo-China. (Cabaton, 1925, 7: 230)

Boreas The blustery god of the north wind gathers the clouds but also scatters them. Son of Eos and Astraios, husband of Orithiyia, and father of Calais and Zetes. Greece. (Cox, 1870: 249; Kerenyi, 1951: 205; Fairbanks, 1907: 169; Pettazzoni, 1956: 153; Ruskin, 1869: 24; Ovid, 1955: 153–154)

Borias The Roman personification of the strong north wind. (Roscher, 1965, 1, 1: 814)

Boroldai Buqu A thunder god, the fourth son of Qoqodai Megun Qubin. The Mongol, Buriat, Siberia. (Curtin, 1909: 119)

Boto One legend names as the wind, child of Tarai and Kot. The Aka-Jeru, Andaman Islands, Bay of Bengal. (Radcliffe-Brown, 1967: 193)

Boža The god of thunder who was given "responsibility for regulating the social and moral conduct of Gurage." Ethiopia. (Shack, 1968: 460n)

Brag btsan dmar po stong gi rje A mountain god and god of lightning. Tibet. (Nebesky-Wojkowitz, 1956, 1: 219)

Bronte(s) The personification of thunder. One of the Cyclopes, son of Uranus and Gaea. Greece. (Fairbanks, 1907: 67; Roscher, 1965, 1, 1: 830)

Brontios A surname of Zeus meaning the Thunderer. Greece. (Roscher, 1965, 1, 1: 830)

'Brug gi sgra sgrog ma A goddess of the weather who lives in the sky. Tibet. (Nebesky-Wojkowitz, 1956, 1: 468)

Budung Yihe Ibi   Beneficent goddess of the mist. The Mongol, the Buriat, Siberia. (Curtin, 1909: 45)

Bugang   With Pandahatan causes lightning and thunder by fighting. The Dusans, Borneo. (Stall, 1925: 945)

Bukpe   A crocodile spirit who causes drought and disease, but whose malevolence can be controlled by ritual. The Nupe, Nigeria. (Nadel, 1954: 27)

Ah Bulen Caan Chac   A Mayan rain god. Mexico. (Thompson, 1970: 254)

Bulhacil^u Talkin   A Lacandon wind god of the east. Mayan, Mexico. (Thompson, 1970: 271)

Bulotu Katoa   The god of hurricanes was invoked to avert them and also drought and famine. The dog was his sacred animal. The Tongans, Polynesia. (Collocott, 1921: 162; Moulton, 1925, 12: 377)

Bumaiyugbug   A weather god, son of Kidul, the thunder. The Ifugao, Philippines. (Barton, 1946: 31)

Bumarali   Lightning Woman lives in the sky in the dry season and travels on thunderclouds in the wet season. Melville Island, Australia. (Mountford, 1955: 129)

Bunabun   "Clouds that Expand"—a god of the atmosphere. The Ifugao, Philippines. (Barton, 1946: 41)

Burias   God of the north wind, equivalent of the Greek Boreas. The Kassites, Near East. (Campbell, 1964: 122)

dBus kyi 'brug lha ga pa   A god of thunder. Tibet. (Nebesky-Wojkowitz, 1956, 1: 296)

Caculha Huracan   The lightning, a god of the creation. The Quiché, Guatemala. (Recinos, 1950: 82, 84)

Caiton   Among some a female sky being who makes the rain. The Andaman Islands, Bay of Bengal. (Radcliffe-Brown, 1967: 145)

Cakak   God of rain and of snow, of the north. The Acoma of New Mexico. (White, 1929–30: 66)

Calla Filatonga   Goddess of the winds. Tonga, Polynesia. (Williamson, 1933, 1: 146)

Cancuen   One of the Tzultacah (earth and thunder gods)—a river. The Mayan Highlands, Guatemala. (Thompson, 1970: 273)

Canopo, Chinemeru   A mountain god who was believed to cause the rain by urinating. The Tanamacos, West Indies. (Lovén, 1935: 619)

Capon   The grandson of Ta Pedn. He makes the thunder at which time blood sacrifices must be made. The Kensieu, Malaya. (Evans, 1937: 180)

Catende   A weather god of Brazil. (Bastide, 1960: 563)

Catequil   The mighty god of thunder and lightning. Peru. (Cohane, 1969: 61; Fiske, 1900: 65; Larousse, 1968: 442)

Tatik Ca?uk   The god of lightning "may bring rain, but can destroy the milpa with the winds that precede the rain or kill man and destroy his house." San Pedro the Martyr is identified with him. The Tzeltal, Mexico. (Nash, 1970: 13, 203)

Cawanaanwi   The south wind. The Fox Indians, Wisconsin. (Jones, 1911: 212)

Cawənəcu   The beneficent and gentle south wind, promoting life and growth of all things. The Naskapi, Labrador. (Speck, 1935: 62–63)

Ccoa, Cacya   A catlike animal spirit of the mountain spirits (among the Kauri-Ausangate), very active and malevolent, who "brings lightning and hail," destroying crops and killing. The Quechua, Peru. (Mishkin, 1946: 464)

Celaeno   One of the Harpies, daughter of Thaumas and Electra. She causes the sky to become overcast. Greece. (Barthell, 1971: 11; Larousse, 1973: 105)

C'ε· o·x́wa   The "Spruce Raingod," a Winter Raingod, a bringer of rain and its accompanying fertility. The Tewa of San Juan, New Mexico. (Laski, 1958: 11)

The Chacs   Gods of the rain and storms, of the milpas and of fertility. Like the Bacabs there are four and each is assigned to a cardinal point, upholding the sky. Yucatec, Mexico. (Morley, 1946: 216, 224; Tozzer, 1941: 112, 137–138; Thompson, 1970: 251)

chahałheeł yimąsii   Rolling Darkness Wind. An evil, bad wind which causes people to plan badly and to do foolish things. The Navaho, Arizona. (McNeley, 1981: 29, 42)

Chahmayic   One of the Tzultacah (earth and thunder gods)—a river. Mayan Highlands, Guatemala. (Thompson, 1970: 273)

Chak-dor "The Wielder of the Thunderbolt." Sikkim. (Sikhim Gazetteer, 1894: 263)

Ah Ch'alelem Caan Chac One of the rain gods, the bringer of lightning. Mayan, Mexico. (Thompson, 1970: 254)

Chambi The supreme sky god "whose voice is the thunder, who gives or withholds rain, and whose hand hurls the lightning." The Congo. (Budge, 1973, 1: 374)

Chaminuka A great tribal spirit of Central Mashonaland considered the god to give them "good rains and bountiful crops." Rhodesia. (Gelfand, 1962: 143)

Chango A god of storms and of thunder and lightning as well as of war. Haiti, Puerto Rico. In Cuba he is also a god of sexuality and virility. West Indies. (Verger, 1957: 337–338; Marcelin, 1950: 81; Gonzalez-Wippler, 1975: 25, 105)

Chang T'ien Fêng Po A god of wind. China. (Day, 1940: 72)

Chaob The wind gods of the Lacandon, the chief of whom is Hunaunic in the east. Mexico. (Thompson, 1970: 271)

The Chauc, Anhel The rain gods/god of the Tzotzil also control(s) the winds. A god of wild animals as well as of sustenance. Mayan, Mexico. (Thompson, 1970: 267–268)

Chauta The god of rain of the Nyanja. Malawi. (Frazer, 1926: 180)

Chemam The god of thunder which he makes by spinning a top. He causes illness and death with his thunderbolts. The Kintak Bong, Malaya. (Evans, 1937: 143, 183)

Chêng T'ien-chün and **Ch'ên T'ien-chün** They, with Chu T'ien-chün, represent "the formidable power of the gods of storms and hurricanes." China. (Werner, 1932: 94)

Chethl The god of thunder or lightning—the Thunderbird—brother of Ahgishanakhou. The Thlinkeets (presumably a variant of Tlingit), British Columbia/Alaska. (Bandroft, 1886, 3: 103, 146)

Ah Ch'ibal Tun Chaacob One of the Mayan rain gods. Mexico. (Thompson, 1970: 255)

the Chicchans The sky Chicchans are giant snake gods of rain and of atmospheric phenomena, four in number, one at each of the cardinal points. They are both beneficial and harmful: the sky Chicchans sending rain for growth and fertility, but also hurricanes; the earth Chicchans, also of snake form, cause landslides and earthquakes. The Chorti (Mayan), Guatemala, Honduras, and El Salvador. (Thompson, 1970: 262; Wisdom, 1940: 393–395, 417)

Chikin Kuh Lacandon god of the west wind. Mayan, Mexico. (Thompson, 1970: 271)

Chi Lung Wang An atmospheric god, one of the Dragon Kings. China. (Day, 1940: 209)

Chin Ko Lao Lung Wang A Dragon King in control of the rain. The T'ang Dynasty, China. (Werner, 1932: 296)

Chin-na-lo One of the Dragon Kings—of waters, of rain, and of atmospheric phenomena. China. (Werner, 1932: 285–286)

Chipiripa, Chipiropa A sky and rain god who controls the atmosphere. Panama. (Bancroft, 1886, 3: 499; Trimborn, 1968: 106; Alexander, 1920: 191)

Chi Po A Chinese god of the wind. (Werner, 1932: 567)

Chiquinaut A god of the wind of the Nicarao. Nicaragua. (Lothrop, 1926: 69; Bancroft, 1886, 3: 491)

Chiuta The supreme being and creator god is also the god of the rain, and is represented by the rainbow. The Tumbuka, the Tonga, The Nkamanga, Rhodesia and Malawi. (Young, 1950: 50–52; Williams, 1936: 259; Frazer, 1926: 183; Mbiti, 1970, 2: 336)

Chiu-t'ien Lei Kung A god of thunder. China. (Werner, 1932: 91)

Chiu T'ien Lei Tsu, Wu Fang Lei Kung, Lei Tsu Ta Ti God of thunder. "His is a mighty charm for diviners and geomancers, for he controls thunder and lightning . . . feared by farmers" because of damage to crops. China. (Day, 1940: 71)

Chuetenshu The north wind brings the cold, the snows, is "the master of the animals" and brings game to hunters. The Waswanipi (Cree) Indians, Quebec. (Feit, 1973: 54)

Churarimunpo The spirit of rain who appears on cloudy, thundery days but no storm breaks. The Mundurucu, Para, Brazil. (Murphy, 1958: 21)

Chusman, Chanzan A god who sends thunder and lightning is considered malignant by some, by others well-disposed. The Patangoro, Colombia. (Kirchhoff, 1948: 346)

Chu T'ien-chün With Ch'ên T'ien-chün and Chêng T'ien-chün reperesents "the formiadable power of the gods of storms and hurricanes." China. (Werner, 1932: 94)

Chuychu The rainbow deity, a servant of the sun. Peru. (Means, 1931: 405)

Cichpan Colel XHelik A Mayan wind goddess. British Honduras. (Thompson, 1970: 272)

Cienga, Chenga A malignant chthonic god who "lets loose whirlwinds and floods of rain, invisibly slays their children, and dries up their flesh." Western Australia. (Tylor, 1891: 290)

Cilkus A malignant god of thunder. The Wailaki, California. (Loeb, 1932: 73)

Circius The god of the northwest wind. Rhone Valley, Gaul. (Renel, 1906: 396; Gray, 1930: 168)

Čišmak A fiend who causes whirlwinds. Iran. (Gray, 1930: 204)

Coatrischie Goddess of water, of winds, and of tempests. Antilles, Haiti, and Puerto Rico. West Indies. (Fewkes, 1903/04: 56; Alexander, 1920: 25; Larousse, 1968: 440)

Cocijo, Cosejo God of rain and water, of lightning, of wind, who "also presided over the cardinal directions." The Zapotec, Oaxaca, Mexico. (Peredo, 1974: 19; Helfritz, 1971: 74; Tozzer, 1957: 114; Krickeberg, 1968: 55; Augur, 1954: 245; Whitecotton, 1977: 159, 162)

Col A spirit of the Nuer associated with rain and lightning. Sudan. (Evans-Pritchard, 1956: 30)

Coliatum Bilik A wind being of the A-Pucikwar. Andaman Islands, Bay of Bengal. (Radcliffe-Brown, 1967: 149)

Con A god of thunder of the Collao was the bringer of rains but also of drought. He was considered a creator god of the coastal area. Peru. (Spence, 1925, 3: 547; Mishkin, 1940: 225; Brinton, 1882: 196)

Corus An Italian wind god. (Keane, 1925, 1: 256)

Cotokinunwu A sky god who wields the lightning and is associated with the clouds. Hopi Indians, Arizona. (Fewkes, 1899: 215; Keane, 1925, 1: 253)

Cotukvnangi, Cotukvnangwuu A weather god, "the Star and Cloud Deity," who gave thunder and lightning to the War Twins. Pueblo Indians, Arizona and New Mexico. (Tyler, 1964: 101–102)

Cuchabiba, Cuchaviva, Cuchavira Goddess of the rainbow to whom offerings of emeralds and beads were made by the ill and by childbearing women. The Chibcha and Muyscas, Colombia. (Kroeber, 1946, 2: 906; Keane, 1925, 3: 515; Brinton, 1882: 150, 223)

Cueravaperi, Cuerohperi The great mother goddess was the goddess of the rains and of water who sometimes sent drought and famine, and to whom human hearts were sacrificed in rainmaking ceremonies. The Tarascan, Mexico. (Craine and Reindorp, 1970: 133, 197; Krickeberg, 1968: 59; Brinton, 1882: 209)

Cuisiabirri Benevolent god of fire, an aspect of Puru, who causes the lightning. The Achagua, the Salivan. Colombia. (Wallis, 1939: 89; Walde-Waldegg, 1936: 40–42; Hernandez de Alba, 1948, 2: 410)

Cuitira The rainmaker of the east who causes fog and mist. The Acoma Indians, New Mexico. (White, 1929/30: 66)

Cul A spirit of the air who sends dreams. The Nuer, Sudan. (Evans-Pritchard, 1956: 32)

Cwol The god of lightning. The Nuer, Sudan. (Huffman, 1931: 56)

The Cyclopes Storm deities, sons of Uranus and Gaea—Arges, the thunderbolt, Brontes, the thunder, Steropes the lightning. Greece. (Fairbanks, 1907: 67; Larousse, 1968: 89–90, 129)

Da A deity or power who is manifest as the rainbow, a serpent symbolizing life and movement, their controlling force. The Fon, Dahomey. (Mercier, 1954: 220; Parrinder, 1949: 40, 52–53; Herskovits, 1938, 2: 189, 201)

Dabaiba The "goddess who controlled the thunder and lightning . . . was also honoured as the mother of the Creator," who was the intermediary between her and mankind. Panama. (Robertson, 1911: 350)

Dadamimaš The Hatti god of the weather whose sons were Inariš and Telepinuš. Asia Minor. (Van Buren, 1943: 82)

Dagan Semitic/Akkadian god of storm and rain, its fertilizing powers in producing grain. Near East. (Jacobsen, 1970: 34; Roberts, 1972: 19)

Daga'shwine'da The "spring wind." The Iroquois Indians, Eastern United States. (Gray, 1925, 7: 422)

Daibiturebo A spirit of rain who also causes high winds. The Mundurucu, Para, Brazil. (Murphy, 1958: 21)

Daibituwatpo A spirit of rain "who brings storms with black clouds." The Mundurucu, Para, Brazil. (Murphy, 1958: 21)

Daiyongdong A god of winds and heavy rains. The Ifugao, Philippines. (Barton, 1946: 62)

Dajoji Panther, god of the west wind, very strong, raises as well as controls storms. The Iroquois, Eastern United States. (Leach, 1949, 1: 275)

Dalbhyesvara The rain god in modern Hinduism who has replaced Indra. India. (Keith, 1917: 233; Crooke, 1894: 38)

Damballa, Damballa Wedo God of the rain and the rainbow is symbolized by the serpent. He is the benevolent god of fecundity and strength. His wife is Aida Wedo. Haiti, West Indies. (Herskovits, 1937, 1: 315–316; Marcelin, 1950: 55, 69, 88; Deren, 1953: 56, 114)

Dam tshig mkha' 'gro ma A goddess invoked for rainfall. Tibet. (Nebesky-Wojkowitz, 1956, 1: 479)

Dan The rainbow serpent god/goddess of the Mahi symbolizes continuity, the vital force, and bestows wealth. Dahomey. (Verger, 1957: 233; Herskovits, 1938, 2: 247)

Dangquico An evil anito who with Makel and Kilang "move the winds that kill instantly." The Apayao, Philippines. (Wilson, 1947: 23)

Datta, Dattas Luwian/Hittite sky and weather god—the reading in Luvian of the two Babylonian ideograms U and IM which represented the Hittite supreme god, spouse of Arinna. Near East. (Ferm, 1950: 88; Gurney, 1952: 138; Eliade, 1958: 88)

Daungen The rainbow goddess is the daughter of Kabunian and Bugan. Philippines. (Jocano, 1969: 62)

Debrong pa-no The god of hail who was invoked and propitiated in their ceremonies. The Lepchas, Sikkim and Tibet. (Nebesky-Wojkowitz, 1956, 1: 475; Gorer, 1938: 204)

Deng, Dengdit A god of the atmosphere, the sky, who is associated with rain, thunder, and lightning. He is invoked for rain and in taking oaths. The Dinka, Sudan. (Parrinder, 1967: 75; Lienhardt, 1961: 104; Butt, 1952: 131–132, 153; Budge, 1973, 1: 375; Gelfand, 1966: 121)

Derra The god of lightning brought fire to the earth. Yap Island, Micronesia. (Furness, 1910: 151)

Dessahi Another name for Pawan Dasseri, the Wind. India. (Elwin, 1949: 82)

Deus Coelestis Baal Hammon after the Punic Wars was worshipped at Carthage under this name as a "Sky-Father and Weather-god." North Africa. (Meyerowtiz, 1958: 130–131)

Dewaite szwenta Lithuanian goddess of rain. (Grimm, 1888: 1458)

Dewy A Canaanite goddess of showers and a consort of Baal. Near East. (Gray, 1957: 42)

Dhakkan, Takkan The rainbow god, a fish/snake-deity of great power, could be malignant or benevolent. The Kabi and Wakka tribes, Queensland, Australia. (Mathew, 1910: 171)

Dierbmes God of thunder of the Lapps of the Kola Peninsula and northern Scandinavia. Same as Tirmes, Thor. (Collinder, 1949: 140; Turville-Petre, 1964: 98; Minn, 1955: 72)

Diewaitis Lithuanian god of thunder. (Grimm, 1888: 1458)

Dinipaan A wind god of the Ifugao. Philippines. (Barton, 1946: 62)

Dione A Greek stellar goddess. As one of the Hyades a harbinger of rain and storm when rising in conjunction with the sun. Daughter of Atlas and Aethra. (Barthell, 1971: 57)

Disako The god of rain to whom offerings are made. The Dakarkari, Nigeria. (Harris, 1938: 129)

Diviriks The Baltic personification of the rainbow. Lithuania. (Queval, 1968: 37; Larousse, 1973: 420)

Dji The rainbow, a sky god, who helps "Xevioso to come to earth." Identified with Aido Hwedo, son of

Mawu and Lisa. Dahomey. (Herskovits, 1938, 2: 107–108)

Djo An omniscient god of the atmosphere, son of Mawu-Lisa, to whom he must give an accounting of his reign. Dahomey. (Herskovits, 1938, 2: 130)

Doam The god of rain of the Burun. Sudan. (Butt, 1952: 160)

Dobeiba The storm goddess vents her anger in thunder and lightning. Human sacrifices are made to her. The Dabeiba, Colombia. (Trimborn, 1968: 102)

Doc-Cu'o'c A benevolent and omniscient god who controls the weather. He bestows success, good crops, virility. Annam. (Cabaton, 1925, 1: 539)

Dogoda Slavic god of the west wind. (Larousse, 1968: 285)

Doli God of rain of the Gallongs (Adi). Northeastern India. (Chowdhury, 1971: 45–46)

Dolon-Khukhu-Tengri One of the seven blue Tengris who bestow the rain, but are not directly invoked. The Buriats, Siberia/Mongolia. (Klementz, 1925, 3: 4)

Domalong-dong The "deity of the northwind." The Bukidnon, Philippines. (Jocano, 1969: 23)

Donar Germanic god of agricultural fertility and god of the elements who expresses his anger with thunder and lightning. (Grimm, 1880: 157, 169; Schoeps, 1961: 105)

Dondonyag "Rain While Sun Shines"—a weather god, son of Kidul. The Ifugao, Philippines. (Barton, 1946: 31)

Dongo The god of thunder and teacher of initiation rites. The Songhay, Upper Niger. (Parrinder, 1967: 74; Larousse, 1973: 528)

Donn The god of the dead is both being as the guardian of crops and cattle and malignant in causing "storms and shipwrecks." Celtic Ireland. (MacCana, 1970: 43)

rDo rje mkha' 'gro ma A goddess invoked for rainfall. Tibet. (Nebesky-Wojkowitz, 1956, 1: 75, 479)

rDo rje shugs ldan A fearful god from whose "nostrils come forth rain-clouds and . . . raging thunder and lightning." Tibet. (Sierksma, 1966: 26)

Drag po'i klog khyung ma A goddess of weather. Tibet. (Nebesky-Wojkowitz, 1956, 1: 468)

Drangoni A benevolent male power who drives off Kulshedra, the evil female power, with thunder and lightning. He may be a man or an animal. Albania. (Durham, 1928: 123)

Drifa Goddess of the "loose drifting snow," daughter of Snior. Norway. (Grimm, 1883, 2: 883)

Dsovean A storm god who "rules supreme in the storm." Associated with Dsovinar. Armenia. (Ananikian, 1964: 46)

Dsovinar A storm goddess associated with Dsovean. Armenia. (Ananikian, 1964: 46)

Duarsani Pat A hill deity invoked to bring rain. The Santals, India. (Mukherjea, 1962: 278)

Dubudubon "Gentle Wind," a god of the Ifugao. Philippines. (Barton, 1946: 34)

Dumalalu A weather and wind god of the Ifugao. Son of Kidul. Philippines. (Barton, 1946: 31, 62)

Dumunguwol A weather god and son of Kidul. The Ifugao, Philippines. (Barton, 1946: 31)

Durgama The "personification of drought"—an *asura* whom Durga promises to destroy. India. (Eliade, 1958: 280)

Dyuok, Djuok The supreme being of the Luo is also a god of the wind. Kenya and Uganda. (Pettazzoni, 1956: 10, 38)

Dzivaguru A great spirit who "first appeared as a man and when he died his spirit became a very powerful rain spirit." The Shona. Rhodesia. (Gelfand, 1962: 9)

Ea A deity who represents a form of thunder. The Maori, New Zealand. (Best, 1924: 175)

Eate The spirit of the tempest, of hurricane winds, of fire, and of floods. The Basques, Spain and France. (Barandiaran, 1972: 71)

Ecalchot God of the wind. Nicaragua. (Bancroft, 1886, 2: 490–491; Larousse, 1968: 440)

Ecke A Teutonic god-giant of wind and water, brother of Fasolt and Abentrot. He is identified with Oegir and rules the waters. (Grimm, 1880: 232; 1883, 2: 636)

Egua The south wind who does not bring rain. The Basques, Spain and France. (Barandiaran, 1972: 72)

Ehécatl   Aztec god of the wind, identified with Quet-zalcóatl. Mexico. (Nicholson, 1967: 28; Krickeberg, 1968: 43; Vaillant, 1962: 149)

Ehlaumel   The thunder, a great deity of the Coast Yuki. California. (Kroeber, 1925: 216)

Eiuga   The supreme being, a sky god, whose voice is the thunder and whose breath is the wind. He causes storms when angry. The Onges, Little Andaman, Bay of Bengal. (Cipriano, 1966: 43)

Elat   The god of the rain, of thunder and lightning. Kenya. (Massam, 1927: 188–189)

ela'tawe gi'pozidit   Sheet lightning. The Penobscot Indians, Maine. (Speck, 1935: 20)

Ele, Ali   The god of lightning, usually male but sometimes female. Andaman Islands, Bay of Bengal. (Radcliffe-Brown, 1967: 145)

Elias   Slavic god of thunder and lightning who controls the rain and the wind, is invoked to withhold hail. Also the Caucasus. (Welsford, 1925, 9: 252; Grimm, 1880: 174)

Enekitsum   The god of snow is invoked to protect from too prolonged frost and snow. The Nootka, Washington and Vancouver Island. (Strange, 1900: 51)

l'Engai Narok   The benevolent god of rain. The Masai, Tanzania. (Dallas, 1931: 40)

Eñketa   The elements are under the control of the supreme sky deity. Congo. (Budge, 1973, 1: 374)

Enlil   One of the chief gods in the Sumerian/Babylonian pantheon—god of the weather and of the winds, particularly the god of the moist winds, "growing weather," of spring. He is both beneficent and destructive, the latter evident in storms. Near East. (Roberts, 1972: 21; Pettazzoni, 1956: 19; Jacobsen, 1946: 184; 1976: 25, 98–99, 100–101)

'Ere'ere-fenua   A goddess of the Society Islands and wife of Rua-tupua-nui. Her appearance foretold "destruction on earth, by storm or by war." Polynesia. (Henry, 1928: 359)

Ernio-aize   The southwest wind is violent, frequently causing damage in the woodlands and the harvests. He brings rains which are heavy when he encounters Mendeal, the northwest wind. Usually blows for nine consecutive days. The Basques, France and Spain. (Barandiaran, 1972: 72)

Erse   Greek goddess of the dew, daughter of Selene and Zeus. (Larousse, 1968: 143)

Esaugetuh Emissee   The pre-existent creator god of the Choctaw Indians who also "appears to be the personification of the wind." Mississippi, Alabama, and Georgia. (Spence, 1925, 3: 568)

Etisoda Hadiwenodadie's   The thunder man brings the rain and is thanked with others at the harvest. The Onandaga Indians, New York. (Waugh, 1916: 22)

Etskituns   The rainbow causes harm to those who may be out while it is shining. The Paez and Moguex, Colombia. (Hernandez de Alba, 1946, 1: 954)

Euros, Eurus   Greek god of the southeast wind. Son of Eos and Astraios. (Kerenyi, 1951: 205; Fox, 1916: 265–266; Barthell, 1971: 51; Salkeld, 1844: 315)

Eya   The god of the West and of the west wind is the courageous second son of Tate, the Wind. Eya is the companion of the Winged God, Wakinyan, whom he is to help "cleanse the world of filthy and evil things." He is disorderly, yet capable of creating "cleanliness out of filth, through the process of change." As Wakinyan lives in the West with Eya, Eya "can close the door of his tipi" and prevent him from travelling out and causing lightning. Their association brings the rain. Eya's bird (messenger) is the swallow whose forked tail symbolizes the lightning; his association is with autumn; his color is yellow, ritual color, black. The Oglala/Lakota, South Dakota. His name is sometimes spelled Iya. (Powers, 1977: 72, 75, 76, 79, 192; Walker, 1980: 72, 225)

Fakafotu   The god of storms and hurricanes expressed his anger in the thunder. Fakaofu, Tokelau, Polynesia. (Lister, 1891: 51; Williamson, 1933: 151)

Farewai   The god of navigation is a forecaster of the weather. Ifalik, Micronesia. (Burrows, 1947/48: 8)

Fasolt   Teutonic god of storms, brother of Ecke and Abentrot, god-giants of wind and water. (Grimm, 1880: 232; 1883, 2: 636)

Fatu-tiri   God of thunder. Tuamotu, Tahiti, Polynesia. (Henry, 1928: 128)

Fatuuratane   God of the thunderbolt. Tahiti, Polynesia. (Henry, 1928: 351)

Faurourou   A goddess of the atmosphere—"the frozen, gilded cloud." Tahiti, Polynesia. (Henry, 1928: 370)

Fei Lien A Chinese god of the wind. (Werner, 1932: 567)

Fêng Po, Fêng Shih God of the wind who was identified with the constellation Sagittarius. He was succeeded by the goddess Feng-p'o-p'o. China. (Ferguson, 1937: 73; Werner, 1932: 126; Larousse, 1968: 384)

Fêng-p'o-p'o Goddess of the wind. China. Maspero, 1963: 275; Larousse, 1968: 384)

Firie The supreme sky god who controls the elements. Congo. (Budge, 1973, 1: 374)

Fisaga The deity of the pleasant wind. Samoa, Polynesia. (Andersen, 1928: 218)

Fjorgynn An old name of the Scandinavian god/goddess of thunder. (Davidson, 1964: 111; MacCulloch, 1964: 228)

Fonge and **Toafa** "two oblong smooth stones," which were given offerings and prayers when fine weather was especially desired. Parents of Saato. Samoa, Polynesia. (Turner, 1884: 24, 25)

Fonn Norse goddess of snow and ice. Daughter of Sniorr. (Grimm, 1883, 2: 631)

Frey, Freyr, Freyer Scandinavian/Teutonic god of weather, of rain and sunshine, whose symbol is the golden boar. He was the god of marriage, of fertility and of plenty. Son of Niord, brother of Freya. His wife was Gerda. (Stern, 1898: 44; Davidson, 1964: 29, 96; Wagner, 1882: 199, 204; Guerber, 1895: 107, 112–113, 120)

Frick, Frau Fiuk A Teutonic goddess of the wind. (Grimm, 1888: 1471)

Fujin A god of the winds. Japan. (Piggott, 1969: 31)

Fulgora An Italian goddess of lightning. (Roscher, 1965, 1, 2: 1559)

Futsu-Nushi-no-Kami A god of lightning as well as a god of war. Japan. (Holtom, 1938: 82, 177; Kato, 1926: 72)

Gaende'sonk "gusts of wind," daughter of Awenhai and Haonhwendjiawa'gi. She became the mother of Teharonhia-wagon and Tawiskaron. Awenhai made the sun from her head, the moon from her body. The Iroquois Indians, Eastern United States. (Gray, 1925, 7: 422)

Galaxaura Greek goddess associated with "calm" in reference to weather. Daughter of Oceanus and Tethys. (Kerenyi, 1951: 41; Roscher, 1965, 1, 2: 1590)

Galta-Ulan-Tengri The god of heat and drought, of fire and of lightning. The Buriats, Siberia. (Klementz, 1925, 3: 4; MacCulloch, 1964: 449)

Galudugud A wind god of the Ifugao. Philippines. (Barton, 1946: 62)

Gangr A Scandinavian storm giant, of the "rain-wind." (Stern, 1898: 121)

Gangs dkar sha med The "White Snow-goddess without flesh"—of terrifying appearance. Tibet. (Tucci, 1980: 166)

Ga-oh The spirit of the winds, though restless and sometimes violent, is considered beneficent and mindful of the wishes of the Great Spirit. He controls the winds and the seasons. The Iroquois and Hurons, Eastern United States. (Morgan, 1904: 151–152; Alexander, 1964: 23; Burland, 1965: 149; Leach, 1949, 1: 441)

Gapa A dragon-headed god of thunder and one of those who determines the destinies of men. Tibet. (Nebesky-Wojkowitz, 1956, 2: 51)

//Gauwa A god associated with thunder and lightning, with wind and rain, with whirlwinds; of questionable character, both evil and good. Invoked for success in hunting. The Bushmen of Southwest Africa. (Marshall, 1962: 238–239; Smith, 1950: 91; Eliade, 1967: 268)

Gavampati A Buddhist "god of drought and wind." India. (Larousse, 1968: 348)

Gbade A thunder god, eighth and youngest child of Sogbo, spoiled and violent tempered. "His is the voice heard in the loudest thunderclaps . . . sends the jagged lightning that kills." He is transported to earth by Aido Hwedo. Dahomey. (Herskovits, 1938, 2: 152, 158)

Gbwesu The god of the muffled thunder who does no harm; fifth child of Sogbo. Dahomey. (Herskovits, 1938, 2: 152, 156)

Gebu The god of rain of the Guaraunos. Orinoco delta, Venezuela. (Lovén, 1935: 582)

St. George Their chief god—a storm and solar god who sends hail as punishment, though he is also beneficent as a god of fertility and healing. The Khevsurs, Caucasus. (Gray, 1925, 12: 485)

geselam'sen   The winds control the destinies of men and animals. The Penobscot, Maine. (Speck, 1935: 21)

Ginitob   A wind god of the Ifugao, Philippines. (Barton, 1946: 62)

Girgire   Sumerian god of lightning. Son of Bilulu. Near East. (Jacobsen, 1970: 58)

Gissen Olmai   The god of the winter wind and weather is invoked to protect reindeer from ice. The Swedish Lapps. (Karsten, 1955: 36)

Glog bdag mo   Tibetan goddess of lightning. (Nebesky-Wojkowitz, 1956, 1: 467)

Glog-gsas   A god of lightning and one of the deities of the four quarters. Nepal. (Snellgrove, 1961: 122, 298)

Gnurluwa   A water snake who makes the rainbow by spitting into the sky. His wife is Munbakuaku, the "dollar bird," who is associated with rain. The Anula, Central Australia. (Spencer, 1904: 631)

Goera   The god of strength wields the thunder and lightning. When a tree is blasted by lightning sacrifices must be made to him at its foot. He is invoked for "health and strength after long illnesses." The Garo, Assam. (Playfair, 1909: 81)

Golgol   A god of the wind. The Ifugao, Philippines. (Barton, 1946: 62)

Gomatia tafo   The rainbow. The Nankanse, the Moshi, Ghana. (Rattray, 1932: 335)

Gonti, Gontiyalamma   A Dravidian goddess associated with the rains. The Malas, India. (Elmore, 1915: 66; Hemingway, 1915: 47–48)

Gos   A god of the Vilela invoked for rain and for "protection against epidemics." Gran Chaco, Argentina. (Métraux, 1946, 1: 356)

Gozio   The god of lightning and of rain. The Sierra Zapotec, Oaxaca, Mexico. (Whitecotton, 1977: 169)

Grom   A youthful Slavic god of thunder. (Grimm, 1883, 2: 883)

Gua   A god of thunder and of blacksmiths. The Gã, Ghana. (Field, 1937: 64, 86; Parrinder, 1949: 30)

Guabancex   Goddess of wind and of water who controls the rain, produces storms when angry. Under her are

Guatauva and Coatrischie. Haiti and Puerto Rico, West Indies. (Lovén, 1935: 603, 617; Fewkes, 1903/04: 56; Alexander, 1920: 25; Larousse, 1968: 440)

Guaigerri   God of the wind, an aspect of Puru. The Salivan, Colombia. (Walde-Waldegg, 1936: 40–41; Wallis, 1939: 89)

Guatauva   A messenger of Guabancex and under her orders in producing rain and wind. West Indies. (Lovén, 1935: 617; Fewkes, 1903/04: 56; Alexander, 1920: 25)

Guicthia   Rainmaker of the west. The Acoma, New Mexico. (White, 1929/30: 66)

Gunu   The beneficent chief god who controlled the elements and bestowed children and crops. The tribes of the area of the confluence of the Niger and Benue rivers, Nigeria. (Mockler-Ferrymnan, 1925, 9: 280)

Ha   The spirit of rain and of surface waters is invoked in fishing as he controls the fish and crocodiles. The Maya, British Honduras. (Thompson, 1930: 65)

Hadad   God of weather and of storms who controls the elements. He was beneficent in sending fertilizing rains, destructive in inflicting floods and storms. His wife was Atargatis. Also called Raman, Rimmon; also an earlier name of Baal. Widespread throughout the Near East. (Macler, 1925, 12: 165; Albright, 1956: 73; Ferguson, 1970: 18; James, 1960: 306; Moscati, 1960: 175; Vriezen, 1963: 56; Cook, 1930: 27)

Hadawinetha   The "fire dragon of storm." The Iroquois Indians, Eastern United States. (Gray, 1925, 7: 422)

Ah hadzen-caan-chaac   A Mayan sky and rain god who makes sharp thunderclaps. Yucatan, Mexico. (Redfield and Villa Rojas, 1962: 115; Thompson, 1970: 254–255)

Hadz' Ku, Tan Hadz' Ku   A Mayan god of the lightning-strike who drives the storm. Lacandon, Mexico. (Thompson, 1970: 266)

Haere   A "personification of the rainbow." The Maori, New Zealand. (Best, 1924: 238)

Hafoza   The spirit of thunder and lightning. The Kamano, Jate, Usurufa, Fore of New Guinea. (Berndt, 1965: 81)

U Hahab Ku   The Lacandon god who is the personification of lightning. Mexico. (Thompson, 1970: 266)

Hahana Ku A god of rain, which he obtains from Menzabac on orders from Hachacyum, but controls the quantity; and hail, from Itzan Noh Ku. The Lacandon, Mexico. (Thompson, 1970: 266)

Hakona-tipu, Ha-koua-tipu A wind god, the blustering south gale. Son of Hine-tu-whenua and father of Pua-i-taha. The Maori, New Zealand. (Andersen, 1928: 375; White, 1887, 1: 28)

Halibubu A god of the atmosphere, the clouds. The Ifugao, Philippines. (Barton, 1946: 40)

Ha-lo, Aka-ku-a-nue-nue The goddess of the rainbow. Maui, Hawaii. (Ashdown, 1971: 66)

Hanish A Mesopotamian storm god. In the Gilgamesh epic "he is apparently portrayed as the low-hanging first line of clouds in a rapidly approaching storm front." Near East. (Roberts, 1972: 30)

hank'o q'awani acacila The malevolent spirit (male) of hail and ice who lives on Amantani Island in Lake Titicaca. The Aymara, Peru. (Tschopik, 1951: 198)

Hanpa A god of the wind-demons. Father of Pazuzu. Asia Minor. (Langdon, 1931: 371)

Ha-nui-o-raki His name means great breath. Son of Raki and Poko-harua-te-po, and father of the winds. The Maori, New Zealand. (White, 1887, 1: 18, 28: Andersen, 1928: 375)

lHa rgod thog 'bebs Tibetan god of the thunderbolt, whose consort is Klu mo dung skyong ma. (Nebesky-Wojkowitz, 1956, 1: 328)

The Harpies Daughters of Thaumas and Electra—Aello, Celaeno, Ocypete, Podarge. They had the bodies of birds with human heads and were originally goddesses of the storm winds, manifest in whirlwinds, but later punished crime and intervened in human destinies. Greece. (Fairbanks, 1907: 169; Kerenyi, 1951: 60–62; Murray, 1935: 218; Larousse, 1968: 146; Ruskin, 1869: 26)

Hau-maringi God of the mist. The Maori, New Zealand. (Andersen, 1928: 374)

Hau-marotoroto God of "Heavy Dew." The Maori, New Zealand. (Andersen, 1928: 374)

Hawa Pawan The wind god of the Baiga. India. (Fuchs, 1952: 616)

Hayachi-no-kami, Haya-Tsu-muji-no-Kami God of the winds, of whirlwinds and typhoons. Japan. (Kato, 1926: 10; Herbert, 1967: 491; Larousse, 1968: 416)

hayoolkaal ashkii Dawn Boy—a good wind in association with people. The Navaho, Arizona. (McNeley, 1981: 29, 82)

Hecat A god of the winds. the Nicarao, Nicaragua. (Lothrop, 1926: 69; Bancroft, 1886, 3: 491)

Hehnoh The god of thunder of the Wyandots (Iroquois). Eastern United States. (Connelley, 1899: 118)

Heloha The spirit of thunder, female. The Choctaw Indians, Louisiana. (Bushnell, 1909: 18; Burland, 1965: 150)

Hema A goddess, the personification of the south wind, daughter of Whai-tiri. Hawaii. (Best, 1924: 153; MacKenzie, 1930: 131)

Heng, De Hi No A sky power, the thunder, who was considered a kindly spirit because he heralded the spring. The Huron, Ontario. (Burland, 1965: 77–78, 149)

Henkhisesui God of the east wind. Egypt. (Budge, 1969, 2: 296; Knight, 1915: 134)

Heno The god of thunder, though punitive with his lightning, was considered beneficent bringing the clouds and rain to cool and refresh the earth. His is also "the voice of admonition and the instrument of vengeance." The Iroquois, Eastern United States. (Morgan, 1904: 149; Bjorklund, 1969: 130–132; Barbeau, 1914: 306–307)

Hera Greek goddess of the atmosphere who, in her dark moods, is a goddess of storms, of thunder and winds. She is the sister/wife of Zeus and a goddess of marriage and of childbirth. Mother of Ares, Hebe, Eileithyia, Hephaestos. (Murray, 1935: 48–50; Cox, 1870: 5, 10, 12; Fairbanks, 1907: 44, 101; Willetts, 1962: 252; Barthell, 1971: 19, 21)

Hermes He was a god of many facets and has been interpreted as a god of the wind, swift as the messenger of the gods. He was associated with the clouds and the mist and their power of concealment, their movement in the skies, which ties in with his role as a god of lying, of dissimulation. He watched over trade and travellers, and conducted the souls of the dead to Hades. Greece. (Fiske, 1900: 32; Keary, 1882: 333; Schoeps, 1961: 131; Barthell, 1971: 33–37; Ruskin, 1869: 32, 36)

Herse   Greek goddess of the dew, the cloud dew. Sister of Pandrosos and Aglauros. (Roscher, 1965, 1, 2: 2591; Crawley, 1925, 4: 700; Ruskin, 1869: 48)

Hevioso   God of thunder and of atmospheric phenomena. The Fon, Dahomey. Also Haiti, Cuba. (Courlander, 1966: 15; Mercier, 1954: 213–214; Verger, 1954: Pl.62)

Hiata-i-reia   "Cloud-holder-garland-decked," a sister of Pele. Hawaii. (Henry, 1928: 576)

Hiata-i-te-pori-o-Pere   "Cloud-holder-kissing-the-bosom-of-Pele," sister of Pele. Hawaii. (Henry, 1928: 576)

Hiata-kaalawamaka, Hiiaka-kaa-lawa-maka   "Flashing-eyed-cloud-holder," sister of Pele. Hawaii. (Henry, 1928: 576; Westervelt, 1963, 2: 70)

Hiata-noho-lani, Hiiaka-noho-lani   "Heaven-dwelling-cloud-holder," sister of Pele. Hawaii. (Henry, 1928: 576; Westervelt, 1963, 2: 70)

Hiata-opio   "Youthful-cloud-holder," sister of Pele. Hawaii. (Henry, 1928: 576)

Hiata-tapu-enaena   "Cloud-holder-of-furnace-red-hot," sister of Pele. Hawaii. (Henry, 1928: 576)

Hiata-wawahi-lani   "Heaven-rending-cloud-holder"— "breaking-the-heavens-for-the-heavy-rain-to-fall," sister of Pele. Hawaii. (Henry, 1928: 576; Westervelt, 1963, 2: 70)

Hiiaka-ka-lei-ia   A cloud goddess of the Pele family. Hawaii. (Westervelt, 1963, 2: 70)

Hiiaka-kapu-ena-ena   A cloud goddess of the Pele family. Hawaii. (Westervelt, 1963, 2: 70)

Hiiaka-makole-wawahi-waa   A cloud goddess of the Pele family. Hawaii. (Westervelt, 1963, 2: 70)

Hikok   One of the names of the thunder god of the Coast Central Pomo. California. (Loeb, 1926, 2: 301)

Hila   God/goddess of the atmosphere and of the cold weather, storms, and drifts. The novice shaman attracts her attention through exposure. The Caribou Eskimo, Canada. (Rasmussen, 1930: 51; Nungak and Arima, 1969: 114; Marsh, 1967: 156)

Hilo n di Algo   A god of the atmosphere—"Ray Floods of the Sun." The Ifugao, Philippines. (Barton, 1946: 41)

Hina-kuluua   A goddess with power over the rain is a daughter of Hina. Hawaii. (Beckwith, 1940: 97)

Hine-i-tapapauta   Goddess of the "gentle western winds that calm the seas." Daughter of Tiu and mother of Hine-tu-whenua. The Maori, New Zealand. (Andersen, 1928: 375; White, 1887, 1: 24, 28)

Hine-kapua   The "Cloud Maid," daughter of Tane and Hine-ahu-one. The Maori, New Zealand. (Best, 1924: 112, 162)

Hine-makohu   The "Mist Maid," daughter of Tane. Also called Hine-pukohu. The Maori, New Zealand. (Best, 1924: 119)

Hine-te-uira   The personification of sheet lightning, daughter of Tane and Hine-ahu-one. The Maori, New Zealand. (Best, 1924: 116, 161)

Hine-tu-whenua   A goddess of the "gentle western winds that calm the seas" with her mother Hine-i-tapapauta. The Maori, New Zealand. (Andersen, 1928: 375; White, 1887, 1: 24, 28)

Hine-wai   The Rain Maid, the personification of light, misty rain. The Maori, New Zealand. (Best, 1924: 156–157)

Hine-whaitiri   The goddess of thunder. The Maori, New Zealand. (Best, 1924: 175)

Hino   *See* **Heno**

Hi-no-Hayabi-no-Kami   Japanese god of lightning. (Holtom, 1938: 102–103)

Hinumbian   A god of rain. The Ifugao, Philippines. (Barton, 1946: 161)

Hkü Te   God of the underworld who appears as the rainbow in the west. He is also a god of judgment. The Karen, Burma. (Marshall, 1922: 223, 225, 228)

Hlkayak   The god who wields the thunder. The Tlingit, British Columbia and Alaska. (Swanton, 1925, 12: 351)

Hlora   "heat"—With Vingnir the foster parents of Thor. They are "the personification of sheet lightning." Teutonic. (Guerber, 1895: 61)

Hodōnni'a   The Aurora Borealis. The Iroquois, Eastern United States. (Gray, 1925, 7: 422)

Ho Hu   A dragon god who provides rain. The Monguors of Kansu, China. (Schram, 1957: 85)

Holda Teutonic goddess of orderliness and good housekeeping, of spinning and the cultivation of flax. She is considered a goddess of weather in that when it snows she is shaking her bed, when it rains she is washing clothes. (Grimm, 1880: 266–272; Guerber, 1895: 54; Cox, 1870: 306)

Homi A god of the heavens who controls the rain, the wind, and the temperature. The Hottentots, South Africa. (Brinton, 1897: 77)

Hopop Caan Chac A Mayan god who causes lightning. Yucatan, Mexico. (Thompson, 1970: 255)

Horagalles The god of thunder. The Samek, the Lapps, Northern Europe. (Karsten, 1955: 24; Collinder, 1949: 143; Turville-Petre, 1964: 98)

Hotoru The god of the winds protects men in travelling and in crossing rivers. The Pawnee, Plains Indians, Nebraska. (Fletcher, 1900/01: 29, 78; Burland, 1965: 149)

Hsiang Fêng Chih Shên The god of "Fragrant Wind." China. (Day, 1940: 72)

Hsing T'ien Chün A god of rain, under Lei Tsu. China. (Werner, 1934: 198)

Hsing Yü Hsien Shih The god of rain. In Chow-wang-miao associated with the wind god Chang T'ien Fêng Po. China. (Day, 1940: 72)

Hsuan-t'an P'u-sa A deity who guards them from hail. The Monguors of Kansu, China. (Schram, 1957: 85)

Huaillepenyi The god of the fog is considered responsible for any deformity a child might be born with. The Araucanians, Chile. (Larousse, 1968: 445)

Hubal An Arabian rain god as well as an oracular god and an archer. (Fahd, 1968: 65, 101)

Hukyangkwu Goddess of "high winds and sandstorms," benevolent only in war when she "bewilders the enemy." The Hopi, Arizona. (Parsons, 1939: 178)

huilli fucha and **huilli kushe** The "god and goddess of the southwind"—considered coastal. the Mapuche, Chile. (Faron, 1968: 65, 66, 69)

Hunaunic A Lacandon god of the east who is the leader of the wind gods. Mexico. (Thompson, 1970: 271)

Hunrakán, Huracan, Hurakan "Heart of Heaven"— A powerful god of the weather in all of its manifesta-

tions. He is the one-footed god from whose foot "in the bowels of the earth" was born the god of maize. He was the devil of an earlier cycle (a demon among the Caribs), but regardless of cycle he is demon or god "of the tempest, rain, lightning bolt, thunder, and the illumination produced by sheet lightning. And good or bad meaning depends exclusively upon the cultural criterion." The Quiché, Guatemala. (Girard, 1979: 35, 110; Recinos, 1950: 82; Brinton, 1868: 156, 196; Nicholson, 1967: 65)

Hurunuku-atea The personification of the north wind. The Maori, New Zealand. (Best, 1924: 153)

Huru-te-arangi Mother of the Snow, Frost, and Ice children, and through her son Tawhirimatea of the Wind children. The Maori, New Zealand. (Best, 1924: 152)

Hu-shen The god of hail is invoked to protect the fields from hail storms. China. (Maspero, 1963: 325; Haydon, 1941: 195; Werner, 1932: 179)

Hushtoli The Storm Wind. The Choctaw Indians, Mississippi. (Brinton, 1868: 51)

Hutchaiui God of the west wind who had the form of a serpent-headed human. Egypt. (Budge, 1969, 2: 296; Knight, 1915: 134)

Hutukau "Wind-Ready-to-Give (buffalo to the people)" is a god of the north and has control in the winter. The Skidi Pawnee, Plains Indians, Nebraska. (Dorsey, 1904, 2: 19–20)

Hu-tu-ri-kot-tsa-ru The wind of the spirits of the dead. The Skidi Pawnee, Plains Indians, Nebraska. (Fletcher, 1903: 13)

Hu-tu-ru-ka-wa-ha-ru The "wind that sends the game." The Skidi Pawnee, Plains Indians, Nebraska. (Fletcher, 1903: 14)

Hututu The rain god of the south, and a warrior god, is important in the Shalako festival (the winter solstice). The Zuñi, New Mexico. (Wilson, 1958: 374; Stevenson, 1901/02: 33; Waters, 1950: 284)

Huwult Makai God of the strong spring winds. The Pima Indians, Arizona and Mexico. (Russell, 1904/05: 251)

The Hyades Daughters of Atlas and Aethra and sisters of the Pleiades. Their appearance usually foretells rain. They are named as Ambrosia, Coronis, Dione, Eudora, Pedile, Phyto, Polyxo. Greece. (Murray, 1935: 171; Barthell, 1971: 57; Larousse, 1968: 144; Roscher, 1965, 3, 2: 2492, 2745)

Ianporungrung The spirit of rain which brings lightning and thunder. The Mundurucu, Para, Brazil. (Murphy, 1958: 21)

Ibmel The supreme god, a somewhat abstract deity, whose name was used to designate "the sun, thunder and the rainbow." His wife was Sergue-Edne. The Lapps, Northern Europe. (Bosi, 1960: 129; Karsten, 1955: 30; Pettersson, 1957: 19, 20)

I'chul ad Angachal A thunder god of the Mayawyaw of Luzon. Philippines. (Lambrecht, 1932: 22)

Icmaeus The name of Zeus as the giver of humidity and rain. Greece. (Roscher, 1965, 2, 1: 117; Frazer, 1926: 48)

Idi A Scandinavian storm giant—"rain-wind." (Stern, 1898: 121)

Idurmer A Semitic god of rain and thunder. Same as Adad. Near East. (Langdon, 1931: 81)

Ignirtoq Goddess of lightning, sister of Kadlu. The Eskimo. Canada. (Boas, 1901: 146)

Iguanuptigili One of the demons of rain and floods. Daughter of Olopurguakuayai. The Cuna Indians, Panama. (Nordenskiold, 1938: 285, 325)

Te Iho-rangi The personification of rain is one of the "regulators of the elements." One of the husbands of Huru-te-arangi and father of the Snow children, Frost children, and Ice children. Son of Papa and Rangi. The Maori, New Zealand. (Best, 1924: 97, 105, 152, 162)

Ikadzuchi-no-Kami The god of thunder. Japan. (Revon, 1925, 9: 236; Holtom, 1938: 107)

Ikâ-eshkin A god who caused the fog which makes things grow. The son of the Dawn. The Apache Indians, Southwestern United States. (Bourke, 1890: 209)

Ikenuwakcom A "being of the nature of a thunder-god." The Chinook, Washington and Oregon. (Spence, 1925, 3: 561)

Ikiyeme The thunder. The Shasta and Athapascan, Oregon. (Farrand, 1915: 211)

Iku A wind-point personified, Southwest by West, which moderates the violence of the cyclones arising in the Northeast. Son of Raka. Mangaia, Polynesia. (Andersen, 1928: 358)

Iku-ikazuchi-no-kami A Japanese thunder god. (Herbert, 1967: 490)

Ileña, Ile-ñeut "Rain-Woman or Dampness-Woman," sometimes given as the wife of the supreme being. The Koryak, Siberia. (Jochelson, 1908: 25)

Ilet The thunder who produces rain and whose arm is the rainbow with which he draws up water. The Ndorobo, Kenya/Tanzania. (Millroth, 1965: 44)

Ilet ne-mie The benevolent thunder god, but not worshipped or given offerings. The Nandi, Kenya. (Hollis, 1909: 41)

Ilet ne-ya The malevolent thunder god who also is not worshipped or given offerings. The Nandi, Kenya. (Hollis, 1909: 41)

Ilhataina Lightning. The Yana Indians, California. (Curtin, 1903: 297)

Ilia God of thunder and lightning of the Ossetes. Caucasus. Same as Elias. (Grimm, 1880: 174)

St. Ilija He drives "off the storm fiends" with thunder and lightning. Likened to Drangoni. Serbia. (Durham, 1928: 123)

Illapa, Ilyapa The god of the weather, malevolent as the bringer of storms, thunder and lightning, but benevolent as the bringer of rain. Peru. (Rowe, 1946: 212, 295; Trimborn, 1969: 129; Markham, 1969: 70)

Ilma A deity of the atmosphere whose daughter is Luonnotar. Finno-Ugric. (Larousse, 1968: 304)

Ilmarinen A god of the atmosphere and the sky, later also worshipped as a god of the wind. He was also a smith-god. Finland. (MacCulloch, 1911: 217, 232; de Kay, 1898: 62; Larousse, 1973: 420; Leach, 1949, 1: 514)

Ilmaris A god who causes bad weather, is destructive of ships. The Samek, Lapland. (Karsten, 1955: 80)

The Iltchi Twelve black winds. The Apache Indians, Southwestern United States. (Bourke, 1890: 209)

Iltchi-dishish "(Black Wind), made the world as it now is . . . ravines and cañons." The Apache, Southwestern United States. (Bourke, 1890: 209)

Iltchi-duklij The "Green or Blue Wind, . . . stayed by him (Iltchi-dishish) while he made the world." The

Apache, Southwestern United States. (Bourke, 1890: 209)

Iltchi-lezoc "Yellow Wind, gave light to the world." The Apache, Southwestern United States. (Bourke, 1890: 209)

Iltchi-lokay The "White Wind, improved on." The light given by Iltchi-lezoc. The Apache, Southwestern United States. (Bourke, 1890: 209)

Ilya A deity of the Muhammadans invoked to avert thunderstorms. Arabia and Near East. (Grimm, 1880: 174)

dIm A Semitic god of the storm invoked in curses against another's ripening grain. Near East. (Roberts, 1972: 151)

Im, U The Hittite god of the storm, husband of Arinna, goddess of the lands. A primeval pair—the sky and earth deities. Near East. (Eliade, 1976, 2: 364)

Imbalili A god of the atmosphere and descendent of Umalgo, the sun. The Ifugao, Philippines. (Barton, 1946: 41)

Imbilbilao A wind god of the Ifugao. Philippines. (Barton, 1946: 62)

Imbunong A god of the atmosphere (clouds) and descendent of Umalgo, the sun. The Ifugao, Philippines. (Barton, 1946: 41)

Im-dugud The Sumerian god of the thundercloud was "portrayed as a lion-headed eagle." Near East. (Jacobsen, 1970: 57; Hamblin, 1973: 116)

Inaiyau God of "winds and storms. He also wielded the thunderbolt and the lightning." The Manobo, Philippines. (Jocano, 1969: 23)

Inango A weather god, son of Kidul, the thunder. The Ifugao, Philippines. (Barton, 1946: 31)

Inanna This versatile goddess is also named as a goddess of thunderstorms and rain and wields control over the thunderbird Im-dugud. Near East. (Jacobsen, 1976: 136)

Inanupdikile The goddess of rain, daughter of Olopurguakua-yai. The Cuna, Panama. (Norkenskiold, 1938: 285, 325)

Inaplihan A weather god—the "Squall"—son of Kidul. The Ifugao, Philippines. (Barton, 1946: 31)

Indra The weather and storm god, god of all atmospheric phenomena. He is the giver of agricultural fertility and the guardian of the eastern quarter of the compass. India/Bali. In Iran he is a demon, the opposite of Asha-Vahishta, who brings "winter torrents . . . and heavy rains" which bring malaria. He also draws people away from virtue and causes neglect of religion. (Crooke, 1894: 38, 288; Banerjea, 1953: 73; Ions, 1967: 16, 73; Cox, 1870, 1: 340–343; Elwin, 1949: 98; Bhattacharji, 1970: 267–270; Covarrubias, 1937: 317; Gray, 1930: 181–182; Huart, 1963: 43; Pandit, 1970: 28)

Ingnirtung Goddess of lightning. The Central Eskimo, Canada. (Boas, 1884/1885: 600)

Inhobhob A god of the wind of the Ifugao. Philippines. (Barton, 1946: 62)

Inhuyung A wind god of the Ifugao. Philippines. (Barton, 1946: 62)

'i·ñi' An undependable and evil deity—Thunder—depicted as a bird. The Navaho, Arizona and New Mexico. (Reichard, 1950: 485)

'i·ñi' djiƚgai Winter Thunder, an undependable deity. The Navaho, Arizona and New Mexico. (Reichard, 1950: 500–501)

Inkanitari God of rain of the Campa. Peru. (Weiss, 1972: 163)

Inkosatana, Inkosazana A goddess of the heavens who is manifested in the "rainbow, the mist and the rain" and the lightning. The Bantu-Swazi, the Zulu, South Africa. (Smith, 1950: 112; Pettersson, 1953: 184–185)

Inkosi pezulu A sky god and god of the weather who causes all celestial phenomena. The Zulu, South Africa. (Pettersson, 1953: 180–182; Schapera, 1937: 263)

Inoltagon A goddess of the winds, wife of Nunanud. The Ifugao, Philippines. (Barton, 1946: 61)

Inublag A wind god of the Ifugao. Philippines. (Barton, 1946: 62)

Inudanan "Rainy Season," and a wind god. The Ifugao, Philippines. (Barton, 1946: 31, 62)

Ipar The north wind. When he meets with Ernio-aize there are violent squalls with hail and sleet. In winter he brings snow; a cold, dry wind in winter. The Basques, Spain/France. (Barandiaran, 1971: 72)

Ipilja-ipilja, Ipilya   The gecko which is very colorful and replaces the rainbow-serpent is the creator of storms, of the thunder and the monsoon rains. Australia. (Mountford, 1958: 155; 1969: 66)

Iris   The Greek goddess of the rainbow causes gentle, fertilizing rains. Daughter of Thaumas and Electra, and messenger of the gods. (Kerenyi, 1951: 60–61; Bulfinch, 1898: 8; Murray, 1935: 181–182; Morford and Lenardon, 1975: 90)

Irpa   A Scandinavian demi-goddess, daughter of Hulda and Odin, who sends "four weather, storm and hail, when implored to do so." (Grimm, 1880: 113, 271; 1883, 2: 637)

Ishkur   The Sumerian storm god—of rain, winds and thunder, whose wife is Shala. Near East. (Jacobsen, 1970: 8, 30; Kramer, 1961: 100; Langdon, 1931: 99)

Ishtar   The goddess of the morning and evening star, of war, is also a goddess of rain. Identified with Inanna. Akkadian/Semitic, Near East. (Jacobsen, 1976: 140)

Ishtohoollo Aba   God of the winter rains. The Creek Indians, Georgia. (Waring, 1965: 53)

St. Isidro   A wind god of the Maya. British Honduras. (Thompson, 1930: 64)

Itsanohk'uh   The "lord of hail, cold, lakes and alligators." The Lacandon, Chiapas, Mexico. (Perera and Bruce, 1982: 307)

itsiipaˀotena   The north wind deity brings suffering. The Nahane (Upper Liard Kaska), Western Canada. (Honigmann, 1954: 101)

ittindi   "Lightning" to whom hoddentin is thrown in invocations. The Apache, Southwestern United States. (Bourke, 1892: 503)

Itur-mer   The storm god of the Amorites. Near East. (Oldenburg, 1969: 51–52, 61)

Itzam   One of the Tzultacah, an earth and thunder goddess whose husband is Siete Orejas, a mountain god. The Maya Highlands, Guatemala. (Thompson, 1970: 273)

Itzamna thul Chac   Mayan god of the clouds. Mexico. (Tozzer, 1941: 146)

Itzan Noh Ku, Itzanaoqu   A Lacandon god of rain, of hail, but also a god of nursing, and a god of "lakes and crocodiles." Mexico. (Thompson, 1970: 266–267, 312; Cline, 1944: 112)

Itzlacoliuhqui, Iztlacoliuhqui   Aztec god of the obsidian knife, a variant of Tezcatlipoca. A god of ice and cold, of avenging justice and of blindness. He was "also Venus as god of dawn." Mexico. (Spence, 1923: 337, 339; Nicholson, 1667: 109; Thompson, 1970: 249; Caso, 1958: 29)

Iya (*see also* **Eya**)   The second son of Tate, the Wind. He demanded to look at Wakinyan which caused him "to become a heyoka, a 'contrary,' who does and sees everything in reverse, because this is the only way to approach the creative force. Thus Iya gains the right to establish himself in the first direction," becoming God of the West and the west wind. The Lakota, Plains Indians. South Dakota. (Jahner, 1977: 35)

Iywa   God of thunder. The Tiv, Nigeria. (Temple, 1922: 302)

Jakuta   Another name for the thunder god, Shango. Nigeria. (Parrinder, 1949: 32; Idowu, 1962: 47, 93)

Jamfi moong   A devil of the high mountains who will be angered if the allium safyou (a wild plant) is gathered with knives rather than with sharpened sticks and will cause hail and thunder. The Lepchas, Sikkim. (Gorer, 1938: 91, 369)

Jao-Chwen   The Dragon of the south.   **Jao-Kyih** The Dragon of the north.   **Jao-Kwang**   The Dragon of the east.   **Jao-Ming**   The Dragon of the west.   **Jao-Ping**   The Dragon of the middle.   All worshipped in times of drought. China. (Du Bose, n.d.: 134)

'Jig rten mkha' 'gro ma   A Tibetan goddess invoked for rainfall. (Nebesky-Wojkowitz, 1956, 1: 479)

Jila Bilik   The East wind. The A-Pucikwar, Andaman Island, Bay of Bengal. (Radcliffe-Brown, 1967: 149)

Jila Puluga   The East wind. Brother of Puluga. The Akar-Bale, Andaman Islands. (Radcliffe-Brown, 1967: 149)

Jisen-olmai   The "hoar-frost man." The Southern Lapps, Northern Europe. (Holmberg, 1925, 7: 799)

Jizo Sama   At Usu (among the Ainu) the Japanese bring out his image for ceremonials to bring rain. (Batchelor, n.d.: 256)

Jokumara   A rain god "supposed to have the power of bringing down the rain in proper time." The Kabbera, Southern India. (Thurston, 1909, 3: 1, 6)

Juhauju The West wind. The Yana Indians, California. (Curtin, 1903: 365)

Jukami The North wind. The Yana, California. (Curtin, 1903: 365)

Jukilauyu The East wind. The Yana Indians, California. (Curtin, 1903: 365)

Julunggul The rainbow snake. Northern Territories, Australia. (Robinson, 1966: 3)

Jupiter Roman sky god and god of the heavens, of the atmosphere and its phenomena. As god of rain he was Jupiter Elicius; as god of lightning Jupiter Fulgus. Later as an ethical and political deity he became god of justice, of fidelity, and of law. (Dumézil, 1966, 1: 108, 179–180; Fairbanks, 1907: 98–99; Jayne, 1962: 429; Schoeps, 1961: 145)

Juppiter Dolichenus A weather god in Anatolia. Asia Minor. (Ferm, 1950: 94; Gurney, 1952: 134)

Juwaju The South wind. The Yana Indians, California. (Curtin, 1903: 365)

Ka· ’añe· o·x̱wa The "Raingod of the Smooth Leaf tree"—a Winter Raingod, bringer of rain and its accompanying fertility. The Tewa, San Juan, New Mexico. (Laski, 1958: 11)

Kabagiyawan A "female spirit, who causes typhoons . . . whenever she strips herself completely." Shamans invoke her with offerings. The Isneg of Luzon, Philippines. (Vanoverbergh, 1953: 98)

Kabeyun Amerindian "father of the four winds." North America. (Emerson, 1884: 25)

Kabeyung The West Wind. The name of Mudjeekawis after he left the people and returned to the west to be with his father, Epingishmook. The Ojibway, Great Lakes area. (Johnston, 1976: 153)

Kabezya-mpungu The elements are controlled by the supreme sky god. Congo. (Budge, 1973, 1: 374)

Kabibonokka A god of the wind and of the north and north wind. Brother of Kabun, Shawano and Wabun. The Algonquin Indians. North America. (Maclean, 1876: 432; Brinton, 1882: 45; Emerson, 1884: 23; Gatschet, 1890: xci)

Kabun God of the west and a wind god. Brother of Wabun, Kabibonokka, Shawano. Algonquin Indians, North America. (Schoolcraft, 1857: 659; Maclean, 1876: 432; Brinton, 1882: 45)

Kadai The thunder god of the Baluga. Philippines. (Pettazzoni, 1956: 319)

Kadlu Goddess of thunder among the Central Eskimo. Canada. (Boas, 1884/1885: 600; Wallis, 1939: 117)

Kagei The god of lightning among the Trang-Patalung. Malaya. (Evans, 1937: 157)

Kagi The god of thunder among the Chong and the Trang-Patalung. Malaya. (Evans, 1937: 147; Pettazzoni, 1956: 324)

Kagolo God of lightning and thunder. The Baganda of Uganda. (Budge, 1973, 1: 377; Cunnigham, 1905: 220)

Kagoro God of thunder. He is also a god of cattle and of their fertility. The Banyoro, Uganda. (Roscoe, 1915: 92)

Kahala, Kahalaopuna, Kaikawahine Anuenue The Rainbow maid. Hawaii. (Westervelt, 1963, 3: 84)

Kahango A god of the Basoga to whom human sacrifice is made to obtain rain. Uganda. (Roscoe, 1915: 255)

Kahit The wind. The Wintu of California. (Curtin, 1903: 3)

Kahuila-maka-keha’i-i-ka-lani God of the lightning flash. Hawaii. (Beckwith, 1940: 48)

Kahukura The personified rainbow. "The upper and darker band . . . is called Kahukura-pango, and the lower one Pou-te-aniwaniwa; the former . . . male, the latter . . . female." His appearance foretold the approach of rain. The Maori, New Zealand. (Best, 1924: 160–161; Andersen, 1928: 428; White, 1887, 1: 4, 41, 43)

Kaila The supreme and creator god is also the god of the weather. The Ihalmiut Eskimo, Canada. (Mowat, 1968: 237)

Kajsa A Swedish goddess of the wind. (Grimm, 1883, 2: 631)

Kaka-sha-ha-no-hase The spirit (male) of the whirlwind. The Delaware Indians, Eastern United States. (Morgan, 1959: 55)

Kakring The god of thunder whose quarrels with Kalapiat produce thunder and lightning. Formosa. (Campbell, 1925, 6: 87)

Kalangi A god of the heavens who is manifest in the west wind and the northwest monsoon with which he fertilizes Lumimuut. The Alfures, Minahassa, Celebes, Indonesia. (Pettazzoni, 1956: 11)

Kalapiat Goddess of lightning who quarrels with Kakring producing thunder and lightning. The Amia. Formosa. (Campbell, 1925, 6: 87)

Kaliba tautau One of the names of the thunder god. The Coast Central Pomo Indians, California. (Loeb, 1926, 2: 301)

Kalihal A wind god of the Ifugao. Philippines. (Barton, 1946: 62)

Kalimatoto The thunder god of the Eastern Pomo. California. (Loeb, 1926, 2: 301)

Kalseru The "rainbow serpent associated with rain and fertility." Northwest Australia. (Leach, 1950, 2: 569)

Kalura A culture hero of the primeval time who was "associated with rain and with spirit children." Australia. (Eliade, 1973: 75)

Kamalo The lightning god of the Awhawzara tribe and the sun god of the Ututu tribe. The Ibo, Nigeria. (Jeffreys, 1972: 730)

Kamaluninga With Kadlu makes thunderstorms. The Eskimo of Cumberland Sound, Canada. (Boas, 1901: 175)

Kami-Shinatsuhiko-no-Mikoto A god of winds. Japan. (Yasumaro, 1928: 7)

Kamo-wake-ikazuchi God of the storm, of rain and thunder. Japan. (Herbert, 1967: 489)

Kanapu The flash of the lightning, child of Te-uira. New Zealand. (White, 1887, 1: 54)

k'ana·'ti The Thunder, Red Man ("Red" only in ceremonial language, otherwise "White"). Father of the Two Little Red Men. The heavy, crashing thunder is his voice, the light metallic, theirs. He is a disease expeller rather than a causer; the enemy of all beings and things of the Dark, Evening Land, the West. The Cherokee, North Carolina and Tennessee. (Mooney and Olbrechts, 1932: 23, 24)

Kanaula The rainbow-man one time lived on earth. He tried to steal fire in order to destroy it, but was thwarted. He then went to the sky to live. North Australia. (Mountford, 1969: 52)

Kana-ula A god of the wind. Hawaii. (Westervelt, 1963, 3: 192)

Kanawana The thunder. The Tapirape, Brazil. (Wagley and Galvao, 1948: 177; Pettazzoni, 1956: 420)

Kane-hekili Kane as god of thunder, also as "flashing lightning." Hawaii. (Beckwith, 1940: 48; Westervelt, 1963, 3: 124)

Kane Kauila Kane as god of lightning. Maui, Hawaii. (Ashdown, 1971: 54)

Kane-pu-a-hio-hio Kane as the whirlwind. Hawaii. (Westervelt, 1963, 2: 5)

Kane-wahi-lani A lightning god of Hawaii. (Alexander, 1968: 63)

Kane wawahi lani The aumakua in the thunder. Hawaii. (Emerson, 1967: 51)

Kani-a-ula A wind deity of Hawaii. (Westervelt, 1912: 110)

Kanna Kamui Beneficial and powerful dragon deities. Thunder is considered the sound of their fighting, and "lightning the flashing of swords." Also considered an individual god of thunder and lightning. The Ainu, Sakhalin and Japan. On Hokkaidu the Thunder God (also plural) assumes serpent or dragon form. With proper reverence gives blessings and no damage; if not, brings misfortune. (Ohnuki-Tierney, 1974: 103–104; Munro, 1963: 17; Philippi, 1982: 149)

Kannakapfaluk The goddess of the sea controls the weather and the seal. The Copper Eskimo, Canada. (Jenness, 1913/18: 188)

Kan Pauah Tun A Mayan god "identified with the gods of rain" and associated with the east. Mexico and Guatemala. (Tozzer, 1941: 137)

Kantjira The "great rain totemic ancestor." Western Aranda, Australia. (Robinson, 1966: 29)

Kape-kape, Kabe-kabe The lightning, son of thunder. Surinam. (Penard, 1917: 258)

Karai-shin Buddhist god of lightning. Japan. (Herbert, 1967: 490)

Karei, Kari The god of thunder and of storms is among some also the supreme god (the Semang, the Jehai) as well as god and judge of the dead (the Semang).

His wife is Manoid (the Djahai, the Jehai), mother of Ta Pedn, Takel, Begrag. Among the Menrik Takel is his wife. The Negritos, Malay Peninsula. (Eliade, 1964: 337; Evans, 1937: 151–152, 157; Roheim, 1972: 19, 20; Moss, 1925: 116; Skeat, 1925, 8: 354; Cole, 1946: 72)

Kari Scandinavian storm giant, god of the atmosphere, the weather and storms. Father of the winds as well as Frosti, Jokull, Snor, Fonn, Drifa, Mioll who represent the snow and the cold. (Stern, 1898: 121; Grimm, 1883, 2: 631–636; Wagner, 1882: 241)

Karifo God of the rain is invoked for successful harvests. The Anfillo Mao, Ethiopia. (Cerulli, 1956: 32)

Karuparabo The spirit of rain, particularly that which is associated with electrical storms and thunder. The Mundurucu, Para, Brazil. (Murphy, 1958: 21)

Bodhisattva Kasarpani A merciful god invoked for control of the weather. Tibet. (Nebesky-Wojkowitz, 1956, 1: 475)

Kasenadu The evil Lightning Man was master of it and the thunder. He killed his sister, the mother of Wachamadi. Wachamadi avenged her by stealing the lightning and thunder from Kasenadu and killing him. The Makiritare, Venezuela. (Civrieux, 1980: 85–86, 90–94)

Kasogonaga A goddess of the rain. The Chaco tribes, Bolivia and Paraguay. (Osborne, 1968: 122)

Kastiatsi The rainbow. The Acoma, Pueblo Indians, New Mexico. (Burland, 1965: 150)

Kasurunra The demoness of thunder. The Toba-Pilaga of the Gran Chaco. Argentina and Paraguay. (Métraux, 1937: 175)

Ka-tash-huaht The evil north wind who brought death. The Seneca (Iroquois), New York. (Smith, 1881/82: 59; Bjorklund, 1969: 132)

Katavi A god of rain and of epidemics whose wife is Wamwelu. The Pimbwe, Tanzania. (Willis, 1966: 59)

Katcinas, Kachinas The important gods and supernaturals invoked for rain, many of whom are also clan ancestors. Pueblo Indians, New Mexico and Arizona. (Fewkes, 1895, 1: 351; White, 1929/30: 64; Ferm, 1950: 370; Waters, 1950: 278)

Katibungalon The rainbow god. The Ifugao, Philippines. (Barton, 1946: 42)

Ka-ua-kuahiwa A goddess of rain, sister of Ku-ka-ohia-a-ka-laka. Hawaii. (Beckwith, 1940: 17)

Kauha The spirit of the morning star provides fine weather. The Ongtong Javanese, Indonesia. (Williamson, 1933: 153)

Ka-uila-nui-maka-heha'i-i-ka-lani The flashing lightning. Hawaii. (Beckwith, 1940: 48)

Kaukura God of the wind Tiu. Rarotonga, Polynesia. (Williamson, 1933, 1: 150)

Kauwila-nui The god of lightning. Also called Kane-kauwila-nui. Hawaii. (Westervelt, 1963, 2: 69, 71)

Ka'wixu God of rain and of storms. The Trumai, Brazil. (Murphy and Quain, 1955: 73)

Kayai A god of thunder and storms, a sky god. Also called Kadai and Bayagaw. The Aeta of Luzon, Philippines. (Pettazzoni, 1956: 318; Wales, 1957: 12)

Kayurankuba The spirit of storms. The thunder is the sound of the wings of the birds whose brilliance is the lightning which he flings to the earth. The Zulu, the Baziba, South Africa. (Werner, 1964: 237; Bray, 1935: 221)

Kazaketsuwake-no-Oshiwo-no-Kami A god who protects from storms. Son of Izanagi and Izanami. Japan. (Herbert, 1967: 264; Yasumaro, 1965: 14)

Kaze-no-Kami A god of wind. Japan. (Holtom, 1938: 208)

Ke-ao-mele-mele Goddess and ruler of the clouds. Hawaii. (Westervelt, 1963, 3: 116, 131)

Ke Kona A deity "who rules the southern storms." Maui, Hawaii. (Ashdown, 1971: 68)

Kє·mina A "Deer Raingod wearing deer horns." A Winter Raingod and a bringer of rain and its accompanying fertility. The Tewa, San Juan, New Mexico. (Laski, 1958: 11)

Kenjo The god of thunder controls the rain. The Jukun, Nigeria. (Greenberg, 1946: 57)

Kesar A weather god who hurls the lightning bolts. Tibet. (Francke, 1923: 6)

Keto A sky god who controls the weather, giving rain and sunshine, and causes thunder (his voice) and lightning. The Bateg, Malaya. (Evans, 1937: 158, 183; Pettazzoni, 1956: 7, 311)

Kevak Xuppi   A deity of the atmosphere—"the personification of some luminous appearance." The Mordvins, the Chuvash, Russia. (Paasonen, 1925, 8: 844)

Kevioso   God of thunder and rain, and of waters. Also called Bade. Brazil. (Costa Eduardo, 1948: 78–79; Bastide, 1960: 567)

Kewa, Kiwi   A god who "lives among the clouds, hurling the lightning and causing the rain." Ethiopia. (Cerulli, 1956: 32)

Kewadin   God of the weather, of the northwind and the north, who was the first of the thunderbirds. He furnished the Ojibwa with food in winter. Minnesota. (Coleman, 1937: 38)

Kewutawapeo   A minor thunder god of the Menomini Indians. Wisconsin. (Skinner, 1913: 74)

Keyemen   The rainbow, who took the form of a serpent, was "the grandfather of aquatic birds." The Arecuna, Guiana. (Levi-Strauss, 1969: 262)

Khabru   A rain and weather god of Fayeng and of Sengmai. Also the god of the countryside. Manipur, India. (Hodson, 1908: 103)

Khagat-Noin   A water deity invoked for fair winds, mild weather, and whatever was needed. Trans Baikal Buriats, Siberia. (Klementz, 1925, 3: 6)

Khanukh   The Wolf, not considered beneficent, controls the fog. The Thlinkeets, Pacific Northwestern North America. (Bancroft, 1886, 3: 146)

Khebieso, Hevioso   The god of thunder and lightning. Also called So. The Ewe, Dahomey and Ghana. (Parrinder, 1949: 31; Ellis, 1890: 37)

Khrag gi ser 'bebs ma   A goddess of weather who lives in the ocean. Tibet. (Nebesky-Wojkowitz, 1956, 1: 468)

Khuno   The god of snow and storm. Peru. (Osborne, 1968: 89)

!Khunuseti   The Pleiades are prayed to for rain and for abundance of food. The Hessaquas (Hottentots), South Africa. (Hahn, 1881: 43)

Khyp   The moon was punished for receiving the truant Khosadam to live with him by being required to "serve

man, for whom he divides the time and also foretells the weather." The Yenisei Ostyaks, Siberia. (Czaplicka, 1925, 9: 579)

Kiassoubangango, Kibouco   The thunder god who was introduced from Angola. Brazil. (Bastide, 1960: 567)

Kidol   The spirit of thunder of the village of Manabo. The Tinguian, Philippines. (Cole, 1922: 301)

Kido-ol   The spirit of thunder in Likuan and Bakaok. The Tinguian, Philippines. (Cole, 1922: 301)

Kidul   The god of thunder and of omens, and also a god of pacification at drinkfests. He takes "the form of a wild boar." The Ifugao, Philippines. (Barton, 1946: 30, 42, 89)

Kiduma   The god of rain and wind, of the thunderstorm. The Basoga, Uganda. (Mbiti, 1970, 2: 328)

kikaawei walason   "our father wind." The Pueblo Indians, Isleta, New Mexico. (Parsons, 1929/30: 342–343)

Kilat   A zoömorphic spirit of the thunder and lightning who takes the form of a horse or carabao. The Bagobo, Philippines. (Benedict, 1916: 39, 45)

Kilat Bagilat   God of lightning, son of Kidul, the thunder. The Ifugao, Philippines. (Barton, 1946: 30)

Kilawit   The spirit of lightning—the flash "from the ground"—in Ba-ay. The Tinguian, Philippines. (Cole, 1922: 301)

Kilesa   The god of the winds and also of war. The Gallas, Ethiopia. (Littmann, 1925, 1: 57)

Kineun   The "Golden Eagle and Chief of the Thunderers." Algonquin Indians, North America. (Alexander, 1964: 48)

Kinilatan   A god of the atmosphere—"Lightninged," descendant of Umalgo, the sun. The Ifugao, Philippines. (Barton, 1946: 41)

Kin-kang   God of rain and protector from demons. A celestial Bodhisattva. Same as Vajrapani. China. (Getty, 1962: 50)

Kiolya   A god of the air, of the aurora borealis. Barrow Point, Alaska. (Keane, 1925, 1: 257)

Kiwanka   The god of the thunderbolt. The Baganda, Uganda. (Budge, 1973, 1: 377; Cunningham, 1905: 218)

Kiwanuka God of thunder and lightning and a python god. Son of Semuganda. The Basoga, Uganda. (Roscoe, 1915: 247; Mbiti, 1970, 2: 118; Mair, 1934: 234; Kagwa, 1934: 122)

Klowe A god of thunder and of blacksmiths. Son of Gbobu and Ohimiya. The Gã in Nungwa, Ghana. (Field, 1937: 27–28)

Koaičo Puluga The west wind, brother of Puluga. The Akar-Bale, Andaman Islands, Bay of Bengal. (Radcliffe-Brown, 1967: 149)

Kobange The guardian of the thunder. The Marshall Islands, Micronesia. (Knappe, 1888: 66)

Kodyam The god of sheet lightning, son of Kidul, the thunder. The Ifugao, Philippines. (Barton, 1946: 30)

Kohu The mist personified, the fog, who with Ika-roa, the Milky Way, some say are parents of the stars. The Maori, New Zealand. (Andersen, 1928: 403; White, 1887, 1: 18)

Kohu-rere "flying mist"—offspring of Tama-nui-a-raki. New Zealand. (White, 1887, 1: 20)

Koico Bilik The west wind. The A-Pucikwar, Andaman Islands, Bay of Bengal. (Radcliffe-Brown, 1967: 149)

Koičor-tong Bilik A wind being of the A-Pucikwar. Andaman Islands, Bay of Bengal. (Radcliffe-Brown, 1967: 149)

Ko'k^{cw}, abalasemwe'su The personification of the evil whirlwind. The Penobscot, Maine. (Speck, 1935: 21)

Kolpia(s) A wind god whose wife is Baau, "night." Father of Aion and Protognonos. Phoenicia, Near East. (Roscher, 1965, 2, 1: 1274; Sayce, 1898: 375–376)

Kongo A god of rain and protector from demons. A celestial Bodhisattva. Same as Vajrapani. Japan. (Getty, 1962: 50)

Konomeru The thunder. Surinam. (Penard, 1917: 256)

Kon-noto-ran-guru An evil sea god who causes storms and wrecks, and drives fish away from fisherman. The Ainu, Japan. (Batchelor, n.d.: 392)

Kopishtaiya Deity of the winter clouds, invoked for health, longevity, and bravery. The Acoma, Pueblo Indians, New Mexico. (Stirling, 1942: 16)

Korude, Korule The god of thunder. North Andaman Islands. Bay of Bengal. (Radcliffe-Brown, 1967: 145)

Kot The omniscient sky god and supreme being is also the god of the wind and causes storms when angry. The Nuer, Sudan. (Pettazzoni, 1956: 10, 38)

Kozah (**Koze** in Palestine) Arabic/Persian god of storms, of rain, and thunder and lightning. (Cook, 1930: 204; Larousse, 1968: 323)

k'ska'sen The west wind who with the other winds rules "human and animal destiny." The Penobscot Indians, Maine. (Speck, 1935: 21)

Ku A deity who represents a form of thunder. The Maori, New Zealand. (Best, 1924: 175)

Kuan Kung A god of many aspects. In Confucianism a god of weather, of healing, and of literature; a god of war of the Taoists; a guardian of Buddhist temples; a god of justice and of prosperity. China. (Day, 1940: 54; Shryock, 1931: 66–67)

Kuan Shen Ren A god of rain. Szechwan, China. (Graham, 1958: 47)

Kubeisek A maker of typhoons at Anu. Truk, Micronesia. (Kramer, 1932: 74)

Ku-holoholo-pali A god of rain and of the forest slopes as well as of canoe builders. Hawaii. (Beckwith, 1940: 15, 16)

Kuidya The thunder—"According to some informants the Thunders are two, a male and a female; they somewhat exceed in size the average spirits, and have light-blue bodies covered with coarse hair." The Cayapa, Ecuador. (Barrett, 1925: 360)

Kujaku-myoo A Buddhist goddess who protects from harm and is invoked for rain during drought. Same as Maha Mayuri, "The Great Peacock Goddess." Japan. (Eliseev, 1963: 436; Getty, 1962: 136; Larousse, 1968: 421)

Ku-ka-ieie A rain and forest god—"of the wild pandanus vine." Hawaii. (Beckwith, 1940: 15)

Ku-ka-ohia-laka A god of the rain and of the forest—"of the ohia-lehua tree"—and worshipped by canoe builders because of its wood. He is also a god of the hula dance. Hawaii. (Beckwith, 1940: 15, 16)

Ku-ke-ao-loa The "long cloud of Ku" who was guardian of the house of clouds. Hawaii. (Westervelt, 1963, 3: 128–129)

Kukulcan The plumed serpent (Quetzalcóatl) is the rain god in one of his functions, and a god of fertility. He is associated with the planet Venus, is the giver of civilization, of justice and order. Mayan, Mexico. (Tozzer, 1941: 128, 133, 23; Schellhas, 1904: 18; Keeler, 1960: 184, 200–201; Nicholson, 1967: 23, 39)

Ah K'ulel The Whirlwind is an assistant solar deity serving Hachäkyum. He is "also called the Sweeper of Our Lord's House." He takes the ashes from the god-pots (where the incense is burned) to Hachäkyum. The Lacandon, Chiapas, Mexico. (Perera and Bruce, 1982: 31)

Kulm The personification of Cold. Esthonia. (Grimm, 1888, 4: 1573)

Kulput A god of the atmosphere, of low clouds, descendant of Umalgo, the sun. The Ifugao, Philippines. (Barton, 1946: 41)

Kulput di Bulan A god of the atmosphere, of "clouds that scurry across the moon." Descendant of Umbulan, the moon. The Ifugao, Philippines. (Barton, 1946: 42)

Kulshedra The "evil female power who strives to destroy mankind with storms and floods." Driven back by Drangoni. Albania. (Durham, 1928: 123)

Ku-mauna A rain and forest god as well as god of the mountain. Hawaii. (Beckwith, 1940: 15)

Ku-moku-hali'i A god of rain and of the forest invoked in cutting trees. Also a god of the land. Hawaii. (Beckwith, 1940: 15, 26)

Kunawiri One of the "personified forms of Cold" who assailed the sons of Papa and Rangi when they emerged. The Maori, New Zealand. (Best, 1924: 95)

Kuni-no-Mihashira A Shinto god of the wind. Japan. (Kato, 1926: 15; Herbert, 1967: 491)

Kunku Chac Mayan god of the initial rains of the season. Mexico. (Thompson, 1970: 254)

Kunmanngur The rainbow serpent god who represents regeneration and fertility. Australia. (Robinson, 1966: 50, 67; Poignant, 1967: 126)

Ku-olono-wao God of the rain and of the deep forest. Hawaii. (Beckwith, 1940: 15)

Kupa-ai-ke'e A forest and rain god and "inventor of the bevel adze" used in canoe-making. Hawaii. (Beckwith, 1940: 15; Emerson, 1968: 53; Keliipio, 1901: 115)

Ku-pepeiao-loa and **Ku-pepeiao-poko** "Big-and small-eared Ku," gods of the rain and of the forest as well as of canoe builders—"gods of the seat braces by which the canoe is carried." Hawaii. (Beckwith, 1940: 15–16)

Ku-pulupulu A god of rain and of the forest worshipped by canoe builders when cutting koa wood. Hawaii. (Westervelt, 1963, 1: 98–99; Beckwith, 1940: 15; Emerson, 1916/17: 24)

Kuraokami God of rain and of snow, a dragon god, born of the blood of Kagu-tsuchi on the sword of Izanagi. Japan. (Herbert, 1967: 271, 481; Kato, 1926: 15; Yasumaro, 1965: 18–19; Holtom, 1938: 96, 102–103)

Kurar-Ichchi The god of the wind. The Yaku, Siberia. (Czaplicka, 1969: 278)

Kürdertše-jumo The god of thunder of the Cheremis. Russia. (Leach, 1949, 1: 215)

Kurobirarinyun The spirit of "steady, slow rain." The Mundurucu, Para, Brazil. (Murphy, 1958: 21)

Kuro-ikazuchi "Black Thunder." Japan. (Herbert, 1967: 274)

Kutya?i "(firewind)," often seen as the whirlwind, actively captured souls at night. He was sponsor of some *puvalam* (Shaman). All contact with Kutya?i was dangerous. The Cahuilla, California. (Bean, 1974: 166)

Kuzah God of storms and rainbows. Apparently a variant of Kozah. Arabia. (Goldziher, 1877: 73)

Kwafo Bommo A widely known god who detects thieves, and who "comes and goes in the form of a strong wind . . . also responsible for sudden whirlwinds and for tempests at sea." The Nzema (Akan), Ghana. (Grottanelli, 1969: 377)

Kwallissay The rainbow "is Mustam-ho's medicine for stopping rain." The Mojave, Arizona. (Bourke, 1889: 182)

Kwartseedie The god of the south wind brings the rain. The Nootka, Washington and Vancouver Island. (Swan, 1869: 92)

Kyaka God of lightning of the Basoga. Uganda. (Mbiti, 1970, 2: 238)

sKyeser The personification of the wind. Tibet. (Francke, 1925, 8: 78)

Kyllang A deity of storms as well as a mountain and a war deity. The Khasi, Assam. (Bareh, 1967: 360)

La'a-maomao Polynesian god of the winds who causes storms. In Samoa, the rainbow, whose position, if appearing in battle, foretold the outcome. (Andersen, 1928; 54, 70; Beckwith, 1940: 86; Alexander, 1968: 63; Turner, 1884: 35)

Labu The "master . . . of lightning." Costa Rica. (Stone, 1962: 57)

Laieikawai The "maiden of the mist." Kauai, Hawaii. (Westervelt, 1963, 2: 57)

Laki Balari The god of thunder and of storms whose wife is Obeng Doh. The Kayans, Borneo. (Hose, 1912: 5)

ᵗLam-shua The spirit of the atmosphere who is believed to control the weather. The Chugach Eskimo, Alaska. (Smith, 1953: 121)

Langaan Goddess of rain and of wind. Mother of Aponitolau. Philippines. (Jocano, 1969: 48)

Langieli A god of the surf and of the wind invoked when there are high seas. Ratak Islands, the Marshalls, Micronesia. (Knappe, 1888: 66)

Lanioaka The aumakua in the lightning. Hawaii. (Emerson, 1967: 51)

La 'nTu Mushen, Makam wa ningsang The god of thunder who commands the clouds, rain, wind, and lightning and to whom sacrifices are made. Son of Phungkam Janun. The Katchins, Burma. (Gilhodes, 1908: 677)

Las kyi mkha' 'gro ma A Tibetan goddess invoked for rainfall. (Nebesky-Wojkowitz, 1956, 1: 479)

Laufakanaa God of the winds. Tonga, Polynesia. (Gifford, 1924: 16)

Lau-ka-ie-ie A goddess of the wind and of the wildwood—"Leaf of the trailing pandanus," sister of Makanikeoe and of Hi'ilawe. Hawaii. (Westervelt, 1912: 110; Beckwith, 1940: 93, 522)

Lauliar The rainbow spirit "who brings storms and destroys canoes at sea unless propitiated." Ifalik, Micronesia. (Burrows, 1947/48: 10)

the Law, Law hpo A group of spirits of the wet season who "regulate the rainfall and reveal themselves in the thunder and lightning" and are responsible for the growth of vegetation. The Karen, Burma. (Marshall, 1922: 230)

Layzn The god of the wind. The Gilyak, Siberia. (Shternberg, 1933: 320)

Lei-chu God of thunder. Southwest China. (Graham, 1961: 161)

Lei-kung The god of thunder punishes those who have committed undetected crimes. China. (Maspero, 1963: 274; Werner, 1932: 242; Larousse, 1968: 383)

u'lei pyrthat The god of thunder. Assam. (Stegmiller, 1921: 410; Gurdon, 1907: 157)

Lei-tsu Ta Ti, Lei Tzu Ta Ti One of the gods of thunder who is worshipped also by cooks, seedsmen, innkeepers, and shoemakers. China. (Shryock, 1931: 162; Werner, 1932: 245; Maspero, 1963: 274: Day, 1940: 165)

Ah-lelem-caan-chaac One of the Mayan Chacks—rain gods—god of lightning. Mexico. (Redfield and Rojas, 1962: 115; Thompson, 1970: 255)

Leme-ish The spirit of thunder, sometimes multiple—as five brothers. They wield the thunderbolt and lightning, were once on earth but were relegated to the sky where they can frighten but not do as much harm. The Klamath, Oregon. (Gatschet, 1890: xc)

Leomatagi A lesser god of Hikutavaki invoked for good winds. Niue, Polynesia. (Loeb, 1926, 1: 161)

Lerpio, Lerpiu A spirit associated with rain, immanent in the tribal rainmaker and intermediary between him and Dangdit, the god of rain. The Dinka, Sudan. (Seligman, 1931: 12; Fraxer, 1926: 309)

Leucetius A Celtic god of lightning and of war, assimilated to Mars. Britain and Gaul. (Renel, 1906: 399; Ross, 1967: 201; Anwyl, 1906: 38–39; MacCulloch, 1911: 27)

lham sua The god of the atmosphere, the sky, controls "the forces of nature, the game supply and the souls of men and animals." On Ninivak, Alaska. (Marsh, 1967: 153)

Libbuwog A god of the atmosphere—clouds that hide the sun. Descendant of Umalgo, the sun. The Ifugao, Philippines. (Barton, 1946: 41)

Libtakan   A god of good weather, of the sunrise and sunset. The Manobo, Philippines. (Jocano, 1969: 23)

Likuve, Likube, Lyuba   The supreme god produces the weather, the rain, but is also responsible for the locusts. The Nyamwezi, Tanzania. (Millroth, 1965: 34–36)

Lima-loa   The "god of the mirage." Hawaii. (Andersen, 1928: 286)

Lino   A goddess of the surf and of the wind invoked when there are high seas. Wife of Langieli. Ratak Islands, the Marshalls, Micronesia. (Knappe, 1888: 66)

Lips   A Greek goddess of the winds—the southeast. (Murray, 1895: 201)

Lisa   A god of the pantheon which controls thunder, rain, and waters. Identified with St. Paul. Maranhão, Brazil. (Costa Eduardo, 1948: 78–79, 84; Bastide, 1960: 567)

Lituvaris   A Lithuanian god of rain. (Welsford, 1925, 9: 241)

Liviac   The lightning. Peru. (Markham, 1969: 70)

Lobanga   The otiose creator god sends the rain. The Labwor, Uganda. (Williams, 1936: 178)

Loko   A god of the pantheon which controls thunder, rain, and waters. Worshipped by Dahomean and Yoruban cults. Maranhão, Brazil. (Costa Eduardo, 1948: 78–79, 81)

Lo-lupe, Olo-pue, Ololupe   A god of the wind who is also a god of sorcery is "invoked in the rite of deification of the dead or restoration of the dead to life. . . . Some say his is an errand of benevolence and not of crime, and that he is sent into the heavens to ensnare the souls of those alone who have done evil." Maui, Hawaii. (Beckwith, 1940: 109, 121)

Lombo   The "King of the Air," who was overcome by Libanza and reduced to slavery. The Upotos, Congo. (Frazer, 1926: 148)

Lono   God of the weather, of atmospheric phenomena. He was also a god of agricultural fertility, and a god of sound. Hawaii, the Society Islands, Polynesia. (Henry, 1928: 117; Beckwith, 1940: 31–33, 350; Mackenzie, n.d.: 320–322)

Lono-o-pua-kau   God of rainbows or rainbow-colored clouds which were "signs of a chief's presence." Hawaii. (Westervelt, 1963, 1: 210–211)

St. Lorenzo   A wind god of the Mayans of British Honduras. (Thompson, 1930: 64)

Lorok   A spirit of the south who was guardian of the winds. The Marshall Islands, Micronesia. (Davenport, 1953: 221–222)

Loubon   He controls the weather and typhoons and is associated with the low waters along the land. Truk, Micronesia. (Bollig, 1927: 12)

Loula   A supreme sky god who controls the elements. Congo. (Budge, 1973, 1: 374)

Lubari   The sky god in his aspect of rain. The Gallas, Ethiopia. (Foucart, 1925, 11: 581)

Lu-chen   The thunder spirit. The Meau, China. (Bernatzik, 1947: 156)

Lugal-banda   The storm-bird who "brought the lightning, the fire of heaven, from the gods to men, giving them at once the knowledge of fire and the power of reading the future in the flashes of the storm." Babylonia, Near East. (Sayce, 1898: 294)

Lugeleng   The god of rain. Yap Island, the Carolines, Micronesia. (Christian, 1899: 385)

Lule   The god of rain as well as "of tears, and of mourning." The Baganda, Uganda. (Cunningham, 1905: 218; Budge, 1973, 1: 377)

Lung Chi   A goddess of mist and dew, and of rain. Daughter of Wang-mu Niang-niang. China. (Werner, 1934: 237)

Lung Wang   One of the dragon gods all of whom are invoked to produce rain. China. (Maspero, 1963: 276; Day, 1940: 72; Shryock, 1931: 116; Schram, 1957: 85)

rLun-lha   Tibetan god of storms and god and protector of the northwest. (Waddell, 1959: 367)

Lykaios   The priest of this god came to Hagno spring on the side of Mount Lykaios with a sacrifice when there was severe drought. Greece. (Eliade, 1958: 202)

Lytuvonis   Lithuanian rain deity. (Gimbutas, 1963: 197)

Machi Olonakuokarialel   In the Nele Sibu chronicle a deity who makes "it rain over the whole earth." The Cuna, Panama. (Nordenskiold, 1938: 309)

Machi Olosuitakipipilel   In the Nele Sibu chronicle a deity who makes the rain fall "only on certain places." The Cuna, Panama. (Nordenskiold, 1938: 309)

Ah Mac Ik   A deity invoked to control the winds when they damage the milpas. The Lacandon (Mayan), Mexico. (Thompson, 1970: 272)

Macom   The god of lightning. The Chol (Mayan), Guatemala. (Tozzer, 1941: 113)

madjigiskat   The personification of "bad weather." The Penobscot, Maine. (Speck, 1935: 22)

Maeke   One of the "personified forms of Cold" who assailed the sons of Papa and Rangi when they emerged from her protection. The Maori, New Zealand. (Best, 1924: 95)

Magaragoi   God of typhoons, wind and rainstorms. Yap Island, the Carolines, Micronesia. (Christian, 1899: 385)

Magbaya   The deity of the west wind. The Bukidnon, Philippines. (Jocano, 1969: 23)

Mahakala   In Tibet a demon of drought. (Waddell, 1959: 368)

Mahiki   A whirlwind demon. Waipio Valley, Hawaii. (Westervelt, 1963, 2: 122)

Mahpiya   A presiding spirit over the atmosphere who receives invocations and shows his pleasure or displeasure "by giving or withholding pleasant weather, rains, storms, frosts and dews or by hot winds sent as punishment." The Lakota/Oglala, Plains Indians, South Dakota. (Walker, 1980: 120)

Maingit   A god associated with "sun shower, rainbow and lightning." Son of Amkidul (Kidul), god of thunder. The Ifugao, Philippines. (Barton, 1955: 224)

Maiyatcuna   Deity of the south and of the drizzling rain. The Acoma, New Mexico. (White, 1929/30: 66)

Makani-kau, Makani-keoe   A god of the wind and also a god of love who reconciles quarreling young couples. Hawaii. (Beckwith, 1940: 93; Westervelt, 1915: 48)

Makani-kona   God of the south wind. Hawaii. (Westervelt, 1963, 3: 193)

Makere-whatu   God of the heavy rains. The Maori, New Zealand. (Best, 1924: 175)

Makila   God of thunder and a sky spirit who with Kuksu was a creator and giver of their culture. The northern Pomo, California. (Loeb, 1926, 2: 301; 1932: 3, 4)

Maku   "damp"—son of Kore-te-matua. His wife was Mahora-nui-a-tea. New Zealand. (White, 1887, 1: 18)

Malahshishinish   Scorpion Woman who makes the thunder. She may be associated with "stars in our constellations of Cygnus and Lyra." The Chumash, California. (Hudson and Underhay, 1978: 152)

Malatha   The god of lightning of the Choctaw Indians. Louisiana. (Bushnell, 1909: 18)

Mamaragan   The spirit of lightning who "During the dry season lives quietly at the bottom of a deep waterhole." During the monsoon season he travels about on thunderclouds. Arnhem Land, Australia. (Mountford, 1955: 129)

Mamareraka   A rain ancestral being of Ragatia. Western Aranda, Australia. (Robinson, 1966: 29)

Te Mamaru   One of the guardians of the heavens who controls the clouds. A son of Papa and Rangi. The Maori, New Zealand. (Best, 1924: 162)

Mamogipug   A wind god of the Ifugao. Philippines. (Barton, 1946: 62)

The Mams   The gods "of thunder and lightning, and, by extension, of the rain" of the Mayas of British Honduras are interwoven and confused with the Tzultacaj(h) and the Chacs. They are also gods of the mountains and the valleys and are their most important deities. (Thompson, 1930: 57, 62)

Mamugipug   A god of the winds. The Ifugao, Philippines. (Barton, 1946: 61)

Mamulion   A god of the atmosphere and a descendant of Umalgo, the sun. The Ifugao, Philippines. (Barton, 1946: 41)

Manannan   The god of the sea was also a god of the wind. Like Odin he possesses a steed, a sword, and a mantle which are symbols of the wind. Ireland. (MacBain, 1917: 122)

Mangu   The spirit of the evening star sends "wind and bad weather." Ongtong Java, Indonesia. (Williamson, 1933: 153)

Maninupdikili One of the demons of rain and floods. Daughter of Olopurguakuayai. The Cuna Indians, Panama. (Nordenskiold, 1938: 285)

Manulul A god of the atmosphere—clouds. A descendant of Umalgo, the sun. The Ifugao, Philippines. (Barton, 1946: 41)

Manungod A god of the wind of the Ifugao. Philippines. (Barton, 1946: 61–62)

Maoa'e-ra'i-aneane "North-east-trade-wind-of-the-clear-sky," chief of all the winds. Society Islands, Polynesia. (Henry, 1928: 364)

Maoake The deity of the northeast wind, child of Raka. Mangaia, Polynesia. (Andersen, 1928: 359)

Maoake-anau The deity of the northeast by north wind, child of Raka. Mangaia, Polynesia. (Andersen, 1928: 359)

Maoake-ma-akarua The deity of the north by east wind, child of Raka. Mangaia, Polynesia. (Andersen, 1928: 359)

Maoake-ta The north-northeast wind—"The Terrible Maoake," the deity of cyclonic winds. Child of Raka. Mangaia, Polynesia. (Andersen, 1928: 359)

Mar A spirit of the air. The Nuer, Sudan. (Evans-Pritchard, 1956: 32)

Mara'amu The south wind. Society Islands, Polynesia. (Henry, 1928: 364)

Marangai The wind from the east. Child of Raka. Mangaia, Polynesia. (Andersen, 1928: 358)

Marangai-akavaine The east-northeast wind—"as Gentle as a Woman." Child of Raka. Mangaia, Polynesia. (Andersen, 1928: 359)

Marangai-anau The wind from the east by north. Child of Raka. Mangaia, Polynesia. (Andersen, 1928: 359)

Marangai-maoake The northeast by east wind. Child of Raka. Mangaia, Polynesia. (Andersen, 1928: 359)

Marapou A deity "who sends the wind and rain and causes storms at sea." Yap Island, Micronesia. (Furness, 1910: 150)

Maratji A very dangerous rainbow spirit, lizard-like and highly colored, spoken of singly and multiply, is associated with water, thunderstorms, rain. Melville Island, Australia. (Mountford, 1958: 155–158)

mardež-awa The "mother of the Wind." The Cheremis, Russia. (Leach, 1949, 1: 98)

Maretkhmakniam The supreme god expresses his wrath with rain and storms and governs the phases of the moon. His wife is Maret-Jikky. The Botocudo, Brazil. (Métraux, 1946, 8: 539–540; Pettazzoni, 1956: 21, 421)

Mari The goddess of thunder and lightning, of rain and drought, is believed to live on mountains and in caves. Her husband is Maju and when he comes to meet her there are furious storms of rain and hail. These are also sometimes caused by her annoyance with the villages. She is considered an oracle, knowing the future, and the mistress of sorcerers. She takes many forms: woman, various animals, a gust of wind, a ball of fire, and sometimes is part animal, part human. Her favored offering is a sheep. The Basques, Spain and France. (Barandiaran, 1972: 159, 164, 272–274, 314)

Maro-maomao God of the wind *Akarua*. Rarotonga, Polynesia. (Williamson, 1933, 1: 150)

Marout The storm wind associated with the northwest. Mongolia. (Percheron, 1953: 63)

Maroya A stone idol invoked with Boinayol for rain. Haiti, West Indies. (Arciniegas, 1971: 6, 7)

Marrgon An ancestral being of lightning and thunder. The Djauan tribe, Australia. (Robinson, 1966: 140–141)

Tatik Martil *See* **San Pedro the Martyr**

The Maruts Gods of the atmosphere, of storms, and of winds. They are also beneficent, bringing rains and being healers. They are the sons of Rudra and Prishni, the dappled cow, and the companions of Indra. Their luminosity indicates knowledge, horses, their power for action, oneness, unity and harmony. On the mental-spiritual plane they "preside over the subtle life-energies and thought-powers. . . . [They] are powers of will and nervous or vital Force that have attained to the light of thought and the voice of self-expression." India. (Ions, 1967: 17; Barth, 1921: 14; Danielou, 1964: 102–104; Jayne, 1962: 171; Pandit, 1970: 51–66)

Maruttas God of the wind. The Kassites of Asia Minor. (Campbell, 1964: 122)

Masi The omnipresent, omniscient "spirit of the air. . . . intractable and hard to deal with." The Caribs of the Barama River, British Guiana. (Gillin, 1936: 158)

Mastan The demon of the southwest wind. Efate, New Hebrides, Melanesia. (MacKenzie, 1930: 125)

Mataaho The personification of distant lightning. The Maori, New Zealand. (Best, 1924: 161)

Matai The deity of the wind, a child of Tane. Society Islands, Polynesia. (Williamson, 1933, 1: 141)

Matapula A deity invoked to control storms and winds, particularly from the north. Tikopia, Polynesia. (Firth, 1967, 2: 330)

Matarisvan A form of lightning and an aspect of Agni as the celestial fire. He later "assumes the distinct new feature of a wind-god pure and simple without trace of any connexion with the fire." India. (Keith, 1917: 36, 89; Bhattacharji, 1970: 187, 190; Macdonell, 1897: 72)

Mata-Upolu The deity of the east wind who brings rain. Samoa, Polynesia. (Andersen, 1928: 218)

Matlalcueje A goddess of rain and of waters who dwells on the mountain. A wife of Tlaloc. Same as Chalchihuitlicue. The Tlascaltecs, Mexico. (Bancroft, 1886, 3: 367; Duran, 1971: 257, 466; Mackenzie, 1924: 240; Humboldt, n.d., 2: 14, 23)

Matnau A goddess of the north wind who dances on the mountain top and causes storms at sea. The Hokkaidu Ainu, Japan. (Philippi, 1982: 168)

Matri A goddess, sometimes single sometimes multiple, associated with the weather and invoked in reference to rain, either too much or too little. The Himalayas. India. (Berreman, 1963: 100–101, 378)

Matsyendranath A god whose basic function was "the yearly bringing of the rains." Nepal. (Snellgrove, 1957: 116)

Matu Deity of the north wind, of tempests. Samoa, Polynesia. (Andersen, 1928: 218)

Mâtu God of the western wind, of the tempest, the storm—"he was but one of several storm-gods . . . spoken of as 'the gods Mâtu.' " With Meri he was absorbed by Rimmon. Akkadian/Babylonian, Near East. (Sayce, 1898: 201–202)

Mawake-nui A guardian of the heavens whose function is to control the clouds. The Maori, New Zealand. (Best, 1924: 162)

Mawali The rainbow in the west, twin brother of Tini. They brought about the annihilating flood saving only two girls as their companions. To look him in the eye brings misfortune in hunting and fishing. The Katawishi, Brazil. (Levi-Strauss, 1969: 247)

Mbon The "Spirit of the Wind . . . may be worshipped only at the national harvest festival (*manau*) and then by the chiefs alone"—the importance being that the winds bring the fertilizing rains. The Kachins, Burma. (Temple, 1925, 3: 22–23; Leach, 1950, 2: 785)

Megha Raja The god of rain. India. (Crooke, 1894: 44)

Melalanuku The god of the wind from the southeast which "has a bad odor . . . because He breaks wind all the time." The Kwakiutl Indians, British Columbia. (Boas, 1935: 140)

Melusine A Bohemian goddess of the wind. (Grimm, 1888: 1470)

Menani A deity representing "a small part of the rainbow appearing just above the horizon" is invoked in the ceremony for children, to make them strong, skillful, successful, brave, and to give them longevity. The entire rainbow is called Anak Raja. The Sea Dyaks, Borneo. (Roth, 1968: 171)

Mendeal The northwest wind who collects the waters of the sea when Egua blows, always lying in ambush and hoping for Egua's carelessness, so that he, Mendeal, can launch his storms on the earth. The Basques, France and Spain. (Barandiaran, 1972: 72)

Mensabak, Menzabac, Metzabac God of the rain and of fresh waters who is identified with the west. He is believed to have created the clouds; to have given the sunset colors by placing copal soot "from an incense pot on a macaw's tail and scattered it in all directions except the south." He is the guardian of the souls of the good. His wife is Naimetzabok. He is also called Yum Canan Zabac. The Lacandon, Mexico. (Cline, 1944: 112; Tozzer, 1941: 125; Thompson, 1970: 265–266; Perera and Bruce, 1982: 271, 308)

Meri A god of the air—"the atmosphere when lighted up by the rays of the sun." Akkadian. Same as Rimmon (Semitic). Near East. (Sayce, 1898: 202)

Mermeut An evil spirit who, with Fasolt, creates storms. Teutonic. (Grimm, 1883, 2: 636)

Mesilipik A god who "seems to be a personification of cold. He lives in the seas between the islands." Ifalik, Micronesia. (Burrows, 1947/48: 12)

Metepur Bilik   A wind being of the A-Pucikwar. Andaman Islands, Bay of Bengal. (Radcliffe-Brown, 1967: 149)

Meulen   God of the whirlwind. The Araucanian, the Mapuche-Huilliche, Chile. (Chamberlain, 1900: 57; Alexander, 1920: 327; Cooper, 1946, 6: 748)

Mfidi   A supreme sky god who controls the elements. Congo. (Budge, 1973, 1: 374)

Menakais   The name of Alquntam used when invoking his "power over both rain and dry weather, and is petitioned for whichever is desired." The Bella Coola, British Columbia. (McIlwraith, 1948, 1: 105)

Min   He is classified as a storm god. His aspect of virility and fertility includes the rains and lightning, the epithet "great bull." His consort is Hathor, the cow. They came from Pwnt on the Indian Ocean. Egypt. (Eliade, 1958: 83, 91)

Mingabion   God of the south and of the south wind. The Ojibwa, Minnesota. (Coleman, 1937: 37)

Minggo Ishto Elva, Minggo Ishto Eloha Alkaiasto   The great god of thunder which noise expresses his anger. The giver of the summer rain. The Creek Indians, Alabama and Georgia. (Swanton, 1928: 486; Waring, 1965: 52)

Min Jok   The goddess who brings the rain. The Lango, Uganda. (Driberg, 1923: 216)

Miochin   God of South mountain, of summer, and of summer-lightning. The Keres, New Mexico. (Tyler, 1964: 166, 227)

Miöll   Norse goddess of the snow and ice, daughter of Snior. (Grimm, 1883, 2: 631)

Misevályue   The mother of the clouds and the rain. She is also the mother of dancing and singing. The Cagaba, the Kogi, Colombia. (Reichel-Dolmatoff, 1949/50: 114)

Mitcinoski Inaniu   The "father of the thunderers." The Menomini, Wisconsin. (Skinner, 1913: 75)

Mizen Caan Chac   One of the Mayan rain gods. Mexico. (Thompson, 1970: 255)

Mlengavuwa   The "Creator of rain." The Tonga, Malawi and Zambia. (Mbiti, 1970, 2: 335)

Mo acha   God of the sea and of calm, fine weather. Brother of Shi acha. The Ainu, Japan. (Batchelor, 1894: 20)

Mogaung Kyawzwe   The spirit of the rains. Burma. (Nash, 1966: 118)

Mo-hou-lo-chia   A dragon-king, a deity of rain, clouds, thunder and lightning. China. (Werner, 1932: 285–286, 319)

Moi-tikitiki   The great god of rain. Aneiteum, New Hebrides, Melanesia. (Williamson, 1933, 2: 181)

Mokosh   A Slavic goddess invoked "in time of drought." Czechoslovakia. (Gimbutas, 1971: 168)

Mo-li Ch'ing   A Taoist god who created whirlwinds and waterspouts. China. (Maspero, 1963: 308)

Mo-li Hai   A Taoist god who controls the winds. China. (Maspero, 1963: 308)

Mo-li Hung   A Taoist god who caused the darkness of clouds and brought rain. China. (Maspero, 1963: 308)

Mo-li-Shou   A deity who regulates the wind and the rain. China. (Maspero, 1963: 308)

Mompaidu   A god of the atmosphere, of clouds. The Ifugao, Philippines. (Barton, 1946: 41)

Monabunab   A god of the atmosphere, son of Umalgo, the sun. The Ifugao, Philippines. (Barton, 1946: 40)

Monabuya   A god of the atmosphere, descendant of Umalgo, the sun. The Ifugao, Philippines. (Barton, 1946: 41)

Monambaiyug   A god of the atmosphere, descendant of Umalgo. The Ifugao, Philippines. (Barton, 1946: 41)

Mo-na-ssu   A dragon-king, a god of rain, the clouds, thunder and lightning. China. (Werner, 1932: 285–286)

Moneiba   A goddess worshipped by the women and prayed to for rain. Hierro, Canary Islands. (Hooten, 1925, 7: 12, 64)

Monhanubangal   A god of the atmosphere, of clouds, and descendant of Umalgo. The Ifugao, Philippines. (Barton, 1946: 62)

Monnutnut   A god of the atmosphere and descendant of Umalgo, the sun. The Ifugao, Philippines. (Barton, 1946: 41)

Monongal A god of winds. The Ifugao, Philippines. (Barton, 1946: 62)

Monsauí Master of the weather—of rain, hail, snow, and wind. The Cagaba, the Kogi, Colombia. (Reichel-Dolmatoff, 1949/50: 113)

Mororoma A god of thunder "who threw lightning from the top of the mountains." The Yurakare, Western Matto Grosso, South America. (Métraux, 1942: 12)

Moroz-ata, Kelme-ata Finno-Ugrian god of frost. The Mordvins, Russia. (Paasonen, 1925, 8: 844)

Mozon Ik, Kakal Mozon Ik The spirit of the whirlwind appealed to at the firing of the milpa. Mayan, Yucatan, Quintana Roo, and British Honduras. (Thompson, 1970: 272)

Mpambe The god of thunder who is sent by Mtanga with the rain. The Yao, Malawi and Mozambique. (Lang, 1968: 234)

Muash The god of the south wind. The Klamath, Oregon. (Chamberlain, 1892: 254; Gatschet, 1890: xci)

Mudjekiwis, Wickano The leader of, or chief thunderer. Spoken of also as a group of deities—"the thunder war gods"—Mudjekiwis, Wapinamakiu, Sawina makiu, Mukomais, Wisikapeo. The Menomini, Wisconsin. (Skinner, 1913: 74–78)

Mu-er-go A god of thunder. The Ch'iang at Ho-p'ingchai, Szechwan, China. (Graham, 1958: 52)

Mugasha Among the Haya he is a god of the lake with control over the wind and the weather. His wife is Nyakarembe. Tanzania. (Taylor, 1962: 142)

Muiñwa God of rain of the Pueblo Indians at Oraibi. Arizona. (Powell, 1979/80: 27)

Mukomais One of the thunderers—a god of hail, of cold, and of storms. The Menomini, Wisconsin. (Skinner, 1913: 75, 77)

Muluc A Mayan god of rain and one of the gods of the new year. Central America. (Nicholson, 1967: 44)

Mumpal The thunder, who is also the creator. Australia. (Brinton, 1897: 81)

Mundur-Tengri The "god of hail, loud thunder, and lightning." The Buriats, Siberia and Mongolia. (Klementz, 1925, 3: 4)

Munume The god who controlled the weather. The Banyoro, Uganda. (Roscoe, 1915: 93)

Munya Slavic goddess of lightning. (Grimm, 1883, 2: 883)

Musoke A god of the atmosphere who with Gulu rules the elements. He makes rain from the water sent up to the clouds by the river divinity Mayanja. The Baganda, Uganda. (Roscoe, 1965: 315; Mbiti, 1970, 2: 119, 138)

Musoki God of the rainbow. Uganda. (Budge, 1973, 1: 377)

Muyusu A serpent deity, the rainbow. The Mundurucu, Brazil. (Levi-Strauss, 1969: 324)

Mvurayakucha The "Morning Dew" whose father is Lumukanda, and mother is Watamaraka. South Africa. (Mutwa, n.d.: 191, 194)

Mwari The supreme being and creator god of the Shona is also considered the god of storms and atmospheric phenomena, the giver of rain. Rhodesia. (Pettersson, 1953: 162–164, 177, 195; Schapera, 1937: 264; Daneel, 1970: 15, 16; Gelfand, 1962: 141)

Nadikiawasin The god of the west and of the west wind is the youngest and most powerful of the winds. The Ojibwa, Minnesota. (Coleman, 1937: 37–38)

Nagawonyi The goddess of drought, and of hunger. It was believed if offerings were made to her rain would fall before reaching home, through her influence with Gulu and Musoke. The Baganda, Uganda. (Mair, 1934: 121, 234; Roscoe, 1965: 315)

Nageswar A snake god who controls the weather. Benares, India. (Crooke, 1894: 267; Martin, 1914: 259)

Nago Shango The god of thunder. Plaisance, Haiti. West Indies. (Simpson, 1945: 44)

Nahse kame "Master of the Dry Season"—the "cut shrimp" constellation. The Desana, Colombia. (Reichel-Dolmatoff, 1971: 74)

Nahse kame turu "Master of the Dry Season"—the "cut shrimp" constellation. The Desana, Colombia. (Reichel-Dolmatoff, 1971: 74)

Nakayaga A god of storms and of whirlwinds. Uganda. (Budge, 1973, 1: 377; Cunningham, 1905: 218)

Na kulu wai lani o Kulanihakoi The god of rain. Hawaii. (Emerson, 1967: 51)

nala'təgwe'sən   The deity of the northeast wind who, with the other winds, rules "human and animal destiny." The Penobscot, Maine. (Speck, 1935, 1: 21)

Nama Burag   "The Spirit of the Thunderstorm." Tasmania. (Worms, 1960: 7)

gNam lcags thog 'bebs ma   A Tibetan goddess of weather. (Nebesky-Wojkowitz, 1965, 1: 468)

Nam mkha'i lha mo sprin tshogs ma   A weather and sky goddess who resides in the northeast. Tibet. (Nebesky-Wojkowitz, 1956, 1: 468)

Nam mkha'i mo tsha gsang snyoms   A weather and sky goddess who resides in the southwest. Tibet. (Nebesky-Wojkowitz, 1956, 1: 468)

Nam mkha'i lha mo tshod 'dzin ma   A weather and sky goddess who resides in the southeast. Tibet. (Nebesky-Wojkowitz, 1956, 1: 468)

Namsáuí   A demon who is "the personification of the storm . . . represents rain, cold, snow, and hail." The Kagaba, Colombia. (Preuss, 1926: 82)

Namulyun d Lagod   A god of winds of the Ifugao. Philippines. (Barton, 1946: 61)

Namwanga   The elements are controlled by the supreme sky god. Congo. (Budge, 1973, 1: 374)

Nanda   A serpent (Naga) king. The Nagas are benevolent and "control the rain-clouds, . . . protect from lightning, bring beneficial showers, or stop too abundant rains." India. (Getty, 1962: 173)

Naac Nanec   The god of the air, son of Nexhequiriac. The Trique tribe, Oaxaca, Mexico. (Valentini, 1899: 38)

Nanginawingiyan   A wind god of the Ifugao. Philippines. (Barton, 1946: 62)

Nanju   A powerful spirit who sends torrential rains and other weather phenomena as punishment. The Dyaks, Borneo. (Pettazzoni, 1957: 21, 332)

Nanna· o·'xwa   The "Aspen Raingod." A Summer Raingod who is a bringer of rain and its accompanying fertility. The Tewa, San Juan, New Mexico. (Laski, 1958: 11)

Nan-t'o   A dragon-king, a deity of rain and thunder and lightning. China. (Werner, 1932: 185–186)

Nanub   The thundercloud, also called Gurub. The Hottentot, South Africa. (Hahn, 1881: 128–130; Schapera, 1951: 380–381)

Nap'o· šu·ⁿ   The "specific name of the god who is probably the Chief Raingod of the Summer people, and whose name refers to the sacred blackish clay used for ceremonial bodypaint." Like the others a bringer of rain and its accompanying fertility. The Tewa, San Juan, New Mexico. (Laski, 1958: 11)

Nappakandattha   A water snake who is the source of the rainbow. The Warramunga, Central Australia. (Spencer, 1904: 631)

Nappatecutli   One of the gods of rain and also the god of the straw and rushes used by mat-makers. Worshipped at Lake Texcuco. Aztec, Mexico. (Spence, 1923: 235, 264; Caso, 1958: 45)

Narama   The dangerous "rainbow-serpent woman, . . . of the Liverpool River area . . . destroys all aborigines who approach her home." Australia. (Mountford, 1958: 155)

Narikabura-no-Kami   A thunder deity worshipped at Katsunu-no-Matsu-no-Wo. Japan. (Yasumaro, 1965: 51)

Narjugaaluk   The shaman's name for the god of air and of weather. The Copper Eskimo, Canada. (Nungak and Arima, 1969: 114)

Narshuk, Narssuk, Nartsuk   God of the weather, of storms, of winds, rain, snow. Also called Sila. The Copper Eskimo, the Iglulik, the Netsilik, Canada. (Rasmussen, 1931: 224; 1932: 29; Nungak and Arima, 1969: 114; Balikci, 1970: 207)

Naru-ikazuchi   "Rumbling Thunder." Japan. (Herbert, 1967: 274)

Naru Kami   A Shinto god of thunder. Japan. (Aston, 1925, 11: 463)

Narvoje   A beneficent spirit of the mist. Geelvink Bay, New Guinea. (Haddon, 1925, 9: 351)

sNa tshogs mkha' 'gro ma   A Tibetan goddess invoked for rainfall. (Nebesky-Wojkowitz, 1956, 1: 479)

Nau-lu   Deity of the sudden showers. Maui, Hawaii. (Ashdown, 1971: 68)

Navuvá   "frost, ice." Created by Gauteóvañ. She is the mother of the evil lakes and marshes. The Kagaba, Colombia. (Preuss, 1926: 66, 84)

Nda-la-a-ssaw-mi   A female wind spirit. The Na-khi, Yunnan Province, China. (Rock, 1947: 287)

Ndjambi (Ndyambi) Karunga   The great sky god and creator-remote, beneficent, therefore requiring no worship. Yet he wields the atmospheric phenomena and is implored to protect them from it and other perils. The Herero, Namibia. (Frazer, 1926: 150–151; Luttig, 1933: 7–9)

ndzuu dja   Beneficent god of the wind invoked to cut off "the roads of sickness" and to help vanquish demons. The Ch'uan Miao of Yunnan Province, China. (Graham, 1937: 74)

Negafok   The spirit of cold weather. Eskimo. Canada. (Burland, 1965: 23)

Nemevonam   The thunder god of the Cheyenne Indians. Minnesota, Dakotas, and Montana. (Powell, 1969: 438)

Nemitcuwəts   The Thunder. The Naskapi, Labrador. (Speck, 1935: 62)

'Nenaunir   God of storms and also of evil. The Masai, Kenya and Tanzania. (Larousse, 1968: 476)

Nenek   The spirit of thunder. The Sakai-Jakun, Malay Peninsula. (Evans, 1923: 207)

Neneme'kiwagi   The Thunderers—four manitous of the cardinal points. The Fox, Wisconsin. (Jones, 1911: 213)

Neoga   "Fawn, the south wind." He was god of the summer winds carrying the fragrant odors and sounds of nature over the land. The Seneca, New York. (Leach, 1950, 2: 788)

Nephele   Greek nymph—"the mist of morning tide"—the personification of clouds. She is powerful because she is benevolent as the cloud which gives the rain, as well as malevolent as the thundercloud. Wife of Athamas. (Cox, 1970, 2: 274; Roscher, 1965, 3, 1: 177)

Newerah   The wind, invoked in illness. The Wichita, Plains Indians, Kansas. (Dorsey, 1904, 1: 20, 296)

Ngala   The supreme god, of the sky, of the atmosphere and all its elements. He is identified with the Islamic Allah. The Bambara, Mali. (Tauxier, 1927: 169, 173)

Ngaliyeyeu   God of the west wind controls the winds and the seas. Pukapuka, Polynesia. (Beaglehole, 1938: 311–312)

Ngaljod, Ngaloit   The rainbow serpent, with whom Kunapipi is sometimes identified, will cause waterholes to overflow and drown people if disturbed. The Oenpelli area, Arnhem Land, Australia. (Eliade, 1973: 112; Mountford, 1958: 155)

Nganga   God of sleet. The Maori, New Zealand. (Andersen, 1928: 206)

Ngberrum   God of thunderstorms. The Bachama, Nigeria. (Meek, 1925, 2: 32)

Ngolyadon   A god of weather. Son of Kidul, the thunder. The Ifugao, Philippines. (Barton, 1946: 31)

Ngumalakngak   "Rattling Thunderer," son of Kidul, the thunder. The Ifugao, Philippines. (Barton, 1946: 30)

Niang-Niang   A mother goddess who is invoked in rites against hail. The Monguor of Kansu, China. (Schram, 1957: 85, 99)

Níaprúakálet   A wind demon who "causes insanity." The Cuna Indians, Panama. (Nordenskiold, 1930: 60–61)

Niarimamau?u   Wind Woman was most lustful. She stole Dove's son and kept him prisoner for years. He escaped with help from others and she was sealed up in a cave and became ?Aano?ovi, Echo. The Chemehuevis, California, Nevada, and Arizona. (Laird, 1976: 158–159)

nibənik'ska'sən   The northwest wind who, with the other winds, rules "human and animal destiny." The Penobscot, Maine. (Speck, 1935, 1: 21)

Niłch'i, ńłtči, Niltci, Niltsi   Wind counsels men, is a helpful deity who "represents the flute and other instruments. One of Wind's functions is to give life (motion)." He is "the means of communication between all elements of the living world"—provided thought, then words. Wind is one, a unity, but with numerous names and various aspects—some good, some bad—and reporting news without regard to good or bad effects. The winds are placed at the cardinal points at the horizon and the sacred mountains of the East, South, West, and North "to guard the earth. . . . to act as messengers for the" deities living there. The Navaho, Arizona and New Mexico. (Reichard, 1950: 497–499; Matthews, 1889: 91; Alexander, 1964: 158; McNeley, 1981: 1, 7–10, 16–18, 21)

niłch'i biyázhí, nłt'či biyájí   Wind's Child, Little Winds, Messenger Winds—singular/plural. The winds sent during one's lifetime which "are thought to provide the means of good Navajo thought and behavior"—as differentiated from the primary good wind provided at birth. These are frequently perceived to be at the earfolds (of people, Holy People, in sand paintings, etc.) giving knowledge, guidance, warning of dangers. The Navajo, Arizona. (McNeley, 1981: 36–9, 77; Reichard, 1950: 500)

niłchi'i diłhił, nltči diłxił Dark Wind—at the east cardinal point—is one of those who are the source of breath; one participating in giving life to Changing Woman and Talking God. Dark Wind is associated with Darkness and "Thus, the fact that bad things happen during Darkness is due to the Wind associated with it." Considered to cause foolishness and illness. The Navajo, Arizona. (McNeley, 1981: 18, 25, 29, 33, 51, 84; Reichard, 1950: 428)

niłch'i dootłizh Blue Wind, associated with the South, comes out of the blueness appearing at dawn; one of the winds by which they breathe. With Dark Wind went to the West and brought back corn and the epidermis of Changing Woman for the creation of the Earth Surface people. The Navajo, Arizona. (McNeley, 1981: 10, 18, 25, 26, 33, 67)

niłch'i łigai White Wind in the West. One of the winds who passed through Changing Woman's body to give her life; also to Talking God. The Navajo, Arizona. (McNeley, 1981: 18, 25, 71)

niłch'i łitso Yellow Wind in the North. One of the winds by which people breathe; placed within them to counsel. The Navajo, Arizona. (McNeley, 1981: 18, 25, 33, 71)

Nimbwi The whirlwind, a god who is the attendant of Umwa. The Jen, Nigeria. (Meek, 1931: 197)

Ninhar Sumerian god of "thunder and rainstorms" whose wife is Ninigara. Son of Ningal and Nanna. Near East. (Jacobsen, 1970: 26)

Ninurta Sumerian god of the south wind and of thundershowers. Near East. (Kramer, 1961: 96; Jacobsen, 1970: 8, 57)

Niptailaq God of the falling show. The Copper Eskimo, Canada. (Nungak and Arima, 1969: 114)

nłtči didjoli· Round Wind, a helpful deity. The Navaho, Arizona/New Mexico. (Reichard, 1950: 462)

nłtči diłxił Black Whirlwind—a pre-existent deity, one of the four primordial beings (in one creation myth). The San Carlos Apache. Arizona. (Goddard, 1918: 7)

ᵋnᵋnalanuxᵘdze "Great-Owner-of-the-Weather." The Kwakiutl, British Columbia. (Boas, 1966: 155)

Nochiu-e-ran-guru and **Nochiu-e-ran-mat** God and goddess of the air and of stellar bodies whose duty was "to attend to the shining and well-being of the stars." The Ainu, Japan. (Batchelor, 1925: 243)

Noho Chac Yum The head of the chac (rain) gods among the Lacandon (Mayan). Mexico. (Tozzer, 1941: 138)

Nohol Iq The south wind. The Maya of Cayo District, British Honduras. (Thompson, 1930: 108)

Norte The west wind. The Maya of the Cayo District, British Honduras. (Thompson, 1930: 108)

Norwan "she is that warm, dancing air which we see close to the earth in fine weather, and which is requisite for plant growth." The Wintu, California. (Curtin, 1903: 70)

Noter A maker of typhoons at Anu. Truk, Micronesia. (Kramer, 1932: 74)

Notos The god of the south wind usually brings rain. Greece. (Barthell, 1971: 52; Kerenyi, 1951: 205; Murray, 1935: 183)

Nous II God of air and fire, a demiurge sent forth by Nous I. Gnosticism. (Delcourt, 1961: 77)

Nts'ai hwa A sky goddess—"girl cloud"—who is invoked to bedim or blind the demons of illness and death in exorcising ceremonies. The Ch'uan Miao of Yunnan Province, China. (Graham, 1937: 74)

Nuitaiku A demon who is persuaded by the priests to remove his face (the Nuitaiku-mask) thereby causing rain. The Kagaba, Colombia. (Preuss, 1926: 73)

Nunanud A god of the winds whose wife is Inoltagon. The Ifugao, Philippines. (Barton, 1946: 61)

Ṇun-loki A sky god associated with rain and lightning, usually benevolent. The Bari, Sudan. (Seligman, 1931: 8)

Nuriel A Hebrew "god of hailstones." Near East. (Woodcock, 1953: 103)

Nuu mea lani The god in clouds. Hawaii. (Emerson, 1967: 51)

Nyakang The divine king, intermediary between man and Juok, is invoked for rain and is associated with the harvest festival. The Shilluk, Sudan. (Seligman, 1931: 4, 5, 11; Gelfand, 1966: 121)

Nyamia The supreme god is also "the god of storms, rain, clouds, lightning etc." The Guinea and Senegambia groups, West Africa. (Larousse, 1968: 483)

Nyanhehwe The chief tribal spirit of Kandeya Reserve is invoked for rain. The Shona, Rhodesia. (Gelfand, 1962: 3, 32)

Nyaro The god of thunder and lightning. The Ngaju, Borneo. (Scharer, 1963: 19)

Nyoṇmo, Nyoṇmo Tchawe God of abundant rain. The Ga, Ghana. (Parrinder, 1961: 16; Field, 1937: 61)

Nzalan The thunder. The Fang, Gabon. (Beier, 1966: 20)

Nzasi The thunder who has dogs and is a hunter. The Wachaga, Africa. (Werner, 1964: 237–238)

Oado A wind god. The Kushana, India. (Hinnells, 1973: 31)

Obumo The god of thunder controls the weather and the rain. Among some he was considered the supreme god and creator. The Ibibio, Nigeria. (Frazer, 1926: 127–128; Williams; 1936: 203)

Ochumare Goddess of the rainbow. Puerto Rico, West Indies. (Gonzalez-Wippler, 1975: 26)

Ocypete, Okypete One of the Harpies, human-headed birds, who were considered the goddesses of the storm winds. Greece. (Barthell, 1971: 12; Kerenyi, 1951: 62)

Odin A Scandinavian god of many aspects. As "the all-pervading spirit of the universe, the personification of the air," he was a god of the sky, of sunlight, of fair as well as violent winds, of storms. (Guerber, 1895: 23; Murray, 1935: 360–362; Stern, 1898: 17; Branston, 1955: 204)

Oghene The supreme being and creator gives them rain and expresses his anger in the thunder. The Isoko, Nigeria. (Welch, 1934: 163)

Ognaling The deity of the south wind. The Bukidnon, Philippines. (Jocano, 1969: 23)

Ogodo The god of thunder. A name of Shango in Porto-Alegre. Brazil. (Bastide, 1960: 291)

Ohob A Mayan rain god of Chenalho. Mexico. (Thompson, 1970: 290)

O-hsiu-lo A dragon god associated with fertilizing rains, with thunder and lightning. China. (Werner, 1932: 285–286; 336)

O-ikazuchi A thunder god who lived in the head of the dead Izanami. Japan. (Herbert, 1967: 274)

Okaga The god of the south and the south wind is warm and kind, generous and fearless. He gives good weather and presides over the production of foods. "His spirit is in the smoke of the sweetgrass." His messenger is the meadowlark, his color red. He is loved by Wohpe (Woope); is the fourth son of Tate, the wind. The Lakota, the Oglala, Plains Indians, South Dakota. (Powers, 1977: 72, 77, 79, 193; Jahner, 1977: 35; Walker, 1980: 72, 121, 127, 197, 221)

Okkupeernis A Slavic god of winds and storms. (Grimm, 1883, 2: 637)

Okparen A tribal deity of the Meitheis invoked for rain. Manipur, India. (Hodson, 1911: 108)

Oloesakinkuapipilel Chief of a city in the afterworld who with Olololelpanilel controls the thunder and sends the rain. The Cuna, Panama. (Nordenskiold, 1938: 309)

Oloesakuingapipiler "Rain god in the realm of the dead." The Cuna, Panama. (Nordenskiold, 1938: 327)

Ololelpanilel An associate of Oloesakinkuapipelel who with him controls the thunder and sends the rain. The Cuna, Panama. (Nordenskiold, 1938: 309)

Oloneylopaniler A god who determines when it shall rain. The Cuna, Panama. (Nordenskiold, 1938: 328)

Olonuptigile, Olonupdikili A daughter of Olopurguakuayai "who guards one of the water containers in the underworld" and is one of the rain demons who sends rain and floods. The Cuna, Panama. (Nordeskiold, 1938: 285, 329)

Olopurguakuayai The chief of the goddesses of rain. The Cuna, Panama. (Nordenskiold, 1938: 285, 330)

Oloyakkuplel In the Nele Tiegun chronicle the "Chief of the winds." The Cuna, Panama. (Nordenskiold, 1938: 331)

Oluga Goddess of thunder and lightning, of storms—the equivalent of Puluga and Biliku. Little Andaman

Island, Bay of Bengal. (Radcliffe-Brown, 1967: 151; Pettazzoni, 1956: 302)

Oma The "storm daemon Oma, with his enormous penis," takes part in the female puberty rites. The Tucuna, Brazil. (Zerries, 1968: 302)

Omowah (Tusayan), **Omowûh** (Hopi) The god of rain. Pueblo Indians, Arizona and New Mexico. (Emerson, 1894: 242, 253)

O-na-p'o-ta-to A dragon god who is "symbolic of fertile rain, rain-sending clouds, thunder and lightning." China. (Werner, 1932: 285–286)

Onditachiae The god of thunder, considered a bird, controlled the rains and winds. The Huron, Great Lakes area. (Tooker, 1964: 82)

Oonawieh (Oonawleh) Unggi The eldest of the wind gods. The Cherokee, North Carolina and Tennessee. (Brinton, 1868: 51; Bray, 1935: 273)

Guede l'Oraille Goddess of storm and of violent death. Haiti, West Indies. (Marcelin, 1950: 196)

Oreithyia The "gentle wind of spring," wife of Boreas, the north wind. Greece. (Fairbanks, 1907: 170)

Orre-orre God of the winds. Son of Tangaroa and Papa. The Society Islands, Polynesia. (Williamson, 1933: 59)

Osasero The "cloud bird" who brings the rain sent by Eschetewuarha. The Chamacoco of the Gran Chaco, Paraguay. (Zerries, 1968: 238)

Oshadagea The beneficent eagle god of the dew and moisture. The Iroquois, Huron, Eastern United States. (Alexander, 1964: 24; Larousse, 1968: 430)

Oshunmare, Oshumare The beneficent rainbow-serpent god. The Yoruba, Nigiera. In Brazil he has healing qualities and is identified with St. Bartholomew. (Lucas, 1948: 170; Landes, 1940: 266; Verger, 1957: 235–236; Bastide, 1960: 570)

O-we-ya-la-so The spirit (male) of the wind. The Delaware Indians, Eastern United States. (Morgan, 1959: 55)

oxuhwa "Cloud Beings." "The *oxuhwa* live below springs or lakes, in the hills or mountains, in the six directions. They are referred to by color, *oxuhwa tsqwe* (blue-green), for the north; *oxuhwa tseyi* (yellow), for the west; *oxuhwa pi'i̧* (red), for the south; *oxuhwa tse'yi* (white), for the east; *oxuhwa no̧hu̧we* (dark), for the zenith; *oxuhwa ta̧ma̧gi* (speckled, all colors), for the nadir." The oxuhwa bring the heavy rains. The Tewa, New Mexico. (Parsons, 1929: 268–269)

O'xwa t'u̧n yo̧n A "general name for the Chief Rain-god of either moiety"—the Winter and Summer people. He, like the others, is a bringer of rain and its accompanying fertility. The Tewa, San Juan, New Mexico. (Laski, 1958: 11)

Oya Goddess of the river Niger and a wife of Shango. She is also a wrathful goddess of storms. The Yoruba, Nigeria. In Cuba and Trinidad she is a goddess of winds and rain. In Brazil given as both male and female and also called Yansan. (Lucas, 1948: 98; Parrinder, 1949: 32–33; Meyerowitz, 1946: 26n; Idowu, 1962: 91; Simpson, 1965: 21; Verger, 1957: 230; 1954: 12, 15, Pl58, Pl59)

Oyandone "Moose, the east wind. He was called by Ga-oh into the sky to blow forth mists and chill from his nostrils, to lead the rains, and break down with his antlers great paths through the forests before storms." The Seneca, New York. (Leach, 1950, 2: 839)

Oye The dry sirroco wind of December and January deified. The Yoruba, Nigeria. (Lucas, 1948: 172; Parrinder, 1949: 55). In Puerto Rico the "Giant god of storms." (Gonzalez-Wippler, 1975: 26)

Padma mkha' 'gro ma A Tibetan goddess invoked for rainfall. (Nebesky-Wojkowitz, 1956, 1: 479)

Paetahi The "land breeze," messenger of Punua-pae-vai. Tahiti, Polynesia. (Henry, 1928: 377)

Pafa'ite The northwest wind. The Society Islands, Polynesia. (Henry, 1928: 364)

Pahikyit The rainbow is considered "to be a beautiful maiden." Also the name of the Morning Star. The Kitanemuk, California. (Hudson and Underhay, 1978: 82)

Pajan The thunder god who rules the clouds and the rain. The Mountain Lapps, Finnmarken and Finland. (Minn, 1955: 71–72)

Pakadringa The "man of the thunderstorms," a totemic person. The Tiwi, Melville Island, Australia. (Mountford, 1958: 37, 42)

Pákaprúakálet A wind demon who causes illness, causes delirium during which the person has visions relating to the sea. The Cuna, Panama. (Nordenskiold, 1930: 60–61)

dPal gyi pho nya las mkhan mo   A messenger goddess "who sends hail and lightning." Tibet. (Nebesky-Wojkowitz, 1956, 1: 303)

Palulukon   The plumed or horned water serpent was a god of fertility, of lightning and rain. The Hopi, Arizona. (Fewkes, 1897: 190; Alexander, 1964: 188; Tyler, 1964: 245)

Pana-ewa   A reptile/man of the forest who sent "fog and rain and wind" to cause people to lose their way. Hawaii. (Westervelt, 1963, 2: 98–99)

Panaiyoikyasi   "Short Rainbow"—a god of beneficent as well as malevolent powers who has "power over the atmosphere" during sunshine, over the earth during rain. The Hopi, Arizona. (Waters, 1963: 71, 75)

Panam Ningthou   A rain and weather god of the Meitheis. Manipur, India. (Hodson, 1908: 103)

Pa-nan-t'o   A dragon-king, a god of fertilizing rains, of thunder and lightning. China. (Werner, 1932: 285–286)

Pandahatan   With Bugang causes lightning and thunder by fighting. The Dusans, Borneo. (Stall, 1925: 945)

Pandrosos   A Greek goddess of dew and of agriculture. Sister of Herse and Aglauros, daughters of Cecrops. (Burns, 1925, 3: 373; Bethe, 1925, 1: 226; Crawley, 1925, 4: 700; Ruskin, 1869: 48)

Panyaroi Rawei   A spirit of the wind. The Ngaju, Borneo. (Scharer, 1963: 204)

Papakitera and **Papakiteua**   Together they control the weather. Tikopia, Polynesia. (Firth, 1967, 2: 208)

Papeekawis   Also called Yenaudizih. He was the god of winds and dancing, much loved and admired, but lonely. "Such was the violence of his dances that he created whirlwinds, breezes, gusts, gales (warm and cold), typhoons, hurricanes." Second of the four sons of Epingishmook. The Ojibway, Great Lakes Area. (Johnson, 1976: 153)

Parawera-nui   The "cold south wind." Wife of Tawhirimatea and the mother of the Wind children. The Maori, New Zealand. (Best, 1924: 152)

Parcuns, Percunus   Baltic god of thunder and rain. Prussia. (Welsford, 1925, 9: 488; Puhvel, 1974: 83)

Pare-arohi   She is "the personification of the quivering appearance of heated air, as seen in summer," which phenomenon is created by the dancing of Tane-rore. The Maori, New Zealand. (Best, 1924: 111, 120)

Parjanya   God of the rain, the clouds, thunder, of hurricanes. He sends the rains giving fertility and renewed life. He is sometimes confused with his father, Dyaus, and later had to cede his place and popularity to Indra. India. (Keith, 1917: 21, 37; Macdonell, 1895: 84; Barth, 1921: 14; Crooke, 1894: 33; O'Flaherty, 1980: 25, 26; Eliade, 1958: 83, 84)

Parom   The thunder god of the Slovaks. (Gimbutas, n.d.: 470)

Pate-hoc-hoo-weh   The spirit (male) of thunder. The Delaware Indians, Eastern United States. (Morgan, 1959: 55)

the Pauahs   Another group of four gods, each associated with a cardinal point and a color, with rain and wind, are understandably at times identified, or merged with the Chacs, the Bacabs. Mayan, Mexico. (Tozzer, 1941: 137; Thompson, 1970: 255)

Pavana   A Hindu god of the winds. India. (Coleman, 1832: 111)

Pawan Daseri   The god of the wind who impregnated Astangi Devi, the mother of Suraj and Chanda. The Agaria, India. (Elwin, 1949: 12, 58)

Pawekone   A minor thunder god of the Menomini Indians. Wisconsin. (Skinner, 1913: 74)

San Pedro the Martyr   The "Lord of Lightning." A cross placed on the door post ensures his protection of the house. The Indians call him Tatik Martil, and also identify him with Tatik Ca?uk. The Tzeltal, Mexico. (Nash, 1970: 13)

Pe-konchi-koro-guru   Benevolent god of rain. The Ainu, Japan. (Batchelor, 1925, 1: 243)

Ah Peku   The thunder god of the Lacandon, Mexico. (Thompson, 1970: 266)

Peṇ k'acinna   The "Deer Raingod who wears deer horns." A Summer Raingod and a bringer of rain and its accompanying fertility. The Tewa, San Juan, New Mexico. (Laski, 1958: 11)

Pepezu   The "Wind God who kidnapped men in the middle of the forest." The Yurakare of the western Matto Grosso, Bolivia. (Métraux, 1942: 12)

Peranu, Peraun The Bohemian god of thunder. (Grimm, 1880: 171; Bray, 1935: 46)

Percunatele A goddess, mother of the thunder. Slavic Poland. (Ralston, 1872: 91)

Perkons, Pehrkons The god of thunder. Latvia. (Grimm, 1880: 171; Gimbutas, n.d.: 466)

Perkunas The Baltic/Slavic god of thunder whose first peals in the spring revivify the earth and awaken her to growth. He is associated with the sacred oak and with the he-goat. He exorcises evil spirits and punishes wickedness. Also spelled Perkuno(s). Lithuania and Prussia. (Gimbutas, n.d.: 466–467, 470–474; Puhvel, 1974: 79; Davidson, 1964: 87; Grimm, 1880: 171; Ralston, 1872: 88)

Perkune Tete Baltic/Slavic mother of the thunder and lightning. (Machal, 1918: 319)

Peroon The god of thunder and lightning. Serbia. (Wallis, 1939: 22)

Perperuna The Balkan god of thunder. Same as Perkunas. (Gimbutas, n.d.: 470)

Persoq The god of the snowstorm. The Iglulik Eskimo. Canada. (Nungak and Arima, 1969: 114)

Perun, Perunu The Slavic god of thunder. He was identified with Parjanya in sending the rain and fertilizing the soil. He was associated with the he-goat and the axe. Oaths taken at treaties were sworn to by him. Many variant spellings. Russia and Czechoslovakia. (Ralston, 1872: 86–88; Gimbutas, 1971: 165–166; Schoeps, 1961: 119; Machal, 1918: 293–294; Welsford, 1925, 9: 252; Leach, 1950, 2: 1026)

Perušan The thunder god. Bulgaria. (Gimbutas, n.d.: 470)

Pethakoweyuk The Thunder Beings who had "the duty of watering the earth and protecting the people against Great Horned Water-serpents and other monsters." The Unami (Lenape) Indians, Eastern United States. (Harrington, 1921: 29)

(mae phra) phai A spirit of wind, both male and female. As a goddess invoked in pregnancy. Thai. (Hanks, 1965: 50)

Pheru A demon of the whirlwind. The Chamars, India. (Briggs, 1920: 134)

Phol A god of the Thuringians and Bavarians who is associated with the whirlwind. He seems to be identified with Paltar, Balder, and if so, must be considered a god of light as well. (Grimm, 1880: 220–228; 1883, 2: 632; 1883, 3: xix)

Pho-lio God of thunder who punishes evil. Kouy-tcheon, China. (Schotter, 1908: 422)

Picker, Piker, Pitkne, and variants The god of thunder is invoked for rain and for good crops. Esthonia. (MacCulloch, 1964: 229; Grimm, 1880: 176; de Kay, 1898: 34, 38)

Pidzu Pennu God of rain of the Kandh (Khond). India. (Crooke, 1925, 7: 649)

Piguerao With his brother Apocatequil (Catequil) the gods of thunder and lightning. He is represented as a bird—the ostrich. Peru. (Chamberlain, 1902: 288; Spence, 1925, 3: 504; Brinton, 1868: 153)

Pileswak The thunder spirits of the Minsi (Lenape) Indians. Eastern United States. (Harrington, 1921: 30)

Pillan The supreme god was also the god of thunder and of fire to whom was attributed lightning, earthquakes, and volcanic eruptions. The Araucanians. Among the Mapuche pillan fucha and pillan kushe are the "god and goddess of thunder or volcanoes." Also called tralkan fucha. His thunder, rain, earthquakes are controlled through propitiation. He is considered a minor Andean deity. Chile and Tierra del Fuego. (Alexander, 1920: 325–326; Osborne, 1968: 116; Cooper, 1946, 6: 745; Loeb, 1931: 545; Faron, 1968: 65, 66, 69)

P'i-lou-po-ch'a A dragon-king, a god "symbolic of fertile rain, rain-sending clouds, thunder and lightning." China. (Werner, 1932: 285–286)

Piorun Slavic god of thunder who sends the rain and fertilizes the earth. Poland. (Ralston, 1872: 86–88; Grimm, 1880: 171; Larousse, 1968: 294)

Piribi Deity of the storm, child of Tarai and Kot. The Aka-Jeru, Andaman Islands, Bay of Bengal. (Radcliffe-Brown, 1967: 193)

Piribri The god of rain lives in the cloud-shrouded mountain peaks and, if offended, causes torrential rains to endanger the traveller. There is a taboo of silence when there. The Jivaro, Ecuador. (Stirling, 1938: 116)

Pirthat Recho The god of thunder of the Mikirs. Assam. (Lyall, 1925, 8: 629)

Pitakamikokiu   Mother of the winds and daughter of Masakmekokiu. The Menomini, Wisconsin. (Skinner and Satterlee, 1915: 241–242)

Piwaruxti   The god of lightning who taught the use of fire-sticks. The Skidi Pawnee, Plains Indians, Nebraska. (Dorsey, 1904, 2: 8, 14)

the Pleiades   Daughters of Atlas and Pleione, sisters of the Hyades. Maia, Taygete, Electra, Alcyone, Celoeno, Merope, Sterope. They "foretold each year by their setting the season of rain and of fertility." Greece. (Fairbanks, 1907: 165; Murray, 1935: 171; Larousse, 1968: 144)

(p)mso'sən   The east wind and one of those ruling "human and animal destiny." The Penobscot, Maine. (Speck, 1935, 1: 21)

Podaga   God of the air of the Elbe Slavs. (Machal, 1918: 292, 355n44; Pettazzoni, 1956: 245)

Podarge   One of the Harpies, human-headed bird goddesses of the storm-winds and tempests. She was the wife of Zephyrus and daughter of Thaumas and Electra. Greece. (Murray, 1935: 218; Barthell, 1971: 11, 12, 51)

Poee-ura, Pue ura   Goddess of rain and of agriculture. East Torajas, Celebes, Indonesia. (Wales, 1957: 95; Downs, 1920: 23–24)

Pogoda   Slavic goddess, or god, of the weather. Also worshipped by agriculturalists. (Czaplicka, 1925, 11: 595; Grimm, 1883, 2: 637)

Pokoharua-te-po   Mother of the winds and storms whose first child was Hanui-o-rangi. First wife of Rangi. The Maori, New Zealand. (Andersen, 1928: 374)

Polednice   A female demon of the whirlwind. Slavic. (Grimm, 1883, 2: 633)

Porguini   The god of thunder of the Mordvins. Russia. (Grimm, 1880: 172)

Pountan   The "night breeze . . . at one and the same time he is a god and a hero." The Marianas, Melanesia. (Larousse, 1968: 454)

Pou-te-aniwaniwa   The female personification of the rainbow, the lower band. *See* **Kahuxura.** The Maori, New Zealand. (Best, 1924: 160–161)

Prahaku, Augiya   The god of the atmosphere and the wind causes hurricanes and floods destroying planta-tions and killing livestock. The Mosquito, Nicaragua and Honduras. (Conzemius, 1932: 126)

Prove, Proven   A god of the Wends with a sacred oak grove dedicated to him in the vicinity of Oldenburg. Possibly a variant name of Perun, the thunder god. (Gimbutas, 1971: 155; Pettazzoni, 1956: 245; Machal, 1918: 295)

Prsni   A goddess of the atmosphere—"perhaps the spotted storm-cloud." The mother of the Maruts by Rudra. India. (Keith, 1917: 39, 53)

pso'sən   The north wind which brings the cold and with the other winds figures in "human and animal destiny." The Penobscot, Maine. (Speck, 1935: 21)

Pua-i-taha   The blustering southwest gale. Son of Hakona-tipu. The Maori, New Zealand. (Andersen, 1928: 375; White, 1887, 1: 28)

Puefou   A god of drought. Niue Island, Polynesia. (Loeb, 1926, 1: 161)

P'u-kao-yun-ch'uang   One of the dragon kings who are responsible for fertilizing rains, for thunder and lightning. China. (Werner, 1932: 285–286)

Puli-ing   "Whistling of the Wind," a god of the winds of the Ifugao. Philippines. (Barton, 1946: 61)

Pulotu, Pulotu Katoa   A god of the weather who controlled hurricanes, rain and drought. Tonga, Polynesia. (Gifford, 1929: 301–302)

Puluga   The chief god who lives in the sky, created all good things, and is judge of the dead. He is a god of the winds, usually of fine weather, but sometimes of violent storms which he uses as punishment. Andaman Islands, Bay of Bengal. (Radcliffe-Brown, 1967: 147, 158–159; Pettazzoni, 1956: 301; Roheim, 1972: 8; Cipriani, 1966: 43)

Puok   The wind gods are destructive as a punitive measure. The Ifugao, Philippines. (Jocano, 1969: 18; Barton, 1955: 141)

Puok ud Daiya   "Strong Wind of the Upstream." The Ifugao, Philippines. (Barton, 1946: 34)

Puok ud Lagod   God of the "Wind of the Downstream Region." The Ifugao, Philippines. (Barton, 1946: 61)

Puok ud Nalamban   "Wind God of Nalamban," and a talisman-activating deity. The Ifugao, Philippines. (Barton, 1946: 78)

Pura The supreme god controls the elements and sends the rain. The Arikena (Carib), Brazilian Guiana. (Zerries, 1968: 243–244)

Purairomba A rain and weather god, and tribal deity of the Angom clan, a tribe of the Meitheis. Manipur, India. (Hodson, 1908: 99, 100, 103)

Purgine, Purgine-pas The god of thunder of the Erza and the Mordvins, invoked for rain and to withhold hail. Russia. (Paasonen, 1925, 8: 844; Pettazzoni, 1956: 256; Gimbutas, n.d.: 470)

P'u-yün-ta-shêng A dragon god of weather and rain, and atmospheric phenomena. China. (Werner, 1932: 285–286)

pwiya The rainbow-serpent of the Kyaka. New Guinea. (Bulmer, 1965: 153)

p'yag-na rdo-rje Tibetan god of rain, a celestial Bodhisattva. Same as Vajrapani. (Getty, 1962: 50)

'Pyag-rdor (Chag dor) The carrier of the thunderbolt is also a rain god. Same as Vajrapani. Western Tibet. (Ribbach, 1940: n.p.)

sPyan-ras-gzigs A mountain god, sometimes invoked in weather-making ceremonies. Identified with Avalokitesvara. Tibet. (Sierksma, 1966: 170; Nebesky-Wojkowitz, 1956, 1: 221, 468)

the P'yo Demons who create the clouds by blowing water into the sky from the ocean and from deep pools. The Karen, Burma. (Marshall, 1922: 231)

qaachehin The wind which comes along the shore—some areas from the northeast, in others from the west-southwest. The Chukchee, Siberia. (Bogoras, 1904/09: 321)

Qailertetang A female servant of Sedna who comes in the fall with good weather and "to make the soul of men calm like the sea." The Eskimo, Cumberland Sound, Baffin Island. (Boas, 1901: 140)

Qakimna A god of the air and of the weather. The Copper Eskimo, Canada. (Nungak and Arima, 1969: 114)

Qebui God of the north wind who is "depicted as a winged four-headed ram, or a winged human figure with four rams' heads." Egypt. (Knight, 1915: 133; Budge, 1969, 2: 295)

Qeralhin, qeyalhin (Koryak) The chief wind of the Chukchee. "In the Kolyma country it is the west wind; in the Chukchee Peninsula, the southwest wind. In both cases it is the most violent wind." Siberia. (Bogoras, 1904/09: 320)

Qorsagai Mergin A god of thunder, the third son of Qoqodai Megun Qubin. The Buriat, Siberia. (Curtin, 1909: 119)

q'otawic'a Grandmother of the Lake (Titicaca) who is associated with the rain and who, some consider, owns the fish. The Aymara, Bolivia. (Tschopik, 1951: 197, 200)

Qozah "was possibly at one time a god of storms." Arabia. (Noldeke, 1925: 660)

Quetzalcóatl The plumed serpent god was a god of the wind and as such was known as Echécatl and Chicunaui eecatl (Nine Wind). He was the planet Venus as the morning star to whom warriors were sacrificed to ensure its reappearance; the beneficent god of life and its cultures. Aztec, Mexico. (Caso, 1958: 14, 22–26; Vaillant, 1962: 143; Burland, 1967: x, 66; Spence, 1923: 117–118, 123, 234; Nicholson, 1967: 45)

Qugen Mergin A thunder god, the second son of Qoqodai Megun Qubin. The Buriat, Siberia. (Curtin, 1909: 119)

Quiateot The god of rain, of thunder and lightning. Son of Omeyateite and Omeyatecigoat. Nicaragua. (Lothrop, 1926: 68; Brinton, 1868: 131)

Quioquascacke A god of the Potomac invoked to control the rain—its lack or its excess. Children were sacrificed to him. Virginia. (Swanton, 1956: 743; McCary, 1979: 58)

Qurende Buqu Qubun A god of thunder, eldest son of Qoqodai Megun Qubin. The Buriat, Siberia. (Curtin, 1909: 119)

Ra The goddess of thunder and lightning of the Maguzawa. Wife of Gajimari. Nigeria. (Greenberg, 1946: 32)

Ra'a God of meteorology, of light rains. Son of Atea (or Te Tumu) and Papa (or Fa'ahotu) and husband of Tu-papa. Tahiti, Society Islands, Polynesia. (Henry, 1928: 160, 357; Buck, 1938: 83)

Rabegodona God of thunder of the Malagasy, Madagascar. (Ruud, 1960: 273)

Rahma A demon of the whirlwind. The Chamars, India. (Briggs, 1920: 134)

Raiden A god of thunder. Japan. (Piggott, 1969: 23)

Rain Spirit A supernatural created in the beginning whose function was to promote growth, but who willfully controlled growth or drought. The Cahuilla, California. (Bean, 1974: 167; Brumgardt and Bowles, 1981: 37)

Raka, Raka-maomao God of the winds and in some areas the father of the winds and storms. Polynesia: Mangaia, Mangareva, Rarotonga; New Zealand. (Williamson, 1933, 1: 13; Buck, 1938, 2: 62; 1938, 1: 426; Best, 1924: 152–153)

Raluvhimba The supreme being and god of the heavens controls all phenomena and so is the god of the rain and storms. The Venda and Shona, Transvaal/Southern Rhodesia. (Pettersson, 1953: 143, 193–194; Schapera, 1937: 264; Smith, 1950: 124–125)

Ramikabe The god of hail of the Malagasy. Madagascar. (Rudd, 1960: 273)

Ramman Assyro/Babylonian god of the weather—of rain, of storms, of thunder and lightning—both beneficent and destructive. He was represented as a bull; his consort was Shala. A god of many names: Adad, Rammanu, Ragimu, Murtazna, Ilhallabu, Murta'imu. Near East. (Jastrow, 1898: 159–161; Cook, 1930: 27; Wallis, 1939: 17; Hommel, 1925, 3: 75; Langdon, 1931: 39)

Ra-pati'a The god of the "Steady-blowing" wind which brings destruction. Society Islands, Polynesia. (Henry, 1928: 357)

Rartear Bilik A wind being of the A-Pucikwar. Andaman Islands, Bay of Bengal. (Radcliffe-Brown, 1967: 149)

Rautupu A deity who represents a form of thunder. The Maori, New Zealand. (Best, 1924: 175)

Ravarabe God of lightning of the Malagasy. Madagascar. (Ruud, 1960: 273)

Ravdna Goddess of thunder and wife of the thunder god. The Finnish Lapps. (MacCulloch, 1964: 230; Holmberg, 1925, 7: 799)

Rayos Lightning—worshipped at sites where it has struck. The Aymara, Bolivia. (Buechler and Buechler, 1971: 91)

Reshef, Resheph, Resh-pu A Syrian/Phoenician god of lightning and thunder who was also considered a god of war and of plague. He was introduced into Egypt as a god of war. Near East. (Herm, 1975: 111; Jayne, 1962: 132; Vriezen, 1963: 52; Macler, 1925, 12: 165; Albright, 1956: 79; Budge, 1969, 2: 280–282; Knight, 1915: 108)

Resim, Onun-pelien The spirit of the rainbow is considered "especially dangerous for seafarers" is also "a sign of death." Truk, Micronesia. (Bollig, 1927: 7, 12)

Ribimbi, Rivimbi The creator god of the Tonga taught them rainmaking. Mozambique. (Pettersson, 1953: 179)

Ribung Linti The "god of lightning and thunderstorms." The Sulod, Central Panay, Philippines. (Jocano, 1969: 19)

Ribut The wind carries the invitation to the spirits of Hades to attend the feast of sacrifice for the deceased. The Dyaks of Sarawak, Borneo. (Sarawak Gazette, 1963: 61; Howell, 1908/10: 39)

Rimmon, Ramman Assyro/Babylonian god of the atmosphere, the god of winds and storms, of thunder and lightning, of rain, for which he was invoked. He punished with inundations. Near East. (Sayce, 1898: 202–205, 209–210; Vriezen, 1963: 57)

Rimwa In Moro "means 'God,' 'rain.'" The Nuba Mountains, Sudan. (Stevenson, 1950: 215)

Rin chen mkha' 'gro ma A Tibetan goddess invoked for rainfall. (Nebesky-Wojkowitz, 1956, 1: 75, 479)

Rlung gi lha mo A deity of the wind. Tibet. (Nebesky-Wojkowitz, 1956, 1: 469)

Rlung gi lha mo Dam tshig sgrol ma A goddess of the wind invoked in pollution eliminating ceremonies. Tibet. (Nebesky-Wojkowitz, 1956, 1: 388)

Rongo With Uenga god of the wind Tokerau. Rarotonga, Polynesia. (Williamson, 1933, 1: 150)

Rongo-mai-tauira The god of lightning as well as of eels and the Will-o-the-wisp. The Moriori, Chatham Island, New Zealand. (Shand, 1894: 90)

Rouanuku The god of light breezes. Mangareva, Polynesia. (Williamson, 1933, 1: 151)

Rudra God of storms and winds and father of the Maruts. In his malevolent aspect he is destructive and brings death and disease. In his benevolent aspect he is helpful, a god of healing, and protector of flocks. India. (Jayne, 1962: 172–173; Dumézil, 1966, 2: 418–419; Cos, 1870, 2: 223; Ions, 1967: 23; Barth, 1921: 14; Bhattacharji, 1970: 112, 131; Danielou, 1964: 192–195)

Ryujin   A dragon god who controls the rain, the thunder, and wind, and is also a god of the sea. Japan. (Herbert, 1967: 482–483; Bunce, 1955: 112; Piggott, 1969: 14)

Saato   A god of fine weather who controlled the rain. Son of Fonge and Toafa, two stone deities. Samoa, Polynesia. (Turner, 1884: 25; Williamson, 1933, 1: 16)

Sadwes   The Manichean goddess of rain who manipulates all that comes from the clouds. Iran. (Dresden, 1961: 354)

Sagade Ugugun   The third spirit of Delquen Sagan Burkan who is invoked "for rain, good crops, and children." His wife is Sanqalin Qaten and they have seven sons and seven daughters. The Buriat, Siberia. (Curtin, 1909: 118)

Sagara   One of the dragon kings who are "symbolic of tile rain, rain-sending clouds, thunder and lightning." China. (Werner, 1932: 285–286)

Saga Wende   A rain deity, a manifestation of Wennam. The Mossi, Upper Volta. (Hammond, 1959: 246)

Saint Jean Baptiste   A god of thunder and lightning. Mirebalais, Haiti, West Indies. (Herskovits, 1937, 1: 281)

Sa'ir, Se'yr, Sa'yr, Su'ayr   A Palmyrene god of storms. Near East. (Fahd, 1968: 48–49)

Sakhil-Torum   A son of Kors-Torum and younger brother of Yanykh-Torum; he is sent to bring rain or good weather, as needed. He has a herd of reindeer in the clouds, laden with casks of water; when spilled, it rains. The Vogul, Siberia. (Czaplicka, 1969: 289)

Sak Iq   The "('white wind') is associated with the east." The Maya, Cayo District, British Honduras. (Thompson, 1930: 108)

Salaman   The god of thunder of the Nzema (Akan). Ghana. (Grottanelli, 1969: 376)

Salit   The lightning flash. The Tinguian in Ba-ay, Philippines. (Cole, 1922: 301)

Salulut Antu Ribut   The "Spirit of the Winds." The Dyak, Borneo. (Chadwick, 1930: 430)

Saman Qan Iq   The "north yellow wind." The Maya, Cayo District, British Honduras. (Thompson, 1930: 108)

Samé   A god who controlled the elements and storms and also taught the people agriculture and magic. Brazil. (Donnelly, 1949: 133)

Sangsang Angai   The god of the wind who breathed into the first two humans, giving them breath to live, but also at the same time "depositing in them the germs of death," thwarting the intention of Ranying Atala who meant to give them immortality. Borneo. (MacKenzie, 1930: 309)

Sangs rgyas mkha' 'gro ma   A goddess invoked for rainfall and "asked to deflect those obstacles against rainfall which are caused by planets and stars." Tibet. (Nebesky-Wojkowitz, 1956, 1: 479)

Santiago   A god of hail and lightning, yet he will also protect the crops. The Quechua, Peru. (Mishkin, 1946: 464)

Santo Frio   The chief of frost and ice. The Cuna Indians, Panama. (Keeler, 1960: 89)

Santo Tomas   He is responsible for bringing the rain. The Tzeltal, Mexico. (Nash, 1970: 45)

Sao'ch'ing Niang   Goddess of the sky, of fine weather, who sweeps the sky clear of clouds after rain, or gathers them in drought. China. (Werner, 1932: 406; Maspero, 1963: 272)

Sarameya(s)   God of the rising wind, of the storm, "who invented music, and conducts the souls of dead men to the house of Hades." Son of Sarama. Vedic India. (Fiske, 1872: 204; Larousse, 1968: 123)

Sarangan-sa-bagtiw   God of the storm. The Bisayan, Philippines. (Jocano, 1969: 20)

Saranjus   A goddess—possibly "the personification of the stormy thunder-cloud." India. (Oldenberg, 1896: 47)

Saranyu   Goddess of clouds, daughter of Tvashtri and wife of Vivasvat; mother of the Asvins. India. (Barth, 1921: 22; Danielou, 1964: 125; Larousse, 1968: 329)

Saru   An Assyrian wind god. Near East. (Sayce, 1898: 200)

Savacou   A Carib "who became a bird and later a star, was attributed control over the thunder and strong winds." The Callinago, Lesser Antilles, West Indies. (Rouse, 1948: 564)

sawaneson The south wind who, with the other winds, rules "human and animal destiny." The Penobscot, Maine. (Speck, 1935, 1: 21)

Sawina makiu "Red or Yellow Thunder"—a chief thunderer of the Menomini. Wisconsin. (Skinner, 1913: 75)

Sa'yatasha The "Rain God of the North" who is the high god of the Shalako festival. The Zuni, New Mexico. (Wilson, 1958: 374; Stevenson, 1901/02: 33)

sbang char zilbu The personification of the rain. Tibet. (Francke, 1925, 8: 78)

Semambu A demon who makes an unearthly and strange noise at night and is supposed to be "a weather guide." The Jakun, Malay Peninsula. (Skeat, 1906: 361)

Semargla Slavic "goddess of cold and frost." (Czaplicka, 1925, 11: 593)

Sendu Bir Dravidian "whistling god, whose voice announces the approaching storm." He causes wind, madness, burning houses and immorality. The Panjab, India. (Crooke, 1925, 5: 3)

Sentiu Guardian of the winds, a servant of Kari. Malay Peninsula. (Skeat, 1906: 178)

sənutsegadən God of the southwest wind which comes along the shore and brings terrible storms. With the other winds he rules "human and animal destiny." The Penobscot, Maine. (Speck, 1935: 21)

Serike God of the winds and the hurricane, yet helpful and beneficent to Indians. Costa Rica. (Stone, 1962: 59)

Set God of drought and the desert, of storms, of mist, of winds. He was the antithesis and adversary of Osiris; a god of evil, of darkness. He was the brother/husband of Nephthys, and associated with the planet Mercury. Egypt. (Budge, 1969, 2: 241, 244, 303; Ames, 1965: 64–65; Knight, 1915: 48, 107, 119; Larousse, 1968: 20)

Setekh A Semitic god adopted in Egypt as a god of war and of storm. He corresponds to Hadad, Teshub. (Cook, 1930: 44, 110)

Sevukulyingaxa Father of the Clouds and of the Rain. The Cagaba, the Kogi, Colombia. (Reichel-Dolmatoff, 1949/50: 115)

Shakemba, Kemba The giver of rain. The Ila, Zambia. (Mbiti, 1970, 2: 331)

Shango Yoruban god of thunder and lightning, of storms—a deified king. Nigeria/Haiti/Trinidad. In Brazil he is also a god of justice and is identified with various Catholic saints. (Idowu, 1962: 89–95; Parrinder, 1967: 72; Lucas, 1948: 98, 103; Meek, 1943: 112; Bastide, 1960: 91, 572; Costa Eduardo, 1948: 84; Verger, 1957: 305–311; Simpson, 1965: 19, 21; Courlander, 1966: 10)

Sharabu Amorite god of heat. Canaan, Near East. (Paton, 1925, 3: 181)

Shawano God of the south and a wind god with his brothers Wabun, Kabun, Kabibonokka. Algonquin Indians, North America. (Brinton, 1882: 45; Maclean, 1876: 432; Schoolcraft, 1857, 5: 409)

Shebui The "south wind, a winged lion-headed human figure." Egypt. (Knight, 1915: 133)

Shên Lung One of the dragon gods who are deities of the waters, the seas, the elements. China. (Werner, 1932: 285–286)

Shi acha A god of the sea, elder brother of Mo acha, who causes the storms and bad weather. The Ainu, Japan. (Batchelor, 1894: 20)

Shih Yüan-shuai The head of the Ministry of Thunder who rewarded good and punished evil. China. (Werner, 1932: 430)

Shinatsuhiko-no-Kami The god of the wind "who drives away the morning mists." Son of Izanagi and Izanami. Japan. (Yasumaro, 1965: 15; Kato, 1926: 15; Holtom, 1938: 111)

Shinatsuhime The goddess of the wind, female counterpart of Shinatsuhiko. Japan. (Herbert, 1967: 490; Holtom, 1938: 181; Kato, 1926: 15)

Shi-nish-e-ran-guru God of the air who inhabits the clouds and controls them. The Ainu, Japan. (Batchelor, 1925, 1: 243)

Shi-nish-e-ran-mat Goddess of the air and the clouds, wife of Shi-nish-e-ran-guru. The Ainu, Japan. (Batchelor, 1925, 1: 243)

Shi-wo-shi A deity who causes the rain. The Ch'iang at Lo-pu-chai, Szechwan, China. (Graham, 1958: 47)

Shotokunungwa A sky and star god who is also a god of lightning and of war—"who initiated the practice of scalping." The Hopi, Arizona. (Parsons, 1939: 178, 181, 184; Tyler, 1964: 81, 98, 101)

Shu   God of the atmosphere and of space, of light (both sunlight and moonlight), and of the dryness associated with the sun. Twin of Tefnut who is his female counterpart. He is god of the first hour of the day, of the first hour of the first day of the Moon; and of the first hour of the night of the thirteenth day of the Moon. Egypt. (Budge, 1969, 2: 87–90, 292, 302; Knight, 1915: 122–123; Ames, 1965: 30, 51)

Shukash   Deity of the whirlwind. The Klamath Indians, Oregon. (Chamberlain, 1892: 254)

Shun Fêng Ta Chi   "God of Favourable Winds" and patron of boatmen. China. (Day, 1940: 110, 166)

Shun I Fu-jên   "The Goddess of Drought (or Famine) and Flood." China. (Werner, 1932: 447)

Sieou Wen-ying   Chinese goddess of lightning and thunder. (Chavannes, n.d.: 29)

Sih'usus, Six?usus   The younger of the Two Thunders—(brothers). He is mischievous and his thunder is less violent. They are benevolent and bring the rains. In some myths Little Thunder is the son of Old Thunder. The Chumash, California. (Hudson and Underhay, 1978: 81, 84, 97, 154; Blackburn, 1975: 106–107)

Sila   God of the air, the weather, and among some, more broadly, their supreme being and god of the universe. The Alaska, Reindeer, Copper, Iglulik, and Caribou Eskimos. (Rasmussen, 1929: 62, 71; Eliade, 1964: 294; Lissner, 1961: 175; Jenness, 1970: 189; Nungak and Arima, 1969: 114; Lantis, 1947: 35)

Silagicsortoq   The spirit of the air who gives fair weather. When he punishes infractions he is known as Inerterisoq. Greenland. (Pettazzoni, 1956: 355)

Silili   A goddess of the atmosphere who is also that of theft. She is dangerous and kills people. Normanby Island, Papua and New Guinea. (Roheim, 1946: 325)

Simbi   God of the rains and of magicians. Haiti, West Indies. (Deren, 1953: 70, 117)

Sinai   One of the wind gods and a servant of Kari. Malay Peninsula. (Skeat, 1906: 207)

Sine Matanoginogi   A goddess of the atmosphere. Normanby Island, Papua and New Guinea. (Roheim, 1946: 325)

Sio Humis   A rain spirit of the Hopi Indians, Arizona. (Burland, 1965: 150)

Snior   Norse god of snow and ice, and son of Kari. Father of Fonn, Drifa, and Mioll, goddesses of the show, and of a son, Thorri. (Grimm, 1883, 2: 631, 883)

Snuskeluts   Personified Cold, an anthropomorphic being. The Bella Coola Indians, British Columbia. (McIlwraith, 1948, 1: 43)

Snutsiaxwanem   A supernatural male who causes whirlwinds. The Bella Coola Indians, British Columbia. (McIlwraith, 1948, 2: 236)

So, Sogbo   An androgynous deity, child of Mawu-Lisa, and the deity of atmospheric phenomena. Mother of the thunder pantheon of deities. He/she is a god of judgment and justice, punitive but also benevolent in giving fertility to humans and fields. An earlier name—Xevioso. The Ewe and Fon, Dahomey. (Herskovits, 1938, 2: 129, 150–151; Williams, 1936: 168; Parrinder, 1949: 31–32)

Sobo   God of meteorological phenomena, particularly of thunder. In Plaisance he is also a god of war as well as of healing. In Mirebalais he is symbolized by the ram. Sometimes in Brazil named as a goddess. Haiti and Brazil. (Marcelin, 1950: 111–112; Herskovits, 1937, 1: 316; Costa Eduardo, 1948: 78–79; Bastide, 1960: 572)

So-chia-lo and **So-chieh-lo**   Two dragon kings—gods of the seas and of fresh waters who are "symbolic of fertile rain, rain-sending clouds, thunder and lightning." China. (Werner, 1932: 285–286, 449)

Songela   A thunder demon who destroys plants by lightning. The Kagaba, Colombia. (Preuss, 1926: 82)

Soteknani   The sky god who provides rain and fertility. The Hopi, Arizona. (Tyler, 1964: 100)

Sovota, Sovon   God of the southwest who controls thunder and brings rain and warm weather. The Cheyenne, Montana and Dakotas. (Powell, 1969: 436)

Spenjaɣrya   The "deity of the whistling, roaring wind, whether with or without rain." Iran. (Gray, 1930: 214)

S'ps'   The "Cold Wind," an anthropomorphic being, whose wife is Atata. The Bella Coola, British Columbia. (McIlwraith, 1948, 1: 43)

Spulviero, Spolviero   Etruscan evil spirit of wind and of tempest. Italy. (Leland, 1963: 79)

Sqwlaltua   Personified Heat, an anthropomorphic being. The Bella Coola, British Columbia. (McIlwraith, 1948, 1: 43)

Ssuawakwak God of the winds who caused thunder. Bolivia and Brazil. (Metraux, 1942: 151; Levi-Strauss, 1948, 1: 379)

Steropes The lightning flash. One of the Cyclopes, son of Uranus and Gaea. Greece. (Fairbanks, 1907: 67; Larousse, 1968: 89, 129)

Stribog Slavonic/Russian god of cold and frost, sometimes the god of winds, sometimes the grandfather of the winds. (Machal, 1918: 301; Grimm, 1883, 2: 631; Czaplicka, 1925, 11: 593; Ralston, 1872: 102; Gimbutas, 1971: 164)

Suepate The trade wind. Efate Island, New Hebrides, Melanesia. (MacKenzie, 1930: 125)

Sugawara The chief of the thunder demons. Japan. (Hori, 1968: 115)

Sumiwowo Little Fog, son of Old Fog. In some myths he is the son of Thunder. The Chumash, California. (Blackburn, 1975: 106)

Summanus An Italian deity of the night sky and god of nocturnal thunder and lightning, similar to Jupiter of the daytime. (Dumézil, 1966, 1: 200; Stewart, 1960: 37; Larousse, 1968: 203)

Susa-no-Wo, Susano-O-no-Mikoto God of storms, of rain and winds. He was assigned to rule over the plains of the sea but preferred to dwell with his mother in the netherworld. Brother of Amaterasu. Japan. (Yasumaro, 1928: 23, 28; Kato, 1926: 15; Holtom, 1935: 81, 109; Haydon, 1941: 200–201)

Susna Deity of drought. India. (Gray, 1930: 225)

Su'u padax The whirlwind spirit/god of the north. The eastern Pomo, California. (Loeb, 1926, 2: 300; Barrett, 1917: 424)

Tak Suwau The younger of two snake brothers (with Tak Tahi) who form the rainbow. His youngest child was the source of rice. The Kintok Bong, Malaya. (Evans, 1937: 167)

Suzaubañ The rainbow, a female demon, who was charged by Gauteóvañ with "the task of devouring all sicknesses." The Kagaba, Colombia. (Preuss, 1926: 65)

Sxk'lätl The "supernatural South Wind of winter who brings storm and snow." The Bella Coola, British Columbia. (McIlwraith, 1948, 1: 44)

Szelanya The mother of the winds. Hungarian. (Szabo, 1925, 6: 873)

Szelkiraly The king of the winds to whom they are subject. Hungarian. (Szabo, 1925, 6: 873)

Szu Hai Lung Wang A dragon-king, a god of the rain. China. (Day, 1940: 209)

Taakwic "Ball Lightning"—son of Tuukumit and Tamaayawut. The Acagchemem, San Juan Capistrano, California. (Boscana, 1933: 180–182)

Tabatzi The god of the morning star is also that of the wind. The Cora Indians, Jalisco, Mexico. (Seler, 1925, 6: 829)

Tafito A god of Fangarere appealed to for control of storms and of wind, particularly the east wind. Tikopia, Polynesia. (Firth, 1967, 2: 106, 330)

Tagaloa fafao A rainbow god "implored to counteract the influence of Tagaloa-motumotu" who is a god of bad luck. Niue, Polynesia. (Loeb, 1926, 1: 162)

Tagaloa fakaolo A rainbow god—when it is very bright, which is a good sign. Niue, Polynesia. (Loeb, 1926, 1: 162)

Tagaloambung The "deity of eastwind." The Bukidnon, Mindanao, Philippines. (Jocano, 1969: 23)

Tagaloamotumotu "(Spotted-rainbow) . . . god of bad luck." Also given as the wife of the god Kalua. Niue, Polynesia. (Loeb, 1926, 1: 162)

Tagaloa tatai (1) "(Near-rainbow), younger brother of Tagaloa fakaolo with the same functions." (2) Also given as a wife of the god Kolua. Niue, Polynesia. (Loeb, 1926, 1: 162)

Tagbanua The "god of rain and supervisor of forest divinities . . . very kind . . . if respected but most ferocious when aroused." The Manobo, Philippines. (Jocano, 1969: 22–23)

Tak Tahi The elder of two snake brothers (with Tak Suwau) who together form the rainbow. The Kintak Bong, Malaya. (Evans, 1937: 167)

Tahu-makaka-nui The personification of the west wind. The Maori, New Zealand. (Best, 1924: 153)

Tahu-mawake-nui The personification of the west wind. The Maori, New Zealand. (Best, 1924: 153)

Tairibu   A goddess of the atmosphere who with Verom-atautoru controlled all the winds and storms which were used as punishment for neglect of the gods. Society Islands, Polynesia. (Ellis, 1853: 329–330)

Tajin   God of rain, or waters, and of the thunderstorm. The Totonacs, Mexico. Same as Tlaloc. (Caso, 1958: 41; Peredo, 1974: 19; Krickeberg, 1968: 24; Nicholson, 1967: 98)

Takamesao   A thunder god of the Menomini Indians. Wisconsin. (Skinner, 1913: 75)

Taka-Okami   A dragon god of rain and of the mountain tops. Japan. (Holtom, 1938: 96; Kato, 1926: 15; Herbert, 1967: 481)

Takatsu-Kami   A Shinto god of thunder. Japan. (Kato, 1926: 15)

Take-mika-dzuchi-no-Wo-no-Kami   A god of war who is also considered a god of thunder. Also called Takefutsu-no-Kami or Toyofutsu-no-Kami. He is again considered a chthonic deity and a god of earthquakes. Japan. (Revon, 1925, 9: 237–238; Holtom, 1938: 105, 177; Yasumaro, 1965: 18–19)

Takiong   A deity who fights with the great snake in the sky to make him release the rains. The fight causes the thunder; his weapon is the lightning. The Adi, Northeastern India. (Chowdhury, 1971: 38)

Taknokwunu   The "spirit who controls the weather." The Fire Clan, Hopi, Arizona. (Waters, 1963: 53)

Takshaka   A dragon-king, god of the seas and fresh waters, of rains and clouds, of thunder and lightning. China. (Werner, 1932: 185–186)

Taliaitupon   A god invoked to stop the hurricane. Tongatabu Islands, Tonga, Polynesia. (Gifford, 1929: 301)

Talitonganuku   God of "waterspouts and whirlwinds." Puka-puka, Polynesia. (Beaglehole, 1938: 312)

Tallai, Talliya   Goddess of the dew, of rain. A daughter of Baal. Canaan, Near East. (Ferm, 1950: 129; Gordon, 1961: 196)

Tama   The thunder deity was a culture hero/shaman and "is associated with lightning, rain, and the rainbow." The Paez, Colombia. (Reichel-Dolmatoff, 1975: 51, 53)

Tamagastad   The god of rain of the Pipil was their chief deity and was considered the son of Omayateite and Omeyacigoat. Nicaragua. (Krickeberg, 1968: 81)

Tama-te-uira   The personification of forked lightning, one of the gods who control the elements. The Maori, New Zealand. (Best, 1924: 99, 105, 161)

Tamats   The god of the morning star is also the god of the wind and messenger of the gods. The Huichol, Jalisco, Mexico. Same as Tabatzi (the Cora). (Seler, 1925, 6: 829; Alexander, 1920: 122)

Tamukujen, Tamukuyen   The omnipresent and omniscient high god of the Didinga is also associated with the rain and the rain-cult. Ethiopia and Sudan. (Cerulli, 1956: 79; Pettazzoni, 1956: 38–39; Mbiti, 1970, 2: 138)

Tana-oa   God of the winds and the sea, of fishing. The Marquesas, Polynesia. (Buck, 1938: 151; Handy, 1923: 245–246)

Tanara   God of thunder of the Yakuts. Siberia. (Grimm, 1888: 1338)

Tanaros, Tanarus   A local thunder god identified with Jupiter. Britain and Gaul. (Davidson, 1964: 86; Ferguson, 1970: 213; Bertrand, 1897: 331)

Tane-hetiri   A thunder god, brother of Pele. Hawaii. (Henry, 1928: 576)

Tane-matua   The personification of "thunder unaccompanied by rain." Father/husband of Hine-titama; their daughter is Hine-rau-wharangi. The Maori, New Zealand. (Best, 1924: 116, 175)

Tane-rore   Son of Hine-raumati and the sun. His dancing creates the hot shimmering air of midsummer which is personified by Pare-arohi. The Maori, New Zealand. (Best, 1924: 111)

Tanganggoa   A malicious god who causes lightning; the servant of Te Hainggi-atua. Rennell Island, Polynesia. (Birket-Smith, 1956: 23)

Tangiia   God of the wind *Muri* and a son of Vatea. Mangaia, Polynesia. (Williamson, 1933, 1: 14, 150)

the Tannan   The thunder people of the Quapaw Indians. Arkansas. (Baird, 1980: 17)

Tanuhatzqu   God of lightning. The Lacandon, Mexico. (Cline, 1944: 112)

Tanupekqu   The god of thunder who announces the coming of rain. The Lacandon, Mexico. (Cline, 1944: 112)

Taoitia-pae-kohu   The name means to cover the hills with fog. An evil offspring of Raki. New Zealand. (White, 1887, 1: 19)

T'ao T'ien Chün   A god of rain, under Lei Tsu. China. (Werner, 1934: 198)

Tapakaumatagi   The god of the winds. Niue Island, Polynesia. (Loeb, 1926, 1: 162)

Ta Pedn, Tapern   The supreme being among some Negrito tribes is the sky and weather god, of thunder and lightning. His relationships and identifications are varied. Malaya. (Evans, 1937: 152–153; Pettazzoni, 1956: 310, 324–340; Shryock, 1931: 337, 340)

Tarai   A wind and storm god associated with the southwest monsoon, with thunder and lightning, the rains. Andaman Islands. Among the Semang of Malaysia sometimes male and the husband of Biliku, other times female and the wife of Biliku or his daughter. (Radcliffe-Brown, 1967: 147–151; Roheim, 1971: 38, 43–44; Cole, 1945: 76)

Taranis, Taranucus, Taranus   Celtic god of thunder to whom the heads of the slain were dedicated or human sacrifices were made by burning. He was identified with Jupiter. Gaul. (Ross, 1967: 66, 136; Anwyl, 1906: 38, 40; Renel, 1906: 404; MacCulloch, 1911: 234; Mac-Cana, 1970: 31)

Taru, Tarhund, Tarhunt   Hattic/Hittite/Luwian weather and storm god whose wife was Wurusemu, daughter Mezzulla, granddaughter Zintuhi. Near East. (Ferm, 1950: 88, 92; Guterbock, 1961: 149; Gurney, 1952: 138; Oldenburg, 1969: 64)

Tate   The Wind or the Atmosphere. "He gave to all the mysterious people their *ton* (influence, or power, . . .)" and "gives his spirit to the sage. The smoke of the sage is strong, and all evil spirits fear it. . . . will fly from it." Tate married Ite. They are the parents of the four winds (at one birth)—Yata, Iya, Yanpa, Okaga—and of Yum, the whirlwind. Ite was unfaithful to Tate, but he so loved her that Skan let him and his sons remain on the world to be near her, the winds, and the cardinal points. The Lakota/Oglala, Plains Indians. South Dakota. (Walker, 1980: 50–54, 99, 127; Jahner, 1977: 35; Pettazzoni, 1956: 384)

Tate Hautse Kupuri   "Mother North-Water" who brings rain and fog from the north and "to whom belong the corn, squashes, beans, flowers, cattle, mules, horses, and sheep." She is a "yellow serpent." The Huichol, Jalisco, Mexico. (Chamberlain, 1900: 306; Seler, 1925, 6: 829)

Tate Kyewimoka   "Mother West-Water"—"a white serpent" who brings rain from the west and "to whom belong deer, corn, and the raven." The Huichol Indians, Jalisco, Mexico. (Seler, 1925, 6: 829; Chamberlain, 1900: 305–306)

Tate Naaliwami   A red serpent goddess of water and rain who wields the lightning and brings the rain from the east. She owns the "cattle, mules, and horses." The Huichol, Jalisco, Mexico. (Chamberlain, 1900: 305; Seler, 1925, 6: 829)

Tate Rapawiyema   "Mother South-Water" and the blue serpent goddess of the rain from the south. She is goddess of the seed-corn. The Huichol, Jalisco, Mexico. (Seler, 1925, 6: 829; Chamberlain, 1900: 306)

Tatetob   A name applied to the Four Winds as One. The Oglala, South Dakota. *See also* **Wani.** (Powers, 1977: 54)

Tatsuta-Hiko and **Tatsuta-Hime**   The god and goddess of the wind invoked for good harvest and worshipped by sailors and fishermen. She was also the goddess of autumn. Japan. (Larousse, 1968: 416; Anesaki, 1937: 234)

Tau-Katau   God of the rain and of the breadfruit tree. Ponape, Caroline Islands, Micronesia. (Christian, 1899: 384)

Tauna   An evil stellar god who created storms and wielded the destructive lightning. Guiana. (Levi-Strauss, 1969: 231)

Tawhaki   God of thunder and lightning and of clouds. New Zealand. (Best, 1924: 161; Andersen, 1928: 173; Larousse, 1968: 449)

Tawhiri-matea   God of the northwest wind and father of the winds and storms. His wife was Parawera-nui, mother of the wind children. The Maori, New Zealand. (Best, 1924: 152, 237; Andersen, 1928: 367, 375; Grey, 1855: 2; White, 1887, 1: 24, 28)

Tawhiri-rangi   A personification of the wind, in one of its aspects. Son of Papa and Rangi. The Maori, New Zealand. (Best, 1924: 152)

Tcenes   The god of thunder was the foremost of the two original beings (He and Nagaicho). He was the "creator of men, many animals, mountains, trees, and springs." The Kato, California. (Kroeber, 1925: 155; Loeb, 1932: 14, 23)

Tciwetənəc The west wind personified. The Naskapi, Labrador. (Speck, 1935: 62)

Tciwetinowinu The spirit of the north wind and of winter, one of the winds "as spirits of the four quarters-forces controlling the universe; the life and growth of man and of animal and plant life." The Naskapi, Labrador. (Speck, 1935: 56, 63)

Tcuwut Makai "Earth Magician (medicine-man or doctor) . . . governs the winds, the rains, etc." The Pima, Arizona and Mexico. (Russell, 1904/05: 251)

Te Alongaoa God of the winds, the south wind, and the seas. Pukapuka, Polynesia. (Beaglehole, 1938: 311–312)

Te Atua Vaelua God of the north wind, one of those controlling the winds and the seas. Pukapuka, Polynesia. (Beaglehole, 1938: 311–312)

Te Awuawu God of the east wind who helps control the winds and the seas. Pukapuka, Polynesia. (Beaglehole, 1938: 311–312)

Tê-ch'a-ch'ia One of the dragon kings, gods of the waters, the rains, the thunder and lightning. China. (Werner, 1932: 285–286)

Te-fatu-tiri A great god of thunder. Tahiti, Polynesia. (Henry, 1928: 376)

Tefnut A lion goddess—"the personification of the moisture of the sky. . . . a goddess of gentle rain and soft wind." She is the female counterpart of Shu, but was also associated at one time with a god Tefen. She is named as the goddess of the second hour of the night of the fourteenth day of the Moon. Egypt. (Budge, 1969, 2: 87–88, 92, 292; Knight, 1915: 125; Larousse, 1968: 13)

Te Hainggi-atua The supreme god as well as the god of thunder. First fruit offerings are made to him of taro and yams. His wife is Mauloko and Tanganggoa is his servant. Rennell Island, Polynesia. (Birket-Smith, 1956: 22–23, 59)

Teisbas, Theispas The god of the air and of the weather forms a triad with Khaldis and Ardinis. The Urartians, Armenaia. (Sayce, 1925, 1: 793; Ananikian, 1964: 11; Cook, 1930: 27; Leach, 1950, 2: 576)

Tekarpada A much worshipped goddess of Formosa whose voice is the thunder "when she scolds her husband for not sending sufficient rain on the earth." (Campbell, 1925, 6: 84)

Tenauka The wind spirit captured the souls of men in daylight hours "and caused death and disease." But on some he conferred the power to heal. The Cahuilla, California. (Bean, 1974: 167; Brumgardt and Bowles, 1981: 37–38)

Teng The "specific name of the Chief Winter Rain-god," a bringer of rain and its accompanying fertility. The Tewa, San Juan, New Mexico. (Laski, 1958: 11)

Teŋo o·xwa A rain god of the Summer people, a bringer of rain and its accompanying fertility. The Tewa, San Juan, New Mexico. (Laski, 1958: 11)

Teocuicani "Divine Singer"—a hill, to which sacrifices are made, adjacent to the volcano Popocatzin. From the clouds around it (due to the volcano) "it gives forth terrible thunder and lightning, so resonant and echoing that it is awesome to hear." The Aztec, Mexico. (Duran, 1971: 257)

Teriya The god of the southwest wind. Sometimes the husband, sometimes the son of Biliku. The A-Pucikwar, Andaman Islands, Bay of Bengal. (Radcliffe-Brown, 1967: 147, 151)

Teshub, Teshup Hurrian/Hittite/Elamite god of the weather and of tempests and giver of rain. His wife was Hebat; his animal, the bull. Near East. (Cook, 1930: 27; Van Buren, 1943: 83; Gurney, 1952: 135; Larousse, 1968: 72, 84; James, 1960: 75, 93)

Te Tonusanga The name of Te Hainggi-atua as the god of thunder. Rennell Island, Polynesia. (Birket-Smith, 1956: 23)

Tetzahuitl, Tetzauhpilli A god of rain worshipped at Cuauhilama, Valley of Anahuac, Mexico. (Reed, 1966: 112)

Te Uira The personification of lightning. Same as Kahuila-o-ka-lani (Hawaii), Te Uira-o-te-Rangi (Maori), Te Kanapu. Polynesia. (Andersen, 1928: 157; White, 1887, 1: 54)

Teu Kweh The goddess of the rainbow of the east. Wife of Hku Te. The Karen, Burma. (Marshall, 1922: 223, 228)

Tezcatlipoca Omniscient and omnipresent god of the Smoking Mirror, a deity of numerous aspects, among them that of a god of "drought, famine, barrenness in the seasons, and plagues." He was a god of darkness—"of the storm of the night." Aztec, Mexico. (Brinton, 1882: 69, 72; Duran, 1971: 110; Spence, 1923: 103; Vaillant, 1962: 142–143)

Thams cad mkha' 'gro ma A goddess invoked for rainfall. Tibet. (Nebesky-Wojkowitz, 1956, 1: 479)

Ong Thoi The Annamese god of the wind. (Cabaton, 1925, 1: 541)

Thonapa A weather and thunder god of the Aymara. Bolivia. Same as Ilyap'a. (Rowe, 1946: 295n)

Thor The red-bearded Scandinavian god of thunder whose attributes were his hammer Mjollnir (the thunder-bolt), Megingjarpar his strength-giving belt, and his gauntlets with which he wielded his hammer. He was destructive with his lightning and in his fighting, but a great benefactor in giving fertility to the earth with the rains, and as protector of the household and of marriages. He was not allowed to cross the bridge Bifrost because of his great weight or the danger from his lightning, and must go around. He was the son of Odin and Jord; as the husband of Iarnsaxa the father of Magni and Modi; as the husband of Sif the father of Lorride and Thrud. (Thorpe, 1851: 21, 22; Guerber, 1895: 21, 43, 64; Davidson, 1964: 84; Murray, 1935: 363–365; Wagner, 1882: 123–124; Snorri Sturluson-Young, 1964: 50, 51)

Thora The great spirit of the Kalahari Bushmen seems to be predominantly beneficent providing rains, abundance of food, and good hunting, though he is also responsible for bad weather, thunder, and famine. Botswana. (Pettazzoni, 1956: 32; Schapera, 1951: 185; Smith, 1950: 90)

Thorri A Norse god of the snow and ice. Son of Snior. (Grimm, 1883, 2: 631)

Thraetaona A god who "has been interpreted as a wind-deity." But in being identified with Thrita he is considered a god of healing. Iran. (Jayne, 1962: 194)

Thrym A mountain and frost giant, god of the thunderstorm. He stole Thor's hammer using it to bargain for Freyja. Scandinavia. (Guerber, 1895: 77; Anderson, 1891: 460; Stern, 1898: 120)

Thugine The rainbow spirit of the Bunya-Bunya. Queensland, Australia. (Howitt, 1904: 431)

Thunar, Donar The Germanic god of the weather is a wrathful and angry god, yet in his peaceful aspect he is a fatherly god of law and order, of landmarks and of marriages. (Grimm, 1880: 166–169; Wagner, 1882: 8, 9)

Thunor A god of thunder and the weather, and also of agricultural fertility. England. (Branston, 1957: 30, 105, 115; Davidson, 1964: 83)

Tien Mu Niang Niang Goddess of lightning who causes fires and produces the flashes with mirrors. China. (Day, 1940: 71; Larousse, 1968: 384; Maspero, 1963: 275)

Tiermes The god of thunder is much worshipped and is believed to have "power over life and death" and over man's health. The Lapps, Northern Europe. (Karsten, 1955: 26, 29; Dioszegi, 1968: 28; MacCulloch, 1964: 218)

Tiipa "(a family god of the Pomare kings) . . . who was supposed to preside over the winds." Tahiti, Polynesia. (Williamson, 1933, 1: 142)

Tilo A remote and evil god of the heavens associated with thunder and storms and rains. He has power over life and death and afflicts with diseases and twin births. The Tonga, South Africa and Mozambique. (Schapera, 1937: 263; Pettersson, 1953: 180, 189, 191; Junod, 1962: 429, 446; Smith, 1950: 113–114; Mbiti, 1970, 2: 80, 335)

Tini The rainbow in the east, twin brother of Mawali (that in the west). They brought about the annihilating flood saving only two girls as their companions. If he is looked in the eye a man becomes so clumsy as to injure himself. The Katawishi, Brazil. (Levi-Strauss, 1969: 247)

Tinia, Tin, Tina The most powerful Etruscan god who ruled over the northeastern segments of the cosmos. His wife was Uni. Other gods could hurl thunderbolts but only from certain directions, while Tinia could hurl them from any part of the heavens. He was the equivalent of Zeus and Jupiter. Italy. (Hamblin, 1975: 92–93; Pallottino, 1975: 145; von Vacano, 1960: 19, 21; Dumezil, 1966, 1: 188)

Tioroa Like Tonga-nui-kaea personifies "ice, snow and hail." The Maori, New Zealand. (Best, 1924: 175)

Tipdak A god of the winds. The Ifugao, Philippines. (Barton, 1946: 61)

Tiptaibitum The spirit of rain which also brings stormy winds with the rain. The Mundurucu, Para, Brazil. (Murphy, 1958: 21)

Tirmes God of thunder of the Lapps of Kola Peninsula. Russia. (Collinder, 1949: 140; Karsten, 1955: 26)

Tishtrya A stellar god, Sirius, who is associated with the rains of fertility and of purification, bringing abundance and healing to all. Iran. (Ananikian, 1925, 1: 798;

Jackson, 1925, 12: 86; Huart, 1963: 42; Jayne, 1962: 195)

Tiu   A wind god who with his father Tawhiri-matea rules the northwest wind. They are the chief wind gods. Father of Hine-i-tapapauta. The Maori, New Zealand. (Andersen, 1928: 375; White, 1887, 1: 24, 28)

Ti'yo Ta'lawi'piki   "yellow snake lightning"—male. The Walpi, Arizona. (Tyler, 1964: 235)

Tjitjara, Aukulia   The rainbow, "the son of the rain" who wants to interfere with it, and has to be "sung" to go away and let it continue raining. The Kaitish, Central Australia. (Spencer, 1904: 630)

t'kelam's n   "cold wind"—one of those who rules "human and animal destiny." The Penobscot, Maine. (Speck, 1935, 1: 21)

T'kul   The spirit of the winds. Coastal Indians, Alaska and British Columbia. (Niblack, 1888: 323)

Tlallíchcatl   The name of Ometéotl "As master of the clouds and heavens over the earth." Aztec, Mexico. (León-Portilla, 1982: 98)

Tlaloc   God of the rain particularly, and of weather generally. In most areas beneficent and a god of growth and vegetation. But in the north he represents the destructive elements of the rain and weather. His wives are variously given as Xochiquetzal, or Matlalcueitl, or Chalchiuhtlicue. Aztec/Olmec. Known also in other areas as Chac (Mayan), Tajin (Totonacs), Cocijo (Mixtecs). Mexico. (Caso, 1958: 41–43; Duran, 1971: 154–155; Spence, 1923: 235–238; Vaillant, 1962: 139–145)

Toafa   *See* **Fonge**

Toahim Makai   A god of thunder. The Pima, Arizona and Mexico. (Russell, 1904/05: 251)

Tobǝkin   A god, the four winds, the messenger of all the gods. The Oglala, South Dakota. (Powers, 1977: 54)

Toerau-ma-ra'i-moana   "North-wind-with-clear-sky," child of Ra-ta'iri and Te-muri. Society Islands, Polynesia. (Henry, 1928: 364)

Tohe Tika, Toutika, Toho-Tika   God of thunder and of violent rains. The Marquesas, Cook Islands, Polynesia. (Buck, 1938: 151; Williamson, 1933, 2: 174; Christian, 1895, 4: 190)

Tohil   The god of rain who also gave fire to the people. The Quiché, Guatemala. (Peredo, 1974: 19; Recinos, 1950: 176, 189; Asturias, 1971: 148, 153)

Toliton   A being who makes the rainbow which is an ill omen foretelling illness. The Aka-Jeru, Andaman Islands, Bay of Bengal. (Radcliffe-Brown, 1967: 146)

Tomai-rangi   A god of mist. The Maori, New Zealand. (Andersen, 1928: 374)

Tomituka   A mythical totemic person—"monsoon rain"—daughter of Kwouk-kwouk. The Tiwi, Melville Island, Australia. (Mountford, 1958: 37)

Tó nenĭli, tó ninili·   Water Sprinkler. The god of rain and the "water-carrier of the gods" controls the waters, but particularly the celestial, precipitated waters, which he causes by sprinkling the waters "in his jar in the four directions." One of his duties is "to extinguish fire made by Black God" (xa·ctče·cjini·), the god of fire. The Navaho, Arizona and New Mexico. (Matthews, 1902: 29; Reichard, 1974: 399, 491–492; Babington, 1950: 216)

Tonganui-kaea   A god of ice, snow, and hail; husband of Huru-te-arangi and father of Parawera-nui. The Maori, New Zealand. (Best, 1924: 152, 175)

Topodu   A god of the pantheon which controls thunder, rain, and waters. The Maranhao, Brazil. (Costa Eduardo, 1948: 78–79)

Tora, Tor   The god of thunder of the Chuvash. Russia. (Grimm, 1888: 1338)

Torom   The god of thunder of the Voguls. Siberia. (Grimm, 1888, 4: 1338)

Toruim   The god of thunder of the Ostyaks. Siberia. (Grimm, 1888, 4: 1338)

Totorobonsu   A deity of the Akan who causes heavy rainfall. Ghana. (Mbiti, 1970, 2: 327)

Toutika   God of the wind *Maoake*. Rarotonga, Polynesia. (Williamson, 1933, 1: 150)

Ah T'oxon Caan Chac   Mayan god of "the fine enduring rain." Mexico. (Thompson, 1970: 255)

Tritopatores, Tritopatreis   A goddess of winds in Attica. Greece. (Roscher, 1965, 5: 1208)

Trnavartta   The demon of the whirlwind. India. (Crooke, 1925, 4: 607)

Tsetse The lightning—one of the creatures vomited forth by Bumba. She caused too much trouble and was banished to the sky. The Boshongo, Zaire. (Eliade, 1967: 91–92)

Tsiguwenungy'ok'uwa The lightning spirit. The Tewa, Pueblo Indians, New Mexico. (Harrington, 1907/08: 49)

Tsijuto'o One of the Thunderers, a rainmaker. The Wyandot. Ohio, Pennsylvania, New York, and Ontario. (Barbeau, 1914: 312)

Tsitsinits, Tsitsanits The chief kachina, created by Iyatiku, lives in the west and controls the summer clouds. The Keresen, Pueblo Indians, New Mexico.

Tsona "When he puts on his garment, there is thunder and lightning and hail storm." The Kwakiutl, British Columbia. (Boas, 1935: 158)

Tsuni Goam, Tsui-Goab God of storms and of rain. He is the beneficent supreme being who lives in the red sky of the dawn. His wife is !Urisis, and son is !Urisib. The Hottentots, South Africa. (Hahn, 1881: 37–38, 127; Schapera, 1951: 376–382; Queval, 1968: 114)

Tukapua A goddess, a personification of clouds. The Maori, New Zealand. (Best, 1924: 105, 114)

Tukaro God of the wind *Parapu*. Rarotonga, Polynesia. (Williamson, 1933, 1: 150)

T'ul Chacs Rain deities "who seemingly produce little or useless rain." The Maya, Mexico. (Thompson, 1970: 212)

Tummu The supreme being is closely associated, or identified, with the rain. The Beirs (Sudan), the Pibor Murle (Ethiopia). (Logan, 1918: 244; Cerulli, 1956: 79)

Tumo-pas A Finno-Ugrian tree god, the oak, who is invoked for rain. The Mordvins, Russia. (Paasonen, 1925, 8: 845)

Tuna-yin A water god invoked for rain. The Waiwai, Brazil. (Fock, 1963: 32)

Tung Lu, Tunluh The god of snow. China. (Werner, 1932: 449; Du Bose, n.d.: 75)

T'unupa The greatly feared god of thunder and lightning. The Aymara, Peru and Bolivia. (Tschopik, 1946: 560; La Barre, 1948: 170)

Tunya The god of the air rules over the universe. Barrow Point Alaska. (Keane, 1925, 1: 257)

Tupa, Tupan The god of thunder and lightning, of the storm. He is the culture hero/chief god who gave them agriculture and fire. The Tupi Indians, Brazil. (Brinton, 1868: 152; Spence, 1925, 2: 837; Métraux, 1948, 3: 128; Bastide, 1960: 573; Wagley and Galvao, 1948, 1: 145, 147)

Tupai A personification of lightning and one of the guardians of the institutions and rituals. The Maori, New Zealand. (Best, 1924: 105, 161)

Turia A beneficent god who was able to manipulate the drought, the rains, and sunshine, interchangeably, was also a god of help in conflict as well as in peace. Samoa, Polynesia. (Turner, 1884: 62)

Turpi The supreme being is the source of rain, and of good and bad weather. The Purekamekran (the northern Ge), Brazil. (Pettazzoni, 1956: 421)

Turris The thunder god, another name of Ukko. Esthonia. (Grimm, 1880: 176)

Turul, Ungku, Nanchet The spirit who creates the thunder. The Sakai, Malay Peninsula. (Evans, 1923: 199)

Tu T'ien, Tu-t'ien Pu-sha A Chinese god of rain. (Werner, 1932: 517)

the Two Thunders Benevolent brothers who make the thunder "playing a hoop-and-pole game in the sky; lightning is created from their eyes, and where it strikes the ground, it makes flint." The elder brother makes "heavy thunder," the younger, Sih'usus, is mischievous and less violent. They bestow rain when their team wins in the peon game; are associated with the Morning Star. The Chumash, California. (Hudson and Underhay, 1978: 82, 84, 97)

Tzahui A god of rain, of water. The Mixtec, Mexico. Same as Tlaloc. (Peredo, 1974: 19; Nicholson, 1967: 98)

The Tzultacah Earth and thunder/rain gods who own and control the thunder and lightning. Each has his/her own mountain where he dwells, although they may be identified also with a spring or river. Unlike the Chacs and other rain gods they are associated with the earth rather than the sky, are invoked for the protection of the maize and cattle, are protectors of game and wildlife, and have some control of disease. The Kekchi, Guatemala. (Thompson, 1970: 272–275)

Ua-nganga The spirit of "Furiously Raging Rain." The Maori, New Zealand. (Andersen, 1928: 374)

Ua-nui "Great Rain." The Maori, New Zealand. (Andersen, 1928: 373)

Uapei The rainbow spirit who "comes on the rainbow to rescue mariners lost at sea." Faraulep and Ifalik, Micronesia. (Burrows, 1947/48: 13)

Ua-roa "Long-continued Rain." The Maori, New Zealand. (Andersen, 1928: 374)

Ua-whatu "Rain turning to Hailstorm." The Maori, New Zealand. (Andersen, 1928: 374)

Uelip The god of thunder whose wife is Lidjeman. The Marshall Islands, Micronesia. (Krämer and Nevermann, 1938: 237)

Uenga With Rongo, god of the wind *Tokerau*. Rarotonga, Polynesia. (Williamson, 1933, 1: 150)

Uenuku-rangi God of the rainbow and also a god of war. The Maori, New Zealand. (Best, 1924: 238)

Ufu Jimi Nu Mee Beneficent weather deity in all that pertains to the growth of vegetation. Okinawa. Ryukyu Islands. (Lebra, 1966: 110)

Ugami-taruni-no-mikoto A local wind god. Japan. (Herbert, 1967: 492)

Uhirangi A personification of clouds. The Maori, New Zealand. (Best, 1924: 175)

'U-kiu-kiu A deity of the northern storms. Maui, Hawaii. (Ashdown, 1971: 68)

Ukko The Baltic god of the atmosphere, of clouds, thunder, and rain is venerated for the fertilizing benefits of the rains. He is associated with the woodpecker, is also called Turris, Picker. His wife is variously named as Akka, Rauni, Maan-Eno. Finland and Estonia. (Krohn, 1925, 6: 24; Larousse, 1968: 304, 307; de Kay, 1898: 37; Grimm, 1880: 176; Turville and Petre, 1964: 98)

Umalaka-ak God of "Rolling Thunder," son of Kidul. The Ifugao, Philippines. (Barton, 1946: 31)

Umalogo-og "Deep-Rolling Thunderer," son of Kidul. The Ifugao, Philippines. (Barton, 1946: 31)

Umalotot A weather god and son of Kidul. The Ifugao, Philippines. (Barton, 1946: 31)

Umiging A god of the winds. The Ifugao, Philippines. (Barton, 1946: 61)

Umlimo God of rain and wind, of thunder and lightning. The Sindebele of Southern Rhodesia. Same as Mlimo of the Kalanga. (Gelfand, 1962: 142)

Umouiui God of the clouds. The Manobo, Philippines. (Jocano, 1969: 23)

Umung-ngul A thunder god, son of Kidul. The Ifugao, Philippines. (Barton, 1946: 31)

Umunuwol A thunder god and son of Kidul. The Ifugao, Philippines. (Barton, 1946: 31)

Ungku The thunder—the same as Yenang, the supreme being. The Sakai, Malaysia. (Cole, 1945: 107)

Urapo Stiquitetu The god of thunder was one of the major gods. He was intermediary between mankind and Omequituriqui. The Manase, Bolivia. (Métraux, 1943: 22)

Urara-e-ran-guru and **Urara-e-ran-mat** God and goddess of the air and of the "lower clouds and fogs." The Ainu, Japan. (Batchelor, 1925, 1: 243)

Urios A surname of Zeus as the giver of favorable sailing winds. Greek/Roman. (Roscher, 1965, 6: 117)

Urtz, Ortz, Ost A sky goddess who is beneficent as the bringer of spring rains, but maleficent as the source also of storms with thunder, lightning, hail, etc. The Basques, France and Spain. (Barandiaran, 1972: 195–196)

Uru A deity who represents "perfect calm," a child of Raka, the god of winds. Mangaia, Polynesia. (Andersen, 1928: 358)

Utpolaka A dragon king, a god of seas and waters, of rain and thunder and lightning. China. (Werner, 1932: 285–286)

vačirbani, modur taghan vacirtu God of rain. Mongolia. Same as Vajrapani, a celestial Bodhisattva. (Getty, 1962: 50)

Varma-ava Mother wind who was invoked "not to damage the corn and hay crops." The Mordvins, Russia. (Paasonen, 1925, 8: 844)

Varpulis A Slavonic god of the wind. (Larousse, 1968: 287)

Vasadr A malignant giant—"the dank and moist," father of Cindloni and grandfather of Vetr. Scandinavian. (Grimm, 1883, 2: 758)

Vasud The icy wind personified. Father of Vindsual. Teutonic. (Guerber, 1895: 17)

Vata, Vayu The god of the winds, of the atmosphere. Vayu represents the divine aspect and is associated with Indra. Vata is the elemental wind, the moving, restless air and is associated with Rudra in bestowing healing, purification, and prosperity. In Iran his beneficial side protects the souls of the righteous, while the harmful seeks man's destruction. India and Iran. (Keith, 1917: 37; Jayne, 1962: 178; Macdonell, 1897: 81–82; Ions, 1967: 17, 80; Banerjea, 1953: 51; Dresden, 1916: 351–352; Gray, 1930: 169–170, 216–217)

Veja Mate, Vejamat The Wind-Mother. Latvia. (Gray, 1930: 168; Larousse, 1973: 422)

Vejopatis The wind god. Lithuania. (Gray, 1930: 168; Leach, 1950, 2: 632)

Veromatautoru Chief of the gods of the atmosphere who with Tairibu controlled all the winds and storms and used them as punishment for the neglect of the gods. Society Islands, Polynesia. (Ellis, 1853: 329–330)

Vetru Slavic wind deity. (Leach, 1950, 2: 1027)

Vidrir A Norse name of Odin as "the weatherer." (Grimm, 1883, 2: 637)

Vii The god of lightning. Serbia. (Bray, 1935: 49)

Vikhor Slavic god of the whirlwind. (Bray, 1935: 49)

Vindloni, Vinsvalr The malignant bringer of the winds. Son of Vasadr and father of Vetr (winter). Norway. (Grimm, 1883, 2: 758)

Vingnir The "winged"—with Hlora (heat), the foster parents of Thor. They are the Teutonic "personification of sheet lightning." (Guerber, 1895: 61)

Vintios, Vintius A Celtic god of the wind identified with Pollux. Gaul. (MacCulloch, 1911: 180; Anwyl, 1906: 39)

Virgin Mary She was associated with Elias and in the Middle Ages was invoked for rain. Serbia. (Grimm, 1880: 174)

Vritra The demon of drought as well as of inclement weather—of thunder and lightning, of mist and hail. An adversary of Indra. India. (Elwin, 1949: 98; Martin, 1914: 282; Macdonell, 1897: 158; Cox, 1870, 2: 326–327)

Vul Assyro/Babylonian god of the atmosphere, destructive with the violent elements, but also beneficial in giving rain, fertility, and abundance. Also a god of canals. Near East. (Rawlinson, 1885: 42–46)

Wabanicu The east wind, greatly feared, deprives man of fish and game. The winds are powerful "spirits of the four quarters—forces controlling the universe; the life and growth of man and of animal and plant life." The Naskapi, Labrador. (Speck, 1935: 62–63)

Wabun God of the east and a god of the winds, the leader of the four brothers: Kabun, Kabibonokka, Shawano. The Algonquin Indians, North America. (Brinton, 1882: 44–45; Maclean, 1876: 432)

Wabunodin God of the east and of the east wind who "taught . . . the use of Grand Medicine." The Ojibwa Indians, Minnesota. (Coleman, 1937: 37)

Wachamadi He became the good Master of thunder and lightning after he destroyed his uncle, Kasenadu, an evil deity, who had killed Wachamadi's mother. Wachamadi stole Kasenadu's Arakusa (his lightning cane) and robbed him of his power. In their conflict Wachamadi used the true Arakusa to kill him, but Kasenadu revived; was finally conquered with the thunder. The Makiritare, Venezuela. (Civrieux, 1980: 90–94)

Sidi Waggag He is invoked for rain. If it falls during the sacrifice it foretells a good year; if not, it is a bad omen. Morocco. (Westermarck, 1926, 2: 157)

Wahkeeyan *See* **Wakinyan**

Waka The "thunder aspect of the sky-god." The Gallas, Ethiopia. (Foucart, 1925, 11: 581)

Waki-ikazuchi "Young Thunder" who dwelt in the left hand of the dead Izanami. Japan. (Herbert, 1967: 274)

Wakinyan, Wahkeeyan, Wahkeenyan, Wahkeon The Winged God, the Thunderbird, lives in the West with Yata, the West Wind. Inyan created him to be "his active associate." His favorite incense is that of leaves of the cedar tree which is used to propitiate him when thunderstorms threaten. As the enemy of water monsters he frequently does battle with Unktahe (the Santees in the Fort Snelling, Minnesota area). As they are well-matched either may win. Here, he is also the main god of war and with Tunkan the most worshipped of their gods.

The Oglala, the Lakota, the Santee, South Dakota and Minnesota. (Lynd, 1889: 168; Eastman, 1962: 212, 229; Walker, 1980: 50, 72, 77, 103, 115, 125; One Feather, 1982: 49; Jahner, 1977: 35; Powers, 1977: 54; Emerson, 1884: 3; Wallis, 1947: 104; Beckwith, 1886, 1: 253)

wakwiyo Wind Woman who is "exorcised . . . by sprinkling ashes in the directions." The Tewa, New Mexico. (Parsons, 1929: 267)

Wala-undayua Lightning-man creates thunderstorms. When the monsoon rains come he travels in the clouds and devastates the land. During the dry season he lives in a deep waterhole. Arnhem Land, Australia. (Mountford, 1965: 58)

Wang-lin-kuan A Taoist god invoked in rites against hail. China. (Schram, 1957: 99)

Wang Yeh A river god invoked for rain. Southwest China. (Graham, 1961: 132)

Wani The Four Winds as one god, "the vitalizer and weather"—Eya, Waziya, Yanpa, Okaga. They were commanded to establish the directions and the seasons, each controlling the weather of his season. The period of time which this took (Wani-yetu, the yeartime, twelve moons) was measured by Wohpe. The Lakota, the Oglala, South Dakota. (Walker, 1980: 50–54, 103)

Wapina makiu "White Thunder," a chief thunderer. The Menomini, Wisconsin. (Skinner, 1913: 75)

Wa skyes A Tibetan wind god. (Nebesky-Wojkowitz, 1956, 1: 469)

Waziya God of the North and the North Wind is "strong and cruel," harmful and pitiless. As the god of winter he brings the cold, snow, ice and frost, death. At times he may be jolly and playful—but still vicious. He "guards the entrance to the dance of the shadows of the north (the aurora borealis)." His color is white, aides are the white owl, the raven, the wolf. The Lakota, South Dakota. (Walker, 1980: 72, 103, 108, 120, 125–126; Beckwith, 1886, 1: 253)

Weda The wind spirit. The Yuchi, South Carolina and Georgia. (Speck, 1909: 102)

Wejamaat "wind-mother." Latvia. *See also* **Veja Mate.** (Welsford, 1925, 9: 241)

Wejopatis Baltic god of the wind. Lithuania and Prussia. (Welsford, 1925, 9: 241; Schrader, 1925, 2: 35)

Wero-i-te-ninihi One of the "personified forms of Cold" who assailed the sons of Papa and Rangi when they emerged from their protection. The Maori, New Zealand. (Best, 1924: 95)

wetcibe The southeast wind—the winds rule "human and animal destiny." The Penobscot, Maine. (Speck, 1935, 1: 21)

Whai-tiri The goddess of thunder who in one myth was said to have separated the earth and the sky through magical incantation. New Zealand. (Mackenzie, n.d.: 197, 211; Andersen, 1928: 157)

Whaitiri-pakapaka A personified form of thunder. The Maori, New Zealand. (Best, 1924: 175)

Whaitiri-papa A deity of the clouds who "represents explosive thunder." The Maori, New Zealand. (Best, 1924: 175)

Whatu God of hailstorms. The Maori, New Zealand. (Andersen, 1928: 205)

Wickano, Mudjekiwis The chief of the thunder gods who had power over the wind, lightning, and rain. The Menomini Indians, Wisconsin. (Skinner, 1915, 1: 74–75)

Widapokwi A goddess invoked for protection from whirlwinds. She also gave them medicine songs. The Yavapai, Arizona. (Gifford, 1932: 232–235)

Wisikapeo One of the thunder gods who brings "cold and storms . . . trouble and danger." The Menomini, Wisconsin. (Skinner, 1913: 75, 77)

Wiwolane Lightning. The Zuñi, Pueblo Indians, New Mexico. (Burland, 1965: 150)

Wolgendze-jumo The god of lightning. The Cheremis, Russia. (Leach, 1949, 1: 215)

Wu Fang Lei Kung A Chinese god of thunder. (Werner, 1932: 569)

Wu-je-nao One of the dragon kings who are gods of waters, seas, rain, and thunder and lightning. China. (Werner, 1932: 285–286)

wulgiskat The personification of good weather. The Penobscot, Maine. (Speck, 1935: 22)

Wuo God of the Harmattan wind, but not worshipped. The Ewe, Dahomey. (Ellis, 1890: 76)

Wuotan, Odin A god of many aspects, among them god of storms and winds. He was primarily the All-father, the god of wisdom, of wars, and of victory. Teutonic. (Guerber, 1895: 23–26; Pettazzoni, 1956: 220–221; Grimm, 1880: 131–134; Keary, 1882: 334–336)

Wu-pien-pu One of the dragon kings, deities of seas and fresh waters and "symbolic of fertile rain, rain-sending clouds, thunder and lightning." China. (Werner, 1932: 285–286)

Wupuki Makai The god of lightning. The Pima Indians. Arizona and Mexico. (Russell, 1904/05: 251)

Wu Tao Ta Shen The "god of the five roads" is considered a "combatant of hailstorms." However, he is greatly feared and his appearance is considered a bad omen. He is revered by the shamans of the Monguors of Kansu. China. (Schram, 1957: 84–85, 97; Day, 1940: 66, 138)

Xango, Xango-Bade The god of thunder and lightning. Belem, Brazil. Xango the Yoruban name, Bade the Dahomean—both used. (Leacock, 1972: 156)

Xascelbai, xascelbahi "Water Sprinkler, the god of rain and snow. Like rain he brings joy and mirth." He acts the clown in ceremonials. The Navaho, Arizona and New Mexico. *See also* **Tó'neníli.** (Waters, 1950: 234; Haile, 1947: 13)

xatso'olγal Flash lightning, a helpful deity. The Navaho, Arizona and New Mexico. (Reichard, 1950: 438)

Xeṇ o·'xwa The "Mountain Lion Raingod, who carried wooden symbols of lightning." A Winter Raingod, and a bringer of rain and its accompanying fertility. The Tewa, San Juan, New Mexico. (Laski, 1958: 11)

Xevioso A sky god and the head of the thunder-god pantheon. *See* **So.** Dahomey. (Herskovits, 1938, 2: 150–151)

X T'up Chac One of the Mayan rain gods who gives rain in abundance. Also called Ah Bulen Caan Chac. Mexico. (Redfield and Rojas, 1962: 115; Thompson, 1970: 254)

Xtoh A Quiché goddess of rain. Guatemala. (Recinos, 1950: 125)

Xucaneb God of cold weather and of the north, the fourth of the chief Mams. The Kekchis, British Honduras. (Thompson, 1930: 59)

Ah Xuce The "spirit which causes the rainbow." Also called Yum Cap. Mayan, Mexico. (Thompson, 1970: 326)

g·Ya' bo byed rgyal po stobs po che The wind god of the Bon. Tibet. (Nebesky-Wojkowitz, 1956, 1: 469)

Ya djaj God of the wind and of the north. The Coast Central Pomo, California. (Loeb, 1926, 2: 301)

Yagut A deity who is the giver of rain and protector of artisans. Yemen. (Fahd, 1968: 191)

Yahal "Cloud-Man," son of Inahitelan (a name of the supreme being). The Koryak, Siberia. (Jochelson, 1980: 24; Czaplicka, 1969: 262)

Ya'hal-na'ut Cloud-Woman, daughter of the supreme being. The Koryak, Siberia. (Jochelson, 1908: 26)

Yahweh The sky god of storms, of power, of covenants—a sovereign god who "maintains his absolute freedom" who can revoke decisions and laws. Hebrew, Near East. (Eliade, 1976, 2: 367)

Yamash God of the north wind. The Klamath, Oregon. (Chamberlain, 1892: 254; Gatschet, 1890: xci)

Yanpa God of the East, of the East Wind, who presides over the day is only invoked "when there is an invocation of the daylight or dawn." He knows all that has been (told by the Sun and the Moon) but not what is to come. He is the third son of Tate, is lazy and disagreeable, does not like to be disturbed. However, he is invoked by the sick for relief from pain and for rest. His aides are the night hawks; his color blue. The Lakota, the Oglala, South Dakota. (Walker, 1980: 72, 103, 121, 126–127; Powers, 1977: 72, 75, 76, 78, 170, 175; Jahner, 1977: 35)

Yao Chi A "goddess of rain and fertility" whose symbol was the rainbow, "Her quintessential spirit." China. (Schafer, 1980: 44)

Ya-o-gah The "north wind, the Bear, leashed at the door of Ga-oh's cave." When unleashed "winter hurricanes sweep across the earth, and the waters freeze." The Seneca, New York. (Leach 1950, 2: 1188)

Yapontca A wind spirit associated with whirlwinds. The Hopi, Oraibi, Arizona. (Titiev, 1972: 253)

Yaru The thunder, father of Wadawadariwa. The Yanomamo, Venezuela and Brazil. (Chagnon, 1968: 48)

Yata The first son of Tate, the Wind, was mean, fearful, and cowardly, and was assigned to the North, the north wind, having lost his birthright to Eya. His messenger was the magpie, his color, white. He is associated with winter and kills everything he comes in contact with. Yet north is the place of *ni*, the life, breath, soul. The Oglala, South Dakota. (Powers, 1977: 72, 75, 76, 78, 175, 191–192; Jahner, 1977: 35)

Yavi   The North wind who "caused the land to become dry." The Cahuilla, California. (Bean, 1974: 167; Brumgardt and Bowles, 1981: 37)

Yaw   The god of thunder and of rain, as well as of war, of the Southern Hebrew tribes, who later became the god of Hebrew monotheism. Canaan, Near East. (Langdon, 1931: 5, 37, 41)

Yaxal Chac   A Mayan rain god. Mexico. (Roys, 1965: 9; Thompson, 1970: 326)

Yeh Ch'a   A dragon king and a god of waters, terrestrial and celestial, of thunder and lightning. China. (Werner, 1932: 285–286)

Yen-k'ou-hai-kuang   A dragon king, a god of terrestrial and celestial waters, of thunder and lightning. China. (Werner, 1932: 285–286)

Yen Kung   A god of sailors who had the "power to calm wind and waves." China. (Ferguson, 1937: 73; Werner, 1932: 590)

Yeη sedo· or **Po·vi yen**   The Silent One, a Raingod of both the Winter and Summer moieties. He is a phallic god with serpent qualities, associated with water and with clouds, silent and rhythmic. He represents the primordial waters while the other Raingods represent that of rain and spiritual blessings. The Tewa, San Juan, New Mexico. (Laski, 1958: 11, 72)

Ye shes mkha' 'gro ma   A goddess invoked for rainfall, consort of mGon po dkar po. Tibet. (Nebesky-Wojkowitz, 1956, 1: 64, 479)

Yetl, Yetlth, Yethl   The raven was the creator of the world and of mankind; a god of the clouds and the fog. The Pacific Northwest Indians, North America. (Harrison, 1891: 22–23; Bancroft, 1886, 3: 149; Maclean, 1876: 438; Brinton, 1897: 159)

Yezo   An evil spirit of the winds and tempest. The Ainu, Japan. (Batchelor, 1894: 24)

Yoalli Ehécatl   Tezcatlipoca as the god of the night wind who searched out evil-doers and was called upon in their confessions. The Aztec, Mexico. (Alexander, 1920: 62; Emerson, 1884: 109)

Yobanua-Borna   God of rain of Puerto Rico and the Antilles. West Indies. (Fewkes, 1903/04: 56; Alexander, 1920: 25)

Yowau   The "Thunder . . . hears everything." The Mountain Nisenan, California. (Pettazzoni, 1956: 366)

Yu-ch'iang   A god of the northern sea. As a wind god he takes the form of a human-headed bird; as a god of the sea that of a fish, but with hands and feet. China. (Werner, 1932: 437; Larousse, 1973: 281–282)

the Yukhun-Shudkhan-Tengris   Nine of the malevolent tengris who cause "destructive hailstorms" and "bloody rain." The Buriats, Siberia and Mongolia. (Klementz, 1925, 3: 5)

Yulunggul   The name for the rainbow-snake in Arnhem Land. Australia. (Poignant, 1967: 131)

Yum, Yumni, Yamni   The youngest and fifth son of Tate, the Wind, who remained childlike, not strong and brave, and had no special place. He is the whirlwind, the little wind, who usually chose to stay with Okaga or Eya, and under the auspices of Wohpe. He was the messenger of many of the supernatural beings; was fickle, and a god of amusement and love. The Oglala, the Lakota, South Dakota. (Powers, 1977: 54, 73, 78, 197; Jahner, 1977: 35; Walker, 1980: 51–54, 127)

Yum Cap   Another name for the spirit of the rainbow, Ah Xuce. Mayan, Mexico. (Thompson, 1970: 327)

Yumchakob   Deity of the "chill rains." Yucatan, Mexico. (Alexander, 1920: 141)

Ah Yum Ikar   The wind gods of the Chorti (Mayan) who distribute the rain. Guatemala. (Thompson, 1970: 265)

Yumo   The omniscient sky god who is the god of the weather. The Cheremis, Russia. (Pettazzoni, 1956: 264)

Yün Chung Chün   Chinese god of the clouds. (Ferguson, 1937: 88)

Yün Hsien   A deity of the atmosphere, of clouds. China. (Day, 1940: 72)

Yun-t'ung   "Little Boy of the Clouds." China. (Larousse, 1968: 384)

Yün-yin-miao-ch'uang and **Yu-po-lo**   Dragon-kings, gods of terrestrial and celestial waters, of thunder and lightning. China. (Werner, 1932: 285–286)

Yü Shih A Chinese god of rain "associated with the constellation Hyades in the south-west." (Ferguson, 1937: 73; Werner, 1932: 602)

Zalakuintana A thunder being, the thunder coming from the coast. The Kagaba, Colombia. (Preuss, 1926: 81)

Zaliyanu Hittite/Luwian mountain goddess who is the giver of rain. Asia Minor. (Guterbock, 1961: 152)

Zantana He causes the drought, the red earth, and is controlled by Sintana. The Kagaba, Colombia. (Preuss, 1926: 70)

Zaparwa The "main god of the Palaians, who . . . may well be a Storm-god." Hittite, Asia Minor. (Guterbock, 1961: 150)

Zayan-Sagan-Tengri The eldest and chief of the western beneficent tengri who is a god of "storms and lightning" which he sends against the evil spirits. The Buriat, Siberia and Mongolia. (Klementz, 1925, 3: 4; Czaplicka, 1969: 283)

Zephyrus God of the mild west wind of spring bringing fair weather. Husband of Chloris and father of Carpo. Son of Eos and Astraios, brother of Boreas and Notus. Greece. (Fairbanks, 1907: 170; Kerneyi, 1951: 205; Murray, 1935: 145, 184; Hesiod-Brown, 1981: 63, 64)

Zeus As the sky god who controls all atmospheric phenomena he was the god of storms, of winds, fair as well as foul, of rain, beneficial as well as destructive, and of thunder and lightning. He was Icmaeus as a god of moisture; Ombrios and Hyetios as rain; Urios of favorable winds; Astrapios of the lightning; Bronton of the thunder. He was the supreme god, the father god, the principle of male generative power—wise, omnipotent, and benevolent. Greece. (Barthell, 1971: 19; Kerenyi, 1951: 158; Fairbanks, 1907: 88; Frazer, 1926: 42–48; Pettazzoni, 1956: 145; Eliade, 1958: 78, 79)

Ziphon A Phoenician god of storms. Near East. (Lucas, 1948: 65)

Zu The Assyrian god of storms who stole "the tablets of destiny" from Enlil. He was symbolized as a bird. (Zimmern, 1925, 2: 315; de Kay, 1898: 104; Hooke, 1963: 61)

Zum Dishin Dirlun Tengeri The second spirit of Delquen Sagan Burkan; invoked "for rain, good crops, and children." The Buriat/Mongol. Siberia. (Curtin, 1909: 118)

PART IV

Terrestrial Deities

12

Animal/Bird Gods

Aaa   A serpent-headed god, the herald of Arit III in the Papyrus of Ani. Egypt. (Budge, 1967: 293)

Āa-maā-kheru   A lion-headed god, the watcher of Arit VII in the Papyrus of Ani. Egypt. (Budge, 1967: 294)

Åana   An ape god appearing in the second hour of the night, in the underworld. Egypt. (Budge, 1969, 1: 211)

Åau   A jackal-headed mummy god of the 5th division of the Tuat. Egypt. (Budge, 1969, 1: 186)

Abalabalin   A god who usually takes the form of a bird of variegated plumage but sometimes that of a dog or a cat. His presence in the house foretells death. The Isneg, Luzon, Philippines. (Vanoverbergh, 1953: 95)

Åb-ta   A serpent god, guardian of the pylon of the 9th division of the Tuat. Egypt. (Budge, 1969, 1: 194)

Abuhene   The scarlet macaw, God of the West, and an evil deity. He is a god of death approached only by the dark shaman. The Warao, Venezuela. (Wilbert, 1973, 1: 5; 1973, 2: X 407)

Abyrga-Mogoi   The king of the snakes. The Buriats, Siberia/Mongolia. (Klementz, 1925, 3: 10)

Acagnikakh   Son of Mahakh and Iraghdadakh. With his sister, both of them half-human, half-fox, the parents of the Aleuts. Alaska. (Bancroft, 1886, 3: 104–105)

Acicenaqu   Another name, "Big-Grandfather," by which the Maritime Koryak call Big Raven, Quikinnaqu. Siberia. (Jochelson, 1908: 17)

Adaba   The tree-frog spirit and master of hunting, which he taught the people. The Arawak, Guiana. (Levi-Strauss, 1973: 166–167; Zerries, 1968: 262)

Aditi   The mother of the gods, particularly of the Adityas, was a cow goddess. India. (Campbell, 1968: 63; Cox, 1870, 1: 333–334; Ions, 1967: 20, 94)

Ag-Ag   The crow, the husband of the sun, lives in the eastern heavens. The Semang of Kedah, Malay Peninsula. (Skeat, 1925, 8: 354). Among the Menik Kaien he is the husband of Klang, the hawk, and father of Tanong, the dragonfly. (Evans, 1937: 163)

Agasu   The leopard god of the Fon. Dahomey. (Parrinder, 1961: 174; Herskovits, 1967, 1: 165). Also Agassou.

Agbolesu   A name of Xevioso (the head of the thunder-god pantheon) as a ram-god. Dahomey. (Herskovits, 1938, 2: 151)

Aguara-tunpa   The fox god of the Chiriguano Indians "is a mythological trickster with some features of a culture hero." Bolivia. (Métraux, 1948, 4: 482; Karsten, 1926: 275; Queval, 1968: 12)

Agunua   A serpent god who is supreme and the creator of the land and sea, of humans, of storms. He provided rain, food, and fire. San Cristoval, Melanesia. (MacCulloch, 1925, 11: 401; Leach, 1949, 1: 28)

Ahat   A cow goddess, a form of Meh-urt or Net. Egypt. (Budge, 1969, 2: 19)

Ahcan Uolcab   A Mayan serpent god invoked with others in ceremonial rites to ensure good crops. Central America. (Bancroft, 1886, 2: 701)

Ahisha   The Great Egret who transforms as Iaranavi (White Man). "As the symbol of the white man, the egret is the master of iron." The Makiritare, Venezuela. (Civrieux, 1980: 70, 175)

Ahishama The troupial bird. One of the star people and the first to arrive in the black night sky, becoming the planet Mars. The Makiritare, Venezuela. (Civrieux, 1980: 113, 114)

Aida Wedo A serpent goddess of the rainbow and of fresh waters. Wife of Damballa. Placated before a marriage. Haiti, West Indies. (Verger, 1957: 235; Herskovits, 1937: 111, 316)

Aido Hwedo The rainbow-serpent god has a dual incarnation—the celestial snake delivers the thunderbolts to earth, the terrestrial snake supports the earth. Dahomey. Porto-Alegre, Brazil. (Herskovits, 1938, 2: 108, 158, 291; Williams, 1936: 165; Bastide, 1960: 289)

A'ikren The "Duck Hawk who lives on top of Sugarloaf Mountain and is guardian spirit to the village of Katimin." The Karok, California. (Leach, 1949, 1: 31)

Ainu Satchiri Kamui The spotted kingfisher is "protector of rivers and their produce." The Ainu, Japan. (Munro, 1963: 38)

Aitvaras A household spirit who appears outside as a flying dragon, in the house as a black cock or cat, and brings the master coins representing the treasures of the earth. He provides wealth but also spreads disease; must be fed omelets and kept well. Once in he is difficult to be rid of but can be slain. Lithuania. (Leach, 1949, 1: 31; Gimbutas, 1975:XLC M126)

Aitwars A thieving dragon or snake god who lives above the earth will burn down houses if angered. He can be benevolent or malevolent. The Nadravians, Prussia. (Welsford, 1925, 11: 422)

Ajatar, Ajattara An evil female dragon spirit of the woods who causes diseases. Finland. (Leach, 1949, 1: 32)

Aker A "double lion-headed earth-god" guards "the gate of the dawn through which the Sun-god passed each morning." Also a god of judgement. Egypt. (Budge, 1969, 1: 33, 325; 1969, 2: 360)

Akhan-maati A serpent god, guardian of the pylon of the 7th division of the Tuat. Egypt. (Budge, 1969, 1: 191)

Aklasu A vulture god of Dahomey. (Herskovits, 1938, 2: 142)

Alakila The Black Bear spirit. He is merciful and feeds the hungry hunter. The Kwakiutl, British Columbia. (Boas, 1935: 161)

Ala-muki A dragon goddess protective of the area of the Waialua River. Hawaii. (MacKenzie, n.d.: 74; Westervelt, 1963, 3: 258)

Ame-no-kaku-no-kami The "heavenly deer Kami." Japan. (Herbert, 1967: 341)

Amii The mouse god around which a death and resurrection ritual is performed. The Akan, Ghana. (Meyerowitz, 1958: 43–5)

Ammon The great ram god of the Berber, the setting sun. Libya. (Bel, 1938: 73; Basset, 1925, 2: 508)

Am-net-f A serpent god, guardian of the pylon of the 11th division of the Tuat. Egypt. (Budge, 1969, 1: 200)

Anamelech A god in the form of a horse worshipped for a time by the Hebrews. Near East. (Seligmann, 1948: 49)

Ananse, Anansi The spider created the sun, the moon, the stars, and the first human to whom Nyame gave life. Ghana. (Queval, 1968: 16). Also the culture hero and trickster. West Indies. (Leach, 1949, 1: 52–53)

Ananta The Hindu serpent god of the cosmic abyss, identified with Vishnu. Same as Sesha. India. (Morgan, 1953: 408; Zimmer, 1955: 12–13, 165)

Andarta A bear goddess and a goddess of victory. Gaul. (MacCulloch, 1911: 213; Dottin, 1925, 12: 692; Ross, 1967: 349)

Angamunggi Bisexual rainbow serpent, "father of men, the giver of life." Australia. (Eliade, 1973: 113–114)

Angont A water serpent who brought sickness, death, and misfortune. The Huron, Ontario, Ohio, Pennsylvania, and New York. (Gray, 1925, 6: 885; Brinton, 1868: 136)

Ȧn-hrȧ A dog-headed god, the watcher of Arit VI in the Papyrus of Ani. Egypt. (Budge, 1967: 294)

Anhush The supernatural mink of the Karok. California. (Elmendorf, 1960: 536)

Ankh-f-em-fent A hawk-headed god, doorkeeper of Arit V in the Papyrus of Ani. Egypt. (Budge, 1967: 294)

Anoshma The Turtle brought earth up out of the depths to create the land. The Maidu, California. (Long, 1963: 201)

Antaboga "Through meditation, the world serpent Antaboga created the turtle Bedawang, on whom lie coiled two snakes as the foundation of the world." Bali, Indonesia. (Covarrubias, 1937: 7)

Anubis, Anpu The jackal god, a god of embalming, guide of the dead to the judgement. Also the "opener of the roads of the North" and god of the Summer Solstice. Egypt. (Budge, 1969, 2: 261–264; Ames, 1965: 80; Knight, 1915: 19)

Anyi-ewo The rainbow serpent of the Ewe. Dahomey. (Mockler-Gerryman, 1925, 9: 275; Ellis, 1890: 47)

Ȧp An ape god, deity of the 9th hour of the 9th day of the Moon. Egypt. (Budge, 1969, 2: 268, 292)

Apep, Apepi A serpent or crocodile god of darkness and night, of storm and evil, eternally warring with the sun god. Egypt. (Budge, 1969, 1: 11, 269; Wallis, 1939: 17; Larousse, 1968: 11, 23)

Āpesh The tortoise god—feared—and associated with darkness and evil. Egypt. (Budge, 1969, 2: 376)

Apet The hippopotamus goddess of childbirth. Also called Ta-urt, Rert, Rertu. Egypt. (Budge, 1969, 2: 109; Knight, 1915: 21; Ames, 1965: 110)

Apis The sacred bull, given variously as a reincarnation of Ptah and of Osiris. At Memphis he is identified with Serapis, and a god of healing. Egypt. (Schoeps, 1961: 70; Jayne, 1962: 54; Ames, 1965: 127; Murray, 1935: 403)

Ap-uat The jackal god Ap-uat is considered with Anubis/Anpu as two forms of one god. They are the openers of the ways—Ap-uat of the North, and Anpu of the South (493)—though Budge has these reversed in the two volumes (264). (Budge, 1969, 1: 206, 493–494; 1969, 2: 264; Knight, 1915: 22)

Apu-sipaya The jaguar god of the Shipaya. Brazil. (Nimuendȧju, 1948, 1: 241)

Aqebi A serpent god of the 2nd division of the Tuat. Egypt. (Budge, 1969, 1: 182)

Ara The primeval creator spirit had the form of a bird, created the heavens, and with Irik created mankind from clay. The Sea Dyaks of Sarawak, Borneo. (Sarawak Gazette, 1963: 21; Nyuak, 1906: 16–17)

Arco A bear goddess. Spain. Same as Artio. (Martinez, 1962: 103–104)

Ari A demon, the iguana, who originated consumption. The Cuna Indians, Panama. (Nordenskiold, 1930: 20–21)

Ariawara A bird god who is generally beneficent, if properly propitiated, is very great, and courageous. He "lives on the world mountain of the east." As the God of Origin he notes each new birth, the beginnings of all things. The Warao, Venezuela. (Wilbert, 1972, 2: 61; Wilbert, 1973, 1: 4)

Ȧri-hes A lion-headed god, son of Tempt. In Aphroditopolis a triad with Osiris-An and Bast-Temt. Egypt. (Budge, 1969, 1: 446, 450)

Arista A bull demon. India. (Crooke, 1925, 4: 607)

Ȧri-su-tchesef Lion-headed doorkeeper of the 9th pylon, the Papyrus of Ani. Egypt. (Budge, 1967: 297)

Arslan-Zon The lion, king of the beasts. The Buriats, Siberia and Mongolia. (Klementz, 1925, 3: 10)

Artio The bear goddess worshipped in Switzerland. (Ross, 1967: 349; Renel, 1906: 393)

Arwe A serpent, the progenitor of the royal line. Ethiopia. (MacCulloch, 1925, 11: 411)

Asar-Hapi A name of Serapis, the bull god. Egypt. (Knight, 1915: 23; Budge, 1969, 2: 195)

Ashke-tanne-mat The Spider Goddess, "Long-Fingered-Woman," has great shamanistic powers and reflects the "social role of women as shamanesses." The Ainu, Hokkaidu, Japan. (Philippi, 1982: 78)

Āshtȧrthet, Ashtoreth A lion-headed goddess. Goddess of horses, of the moon, and of war—introduced from Syria into Egypt. (Budge, 1969, 2: 278–279)

Asibisidosi The spirit of the whirlwind or tornado—"a brown insect"—brings misfortune to those who see it. The Ojibwa, Minnesota. (Coleman, 1937: 38)

Asima A god of the Emathites, represented as a goat, was worshipped for a time by the Hebrews. Near East. (Seligmann, 1948: 49)

'Aska' Also Huhaw. Coyote of the Middle World who often visited the Upper World where Sky Coyote, Shnilemun, lived. The Chumash, California. (Hudson and Underhay, 1978: 102–103, 150–151)

Astas The raven, the principal culture hero of the Carrier Indians. British Columbia. (Boas, 1898: 47)

Astika Muni   A serpent god. The Agarwalas, India. (Keane, 1925, 2: 124)

Asus   The bat spirit who decapitates people. The Matako of the Gran Chaco. Argentina. (Métraux, 1939: 48)

Atargatis   The Nabataean mother goddess was represented as having the tail of a fish or of a dolphin. At Ascalson, coast of Palestine. Near East. (Schafer, 1980: 38)

Atek-au-kehaq-kheru   A jackal-headed god, doorkeeper of Arit VI, the Papyrus of Ani. Egypt. (Budge, 1967: 294)

'Atheh   A Cilician lion goddess associated with Baal at Tarsus. Asia Minor. (Frazer, 1961: 162)

Audhumbla, Audhumla   The primeval cow who emerged from the melting ice and nourished the frost-giant Ymir. After which, to satisfy herself, she licked the salt ice and revealed and freed Buri. Scandinavia. (Guerber, 1895: 11; Grimm, 1883, 2: 559)

Aurt   An ape-headed god appearing with the mummified Osiris. Egypt. (Budge, 1969, 2: 134)

Auschkaut, Ausschauts   A Baltic serpent god and god of healing, the mightiest god of the Sudavians, in Samland. (Welsford, 1925, 11: 42–442)

Avaiyo   The water serpent was invoked for flooding rains for use in irrigation. The Pueblo Indians, New Mexico. (Tyler, 1964: 245; Fewkes, 1895, 1: 372)

Avanyo   The water serpent god of the Tewa who controls floods, earthquakes, and landslides. New Mexico. (Parsons, 1939: 184–185)

Awahili   The sacred eagle of the Cherokee Indians. North Carolina, Tennessee. (Burland, 1965: 150; Cohane, 1969: 135)

al-'Awf   A bird god of omens and divination. Arabia. (Fahd, 1968: 49; Abercrombie, 1972: 4)

Awudu   The horned black splitting snake is invoked to intercede with the senior god for rain, more fish, etc., and also is associated with the corn planting. The Gă in Temma, Ghana. (Field, 1937: 11, 12, 21)

?Aya   Desert tortoise, Turtle. Lesser chief, companion and partner to Gila Monster ?Itcivi. ?Aya was "symbolic of the spirit of the people"—representing toughness, determination, endurance. The Chemehuevis. California, Nevada, and Arizona. (Laird, 1976; 116, 168)

Ayida Oueddo   Serpent goddess of the rainbow and of sweet waters, a goddess of fertility and of atmospheric phenomena. Wife of Damballah Oueddo. Haiti and Cuba, West Indies. (Marcelin, 1950: 69, 88; Deren, 1953: 115)

Azaga-suga   The goat god, associated with Mul-lil at Nipur. Babylonia. Near East. (Sayce, 1898: 386)

Azazel   Goat god of the Hebrews to whom a goat was sacrificed as a "sin offering." Near East. (Robertson, 1911: 106; Langdon, 1931: 356; Leach, 1949, 1: 99)

Ba   (1) A serpent god, a form of Set. (2) The "World-Soul" symbolized by a "bearded man-headed hawk," identified with a number of gods. Egypt. (Knight, 1915: 27; Budge, 1969, 1: 481; 1969, 2: 299)

Baba Tsutu   The jaguar god of the Araona. The Takanan. Bolivia. (Métraux, 1942: 41)

Bacchis   The bull-god at Hermonthis. Egypt. (Budge, 1973, 1: 398)

Bach-ho   The "Spirit of the West—the White Tiger." China. (Scott, 1964: 307)

Bagea-bonga   A maleficent tiger deity widely worshipped in India. (Majumdar, 1950: 255, 259)

Bagharra Deo   The tiger god worshipped "for the protection of cattle from wild animals." The Kawar, Central Provinces, India. (Russell, 1916, 3: 399)

Bagh Deo   Tiger god of Hoshangabad. India. Same as Waghdeo of Berar. (Crooke, 1894: 322)

Bagheswar   The tiger deity of Mirzapur. India. Also of the Bharia. (Crooke, 1894: 322; Russell, 1916, 2: 248)

Baghisvar   The tiger god of the Gonds. Bengal. (Crooke, 1925, 2: 486)

Baghsunath, Baghsu Nag   A snake god, guardian of cattle and of water springs. The Kangra, India. (Crooke, 1894: 264)

Baghut Bonga   The tiger spirit worshipped so as not to kill the cattle. The Santals, India. (Mukherjea, 1962: 282)

Bai   A ram god identified with Osiris. Also the personification of "soul." Egypt. (Budge, 1969, 2: 154, 328–329; Gardiner, 1925, 9: 787)

Baigona A mythical snake from whom "authorized practitioners, baigona, claim to have control of rain, practise massage, employ two drugs, and regulate the affairs of the natives." The Kworafi or Korapi, New Guinea. (Haddon, 1925, 9: 346)

Bali Flaki A carrion hawk omen deity "observed during the preparation for and conduct of war." Messenger of Bali Penyalong. The Kenyahs, Borneo. (Hose, 1912: 15, 18)

Bali Penyalong Crocodile god of the Punans. Borneo. (Same name as the Supreme Being of the Kenyahs.) (Hose, 1912: 84)

Bali Sungei A river-serpent god who causes boats to capsize. The Kenyahs, Borneo. (Hose, 1912: 16; MacCulloch, 1925, 11: 401)

Ba-neb-Tattu Ram god of Tattu (Mendes). A god of virility and a phallic god whose female counterpart is Hat-mehit, their son Heru-pa-khart. Egypt. (Budge, 1969, 1: 103; 1969, 2: 64–65)

Banraja A tiger god and "lord of the wood." The Kisans and Santals, India. (Crooke, 1925, 2: 486; Grierson, 1925, 2: 554)

Barewa The antelope spirit. To hunt them successfully he must be allowed to possess (a person). The Maguzawa, Nigeria. (Greenberg, 1946: 35)

Basava A bull god worshipped on Mondays by the Lingayats; believed to bring rain to relieve the drought. Karnataka, India. (Ishwaran, 1974: 30–34)

Bast, Bastet As a cat-headed deity she is the goddess of the moon and of childbirth, mother of Khensu. As a lioness she is solar goddess, of the sun's beneficent warmth, and a goddess of fire. Egypt. (Budge, 1969, 1: 444–448, 518; Ames, 1965: 104; Knight, 1915: 30; Jayne, 1962: 84)

Basuk Nag, Vasuki The chief of the snake gods. India. (Crooke, 1894: 268; Briggs, 1920: 123)

Bathala, Batala, Bahala, Badlao, Batla A bird god of the Pampanga, and of the Tagalog among whom he is also the chief god and creator, "just and merciful" but also punitive. Philippines. (Kroeber, 1918, 2: 40; Jocano, 1969: 8, 9)

Bedawang The turtle created by Antaboga to support the two snakes who are the "foundation of the world." He is considered to be in the underworld. Bali, Indonesia. (Covarrubias, 1937: 7)

Beelzebub The Lord of Flies was worshipped by the Canaanites because his "temple was never polluted by these unclean insects." Near East. (Seligmann, 1948: 47)

Béeze The jaguar god is also the god of riches. The Zapotec, Oaxaca, Mexico. (Augur, 1954: 244)

Bekebeka-a-Tama A white "flying-fox god . . . whose appearance is an omen of disaster." Tonga, Polynesia. (Collocott, 1921: 230)

Bennu The phoenix is considered the soul of Ra and of Osiris, is identified with the rising sun. Egypt. (Knight, 1915: 31; Budge, 1969, 1: 96–97; 1969, 2: 329)

Benth An ape god of the 2nd hour of the night. Egypt. (Budge, 1969, 1: 211)

Ber Ninib as the "lord of the wild boar." Babylonia. Near East. (MacKenzie, 1930: 267)

Beru A butterfly demoness who takes part in female puberty rites. The Tucuna, Brazil. (Zerries, 1968: 302)

Bhainsasur(a) A buffalo water god who lives in a pool in Mirzapur and must be propitiated before fishing. In some areas he "is a stone placed in every field . . . worshipped when a cow runs dry or the milk goes bad." India. (Crooke, 1925, 11: 872; 1925, 12: 716)

Bhajang A snake god of Kathiawar. India. (Crooke, 1894: 135)

Biri The monkey spirit. To hunt them successfully he must be allowed to possess (a person). The Maguzawa, Nigeria. (Greenberg, 1946: 35)

Bisan The "Spirit of Camphor: a female spirit which assumes the form of a cicada" and is propitiated by camphor hunters. Malaya. (Leach, 1949, 1: 145)

biu si The "spirit mother of the tapir." The Mundurucu, Para, Brazil. (Murphy, 1958: 141)

Blanga A zoomorphic deity of the Bagobo "distinguished by enormous branching horns." Philippines. (Benedict, 1916: 40)

Bodari The skunk spirit. To hunt them successfully he must be allowed to possess. The Maguzawa, Nigeria. (Greenberg, 1946: 35)

Bokoomeerlekuluk A deity with the body of a fox and a human head but with tusks, who lives on the bottom of the sea and gives seals to the Eskimo. Baffin Land, Canada. (Bilby, 1923: 267)

Budi One of the creatures, the goat, vomited forth by Bumba. Budi "produced every beast with horns." The Bushongo, Zaire. (Eliade, 1967: 91)

Bugan Among the Igorot sometimes the goddess of locusts. Philippines. (Kroeber, 1918, 2: 44)

Bugios Named as possibly a goat god of Lorraine. Gaul. (Renel, 1906: 395)

Bukpe A malevolent crocodile god who causes disease and drought. He can be controlled through ritual. The Nupe, Nigeria. (Nadel, 1954: 27)

Buñkuei The daughter of Gauteóvañ and sister of Híuika "is designated as a deer, who turns into human form at will." She produced "the coca leaves which are chewed for eating lime." Is also associated with fire and "the brightness of day." The Kagaba, Colombia. (Preuss, 1926: 66)

Buto A serpent goddess of Lower Egypt. (Ames, 1965: 87; Keeler, 1960: 45; Larousse, 1968: 29)

Buxa-Noyon The bull god, part bull, part man. Son of Esege Malan and the ancestor of the Buryats. Siberia. (Krader, 1954: 339–341)

Cadaraki A snake spirit. To hunt them successfully he must be allowed to possess (a person). The Maguzawa, Nigeria. (Greenberg, 1946: 35)

Cagn, Kaang An insect god, the mantis, is the great god, the creator or fashioner of all things. His wife is Coti, sons are Cogaz and Gewi. The Bushmen, Namibia, Lesotho. (Lang, 1887: 175; Kato, 1926: 62; Smith, 1950: 89; Larousse, 1968: 476)

C'Ahaual Queh God of the stags—the "symbol of disappearance and of farewell." The Quiché (Mayan), Guatemala. (Recinos, 1950: 205)

Cakix The macaw, a god of the Zotzil. Mexico. (Alexander, 1920: 181)

Camazotz, Camalzotz, Chakitzam The celestial vampire bat god—a god of death—greatly feared, powerful and malignant. He is the descending god, god B, with the face of a bat, come to decapitate the Maize god. "It is well known that god B is the figure of the Agrarian god called Chac or Itzamná." The Quiché, Guatemala. (Nicholson, 1967, 47; Girard, 1979: 186–188, 345; Recinos, 1950: 1950: 90, 149–150)

Canam Lum "Serpent of the Earth, . . . Guardian of the Soil." The Maya of Chiapas, Mexico. (Alexander, 1920: 133; Thompson, 1970: 321)

Capa The "Spirit of the Beaver was the patron of work, provision, and of domestic faithfulness." The Lakota, the Oglala. South Dakota. (Walker, 1980: 121)

Capac Apu Amaru The serpent deity of the Anti-Suyu. Northeast Peru. (Trimborn, 1968: 123)

Capai A spirit shaman, the *Kakuh*-bird, created by Pedn. His wife was Pa'ig. The Kensieu (Negritos), Malaya. (Evans, 1937: 160)

Carancho A falcon demiurge and culture hero. The Toba-Pilaga, Paraguay and Argentina. (Levi-Strauss, 1969: 100; 1973: 98)

Cashinducua The jaguar god to whom ceremonial houses are dedicated. The Cóqui (Kogi), Colombia. (Reichel-Dolmatoff, 1965: 149)

Caugh The raven god and creator deity of the Tsimshians. British Columbia. (Deans, 1891: 34)

Ccoa, Cacya A malevolent catlike mountain spirit who destroys with lightning and hail. The patron of sorcerers. The Quechua, Peru. (Mishkin, 1946: 464)

Cetan The Hawk spirit exemplified and controlled the qualities of swiftness and endurance. The Lakota, the Oglala. South Dakota. (Walker, 1980: 122)

Ông Cha Sir Stag is sacrificed to and invoked not to damage the fields of rice. Annam. (Cabaton, 1925, 1: 541)

Chac-Mumul-Ain, Itzam Cab Ain The earthly crocodile/iguana god, a terrestrial manifestation of Itzam Na, "Iguana House," the Maya Universe. Mexico and Guatemala. (Roys, 1949: 160; Thompson, 1970: 218)

Chakitzam *See* **Camazotz**

Chamalcan The principal god of the Cakchiquels who took the form of a bat. Guatemala. (Bancroft, 1886, 3: 483; Recinos, 1950: 180)

Ông Chang Sir Boar or Sir Wild Buffalo is invoked not to damage the fields or the harvest. Annam. (Cabaton, 1925, 1: 541)

Chaska The chapparal cock god of the Sia. Pueblo Indians. New Mexico. (Fewkes, 1895, 2: 127–8)

The Chembel k'uh The lesser gods who live in the highest heaven frequently take the form of a jaguar. The Lacandon, Mexico. (Perera and Bruce, 1982: 85–86, 115, 272)

Chethl The thunderbird, brother of Ahgishanakhou. The Thlinkeets, British Columbia and Alaska. (Bancroft, 1886, 3: 103, 146) *See also* **Yehl, Yetl.**

Chíchipáchu An illness demon, half-dog, half-woman, who causes an eclipse by devouring the moon. The Cuna, Panama. (Nordenskiold, 1930: 20–21)

Chíchipáchuored A demon who is a "black and rotund dog" causes obstructions in childbirth. The Cuna, Panama. (Nordenskiold, 1930: 20–21)

China The supernatural mole of the Sia. Pueblo Indians, New Mexico. (Fewkes, 1895, 2: 128)

Ch'ing-wa Shên A frog deity "worshipped for commercial prosperity and prevention and healing of sickness." China. (Werner, 1932: 84–5)

chironnup kamui The fox deity of the Hokkaidu Ainu. Japan. (Philippi, 1982: 46)

The Chokchebi The weasel gods of luck. Korea. (Clark, 1932: 205)

Chu Ch'iao Shên Chün "Vermilion Sparrow of the South" is associated with fire and thought capable of controlling its ravages. Also known as Nan Fang Chu Chiao. China. (Day, 1940: 72)

Chu-dieu The "Spirit of the South, . . . the Red Sparrow." China. (Scott, 1964: 307)

Ch'ung Wang The god of insects. North China. (Gamble, 1954: 400)

Cin-an-ev The Wolf, culture hero/trickster of the Ute Indians. Utah. (Leach, 1949, 1: 233)

Cin-au-av Wolf gods of the Kaibabit. Northern Arizona. (Powell, 1879/80: 28)

Cinawavi Coyote. A transformer who assumed the forms of man, water-spider, and coyote. He and Wolf helped Hutsipamamauʔu in the creation of the earth, Coyote measuring east-west distances until it was considered large enough. Coyote and Pooʔwavi (Louse) became the parents of all of the Indian tribes. Wolf and Coyote were also the "pattern-setters" for mankind; the people chose to follow Coyote's way. He "embodies *all*

the human traits: cowardice and incredible daring; laziness and patient industry or frantic exertion; foolishness and skillful planning; selfishness and concern for others." He has a sense of humor rather than dignity; was the one to decide man should reproduce sexually rather than by magic (as suggested by Wolf). Coyote had a wife, one son, and three daughters, with one of whom he had incestuous relations—she becoming ill unto death. The shaman cured her, publicly denouncing Coyote, and in disgust they (the six—wife, shaman, children) left for the sky while Coyote was gone—becoming the Pleiades. Cinawavi is the younger brother of Tivatsi. The Chemehuevis, California, Nevada, and Arizona. (Laird, 1976: 45, 148–152, 156–157, 192, 231)

Ciuacoatl An Aztec serpent and earth goddess, of war and adversity, of childbirth. Also known as Tonantzin, Quilaztli, Yaociuatl. Mexico. (Spence, 1923: 179–182; Nicholson, 1967: 112; Alexander, 1920: 75; Thompson, 1970: 177–178; Bancroft, 1886, 3: 352, 363)

Con tram nu'o'c The water buffalo who "causes the waters to divide before it." Annam. (Cabaton, 1925, 1: 541)

Ông Cop The tiger god who was feared and worshipped. Annam (Cabaton, 1925, 1: 541)

Cuauhtemoc The name of Tonatiuh as the evening sun—"the eagle who fell." Mexico. (Caso, 1958: 33)

Cuauhtlehuanitl The name of Tonatiuh as the morning or rising sun—"the eagle who ascends." Mexico. (Caso, 1958: 33)

Curicaveri A beneficent god who takes the form of a white eagle and is associated with successful wars and deeds. He is identified with Huitzilopochtli. The Chichimecs, the Tarascan. Mexico. (Krickeberg, 1968: 58; Craine and Reindorp, 1970: 55, 104, 130, 58; Alexander, 1920: 60)

Da The serpent god, manifest in the rainbow, is interpreted as the principle of movement, of the fluidity of life and its fortunes. Dahomey. (Herskovits, 1938, 2: 189, 201; Mercier, 1954: 220, 217; Parrinder, 1949: 40, 52–53)

Daboa, Dangbe Variant names of the snake divinity. Whydah, Dahomey. (Herskovits, 1938, 2: 245–246; Parrinder, 1949: 50)

Dai-Ja The serpent/dragon god. Idzumo, Japan. (Casanowicz, 1926: 1)

Damballa(h), Damballa Wedo Benevolent serpent god of rivers and springs and of atmospheric phenomena. Also a god of fecundity and strength. Identified with St. Patrick. His wife is Ayida (Aida Wedo). Haiti, West Indies. (Herskovits, 1937, 1: 315–316; Deren, 1953: 56, 114–115; Marcelin, 1950: 55–56, 69, 88; Verger, 1957: 235)

Damisa The leopard spirit. To hunt them successfully he must be allowed to possess. Husband of Kyanwa. The Maguzawa, Nigeria. (Greenberg, 1946: 35)

Damona A Celtic cow goddess associated with Borvo. Gaul. (MacCana, 1970: 32; Jayne, 1962: 513; Renel, 1906: 396)

Dan The rainbow serpent god who symbolizes continuity, the vital force. He is the protector of abnormal children, and also bestows wealth. The Mahis, Dahomey. (Verger, 1954: Pls 130, 135–136; 1957: 233; Herskovits, 1938, 2: 247)

Dangbe, Dang-ghi The benevolent python god, particularly strong at Whydah. Dahomey. Also Brazil. (Herskovits, 1967, 1: 182–183; Parrinder, 1949: 51; Verger, 1957: 511)

Dauarani Goddess of the forest, a serpent deity, and goddess of male artisans, particularly canoe-makers. The Winikina-Warao, Venezuela. (Wilbert, 1973: 5; 1972, 2: 61)

Dawaik The rhea spirit is the master and protector of the flocks of birds and punishes over-killing. The Toba, Gran Chaco, Argentina and Paraguay. (Zerries, 1968: 263; Métraux, 1937: 175)

Dengei A serpent god who taught the boat-builders the art of canoe making. Fiji, Melanesia. (Fison, 1904: 27)

Deung Adok A "great white cow," who was created by Jo-uk, rose out of the Nile. She was the ancestress of the Shilluk kings. Sudan. (Budge, 1973, 1: 403)

Dharam Raj A deity who has been described as a snake god or a man with the tail of a fish. Bengal. (Briggs, 1953: 553–4)

Dila The jackal spirit. To hunt them successfully he must be allowed to possess. The Maguzawa, Nigeria. (Greenberg, 1946: 35)

Dinewan The "personified emu . . . chief of birds." The Eulayhi (Ualayi). New South Wales, Australia. (Leach, 1949, 1: 313)

Dionysus The Greek god of vegetation, of the vine, is sometimes depicted as a bull or as a goat. (Kerenyi, 1951: 109; Younger, 1966: 117–118; Willetts, 1962: 220; Frazer, 1960: 453)

Djungun A culture hero, in the form of a small night bird of the primeval time, who became the star Beta Gemini. Australia. (Eliade, 1964: 64–65)

Djwij'ahnu A god who appeared as a human, a snake, or a jaguar. Ghana. (Ellis, 1887: 40–41; MacCulloch, 1925, 11: 400)

Dorina The hippopotamus spirit. To hunt them successfully she must be allowed to possess. The Maguzawa, Nigeria. (Greenberg, 1946: 36)

Dtu-p'er Khyu-t'khyu Garuda—worshipped in the vicinity of Ha-ba Snow peak. Yunnan Province, China. (Rock, 1947: 262)

Dyabdar The serpent who helped in the formation of the earth. He formed the river beds with his sinuous crawl. The Evenks, Siberia. (Michael, 1963: 166)

Echdae Celtic horse god. Ireland. (Ross, 1967: 326)

Echidna Half-woman, half-serpent, daughter of Phorcys and Keto. Wife of Typhoeus and mother of numerous monsters. Greece. (Kerenyi, 1951: 51)

Ek Balam Chac Black tiger of the fields was worshipped with others in agricultural ceremonies. Mayan, Mexico. (Bancroft, 1886, 2: 701; Tozzer, 1941: 60)

Ek Cocah Mut The "black Coc bird," a god which "appears in the Chumayel." A title of ItzamNa meaning "star" and "presumably identified with the Pleiades and conjecturally other constellations." Mayan, Mexico. (Tozzer, 1941: 145; Thompson, 1970: 214)

'Elepaio The bird form of the goddess Lea in which she passes judgment on the soundness of the tree felled for a canoe. Oahu, Hawaii. (Westervelt, 1963, 1: 100; Beckwith, 1940: 91)

Emisiwaddo She is "identified as the *cushi*-ant," a wife of Kururumany. The Arawak, Guiana. (Alexander, 1930: 259)

Eno The name of Eyacque (Coyote) after it was changed to indicate his thievery and cannibalism. The Acagchemem, San Juan Capistrano, California. (Boscana, 1933: 28)

Epona The Celtic horse goddess, guardian of horses, was also associated with birds and had widespread worship. Gaul and Britain. (Ross, 1967: 198, 267; Renel, 1906: 397; MacCulloch, 1911: 213)

Erechtheus The serpent guardian of the Acropolis at Athens. Greece. (Guthrie, 1950: 228)

Ernutet The goddess of plenty, of the harvest, is a cobra or a cobra-headed woman. Egypt. (Gardiner, 1925, 9: 789; Younger, 1966: 43)

Eyacque The name of Coyote before it was changed to Eno. The Acagchemem, California. (Boscana, 1933: 28)

Faiga'a A goddess of whom the light-colored heron is the incarnation. Companion of Jiji. Tongans, Polynesia. (Collocott, 1921: 232)

Fakailoatonga A god who takes the form of a shark or a kingfisher. Vavau Island, Tonga, Polynesia. (Gifford, 1929: 311)

Frimene Sister of Nuna from whom she stole the *Huehanna* (like a large egg) filled with good people from heaven. She fled from him as far as the Orinoco River which she could not cross; there she transformed herself into Huiio, the great snake. The egg was broken open on a rock in the river and those within became fishes, water snakes, etc. The Makiritare, Venezuela. (Civrieux, 1980: 48–53)

Fu Hsi "(Subduer of Animals), a sage . . . said to have taught men how to hunt and cook, to make nets." His sister or consort is Nu-kua and "like her, a proto-musician and creator spirit." They have human torsos "but merge below into serpent tails." Han Period. China. (Bodde, 1961: 386; Schafer, 1980: 40–61)

Gadiu A snake god who is armed with bows and arrows. Rossell Island, Melanesia. (Armstrong, 1923/24: 2)

Ga-gaah The Crow who brought corn to man. The Iroquois, Eastern United States. (Leach, 1949, 1: 429–430)

Gajimari The rainbow serpent takes the form of a snake on earth and of the rainbow in the sky. He causes stomach trouble and a black sheep is sacrificed to him. His wife is Ra. He is the oldest son of Babban Maza and 'Inna. The Maguzawa, Nigeria. (Greenberg, 1946: 31)

Gajkaran The elephant god—a sign representing him is tattooed on the upper part of the foot and is expected to "enable them to bear weight." The Gonds, Central Provinces, India. (Russell, 1916, 3: 125–126)

Galaru The rainbow serpent. Australia. (Eliade, 1973: 77n)

Ganda Bumba The crocodile, one of the creatures vomited forth by Bumba. He created "serpents and the iguana." The Bushongo, Zaire. (Eliade, 1967: 91)

Ganesha The elephant-headed god of wisdom, the remover of obstacles. His vehicle, the rat, symbolizes perseverance. He provides good fortune and prosperity, is invoked on all undertakings. Son of Siva and Parvati. India. (Martin, 1914: 191, 193; Crooke, 1894: 50, 104, 287; Banerjea, 1953: 51–52, 62, 71, 408; Tod, 1920: 688; Larousse, 1968: 376; Ions, 1967: 100; Murray, 1935: 392; Russell, 1916, 2: 124; Barth, 1921: 164; Brown, 1961: 306)

Gaphu A king of the serpent of water spirits. The Sherpas, Nepal. (Furer-Haimendorf, 1964: 267)

Garuda Part-bird, part-human god upon whom Vishnu rides. The enemy of evil. India, Nepal, and Tibet. (Ions, 1967: 101; Burrows, 1972: 36; Heeramaneck, 1966: 78; Dubois, 1906: 639)

Gatoya The horned water serpent, the god of waters and of floods. The Acoma and Keresan, Pueblo Indians, New Mexico. (Parsons, 1939: 185; Tyler, 1964: 245)

Gavião A hawk god—a lesser god interested in a good time. Belem, Brazil. (Leacock, 1972: 157, 168)

Gazi Mian The king of the serpents is worshipped for immunity from snakebite. The Sansiyas, India. (Briggs, 1953: 481)

Gbekze A monkey-headed god, a "judge of all souls." The Baule, Ivory Coast, Africa. (Abbate, 1972: 48)

Gbobu A beneficent deity believed to have once been a leopard god. The Gã in Nungwa, Ghana. (Field, 1937: 27, 29)

gha'ashkidi, γa·áckidi· Hunchback God is possibly "a deified mountain sheep." "Matthews defines him as 'a god of harvest, a god of plenty, a god of mist.'" The Navaho, Arizona and New Mexico. (Reichard, 1950: 443)

ghoneshch'indi, γó·ne·ctčį·di· The cicada, a helpful deity with much power. The Navaho, Arizona and New Mexico. (Reichard, 1950: 419)

Ghora Dev The horse god. The Bhils, the Rajput tribes of Gujarat. India. (Grierson, 1925, 2: 555; Crooke, 1925, 5: 8)

γorsikidi· Measuring Worm, a helpful deity. The Navaho, Arizona and New Mexico. (Reichard, 1950: 448)

Gilgildokwila The lark, the giver of long life, who initiates shamans. The Kwakiutl at Rivers Inlet. British Columbia. (Boas, 1966: 135)

Ginitsoh, Gintsoh "Big-prairie-hawk," a helpful deity. The Navaho, Arizona and New Mexico. (Reichard, 1950: 393)

Giwa Elephant spirit. To hunt them successfully he must be allowed to possess. The Maguzawa, Nigeria. (Greenberg, 1946: 35)

Giwoitis A Slavonic domestic spirit in the form of a lizard. (Larousse, 1968: 290)

Glykon A serpent venerated as a god, depicted with a human head. Roman. (Roscher, 1965, 1, 2: 1692)

Gni sungsung A wild dog deity of the third generation of deities, child of Ningthoi and Ningsin. The Katchins, Burma. (Gilhodes, 1908: 676)

Gnurluwa A water snake god who creates the rainbow by spitting into the sky, which brings the rain. His consort is Munbakuaku, the "dollar bird." The Anula, Central Australia. (Spencer, 1904: 631)

Goba The mantis god of the Bushmen. Orange Free State. (Schapera, 1951: 181)

Gonaldjictco xastin An insect deity, one of the four creators of the earth and sky in one version of the creation myth. San Carlos Apache, Arizona. (Goddard, 1918: 27)

Gopehohan, Bhatidev The "god of serpents" who can alleviate snakebite. The Bhils, India. (Naik, 1956: 180)

Gorakh Nath A snake god worshipped by snake charmers. India. (Skafte, 1979: 124)

Guaca The jaguar god. The Nutibara, Colombia. (Steward, 1948, 1: 17)

Guga A snake god associated with their control and "protection from snake-bite." Also called Zahra Pir. The Chamars, India. (Briggs, 1920: 123; Crooke, 1894: 133)

gwax^ugwaxwalanux^usiwe A raven deity with a room in the house of the Cannibal Spirit, "who eats the eyes of the victims of the cannibal." The Kwakiutl, British Columbia. (Boas, 1935: 142)

Ha An Egyptian serpent-headed god. (Knight, 1915: 34)

Haele Feke The octopus god was said to change "into a lizard when travelling overland." Tonga, Polynesia. (Collocott, 1921: 231; Gifford, 1929: 308)

Hagulak The "sea grizzly bear." The Tsimshian, British Columbia. (Swanton, 1925, 12: 465)

Hai A serpent god, a name by which Apep is called. Egypt. (Budge, 1969, 2: 246, 367)

Hak-ti tash-a-na The mountain lion, hunter god of the north. The Zuñi, Mexico. (Cushing, 1881/82: 25)

Halulu A cannibalistic bird/god or bird/man. Lanai, Hawaii. (Beckwith, 1940: 92; Westervelt, 1915: 68; Emory, 1924: 12)

Hanei The son of Karei became "a tiger who dwells in the forest." The Menri (Semang), Malaya. (Schebesta, 1927: 274)

Hannat The snake goddess who "could taste of the fruit of the tree" (of knowledge). (Eliade, 1958: 285)

Hanuman, Hanumat The monkey god, a god of wisdom and beneficence, of speed and strength. Among the Gond they tattoo his image on "the outer side of each upper arm" to make the arms strong for carrying. He drives away evil spirits and is invoked for fertility. India. (Crooke, 1894: 33, 51–52; Ions, 1967: 102; Martin, 1914: 226; Russell, 1916, 3: 126)

Hap, Apis Predynastic sacred bull, during the Ptolemaic period merged with Osiris (as the bull of the underworld) to form the god Serapis. Also called Asar-Hapi. Egypt. (Budge, 1969, 1: 26; 1969, 2: 349)

Hapay-Can An evil serpent god "who draws people to him with his breath and kills them." The Lacandon, Mexico. (Roys, 1949: 161)

Hapikern An evil snake god. The Maya of Yucatan, Mexico. (Cline, 1944: 112, table 1)

Ha-pu'u A dragon goddess and goddess of the forest. She and Hau-ola, in the form of stones, are protective of children from evil when their navel cords are buried under the stones. Nuuanu Valley, Oahu, Hawaii. (Mackenzie, n.d.: 74; Westervelt, 1963, 3: 258)

Hari Sinh A snake godling of India. (Crooke, 1894: 269)

Harsiesi A deity shown with numerous animal representations. Egypt. (Knight, 1915: 38)

Hatee Supernatural "Bird of the North." The Sia, Pueblo Indians, New Mexico. (Fewkes, 1895, 2: 127)

Hathor The celestial cow and sky goddess—a goddess of love and childbirth, of joy and the arts, the great mother goddess who represents the continuous productivity of nature. As a goddess of the underworld she was benevolent, taking the deceased under her protection. Egypt. (Knight, 1915: 39; Budge, 1969, 1: 429–435; Neumann, 1955: 153–154; Jayne, 1962: 58; Ames, 1965: 76)

Hatuibwari The Winged Serpent, the dragon god and creator. San Cristoval. The supreme being also. The Arosi, Melanesia. (MacKenzie, 1930: 90, 177; Leach, 1949, 1: 485)

Hau-ola A dragon goddess and forest deity, now in the form of a stone believed to protect children from evil when their navel cords are buried beneath it. Nuuanu Valley, Oahu, Hawaii. (MacKenzie, n.d.: 74; Westervelt, 1963, 3: 258)

Haya The deer spirit, one of the first beings. The Yanomamo, Venezuela and Brazil. (Chagnon, 1968: 46)

Hebi An Egyptian lion god. (Budge, 1969, 2: 362)

Hehaka The "Spirit of the Male Elk presided over sexual relationship." The Lakota and Oglala, Plains Indians. South Dakota. (Walker, 1980: 121)

Hekenth A lion-headed goddess of the 7th hour of the night. Egypt. (Budge, 1969, 1: 234)

Hemaskas A supernatural being identified with Raven. The Bellabella and Rivers Inlet tribes. British Columbia. (Boas, 1909/10: 584)

Henga The sacred eagle of the Osage. Plains Indians, Missouri and Kansas. (Burland, 1965: 149)

Hentet-Arqiu A hippopotamus goddess, the doorkeeper of the 5th pylon in the Papyrus of Ani. Egypt. (Budge, 1973, 1: 296)

Heptet A snake-headed goddess who was associated with the resurrection of Osiris. Egypt. (Budge, 1969, 2: 131)

Heqet, Hequet A frog-headed goddess, the "symbol of generation, birth and fertility"—a form of Hathor and also of Nut. Egypt. (Budge, 1969, 2: 136, 109, 378)

Her-shef A form of Khnemu as a ram-headed god. God of strength and bravery, a solar god. His female counterpart is Atet or Mersekhnet. Egypt. (Casson, 1965: 108; Knight, 1915: 45; Budge, 1969, 2: 58, 60–61)

Her-tept A snake-headed goddess who attends the mummified Osiris. Egypt. (Budge, 1969, 2: 134)

Hert-Ketit-s A lion-headed goddess of the 11th hour of the night who destroyed the fiends in the pit of Hatel—in the Underworld. Egypt. (Budge, 1969, 1: 255)

Heru, Horus The hawk god, the personification of the heavens. Egypt. (Budge, 1969, 1: 40, 78, 466)

Heru-merti A hawk-headed god, "Horus of the Two Eyes." Egypt. (Budge, 1969, 1: 469–70)

Heru-neb-Mesen A lion god. Egypt. (Budge, 1969, 2: 362)

Heru-sekha An Egyptian cow goddess. (Budge, 1969, 2: 212)

Hesamut A hippopotamus goddess (Reret) identified with Draco as a star goddess. Egypt. (Budge, 1969, 2: 312)

Hes-nefer-Sebek A crocodile-headed god with whom Ar-hes-nefer is identified. Egypt. (Budge, 1969, 1: 464)

Hetepui A serpent god of the 6th hour of the night in the underworld whose duty was to destroy the enemies of Khepera. Egypt. (Budge, 1969, 1: 230)

Hetet An ape god, and god of the 11th hour of the 11th day of the Moon. Egypt. (Budge, 1969, 2: 213, 292)

Hine-karoro The seagull personified. The Maori, New Zealand. (Best, 1924: 176)

Hine-tara The personified tern. The Maori, New Zealand. (Best, 1924: 176)

Hirava The peacock deity. The Thakur, India. (Chapekar, 1960: 87)

Hiyovinya?aivyatsiwi Dove-human transformations. The two Dove Boys (which had been one, and were split to be two); grandsons of Yu?uravatsi and Win?namakasaama?-apitsi. Their appearance as two was the sign for the Coyote people to go to war against Gila Monster (?Iitcivi) and Turtle (?Aya), acting as guides to the camp. The Chemehuevis, California, Nevada, and Arizona. (Laird, 1976: 170–182)

Hnaska The "Spirit of the Frog was the patron of occult powers." The Lakota and Oglala, Plains Indians, South Dakota. (Walker, 1980: 122)

Hocboa The supernatural chapparal cock. The Walpi, Pueblo Indians, Arizona. (Fewkes, 1895, 2: 128)

Hohottu The rust-colored pygmy owl is a great shaman's helper. He lives in the "sixth Heaven." The Makiritare, Venezuela. (Civrieux, 1980: 180)

Holhol, *also* **Xolxol** A supernatural being associated with the California condor as well as with Mars. The condor's reddish-orange head and Holhol's ability to travel at supernatural speeds suggested the noticeably rapid movement of Mars at times. He was an excellent sorcerer with powers of locating lost people, articles, etc., and was often requested to locate Slo'w, the Golden Eagle. Holhol was one of the eaters of the dead, clearing the world of foulness. He is the equivalent of Tsikolkol of the Pomo, and like him, wears a feather cloak or suit. The Chumash, California. (Hudson and Underhay, 1978: 84, 91–93; Blackburn, 1975: 29, 38)

Honani The supernatural badger of the Walpi, the Hopi, who taught them herbs and plants for curing. Pueblo Indians, Arizona. (Fewkes, 1895, 2: 128; Waters, 1963: 56)

Honauwuh The supernatural bear of the Walpi, Arizona. (Fewkes, 1895, 2: 128)

Horbehudti The Sparrow-hawk, a form of Horus, who did battle for Ra. Egypt. (Frazer, 1926: 594)

horokew kamuy The wolves, mountain deities, and guardians of the Ainu, had great powers for curing illness. Sakhalin. (Ohnuki-Tierney, 1974: 97)

Horus The personification of the heavens was a hawk-headed man or lion. Egypt. (Knight, 1915: 48; Budge, 1969, 1: 78, 467)

Hoy A bird, or bird-like, supernatural being who lives alone in "the Upper-most World" and possibly represented a planet or star. The Chumash, California. (Hudson and Underhay, 1978: 96)

Huang Nan Chih Chen Shen The "God of Locusts, . . . [invoked] for rain to kill the locusts." Anking, China. (Shryock, 1931: 155)

Huiio The supernatural anaconda, Mistress of the Water and of the River, and the Mistress of Lake Akuena in the highest Heaven, Kahuna. Frimene changed herself into the Great Snake in fleeing from Nuna when she reached the Orinoco and couldn't cross. The Makiritare, Venezuela. (Civrieux, 1980: 51–3, 180)

Huit, Huiti The god of the sphinx. Egypt. (Budge, 1969, 1: 348)

Huliamma The tiger goddess of Mysore. India. (Whitehead, 1916: 24)

Humse kamuy The owls are considered mountain deities and guardians of the Ainu and their settlements. They help lost people to find their way, can dispel diseases, and predict successful bear hunting. Sakhalin. (Ohnuki-Tierney, 1974: 97)

Hu Nonp The Bear God was "the patron of wisdom," the teacher to the shamans of their secrets and their language, *Tobtob,* as well as the medicines. The Lakota and Oglala, South Dakota. (Walker, 1980: 50–1, 128)

huntu katt! katten The rock rabbit, wife of kaggen, the mantis. The Cape Bushmen, South Africa. (Schapera, 1951: 177)

Huri (or Furi) kamui A huge, ferocious, and malevolent bird deity. Sometimes a pair. The Ainu, Japan. (Philippi, 1982: 165; Munro, 1963: 22)

Hurumanu The origin and personification of sea birds. The Maori, New Zealand. (Best, 1924: 97, 176)

Huwaka The serpent god of the heavens, associated with the sun. The Sia, Pueblo Indians, New Mexico. (Fewkes, 1895, 2: 126; Parsons, 1939: 185)

Iarakaru The capuchin monkey into which he was transformed as punishment for releasing darkness upon the earth. This occurred when Iarakaru opened the *chakara* of Nadeiumadi, his uncle, which contained his powers and also the night. The Makiritare, Venezuela. (Civrieux, 1980: 24, 25)

Ikaina The serpent god at Isleta is associated with the sun. Pueblo Indians, New Mexico. (Parsons, 1939: 185)

Ikenga A ram-headed god of the Ibo was originally the god of head-hunters but became that of the craftsmen, of the skills of the hands, as well as one of good luck. Nigeria. (Jeffreys, 1972: 723; Sierksma, 1960: 23, 25)

Ikto, Iktomi Grandfather Spider "named all people and animals, and he was the first to use human speech," The Tetons, Wyoming, Montana, and Dakotas. (Unktomi in Santee). *See also* **Inktomi.** (Dorsey, 1889: 134)

Ilari-Edutzi, Baba-guaro   The wild pig god of the Araona, The Takanan. Bolivia. (Métraux, 1942: 41)

Imbulu Man   A bird goddess sent down from the sky who was the mother of humans. The Battak, Sumatra. MacKenzie, 1930: 311)

Im-dugud   The thunderbird god, an early form of Ninurta/Ningirsu, "was portrayed as a lion-headed eagle" and represented the force of the storm cloud. Near East. (Jacobsen, 1976: 128; Hamblin, 1973: 116)

'Imoa   A rodent god, the "Rat, the Mouse" who was the husband of Papamavae and father of Salasala. Samoa, Polynesia. (Williamson, 1933, 1: 8)

Inari-sama   The fox god is believed to be a god of human and agricultural fertility. Takashima, Japan. (Norbeck, 1954: 124)

Inkisi   The "great water-snake" of the Ipurina. The last resort when hope has been given up in illness. Brazil. (Chamberlain, 1925, 4: 740)

Inktomi   The Spider—the culture hero, trickster, and transformer is responsible for the creation of time and space, of the naming of things, of language. Son of Inyan and Wakinyan; older brother of Iya. The Oglala, Plains Indians, South Dakota. *See also* **Iktomi, Ikto** (Powers, 1977: 53–55, 79, 83, 84)

Iphemedeia   A "Dove Goddess" to whom offerings were made at shrines honoring Zeus, Poseidon (with whom she seems to be associated), herself, and others. Mycenea, Greece. (Chadwick, 1976: 95; Samuel, 1966: 89, 94)

Ipilja-ipilja, Ipilya   On Groote Eylandt, the gecko, a lizard, "takes the place of the rainbow-serpent." A deity associated with atmospheric phenomena, the creator of "thunderstorms and the monsoon rains." Australia. (Mountford, 1958: 155; 1969: 66)

Irik   Primeval creator spirit, in the form of a bird, who created the earth. With Ara, created mankind from clay. The Sea Dyaks of Sarawak, Borneo. (Nyuak, 1906: 16, 17; Sarawak Gazette, 1963: 21)

Isauwuh   Supernatural coyote of the Walpi. Pueblo Indians, Arizona. (Fewkes, 1895, 2: 128)

isepo kamui   The hare deity of the Hokkaidu Ainu. Japan. (Philippi, 1982: 46)

Ishits   The supernatural scarabaeus of the Sia. Pueblo Indians, New Mexico. (Fewkes, 1895, 2: 128)

Ish-khanna   A scorpion goddess. Babylonia, Near East. (Hommel, 1925, 3: 78)

Iso kamuy   The bear, the supreme deity of the Ainu, their guardian, protective of their welfare and giving them food. Sakhalin. (Ohnuki-Tierney, 1974: 90)

Itciai   The jaguar god, creator of the river waters. Brother of Kuma and Puana. The Yaruro, Venezuela. (Hernandez de Alba, 1948, 4: 462; Petrullo, 1939: 245)

?Itcivi   Gila Monster, the High Chief and an Immortal. His companion and partner was ?Aya, Turtle. They instructed and cared for the people, taught them to store food for lean times. The Chemehuevi, California, Nevada, and Arizona. (Laird, 1976: 168)

Itseyeye   The coyote, chief of the animals. The Nez Perce, Columbia River basin, Washington and Oregon. (Spinden, 1908: 13)

Itzam   Among some Mayan a crocodile deity. Mexico and Guatemala. (Tozzer, 1941: 192)

Itzpapalotl   The "Obsidian Knife Butterfly" goddess, a fierce earth mother, and a stellar and agricultural deity. The Chichimec and Aztec, Mexico. (Vaillant, 1962: 150; Spence, 1923: 225–227)

Iwa   The alligator spirit, one of the first beings, who possessed fire and was tricked into releasing it. His wife is Bruwaheiyoma. The Yanomano, Venezuela and Brazil. Chagnon, 1968: 46)

Jalodeh   The crocodile god invoked for protection in traveling on lagoons. The Ewe, Dahomey and Ghana. (Ellis, 1890: 71)

Japetequara, Caboclo Velho   A god of local Indian origin identified with the alligator. A god of the forest and of hunting. Belem, Brazil. (Leacock, 1972: 141–142, 148)

Jararaca   The snake spirit. The Paressi, Mato Grosso, Brazil. (Zerries, 1968: 308)

Jassuju   A goddess in the form of a frog who with her brother Lujjuphu were the parents of the human race. The Dhammai, Northeast India. (Long, 1963: 106)

Jata, Bawin Jata Balawang Bulau   The watersnake who lives in the primeval waters. With Mahatala she forms a dual supreme being—he of the upperworld, she of the underworld. They represent the duality of all things—life and death, good and evil, war and peace, etc. She participated with him in the creation period. Though she is beneficent in some ways, she is also the destroyer. The Ngaju, Borneo. (Scharer, 1963: 15–28, 88, 126)

Jaur Singh, Jewar   A snake god of India. (Crooke, 1894: 269)

Jem-wos-aika   The bear god, brother of Mir-susne-xum. The Vogul, Siberia. (Roheim, 1954: 27)

Jiji   A minor goddess of whom the dark-colored heron is the incarnation. The Tongas, Polynesia. (Moulton, 1925, 12: 377; Collocott, 1921: 232)

Julunggul   A rainbow snake goddess of the Northern Territory. Australia. (Poignant, 1967: 133; Eliade, 1973: 102)

'Kaang   *See* **Cagn.**

Kabamba   A python god of the Basoga. Son of Semuganda. Uganda. (Roscoe, 1915: 247)

Ka-Di   A serpent mother goddess at Dir—"lady of life." Near East. (Roheim, 1972: 171)

Kado   The crocodile spirit. To hunt them successfully he must be allowed to possess. The Maguzawa, Nigeria. (Greenberg, 1946: 36)

K'adowi   A double-headed mountain snake. The Pueblo Indians of Santa Domingo, New Mexico. (Parsons, 1939: 185)

Kagauraha   A serpent goddess who is offered first-fruits and is invoked for "relief from sickness, from bad seasons." San Cristoval, Melanesia. (MacCulloch, 1925, 11: 401)

Kaggen   Another name for the mantis god, Cagn. (Schapera, (1951: 177)

Kahausibware   A snake goddess who created animals, fruits, and vegetables, but is not worshipped. The Solomon Islands, Melanesia. (Codrington, 1881: 298)

Ka-hemhem   A lion god of the 6th hour of the night in the underworld. Egypt. (Budge, 1969, 1: 228)

Kailung   A serpent god of the Ahir. Panjab Hills, India. (Crooke, 1925, 1: 233)

Ka-'iwa-ka-la-meha   A bird/woman kupua of Hawaii. (Westervelt, 1963, 1: 224)

Kajira   A bird deity invoked at the beginning of the rice-farming season. The Sea Dyaks, Borneo. (Roth, 1968: 174)

Kak, Kakamtch   The Raven who is "Fate personified" and changes people into rocks "who act antagonistically to his or his allies' interests." The Klamath, Oregon. (Gatschet, 1890: xci, civ)

Kakan   Wolf god of the east. The Sia, New Mexico. (Fewkes, 1895, 2: 127)

Kali   She is sometimes represented with the head of a jackal. India. (O'Flaherty, 1980: 262)

Kalicknateck   An evil spirit "who seems a faithful reproduction of the great thunder-bird of the north," catches and eats whales. Trinity River, California. (Bancroft, 1886, 3: 176)

Kalki   The future incarnation of Vishnu takes the form of a white horse. India. (Crooke, 1894: 288; Martin, 1914: 117)

Kaiseru   The "rainbow serpent associated with rain and fertility." Northwest Australia. (Leach, 1950, 2: 569)

Kama-pua'a   The hog god who "embodies the idea of unbridled passion and mighty brute force." He transformed as man/hog/fish/plants. He and Pele were happily married for a time. Hawaii. (Beckwith, 1940: 201–202; Emerson, 1968: 43, 50; MacKenzie, n.d.: 348–349)

Kamotaketsu-numi   The crow god of a Shinto shrine in Kyoto. Guide of the Emperor Jimmu. Japan. (Kato, 1926: 60)

kamui-chikap-kamui   *See* **Kotan-kor-kamui.**

Kamurai   A serpent and earthquake god whose movement causes tremors and whose breathing causes the wind and the churning oceans. The Yami, Formosa. (Del Re, n.d.: 70)

Kamuʷaantsi   Young Jackrabbit. He and Tavoʷaatsi showed Tavutsi where and how they obtained water and food in their desolate region, whereupon these necessities were released from their confinement and/or scarcity. The Chemehuevi, California, Nevada, and Arizona. (Laird, 1976: 152–154)

Kanavi Cheda   A cobra spirit with five hoods. The Thakur, India. (Chapekar, 1960: 88)

Kane-kua'ana   A dragon goddess of Ewa lagoon (Pearl Harbor) is worshipped by oyster gatherers and brings prosperity. Hawaii. (Westervelt, 1963, 3: 258; Beckwith, 1940: 126)

Kanthaka   The horse of the Future Buddha which died of grief, "and was reborn in the Heaven of the Thirty-three" as a god. Burma. (Zimmer, 1955: 192)

Kapa-Chiri, kapachir kamui   The eagle god. The claws of white-tailed eagles were used as fetishes to cure snakebite. The Ainu, Japan. (Batchelor,n.d.: 225–226; Philippi, 1982: 46)

Kapap Kamui   The bat god, very wise. The Ainu, Japan. (Batchelor,n.d.: 396)

Kararat   The Carrion Crow Goddess, an "auspicious" deity who amuses herself by dancing and shedding good things—acorns, chestnuts. The Hokkaidu Ainu, Japan. (Philippi, 1982: 66)

Karkotaka   The King of the serpents which are considered weather deities. India and Nepal. (Keith, 1917: 241; Crooke, 1894: 23)

Karoshimo   The Toad god, the supreme kanobo, and the God of the South. He is beneficent if continuously placated with offerings of *"moriche* flour, fish or crabs, and incense" and more particularly of tobacco smoke, the proper food of the gods. The Warao, Venezuela. (Wilbert, 1973, 1: 3, 4; 1972, 2: 61)

Kartal Deo   A snake god of the Arakh. India. (Crooke, 1925, 1: 73)

Karua   The cobra—a family god among the Bharias. Central Provinces, India. (Russell, 1916, 2: 247)

Kashindukua   A jaguar god and a great shaman who was considered benevolent even though he devoured people. The Kogi, Colombia. (Reichel-Dolmatoff, 1975: 55–59)

Kaspanna   Serpent god of the west. The Sia, Pueblo Indians, New Mexico. (Fewkes, 1895, 2: 126)

Kato'ya   The black snake god, guardian of "the west and night." The Hopi, Arizona. (Waters, 1963: 50)

Kauyumarie   The deer god who is assistant to Tatewari and to the shamans. Another aspect—Maxa Kwaxi. The Huichol, Mexico. (Furst, 1972: 80, 146–149; 1973: 38)

Kawao   The wife of Manuwa, the jaguar, transformed as a toad. She had the secret of fire which she kept in her stomach, and was the only one who could cook. She was the foster mother of Shikiemona and Iureke who finally learned her secret of fire, then killed her, making her into a stew for Manuwa, as they were planning to kill the boys. The Makiritare, Venezuela. (Civrieux, 1980: 55, 56)

Kawas   The beneficent brown eagle controls the waters and protects the Pawnee in crossing them. In the Hako ceremony "represents the feminine principle, the night, the moon." Nebraska. (Fletcher, 1900/01: 42, 75–77)

ke   The bear divinity of the west, a powerful medicine animal. The Tewa, New Mexico. (Harrington, 1907/08: 43)

ke'a   The badger divinity of the south, a powerful medicine animal. The Tewa, New Mexico. (Harrington, 1907/08: 43)

Ke-ao-lewa   "The-moving-cloud," a sky deity who takes the form of a bird/woman and is ruler of the birds. Ancestress of Lepe-a-moa. Honolulu, Hawaii. (Westervelt, 1912: 107; 1963, 1: 207, 228)

Keb   The "ancient Goose-god, who produced the cosmic egg." The earth god. Egypt. (Budge, 1973, 1: 60, 79)

Kele   The wolf deity. The Wintun, California. (Chamberlain, 1905: 115)

Kena   The gannet goddess. Her sons by Vie Moko introduced tattooing. Easter Island, Polynesia. (Métraux, 1940: 316)

Keneu   The golden eagle, chief representative of Hino, the thunderer. The Iroquois, Eastern United States. (Alexander, 1964: 25)

Kenyalong   The great hornbill whose feast is associated with war and is celebrated only by those who have taken enemy heads. The Iban Dyaks, Sarawak, Borneo. (Nyuak, 1906: 421)

Keowuch   A supernatural animal. The Sia, New Mexico. (Fewkes, 1895, 2: 128)

Keri   The White Condor, a remote and powerful rival of the creator/culture hero. The Mosetene, Bolivia. (Métraux, 1946, 2: 114)

Kesorap Kamui   A beneficent mythical bird deity. The Ainu, Japan. (Munro, 1963: 22)

Ketq Skwaye   Grandmother Toad, a creator goddess of the Huron Indians. Ontario, Ohio, Pennsylvania, and New York. (Burland, 1965: 149)

Ketutor The turtle-dove, the source of rice. Youngest child of Tak Suwau. The Kintak Bong, Malaya. (Evans, 1937: 168)

Ke-utchish, Ke-utchiamtch The deified gray wolf. The Klamath, Oregon. (Chamberlain, 1892: 254; Gatschet, 1890: cii)

Keya The "Spirit of the Turtle was the guardian of life and patron of surgery and controlled accidents." The Lakota, the Oglala. South Dakota. (Walker, 1980: 122)

Keyemen The rainbow serpent—The "grandfather of aquatic birds." The Arecuna, Guiana. (Levi-Strauss, 1969: 262)

khaengy The mountain lion divinity of the north—a very powerful medicine animal. The Tewa, New Mexico. (Harrington, 1907/08: 43)

mKha-lding The equivalent of Garuda, part bird, part human. Nepal. (Snellgrove, 1961: 286)

mKha' lding gser mig 'khyil ba A *garuda,* a protective deity invoked in magic ceremonies. Tibet. (Nebesky-Wojkowitz)

Khanderav A deity of the Thakur represented as a tiger. India. (Chapekar, 1960: 87–8)

Khanukh The wolf who controls fog. He is older than Yehl from whom he stole fresh water and is not considered beneficent. The Thlinkeets, Pacific Northwest, North America. (Bancroft, 1886, 3: 101, 146)

Khas An Egyptian lion-headed god. (Budge, 1969, 2: 269)

Khatru The "Icheumon god, who was probably venerated in connection with the supposed virtues of the animal as a destroyer of snakes and the eggs of crocodiles." Egypt. (Knight, 1915: 60)

Khent-Heru A god, a black hawk, of the 10th hour of the night—in the underworld. Egypt. (Budge, 1969, 1: 246)

Khenti Amenti A wolf god. Egypt. (Larousse, 1968: 17)

Khepera The beetle god, self-produced, was a god of creation and resurrection. As a solar god he represents the sun when about to rise. Egypt. (Knight, 1915: 62; Budge, 1969, 1: 294–295, 471; 1969, 2: 379)

Khnemu-Khnum A ram-headed god, a creator god who made the gods and fashioned man on the potter's wheel. He absorbed the attributes of Ra, Shu, Qeb or Seb, and Osiris and as such was called Sheft-Hat "with four rams' heads upon a human body . . . [symbolizing] fire, air, earth, and water." Egypt. (Knight, 1915: 64; Budge, 1969, 1: 463; 1969, 2: 50–51; Casson, 1965: 106)

Khut A serpent goddess associated with Ra (encircling the disk of the sun); a name of Isis as "the light-giver" during the first part of the year. Egypt. (Budge, 1969, 1: 323; 1969, 2: 216)

Khu-tchet-f A hawk god, doorkeeper of the 8th pylon, the Papyrus of Ani. Egypt. (Budge, 1973, 1: 297)

Khwini A supernatural bird who has great shamanistic powers. The Nutka, Vancouver Island, Canada. (Sapir, 1925, 12: 594)

Kiha-nui-lulu-moku A reptile guardian of Paliuli. Hawaii. (Beckwith, 1940: 348)

Kiha-wahine A Maui chiefess who became a mo'o (reptile) goddess, half-woman, half-reptile, and lives in fish ponds on Maui and Kauai. If fish are caught while she is at home they will be bitter. Hawaii. (Beckwith, 1940: 125–6; Emerson, 1968: 42; Westervelt, 1963, 3: 258–259)

Kilat A horse or carabao spirit of the sky is the thunder and lightning spirit. The Bagobo, Philippines. (Benedict, 1916: 39, 45)

Kilioe A dragon god on Kauai. Hawaii. (Westervelt, 1963, 3: 258)

K'imbol A serpent god of the Lacandon. Mexico. (Cline, 1944: 112, table 1)

kimun kamui The Bear—"the supreme land deity" of the Ainu. Hokkaidu, Japan. (Philippi, 1982: 83)

Kintu A python god, son of Semuganda. The Basoga, Uganda. (Roscoe, 1915: 247)

Kiriamagi A serpent god of evil who tempted men. The Wapare or Wasu. Tanzania. (Frazer, 1926: 201)

Kiwanuka A python god and a deity of thunder. Son of Semuganda. The Basoga, Uganda. (Roscoe, 1915: 247; Mbiti, 1970, 2: 118)

Klang (1) The hawk, younger brother of Jalang and Jamoi. The Kintak Bong, Malaya. (Evans, 1937: 143)

(2) The hyena god of the Gã in Kpong. Ghana. (Field, 1937: 77)

Klictso   The great snake deity of the Navajo Indians. Arizona and New Mexico. (Matthews, 1889: 91)

Klu bdud g·yag mgo can   A local protective deity with "the form of a wild yak." Tibet. (Nebesky-Wojkowitz, 1956, 1: 153)

Ko   A goddess, the mantis, who sometimes informs hunters where game is. The Bushmen, Orange Free State. (Schapera, 1951: 181–182)

Kodapen   A horse god of the Gonds. India. (Crooke, 1894: 319)

Koe   A dragon god of Kauai. Hawaii. (Westervelt, 1963, 3: 258)

Kogang   A zoomorphic *buso* who takes several shapes. The Bagobo, Philippines. (Benedict, 1916: 40)

Kohai   Bear god of the west. The Sia, Pueblo Indians, New Mexico. (Fewkes, 1895, 2: 127)

Kohone   A supernatural animal of the Walpi. Pueblo Indians, Arizona. (Fewkes, 1895, 2: 128)

Kokopilau   The locust, the Humpbacked Flute Player, the carrier of seeds and also the representative of human reproduction. The Hopi, Arizona. (Waters, 1963: 45–46)

Kokyanwuqti, Kohkang Wuhti, Kokyangwuti   Spider Woman, mother earth, and creator of plants, birds, and animals. The Hopi, Arizona. Same as Sussistinnako (Sia). (Fewkes, 1920: 605;

Kolowisi   The horned serpent, god of underground waters, controls floods, earthquakes, and landslides. Considered also a god of lightning and of fertility. The Zuni, New Mexico. (Bunzel, 1929/30: 487; Parsons, 1939: 184–85; Alexander, 1964: 188)

Komau   A giant bird spirit, male, who "steals people and their possessions." The Tinguian, the Ilocano, Philippines. (Cole, 1922: 301)

Kondole   The Whale. The man who was "the sole owner of fire" was selfish, not sharing. The people, in anger, speared him in the skull. All were transformed into animals, birds, etc. Kondole became the whale, spouting water through the spear wound. Encounter Bay, Australia. (Mountford, 1969: 40)

Konipha   A snake god worshipped by snake charmers. India. (Skafte, 1979: 124)

Kono Bumba   The tortoise, one of the creatures vomited forth by Bumba, who created other like creatures. The Bushongo, Zaire. (Eliade, 1967: 91)

Konowaru   The frog, a transformer, who possessed curing properties. The Caribs of the Barama River, British Guiana. (Levi-Strauss, 1973: 167)

Kopecho   The Frog-Woman is the arbiter of the destination (happy or tormenting) of the dead. The Yupa, Venezuela. (Wilbert, 1974: 5, 6, 25)

Koquira   Serpent god of the south. The Sia, Pueblo Indians, New Mexico. (Fewkes, 1895, 2: 126)

Koroha   The honey bee—maker of honey and sweet drinks. The Warao, Venezuela. (Levi-Strauss, 1973: 155)

Kotan-kor-kamui   The Owl God in the early period was considered the protector of human beings and ruler of the land. Also called kamui-chikap kamui. In some regions he was second in worship to the Fire Goddess. There are six owl brothers. The youngest is the largest and brings good luck, sometimes wealth. The Hokkaidu Ainu, Japan. (Philippi, 1982: 10, 101, 108, 137)

Koy Bumba   The leopard, one of the creatures vomited forth by Bumba. The Bushongo, Zaire. (Eliade, 1967: 91)

Ku-aha-ilo   A parentless dragon/man demon whose wife is Hi'ilei. Hawaii. (Westervelt, 1963, 3: 163, 165, 170)

Kududu   A giant toad which supports the sky on its back. The Shipaya, Brazil. (Zerries, 1968: 288)

Kuinadi   The collared trogon, "a beautiful bird, old and wise," is the master of the *moriche,* and a counsellor of Wachamadi. The Makiritare, Venezuela. (Civrieux, 1980: 90, 91, 185)

k'ujo   The wolf divinity of the east, a powerful medicine animal. The Tewa, New Mexico. (Harrington, 1907/08: 43)

Kukauahi   The god of owls was a good omen in time of danger. Hawaii. (Alexander, 1967: 64)

Kulabel   The rainbow snake who bestows upon the medicine man his powers. The Lunga and Djara tribes, Australia (Eliade, 1973: 156)

Kuli A dog god. Futuna Island, Melanesia. (Smith, 1892: 44)

Kumaphari A jaguar god who at first had human shape, was a culture hero/creator god who "stole fire from the tapir hawk and created man from arrow-reeds." The Shipaya, Brazil. (Nimuendaju, 1948, 1: 241; Zerries, 1968: 288; Levi-Strauss, 1969: 141)

Kumuhea The *enuhe,* the cutworm, is "an *aumakua* of ill omen," a monster who lived in a cave on Hawaii Island and took the form of a man. When he was slain, "From him sprang the hordes of *peluas* and other worms so destructive to vegetation, also the loli [sea-cucumber] and allied forms of marine life." Son of Ku. Hawaii. (Emerson, 1967: 48; Beckwith, 1940: 135)

Kumukahi The plover god, bird or man at will. Hawaii. (Beckwity, 1940: 119)

Kuna The dragon god of Nuuanu Valley. Oahu, Hawaii. (Westervelt, 1963, 1: 90)

Kunapipi The snake mother fertility goddess of Arnhem Land. Australia. (Eliade, 1973: 112; Robinson, 1966: 37)

Kundalini A serpent goddess. India. (O'Flaherty, 1980: 54)

Kunmanngur The rainbow serpent god, a creator and a god of fertility. The Murinbata tribe, Australia. (Robinson, 1966: 50, 67; Poignant, 1967: 126)

Kurtz The supernatural antelope. The Sia, Pueblo Indians, New Mexico. (Fewkes, 1895, 2: 128)

Kutkh The raven-creator god was associated with the cultural gifts of mankind. The Itel'mens (Kamchatka), Siberia. (Michael, 1963: 210; Antropova, 1964: 880)

Kuyqinnaqu The Raven, the chief deity of the Koryak. Siberia. (Bogoras, 1904/09: 315)

Kwahu The supernatural eagle. The Walpi, Pueblo Indians, Arizona. (Fewkes, 1895, 2: 128)

Kwaklya A snake spirit. To hunt them successfully he must be allowed to possess. The Maguzawa, Nigeria. (Greenberg, 1946: 35)

Kwanantsitsi Red-Tailed Hawk—"the ideal Chemehuevi hunter and warrior, who also possesses considerable shamanistic powers." The Chemehuevi, California, Nevada, and Arizona. (Laird, 1976: 165–168, 218)

Kwataka The "Bird-man," a sky and war god, is invoked for rain and snow, for agricultural fertility and abundance. The Hopi, Arizona. (Fewkes, 1899: 529, 533)

Kwatoko The eagle, the killer bird, is associated with the zenith. The Zuñi, Oraibi, Sia, Acoma. Among the Hopi he is guardian of the Eagle Clan and his feathers carry prayers to the Sun. Arizona and New Mexico. (Parsons, 1939: 178, 186–7; Waters, 1963: 68–69)

K!wek!waxawe' A name for the raven—"Great Inventor." Also called Hemaskas. The Rivers Inlet tribe, British Columbia. (Boas, 1909/10: 584)

Kwelopunyai The toad, the midwife of the earth mother. The Cuna, Panama. (Keeler, 1961: 30)

Kwenmastili Grasshopper, the messenger of Olowaipippilele. The Cuna, Panama. (Keeler, 1960: 56)

Kwewe The supernatural wolf of the Walpi. Pueblo Indians, Arizona. (Fewkes, 1895, 2: 128)

Kwouk-kwouk The frog woman, mother of Pakadringa and Tomituka, Buerali—the weather supernaturals. The Tiwi, Melville Island, Australia. (Mountford, 1958: 37, 42)

Kyanwa The cat spirit. To hunt them successfully she must be allowed to possess. Wife of Damisa. The Maguzawa, Nigeria. (Greenberg, 1946: 35)

Ladon A dragon, son of Phorcys and Keto, who was a "guardian of the golden apples of the Hesperides," assisting the three Hesperides. Later, in one legend, he was made the constellation Draco by Hera. Greece. (Barthell, 1971: 11, 58)

Lagarto A "giant lizard spirit" inhabits the turbulent waters of streams and kills unwary bathers. The Chorti, Guatemala. (Wisdom, 1940: 409)

Lakin Chan God K—"serpent of the east . . . creator of men and of all organic life . . . founded the Maya culture." Guatemala and Mexico. (Nicholson, 1967: 127)

Lani-wahine A lizard goddess who takes human form to foretell disaster. Oahu, Hawaii. (Beckwith, 1940: 126)

Lassoo-fo moong A man-eating bird devil who was killed by Rumnam (a mythological hero), and from whose scattered flesh came "leeches and mosquitoes, and the small predatory bird kar-hu-fo." The Lepchas, Sikkim. (Gorer, 1938: 55)

Leatualoa   The centipede god whose actions predicted death, if it crawled under the mat, or recovery, if on top of the mat. Samoa, Polynesia. (Turner, 1884: 69)

Lejman   The "first living beings were two worms, Wulleb and Lejman, living together in a shell . . . [They] raised the top shell to make the sky; the lower shell became the earth." The Marshall Islands, Micronesia. (Leach, 1956: 183)

Lepe-a-moa   A bird/girl who had an ancestress, Ke-ao-lewa, who was a bird/woman and a sky sorceress. Hawaii. (Beckwith, 1940: 428; Westervelt, 1963, 1: 206–208)

ɫé·tcạ·'í (letcan'i)   A dog deity of bad luck. The Navaho, Arizona and New Mexico. (Reichard, 1950: 430)

Le-tkakawash   A bright red or yellow bird who represents "the bright sky at moonrise or sunrise." Mother of Aishish. The Klamath, Oregon. (Gatschet, 1890: lxxxv)

Lik   A supernatural serpent "who carries fish within his tail." If someone finds him stranded on dry ground during the winter and carries him back to a lagoon he promises them many fish whenever they ask for them, but only if the secret is kept. The Toba, Argentina. (Métraux, 1969: 59)

Limbago   A "long-necked quadruped" zoomorphic *buso* which is a carrier of illness. The Bagobo, Philippines. (Benedict, 1916: 40)

Limik   A falcon god—"silent, determined, wise, a warrior." The Yokuts, California. (Kroeber, 1925: 510)

Linda   A bird goddess—the swan—wife of Kalev and mother of Kalevipoeg. Finland. (de Kay, 1898: 73, 215)

Lube, Lupe   The dove, female twin of Hemoana (or Tukuhali), fourth pair born of Touia-a-Futuna, the primordial parent-rock. Goddess of the forest and the land. The Tongans, Polynesia. (Collocott, 1921: 152–153; Williamson, 1933, 1: 10; Moulton, 1925, 12: 376, 379)

Lugalbanda   A bull god of Uruk whose consort is Nin-sun. Sumer, Near East. (Jacobsen, 1970: 8)

Luisi   The hyena god. The Baganda, Uganda. (Cunningham, 1905: 218; Budge, 1973, 1: 377)

Lujjuphu   A god in the form of a frog who with his sister, Jassuju, were parents of humans. The Dhammai, Northeast India. (Long, 1963: 106)

Luk   The deified grizzly bear, female, sometimes male. The Klamath Indians, Oregon. (Gatschet, 1890: cii; Chamberlain, 1892: 254)

Luk   A black nocturnal bird was a god of death and disease as well as the patron of thieves and robbers. Yap Island, the Carolines, Micronesia. (Christian, 1899: 384–385)

Lupe   The Dove, child of Malamanganga'e and Malamangangaifo. Wife of Papatu and mother of A'alua. Samoa, Polynesia. (Williamson, 1933, 1: 8)

Maboya, Mapoia   A snake god who causes hurricanes and is the guardian deity of the shaman. The Carib, West Indies. (Alexander, 1920: 38)

Maçat, Mazat   The deer god is the god of the chase. The Nicarao, Nicaragua. (Bancroft, 1886, 3: 492; Lothrop, 1926: 70)

Ma-cha Shên   The goddess of locusts is worshipped primarily in the north of China. (Leach, 1950, 2: 641; Werner, 1932: 341)

Mafdet   A cat goddess or god who keeps the "Hall of Life" clear of snakes. Egypt. (Hornblower, 1943: 85)

Magar   A Dravidian crocodile god worshipped annually as a protection against crocodiles and also against illness. Baroda, India. (Crooke, 1925, 5: 9)

Magni Wunlang Manang Wumphrang   The embryonic elephant deity, of the second generation of deities. Child of Kring-Krong wa and Ynong majan. The Katchins, Burma. (Gilhodes, 1908: 675)

Magobwi   A snake god of Uganda. (Cunningham, 1905: 218)

Mahabir   The equivalent of Hanuman. India. (Crooke, 1894: 51; Russell, 1916, 4: 82)

Mahakh   The bitch-mother of the Aleuts. The mother, by Iraghdadakh, of "two creatures, male and female, half man, half fox" who became the parents of the human race. Alaska. (Bancroft, 1886, 3: 104–105)

Mahatala   The hornbill forms a dual supreme being with Jata, the watersnake. They represent the total divinity, the duality of all things—"Upperworld and Underworld, man and woman, sun and moon, sacred spear and sacred cloth, good and evil, life and death, war and peace, etc." He is the creator, assisted by Jata. His full name, Ranying Mahatala Langit, is that used in the priesthood. The Ngaju, Borneo. (Scharer, 1963: 14–22, 26, 27)

Mahes A lion god who is associated with the dead. Egypt. (Knight, 1915: 67; Budge, 1969, 2: 362)

Maitubo The shrew god of the earth. The Sia, Pueblo Indians, New Mexico. (Fewkes, 1895, 2: 127)

Mai-tu-pu The mole god of the lower regions. The Zuñi, New Mexico. (Cushing, 1881/82: 20)

Makatcatsi Horned Toad, a desert Immortal. The Chemehuevi, California, Nevada, and Arizona. (Laird, 1976: 160)

Mamala A lizard- crocodile- or shark-woman. Wife of Ouha, the shark-man/god. Oahu, Hawaii. (Westervelt, 1963, 1: 52)

Mamili A zoomorphic *buso*—"king of snakes." The Bagoba, Philippines. (Benedict, 1916: 39)

Manasa The snake goddess, protective against their bites. The special guardian deity among the Mal. India. (Crooke, 1894: 135; 1925, 8: 344; Martin, 1914: 258–259)

Mane Manchi, or Mane Manchamma A serpent goddess of Mysore. India. (Whitehead, 1916: 85)

Manager-kunger-kunja The lizard creator god and the teacher of culture. The Western Aranda, Australia. (Leach, 1956: 192)

Manito Wabos The rabbit god of the east, a god of light and of the dawn. The Cherokee, North Carolina and Tennessee. (Spence, 1925, 3: 503–504)

Manuseu The "sacred swan" who dwells in the heavens. The Menomini, Wisconsin. (Skinner, 1915: 78)

Manuwa A man who transformed as a jaguar and ate humans. His wife was Kawao whom he ate when her foster sons, Shikiemano and Iureke, killed her and served her to him as a stew. The Makiritare, Venezuela. (Civrieux, 1980: 55, 62)

Mapeun Supernatural bird of the south. The Sia, Pueblo Indians, New Mexico. (Fewkes, 1895, 2: 127)

Marici The goddess of the dawn was worshipped by a Buddhist sect in the north as a pig goddess—"the Diamond Sow." India. (MacKenzie, 1930: 260)

Marina A zoomorphic *buso*—"an arboreal animal with a snake-like body, that climbs by means of long arms." The Bagobo, Philippines. (Benedict, 1916: 40)

Maruti Another name for Hanuman (Hanumat), the monkey god. India. (Ghurye, 1962: 4; Chapekar, 1960: 89)

Masichu'a The Gray Horned Snake god and guardian of the north. The Hopi Indians, Arizona. (Waters, 1963: 50)

Maskikhwsu The toad woman, a "woods spirit, is a seducer of men and children . . . though her intentions are good, an involuntary baleful influence soothes it into a sleep from which there is no awakening." The Penobscot, Maine. (Speck, 1935: 16)

Mat Chinoi A serpent deity who controls the Chinoi class or group of spirits. The Negritos, Malay Peninsula. (Eliade, 1964: 340)

Mato Piseo The "Great Panther"—a power of the earth. The Menomini, Wisconsin. (Skinner, 1915, 1: 207)

Mati A cat-headed goddess of the 11th division of the Tuat. Egypt. (Budge, 1969, 1: 201)

Mato "The Spirit of the Bear which presides over love and hate and bravery and wounds and many kinds of medicines. He was the patron of mischief and fun." The Oglala, South Dakota. (Walker, 1980: 121)

Matshikitshiki The great sea-serpent god who fished up the island of Aniwa and of whom the people lived in terror. New Hebrides, Melanesia. (Williamson, 1933, 2: 181)

Mawiang A "ferocious double-headed dog" who guards the road to the afterworld and must be propitiated. The Milanows, Borneo. (De Crespigny, 1875: 35)

Maw law kwi "The king of the crocodiles," considered one of the P'yo demons. The Karen, Burma. (Marshall, 1922: 231)

Mayanja The leopard god of the Baganda. Uganda. (Cunningham, 1905: 215)

Maykiya The eagle spirit. To hunt them successfully he must be allowed to possess. The Maguzawa, Nigeria. (Greenberg, 1946: 36)

Mbasi A snake god who married Konjini, producing an egg which in turn produced the first human pair.

Rossel Island, Melanesia. (Armstrong, 1923/24: 2; MacKenzie, 1930: 148)

Mbatingasau   The hawk god of Ndreketi. Lau Islands, Melanesia. (Hocart, 1929: 198)

Mbulakambiri   A white striped rat is the god of Vanravua. Lau Islands, Melanesia. (Hocart, 1929: 197)

Mbyung   A snake god who threw stones as his weapons. Rossel Island, Melanesia. (Armstrong, 1923/24: 18,19)

Mea Moa   A bird god of Easter Island. Polynesia. (Gray, 1925, 5: 133)

Mehen   A serpent goddess of the 2nd division of the Tuat. Egypt. (Budge, 1969, 1: 180)

Mehenet   A serpent goddess with whom Sekhet is identified. Egypt. (Budge, 1969, 1: 515)

Mehurt   A cow goddess of the primeval time. Egypt. (Neumann, 1955: 154; Knight, 1915: 68)

Menat   A lion goddess, also worshipped by Arabians. Egypt. (Budge, 1969, 2: 289, 362)

Mendjangan Seluang   A deer god, "the totemic animal of the descendants of Madjapahit." Bali, Indonesia. (Covarrubias, 1937: 92)

Menhet   A lioness-headed goddess with whom Bast was identified in Nubia. A name of Isis in Heliopolis. Egypt. (Knight, 1915: 69; Budge, 1969, 1: 446; 1969, 2: 213)

Menrot   The "Great Stallion is the ancestor of the nation." Father of Hunor and Magor. Hungary. (Roheim, 1954: 9)

Merkyut   The Bird of Heaven invoked in ceremonies of sacrifice to Bai-Yulgen. The Altaians, Siberia. (Czaplicka, 1969: 298–300)

Mertseger   A "snake-goddess of the Theban necropolis," benevolent but also punitive. Egypt. (Ames, 1965: 114)

Meru   A python god of the Basoga. Son of Semuganda. Uganda. (Roscoe, 1915: 247)

Mer-ur, Mnevis   The predynastic sacred bull of Heliopolis, believed to represent the sun. Egypt. (Budge, 1969, 1: 26; 1969, 2: 351)

Meskheti   A bull god and a star god—the Great Bear. Egypt. (Budge, 1969, 2: 312)

Meskwa   A name for Raven. Vancouver Island, British Columbia. (Boas, 1909/10: 584)

Mes-Ptah   A lion-headed deity, the doorkeeper of the 2nd pylon of the Papyrus of Ani. Egypt. (Budge, 1973, 1: 295)

Messon   The Great Hare, the Algonquin creator, is also the god of all animal life. The Montagnais, Labrador and Quebec. (Drahomanov, 1962: 19; Alexander, 1964: 32)

Messou   The Great Hare, creator of the earth. Also called Manibojo, Michabo, and Nanabojou. The Algonquin. Ontario, Ohio, Pennsylvania, and New York. (Dragomanov, 1961: 19, 22)

Metot-ush Kamui   The bear god of the Saru and Mukawa Districts. The Ainu, Japan. (Munro, 1963: 13)

Metsi   Coyote—a transformer and trickster. The Yana, California. (Curtin, 1903: 325, 335)

Mica   The Coyote is the spirit of cowardice, of malevolent mischief, and of thievery. He is a friend of Iktomi, and like him, fears the sweat lodge. The Oglala, South Dakota. (Walker, 1980: 121, 129, 242)

Michabo   The Great Hare, creator of the earth, the god of light, of the weather and of culture. The Algonquin, United States. (Brinton, 1882: 47; Fiske, 1900: 73, 154; Spence, 1925, 4: 127; Dragomanov, 1961: 19, 22; Brinton, 1868: 166; Larousse, 1968: 427)

Milapukala   The totemic cockatoo created many of the animals and foods. The Tiwi, Melville Island, Australia. (Mountford, 1958: 37, 53)

Miloli'i   A dragon god of Kauai. Hawaii. (Westervelt, 1963, 3: 258)

Minokawa   An enormous bird who swallows the moon causing the eclipse. The Bagobo, Philippines. (Benedict, 1916: 40, 47)

Misabos   The Great Hare of the Ojibwa. Minnesota and Ontario. (Hallowell, 1967: 218)

Mixcoatl   The Cloud Serpent was associated with the Milky Way and with lightning. He was also a god of the chase. The Chichimecs and the Aztec. Mexico. (Caso, 1958: 31, 37; Brinton, 1868: 51; Spence, 1923: 181, 312, 319)

Moccus The Celtic swine god, identified with Mercury. Gaul. (Renel, 1906: 401; MacCulloch, 1911: 24)

Moho-Koko-Ko-ho An owl deity who ruled in the north. The Winnebago, Wisconsin. (Emerson, 1884: 8)

Moire Mat The spider goddess is invoked in house-warming ceremonies. The Ainu, Japan. (Munro, 1963: 79, 80)

Mokaitc The cougar god of the north. The Sia, Pueblo Indians, New Mexico. (Fewkes, 1895, 2: 127)

Mokiach The lion god and a god of hunting. The Keresan, New Mexico. (Tyler, 1964: 213)

Moko (1) The lizard god of Mangaia. Polynesia. (Andersen, 1928: 146) (2) The lizard woman. The sons of herself and Vie Kena introduced tattooing. Easter Island, Polynesia. (Métraux, 1940: 316)

Moko-Hae "Chief of the lizard gods, hostile to mankind; producers of internal ailments and racking pains." The Marquesas, Polynesia. (Christian, 1895: 190)

Moko-hiku-aru A lizard god and a wizard god, a guardian of the sacred axe Te Awhio-rangi. New Zealand. (MacKenzie, n.d.: 59, 60)

Moko-huruhuru The glow worm personified. The Maori, New Zealand. (Best, 1924: 95)

Moko-nui An evil lizard diety. The Maori, New Zealand. (Andersen, 1928: 146)

Moko-titi An evil lizard deity of the Maori. New Zealand. (Andersen, 1928: 146)

Mokuhinia A lizard goddess of Maui, Hawaii. (Beckwith, 1940: 126)

Moltinus A sheep god at Saone-et-Loire. Gaul. (Renel, 1906: 401)

Mönetta The scorpion, one of the star people, who became the constellation Ursa Major. The Makiritare, Venezuela. (Civrieux, 1980: 114)

Month A falcon god. Egypt. (Larousse, 1973: 51)

Mo'o-inanea A dragon goddess, who "cared for the first children of the gods," was also described as a man-eating deity. Hawaii. (Westervelt, 1963, 3: 116–117; Beckwith, 1940: 71, 78, 127)

Mo'o-lau A great dragon god. Kohala District, Hawaii. (Westervelt, 1963, 2: 122)

Mo'o-uri The black lizard god "who showed himself in the lowering sky along the horizon; he guided those who sailed from the low islands." Tahiti, Polynesia. (Henry, 1928: 377)

Mora A demoness who takes "the form of a butterfly, and oppresses the breathing of sleepers at night." She also sometimes takes the form of a horse, or of a tuft of hair. Serbia, Montenegro, Bohemia, and Poland. (Ralston, 1872: 133)

moyuk The racoon-dog deity of the Ainu. Hokkaidu, Japan. (Philippi, 1982: 46)

Müdo The great potoo—"One of the three great bird spirits living in the sixth Heaven, Matawahuña. Despite his position as one of the most powerful shaman helpers, Müdo is often made fun of because of his ugliness." Brother of Wanadi. The Makiritare, Venezuela. (Civrieux, 1980: 52, 188)

Mumbo A serpent god of the Luo. Kenya. (Davidson, 1969: 273)

Munekiachu The dog demon who tries to interfere with parturition. The Cuna, Panama. (Nordenskiold, 1938: 370)

Mush A Sumerian/Akkadian serpent god who is associated with earth fertility and solar heat. Near East. (Langdon, 1931: 90)

Musiu birbiks A Litu-Prussian divinity—the fly pest. (Schrader, 1925, 2: 31)

Muut The messenger of death created by Mukat frequently appeared as an owl whose hooting foretold death. Muut was regarded "as both a blessing and a bringer of sadness." The Cahuilla, California. (Brumgardt and Bowles, 1981: 37; Bean, 1974: 167)

Muyi The supernatural mole of the Walpi. The Pueblo Indians, Arizona. (Fewkes, 1895, 2: 128)

Muyusu The rainbow serpent deity of the Mundurucu. Brazil. (Levi-Strauss, 1969: 324)

Mwanga A serpent god invoked for children. Also a god of divination of the future. The Bagesu and the Baganda, Uganda. (Roscoe, 1915: 179; Cunningham, 1905: 216; Budge, 1973, 1: 377)

na'acdjêi· 'esdzá· Spider woman is both beneficial and destructive—at times having to be subdued. "She is a symbol of the textile arts, having taught man weaving; she requires woven fabrics as offerings." The Navaho, Arizona and New Mexico. (Reichard, 1950: 467–468)

na'actcidi· The badger, a very powerful and helpful deity. The Navaho, Arizona and New Mexico. (Reichard, 1950: 382)

Naat A zoomorphic *buso,* the deer, with one good and one bad horn. The Bagoba, Philippines. (Benedict, 1916: 39)

na'azisi Pocket Gopher, a helpful deity of the Navaho. Arizona and New Mexico. (Reichard, 1950: 457)

Nabia A jaguar goddess, mother of Namaku by Noánase. The Kogi, Colombia. (Reichel-Dolmatoff, 1975: 57)

Naga Busai A monstrous serpent of the primeval waters upon whose head Hatala poured out the earth. Borneo. (MacKenzie, 1930: 308)

Naga Padhoa A serpent deity of the Bataks of Silindung. Sumatra, Indonesia. (Coleman, 1832: 365)

Naga-rajah A Dragon King, a protector of monasteries. China. (Edkins, 1880: 207)

Nag Deo The cobra god of the Baiga, the Barai, and the Kirar. Among the Gond they believe that killing and eating one during the first month of the rains will "protect them from the effects of eating any poisonous substance." India. (Russell, 1916, 2: 86, 194; 1916, 3: 101, 491)

Nagdev A serpent god of the Bhils. Bombay Province, India. Naik, 1956: 172)

Nag Dewata A snake god worshipped and thanked by the snake charmers when they have caught a snake "by drinking and eating sweets together. . . . All snakes are physical manifestations" of him. India. (Skafte, 1979: 124)

Nageswar The serpent god of Benares controls the weather. India. (Crooke, 1894: 267; Maetin, 1914: 259)

Nagoba A guardian snake god of the Deccan. India. (Crooke, 1925, 11: 414)

Nag Raja A snake and household god of the Himalayas. If a snake is injured in any way while working the fields, work must stop and retribution be made. India. (Berreman, 1963: 372–373)

Nahengan A supernatural animal power "similar to a grizzly bear." The Tsimshians, British Columbia. (Boas, 1909/10: 555)

Nai A serpent god and god of the 22nd day of the month. Egypt. (Budge, 1969, 1: 23; 1969, 2: 322)

Naicje'etcó diǐxiǐn "Large black spider," one of four creator deities. The San Carlos Apache, Arizona. (Goddard, 1918: 27)

Nak An Egyptian serpent god. (Budge, 1969, 1: 335)

Naľuletcu diǐxiǐn Black Big Spider—pre-existent. One of the four primordial beings. The San Carlos Apache, Arizona. (Goddard, 1918: 7)

Nama An evil and malevolent hyena god of the Bambara. Mali. (Tauxier, 1927: 179–180, 303)

Namaku A jaguar god, son of Noánase and Nabia. The Kogi, Colombia. (Reichel-Dolmatoff, 1975: 45, 57)

Namcu The sacred eagle, the messenger of the gods to men. The Araucanian, Chile. (Emerson, 1884: 37)

Nanabojou Another name for Michabo, the Great Hare. The Algonquin Indians, Eastern United States. (Dragomanov, 1961: 19; Brinton, 1897: 70)

Nanda The "Nagaraja, king of the serpents." India. (Getty, 1962: 173)

nangkhaengy The gopher deity of the underground, a powerful medicine animal. The Tewa, Pueblo Indians, New Mexico. (Harrington, 1907/08: 43)

Nan-kieil-ilil-man "God of the *Kieil*—a large black lizard with red spots, . . . considered 'uncanny', from its savage disposition." Ponape, Caroline Islands, Micronesia. (Christian, 1899: 382)

Nankilalas Raven, a supernatural being of the Haida. British Columbia. (Boas, 1909/10: 584)

Nantotsuelta, Nantosvelta A Celtic goddess associated with domesticity as a dovecote and with war as a raven. Britain and Gaul. (Ross, 1967: 219, 244; Renel, 1906: 401)

Nappakandattha A watersnake and the source of the rainbow. The Warramunga, Central Australia. (Spencer, 1904: 631)

Narama The rainbow-serpent goddess who is dangerous to aborigines. Liverpool River area, Australia. (Mountford, 1958: 155)

Narasiṃhi A lion-headed goddess. India. (O'Flaherty, 1980: 262)

Nareau The Ancient Spider was pre-existent and "commanded sand and water to bear children." Among them was Nareau, the Younger, who killed Nareau, the Elder, and made the sun and moon from his eyes. The Gilbert Islands, Micronesia. (Leach, 1956: 183; Poignant, 1967: 71)

Narpajin The rainbow snake goddess, whose upper portion was a woman and lower a snake, from whom were stolen the ritual songs and law. The Murinbata tribe, Australia. (Robinson, 1966: 71)

Narsinghswami The "man-lion incarnation of Vishnu" worshipped by the Namaddar. Central Provinces, India. (Russell, 1916, 4: 156)

Nasr A vulture god, a deity of the Himyarites, the Sabaeans. Arabia and Persia. (Noldeke, 1925, 1: 662–663; Fahd, 1968: 132; Smith, 1969: 226; Larousse, 1968: 323)

Nata A cobra deity of the Coorgs. South India. (Srinivas, 1952: 160)

Na·tsedlozi· The roadrunner, a helpful deity. The Navaho, Arizona and New Mexico. (Reichard, 1950: 462)

Nāu A serpent god of Egypt. (Knight, 1915: 75; Budge, 1969, 1: 267)

Naxa Mountain Sheep. A shaman's helper. The Chemehuevi, California, Nevada, and Arizona. (Laird, 1976: 112, 207)

Náybemunéki A snake demon who causes difficulties in childbirth. The Cuna, Panama. (Nordenskiold, 1930: 60–61)

Ndamathia A snake god of the Mathioya River who when sacrificed to provides abundant rains. The Kikuyu, Kenya. (Willoughby, 1932: 10, 11)

Ndengei Originally a deified ancestor who became a serpent god symbolizing eternity. He lives in a mountain cave and his movement causes earthquakes. He and his son, Rokomautu, were believed to be creator deities. Fiji Islands, Melanesia. (Thomson, 1925, 1: 443; 1925, 6: 14; MacKenzie, 1930: 95; Poignant, 1967: 94)

Nefer-Tem A lion-god, son of Ptah and Sekhet, a god of the rising sun. Egypt. (Knight, 1915: 74–75; Budge, 1969, 1: 514, 521; 1969, 2: 362)

Neha-hra A serpent deity of Egypt. (Budge, 1969, 1: 231)

Nehebka(u) A serpent goddess and one of the judges of the dead. Egypt. (Hambly, 1929: 663; Budge, 1969, 2: 62)

Nekau A cow-headed deity, the doorkeeper of the fourth pylon, Papyrus of Ani. Egypt. (Budge, 1973, 1: 296)

Nekhebet A vulture goddess, twin sister of Uatchet, and goddess of the south, also a goddess of childbirth. She was identified with Hathor and also with Isis and as such was the mother of the sun-god. Egypt. (Jayne, 1962: 72; Knight, 1915: 79–80; Ames, 1965: 87; Budge, 1969, 1: 438–440)

Nekilstlus, Nekilstlas The benevolent raven god, the creator of all things. Same as Yelt. The Haida, British Columbia. (Maclean, 1876: 438; Niblack, 1888: 378)

Nemcatacoa, Nencatacoa A bear god and a god of weavers, painters of cloth, and of drunkenness. The Chibcha, Colombia. (Kroeber, 1946: 906; Reichel-Dolmatoff, 1975: 45; Alexander, 1920: 204)

Nenstalil "Grizzly-Bear-of-the-Door" has a room in the house of the Cannibal Spirit and is watchman of the house. The Kwakiutl, British Columbia. (Boas, 1935: 142, 160)

Nepokwai'i, Kokopelli The insect kachina—"a hunter who seduces girls or makes them bridal moccasins and whose 'hump' is really a gift-containing sack." The Hano-Hopi, Pueblo Indians, Arizona. (Parsons, 1939: 191–192)

Ngaloit The rainbow serpent of the Oenpelli area who, if disturbed, will cause waterholes to overflow and drown people. Australia. (Mountford, 1958: 155)

Nga sungsung A wild animal resembling a buffalo, of the third generation of deities. Child of Ningthoi and Ningsin. The Katchins, Burma. (Gilhodes, 1908: 676)

Nikaiva Believed to be a crocodile goddess who lives in the river and to whom a live sheep is sacrificed. The Shilluk, Sudan. (Butt, 1952: 64)

Nin-ezen xLa A bull god of Kiabrig. His consort is Nin-e-i-garak. Sumer, Near East. (Jacobsen, 1970: 7)

Ningpaum Wunlang Pauchen Wunphrang The embryonic bison of the second generation of deities. The Katchins, Burma. (Gilhoes, 1908: 675)

Ningublaga The bull god and city god of Kiabrig. Near East. (Jacobsen, 1976: 25)

Ninmar A bird goddess and city goddess of Guabba. Daughter of Nanshe. Sumer, Near East. (Jacobsen, 1970: 23)

Ninsun A cow goddess and city goddess of Kullab. Wife of Lugalbanda and mother of Gilgamish. Sumer, Near East. (Jacobsen, 1970: 8, 26; Langdon, 1931: 115; Pettazzoni, 1956: 84)

Ninzi Wunland Tetsin Wunphrang The embryonic sparrow hawk of the second generation of deities. The Katchins, Burma. (Gilhodes, 1908: 675)

Noánase A jaguar god and a shaman, son of Kashindukua. He too devoured people and was killed by his uncle Búkuase, but he still lives and will return. The Kogi, Colombia. (Reichel-Dolmatoff, 1975: 55–58)

Noho-a-mo'o A dragon god of Hilo. Hawaii. (Westervelt, 1963, 2: 121)

Noitu A jaguar/woman goddess, wife of Mavutsine and mother of Kuat (the sun) and Yai (the moon). The Camayura, Mato Grosso, Brazil. (Oberg, 1953: 53; Weyer, 1961: 134)

Ñomo The mistress and the mother of the snakes in the sky (there were none on earth). She was beautiful but evil, and mistress of the poisons. Her children became poisonous snakes when she sent them to earth. She captures the souls of those bitten by her sons with a draught of forgetfulness. The Makiritare, Venezuela. (Civrieux, 1980: 88, 188)

Nongwa A snake god whose only weapons were fingers. Rossel Island, Melanesia. (Armstrong, 1923/24: 2)

Nukaima The serpent spirit whose wife is Kamuteriro. The Paressi, Brazil. (Métraux, 1948, 4: 358; Zerries, 1968: 307)

Nü Kua, Nü Wa A beautiful and powerful goddess "commonly represented as half serpent, half woman," sometimes as a rainbow dragon, sometimes simply a woman. Her name implies association with ponds, rain pools, water generally and the animals that live in or near them, indicating the possibility also of interpreting her as a frog or snail goddess. She is considered the creator of man a goddess of wind and of wind instruments. Her twin or consort, Fu Hsi, is "like her, a proto-musician and creator spirit." China. (Schafer, 1980; 37–41, 61–62; Werner, 1934: 81; Bodde, 1961: 386, 388–389) Also Nu Kua Shih.

Nulla Pambu A serpent god of India. The cobra. (Miller, 1970: 406)

Numlang Wunlang Khaka Wunphrang The embryonic crow-raven of the second generation of deities. The Katchins, Burma. (Gilhodes, 1908: 675)

Nunusomikeeqonem The mother of Alkuntam "is described as a Cannibal, who inserts her long snout in the ears of man, and sucks out his brain. Eventually she was transformed into the mosquito." The Bella Coola, British Columbia. (Boas, 1898: 30)

Nupuri-kor(o)-kamui The wise and gentle bear gods, who are friendly toward humans and sometimes take human form, are worshipped. They are mountain gods; they can be violent if there is a misunderstanding. In contrast, the Nupuri-kesh-un-guru, or arsarush, are wild and ferocious monster bears and are not worshipped. The Ainu, Japan. (Batchelor, n.d.: 123; Philippi, 1982: 115)

Nut The cow and sky goddess from whose back Ra raised himself into the sky. Daughter of Shu and Tefnut and wife of Seb; mother of Osiris and Isis, Set and Nephthys. She is also considered the female counterpart of Nu. Egypt. (Knight, 1915: 88; Ames, 1965: 53; Budge, 1969, 1: 283–4, 367; 1969, 2: 100)

Nyani'manus A malevolent tiger spirit of the Sakai. Malay Peninsula. (Skeat, 1906: 247)

Nyanyi Bumba The white heron—one of the creatures vomited forth by Bumba. He created all birds except the kite. The Bushongo, Zaire. (Eliade, 1967: 91)

Nyukuadn A snake and water god who causes the rains and floods. The Botocudo, Brazil. (Nimuendaju, 1946: 111)

O-Dotsu A snake god at Takashima. Japan. (Norbeck 1954: 132)

Ogediga A python—"the tribal- and war-god" of the Brass River people. West Africa. (MacCulloch, 1925, 11: 400)

Oka The jaguar of the sky-world whose mother is Mero and brother is Kuara. The Bakairi, Brazil. (Alexander, 1920: 312)

Oke The chief god and creator among the Potomac takes the form of a great hare. Virginia. (Swanton, 1946: 743, 749)

O-ke-hée-de The Owl, the Evil Spirit. The Mandan, North Dakota. (Catlin, 1967: 59)

Okuchi-no-Kami The Shinto wolf god. Japan. (Kato, 1926: 18)

Olaga A local snake god of Calabar. Nigeria. (Mac-Culloch, 1925, 11: 411)

O le Lulu "[The owl] was regarded as a war spirit on Ofu." Manua (Samoa), Polynesia. (Mead, 1930: 208)

Oloopanilel The "Ant-bear . . . Chief in the realm of the dead," whose wife is Oloakindili. The Cuna, Panama. (Nordenskiold, 1938: 329)

Olopaikkalilel "Chief of the white apes." The Cuna, Panama. (Nordenskiold, 1938: 329)

Olopak-kukulor The chief of the ants who has charge of Pili-Baabakka (the eighth layer of the heavens). The Cuna, Panama. (Nordenskiold, 1938: 161; Keeler, 1960: 90)

Olopanieginalilel A heron god whose wife is Olopindilisop. The Cuna, Panama. (Nordenskiold, 1938: 301)

Onditachiae The thunderbird god controlled the weather. The Huron, Eastern United States. (Tooker, 1964: 82)

Onkoy The supreme god of the Chavin "is a hybrid, both male and female, half-feline and half-reptile." Associated with the constellation of the Pleiades. Peru. (Flornoy, 1958: 83)

Opaskwusiu The vulture, servant of the thunderers. The Menomini, Wisconsin. (Skinner, 1913: 78)

Opigielguoviran A "dog-like being." The Antilles, West Indies. (Alexander, 1920: 25)

Ora The jaguar spirit of the Yanomamo. Venezuela and Brazil. (Chagnon, 1968: 46)

Orseley Tiger god of the Bondo. India. (Elwin, 1950: 151)

Osabu A snake god of the Gã in Labadi. Among the Gã in Kpong he is associated with the leopard. Ghana. (Field, 1937: 40, 77)

Oshadagea The Dew Eagle, an assistant of Hino, who provides moisture and also quenches the destruction of the Fire Spirits. The Iroquois Indians, Eastern United States. (Alexander, 1964: 24; Larousse, 1968: 430)

Osiris-Keb "Osiris fused with the ancient Goose-god, who produced the cosmic egg." Egypt. (Budge, 1973, 1: 60)

Osiris-Neb-Heh As a bennu-headed mummy he represents the god of the eternity of existence. Egypt. (Budge, 1973, 1: 60)

Otava The Great Bear, a Finno-Ugric celestial deity. (Larousse, 1968: 304)

Ouroboros The serpent, both good and bad, "worshipped by several sects of the Ophites" and who "planted in man's heart the yearning for knowledge." Gnosticism. (Seligmann, 1948: 106, 134)

Owufu The black snake god of the Gã in Nungwa. Ghana. (Field, 1937: 27)

Paatsatsi Bat, son-in-law of Coyote, had magic power that "quickly froze water into ice" by which he cured burns. As a shaman's helper he could confer these powers on them. The Chemehuevi, California, Nevada, and Arizona. (Laird, 1976: 113, 182–192)

Padang Lapu Mana Puthung The great serpent who causes earth-quakes with his movements is controlled by Ningkong wa. The Katchins, Burma. (Gilhodes, 1908: 673)

Pakhangba Among the Meitheis an ancestor god who manifests himself as a snake. Assam. (Crooke, 1925, 11: 413)

Palulukoñ, Palulukoñti The plumed serpent deity, a god of fertility and of rain. The Patki, the Tusayan, and the Hopi. Arizona. (Fewkes, 1897: 190; Alexander, 1964: 188; Tyler, 1964: 245)

Pana'ewa A reptile/man deity of the forest who caused people to lose their way with fogs and rain. Hawaii. (Westervelt, 1963, 2: 98–99)

Pangi A river god who is an anaconda and lives in the cataract of the Marañon. There is a taboo of silence in traveling through the gorge. The Jivaro, Ecuador. (Stirling, 1938: 116)

Papagado A benevolent snake god of the Bush Negroes. Dutch Guiana. (MacCulloch, 1925, 11: 400)

Papawa Bear, aunt of Wolf and Coyote. "As a shaman's familiar, the bear confers great strength." The Chemehuevis, California, Nevada, and Arizona. (Laird, 1976: 113, 192–193)

Parauri A female being who personifies the parson bird. By Tane she was the mother of "the *koko* and other forest birds." The Maori, New Zealand. (Best, 1924: 114, 176)

Pashkuru Kamui The crow deity of the Ainu. Japan. (Munro, 1963: 22)

Pasikola The rabbit, trickster god of the Creek Indians. Alabama and Georgia. (Burland, 1965: 150)

pa yel bu A serpent god of the Lepchas. Sikkim. (Siiger, 1967: 192)

Pekhet(h) A cat or lioness goddess of Egypt. (Budge, 1969, 1: 517; Larousse, 1968: 37)

Pena Verde A god "identified with the blue macaw." Belem, Brazil. (Leacock, 1972: 150)

Penkye Otu Among the Akan he is incarnate in the antelope and is dangerous. He is asked to foretell the coming year. Among the Effutu he is the beneficent chief god protective of their welfare. Ghana. (Meyerowitz, 1958: 39–42; Wyllie, 1966: 478)

Ix Pic Tzab A Mayan serpent goddess. Mexico. (Thompson, 1970: 328)

Pilang Kuntung Usang A Great Bird, child of Samni and Ning-pang majan. The Katchins, Burma. (Gilhodes, 1908: 673)

Pili The lizard is god of agriculture as well as of fishing and is "associated with the origin of kava, sugar cane, and taro." Manua (Samoa), Polynesia. (Mead, 1930; 158–59)

Pili-a-mo'o A dragon god of Hilo. Hawaii. (Westervelt, 1963, 2: 121)

Pilo'i "The rat child." Born of Po-hiolo and Po-ne'a-aku. Hawaii. (Leach, 1956: 170)

Pipa A snake godling of India. (Crooke, 1894: 269; Elwin, 1949: 163)

Piwichen A winged serpent supernatural being of the Mapuche-Huilliche (Araucanians). Chile. (Cooper, 1946, 6: 753)

P'laiwash The deified golden eagle, but not as respected as Raven. The Klamath, Oregon. (Gatschet, 1890: civ)

Pohichio A dog spirit, father and ruler of the forest spirits. The Chamacoco of the Gran Chaco, Argentina. (Zerries, 1968: 238, 305)

Pongo Bumba The crested eagle, one of the creatures vomited forth by Bumba. The Bushongo, Zaire. (Eliade, 1967: 91)

Poo?wavi Louse. A beautiful woman who agreed to accept Coyote, and they became the parents of all Indian tribes. (A difficult task as she had a "toothed vagina"). The Chemehuevi, California, Nevada, and Arizona. (Laird, 1976: 149–152)

Posew'a Coyote—"generally the trickster" but sometimes "acts as go-between for the kachina and the towns people." He also has prophetic qualities. The Tewa, New Mexico. (Parsons, 1929: 275)

Prithivi The earth is represented as a "variegated cow." She is the wife of Dyaus—the primeval parents—and the mother of all things. She is associated with patience. India and Bali. (Danielou, 1964: 87; Keith, 1917: 16; Martin, 1914: 29; Cox, 1870, 1: 328; Levi, 1933: xxiii)

Pua'a-akua The hog-god—the name of Kama-pua'a, the kupua, when he appeared in the form of a pig. Oahu, Hawaii. (Westervelt, 1963, 2: 45)

Puana The watersnake who helped created the world. Brother of Kuma, the moon, and Itciai, the jaguar. The Yaruro, Venezuela. (Kirchhoff, 1948, 2: 462)

Pueo-nui-akea Beneficent owl god who gave warning of danger and aided the prisoner to escape. Maui, Hawaii. (Beckwith, 1940: 124; Emerson, 1968: 44)

Pueo nui o Kona The owl god of Kona, where he is revered as a family god, warns them in time of danger, assists prisoners to escape. Hawaii. (Emerson, 1967: 44)

Puke An evil serpent god who is also a god of wealth, and will burn down houses if angered. Latvia. (Welsford, 1925, 11: 422)

Pulleyar The elephant god, a phallic deity, is worshipped in rites emphasizing male procreation and also the fertility "of crops and women and the health of young children." The Sinhalese Buddhists, Ceylon. (Leach, 1958: 303; 1968: 35)

Punaweko The origin of and personification of land birds. The Maori, New Zealand. (Best, 1924: 97, 176)

Pungatu A zoomorphic *buso*, a "fat quadruped, with a birdlike head, and several humps on his back." The Bagobo, Philippines. (Benedict, 1916: 40)

Pupula The lizard. He took the fetal-positioned humans and gave them flexibility and dexterity, then taught them their culture. The Pindupi and Jumu, Australia. (Leach, 1956: 191)

Pwiya The rainbow serpent of the forest. The Kyaka, New Guinea. (Lawrence-Bulmer, 1965: 153)

The P'yo Dragon or serpent demons who "blow the water up from the ocean and produce the clouds" for rain. The Karen, Burma. (Marshall, 1922: 231)

Qebh A ram-headed god, the name of Khnemu as the early god of the Nile. Egypt. (Budge, 1969, 2: 50)

Qebhsennuf One of the gods of the underworld and a son of Horus. As a god of the Canopic Jars, he is the hawk-headed god guarding the liver and the gall bladder, assisted by Serqet. As god of the Cardinal Points, he represents the West. Egypt. (Knight, 1915: 35; Budge, 1969, 1: 456, 491–492; Ames, 1965: 48)

Qeq-hauau-ent-pehui A jackal-headed god, doorkeeper of Arit III in the Papyrus of Ani. Egypt. (Budge, 1967: 293)

Qerhet An Egyptian snake god. (Budge, 1969, 1: 353)

Qo'icini'mith A supernatural being identified with Raven. The Nootka, Washington and British Columbia. (Boas, 1909/10: 584)

Quetzalcóatl The plumed serpent, god of civilization and of knowledge. As the wind god he was called Ehécatl, was god of the east and of the 9th hour of the day. He was the god of the planet Venus as the morning star. Mexico. (Caso, 1958: 14, 22–26; Alexander, 1920: 54, 57; Vaillant, 1962: 140, 143, 148; Spence, 1923: 118, 123; Nicholson, 1967: 31, 45)

Quikinnaqu The Raven deity "as organizer of the universe, . . . the assistant of the Supreme Being" brought order to human affairs and taught man hunting and the use of fire. The Koryak, Siberia. (Jochelson, 1904: 416–417; Czaplicka, 1969: 262–264)

Quissera Serpent god of the east. Sia, Pueblo Indians, New Mexico. (Fewkes, 1895, 2: 126)

Racumon A man-headed snake who is a god of war and a stellar god. The Carib. Guiana. (Tyler, 1964: 102)

Raharariyoma A snake-like river monstress who causes people to drown. The Yanomamo, Venezuela and Brazil. (Chagnon, 1968: 47)

Raja Sial The watersnake, the epitome of evil, who brings misfortune and failure. The Ngaju, Borneo. (Scharer, 1963: 20, 129)

Rakaiora A deity who represents the lizard. The Maori, New Zealand. (Best, 1924: 238)

Rannut, Rannu, Renenet, Renenutet A serpent goddess or a lioness goddess—a deity of nursing, of fertility and the harvest, of plenty. Egypt. (Knight, 1915: 105; MacCulloch, 1925, 11: 402; Budge, 1969, 2: 144, 362; 1967: cxxv; Younger, 1966: 31; Jayne, 1962: 86)

Rarog, Rarach A "supernatural falcon and fiery dwarf" who takes the form of a whirlwind or an animal. Czech and Slovak. (Leach, 1950, 2: 1026)

Rato A serpent and water demon invoked for success in fishing. Taulipang, Guiana. (Métraux, 1949: 566; Zerries, 1968: 264)

Ratu-mai-mbulu A serpent god, a chthonic god who causes things to grow and the sap to rise in the trees. Fiji and New Guinea. (MacCulloch, 1925, 11: 401; Thomson, 1925, 6: 15; Frazer, 1961: 90)

Raudalo The King of the snakes who lived on the mountain Tauaga and who caused the waters of the great flood to recede. New Guinea. (MacKenzie, 1930: 152)

Renenet *See* **Rannut**

Reret A hippopotamus goddess who restrains the evil influences of Set. She is also a star goddess identified with Draco. Egypt. (Knight, 1915: 107; Budge, 1969, 2: 249, 312)

Reri A serpent god of the 12th division of the Tuat. Egypt. (Budge, 1969, 1: 203)

Rhiannon, Riannon A mare goddess, wife of Pwyll and mother of Pryderi. Later, the wife of Manawyddan. She is also associated with birds. Wales. (Sjoestedt, 1949: 18; O'Rahilly, 1946: 293; Ross, 1967: 225; MacCana, 1970: 55)

rikun kanto ta horkeu kamui "The Wolf God of the Upper Heavens." The Hokkaidu Ainu, Japan. (Philippi, 1982: 75)

Dona Rosalina A snake goddess identified as the Cobra Grande da Lagoa, daughter of Japetequara. Belem, Brazil. (Leacock, 1972: 141–142)

Rumba Wunlang Sharanng Wunphrang The embryonic tiger, of the second generation of deities. Child of Kringkrong wa and Ynong majan. The Katchins, Burma. (Gilhodes, 1908: 675)

Rumba Wunlang Trapru Wunphrang The embryonic bear, of the second generation of deities. Child of Kringkrong wa and Ynong majan. The Katchins, Burma. (Gilhodes, 1908: 675)

Rupe A deity who personifies the pigeon. The Maori, New Zealand. (Best, 1924: 176)

Ruu A pig-like zoomorphic deity who lives underground and steals strength, causing weakness. The Bagobo, Philippines. (Benedict, 1916: 40)

Ryujin A dragon god who controls the thunder, rain, and wind. Japan. (Herbert, 1967: 482; Bunce, 1955: 112)

Sa An ape god, a deity of the 10th hour of the 10th day of the Moon. Egypt. (Budge, 1969, 2: 292)

Sa bdag 'brong nag po "black wild yak"—A deity of the *sa bdag* class, malevolent deities who cause illness. Tibet. (Nebesky-Wojkowitz, 1956, 1; 192)

Sabimochi-no-Kami Shinto crocodile god. Japan. (Kato, 1926: 19)

Saci Cerere The "fire-snake, who protects the country from fire." The Tupi, Brazil. (Spence, 1925, 2: 837)

Safolo A serpent god of the royalty. The Bambara, Mali. (Tauxier, 1927: 213)

Sakrabundu The "political" god was originally a sky and fertility deity, an antelope god. In the Bono kingdom he deteriorated to "smelling out witches and black magic . . . " and became a political tool for destroying people and maintaining power. Ghana. (Meyerowitz, 1958: 124–125)

Sakti-f A ram-headed deity, the doorkeeper of the 7th pylon, the Papyrus of Ani. Egypt. (Budge, 1967: 297)

Sala A Babylonian "goddess of reptiles," wife of Rimmon. (MacCulloch, 1925, 11: 402)

Sambhar Deo The deified *sambhar* stag who is worshipped to prevent damage to crops. He controls the wild animals of the forest. Central Provinces, India. (Russell, 1925, 3: 314)

Sang grong mung A demon, half-human, half-ape, lived with his wife in "deep, dark caverns in the hills," and lived on human flesh. The Lepchas, Sikkim. (Nebesky-Wojkowitz, 1952: 28)

Šaq *See* **Shaq**

Saracura The water-hen who rebuilt the earth after the flood. The Ge, Brazil. (Spence, 1925, 2: 838)

Sata An Egyptian serpent god. (Budge, 1969, 2: 377)

Satchini Kamui The kingfisher, a deity protective of fish. The Ainu, Japan. (Munro, 1963: 22)

Saulal A deity, half-man, half-lawud (a sea creature), is god of the underworld as well as creator of the universe. Ifalik, Micronesia. (Burrows, 1947/48: 2)

Sebek, Sebek-Ra, Sebak A crocodile-headed god who when associated with Set has an evil reputation; as identified with Ra, a form of sun god and considered beneficent, a god helpful to the deceased. Egypt. (Knight, 1915: 112; Larousse, 1968: 33; Budge, 1969, 1: 345, 356)

Sebi A serpent god of the 12th division of the Tuat. Egypt. (Budge, 1969, 1: 203)

Sede-tsiak Coyote—creator of man, animals, and plants. He taught men their culture. The Patwin Indians, California. (Kroeber, 1932: 304–5)

Sedit Coyote. Among the Wintu he introduced death and thwarts the efforts of Olelbis. California. (Curtin, 1903: 163; Muller, 1968: 225)

Sef A lion god, "Yesterday," guardian (with Tuau, "Today") of the tunnel through which the sun passes at night. Egypt. (Budge, 1969, 2: 361)

Segep Coyote, not very important among the Yurok. California. (Kroeber, 1925: 74)

Seh The supreme god, represented by the leopard. Dahomey. (Williams, 1936: 122)

Sekhem-Matenu-sen, Ates-sen A hare-headed god, the doorkeeper of Arit VII, the Papyrus of Ani. Egypt. (Budge, 1967: 294)

Sekhen-ur A ram-headed god, guardian of the 10th pylon in the underworld. Egypt. (Budge, 1969, 1: 177)

Sekhet A lioness-headed goddess, female counterpart of Ptah and mother of I-em-hetep with whom she forms a triad at Memphis. Goddess of the West; of the fourth hour of the fourth day of the Moon; of the fourth month of the year. She is one of the goddesses who cares for the Eye of Horus. Egypt. (Budge, 1969, 1: 114, 126, 248, 514)

Sek Naga A snake god of the Gonds. India. (Crooke, 1925, 11: 414)

Sekur, Sakar A zoomorphic deity, a big-eared quadruped, of the Bagobo. Philippines. (Benedict, 1916: 40)

Selket, Serqet, Selqet The scorpion goddess who is associated with Qebhsennuf in guarding the Canopic vase containing the intestines, in the embalming ceremony. A protector of conjugal union as well as of the dead. Egypt. (Casson, 1965: 114; Knight, 1915: 116; Budge, 1969, 1: 456)

Selwanga The python deity, a god of the Majusi River and the giver of children. The Baganda, Lake Victoria, Uganda. (Willoughby, 1932: 12; Roscoe, 1965: 320–321)

Semenia The chief of the bird people who could transform as bird/human is the red-billed scythebill, is also the Master of the Earth's food. He was created by Wanadi to help the old people (human/animal). He taught them to clear trees, making conucos (clearings), and cultivation. He brought order, cooperation, food, etc. When he had them cut down the Marahuaka tree (its roots were in the sky), the rains came from the heavens forming the rivers. Its trunk broke into three parts, forming the mountains. Later the bird people retired to the sky to live. The Makiritare, Venezuela. (Civrieux, 1980: 132–36, 143, 190)

Semuganda The python god of death is invoked by women for children and by men for wealth and prosperity. The Basoga, Uganda. (Roscoe, 1915: 247)

Serakh A snake god and a god of corn. Babylonia. (Mac Culloch, 1925, 11: 402)

Serapis A god of the underworld formed by the merging of Hap (Apis), the sacred bull, with Osiris as Bull of the Underworld. Established at Alexandria and at Memphis for the Greeks and the Egyptians. (Budge, 1969, 1: 26; 2: 195, 198; Jayne, 1962: 77–78; Murray, 1935: 404; Schoeps, 1961: 70)

Seremo A giant eagle, a guardian for the Master of Animals, "devours all hunters" who kill more than they require for food. The Yupa, Venezuela. (Wilbert, 1974: 38)

Seres-hra A dog-headed watcher of Arit III in the Papyrus of Ani. Egypt. (Budge, 1967: 293)

Seres-tepu A hawk-headed god, the watcher of Arit IV in the Papyrus of Ani. Egypt. (Budge, 1967: 293)

Serisa A star god, a crocodile. Egypt. (Budge, 1969, 2: 312)

Serqet *See* **Selket**

Sesenet-khu A lion-headed goddess of the 2nd hour of the night, in the underworld. Egypt. (Budge, 1969, 1: 211)

Sesha Naga The great serpent god. Also called Ananta. India. (Crooke, 1894: 268; Larousse, 1968: 363)

Seta A serpent deity in the Papyrus of Ani. Egypt. (Budge, 1967: 337)

Set-hra A snake god, guardian of the pylon of the 8th division of the Tuat. Egypt. (Budge, 1969, 1: 192)

Sethu A serpent god, guardian of the pylon of the 10th division of the Tuat. Egypt. (Budge, 1969, 1: 196)

Shai, Shay The personification of destiny was represented at various times as a god in human form, as a ram, and as a serpent. Egypt. (Gardiner, 1925, 9: 787, 789; Budge, 1973, 1: 43; Casson, 1965: 111)

Shai'i Eagle initiate, spirit of the north. The Northern Pomo, California. (Loeb, 1926, 2: 301)

Shanker Bho-la A snake god of the snake charmers. India. (Skafte, 1979: 124)

Shaq, Šaq Turtle. For a time he was *wot* (chief) of the Land of the Dead, Šimilaqša. "He was still a man then and a great runner." Coyote challenged him to a race around the world, but instead had Sih'usus run and himself acted as referee. Through trickery they won and Shaq was killed. The Chumash, California. (Hudson and Underhay, 1978: 83, 84; Blackburn, 1975: 112)

Shel gyer (pr. **Shêgyer**) A creation deity—"the yak descends from heaven on to the mountain and thus goes out into the world. Thereupon he tears with his horns the mountains to right and left, and the earth becomes covered with flowers. . . . With this the creation is completed." The Bon, Tibet. (Tucci, 1980: 220)

Sheli The mammoth created earth for man to live on. The Evenks, Siberia. (Michael, 1963: 166)

Shemti An Egyptian serpent god. (Budge, 1969, 1: 194, 347)

Shenty A cow goddess associated with agricultural rites. Egypt. (Frazer, 1961: 87–8)

Sheta A tortoise god of Egypt. (Budge, 1969, 2: 376)

She-wang A serpent god of China. (Werner, 1932: 416)

Shitumbe Kamui The black fox deity "has a special earmark if entirely reliable." The Saru and Mukawa districts. The Ainu, Japan. (Munro, 1963: 13, 21)

Shnilemun The otiose Sky Coyote is very benevolent toward mankind and watches over them although he just stays up there and thinks. He was much involved with the creation of humans after the Flood destroyed the world, was "opposed to the institution of death," wanting to rejuvenate the old by throwing them into a lake. There is suggested identification with Polaris or with Aldebaran. The Chumash, California. (Hudson and Underhay, 1978: 84, 101; Blackburn, 1975: 30, 32, 37, 92)

Shuahkai Supernatural "small black bird with white wings." Sia, Pueblo Indians, New Mexico. (Fewkes, 1895, 2: 128)

Shumaikoli The supernatural Dragonfly. Among the Zuñi believed to cause children to have sore eyes; among the Hano and Laguna, a deity of blindness, of deformity. Pueblo Indians, New Mexico. (Parsons, 1939: 191, 208)

Shurtsunna The coyote deity of the Sia. Pueblo Indians, New Mexico. (Fewkes, 1895, 2: 128)

Shuwakai Supernatural bird of the east. Sia, New Mexico. (Fewkes, 1895, 2: 127)

Siju A frog god, a deified human, who, in return for attention and care, promised them victory and protection from illness and misfortune. The Dyak, Borneo. (MacKenzie, 1930: 334)

Sika The supernatural Locust. Sia, Pueblo Indians, New Mexico. (Fewkes, 1895, 2: 128)

Simargl A Slavic bird god, possibly an eagle or a winged griffin, and thought to come from the Sarmatians. Russia. (Gimbutas, 1971: 164)

Sinchlep The beneficent coyote deity of the Flathead Indians. Inland British Columbia and Washington. (Clark, 1966: 64)

Singalang Burong Manifested as a hawk. The god of war and chief of the gods. The Sea Dyaks, Borneo. (Gomes, 1911: 196; Sarawak Gazette, 1963: 14; Brinton, 1897: 158; Roth, 1968: 179)

Sinjep Wunlang Lapu Wunphrang The embryonic serpent of the second generation of deities. Child of Kringkrong wa and Ynong majan. The Katchins, Burma. (Gilhodes, 1908: 675)

Sinnilktok A split deity, one side woman, one side dog. She is benevolent, providing seals and healing the sick. The Eskimo, Baffin Land, Canada. (Bilby, 1923: 265)

Sinpi-u A great bird, child of Samni and Ningpang majan. The Katchins, Burma. (Gilhodes, 1908: 673)

Sis Nag A cobra god who causes earthquakes when he shakes his head. The Chamars, India. (Briggs, 1920: 123–124)

Sisika The supernatural Swallow. Sia, Pueblo Indians, New Mexico. (Fewkes, 1895, 2: 128)

sisiul, xtsaltsalosem A snake or fish deity which lives in the saltwater pond where Qamaits bathes. When it descends to the earth it causes landslides. The Bella Coola Indians, British Columbia. (Boas, 1898: 28)

Sisiutl The double-headed snake, a beneficent totemic being. However, it can transform into a fish whose flesh is deadly. "Pieces of its body, owned by shamans, are powerful medicine." The Kwakiutl, British Columbia. (Alexander, 1964: 243)

Skämsem The raven deity of the Tsimshian. British Columbia. (Swanton, 1925, 12: 465)

Skasa-it "Robin," the elder brother of Blue Jay. The Chinooks, Washington and Oregon. (Spence, 1925, 3: 561)

Skatowe The plumed serpent god of the north. Sia, Pueblo Indians, New Mexico. (Fewkes, 1895, 2: 126; Parsons, 1939: 185)

Skel, Skelmtch The deified marten, older brother of Teashkai (Tchashgai), the weasel. He is a transformer—bird, another animal, old woman, etc. The Klamath, Oregon. (Gatschet, 1890: lxxxii, ci, cii; Chamberlain, 1892: 254)

Skule The meadowlark, sister of Skel, and wife of the eldest of the Thunders. The Klamath Indians, Oregon. (Gatschet, 1890: xc)

Skyamsen The thunderbird of the Tlingit. British Columbia and Alaska. (Burland, 1965: 148)

Slo'w Golden Eagle remained in the sky, thinking, was prescient. He was associated with death and afterlife, lived in the sky where the bones of the dead were, and was possibly the wot (chief) of Shimilaqsha, the land of the dead. With Condor and Buzzard he "removed the foulness from the world." He was also associated with the Sun, with whom he played the nightly peon game against Sky Coyote and Morning Star, and whom he represented in the winter solstice ceremony. His great wings support the Upper World. When he stretches it causes the phases of the moon and/or eclipses. The Chumash, California. (Hudson and Underhay, 1978: 52, 81, 84–85, 90; Blackburn, 1975: 30, 92)

Snilemun *See* **Shnilemun**

Snoolexelts Alkuntam The deer. "The foolish son" of Alkuntam. The Bella Coola, British Columbia. (Boas, 1898: 32)

Sowinna Supernatural deer. The Walpi, Pueblo Indians, Arizona. (Fewkes, 1895, 2: 128)

Succoth Benoth A goddess who "was represented as a hen with her chicks." Worshipped for a time by the Hebrews. (Seligmann, 1948: 49)

Suen A monkey deity and a household god. Taiwan. (Jordan, 1972: 110–11)

Sulak The condor who is associated with the south. The Pomo Indians, California. (Gifford, 1926: 353–354)

Sumari kamuy The fox, a mountain deity, like the bear is captured as a cub and ceremonially treated. Can be good (warn of a death), or bad (bewitch). The Ainu, Sakhalin. (Ohnuki-Tierney, 1974: 97)

Sumukha A serpent god and husband of Gunakesi. India. (Keith, 1917: 132)

Sungmanitu The Wolf Spirit presides over hunting and war. If a wolf is shot with a gun it will not function the next time used, if shot from a horse, the horse will go lame. The Oglala, North and South Dakota. (Walker, 1980: 121, 160)

Sun Hou-tzū The monkey god who "represents human nature, which is prone to all evil." After many exploits he repented and "endeavored to suppress evil and cherish virtue . . . subjugated evil spirits . . . [and was] appointed God of Victorious Strife." China. (Werner, 1934: 325, 368)

Sunka "The Spirit of the Dog presided over friendship and cunning." The Oglala, South Dakota. (Walker, 1980: 121)

Sussistinnako Spider Woman, the mother goddess and creator. Pueblo Indians, Arizona and New Mexico. (Fewkes, 1895, 2: 123n; Stirling, 1942: 1; Parsons, 1939: 192)

Suvinengge The vulture god who is believed to deliver the sacrifices to the gods and to indicate if they are acceptable. Dahomey. (Herskovits, 1938, 2: 140; Leach, 1950, 2: 1090–1091)

Tak Suwau The younger of two snake brothers (with Tak Tahi) who form the rainbow. The Kintak Bong, Malaya. (Evans, 1937: 167)

Ta'aroa-i-manu-i-te-a'a A bird god of the Society Islands. Polynesia. (Henry, 1928: 384)

Tabung The dragonfly who reveals to Tapern when men sin and punishes them with flooding and drowning. The Lanoh, Malaya. (Evans, 1937: 145)

Tagati A snake goddess of South Africa introduced by the Phoenicians. (Mutwa, 1966: iv)

sTag-lha A tiger god invoked for protection by the p'on-pos. Nepal. (Snellgrove, 1961: 51, 288)

sTag-lha-me-'bar A tiger god and guardian deity. The Bon religion, Tibet. (Nebesky-Wojkowitz, 1956, 1: 311–2; Hoffman, 1956: 104)

Tak Tahi The elder of two snake brothers who together form the rainbow. (Tak Suwau). The Kintak Bong, (Evans, 1937: 167)

Tahobn, Taheum The dung beetle brought the earth up from the depths of the water. The Menik Kaien and Kintak Bong, Malaya. (Evans, 1937: 143, 159; Long, 1963: 210)

Taipan The rainbow serpent, god of healing and controller of life and death. The Munkan, North Queensland, Australia. (McConnel, 1957: 12, 111; Poignant, 1967: 125)

Tajuk A snake, guardian and controller of underground waters, causes floods. The Lanoh, Malaya. (Evans, 1937: 174)

rTa khyung 'bar ba A deer skull is used to hold offerings to him to drive away hostile beings. He is represented with a horse's head and the face of a khyung (a mythical bird). Tibet. (Tucci, 1980: 273, n. 24)

Taksaka A sky serpent "who has legs and wings." Bali, Indonesia. (Covarrubias, 1937: 7)

Ong Tam Sir Silk-Worm. Annam. (Cabaton, 1925, 1: 541)

Tañe The supernatural Deer. Sia, Pueblo Indians. New Mexico. (Fewkes, 1895, 2: 128)

Tane-manu The god Tane manifested as a red bird. Society Islands, Polynesia. (Henry, 1928: 540)

Tango da Pará "The tangaru-pará songbird." A healing god, sometimes identified with Guapindaia. Belem, Brazil. (Leacock, 1972: 135, 168)

Tanong The dragonfly who lives in the sun as caretaker. Son of Ag-ag and Klang. The Menik Kaien, Malaya. (Evans, 1937: 163)

Tantivaiyipatsi Southern Fox was gregarious—he traveled and visited. He shot arrows as he went and when pulled out, water gushed forth providing wells and springs. The Chemehuevis, California, Nevada, and Arizona. (Laird, 1976: 159)

Tapinare A god of healing identified with the jaguar. Belem, Brazil. (Leacock, 1972: 135)

Tarapila An Estonian owl god. (de Kay, 1898: 172–173; Grimm, 1883, 2: 669)

Tartaruga da Amazonas A turtle deity, child of Japetequara. Belem, Brazil. (Leacock, 1972: 141, 168)

Tatanka The Buffalo God is the patron of health, fecundity, and guardian of women; of ceremonies, of hospitality; of provisions and hunting; of virtue and industry. He is pleased by generosity, frowns on stinginess. He controls the loves and hates of all men and animals. The Oglala and Lakota. North and South Dakota. (Walker, 1980: 50, 67, 121, 197, 222; Powers, 1977: 54)

Tate Hautse Kupuri The yellow serpent goddess who "brings rain from the North" and to whom belong "the corn, squashes, beans, flowers, cattle, mules, horses, and sheep." The Huichol, Mexico. (Seler, 1925, 6: 829; Chamberlain, 1900: 306)

Tatei Werika 'Uimari The "celestial eagle mother" with whom the Virgin of Guadalupe is identified. The Huichol, Mexico. (Furst, 1972: 139)

Tate Kyewimoka The white serpent goddess "who brings rain from the West," and to whom belong "deer, corn, and the raven." The Huichol, Mexico. (Chamberlain, 1900: 305–306; Seler, 1925, 6: 829)

Tate Naaliwami The red serpent goddess "who brings rain from the East," to whom belongs "cattle, mules and horses." The Huichol, Mexico. (Chamberlain, 1900: 305; Seler, 1925, 6: 829)

Tate Rapawiyema The blue serpent goddess "who brings rain from the South" and "to whom belongs the seed-corn." The Huichol, Mexico. (Seler, 1925, 6: 829; Chamberlain, 1900: 306)

Tatotsi Mara Kware The chief deer god is also a god of fire. The Huichol Indians, Mexico. (Seler, 1925, 6: 828; Chamberlain, 1900: 305)

Ta-urt, Taueret An ancient mother goddess, the hippopotamus, and goddess of childbirth. Egypt. (Neumann, 1955: 153; Budge, 1969, 2: 30, 359; Knight, 1915: 124)

Tavahuk^{w}ampi Sun Spider (black widow spider), grandfather of Wildcat, lived in the sky; is associated with "guardianship of the 'sky-hole'". He played with the rabbits in the sky in the nightly peon game. The Chemehuevi, California, Nevada, and Arizona. (Laird, 1976: 90, 155)

Tavamuhuumpitsi Day Owl, a deity of the Chemehuevis. California, Nevada, and Arizona. (Laird, 1976: 90)

Tavo^{w}aatsi Young Cottontail Rabbit. With Kamu-^{w}aantsi, showed Tavutsi where and how they obtained water and food, whereupon these necessities were released from their confinement and/or scarcity. The Chemehuevi, California, Nevada, and Arizona. (Laird, 1976: 152–154)

Tavutsi Cottontail Rabbit. In ancient times the sun was very hot. He reduced its heat by throwing a stone at it, breaking off huge chunks. Tavo^{w}aatsi and Kamu^{w}aantsi demonstrated how they got food and water, and Tavutsi, again with a rock, caused the Immortal Water to splash all over forming the streams, lakes, etc. In the same fashion he smashed Immortal Yucca Date providing the species of yucca for food. Then he broke open the rock which contained the seeds for other plants. The Chemehuevi, California, Nevada, and Arizona. (Laird, 1976: 152–154)

Ta-vwots, Ta-vwotz, Ta-wats The hare god who "established the seasons and days," whose arrow was the lightning. The Shoshone, Ute Indians, Western United States. (Lowie, 1909: 231; Emerson, 1884: 80; Powell, 1879/80: 24)

Tawataho   A snake god of the Snake Clan who "governs the Above." The Hopi, Arizona. (Waters, 1963: 50)

Tayau Sakaimoka   The serpent god, "assistant of Father Sun." The Huichol, Mexico. (Seler, 1925, 6: 829)

Tcaapani   The bat deity of the Navajo Indians. Arizona and New Mexico. (Matthews, 1889: 91)

Tchashkai, Tchashgai   The deified weasel, younger brother and servant of Skel. The Klamath Indians, Oregon. (Gatschet, 1890: lxxxiii, ci)

Tchkel   The deified pine-marten. Same as Skel. The Modoc, Oregon. (Gatschet, 1890: lxxxiii)

Tcikwelagwe   A bird spirit of the Penobscot Indians. Maine. (Speck, 1935, 1: 15)

Tcua-wuti   A snake goddess of the underworld who became the wife of White-corn (Kwe-teat-ri-yi), a culture hero type. This was the origin of the snake order. She could cause rain by invoking the Rain-god of her country. The Moquis, Arizona. (Stephen, 1888: 114)

Tcubio   The supernatural antelope. The Walpi, Arizona. (Fewkes, 1895, 2: 128)

Teashkai   The deified weasel, brother of Skel, the marten. The Klamath, Oregon. (Chamberlain, 1892: 254)

Teb-hra-keha-kheft   A snake-headed god, herald of Arit V in the Papyrus of Ani. Egypt. (Budge, 1967: 294)

Tefen   A scorpion god who protected Isis with the infant Horus. He is associated with Tefnut in the Unas Texts. Egypt. (Budge, 1969, 1: 487; 1969, 2: 92)

Tefnut   Sometimes a lioness. The goddess of the dew and rain, twin of Shu. She was earlier associated with Tefen. Also the goddess of the 2nd hour of the night of the 14th day of the Moon. Egypt. (Knight, 1915: 125; Ames, 1965: 51; Budge, 1969, 2: 87–88, 92, 292)

Tejaji   A snake deity who protects from snakebite. Marwar, India. (Crooke, 1894: 135)

Teka-hra   A serpent guard of the 5th division of the Tuat. Egypt. (Budge, 1969, 1: 186)

Tel Cuzan   The swallow god of the Mayan at Cozumel. Yucatan, Mexico. (Thompson, 1970: 311)

Tenan-tomgin   The "Big-Raven," the benevolent and powerful creator. The Chukchee, Siberia. (Bogoras, 1904/09: 314, 319; Czaplicka, 1969: 257)

Tent   A ram-headed god of the 11th hour or division of the Tuat. Egypt. (Budge, 1969, 1: 200)

Tenyelang   The Hornbill "becomes a god, or the representative of a god, to assist all those who adore it and it is believed . . . able to confound their enemy and vanquish them." It receives offerings after the taking of a head in battle. The Iban, Borneo. (Howell, 1908/10: 49)

Tepeyollotl, Tepeyolohtli   A jaguar god, a god of caverns and the underground, believed to cause earthquakes. Mexico. (Vaillant, 1962: 150; Spence, 1923: 167; Alexander, 1920: 54, 79; Thompson, 1970: 293; Burland, 1967: 87)

Te-pi   The Wild Cat-Hunter god of the south. The Zuñi, New Mexico. (Cushing, 1881/82: 27)

Thang-long   The Blue Dragon who is the "Spirit of the East." China. (Scott, 1964: 307)

Thla-k'is-tchu, Sus-ki   The name of Coyote (Sus-ki) as the Hunter god of the West. The Zuñi Indians, New Mexico. (Cushing, 1881/82: 20)

Thlen   A serpent spirit who must be propitiated with human blood. The Khasi, Assam. (Bareh, 1967: 357–358)

Thole   The spider deity, a variant of Tore, the god of the forest. The Pygmy Babinga, Zaire. (Pettazzoni, 1956: 32)

Tho-Xe   The buffalo bull, seemingly a supernatural, who became the symbol of the gentle Sky People. He had "given them corn and squash and sinew and robes and bedding and lodges and food and utensils" when they first came to earth from the sky. The Osage, Lower Missouri River Basin. (Mathews, 1982: 39)

Thusandi   A serpent princess who was the ancestress of the Palaung. Burma. (Scott, 1964: 276–277)

Ông Ti   Sir Rat is invoked by farmers and sailors not to damage their fields and their boats. Annam. (Cabaton, 1925, 1: 541)

Tiami   The eagle god of the heavens. The Sia, New Mexico. (Fewkes, 1895, 2: 127)

Tihiya   Deer, a shaman's helper. The Chemehuevis, California, Nevada, and Arizona. (Laird, 1976: 112, 207)

Timbalung   A zoomorphic mountain deity who causes abdominal diseases. The Bagobo, Philippines. (Benedict, 1916: 39)

Tingang   The hornbill. A name of the supreme deity, a manifestation of Mahatala. The Ngaju, Borneo. (Scharer, 1963: 13–4, 33)

Tivatsi   Wolf. He covered the earth Hutsipamamuʔu was creating from north to south to tell when it was large enough. He and Coyote were "assistant creators of and pattern-setters (potential and actual, respectively) for mankind." When appearing in human form he was the "noble, perfect man" but primarily the model for the shaman. He possesses foreknowledge and prefers to accomplish things by magic. Older brother of Ciɨnawavi. The Chemehuevi. California, Nevada, and Arizona. (Laird, 1976: 45, 148, 192, 230–231)

Tjak   A human-faced bird who lives in the Perfumed Sky. Bali, Indonesia. (Covarrubias, 1937: 7)

tlaqwagi'layugwa   "Copper-Maker-Woman," daughter of Qomogwa, who appears "as a white bird that smells like copper." The Kwakiutl, British Columbia. (Boas, 1935: 130)

Tlatocaocelocelotl   The tiger king. Mexico. (Bancroft, 1886, 3: 398)

Tlkelikera   The supernatural mole, sister of Wohpeku-meu. The Yurok Indians, California. (Kroeber, 1925: 74)

Tlotli   The Hawk, the messenger of the gods on earth to their mother Citlalicue. Mexico. (Bancroft, 1886,3: 58)

Toahitu   A god created by Taʻaroa who had the form of a dog and protected those who were in "danger of falling from rocks and trees." Society Islands, Polynesia. (Ellis, 1853: 326; Mackenzie,n.d.: 283; Williamson, 1933, 1: 59)

Tobi   The snake deity, the source of cultivated plants. The Shipaya, Brazil. (Nimuendaju, 1948, 1: 241)

Tohouh   The supernatural cougar. The Walpi, Pueblo Indians, Arizona. (Fewkes, 1895, 2: 128)

Tokchi'i   A serpent god of the Snake Clan, the guardian of the east. The Hopi, Arizona. (Waters, 1963: 49)

Tonatiuh   The sun god "was looked upon by the Aztecs as an eagle." As the morning sun he was Cuauhltehuanitl; as the evening sun, Cuauhtemoc. Mexico. (Caso, 1958: 32–33)

Tongaiti   The third son of Vatea and Papa had the form of "the white and black spotted lizard." His wife is Ari. Mangaia, Polynesia. (Andersen, 1928: 376–377; Buck, 1938: 110, 114; Williamson, 1933, 1: 14)

Tonu-uta   The land turtle, male twin of Tonu-tai, female; the third pair born of Touiafutuna. Tonga, Polynesia. (Williamson, 1933, 1: 10)

Tootooch   The thunderbird. In one legend the wife of Quawteaht, and the parents of man. The Ahts, Vancouver Island, British Columbia. (Bancroft, 1886, 3: 96)

topétine   Mother of nU'/tapa. She takes the form of a jaguar. She was the possessor of fire which was stolen from her by dyoi. The Tukuna, Brazil and Peru. (Nimcendaju, 1952: 122–123, 130)

Torngarsoak   Among the Eskimo of Labrador he has the form of an enormous white bear who "rules over wild game." (Larousse, 1973: 446)

Toste, Teotost   The rabbit god and the god of the chase. The Nicarao, Nicaragua. (Bancroft, 1886, 3: 492; Lothrop, 1926: 70)

Touch   A god of the mountains and of the underground who takes the form of various animals. He sends to each child an animal protector. California. (Bancroft, 1886, 3: 167–168)

tse   The eagle divinity of the Tewa, a powerful medicine animal. New Mexico. (Harrington, 1907/08: 43)

Tsetsesgin   The grizzly bear supernatural who gives the grizzly bear dance in exchange for the return of his mask which is his "means of obtaining food." The Kwakiutl, British Columbia. (Boas, 1935: 160)

tsi̧ 'ayáhi·   The Woodbeetle, a helpful deity. The Navaho, Arizona and New Mexico. (Reichard, 1950: 502)

Tsitsshrue   The water serpent god who controls floods, earthquakes, landslides. The Keres, New Mexico. (Parsons, 1939: 184–185)

tsiya·γo·ji·   The Meadowlark, an undependable deity. The Navaho, Arizona and New Mexico. (Reichard, 1950: 448)

tsi̧yikali·   The Woodpecker, a helpful deity. The Navaho, Arizona and New Mexico. (Reichard, 1950: 502)

Tsmok   A snake, a beneficent household spirit to those who treat it well. Slavic Russia. (Welsford, 1925, 11: 422; Ralston, 1872: 123–125)

Tuamutef A jackal-headed son of Horus, a god of the underworld and of the Canopic Jars, guardian of the heart and lungs, assisted by the goddess Net. As a god of the Cardinal Points he represents the East. Egypt. (Budge, 1969, 1: 145, 158, 456, 492; Knight, 1915: 34)

Tuau A lion god, "To-day," guardian with Sef of the tunnel through which the sun passes at night. Egypt. (Budge, 1969, 2: 361)

Tukumumuuntsi Mountain Lion, a deity of the Chemehuevis. California, Nevada, and Arizona. (Laird, 1976: 148)

Tulugaak The raven god, creator of the earth. North Alaskan Eskimo. (Spencer, 1959: 257)

Tu-lu-kau-guk The raven/man god, creator of the earth. Bering Strait Eskimo. (Nelson, 1896/97: 425)

Tulungusaq The Crow Father—a creator. The Swallow existed before him. Tulungusaq fashioned vegetation, animals, and men from clay. He supplied the earth with light (sun and moon); also produced stars. As a culture hero he taught men construction and hunting and fishing. The Eskimo, Alaska. (Larousse, 1973: 441)

Tu-mataika The personification of the brown parrot. The Maori, New Zealand. (Best, 1924: 176)

Tunder Ilona The Hungarian swan-goddess, consort of Gander-Chief. (Roheim, 1954: 63)

Tuon-pas The Finno-Ugrian swine-god. The Mordvins, Russia. (Paasonen, 1925, 8: 846)

Tuopi Badger god of the south. Sia, Pueblo Indians, New Mexico. (Fewkes, 1895, 2: 127)

Tu-tangata-kino A wizard god who has the form of a lizard and is a guardian of the sacred axe, Te Awhiorangi. He is also the cause of stomach pains. New Zealand. (White, 1887, 1: 96; Mackenzie, n.d.: 59–60)

Tuwachu'a The sand or sidewinder snake god, guardian of the Below. Hopi Indians, Arizona. (Waters, 1963: 50)

Txamsem The Raven, to whom they "ascribe the origin of daylight, fire, water, tides, fresh water, the olachen, etc." The Tsimshian, British Columbia. (Boas, 1935: 180)

Tyi wara The god of the young fieldworkers is invoked for strength, health. A "supernatural being, half man and half animal—usually a roan antelope—who long ago taught men to farm." The Bambara, Mali, Niger, and Senegal. (Tauxier, 1927: 325; Imperato, 1975: 70)

Tziminchac A wounded horse left by Cortes, deified as a "god of thunder"—Cortes having fired from his back. Guatemala. (Bancroft, 1886, 3: 483)

Uamemti An Egyptian serpent god. (Budge, 1969, 1: 198)

Uatchet A serpent goddess, sometimes winged, goddess of the North, goddess of the 5th hour of the 5th day of the Moon, and a goddess of the dead as a "destroyer of the foes of the deceased." Twin sister of Nekhebet. Also called Ap-taui. Egypt. (Knight, 1915: 79; Budge, 1969, 1: 439–444; 1969, 2: 292)

Ubag A zoomorphic deity, a horse with a hump, which causes mortal illness. The Bagobo, Philippines. (Benedict, 1916: 40)

Uga-jin A human-headed serpent deity of Kamakura. Japan. (Getty, 1962: 173; Larousse, 1973: 326)

Uis Meto The python, a god of the earth. Timor, Indonesia. (Middelkoop, 1960: 24)

Uis Oe The crocodile, a god of the water. Timor, Indonesia. (Middelkoop, 1960: 24)

Ungud A great snake, can be either sex or androgynous, is associated with the earth as well as with waters, and gives the medicine man his powers. With Wallanganda the creator of all things. The Unambal, Australia. (Eliade, 1964: 68–79)

'Ungulu The vulture spirit of the Maguzawa. Nigeria. (Greenberg, 1946: 36)

Unktomi *See also* **Iktomi.** The Spider, who may also be like a goblin, is the spirit of practical jokes and pranks, can use magical powers "over persons and things." The Oglala, South and North Dakota. (Walker, 1980: 122)

Unnu, Un The hare god whose female counterpart is Unnit. God of the city of Unnu. (Hermopolis). Egypt. (Budge, 1969, 1: 427)

Upuaut, Upwaut, Upwawet The wolf-headed or canine god, the "Opener of the Way," guides warriors and the dead, and the sun through the night. Egypt. (Casson, 1965: 46, 82; Campbell, 1962: 56, 75; Anthes, 1961: 32, 73)

Uraro The toad god and a god of the south, is the companion of Karoshimo, the senior god of the south. They are "the most powerful of the Warao pantheon." Venezuela. (Wilbert, 1973, 1: 3, 4)

Urt-hekau A lion god or goddess "said to be the 'protective power of the Eye of Horus' " Egypt. (Knight, 1915: 133; Budge, 1969, 1: 456; 1969, 2: 362)

Uset A dog-headed god, herald of Arit II in the Papyrus of Ani. Egypt. (Budge, 1967: 292)

Ushumgalanna A sky-serpent dragon deity, one of the dying gods. Asia Minor. (Langdon, 1931: 178–179)

U Thlen A serpent god to whom human sacrifices were made. Assam. *See also* **Thlen.** (Crooke, 1925, 11: 413; Hodson, 1908: 101; Barkataki, 1969: 37)

U tunsung A wild fowl, of the third generation of deities. Child of Ningthoi and Ningsin. The Katchin, Burma. (Gilhodes, 1908: 676)

Vaghacha Kunvar, Vaghdev A Dravidian tiger god to whom a bullock is sacrificed. The Bhils of Khandesh, India. (Crooke, 1925, 5: 15; Grierson, 1925, 2: 554)

Vaghya The tiger god of the Thakur. India. (Chapekar, 1960: 87)

Vajra-Vārāhī The "adamantine female boar" is the partner of Vajradāka. Tibet. (Snellgrove, 1957: 207)

Varaha Avatar of Vishnu, his third incarnation, as a boar. India. (Ions, 1967: 48; Martin, 1914: 112)

Vasuki, Basuk Nag An important snake god who helps Shiva overcome demons. India. (Crooke, 1894: 268; Ions, 1967: 108; Martin, 1914: 259)

Vigneshwara A name of Ganesha, the elephant-headed god. India. (Dubois, 1906: 631–632)

Voc A hawk god, messenger of Huracan. The Quiché, Mexico and Guatemala. (Recinos, 1950: 173)

Ông Voi The elephant god is worshipped for his strength and modesty. Annam. (Cabaton, 1925, 1: 541)

Votan A Mayan culture hero and snake god, widespread in Chiapas, Cholula, Oaxaca, is associated with Quetzalcóatl. Mexico. (Bancroft, 1886, 3: 450–454; Brinton, 1882: 212–214; Spence, 1923: 133)

Vrisha Kapi A monkey god of the Veda. India. (Crooke, 1894: 51; Ghurye, 1962: 2)

Vritra, Vrtra An atmospheric serpent demon—the demon of drought who uses thunder, lightning and hail as his weapons—is continuously at war with Indra, who forces him to release the rains. Also called Ahi. India. (Macdonell, 1897: 158; Elwin, 1949: 98; Cox, 1870, 2: 326; Martin, 1914: 282)

Wabiskinitapasos The "sacred white deer" is invoked by hunters "[who with Wabiskuitnama] have charge over all things on earth and in the water." The Menomini, Wisconsin. (Skinner, 1913: 156)

Wabiskiu A swan deity invoked in the rain dance. The Menomini, Wisconsin. (Skinner, 1915, 1: 207)

Wabiskuitnama The "sacred white beaver [assistant of Wabiskinitapasos] who have charge over all things on earth and in the water" The Menomini, Wisconsin. (Skinner, 1913: 156)

Wabosso, Wabasso The white rabbit god of the north. The Potawatomi, Michigan and Wisconsin. (Schoolcraft, 1857, 1: 317; Maclean, 1876: 427; Emerson, 1884: 337; Alexander, 1964: 41)

Wacabe The Black Bear, a tutelary spirit who represents "strength and courage" as well as "old age and longevity." The Osage, Lower Missouri River Basin. (Leach, 1949, 1: 146)

Wachedi Master of the tapirs. The Makiritare, Venezuela. (Civrieux, 1980: 139)

Wade The beneficent "grandfather of all the sloths" took human or sloth form. He was "Wanadi's teacher and friend and the most powerful shaman from amongst the 'old people'." The Makiritare, Venezuela. (Civrieux, 1980: 30, 192)

Waghai Devi A tiger goddess. Berar, India. (Crooke, 1894: 322)

Waghdeo A tiger godling. Berar, India. (Crooke, 1894: 322)

Waghdev A tiger god who causes injury because easily displeased. The Bhils, Bombay Province, India. (Naik, 1956: 172, 179–180)

Waiabskinit Awase The White Bear, a god of evil. The Menomini, Wisconsin. (Skinner, 1913: 81, 88)

Waillepen A "calf-sheep" supernatural being. The Mapuche-Huilliche (Araucanians), Chile. (Cooper, 1946: 753)

Wakimowit The chief of the bears invoked with others in the rain dance. The Menomini, Wisconsin. (Skinner, 1915, 1: 207)

Wakinyan The Thunderbird is propitiated when storms threaten. He lives in the West with Yata, the West Wind, is the enemy of, and fights, the water monsters. The Lakota, South and North Dakota. (Walker, 1980: 72, 77, 103, 115, 125)

Wali-manoanoa A lizard goddess influential in government. Hawaii. (Beckwith, 1940: 126–7)

Walinu'u A lizard goddess "upon whom depends the prosperity of the government." Hawaii. (Beckwith, 1940: 126–127)

Wambli "The Spirit of the Eagle presided over councils, hunters, war parties, and battles." The Oglala, South and North Dakota. (Walker, 1980: 122)

Wanadi Wanadi Tonoro, the crimson-crested woodpecker, is Wanadi's double whose form he frequently assumes. The Makiritare, Venezuela. (Civrieux, 1980: 193)

Wanakyudy'a The water serpent god. The Jemez, Pueblo Indians, New Mexico. (Parsons, 1939: 184)

Wang Ta-hsien The God of White Ants. China. (Werner, 1932: 566)

Wapa Tcua A rattlesnake deity of the Moquis. Arizona. (Stephen, 1888: 110)

Warowaro The Butterfly god, generally beneficent, gives fertility, longevity, health, etc., is also god of the north. The Warao, Venezuela. (Wilbert, 1973: 61)

Wash, Washamtch The deified coyote. The Klamath, Oregon. (Gatschet, 1890: cii; Chamberlain, 1892: 254)

Wa sungsung A wild animal resembling a pig, of the third generation of deities. Child of Ningthoi and Ningsin. The Katchins, Burma. (Gilhodes, 1908: 676)

Wawatsari A deer god—"the Deer-Peyote." The Huichol, Jalisco, Mexico. (Furst, 1972: 141)

Wawi The rainbow serpent from whom the medicine man gains powers. The Wiradjuri, Australia. (Eliade, 1973: 155)

Wekwek A hawk or falcon god. The Nisenan, the Miwok, California. Same as Katit. (Kroeber, 1932: 303)

the wemawe The "Beast Gods. . . . These are the beasts of prey and partake of their rapacious nature. They are the most dangerous and violent gods in the Zuñi pantheon. They are the priests of long life, . . . the givers of medicine, . . . the source of black magic." New Mexico. (Bunzel, 1929/30: 528)

wen arsarush An evil bear god, who seems to be a famine god withholding food from humans, was overcome, and his hoards dispersed, by the culture hero. The Ainu, Japan. (Philippi, 1982: 162)

We-sa-pa-ktean-ka-han The serpent deity is especially important. The Quapaw, Arkansas. (Baird, 1980: 17)

White Buffalo Calf Woman She gave them their seven great ceremonies: the "sun dance, vision quest, sweat lodge, spirit keeping, Hunkayapi, a women's puberty ceremony, and the sacred ball game." The Oglala, South and North Dakota. (Powers, 1977: xx, 49)

Wiabskinit Matc Piseu The "white underground panther" invoked by hunters. The Menomini Indians, Wisconsin. (Skinner, 1913: 149)

Wigit The raven, a celestial god, determines the longevity of the newborn. The Haida, British Columbia. (Alexander, 1964: 252)

Win?namakasaama?apitsi An immortal who took bird form. A grandmother of the Dove Boys. The Chemehuevis. California, Nevada, and Arizona. (Laird, 1976: 170–182)

Wodoi A culture hero in the form of a small nightbird, of the primeval time, who became the star Alpha. Australia. (Eliade, 1964: 74–75)

Wollunqua A mythical snake who is dangerous and attacks people; a totemic ancestor but not invoked for increase of its kind, as is usual with totems. The Warramunga, Central Australia. (Spencer, 1904: 266–227)

Wonambi The great snake who swallows the initiate medicine man, then regurgitates him. Tribes of the western desert, Australia. (Eliade, 1973: 141)

Woope The name of White Buffalo Woman among the Lakota. She brought the message from Wakan-Tanka to Tate that his sons were to establish the directions and live there. South and North Dakota. (Jahner, 1977: 35)

Wowta An evil-tempered frog spirit. She assumes human form. The Warau, Guiana. (Brett, 1868: 394)

Woy   A type of hawk who warns and informs the supernaturals of what is happening. Brother of Momoy. The Chumash. California. (Blackburn, 1975: 106, 113)

Wulieb   The primeval beings were two worms, Wulleb (male) and Lejman, "living together in a shell . . . raised the top shell to make the sky; the lower shell became the earth." The Marshall Islands, Micronesia. (Leach, 1956: 183)

Xalpen   The spirit of an initiation ceremony of men and boys "was a huge worm crawling on the earth." The wife of Soorte. The Ona, Tierra del Fuego. (Zerries, 1968: 306)

xazaitsosi.   The chipmunk, a helpful deity. The Navaho, Arizona and New Mexico. (Reichard, 1950: 419)

Xiuhcoatl   The fire snake, the "turquoise snake," a form of Quetzalcóal. Mexico. (Vaillant, 1962: 143; Tozzer, 1957: 116)

Xolxol   *See* **Holhol**

xuxaw   *See* **'Aska'**

Yaai   Serpent god of the earth. Sia, Pueblo Indians, New Mexico. (Fewkes, 1895, 2: 126)

yaoshkep kamui   Spider goddesses worshipped by women are sometimes the companion spirits of shamanesses, invoked in childbirth. The Ainu of Hokkaidu, Japan. (Philippi, 1982: 78)

Yehl, Yel, Yetl, Yethl   The raven, a demiurge and benefactor, yet at the same time a trickster. The Haida, Thlinkeets, Tlingit, British Columbia. (Boas, 1909/10: 584; Brinton, 1882: 228–229; Knapp and Childe, 1896: 153; Bancroft, 1886, 3: 98, 115; Maclean, 1876: 438; Harrison, 1891: 22–23)

Yum Ah Say   The "lord of the leaf-cutter ants." The Lacandon, Chiapas, Mexico. (Perera and Bruce, 1982: 311)

Yum Ch'om   The lord of the vultures and of the buzzards. The Lacandon, Chiapas, Mexico. (Perera and Bruce, 1982: 311, 134)

Yurlunggur   The rainbow snake, a deity of duality—male/female, creator/destroyer, good/evil; also a symbol of fertility. Known by various names across Australia. (Poignant, 1967: 119, 124–125; Eliade, 1973: 100–102)

Yu tunsung   A wild animal resembling a rat, of the third generation of deities. Child of Ningthoi and Ningsin. The Katchins, Burma. (Gilhodes, 1908: 676)

Yu?uravatsi   An immortal who took bird form. A grandmother of the Dove Boys. The Chemehuevi, California, Nevada, and Arizona. (Laird, 1976: 170–182)

Zacuán   The turpial bird which is a god of the Cakchiquels. Guatemala. (Recinos and Goetz, 1974: 56n.52)

Zaki   The lion spirit. To hunt the lion successfully he must be allowed to possess. The Maguzawa, Nigeria. (Greenberg, 1946: 35)

Zaqui-Nimá-Tziís   The white coatimundi goddess, consort of Nim-Ac. The Quiché, Mexico and Guatemala. (Recinos, 1950: 78n.3)

Zayahung Yihe Zayasha   The hedgehog was the creator and the wisest of gods. The Buriat, Mongol. Siberia. (Curtin, 1909: 45)

Zinhu   A monkey god was "sacred to twins." Whydah, Dahomey. (Herskovits, 1967, 1: 182)

Zogphu   A king of the *lu* (serpent or water spirits). The Sherpas, Nepal. (Furer-Haimendorf, 1964: 267)

Zotz   *See* **Camazotz**

Zu   A god who stole the tablets of destiny from Bel (Mullil) and fled with them to the mountains. Because his fellow-gods refused to slay him he was transformed into a bird and exiled. "The 'divine storm-bird' served to unite the two species of augury which read the future in the flight of birds and the flash of lightning." Babylonia. Near East. (Sayce, 1898: 297–299; de Kay, 1898: 104; Hooke, 1963: 61)

Zuzeca   "The Spirit of the Snake presided over the ability to do things slyly, to go about unknown and unseen, and of lying." The Oglala, South and North Dakota. (Walker, 1980: 122)

13

Earth Gods:
Land, Soil, Earthquakes

Ackwin The earth goddess to whom offerings are made "at the various ceremonies, particularly at the medicine dance and the war-bundle feasts." The Winnebago, Wisconsin. (Emerson, 1884: 91; Radin, 1915/16: 286)

Aganju God of the soil whose sister/wife is Yemaja; parents of Orungan. Son of Obatala and Odudua. The Yoruba, Nigeria. (Frazer, 1926: 120; Meek, 1925: 29; 1943: 112)

Ahgishanakhou A chthonic goddess who guards the pillar which supports the earth. The Thlinkeets, Pacific Northwest. (Bancroft, 1886, 3: 103–104)

Ahk tun o wihio A beneficent chthonic god invoked for growth of food and herbs and for abundant water. The Cheyenne Indians, Minnesota and the Dakotas. (Grinnell, 1962: 88, 89)

Aje An earth spirit of the Idoma. Nigeria. (Mbiti, 1970, 2: 119)

Aker The "great double lion-headed earth-god . . . supposed to guard the gate of the dawn through which the Sun-god passed each morning." A god of judgment. Egypt. (Budge, 1969, 1: 33, 325; 1969, 2: 360)

Akosa Sapata, Akossi-Sapata An earth god who inflicts skin diseases as punishment or relieves them as a reward. Maranhão, Belem. Brazil. (Costa Eduardo, 1948: 78; Leacock, 1972: 161)

Ala, Ale The earth and mother goddess of the Ibo. A goddess of morality and laws as well as of the underworld. Also the goddess of fertility. Among some tribes the wife of Amade Onhio. Nigeria. (Parrinder, 1961: 37; 1967: 78; Meek, 1931: 179; Talbot, 1967: 58, 60–61; Uchendu, 1965: 95–96)

Alalkomenia A Boeotian earth goddess whose sisters are Thelxinoia and Aulis. Greece. (Roscher, 1965, 1, 1: 222)

Alepalaxtnaix A giant in the east holds a stone bar to which the earth is attached. When he shifts his grip—earthquake. The Bella Coola Indians, British Columbia. (Boas, 1898: 37)

Alo The earth, wife of Eze Chite Okike, the sun, and mother of Igwe, the sky. Together they form a triad. The Abadja tribe of the Ibo, Nigeria. (Jeffreys, 1972: 730)

Alosaka, Muyinwu An earth or chthonic god—the "symbolic personification of the earth." He is the "Germinator," a god of fertility and of vegetation. The Hopi Indians, Arizona. (Fewkes, 1920: 592, 604; Tyler, 1964: 19, 20; Waters, 1963: 190)

Altor A Roman earth god, "the Nourisher," associated with the earth mother Tellus. (Dumézil, 1966, 1: 374; Frazer, 1926: 329–330)

Ama An earth goddess and a goddess of the underworld, in its chthonic aspect as nourisher as well as of the place to which men return at death. She rules over Kindo, the underworld, and is a goddess of justice and righteousness. The Jukun, Nigeria. (Meek, 1943: 110, 113;1931: 190, 208–9)

Amakiri The earth goddess at Ogu and among the Okrikan. Nigeria. (Talbot, 1967: 120; Meek, 1931: 191)

Ammal A goddess of the Pariyas who "represents Parvati as the Earth Mother." Beneficent as well as malevolent. The Doms, India. (Briggs, 1953: 538)

An Alai Chotoun, An-Darkhan-Khotun Mother earth, a goddess of vegetation, of nature, is also a creator. The Yakut, Siberia. (Eliade, 1964: 187; Czaplicka, 1969: 278; MacCulloch, 1964: 459)

Ande He supports the earth in one hand. When he shifts it to the other it causes earthquakes. The Komkane, New Guinea. (Aufenanger, 1962: 2, 3)

Ane The earth goddess of the Ezza tribe of the Ibo. Nigeria. (Jeffreys, 1972: 730)

Ang An earth god of the Meau. China. (Bernatzik, 1947: 156)

Ani The earth. With Okuke she is concerned with fertility and childbirth. She is as well the goddess of the farming cycle, of morality, and of the afterworld. The northern Ibo, Nigeria. (Horton, 1956: 20–23)

Aninito ad Chalom A chthonic goddess who makes the earthquakes. The Mayawyaw, northern Luzon, Philippines. (Lambrecht, 1932: 22)

Anyigba The earth goddess of the Ewe-speaking people. She is the giver of human and agricultural fertility, of good fortune in trade, hunting, and war. She will inflict disease, but also heals. Togo. (Frazer, 1926: 414)

Apia A Scythian goddess equated with Ge (Gaea) and with Armaiti, and as such would be an earth goddess. (Gray, 1930: 50; Minns, 1913: 85)

Arinna "The 'queen of the lands' . . . and her husband U or Im, the god of storm," were the primeval pair, earth and sky. The Hittite, Near East. (Eliade, 1976, 2: 364)

Armaiti An androgynous deity, but usually female, a goddess of the earth, of fertility and reproduction. Iran. (Littleton, 1965: 99; Haydon, 1941: 68; Gray, 1930: 220)

Arsay, Arsy, Arsai The third daughter of Ba'al (by Y'bdr) who is associated with the earth as well as the underworld. Canaan, Near East. (Albright, 1968: 144; Oldenburg, 1969: 77; Gordon, 1961: 196)

Aruru An Akkadian, Sumerian, and Babylonian earth and mother goddess and creator of man. Near East. (Jastrow, 1898: 448; Langdon, 1931: 12; Kramer, 1961: 121)

Asakana The "spirit of the land" who lives in a sacred grove. The Nankanse, Ghana. (Rattray, 1932: 307)

Asapurna An earth goddess "who fulfills desire." India. (Leach, 1949, 1: 79)

Asase, Asase Afua, Asase Yaa The earth mother and goddess of the soil is also a goddess of the underworld. Wife of Nyame (Nyankopon). The Ashanti and the Akan, Ghana. (Queval, 1968: 16; Parrinder, 1949: 27, 39; Clarke, 1930: 438; Danquah, 1944: 45; Meyerowitz, 1958: 28, 136)

Ascensus A Roman god of the gradual elevation of terrain and of mountain slopes. (Roscher, 1965, 2, 1: 193)

'asdzá·nádle·hé, asdzáán nádleehé, Estsanatlehi Changing Woman, the earth mother, goddess of morality, of peace. She "decreed fertility and sterility." Her epidermis "along with such jewels as white shell, turquoise, abalone, and jet" were used in the creation of humans. The Navaho, Arizona and New Mexico. (Reichard, 1950: 406–413, 431; McNeley, 1981: 24–26)

Asherah An earth goddess of the Syrians, associated with the corn cult. Among others a goddess of the sea. (James, 1960: 87)

Asherat(h) An earth mother, symbolizing "the fruitful earth, or fertility in general" as well as a goddess of the sea and of wisdom. Given as the wife and counsellor of El, or of Baal, but also as the mother of Baal. Phoenicia and Canaan. Near East. (Herm, 1975: 109; Ferm, 1950: 125; Larousse, 1968: 76, 78)

Asia The earth goddess of the Guinea and Senegabia groups of people. West Africa. (Larousse, 1968: 483)

Atabei An earth goddess of the West Indies with many variant names: Attabeira, Apito, Siella, Suimado, Mamona, Guacarapita, Liella, Guimazoa. (Fewkes, 1903/04: 55; Alexander, 1920: 24–25; Rouse, 1948: 538)

Atugan An earth-mother goddess of the Mongols. Siberia. (Queval, 1968: 21)

Autran A goddess, sister or daughter of Aluelap, rules the earth and is the mother of mankind. She established sexual tabus. Ifalik, Micronesia. (Burrows, 1947/48: 3)

Auxesia An earth goddess and goddess of fertility and of crops. Greece. (Jayne, 1962: 315; Willetts, 1962: 52)

Awehai, Awenhai The earth mother was originally a celestial being, the wife of Haonhwendjiawagi (Dehavenjawa), and was cast out of the skies because of suspected infidelity. She took with her all the things which are on the earth. Mother of Gaendesonk. The Iroquois, Eastern United States. (Gray, 1925, 7: 422; Keeler, 1960: 14)

Awitelin Tsita The earth mother, created by Shiwa-notka. The Zuñi, New Mexico. (Stevenson, 1898: 34; Cushing, 1891/92: 379)

Azele Yaba The earth goddess, wife of Nyamenle. If either is blasphemed he or she must be propitiated immediately or punishment will result. The Nzema, Ghana. (Grottanelli, 1967: 37–39; 1969: 372)

Baalipenu The earth spirit of the Konds. India. (Schulze, 1912: 15)

Baginda Ilijas The guardian of the land. Java, Indonesia. (Geertz, 1960: 40)

Bangla-ong A chthonic deity of the Kabuis of Manipur. India. (Hodson, 1911: 128)

Banua The earth deity and chief deity of the Batak. Philippines. (Kroeber, 1918, 2: 43)

Baski Mata A goddess who stands on her head on a lotus flower at the bottom of the sea and supports the earth on her feet. When she tires and shifts position there is an earthquake. The Bhuiya, India. (Elwin, 1949: 28–29)

Basmoti The earth goddess of Orissa. India. (Elwin, 1954: 635)

Basuki, or Basumata The earth goddess who is worshipped for agricultural prosperity. The Santals, India. (Mukherjea, 1962: 280; Elwin, 1954: 635)

Basumati The earth mother to whom offerings are made at the planting and harvest seasons. The Juangs, Bengal. (Crooke, 1925, 2: 482; Frazer, 1926: 617)

Batoo Bedano The god of earthquakes. Nias, Oceania. (Frazer, 1961: 202)

Bela Pinnu The earth god or goddess of the Kond. India. (Elwin, 1954: 635)

Belitili *See* **Ninhursaga.** (Jacobsen, 1970: 30)

Berchte, Berchta Teutonic earth goddess who foretells both good and bad. Berche in Bavaria, Perchta, Perchtel in the Salzburg mountains. Berchtli in Switzerland. (Grimm, 1880: 277, 279; Wagner, 1882: 6, 116)

Berecynthia Celtic earth mother and goddess of fertility. Gaul. (MacCulloch, 1911: 44; Ferguson, 1970: 15)

Bhairon A godling of the land—Bhairoba in Bombay, Bhaironnath in Benares. India. (Crooke, 1894: 67)

Bhudevi The benevolent aspect of the earth goddess—also known as Dharti Mai, Basundhara, Ambabachi, Basumati, Thakurani. Bengal. (Crooke, 1925, 2: 484)

Bhuia A beneficent god of the soil who is associated with agriculture and is invoked regarding the rains, either too much or too little. The Himalaya, India. (Berreman, 1963: 100–101, 108, 379)

Bhumi Devata The earth goddess of the Poroja. Also known as Jakar Devata. Southern India. (Thurston, 1909, 6: 215)

Bhumiya Beneficent god of the soil "worshipped after the harvests, at marriages, and on the birth of a male child." Delhi, India. (Crooke, 1894: 44, 66–7; Briggs, 1920: 155)

Bhumiya Rani The goddess of the soil, the equivalent of Bhumiya. Oudh, India. (Crooke, 1894: 65)

Bhumme Nari A goddess of the earth. One of the Nagas. India. (Coleman, 1832: 254)

Bhuyian The earth goddess of the Doms. An aspect of Devi. India. (Briggs, 1953: 529)

Bimbeal, Binbeal Bunjil, his father, gave him "power over the earth." The Kulin, Australia. (Eliade, 1958: 42)

Bonmazo The guardian of the earth. Burma. (Nash, 1966: 118)

Britomartis, or Dyktynnan Goddess of the earth and of wild animals, and goddess of Mount Dikte. Crete. (James, 1960: 99; Neumann, 1955: 275; Kerenyi, 1951: 147)

aBru-gu-ma An earth goddess who is sometimes named as the daughter of brTan-pa. Wife of Kesar. Tibet. (Francke, 1923: 9)

Buluc Ch'abtan An earth god who "seems to have much to do with the inauspicious destinies which are predicted." The Maya, Mexico. (Roys, 1949: 160; Thompson, 1970: 295)

Burha-Burhi The "androgynous form of the Earth-deity." Bengal. (Crooke, 1925, 2: 487)

Bursung The earth mother, both benevolent and destructive—feeds and starves, creates life and receives the dead. She is also a goddess of fecundity. The Bondo, India. (Elwin, 1950: 152; Wales, 1957: 32)

Caban Earth. As "a goddess is an extruded part or hypostasis of Hunrakán, the god of Heaven." The Quiché, Guatemala. (Girard, 1979: 35)

Cabrakan *See* **Caprankán**

Caillech Bherri A Celtic goddess of the land, a divine ancestress. A goddess of sovereignty. Ireland and Scotland. (MacCana, 1970: 94)

Canam Lum Mayan "Serpent of the Earth," "Guardian of the Soil." Chiapas, Mexico. (Alexander, 1920: 133; Thompson, 1970: 321)

Caprakán, Cabrakan God of Earthquakes. Son of Vukup Cakix and Chimalmat; brother of Zipacná. His death, caused by magic used by Hunahpú and Ixbalamqué, "ends the era of the giants." The Quiché, Guatemala. (Girard, 1979: 67, 82, 84; Krickeberg, 1968: 79)

Chaabou Virgin earth goddess of the Nabataeans. Mother of Dusares. Near East. (Langdon, 1931: 16–18)

Chibchachum An earth god who was banished to the underground for flooding the valley of Bogota. Henceforth he supported the earth on his shoulders; his restlessness causes earthquakes. He was also considered the god of merchants and craftsmen, and of laborers. The Chibcha, Colombia. (Trimborn, 1968: 91; Kroeber, 1946: 908; Osborne, 1968: 112)

The Chicchans The earth Chicchans have the form of serpents and are both beneficial and harmful. They send the rain for growth, but they also cause earthquakes, landslides, and hurricanes. The Chorti, Guatemala. (Wisdom, 1940: 394–395, 417; Thompson, 1970: 262)

Chö A Chinese god of the earth. (Chavannes, n.d.: 439)

Chthon The fertile earth personified. Greece. (Roscher, 1965, 1, 1: 906)

Chulmetic The earth goddess of the Tzeltal. Mexico. (Villa Rojas, 1969: 222)

Chup, Chupu, Shup The earth goddess, known ritually as Hutash, had three aspects—"wind, rain, and fire." She "possessed will, reason, emotions, and power; . . . provided all living things with food." Mother of the Indians. The Chumash, California. (Hudson and Underhay, 1978: 22, 45)

Cihuacoatl, Ciuacoatl Serpent earth goddess of the Aztec. Goddess of "women who died in childbirth." She was also predictive of war. Mexico. (Caso, 1958: 54; Spence, 1923: 154, 181; Alexander, 1920: 75; Thompson, 1970: 117–118)

Cizin *See* **Kisin**

Coatlicue The Aztec earth goddess of the serpent skirt. Mother of Huitzilopochtli. She represents love as well as destruction. Mexico. (Caso, 1958: 12, 13, 53, 54; Spence, 1923: 154, 183; Vaillant, 1962: 148)

Coquehuilia The god of "the center of the earth," is worshipped in Macuilxochitl. The Zapotec, Oaxaca, Mexico. (Whitecotton, 1977: 157)

Cotys, Cottyto A Phrygian Earth goddess. Either she or Bendis is named as the wife of Sabazius. Asia Minor. (Larousse, 1968: 160)

Cuch Uinahel Balumil Four gods who support the earth and whose movement causes earthquakes. The Tzotzil, Mexico. (Thompson, 1970: 346)

Cupra A benevolent earth and death goddess revered in Umbria and Picenum. Italy. (Roscher, 1965, 1, 1: 931)

Cybele The Great Mother, as Earth symbolized by a stone, "is the mother of stones, of stone implements, and of fire." As a goddess of earth and fertility, of agriculture, she is also "frequently associated with a vegetable symbol." Phrygia, Near East. (Neumann, 1955: 260–261)

Daban-Sagan-Noin A benevolent old god of the earth whose wife is Deleyte-Sagan-Khatun. The Balagan, Buriats. Siberia and Mongolia. (Klementz, 1925, 3: 11; Czaplicka, 1969: 284)

Dagan Assyrian god of the earth later absorbed by, or identified with, the Babylonian Bel. (Jastrow, 1898: 209; Paton, 1925, 4: 6, 338)

Dagau A goddess who lives at the pillars of the world and who has a python which she causes to writhe around the pillars causing earthquakes. She is also the "goddess of rice, and she can make the soil infertile and diminish the amount of rice in the granaries" if displeased. The Manobo, Philippines. (Raats, 1969: 20)

Dagda A father-figure, multi-purpose god. A god of the earth, its fertility and growth, as well as a sky and atmospheric god. He was a protector and leader in war, "law-giver in times of peace," wise and benign. His wife or mistress was Boann. Celtic Ireland. (Ross, 1967: 166;

Squire, 1906: 54–55; MacCulloch, 1911: 72, 78, 81; MacBain, 1917: 121)

Dam-kina, Dav-kina An earth goddess, the personification of the earth, consort of Ea and mother of Marduk. Babylonian. Near East. (Jastrow, 1898: 64, 143; Sayce, 1898: 139)

Demeter Goddess of the earth, of the soil and its fertility, of the ripe corn; the nourisher of all life; guardian of the wealth of the earth. Daughter of Cronus and Rhea, sister/wife of Zeus, mother of Persephone. Greece. (Cox, 1870, 2: 307–308; Frazer, 1960: 134, 456, 461; Jayne, 1962: 316–317; Larousse, 1968: 150; Hesiod-Brown, 1981: 66, 78, 79)

Dessra, Derra God of earthquakes and of fire. Yap Islands, the Carolines, Micronesia. (Christian, 1899: 385)

Dharitri, Dharti Mata The bountiful earth and mother goddess worshipped throughout the agricultural season. India and Tibet. (Crooke, 1894: 13, 17, 18; Fuchs, 1952: 610–616; Waddell, 1959: 344; Martin, 1914: 247; Briggs, 1920: 155; Elwin, 1939: 58; Russell, 1916, 2: 85)

Dharni Deota The earth god is the head of the pantheon of the Khond (Kandh). Formerly a goddess—Tari (or Bera) Pennu. India. (Russell, 1916, 3: 473; Crooke, 1925, 7: 650; Frazer, 1926: 385)

Dharni Pinnu Mother earth of the Kond. India. (Elwin, 1949: 42)

Dibia-Sagan-Noin The god of the earth. The Buriats, Siberia. (Klementz, 1925, 3: 9)

Din ding ka The earth, child of Samni and Ningpang majan. The Katchins, Burma. (Gilhodes, 1908: 673)

Djawuwel The spirit of the earth. Northern Pomo Indians, California. (Loeb, 1926, 2: 301)

Dongar Pat The "hill-godling who prevents earthquakes and volcanic eruptions, and keeps off frost." Central Provinces, India. (Russell, 1925, 3: 314)

Drebkullis Baltic god of earthquakes. Lithuania and Latvia. (Welsford, 1925, 9: 241; Grimm, 1888: 1542)

Dugbo The earth goddess, mother of all vegetation, and wife of Yataa. The Kono, Sierra Leone. (Parsons, 1950: 270)

dunna musun The "mistress of the earth, . . . the cult of old women, protectresses of the roads to the realm of the dead." The Evenki, Siberia. (Dioszegi, 1968: 469–470)

Dyabu fafa The earth deity, with Dyabu lara forms a duality. Aru Island (the Moluccas), Indonesia. (Pettazzoni, 1956: 335–336)

Dzari The earth mother, giver of life. The Kaean, New Guinea. (Meiser, 1963: 905–906)

Ehe Tazar Mother earth of the Buriat. Siberia. (Curtin, 1909: 39)

Eingana A serpent/earth/mother goddess, the giver of life and fertility. The Djauan tribe, Northern Territory, Australia. (Robinson, 1966: 34, 35)

Eithinoha The earth mother whose daughter is Onatah, the corn or wheat goddess. The Iroquois Indians, Eastern United States. (Alexander, 1964: 27; Larousse, 1968: 430)

Eji An earth spirit to whom offerings are made to insure the agricultural prosperity. The Egede, Nigeria. (Armstrong, 1955: 146)

Eluku-Oro The "genius of the earth—a death-dealing spirit." The Yoruba, Nigeria and Dahomey. (Williams, 1964: 142)

En-Gop The god of the earth. The En-jemusi, Kenya. (Beech, 1911: 19)

Erce A Teutonic earth goddess. (Grimm, 1883, 2: 641; Turville-Petre, 1964: 188)

Erda A Germanic earth goddess. (Grimm, 1880: 250)

Erkir, Armat An Armenian earth goddess. (Ananikian, 1964: 35)

Erra A chthonic god, the personification of the "scorched earth" resulting from fire. He is associated with Mamma, goddess of fertility, representing the burning of fields to maintain the yield. He is also portrayed as "a warrior whose main weapon is famine." Hence, he is both beneficent and destructive. Semitic/Akkadian. Near East. (Roberts, 1972: 24–6; Jacobsen, 1970: 35)

Esceheman The earth, "Our Grandmother." The Cheyenne, the Dakotas and Minnesota. (Powell, 1969: 437)

Esesar The earth goddess, wife of Ebore. The Gbanya, Ghana. (Rattray, 1932: 43–45)

Eth Etruscan god of nature and the earth, associated with the southeast division of the sky and with haruspicy. Italy. (Hamblin, 1975: 95; Pallottino, 1975: 145)

Etogon The earth goddess of the Monguors of Kansu. China. (Schram, 1957: 113)

Etugen The earth goddess of the Mongols. Siberia and Mongolia. (Czaplicka, 1969: 355)

Fakahotu The earth mother, goddess of plant life. Tuamotus, Polynesia. (Poignant, 1967: 31; Stimson, 1933: 20, 59)

Fatou The earth. Society Islands, Polynesia. (Williamson, 1933, 1: 148)

Fauna A Roman goddess "personifying the earth and its fertility, was originally an agricultural and prophetic divinity who bestowed health and blessing." Wife or daughter of Faunus. (Jayne, 1962: 421; Fairbanks, 1907: 248)

Fincenu Goddess of the land (region) of the same name. Sister of Cenufana. Colombia. (Trimborn, 1968: 104)

Fiorgyn, Fjorgyn A Norse earth goddess. Also called Hlodyn, and may also be identified with Jord, as both are named as the mother of Thor. (Grimm, 1880: 256; Turville-Petre, 1964: 97; Davidson, 1964: 111)

Frig Mother earth and goddess of agricultural fertility. England. (Branston, 1957: 127)

Frigg(a) The Germanic Mother earth, personifying the fertile summer earth, wife of Wodan and mother of the gods. She represents law and order, particularly as it pertains to agriculture. (Thorpe, 1851: 167, 231; Anderson, 1891: 236–237; Wagner, 1882: 6)

Furrina An Etruscan goddess believed to be an Earth Mother. Italy. (Altheim, 1937: 117)

Gaea, Gaia, Ge Earth, second to come into being, after the Void (Chaos). She is the earth as form, structure, is the source of "the whole realm of Being." She produced the starry Sky, the mountains, the "barren waters." As the wife of Ouranos she became the mother of the twelve Titans—Oceanus, Coeus, Crius, Hyperion, Iapetus, Theia, Rhea, Themis, Phoebe, Mnemosyne, Tethys, Cronus; the Cyclopes—Brontes (Thunder), Steropes (Lightning), Arges (Bright); and the Hecatonchires—Cottus (the striker), Briareus (the strong), and Gyes (the "bemembered"). Gaea instigated the cas-

tration of Ouranos (by Cronus, their son) and from the drops of blood which fell on the earth she later gave birth to the Erinyes. Pontus (Sea) also united with Earth producing Thaumas, Phorcys, Ceto and Eurybia. Subsequently Gaea was supplanted by other earth goddesses— Hera, Demeter, Persephone. Greece. (Hesiod-Brown, 1981: 16, 56–60; Eliade, 1976, 2: 358–359; Kerenyi, 1951: 21; Delcourt, 1961: 17; Fairbanks, 1907: 142; Morford & Lenardon, 1975: 19, 20, 21, 25, 86, 89, 90)

Gai matutsi The earth initiate of the Eastern Pomo Indians. California. (Loeb, 1926, 2: 300)

Ga-Tum-Dug One of the names of the earth mother at Lagash. Others—Innini, Ninjursag. Babylonia. Near East. (Larousse, 1968: 61)

Gau An earlier name for the earth goddess, prior to Prithivi. India. (Keary, 1882: 118)

Geb The earth god whose sister/wife is Nut. Same as Seb, Keb. Egypt. (Ames, 1965: 52; Larousse, 1968: 14; Branston, 1957: 182)

Ghadsaryn, or Gadsar-un The "Spirit, or 'Owner,' of the Earth." The Mongol do not practice agriculture because it would be disturbing to earth. Gobi Desert. (Montell, 1940: 79)

Giô The earth deity of the Tigong. Nigeria. (Meek, 1931: 180)

Grilya Burhin An old woman who supports the middle of the world on her head. When her husband insists on lying with her there is an earthquake. The Dhoba. India. (Elwin, 1949: 34)

Ha'arts The earth, with thom the serpent of the Nadir is associated. Hopi Indians, Arizona. (Tyler, 1964: 239)

Haenovaiurua The "god of quagmire," also called Oa hivari. Tahiti, Polynesia. (Henry, 1928: 376)

Hahaiwuqti An earth and mother goddess of the Tusayan, Pueblo Indians. Arizona. Same as Utset. (Fewkes, 1895, 2: 123; 1893/94: 291)

hai'ya'a'ai ha'wil, ha 'wilume The "Land Chief" invoked with others during bathing rituals. The Nootkan tribes, British Columbia and Washington. (Drucker, 1951: 152)

Hakahotu The earth mother and the female principle. Wife of Atea—primary parents of Tongarevans. Polynesia. (Buck, 1932, 2: 85)

Haniyasu-hiko-no-Kami   God of the earth, and as the god of clay also the god of potters. Japan. (Yasumaro, 1928: 8, 9; Herbert, 1967: 476; Kato, 1926: 141)

Haniyasu-hime-no-Kami   Goddess of the earth, of clay, and so also of potters. Japan. (Yasumaro, 1928: 9; Herbert, 1967: 267, 476)

Hayicanak   The "Old-woman-underneath" the earth who causes earthquakes. The Tlingit, British Columbia and Alaska. (Swanton, 1904/05: 452; Boas, 1909/10: 732)

Hea   The earth, a goddess of wisdom. Mesopotamia, Near East. (Seligmann, 1948: 23, 35)

Heou t'ou   A deified human worshipped as a god of the earth. China. (Chavannes, n.d.: 504)

Hine-one   The Sand Maid, daughter of Rangahua, who was assigned to protect Mother Earth from Hine-moana. The Maori, New Zealand. (Best, 1924: 154, 263)

Hine-tu-a-hoanga   The "Sandstone Maid," daughter of Rangahua. Also "a personification of the grindstone," a goddess of stone-grinders. The Maori, New Zealand. (Best, 1924: 163; Mackenzie, n.d.: 37)

Hine-tu-a-kirikiri   The "Gravel Maid" assigned to protect mother earth from Hine-moana. The Maori, New Zealand. (Best, 1924: 154, 263)

Hine-tuoi   A deity who represents volcanic phenomena. The Maori, New Zealand. (Best, 1924: 175)

Hishikoyatsaspa   An earth goddess. The Sia, New Mexico. (Fewkes, 1895, 2: 123)

Hkrip Hkrawp   A god who "represented earth." The Kachin, Burma. (Scott, 1964: 263)

Hlodyn   A Norse earth goddess. Also called Fiorgyn. (Grimm, 1880: 256)

Hludana   Germanic earth goddess. Same as Hlodyn. (Grimm, 1880: 257)

Hopokike-ush   A land demon who causes landslides and rocks to fall. The Ainu, Japan. (Batchelor, 1925, 1: 244)

Hoshi-no-kamikakaseo   A Japanese earthly deity. (Yasumaro, 1928: 75)

Hou-t'u   The god of the earth in early China. During the Ming dynasty the deity was transformed into a god-

dess. (Ferguson, 1937: 67; Campbell, 1962: 432; Day, 1940: 66)

Hou T'u Kuo Huang   The goddess of the earth since the Ming dynasty. China. (Day, 1940: 59)

Hsi gu maw ya, Maw ya   The brother of Y'wa. He supports the world on his shoulders and his movements cause the earthquakes. The Karen, Burma. (Marshall, 1922: 230)

Huallallo Caruincho   The god of the land whose strength lay "in fire." The coastal highlands of Peru. (Alexander, 1920: 227; Osborne, 1968: 93, 96)

Huemac   A name applied to a god of earthquakes who is perhaps to be identified with Quetzalcóatl. Mexico. (Bancroft, 1886, 3: 269, 284; Brinton, 1897: 82; 1882: 109)

Humba   An earth god of the Elamites. Near East. (Langdon, 1931: 255)

H'Uraru   The earth, who is also called Atira (Mother), and who is omniscient, the guide of all conduct. The Pawnee, Plains Indians, Nebraska. (Alexander, 1964: 91)

Hutash   *See also* **Chup.** Earth—to whom the harvest ceremony is dedicated; allied with a St. Michael celebration. The Chumash, California. (Hudson and Underhay, 1978: 24, 45)

Huzru wuqti   Another name of the earth goddess of the Tusayan. Arizona. (Fewkes, 1895, 2: 123)

Ibu Pertiwi   Mother earth and goddess of fertility who was raped by Wisnu to "give birth to rice." Bali, Indonesia. (Grader, 1960: 167; Covarrubias, 1937: 70, 317)

Idunn, Iduna   A Scandinavian earth goddess representing the earth's seasons. She is the goddess of immortality, guardian of the apples restoring youth. Wife of Bragi. (Stern, 1898: 84; Wagner, 1882: 173; Davidson, 1964: 165; MacCulloch, 1964: 178)

ihp'en   The "earth-god, . . . the personification of the earth, the soil, plant growth, and riches and property in general." He is identified with St. Manuel. Consort of icq'anan. The Chorti, Guatemala. (Wisdom, 1940: 402)

Ii   The earth goddess of the Margi, the mother of the crops. Nigeria. (Meek, 1931: 180)

Ilamatecuhtli   An ancient and primeval goddess of the earth and of maize. She is the patroness of old women. Aztec, Mexico. (Vaillant, 1962: 149; Spence, 1923: 233)

Ilat, Allat, Hallat In North Arabia she is the earth-mother and mother goddess. In South Arabia, she is the sun goddess and mother goddess. (Langdon, 1931: 15; Bhattacharji, 1970: 225)

Indara The earth goddess. With Ilai, the maker of men. Central Celebes, Indonesia. (Kruijt, 1925, 7: 248; Kern, 1925, 8: 347)

Innini Sumerian and Babylonian earth goddess who was, however, also considered the goddess of the planet Venus, a goddess of water and of war. Near East. (Langdon, 1931: 5, 14, 93; Mercer, 1925, 12: 700, 709; Larousse, 1968: 61)

Intombangol The "earth rests on two huge serpents, male and female, . . . who lie so as to form a cross. Their mouths are below the water at the point where earth and sky meet. When they move they cause earthquakes; when they breathe they cause the winds; if they pant they cause violent storms. They do not fall for they are held up by Magbabáya tominapay." The Bukidnon, Mindanao, Philippines. (Cole, 1956: 97)

Ioio-whenua A deity who represents earthquakes and volcanic activity. The Maori, New Zealand. (Best, 1924: 175)

Irungu God of the earth and of the forest who formed the earth and its features, "and peopled them with animals." Tanzania. (Frazer, 1926: 426; Taylor, 1962: 142, 147)

Isong The earth goddess and goddess of fertility. The Ibibio, Nigeria. Same as Obasi Nsi (Ekoi). (Parrinder, 1949: 38; Frazer, 1926: 128)

Itchita The goddess of the earth who lives in the white birch trees and is protective of men from illness, with the help of her spirit servants. The Yakuts, Siberia. (Larousse, 1973: 435)

Itzcueye An earth goddess of the Pipil, a Nahuatlan tribe. Nicaragua. (Alexander, 1920: 184)

Iwasubime-no-Kami The goddess of sand, daughter of Izanagi and Izanami. Japan. (Yasumaro, 1965: 14)

Ixuixiwi "Our mother, the earth." The Iowa Indians. Iowa, Missouri, and Minnesota. (Skinner, 1920: 192)

Izanami A goddess, the personification of the earth, who with her brother/husband produced the islands of Japan, and were the parents of other gods. She became the goddess of the underworld. Japan. (Holtom, 1938: 81, 109; Yasumaro, 1928: 3, 19; Haydon, 1941: 202)

ja-neb'a Benevolent mother earth. The Samoyeds, Siberia. (Dioszegi, 1968: 462)

Janun dingding ka The earth, almost formed, a fourth generation deity, child of Ningsang Woishun and Phung-kam Janun. The Katchins, Burma. (Gilhodes, 1908: 677)

Jar-Sub A land and water deity of the Teleuts. Siberia. (MacCulloch, 1964: 462)

Jhankara The "god of the land, rainfall, and crops" to whom a cow is sacrificed. The Gadaba, Southern India. (Thurston, 1909, 2: 242, 250)

jii nu kami, jiitchi The earth kami. Okinawa. (Lebra, 1966: 219)

Jo Kan A very powerful and beneficial god of the earth. Siberia. (Casanowicz, 1924: 417)

Joli-Tarem The earth mother and giver of life. Sister of Numi-Tarem. Vogul, Siberia. (Pettersson, 1957: 20–21; Roheim, 1954: 31)

Jord The "primitive earth," daughter of Nott and Anar, and the mother of Thor as the wife of Odin. Teutonic. (Guerber, 1895: 15, 43; Grimm, 1883, 2: 735; Wagner, 1882: 31, 123, 237)

Juiup An earth god and a deity of evil in opposition to Kij. Guatemala. (Bancroft, 1886, 3: 482)

ka jumai The "demoness of earthquakes." The Khasi, Assam. (Stegmiller, 1921: 422)

Juyutikah An earth god of the Quiché. Guatemala. (Thompson, 1970: 275)

Kadru The earth, one of the wives of Kasyapa. India. (Zimmer, 1955: 52)

Kahuone Goddess of the sands, wife of Tiki. The Marquesas, Polynesia. (Williamson, 1933, 2: 174)

Kaila The "Earth . . . a mysterious shadowy power of incalculable energies and influences, rather mischievous and wicked than beneficial to mankind." The Klamath, Oregon. (Gatschet, 1890: xci; Chamberlain, 1892: 254)

Kai-matutsi "earth-occupation" who lived below—the nadir. The Pomo, California. (Barrett, 1917: 424)

Kakdzyamu God of the taiga. The Orochi, Siberia. (Ivanov, Smolyak and Levin, 1964: 757)

Kalcheng, Kalcegn An earth goddess invoked for relief and intercession with Tapern in thunderstorms. The Menik Kaien and Kintak Bong, Malaya. (Evans, 1937: 172)

Kaliog A deity of earthquakes, of the underworld. The Ifugao, Philippines. (Barton, 1955: 141)

Kaltas, Kaltes Goddess of the earth and of birth who takes the form of a goose or a hare, and is associated with Numi-Torum (Numi-Tarem). The Ob-Ugrian, Vogul, Ostyak. Siberia. (Michael, 1963: 208; Roheim, 1954: 27)

Kamurai An earthquake god who causes the universe to tremble when he coils himself—a serpent. The Yami, Formosa. (Del Re, n.d.: 70)

Kane-huli-honua A god of earthquakes and volcanic eruptions. Hawaii. (Westervelt, 1963, 2: 71)

Kane-lulu-moku (honua), Kane-ruru-honua God of earthquakes. Hawaii. (Beckwith, 1940: 566)

Kane-pohaku-ka'a Another name of the earthquake god. Hawaii. (Westervelt, 1963, 2: 71)

The karuhua The sons of the gods kupuka fucha and kupuka küshe. They are beneficent minor deities associated with the earth and benefiting mankind through the intermediaries—the ancestral chiefs. The Mapuche, Chile. (Faron, 1968: 66, 67)

Kathshchar-Ekva The earth goddess of the Mansi. Sister of Numi-Torum. Siberia. (Michael, 1963: 209)

Ka Wunphrang The embryonic earth, child of Kringkrong wa and Ynong majan. Of the second generation of deities. The Katchins, Burma. (Gilhodes, 1908: 675)

Keb The earth god—The "ancient Goose-god, who produced the cosmic egg." Egypt. (Budge, 1973, 1: 60, 79)

Kenjo The god of the land who is offered first fruits. He is a patron of hunters and of war, and among some the god of thunder and rain. The Jukun, Nigeria. (Meek, 1931: 201, 265–266; Greenberg, 1946: 57)

Khermata A Dravidian earth goddess identified with Devi. India. (Crooke, 1925, 5: 7; Russell, 1916, 4: 81)

Khetrpal, Bhumiya An earth god and guardian of boundaries. Gujarat, Bengal. (Crooke, 1925, 2: 484; 1925, 11: 872)

Khon-ma "Old mother" earth controls the earth spirits/demons, is "the guardian of the earth's doors." The ceremony for barring the demons is directed to her. "She rides upon a ram, and is dressed in golden yellow robes. . . . She holds a golden noose, and her face contains eighty wrinkles." Tibet. (Waddell, 1959: 484–486)

Ki An ancient Sumerian earth goddess—later supplanted by Nin-tu, Ninhursaga, Ninmah. The mother of Enlil by An. Near East. (Jacobsen, 1946: 158; Kramer, 1967: 110; Ferm, 1950: 57)

Kildisin A Finno-Ugric goddess of birth who is also a deity of the earth, and of the corn. The Votiaks, Russia. (MacCulloch, 1964: 258)

Kilu Dravidian chthonic spirits who destroy crops and must be propitiated. The Abor, Tibet and India. (Crooke, 1925, 1: 33)

kimun kamui The bear is the supreme god of the land. The Hokkaidu Ainu, Japan. (Philippi, 1982: 83)

Kine-dene The earth-mother goddess of the Minyong Abors. Assam. (Furer-Haimendorf, 1954: 594)

Kine-Nane An earth goddess, a chthonic deity, who represents "universal motherhood," and is associated with fertility and abundance. The Adi, Northeastern India. (Chowdhury, 1971: 113–114)

Kisin The evil god of earthquakes and of the part of the underworld called Metlán. He is the servant of Sukukyum and punishes sinners. The Chol and the Lacandon, Mexico. (Cline, 1944: 112; Tozzer, 1941; 132; Alexander, 1920: 141; Perera and Bruce, 1982: 176, 308)

Kitaka The god of the earth. Among the Baganda he is made offerings by women to ensure abundant crops, and by the king regarding condemned people "to destroy their bodies and spirits so that they could not return to harm the king." (Roscoe, 1965: 312–13). Among the Basoga he is also the god of earthquakes which he causes when he passes through the land. He is followed by Kibaho, who causes plague and illness. Uganda. (Roscoe, 1915: 250–251)

Kjoni-samptni The god of the earth of the Uru. Bolivia. (LaBarre, 1941: 521)

Kokyanwuqti Tusayan mother earth, Spider Woman. Same as Sussis-tinnako (Sia). Arizona. (Fewkes, 1895, 1: 356; Waters, 1963: 166)

Koliog "Earthquake," a god of the underworld. Offspring of Mayogyog. The Ifugao, Philippines. (Barton, 1946: 34)

Kotan-kor-kamui The Owl God in the early period was considered the protector of humans and the ruler of the land. The Hokkaidu Ainu, Japan. (Philippi, 1982: 10, 101)

Kow Lung A guardian deity of the land. China. (Du Bose, n.d.: 139)

ku The "god of Earth and of Maize." The Tlapanecs, Guerrero, Mexico. (Girard, 1979: 108)

Kujum-Chantu Mother earth whose "eyes became the Sun and Moon." India. (Long, 1963: 35)

Te Kuku A deity who represents "earthquakes and volcanic phenomena." The Maori, New Zealand. (Best, 1924: 175)

Ku-moku-hali'i A god of the land, of the forest, and the rain, who is invoked in cutting trees. Hawaii. (Beckwith, 1940: 15, 26)

Kuni-no-Tokotachi-no-Kami "The Earthly-Eternally-Standing Deity." Japan. (Hori, 1968: 4; Yasumaro, 1928: 65)

Kunitsukami Uzuhiko An earthly deity—"the process of 'material' creation (i.e. physical, vital and mental) had been completed by" him. Japan. (Yasumaro, 1928: 96; Herbert, 1967: 334)

Kupo A god of the soil, a chthonic deity, who helps the crops to grow. The Akim-Kotoku, Ghana. (Field, 1948: 180–181)

sKyabs-mdun "The highest deity of the earth is Mother sKyabs-mdun, ''helpful spouse.' She seems to be identical with the goddess of the earth brTan-ma . . . or brTar-byed-ma." Her role as an active earth goddess is transferred to aBru-gu-ma, the wife of Kesar. Tibet. (Francke, 1923: 7)

Kye-phang A god of the soil, at Lahul. Tibet. (Snellgrove, 1957: 176)

Labosum God of the earth of the Saora. Orissa, India. (Elwin, 1954: 638)

Lai-oid An earth goddess, wife of Jawait, who causes the underground waters to rise destroying "the houses of those who have offended the deities." The Bateg, Malaya. (Evans, 1937: 146)

Larunaen The god who causes earthquakes also created the earth, is father of all things, and provides man with all his needs. His sister/wife is Hintabaran. New Ireland, Melanesia. (Cox, 1913: 195–196)

Latu hila la balaa Mother earth of Watubela Island. Indonesia. (Frazer, 1926: 667)

Lauma Lithuanian goddess of the earth and of weaving. (Grimm, 1888, 4: 1369)

Laxoo The god of earthquakes. The Sierra Zapotec, Oaxaca, Mexico. (Whitecotton, 1977: 169)

Lebie-pogil The Owner of the Earth is over all the lesser related spirits, and is appealed to by the shaman before the hunt. He gives the soul of a reindeer (which indicates good hunting) or of a bull (bad hunting). The Yukaghir, Siberia. (Jochelson, 1900/02: 144–145, 210)

Lengbin The god of the earth of the Ahom. Tai. (Gurdon, 1925, 1: 236)

Lengdin The goddess of the earth of the Ahom. Tai. (Gurdon, 1925, 1: 236)

Lethn A deity of nature and the earth associated with the east/southeast in the divisions of the sky, and who appears on "the bronze liver of Piacenza" used in divination. Etruscan, Italy. (Hamblin, 1975: 95; Pallottino, 1975: 145)

Lethns An Etruscan earth and nature deity associated with the west/southwest in the divisions of the sky and whose name appears in relation to the "bronze liver from Piacenza" used in divination. Italy. (Pallottino, 1975: 145; Hamblin, 1975: 95)

Lobo The earth deity of the Savara. Southern India. (Thurston, 1909, 6: 336)

Lofia A deity considered by some to cause earthquakes. Tonga and Samoa, Polynesia. (Williamson, 1933, 2: 213)

Loowe An earth god who brought people and animals from the underworld, and is associated with "fertility and vigor," also with caves. South Africa. (Willoughby, 1932: 74, 76; Schapera, 1937: 269–70)

Lumimuut The earth goddess, who was impregnated by the god of the west wind, is the mother of all things and with her son/husband Toar the parents of mankind. The Alfures and the Minahassans, Celebes, Indonesia. (Keane, 1925, 1: 254; Pettazzoni, 1956: 11; Raats, 1969: 20)

Lur, Lurbira   The Earth is considered the mother of the sun and the moon, and the vital force of the vegetable kingdom. She contains the treasures of the earth. The Basques, Spain and France. (Barandiaran, 1972: 149)

Luumkab   Minor deities who are associated with the earth, with stones. The Lacandon, Mexico. (Perera and Bruce, 1982: 308)

Maanhaltija   The earth spirit whose consent must be obtained before building. Finland. (Krohn, 1925, 6: 24)

Machandri   Mother earth who is invoked at the end of the sowing to promote fertility. Hoshangabad, India. (Crooke, 1894: 31)

Maddar-ahkku   The earth mother was also a goddess of healing and of childbirth. The Lapps. (Minn, 1955: 72)

Ma Dharti   Mother earth who is worshipped on building a house, in sacrifices to the dead, and during the harvest. The Bhils, India. (Naik, 1956: 185)

Madji ahan-do   An evil spirit who causes earthquakes. The Penobscot, Maine. (Speck, 1935: 5, 21)

Mafui'e, Mafue   God of earthquakes and of fire, from whom Ti'iti'i obtained fire for the Samoans, inhabits the volcanic region below. Polynesia. (Andersen, 1928: 216; Williamson, 1933, 2: 184, 186; Mead, 1930: 158; Stair, 1897: 211)

Mafuike   The god of earthquakes. Futuna. On Fakaofo Island a goddess, and from whom fire was obtained. Polynesia. (Burrows, 1936: 106; Smith, 1892: 35; 1920: 147)

Magbabáya tominapay   The "spirit who lives under the earth and supports it with his hands. . . . Only slightly inferior to" Diwata Magbabáya. The Bukidnon, Mindanao, Philippines. (Cole, 1956: 93)

Magna Mater   Cybele, Phrygian mother goddess, was brought to Rome, as a black stone, from Pessinus in Phrygia and worshipped at the time of Hannibal's invasion. Italy. (Morford and Lenardon, 1975: 416)

Mah   A Sumerian and Akkadian earth-mother goddess, sister of Enlil; the creator of man from clay, and a goddess of childbirth as well as of animal fertility. Near East. (Langdon, 1931: 109–110)

Maja   The earth goddess and mother of the Indian race. The Sioux, Plains Indians, Minnesota to Rocky Mountains. (Dorsey, 1892: 293)

Maju   A chthonic spirit, husband of Mari, who causes hailstorms when he leaves his cavern to join her. The Basques. France and Spain. (Barandiaran, 1972: 155)

Maka, Maka-akan   The Earth was created by Inyan from a part of himself; is the second of the superior gods. She is the ancestress of all on earth and the provider for all. She shows her pleasure or displeasure (of invocations, sacrifices) by giving good or bad seasons, plenty or scarcity of production. She "presides over the medicines that come from the earth and gives to them potencies for good or evil" relative to her pleasure and/or the skill of the shaman and his invocations. Among some people it is believed in the creation of animals she, with Woope, fashioned those "having claws and blunt teeth." The Lakota, Plains Indians, South Dakota. (Walker, 1980: 50, 51, 107, 120; Jahner, 1977: 34; Powers, 1977: 54; One Feather, 1982: 49)

Makiutija   The spirit of the earth appears as a large lizard. The Kapauku Papuans, New Guinea. (Pospisil, 1958: 33)

Mama Allpa   An earth goddess. Peru. (Brinton, 1868: 223)

Mama Latay   Mother of the Earth, identified with St. Veronica. The Shango Cult, Trinidad. (Simpson, 1965: 19, 22)

Mama Nono   The earth, a mother goddess of the Caribs of the Antilles. West Indies. (Spence, 1925, 2: 836)

Mama Pacha   The earth goddess of the Chincha invoked for good harvests. Peru. (Alexander, 1920: 224; Markham, 1969: 133)

Manamoan   A goddess of childbirth and associated with the earth. The Mandaya (Mindanao), Philippines. (Raats, 1969: 20)

Ma-ndɔə   The earth goddess, wife of Ngewə. The Mende, Sierra Leone. (Harris, 1950: 279)

Manoid   The earth goddess, wife of Karei. He communicates with her by lightning. They are propitiated for sins by pouring blood on the ground for her, by flicking it toward the sky for him. The Djahai, and Jehai, Indonesia. (Evans, 1937: 152; Roheim, 1972: 20, 23; Pettazzoni, 1956: 312–313)

ya Manoij   The goddess who was "ruler of the lower world"—the earth as against the heavens ruled by Ta Ped'n. The Semang, Malaya. (Schebesta, 1957: 33)

St. Manuel   Identified with ihp'en, the earth god. The Chorti, Guatemala. (Wisdom, 1940: 401–402)

Marinette   A goddess of the earth, wife of Ti-Jean Petro. The "major and violent female of the Petro nation." Haiti. (Deren, 1953: 63, 83, 138)

Masakamekokiu   The earth—"grandmother of everything that breathes." The Menomini, Wisconsin. (Skinner and Satterlee, 1915: 241)

Mastor-ava   Finnon-Ugrian earth mother invoked for good harvest and health. She is worshipped immediately after the sky god. The Erza and the Moksha. Russia. (Paasonen, 1925, 8: 844; Leach, 1949, 1: 96)

Mastor-pas   In some areas the earth is male and malignant, invoked "to bring their enemies to destruction." The Mordvins, Russia. (Paasonen, 1925, 8: 845)

Mati-Syra-Zemlya   Slavic mother earth, described as "the cold," "the moist," who was invoked as a witness to oaths and in settling disputes, for protection from illness and misfortunes. Russia. (Schrader, 1925, 2: 38; Larousse, 1968: 287)

Ma-ukuuku   "white clay"—a wife of Raki. The Maroi, New Zealand. (White, 1887, 1: 21)

Mbache   The earth goddess, wife of Ppahia. The Yachi, Nigeria. (Armstrong, 1955: 150)

Mebuyan   A goddess associated with the earth and with rice. She refused to go to the heavens with her brother, Lumabat, and instead descended into the earth with her bowl of rice, dropping grains as she went. She represents the rhythm of life and death controlled from the underworld by her shaking of the tree "on which all life hangs, thus causing death on earth." As such she is a goddess of the dead and of the underworld, Gimokudan. The Bagobo, Philippines. (Raats, 1969: 21, 24, 32–34)

Meder, Medr   Semitic mother earth. Ethiopia. (Moscati, 1960: 225). The earth god of the South Arabians of Aksum, Ethiopia. (Langdon, 1931: 11). The "god (or goddess) of the earth." Forms a triad with 'Astar and Beher. (Littmann, 1925, 1: 57)

Ratu Medrwe Karang   The Owner of the Ground. Bali, Indonesia. (Covarrubias, 1937: 94)

melande-awa   "Mother of the Earth." The Cheremis, Russia. (Leach, 1949, 1: 98)

Mesakamigokwaha   The earth mother of the Sauk, the Fox. Wisconsin. (Skinner and Satterlee, 1915: 241)

Mi-bou-do   Mother earth of the Lo-lo p'o. Yunnan, China. (Frazer, 1926: 81)

Mif-yz   The beneficent god of the earth. The Gilyaks, Siberia. (Klementz, 1925, 6: 225; Dioszegi, 1968: 407)

Mkissi nssi   "He or she appears to be an embodiment of the earth viewed in its productive and fertilizing aspect." Generally spoken of as male. The Bafioti, Gabon. (Frazer, 1926: 418)

Mlum Mukyam   An earth deity born of Itpomu and Debu. The Lepchas, Sikkim. (Gorer, 1938: 223)

Moekilai-puka   One of four gods who "ruled the earth." Vaitupu (Ellice Islands), Polynesia. (Williamson, 1933, 2: 102)

Moitjinka   An earth mother, the equivalent of Kunapipi. The Munrinbata, Australia. (Robinson, 1966: 125)

Mo'n-Sho'n   Sacred Mother Earth to where the Little Ones of the Sky were sent to live by Wah'-Kon-Tah. The Osage, Lower Missouri River Basin. (Mathews, 1982: 9, 10, 400, 529)

Móooi   The god who supports the earth. When he turns it causes earthquakes. Tonga, Polynesia. (Frazer, 1961: 201)

Morufonu   A god who holds the world steady. When he shifts his weight, there are tremors. His wife is Jugumishanta and they are the parents of all, among them Wajubu, the moon, and Wainako, the sun. The Kamano, the Usurufa, the Jate, and the Fore, New Guinea. (Berndt, 1965: 80)

Moumousia   One of four gods who "ruled the earth." Vaitupu (Ellice Islands), Polynesia. (Williamson, 1933, 2: 102)

M'ox   A Mayan earth god. The Quiché, Guatemala. (Thompson, 1970: 220)

The Mundo   The Earth deity before whom a person destined to be a daykeeper (calendar diviner) must appear and bring gifts to the shrine. Guatemala. (Tedlock, 1982: 53)

Musisi   A chthonic god who is god of earthquakes. Father of Mukasa. The Baganda, Uganda. (Roscoe, 1965: 313; Cunningham, 1905: 215; Werner, 1964: 130)

Muyinwu   An earth or germ god—of fertility, germination, and growth. The Hopi Indians, Arizona. (Fewkes, 1920: 592; 1901: 215)

Muyinwu-wuqti A Tusayan earth goddess. Pueblo Indians. Arizona. (Fewkes, 1895, 1: 350)

Nabinge The earthquake god of the Banyankole and the Bakyiga. Among the latter he is also associated with plague and disease. Uganda. (Roscoe, 1923: 25; Frazer, 1926: 425)

Nachigai The earth goddess, also known as Etugen, was invoked for good weather, abundance of crops and animals, and for prosperity. The Mongols. (Phillips, 1969: 34)

Naëstsán The earth goddess of the Navaho whose husband was Yadilyil, the sky. Arizona and New Mexico. (Matthews, 1902: 739)

nahosdzáán (*see also* **Naëstsán, naxa'asdzá·n**) Earth Woman. The wind within her provides life and guidance to those of the underworld as well as to earth's surface people. The winds (Words One, Two, Three, and Four), which she established at the cardinal points, are those by which man is guided in his thoughts and actions, his capabilities. They are the same as the inner wind received at conception. She is the wise owner and regulator of all living things. The Navaho, Arizona, and New Mexico. (McNeley, 1981: 15–17, 28, 81)

Nai-no-Kami God of earthquakes. Japan. (Herbert, 1967: 490; Larousse, 1968: 416)

Namazu A "monstrous catfish" who supports the islands on his back, a god of earthquakes. Japan. (Sierksma, 1960: 28, 51)

Nanaolonupippisopi The earth mother on the third layer of heaven. The Cuna, Panama. (Keeler, 1960: 46)

Nanga Baiga God of the earth and the animals. He and his wife, Nanga Baigin, helped stabilize the earth at the creation. The Baiga and the Agaria, India. (Elwin, 1939: 307, 313; 1949: 12)

Nanga Baigin Goddess of the earth and wife of Nanga Baiga. The Baiga and the Agaria, India. (Elwin, 1939: 313; 1949: 12)

Nangkwijo The earth, wife of Makowasendo, the sky. The Tewa, New Mexico. (Harrington, 1907/08: 51)

Nang Tholani Goddess of the earth. Laos. (Deydier, 1952: 30)

na rip bu A "deity who created the different kinds of soil, i.e. both the cultivable soil and the stony soil." The Lepchas, Sikkim. (Siiger, 1967: 143)

Natigai, Natigay The god of the earth, of crops, of cattle, of children. The Tartar and the Mongols, Siberia. (MacCulloch, 1964: 460; Crooke, 1894: 14)

naxa'asdzá·n The earth woman, a helpful deity, who represents growth. The Navaho, Arizona and New Mexico. (Reichard, 1950: 431–32)

Ndara Goddess of the earth and of the underworld who supports the earth on her head. Her slightest movement causes earthquakes. The carrying of the earth is also attributed to others, Toralindo (a giant buffalo) and Bagina Ali (Mohammed's son-in-law). Celebes, Indonesia. (Adriani and Kruyt, 1950: 370–371; Pettersson, 1957: 27; Downs, 1920: 9, 12; Pettazzoni, 1956: 333)

Ndengei A serpent god whose turning causes earthquakes. Among some he is the creator of mankind. Fiji Islands, Melanesia. (Thomson, 1925, 6: 14; Poignant, 1967: 94)

Ndoi The earth goddess, wife of the supreme god Ngewo. The Mende, Sierra Leone. (McCulloch, 1950: 39)

Neiterogob An earth goddess of the Masai. Kenya and Tanzania. (Larousse, 1973: 523)

Nerthus Teutonic earth-mother goddess, the symbol of fruitfulness. A goddess of peace and tranquility. Sometimes considered the sister of, or identified with, Njord. (MacCulloch, 1964: 102–103; Grimm, 1880: 251–252; Stern, 1898: 61; Turville-Petre, 1964: 171)

Netcensta The earth mother who also supports it and whose shifting when tired causes earthquakes. The Tahltan, British Columbia. (Teit, 1919: 227)

Ngun lo kak A malevolent aspect of Ngun as the god of the earth, "associated with cultivation." The Bari and the Pojulu, Sudan. (Huntingford, 1953; 42, 70)

ni' The earth, a helpful deity, identified with Changing Woman. The Navaho, Arizona and New Mexico. (Reichard, 1950: 431)

Niatha The wise and beneficent "owner of all the land," whose blessings are requested. The Arapahoe, Colorado. (Grinnell, 1972: 89)

Nigoubub A female spirit in the form of an eel "at whose breast the earth rests. When she turns, the earth trembles." Truk Island, Micronesia. (Bollig, 1927: 12)

Ningtangr A being who steadies the post at the end of the world which supports the sky. His inattention causes earthquakes. The Ao Naga, India. (Elwin, 1949: 14)

Ninhursag The Sumerian earth-mother goddess who represented the source of all life, the earth's fertility, even to the capacity of the rocky ground and the desert to produce life. She was the mother of Ninsar, or Ninmu, the goddess of plants, by Enki. Near East. (Kramer, 1961: 101; James, 1960: 78; Hooke, 1963: 33; Jacobsen, 1970: 30)

Ninisan A deity worshipped as the earth "but seems capable of a wider meaning, including the universe." the Hupa, California. (Goddard, 1925, 6: 882)

Nin-ki A chthonic goddess, "Lady Earth," associated with Enki. Near East. (Jacobsen, 1976: 122, 270)

Ninmah Another name of Ninhursag. (Jacobsen, 1970: 30; Kramer, 1961: 104, 121)

Nkike The earth goddess of the Mbolli. Nigeria. (Talbot, 1967: 100)

Nokomis The goddess of the earth, the giver of life. Grandmother of Manabozho. The Algonquin Indians, United States. (Alexander, 1964: 27, 39; Larousse, 1968: 428)

Nono The Earth was like a part of the Sky, but no one lived there, there was nothing. The Makiritare, Venezuela. (Civrieux, 1980: 21)

Notasqa-vairgin God of the nadir, the "earth-being." The Chukchee, Siberia. (Bogoras, 1904/09: 305)

Ntoa A state god/goddess whose planet is Venus. In the female aspect a goddess of the "Fertile Earth." This deity is a participant in death/rebirth ceremonies. The Akan, Ghana. (Meyerowitz, 1958: 49, 57, 89)

Nuliajuk Goddess of both the sea and the land and of all animals. The Netsilik and the Mackenzie Eskimo, Canada. (Balikci, 1970: 205–206; Rasmussen, 1931: 224)

Nungui The earth mother, important in agricultural growth, and the giver of culture. The Jivaro, Ecuador and Peru. (Harner, 1972: 70, 74–75; Karsten, 1926: 300–301; Hatt, 1951: 879; Weyer, 1961: 122)

Nurkami God of the nadir, the earth. The Sia, Pueblo Indians, New Mexico. (Fewkes, 1895, 2: 126)

Nutenut The Earth who is the owner of the world under the sea. The Chukchee, Siberia. (Bogoras, 1904/09: 306)

Nyohwe Ananu An earth goddess, wife/twin of Dada Zodji, parents of the earth gods. Abomey. (Herskovits, 1938, 2: 129, 139)

Nzambi-si The earth mother. Lower Congo, Africa. (Werner, 1964: 125)

Obasi Nsi, Obassi Nsi The beneficent earth goddess who gives them food while alive and receives them in the afterworld when dead. The Ekoi, Nigeria and Cameroon. (Meek, 1931: 180; Parrinder, 1949: 38; Frazer, 1926: 131–132)

Oda-no-Mikoto God of the earth and of the rice field. Also known as Otsuchi-no-Mi-oya-no-Kami, Saruta-hiko, Yachimata-no-Kami, Sae-no-Kami, and Dosojin. Japan. The second important deity of Fushimi-Inari Shrine. (Czaja, 1974: 258)

'Og-gis-bdag Mother earth, goddess of the Nadir. Same as Ananta. Tibet. (Waddell, 1959: 367)

Ogo A deity of discord created by Amma, and twin of Nommo, "associated with the arid, unproductive earth." The Dogon, Mali and Upper Volta. (Paulme, 1973: 92)

Oho-na-mochi The chief Shinto earth god. To him (and Sukuna-bikona) "is attributed the origin of the art of medicine and of charms against the powers of evil." Japan. (Aston, 1925, 11: 463, 466)

Oho-toko-nushi-no-kami Known as the "great-earth-master-deity." Japan. (Czaja, 1974: 166)

Oikumene Greek personification of the earth. (Roscher, 1965, 3, 1: 748)

Okunimitama-no-kami A god of the land and the guardian deity of Yamato Province. Japan. (Yasumaro, 1965: 51; Herbert, 1967: 332)

Olokukurtilisop The earth mother and fertility goddess whose son and consort is Olowaipippilele, the sun god. They produced mankind, sacred plants, animals. The Cuna, Panama. (Keeler, 1960: 11, 46)

Olomakriai An earth mother, wife/sister of Olotwalikippilele, the moon god. Parents of the sun and stars. The Cuna, Panama. (Keeler, 1960: 147)

Omahank-Chika The malignant and "evil one of the earth." The Mandan, North Dakota. (Wied-Neuwied, 1843: 360)

Omusisi The earthquake god of some of the Banyankole. Others say it is Nabinge. Uganda. (Roscoe, 1923: 25)

One Kea The sand goddess, "White Sands," who takes away the beach sands in the autumn and returns them "glistening clean" in the spring. Her male counterpart is One-uli. Hawaii. (Ashdown, 1971: 29)

One-uli "Dark Sands," who inspects the beaches of the oceans with One Kea. Hawaii. (Ashdown, 1971: 29)

Onile The Owner of the Earth and giver of life, but also the goddess of the dead who come to her domain. The Yoruba, Dahomey and Nigeria. (Williams, 1964: 140; Morton-Williams, 1964: 245)

Onuava A nature goddess associated with the earth—at Gironde. Gaul. (Renel, 1906: 402; Ferguson, 1970: 214)

Otokonushi-no-Kami Shinto god of the lands. Japan. (Kato, 1926: 82)

Otsuchi-no-Kami A god of the earth. Also called Tsuchi-no-Mioya-no-kami. Japan. (Yasumaro, 1965: 51, 52; Herbert, 1967: 332–3)

Otygen Mother earth. The Mongol, Siberia. (MacCulloch, 1964: 453)

Paabothkwe Omniscient mother earth. The Shawnee, Lower New York, New Jersey, and Delaware. (Pettazzoni, 1956: 13)

Pacha-mama The earth mother and goddess of fertility who controls all agricultural products. The Uru, Chipaya, Aymara, and Inca. Peru and Bolivia. (Rowe, 1946: 295; Tschopik, 1946: 559; 1951: 192; LaBarre, 1946: 582–583; Nash, 1972: 54)

Panku An old god of the Tami who causes earthquakes. New Guinea. (Frazer, 1961: 198)

Panlinugun The chief god of Idadalmunon, the Underworld, and the god of earthquakes. The Sulod, Philippines. (Jocano, 1969: 19)

Papa (1) Also Papa-tu-a-nuku. The earth, with Rangi, the sky father, the primordial parents from whom all else came. The Maori. In the Society Islands she is the wife of Atea (or Te Tumu) and in Mangaia, the wife of Vatea. Polynesia. (Best, 1924: 86; Grey, 1855: 1, 5; Andersen, 1928: 355, 360, 367; Buck, 1938: 83, 110) (2) Among the Cuna Indians—"the earth which feeds us we call *papa*." Panama. (Nordenskiold, 1938: 129)

Pekujike The earthquake god is believed to have created the world, and is also a god of the afterworld with whom the ghost must contend. The Naga of Manipur, India. (Hodson, 1911: 127, 161)

Ih P'en An androgynous deity of the soil, the "personification of the earth and patron of plant growth, fertility, family life, property, and other wealth." In the male aspect, "the consort of Ix Kanan, female spirit of the bean." Also called Tulanta. The Chorti, Guatemala. (Thompson, 1970: 294)

Pezelao, Bezelao The god of the earth as well as god of death and of the underworld. The Zapotec, Oaxaca, Mexico. (Whitecotton, 1977: 158, 169)

Phuplans Etruscan "god of earth and all earth's products, who is well compared with Dionysus and Bacchus." The god of Pupluna. Italy. (Rawlinson, 1885: 123)

Pillan The supreme being and god of thunder, giver of fire, was also the god of earthquakes and volcanic eruptions. The Araucanians. Among the Mapuche, pillan fucha and pillan kushe are the god and goddess of volcanoes and thunder. Earthquakes and the elements are controlled through propitiation. Chile and Tierra del Fuego. (Loeb, 1931: 545; Osborne, 1968: 116; Alexander, 1920: 325–326; Cooper, 1946, 6: 745–747; Faron, 1968: 65, 66, 69)

Pitao-Xoo The god of earthquakes. Oaxaca, Mexico. (Bancroft, 1886, 3: 457; Whitecotton, 1977: 169)

Poseidon The god of the sea was also the god of earthquakes, worshipped in the hope that he would stabilize the land. Greece. (Ferguson, 1970: 38; Frazer, 1961: 195–196; Larousse, 1968: 133; Chadwick, 1976: 86, 96; Hesiod-Brown, 1981: 66)

Potnia A goddess worshipped at Pylos—presumably an earth goddess. Also associated with smiths. Greece. (Chadwick, 1976: 92–93; Samuel, 1966: 60, 90–91)

Prah Thorni The goddess of the earth. Cambodia. (Marchal, 1963: 206)

Prithivi The earth, wife of Dyaus—the "primeval parents"—the mother of all things. She is associated with patience, and is represented as a "variegated cow." India and Bali. (Danielou, 1964: 87; Keith, 1917: 16; Martin, 1914: 29; Cox, 1870, 1: 328; Levi, 1933: xxiii)

Protogenia A Greek earth goddess. (Roscher, 1965, 3, 2: 3182)

Pruvisana A god who supports the earth and causes earthquakes. The Achagua, Venezuela and Colombia. (Hernandez de Alba, 1948, 2: 410)

Puivisana The god of earthquakes, an aspect of Puru. The Salivan, Colombia. (Walde-Waldegg, 1936: 40–41; Wallis, 1939: 89)

Pulang Gana The god of the earth, of the soil, and of all aspects of rice farming. With Raja Sua also the creators of heaven and earth. The Sea Dyaks, Borneo. (Roth, 1968: 174, 177; Gomes, 1911: 196; Sarawak Gazette, 1963: 16, 133)

Punauaga Olopunalisop The goddess of earthquakes, wife of Oloikanipipilel. Later the wife of Ibelele. The Cuna, Panama. (Nordenskiold, 1938: 327, 332)

Purgyul A god of the soil. Tibet. (Snellgrove, 1957: 176)

Puškaitis An earth god "living under elderberry bushes" who on receiving offerings would send his subterranean spirits to bring "plenty of corn and did the household work." Lithuania. (Gimbutas, 1963: 194)

Quilaztli A goddess of the earth and "of women who died in childbirth," worshipped at Cuauhilama, Valley of Anahuac. Another name of Cihuacoatl. Mexico. (Reed, 1966: 112; Bancroft, 1886, 2: 269)

Rab brtan ma A Tibetan earth goddess. (Nebesky-Wojkowitz, 1956, 1: 294)

Rabie A goddess "associated with the moon and the earth." Wife of Tuwale. The Wemale, Philippines. (Raats, 1969: 49)

Rakahore The personification of rock, son of Tuamatua and Takoto-wai, and protector of Papa from the attacks of Hine-moana. The Maori, New Zealand. (Best, 1924: 154–155; Andersen, 1928: 285)

Ramchandi Some consider her "the personification of Mother Earth." The Kolta, Central Provinces, India. (Russell, 1916, 3: 541)

ka ram-ew The goddess of earth. The Khasi, Assam. (Stegmiller, 1921: 410)

Rangahua The personification of stones, offspring of Tuamatua and Takoto-wai, and spouse of Tu-maunga—parents of the sand and gravel maidens. The Maori, New Zealand. (Best, 1924: 99; Andersen, 1928: 104)

Ah Raxa Lac God of the earth. The Quiché, Guatemala. (Recinos, 1950: 78)

Reh-be An earth god of the Ch'iang at Ts'u-sha Ji Geh and at Ch'ing-p'o Ji Geh. Szechwan, China. (Graham, 1958: 71)

Rhea Mother earth—daughter of Uranus and Gaea, wife of Cronus, mother of Hestia, Demeter, Hera, Hades, Poseidon, and Zeus. Greece and Crete. (Kerenyi, 1951: 21–22; Cox, 1870, 2: 312; Barthell, 1971: 12, 14; Fairbanks, 1907: 91)

Rinda, Rindr A Scandinavian earth goddess representing the surface of the earth. As a wife of Odin she represents the winter earth when it is unfruitful. Mother of Vali. (Guerber, 1895: 43, 185; Grimm, 1880: 251; Wagner, 1882: 31, 237)

Ro-bo-shi An earth deity of the Ch'iang at Lo-pu-chai. Szechwan, China. (Graham, 1958: 47)

Ru', Ruaumoko The "god of earthquakes, was never born, but still lives within Papa, and ever and anon struggling for light and air." The Maori, Polynesia. (Andersen, 1928: 375; White, 1887, 1: 21)

Ru-be-sei An earth god "who controls the earth and the soil, causes rain and good crops," and is protective of the people. In some places, female. The Ch'iang at Hop'ing-chai. Szechwan, China. (Graham, 1958: 47, 60)

Rusor A Roman earth god associated with Tellus. He represents the revolving, cyclic feature of nature. Italy. (Dumézil, 1966, 1: 374; Frazer, 1926: 330)

Saba-faat-chaum An earth deity born of Itpomu and Debu. The Lepchas, Sikkim. (Gorer, 1938: 223)

Sa bla dog rum (pr. **Sala Dokrum**), **Sa yi lha 'od** The Bon earth god, consort of Sa rgyal dong gi dbal mo. Tibet. (Tucci, 1980: 218)

Sagbata, Sakpata He is part of the sky pantheon as the eldest son of Mawu and Lisa, but in descending to the earth he is an earth god and head of that pantheon which rules the earth. This entire pantheon is identified with smallpox, which is used as punishment. Dahomey and Brazil. (Herskovits, 1938, 2: 129–36; Bastide, 1960: 571; Parrinder, 1949: 41–42; Mercier, 1954: 222, 231; Verger, 1954: 184)

Sa'i lha mo Sangs rgyas spyan ma A goddess of the earth invoked in pollution eliminating ceremonies. Tibet. (Nebesky-Wojkowitz, 1956, 1: 388

Sakyuen-faat-it An earth deity born of Itpomu and Debu. The Lepchas, Sikkim. (Gorer, 1938: 223)

Sangvo Nimu An earth spirit, one of the wives of Adoo Yook and Alau Yook, by whom they are fertilized with rice, millet and maize. The Lepchas, Sikkim. (Gorer, 1938: 237)

Sansari Mai The earth mother who is also the goddess of thieves, invoked by them before undertaking a raid. The Doms, India. (Keane, 1925, 2: 123; Briggs, 1953: 530)

Saptapetala An earth goddess of Bali. Indonesia. (Belo, 1953: 53)

Sarapat The spirit of the soil of the Jakun. Malay Peninsula. (Skeat, 1906: 182)

Sa rgyal dong gi dbal mo (pr. **Sagyel Dong-gi Welmo**) Bon earth goddess, consort of Sa bla dog rum. Tibet. (Tucci, 1980: 218)

Sasabonsum A malignant and cannibalistic earth god and god of earthquakes after which, among the Ashanti, human sacrifices were made to appease him. Ghana. (Mockler-Ferryman, 1925, 9: 277; Frazer, 1961: 201; Ellis, 1887: 34–35)

Sa the(l) nag po The black earth, a seven-headed demon, is the personal attendant of Khön-ma, the "Old Mother." Also named as Sa thil smug po. Tibet. (Nebesky-Wojkowitz, 1956, 1: 98; Waddell, 1959: 484)

Saweigh A chthonic goddess who lives in the earth with Melu. A co-creatress. The Bilaan, Philippines. (Raats, 1969: 34)

Sa-yi-lha-mo An earth goddess of Sikkim. (Gazeteer of Sikhim, 1894: 368)

Sa yi lha 'od (pr. **Sayi Lha-ö**), **Sa bla dog rum** Earth god of the Bon. Tibet. (Tucci, 1980: 218)

Seb God of the earth, of its surface and its vegetation as well as of the underground, and as such a god of tombs. He was the son of Shu and Tefnut and brother/husband of Nut—together the parents of Isis and Osiris, of Set and Nephthys. Egypt. (Knight, 1915: 109–110; Budge, 1969, 2: 94–99; Bulfinch, 1898: 367)

Sedi The earth goddess of the Minyong, the Adi. She represents the female principle, is the wife of Melo, the sky, with whom she forms a dual deity, Sedi-Melo, credited with the creation. Northeast India. (Long, 1963: 106; Chowdhury, 1971: 75, 78, 105)

Seismos The personification of earthquake. Greece. (Roscher, 1965, 4: 640)

Selva An Etruscan god of nature and of the earth associated with the southwest and with divination by haruspicy. Italy. (Hamblin, 1975: 95; Pallottino, 1975: 145)

sengi-mama A goddess who rules the earth, the taiga, and the game. The Nanai, Siberia. (Dioszegi, 1968: 470)

Shadip The name of Phungkam Janun after she died and became mistress of the earth. She sends the rainbow in response to Woishun's rain. The Katchins, Burma. (Gilhodes, 1908: 679)

She God of the soil. China. (Maspero, 1963; 271; Peeters, 1941: 9)

Shidkin-kede The goddess of the earth of the Minyong Abors. Assam. (Furer-Haimendorf, 1954: 593; Chowdhury, 1970: 112–113)

Shir-kor-kamui A goddess who rules the earth. The Ainu, Japan. (Philippi, 1982: 177)

Naac Shishec The earth god, son of Nexhequiriac. The Trique, Oaxaca, Mexico. (Valentini, 1899: 38)

Sichi Mother earth who is also the creator. Same as Sedi. The Gallongs (Adi), Northeastern India. (Chowdhury, 1971: 115–116)

Sis Nag A cobra god who causes earthquakes in shaking his head. The Chamars, India. (Briggs, 1920: 123–124)

Sita An earth goddess and wife of Rama. The divinity of both is ambiguous. India. (O'Flaherty, 1980: 79, 80)

Sitking-Kedding The earth, wife of Peddo-Dodum, the sky, and mother of Doini and Pollo. The Bori (Adi), Northeastern India. (Chowdhury, 1971: 76)

Siwash The god of the earth of the Saboba Indians. California. (Beckwith, 1940: 84; James, 1902: 36)

Sninia A being "who lives amid the ice in the far north; he grasps a rope to which the earth is fastened, and he keeps it steady by maintaining a tension on the rope to hold the world against his feet. When he tightens the rope it causes an earthquake." The Bella Coola, British Columbia. (McIlwraith, 1948, 1: 23, 42)

Solang A terrestrial god and patron of canoe building. Son of Palulap and brother of Ialulwe. Ulithi and the

Carolines, Micronesia. (Lessa, 1966: 59; Poignant, 1967: 80)

Spenta Armaiti The spirit and guardian of the earth. An abstract deity—"Holy Harmony." Iran. (Williams Jackson, 1925, 1: 384–385; Huart, 1963: 41; Larousse, 1968: 317)

Subbu-Khai-Thung The earth. Dhammai (Miji), Northeast India. (Long, 1963: 105)

Suk-dum-lung-ming An earth deity born of Itpomu and Debu. The Lepchas, Sikkim. (Gorer, 1938: 223)

Tagma-sa-yuta The "lord of the earth." The Subanun of Zamboanga, Philippines. (Jocano, 1969: 24)

Tailtiu A Celtic earth mother. Ireland. (Puhvel, 1970: 170)

Takel A chthonic goddess who is one of the guardians of "the roots of the pillar which supports the heavens." Among the different tribes she has different relationships. The Negritos of Malaya. (Evans, 1937: 157, 177)

Takemikaduchi-no-Wo-no-Kami A god of earthquakes and a god of the underground. Japan. (Revon, 1925, 9: 237–238)

Takotsi Nakawe Goddess of the earth and of growth, who owns the earth. The Huichol, Mexico. (Seler, 1925, 6: 829; Alexander, 1920: 122)

Talatumsi The earth goddess of the Walpi, associated with the new-fire ceremony and with the dawn. The Hopi, Arizona. (Fewkes, 1895, 1: 350; 1900: 97, 120)

Tallur Muttai The earth mother of the Gondi-Koya. Orissa, India. (Elwin, 1954: 641)

Talyeu Nimu An earth spirit, one of the wives of Adoo Yook and Alau Yook, by whom they are fertilized with rice, millet, and maize. She takes part in the harvesting of the rice. The Lepchas, Sikkim. (Gorer, 1938: 237, 240)

Tamaayawut The earth, sister/wife of Tuukumit—parents of all things. The mountain Acagchemem, San Juan Capistrano, California. (Boscana, 1933: 115–116)

Tamayowut The earth, the female principle. With brother Tukomit, the creators of the things and features of the world—animated an inanimated—through birth. The Luiseño, California. (Kroeber, 1925: 677–678)

Tana Ekan The earth, female counterpart of Lera-Wulan, the supreme being. East Flores and Solor Islands, Indonesia. (Pettazzoni, 1956: 334)

Tanah The earth deity. Solor Island, Indonesia. (Frazer, 1926: 660)

Tang Ching T'u Ti A god of the soil. China. (Day, 1940: 208)

brTan-ma A goddess of the earth with whom sKyabs-mdun is identified. Tibet. (Francke, 1923: 7)

Tanowish The earth, mother of all things. La Jolla Indian Reserve Indians, California. (DuBois, 1904: 185)

Tapufatu One of four gods who "ruled the earth." Vaitupu (Ellice Islands), Polynesia. (Williamson, 1933, 2: 102)

Tari Pennu A malevolent earth goddess who caused disease and death, misfortunes, to whom human sacrifices were made. India. (MacCulloch, 1925, 8: 51; Robertson, 1911: 109; Martin, 1914: 29; Russell, 1916, 3: 473–475; Thurston, 1909, 3: 372)

Taru Pennu The earth god of the Kandhs of Kandhmals. India. (Crooke, 1925, 7: 649)

Ta-tenen, Tenen, Tatunen The primeval earth god. Budge suggests that he "must be the god of inert but living matter of the earth." Ptah is sometimes identified with him. Egypt. (Anthes, 1961: 61; Budge, 1969, 1: 508–509; Larousse, 1968: 36)

Tega The earth goddess, wife of We. The Kasene, Ghana. (Rattray, 1932: 45)

Tekkeitserktok A very powerful god of the land, and of the deer. Invoked by hunters. The Eskimo, Canada. (Bilby, 1923: 265; Larousse, 1968: 426)

Teleglen-Edzen The goddess of the surface of the earth. Also called Altan-telgey. The Mongols, Siberia and Mongolia. (Klementz, 1925, 3: 11)

Tellumo A Roman earth god associated with the earth mother Tellus. A god of fecundity, of the production of the seed. Italy. (Dumézil, 1966, 1: 374; Jayne, 1962: 422; Frazer, 1926: 329; Larousse, 1968: 210)

Tellus Roman goddess of the earth and of its fertility. Closely associated with Ceres to whom many sacrifices were made jointly. Italy. (Dumézil, 1966, 1: 194, 240; Fairbanks, 1907: 175; Altheim, 1937: 120; Frazer, 1926: 328–334)

Tenga The goddess of the earth, of morality and justice. Among the various tribes the wife of Wenda, Nwende, Wene (Yini), Nwene. Upper Volta, Senegal, and Ghana. (Rattray, 1932: 45; Frazer, 1926: 403; Greenberg, 1946: 45)

Tenga Wende The terrestrial manifestation of Wennam who receives sacrifices and is invoked for good fortune, "good health, heavy rains, and a successful harvest." The Mossi, Upper Volta. (Hammond, 1959: 246, 249)

Ten'gono The powerful earth goddess, wife of Yini, the sky god. The Nankanse, Ghana. (Rattray, 1932: 320)

St. la Terre The earth. Mirebalais, Haiti. (Herskovits, 1937, 1: 281)

Terupe One of four gods who "ruled the earth." Vaitupu (Ellice Islands), Polynesia. (Williamson, 1933, 2: 102)

Teteoinnan An earth goddess and the mother of the gods. A name of Coatlicue. The Aztec, Mexico. (Caso, 1958: 53; Hatt, 1951: 871; Burland, 1967: 75)

Teteu The god of earthquakes. The Pageh Islands, Mentawei Islands, Indonesia. (Loeb, 1929: 188)

Thadha Pennu The earth goddess, represented as a peacock to whom sacrifices were made for favorable crops. The Goomsur, India. (Robertson, 1911: 109; Thurston, 1909, 3: 372)

Thakurani Mai An earth goddess of the Central Provinces. Sometimes male, as Thakur Deo. India. (Russell, 1916, 3: 473)

Tho Chu The god of the earth is invoked to protect crops in the field, particularly from thieves. Annam. (Cabaton, 1925, 1: 539)

Tho Than The "Spirit of the Soil" to whom offerings are made in propitiation for taking one of his animals. Annam. (Cabaton, 1925, 1: 539)

Ti-Kuan The "Agent of Earth" who records all acts, good and bad, and who has the power to remit sins. China. (Maspero, 1963: 342; Larousse, 1968: 391; Day, 1940: 137)

Tillili A variant name of the primordial earth, consort of Alala. Together identified with Lukhma and Lakhama. Babylonia, Near East. (Sayce, 1898: 251, 248–249)

Ti Mu The earth mother and goddess of growth. China. (Graham, 1961: 202; Day, 1940: 163; Graham, 1928: 44)

Tinggfame The god of sand who punishes by sending sandstorms. Dahomey. (Herskovits, 1938, 2: 142)

Tintai, Tinten The earth goddess. Wife of Wea. The Isal, Ghana. (Rattray, 1932: 45)

Titaea An earth goddess of the Greeks who gave the tree of golden apples to Zeus and Hera. (Murray, 1935: 174)

Tlallamánac An aspect of Ometéotl as " 'she who sustains and upholds the earth.' " The Aztec, Mexico. (Léon-Portilla, 1982: 98)

Tlaltecuhtli The earth god symbolized by the alligator, the frog, or the toad. The Aztec, Mexico. (Caso, 1958: 53; Alexander, 1920: 54, 80; Duran, 1971: 261; Vaillant, 1962: 146)

Tlazolteotl An earth goddess and a goddess of love and sexuality, of childbirth. She was the goddess of filth, as the devourer of which, in consuming men's sins, she performed an act of purification. The Aztec, Mexico. (Caso, 1958: 55–56; Vaillant, 1962: 146, 148; Spence, 1923: 165, 168; Nicholson, 1967: 113; Thompson, 1970: 246; Alexander, 1920: 54, 78)

To'a-hiti-o-te-vao The "land" aspect of the god To'a-hiti-mata-nui. He was protective of those who ventured deep into the valleys. Tahiti, Polynesia. (Henry, 1928: 379)

Toara-lino A god who lives under the earth and is invoked for children. The Toradja, Celebes, Indonesia. (Adriani and Kruyt, 1950: 348)

təbixw The earth, whose function is "to discourage or punish evil." The Twana, Washington. (Elmendorf, 1960: 530–531)

Toci An earth goddess, "Our Grandmother." A name of Coatlicue. The Aztec, Mexico. (Caso, 1958: 53; Duran, 1971: 229)

Toikunrari-kuru, Toikunrari-mat (wife) Demons of the land who are considered the friends of hunters and are invoked in danger. The Ainu, Japan. (Batchelor, 1925, 1: 244)

Tomaiyowit The earth who, through her brother the sky, Tuk-mit, became the mother of all things. The

Luiseño Indians, California. (Du Bois, 1904: 52–53; Strong, 1929: 327; White, 1963: 140)

Toyokumonu-no-Kami   An earthly deity "manifesting the steamy atmosphere of the earth." Japan. (Yasumaro, 1928: 2; 1965: 10)

Tuanuku   Another name for Papa, the earth. The Maori, New Zealand. (Best, 1924: 174)

Tumayowit   The earth god. With Mukat, the creator of all things. They instituted death and retired to the underworld. The Cupeño Indians, California. (Kroeber, 1925: 692)

The T'u Ti   The earth gods, the personification of the energies of the earth, the gods of localities. There is a hierarchy of these gods: the family, the canton, the arrondissement, and the principalities. China. (Shryock, 1931: 26; Chavannes, n.d.: 437–443; Larousse, 1968: 387; Werner, 1932: 527)

T'u Ti Chêng Shên   A "Village God of the Soil." China. (Day, 1940: 208)

T'u Ti Fu Jên   A land tutelary, wife of T'u Ti Lao Yeh. China. (Day, 1940: 65)

T'u Ti Lao Yeh   A local god of the earth, of the soil. His wife is given variously as T'u Ti Fu Jen and T'u Ti nai-nai. China. (Day, 1940: 65; Ferguson, 1937: 64, 66)

T'u Ti nai-nai   A goddess of the earth, of the soil. Wife of T'u Ti Lao Yeh. China. (Ferguson, 1937: 66)

T'u Ti Shen   The "national god of the soil." Mortals were deified as him, e.g. Ko Lung. China. (Ferguson, 1937: 62). A god of the earth of the Monguors of Kansu. (Schram, 1957: 86)

Tuwapontumsi   "Earth-woman" to whom offerings are made at the new-fire ceremony in November. The Hopi, Arizona. (Fewkes, 1895, 1: 352)

Uban Sanane   Grandmother earth, associated with Uban Langi, the sky god. Buru Island (the Moluccas), Indonesia. (Pettazzoni, 1956: 334)

U-ieng-kong   The Earth god who is worshipped by fishermen for protection from drowning. Taiwan. (Diamond, 1969: 97)

Uis Meto   The python god of the Dry Land. Timor, Indonesia. (Middelkoop, 1960: 24)

Uitzailic   An earth god of the Chuh. Mexico. (Thompson, 1970: 275)

Uligin Sagan Deda   The "revered pure earth." The Buriat, Mongol. Siberia. (Curtin, 1909: 45)

The Unkcegila   Dangerous and threatening "Spirits of the Land" who may be propitiated ritually "and especially by the aroma of sweetgrass and sage, and the smoke of a pipe." The Oglala, South and North Dakota. (Powers, 1977: 55)

Upunusa   Grandmother Earth—the female principle, fertilized by Dudilaa. Leti, Moa, and Lakor Islands, Indonesia. (Hartland, 1925, 9: 822; Frazer, 1926: 660)

Upu Tapene   The earth goddess invoked with Upu Langi in oath-taking. Ceram (Molucca Islands), Indonesia. (Pettazzoni, 1956: 334)

Upu Ume   Mother earth who is invoked with Upu Lanito in oath-taking. Ambon Island (Moluccas), Indonesia. (Pettazzoni, 1956: 334–335)

Usert   A goddess known at Thebes as an earth deity. Egypt. (Budge, 1969, 2: 216)

Usi-Afu   A goddess of the earth, of fertility and growth. Wife of Usi-Neno. Timor, Indonesia. (Eliade, 1959: 124; Frazer, 1926: 657)

Usif Pah   God of the earth. Timor, Indonesia. (Middlekoop, 1960: 24)

Usi-Pasha   A god of the earth, considered an evil spirit. Timor, Indonesia. (Frazer, 1926: 658)

Utset   An earth mother and corn goddess. The Sia, Pueblo Indians, New Mexico. (Parsons, 1939: 182; Fewkes, 1895, 2: 123)

Vikesi   A goddess of the earth, wife of Sarva and mother of Angaraka. India. (Danielou, 1964: 205)

Wathoundaye   An earth goddess. Burma, Thailand, and Cambodia. (Spiro, 1967: 46)

Te Wawau   One of those representing "earthquakes and volcanic phenomena." The Maori, New Zealand. (Best, 1924: 175)

Wuon lowo   "Owner of the earth." The Luo, Kenya. (Mbiti, 1970, 2: 332)

Xaratanga A Tarascan goddess who personifies the earth and its fruitfulness, and is also a goddess of "conception and birth." Mexico. (Kickeberg, 1968: 59)

Xquic, Ixquic Born in the underworld, the daughter of Cuchumaquic, she became the human mother of Hunahupú and Ixbalamqué, sons of the Ahpú skulls. On being sentenced to die, because of her pregnancy, she converts her four executioners and they ascend to the earth, becoming the earth goddess and her servants. The Quiché, Guatemala. (Girard, 1979: 113–114, 122–123)

Yahval Balamil The Owner of the earth who controls the rain, lightning, the crops, and all the products of the earth. The Zinacantecans of Chiapas, Mexico. (Vogt, 1970: 6)

Yak The earth mother who lives underground. Mother of Ta Ponn. The Semang of Kedah, Malay Peninsula. (Skeat, 1925, 8: 354)

Ya-nebya Benevolent mother earth, particularly helpful to women, especially in childbirth. The Nentsy, Siberia. (Prokof'yeva, 1964: 564)

Ya-un-Kamui The gods of the land. The Ainu, Japan. (Batchelor, 1925, 1: 240)

Yin Shên The god of the element earth. China. (Du Bose, n.d.: 72; Werner, 1932: 594)

Yolotlicue An earth goddess who wears a skirt of hearts. Mexico. (Museum of Anthropology, Mexico City, 1973)

Yurugu A "being of the night" to whom "the dry, uncultivated, uninhabited earth belongs." Death is associated with him; he represents the creation of disorder. The Dogon, Mali and Nigeria. (Griaule and Dieterlen, 1954: 87, 93)

Zam A goddess of the earth associated with Ashtat and Amurdat. Iran. (Gray, 1930: 172; Larousse, 1973: 194)

Zapotlantenan An earth goddess of the valley of Zapotlan, "said to have been the inventor or discoverer of turpentine." Mexico. (Spence, 1923: 229)

Ze-beh The earth god of the Ch'iang at Ta-er-p'i. Szechwan, China. (Graham 1958: 70)

Zem The earth, a lesser Persian god. (Huart, 1963: 42)

Zemeluks Lithuanian "god of the earth and of those buried in it." (Gray, 1930: 179)

Zemes Mate The great mother earth. Latvia. (Gimbutas, 1963: 191; Gray, 1930: 172)

Zemininkas, Zempattys, Zemepatis The earth as a god, the god of the homestead. Lithuania; Latvia. (Welsford, 1925, 9: 242; Gray, 1930: 179; Gimbutas, 1963: 192)

Zemyna, Zemynele The earth-mother goddess, the source of all life. She is "associated with plant life, fields and hills" and the minor deities who carry out her functions. Lithuania. (Gimbutas, 1958: 97; 1963: 191; Welsford, 1925, 9: 242; Leger, 1925, 1: 466)

Zipacná The Earth god of the giant people, a maker and mover of mountains. He was finally killed by Hunahpú and Ixbalamqué who lured him into a cave and then crushed him with a mountain. Son of Vukup Cakix and Chimalmat; brother of Caprakán. The Quiché, Guatemala. (Girard, 1979: 67, 75, 79, 80)

Zre-beh A god of the earth of the Ch'iang at Ta-yeh-p'ing. Szechwan, China. (Graham, 1958: 70)

14

Fire Gods:
Elemental, Domestic

A-ba-sei A god of fire, one of the legs of the three-legged Ch'iang stove. The others are A-ta-sei and Mo-go-i-shi. The Ch'iang, Szechwan, China. (Graham, 1958: 49)

Abera-ra-shut A deity dwelling below the hearth. The Ainu, Japan. (Munro, 1963: 38)

Abi Son of Gbadu—"Becoming the ashes of the fire," punishes those women disrespectful of Minona. Dahomey. (Herskovits, 1938, 2: 204–205)

Agin Deo The god of fire on whom oaths are sworn. The Baiga, India. (Elwin, 1939: 66)

Agni The simple god of fire in Bali, in Mongolia. In India his manifestation is complex. As the celestial fire he is manifest in the heat and light of the sun and descends to earth as the lightning, an atmospheric form. His terrestrial form is the fire within the earth, the fire of the hearth. His mystical form is the sacrificial fire of worship through which he receives the offering or the soul and returns them to the heavens. He is considered present in other symbolic forms—combustion, digestion, passion. He is the beneficent protector of the home, its welfare and prosperity. (Keary, 1882: 101–102; Basak, 1953: 93; Danielou, 1964: 63–64; Percheron, 1953: 63; Friederich, 1959: 51)

Agyasur The god of fire of the Agaria. India. Same as Agin Deo. (Elwin, 1942: 117)

Ahpú The god of fire, considered the oldest god in the pantheon, "preexists the agrarian deities." He is the father of Hunahpú, the god of Maize. The Quiché, Guatemala. (Girard, 1979: 91, 92)

Ai-la'au A fire god who was there when Pele arrived. He is a destructive god but also in part a creative force—through volcanic eruption increasing the land. Hawaii. (Westervelt, 1963, 2: 1, 2)

Amatsu-hikone A deity of fire, a god created by Susano-wo. Japan. (Yasumaro, 1928: 32; 1965: 27–28; Herbert, 1967: 294)

Ame-no-Hohi A god of fire, and a god sent to rule "The land of luxuriant reed plain and rich crops and everlasting prosperity." Japan. (Yasumaro, 1965: 28, 52)

Ammi-seshet A goddess of fire. Egypt. (Budge, 1969, 1: 519)

Ao-ao-ma-ra'i-a- The father of fire whose wife is Ma-hui-e. Tahiti, Polynesia. (Henry, 1928: 427)

Apemeru-ko-yan-mat *See* **Huchi**

Aspelenie The goddess of the hearth. Litu-Prussian. (Schrader, 1925, 2: 34)

Atar The god of fire, son of Ahura Mazda; as the celestial fire the light of the heavens, the thunderbolt; as the terrestrial fire that latent in the wood, the fire of the hearth. Iran. (Huart, 1963: 41; Gray, 1930: 66; Haydon, 1941: 69; Hinnells, 1973: 37)

A-ta-sei A god of fire, one of the legs of the three-legged Ch'iang stove. The others are A-ba-sei and Mo-go-i-shi. The Ch'iang, Szechwan, China. (Graham, 1958: 49)

Au Mujaupa The "master of fire." The Yana Indians, California. (Curtin, 1903: 365)

Ayaba Goddess of the hearth and guardian of the food. Daughter of Mawu and Lisa. Dahomey. (Herskovits, 1938, 2: 109)

Bast, Bastet As a lioness-headed goddess she is a goddess of fire, the personification of the power of the heat of the sun, its warmth and germinating power. As a cat-headed deity she is a goddess of the moon and a goddess of childbirth. Egypt. (Budge, 1969, 1: 444–447, 518; Jayne, 1962: 84; Ames, 1965: 104; Knight, 1915: 30)

Batoyi The spirit who "animates the fire." Son of Mak'era and husband of Randa. An ash-colored cock is sacrificed to him. The Maguzawa, Nigeria. (Greenberg, 1946: 34)

Beal, Beil A Celtic god of light or fire who was celebrated at the needfire rites and the festivals on the first of May. Ireland. (Grimm, 1883, 2: 613–614)

Bel The Turkic "owner of the hearth." Central Asia. (Czaplicka, 1925, 12: 482)

Belchans The Etruscan god of fire, associated with the East in the divisions of the universe. Italy. (Hamblin, 1975: 92)

Bhasmāsura The lustful "Demon of Ashes." India. (O'Flaherty, 1980: 137, 230)

Bhuranyu A Vedic fire god. India. (Cox, 1870, 2: 195)

Bitsis Lizin "Black Body." The equivalent of Hastsezini of the Navahos, who is a god of fire. Pueblo Indians, Arizona and New Mexico. (Long, 1963: 51)

Batara Brahma The "lord of fire." Bali, Indonesia. (Franken, 1960: 298)

Briganti Mac Bain cites Stokes as proving she is "a fire-goddess; she was born at sunrise; her breath revives the dead; a house in which she stays flames up to heaven; she is fed with the milk of a white red-eared cow; a fiery pillar rises from her head, and she remains a virgin like the Roman goddess, Vesta." Britain. (Mac Bain, 1917: 130)

Brigindo Celtic goddess of fire and the hearth, of poetry. Gaul. Same as Brigit, Brigantia. (Squire, 1906: 228, 277; Jayne, 1962: 513)

Brigit Goddess of the sacred (perpetual) fire and of the household fire. She is a triple goddess with her attributes distributed through fire, healing, poetry, smith-work, and fecundity and childbirth. Ireland. (Mac Bain, 1917: 129–130; Ross, 1967: 206, 360; Jayne, 1962: 513; MacCulloch, 1911: 69; Squire, 1906: 56)

Chakekenapok The flint stone man, the source of fire, son of the Great Spirit. The Potawatomi, the Tusans, the Algonquin Indians, Upper Mississippi Valley and Great Lakes. (Alexander, 1964: 41; Maclean, 1876: 427; Brinton, 1868: 167)

Chantico A goddess of fire—of the domestic hearth and of the volcanic. She is associated with the water-sun age, the volcanic fire which will end it. The emblem shown on her head, a torrent of fire and water, associated her also with war. Beyond this she is also considered a goddess of goldsmiths. The Aztec, Mexico. (Vaillant, 1962: 149; Krickeberg, 1968: 44; Spence, 1923: 282–283)

Cherruve A god of fire, "originator of the comets and of meteors." The Araucanian Indians, Chile. (Chamberlain, 1900: 57)

Chicomecoatl, Chantico Among the Xochimilcas and the Acolhuas she is a goddess of the hearth and of fecundity. Mexico. (Reed, 1966: 112)

Chieh The deity of the hearth varies from male to female and is sometimes a couple. When the hearth and the fire are considered separately, the first is female, the second male. China. (Schram, 1957: 123)

Ch'ih Ching-tzu The "principle of spiritual fire, . . . fire personified." China. (Werner, 1932: 196)

Chohyung The god of the element fire. Also a god of the compass—the south. China. (Du Bose, n.d.: 72, 327)

Chu Jung, Chu Fung The God of Fire causes/prevents conflagrations; is propitiated for their control; taught the arts of purification, of forging, of metal-working. He is, as well, god of the South, which he governs, of summer, of the fourth month. He is sometimes "represented as an animal with a human face." China. *See also* **Huo Shen.** (Day, 1940: 66; Werner, 1932: 196, 450; 1934: 81, 238; Campbell, 1962: 396, 432; Ferguson, 1937: 76; Williams, 1976: 206–207)

Cuati Edutzi The fire god of the Takanan. The Araona, Bolivia. (Métraux, 1942: 41)

Cuisiabirri The benevolent god of fire who also causes lightning and rouses Puivisana, the earthquake. He is not an independent god but an aspect or emanation of Puru, and is invoked as intercessor with him. The Salivan, Colombia. Also the god of fire of the Achagua of Venezuela and Colombia. (Walde-Waldegg, 1936: 40–42; Wallis, 1939: 89; Hernandez de Alba, 1948, 2: 410)

Dessra, Derra   The god of fire and of earthquakes. Yap Islands, the Carolines, Micronesia. (Christian, 1899: 385)

Dik   Sir Prawn "who first produced or obtained fire." The Aka-Cari, Andaman Islands, Bay of Bengal. (Radcliffe-Brown, 1967: 189)

Dinstipan   A Lithuanian hearth god "who directed the smoke up the chimney." (Crawley, 1925, 6: 562)

Dso   The god of fire who shows his anger by burning property. The Ewe, Dahomey and Ghana. (Mockler-Ferryman, 1925, 9: 278; Ellis, 1890: 46)

Einmyria   Norse goddess of ashes, daughter of Loki and Glut, sister of Eisa. (Guerber, 1895: 199)

Eisa   "Embers"—a daughter of Loki and Glut. Norse. (Guerber, 1895: 199)

fadza-mama   An old woman who was mistress of the fire. The Nanai, Siberia. (Dioszegi, 1968: 471; Levin and Potapov, 1964: 712)

Fa· tege 'eno   "The clowns pray not only to the watersnake but also to Fa· tege 'eno, the youthful Firegod whose ash clouds will help them perceive the approaching Great Ones [the Raingods]. I feel that this Firegod is symbolically a sex god, and the use of ashes may be interpreted as a reference to the resurrection and rejuvenation of all living things." The Tewa, San Juan, New Mexico. (Laski, 1958: 87)

Frobagh   A deity of terrestrial fires, associated with Atar. Persia. (Huart, 1963: 42)

Kamui Fuchi, Kamui Fuji   The goddess of the fire, of the hearth, the most revered of the kamui. The Ainu, Japan. (Munro, 1963: 14–17; Batchelor, 1925, 1: 242)

Gabjaujis   The fire god of the kiln "was offered a cock at the end of the threshing, because the kiln was heated all the time during threshing." Lithuania. (Leach, 1950, 2: 633)

Gabija   Goddess of the fire and of the hearth, protectress of it and the family. The fire must never be extinguished. Lithuania. (Gimbutas, 1963: 204; 1975: XLC M126; Leach, 1950, 2: 633)

Galai-Khan   The fire god is also called Gali-Edzin and Ut. The Mongols, Siberia. (MacCulloch, 1964: 456)

Galta-Ulan-Tengeri   The god of fire, of heat and drought, as well as of lightning. The Buriats, Siberia. (MacCulloch, 1964: 449; Klementz, 1925, 3: 4)

Gibil   Assyrian and Babylonian god of fire and of healing, of purifying fires and of symbolic magic "which destroyed demons of disease." Near East. (Jayne, 1962: 121; Langdon, 1931: 100–102; Jastrow, 1898: 220; Sayce, 1898: 181)

Girru   The god of fire—personified—as well as the sacrificial purifying fire and the mundane fire of the crafts. Babylonia, Near East. (Zimmern, 1925, 2: 312)

dGra lha thab lha g·yu mo   A goddess of the hearth. Tibet. (Nebesky-Wojkowitz, 1956, 1: 330)

Grande Ezili   Goddess of the hearth and of sweet waters. She is beneficent and personifies wisdom. Identified with Ste. Anne. Haiti. (Marcelin, 1950: 93, 95)

Guih-teuct-li   The god of fire; also the god of the year and of the planets. Also called Ix-coz-auh-qui. Mexico. (Schoolcraft, 1857: 641)

Hastsezini   The god of fire who is the same as Bitsis Lizin of the Pueblo Indians. The Navaho, Arizona and New Mexico. (Matthews, 1902: 26; Babington, 1950: 216; Long, 1963: 51)

Hephaestus, Hephaistos   The god of terrestrial fire, of volcanic as well as the constructive fire used in the many crafts. The deformed forger son of Hera. Greece. (Jayne, 1962: 317–318; Murray, 1935: 85–87; Cox, 1870, 2: 197; Kerenyi, 1951: 155)

Hestia   Greek goddess of the house fire, protectress of the home. She was a virgin goddess, eldest daughter of Rhea and Cronus. (Murray, 1935: 77–78; Kerenyi, 1951: 91; Cox, 1870, 2: 196; Larousse, 1968: 136)

Hihayabi-no-Kami   A goddess manifest in the fire. Japan. (Yasumaro, 1965: 18–19; Herbert, 1967: 271)

Hina-ke-ahi   A daughter of Hina who "has power over fire." Hawaii. (Beckwith, 1970: 97)

Hina-mahuia   A daughter of Hine and fire goddess of Mafuie. Polynesia. (Beckwith, 1970: 97)

Hine-i-tapeka   A goddess of subterranean fire. New Zealand. (Best, 1924: 152; Andersen, 1928: 218)

Hine-kaikomako The "Fire-maid" who is personified in the kaiko mako tree. New Zealand. (Best, 1924: 176; Andersen, 1928: 217–218)

Hi-no-Kami The god of fire. Japan. (Herbert, 1967: 393; Holtom, 1938: 208)

Hi-no-Yagihayawo-no-Kami The god of fire. Japan. Also called Hi-no-Kagabiko, Hi-no-kagu-tsuchi. (Yasumaro, 1965: 16; Herbert, 1967: 266)

Ho djaj "Fire man." The Coast Central Pomo Indians, California. (Loeb, 1926, 2: 301)

Ho-Lih-Ta-Ti The god of fire. China. (Du Bose, n.d.: 389)

Ho-Musubi-no-Kami The god of fire. Another name of Kagu-Tsuchi. Japan. (Kato, 1926: 9; Holtom, 1938: 111)

Ho Shen The god of fire who punishes wrongdoing with fires. His temple in Anking is used by Fortune Tellers' and Barbers' Guilds. He is also the patron of sellers of firecrackers. China. *See also* **Huo Shen, Chu Jung.** (Shryock, 1931: 33, 121; Graham, 1961: 186; Ferguson, 1937: 76)

Huchi, Fuji The goddess of fire, both the hearth and volcanic. She is the beneficent protector of the hearth and home; tends to the cooking and purifies "the body from disease." She is the first approached in all prayers, takes predominance in all worship, and acts as intermediary between man and the gods. Her full name is Apermeru-ko-yan-mat. The Ainu, Japan. (Batchelor, n.d.: 175–179; Philippi, 1982: 60–61, 69, 108)

Huehueteotl The beneficent old god of the fire who is associated with the night and is also a god of the year. The Aztec, Mexico. (Caso, 1958: 28; Reed, 1966: 31; Nicholson, 1967: 30)

Hui Lu A popular god of fire who had fire-birds which he let out to set conflagrations. China. (Werner, 1934: 238–39)

Huo Shen The god of destructive fire. Also called Huo Te Hsing Chün, Huo Te Ta Chun, Hwo Shen in Confucianism. He is also worshipped by the guild of Pork Shops in North China. *See also* **Chu Jung.** (Day, 1940: 72, 89; Chavannes, n.d.: 100; Gamble, 1954: 409; Burgess, 1928: 180; De Groot, 1925, 4: 14)

Huo Te Hsing Chün The god of fire who is identified with the planet Mars. China. (Day, 1940: 162, 209)

Hutasana A god of fire, father of Kumara (Skanda) by Ganga. Rajasthan, India. (Tod, 1920: 693)

Hwa Kwang Buddhist and Taoist god of fire who is "connected with light . . . not originally a human being, but a lamp. . . . He is the form and soul of fire." China. (Ball, 1925, 8: 51)

Ibissa Sayto The evil spirit of fire to whom black goats are sacrificed. The Galla, Ethiopia. (Huntingford, 1955: 75)

Ikutsu-hikone A god of fire created by Susano-o-no-Mikoto. Japan. (Yasumaro, 1965: 27, 28; Herbert, 1967: 294)

Inchanyi The god of fire of the Barundi. Burundi. (Mbiti, 1970, 2: 328)

Ira-whaki The "fire-revealer" whose wife is Hine-kaikomako. New Zealand. (Andersen, 1928: 218)

Ishto-hoollo Aba The "omnipresent Spirit of fire and light;" lives in the heavens. The Creek Indians, Alabama and Georgia. (Swanton, 1928: 483)

Ishum Beneficent god of fire, messenger and companion of Erra (Irra). Babylonia, Near East. (Roberts, 1972: 40–41; Kramer, 1961: 127; Cook, 1930: 150)

Itzam Cab An aspect of Itzam Na as a fire god. The Maya, Yucatan, Mexico. (Thompson, 1970: 229)

Ixcozauhqui The god of fire and lord of the year. A name of Xiuhtecuhtli. The Aztec, Mexico. (Caso, 1958: 28; Duran, 1971: 177)

Jagaubis A Lithuanian god of fire. (Welsford, 1925, 9: 241)

Kaak The Lacandon god of fire also sends fever, yet again, is the protector of travelers along trails from snakes and jaguars. *See also* **Qaq.** Mexico. (Thompson, 1970: 312–14)

Kagutsuchi-no-Kami The god of fire, of conflagrations. The same as Ho-musubi. Japan. (Kato, 1926: 9; Herbert, 1967: 483; Yasumaro, 1928: 8)

Kai King Arthur's steward who is "no less than the British Vulcan, the fire-god." (MacBain, 1917: 99)

Kakal Ku A Mayan god of fire. Yucatan, Mexico. (Thompson, 1970: 323)

Ka-poha-i-kahi-ola God of explosions in volcanic eruptions. Hawaii. (Westervelt, 1963, 2: 71; Beckwith, 1940: 167)

Karandi A demon fire god who "makes himself known by arson." The Bondo, India. (Elwin, 1950: 155)

Kasindukua A fire demon who has human as well as puma form. He "is supposed to devour sickness . . . but, instead eats people." Son of Gauteóvañ. The Kagaba, Colombia. (Preuss, 1926: 79)

Katen A god of purifying fire. Japan. (Eliot, 1935: 139)

kefeliu The old woman of the fire—of the kiva as well as of the home. The Pueblo Indians, Isleta, New Mexico. (Parsons, 1929/30: 343)

Kengra Barsa "Father of fire and of all the heavenly bodies." Son of Salgong and Apongma. The Garos, Tibet and Burma. (Keane, 1925, 2: 122)

Keoahi-kama-kaua A volcanic god of Kilauea. Hawaii. (Beckwith, 1940: 167; Westervelt, 1963, 2: 71)

Ke-ua-a-ke-po "Rain of fire"—a god of the Pele fire family. Hawaii. (Beckwith, 1940: 167; Westervelt, 1963, 2: 71)

Kiech Goddess of fire and of the 13th day of the calendar. The Chimalteco, Guatemala. (Wagley, 1949: 70)

Kuma A goddess who owned the fire which was stolen by a fish. The Yaruro, Venezuela. (Métraux, 1969: 112)

Kumanokusubi, Kumanukusubi A god of fire created by Susano-wo. Japan. (Yasumaro, 1928: 32; 1965: 27; Herbert, 1967: 294)

kutug:a "Mistress of the fire." The Negidals, Siberia. (Dioszegi, 1968: 471)

k!waxLala The "spirit of the fire." The Kwakiutl, British Columbia. (Boas, 1966: 139)

Laki Pesong The god of fire of the Kayans. Borneo. (Hose, 1912: 5)

Lateranus Roman god of the kilns for making bricks and chimneys and stoves. (Roscher, 1965, 2, 1: 201)

Ka Lei Khuri A hearth deity of the Khasi. Assam. (Bareh, 1967: 375)

Locid-epie Grandmother of the fire. The Yukaghir, Siberia. (Jochelson, 1900/02: 217)

Locin-pogil The owner of the hearth fire who moves with the family. He warns them not to move (by a crackling noise) if "misfortune or famine is awaiting them." The Yukaghir, Siberia. (Jochelson, 1900/02: 154)

Logi Scandinavian god—the natural untamed fire. Son of Forniot(r), counterpart of Loki. (Grimm, 1880: 241; Stern, 1898: 121; Wagner, 1882: 241)

Lo Hsüan "President of the ministry of Fire." China. (Werner, 1932: 279)

Loki An early Scandinavian god of the hearth at which time his wife was Glut (glow). They had two daughters Eisa (embers) and Einmyria (ashes). He later became a god of deceit and mischief even though entertaining and fun-making. His second wife was Angurboda, who was the mother of Hel, Fenris, and Jormungander. His third wife was Sigyn, the mother of Wali and Narwi. (Guerber, 1895: 198–200; Wagner, 1882: 249–250; Stern, 1898: 100–101; Snorri Sturluson, 1964: 56; Davidson, 1965: 177)

Lono-makua A god of earth fires. "Pele's fire keeper as represented in the fire sticks, a symbol of fertilization." Hawaii. (Westervelt, 1963, 2: 51, 137; Beckwith, 1940: 170)

Lu Huo The god of the stove fire, beneficent. China. (Day, 1940: 89)

Ka Lukhimai A hearth deity of the Khasi. Assam. (Bareh, 1967: 375)

Mafui'e The god of fire and of earthquakes. Samoa, Polynesia. (Williamson, 1933, 2: 184, 186; Andersen, 1928: 216)

Ma-hui-e Wife of Ao-ao-ma-ra'i-a. She perpetuated the fire he made. Society Islands, Polynesia. (Henry, 1928: 427, 429)

Mahuika A goddess of the underworld, the personification of fire. Sister of Hine-titama. The Maori, New Zealand. (Best, 1924: 146–147; Andersen, 1928: 204, 217)

Mahu-ike God of the underworld and of fire from whom Maui obtained it. The Marquesas, Polynesia. (Handy, 1923: 246; Buck, 1938: 153). In Rarotonga a chthonic goddess of fire. (Poignant, 1967: 46)

Maklium-sa-bagidan God of fire and a deity of the sky world. The Bisayan, Panay, Philippines. (Jocano, 1969: 20)

Masau'u, Masauwu(h) Predominantly a god of death and of the underworld. He is also a god of fire whose heat causes crops to grow. The Hopi, Arizona. (Fewkes, 1902: 21; Tyler, 1964: 3, 4, 8; Parsons, 1939, 1: 170, 179)

Maui Motu'a The father of Maui Atalanga and grandfather of Maui Kijikiji. He is the guardian of the fire the latter stole from the underworld. The Tongans, Polynesia. (Collocott, 1921: 153; Moulton, 1925, 12: 376)

Me'ilha mo Gos dkar mo A goddess of fire invoked in pollution eliminating ceremonies. Tibet. (Nebesky-Wojkowitz, 1956, 1: 388)

Mela The god of fire to whom offerings are made at the cremation pyre. The Sherpas, Nepal. (Furer-Haimendorf, 1964: 233)

Me-lha The god of fire and protector of the Southeast. He drives away evil spirits. Tibet. (Schlagintweit, 1969: 207; Waddell, 1959: 367, 593; Nebesky-Wojkowitz, 1956, 1: 366)

Memdeye-Ecie Beneficent "Father-Fire" lives in the eastern sky. The Yukaghir of Upper Kolyma, Siberia. (Jochelson, 1900/02: 140–141)

Mika-haya-hi-no-kami The manifestation of fire, a god born from the blood of Kagu-tsuchi. Japan. (Herbert, 1967: 271; Yasumaro, 1965: 19)

Mo-bo-sei The god of fire "who controls fire in the home and prevents it from burning the house." The Ch'iang at Ho-p'ing-chai, Szechwan, China. (Graham, 1958: 48)

Mo-go-i-shi A god of fire, one of the legs of the three-legged Ch'iang stove. The others are A-ba-sei and A-ta-sei. The Ch'iang, Szechwan, China. (Graham, 1958: 49)

Moko-fulu-fulu The chief of "the first heaven below" who is the possessor of fire. Niue Island, Polynesia. (Williamson, 1933, 2: 88)

myjkudy The "master of fire." The Negidals, Siberia. (Dioszegi, 1968: 471)

Nairyosangha The "god of fire and messenger between gods and men; associated with Atar in the Avesta." Iran. (Leach, 1950, 2: 780)

Nalibikax One story gives him as the owner of fire. The Kwakiutl, British Columbia. (Boas, 1935: 138)

Naq pu God of the ninth day of the calendar and the "owner of fire. . . . Fires come to burn down houses on this day." The Chimalteco, Guatemala. (Wagley, 1949: 70)

Nay-Ekva Goddess of fire, sister of Numi-Torum. The Mansi, Siberia. (Michael, 1963: 209)

Ndauthina The god of fire is quite an all-purpose god, being a god of light, of seafaring, of war, and of adulterers. Fiji, Melanesia. (Thomson, 1925, 6: 15; MacCulloch, 1925, 8: 50; Hocart, 1929: 196)

Niha-taka-tsu-hi-no-Kami and **Niha-tsu-hi-no-kami** They seem to be identical as the god of the "fire in the yard." Japan. (Herbert, 1967: 332–333)

Nina An Inca god of fire. Peru. (Larousse, 1968: 442)

nōnɬtsēᶜstalaɬ The "Fire-Dancer," a supernatural with a room in the house of the Cannibal Spirit. The Kwakiutl, British Columbia. (Boas, 1935: 142)

Nusk(u), Nuzku The fire god is invoked "to destroy the demons of disease by fire." He was originally a solar deity. According to some he is the personification of the crescent moon and the son of Sahar and Nikkal. He is also the messenger of the gods. Assyria, Babylonia, and Syria. (Macler, 1925, 12: 166; Jayne, 1962: 126; Jastrow, 1898: 220–221; Cook, 1930: 120; Sayce, 1898: 118–119)

Ogon Slavic god of the fire, particularly of the hearth. Son of Svarog. Russia. (Ralston, 1872: 85–86)

Okitsuhiko and **Okitsuhime** God and goddess of the furnace and of the kitchen, the kitchen range. Japan. (Herbert, 1967: 332, 498; Yasumaro, 1965: 51)

Ot The beneficent goddess of fire. The Khahass, Siberia. Among the Mongols she is invoked at marriage ceremonies. (Queval, 1968: 116; Larousse, 1973: 435)

ot änä "Mother-fire" who is given a part of each meal "as protectress of the family." The Altai, Siberia. (Dioszegi, 1968: 466)

pahpobi kwiyo "Fire is a supernatural. . . . Fire flower woman. . . . She is prayed to in infant naming ritual and in connection with hunting." The Tewa, New Mexico. (Parsons, 1929: 267)

Pahte enu Fire boy who "is prayed to by the *kossa* of San Juan for a good day when they are going out to play." The Tewa, New Mexico. (Parsons, 1929: 267)

Panike Slavic goddess of fire. Prussia. (Gimbutas, 1963: 204)

Panu A Finnish god of fire. (Welsford, 1925, 9: 241)

Pasiko A deity who "brought fire to men on earth." The Lakalai, New Britain, Melanesia. (Valentine, 1965: 183)

Pattini A goddess "regarded as the source of fire in the universe; she is propitiated not only by a cooling ritual (the boiling of milk) but by the *telling of her myths,* which is said to have the power to cool her anger" which pleases her and is a measure of "relief and reassurance." She originated in South India. Sri Lanka. (O'Flaherty, 1980: 96, 275)

Pavaka The "Purifier," an aspect of fire, son of Agni and Svaha. India. (Danielou, 1964: 88)

Pavamana The "Purifying," an aspect of fire, son of Agni and Svaha. India. (Danielou, 1964: 88)

Pele Goddess of volcanoes and volcanic fires, of the lava flow. She is the head of the Pele family of volcano deities. Hawaii. (Beckwith, 1940: 167; Emerson, 1968: 43; Poignant, 1967: 44)

Pere Goddess of terrestrial fire, of volcanoes. Daughter of Mahu-ike. Society Islands, Polynesia. (Williamson, 1933, 2: 215; Henry, 1928: 359; Poignant, 1967: 46)

Phai The god of fire. The Ahom, Tai. (Gurdon, 1925, 1: 236)

(mae phra) phloeng The spirit of fire, both male and female. As a goddess she is invoked in pregnancy. Thailand. (Hanks, 1964: 50)

Phoroneus The "discoverer or bestower of fire . . . the fire itself." Son of Inachos and Melia. Greece. (Cox, 1870, 2: 195; Fox, 1916: 16; Keightley, 1838: 405)

Pillan The supreme god and god of thunder and of fire, the source of volcanic eruptions, of earthquakes, and of the lightning. The Araucanians, Chile and Tierra del Fuego. (Loeb, 1931: 545; Alexander, 1920: 325–326; Cooper, 1946, 2: 747)

Pohila "Fire child," the source of spontaneous fire. Son of Yonot. The Wintu, California. (Curtin, 1903: 12)

Polengabia Lithuanian goddess of the "bright hearth." (Welsford, 1925, 9: 241)

Ponyke Lithuanian goddess of fire. (Welsford, 1925, 9: 241)

poza-mama The "mistress of the fire." The Amur Ulchi, Siberia. (Dioszegi, 1968: 471)

Prometheus A titan who stole fire from Zeus and bestowed it on mankind for his use and benefit. Son of Iapetos and Clymene. Greece. (Kerenyi, 1951: 214–215; Cox, 1870, 2: 210; Fairbanks, 1907: 80; Bulfinch, 1898: 20–21)

Pufine i Ravenga "The fire [was] more especially [under the control] of Pufine i Ravenga, a female deity, known in this particular function as Ruataka." As an oven deity she was called Raupenapena. Tikopia, Polynesia. (Firth, 1967, 2: 348, 445)

Pyr A Greek god of fire. (Roscher, 1965, 3, 2: 3332–3333)

Qaq "God of fire; cares for arrows; protects pilgrims." The Lacandon, Mexico. *See also* **Kaak.** (Cline, 1944: 112)

Randa A goddess who starts fires which her husband Batoyi "blows into conflagrations." A chicken is sacrificed to her. The Maguzawa, Nigeria. (Greenberg, 1946: 35)

Raupenapena A name of Pufine i Ravenga as an oven goddess. Tikopia, Polynesia. (Firth, 1967, 2: 445)

Rekhi A god of fire. Egypt. (Budge, 1969, 1: 343)

Ruataka A name of Pufine i Ravenga as the controller of fire. Tikopia, Polynesia. (Firth, 1967, 2: 348)

Ruau-moko God of subterranean fire, of volcanoes and earthquakes. The Maori, New Zealand. (Best, 1924: 100, 237; Andersen, 1928: 288)

Sabaga The goddess of fire of the Yakuts. Siberia. (MacCulloch, 1964: 454)

Saci Cereré The fire-snake who is under Jacy and "protects the country from fire." The Tupi, South Brazil. (Spence, 1925, 2: 837)

Safa The god of the hearth-chain by whom oaths are sworn. The Ossetes, Caucasus. (Morgan, 1888: 383, 391)

Sakhadai   The god of fire of the Buriats. Also Sakhidai-Noin, whose wife is Sakhala-Khatun. Siberia. (MacCulloch, 1964: 454; Klementz, 1925, 3: 4, 11)

Sakhala, Sakhala-Khatun   The goddess and ruler of the fire with her husband Sakhadai (Sakhidai-Noin). The Buriats, Siberia. (MacCulloch, 1964: 454; Klementz, 1925, 3: 4)

Sakhri nad, Chulahi nad   The spirit of the hearth. The Oraon, India. (Roy, 1928: 72)

Savul   The fire-stick was deified as an individual god. Babylonia, Near East. (Sayce, 1898: 181)

Setcheti   An Egyptian fire god. (Budge, 1969, 1: 347)

Sethlans   Etruscan god of fire, god of smiths—the artificer of the gods. Same as Vulcan, Hephaestus. Italy. (Rawlinson, 1885: 123; von Vacano, 1960: 19, 110; Pallottino, 1975: 142; Roscher, 1965, 4: 785)

Shahli milo   The god of fire, identified with the sun which is not addressed except as fire. The Choctaw Indians, Mississippi. (Spence, 1925, 3: 567–568)

Shulawitsi   The youthful god of fire and also of maize and hunting. He is a messenger for the sun. The Zuñi, New Mexico. (Parsons, 1939: 175, 205; Tyler, 1964: 25; Stevenson, 1901/02: 33; Waters, 1950: 283–284)

Suci   "Purity"—an aspect of fire, son of Agni and Svaha. India. (Danielou, 1964: 88)

Suhui Kak, Suhuy Kak   Goddess of the virgin or new fire and also a goddess of healing. The Maya, Mexico and Guatemala. (Tozzer, 1941: 153; Roys, 1965: 159)

Sung Wu-chi   "The God of the Flame." China. (Werner, 1932: 471)

Surtr   A Teutonic fire giant who guarded "Muspellsheim, the home of elemental fire." He threatened to destroy the world—at Ragnarok—and did, leaving only a few survivors among the gods. (Guerber, 1895: 10, 267–270; Branston, 1955: 201)

Svarozic, Svarozhigh, Svaroziczu   Slavic god of fire, of celestial fire and of the hearth. Son of Svarog. Russia. (Machal, 1918: 298; Queval, 1968: 107; Gimbutas, 1971: 162; Welsford, 1925, 9: 252)

ta ho lu pin   The spirit of fire whose function is its care. The Miao, China. (Bernatzik, 1947: 166)

Talatumsi   A goddess associated with the new-fire ceremony. The Walpi, Arizona. (Fewkes, 1900: 97)

Tama-ehu   "Blond-child . . . chief of fire gods." He is also a god of salamanders. Also known as Tama-tea. Society Islands, Polynesia. (Henry, 1928: 377, 391)

Tanunapat   An aspect of Agni as the fire latent in the fuel. India. (Bhattacharji, 1970: 187)

Tartois Kibirksztu   " 'A charmer of sparks, a god who withstands fire'." Lithuania. (Welsford, 1925, 9: 241; Schrader, 1925, 2: 32)

Tatevali, Tatewari   The god of fire, Our Grandfather, is their principal god; a god of life and of health "to whom belong the macaw, the royal eagle, the cardinal-bird, the tiger, the lion, and the opossum,—also herbs and grass." He is the shaman of the gods, healing them as the mortal shaman, cures his people with his help; the god of the shaman, particularly those of healing and prophesying. The Huichol Indians, Mexico. (Seler, 1925, 6: 828; Wilbert, 1972: 80, 140; Furst, 1973: 37; Alexander, 1920: 121; Chamberlain, 1900: 305)

Tatotsi Mara Kwari   A secondary fire god, or another form of Our Grandfather, "considered to be the spark produced by striking flint, and is the chief deer-god." The white-tailed hawk belongs to him. The Huichol, Mexico. (Seler, 1925, 6: 828; Chamberlain, 1900: 305)

Thab-lha   The god of the hearth who can increase one's wealth, but who punishes neglect with illness and misfortune. Tibet. (Hoffman, 1956: 20; Nebesky-Wojkowitz, 1956, 1: 296, 332)

Thab lha g·ui mo   The goddess of the hearth. Tibet. (Nebesky-Wojkowitz, 1956, 1: 202)

T'ien Huo   A minor Chinese fire god. (Day, 1940: 71)

Ti Huo   A minor fire god. China. (Day, 1940: 71)

togo musun   The " 'mistress of the fire' . . . the mother of the clan, . . . head of the tent, . . . protectress of the souls of the members of the clan." The Evenki, Siberia. (Dioszegi, 1968: 468)

Tohil   God of rain and of thunder who gave fire to the people. The Quiché, Guatemala. (Recinos, 1950: 176, 189; Asturias, 1971: 148, 153)

Tol-ava   Finno-Ugrian goddess of fire. The Mordvins, Russia. (Paasonen, 1925, 8: 845; Leach, 1949, 1: 96)

Tsao-Chen The hearth spirit of the Meau. China. (Bernatzik, 1947: 156)

Tsao Shen The god of the hearth who reports to Heaven on the families. He controls their welfare. A common name of Tung Chu Szu Ming. China. (Ferguson, 1937: 74; Day, 1940: 86–7)

Tsao-wang The god of the hearth who keeps family records—the acts and words of the members. China. (Larousse, 1968: 389)

tul-awa "Mother of Fire." The Cheremis, Russia. (Leach, 1949, 1: 98)

tul-wodez The "spirit of fire." The Cheremis, Russia. (Leach, 1949, 1: 215)

Tung Chu Szu Ming Also known as Tsao Shen. The god of the kitchen range, an important household deity, who controls the welfare and observes the conduct of the family. China. (Day, 1940: 86–87)

Uggunsmate, Uguns mate The goddess of the fire. Latvia. (Gimbutas, 1963: 204; Welsford, 1925, 9: 242; Leach, 1950, 2: 608)

Ulakhany The god of fire of the Yakuts. Siberia. (MacCulloch, 1964: 454)

Unchi Ahchi Goddess of the hearth—"Fire Grandmother"—who is their protector and mediator with the gods. The Ainu, Sakhalin, Siberia. She is also a goddess of the shore. (Ohnuki-Tierney, 1974: 89)

Uot-ichchite God of fire (sometimes considered as seven brothers). The Yakuts, Siberia. (Tokarev and Gurvich, 1964: 281)

Ut Goddess of the fire, of the hearth. The Mongols, Siberia. (MacCulloch, 1964: 453)

Vesta The virgin goddess of the hearth fire, both household and the public hearth of the City of Rome with its continuous flame. (Dumézil, 1966, 1: 315; Schoeps, 1961: 147; Murray, 1935: 77–79; Larousse, 1968: 204)

Vulcan, Volcanus The god of fire in both its constructive (e.g., the smith's crafts, the hearth) and destructive (volcanic, lightning) forms. Italy. (Dumézil, 1966, 1: 320; Altheim, 1937: 119, 150; Murray, 1935: 85, 87; Keary, 1882: 133)

Wun Lawa Makam The Nat who possessed fire and taught man how to make it with two sticks of bamboo. The Katchins, Burma. (Gilhodes, 1908: 689–90)

xa·ctčé·cjini·, xasceszini Black God, the god of fire who "represents the being in control of fire and fire-making rather than fire itself." The Navaho, Arizona and New Mexico. (Reichard, 1950: 399; Haile, 1947: 13,22)

Xiuhtecuhtli The god of fire presides over the hearth of the universe, its center, and in like manner occupies the central position among the cardinal points. He is god of the year and of the first hour of the night and of the morning. The Aztec, Mexico. (Caso, 1958: 28, 38; Alexander, 1920: 53; Bancroft, 1886, 3: 384–388; Vaillant, 1962: 149; Spence, 1923: 272, 278)

Yegiled-eme'i The goddess of fire invoked by the shaman in healing. The Yukaghir of Yassachnaya River area, Siberia. (Jochelson, 1900/02: 202)

Yen-ti A Bodhisattva and a god of fire. Szechwan, China. (Wood, 1937: 173)

Yota-anit The god of fire of the Naragansetts. Connecticut. (De Forest, 1853: 24; Skinner, 1913: 91)

15

Fresh Water Gods:
Rivers, Lakes, Irrigation, Curative

Abarbarea A water nymph, daughter of Oceanus and Tethys. Greece. (Barthell, 1971: 42)

Aberewa Awukuwa The river Aberewa, the mother of Twe (Bosomtwe). The Ashanti, Ghana. (Rattray, 1923: 61)

Abu-mehsu Goddess of the river of that name, wife of Bobowissi. The Nzema (Akan), Ghana. (Mockler-Ferryman, 1925, 9: 277; Ellis, 1887: 31; Grottanelli, 1969: 375)

Abzu Babylonian god of sweet waters. Variant of Apsu. Near East. (Kramer, 1967: 107)

achachilas Lake and mountain spirits of the Aymara. Bolivia. (Buechler and Buechler, 1971: 91)

Acheloos, Acheloüs The great river god, "the father of all fresh-water springs" and as such associated with health and with the hygienic qualities of water. He is described as a man with a horned head with the "lower body consisting of a serpent-like fish." The paternity of the sirens is sometimes attributed to him. Son of Oceanus and Tethys. Greece. (Kerenyi, 1951: 56; Hesiod-Brown, 1981: 63; Thramer, 1925, 6: 548; Roscher, 1965, 1, 1: 6, 7)

Acheron A river of the underworld. He was personified as a son of Gaea and banished to the underworld for giving water to the Titans in their battle against Zeus. Greece. (Roscher, 1965, 1, 1: 9, 11; Larousse, 1968: 165)

Acionna A goddess of wells, near Orleans. Gaul. (MacCulloch, 1911: 182; Bertrand, 1897: 195)

Adamisil Wedo A water goddess identified with Ste. Anne. Also called Si Adaman. Mirebalais, Haiti, West Indies. (Herskovits, 1937: xvi, 280)

Adjakpa The guardian of the drinking water. A son of Mawu and Lisa. Dahomey. (Herskovits, 1938, 2: 109)

Adjasou A powerful god who "makes water rise in springs." Haiti, West Indies. (Simpson, 1971: 511)

Adranga A deity of the rivers. The Alur, Uganda. (Butt, 1952: 177)

Adumu The chief water spirit is the father of pythons. The Ibo and the Ibiblio, Nigeria. (Parrinder, 1961: 52)

Adzi-anim A bird-sized friendly god who helps "find good water, by means of birds." Gold Coast, West Africa. (Mockler-Ferryman, 1925, 9: 278; Ellis, 1887: 40)

Aeas A Greek river god. (Ovid, 1955: 44)

AEnicidu A water god, particularly of inopportune rains and floods. The Arawak, Guiana. (Im Thurn, 1883: 365)

Afuru A water god—"the thief of the water people." The Kalabari, Nigeria. (Horton, 1960: 44)

Aganippe A spring nymph of Mount Helicon whose waters were inspirational. Greece. (Larousse, 1968: 149)

Agassou Gnenin, Djeme A powerful god of sweet waters who is also a god of healing. He is represented by a crab; is identified with St. Esprit or St. Augustin. Haiti, West Indies. (Marcelin, 1950: 127)

Agayu A river deity of the Yoruba. Nigeria. (Courlander, 1973: 234)

Agionna A spring deity, near Orleans. Gaul. (Renel, 1906: 391)

Agiri A water god of "ruthless nature." The Kalabari, Nigeria. (Horton, 1960: 31, 36)

Agəlibemu A water spirit whom some describe as a monster frog, others as a giant lizard-like monster. The Penobscot Indians, Maine. (Speck, 1935: 15)

Ahokpo The lagoon god of Akatekyi whose crocodiles obey him and avenge offenses. The Nzema (Akan), Ghana. (Grottanelli, 1969: 377)

Ahti, Ahto, or **Lemminkainen** The god of waters who is helpful to fishermen. His wife is Vellamo. Finland. (Larousse, 1968: 304; de Kay, 1898: 114; Leach, 1949, 1: 30)

Ahuic and **Aiauh** Names of Chalchihuitlicue, goddess of waters, referring to "its motion, now to one side, now to the other." Mexico. (Bancroft, 1886, 3: 367)

Ahurani A water goddess invoked "for health and healing, for prosperity and growth." Her offerings must be made by day. Iran. (Jayne, 1962: 187; Gray, 1930: 131)

Airo A water god, the protector of the fountain. Spain. (Martinez, 1962: 167–168)

Aisepos A river god, son of Oceanus and Tethys. Greece. *See also* **Asopus.** (Roscher, 1965, 1, 1: 197)

Aitan Goddess of the stream. The Khasi, Assam. (Gurdon, 1907: 157)

Aizan A god of water who also gives knowledge of healing. Haiti, West Indies. (Herskovits, 1937 : 151, 316)

Akis, Acis A river god of Mount Etna, son of a faun and the nymph Symaithis. Sicily, Italy. (Roscher, 1965, 1, 1: 210)

Akom A river god of the Akim-Kotoku. Ghana. (Field, 1948: 156)

Akora A river god of the Akim-Kotoku. Ghana. (Field, 1948: 202)

Akragas A river god, son of Zeus and Asterope. Sicily, Italy. (Roscher, 1965, 1, 1: 213)

Akwakule A river god. Ghana. (Rattray, 1932: 158)

Alalalahe A god associated with floods. Hawaii. (Beckwith, 1932: 182)

Alaunos A river god. Gaul. (Renel, 1906: 392)

Albunea A fountain nymph near Tivoli. Italy. (Roscher, 1965, 1, 1: 224)

Alein, Aleyin A god of springs and underground waters as well as of rain. Generally given as a son of Ba'al. He forms a conflict pair with Mot, but of opposites rather than of good and bad. Syria, Phoenicia, and Palestine. (Schaeffer, 1966: 305; James, 1960: 87; Haydon, 1941: 219; Larousse, 1968: 76)

Alαmbégwi·no'si·s Deep pools of rivers and lakes are inhabited by "man-like dwarfish" beings whose appearance foretells a death by drowning. The Penobscot Indians, Maine. (Speck, 1935: 13)

Alpheios, Alpheius, Alpheus The god of the largest river of the Peloponnesus. Son of Oceanus and Tethys. Greece. (Roscher, 1965, 1, 1: 256; Larousse, 1968: 149; Hesiod-Brown, 1981: 62)

Amaltheia A Greek nymph of spring waters, associated with Apollo. (Fairbanks, 1907: 147)

Amana A water goddess whose body ends as a serpent. She is associated with the Pleiades. She meets the novice shaman and gives him "charms and magical formulas." The Carib Indians, Surinam. (Zerries, 1968: 246–247; Eliade, 1964: 129)

Amanzule A famous god on the coast, originally a river god, but turned "to the sea in a strikingly modern fashion" by having a motorboat with which he patrols the coast and lures European boats on to the shoals by signals with lights. The Nzema (Akan), Ghana. (Grottanelli, 1969: 377)

Ameipicer A goddess of a fountain, or spring. Spain. (Martinez, 1962: 169)

Amelenwa The river goddess of Atuabo who rules other gods, is ruthless and does not forget offenses. Wife of Bulakpole. The Nzema (Akan), Ghana. (Grottanelli, 1969: 375–376)

Ame-no-ku-hiza-mochi-no-kami, Ame-no-Kuizamochi-no-Kami "Heavenly Kami water-drawing-gourd-possessor." A god of watering. Japan. (Yasumaro, 1965: 15; Herbert, 1967: 265)

Ame-no-Mikumari-no-Kami   God of irrigation. Japan. (Yasumaro, 1965: 15; Herbert, 1967: 265)

Ame-no-Tsudohechine-no-Kami   The "deity of accumulating water." Consort of Fuka-fuchi-no-mizu-yarehana. Japan. (Yasumaro, 1965: 36; Herbert, 1967: 317)

Ameucn   An aquatic god. Spain. (Martinez, 1962: 169)

Ameucni   A deity of curative waters. Leon, Spain. (Martinez, 1962: 169)

a mik ka ta bo   A dangerous demon "with only one eye . . . has the habit of gliding along the surface of rivers and brooks." The Lepchas, Sikkim. (Siiger, 1967: 180)

Amimitl   A goddess "of floating gardens and canals;" worshipped at Cuauhilama. Valley of Anahuac, Mexico. (Reed, 1966: 112)

Amisakyi   A river god. Ghana. (Field, 1948: 204)

Ampah   A lagoon god who protects the fishing industry of Moree. Gold Coast, West Africa. (Ellis, 1887: 49, 50)

Amphiro   A goddess associated with flowing water. Daughter of Oceanus and Tethys. Greece. (Kerenyi, 1951: 41)

Amphrysus   A Greek river god. (Ovid, 1955: 44)

Anahita   A river goddess and goddess of sacred waters. She is the beneficent goddess of the fecundity of all living things, a goddess of childbirth and of virility, of health. She is associated with the planet Venus. Iran. (Dumézil, 1966, 1: 302; Jayne, 1962: 189–190; Dresden, 1961: 353; Huart, 1963: 38, 42; Larousse, 1968: 311, 313; Hinnells, 1973: 32)

Anavatapta   A dragon-king, a guardian of all waters. China. (Werner, 1932: 9)

Anchicara   A well-god. Peru. (Trimborn, 1968: 126)

Andjalui   The spirit of fresh water, husband of Wuriupranala and father of Wuriuprinili. The Tiwi, Melville Island, Australia. (Mountford, 1958: 25, 31, 42)

Angu   A river god of the Nzema. Ghana. (Grottanelli, 1969: 397)

Anqet, Anuqet   A river goddess, "the personification of the waters of the Nile" at Elephantine, where she forms a triad with Khnemu and Sati. She is a goddess of

life, of health, of joy. Egypt and Sudan. (Budge, 1969, 2: 57–58; Knight, 1915: 17, 126; Ames, 1965: 108; Jayne, 1962: 53)

Apa, Apah, Apas   The beneficent and loving goddesses of the waters, cleansing and purifying, giving remedies and healing, health and wealth, long life and immortality. India. (Macdonell, 1897: 85; Jayne, 1962: 162)

Apam Napat   "Child of the Waters," a god of the fertilizing waters which he apportions. He is also associated with the lightning and here identified with Agni in India. Iran. (Macdonell, 1897: 70; Gray, 1930: 133–134, 221; Keith, 1917: 36, 43)

Apidanus   A Greek river god. (Ovid, 1955: 44)

Apo   An Ashanti water god, son of 'Nyame. Ghana. (Clarke, 1930: 446–448)

Apo   The waters, the equivalent of the Indian Apas. "Sacrifice to them may be made only between sunrise and sunset, oblations at any other time being a most grievous sin." Iran. (Gray, 1930: 136; Huart, 1963: 42)

Apozonallotl and Acuecuejotl   Names of Chalchihuitlicue "which mean the swelling and fluctuation of water." The Aztec, Mexico. (Bancroft, 1886, 3: 367)

Appias   The nymph of a fountain in the Forum of Rome. Also called Minerva Appias. Italy. (Roscher, 1965, 1, 1: 468)

Apsu   The god of the sweet waters of the primordial ocean whose consort was Tiamat. Son was Mummu. Babylonia, Near East. (James, 1960: 208; Kramer, 1961: 120; Jastrow, 1898: 411)

Aranzah   Hittite and Hurrian goddess of the river Tigris. Near East. (Littleton, 1970, 2: 96)

Ardeskos, Ardescus   A river god, son of Oceanus and Tethys. Greece. (Roscher, 1965, 1, 1: 474; Hesiod-Brown, 1981: 63)

Ardvi Vaxsha   A "local eastern Persian goddess of water and moisture, related to the great Ardvi Sura Anahita." (Hinnells, 1973: 52)

Aredvi   Goddess of waters and of "human generation and birth." Iran. (Gray, 1930: 55)

Arethusa   One of the Nereids, a daughter of Nereus and Doris. A nymph in Elis and follower of Artemis. She was loved by the river god Alpheus, and, to escape his attentions, was changed by Artemis into a spring which flowed underground to arise in Ortygian Sicily. Greece. (Fairbanks, 1907: 148; Larousse, 1968: 146; Prentice Hall, 1965: 18; Ovid, 1955: 129–133)

Argyra A nymph of a spring in Achaja. Greece. (Roscher, 1965, 1, 1: 540)

Arnemetia A goddess of curative waters in Britain. (Ross, 1967: 218)

As-ava A Finno-Ugrian water goddess. The Mordvins, Russia. (Paasonen, 1925, 8: 845)

Ashadu A lagoon god, a child of Odame. The Gã in Labadi, Ghana. (Field, 1937: 57)

Asopus, Aesepus, Aisepos A river god of Boeotia. Ancestor of the people of Sicyon. Greece. (Fairbanks, 1907: 147; Prentice Hall, 1965: 21; Larousse, 1968: 126, 149; Hesiod-Brown, 1981: 63; Roscher, 1965, 1: 197)

Asra A goddess of water who lives near rivers. India. (Russell, 1925, 3: 314)

Assaecus A water god. Portugal. (Martinez, 1962: 171)

Asterion A Greek river god, father of Akraia. (Roscher, 1965, 1, 1: 213)

Asubonten The spirit of the ford, the river crossing. A son or emanation of Tano. The Ashanti, Ghana. (Rattray, 1923: 200)

Atengabona A river spirit of the Nankanse. Ghana. (Rattray, 1932: 307)

Atete The goddess of fertility is also considered a water spirit inhabiting rivers. The Galla, Ethiopia. (Huntingford, 1955: 76; Bartels, 1969: 407; Rossini, 1925, 6: 491)

Athtar A god of irrigation, of wells. Syria, Canaan, and Arabia. (Driver, 1956: 20; Crawford, 1957: 23; Smith, 1969: 100)

Atlacamani A name of Chalchihuitlicue as goddess of waters—"the storms excited thereon." The Aztec, Mexico. (Bancroft, 1886, 3: 367)

Atlahuac A goddess "of floating gardens and canals" worshipped at Cuauhilama, Valley of Anahuac. Mexico. (Reed, 1966: 112)

Attar, Attr The morning star, Venus, was also the god of irrigation and the giver of autumn and spring rains. Canaan, Near East. (Gray, 1957: 12, 21; Oldenburg, 1969: 39)

Aturrus An aquatic as well as a chthonic god. Spain. (Martinez, 1962: 170)

Aungpinle Boubongyi The guardian of the reservoir, a god of water "propitiated daily during the transplanting and the harvesting seasons." Burma. (Spiro, 1967: 106)

Autrimpas A Slavic god of the lakes and of the sea. Prussia. (Gimbutas, 1963: 197; Puhvel, 1974: 83)

Avantia, Aventia A water goddess associated with Grannos. Gaul. (Bertrand, 1987: 195; MacCulloch, 1911: 43, 182)

Avanyo, avanyu sen^do The horned water serpent controls river waters and sends water from the mountains for irrigation. The Tewa, New Mexico. (Parsons, 1929: 274; 1939: 184)

Avicantus A stream god of the Gard. Gual. (Renel, 1906: 393)

Avrejo A god of the pantheon which controls thunder, rain, and waters. Maranhão, Brazil. (Costa Eduardo, 1948: 78–79)

Avrekete A god of the pantheon which controls all waters, celestial and terrestrial. Brazil. (Costa Eduardo, 1948: 78–79)

Awa-an A water spirit of the Tinguian. Philippines. (Cole, 1922: 342)

Axios, Axius A river god of Macedonia. Greece. (Roscher, 1965, 1, 1: 742; Barthell, 1971: 44)

Axona Goddess of the river Aisne. Gaul. (Anwyl, 1906: 38)

Axwaga Second child of Agbe and Naete, deities of the sea. He was an evil god and was banished by Agbe to the land where he transformed himself into a river. Dahomey. (Herskovits, 1938, 2: 152, 155)

Ayensu A God of the Ayensu river who improves man's well-being and health. The Effutu, Ghana. (Wyllie, 1966: 479)

Ayida Oueddo The goddess of the rainbow and of sweet waters who is represented by a serpent. She is a goddess of fertility and of atmospheric phenomena; is the wife of Damballah Oueddo, but also the mistress of Agoue. Haiti, West Indies. (Marcelin, 1950: 69, 70, 88)

Ayizan Velequete Goddess of sweet waters, of marketplaces, public places, doors and gateways, etc. She is the wife of Legba, is represented by a serpent, and is an exorciser and purifier. Haiti, West Indies. (Marcelin, 1950: 29, 34)

'Ayya A Semitic god who, through his identification with Ea, Enki, is believed to be a "god of fresh-water springs." Near East. (Roberts, 1972: 21, 57)

Azaka Mede The "spirit of a a stream which the dead must cross" at Arada. A river god at Mirebalais. Haiti, West Indies. (Courlander, 1966: 15; Herskovits, 1937, 1: 280)

Bachue A beneficent goddess who emerged from a lake with her three-year-old son whom she later married in order to populate the land. She is a goddess of agriculture, protective of the crops. She and her son transformed into serpents and returned to the lake. The Chibcha, Colombia. (Osborne, 1968: 110; Kroeber, 1946: 908; Keane, 1925, 3: 515)

Bacurdus A local Rhine god of Cologne. Germany. (Renel, 1906: 393; Roscher, 1965, 1, 1: 745)

The Bà-Dú'c-Chúa The "Three Mothers . . . represent . . . the Spirit of the Forests, the Spirit of the Waters, and the Spirit of the Air and Sky." Annam. (Cabaton, 1925, 1: 539)

Bagil A spirit who controls running waters. The Eastern Pomo, California. (Loeb, 1926, 2: 302)

Baginda Chilir Guardian of the water. Java, Indonesia. (Geertz, 1960: 40)

Balintawag A female river spirit of a pool below Sabangan. The Isneg, Luzon, Philippines. (Vanoverbergh, 1953: 82)

Bali Sungei A river god who takes the form of a serpent and causes boats to capsize. The Kenyahs, Borneo. (Hose, 1912: 16; MacCulloch, 1925, 11: 401)

Bamusehua A god of water. The Sinaloas, Mexico. (Bancroft, 1886, 3: 180)

dBang bsdud ma An evil lake goddess who "causes illnesses of the blood." Tibet. (Nebesky-Wojkowitz, 1956, 1: 307)

Bangputtis, Banputys A god of water and also a storm god. Lithuania. (Welsford, 1925, 9: 241; Gimbutas, 1963: 197)

Bansura A river god "who protects fish from evil spirits." India. (Briggs, 1953: 555)

Bateia A water nymph, daughter of Oceanus and Tethys. Greece. (Barthell, 1971: 42)

Batoer Goddess of the sacred lake. Wife of Goenoeng Agoeng. Bali, Indonesia. (Belo, 1953 : 8)

Baunan A spirit of the swamp. The Sakai, Malay Peninsula. (Skeat, 1906: 182)

Bea A river god, son of 'Nyame. Ghana. (Rattray, 1923: 146)

Behnya God of the river of the same name and a god of war of the Elminas. His wife is Nana enna. Elmina District, Gold Coast, West Africa. (Ellis, 1887: 53)

Bel-Ashur A name of Ea as a water god of Chaldea. Near East. (Dragomanov, 1961: 31)

Belisama A river goddess associated with the Mersey or the Ribble river. She was identified with Minerva. Britain. (Anwyl, 1906: 37; MacCulloch, 1911: 41)

Bel-Merodach A name of Ea as a water god of Chaldea. Near East. (Dragomanov, 1961: 31)

Be'u'byin chu yi zhags pa can A god who "is said to dwell in the middle of rivers and lakes—but apparently also on coracles and ferry-boats." Tibet. (Nebesky-Wojkowitz, 1956, 1: 292)

Bhainsasura A water god, "the buffalo demon," who lives in a pool in Mirzapur and must be propitiated before fishing. India. (Crooke, 1925, 12: 716)

Bia A river god who is the eldest son of the supreme god, and brother of Tano. Ghana. (Parrinder, 1949: 46)

Binunlunan A male spirit who "lives under water in a cave in the river, between Bayag and Sabangan." The Isneg, Luzon, Philippines. (Vanoverbergh, 1953-: 82)

Bisangolan A god who keeps the rivers free of jamming by logs and refuse and prevents floods. The Tinguian, Philippines. (Cole, 1922: 299)

Ka blei sam um A river goddess to whom offerings are made before the casting of nets, also "when the umbilical cord . . . falls off." The Khasis, Assam. (Gurdon, 1914: 114, 124)

Boand, Boann The goddess of the river Boyne and wife of Nechtan. She is the mother of Mac and Og (Oenghus, Angus) by Dagda. Ireland. (Sjoestedt, 1949: 41; MacCulloch, 1911: 81; MacCana, 1970: 33; Squire, 1906: 55, 141)

Bolbe Goddess of the lake Bolbe at the bay of Strymon. Greece. (Roscher, 1965, 1, 1: 789)

Boni A river deity near Krachyi. Ghana. (Field, 1948: 203)

Bormana A goddess of hot springs, associated with Bormanus or Apollo. Bouche-du-Rhone, Gaul. (Renel, 1906: 394; MacCulloch, 1911: 43, 182)

Bormanicus A Celtic god of "healing springs and health resorts." Portugal. (Jayne, 1962: 512; Rocher, 1965, 1, 1: 814)

Bormanus, Bormo, Borvo A god of hot springs identified with Apollo. Gaul. (Renel, 1906: 394–395; Anwyl, 1906: 40; MacCulloch, 1911: 26; Jayne, 1962: 512; MacCana, 1970: 32)

Bormonia A goddess of a healing fountain at Bourbon-Lancy. Gaul. (Roscher, 1965, 1, 1: 815)

Borvonia A goddess of a healing fountain. Gaul. Roscher, 1965, 1, 1: 815)

Bosom-Pra A clan god associated with the Pra river who inspired them "to be as resolute and tenacious" as the river. The Akan, Ghana. (Meyerowitz, 1958: 99)

Bosomtwe The spirit of Lake Bosomtwe and a clan god whose members try to be "as calm and tolerant and their souls as immaculate" as the lake. A fowl is offered for plentiful fish. Son of 'Nyame and Aberewa Awukuwa. The Akan, Ghana. (Meyerowitz, 1958: 99; Rattray, 1923: 60, 61, 146)

Brixia, Bricia A goddess associated with waters and with Luxovius. Gaul. (Renel, 1906: 395; MacCulloch, 1911: 43)

Buk A goddess of rivers and streams and considered the source of life. She is the mother of Deng and two daughters, Candit and Nyaliep. The Nuer, Sudan. (Evans-Pritchard, 1956: 31–32, 45)

Bulalakau The "spirit or spirits of the water . . . have their home in the center of the sea but they also frequent springs, streams and rivers. . . . One of these spirits is responsible for drowning." The Bukidnon, Mindanao, Philippines. (Cole, 1956: 94, 99)

Bunad A spirit of a river pool at Pannun. The Isneg, Luzon, Philippines. (Vanoverberg, 1953: 85)

Burhi Thakurani Goddess of the river Tista. Bengal. (Crooke, 1925, 2: 483)

Čacc-olmai, Čacce-olmai, Čacce-haldde A god representing the element of water who received sacrifices. The Lapps, Northern Europe. (Collinder, 1949: 145; Leach, 1949, 1: 475)

Cada The god of Lake Cada. The Pimbwe, Tanzania. (Willis, 1966: 59)

Caicus A river god possessed of the gift of healing. Son of Oceanus and Tethys. Mysia, Asia Minor. (Fairbanks, 1907: 147; Hesiod-Brown, 1981: 63)

Caliadne A water nymph, daughter of Oceanus and Tethys. Greece. (Barthell, 1971: 42)

Callirrhoe A water nymph, daughter of Oceanus and Tethys. Greece. (Murray, 1895: 188; Barthell, 1971: 41)

The Camenae Roman fountain nymphs. The name was also applied to the Muses. (Bulfinch, 1898: 220; Prentice Hall, 1965: 30)

Camise A Roman spring nymph named as a wife of Janus and the mother of Tiberinus. (Fairbanks, 1907: 247)

Candit A goddess associated with streams. Daughter of Buk. The Nuer, Sudan. (Evans-Pritchard, 1956: 31)

Carpundia, Carpunda A well goddess. Gaul. (MacCulloch, 1911: 182; Bertrand, 1897: 195)

Cassotis Greek nymph of a prophetic spring on Parnassus. (Larousse, 1968: 149)

Castalia A nymph of a prophetic spring at Delphi. Greece. (Larousse, 1968: 149; Prentice Hall, 1965: 32)

Ca Yum Santa Cruz "Among the postconquest gods, the cross is considered as a water deity personified as Ca Yum Santa Cruz, ''Our Lord, The Holy Cross,' or as Yax Cheel Cab, 'the first tree of the world.' We have seen that the latter refers to the ceiba." Mayan, Central America. (Tozzer, 1957: 201)

Celiborca A goddess of thermal waters. Spain. (Martinez, 1962: 174)

Cephisus A river god of Boeotia. Father of Narcissus. Greece. (Fairbanks, 1907: 147; Murray, 1935: 173; Larousse, 1968: 149)

Chalchiuhcueye The goddess of "the fourth element, Water." The Aztec, Mexico. (Duran, 1971: 261, 263)

Chalchiuhtlicue The goddess of waters, of lakes and rivers, of the sea is invoked by fishermen and all those involved with the water. She is a goddess of purification from sins as well as having medicinal qualities. As a calendrical deity her name is "Eight Malinalli." She is patroness of the fifth day, Coatl, (the serpent), of the 20-day series, Tonalpouhalli. The Aztec, Mexico. (Caso, 1958: 44; Burland, 1967: 88; Vaillant, 1962: 139, 145; Spence, 1923: 130, 260–1; Alexander, 1920: 54)

Ch'a-'lha The god of waters and protector of the west quarter was "formerly the god of the Sky." Same as Varuna. Tibet. (Waddell, 1959: 367)

Chang Lung A dragon-king, a tutelary deity "of seas, rivers, lakes, and waters generally." China. (Werner, 1932: 294, 285–286)

Ch'ang-yüan A dragon-king and the god of the river Huai. China. (Werner, 1932: 437)

Chariclo A water nymph, wife of Cheiron, and the daughter of Oceanus, Apollo, or Perses. Greece. (Barthell, 1971: 42, 59; Roscher, 1965, 1, 1: 872)

Chavisana The god of waters, an emanation of Puru, and invoked as an intercessor with him. The Salivan, Colombia. (Walde-Waldegg, 1936: 40–41; Wallis, 1939: 89)

Ix Chel A water goddess, and, as such, malevolent. She is responsible for all destruction through water—floods, cloudbursts, etc. As a benevolent deity she is a goddess of pregnancy and childbirth, of medicine, and of weaving. She is the moon goddess and the wife of Itzamna. The Mayan, Yucatan, Mexico. (Morley, 1946: 223, 230; Tozzer, 1941: 10, 154; Thompson, 1970: 242; Nicholson, 1967: 115)

Chia The moon goddess was "also goddess of water and flooded the earth out of spite." The Muyscas, Colombia. (Brinton, 1868: 134; Kroeber, 1946: 906)

Chia-lou-lo A dragon-king, a deity of all waters. China. (Werner, 1932: 58, 285–286)

Ch'ien-t'ang The principal god of rivers. China. (Werner, 1934: 219)

Chili The god of water of the Daphla. Bengal and Assam. (Crooke, 1925, 4: 399)

Ching A river spirit worshipped by the Berom. Nigeria. (Meek, 1925: 24)

Ch'ing A dragon-king, god of the river Chi. China. (Werner, 1932: 437)

Ch'ing-ching-sê A dragon-king, a god of all waters. China. (Werner, 1932: 82, 285–286)

Ching Ch'üan Tung Tzŭ The "Spirit of the Well." China. (Day, 1940: 41)

Chin-na-lo A dragon-king, a god of all waters generally. China. (Werner, 1932: 80, 285–286)

Chiuka-pinne-Kamui-Rametok "Valiant and Divine Male Current." A river demon that inhabits rapids and rough waters. The Ainu, Japan. (Batchelor, n.d.: 390; 1925, 1: 244)

Chiu-rang Guru Female river spirits inhabiting rapids and rough waters, also associated with waterfalls. The Ainu, Japan. (Batchelor, n.d.: 390; Munro, 1963: 20)

Chiu-range guru A river demon, a deity of the current. The Ainu, Japan. (Batchelor, 1925, 1: 244)

Chiu-rape Guru (male) and **Chui-rape Mat** (female) Together they "control the undercurrent" in the river. Assistants of Wakka-ush Kamui. The Ainu, Japan. (Munro, 1963: 20)

Chi-wash Kamui A deity who controls "the waters at the mouth of the river" and is protective of fishing boats in the area. Assistant to Wakka-ush Kamui. The Ainu, Japan. (Munro, 1963: 20, 43)

Chiwashekot-mat Goddess of the mouths of rivers, at the mingling of the salt and fresh waters. She is protective of the fish going in and out and guides them to spawning. The Ainu, Japan. (Batchelor, n.d.: 391; 1925, 1: 244)

Chiwash-kor-kamui Goddess of the River Rapids. She and Wakka-ush-kamui saved mankind from famine and taught them how to prevent them "by observing the proper hunting and fishing rituals." The Ainu, Hokkaidu, Japan. (Philippi, 1982: 99, 101)

Chiwash-koro Kamui Deity of the surf of the river mouth. The Ainu, Japan. (Munro, 1963: 20)

Chokesuso A goddess of irrigation channels and of fertility, associated with Anchicara, the well god. Peru. (Trimborn, 1968: 125–126; Alexander, 1920: 232)

Chrysas God of a river of the same name. Sicily, Italy. (Roscher, 1965, 1, 1: 900)

Chrysorrhoa A river god near Damascus. Syria. (Smith, 1969: 171)

Ch'uan Hou A goddess of streams and a variant name of the goddess T'ien Hou, goddess of the sea. China. (Ferguson, 1937: 72)

Chu'i lha mo Mamaki A goddess of the water invoked in pollution-eliminating ceremonies. Tibet. (Nebesky-Wojkowitz, 1956, 1: 388)

Chu lcam (rgyal mo) (pr. **Chhucham Gyelmo**) A goddess of the waters. Mother of bsKal med 'bum nag (born from the black egg), also of the 18 srid pa'i ming sring. Consort of Ye smon rgyal po. Bon religion. Tibet.

Chu lha (pr. **Chhulha**) The Bon "water-god . . . from whom serpents come." Tibet. (Tucci, 1980: 218)

Chu 'phrul can An evil lake goddess who causes jaundice. Tibet. (Nebesky-Wojkowitz, 1956, 1: 307)

Chu-roro Guru The deity of the deep waters above rapids. The Ainu, Japan. (Munro, 1963: 20)

Ciaga A "water god, who shared in the creation." Nicaragua. (Larousse, 1968: 440)

Clairmé, Mait' Clairmé A river god, husband of Mme. Clairmé and father of Clairmézine. Mirebalais, Haiti, West Indies. (Herskovits, 1937, 1: 312, 317)

Mme. Clairmé A river goddess, wife of Clairmé. Mirebalais, Haiti. Herskovits, 1937, 1: 317)

Clairmézine A river goddess, daughter of Clairmé. Mirebalais, Haiti, West Indies. (Herskovits, 1937, 1: 317)

Cleochareia A water nymph, daughter of Oceanus and Tethys. Greece. (Barthell, 1971: 42)

Clitumnus An Umbrian river god with oracular and healing qualities. Italy. (Jayne, 1962: 420; Roscher, 1965, 1, 1: 912)

Clota Goddess of the river Clyde. Scotland. (MacCulloch, 1911: 43; Ross, 1967: 21)

Clutoida A spring nymph at Nièvre. Also called Dirra. Gaul. (Renel, 1906: 396; MacCulloch, 1911: 70)

Clutonda A water goddess at Mesves. Gaul. (Bertrand, 1897: 195, 332)

Coatrischie A goddess of water and wind who causes the streams to rush destructively down the mountains into the lowlands. A subordinate of Guabancex. Haiti, Puerto Rico, and the Antilles, West Indies. (Fewkes, 1903/04: 56; Lovén, 1935: 617; Larousse, 1968: 440)

Condatis A local god of thermal waters, of the confluence of streams. Britain. (MacCana, 1970: 50; Ross, 1967: 182)

Cnenili The water god of the Navajo. Arizona and New Mexico. (Chamberlain, 1894: 193)

Coventina (1) A prophetic aquatic and chthonic goddess. Spain. (Martinez, 1962: 190–194) (2) The "patron goddess of the sacred well at Carranburgh, Northumberland." Britain. (Ross, 1967: 207)

Creusa A water nymph, daughter of Oceanus and Tethys and wife of Peneius, a river god in Thessaly. Greece. (Barthell, 1971: 42, 47)

Naac Cunma The god of water. Son of Nexhequiriac. The Trique, Oaxaca, Mexico. (Valentini, 1899: 38)

brDa'i 'phrad An evil lake goddess who "sends madness to her enemies." Tibet. (Nebesky-Wojkowitz, 1956, 1: 307)

da mik The "god of the rivers and of fishing in the rivers." The Lepchas, Sikkim. (Siiger, 1967: 141)

Dewi Danu A goddess of rivers and lakes. Bali, Indonesia. (Covarrubias, 1937: 9, 317; Friederich, 1959: 43)

Danuvius A Celtic river god. (MacCulloch, 1925, 3: 295)

Darantan An evil river anito who causes drownings. The Apayao, Philippines. (Wilson, 1947: 23)

Dara Rambai Geruda A water goddess who aids good divers, but who can also be harmful and cause death by drowning. The Iban Dyaks of Sarawak, Borneo. (Sarawak Gazette, 1963: 135)

Dariwa-wakan   The spirit of a river pool at Bana. The Isneg, Luzon, Philippines. (Vanoverbergh, 1953: 83)

Dasara   A goddess of the Ganges river. India. (Basak, 1953: 96)

Da Sindji   The guardian of the drinking water, an earth god, son of Dada Zodji and Nyohwe Ananu. Dahomey. (Herskovits, 1938, 2: 140)

Data   A water goddess, sister of Sabo and girlfriend of Agiri. The Kalabari, Nigeria. (Horton, 1960: 31)

Da Tokpo   The guardian of the earth's waters. Second son of Dada Zodji. Dahomey. (Herskovits, 1938, 2: 139)

Densu   A river god of Ghana. (Field, 1948: 203)

Deog Ian   A malevolent spirit of river sources who causes dropsy. The Malanau, Land Dyaks, Borneo. (De Crespigny, 1875: 35; Roth, 1968: 166)

Deva   A goddess of the river Dee. Britain. (Anwyl, 1906: 37)

Diiona   A deified river. Gaul. (Renel, 1906: 397)

Dirke   Greek nymph of a spring in Thebes. Daughter of Acheloos. (Roscher, 1965, 6: 861)

Dirson   The spirit of the source of the Sinaligan river. The Isneg, Luzon, Philippines. (Vanoverbergh, 1953: 84)

Diuturna   Roman "goddess of still waters and of rivers." Latium. (Larousse, 1968: 210)

Divona   A river goddess at Cahors and Bordeaux. Gaul (MacCulloch, 1911: 43; Bertrand, 1897: 195, 332)

Djanuken   The water god who is propitiated to do no harm and to bring luck in fishing. Truk Islands, Micronesia. (Krämer, 1932: 142)

Djok Matar   A spirit of the lake. The Alur, Uganda. (Butt, 1952: 177)

Dobayba   The goddess of water and mother of mankind. Darien, Panama. (Brinton, 1868: 123)

Dodo   A cannibalistic water spirit. The Maguzawa, Nigeria. (Greenberg, 1946: 37)

Dodone   A water nymph, daughter of Oceanus and Tethys. Greece. (Roscher, 1965, 1, 1: 1191)

Domfe   The water spirit who came "down to earth with rain and wind and the first food-bearing seeds." The Kurumba, Volta and upper Niger. (Larousse, 1973: 528)

D/Taban   A deified river "probably to be identified with the modern Ab-i-Neft or Ab-i-Gangir." Semitic. Near East. (Roberts, 1972: 18)

Duamaliue   A mother of rivers and also of field crops. She is "the source lake of the Rio Noavaka and Nuameiži." The Kagaba, Colombia. (Preuss, 1926: 84)

bDud mo gshin rje lag brgya ma   A lake goddess who is invoked for protection from hail and lightning. Tibet. (Nebesky-Wojkowitz, 1956, 1: 72, 244)

bDud mo gshin rje mgo dgu ma, bDud mo gsod byed ma, bDud mo phung khrol ma   Lake goddesses invoked for protection from hail and lightning. Tibet. (Nebesky-Wojkowitz, 1956, 1: 72, 244)

Duminea   A water god of the village of Soku. The Kalabari, Nigeria. (Horton, 1960: 50)

Durbedicus   A god of waters. Spain. (Martinez, 1962: 174)

Durius, Duris   A god of the river of the same name found on an inscription at Oporto. Portugal. (Roscher, 1965, 1, 1: 1205)

Durul   A deified river of the Semites "probably to be identified with the Turnat." Near East. (Roberts, 1972: 19)

Durus   God of the river Duero. Portugal. (Martinez, 1962: 174–5)

Dwurumprem   The deity of a river near Tafo. Ghana. (Field, 1948: 204)

Dyevae   A water spirit who participates in female puberty rites. The Tucuna. Brazil. (Zerries, 1968: 302)

Dzroko   A water god of the Gã in Kpong. Ghana. (Field, 1937: 78)

Ea, Enki   The Sumerian/Assyrian/Babylonian god of the underground waters. In association with its use he was a god of purification, of healing, of medicine. The unfathomable depths and unpredictability of the waters led to the concept of Ea/Enki as a god of wisdom and deep knowledge, of understanding. He was considered a demiurge, the organizer of the universe and the earth, becoming a god of civilization and of culture, of the crafts and the arts. He was god of the month Iyyar (Semitic) and Airu (Sumerian). Near East. (Jastrow, 1898: 61–62, 133–137, 462; Kramer, 1950: 60; 1961: 98, 120–122; 1967: 100–103; Jacobsen, 1946: 160; 1970: 21–22; James, 1960: 211; Dragomanov, 1961: 31; Langdon, 1931: 106; Jayne, 1962: 119; Hommel, 1925, 3: 74; Sayce, 1898: 104, 133, 139)

Edovius   A Celtic aquatic god named on an inscription at Caldas de Reyes. Spain. (Roscher, 1965, 1, 2: 1215; Martinez, 1962: 175)

Egeria   A spring nymph who was associated with Diana and was offered sacrifices for an easy childbirth. Italy. (Dumézil, 1966, 2: 408; Fairbanks, 1907: 253; Frazer, 1960: 4, '193)

Eholie   A river god of the Ashanti. Ghana. (Parrinder, 1949: 53)

Ekaki   A water god of the Kalabari. Nigeria. (Horton, 1960: 23)

Elusu   The guardian goddess "of the bar between the Lagos lagoon and the Bight of Benin." Wife of Olokun. She "is covered with fish scales from below the breasts to the hips." The Yoruba, Nigeria. (Lucas, 1948: 164; Wallis, 1939: 61)

Emanjah, Amanjah, Omanjah   The goddess of the river who is "thought of as a nurse and as a teacher of children." She is identified with St. Anne or St. Catherine. The Shango Cult, Trinidad, West Indies. (Simpson, 1965: 18, 20)

Enbilulu   A Sumerian god of irrigation and of canals, of drinking places, who was placed in charge of these Tigris-Euphrates waters by Enki. Near East. (Jacobsen, 1970: 57; Kramer, 1950: 60; 1961: 99)

Enhydria   The personification of the abundance of water. Greece. (Roscher, 1965, 1, 1: 1249)

Enipeus   The god of a river in Thessaly. Greece. (Prentice Hall, 1965: 49; Roscher, 1965, 1, 1: 1249)

Enki   *See* **Ea**

Ephydateia   A water nymph, daughter of Oceanus and Tethys. Greece. (Barthell, 1971: 42)

Erh Lang   (1) A god of Szechwan, "constructor of the Chengtu irrigation system . . . the controller of rivers." China. (Wood, 1937: 167, 173) (2) God of the Hsining river who is also the protector from hail, to insure which

protection and to receive his "blessings upon the crops" the goddesses periodically visit him overnight. The Monguors of Kansu, China. (Schram, 1957: 102–103)

Eridanus   A river god of Attica. Son of Oceanus and Tethys. Greece. (Barthell, 1971: 45; Hesiod-Brown, 1981: 62)

Erinle   A local river deity. Nigeria. (Courlander, 1973: 235)

Erua   A Babylonian water goddess "regarded as the daughter of Ea." She became merged with Sarpanitum. Near East. (Jastrow, 1898: 123)

Erymanthos   The god of the river of the same name. Greece. (Roscher, 1965, 1, 1: 1373)

Euenus   A river god, son of Oceanus and Tethys. Greece. (Hesiod-Brown, 1981: 63)

Euneike, Eunike   A Nereid, a spring/fountain nymph, daughter of Nereus and Doris. Greece. (Kerenyi, 1951: 64; Roscher, 1965, 1, 1: 1404)

Eurotas   A river god of Laconia. Greece. (Barthell, 1971: 45)

Ežerinis   A deity of lakes. Lithuania. (Gimbutas, 1963: 197)

Ezili, Ezili Freda Dahomey   The goddess of sweet waters is also the goddess of beauty and of love, of coquetry. As the mistress of Agoue T'Arroyo she is goddess of the sea, as that of Damballah, the goddess of sweet waters. Haiti, West Indies. (Marcelin, 1950: 77, 79, 88)

Faro   The god of water. "Two great spirits, Pemba and Faro, whose interaction spells conservation and change. . . . Faro, master alike of Water and the Word . . . is the shaper and reorganiser of the world." The Bambara, Mali, Niger, and Senegal. (Davidson, 1969: 173; Tauxier, 1927: 142; Queval, 1968: 40)

Fêng I   A god of waters. "Sometimes identified with the God of the Yellow River." China. (Werner, 1932: 126; Ferguson, 1937: 90; Schafer, 1980: 70)

Ferentina   A spring/fountain nymph and a goddess of protection of the Latin League. Italy. (Roscher, 1965, 1, 2: 1475; Prentice Hall, 1965: 54)

Fons   A Roman god of springs, son of Janus and Juturna. (Dumézil, 1966, 1: 388; Fairbanks, 1907; 247; Roscher, 1965, 1, 2; 1496)

Fontis Agineesis A god of a spring, the source of the river Borma. Spain. (Martinez, 1962: 168)

Frovida A goddess of rivers—altar found in Braga. Spain. (Martinez, 1962: 176)

Fucinus A Roman lake god. (Roscher, 1965, 1, 2: 1558)

Fukafuchi-no-Miduyarehana-no-Kami A god of watering. Japan. (Yasumaro, 1965: 36; Herbert, 1967: 317)

al-Gadd A divinity of wells. Arabia. (Fahd, 1968: 78–79)

Gajan Ghotho A water god of the Bhils. Son of Megh Raja and Kali Badli. India. (Naik, 1956: 181)

Galaxaura A water nymph, daughter of Oceanus and Tethys. Greece. (Murray, 1895: 188; Kerenyi, 1951: 41)

Gamainha A feared water demon. The Manao, Amazon Basin. Brazil. (Métraux, 1946, 6: 711)

Ganga The benevolent goddess of the Ganges River, eldest daughter of Himavat and Mena. India. (Crooke, 1894: 108; Martin, 1914: 213–214)

Gangaji The goddess of the river to whom sacrifices are made. The Patni boatmen, Bengal. (Crooke, 1925, 2: 483)

Gangamma The goddess of water who is also protective against smallpox. The Telugu, Southern India. (Whitehead, 1916: 21, 22)

Betara Gangga The god of water invoked in the bathing and cleansing ceremonies of the gods. Bali, Indonesia. (Belo, 1953: 39)

Dewi Gangga A goddess of rivers and lakes, a wife of Siwa. Bali, Indonesia. (Covarrubias, 1937: 317)

Gaphu A king of the lu (serpent or water spirits). The Sherpas, Nepal. (Furer-Haimendorf, 1964: 267)

Garha Era A water god who is thought to cause sickness. The Kols, India. (Crooke, 1894: 25)

Gasani The chief god of the Bakene who is a god of water as well as a sky god, and who is invoked in illness. Uganda. (Roscoe, 1915: 154, 249)

Gelas A highly esteemed river god. Greece. (Roscher, 1965, 1, 2: 1608)

Gestinanna An early name of Nina as " 'queen of waters' . . . a fish-goddess." Babylonia, Near East. (Mercer, 1925, 12: 709)

Ghatoia Deo, Ghotoiya The god of the river crossing, the ghat (landing-place) who is invoked for protection from snakes and crocodiles. The Dhimar, the Dhobis, Central Provinces, India. (Russell, 1916, 2: 507, 521; Crooke, 1925, 11: 872)

Glang djy A demon who "often drowns people in creeks and rivers." The Ch'uan Miao, China. (Graham, 1937: 63)

Godavari A river goddess. India. (Putman, 1971: 449)

Grande Ezili A beneficent old goddess of sweet waters and of the hearth who personifies wisdom. She is Maitresse Ezili in old age; is identified with Ste. Anne. Haiti and West Indies. (Marcelin, 1950: 93, 95)

Granikos, Granicus A river god in Mysia, son of Oceanus and Tethys. Asia Minor. (Roscher, 1965, 1, 2: 1738; Hesiod-Brown, 1981: 63)

Grannos A god of thermal springs and a healing deity, widely known. He is usually associated with Sirona and equated with Apollo. Gaul—known also in Britain, Scotland, and Sweden. (Jayne, 1962: 515; MacCana, 1970: 32; MacCulloch, 1911: 26; Ross, 1967: 377)

Graselus The god of the fountain of Grosel. Gaul. (Renel, 1906: 171, 398)

Guabancex A goddess of waters, of winds and storms, who has two subordinates—Guatauva and Coatrischie. Haiti and Puerto Rico. West Indies. (Fewkes, 1903/04: 56; Lovén, 1935: 603, 167; Alexander, 1920: 25)

Gucumatz Among the Cakchiquel this deity is associated with water. Guatemala. (Recinos and Goetz, 1974: 59, n. 62)

'Gying dkar ma An evil lake goddess who afflicts with dropsy. Tibet. (Nebesky-Wojkowitz, 1956, 1: 307)

Ha The spirit of rain and of surface water who controls the fishes and crocodiles and is invoked in fishing. He functions under the Chacs. The Mayan, British Honduras. (Thompson, 1930: 65)

Ông Hà Bà The god of the river to whom sacrifices are made before launching a new junk. Annam. (Cabaton, 1925, 1: 541)

Hagno   A fountain nymph of Arcadia, on Mt. Lycaion. Greece. (Roscher, 1965, 1, 2: 1815)

Hai-lung-wang   The great water god of the Miao. China. (Wang, 1948: 67)

Haliakmon   The god of a large river of Macedonia. Son of Oceanus and Tethys. Greece. (Roscher, 1965, 1, 2: 1820; Hesiod-Brown, 1981: 63)

Halitaia   The personification of the spring/fountain of Ephesos. Greece. (Roscher, 1965, 1, 2: 1822)

Halys   God of the river Halys. Asia Minor. (Roscher, 1965, 1, 2: 1824)

Hap, Hapi   Two gods of this name. The god of the Nile who is a god of fertility and nourishment. When depicted as the northern Nile he wears a crown of papyrus, when the southern or upper Nile, one of the lotus. The other god is a son of Horus and a god of the underworld. Egypt. (Knight, 1915: 36; Budge, 1969, 1: 177–178; 1969, 2: 43)

Hap-Meht   The god of the northern Nile whose female counterpart is considered to be Uatch-ura. Egypt. (Budge, 1969, 2: 43, 47)

Hap-Reset   The god of the southern Nile's female counterpart is considered to be Nekhebet. Egypt. (Budge, 1969, 2: 43, 47)

Hattar-koro Kamui   The deity of the deepest depths of the river. The Ainu, Japan. (Munro, 1963: 20)

Haurvatat   One of the Amesha Spentas who represents Health. He is protective of the waters, of vegetation and animals. He is associated with Ameretat in being concerned with the physical well-being of the people, in life as well as in death. Iran. (Jayne, 1962: 185; Littleton, 1965: 99; Gray, 1930: 51–52; Huart, 1963: 41)

Hawt   The spirit of water who was transformed into the lamprey eel. He was the great musician (the flute). The Wintun Indians, California. (Chamberlain, 1905: 115; Curtin, 1903: 121, 199, 508)

Haya-Aki-tsu-Hiko-no-Kami   A god of streams, of river mouths, of estuaries, of harbors. Japan. (Holtom, 1938: 181; Kato, 1926: 141; Herbert, 1967: 264)

Haya-akitsu-hime   A goddess of river mouths, estuaries, and harbors. Japan. (Herbert, 1967: 480; Yasumaro, 1928: 7)

Hebros   A river god in Thrace. Balkan Peninsula. (Roscher, 1965, 1, 2: 1871)

Hekes   "... 'lord of the mouth of the rivers,' is a rarely met god with stellar characteristics." Egypt. (Mercer, 1925, 12: 711)

Helice   A water nymph, daughter of Oceanus and Tethys. Greece. (Barthell, 1971: 41–42)

Heng chan, Tch'en Hao   God of the Peak of the North who presides over waters and all four-footed animals. China. (Chavannes, n.d.: 4, 418)

Hep   A very ancient name for the god of the Nile, Hap. Egypt. (Budge, 1969, 2: 42)

Heptaporos, Heptaporus   A Mysien river god, son of Oceanus and Tethys. Asia Minor. (Roscher, 1965, 1, 2: 2074; Hesiod-Brown, 1981: 62)

Herkyna   Nymph of a river in Boeotia, associated with Trophonios at the oracular grotto at Lebadeia. Greece. (Eliade, 1967: 244; Roscher, 1965, 1, 2: 2300)

Hermus, Hermos   A river god, son of Oceanus and Tethys. Asia Minor. (Hesiod-Brown, 1981: 63; Roscher, 1965, 1, 2: 2436)

Hiberus   God of the river Iberus. Italy. (Roscher, 1965, 1, 2: 2654)

Hi'ilawe   The god of "the wonderful misty falls of Waipio." Hawaii. (Westervelt, 1963, 3: 47)

Hine-i-te-huhi   The Swamp Maid. The Maori, New Zealand. (Best, 1924: 177, 495)

Hine-i-te-repo   A personification of swamps. The Maori, New Zealand. (Best, 1924: 177)

Hipparis   A horned river god shown on a coin of Kamarina. Greece. (Roscher, 1965, 1, 2: 2665)

Hippo   A water nymph, "like a swift current;" daughter of Oceanus and Tethys. Greece. (Murray, 1895: 188; Roscher, 1965, 1, 2: 2666)

Hippophoras   A river god shown on coins from Pisidia. Asia Minor. (Roscher, 1965, 1, 2: 2690)

hitha-kal   A lake spirit of the Chukchee. Siberia. (Bogoras, 1904/09: 286)

la-Hkima Oqla A very dangerous female jenn who lives in the river Buzemlan and who rules over many other evil jenn. Morocco. (Westermarck, 1920: 128)

Hler A storm giant who represents the element of water, in its "violent, untamed nature." An older name of Oegir. Scandinavia. (Stern, 1898: 121; Grimm, 1880: 240–1)

Ho Hsiu-chi A dragon-king, deities "of seas, rivers, lakes, and waters generally." China. (Werner, 1932: 158, 285–286)

Ho Ku The female spirit of the Han, a large tributary of the Yang-tzŭ. China. (Werner, 1932: 440)

Ho Pai Shui Kuan The "ruler of canal waters." China. (Day, 1940: 48)

Ho Po The god of the Yellow River. China. (Ferguson, 1937: 90)

Horokariyep The spirit (female) of the eddy. The Ainu, Japan. (Batchelor, n.d.: 389)

Ho Shen A river god of north China. (Gamble, 1954: 400)

Hsiang Chün The "god of the waterways of Hsiang (modern Hunan)." China. (Ferguson, 1937: 88)

Hsiao Kung The protective deity of rivers. China. (Werner, 1932: 166)

Hsüan Ming The god of the element Water, associated with the north. The Han period. China. (Campbell, 1962: 432)

Huan-t'ien Shang-ti The "Supreme Lord of the Dark Heaven, . . . rules over the northern quarter of the sky and the world, is the ruler of water among the five elements, and lastly, drives away evil spirits." China. (Maspero, 1963: 339)

Huiio Mistress of Lake Akuena in the highest Heaven, Kahuña. As the supernatural anaconda she is the Mistress of the Water, of the Orinoco River. Prior to this she was Frimene who stole the *Huehanna* from Nuna and in fleeing transformed herself into Huiio. The Makiritare, Venezuela. (Civrieux, 1980: 51–53, 180)

Hydor A god personifying water. Greece. (Roscher, 1965, 1, 2: 2769)

Hypereia A nymph of a spring/fountain of the same name. Greece. (Roscher, 1965, 1, 2: 2841)

Hypsas God of the river of the same name. Greece. (Roscher, 1965, 1, 2: 2852)

Iasis The nymph of a healing spring/fountain in Elis. Greece. (Roscher, 1965, 2, 1: 63; Thramer, 1925, 6: 548)

Iberus A river god. Spain. (Martinez, 1962: 175–176)

Icauna Goddess of the river Yonne. Gaul. (MacCulloch, 1911: 43; Bertrand, 1897: 195; Renel, 1906: 398)

Id Goddess of "pure waters," and "according to Brünnow . . . was the mother of Ea." Babylonia, Near East. (Thompson, 1903: 19, 27)

Igbo A water god, extravagant and lascivious. The Kalabari, Nigeria. (Horton, 1960: 31)

Igoni An old water goddess of the Kalabari. Nigeria. (Horton, 1960: 31)

Ihturi God of the Sirwi and Kakum rivers, malevolent toward others, but considered friendly toward the Elminas and Ashantis. Gold Coast, West Africa. (Ellis, 1887: 51)

I'ke Ningthou With I-rai Leima, the "gods of all the waters of Manipur." India. (Shakespear, 1913: 85)

Ikir-bonga A god "who rules over wells and sheets of water." The Mundas, India. (Crooke, 1925, 9: 2)

Iku-wi-no-kami God of the household waters. Japan. (Herbert, 1967: 497)

Ileguwan A male spirit of the source of the Lassiyan brook who resents intrusion, and which he punishes with sterile ears on the palay. The Isneg, Luzon, Philippines. (Vanoverbergh, 1953: 87)

Ilissos God of the river of the same name in Ithaca. Greece. (Roscher, 1965, 2, 1: 119)

Ilixo A god of the thermal springs at Bagnères-de-Lucon. Gaul. (Jayne, 1962: 520; Roscher, 1965, 2, 1: 119)

Imanja A goddess of waters in general, a mermaid, of Yoruban origin. Belem, Brazil. (Leacock, 1972: 157–158)

Imbrasos God of the river of the same name in Samos. Greece. (Roscher, 1965, 2, 1: 122)

Imo   Goddess of the Imo river at whose shrine oaths are sworn. At the annual rites she is invoked for children, prosperity, etc. The Igbo, Nigeria. (Uchendu, 1965: 97)

Imul   The spirit of a waterfall of the same name on the Baliwanan river. The Isneg, Luzon, Philippines. (Vanoverbergh, 1953: 88)

Inachus   A river god of Argos, father of Io. He was a god of arbitration. Greece. (Fairbanks, 1907: 147; Larousse, 1968: 149; Barthell, 1971: 45, 289; Bulfinch, 1898: 40)

Inan oinan   The "Mother of Rivers, or Waters" who is beneficent if properly protitiated and if no ritual sin has been committed. Pageh, Mentawei Islands, Indonesia. (Loeb, 1929: 188)

Innini   The Sumerian/Babylonian earth goddess was the embodiment of the "female principle of Heaven" and associated with the planet Venus. She was a water goddess "represented with serpents and blades of grass," as well as a goddess of war identified with Ishtar. Near East. (Mercer, 1925, 12: 700, 709; Langdon, 1931: 5, 93)

Iphianassa   A water nymph, daughter of Oceanus and Tethys. Greece. (Barthell, 1971: 42)

Iqamiaitx   A goddess of waters. Same as Itclixyan. The Chinook, Oregon and Washington. (Spier and Sapir, 1930: 236)

I-rai Leima   With I'ke Ningthou, "the gods of all the waters of Manipur." India. (Shakespear, 1913: 85)

Irungu   Among the Zinza a god of "the forest and the lake." Tanzania. (Taylor, 1962: 147)

Ismenos   God of the river of the same name close to Thebes. Son of Oceanus and Tethys or of Apollo and Melia. Greece. (Roscher, 1965, 2, 1: 551)

Ister   A river god, son of Oceanus and Tethys. Greece. (Hesiod-Brown, 1981: 62)

Istros   A river god who is depicted with horns. Son of Oceanus and Tethys. Greece. (Roscher, 1965, 2, 1: 555)

Itclixyan   Goddess of the Columbia River waters. Guardian of "fishermen and hunters of water animals." The Wishram, Oregon and Washington. (Spier and Sapir, 1930: 236)

Itcxiun   A water monster "living in the big whirlpools and eddies of the Columbia was also a guardian." The Wishram, Oregon and Washington. (Spier and Sapir, 1930: 236)

Itumbalombe   A female water spirit who is generous and helps supply children. The Nkundu, Zaire. (Hulstaert, 1938: 440)

Itzan Noh Ku   A god of "lakes and crocodiles." He cares for the sick, but also produces hail. The Lacandon, Mexico. (Thompson, 1970: 266–267)

Ivaos   God of the healing springs of Evaux. Gaul. (Renel, 1906: 399; Jayne, 1962: 520; Roscher, 1965, 2, 1: 766)

Ivat   A water spirit of the Kamauira. Xingu River, Brazil. (Villas Boas, 1973: 158)

Ivilia   A goddess of medicinal springs. Spain. (Martinez, 1962: 198)

Iyafo   A water god. The fish in the rivers he inhabits are sacred. The Ibo, Nigeria. (Wallis, 1939: 62)

The Jakui   Important water spirits of rivers and lagoons who make beautiful music on flutes, and after whom the jakui flute of the natives is named. The Kamauira, Xingu River, Brazil. (Villas Boas, 1973: 111–121, 257)

Jakuiaep   A male water spirit of the river bottom. The Kamauira, Brazil. (Villas Boas, 1973: 257)

Jal Deo   The water god by whom oaths are sworn. The Baiga, India. (Elwin, 1939: 66)

Jalkamni   A water deity, sometimes male, sometimes female. Orissa, India. (Elwin, 1954: 637)

Jata Rohini   A water demon of the river Karsa in Mirzapur who is invoked for rain, good harvests and good health. India. (Crooke, 1894: 24)

Jên-fei-jên-têng   A dragon-king, a deity of "seas, rivers, lakes, and waters generally." China. (Werner, 1932: 208, 285–286)

Jonjari (male) and **Jonjaringan** (female)   Beneficent spirits of mineral springs. The Kabi and Wakka tribes, Queensland, Australia. (Mathew, 1910: 170)

Jori Pennu   The god of streams. The Kandh, Bengal. (Crooke, 1925, 7: 649)

Jumna Ji   A benevolent river goddess. India. (Crooke, 1894: 35)

Juturna A nymph of healing springs sometimes named as the wife of Janus and the mother of Fons. Rome. (Jayne, 1962: 452; Fairbanks, 1907: 247, 253; Dumézil, 1966, 1: 388)

kaa nu kami The deity of a well or spring. Okinawa. (Lebra, 1966: 219)

Kaene A river spirit of the Kono concerned particularly with the sons of chiefs. Sierra Leone. (Parsons, 1950: 271)

Kahaku A river god whose name "is often found on edgetiles . . . to protect against fires." Japan. (Herbert, 1967: 479)

Kaikos A river god, son of Oceanus and Tethys, in Mysia. Asia Minor. *See also* **Caicus.** (Roscher, 1965, 2, 1: 894)

Ka-Jum The water spirit who is the father of fish and is invoked in hunting and fishing rituals and ordeals. The Oyana, French Guiana. (Zerries, 1968: 263)

Kal' Adumu A water deity of the Santa Barbara River. The Kalabari, Nigeria. (Horton, 1960: 25)

Kaleon A Greek river god. (Roscher, 1965, 2, 1: 925)

Kali Vijal A water deity of the Bhils. Child of Megh Raja and Kali Badli. India. (Naik, 1956: 181)

Kalliphaeia A nymph of a healing fountain in Elis. Greece. (Thramer, 1925, 6: 548)

Kallirhoe A goddess associated with flowing water, daughter of Oceanus and Tethys. Greece. (Kerényi, 1951: 41; Roscher, 1965, 2, 1: 929)

Kalunga The "water goddess of the mayomberos" (black witches). Puerto Rico. West Indies. (Gonzalez-Wippler, 1975: 107)

Kalykadnos A Greek river god. (Roscher, 1965, 2, 1: 939)

Kameinan An evil water spirit of Pageh Island. Mentawei Islands. Indonesia. (Loeb, 1929: 188)

Kamui natne-po The guardian goddesses of the waters. The Ainu, Japan. (Batchelor, n.d.: 389)

Kamui po-teke The divinities of the tributaries of the rivers. The Ainu, Japan. (Batchelor, n.d.: 389)

Ka-mu-iu-dr-ma-giu-iu-e-ba "Mother of the Waters"—a great goddess who "was wooed by the rattlesnakes, and bore two sons Ha-ma-u-giu-iu-é-ba, or 'Children of the Waters.' " They killed the rattlesnakes and led the Indians into the canyon. The Havasupai, Arizona. (Cushing, 1882: 558)

Kane i ka wai e ola "The *aumakua* in the water." Hawaii. (Emerson, 1967: 51)

Ka'nini The spirit of a prophetic cult phenomenon— the "Great Mother from the Water, who, in a series of pantomines, swallowed all the whites." Australia. (Eliade, 1973: 180)

Kan-ta-p'o A dragon-king, a deity of all waters generally. China. (Werner, 1932: 214, 285–6)

Kapros A river god. Asia Minor. (Roscher, 1965, 2, 1: 955)

Kárldikukui Mother of the water. The Cagaba, the Kogi. Colombia. (Reichel-Dolmatoff, 1949/50: 114)

Karmeios A river god. Phrygia, Asia Minor. (Roscher, 1965, 2, 1: 960)

Karokung A very amorous female spirit who lives in rivers and causes fever and chills in men. The Bagobo, Philippines. (Benedict, 1916: 38, 226)

Karunga, Kalunga The aspect of the dual god Ndjambi Karunga which relates to the earth, water, and the netherworld. They are combined, yet separate. The Herero, Namibia. (Luttig, 1933: 7–9; Pettersson, 1953: 169, 74)

Kasaray-sarayan-sa-silgan The deity of the streams. The Bisayan, Philippines. (Jocano, 1969: 20)

Kasila A water spirit of the Sherbro, Bullom, and Krim who is considered responsible for "floods, upset canoes, and various ills that beset fishermen." Sierra Leone. (McCulloch, 1950: 83)

Ka-silim A Babylonian river goddess. Near East. (Hommel, 1925, 3: 75)

Katarrhaktes A Greek river god. (Roscher, 1965, 2, 1: 1002)

Katarwiri A malignant river goddess to whom sacrifices of women were made. Wife of Tando. The Ashanti and northern Tshi. Ghana. (Ellis, 1887: 33; Mockler-Ferryman, 1925, 9: 277)

Kaveri A river goddess, a manifestation of Parvati. The Coorgs, Southern India. (Srinivas, 1952: 217; Putman, 1971: 449)

Kawaj A god of water and of boatmen. Same as Khwaja Khizr, Raja Kidar. Bengal. (Crooke, 1894: 26; Keith, 1917: 235)

Kawakami-no-kami A river god whose shrine is located at its source. Japan. (Holtom, 1938: 100)

Kaweshawa The daughter of the master of fish. In the water she was a fish, out of water a beautiful woman. She lived in the Kasuruña Rapids and her permission was needed to fish there. Wife of Wanadi. The Makiritare, Venezuela. (Civrieux, 1980: 32–43)

Kaxshikuáma Mother of the stream. The Cagaba, the Kogi. Colombia. (Reichel-Dolmatoff, 1949/50: 114)

Kayalil Daivam The "deity of backwaters." The Izhavas, Southern India. (Thurston, 1909, 2: 401)

Kaystros, Kaystrios The god of a river of the same name, near Ephesus. Asia Minor. (Roscher, 1965, 2, 1: 1008)

Kazanes A Greek river god. (Roscher, 1965, 2, 1: 1009)

Kebren, Cebren A river god in Troas. Asia Minor. (Roscher, 1965, 1, 1: 658; Prentice Hall, 1965: 101; Barthell, 1971: 44)

Kenchreios A river god. Greece. (Roscher, 1965, 2, 1: 1030–1031)

Kephissos A river god, son of Oceanus and Tethys. Greece. *See also* **Cephisus.** (Roscher, 1965, 2, 1: 1114–1115)

Kestros A river god. Greece. (Roscher, 1965, 2, 1: 1177)

Keteios A river god. Greece. (Roscher, 1965, 2, 1: 1177)

Kevioso Also called Bade. God of "thunder, rain and all bodies of water." Brazil. (Costa Eduardo, 1948: 78–79)

Khala Kumari A water goddess to whom fishermen sacrifice "first-fruits." Bengal. (Crooke, 1925, 2: 483)

Khanukh The Wolf—the possessor of fresh water from whom Yehl stole it. He controls the fog. The Thlinkeets, British Columbia. (Bancroft, 1886, 3: 101, 146)

Kharhariai-Noin A water god, son of Khaga-Tai-Noin. Lake Baikal, Siberia. (Klementz, 1925, 3: 6)

Khnemu, Khnum Originally a river god, of the First Cataract of the Nile. Identified with Hapi as the controller of the waters. He is a ram-headed god, head of the triad of Elephantine. He fashioned gods and men on his potter's wheel. He absorbed attributes of Ra, Shu, Qeb, and Osiris, and as such was called Sheft-Hat—depicted "with four rams' heads upon a human body . . . [symbolizing] . . . fire, air, earth, and water." Egypt. (Knight, 1915: 64; Budge, 1969, 2: 49–53; Casson, 1965: 106)

Khwaja Khizr, Khwaja Khidr A god of water and of boatmen, adopted from Islam. India. (Crooke, 1894: 26; Briggs, 1920: 199; Crooke, 1925, 12: 717; 1925, 2: 483)

Kidi A deity of a hot spring. The Pimbwe, Tanzania. (Willis, 1966: 59)

Kieou-long A river deity. China. (Chavannes, n.d.: 90)

Kikum The "spirit from the water and the interpreter for Kukluknam" (the spirit of the sun dance). The Kutenais, Northern Rockies, United States. (Clark, 1966: 155)

Kilbos A Greek river god. (Roscher, 1965, 2, 1: 1184)

Kinomata-no-Kami God of the tree fork and also a god of wells. Also called Ni-wi-no-kami. Japan. (Herbert, 1967: 326–327; Yasumaro, 1965: 41–42)

Kissiang A river goddess. China. (Du Bose, n.d.: 72)

Kjotsamptni A god of Lake Titicaca. The Uru, Bolivia. (LaBarre, 1941: 521)

Kladeas A river god. Greece. (Roscher, 1965, 2, 1: 1209)

Kladeos The god of the river of the same name, near Olympia. Greece. (Roscher, 1965, 2, 1: 1210)

Kochiu-tunash guru A river demon, a god of the swift current. The Ainu, Japan. (Batchelor, 1925, 1: 244)

Kogamis A Greek river god. (Roscher, 1965, 2, 1: 1265)

Kokobi The goddess of the permanent pool of the village's household water supply, but which is forbidden during the rainy season because snakes come to live in the adjacent grove. The Effutu, Ghana. (Wyllie, 1966: 479)

Kole A lagoon god associated with the corn planting. The Gã in Accra. Ghana. (Field, 1937: 85–86, 89)

Kolowisi The horned water snake, the god of terrestrial waters who controls floods, earthquakes and landslides. He punishes promiscuity. The Zuñi, New Mexico. (Bunzel, 1929/30: 487; Parsons, 1939: 184–185)

Kona The name of the supreme power which is also the word for rain, and so he is associated with water and rivers. The Mount Hagen tribes of New Guinea. (Gitlow, 1947: 52)

Konupki-ot-guru River demons who dwell in the muddy waters near the banks of streams. The Ainu, Japan. (Batchelor, 1925, 1: 244)

Kottor-krabah A god of wells. Gold Coast, West Africa. (Ellis, 1887: 42)

Kou T'u Ti An aspect of T'u Ti as protector of drainage ditches. China. (Day, 1940: 67)

Krathis A river god. Greece. (Roscher, 1965, 2, 1: 1410)

Krimisos A river god personified as a bear or a dog. Sicily, Italy. (Roscher, 1965, 2, 1: 1430)

Kuamalíue The "source lake of the Rio Guamaka, gives too much water: 'Kuamalíue, the mother of the rivers, was wont to think up evil against the field crops.'" The Kagaba, Colombia. (Preuss, 1926: 84)

Kuihping A river god of China. (Du Bose, n.d.: 72)

Kul An evil water spirit who lives in deep waters. The Ziryen. He is also known among some Ostyak and Vogul. Finno-Ugrian. (Leach, 1950, 2: 594; Larousse, 1968: 307)

Kum-zer roong The deity of curative hot streams. The Lepchas, Sikkim. (Gorer, 1938: 223)

Kuni-no-Kuizamochi-no-Kami A goddess of watering. Japan. (Yasumaro, 1965: 15; Herbert, 1967: 265)

Kuni-no-Mikumari-no-Kami A goddess of irrigation, of water. Japan. (Yasumaro, 1965: 15; Herbert, 1967: 265)

Kupli A water goddess invoked in a fertility rite held in the month of June. The Khasi, Assam. (Bareh, 1967: 355)

Kura-Midzuha-no-Kami, Kuramitsuha-no-Kami "Dark-Water-Swift-Deity," a deity of running waters. Born of the blood of Kagu-tsuchi. Japan. (Yasumaro, 1965: 18, 19; Holtom, 1938: 102–3; Herbert, 1967: 271)

ya Ku-ung The "primeval water itself and is identical with *ya Lanig*." the Semang, Malaya. (Schebesta, 1957: 36)

Kweku Mbonyi A deity who dwells in the Muni Lagoon and is the spokesman for Penkye-Otu. The Effutu, Ghana. (Wyllie, 1966: 478)

Kwela A lake deity of the Fipa. Tanzania. (Willis, 1966: 31)

K'we-swa-sei A creek god at Ho-p'ing-chai. The Ch'iang, Szechwan, China. (Graham, 1958: 52)

Kw'e-we-bo A creek god at Ch'i-p'a-u. The Ch'iang, Szechwan, China. (Graham, 1958: 71)

Labento An evil spirit who lives in the waterhole. Marshall Islands, Micronesia. (Erdland, 1914: 313)

Lacubegus An aquatic god named on an altar found in Ujue, now in Pamplona. Spain. (Martinez, 1962: 176–177)

Ladon A river god, son of Oceanus and Tethys and father of Daphne. Also the father of Metope, Telphusa, and Themis by Stympalis. Greece. (Kerenyi, 1951: 140; Barthell, 1971: 43, 46; Larousse, 1968: 149; Hesiod-Brown, 1981: 63)

Lahe God of the spring Matahiva. Ha'afeva Island, Tonga. Polynesia. (Gifford, 1929: 307)

Lakai Akani The "spirit of the waters, the creeks, and rivers." The Barama River Caribs, British Guiana. (Gillin, 1936: 158)

dut Langshol The demon "of a lake or pond in the neighborhood of a bridge crossing the Tista." A soldier of kong chen. The Lepchas, Sikkim. (Siiger, 1967, 2: 144)

Laodice A "water nymph, mother of Niobe." Greece. (Prentice Hall, 1965: 80)

Lathon, Lethon A river god depicted with horns. Greece. (Roscher, 1965, 2, 2: 1903)

Latis "Goddess of the bog or pool." Celtic Britain. (Ross, 1967: 31)

Leewa A dangerous river spirit "who sucked the bather into pools and eddies, and sent forth devastating water spouts and hurricanes." Honduras. (Bancroft, 1886, 3: 497)

ka 'lei aitan Goddess of the river (apparently the same as Aitan). The Khasi, Assam. (Stegmiller, 1921: 410)

U lei umtong The god of water "used for drinking and cooking purposes" is propitiated annually to ensure its purity. The Khasis, Syntengs, Assam. (Gurdon, 1907: 106; 1914: 106; Stegmiller, 1921: 408)

Lemminkainen, Ahti The god of waters and the god of love whose female counterpart is Lemmetar. Finland and Estonia. (de Kay, 1898: 61–62, 114; Grimm, 1888, 4: 1361)

Lenju A stream goddess of the Khasi. Assam. (Bareh, 1967: 360)

Lepeh One of the grandmothers who lives under the earth and sometimes causes the waters to rise out of the earth, bringing floods. The Negritos, Malaya. (Evans, 1937: 142–143, 173; 1923: 148–149)

Lethaios A Greek river god. (Roscher, 1965, 2, 2: 1956)

Li-Au-en-pon-tan Goddess of the Palikalao river. Ponape, Caroline Islands, Micronesia. (Christian, 1899: 384)

Lilaia A Greek water nymph. (Roscher, 1965, 2, 2: 2048)

Limnaea A name of Artemis as a goddess of swamps and lakes. Greece. (Roscher, 1965, 2, 2: 2050; Murray, 1935: 123)

Limnades Dangerous "nymphs of lakes, marshes, and swamps" who lure travelers. Greece. (Murray, 1935: 171)

Limyros A river god of Lycia. Asia Minor. (Roscher, 1965, 2, 2: 2052)

Ling p'ai God of the river Nai. China. (Chavannes, n.d.: 101, 548)

Lin Ts'ên "The Spirit of Ponds." China. (Werner, 1932: 440)

Liting ud Naltang " 'Water of Naltang'—said to be the source of the Kababuyan River." The Ifugao, Philippines. (Barton, 1946: 46)

Lo Shen Goddess of the river Lo. China. (Ferguson, 1937: 34)

The Lu Water gods and nymphs who appear as snakes or in combinations with human bodies dwell "in the depths of the earth, in rivers, lakes, and marshes, but also up in the air." Western Tibet. (Ribbach, 1940: 42)

Luandinha A water goddess of the Amazon said to be a snake. Ita, Brazil. (Wagley, 1964: 228)

Lumagonong A male river spirit who lives below Sabangan and who possesses shamans. The Isneg, Luzon, Philippines. (Vanoverbergh, 1953: 82)

Lung Wang A dragon-king. There are deities of all waters, but Lung Wang is primarily a god of rain. China. (Day, 1940: 72–74; Shryock, 1931: 116; Werner, 1932: 286; Maspero, 1963: 276; Schram, 1957: 85)

Lupianae An aquatic god. Spain. (Martinez, 1962: 177)

Lusingi Garbo A lake demon near the Pemayangtse Monastery. The Lepchas, Sikkim. (Siiger, 1967: 142)

Luxovius God of the thermal springs at Luxeuil, Haute-Saone. Gaul. (Jayne, 1962: 520; Renel, 1906: 400; MacCulloch, 1911: 43)

Maching nu Sinwadu Guardian of fountains. The Katchins, Burma. (Gilhodes, 1908: 679)

Machin Tungku The mother of water, daughter of Phungkam Janun. The Katchins, Burma. (Gilhodes, 1908: 678)

Madeda A malevolent water god of the village of Dakala who claims sacrificial victims by drowning. The Bambara, Mali, Niger, and Senegal. (Tauxier, 1927: 142)

Maeander, Maiandros A river god in Phrygia. Son of Oceanus and Tethys. Asia Minor. (Roscher, 1965, 2, 2: 2241; Larousse, 1968: 149; Hesiod-Brown, 1981: 62)

Magdan-durunoon The "lord of hidden lakes." The Bisayan, Panay, Philippines. (Jocano, 1969: 20)

Ma Gonga God of water. The Santals, India. (Mukherjea, 1962: 210)

Mahisoba A water god who takes the form of a buffalo and demands propitiation. India. (Crooke, 1894: 25)

Malaki t'Olug Waig, Malaki t'olu k'Waig A male spirit associated with the element of water. An omnipotent and omniscient god, the "highest ideal of goodness and of purity" to whom occasional human sacrifice was made. The Bagobo, Philippines. (Benedict, 1916: 15, 20, 94; Raats, 1969: 85)

Malumbe A water deity of the Baila. South Africa. (Willoughby, 1932: 8)

Manasvin A dragon-king, a god of all waters. China. (Werner, 1932: 305, 285–6)

Manideakdili A woman who guards the river Capikundiual under the earth, in the Nele Sibu chronicle. The Cuna Indians, Panama. (Nordenskiold, 1938: 319)

Maniingili Female guardian of the river Marikundiual under the earth. The Nele Sibu chronicle. The Cuna, Panama. (Nordenskiold, 1938: 319)

Marghet A male evil spirit of the inland waters who causes people to disappear in the waters by drowning. The Wheelman tribe, Southwestern Australia. (Hassell-Davidson, 1936: 703)

Marsyas A river god in Phrygia. Asia Minor. (Larousse, 1968: 161; Bray, 1935: 95)

Matlalcueitl, Matlalcueye The goddess of the green skirt is a mountain goddess (Malinche) and a goddess of vegetation, of waters, and of rain. She is the second wife of Tlaloc. Mexico. (Reed, 1966: 131; Caso, 1958: 42; Duran, 1971: 257, 466; Mackenzie, 1924: 240)

Matrona Goddess of the river Marne. Gaul. (Mac-Cana, 1970: 33; Renel, 1906: 400; Bertrand, 1897: 195)

Maung Ingyi A water spirit who causes death by drowning. The Burmans and Talaings, Burma. (Temple, 1925, 3: 23)

Mayanja A minor river and lake divinity who sends water to the clouds, which Musoke returns as rain. The Ganda, Uganda. (Mbiti, 1970, 2: 138)

Mayarani A goddess associated with water. India. (Ghurye, 1962: 252)

Mbomb Ipoku The god of the lake from whom the grand chief draws his authority. Zaire. (Putman and Elisofon, 1973: 406)

Mearatsim A male water spirit "associated with the flute spirit Jakui." The Kamaiura, Xingu River, Brazil. (Villas Boas, 1973: 160, 260)

Mem Loimis Goddess of water and wife of Olelbis, mother of Wokwuk and Kut. The Wintu, California. (Curtin, 1903: 51, 52)

Meret A water goddess associated with Mut. Egypt. (Mercer, 1925, 12: 712)

Mesabai, Mesako A goddess associated with water. India. (Ghurye, 1962: 252)

Mesma A nymph of a mineral spring. Greece. (Roscher, 1965, 2, 2: 2842)

Messeis A nymph of a mineral spring in Thessaly. Greece. (Roscher, 1965, 2, 2: 2844)

Metope A water nymph, daughter of Ladon and Stymphalis, and wife of Asopus. Greece. (Barthell, 1971: 43, 46)

Metzabok, Mensabak God of fresh waters and of rain who is identified with the west, where the Tsinqu are his servants. The Lacandon, Mexico. (Cline, 1944: 112; Tozzer, 1941: 125)

Michininsi The god of waters to whom dogs are sacrificed. The Algonquin Indians, United States. (Wallis, 1939: 117)

Midzuha-no-Me-no-Kami A goddess of water. Japan. (Holtom, 1938: 104)

Midzu-no-Kami A god of water. Japan. (Holtom, 1938: 208)

Mi Fei The spirit of the river Lo, also named Queen Chên. China. (Werner, 1932: 439)

Mii-no-Kami "The god of wells." Japan. (Larousse, 1968: 416)

miji-gami A water deity of Okinawa. The Ryukyu Islands. (Lebra, 1966: 220)

Mimir Scandinavian guardian of the well at Gjallarhorn under Yggdrasill. This well represents the "source of wisdom . . . prehistoric facts, primeval truth, the knowledge that transcends human records and intelligence." (Stern, 1898: 11; Branston, 1955: 147, 150; Davidson, 1964: 166; Anderson, 1891: 229–230; Mac-Culloch, 1964: 167–168)

Minato-no-Kami God of the river mouths. Japan. (Herbert, 1967: 264)

Minti Dara Bunsu A water goddess who aids good divers but who can also be harmful, causing death by drowning. The Iban Dyaks of Sarawak, Borneo. (Sarawak Gazette, 1963: 135)

Mintuchi Kamui A water nymph invoked in the exorcism of troubles brought on by Pauchi Kamui. The Ainu, Japan. (Munro, 1963: 101–102)

Mirsu God of irrigation. Babylonia. Near East. (Langdon, 1931: 191)

Mishima-no-mizo-kui-hime The "goddess of the 'Water-channel-piles', sometimes called Tama-kushi-hime, a wife of Koto-shiro-nushi." Japan. (Herbert, 1967: 479)

Mitsuha-no-me-no-Kami A god of irrigation. Japan. (Yasumaro, 1965: 16, 17)

Mi-wi-no-kami The god of wells, also known as Ki-no-mata-no-kami. Japan. (Herbert, 1967: 327)

Mizuha-no-Me A goddess of water. Japan. (Kato, 1926: 140; Herbert, 1967: 268)

Mizu-maki-no-kami A deity of water sprinkling. Japan. (Herbert, 1967: 333)

Mizu-tsu-hime A goddess of water. Japan. (Herbert, 1967: 480)

Mo-hou-lo-chia A dragon-king, a deity of all waters generally. China. (Werner, 1932: 285–286, 319)

Molou God of waters. Togoland. (Verger, 1954: 17)

Mo-na-ssŭ A dragon-king, a deity of all waters. China. (Werner, 1932: 285–286, 319)

Mugasha God of the lake (Victoria), or water. The Zinza, the Haya, the Bahina, the Ziba. Uganda and Tanzania. (Taylor, 1962: 142, 147; Larousse, 1973: 523; Millroth, 1965: 109)

Mugizi God of Lake Albert to whom offerings are made before crossing by canoe. The Banyoro, Uganda. (Roscoe, 1915: 92)

Muialha God of the Jatate River. The Lacandon, Mexico. (Thompson, 1970: 324)

Muige The spirit of the Sezibwa river. South Africa. (Willoughby, 1932: 13)

Mukasa The benevolent and great deity of Victoria Nyanza, sometimes male, sometimes female. He/she could control the raging storms, give safe passage, provide abundance of fish and food, and care for the ills of mankind. The Baganda, Uganda. (Cunningham, 1905: 79, 215; Roscoe, 1965: 290–291, 300; Parrinder, 1967: 89; Willoughby, 1932: 56; Millroth, 1965: 108)

Mulgewanke A "water spirit . . . half man, half fish . . . " to whom is attributed the "booming sound which is heard frequently in Lake Alexandrina." The Narrinyeri, South Australia. (Woods, 1879: 62)

Muni Mental Batu A water goddess who aids good divers but who can also be harmful and cause death by drowning. The Iban Dyaks of Sarawak, Borneo. (Sarawak Gazette, 1963: 135)

Muru A river god. Ghana. (Field, 1948: 202)

Mygdonios A Greek river god. (Roscher, 1965, 2, 2: 3301)

Nabia A personified river. Spain. (Martinez, 1962: 178, 185)

Nabia Elaesurraega A personified river. Spain. (Martinez, 1962: 179, 185)

Naga A malevolent river spirit who afflicts with disease. The Malanau, Land Dyaks, Borneo. (Roth, 1968: 166; De Crespigny, 1875: 35)

Naga Era A water god of the Kols. India. (Crooke, 1894: 25)

Nage-bonga A beneficent river goddess. However, if she is offended she causes "conjunctivitis, and diseases of the ear." The Hos, India. (Majumdar, 1950: 252, 254, 257)

Nagera The water goddess who saved the boy and girl created by Singbonga and Chando from the fire sent to destroy them for their "sin" (copulation), and so mankind was saved. The Yernga Kol, India. (Elwin, 1949: 50)

Nagodya A goddess of the lake, daughter of Mukasa, to whom sacrifices were made at Tambiro. The Baganda, Uganda. (Cunningham, 1905: 218; Budge, 1973, 1: 377)

Nai-orun Kamui The goddess of springs and pools in valleys. The Ainu, Japan. (Munro, 1963: 20)

Nakawomba The spirit of the river Wajale. The Baganda, Uganda. (Roscoe, 1965: 318)

Nakk A water spirit who assumes various forms, usually human or animal, and may appear in either sex. When female, called Nakineiu. He lures people as his victims and "his appearance predicts drownings." Estonia. (Leach, 1950, 2: 780; Bray, 1935: 45–46)

Nakki The water spirit who "is represented as a man of unusual size. Sometimes he is half man and half animal, with horse feet." The female is Nakinneito, who is a beautiful woman with "big breasts which she can throw over her shoulders." Finland. (Leach, 1950, 2: 781; Larousse, 1968: 308; Bray, 1935: 45–46)

Nam A river god involved with "the phenomenon of possession and its treatment." The Lango, Uganda. (Driberg, 1923: 220)

Nana Buruku An ancient goddess of waters identified with St. Anne. Mother of Omolu Obaluaiye. Brazil. (Verger, 1957: 274)

Nanan A goddess of waters who lives at the bottom of rivers. The unattractive first wife of Oshala and mother of Omolu, Loko, and Oshunmare. Identified with St. Anna. Brazil. (Landes, 1940: 264)

Nan-t'o A dragon-king, a god of waters. China. (Werner, 1932: 285–286, 326)

Narmada A river goddess of Northern India. (Crooke, 1894: 39; Putman, 1971: 449)

Naru A Babylonian river god. Near East. (Roberts, 1972: 46; Mercer, 1925, 12: 710)

Nas chu spyi 'om klung gi bdag A river god who may cause illness. Tibet. (Nebesky-Wojkowitz, 1965, 1: 305)

Navia A Gallacian aquatic goddess. Spain. (Martinez, 1962: 179; Roscher, 1965, 3, 1: 42)

Navia Arconunieca A water goddess. Spain. (Martinez, 1962: 180)

Ndaduma "Father Niger," a river god. The Nupe, Nigeria. (Nadel, 1954: 27)

Ndjambi Karunga *See* **Karunga**

Nechtan A water god whose wife is Boand (Boann). Another name of Nuadu. Ireland. (O'Rahilly, 1946: 320, 516; Sjoestedt, 1949: 41; MacCana, 1970: 33)

Neis A Greek water nymph. (Roscher, 1965, 3, 1: 103)

Nekke A water spirit who foretold misfortune. The Lapps. Northern Europe. (Holmberg, 1925, 7: 798)

Nemausos A spring/fountain deity at Nimes. Gaul. (Ferguson, 1970: 69; Renel, 1906: 401; MacCulloch, 1911: 40)

Nerius God of a hot springs at Néris-les-Bains. Gaul. (Roscher, 1965, 3, 1: 273; Renel, 1906: 402)

Nessus A river god, son of Oceanus and Tethys. Greece. (Hesiod-Brown, 1981: 63)

Nestos A river god in Thrace, father of Kallirrhoe. Greece. (Roscher, 1965, 3, 1: 298)

Netapu A spirit of the source of the river Awan at Aniwara. The Isneg, Luzon, Philippines. (Vanoverbergh, 1953: 84)

Netekwo A stream god who guides the priest in counteracting witchcraft. The Nzema, Ghana. (Grottanelli, 1969: 392, 397)

Netlang The water god who is invoked when "setting out on a journey." He brings disease; is the husband of Loa. The Iraku, Tanzania. (Millroth, 1965: 23)

Ngassa The god of Lake Victoria sends storms and is sacrificed to by sailors. He is beneficent as the god of fishes, providing fishermen with a good catch. Tanzania. (Millroth, 1965: 109–110)

dNgul chu'i dge bsnyen rdo rje dpal A river god who may cause illness. Tibet. (Nebesky-Wojkowitz, 1956, 1: 305)

Ngurvilu A god of rivers and lakes. The Araucanians, Chile. (Larousse, 1968: 445)

Ngwilo God of the falls of the river Msadya. The Pimbwe, Tanzania. (Willis, 1966: 60)

ka niangriang A water deity said to cause "disease of the navel of a child." The Khasis, Assam. (Gurdon, 1914: 124)

Nina Originally a water goddess, a daughter of Ea, she was as well a goddess of destinies and of war. As Gestinanna she was a fish goddess. Babylonia, Near East. (Jastrow, 1898: 86–87; Mercer, 1925, 12: 709; Pinches, 1925, 12: 44)

Nin-akha-kuddu A water goddess and a goddess of purification associated with Ea. Also known as Ninkarrak and Gula. Babylonia, Near East. (Mercer, 1925, 12: 710)

Ningirsu   The "tamer of the raging waters" and a god of irrigation, a patron of the city of Lagash, and also a god of war. Son of Enlil. Babylonia. Near East. (Campbell, 1964: 117–119; Larousse, 1968: 60)

Ninhabursildu   A Babylonian fountain goddess. Near East. (Mercer, 1925, 12: 710)

Nitat-unarabe   An evil goddess of swamps, of fens and marshes, and mother of many demons. The Ainu, Japan. (Batchelor, 1925, 1: 243)

Njalagobe   The spirit of Lake Victoria. The Bantu Kavirondo, Kenya. (Millroth, 1965: 108)

Nodinus   An Italian river god. (Roscher, 1965, 3, 1: 446)

Nodəmhkenoweth   "Grabbing-from-beneath-the-water, is a creature of the pools, half fish and half human." The Penobscot, Maine. (Speck, 1935, 1: 13)

Nommo   The spirit of the pools. Mali and Upper Volta. (Paulme, 1940: 344)

Nonissus   God of the springs of l'Armancon (Essey). Gaul. (Renel, 1906: 402)

No-we   The "god of the lagoon Denham Waters, particularly hostile to criminals." Dahomey. (Mockler-Ferryman, 1925, 9: 279)

nrop-lik   "Man-of-the-Water," who provided an abundance of fish to those with whom he was pleased. The Toba and Pilagá, Argentina. (Métraux, 1969: 50)

Nu, Fu, Nufu   A river god considered by some to be the ancestor of the people to whom he gave cattle. The Fulani, Nigeria. (Webster, 1931: 238)

Nuadu   God of the river Boyne where the "Salmon of Wisdom" was to be found. Ireland. (O'Rahilly, 1946: 320)

Nuaneneumañ   The lake source of the river Nuameiži of the Kagaba at San Miguel. Daughter of Maneneumañ and Mukulyinmakú Seižankua. Colombia. (Preuss, 1926: 68)

Nudimmud   A name of Ea/Enki, the god of waters and of wisdom, as representing the earth, and as a creator god. Babylonia and Sumer. Near East. (Jacobsen, 1946: 185; 1970: 22)

Nü Kua, Nü Wu   A powerful goddess frequently depicted as half-woman, half-serpent, with a scaly tail. She is associated with ponds and rain pools, and the moist slippery animals found nearby. China. (Schafer, 1980: 37–41)

Nummo   Twin celestial spirits who were the personification of all waters, and were celestial blacksmiths as well. The Dogon, Mali and Upper Volta. (Parrinder, 1967: 23, 27)

Nunkályisaka   A mother of the lake. The Cagaba, the Kogi, Colombia. (Reichel-Dolmatoff, 1949/50: 114)

Nupki-ot-guru and **Nupki-ot-mat**   A river demon and his wife who live near the river's edge and make the waters muddy and "tear down the banks." The Ainu, Japan. (Batchelor, n.d.: 389)

Nyaliep   A goddess associated with streams, a daughter of Buk. The Nuer, Sudan. (Evans-Pritchard, 1956: 31)

Nyalwe   A river spirit to whom animal sacrifices are offered near the end of initiation ceremonies for boys. The Kono, Sierra Leone. (Parsons, 1950: 271)

Nyani'tiu   A malevolent river or water spirit. The Sakai, Malay Peninsula. (Skeat, 1906: 247)

Nycheia   A nymph of a river source of Taphos. Daughter of Oceanus and Tethys. Greece. (Roscher, 1965, 3, 1: 491)

Nyukua·dn   "The great snake . . . lord of the water," who causes rains and floods. The Botocudo, Brazil. (Nimuendaju, 1946, 2: 111)

Oa-he-vari   A god of boggy grounds. Tahiti, Polynesia. (Henry, 1928: 376)

Oba   Yoruban goddess of the river Oba who in Africa is "the protectress of prostitutes," but not in the Americas. A wife of Shango. Nigeria, Brazil, and Puerto Rico. (Verger, 1957: 413; Gonzalez-Wippler, 1975: 25, 105; Bastide, 1960: 290, 569; Lucas, 1948: 98)

Obrimas   A river god of Phrygia. Asia Minor. (Roscher, 1965, 3, 1: 595)

Oceanus, Okeanos   The great stream which encircled Gaea and was the source of all waters, the father of the water deities by his sister/wife Tethys. The eldest of the Titans, son of Uranus and Gaea. Greece. (Kerenyi, 1951: 15, 21, 160; Barthell, 1971: 12, 13, 41; Murray, 1935: 161; Larousse, 1968: 88, 146; Hesiod-Brown, 1981: 56, 57, 62, 63)

Oeroe Goddess of the river of the same name. Daughter of Asopos. Greece. (Roscher, 1965, 3, 1: 682)

Ogbame A lagoon god among the Gã in Labadi. Among others a war god. Ghana. (Field, 1937: 13, 65, 57)

O-hsiu-lo A dragon-king, a deity of all waters generally. China. (Werner, 1932: 285–286, 336)

Oiara A water deity of the Amazonian Tupi. Brazil. (Spence, 1925, 2: 838)

Oibon-eciye The owner/father of the Oibon (Omulevka) river. The Yukaghir, Siberia. (Jochelson, 1900/02: 145)

Ojid-emei "Water-mother" invoked for safe passage at the spring breakup of the Yassachnaya river. The Yukaghir, Siberia. (Jochelson, 1900/02: 217)

Ojin-pogil The "Owner of the fresh Waters" and overall the lesser pogil of the waters. The Yukaghir, Siberia. (Jochelson, 1900/02: 144–145)

Oknama A spirit of the river mouths who is protective of men. Costa Rica. (Stone, 1962: 61)

oko: yumo A water spirit dangerous to young girls, who "causes illness or even death." The Maroni River Caribs, Surinam. (Kloos, 1969: 901)

Okwa naholo The spirits of "deep pools in rivers and bayous." The Choctaw, Louisiana. (Bushnell, 1909: 31)

Okyrhoë, Ocyrhoë, Okyrrhoë Daughter of Oceanus and Tethys. She is associated with "mobility . . . [of] water, wind and wave." Greece. (Kerenyi, 1951: 41; Roscher, 1965, 3, 1: 828)

Olodeakdili Female guardian of the river Siakundiual under the earth, in the Nele Sibu chronicle. The Cuna Indians, Panama. (Nordenskiold, 1938: 319)

Oloingili Female guardian of the river Kaikundiual under the earth, in the Nele Sibu chronicle. The Cuna, Panama. (Nordenskiold, 1938: 319)

Olokikadiryae A goddess of the fourth layer of the underworld, a wife of Oloueliptol. They are guardians of the river Kulikundiual where they await the arrival of the dead, in the Nele Sibu chronicle. The Cuna, Panama. (Nordenskiold, 1938: 297)

Olosa A beneficent lagoon goddess who is the wife/sister of Olokun. The Yoruba, Nigeria. (Lucas, 1948: 98, 167; Parrinder, 1949: 45; Wyndham, 1921: 22)

Oloueliptol Guardian of the river Kulikundiual in the fourth layer of the underworld. His wives are Punauagaui-sogdili and Olokikadiryae. The Nele Sibu chronicle. The Cuna, Panama. (Nordenskiold, 1938: 297)

O(o)luksak God of the lakes through whom shamans work. The Eskimo. Canada. (Bilby, 1923: 265; Larousse, 1968: 426)

Ombwiri A "genie of water courses or the sea, associated with the search for fortune." The Fang, Gabon. (Fernandez, 1972: 241)

O-mizu-nu-no-kami "Great Water-master Kami," whose wife is Fute-mimi-no-kami. Japan. (Herbert, 1967: 317)

Ompombinanga God of the mouth of the river. The Toradja, Celebes, Indonesia. (Adriani and Kruyt, 1950: 282)

O-na-p'o-ta-to A dragon-king, a deity of "seas, rivers, lakes, and waters generally." China. (Werner, 1932: 285–286, 338)

Onmun-emei The owner/mother of the Kolyma river, subject to Ojin-pogil. The Yukaghir, Siberia. (Jochelson, 1900/02: 145)

Oraendos A river god of Pisidia. Asia Minor. (Roscher, 1965, 3, 1: 938)

Orang Bunyan A spirit of the swamp. The Jakun, Malay Peninsula. (Skeat, 1906: 182)

Orehu The "Water Mother . . . versed in herbal medicine." The Arawaks, West Indies. (Lovén, 1935: 569)

Orontes A river god. Phoenicia. Near East. (Cook, 1930: 191)

Oshun Goddess of the river Oshun and wife or mistress of Shango. The Yoruba, Nigeria. Known also in Brazil, Cuba, and Trinidad. (Wyndham, 1921: 10, 60; Parrinder, 1961: 45; Wescott, 1962: 343; Verger, 1957: 411; 1954: 15; Bastide, 1960: 570; Gonzalez-Wippler, 1975: 25–26, 115)

Otaminni A river god whose wives are Ogori, Ocham, and Wujere. Nigeria. (Talbot, 1967: 12, 24)

ötkel los The water god, "stingy and covetous," who will rob or is punitive if offerings are not adequate, refusing fish, sending diseases, or causing drownings. The Selkup (Samoyed), Siberia. (Donner, 1926: 51, 70)

Otskahakakaitshoidiaa A goddess of waters and of its creatures, who has cleansing and healing powers. The Wichita, Kansas. (Dorsey, 1904, 1: 19)

Outego-Lous God of waters. The Ostyaks, Siberia. (Bertrand, 1897: 87)

Ovia A river goddess and a wife of Shango. Benin, Nigeria. (Parrinder, 1949: 45)

Owu Akpana A water god who took the form of a shark and devoured people. The Kalabari, Nigeria. (Horton, 1960: 16)

Owuampu A water spirit of the Agberi. Nigeria. (LACMA, n.d.: 73)

Oya Goddess of the Niger River and a wife of Shango. She is fierce and bearded, yet comely, and is associated with storms. The Yoruba, Nigeria. She is known also in Cuba, Puerto Rico, Trinidad (where she is identified with St. Catherine or St. Philomena), and Brazil. (Parrinder, 1949: 32–33; Lucas, 1948: 98; Idowu, 1962: 91; Simpson, 1965: 19, 21; Gonzalez-Wippler, 1975: 25, 115; Verger, 1957: 230; 1954: 12, 15; Meyerowitz, 1946: 26n)

Paakniwat The owner of the springs and watering places from whom permission must be requested for their use. He sometimes sponsors a *puvalam* (shaman). The Cahuilla, California. (Brumgardt and Bowles, 1981: 37; Bean, 1974: 167)

Pae Devi, Pa Janjali The goddess of all waters, both salt and fresh, and of all fish and water animals. The Bhils, India. (Naik, 1956: 181, 187)

Pai A water demon of the Shipaya. Brazil. (Nimuendaju, 1948, 1: 241)

Pa Janjali *See* **Pae Devi**

Palpukawil A water demon sometimes appearing as a waterspout, "and was associated with thunderclouds." The Cahuilla, California. (Bean, 1974: 167)

Pamisos God of the river of the same name. Greece. (Roscher, 1965, 3, 1: 1345)

Pa-nan-t'o A dragon-king, a deity of all waters. China. (Werner, 1932: 285–286, 352)

Panchagara A river deity. Haiti, West Indies. (Courlander, 1966: 10)

Pangi The "great anaconda River God, dwells a captive in the Pongo Manseriche, the great cataract of the Marañon." There is a taboo of silence in traveling through the gorge. The Jivaro, Ecuador. (Stirling, 1938: 116)

Panjer-roong With **Pantsong-roong,** deities of the Rungit River. The Lepchas, Sikkim. (Gorer, 1938: 223)

Pantsong-roong *See above*

Pan-utka Guru A deity of the rapids in streams. The Ainu, Japan. (Munro, 1963: 20)

Pape-hau "Cool-water," a god associated with Ta'aroa. Society Islands, Polynesia. (Henry, 1928: 581)

Pape-rurua "Sheltered-water," a god associated with Ta'aroa. Society Islands, Polynesia. (Henry, 1928: 581)

Para-whenua-mea The mother of waters, daughter of Tane and Hine-tu-pari-maunga, and first wife of Kiwa. The Maori, New Zealand. (Best, 1924: 114, 154)

Parthenios, Parthenius A river god, son of Oceanus and Tethys. Greece. (Roscher, 1965, 3, 1: 1650; Hesiod-Brown, 1981: 63)

Parusni A river deity. India. (Macdonell, 1897: 86)

Patrimpas, Potrympas A Slavic and Baltic "god of rivers and springs." (Gimbutas, 1963: 197; Puhvel, 1974: 83; Machal, 1918: Pl.xxxvii)

Pegai A river god near Damascus. Syria. (Smith, 1969: 171)

Pelib A water god. Mirebalais, Haiti, West Indies. (Herskovits, 1937, 1: 158)

Peneois, Peneios, Peneus, Peneius A river god of Thessaly, son of Oceanus and Tethys, and father of Daphne. Greece. (Kerenyi, 1951: 140; Bulfinch, 1898: 30–32; Roscher, 1965, 3, 2: 1898; Hesiod-Brown, 1981: 63)

Penyadin "A water demon, with the head of a dog and the mouth of a crocodile. It sucks blood from the thumbs and big toes of human beings, thus causing death." The Mantra, Malay Peninsula. (Skeat, 1906: 323)

Permessos God of the river of that name. Greece. (Roscher, 1965, 3, 2: 1980)

Pet-etok-mat Goddesses of the sources of rivers, worshipped to maintain the flow. The Ainu, Japan. (Batchelor, n.d.: 388)

Pet-ru-ush-mat Goddesses of the rivers who watch over the entire course, and to whom offerings are made for protection on the rapids and for good fishing. The Ainu, Japan. (Batchelor, n.d.: 389; Czaplicka, 1969: 274)

Phasis A river god in Colchis. Son of Oceanus and Tethys. Near East. (Roscher, 1965, 3, 2: 2287; Hesiod-Brown, 1981: 62)

Pidasos A river god in Lydia. Asia Minor. (Roscher, 1965, 3, 2: 2496)

pi-hsi A "god of the rivers, to whom enormous strength is attributed." Depicted as a tortoise. China. (Williams, 1976: 405)

Pijju-Bibenj A god of water "providing both rain from the sky and water from a spring." Orissa, India. (Elwin, 1954: 640)

P'i-lou-po-ch'a A dragon-king, a deity of all waters. China. (Werner, 1932: 285–286, 275)

P'ing Chiang Ta Shên God of the Peaceful River worshipped to avoid inundation. China. (Day, 1940: 42)

Pingee A river god. China. (Du Bose, n.d.: 72)

Pir Bhadr A water godling worshipped by fishermen and boatmen. India. (Crooke, 1925, 5: 3)

Pirene A fountain nymph at Corinth. Greece. (Larousse, 1968: 150)

Pleistos A river god near Delphi. Greece. (Roscher, 1965, 3, 2: 2563)

Plexaure A water nymph—"like a dashing brook"—daughter of Oceanus and Tethys. Greece. (Murray, 1895: 188; Kerenyi, 1951: 41)

Porpax A river god in Sicily. Italy. (Roscher, 1965, 3, 2: 2778)

Potamia Artemis as a river goddess. Greece. (Murray, 1935: 123)

Potamos A river god, the Thymbris. Greece. (Roscher, 1965, 3, 2: 2900)

Pra(h) A river god considered malignant because of drownings. Sometimes a goddess. Ghana. (Ellis, 1887: 64–66; Field, 1948: 152)

Premnosia A Greek spring or fountain nymph. (Roscher, 1965, 3, 2: 2935)

Prymno A water nymph—"like a cascade"—daughter of Oceanus and Tethys. Greece. (Murray, 1895: 188; Roscher, 1965, 3, 2: 3192)

Pujio A water demon who keeps the soul of a man and causes illness. Bolivia and Argentina. (Chamberlain, 1925, 4: 740)

P'u-kao-yun-ch'uang A dragon-king, a deity of waters generally. China. (Werner, 1932: 285–286, 385)

Punauaga Oloeaydili A female guardian of a river in the realm of the dead. The Cuna Indians, Panama. (Nordenskiold, 1938: 331)

Punauaga Oloesgidili Female guardian of the river Osikundiual under the earth. The Nele Sibu chronicle. The Cuna, Panama. (Nordenskiold, 1938: 319)

Punauaga Oloniskidilisop Female guardian of the Cacao River in the realm of the dead. The Cuna Indians, Panama. (Nordenskiold, 1938: 331)

Punauaga Olouagaidili Female guardian of the river Kuilubkundiual under the earth. The Nele Sibu chronicle. The Cuna, Panama. (Nordenskiold, 1938: 319)

Punauaga Uisogdili Goddess of the fourth layer of the underworld and one of the wives of Oloueliptol. They are guardians of the river Kulikundiual and await the arrival of the dead. The Nele Sibu chronicle. The Cuna, Panama. (Nordenskiold, 1938: 297)

Punua-moe-vai The water god who is worshipped to prevent heavy rains. Society Islands, Polynesia. (Henry, 1928: 161)

P'u-yün-ta-shêng A dragon-king, a deity "of seas, rivers, lakes, and waters generally." China. (Werner, 1932: 285–286, 388)

Pydes God of the river of the same name in Pisidia. Asia Minor. (Roscher, 1965, 3, 2: 3283)

The P'yo These are "demons, usually in the form of dragons or serpents, that blow the water up from the ocean and produce the clouds" for rain. "They preside over the deep pools of streams." The Karen, Burma. (Marshall, 1922: 231)

Qebh A name of Khnemu as the early god of the Nile. A ram-headed god. Egypt. (Budge, 1969, 2: 50)

q'otawic'a Grandmother of the Lake (Titicaca) who is associated with the rain, and who owns the fish, according to some people. The Aymara, Bolivia. (Tschopik, 1951: 197, 200)

U Qux Cho The spirit of the lake. The Quiché, Guatemala. (Recinos, 1950: 78)

Rakembaranu A water nymph, ancestress of the Sihanaki family. The Bara, Madagascar. (Lessa, 1961: 156)

Ramasondi A water god of India. (Crooke, 1925, 12: 717)

Rav-ava A water goddess, "mother Volga." The Mordvins, Russia. (Paasonen, 1925, 8: 845)

Ravgga A water spirit who foretold misfortune. The Lapps. Northern Europe. (Holmberg, 1925, 7: 798)

Reva An aquatic goddess, the "personification of running waters." Spain. (Martinez, 1962: 184–185)

Revelanganidaegus An aquatic deity named on an altar found in Idanha. Spain. (Martinez, 1962: 185–186)

Revelanganitaecus An aquatic deity named on an altar in Porenca. Spain. (Martinez, 1962: 186–187)

Rhenus The deified Rhine. Gaul. (Renel, 1906: 403; Roscher, 1965, 4: 99)

Rhesus A river god, son of Oceanus and Tehys. Greece. (Hesiod-Brown, 1981: 63)

Rhodanos A river god of Gaul. (Roscher, 1965, 4: 112)

Rhodeia, Rhodea A water nymph, daughter of Oceanus and Tethys. Greece. (Murray, 1895: 188; Kerenyi, 1951: 41; Hesiod-Brown, 1981: 63; Roscher, 1965, 4: 113)

Rhodios, Rhodius God of the river of the same name in Troas. Asia Minor. Son of Oceanus and Tethys. (Roscher, 1965, 4: 113; Hesiod-Brown, 1981: 63)

Rhodope A fountain nymph of Thrace. Daughter of Oceanus and Tethys. Greece. (Roscher, 1965, 4: 115; Prentice Hall, 1965: 129)

Rhyndakos A god of a river of the same name. Asia Minor. (Roscher, 1965, 4: 126)

Ru-esan-koro Guru A river deity of the "lower reaches." The Ainu, Japan. (Munro, 1963: 20)

Runkta A god of "the stream where people went to bathe." The Bondo, India. (Elwin, 1950: 151)

The Rusalka Female water spirits who are beautiful, but dangerous to those who join them in the water. They are associated with spinning and weaving and "are fond of . . . washing linens," which in some places must be supplied them. They are potentially beneficent but to a greater extent dangerous. Russia. (Ralston, 1872: 139–141)

Sabrina Goddess of the river Severn. Britain. (Ross, 1967: 21; MacCulloch, 1911: 43)

Sa-buru A dangerous demon huntsman who "dwells in lakes and river-pools" and causes his dogs to pursue and attack men. The Mantra, Malay Peninsula. (Skeat, 1906: 323)

Sagara A dragon-king, a deity of all waters. China. (Werner, 1932: 285–286, 397)

Sagras God of the river of the same name in Kaulonia. Italy. (Roscher, 1965, 4: 275)

Sahim A demon of a pond in the Tingbung area. The Lepchas, Sikkim. (Siiger, 1967: 144)

sak-somo-ayep A dragon god. They live "in lakes or swamps" and emit "a terrible stench." They are occasionally "companion spirits of shamanesses." The Ainu, Hokkaido, Japan. (Philippi, 1982: 154)

Sakumo The god of the great Sakumo lagoon, who is their most important deity, is associated with the corn planting. The Gã in Accra and in Temma. Ghana. (Field, 1937: 10, 21, 86–87, 89)

Saku-wi-no-kami The god of household waters, "of the blessing well." Japan. (Herbert, 1967: 497)

Salama A river god of Spain. (Martinez, 1962: 188–189)

Salmacis A water nymph whom the gods united bodily with Hermaphroditus, creating a bisexual being. Greece. (Larousse, 1968: 149; Prentice Hall, 1965: 67, 130; Roscher, 1965, 4: 290)

Sangarios, Sangarius God of the river of the same name. Son of Oceanus and Tethys. His wife is Evagora. Asia Minor. (Kerenyi, 1951: 89; Barthell, 1971: 48; Roscher, 1965, 4: 334; Hesiod-Brown, 1981: 63)

Sao Kang The god of a lake in the center of the city to whom four virgins were married (no longer done) at a festival about the beginning of the rain, though they returned home later. Kengtung, Siam. (Scott, 1964: 334–335)

Sarak Kamui An evil river goddess who is the cause of "all river accidents." The Ainu, Japan. (Batchelor, 1894: 20; Czaplicka, 1969: 274)

Sarasvati The great river goddess of the river of that name who purifies and cleanses, a goddess of fertile waters who bestows wealth, vitality, and offspring. It is only later that she became the goddess of eloquence and wisdom and the wife of Brahma. India and Bali. (Getty, 1962: 127; Larousse, 1968: 345; Hooykaas, 1964: 21–23; Banerjea, 1953: 10; Ions, 1967: 81, 89; Dowson, 1961: 284; Jayne, 1962: 173)

Sarkin Rafi A river god who causes " 'cold' through dampness" and to whom a "black cock with white patches" is sacrificed. The Maguzawa, Nigeria. (Greenberg, 1946: 3)

Sarnus God of the river of the same name in Campania, Italy. (Roscher, 1965, 4: 387)

Satet Goddess of the inundation and of fertility. She is associated with the current of the Nile river and is a guardian of the Cataracts. Egypt and Sudan. (Knight, 1915: 108; Budge, 1969, 2: 50, 55; Ames, 1965: 108)

Satnioeis A river god. Greece. (Roscher, 1965, 4: 422)

Savus The god of a river in Noricum. Austria. (Roscher, 1965, 4: 533)

Sayin "Master-of-the-Water." The Toba and the Pilagá, Argentina. (Métraux, 1969: 50)

Scamander The god of a river near Troy, whose wife is Idaea. Son of Oceanus and Tethys. Asia Minor. (Barthell, 1971: 48; Prentice Hall, 1965: 131; Hesiod-Brown, 1981: 63)

Sebeithos, Sebethos God of the river of the same name, near Naples. Italy. (Roscher, 1965, 4: 579)

Sedaw Thakmina The guardian goddess of the irrigation waters at Sedaw and the surrounding lands. The Yeigyi, Burma. (Spiro, 1967: 105–106)

Segeta A goddess of healing springs. Loire, Gaul. (Jayne, 1962: 520; Renel, 1906: 404; Roscher, 1965, 4: 599)

Segomanna Possibly a goddess of springs. Gaul. (Roscher, 1965, 4: 599)

Selu A malicious water spirit who causes stomachaches and other ills. The Dafla, Assam. (Stonor, 1957: 6)

Sequana Goddess of the river Seine who practiced healing at its source. Gaul. (Ross, 1967: 339; Jayne, 1962: 520; Renel, 1906: 404; MacCulloch, 1911: 43)

Seragendi God of the waters of Hawkbell Island who was invoked in the ceremony for children to make them strong, skillful, successful, brave, and to give them longevity. The Iban Dyaks of Sarawak, Borneo. (Roth, 1968: 170; Sarawak Gazette, 1963: 133)

gSer chu 'bri klung dge bsnyen A river god who may cause illness. Tibet. (Nebesky-Wojkowitz, 1956, 1: 305)

Sewakaao A deity of the Lake Tanganyika shore. The Fipa, Tanzania. (Willis, 1966: 31)

Shên Lung A dragon deity who controls the waters, both in their beneficent and destructive forms. China. (Werner, 1932: 285–286, 419)

Shivaldungáya A mother of the lake. The Cagaba, the Kogi. Colombia. (Reichel-Dolmatoff, 1949/50: 114)

Shui Chün A "ruler of water . . . who rides on a horse in the water and has a human form." China. (Ferguson, 1937: 73)

Shui I A god of waters. China. (Ferguson, 1937: 90)

Shui-kuan The god and controller of waters. China. (Day, 1940: 137; Graham, 1958: 52; Maspero, 1963: 342; Werner, 1932: 446)

Shui-mu Niang-niang The goddess of waters who caused inundations. China. (Werner, 1932: 444; Schram, 1957: 85)

Shui-p'ing Wang The "God of Tranquil Waters," is also the god of Lake T'ai. China. (Werner, 1932: 440)

Shui Shên The god of waters. China. (Ferguson, 1937: 90; Day, 1940: 72)

Shui Tê Hsing Chün The "star god of water," who is invoked for rain and for relief from floods. China. (Day, 1940: 72)

Siannus A deified thermal spring, a god assimilated to Apollo. Mont-Dore, Puy-de-Dome, Gaul. (Renel, 1906: 404; MacCulloch, 1911: 26; Bertrand, 1897: 147)

Siao A river deity of China. (Chavannes, n.d.: 90)

Siburu A spirit of the swamp. The Sakai and the Jakun, Malay Peninsula. (Skeat, 1906: 182)

Siguanaba A dual-sexed deity, though usually a woman. She is guardian of streams and of fish and attacks fishermen, so they usually go in groups. She seduces men and terrifies them by her transformation, causing insanity. The Chorti, Guatemala. (Wisdom, 1940: 407)

Silenus In Lydia, Asia Minor, he is described as a spirit "of fertilizing fountains, streams, marshy land, and luxuriant gardens, as well as the inventor of such music as was produced by the syrinx (Pan's pipe) and the double flute." In Greece he was a satyr of great wisdom and the tutor of Dionysus, and was a great lover of wine. (Murray, 1935: 158–159; Larousse, 1968: 161, 168; Prentice Hall, 1965: 133)

Silonsaclus A water deity of Spain. (Martinez, 1962: 189)

Simbi The god of sweet waters, patron of ferrymen, and also a god of healing and of magicians. His wife is Maman Simbi. Haiti, West Indies. (Deren, 1953: 70, 117; Marcelin, 1950: 13, 16)

Maman Simbi Goddess of springs and wife of Papa Simbi. Haiti, West Indies. (Marcelin, 1950: 15)

Simois, Simoeis A river god, near Troy in Mysia. Asia Minor. Son of Oceanus and Tethys. (Barthell, 1971: 49; Roscher, 1965, 4: 879; Hesiod-Brown, 1981: 63)

Sinann, Sinnan Goddess of the river Shannon. Ireland. (Ross, 1967: 21; MacCulloch, 1911: 43)

Sindhu Goddess of the river Indus. India. (Macdonnell, 1952: 25; Putman, 1971: 449)

Singraj Goddess of the spring and the falls. The Bondo, India. (Elwin, 1950: 151)

La Sirène Goddess of the sea and of sweet waters and wife of Agwe. She is identified with Notre Dame de Grace. Haiti, West Indies. (Marcelin, 1950: 119; Deren, 1953: 120; Herskovits, 1937, 1: 279)

Sirona A deified fountain in Gironde, and a goddess associated with Grannus. Gaul. (Renel, 1906: 404; MacCana, 1970: 32; Bertrand, 1897: 195; MacCulloch, 1925, 3: 280)

Sitalamma A water goddess of Southern India. (Whitehead, 1916: 22)

Smardos A youthful river god found on coins of Phokaia. Greece. (Roscher, 1965, 4: 1081)

So-chia-lo A dragon-king, a deity of all waters generally. China. (Werner, 1932: 285–286, 449)

So-chieh-lo A dragon-king, a deity of all waters generally. China. (Werner, 1932: 285–286, 449)

Soio A deified spring in Ardèche. Gaul. (Renel, 1906: 404)

Sompallwe A god of the water, a lake spirit, invoked for good fishing. The Araucanians, Chile. (Zerries, 1968: 264)

Sooga Pennu A god of fountains. The Kandh, Bengal. (Crooke, 1925, 7: 649)

Souconna Celtic goddess of the Saône. Gaul. (MacCana, 1970: 50)

Maît' Source The "Master of the Stream." Mirebalais, Haiti, West Indies. (Herskovits, 1937, 1: 161)

Spercheius, Spercheios God of the river of the same name. Thessaly, Greece. (Roscher, 1965, 4: 1292; Barthell, 1971: 49)

Strymon A river god of Macedonia. Son of Oceanus and Tethys and father of Evadne by Neaera, and of Rhesus by Euterpe. Greece. (Barthell, 1971: 49; Hesiod-Brown, 1981: 62)

sug tayykh The water, to whom prayers were addressed. The Kachin, Siberia. (Potapov, 1964: 357)

Sul, Sulla, Sulis Goddess of the hot springs at Bath. Britain. A goddess of healing in Gaul. Equated with Minerva. (Ross, 1967: 175, 190; MacCana, 1970: 34; Jayne, 1962: 519; MacCulloch, 1911: 41, 125)

Suláliue Goddess of the "lake of song or of prophecy . . . the source lake of the Rio Palomino." Daughter of Maneneumañ and Mukulyinmakú Seizankua. The Kagaba at San Miguel, Colombia. (Preuss, 1926: 68)

Sumalongson The "god of the rivers and seas." The Sulod, Central Panay, Philippines. (Jocano, 1969: 19)

Sumba Some call him the spirit of the Lake (Victoria) and some put him "in charge of the lake fish." The Bantu Kavirondo, Kenya. (Millroth, 1965: 108)

gSum brag ma An evil lake goddess who causes dysentery. Tibet. (Nebesky-Wojkowitz, 1956, 1: 307)

Sungei A river spirit of the Jakun and the Besisi who "haunts the sources of the rivers." Malay Peninsula. Among the Berembun tribes they are plural and evil, "inflicting diseases, and feeding on the human soul." (Skeat, 1906: 182, 303, 359)

Sungui The spirit of water and of water life whose domain is of "a multi-colored but predominantly red spectrum." The Canelos Quichua, Ecuador. (Whitten, 1978: 95, 97)

Suqamuna A deity of the Elamites "explained by the Babylonians as 'Merdoch of water-channels'." Near East. (Pinches, 1925, 5: 251)

Sutudri A river goddess of India. (Macdonell, 1897: 86)

Symaithos A river god of Sicily. Italy. (Roscher, 1965, 4: 1626)

Szullinnis, Szullinnus A god of wells. Lithuania. (Schrader, 1925, 2: 32; Welsford, 1925, 9: 241)

Tagitsu-hime A river goddess of Japan, and also a goddess of seafaring. (Herbert, 1967: 479; Yasumaro, 1965: 27)

Tagma-sa-uba The "lord of the rivers." The Subanun of Zamboanga, Philippines. (Jocano, 1969: 24)

Tajuk A snake, guardian and controller of underground waters, who causes floods. The Negritos (Lanoh), Malaya. (Evans, 1937: 174)

Taki-Tsu-Hiko A waterfall or cataract god. Japan. (Herbert, 1967: 480; Larousse, 1968: 416)

Takshaka A dragon-king, a deity of all waters generally. China. (Werner, 1932: 285–286, 485)

Tala, Telehe A popular spirit of the Omo River and an important deity to whom chickens and goats are sacrificed to prevent illness. Ethiopia. (Cerulli, 1956: 113–114)

Tameobrigus A river god named on an altar found at the confluence of the Duero and Tamaga rivers. Spain. (Martinez, 1962: 190)

Tanais God of the river of the same name. (The Don River in Russia). Son of Oceanus and Tethys. (Roscher, 1965, 5: 73)

Tando A malignant river god to whom seven men and seven women were sacrificed at a time. He vented his anger with storm and pestilence. The Ashanti, Gold Coast, West Africa. (Ellis, 1887: 32–33; Budge, 1973, 1: 371)

Tano The great river god, son of 'Nyame, was credited with creation. Ghana and Togo. (Parrinder, 1949: 30, 46, 63; Field, 1948: 153; Clarke, 1930: 446–448; Rattray, 1923: 146, 183)

Ta-oun-ya-wat-ha The god of rivers of the Onondaga Indians. New York. (Beauchamp, 1888: 201)

Tapati "The river Tapti personified as a daughter of the Sun by Chhaya." India. (Dowson, 1961: 318)

Tarsos God of the river of the same name, in Cilicia. Asia Minor. (Roscher, 1965, 5: 119)

Taru Goddess of water. The Botocudos, Brazil. (Brinton, 1868: 123)

Tatrsaki Makai "Foam Magician, causes the river to rise and bear foam upon its waves in the month succeeding the month of wind." The Pima, Arizona and Mexico. (Russell, 1904/05: 251)

Tavari A "water spirit . . . which is associated with the jakui flute." The Kamaiura, Xingu River, Brazil. (Villas Boas, 1973: 267)

Tchou A river deity. China. (Chavannes, n.d.: 90)

Te-ch'a-ch'ia A dragon-king, a deity of all waters generally. China. (Werner, 1932: 285–286, 492)

Tegid Voel God of Lake Tegid and husband of Cerridwen, father of Creirwy, Morvran, Avagddu. Wales. (MacCulloch, 1911: 116)

Telesto A nymph of cool springs and also a "goddess of initiations into mysteries." Daughter of Oceanus and Tethys. Greece. (Murray, 1895: 188; Kerenyi, 1951: 41)

Telmissos I A river god of Greece. (Roscher, 1965, 5: 346)

Telo A deified spring of the Dordogne. Gaul. (Renel, 1906: 405)

Tembris God of the river of the same name. Greece. (Roscher, 1965, 5: 351)

Tethys Goddess of the waters. A Titaness, daughter of Uranus and Gaea, sister/wife of Oceanus, and mother of all the streams, of the Oceanides, and the Naiads.

Greece. (Barthell, 1971: 41; Kerenyi, 1951: 15–16; Prentice, Hall, 1965: 140)

Therma Nymph of the warm springs of Apameia. Greece. (Roscher, 1965, 5: 655)

Thermaia Surname of Artemis as a goddess of warm springs, giving health. Greece. (Roscher, 1965, 5: 655)

Thothi Vijal A water god of the Bhils. India. (Naik, 1956: 181)

Thuy-Tinh-công-Chúa "Star of the Waters," the first of the five great fairies who head the female spirits. Annam. (Cabaton, 1925, 1: 539)

Thymbris A nymph of a river of the same name, in Troy. Asia Minor. (Roscher, 1965, 5: 924)

Tiberinus God of the Tiber river who was "occasionally referred to as a healing deity, since he was able, when propitiated, to heal the diseases which his waters were supposed to bring." His mother was Camise, a spring nymph. Italy. (Jayne, 1962: 440; Fairbanks, 1907: 247; Larousse, 1968: 214)

Tiburtus God of the river Anio. Italy. (Prentice Hall, 1965: 143)

Tieholtsodi The god of waters—surface, underground, and oceanic. The Navajo, Arizona and New Mexico. (Matthews, 1902: 29; Alexander, 1964: 157)

Tikoloshe, Hili A malevolent water spirit, a trickster and seducer. The Xosa, South Africa. (Willoughby, 1932: 2, 279)

Tinggi A spirit of the swamp. The Sakai and the Jakun. Among the Mantra he inhabits the headwaters of streams. Malay Peninsula. (Skeat, 1906: 182, 323)

Tingoi A female nature spirit who lives in the depths of rivers. The Mende, Sierra Leone. (Gelfand, 1966: 125)

Tirukala The "active, the working side of water as a personage, the widener of valleys, the pusher apart of mountains, the maker of all streams and rivers. Tirukala works without ceasing, he sings as he labors, and never eats food of any kind." The Yana, California. (Curtin, 1903: 522)

Titaresios God of the river of the same name. Greece. (Roscher, 1965, 5: 1020)

tjas-olmai The god of waters, of lakes, and of fishing. Lapland. (Bosi, 1960: 132; Dioszegi, 1968: 28)

Tlaloc The god of waters and of vegetation is more commonly known as the god of rain and of thunder and lightning, generally beneficent, but at times destructive. He is known as Chac (Mayan), Tajin (Totonacs), Cocijo (Mixtecs). The Aztec, Toltec. Mexico. (Caso, 1958: 41–43; Burland, 1967: x; Vaillant, 1962: 139–140, 145; Duran, 1971: 154–155; Krickeberg, 1968: 41; Spence, 1923: 238)

tó 'asdzá·n A water goddess who "presides over all small tributaries. Rain is her child." The Navaho Indians, Arizona and New Mexico. (Reichard, 1950: 493)

tó biyájí Water's child. "Said by Father Berard to be spring water and by Matthews to be the splash of rain falling into a quiet pool." The Navaho, Arizona and New Mexico. (Reichard, 1950: 493)

Togbo A water god near Porto Novo, where "trial by ordeal of water" was conducted. Slave Coast, West Africa. (Mockler-Ferryman, 1925, 9: 279)

Tokpodun A sea and sky goddess, third child of Naete and Agbe, who "was so dismayed by the brutality of her brothers" that she left the sea and changed herself into a river—near Whydah. Dahomey. (Herskovits, 1938, 2: 152, 155)

tó niñili· Water Sprinkler, who controls deep and underground waters, and rain, is associated with Black God and with Talking God. One of his duties "is to extinguish fire made by Black God." The Navaho, Arizona and New Mexico. (Reichard, 1950: 491–492)

Tonu God of the spring Matahiva. Ha'afeva Island, Tonga, Polynesia. (Gifford, 1929: 307)

Toosib, Toosep The god of water. The Hottentot, South Africa. (Hahn, 1881: 54; Willoughby, 1932: 2n)

Topielec The Master of Waters. Poland. Same as Vodyanik (Russian). (Machal, 1918: 270)

Totole A lagoon goddess of the Gā in Nungwa. Ghana. (Field, 1937: 27)

Trita A water god and a god of the atmosphere, closely associated with Indra. He is also associated with Soma, the drink of immortality. India. (Macdonell, 1897: 67–69; Danielou, 1964: 138; Dowson, 1961: 321)

Tsakan A water demon who causes illness. The Cora Indians, Mexico. (Chamberlain, 1925, 4: 740)

Tsala God of the Omo River to whom sacrifices of chickens and sheep are made. The Zala, Ethiopia. (Cerulli, 1956: 114; Mbiti, 1970, 2: 126)

Tsantsalyineumañ Source lake of the Rio Huachaca, daughter of Maneneumañ and Mukulyinmankú Seižankua. The Kagaba, San Miguel, Colombia. (Preuss, 1926: 68)

Tsar Morskoi The king of waters, surface and subterranean. Russia. (Ralston, 1872: 148)

Tshadze-jielle The water spirit of the Russian Lapps. (Holmberg, 1925, 7: 798)

Tshatse-neida (western), **Tshadze-ienne** (eastern) The "water mother" of the Lapps. (Holmberg, 1925, 7: 798)

Tshatse-olmai The "water man" to whom offerings are made to avert danger and damage when traveling by water. Also for success in fishing. The southern Lapps. (Holmberg, 1925, 7: 798)

mTsho sman g·yu thang cho longs ma A lake goddess of Tibet. (Nebesky-Wojkowitz, 1956, 1: 201)

mTsho sman gzi ldan ral gcig ma A lake goddess of Tibet. (Nebesky-Wojkowitz, 1956, 1: 201)

mTsho sman klu yi rgyal mo A lake goddess who dwells in the mTsho sngon khri shor. Tibet. (Nebesky-Wojkowitz, 1956, 1: 201)

mTsho sman mthing gi lha mo, mTsho sman nyi ma'i byan goig ma Lake goddess of Tibet. (Nebesky-Wojkowitz, 1956, 1: 201)

mTsho sman rgyal mo mkhro'i gtso A queen of the *mtsho sman* goddesses who dwell in lakes. Tibet. (Nebesky-Wojkowitz, 1956, 1: 200)

mTsho sman ru phyug rgyal mo A queen of the *mtsho sman* goddesses who dwell in lakes, and "apparently the sister, or perhaps the *sakti,* of the Khyung lding nag po." Tibet. (Nebesky-Wojkowitz, 1956, 1: 200)

tsooli-qaa A water monster, grandson of soxpekomaw· the culture hero. The Yurok, California. (Waterman, 1920: 258)

Tsunaga-wi-no-kami "Kami of the long-rope well," a god of household waters. Japan. (Herbert, 1967: 497)

Tuima A river goddess "coming to be identified with the Ganga." The Tiparas, Bengal. (Crooke, 1925, 2: 481)

Tukun-wawa-samptni Goddess of the lake. The Uru, Bolivia. (LaBarre, 1941: 521)

Tunga A water spirit of the Maguzawa. Nigeria. (Greenberg, 1946: 36)

Turanga A river god "invoked before fishing expeditions." New Zealand. (Poignant, 1967: 27)

Turiacus An aquatic deity. Spain. (Martinez, 1962: 196–197)

Túrliue The source lake of the Rio Surivaka, and "the mother of the field crops, the temple, the festive ornaments, and all things." The Kagaba, Colombia. (Preuss, 1926: 84)

Tursas A Finno-Ugric water spirit associated with Ahti. Harmful. (Larousse, 1968: 304)

Twe The god of Lake Bosomtwe. Ghana. (Parrinder, 1967: 86)

Tweneboa The god of a river near Achiase. Ghana. (Field, 1948: 156)

Twi A lake deity of the Akim-Kotoku. Ghana. (Field, 1948: 202)

The Tzultacaj Deities of agriculture, of water, of lightning, benevolent in opposition to the Mams with whom they are sometimes confused. The hot springs are considered female Tzultacaj. Sometimes a singular deity, male. The Kekchis, British Honduras. (Thompson, 1930: 59–62)

Tzultacca "Especially venerated by the traveller. He is the god of the forest, of water, and of animals to whom the wayfarer every morning and evening burns copal in a large leaf and offers a prayer, especially for game." The Kekchi, British Honduras. (Tozzer, 1941: 107)

Udan A spirit of brooks who "causes them to swell very much, even after a light rain." The Isneg, Luzon, Philippines. (Vanoverbergh, 1953: 98)

udensmate Latvian "mother of the water." (Leach, 1950, 2: 608)

U Iale A water god to whom human sacrifices were made annually. The Khasi, Assam. (Bareh, 1967: 356)

Uis Oe   A crocodile god, Lord of the Water. Timor, Indonesia. (Middelkoop, 1960: 24)

The Ukhan Khans   Water divinities who are invoked to intercede with the Dolon-Khukhu-Tengri for rain. The Buriats, Siberia and Mongolia. (Klementz, 1925, 3: 4)

U lei umtong   The god of water of the Khasis and the Syntengs. Assam. (Gurdon, 1914: 106)

Uli-po'ai-o-ka-moku   A water goddess of Hawaii. (Beckwith, 1940: 541)

Ulumandiañ   Source lake of the Rio Don Diego. Daughter of Maneneumañ and Mukulyinmakú Seižan-kua. The Kagaba at San Miguel, Colombia. (Preuss, 1926: 68)

Umtisong   A water deity of the Khasi. Assam. (Bareh, 1967: 360)

Umugassa, Mugascha   God of streams and of rain. Uganda. (Meyer, 1916: 184–185)

Unk   The goddess of waters was created by Maka as a companion but she was contentious, and so, banished. The "ancestress of all evil beings." She was the mother of Iya by Inyan, and incestuously (Unk and Iya) the mother of Gnaski. The Lakota and the Oglala, South Dakota. (Walker, 1980: 50–51)

Unktaghe, Unktahe, Onkteri   The serpent god of waters, associated with medicine, magic, and the use of colors. In the vicinity of Fort Snelling, Minnesota, he is a great fish with horns. If seen it is "always a sign of trouble." He and the Thunderbird frequently fight and as both are very powerful, either may win. The Dakotah Indians. Minnesota to Montana and Wyoming. (Maclean, 1876: 438; Emerson, 1884: 41, 45; Schoolcraft, 1857, 3: 485; Beckwith, 1886: 253; Eastman, 1962: xxxi, 53, 118, 160–161)

Unktehi   The spirit of waters deals with those who have been cowardly or mean during life—when they are traveling to the land of shades. He is malicious, is involved with drowning and water accidents, floods, and fouls the water. As a general term, "Unktehi are like animals" living in waters and swamps. They have supernatural use of their horns and tails, and the long hair on their neck and head is *wakan*. They are dangerous and destructive of living things. The Lakota. (Walker, 1980: 108, 122–123) The dangerous and threatening water spirits may be ritually appeased by "the aroma of sweetgrass and sage, and the smoke of a pipe." The Oglala, South Dakota. (Powers, 1977: 55)

Unun-eme'i   The goddess/mother of the Korkodon river. The Yukaghir, Siberia. (Jochelson, 1900/02: 217)

Upinis, Uppinis   A Lithuanian river god to whom "white sucking-pigs were offered" to keep the water clear. (Gimbutas, 1963: 197; Welsford, 1925, 9: 241)

Ura   A well or spring goddess of the Gard. Gaul. (MacCulloch, 1911: 182; Renel, 1906: 405; Bertrand, 1897: 195, 332)

Urai Uka   A god of the lakes and rivers. The Kayans, Borneo. (Hose, 1912: 5)

Urnia   A water goddess at Ourne. Gaul. (Renel, 1906: 405; Roscher, 1965, 6: 121)

utkyl' loz   The god of water of the Selkups. Siberia. (Prokof'yeva, 1964: 601)

Uto   Goddess of the protection of the delta. Also a goddess of oracles. Lower Egypt. (Roscher, 1965, 6: 142)

Utoplec   Slavic half-fish, half-man water demon of the underworld (water) kingdom for whom drowned people are a tribute. One should not help the drowning as he will take revenge. Poland. (Gimbutas, 1975: XLC M126)

Utpolaka   A dragon-king, a deity of all waters generally. China. (Werner, 1932: 285–286, 540)

Uwan   The malignant mother of water who controls the rivers and their creatures. She causes illness; is also called Upore and Uzare. The Tenetehara, Brazil. (Wagley and Galvao, 1948, 1: 145)

Uwanami   The water spirits and rain makers of the Zuñi, New Mexico. (Bunzel, 1929/30: 487, 513)

Vai   God of Fresh Water, son of Ilu and Mamao. The Malietoa, Upolu, Samoa, Polynesia. (Williamson, 1933, 1: 4)

Va-kul   Harmful water genies, male or female, of the Finno-Ugric Zyrians. Russia. (Larousse, 1968: 307)

Varuna   A god whose functions and importance varied with different times. During one period he functioned as the god of waters, of the seas, and was associated with the West. Earlier he was a sovereign god of the heavens, a god of light, controlling the universe and guardian of all order both cosmic and moral; was a god of righteousness and justice, punitive yet forgiving. During another period he became the god of the night sky, associated with the darkness and its malevolent aspects. Also a god of death.

India, Bali, and Mongolia. (Keith, 1917: 22–26; Banerjea, 1953; 29, 53, 73; Ions, 1967: 14–15, 79; Bhattacharji, 1970: 27, 33; Danielou, 1964: 118–121, 130; Percheron, 1953: 62; Macdonell, 1897: 20–26; Hooykaas, 1964: 48; Martin, 1914: 41, 44; Dubois, 1906: 633)

Vasio   Celtic name of a spring god of Vaison in the Vaucluse. Gaul. (Roscher, 1965, 6: 166; Renel, 1906: 405; MacCulloch, 1911: 40)

Ved-ava, Vedmastor-ava, Ved-azerava (Moksha) Finno-Ugrian mother of water who is also a goddess of fecundity—human, animal, and vegetable. The Mordvins, Russia. (Paasonen, 1925, 8: 845; Leach, 1949, 1: 96)

Veden Emo   The " 'mother of the water,' who 'guided fish into the net.' " Finland. (Krohn, 1925, 6: 24)

Veden-kan   The "prince of water" of the Erza (Mordvins). Russia. (Paasonen, 1925, 8: 845)

Ved-eraj, Vetsa-eraj   A malignant water god of the Mordvins, Russia. (Paasonen, 1925, 8: 845)

Venilia   A Roman spring nymph named as a wife of Janus, and the mother of Canens. (Fairbanks, 1907: 247)

Vercana   Goddess of a spring of the same name in the Belgian part of Gaul. (Roscher, 1965, 6: 211)

Verdatchamma   A goddess associated with the Cumbum irrigation tank, to whom human sacrifice was made. India. (Elmore, 1915: 71)

Vetehinen   A Finno-Ugric water genie, "generally harmful," who was associated with Ahti. (Larousse, 1968: 304)

Vipas   A river goddess of India. (Macdonell, 1897: 86)

Vishnu   In Bali, Vishnu, the great Indian preserver of the world and corrector of evils through his many avatars, is worshipped as a god of waters. Indonesia. (Coleman, 1832: 349; Friederich, 1959: 44; Martin, 1914: 82, 95; Banerjea, 1953: 54–55)

Visuna   A goddess probably associated with the healing springs of Baden Baden. Gaul. (Roscher, 1965, 6: 350)

Vit-Khon   A beneficent water god who has charge of the fishes. The Vogul, Siberia. (Czaplicka, 1969: 290)

Vit-Kul   A "dark spirit" of the water. The Vogul, Siberia. (Czaplicka, 1969: 290)

Viz-anya   "Water-mother" whose appearance "always foretold misfortune." The Magyar, Hungary. (Larousse, 1968: 307)

Vizi-ember   "Water-man"—a spirit of rivers and lakes who sometimes required human victims. The Magyar, Hungary. (Larousse, 1968: 307)

Vizi-leany   A young female water spirit whose appearance "always foretold misfortune." The Magyar, Hungary. (Larousse, 1968: 307)

Vodeni Moz   The master of waters of the Slovenians. Same as Vodyanik (Russian). (Machal, 1918: 270)

Vodnik   The Bohemian master of waters. Same as Vodyanik (Russian). (Machal, 1918: 270)

Vodyanik, Vodyanoy, Vodyany   Slavic god of waters who, when amiable, bestows many fish and gives safe journeys to mariners, but when ill-tempered causes dangerous upsets and drownings. Russia. (MacCulloch, 1964: 270; Machal, 1918: 270–271; Ralston, 1872: 151–152)

Volturnus   An old Roman god of a river in Campania. Italy. (Dumézil, 1966, 1: 105; Roscher, 1965, 6: 370; Prentice Hall, 1965: 149)

Voysi nyaali   The god of water who is invoked for success in hunting and fishing. The Ul'chi, Siberia. (Ivanov, Smolyak, and Levin, 1964: 730)

Vu-kutis   A Finno-Ugrian water spirit who "fought disease." The Votyaks, northern Ural Mountains, Russia and Siberia. (Larousse, 1968: 308)

Vu-murt   A male water spirit of the Votyak, considered evil and feared. It is considered ill-fortune to meet him. However, he can be "helpful to fishers and millers." Sacrifices are made to him for purposes of rain, of fertility, of health, and good fishing. Russia and Siberia. (Larousse, 1968: 307; Leach, 1950, 2: 1163)

Vu-nuna   A benevolent and protective water spirit of the Wotyaks. Russia and Siberia. (Larousse, 1968: 307)

Vuvozo   A harmful water spirit. The Votyaks. Russia and Siberia. (Larousse, 1968: 307)

Wah-Sha-She   The god of the "waters of the earth." He gave his name to the water people and they, in turn, became the name givers of the other groups of people. The Osage, Lower Missouri River Basin. (Mathews, 1982: 12)

Wai-o "Water sufficient," father of Wai-o-whaka-tangata. New Zealand. (White, 1887, 1: 32)

Wai-o-nuku "Water of earth," offspring of Raki and Papa-tu-a-nuku. New Zealand. (White, 1887, 1: 21)

Wai-o-raki "Water of heaven," offspring of Raki and Papa-tu-a-nuku. New Zealand. (White, 1887, 1: 21)

Wai-o-whaka-tangata "Sufficient water for man," son of Wai-o and father of Te-anu-mahana. New Zealand. (White, 1887, 1: 32)

aWakka-ush-kamui Goddess of the waters, with Chiwash-kor-kamui, saved mankind from the famine and taught him proper observances for "hunting and fishing rituals." Also called Petru-ush-mat. The Ainu, Hokkaidu, Japan. (Philippi, 1982: 69, 99) The good and evil spirits of the rivers from the source to the sea. The Ainu, Japan. (Batchelor, n.d.: 387)

wak'tcexi A male water monster whose evil side is to be feared, but whose beneficent side bestows great blessings. The Winnebago, Wisconsin. (Radin, 1915/16: 287–288)

Walula A serpent god who controls the river and is easily offended, to whom pinole is offered. The Tarahumara, Mexico. (Lumholtz, 1902: 402; Bennett and Zingg, 1925: 122)

Wamala The god responsible for the formation of a river which fed and formed Lake Wamala. A prominent god, son of Musisi. The Baganda, Uganda. (Roscoe, 1965: 314)

Wampembe A deity of the Lake Tanganyika shore. The Fipa, Tanzania. (Willis, 1966: 31)

Wang E A deified hero, "the god of boatmen." Szechwan, China. (Graham, 1928: 74)

Wang I A river god "who also helps lumbermen in the forests." Szechwan, China. (Graham, 1958: 52)

Wang Yeh A river god and god of boatmen who is invoked for rain. Southwest China. (Graham, 1961: 132)

Wao A goddess of springs. Maui, Hawaii. (Ashdown, 1971: 17)

Wa-o-tun-oo-wase The water spirit, who has the body of a woman with the tail of a fish, is present in every drop of water and is responsible for drownings. The Delaware Indians, Eastern United States. (Morgan, 1959: 55)

Were Deity of the river Malaba. The Kavirondo, South Africa. (Willoughby, 1932: 12)

Wisnu The god of waters and of rains, of fertility and prosperity, as well as "lord of the underworld." He is the patron god of the north. His wife is Dewi Sri, daughter Dewi Melanting. Bali, Indonesia. *See also* **Vishun.** (Covarrubias, 1937: 317, 296; Grader, 1969, 1: 158, 219)

Wu-jê-nao A dragon-king, a deity of all waters generally. China. (Werner, 1932: 285–286, 572)

Wu-pien-pu A dragon-king, a god of all waters. China. (Werner, 1932: 285–286, 574)

wüt-awa The "mother of Water." The Cheremis, Russia. (Leach, 1949, 1: 98)

Wutszeseu The "God of the Wave . . . was drowned in the River Seu. Merchants on long journeys worship him." China. (Du Bose, n.d.: 328)

wüt-wodež, wüt-oza The spirit of water—evil. The Cheremis, Russia. Also wüt-oza. (Leach, 1949, 1: 215)

Wu-tzŭ Hsü God of the Yang-tzŭ river. "He is the personification of vengeance, a thing sacred in China." Werner, 1932: 577)

xa·ctčé·dó·dí (xashchedodi) "Said to be another name for Water Sprinkler" (tó niṅili·). The Navaho, Arizona and New Mexico. (Reichard, 1950: 504)

Xa matutsi The water god of the west. Eastern Pomo, California. (Loeb, 1926, 2: 300; Barrett, 1917: 424)

Xanthos River god in Troas. Another name for Scamander. Asia Minor. (Roscher, 1965, 6: 520; Prentice Hall, 1965: 150)

Xixiquipilhui A name of Chalchihuitlicue as "the alternate rising and falling of the waves." Mexico. (Bancroft, 1886, 3: 367)

Xok "Mythical merman; a supernatural water being who is said to inhabit deep lakes and rivers and to carry away women who bathe in them." The Lacandon, Mexico. (Perera and Bruce, 1982: 310)

yabahen The guardian of the river. The Tzeltal, Mexico. (Blom and La Farge, 1927: 368)

Yaca-mama The "mother of the streams" hinders their passage, and is embodied in the anaconda. Issa-Japura District, Brazil. (MacCulloch, 1925, 11: 402)

Yacu-mámam The god of rivers and rain arbitrarily and willfully controls destructive floods and beneficial rains. He transforms from tapir to anaconda to frog, and so these three animals are never molested for fear of his anger. The Jivaro, Ecuador. (Up de Graff, 1923: 216–217)

Yahammu A water god, one of their highest deities. The Yurak Samoyed, Siberia. (Czaplicka, 1925, 11: 175)

Yami, Yamuna Goddess of the river Yamuna (Jumna) and twin sister of Yama. India and Tibet. (Martin, 1914: 60; Bhattacharji, 1970: 217–218; Sierksma, 1966: 204–207; Ions, 1967: 80)

Yanki-murt A harmful water spirit of the Votyaks. Russia and Siberia. (Larousse, 1968: 307)

Yao Chi The "Turquoise Courtesan." A water goddess whose home was on Wu shan, "Shamanka Mountain," Yangtze area, though her home locale does vary and is uncertain. The "most delectable but most deceptive, the most alluring but most unreliable" of the water goddesses. China. (Schafer, 1980: 43)

Yeh Ch'a A dragon-king, a deity of all waters generally. China. (Werner, 1932: 285–286, 589)

Yeman gnyem The beneficent god of the mouth of the Ob River, who is a god of fish and of travelers. The Ostyaks, Siberia. (Czaplicka, 1925, 9: 577)

Yemaja, Yemanja Goddess of sweet waters and of the sea. She is the sister/wife of Aganju. Nigeria and Brazil. (Meek, 1943: 112; Parrinder, 1961: 45; Verger, 1954: 15, 187, Plate 119; Landes, 1940: 264; Bastide, 1960: 573)

Yen A river deity of China. (Chavannes, n.d.: 90)

Yen-k'ou-kuang A dragon-king, a deity "of seas, rivers, lakes, and waters generally." China. (Werner, 1932: 285–286, 590)

Yen sedo Classed with the rain gods, though he represents the primordial waters, while the other rain gods represent that of rain and spiritual blessings. The Tewa, San Juan, New Mexico. (Laski, 1958: 11, 72)

Yer Kaniya A water goddess to whom the clan god is committed when he gets old, for her to care for. Bastar, India. (Elwin, 1943: 99)

yonwi ganeidon Long Human Being. The river. He sends disease if insulted with pollution of any kind. He is invoked for longevity and in divination and incantation ceremonies. The Cherokee, North Carolina and Tennessee. (Mooney and Olbrechts, 1932: 22–23, 191–192)

Ysituu God of the river and of all its creatures. The Manasi, Bolivia. (Métraux, 1943: 22)

Yum klu mo yaksa nag mo The mistress of the *klu mo*, the female water spirits. Tibet. (Nebesky-Wojkowitz, 1956, 1: 287)

Yum mchog brgya byin sras mo gnam mtsho sman A lake goddess who lives in the Byang thang gnam mtsho. Tibet. (Nebesky-Wojkowitz, 1956, 1: 201)

Yumud The water god of the Manobo. Philippines. (Jocano, 1969: 23)

Yunwi Gunahita The god of rivers who was invoked on all important occasions. The Cherokee, North Carolina and Tennessee. (Mooney, 1885/86: 1, 2)

Yün-yin-miao-ch'uang A dragon-king, a deity of all waters generally. China. (Werner, 1932: 285–286, 612)

Yu-po-lo A dragon-king, a deity of all waters generally. China. (Werner, 1932: 285–286, 597)

Ywan A male water deity who punishes with illness. The Tenetehara, Maranhão, Brazil. (Wagley and Galvão, 1949: 98, 103)

Zer-panitum The "lady of the abyss," consort of Marduk as a water god, and a god of the abyss. Babylonia, Near East. (Mercer, 1925, 12: 709)

Zeuxippe A water nymph, daughter of Oceanus and Tethys. Greece. (Barthell, 1971: 42)

Zin-kibaru A water spirit who ruled over the fish and other creatures of the waters. Ghana. (Parrinder, 1967: 87; Larousse, 1973: 528)

16

Metals:
Mines, Minerals, Treasures

Agekai A god of Easter Island who with Hepeue produced obsidian. Polynesia. (Gray, 1925, 5: 133)

Ahisha The Great Egret of the Makiritare is the "master of iron." Venezuela. (Civrieux, 1980: 70, 175)

Ancanco An "evil old dwarf" who is the owner of "veins and deposits of gold and silver, as well as objects made of these metals." The Aymara, Peru. The Aymara of Bolivia believe he causes sickness and death. (Tschopik, 1951: 200)

Awiche A spirit, an old woman, who is present in the mines. Bolivia. (Nash, 1972: 54)

Ba In Egypt there are several gods of this name, one of whom is a god of iron. (Knight, 1915: 28; Budge, 1969, 2: 393)

Chakekenapok The "Flint Man," the provider of fire. The Tusans and the Potawatomi. Lakes Michigan and Superior. (Alexander, 1964: 41; Maclean, 1876: 427; Brinton, 1868: 167)

Corpa "Ores in general were addressed as Corpa . . . [and] . . . implored . . . for a plentiful yield." The Colonial Quechua, Peru. (Kubler, 1946: 397)

Coya The "gold mines . . . implored, as huacas, for a plentiful yield." The Colonial Quechua, Peru. (Kubler, 1946: 397)

Datoh A god worshipped by the miners as the guardian of the mines and the laborers, their safety. The Chinese, Malaya. (Siew, 1953: 27)

Dawiskula Flint was ogrelike, frightful, and appealed to in childbirth to frighten the baby into hurrying in being born. Also the "dreaded enemy of all the mythic animal world because it was with flint that man pointed his deadly arrows." The Cherokee, North Carolina and Tennessee. (Mooney and Olbrechts, 1932: 277–279)

dGe ri lcam dral A guardian deity who is a god of treasures. Tibet. (Nebesky-Wojkowitz, 1956, 1: 254)

Gohantone The god of iron of the Yuchi of South Carolina and Georgia. (Speck, 1909: 102)

Gu God of iron, of metal, as well as a god of war. Dahomey. (Herskovits, 1938, 2: 107; Parrinder, 1967: 79, 83; Mercier, 1954: 222)

Ham-trhang A god of treasures. Tibet. (Snellgrove, 1957: 243)

Hathor The cow-goddess is also considered a personification of jade. Egypt. (Mackenzie, n.d.: 46)

hatukaci acacila The owner of the salt, at Ilave. The Aymara, Peru. (Tschopik, 1951: 201)

Hepeue A goddess who, with Agekai, produced obsidian. Easter Island, Polynesia. (Gray, 1925, 5: 133)

Hevyoso The thunder god is, like Gu, a god of iron. The Fon, Dahomey. (Mercier, 1954: 213, 222)

tHli'akwa The god of turquoise, of Turquoise Mountain. The Zuñi, New Mexico. (Tyler, 1964: 185–186)

Houa chan God of the Peak of the West who presides over all metals and all feathered flying animals. Also called Kiang T'ou. China. (Chavannes, n.d.: 4, 410)

Huari The god of the earth's treasures who persuaded men to abandon the fields and come to mine in the caves. Bolivia. (Nash, 1972: 52)

Huixtocihautl, Uixtocihuatl Goddess of salt and of water, sister of the rain gods, and a wife of Tezcatlipoca. The Aztec, Mexico. (Caso, 1958: 44, 69; Bancroft, 1886, 2: 325; Vaillant, 1962: 149)

Ichma, or **Linpi** "Mercury and its ores were adored . . . [and] implored . . . for a plentiful yield." The Colonial Quechua, Peru. (Kubler, 1946: 397)

Ju Shou God of metal who is associated with the west. China. (Campbell, 1962: 432)

Kana-Yama-Hiko God of minerals, of metals. Japan. (Yasumaro, 1965: 16–17; 1928: 8; Herbert, 1967: 268)

Kana-Yama-Hime Goddess of metals, of minerals. Japan. (Yasumaro, 1928: 8; 1965: 16–17; Herbert, 1967: 268)

Kane-no-Kami Japanese god of metals. (Holtom, 1938: 209)

Kansasur Deota The "godling . . . of brass" by whom the Byadh Nats swear. The Doms, India. (Briggs, 1953: 387)

Kant Jan Goddess/mother of precious stones. Daughter of Phungkam Janun. The Katchins, Burma. (Gilhodes, 1908: 678)

Kantli Duwa God/father of precious stones. Son of Phungkam Janun. The Katchins, Burma. (Gilhodes, 1908: 678)

Keufang The god of the element gold. China. (Du Bose, n.d.: 72)

Khshathra Vairya One of the Amesha Spentas who had metals under his control. Iran. (Haydon, 1941: 68; Huart, 1963: 41; Larousse, 1968: 317)

Kiang T'ou, Houa chan God of the Peak of the West who presides over all metals and all feathered flying animals. This is Houa chan's personal name. China. (Chavannes, n.d.: 419–420)

Koelasur The "godling . . . of charcoal is . . . both male and female." The Agaria, India. (Elwin, 1942: 123–124)

L!äqwag·iᶜlayugwa (tl'aqwagi'layugwa) "Copper-Maker-Woman." Daughter of Q!omogwa. She "appears as a white bird that smells like copper." The Kwakiutl, British Columbia. (Boas, 1935: 130)

Loha Deota God of iron in Orissa. India. (Elwin, 1954: 638)

Loha Pennu The god of iron and of war who directs the arrows of his followers and protects them from enemies. Bengal and Madras. India. (Crooke, 1925, 7: 649, 651; Leach, 1949, 1: 75)

Lohasur God/goddess of iron and of smiths. The Agaria, India. (Elwin, 1942: 88, 106; Keane, 1925, 2: 123)

Mama The "silver mines and their metals . . . implored, as huacas, for a plentiful yield." The Colonial Quechua, Peru. (Kubler, 1946: 297)

Minaxáldu Father of the Mines. The Cagaba and the Kogi, Colombia. (Reichel-Dolmatoff, 1949/50: 115)

Nin-kurra A minor Babylonian mountain god of the Hammurabi period, the patron of stone quarriers. Assistant to Ea. Near East. (Jastrow, 1898: 171, 178)

Noub, Nubt The personification of gold, a goddess identified with Hathor. Egypt. (Gardiner, 1925, 9: 791; Mackenzie, n.d.: 46)

Ogillon Yoruban god of certain metals and of smiths. Brazil. (Bastide, 1960: 569)

Ogun, Oggun God of iron and of minerals, of smiths, of war and hunting. The Yoruba, Nigeria. Also Cuba, Haiti, Trinidad, and Puerto Rico. (Idowu, 1962: 85–87; Parrinder, 1967: 79; Morton-Williams, 1964: 249–251; Courlander, 1966: 10; Verger, 1957: 174; Simpson, 1965: 20; Gonzalez-Wippler, 1975: 108–109)

Ông Wuhti The goddess of salt who is also believed to predict the seasons. The Hopi, Arizona. (Titiev, 1972: 131; Tyler, 1964: 190)

Pien Ho God of jade and of precious stones as well as the rough gems. God of jewellers. China. (Maspero, 1963: 332; Du Bose, n.d.: 329; Werner, 1932: 378)

Plouton, Ploutos, Plutus, Pluto As Hades he is the god of the dead, of burial. As Pluto, the god of the wealth of and in the earth; a chthonic god rather than of the underworld. Greece. (Cox, 1870, 2: 307; Fairbanks, 1907: 235; Campbell, 1964: 14–15; Murray, 1935: 58)

Pounamu A shark god, twin of Poutini, "a personification of jade." (Jade is supposed to form in a soft state inside of the shark and harden on exposure to air.) Son of Tangaroa and Anu-matao. New Zealand and Polynesia. (Mackenzie, n.d.: 46; White, 1887, 1: 34)

Poutini A shark god, twin of Pounamu, and "a personification of jade." In a "Taranaki version of this myth," Poutini is a goddess, but still associated with jade. New Zealand, Polynesia. (Mackenzie, n.d.: 36–37, 46, 52–53)

Q!omogwa A god of the sea who is the owner of copper and of herrings. He is "identified with the double-headed serpent." He is the father of Extsemalagilis and L!aqwagiєlayugwa. He is "also called L!aqwag.iєla, Copper-Maker." The Kwakiutl, British Columbia. (Boas, 1935: 125–31)

Raja Ontong God of wealth, of gold, of precious stones which he gives to mankind. The Nagju, Borneo. (Scharer, 1963: 20)

Téiku Father of the Gold, also a Father of the Canoe. The Cagaba and the Kogi, Colombia. (Reichel-Dolmatoff, 1949/50: 113, 115)

Thesauros The personification of treasures, servant of Pluto. Greece. (Roscher, 1965, 5: 677)

Tinjeg The "lord of iron." The Semang, Malaya. (Schebesta, 1927: 219)

tl'aqwagi'layugwa *See* **L!aqwag·iєlayugwa**

Uixtocihuatl *See* **Huixtocihuatl**

Urcaguary, Urcaguai The Inca god of the earth's riches was represented as a snake. Peru. (MacCulloch, 1925, 11: 402; Larousse, 1968: 443)

Xibalbay The Cakchiquel cardinal-point god of the west was associated with obsidian. Guatemala. (Mackenzie, n.d.: 56)

Xshathra One of the Amesha Spentas, "Power," who is the patron of metal, especially that of instruments of war. Iran. (Littleton, 1965: 98–99)

Yen Tsu "The patron deity of the salt-pits of Yunnan." China. (Werner, 1932: 593)

17

Nature Gods:
Forest, Hills, Mountains, Stones, Trees

Abeh, Ebih A deified mountain or hill upon which the city of Assur was built. Assyria. (Van Buren, 1943: 77; Roberts, 1972: 12)

Abeka The deity of a Fanti hill. The Akim-Kotoku, Ghana. (Field, 1948: 104)

Abellio God of the apple tree. The Pyrenees region, Gaul. (Larousse, 1973: 339)

Abna-intswakhwe The god of the woods invoked for protection while there. The Abkhasians, Caucasus. (Janashia, 1937: 151)

Aceio A deified mountain in the Pyrenees near Bagnere-de-Bigorre, Gaul. (Renel, 1906: 391)

achachilas Spirits of lakes and mountains. The Aymara, Bolivia. (Buechler and Buechler, 1971: 91)

Acomani A mountain god of the Callawayas. Northeast of Lake Titicaca, Bolivia. (McIntyre, 1973: 754)

Aconcagua The Chilean volcano to whom animals and humans were sacrificed. (Karsten, 1926: 333)

Adaa A wood spirit who sometimes resides in the fruit-bat. The Kapauku Papuans, New Guinea. (Pospisil, 1958: 33)

Adados An "altar in Rome mentions the god Adados of Libanos and the god Adados of the mountain-top." (Cook, 1930: 219)

Jok Adongo An aspect of Jok associated with sacred and tabu trees approached as oracles. The Lango, Uganda. (Driberg, 1923: 218)

Adsyla-intswakhwe God of the tree, invoked to protect children from falling off trees and injuring themselves. The Abkhasians, Caucasus. (Janashia, 1937: 141)

Aegipanes Greek deities of the forest, pan-like, sometimes called Panisci. (Murray, 1935: 151)

Ahcanankakabool A Mayan god, guardian of the woods. Santa Cruz, Guatemala. (Gann, 1915: 47–8)

Aja A beneficent goddess of the forests who teaches mortals "the medicinal properties of herbs and plants." Nigeria. (Mockler-Ferryman, 1925, 9: 280; Lucas, 1948: 153)

Ajatar, Ajattara An evil female dragon spirit of the woods "who suckles snakes and produces diseases." Finland. (Leach, 1949, 1: 32)

Aka'aka A mountain god of Manoa Valley, Hawaii. (Westervelt, 1963, 3: 88)

Akathaso The nat of the treetops. Burma. (Temple, 1925, 3: 23)

Akraia A name of Hera as the goddess of the hilltops. Greece. (Fairbanks, 1907: 100)

Alambrima A deified mountain near Piarre, Hautes-Alpes. Gaul. (Renel, 1906: 392)

Alisanos A Celtic god of the rocks. (MacCana, 1970: 50)

Alno Ka'ekade A spirit of the wild. "The neck-twisters." The Fulani, Nigeria. (Webster, 1931: 242)

Amasanga The forest spirit of the Canelos Quichua. Ecuador. (Whitten, 1978: 95)

Amni Chialip A mountain god, one of "five chief spirits, owners of the country." The Monguors, Kansu, China. (Schram, 1957: 114)

Amni Chokker A mountain god, one of "five chief spirits, owners of the country," who are also worshipped in the monasteries of the Yellow Sect. The Monguors, Kansu, China. (Schram, 1957: 114)

Anala Goddess of food and milk-yielding trees, daughter of Surabhi. India. (Mackenzie, 1924: 173)

anchanchus "Evil place spirits usually associated with caves." The Aymara, Bolivia. (Buechler and Buechler, 1971: 91)

Angamucuracha The Michoacan gods of the mountains. Mexico. (Craine and Reindorp, 1970: 104)

Anhanga A malignant forest demon who hunts rubber gatherers and hunters. Usually takes the form of a fowl and is protective of field game. The Ita and the Tupi, Brazil. (Wagley, 1964: 234; Spence, 1925, 2: 837)

Anjan Deo The forest god in the Nimar District. Central Provinces, India. (Russell, 1925, 3: 314)

Apo Bolinayen A great mountain god of the Philippines. (Jocano, 1969: 146–147)

Appuppan A mountain deity who must be appeased. The Kurava, Southern India. (Thurston, 1909, 4: 124)

Apunga A goddess with whom Tane mated and "produced small plants." The Maori, New Zealand. (Best, 1924: 114)

The Apus Mountain spirits which "can be manipulated." In some areas they are considered guardian deities. The Quechua, Peru. (Mishkin, 1946: 463)

Aranyani Goddess of the jungle, the forests, and the "mother of beasts." India. (Macdonell, 1897: 154)

Arduinna The goddess of the Ardennes Forest. Gaul. (Renel, 1906: 393; MacCulloch, 1911: 43)

Arezura An Iranian volcano deity. (Gray, 1930: 165)

Argiope A nymph of Mt. Parnass, daughter of Teuthras. Greece. (Roscher, 1965, 1, 1: 501)

Aroni A benevolent/malevolent god of the forests and of medicine, who when confronted boldly will initiate "into medicinal lore." Nigeria. (Lucas, 1948: 155; Greenberg, 1946: 58; Mockler-Ferryman, 1925, 9: 280)

Artemis Early on, a goddess of nature, of lakes and rivers, of woods, of wild life. Greece. (Leach, 1949, 1: 76)

Ascensus Roman god of the gradual elevation of terrain and of mountain slopes. (Roscher, 1965, 2, 1: 193)

Ashkha-intswakhwe The god of the mountains to whom shepherds make offerings when taking the cattle to the mountains. The Abkhasians, Caucasus. (Janashia, 1937: 148)

Asia-Bussu The god of the bush of the Guinea and Senegambia groups. West Africa. (Larousse, 1968: 483)

Asteheyta A cave goddess of the Isle of Fer. Canary Islands. (Basset, 1925, 2: 507)

Asthbhuja An eight-armed devi worshipped in connection with the Kaimur and Vhindhyan mountain ranges. India. (Crooke, 1894: 36)

The Aswatta The beautiful and sacred pagoda fig tree worshipped by the Brahmins. It gives great shade and is "considered to possess health-giving properties." It is associated with Vishnu. India. (Dubois, 1906: 652–653)

Atalante Arcadian Artemis as a mountain nymph. She takes various forms. Greece. (Roscher, 1965, 1, 1: 664)

Ata-tangi-rea A goddess upon whom Tane "begat the *maire-rau-nui . . .* tree." New Zealand. (White, 1887, 1: 143)

Atoja A powerful mountain goddess who controls the rain and whose shrine is used in rain-making. The Aymara, Peru. (Tschopik, 1951: 195, 197)

Atua i te Uruao "The God in the Woods." Associated with the sacred canoe. Tikopia, Polynesia. (Firth, 1967, 2: 98, 155)

The Aukis Mountain spirits which in some areas are associated with cultivation. They are invoked by the sorcerer for help in curing and in divination. The Quechua, Peru. (Mishkin, 1946: 463, 469)

Ausangate A mountain near Cuzco which is widely worshipped. Peru. (Rowe, 1946: 296)

Avaro The powerful god of the "sacred avaro (Premna tahi-tensis) tree, which has a speckled bark in consequence. Doctors invoked him to heal patients afflicted with rashes." Tahiti, Polynesia. (Henry, 1928: 378)

A wo dge mjo A Tibetan mountain deity. (Nebesky-Wojkowitz, 1956, 1: 229)

Aw-wua-wua A mountain god, brother of Sa-ddo and La-gkyi-la-khu. The Na-khi, Yunnan Province, China. (Rock, 1947: 269)

Aya The python god of a sacred grove. The Gã in Kpong, Ghana. (Field, 1937: 77)

Ayiravalli A mountain deity who must be appeased. The Kurava, Southern India. (Thurston, 1909, 4: 124)

Ayug The "spirit of a magic tree"—a very powerful shaman's helper. The Taulipang, Guyana. (Zerries, 1968: 314)

Baban-awan A spirit of a "solitary big tree . . . under whose shade travellers take their rest." The Isneg, Luzon, Philippines. (Vanoverbergh, 1953: 93)

Bacax A cave god of the vicinity of Cirta. Algeria. (Ferguson, 1970: 215)

Badhan A hill spirit of the Doms and guardian of cattle. India. (Briggs, 1953: 480)

The Bà-Dú'c-Chúa The "Three Mothers . . . represent . . . the Spirit of the Forests, the Spirit of the Waters, the Spirit of the Air and Sky." Annam. (Cabaton, 1925, 1: 539)

Bago A spirit of the bush. The Isneg, Luzon, Philippines. (Vanoverbergh, 1953: 81)

Baj Bajaniai A benevolent spirit of the deep forest who " 'gives' furry animals and certain birds." The Yakuts, Siberia. (Larousse, 1973: 437)

Bakayauwan The beneficent mountain spirits who are "friendly and helpful to the hunters." The Ifugao, Philippines. (Jocano, 1969: 16)

Balanyan A malevolent spirit of the woods who afflicts with diseases. The Milanows, the Malanau, and the Land Dyaks, Borneo. (Roth, 1968: 166; De Crespigny, 1875: 35)

Bal yul gser phug A mountain god of the Bonpos in the Bal yul region. Tibet. (Nebesky-Wojkowitz, 1956, 1: 229)

Bana Sankari A goddess of the forests. The Lambadi, Southern India. (Thurston, 1909, 4: 226)

Banga-jaudi A spirit of the wild. The Fulani, Nigeria. (Webster, 1931: 242)

Banjari A tutelary goddess who is invoked for protection from danger while in the forest. The Banjaras, Central Provinces, India. (Russell, 1916, 2: 176)

Banji-banmang An evil spirit of the forest and the air who "kills men . . . and drinks their blood." The Minyong Abors, Assam. (Furer-Haimendorf, 1954: 599)

Banraj, Banraja A god of the forest and a tiger god. The Musahar, the Kisans, and the Santals, India. (Wallis, 1939: 49; Grierson, 1925, 2: 554; Crooke, 1925, 2: 486)

Bansapti Goddess of the woods who causes fruit trees to bear, and bulbs to grow, and influences the productivity of all things and animals useful to man. The Musahar, India. (Wallis, 1939: 49)

Bar, Pa-Bar A Syrian god of the mountain and the burning desert, as well as a god of war. Introduced into Egypt. (Budge, 1969, 2: 281; Mercer, 1925, 12: 703)

Bara Deo, Bara Pen The chief god of the Gond and the Baiga who is associated with the sacred saja tree and whose offering is a white bull. India. (Elwin, 1939: 56–57; 1949: 433)

Baram, Baram Deo A forest deity venerated as the head of the pantheon of the Juangs. Bengal. Among the Dhimar he is the "spirit of the banyan tree." (Crooke, 1925, 2: 482; Russell, 1916, 2: 507)

Barutugala Yaka A rock spirit associated with the peak of the same name. The Sinhalese Vedda, Ceylon. (Seligmann and Seligmann, 1911: 170)

Basajaun, Baxajaun A spirit of the forest who is also the protector of the flocks of sheep. His presence is announced by the shaking and sounding of the bells of the ewes, which indicates they are safe from wolves. The Basques, Spain and France. (Barandiaran, 1972: 57, 420)

dŭt Basunam gye The mung of "kam fón name of a rock above Sakyang, near Talung, west of Tingbung;" and also the mung of a "pond or lake near Chumbi." The Lepchas, Sikkim. (Siiger, 1967, 2: 122–123)

Batur, Gunung Batur A volcano worshipped by the blacksmiths of Bali. Indonesia. (Covarrubias, 1937: 201)

Bele Alua   A tree goddess, the *enyenwa*, who is the wife of Bobo Arisi. The Nzema (Akan), Ghana. (Grottanelli, 1969: 376–379)

Belit   The "female principle of nature," designated variously as the consort of Bel, of Ashur, and of Ea. Assyria and Babylonia. (Seligmann, 1948: 100; Jastrow, 1898: 226)

Bergimus   A mountain god of the Po Valley. Italy. (Roscher, 1965, 1, 1: 783; Conway, 1925, 7: 460)

Bettada Chicama   The "mother of the hill." The dead appear in dreams and direct that offerings be made to her, and unless done she causes illness. The Kurumba, Southern India. (Thurston, 1909, 4: 164)

Bhillet   A hill god worshipped by the Bheels. India. (Coleman, 1832: 375)

Bikut   A spirit of the bush to whom offerings are made by those helped when lost. The Isneg, Luzon, Philippines. (Vanoverbergh, 1953: 98)

Bilikonda   A deity of the forest. The Ngombe, Zaire. (Mbiti, 1970, 2: 333)

Birzulis   God of the birch tree. Lithuania. (Welsford, 1925, 9: 241)

Bok   A famous local hill spirit of the confluence of the Scrim and Pacho Rivers. Ethiopia. (Cerulli, 1956: 49)

Bommaso   The spirit of the "roots of trees." Burma. (Temple, 1925, 3: 23)

Bontĭálon   One of the Kaliga-ŏn. The Bukidnon, Mindanao, Philippines. (Cole, 1956: 96)

Brag btsan dmar po stong gi rje   A mountain god and a god of lightning. Tibet. (Nebesky-Wojkowitz, 1956, 1: 219)

Brag dkar bya rgod   A mountain deity of the Bonpos. Tibet. (Nebesky-Wojkowitz, 1956, 1: 229)

Bril phrom rdo rje g·yu drung   A mountain god ruling the 'Bring zla sgang ridge. Tibet. (Nebesky-Wojkowitz, 1956, 1: 225)

'Brog gnyan 'phya ba   A Tibetan mountain deity. (Nebesky-Wojkowitz, 1956, 1: 230)

Buba   A spirit of the wild of the Fulani. Nigeria. (Webster, 1931: 242)

Budu   The deity of a Fanti hill. The Akim-Kotoku, Ghana. (Field, 1948: 204)

Bugabor   God of the forest of the Bondo. India. (Elwin, 1950: 151)

Bukit Kiwa Tengen   A dual god of the mountain, the Left and the Right, and sometimes called separately Ratu Puchak and Ratu Pemeneh. Pura Besakih, Rendang District, Bali. Indonesia. (Goris, 1969: 86)

bukLbru   Lord of the peak between Talamanca and Ujarras, who must be appeased to protect travelers. The Bribri and the Cabecar, Costa Rica. (Stone, 1962: 52)

Bulahao   A nocturnal mountain deity who causes illness. The Ifugao, Lahmaiyan, Philippines. (Barton, 1946: 82)

Bura Deo   God of the forest and of the saj tree, whose offerings are usually goats and pigs. Oaths are sworn in his name, and he is invoked for the purification of wounds. The Baiga and the Gonds. India. Same as Bara Deo. (Russell, 1916, 2: 6, 85; 1916, 3: 30, 97, 99, 103)

Burasa   A god of the forest of the Tiparas. Bengal. (Crooke, 1925, 2: 481)

The Burkans   Hill gods of the Buriat. The Mongol, South Siberia. (Curtin, 1909: 44)

Bya ma bye ri   A mountain deity of the Bonpos in the Ag ta rong region. Tibet. (Nebesky-Wojkowitz, 1956, 1: 229)

Byang gi gangs dkar   A mountain deity who causes illness. Tibet. (Nebesky-Wojkowitz, 1956, 1: 230)

Byang gi gnyan chen thang lha   A mountain god believed to be the son of 'O degung rgyal. Tibet. (Nebesky-Wojkowitz, 1956, 1: 208–9)

Bya rgod spung ri   A mountain god of the Bonpos in the rGya gar region. Tibet. (Nebesky-Wojkowitz, 1956, 1: 229)

Cagiris   A deified mountain, Cagire, in the Haute-Garonne. Gaul. (Renel, 1906: 395)

Camainha pichene   A forest demon feared by the Manaro. Amazon Basin, Brazil. (Métraux, 1948, 6: 711)

Canan Kax   A Mayan guardian of the forests. Mexico. (Thompson, 1970: 321)

Candamius God of the mountain Candanedo. Spain. (Martinez, 1962: 87)

Canotedan, Canotidan God of the forest of the Dakotah Indians who mischievously lures hunters into the woods with animal voices, then frightens them by revealing himself. United States and Canada. (Beckwith, 1886: 253; Lynd, 1889: 153–154; Eastman, 1962: xxxi)

The Canoti Dangerous and threatening "Forest-Dwelling Spirits" who may be ritually guarded against. The Oglala, South Dakota. (Powers, 1977: 55)

Carrus A mountain deity of the Basses-Alpes, and a war god assimilated to Mars. Gaul. (Renel, 1906: 395; MacCulloch, 1911: 27)

Castitas Minerva as the goddess and protectress of the olive trees. Italy. (Roscher, 1965, 1, 1: 856)

Chah-o-ter(teer)-dah A forest god of the Dakotah Indians. United States and Canada. (Schoolcraft, 1957, 3: 486; Emerson, 1884: 29)

Chao Wu-chen A mountain god and also a god of epidemics. China. (Werner, 1934: 242)

Chattan A mountain deity who must be appeased. The Kurava, Southern India. (Thurston, 1909, 4: 124)

Chavar A mountain deity of the Kurava who must be appeased. Southern India. (Thurston, 1909, 4: 124)

Che A Mayan spirit of the forest and of vegetation who has some control over the forest game animals. British Honduras. (Thompson, 1930: 65)

Chigaeshi-no-Okami A deified stone, the "Great Deity who prevented the Goddess Izanami of the Underworld from returning to the upper earth." Japan. (Kato, 1926: 28)

chikisani kamui The Elm Goddess is the mother of the culture hero, Aeoina-kamui, by Pa-kor-kamui, the Pestilence God, or by a sky god. The Ainu, Japan. (Philippi, 1982: 202)

Chikuni Kamui The gods of the trees. The Ainu, Japan. (Batchelor, 1925, 1: 240)

Chimborazo A volcano god who, with Tungurahua, was believed to be the ancestor of the Puruha. He was considered the source of disease but was also invoked for its cure. Ecuador. (Murra, 1946, 1: 798; Karsten, 1926: 331)

Ching-chü-kung The greatest mountain god of the Miao. China. (Wang, 1948: 67)

Chin Mu A mountain goddess. China. (Werner, 1934: 183)

Chiton A spirit of the forest who is sometimes considered beneficent, other times malevolent. The Kachins, Burma. (Temple, 1925, 3: 22–3)

Chochering A mountain god of the Everest group. The Sherpa, Nepal. (Furer-Haimendorf, 1955: 50)

Chogaro A mountain god of the Everest group. The Sherpa, Nepal. (Furer-Haimendorf, 1955: 50)

Chola Pacho The goddess of the sacred grove, the portion of the forest left standing when it is cleared. "She is credited with the power of giving rain and consequently good crops." The Oraon, Central Provinces, India. (Russell, 1916, 4: 311)

Chomolongo The "goddess of Mount Everest." The Sherpa, Nepal. (Furer-Haimendorf, 1955: 50)

Chourimala Iyappan, or Sastha A deity of the woods of the Valans. Southern India. (Thurston, 1909, 7: 288)

Choyo A mountain god of the Everest group. The Sherpa, Nepal. (Furer-Haimendorf, 1955: 50)

Chrysopeleia A Greek tree nymph who lived in an oak and was endangered by a flooding river which Argos deviated. (Roscher, 1965, 1, 1: 905)

Chulla-Chaquicuna The invisible god of the forest who has the "form of a man with one human and one jaguar's foot." The Jivaro, Ecuador. (Up de Graff, 1923: 216–217)

Clivicola A Roman goddess of the slopes of the mountains. (Roscher, 1965, 2, 1: 195)

Cod pan mgrin bzang ma A mountain goddess who is depicted as red and "holding a jewel and a treasure box." Tibet. (Nebesky-Wojkowitz, 1956, 1: 30, 177–178)

Coen, Koin An evil spirit of the woods who expresses his anger with thunder. The Gringai, Southeast Australia. (Howitt, 1904: 431, 496)

Cog la mtshal rtse A mountain god of the Bonpos in the Hor yul region. Tibet. (Nebesky-Wojkowitz, 1956, 1: 229)

Cog la tshal rtse   A mountain god of Tibet. (Nebesky-Wojkowitz, 1956, 1: 221)

Coinquenda   Roman goddess of the pruning of trees, the removal of damaged portions, is also invoked in expiatory rites in the removal of trees in sacred places. (Dumézil. 1966, 1: 35; Roscher, 1965, 2, 1: 195)

Collatina   Roman goddess of the hills. (Roscher, 1965, 2, 1: 195; Altheim, 1937: 145)

Coombar Jannock   A male spirit of the deep forests, originally human, who seized and killed men who came looking for sticks for spears. The Wheelman, Southwest Australia. (Hassell, 1936: 703–704)

Coropuna   A mountain peak of Peru, widely worshipped. (Rowe, 1946: 296)

Corupira, Corropira, Curupira   God of the forest and the bush and protector of game animals, punishing the inordinate hunter. Brazil. (Bastide, 1960: 564; Wagley, 1964: 225; Costa Eduardo, 1948: 83; Fock, 1963: 93; Wilbert, 1974: 39; Métraux, 1949: 567)

Cotopaxi   A volcano deity who was a source of disease, but was also invoked for cures. Ecuador. (Karsten, 1926: 331)

C'oxol   As a Mam (yearbearer), he is the spirit of the sacred mountain of the east—Quilaja—who taught the leaders about the solar calendar, the proper customs for the town and patrilineal shrines, about commercial customs. He is also the Red Dwarf who strikes the "lightning" into the blood of the diviners. He is the "gamekeeper and guardian of the Mundo." Momostenango, Guatemala. (Tedlock, 1982: 147–148).

Cuvto-ava   Finno-Ugrian "tree-mother" who was asked for pardon for injuries to her. The Mordvins, Russia. Paasonen, 1925: 845)

Cybele   Phrygian mountain goddess also associated with the earth and with fertility. Introduced into Greece and Rome. (MacCulloch, 1925, 8: 864; Murray, 1935: 33; Willetts, 1962: 113; Hadas, 1965: 127; Fairbanks, 1907: 142–144; Frazer, 1960: 404)

Dafto   The evil spirit of *sang fyok* "pond between Nung and Namprik in the Tingbung area." The Lepchas, Sikkim. (Siiger, 1967, 2: 122)

Dagigón   One of the Kaliga-ón. The Bukidnon, Mindanao, Philippines. (Cole, 1956: 96)

Dag lha sgam bu   A mountain deity of the Bonpos in the dGe yul region. Tibet. (Nebesky-Wojkowitz, 1956, 1: 229)

Dalong   A malevolent woods spirit who causes illness. The Malanau (Milanow) and the Land Dyaks, Borneo. Indonesia. (Roth, 1968: 166; De Crespigny, 1875: 35)

Danga   A spirit of the wild. The Fulani, Nigeria. (Webster, 1931: 242)

dang du   A mountain demon of the Lepchas. Sikkim. (Siiger, 1967, 1: 189)

Dano gauk   A mountain spirit of the Eastern Pomo, California. (Loeb, 1926, 2: 302)

Dapwanay   The god of Mt. Posoey who watches over the game there. The Tinguian, Philippines. (Cole, 1922: 336)

Dar 'dzin skyes ri mthon po   A mountain god of Tibet. (Nebesky-Wojkowitz, 1956, 1: 214)

Dasiri   A tree god, protector of the village from evil spirits, from illness and from wild beasts, is appealed to by women who fear sterility and for protection from the dangers and accidents of pregnancy. The Bambara, Mali. (Tauxier, 1927: 164, 335, 362)

Daterata   The diva "who guards the eastern side of Mt. Meru, controls the evil nats." Burma. (Spiro, 1967: 44)

Dauarani   The serpent goddess of the forest is the "patron of male artisans, especially canoe makers." If the dead craftsman has observed all the ethical rules, he will gain immortality and life in her domain. The Winikina-Warao, Venezuela. (Wilbert, 1972, 2: 61; 1973, 1: 5)

Deavoavai   A spirit of the woods, male, who furnished an abundance of food. The Tacana, Bolivia. (Levi-Strauss, 1973: 336–337)

Deswali   A forest god who lives in the sacred grove, left from the clearing of the forest. He is "responsible for the crops, and receives an offering of a buffalo at the agricultural festival." The Kol and the Munda, Central Provinces, India. (Russell, 1916, 3: 513; 1916, 4: 15)

Dev Anjwo, Dev Hatrio, Devtokario   Hill gods of the Rajpipla Bhils. India. (Naik, 1956: 181)

Dive zeny   A Slavic female spirit of the woods. Bohemia. (Mansikka, 1925, 4: 628)

rDo gling yul gangs chen A mountain god, an aspect of Gangs chen mdzod lnga, worshipped as a local protective deity by the Buddhists of Darjeeling. Tibet and India. (Nebesky-Wojkowitz, 1956, 1: 219)

Doig A malevolent spirit of the woods who afflicts with diseases. The Milanow (Malanau) and the Land Dyaks, Borneo. (De Crespigny, 1875: 35; Roth, 1968: 166)

Dongar Dai A goddess of the forest and of the hills. Orissa, India. (Elwin, 1954: 636)

Dongar Deo A god of the hills, a stone god placed "on the boundary; he is believed to avert calamities for the coming year." Betul District, India. (Crooke, 1925, 11: 872). Among the Korku of Central Provinces, offerings are made him of "cocoanuts, limes, dates, vermillion and a goat." (Russell, 1916, 3: 559)

Dongar Pat The "hill-godling who prevents earthquakes and volcanic eruptions, and keeps off frost." Central Provinces, India. (Russell, 1925, 3: 314)

sDong grogs zhal dkar gnyan po A Tibetan mountain god. (Nebesky-Wojkowitz, 1956, 1: 214)

Dongor Gomoij A god of the jungle. The Kurkus (Munda), India. (Drake, 1925, 7: 761)

rDo rje dpal gyi yum (pr. **Dorje Pêgyi yum**) The liturgical name of a terrible mountain goddess whose name was formerly Rong gi Jo mo kha rag. Tibet. (Tucci, 1980: 166)

rDo rje drag mo rgyal A mountain goddess and a protective deity, a guardian of the Buddhist doctrine. Tibet. (Nebesky-Wojkowitz, 1956, 1: 182, 190)

rDo rje dril dkar dar thod can A mountain god ruling the Tshab sgang ridge. Tibet. (Nebesky-Wojkowitz, 1956, 1: 226)

Dototam Mischievous but not evil god of the mountains. The Yenesei Ostyaks, Siberia. (Czaplicka, 1925, 9: 579)

Dra-lha, dgra-lha A mountain god—of the mountain called Jang-ri-mug-po. Tibet. (Rock, 1947: 185)

The Dryades Greek deities of the trees and woods. (Murray, 1935: 170; Bulfinch, 1898: 18)

Du-ba-gyap A mountain god and protective deity. Nepal. (Snellgrove, 1961: 92)

Duc Ba, Duc Thanh Ba, Ba-Duc Chua "In Annamese belief, the Three Mothers who represent the Spirit of the Forests, the Spirit of the Air, and the Spirit of the Waters," worshipped mostly by women. Tonkin, Vietnam. (Leach, 1949, 1: 329)

bDud btsan dpa' bo hum ri A mountain god, of Mt. Pahunri. Sikkim and Tibet. (Nebesky-Wojkowitz, 1956, 1: 219)

bDud kyi dge bsnyen A mountain god and guardian of commandments. Tibet. (Nebesky-Wojkowitz, 1956, 1: 220)

bDud mo rno myur A Tibetan mountain goddess. (Nebesky-Wojkowitz, 1956, 1: 221)

Duende A dwarf, dual-sexed deity of the Chorti who is "considered man and wife." A god of the hills and valleys. Those who want more property make a pact with him wherein at the end of ten years, Duende claims a son of the man as his servant. Guatemala. (Wisdom, 1940: 408)

Dulyunon A nocturnal mountain deity at Talimutok who causes illness. The Ifugao, Philippines. (Barton, 1946: 82)

Dumakulem A hunter god and "guardian of created mountains." The Tagalog, Philippines. (Jocano, 1969: 9)

Dumbar God of the sacred grove. The Bondo, India. (Elwin, 1950: 151)

Duminhug A nocturnal mountain deity at Kapugan who causes illness. The Ifugao, Philippines. (Barton, 1946: 82)

Dungardeo A mountain god of the Kurkus. India. (Crooke, 1894: 35)

Dungaryadev A hill god of the Bhils of Bombay Province. India. (Naik, 1956: 172)

Dwirebi A deified rock which at one time could talk and out of which rises a river. The Akim-Kotoku, Ghana. (Field, 1948: 203)

Dziwozony A Slavic female spirit of the woods. Poland. (Mansikka, 1925, 4: 628)

Dzo-an-p'u A mountain god of the Hli-khin people. Southwest China. (Rock, 1947: 398)

Ebangala A deity of the Ngombe "who began the forest." Zaire. (Mbiti, 1970, 2: 333)

Echo A mountain nymph who was a servant of Hera and was deprived by her of speech (leaving her only the power to repeat) because of her loquacity. Greece. (Murray, 1935: 172; Larousse, 1968: 162; Ovid, 1955: 83)

Edinkira A tree and nature god invoked to take away illness. The Ashanti, Ghana. (Wallis, 1939: 118; Clarke, 1930: 448)

Edinkra A bisexual goddess of a sacred grove at Nkoranza. The Akan, Ghana. (Meyerowitz, 1958: 38)

Elagabal, Elagabalus A mountain god who is also a solar deity and is worshipped in a temple as a "large black conical stone." Syria. (Cook, 1930: 159; Frazer, 1926: 496, 498)

El-Shaddai Yahweh as a mighty mountain god. Palestine. (Haydon, 1941: 222)

Erem-chauga-la A malevolent forest spirit. Andaman Islands, Bay of Bengal. (Temple, 1925, 1: 468; Radcliffe-Brown, 1967: 163)

Fagus The god of beech trees. Gaul. (Renel, 1906: 398)

Fanio Etruscan form of Faunus. Italy. (Leland, 1963: 100)

Fatunu'u A god invoked "to possess his axe" in felling timber. Tahiti, Polynesia. (Henry, 1928: 484)

Faunus An ancient and lascivious god of the woodlands and hills, of livestock and pasturage and fields, to which he gave fertility. Italy. (Dumézil, 1966, 1: 344–345; Jayne, 1962: 422; Fairbanks, 1907: 247–248; Murray, 1935: 153)

Firaguli A mountain god of Karonga. Originally mortal, he became a minor deity with little powers. Tanzania. (Willoughby, 1932: 10; Mackenzie, 1925: 187)

rGad stod kyi jo bo 'gyog chen A mountain god of Tibet. (Nebesky-Wojkowitz, 1956, 1: 208–209)

sGam po dpal ri A mountain god of the Dvags po District. Tibet. (Nebesky-Wojkowitz, 1956, 1: 221)

Gang ba bzang po A mountain god who lives on the gNod sbyin gang bzang mountain and who rules over the deities of Tsang province. He is believed to be the son of 'O de gung rgyal and is the consort of sByin ma. He is also one of the gods of wealth. Tibet. (Nebesky-Wojkowitz, 1956, 1: 69, 74, 203, 208–209,221)

Gangkar Shame A mountain goddess "clothed in glacier ice carrying a blood-spattered banner." Tibet. (Nebesky-Wojkowitz, 1956, 2: 33)

Gangs chen mdzod lnga A mountain god of Sikkim. (Nebesky-Wojkowitz, 1956, 1: 217)

Gangs dkar rgyal po A mountain god of the Bonpos. Tibet. (Nebesky-Wojkowitz, 1956, 1: 229)

Gaokerena A deified mythic plant or tree. Iran. (Gray, 1930: 145)

Gar Goddess of the mountain of this name in the Pyrenees. The Basques, France and Spain. (Barandiaran, 1972: 93)

Garra A deified mountain—Pic du Gard, Haute-Garonne. Gaul. (Renel, 1906: 398)

Gasain Era The goddess of a sacred grove who is worshipped at the foot of the Mowah tree. An important guardian deity. The Santal, India. (Biswas, 1956: 135–138)

Gaueteaki A goddess—a "square column or rough white stone, about a foot high." Bellona Island, British Solomon Islands, Melanesia. (Bradley, 1956: 333)

Gaugano A god—a "smooth black conical stone, rounded at the top and about two feet high." Bellona Island, British Solomon Islands, Melanesia. (Bradley, 1956: 333)

Gdas A cave deity of the Berbers. North Africa. (Basset, 1925, 2: 507)

dGe bsnyen 'bo rong A Tibetan mountain deity. (Nebesky-Wojkowitz, 1956, 1: 230)

dGe bsnyen ston ka rgyal mtshan A mountain deity of Tibet. (Nebesky-Wojkowitz, 1956, 1: 229)

Getah A tree spirit of the Jakun and the Besisï. Malay Peninsula. (Skeat, 1906: 182)

Gharu A tree spirit—the "Eaglewood Demon." The Jakun and the Besisi, Malay Peninsula. (Skeat, 1906: 182, 302)

Giraitis Lithuanian god of the forests. (Gimbutas, 1963: 194)

Giriputri Sri as the mountain goddess. Bali, Indonesia. (Grader, 1960: 167; Covarrubias, 1937: 317)

Girisa A mountain god of the Khmer. Cambodia. Same as Siva. (Wales, 1957: 129–130)

Ông Góc "Sir Tree-trunk"—invoked and sacrificed to to prevent collision with or damage from tree trunks in the water. Annam. (Cabaton, 1925, 1: 541)

Goenoeng Agoeng The god of the highest mountain whose mountain is the abode of the gods. His wife is Batoer. Bali, Indonesia. (Belo, 1953: 8, 23)

Gologóndo One of the most powerful of the Kaliga-ón. The Bukidnon, Mindanao, Philippines. (Cole, 1956: 96)

Goiabeira A tree god. Belem, Brazil. (Leacock, 1972: 130)

mGon po 'brong ri A mountain god in bSer yul. Tibet. (Nebesky-Wojkowitz, 1956, 1: 229)

Gossa Pennu A god of the forest. The Kandh, Bengal. (Crooke, 1925, 7: 649)

Grid(r) A Scandinavian mountain giantess, and mother of Vidar by Odin. (Stern, 1898: 120; Anderson, 1891: 337)

sGrog chen A mountain god of Tibet. (Nebesky-Wojkowitz, 1956, 1: 216)

Grogs byed mgo dkar mgo sngon A Tibetan mountain god. (Nebesky-Wojkowitz, 1956, 1: 214)

Gubarra The "lady of the mountain," consort of Mâtu. Babylonia, Asia Minor. (Sayce, 1898: 201)

Gunung Agung The most sacred and highest mountain of the East. Bali, Indonesia. (Covarrubias, 1937: 6)

rGyam rgyal rdo ti gangs dkar A mountain god ruling the lHo zla sgang ridge. Tibet. (Nebesky-Wojkowitz, 1956, 1: 225)

Gyrstis A Lithuanian god of the wood. (Welsford, 1925, 9: 241)

Ha-bo-gans-bzan, gNod-sbyin-gan-bza A deified mountain on the west. Tibet. (Waddell, 1959: 371)

lHa btsun bu le A mountain deity. Tibet. (Nebesky-Wojkowitz, 1956, 1: 229)

lHa btsun ku le A mountain god of the north. Tibet. (Nebesky-Wojkowitz, 1956, 1: 209)

lHa'i dge bsnyen A mountain god and a guardian of commandments. Tibet. (Nebesky-Wojkowitz, 1956, 1: 220)

haldde The "spirit of nature. . . . The word is often found in combination, as for example: mära-haldde—the spirit of the sea, čacce-haldde—the spirit of the water." The Lapps, Northern Europe. (Leach, 1949, 1: 475)

Hani-yama-Hime "Clay Mountain Lady," and earth goddess, a daughter of Izanami. Japan. (Holtom, 1938: 116)

Haokah *See* **Heyoka**

Ha-pu'u A dragon goddess and goddess of the forest, Nuuanu Valley. She and Hau-ola in the form of stones are protective of children from evil when their navel cords are buried under the stones. Oahu, Hawaii. (Mackenzie, n.d.: 74; Westervelt, 1963, 3: 258)

lHa rabs shams po A mountain god and chief of the gods of the countryside. Tibet. (Nebesky-Wojkowitz, 1956, 1: 268, 282)

Harayamatsumi-no-Kami The god of the plain. (Yasumaro, 1965: 19). The owner of the woodland mountains. (Herbert, 1967: 469). Japan.

lHa ri gyang te A mountain deity of the Bonpos in the rGong po rong region. Tibet. (Nebesky-Wojkowitz, 1956, 1: 229)

Hari-sa-bukid A benevolent god of the "mountain-top of Kanlaon in Buglas," who allowed people to plant tobacco on the mountainside up to a certain level. When over the years they went farther, he exploded and sent a flow of mud lava. The Philippines. (Jocano, 1969: 68–9)

lHa ri spo mthon A mountain god of the Bonpos in the sTag gzig region. Tibet. (Nebesky-Wojkowitz, 1956, 1: 229)

Hátei Sexanduna Father of the hills. The Cagaba and the Kogi, Colombia. (Reichel-Dolmatoff, 1949/50: 115)

Hátei Tumu Father of the stones. The Cagaba and the Kogi, Colombia. (Reichel-Dolmatoff, 1949/50: 115)

Hau-ola A dragon goddess and forest deity, now in the form of a stone, who protected children from evil when their navel cords were buried under the stone. Nuuanu Valley, Oahu, Hawaii. (Mackenzie, n.d.: 74; Westervelt, 1963, 3: 258)

Hawaj   A hill deity of the Rajpipla Bhils. India. (Naik, 1956: 181)

Hayamato-no-Kami   A mountain god of the lower slopes. Japan. (Yasumaro, 1965: 19, 51; Herbert, 1967: 332, 469)

Hay-Tau   A Phoenician god of forest vegetation. Near East. (Larousse, 1968: 74)

Hazzi   A Hatti and Hurrian mountain god. Asia Minor. (Akurgal, 1969: 267; Van Buren, 1943: 82; Cotenau, 1948: 137)

Hejkal   A Slavic forest spirit. Bohemia. (Mansikka, 1925, 4: 628)

Helike   A Grecian nymph—the "willow." (Barns, 1925, 12: 452)

Heng Shan   Of the five sacred mountains in China, two are named Heng Shan; one in Hopeh province and one in Hunan province. In Hunan he is God of the Peak of the South; in Shansi, Hopeh, God of the Peak of the North. (Maspero, 1963: 278; Peeters, 1941: 10)

Her-sha-s   A goddess of the blazing desert. Egypt. (Budge, 1969, 1: 256)

Heyoka, Haokah   The antinatural god of the prairies, in whom all is in opposites. When he is happy he sighs and groans, when sad he laughs, when he is cold he sweats, when hot he shivers. The Heyoka are also a class of people who do things differently, contrary to normal, who have seen "Wakinyan or any of his lieutenants in a vision," which causes them to become *heyoka*. Wakinyan hates them, commands them to do things, and to kill. Some believe they afflict with "skin diseases and sore eyes." But they are very *wakan* and also have good medicine, can cause clouds to disperse. Among some he is a giant, revered and feared, invoked when attempting deeds of valor. A warrior believes that if "he dreams of Haokah, calamity is impending and can only be avoided by some sort of sacrifice." To see him can bring good luck in hunting. The Dakota, Plains Indians, United States and Canada. (Beckwith, 1886: 253; Wallis, 1947: 112; Walker, 1980: 72, 101, 105, 129, 141, 156, 187; Eastman, 1962: 208–209, 243; Lynd, 1889: 158)

Hiisi   A Finnish god of the forest and "guardian spirit of the sacrificial grove." (Krohn, 1925, 6: 24)

Himavan(t), Himavat, Himalaya   The god of the Himalaya mountains, father of Parvati, Ganga, and Uma. India. (Ions, 1967: 91, 109; Keith, 1917: 115; Martin, 1914: 214; Coleman, 1832: 382)

Hina-ulu-'ohi'a   Goddess of the ohia tree, of the forest growth. Hawaii. (Beckwith, 1940: 16; Westervelt, 1963, 3: 37)

Hine-kaikomako   Goddess of the fir tree, a child of Tane. The Maori, New Zealand. (Best, 1924: 176; Andersen, 1928: 217)

Hine-maunga   A goddess of the mountains and a wife of Tane. The Maori, New Zealand. (Best, 1924: 95, 154, 163)

Hine-one   The Sand Maid, daughter of Rangahua, who was assigned to protect Mother earth from Hine-moana. The Maori, New Zealand. (Best, 1924: 154, 163)

Hine-tu-a-kirikiri   The Gravel Maid, daughter of Rangahua, who was assigned to protect Mother Earth (Papa) from Hine-moana. The Maori, New Zealand. (Best, 1924: 154, 163)

Hine-waoriki   A goddess who "personifies the white pine." The Maori, New Zealand. (Best, 1924: 176)

Hinolóban   One of the Kaliga-ón. The Bukidnon, Mindanao, Philippines. (Cole, 1956: 97)

Hiriadeva   The Kurumba worship a "rough stone . . . setting it up either in a cave, or in a circle of stones," to which they sacrifice a goat. Southern India. (Thurston, 1909, 4: 167)

Horupenu   A hill spirit of the Konds. India. (Schulze, 1912: 14)

Houa chan, Hua-shan   God of the Peak of the West. He presides over all metals and all feathered flying animals. China. (Chavannes, n.d.: 4, 420; Maspero, 1963: 278; Peeters, 1941: 10)

Huanacauri   A "spindle-shaped unwrought stone on Huanacauri hill near Cuzco, which was believed to represent one of Manco Capac's brothers . . . and was a special protector of the Inca royal family," to whom llamas were sacrificed in the puberty ceremonies for youths asking permission to become warriors. Peru. (Rowe, 1946: 296; Means, 1931: 378)

Humintang   A mountain deity. Pechanigayan, Bali. Indonesia. (Goris, 1969, 2: 99)

hun ahau   A guardian of the mountains. The Tzeltal, Mexico. (Blom and La Farge, 1927: 368)

Huntin   God of the "silk-cotton and odum, or poison, trees," to whom offerings are made in times of illness. His messenger is the owl. The Ewe, Dahomey. (Ellis, 1890: 49–50; Mockler-Ferryman, 1925, 9: 278)

Huri-mai-te-ata   The mother of the tea tree. New Zealand. (White, 1887, 1: 27)

Iavure-cunha   A female spirit of the forest. Xingu River area, Brazil. (Villas Boas, 1973: 59, 256)

Ibago   A god who "caused bamboos and other trees to grow on the islands (i.e. Kashotô, Kôtôsho and possibly Taiwan itself). The god then ordered the wind to blow first in one direction and then in the other until the bamboo split open. First a woman sprang out of it, then a man." Formosa. (Del Re, n.d.: 45)

Idafe   A "rock six hundred feet high, like an immense obelisk, which was deified," and to which offerings were made. La Palma, Canary Islands. (Cook, 1900: 492; Hooten, 1925: 12)

Ifru   Possibly a god of caverns. The Berbers, Algeria. (Basset, 1925, 2: 507; Ferguson, 1970: 215)

Ihi   A beneficent goddess, guardian of the breadfruit tree. The Marquesas, Polynesia. (Christian, 1895: 190)

Ikal Ajau   A mountain to which masses are offered. The Tzeltal, Mexico. (Villa Rojas, 1969: 221)

Ikoro-koro-guru   A god who is guardian of the forests and the mountains and of those animals which are worshipped. The Ainu, Japan. (Batchelor, 1925, 1: 243)

ima: wale   The "spirit of the forest, . . . is a menace" to girls. The Maroni River Caribs, Surinam. (Kloos, 1969: 901)

Imbabura   A mountain god who courts the mountain goddess Wami Rasu. The Peguche, Ecuador. (Parsons, 1940: 221)

Imbarakoinona   The "god of the forest-silence." The Malagasy, Madagascar. (Ruud, 1960: 273)

Inacho   A goddess of the woods. Ponape, Caroline Islands, Micronesia. (Christian, 1899: 384)

Inglong-pi   A mountain god who is invoked for prosperity and to avert misfortune. The Mikirs, Assam. (Lyall, 1925, 8: 630)

Injha, Vindhya Devi   The guardian deity of the Vindhyan hills. The Injhwar, Central Provinces, India. (Russell, 1916, 3: 214)

Inyan   "Inyan (Rock) had no beginning for he was when there was no other. His spirit was Wakan-Tanka (the Great Mystery), and he was the first of the superior gods." He was an omniscient, omnipresent "primal power"—the source of all things—yet "he was soft and shapeless." His power was in his blue blood. He created Maka (Earth) from a part of himself and gave her a spirit—Maka-akan. In doing so he opened his veins and his blood flowed out from him, becoming the blue waters; and he "became hard and powerless." Inyan had two sons: Ksa, God of Wisdom, but demoted to Imp of Mischief, and Iya—"utterly evil and the chief of all evil beings." Inyan was invoked more than any other god as the Spirit of the Rocks—as such very powerful. He gave them the buffalo. The Lakota and the Oglala, South Dakota. (Walker, 1980: 50–52, 102, 118, 124; Jahner, 1977: 33, 34; Powers, 1977: 54)

Irimal   A hill deity, male, of the Rajpipla Bhils. India. (Naik, 1956: 181)

Irnini   A goddess of the cedar mountain. Asia Minor. (Langdon, 1931: 252)

Irungu   A god of the forest, of the bush, of the lake, and a guardian of travelers. The Haya and the Zinza, Tanzania. (Taylor, 1962: 142, 147)

I-Takeru-no-Mikoto   A god of the trees and the forest, a son of Susano-Wo with whom he planted various of the trees. Japan. (Holtom, 1938: 129; Yasumaro, 1965: 39; Herbert, 1967: 492)

Itweelele   A hill deity of the Fipa. Tanzania. (Willis, 1966: 31)

Iwasubime-no-Kami   The goddess of sand, daughter of Izanagi and Izanami. Japan. (Yasumaro, 1965: 14)

Iztaccihuatl   Goddess of the snow-capped mountain, the wife of Popocatepetl. The Aztec, Mexico. (MacCulloch, 1925, 8: 863; Caso, 1958: 21; Duran, 1971: 248)

Jahira Buru   Beneficent goddess of the sacred grove, the wife of Dessauli. The Hos, India. (Majundar, 1950: 256, 275)

Jakri Babiro   A mountain god at Tibrikot village. Nepal. (Snellgrove, 1961: 27, 29)

'Jam dpal dbyyangs   A mountain god. Tibet. (Nebesky-Wojkowitz, 1956, 1: 221)

Jamfi moong   A wild plant, a devil of the high mountains. When gathered, the "allium *safyou* . . . must be dug up with sharpened sticks," not knives, or he "will be angry and throw sticks at the collectors and cause hail and thunder." The Lepchas, Sikkim. (Gorer, 1938: 91, 369, 470)

lJang ra smug po   A mountain god of the Bonpos in the Li yul region. Tibet. (Nebesky-Wojkowitz, 1956, 1: 229)

'Jang ri smug po   A mountain god, leader of the *sa bdag* (malevolent deities who cause illnesses) of the 'Jang country. Tibet. (Nebesky-Wojkowitz, 1956, 1: 221)

Japetequara   A god of the forest and of hunting who is identified with the alligator. Belem, Brazil. (Leacock, 1972: 141–2, 148)

Jarina   A tree goddess who is gay and playful and fond of drinking. Belem, Brazil. (Leacock, 1972: 140, 168)

Jharkhandi   A forest god worshipped "in the month of Chait, and until this rite has been performed they do not use the leaves or fruits of the palas, aonla or mango trees." The Nahal, Central Provinces, India. (Russell, 1916, 4: 260)

Jibbi-Jang-Sangne   A mountain goddess. Dhammai, Northeast India. (Long, 1963: 105)

Jili   A spirit of the wild. The Fulani, Nigeria. (Webster, 1931: 242)

Jimu Tayang   The "spirit of the high mountains." The Adi (Shimongs), Northeastern India. (Chowdhury, 1971: 72)

Jipi   The spirit (male) of the mountain of the same name (east of Compi) to whom offerings are made when there are abortions, miscarriages. If this is not done, hail may come and ruin the fields. The Aymara, Bolivia. (Buechler and Buechler, 1971: 93)

Jo bo g·yul rgyal   A mountain god believed to be the son of 'O de gung rgyal. Tibet. (Nebesky-Wojkowitz, 1956, 1: 208–9)

Jo bo g·ya' spang, Jo bo gze rgyal, Jo bo la bcas, Jo bo mchim lha, Jo bo nges sum   Mountain deities of Tibet. (Nebesky-Wojkowitz, 1956, 1: 224, 230)

Jo mo lha ri   A mountain goddess of the vicinity of the Bhutanese border. Tibet. (Nebesky-Wojkowitz, 1956, 1: 220)

Jo mo nag ri   A mountain deity of Tibet. (Nebesky-Wojkowitz, 1956, 1: 229)

Juan Noq   The god of the volcano Santa Maria. He is also the god of smallpox, and the spirits of the dead have to work for him rebuilding his house. The Chimalteco, Guatemala. (Wagley, 1949: 59, 60)

Jubbu-Jang-sangne   A mountain goddess, daughter of the earth and sky, sister of Subjang-Gnoi-Rise. The Dhammais, Northeast India. (Chowdhury, 1971: 76)

Jurema   A tree goddess, the head of the Jurema line of deities. The jurema is a sacred tree from which is concocted a "vision-inducing narcotic." Belem, Brazil. (Leacock, 1972: 147, 168)

ka bong   A mountain demon of the Lepchas. Sikkim. (Siiger, 1967: 141)

Kahoupokane   "Possibly the goddess of the mountain Hualalai, controlling the snows" which fall upon it. Hawaii. (Westervelt, 1963, 2: 57)

Kaikupake'e   A forest god of Hawaii. (Beckwith, 1940: 465)

Kakaho   "Reed-grass," an offspring of Atea. The Marquesas, Polynesia. (Christian, 1895: 189)

Kalabawan   A spirit of a tree on the top of a mountain who causes heavy rains if approached. The Isneg, Luzon, Philippines. (Vanoverbergh, 1953: 83)

Kali   She is worshipped by the Eravallar for protection while living in the forest. Offerings are made to her in plowing, sowing, and reaping. Southern India. (Thurston, 1909, 2: 215–216)

The Kaliga-ón   Sixteen "powerful spirits who dwell in high hills or mountains, particularly volcanoes." They are: Bontíalon, Dagingón, Gologóndo, Hinolóban, Korongon, Lantangón, Laulau-ōn, Liga-ón, Linankóban, Masaubasau, Moyoñ-boyoñ, SapawEn, Sayobánban, SEgkarón, Tagalamboñ, Tambolón. The Bukidnon, Mindanao, Philippines. (Cole, 1956: 96–97)

Kaliyani   A mountain goddess of the Kadan. India. (Hermanns, 1955: 146)

Kalotkot   A nocturnal mountain deity who causes illness. The Ifugao, Amuging, Philippines. (Barton, 1946: 82)

Ka-meha-i-kana   A name of Haumea as goddess of the breadfruit tree. Hawaii. (Beckwith, 1940: 281; Westervelt, 1963, 1: 29)

Kamina A tree deity of the village of Mpimbwe. The Pimbwe, Tanzania. (Willis, 1966: 60)

kam li gen A god "who has his dwelling in a rock at Tingbung." The Lepchas, Sikkim. (Siiger, 1967, 1: 169)

Kamubalu A mountain demon. Palicur, South America. (Métraux, 1949: 566)

Kanank'ax, Kanancash The guardian of the forest who lives in the "tree from whose bark clothes are made." His permission should be requested before cutting down a mahogany tree. If a man was invited to tarry with an Xtabay (seductive nymphs), he must not stay too long and was advised to spend the night with Kanank'ax to receive his blessing. Then he may see the Xtabay again. The Lacandon, Mexico. (Cline, 1944: 112; Gann, 1915: 48; Perera and Bruce, 1982: 86, 160, 307)

Kan-ch'en-mdsod-lna A mountain god of Tibet. (Waddell, 1959: 370–371)

Kane-kulana-ula A god who takes the form of a tree. Hawaii. (Westervelt, 1963, 3: 114)

Kangchenjunga (Gangs-chen-mdzod-lnga), Kanchinjunga A mountain god. Another name of Kan-ch'en-mdsod-lna. Tibet and Sikkim. (Hoffman, 1956: 19; Waddell, 1959: 371; Nebesky-Wojkowitz, 1956, 2: 30–31)

Kang-chhen sdo-nga A benevolent mountain god. Sikkim. (Gazeteer of Sikkim, 1894: 263–264)

Kanimpana Father of the trees. The Cagaba and the Kogi, Colombia. (Reichel-Dolmatoff, 1949/50: 112)

Kanni A very malevolent deity who lives in big trees, so the Savara "never cut in groves which this deity is supposed to haunt." Southern India. (Thurston, 1909, 6: 333)

Kaohelo A goddess from whose body "grew the ohelo bushes so abundant on volcanic mountainsides." Sister of Pele. Hawaii. (Beckwith, 1940: 99)

Kapeembwa A rock deity of the coast of Lake Tanganyika. The Lungu, Tanzania. (Willis, 1966: 46)

Kapor A tree spirit of the Jakun and the Besisi. Malay Peninsula. (Skeat, 1906: 182, 302)

Ka-pu-o-alakai A goddess of the forest and of canoe builders "who presided over the knot (pu or pua) by which the guiding ropes (ala-kai) were held to the canoe." Hawaii. (Beckwith, 1940: 16)

Kara-no-Kami A god of trees in the *Kojiki*, generally identified with Iso-takeru of the *Nihongi*. Japan. (Yasumaro, 1965: 51; Herbert, 1967: 332)

Karimalai Gopuram (Aiyappan) A mountain god who is protective against wild beasts and snakes and who provides game for the hunter. The Kadan, India. (Hermanns, 1955: 145–146)

dKar-mo A mountain goddess of southwest China. (Rock, 1946: 383)

kar nit kar song A mountain demon invoked at the Cherim ceremonies "at the beginning of the rains and at the beginning of winter," to spare them from illness and death. The Lepchas, Sikkim. (Siiger, 1967, 1: 187–190; 1967, 2: 142)

Kasari A spirit of the wild. The Fulani, Nigeria. (Webster, 1931: 242)

Kashiwa-no-Kami The god of oak trees. Japan. (Larousse, 1968: 417)

Kasunsuli A god of the forest. The Baganda, Uganda. (Roscoe, 1965: 322)

Katanda A tree god of the village of Mbede. The Pimbwe, Tanzania. (Willis, 1966: 60)

Katiyatikal The mountain gods of the Kuravas. Southern India. (Thurston, 1909, 4: 124)

Kattarpar God of ravines. Central Provinces, India. (Crooke, 1894: 35)

Kave-Au A beneficent god of the breadfruit tree. The Marquesas, Polynesia. (Christian, 1895: 190)

Kayakan Kandheki A mountain god of southwest India. (Hermanns, 1955: 146)

Kayeye A lesser deity associated with rocks on the shore of Lake Tanganyika. The Lungu, Tanzania. (Willis, 1966: 46)

kazyng tayykh The birch tree to whom prayers were addressed. The Kachin, Siberia. (Potapov, 1964: 357)

Ketsa The spirit of a steep rock "which rises in midstream near Jebba Island." The Nupe, Nigeria. (Nadel, 1954: 27)

Kha ba dkar po A mountain god of the Bonpos in the Tsha ba rong region. Tibet. (Nebesky-Wojkowitz, 1956, 1: 229)

Kha ba gang bzang A mountain deity of the Bonpos in the dBus and gTsang regions. Tibet. (Nebesky-Wojkowitz, 1956, 1: 229)

Kha ba klo 'dril A mountain deity of Tibet. (Nebesky-Wojkowitz, 1956, 1: 229)

Khabru The god of the countryside as well as a rain and weather god. The Fayeng and Sengmai Meitheis, Manipur, India. (Hodson, 1908: 103)

Kha shag smug ri A mountain god of the Bonpos in the mGo yul region. Tibet. (Nebesky-Wojkowitz, 1956, 1: 229)

Kha sha snyu ri A mountain god, chief of the *sa bdag* deities, malevolent deities causing illnesses, of the Mon country. Tibet. (Nebesky-Wojkowitz, 1956, 1: 221)

Kha'y-taw The "Egyptian patron of the forests of Lebanon." (Albright, 1968: 147)

'Khor lo bde mchog A mountain deity of Tibet. (Nebesky-Wojkowitz, 1956, 1: 222)

Khumbu-yulha A mountain god and the principal deity of the Khumbu area, to whom the gods of the soil are attendants. The Sherpas, Nepal. (Furer-Haimendorf, 1964: 22;, 127, 198)

Khyung 'dus A mountain god. Tibet. (Nebesky-Wojkowitz, 1956, 1: 427)

Khyung tho ri; Khyung tho dung ri A mountain god and divine ruler of the sPo bo region. Tibet. (Nebesky-Wojkowitz, 1956, 1: 221, 227)

Kiang T'ou Another name of Houa chan, the god of the Peak of the West. China. (Chavannes, n.d.: 419–420)

Kijimung A mischievous male tree spirit of the banyan trees. Okinawa, the Ryukyu Islands. (Lebra, 1966: 30)

Kilaimo A nocturnal forest spirit. The Bacairi, Mato Grosso, Brazil. (Altenfelder, 1950: 266)

Kili-unan A spirit of the woods who causes illness and death. Ponape, Caroline Islands, Micronesia. (Christian, 1899: 384)

Kim-un Kamui The god of the high mountains, the bear. The Ainu, Japan. (Munro, 1963: 10, 31)

Ki-no-Kami A Japanese god of trees. (Holtom, 1938: 209)

Kinomata-no-Kami The god of the tree fork and a god of wells. Also called Mi-wi-no-kami. Japan. (Yasumaro, 1965: 41–42; Herbert, 1967: 326–327)

Kitasamba God of the mountain. The Konjo, Uganda. (Taylor, 1962: 94)

Kithairon A Greek mountain god. (Kerenyi, 1951: 97)

Klu bdad khyags pa dkar po A Tibetan mountain deity. (Nebesky-Wojkowitz, 1956, 1: 229)

Klu'i dge bsnyen A mountain god and a guardian of commandments. Tibet. (Nebesky-Wojkowitz, 1956, 1: 220)

Klu sras bu lu A mountain god of Tibet. (Nebesky-Wojkowitz, 1956, 1: 220)

Koana A forest god of the Gã in Accra. Ghana. (Field, 1937: 87)

Kolias A goddess of the foothills. Greece. (Roscher, 1965, 2, 1: 1269)

Kong chen The god of Mount Kanchenjunga. He is the national war god and the protector of the country, as well as being associated with the individual and the family. The Lepchas, Sikkim. (Siiger, 1967, 1: 43, 190; 1967, 2: 142)

Kongtsun Demo A mountain goddess "armed with a magic dart and mounted on a turquoise-maned horse." Tibet. (Nebesky-Wojkowitz, 1956, 2: 33)

Kootti Pennu The god of ravines of the Kandh. India. (Crooke, 1925, 7: 649)

Kope-lobo A forest demon who attacks lone hunters. Maranhão, Brazil. (Wagley and Galvão, 1949: 103)

Kore, Kote A malevolent tree god with a hyena head and cruel and obscene rites. Also a god of the brush and of vegetation. The Bambara, Mali. (Tauxier, 1927: 158–159)

Korongon One of the Kaligaón. The Bukidnon, Mindanao, Philippines. (Cole, 1956: 96)

Kətadən A mountain spirit, of Mount Katahdin. The Penobscot, Maine. (Speck, 1935: 76)

Koti Rani A godling of nature "embodied in the locusts," usually found on Chainpur hill. India. (Crooke, 1894: 36)

Kovave An evil mountain god, omnipotent in the fortune of travelers into the interior. He is also important in initiation rites. The Elema and the Ipi, Papuan Gulf, New Guinea. (Holmes, 1902: 430; Haddon, 1925, 9: 342)

Kozah, Koze A mountain god and a god of thunder, of storms. Arabia, Persia, and Palestine. (Cook, 1930: 204; Larousse, 1968: 323)

bKra bzang zhing skyong, bKra shis lha brag dkar po Mountain gods of Tibet. (Nebesky-Wojkowitz, 1956, 1: 220, 214)

Krumai A goddess of the snow mountains who is popular because of the "comical dance in her honour, which invariably ends the performances at the regular ceremonies." The Kafir, Kafiristan. (Robertson, 1925, 7: 635–636)

Kuari Pen The guardian of the jungle. Bastar, India. (Elwin, 1943: 100)

sKu bla g·yu rtse A mountain deity of the Bonpos in the Bu 'bor sgang region. Tibet. (Nebesky-Wojkowitz, 1956, 1: 229)

Ku-holoholo-pali God of the forest slopes and of canoe builders who helps in carrying the canoe to water. Also a god of rain. Hawaii. (Beckwith, 1940: 15, 16)

The Kuilob Kaaxob The gods of the forests are also gods of agriculture as related to the clearing of the land. The Mayan, Yucatan, Mexico. (Redfield and Rojas, 1962: 113; Thompson, 1970: 291)

Te Kui-u-uku The mother of the *matai* tree. New Zealand. (White, 1887, 1: 27)

Ku-ka-'ie'ie God "of the wild pandanus vine"—a rain and forest god. Hawaii. (Beckwith, 1940: 15)

Ku-ka-'ohi'a-laka God of the ohia-lehua tree worshipped by canoe builders because of its hard wood. A forest and rain god, as well as the god of the hula dance. Hawaii. (Beckwith, 1940: 15, 16)

Ku-ku-matz With his brother Tochipa, associated with volcanoes. Apparently a vestige of Gucumatz of Guatemala. Sons of the earth and the sky. The Mojave, Arizona. (Bourke, 1889: 178; Alexander, 1964: 179–180)

Kuku-no-chi The god of trees, the trunks. Japan. (Yasumaro, 1928: 7; Kato, 1926: 17; Larousse, 1968: 417)

Kuku-no-Kami Stern Elder Deity, the god of trees, is combined with Kaya-no-Hime-no-Kami, the "goddess of grasses and weeds," to make Ugadama at one shrine (Inari). "These two presences show that the primary spirits of the Inari pantheon include both the deity food and the watchful guardian of the home. Inasmuch as Japanese houses use timbers for structural frames, grasses for tatami mats, and rushes for thatching," carpenters are among their "most ardent worshipers." Japan. (Czaja, 1974: 257)

sKu-la k'a-ri A deified mountain on the south. Tibet. (Waddell, 1959: 371)

sKu la mkha' ri One of the chief mountain gods, whose residence is in the south. Tibet. (Nebesky-Wojkowitz, 1956, 1: 203)

Kulde A nocturnal mountain deity who causes illness. The Ifugao, Philippines. (Barton, 1946: 82)

Ku-makua A tree god of Hawaii. (Beckwith, 1940: 26)

Ku-mauna A god of the mountain and a rain and forest god. Hawaii. (Beckwith, 1940: 15, 17)

Ku-moku-hali'i A god of the land, of the forest and the growth of trees. Invoked in their felling, and for success when planting by agriculturists. Hawaii. (Beckwith, 1940: 15, 26; Alexander, 1967: 90)

Kun bzang ma A mountain goddess of Tibet. (Nebesky-Wojkowitz, 1956, 1: 215)

Kun-ga-gyap A mountain god and a local protective deity. Shimen, Nepal. (Snellgrove, 1961: 92)

Kuni-no-Kurado-no-Kami A deity of the valley. Japan. (Yasumaro, 1965: 15, 16; Herbert, 1967: 266)

Kuni-no-Saduchi-no-Kami A deity of the "slope road," of the passes. Japan. (Yasumaro, 1965: 15, 16; Herbert, 1967: 247, 265)

Kuni-no-Sagiri-no-Kami "God of Earthly Mist," and a deity of the boundaries. Japan. (Yasumaro, 1965: 15, 16; Kato, 1926: 132; Herbert, 1967: 266)

Ku-olono-wao God of the deep forest and of rain. Hawaii. (Beckwith, 1940: 15)

Kupa-ai-ke'e Primarily a god of canoe builders, of the adzing of the interior, but also a god of the forest and the rain. Hawaii. (Beckwith, 1940: 15; Emerson, 1968: 53; Keliipio, 1901: 115)

Ku-pepeiao-loa and **Ku-pepeiao-poko** "Big- and small-eared Ku"—names of Ku as a forest and rain god. Also a god of canoe builders—"of the seat braces by which the canoe is carried." Hawaii. (Beckwith, 1940: 15, 16)

Ku-pulupulu A god of the undergrowth, of the forest and the rain. Also a god of canoe builders worshipped when cutting the koa wood. Hawaii. (Beckwith, 1940: 15; Westervelt, 1963, 1: 98–99; Emerson, 1916/17: 24)

Ku-raki Mother of the white pine tree. New Zealand. (White, 1887, 1: 27)

Kurayamatsumi-no-Kami A god of the mountain and of the valley. Japan. (Yasumaro, 1965: 19; Herbert, 1967: 271, 470; Holtom, 1938: 102–103)

Kur Ent A benevolent spirit of the woods. The Mount Hagen tribes, New Guinea. (Gitlow, 1947: 52)

sKu rgyal she ne A mountain god ruling the Zal mo sgang ridge. Tibet. (Nebesky-Wojkowitz, 1956, 1: 225)

Kurupira *See* **Corupira**

Te-ku-whaka-hara The "mother of the totara tree." New Zealand. (White, 1887, 1: 27)

Kwimba A deity "associated with the hill or mountain of that name." The Bungu, Tanzania. (Willis, 1966: 71)

Kwinyawa A mountain spirit, patron of the shamans and giving them curing powers. The Walapai, Arizona. (MacKennan, 1935: 186)

Kwoth ngopna "spirit of the fig-tree." The Nuer, Sudan. (Evans-Pritchard, 1953: 205)

sKye ri gnyen po A mountain deity of the Bonpos of the Tsong kha region. Tibet. (Nebesky-Wojkowitz, 1956, 1: 229)

sKyid shod zhog lha phyug po A mountain god of Tibet. (Nebesky-Wajkowitz, 1956, 1: 208–209)

sKyi shod rdzong btsan zangs khrab can A god of the woods whose attributes are a lance and a snare. Tibet. (Nebesky-Wojkowitz, 1956, 1: 265)

Kyllang A deity of the mountain and of storms, as well as of war. The Khasi, Assam. (Bareh, 1967: 360)

La-gkyi-la-khu A mountain god of the Na-khi of Yunnan Province. He is also the protector of the sorcerer. China. (Rock, 1947: 269; 1959: 797)

Laiching A hill god of the Meitheis of Manipur. Assam. (Hodson, 1908: 98)

la mi yong, long mi yong, lang di yang rang gon Mountain demons of the Lepchas. Sikkim. (Siiger, 1967, 2: 142)

lang gom A mountain demon of the vicinity of Talung Monastery. The Lepchas, Sikkim. (Siiger, 1967, 2: 142)

lang ko, lang kor, lang song Mountain demons of the Lepchas. Sikkim. (Siiger, 1967, 2: 142)

Lang (Long) Targe Marpa The mung "of a lake or tarn below kam fon." The Lepchas, Sikkim. (Siiger, 1967, 2: 122, 142)

lang yi A mountain demon of the Lepchas. Sikkim. (Siiger, 1967, 2: 142)

Lantangón One of the Kaliga-ón. The Bukidnon, Mindanao, Philippines. (Cole, 1956: 97)

Lantaxan Chief of the spirits who live on Mt. Dakulub. The Isneg, Luzon, Philippines. (Vanoverbergh, 1953: 93)

Larocus A god of a mountain range. Spain. (Martinez, 1962: 79)

Lau-ka-'ie-'ie A "goddess of the wildwood." Hawaii. (Beckwith, 1940: 93, 522)

Laulau-ón One of the Kaliga-ón. The Bukidnon, Mindanao, Philippines. (Cole, 1956: 96)

Lei Shillong The god of Shillong Peak. The Khasis, Assam, India. (Barkataki, 1969: 37)

Lekennat A bush spirit. The Marshall Islands, Micronesia. (Erdland, 1914: 314)

Le pepe-en-wal A god of the jungle and the wilderness. Ponape, Caroline Islands, Micronesia. (Christian, 1899: 382)

Lesni Zenka Slavic wood nymphs "both kindly and dangerous . . . their love, like that of divine beings generally, is apt to be dangerous to mortals." (Machal, 1918: 260)

Lha-steng-gzhi-bdag-kha-drag-rdo-rje (shortened to **Kha-dra**) A mountain god and protective of Wa-chin. Southwest China. (Rock, 1947: 382)

Li-ara-katau   A goddess of the woods. Ponape, Caroline Islands, Micronesia. (Christian, 1899: 406)

Libuwat   A spirit of the thickets who may cause death by devouring a person's kidneys. The Isneg, Luzon, Philippines. (Vanoverbergh, 1938: 237)

Liekkio   A Finnish forest deity "who 'presided over plants, roots, and trees.' " (Krohn, 1925, 6: 24)

Liga-ón   One of the Kaliga-ón. The Bukidnon, Mindanao, Philippines. (Cole, 1956: 96)

Likant-en-Arum, Likant-e-rairai   Goddesses of the woods. Ponape, Caroline Islands, Micronesia. (Christian, 1899: 384)

Lilinoe   The goddess of Haleakala who could control its eruptions. Maui, Hawaii. (Westervelt, 1963, 2: 56; Alexander, 1968: 63)

Li-mot-a-lang   A goddess of the woods. Ponape, Caroline Islands, Micronesia. (Christian, 1899: 384)

Linankóban   One of the Kaliga-ón. The Bukidnon, Mindanao, Philippines. (Cole, 1956: 96)

Lityss   A forest spirit who "has fur like a bear, and leaves tracks like a reindeer." The Yenisei Ostyaks, Siberia. (Czaplicka, 1925, 9: 579)

Ljesyj, or Ljesovik   A spirit of the forest. Slavic Russia. (Mansikka, 1925, 4: 628)

Loko   The god of trees, which have souls and are attributed to have powers of healing and magic, to whom offerings are made in illness. Dahomey. (Herskovits, 1938, 2: 108–109; Ellis, 1890: 49–51; Mockler-Ferryman, 1925, 9: 278; Parrinder, 1961: 11)

Lo-lo-sei   God of the snow mountains and of the vegetation at the snowline. The Ch'iang, Ho-p'ing-chai, Szechwan, China. (Graham, 1958: 47)

ka Longkhuinruid   A household god of the Syntengs who became a forest deity. Assam. (Gurdon, 1907: 109)

Lube   "Dove," goddess of the land and of the woods. Twin of Hemoana, one of the primal pairs. The Tongans, Polynesia. (Moulton, 1925, 12: 376, 379; Collocott, 1921: 152–153)

Lukensa   A tree deity of the village of Mpimbwe. The Pimbwe, Tanzania. (Willis, 1966: 60)

luk ni lang bong   A mountain deity of the vicinity of the Talung Monastery. The Lepchas, Sikkim. (Siiger, 1967, 2: 142)

lung ji   A malevolent jungle demon. The Lepchas, Sikkim. (Siiger, 1967, 1: 178)

Lyeshy   A malicious forest spirit who takes different forms and is gigantic or minute at will. He is the protector of birds and wild animals and must have offerings to ensure the hunter of success. He will cause them and travelers to lose their way. Russia. (Ralston, 1872: 153–157)

Ma-chen Pomra, rMa-chen spom-ra   A ferocious and powerful god of the mountain Amne Ma-chen. Tibet. (Nebesky-Wojkowitz, 1956, 2: 34–35; Sierksma, 1966: 272)

Machil' loz   The god of the forest. The Selkups, Siberia. (Prokof'yeva, 1964: 601)

rMad gnyan spom ra   A mountain god of the Bonpos in the mDo smad region. Tibet. (Nebesky-Wojkowitz, 1956, 1: 229)

Madremonte   Goddess of the forest, protective of the animals. The Central Cordillera, Colombia. (Reichel-Dolmatoff, 1971: 80)

sMad shod rdo rje mu nam   A god of the woods whose attributes are "a lance with a banner and a jewel." Tibet. (Nebesky-Wojkowitz, 1956, 1: 266)

dMag bskul gnyan rje gong sngon   A mountain god of Tibet. (Nebesky-Wojkowitz, 1956, 1: 214)

dMag dpon dgra 'dul   A mountain god of Tsha ba sgang. Tibet. (Nebesky-Wojkowitz, 1956, 1: 221)

Magduwaraw   The spirit "who planted the wild *taraw* palms." The Isneg, Luzon, Philippines. (Vanoverbergh, 1953: 98)

Ma g·yo ko ba   A mountain deity of the Bonpos in the dNgul rdza sgang region. Tibet. (Nebesky-Wojkowitz, 1956, 1: 229)

Maichina   "Oak of the South." The Sia, Pueblo Indians, New Mexico. (Fewkes, 1895, 2: 127)

Mainpat   A mountain deity of the Korwas and Kurs. India. (Crooke, 1894: 35)

Makatata "Parent of stones," child of Takoto-wai and Tuamatua. The Maori, New Zealand. (Best, 1924: 163, 501)

Makatiti "Parent of Gravel," child of Takoto-wai and Tuamatua. The Maori, New Zealand. (Best, 1924: 163)

Maklium-sa-twan A deity of the sky world—"lord of the plains and valleys." The Bisayan, Central Panay, Philippines. (Jocano, 1969: 20)

Makuko A forest spirit on whom "mask and mime" are used to bring it and the animals under the power of the hunters. The Cubeo and the Caua, Colombia. (Zerries, 1968: 301)

Malaki Lisu Karan A spirit who lives in densest meadow growth. The Bagobo, Philippines. (Benedict, 1916: 22)

Malakoran A hill deity—a "divine couple" with Malakoratti. The Kadar, Southwest India. (Ehrenfels, 1952: 163)

Malakoratti *See* **Malakoran**

Mali Bebur A god of the forest "who has some control over tigers." The Bondo, India. (Elwin, 1950: 155)

Mampadurei The "mother of the forest." Romania. (Roheim, n.d.: 58)

Mamony A Slavic female spirit of the woods. Poland. (Mansikka, 1925, 4: 628)

The Mams Mayan gods of the mountains and the plains. Though lesser deities, they are very important because of their extensive functions—as gods of the weather, of agriculture, of hunting and fishing. Among the Kekchi they are considered malevolent, destructive of crops and the bringers of pestilence. British Honduras. (Thompson, 1930 : 57–62)

Mandwa Rani Goddess of the Mandwa hill who helps people lost in the forest to find their way or provides them with food and water. The Kawar, Central Provinces, India. (Russell, 1916, 3: 399)

Mangar Pat A hill god of the Santals to whom human sacrifices were made at one time. India. (Mukherjea, 1962: 277)

Maqen Bomra The mountain god of the peak of Anye-maqen (Amne Machin—region of Qinghai-China). The Gologs. Tibet. (Rowell, 1982: 244–247)

Maranaywa A malevolent forest demon, the owner of the forest and its animals, who causes illness and misfortune and who punishes overkilling by hunters. The Tenetehara, Brazil. (Wagley and Galvão, 1949: 98; Levi-Strauss, 1969: 85)

Marang Buru Dravidian god of the mountain and of rain from whom the women of the Santals gained the art of witchcraft, though it was meant for the men. He is invoked during drought and epidemics. Also the Mundas and the Hos. India. (Mukherjea, 1962: 275, 292; Biswas, 1956: 117; Crooke, 1894: 35; Wales, 1957: 45; Majumdar, 1950: 262; Russell, 1916, 3: 512)

Marbod The "deity represented by the branch of the creeper," used to sweep out the house in the rainy season—to sweep away all illnesses and insects. The Teli, Central Provinces, India. (Russell, 1916, 4: 550)

Marjing A hill god of the Meitheis of Manipur. India. (Hodson, 1908: 111)

Markam The god of the mango tree. The Gonds, Central Provinces, India. (Russell, 1916, 3: 61)

sMar mo ngang rdzongs A mountain deity of the Bonpos in the sMar khams sgang region. Tibet. (Nebesky-Wojkowitz, 1956, 1: 229)

Marsyas-Masses A god associated with the mountain Massis, a skillful flutist. Armenia. (Ananikian, 1964: 62)

Maruta A mountain deity who must be appeased. The Kurava, Southern India. (Thurston, 1909, 4: 124)

Maryang Makiling Some consider her the goddess of Mount Arayat. Luzon, Philippines. (Jocano, 1969: 124)

Ma sangs g.ya' spang rdza rgyal A mountain god ruling the lHo zla sgang ridge. Tibet. (Nebesky-Wojkowitz, 1956, 1: 225)

Ma sangs khyung 'dus A mountain god and a protective deity. Tibet. (Nebesky-Wojkowitz, 1956, 1: 224)

Masaubasau One of the Kaliga-ón. The Bukidnon, Mindanao, Philippines. (Cole, 1956: 96)

Masaya A goddess of the volcano who caused earthquakes and to whom human sacrifices were made. The Dirans, Nicaragua. (Bancroft, 1886, 3: 493; Larousse, 1968: 440)

Massou-Lous God of the woods. The Ostyaks, Siberia. (Bertrand, 1897: 87)

359

Masta A mountain god of a Tibrikot village. Nepal. (Snellgrove, 1961: 27)

masterko A god of the forest and rivers invoked for assistance in fishing. The Nenets (Samoyed), Siberia. (Struve, 1880: 795)

Matan A mountain deity who must be appeased. The Kurava, Southern India. (Thurston, 1909, 4: 124)

Matar Kubile A Phrygian mountain-mother goddess. Asia Minor. Equated with Rhea (Greek). (Kerenyi, 1951: 82)

Matlalcueye Goddess of the mountain, of the rain and of waters. The wife of Tlaloc. The Tlascaltecs, Mexico. (Duran, 1971: 257, 466; Bancroft, 1886, 3: 367; Mackenzie, 1924: 240)

Matsiakwana A cave god of the Maganana tribe. Northern Transvaal, South Africa. (Willoughby, 1932: 35)

Matsieng, Matsien A cave god sometimes invoked for rain and abundance. The Tswana, South Africa. (Schapera, 1937: 269–70; Willoughby, 1932: 74)

Maut "Mother Nature," the representation of nature; the wife of Ammon. Egypt. (Rawlinson, 1885: 23; Murray, 1935: 399)

Mawaragala Yaka A rock spirit associated with the peak of the same name. Sinhalese Vedda, Ceylon. (Seligmann and Seligmann, 1911: 170)

Ma zhing khyung rtse A mountain god. Also known simply as Khyung rtse. Tibet. (Nebesky-Wojkowitz, 1956, 1: 215–216)

Mbembu A tree deity of the village of Mpimbwe. The Pimbwe, Tanzania. (Willis, 1966: 60)

Medeine The goddess of the forest. Lithuania. (Gimbutas, 1963: 194; Leach, 1950, 2: 631)

Medeinis The god of the woods. Lithuania. (Schrader, 1925, 2: 36)

Mehaluku Yakini A rock spirit "associated with a rock Batugala near Alutnuwara." The Sinhalese Vedda, Ceylon. (Seligmann and Seligmann, 1911: 170)

Meiden A hare god and a deity of the woods and its animals. Lithuania. (Queval, 1968: 71; Larousse, 1973: 420)

Mejdejn A Baltic goddess of woodlands. (Puhvel, 1974: 78)

Melapi A fearful wood demon. The Narrinyeri, South Australia. (Woods, 1879: 62)

Melia The nymph of the ash tree. Mother of Amycus by Poseidon. Greece. (Fairbanks, 1907: 79)

Me-p'ok-sei The god of a great pine tree of a temple of the Ch'iang, worshipped as the chief god of Ru-ta-chai. Offerings are made to it. Szechwan, China. (Graham, 1958: 51)

Meschamaat A Slavic goddess of the forest. Latvia. (Machal, 1918: 260)

Mesitch A god of the woods and of hunting. The Tcherkass (Circassians), Russia. (Grimm, 1880: 215)

Monduntug A nocturnal mountain deity who causes illness. The Ifugao, Philippines. (Barton, 1946: 82)

Montinus A Roman god of the mountains. (Roscher, 1965, 2, 1: 204)

Moo-tii "The tutelary god of the *eva* tree, which produces a powerfully poisonous fruit, much in request for suicides, especially amongst women crossed in love or suffering from jealousy." The Marquesas, Polynesia. (Christian, 1895: 190)

Mousso-ka-dyri A tree deity, protector of women and young girls. The Bambara, Mali. (Tauxier, 1927: 164)

Moyoň-boyoň One of the Kaliga-ón. The Bukidnon, Mindanao, Philippines. (Cole, 1956: 97)

Mtombwa A lesser deity associated with rocks on the Lake Tanganyika shore. The Lungu, Tanzania. (Willis, 1966: 46)

Mubiru A forest god of the Baganda. Uganda. (Roscoe, 1965: 322)

Mumpani A friendly woods spirit who protects people from the Minungara, two unfriendly sky beings who try to kill. The Mara, Gulf of Carpentaria, Australia. (Roheim, 1972: 68; Spencer, 1904: 502)

Mumuhanga, Mu-mu-whango A wife of Tane, mother of the *totara* tree. The Maori, New Zealand. (White, 1887, 1: 142; Best, 1924: 114)

Munduntug   Malevolent mountain spirits who haunt hunters and cause them to get lost. The Ifugao, Philippines. (Jocano, 1969: 16)

Mungilamma   The bamboo goddess. The Paraiyans, Southern India. (Thurston, 1909, 6: 105)

dMu rje lha gnyan   A mountain god of the Bonpos in the rGyal mo rong region. Tibet. (Nebesky-Wojkowitz, 1956, 1: 229)

Mur-mi-si   A mountain god of the Lolos. Southwest China. (Graham, 1961: 83)

Murti   A mountain deity who must be appeased. The Kurava, Southern India. (Thurston, 1909, 4: 124)

Murugan   A god of the hills who rides a peacock. Identified with Subrahmanya. The Tamils, India. (Aiyangar, 1914: 285–6; Larousse, 1973: 269)

Muttusaikla   Chief of the black wax resin tree. The Cuna, Panama. (Keeler, 1960: 88)

Mutua Deo   "Is represented by a heap of stones within the village and receives a pig for a sacrifice, besides special oblations when disease and sickness are prevalent." The Korku, Central Provinces, India. (Russell, 1916, 3: 559)

Muur   A forest god of the Lacandon. Chiapas, Mexico. (Thompson, 1970: 324)

Mu xa hkleu   The god of the banyan tree. The Karen, Burma. (Marshall, 1922: 224)

Muzamuza   A malicious female spirit of the woods who is ruinous to men, causing them to disappear or driving them mad. The Sema Nagas, India. (Hutton, 1968: 197)

Mwenembago   God of the forest in Uzaramo. Africa. (Werner, 1964: 242)

Nabambe   A god of the forest who sharpens the hunters senses and protects them from wild animals. The Baganda, Uganda. (Roscoe, 1965: 322)

Nading   A nature god of the Gã in Accra. Ghana. (Field, 1937: 89)

Nagyoro   A spirit of the wild. The Fulani, Nigeria. (Webster, 1931: 242)

Naka-Yama-Tsu-Mi   "Middle Mountain-kami," a god of the slopes. Japan. (Herbert, 1967: 470; Larousse, 1968: 416)

nam bu   A mountain demon of the Lepchas. Sikkim. (Siiger, 1967, 2: 143)

Namni   A Hatti mountain god. Asia Minor. (Van Buren, 1943: 82; Cotenau, 1948: 137)

Nanchau-en-chet   The "lord of the morasses and salt marshes, dwelling in the body of the *kaualik* or blue heron." Ponape, Caroline Islands, Micronesia. (Christian, 1899: 384)

gÑan-ch'en Tan   The malignant "local demon of the red hill near Lhaŝa." Tibet. (Waddell, 1959: 372)

Nanda Devi   A Himalayan mountain goddess. India. (Crooke, 1894: 35)

Nanni   A deified mountain of the Hittite. Anatolia. (Akurgal, 1969: 267)

Nanyolwa   A rock god of the village of Manga. The Pimbwe, Tanzania. (Willis, 1966: 60)

Napasaikla   Chief of the palm trees. The Cuna, Panama. (Keeler, 1960: 88)

na rim   A mountain demon of the Lepchas. Sikkim. (Siiger, 1967, 2: 143)

gNas kha ba dkar po   A mountain god in eastern Tibet. (Nebesky-Wojkowitz, 1956, 1: 230)

The Natue   The "Grandmothers, patronesses of the moriche palm, . . . [of] great nutritional and material value." They are also goddesses of the winter solstice. The Winikina-Warao, Venezuela. (Wilbert, 1973: 6)

Nemestrinus   Roman god of forests and groves. (Roscher, 1965, 2, 1: 207)

Nevada de Sajama   A mountain deity of the Chipaya. Bolivia. (LaBarre, 1946: 583)

rNga la stag rtse   A mountain god in bSer smad. Tibet. (Nebesky-Wojkowitz, 1956, 1: 229–230)

Ngazo   A jungle spirit. The Lhota Nagas, India. (Mills, 1922: 115)

sNgo la g·yu rtse   A beneficent mountain god who averts obstacles, destructive magic, illness, bad omens. Tibet. (Nebesky-Wojkowitz, 1956, 1: 202, 215)

Ngom rgyal mtsho bkra   A mountain god who rules the Zal mo sgang ridge. Tibet. (Nebesky-Wojkowitz, 1956, 1: 225)

Nibu-tsu-hime The goddess of Mount Koya. Japan. (Hori, 1968: 168)

Nikolosa A tree deity of the village of Mamba. The Pimbwe, Tanzania. (Willis, 1966: 60)

Nila An evil tree god who lives "in hollow Pterocarpus trees" and kills people who come near. The A-Pucik-war, Andaman Islands. Bay of Bengal. (Radcliffe-Brown, 1967: 163; Haddon, 1925, 9: 272)

Ninhursaga Goddess of the foothills, of the stony ground, and of the desert areas. Wife of Enlil and mother of Emesh (summer), Enten (winter), and Ninurta or Ningirsu. She is the goddess of the wildlife of the foothills. In another tradition she is the sister of Enlil and the wife of Shulpae. She is also associated with domestic herd animals and is the mother of Lisina, a donkey goddess. As the mother of the animals she is named Nintur, and is a goddess of birth. Near East. (Jacobsen, 1976: 104–105, 107)

Nin-kharsak Goddess of the mountain and mother of the gods. A wife of Mul-lil (Bel). Babylonia, Near East. (Sayce, 1898: 151; Jastrow, 1898: 55)

Ninkurra A mountain goddess, daughter of Enki and Ninsar, and mother, by Enki, of Uttu. Near East. (Jacobsen, 1976: 112–113)

Nkulu A grove deity of the Fipa. Rukwa Valley, Tanzania. (Willis, 1966: 31)

Nlung Wunlang Lung Chaupha Wunphrang The embryonic rock, of the second generation of deities. Child of Kring-krong wa and Ynong majan. The Katchins, Burma. (Gilhodes, 1908: 675)

gNod sbyin gangs bzang A mountain god of the west of Tibet. (Nebesky-Wojkowitz, 1956, 1: 203)

gNod sbyin rgyal thang A Tibetan mountain god. (Nebesky-Wojkowitz, 1956, 1: 221)

Nongmaiching A hill god of the Meitheis. Manipur, Assam, India. (Hodson, 1908: 111)

Nongshaba The "greatest of the . . . forest gods." In the primeval universe he is credited with producing light. Manipur, India. (Shakespear, 1913: 81, 85)

Ntamaso A god of the forest who with Nabambe sharpened the senses of the hunters and protected them from wild animals. The Baganda, Uganda. (Roscoe, 1965: 322)

Nunuoska One of the subjects of their dances—"Mother-Nature, giving birth to the flowers and trees in the spring." The Bella Coola, British Columbia. (McIlwraith, 1948, 2: 196)

Nupka-ush-mat (Yamni huchi) The "Chestnut-tree Grandmother," a goddess from the Upper Heavens who lived on earth for a time. The Ainu, Japan. (Philippi, 1982: 261–268)

Nupuri Kamui, nupuri-kor-kamui, nuburi-kamui The god of the mountain who provided the Ainu with food. The Inau Cult. Among the Ainu of Hokkaidu, the mountain god was also a wise and friendly bear god. Japan. (Sternberg, 1906: 426; Batchelor, 1925, 1: 240; Philippi, 1982: 115)

gNyan chen g·yu rtse A mountain god ruling the Shar zla sgang ridge. Tibet. (Nebesky-Wojkowitz, 1956, 1: 224)

gNyan chen thang lha (pr. **Nyenchen Thanglha**) Also just Thang lha. The most important and most popular of the gods of the mountains. He rules the great gNyan chen thang lha range of northern Tibet. He is also "believed to be a guardian of treasures," is a protector of the Buddhist laws, fighting evil powers. He became a Bodhisattva. Tibet. (Sierksma, 1966: 274; Nebesky-Wojkowitz, 1956, 1: 94, 205–206; Tucci, 1980: 164)

Nyangkomli A god of a grove of the Gã in Kpong. Ghana. (Field, 1937: 77)

Nyani' jehu A very dangerous tree spirit. The Sakai, Malay Peninsula. (Skeat, 1906: 247)

Nyani' s'rak A malevolent spirit of the jungle. The Sakai, Malay Peninsula. (Skeat, 1906: 247)

gNyan ljang rdo rje blo gros A mountain god ruling the 'Bring zla sgang ridge. Tibet. (Nebesky-Wojkowitz, 1956, 1: 225)

gNyan rje gung sngon, Nye gnas lcang dkar Mountain gods of Tibet. (Nebesky-Wojkowitz, 1956, 1: 215)

Nyyrikki A minor Finno-Ugric god of the woods whose father is Tapio. (de Kay, 1898: 39; Larousse, 1968: 304)

Obo A nature god of the Gã in Accra. Ghana. (Field, 1937: 89)

'O de gung rgyal, Ode Gunggyel An ancient mountain god of the region south of 'Ol kha, father of gNyan chen thang lha, and chief of the sa bdag (malevolent deities who cause illness) of Myang po. He is "regarded . . . as the first king, originating from heaven." The Bon religion. Tibet and Sikkim. (Nebesky-Wojkowitz, 1956, 1: 208, 221; 1956, 2: 32; Snellgrove, 1957: 239; Tucci, 1980: 218, 226)

Odoyamatsumi-no-Kami God of the mountainside. Japan. (Yasumaro, 1965: 19; Herbert, 1967: 470)

Oeoe God of the pandanus and its fruit. The Marquesas, Polynesia. (Christian, 1895: 190)

Ogbenai God of the chadzo tree. The Gã in Temma, Ghana. (Field, 1937: 12)

Oho-yama-tsu-mi The supreme mountain god. Japan. (Revon, 1925, 9: 237)

Oiwa Daimyojin A Buddhist and Shinto god of rock. Japan. (Herbert, 1967: 477; Larousse, 1968: 417)

'Okuwapi " 'Red cloud'. . . . The father of the War Gods . . . lives on top of Sandia Mountain." The Tewa, New Mexico. (Harrington, 1907/08: 47)

Okuyamatsumi-no-Kami God of the heart of the mountain. Japan. (Yasumaro, 1965: 19; Herbert, 1967: 470)

Olie Dungar A hill deity of the Rajpipla Bhils. India. (Naik, 1956: 181)

Oloba The spirit of the Owerri bush. Nigeria. (Talbot, 1967: 12)

Olopenkekelel A god of the afterworld who is the guardian of all trees. The Cuna, Panama. (Nordenskiold, 1938: 329)

Olu-Igbo God of "the bush country and the forest" to whom the animals turn for help. The Yoruba, Nigeria. (Courlander, 1973: 28, 172)

Omalagad "In the *Panalikot* ceremony he is recognized as chief of the spirits of the rocks, cliffs and trees." He is a god of hunters. The Bukidnon, Mindanao, Philippines. (Cole, 1956: 95)

Omiwa A god who lives on Mount Mimoro. Japan. (Larousse, 1968: 412)

Onufrius A Slavic forest spirit. Russia. (Mansikka, 1925, 4: 628)

Onyai God of the silk-cotton tree of the Gã in Nungwa and in Accra. Ghana. (Field, 1937: 29, 86)

Ooyarraksakju A beneficent female spirit whose home is in rocks and boulders. The Eskimo, Baffin Land, Canada. (Bilby, 1923: 209)

Oros A Greek mountain god. (Roscher, 1965, 3, 1: 1058)

Ortik The god of the mountaintop is invoked if Yamal is unable to help with fishing. The Nenets (Samoyed), Siberia. (Struve, 1880: 795)

Osain, Osai, Ossaim A god of the forest and of herbs, of herbal magic (in Puerto Rico). Identified with St. Francis. Brazil, Trinidad, Cuba, and Puerto Rico. (Landes, 1940: 266; Simpson, 1965: 19, 37; Bastide, 1960: 570; Costa Eduardo, 1948: 84; Verger, 1957: 230; Gonzalez-Wippler, 1975: 86–87)

Ossa Female personification of the mountain Ossa. Greece. (Roscher, 1965, 3, 1: 1230)

Oto-madoiko-no-Kami and **Oto-matoiko, Oto-madoime-no-Kami** and **Otomatoime** God and goddess of the slopes and the gentle folds of the mountains. Japan. (Yasumaro, 1928: 7, 8; 1965: 15, 16; Herbert, 1967: 266, 471)

Oyamakui-no-Kami A great mountain god worshipped on Mt. Hie in Chikatsuaumi Province. Also called Yamasuye-no-Onushi-no-Kami. Japan. (Yasumaro, 1965: 51; Herbert, 1967: 332)

Oyamatsumi-no-Kami God of the mountains, son of Izanagi and Izanami. His wife is Kayanuhime-no-Kami and they are the parents of many deities of the hills and valleys. Japan. (Yasumaro, 1928: 7, 8; Kato, 1926: 72; Holtom, 1938: 104)

Ozteotl A god of caves, an aspect of Huitzilopochtli. Mexico. (Reed, 1966: 128)

pa cyor pa tang A mountain demon of the Lepchas. Sikkim. (Siiger, 1967, 2: 143)

pa dim A mountain god and very popular deity as he protects mankind from the *mung*, who cause illness and death, evil and misfortune. The Lepchas, Sikkim. (Siiger, 1967, 1: 169, 175; 1967, 2: 143)

Paikutlatha A god—"a projecting rock overhanging a slab of rock, on which are two stones set up on end." The Kadir, Southern India. (Thurston, 1909, 3: 21)

Pakavan, Pakavati Mountain deities who must be appeased. The Kurava, Southern India. (Thurston, 1909, 4: 124)

pa ki, pa li yang Mountain demons of the Lepchas. Sikkim. (Siiger, 1967, 2: 143)

dPal ldan mgon po nag po chen po A Tibetan mountain god, the mountain near Siliguri, India. (Nebesky-Wojkowitz, 1956, 1: 219)

Pal Nibach God of the taiga and the mountains and of their animals. The Gilyaks, Siberia. (Lissner, 1961: 231)

Pal' n'igyvyn "The master of the mountains and of the taiga." The Gilyak, Siberia. (Shternberg, 1933: 320)

Pal-yz' God of the taiga and of the mountains who rules over all the beasts and allots them to man. The Nivkhi and the Gilyak, Siberia. (Ivanov, Smolyak and Levin, 1964: 778; Shternberg, 1933: 55)

Pana-'ewa A reptile/man of the forest who sends adverse weather to cause people to lose their way. As the fog he is called Kino-'ohu. Hawaii. (Westervelt, 1963, 2: 98–100)

Pancenu God of the region of the same name. Colombia. (Trimborn, 1968: 104)

pan dong, pan dong cyu A mountain god invoked at the Cherim ceremonies "at the beginning of the rains and at the beginning of winter," to spare them from illness and death. Husband of pan song. The Lepchas, Sikkim. (Siiger, 1967, 1: 187–190; 1967, 2: 90, 96, 143)

pan grim, ta lom pan grim A mountain god of a peak southeast of Kanchenjunga. The Lepchas, Sikkim. (Siiger, 1967, 2: 98)

Paninduela The totemic eucalyptus tree, wife of Tukimbini, who created the features of their country, the animals, and the water plants. The Tiwi, Australia. (Mountford, 1958: 36, 42)

pan jing A mountain demon of the Lepchas. Sikkim. (Siiger, 1967, 2: 143)

pan song, pan song cyu A mountain goddess invoked at the Cherim ceremonies "at the beginning of the rains and at the beginning of winter," to spare them from illness and death. Wife of pan dong. The Lepchas, Sikkim. (Siiger, 1967, 1: 187–190; 1967, 2: 90, 143)

Paplawe A tree as a nature god. The Gã, Accra, Ghana. (Field, 1937: 89)

Parga The beneficent spirit of the forest who controls the game and gives his allotted share to each man. The Selkup (Samoyed), Siberia. (Donner, 1926: 70)

Parvati As a mountain goddess, the wife of Siva is identified with the Himalayan peak Nanda Devi. India. (Crooke, 1894: 35; Keith, 1917: 236; Russell, 1916, 4: 14)

Parya A forest spirit of the Tym River. The Samoyed, Siberia. (Czaplicka, 1925, 11: 177)

Pastoria(nen)sis A mountain deity of Tunisia. (Basset, 1925, 2: 506)

pa tet A mountain demon of the Lepchas. Sikkim. (Siiger, 1967, 2: 143)

Pat Sarna A mountain god, fourth in importance in the pantheon. The Mundas, India. (Crooke, 1925, 9: 2)

Pa'u-o-Pala'e The goddess of ferns. Hawaii. (Westervelt, 1963, 2: 97)

pa wo hung ri The demon "of the mountain peak Pauhunri." Younger brother of kong chen. His wife is Samo Gajong. The Lepchas, Sikkim. (Siiger, 1967, 1: 175; 1967, 2: 143)

Payer A hill god of the Bhils, son of Raja Pantha by Pandhar. India. (Naik, 1956: 180)

pa zor A mountain demon of the Lepchas. Sikkim. (Siiger, 1967, 2: 143)

Pecmo A mountain god of the Mayan highlands who protects "from fevers and snake bites." Guatemala. (Thompson, 1970: 273)

Pedro Angaço The god in charge of the spirits of the forest of Codó in Maranhão. Belem, Brazil. (Leacock, 1972: 130)

Pele Goddess of volcanoes and of fire. She "symbolised woman at her most destructive." Her form was usually that of an ugly old hag, but she could assume that of a beautiful woman. Hawaii. (Beckwith, 1940: 167; Emerson, 1968: 43; Andersen, 1928: 267; Poignant, 1967: 44)

Pemule A friendly spirit of the vicinity of Mt. Katahdin. The Penobscot, Maine. (Speck, 1935, 1: 15)

sPen dkar A mountain god of Tibet. (Nebesky-Wojkowitz, 1956, 1: 215)

sPe ni ri bkra   A mountain god of the Bonpos in the Bod yul region. Tibet. (Nebesky-Wojkowitz, 1956, 1: 229)

Pepe   A fearful wood demon of the Narrinyeri. South Australia. (Woods, 1879: 62)

Peregun 'Gbo   A forest god who "caused the forest to bring forth birds and beasts." The Yoruba, Nigeria. (Wyndham, 1919: 124–125; 1921: 35)

Pesi   An Egyptian goddess of the desert. (Budge, 1969, 1: 256)

Pe Tum Moi   A spirit of the bush who appears as a frog and also as a tiger. The Miao, China. (Bernatzik, 1947: 167)

Phying dkar ba   A mountain god "said to be an 'emanation' of the mountain god rMa chen spom ra." Tibet. (Nebesky-Wojkowitz, 1956, 1: 203)

Physis   A Greek goddess of nature. (Roscher, 1965, 3, 2: 2488)

Pichon   A mountain god, guardian of the mountain of that name. The Chimalteco, Guatemala. (Wagley, 1949: 55)

Pichupichuni   A mountain deity of the Aymara. Peru. (Tschopik, 1951: 195)

Pien-pogil   "The owner of the mountain." The Yukaghir, Siberia. (Jochelson, 1900/02: 145)

Pion   A Greek mountain god. (Roscher, 1965, 3, 2: 2510)

P'i-ru-sei   A deity who rules and protects the forests and its wildlife. The Ch'iang, Ho-p'ing-chai. Szechwan, China. (Graham, 1958: 47)

Pisosag   A spirit of the bush, a man-killer. The Isneg, Philippines. (Vanoverbergh, 1953: 99)

Piyumari   A reasonably benevolent spirit of the land and the forest. The Caribs, Barama River, British Guiana. (Gillin, 1936: 158)

Poananga   A child of Tane representing the clematis. The Maori, New Zealand. (Best, 1924: 176)

Poeninus   A god of the Pennine Alps, assimilated to Jupiter. Gaul. (Renel, 1906: 403; MacCulloch, 1911: 39)

Pohichio   The "dog daemon," father and ruler of the forest spirits born by Eshetewuarha, his consort. The Chamacoco and the Gran Chaco, Paraguay and Brazil. (Zerries, 1968: 238, 305)

Poli-'ahu   The goddess of Mauna Kea, also called the snow goddess. Hawaii. (Beckwith, 1940: 87; Westervelt, 1963, 3: 127; 1963, 2: 55)

Popali   A spirit of the forest, also a phallic and fertility spirit. The Cubeo, Colombia. (Zerries, 1968: 280)

Poptyo Dungar   A hill god of the Rajpipla Bhils. India. (Naik, 1956: 181)

Popocatepetl   "Smoking Mountain"—also called Popocatzin, whose wife was nearby Iztaccihuatl. Mexico. (Duran, 1971: 250, 253, 452; MacCulloch, 1925, 8: 863)

Poramai, Poru Mai   Goddess of the jungle of the Nadiya. India. (Crooke, 1894: 72; Keith, 1917: 238)

Poroshir   God of that mountain. The Ainu, Hokkaidu, Japan. (Philippi, 1982: 214)

sPos ri ngad ldan   A mountain god of the Bonpos in the Zhang zhung region. Tibet. (Nebesky-Wojkowitz, 1956, 1: 229)

Pox (Agave)   The aunt of Six?usas and Sumiwowo. The Chumash, California. (Blackburn, 1975: 119)

Proven   A Slavic god with a sacred oak grove dedicated to him. (Machal, 1918: 295; Gimbutas, 1971: 155)

Puahou   A child of Tane representing the parapara tree. The Maori, New Zealand. (Best, 1924: 176)

P'u-ber-shi   A tree god of the Ch'iang at Yang-tzu-lin. Szechwan, China. (Graham, 1958: 86)

Pukdjinskwesu   A repulsive old woman spirit of the forest. The Penobscot, Maine. (Speck, 1935, 1: 17)

Purainha   The godling of the lotus plant. The Kawar, Central Provinces, India. (Russell, 1916, 3: 400)

Puszaitis   Lithuanian god of the pine tree. (Schrader, 1925, 2: 36)

Pu-whakahara   A goddess who, fertilized by Tane, produced various trees. The Maori, New Zealand. (White, 1887, 1: 142–143; Best, 1924: 114)

sPyan-ras-gzigs A mountain god of Tibet. Same as Avalokitesvara. (Nebesky-Wojkowitz, 1956, 1: 221; Sierksma, 1966: 170)

sPyid bdud rgyal gu rum rtse A mountain god of Tibet whose attributes are a lance and a sword of crystal. (Nebesky-Wojkowitz, 1956, 1: 224)

Ra-beh A cliff god of the Ch'iang at No-to-ch'i. Szechwan, China. (Graham, 1958: 71)

Ra-dzu-shi The "god of the pointed cliff" of the Ch'iang at Yen-men. Szechwan, China. (Graham, 1958: 86)

Rakahore The personification of rock, son of Tua-matua and Takotowai, and the protector of Papa from the attacks of Hine-moana. The Maori, New Zealand. (Best, 1924: 154–155; Andersen, 1928: 285)

rak sot lang dong A mountain demon in the vicinity of the Talung Monastery. The Lepchas, Sikkim. (Siiger, 1967, 2: 144)

Rangahua A deity representing stones, spouse of Tu-maunga; parents of the Gravel Maid and the Sand Maid. The Maori, New Zealand. (Best, 1924: 99)

rang dyang, rang gang Mountain demons invoked at the Cherim ceremonies "at the beginning of the rains and at the beginning of winter," to spare them from illness and death. Sikkim. (Siiger, 1967, 2: 144)

Ratnomal A hill god of the Rajpipla Bhils. India. (Naik, 1956: 181)

Rau-'ata-mea "Leaf-of-pink-stem," a goddess of the forest, daughter of Ta'aroa and Papa-raharaha. Tahiti, Polynesia. (Henry, 1928: 374)

Rau-'ata-'ura "Leaf-of-red-stem," a goddess of the forest, daughter of Ta'aroa and Papa-raharaha. Tahiti, Polynesia. (Henry, 1928: 374)

Rau-'ata'ati "Prickly-leaf," a goddess of the forest, and daughter of Ta'aroa and Papa-raharaha. Tahiti, Polynesia. (Henry, 1928: 374)

Rau-penapena "Protecting-leaf," a goddess of the forest. Tahiti, Polynesia. (Henry, 1928: 374)

Rayer A hill god, son of Raja Pantha by Pandhar. The Bhils, India. (Naik, 1956: 180)

Raz-ajk The "grass mother." The Lapps, Kola Peninsula, Russia. (Holmberg, 1925, 7: 799; Collinder, 1949: 140)

Re-beh A local god, a large rock, worshipped by the Ch'iang. Szechwan, China. (Graham, 1958: 71)

Rekhit An Egyptian goddess of the blazing desert. (Budge, 1969, 1: 256)

Renerungen A mountain god with a family of friendly deities. The Bagobo, Philippines. (Benedict, 1916: 24)

Rerangala Yaka A rock spirit associated with the peak of the same name. The Sinhalese Vedda, Ceylon. (Seligmann and Seligmann, 1911: 170)

Rerenoa A goddess with whom Tane mated and "produced epiphytic plants." The Maori, New Zealand. (Best, 1924: 114)

Ri bo rtse lnga bya rkang can A mountain god and ruler of the rGya nag region. Tibet. Nebesky-Wojkowitz, 1956, 1: 226)

Robur Celtic god of the oak tree. Pyrenees, France and Spain. (Larousse, 1973: 339)

Rong gi Jo mo kha rag (pr. **Rong-gi Chomo Kharak**) The original folk religion name of rDo rje dpal gyi yum, a mountain goddess. Tibet. (Tucci, 1980: 166)

Rong lha rgyal mtshan A mountain god, head of the *sa bdag* (malevolent deities who cause illness) of the Rong district. Tibet. (Nebesky-Wojkowitz, 1956, 1: 221)

Ronkini A hill goddess who used to require human sacrifices. The Santals, India. (Mukherjea, 1962: 279)

Ronomal A hill god of the Rajpipla Bhils. India. (Naik, 1956: 181)

Rosna A dangerous goddess, owner of the volcano Tajalmulco. The Chimalteco, Guatemala. (Wagley, 1949: 59)

Ru-beh A cliff god of the Ch'iang at Kan-ch'i. Szechwan, China. (Graham, 1958: 71)

Ru-di God of the Ra Ge Ji Geh cliffs. The Ch'iang, Szechwan, China. (Graham, 1958: 71)

Rupa Mal A hill god of the Rajpipla Bhils. India. (Naik, 1956: 181)

Ruru-tangi-akau Child of Tane personifying the *ake* tree. The Maori, New Zealand. (Best, 1924: 176)

Rusina   Roman goddess of the fields, the open country. (Roscher, 1965, 2, 1: 220; Hadas, 1965: 122)

Sa-bpi zher nv-lv   A mountain deity (Zhi-da-mung-po of Tibet). The Na-khi, Yunnan Province, China. (Rock, 1947: 41)

Sa-ddo, San-to, San-t'an, Sa-tham   The mountain god of the Li-chiang snow range whose wife is Gkyi-chi-ndzer-dto, and concubine Gkyi-chi-ndzer-mun. The Na-khi, Yunnan Province, China. (Rock, 1947: 87, Pls. 61, 62)

Sagami   A "Deity of the Sea or Deity of the Mountains." Japan. (Czaja, 1974: 31)

sa hyur   A mountain demon of the Lepchas. Sikkim. (Siiger, 1967, 2: 144)

Saigo   A spirit of the wild—"the neck-twisters." The Fulani, Nigeria. (Webster, 1931: 242)

Sai-jo   The "god of pointed cliffs among mountains" at T'ung-lin-shan. The Ch'iang, Szechwan, China. (Graham, 1958: 71)

Saisho   God of Tai-san mountain. Japan. (Puini and Dickens, 1880: 450)

Sait   A goddess of the blazing desert. Egypt. (Budge, 1969, 1: 256)

Saka-no-Mi-Wo-no-Kami   A god of the slopes and declivities of mountains and hills. Japan. (Herbert, 1967: 470; Larousse, 1968: 416)

Salagrama   A stone greatly honored among family possessions and worshipped daily, as it has the power of forgiveness of sins. Considered a metamorphosis of Vishnu, but partakes of all other deities. India. (Dubois, 1906: 649)

Salevao   God of the rocks. Samoa, Polynesia. (Williamson, 1933: 5)

sa ling sa tho gen   A mountain demon of the Lepchas. Sikkim. (Siiger, 1967, 2: 144)

Saman   God of Sri Pada peak. Ceylon. (Obeyesekere, 1974: 77–8)

sa mok sa bok   A mountain demon of the Lepchas. Sikkim. (Siiger, 1967, 2: 144)

Sanbai-sama   A god of the mountains who lives among the peaks most of the year. He descends to the valleys in June as god of the rice fields at the time of the transplanting ritual, the Mibu Ohana-taue, when he is invoked for a good crop. Chiyoda, Japan. (Lee, 1978: 78, 85)

San Francisco ipoq'apaqa   A mountain spirit considered by some to be the "owner of all llamas, alpacas, and vicunas," to whom the blood is offered to maintain the supply. The Aymara, Peru. (Tschopik, 1951: 199)

sang cer mit, sang kyon dang zot   Mountain demons of the Lepchas. Sikkim. (Siiger, 1967, 2: 144)

Sangrama   God of the Himalaya. The Tiparas, Bengal. (Crooke, 1925, 2: 481)

The Sansin   The mountain gods who were fertility deities—worshipped after the harvest. Korea. (Clark, 1932: 200)

Saokenta   A deified mountain. Iran. (Gray, 1930: 165)

Saoruli   A hill god of the Bondo. India. (Elwin, 1950: 151)

SapawEn   One of the Kaliga-ón. The Bukidnon, Mindanao, Philippines. (Cole, 1956: 96)

Sapun   A Mesopotamian mountain god. Near East. (Cook, 1930: 120)

Saputan   Goddess of the volcano of that name. Northern Minahassa, Celebes, Indonesia. (MacKenzie, 1930: 330)

sa rong   A mountain demon of the Lepchas. Sikkim. (Siiger, 1967, 2: 144)

Saru Pennu   A mountain god. The Khandhs, Bengal. (Crooke, 1925, 2: 482)

Sasthan   The forest god, chief deity of the Kanikar. Southern India. (Thurston, 1909, 3: 169)

Saxit   A spirit of the bush, a man-killer. The Isneg, Luzon, Philippines. (Vanoverbergh, 1953: 99)

Sayobánban, SEgkarón   Two of the Kaliga-ón. The Bukidnon, Mindanao, Philippines. (Cole, 1956: 96, 97)

Seikkaso   The *nat* of the tree trunks. Burma. (Temple, 1925, 3: 23)

Seleleding   A god "who has charge of the highlands straight and well defined" and who is invoked in the ceremony for children to make them strong, skillful, successful, brave, and to give longevity. The Sea Dyaks, Borneo. (Roth, 1968: 170)

Seleledu A god "who has charge of the little hills," and who is invoked in the ceremony for children to make them strong, skillful, successful, brave, and to give longevity. The Sea Dyaks, Borneo. (Roth, 1968: 170)

Selva An Etruscan god of nature and the earth who is associated with the southwest and also with divination by haruspicy. Italy. (Pallottino, 1975: 145; Hamblin, 1975: 95)

bSe mi 'brong ri smug po A mountain god ruling the Shar zla sgang ridge. Tibet. (Nebesky-Wojkowitz, 1956, 1: 224)

Sengen-Sama The goddess of Fujiyama. Japan. (Larousse, 1968: 416)

Seng-ge ga-mu The mountain goddess of the Hli-khin. Southwest China. Same as dKar-mo. (Rock, 1947: 383)

Seng-ge kar-mo A mountain goddess, "the White Lioness," who possesses lamas at the Yung-ning Lamasery. (Yung-ning, China. (Rock, 1959: 817)

Seng ge rgyab bsnol A mountain god of the Bonpos in the Bya ba sgrub pa'i gnas ri region. Tibet. (Nebesky-Wojkowitz, 1956, 1: 229)

Seng ge sgra li A mountain god of the Bonpos in the Ge sar gyi yul region. Tibet. (Nebesky-Wojkowitz, 1956, 1: 229)

Sentshadi A cave god at Kanye. Bechuanaland. (Willoughby, 1932: 36)

Septemontius A god protective of the hills of Rome. (Roscher, 1965, 2, 1: 222)

Seragendah A god "who has charge of the stiff clay earth" and who is invoked in the ceremony for children to make them strong, skillful, successful, brave, and to give longevity. The Sea Dyaks, Borneo. (Roth, 1968: 170)

Setsalänl Echo—regarded as an anthropomorphic male. The Bella Coola, British Columbia. (McIlwraith, 1948, 1: 46)

Sexsarbor A tutelary god of trees. Acquitaine, Gaul. (Roscher, 1965, 4: 789)

Shan Shên Chih Wei A mountain spirit. China. (Day, 1940: 206)

Shan Shen T'u Ti A mountain and earth god to whom "offerings must be made at the time a new grave is located" or at the time of graveside ancestral sacrifices. China. (Day, 1940: 31, 67; Schram, 1957: 86)

Shan Wang The mountain god and patron of hunters. In some areas he is the supreme god as well. The Ch'iang, Szechwan, China. (Graham, 1958: 45, 52: 1961: 186)

Shar gyi rma chen spom ra, She'u mkha' ri Mountain gods believed to be the sons of 'O de gung rgyal. Tibet. (Nebesky-Wojkowitz, 1956, 1: 208–9)

Shigiyamatsumi-no-Kami The god of the thick mountain forest. Japan. (Yasumaro, 1965: 19; Herbert, 1967: 470)

Shiki-yama-tsu-mi "Mountain-foundation Kami." Japan. (Herbert, 1967: 470)

Shirampa-kamui The deity who rules the trees. The Ainu, Hokkaidu, Japan. (Philippi, 1982: 177)

Sho-ichi Kimyo Dai-Myojin "First-class Marvelous Great Enlightened Deity"—a tree deity (the pine) worshipped mostly by women. Near Kyoto, Japan. (Czaja, 1974: 183)

Shwisinihanawe "Aspen of the East." The Sia, Pueblo Indians, New Mexico. (Fewkes, 1895, 2: 127)

Shwitirawana "Pine of the West." The Sia, Pueblo Indians New Mexico. (Fewkes, 1895, 2: 127)

Siete Orejas A mountain god of the Maya highlands. Guatemala. (Thompson, 1970: 273)

Siliniets A Slavic god of the forest. Poland. (Larousse, 1968: 291)

Silvanus Roman god of the forests who was protective of the hunter and of shepherds and their flocks, which he extended also to the homestead and agriculture. He was known also in Gaul. (Fairbanks, 1907: 248–249; Jayne, 1962: 439; Murray, 1935: 157; MacCulloch, 1911: 36–37)

Sindar A mountain god of the Bagobo. Philippines. (Benedict, 1916: 24)

Sinukuan A forest and mountain god whose hideout is Mount Arayat. Luzon, Philippines. (Jocano, 1969: 124)

S'iring A wood demon of the Bagobo. Philippines. (Benedict, 1916: 249)

Siyol   A mountain spirit of the Isneg. Luzon, Philippines. (Vanoverbergh, 1953: 82)

sku-la k'a-ri   A deified mountain on the south. Tibet. (Waddell, 1959: 371)

So-bat   A sad spirit who lives on top of a tree-shaded mountain. The Isneg, Luzon, Philippines. (Vanoverbergh, 1953: 93)

Solo   A nature god of the Gã in Accra. Ghana. (Field, 1937: 89)

Song kao, Yun Yang   The mountain of the center (of the five major mountain gods) who presides over the land and over domestic animals. China. (Chavannes, n.d.: 3, 418)

Soro Pennu   The hill god of the Kandh. Bengal. (Crooke, 1925, 7: 649)

Srahmantin   A goddess who dwells in bombax trees and captures people whom she retains for a time and trains as her priests, priestesses. The Ashanti, Ghana. (Ellis, 1887: 36; Mockler-Ferryman, 1925, 9: 277–278)

Sras smon pa don grub   A mountain god. Tibet. (Nebesky-Wojkowitz, 1956, 1: 215)

Srid pa chags pa'i lha dgu   A mountain god of Tibet. (Nebesky-Wojkowitz, 1956, 1: 224)

Srid pa'i lha chen gnyan gyi gtso   An aspect of gNyan chen thang lha. A mountain god. Tibet. (Nebesky-Wojkowitz, 1956, 1: 207)

Ssan-ddo, Boa-shi Ssan-ddo   A mountain god and protector of the sorcerer. The Nakhi, China and Tibet. (Rock, 1959: 797)

Stabai   A deity who lives in stones. The Lacandon, Mexico. (Cline, 1944: 112, Table 1)

Subjang-Gnoi-Rise, Sujang-Gnoi-Rise   A mountain god, son of the earth and sky and brother of Jubbu-Jang-sangne. Dhammai, Northeast India. (Chowdhury, 1971: 76; Long, 1963: 105)

Sudaung   A spirit of the Land Dyaks "who lives amid the clefts and holes of the rocks on the hills." Mount Peninjauh, Borneo. (Roth, 1968: 166)

Sumu Mung   A demoness who lures and seduces young men and who attacks people alone in the forest at night. The Lepchas, Sikkim. (Nebesky-Wojkowitz, 1956, 2: 135–136)

Su-mu-sei   A god of the forests and protector of its wildlife. The Ch'iang, Ho-p'ing-chai, Szechwan, China. (Graham, 1958: 47)

Sung-shan   The god of the Central Peak (of five mountains) in Honan. China. (Peeters, 1941: 10; Maspero, 1963: 278)

Surrupira, Curupira   A god, protective of the forests. Maranhão, Brazil. (Costa Eduardo, 1948: 83)

Suttung   A Scandinavian mountain giant. (Stern, 1898: 120)

gTad dkar 'gro bzang ma   A Tibetan mountain goddess. (Nebesky-Wojkowitz, 1956, 1: 177–178)

Tagalambón   One of the most powerful of the Kaligaón. The Bukidnon, Mindanao, Philippines. (Cole, 1956: 97)

tag tayykh   The mountains—to whom prayers were addressed. The Kachin, Siberia. (Potapov, 1964: 357)

T'ai Chan, T'ai Shan   The great mountain god. His early worship was as a god of the clouds and rain, of the land and harvest. He later was the origin of all life and a god who received and judged the dead. China. (Day, 1940: 120; Chavannes, n.d.: 8, 13, 28, 45, 268; Haydon, 1941: 193–194; Peeters, 1941: 10)

Taivam   A mountain deity who must be appeased. The Kurava, Southern India. (Thurston, 1909, 4: 124)

T'ai-yo ta-ti   A name of the great mountain T'ai-shan, the Peak of the East. China. (Maspero, 1963: 278)

Takalu   A powerful spirit of Loi Seng Hill. The Palaungs, Burma. (Temple, 1925, 3: 23)

tak cyom, ta kri   Mountain demons of the Lepchas. Sikkim. (Siiger, 1967, 2: 145)

Taksol   The demon of a rock in the Tingbung area. The Lepchas, Sikkim. (Siiger, 1967, 2: 122, 145)

Ta La   The goddess who dwells on the sacred mountain Thaw Thi. The Karen, Burma. (Marshall, 1922: 262)

Talal   A nocturnal mountain deity who causes illness. The Ifugao, Amuyung, Philippines. (Barton, 1946: 82)

Talali   A spirit of Mt. Agamamatan. The Isneg, Luzon, Philippines. (Vanoverbergh, 1953: 84)

Taman(mal) A hill god of the Bhils who is invoked in cases of snakebite. Son of Raja Pantha by Pandhar; husband of Thewal and Newal. India. (Naik, 1956: 180, 187)

Tambolón One of the Kaliga-ón. The Bukidnon, Mindanao, Philippines. (Cole, 1956: 97)

Tame Deities of the "untravelled jungles" who "misled travellers to their doom." The Manobo, Philippines. (Jocano, 1969: 22–23)

Ta Mensa An important nature deity of the Ashanti. Ghana. (Parrinder, 1961: 53)

Tane, Tane-mahuta The god of the forests, of all its vegetation and creatures. He was also the god of light. The Maori, Moriori, and elsewhere in Polynesia. (Best, 1924: 236; Shand, 1894: 89; Hongi, 1920: 26; Buck, 1938: 28–30, 264–265; Poignant, 1967: 39; Grey, 1855: 2)

tang dong A mountain demon of the Lepchas. Sikkim. (Siiger, 1967, 2: 145)

T'an-lha A deified mountain in the north. Tibet. (Waddell, 1959: 371)

Ta-no-kami A mountain god who comes down during the rice-growing season. In some regions he is identified with Yama-no-kami. Japan. (Herbert, 1967: 499)

Tao sa salup A nature spirit—"man of the forest." The Bukidnon, Mindanao, Philippines. (Cole, 1956: 96)

Tapio The god of the woods who provides hunters with game. He is represented by the woodpecker. Finland. (de Kay, 1898: 38; Collinder, 1949: 140; Krohn, 1925, 6: 24)

rTa shod dpang mto rgyal ri A god of the woods. Tibet. (Nebesky-Wojkowitz, 1956, 1: 266)

tat kri A mountain *mung* invoked at the Cherim ceremonies to spare them from illness and death. The Lepchas, Sikkim. (Siiger, 1967, 1: 187–190; 1967, 2: 97)

Tauwhare-kiokio The mother of the tree ferns impregnated by Tane. The Maori, New Zealand. (Best, 1924: 114)

Tch'ong Li The personal name of the Peak of the South, Heng chan. China. (Chavannes, n.d.: 419)

Tege A demon of the woods whose wife is Ukwaanija. He is a helper of the shamans and often resides in the Pugaago parrot. The Kapauku Papuans, New Guinea. (Pospisil, 1958: 24, 33)

Tekam The teak tree, a god of the Gonds. Central Provinces, India. (Russell, 1916, 3: 61)

Teluk Biyu A mountain god of Rendang District. Bali, Indonesia. (Grader, 1969, 1: 138)

Thangjing A hill god of the Meitheis. Manipur, India. (Hodson, 1908: 111)

Thang-lha (1) The god of the mountain range of that name. Tibet. (Hoffman, 1956: 18). (2) The god of the plains. The Sherpas of Nepal. Also Tibet. (Furer-Haimendorf, 1965: 232; Snellgrove, 1957: 176)

Thang lha yar bzhugs A mountain god of the Bonpos in the mDo stod region. Tibet. (Nebesky-Wojkowitz, 1956, 1: 229)

mThing gi zhal bzang ma A mountain goddess and a goddess of divination. Tibet. (Nebesky-Wojkowitz, 1956, 1: 177–178, 180)

Thliwale A mountain god of the Isletans. The Pueblo Indians, New Mexico. (Parsons, 1939: 176)

Thog la rgom po A mountain deity of the Bonpos in the Tsha ba sgang region. Tibet. (Nebesky-Wojkowitz, 1956, 1: 229)

mThu dpung spos ri zlum po A mountain god of Tibet. (Nebesky-Wojkowitz, 1956, 1: 214)

Tigbalan A forest demon of the Tagalo-Bisaya who was highly respected. Philippines. (Best, 1892: 197)

Tinggfame A god who controls the sand and sends sandstorms as punishment. Dahomey. (Herskovits, 1938, 2: 142)

Tipi A nocturnal mountain deity who causes illness. The Ifugao, Gonhadan, Philippines. (Barton, 1946: 82)

Tiru-vengadam God of the Tirupati Hills. The Tamils, India. (Aiyangar, 1914: 302)

Ti se lha btsan The god of Mt. Kailas. Tibet. (Nebesky-Wojkowitz, 1956, 1: 223)

Tismar A deified rock in the district of Galdar. Great Canary Island. (Basset, 1925, 2: 507)

Tlapaltecatl A mountain god in Tlaxcala propitiated with Matlalcueye. The Aztec, Mexico. (Duran, 1971: 257)

Tmolus   A mountain god. Lydia, Asia Minor. (Bulfinch, 1898: 61; Morford and Lenardon, 1975: 150, 172)

To-chi-pa   A god associated with volcanoes. Brother of Ku-ku-matz, sons of the earth and sky. They came from the far west. The Mojave, Arizona. (Bourke, 1889: 178)

Tokiaa   The dangerous goddess of the volcano Tacana. The Chimalteco, Guatemala. (Wagley, 1949: 59)

Nana Tongo   A hill god who was a deity of the fertility of men and cattle, and of agricultural growth. The Akim-Kotoku, Ghana. (Field, 1937: 180)

sTong ri dkar po   A Tibetan mountain deity. (Nebesky-Wojkowitz, 1956, 1: 229)

Tonko   A spirit of the wild. The Fulani, Nigeria. (Webster, 1931: 242)

Topochi   A great tree god who was wise and had the power of healing. Son of Shirampa. The Ainu, Japan. (Batchelor, n.d.: 352)

Tore   Among the Ituri Pygmies the god of the forest and "of the lower animals." Zaire. (Pettazzoni, 1956: 31)

Toro-i-waho   A child of Tane representing vines. The Maori, New Zealand. (Best, 1924: 176)

Trikurat, or **Kyam**   A beneficent forest spirit, helpful to hunters. The Kachins, Burma. (Temple, 1925, 3: 22)

Tsa   A mountain demon who spreads illnesses and is propitiated to prevent them. The Nda-pa, Yunnan, China. (Rock, 1959: 804)

bTsan gyi dge bsnyen   A mountain god and guardian of commandments. Tibet. (Nebesky-Wojkowitz, 1956, 1: 220)

bTsan zangs ri 'khyil pa   A mountain deity. Tibet. (Nebesky-Wojkowitz, 1956, 1: 229)

Tseh-zhooh-skah-hah   A god of nature, of the forest. The Wyandot. Ohio, Pennsylvania, New York, and Ontario. (Connelley, 1899: 118)

Tsha ba'i brtan ma chen mo   A mountain goddess ruling the Tshab sgang ridge. Tibet. (Nebesky-Wojkowitz, 1956, 1: 226)

Tsuma-tsu-hime   A daughter of Susano-wo and a planter of trees. Japan. (Herbert, 1967: 332)

Tuamatua   The personification of stones, a guardian of shellfish and seaweed; spouse of Takoto-wai; parents of Rakahore, Makatiti, Rangahua, and Makatata. The Maori, New Zealand. (Best, 1924: 155, 163)

Tui-chimbal   Guardian deity of the cypress grove at Chimaltenango. The Chimalteco, Guatemala. (Wagley, 1949: 55)

Tui Fiji   The god of the *fehi* tree used for making spears and canoes. Tonga, Polynesia. (Collocott, 1925: 232)

Tui-pich-jap   A mountain god and its guardian. The Chimalteco, Guatemala. (Wagley, 1949: 55)

Tui-sakahap   A mountain god and its guardian. The Chimalteco, Guatemala. (Wagley, 1949: 55)

Tukan   An Amerindian stone god. Canada. (Maclean, 1876: 438)

The Tulasi   A plant venerated for its virtues and cultivated in homes, is offered "daily prayers and sacrifices." It is considered the wife of Vishnu. It bestows pardon of sins and purification. India. (Dubois, 1906: 649–650)

Tule   A variant name of Tore, god of the forest. The Banziri, Central African Republic. (Pettazzoni, 1956: 32)

Tumo-pas   Finno-Ugrian god of the oak tree, invoked for rain. The Mordvins, Russia. (Paasonen, 1925, 8: 845)

Tungurahua   A volcano goddess from whom, with Chimborazo, the Puruha and the Panzaleo claim descent. Ecuador. (Murra, 1946: 798; Trimborn, 1968: 97)

Tung Yo, Tung-yoh shen   Another name for the Eastern Peak, T'ai Shan mountain. China. (Shryock, 1931: 91; Ferguson, 1937: 71; De Groot, 1925, 4: 14)

Tunkan   The Stone God (Inyan). The oldest and most popular of the gods among the Minnesota Dakotas is part of their everyday worship. (Lynd, 1889: 159, 168)

Ah T'up   Mayan chief of the forest gods. The Yumil Qasob, Cayo District, British Honduras. (Thompson, 1930: 107)

Tupa   The god of "rocks and mountains." The Marquesas, Polynesia. (Handy, 1923: 246)

Tuulikki   A goddess of the woods, daughter of Tapio. Finno-Ugric. (Larousse, 1968: 304)

Tu-wae-rore The mother of the *kahika-tea, rimu,* and *tane-kaha* trees, by Tane. New Zealand. (White, 1887, 1: 143)

Tz'u-shan Chang Ta-ti The god of Mount Tz'u. China. (Werner, 1932: 536)

Tz'u Shan Ta Ti "The spirit of the hill where the ancestral hall stands." To avoid harm they give it attention. China. (Day, 1940: 41)

Ubanan A nocturnal mountain deity who causes illness. The Ifugao, Philippines. (Barton, 1946: 82)

Udyo Dungar A hill god of the Rajpipla Bhils. India. (Naik, 1956: 181)

Ugtsho Yamasil A mountain goddess of red color who is depicted on a nine-headed tortoise. Tibet. (Nebesky-Wojkowitz, 1956, 2: 33)

Ui-roa A god, son of Ira-tu-roto and Waha-mata-reka, who planted the things which became the permanent trees, grasses and roots. New Zealand. (White, 1887, 1: 32–33)

u kuil kaax A Mayan forest deity. Mexico. (Redfield and Rojas, 1962: 113)

U'lei Shillong The powerful god of Shillong peak. Assam, India. (Gurdon, 1914: 115; Bareh, 1967: 360)

Ulurkura A friendly spirit of the woods who protects them from the ill-disposed sky spirits, the Mundagadji. The Bimbinga, Gulf of Carpentaria, Australia. (Roheim, 1972: 68; Spencer, 1904: 501)

Untaantwa A hill deity of the Fipa. Tanzania. (Willis, 1966: 31)

Ure Amaka God of the forest who is protective of the animals. The Tungus, Siberia. (Lissner, 1961: 240)

Usat A spirit of the Cordillera Mountains. The Isneg, Luzon, Philippines. (Vanoverbergh, 1953: 84)

Ushidarena A deified mountain. Iran. (Gray, 1930: 165)

u'suid bri, u'suid khlaw A forest spirit to whom offerings are made "when the umbilical cord . . . falls off." The Khasis, Assam, India. (Gurdon, 1914: 124)

U Symper A hill god of the Khasis who is propitiated in illness. Assam, India. (Gurdon, 1914: 115–116)

u tcur witsir A dual-sexed, evil and terrifying deity of the high mountains who causes insanity. The Chorti, Guatemala. (Wisdom, 1940: 408–409)

Vaital Dev A hill god in Gujarat represented by a stone. India. (Crooke, 1925, 11: 872)

Valapan A mountain god of the Kunnuvan, worshipped more than their other gods. Southern India. (Thurston, 1909, 4: 122)

Vallonia Roman god of the valleys. (Altheim, 1937: 145; Hadas, 1965: 122)

Vanaspati In the Rig Veda there is a cult for him as "lord of plants." India. (Eliade, 1958: 278)

Vanaspati Mai Goddess of the forest. Northwest Provinces, India. (Keith, 1917: 238)

Vare-jielle A spirit of the woods. The Lapps, Northern Europe. (Holmberg, 1925, 7: 798)

Veniyu yeyu The god of the mountains to whom turkeys were sacrificed for rain. The Zapotec, Oaxaca, Mexico. (Beals, 1935: 189)

Vidar Teutonic god of the primeval forest, the strong and silent god, son of Odin and Grid. (Guerber, 1895: 147; Anderson, 1891: 337–339)

Vilcanota A widely worshipped mountain peak. The Quechua, Peru. (Rowe, 1946: 296)

Vimenya A deified rock in the district of Telde. Great Canary Island. (Basset, 1925, 2: 507)

Vindhya, Vindhyesvari The goddess of the Vindhyan range of mountains. India. (Crooke, 1894: 36; Ions, 1967: 109)

Vir-ava The goddess of the forest. The Mordvins, Russia. (Paasonen, 1925, 8: 845; Leach, 1949, 1: 96)

Vire-pavas The Finno-Ugrian god of the forest among the Mokshas. Russia. (Passonen, 1925, 8: 845)

Vosegus The god of the Vosges mountains and protective of the forests. Gaul. (Renel, 1906: 406; MacCulloch, 1911: 39; Roscher, 1965, 6: 327)

Waghan (mal) A hill god of the Bhils. India. (Naik, 1956: 180)

Waiau A snow goddess of Mauna Kea. Hawaii. (Westervelt, 1963, 2: 56)

Wa-la-gyap   A mountain god and protective deity. Yangtsher, Nepal. (Snellgrove, 1961: 92)

Wami Rasu   A mountain goddess courted by the mountain Imbabura. The Peguche, Ecuador. (Parsons, 1940: 221)

Wao   The goddess of the Upland Forests and of water-springs. Maui, Hawaii. (Ashdown, 1971: 17)

Wendigo   A greatly feared forest god of the northern Indians. Canada. Same as Wenigo of the Ihalmiuk Eskimo. (Mowat, 1968: 239)

Wenigo   A cannibalistic forest god whose only beneficial influence is that he keeps them from venturing into the forest areas where their enemies lurk. The Ihalmiuk Eskimo, Canada. (Mowat, 1968: 239)

Wikame   A very powerful mountain spirit, patron of the shamans, who gives them curing powers. The Wala-pai, Arizona. (MacKennan, 1935: 186)

Winyakaiva   A mountain spirit of the Walapai who gives the shamans curing powers. The Walapai, Arizona. (MacKennan, 1935: 186)

Wirulaka   The guardian of the south of Mount Meru. Burma. (Spiro, 1967: 44n)

Wirupeka   The guardian of the western side of Mount Meru who "controls the mythical garuda birds . . . and . . . serpents." Burma. (Spiro, 1967: 44n)

Witz-Ailik   A Mayan mountain and valley deity. The Chuj, British Honduras. (Thompson, 1930: 57)

Wua-zhu Pu-na   The mountain god of the Ch'ien-so T'u-ssu. Southwest China. (Rock, 1947: 383)

Wuteiatəkw   " 'Heart of tree' [sap] . . . "—a personified supernatural force. The Naskapi, Labrador. (Speck, 1935: 62)

Xasila   A malevolent mountain spirit who may cause death by devouring a person's kidneys. The Isneg, Luzon, Philippines. (Vanoverbergh, 1938: 237)

Xtabai, Xtabay   "A goddess who resides in the rocks of the forest." The Lacandon, Mexico. (Thompson, 1930: 66) Minor seductive goddesses or nymphs of the forest. If a man is invited by one to tarry with her, he must never stay too long, and after should spend the night with Kanank'ax to receive his blessing if he wants to see her again. The Lacandon, Mexico. (Perera and Bruce, 1982: 160, 310)

Yab 'od de gung rgyal   A mountain god of Tibet. (Nebesky-Wojkowitz, 1956, 1: 208–209)

Yakaw   A spirit "who always remains in a standing position on a certain mountain that is covered with cogon grass." The Isneg, Luzon, Philippines. (Vanoverbergh, 1953: 93)

Yaluk   A Mayan mountain and valley god, one of the Mams who are thunder and rain gods. The Mopan of British Honduras and the Kekchi of Guatemala. (Thompson, 1970: 349)

Yamagami-sama   A mountain god at Takashima. Japan. (Norbeck, 1954: 129)

Yama-no-Kami   God of the mountains who descends (as a snake) in the spring and becomes Ta-no-Kami, the god of the rice fields. Phallic deities protective and productive of agriculture. In the fall Ta-no-Kami returns to the mountains as Yama-no-Kami. Japan. (Herbert, 1967: 499; Hori, 1968: 67–68; Czaja, 1974: 50, 167)

Yametsuhime   A Shinto mountain goddess. Japan. (Kato, 1926: 16)

Yapum   God of the woods and the trees who controls the animals and frightens people. The Daphlas and the Mikirs, Bengal and Assam. (Crooke, 1925, 4: 399)

Yar lha sham po   The god of the mountain range of the same name. A protective deity. His consort is Thog gi bu yug. Also Yar lha z'an-po. Tibet. (Nebesky-Wojkowitz, 1956, 1: 95, 203–204; Waddell, 1959: 371; Hoffman, 1956: 18)

Yar lung gi yar lha sham po   Apparently a variant name of Yar lha sham po above. Tibet. (Nebesky-Wojkowitz, 1956, 1: 208–209)

Yifula   A mountain god of the Monguors of Kansu. China. (Schram, 1957: 149)

Yocahuguama   The "yucca spirit." The Taino, West Indies. (Alexander, 1920: 35)

Yolin-pogil, Yobin-pogil   The god of the forest who is beneficent and gives game if moderate in hunting, but will kill the hunter if he overkills. The Yukaghir, Siberia. (Jochelson, 1900/02: 145, 150)

Yon-tra T'u-bbu   A mountain god who rides a white horse "and is accompanied by a white dog and a white rooster." The Tso-so, Southwest China. (Rock, 1947: 422)

Yüan Ling Shu Shên "Park Trees Spirit." China. (Day, 1940: 206)

Yumi Kaax The god of the forest and of hunting who kidnaps young people. Those who return possess "wonderful powers." British Honduras. (Muntsch, 1943: 33)

Yum K'ax Among the Lacandon he is a "dangerous and exacting" supernatural of the forest. Among Mayas of the Peninsula he is "the benevolent corn god." Mexico. (Perera and Bruce, 1982: 311)

Yun Yang The name of the Peak of the South, Song chan, China. (Chavannes, n.d.: 418)

g·Yu ri sngon po A mountain god of the Bonpos in the 'Jang yul region. Tibet. (Nebesky-Wojkowitz, 1956, 1: 229)

Zaliyanu Luwian and Hittite mountain goddess who gives rain and is said to be the wife of Zaskhapuna. Asia Minor. (Guterbock, 1961: 152)

Zangs mdog dpal ri A mountain god of the Bonpos in the rNga yab gling region. Tibet. (Nebesky-Wojkowitz, 1956, 1: 229)

Zaquicoxol The "spirit of the Volcano of Fire"—Volcano of Fuego—and guardian of the road passing between it and Hunahpú. The Cakchiquels, Guatemala. (Recinos and Goetz, 1974: 61)

gZha brag lha rtse A mountain deity of the Bonpos in the Rab sgang region. Tibet. (Nebesky-Wojkowitz, 1956, 1: 229)

Zhabs ra dkar po, Zhang po gnyan dmar Mountain gods of Tibet. (Nebesky-Wojkowitz, 1956, 1: 229, 216)

Zhi-da-mung-po, gzhi-bdag-smug-po A mountain deity of Tibet. (Rock, 1947: 41)

Dz'ibaan Na A Mayan "guardian of the mountains and hunting." He is also a healing deity; is the younger brother of Menzabac. Mexico. (Thompson, 1970: 327)

Zipacna The god of the volcano. The Maya, Guatemala. (Krickeberg, 1968: 79)

Zla btsan gnyan po tshe dbang rtsal A mountain god ruling the dNgul Zla sgang ridge. Tibet. (Nebesky-Wojkowitz, 1956, 1: 225)

Zuttibur Slavonic forest god. (Larousse, 1968: 291)

18

Sea Gods:
Surf and Coastline, Seafarers and Navigation

Aba-Khatun Goddess of the sea. The Olkhonian Buriats (Baikal), Siberia and Mongolia. (Klementz, 1925, 3: 11)

Abd al-Qadir al-Jilani In India a Muhammadan sea saint and a guardian and ruler of the Arabian Sea. (Crooke, 1925, 12: 718)

Abe A goddess who "controls waters of the sea." Daughter of Sogbo. Brazil. (Costa Eduardo, 1948: 79; Bastide, 1960: 559)

Abena Budu "A goddess who resides in a white rock in the sea," which fishermen must not pass over at high tide for fear of misfortune. "If the gods require the *sunsum* of a woman for their use," she sees to someone's drowning. The Effutu, Ghana. (Wyllie, 1966: 478)

Abroh-ku A friendly "god of the surf which breaks upon the landing-place." Once considered malignant. Cape Coast, Ghana. (Mockler-Ferryman, 1925, 9: 278; Ellis, 1887: 45)

Acaste, Akaste One of the Greek Oceanides, daughter of Oceanus and Tethys. (Barthell, 1971: 41; Kerenyi, 1951: 41)

Admete "Untamable." Daughter of Oceanus and Tethys. Greece. (Kerenyi,. 1951: 41; Roscher, 1965, 1, 1: 67)

Aegir, Aeger God of the deep and wild sea, omnipotent in his realm, who caused the great tempests as well as stilled them. His sister/wife is Ran and their nine daughters are the Wave Maidens. Scandinavia. (Guerber, 1895: 171–178; Anderson, 1891: 343; Davidson, 1964: 128–129)

Aequorna Probably a goddess of seafarers and traders. Italy. (Roscher, 1985, 1, 1: 86)

Aethra One of the Oceanids and a wife of Atlas. Mother of the Hyades: Ambrosia, Coronis, Dione, Eudora, Pedile, Phyto, Polyxo, and one son, Hyas. Greece. (Barthell, 1971: 41, 57)

Afrekete A goddess of the sea who guards its riches. Daughter of Agbe and Naete, and like other "youngest" children of African pantheons, she is very knowing and a trickster. Dahomey. (Herskovits, 1938, 2: 155- 156)

Agaue, Agave A Nereid, "the noble," "illustrious," a daughter of Nereus and Doris. Greece. (Kerenyi, 1951: 64; Roscher, 1965, 1, 1: 99; Hesiod-Brown, 1981: 86)

Agbe A sea/sky god, third son of Mawu and Lisa, and head of the sea pantheon. He and his twin/wife Naete were assigned to control the waters. When lightning strikes at sea it is done by him, when on land, by Sogbo. Dahomey. (Herskovits, 1938, 2: 105, 129–130; Verger, 1954: 265)

Agboγu First child of Agbe and Naete. They are sea and sky gods as they live at the horizon of the ocean. Agbogu was assigned to watch over his mother, Naete. Dahomey. (Herskovits, 1938, 2: 152, 154)

Ageb "A god of the deep." Egypt. (Mercer, 1925, 12: 711)

Agoué, Agwé God of the sea and its islands, of fishermen. Husband of La Sirene "(the sea aspect of the Goddess of Love, Erzulie)." Haiti. West Indies. (Deren, 1953: 119–120; Marcelin, 1950: 103, 108; Verger, 1957: 235)

Agwe Woyo A god of the sea—one of the group of Rada deities who can endow with "the knowledge of healing and helping." Father of Agweto and Agweta Woyo. Haiti. West Indies. (Herskovits, 1937: 151, 317)

Ahti, Ahto Finnish god of the sea, of waters. Also called Lemminkainen and, as such, god of love. (Grimm, 1888: 1361; de Kay, 1898: 114; Larousse, 1968: 304)

Ahtoh-enteffi Malignant god of the surf on the Gold Coast. Ghana. (Ellis, 1887: 45; Mockler-Ferryman, 1925, 9: 278)

Aihu-moana A sea deity of the Maori. New Zealand. (Andersen, 1928: 105)

Air The "foam on a rough sea," child of Tarai and Kot. Aka-Jeru, Andaman Islands. Bay of Bengal. (Radcliffe-Brown, 1967: 193)

Lälla 'Aiša A jenn saint of the sea at Tangier. Morocco. (Westermarck, 1920: 39)

Akkruva, Avfruvva A sea goddess whose lower half was fish, upper human. The Lapps, Northern Europe. (Holmberg, 1925, 7: 798)

Aktaia, Actaea One of the Nereids, goddess of the shores. Greece. (Fairbanks, 1907: 56; Kerenyi, 1951: 64; Hesiod-Brown, 1981: 86)

Akua-pehu-'ale "God-of-the-swollen-billows"—a cannibalistic kupua (man/animal). Hawaii. (Westervelt, 1912: 106; 1963, 1: 205)

Akum-brohfo A marine god who drowns whites and saves blacks. Cape Coast, Ghana. (Ellis, 1887: 46)

'Alahtin The moon goddess causes the movements of the sea. The Chumash, California. (Hudson and Underhay, 1978: 75)

Alarum tayaruu, Alarum isuu A deity of the sea of indeterminate sex, "which if seen by people portends danger at sea." The Aleuts, Alaska. (Marsh, 1967: 154)

Alimede One of the Nereids, daughter of Nereus and Doris. Greece. (Barthell, 1971: 12)

Alis-i-tet, Toutop The Lamotrek god of the sea and of fishes. The Carolines, Micronesia. (Christian, 1897: 198)

Aliu-sat, Pon-norol God of the sea and of fishes. Satarval, the Carolines, Micronesia. (Christian 1897: 198)

Aluelap The protector of the ship navigators of Pis. Truk, Micronesia. (Krämer, 1932: 90)

Alulue, Aluluei God of sailors on Truk Island. In the Carolines the teacher and god of navigation. Micronesia. (Pettazzoni, 1956: 348; Poignant, 1967: 80; Burrows, 1947/48: 8)

Amanikable God of the sea of the Tagalog. Philippines. (Jocano, 1969: 9)

Amphinome One of the Nereids. Greece. (Roscher, 1965, 3, 1: 207)

Amphiro A goddess associated with flowing water. Daughter of Tethys and Oceanus. Greece. (Kerenyi, 1951: 41; Hesiod-Brown, 1981: 87)

Amphitrite Goddess of the sea, of the foaming waves, of sea monsters. She is one of those able to calm the stormy seas and winds. Daughter of Nereus and Doris, wife of Poseidon, and mother of Triton and Rhodes. Greece. (Barthell, 1971: 12; Kerenyi, 1951: 64, 186–187; Fairbanks, 1907: 155; Hesiod-Brown, 1981: 60, 79, 87)

Ampithoe One of the Nereids. Greece. (Roscher, 1965, 3, 1: 207)

Anabarima "Father of the Waves" and a god of the north. The Winikina-Warao, Venezuela. (Wilbert, 1973: 4)

Anavigak, Unaviga The sea goddess of the Eskimo at Pond Inlet in north Baffin. The two names "may or may not be different renderings of the same word." Canada. (Nungak and Arima. 1969: 113)

Angeyja A Scandinavian giantess/goddess of the waves. One of nine sisters who were the mothers of Heimdall by Odin. Daughter of Ran and Aegir. (Anderson, 1891: 344, 440; Turville-Petre, 1964: 147–148, 152; MacCulloch, 1964: 152–155)

An-kung God of sailors and protector of people. China. (Werner, 1934: 165)

anqa-kal A sea spirit with "the body of a fish, with a very large shaggy head." The Chukchee, Siberia. (Bogoras, 1904/09: 286)

anqaken-etinvilan "Master of the Sea" to whom reindeer are sacrificed. The Koryak, Siberia. (Czaplicka, 1969: 264, 353)

anqa-naut A sea goddess given at times as the wife of the supreme being. The Koryak, Siberia. (Jochelson, 1908: 25)

Anrur-un-kamui God of the western seaboard of the island of Hokkaido. Japan. (Philippi, 1982: 214–215)

Antrimpus God of the sea of the Sudavians in Samland. Prussia. Same as Autrimpus. (Welsford, 1925, 9: 488; Puhvel, 1974: 83)

Anubis At Delos he, Isis, and Serapis (Egyptian deities) are invoked as protectors of vessels from the dangers of the sea by merchants and sailors. Greece. (Duprez, 1970: 52–53)

Anu en marasi The god of navigation and a god of the rainbow. The Carolines (Namokuk), Micronesia. (Lessa, 1961: 32)

Anuputsaditk A "supernatural being who regulates the height of tides in rivers." The Bella Coola, British Columbia. (McIlwraith, 1948, 2: 579)

Anu-set The sea god of the Mortlock Islanders. Caroline Islands, Micronesia. (Keane, 1925, 2: 242)

Te Anu-ti-Ananua The god of the ocean. The Marquesas, Polynesia. (Christian, 1895: 189)

Aoa-lala A sea being who with Ngao-ngao-le-tai was to people the sea. Samoa, Polynesia. (Mackenzie, n.d.: 266)

Apita'aiterai A demon of the sea. Tahiti, Polynesia. (Henry, 1928: 477)

Apseudes One of the Nereids. Greece. (Kerenyi, 1951: 66; Roscher, 1965, 3, 1: 207)

Aramara God of the sea of the Huichol Indians. Mexico. (Peredo, 1974: 19)

Arnaaluk takannaaluk (Takannakapsaaluk), Arnaluk takanaluk Goddess of the sea and of sea animals. She is called Tanakapsaluk as "the terrible one down there." Her name is sometimes reversed as Takanaluk arnaluk. The Iglulik Eskimo, Canada. (Rasmussen, 1929: 62–63; Nungak and Arima, 1969: 113)

Arnakapfaluk, Arnakapshaaluk Goddess of the sea, "mother and guardian of the sea beasts." She is the source of taboos. Her husband is Igpiarjuk (Ikparyuak). The Copper Eskimo, Canada. (Jenness, 1913/18: 189; Nungak and Arima, 1969: 113; Rasmussen, 1932: 22, 24)

Aruna Hittite god of the sea. Asia Minor. (Cotenau, 1948: 121)

Asherah, Asherat (Phoenician) Goddess of the sea and wife of El, sometimes of Baal. She is considered a goddess of fertility—of mankind and of vegetation. Canaan, Asia Minor. (Schoeps, 1961: 63; Gray, 1964: 123; Patai, 1967: 32–35, 52; Vriezen, 1963: 51; Hooke, 1963: 81; Herm, 1975: 108–109)

Ashiakle A lesser sea goddess of the Gā in Accra. Ghana. (Field, 1937: 86)

Asia (1) Daughter of Oceanus and Tethys and mother of Atlas, Prometheus, Epimetheus, and Menoitios. (2) Daughter of Nereus and Doris. *See also* **Clymene**. Greece. (Kerenyi, 1951: 41; Roscher, 1965, 1, 1: 609)

Asterope An Oceanid, mother of Akragas by Zeus. Greece. (Roscher, 1965, 1, 1: 658)

Atla One of the nine "wave maidens" who were the mothers of Heimdall. Daughter of Aegir and Ran. Scandinavian. (Guerber, 1895: 137; Anderson, 1891: 440)

atui-kamui "Master of the sea." With chup-kamui and nuburi-kamui, their most important deities "who supply them with the main objects of subsistence—beasts, fish, sea-animals." The Inau Cult. The Ainu, Japan. (Sternberg, 1906: 426)

Augeia One of the Scandinavian "wave maidens" and one of the nine giantesses who were the mothers of Heimdall. (Guerber, 1895: 137)

Aulanerk An Eskimo god of the sea who makes the waves. Canada. (Bilby, 1923: 266; Larousse, 1968: 426)

Aurgiafa One of the Scandinavian "wave maidens" who were the mothers of Heimdall. (Guerber, 1895: 137)

Autonoe One of the Nereids, daughter of Nereus and Doris, "giver of inspiration." Wife of Aristaios and mother of Aktaion. Greece. (Kerenyi, 1951: 65, 145; Roscher, 1965, 1, 1: 737)

Autrimpas Slavic god of the sea and of large lakes. Prussia. Same as Antrimpus. (Gimbutas, 1963: 197; Puhvel, 1974: 83)

Avlekete Goddess of the sea at the port of Cotonou. The Fon and the Ge. Dahomey. (Parrinder, 1949: 46)

Avrikiti God of the sea worshipped by fishermen in the vicinity of Whydah. The Ewe, Dahomey. (Ellis, 1890: 67; Mockler-Ferryman, 1925, 9: 278)

Awanagi-no-Kami God of the foam. Son of Izanagi and Izanami. Japan. (Herbert, 1967: 252, 264; Yasumaro, 1965: 15)

Awanami-no-Kami Goddess of the foam. Daughter of Izanagi and Izanami. Japan. (Herbert, 1967: 252, 264; Yasumaro, 1965: 15)

Awa-nui-a-rangi (Kai-tangata) "Great River of Heaven" who "may have been an older god of the sea and ancestor of fish than Tangaroa." Married Whai-tiri. New Zealand. (Mackenzie, n.d.: 297)

Awasaku-mitama "The foaming spirit." The name of Saruda-biko-no-Kami after he had sunk to the bottom "when the water was foaming freshly." Japan. (Yasumaro, 1965: 63)

Axwaga A sea and sky god—one of those who live at the horizon. The second child of Naete and Agbe who was malignant, causing boats to sink. Agbe banished him. He settled on the land, and finally turned himself into a river. Dahomey. (Herskovits, 1938, 2: 152, 155)

Bangputys, Bangputtis Lithuanian god of the sea, or water, who is also god of storms and of waves. (Gimbutas, 1963: 197; Welsford, 1925, 9: 241)

Bardoyats Slavic "god of ships." Prussia. (Gimbutas, 1963: 197)

Baruna A god of the sea. Also called Batara Tengahing Segara. Bali, Indonesia. (Friederich, 1959: 45; Grader, 1969, 2: 180)

Beher Semitic god of the sea, forming a triad with Astar and Medr. Some consider him a war god and identify him with Mahren. Ethiopia. (Littmann, 1925, 1: 57; Moscati, 1960: 225)

Beroe One of the Nereids. Greece. (Roscher, 1965, 1, 1: 784)

Bokoomeerlekuluk A deity who lives on the bottom of the sea, gives seals to the Eskimo, and has the body of a fox and the head of a human, but with tusks. Baffin Land, Canada. (Bilby, 1923: 267)

Bons'ahnu A malignant marine god of the Elmina District to whom human sacrifices were made. Gold Coast, Ghana. (Ellis, 1887: 52)

Bonsu The whale who is the incarnation of the sea god and to whom offerings of corn are made. The Fante and the Gã. Ghana. (Parrinder, 1949: 47)

Sidi Boqnadel A jenn saint of the sea at Tangier. Morocco. (Westermarck, 1920: 39)

Bosumabla A lesser sea goddess of the Gã in Accra. Ghana. (Field, 1937: 86)

Bozomgboke A reef god who is the "opponent and punisher of all impurity," who has other gods under him who were invoked "to cure diseases and detect thieves." The Nzema (Akan), Ghana. (Grottanelli, 1969: 376)

Brizo A goddess invoked for the protection of ships. Also a goddess of dreams. Greece. (Roscher, 1965, 1, 1: 829)

Dewa Taksu Bungkah Karang A lesser god of the sea whose responsibility is "the task of cleaning up coral reefs and promoting shipping." Bali, Indonesia. (Franken, 1960: 224)

Bylgja A Scandinavian goddess of the sea representing "the swell." Daughter of Aegir and Ran. (Eliade, 1958: 206)

Callirrhoe, Kallirhoe One of the Oceanids, "Beautiful Stream"—referring to the sea. Daughter of Oceanus and Tethys. Greece. (Barthell, 1971: 41; Kerenyi, 1951: 41; Roscher, 1965, 2, 1: 919; Hesiod-Brown, 1981: 87)

Calounga Bantu goddess of the sea (in Rio de Janeiro) and goddess of death (in Maranhão). Brazil. (Bastide, 1960: 401, 562)

Calypso, Kalypso Given both as a Nereid and as an Oceanid. She is associated with sheltering caves. Greece. (Kerenyi, 1951: 41; Roscher, 1965, 3, 1: 207; Larousse, 1968: 150; Hesiod-Brown, 1981: 63)

Ca nuoc The dolphin—worshipped by sailors—whom they believe can save them when shipwrecked. Annam. (Cabaton, 1925, 1: 541)

Castor *See* the **Dioscuri**

Cerceïs, Kerkeis One of the Oceanids, daughter of Oceanus and Tethys. Greece. (Roscher, 1965, 2, 1: 1166; Kerenyi, 1951: 41; Barthell, 1971: 41)

Ch'ao Shen God of the tide at Hangchow. China. (Day, 1940: 43)

Cho: haykuh An important sea deity, protector and guardian of boats in storms, has a sea-mammal form. The Ainu, Sakhalin, Siberia. (Ohnuki-Tierney, 1974: 89, 100–101)

Choro   A Greek Nereid. (Roscher, 1965, 1, 1: 898)

Christalline   An evil sea goddess identified with St. Philomena. Mirebalais, Haiti, West Indies. (Herskovits, 1937, 1: 280)

Chryseis   An Oceanid, daughter of Oceanus and Tethys. Greece. (Hesiod-Brown, 1981: 63; Kerenyi, 1951: 41)

Chu-ch'eng, Chu Jung   The god of the Southern Sea is also god of the south and rules summer. China. (Werner, 1932: 196; Day, 1940: 66; Campbell, 1962: 432)

Chu-liang, Chohliang   The ruler of the Western Sea. China. (Werner, 1932: 437; Du Bose,n.d.: 71)

Chusor   A god who "ruled over the sea with Asherat and watched over the punctual succession of the seasons." Phoenicia. Near East. (Herm, 1975: 111)

Cinei-new   A goddess of the sea, wife of Keretkun. The maritime Chukchee, Siberia. (Czaplicka, 1969: 257)

Clymene, Klymene   (1) An Oceanid, daughter of Oceanus and Tethys, mother of Atlas, Menoitios, Epimetheus, and Prometheus by Iapetos, mother of Aegle and Phaethon by Helios. (2) A Nereid, daughter of Nereus and Doris. (3) A nymph, daughter of Zeus and Gaea. Greece. (Barthell, 1971: 41, 54–55, 151; Kerenyi, 1951: 41, 161, 208; Roscher, 1965, 2, 1: 1227; Morford and Lenardon , 1975: 39)

Clytie, Klytia   An Oceanid, daughter of Oceanus and Tethys. Greece. (Barthell, 1971: 41; Kerenyi, 1951: 41; Roscher, 1965, 2, 1: 1245)

Cobun-pogil'   The "Owner of the Sea" and ruler over all the lesser pogil' of the inlets, etc. The Yukaghir, Siberia. (Jochelson, 1900/02: 144–145)

Coha   God of the seas "and associated with the South." The Kekchis, British Honduras. (Thompson, 1930: 59)

Couroumon   A star which "controlled the tides and caused the heavy waves which upset canoes." The Callinago, Lesser Antilles, West Indies. (Rouse, 1948: 564)

Cudjo   A friendly reef god "between Cape Coast Castle and Acquon Point." Once malevolent. Gold Coast, Ghana. (Ellis, 1887: 45; Mockler-Ferryman, 1925, 9: 278)

Cymatolege   A Nereid who "is able to calm the waves of the dark sea and the blasts of stormy winds." She is also associated with the "art of sailing." Daughter of Doris and Nereus. Greece. (Hesiod-Brown, 1981: 60, 86)

Cymo   One of the Nereids, associated with waves. Daughter of Nereus and Doris. *See also* **Kymo.** Greece. (Barthell, 1971: 12; Hesiod-Brown, 1981: 60, 86)

Cymodoce   *See also* **"K".** One of the Nereids—one of those able to calm the waves of the sea and the winds; also associated with the "art of sailing." Greece. (Barthell, 1971: 12; Hesiod-Brown, 1981: 60, 86)

Daeira   One of the Oceanids, daughter of Oceanus and Tethys. Greece. (Barthell, 1971: 41; Roscher, 1965, 1, 1: 933)

Darya Pir   A Muhammadan saint/sea god to whom offerings are made. India. (Crooke, 1925, 12: 718)

Deianeira   A daughter of Nereus and Doris, a sea nymph. Greece. (Roscher, 1965, 1, 1: 976)

Deino   One of the Graiai, daughters of Ceto and Phorcys, the "personifications of the white foam of the sea." Greece. (Roscher, 1965, 1, 2: 1729, 1731; Barthell, 1971: 11; Kerenyi, 1951: 46)

Deiopeia   A Greek Nereid. (Roscher, 1965, 1, 1: 980)

Dero   A Greek Nereid. (Roscher, 1965, 1, 1: 992)

Dexamene   A Nereid. Greece. (Roscher, 1965, 1, 1: 998)

Diamichius   A deified human, whose mortal name was Chrysor, invented the fishing boat and equipment and was the first to sail. Near East. (Langdon, 1931: 54)

Dione   One of the Oceanids, daughter of Oceanus and Tethys, and mother of Aphrodite by Zeus. Greece. (Barthell, 1971: 31, 41; Larousse, 1968: 130; Kerenyi, 1951: 40)

The Dioscuri—Kastor and **Polydeukes, Castor** and **Pollux**   The Greek/Roman divine twins of numerous functions. That in relationship to the sea was to protect sailors and travelers at sea and to assist those suffering shipwreck. (Barthell, 1971: 150; Kerenyi, 1951: 107; Larousse, 1968: 188–190, 215)

Don Battyr   God of the sea of the Ossets. Caucasus. (Littleton, 1965: 127)

Doris   (1) One of the Oceanids, daughter of Oceanus and Tethys. She is the wife of Nereus and mother of the

Nereids, sea goddesses who are associated with "gifts and wealth." (2) A Nereid, daughter of Nereus and the Oceanid Doris. Greece. (Kerenyi, 1951: 41; Barthell, 1971: 11, 41; Larousse, 1968: 146; Hesiod-Brown, 1981: 60, 86–87)

Doto One of the Nereids, associated with the beneficence and generosity of the sea. Greece. (Kerenyi, 1951: 64; Roscher, 1965, 1, 1: 1200; Hesiod-Brown, 1981: 60, 86)

Drafn A Scandinavian sea goddess—"the waves seizing and dragging things along with them." Daughter of Aegir and Ran. (Eliade, 1958: 206)

Drimo A Nereid. Greece. (Roscher, 1965, 1, 1: 1202)

Drymo A Nereid. Greece. (Roscher, 1965, 1, 1: 1203)

Dylan A Celtic sea god, god of the waves. Son of Arianrhod. (MacCulloch, 1911: 110)

Dynamene One of the Nereids. Greece. (Kerenyi, 1951: 64; Roscher, 1965, 1, 1: 1208)

'Ea A great red turtle—a "kupua of the ocean." Hawaii. (Westervelt, 1963, 3: 212)

Eagor The Anglo-Saxon name of the sea god, Aegir. Britain. (Guerber, 1895: 173)

Ecke A Norse god of the tide and of the waves, and also of wind. Brother of Abentrot and Fasolt. He is identified with Oegir. (Grimm, 1880: 232; 1883, 2: 636)

Egia One of the Scandinavian "wave maidens," and one of the nine giantesses who were the mothers of Heimdall. (Guerber, 1895: 137)

Eidyia One of the Oceanids. Greece. (Barthell, 1971: 41)

Eione One of the Nereids, a goddess of the shore. Greece. (Kerenyi, 1951: 65; Roscher, 1965, 1, 1: 1221; Hesiod-Brown, 1981: 60, 86)

Eistla Scandinavian giantess/goddess of the waves. She was one of the nine wave-maiden daughters of Aegir and Ran, who were the mothers of Heimdall by Odin. (Anderson, 1891: 440, 443; Turville-Petre, 1964: 147–148, 152; MacCulloch, 1964: 152–155)

Elektra Daughter of Oceanus and Tethys and mother of Iris and the Harpies by Thaumas. Greece. (Kerenyi, 1951: 41, 60; Roscher, 1965, 1, 1: 1234; Hesiod-Brown, 1981: 60, 63)

Sainte Elisabeth A goddess of the sea, associated with Agoue. Her husband is given as Nouvelle, an escort of Agoue. She may be the same as Ezili. Haiti, West Indies. (Marcelin, 1950: 90)

Enyo One of the Graiai, daughters of Ceto and Phorcys, who are goddesses of the sea and considered "personifications of the white foam of the sea." Enyo was also a goddess of war and its devastation, a companion of Ares. Greece. (Roscher, 1965, 1, 2: 1729; Kerenyi, 1951: 45; Barthell, 1971: 11, 28; Murray, 1935: 214)

Erato (1) One of the Nereids, daughter of Nereus and Doris. (2) Erato, a daughter of Zeus and Mnemosyne, is one of the Muses. Greece. (Roscher, 1965, 3, 1: 207; Kerenyi, 1951: 64)

Etna An Oceanid who bore twins to Hephaestus—"the Palici, the Dioscuri of Sicily." Greece and Italy. (Larousse, 1968: 128)

Et-nekha-Aga-nekha The sea god of the Abkhasians who must be respected. Caucasus. (Janashia, 1937: 148)

Euagora One of the Nereids. Greece. (Kerenyi, 1951: 65; Roscher, 1965, 1, 1: 1392) *See* **Evagora**

Euarne One of the Nereids. Greece. *See* **Evarne** (Roscher, 1965, 1, 1: 1396; Kerenyi, 1951: 65)

Eucrante, Eukrante, Eukrate One of the Nereids, a goddess of waves. Greece. (Barthell, 1971: 12; Hesiod-Brown, 1981: 60, 86; Kerenyi, 1951: 64; Roscher, 1965, 1, 1: 1401)

Eudia A Nereid. Greece. (Roscher, 1965, 1, 1: 1398)

Eudora (1) A Nereid, daughter of Nereus and Doris, associated with gifts. (2) An Oceanid, "Good Giver," associated with blessings. Greece. (Kerenyi, 1951: 41, 64; Hesiod-Brown, 1981: 60, 63, 86, 87; Roscher, 1965, 3, 1: 207)

Eulimene One of the Nereids, associated with "the art of sailing"—"she of good haven." Greece. (Kerenyi, 1951: 64; Roscher, 1965, 1, 1: 1401; Hesiod-Brown, 1981: 86)

Eumolpe A Nereid. Greece. (Roscher, 1965, 1, 1: 1402)

Eunike, Euneike One of the Nereids, daughter of Nereus and Doris. "She of happy victory." Greece. (Kerenyi, 1951: 64; Roscher, 1965, 1, 1: 1404)

Eupompe   One of the Nereids. "Good Voyage," as related to sailing. Greece. (Roscher, 1965, 1, 1: 1409; Kerenyi, 1951: 65; Hesiod-Brown, 1981: 60, 86)

Europa   An Oceanid, daughter of Tethys and Oceanus. Greece. (Hesiod-Brown, 1981: 63)

Eurybia   A goddess who represented the sea's "resistless might." Daughter of Pontus and Gaea; sister of Ceto, Phorcys, Nereus, Thaumas; wife of Crius and mother of Astraeus, Pallas, Perses. Greece. (Fairbanks, 1907: 149; Barthell, 1971: 10, 50; Kerenyi, 1951: 34)

Evagora   One of the Nereids, daughter of Nereus and Doris, wife of Sangarius and mother of Hecuba. Greece. (Barthell, 1971: 12, 48)

Evarne   One of the Nereids. Greece. (Barthell, 1971: 12)

Ewuraba   A "goddess who lives in a rock in the sea." She has earthenware pots with oil and wicks with which she provides light for the conferences of the gods. The Effutu, Ghana. (Wyllie, 1966: 478)

Eyrgjafa   A Scandinavian giantess/goddess of the waves, one of the nine wave-maiden daughters of Aegir and Ran, who were the mothers of Heimdall by Odin. (Turville-Petre, 1964: 147–148, 152; Anderson, 1891: 344, 444; MacCulloch, 1964: 152, 155)

Maitresse Ezili   Goddess of beauty, of love, of coquetry. As the mistress of Agoue T'Arroyo she is a goddess of the sea; as that of Damballah, goddess of sweet waters. Haiti, West Indies. (Marcelin, 1950: 77–79)

Fakana-tua   A son of Huanaki who with others ruled over the aspects of the ocean and the coastline. Niue-Fekai, Polynesia. (Pulekula, 1903: 26)

Farewai   A god of navigation and forecaster of the weather. Ifalik, Micronesia. (Burrows, 1947/48: 8)

Fasolt   A god/giant of wind and water, of tides and waves, and of storms. Brother of Ecke and Abentrot. Norse. (Grimm, 1880: 232; 1883, 2: 636)

Sidi Fat Meimun   A jenn saint of the sea at Tangier. Morocco. (Westermarck, 1920: 39)

Feng Hsiu-ch'ing   The "sovereign lord of the Eastern Seas" whose wife is Chu Yin-e. China. (Werner, 1932: 437)

Fotokia   A reef god at Niue Island. Polynesia. (Loeb, 1926, 1: 161)

Funa-dama   God/goddess of seafaring, of boats, of fishermen. Japan. (Herbert, 1967: 483; Norbeck, 1954: 129–130)

Fu-tsang Lung   The "Dragon of the Hidden Treasures," a god of the seas and of waters generally. China. (Werner, 1932: 144, 285–286)

Galateia   One of the Nereids, beloved by Polyphemus. Greece. (Kerenyi, 1951: 64; Fairbanks, 1907: 150; Hesiod-Brown, 1981: 60, 87)

Galaxaura   Daughter of Oceanus and Tethys associated with "calm" in reference to weather and to the sea. Greece. (Kerenyi, 1951: 41; Roscher, 1965, 1, 2: 1590; Hesiod-Brown, 1981: 63, 87)

Galene   One of the Nereids associated with the quietness of the sea—mirrorlike. Greece. (Roscher, 1965, 1, 2: 1590; Kerenyi, 1951: 64; Hesiod-Brown, 1981: 60, 86)

Gardoayts, Bardoayts, Perdoytus   A Baltic god of seafarers. (Puhvel, 1974: 83)

Gbeyogbo   Fifth child of Naete and Agbe—"the god of the receding surf, is the most evil of all the Sea deities." Dahomey. (Herskovits, 1938, 2: 152, 155)

Geofon   Anglo-Saxon god of the sea. (Grimm, 1883, 2: 565)

Gin   A malignant spirit of the sea who afflicts with diseases. The Land Dyaks, Borneo. (De Crespigny, 1875: 35; Roth, 1968: 166)

Gjalp, Gialp   One of the Scandinavian "wave maidens," daughters of Ran and Aegir, the nine sister/giantesses who were the mothers of Heimdall by Odin. (Guerber, 1895: 137; Anderson, 1891: 344, 447; Turville-Petre, 1964: 147–148, 152)

Glaucus   A mortal who acquired immortality by eating certain herbs and became a marine deity, and upon whom Apollo bestowed the gift of prophecy. Greece. (Fairbanks, 1907: 150; Laroussee, 1968: 147)

Glauke   One of the Nereids, the mirror of the sea full of splendor and light. Greece. (Roscher, 1965, 1, 2: 2675; Kerenyi, 1951: 64)

Glaukonome One of the Nereids who reflects mastery of the sea in sailing—"the dweller in the green sea." Greece. (Kerenyi, 1951: 65; Roscher, 1965, 1, 2: 1677; Hesiod-Brown, 1981: 60, 86)

Gonaqadet A sea god who "brings power and fortune to all who see him." The Tlingit, British Columbia. (Emmons, 1907: 330)

The Graiai Goddesses of the sea who were "personifications of the white foam of the sea." They had the shape of swans, and one tooth and one eye in common. They were always old and gray-haired from birth on. Deino, Enyo, and Pemphredo. Daughters of Ceto and Phorcys. Greece. (Roscher, 1965, 1, 2: 1729, 1731; Barthell, 1971: 11)

Greip One of the Scandinavian giantess/goddesses of the waves, the daughters of Aegir and Ran, who were the mothers of Heimdall by Odin. (Turville-Petre, 1964: 147–148, 152; Guerber, 1895: 137; Anderson, 1891: 344, 447; MacCulloch, 1964: 152–155)

Guabonito Goddess of the sea. Haiti, West Indies. (Alexander, 1920: 261)

Gutufolo A god of the "opening in the reef, . . . invoked when fishing." A lesser god of Tuapa. Niue Island, Polynesia. (Loeb, 1926: 161)

Halia One of the Nereids. She reflects the saltiness of the sea as an aspect of its substance. The personified sea at Rhodes. Greece. (Kerenyi, 1951: 64; Roscher, 1965, 1, 2: 1819; Hesiod-Brown, 1981: 60, 86)

Halimede One of the Nereids, "the sea-goddess of good counsel." Like Halia she relates to the salty aspect of the sea. Greece. (Kerenyi, 1951: 65; Roscher, 1965, 1, 2: 1821; Hesiod-Brown, 1981: 60, 86)

Halosydne Goddess of the sea or the sea itself. Also a surname of Thetis. Greece. (Roscher, 1965, 1, 2: 1823)

Haramara Goddess of the Pacific Ocean. The Huichol, Mexico. (Furst, 1971: 173)

Harsiddh Mata A goddess of the seashore. "It is said . . . that she used to swallow all the vessels that passed by." Rajasthan, India. (Tod, 1920: 681)

Havilia A child of Huanaki who with others ruled over the aspects of the ocean and coastline. Niue-Fekai, Polynesia. (Pulekula, 1903: 26)

Haya-akiduhiko-no-Kami, Haya-Akitsuhi-no-Mikoto, Haya-Akitsu-Hiko-no-Kami God of harbors, of river mouths, of estuaries, of rivers. Son of Izanagi and Izanami. Japan. (Yasumaro, 1965: 14; Holtom, 1938: 181; Herbert, 1967: 264; Kato, 1926: 141)

Haya-akiduhime-no-Kami, Haya-akitsu-hime Goddess of harbors, of river mouths, of estuaries, of rivers. Daughter of Izanagi and Izanami. With Haya-akiduhiko the parents of Awanagi-no-Kami, Awanami-no-Kami, Tsuranagi-no-Kami, Tsuranami-no-Kami, Ame-no-Kuizamochi-no-Kami, Kuni-no-Kuizamochi-no-Kami. Japan. (Yasumaro, 1965: 14, 15: Herbert, 1967: 264; Yasumaro, 1928: 7)

Hetsukaibera-no-Kami A god of the middle beach and also a god of purification, born of the bracelet of Izanagi. Japan. (Yasumaro, 1965: 23; Herbert, 1967: 279)

Hetsunagisabiko-no-Kami God of the outer beach and also a god of purification, born of the bracelet of Izanagi. Japan. (Yasumaro, 1965: 23; Herbert, 1967: 279)

Hezakaru-no-kami God of the inner beach and also a god of purification, born of the bracelet of Izanagi. Japan. (Yasumaro, 1965: 23; Herbert, 1967: 279)

Hina-ke-kai A kupua daughter of Hina who has power over the sea. Hawaii. (Beckwith, 1940: 97)

Hina-lua'i-koa A goddess of the sea. Hawaii. (Beckwith, 1940: 223)

Hina-opuhala-koa A "goddess of the corals and spiny creatures of the sea" who sometimes takes the form of a reef or a woman. Hawaii. (Beckwith, 1940: 219)

Hine-moana An ocean goddess who would engulf canoes if tapu had been broken during their construction, unless they were protected by the other gods. The Maori, New Zealand. (Best, 1924: 255)

Hine-one The Sand Maid assigned to protect Mother Earth from Hine-moana. Daughter of Rangahua. The Maori, New Zealand. (Best, 1924: 154, 163)

Hine-tu-a-tai The "daughter of the sea-coast" and wife of Ta-whaki. They are the parents of the various fishes. New Zealand. (Mackenzie, n.d.: 213)

Hippo A water nymph associated with horses, and with swift currents. Daughter of Tethys and Oceanus. Greece. (Kerenyi, 1951: 41; Murray, 1895: 188; Hesiod-Brown, 1981: 63; Roscher, 1965, 1, 2: 2666)

Hipponoe One of the Nereids—"unruly as a mare," relating to the "moods of the sea." Greece. (Kerenyi, 1951: 65; Roscher, 1965, 1, 2: 2689; Hewiod-Brown, 1981: 60, 86)

Hippothoe One of the Nereids—"swift as a mare" as relating to the "moods of the sea." Greece. (Roscher, 1965, 1, 2: 2692; Kerenyi, 1951: 65; Hesiod-Brown, 1981: 60, 86)

Hiro A god of the seas who could control storms. He was also a god of thieves. Tahiti, Polynesia. (Ellis, 1853: 328, 333)

Hitkoktak With Ikparyuak, friendly toward men and would provide seals. They live in the sea with Arnakap-faluk, the Copper Eskimo of Bathhurst Inlet. Canada. (Jenness, 1913/18: 189)

Ho Hsiu-chi A dragon-king, a god of the seas and of waters generally. China. (Werner, 1932: 158, 285–286)

Hrafn A sea goddess—"the despoiler." Daughter of Aegir and Ran. Scandinavian. (Eliade, 1958: 206)

Hsi Hai God of the Western Sea. China. (Ferguson, 1937: 70)

Hsuan Ming God of the Northern Sea, also known as Yu-chiang. He is also named as a god of the kidneys. China. (Werner, 1932: 219, 437)

Hu, Wu God of the sea of the Fon, the Ewe. Same as Agbe. Dahomey. (Ellis, 1890: 63; Parrinder, 1949: 45; Mockler-Ferryman, 1925, 9: 2780

Humitau A "sea maiden guard of Tau-mariu, lord of the sea." She was kidnapped by Aponi-tolau which caused "the great flood." The Tinguian, Philippines. (Jocano, 1969: 47)

Iaira A Nereid, daughter of Nereus and Doris. Greece. (Roscher, 1965, 2, 1: 1)

Ianassa One of the Nereids. Greece. (Roscher, 1965, 2, 1: 14)

Ianeira, Ianira 1) An Oceanid, daughter of Oceanus and Tethys. 2) A Nereid, daughter of Doris and Nereus. Greece. (Kerenyi, 1951: 41; Roscher, 1965, 2, 1: 14; Hesiod-Brown, 1981: 63)

Ianthe An Oceanid, daughter of Oceanus and Tethys. Greece. (Roscher, 1965, 2, 1: 4; Kerenyi, 1951: 41)

Ichar-tsirew A marine goddess who promotes peace in the household and safety in childbirth. Gold Coast, Ghana. (Ellis, 1887: 45–46)

Ichiki-shima-hime-no-mikoto A goddess of seafarers, created by Amaterasu, or a daughter of Susano-o-no-Kami. She is also called Sayoribime-no-Mikoto. Japan. (Yasumaro, 1928: 32; 1965: 27; Kato, 1926: 70; Herbert, 1967: 483)

Idyia, Eidyia An Oceanid, daughter of Oceanus and Tethys. Greece. (Kerenyi, 1951: 41; Roscher, 1965, 2, 1: 108)

Iemanja *See* **Yemanja**

Ikparayauk With Hitkoktak, friendly toward men and would provide seals. They live in the sea with Arnakap-faluk, the Copper Eskimo of Bathhurst Inlet, Canada. (Jenness, 1913/18: 189)

Ilekerep God of the sea lanes invoked by navigators for guidance. Ifalik, Micronesia. (Burrows, 1947/48: 9)

Imam-shua Goddess of the sea and of sea animals who is invoked for game and good weather. The Chugach Eskimo, Alaska. (Marsh, 1967: 154; Birket-Smith, 1953: 121)

Imd(r) Scandinavian goddess of the waves, one of the nine daughters of Aegir and Ran, who were the mothers of Heimdall by Odin. (Anderson, 1891: 344, 451; MacCulloch, 1964: 152–155; Turville-Petre, 1964: 147–148, 152)

Inawen A pregnant sea goddess to whom offerings are made of "the blood of a chicken mixed with rice." The Tinguian, Philippines. (Cole, 1922: 299)

Indech A Celtic god of the deep seas and a king of the Fomors. He was associated "with vastness, darkness, and monstrous births." Ireland. (Squire, 1906: 48)

Ione A Nereid. Greece. (Roscher, 1965, 2, 1: 292)

Isis At Delos she, Anubis, and Serapis are invoked as protectors of vessels from the dangers of the sea by merchants and sailors. Greece. (Duprez, 1970: 52–53)

Jajyik-Kan, Jajyk Kan A god of the sea who is helpful to the shaman in his ecstatic journey and who mediates between the sky god and mankind. The Altaians, Siberia. (Eliade, 1964: 88; Roheim, 1954: 60)

Jalyintána Father of the sea. The Cagaba and the Kogi, Colombia. (Reichel-Dolmatoff, 1949/50: 115)

Jamaina A goddess of salt water and the most popular of the mermaid goddesses. Belem, Brazil (Leacock, 1972: 157–158)

Jandira A goddess of the sea and of the Rei Turquia family of gods. Belem, Brazil. (Leacock, 1972: 131, 342)

Jarnsaxa, Iarnsaxa One of the Scandinavian "wave maidens," daughters of Ran and Aegir, the nine sister/giantesses who were the mothers of Heimdall by Odin. Also given as the first wife of Thor and the mother of Magni and Modi. (Anderson, 1891: 344, 451; Guerber, 1895: 64, 137; Grimm, 1880: 321; 1883, 2: 530; Turville-Petre, 1964: 147–148, 152; MacCulloch, 1964: 152–155)

Lalla Jmila A jenn saint of the sea at Tangier. Morocco. (Westermarck, 1920: 39)

Juras mate, Jurasmat Latvian "mother of the sea." (Leach, 1950, 2: 608; Gimbutas, 1963: 197; Larousse, 1973: 422)

Jurua An "evil spirit of the sea." North Andaman Island, Bay of Bengal. (Leach, 1950, 2: 564)

Juruwin An evil sea spirit of the Andaman Islands. He devours the drowned and sometimes causes fishermen to have cramps or illness. Bay of Bengal. (Temple, 1925, 1: 468; Leach, 1950, 2: 564)

Kai-pe-chupka-un-kuru A benevolent god of the sea—usually in the form of a large fish. The Ainu, Japan. (Batchelor, 1925, 1: 244)

Ka'ipo Goddess of "the Deep Sea," sister of Pele. Maui, Hawaii. (Ashdown, 1971: 17)

Kai-pok-un-guru A demon of the sea who with his wife " 'reside(s) under the surf' upon the seashore." The Ainu, Japan. (Batchelor, 1925, 1: 244)

Kallianassa A Greek Nereid. (Roscher, 1965, 3, 1: 207)

Kallianeira A Greek Nereid. (Roscher, 1965, 3, 1: 207)

Kalunga "Both the sea and a Supreme Lord." The Bakongo. Among the Ovimbundu he is "associated with the sea, death, and the grave, but he is never thought of as the Supreme Being," as with many peoples. Zaire. (White, 1961: 32; McCulloch, 1951: 72)

Kamihaya-akitsu-hiko God of harbors who controls the land areas, while Haya-akitsu-hime controls that of the sea. Japan. (Yasumaro, 1928: 7)

Kanapu A god of the western seas. Pukapuka, Polynesia. (Beaglehole, 1938: 315)

Kane-huli-koa A god of the sea who is associated with the coral reefs. Hawaii. (Alexander, 1968: 63; Westervelt, 1963, 2: 71)

Kanhaiya God of navigators. India. (Tod, 1920: 611)

Kannakapfaluk The goddess of the sea who controls the seal and the weather. Her assistant is Unga. The Copper Eskimo, Canada. (Jenness, 1913/18: 188)

Kanni Amma A "virgin village-goddess with great power at sea" who is propitiated on launching rites and undertaking voyages. Sometimes a collective deity, the Kanniammar. South India and Ceylon. (Hornell, 1943: 124)

Kanugu A sea god of the Tlingit (Tahlton) invoked for good weather. British Columbia. (Teit, 1919: 201)

Kapää A sea goddess—wife of Peave and mother of Keloguei and Keheari. Ongtong Java, Indonesia. (Chadwick, 1930: 441)

Karaeng lowe A god of the sea and a phallic god who controls fortune, good and evil, and is invoked for health, children, good harvests. Southern Celebes, Indonesia. (Kruijt, 1925, 7: 250; Hartland, 1925, 9: 818)

Kara-ma-kuna A fearsome goddess of the sea who guards the afterworld, Bouru. Micronesia. (MacKenzie, 1930: 170)

Kaukau One of the "guardians of the realm of Hinemoana, the Ocean Maid." With Te Arawaru the parents of cockles, etc. The Maori, New Zealand. (Best, 1924: 105, 155)

Kavna A name of Nuliayuk, the sea goddess. The coastal Iglulik Eskimo, Canada. (Nungak and Arima, 1969: 113)

Ke-au-ka God of the "Moving-seas." Hawaii. (Westervelt, 1963, 2: 5)

Ke-au-miki God of the "strong-current," son of Nakulakai and Nakula-uka. Hawaii. (Westervelt, 1963, 2: 5; 1963, 3: 164)

Kees-du-je-al-ity Kah, Keesshusaah Ankow A powerful evil spirit of the Tlingit who was "master of the tides." British Columbia. Same as Setlm-ki-jash (Haida). (Niblack, 1888: 379)

Keheari A sea goddess, daughter of Peave and Kapää, whose brother is Keloguei. Ongtong Java, Indonesia. (Chadwick, 1930: 441)

Keloguei A sea god, son of Peave and Kapää, and brother of Keheari. Ongtong Java, Indonesia. (Chadwick, 1930: 441)

Kenchreias Personification of the ports of Corinth, a son of Poseidon. Greece. (Roscher, 1965, 2, 1: 1030)

Kenchreios (1) a river god. (2) A son of Poseidon, with Kenchreias the personification of the ports of Corinth. Greece. (Roscher, 1965, 2, 1: 1030–1031)

Keretkun God of the sea and of sea animals—fierce, but can be beneficent. His wife is Cinei-new. He is also called Peruten. The Chukchee, Siberia. (Bogoras, 1904/09: 289, 316–317; Antropova and Kuznetsova, 1964: 823; Czaplicka, 1968: 257)

Khwaja Khizr, Khwaja Khidr God of the sea and of rivers, protective of seafarers. Adopted from Islam. Bengal. (Crooke, 1925, 2: 483; 1925, 12: 717; Briggs, 1920: 199; Crooke, 1894: 26)

Kingoatseak A god of the sea who looks like a dog, cannot surface. The Eskimo, Baffin Land, Canada. (Bilby, 1923: 265)

Kiwa God, guardian, and controller of the ocean, whose wife is Hine-moana. Son of Rangi and Papa. The Maori, New Zealand. (Downes, 1920: 31; Best, 1924: 97, 154, 237)

Klymene *See* **Clymene**

Kolga A Scandinavian sea goddess who represents "the untamed sea." Daughter of Aegir and Ran. (Eliade, 1958: 206; MacCulloch, 1964, 2: 190)

Komokoa God of the sea and of the drowned. He is protective of seals. Pacific Northwest, North America. (Alexander, 1964: 244)

Kompira A god protective of sailors, as well as a god of prosperity. Japan. (Eliseev, 1963: 435; Norbeck, 1954: 131; Eliot, 1935: 138)

Ko-noto-ran-guru An evil sea god who causes storms and wrecks, and drives fish away from fishermen. The Ainu, Japan. (Batchelor, n.d.: 392)

Koodjaunuk A benevolent god who "lives at the bottom of the sea" and surfaces when invoked by the shaman. He is not feared, is of good intentions. The Eskimo, Baffin Land, Canada. (Bilby, 1923: 267–268)

Kou Mang God of the Eastern Sea. China. (Werner, 1932: 437)

Kou-ta Ch'iu-po God of the Western Seas whose wife is Ling Su-chien. China. (Werner, 1932: 437)

Kranto A Nereid, daughter of Nereus and Doris. Greece. (Roscher, 1965, 2, 1: 1407)

Kuang-jun The dragon-king of the Western Sea. China. (Maspero, 1963: 277)

Kuang-li Lung-wang Ta-ti The dragon-king of the Southern Sea. China. (Werner, 1932: 433; Maspero, 1963: 277)

Kuang-she The dragon-king of the Northern Sea who "increases generosity." China. (Maspero, 1963: 277)

Kuang-te Lung-wang Ta-ti The dragon-king of the Eastern Sea who "increases virtue." China. (Werner, 1932: 433; Maspero, 1963: 277)

Kuang-tse Lung-wang Ta-ti The dragon-king of the Northern Sea. China. (Werner, 1932: 433)

Kuan-jun Lung-wang Ta-ti The dragon-king of the Western Sea. China. (Werner, 1932: 433)

Kuttiyandavan A god of the sea invoked before fishing. The Pattanavan, Southern India. (Thurston, 1909, 6: 182)

Kutun God of the reef and of its creatures. Ponape, the Carolines, Micronesia. (Christian, 1899: 381)

Kymata Personifications of waves. Greece. (Roscher, 1965, 2, 1: 1702)

Kymathea A Nereid. Greece. (Roscher, 1965, 2, 1: 1702)

Kymatolege One of the Nereids—"the wave-stiller." Greece. *See also* **Cymatolege**. (Kerenyi, 1951: 65; Roscher, 1965, 2, 1: 1702)

Kymo One of the Nereids, a goddess of the waves. Greece. *See also* **Cymo.** (Kerenyi, 1951: 65; Roscher, 1965, 2, 1: 1703)

Kymodoke One of the Nereids—"the wave-gatherer." Greece. *See also* **Cymodoce.** (Kerenyi, 1951: 65; Roscher, 1965, 2, 1: 1703)

Kymothoe, Cymothoe One of the Nereids, a goddess of waves. Greece. (Kerenyi, 1951: 64; Fairbanks, 1907: 56)

Kyushin The god of the South Sea. China. (DuBose, n.d.: 71)

lafken fucha and **lafken kushe** God and goddess of the sea among some of the Mapuche, Chile. (Faron, 1968: 65)

laf-kenche God of the sea among all of the Mapuche. Chile. (Faron, 1968: 69)

Lageiki A powerful, wicked, and licentious god of the sea. Niue Island, Polynesia. (Loeb, 1926, 1: 161–4)

Lageikiua A child of Huanaki who with others ruled over the aspects of the ocean and coastline. Niue-Fekai, Polynesia. (Pulekula, 1903: 26)

Lagitaitaia A lesser god of Hikutavaki who calmed the seas after a hurricane. Niue Island, Polynesia. (Loeb, 1926, 1: 161; Pulekula, 1903: 26)

Laidekjet The god of the sea. The Marshall Islands, Micronesia. (Krämer and Nevermann, 1938: 239)

Lakhmya A sea spirit of the Son Kolis of Bombay. India. (Punekar, 1959: 161)

Lampra, Khabdi A deity of the Tiparas "who rules sky and ocean." Bengal. (Crooke, 1925, 2: 481)

Langieli With his wife Lino, "gods of the surf and the wind." They are invoked when there are high seas. Ratak, the Marshall Islands, Micronesia. (Knappe, 1888: 66)

Laomedeia One of the Nereids. Greece. (Kerenyi, 1951: 65; Roscher, 1965, 2, 2: 1843)

Latmikaik A goddess who lives at the bottom of the sea. She and Tpereakl are "the origin of all life." Mother of two sons and the fish. Pelew (Paulau) Islands, Micronesia. (Larousse, 1973: 508)

Leiagora, Leiagore One of the Nereids. Greece. (Kerenyi, 1951: 65; Roscher, 1965, 2, 2: 1933)

Leomatagi A god of Hikutavaki invoked for good winds. A child of Huanaki who with others ruled over the aspects of the ocean and coastline. Niue-Fekai, Polynesia. (Loeb, 1926, 1: 161; Pulekula, 1903: 26)

Ler, Llyr Celtic god of the sea and the father of Manannan. His first wife was Aobh, daughter of Bodb Dearg; his second was Aoife, another daughter. The latter transformed her stepchildren into swans. Ireland. (MacCulloch, 1911: 86; 1918: 51)

Leucippe One of the Oceanids, associated with Persephone. Greece. (Barthell, 1971: 41; Roscher, 1965, 2, 2: 1987)

Leucothea A mortal named Ino, daughter of Cadmus. She became a goddess of the sea and of seafarers, protecting them from shipwreck. Mother of Palaemon. Greece. (Murray, 1935: 164–165; Bulfinch, 1898: 219; Morford and Lenardon, 1975: 170, 266)

Li-arongorong-pei A goddess of the sea on Ngatik (Ponape). Caroline Islands, Micronesia. (Christian, 1899: 384)

Liavaha (1) A fish god at Hikutavaki who "made the seas calm after a hurricane." Niue. (Loeb, 1926, 1: 161) (2) A child of Huanaki who with others ruled over the aspects of the ocean and coastline. Niue-Fekai, Polynesia. (Pulekula, 1903: 26)

Limnoreia A Greek Nereid. (Roscher, 1965, 3, 1: 207)

Lino With her husband Langieli, "gods of the surf and the wind." They are invoked when there are high seas. Ratak, the Marshall Islands, Micronesia. (Knappe, 1888: 66)

Llyr Welsh equivalent of Ler.

Loulemwau A god of navigation and of the canoe. Ifalik, Micronesia. (Burrows, 1947/48: 9)

Lowa, Loa A being who "lived on the sea." From a tumor on his leg emerged Wulleb and Limdunanij. The Marshall Islands, Micronesia. (Krämer and Nevermann, 1938: 238)

Lugeilang, Luk-e-ling God of navigation and of seafarers. Yap Islands, the Carolines, Micronesia. (Christian, 1899: 384)

Luyong Baybay The goddess who controlled the tides is the wife of Paigrab, and also a goddess of the underworld. The Sulod, Philippines. (Jocano, 1969: 19)

Lykorias One of the Nereids. Greece. (Roscher, 1965, 2, 2: 2183)

Lysianassa One of the Nereids. Greece. (Kerenyi, 1951: 65; Roscher, 1965, 2, 2: 2211)

Ma'atahi A god of the sea. Tahiti, Society Islands, Polynesia. (Henry, 1928: 359)

Madai God of sailors and of fishermen, also of fishes. Yap Islands, the Carolines, Micronesia. (Christian, 1899: 385)

Mahilane The sea personified and apparently the equivalent of Makaneta. South Africa. (Willoughby, 1932: 5)

Ma-hsien A "Spirit of the Sea, represented as a unicorned dragon." China. (Werner, 1932: 434)

Maira One of the Nereids. Greece. (Roscher, 1965, 2, 2: 2285)

Makaneta *See* **Mahilane**

Maklium-sa-tubig God of the sea. The Bisayan (Panay), Philippines. (Jocano, 1969: 20)

Mama Cocha, Mama qoca Goddess of the sea. The Inca and the Chincha, Peru. (Rowe, 1946, 2: 295; Alexander, 1920: 224; Hatt, 1951: 878; Markham, 1969: 133)

Mama Salma A Muhammadan sea saint, a guardian of the sea and ruler of the Persian Gulf. India. (Crooke, 1925, 12: 718)

Mambang Tali Harus The "god of mid-currents." Malay Peninsula. (Skeat, 1925, 8: 354)

Manannan Celtic god of the sea, "particularly . . . between northeast Ireland and Britain." Also god of "the island otherworld." His wife was Fand. Son of Ler. Ireland. (Ross, 1967: 285; MacCulloch, 1918: 86, 88; Mac Cana, 1970: 69)

Manquian An important mythical local deity of the coastal Mapuche. He was a fisherman whose feet became entrapped by two rocks. In spite of shamanistic rituals he gradually turned to stone. Now they believe he is "fisher of souls, lord of the sea, and that they are Manquian's 'people'." Chile. (Faron, 1968: 69, 70)

mara-halddo The "spirit of the sea." The Lapps, Northern Europe. (Leach, 1949, 1: 475)

Mari amma Primarily the goddess of smallpox, but in South India and Ceylon also known as a "protectress of seafarers." (Hornell, 1943: 121; Martin, 1914: 253; Whitehead, 1916: 26–28)

Mariana A very popular goddess of Belem—"special protector of sailors and of the Brazilian Navy," as well as a goddess of healing, of childbirth, and of love. Brazil. (Leacock, 1972: 133–134)

Marulupolamma The sea goddess of the Vada. India. (Thurston, 1909, 7: 262)

Masara-koro Kamui The spirit of "the shore just above high tide mark," protective of fishing boats. The Ainu, Japan. (Munro, 1963: 43, 67)

Ma Tsu A goddess protective of sailors. China. (Mac Lagan, 1925, 6: 646)

Matsu Goddess of the sea. Taiwan. (Grove, 1982: 94)

Ma Tsu P'o The goddess of the ocean, of the Southern Sea, and of sailors is invoked for "fine weather and safe conduct," as she controls the elements. China. (Day, 1940: 84; De Groot, 1925, 4: 14; Williams, 1976: 336–337)

Melicertes A mortal, son of Ino (Leucothea), who became a sea god who brought ships safely into port. His name as a deity was Palaemon, called by the Romans Portunus. Greece. (Roscher, 1965, 2, 2: 2632; Fairbanks, 1907: 150; Murray, 1935: 165; Morford and Lenardon, 1975: 170, 266)

Melite (1) One of the Nereids. (2) An Oceanid and companion of Persephone. Greece. (Kerenyi, 1951: 64; Roscher, 1965, 2, 2: 2643; Hesiod-Brown, 1981: 60, 86)

Mellih A Phoenician god of sailors and fishermen. Near East. (Paton, 1925, 9: 893)

Melkart, Melqart A Phoenician solar god, city god of Tyre, and seemingly also a god of the sea. Near East. (Larousse, 1968: 81; Moscati, 1960: 114)

Menestho An Oceanid, daughter of Oceanus and Tethys. Greece. (Kerenyi, 1951: 41; Roscher, 1965, 2, 2: 2793)

Menippe One of the Nereids—"the courageous mare," relating to the "moods of the sea." Greece. (Kerenyi,

1951: 65; Roscher, 1965, 2, 2: 2793; Hesiod-Brown, 1981: 60, 86)

Messapus The Illyrian name of Poseidon as he was worshipped in Falerii. Italy. (Altheim, 1937: 154)

Metileru A sea demon who carries off the souls of the ill "in his canoe of flame" when the winds are from the east. Faraulep, Micronesia. (Burrows, 1947/48: 13)

Mγntɬato·snγm "Tide-Measurer," who controls the height of the tides. The Bella Coola, British Columbia. (Mc Ilwraith, 1948, 2: 237)

Mitg The spirit of the sea of the Itel'mens. Siberia. (Antropova, 1964: 880)

Mo acha The benevolent god of the calm and peaceful sea. Brother of Shi acha. The Ainu, Japan. (Batchelor, 1925, 1: 242)

Moana-nui-ka-lehua A sea goddess of Hawaii. (Beckwith, 1940: 176)

Mongotohoro A god of the sea who lived on "the reef flat where people walk" and was regarded with affection. One of their main gods. Kapingamarangi, Polynesia. (Emory, 1965: 202, 216)

Mor'ava Finno-Ugrian "sea-mother." The Mordvins, Russia. (Paasonen, 1925, 8: 845)

Morgen A Celtic sea god. (MacCulloch, 1911: 178)

Sidi Muhammed l-Bhar The "sea is itself personified as a saint" of this name to whom sacrifices are made of a silver coin in gales at sea. Morocco. (Westermarck, 1926, 1: 50, 90)

Mutering Segara "Lord Churning the Sea." Bali, Indonesia. (Grader, 1969, 1: 172)

Mwarisepa, or Morisepa A spirit who is supposed to help mariners lost at sea, but there is little faith in him. Ifalik, Micronesia. (Burrows, 1947/48: 13)

Naete Twin and wife of Agbe, children of Mawu-Lisa. They and their children are sea and sky gods, as they live on the horizon where sea and sky meet. She also inhabits rivers. Dahomey. (Herskovits, 1938, 2: 129–130, 151–152, 160)

Nai A sea god who is also associated with corn planting. the Gā in Accra, Ghana. (Field, 1937: 69, 89)

Nakadutsu-no-Wo-no-Mikoto, Naka-tsu wata-dzu-mi, Nakatsuwata-tsumi-no-Kami, Nakazutsu-no-o A god of the sea and of seafaring. With Uha-tsu (Uwazutsu-no-o) and Soko-tsu (Sokozutsu-no-o), frequently worshipped and treated as one and invoked for prosperous voyages. Japan. (Aston, 1925, 11: 466; Yasumaro, 1965: 24; Kato, 1926: 70)

Nakorut A name of the sea goddess, giver of sea animals. The Copper Eskimo, Canada. (Nungak and Arima, 1969: 113)

Na-maka-o-ka-hai, Na-maka-haha'i A goddess of the sea who rules its surface. Daughter of Haumea, sister and enemy of Pele. Hawaii. (Westervelt, 1963, 2: 8, 9; Ashdown, 1971: 69; Beckwith, 1940: 171)

Nang Mekhala A deity of the sea. Laos. (Deydier, 1952: 30)

Nanoquaqsaq The equivalent of Sedna among the Akuliarmiut of Baffin Land. Canada. (Boas, 1884/85: 587)

Nati A god of the sea and its fish worshipped particularly by fishermen. The Ewe in the vicinity of Whydah, Dahomey. (Ellis, 1890: 66–67; Mockler-Ferryman, 1925, 9: 278)

Ndauthina The god of seafarers and fishermen is also a god of fire and of light. Also a god of war. Lau Islands, Fiji, Melanesia. (Thomson, 1925, 6: 15; MacCulloch, 1925, 8: 50; Hocart, 1929: 196)

Neguno God of the sea of the Zambal. Philippines. (Jocano, 1969: 160)

Nehalennia A Belgian or Frisian goddess of seafarers and traders on the island of Walcheren. (Ross, 1967: 339; Grimm, 1880: 257; Wagner, 1882: 107)

Nemertes One of the Nereids—"the truthful." Greece. (Kerenyi, 1951: 65; Roscher, 1965, 3, 1: 117)

ɛnɛmxx·álig·iu, 'nəmxxaligiu A sea monster "similar to a giant halibut" who lives at the bottom of the sea and has seals for dogs. "When it arises the water becomes shallow and dangerous tides begin to flow." The Kwakiutl, British Columbia. (Boas, 1935: 128)

Neptune An early Roman god believed to have been a god of moisture and water invoked during drought. With the introduction of Poseidon and being identified with him, Neptune became god of the sea as well as of fresh waters. (Fairbanks, 1907: 159; Jayne, 1962: 435; Bulfinch, 1898: 7, 218)

The Nereids, The Dorides The daughters of Nereus and Doris were sea goddesses and also oracular. Primarily they represent all beauty and inspire love. With the Oceanids they are representative of law and justice in the universe. (Kerenyi, 1951: 64–66; Murray, 1935: 163, 171; Hesiod-Brown, 1981: 30, 31) They are: Agaue (Agave), Aktaia (Actaea), Alimede, Amphinome, Amphitrite, Ampithoe, Apseudes, Arethusa, Autonoe, Beroe, Choro, Cymo, Cymodoce, Deianeira, Deiopeia, Dero, Dexamene, Doto, Drimo, Drymo, Dynamene, Eione, Erato, Euagora (Evagora), Euarne (Evarne), Eucrante, Eudia, Eudora, Eukrante, Eulimene, Eumolpe, Eunice (Eunike), Eupompe, Galatea, Galene, Glauce, Glauconome, Halia, Halimede, Hipponoë, Hippothoë, Iaira, Ianassa, Ianeira, Ione, Kale, Kallianassa, Kallianeira, Kalypso, Kranto, Kymathea, Kymatolege, Kymo, Kymothoe, Laomedea, Leagora, Lycorias, Lysianassa, Maira, Melite, Menippe, Nausithoe, Nemertes, Nesaia, Neso, Oreithyia, Panopea, Pasithea, Pasithoë, Pherousa, Phyllodoke, Plexaura, Ploto, Polynoe, Pontomedusa, Pontopereia, Pronoe, Protho, Proto, Protomedea, Psamathe, Sao, Speio (Speo), Thalaeia, Themisto, Thetis, and Thoë.

Nereus God of the sea renowned for his benevolence, truthfulness, trustworthiness and wisdom. Son of Pontus and Gaea and brother of Ceto, Eurybia, Phorcys, and Thaumas. His wife was Doris, a daughter of Oceanus. They were the parents of the Nereids. Greece. (Kerenyi, 1951: 34, 45; Cox, 1870, 2: 256; Barthell, 1971: 10–12; Bulfinch, 1898: 219)

Nerites The only son of Nereus who was the lover of Aphrodite while she lived in the sea. When he refused to go with her to Olympus she transformed him into a cockle. Greece. (Kerenyi, 1951: 70; Roscher, 1965, 3, 1: 272)

Nesaia, Nesaea One of the Nereids—"the dweller on islands." Greece. (Kerenyi, 1951: 64; Roscher, 1965, 3, 1: 278; Hesiod-Brown, 1981: 30, 60, 86)

Neso One of the Nereids—"the island-goddess." Greece. (Kerenyi, 1951: 65; Roscher, 1965, 3, 1: 279; Hesiod-Brown, 1981: 86)

Nestis A sea and fish god who gives nutrition to all Sicily. Italy. (Roscher, 1965, 3, 1: 287)

Nethun, Nethuns An Etruscan god identified with Neptune. Italy. (Dumézil, 1966, 2: 673; Pallottino, 1975: 100)

Ngao-ngao-le-tai With Aoa-lala, created by Tangaloa "that they two may people the sea." Samoa, Polynesia. (Mackenzie, n.d.: 266)

Ni The ocean—invoked for abundance of fish and for protection from drowning. The Chimu, Peru. (Rowe, 1948: 50; Markham, 1969: 122; Alexander, 1920: 223)

Nimmoi The spirit of the sea. Truk, Micronesia. (Gladwin and Sarason, 1953: 66)

Ninbubu Ea as the god of sailors. Sumer, Near East. (Langdon, 1931: 105)

Nirivik A goddess who calms the sea. The Tikirarmiut, Alaska. In Greenland she is the goddess of the sea and of the food supply. (Marsh, 1967: 154–157)

Nisoukepilen A female spirit, half-eel, half-human, who is the guardian of the sea. She lives in the sacred lake. Truk, Micronesia. (Bollig, 1927: 3)

Njai, or **Ratu Loro Kidul** Goddess of the sea who is much revered. Java, Indonesia. (Kruijt, 1925, 7: 250; Mac Leish, 1971: 29)

Njord(r), Niordr Benevolent god of the sea who calmed its wildness and controlled the winds. He was a god of seafarers protective of trade and fishing, bestowing wealth on men. As a Vanir god he was the father of Frey and Freya, who with him went as hostages to dwell in Asgard after the war between the Aesir and Vanir. His wife was Nerthus. Among the gods of Asgard he became the husband of Skadi and they were the "personifications of summer and winter." He was invoked to bring the summer warmth and a plentiful harvest. Scandinavia. (Guerber, 1895: 107–110; MacCulloch, 1964: 101–102; Grimm, 1880, 1: 217–218; Wagner, 1882: 183–184; Davidson, 1964: 29, 106; Snorri Sturluson, 1964: 51)

Noäkx̣nɣm A supernatural sea being who is believed to bring the salmon and the berries from the far west. He comes for the kusiut dances; can destroy men but pays them little attention. The Bella Coola, British Columbia. (McIlwraith, 1948, 1: 53–54)

Nodon A god of the depths of the sea who had a temple in Gloucestershire. Britain. Same as Nudd (Wales). (MacBain, 1917: 90; Squire, 1906: 253; Roscher, 1965, 3, 1: 446)

Nootaikok A benevolent "spirit of icebergs" who provides the Eskimo with seals. Canada. (Bilby, 1923: 268; Larousse, 1968: 426)

Nuada A god of the seas and one of the great gods of the Tuatha De Danann. He lost a hand in battle. It was replaced with a silver one by Diancecht, then completely restored by Miach. Celtic Ireland. (Squire, 1906: 51–52, 74–81; MacBain, 1917: 109, 130–131)

Nudd A god of the depths of the sea and of its treasures, not of the sea proper. He is identified with Nuada, Nodon. Wales. (MacBain, 1917: 91, 95; Squire, 1906: 252–253; MacCulloch, 1911: 115)

Nuki-i-te-tafa-tai "Gods of the sea foam." Tikopia, Polynesia. (Firth, 1967, 2: 293)

Nuliajuk, Nulijajuk Goddess of the sea and of the land, and "mother of all animals," both sea and land. The Netsilik and the Mackenzie Eskimo, Canada. (Balikci, 1970: 205–206; Rasmussen, 1931: 224; Ostermann, 1942: 56)

Nulirahak An "old woman living at the bottom of the sea" to whom sacrifices are offered. The Eskimo, Indian Point. (Bogoras, 1904/09: 318)

Nyange A devil associated with the sea who causes madness and who is worshipped, propitiated, and exorcised with a cult of dancing. His symbol is a trident. The Hadimu, Zanzibar. (Ingrams, 1925: 140)

Nyevile The sea personified is invoked for good fishing. Azele Yaba is sometimes named as his wife. The Nzema (Akan), Ghana. (Grottanelli, 1967: 38–40)

Nyongmo Tshawe Among the Gã in Teshi he is a sea god. Chana. (Field, 1937: 73)

Oatuatafu God of the channel in the reef. Matautu, Tikopia, Polynesia. (Firth, 1967, 2: 368)

Obaji, Obazi A god of the sea. Nigeria. (Talbot, 1967: 120)

Obotu A lesser sea god of the Gã in Accra. Ghana. (Field, 1937: 86)

Oc A sea god who "lives on lonely islands, comes at night to the inhabited ones and devours children." Truk, Micronesia. (Krämer, 1932: 319)

The Oceanids Sea and fresh water deities, daughters of Oceanus and Tethys. They are associated either with features of the sea and/or with favorable influences in the life of man such as wealth, statesmanship, success. The lists of Oceanids and Nereids are very similar, but Oceanids "are specifically related to the dispensation of Zeus . . . with the help of Lord Apollo and of their brothers the Rivers, bring young boys to manhood." They and the Nereids help with the dispensation of justice; promote the arts; represent all beauty. Greece. (Murray, 1935: 160, 170; Barthell, 1971: 41; Larousse, 1968: 146; Hesiod-Brown, 1981: 29–31) They are:

Abarbarea, Acaste, Admete, Aethra, Amphiro, Asia, Asterope, Bateia, Caliadne, Callirrhoe (K), Calypso, Cerceis (Kerkeis), Chariclo, Chryseis, Cleochareia, Clymene, Clytie (Klytia), Creusa, Daeira, Dodone, Doris, Eidyia (Idyia), Elektra, Ephydateia, Etna, Eudora, Europa, Eurynome, Galaxaura, Helike, Hippo, Iache, Ianeira, Ianthe, Iphianassa, Kapheira, Leucippe, Limnoreia, Liriope, Meliboea, Melite, Melobosis, Menestho, Metis, Nycheia, Ocyrhoe, Paregoros, Peitho, Periboea, Perse (Perseis), Petraia (Petraea), Phaino, Philyra, Pleione, Plexaura, Plouto, Polydora, Polyxo, Prymno, Rhodeia, Rhodope, Telesto, Thoe, Tyche, Xanthe, Zeuxippe, and Zeuxo.

Oceanus One of the Titans, son of Uranus and Gaea. He was considered the great stream encircling the earth. With his sister/wife Tethys, the gods of the oceans and the fresh waters and parents of the other sea and water deities. Greece. (Barthell, 1971: 11–13, 41; Murray, 1935: 160–161; Larousse, 1968: 146; Hesiod-Brown, 1981: 56–57, 62–63)

Ocory A sea god who "shines like fire at night; he is said to dig up the bodies buried on the beach and devour them at sea." Truk, Micronesia. (Krämer, 1932: 319)

Oegir, Ogir Variants of Aegir.

Oho-wata-tsu-mi, O-Wata-Tsu-Mi The greatest of the sea gods who precedes Susa-no-wo. First son of Izanagi and Izanami. Japan. (Revon, 1925, 9: 236; Yasumaro, 1928: 7; Yasumaro, 1965: 14)

Okita Myojin A goddess—protectress of the embankment against the sea. A deified human. Japan. (Kato, 1931: 127)

Okitsukaibera-no-Kami "The deity of the water between far off sea and strand." Japan. (Yasumaro, 1965: 23)

Okitsunagisabiko-no-Kami God of the strand. Japan. (Yasumaro, 1965: 23)

Okizakaru-no-Kami God of "the far off sea." Japan. (Yasumaro, 1965: 23)

Okura-nushi A god of the Bay of Oka, active and sometimes hostile. Japan. (Herbert, 1967: 480)

Okyroe, Okyrrhoe Daughter of Oceanus and Tethys and associated with the "mobility . . . [of] water, wind and wave." Greece. (Kerenyi, 1951: 41; Roscher, 1965, 3, 1: 828)

Olokoun   Yoruban god of the sea. Brazil. (Bastide, 1960: 570)

Olokun   God/goddess of the sea, also of wealth and of fertility. Sex varies in different areas. The Yoruba, Nigeria. In Puerto Rico, a hermaphrodite and ruler of "a great retinue of mermaids and tritons." (Idowu, 1962: 14; Parrinder, 1949: 45; Lucas, 1948: 98; Gonzalez-Wippler, 1975: 26)

Oluk   The "spirit of driftwood" is important to seafarers because of the fish which stay close to the driftwood. If he is angered there will be no fish, but danger from sharks. Truk, Micronesia. (Bollig, 1927: 13, 27)

Ombwiri   A "genie of water courses or the sea, associated with the search for fortune." The Fang, Gabon. (Fernandez, 1972: 241)

O Ming   The "Spirit of the Eastern Sea." Also known as Koumang. China. (Werner, 1932: 437)

Oomarreeo   The "god and creator of the seas." Son of Tangaroa and Papa. Society Islands, Polynesia. (Williamson, 1933: 59)

Opo   Ashanti god of the sea. Ghana. (Parrinder, 1949: 47; Clarke, 1930: 438; Rattray, 1923: 146)

Oreithyia   Daughter of Nereus and Doris and wife of Boreas, the north wind. Greece. (Fairbanks, 1907: 170; Roscher, 1965, 3, 1: 207)

'Oropa'a   The great god of the ocean who swallows people and canoes and whose messenger is the whale. Son of Tumunui and Papa-raharaha. Tahiti, Polynesia. (Henry, 1928: 165, 344, 358)

Orusandiamma   A sea goddess worshipped by fishermen on the east coast. Sister of Ramasondi. India. (Crooke, 1925, 12: 717)

Ota-patche-guru   A demon of the sea who with his wife causes the sand to fly. The Ainu, Japan. (Batchelor, 1925, 1: 244)

Ot's'uved-azerava   A goddess of the seas, of all waters. The Moksha (Mordvins), Russia. (Paasonen, 1925, 8: 845)

O-Wata-Tsu-Mi   The greatest of the sea gods, first born of Izanagi and Izanami. He is "also known as the Old Man of the Tide, Shio-Zuchi." Japan. (Yasumaro, 1928: 7; Holtom, 1938: 181; Larousse, 1968: 416)

Oxun   A mermaid goddess of Yoruban origin. Belem, Brazil. (Leacock, 1972: 157–158)

Oyeni   A sea god of the Gã in Accra. Ghana. (Field, 1937: 69)

Pae Devi, Pa Janjali   The goddess who controls the Seven Seas and is goddess of fish and of water animals. She is invoked in cases of evil eye. Her husband is Sunagi Moru. The Bhils, India. (Naik, 1956: 181, 187)

Pahuanuiapita'aiterai   A demon of the sea. Tahiti, Polynesia. (Henry, 1928: 470)

Palaemon, Melicertes   A god of the sea and of sailors, protective from shipwreck. He and his mother, Ino (Leucothea), were deified mortals. Greece. (Bulfinch, 1898: 220; Fairbanks, 1907: 150; Morford and Lenardon, 1975: 170, 266)

Paluelap   A god of navigation. Ifalik, Micronesia. (Burrows, 1947/48: 8)

Panda   Goddess of the sea, equivalent of Yemanja. Brazil. (Bastide, 1960: 570)

Panopeia, Panope, Panopea   One of the Nereids, "Panorama"—a daughter of Nereus and Doris. Greece. (Kerenyi, 1951: 64; Roscher, 1965, 3, 1: 1538; Hesiod-Brown, 1981: 60, 86)

Pasithea   One of the Nereids, a goddess of the sea. Greece. (Roscher, 1965, 3, 2: 1674; Kerenyi, 1951: 64; Hesiod-Brown, 1981: 60, 87)

Pasithoë   "All-fast," an Oceanid associated with the sea. Greece. (Hesiod-Brown, 1981: 63, 87; Kerenyi, 1951: 41; Roscher, 1965, 3, 2: 1674)

Patesi-Gal-Zuab   A Babylonian god of the sea invoked in exorcising demons. Near East. (Thompson, 1903: 35)

Paump'agussit   "The Sea." The Narraganset, Massachusetts and Rhode Island. (Skinner, 1913: 91)

Peave   The god of the ocean who if properly treated gives abundance of fish. If not, he "sends floods and storms." His wife is Kapãa; father of Keloguei and Keheari. Ongtong Java, Indonesia. (Chadwick, 1930: 441)

Pelagos   A god of the sea, son of Gaea and Aither. Same as Pontos. Greece. (Roscher, 1965, 3, 2: 1816)

Pemphredo   One of the Graiai, daughters of Ceto and Phorcys. A sea goddess representing the white foam. Greece. (Kerenyi, 1951: 45; Barthell, 1971: 11)

Perdoytus A god of seafarers. Lithuania. Other names are Bardoayts, Gardoayts. (Puhvel, 1974: 83)

Pereba A half-human, half-fish goddess of the sea. The Effutu, Ghana. (Wyllie, 1966: 478)

Perseis, Perse One of the Oceanids, wife of Helios and mother of Aega, Circe, Pasiphae, Aeetes, and Perses. Greece. (Barthell, 1971: 41; Larousse, 1968: 142)

Te Petipeti A sea deity of the Maori. New Zealand. (Andersen, 1928: 104)

Petraia, Petraea An Oceanid—"Rocky," in association with the sea. Daughter of Tethys and Oceanus. Greece. (Hesiod-Brown, 1981: 63, 87; Kerenyi, 1951: 41)

Pherousa, Pherusa One of the Nereids and also the name of one of the Horai. Greece. (Kerenyi, 1951: 64; Roscher, 1965, 3, 2: 2299)

Phorcys One of the old gods of the sea representing its wildness. Usually given as the son of Pontus and Gaea. He was the brother of Nereus, Thaumas, Eurybia and Ceto, who was also his wife and the mother of the Graiai. Greece. (Kerenyi, 1951: 42; Fairbanks, 1907: 149; Barthell, 1971: 10, 11)

Phyllodoke One of the Nereids. Greece. (Roscher, 1965, 3, 2: 2487)

Plexaura Daughter of Oceanus and Tethys, associated with "whipping wind." Also given as a Nereid, Plexaure. (Kerenyi, 1951: 41; Roscher, 1965, 3, 1: 207; 1965, 3, 2: 2564; Hesiod-Brown, 1981: 63, 87)

Ploto One of the Nereids—"the swimmer." She is also associated with the "art of sailing." Greece. (Kerenyi, 1951: 64; Roscher, 1965, 3, 2: 2565; Hesiod-Brown, 1981: 60, 86)

Plouto Daughter of Oceanus and Tethys, associated with "gifts and wealth." Greece. (Kerenyi, 1951: 41; Hesiod-Brown, 1981: 63)

Poakwa The sea as a deity. Akim-Kotoku, Ghana. (Field, 1948: 152)

Pollux, Polydeukes *See* **The Dioscuri**

Polynoe One of the Nereids—"giver of reason." Greece. (Kerenyi, 1951: 65; Roscher, 1965, 3, 1: 207)

Pontomedusa A Greek Nereid. (Roscher, 1965, 3, 1: 207)

Pontopereia One of the Nereids—"the seafarer." Greece. (Kerenyi, 1951: 65; Roscher, 1965, 3, 2: 2758)

Pontus, Pontos The personification of the sea. Son of Gaea (alone) and with her the parents of Ceto, Eurybia, Phorcys, and Nereus. Greece. (Barthell, 1971: 10, 11; Kerenyi, 1951: 34; Cox, 1870, 2: 256; Larousse, 1968: 146)

Portunus Roman god of the sea and of harbors. Same as Palaemon. (Fairbanks, 1907: 150; Bulfinch, 1898: 220; Larousse, 1968: 200)

Poseidon An early aspect of his was that of a god of horses, of horsemanship and of fertility, at which time his wife was Demeter. An alliance with Medousa produced Pegasus who sprang from her neck when her head was severed by Perseus. He, Poseidon, became ruler of the sea and of waters in his marriage with Amphitrite, in which aspect he is best known. He was also god of earthquakes and invoked to stabilize the land. Son of Rhea and Cronus, brother of Zeus. Greece. (Kerenyi, 1951: 22, 181–185; Cox, 1870, 2: 262; Frazer, 1961: 195–196; Fairbanks, 1907: 55, 153; Campbell, 1964: 153; Ferguson, 1970: 38)

Posidaeia A goddess of the Pylians who seems to be a consort or female counterpart of Poseidon. Mycenean. Greece. (Samuel, 1966: 90, 91; Chadwick, 1976: 94)

Pronoe One of the Nereids—"the provident." Greece. (Kerenyi, 1951: 65; Roscher, 1965, 3, 2: 3119)

Proteus Given as the son of Oceanus or of Poseidon. He was a god of the sea with powers of metamorphosis, and the herder of Poseidon's seals. He was fickle but also wise, knowing the depths of the sea, the location of the fish, and having knowledge of past events. Greece. (Cox, 1870, 2: 256; Kerenyi, 1951: 43–44; Fairbanks, 1907: 57; Larousse, 1968: 147)

Protho A Nereid. Greece. (Roscher, 1965, 3, 1: 207)

Proto One of the Nereids. Greece. (Kerenyi, 1951: 64; Roscher, 1965, 3, 2: 3181)

Protomedeia One of the Nereids. Greece. (Kerenyi, 1951: 64; Roscher, 1965, 3, 2: 3186)

Prymno Daughter of Oceanus and Tethys, associated with "the ship's stern." Greece. (Kerenyi, 1951: 41; Roscher, 1965, 3, 2: 3192)

Psamathe One of the Nereids—"the sand-goddess." Mother of Phokos by Aiakos. Greece. (Kerenyi, 1951:

65; Roscher, 1965, 3, 2: 3194; Hesiod-Brown, 1981: 60, 81, 86)

Pu Tafatai A god of seafaring. Also known as Takatosi. Tikopia, Polynesia. (Firth, 1967, 2: 223)

Qadirwali Sahib A Muhammadan sea saint on the Coromandel coast helpful to sailors. India. (Crooke, 1925, 12: 718)

Q'omogwa The wealthy god of the sea "also called L!aqwag.i la, Copper-Maker." He is "the owner of copper . . . and . . . identified with the double-headed serpent." He is the father of Extsemalagilis and L!aqwag.i layugwa (tl'aqwagi'layuga). The Kwakiutl, British Columbia. (Boas, 1935: 125–131)

Qomoqwa The lord of the supernatural sea beings, counterpart of Alquntam. These beings can "cause death, but they are usually regarded as uncanny rather than dangerous." Qomoqwa is regarded "with unmixed awe." He is cannibalistic, will cause drownings, suck canoes under, etc. The Bella Coola, British Columbia. (McIlwraith, 1948, 1: 51, 52)

Quiamucame The "goddess of sea water." The Huichol, Mexico. (Peredo, 1974: 19)

u Qux Palo The "spirit of the sea." The Quiché, Guatemala. (Recinos, 1950: 78)

Raeapua, Laeapua A god of the sea, a fish god, worshipped by fishermen. Lanai and Molokai, Hawaii. (Emory, 1924: 13; Beckwith, 1940: 452)

Rambha A goddess of the sea, "the queen of the naiads or Apsaras." India. (tod, 1920: 675)

Ran Scandinavian goddess of the sea, sister and wife of Aegir (Oegir) and mother of the nine wave maidens: Gjalp (Gialp), Greip, Eistla, Eyrgjafa (Aurgiafa), Ulfrun, Angeyja, Imd(r), Atla, and Jarnsaxa (Iarnsaxa); variants Egia, Augeia, Sindur. She entrapped men in her net and drew them to her realm. She was the goddess of death of those who drowned. (Guerber, 1895: 137–139, 172; Grimm, 1880: 311; Davidson, 1891: 129; Turville-Petre, 1964: 147–148; Anderson, 1891: 271, 344, 440)

Rangitafu A sea god who "presided over shipwrecks" and was represented by "a block of whinstone." New Hebrides, Melanesia. (Mackenzie, n.d.: 141)

Po Rayak God of the waves, "or the whale-god." The Chams, Annam and Cambodia. (Cabaton, 1925, 3: 342)

Rengasami A god of seafarers. Ceylon. (Hornell, 1943: 121)

Rep un Kamui Given as singular and plural. As a duality two brothers, gods of the sea, the younger Mo acha is beneficient, the elder Shi acha is evil. (Czaplicka, 1969: 273–4) As "the chief sea-god . . . identified with the grampus, which is able to kill whales and is therefore a creature of immense power." (Munro, 1963: 36) The supreme god of the sea takes the form of a killer whale and rules the food animals of the sea. As such he is known as Rep-un-riri-kata inao uk Kamui. The Ainu, Japan. (Batchelor, 1925, 1: 240, 244; Philippi, 1982: 63, 83)

Rhodeia An Oceanid, companion of Persephone. Greece. (Kerenyi, 1951: 41; Roscher, 1965, 4: 113)

Riuta A god of the reef. Kapingamarangi, Polynesia. (Emory, 1965: 202)

Rona A goddess of the sea who dwells far out. Mother of Mongotohoro and Mongohenua. Kapingamarangi, Polynesia. (Emory, 1965: 201–2). Among the Maori she is the goddess who controls the tides—the moon. New Zealand. (Best, 1924: 97, 110)

Rongo-maitaha-nui A sea deity of the Maori, New Zealand. (Andersen, 1928: 104)

Rua-hatu, Rua-hatu-tini-rau God of the sea and of fishermen. He had a human body with the tail of a fish. Tahiti, Society Islands, Polynesia. (Henry, 1928: 80, 148, 358; Larousse, 1968: 449; Ellis, 1853: 328)

Ruamano A god of the ocean. The Maori, New Zealand. (Best, 1924: 238)

Rua-puna A god of the ocean. Tahiti, Polynesia. (Henry, 1928: 377)

Ruko God of the sea and of the watery underworld. Merir, West Caroline Islands, Micronesia. (Wallis, 1939: 239)

Rutapa A god of the reef. Kapingamarangi, Polynesia. (Emory, 1965: 202)

Ryujin A dragon-god of thunder and rain, is also considered a god of the sea. Japan. (Piggott, 1969: 14; Herbert, 1967: 482–483; Bunce, 1955: 112)

Sagami A "Deity of the Sea or Deity of the Mountains." Japan. (Czaja, 1974: 31)

Sagara (1) A dragon-king, a god of the seas and of fresh waters. China. (Werner, 1932: 285–286, 397) (2) "Another god of the sea . . . distinct from Varuna." India. (Jacobi, 1925, 2: 806)

Sagol (former name **Valur**) A god of navigation and of the fish "who guides navigators." Ifalik, Micronesia. (Burrows, 1947/48: 49)

Saiol A spirit of the sea who causes seasickness. Ifalik, Micronesia. (Burrows, 1947/48: 11)

Salacia A Roman goddess of the sea associated with Neptune. (Dumézil, 1966, 1: 389; Murray, 1935: 57)

Sami The sea, son of Ilu and Mamao. The Malietoa, Upolu, Samoa. Polynesia. (Williamson, 1933, 1: 4)

Sango The god of the lagoon where salt is obtained. The Gã in Nungwa. Ghana. (Field, 1937: 27)

Sao One of the Nereids—"the rescuer." "Safety" in association with sailing. Greece. (Kerényi, 1951: 64; Roscher, 1965, 4: 335; Hesiod-Brown, 1981: 60, 86)

Saxo Fourth child of Naete and Agbe, a sea and sky deity, as they live at the horizon. He "inhabits the incoming waves and it is he who makes the sea rise." Dahomey. (Herskovits, 1938, 2: 152, 155)

Sedna The goddess of the sea and of the sea animals is the supreme deity. She controls man's destiny and sends "sickness, bad weather, and starvation" if taboos are broken. If observed, animals are plentiful. As the ruler of Adlivun, where souls go after death, she is called Idliragijenget. The Central Eskimo, Canada. (Boas, 1907: 119921; 1884/85: 583, 588; Queval, 1968: 103; Thompson, 1968: 3; Lantis, 1950: 323)

Segara God of the sea. Bali, Indonesia. (Coleman, 1832: 349)

Segur A god of navigation. Son of Aluluei. Ifalik, Micronesia. (Burrows, 1947/48: 9)

Se-ka-jec-ta A spirit of the tide propitiated for good winds and calm seas. The Nootka, Washington and Vancouver Island. (Swan, 1869: 87)

Selsats A sea god who causes the tides. The Bella Coola, British Columbia. (Boas, 1898: 37)

Semoana A sea god of the Tafua group. Tikopia, Polynesia. (Firth, 1967, 2: 130)

Serapis In the Near East and the Grecian Islands he is a protector of navigation, as well as a god of healing and of fecundity. (Duprez, 1907: 52, 53, 73)

Setlm-ki-jash God of the tides, an evil spirit of great power. Uncle of Yetl, and the equivalent of the Tlingit Kees-du-je-al-ity Kah. The Haida, British Columbia. (Niblack, 1888: 379)

Shi acha A god of the sea, the restless, turbulent, and dangerous sea, causing storms, shipwrecks, and drowning. Elder brother of Mo acha. The Ainu, Japan. (Batchelor, 1925, 1: 242; 1894: 20)

Shih-ch'ih God of the Southern Seas whose wife is I I-liao. China. (Werner, 1932: 437)

Shiho-tsuchi-no-kami A god of the sea, a salt deity. Japan. (Chadwick, 1930: 437)

Shih-yü Chang-li God of the Northern Seas whose wife is Chieh Lien-ch'iao. China. (Werner, 1932: 437)

Shio-Zuchi The name of O-Wata-Tsu-Mi as god of the tide. Japan. (Larousse, 1968: 416)

Shiwotsuchi-no-Kami A deity of navigation. Japan. (Yasumaro, 1955: 66)

Shony A Celtic sea god to whom offerings are made for bountiful returns. The Lews (part of an island). (MacBain, 1917: 170–171)

Sindur One of the Scandinavian "wave maidens" and one of the nine giantesses who were the mother of Heimdall. (Guerber, 1895: 137)

Sirara Enki "sets up the rules for the sea and places the goddess Sirara in charge of it." Sumer, Near East. (Kramer, 1950: 60)

Si Raya The "spirit of the sea from low-water mark to mid-ocean." Malaya. (Leach, 1950, 2: 119)

La Sirene Goddess of the sea and of fresh waters— "the sea-aspect of the Goddess of Love, Erzulie." The wife of Agwe or of Agoue T'Arroyo. Identified with Notre Dame de Grace. Haiti, West Indies. (Herskovits, 1937, 1: 279; Deren, 1953: 120; Marcelin, 1950: 119)

Si-tcom'pa Ma-so-its The "grandmother goddess of the sea, brought up mankind from beneath the waves in a sack." The Kaibabit (Kaibab Plateau), Arizona. (Powell, 1879/1880: 28)

Sjojungfru "Lady of the Sea." The Lapps, Northern Europe. (Holmberg, 1925, 7: 798)

Sjora Swedish goddess of the sea, equivalent of Ran. (MacCulloch, 1964: 191)

Sokodutsu-no-Wo-no-Mikoto A Japanese seafaring deity. (Yasumaro, 1965: 24)

Sokotsuwatatsumi-no-Kami A god of the sea bottom and a seafaring deity. He is also a god of purification, born of Izanagi's bathing after his return from Yomi. With Naka-tsu-wata-dzu-mi and Uha-tsu-wata-dzu-mi, frequently worshipped and treated as one, and invoked for prosperous journeys. Japan. (Aston, 1925, 11: 466; Yasumaro, 1965: 24; Herbert, 1967: 279)

Sokozutsu-no-o A sea god who forms a triad with Uwazutsu-no-o and Nakazutsu-no-o and together known as the "Sea-God of Suminoe" and protector of seafarers. Japan. (Kato, 1926: 70) *See also above.*

Speio, Speo One of the Nereids and a goddess of caves. Greece. (Kerenyi, 1951: 64; Fairbanks, 1907: 56; Hesiod-Brown, 1981: 60, 86)

Stolos The personification of navigation. Male. Greece. (Roscher, 1965, 4: 1538)

Sumiyoshi-Myojin A god of seafarers. Japan. (Yasumaro, 1928: 84)

Sumudra, Samudra The sea personified and worshipped. India. (Coleman, 1832: 396)

Sxlo·xíʔ A supernatural sea creature "about the size of a seal, brown in colour, and of jelly-like substance," whose poison is very dangerous, frequently causing death (in contact with itself or through poisoning clams and sea foods). The Bella Coola, British Columbia. (McIlwraith, 1948, 1: 54)

Ta'aroa At Opoa he is a lesser departmental god in charge of "marine affairs and fishing." Son of Atea and Papa. Tahiti, Polynesia. (Buck, 1938: 83–84)

Tafehemoana A god of the sea, "most powerful . . . after Lage-iki." Niue Island, Polynesia. (Loeb, 1926, 3: 161)

Tagaloa leo 'ava Tagaloa as a god of the sea, a patron of fishermen. Manua (Samoa), Polynesia. (Mead, 1930: 159)

Tagaloafofoa, Tagaloalahi, and **Tagaloauluulu** Goddesses who "were friendly with the winds, and if they

agreed to destroy the beaches they carried them away into the ocean." Niue Island, Polynesia. (Loeb, 1926, 1: 162)

Tagaloa-pupu-ki-maka A son of Huanaki, one of those who ruled over the aspects of the ocean and coastline. Niue-Fekai, Polynesia. (Pulekula, 1903: 26)

Tagaloauluulu *See* **Tagaloafofoa**

Tagaroa God of the ocean, son of Atea and Fakahotu. Anaa Island, Tuamotu, Polynesia. (Stimson, 1933: 20)

Tagitsu-hime A goddess of seafaring, created by Amaterasu-Omikami. Japan. (Yasumaro, 1965: 27; 1928: 32)

Tagma-sa-dagat God of the sea. The Subanun, Zamboanga, Philippines. (Jocano, 1969: 24)

Taha-uru God of the sea coasts. Tahiti, Polynesia. (Henry, 1928: 378)

Tahbi A malignant god of the sea of the Cape Coast area who causes drowning. Gold Coast, Ghana. (Ellis, 1887: 44; Mockler-Ferryman, 1925, 9: 278)

Tahbi-yiri A malignant marine goddess, wife of Tahbi, and like him, also drowns people. Gold Coast, Ghana. (Ellis, 1887: 44; Mockler-Ferryman, 1925, 9: 278)

Tairnana nigivyn God of the sea who created rivers. Sakhalin, Siberia. (Michael, 1963: 219)

Takaaho One of "the guardians of the ocean"—the personification of sharks. The Maori, New Zealand. (Best, 1924: 155, 177)

Takanakapsaluk Goddess of the sea and of its animals who provides man with all the good things indispensible to him, but also sends storms and misfortunes as punishment. She is visited by the shamans at the bottom of the sea to ensure game and also in healing seances. The dead go to her abode where she judges their destination— Udlormiut (the Land of Day, of the Moon Spirit), or Qimiujarmiut (the Narrow Land). The Iglulik Eskimo, Canada. (Rasmussen, 1929: 56, 94; Eliade, 1964: 289, 294; Nungak and Arima, 1969: 113; Rasmussen, 1958: 388)

Take-mi-nakata A god of seafarers whose wife is Yasaka-tome-no-mikoto. Japan. (Herbert, 1967: 345)

Takiribime-no-Mikoto A goddess of seafaring, wife of Okuninushi-no-Kami and mother of Kamo-no-Okami. Japan. (Yasumaro, 1965: 27, 28, 48)

Talimainuku   A sea god of Liku, father of the war gods Fakata-fetau and Fakalagalaga. Niue Island, Polynesia. (Loeb, 1926, 1: 162–163) One of those who ruled over the aspects of the ocean and coastline. Niue-Fekai. (Pulekula, 1903: 26)

Tamauanu'u   A marine deity. Samoa, Polynesia. (Turner, 1884: 26, 27)

Tamayorihime   A sea goddess, wife of Ugaya-fuki-aezu. She is also worshipped as a goddess of childbirth. Japan. (Herbert, 1967: 370, 388)

Tamtu   A god of the sea, the equivalent of, or another name for, Yam. Canaan, Near East. (Albright, 1968: 144)

Tamwinibegw   A personified supernatural force— " 'deepest part of the sea'." The Naskapi, Labrador. (Speck, 1935: 62)

Tana-oa   God of the sea, of the winds, and of fishing. The Marquesas, Polynesia. (Handy, 1923: 245–246; Buck, 1938: 151)

Tanaroa, Kanaloa   God of the southern ocean, of seafarers, and of fishermen. Also god of night. Hawaii. (Melville, 1969: 25, 35)

Tane-ere-tui   A god personified in the breakers. Son of Raka, and twin of Tikokura. Hervey Islands, Polynesia. (Williamson, 1933: 147)

Tangaroa   God of the ocean and all of its creatures, father of fish and reptiles, the patron of fishermen. "Of special interest is his connexion with jade which . . . was regarded as a fish." His wife was Anu-matao and of their twin sons, Pounamu was the personification of jade, and Poutini its guardian. As controller of the tides his name was Tangaroa-whakamau-tai, in which duty he was assisted by Rona, the goddess of the moon. The Maori, New Zealand, the Marquesas, Hawaii. On Easter Island he took the form of a seal. Polynesia. (Mackenzie, n.d.: 301; Best, 1924: 97; Pettazzoni, 1956: 344; Métraux, 1940: 310; Poignant, 1967: 39; Andersen, 1928: 368, 370; White, 1887, 1: 1, 23)

Tangata-no-te-moana   God of the sea and of its fish. He was also a god of the underworld where he cared for the vegetation. Pukapuka, Polynesia. (Beaglehole, 1938: 313)

Taufa   A god of the sea and of the land. As the former he manifests himself as a shark (Taufa-tahi), as the latter as Taufa-uta with no sacred animal. Tonga, Polynesia. (Collocott, 1921: 229; Gifford, 1929: 288, 298)

Tau-mariu   God of the sea of the Tinguian. Philippines. (Jocano, 1969: 47)

Tawhaki   A god associated both with the sky and the sea. In the latter his wife was "Hine-tu-a-tai (daughter of the sea-coast) and their family were fishes." Polynesia. (Mackenzie, n.d.: 211–213)

Tayrnadz, Tol'yz'   A god of the sea who "lives on the bottom of the Sea of Okhotsk." He controls the distribution of the salmon. The Nivkhi and the Gilyak, Siberia. (Ivanov, Smolyak and Levin, 1964: 778; Shternberg, 1933: 55)

Te Alongaoa   God of the seas and of the south wind. Pukapuka, Polynesia. (Beaglehole, 1938: 311–312)

Te Amafakaro   A god of "the drifting foam on the sea." Associated with ceremonies to "quell the wind." Tikopia, Polynesia. (Firth, 1967, 2: 292–293)

Te-a'u-roa   A god of the sea. Tahiti, Polynesia. (Henry, 1928: 528)

teemu   The sea god personified as the killer whale. The Orochi, Siberia. (Ivanov, Smolyak and Levin, 1964: 757)

Te-fatu   God of the ocean and of the Canoe Builders Marae, invoked in the launching. Tahiti, Society Islands, Polynesia. (Henry, 1928: 122, 146)

Batara Tengahing Segara   "God in the midst of the Sea." Same as Batara Baruna. Bali, Indonesia. (Grader, 1969, 2: 180)

Terukken   A sea god—"most important because he lives in the shallow island-waters where the women generally fish. For that reason they must not have had sexual intercourse for at least three days before they go fishing. Punishment, illness, especially elephantiasis." Truk, Micronesia. (Krämer, 1932: 319)

Tethra   A Celtic sea god and a god of war. Ireland. (MacCana, 1970: 72; MacCulloch, 1911: 59)

Tethys   A Titaness, daughter of Uranus and Gaea, wife/sister of Oceanus, and mother of the streams and rivers with their gods, the Oceanids, the Naiads. Greece. (Kerenyi, 1951: 15–16; Barthell, 1971: 41; Hesiod-Brown, 1981: 56–57, 62–63)

Teum   God of the sea to whom sacrifices were made in the spring when the ice broke, and in the fall after the salmon run. The Oroks, Siberia. (Ivanov, Smolyak and Levin, 1964: 764)

Thagimasadas, Thamimasadas A god of the Royal Scythians equated with Poseidon, but whether as a sea god or a horse god is undetermined. (Minns, 1913: 85; Pettazzoni, 1956: 185)

Thalaeia One of the Nereids. Greece. (Roscher, 1965, 3, 1: 207)

Thalassa Erythra Greek personification of the Red Sea. (Roscher, 1965, 5: 447)

Thaumas An old god of the sea, son of Pontus and Gaea and brother of Ceto, Nereus, Eurybia, Phorcys. His wife was Elektra, daughter of Oceanus, and their daughters were Iris, Arce, Aello, Ocypete, Celaeno, Podarge—the last four the Harpies. Greece. (Kerenyi, 1951: 34, 60; Barthell, 1971: 10, 12; Fairbanks, 1907: 149; Hesiod-Brown, 1981: 60)

Themisto One of the Nereids. Greece. (Kerenyi, 1951: 65; Roscher, 1965, 5: 609)

Thetis A goddess of the sea, daughter of Nereus and Doris. As the wife of Peleus, a mortal, she became the mother of Achilles. Greece. (Kerenyi, 1951: 16, 64, 225; Barthell, 1971: 12; Larousse, 1968: 95, 136, 179; Hesiod-Brown, 1981: 60, 81, 87)

Thoë (1) A daughter of Oceanus and Tethys associated with "speed . . . [of] . . . water, wind and wave." (2) A Nereid, daughter of Nereus and Doris, associated with speed in sailing. Greece. (Kerenyi, 1951: 41, 64; Roscher, 1965, 5: 823; Hesiod-Brown, 1981: 60, 63, 86, 87)

T'hôm The "personification of the 'watery deep'." Same as Tiamat (Babylonian). Hebrew. Near East. (Jastrow, 1898: 411)

Tiamat The sea, "a personification . . . of primaeval chaos" who created the first monstrous beings. Assyro/Babylonian. Near East. (Drahomanov, 1961: 32; Jastrow, 1898: 409)

Tieholtsodi The god of the "ocean, rivers, and lakes," as well as the "waters beneath the earth." The Navajo, Arizona and New Mexico. (Matthews, 1902: 29; Alexander, 1964: 157)

T'ien Fei A goddess of sailors and of navigation invoked for safe passage as well as for children. China. (Werner, 1932: 503)

T'ien Hou The goddess of heaven is also goddess of sailors and navigators, worshipped for protection and suc-

cess in fishing. China. (Day, 1940: 92, 110; Maspero, 1963: 329; Shryock, 1931: 79; Larousse, 1968: 395; Ferguson, 1937: 72; Werner, 1934: 165)

Tikokura God of the "storm wave," son of Raka, and twin of Tane-ere-tui. Hervey Islands, Polynesia. (Williamson, 1933: 147)

Tinirau God of the ocean and ruler of fish and sea animals. Son of Tangaroa, husband of Hina-uri. Polynesia. (Hongi, 1920: 26; Poignant, 1967: 50; Andersen, 1928: 246–247; Best, 1924: 155–156)

Tino-rua God of the ocean and of fishermen. Society Islands, Polynesia. (Buck, 1938: 70; Henry, 1928: 148, 359)

Tipeva God of the western seas. Pukapuka, Polynesia. (Beaglehole, 1938: 315)

Tiwawe One of the main gods of Kapingamarangi, who "dwelt in the ocean . . . where waves break as they near the reef." Invoked in fishing. Polynesia. (Emory, 1965: 200–202)

Tokoyoto The crab—"the master of the sea." In some myths the father of Miti. The Koryak, Siberia. (Jochelson, 1908: 20)

Tol God of the sea and the sea itself. The Gilyak, Siberia. (Czaplicka, 1969: 271)

Toll Nibach God of the sea and of all its creatures. The Gilyak, Siberia. (Lissner, 1961: 231)

Tol yz, Toll-yz Beneficent god of the sea, of waters. The Nivkhi (Gilyak), Siberia. (Dioszegi, 1968: 407; Klementz, 1925, 6: 225)

Tori-no-Iwakusu-fune-no-Kami, Tori-no-iha-kusu-bune-no-kami God of "Marine transportation." Also called Ame-no-Torifune-no-Kami. Son of Izanagi and Izanami. Japan. (Yasumaro, 1965: 16; Herbert, 1967: 266)

Torone One of the Oceanids, daughter of Oceanus and Tethys, and a wife of Proteus. Greece. (Barthell, 1971: 41, 145)

Totoloa A "god of the eastern seas." Pukapuka, Polynesia. (Beaglehole, 1938: 315)

t'otowaxsemalaga A sea being—"Swell-Woman . . . who gives the crab of the war dance" to a novice. The Kwakiutl, British Columbia. (Boas, 1935: 131)

Toyotama-hiko-no-Mikoto   The god of the sea, father of Toyo-tama-hime. Japan. (Yasumaro, 1928: 86–87; Herbert, 1967: 379)

Triton   God of the sea, half-fish, half-man, who personified the roaring of the sea and "rules the bottom of the sea." At the end of the fifth century he became pluralized—"the untamed nature of the sea, the music of its waves, and its rapid changes, all are reflected in the character of the Tritons." Greece. (Kerenyi, 1951: 187; Fairbanks, 1907: 156; Murray, 1935: 163–164; Hesiod-Brown, 1981: 79)

Tsar Morskoi   The "Marine or Water King, who dwells in the depths of the sea, or the lake, or the pool, and who rules over the subaqueous world." Slavic Russia. (Ralston, 1872: 148)

Tsubura-hime   A goddess of the Bay of Oka. Japan. (Herbert, 1967: 480)

Tuara'atai   A god of the sea created by Tangaroa (Ta'aroa). Society Islands, Polynesia. (Henry, 1928: 359; Williamson, 1933: 59; Ellis, 1853: 326, 328)

Tu-ariki   A god who "dwelt in the ocean" far from shore. Possibly a creator god. Kapingamarangi, Polynesia. (Emory, 1965: 202)

Tu-hina-po   A god of the sea, a guide over the ocean, to whom seaweed is the offering. New Zealand. (White, 1887, 1: 40)

Tuma-tahi   A demon of the sea. Tuamotu, Polynesia. (Henry, 1928: 524)

Tung Hai   God of the Eastern Sea. China. (Ferguson, 1937: 70)

Tupe-io-ahu   A demon of the sea. Tahiti, Polynesia. (Henry, 1928: 472)

Tupiecha   The god of the sea. Mexico. (Craine and Reindorp, 1970: 225)

Tutumatua   An ancient god of Naitombo "who lives on the shore and is often seen." Lau Islands, Fiji, Melanesia. (Hocart, 1929: 191)

Uha-tsu-wata-dzu-mi   "Upper-sea-body." A sea god who was produced when Izanagi "washed in the sea after his return from Yomi." With Naka-tsu wata-dzu-mi and Soko tsu wata-dzu-mi, frequently worshipped and treated as one and invoked for prosperous voyages. Japan. (Aston, 1925, 11: 466)

Ulfrun   One of the Scandinavian "wave maidens"—the nine sister/giantesses who were the mothers of Heimdall by Odin. Daughter of Ran and Aegir. (Guerber, 1895: 137; Anderson, 1891: 344, 460; MacCulloch, 1964: 152–155; Turville-Petre, 1964: 147–148, 152)

Umale okun   A deity of the sea of the Itsekiri. Nigeria. (Mbiti, 1970, 2: 119)

unjami   A deity of the sea. Okinawa, Ryukyu Islands. (Lebra, 1966: 224)

Unktehi   The Sea God had a female counterpart and they are the parents of all the Unktehi "now scattered through the waters and upon the face of the earth." He is considered by the Medicine Dance group as the greatest deity. He taught the medicine men the colors and patterns to use in worship. The Dakota, Minnesota. (Lynd, 1889: 155, 159, 170)

Urpihuachac   Goddess of the sea who controlled the fish and had them in a pond. Uira-cocha emptied them into the sea when he was enraged over the flight of her daughters as doves. Peru. (Alexander, 1920: 229; Markham, 1969: 131)

Utariki   One of the main gods of Kapingamarangi who "dwelt in the ocean." Polynesia. (Emory, 1965: 202)

Uwadutsu-no-Wo-no-Mikoto   A seafaring deity. Japan. (Yasumaro, 1965: 24)

Uwatsuwatatsumi-no-Kami   A seafaring deity. Japan. (Yasumaro, 1965: 24)

Uwazutsu-no-o   With Nakazutsu-no-o and Sokozutsu-no-o, a trio of gods who later became "known as the Sea-God of Suminoe," protector of seafarers. Japan. (Kato, 1926: 70)

Vahine-mau-i-te-pae-fenua   A goddess who guarded the seashore "so that it might not be subverted into the shoals." Tahiti, Polynesia. (Henry, 1928: 378)

Varuna   One of his later and lesser aspects is that of a god of the ocean, of the sea-coast, of waters. India. In Bali he was god of the sea, worshipped and invoked in cremation ceremonies. (Jolly, 1925, 4: 754; Aiyangar, 1914: 285; Danielou, 1964: 118–121; Martin, 1914: 44; Levi, 1933: xiv; Hooykaas, 1964: 48; Banerjea, 1953: 73)

Vave'a   God of waves who caused "breakers out at sea and on the reefs." Tahiti, Polynesia. (Henry, 1928: 377)

Vellamo "Goddess of the sea and of the waters; the wife of Ahti." Finland. (Leach, 1950, 2: 1155)

Vetal God of the sea and a village god. The son Kolis, Bombay, India. (Punekar, 1959: 160–161)

La Vierge Caridad The goddess of the sea—probably the same as Ezili, associated with Agoué. Haiti, West Indies. (Marcelin, 1950: 89)

Vourukasha The deity of the sea—"also, the heavenly lake whose waters supply the world and in the middle of which grows the Tree of Life." Persia. (Leach, 1950, 2: 1163)

Wainui Among some the ocean is personified as Wainui who becomes the wife of Rangi. New Zealand. (Best, 1924: 153–4)

waoyakila A sea being—"the Tide-Woman . . . who appears first like quartz, then like the shadow of a person which finally assumes substance." The Kwakiutl, British Columbia. (Boas, 1935: 131)

Wareleng God of sailors and fishermen, of fishes. Yap Islands, the Carolines, Micronesia. (Christian, 1899: 385)

Wata-tsu-mi God of the sea and of seafarers, son of Izanagi and Izanami. Also known as Nakatsuwatatsumi-no-Kami. Japan. (Yasumaro, 1965: 24, 66; Herbert, 1967: 371)

The Wave Maidens Nine Scandinavian giantess/goddesses of the waves, daughters of Ran and Aegir, who were the mothers of Heimdall by Odin. Most frequently they are given as: Angeyja, Atla, Eistla, Eyrgjafa, Gjalp, Greip, Jarnsaxa, Imd(r), and Ulfrun; but variants of Egia, Augeia, Sindur, and Aurgiafa are also named. (Guerber, 1895: 137–139; Anderson, 1891: 344, 440; MacCulloch, 1964: 152–155; Turville-Petre, 1964: 147–148, 152; Snorri Sturluson, 1964: 54)

Waz-wer Personification of the sea. Egypt. (Gardiner, 1925, 9: 792)

Weka-i-te-ati-nuku A god of the ocean who guided them over the ocean, to whom seaweed is the offering. New Zealand. (White, 1887, 1: 40)

Wên Chung A god who rules the tides with Wu (Yüan) Yün. China. (Werner, 1932: 501; Du Bose, n.d.: 132)

Wëriëng A god of navigation and "of the sea-birds who guide navigators." Ifalik, Micronesia. (Burrows, 1947/48: 9)

Wuming God of the East Sea. China. (Du Bose, n.d.: 71)

Wu (Yüan) Yün A god who rules the tides with Wên Chung. China. (Werner, 1932: 501; Du Bose, n.d.: 132)

Yaexoeqoa A god who lives at the bottom of the sea and gave them the tides. The Bellabella and Rivers Inlet people, British Columbia. (Boas, 1909/10: 657)

Yaik Kan God of the sea of the Altaians. Siberia. (Eliade, 1964: 193)

Yam, Yamm, Yam-Nahar God of the sea, of rivers, and of underground waters. Canaan, Phoenicia, and Syria. (Vriezen, 1963: 53; Driver, 1956: 12, 13, 20; Hooke, 1964: 81; Gordon, 1961: 191)

Yang Hou A god of the sea, of the waves. China. (Werner, 1932: 433)

Yaryik The "Jersu prince of the seas, is best able, by driving waterfloods, to force the return of the abducted soul and to drive the soul of the departed to the netherworld." (All in the purification of the soul—through the shaman.) Siberia. (Casanowicz, 1924: 430)

Yemanja Goddess of salt waters and of sweet waters, and mother of the gods. Brazil. (Verger, 1954: 15, 187; Bastide, 1960: 573; Landes, 1940: 264)

Yemaya Goddess of the sea, of the waters, and the universal mother, representing maternity and womanhood. She was forced into an incestuous relationship by her brother, Aganyu, and was the mother of Orungan. Aganyu died of her curse and she of sorrow. Puerto Rico, West Indies. (Gonzalez-Wippler, 1975: 15, 24–25, 111–113; Verger, 1957: 294; Courlander, 1966: 10)

Yen Kung God of sailors. China. (Werner, 1932: 590)

Yen P'ing Tzu A deified mortal who is god of the tide of the village of Weng Chia Shan. China. (Day, 1940: 43)

Yu-chiang God of the North Sea and also a god of the sea wind. Also known as Hsuan-ming. China. (Du Bose, n.d.: 71; Werner, 1932: 437; Larousse, 1973: 281–282)

Zeus Kasius A god of seamen, encouraging them at the estuary or promontory. Spain. (Cook, 1930: 158)

Zeuxo An Oceanid, daughter of Tethys and Oceanus. Greece. (Hesiod-Brown, 1981: 63)

Zulaimah A Muhammadan sea saint, guardian of the sea and ruler of the Red Sea. India. (Crooke, 1925, 12: 718)

PART V

Life/Death Cycle Deities

19

Life:
Birth, Procreation, Soul (in life), Longevity

Abnoba   Goddess of the Black Forest and a goddess of childbirth who is identified with Diana. She is the Black Forest deified. Celtic Gaul. (Renel, 1906: 391; Jayne, 1962: 519)

Acat   The "God of Life" who shaped the fetus. Also the god of tattooers. The Maya, Yucatan, Mexico. (Bancroft, 1886, 3: 467; Thompson, 1970: 313)

Acek   A name of Nialic, possibly his female counterpart, who is considered responsible for "barrenness, pregnancy, the care of the embryo child, and giving it life." The Padang Dinka, Sudan. (Butt, 1952: 131)

Acna, Akna   Goddess of the moon and goddess of childbirth—in this latter capacity also called Ixchel. Wife of Chi Chac Chob (Ah Kan Chob). The Lacandon, Mexico. (Tozzer, 1941: 148; Thompson, 1970: 241–242)

Agashi   The "principal god of child-birth, by whom both sexes make oath." The Tiv, Nigeria. (Temple, 1922: 301)

Agbasia   A West African god who is the giver of children, and to whom a child acquired through his shrine is dedicated. (Frazer, 1961: 79)

Ahkushtal   A Mayan deity of birth. Yucatan, Mexico. (Alexander, 1920: 141)

Ahumbe   A god of childbirth. The Tiv, Nigeria. (Temple, 1922: 302)

Ajysyt   A goddess of fertility and of birth, which she assists, brings the soul for the child. The Yakut, Siberia. (Jochelson, 1933: 105; MacCulloch, 1964: 399; Dioszegi, 1968: 468)

Akwatia Kosie Kwaku, Atia   A god of birth of the Akan. Son of Ameyaa. Ghana. (Meyerowitz, 1958: 34)

Alemona   A Roman deity who cares for the well-being of the fetus. (Jayne, 1962: 497)

Altjira nditja   Eternal Youth. The Aranda, Australia. (Eliade, 1976, 1: 28)

Ama   The second-highest deity of the Jukun, considered the creative aspect of Chido, in some ways identified with him, but in others quite a separate deity. One aspect is that of goddess of childbirth, others—an earth goddess and a goddess of the underworld. Nigeria. (Meek, 1931: 178–179, 189–190)

Amitāyus, Ts'e-dpag-med   The "Buddha of Infinite or Eternal Life;" confers longevity. Tibet. (Waddell, 1959: 350–352, 414)

Anahit   A goddess of fecundity and of childbirth, protective of children. She is one of the seven chief deities and the most popular, forming a triad with Aramazd and Vahagn. As goddess of fertility she is associated with orgiastic religion and prostitution, but also is regarded as the great mother goddess representing sobriety and the giver of life to the nation. She is the daughter of Aramazd, sister of Mihr and Nane. Armenia. (Ananikian, 1964: 17, 28)

Anahita   A goddess of waters, of rivers, of all nature; of fertility, childbirth, and nursing; of virility, strength, and of health; and, as a planetary goddess, Venus. Iran. (Jayne, 1962: 189–190; Dumézil, 1966, 1: 302; Dresden, 1961: 353; Huart, 1963: 38, 42)

Änäm jajuci   The "goddess who gives the child its soul at birth." The Teleuts, Siberia. (Pettersson, 1957: 29)

Anauk Medaw   An auk nat associated with childbirth. Burma. (Nash, 1966: 126)

Ańchumunéki   A demon who causes a child to be born feet first. The Cuna, Panama. (Nordenskiold, 1930: 60–61)

Anghairya   An Iranian goddess of birth. (Gray, 1930: 133)

Anje-a   The god "who puts babies into women." Also the guardian of souls which he tends until ready for rebirth. Queensland, Australia. (Frazer, 1961: 103; Leach, 1949, 1: 63)

Anqet, Anuqet   A goddess of life and childbirth, of health and joyousness. A Nubian goddess introduced into Egypt. At Elephantine, a goddess of the Nile and its fertile waters; she forms a triad with Khnemu and her sister Satet (Sati). (Jayne, 1962: 53; Budge, 1969, 2: 50, 57–58)

Antevorta   A Roman goddess of birth associated with a favorable presentation at delivery. Porrima and Prorsa "were practically identical" with her. She was also a goddess of prophecy, of destiny, and represented the waxing moon. (Dumézil, 1966, 1: 393; Jayne, 1962: 494; Pettazzoni, 1956: 168; Roscher, 1965, 2, 1: 192)

Anumati   A Vedic goddess of childbirth and procreation who forms the child, and is invoked for offspring. She is associated with the moon "as representing the day before full-moon." She is the daughter of Angiras and Sraddha. India. (Gray, 1930: 59; Jayne, 1962: 160; Danielou, 1964: 319; Macdonell, 1897: 119)

Apame   A god who punishes the breaking of taboos, resulting in the birth of *Amu* children (pre-puberty intercourse, non-observance of the three menses period following a birth, any irregular conception). The Tzema (Akan), Ghana. (Grottanelli, 1969: 389)

Apet   The hippopotamus goddess of childbirth. Other names—Rert, Rertu, Taurt, and Taueret. Egypt. (Knight, 1915: 21; Ames, 1965: 110)

Apim   A god invoked after the birth of an abnormal child and beseeched for a normal one. The Nzema (Akan), Ghana. (Grottanelli, 1969: 387)

Ardaul-due   Father of the Stone of Coitus. The Cagaba and the Kogi, Colombia. (Reichel-Dolmatoff, 1949/50: 115)

Arduinna   Celtic goddess of childbirth and goddess of the sacred Ardennes Forest. Gaul. (Jayne, 1962: 519; Renel, 1906: 393)

Art Toyon Aga   God of "light and life"—an aspect of the chief of the sky gods. The Yakut, Siberia. (Czaplicka, 1925, 12: 828; Eliade, 1964: 186–187)

Asapura   A goddess who gives children. Gujarat, India. (Crooke, 1894: 70)

Asase Afua   "Goddess of Procreation," and of the fertile earth. Her planet is Venus, and her day is Friday. The Akan, Ghana. (Meyerowitz, 1958: 28, 83; Danquah, 1944: 45)

'asdzá· nádle·hé   Changing Woman controls the reproduction and birth, the fertility and/or sterility of all that exists. The Navaho, Arizona. (Reichard, 1950: 406–413)

Atete   Goddess of fertility of men and animals and of childbirth. Her annual festival is in September. Some consider her the creator of the world, allocating to men the spear and shield, and to women the needle and household goods. The Galla, Ethiopia. (Bartels, 1969: 407, 411; Rossini, 1925, 6: 491; Huntingford, 1955: 76)

Ave i le tala   A god of childbirth invoked for the safety of the patient. Samoa, Polynesia. (Turner, 1884: 24)

Ayisit   The goddess of birth of the Tatars and Yakut. Siberia. Same as Umai (Altai). (Czaplicka, 1925, 12: 482)

Ayt 'ar   A great god of procreation and fertility, particularly with regard to the breeding of cattle." He is the chief of a number of gods who represent his various aspects. The Abkhasians, Caucasus. (Janashia, 1937: 121, 129)

Ayusi, čaghlasi ügei nasutu   God of longevity, "Buddha of Eternal Life." Same as Amitayus. Mongolia. (Getty, 1962: 39)

Bagbo   A deity associated with a charm to insure longevity. Dahomey. (Herskovits, 1938, 2: 271)

Bajang   A birth demon of the Blandas. Also known to the Malays. The Malay Peninsula. (Skeat, 1906: 14)

Balaji   A deity to whom "offerings of money are made . . . for the bestowal of children." The Lambadi, Southern India. (Thurston, 1909, 4: 229–230)

Balin   The god who gave a soul to the man created by Barasiluluo. Nias, Indonesia. (MacKenzie, 1930: 329)

Balitok and **Bugan**   A god and goddess of obstetrics, considered jointly. The Ifugao, Philippines. (Barton, 1946: 88)

Bali Urip The god of life of the Kenyaks. Borneo. (Hose, 1912: 14)

Bangauwan A god of reproduction of the Ifugao. Philippines. (Barton, 1946: 32)

Bast, Bastet Cat-headed goddess of childbirth and the healing arts, goddess of the moon and mother of Kensu, a lunar god. She was joyous and pleasure-loving. As a lioness she was a solar goddess representing the warmth and generating powers of the sun. Egypt. (Budge, 1969, 1: 444–448, 518; Knight, 1915: 30; Jayne, 1962: 84)

Bes A dwarf god introduced into Egypt—possibly Nubian—who has numerous aspects, one of which is that of a god of childbirth and protector of children. He is probably most known as a god of the pleasures, of music, dancing, etc. His belligerent aspect is expressed as a god of war and of fighting. Known also in Carthage. (Knight, 1915: 32; Jayne, 1962: 55; Budge, 1969, 2: 284–285)

Binantiao ud Kabunian An obstetrics deity of the Ifugao. Philippines. (Barton, 1946: 88)

Bolang A god of reproduction of the Ifugao. Philippines. (Barton, 1946: 45)

Brigit A triple goddess—of fecundity, childbirth and healing, of the arts and poetry, and of smiths. She is the daughter of Dagda and the wife of Bres. Ireland. (Jayne, 1962: 513; Ross, 1967: 206, 226, 360; MacCulloch, 1911: 58, 69)

Bugan inIntongnin A goddess of reproduction of the Ifugao. Wife of Intongnin. Philippines. (Barton, 1946: 46)

Bugan inNgilin A goddess of reproduction—beneficent, but can cause illness. Wife of Ngilin. The Ifugao, Philippines. (Barton, 1946: 44)

Bugan inWigan A goddess of reproduction, sister/wife of Wigan. The Ifugao, Philippines. (Barton, 1946: 45)

Buhlong Kahlangan ud Tinok A god of obstetrics. The Ifugao, Philippines. (Barton, 1946: 88)

Candelifera A Roman goddess who "lighted and carried the candles during confinement." A goddess of the actual birth. (Jayne, 1962: 494; Ferguson, 1970: 68)

Carmenta, Carmentis Etruscan/Roman goddess of pregnancy and of birth who prophesied for the child. (Jayne, 1962: 444; Dumézil, 1966, 1: 392–393; Leland, 1963: 62; Pettazzoni, 1956: 168)

Chakwena A name of Kuyapalitsa as a goddess of childbirth. the Zuñi, New Mexico. (Tyler, 1964: 188)

Ch'ang shêng-fo Chinese name of Amitayus, the "Buddha of Eternal Life." (Getty, 1962: 39)

(Ix) Chel The Mayan moon goddess and goddess of procreation, pregnancy and childbirth, as well as of medicine. She is also considered a destructive water goddess causing floods and cloudbursts. Mexico. (Morley, 1946: 223, 230; Tozzer, 1941: 10, 154; Thompson, 1970: 242)

Chhath, Chhathi A Dravidian deity who in the United Provinces is worshipped as "the impersonated sixth day after birth, when . . . the child is likely to be attacked by infantile lockjaw." India. (Crooke, 1925, 4: 853)

Chien-t'an The deity who delivers male offspring to the mother. China. (Werner, 1932: 35)

Chi'i-lin-sung-tzu A deity who provides sons. Southwest China. (Graham, 1961: 130)

Chikerimunéki The "snake-star demon" who causes difficulties in childbirth, when "the vagina refuses to open up." The Cuna Indians, Panama. (Nordenskiold, 1920: 60–61)

Chordeva A "birth-fiend, who comes in the form of a cat and worries the mother or tears her womb; so cats are not allowed in the birth-chamber." The Chamars, India. (Briggs, 1920: 134)

Chui-shen-niang-niang A goddess of childbirth worshipped for an easy delivery. Southwest China. (Graham, 1961: 33)

Ch'u Tsai Chang A Tu Di deity invoked to save mothers from calamities after childbirth. Szechwan, China. (Graham, 1928: 18)

Cihuacoatl, Cioacoatl, Ciuacoatl A serpent earth goddess of birth and death (those who die in childbirth), invoked in difficult deliveries. Known by numerous other names or titles, among them Tonantzin. Xochimilco and Colhuacan, Mexico. (Caso, 1958: 54; Bancroft, 1886, 2: 269; Spence, 1923: 179, 183; Vaillant, 1962: 148)

Comitia A Roman goddess who "was assimilated to, if she was not identical with Carmentis as a deity of childbirth and a healing goddess." (Jayne, 1962: 445)

Cuchabiba, Cuchavira, Cuchaviva Primarily the goddess of the rainbow, of rain and of waters, but a major function was also in healing the sick and protecting women in childbirth. She was associated with Bochica. The Muyscas and the Chibchas of Colombia. (Keane, 1925, 3: 515; Brinton, 1882: 150, 223; Kroeber, 1946, 2: 906)

Ah Cuxtal   God of birth of the Lacandon. (Mayan). Mexico. (Thompson, 1970: 322)

Da, Danbira   A Dahomean god introduced into Brazil as a god of life and fecundity. (Bastide, 1960: 564)

Dada   "God of unborn children and of gardens. He is represented by a pumpkin embellished with seashells." Identified with Our Lady of Mount Carmel. Puerto Rico, West Indies. (Gonzalez-Wippler, 1975: 26–27)

Daga   A god of reproduction. The Ifugao, Philippines. (Barton, 1946: 45)

Dalog   A god of reproduction of the Ifugao. Philippines. (Barton, 1946: 46)

Decima   One of the Parcae, the fates, and a goddess of life and birth who, with Nona, "presided over different months of birth." Italy. (Branston, 1957: 60, 64; Jayne, 1962: 495)

Deverra   A Roman guardian deity of the broom, protective of the new mother and child from Silvanus. (Dumézil, 1966, 2: 616; Jayne, 1962: 436; Ferguson, 1970: 68)

Dhatr, Dhatri   One of his aspects is that of a god of procreation invoked for offspring and for longevity. India. (Jayne, 1962: 169–170; Macdonell, 1897: 115)

Diana   A virgin goddess, yet a goddess of procreation and fertility, of women and of childbirth. She was as well a goddess of the woods and a goddess of treaties. Italy. (Frazer, 1960: 9; Fairbanks, 1907: 140; Jayne, 1962: 442; Dumézil, 1966, 2: 407–411)

Diroa-mahse   A beneficent god created by the Sun as a protector of the world. He is invoked to protect the new-born child from Vai-mahse, who is enraged by any flow of blood. The Desana, Colombia. (Reichel-Dolmatoff, 1971: 27–28, 140, 147)

Ditidit   A god of reproduction of the Ifugao. Philippines. (Barton, 1946: 45)

Di Tsang Wang   A Tu Di deity invoked to save mothers from calamities after childbirth. Szechwan, China. (Graham, 1928: 18)

Dudhyo Her   At childbirth, offerings are given to the deity of milk. The Bhils, India. (Naik, 1956: 185)

Egeria   A Roman fountain or spring nymph invoked for easy childbirth, who "foretold the fate of new-born babies." Wife of Numa. (Dumézil, 1966, 2: 408; Frazer, 1960: 4; Larousse, 1968: 210)

Eileithyia   Greek and Cretan goddess of childbirth, daughter of Hera and Zeus. She was in attendance at Apollo's birth. She could be malignant and cause delay or difficulties. (Jayne, 1962: 320; Kerenyi, 1951: 98; Willetts, 1962: 52, 169)

Elle Yakini   A female spirit invoked for protection during pregnancy and given offerings after childbirth. The Vedda, Ceylon. (Seligmann and Seligmann, 1911: 174)

Epaphos   An ancient Greek god who "assisted at childbirth by the laying-on of hands." Son of Io and Zeus. (Jayne, 1962: 323)

Erditse   The goddess of maternity. The Basques, Spain and France. (Leach, 1949, 1: 117)

Februa   A Roman "goddess of purification who presided over the delivery of the after-birth and over purgation." (Jayne, 1962: 495)

Februus   A name of Faunus as a god of impregnation. Februus is also identified with Dis Pater as a god of the dead. Italy. (Altheim, 1937: 132; Jayne, 1962: 424)

Fluonia, Fluona   A minor Roman deity who "stopped the menses after conception and prevented hemorrhages during pregnancy." (Jayne, 1962: 495)

fo grong thing   The creator god of the Lepchas whose wife is na zong nyu. He is also a god of procreation. Sikkim. (Siiger, 1967: 41, 92, 141)

Fukurokiyu   One of the seven gods of happiness, a god of long life and of wisdom. Japanese Buddhism. (Eliot, 1935: 140; Larousse, 1968: 422; Piggott, 1969: 59)

Gaiyun   A goddess of reproduction, beneficent, though she can cause illness and death. She is also a minor goddess of war. Wife of Pinyuhon. The Ifugao, Philippines. (Barton, 1946: 44, 75)

Gan Gaur   A goddess invoked by women for the longevity of their husbands. Village of Nimkhera, Madhya Pradesh, India. (Jacobson, 1977: 282)

Gasani Among the Basoga the god who controls births, and to whom twins are attributed. Uganda. (Roscoe, 1915: 249)

Gatui ud Lagod A god of reproduction of the Ifugao. Also invoked for cures in illness. Philippines. (Barton, 1946: 45, 71)

Gaulchováng The omnipresent and beneficent Universal Mother who presides over birth and its ceremonies. In this aspect she "appears in her bat transformation." The Cagaba and the Kogi, Colombia. (Reichel-Dolmatoff, 1949/50: 88, 90, 173)

Gazi Mian A godling of the Doms worshipped in Benares for children, and to whom offerings are made after childbirth. India. (Briggs, 1953: 481)

Gek rum The god of birth of the Lepchas. Sikkim. (Gorer, 1938: 290)

Genetyllis A Greek goddess of childbirth, later identified with other goddesses—Aphrodite, Hekate, and Artemis. (Jayne, 1962: 323)

Genita Mana A Roman goddess with "power over life and death, . . . great influence over child-birth." Also invoked to spare the family from death. (Jayne, 1962: 449; Fairbanks, 1907: 238)

Ghazi Miyan A household deity of the Kalwars worshipped especially at childbirth. India. (Crooke, 1925, 7: 643)

Gin Kang Seo A Tu Di deity invoked to save mothers from calamities after childbirth. Szechwan, China. (Graham, 1928: 18)

Ginumon A beneficent god of reproduction, but who can nevertheless cause illness and death. The Ifugao, Philippines. (Barton, 1946: 44)

dGra lha ma lha bu rdzi Tibetan "goddess of maternity, who influences the birth of children." (Nebesky-Wojkowitz, 1956, 1: 330)

Gumitang A god of reproduction, and also a guardian of property and prestige. The Ifugao, Philippines. (Barton, 1946: 44, 58)

Gungu An ancient goddess of procreation and childbirth, associated with the phases of the moon. India. (Barth, 1921: 25; Jayne, 1962: 160)

Gunu The beneficent chief god who is the "provider of children and crops and controller of the elements" to the tribes of the confluence of the Niger and Benue rivers. Nigeria. (Mockler-Ferryman, 1925, 9: 280)

Guru Asara The "provider of long life and disciple of Guru Rimpoche." The Sherpas, Nepal. (Furer-Haimendorf, 1964: 233)

Gwenhwyfar A Celtic goddess of childbirth and fertility. Wales. (Ross, 1967: 206)

Hathor A cow-headed goddess among whose many functions and aspects is that of goddess of love and of childbirth, the patroness of women. Egypt. (Jayne, 1962: 58; Ames, 1965: 76; Keeler, 1960: 128)

Haumea Goddess of childbirth and of fertility, and goddess of uncultivated foods. Mother of Pele. Hawaii. (Beckwith, 1940: 283, 185; Poignant, 1965: 45)

Heket, Heqet A frog-headed goddess of childbirth, generation, and fertility. Also associated with the birth of the sun each morning. Egypt. (Knight, 1915: 44; Ames, 1965: 111; Budge, 1969, 2: 378)

Hema Goddess of the power of procreation. Daughter of Whai-tiri and Kai-tangata; wife of Hu-aro-tu (or Ara-whita-i-te-rangi) and mother of Karihi, Pupu-mai-nono, and Ta-whaki. New Zealand. (White, 1887, 1: 54; Mackenzie, n.d.: 211, 298)

Hera, Here Greek goddess of fertility and childbirth, of marriage, women, and chastity. She was sister/wife of Zeus, and as his female counterpart, a goddess of the atmosphere wielding thunder and lightning, storms and winds. She was the daughter of Kronos and Rhea, and mother of Ares and Hephaistos, Hebe and Eileithya. (Fairbanks, 1907: 44, 101; Cox, 1870, 2: 5, 10–12; Kerenyi, 1951: 95, 98; Barthell, 1971: 19–21)

Hina-te-iwaiwa Maori goddess of the moon and of childbirth invoked for easy delivery. New Zealand. (Hongi, 1920: 27)

Hina-uri Polynesian goddess of the moon and of childbirth, sister of Maui and wife of Tini-rau. (Andersen, 1928: 212, 236–237, 247)

Hinobhob A god of reproduction of the Ifugao. Philippines. (Barton, 1946: 44)

Hituayuta God of generation, of propagation. The Mixtec, Mexico. (Caso, n.d.: 51)

Hsieh Jên Hsing Chün "A star goddess of childbirth." China. (Day, 1940: 93)

Hsieh Kuang Hsing Chün A god invoked for easy childbirth. China. (Day, 1940: 93)

Hsien Wêng Chinese god of longevity. (Werner, 1932: 435)

Humilak A god of reproduction of the Ifugao. Philippines. (Barton, 1946: 44)

Ibabasag A goddess of pregnant women invoked in childbirth. The Bukidnon, Philippines. (Jocano, 1969: 23; Cole, 1956: 96)

Ichar-tsirew A marine goddess who promotes peace in the household and safety in childbirth. The Gold Coast, Ghana. (Ellis, 1887: 45–46)

Ichigi A god of childbirth. The Tiv, Nigeria. (Temple, 1922: 302)

Ifa The "god of divination, who causes pregnancy, and presides over births." The Yoruba, Nigeria. (Budge, 1973, 1: 373). In Puerto Rico he is the god of fertility and gives his help to all women who desire children. West Indies. (Gonzalez-Wippler, 1975: 27–28)

Igbo A god of childbirth among the Tiv. Nigeria. (Temple, 1922: 302)

Iha-naga A goddess of longevity and a consort of Ninigi, by whom she was rejected in favor of her beautiful younger sister, Kono-hana-sakuya-hime. For this the princess lost the blessing of long life. Japan. (Herbert, 1967: 364–366)

Ihik A god of reproduction of the Ifugao. Philippines. (Barton, 1946: 46)

Il A high Akkadian god "who is interested in man's welfare, and who is particularly active in the giving of children." Near East. (Roberts, 1972: 34)

Ilithya *See* **Eileithyia**

Impinditan A god of reproduction of the Ifugao. Philippines. (Barton, 1946: 44)

Indagarra The god of procreation worshipped by the Batwa. Barundi. (Meyer, 1916: 189)

Indangunay A god of reproduction of the Ifugao. Philippines. (Barton, 1946: 46)

Indra In all aspects of his attributes and powers, he manifests total involvement with the life force and its promotion. India. (Eliade, 1958: 84–86)

Inhilap A god of reproduction, beneficent, but can cause illness and death. The Ifugao, Philippines. (Barton, 1946: 50)

Inlingay ud Kabunian An obstetrics deity of the Ifugao. Philippines. (Barton, 1946: 88)

Intercidona Roman goddess of pregnancy and childbirth, and of children; protective of the new mother (with Deverra and Pilumnus) from evil spirits and from Silvanus. Also goddess of the axe and of firewood. (Jayne, 1962: 436, 495; Dumézil, 1966, 2: 616)

Intongnin A god of reproduction of the Ifugao. Philippines. (Barton, 1946: 45)

Inumban A god of reproduction of the Ifugao. Philippines. (Barton, 1946: 45)

Inuus An early Italian god of procreation associated with the breeding of animals, then extended to include human coition. Identified with Faunus. (Jayne, 1962: 424; Roscher, 1965, 2, 1: 262; Murray, 1935: 150)

Iresu Kamui A deity invoked "for children and in childbirth." A variant of Kamui Fuchi and identified with Uare Kamui. Also called Usarawa Kamui. The Ainu, Japan. (Munro, 1963: 34–35)

Iroijdrilik A god of reproduction of all living things. Marshall Islands, Micronesia. (Davenport, 1953: 222)

Ishtar Goddess of love and of childbirth, of healing and of fertility. Her absence in search of Tammuz in the netherworld causes temporary sterility on earth. Assyria and Canaan, Near East. (Jayne, 1962: 122; Driver, 1956: 10; Seligmann, 1948: 30)

Istsel Goddess of childbirth. Wife of Aquantsob. The Lacandon, Mexico. (Cline, 1944: 112) *See* **(Ix) Chel.**

Iuno Lucina *See* **Juno**

Ixchebelyax Mayan goddess of the moon, who is also a goddess of childbirth as well as of basketry and weaving. Cozumel, Yucatan, Mexico. (Krickeberg, 1968: 70)

Ixchel *See* **(Ix) Chel**

Jirong A god of procreation and birth, but who also causes sickness, accident, and death. The Land Dyaks, Borneo. (Roth, 1891: 165)

Juksakka Goddess of birth who could change a girl to a boy before birth, and goddess and guardian of children, protecting them from mishaps. The Lapps, Northern Europe. (Pettersson, 1957: 33; MacCulloch, 1964: 254; Bosi, 1960: 134; Collinder, 1949: 169)

Jumon-ava Finno-Ugric goddess "of childbirth and marriage." The Cheremiss, Russia. (MacCulloch, 1964: 258)

Juno Roman goddess of birth and of women. As Iuno Lanuvina she is a goddess of conception; as Iuno Lucina (or Juno Sospita) a goddess of confinements and protector of children; as Juno Populonia she "watched over the multiplication of the race." (Jayne, 1962: 323, 424, 442; Larousse, 1968: 203–204; Dumézil, 1966, 1: 291, 294; Murray, 1935: 51)

Jurojin One of the seven gods of happiness, of good luck, and a god of long life. Japanese Buddhism. (Puini and Dickins, 1880: 446–448; Eliot, 1935: 140; Larousse, 1968: 422; Piggott, 1969: 59)

Kabigat A god of reproduction of the Ifugao. Philippines. (Barton, 1946: 45)

Kahlangan ud Tinok A god of childbirth of the Ifugao. Philippines. (Barton, 1946: 87)

Kailu A god of abortion, worshipped by women after childbirth. The Ahir, Panjab Hills, India. (Crooke, 1925, 1: 233–4)

Kalika A goddess of childbirth beseeched by barren women for children. The Tharus, India. (Briggs, 1953: 531)

Kaltas-anki A goddess of birth, protective of mother and child, who "gives the child its soul" and determines its longevity. The North Ostyak, Siberia. (MacCulloch, 1964: 260; Pettersson, 1957: 22)

Kalteš Goddess of birth and an earth goddess who can take the form of a goose or a hare. She is associated with Numi-Tarem; their son is Mir-susne-xum. The Vogul and the Ostyak, Western Siberia. (Roheim, 1954: 27)

ka tu' Goddess of childbirth and of the moon. She is also a goddess of agricultural fertility. The Chorti, Guatemala. (Wisdom, 1940: 400)

Keya "The Spirit of the Turtle was the guardian of life and patron of surgery and controlled accidents." The Lakota and the Oglala, South Dakota. (Walker, 1980: 122)

Khem, Amsu, Min God of reproduction, "the personification of the power of generation." The god of

Qebti (Coptos), capital of the nome of Herui. Egypt. (Budge, 1969, 2: 17, 97; Emerson, 1894: 250)

Khumbaba Sumerian deity of pregnant women. Near East. (Keeler, 1960: 155)

Kildisin Finno-Ugric goddess of birth and also "of the earth, of the corn, and of children." The Votiaks, Siberia. (MacCulloch, 1964: 258)

Kilkilang A god of reproduction of the Ifugao. Philippines. (Barton, 1946: 45)

Kilut A god of reproduction. The Ifugao, Philippines. (Barton, 1946: 46)

Kintu A python god and a deity helpful in childbirth. The son of Semuganda. The Basoga, Uganda. (Roscoe, 1915: 247; Mbiti, 1970, 2: 118)

Kir A malevolent male spirit "who dries up the breasts of nursing women." Truk, Micronesia. (Bollig, 1927: 13)

Klote A god of the Gã in Osu invoked in pregnancy rites. Ghana. (Field, 1937: 64, 168)

Klu bdud nag po mgo dgu A Bon god of birth whose neglect can cause illness, calamity, etc. Tibet. (Nebesky-Wojkowitz, 1956, 1: 305)

Ko Ku "The midwife and bringer of children." China. (Werner, 1932: 220)

kolkolibag "Spirits of birth" who can cause difficult labors unless propitiated. The Ifugao, Philippines. (Jocano, 1969: 18)

Kôshart(u) Goddess of childbirth and feminine counterpart of Koshar. Canaan, Near East. (Albright, 1968: 138)

Koyasu Kannon Goddess of easy childbirth and protector of children. Japan. (Getty, 1962: 97; Hori, 1968: 39)

Kuan Shi Yin A goddess who saves mothers from calamities after childbirth. Szechwan, China. (Graham, 1928: 19)

Kubai-khotun Goddess of birth, of life, and of destiny. Another name—Ajysyt. The Yakuts, Siberia. (Pettersson, 1957: 28)

Kugu shotshen-ava Finno-Ugric goddess of birth. The Cheremiss, Russia. (MacCulloch, 1964: 258)

Kumulikil   A god of reproduction of the Ifugao. Philippines. (Barton, 1946: 47)

Jin Kuwak   A harmless birth spirit of the Jakun. The Malay Peninsula. (Skeat, 1906: 183)

Kybai-Khotun   Variant of Kubai-khotun, above.

Ladu   A god of reproduction of the Ifugao. Philippines. (Barton, 1946: 47)

La-ik   A god of reproduction of the Ifugao. Philippines. (Barton, 1946: 47)

Laima   Baltic goddess of women and marriage, of childbirth, and protector of young girls and their chastity. She is a goddess of destiny and with Dievas determines the length of life of each being; is the personification of happiness, good fortune. Latvia and Lithuania. (Jonval, 1929: 18–21; Gimbutas, 1963: 197; Queval, 1968: 66; Grimm, 1880: 416)

Laki Ju Urip   The most important of the "three gods of life." The Kayans, Borneo. (Hose, 1912: 5)

Laki Kalisai Urip   One of the "three gods of life." The Kayans, Borneo. (Hose, 1912: 5)

Laki Makatan Urip   One of the "three gods of life." The Kayans, Borneo. (Hose, 1912: 5)

Langhui   The birth demon of the Blandas. Malay Peninsula. (Skeat, 1906: 296)

H. Langhwe   A malevolent birth spirit of the Jakun. Malay Peninsula. (Skeat, 1906: 183)

Langsuir   A birth demon of the Malay, similar to Langhui of the Blandas. Malay Peninsula. (Skeat, 1906: 13)

Lapug   A god of reproduction of the Ifugao. Philippines (Barton, 1946: 45)

(rgyal po) Li byin ha ra   A god of birth whose neglect can cause illness, calamity, etc. Tibet. (Nebesky-Wojkowitz, 1956, 1: 305)

Liting ud Inude   A god of reproduction of the Ifugao. Philippines. (Barton, 1946: 46)

Liting ud Naltang   A god of reproduction of the Ifugao. Also "said to be the source of the Kababuyan River." Philippines. (Barton, 1946: 46)

Locheia, Lecho   Spartan goddess of childbirth. Greece. (Jayne, 1962: 322)

Lotang   A god of reproduction of the Ifugao. Philippines. (Barton, 1946: 46)

Lucele   God of life of the Lala. Zambia. (Mbiti, 1970, 2: 332)

Lucina   *See* **Juno**

Ludulud   A god of reproduction of the Ifugao, Philippines. (Barton, 1946: 47)

Lu-hsing   A star god representing happiness and long life, also providing prestige and monetary prosperity. China. (Maspero, 1963: 344–345; Day, 1940: 95)

The Luonnotar, The Synnytar   The three ancient goddesses of birth. Finland. (MacCulloch, 1964: 257; Bray, 1935: 44)

Luplup   A god of reproduction of the Ifugao. Philippines. (Barton, 1946: 46)

Maddar-akko, Madder-akka   Earth/Mother goddess and goddess of childbirth. Radien entrusted to her the spirit or soul of the child which she nurtured until ready for birth, when she gave it to Sar-akka to transfer to the woman. She is the mother of the three goddesses of childbirth: Sar-akka, Juks-akka, and Uks-akka; and the wife of Maderatja. The Lapps, Northern Europe. (Bosi, 1960: 133–134; Collinder, 1949: 168–169; Karsten, 1955: 38–40; Pettersson, 1957: 18)

Maderatja   The "god of conception and birth." Husband of Maddar-akko. He is also considered the creator of men and of animals. The Lapps, Northern Europe. (Pettersson, 1957: 18)

Mah   A most important Earth Mother—goddess of childbirth, of animal fertility, and creator of man from clay. Types or aspects of her are: Gula, Bau, Erishkigal, Ninmah, Ninhursag, Nintur, Ninmea, and Ninsikilla. She is the sister of Enlil. Near East. (Langdon, 1931: 109–110)

Mam   Goddess of childbirth. Yap Islands, the Carolines, Micronesia. (Christian, 1899: 385)

Mama fo Gro   An Earth Mother who is invoked in childbirth and particularly in difficulty in raising children, where many have been lost. The Paramaribo Negroes, Surinam. (Leach, 1950, 2: 668)

Mamaiyabaiyang   A god of reproduction who "causes lascivious dreams with orgasm; these are believed to foretell conception." The Ifugao, Philippines. (Barton, 1946: 44)

Mamaiyu   A god of reproduction of the Ifugao. Philippines. (Barton, 1946: 46)

Mamalompon   A god of reproduction of the Ifugao. Philippines. (Barton, 1946: 44)

Mama Quilla, Mama-Kilya   The Inca moon goddess, sister/wife of Inti, the sun. She is the goddess of love and marriage, of childbirth and of children. Peru. (Brinton, 1868: 132; Rowe, 1946, 2: 295; Larousse, 1968: 442)

Mamatug ud Daiya   An obstetrics deity who "dam(s) the birth canal." The Ifugao, Philippines. (Barton, 1946: 88)

Mami   An Akkadian/Assyro/Babylonian goddess who fashioned man from clay, and who is invoked at the onset of childbirth. Near East. (Langdon, 1931: 12; Larousse, 1968: 62–63)

Mamitapit   A god of reproduction of the Ifugao. Philippines. (Barton, 1946: 44)

Mamma   Semitic goddess of fertility, a mother goddess who is "the divine midwife during human childbirth." Near East. (Robert, 1972: 24, 44)

Mamukok, Mamuyabuya, and **Manabung**   Gods of reproduction of the Ifugao. Philippines. (Barton, 1946: 45, 44, 46)

Manamoan   A goddess of the earth who is associated with childbirth. The Mandaya, Mindanao, Philippines. (Raats, 1969: 20)

Mang Chin'i   "The Goddess of the Womb . . . worshipped to ensure safe child-birth." China. (Werner, 1932: 567)

Mangoñoyamo   The female servant of Panglang. Together they are protective of "midwives, pregnant women, and unborn children." The Bukidnon, Philippines. (Cole, 1956: 95)

Manungal   Mesopotamian goddess of childbirth, of midwifery. Near East. (Jacobsen, 1970: 322)

Ma-ongong and **Mapatung**   Gods of reproduction of the Ifugao. Philippines. (Barton, 1946: 46)

Marassa Jumeaux   Twin deities of African origin who are invoked at childbirth for an easy delivery. They also cause illnesses. Haiti, West Indies. (Deren, 1953: 40, 312;: Simpson, 1945: 44; Marcelin, 1950: 125)

Marei-kura   A goddess of midwifery as well as of plaiting and weaving. Anaa Island, Tuamotus, Polynesia. (Stimson, 1933: 25)

Mariana   A goddess of healing and childbirth, and of love. She is also "special protector of sailors and of the Brazilian Navy." She is the daughter of Rei Turquia, and twin of Mariano. Belem, Brazil. (Leacock, 1972: 131–134)

Masawu, Masauu, Eototo   "The Fire God, besides being a god of life, is likewise the Skeleton God or God of Death, because his realm, like that of the Sun God, is the Underworld where live the breath bodies of the dead." The Hopi, Arizona. (Fewkes, 1902: 21; 1920: 596)

Matabai   A powerful mother goddess whom the women invoke for children, particularly "at the Havan, a nine-day sacred-fire ceremony in December." Village of Nimkhera, Madhya Pradesh, India. (Jacobson, 1977: 282)

Mata Januvi   A goddess of births. The Rajputs, India. (Crooke, 1894: 72)

Matbang   A god of reproduction of the Ifugao. Philippines. (Barton, 1946: 46)

Mati Anak   Malevolent and deadly demon of stillbirth. The Jakun and the Besisi, Malay Peninsula. (Skeat, 1906: 183, 304)

Mbale   A god invoked for offspring. The Baganda, Uganda. (Roscoe, 1965: 316)

Meskhenit, Meshkent   Goddess of the moment of birth, and also a goddess of fate, foretelling the child's future. She is also a goddess of the underworld, accompanying the dead soul for judgment. Egypt. (Jayne, 1962: 85–86)

Meztli, Metztli   Aztec goddess of the moon and of generation, protective in childbirth. Also a goddess of love and marriage. She has a malignant side as "the goddess of the night, the dampness, and the cold." Also called Teczistecatl. Mexico. (Brinton, 1868: 132; Bancroft, 1886, 3: 111; Spence, 1923: 309)

Miao gih Shiang A Tu Di deity invoked to save mothers from calamities after childbirth. Szechwan, China. (Graham, 1928: 18)

Mi Leh Fuh A Tu Di deity invoked to save mothers from calamities after childbirth. (Maitreya). Szechwan, China. (Graham, 1928: 18, 63)

Mommukun A beneficent god of reproduction, yet can cause illness and death. The Ifugao, Philippines. (Barton, 1946: 44)

Monahal A god of reproduction. Also a minor god of war. The Ifugao, Philippines. (Barton, 1946: 45, 75)

Mongahid At Kalinugan he is a god of reproduction; at Namtogan, a god of agriculture. The Ifugao, Philippines. (Barton, 1946: 36, 38, 44)

Monkilub An obstetrics deity "responsible for abnormal presentations." The Ifugao, Philippines. (Barton, 1946: 88)

Monlihli A god of reproduction of the Ifugao. Philippines. (Barton, 1946: 45)

Monliktag A god of reproduction as well as a god of weaving. Son of Monkulabe. The Ifugao, Philippines. (Barton, 1946: 30, 45)

Monlita ud Daiya An obstetrics deity who may "dam the birth canal." The Ifugao, Philippines. (Barton, 1946: 88)

Montadu A god of reproduction of the Ifugao. Philippines. (Barton, 1946: 45)

Montalug A beneficent god of reproduction, but can cause illness and death. The Ifugao, Philippines. (Barton, 1946: 44)

Monulat An obstetrics deity who blocks the vagina. The Ifugao, Philippines. (Barton, 1946: 88)

Móromunéki The "great turtle demon" who causes obstructions in delivery of the child. The Cuna, Panama. (Nordenskiold, 1930: 60–61)

Mu An important goddess of the San Blas Cuna Indians who is particularly concerned with pregnancy and birth, with the formation of the foetus and its characteristics. Panama. (Stout, 1947: 41; Nordenskiold, 1938: 368, 372)

Mu Alesop and **Mu Aligisai** Goddesses of the kingdom of the dead concerned "with the creation of human life." The Cuna, Panama. (Nordenskiold, 1938: 372 372)

Munékiáchu The "dog demon" who causes difficulties in childbirth. The Cuna, Panama. (Nordenskiold, 1930: 60–61)

Munékitáyma The "alligator demon" who causes difficulties in childbirth. The Cuna, Panama. (Nordenskiold, 1930: 60–61)

Munékitulup The "lobster demon" who "holds fast the child when it appears feet foremost at birth." The Cuna, Panama. (Nordenskiold, 1930: 60–61)

Mun kung The protective "guardian spirit of life." The Lepchas, Sikkim. (Nebesky-Wojkowitz, 1952: 30)

Mu Olokundil, Mu Olotagisop, Mu Olotakiki, and **Mu Sobia** Goddesses of the kingdom of the dead who are concerned "with the creation of human life." The Cuna Indians, Panama. (Nordenskiold, 1938: 372)

The Mü xa Celestial beings whose king is Mü xa do. They function as deities of birth. The Karen, Burma. (Marshall, 1922: 223–224)

Mü xa do The king of the Mü xa, celestial beings concerned with birth. He creates men and his inattention at times is responsible for the cripples and defectives. He is protective when propitiated. The Karen, Burma. (Marshall, 1922: 223–224, 248)

Muyt A goddess of generation and an abstract deity— the personification of " 'seed,' of human beings and animals." Egypt. (Gardiner, 1925, 9: 791)

Mylitta Assyrian goddess of fertility and procreation. Near East. (Prentice Hall, 1965: 93)

Nã Afiye The "goddess of births" of the Gã in Osu and in Nungwa, invoked in pregnancy rites. She is associated with the lagoon god. Ghana. (Field, 1937: 64, 27, 168)

Nã Bake A goddess invoked in pregnancy rites. Wife of Nadu. The Gã in Osu, Ghana. (Field, 1937: 64, 168)

Naëstsan, nahosdzáán Earth Woman is the source of the winds which control life; of " 'the wind standing within us' which enters in the process of reproduction." She is the important regulator of the life of all breathing things. The Navajo, Arizona. (McNeley, 1981: 15–17, 28)

Na-ina A goddess of reproduction at Kapungahan. Also a minor goddess of war. The Ifugao, Philippines. (Barton, 1946: 45, 75)

Ñaiñinen The Supreme Being—"Universe, World," is also known by numerous other names or titles, and is sometimes identified with the sun. He "is particularly concerned in birth. He sends the souls of the new-born into the wombs of their mothers" and determines the length of life. The Koryak, Siberia. (Jochelson, 1908: 24, 26)

Nalwanga A goddess whose function was to assist barren women to become pregnant. Wife of Mukasa. The Baganda, Uganda. (Roscoe, 1965: 301, 322)

Nalygyr-Aissyt-Khotun A benevolent sky goddess who is goddess of childbirth. The Yakut, Siberia. (Czaplicka, 1969: 277)

Nama djang ad Anga chal A god of the Skyworld who creates fetuses. The Mayawyaw, Northern Luzon, Philippines. (Lambrecht, 1932: 22)

Nama djang ad Chalom A goddess of the Underworld who creates fetuses. The Mayawyaw, Northern Luzon, Philippines. (Lambrecht, 1932: 22)

Nan Goddess of human procreation. The Abkhasians, Caucasus. (Janashia, 1937: 145)

Nana Olokegepiai A goddess of the kingdom of the dead who is involved with the formation of human life. The Cuna, Panama. (Nordenskiold, 1938: 372)

Nana Olomaguyriai A goddess of the kingdom of the dead who is concerned with the formation of humans in the womb. The Cuna, Panama. (Nordenskiold, 1938: 372)

Nan Chi Hsien Weng A god of long life and of good fortune, associated with the South Pole. China. (Day, 1940: 27, 84; Werner, 1932: 324–325)

Natio, Nascio A goddess of birth who was "supplanted by Iuno Lucina." Italy. (Jayne, 1962: 454; Roscher, 1965, 3, 1: 22)

Náybemunéki The "snake demon" who causes difficulties in childbirth. The Cuna, Panama. (Nordenskiold, 1930: 60–61)

Na Yo Goddess of birth of the Gã in Temma. She was introduced from Kpeshi, and then became the wife of Sakumo. She is also associated with the planting of corn. Ghana. (Field, 1937: 11, 21)

na zong nyu Goddess of birth and procreation invoked at childbirth to give the child longevity and good health.

Wife of fo grong thing. The Lepchas, Sikkim. (Siiger, 1967: 61, 68, 79, 122)

Nekhebet, Nekhbet Goddess of childbirth and nurse of kings. She is a vulture goddess, twin sister of Uatchet and wife of Khent-Amenti. She is also goddess of the South. Egypt. (Jayne, 1962: 72; Budge, 1969, 1: 438–440; Knight, 1915: 79)

Ngakola A god "who breathed life into the first man fashioned by his father." Central African Republic. (Larousse, 1973: 530)

Ngilin A god of reproduction of the Ifugao. He is also a minor god of war, and a "harassing" deity invoked by creditors. Philippines. (Barton, 1946: 44, 75; 1955: 131)

Niang-niang sung-tzu A goddess of the Na-khi who brings children. Yunnan Province, China. (Rock, 1947: 183)

Nijusanya-sama Deity of easy delivery in childbirth and guardian of good fortune. Japan. (Hori, 1968: 67)

Nilchi Wind, Air, Atmosphere. A holy being, the Holy Wind, which gives life and motion to all living things, through which "the Navajo Soul is linked to the immanent powers of the universe." The Navajo, Arizona. (McNeley, 1981: 1, 7)

Ninmah A Sumerian goddess of birth, identified with Ninhursag. Near East. (Hooke, 1963: 29; Kramer, 1961: 104, 121)

Nintu, Nintud Sumerian goddess of birth identified with Ninhursaga, and also called Aruru. She is the sister of Enlil. Near East. (Kramer, 1961: 100; Jacobsen, 1970: 18, 30)

Nintur A name of Ninhursaga as the former of the fetus, the midwife, the goddess of birth. Near East. (Jacobsen, 1976: 107–109)

Niya Life or Breath, a class 4 deity of the Oglala (Plains Indians), South Dakota. (Powers, 1977: 54)

Njakomba, Mbombianda The god who makes the procreation of children possible, though sometimes this is through the work of the bilima (spirits). He is the supreme being and creator. The Nkundo, Zaire. (Hulstaert, 1938: 12, 439)

Nkulo, Nkulu A god whose chief function was "to assist women to have children." The Baganda and the Banabuddu. Uganda. (Roscoe, 1965: 316; Cunningham, 1905: 67)

413

Nohuichana A "goddess of childbirth and children, the goddess of creation." She was also a goddess of hunting and fishing, and of weaving. The Zapotec, Sola, Oaxaca, Mexico. (Whitecotton, 1977: 164)

Nona One of the Roman Parcae, fates, who with Decima determined "the proper date of birth." (Jayne, 1962: 495; Branston, 1957: 60, 64)

Nuang ud Lagod A god of reproduction of the Ifugao. Philippines. (Barton, 1946: 45)

Nuexqemalsaix A goddess who rocks the unborn young of humans and animals in a cradle. When she stops rocking, Senx sends them to be born. Also called Semsemeltstas Senxalaolela. The Bella Coola Indians, British Columbia. (Boas, 1898: 31)

Numeria The goddess of easy childbirth is also "the goddess of counting." Italy. (Jayne, 1962: 495)

Nyabahasa, Nyabibuya, and **Nyabingi** Goddesses who are helpful to women in childbirth and of assistance in cases of sterility. The Konjo and the Kiga, Uganda. (Taylor, 1962: 94)

Nyakala A goddess of fertility and of childbirth invoked to remove sterility. Very powerful and dangerous. The Amba, Uganda and Zaire. (Taylor, 1962: 86; Middleton, 1967: 39)

Nyingwan Mebege The moon goddess and goddess of procreation represents "the female principle of the universe." The major deity of the Bwiti Cult. The Fang, Gabon. (Fernandez, 1972: 241, 247)

Obban The goddess of reproduction of the Bontok and Kankanay of Northern Luzon. Daughter of Lumauwig and Bugan. Philippines. (Jocano, 1969: 15)

Obu A god of the Gã in Osu, invoked in pregnancy rites. Ghana. (Field, 1937: 168)

Odame The "goddess of birth and death." The Gã in Nungwa, Ghana. (Field, 1937: 28)

Ohmahank-Numakshi The god of life—the most exalted and most powerful of their supernatural beings. The Mandan Indians, North Dakota. (Wied-Neuwied, 1843: 359)

Olnob A god of reproduction of the Ifugao. Philippines. (Barton, 1946: 46)

Olotagiki and **Olotagisop** "In the realm of the dead. Gives the body its functions, the breathing, the hear-

ing and so forth." The Cuna, Panama. (Nordenskiold, 1938: 330)

Ombepo A god "whose name means 'wind', 'breath', or 'spirit' ." An aspect of Mukuru as the creator of the soul. The Herero, Namibia. (Luttig, 1933: 24, 83)

Onekh The personification of " 'life,' depicted as a Nile-god." Egypt. (Gardiner, 1925, 9: 790)

Opigena A Roman goddess associated with the cult of Iuno Lucino, aiding in childbirth. (Jayne, 1962: 394)

Orongo A manifestation or aspect of Jok which "is concerned with the souls or *tipo* of human beings and animals." It is probable "that Orongo is the universal spirit from which the individual *tipo* derives its separate, though not entirely independent, origin." The Lango, Uganda. (Driberg, 1923: 220)

Oshala A sky god and god of procreation. He has two forms: as Oshagiyan, a warrior dressed in white, and as Oshaloufan. He is an "old" god with two wives: Nanan, the mother of Omolu, Loko, and Oshunmare; and Yemanja. He is the father of Shango. Equivalent of Obatala. Brazil—vicinities of Bahia and Porto-Alegre. (Verger, 1954: 15–16; Bastide, 1960: 268, 570; Landes, 1940: 264)

Our Lady of Sorrows Goddess of childbirth at Ita. Brazil. (Wagley, 1964: 223)

Oyamakui One of his aspects is that of a protector of childbirth. He is a mountain god (Mt. Hie in Chicatsuaumi Province), is also "specially worshipped by industrialists." He is the son of Otoshi-no-Kami and Ame-shiru-Karu-mizu-hime; is considered to be bisexual. Japan. (Yasumaro, 1965: 51; Herbert, 1967: 332, 470–471)

Palahik A god of reproduction of the Ifugao. At Kalinugan he is an agricultural deity. Philippines. (Barton, 1946: 37, 45)

Panglang She and her servant Mangoñoyamo "care for midwives, pregnant women, and unborn children." The Bukidnon, Philippines. (Cole, 1956: 95)

Pan-quetzal-itztli A "life-giving" goddess of the Aztec. In her association with Huitzilopochtli she is a war goddess. Mexico. (Mackenzie, 1924: 228 plate)

Panthoibi Goddess of birth and death, and associated with the sun. Wife of Khaba. The Meitheis, Manipur, Assam. (Hodson, 1908: 97)

Parca A Roman goddess of birth. With Nona and Decima, goddesses of destiny, determing that of the child "about one week after birth." Now considered the name of the group as goddesses of destiny, Parcae. (Jayne, 1962: 498; Roscher, 1965, 2, 1: 210)

Partula Roman deity of the delivery in childbirth. (Jayne, 1962: 496; Ferguson, 1970: 68)

Pata Yaku Three yaku who are invoked for safe pregnancy and childbirth. The Vedda, Ceylon. (Seligmann and Seligmann, 1911: 248)

Patit di upud Pumupud An obstetrics deity of the Ifugao. Philippines. (Barton, 1946: 88)

P'ei-t'ai Niang-niang A goddess of conception. China. (Werner, 1932: 475)

Perna Possibly an Oscan goddess of birth. Italy. (Roscher, 1965, 3, 2: 1980)

Persephone One of her functions was that of a healing goddess and goddess of childbirth associated with Damia and Auxesia. As Kore, daughter of Demeter and Zeus, she was goddess of the seed corn, and was kidnapped by Pluto to be his queen of the underworld where she spent a portion of each year. Greece. (Frazer, 1960: 456; Kerenyi, 1951: 113, 459–461; Jayne, 1962: 343)

Dewi Pertimah A Javanese goddess to whom offerings are made prior to the birth of a child. Indonesia. (Geertz, 1960: 39)

Peruda, Ruda God of love and of procreation. The Tupi. Among the Tupi-Guarani he is also a creator god. Brazil. (Spence, 1925, 2: 837; Sykes, 1952: 169)

Picumnus Roman god of matrimony, protective of women in childbirth and of the newborn, driving away evil spirits and promoting the development and growth of the child. He is also a god of agriculture and of fertilization. (Jayne, 1962: 436; Prentice Hall, 1965: 120; Dumézil, 1966, 2: 616)

Pilumnus Twin of Picumnus with the same attributes in regard to the family. They are associated with Intercidona and Deverra. Italy. (Larousse, 1968: 220; Jayne, 1962: 436; Dumézil, 1966, 2: 616)

Pinudan A god of reproduction of the Ifugao. Philippines. (Barton, 1946: 44)

Pinyuhan A beneficent god of reproduction, but who can cause illness and death. Also a minor god of war and

a harasser of debtors. His wife is Gaiyun. The Ifugao, Philippines. (Barton, 1946: 44, 75; 1955: 131)

Po-ne'e-aku "Night-receding." With Po-neie-mai, deities of birth. They are the seventh pair born in the primordial night; the parents of the dog and of the birth of light, of plant life. Hawaii. (Leach, 1956: 170)

Porrima A Roman goddess of birth who looks toward the position of the fetus. Also a goddess of destiny, looking into the future. Same as Antevorta. (Roscher, 1965, 2, 1: 216; Dumézil, 1966, 1: 393)

Postvorta A Roman goddess associated with breech presentations in childbirth, a companion of Carmentis. She was prophetic of the future; represented the waning moon. (Jayne, 1962: 496; Dumézil, 1966, 1: 393; Pettazzoni, 1956: 168; Roscher, 1965, 2, 1: 216)

Prorsa A Roman goddess similar to Antevorta, which see. (Roscher, 1965, 2, 1: 218)

Ptai A deity "charged with the care of the foetus." Egypt. (Ames, 1965: 112)

Pumupud A god of childbirth who "blocks the passage of the foetus." The Ifugao, Philippines. (Barton, 1946: 87)

Pungan A god of reproduction of the Ifugao. Philippines. (Barton, 1946: 45)

P'ushien Fuh A Tu Di deity invoked to save mothers from calamities after childbirth. Szechwan, China. (Graham, 1928: 18)

Radien-Kiedde He gave the soul to Maddar-akka to care for "until it assumed bodily form," after which she delivered it to Sarakka to pass on to the human mother. He is the son of Radien Atzhie. The Lapps, Northern Europe. (Bosi, 1971: 133–134; Pettersson, 1957: 18)

Rahnyo Her A deity of life to whom offerings are made at childbirth. The Bhils, India. (Naik, 1956: 185)

Rajamma A goddess who "blesses barren women with children" and fishermen with large catches. The Jalari, the Vada, and the Oriya Kumbaro, Southern India. (Thurston, 1909, 2: 446; 4: 117; 7: 261)

Raka Goddess of procreation and childbirth and also goddess of the full moon. Daughter of Angiras and Sraddha. India. (Jayne, 1962: 160; Macdonell, 1897: 125; Danielou, 1964: 319; Barth, 1921: 25)

Ruremabibondo A deity of the Barundi—"Maker of children." Burundi. (Mbiti, 1970, 2: 328)

Samaiya A goddess of the Doms invoked with offerings at childbirth, during teething, and in illness. She is the wife of Gandak. India. (Crooke, 1925, 4: 841; Briggs, 1953: 466)

Sampny nang Goddess of life. Daughter of Ningpang. The Katchins, Burma. (Gilhodes, 1908: 674)

San Kuan Ta Ti A Taoist deity of long life. China. (Day, 1940: 137)

Sar-akka A goddess of childbirth, particularly charged with the girls to be born, with the transfer of the child from Maddar-akka to the mother, and with the birth itself. She is also goddess of the birth of the reindeer. Daughter of Maddar-akka. The Lapps, Northern Europe. (Bosi, 1960: 134; Pettersson, 1957: 253; Larousse, 1968: 308; Karsten, 1955: 38, 40)

Sasthi A goddess who is "apparently a personification of the spirit presiding over the critical sixth day after the birth of a child." India. (Keith, 1917: 246)

Sa'yatasha The god of rain of the north is also the bringer of longevity. He is important in the Shalako ceremonial of the winter solstice. The Zuñi, New Mexico. (Waters, 1950: 283; Wilson, 1958: 374)

Seatakán Mother of the Coitus. The Cagaba and the Kogi, Colombia. (Reichel-Dolmatoff, 1949/50: 114)

Seijaldyue Mother of the First Menstruation. The Cagaba and the Kogi, Colombia. (Reichel-Dolmatoff, 1949/50: 114)

Selampandai The god who forms the unborn child in the womb. The Sea Dyaks, Borneo. (Sarawak Gazette, 1963: 14, 16; Howell, 1908/10: 8)

Sembu Mahadeo A supreme being who provides the life substance for the embryo and when this leaves, death occurs. Same as Bhagavan. The Raj Gonds, India. (Furer-Haimendorf, 1974: 243, 250)

Sergue-Edne A goddess who creates souls and delivers them to Maddar-akka to be "given a body." Wife of Ibmel. The Lapps, Northern Europe. (Pettersson, 1957: 19–20)

Setlocenia Celtic "Goddess of Long Life." Britain. (Ross, 1967: 378)

Shashthi A goddess of women and of childbirth, the giver of and guardian of children. Bengal. (Martin, 1914: 251; Briggs, 1953: 532; Crooke, 1894: 82)

Shel gyi khrab can A god of birth whose neglect can cause illness and calamity. Tibet. (Nebesky-Wojkowitz, 1956, 1: 306)

Shêng Ch'an Kuei "The Demon of Maternity." China. (Werner, 1932: 420)

Shi-nun-manuri The chief goddess of the foruth plane of the heavens, where all the deities are goddesses. They control and supervise the birth of the sexes (equalizing them), and determine longevity. The Yami, Formosa. (Del Re, n.d.: 64)

Shou Hsing A stellar god, Canopus in the constellation Argo, is a god of longevity, of happiness, and of high position. China. (Day, 1940: 95; Werner, 1932: 431; Maspero, 1963: 344; Williams, 1976: 209, 371)

Shou-lao A Chinese Taoist god of longevity. (Switzer, 1971: 853)

Shou-shên A stellar god—Canopus—who determines the length of life. Also known as "the Ancient of the South Pole." China. (Maspero, 1963: 345)

Shu K'ong Chang A Tu Di god invoked to save mothers from calamities after childbirth. Szechwan, China. (Graham, 1928: 18)

Siki The deity of childbirth. The Daphla, Bengal and Assam. (Crooke, 1925, 4: 399)

Sinavali, Sinivali A Vedic goddess of fecundity and childbirth who forms the child in the womb, is invoked for offspring and for easy birth. She is the goddess of the "first day of the new moon." Daughter of Angiras. India. (Elwin, 1950: 157; Danielou, 1964: 319; Barth, 1921: 25; Gray, 1930: 59)

Ski-pas A Finno-Ugric god of procreation. The Erza (Mordvins), Russia. (Paasonen, 1925, 8: 844)

Soko-ni Fuchi A deity who aids Uari Kamui in the purification of the house in difficult childbirth. The Ainu, Japan. (Munro, 1963: 49)

Soumöröges A god who is both loved and hated by the women "for the children's souls are subject to him. He brings them and takes them away again upon the death of the child." Truk, Micronesia. (Bollig, 1927: 12)

Srog gi lha The "god of life" who is protective of worshippers and their prosperity. Tibet. (Nebesky-Wojkowitz, 1956, 1: 327)

Sti-per-sei A goddess "who protects women and girls in matters connected with childbirth." The Ch'iang, Ho-p'ing-chai, China. (Graham, 1958: 48)

Sumúldo "Mother of the Breasts," invoked for full breasts when pregnant and for release from discomfort when time for drying up. The Cagaba and the Kogi, Colombia. (Reichel-Dolmatoff, 1949/50: 173)

Sung-tsi niang-niang A goddess invoked as the giver of children, particularly of sons, though she is charged with delivering female children as well. China. Also spelled Sung-Tzi (Tzu) niang-niang. (Shryock, 1931: 79, 82; Day, 1940: 33, 92; Werner, 1932: 35)

Sung-tzu-lung-wang A dragon King, giver of sons. Southwest China. (Graham, 1961: 130)

Sung Tzu Kuan-yin Avalokitesvara as a deity of fertility and the giver of offspring. China. (Getty, 1962: 80; Day, 1940: 27)

Syt-kul-amine Goddess of birth of the Buryats. Siberia. (Pettersson, 1957: 29)

Lalla Ta bullat Her gravesite helps pregnant women in difficult deliveries. Morocco. (Westermarck, 1926, 1: 69)

T'ai Chün Hsien Niang Goddess of easy childbirth. China. (Day, 1940: 93)

T'ai Shan A very important mountain god who was in control of the earth and the elements. He became a god of birth (life) and death, invoked for sons, and success; and later became judge of the dead in the seventh court. China. (Day, 1940: 120–121; Haydon, 1941: 193–194)

Takán-kukui Father of the Sperm. The Cagaba and the Kogi, Colombia. (Reichel-Dolmatoff, 1949/50: 115)

Talomasim A spirit of evil influence at the time of childbirth. The mother can be protected from illness by a "piece of ginger" placed on her knife, which she always carries in her headband. The Isneg, Luzon, Philippines. (Vanoverbergh, 1936: 93)

Tamayoribime A goddess of childbirth as well as a goddess of the sea. She is the wife of Ugaya-fuki-aezu and sister of Toyotamabime. Japan. (Yasumaro, 1965: 71; Herbert, 1967: 370, 388)

Ta-nai Fu-jên A goddess who hastens childbirth. Also known as Ts'ui-shêng Shêng-mu. China. (Werner, 1932: 474–475)

Tano A god of procreation, of sexuality, of fertility. He is represented by the duiker-antelope, the bush-goat, crocodiles, and catfish. The Akan, Ghana. (Meyerowitz, 1958: 48, 50)

Tao-mu A goddess of longevity, a northern stellar deity. China. (Puini and Dickins, 1880: 448)

Tate Tulirikita The "goddess of conception and birth." The Huichol, Jalisco, Mexico. (Seler, 1925, 6: 829)

Ta-urt, Taueret Ancient hippopotamus goddess of fertility and of birth. Known also as Api, Apet, Opet, Rert, Rertu, Sheput. Egypt. (Budge, 1969, 2: 30, 359; Knight, 1915: 124)

Tciakwenaoka A "goddess who protects women in labour and brings fruitfulness." The Zuñi, New Mexico. (Muller, 1968: 208)

Tepkanuset The moon, wife of the sun. She is protective of women in childbirth, of "life from the malignant night air." The giver of children "and the milk to feed them." The Micmac, Maritime Provinces, Canada. (Wallis, 1955: 143–144)

Te-tu-a-Hatu The god of childbirth. The Marquesas, Polynesia. (Christian, 1895: 190)

Te Vaerua "The breath, or the life." Second deity of the very beginning—after Te ake-ia-roe. Hervey Islands, Polynesia. (Westervelt, 1963, 1: 3)

Thoueris A variant of Ta-urt.

Thovela, Thovele A beneficent god who is protective of unborn children, pregnant women and marital happiness, as well as of strangers and travelers within the country. The Bawenda, Transvaal. (Hartland, 1925, 2: 364; Wessman, 1908: 80)

T'ien Sheng A god of birth invoked for easy childbirth. China. (Day, 1940: 93, 211)

Tih'kuyi Goddess of childbirth and of generation, both human and animal, as well as goddess of hunting and of game. The Hopi, Arizona. (Tyler, 1964: 133, 188; Leach, 1950, 2: 1113)

Tiwad ud Lagod An obstetrics deity who opens up the obstructed birth canal. The Ifugao, Philippines. (Barton, 1946: 88)

Tlazolteotl An earth goddess of great sexuality and fecundity, in conjunction with which she was considered as well a goddess of birth. Mexico. (Spence, 1923: 169; Thompson, 1970: 246)

Toa-miru The "goddess of childbirth and the guide of souls." She lives in the underworld of Pouaru. Mangareva, Polynesia. (Buck, 1938: 426)

Torom anki The goddess of birth of the North Ostyak. Siberia. (Pettersson, 1957: 22)

ts'e-dpag-med, Tsepagmet God of longevity, the "Buddha of Eternal Life." Same as Amitayus. Tibet. (Schlagintweit, 1969: 98; Getty, 1962: 39)

Tse-pa-med God of longevity, of "Unlimited Life." Sikkim. (Gazetteer of Sikhim, 1894: 263)

tsering mo A god of the Lepchas invoked for "long life and prosperity." Sikkim. (Siiger, 1967: 115)

Ts'uai-shen-niang-niang A goddess of childbirth and giver of sons. Southwest China. (Graham, 1961: 130)

Tsua Sen Niang Niang A goddess of childbirth, of easy delivery. Szechwan, China. (Graham, 1928: 17)

Ts'ui Sheng Goddess of midwifery and of easy childbirth. China. (Werner, 1932: 523–524)

Tuiteke A beneficent sky spirit who taught humans how to have natural childbirth. Prior to this it was by Caesarean section. Kapingamarangi, Polynesia. (Elbert, 1949: 244)

Tumaladyu A god of reproduction. The Ifugao, Philippines. (Barton, 1946: 45)

Ture A god of childbirth of the Tiv. Nigeria. (Temple, 1922: 302)

Tuwa'boñtumsi A goddess, Sand Altar Woman, created by Huruing Wuhti. She is the female counterpart of Muingwu. A goddess of "human fecundity," also called Childbirth Water Woman. The Hopi, Arizona. (Tyler, 1964: 82)

Uari Kamui In the presence of impurities, as in childbirth, a second fire is kindled which is tended by Uari Kamui, to purify the house. The Ainu, Japan. (Munro, 1963: 17)

Ugayafukiaezu A god who, among his diverse functions, is considered a "protector of . . . childbearing and breast-nursing." Son of Hiko-ho-ho-demi and Toya-tama-hime. Japan. (Herbert, 1967: 370, 388; Kato, 1926: 60)

Uks-akka A goddess of childbirth who controlled the sex of the child and could change it from girl to boy. She was a guardian of children after birth. Daughter of Maddar-akka. The Lapps, Northern Europe. (Pettersson, 1957: 33; MacCulloch, 1964: 254; Karsten, 1955: 38, 41)

Umai Goddess of childbirth and of children. Sometimes identified with Ayisit. The Altai-Turks, Central Asia. (Czaplicka, 1925, 12: 482; Queval, 1968: 116; Potapov, 1964: 444)

Umbumabakal A god of reproduction of the Ifugao. Philippines. At Taiyup also a minor god of war. (Barton, 1946: 45, 75)

Umilong A god of reproduction of the Ifugao. Philippines. (Barton, 1946: 46)

Upud Kahlangan ud Tinok An obstetrics deity of the Ifugao. Philippines. (Barton, 1946: 88)

Uri (1) A birth demon of the Blandas. Malay Peninsula. (Skeat, 1906: 296) (2) **(hantu) uri** An "evil spirit of the after-birth connected with the caul, is held responsible for the gurgle (agah) of an infant during sleep." Malaya. (Gimlette, 1929: 25)

Uzoit, Uazit, Buto A serpent goddess, goddess of childbirth, and goddess of the north. Sister of Nekhbet. Egypt. (Jayne, 1962: 84–85)

Vagneg-imi A Finno-Ugric goddess of birth and of fate, determining the length of the child's life. Vicinity of Surgut. U.S.S.R. (MacCulloch, 1964: 260)

Vajar Mata A goddess of the Bhils invoked for offspring. A wife of Siva. India. (Grierson, 1925, 2: 556)

Vajrasattva The Adamantine, the Everlasting, who "purifies the soul from sin." T., rDo-rje dSems-pa. Tibet. (Waddell, 1959: 414)

Virbius A Roman "deity associated with child-birth in the cults of Diana and Egeria." (Jayne, 1962: 455)

Vita Roman personification of life. (Roscher, 1965, 6: 350)

Vitumnus A Roman deity who gives the child life. (Dumézil, 1966, 1: 34; Jayne, 1962: 496)

Walla-gudjail-uan A deity of birth who delivers the babies to their rightful mothers. Australia. (Reed, 1965: 60)

Wohpekumeu An erotic philanderer "but also . . . originator of childbirth." Previously women had one child and died. The Yurok, California. (Elmendorf, 1960: 536)

Xaratanga A Tarascan goddess of "conception and birth . . . the patron of the steam baths taken . . . to promote an easy labour." She is the mother of Manovapa. Michoacan, Mexico. (Bancroft, 1886, 3: 445–446; Krickeberg, 1968: 59)

Xochiquetzalli A "goddess of pregnancy and the protector of unborn children," as well as "goddess of domestic labor, the harvest, the 'New Fire' and flowers." Wife of Xochipilli. Valley of Anahuac, Mexico. (Reed, 1966: 96, 112)

Xuchicaltzin God of the bath in whose care and protection pregnant women were placed as they neared confinement. Mexico. (Bancroft, 1886, 2: 268)

Yagtač-vairgin The benevolent "Life-giving Being" of the Chukchee. Siberia. (Bogoras, 1904/09: 314)

Ya-nebya Benevolent mother earth is particularly helpful to women, especially in childbirth. The Nentsy, Siberia. (Prokof'yeva, 1964: 564)

Yanga-nama:Ka Deity of boy babies. The Munkan, Australia. (McConnel, 1957: 12)

Yang T'ai Chün A goddess of easy childbirth. China. (Day, 1940: 93)

Yárbimunéki The "eel demon. When this demon has been at work, the child at birth comes out sideways." The Cuna, Panama. (Nordenskiold, 1930: 60–61)

Yáukamunéki The "turtle demon" who causes difficulties in childbirth. The Cuna, Panama. (Nordenskiold, 1930: 60–61)

Yi-mu-sei A goddess protective during pregnancy and childbirth, also of children. Giver of sons. The Ch'iang, Ho-p'ing-chai, China. (Graham, 1958: 47)

Yoalticitl A mother goddess, of the baths, of childbirth, and of the cradle. Invoked in difficult childbirth. Mexico. (Bancroft, 1886, 2: 268, 275; 3: 363)

Za A deity controlling "all births, of both man and animals." The Na-khi, Yunnan Province, China. (Rock, 1947: 78)

Ziva Slavic goddess of life. (Machal, 1918: 117 Plate xxxiv; Bray, 1935: 51)

Zywie Goddess of life invoked for longevity and health. Same as Ziva. Poland. (de Kay, 1898: 116; Bray, 1935: 51)

20

Mankind:
Men, Women, Children, Youth, Age

Abeona A minor Roman goddess of children, protective of their activities. (Roscher, 1965, 1, 1: 3; Dumézil, 1966, 1: 34; Jayne, 1962: 496)

Abuk A goddess who "presides over the occupations of women," primarily agricultural. The Dinka, Sudan. (Lienhardt, 1961: 89, 160)

Acaste One of the Oceanids who, with the help of Apollo and their brothers the rivers, were assigned by Zeus to "bring young boys to manhood." Greece. (Hesiod-Brown, 1981: 30, 63)

Achali A secret guardian god of the Santal males whose name is known only to the head of the family and his eldest son. India. (Mukherjea, 1962: 283; Biswas, 1956: 135)

Achrael A benevolent god protective of and worshipped by women. India. (Crooke, 1925, 9: 2; Roy, 1928: 16, 67)

Acraeli A god who is concerned with "the interests of married women." If she steals from her parents to benefit her husband's home, he "punishes the household by bringing illness and even death." The Santals, India. (Mukherjea, 1962: 282)

Adeona A minor Roman goddess of children. With Abeona, protective of their activities. (Roscher, 1965, 1, 1: 67; Dumézil, 1966, 1: 34; Jayne, 1962: 496)

Admete A daughter of Oceanus and Tethys—among the Oceanids assigned by Zeus, with the help of Apollo and the river gods, to "bring young boys to manhood." Greece. (Hesiod-Brown, 1981: 63)

Ahnt ahs Pok A goddess of girls to whom offerings of dew are made. Daughter of Ahnt Kai. The Seris, Sonora, Mexico. (Coolidge, 1939: 100, 110)

Ahnt Kai The goddess of women and children who "taught women to dance and sing" and who is the only one who can tell them when to dance a Fish Dance. She is the daughter of the Sun and mother of Ahnt ahs Pok. She cures snakebite. The Seris, Sonora, Mexico. (Coolidge, 1939: 100, 109–110)

Ami rum A god of women who is also the god of riches. The Lepchas, Sikkim. (Gorer, 1938: 150)

Angus Mac-ind-oc Gaelic god of "Youth or Perfection," a god of love and lightheartedness. Son of Dagda. Ireland. (MacBain, 1917: 130; Squire, 1906: 56)

Aranya, Jamai Sashthi A goddess "who ensures the health of children and cures barrenness." Bengal. (Crooke, 1925, 2: 487)

Asia One of the Oceanids assigned by Zeus, with the help of Apollo and the river gods, to "bring young boys to manhood." Greece. (Hesiod-Brown, 1981: 63)

Atete A goddess protective of women, and a goddess of fertility and childbirth. The Galla, Ethiopia. (Littmann, 1925, 1: 57; Rossini, 1925, 6: 491; Bartels, 1969: 407; Huntingford, 1955: 76)

Atua Fafine A goddess, tutelary deity of women, who is particularly protective in the raising of the sacred yam. Tikopia, Polynesia. (Firth, 1967, 2: 143, 396)

Averruncus A Roman deity "who guarded women during parturition and afterwards from the assaults of Silvanus." (Jayne, 1962: 494)

Bab(a)ia A goddess of children, of childish babbling. Damascus, Near East. (Roscher, 1965, 1, 1: 744)

Baba Yaga An ancient Slavic being who kills children, is associated with the world of the dead, and sometimes appears as a witch. Russia. (Gimbutas, 1975: XLC M126; Mansikka, 1925, 4: 623)

Bahara A secret family god whose name is only known by the male and ultimately disclosed to the eldest son. Men only can participate in the sacrifices. The Santals, India. (Mukherjea, 1962: 283)

Benelaba A god for men only to whom were sacrificed "dogs, turkeys, quail and male slaves captured in war." His wife was Jonaji Belachina. The Zapotec, Coatlán, Oaxaca, Mexico. (Whitecotton, 1977: 158–159)

Benih Lela Punggang Tengian Dara Bintang Tiga Datai Ka Jelan A goddess who grants women the ability to be expert in weaving, etc. Daughter of Pulang Gana. The Dyaks, Sarawak, Borneo. (Sarawak Gazette, 1963: 79)

Bes A Nubian/Egyptian dwarf god among whose many functions is that of protector of children and youths. (Budge, 1969, 2: 276, 284–285; Jayne, 1962: 55)

Bona Dea A goddess who was "essentially a deity of women, symbolizing their fertility." She was also a prophetic goddess foretelling the future. Same as Fauna. Rome. (Jayne, 1962: 418–419); Fairbanks, 1907: 248)

Bunsu Kamba A god of the Sea Dyaks invoked in the ceremony for children to make them strong, skillful, successful, brave, and to give them longevity. Borneo. (Roth, 1968: 171)

Bunsu Rembia Abu A god of the Sea Dyaks invoked in the ceremony for children to make them strong, skillful, successful, and grave, and to give them longevity. Borneo. (Roth, 1968: 171)

Carmenta, Carmentis Roman goddess of women and of childbirth, guardian of children for whom she made prophecies. (Pettazzoni, 1956: 168; Dumézil, 1966, 1: 392–393; Leland, 1963: 62; Jayne, 1962: 444–445)

Catius A minor Roman deity—"a protector of boys, awakened and molded the child's intellect." (Jayne, 1962: 497)

Champa denagarh A secret god of the Santal male whose name is known only to him and his eldest son. India. (Mukherjea, 1962: 283)

Chandi The "goddess of bachelors," who are the only ones who can make sacrifices to her. She is a goddess of hunting and of war and appears in various forms—a tiger, elephant, snake. The Oraons, India. (Roy, 1928: 16, 61, 64; Rahmann, 1952: 882)

Chiconahuizcuintli The "god of the aged," worshipped at Cuauhilama, Valley of Anahuac, Mexico. (Reed, 1966: 112)

Chng-bu A goddess protective of small children. Taiwan. (Diamond, 1969: 98)

Cilera-balanda The guardian of orphans. The Tumbuka, Malawi. (Mbiti, 1970, 2: 336)

Clymene and **Clytie** Among those Oceanids assigned by Zeus to "bring young boys to manhood"—with the help of Apollo and their brothers, the river gods. Greece. (Hesiod-Brown, 1981: 63)

Cuba Roman goddess of infancy and of childhood. (Jayne, 1962: 497; Roscher, 1965, 2, 1: 196)

Cunina A Roman deity of the cradle and invoked where women feared sterility. (Dumézil, 1966, 1: 34; Ferguson, 1970: 68; Jayne, 1962: 443)

Curitis A minor Roman goddess protective of married women, promising them healthy children. She was also a goddess of festivals and joyousness. (Jayne, 1962: 494; Hadas, 1965: 73)

Daena The daughter of Ahura Mazda and Armaiti is the guardian of women. Iran. (Gray, 1930: 70)

The da-lha Personal deities whose worship helps overcome enemies. Also vulgarly called dab-lha. Tibet. (Waddell, 1959: 375)

Daraxodan A benevolent male spirit who looks after the baby. The Isneg, Luzon, Philippines. (Vanoverbergh, 1936: 98)

Dekla A Baltic goddess and guardian of the newborn who "grieved over the birth of a baby who was destined to have an unhappy life." Latvia. (Queval, 1968: 32; Gimbutas, 1963: 198)

Deswali A secret god of the Santal male whose name is known only to him and his eldest son, but also a household god invoked at various festivals. India. (Mukherjea, 1962: 283; Biswas, 1956: 135)

Dhanghara A secret and guardian god of the male Santal whose name is known only to the man and his eldest son. India. (Mukherjea, 1962: 283; Biswas, 1956: 135)

Dharamsore A secret family god whose name is known only to the head of the family and is ultimately disclosed to the eldest son. Men only can participate in the sacrifices. The Santals, India. (Mukherjea, 1962: 283)

Dinan A spirit of the Isneg who "seizes newborn babes." Luzon, Philippines. (Vanoverbergh, 1953: 100)

Doh Tenangan The wife of Laki Tenangan. She is worshipped especially by women. The Kayans, Borneo. (Hose, 1912: 6)

Domiduca A Roman goddess who with Juno Iterduca supervises Abeona and Adeona, who watch over children going to and from school. (Dumézil, 1966, 1: 34; Jayne, 1962: 497)

Duarseri A secret god of the male Santal whose name is known only to him and his eldest son. India. (Mukherjea, 1962: 283)

Durgamma A goddess of Telangana who is protective of children. India. (Mudiraj, 1970: 49)

Educa, Edusa, Edula A Roman deity of children—from birth on—who watches over their nourishment. (Dumézil, 1966, 1: 34; Jayne, 1962: 497; Altheim, 1937: 145)

Emanjah A goddess of the Shango Cult identified with St. Anne, or St. Catherine, considered "as a nurse and as a teacher of children." Trinidad, West Indies. (Simpson, 1965: 18, 20)

Entelanying A beneficent goddess who makes men "invulnerable against the weapons of the enemies" and empowers "women to weave and to work the ornamental patterns on the native cloth." The Iban Dyaks, Sarawak, Borneo. (Sarawak Gazette, 1963: 136)

Êpet, Uêret A goddess who protects children from birth through childhood. Egypt. (Jayne, 1962: 57)

Fabulinus A minor Roman deity who "awakened the understanding" and taught the child to speak. (Jayne, 1962: 497; Ferguson, 1970: 68)

Farinus A Roman god protective of children in their youth. (Roscher, 1965, 2, 1: 198)

Florentes The personification of the blooming and also of the strength of youth. Roman. (Roscher, 1965, 1, 2: 1487)

Garsinka A secret and guardian god of the male Santal whose name is known only to him and his eldest son. India. (Biswas, 1956: 135; Mukherjea, 1962: 283)

Geras The personification of old age, a monster of wickedness, and a child of Nyx. Greece. (Roscher, 1965, 1, 2: 1628; Barthell, 1971: 8; Hesiod-Brown, 1981: 59)

Gitir A beneficent goddess who makes men "invulnerable against the weapons of their enemies" and empowers "women to weave and work the ornamental patterns on the native cloth." The Iban Dyaks, Sarawak, Borneo. (Sarawak Gazette, 1963: 136)

Gosainera A secret family deity whose name is known only to the head of the family who ultimately discloses it to the eldest son. Men only can participate in the sacrifices. The Santals, India. (Mukherjea, 1962: 283)

sGrol ma Tara. She shelters men from danger from: "lions, elephants, fire, snakes, thieves, water, epidemics, enemies." Tibet. (Tucci, 1980: 43, n.)

Guyak A god of the Sea Dyaks who dwells in the Pleiades and who is invoked in the ceremony for children to make them strong, skillful, successful, brave, and to give them longevity. Borneo. (Roth, 1968: 171)

Hariti A Hindu goddess, originally cannibalistic, who upon conversion to Buddhism became the protectress of children. Known in India, China, Japan, Nepal, Tibet, Java, and Chinese Turkestan. (Getty, 1962: 84; Zimmer, 1955: 135)

Hebe Greek goddess of youth, daughter of Zeus and Hera, and for a time the cup-bearer of the gods. She was the wife of Heracles. (Cox, 1870, 2: 12; Barthell, 1971: 30–31; Fairbanks, 1907: 48; Larousse, 1968: 137)

Heqet An Egyptian frog-headed goddess, wife of Khnum (Khnemu), goddess of fertility and birth, and of the cradle. (Jayne, 1962: 85; Budge, 1969, 2: 136, 378; Knight, 1915: 44)

Heru-pa-khart Before taking on the aspects of a sun-god, he was a god of youth and vigor. Egypt. (Budge, 1969, 1: 495)

Ho Hsien-ku The Taoist patroness of women. China. (Peeters, 1941: 31)

Pitao Huichaana, Huiçana The goddess of children is also the creatress of men and animals, and a goddess of fishing. The Valley Zapotec, Oaxaca, Mexico. (Whitecotton, 1977: 169)

Huichanatao A goddess associated with children whose male counterpart is Pitao Cozaana. The Zapotec, Oaxaca, Mexico. (Whitecotton, 1977: 158)

Ibeji Guardian deity of twins. The Yoruba, Nigeria and Dahomey. (Wallis, 1939: 60; Mockler-Ferryman, 1925, 9: 280; Courlander, 1973: 236)

Ibeyi "Twin gods who protect infants." Identified with St. Cosme and St. Damian. Puerto Rico, West Indies. (Gonzalez-Wippler, 1975: 27, 28)

Ibillekpari The protector of women. Cross River, Nigeria. (Mockler-Ferryman, 1925, 9: 280)

Idunn Scandinavian goddess of immortal youth, the guardian of the apples of immortality which restored youth to the gods. (MacCulloch, 1964: 178; Wagner, 1882: 173; Davidson, 1964: 165)

Indai Abang A beneficent goddess who makes men "invulnerable against the weapons of their enemies," and empowers "women to weave and to work the ornamental patterns on the native cloth." The Iban Dyaks, Sarawak, Borneo. (Sarawak Gazette, 1963: 136)

Intercidona Goddess of the axe who with Deverra and Pilumnus protected women in childbirth and the newborn from evil spirits and from Silvanus. Rome. (Dumézil, 1966, 2: 616; Jayne, 1962: 436; Larousse, 1968: 220)

Isengowa A deity worshipped by the Haya women of Karagwe. Tanzania. (Taylor, 1962: 142)

Iterduca An aspect of Juno wherein, with Domiduca, she supervises Abeona and Adeona in seeing children to and from school. Rome. (Dumézil, 1966, 1: 34; Jayne, 1962: 497)

Iuventas *See* **Juventas**

Ixcuiname A four-fold goddess identified with Tlazolteotl who represents the four stages of women's maturity. Aztec, Mexico. (Alexander, 1920: 79)

Ixtlilton A god of children and of health. Mexico. (Reed, 1966: 96; Bancroft, 1886, 3: 409; Helfritz, 1971: 158)

jer mu A god whose wife is kam mu. They are invoked to protect "the hands, legs, eyes, and ears of" children; are considered the creators of cardamom. The Lepchas, Sikkim. (Siiger, 1967: 69)

jer thing A god invoked to guide and protect children. The Lepchas, Sikkim. (Siiger, 1967: 68)

Jhulan Devi Goddess of the cradle. After childbirth a woman can have Jhulan's image tattooed on her body where the child's body rests against her in its sling— which "supports and protects the child." The Gonds, India. (Russell, 1916, 3: 101, 127)

Joda A deity worshipped by women to whom offerings are made for feminine "health and happiness." Oraon, India. (Roy, 1928: 16, 68)

Jonaji Belachina, Xonaxi Peochina Coyo A goddess worshipped by women only. The wife of Benelaba. She is offered sacrifices similar to his. The Zapotec, Coatlán, Oaxaca, Mexico. (Whitecotton, 1977: 159)

Juks-akka Goddess and guardian of children, particularly of boys. She could transform a girl in the womb into a boy. The Lapps, Northern Europe. (Bosi, 1960: 134; Dioszegi, 1968: 30; Karsten, 1955: 41; Pettersson, 1957: 33; Collinder, 1949: 169)

Juno Goddess of women and of marriage, of birth, and guardian of all females from birth to death. Italy. (Cox, 1870, 2: 13; Dumézil, 1966, 1: 291; Fairbanks, 1907: 102–103; Larousse, 1968: 204)

Juventas, Iuventas Goddess of youth and its development, "patroness of those who had put on the toga for the first time." Rome. (Jayne, 1962: 498; Carter, 1925, 9: 797; Littleton, 1965: 77; Dumézil, 1966, 1: 200–201; 1966, 2: 617)

K'ai Kuan Hsing A deity whose "sole function is to assist children through the peculiarly trying periods of early infancy and adolescence." China. (Day, 1940: 94)

kam mu A goddess who, with her husband jer mu, was invoked to protect "the hands, legs, eyes, and ears of" children. The Lepchas, Sikkim. (Siiger, 1967: 69)

Kandoo moong "With women . . . the physical signs of puberty . . . are believed only to occur through the external influence either of a man or of a supernatural named Kandoo moong . . . [whose visit] is considered to be a sign of good luck." The Lepchas, Sikkim. (Gorer, 1938: 315)

ka thong fi, Katong Fi   A god and guardian of women "who visits women in their dreams and copulates with them at the time of their menses; this dream-copulation is meant to continue throughout life, and should a month pass without this dream it means that the woman is shortly going to die." The Lepchas, Sikkim. (Gorer, 1938: 150; Siiger, 1967: 92)

Ketkomkudra   A secret guardian god of the male Santal whose name is known only to him and his eldest son. India. (Mukherjea, 1962: 283; Biswas, 1956: 135)

Kildisin   A Finno-Ugric goddess of birth and of children, as well as of the earth and the corn. The Votyaks, Russia and Siberia. (MacCulloch, 1964: 258)

Kiranga, Riangombe   A god who is partial to twins and is likely to take one or both. He is therefore invoked at their birth for their well-being. He is the ruler over all material things and of the lesser demons and is the god to whom the people turn. The Rundi, Burundi. (Meyer, 1916: 33, 170, 186)

Kishi-Mojin, Kishi-Bojin   The name of Hariti in Japan. *See also* **Koyasu Kannon.** (Eliot, 1935: 138; Getty, 1962: 86)

Knaritja   An emu-footed sky god "who is also the Eternal Youth." The western Aranda, Australia. (Eliade, 1973: 30–32)

Kourotrophos   A Samian goddess, protector of the newborn. Greece. (Jayne, 1962: 323)

Koyasu Kannon   The Buddhist goddess Hariti in her saintly aspect is worshipped under this name—a goddess of childbirth and of children. Japan. (Getty, 1962: 86; Hori, 1968: 39)

Kudracandi   A secret and guardian god of the male Santal whose name is known only to him and his eldest son. India. (Mukherjea, 1962: 283; Biswas, 1956: 135)

Kudraj   Like the above, a secret god of the male Santal. India. (Mukherjea, 1962: 283; Biswas, 1956: 135)

Kumara   The god and guardian of infants and children who is honored at their ceremonies. Bali, Indonesia. (Covarrubias, 1937: 317; Hooykaas, 1964: 48)

Kwako   A deity worshipped by the Haya women at Karagwe. Tanzania. (Taylor, 1962: 142)

Laglagemin   A benevolent spirit with the form of a bird who looks after ill-cared-for children. The Isneg, Luzon, Philippines. (Vanoverbergh, 1936: 98)

Laima   Goddess of women—in their work, in childbirth, the protector of young girls and their chastity, of orphans. She is also the goddess of destiny, determining one's fortune and length of life. Latvia and Lithuania. (Jonval, 1929: 18–21; Gimbutas, 1963: 197; Grimm, 1880: 416; Queval, 1968: 66)

Lakshmi   The goddess of youth and of beauty. Sakti of Vishnu. Cambodia. (Marchal, 1963: 210)

Leto   Greek goddess of healing, of childbirth, and guardian of children. As a wife of Zeus and mother of Apollo and Artemis, she represents wifely purity and motherly love. (Kerenyi, 1951: 35, 91; Jayne, 1962: 338; Rawlinson, 1885: 151)

Levana   A Roman goddess, guardian of the newborn and the acknowledgement of their legitimacy. (Roscher, 1965, 2, 1: 201; Jayne, 1962: 498)

Lhesania   A god worshipped by children in the celebration of spring. The Himalayas, India. (Berreman, 1963: 377)

Lilachangi   A secret and guardian god of the male Santal whose name is known only to the man and his eldest son. India. (Mukherjea, 1962: 283; Biswas, 1956: 135)

Lin-cui-hu-zin   A goddess, the protector of children, is invoked for aid in illness. Taiwan. (Diamond, 1969: 103)

Locutius   A minor Roman god of childhood who "taught the child to speak correctly." (Jayne, 1962: 498; Roscher, 1965, 2, 1: 203)

Mabon   "Divine Youth," son of Modron, and the equivalent of Maponos. Wales and Britain. (Ross, 1967: 208; MacCana, 1970: 33; Squire, 1906: 328)

Macuilcalli   God of virgins, worshipped at Cuauhilama. Valley of Anahuac, Mexico. (Reed, 1966: 112)

Magba   A god, guardian of women, who gives or withholds children according to their actions. Dahomey. (Herskovits, 1938, 2: 140)

Mahm-m   A goddess of women. The Seris, Sonora, Mexico. (Coolidge, 1939: 100)

Maponos   A god of youth, of poetry and music, and identified with Apollo. Britain and Gaul. (Reed, 1967: 208; MacCana, 1970: 32; Anwyl, 1906: 40)

Mater Matuta   A Roman goddess of matrons and children. Also a goddess of the dawn whose feast is the

Matralia and is celebrated by matrons. (Altheim, 1937: 126; Jayne, 1962: 453; Dumézil, 1966, 1: 50–51)

Mater Montana A Roman goddess of infants. (Tod, 1920: 664)

Megit A deity of the heavens who is invoked in the ceremony for children to make them strong, skillful, successful, brave, and to give them longevity. The Sea Dyaks, Borneo. (Roth, 1968: 171)

Megu God of the evening star who is invoked in the ceremony for children to make them strong, skillful, successful, brave, and to give them longevity. The Sea Dyaks, Borneo. (Roth, 1968: 171)

Menani A deity of the rainbow, "a small part . . . appearing just above the horizon," who is also invoked in the ceremony for children to make them strong, etc., as Megit and Megu. The Sea Dyaks, Borneo. (Roth, 1968: 171)

Mendong A beneficent goddess who makes men "invulnerable against the weapons of their enemies" and empowers "women to weave and to work the ornamental patterns on the native cloth." The Iban Dyaks, Sarawak, Borneo. (Sarawak Gazette, 1963: 136)

Mhaya A goddess worshipped primarily by women who have been "deserted by their lovers." Tanzania. (Taylor, 1962: 142)

Minona A goddess of magic, both good and evil, and also the protectress of women. Dahomey. (Herskovits, 1938, 2: 260)

Mlezi Among the Chewa the guardian of children. Malawi. (Mbiti, 1970, 2: 329)

Mo lha (mo), phug lha The goddess/god of women, protecting them and living in the area of their activities. The house god of the interior; the god of the female line; also the god of the left armpit. "The phug lha also controls the property of the family, especially the livestock." Tibet. (Nebesky-Wojkowitz, 1956, 1: 327; Tucci, 1980: 187–188)

Morey ba Goddess of women. Fer, Canary Islands. (Basset, 1925, 2: 511)

Mousso-ka-dyri A tree deity, protector of women and young girls. The Bambara, Mali. (Tauxier, 1927: 164)

Muckquachuckquand, Muckachuckwand The Narragansett Indian god of children. Connecticut. (Skinner, 1913: 91; De Forest, 1853: 26)

Mukrang A house-god associated with Hemphu. They are "preservers of men." The Mikirs, Assam. (Lyall, 1925, 8: 629)

Nabuzana A goddess who was a patroness of women and assisted in childbirth. The Baganda, Uganda. (Roscoe, 1965: 317–318)

Nahualpilli The "god of the young" worshipped at Cauahilama. Valley of Anahuac, Mexico. (Reed, 1966: 112)

Nai Mu A "goddess of wet nurses" and a protector of children. China. (Day, 1940: 93)

Nana enna A goddess of the Elmina District who protects women whose men are at war. Wife of Behnya. Gold Coast/Ghana. (Ellis, 1887: 53)

N'Goni A tree god and god of children. The Bambara, Mali. (Tauxier, 1927: 389)

Niang-Niang A goddess of children invoked also in rites against hail. The Monguor, Kansu, China. (Schram, 1957: 85, 99)

Nirmali A goddess of the Kafir who is protective of children and women in childbirth. Kafiristan. (Robertson, 1925, 7: 635–636)

Nohuichana A goddess of children and of childbirth who is also a goddess of hunting and fishing, of weaving. The wife or female counterpart of Pitao Cozaana. The Zapotec, Sola, Oaxaca, Mexico. (Whitecotton, 1977: 164)

N'tomo A god of adolescents, of the rites of circumcision and excision. The Bambara, Mali. (Tauxier, 1927: 324–325)

Nu'akea Goddess of nursing and guardian of the child's welfare; associated with the "ceremony for weaning a boy child." Hawaii. (Beckwith, 1940: 32–33)

Nundina A goddess of infants, of their naming and their acceptance—the girls on the eighth day, the boys on the ninth. Roman. (Jayne, 1962: 498; Roscher, 1965, 2, 1: 208)

Nyauleza The supreme judge, worshipped by the woman of Karagwe. The Haya, Tanzania. (Taylor, 1962: 142)

Obatala The "shaper of infants in the wombs of humans and, by extension, the special protector of all who are mal-formed." The Yoruba, Nigeria. (Courlander, 1973: 6, 10)

Ocyrrhoe, Okyrrhoe A daughter of Oceanus and Tethys—one of those assigned by Zeus to "bring young boys to manhood" with the help of Apollo and the river gods. Greece. (Hesiod-Brown, 1981: 63)

Ohur A deity "who saves women from widowhood." The Agarwalas, India. (Keane, 1925, 2: 124)

Ong-ia, Ti-Ong-ia A god with healing powers, protective particularly of children from illness. Taiwan. (Diamond, 1969: 99)

Opis A Roman deity of children from birth on. (Dumézil, 1966, 1: 34)

Oshoun A goddess of youth and of waters, sometimes given as the wife of Oshossi. Brazil. (Landes, 1940: 265)

Paiyatuma God of youth and of clowns—irresponsible. Sometimes a collective or multiple god. The Zuñi Indians, New Mexico. (Parsons, 1939: 170, 177)

Palilítan A "young male spirit for whom the miniature cradle is hung over a new-born child. It is his duty to protect the infant from sickness and danger. He is a servant of Panglang." The Bukidnon, Mindanao, Philippines. (Cole, 1956: 95)

Panchananda A deity who is protective of children from illness. Bengal. (Crooke, 1925, 2: 487)

Pao Tung Chiang Chün A guardian of children. China. (Day, 1940: 93)

Paventia, Paventina A goddess protective of the fears in children. Roman. (Roscher, 1965, 2, 1: 213; Dumézil, 1966, 1: 34; Jayne, 1962: 498)

Peitho "Persuasion," an Oceanid. Among those assigned by Zeus to "bring young boys to manhood." She was associated with the "qualities of human leadership." Greece. (Hesiod-Brown, 1981: 63, 87)

P'ei-Yang Goddess of nourishment and guardian of children. China. (Day, 1940: 93)

Pên Ming Hsing Chün A star god, patron of males. China. (Day, 1940: 94)

Perseis Among those Oceanids assigned by Zeus to assist in bringing "young boys to manhood." Greece. (Hesiod-Brown, 1981: 63)

Phoebus Apollo That aspect of Apollo as a god of youth and beauty, of music. Son of Leto and Zeus and twin of Artemis. Greece. (Kerenyi, 1951: 35, 139; Murray, 1935: 104–105)

Pho lha, the p'o lha A personal guardian god of men whose power resides in the right armpit, worshipped for longevity and protection from accident. He is also concerned with the protection of the exterior of the house. Tibet and Sikkim. (Nebesky-Wojkowitz, 1956, 1: 264, 327; Gazetteer of Sikhim, 1894: 353; Waddell, 1959: 375)

Pichanto A goddess associated with children and the intermediary with Pichana Gobeche. Her male counterpart is Pitao Cozaana. The Zapotec, Chichicapa, Oaxaca, Mexico. (Whitecotton, 1977: 158)

Picumnus Roman god of infants, the protector of the newborn from illness and the promoter of growth and development. Twin of Pilumnus. (Dumézil, 1966, 2: 616; Jayne, 1962: 436; Murray, 1935: 154)

Pi-hia-yüan-kün A Taoist goddess of the clouds, "protectress of women and children." China. (Maspero, 1963: 282, 350)

Pilumnus A god of the family and of infants. With Intercidona and Deverra, the protectors of the new mother and infant from assaults by evil spirits and Silvanus. Twin of Picumnus. Roman. (Dumézil, 1966, 2: 616; Jayne 1962: 436; Murray, 1935: 154)

Pof The god of women and of lovemaking. Yap Islands, the Carolines, Micronesia. (Christian, 1899: 385)

Potina A Roman goddess who presided over the nourishment of children. (Jayne, 1962: 499; Altheim, 1937: 145; Ferguson, 1970: 68)

Puyu A beneficent goddess who makes men "invulnerable against the weapons of their enemies" and empowers "women to weave and to work the ornamental patterns on the native cloth." The Iban Dyaks, Sarawak, Borneo. (Sarawak Gazette, 1963: 136)

sPyan ras gzigs Same as Avalokitesvara. A particular helper of mankind called upon in all situations. He "accompanied and comforted the Tibetan on his entire path through life." Tibet. (Tucci, 1980: 105)

Radau A god of the Milky Way invoked in the ceremony for children to make them strong, skillful, successful, brave, and to give longevity. The Sea Dyaks, Borneo. (Roth, 1968: 171)

Renenet, Renenit, Rannut A lioness goddess of maternity and of nursing. She named the infant and gave him his personality and fortune. Egypt. (Knight, 1915: 105; Ames, 1965: 111; Gardiner, 1925, 9: 791; Larousse, 1968: 38)

Renpet The "goddess of the year, the goddess of spring-tide and of youth." Egypt. (Ames, 1965: 111)

Rumina Roman goddess of nursing, invoked when women feared sterility. (Jayne, 1962: 443, 499; Ferguson, 1970: 68)

Samazi A beneficent spirit of the Rengma Nagas, protective of small children. India. (Mills, 1937: 170)

The Samsin Three spirits who were the guardians of small children and worshipped by women desiring a child. Korea. (Clark, 1932: 206)

San Fu Jên The " 'Three Matrons' who help women in times of special need." China. (Day, 1940: 22)

Sar-akka A Finno-Ugric goddess of women in all their functions, but primarily a goddess of childbirth. The Lapps, Northern Europe. (Karsten, 1955: 38, 40; Dioszegi, 1968: 30; Pettersson, 1957: 18, 31; MacCulloch, 1964: 253; Bosi, 1960: 134)

Seleleding, Seleledu, Selingiling Three gods of the Sea Dyaks invoked in the ceremony for children to make them strong, skillful, successful, brave, and to give longevity. Borneo. (Roth, 1968: 170–171)

Senecta, Senectus Personification of old age. Daughter of Erebos and Nyx. Greece. (Roscher, 1965, 4: 710)

Sengungong A god "who has charge of the full-grown knotted branches" and also is invoked in the ceremony for children to make them strong, skillful, successful, brave, and to give longevity. The Sea Dyaks, Borneo. (Roth, 1968: 171)

Sentia A Roman goddess of childhood providing the child with "discernment and wisdom." (Roscher, 1965, 2, 1: 222; Jayne, 1962: 499)

Sentinus A Roman deity who gives the child in the womb the sense of feeling. (Roscher, 1965, 2, 1: 222; Dumézil, 1966, 1: 34; Jayne, 1962: 496)

Seragendah An earth god of the Sea Dyaks who is invoked in the ceremony for children to make them strong, skillful, successful, brave, and to give longevity. Borneo. (Roth, 1968: 170)

Seragendi A god of the waters and streams who is invoked in the ceremony for children to make them strong, etc., as in the above. The Iban Dyaks, Sarawak, Borneo. (Roth, 1968: 170; Sarawak Gazette, 1963: 133)

Shasthi A Hindu goddess of women and children, of childbirth. India. (Crooke, 1894: 82; Banerjea, 1953: 69; Briggs, 1953: 532; Martin, 1914: 251)

She-p'er An ancestress who is helpful to women and girls. The Ch'iang, Lo-pu-chai, Szechwan, China. (Graham, 1958: 49)

Simei A goddess of women and protective in births. Sister/wife of Ple. The Semong (Senoi), Malaya. (Schebesta, 1954: 262, 266; Skeat, 1906: 213–214)

Singgar A beneficent goddess who makes men "invulnerable against the weapons of their enemies" and empowers "women to weave and to work the ornamental patterns on the native cloth." The Iban Dyaks, Sarawak, Borneo. (Sarawak Gazette, 1963: 136)

Sowika The god protective of children. The Hopi, Oraibi, Arizona. (Titiev, 1971: 277)

Squauanit "The Woman's God." The Narragansett, Rhode Island. (Skinner, 1913: 91)

Statanus, Statilinus, and **Statina** Roman deities who taught the children to stand and walk. (Roscher, 1965, 2, 1: 224; Jayne, 1962: 499; Ferguson, 1970: 68)

Stimula Roman goddess of stimuli and sensitivity to them. (Jayne, 1962: 499; Roscher, 1965, 2, 1: 226)

Strenia A goddess protective of youth. Also a goddess of health. Italy. (Roscher, 1965, 2, 1: 227; Jayne, 1962: 440)

Sung Tzŭ Chinese goddess of children. (Day, 1940: 93)

Taua A goddess and guardian of women consulted in times of danger or in cases of antisocial conduct. Pukapuka, Polynesia. (Beaglehole, 1938: 309)

Tebaran A god associated with the moon who is invoked in the ceremony for children to make them strong, skillful, successful, brave, and to give longevity. The Sea Dyaks, Borneo. (Roth, 1968: 171)

Telpochtli Tezcatlipoca as the god of youth. The Aztec, Mexico. (Alexander, 1920: 62; Duran, 1971: 476)

T'ien Hsien   A goddess protective of children. China. (Day, 1940: 93)

Tohar-tsireur   A goddess who "resides in a rock close to Cape Coast" and is protective of women. Ghana. (Mockler-Ferryman, 1925, 9: 278)

Tse-Sun   A goddess of posterity and a protector of children. China. (Day, 1940: 93)

Ts'i Ma Niang Tsai   A sky goddess who is merciful and helpful to unfortunate children. The Ch'uan Miao, Southwest China. (Graham, 1937: 62)

Lalla Tsuglhair   A saint whose sanctuary "is only visited by women and children," by supplicants, as well as those recovered from illness. Morocco. (Westermarck, 1926, 1: 81)

Umai, Umaj   A goddess of children, of cradles, of childbirth. The Altai Turks, Central Asia. (Potapov, 1964: 444; Dioszegi, 1968: 463; Queval, 1968: 116; Czaplicka, 1925, 12: 482; Larousse, 1973: 435)

Vagitanus   A minor Roman deity of the breathing and first cries of the infant. (Jayne, 1962: 496; Ferguson, 1970: 68)

Vaticanus   A minor Roman deity of children—"the maker and developer of the human voice," stimulating the first wails. (Jayne, 1962: 499; Dumézil, 1966, 1: 34)

Virgen del Rosario   She is "considered the patron of women" and is at times identified with the moon. The Zinacanticos, Chiapas, Mexico. (Vogt, 1970: 8)

Voleta   A Roman goddess of childhood and also of will and strength of mind. (Roscher, 1965, 2, 1: 232)

Volumna and **Volumnus**   Goddess and god of childhood and of will power who induce morality in the child. Roman. (Jayne, 1962: 499; Roscher, 1965, 2, 1: 232)

Wolera   "Caretaker of Children." Same as Mlezi. Malawi. (Mbiti, 1970, 2: 329)

Yalatandin   The protector of "solitary women in the meadows." The Bagobo, Philippines. (Benedict, 1916: 22)

Yalode   A goddess worshipped especially by women, who offer her cowrie shells and a ram in the Yam festival. Dahomey. (Herskovits, 1938, 1: 37; 1938, 2: 155)

Yid-'prog-ma   Tibetan name of the Buddhist goddess Hariti. (Getty, 1962: 84–86)

Yoalticitl   A goddess of the cradle as well as of childbirth and the sweatbaths. Mexico. (Bancroft, 1886, 3: 275, 268)

21

Fertility:
Animal, Vegetable, Phallic

Agathos Daemon, Agothodaemon   An ancient Greek fertility god who takes the form of a snake. He was the personification of the beneficence of nature, especially of vineyards, and was also considered a god of good fortune like his consort Agathe Tyche. (Ferguson, 1970: 82; Roscher, 1965, 1, 1: 98; Campbell, 1968: 17)

Aine   A Celtic goddess of fertility, associated with waters—wells and springs. Ireland. (Ross, 1967: 219; MacCulloch, 1911: 70)

Aisyt, Ayyysyt, Ayisit   An important goddess of fertility, of procreation, and of childbirth, invoked especially for sons. She leads the soul to the child. The Yakut, Siberia. (Eliade, 1964: 80; Tokarev and Gurvich, 1964: 280; Jochelson, 1900/02: 160)

Ala   The goddess of fertility is also the goddess of the earth and of the underworld, the goddess of morality whose name is invoked in oaths. The Ibo, Nigeria. (Parrinder, 1967: 78; 1949: 37; Meek, 1943: 113; Jeffreys, 1972: 730)

Alasho-funfun   A goddess of fertility associated with the festival of Okebadan. The Ibadan, Nigeria. (Parrinder, 1951: 57)

Ale   The same as Ala. The Etche Ibo, Nigeria. (Talbot, 1967: 58, 60; Williams, 1936: 203)

Alosaka   A god of fertility, of germination, of animals and of vegetation; a horned god and a god of the earth. The Hopi, New Mexico. (Fewkes, 1899: 534, 539; 1920: 592, 604; Waters, 1963: 190)

Amado Oha   As the source of rain he is considered a god of fertility—of crops and for children. He is primar-ily the storm god of the Ibo. Nigeria. (Parrinder, 1949: 33; Williams, 1936: 213)

Ammon   An oracular sky and fertility god of Shiwa. A ram god who in his solar aspect later became the supreme god. He represented the setting sun. Libya. (Meyerowitz, 1958: 139–141; Basset, 1925, 2: 508; Bel, 1938: 73)

Amon   A deity of various attributes and functions. As a phallic deity he was a god of fertility and of reproduction. Egypt. (Casson, 1965: 89; Larousse, 1968: 29)

Amra   The sun goddess, a part of Ayt'ar, was invoked for fertility. The Abkhasians, Caucasus. (Janashia, 1937: 127–128)

Amsu, Min, or Khem   A god of virility and of reproduction whose female counterpart is Nephthys. Egypt. (Budge, 1969, 2: 258, 507; Knight, 1915: 15)

Anahit   A goddess adopted from the Persians. She is a goddess of fecundity and childbirth; as a goddess of fertility she is associated with orgiastic religion and prostitution, but is also regarded as the great mother goddess. She is the most popular of the seven chief deities, daughter of Aramazd and sister of Mihr and Nane. Here she is not associated with water or with the planet Venus. Armenia. (Ananikian, 1925, 1: 797; 1964: 17, 18, 28; Gray, 1930: 23)

Anahita, Anaita   A river goddess who is a goddess of fertility, of the fecundity of nature, of virility, of childbirth, and of nursing. As a goddess of strength she is invoked by warriors. She is associated with the planet Venus. Iran. (Dumézil, 1966, 1: 302; Dresden, 1961: 353; Jayne, 1962: 189–190; Fairbanks, 1907: 132; Huart, 1963: 38, 42)

Anat(h)   A goddess of the fertility of the soil, a goddess of love and sex, virginal yet wanton. She was primarily a goddess of war, ruthless, bloodthirsty, and cruel, associated with Baal, usually as his sister but sometimes as a daughter, a wife. In these latter relationships she was also named in association with El. She is identified at times with Astarte and Asherah. Canaan, Phoenicia, and Syria. (James, 1960: 89; Moscati, 1960: 114; Oldenburg, 1969: 87–89; Crawford, 1957: 25; Albright, 1956: 74, 77; Vriezen, 1963: 51; Patai, 1967: 53, 61–62; Larousse, 1968: 76; Gray, 1964: 123–124)

Anderon   A god of fecundity, protector of livestock and of women. Spain. (Martinez, 1962: 97)

Aningat, Aningap   The moon, a god of fertility and of fruitfulness, the guardian of morals, and though he punishes, is not feared but considered beneficent. The Iglulik Eskimo, Canada. (Rasmussen, 1929: 62–63, 73–75)

'anłtáni·   Cornbeetle—a helpful deity, "the symbol of female generative power, may be represented as male or female." The Navaho, Arizona and New Mexico. (Reichard, 1950: 422)

Anqet, Anuqet   A Nubian goddess, deity of fertility and of childbirth, of life, health, and joy. She was a goddess of the Nile and formed a triad at Elephantine with Khnemu and Sati. Egypt. (Budge, 1969, 2: 50, 57–58; Jayne, 1962: 53)

a nyit a jom   A female assisting in the creation of seeds. A ma yel being—"creators of the fertility of the fields." The Lepchas, Sikkim. (Siiger, 1967, 1: 91; 1967, 2: 40)

Aphrodite   As a Phoenician goddess introduced into Greece, she was a goddess of fertility and fruitfulness, of motherhood, as well as a goddess of love and of licentious rites. (Frazer, 1960: 384; Barthell, 1971: 31–32)

Apocatequil   As the god who produced thunder and lightning, he was considered a god of fertility of the fields. Twin of Piguerao. The Huamachuco Indians, Peru. (Brinton, 1868: 153; Métraux, 1946, 2: 120)

Are   A god invoked in fertility or prosperity ceremonies. The Ora, Nigeria. (Clarke, 1944: 93)

Aritimi   An Etruscan goddess, the equivalent of Artemis, as a goddess of fertility and of the hunt. Italy. (Hamblin, 1975: 87)

Armaiti   A Zoroastrian deity, "an androgynous figure (but more female than male) conceived as the patron (-ess) of the earth," who represents fertility, and is considered an earth goddess. Daughter of Ahura Mazda. Iran. (Littleton, 1973: 77, 177; Gray, 1930: 47–48, 220)

Artemis   At Ephesus in Asia Minor, she was primarily a goddess of fertility served by eunuchs who castrated themselves in orgiastic rites. In early Greece she was also a goddess of fertility, subsequently becoming goddess of the hunt and of wild beasts, and a goddess of the moon and of childbirth. (Frazer, 1960: 8, 406; Larousse, 1968: 122, 110)

Aruarani   "Mother of Moriche Flour." Goddess of "sustenance and fertility," and of hammock makers. The Winikina-Warao, Venezuela. (Wilbert, 1973: 6, 28)

Asha Vahishta   A god who increases the productivity of agriculture and of animals. He is also the guardian of the fire. Iran. (Gray, 1930: 38; Williams Jackson, 1925, 1: 385; Huart, 1963: 41)

Asherah   In Canaan/Palestine, a goddess of fertility and of childbirth, and a mother goddess. She was originally a goddess of the sea. Near East. (Patai, 1967: 52; Gray, 1964: 123; Schoeps, 1961: 63; Sayce, 1898: 256; Oldenburg, 1969: 29–31)

Ashi   A goddess of fertility and of abundance as well as of healing. Also, "as the personification of retribution, sees that each man receives his proper 'share' in the hereafter rather than" in this world. Iran. (Jayne, 1962: 190; Haydon, 1941: 67; Littleton, 1965: 124)

Astarte, Ashtart, Ashtaroth   Goddess of fertility, of love, and of sex—representing the reproductive powers of nature. She was also a goddess of war as Venus of the morning. In Phoenicia she was a goddess of sacred prostitution. Canaan, Syria, and Phoenicia. Near East. (Jayne, 1962: 133; Vriezen, 1963: 52; Albright, 1956: 75; Moscati, 1960: 114; Langdon, 1931: 25; Ferm, 1950: 125–126; Oldenburg, 1969: 42–43)

Atargatis   A Nabataean mother goddess represented as having the tail of a fish or a dolphin. She had "power over the fertility of living things, was worshipped at Ascalon on the coast of Palestine." Near East. (Schafer, 1980: 38)

Atete   A goddess of fertility of men and animals, and of childbirth, protective of women. Some consider her the creator. The Galla, Ethiopia. (Littmann, 1925, 1: 57; Rossini, 1925, 6: 491; Bartels, 1969: 407; Huntingford, 1955: 76)

'Attrt   *See* **Astarte**

Auge   A goddess of heat and of fertility. Spain. (Martinez, 1962: 105)

Auschauts, Auschkaut   Baltic god of fertility and of healing, a serpent god. The Sudavians, Samland. (Puhvel, 1974: 83; Welsford, 1925, 11: 421–422)

Auxesia   A goddess of fertility and of growth, associated with crops. Greece. (Jayne, 1962: 315; Willetts, 1962: 52)

Ayt'ar   A "great god of procreation and fertility, particularly with regard to the breeding of cattle." The chief god of a group (Jabran, Zhwabran, Aleshkintr, Amza, Amra, Anap'a-naga, Atchshe-shyashyana) who represent various aspects of him. The Abkhasians, Caucasus. (Janashia, 1937: 121, 129)

Azer-ava   The goddess of fruitfulness is also a sky goddess, the bringer of rain. The Mordvins, Russia. (Paasonen, 1925, 8: 844; MacCulloch, 1964: 258)

Baal   The storm and rain god was equally important as a god of fertility and generation, representing the male productive principle. His female counterpart or consort is variously given as Anath, Astarte, Ashera. In Lybia he is known as Baal-Hamon. Canaan, Syria, and Phoenicia. Near East. (Gordon, 1961: 184–185; Albright, 1956: 73–74; Driver, 1956: 5, 20–21; Vriezen, 1963: 51; Meyerowitz, 1958: 130–131)

Baba   God of the phallus, eldest son of Osiris. Egypt. (Budge, 1969, 2: 91)

Bai Ulgan (Ulgen, Ulgon)   The god of the fertility of animals and of crops is also a god of the atmosphere. He is second under Kaira Kan. Horses are sacrificed to him. The Altaic, Siberia. (Eliade, 1964: 198; Casanowicz, 1924: 417; Ferm, 1950: 300; Wales, 1957: 71)

Baklum Chaam   A phallic god, a god of the fertility of the fields and of animals. The Mayan, Yucatan, Mexico. (Bancroft, 1886, 3: 467)

Ba-neb-Tattu, Ba-neb-Tettu   The ram-god of Tattu. A god of virility, a phallic god, whose female counterpart is Hat-mehit; their son is Heru-pa-khart. Egypt. (Budge, 1969, 1: 103; 2: 64–65)

Bara Kumba   With Rani Kajhal, a pair worshipped for the fertility of the earth mother. They are tree and fertility deities who are invoked at marriage rites and to whom sacrifices are made before the harvest. The Pavras, India. (Crooke, 1925, 5: 5)

Belet   A god of the fertility of men and of cattle, as well as the growth of corn. The Nuba, Sudan. (Seligman, 1925, 9: 403)

Bendis   Thracian/Phrygian moon goddess who is also a goddess of fertility in nature. Greece and Asia Minor. (Fairbanks, 1907: 133; Larousse, 1968: 111, 160; Grimm, 1888: 1398)

Berecynthia, Berecyntia   A Celtic earth mother and goddess of agricultural fertility. Gaul (Ferguson, 1970: 15; MacCulloch, 1911: 44)

Berejya   Iranian god of agricultural (grain) fertility. (Gray, 1930: 140)

Bhimai   A rain and sky god associated with agricultural fertility. India. (Elwin, 1950: 141)

Buanann   A Celtic goddess of fertility and a warrior-mother-goddess. Wales. (Ross, 1967: 228; MacCulloch, 1911: 73)

Butu-Ulisiwa   A phallic god worshipped by the Ulisiwa as the source of fertility in women is also the source of good fortune at sea, and of victory in war. Ambon and Uliasa (Moluccas), Indonesia. (Hartland, 1925, 9: 818)

Cernunnos   Celtic horned god of animals, of fertility and of abundance. Gaul, Britain, and Ireland. (MacCulloch, 1964: 35; Ross, 1967: 131, 137; MacCana, 1970: 47)

Chango   A god of virility and strength, of lightning and thunder, also of sexuality. He is identified with Saint Barbara, and is a hermaphroditic deity. Cuba, West Indies. (Verger, 1957: 337; Marcelin, 1950: 81)

Chicomecoatl, Chantico   A goddess of fecundity and of the hearth among the Xochimilcas, the Mexicas, and the Acolhuas. Mexico. (Reed, 1966: 112)

Choque Suso, Chokesuso   A goddess of fertility and of the irrigation channels. Peru. (Trimborn, 1968: 125–126; Alexander, 1920: 232)

Cromm Cruaich   Celtic god of fertility. Ireland. (MacCulloch, 1911: 57)

Cybele   Phrygian orgiastic fertility goddess, mother of the gods, and a mountain goddess. Known also in Greece and Rome. (Frazer, 1960: 403; Hadas, 1965: 127; Fairbanks, 1907: 142–4; MacCulloch, 1925, 8: 864)

Cymidei Cymeinfoll   A Celtic goddess of "fertility and warlike vigour." Britain. (MacCana, 1970: 86)

Da Agboku   A god of the fertility of the fields. Son of Dada Zodji and Ananu. Dahomey. (Herskovits, 1938, 2: 143)

Dagda   Celtic god of the earth and its fertility. A tribal god of virility, "lawgiver in times of peace, protector in times of danger." Ireland. (Ross, 1967: 166; MacCulloch, 1911: 72, 78)

Dagoi   A guardian demon who controls human and vegetal fertility or barrenness and must be propitiated to avert mis- or ill-fortune. The Bondo, India. (Elwin, 1950: 158)

Dagon, Dagan   An earth god and a god of agriculture, of grain, of fertility. In Assyria he is a judge of the dead in the lower world, associated with Nergal and Misharu. Canaan, Phoenicia, and Euphrates Valley. (Albright, 1968: 124, 143; Ferm, 1950: 124; Vriezen, 1963: 52; Langdon, 1931: 78, 80; Paton, 1925, 4: 388)

Dakin   With Darhar, a pair to whom offerings are made for the fertility of the earth mother. The Kharwars, Palamau. India. (Crooke, 1925, 5: 5)

Dame   A sky fertility god of the Akan at Nkoranza. Ghana. (Meyerowitz, 1958: 73)

Damoia   A Greek goddess of fertility. (Willetts, 1962: 52)

Darhar   *See* **Dakin**

Dea Domnann   MacCulloch suggests that this is a chthonic goddess and possibly also of the earth's fertility. Celtic Ireland. (MacCulloch, 1911: 59; 1925, 3: 282)

Demeter   Goddess of agriculture (of corn particularly), of fertility, and of the earth's abundance. She was the mother of Persephone by Zeus. Greece. (Jayne, 1962: 316–317; Fairbanks, 1907: 93, 171; Frazer, 1960: 134, 456, 460)

Deoharin   With Dih worshipped for the fertility of the earthmother. India. (Crooke, 1925, 5: 5)

Dharma Thakur   A god of various aspects, among them that of fertility and prosperity. He is invoked for the healing of numerous diseases. Bengal. (Maity, 1971: 81–83; Elwin, 1950: 135)

Dih   *See* **Deoharin**

Dinditane   A deity of agricultural fertility. The Huli, Southern Highlands, New Guinea. (Glasse, 1965: 43)

Djanggawul   A collective name for three ancestral divine beings—a brother and two sisters. The name is used also as the brother's name, who is also known as Gundanguru and Balwadjar; the elder sister Bildjiwuraroiju, or Reiwurjan, or Ganinjara; the younger sister Miralaidj (Malalait, Mandalaidj) or Djurdjunga, or Balmabalma. The sisters are goddesses of fertility, "eternally pregnant." All are associated with water and instituted the rituals and ceremonies. Arnhem Land, Australia. (Berndt, 1952: 1–5, 26; Poignant, 1967: 130–131; Eliade, 1973: 63)

Donar   Germanic god of agricultural fertility, and of thunder and rain. Same as Thor, Thunor. (Grimm, 1880: 157, 164, 166; Schoeps, 1961: 105)

Dosojin   A phallic deity, benevolent and understanding, easily approached, and frequently appearing as a couple usually identified as Saruta-hiko and Uzume. Phallic deities should not be considered obscene. The Dosojin couple express generation, the creative impulse, fecundity and prosperity. As a god of agriculture he is found at crossroads leading to the rice fields, or on their edges, protecting the crops from insects and other natural hazards. As a preventive and protective deity, a god of the roads, he is placed on the village borders, paths, bridges, and facing the mountain from which evil spirits come, watching over travelers and villagers alike. As a god of fecundity and sexuality he is worshipped for marriages, offspring, and a happy sex life. Also called Saeno-Kami. Japan. (Kato, 1926: 31; Hori, 1959: 414; Bunce, 1955: 112; Czaja, 1974: 28–30, 41–50)

Dshesyugei-Ayi   A deity of the Yakut who gives them food and "increase of cattle and horses." Siberia. (Jochelson, 1933: 46)

Dumuzi, Dumuzid   The shepherd god, a "god of fertility and new life," the shepherd aspect of the dead and rising deity. He represents the life-giving powers in the fresh milk of spring. When this season ends, he dies. Same as Tammuz. Sumerian. Near East. (Jacobsen, 1970: 41, 56, 327; James, 1960: 78; Kramer, 1950: 100)

Dumuzi(d)-abzu(k)   Sumerian goddess of fertility and of new life in the marshlands. Equated with Tammuz as a "god of fertilizing waters." Near East. (Jacobsen, 1970: 23; Mercer, 1925, 12: 710)

Dzidzielia   Slavic goddess of fertility and of marriage. (Czaplicka, 1925, 11: 594)

Eingana   A snake goddess, the earth mother and goddess of fertility. The Djauan, Northern Territories, Australia. (Robinson, 1966: 34–35)

Eja A phallic god and god of fertility associated with the goddess Ekumoke. He is protective of men and their property from lightning. The Ibo and the Ekoi, Nigeria. (Hartland, 1925, 9: 821; Talbot, 1967: 80)

Ekeko, Ekkekko "Probably an ancient fertility god" reduced to the status of a household god and a god of good luck. The Aymara, Peru. (Trimborn, 1968: 129, 140; Osborne, 1968: 88)

Eklinga A phallic god (identified with Isvara). With Gauri, the patrons in fertility ceremonies. India. (Crooke, 1925, 5: 5; Tod, 1920: 598)

Ekumoke A fertility goddess associated with Eja. Nigeria. (Talbot, 1967: 80)

Elo A god invoked for the fertility of cattle. He also sends the rains. The Nuba, Sudan. (Seligman, 1925, 9: 403)

Enda Semangko A goddess of fertility, also of health, and of "success in warfare." The Kyaka, Western Highlands, New Guinea. (Bulmer, 1965: 136, 150)

Enki Sumerian god of wisdom and of fresh waters, and as such a god of the fertility of the fields. Near East. (Kramer, 1961: 98; Jacobsen, 1946: 160)

Erin(is) pater A Roman god in close relationship to Vesuna; probably a god of fertility. (Roscher, 1965, 1, 1: 1310)

Eurynome Greek goddess of animal and vegetable fertility; mother of the Charities as a wife of Zeus. (Fairbanks, 1907: 93, 104; Kerenyi, 1951: 40)

Ezum Mezum Goddess of fertility. The female of the Ibudu (the male-female fertility symbol) at Amaii in Abaw District. Nigeria. (Talbot, 1967: 78)

Fa-ā "Amen in his character of the god of generation and reproduction." Egypt. (Budge, 1969, 2: 21)

Fascinus A Roman god of the phallus, guardian of the home and protective against evil and from illness (as a healing deity). (Jayne, 1962: 421)

Fauna, Fatua, Bona Dea Wife, daughter, or sister of Faunus. She personifies "the earth and its fertility." She was also prophetic. Roman. (Jayne, 1962: 421; Dumézil, 1966, 1: 350; Fairbanks, 1907: 248)

Faunus, Fatuus Roman god of fields and flocks and of their fertility. As Fatuus he was a god of prophecy. (Fair-

banks, 1907: 247–248; Dumézil, 1966, 1: 344–345; Bulfinch, 1898: 16)

Faustitas Roman goddess of the verdant fields, of their fruitfulness. (Roscher, 1965, 1, 2: 1461)

Fecunditas A goddess who was the personification of the fertility of the Roman empresses. An abstract concept of fertility and of impregnation. (Roscher, 1965, 1, 2: 1471; Jayne, 1962: 424)

Fiyn A deity invoked for fertility of women, herds, and crops, for prosperity and for protection from harm. The Bum, Nigeria. (Williams, 1936: 207)

St. Foutin "By tradition the first bishop of Lyons," who was worshipped by the Gauls as a phallic god "for the purpose of obtaining offspring or curing impotence and sexual disease." (Hartland, 1925, 9: 817)

Frey A solar god and god of sunshine and rain, of fruitfulness and fertility, of love and marriage, of peace and plenty. His wife is Gerda; his symbol the golden boar. The much-loved god of the Scandinavians. (Branston, 1955: 53, 132–133; Stern, 1898: 44; Wagner, 1882: 189, 199; Guerber, 1895: 112–113; Davidson, 1964: 29, 96; Turville-Petre, 1964: 166, 173–175)

Freya, Freyja Scandinavian goddess of fertility, of love. She is the sister of Frey with whom she rode, scattering abundance on mankind, and daughter of Njord. As the leader of the Valkyries she claimed one-half of the dead in battle. As the wife of Odr she was the mother of Hnoss and Gersemi. (Guerber, 1895: 124–128; MacCulloch, 1964: 120–123; Grimm, 1880: 299–366; Snorri Sturluson, 1964: 53; Turville-Petre, 1964: 159, 175–178)

Fricco Teutonic phallic god. (Schrader, 1925, 2: 51)

Frig In England Mother Earth, goddess of the fertility of the fields, wife of Woden. (Branston, 1957: 126–127)

Frigg(a) Incidentally she was a goddess of fertility. Primarily her function was that of goddess of marriage and of conjugal love, and goddess of the cultivated and fertile earth. As the second wife of Odin she was the mother of Balder, Hermod, and Tyr. In Germany she and Freya are identified, elsewhere in Scandinavia they are separate goddesses. (Grimm, 1880: 299–304; Anderson, 1891: 236–237; Thorpe, 1851: 167; Wagner, 1882: 209; Guerber, 1895: 43, 47, 108, 124)

Fro, Froho Teutonic form of Frey. God of fertility and generation, of summer sunshine and showers. (Grimm, 1883, 3: xix; 1880: 216; Guerber, 1895: 112)

Funado A phallic god associated with agriculture. Also a god of travel, of the roads, protective of men. Japan. (Kato, 1926: 31; Revon, 1925, 9: 237; Herbert, 1967: 495)

Gansam A Dravidian phallic god associated with Devi, to whom offerings are made jointly for the fertility of the earth mother. Northern India. (Crooke, 1925, 5: 5)

Gefjun, Gefion Scandinavian goddess of virgins and of agriculture. On the island of Seeland (Zealand) she is venerated as a goddess of fertility and for having ploughed the island out from Sweden. Denmark. (Thorpe, 1851: 34; Anderson, 1891: 240–241; Davidson, 1964: 45; Larousse, 1968: 274; Turville-Petre, 1964: 188)

Gouri, Isani A goddess of agricultural and human fertility, as well as of abundance. Hindu India. (Frazer, 1960: 398–399)

Guerlichon, Grelichon A phallic god worshipped at Bourges for children and to cure "impotence and sexual disease." Gaul. (Hartland, 1925, 9: 817)

Guignolet A phallic god worshipped at Brest for children, for "curing impotence and sexual disease." Gaul. (Hartland, 1925, 9: 817)

Gula Secondarily a goddess of fertility. She is a goddess of health, of healing, who would cause disease but also remove it; a goddess of the underworld and associated with immortality. Gula is also known as Ninkarrak, Da-mu-gal, and sometimes identified with Bau, and is the consort of Ninib. Akkadian/Assyrian/Babylonian. Near East. (Jastrow, 1898: 60, 166, 173–175; Jayne, 1962: 121; Campbell, 1964: 13, 14; Landgon, 1931: 182)

Gwenhwyfar Celtic goddess of fertility and of childbirth. The wife of Arthur. Wales. (Ross, 1967: 206; Larousse, 1968: 232)

Gwon, Bom God of fertility as well as of justice. The Angas, Nigeria. (Meek, 1925: 30; Williams, 1936: 215)

Hanuman Beneficent monkey god of virility and fertility invoked for offspring and to remove barrenness. He is also a god of great learning. India. (Crooke, 1894: 33, 52; Martin, 1914: 226; Ions, 1967: 102)

Hapi, Hap There are two gods of this name. This Hapi is God of the Nile and of fertility and nourishment. Egypt. (Budge, 1969, 2: 43; Knight, 1915: 36)

Harinaigameshin A deer-headed god of fertility of Jainism. India. (Kramer, 1961: 318)

Haumea A goddess of fertility and of childbirth, also of uncultivated foods. She is sometimes destructive. The mother of Pele. Hawaii. (Beckwith, 1940: 185, 283, 290; Poignant, 1967: 45)

Hawwah Semitic goddess of fertility. Near East. (Cohane, 1969: 99)

Hinglajin A goddess of the fertility of crops. The Pardhan, Mandla District, India. (Elwin, 1949: 442)

Huligamma A goddess for whom "men who are or believe themselves impotent will vow to dress as women and serve the goddess in the hope of recovering their virility." India. (Frazer, 1961: 271n)

Ibu Pertiwi Mother Earth. The name of Sri as a goddess of "the fertility of the soil." Bali, Indonesia. (Grader, 1960: 167; 1969: 160)

Icelaca A phallic deity to whom "the natives offered blood drawn from the organs of generation," and who was the deity before whom boys were circumcised. Cezori, Honduras. (Bancroft, 1886, 3: 506)

Ifa The god of fertility who helps women desiring children. Identified with Saint Anthony of Padua. Puerto Rico, West Indies. (Gonzalez-Wippler, 1975: 27–28)

Iho A deity who could overcome sterility in women. New Zealand. (Pettazzoni, 1956: 11)

Ikapati The goddess of fertility of fields and of herds was also a goddess of cultivated foods and of prosperity. The Tagalog, Philippines. (Jocano, 1969: 10)

Ilbaba One of the Assyro/Babylonian "war and storm-gods, temperamental bringers of fertility and victory." Near East. (Oppenheim, 1950: 70)

Imana The highest deity of the Batussi is also a god of fertility. Burundi. (Meyer, 1916: 87)

Indra As a weather god bringing rain and sunlight he is also a god of fertility. India. (Danielou, 1964: 106; Ions, 1967: 15–16; Crooke, 1894: 38, 288; Bhattacharji, 1970: 267–270)

Ishtar As a Semitic goddess she was "the fruitful goddess of the earth," of fertility and of love and childbirth. Babylonia, Near East. (Jayne, 1962: 122; Sayce, 1898: 259–266)

Isong Goddess of the earth who is "responsible for the fertility of the crops." The Ibibio, Nigeria. (Parrinder, 1949: 38; Frazer, 1926: 128)

Itzama The moon god and god of fertility. The Cuna, Panama. (Keeler, 1960: 200)

Iwanaga-hime An "ancient phallic goddess," daughter of Oyama-tsumi and sister of Konohana-no-Sakuyabime. Japan. (Yasumaro, 1965: 64; Holtom, 1938: 209)

Juno Caprotina Roman goddess of fertility. (Murray, 1935: 51)

Juno Coelestis Goddess of fecundity, of debauchery, and of sacred prostitution. The Berber, North Africa, adopted from the Roman. (Bel, 1938: 78)

Kagoro A god of cattle and of their fertility. The Banyoro, Uganda. (Roscoe, 1915: 92; Mbiti, 1970, 2: 117)

Kaldyni-mumas A Finno-Ugric goddess of fertility invoked for children and for marriage. The Votyak, Russia and Siberia. (MacCulloch, 1964: 258)

Kan Pauah Tun A Mayan god "identified with the gods of rain, hence of fertility." Central America. (Tozzer, 1941: 137)

Karaeng lowe A phallic god and a god of the sea—a powerful god who controls life and death, good or bad fortune, health and prosperity. Southern Celebes, Indonesia. (Kruijt, 1925, 7: 250; Hartland, 1925, 9: 818)

Kanisini Laksmi as "the cow-dung goddess" among the rice-growing people—giving fertility to the soil and good crops. India. (Bhattacharji, 1970: 161)

ka tu' Goddess of the moon, of agricultural fertility, and of childbirth. The Chorti, Guatemala. (Wisdom, 1940: 400)

Kem A phallic deity of West Africa. (Zabarowski, 1894: 328)

Khazang The supreme being and creator who is invoked for the fertility of man and animals, for protection from illness and death, and for prosperity. The Lakher, Assam. (Wallis, 1939: 145; Pettazzoni, 1956: 293, 296)

Khensu Nefer-hetep A form of Khensu as a lunar god who "ruled the month," promoted the fertility of animals and the growth of vegetation. Egypt. (Budge, 1969, 2: 37)

Khensu-pa-khart A form of Khensu as a god of conception and fertility in women and cattle. Egypt. (Budge, 1969, 2: 35)

Kine-Nane A chthonic earth goddess associated with fertility and productivity, with abundance. The Adi, Northeastern India. (Chowdhury, 1971: 113–114)

Kokopelli Frequently a phallic figure, suggesting a god of fertility. The Pueblo Indians, Arizona and New Mexico. (Hawley, 1937: 644–645; Titiev, 1939: 91, 98)

Kolowisi, Koloowisi The horned water serpent, god of fertility invoked in rites for the longevity of one's children. He punishes promiscuity, is sometimes purely a phallic symbol. He is also a god of lightning and controls floods, earthquakes and landslides. The Zuñi, New Mexico. (Tyler, 1964: 245–247; Alexander, 1964: 188; Parsons, 1939: 184–185)

Konsei-Daimyojin, Konsei Myojin A Shinto phallic god associated with agriculture and with Dionysian festivals. Japan. (Kato, 1926: 31; Revon, 1925, 9: 239)

Kuai A culture hero and fertility god of the Kabeua (Arawak). Brazil. (Alexander, 1920: 294)

Kunado A phallic god—"originally a symbol of the procreative power, the phallus came to represent lusty animal vigour generally, the foe to death and disease. Hence its use as a magical appliance to repel pestilence." He was also a god of roads, and a god of divination. Japan. (Aston, 1925, 11: 467; Herbert, 1967: 495; MacCulloch, 1925, 4: 334)

Kunapipi Goddess of fertility, mother of the Waugeluk sisters. The Leagulawulmirree, Australia. (Robinson, 1966: 37)

Kunmanngur The rainbow snake, a creator, and a god of fertility. One of those who send "spirit children." The Murinbata, Northern Territories, Australia. (Robinson, 1966: 50, 67; Poignant, 1967: 126; Eliade, 1973: 39)

Kuwai A god of fertility and of vegetation; also a culture hero and creator. The Cubeo and the Tucano. Brazil and Colombia. (Zerries, 1968: 255; Goldman, 1948, 3: 794; Levi-Strauss, 1973: 223)

Kwigbe A deity of fertility in women. The Kono, Sierra Leone. (Parsons, 1950: 270)

Lahmu In Canaan a god of fertility. He is among the primordial beings in Babylonian myth, twin of Lahamu, the first pair born to Apsu and Tiamat. Near East. (Paton, 1925, 3: 184; Long, 1963: 81)

Lake Ivong A sea god invoked at the Bunut festival seemingly for the fertility of women and of the soil. The Sea Dyaks, Borneo. (Roth, 1891: 126)

al-Lat An Arabian goddess of fertility identified with Venus, the Morning Star. (Fahd, 1968: 111, 118–119)

Latsapa A beneficent deity of fertility. The Sema Nagas, India. (Hutton, 1968: 196)

Legba A phallic god, as mortal sexuality, and also as the cosmic creative force. He is the messenger and intermediary between man and the gods, has knowledge of all languages, and is closely associated with *Fa* (Destiny) as the youngest and trickster son of Mawu, whom she sent to help man manipulate his fate through accident. Dahomey. (Deren, 1953: 96–97; Williams, 1936: 165; Ellis, 1890: 41–45; Parrinder, 1967: 21, 91; Herskovits, 1938, 2: 109, 201, 205; 1937: 30–31)

Leto Phytia The "goddess of growing things"— changed a little girl (Leucippos) into a boy, providing her with the male sex organ at the request of the mother, Galatea, as her husband would not accept a girl child. Crete, Greece. (Delcourt, 1961: 4, 5)

Liber A Roman god of fertility in all aspects, god of the male generative process, in some cults assuming a phallic nature. As an agricultural deity he presides over the fertility of the fields and is associated with the life and death of vegetation. (Dumézil, 1966, 1: 378; Altheim, 1937: 125–126; Jayne, 1962: 431; Larousse, 1968: 209)

Libera Roman goddess of the female generative process, of fertility in all its aspects, invoked where men feared impotency. With her husband Liber she presides "over the family and granting the blessing of children." (Dumézil, 1966, 1: 378; Jayne, 1962: 431, 443; Fairbanks, 1907: 191)

Lono A god of weather, of agriculture and of fertility. With Kane and Kanaloa, creators of heaven and earth, forming a triune composite god known as Akua-kahikolu. His sister/wife is Laka. Hawaii. (Beckwith, 1940: 31–33; 1932: 174; Mackenzie, n.d.: 320–322; Poignant, 1967: 38)

Loowe An earth god associated with caves, a god of fertility invoked for rain and good crops. The Tswana, South Africa. (Schapera, 1937: 269–270; Willoughby, 1932: 74–76)

Ma Goddess of fertility in nature—Lady of the Beasts. Asia Minor. Introduced to Rome as a goddess of fruitfulness. (Fairbanks, 1907: 133; Neumann, 1955: 275; Larousse, 1968: 220; Dumézil, 1966, 2: 489)

Maan-Eno Estonian goddess of fecundity and of harvest. Wife of Ukko. (Larousse, 1968: 307)

The Macha A trio of Celtic goddesses—of fertility in nature as well as goddesses of war. Their animal motif is the crow. Ireland. (Ross, 1967: 206, 219; MacCana, 1970: 91)

Mahui God of fertility and of abundance, believed to be present from October to May. The Marquesas, Polynesia. (Rivers, 1915: 433)

Maia Roman goddess of agricultural fertility for whom the month of May was named. A "goddess of growth and the spring season." (Dumézil, 1966, 1: 240; Madden, 1930: 78; Leach, 1950, 2: 666)

Malakbel At Palmyra a solar god and god of fertility. Syria. (Vriezen, 1963: 67; Cook, 1930: 219–220; Langdon, 1931: 37)

Mamma A Semitic goddess of fertility and of childbirth. Given as the wife of Erra as well as of Nergal. Near East. (Roberts, 1972: 24, 44)

Manawyddan ab Llyr A Celtic god of fertility (probably agricultural) and of craftsmanship. Son of Llyr. Wales. (Larousse, 1968: 231; MacCulloch, 1911: 101)

Marnas An important god of Gaza—of fertility and of growth. Near East. (Cook, 1930: 181, 185)

Mas, Mar, Maso An Etruscan god of virility, of marriage, as well as of the fertility of nature—crops and harvest. Italy. (Leland, 1963: 49–51)

Masewi Among the Keres he and Oyoyewi are gods of fertility, providing rain. The Pueblo Indians, Arizona and New Mexico. (Parsons, 1939: 247)

Matlalcueitl The Tlaxcalan mountain, goddess of waters and of fertility. Second wife of Tlaloc. Mexico. (Reed, 1966: 131; Caso, 1958: 42)

Maweno A "goddess of fruitfulness." The Angami Nagas, India. (Hutton, 1921: 182)

Mayahuel, Mayauel Primarily goddess of the maguey plant from which pulque is made, an intoxicating drink. She is also a goddess of fertility. Aztec, Mexico. (Vaillant, 1962: 149; Spence, 1923: 297; Duran, 1971: 176n; Nicholson, 1967: 69)

The Mayel Seven mythical brothers who provide agricultural fertility and are invoked at the time of sowing and of harvesting. Each is the patron of some special grain. Some of their names are Mayel Yook, Mi-tik, Tom-tik, Adoo Yook, Alau Yook. The Lepchas, Sikkim. (Siiger, 1967, 1: 90; 1967, 2: 143; Gorer, 1938: 236–238)

Dewi Melanting A goddess of fertility, "of seeds, gardens, and markets." She is the daughter of Wisnu and Dewi Sri, and like Persephone lives 50 percent of the time below ground and 50 percent above. Bali, Indonesia. (Covarrubias, 1937: 46, 71, 317)

Meme A Semitic goddess of fertility and of healing as identified with Ninkarrak and Gula. Near East. (Roberts, 1972: 45)

Mendes The goat god of ancient Egypt who was first "worshipped merely as a personification of the procreative energy." (Eastlake, 1883: 261–262; Prentice Hall, 1965: 88)

Min Egyptian god of virility and of fertility, both animal and vegetable. He was also a god of roads and of travelers in the desert. (Ames, 1965: 108–109; Anthes, 1961: 32; Budge, 1969, 1: 507; Cook, 1930: 106n; James, 1960: 71–72)

Mkissi nssi, or **Bunssi** A god of fertility of the earth and of the distribution of the rain. The Bafioti, Loanga and Gabon. (Frazer, 1926: 418)

Mohan Sylgylax A deity appealed to "to cure barrenness." The Yakut, Siberia. (Jochelson, 1933: 107)

Mokoši "The only goddess of the Kievan official pantheon, Mokoši, literally moist. . . . The Iranian Ardvi (moist) Sura Anahita is particularly close to Mokoši: both of them protect semen, child-bearing, and sheep-breeding." Russia. (Leach, 1950, 2: 1027)

Morė, Kotrė The personification of agricultural fertility. Lithuania. (Leach, 1950, 2: 632)

Mui'ingwa, Muingwu, Muiyinwu A chthonic god of fertility, of germination, of vegetation who gave mankind the seeds for his crops. The Hopi, Arizona. (Parsons, 1939: 178; Tyler, 1964: 19, 20, 82, 126; Fewkes, 1900: 125)

Mukta Devi A wife of Dharma Thakur invoked for fertility. Bengal. (Maity, 1971: 92–93)

Mush A Sumerian/Akkadian serpent god who is associated with "the generative powers of the earth and the heat of the sun." Near East. (Langdon, 1931: 90)

Muyinwu(h) God of the earth, of fertility, of germination, of growth. Hopi. Among the Tusayan Hopi a goddess, and also a deity of the underworld. Arizona. (Fewkes, 1920: 592; 1901: 215; 1893/94: 259)

Mylitta Assyro/Babylonian "goddess of fertility and procreation." Near East. (Prentice Hall, 1965: 93; Leach, 1950, 2: 776)

Nerthus Teutonic earth mother who is the symbol of fruitfulness, a goddess of peace and tranquillity. In Germany she is identified with Frigga, but in Scandinavia she is a separate goddess and the sister/wife of Niord before he was transferred as hostage to Asgard. (Grimm, 1880: 251–252; Guerber, 1895: 108; MacCulloch, 1964: 102–103; Stern, 1898: 61)

Ningo Baghiya A guardian of crops—"the phallic tiger, to whom, when the grain is ripe, the first five handfuls . . . are offered." The Majhwars, Mirzapur, India. (Crooke, 1925, 5: 5)

Ninni An early goddess of fertility and generation who was merged with Innanna. She was also identified with Ishtar as a goddess of war. Babylonia, Near East. (Jastrow, 1898: 80; Mercer, 1925, 12: 700)

Njord, Niord The god of the sea and of seafarers, of riches, is also a god of fertility and of seasonal growth. Scandinavia. (Turville-Petre, 1964: 162–165; Branston, 1955: 131–132)

Nü Kua As a goddess of rain and associated with water she is also considered a goddess of fertility. China. (Schafer, 1980: 37)

Nyakala A goddess of fertility and childbirth, a powerful goddess whose house was a haven for those pursued during war. The Amba, Uganda and Zaire. (Middleton, 1967: 39; Taylor, 1962: 86)

O-ichi-hime A goddess of human and of agricultural fertility. The "phallic counterpart of Saruta-hiko." Japan. (Czaja, 1974: 259–261)

Okuke A god of fertility, of childbirth, and health. The Northern Ibo, Nigeria. (Horton, 1956: 20)

Olokukurtilisop Earth mother and goddess of fertility whose consort and son is Olowaipippilele, the sun god. She influences the lives of men both on earth and in the afterlife. She is also called Achamommor and Nan Tummat. The Cuna, Panama. (Keeler, 1960: 11, 46, 114, 197)

Ops Sabine/Roman goddess of agricultural fertility and abundance; also honored in human childbirth and growth. She is associated with Consus and also with Faunus. Italy. (Jayne, 1962: 454–455; Dumézil, 1966, 1: 49, 156; Fairbanks, 1907: 250; Larousse, 1968: 208)

Osiris In his earliest form, a primitive god of fertility and of vegetation, the life and death cycle of agriculture. He is also represented as an early tree god with the same relation to resurrection. Egypt. (Frazer, 1960: 420, 442; Casson, 1965: 72, 184; Roheim, 1929: 191; Budge, 1969, 2: 139; Ames, 1965: 54–56)

Oyoyewi With his brother Masewi a god of fertility, providing rain. Son of Iyatiku. The Keresan, Pueblo Indians, New Mexico. (Parsons, 1939: 243, 247)

Page abe The omnipotent Sun Father whose creating, fertilizing element is considered solar semen, bestowing fertility on all things. The "Creator of the Universe." The Desana, Colombia. (Reichel-Dolmatoff, 1971: 41–42, 48)

Palulukoñ, Palulukang The plumed water serpent—a god of fertility and of lightning, of rain. His Zuñi counterpart is Kolowisi. The Hopi, Arizona. (Alexander, 1964: 188; Tyler, 1964: 245)

Pamuri-mahse The "personification of a phallus that ejaculates, a new creator, sent by the Sun to populate the earth." His vehicle, the snake-canoe, is feminine in character. He brought the men created by Page abe from Ahpikondia (Paradise) to the earth level and gave the different tribes their identifying objects. The Desana, Colombia. (Reichel-Dolmatoff, 1971: 25–27, 55)

Pattini A goddess who presides over fertility. Ceylon. (Leach, 1968: 35)

Pdry A goddess of fertility and of mist. Canaan, Near East. (Gray, 1957: 42, 140)

Pe Goddess of the moon and of fecundity. The Pygmies, Zaire and Gabon. (Eliade, 1959: 149)

Peko The god of fertility invoked in the fall for the protection of the domesticated animals and the crops; in the spring for the fertility of the fields and the crops. Estonia. (Leach, 1950, 2: 850)

Ih P'en Chorti god of the soil, of fertility and growth, as well as of "family life, property, and other wealth." Guatemala. (Thompson, 1970: 294)

Penaban Sari A pair—male and female—of benevolent chthonic deities of fertility to whom offerings of crops are made. Bali, Indonesia. (Grader, 1969, 1: 140, 158–160)

Pergubrius A Baltic god of agriculture and fertility as well as of healing. Lithuania and Latvia. (Puhvel, 1974: 83; Welsford, 1925, 9: 242)

Piluitus, Pilwittus, Piluuytis A Baltic god or goddess of fertility, of agriculture and harvests as well as of healing. Lithuania, Latvia, and Prussia. (Welsford, 1925, 9: 242, 488; Puhvel, 1974: 83)

Poere A god (a stone) who was a god of the fertility of food products; also a god of artisans. Rapa Island, Polynesia. (Buck, 1938: 173)

Popali A phallic fertility spirit who was also a forest spirit. The Cubeo, Colombia. (Zerries, 1968: 280)

Poseidon Prior to being god of the sea and of storms, he was a god of fertility, of horses and horsemanship. Greece. (Fairbanks, 1907: 55, 153; Larousse, 1968: 133)

Potrimpus, Potrympus A Slavic/Baltic god of rivers and springs, of vegetation and fertility, of healing and good fortune. (Puhvel, 1974: 83; Machal, 1918: Plate XXXVII)

Priapos, Priapus A phallic god, of the fertility of vegetation and of animals, of the principle of abundance and prosperity. He was the son of Aphrodite with paternity variously attributed to Dionysus, Hermes, Adonis, Zeus. He was "simply a personification of the phallus." From deformed, grotesque masculinity he was beautified and feminized and became "identical with Hermaphrodite." Yet he maintained more individuality. As a country deity, representing the phallus, he was venerated and represented in "farmsteads by a great yew," with the capacity to ward off evil, to indicate possessiveness and to bestow fecundity. Near East, Greece, and Rome. (Kerenyi, 1951: 176; Larousse, 1968: 161; Murray, 1935: 148–149; Morford and Lenardon, 1975: 99; Delcourt, 1961: 50–52)

Prithivi Goddess of earth and of fertility, mother of all things in all forms. India. (Ions, 1967: 15, 96; Danielou, 1964: 87)

Pulleyar A phallic god of sexuality and fertility—of humans, cattle, crops. The equivalent of Ganesha, Pillaiyar (Tamil). Ceylon. (Leach, 1958: 303, 309–311)

Rangda A chthonic goddess of fertility, of sexuality and lust, associated with black magic in charms and potions. She is also a "goddess of the temple of the dead." Bali, Indonesia. (Grader, 1969, 1: 155–156)

Rani Kajhal With Bara Kumba, a pair worshipped for the fertility of the earth mother—sacrificed to before the harvest, and invoked at marriage rites. Tree deities. The Pavras, India. (Crooke, 1925, 5: 5)

Rara-taunga-rere A child of Tane who "represents the fruitfulness of trees." The Maori, New Zealand. (Best, 1924: 176)

Rongo God of agricultural fertility, germination, and reproduction as well as a god of peace and of plenty. The Maori, New Zealand. (Best, 1924: 105, 236; Howells, 1948: 222)

Sabazios Phrygian/Thracian god of the fertility of nature, of vegetation, equated with or identified with Dionysos. Greece and Asia Minor. (Ananikian, 1964: 12–13; Jayne, 1962: 346)

Sae-no-Kami A phallic god associated with agriculture. He is also a god of roads. Japan. (Kato, 1926: 31; Holtom, 1938: 208)

Sagade Ugugun The third spirit of Delquen Sagan Burkan, invoked "for rain, good crops and children" and as such could be considered a god of fertility. His wife is Sanqalin Qaten. The Mongol, Buriat, Siberia. (Curtin, 1909: 118)

Sahi-no-kami Phallic deities worshipped at crossroads and friendly toward travelers. Japan. (MacCulloch, 1925, 4: 332)

Saljong A god of fertility, who is responsible for the crops and the harvests, is represented by the sun. The Garos, Assam. (Barkataki, 1969: 27; Playfair, 1909: 81)

Sanda A Hittite god of fertility. Near East. (Ananikian, 1964: 379n)

Sandan, Sandes, Sanda A Cappadocian and Cilician god of fertility who at Tarsus is the son of Baal and forms a triad with him and Atheh. Asia Minor. (Frazer, 1961: 161–171)

The Sansin Mountain gods who were also fertility gods. Korea. (Clark, 1932: 200)

Saranyū A pre-Vedic goddess who was the wife of Vivasvant. In one version of myth "she is a figure of fertility, the goddess who unites with the king in order to produce immortal progeny." India. (O'Flaherty, 1980: 184)

Saruta-hiko A phallic god associated with agriculture and also with the crossroads, considered a god of good luck. Japan. (Kato, 1926: 31; Holtom, 1938: 183; MacCulloch, 1925, 4: 332; Herbert, 1967: 356, 359)

Satet, Sati A goddess of fertility and of the inundation. The female counterpart of Khnemu with whom (and her sister Anqet) she forms a triad. Egypt. (Cook, 1930: 145; Budge, 1969, 2: 49, 55; Knight, 1915: 108)

Seri The goddess of fertility of the Kelantan. Malaya. (Hill, 1951: 64)

Shapash, Špš The sun goddess is also a goddess of fertility, "a great blessing for crops" when associated with Baal. But when "in the power of Mot . . . Špš can destroy the fields, burning the crops." Canaan, Near East. (Oldenburg, 1969: 20, 94; Albright, 1956: 83)

Shimunenga A god who is considered the "giver of virility to males" and is invoked for protection from lions and pestilence. The ba-Mala, Rhodesia. (Smith, 1920: 180, 189)

Shushtee Hindu goddess of fecundity. India. (Coleman, 1832: 396)

Šicun The Potency, a class-4 deity of the Oglala, Plains Indians, South Dakota. (Powers, 1977: 54)

Sif The golden-haired wife of Thor is considered a goddess of fertility as well as of love and loveliness. Scandinavia. (Branston, 1955: 122; Davidson, 1891: 84; Grimm, 1880: 309)

Sinavali Vedic goddess of fecundity and easy birth, daughter of Angiras. She represents "the first day of the new moon, giver of fecundity." India. (Danielou, 1964: 319; Elwin, 1950: 157)

Siva INDIA—The phallic god, god of fertility, representing the creative energies of all of nature as well as its destructive and cruel forces, expressed in birth, death, and rebirth. (Schoeps, 1961: 162; Martin, 1914: 168; Danielou, 1964: 192: Banerjea, 1953: 161–162)
BALI—The supreme god and god of light whose symbol is the linga. He is "the source of all life, the synthesis of the creative and generative powers in nature." (Goris, 1960, 2: 123; Friederich, 1959: 43; Covarrubias, 1937: 290; Grader, 1969, 2: 92)
CAMBODIA—Here Siva never has destructive connotations, and here the linga symbol represents "the creative energy of the powers of nature; the sexual idea that may be attributed to it is incorrect if we halt on this particular concept alone; in Oriental symbolism it is one of the expressions of the intense life that ends in absorption into the godhead." (Marchal, 1963: 210–211)

So, Xevioso A god of several aspects among which is that of providing for fertility in humans. He is considered an androgynous deity in having given birth to the gods of the Xevioso pantheon. He is primarily known as the thunder god. The Ewe, Dahomey. (Herskovits, 1938, 2: 129, 150–151; Parrinder, 1961: 32)

Song tseu niang niang, Tseu souen nai nai A goddess who gives children. China. (Chavannes, n.d.: 32)

Dewi Sri The goddess of rice is also the goddess of fertility and abundance, of beauty. Bali, Indonesia. (Covarrubias, 1937: 317; Friederich, 1959: 47; Hooykaas, 1964: 22)

Sung Tzi Liang Liang A goddess who gives male children. Anking, China. (Shryock, 1931: 82)

Sura A benevolent god to whom the seeds (in baskets) of men and animals were entrusted. Panama. (Alexander, 1920: 193)

Tamfana A Germanic deity—"apparently a goddess of fertility, of harvest." The Marsi. (MacCulloch, 1964: 17, 195; Pettazzoni, 1956: 245)

Tammuz Primarily a god of death and resurrection, of agricultural death and rebirth, but also a god of fertility, and represented by a tree. Sumerian/Babylonian/Syrian. Near East. (Vriezen, 1963: 39, 40; Hooke, 1963: 41; Wales, 1957: 31; Frazer, 1960: 379)

Tanit Pene Baal The moon goddess and goddess of fecundity who is considered bisexual in having given "birth to the universe without the help of a male partner." The Berbers, Carthage. (Bel, 1938: 75, 78; Meyerowitz, 1958: 130–131)

Ta-no-Kami With Yama-no-Kami—phallic deities, who are protective and productive of agriculture and take serpent form. Yama-no-Kami descends from the mountains and becomes Ta-no-Kami in the spring. He, in turn, returns to the mountains in the fall as Yama-no-Kami. Japan. (Czaja, 1974: 50, 167)

Tarku A god of Amurru, of the fertility of vegetation, and of the harvest. Near East. (Younger, 1966: 120)

Tatqeq Goddess of the moon and the giver of fertility in women. The Netsilik Eskimo, Canada. (Balikci, 1970: 207)

Taubewa Chief of the underworld people. He and his wife, Sinekili, own all the food. He seems to be an aspect of Yaboaine as a phallic god—his "semen is the yam."

Normanby Island, Papua, New Guinea. (Roheim, 1946: 331)

Tekha Shara Matzkala God of fecundity as well as of the dance and of wealth. He is visited by the shamans on their ecstatic journeys. The Buryat and the Teleut, Siberia. (Eliade, 1964: 75)

Tellumo, Telluno An earth god and god of fecundity, the personification of the earth as the producer of seeds. He is associated with Tellus, but not forming a pair. Rome. (Frazer, 1926: 329; Dumézil, 1966, 1: 374; Larousse, 1968: 210)

Tellus Goddess of the earth and of its fertility to whom pregnant cows and sows were sacrificed to ensure fertility and abundance, many to her and Ceres jointly. Rome. (Dumézil, 1966, 1: 194, 240; Frazer, 1926: 328–334; Larousse, 1968: 205; Fairbanks, 1907: 175)

Tengri The great heaven god. As Blue Tengri he "gives to the earth fruitfulness and productivity." The Mongols and the Kalmucks, Siberia. (MacCulloch, 1964: 391–392; Phillips, 1969: 34)

Ters A phallic god "whose figure appeared over the gateway to the church of St. Walburga, in the Rue des Pecheurs at Antwerp." Belgium. (Hartland, 1925, 9: 817)

Thor Scandinavian god of thunder and, as the bringer of rain, a god of agriculture and the fertility of the earth. His wife is the earth goddess Sif. (Davidson, 1964: 84; Branston, 1955: 121; Stern, 1898: 29, 31)

Thoueris Egyptian hippopotamus goddess, of fertility and childbirth. (Casson, 1965: 75)

T'ien Kung Ti Mu The "god and goddess of fertility of the fields." China. (Day, 1940: 106)

Tintibane A cave god and a god "of fertility and of vigor," invoked for rain and the fertility of the crops, and also for strength and success in war. The Tswana and the Bantu, South Africa. (Willoughby, 1932: 39, 74, 76; Schapera, 1937: 269–270)

Tishtrya A stellar deity, Sirius, the Dog Star, who controls the rain, and as such brings fertility to the earth as well as to men and animals. Iran. (Ananikian, 1925, 1: 798; Gray, 1930: 116, 223; Huart, 1963: 42; Jackson, 1925, 12: 86)

Turan Etruscan goddess of fertility identified with Aphrodite. Italy. (Dumézil, 1966, 2: 447; von Vacano, 1960: 11; Roscher, 1965, 5: 1284)

Tutunus, or **Muntunus**   An early Greek name for the phallic god Priapos. (Bhattacharji, 1970: 180)

Tuwabontumsi, Tiwakpomatamsi   A goddess, Sand Altar Woman, created by Huruing Wuhti. She is the female counterpart of Muingwu; a goddess of "human fecundity," and is also called Childbirth Water Woman. The Hopi, Arizona. (Tyler, 1964: 82)

Umaj, Umai   Goddess of fertility and of children, also of childbirth. The Altai Turks, and the Shors, Siberia. (Dioszegi, 1968: 463; Potapov, 1964: 444; Czaplicka, 1925, 12: 482; Queval, 1968: 116)

U-mo   A god of fertility (human) of the Ch'iang at Lo-pu-chai. Szechwan, China. (Graham, 1958: 49)

Upulero   The supreme god, the sun, and the male principle who impregnates mother earth. A phallic god invoked to increase the fertility and abundance of humans and animals, of harvests, and of fishing. Moluccas Islands and Babar Archipelago, Indonesia. (Hartland, 1925, 9: 822; Kern, 1925, 8: 347; Maity, 1971: 92)

Ushumgalanna   An ancient serpent god of the "dying god" group and a god of the fertility of the earth. Asia Minor. (Langdon, 1931: 178–179)

Usi-Afu   Goddess of the earth, its personification, and wife of Usi-Neno; a goddess promoting fertility and growth. Timor, Indonesia. (Frazer, 1926: 657; Eliade, 1959: 124)

Usi-Neno   God of the sun, its personification, and the male principle, who with his wife Usi-Afu are the source of "fertility and growth." Timor, Indonesia. (Frazer, 1926: 657; Eliade, 1959: 124)

Vadhi Devata   The "god of increase" to whom offerings are made at marriages. The Banjara, Kathiawar, India. (Crooke, 1925, 2: 347)

Vai-mahse   Two beings created by the sun, one for animals and one for fish. As master of animals, the owner of the animals and the herbs of the forest is "a phallic being in charge of the fertility of the game animals." Some of the shamans obtain their powers from him rather than from Viho-mahse. He is aggressive sexually and dangerous to women. The Desana (Tukano), Colombia. (Reichel-Dolmatoff, 1971: 28, 51, 80–85; 1975: 83)

Varalden-olmai, Veralden-olmai   The supreme being and god of the fertility of all things. The Lapps, Northern Europe. (Bosi, 1960: 105, 132; Karsten, 1955: 47–48; Dioszegi, 1968: 28; MacCulloch, 1964: 250)

Ved-ava, Vedmastor-ava, Ved-azerava   "Water mother" (seem to be many individual deities) goddess of agricultural and animal and human fecundity. The Mordvins, Moksha River, Russia. (Paasonen, 1925, 8: 845)

Wamara   A god of fertility and of abundance. On the birth of twins the elder is dedicated to him. The Banyankole and the Nyankore. Uganda. Roscoe, 1923: 23–24; Taylor, 1962: 111)

Wandatilepu   An agricultural fertility god. The Huli, Southern Highlands, New Guinea. (Glasse, 1965: 43)

Warunsasadun   A goddess, consort of Kinorohingan, who "killed her own child and buried it in the earth, thus making the soil fertile and productive." The Dusun, Borneo. (Raats, 1969: 21)

The Wawalag, Wauwalak   Sisters, goddesses of a fertility cult. They were guilty of primordial sin—of incestuous copulation, so instituting sexual relationships. To repent, they taught mankind the ritual ceremonies through which he is purified. Australia. (Eliade, 1973: 111; Poignant, 1967: 133)

Wisnu   God of the rains, of waters and bestower of fertility and prosperity. He is the guardian god of the north. His wife is Dewi Sri, daughter Dewi Melanting. He commonly forms a trinity with Brahma and Iswara. Bali, Indonesia. (Covarrubias, 1937: 290, 317; Grader, 1969, 1: 158, 219n)

Xopancalehuey Tlalloc   The "presiding god of spring," considered a phallic god. Mexico. (Bancroft, 1886, 2: 505)

Yachimata-hiko   A phallic god associated with agriculture and with Dionysian festivals. He is also a god of the crossroads, of travel—protective and friendly to travelers. Japan. (MacCulloch, 1925, 4: 332; Kato, 1926: 31; Revon, 1925, 9: 237)

Yachimata-hime   A phallic goddess associated with agriculture and with Dionysian festivals. Also a protective goddess of travel, of the crossroads. Japan. (MacCulloch, 1925, 4: 332; Kato, 1926: 31; Revon, 1925, 9: 237)

Yama-no-Kami   The god of the mountains, as a phallic deity, descends in the spring to the plains becoming Ta-no-Kami. Japan. (Czaja, 1974: 50, 167)

Yao Chi   A goddess of rain and fertility. . . . The rainbow was, therefore, both her symbol and her quintessential spirit." China. (Schafer, 1980: 44)

Yarilo   Slavonic god "of springtime and fecundity . . . of carnal love." (Larousse, 1968: 294–295)

Yeman'gnyem   Beneficent god of the fertility of the river, of fish, from the mouth of the Ob River. Also a god of travelers and common to all Ostyaks. He is also called Yega-tei-igenen. Siberia. (Czaplicka, 1925, 9: 577)

Yen sedo   A phallic god with serpent qualities, associated with water and with clouds, silent and rhythmic. He represents the primordial waters. The Tewa, New Mexico. (Laski, 1958: 11, 72)

Zamna, Itzamna   A god of fertility and of rain as well as the god of civilization and the culture of the Yucatec. The Mayan, Mexico. (Alexander, 1920: 131, 134; Bancroft, 1886, 3: 462–463; Brinton, 1868: 160)

Zelus   A god of agricultural fertility. Lithuania. (Gray, 1930: 140)

Zeus   As the god who controls the rains, he is also the source of agricultural fertility. Greece. (Eliade, 1958: 78, 79)

22

Disease Gods:
Accident

Aan Arbatyy Toyon, Arkhakh Toyon A deity of the Yakuts who caused consumption. Siberia. (Tokarev and Gurvich, 1964: 279)

Abalouaie, or **Obalouaye** Yoruba god of smallpox in Brazil. (Bastide, 1960: 559)

The Abat "Spirits who cause sore feet and headache." The Tinguian, Philippines. (Cole, 1922: 299)

Abong A malignant spirit who afflicts with ague and fever. The Milanow (Malanau), Land Dyaks, Borneo. (Roth, 1968: 166; De Crespigny, 1875: 35)

Achupinakolet A demon who causes hiccups. The Cuna, Panama. (Nordenskiold, 1938: 404)

Áchuprúakáletkíniti A wind demon who causes illness. The Cuna, Panama. (Nordenskiold, 1930: 60–61)

Adan Tagni A god who causes leprosy; son of Da Zodji. Dahomey. (Verger, 1957: 239)

Adasha A minor tutelary god who is feared as the cause of leprosy and fires. He receives gifts and libations and participates in the rites opening the salt season. The Jukun, Nigeria. Meek, 1931: 275)

Ademat An evil anito who "gives a fatal illness." The Apayao, Philippines. (Wilson, 1947: 23)

Ag-aganney A mischievous female spirit who sits by the road and strikes people on the legs causing tumors. The Kankanay, Luzon, Philippines. (Vanoverbergh, 1972: 86)

Agbadu A deity who causes rheumatism and arthritis. The Jukun, Nigeria. (Greenberg, 1946: 61)

Agbogbodji A god who causes elephantiasis and who drowns those who have done wrong. Dahomey. (Herskovits, 1938, 2: 140)

Aglossunto, Aglosunto, Aglosuto A god who causes incurable sores or wounds. He is also a god of magic and charms which he bestows on men through the priests. Son of Kohosu and Nyohwe Ananu and twin of Gbossou Zouhon. Dahomey. (Herskovits, 1938, 2: 140, 259; Verger, 1954: 184; 1957: 239)

Agwani A fire goddess who causes fever. Sister of Sitala. India. (Crooke, 1894: 80; Briggs, 1920: 138)

Agyo Khambe A god of fever invoked for its relief. The Bhils, India. (Naik, 1956: 187)

Ahal Canya A god of disease. The Cakchiquel, Guatemala. (Recinos, 1950: 111)

Ahalgana A god of the underworld who causes dropsy. The Quiché, Guatemala. (Recinos, 1950: 110)

Ahalpuh A god of the underworld who causes disease—"to make men swell and make pus gush forth from their legs." The Quiché, Guatemala. (Recinos, 1950: 110)

Ahosu Ganwha A god who causes swelling which causes death. Son of Kohosu and Nyohwe Ananu. Dahomey. (Verger, 1957: 239)

Ajo-ase A god of cholera whose offering is "two fowls and many eggs." The Mikirs, India. (Stack and Lyall, 1908: 32)

Akasi A god of sickness and of health. The Zambal, Philippines. (Jocano, 1969: 14)

Akatokae   A minor god of evil who causes illness. Mangareva, Polynesia. (Buck, 1938: 425)

Akhkhazzu   The demon of jaundice. The Gypsies, Babylon, Near East. (Clebert, 1967: 195)

Akhye Zoshan   The god of smallpox whose wife is Khania Shkwakwa. The Abkhasians, Caucasus. (Janashia, 1937: 153)

Akknivayravan   A male evil spirit who inflicts illness and pain as well as misfortune. The Pulaya (Cochin), India. (Thaliath, 1956: 1034)

Akosa Sapata, Akossi   An earth deity who inflicts skin diseases as punishment or relieves from them as reward. Belem, Maranhão, Brazil. (Costa Eduardo, 1948: 78; Leacock, 1972: 161)

Aku-Maga   A god who may cause illness; sacrifices must be made to him if he allows recovery. He is primarily the god of the buttock dance and a god of sexuality. The Jukun, Nigeria. (Meek, 1931: 255, 273–274; Greenberg, 1946: 58)

Akura   A deity who causes abdominal trouble. The Jukun, Nigeria. (Greenberg, 1946: 61)

Alalayo   A deity who inflicts with illness. The Kankanay, Luzon, Philippines. (Vanoverbergh, 1972: 87)

Aldúna Kálda-bauku   A master of sicknesses. The Cagaba and the Kogi, Colombia. (Reichel-Dolmatoff, 1949/50: 113)

Alibay   A spirit who is harmful to women in childbirth and must be propitiated. The Kankanay, Luzon, Philippines. (Vanoverbergh, 1972: 86)

Alimuwo-na   A god of boils and abscesses. The Ifugao, Philippines. (Barton, 1946: 64)

Aloge, Alogbwe   A Dahomean god of smallpox. Son of Sapata. Brazil. (Bastide, 1960: 560; Costa Eduardo, 1948: 78)

Alulevalu   "Chief of the spirits who live ashore, in the trees, and inflict disease on those who disobey the chiefs or shirk communal labor." Ifalik, Micronesia. (Burrows, 1947/48: 11)

Amal   A Sumerian god—"dAmal-gig-du-ga, "disease-decreeing dAmal," who is identified with the Akkadian dBennu. Near East. (Jacobsen, 1970: 420)

a mik ka ta bo   A dangerous one-eyed demon who prowls at night and who "has the habit of gliding along the surface of rivers and brooks." If his shadow falls on a man it causes illness; if met face to face, instant death. He is the only mung to whom a goat is sacrificed, never to a god. The Lepchas, Sikkim. (Siiger, 1967, 1: 180–181)

Amimitl   A goddess "associated with dysentery" who is also goddess "of floating gardens and canals," worshipped at Cuauhilama. Mexico. (Reed, 1966: 96, 112)

Ammal   A goddess who is the cause of smallpox and skin diseases. The Tamil, Ceylon. (Seligmann and Seligmann, 1911: 336)

Ančančo   The Aymara in Bolivia believe him the source of illness and death. Among the Peruvian Aymara, he is the owner of gold and silver. (Tschopik, 1951: 200)

Angar Mata   The deity of smallpox of the Korwas. India. (Majumdar, 1950: 277)

Angarmati Bhawani   A goddess who causes sunstroke. India. (Briggs, 1953: 529–530)

Angina   The goddess of quinsy sore throat who was "invoked for its cure." Rome. (Jayne, 1962: 461)

Angiyu   A god of dysentery of the Ifugao. Philippines. (Barton, 1946: 63)

Angont   A monstrous water serpent who was the source of sickness, death, and other misfortunes. The Iroquois and Huron, Ontario and Michigan. (Gray, 1925, 6: 885; Brinton, 1868: 136)

Ango ud Latapango   A place spirit at Latapango who steals the "souls of rice and men, causing death" and illness. Also the owner of game in the vicinity. The Ifugao, Philippines. (Barton, 1946: 85)

Anguan   An evil anito who "hunts men with dogs and gives one a headache from which he may die." The Apayao, Philippines. (Wilson, 1947: 23)

Aniku, Inikuan   A god of dysentery. The Ifugao, Philippines. (Barton, 1946: 63)

Ankalamma   A deity worshipped for protection from epidemic disease. The Lambadi, Southern India. (Thurston, 1909, 4: 230)

Ankamma   The "goddess of cholera and disease generally." Ellore District, India. (Whitehead, 1916: 22)

Anlu-lebie-landet numakiedeil emei   Goddess of smallpox. Her name means "out from the Russian country here settled mother." The Yukaghir, Siberia. (Jochelson, 1900/02: 218)

Anoano   A goddess who caused insanity in women. The Marquesas, Polynesia. (Handy, 1923: 247)

Antai   A mother goddess who causes as well as protects from whooping cough. The Gujarat, India. (Crooke, 1894: 70)

Aoutaerohi   A demon of disease of the Huron Indians. Ontario and Michigan. (Gray, 1925, 6: 885)

Apang moong   A devil of genitourinary diseases. The Lepchas, Sikkim. (Gorer, 1938: 232)

Apenaweni   The "spirit of sickness." The Sacs and the Foxes. Wisconsin and Iowa. (Chamberlain, 1925, 4: 740)

A po kun sdud   A king of the *bdud* gods who causes fits of unconsciousness. Tibet. (Nebesky-Wojkowitz, 1956, 1: 275)

Apollo   As one of his aspects he could cause plague and death, but as a god of healing could also deliver from them. Greece. (Jayne, 1962: 223; Thramer, 1925, 6: 545; Barthell, 1971: 24–26)

Ari   A demon, the iguana, who originated consumption. The Cuna, Panama. (Nordenskiold, 1930: 20–21)

Arot moong   A devil who takes the form of a red butterfly and causes illness. When a violent death is caused by Arot, ceremonies should be conducted annually forever because violent death "is infectious and hereditary." The Lepchas, Sikkim. (Gorer, 1938: 221, 352)

Asag   A Sumerian "demon of sickness and disease." Near East. (Kramer, 1961: 105)

Asakku, Ashakku   A god of fever, of tuberculosis, of plague. Babylonia, Near East. (Thramer, 1925, 6: 541; Clebert, 1967: 195; Langdon, 1931: 372)

Asmaram   A male evil spirit who causes illness. The Pulaya, India. (Thaliath, 1956: 1044)

Atlatonan   Goddess of lepers who also caused physical birth defects and people to suffer from sores. The Aztec, Mexico. (Alexander, 1920: 64)

Auixa Hátei   Father of the Dysentery. The Cagaba and the Kogi. Colombia. (Reichel-Dolmatoff, 1949/50: 115)

Avanagadan   A male evil spirit who causes "sickness, pain, misfortune." The Pulaya (Cochin), India. (Thaliath, 1956: 1033–1034)

'Awwa   A spirit who causes swelling and also possesses people. The Maguzawa, Nigeria. (Greenberg, 1946: 33)

Ayo   A deity of the Jukun who causes ophthalmia. Nigeria. (Greenberg, 1946: 61)

Azoani   A god of smallpox. Brazil. (Bastide, 1960: 560; Verger, 1954: 16)

Babaluaye   A god of contagious skin diseases identified with St. Lazarus. "His symbol is a pair of crutches and he is represented by a leprous old man accompanied by two dogs." Cuba and Puerto Rico, West Indies. (Verger, 1957: 255; Gonzalez-Wippler, 1975: 27)

Badi Mata   A goddess of smallpox who attacks children. Bengal. (Crooke, 1925, 2: 485)

Bai Haldahin (Hardahin)   A goddess of disease who "causes a yellow vomit." The Baiga, India. (Elwin, 1939: 364)

Baihi   A goddess who causes madness. The Baiga, India. (Elwin, 1939: 364)

Balanan   A malevolent god of madness. The Kayans, Borneo. (Hose, 1912: 5, 6)

Balanian   A god who afflicts with arthritis. The Ifugao, Philippines. (Barton, 1946: 69)

Balanyan   A malignant spirit of the woods who afflicts with diseases. The Milanows (Malanau), Land Dyaks, Borneo. (De Crespigny, 1875: 35; Roth, 1968: 166)

Balingen-ngen   A spirit who causes "Illness, sore feet, headache, and bad dreams." The Tinguian, Philippines. (Cole, 1922: 300)

Balitok nak Magnad   A god who attacks the liver. Son of Magnad. The Ifugao, Philippines. (Barton, 1946: 65)

Bamusayi   A lame forest spirit who causes men to be impotent and women to be frigid. The Maguzawa, Nigeria. (Greenberg, 1946: 33)

Bangara   A god of fever. The Kols, Chaibasa, India. (Crooke, 1894: 87)

U Bangjang   A forest demon/god who brings illness. Sacrifices are made by the roadside. The Khasi, Assam. (Gurdon, 1907: 196)

Barah Sisip A powerful demon of disease who causes internal abscesses. The Mantra, Malay Peninsula. (Skeat, 1906: 322)

Barah Terkilir A demon of disease who causes external ulcers. The Mantra, Malay Peninsula. (Skeat, 1906: 322)

Baram-bonga A maleficent deity who causes smallpox and cattle diseases. The Hos, India. (Majumdar, 1950: 260)

Basanti A goddess of disease and sister of Sitala. She is called the "yellow goddess" because of the color of the skin in certain diseases. India. (Crooke, 1894: 80; Briggs, 1920: 138)

Bauri Bai A goddess of disease who causes madness. The Baiga, India. (Elwin, 1939: 364)

Benisalsal An unpleasant and mischievous spirit who "causes illness, sore feet, headache, and bad dreams." The Tinguian, Philippines. (Cole, 1922: 300, 323)

Bennu An Akkadian "God of epilepsy(?)" identified with the Sumerian Amal. Near East. (Jacobsen, 1970: 420)

Bhagadevi A goddess who "protects the community from cholera." The Jalari and the Vada, Southern India. (Thurston, 1909, 2: 446; 7: 261)

Bhagavati A goddess of smallpox of the Kol. Also called Khermai. India. (Elwin, 1949: 344)

Bhagavatiamman A malevolent goddess of smallpox of the Trichinopoly District, India. (Hemingway, 1907: 90)

Bhageseri One of the six sisters of Sitala, goddesses of "eruptive diseases." The Doms, India. (Briggs, 1953: 531)

Bibi An old goddess of disease—"Cholera itself." She also can cause other illnesses, but is not totally harmful if properly worshipped and appeased, given due honors. She is invoked for health. The Gypsies. (Trigg, 1973: 185–187)

Bijungo A god of the plague. The Basoga, Uganda. (Roscoe, 1915: 247)

Bisagit The "spirit of smallpox" from whom Kinharingan and Munsumundok procured earth in exchange for half of the people—the creation myth. The Dusuns, North Borneo. (Evans, 1923: 47; MacKenzie, 1930: 336)

Bisari A malevolent goddess who causes ophthalmia. The Kachhi, India. (Crooke, 1925, 7: 634)

Bitoso A demon, son of Ana and the King of Devils. He is a multiheaded worm who causes headaches, stomachaches, loss of appetite; the husband of Schilalyi. (Trigg gives Schilayi [sic] as male). The Gypsies, Transylvania. (Clebert, 1967: 185; Trigg, 1973: 164)

Bo Gaha Yaka A tree yaka, the bo tree, who sends illness. The Sinhalese Vedda, Ceylon. (Seligmann and Seligmann, 1911: 170)

Bolot-Sagan-Noyon The god of "the disease common in their district, *Sibirskaya yazva* (called in Buryat *bomo*)." The Buryat, Balagan, Siberia. (Czaplicka, 1969: 286)

Bosouko A Dahomean god of smallpox. Brazil. (Bastide, 1960: 561)

Botono An evil spirit "of the common cold" who can also cause death. The Yupa, Venezuela. (Wilbert, 1974: 99–100)

Budyah Goddess of smallpox. Australia. (Crooke, 1894: 78)

Bugan inMagnad A goddess who attacks the liver. Wife of Magnad. The Ifugao, Philippines. (Barton, 1946: 65)

Bugan inPati A goddess who exacts sacrifices by inflicting disease. The Ifugao, Philippines. (Barton, 1946: 70)

Bukpe A male crocodile spirit who causes disease and drought, but whose malevolence can be controlled by ritual. The Nupe, Nigeria. (Nadel, 1954: 27)

Bumabala A god of boils and abscesses. The Ifugao, Philippines. (Barton, 1946: 65)

Bumagang A god of boils and abscesses. The Ifugao, Philippines. (Barton, 1946: 65)

(Jin) Bumi He sends illnesses and causes death "but his power is entirely derived from Pirman." The Benua, Malay Peninsula. (Skeat, 1906: 349–350)

Bumintol A god of boils and abscesses. The Ifugao, Philippines. (Barton, 1946: 64)

Bungbungaan A god of boils and abscesses—when they are ripe. The Ifugao, Philippines. (Barton, 1946: 65)

Burhi Mata, Thakurani Mata The "goddess of small-pox and rinderpest." She is offered flowers and incense during an epidemic, but if she doesn't alleviate it they abuse her. The Gadbas, India. (Russell, 1916, 3: 11)

hantu buta The evil spirit of blindness. Malaya. (Gimlette, 1929: 25)

Butagian A god who afflicts with arthritis. The Ifugao, Philippines. (Barton, 1946: 69)

Butham A male evil spirit who causes illness. The Pulaya (Cochin), India. (Thaliath, 1956: 1044)

Buth Arvila A male evil spirit who causes illness. The Pulaya (Cochin), India. (Thaliath, 1956: 1044)

ka byrdaw A demoness who causes attacks of cramps. The Khasi, Assam. (Stegmiller, 1921: 411)

Cajanja A god of smallpox. Brazil. (Bastide, 1960: 562)

Calalukise An illness demon who originated rheumatism. The Cuna, Panama. (Nordenskiold, 1930: 20–21)

Chal, Chalnad A god who is worshipped only when plague attacks the village. The Mal, India. (Crooke, 1925, 8: 344–5)

Chamariya The most malignant of the goddesses of smallpox, elder sister of Sitala. India. (Lillingston, 1925, 3: 353; Crooke, 1894: 81; Briggs, 1920: 138)

Chang Yuan-po The deity of the "Spring Plague." China. (Werner, 1932: 560)

Chang Yuan-Shuai One of the gods of smallpox. China. (Werner, 1932: 42)

Chankpana The god of smallpox whose messengers are the flies and mosquitoes. "His symbol is a red and white cane." Puerto Rico. West Indies. (Gonzalez-Wippler, 1975: 26)

Chao Kung-ming God of the "Autumn Plague," but also worshipped by merchants as a god of wealth. China. (Werner, 1932: 44, 515, 560)

Chao Wu-chên A god of epidemics, one of the Wu Yüeh, and also a mountain god. China. (Werner, 1934: 242)

Chapanan One of the names of the Yoruba god of smallpox. Brazil. (Bastide, 1960: 563)

Chavandi A male evil spirit who inflicts "sickness, pain, misfortune." The Pulaya (Cochin), Indoa. (Thaliath, 1956: 1034)

Chemam The god of thunder who causes illness and death with his thunderbolts. The Kintak Bong Negritos, Malaya. (Evans, 1937: 143, 183)

Chen Shen God of measles. Son of Tou-shen Niang-Niang. China. (Werner, 1932: 46; Maspero, 1963: 361)

Chhath, Chhathi A Dravidian deity worshipped in the United Provinces as "the impersonated sixth day after birth, when . . . the child is likely to be attacked by infantile lockjaw." India. (Crooke, 1925, 4: 853)

Chíchipáchu An illness demon and "the dog of the night—who is half dog and half woman. When this demon starts eating the moon, an eclipse takes place." The Cuna, Panama. (Nordenskiold, 1930: 20–21)

Chíchipáchuored An illness demon—a "black and rotund dog . . . that obstruct(s) child-birth in women." The Cuna, Panama. (Nordenskiold, 1930: 20–21)

Chika A demon who causes excruciating abdominal pains, severe colic at night. The Mantra, Malay Peninsula. (Skeat, 1906: 324; Gimlette, 1929: 25)

Chilkin Piri Goddess of stomach pains. The Baiga, India. (Elwin, 1939: 364)

Chingan Mata A goddess of disease who causes crippling rheumatism. The Baiga, India. (Elwin, 1939: 365)

Ching Feng Szu A god of disease—"Convulsions Controller." China. (Day, 1940: 205)

Ch'i Shang Chih Shen A "spirit of seven injuries to eyes, nose, ears, mouth, hands, feet, and heart." China. (Day, 1940: 44)

Ch'i T'ou She A god of disease. "Seven-Headed Snake Charm." China. (Day, 1940: 205)

Ch'iu She "Autumn Snake Charm," a god of disease. China. (Day, 1940: 205)

Chiu T'ou She "Nine-Headed Snake Charm," a god of disease. China. (Day, 1940: 205)

Chondu A minor disease godling who causes the itch. Chaibasa, India. (Crooke, 1894: 87)

Chonu The god who punishes incest by making the man impotent. Dahomey. (Herskovits, 1938, 2: 140)

Chou Hsin God of the star Shih'o who is "Overseer of Epidemics of the East." China. (Werner, 1932: 92, 560)

Chung Shih-kuei God of the "Winter Plague." China. (Werner, 1932: 560)

Chung Yang Ch'ang Szu "Central Pestilence Demon." China. (Day, 1940: 206)

Ch'un She "Spring Snake Charm," a god of disease. China. (Day, 1940: 205)

Churakuzhi A male evil spirit who inflicts "sickness, pain, misfortune." The Pulaya (Cochin), India. (Thaliath, 1956: 1034)

Churelin Mata A goddess of disease who causes impotency in young men. The Baiga, India. (Elwin, 1939: 365)

Chu T'ien-lin "Overseer of Epidemics of the South." China. (Werner, 1932: 560)

Chyong moong A male devil exorcised in illness through the Dumbu Soong ceremony. The Lepchas, Sikkim. (Gorer, 1938: 472, 476)

Cigoro A goddess who causes "eyesickness," a wife of 'Dan Galadima. The Maguzawa, Nigeria. (Greenberg, 1946: 38)

Cuchi A god who takes the form of a snake or a bird and causes illness. Australia. (Brinton, 1897: 80)

Dada Zodji, Da Zodji God of smallpox, of dysentery, and vomiting who sends epidemics as a scourge because he "detests black magic." He is the twin and husband of Nyohwe Ananu. Dahomey. (Herskovits, 1938, 2: 139, 287; Verger, 1957: 239; Mercier, 1954: 231)

Dade moong An "evil spirit sent by an enemy" who causes illness. Also called Nanjet moong and Tomloong Deut moong. The Lepchas, Sikkim. (Gorer, 1938: 471)

Dagdagamiyan A female spirit who causes illness in children if they play near the harvesting. The Isneg, Luzon, Philippines. (Vanoverbergh, 1941: 337)

Daguya-yappan A spirit who afflicts with sleeping sickness. The Isneg, Luzon, Philippines. (Vanoverbergh, 1953: 98)

Dako A god who afflicts with malaria. The Ifugao, Philippines. (Barton, 1946: 70)

Dalit A god of dysentery. The Ifugao, Philippines. (Barton, 1946: 63)

Dalong A malevolent woods spirit who causes illness. The Malanau (Milanow) and the Land Dyaks, Borneo. (Roth, 1968: 166; De Crespigny, 1875: 35)

Daludalum A god who causes blindness, and a god of sorcery. The Ifugao, Philippines. (Barton, 1946: 40)

Dangira A goddess who causes itch. The Maguzawa, Nigeria. (Greenberg, 1946: 38)

'Dan Musa A god who causes constipation, and those who are possessed by him wriggle on their bellies like a snake. A speckled cock is sacrificed to him. The Maguzawa, Nigeria. (Greenberg, 1946: 32)

Dapeg A spirit who causes "illness, sore feet, headache, and bad dreams," but who also kills people. The Tinguian, Philippines. (Cole, 1922: 300, 323)

Darantan An evil river anito who causes drownings. The Apayao, Philippines. (Wilson, 1947: 23)

(Po Yan) Dari A nature goddess who is a goddess of disease though at Phan-ri "she cures fever in little children." The Chams, Annam and Cambodia. (Cabaton, 1925, 3: 342)

Dariya A goddess who causes "hysteria 'laughing madness'" The Maguzawa, Nigeria. (Greenberg, 1946: 39)

Dayom Pano A devil of illness. The Lepchas, Sikkim. (Morris, 1938: 158)

Deog Ian A malevolent spirit of the sources of rivers who causes dropsy. The Malanau and the Land Dyaks, Borneo. (Roth, 1968: 166; De Crespigny, 1875: 35)

Deut moong A fever devil who in illness is exorcised in the Dumbu Soong ceremony. At the end of life he "quarrels" for the soul of the person, as to his living or dying. The Lepchas, Sikkim. (Gorer, 1938: 469, 472)

Dhahu Dhukan A goddess of disease who "causes sudden pains in the chest." The Baiga, India. (Elwin, 1939: 365)

Dhaman Mal A god invoked in cases of snakebite. The Bhils, India. (Naik, 1956: 187)

Diarrhoea Goddess of that illness. The Gypsies, India. (Clebert, 1967: 195)

Didi Thakurani A disease deity of Bardwan. Bengal. (Crooke, 1925, 2: 485)

Dinawagan Wife of Hatan. They are invoked for help—"especially in sickness." The Apayao, Philippines. (Wilson, 1947: 20)

Dispirir Mata Goddess of syphilis. The Baiga, India. (Elwin, 1939: 363)

Diu A spirit of cattle plague; apparently comes from the Dinka, as more known to the west of the Nile. The Nuer, Sudan. (Evans-Pritchard, 1956: 29, 30)

Doam moong The devil of leprosy. The reason it is incurable is that he is the only devil who did not take the oath administered by Komsithing to leave man alone if sacrifices are made. The Lepchas, Sikkim. (Gorer, 1938: 224)

Dobrochot A demon of disease (singular and plural) to whom in illness an offering is made at night at the cross-road. Slavic Russia. (Mansikka, 1925, 4: 625)

Doig A malevolent spirit of the woods who afflicts with diseases. The Milanow (Malanau) and the Land Dyaks, Borneo. (De Crespigny, 1875: 35; Roth, 1968: 166)

rDo rje legs pa ging gi gtso A god who causes illness in children as well as ill-feeling and bad weather. Tibet. (Nebesky-Wojkowitz, 1956, 1: 283)

ka Duba The female spirit of fever. The Khasis and the Syntengs, Assam. (Gurdon, 1914: 107; Stegmiller, 1921: 411)

Duhkharni Mai One of the six sisters of Sitala, goddesses of "eruptive diseases." The Doms, India. (Briggs, 1953: 531)

Duna A spirit who causes fever. He is "dog-like in appearance; a person possessed by him barks like a dog." A black cock or black goat is sacrificed to him. The Maguzawa, Nigeria. (Greenberg, 1946: 32)

Durga Mata The goddess of smallpox. The Kamar, Central Provinces, India. (Russell, 1916, 3: 328)

Durpatta Mata A goddess of disease who prevents childbirth, killing both child and mother. The Baiga, India. (Elwin, 1939: 364)

Dwopi An evil household spirit who can cause madness. The Chins, Burma. (Temple, 1925, 3: 25)

Ehre'er, E'hrip The god of colic. The Chukchee, Siberia. (Bogoras, 1904/09: 298)

Ellamma Vows are taken for her when children fall ill. The Donga Dasari, Southern India. These are religious mendicants and thieves, and sacrifices are made to her and to Huligavva before a thieving expedition. (Thurston, 1909, 2: 192–193)

Era Babylonian god of plague. Near East. (Bhattacharji, 1970: 64)

Erh T'ou She "Two-Headed Snake Charm," a god of disease. China. (Day, 1940: 205)

Febris Roman goddess of fever, which she also healed by the "purifying fire within the body." (Jayne, 1962: 462; Schoeps, 1961: 148; Madden, 1930: 33–34)

Feng Hsieh Szu "Wind Disease Carrier," a god of disease who causes colds and fever as well as madness. China. (Day, 1940: 39, 205)

St. Foutin "By tradition the first bishop of Lyons," who was worshipped by the Gauls as a phallic god to cure "impotence and sexual disease," as well as for offspring. (Hartland, 1925, 9: 817)

Gabbuwa A malevolent spirit who causes illness. The Isneg, Luzon, Philippines. (Vanoverbergh, 1941: 290)

Gaiyaman A god of dysentery. The Ifugao, Philippines. (Barton, 1946: 63)

Gaizkiñ A malignant spirit which causes mysterious illnesses in children by incarnating himself in the feathers of the pillow on which they sleep. The Basques, Spain and France. (Barandiaran, 1972: 93)

Galadevi A goddess who causes mumps. The Baiga, India. (Elwin, 1939: 365)

Gampa The god of measles. Son of Woeadja. The Toradja, Celebes, Indonesia. (Downs, 1920: 21; Adriani and Kruyt, 1950: 205)

Gangammal The goddess of cholera. The Paraiyans, Southern India. (Thurston, 1909, 6: 106)

Ganga-sabota A deity who causes "pneumonia, fever and vomiting." The Bondo, India. (Elwin, 1950: 155)

Gangngo, Gango A god who afflicts with rheumatism; he is also a guardian of property and prestige. The Ifugao, Philippines. (Barton, 1946: 57, 70)

Garang A sky god who causes minor indispositions and is invoked for their relief. The Dinka, Sudan. (Lienhardt, 1961: 56–57, 83–86)

GaRba A god who causes "soreness of the back and neck," to whom a brown goat is sacrificed. The Maguzawa, Nigeria. (Greenberg, 1946: 34)

Gardhavan A male evil spirit who causes illness. The Pulaya (Cochin), India. (Thaliath, 1956: 1044)

Gargasi The malevolent head of the bad spirits who causes epidemics as well as other misfortunes. The Sea Dyaks, Sarawak, Borneo. (Sarawak Gazette, 1963: 17)

Gasang A malevolent spirit who causes drowsiness. The Mosangs of the Tangsas, India and Burma. (Dutta, 1959: 67)

Gata A deity who inflicts diseases of the eye. He is also a guardian of property and prestige. The Ifugao, Philippines. (Barton, 1946: 57)

Gebu Tabrong Pano A god who punishes quarreling with aches and pains. He also causes colds. The Lepchas, Sikkim. (Gorer, 1938: 473; Siiger, 1967: 141)

Ghatchindan A goddess of disease who "catches cattle by the throat." The Baiga, India. (Elwin, 1939: 364)

Gin A malignant spirit of the sea who afflicts with diseases. The Milanow (Malanau) and the Land Dyaks, Borneo. (De Crespigny, 1875: 35; Roth, 1968: 166)

Gobgob-an-na A god of boils and abscesses. The Ifugao, Philippines. (Barton, 1946: 64)

Gohem A god of cholera. Chaibasa, India. (Crooke, 1894: 87)

Goje A spirit who causes leprosy, cough, and ulcers. The Maguzawa, Nigeria. (Greenberg, 1946: 37)

Gomogopos A god who causes as well as cures stomach troubles. The Tinguian, Philippines. (Cole, 1922: 340)

Gongbu A devil who causes distended stomachs in children. The Lepchas, Sikkim. (Gorer, 1938: 474)

Grib bdag chen mo A black goddess—"the great pollution-mistress." Tibet. (Nebesky-Wojkowitz, 1956, 1: 388)

Grib bdag rgyal po The "king of the masters of pollution." Tibet. (Nebesky-Wojkowitz, 1956, 1: 307)

Grotak Demon of stomachache. The Jakun, Malay Peninsula. (Skeat, 1906: 183)

Gualichu A spirit of evil who is responsible for "sickness and death," but who can be beneficent. The Puelche and the Araucanian, Argentina. (Alexander, 1920: 335; Cooper, 1946, 1: 167)

Guerlichon, Grelichon A phallic god worshipped for children and to cure "impotence and sexual disease." Bourges, Gaul. (Hartland, 1925, 9: 817)

Gugulu-na A god of boils and abscesses. The Ifugao, Philippines. (Barton, 1946: 65)

Guignolet A phallic god worshipped at Brest for children and for the cure of "impotence and sexual disease." Gaul. (Hartland, 1925, 9: 817)

Gukguk-na A god of boils and abscesses when they harden. The Ifugao, Philippines. (Barton, 1946: 65)

Gula A great goddess of healing and of health, yet at times she would perversely inflict disease. Akkadia, Assyria, and Babylonia, Near East. (Jayne, 1962: 121; Jastrow, 1898: 166, 175; Langdon, 1931: 182)

Gulsalia Mata Goddess of smallpox. Bengal. (Crooke, 1925, 2: 485)

Gumongo A spirit of plague and diseases. California Indians. (Larousse, 1968: 436)

Gurang A deity of disease who "torments with bellyache." The Bondo, India. (Elwin, 1950: 155)

Gurgu A lame forest spirit, a hunter, who causes lameness. A dwarf cock is sacrificed to him. The Maguzawa, Nigeria. (Greenberg, 1946: 34)

rGyal po 'od lha dkar po A god of the retinue of Pe har—of the rgyal po class, illness bringing deities. Tibet. (Nebesky-Wojkowitz, 1956, 1: 128)

Gyalpo Shuk-din A demon at Pemiongchi who afflicts with illness and accident. Sikkim. (Gazeteer of Sikhim, 1894: 261)

rGyal po tshangs pa A form of Tsangs pa as a god causing illness. Tibet. (Nebesky-Wojkowitz, 1956, 1: 145)

Gyangya'di A goddess causing sleeping sickness. Wife of 'Dan Galadima. The Maguzawa, Nigeria. (Greenberg, 1946: 39)

'Gying dkar ma   An evil lake goddess who causes dropsy. Tibet. (Nebesky-Wojkowitz, 1956, 1: 307)

Ha'aro-mata-rai   God of blindness. Tahiti, Polynesia. (Henry, 1928: 380)

lHa chen nam dbang phyug   A form of Mahadeva believed to be harmful and to send madness. Tibet. (Nebesky-Wojkowitz, 1956, 1: 269)

Hadphoran Marhi   Goddess of smallpox. The Baiga, India. (Elwin, 1939: 364)

Hadui   God of illness and death who was conquered by Teharon-hiawagon and promised to provide cures for the diseases; the origin of the mask-faces society for exorcising disease. The Iroquois, Eastern United States. (Gray, 1925, 7: 422; Alexander, 1964: 37)

Hagaang   A god of dysentery. The Ifugao, Philippines. (Barton, 1946: 63)

Hagagian   "Limping Gait"—a god who afflicts with arthritis. The Ifugao, Philippines. (Barton, 1946: 69)

Haialilaqs   The "spirit of pestilence." The Tsimshian Indians, British Columbia. (Boas, 1909/10: 546)

Halibongbong   A god of sorcery who causes convulsions, fits, and epilepsy. The Ifugao, Philippines. (Barton, 1946: 40–41)

Halimudong   A god who punishes infractions of enemy taboos with illness. The Ifugao, Philippines. (Barton, 1946: 53)

Hamoran   One of the most powerful of the demons of disease. The Mantra, Malay Peninsula. (Skeat, 1906: 322)

Hanake   "Also called Niho-Oa, an evil deity who inflicted paralysis and all wasting sicknesses." The Marquesas, Polynesia. (Christian, 1895: 190)

Hara   A name of Siva as the devastating destroyer "identified with sickness and death, . . . destroys indiscriminately the good and the bad." India. (Danielou, 1964: 196–197)

Harda, Hardaur Lala   A god of cholera in various areas, but in Bundelkhand he is a wedding godling. India. (Crooke, 1894: 88; Martin, 1914: 256–257; Briggs, 1953: 477)

Harduli Gomoij   God of cholera of the Kurkus (Munda). India. (Drake, 1925, 7: 761)

Heisei   The "Master of Sickness" depicted with a tiger face. He sends sickness as punishment for offenses committed or for negligence of rituals and offerings. He is omnipresent, is associated with death and with the west; his symbols—"the snake, the arrow, the crab." He is a god of sexuality who sends dreams and through them attempts to seduce. The Cagaba and the Kogi, Colombia. (Reichel-Dolmatoff, 1949/50: 89–91, 142)

Hemphy Arnam   A god invoked for relief from sickness. The Mikirs, Assam. (Barkataki, 1969: 58–59)

Herabe   A god who can "cause temporary or permanent insanity." The Huli, New Guinea. (Glasse, 1965: 35)

Hibalot   A spirit who causes intestinal ulcers. The Ifugao, Philippines. (Jocano, 1969: 17)

Hinalokhokan   A god who punishes infractions of enemy taboos with illness, difficulty in breathing. The Ifugao, Philippines. (Barton, 1946: 52)

Hinigaan   A god who punishes infractions of enemy taboos with illness. The Ifugao, Philippines. (Barton, 1946: 52)

Hinigalan   A god of dysentery. The Ifugao, Philippines. (Barton, 1946: 63)

Hinipaiyan   A god who causes illness for breaking enemy taboos. The Ifugao, Philippines. (Barton, 1946: 52)

Hinukbut   A god who punishes infractions of enemy taboos with a weakening cough. The Ifugao, Philippines. (Barton, 1946: 52)

Hinumban   A god who punishes infractions of enemy taboos with illness. The Ifugao, Philippines. (Barton, 1946: 52)

Hinumbian   A god who attacks the liver. He is also a rain god. The Ifugao, Philippines. (Barton, 1946: 65; 1955: 161)

Hlamen Djémé rum   A "god when pleased a devil when angry." He causes illness. The Lepchas, Sikkim. (Gorer, 1938: 472)

Hmin   A demon who, if encountered, drives one mad. Burma. (Temple, 1925, 3: 23; Leach, 1950, 2: 785)

hocere'un wahira   "Disease-giver." An "approximate translation of his name, . . . a very peculiar figure, . . . dealing out death from one side of his body and life from the other. He is preeminently a guardian spirit who only appears to the bravest and holiest fasters. His specific blessings seem to be connected with war and the curing of disease." The Winnebago, Wisconsin. (Radin, 1915/16: 287)

Homohomok-na   A god of dysentery. The Ifugao, Philippines. (Barton, 1946: 63)

Hsiang Yuan-ta   The "Summer Plague." China. (Werner, 1932: 560)

Hsia She   "Summer Snake Charm," a god of disease. China. (Day, 1940: 205)

Hsi Fang Ch'ang Szu   "Western Pestilence Demon." China. (Day, 1940: 206)

Hsi Wang Mu   As an early deity she "was the fearsome, tiger-toothed mistress of plague and disaster." From this ogress she subsequently became "the guardian-goddess of the herb of immortality," presumably because in dispensing sickness and death she could also withdraw them. China. (Larousse, 1973: 284)

Huang Ying-tu   A god of epidemics, one of the Wu Yüeh. China. (Werner, 1934: 242)

Hugenda   A god who attacks pregnant women. A part of the deity "lodges itself in the internal organs of the foetus." The Huli, New Guinea. (Glasse, 1965: 36)

Hul-ater   A god who made man subject to illness. The Vogul, Siberia. (Pettersson, 1957: 21)

Huligavva   A goddess for whom "vows are undertaken . . . when children fall ill." The Donga Dasari are religious mendicants and thieves, and sacrifices are made to her before an expedition. Southern India. (Thurston, 1909, 2: 192–193)

Hulka Devi   A goddess of cholera and of vomiting. Bengal. (Crooke, 1894: 94; Martin, 1914: 256)

Hulki Mai   Goddess of cholera and of smallpox. The Chamars and the Nats. India. (Briggs, 1920: 154; 1953: 531)

Humapiping   A god of boils and abscesses. The Ifugao, Philippines. (Barton, 1946: 65)

Humubut   A god who punishes infractions of enemy taboos with illness. The Ifugao, Philippines. (Barton, 1946: 53)

Hunding   A god, son of Umalgo, who punishes infractions of enemy taboos with illness. The Ifugao, Philippines. (Barton, 1946: 53)

Hung Sha Shang Szu   Demon of plague. China. (Day, 1940: 44)

Imalbi   A spirit who causes eye trouble. The Tinguian, Philippines. (Cole, 1922: 338)

Inahuan, Inipaiyan, and **Inipingan**   Gods of dysentery. The Ifugao, Philippines. (Barton, 1946: 63)

Inoklingan   A god who punishes infractions of enemy taboos with phlegm. The Ifugao, Philippines. (Barton, 1946: 52)

Inukukan   A god who punishes infractions of enemy taboos with illness—resembling tuberculosis. The Ifugao, Philippines. (Barton, 1946: 52)

Inyahyahan   A god who punishes infractions of enemy taboos with breathlessness. The Ifugao, Philippines. (Barton, 1946: 52)

Ipamahandi   The "goddess of accident." The Bukidnon, Philippines. (Jocano, 1969: 23)

Irra   An Akkadian god of pestilence and destruction, of evil. Near East. (Kramer, 1961: 127; MacCulloch, 1964: 137–139)

Iteyun   A male spirit of epilepsy, a ground spirit. The Chukchee, Siberia. (Bogoras, 1904/09: 293)

I T'ou She   "One-Headed Snake Charm," a god of disease. China. (Day, 1940: 205)

Iumetun   A male ground spirit who lives in the desert and "causes a nervous disease bearing the same name." The Chukchee, Siberia. (Bogoras, 1904/09: 293)

Iya   The "utterly evil" son of Inyan is believed to cause headaches and paralysis. The Lakota, Plains Indians, South Dakota. (Walker, 1980: 51, 141)

Iyappaswami   A "stone set up beneath a teak tree, and worshipped as a protector against various forms of sickness and disease." The Kadir, Southern India. (Thurston, 1909, 3: 21)

Jalia   In some areas male, others female, but a very malevolent deity who causes illness and death, but can be appeased. The Savara, Southern India. (Thurston, 1909, 6: 331–2)

452

Jalpa Mai Goddess of the plague and of death. The Basors, Jubbulpur, India. Same as Mari Mai. (Briggs, 1953: 531)

Jambha A "Vedic godling of disease, was supposed to cause the tismus of infants." India. (Jolly, 1925, 4: 754)

Jammarke A god who causes diarrhea. He is also the patron of boxers. His wife is Makasa. The Maguzawa, Nigeria. (Greenberg, 1946: 34)

Jappi Mata A goddess who causes sleeping sickness. The Baiga, India. (Elwin, 1939: 365)

Jechit A disease spirit who causes "blood dysentery." The Tangsas, India and Burma. (Dutta, 1959: 67)

Jimalingan Invoked in time of illness. The Apayao, Philippines. (Wilson, 1947: 23)

u jingbih-u lasam The devil who causes sickness of the mouth and teeth. The Khasi, Assam. (Stegmiller, 1921: 411)

Jogini A deity of disease. Orissa, India. (Crooke, 1925, 2: 485)

Jok Adongo, Jok Orongo, Jok Abong, Jok Orogo Manifestations of Jok as diseases giving the appearance of madness. Jok Adongo is also a manifestation of Jok in association with trees. The Lango, Uganda. (Butt, 1952: 104–105)

Jok Omarari A manifestation of Jok as causing bubonic plague. The Lango, Uganda. (Butt, 1952: 104)

Juan Noq The god of the volcano Santa Maria sends illness, is a god of smallpox. The spirits of the dead have to work for him, rebuilding his house. The Chimalteco, Guatemala. (Wagley, 1949: 51, 60)

Jum chang A spirit who causes disease and is also a household deity. The Ron-Rangs (Tangsas), India and Burma. (Dutta, 1959: 67, 92)

Jvaraharesvara A deity of malaria who also helps alleviate the fever. Benares, India. (Crooke, 1894: 87)

Jwara Narayan God of fever. Bengal. (Crooke, 1925, 2: 485)

Jyestha Alaksmi The "southern counterpart of the northern Sitala (goddess of smallpox)." She is described as of an "aged and decrepit appearance indicating that she symbolized decay." India. (Bhattacharji, 1970: 89, 90)

Kabuga God of smallpox. The Ifugao, Philippines. (Barton, 1946: 70)

ka cu/tsu lom An evil spirit who causes children to be ill. The Lepchas, Sikkim. (Siiger, 1967: 142)

Kahu-kura The "god of travellers, war, life, disease, and death" who must be invoked in illness. He is now represented by the rainbow. "The upper and darker band . . . is called Kahukura-pango, and the lower one Pou-te-aniwaniwa; the former . . . male, the latter . . . female." The Maori, New Zealand. (White, 1887, 1: 4, 41, 43; Best, 1924: 160–161)

Kairadeshahi A goddess of disease who causes still-birth. The Baiga, India. (Elwin, 1939: 364)

Kakading A deity who inflicts with illness. The Kankanay, Luzon, Philippines. (Vanoverbergh, 1972: 87)

K'ak'ari A god who causes pneumonia, to whom a red and white goat is sacrificed. He takes the form of a snake. Son of 'Dan Musa and Ricana. The Maguzawa, Nigeria. (Greenberg, 1946: 32)

Kalachandi A mischievous male spirit who causes epidemics among "men or cattle, unless propitiated." The Santals, India. (Mukherjea, 1962: 281)

Kalae A poison god who caused diseases. Hawaii. (Westervelt, 1963, 3: 96)

Kalai-pahoa The posion god. Maui, Hawaii. (Beckwith, 1940: 109; Westervelt, 1915: 108)

Kalalukise The demon of rheumatism. The Cuna, Panama. (Nordenskiold, 1938: 400)

Kalamahichandi A mischievous female spirit who brings "epidemics to men or cattle, unless propitiated." The Santals, India. (Mukherjea, 1962: 281)

Kalamau A god who caused illness and death. Central Celebes, Indonesia. (Downs, 1920: 22)

The kalau Evil spirits who cause illness and death. As an individual, a god of evil who intercepts the sacrifices made by the shaman to the supreme being for cures, causing the patient to die. The Koryak, Siberia. (Jochelson, 1904: 417–418; Eliade, 1964: 249- 250)

Kalda-bauku Father of the Fever. The Cagaba and the Kogi, Colombia. (Reichel-Dolmatoff, 1949/50: 115)

Kalda-bauku báxe Father of the Black Fever. The Cagaba and the Kogi, Colombia. (Reichel-Dolmatoff, 1949/50: 115)

Kalda-bauku búchi Father of the White Fever. **Kalda-bauku tashi** Father of the Blue Fever. **Kalda-bauku tśeshi** Father of the Red Fever. The Cagaba and the Kogi, Colombia. (Reichel-Dolmatoff, 1949/50: 115)

Kali The "goddess who presides over the infectious diseases, cholera and smallpox. She is a virgin goddess, whom no quantity of blood can satisfy." Sacrifices are made to her during epidemics. The Nayar, India. (Thurston, 1909, 5: 401; Martin, 1914: 256)

Kalu Kumara Yaka A Sinhalese demon, the "black prince" (whose female counterpart is Mohini Yakkhini). He causes sterility and menstrual disorders in females, difficulties and fever in pregnancies, and erotic dreams. Ceylon (Sri Lanka). (Leach, 1950, 2: 569; Ames, 1978: 46)

Kaluvaliamma Goddess of epidemics as well as of travelers. She is propitiated upon return. India. (Briggs, 1953: 537-8)

Kamang A demon of disease who lives in the ground and "causes inflammation and swellings both in the hands and feet." The Mantra, Malay Peninsula. (Skeat, 1906: 323)

Kamthi Mata A goddess of the plague. India. (Briggs, 1930: 136)

kam yu lom A demon who brings illness to children. The Lepchas, Sikkim. (Siiger, 1967, 2: 142)

Kanagian A god who afflicts with arthritis. The Ifugao, Philippines. (Barton, 1946: 69)

Kandundu A powerful spirit of the Ovimbundu—"the spirit of dreaming who makes swellings on the body." Angola. (McCulloch, 1952: 36)

Kankar Mata "The most dreaded" of the seven goddesses of smallpox. Bengal. (Crooke, 1925, 2: 485)

Kan kubul The yellow cacique bird. When an atmospheric condition causing "yellowish light" before dusk occurs, he is aboard causing all their diseases, as well as injuring the maize. British Honduras. (Muntsch, 1943: 35, 36)

Kapialu The demon of fever. The Mantra, Malay Peninsula. (Skeat, 1906: 333)

Kapi-ap A god who inflicts disease in order to exact sacrifice. The Ifugao, Philippines. (Barton, 1946: 70)

Kapni Piri A goddess who causes ague. The Baiga, India. (Elwin, 1939: 364)

Karama The youngest and jealous wife of 'Dan Galadima who causes eyesickness. The Maguzawa, Nigeria. (Greenberg, 1946: 38)

Karambaoe A name of the Pox Spirit. Others: Woeadja, Toring-ka. Celebes, Indonesia. (Adriani and Kruyt, 1950: 204)

Karo moong A devil causing illness through "enmity and jealousy." The Lepchas, Sikkim. (Gorer, 1938: 472)

Karokung A river goddess who causes fever and chills in men. The Bagobo, Philippines. (Benedict, 1916: 38, 226)

Karukutty A male evil spirit who inflicts with "sickness, pain, misfortune." The Pulaya (Cochin), India. (Thaliath, 1956: 1034)

Karuvilli A demon who possesses people, taking the form of fever. The Karimpalan, Southern India. (Thurston, 1909, 3: 250)

Kasi Baba A godling who causes disease in cattle. Bengal. (Crooke, 1894: 93)

Kassaúgu A Master of Sicknesses and also a Father of the Civilized Ones. The Cagaba and the Kogi, Colombia. (Reichel-Dolmatoff, 1949/50: 113, 115)

Kasviš A demon of disease. Iran. (Gray, 1930: 207)

Katai God of smallpox and other diseases, which he also cured. In some areas male with a wife, Wamwelu; in others female. The Fipa, Tanzania. (Willis, 1966: 30–1)

Katau The spirit of smallpox. The Metako, Argentina. (Métraux, 1939: 47)

Katavi The god of epidemics and of rain, whose wife is Wamwelu. The Pimbwe, Tanzania. (Willis, 1966: 59)

Kateri A "forest goddess who sends cholera and similar diseases." She is propitiated by pregnant women. India. (Elmore, 1915: 47)

Ka-tumbohan The demon of smallpox. The Mantra, Malay Peninsula. (Skeat, 1906: 323)

Kaumpuli God of plague who also causes swollen glands. The Baganda, Uganda. (Cunningham, 1905: 215; Roscoe, 1965: 309; Willoughby, 1932: 56; Kagwa, 1934: 121)

hantu kelumbohan An evil spirit who brings small-pox. Malaya. (Gimlette, 1929: 25)

Kembang Buah The demon of headache. The Jakun, Malay Peninsula. (Skeat, 1906: 183)

Kembong An evil spirit who is the cause of stomach pains and distended abdomens as well as headache. Malaya. (Skeat, 1906: 323; Gimlette, 1929: 25)

Kempunan A demon of disease who "causes pains and accidents to persons" who have not been able to satisfy a craving for a particular food. The Mantra, Malay Peninsula. (Skeat, 1906: 323)

Kha la me 'bar ma A goddess of illness. Tibet. (Nebesky-Wojkowitz, 1956, 1: 308)

Khania Shkwakwa Goddess of smallpox, wife of Akhye Zoshan. The Abkhasians, Caucasus. (Janashia, 1937: 153)

Kha stongs me 'bar A king of the *bdud* gods. He causes fits of unconsciousness. Tibet. (Nebesky-Wojkowitz, 1956, 1: 275)

Khermai Among the Kol the goddess of smallpox. India. (Elwin, 1949: 344)

Khesa An especially feared evil spirit of the Ron-Rangs who causes diseases. The Tangsas, India and Burma. (Dutta, 1959: 67)

ka Khlam The demoness of cholera. The Khasis and the Syntengs, Assam. (Gurdon, 1914: 107; Stegmiller, 1921: 411)

Khuavang A god whom to see causes illness. The Lushai, Bengal and Assam. (Shakespear, 1912: 61; Hodson, 1925, 8: 197)

Kibaho A god of plague and illnesses who follows the earthquake god, Kitaka, when he passes through the land; must be propitiated to avert the diseases. The Basoga, Uganda. (Roscoe, 1915: 251)

Kiha-wahine A dragon goddess, human above the waist, reptile below, who causes illness. Hawaii. (Emerson, 1968: 42; Beckwith, 1932: 169)

Kikiba-an A spirit "who causes illness, sore feet, headache, and bad dreams." The Tinguians, Philippines. (Cole, 1922: 300)

Kinoptiu ud Ubub A deity who steals the "souls of rice and men, causing death" and illness. He is also owner of game in the vicinity. The Ifugao, Philippines. (Barton, 1946: 85)

Kinoyama-sama A god of epidemics at Takashima. Japan. (Norbeck, 1954: 133)

Kinulhudan A god of dysentery. Also a god of weaving. The Ifugao, Philippines. (Barton, 1946: 29, 63)

Kinulidangan A god of dysentery. The Ifugao, Philippines. (Barton, 1946: 63)

Kipu-Tytto A goddess of illness, daughter of Tuoni and Tuonetar. The Finno-Ugric. (Larousse, 1968: 306)

Kivutar Finno-Ugric goddess "of pain and disease." (Larousse, 1968: 306)

Klu bdud dom nag sdig pa'i mgo bo can A scorpion-headed god who causes illness. Tibet. (Nebesky-Wojkowitz, 1956, 1: 286)

Klu bdud 'gram nag ral pa can, Klu bdud gser gyi 'phrog zhu can, and **Klu bdud gtsang pa sbrul mgo can** Malevolent gods who cause illness. Tibet. (Nebesky-Wojkowitz, 1956, 1: 286)

Klu bdud khri stong ral pa The leader of nine klu bdud brothers, "malevolent beings, who cause bilious diseases, leprosy, dropsy, sudden pain, the vomiting of blood, etc." Tibet. (Nebesky-Wojkowitz, 1956, 1: 286)

Klu bdud nyu le nyab kyi lag ring, Klu bdud stag dgu nam mkha' lding, Klu bdud tsang pa'i mgo dgu, and **Klu bdud zhags pa dgur bcings** Malevolent gods who cause illness. Tibet. (Nebesky-Wojkowitz, 1956, 1: 286)

Koemobo The "master of dropsy." Son of Woeadja. The Toradja, Celebes, Indonesia. (Adriani & Kruyt, 1950: 205)

Kohosu God of smallpox whose wife is Nyohwe Ananu. Dahomey. (Verger, 1957: 239)

Kokkalamma The goddess of coughs at Bangalore. Mysore, India. (Whitehead, 1916: 23)

kom si lom A demon who causes diseases in children. The Lepchas, Sikkim. (Siiger, 1967: 142)

rKong rje brang dkar A god, of black color, who causes fits of unconsciousness. Tibit. (Nebesky-Wojkowitz, 1956, 1: 274)

Kopea A minor evil god who causes sickness and lives in the underworld Te Matagi. Mangareva, Polynesia. (Buck, 1938, 1: 425)

Kukwobolitomi A spirit who causes miscarriages. The Sema Nagas, India. (Hutton, 1968: 198)

Kuladut ud Dungudungu A deity who steals "souls of rice and men, causing death" and illness, and loss of rice from the granary. He is also owner of game in the vicinity. The Ifugao, Philippines. (Barton, 1946: 85)

Kulbung ud Baiyun A deity who steals "souls of rice and men, causing death" and illness, and loss of rice from the granary. He is also the owner of game in the vicinity. The Ifugao, Philippines. (Barton, 1946: 86)

Kulde A nocturnal mountain deity who causes illness. The Ifugao, Philippines. (Barton, 1946: 82)

Kuleswari A goddess of "eruptive diseases," sister of Sitala. The Magahiyas, Gaya, India. (Briggs, 1953: 531)

Kumiyake A god of boils and abscesses—the "Itcher." The Ifugao, Philippines. (Barton, 1946: 65)

Kumobo A deity of dropsy, child of Sagala. Central Celebes, Indonesia. (Downs, 1920: 21)

Kure A god who causes headache and loss of soul, considered as a hyena. A red cock or red male goat is sacrificed to him. He is the son of Babban Maza and 'Inna; his wife is 'UwaRdawa. The Maguzawa, Nigeria. (Greenberg, 1946: 33)

Kwali, Ndawula God of smallpox. The Ganda, Uganda. (Mair, 1934: 234)

Kweraak Kutar "Blind-Old-Man" who is evil and the source of sickness. The Yuma, Arizona. (Harrington, 1908: 328)

u Kyrtep The devil who causes blindness. The Khasi, Assam. (Stegmiller, 1921: 411)

Labartu The "demon of accidental abortion." The Gypsies, Babylon, Near East. (Clebert, 1967: 195)

Lake jarub An evil spirit who causes chest pains. The Marshall Islands, Micronesia. (Erdland, 1914: 313)

Lalbai Phulbai "Dear flower lady"—a stone worshipped during cholera epidemics. India. (Crooke, 1925, 11: 874)

Lamashtu A Babylonian demoness (Lamme, Sumerian) who "destroyed children with plague." Daughter of Anu. Near East. (Langdon, 1931: 112, 358)

Lamdakbar An evil spirit who causes headache. The Marshall Islands. Micronesia. (Erdland, 1914: 313)

Lamkariya A goddess of disease and a sister of Sitala. India. (Crooke, 1894: 80; Briggs, 1920: 138)

Lango A god of disease except for epilepsy or demoniacal possession. A manifestation of Jok. The Lango, Uganda. (Driberg, 1923: 220)

Langteun-a-nyon A female devil who causes headache and eyeache. The Lepchas, Sikkim. (Gorer, 1938: 186)

Lanij A sky deity who causes the illness mijlan. The Marshall Islands, Micronesia. (Spoehr, 1949: 245)

Laolao ud Huminal A deity who steals "souls of rice and men, causing death" and illness, and loss of rice from the granary. Also owner of game in the vicinity. The Ifugao, Philippines. (Barton, 1946: 86)

u lasamdoh The devil who causes swelling of the joints and hoarseness. The Khasi, Assam. (Stegmiller, 1921: 411)

Lawulleb An evil spirit who causes headaches. The Marshall Islands, Micronesia. (Erdland, 1914: 313)

Leoij A sky deity who causes the illness mijlan. The Marshall Islands, Micronesia. (Spoehr, 1949: 245)

Leroro An evil spirit who punishes with coughing. The Marshall Islands, Micronesia. (Krämer and Nevermann, 1938: 237–238; Erdland, 1914: 313)

Lewa Levu A female cult spirit who inflicted disease as punishment for trespassing on the sacred ground. Fiji, Melanesia. (Spencer, 1941: 30)

Lha-mo, Dpal-ldan Lha-mo A malignant goddess, wife of Shinje, who controls and releases the demons of disease. Tibet. (Waddell, 1959: 364; Schlagintweit, 1969; 112; Hackin, 1963: 166; Sierksma, 1966: 163)

Lho moong A devil to be exorcised in illness through the Dumbu Soong ceremony. The Lepchas, Sikkim. (Gorer, 1938: 472)

Liaw   A deity of the Kankanay who inflicts with illness. Luzon, Philippines. (Vanoverbergh, 1972: 87)

Li Chi   "Overseer of Epidemics of the West." China. (Werner, 1932: 560)

Li Chi Szu   A god of disease—"Dysentery Controller." China. (Day, 1940: 205)

Lichoradka   "The demon of fever is believed to be one of the three, seven, twelve, or seventy-seven so-called Lichoradka-sisters." May be represented as young and beautiful or old and ugly. Offerings are made. White Russian. (Mansikka, 1925, 4: 625)

Lihaiyung   A god of headaches. The Ifugao, Philippines. (Barton, 1946: 66)

Lilyi   A demoness with the body of a fish and a human head causes catarrhal disease. Second child of Ana, and wife of Melalo. The Gypsies, Transylvania. (Clebert, 1967: 184; Trigg, 1973: 164)

Limbago   A zoomorphic spirit, a "long-necked quadruped, that carries sickness wherever he goes." The Bagobo, Philippines. (Benedict, 1916: 40)

Limsirwali   A malevolent spirit who causes diseases. The island of Keisar, the Moluccas, Indonesia. (Hartland, 1925, 4: 413)

Linihong   A god of headaches. The Ifugao, Philippines. (Barton, 1946: 66)

Loi   A deity who causes illness and possesses people. The Dinka and the Agar, Sudan. (Leinhardt, 1961: 56–57)

Lolmischo   A demon who causes eczema. Husband of Minceskro, son of Ana and the King of Devils. The Gypsies, Transylvania. (Clebert, 1967: 185; Trigg, 1973: 164)

Lom-doon moong   The devil of jaundice. The Lepchas, Sikkim. (Gorer, 1938: 479)

Loo moong   A devil who causes skin disease, wife of Sabdok. The Lepchas, Sikkim. (Gorer, 1938: 78)

Lu   A malignant and cannibalistic spirit who causes illness and death to ensure his food supply—corpses. He is propitiated with offerings during illness. The Red Karens, Burma. (Temple, 1925, 3: 25–26)

Lugal-gira   An aspect of Nergal as a god of pestilence and war. The Elamites, Near East. (Jastrow, 1898: 172; Pinches, 1925, 5: 251)

Luk   A god of disease and death and also a patron of thieves and robbers. He is "incarnate in the orra," a black night bird. Yap Islands, the Carolines, Micronesia. (Christian, 1899: 384–385)

Lum dong moong   A devil who causes illness and takes the form of a pig. The Lepchas, Sikkim. (Gorer, 1938: 221; Morris, 1938: 121)

Lupagan   A god of dysentery. The Ifugao, Philippines. (Barton, 1946: 63)

Lu T'ou She   "Six-Headed Snake Charm," a god of disease. China. (Day, 1940: 205)

Lu Yueh, Lu Yo   "President of the Ministry of Epidemics." China. (Werner, 1932: 298, 560)

Magali   A deity considered responsible for outbreaks of cholera, "represented by an upright stone." The Kotas, Southern India. (Thurston, 1909, 4: 13)

Magnad ud Dukligan   A deity which attacks the liver. The Ifugao, Philippines. (Barton, 1946: 65)

Mahadama   A village god, also called Daha-Pachcho, who inflicts epidemics and death, and to whom formerly human sacrifices were made. Oraon, India. (Roy, 1928: 15, 50, 52)

Mahakali   A form of Kali as "the cause of the prevalence of cholera." India. (Whitehead, 1916: 25)

Mahakola Sanniya Yaka   The "demon of delirious and convulsive states, the particularly hideous and powerful leader of the eighteen *sanni*, personifications of the terrible maladies they cause." Sri Lanka (Ceylon). (Ames, 1978: 46)

Mahari, Mariatha   Goddess of smallpox. The Irulas, the Neilgherries, India. (Shortt, 1868: 64)

Mahasona Yaka   The "great cemetery demon," who lies in wait for mourners at graveside rituals. He causes "cholera, smallpox, and dysentery." Sri Lanka (Ceylon). (Ames, 1978: 45)

Mai   God of sickness. Tahiti, Polynesia. (Henry, 1928: 213)

Maikiroa   One of those who controls diseases. The Maori, New Zealand. (Best, 1924: 105)

Maile   A spirit who causes dizziness and vertigo. Ponape, Caroline Islands, Micronesia. (Christian, 1899: 384)

Makaptan God of sickness. Husband of Sidapa with whom he rules the earth. The Bisayan, Central Panay, Philippines. (Jocano, 1969: 20)

Makasa A bush spirit who causes diarrhea. Wife of Jammarke. The Maguzawa, Nigeria. (Greenberg, 1946: 34)

Makialte A guardian of property and prestige, but also afflicts the liver. The Ifugao, Philippines. (Barton, 1946: 58)

Makibaba A guardian of property and prestige, but also afflicts the teeth. The Ifugao, Philippines. (Barton, 1946: 58)

Makibotli A guardian of property and prestige, but also afflicts the penis. The Ifugao, Philippines. (Barton, 1946: 58)

Makidapan A guardian of property and prestige, but also afflicts the feet. The Ifugao, Philippines. (Barton, 1946: 58)

Makigitang A guardian of property and prestige, but also afflicts the waist. The Ifugao, Philippines. (Barton, 1946: 58)

Makihoki A guardian of property and prestige, but also afflicts the legs. The Ifugao, Philippines. (Barton, 1946: 58)

Maki-inga A guardian of property and prestige, but also afflicts the ears. The Ifugao, Philippines. (Barton, 1946: 58)

Makilulug A guardian of property and prestige, but also afflicts the knees. The Ifugao, Philippines. (Barton, 1946: 58)

Makimata A guardian of property and prestige, but also afflicts the eyes. The Ifugao, Philippines. (Barton, 1946: 58)

Makinul A god of hunting who also attacks the liver. The Ifugao, Philippines. (Barton, 1946: 65)

Makitaglang A guardian of property and prestige, but also afflicts the side. The Ifugao, Philippines. (Barton, 1946: 58)

Maki-ulu A guardian of property and prestige, but also afflicts the head. The Ifugao, Philippines. (Barton, 1946: 58)

Makupu-ahi A lesser god of evil who caused illness, lived in the underworld Te Matagi. Mangareva, Polynesia. (Buck, 1938, 1: 425)

Malam 'Alhaji A Mohammedan spirit who causes cough. His wife is Sarawniya. The Hausa, Nigeria. (Greenberg, 1946: 63)

Mamahauwat, Mamahok, and **Mamatukul** Gods of dysentery. The Ifugao, Philippines. (Barton, 1946: 63)

hantu mambang The evil spirit of jaundice. Malaya. (Gimlette, 1929: 25)

Mamoo moong A female devil invoked in ceremonies to avert illness. The Lepchas, Sikkim. (Gorer, 1938: 229)

Mamoo Takloong A female devil exorcised in illness through the Dumbu Soong ceremony. The Lepchas, Sikkim. (Gorer, 1938: 472)

Ma mo sgam pa ma A goddess who causes illness. Tibet. (Nebesky-Wojkowitz, 1956, 1: 269–270)

Mamulul, and **Managad** Gods of dysentery. The Ifugao, Philippines. (Barton, 1946: 63)

Mangagaway A goddess who brought disease and death, an agent of Sitan. The Tagalog, Philippines. (Jocano, 1969: 11)

Mangalamai One of the six sisters of Sitala, goddesses of "eruptive diseases." The Magahiyas in Gaya (Doms), India. (Briggs, 1953: 531)

Maniktik, Manugub, and **Manulidang** Gods of dysentery. The Ifugao, Philippines. (Barton, 1946: 63, 64)

Manulit "Makes boring pains"—a god of dysentery. The Ifugao, Philippines. (Barton, 1946: 63)

Mapito-iti A lesser god of evil who causes sickness, lives in the underworld Te Matagi. Mangareva, Polynesia. (Buck, 1938, 1: 425)

Maraki A lesser goddess who causes cholera. Gujarat, India. (Crooke, 1894: 70)

Maramma Goddess of cholera in Mysore. India. (Whitehead, 1916: 23)

Marana ywa A male forest demon of the Tenetehara who is malevolent and causes illness and insanity, poor hunting and fishing. He is the owner of the forest and its animals and punishes those who overkill. Maranhão, Brazil. (Wagley and Galvão, 1949: 98, 102)

Mardi Deo God of cholera. Orissa, India. (Elwin, 1954: 639)

Marhai Mata The goddess of smallpox and cholera. The Kunbi and the Kurmi, Central Provinces, India. (Russell, 1916, 4: 38, 81)

Mari, Mariai, Mariamma Goddess of cholera, of smallpox, of epidemic diseases among many peoples in India. (Briggs, 1953: 535–536; Srinivas, 1952: 235; Whitehead, 1916: 26–28; Beals, 1964: 105; Ghurye, 1962: 243, 257; Thurston, 1902, 2: 385)

Mari Bhavani Brahman goddess of pestilence, of death. India. (Crooke, 1894: 94)

Maridamma, Maridiamma A malevolent goddess, the bringer of disease, who is propitiated during cholera epidemics. India. (Whitehead, 1916: 25; Hemingway, 1915: 48)

Marie-aimée A malevolent/benevolent goddess associated with disease, and a variant of Mariamma. Martinique, West Indies. (Horowitz, 1963: 340)

Mari Mai Goddess of cholera, "Mother of Death," a form of Kali among the Doms. She is worshipped as well "for good crops." India. (Briggs, 1953: 528, 530; Martin, 1914: 256)

Mari Mata The goddess of cholera in Berar who "regulates the spread of the disease." Also of the Banjara. India. (Crooke, 1894: 88; Russell, 1916, 2: 177)

Mariyattal The goddess of smallpox, sometimes also of cholera. The Paraiyans, Southern India. (Thurston, 1909, 6: 106)

Mariyayi The goddess of cholera. The Malayali, Southern India. (Thurston, 1909, 4: 431)

Maruta The "spirit of smallpox, receives special worship." The Tandan, Southern India. (Thurston, 1909, 7: 11)

Masan Among the Himalayan Doms the god of the graveyard and the burning ghats also causes disease. India. (Crooke, 1925, 4: 841; Briggs, 1953: 528–529)

Mata The goddess of smallpox and cholera to whom sacrifices are made. The Bhils, the Hos, the Bhunjia, and the Korku. India. (Elwin, 1954: 639; Majumdar, 1950: 277; Russell, 1916, 2: 327; 1916, 3: 559)

Mata Bangta The demon of cholera among the Bondo. India. (Elwin, 1950: 155)

Matangi Sakti, Matamgi A goddess of disease associated with smallpox. She takes numerous forms, e.g. Sitala Devi. India. (Crooke, 1894: 84; Briggs, 1953: 538, 471)

Matawali As an individual, or jointly with Herabe and Podadeli, causes "temporary or permanent insanity." The Huli, New Guinea. (Glasse, 1965: 35)

Maura Mata A goddess of disease who causes fits in children. The Baiga, India. (Elwin, 1939: 364)

Mayakutti A male evil spirit who inflicts "sickness, pain, misfortune." The Pulaya (Cochin), India. (Thaliath, 1956: 1034)

Mayavva A goddess propitiated by the people of Sivapur "to cure chicken pox and other childhood diseases." India. (Ishwaran, 1974: 30)

Mayramu A goddess who "causes a sickness in which the person's arms look as though they had been burnt in spots." The Maguzawa, Nigeria. (Greenberg, 1946: 39)

Mboli The supreme being and creator also causes disease and death. The Zande, Congo. (Williams, 1936: 119)

(Jero Gede) Mechaling The demon of cholera. Bali, Indonesia. (Franken, 1960: 38)

Mefitis The noxious earth vapours personified as a goddess and invoked for protection from them and attendant illnesses. Considered by some as male. Also invoked for cure when exposed. Italy. (Jayne, 1962: 463; Frazer, 1961: 204)

Melalo A demon who causes people to lose their reason, and at times, even to the violence of "rape and murder." He takes the form of a two-headed bird with "dirty green plumage;" is the eldest son of Ana and the King of Devils. His wife is Lilyi. The Gypsies, Transylvania. (Clebert, 1967: 184; Trigg, 1973: 164)

Mering Tandok The leader of the female group of smallpox demons. Malaya. (Gimlette, 1929: 88)

Mering Tanu The leader of the male group of smallpox demons. Malaya. (Gimlette, 1929: 88)

Migséxa-due Brother of Pain. The Cagaba and the Kogi. Colombia. (Reichel-Dolmatoff, 1949/50: 113)

Mi nag spres mgo can   One of the *bdud* gods who cause fits of unconsciousness. Tibet. (Nebesky-Wojkowitz, 1956, 1: 275)

Minceskro   A demoness who causes diseases of the blood. She is the daughter of Ana and the King of Devils; the wife of Lolmischo; the mother of the devils of smallpox, scarlet fever, measles. The Gypsies, Transylvania. (Clebert, 1967: 185–6; Trigg, 1973: 164–165)

Mindi   A serpent god who sends diseases. "Smallpox is called Mindi's dust; the scars Mindi's scales." Australia. (Bray, 1935: 233)

Mirgi Devi   Goddess of epilepsy. The Baiga, India. (Elwin, 1939: 364)

Miroi Deo   A stone god, a god of boundaries who is worshipped in times of sickness. Central Provinces, India. (Crooke, 1925, 11: 872)

Mohini Yakkhini   The female form of Kalu Kumara. "The succubus visits young bachelors at night, causing nocturnal emissions. She drives young men to distraction or hysteria." Sri Lanka (Ceylon). (Ames, 1978: 46)

Moko-Hae   The chief of the malevolent lizard gods who are responsible for internal ailments and racking pains. The Marquesas, Polynesia. (Christian, 1895: 190)

Mombakaiyauwan   A god who attacks the liver, and is also a minor deity of war. The Ifugao, Philippines. (Barton, 1946: 65, 75)

Mombalai-yi and **Monduntug**   Nocturnal mountain deities who cause illness. The Ifugao, Philippines. (Barton, 1946: 82)

Moreko-Turuiko   A high village deity—actually "a group of bonga—five brothers and six sisters" who are offered sacrifice at times of illness, of epidemics, and cattle disease. The Santal, Bihar, India. (Kochar, 1966: 246, 249)

Moti Mata   Pearl Mother—a stone worshipped during cholera epidemics. India. (Crooke, 1925, 11: 874)

Munekiachu   The "dog demon" who tries to interfere with parturition. The Cuna, Panama. (Nordenskiold, 1938: 370)

Murdo   The deity of smallpox of the Kandhs of Madras. India. (Crooke, 1925, 7: 651)

Mutai   A god who inflicts disease. Futuna Island, Polynesia. (Burrows, 1936: 107)

Mutnyam Chen   A "demon which causes shooting pains, shortness of breath, and pains in the heart." The Lepchas, Sikkim. (Morris, 1938: 145)

Mutua Deo   A minor disease godling who sends epidemics and fevers. Hoshangabad, India. (Crooke, 1894: 88)

Mutyalamma, Mathyalamma   The goddess of chicken pox, smallpox, and cholera who is worshipped to avert illness. The Telangana, the Koyi, the Konda Dora, and the Koya, India. (Mudiraj, 1970: 49; Thurston, 1909, 3: 355; 4: 58)

Mwawa   A god of evil who inflicts with smallpox. The Wakulwe and the Kuulwe, Tanzania. (Frazer, 1926: 194; Willis, 1966: 66)

sMyo kha'i mkhar nag zo ra   A god who is "apt to cause illnesses." Tibet. (Nebesky-Wojkowitz, 1956, 1: 305)

Nabinge   Among the Bakyiga the earthquake god is also associated with "the outbreak of plague or other sickness." Uganda. (Frazer, 1926: 425)

Nad-bdak Remati   A god of illness who is also invoked in divination. Sikkim and Tibet. (Gazeteer of Sikhim, 1894: 334; Waddell, 1959: 470)

Naga   A malignant river spirit who afflicts with diseases. The Milanow (Malanau) and the Land Dyaks, Borneo. (Roth, 1968: 166; De Crespigny, 1875: 35)

Na Gaha Yaka   A tree yaka, the na tree, who sends illness. The Sinhalese Vedda, Ceylon. (Seligmann and Seligmann, 1911: 170)

Nage-Era   Sister of Singbonga, who rescued two humans from his destructive wrath, and only gave them up on his promise to never again destroy man. She received as her share of mankind those "persons who might have leprous sores or marks on their bodies." Since then she has been known to cause leprosy and skin disease to increase her number. The Munda, India. (Elwin, 1949: 24, 412)

Naigamesa   A demon of disease who attacks children. India. (Jolly, 1925, 4: 753)

Naikin Bai   A goddess of disease who causes plagues to attack cattle. The Baiga, India. (Elwin, 1939: 364)

Nalongo   An important goddess who is invoked when epidemics strike. The Bosoga, Uganda. (Roscoe, 1915: 246)

Nalwun An evil spirit who lives in the veranda and causes sterility in women. The Chins, Burma. (Temple, 1925, 3: 25)

Namamdamma A village goddess who is worshipped to avert cholera and cattle disease and is offered a goat as sacrifice. The Kannadiyan, Southern India. (Thurston, 1909, 3: 214)

Namtar(u) The Akkadian/Assyro/Babylonian god of fate, of death; attacks the throat; is a god of the plague. He is the son of Enlil and Ereshkigal. Near East. (Kramer, 1961: 124; Langdon, 1931: 357, 364, 372; Larousse, 1968: 64; Sayce, 1898: 147, 306)

gNam the dkar po A god who brings illness. Tibet. (Nebesky-Wojkowitz, 1956, 1: 98)

gNam the'u dkar po An evil god causing ill-feeling, bad weather, and illness in children. Tibet. (Nebesky-Wojkowitz, 1956, 1: 283)

Nan Fang Ch'ang Szu "Southern Pestilence Demon." China. (Day, 1940: 206)

Naono An evil spirit who "lives in the wall, and causes fever and ague." The Chins, Burma. (Temple, 1925, 3: 25)

Napchut A malevolent spirit of the Ron-Rangs who is especially feared and who causes diseases. The Tangsas, India and Burma. (Dutta, 1959: 67)

Narayani Mai One of the six sisters of Sitala, goddesses of "eruptive diseases." The Magahiyas, Gaya; the Doms, India. (Briggs, 1953: 531)

Nason-kudra An evil spirit who must be propitiated to prevent him from bringing epidemics among men and cattle. The Santals, India. (Mukherjea, 1962: 281)

Nawang An evil spirit who causes stomach pains, vomiting, and diarrhea. He also preys on the souls of the dead. The Garo, Assam. (Playfair, 1909: 82)

Ndaulo God of smallpox. The Banyoro, Uganda. (Roscoe, 1915: 91)

Negra A minor disease godling—of indigestion. Chaibasa, Bibar, India. (Crooke, 1894: 87)

Nen'vetgyyn'yn A harmful deity of the Koryaks who caused weakness and disease in men. Siberia. (Antropova, 1964: 868)

Nergal A god of destruction—of pestilence and death, of war and of fire. He is usually associated with the planet Mars. He became god of the underworld in marrying Ereshkigal. Akkadia, Assyria, Babylonia, and Sumer, Near East. (Seligmann, 1948: 30; Jastrow, 1898: 66–67, 459; Cook, 1930: 121; Bhattacharji, 1970: 64; Schoeps, 1961: 58)

Nerra Babylonian god of plague, identified with Nergal. Near East. (Sayce, 1898: 206, 372)

Ngulete A malevolent god who causes illness but can be appeased. Sometimes used as a general term for evil spirits. The Kakwa, Sudan. (Huntingford, 1953: 55; Mbiti, 1970, 2: 125)

Ni An important deity who causes leprosy. Son of Honabe and Timbu. The Huli, New Guinea. (Glasse, 1965: 33–35)

Nia Kilu A great devil of disease. The Cuna, Panama. (Keeler, 1960: 87)

ka niangriang A demoness who causes illnesses in children, "especially in the navel." The Khasi, Assam. (Stegmiller, 1921: 411)

Nia Poni Ekwali A disease devil of the Cuna Indians. Panama. (Keeler, 1960: 89)

Nia Poni Kwentuli A disease devil of the Cuna Indians. Panama. (Keeler, 1960: 89)

Níaprúakálet A wind demon who causes insanity. The Cuna, Panama. (Nordenskiold, 1930: 60–61)

Nia Siren A disease devil of the Cuna, Panama. (Keeler, 1960: 87)

Nia Tusi A disease devil who causes boils and carbuncles. The Cuna, Panama. (Keeler, 1960: 89)

Nipong A malignant spirit who causes diseases of women "and attacks men also with haemorrhage and colic, which cause the sufferer to roll about like a woman in travail." The Abor, Tibet and India. (Crooke, 1925, 1: 33)

Nokpi An evil spirit who lives in the veranda and causes sterility in women. The Chins, Burma. (Temple, 1925, 3: 25)

Nomkubulwane A goddess of the heavens who afflicts people with sickness and must be propitiated. The Swazi, Swaziland. (Pettersson, 1953: 187)

Nukalamma A goddess worshipped to avert sickness, smallpox. Southern India. (Thurston, 1909, 2: 446; Francis, 1907: 74)

Nuñda The moon is considered to cause blindness. The Cherokee, North Carolina and Tennessee. (Mooney and Olbrechts, 1932: 22)

Nunv The god of leprosy of the district of Langch'u T'u-ssu. Southwest China. (Rock, 1947: 433)

Nurbia An Etruscan "spirit of disease, who is invoked while preparing the stone of health, or a pebble used to cure rheumatism." Italy. (Leland, 1963: 135)

Nu She "Female Snake Charm," a goddess of disease. China. (Day, 1940: 205)

Nyambi The creator god to whom the souls return at death. He permits the people to be afflicted with *mandengure*, an illness and a form of madness, and the *mandengure* ceremony is performed to alleviate and cure it. The Hambukushu, Ngamiland, Botswana. (Larson, 1971: 57–60)

Obá A minor disease godling of cholera, of pestilence. Same as Mari Bhavani. Mirzapur, India. (Crooke, 1894: 94)

Odichathan, Odikali, and **Odimaya** Male evil spirits who cause illness. The Pulaya (Cochin), India. (Thaliath, 1956: 1044)

Odyne The personification of pain—female. Greece. (Roscher, 1965, 3, 1: 602)

ogan'elu The spirit of smallpox, important during epidemics. The Igbo, Nigeria. (Uchendu, 1965: 100)

Ojuku A god of smallpox of the Ibo. Nigeria. (Parrinder, 1949: 44)

Ola Bibi, Ola Chandi Goddess of cholera. Bengal. (Crooke, 2936, 3: 485)

O le nifo loa A "disease-making god." Samoa, Polynesia. (Turner, 1884: 41)

Omaha An evil power "possessing the shape of a grizzly bear, is invisible, . . . bringing sickness and misfortune on mankind." Trinity River area, California. (Bancroft, 1886, 3: 176)

Omarari God of the bubonic plague, an aspect of Jok. The Lango, Uganda. (Driberg, 1923: 221)

Omauwa One of the first beings who, after the flood, "became an enemy to the Yanomamo. Today he sends hiccups, sickness, and epidemics." Venezuela and Brazil. (Chagnon, 1968: 47)

Omolu, Omoulou God of smallpox and of contagious diseases. Bastide says that he has gradually become a god of medicine. He is the son of Nana and Oshala. His wife is Oba. He is identified with the noonday sun and with St. Lazarus and St. Rocque. Bahia, Brazil. (Bastide, 1960: 570, 355; Verger, 1954: 15; Landes, 1940: 264–266)

Osaka A goddess who caused stomach ailments because people were using her grove for burials. When they stopped the illnesses ceased. The Effutu, Ghana. (Wyllie, 1966: 479)

Osanoha Creator of animals and also of diseases; evil counterpart of Osanowa. The Edo, Benin, Nigeria. (Frazer, 1926: 126–7)

Paduka A malevolent ancestor spirit who brings illness. He also "taught them their ritual." The Kankanay, Luzon, Philippines. (Vanoverbergh, 1972: 79)

Pai Hu Shang Szu Chinese demon of pestilence. (Day, 1940: 44)

Påkaprúakálet A wind demon who causes illness. "When a person is delirious and sees a ship, or something pertaining to the sea, then this demon is at the root of it." The Cuna, Panama. (Nordenskiold, 1930: 60–61)

Pakoro Kamui, Pa-kor-kamui As an individual the God of Pestilence, of smallpox, of cholera, and chief of the pestilence gods, the *pa-kor-kamui,* who "come in the form of flocks of little birds." They are also called the Traveling Gods. Pakoro Kamui is also called Oripak Kamui. The Ainu, Japan. (Philippi, 1982: 63, 202, 204, 371; Munro, 1963: 25)

Pan-chen Goddess of scarlet fever. China. (Day, 1940: 93)

Pansahi Mata Goddess of smallpox who attacks "children under the age of seven." Bengal. (Crooke, 1925, 2: 485)

Pan Shen God of black smallpox. China. (Maspero, 1963: 361; Werner, 1932: 354)

Pari A demon who "fastens upon the wound and sucks the blood, and this is the cause of the blood's flowing." The Mantra, Malay Peninsula. (Skeat, 1906: 324)

Pa T'ou She "Eight-Headed Snake Charm," a god of disease. China. (Day, 1940: 205)

Pauchi Kamui A deity "held responsible for gastralgia, food poisoning, insanity, and epidemics of frenzied dancing," as well as for psychological troubles. The Ainu, Japan. (Munro, 1963: 25, 102)

payekai kamui A name of the *pa-kor-kamui* (pestilence gods) as the Traveling Gods. The Ainu, Japan. (Philippi, 1982: 240)

Pazuzu Babylonian " 'Lord of the wind demons,' spreading fever and cold and other disease." Son of Hanpa. Near East. (Langdon, 1931: 371; Bray, 1935: 152)

Pei Fang Ch'ang Szu "Northern Pestilence Demon." China. (Day, 1940: 206)

hantu pekak The evil spirit of deafness. Malaya. (Gimlette, 1929: 25)

Pharka Undharan Mata A goddess of disease. The Baiga, India. (Elwin, 1939: 365)

Phoki Mata A goddess of disease who inflicts dysentery upon the cattle. The Baiga, India. (Elwin, 1939: 365)

Phulmata Goddess of smallpox who attacks "children under the age of seven." Bengal. (Crooke, 1925, 2: 485)

Phulmati A goddess of disease who inflicts a mild form of smallpox. Younger sister of Sitala. India. (Briggs, 1920: 138; Crooke, 1894: 81)

Pinahikangan and **Pinatitan** Gods of dysentery. The Ifugao, Philippines. (Barton, 1946: 63)

Pirah A minor evil spirit who causes eye diseases. The Dafla tribes, Assam. (Stonor, 1957: 7)

Pishuni, Pishumi An evil spirit who brings disease and also temptations. The Acoma, Pueblo Indians, New Mexico. (Stirling, 1942: 12, 28; Burland, 1965: 150)

Piti The "rheum-spirit"—male. The Chukchee, Siberia. (Bogoras, 1904/09: 297)

Plague-amma A deity worshipped and propitiated for protection from cattle plague. India. (Whitehead, 1916: 16)

Pochamma Goddess of smallpox. The Telangana, India. (Mudiraj, 1970: 49)

Podadeli A god who, individually or in conjunction with Matawali and Herabe, causes insanity. The Huli, New Guinea. (Glasse, 1965: 35)

Polamde A disease godling, sister of Sitala, who "makes the patient soft or flabby." India. (Crooke, 1894: 80)

Poleramma A boundary goddess, but also a goddess of smallpox among the Telugu. India. (Elmore, 1915: 18–19; Whitehead, 1916: 22)

Polibogi One of the Dahomean names of the god of smallpox. Brazil. (Bastide, 1960: 571)

hantu polong An evil spirit of many diseases. Malaya. (Gimlette, 1929: 51)

Poni Machi Olotewikinya A disease devil of the Cuna Indians. Panama. (Keeler, 1960: 89)

Poreskoro A hermaphroditic deity, born of the Queen of Fairies and the King of Devils, who causes epidemics of plague, cholera, and also parasitical diseases; depicted with "four cat's heads and four dog's heads, with a tail like a snake with a forked tongue." The Gypsies, Transylvania. (Clebert, 1967: 186; Trigg, 1973: 165)

Poxlom, Pozlom A Mayan god "seemingly of disease." The Tzeltal, Mexico. (Thompson, 1970: 325)

Prom The god of diseases of the Daphla. Bengal and Assam. (Crooke, 1925, 4: 399)

Pufine ma Twin goddesses, Mafurere and Nau Taufiti, of disease and evil. Korokoro, Tikopia, Polynesia. (Firth, 1967, 1: 85, 90)

Pujio A water demon who keeps the soul of a man and causes disease and illness. Bolivia and Argentina. (Chamberlain, 1925, 4: 740)

Pulit A god of dysentery of the Ifugao, Philippines. (Barton, 1946: 63)

Pumagang A god of dysentery and also of a "condition in which food will not stay on the stomach." The Ifugao, Philippines. (Barton, 1946: 63)

Pumihdol A god of boils and abscesses. The Ifugao, Philippines. (Barton, 1946: 64–65)

Pumilangat A god of boils and abscesses who inflicts "Redness of Inflammation." The Ifugao, Philippines. (Barton, 1946: 57, 65)

Pumsang A malevolent spirit who causes evil—"hits the brain." The Mosangs of the Tangsas, India and Burma. (Dutta, 1959: 67)

Pumtu A deity who inflicts stomach trouble, but who is also a guardian of property and prestige. The Ifugao, Philippines. (Barton, 1946: 57)

Pumupud A god of childbirth who "blocks the passage of the foetus." The Ifugao, Philippines. (Barton, 1946: 87)

Pungal An evil anito who "causes sickness and death." The Apayao, Philippines. (Wilson, 1947: 23)

Putu A god who afflicts with "Flux." The Ifugao, Philippines. (Barton, 1946: 70)

sPyi phyir phur byed A god who causes fits of unconsciousness. Tibet. (Nebesky-Wojkowitz, 1956, 1: 275)

Pyretos Greek deity of fevers. Same as Febris. (Roscher, 1965, 3, 2: 3345)

Rahabasin Mata A goddess of disease who causes illness from fear. The Baiga, India. (Elwin, 1939: 365)

Raja Puru, Raja Peres God of diseases and epidemics, but is also credited with having taught men their crafts. The Ngaju, Borneo. (Scharer, 1963: 20–21, 52)

Rak The demon of cholera. The Sakai, Malay Peninsula. (Skeat, 1906: 288)

Rakat Soka A godling, male, "who is the enemy of children, drinking their blood, and making them grow weak." Central Provinces, India. (Russell, 1925, 3: 314)

Raksin Mata A goddess of disease who "causes itch with large sores." The Baiga, India. (Elwin, 1939: 365)

Rangren A malevolent spirit of the Ron-Rangs who causes fever and headache. The Tangsas, India and Burma. (Dutta, 1959: 67)

Rašap "Flame"—a god of pestilence. His name "may very possibly be the high fever which accompanies many epidemic diseases." Asia Minor. (Roberts, 1972: 48)

Rathu A deity who causes pains in the neck. The Savara, Southern India. (Thurston, 1909, 6: 333)

Raxie A god of the Male Paharias who is invoked in times of epidemics. India. (Crooke, 1925, 5: 13)

Reshef, Resheph A god of the underworld who destroyed men through plague and pestilence and war—a god of mass destruction. Canaan and Phoenicia, Near East. (Gray, 1969: 81–82; 1964: 123; Vriezen, 1963: 52; Albright, 1968: 139)

Ricana A goddess who causes eye infections to whom a "black chicken with gray neck" is sacrificed. The Maguzawa, Nigeria. (Greenberg, 1946: 32)

ka Rih The female devil of malarial fever. The Khasis and the Syntengs, Assam. (Gurdon, 1914: 107)

Riri Yaka The "blood demon" is a grave robber, devouring bodies, and "is thought to cause fevers, stomach pains, headaches, and hysteria, and is associated with diseases and injuries that result in loss of blood." Sri Lanka (Ceylon). (Ames, 1978: 45)

Rota, Ruto, Rutu An evil god of disease and of torment, of death and of the underworld. He is propitiated during epidemics. The Lapps, Northern Europe. (Pettersson, 1957: 9, 132, 152; Dioszegi, 1968: 30; Karsten, 1955: 40, 53; Holmberg, 1925, 7: 798; MacCulloch, 1964: 75–76)

Ršp The "power of pestilence and death." Canaan, Near East. (Gray, 1957: 137)

Rugo Deity of cholera. The Kandhs, Madras, India. (Crooke, 1925, 7: 651)

Sabdok moong As an individual he can cause lack of sons; his wife is Loo moong. As a multiple deity, devils who cause skin disease. The Lepchas, Sikkim. (Gorer, 1938: 77–78, 231)

Sagala The god of smallpox of Central Celebes. Indonesia. (Downs, 1920: 20)

Sagbata God of smallpox. As the eldest son of Mawu and Lisa he is a sky god, but in descending to the earth became an earth god and the head of the Earth Pantheon, all of whom are identified with smallpox. Dahomey. In Brazil he is an earth god and god of smallpox. (Herskovits, 1938, 2: 129, 135–136; Howells, 1948: 226–227; Bastide, 1960: 571)

Saiol A "sea-spirit who inflicts sea-sickness." Ifalik, Micronesia. (Burrows, 1947/48: 11)

sak cum (tsum) sak par A demon who brings illness to children. The Lepchas, Sikkim. (Siiger, 1967: 144)

Sakngam A disease spirit who causes stomach trouble. The Tangsas, India and Burma. (Dutta, 1959: 67)

Sakpata   A variant of Sagbata.

Salar   A demon of disease. The Mantra, Malay Peninsula. (Skeat, 1906: 324)

Sangkoi   A malevolent spirit of diseases. The Tangsas, India and Burma. (Dutta, 1959: 67)

Sankata   One of the six sisters of Sitala, goddesses of "eruptive diseases." The Magahiyas, Gaya, India. (Briggs, 1953: 531)

Sansari Mai   An earth goddess and a goddess of thieves. Among the Doms of Gaya she is identified with Jagadamba as a goddess of smallpox. India. (Briggs, 1953: 530; Keane, 1925, 2: 123)

San T'ou She   "Three-Headed Snake Charm," a god of disease. China. (Day, 1940: 205)

Sapata   A variant of Sagbata.

sap dok a mu   A demon of skin diseases and itching as well as of death. The Lepchas, Sikkim. (Siiger, 1967: 144)

Sarawniya   A female spirit who causes "impotence in men; cessation of menstruation in women." She is the wife of Malam 'Alhaji. The Maguzawa, Nigeria. (Greenberg, 1946: 37)

Sarisano   A god of evil who is propitiated as the sender of diseases. Formosa. (Campbell, 1925, 6: 84)

Sarkin 'Aljan   "King of the jinn" who causes headache. Human sacrifices were made to him in some tribes. The Maguzawa, Nigeria. (Greenberg, 1946: 29, 30)

Sarkin Ruwa   A water spirit who causes ear illnesses. The Maguzawa, Nigeria. (Greenberg, 1946: 36)

Sat Matra   A stone deity, "mother of truth," who was worshipped with offerings at outbreaks of cholera. India. (Crooke, 1925, 5: 12)

Satvai   The goddess of smallpox of the Mahars. India. (Briggs, 1953: 533)

Scabies   Supposedly the personification of itching skin diseases and invoked for relief. A questionable Roman goddess. (Jayne, 1962: 463–464)

Schilalyi   A white mouse demon, daughter of Ana, who causes colds and fever. She is the wife of Bitoso. Trigg cites as male and spells it Schilayi. The Gypsies, Transylvania. (Clebert, 1967: 185; Trigg, 1973: 164)

Sedhu Lala   A disease god associated with Sitala. India. (Crooke, 1894: 80)

bSe'i skyes bu shogs can sdud   A god who causes fits of unconsciousness. Tibet. (Nebesky-Wojkowitz, 1956, 1: 275)

Sekhmet   A lion-headed goddess who caused and cured epidemics. She had other capacities as a goddess of healing, of bone-setters, as well as being a goddess of war and of vengeance. She is generally associated with Ptah. Egypt. (Casson, 1965: 73, 75; Schoeps, 1961: 70; Jayne, 1962: 76; Ames, 1965: 101–102)

Selday   A god who causes sore feet and must be propitiated for relief. He will also send severe illness to the village if a piglet's blood is not offered him at the open gravesite. The Tinguian, Philippines. (Cole, 1922: 300)

Selu   A malicious water spirit who causes stomachache as well as other misfortunes. The Dafla tribes, Assam. (Stonor, 1957: 6)

Shang Yen Ta Shen   A god of sudden heart failure. China. (Day, 1940: 43)

Shankpana, Shopona, Shapana   God of smallpox and of the earth. When called Olode he is beneficial, preserving the seed. The Yoruba, Nigeria. In Brazil, as Shapana(n) (same as Sagbata), he is god of all skin diseases which he also cures. (Idowu, 1962: 47, 95; Meek, 1925, 2: 29; Parrinder, 1949: 41; Morton-Williams, 1964: 251; Costa Eduardo, 1948: 82)

Sha Shen   A god of disease, of measles, of scarlatina, headache, indigestion, who is invoked and called "Cholera Controller." China. (Werner, 1932: 408; Day, 1940: 205; Maspero, 1963: 361)

Sher moong   A male devil to be exorcised in illness through the Dumbu Soong ritual. The Lepchas, Sikkim. (Gorer, 1938: 472, 476)

Shih Hsiang Kung   A god of disease "considered very effective in general cures." China. (Day, 1940: 39, 205)

Shook-sor moong   A devil who causes heart pain but cannot kill humans, only animals. The Lepchas, Sikkim. (Gorer, 1938: 407)

Shopona, Sopona   The god of smallpox. The Yoruba, Nigeria. *See also* **Shankpana.** (Johnson, 1921: 28; Forde, 1951: 30; Morton-Williams, 1964: 251n)

Shumaikoli The supernatural dragonfly. Among the Zuñi believed to cause children to have sore eyes. Among the Hano and Laguna Indians, the "kachina of blindness or deformity." New Mexico. (Parsons, 1939: 191, 208)

ka shwar A demoness who causes convulsive cramps. The Khasi, Assam. (Stegmiller, 1921: 411)

Siag A malignant spirit of fever and ague. The Malanau (Milanow) and the Land Dyaks, Borneo. (Roth, 1968: 166; De Crespigny, 1875: 35)

u Siem niang thylliew, u siem thylliew The god of smallpox, "not . . . appeased in any way." The Khasi, Assam. (Gurdon, 1914: 108; Stegmiller, 1921: 411)

Simungala, or Ilimingala A demon who causes destruction by locusts, and smallpox and epidemics. The Sukuma-Nyamwezi, Tanzania. (Mbiti, 1970, 2: 119–120)

Singi-Arke The proper name of Mahaprabhu, the supreme being. He is "not entirely benevolent," as he may cause high fever and convulsions in children. The Bondo, India. (Elwin, 1950: 133–135, 144)

Sipsang A malevolent spirit who causes fever and to whom sacrifices are made. The Tangsas, India and Burma. (Dutta, 1959–67)

Sitala The goddess of smallpox may cause it or protect from it. She is an ambivalent and powerful goddess capable of "pestilence and mindless destruction," but also of providing "life-giving reassurance through her *pervasive presence*" if her ambivalence is fully accepted, and may bring blessings and rebirth. She is also known as Jag Rani, Maha Mai, Jagadamba, Phapholewali, Kalejewali, Ugali Mata, Thandi. Her sisters are variously given as: Masani, Basanti, Maha Mai, Polamde, Lamkariya, Agwani—or Phulmati, Chamariya, Durga Kali, Maha Kali, Bhadra Kali. India. (Crooke, 1894: 69–82; Martin, 1914: 253–254; Ions, 1967: 97; Russell, 1916, 2: 159; O'Flaherty, 1980: 279–280)

Sitla Mata The smallpox deity who must be propitiated with offerings. Kashmir. (Lawrence, 1895: 264)

Sitsang A malevolent spirit who causes pain. The Mosangs of the Tangsas, India and Burma. (Dutta, 1959: 67)

Si Wang Mu Goddess of the West. As an ancient deity she was a goddess of epidemics who could also avert or cure them. China. (Maspero, 1963: 382; Mackenzie, 1924: 217)

Sonsang A malevolent spirit who causes headache. The Mosangs of the Tangsas, India and Burma. (Dutta, 1959: 67)

Sonsi Deity of chickenpox, child of Sagala. Central Celebes, Indonesia. (Downs, 1920: 21)

Sor moong A female devil who causes illness, miscarriage, and violent death. The Lepchas, Sikkim. (Gorer, 1938: 221, 232, 285)

Sorisi The god of chickenpox. Son of Woeadja. The Toradja, Celebes, Indonesia. (Adriani & Kruyt, 1950: 205)

Sotu The god of dumbness. The Daphla, Bengal and Assam. (Crooke, 1925, 4: 399)

Sowa-Sowa A devil who causes chills. The Cuna Indians, Panama. (Keeler, 1960: 89)

u 'suid briew, u 'suid ngon The "devil who attacks people in the early morning and causes stitches in the side or hoarseness." The Khasi, Assam. (Stegmiller, 1921: 411)

u 'suid-kynta-maram The "devil who makes headaches." The Khasi, Assam. (Stegmiller, 1921: 411)

u 'suid-um A water devil who causes sterility and miscarriage in women. The Khasi, Assam. (Stegmiller, 1921: 411)

Sukhajamma A goddess of smallpox and measles with a shrine at Bangalore, Mysore. India. (Whitehead, 1916: 23)

gSum brag ma An evil lake goddess who causes dysentery. Tibet. (Nebesky-Wojkowitz, 1956, 1: 307)

Sunchoremene Greek deity of smallpox who is also called Eulogia. (Crooke, 1894: 78)

Sunkalamma A goddess of measles and smallpox worshipped in the Cuddapah, Kurnool, and Bellary Districts. India. (Whitehead, 1916: 73, 77)

Susime A goddess associated with the moon who causes, as well as cures, blindness and lameness. The Garo, Assam. (Playfair, 1909: 82–83)

Suzaubañ The rainbow, a female demon, was charged by Gauteóvañ with "the task of devouring all sicknesses. She herself also represents sickness and with it the fever-heat related to fire." The Kagaba, Colombia. (Preuss, 1926: 65)

Swen A demon who causes convulsions. The Mantra, Malay Peninsula. (Skeat, 1906: 324)

ka syrtieh A "demoness, who cuts and scratches and files and saws, i.e., through inner pains." The Khasi, Assam. (Stegmiller, 1921: 422)

Szu T'ou She "Four-Headed Snake Charm," a god of disease. China. (Day, 1940: 205)

Tabla A "god of wealth and disease." The Mishmis, Assam. (Crooke, 1925, 8: 697)

Tabungao and **Tabuyug-na** Gods of boils and abscesses. The Ifugao, Philippines. (Barton, 1946: 65)

sTag mgo can A god who causes fits of unconsciousness. Tibet. (Nebesky-Wojkowitz, 1956, 1: 275)

tak pu A demon who causes genital diseases. The Lepchas, Sikkim. (Siiger, 1967: 145)

ta kra A demon who causes venereal diseases. The Lepchas, Sikkim. (Siiger, 1967: 145)

Talapi A spirit who caused contagious diseases. Central Celebes, Indonesia. (Downs, 1920: 30)

Tamaki, Hangatamaki A god who afflicted with disease. Uvea, Polynesia. (Burrows, 1937: 85)

ka Taroh A demoness believed to cause delirium. The Khasis and the Syntengs, Assam. (Gurdon, 1914: 107)

Tcaridyi A demoness, daughter of Ana, who has the form of a "small hairy worm." She penetrates the body causing "burning fevers, and especially puerperal fever to women in childbirth." Wife of Tculo. The Gypsies, Transylvania. (Clebert, 1967: 185; Trigg, 1973: 164)

Tculo A demon, son of Ana and the King of Devils. He looks "like a little ball covered with prickles and would enter the human stomach to bring about violent pains, especially in pregnant women." His wife is Tcaridyi. The Gypsies, Transylvania. (Clebert, 1967: 185; Trigg, 1973: 164)

Teggi The spirit of the cough. The Chukchee, Siberia. (Bogoras, 1904/09: 297)

Tegha-aghuzuwu God of delirium. The Sema Nagas, India. (Hutton, 1968: 198)

Tena-ranide The "Spirit of Plague . . . Death itself." The Tinne (northern Athapascan), Canada. (Alexander, 1964: 78)

Te-oho-o-te-ku'a The deity of leprosy. The Marquesas, Polynesia. (Handy, 1923: 247)

Tertiana A goddess of three-day recurrent fever. Britain. (Roscher, 1965, 5: 392)

Thakurani Bakorani, Thakurani Mata The goddess of "smallpox and rinderpest" who is offered flowers and incense when these illnesses are "prevalent among men and cattle," but is abused if the epidemic is not alleviated. The Gadbas and the Bondo. India. (Elwin, 1950: 155; Russell, 1916, 3: 11)

Theng-thon A god who is considered responsible for recurrent illnesses—"he is propitiated with a goat and a pig, or two or three fowls." The Mikirs, India. (Stack and Lyall, 1908: 32)

thung cu (tsu) lom A demon who afflicts children with disease. The Lepchas, Sikkim. (Siiger, 1967, 2: 66, 145)

u thynrai A demon who causes illness to worsen. The Khasi, Assam. (Stegmiller, 1921: 411)

T'ien Po-hsüeh A god of epidemics, one of the Wu Yüeh. China. (Werner, 1934: 242)

ka tihar A demoness who causes severe colic. The Khasi, Assam. (Stegmiller, 1921: 411)

Ti'ipa A god who caused barrenness in women. He was also considered a god of the winds. Tahiti, Polynesia. (Henry, 1928: 377; Williamson, 1933, 1: 142)

Tilo A god of the heavens, an impersonal power who is associated with misfortunes—the birth of twins (a calamity), convulsions and other illnesses, with storms, hail, locusts, and the control of life and death. Various Tonga tribes, South Africa and Mozambique. (Schapera, 1937: 263; Smith, 1950: 113–114; Pettersson, 1953: 180, 189, 191)

Timbalung A mountain spirit who brings diseases of the belly. The Bagobo, Philippines. (Benedict, 1916: 39)

Tinamatam A headache deity "referring probably to deranged or defective vision." The Ifugao, Philippines. (Barton, 1946: 66)

Tinikmal A god of headaches. The Ifugao, Philippines. (Barton, 1946: 66)

Tipi A nocturnal mountain deity who causes illness. The Ifugao, Philippines. (Barton, 1946: 82)

Todtod-o A spirit of retching. The Kankanay, Luzon, Philippines. (Vanoverbergh, 1972: 87)

Tonga-hiti God of headache. The Maori, New Zealand. (Andersen, 1928: 164)

Toringka A name of the Pox Spirit. Others: Woeadja, Karambaoe. Celebes, Indonesia. (Adriani and Kruyt, 1950: 204)

Tororut God of the sky, the supreme being, who sends diseases of cattle as punishment for sins. The Suk, Kenya. (Pettazzoni, 1956: 6; Beech, 1911: 19)

Tou-Chen Goddess of smallpox. China. (Day, 1940: 93)

Tou Shen, Tou Hua Wu Sheng God and controller of smallpox and measles. China. (Day, 1940: 205; Werner, 1932: 40)

Tou-shen Niang-niang Goddess of smallpox. She is also "especially charged with the punishment of infanticide." China. (Werner, 1932: 512; Maspero, 1963: 361)

Tow A malignant spirit of the woods who afflicts with diseases. The Milanow (Malanau) and the Land Dyaks, Borneo. (Roth, 1968: 166; De Crespigny, 1875: 35)

Tsa A mountain demon who roams about dispersing illness if not propitiated. The Nda-pa, Yung-ning, China. (Rock, 1959: 804)

Ts'ai Wên-chü A god of epidemics, one of the Wu Yüeh. China. (Werner, 1934: 242)

Tsakan A water demon who causes illness. The Coras, Mexico. (Chamberlain, 1925, 4: 740)

bTsan mgo dmar po A god who causes fits of unconsciousness. Tibet. (Nebesky-Wojkowitz, 1956, 1: 275)

bTsan po phung kha nag po A god of the retinue of Pe har, of the rgyal po class of illness-bringing deities. Tibet. (Nebesky-Wojkowitz, 1956, 1: 128)

Tshuma A "female personification of the plague" who takes the form of an owl. Russia. (Roheim, n.d.: 75)

Tsi'u dmar po An important protective deity, guardian of Samye. He causes illness and madness among enemies. His wife is lHa mo hrol mo spyan gcig ma. Tibet. (Nebesky-Wojkowitz, 1956, 1: 95, 167)

Tung Fang Ch'ang Szu "Eastern Pestilence Demon." China. (Day, 1940: 206)

Tung Hung-wên A god of epidemics, one of the Wu Yüeh. China. (Werner, 1934: 242)

Tung She "Winter Snake Charm," a god of disease. China. (Day, 1940: 205)

Turua A forest spirit who sometimes causes hemorrhaging and serious illness. The Xingu River area Indians. Brazil. (Villas Boas, 1973: 269)

Ubag A zoomorphic spirit, a horse with a hump, who causes mortal illness. The Bagobo, Philippines. (Benedict, 1916: 40)

Ubanan A nocturnal mountain deity who causes illness. The Ifugao, Philippines. (Barton, 1946: 82)

Uddyo-na A god of boils and abscesses. The Ifugao, Philippines. (Barton, 1946: 65)

Ujali Mata A goddess of disease, a name of Sitala Mata in the Muzaffarnagar District. India. (Briggs, 1920: 137)

Ukuk A god who afflicts with consumption. The Ifugao, Philippines. (Barton, 1946: 70)

Ulu A god of headache. The Ifugao, Philippines. (Barton, 1946: 70)

Ululok-na and **Umaladang** Gods of dysentery. The Ifugao, Philippines. (Barton, 1946: 63)

Umariya Mata A goddess of cholera. The Chamars, India. (Briggs, 1920: 136)

Uminga A god of boils and abscesses. The Ifugao, Philippines. (Barton, 1946: 65)

Umlenzengamuye A one-legged sky god who appears rarely and only for women. He comes in the mist and causes fevers, is sacrificed to and propitiated. The Swazi, Swaziland. (Pettersson, 1953: 180, 188; Smith, 1950: 111)

Ura Babylonian god of the plague. Near East. (Thompson, 1903: xlvii)

Urom A malignant spirit who attacks at night causing stomach pains and headaches. The Abor, Tibet and India. (Crooke, 1925, 1: 33)

Ushnu A male evil spirit who inflicts "sickness, pain, misfortune." The Pulaya (Cochin), India. (Thaliath, 1956: 1034)

Ututog-na   A god of dysentery and retching. The Ifugao, Philippines. (Barton, 1946: 63)

Uusibugua   The spirit of illness lives in the sea. The Cuna, Panama. (Nordenskiold, 1938: 403)

'UwaRdaw   "Mother of all the forest spirits." She causes paralysis and "a red childless she-goat" is sacrificed to her. She is the wife of Kure. The Maguzawa, Nigeria. (Greenberg, 1946: 33)

Vajrapani   A celestial Bodhisat who "saves from accident and bodily injury." Tibet. (Waddell, 1959: 414)

Vammatar   "Finno-Ugric goddess of pain and disease." (Larousse, 1968: 306)

Varuna   The god of righteousness finds a place in this category as the sender of fever and dropsy as punishment for sins; is invoked for their relief. India. (Jolly, 1925, 4: 754; Jayne, 1962: 177–178)

Vayaravan   A male evil spirit who inflicts "sickness, pain, misfortune." The Pulaya (Cochin), India. (Thaliath, 1956: 1034)

Vihara Deyo   A spirit believed to send sickness and invoked for renewed health. The Sinhalese Vedda, Ceylon. (Seligmann and Seligmann, 1911: 176)

Wade   A forest spirit who causes swelling, to whom a dwarf cock is sacrificed. Son of Kure and 'UwaRdawa. The Maguzawa, Nigeria. (Greenberg, 1946: 34)

Wamala   The first son of Musisi is associated with conjunctivitis and is invoked in times of sickness and plague, whether of men or animals. Uganda. (Kagwa, 1934: 114; Roscoe, 1915: 90)

Wanurú   The "spirit of sickness and of death." A term also used for all the spirits of the dead. The Goajiro, Colombia. (Pineda Giraldo, 1950: 25)

Wen chen   A god of epidemics. China. (Chavannes, n.d.: 102)

Wen Shen   A god of disease, of epidemics. Anking, China. (Shyrock, 1931: 91; Gamble, 1954: 419)

Wen Yuan Shuai   A god of the plague. China. (Day, 1940: 24)

Winanglihan   A god of dysentery. The Ifugao, Philippines. (Barton, 1946: 63)

Woeadja   A name of the Pox Spirit. Others: Karambaoe and Toringka. Father of Sorisi, Koemobo, Gamba, Boeti, Dato. The Toradja, Celebes, Indonesia. (Adriani and Kruyt, 1950: 204–205)

Wu Se She   "Five Color Snake Charm," a god of disease. China. (Day, 1940: 205)

Wu T'ou She   "Five-Headed Snake Charm," a god of disease. China. (Day, 1940: 205)

The Wu Yüeh   Five gods of epidemics who are also mountain gods. They "are stellar devils whom Yü Huang sent to be reincarnated on earth"—T'ien Po-hsüeh, Tung Hung-wên, Ts'ai Wên-chü, Chao Wu-chên, Huang Ying-tu. They were scholars and became musicians in the court of Li Shih-min. China. (Werner, 1934: 242–243)

Xolotl   The evening planet Venus, twin of Quetzalcoatl. He is a god of sickness, of abortions, of the malformed, as well as the god of the ball courts. Mexico. (Reed, 1966: 95; Alexander, 1920: 82; Caso, 1958: 18, 24)

Yang Wên-hui   "Overseer of Epidemics of the North." China. (Werner, 1932: 560)

Yarbimuneki   The "eel demon" who attempts to interfere with parturition. The Cuna, Panama. (Nordenskiold, 1938: 370)

Ywan   A male water deity who punishes with illness. The Tenetehara, Maranhão, Brazil. (Wagley and Galvão, 1949: 98, 103)

23

Death Gods:
the Dead, Soul (in death), Funereal, Embalming, Cemeteries

Abuhene The Scarlet Macaw—God of the West, who represents the setting sun, is the god of death, of the underworld, of dark shamanism. He is an evil deity who can be approached only by the hoarotu, the dark shaman, who must feed him the livers of humans, who must maintain contact with the West for the people to live. The Warao, Venezuela. (Wilbert, 1973, 1: X407; 1973, 2: 5)

Acolnauacatl, Acolnahuacatl A god of the dead, another name of Mictlantecutli. The Aztec, Mexico. (Alexander, 1920: 80; Caso, 1958: 64)

Agaman Nibo A goddess of the dead, mother of Baron Samedi. Haiti, West Indies. (Marcelin, 1950: 198)

Aiaru A goddess who foretells the approach of death. Tahiti, Polynesia. (Henry, 1928: 416)

Aki A god of death who enters the body and slowly kills. The Jukun, Nigeria. (Meek, 1931: 201)

Aku Ashe Ki A tutelary god who is concerned "with death and burial rites." The Jukun, Nigeria. (Meek, 1931: 276)

Akwa The object of many private cults who seems to be a god of the dead. The Jukun, Nigeria. (Meek, 1931: 201, 227)

Ament, Amentet A goddess of the necropolis who welcomes the dead. A name of Isis as goddess of the underworld in her role of the transformation of the dead for entry to the realm of Osiris. Ament was originally a goddess of Libya, the personification of the west. When death became associated with the west, she became a goddess of the underworld. Egypt. (Gardiner, 1925, 9: 787, 792; Budge, 1969, 2: 1, 216; Knight, 1915: 57–58; Larousse, 1968: 17)

a mik ka ta bo A dangerous one-eyed demon who prowls at night, and who, if met face to face, causes instant death. He is the only mung to whom a goat is sacrificed, never to a god. The Lepchas, Sikkim. (Siiger, 1967, 1: 180–181)

Amma The great creator god to whom souls go on death. Mali. (Paulme, 1940: 496)

Amset, Amseth A funereal god. As one of the four sons of Horus, the gods of the Canopic jars, he protects the stomach and the large intestines with the help of Isis. He is also god of the cardinal point of the South. Variant names: Imset, Mestha. Egypt. (Budge, 1969, 1: 158, 456, 491–492)

Anagui An aspect of Eleggua—The "guardian of the cemetery's doors." Puerto Rico, West Indies. (Gonzalez-Wippler, 1975: 103)

Androctasia Murder and Manslaughter, singular/plural, daughter(s) of Eris. Greece. (Barthell, 1971: 8; Roscher, 1965, 1: 34; Hesiod-Brown, 1981: 59)

Anguta The supreme being and creator, father of Sidne, Sedna. He carries the dead to Adlivun where she lives and where the dead remain for a year before going to other afterworlds. The Nugumiut, Frobisher Bay, Baffin Island, Canada. (Boas, 1884/85: 583; MacCulloch, 1925, 11: 825)

An-her, Anhur An early god of the dead prior to Osiris, and also a god of war. Abydos, Egypt. (Knight, 1915: 16; Mercer, 1925, 12: 702; Budge, 1969, 1: 172)

Anubis, Anpu The jackal god of the dead, of embalming, and of judgment in the underworld. He is the guardian of tombs and guide of the dead, protecting them and participating in the weighing. Son of Nephthys and Osiris, or Set. Egypt. (Knight, 1915: 19–20; Budge, 1969, 2: 261–264; Ames, 1965: 66, 80)

Arman   The god of death. Karakirgis. (Pettersson, 1957: 164)

Arot, a rot a fung mung   A devil who appears "as a red butterfly," causes illness, sudden and violent death, suicides. When death is caused by Arot, ceremonies should be conducted annually forever because violent death "is infectious and hereditary." The Lepchas, Sikkim. (Gorer, 1938: 221, 352; Siiger, 1967, 1: 70; 1967, 2: 35; Morris, 1938: 121)

Asar   A name of Osiris, the god of the dead. Egypt. (Budge, 1969, 1: 113)

Astes   A god associated with death, named in the Book of the Dead. Egypt. (Knight, 1915: 24; Budge, 1969, 2: 325)

Asto-viŏatu   A demon who "destroys life . . . the deity of the death agony." Iran. (Gray, 1930: 201)

Ataecina   A goddess of the dead, and a goddess of the city of Turobriga. Iberia (Spain). (Martinez, 1962: 141–146)

a'tɫät·iaiutɫ   A male chthonic spirit who "sometimes comes at dusk to cause death by carrying away a man's spirit." The Bella Coola, British Columbia. (McIlwraith, 1948, 1: 49)

Avimadye   A god who concerns himself with the dead. Dahomey. (Herskovits, 1938, 2: 142)

Azagon La Croix   An aspect of Ghede, the god of the dead, "mainly related to the cemetery and to magic." Haiti, West Indies. (Deren, 1953: 303)

Baba Yaga, Baba-jaga   A very old Slavic being, well-preserved in Russia, who is the mother of the evil spirits and is associated with the world of the dead, the bones of the dead, kills children. She appears as a witch and is also associated with animals. (Mansikka, 1925, 4: 623; Bray, 1935: 41; Gimbutas, 1975: XLC M126)

Bakaowa ud Haitan   A deity at Haitan who causes death and illness. He is also owner of game. The Ifugao, Philippines. (Barton, 1946: 85)

Baladung ud Inhungduwan   A deity of Inhungduwan who causes death and illness, is also the owner of game. The Ifugao, Philippines. (Barton, 1946: 85)

Balle bide   "Death personified." The Dogon, Mali. (Paulme, 1940: 496)

Bamoo   A female devil who foretells death. The Lepchas, Sikkim. (Gorer, 1938: 375)

Banbanilag ud Tano   A deity at Tano who causes illness and death, and is also owner of game in the vicinity. The Ifugao, Philippines. (Barton, 1946: 85)

dBang gi ghsin rje   A form of Yama, the god of death. Tibet. (Nebesky-Wojkowitz, 1956, 1: 83)

Baron Cimitière   One of the gods of the dead, ruler and guardian of cemeteries, who receives the dead from Baron La Croix. Haiti, West Indies. (Deren, 1953: 102; Marcelin, 1950: 146, 173)

Baron La Croix   One of the gods of the dead and of cemeteries. He seeks out the dead and accompanies them to the cemetery. Also called Azagon La Croix. Haiti, West Indies. (Deren, 1953: 303; Marcelin, 1950: 146, 172)

Baron Piquant   An aspect of Ghede, and as such a god of the dead. Haiti, West Indies. (Deren, 1953: 112)

Baron Samedi   Father and chief of the Guédé (gods of the dead and of cemeteries). He is also god of the crossroads and of black magic as it relates both to death and to the crossroads. He is equated with Ghede. Haiti, West Indies. (Marcelin, 1950: 153; Herskovits, 1937: 247; Deren, 1953: 69, 103)

Bayang Lasa   The deity who carries the souls of the dead to Pulan Buah, the afterworld (Fruit Islant). The Mantra, Malay Peninsula. (Skeat, 1906: 321)

Bhairavi   A goddess who represents the power of death which begins from the very beginning of existence. India. (Danielou, 1964: 281–282)

Bibengkulan ud Akdangan   A deity at Akdangan who causes illness and death. The Ifugao, Philippines. (Barton, 1946: 85)

Bilé   A god of death and of the underworld. Ireland. (Squire, 1906: 51, 65)

Bimaiyuong ud Buyugan   A deity at Buyugan who causes death and illness. The Ifugao, Philippines. (Barton, 1946: 85)

Bolang   A deity who ends either life or death, invoked at funerals. He is also a god of reproduction. The Ifugao, Philippines. (Barton, 1946: 45, 84)

Bowa, Alibowa A "spirit who feeds on dead bodies," who must be kept away by placing various objects on the grave. The Isneg, Luzon, Philippines. (Vanoverbergh, 1938: 252)

Bozaloshtsh A Slavic demoness who conveys "the message of death." The Wends, East Germany. (Mansikka, 1925, 4: 627; Leach, 1949, 1: 160)

Brimo A goddess of death without mercy. Thessaly, Greece. (Roscher, 1965, 3, 1: 595)

Britisse Jean-Simon Elder brother of the Guédé. He presides over the tribunal of the dead and is a severe judge. Haiti, West Indies. (Marcelin, 1950: 194)

Bun The god of death of the Olchi. Siberia. (Pettersson, 1957: 142)

Bundjil miri, Bundulmiri The god of the dead, said to be the son of Wolaro. Kimberley, Northwest Australia. (Eliade, 1973: 193; Capell, 1939: 385)

Calounga Bantu goddess of the sea and of death. In Maranhão considered a goddess of death. In Rio de Janeiro, a goddess of the sea. Brazil. (Bastide, 1960: 401, 562)

Camé The god of death. The Quiché, Guatemala. (Girard, 1979: 219)

Capuari The god of death. The Takanan, Araona. Bolivia. (Métraux, 1942: 41–42)

Cel Etruscan god of death and of the underworld, associated with the west. Italy. (Hamblin, 1975: 95)

Chalmecacihuatl A goddess of the dead, wife of Tzontemoc. Mexico. (Caso, 1958: 64)

Charon The Greek god who rowed the dead across the river Styx. (Barthell, 1971: 9; Prentice Hall, 1963: 34)

Charun, Churun The Etruscan god of death who conducted men to the underworld—a much more aggressive and active demon than his Greek counterpart. Italy. (Hamblin, 1975: 109; Dumézil, 1966, 2: 693; Fairbanks, 1907: 238)

Chawthang The "spirit of the dead." The Tangsas, India and Burma. (Dutta, 1959: 67)

Chibiabos A god with the qualities of a psychopomp—escorting the departed souls, assisting and guiding them on the way to the afterworld in the west. Younger brother

of Wi'ske. The Potawatomi, Michigan and Wisconsin. (Ritzenthaler, 1970: 43; Edmunds, 1980: 20)

Chinde A malignant spirit of the Navaho who causes death. Arizona and New Mexico. (Hartland, 1925, 4: 413)

Chin-ni The death spirit of women, whose servant is Minang. Malay Peninsula. (Skeat, 1906: 217)

Chodala Bhadrakali A graveyard deity charged, in the rites for the dead, to stay away for seven days. Also invoked to release the spirit of the dead. The Pulaya, India. (Thaliath, 1956: 1047, 1050)

Christ God of the dead. The Khevsurs, Caucasus. (Gray, 1925, 12: 485)

Chutsain The personification or spirit of death who received the souls of the dead. The Tinneh, Pacific Northwest, Canada. (Bancroft, 1886: 142, 518)

Chyom The "devil who causes people to die by falling from a tree or cliff." The Lepchas, Sikkim. (Gorer, 1938: 234)

Cihuacoatl, Ciuacoatl A serpent and earth goddess, considered the mother of the human race, was a goddess of childbirth but also of death, of those who died in childbirth. Xochimilco and Colhuacan, Mexico. (Duran, 1971: 210, 472; Caso, 1958: 54; Emerson, 1884: 119)

Cilens An Etruscan deity of death and the underworld, associated with the north. Italy. (Hamblin, 1975: 95)

Citsel (Citzil) Bac A god of death of the Tzotzil. Mexico. (Thompson, 1970: 117)

Cocohuame Death—the most venerated of the gods of the Sinaloas. Mexico. (Bancroft, 1886: 180)

Coquechila, Coqueehila (in Sola) The god of death and of the underworld among some Valley Zapotecs. His wife is Xonaxihuilia. Oaxaca, Mexico. (Whitecotton, 1977; 158, 164)

Coqui Bexelao (Bezelao) The god of death and of the underworld among some Valley Zapotecs. Husband of Xonaxi Quecuya. Oaxaca, Mexico. (Whitecotton, 1977: 158)

cos-rgyal *See* gSin-rje. Tibet.

Cukit " 'Very wicked' but very respected." If he wins the game of peon against the Sun, it results in deaths and wars. He is also associated with Datura. Same as Tsukit (Yokuts) and Chukit (Fernandeno and Gabrielino). The Kitanemuk, California. (Hudson and Underhay, 1978: 33, 57)

Cumhau A death god, a variant of Hunhau. The Mayan, Mexico and Guatemala. (Tozzer, 1941: 132; Thompson, 1970: 303)

Cupay (Supay) God of the dead and the underworld ("land of shades") where those not qualified for the land of the Sun must go. Peru. (Brinton, 1868: 61, 251–252)

Cupra An earth and benevolent death goddess revered in Umbria. Italy. (Roscher, 1965, 1, 1: 931)

Cvlalp An Etruscan god of death and the underworld, associated with the northeast. Italy (Hamblin, 1975: 95)

dadungut Guardians of the tombs. The Ifugao, Philippines. (Jocano, 1969: 17)

Dago, Degup A demon who "haunts graves, and assumes the shape of deer." The Mantra, Malay Peninsula. (Skeat, 1906: 324)

Batara Gede Dalem The god of the dead. Bali, Indonesia. (Franken, 1960: 380)

Dangquico With "Makel, and Kilang move the winds that kill instantly." An evil anito. The Apayao, Philippines. (Wilson, 1947: 23)

Dara Rambai Geruda A water goddess who aids good divers, but who can also be harmful and cause death by drowning. The Iban Dyaks, Sarawak, Borneo. (Sarawak Gazette, 1963: 135)

Dé A god who looks after the dead and who is invoked to help conduct souls to heaven. The Lepchas, Sikkim. (Gorer, 1938: 231, 357)

Dea Muta Roman goddess of the dead. (Fairbanks, 1907: 238)

Debdib ud O-ong A deity at O-ong who causes illness and death. The Ifugao, Philippines. (Barton, 1946: 86)

Deuse The all-powerful god who causes the deaths of those too aged to live. Nicobar Islands, Bay of Bengal. (Man, n.d.: 158)

Deut A devil who "quarrels" for the soul of the person at the end of life—as to his living or dying. The Lepchas, Sikkim. (Gorer, 1938: 469)

Dichali A minor deity of disease and death. Chaibasa, India. (Crooke, 1894: 87)

Diva Angerona A Roman goddess of the dead. (Altheim, 1937: 115)

Donn Celtic god of the dead, both "benign and terrible." Ireland. (MacCana, 1970: 43; Pettazzoni, 1956: 199)

Drag gi gshin rje A form of Yama, god of the dead. Tibet. (Nebesky-Wojkowitz, 1956, 1: 83)

Druj Nasu The "corpse demon, who is the personification of the spirit of corruption, decomposition, contagion and impurity." Persia. (Hinnells, 1973: 56)

Duamutef A variant spelling of Tuamutef, one of the four sons of Horus who are gods of the Canopic jars. He is guardian of the stomach with the help of Neith—in the underworld. Egypt. (Ames, 1965: 48)

Dumudui A deity who preys on the souls of those just dead, particularly murdered persons. The Ifugao, Philippines. (Barton, 1946: 73)

Dupapp "He it is who absorbs the decayed matter (*saxó*) that flows from the nose and mouth of the deceased." The Isneg, Luzon, Philippines. (Vanoverbergh, 1938: 245)

Durga The goddess of death who delivers the souls of the dead to Yama for judgment. She is the malevolent and destructive aspect of Uma. Bali, Indonesia. (Covarrubias, 1937: 317, 291; Hooykaas, 1964: 68)

The Dur khrod bdag po A "pair of skeletons appearing in the retinue of Yama." The god of death. They are important protective deities. Tibet. (Nebesky-Wojkowitz, 1956, 1: 95)

Dur khrod bdag po lcam dral The god of the cemetery—"a white skeleton," considered a form of Yama, the god of the dead. Tibet. (Nebesky-Wojkowitz, 1956, 1: 86)

Dur khrod kyi bdag mo khros ma nag mo Goddess of the cemetery who controls the gods of hail. Tibet. (Nebesky-Wojkowitz, 1956, 1: 469)

Dur khrod lha mo A goddess of the cemetery identified with Ekajata. Tibet. (Snellgrove, 1957: 236)

Dŭt mung With his wife Sŭ mo mung, "killed lonely travellers and ate their flesh." The Lepchas, Sikkim. (Nebesky-Wojkowitz, 1952: 28)

Edshu A god of death of the Yoruba. Nigeria. (Deren, 1953: 292)

Emma-o God of death and god of judgment in the underworld, assigning sinners to the various parts of hell. Japan. (Getty, 1962: 152–153; Eliseev, 1963: 424; Eliot, 1935: 140)

Endovellicus A funereal god, and god of the dead or of the underworld. Spain. (Martinez, 1962: 147, 159)

Ereshkigal Goddess of death and darkness, of the underworld. She married Nergal and made him god of the dead. She is the sister of Inanna. Akkadia, Babylonia, and Sumer, Near East. (Kramer, 1962: 105, 113, 124; James, 1960: 179)

Erlen (Erlik) Khan God of the dead, causer of natural sickness and death. The Buryat, Siberia. (Krader, 1954: 332)

Erlik, Erlik Khan A god of evil and corruption causing "all misfortunes, from poverty to death." A god of the underworld and of the dead. The Altai, Turco-Tatar, Siberia. (Casanowicz, 1924: 417–418; Chadwick, 1936: 94, 106; Potapov, 1964: 325)

erlik qan Mongolian god of the dead, equated with Yama. A Dharmapala and Defender of the Law. (Getty, 1962: 152)

Ettsuñe A "supernatural being who is perhaps a personification of death." When a medicine man captures the wandering soul of the sick person, he forces the deity "to enter the patient" to replace it. The Hare-skins, Canada. (Hartland, 1925, 4: 412)

Fên Mu T'u Shên Chün Guardian of grave mounds. China. (Day, 1940: 209)

Gaiyun A goddess who ends either life or death, and is invoked at funerals. The Ifugao, Philippines. (Barton, 1946: 84)

Genita Mana A Roman goddess with "power over life and death," invoked to spare the family from death. (Jayne, 1962: 449; Fairbanks, 1907: 238)

Ghede, Gede "The idea of death as virile and fecund is found . . . in modern Haiti, where Ghede the god of the dead is a phallic corpse, 'both tomb and womb'." He is just, and decides whether someone is really to die. Haiti, West Indies. (Sierksma, 1966: 205; Herskovits, 1937: 247, 318)

Giltinie A god of death. Lithuania. (Gray, 1930: 202)

Ginumon A beneficent god, but a cause of illness and death. The Ifugao, Philippines. (Barton, 1946: 44)

Goigecko God of death of the Bondo. Koraput District, India. (Elwin, 1949: 416)

Gol A spirit who causes death. Ifalik, Micronesia. (Burrows, 1947/48: 11)

Golarai God of death of the Kuki. Tibet and Burma. (Keane, 1925, 2: 122)

Gora dai leng A god of vengeance, punishing dead sinners. Yap, Caroline Islands, Micronesia. (Christian, 1899: 385)

Grande Brigitte Goddess of the dead and of cemeteries. She is the wife of Baron Samedi and mother of Les Guédé, and is as powerful as her husband. Haiti, West Indies. (Marcelin, 1950: 146, 177)

Grand'-Pois One of the family of the gods of the dead. Haiti, West Indies. (Marcelin, 1950: 198)

Grogoragally The beneficent sun god presents the soul of the dead to the supreme being. The Wiradjuri-Kamilaroi, Southwest Australia. (Eliade, 1959: 120, 126)

Gsang-sgrub A form of Yama, the god of death. Tibet. (Getty, 1962: 153)

Guayavacunnee God of the dead, but also the supreme being—benevolent but remote. The Puelche, Patagonia. The Guaya-vacuni and the Tehuelcho, Tierra del Fuego. (Cooper, 1946, 1: 157; Lissner, 1961: 99; Grubb, 1925, 9: 597)

The Guédé Gods of the dead and of cemeteries whose parents are Grande Brigitte and Baron Samedi. Haiti, West Indies. (Marcelin, 1950: 145)

Guédé-Hou, or Houn One of the family of the gods of the dead. Haiti, West Indies. (Marcelin, 1950: 198)

Guingelda Master of the Burial. The Cagaba and the Kogi, Colombia. (Reichel-Dolmatoff, 1949/50: 113)

rGyas pa'i gshin rje A form of Yama, the god of the dead. Tibet. (Nebesky-Wojkowitz, 1956, 1: 83)

Hades, Pluto God of death and of the underworld—as Hades god and judge of the dead, as Pluto, benevolent god of agricultural fertility and of the earth's treasures.

He stole his niece Persephone to be his wife. Greece. (Kerenyi, 1951: 231–232; Fairbanks, 1907: 235)

Hadui Iroquois god of disease and death who was overcome and forced to cure the diseases he caused. This event was the origin of the Mask-faces society for exorcising disease and death. Eastern United States. (Gray, 1925, 7: 422; Alexander, 1964: 37)

Haetsh God of the dead of the Kamchadals. Kamchatka. (Lang, 1968: 205)

Hap, Hapi A funereal god, protector of the body of the deceased. One of the four sons of Horus. As a god of the Canopic jars he is assisted by Nephthys in protecting the "small viscerae." As a Cardinal god he is the god of the north. Egypt. (Budge, 1969, 1: 158, 456, 491–492; Knight, 1915: 34)

Hara An aspect of Siva as Death—Disease. India. (Danielou, 1964: 196–197)

Hathor The great cow goddess is both celestial and chthonic. As a goddess of the underworld she is a beneficent goddess of death who helps and protects the deceased in striving to attain everlasting life. Egypt. (Jayne, 1962: 58; Budge, 1969, 1: 434–435; Neumann, 1955: 53–54)

Hdur-gsas-spa-po A deity who teaches funeral ceremonies, burials, and methods to subdue demons. Tibet. (Li An-che, 1948: 39)

Hel Goddess of death and of the underworld (Niflheim)—of those who die on land, as opposed to Ran who is goddess of those who die at sea. Hel is the daughter of Loki and the giantess Angurboda. Scandinavia. (Grimm, 1880: 312–313; Wagner, 1882: 150; Stern, 1898: 6)

Hikuleo Goddess/god of the dead, ruler of Pulotu, the world of the dead (also called the dwelling place of the gods). Tonga, Polynesia. (Collocott, 1921: 152–153; Burrows, 1937: 85; Gifford, 1929: 287)

Hine-nui-te-po As Hine-a-tauira she was unknowingly the daughter/wife of Tane. On learning the relationship she fled to the underworld taking the name of Hine-nui-te-po as goddess of death, of night, and of the underworld. She was the mother of Po-uriuri, Po-tangotango, and Pare-kori-tawa. The Maori, New Zealand. (Andersen, 1928: 212, 409–411; Henry, 1928: 466; Best, 1924: 116, 323)

Hit rum The "Mun god who looks after the new-born dead," invoked to help conduct souls to heaven. The Lepchas, Sikkim. (Gorer, 1938: 231, 357)

Hlamin Jimen A "god when pleased and a demon when angry," who sometimes detains the soul of the dead. The Lepchas, Sikkim. (Morris, 1938: 144)

Holler "Frisian god of the dead." North Sea Islands. (Rhys, 1912: 177)

Hun-Came A god of death and of the underworld where the black road leads to his residence. With Vucub-Came the supreme judges of the council of the lords of the underworld (Xibalba). The Quiché, Guatemala. (Recinos, 1950: 109–110; Krickeberg, 1968: 79; Girard, 1979: 95)

Hunhau, Hun Ahau, Ahpuch God of death and of the underworld (Mitnal). The Mayan, Mexico. (Schellhas, 1904: 13; Thompson, 1970: 302)

Ikal Ahau A death god of the Tzotzil. Mexico. (Thompson, 1970: 323)

Ilamatecuhtli A goddess of death. The Terrible Mother goddess with the knives and "vagina dentata." She was also the "old" mother goddess, of the old, dry corn, and the female counterpart of Huehueteotl. The Aztec, Mexico. (Caso, 1958: 47; Neumann, 1955: 167–168; Krickeberg, 1968: 44)

Illike Nga A malevolent male spirit who causes death by taking a man's soul-life. The Yurak Samoyed, Siberia. (Czaplicka, 1925, 11: 176)

Imbagaiyon ud Lingaiyan, Imbagyan A messenger of death and a conductor of souls. The Ifugao, Philippines. (Barton, 1946: 86; Jocano, 1969: 17)

Imset, Imsety *See* **Amset.**

Inhilap A god who can cause illness and death, though he is a beneficent god of reproduction. The Ifugao, Philippines. (Barton, 1946: 44)

Ixpuzteque A god of the dead whose wife is Nesoxochi. The Aztec, Mexico. (Caso, 1958: 64)

Jameakka Finno-Ugric goddess of death and of the underworld (Jabmeanimo). She "brought illness and death to men and animals." The Lapps, Northern Europe. (Pettersson, 1957: 43, 161; Karsten, 1955: 107)

Jam Raja, Jammasum, Jomma Kittung, Jam Deota God of death of Orissa. India. Same as Yama. (Elwin, 1954: 637)

Jawait Among the Bateg Negritos he is a god who greets "the souls of dead shamans." His wife is Lai-oid.

At Lata Lang on the Cheka River he is considered to meet all the dead with games, food, and flowers. With the Batek Negritos of Pahang he is the sky god whose wife is Geles. Malaya. (Evans, 1937: 146, 262; Pettazzoni, 1956: 326)

Jene   A god of the dead—the married or aged. Japan. (Coleman, 1832: 341)

Jizo (Kshitigarbha)   A god who conducts the souls of the dead, and is particularly protective of children. Toward the living he is protective of all sufferers, as well as of warriors, travelers, pregnant women. Japan. (Getty, 1962: 34, 102, 105; Clark, 1932: 55; Piggott, 1969: 20; Eliseev, 1963: 432–434)

Jok Orongo   Jok as the "patron of souls." The Lango, Uganda. (Frazer, 1926: 296)

Jom   God of the dead of the Mikirs. Assam. (Lyall, 1925, 8: 629)

Jom Raja   The god of death whose abode is Norok. The Santals, India. (Mukherjea, 1962: 194, 229)

Kalaman   An evil god who caused illness and death. Central Celebes, Indonesia. (Downs, 1920: 22)

Kalau   As an individual he is a god of death and of evil who intercepts the sacrifices made by the shaman to the supreme being for cures, causing the patient to die. As a group—evil spirits who cause illness and death. The Koryak, Siberia. (Eliade, 1964: 249–250; Jochelson, 1904: 417–418)

Kalma   Finno-Ugric personified Death, god of tombs. (Bray, 1935: 43; Larousse, 1968: 306)

Kalubdur   One of the four tutelary spirits who seek out and transport the souls of the dead. In the chronicle of Nele Sibu. The Cuna, Panama. (Nordenskiold, 1938: 295)

Kalung   "Death personified." Angola. (Werner, 1964: 117)

Kanaima   A god of death, of murderers, of vengeance. The Acawoios, Guiana. (Brett, 1880: 152–153)

Kanda Swami or **Skanda**   The god of the dead, also known as "the Kataragam God." The Bandaraduwa community of the Vedda, Ceylon. (Seligmann and Seligmann, 1911: 154)

Ka-'onohi-o-ka-la   In some traditions "(the eye-ball of the sun) conducted the souls of heroes to a heaven in or beyond the clouds." Hawaii. (Alexander, 1967: 103)

Kapo   A goddess of death on Maui and a sorceress, who, through possession of the ancestor gods, "gives commands or foretells events." She is also goddess of the hula—sometimes depicting "grace and beauty," and at others "darkness and lust." Hawaii. (Beckwith, 1940: 113, 187; Westervelt, 1915: 98, 140; Emerson, 1916/17: 24–25)

Kapu Mate   A goddess of the dead and of graves. The Letts. Latvia. (Leger, 1925, 1: 466; Gray, 1930: 194)

Kapunan   An evil anito who "gives sudden death by hemorrhage." The Apayao, Philippines. (Wilson, 1947: 23)

Karasaw   A spirit who may snatch the corpse (if unguarded) and devour it. The Isneg, Luzon, Philippines. (Vanoverbergh, 1938: 232)

Kari   God and judge of the dead, the giver and taker of life. He is the supreme and creator god as well as god of thunder and storms, which he sends as punishment. The Semang, Malay Peninsula. (Skeat, 1906: 177–178; Cole, 1945: 72; Moss, 1925: 116; Eliade, 1964: 337)

Ka-tash-huaht   The north wind, an evil spirit who brought death. The Seneca (Iroquois), New York. (Smith, 1881/82: 59; Bjorklund, 1969: 132)

Kati Ankamma   Goddess of the cremation and burial grounds who feeds on corpses and kills children and cattle. India. (Elmore, 1915: 39)

Kechira   A god who classifies the dead "according to merit . . . or the manner of death." The Naga, Manipur, India. (Hodson, 1911: 161; MacCulloch, 1925, 11: 824)

Ker   A Greek goddess of death. (Bhattacharji, 1970: 86)

Keyuri   A cemetery goddess. India. (Evans-Wentz, 1960: 142)

Kibuka   The "personification of the unexpectedness of death." Also a god of war. South Africa. (Mutwa, 1966: iii; Roscoe, 1965: 275; Junod, 1962: 409)

Kikadur   One of the four tutelary spirits who seek out and transport the souls of the dead. In the chronicle of Nele Sibu. The Cuna, Panama. (Nordenskiold, 1938: 295)

Kinoptiu ud Ubub A deity at Ubub who causes illness and death. The Ifugao, Philippines. (Barton, 1946: 85)

Kisin The god of death and of earthquakes is chief of the part of the underworld called Metlán. Earlier he was not considered particularly malevolent, but now very much so as he "is associated with criminal violence, theft, lying and all kinds of ill tidings." The Lacandon, Mexico. (Perera and Bruce, 1982: 86, 102–103, 308)

Kiyamat-tora Beneficent god of death who helps the righteous into the life beyond. The Cheremiss, Russia. (MacCulloch, 1964: 75)

Kokwiteit A deity of the Yokuts responsible for the existence of death. California. (Kroeber, 1925: 510)

Komakadong An evil spirit which snatches the bodies of the dead. The Dusuns, North Borneo. (Evans, 1923: 14)

Komokoa God of the sea and of the drowned. He is the protector of seals. Pacific Northwest Indians, North America. (Alexander, 1964: 244)

Kshitigarbha A Buddhist Bodhisattva. The "conductor of souls" and a god of the dead, who intercedes for them with the judges in the lower world. He is Ti-tsang p'u-sa in China, Jizo in Japan. Known also in Chinese Turkestan and Central Asia. (Getty, 1962: 34, 102; Hackin, 1963: 248)

Ku The personification of death, sent into the world by Mawu because she was challenged by Awe, who knew the art of curing. Now Awe and Ku are friends. Dahomey. (Herskovits, 1938, 2: 258–259)

Kubur Demon of tombs and graves. The Jakun, Malay Peninsula. (Skeat, 1906: 183, 244)

Kudulimayahe A "god who commanded death." Dahomey. (Herskovits, 1938, 2: 142)

Kuinyo An evil spirit of death. Australia. (Bray, 1935: 232)

Kukitat The god who caused death, also dissension. Younger brother of the creator, Pakrokitat. The Serrano, California. (Kroeber, 1925: 619)

Kuladut ud Dungudungu A deity at Dungudungu who causes illness and death. The Ifugao, Philippines. (Barton, 1946: 85)

Kulbung ud Baiyun A deity at Baiyun who causes illness and death. The Ifugao, Philippines. (Barton, 1946: 86)

Kulmu Etruscan god of the tomb. Italy. (Rawlinson, 1885: 126)

Kume A goddess associated with Nau Taufiti, her sister, in the cleansing of the spirit of the dead for participation in the afterlife. Tikopia, Polynesia. (Firth, 1967, 1: 89, 90)

Kutaw The ferryman who conducts the soul across "the great pond . . . to the realm of the dead." He may be arbitrary in his ferrying if the proper procedures have not been followed. The Isneg, Luzon, Philippines. (Vanoverbergh, 1938: 227)

Lamiyad, or **Lalamiyadan** A spirit of the Isneg "whose victims die instantly." Luzon, Philippines. (Vanoverbergh, 1953: 90)

Laolao ud Huminal A deity at Huminal who causes illness and death. The Ifugao, Philippines. (Barton, 1946: 86)

Las gshin dmar po khrag mdog A form of Yama (the god of the dead) who is blood-red. His attributes are a thunderbolt and a snare. His consort is Dus mtshan ma. Tibet. (Nebesky-Wojkowitz, 1956, 1: 84)

Las gshin dmar po ma ru rtse bzhis skor ba A form of Yama, red and fierce. His attributes are a sword and a wind-wheel. His consort is "the black-coloured . . . Ekajati." Tibet. (Nebesky-Wojkowitz, 1956, 1: 84)

Las gshin lha bcu gsum A form of Yama. Tibet. (Nebesky-Wojkowitz, 1956, 1: 84)

Las kyi gshin rje A buffalo-headed form of Yama, golden-yellow, whose attributes are a skull-headed club and a black snare. Tibet. (Nebesky-Wojkowitz, 1956, 1: 85)

Latura The god of the dead, brother of Lowalangi, the sky god. Nias Island, Indonesia. (Leach, 1950, 2: 606)

Lauon, Laon An ancient god who punished mankind with death for killing his "most beautiful fish" and picking "the most luscious fruit" from his particular tree. The Tagalo-Bisaya, Philippines. (Best, 1892, 1: 200)

Laverna An Etruscan goddess of death. The Roman deity is a "goddess of lawful or unlawful gain" and is invoked by thieves. Italy. (Herbig, 1925, 5: 535; Prentice Hall, 1965: 81; Keane, 1925, 2: 123)

Lemures (Roman), **Lemuri** (Etruscan)   Spirits of churchyards. Italy. (Leland, 1963: 95)

Leta Ahuila   The god of death, of the underworld, of the Zapotec in Sola. Same as Pezelao. He "apparently had both male and female refractions: Coqueehila, the lord of the underworld, and his wife Xonaxihuilia." Oaxaca, Mexico. (Whitecotton, 1977: 164)

Libentina   Goddess of the dead—records of death were kept in her temple. Italy. (Roscher, 1965, 2, 1: 201)

Libitina   An old Italian "goddess of corpses and burials," and of funerals. (Prentice Hall, 1965: 83; Larousse, 1968: 213)

Likuthava   An easily offended goddess of Valelailai who killed men. Lau Islands, Fiji. (Hocart, 1929: 190)

Limenolol   An evil spirit "who causes death by bewitching the head." The Marshall Islands, Micronesia. (Erdland, 1914: 313)

Litsowo   A deity who captures and devours dead souls. The Sema Nagas, India. (Hutton, 1968: 197)

Loa   The sun goddess who also "brings death to the people." The Iraku, Tanzania. (Millroth, 1965: 23)

Lobag   A conductor of souls when summoned by deities, ancestors, or relatives. Son of Imbagaiyon. The Ifugao, Philippines. (Barton, 1946: 86)

Lojibwineamen   The god of death who lives in the north and kills each thing individually. Marshall Islands, Micronesia. (Davenport, 1953: 221–222)

Lolupe   A deity who conducted and assisted the spirits of the dead chiefs in their journey to the afterworld. Hawaii. (Alexander, 1967: 103)

Lo Yuyang   God of the soul. China. (Du Bose, n.d.: 327)

Lu   An evil spirit of the Red Karens who lives on corpses and appeases his appetite by causing disease and death. Burma. (Temple, 1925, 3: 25)

Lufu, or **Lirufu**   Death personified. The Basumbwa, Tanzania. (Werner, 1964: 174)

Lug   A god of death who catches ghosts during full moon and gives them to Nomou to devour. So all the dead do not get to Falraman, "the great sky-house of Yalafath." Yap Island, Micronesia. (MacKenzie, 1930: 172–173; Müller, 1917: 308)

Luk   "The god of death and disease; . . . incarnate in the *orra,* a black bird of nocturnal habits." Also a god of thieves and robbers. Yap Island, the Carolines, Micronesia. (Christian, 1899: 384–385)

Lule   A god of mourning and tears, as well as of rain. The Baganda, Uganda. (Cunningham, 1905: 218)

Lumok   A deity who preys on the souls of those just dead, particularly murdered persons. The Ifugao, Philippines. (Barton, 1946: 73)

Machi Olopigiñalilel   A guide of the dead, in the Nele Sibu chronicle. The Cuna, Panama. (Nordenskiold, 1938: 303; Keeler, 1960: 87)

Machi Oloyapipilel   A guide of the dead in the Nele Sibu chronicle. The Cuna, Panama. (Nordenskiold, 1938: 303; Keeler, 1960: 87)

Madanal te una   A deity invoked in post-entombment rites for the dead. The Ifugao, Philippines. (Barton, 1946: 74)

Magahal te laiya   A deity invoked in post-entombment rites for the dead. The Ifugao, Philippines. (Barton, 1946: 74)

Magtatangal   A goddess who caused death from fright. Sister of Silangan. The Tagalog, Philippines. (Jocano, 1969: 12)

Mahasona Yaka   The " 'great cemetery demon,' lies in wait for people burying their dead." He causes illness. Ceylon (Sri Lanka). (Ames, 1978: 45)

Makalay   An evil spirit, in form like a kangaroo or a unicorn, the sight of whom is frequently a cause of death. The Yurok, California. (Powers, 1877: 63; Bancroft, 1886, 3: 176)

Maknyam   The demon of death. The Lepchas, Sikkim. (Gorer, 1938: 92; Siiger, 1967: 143)

Makupu   A goddess associated with funerals. Tikopia, Polynesia. (Firth, 1967, 1: 103)

Malhong te ginga   A deity invoked in post-entombment rites for the dead. The Ifugao, Philippines. (Barton, 1946: 74)

Malulugan te balat   A deity invoked in post-entombment rites for the dead. The Ifugao, Philippines. (Barton, 1946: 74)

Ma-mien   A horse-headed god who comes to collect the soul when the register of death indicates his life is over. The door god verifies the "warrant" before allowing him to enter. China. (Larousse, 1968: 399)

Mampes   The god who meets the good dead and conducts them to the island of Belet, and is also the guardian of the bridge which leads to it. The Semang, the Menik Kaien, and the Kintak Bong, Malaya. (Evans, 1937: 257, 263; Eliade, 1964: 281)

Mana   Etruscan goddess of "the souls of the dead." Italy. (Altheim, 1937: 117)

Mandait   The spirit of souls. The Manobo, Philippines. (Jocano, 1969: 23)

Manduyapit   The ferryman who transported the souls of the dead to the afterworld. The Manobo, Philippines. (Jocano, 1969: 23)

Mangagaway   A goddess who brought disease and death. The Tagalog, Philippines. (Jocano, 1969: 11)

Manlaton   The god of death, who eats the kidneys of those dead which have not been taken by other spirits. The Isneg, Luzon, Philippines. (Vanoverbergh, 1938: 237)

Mantuona   An Etruscan goddess of the dead associated with Mantus. Italy. (Altheim, 1937: 118)

Manturna   An Etruscan goddess of death. Italy. (Herbig, 1925, 5: 535)

Mantus   An Etruscan god of death and of the underworld. Italy. (Altheim, 1937: 118; von Vacano, 1960: 148; Herbig, 1925, 5: 523; Fairbanks, 1907: 238)

Ma-o-ma-ka-nen   A beneficent spirit who accompanies the dead on his journey to the afterworld. The Batak, Palawan, Malaysia. (Cole, 1945: 70)

Mara   Buddhist god of death and of evil. China. (Werner, 1932: 307; Campbell, 1962: 219)

Maraya   The god of death. The Sinhalese, India and Ceylon. (Ames, 1964: 24; Yalman, 1964: 130; 1966: 213)

Mari Bhavani   Brahman goddess of death. The equivalent of Oba in Mirzapur. India. (Crooke, 1894: 94)

Mari Masan   The deity of the cremation grounds. The Doms, United Provinces, India. (Crooke, 1925, 4: 841)

Maru-a-nuku   A goddess, guardian of the entrance to Kororupo, who leads ghosts to the underworld. Anaa Island, Tuamotus, Polynesia. (Stimson, 1933: 25)

Maru-a-roto   A goddess, guardian of the entrance to Kororupo, who leads ghosts to the underworld. Anaa Island, Tuamotus, Polynesia. (Stimson, 1933: 25)

Guédé Masaka   A god of the dead and of cemeteries—a grave-digger, assistant of Guédé Nibo. Haiti, West Indies. (Marcelin, 1950: 194)

Masan   God/goddess of the cremation grounds—considered by some as male, others as female. The Doms, India. (Crooke, 1925, 4: 841; Briggs, 1953: 528–529)

Masani   A goddess of cremation and of burial grounds. Also a goddess of disease and a sister of Sitala. India. (Crooke, 1894: 80; Briggs, 1920: 133, 137)

Masauu, Masauwu   Hopi god of death, of the underworld, and of the earth's surface. As the latter he is a god also of fertility and a germ god. He is beneficent and friendly as a god of fire whose heat causes crops to grow. Among some clans he is known as Eototo. Arizona. (Fewkes, 1902: 21; Hatt, 1951: 859; Parsons, 1939, 1: 170, 179; Tyler, 1964: 3, 4, 8, 19)

Maso Mung   A demon who brings death to the Lepchas. Sikkim. (Nebesky-Wojkowitz, 1956, 2: 135)

Mate   "Death"—whose wife is Iro Puget. Banks Island, Melanesia. (Bray, 1935: 248)

Mathunda   The creator god, but also associated with death and destruction. The Sandawe, Tanzania. (Raa, 1969: 25, 47)

Matu   God of the dead. The Bambuti, Zaire. (Mbiti, 1970: 117)

Maung Ingyi   A water nat who "causes death by drowning." The Burmans and the Talaings, Burma. (Temple, 1925, 3: 23)

Ma Us Amkiunic   The death god of the Kekchi of Chamelco. Guatemala. (Thompson, 1970: 303)

Mǎ zom mung   A spirit who takes "the form of a huge black dog . . . frequently held responsible for the death of a person." The Lepchas, Sikkim. (Nebesky-Wojkowitz, 1952: 28)

Mboli The supreme being and creator of the Zande, who also causes disease and death. Congo. (Williams, 1936: 119)

Mehenit A form of Net wherein she provides the linens and arrays the dead in them. Egypt. (Budge, 1969, 1: 462)

Memelú An "evil spirit which caused the death of children." The Betoi, Colombia. (Hernandez de Alba, 1948: 398)

Meng P'o The goddess of the Broth of Oblivion which the dead spirits must drink before being reborn. China. (Maspero, 1963: 368; Werner, 1932: 312)

Merodach The god of heaven and earth, the mediator between gods and men, the divine king, was at an earlier time a god of death associated with the dog—the hounds of death. Babylonia. Near East. (Sayce, 1898: 95–8, 388)

Meskhenet, Meskhenit, Meshkent Goddess of the funeral chamber who accompanied the dead soul for judgment, testifying in his behalf. She is more usually a goddess of rebirth and of destiny in that she predicts the future of the newborn. Egypt. (Knight, 1915: 71–72; Jayne, 1962: 85–86; Budge, 1969, 2: 144, 285; Ames, 1965: 111)

Mestha, Mest, Mesti, Amset, Imset One of the four sons of Horus. As a god of the Canopic jars in the underworld, he guards the stomach and large intestines. As a god of the cardinal points he represents the south. Egypt. (Knight, 1915: 35; Budge, 1969, 1: 492)

Mianikotoibo God of the dead and ruler "of all Cubeo souls and all macaws; this last suggests that the souls . . . may actually be identified with macaws." He is a deformed deity whose wife is Wanio. He is the brother of Homanihiko and Kuwai. The Cubeo and the Tucano, Colombia. (Zerries, 1968: 255)

Micapetlacalli A goddess of the dead, wife of Nextepeua. The Aztec, Mexico. (Caso, 1958: 64)

Mictecacihuatl, Mictlantecihuatl Goddess of the dead and of the underworld. Wife of Mictlantecuhtli. The Aztec, Mexico. (Vaillant, 1962: 147; Alexander, 1920: 80; Nicholson, 1967: 26; Sykes, 1952: 141)

Mictlantecuhtli God of the dead and of the underworld whose wife is Mictecacihuatl. He was god of the north, and god of the eleventh hour of the day; as god of the underworld, the god of the fifth hour of the night. Also called Tzontemoc and Acolnauacatl. The Aztec, Mexico. (Alexander, 1920: 54, 57, 80; Vaillant, 1962: 140; Spence, 1923: 327, 331)

Mihr With Sraosh and Rashnu "weigh the soul," and sit in judgment. Persia. (Larousse, 1973: 198)

Milómaki A boy from the sky who brought death to the people, but also was the source of wondrous music. When he sang all came to listen, but those who "then ate fish died instantly." They sacrificed him by burning and from his ashes a palm tree grew. From its wood the people make flutes. The Yurupai, Brazil. (Roheim, 1925: 185; Alexander, 1920: 294)

Milu God of death and of the underworld. Hawaii. He is the equivalent of Miru of the Maori. In some areas of Polynesia, a goddess. (Andersen, 1928: 305; Beckwith, 1940: 114; Poignant, 1967: 63)

Minti Dara Bunsu A water goddess who aids good divers, but who can cause harm and death by drowning. The Iban Dyaks, Sarawak, Borneo. (Sarawak Gazette, 1963: 135)

Miru On Paumotu, god of night and of the souls of the dead. On Mangaia, the cannibalistic goddess of the underworld. Female on Rarotonga, and among the Maori; male on Paumotu and in Hawaii. Polynesia. (Andersen, 1928: 121; Williamson, 1933, 2: 80, 171; Buck, 1938: 111)

Misik thang A malevolent spirit of the Lungris who causes accidental deaths of all kinds. The Tangsas, India and Burma. (Dutta, 1959: 67)

Mommukun A god of reproduction who also causes illness and death. The Ifugao, Philippines. (Barton, 1946: 44)

Monkuhubu A god associated with violent death. Descendant of Umalgo, the Sun. The Ifugao, Philippines. (Barton, 1946: 41)

Montalug A beneficent god of reproduction who, however, can cause illness and death. The Ifugao, Philippines. (Barton, 1946: 44)

Morana A Slavic goddess of death and of winter. Bohemia. (Bray, 1935: 45)

Moros A personification of unfortunate destiny and of violent death. Son of Nyx. Greece. (Roscher, 1965, 2, 2: 3215)

Mors The inexorable god of death, also associated with the underworld. Twin brother of Sleep. They are the sons of Nyx though sometimes named as sons of Earth and Tartarus. He is also called Thanatos, which see. Greece. (Bulfinch, 1898: 488; Gray, 1935: 97; Roscher, 1965, 2, 2: 3220)

Mot, Muth A god of death, of drought and sterility, and of the dead seed, but representing its death and rebirth, and so a god of fertility, of vegetable dormancy. Canaan, Syria, and Phoenicia, Near East. (Vriezen, 1963: 51; Crawford, 1957: 19; Albright, 1956: 86–87; James, 1960: 88; Paton, 1925, 3: 182)

Mout An Egyptian personification of death. (Gardiner, 1925, 9: 791)

Moyotsung God of the dead of the Ao Nagas. India. (Mills, 1926: 228)

Mrtyu Given variously as a god or goddess of death. Compassionate, she did not wish to kill and so her tears were changed by Brahman into fatal diseases. India. (Bhattacharji, 1970: 56; Gray, 1930: 202; Danielou, 1964: 138)

Mungu A benevolent god, but also associated with death. The Epulu (Pygmies), Zaire. (Turnbull, 1965: 237)

Muni Mental Batu A water goddess who aids good divers, but who can also be harmful and cause death by drowning. The Iban Dyaks, Sarawak, Borneo. (Sarawak Gazette, 1963: 135)

Muut The messenger of death, created by Mukat to prevent overpopulation, frequently appeared as an owl whose hooting foretold death. He was regarded "as both a blessing and a bringer of sadness." The Cahuilla, California. (Brumgardt and Bowles, 1981: 37; Bean, 1974: 167)

Naenia Roman goddess of lamentation over the dead. (Salkeld, 1844: 314; Roscher, 1965, 3, 1: 2)

Nagi, Nagila The Shade, or Apparition. The Shade-like. Class 4 deities of the Oglala. Plains Indians, South Dakota. (Powers, 1977: 54)

Namtar Akkadian god of death, of fate, whose wife is Hushbishag. Near East. (Kramer, 1961: 124; Langdon, 1931: 161)

Nang sgrub srin gi gdong can A form of Yama whose attributes are a chopper and a skull-cup. Tibet. (Nebesky-Wojkowitz, 1956, 1: 82)

Nasu A demoness, the carrion, who "represents the corruption of corpses." Persia. (Huart, 1963: 43; Schoeps, 1961: 87; Gray, 1930: 211)

Nau Taufiti A goddess associated with Kume in cleansing of the dead spirit for participation in the after-life. Also called Mafutoka, Rautoro. The wife of Rata. Tikopia, Polynesia. (Firth, 1967, 1: 87–90)

Naxpatao Guardian of the dead of the Menomini, brother of Manabus. Together they gave medicine bundles to man and the powers to use them. Wisconsin. (Skinner, 1913: 200; 1915: 86, 132)

Necessitas A goddess associated with death and with destiny. Italy. (Roscher, 1965, 3, 1: 70–72)

Neheb-ka A serpent goddess who provided the dead with the divine food; one of the 42 judges or assessors of the dead for the goddess Maat; also directs the way to the underworld. Egypt. (Hambly, 1929: 663; Budge, 1969, 1: 419; 1969, 2: 62)

Nephthys, Nebt-het Egyptian goddess of "the death which is not eternal," of night and of darkness. She is the daughter of Nut and Seb, the sister/wife and female counterpart of Set. Though Set killed Osiris, their brother, she helped Isis in bringing about his resurrection—as a deity of magic and of healing. (Budge, 1969, 2: 254–258; Knight, 1915: 83–84; Jayne, 1962: 73–74)

Nergal An Akkadian/Sumerian/Babylonian god of destructive forces—of the sun, of war, of pestilence, and of fire—which cause the death of mankind and of vegetation. He became the god of the dead in marrying Ereshkigal, and judge of souls. He is god of the planet Mars (or Saturn), and of the month Kislev (Semitic), or Kisilimu (Sumerian). Near East. (Jastrow, 1898: 66–68, 459, 463; Hommel, 1925, 3: 75; Langdon, 1931: 147; Seligmann, 1948: 30)

Nesoxochi A goddess of the dead and the wife of Ixpuzteque. Aztec, Mexico. (Caso, 1958: 64)

Nextepeua A god of the dead whose wife is Micapetlacalli. The Aztec, Mexico. (Caso, 1958: 64)

Ngaa The god of death and of illness. Son of Num. The Nentsy and the Yurok-Samoyed, Siberia. (Pettersson, 1957: 21; Prokof'yeva, 1964: 564)

Ngumatol te aba A deity invoked in post-emtombment rites for the dead. The Ifugao, Philippines. (Barton, 1946: 74)

Nibo An hermaphroditic deity of the dead and of tombs, protector of the living as well as the dead, and invoked for news of the living who are away, and of the dead. Haiti, West Indies. (Marcelin, 1950: 146, 181, 183, 186; Simpson, 1945: 43)

Nifoloa A "vindictive long-toothed demon whose bite caused death." Samoa, Polynesia. (Grattan, 1948: 131)

Naac Nimá God of death of the Trique Tribe of Oaxaca. Son of Nexhequiriac. Mexico. (Valentini, 1899: 38)

Nipa The "Moon as Goddess of Night, Death, Cold, Sleep." The Algonquin Indians, Eastern North America. (Bray, 1935: 273)

Nirriti Goddess of death, destruction, and misery, the female counterpart of Yama. She is guardian of the southwest quarter of the compass. India. (Bhattacharji, 1970: 8, 81; Danielou, 1964: 138; Dowson, 1961: 223)

Nirrta, Nirritu The masculine aspect of Nirriti, representing death, destruction and misery. Son of Kasyapa. India. (Danielou, 1964: 137; Sykes, 1952: 154)

Niu-t'ou An ox-headed deity, one of those who comes to collect the souls when the register of Death indicates life is over. His "warrant" must be verified by the Door God. China. (Larousse, 1968: 399)

Noatch The "supreme evil spirit" who haunted the burial grounds to intercept the souls of the dead as they left the grave to go to the afterworld. The Wheelman, Southwest Australia. (Hassell, 1936: 702)

Nomou A god who devours the ghosts (souls?) caught by Lug and given to him. Yap Island, the Carolines, Micronesia. (MacKenzie, 1930: 172–173)

Nouvavou, or **Nouvavon** One of the gods of the dead and of cemeteries—a beggar, often ridicules. Haiti, West Indies. (Marcelin, 1950: 197)

Nuizarom-Paz God of the dead, and yet protective of the Mordvin people. Russia. (Roheim, 1954: 62)

Nuskiaχɛk The "supernatural lord of the land of ashes, . . . has a huge salmon-weir in which he catches the corpses of those drowned either in the rivers or the ocean; they serve him as food, in fact, they are his salmon." The Bella Coola, British Columbia. (McIlwraith, 1948, 2: 468)

Nya A Slavonic god, the equivalent of the Greek Pluto. (Leger, 1925, 1: 466)

Nyamenle Though a sky god and created by Edenkema, "he is equated with Edenkema as the master and sender of death." His wife is Azele Yaba. The Nzema (Akan), Ghana. (Grottanelli, 1956: 33–41)

Odame Goddess of death as well as of birth. The Gã, Nungwa, Ghana. (Field, 1937: 28)

Odin Among his many functions the Scandinavian All-Father had that of a god of the dead, of those fallen in battle and of the hanged. (Davidson, 1964: 27–29, 48–51; Guerber, 1895: 25–26; Turville-Petre, 1964: 35–45, 54; Schoeps, 1961: 105)

Olouiuidur One of the four tutelary spirits who seek out and transport the souls of the dead. In the chronicle of Nele Sibu. The Cuna, Panama. (Nordenskiold, 1938: 295)

Guédé l'Oraille Goddess of storm and of violent death. Haiti, West Indies. (Marcelin, 1950: 196)

Orcus Greek/Roman god of death and of the underworld. He brings death both gently and violently. (Fairbanks, 1907: 237; Frazer, 1961: 231n; Larousse, 1968: 213)

Osiris As a god of the dead and of the underworld, he is judge of the dead, and bestows on his followers a life of abundance after death. As a god of vegetation he represents the fertility of the Nile, the sprouting and harvest of crops. Through both he is the god of death and resurrection. Brother/husband of Isis, son of Seb and Nut. Egypt. (Frazer, 1960: 420–421, 442–443; Casson, 1965: 54; Budge, 1969, 2: 115, 118, 139)

Osooso Goddess of suicides. With Makunai (female) and Horomorun and Konopia (males), the original kupuna ancestors of the Eagle-people, a sib. The Siuai, Bougainville, Solomon Islands, Melanesia. (Oliver, 1967: 57, 67)

Ouki One of the family of the gods of the dead. Haiti, West Indies. (Marcelin, 1950: 198)

Oxlahun Tox A "Tzeltal demon, presumably a death god." Mexico. (Thompson, 1970: 325)

Pales An Etruscan god associated with cremation. Italy. (Altheim, 1937: 136)

P'ang Ch'e, P'ang Chiao, and **P'ang Chu** The three "Goddesses of the Corpse." China. (Werner, 1932: 107)

Panthoibi Goddess of death and of birth. Wife of Khaba. The Meitheis, Manipur, Assam. (Hodson, 1908: 97)

Pap Olokupilele   God of the cemetery. The Cuna, Panama. (Keeler, 1960: 91)

Patollo, Patollus   God of death, of the underworld. Prussia. (Fisher, 1970: 149; Machal, 1918: Plate XXXVII)

Paugak   The personification of death. The Algonquin Indians, Eastern North America. (Schoolcraft, 1857, 6: 660)

Pawul   The demon of graves. The Blandas, Malay Peninsula. (Skeat, 1906: 105)

Pecols   A god associated with death. It is "possible that he is a personification of the land of the dead." Old Prussian. (Welsford, 1925, 9: 489; Puhvel, 1974: 83)

Penyadin   A water demon who causes death by sucking blood. The Mantra, Malay Peninsula. (Skeat, 1906: 323)

Pezelao, Bezelao   The god of death, of the underworld, as well as a god of the earth. The Zapotec, Oaxaca, Mexico. (Whitecotton, 1977: 158, 169; Bancroft, 1886: 457; Hagar, 1925, 1: 436)

Phersu   An Etruscan god of death. Italy. (Altheim, 1937: 158)

Phonos   Murder personified, a child of Eris. Greece. (Hesiod-Brown, 1981: 59; Barthell, 1971: 8; Roscher, 1965, 3, 2: 2423)

Phyi-sgrub   A form of Yama who is "protector of the Yellow Bonnets (Ge-lugs-pa sect)." Tibet. (Getty, 1962: 153)

Pickollos   An Old Prussian god associated with death. (Welsford, 1925, 9: 489)

Pimukvul   The personification of death. The Acagchemem, San Juan Capistrano, California. (Boscana, 1933: 75, 198)

Pinyuhan   A god of reproduction, beneficent, but also can cause illness and death. The Ifugao, Philippines. (Barton, 1946: 44)

Pluto, Plouton   Greek/Roman god of the dead and of the underworld, identified with Hades and with Dis. However, he is the benevolent chthonic god of agriculture and of the earth's treasures, rather than a threatening god of death. (Cox, 1870, 2: 307; Bulfinch, 1898: 7, 14; Fairbanks, 1907: 235)

Pogtan   One of the "Ending Deities" who end "either life or death . . . [and] are invoked in funeral rites." The Ifugao, Philippines. (Barton, 1946: 84)

Pradjapati   The name of Brahma (god of fire) "as lord of cremation." Bali, Indonesia. (Covarrubias, 1937: 317)

Proserpina   Roman goddess of the dead as wife of Pluto, but more importantly the goddess of agricultural fertility, of seeds and their sprouting. Same as Persephone. (Frazer, 1960: 461; Bulfinch, 1898: 12; Fairbanks, 1907: 180)

Pua   A god/goddess of death on Maui, but also has medicinal powers. Hawaii. (Westervelt, 1915: 98, 111; 1963: 111)

Ah Puch, Pucuh, Hunhau, Yum Cimil, Xibalba, Cumhau   The malevolent Mayan god of death, ruler of Mitnal in the underworld. He is the Ma Us Amkuinic of the Kekchi, and Pucuh of the Tzeltal, Tsotzil, and Tojolabal. Mexico and Guatemala. (Thompson, 1970: 303; Morley, 1946: 216)

Purukupali   The god who decreed death for all creation because of the death of his son Djinini. His wife is Bima. He is the son of Mudungkala and brother of Wuriupranala and Murupiangkala. The Tiwi, Melville Island, Australia. (Mountford, 1958: 24–25, 29)

Qebhsennuf   A hawk-headed god, one of the four sons of Horus who are the gods of the Canopic jars in the afterworld. He is assisted by Serqet (Selket) in guarding the (variously given) liver and gallbladder, or the intestines. As a god of the cardinal points he represents the west. He is also god of the fourth hour of the day and of the night. Egypt. (Knight, 1915: 35; Budge, 1969, 1: 456, 491; 1969, 2: 294; Larousse, 1968: 40)

Ran   A Teutonic goddess of the sea as well as of death—of those perishing at sea. She is cruel and dangerous, entrapping men in her net and drawing them to her realm. She is the wife of Aegir and the mother of the nine wave maidens, who are the mothers of Heimdall. (Grimm, 1880: 311; Guerber, 1895: 172; Davidson, 1964: 129)

Rangda   One of her aspects is that of "the goddess of the temple of the dead." She is a manifestation of Durga, as a goddess sexually obvious and lustful and associated with black magic and love potions. Bali, Indonesia. (Grader, 1969, 8: 155–156)

Ravuravu   Fijian god of murder. Melanesia. (Thomson, 1925, 1: 444)

Rīri Yakā In various human and animal forms, the blood demon digs up the graves of the newly buried to devour the flesh or suck the blood. Sri Lanka (Ceylon). (Ames, 1978: 45)

Ro kha ma A goddess who lives in cemeteries. Tibet. (Nebesky-Wojkowitz, 1956, 1: 271)

Rot A devil "who causes people to commit suicide." The Lepchas, Sikkim. (Gorer, 1938: 234)

Rota, Rutu God of death and disease, and of the underworld, Ruto-aibmo. The Lapps, Northern Europe. (Holmberg, 1925, 7: 798; Dioszegi, 1968: 30; Karsten, 1955: 40, 53)

Ršp The "power of pestilence and death." Canaan. (Gray, 1957: 137)

Sa A goddess who "protects his members"—of the deceased. Egypt. (Budge, 1969, 1: 425)

(Chinoi) Sagar A goddess encountered by the souls of the dead on the way to Belet, the afterworld. Malay Peninsula. (Eliade, 1964: 281)

Salmoxis *See* **Zalmoxis.**

Sandé If this moong causes death, ceremonies of disinfection must be carried out immediately. The Lepchas, Sikkim. (Gorer, 1938: 350)

San Hsing "The Noxious God . . . takes the dead man's soul and brings it back home." China. (Werner, 1932: 333)

Sä·tma A dreaded male supernatural who wears a nose-ring and is responsible for sudden death, accidents, etc. The Bella Coola, British Columbia. (McIlwraith, 1948, 1: 49)

Savea, Savea Si'uleo The god of the dead and of judgment in the underworld, Pulotu. Samoa, Polynesia. (Moss, 1925: 114; Williamson, 1933, 1: 5: 1933, 2: 155)

Seker A hawk-headed, mummy-form god of the dead merged with Ptah and Osiris as Ptah-Seker-Asar. They form the "symbol of resurrection from the dead." A god of the Hennu boat in the underworld, and god of the fourth and of the seventh hours of the night. Egypt. (Knight, 1915: 113; Budge, 1969, 1: 217, 506–507; 1969, 2: 117, 301, 503)

Selket, Selqet, Serqet A scorpion goddess of the embalming of the dead, protectress, with Qebhsennuf, of the Canopic jar containing the intestines or the liver and gallbladder (variously given) of the deceased. She is also the "guardian of conjugal union." Egypt. (Casson, 1965: 114; Larousse, 1968: 39, 40; Budge, 1969, 1: 198, 456)

Semmesmaat A goddess "referred to as the keeper of the grave." Latvia. (Welsford, 1925, 9: 242)

Semuganda A python god of death who is invoked by women for children, and by men for wealth and property. The Basoga, Uganda. (Roscoe, 1915: 247)

Shadapinji The messenger of death (from Nyambi) with whom evil people have to live when they die. The Hambukushu, Ngamiland. Botswana. (Larson, 1971: 57)

Shidook When death is caused by this moong ceremonies are performed "two months after the death." The Lepchas, Sikkim. (Gorer, 1938: 351)

gShin rje, Shinje, Shinje-chogyal, gSin rje The god of the dead and their impartial judge. Same as Yama. gSin rje is also a term denoting a whole class of death-bringing demons. Tibet and Nepal. (Nebesky-Wojkowitz, 1956, 1: 82; Schlagintweit, 1969: 93; Furer-Haimendorf, 1964: 195, 247; Evans-Wentz, 1960: 35–37; Waddell, 1959: 367; Tucci, 1980: 194–195)

Shom mung A malignant spirit responsible for accidental death, suicide, and murder. He captures the soul and prevents it from going to the other world; must be forced to relinquish it. The Lepchas, Sikkim. (Nebesky-Wojkowitz, 1952: 29)

Sidapa Goddess of death, one of the chief deities of the Bisaya, who with her husband, Makaptan, ruled over Kamariitan, the earth section of the Bisayan world of deities. Philippines. (Kroeber, 1918: 43)

Mademoiselle Similia One of the family of the gods of the dead. Haiti, West Indies. (Marcelin, 1950: 198)

Siquani A god of the dead who "presides over the souls of children." Japan. (Coleman, 1832: 341)

Sixsekilaix A deity who controls the death of men and of animals. The Bella Coola, British Columbia. (Boas, 1898: 30)

Skwanät·äm·a "The Female Mourner." Her wailing is an omen of death. Yet—"as she cries she ejects mucus from her nose, which solidifies into a glass-like substance about a foot in length. Anyone who sees her should take the transformed mucus, and wrap it in some article of clothing; it will bring him good fortune." The Bella Coola, British Columbia. (McIlwraith, 1948, 1: 535)

ka smer A demoness of violent death. The Khasi, Assam. (Stegmiller, 1921: 411)

Smertis A Lithuanian god of death who "comes as a warrior with sword and pike." (Grimm, 1883, 2: 846)

Sokar, Sokaris A god of the dead and of the grave. Egypt. (Schoeps, 1961: 70)

Songkam God of death and god of the evil spirits. The Nagas, Cachar, India. (Elwin, 1969: 423)

Sor The demon of violent death, and also the cause of illness and miscarriages. The Lepchas, Sikkim. (Gorer, 1938: 221, 232, 285)

Guédé-Souffrance-Latrine One of the family of the gods of the dead. Haiti, West Indies. (Marcelin, 1950: 198)

Spinagaralu The locust larva who was the originator of death. The Wiyot, California. (Kroeber, 1925: 120)

Srinmo A demoness of death. Tibet. (Neumann, 1955: 234)

Srog bdag mo Goddess and chief of the gshin rje mo deities who are demonesses of death. Tibet. (Nebesky-Wojkowitz, 1956, 1: 267)

Sroš A deity associated with the souls of the dead. Iran. (Gray, 1930: 107)

Stro-je A god of the Ch'iang at Lo-pu-chai "who controls people's souls. People worship him when they are worried lest their souls depart and they die." Szechwan, China. (Graham, 1958: 49)

Sǔ mo mung With her husband, Dǔt mung, "killed lonely travellers and ate their flesh." She also seduced young men. The Lepchas, Sikkim. (Nebesky-Wojkowitz, 1952: 28)

Supai, Supay A chthonic deity, a god of death. The Inca, Peru. (Larousse, 1968: 444; Rhys, 1937: 163)

Surma A Finno-Ugric monster—the "personification of fatal destiny or of violent death." (Larousse, 1968: 306)

Swadha Goddess of funeral ceremonies. India. (Coleman, 1832: 397)

Sxaiaxwax A malevolent deity who attacks men and seduces young girls. His "coming almost invariably brings death." He is so evil "shamans can rarely cure anyone visited by him." However, on occasion he can be beneficial—making a man a shaman, or easing childbirth. The Bella Coola, British Columbia. (McIlwraith, 1948, 1: 47–49)

Ix Tab The Mayan goddess of suicide and of the gallows. Those who committed suicide were believed to go directly to Paradise. Mexico. (Morley, 1946: 221, 231; Tozzer, 1941: 132, 310; Nicholson, 1967: 122)

Tahquitz, Tawquish, Taqwuš An evil god, originally good, to whom Mukat gave many powers expecting them to be used beneficially, but Tahquitz grew to use them harmfully, stealing souls and causing misfortunes, diseases and death. He took numerous forms: "old man, a blue flame, or a meteor"—the latter came to be taken as an omen of death. Yet, he also conferred upon some people the power to heal. He lived on San Jacinto Peak. The Cahuilla, California. (Brumgardt and Bowles, 1981: 34–38; Bean, 1974: 166)

T'ai Shan A very important mountain god who became god of birth (life) and death, invoked for sons and success. He then became judge of the dead. China. (Haydon, 1974: 193–194; Day, 1940: 120–121)

Ta-iti A god of mourning in Tahiti. Polynesia. (Henry, 1928: 378)

Tarp-eia An Etruscan goddess of death. Italy. (Herbig, 1925, 5: 535)

Tatan bak "Father of bones." A god of death of the Cakchiquel. Guatemala. (Recinos, 1950: 111)

Tatan holom "Father of skulls." A god of death of the Cakchiquel. Guatemala. (Recinos, 1950: 111)

Tauptú The "hawk of death who lives in the sky. . . . Shooting stars are caused by tauptú defecating at night. . . . [He] does not cause illness, but when people get sick he begins to eat away the flesh and finally kills them and eventually takes their bones to his abode in the sky." The Nambicuara, Brazil. (Oberg, 1953: 99, 100)

Taxet A god in the sky to whom go those killed in battle or murdered. The Haida, British Columbia. (Chamberlain, 1925, 6: 473; Alexander, 1964: 253)

Te-meharo The god of strangulation. Tahiti, Polynesia. (Henry, 1925: 376)

Tena-ranide "Death itself." The Tinne, Northern Athapascan Indians, Canada. (Alexander, 1964: 78)

Teoyaomique, Teoyamaqui, Teoyaomqui, Teoyaoim-qui Goddess of the warrior dead who carried them to paradise. She was the consort of Huizilopochtli. Also the deity of the enemy warriors who were sacrificed to the sun. Some name as a god. Mexico. (Bancroft, 1886: 398; Alexander, 1920: 54; Bourke, 1892: 484; Caso, 1958: 59)

Tha-ma The god who judges the dead. The Karens, Burma. (McMahon, 1876: 141)

Thanatos, or Mors Death, the son of Nyx or some say Earth and Tartarus, twin brother of Hypnos. He is regarded as the more opportune or appropriate form of death (than Mors) and "as a personification of endless repose." Greece. (Murray, 1935: 222–224; Barthell, 1971: 8; Larousse, 1968: 166; Hesiod-Brown, 1981: 59)

Thupltha An Etruscan goddess who may be a goddess of death or may be a goddess of benediction and healing. Italy. (Roscher, 1965, 5: 909)

Tia The god of violent death. The Haida, British Columbia. (Chamberlain, 1925, 6: 473)

Ti-Canmil, Petit Camille One of the family of the gods of the dead. Haiti, West Indies. (Marcelin, 1950: 198)

Tiki On Rarotonga (Cook Islands) he is judge of the dead and god of Paradise. Polynesia. (Moss, 1925: 114)

'Ti Kita A goddess of the Petro group of deities who is "associated with the cult of magic and the dead." Haiti, West Indies. (Herskovits, 1937: 144, 319)

Guédé Ti-Ouare The chief-of-state of the Guédé (gods of the dead and of cemeteries). Also a healing god. Haiti, West Indies. (Marcelin, 1950: 197)

Ti-tsang p'u-sa, Ti-tsang Wang p'u-sa The Buddhist Bodhisattva of compassion and mercy, intercessor for the dead and saviour of souls, leading them to the heaven of Amitabha. Same as Kshitigarbha. China. (Werner, 1932: 497; Getty, 1962: 104–105; Day, 1940: 124–125)

Tluscv An Etruscan deity of death and of the under-world, associated with the west. Italy. (Hamblin, 1975: 95)

Todote God of death and of evil. Son of the sky and earth. The Ent-Samoyed, Siberia. (Larousse, 1973: 435)

Toglai The first man, who was considered by some as judge of the dead. The Bagobo, Philippines. (MacKenzie, 1930: 306)

Tokákami A god of death and of the underworld. The Huichol, Mexico. (Chamberlain, 1900: 306; Alexander, 1920: 122)

Topiehe A bird of the Mato Grosso who "when killed, steals the person's shadow," which causes the death of the individual. The Bacairi, Brazil. (Abreu, 1938: 268; Altenfelder, 1950: 266)

Tore The god of death among the Bambuti who "loves the dead more than the living." Zaire. (Mbiti, 1970, 2: 37, 117)

Toxayon A benevolent guardian of the tomb of the dead—for three nights. The Isneg, Luzon, Philippines. (Vanoverbergh, 1938: 254)

Tse-gu-dzih The chief patriarch in the sky who "gave the boon of death to the world." The Lolos, western China. (Henry, 1903: 105)

Tshe bdag nag po A demon of death. Tibet. (Nebesky-Wojkowitz, 1956, 1: 269)

Ts'in-kuang-wang God of the first Court of Hell and head of the other nine, who evaluates the merits and demerits of the dead. China. (Chavannes, n.d.: 96; Maspero, 1963: 364)

Tuamutef Jackal-headed son of Horus. As a god of the Canopic jars in the underworld he is assisted by Net in protecting the heart and lungs in embalming. As a god of the cardinal points he represents the east. He is god of the third hour of the day and of the night. Egypt. (Budge, 1969, 1: 158, 456, 492; 1969, 2: 145; Knight, 1915: 34)

Tudung A deity invoked in post-entombment rites for the dead. The Ifugao, Philippines. (Barton, 1946: 74)

Tuhan Di-Bawah God of the lower world who created the earth and instituted death to control population. The Jakun and the Mantra, Malay Peninsula. (Skeat, 1906: 179–180, 322; Cole, 1945: 119)

Tulupaligualel One of the four tutelary spirits who seek out and transport the souls of the dead. In the chronicle of Nele Sibu. The Cuna, Panama. (Nordenskiold, 1938: 295)

Tuwale He is "a spirit who eats bats, and whenever he eats one a man on earth dies." The Wemale, Philippines. (Raats, 1969: 49)

u tynjang The "lame devil who lives in the thicket and tickles people to death." The Khasi, Assam. (Stegmiller, 1921: 411)

ka Tyrut A goddess of violent death to whom offerings of a black hen (if death is by the sword) and sows are made. The Khasi, Assam. (Gurdon, 1907: 136; Stegmiller, 1921: 411)

Tzontemoc A god of the dead whose wife is Chalmecacihuatl. Another name of Mictlantecutli. The Aztec, Mexico. (Caso, 1958: 64; Alexander, 1920: 80)

Uac Mitun Ahau A Mayan god of death and of the "sixth hell" in the underworld. Mexico. (Tozzer, 1941: 147; Thompson, 1970: 228)

Uggae A Babylonian god of the dead. Near East. (Littleton, 1970, 2: 111)

Umm s-Subyan A name of Tab'a as a killer of infants. She is also known in the east—in Egypt, Kordofan, and Mecca. Morocco. (Westermarck, 1926, 1: 400–402)

Um Ut Anubis as god of embalming and mummification. Egypt. (Knight, 1915: 20)

Unhcegila Dragon-like creatures of the land who are responsible for "mysterious disappearances or death." "Their power lies in their tails and if they lose their tails they are weak and foolish and can do no harm." The females of the Unktehi. The Lakota, South Dakota. (Walker, 1980: 108, 122)

Urur In the Egyptian mortuary rituals—"The god Urur gives thee the fluid of life." (Roheim, 1972: 163)

Vata Papuan god of death and of disease. Melanesia. (Bray, 1935: 251)

Vayu The wind, who is benevolent in aiding "the just man to surmount obstacles on his journey after death" and as a destroyer of evil, but is also malevolent as the source "of death in the storm." Persia. (Hinnells, 1973: 31; Larousse, 1973: 192)

Velinas, Velnias The god of the dead and the underworld is a dangerous and punitive deity who lives deep in swamps and lakes and lures people to their death by drowning. It is instant death to see him. He takes the form of a serpent, which indicates his dual character. Besides being a god of death he is the god of wealth and trade, of cattle and fertility, and is helpful to the poor. Lithuania. (Gimbutas, 1974: 87–92)

Velu Mate, Velumate Lettish goddess of the dead and of the underworld. Latvia. (Gray, 1930: 194; Leach, 1950, 2: 608)

Viduus Roman god who separated body and soul at death. (Roscher, 1965, 2, 1: 231; Prentice Hall, 1965: 149)

Vielona Lithuanian goddess of the dead. (Leger, 1925, 1: 466)

Vucub-Came God of death and of the underworld. The Maya, Guatemala. (Krickeberg, 1968: 79; Recinos, 1950: 109–110)

Walumbe God of death of the Baganda, the Ganda, the Basoga (among the latter he is also called Semuganda). Son of Gulu. Uganda. (Mbiti, 1970, 1: 37, 118–119; Roscoe, 1965: 315; Werner, 1964: 117; Feldman, 1963: 85)

Wamara Among the Haya he is the supreme deity, as well as god of the souls of the dead. Elsewhere he is a god of fertility and of abundance. Uganda and Tanzania. (Taylor, 1962: 111, 142)

Wanio A goddess of the dead, wife of Mianikotoibo. The Cubeo and the Tucano, Colombia. (Zerries, 1968: 255)

Wanman'-Mindo One of the family of the gods of the dead. Haiti, West Indies. (Marcelin, 1950: 198)

Wertspit The "locust larva" who introduced death. The Yoruk, California. (Kroeber, 1925: 74)

Whiro God of death and evil, of darkness, the antithesis of Tane. He is also the god of thieves. The Maori, New Zealand. (Best, 1924: 107, 237; Andersen, 1928: 115)

Wirwer An evil spirit who may snatch an unguarded corpse and devour it. This can be prevented by sticking a spear in the tomb. The Isneg of Luzon. Among the Apayao he will dig up the corpse to eat it. Philippines. (Vanoverbergh, 1938: 232, 252; Wilson, 1947: 23)

Woden The Teutonic high god who was in one of his aspects the god of death. In others he was a god of war, of wisdom, of fate and of storms. Germany and England. Same as Odin, Wotan, Wodan. (Larousse, 1968: 253–254; Davidson, 1964: 69; Wagner, 1882: 5, 6; Branston, 1957: 87–90; Turville-Petre, 1964: 70–72)

Wolgara A god of the Wardoman who judges the dead. He also "kills" and revives the aspiring medicine man. Australia. (Eliade, 1973: 145)

Wu-er-yeh A god who conducts the souls of the dead to the afterworld to be judged. Southwest China. (Graham, 1961: 180)

Wuluwait   The boatman who takes the spirit of the dead to Purelko, an island, "the aboriginal 'heaven.'" Australia. (Mountford, 1965: 62)

Wun   God of death, brother of Venin. The Bachama, Nigeria. (Meek, 1930: 324)

Xiba   A name of the Mayan death god. Mexico and Guatemala. (Thompson, 1970: 303)

Xic   A god of the underworld who brought sudden death to men. The Quiché, Guatemala. (Recinos, 1950: 110)

Ximbanonan   A spirit who revives the recently dead if he wishes to help. The Isneg, Luzon, Philippines. (Vanoverbergh, 1953: 97)

Xipe Totec   The flayed god. "In the Codex Borgia, Xipe is shown in his character of the patron god of the warrior's death by combat, or the stone of sacrifice." Primarily he is the god of the seed and of its planting and represents the renewal of life. The Aztec, Mexico. (Spence, 1923: 204, 218; Burland, 1967: xi; Vaillant, 1962: 149)

Xonaxi Huilia, Xonaxihuilia   The goddess of death and of the underworld—in some towns—whose husband was Coquechila. The Zapotec, Oaxaca, Mexico. (Whitecotton, 1977: 158)

Xonaxi Quecuya   Goddess of death and of the underworld. Wife of Coqui Bexelao. The Zapotecs at Mitla (Coqui Bezelao, the southern Zapotecs). She is also called Xonaxi Huilia in other towns. Oaxaca, Mexico. (Whitecotton, 1977: 158)

Yabme-akka   A variant spelling of Jameakka, Jabmeakka.

Yahira   God of death and of vengeance. Also god of the north. The Guarani, Paraguay and Brazil. (Métraux, 1948: 90)

Yama   God and judge of the dead. A solar god as a son of Vivasvat, the sun, and also god of the south of the compass. Variant names: Dharma, Antaka, Mrtyu, Kala. India, Cambodia, Bali, Mongolia, Tibet, and Korea. (Percheron, 1953: 62; Marchal, 1963: 203; Bhattacharji, 1970: 47–64; Sierksma, 1966: 115; Banerjea, 1953: 53, 73; Moes, 1983: 127)

Yum Cimil (Kimil), Hunhau, Ah Puch, Kisin   Mayan god of death and of the underworld. The name used at present in Yucatan. Mexico. (Morley, 1946: 227; Tozzer, 1941: 32; Bray, 1935: 287)

Yungayung   A deity invoked in post-entombment rites for the dead. The Ifugao, Philippines. (Barton, 1946: 74)

Zalmoxis, Salmoxis   God of the dead and of the underworld of the Getae or Dacians. Romania. He is also a supreme sky god, and a bear god. Romania and Thrace. (Eliade, 1964: 390; 1967: 66)

Guédé Zarignin   One of the family of the gods of the dead and of cemeteries. Haiti, West Indies. (Marcelin, 1950: 198)

Zhi ba'i gshin rje   A form of Yama, the god of the dead. Tibet. (Nebesky-Wojkowitz, 1956, 1: 83)

Zhing skyong   Protective god of the cemetery whose consort is Dus mtshan ma. Tibet. Same as Kshetrapala. (Nebesky-Wojkowitz, 1956, 1: 39–42)

Zombu   The "devil which causes death, and which can be heard on the day of burial and also on the anniversary of the death." The Lepchas, Sikkim. (Gorer, 1938: 375)

24

Afterworld/Underworld: Judgment, Soul (in death)

Abuhene God of death and ruler of the underworld. He is the scarlet macaw, the god of the west and of dark shamanism; as such he eats the liver of humans (not tobacco smoke as the other gods do) which the dark shaman must obtain for him. He represents the setting sun. The Warao, Venezuela. (Wilbert, 1973, 1: 5; 1973, 2: X407)

Abyang Durunuun "Goddess of charms" in the underworld. Assistant to Sumpoy and Magyan. The Bisayan, Philippines. (Jocano, 1969: 21)

Aeacus One of the three judges of the underworld, the judge "of the Europeans." Greece. (Morford and Lenardon, 1975: 246; Leach, 1950, 2: 936)

Ahalgana A god of the underworld who causes dropsy. The Quiché, Guatemala. (Recinos, 1950: 110)

Ahalmez A god of the underworld who brings disaster to men. The Quiché, Guatemala. (Recinos, 1950: 110)

Ahalpuh A god of the underworld who causes disease—"to make men swell and make pus gush forth from their legs." The Quiché, Guatemala. (Recinos, 1950: 110)

Ahaltocob A god of the underworld who brings misery and disaster to men. The Quiché, Guatemala. (Recinos, 1950: 110)

Ahbubu A god of the underworld, offspring of Mayogyog. The Ifugao, Philippines. (Barton, 1946: 34)

Aita An Etruscan god of the underworld, paired with Phersipnai. Same as Eita. Italy. (Pallottino, 1975: 143)

Akaanga Servant of Muru who catches the souls of the dead in nets. Rarotonga (Miru in Mangaia), Polynesia. (Williamson, 1933, 2: 26, 30)

Akaranga A god of the underworld who devours the dead, except those dying in battle. Hervey Island (Cook Islands), Polynesia. (Eliade, 1958: 137)

Akasha Garbha (Nam-mkhahi-snying-po) A Bodhisattva who appears on the third day of the Bardo of Karmic Illusions with Rana-Sambhava, in the testing period after death. Tibet. (Evans-Wentz, 1960: 111)

Akodau A goddess of the underworld of the Nabaloi. Philippines. (Moss, 1920: 283)

Ala Buuray Toyon The same as Arsan-Duolai, god of the underworld. The Yakuts, Siberia. (Tokarev and Gurvich, 1964: 279)

Allara-Ogonur Evil spirit of the underground, of the far north. The Yakut, Siberia. (Czaplicka, 1925, 12: 828)

Allatu Goddess of the underworld and of the dead, who also acts in judgment. A consort of Nergal. Same as Ereshkigal. Assyria/Babylonia/Carthage. (Cook, 1930: 121–122; Frazer, 1960: 379; Rhys, 1937: 8; Wallis, 1939: 255)

Allatum A chthonian goddess, "same as Arsay, daughter of Baal." Ugarit, Canaan. (Albright, 1968: 143; Jacobsen, 1970: 35)

Ama Goddess of the underworld, of darkness. The Ostyak, the Yurak, and the Samoyed, Siberia. (Eliade, 1964: 226)

Áma   A god of the eleventh hour of the night in the Book of That Which is in the Underworld. Egypt. (Budge, 1969, 1: 250)

Ament   Consort and female counterpart of Amen, as the second pair of the primeval gods. A name of Isis as goddess of the underworld, where she took part in the transformation of the dead into the form they would have in the Realm of Osiris. Originally a Libyan goddess. Egypt. (Budge, 1969, 2: 1, 216; Larousse, 1968: 17; Knight, 1915: 57–58)

Amenti   Goddess of the underworld as a chthonic deity, associated with fertility. Egypt. (Emerson, 1894: 243)

Amitabha   In the underworld he appears on the fifth day of the Bardo of the Teaching of Wisdom, that of All-Discriminating Wisdom—the testing period following death; and again on the fourth day of the Bardo of Karmic Illusions, with the goddess Gös-dkar-mo; also on the sixth day of the Bardo of Karmic Illusions, in the testing period following death. Tibet. (Evans-Wentz, 1960: 9, 113, 120)

Amogha-Siddhi   From him emanates one of the five elements—"air, or aggregate of volition." He appears on the fifth day of the Bardo of Wisdom Teachings—that of "All-Performing Wisdom, which gives perseverance and unerring action in things spiritual" in the testing period following death; again on the fifth day of the Bardo of Karmic Illusions with the goddess Sgrolma; and also on the sixth day of the Bardo of Karmic Illusions. Tibet. (Evans-Wentz, 1960: 9, 16, 116, 120)

Anatalik   God of the lower world who punishes the transgression of taboos. Father of Nyliayoq. The Hudson Bay Eskimo, Canada. (Wallis, 1939: 216)

Antaboga, *also* **Basuki** or **Gasuki**   The world serpent, guardian of the netherworld, who created the turtle which, with two snakes, supports the world. Bali, Indonesia. (Covarrubias, 1937: 7, 317)

Apuat   Jackal-headed god of the underworld and of the dead. A variant of Anubis/Anpu—two forms of one god, and yet "each a distinct god of the dead." Apuat is the "opener of the roads of the North," and the god of the winter solstice. Egypt. (Budge, 1969, 1: 494; 1969, 2: 264)

Arawn   God of Annwfn, the Celtic otherworld. Wales. (Ross, 1967: 338; Bray, 1935: 5: Rhys, 1937: 14)

Ärlik   God of the underworld who "sent illness to man." The Altai-Tatars, Siberia. (Pettersson, 1957: 163)

Arsan-Duolai   God of the underworld and of the dead. The Yakut, Siberia. (Pettersson, 1957: 142; MacCulloch, 1964: 486; Jochelson, 1933: 103)

Arsay   Goddess of the underworld, daughter of Baal, and equivalent of Allatum. Ugarit, Canaan. (Albright, 1968: 144)

Arud   Goddess of the underworld of the Sakai—Jakun of the Tekai River. Malay Peninsula. (Moss, 1925: 116)

Asaase Aberewa   A form of Nyame as a scorpion and serpent, "the Thursday-goddess of the Underworld," symbolizing death and rebirth. The Akan, Ghana. (Meyerowitz, 1958: 134)

Asase Yaa   Goddess of the earth—the barren soil—and apparently chthonic in her identification with the underworld. She is honored at the planting season, and "during conception rites and at funerals." The Akan, Ghana. (Evans, 1950: 247; Meyerowitz, 1958: 28)

Asharay-bioho   The chief god of the underworld, ruler over the demons. The Yakut, Lena Basin, Siberia. (Keane, 1925, 2: 121)

Astvihat   Zoroastrian demon of death who accosts the soul of the dead on the way to the Cinvat Bridge—en route to the netherworld. Iran. (Eliade, 1967: 360)

Atua-mangumangu   A god of the underworld, the "Emaciated-god." Futuna Island, Polynesia. (Burrows, 1936: 107)

Atua-mata-lu   "Two-eyed-god," a god of the underworld. Futuna Island, Polynesia. (Burrows, 1936: 107)

Atua-mata-tasi   "One-eyed-god," a god of the underworld. Futuna Island, Polynesia. (Burrows, 1936: 107)

Atum, or **Adum**   A goddess of the underworld, consort of Resheph. Canaan. (Albright, 1968: 140)

Aturrus   A chthonic god as well as an aquatic god. Spain. (Martinez, 1963: 170)

Avia Larvarum   A goddess of the underworld, a terrifying figure, mother or grandmother of ghosts. Italy. (Roscher, 1965, 1, 1: 741)

Aygnan   The evil spirit of the Tupinambas who carries away the unpatriotic, cowardly dead to torment them. Brazil. (Taylor, 1891: 289; MacCulloch, 1925, 11: 825)

A-zi-mu-a A Mesopotamian chthonic goddess, wife of Ningishzida. A deity born of Ninhursaga to heal Enki's arm. Near East. (Jacobsen, 1970: 324; 1946: 172)

Bahiwag A god of the underworld of the Ifugao. Philippines. (Barton, 1946: 33)

Balo Adat Chief god of the underworld who receives the soul of the dead. The Milano (Muka), Indonesia. (Moss, 1925: 113)

Balu Adad A goddess of the Milanows who conducts the souls of the dead to the afterworld. Borneo. (De Crespigny, 1875: 35)

Bapa nibadabadia The guardian of heaven and the interrogator of souls. The Karo Battak, Indonesia. (Kruijt, 1925, 7: 245)

Barastyr Beneficent and merciful god of the afterworld invoked to care for the deceased. The Ossetes, Caucasus. (Morgan, 1888: 385)

Batu-beana A chthonic god of Nias. Indonesia. (Keane, 1925, 2: 238)

Beli A Celtic god of the underworld. Britain. (Squire, 1906: 120)

Belili A very ancient goddess of the underworld, consort of Alala and sister of Tammuz. She is also a moon goddess and goddess of love. Sumer and Babylonia, Near East. (Jastrow, 1898: 417; Larousse, 1968: 64; Sykes, 1952: 32–33; Kramer, 1961: 114)

Bilé A Celtic god of death, of the underworld. Ireland. (Squire, 1906: 51, 65)

Bolafagina God of Kolapapauro, the afterworld—located on the island of Laulau. Solomon Islands (Ysabel), Melanesia. (Codrington, 1881: 308)

Brave, Brav A Vodun deity, god of the underworld, and an aspect of Ghede. Plaisance, Haiti, West Indies. (Simpson, 1945: 41; Deren, 1953: 82, 303)

Britomartis As a chthonic goddess she is the guardian of the dead. She is also called Dictynna and, as such, is a mountain goddess—of Mount Dikte. She has other aspects as well: an earth/mother goddess, goddess of trees and of wild beasts. Crete and Greece. (Kerenyi, 1951: 147; James, 1960: 99; Willetts, 1962: 182; Neumann, 1955: 275–276)

Burha Nang Ruler of the lower world. The Baiga, Central India. (Fuchs, 1952: 608)

Butza Uri A dwarf god on a large lake who receives the souls of the dead and "transports them in a large canoe" to Hoatziqui. The Opata, Sonora, Mexico. (Johnson, 1949: 34)

Bwebweso A deity who receives those dead by suicide, of old age, or through a sorcerer. Normandy Island, Papua, Indonesia. (Roheim, 1946: 223)

Carna Roman goddess of the vital organs. In life, as a goddess of health, she protected particularly infants and women in childbirth. As a goddess of the underworld she had charge of the heart and digestive organs. (Jayne, 1962: 459; Fairbanks, 1907: 253)

Cel An Etruscan god of death and the underworld, associated with the west. Italy. (Hamblin, 1975: 95)

Cernunnos The Celtic horned god was named as a god of the underworld, but was primarily a god of fertility and abundance, and of animals. Gaul, Britain, Ireland, and Italy. (Ross, 1967: 83, 131; MacCana, 1970: 47; MacCulloch, 1964: 35, 137)

Chags-kyu-ma The shakti, or female counterpart, of Vijaya (rNam-par-rgyal-va). She is the doorkeeper of the east and appears on the sixth day of the Bardo of Karmic Illusions in the testing period following death. Tibet. (Evans-Wentz, 1960: 120)

Chamiabac A god of the underworld who causes men to waste away to skin and bones. The Quiché, Guatemala. (Recinos, 1950: 110)

Chamiaholom A god of the underworld who causes men to waste away to skin and bones. The Quiché, Guatemala. (Recinos, 1950: 110)

Charon, Churun The ferryman of the River Styx who transported the dead across the river to Hades. Greece. As an Etruscan god of death he was a much more aggressive and active demon of the underworld, conducting the souls to the underworld. Italy. (Fairbanks, 1907: 238; Hamblin, 1975: 109; Barthell, 1971: 9; Dumézil, 1966, 2: 693)

Chayer An unterrifying god of the afterworld where those who die a natural death—in bed—go. The Ahts, Vancouver Island, Canada. (Bancroft, 1886: 521)

Chayfi God of Zazarraguan (Sasalaguan) where those who died violently went and were tormented. The Chamorro, Guam. (Safford, 1902: 716; Beardsley, 1964: 90)

Chiao Mien Kuei Wang "Scorch-Face Demon-King," a god of the underworld, of torture. China. (Day, 1940: 215)

Chiao Tan "Porter of the Gate," a god of the underworld. China. (Day, 1940: 215)

Chiawat The demon who is allowed to "plague the inmates" of the otherwise pleasant afterworld. The Pima Indians, Arizona and Mexico. (Bancroft, 1886: 527)

Ch'ih Ching Chung Liang Wang T'ien Chun "Spirit Ruler and Consumer," one of the Imps of Torture of the underworld. China. (Day, 1940: 215)

Yak Chin The goddess in charge of Paradise, Laud. The Lanoh (Negritos), Malay. (Evans, 1937: 258)

Ch'in Kuang Wang The king and judge of the First Court of Hell. "He keeps the register of the living and the dead, and measures the length of men's lives." China. (Day, 1940: 89; Werner, 1932: 80)

Chipiopos, Chipiapoos God and ruler of the afterworld of the Tusans. Among the Potawatomi he is also god of the dead. Midwest, Lake Michigan and Lake Superior. (Maclean, 1876: 427; Alexander, 1964: 41)

Ch'i Tien T'ai Shan Ta Wang A god of the underworld, one of the kings of the ten courts. China. (Day, 1940: 214)

Chiu Ch'a Kung Kuo "Examiner of Merits," a god of the underworld. China. (Day, 1940: 215)

Chiu Tien Tu Shih Ta Wang A god of the underworld, King of the Ninth Court. China. (Day, 1940: 214)

Chuan Lun (wang) King of the Tenth Court of Hell, who controls the wheel of transmigration and determines the level of rebirth. China and Central Asia. (Hackin, 1963: 249; Maspero, 1963: 368; Werner, 1932: 95; Day, 1940: 121–122)

Ch'u Chiang Wang, Chu-kiang wang The King of the Second Court of Hell who detects and punishes wrongdoing—dishonesty, fraud, and ignorance which causes harm to living beings. China. (Hackin, 1963: 248–249; Maspero, 1963: 365; Werner, 1932: 94; Day, 1940: 121)

Chu Fen Chu Che "Sawing Asunder Demon"— an Imp of Torture of the underworld. China. (Day, 1940: 215)

Chui Hun Shih Che "Pursuer of Souls," a god of the underworld. China. (Day, 1940: 215)

Chunguy The god of hell, son of Nexhequiriac. The Trique, Oaxaca, Mexico. (Valentini, 1899: 38)

Chusman, Chusma, Chanzan A god of the underworld, malevolent, causing disease, famine, and storms. Some considered he was a sky god and benevolent, communicating with mankind through the shaman. The Patangoro, Colombia. (Kirchhoff, 1948: 346; Trimborn, 1968: 95)

Cilens An Etruscan god of death and the underworld, associated with the north. Italy. (Hamblin, 1975: 95)

Cizin, Kisin A Mayan god of death and of the underworld, as well as an earthquake god. Yucatan to Pokoman territory, Mexico. (Thompson, 1970: 310–313, 338)

Coquechila, Coqueehila The god of the underworld and of death among some Valley Zapotecs. His wife was Xonaxi Huilia. Oaxaca, Mexico. (Whitecotton, 1977: 158)

Coqui Bexelao (Bezelao) God of the underworld and of death whose wife was Xonaxi Quecuya. Also called Coquechila in some towns. The Zapotecs, Mitla, Oaxaca, Mexico. (Whitecotton, 1977: 158)

Coventina In Spain she was a chthonic goddess as well as an aquatic and prophetic deity. (Martinez, 1962: 190–194)

Cuchumaquic A god of the underworld who caused violence among men. He was the father of Xquic, who was the mother of Hunahpu and Xbalanque. The Quiché, Guatemala. (Recinos, 1950: 110, 119, 124)

Cu Roi God of the underworld and king of the realm where Irish heroes went. (Cohane, 1969: 246)

Cvlalp An Etruscan god of death and the underworld, associated with the northeast. Italy. (Hamblin, 1975: 95)

Dagon A judge of the dead in the lower world with Nergal and Misharu, also associated with Enlil. Assyria. Elsewhere he is primarily a god of grain, of fertility. Near East. (Langdon, 1931: 78, 80; Gray, 1964: 122; Vriezen, 1963: 52; Albright, 1968: 124)

Dalyunan A god of the underworld, only invoked in sickness rites. Offspring of Mayogyog. The Ifugao, Philippines. (Barton, 1946: 34)

Damoh, Dangoh   A god of the underworld of the Cape Hottentots. South Africa. (Schapera, 1951: 387)

Dea Domnann, Dea Domnu   A Formorian goddess of the underworld "and probably also of fertility." Celtic Ireland. (MacCulloch, 1911: 59; Rhys, 1937: 57)

Dea Muta   Roman goddess of the underworld and of the dead, "identified with Larunda the mother of the Lares." (Fairbanks, 1907: 238; Roscher, 1965, 1, 1: 975)

Dhupema (Sanskrit, **Dhupa**; Tibet, **bDug-spös-ma**) A female Bodhisattva who appears on the third day of the Bardo of Karmic Illusions with Ratna-Sambhava in the testing period following death. Tibet. (Evans-Wentz, 1960: 111)

Dis, Dispater   A Roman god of death and of the underworld, husband of Proserpina. In Gaul his aspect is more chthonian, a god of the dead and of the underworld, but also the progenitor of mankind and a god of fertility. (MacCulloch, 1911: 22, 31–32; Anwyl, 1906: 66; Fairbanks, 1907: 237; Larousse, 1968: 211)

djabani, djaabani, djaaban   A deity of the lower world, a guardian and helpful; male and/or female. The Navaho, Arizona and New Mexico. (Reichard, 1950: 383)

Djata   A god of the underworld of the Ngadju Dyaks. Borneo. (Wales, 1957: 78)

Djēwmé   The goddess of the afterworld, leader of the warria, a class of important spirits of the dead. She and they lead the dead to onosobert in the sky, but to pass through her house on the way, offerings of pork are required. She is the owner of all of the animals, fish, birds, etc. The Kaowerabedj, New Guinea. (Oosterwal, 1963: 4, 5)

Dri-ch'a-ma, Dri-chha-ma   A female Bodhisattva who appears with Amogha-Siddhi on the fifth day of the Bardo of Karmic Illusions in the testing period following death. Tibet. (Evans-Wentz, 1960: 116; Waddell, 1959: 366)

Dril-bu-ma   Shakti of Amrita-Dhara (bDud rtsi 'khyil ba). She is the doorkeeper of the north and appears on the sixth day of the Bardo of Karmic Illusions in the testing following death. Tibet. (Evans-Wentz, 1960: 120)

Druj   Iranian goddess of the underworld. (Gray, 1930: 194)

bDud rtsi 'khyil ba (Skt. Amrita-Dhara)   A god "whose function is to transmute all things into nectar . . . esoterically, 'voidness'. He is the Door-keeper of the North." He appears on the sixth day of the Bardo of Karmic Illusions in the testing period following death. His shakti is Dril-bu-ma. Tibet. (Evans-Wentz, 1960: 120)

bDug-spös-ma   *See* **Dhupema**

Dumaluplup   "Bubbling Evenly." A god of the underworld, offspring of Mayogyog. The Ifugao, Philippines. (Barton, 1946: 34)

Eita   Etruscan god of the underworld, husband of Persipnei. Italy. (Dumézil, 1966, 2: 692; Larousse, 1968: 211)

Emma-o (Yama-raja)   Buddhist god of the underworld and judge of the dead, assigning sinners to the various parts of hell. Japan. (Eliseev, 1963: 424; Getty, 1962: 152–153; Rhys, 1937: 62)

Empousa   A monster demon of the lower world whose task was to punish sinners. Equated with Skylla and Lamia. Greece. (Kerenyi, 1951: 42; Barthell, 1971: 8)

Endovellicus   A god of the dead or of the underworld. Spain. (Martinez, 1962: 159)

Ereshkigal, Allatu   Goddess/queen of the underworld, of darkness, and of death. She married Nergal, making him a god of the dead. Near East. (Kramer, 1961: 107, 124; James, 1960: 179; Larousse, 1968: 64)

Erh Tien Ch'u Chiang Wang   A god of the underworld, king of the Second Court of Hell. China. (Day, 1940: 214)

The Erinyes   Allekto, Tisiphone, Megaira. Goddesses of the underworld whose function was to avenge and punish wrongdoing, to guard and uphold social and natural laws. As the latter they were called the Eumenides. Greece. (Kerenyi, 1951: 48; Fairbanks, 1907: 239; Willetts, 1962: 198)

Erlik Khan   God of the underworld and ruler of all the evil spirits. A god of corruption and evil, the source of all misfortune and causing men to sin. Siberia, Central Asia, and parts of China. (Casanowicz, 1924: 417–418; Potapov, 1964: 325; Schram, 1957: 80; Chadwick, 1936: 94, 106; MacCulloch, 1964: 487)

Erra   An Akkadian chthonian god. Near East. (Jacobsen, 1970: 35)

Eurynomos A demon of the lower world who devoured the dead. Greece. (Altheim, 1937: 118; Barthell, 1971: 8)

Eve "Phoenician inscriptions invoke a goddess Eve who seems to have been a goddess of the underworld . . . probably identical with Ishtar, 'the great mother serpent'." Near East. (Roheim, 1972: 171)

Fen Ch'ih Chu Che "Miry Manure Pond Demon"—an Imp of Torture of the underworld. China. (Day, 1940: 215)

Feng Tu Ta Ti In Szechwan, lord of the underworld. China. (Day, 1940: 119)

Frehzisht Zoroastrian demon of the netherworld who accosts the soul of the dead en route to Cinvat Bridge for judgment. Iran. (Eliade, 1967: 360)

Fudno, Fuodno God and ruler of the underworld, another name for Ruto. The Lapps and the Samek, northern Europe. (Karsten, 1955: 107; Holmberg, 1925, 7: 798)

Gaffer Engkoh, or **Jongkoh** A divine ancestor of the Besisi who is chief of their Paradise. He dwells in the moon. Malay Peninsula. (Skeat, 1906: 300)

The Gayak A pair, male and female, who rule the underworld, the abode of the dead. The Bera, Malay Peninsula. (Evans, 1923: 209)

Gendui Lanyut Goddess of hell whose function is "washing human souls." The Sakai, Malay Peninsula. (Skeat, 1906: 239)

Ghasmari A wrathful dark-green goddess who appears from the southwest on the thirteenth day of the Bardo of Karmic Illusions, in the testing period following death. Tibet. (Evans-Wentz, 1960: 142)

Ginitok A god of the underworld who possesses priests. The Ifugao, Philippines. (Barton, 1946: 33)

Goeroe ri Seleng God of the underworld whose daughter Njilitimo was the ancestress of the people. Brother of Sangkoeroewira. The Buginese, Indonesia. (Alkema and Bezemer, 1927: 189)

Gomogonal The "spirit of a man who lived in the 'first times.' He now has his home on Mount Balatocan where he looks after the spirits (*gimokod*) of the dead." The Bukidnon, Mindanao, Philippines. (Cole, 1956: 95)

Gös-dkar-mo Shakti of Amitabha with whom she appears on the fourth day of the Bardo of Karmic Illu-

sions, in the testing period following death. Tibet. (Evans-Wentz, 1960: 70, 113)

Gugurang A god of the lower world of the Bisaya. Also a god of the Bikol. Philippines. (Kroeber, 1918: 40)

Gumanob A god of the underworld who "possesses [a] priest and causes him to count victims awaiting sacrifice." Offspring of Mayogyog. The Ifugao, Philippines. (Barton, 1946: 34)

Gushojin A secretary of the god of the underworld, Emma-o, "who consulted registers and reported to him on the good and bad acts committed by each individual." Japan. (Larousse, 1973: 332)

Gwynn Welsh/British god of the underworld and of the dead. Son of Nudd. (MacCulloch, 1911: 115; Rhys, 1937: 77; Wallis, 1939: 28)

Hades, Pluto, Plouton Greek/Roman god of the underworld, son of Chronus and Rhea, brother of Zeus and Poseidon. As Hades he was god of the dead, of burial, and to be feared as judge. As Pluto his aspect was that of a beneficent chthonic god, giver of fertility and of the treasures under the earth. (Fairbanks, 1907: 235; Murray, 1935: 58; Kerenyi, 1951: 231; Cox, 1870, 2: 307, 320)

haⱡasō's ha'wiⱡ The chief of the underworld, sometimes considered "Four Chiefs," called upon "in prayers during bathing rituals." The Nootkan, Washington and Vancouver Island. (Drucker, 1951: 152)

Halja, Hali Teutonic variant of Hel as a protective goddess of the dead in the underworld. (Grimm, 1883, 2: 889)

Hanau Goddess of the underworld and wife of Tonofiti. The Marquesas, Polynesia. (Handy, 1923: 246)

Han Ping Chu Che "Freezing in Ice Demon," an Imp of Torture of the underworld. China. (Day, 1940: 216)

Hapi, Hap One of the four sons of Horus who were the gods of the Canopic jars in the underworld. He was the protector, with Nephthys, of that containing the small intestines. As a god of the cardinal points he was god of the north. Egypt. (Budge, 1969, 1: 158; 1969, 2: 456, 491; Knight, 1915: 34)

Hecate, Hekate Goddess of the underworld, of darkness, and of night, who had powers of magic and sorcery. As an early Thracian moon goddess, she partook of the powers of the heavens and the earth, bestowing prosperity and wisdom. She is variously given as the daughter of Nyx and Tartarus, or of Asteria and Perses. She is the mother of Skylla by Phorcys. Greece. (Kerenyi, 1951: 35–36; Murray, 1935: 76; Fairbanks, 1907: 138–139; Neumann, 1955: 170; Jayne, 1962: 326)

The Hecatoncheires   Cottus, spokesman for the three, Briareus and Gyes, each with 50 heads and 100 hands, were the sons of Gaea and Uranus. They were monstrous and horrible, strong and bold. Uranus chained them and confined them to the underground from which they were released by Zeus. They gave him their allegiance and fought for him in the war with the Titans. They later acted as the guardians of Tartarus. Greece. (Hesiod-Brown, 1981: 57, 70–71, 73)

Hel   Scandinavian goddess of the underworld and of death—of those who died on land and without shedding blood, as opposed to those dying in battle or at sea. She rules over Niflheim where she distributes the dead among its nine worlds. She is not unkindly to the innocent, but inexorable. She is the daughter of Loki and Angurboda. (Anderson, 1891: 289, 387; Stern, 1898: 6, 61; Grimm, 1880: 312; Snorri Sturluson, 1964: 56)

Hetgwaulana   The god of darkness (a supreme deity) who lives in the lower regions (Hetgwauge) where the wicked go. He is not feared, but worshipped, and invoked for curses on enemies. The Haida, British Columbia. (Harrison, 1891: 16, 18)

Hihr   A Zoroastrian deity, beneficial; one of the mediators the soul encounters at the Cinvat Bridge in being judged as to his destination. Iran. (Eliade, 1967: 360)

Hina-Mataone   The queen of the underworld. The Marquesas, Polynesia. (Christian, 1895: 190)

Hine-a-te-ao   A goddess and guardian of the entrance to the netherworld. The "daughter of light" who was charged with the area between day and night. The Maori, New Zealand. (Andersen, 1928: 409)

Hine-a-te-po   Goddess and guardian of the entrance to the netherworld. The "barrier between night and day." The Maori, New Zealand. (Andersen, 1928: 409)

Hine-nui-te-po   As Hine-a-tauira, or Hine-titama, she was unknowingly the daughter/wife of Tane. On learning of the relationship she fled to the underworld, taking the name of Hine-nui-te-po as goddess of death, of night, and of the underworld. The Maori, New Zealand. (Best, 1924: 116, 323; Andersen, 1928: 212, 409–411; Henry, 1928: 466)

Hine-ruaki-moe   A goddess of the netherworld, guardian of the darkness. The Maori, New Zealand. (Andersen, 1928: 409)

Hjam-dpal, hdjam-dpal   The equivalent of Manjusri, the "God of Transcendent Wisdom." He appears on the fourth day of the Bardo of Karmic Illusions with Amitabha, in the testing period following death. Tibet. (Evans-Wentz, 1960: 113; Getty, 1962: 110)

Hku Te   God, ruler, and judge of sinners of the underworld. He appears as the rainbow in the west. The Karen, Burma. (Marshall, 1922: 223–228)

Hoatziqui   An old goddess who lives on the south shore of the lake crossed by the souls of the dead. She receives them and "swallows the souls one by one, save those she finds with painted faces, like the Pima. These she rejects . . . [and] throws them into the lake. Those she swallows live a life of plenty in her belly." The Opata, Sonora, Mexico. (Johnson, 1949: 34)

Honing   The ruler of Paradise (Ru'no'no), but he is also concerned with human affairs. His brothers are Komarara, Hokeru, and Komakiki. The Siuai, Bougainville, Solomon Islands, Melanesia. (Oliver, 1967: 41, 60, 66, 495)

Horon   A lesser god worshipped in Canaan, considered by some to be possibly a chthonic deity. A god invoked in curses. Near East. (Driver, 1956: 5; Gray, 1957: 133; Vriezen, 1963: 53; Oldenberg, 1969: 43)

Hphreng-ba-ma, Mahlaima   (Sanskrit, **Mala**) A female Bodhisattva who appears on the third day of the Bardo of Karmic Illusions with Ratna-Sambhava, in the testing period following death. Tibet. (Evans-Wentz, 1960: 111)

Hsing Fang   A god of the underworld—"Chief of Judiciary," an administrative department. China. (Day, 1940: 215)

Hsueh Hu Niang Niang   The "goddess who saves from the 'Pool of Blood' in the nether world." China. (Day, 1940: 29)

Hsueh K'ang   "Bloody Pool Demon," an Imp of Torture of the underworld. China. (Day, 1940: 216)

Huang Fan Shen Chun   "Guide to Chief Gods," a god of the underworld. China. (Day, 1940: 215)

Hu Fang   "Chief, Board of Census," an administrative department of the underworld. China. (Day, 1940: 215)

Hun-Came God of the underworld, Xibalba, where the black road leads to his residence. With Vucub-Came the supreme judges of the council of the lords of the underworld. The Quiché, Guatemala. (Recinos, 1950: 109–110; Girard, 1979: 95)

Hunhau, Hun-Ahau God of death and of the underworld, Mitnal. A manifestation of Ah Puch. The Mayan, Mexico. (Schellhas, 1904: 13; Morley, 1946: 221; Nicholson, 1967: 120)

Hushbishag Wife of Namtar. She "keeps the tablets of Arallu," the land of darkness, "on which the hour of death of every man is written." Akkad, Near East. (Langdon, 1931: 161)

Hyesemmigadon A Greek chthonic god whose name was found in a Greek magic papyrus. Also mentioned as Hermanubis. (Roscher, 1965, 1, 2: 2771)

Ibu Goddess of the dead and of the afterworld. The Manobo, Philippines. (Jocano, 1969: 23; Raats, 1969: 20)

Idliragijenget A name of Sedna, the supreme being, as "the mistress of one of the countries to which the souls go after death." The Central Eskimo, Canada. (Boas, 1884/85: 583, 588)

Igorobandur The chief of the realm of the dead. His wife is Oloubikunyahi. The Cuna, Panama. (Nordenskiold, 1938: 324)

Impatibu n Ginumon As a god of the underworld, the offspring of Mayogyog. The Ifugao, Philippines. (Barton, 1946: 33)

Indo i laoe Goddess of the underworld who brought the grain to the rice. Sister of Indo i losi. Celebes, Indonesia. (Downs, 1920: 25)

Irkalla Babylonian goddess of the underworld, equated with Allat. Near East. (Langdon, 1931: 259; Thompson, 1903: xxviii; Hooke, 1963: 52; Sayce, 1898: 154)

Irodjerilik, Irojrilik The god of the pleasant afterworld who rules the souls of the good. He is also a god of increase as well as of the west. The Marshall Islands, Micronesia. (Knappe, 1888: 66–67; Kramer and Nevermann, 1938: 238)

Išar Believed to be a Semitic god of the underworld and probably a judge of the dead. Near East. (Roberts, 1972: 36–37)

Istustaya Hattic-Hittite goddess of the underworld who, with Papaya, spins the thread of life. Asia Minor. (Guterbock, 1961: 149)

Ita-nga-ta A vindictive deity of O le nu'u-o-nonoa, "the land of the bound;" one of the places of the dead, or the underworld Sa-le-Fe'e. Samoa, Polynesia. (Stair, 1897: 217)

I Tien Ch'in Kuang Wang A god of the underworld, king of the first of the courts. China. (Day, 1940: 214)

I Wan Kuan Wen "Collector of (Burned) Monies," a god of the underworld. China. (Day, 1940: 215)

Izanami The earth goddess, wife/sister of Izanagi, who after her death became goddess of the underworld. They were the creators of the islands of Japan. (Yasumaro, 1965: 19; Haydon, 1941: 202; Holtom, 1938: 109)

Jabmeks, Jabmi-akko, Jami-Ajmo-Ollmaj, Jame-akka Goddess of the dead and of the underworld. The Lapps, Northern Europe. (Holmberg, 1925, 7: 798; Karsten, 1955: 107; Pettersson, 1957: 152)

Jal-najer, or **Hul-ater** Finno-Ugric god of the underworld of the Vogul. Russia. (Pettersson, 1957: 162)

Ja Puteu The " 'great sorceress' of the underworld . . . the wife or mother of the celestial Supreme Being." The Ple, Malaya. (Pettazzoni, 1956: 314)

Jata, Bawin Jata Balawang Bulau Also known as Tambon. Goddess of the underworld or the "primeval waters." She is manifested as the watersnake. With Mahatala she is concerned with the creation of the world and of humans. The Ngaju, Borneo. (Scharer, 1963: 14–16, 23, 27)

Jih Hsun Ch' "Demon Inspector of Day," a god of the underworld. China. (Day, 1940: 215)

Jih Yu Shen "God of the Daytime," a god of the underworld. China. (Day, 1940: 215)

Jizo, Kshitigarbha As the Compassionate God he is associated with the underworld as the conductor of souls, as the helper of sufferers and the special protector of children, alive or dead; the patron of women and children and of travelers. Japanese Buddhism. (Getty, 1962: 102, 105; Piggott, 1969: 20; Eliseev, 1963: 432–434; Rhys, 1937: 97; Clark, 1932: 55)

lJogspo King of Yogklu, the underworld. Tibet. (Francke, 1925, 8: 76)

Kabes Semen God of the underworld—"at once benevolent, powerful and terrifying." The Mejbrat, New Guinea. (Elmberg, 1955: 42)

Kaboi The culture hero ancestor god of the Caraja who discovered the surface of the earth and made it possible for the people to emerge from the underworld. He stayed below because he detected the presence of death on the surface. Brazil. (Levi-Strauss, 1969: 149–150; Lipkind, 1940: 248–249; Spence, 1925, 2: 838)

Kahoali'i A god of the underworld who demanded an offering of a human eyeball, which was "swallowed in a cup of awa." A chief could invoke this law when possessed by him. Hawaii. (Beckwith, 1970: 50, 61)

Kaina God of Mapua, the afterworld for warriors and great hunters. The Koriki, New Guinea. (Wallis, 1939: 241)

Kakramal Kunwar A giant crab who guards the entrance to Utra khand, the lower world. The Baiga, India. (Fuchs, 1952: 611)

Kala God of the underworld who "created the light and Mother Earth, over which extends a layer of water" (in the creation myth). He is also called a god of evil, of darkness, as the destructive aspect of Siwa. Bali, Indonesia. (Covarrubias, 1937: 7, 317; Friederich, 1959: 39, 43)

Kala-Purusha An attendant who executes the commands of Yama, the judge of the dead. India. (Martin, 1914: 61)

Kalekamo The guardian of heaven who questions and judges the souls. Nias, Indonesia. (Kruijt, 1925, 7: 245)

Ka-moho-ali'i The great shark god and god of sorcery, older brother of Pele, was also considered an underworld deity. Hawaii. (Beckwith, 1940: 51, 90, 105, 169; Emerson, 1968: 46)

Kanaloa God of the squid, the leader of the rebellious spirits who, in defeat, were cast down into Po, the underworld, where he became known as Milu. Hawaii. (Beckwith, 1940: 60; Henry, 1928: 345; Mackenzie, n.d.: 288)

Kara-ma-kuna A goddess of the sea who was guardian of Bouru, the land of the dead. Micronesia. (MacKenzie, 1930: 170)

Karunga The aspect of the dual-named god Ndjambi Karunga which is "god of the earth, water and netherworld," a god of death. His wife is Musisi. The Herero, Namibia. (Luttig, 1933: 7–9)

K'daai Maqsin A god of evil and of the underworld where he is chief blacksmith, from whom the blacksmiths get their craft. He also introduced shamans to the world. The Yakut, Siberia. (Popov, 1933: 260; Eliade, 1964: 470)

Kerima The White Kerima—a wrathful goddess appearing from the east on the thirteenth day of the Bardo of Karmic Illusions, in the testing of the dead. Tibet. (Evans-Wentz, 1960: 142)

Kermo Deota God of the underworld from whom the boar (after the flood) stole earth and trees to reform the world. The Bondo, India. (Elwin, 1949: 33)

Kesu Raja The god of the underworld who helped dry out the earth after the flood, but also finally induced the mother to marry her son (survivors of the flood) and repopulate the earth. The Gadaba, India. (Elwin, 1949: 36)

Khara-Eren-Noyon Ruler of Khalga where the black shamans go after death. The Buryat, Siberia. (Czaplicka, 1969: 285)

Khulater, Jal-najer, Hul-ater Finno-Ugric god of the land of the dead. The Voguls, Russia. (MacCulloch, 1964: 77; Pettersson, 1957: 162)

!khutse Benevolent god of the afterworld to whom those who die a "good death" go and live a good life. The Auen and Naron Bushmen, South Africa. (Schapera, 1951: 168)

Kigipe The chief of the underworld mentioned in the Nele Tiegun chronicle. The Cuna, Panama. (Nordenskiold, 1938: 325)

Kine-Nane A chthonic goddess of the underworld associated with fertility and productivity. The Adi, Northeastern India. (Chowdhury, 1971: 113–114)

Kiru A god of the underworld who devours the dead, other than those dying in battle. Hervey Island (Cook Islands), Polynesia. (Eliade, 1958: 137)

Kisin God of the underworld and of earthquakes. A god of evil, servant of Sukukyum. The Chol and the Lacandon, Mexico. (Tozzer, 1941: 132; Cline, 1944: 112; Alexander, 1920: 141)

iKombengi A god of evil, of the underworld and the night. He created men at the behest of iLai, and is invoked for good rice crops. The Toradjas, Celebes, Indonesia. (Downs, 1920: 14, 16, 23, 45; Pettersson, 1957: 27)

Kopecho The Frog-Woman. Before her transformation she caused one of the original two suns that shone alternately to become less bright, to be the moon. He in turn caused her to change into a frog. She is the arbiter of the destination (happy or tormenting) of the dead on the route to the otherworld, determined by their skill in basket weaving. The Yupa, Venezuela. (Wilbert, 1974: 5, 6, 25)

Kou Hsiao Szu "Accountant, Debt-Canceller," a god of the underworld. China. (Day, 1940: 215)

Kuahailo A god who, with Ka'onohiokala, conducted the souls of the chiefs to the afterworld. Hawaii. (Mackenzie, n.d.: 115)

K'u Li "Assistant Treasurer," a god of the underworld. China. (Day, 1940: 215)

Kul Odyr, Kul-oter A god of the underworld who lived north of the mouth of the Ob River, a god of darkness and of evil who spoiled the creation of man, making him less than perfect. The Ostyak and the Vogul, Siberia. (Czaplicka, 1925, 9: 577; 1969: 289–290; MacCulloch, 1964: 376)

Kuma The great and beneficent mother goddess, the moon, who created all things with the help of her brothers Puana and Itciai, and rules the afterworld where all go after death to live a life of fullness and enjoyment. The Yaruro, Venezuela. (Petrullo, 1939: 241; Kirchhoff, 1948: 462; Métruax, 1946, 2: 115; Sierksma, 1960: 14)

Kung Fang A god of the underworld where he is administrator of the Board of Public Works. China. (Day, 1940: 215)

Kuwatawat "Guardian of the entrance to the underworld." The Maori, New Zealand. (Best, 1924: 97)

Labraid A Celtic god of the otherworld. Ireland. (O'Rahilly, 1946: 103)

Lamia A demon of the lower world who snatched and slaughtered children. Greece. (Barthell, 1971: 8, Roscher, 1965, 2, 2: 1818)

Langkoda The interrogator of souls and guardian of the afterworld. He is also a smith who sometimes places the soul of the dying in his bellows, causing a long death agony. If he places it in the center of his furnace, the individual "has a violent but short death bed." He is instructed in this by the gods. Fiji, Celebes, Indonesia. (Moss, 1925: 112; Kruijt, 1925, 7: 245; Adriani and Kruyt, 1950: 460, 468)

Lature Dano A god of the underworld, of death and evil, of all things of a dark nature. Son of Sirao and brother of Lowalangi. North and Central Nias, Indonesia. (Suzuki, 1959: 7, 10)

Le-hev-hev Goddess of the underworld, the dark aspect of the mother goddess. Malekula, New Hebrides, Melanesia. (Neumann, 1955: 173–174)

Yak Lepeh One of the grandmothers who live under the earth, and sometimes cause the waters to rise out of the earth. Wife of Tak Tinjeg. The Kintak Bong and the Menik Kaien, Malaya. (Evans, 1937: 142–143, 173)

Leta Ahuila God of the underworld and of death in Sola who "apparently had both male and female refractions: Coqueehila, the lord of the underworld, and his wife Xonaxihuilia." Same as Pezelao. Oaxaca, Mexico. (Whitecotton, 1977: 164)

Lghags-sgrog-ma The shakti of Hayagriva (rTamgrin-rgyal-po). She is a doorkeeper of the west, and appears on the sixth day of the Bardo of Karmic Illusions in the testing period following death. Tibet. (Evans-Wentz, 1960: 120)

Li-char A goddess, guardian of Pueliko, the underworld. Ponape, Caroline Islands, Micronesia. (Christian, 1899: 383)

Li-cher "Lady of the torch," a guardian of Pueliko, the underworld. Ponape, Caroline Islands, Micronesia. (Christian, 1899: 383)

Li Fang 1) A god of the underworld—"Chief, Civil Service Board," an administrative department; 2) "Chief, Board of Rites," an administrative department. China. (Day, 1940: 215)

Ligifo A goddess who "counts the leaves that have fallen from the tree of life. Then she goes to the door of heaven and directs the souls to the house of Lug," the god of death. Yap Islands, Micronesia. (Müller, 1917: 319)

Liu Tien Pien Ch'eng Wang A god of the underworld, the king of the sixth of the ten courts. China. (Day, 1940: 214)

Lorok The guardian of a reef on Narikrik Island which the ghost must cross on the way to Eorerok, their Paradise. He is also responsible for the winds. The Marshall Islands, Micronesia. (MacKenzie, 1930: 171; Davenport, 1953: 221–222)

Loz A deity of the underworld, Meslam or Aralu, ruling with Nergal and Ninmug. Babylonia, Near East. (Sykes, 1952: 128)

Lu Kung Pai Hu "General of Demons," of the underworld. China. (Day, 1940: 216)

gLu-ma Ghirdhima, Sanskrit, **Gita** A goddess of music and song. A female Bodhisattva who appears with Amitabha on the fourth day of the Bardo of Karmic Illusions in the testing period following death. Tibet. (Evans-Wentz, 1960: 113; Waddell, 1959: 366)

Lutsiper A Slavic god of hell where he lives with his wife and attendants "torturing the souls of the dead." (Mansikka, 1925, 4: 623)

Luyung Kabig A goddess who "controlled the stream of snakes at the entrance of the Underworld." The Sulod, Philippines. (Jocano, 1969: 19)

Maa-ha-f The ferryman of the Lake of Kha who was told by Ra which souls were to be carried across. Egypt. (Budge, 1973, 1: 134)

Magsanladung Biday Deity of the underworld whose parents are Luyong Baybay and Paigrab. The Sulod, Philippines. (Jocano, 1969: 19)

Magyan A god of the underworld, Kasakitan, who transported the souls of the dead. Brother of Sumpoy and Makaptan. The Bisayan, Panay, Philippines. (Jocano, 1969: 20)

Mahlaima, Hphreng-ba-ma, Sanskrit, **Mala** A female Bodhisattva who appears on the third day of the Bardo of Karmic Illusions with Ratna-Sambhava, in the testing period following death. Tibet. (Evans-Wentz, 1960: 111)

Makawalang A goddess and guardian of the afterworld. The Minahassa, northern Celebes, Indonesia. (Kruijt, 1925, 7: 245; MacKenzie, 1930: 330)

Makea-tutara A god of the Maori who lives in the netherworld, and who is the father of Maui—Ru among the Mangaian. Polynesia. (Andersen, 1928: 192, 214)

Maligang A guardian of the entrance to the afterworld. The Punans, Borneo. (Moss, 1925: 113)

Ma Mien A horse-faced or horse-headed god. With Niu T'ou "the two chief constables of Hell," he collects the souls of the dead when the register indicates the life is over. A god of vengeance who punishes the wicked. China. (Werner, 1934: 268; Larousse, 1968: 399; Eastlake, 1883: 272, 279–280)

Mampes Guide of the dead and guardian of the bridge leading to the island of Belet, the land of the "good" dead. The Menik Kaien. Among the Kintak Bong he is the guardian of the land of the dead and meets the dead on their arrival. Malaya. (Evans, 1937: 257, 263; Eliade, 1964: 281)

Mania, Mana Goddess of the underworld and considered the mother of the Manes and also of the Lares. Italy. (Altheim, 1937: 117–118; Leland, 1963: 51)

Manolge inBahiwag A goddess of the underworld, wife of Bahiwag. The Ifugao, Philippines. (Barton, 1946: 33)

Mantus An Etruscan god of the underworld and of death. Italy. (Herbig, 1925, 5: 534; Fairbanks, 1907: 238; Altheim, 1937: 118; von Vacano, 1960: 148)

Manua A god of the underworld supplanted by Milu. His sister is Uli and brother Wakea. Hawaii. (Beckwith, 1970: 114, 155)

Maquetaurie Guayava God of the land of the dead, called Coaybay. Haiti, West Indies. (Arciniegas, 1971: 7)

Maru-a-nuku Goddess and guardian of the entrance to Kororupo, who leads the dead to the underworld. Anaa Island, Tuamotus, Polynesia. (Stimson, 1933: 25)

Maru-a-roto A goddess and guardian to the entrance to Kororupo, who leads the dead to the underworld. Anaa Island, Tuamotus, Polynesia. (Stimson, 1933: 25)

Masaw God of death and the underworld during the third world of the Hopi. In the fourth world, he is guardian, protector and caretaker. Arizona. (Waters, 1963: 28)

Maseken A god of the underworld of the Nabaloi. Philippines. (Moss, 1930: 283)

Masolokuirgikalilel A god of the underworld whose wife is Olouiknidilisop—in the Nele Tiegun chronicle. The Cuna, Panama. (Nordenskiold, 1938: 326)

Mateczungua The master of "the icy regions of the north where perpetual snow prevails" (in the afterworld), where the souls come from and to which they return to "expiate their sins" before returning to the southern regions, which are pleasant. The Siouan, South Carolina. (Swanton, 1946: 759)

Math A benevolent Celtic god of the underworld, a god of justice and wisdom, of wealth and magical lore, the latter of which he taught to his nephew Gwydion. Wales. (Squire, 1906: 260; MacCulloch, 1911: 105)

Maui God of the underworld in areas of Polynesia. In some places the god of Lolofonua, the place of the less fortunate dead; in others of Bulotu (Paradise). He is also called Maui Atalanga. (Williamson, 1933: 11, 108; Fison, 1904: 139; Collocott, 1921: 152–153)

Mawiang A "ferocious double-headed dog" who guards the road to the afterworld and must be propitiated. The Milanows, Borneo. (De Crespigny, 1875: 35)

Maya God of the underworld, Sutala. India. (Danielou, 1964: 315)

Mebuyan Goddess of death and of the underworld, Gimokudan. She represents the rhythm of life and death controlled from the underworld by her shaking of the tree "on which all life hangs, thus causing death on earth." The Bagobo, Philippines. (Raats, 1969: 21, 32–34)

Menthe A Greek nymph of the underworld. Also called Nais. (Roscher, 1965, 2, 2: 2801)

Meshkent, Meskhenit Goddess of the underworld and of the funeral chamber who accompanied the dead to judgment. She is also a goddess of birth and of children, predicting their future. Egypt. (Budge, 1969, 2: 144; Jayne, 1962: 85–86; Ames, 1965: 111)

Meslamtaea Sumerian god of the underworld, son of Ninlil and Enlil. His wife is Ereshkigal. Same as Nergal. Near East. (Jacobsen, 1970: 32–34)

Mestha, Mesthi, Amset One of the four sons of Horus, a funereal god. As a god of the Canopic jars in the underworld he is protector of the stomach and large intestines. As a god of the cardinal points he represents the south. Egypt. (Budge, 1969, 1: 492; Knight, 1915: 35)

Mictanteot, Miquetanteot, Miqtanteot God of the underworld. Nicaragua. Same as Mictlantecuhtli of Mexico. (Lothrop, 1926: 70; Bancroft, 1886, 3: 492; Larousse, 1968: 440)

Mictecacihuatl, Mictlantecihuatl Goddess of the underworld and of the dead with her consort Mictlantecuhtli. Goddess of the fifth hour of the night. The Aztec, Mexico. (Vailland, 1962: 147; Spence, 1923: 233; Burland, 1967: ix)

Mictlantecuhtli God of the Land of the Dead, Mictlan, who presided over the north zone of the universe, though sometimes associated with the south. As god of the dead,

the god of the eleventh hour of the day; as of the underworld, the god of the fifth hour of the night. His wife is Mictecacihuatl. The Aztec, Mexico. (Vaillant, 1962: 140, 147; Alexander, 1920: 54, 57; Spence, 1923: 327, 331; León-Portilla, 1982: 34, 99)

Milkath A chthonic goddess associated with Allath and Hawwath. Carthage. (Cook, 1930: 201)

Milu God of the underworld and of death. Hawaii. In some areas a goddess. Same as Miru of the Maori. Polynesia. (Beckwith, 1932: 48; 1940: 114; Andersen, 1928: 305; Westervelt, 1915: 99)

Minos One of the three judges (with Rhadamanthus and Aeacus) of the underworld. He had the deciding vote. Son of Zeus and Europa. (Morford and Lenardon, 1975: 246; Leach, 1950, 2: 936)

Miru Goddess of the underworld, Avaiki. On Rarotonga the mother of Tau-titi; on Mangaia, mother of Kumu-Tonga-I-Te-Po and Karaia-I-Te-Ata. Polynesia. (Andersen, 1928: 121; Williamson, 1933: 171; Sykes, 1952: 142)

Misharu In Assyria he is a judge of the dead, associated with Nergal and Dagan. In Babylonia he is an abstract god representing rectitude, law, and the son of Shamash. Near East. (Langdon, 1931: 80; Ananikian, 1964: 40; Larousse, 1968: 58)

Modgud(r) A goddess who guards the Giallar-bru (the bridge of death) leading to the underworld. Norse. (Guerber, 1895: 288; Grimm, 1883, 2: 802; Branston, 1955: 92)

Mo Hsi Chu Che "Grinder into Tidbits," an Imp of Torture of the underworld. China. (Day, 1940: 215)

Montakwet The guardian of the gate to Telmikish, as well as the examiner and tester of the spirit attempting to pass through the moving mountains which crush those not qualified. The Cahuilla, California. (Brumgardt and Bowles, 1981: 14, 39–40)

Mo Pi Shih Che "Arrester of Souls," a god of the underworld. China. (Day, 1940: 215)

Moso A vindictive deity of one of the lands of the dead, O le nu'u-o-nonoa. Samoa, Polynesia. (Stair, 1897: 217)

Mot A chthonic god, of drought, of death and sterility of corn and vegetation, yet with the implication of rebirth. Canaan and Syria. (Crawford, 1957: 19;

Albright, 1956: 86–87; Vriezen, 1963: 51; Hooke, 1963: 84; Oldenberg, 1969: 19, 36, 38)

Mubben   A deity of the underworld of the Samek. Lapland. (Karsten, 1955: 107)

Mui'ingw   "Father of the underworld;" but in the chthonic sense of a god of vegetation and growth. The Hopi, Arizona. (Parsons, 1939: 178; Waters, 1963: 174)

Mukuru   The north where he lives is closely associated with water and the netherworld, the area of birth, death, and rebirth, where the sun dies and rises each day. He is a god of good/evil duality and identified with Kurunga, but as living in the netherworld he is a separate entity. The Herero, Southwest Africa. (Luttig, 1933: 3, 13–14)

Mul-lil   The old Akkadian name of Bel. He was the supreme god and creator at Nipur, but still retained his aspects as a god of the lower world "whose messengers were diseases and nightmares and the demons of the night." Near East. (Sayce, 1898: 125, 145–147)

Mul-nigi   A god of Hades, brother of Adar and son of Mul-lil. Same as Irkalla. Near East. (Sayce, 1898: 154)

Mulua Satene   Goddess of the afterworld and of the dead. She sends children to the earth to be born and to finally die to populate the underworld. The Wemale, Ceram, Indonesia. (Raats, 1969: 21, 34)

Muyiñwuh   Tusayan goddess of the underworld, of germs. Pueblo Indians, Arizona. (Fewkes, 1893/94: 259)

Naing-Naing   God of the underworld of the Tembeh. Malay Peninsula. (Skeat, 1906: 286)

Nam-mkhahi-snying-po, Akasagarbha   A Bodhisattva who appears on the third day of the Bardo of Karmic Illusions with Ratna-Sambhava, in the testing period after death. Tibet. (Evans-Wentz, 1960: 111; Getty, 1962: 101)

rNam-par-rgyal-va   The "Doorkeeper of the East" who appears on the sixth day of the Bardo of Karmic Illusions in the testing period following death. His shakti is Chags-kyu-ma. Tibet. (Evans-Wentz, 1960: 120)

Nanga-Nanga   The guardian god of the afterworld who is opposed to bachelors and tries to thwart their entrance. Fiji, Melanesia. (Moss, 1925: 201)

sNang-gsal-ma, Skt. Aloka   She "personifies (or symbolizes) light." A female Bodhisattva who appears with Amitabha on the fourth day of the Bardo of Karmic

Illusions in the testing period following death. Tibet. (Evans-Wentz, 1960: 113)

Nan Nu Ming I   A demon of the underworld—among the Imps of Torture. China. (Day, 1940: 216)

Ndara   A chthonic earth goddess whose husband is Toaralino. East Torajas, Celebes, Indonesia. (Downs, 1920: 9, 12; Wales, 1957: 78)

Nentcha   A deity of the underworld who with Hathor encourages the deceased to do battle with Apep. Egypt. (Budge, 1969, 1: 436)

Nergal   Originally a solar god representing the sun's destructive forces. In marrying Ereshkigal he became god of the underworld and of death, a god of disasters—plague, war, drought. Identified with the planet Mars. Near East. (Cook, 1930: 121; Seligmann, 1948: 30; Jastrow, 1898: 66–68, 171, 459; Schoeps, 1961: 58; James, 1960: 179; Sayce, 1898: 47, 197)

Neti   Sumerian guardian of the entrance to the underworld. Near East. (Moscati, 1962: 34)

Nga   God of the underworld of the Yuroks. Russia. (Queval, 1968: 75)

Nggalevu   The chief god of the spirit-land who lives in the volcano on which is the entrance to the underworld. Lepers Island, New Hebrides, Melanesia. (Moss, 1925: 33)

Nin-Anna   Babylonian goddess—"Scribe of the Underworld." Near East. (Thompson, 1903: 11)

Ninazu   A Sumerian "chthonic god combining death- and life-giving powers . . ." whose wife is Ningirda. Son of Enlil and Ninlil. Near East. (Jacobsen, 1970: 9, 24, 32; Kramer, 1950: 58)

Ningishzida   A god of healing and also a god of the underworld whose wife is Ninazimua. Son of Ninazu and Ningirda. He is at times identified with Nin-girsu and Nin-ib. Sumer and Babylonia, Near East. (Keeler, 1960: 219; Jacobsen, 1970: 24; Jastrow, 1898: 92; Zimmer, 1955: 53)

Ninmug   Another name of Ereshkigal, Allatu. Babylonia. Near East. (Sykes, 1952: 154)

Niu-t'ou   An ox-headed god. With Ma Mien "the two chief constables of Hell." He is one of those who collects the souls when the registry of Death indicates that life is over. China. (Werner, 1934: 268; Larousse, 1968: 399)

Nuliayoq Goddess of the lower world and daughter of Anatalik. The Hudson Bay Eskimo, Canada. (Wallis, 1939: 216)

Nuη A deity or power of dual aspect: Nuη-loki of the sky and the superior, and Nuη-lukak, a chthonic god associated with the earth, with cultivation and growth. The Bari, Sudan. (Seligman, 1931: 7, 8)

Nunu A Semitic god who is "closely tied to Enmešara" and is clearly an underworld deity. Near East. (Roberts, 1972: 47)

Nyeli-thub "God of Nyela, the sphere of hell." The Sherpas, Nepal. (Furer-Haimendorf, 1964: 232)

Nyja A Slavic god, the equivalent of Pluto. Poland. (Machal, 1918: 355, n. 44)

Obassi Nsi The earth goddess, beneficent and good, provides them with food and receives them in "the world under the earth, when they die." The Ekoi, Nigeria and Cameroons. (Frazer, 1926: 131–132; Meek, 1931: 180)

Oblivio Roman goddess of forgetfulness, of the underworld. Daughter of Nox and Erebus. (Roscher, 1965, 2, 2: 1957; 1965, 3, 1: 595)

Oloegekinyaligu "Guard of the coffee river in the realm of the dead." The Cuna, Panama. (Nordenskiold, 1938: 327)

Oloesakinkuapipilel Chief of a city in the afterworld who with Ololelpanilel "control the thunder" and send down the rain. The Cuna, Panama. (Nordenskiold, 1938: 309)

Oloesakuingapipler "Rain god in the realm of the dead." The Cuna, Panama. (Nordenskiold, 1938: 327)

Oloibakilel "The chief for Kalu Ibakki that is located in the east in the second (?) layer of the underworld." In the Nele Tiegun chronicle. The Cuna, Panama. (Nordenskiold, 1938: 327)

Oloikanipipilel, Oloikanilel A god of the eighth layer of the underworld who is the antagonist of Ibelele. His wife is Punauaga Olopunalisop and causes earthquakes. The Cuna, Panama. (Nordenskiold, 1938: 327)

Oloinpalilele "Chief of fishes in the underworld." The Cuna, Panama. (Nordenskiold, 1938: 328)

Olokanigidilisop A "woman who guards a tree in the underworld." The Cuna, Panama. (Nordenskiold, 1938: 328)

Olokerkikalilel, Olokerkekkalilel A god of the underworld in the Nele Tiegun chronicle. The Cuna, Panama. (Nordenskiold, 1938: 328)

Olokikadiryae A goddess of the fourth layer of the underworld, a wife of Oloueliptol. They are guardians of the river Kulikundiual where they await the arrival of the dead—in the Nele Sibu chronicle. The Cuna, Panama. (Nordenskiold, 1938: 297)

Olokuadile "Guards one of the water containers in the underworld. Husband to one of the female guards." The Cuna, Panama. (Nordenskiold, 1938: 328)

Olokunnikkalilel A "Chief in the underworld" in the Nele Tiegun chronicle. The Cuna, Panama. (Nordenskiold, 1938: 328)

Oloneylopaniler "In the realm of the dead he gives orders as to when it shall rain." The Cuna, Panama. (Nordenskiold, 1938: 328)

Olonuptigile "A woman who guards one of the water containers in the underworld." In the Tiegun chronicle. The Cuna, Panama. (Nordenskiold, 1938: 329)

Oloopanilel "Ant-bear . . . Chief in the realm of the dead." His wife is Oloakindili. In the Nele Organ and Nele Pailibe chronicles. The Cuna, Panama. (Nordenskiold, 1938: 329)

Olopenkekelel A god of the realm of the dead who "looks after all trees on the earth." The Cuna, Panama. (Nordenskiold, 1938: 329)

Olopioidigine The chief of the ants in the afterworld. His wife is Punauaga Olokurgililiae—in the Nele Sibu chronicle. The Cuna, Panama. (Nordenskiold, 1938: 311)

Olotagiki "In the realm of the dead. Gives the body its functions, the breathing, the hearing and so forth," as does Olotagisop. The Cuna, Panama. (Nordenskiold, 1938: 330)

Olotagisop The same information as above.

Oloueaidili Goddess of the fourth layer of the underworld. Wife of Uuakua, in the Nele Sibu chronicle. The Cuna, Panama. (Nordenskiold, 1938: 297)

Oloueliptol Guardian of the river Kulikundiual in the fourth layer of the underworld. His wives are Punauagauisogdili and Olokikakiryae. They "await the arrival of the dead." The Nele Sibu chronicle. The Cuna, Panama. (Nordenskiold, 1938: 297)

Olouigipipilele The chief of all the evil spirits of the underworld and the "owner of the water container." The high god informs him when there will be eclipses, earthquakes, floods, storms. The Nele Tiegun Chronicle. The Cuna, Panama. (Nordenskiold, 1938: 285, 330–331)

Olouiknidilisop Goddess of the underworld and wife of Masolokuirgikalilel in the Nele Tiegun chronicle. In the Nele Sibu chronicle she is the wife of Olokuirgikalilel, chief of rabbits. The Cuna, Panama. (Nordenskiold, 1938: 301, 326)

Olouiuidur One of the four tutelary spirits who seek out and transport the souls of the dead. In the chronicle of Nele Sibu. The Cuna, Panama. (Nordenskiold, 1938: 295)

Oloyakunalele A "Chief in the underworld" in the Nele Tiegun chronicle. The Cuna, Panama. (Nordenskiold, 1938: 330)

Oloyeginyalilel A "Chief in the underworld" in the Nele Tiegun chronicle. The Cuna, Panama. (Nordenskiold, 1938: 330)

O-mi-t'o Fo The Buddha of the Western Paradise and the conductor of souls. China. (Wood, 1937: 164; Edkins, 1880: 208; Werner, 1934: 119–120)

On God of the land of the dead, Amnodr, "believed to have created the Todas and their buffaloes." India. (Rivers, 1925, 12: 354; MacCulloch, 1925, 11: 824)

Op A Syrian god of the underworld. (Albright, 1968: 142)

Orcus Roman/Greek god of the underworld and of death which he brings both gently and violently. (Fairbanks, 1907: 237; Larousse, 1968: 213; Frazer, 1961: 231)

Orphne Greek personification of the dark of the underworld. Female. (Roscher, 1965, 3, 1: 1207)

Osiris God of the underworld and judge of the dead, bestowing on his followers a resurrection in the form of a life of abundance after death. He is thought to be an early river god identified with Hap, the Nile God, and a god of vegetation wherein he again represents death and rebirth. With his brother Set, who slays him, they represent the struggle between drought and fertility. Isis, his sister/wife, revives him. As god of the dead he represents the sun at night. He is the son of Seb and Nut, is a god of the south, and is god of the planet Venus. Egypt. (Budge, 1969, 2: 42, 117–118, 122, 139, 303; Frazer,

1960: 420–422, 442–443; Knight, 1915: 90; Ames, 1965: 56; Bulfinch, 1898: 367)

Oupu Goddess of the afterworld for the good. Tahuata, the Marquesas, Polynesia. (Williamson, 1933, 2: 42)

Owasse The "Bear and Chief of the Underground People." The Algonquian Indians, Eastern United States. (Alexander, 1964: 48)

Pahuamo "Guardian of the gate of the middle Hades." The Marquesas, Polynesia. (Handy, 1923: 246)

Paidogo God and ruler of the afterworld (on the island of Watum) where all the people go—good and bad. Murua or Woodlark Island, Melanesia. (MacCulloch, 1925, 11: 821)

Paigrab God of the underworld of the Sulod. Husband of Luyong Baybay, father of Magsanladung Biday. Philippines. (Jocano, 1969: 19)

pan·a The goddess of heaven to whom the souls of the dead go to be reborn and returned to the earth by the moon to become other humans or animals. The Padlermiut Eskimo, Canada. (Rasmussen, 1930: 79)

Panlinugun Chief god of Idadalmunon, the underworld. He is also god of earthquakes. The Sulod, Philippines. (Jocano, 1969: 19)

P'ao Lao Chu Che "Hot Pillar Roasting Demon," a god of the underworld, an Imp of Torture. China. (Day, 1940: 215)

Pao Wei Shen Chun "Guide to Chief Gods," a god of the underworld. China. (Day, 1940: 215)

Papaya With Istustaya "the primeval Netherworld goddesses," who spin the thread of life. Hattic/Hittite. Near East. (Guterbock, 1961: 149)

Pa She Chu Che "Tongue Extractor Demon," an Imp of Torture of the underworld. China. (Day, 1940: 215)

Patan A Mayan god of the underworld who brought sudden death to men. The Quiché, Guatemala. (Recinos, 1950: 110)

Pa Tien P'ing Teng Wang A god of the underworld, king of the eighth court. China. (Day, 1940: 214)

Patollus A Slavic deity of the underworld. Prussia. (Machal, 1918: Plate xxxvii)

Peres Also called Angoi. A god of the underworld who is identified with Jata in his desire "to destroy the good works of Mahatala." He introduced death into the creation of man. The Ngaju, Borneo. (Scharer, 1963: 22–23) Among the Ot Danum he is also associated with the underworld. He interfered with Pahatara's creation of man by convincing Anin Bamban, Pahatara's wife, that man should be mortal and die or there would be overcrowding. Pahatara agreed. (Raats, 1969: 27)

Persephone A goddess who became queen of the netherworld when kidnapped by Pluto. As the daughter of Demeter, her name was Kore. As such she was goddess of the seed corn. She was also a healing deity and a goddess of childbirth. Greece. (Frazer, 1960: 380, 456; Kerényi, 1951: 113, 461; Jayne, 1962: 343)

Persipnei, Phersipnai Etruscan goddess of the underworld and the wife of Eita, Aita. Same as Persephone. Italy. (Larousse, 1968: 211; Roscher, 1965, 3, 2: 2298; Pallottino, 1975: 143)

Petali A wrathful black goddess who appears from the north on the thirteenth day of the Bardo of Karmic Illusions, in the testing period following death. Tibet. (Evans-Wentz, 1960: 142)

Pezelao God of the underworld and of death, as well as a god of the earth. The Zapotec, Oaxaca, Mexico. (Whitecotton, 1977: 169)

Phyag-na rdo-rje, Vajrapani, (Sanskrit) A Bodhisattva who appears with Amogha-Siddhi on the fifth day of the Bardo of Karmic Illusions, in the testing period following death. Tibet and Nepal. (Evans-Wentz, 1960: 116; Snellgrove, 1961: 288)

Pien Ch'eng (Wang) King of the Sixth Court of Hades who punishes for sacrilege, disrespect for the gods, obscenity. China and Central Asia. (Maspero, 1963: 366; Werner, 1932: 377; Chavannes, n.d.: 96)

P'ing Teng Buddhist god of the Eighth Court of Hell who punishes for lack of filial piety. China. In Central Asia, P'ing-teng Tu-shi. (Maspero, 1963: 367; Day, 1940: 121; Chavannes, n.d.: 96)

Potoro A god of the underworld "who chained men." The Marquesas, Polynesia. (Williamson, 1933, 2: 41)

Prajapati In Bali he is a god of the netherworld who controls the souls of the dead until liberated by appropriate rituals. Indonesia. (Grader, 1969: 142)

Pramoha A wrathful red goddess who appears from the west on the thirteenth day of the Bardo of Karmic

Illusions, in the testing period following death. Tibet. (Evans-Wentz, 1960: 142)

Proserpina Roman goddess of the underworld as the wife of Pluto. However, she is primarily the goddess of the seed corn and of fecundity. (Frazer, 1960: 461; Bulfinch, 1898: 12, 74; Fairbanks, 1907: 180)

Pryderi A chthonic god associated with the earth's fertility rather than with a gloomy underworld. Son of Pwyll and Rhiannon. Wales. (MacCulloch, 1911: 112; Larousse, 1968: 232; Bray, 1935: 17)

Ah Puch Mayan god of death and malevolent ruler of Mitnal, the lower level of the underworld. Also known as Hunhau, Yum Cimil. Mexico and Guatemala. (Morley, 1946: 216; Thompson, 1970: 303)

Pukkase A wrathful red goddess who appears from the southeast on the thirteenth day of the Bardo of Karmic Illusions, in the testing period following death. Tibet. (Evans-Wentz, 1960: 142)

Pulang Gana As a god of the land of the dead he must be propitiated on the arrival of a new corpse. However, he is primarily a god of the soil and of agriculture, particularly all phases of rice farming. Among the Iban he is also, with Raja Sua, creator of heaven and earth. The Sea Dyaks, Borneo. (Roth, 1891: 121; Sarawak Gazette, 1963: 16, 133; Gomes, 1911: 196; Nyuak, 1906: 177)

Punauaga Oloeaydili Female guardian of "a river in the realm of the dead." The Cuna, Panama. (Nordenskiold, 1938: 331)

Punauaga Oloesgidili Female guardian of the river Osikundiual under the earth. The Nele Sibu chronicle. The Cuna, Panama. (Nordenskiold, 1938: 319)

Punauaga Oloibiyalisop Female guardian of "a tree in the realm of the dead." The Cuna, Panama. (Nordenskiold, 1938: 331)

Punauaga Olokurgililiae Wife of the chief of the ants in the afterworld. The Cuna, Panama. (Nordenskiold, 1938: 311)

Punauaga Oloniskidilisop Female guardian of the "Cacao River in the realm of the dead." The Cuna, Panama. (Nordenskiold, 1938: 331)

Punauaga Olouagaidili Female guardian of the river Kuilub-kundiual under the earth. The Nele Sibu chronicle. The Cuna, Panama. (Nordenskiold, 1938: 319)

Punauagauisogdili Goddess of the fourth layer of the underworld and one of the wives of Oloueliptol, who are guardians of the river Kulikundiual and await the arrival of the dead. The Nele Sibu chronicle. The Cuna, Panama. (Nordenskiold, 1938: 297)

Puntasbas Phrygian god of the underworld, protector of the tombs. Asia Minor. (Roscher, 1965, 3, 2: 3281)

Pwyll A deified mortal who became a god of the Otherworld in exchanging places with Arawn, the King of the Otherworld, and assuming his role as a god of death. His wife is Rhiannon; son of Pryderi. Wales. (MacCana, 1970: 180; Larousse, 1968: 232)

Qebhsennuf One of the four sons of Horus who, as a god of the underworld and a god of the Canopic jars, had charge of the liver and the gall bladder of the deceased, assisted by the goddess Serqet. A hawk-headed god, he represents the West and is god of the fourth hour of the day and of the night. Egypt. (Budge, 1969, 1: 456, 491–492; 1969, 2: 294; Knight, 1915: 35)

Quexuga The lame ruler of the southern regions in the afterworld, a region of joy and reunion. The Siouan Indians, South Carolina. (Swanton, 1946: 759)

Quicré A Mayan god of the underworld. The Quiché, Guatemala. (Recinos, 1950: 141)

Quicrixcac A Mayan god of the underworld. The Quiché, Guatemala. (Recinos, 1950: 141)

Quicxic A Mayan god of the underworld. The Quiché, Guatemala. (Recinos, 1950: 141)

Raja Puru, Raja Peres A deity of the underworld, a spirit of illness and disease. The Ngaju, Borneo. (Scharer, 1963: 21)

Rashnu "Truth." With Mithra and Sraosha a triad who act as the judges of the dead. Persia. (Hinnells, 1973: 62; Huart, 1963: 42; Haydon, 1941: 67, 79; Dresden, 1961: 348)

Rati-mbati-ndua The "god of hell in various parts of Fiji, is a man with only one tooth (which is the meaning of his name) with which he devours the dead, while instead of arms he has wings with which he can fly through space like a burning meteor." Melanesia. (Larousse, 1968: 450)

Ratna-Sambhava From him emanates one of the five elements—"earth, or aggregate of touch." He appears on the third day of the Bardo of Wisdom Teachings—that of the Wisdom of Equality—in the testing period following death; and again on the third day of the Bardo of Karmic Illusions with the goddess Sangyay-Chanma (Sangs-rgyas-spyan-ma). He appears also from the south on the sixth day of the Bardo of Karmic Illusions. Tibet. (Evans-Wentz, 1960: 9, 16, 111, 120)

Resheph, Reshef A god of the underworld, but primarily a god of disaster through war, plague, and the natural elements of fire, drought, lightning. Identified with Mot. Canaan and Phoenicia, Near East. (Albright, 1968: 139; Jayne, 1962: 132; Gray, 1964: 123)

Rhadamanthus One of the three judges (with Minos and Aeacus) of the underworld, "especially, according to Plato, judge of the Asiatic dead, or the overlord of the Elysian fields. . . . Rhadamanthus did not die like other mortals but was taken directly to Elysium." Son of Zeus and Europa, brother of Minos, and husband of Alcmena. Greece. (Morford and Lenardon, 1975: 246, 335; Leach, 1950, 2: 936)

Rhiannon, Riannon Goddess of birds and horses. As the wife of Pwyll she became a goddess of the Otherworld. She was the mother of Pryderi by Pwyll. After Pwyll's death she became the wife of Manawyddan. Wales. (Ross, 1967: 225, 268; MacCana, 1970: 55; MacCulloch, 1911: 110–111)

Rogo A god of the underworld and of agriculture in Mangareva. Son of Tagaroa and Haumea. Polynesia. (Buck, 1938: 422)

Roma-Tane The god of Paradise who judged which souls were to be allowed to enter. Tahiti, Polynesia. (Henry, 1928: 173, 378; Poignant, 1967: 26)

Rota, Ruto, Rutu An evil god of the underworld, of death, and of disease. Lapland, Northern Europe. (Dioszegi, 1968: 30; Karsten, 1955: 40–53; Pettersson, 1957: 9, 132; MacCulloch, 1964: 75–76)

Rua-kumea With Rua-toia conducts the souls of the dead to the underworld. The Maori, New Zealand. (Best, 1924: 325)

Rua-toia A deity who with Rua-kumea is "said to conduct souls of the dead down the way called Tahekeroa, that leads to the underworld." The Maori, New Zealand. (Best, 1924: 325)

Ruau-moko A god of the underworld associated with earthquakes and with the change of seasons. Polynesia. (Best, 1924: 237; Andersen, 1928: 288)

Ruko God of the underworld and of the sea. Merir, West Caroline Islands, Micronesia. (Wallis, 1939: 239)

Sagar Goddess on the bridge to Belet, the land of the dead. The Grik (Negritos), Malaya. (Evans, 1937: 145, 257)

Sama Bolowa Goddess of the underworld of the Nzema (Akan); though powerful, not one of the high gods. Ghana. (Grottanelli, 1967: 40)

Samanta-Bhadra, Kuntu-bzang-po "This is not the Adi-Buddha Samanta-Bhadra, but the spiritual son of the Dhyani Buddha Vairochana." A Bodhisattva who appears on the third day of the Bardo of Karmic Illusions with Ratna-Sambhava, in the testing period following death. Tibet. (Evans-Wentz, 1960: 111)

Sangiang A god to whom the souls of the dead journey. The Dyak, Borneo. (Eliade, 1964: 285)

Sangs-rgyas-spyan-ma Shakti of Ratna-Sambhava with whom she appears on the third day of the Bardo of Karmic Illusions in the testing period following death. Tibet. (Evans-Wentz, 1960: 70, 111)

Santaramet Armenian goddess of the underworld. (Ananikian, 1964: 35)

San Tien Sung Ti Wang A god of the underworld, king of the third of the ten courts. China. (Day, 1940: 214)

Sataran Sumerian chthonic deity of Etummal, identified with Damu. Near East. (Jacobsen, 1970: 324)

Saulal The god of the underworld who is half man, half lawud (a sea creature) is also the creator of the universe. Ifalik, Micronesia. (Burrows, 1947/48: 2)

Seb, Geb, Keb God of the underworld and of tombs, as well as god of the surface of the earth and its vegetation. Son of Shu and Tefnut; brother/husband of Nut; father of Isis and Osiris, Set and Nephthys. God of the third hour of the night and of the fifteenth day of the moon. Egypt. (Budge, 1969, 2: 94–99, 292; Knight, 1915: 109–110; Bulfinch, 1898: 367)

Sedna The supreme being and goddess of the sea and its animals. Among the Central Eskimo she is also goddess of the land of the dead, in which case she is invoked as Idliragi-jenget. Canada. (Boas, 1884/85: 583; Queval, 1968: 103; Thompson, 1968: 3)

Sehuiab A god to whom the souls of the dead go to live in the east. Son of the creator. The Pima, Arizona and New Mexico. (Bancroft, 1886, 3: 527)

Serapis A god of the underworld introduced by Ptolemy I, combining Osiris and the Apis Bull, as a deity for the Greeks and the Egyptians at Memphis. He was also a god of healing. (Budge, 1969, 2: 195, 198; Jayne, 1962: 77)

Setesuyara Goddess of the underworld. Bali, Indonesia. (Covarrubias, 1937: 7)

sgrib-pa rnam-sel Sarvanivarana-Vishkambhin, a Dhyani-Bodhisattva. He appears with Amogha-Siddhi on the fifth day of the Bardo of Karmic Illusions in the testing period following death. Tibet. (Getty, 1962: 106; Evans-Wentz, 1960: 116)

sgrol-ma, Tara (Sanskrit) Shakti of Amogha-Siddhi, with whom she appears on the fifth day of the Bardo of Karmic Illusions in the testing period following death. Tibet. (Evans-Wentz, 1960: 70, 116; Waddell, 1959: 150)

Sheol An ancient Semitic personification of the underworld. Canaan. Near East. (Paton, 1925, 3: 181)

She P'o Chiang Chun "Catcher of Souls," a god of the underworld. China. (Day, 1940: 215)

Shinje-chho-gyal, Charma-Raja God and impartial judge of the dead. Tibet and Sikkim. (Evans-Wentz, 1960: 35–37)

gShin rje gshed, Yamantaka (Sanskrit) Protector of the religious law. He is "the wrathful aspect of Avalokitesvara." He appears on the sixth day of the Bardo of Karmic Illusions in the testing period following death. Tibet. (Evans-Wentz, 1960: 210; Nebesky-Wojkowitz, 1956, 1: 23)

Shozu-ga no Baba A goddess, "(the guardian of the crossroads on the journey of the soul) . . . where the three ways of transmigration begin." Japan. (Anesaki, 1937: 240, Plate XI)

Siguinarugan A giant of the underworld who with Simuran guards the kanitu-nituhan gates. Assistant to Sisiburanen. Unredeemed souls are eventually fed to the guards. The Bisayan, Philippines. (Jocano, 1969: 20)

Simuran A giant in the underworld, a guard "of the kanitu-nituhan gates," to whom unredeemed souls are eventually fed. The Bisayan, Philippines. (Jocano, 1969: 20)

Sisiburanen A god of the underworld who treated all souls impartially, but if no sacrifice was made for the souls of the dead, they were kept for years and eventually fed to Simuran and Siguinarugan. The Bisayan, Philippines. (Jocano, 1969: 20)

Sitan   God of the lower world who punished the sinful at "Kasanaan, the village of grief and affliction." Maca is the afterworld of the good. The Tagalog, Philippines. (Jocano, 1969: 11)

Smasha, Smashali   A wrathful dark-blue goddess who appears from the northeast on the thirteenth day of the Bardo of Karmic Illusions, in the testing period following death. Tibet. (Evans-Wentz, 1960: 142)

Solal   The god of the netherworld. Yap, Ulithi. On the latter he is also "patron of the public fish magicians of the atoll." The Carolines, Micronesia. (Lessa, 1966: 60; Müller, 1917: 308)

spyan-ras-gzigs   Same as Avalokitesvara. He appears on the fourth day of the Bardo of Karmic Illusions with Amitabha, in the testing period following death. Tibet. (Evans-Wentz, 1960: 113; Hackin, 1963: 161)

Sraosha, Sros   As the guide of the dead to the afterworld he is guardian of the interim period before judgment, over which he presides with Mithra and Rashnu. Iran. (Hinnells, 1973: 52, 53, 62; Huart, 1963: 42; Haydon, 1949: 79; Dresden, 1961: 348)

Styx   A river goddess, the most renowned of the daughters of Oceanus and Tethys. She is the goddess of oaths and is associated with the underworld. She is the wife of Pallas and the mother of Bia, Cratos, Nike, and Zelus, whom she pledged with herself to assist Zeus in his war with the Titans. Greece. (Barthell, 1971: 15; Kerenyi, 1951: 34–35, 42; Larousse, 1968: 165)

Sucunyum, Sukunkyum, Sukukyum, Sukunyum   A god of the underworld who carries the sun on his shoulders during the night. Souls pass through his hands on the way to judgment. His part of the underworld is a beautiful place with forests, animals, etc. The average good person stays in his place if he approves of him. The Lacandon, Mexico. (Thompson, 1970: 240, 303; Cline, 1944: 112, 108; Perera and Bruce, 1982: 176–177, 309)

u 'suid-lam-iap   A deity who conducts the souls of the dead to the other world. The Khasi, Assam. (Stegmiller, 1921: 411)

Sumpay Pako-pako   A deity of the underworld and messenger of Sumpoy and Magyan. The Bisayan, Philippines. (Jocano, 1969: 21)

Sumpoy   God of the underworld, Kasakitan. He took the souls brought by Magyan, his brother, to "a region

called kanitu-nituhan" and delivered them to Sisiburanen. The Bisayan, Philippines. (Jocano, 1969: 20)

Sung Ti (Wang), Song Ti   God of the Third Court of Hell who punishes injustice and subordination with fire and hot water. China and Central Asia. (Hackin, 1963: 249, 365; Day, 1940: 121)

Susa-no-Wo   He was made god of the sea and of storms by his father, Izanagi, but chose to abandon this realm in favor of living in the netherworld with his mother. Brother of Amaterasu and father of Okuni-Nushi-no-Mikoto. Japan. (Schoeps, 1961: 215; Yasumaro, 1965: 28; Holtom, 1938: 81, 147)

Tahit, Tabit   God of the afterworld of the north where those who meet a violent death go. He is also a god of fate as he determines those who will die in battle, the sex of children, and whether a woman shall die in childbirth. The Tlingit, British Columbia and Alaska. (Alexander, 1964: 249; Wallis, 1939: 218)

Tambon   Goddess of the underworld, known also as Bawin Jata Balawang Bulau, or simply Jata. The Ngaju, Borneo. (Scharer, 1963: 14, 15)

Tamek-vui   Finno-Ugric god of the world beyond. (MacCulloch, 1964: 75)

rTa-mgrin-rgyal-po   "Skt. Hayagriva: 'Horse-necked King', the Door-keeper of the West." He appears on the sixth day of the Bardo of Karmic Illusions in the testing period following death. His Shakti is Lghags-sgrog-ma. Tibet. (Evans-Wentz, 1960: 120)

Tangata-no-te-moana   God of the underworld, the gardner, and god of the sea in charge of the fish. A very powerful deity. Pukapuka, Polynesia. (Beaglehole, 1938: 313)

Tartarus, Tartaros   One of the four (the third) primeval beings. He encompasses all of the lower world where all the dead go, not just representative of the punishment of sinners. Greece. (Barthell, 1971: 7; Cox, 1970, 2: 206, 323)

Tatusiso   A god who guards the bridge to the afterworld and guides the soul to the Land of the Gods. As an unkempt god he asked young men to delouse him. If they refused he sometimes threw them into the river "causing rain and floods on earth." The Manasi, Bolivia. (Métraux, 1943: 27)

Tch'ou-kiang   One of the Kings of Hell. China. (Chavannes, n.d.: 96)

Tcua-wuti A snake goddess of the underworld who became the wife of White-corn (Kwe-teat-ri-yi)—a culture-hero type. This was the origin of the snake order. Tcua-wuti could cause rain by invoking the rain god of her country. The Moquis, Arizona. (Stephen, 1888: 114)

Te Agai-a-tui A god of the underworld Te Matagi. Mangareva, Polynesia. (Buck, 1938: 425)

Teailoilo A god of the underworld, observer at the gate of heaven. Futuna, Polynesia. (Burrows, 1936: 107)

Tecolotl An Aztec god of the underworld. Mexico. (Bray, 1935: 284)

Te Etua-tapu-o-ako A god of the underworld Te Matagi. Mangareva, Polynesia. (Buck, 1938: 426)

Te Ika-tohara A god of the underworld Te Matagi. Mangareva, Polynesia. (Buck, 1938: 425)

Teikihaaotepo A god and guardian of the lower world. The Marquesas, Polynesia. (Handy, 1923: 246)

Telmikish A place in the East to which the spirits of the dead go—provided by Mukat. The Cahuilla, California. (Brumgardt and Bowles, 1981: 14)

Te Maguru A god of the underworld Te Matagi. Mangareva, Polynesia. (Buck, 1938: 426)

Te-mai-rihau-o-Rogo God "of all things beneath the earth, . . . in the Night-realm." Anaa Island, Tuamotus, Polynesia. (Stimson, 1933: 24)

Te Ma-tapuariki A god of the underworld Te Matagi. Mangareva, Polynesia. (Buck, 1938: 426)

Te Rupe A god of the underworld Te Matagi. Mangareva, Polynesia. (Buck, 1938: 426)

Tetewan Goddess of the netherworld, of darkness, and of the night sky. The Cora, Nayarit, Mexico. (Pettazzoni, 1956: 405)

té·xo·ɫtsó·di· Water Monster, an undependable deity of the lower world. The Navaho, Arizona and New Mexico. (Reichard, 1950: 490)

Themba The ferryman who carries the souls of the dead to the afterworld. Fiji, Melanesia. (Moss, 1925: 106)

Thenenet A goddess of the underworld and a goddess of Hermonthis with whom Hathor was identified. Also Isis. Egypt. (Budge, 1969, 1: 431; 1969, 2: 213, 216)

Thevathat God of the underworld, brother of Sommonacodom. Siam. (Bray, 1935: 175)

Ti Chang One of the Gods of Hell. Szechwan, China. (Graham, 1958: 52)

Tieholtsodi Variant spelling of té·xo·ɫtsó·di· (Burland, 1967: 105)

Tihpiknits The god of the afterworld of the Yokuts. The rattlesnake is his secretary, spies on the Yokuts and reports on them to Tihpiknits. If he wins in the celestial game played between him and Coyote, people die. California. (Latta, 1949: 210; Hudson and Underhay, 1978: 33)

Tiki (1) The king of the underworld. The Marquesas, Polynesia. (Christian, 1895: 190) (2) The god of Paradise who is judge of the dead. Rarotonga (Cook Islands), Polynesia. (Moss, 1925: 114)

Ting Huo Chu Che "Boiling Cauldron Demon," an Imp of Torture of the underworld. China. (Day, 1940: 215)

Tinukud A god of the underworld, offspring of Mayogyog. The Ifugao, Philippines. (Barton, 1946: 33)

Ti-tsang, Ti-tsang p'u-sa, Ti-Ts'ang Wang God of Hades, over the kings of the ten courts, who is also the earth god. He does not sit in judgment, but rather is merciful and compassionate, protective of children, and rescuing souls from the torments of hell. Same as Kshitigarbha. China. (Du Bose, n.d.: 270, 305; Edkins, 1880: 242; Werner, 1932: 497; Getty, 1962: 104–105; Maspero, 1963: 375; Day, 1940: 120–124; Williams, 1976: 400–401)

Tluscv An Etruscan deity of death and of the underworld, associated with the west. Italy. (Hamblin, 1975: 95)

Toa-miru A goddess of the underworld of Pouaru—the beneficent "goddess of childbirth and the guide of souls." Mangareva, Polynesia. (Buck, 1938: 426; Williamson, 1933, 2: 80)

Toaralino A god of the lower world, husband of Ndara. Celebes, Indonesia. (Downs, 1920: 9)

Tokakami God of death and of the underworld. The Huichol, Jalisco, Mexico. (Alexander, 1920: 122; Chamberlain, 1900: 306)

Tokonaka The Agave spirit sentinel who meets "the breath body" of the dead on its way to the "place of

Emergence" (their origin to which they return) and judges where he is to go. The Hopi, Arizona. (Parsons, 1939: 216)

Tonofiti A god who separated the earth and sky and then "became a god of the underworld." His wife is Hanau. The Marquesas, Polynesia. (Handy, 1923: 245–246)

Topileta God of the underworld and guardian of the route to it. He causes earthquakes, and also is a lustful god who satisfies his desires on the female spirits of the dead. Tuma Island, Trobriand Islands, Indonesia. (Roheim, 1972: 153; Moss, 1925: 114; Wallis, 1939: 241)

Tou-che One of the Kings of Hell. China. (Chavannes, n.d.: 96)

Toy-kamui The "master of the subterranean world." The Ainu and the Inau Cult, Japan. (Sternberg, 1906: 426)

Triptolemus Foster child of Demeter and Persephone, "said to have brought Demeter's gift of grain into the world," and her messenger in restoring the fertility of the earth. As associated with Persephone, a god of the underworld. Greece. (Campbell, 1964: 49; Morford and Lenardon, 1975: 210)

Trophonios A chthonic god of Boeotia, a god of fertility, oracular, and also an early minor god of healing. Greece. (Jayne, 1962: 351; Guthrie, 1950: 223–231; Tyler, 1964: 9)

Tsaaiyahatl Ruler of the world of the dead. The Tillamook, Oregon. (Boas, 1923: 11)

Tsandhali A wrathful yellowish-white goddess who appears from the northwest on the thirteenth day of the Bardo of Karmis Illusions, in the testing period following death. Tibet. (Evans-Wentz, 1960: 142)

Tseurima A wrathful yellow goddess appearing from the south on the thirteenth day of the Bardo of Karmic Illusions, in the testing period following death. Tibet. In India a cemetery goddess. (Evan-Wentz, 1960: 142)

Ts'in-kuang-wang God of the First Court of Hell who evaluates the merits and demerits of the dead. China. (Maspero, 1963: 364; Chavannes, n.d.: 96)

Tso Tsao Szu Che "Left Side Police Runner," a god of the underworld. China. (Day, 1940: 215)

Tuamutef A god of the underworld, jackal-headed son of Horus. As a god of the Canopic jars, he guards the heart and lungs of the dead, assisted by Net. As a god of the cardinal points he represents the east. He is also the god of the third hour of the day and of the night. Egypt. (Budge, 1969, 1: 145, 158, 456, 492; 1969, 2: 294; Knight, 1915: 34)

Tua-te-Ahu-tapu The "Marquesan Cerberus, the grim porter of Hades." Polynesia. (Christian, 1895: 190)

Tuchulcha An Etruscan demoness, a Fury of the underworld, associated with Charun. Italy. (Hamblin, 1975: 109; Roscher, 1965, 5: 1281; Larousse, 1968: 211; Dumézil, 1966, 2: 694)

Tuhan Di-Bawah God of the lower world who created the earth, and who instituted death to control the population. The Jakun, Malay Peninsula. (Skeats, 1906: 179–180; Cole, 1945: 119)

Tui Tao Chu Che "Pounding in Mortar Demon," a deity of the underworld. China. (Day, 1940: 215)

Tungkung Langit A god of the underworld who supports the world—not the same as the god of the upperworld of the same name. His wife is Luyung Kabig. The Sulod, Philippines. (Jocano, 1969: 19)

Tung Yueh Ta Ti A god of the underworld. China. (Day, 1940: 119)

Tuonetar Finno-Ugric queen of the underworld, wife of Tuoni and mother of Kipu-Tytto and Loviatar. Finland. (Larousse, 1968: 306)

Tuoni God of the underworld, Tuonela, whose wife is Tuonetar, and his daughters Kipu-Tytto and Loviatar. Finno-Ugric. Finland. (Larousse, 1968: 306)

Turngarsoak God of the spirit world and also god of sea animals. Husband of Superguksoak. The Labrador Eskimo, Canada. (Marsh, 1967: 156)

Tu Shih King of the Ninth Court of Hell where suicides are sent. He also punishes "incendiaries, abortionists, obscene painters or writers." China. (Day, 1940: 121–122; Maspero, 1963: 367)

Tutae-avae-toetoe God of Hades who keeps "guard over buried victims for 'Oro, the manslayer." Society Islands, Polynesia. (Henry, 1928: 319, 375)

Tu-ta-horoa The god who was guardian of the roads to Paradise and to Po (the netherworld), and who pointed the direction to be taken, or sometimes gave an extension of life. Tahiti, Society Islands. Polynesia. (Henry, 1928: 201, 378)

Tu-ti Wang   God of the Eighth Court of Hell, sometimes given as of the Ninth Court. China. (Werner, 1932: 527)

Uac Mitun Ahau   Mayan god of the underworld and of death—"Lord of the sixth hell." A title of Ah Uoh Puc as "lord of the underworlds." Mexico. (Tozzer, 1941: 147; Thompson, 1970: 228; Krickeberg, 1968: 70)

Ukunaibe   "Rattlesnake. Chief in the underworld." In the Nele Tiegun chronicle. The Cuna, Panama. (Nordenskiold, 1938: 332)

Ungap   A goddess, guardian to the entrance of the afterworld, who can be bribed. The Punans, Borneo. (Moss, 1925: 113)

Ah Uoh Puc   Mayan "spirit of destruction," a god of the underworld. He was also called Uac Mitun Ahau, and as such was represented as a skeleton. Mexico. (Krickeberg, 1968: 70)

Urken Rimpoche   In the afterworld he meets the dead and sends them on one of the seven paths according to their merits. Same as Padmasambhava. The Sherpas, Nepal. (Furer-Haimendorf, 1964: 156, 209)

Vagodonnaegus   A god of the underworld. Spain. (Martinez, 1962: 164–165)

Vahram   A Zoroastrian deity of the netherworld who accompanies the soul on the route to Cinvat Bridge for judgment. Iran. In Armenia he was the equivalent of "Verethraghna, the genius of victory." (Eliade, 1967: 360; Ananikian, 1925, 1: 799)

Vairochana   The celestial Buddha appears on the first day of the Bardo plane—after death—on the journey of the soul through the testing period. He appears also "from the Central Realm of the Spreading Forth of Seed" on the sixth day of the Bardo of Karmic Illusions. Tibet. (Evans-Wentz, 1960: 15, 119)

Vajra-Sattva   Following death the individual soul proceeds through the Bardo plane of the testing period. On the second day Vajra-Sattva appears; also on the sixth day of the Bardo of Karmic Illusions, coming from "the Eastern Realm of Pre-eminent Happiness." Tibet. (Evans-Wentz, 1960: 15, 119)

Vanth   An Etruscan goddess of the underworld who records fates and is associated with the spirit of death,

Charun. Italy. (Herbig, 1925, 5: 536; Dumézil, 1966, 2: 694; Larousse, 1968: 211)

Vedius   A deity associated with the underworld, the ruler of the Manes. Italy. (Dumézil, 1966, 1: 170; Weinstock, 1946: 105)

Veiovis, Vediovis   An Etruscan/Roman god of the underworld who watched over the relationship between master and slave and also that of asylum, and judged the evil spirits. He appears in region fifteen of the heavens in the Cosmic System of the Etruscans (Martianus Capella). Italy. (Altheim, 1937: 132–133, 262; Weinstock, 1946: 105)

Velinas, Velnias, Velas, Vels   The god of the dead and of the underworld whose realm is in the depths of swamps and lakes. To satisfy his need for human blood he lures people to their deaths by drowning, hanging, or fright. He is "the creator of snakes, toads, frogs, other crawling creatures," as well as black animals and birds. He assumes many forms, most frequently that of a snake, which represents his versatility and his dangerous unpredictability. As a god of cattle and of fertility, of wealth and of trade, of magic and of clairvoyance, he is frequently beneficent, helping the poor and the good. But primarily his blacker side rules. His name of Velinas must not be used because of taboos—among those which are used: Pikulas, Piktis, Ragius, Balinis, Kirnis, and numerous others. Lithuania. (Gimbutas, 1974: 87–92)

Vels   Latvian "god of the underworld and guardian of cattle." (Gimbutas, 1971: 167)

Vetis   An Etruscan deity of the underworld associated with the northwest. Italy. (Hamblin, 1975: 95; Roscher, 1965, 6: 277)

Vizarsh, Vizaresa   A demon of the netherworld who transports the souls of the wicked and inflicts pain, misery, etc. on them. Iran. (Eliade, 1967: 361; Gray, 1930: 217)

Vizisht   A demon of the netherworld who accosts the soul en route to Cinvat Bridge for judgment. Iran. (Eliade, 1967: 360)

Vucub-Came, Vukup Camé   God of death and of the underworld, Xibalba. With Hun-Came the supreme judges of the council of the lords of the underworld. The Quiché, Guatemala. (Recinos, 1950: 109–110; Krickeberg, 1968: 79; Girard, 1979: 87)

Wadawadariwa   A spirit on the route to the afterworld, *hedu*, who questions the soul as to its generosity while on earth. If the answer is no he sends them to *shobari waka,* where they "burn eternally." The Yanomamo, Venezuela and Brazil. (Chagnon, 1968: 48)

Waiabskinit Awase   The "white bear," chief of the gods of the lower world. He is "the essence of evil." The Menomini, Wisconsin. (Skinner, 1913: 13, 88)

Wai Tsao Szu Che   "Outside Police Runner," a god of the underworld. China. (Day, 1940: 215)

Warrugura   An evil spirit of the Watchandi who lives in the lower regions. Australia. (Tylor, 1891: 292)

Wu Ch'ang Shih Che   "Assistant Detective," a god of the underworld. China. (Day, 1940: 215)

Wu Kuan   God of the Fourth Court of Hell who punishes the "miserly rich," defrauders, falsifiers, and thieves. China and Central Asia. (Maspero, 1963: 365; Day, 1940: 121; Hackin, 1963: 249)

Wuluwait   The boatman who carries the spirit of the dead to the island Purelko, their heaven. Australia. (Mountford, 1965: 62)

Wu Tien Yen Lo Wang   A god of the underworld, fifth King of the ten courts. China. (Day, 1940: 214)

Xic   A god of the underworld who brought sudden death to men. The Quiché, Guatemala. (Recinos, 1950: 110)

Xiquiripat   A god of the underworld "who caused the shedding of blood of the men." The Quiché, Guatemala. (Recinos, 1950: 110)

Xonaxi Huilia   The goddess of the underworld and of death—in some towns—whose husband is Coquechila. The Zapotec, Oaxaca, Mexico. (Whitecotton, 1977: 158, 164)

Xonaxi Quecuya   Goddess of the underworld and of death of the Valley Zapotecs at Mitla. Wife of Coqui Bexelao. Same as Xonaxi Huilia. Oaxaca, Mexico. (Whitecotton, 1977: 158)

Xul-ater   Vogul god of the underworld. Western Siberia. (Roheim, 1954: 35)

Yama   God of the underworld and of death, impartial judge of the dead. Son of Vivaswat, the sun, and associated with the south. Hinduism/Buddhism. In the latter his names are: gSin-rje (Tibet), erlik qan (Mongolia), Yen-lo-wang (China), Emma-o (Japan). He is also known in Bali, Cambodia, Korea. (Friederich, 1959: 49, 50; Percheron, 1953: 62; Waddell, 1959: 367–368; Hackin, 1963: 169; Getty, 1962: 152; Grosvenor, 1969: 697; Marchal, 1963: 203; Danielou, 1964: 130; Moes, 1983: 127)

Yeh Hsun Ch'a   "Demon Inspector of Night," a god of the underworld. China. (Day, 1940: 215)

Yeh Yu Shen   "God of the Night-time," a god of the underworld. China. (Day, 1940: 215)

Yen-lo Wang   God of the Fifth Court of Hell who judges and punishes for religious sins, murder, incredulity, lust, rape, prostitution. Same as Yama. China. (Maspero, 1963: 366; Hackin, 1963: 249; Day, 1940: 69, 98, 121, 124)

Yen-wang-yeh   God of the First Court of Hell who judges the dead and, where punishment is due, assigns them to the proper court. China. (Larousse, 1968: 398)

Yidak-thub   "God of Yidak-yul, the sphere of suffering spirits." The Sherpas, Nepal. (Furer-Haimendorf, 1964: 232)

Yin Yang Kuan   A god of the underworld who is the gatekeeper between life and death and guide of the soul to the first court, where a man is judged. From there the appropriate Imp of Torture leads him to his assigned place of torment. China. (Day, 1940: 122, 215)

Yomo-tsu-Okami   Izanami as the goddess of the underworld. Japan. (Kato, 1926: 17; Holtom, 1938: 112)

Yu Chu Ling Kuan   "Grand Marshall of Soul," a god of the underworld. China. (Day, 1940: 215)

Yum Cimil   God of the underworld and of death. The Mayan, Yucatan. Other names: Kisin, Ah Puch, Hunhau. Mexico. (Morley, 1946: 227; Tozzer, 1941: 132)

Yumna   God of the underworld. Korea. (Clark, 1932: 119)

Yun Te Ch'ao Wang   "Wealth God for the Dead," a god of the underworld. China. (Day, 1940: 215)

Yu Tsao Szu Che   "Right Side Police Runner," a god of the underworld. China. (Day, 1940: 215)

Zhags-pa-ma, Pashadhari (Sanskrit) The shakti of Yamantaka. She appears on the sixth day of the Bardo of Karmic Illusions in the testing period following death. She is a doorkeeper of the south. Tibet. (Evans-Wentz, 1960: 120)

Zhal-zas-ma Also called Nidhema. A female Bodhisattva who appears with Amogha-Siddhi on the fifth day of the Bardo of Karmic Illusions in the testing period following death. Tibet. (Evans-Wentz, 1960: 116)

25

Resurrection/Rejuvenation Deities

Adonis God of vegetation and of fertility who represents the death and resurrection of nature, spending half the year on earth, half in the underworld. Asia Minor. In Greece he is the beloved of Aphrodite with whom he spends a third of the year, a third by himself, and a third with Persephone in the underworld. (Schoeps, 1961: 64; Frazer, 1960: 380; Kerenyi, 1951: 76; Fairbanks, 1907: 207; Moscati, 1960: 114; Larousse, 1968: 81, 84)

Akipe A benevolent deity who takes people to eternity and when he returns them they "appear in good health as if nothing had happened." Considered particularly to be the experience of witch doctors, but happens to others also. The Turkana, Kenya. (Penley, 1930: 139–140)

Asaase Aberewa The "Thursday-goddess of the Underworld" who is represented by the scorpion and the serpent, which symbolize "not only death but rebirth." The Akan, Ghana. (Meyerowitz, 1958: 134)

Attis Phrygian god of vegetation, with death at the harvest, and resurrection each spring; the beloved of Cybele. Asia Minor. (Frazer, 1960: 403, 409; James, 1960: 97; Larousse, 1968: 150)

Baal The storm king as the giver of rains and dew was a god of fertility, of the vegetation cycle, a death and resurrection god. Slain by Mot, all vegetation mourned Baal until his revival in the spring. Canaan, Phoenicia, and Syria. (Albright, 1956: 73–74; Gordon, 1961: 814–815, 211; Crawford, 1957: 19, 23; Herm, 1975: 108–110)

Chipi The deity of death and rebirth. Oaxaca, Mexico. (Doty, 1977: 63)

Dionysus A god of vegetation as well as wine. He spends a portion of each year underground and returns with, or brings, the spring. He is depicted as a bull or a goat; is usually named as the son of Zeus and Semele.

Greece. (Frazer, 1960: 450–453; Kerneyi, 1951: 158, 109; Fairbanks, 1907: 58, 190; Jayne, 1962: 318)

Dumuzi, Dumuzid The shepherd god, the shepherd aspect of the dead and rising deity, representing the life-giving powers in the fresh milk of spring. When this season ends, he dies. Mesopotamia, Near East. (Jacobsen, 1970: 56, 327; Kramer, 1950: 100; Sayce, 1898: 221, 231)

Dushara, Dusares An Arabian earth god, consort of Atargatis. "The king who dies and is reborn." (Ferguson, 1970: 17)

Estsanatlehi, Estsunnadlehi A goddess, "Changing Woman," who has the power to rejuvenate herself when she grows old, becoming a baby and growing again. She is the goddess of fruitfulness and of nature's abundance; the wife of the sun god (Johanoai, Tshohanoai); lives in the west. She is the creator of people. The Navaho, Arizona and New Mexico. (Mattews, 1890: 89, 95; Alexander, 1964: 157; Babington, 1950: 210–212; Newell, 1896: 216; Burland, 1965: 112–113; Goodwin, 1939: 5)

Haweniu, Hawenneyu The Great Spirit and creator who had the power of rejuvenating men, giving them great powers. The Iroquois Indians, Eastern United States. (Parker, 1910: 473; Morgan, 1904: 147)

Heqet, Hequet A frog-headed goddess of fertility and rebirth, also "associated with the Egyptian idea of resurrection." (Knight, 1915: 44; Budge, 1969, 2: 378)

Hor-m-akhet, Harmakhis (Greek) Horus of the Horizon, the "personification of the rising sun and a symbol . . . of resurrection." Egypt. (Casson, 1965: 70)

Hunahpú He, with his twin Xbalanque (Xblamqué), was conquered by the powers of the underworld, but rose again "to overcome and destroy the powers of death and hell (Xibalba)." As the maize god he gives his life to feed the people when he is beheaded in Xibalba—symbolically the death and regeneration deity. The twins were the children of Xquiq who was impregnated by the spittle of Hunhun-Ahpu. The Quiché, Guatemala. (Brinton, 1868: 258; Recinos, 1950: 119, 124; Thompson, 1970: 237; Girard, 1979: 114, 186, 227)

Idunn The goddess of immortality, the guardian of the apples which maintain the youth of the gods. Scandinavia. (Turville-Petre, 1964: 186; MacCulloch, 1964: 178; Davidson, 1964: 165; Wagner, 1882: 173)

Jalandhara A demon of extraordinary strength and powers who made war on the gods, but was finally defeated by Siva and his wives. He "received from Brahma himself the power of resurrecting the dead." India. (Larousse, 1968: 337)

Jara-meng The moon goddess who has powers of rejuvenation—ages and then becomes young again. The Semang, Lenggong, North Perak, Indonesia. (Pettazzoni, 1956: 339)

Khepera, Kheper, Khepri The beetle or scarab god, a god of creation and resurrection. He is a solar god, a form of Ra, representing the sun in its primeval rising as well as in its daily appearance. Egypt. (Budge, 1969, 1: 294, 298, 355; 1969, 2: 379; Long, 1963: 76; Casson, 1965: 27, 50; Knight, 1915: 62)

Ma'i-ola A tree god whose powers could restore life, as an antidote for the poison-god Kalai-pahoa. Hawaii. (Westervelt, 1963, 3: 109)

Mot In Syria and Phoenicia he is a vegetation/harvest god, representing death and rebirth, the seed in its dormant state, which then sprouts and rises. With Aleyin he forms a conflict pair, of opposites rather than of good and bad. He represents the drought of summer; is also considered a god of the underworld, of death, and of sterility. Near East. (Crawford, 1957: 19; James, 1960: 88; Vriezen, 1963: 51)

Mululil A "dying god, comparable with Dumuzi." Son of Ninhursaga and Shulpae. Sumer, Near East. (Jacobsen, 1970: 30)

Nafanua A goddess of the bathing place Vaiola, "the water of life," in the afterworld—the source of rejuvenation. Samoa, Polynesia. (Williamson, 1933, 1: 334)

Ntoa A god/goddess whose planet is Venus. He/she "is expressed in the goat (sex, life), and the dog (death and

resurrection)." In cult rituals, a participant in death/rebirth ceremonies. The Akan, Ghana. (Meyerowitz, 1958: 49, 57)

Osiris Originally a nature god, he represented the harvest and death of vegetation, then the sprouting or rebirth of the grain. With Set he forms a pair of opposites—of drought and fertility, of darkness and light. Later he became god and judge of the dead where he is again the symbol of resurrection and the hope of a happy afterlife. He was slain by Set, then resurrected by his wife Isis. Egypt. (Frazer, 1960: 442–443; Casson, 1965: 54; Ames, 1965: 56; Budge, 1969, 2: 118, 139; Larousse, 1968: 16)

Seker An older Egyptian god absorbed by Ptah (Ptah-Seker) and with Osiris forming a triad Ptah-Seker-Asar wherein they form the "symbol of resurrection from the dead." (Budge, 1969, 2: 506–507)

Taema A goddess of Vaiola, "the water of life," a bathing place in the afterworld—the source of rejuvenation. Samoa, Polynesia. (Williamson, 1933, 1: 334)

Tammuz A Sumerian/Babylonian god of vegetation, representing the cycle of life and death in nature. He was the spouse/lover of Ishtar by whom he was rescued each year from the netherworld. A tree god. Same as Adonis, Dumuzi. Near East. (Vriezen, 1963: 39, 40; Jacobsen, 1970: 73; Wales, 1957: 31; Hooke, 1963: 41; Frazer, 1960: 379)

Tezcatlipoc "Smoking Mirror." As the Red Tezcatlipoca (Xipe or Camaxtle) he is associated with vegetation, a death and resurrection god who lives for a year in the person of a young man and is then sacrificed, being replaced by another young man—the new growth. Basically Tezcatlipoca is a god of many aspects: e.g., solar, war, cardinal points. Mexico. (Vaillant, 1962: 142–149; Frazer, 1960: 680–682; Keeler, 1960: 122)

Tilafainga A goddess of Vaiola, "the water of life," the source of rejuvenation in the afterlife. Samoa, Polynesia. (Williamson, 1933, 1: 334)

Xbalanque Twin of Hunahpu, sons of Xquiq, who was impregnated by the spittle of Hun-Hunahpu. They were overcome by the powers of the underworld, but succeeded in their struggle against them and rose again in turn to overcome the gods of death and of Xibalba, the underworld. The Quiché, Guatemala. (Recinos, 1950: 119, 124; Thompson, 1970: 234; Brinton, 1868: 258)

PART VI

Economic Activities

26

Agriculture/Vegetation Deities

Ab   An Egyptian grain god. (Budge, 1973, 1: 58)

Abad   A spirit of the rice harvest helpful to the reapers. The Isneg, Luzon, Philippines. (Vanoverbergh, 1941: 337)

Abalud   A spirit of the harvest time to whom betel is offered. The Isneg, Luzon, Philippines. (Vanoverbergh, 1941: 337)

Abanna   The yam god at Awakande whose wife is Ekpaga and daughter is Oka. Cross River region, Nigeria. (Mockler-Ferryman, 1925, 9: 280)

Abellio   God of the apple-tree. The Pyrenees region. Gaul. (Larousse, 1973: 339)

Abu   Sumerian god of vegetation, created to serve man. Asia Minor. (Langdon, 1931: 202)

Abundantia   A Roman goddess of agricultural prosperity, one of the earliest personifications of abundance. (Ferguson, 1970: 73; Roscher, 1965, 1, 1: 3)

Abuwes   A spirit offered rice pudding at the beginning of the harvest and invoked to go away. The Isneg, Luzon, Philippines. (Vanoverbergh, 1941: 346)

Ach Bilam   The Lacandon make pilgrimages to his shrine before burning their milpas. Mexico. (Thompson, 1970: 319–320)

Achita   A god of agriculture of the Tiv. Nigeria. (Temple, 1922: 302)

Aden   A sky god, second son of Sogbo, who gives the fine rain beneficial to fruit trees of which he is guardian. Dahomey. (Herskovits, 1938, 2: 152, 156; 1933: 21)

Adolenda   A minor Roman goddess of agriculture—for the removal of trees, especially those of the temple of Dea Dia. (Ferguson, 1970: 69; Roscher, 1965, 1, 1: 69)

Adonis   God of vegetation and of fertility symbolizing the vegetation cycle of death and resurrection. He represented the fruitfulness of the earth, "was manifest in the seed of corn." Greece, Phoenicia, Canaan, and Syria. (Cox, 1870, 2: 7; Fairbanks, 1907: 207; Moscati, 1960: 114; Larousse, 1968: 81)

Adoo Yook   One of the two oldest of the Mayel (with Alau Yook). Their so-called wives are Talyeu Nimu and Sangvo Nimu who are earth spirits and whom they fertilize with rice, millet, and maize. The Lepchas, Sikkim. (Gorer, 1938: 237)

Aggayen   A guardian of the rice and the granary. The Isneg, Luzon, Philippines. (Vanoverbergh, 1941: 297)

Agkebaan   Unlike the other spirits he is not concerned with rice "but kills unmercifully anybody who dares steal products of the garden that have been left behind after the general harvest." The Isneg, Luzon, Philippines. (Vanoverbergh, 1941: 363)

Aglalannawan   A spirit of the rice harvest who is helpful to the reapers. The Isneg, Luzon, Philippines. (Vanoverbergh, 1941: 337)

Aglauros, Agraulos   An ancient goddess of agriculture, later identified with Athene and Demeter. She is a goddess of the dew and sister of Herse and Pandrosos. Greece. (Bethe, 1925, 1: 226; Roscher, 1965, 1, 1: 106)

Agras   God of turnips of the eastern Finns, implored for abundance, Finland. (Krohn, 1925, 6: 25)

Agroi   Finnish god of turnips, and also god of twins. (MacCulloch, 1964: 244)

Agroueros, Agrotes   A Phoenician god of agriculture. Byblus, Near East. (Cook, 1930: 165)

Ague   God of herbs and foliage. Brazil. (Bastide, 1960: 560)

Aha Njoku   The very powerful yam spirit. "She acts as a social sanction which controls the behavior of women in the home, the farm, and the ba—a storage place for yams." The Igbo, Nigeria. (Uchendu, 1965: 98–99)

Ahbuluc Balam   A god invoked with Chichac Chob, Ek Balam Chac, and Ahcan Uolcab in ceremonial rites to ensure good crops. The Mayan, Mexico and Guatemala. (Bancroft, 1886, 2: 701)

Ahcan Uolcab   A Mayan serpent god invoked with others in ceremonial rites to ensure good crops. Mexico and Guatemala. (Bancroft, 1886, 2: 701)

Ahn tee up   "Wants a flower." A god who makes "the flowers grow." The Seris, Sonora, Mexico. (Coolidge, 1939: 204)

Aiyanar   In Southern India a popular village god who is guardian of the fields and protective of the crops, helped by his wives Purani and Pudkala. (Geden, 1925, 1: 257)

Aiyang   God of agriculture of the Seiyawa. Nigeria. (Meek, 1925: 28)

Aji Ti Brani Ngilah Bulan Suka Raja Rengayan   With Pulang Gana, his father-in-law, he gives "to the men charms for obtaining padi" (rice). He is the husband of Benih Lela Punggang Tengian Dara Bintang Tiga Datai Ka Jelan. The Dyaks, Sarawak, Borneo. (Sarawak Gazette, 1963: 79; Howell, 1908/10: 40)

Ajokko-Ji, Njokkoji   The yam spirit. Nigeria. (Talbot, 1967: 99)

Aka-kanet   God of grain and fruit, protective of their harvest. The Araucanians, Chile. (Rhys, 1937: 7; Brinton, 1868: 61; Bray, 1935: 288)

Akinchob   The god of corn protects the milpa and also men. He is the son-in-law of Hachakyum, the creator. The Lacandon, Chiapas, Mexico. (Perera and Bruce, 1982: 305)

Akuma   A guardian god of the Jukun who receives offerings of thanks for the crops at the harvest. Nigeria. (Meek, 1931: 272–3)

Ala Tala   A boy who was born to be sacrificed—from his head came the coco palm, from his body the water buffalo. Middle Celebes, Indonesia. (Hatt, 1951: 887)

Alau Yook   With Adoo Yook the two oldest of the Mayel. They fertilize the earth spirits Talyeu Nimu and Sangvo Nimu with rice, millet, and maize. The Lepchas, Sikkim. (Gorer, 1938: 237)

Alijan-Baal   A vegetation deity "equated with the grain that is sowed in the field, subsequently reaped and threshed, winnowed and finally baked into bread." Canaan, Near East. (Schoeps, 1961: 64)

Alindaiyu   An agricultural deity at Nagadangan. The Ifugao, Philippines. (Barton, 1946: 37)

Alindodoay   A female rice spirit invoked during the harvesting. The Isneg, Luzon, Philippines. (Vanoverbergh, 1941: 297, 343)

Alipugpug   A very helpful spirit to a farmer clearing a field. Manifests himself in eddies or whirls of wind. The Isneg, Luzon, Philippines. (Vanoverbergh, 1941: 309)

Alipundan   A spirit of the rice harvest time who "causes the reapers' toes to get sore all over and swell." The Isneg, Luzon, Philippines. (Vanoverbergh, 1941: 337)

Sidi Ali uMhammd   The patron saint of the Igliqa and the Ait Wauzgit who is given "the first basket (taryalt) of any kind of corn" at the harvesting. Morocco. (Westermarck, 1926, 1: 179, 238)

'Alo'alo   A god of vegetation and of harvest. He is primarily a god of weather to whom offerings are made for good weather and fertility. The Tongans, Polynesia. (Moulton, 1925, 12: 377; Mariner, 1820: 385)

Alosaka   The Germ God, a god of seeds. *See* **Muingwu.** The Hopi, Arizona. (Fewkes, 1920: 592; Tyler, 1964: 126–127)

Alpena   An Etruscan goddess of flowers associated also with rainbows and clouds, with air and light. Italy. (Leland, 1963: 119)

Amaethon   Celtic god of agriculture, of farming, who also brought useful animals to earth. Son of Don. (Anwyl, 1906: 35; MacCulloch, 1911: 107; Rhys, 1937: 8)

Ama-ushumgal-anna   An aspect of Tammuz as deity of the date palm. Sumer, Near East. (Jacobsen, 1970: 83)

Ambabai A goddess associated with sprouting and sowing rites at Pandharpur. India. (Frazer, 1961: 243)

Ambungan The "guardian of the rice harvest." The Apayao, Philippines. (Wilson, 1947: 22)

Ame-no-tajikara-wo The priests of his temples "hold that he was originally a god of agriculture." His popular aspect is as a god of war and of strength. Japan. (Herbert, 1967: 305)

Amerodat, Ameretat "Immortality," the protectress of vegetation and of waters. She is associated with Haurvatat. Iran. (Gray, 1930: 221; Dumézil, 1970: 53; Littleton, 1965: 99; Hinnells, 1973: 52; Huart, 1963: 41)

Ampelos The personification of the grapevine. Thrace. (Roscher, 1965, 1, 1: 292)

Anala Goddess of trees yielding pulpy fruits and milk such as the date, the coconut, etc. Daughter of Surabhi. India. (Mackenzie, 1924: 173)

Anap An evil spirit of the rice harvest time who kills. The Isneg, Luzon, Philippines. (Vanoverbergh, 1941: 337)

Anat A benevolent female spirit who helps the reapers of the rice harvest. The Isneg, Luzon, Philippines. (Vanoverbergh, 1941: 337)

A-neb A protector of the rice fields who lives at the edge. The Isneg, Luzon, Philippines. (Vanoverbergh, 1941: 300)

Anglabbang A spirit offered betel and invoked for support in storing the rice in the granary. The Isneg, Luzon, Philippines. (Vanoverbergh, 1941: 361)

Annadeo A god of grain. Agaria, India. (Elwin, 1942: 93)

Annadeva The " 'giver of food'." India. (Tod, 1920: 617)

Anna Kuari A goddess of crops worshipped during the threshing of grain. Also a goddess of good fortune. Chota Nagpur, India. (Frazer, 1960: 503; Elwin, 1949: 435; Russell, 1916, 4: 312)

Anna-Purna A beneficent goddess who provides food. A form of Parvati. Tanjore, Bengal. The corn goddess of the Bania. India. (Ghurye, 1962: 243, 258; Coleman, 1832: 97; Dowson, 1961: 17; Russell, 1916, 2: 125, 506)

Annona Roman goddess of crops and of harvests. (Carter, 1925, 9: 799; Roscher, 1965, 1, 1: 360)

Anrixad A benevolent male spirit of the rice harvest time who increases the crop. The Isneg, Luzon, Philippines. (Vanoverbergh, 1941: 337)

Anura The spirit of the tobacco seeds. The Arawak, Guiana. (Levi-Strauss, 1973: 426)

Anyi Lawang A god of the harvest. The Kayans, Borneo. (Hose, 1912: 5)

Apai Mapai A god invoked at the beginning of the rice farming season. The Sea Dyaks, Borneo. (Roth, 1968: 174)

Aphowo A spirit of the harvest. The Sema Nagas, India. (Hutton, 1968: 198)

Aran A spirit offered rice pudding at the beginning of the harvest and invoked to go away. The Isneg, Luzon, Philippines. (Vanoverbergh, 1941: 346)

Ariki-noanoa The god of the fern-root—"the food for times of commotion and war." New Zealand. (White, 1887, 3: 97)

Aristaeus, Aristaios A god of agriculture, of flocks and herds, as well as of healing. Son of Apollo and Kyrene. Greece. (Jayne, 1962: 310 310); Kerenyi, 1951: 142; Thramer, 1925, 6: 546)

Arkamtse-lha-tsen karbu A god of the soil of the Sherpas. Vicinity of Tangnak, Nepal. (Furer-Haimendorf, 1964: 22)

Arnam-paro A god worshipped at the beginning of the cultivation season and invoked for prosperity and to avert misfortune. The " 'hundred-god'." He "takes a hundred shares of rice, rice-flour, betel-nut." The Mikirs, Assam. (Lyall, 1925, 8: 629–630)

Aruarani "Mother of Moriche Flour" and goddess of "sustenance and fertility." She is also the patron goddess of the women hammock makers. The Winikina-Warao, Venezuela. (Wilbert, 1973: 6, 28)

Arurin A female spirit of the rice harvesting who must have a share at meals to insure the harvest. The Isneg, Luzon, Philippines. (Vanoverbergh, 1941: 337)

Asari A god of agriculture of Syria. (Sykes, 1952: 18)

Ashingyi A spirit propitiated for good rice crops and harvest. Burma. (Nash, 1966: 126)

Ashnan   Sumerian/Babylonian goddess of grain. Near East. (Mercer, 1925, 12: 709; Langdon, 1931: 191; Ferm, 1950: 60; Oldenburg, 1969: 48)

Asu Mainao   Goddess of the *asu* crop. The Kacharis, Assam. (Endle, 1911: 37)

Atea   The god of agriculture, of husbandry, "who brought good seasons with refreshing rains." The Marquesas, Polynesia. (Christian, 1895: 189)

Atira   Mother Corn, who is the leader of the Hako ceremony which is for achieving children, longevity, abundance, happiness and peace. She is the wife of Tirawa. The Pawnee, Plains Indians, Nebraska. (Fletcher, 1900/01: 26, 44–46; Dorsey, 1904: 3; Grinnell, 1893: 114–115)

Attis   A tree spirit, the pine, who is god of vegetation and of fertility, the death and resurrection cycle. In Phrygia he is the "beloved of Cybele." Asia Minor. (Frazer, 1960: 403, 409; James, 1960: 97)

Atua Fafine   A goddess protective of the women in "the Work of the Yam." She is the goddess of women generally; is the mother of Matapula. Tikopia, Polynesia. (Firth, 1967, 2: 143, 330, 396)

Atua-metua   A parent god of the Creation Chant who produced the coconut, the *toro-miro* tree, and green leaves. Easter Island, Polynesia. (Métraux, 1940: 321: Buck, 1938: 225)

Auschleuts   A deity of the Sudavians in Samland "invoked when there was a poor harvest." Old Prussian. (Welsford, 1925, 9: 488)

Auxesia   A Greek goddess who promotes the growth of crops and is a goddess of fertility. (Jayne, 1962: 315; Prentice Hall, 1965: 25; Willetts, 1962: 52)

Axomama   The "Potato-mother." Peru. (Karsten, 1926: 319)

Aya-Eke   Goddess of the Yam Cult. Nigeria. (Talbot, 1967: 113)

Azacca, Azaka Mede   A god of agriculture and also a protector of travelers. Identified with St. Isidore and with St. Charles Barromee. Haiti, West Indies. (Deren, 1953: 56; Marcelin, 1950: 85)

Azag   The "king of plants." Son of An and Ki. Near East. (Jacobsen, 1976: 95)

baäbai   Grandmother rice of the Tsou of Formosa. (Er-wei, 1959: 537)

Baal   Among Cilician gods he forms a triad with Atheh and Sandan as "the god of the corn and the vine." In Syria he is a god of rain and of cultivation, of fertility, as well as of the weather. Near East. (Frazer, 1961: 160, 170–171; Crawford, 1957: 19, 23–24)

Babalasinnud   A spirit of the rice harvest time who "lives in the *sixay-hut*" of the rice fields. The Isneg, Luzon, Philippines. (Vanoverbergh, 1941: 337)

Bachue   A goddess of agriculture and of crops. She was an earth mother goddess who rose from a lake with her son. Also called Fura-chogue. The Chibcha, Colombia. (Hatt, 1951: 878; Alexander, 1920: 204; Kroeber, 1946, 2: 908; Keane, 1925, 3: 515; Osborne, 1968: 110)

Bakakaw   A spirit of the rice fields important at the time of planting. The Isneg, Luzon, Philippines. (Vanoverbergh, 1941: 316)

Bakashili   A god of the Kurama of Southern Kauru District invoked at the time of planting. Nigeria. (Gunn, 1956: 55)

The Balams   Usually four. Mayan deities who guard the milpas and the entrances to the villages. Mexico. (Redfield and Rojas, 1962: 112; Thompson, 1970: 291)

Balang Tamak   A god of agriculture, protective of the crops and livestock. Bali, Indonesia. (Grader, 1969: 177–178)

Balawi   A mountain spirit who protects the huts of the rice fields and who "must be propitiated by" offerings to prevent illness. The Isneg, Luzon, Philippines. (Vanoverbergh, 1941: 321)

Balulung   A granary idol deity invoked to increase the stored rice. The Ifugao, Philippines. (Barton, 1946: 81)

Bang lha   God of the store-room who increased the food supply and property. A dgra lha deity who is protective of worshippers and their prosperity. Tibet. (Nebesky-Wojkowitz, 1956, 1: 328, 333)

Baroyan   A malevolent spirit who causes the farmer to be unable to perform, or causes aching, or even madness. The Isneg, Luzon, Philippines. (Vanoverbergh, 1941: 290)

Barpahari   A god of vegetation of the Asurs. India. (Rahmann, 1952: 875)

Basuki, Basumata A deity worshipped "for the welfare of agriculture, during the month of Ashar." The Santals, India. (Mukherjea, 1962: 280)

Batara Invoked for abundant rice harvest. This highest spirit is dual: one above who watches and directs, and the other below who rules over the other spirits and is under the Batara above, though they are of equal capacities. The Iban Dyaks, Sarawak. Borneo. (Sarawak Gazette, 1963: 132–133, 147; Nyuak, 1906: 177)

Battug A spirit who is offered rice pudding at the beginning of the harvest and invoked to go away. The Isneg, Luzon, Philippines. (Vanoverbergh, 1941: 346)

Batu Gawa, Batu Imu, Batu Nyanggak, Batu Nyantar, and **Batu Nyantau** Gods invoked at the beginning of the rice-farming season. The Sea Dyaks, Borneo. (Roth, 1968: 174)

Begbalel A guardian of the taro fields who controls the yield of the crops. Yap Islands, Micronesia. (Furness, 1910: 150)

Sidi Bel 'Abbas Cairns are dedicated to him at the time of threshing to obtain the westerly wind. He is also invoked in the measuring of the grain. Morocco. (Westermarck, 1926, 2: 231–238)

Belet An ancestral spirit who "sends rain . . . and causes the corn to grow." He is also a deity of fertility. The Nuba, Sudan. (Seligman, 1925, 9: 403)

Belun Beneficent old god of the fields "who helps the reapers and bestows rich presents upon them." He also helps those who are lost. The White Russians. (Machal, 1918: 269)

Berejya A god of agricultural (grain) fertility. Iran. (Gray, 1930: 140)

Berhta, Bertha, Perahta Teutonic goddess of agriculture and of ploughs who watches over the plants with the help of the children in her care—"the souls of unborn children, and of those who die unbaptized." She is also goddess of spinning, rewarding the diligent and punishing the careless. She is called the White Lady, the bright and luminous, reflecting her beneficence. In Mecklenburg she is known as Frau Gode, in Holland as Vrou-elde. Germany, Austria, and Switzerland. (Grimm, 1880: 214, 272–279; Guerber, 1895: 58–59)

Besua An Egyptian grain god. (Budge, 1973, 1: 58)

Betao Yazobi "God of Maize and All Food; and God of Abundant Sustenance." The Sierra Zapotec, Oaxaca, Mexico. (Whitecotton, 1977: 169)

Bhainsasur The buffalo demon to whom sacrifices are made for good crops and for their protection. The Kol and the Kumhar, India. (Russell, 1916, 3: 513; 1916, 4: 8)

Bhairom, Bhairon A godling of the land, "protector of the fields and of cattle." The Chamars, India. (Briggs, 1920: 156; Crooke, 1894: 67)

Bhandarin Goddess of agriculture of the Gadbas. Central Provinces, India. (Russell, 1916, 3: 11)

Bhasmasur A deity of the Gonds worshipped at the Bidri festival celebrated before the sowing of the seeds. India. (Kurup, 1970: 162)

Bhimsen The chief god of the Bidri festival celebrated before the sowing of the seed. The Gonds, India. (Kurup, 1970: 162)

Bhitari A deity protective of the crops. The Doms, India. (Briggs, 1953: 555)

Bhora Pennu The "god of new fruits produced on trees or shrubs." The Kandh, Bengal. (Crooke, 1925, 7: 649)

Bhuia A beneficent god of the soil, of agriculture, of crops. The Himalaya, India. (Berreman, 1963: 100–101)

Bhutuwa A deity worshipped at the Bidri festival celebrated before the sowing of seeds. The Gonds, India. (Kurup, 1970: 162)

Biku Indu Antu A goddess of the Iban Dyaks invoked for an abundant rice harvest. Sister of Batara. Sarawak, Borneo. (Sarawak Gazette, 1963: 135, 147; Nyuak, 1906: 177)

Binu-silan A benevolent spirit of the rice harvesting who helps the reapers. The Isneg, Luzon, Philippines. (Vanoverbergh, 1941: 337)

Boarmia A surname of Athena as inventor of the plow. Boeotia, Greece. (Roscher, 1965, 1, 1: 788)

Bolon Dzacab, Bolon Zacab A Mayan god of vegetation and of crops worshipped in kan years with Kanu Uayeyab in agricultural ceremonies. Yucatan, Mexico. (Bancroft, 1886, 2: 702–703; Thompson, 1970: 227)

Bolon Mayel A god of the Chumayel creation legend associated "with flowers and honey." Mexico. (Thompson, 1970: 320)

Bombason A minor spirit of the rice. The Dusans, Borneo. (Stall, 1925: 945)

Bonsu Younger brother of Teng, a sky god, who watches over the fruits and flowers. The Bateg, Malay Peninsula. (Evans, 1937: 146)

Bonus Eventus A Roman god who was first a god of agriculture and of the harvests. Later his functions became more generalized. (Carter, 1925, 9: 797; Larousse, 1968: 214)

Boorbi Pennu The "goddess of new vegetation and first fruits." The Kandh, Bengal. (Crooke, 1925, 7: 649)

Bope-joku The god of the planting of the maize. Son of Burekoibo. The Bororo, Brazil. (Levi-Strauss, 1973: 311)

Boreawa, Bore The spirit of plantains (not truly a god). The Yanomamo, Venezuela and Brazil. (Chagnon, 1968: 45)

Sidi bou Jma' Patron of harvesters. Morocco. (Basset, 1920: 68)

Bounmagyi A female spirit "associated with agriculture, . . . propitiated at the harvest . . . either on the threshing floor or in the granary." The Yeigyi, Burma. (Spiro, 1967: 50)

Braciaca Celtic god of malt. Gaul and Britain. (Schrader, 1925, 2: 36; MacCulloch, 1911: 28; Ross, 1967: 181)

Buan A malicious male spirit who lurks to destroy plants in the rice fields and must be driven away. The Kankanay, Luzon, Philippines. (Vanoverbergh, 1972: 87)

Bugan inBulul An agricultural goddess of the Ifugao, wife of Bulul and daughter of Nagalong at Nagubatan. Philippines. (Barton, 1946: 36)

Bughin An Etruscan spirit, both good and evil, who controlled the condition of the grain, caused rust in wheat. Italy. (Leland, 1963: 116–117)

Bulibuli A granary idol deity invoked to increase the stored rice. The Ifugao, Philippines. (Barton, 1946: 81)

Bulotu Katoa A god of agriculture and of hurricanes. He was invoked to prevent drought and famine, and hurricanes. The Tongans, Polynesia. (Collocott, 1921: 162; Moulton, 1925, 12: 377)

Buluhan An agricultural deity at Namtogan. The Ifugao, Philippines. (Barton, 1946: 37)

Bulul A granary god at Namtogan. The Ifugao, Philippines. (Barton, 1946: 36)

Bumadi An agricultural spirit of the earth. The Burmans and the Talaings, Burma. (Temple, 1925, 3: 23)

Bumigi A rice-pest deity. The Ifugao, Philippines. (Barton, 1946: 14)

Bunsu Kamba God of "the plants of thin *maram*." The Sea Dyaks, Borneo. (Roth, 1968: 171)

Bunsu Rembia Abu A god "who has charge of the bends of the wide-spreading *tapang* branches." The Sea Dyaks, Borneo. (Roth, 1968: 171)

Burekoibo The spirit of the maize fields, father of Bope-joku. The Bororo. Brazil. (Levi-Strauss, 1973: 311)

Cacaguat God of the cacao and its culture. The Nicarao, Nicaragua. (Lothrop, 1926, 8, 1: 70; Bancroft, 1886, 3: 492)

Cachimana A vegetation god who ripens the crops and controls the seasons. The Orinoco Region, Venezuela. (Alexander, 1920: 259; Karsten, 1926: 302, 310)

Caepol A god of vegetation, believed the same as Caepus. Spain. (Martinez, 1962: 67)

Caepus A god of vegetation, protector of fruits and vegetables. Portugal. (Martinez, 1962: 66)

Calako Mana The beneficent corn maiden. The Hopi, Arizona. (Fewkes, 1920: 604)

Canan Er "Guardian of the Milpas." The Mayan, Mexico. (Thompson, 1970: 321)

Canan Semillaob Mayan "Guardian of the Seed." Mexico. (Thompson, 1970: 321)

Carpo Greek goddess of fruits and of the harvest; one of the Horae—Autumn. Daughter of Zephyrus and Chloris. (Burns, 1925, 3: 373; Fairbanks, 1907: 170; Murray, 1935: 142)

Castitas Minerva as the goddess of the olive trees. Italy. (Roscher, 1965, 1, 1: 856)

Cavi The spirit of the maize who also takes part in female puberty rites. The Tucuna, Brazil. (Zerries, 1968: 302)

Centeotl The god/goddess of maize and of agriculture. The Aztec, Nahuatl. Among the Totonacs a goddess, where she was loved and required no human sacrifices as among the Aztecs. As a male, the son of Tlazolteotl. Mexico. (Bancroft, 1886, 3: 349–351; Caso, 1958: 46, 54; Vaillant, 1962: 145, 148; Thompson, 1970: 289; Brinton, 1868: 134–135)

Cep-kalwari-cici God of potatoes of the Uru. Bolivia. (La Barre, 1941: 521)

Ceres Roman goddess of agriculture, of the growth of plant life, of crops. Mother of Proserpine. Same as Demeter. (Altheim, 1937: 120; Fairbanks, 1907: 175; Cox, 1870, 2: 308; Dumézil, 1966, 1: 390, 430; Bulfinch, 1898: 67)

Cerus A Latin "god of the growth of grain." Italy. (Gray, 1930: 140)

Chade A goddess of abundance, associated with the corn planting. The Gã, Temma, Ghana. (Field, 1937: 21, 61)

Chahal, Chajal The protector of the cornfields who is also responsible for the sprouting of the seeds and their growth. The Quiché, Guatemala. (Recinos, 1950: 125; Girard, 1979: 132)

Chamconda Mata A harvest goddess of the Bheels. India. (Coleman, 1832: 377)

Chaminuka A tribal spirit who provides plentiful rains and abundant crops. Rhodesia (Central Machonaland). (Gelfand, 1962: 143; 1966: 38)

Chermatiya Deo God of "good crops" who instituted dancing in worship. The Dhanwar, India. (Elwin, 1949: 482)

Cherri-chou-lang A deity responsible for the presence of the kava plant. Ponape, the Carolines, Micronesia. (Christian, 1899: 382)

Che-wara The antelope, god of agriculture of the Bambara. Mali. (LACMA, Art of Black Africa, n.d.: Item 66)

Chi The spirit of the seed. China. (Peeters, 1941: 9)

Chiao Kuan A god of the bean-curd makers and sellers. China. (Werner, 1932: 65; Leach, 1949, 1: 123)

Chiawitsa-kyung karbu A god of the soil of the Sherpas. Above Maralung. Nepal. (Furer-Haimendorf, 1964: 22)

Chicomecoatl "Seven Serpents." Goddess of maize, of all foods, of the crops and the harvests. Also called Chal-chiuhcihuatl, Xilonen, and identified with Tonacaciuatl, Xochiquetzal, Xumoco, Tonacadigua. She was benevolent but also malevolent in allowing barren years. She was considered the female counterpart of Cinteotl. The Aztec, Mexico. (Alexander, 1920: 75; Bancroft, 1886, 3: 421; Duran, 1971: 221–222; Spence, 1923: 151)

Chi Ming God of the five grains. China. (Day, 1940: 106)

Ching Ling Tzu The god of tea in North China. (Werner, 1932: 492)

Chitkuar Devi The goddess of the threshing-floor to whom a chicken and a pig are offered. The Gonds, Central Provinces, India. (Russell, 1916, 3: 107)

Chloe A name of Demeter as the protector of green sprouts. Greece. (Roscher, 1965, 1, 1: 896)

Chloris Greek goddess of vegetation, of buds and flowers. Wife of Zephyrus and mother of Carpo. One of the Horae—Spring. (Fairbanks, 1907: 170; Murray, 1935: 145)

Chorabudi, Choradubi The benevolent protector of the crops is offered first fruits, and sacrifices are made to him. The Garo, Assam. (Playfair, 1909: 81; Barkataki, 1969: 27)

Chou-nach-en-chen God of the sugar cane. Ponape, the Carolines, Micronesia. (Christian, 1899: 381)

Chung Tso A god protective of "germinating seeds and growing vegetation." China. (Day, 1940: 106)

Cinteotl A variant spelling of Centeotl. The god of maize, son of Tlazolteotl and husband of Xochiquetzal. The Aztec, Mexico. (Spence, 1923: 174; Alexander, 1920: 54; Nicholson, 1967: 46)

Cocamama The mother of the coca. Peru. (Markham, 1969: 133; Karsten, 1926: 319)

Cohuy God of maize. The Mixtec, Oaxaca, Mexico. (Caso, n.d.: 51)

Commolenda A minor Roman agricultural deity for the removal of trees, one of those invoked in expiatory rites when it was necessary to remove trees from the temple of Dea Dia. (Dumézil, 1966, 1: 35; Ferguson, 1970: 69)

Conditor A Roman agricultural deity in charge of storing the produce. (Dumézil, 1966, 1: 35; Campbell, 1964: 321)

Coniraya Also called Con. A creator god who in a culture hero aspect "was responsible for the system of agricultural terracing and irrigation." Also a solar god. The coastal region of Peru. (Métraux, 1949, 5: 560; Mishkin, 1940: 226; Osborne, 1968: 96)

Consus An Italian god of antiquity, associated with Ops, but not as consort. An agricultural god who watched over the harvested and stored crops. (Dumézil, 1966, 1: 49, 267; Fairbanks, 1907: 250; Schoeps, 1961: 146)

Convector A Roman agriculture and harvest god in charge of collecting and carting the cut grains. (Roscher, 1965, 2, 1: 196; Dumézil, 1966, 1: 35; Campbell, 1964: 321)

Copan The youthful god of corn. Honduras. (Morley, 1946: Frontespiece)

Coqueelaa The "god of the cochineal harvest" to whom a white hen is sacrificed "on planting the nopal cactus, or on gathering the cochineal." The Zapotec, Sola, Oaxaca, Mexico. (Whitecotton, 1977: 164)

Cordelia The goddess of summer flowers who was fought over every first of May by Gwythyr (represents the powers of the air) and Gwynn (represents the underworld). Daughter of Lir, the sea god. Britain. (MacBain, 1917: 92–93, 99)

Core *See* **Kore.** Another name for Persephone. (Schoeps, 1961: 134)

Cozobi The god of maize and of abundant food. Next in importance to Cocijo. The Zapotec, Oaxaca, Mexico. (Krickeberg, 1968: 55; Whitecotton, 1977: 162)

Cronus One of the Titans, successor of Ouranos, his father, and succeeded in turn by his son Zeus. He was a god of the harvest, and of the maturing of all life. His sister/wife was Rhea, mother of Hestia, Demeter, Hera, Hades, Poseidon, and Zeus. Greece. (Murray, 1935: 25; Barthell, 1971: 13–16)

Curche (1) A Baltic divinity, an insect parasite of grain, invoked to allay its ravages. (Queval, 1968: 31)

(2) A goddess of food and drink who was replaced by Gurcho. Old Prussian. (Welsford, 1925, 9: 488)

Dada God of vegetables, of vegetation. Son of Orungan and Yemaja. The Yoruba, Nigeria. (Meek, 1925: 29; Lucas, 1948: 98)

Dadal God of vegetables, introduced from Africa, who has almost been displaced by Azacca. Haiti, West Indies. (Deren, 1953: 69)

Dagaiyupun A granary idol deity believed to be able to increase the stored rice. The Ifugao, Philippines. (Barton, 1946: 81)

Dagon, Dagan God of grain, of vegetation, of crops, and a god of fertility. Canaan and Babylonia. Near East. (Ferm, 1950: 124; Albright, 1956: 74; 1968: 124; Langdon, 1931: 78; Paton, 1925, 4: 388; Schoeps, 1961: 57; Oldenburg, 1969: 48, 54)

Dagau The goddess of rice who "can make the soil infertile and diminish the amount of rice in the granaries" if displeased. The Manobo, Philippines. (Raats, 1969: 20)

Dagundun A granary idol deity believed able to increase stored rice. The Ifugao, Philippines. (Barton, 1946: 81)

Dais A goddess who personified a plentiful meal. Greece. (Roscher, 1965, 1, 1: 939)

Daliman A spirit who is offered betel to stay away during the rice harvesting. The Isneg, Luzon, Philippines. (Vanoverbergh, 1941: 337)

Damia, Damoia A goddess of the cornfield and of crops, of fertility as well as of childbirth. Associated with Auxesia. Greece. Her worship spread to parts of Italy where she was identified with Bona Dea. (Jayne, 1962: 316; Willetts, 1962: 52; Roscher, 1965, 1, 1: 943)

Damu A god of vegetation, of fertility and new life, who dies and returns. He was also the city-god of Girsu. Son of Ningishzida and Ninazimua. Sumer, Near East. (Jacobsen, 1970: 24, 324, 327)

Damubir A deified human to whom offerings are made at the time of the harvest. The Kahar, Bengal. (Crooke, 1925, 7: 636)

Damulag A god responsible "for keeping the flowers of the rice plants from being blown away by hurricanes." Brother of Dumagan. The Zambal, Philippines. (Jocano, 1969: 15)

Dantu   A god associated with the planting of the corn. The Gā, Accra, Ghana. (Field, 1937: 89)

Dapinay   A guardian of the rice and the granary. The Isneg, Luzon, Philippines. (Vanoverbergh, 1941: 297)

Daramiam   A male spirit of the rice fields who is offered food from every meal taken at the *sixay-hut*. The Isneg, Luzon, Philippines. (Vanoverbergh, 1941: 338)

Darapaypay   A spirit offered betel at the rice harvesting and invoked to be present. The Isneg, Luzon, Philippines. (Vanoverbergh, 1941: 352)

Darikokko   A guardian of the rice and the granary. The Isneg, Luzon, Philippines. (Vanoverbergh, 1941: 297)

Darupaypay   A spirit who consumes the rice stored in the field hut before being taken to the granary. The Isneg, Luzon, Philippines. (Vanoverbergh, 1941: 338)

Darzamat   "Mother of the garden." Latvia. (Larousse, 1973: 422)

Datan   Slavic god of the tilling of the soil. Poland (Larousse, 1968: 291)

Dawiliyan   A spirit of the rice harvesting who helps the reapers. The Isneg, Luzon, Philippines. (Vanoverbergh, 1941: 338)

Deferunda   A minor Roman agricultural deity for the removal of trees, invoked in expiatory rites when it was necessary to remove trees at the temple of Dea Dia. (Ferguson, 1970: 69; Dumézil, 1966, 1: 35)

Dekat   A spirit of the rice harvesting who "accompanies the reapers." The Isneg, Luzon, Philippines. (Vanoverbergh, 1941: 338)

Demeter   Greek goddess of vegetation and of the corn, the ripe corn, and of the fruits of the land. She is the daughter of Rhea and Cronus and the wife of Poseidon by whom she is the mother of Despoina and Orion. However, she is a goddess of numerous loves. By Zeus she is the mother of Persephone, the goddess of the seed corn. By Iasion she is the mother of Plouton, the god of the earth's treasures, and she assumes a chthonic aspect as guardian of the earth's wealth. She also became a goddess of the social order, of "peace and justice." (Cox, 1870, 2: 307–308; Fairbanks, 1907: 93, 173–174; Kerenyi, 1951: 22, 113; Frazer, 1960: 134, 456, 460)

De-o-ha-ko   Three sister spirits, of the corn, the bean, and the squash. The corn is Onatah. The Iroquois Indians, Eastern United States. (Morgan, 1904: 152; Leach, 1949, 1: 307)

Dessauli   One of his aspects is that of the god of the harvest. The Hos, India. (Majumdar, 1950: 257)

Devi Kanail   A deity of the Bheels invoked to ripen the corn. India. (Coleman, 1832: 379)

Dewi Çri   Goddess of "the wet rice." Java and Bali, Indonesia. (Hatt, 1951: 885)

Dharmer Gosain   The sun (head of the pantheon) worshipped at the beginning of the harvest, and also in times of misfortune. The Mal, India. (Crooke, 1925, 8: 344)

Dinkom ud Malui   An agricultural deity of the Ifugao. Philippines. (Barton, 1946: 38)

Dionysus, Dionysos   God of vegetation, particularly the vine and cultivated trees, who represents the death and rebirth cycle, spending a portion of each year underground and bringing the spring. He is generally named as the son of Zeus and Semele. Greece and Thrace. (Frazer, 1960: 450–452; Kerenyi, 1951: 256; Fairbanks, 1907: 58; Murray, 1935: 128–129)

Di-ran   A spirit offered rice pudding at the beginning of the harvest and invoked for good luck. The Isneg, Luzon, Philippines. (Vanoverbergh, 1941: 346)

Dizane   A goddess of the Kafir who "protects the growing wheat crop." If a son is born they sacrifice a goat to her. Kafiristan. (Robertson, 1925, 7: 635–636)

Doanashívuldue   A father of the plants. The Cagaba and the Kogi. Colombia. (Reichel-Dolmatoff, 1949/50: 115)

Doliku   A god of the fields. Son of Dada Zodji and Ananu. Dahomey. (Herskovits, 1938, 2: 143)

Do-raw   A spirit invoked or propitiated at the beginning of the planting of a field. Particularly detrimental to a good harvest. The Isneg, Luzon, Philippines. (Vanoverbergh, 1941: 315)

Doruwanaw   A spirit to whom betel is offered at the beginning of the rice harvest. The Isneg, Luzon, Philippines. (Vanoverbergh, 1941: 338)

Dosojin   As a deity of agricultural fertility and protector of the rice fields he is frequently located at edges of fields or at the crossroads leading to them. Often presented as a couple. Japan. (Czaja, 1974: 41, 50)

Duamaliue   The mother of the rivers is also the mother of the field crops. The Kagaba, Colombia. (Preuss, 1926: 84)

Duillae   Goddesses of nature, protectors of vegetation. Spain. (Martinez, 1962: 68)

Dumagan   A god who provides a good rice harvest. The Zambals, Philippines. (Jocano, 1969: 15)

Dumakdak   An agricultural god at Namtogan. Son of Mongahid. The Ifugao, Philippines. (Barton, 1946: 37)

Dumanal   "Bud Wormer"—A god who "kills the growing shoot." The Ifugao, Philippines. (Barton, 1946: 31)

Dumangan   A god of good harvests, husband of Idianale and father of Dumakulem and Anitun Tabu. The Tagalog, Philippines. (Jocano, 1969: 9)

Duminxiw   A spirit of the rice harvesting time who accompanies the reapers and increases the rice. The Isneg, Luzon, Philippines. (Vanoverbergh, 1941: 338)

Dummasisi   A spirit residing at Dago Masi who is offered betel and importuned to go away during rice harvesting. The Isneg, Philippines. (Vanoverbergh, 1941: 352)

Dumolpop   A god who is harmful to the rice. The Ifugao, Philippines. (Barton, 1946: 31)

Dunggali   A deity invoked for stolen rice, and offered betel. The Isneg, Philippines. (Vanoverbergh, 1941: 361)

Duwakaw   A spirit of the rice fields who lives there. The Isneg, Luzon, Philippines. (Vanoverbergh, 1941: 338)

Ebisu   One of the seven gods of happiness, of good luck. He is also a god of good harvests and of fishermen. Japan. (Hori, 1968: 68; Eliot, 1935: 140; Herbert, 1967: 511–512)

Egitummal   A goddess of grain and the city-goddess of Tummal. Sumer, Near East. (Jacobsen, 1970: 32)

Egres   A Finno-Ugric deity "who created peas, beans, and turnips, and brought forth cabbage, flax, and hemp." (Krohn, 1925, 6: 25)

Ek Balam Chac   Black Tiger of the fields—worshipped with Chichac Chob, Ahcan Uolcab, and Ahbuluc Balam in agricultural ceremonies. The Mayan, Mexico. (Bancroft, 1886, 2: 701; Tozzer, 1951: 60)

Elaiji-nyou   God of cardamum (from Nepal) "whom the Lepchas equate with Maknyam moong, the devil of death." Sikkim. (Gorer, 1938: 92, 238)

Enkimdu   The farmer god, the god of the irrigation dikes and canals, whom Enki placed in charge of the plow and the yoke. Sumer, Near East. (Ferm, 1950: 60; Jacobsen, 1946: 180–181; Kramer, 1961: 100, 107)

Ennunsilimma   A Sumerian/Babylonian gardener god in the service of Anu. Near East. (Langdon, 1931: 385, n. 136)

Ernutet   A cobra, or cobra-headed, goddess of the harvest. Egypt. (Gardiner, 1925, 9: 789)

Estsanatlehi   Changing Woman, who represents nature's seasonal cycle, ever growing old and becoming young again. She is a goddess of fruitfulness and abundance having given mankind food plants and seeds. She is the wife of Tsohanoai and mother of Nayenzgani; lives in the west from where the rains come. The Navaho, Arizona and New Mexico. (Matthews, 1902: 19, 31–32; Alexander, 1964: 157; Babington, 1950: 210–212)

Ests'unnadlehi   Changing Woman—Among the White Mountain Apache she is the most important goddess who is protective of the crops. Arizona. (Goodwin, 1939: viii, 5)

Esus   A Celtic god of vegetation, usually shown as a woodcutter, to whom human sacrifices were offered "by hanging on a tree." He is also named as a god of war. (MacCulloch, 1925, 3: 280; 1911: 36, 234; MacCana, 1970: 31; Grimm, 1880: 204)

Ezinu   In Sumer goddess of the grain, its capacity for growth as a seed and the grain itself. In the Assyro/Babylonian pantheon a god of grain. Near East. (Jacobsen, 1970: 3, 32, 36; Oldenburg, 1969: 48)

Fai, Fai-malie   The mother of yams. Tonga, Polynesia. (Collocott, 1921: 231)

Fakahotu   Goddess of plant life and food, an earth goddess. Tuamotu, Polynesia. (Stimson, 1933: 20, 59; Poignant, 1967: 31)

Faraguvaol   A vegetation deity which takes the form of a "tree-trunk with the power of wandering at will." The Antilles, West Indies. (Alexander, 1920: 25)

Fauna   Wife, daughter, or sister of Faunus. She "was originally an agricultural and prophetic divinity who bestowed health and blessing." Identified with Bona

Dea. Italy. (Fairbanks, 1907: 248; Dumézil, 1966, 1: 350; Jayne, 1962: 421)

Faunus Roman agricultural deity and god of fields as well as of woodlands, of shepherds and their flocks, of their fertility. As a prophetic god he was known also as Fatuus. His sister, wife, or daughter was Fauna. (Murray, 1935: 153; Fairbanks, 1907: 247–248; Larousse, 1968: 207)

Faustitas A Roman goddess of the verdant fields, their fruitfulness. (Roscher, 1965, 1, 2: 1461)

Fejokoo A god of Abo who supplied the yams. Nigeria. (Mockler-Ferryman, 1925, 9: 280)

Feronia A goddess of spring flowers and of vegetation, of harvests. She is a goddess of the taming of the wild forces of nature's vegetation, and represents the fertility of nature. In another aspect she is the goddess of the freedom of slaves. Italy. (Jayne, 1962: 425; Altheim, 1937: 255; Dumézil, 1966, 2: 414–417; Fairbanks, 1907: 251)

Flora An ancient Italian goddess of flowers, protectress of all flowering plants, and a goddess of spring. (Fairbanks, 1907: 251; Altheim, 1937: 122; Dumézil, 1966, 1: 270; Larousse, 1968: 210)

Fluusa Oscan variant of Flora. Italy. (Conway, 1925, 7: 458)

Fonge and **Toaf** "Two oblong smooth stones" are believed to promote the growth of yams. Samoa, Polynesia. (Turner, 1884: 24, 25)

Fructesea Roman goddess of fruit. (Roscher, 1965, 2, 1: 199)

Fura-chogue *See* **Bachue**

Ga'askidi, γá·'ackidi·, Ganaskidi A god of harvest and of plenty, as well as of mist. He is called the Hunchback God either because of a hump containing the seeds of vegetation or in association with the mountain sheep. The Navaho, Arizona and New Mexico. (Reichard, 1950: 443; Matthews, 1902: 13; Chamberlain, 1894: 188; Haile, 1947: 13; Babington, 1950: 216)

Gabjauja God of the granary. Lithuania. (Gray, 1930: 155)

Gamal Gibak A granary idol deity believed able to increase stored rice. The Ifugao, Philippines. (Barton, 1946: 81)

Ganagan A granary idol deity believed able to increase stored rice. The Ifugao, Philippines. (Barton, 1946: 81)

Ganaskidi *See* **Ga'askidi**

Gangadevi The "name of the rice after transplantation" in relation to Sri as goddess of rice. Bali, Indonesia. (Levi, 1933: xxviii)

Gansam Deo A deified hero of the Doms who is a protector of crops. His wife is Banspati Ma. India. (Briggs, 1953: 473–474)

Gaue A Germanic goddess to whom offerings are made in harvesting the rye. (Grimm, 1880: 252)

Gauri Goddess of the yellow corn. She is worshipped with Ganesh at wedding ceremonies in the Central Provinces; is a patron deity with Eklinga in fertility ceremonies in Rajputana. India. (Russell, 1916, 2: 125; Crooke, 1925, 5: 5; Tod, 1920: 660, 665)

Gbosuzogo God of the fields. Dahomey. (Herskovits, 1938, 2: 140)

Gefjun A Scandinavian goddess of agriculture, of the plough, of fertility. She was also goddess of virgins, and of oaths. (Anderson, 1891: 240–241; MacCulloch, 1964: 180–181; Branston, 1955: 152–153; Turville-Petre, 1964: 188; Davidson, 1964: 45, 113)

dGe lha A dgra lha deity, protective of worshippers and their prosperity, bestowing good harvests. Tibet. (Nebesky-Wojkowitz, 1956, 1: 328, 333)

Geshtin Sumerian/Babylonian goddess of the vine. Near East. (Younger, 1966: 31; Larousse, 1968: 61)

Ghanan God of maize, of husbandry. May be identical to Kan or Yum Kaax. The Mayan, Mexico and Guatemala. (Schellhas, 1904: 25; Sykes, 1952: 84)

Ghat A deity worshipped at the festival Bidri celebrated before the sowing of seeds. The Gonds, India. (Kurup, 1970: 162)

Ghatauriya Baba A deity worshipped in the planting of melons, along with Siloman Baba and Madho Baba. The Kahar, United Provinces, India. (Crooke, 1925, 7: 637)

Gil An Assyro/Babylonian god of grain. Near East. (Jacobsen, 1970: 36)

Gila A guardian spirit of the corn. The Kulu, Northern Nigeria. (Meek, 1934: 263)

Girinatha   The "name of the young plant" in relation to Sri as goddess of rice. Bali, Indonesia. (Levi, 1933: xxviii)

Gishbare   A minor god under Ningirsu "charged with making the fields yield, causing the water to rise in the canals, and filling the temple granaries." Lagash, Near East. (Jacobsen, 1946: 203)

Gurcho   A Baltic god of agriculture and of food and drink who replaced the feminine form of Curche. Old Prussian. (Welsford, 1925, 9: 242, 488)

Gurrana Minari   God of vegetation, of the cultivated fields. The Achagua, Colombia and Venezuela. (Hernandez de Alba, 1948, 4: 410; Zerries, 1968: 245)

Guyeyap   A spirit who helps with the counting of the bundles of rice. The Isneg, Luzon, Philippines. (Vanoverbergh, 1941: 357)

Gyhldeptis   A vegetation spirit of the Northwest Coast. North America. (Burland, 1965: 148)

Hachiman   A god named as a god of agriculture and of fishing, but who is primarily known as a god of war. Japan. (Bunce, 1955: 124; Holtom, 1938: 173; Piggott, 1969: 47)

Haia   Sumerian god of stores. Near East. (Jacobsen, 1970: 32)

Hakumani   A goddess of the *hiapo* cutting. Niue, Polynesia. (Loeb, 1926: 164)

Hakumyi   A spirit helpful in gardening. Brazil, Paraguay, and Bolivia. (Métraux, 1948, 1: 352)

al-Halasa   An Arabian goddess of agriculture. (Fahd, 1968: 67)

Halkod   An agricultural deity at Pinuyuk. Protector of fruit trees. The Ifugao, Philippines. (Barton, 1946: 37)

Hamori   A god protective of tree leaves. Japan. (Herbert, 1967: 492; Larousse, 1968: 417)

Hamuri   Goddess of the coconut tree. Tahiti, Polynesia. (Henry, 1928: 421)

Han Hsiang-tzu   One of the Eight Immortals (about 820 A.D.) "credited with the power of making flowers grow and blossom instantaneously." Also a patron of musicians with the flute as emblem. China. (Williams, 1976: 155)

Han Tsu   A deity who distributes buckwheat seed. In some areas a god of silkworms. Ting Hsien, North China. (Gamble, 1954: 418, 420)

Hariyali   A goddess who "guards the crops for hunters." She is worshipped in the month of Sawan. India. (Briggs, 1953: 555)

Hariyari Mata   A goddess to whom sacrifices are made at the time of the sowing and the harvesting. A guardian of the crops. The Majhwars, India. (Crooke, 1925, 5: 5)

Has-gueme   The goddess of corn who can foretell the crop. The Delaware, Eastern United States. (Morgan, 1959: 55, 56)

Hastseyalti   "According to some shamans he is a god of corn," but there are others. He is primarily a god of solar attributes, of the dawn, of the east. He is called Talking God. The Navaho, Arizona and New Mexico. *See also* **xa·ctce·ltihi, xašč'eltˣi'i.** (Matthews, 1902: 9, 11; Babington, 1950: 18–19; Pepper, 1908: 178)

Hatipowa   God of agriculture of the Bheels. India. (Coleman, 1832: 382)

Hatukaci acacila   The owner of the salt. The Aymara, Peru. (Tschopik, 1951: 201)

Hau-lani   A plant goddess, daughter of Hina and sister of Hau-nu'u. Hawaii. (Beckwith, 1940: 207)

Haumea   A goddess of fertility, of uncultivated foods and vegetation, who is also associated with childbirth. She is identified or equated with numerous others— Papa, Pele, La'ila'i; is a goddess of numerous forms and "rebirths." She returns to Nu'umealani, the land of the gods, "and changes her form from age to youth and returns to marry with her children and grandchildren. Hawaii. (Beckwith, 1940: 185, 276, 278, 289)

Haumia, Hau-mia   (1) "As goddess of the fernroot she is invoked to ward off witchcraft." The Maori, New Zealand. (Beckwith, 1940: 289) (2) "God of the fernroot." Son of Tama-nui-a-raki. New Zealand. (White, 1887, 1: 1, 20)

Haumia-tikitiki   The god of uncultivated food plants. A son of Rangi and Papa. The Maori, New Zealand. (Best, 1924: 237; Andersen, 1928: 368; Grey, 1855: 3)

Hau-nu'u   A plant goddess, daughter of Hina and sister of Hau-lani. Hawaii. (Beckwith, 1940: 207)

Haurvatat   Usually associated with Ameretat as protectors of vegetation, animals, and water, as guardians of "wholeness," of "health." Iran. (Gray, 1930: 51–52; Huart, 1963: 41)

Hegemone The goddess of the growth of plants to fruition. Greece. (Burns, 1925, 3: 373)

Heket Frog-headed goddess "who, it seems, symbolised the embryonic state when the dead grain decomposed and began to germinate." She is primarily a birth divinity. Egypt. (Ames, 1965: 111; Budge, 1969, 2: 378)

Henbi, Heneb A god of grain and produce, and of vineyards. Egypt. (Budge, 1969, 2: 63; Knight, 1915: 43)

He-no The thunder god and giver of rain is also god of vegetation who is invoked at the time of sowing and thanked at the harvest. He protects the crops and ripens the harvest. The Iroquois, Eastern United States. (Barbeau, 1914: 306–309; Morgan, 1904: 149, 188; Bjorklund, 1969: 130–132)

Hera The queen of the heavens was a goddess of vegetation in the Argos District. Greece. (Schoeps, 1961: 129)

Herse A goddess of agriculture, of the growth of the crops. She is also goddess of the dew. Greece. (Crawley, 1925, 4: 700; Bethe, 1925, 1: 226; Roscher, 1965, 1, 2: 2591)

Her-she-tuati A god of plowing and irrigation. Egypt. (Budge, 1969, 1: 244)

Hetch-a An Egyptian grain god. (Budge, 1973, 1: 58)

Himalia Goddess of the benediction of the harvest. Greece. (Roscher, 1965, 1, 2: 2659)

Himalis Surname of Demeter of Syracuse. Goddess of abundance in grinding the grain. Greece. (Roscher, 1965, 1, 2: 2659)

Hinabwakan An agricultural god at Namtogan. The Ifugao, Philippines. (Barton, 1946: 36)

Hina-puku-'ai "Goddess of vegetable food." Oahu, Hawaii. (Beckwith, 1940: 69)

Hine-raumati Goddess of the summer, a wife of the sun who lives with her half of the year. She "is concerned with the cultivation of food products, and the fruits of the forest." The Maori, New Zealand. (Best, 1924: 110)

Hine-rau-wharangi A goddess, the personification of vegetable growth, daughter of Tane and Hine-titama and

wife of Te Kawe-kairangi. The Maori, New Zealand. (Best, 1924: 116, 155)

Hinigaiyan An agricultural deity at Kalinugan. A god of the dispersal of locusts. The Ifugao, Philippines. (Barton, 1946: 37)

Hinumbian ud Daiya A granary idol deity believed able to increase stored rice. The Ifugao, Philippines. (Barton, 1946: 82)

Hirkulyo A great god of agriculture. The Bhils, India. (Naik, 1956: 178)

Hobang A granary idol deity believed able to increase stored rice. The Ifugao, Philippines. (Barton, 1946: 81)

Hobnil The Bacab of the East is the chief god of the apiarists; the other Bacabs to a lesser extent. He is also feted by cacao plantation owners. The Mayan, Mexico. (Bancroft, 1886, 2: 699; Tozzer, 1941: 157, 164; Thompson, 1970: 276–277)

Hoi-tini The "goddess of the yam and *ti* plant." The Marquesas, Polynesia. (Christian, 1895: 190)

Homshuk The personification of maize at Vera Cruz. Mexico. (Nicholson, 1967: 64)

Horta Possibly an Etruscan goddess of gardens. Italy. (Leland, 1963: 138)

Hostilina Roman goddess of the grain beards. (Hadas, 1965: 122)

Hou Chi A patron deity of agriculture. China. (Werner, 1932: 415; Peeters, 1941: 9)

Hou-tsi God of crops and of cereals. China. (Maspero, 1963: 325)

Hpi Bi Yaw Goddess of vegetation, of the crops, of the paddy. The Karen, Burma. (Marshall, 1922: 210, 226)

Hsien Nung A Chinese god of agriculture. (Werner, 1932: 6)

Hsien Sê A Chinese god of agriculture. (Werner, 1932: 6)

Hua Hsien "Taoist Goddess of Flowers." China. (Williams, 1976: 191)

Huai Nan Tzu A god of the bean-curd makers and sellers. China. (Werner, 1932: 183; Day, 1940: 110; Graham, 1961: 186)

Huang Nan Chih Chen Shen The god of locusts invoked by agriculturalists for rain to kill them. Anking, China. (Shryock, 1931: 155)

Huang Shi The deity of cotton in Canton and Fukien. China. (Maspero, 1963: 325)

Hua Shen Sheng Chung The god of flowers. China. (Day, 1940: 41)

Huixtocihuatl The goddess of salt and of water, a wife of Tezcatlipoca. Mexico. (Caso, 1958: 69, 44; Vaillant, 1962: 149; Bancroft, 1886, 2: 325)

Huldáma A Mother of the maize. The Cagaba and the Kogi. Colombia. (Reichel-Dolmatoff, 1949/50: 114)

Hunahpú As the god of maize his beheading in Xibalba, the underworld, symbolizes death and regeneration. He is also known as Ce Acatl. The Quiché, Guatemala. (Girard, 1979: 186, 221, 227)

Huntin God of the bombax tree who destroys those who offend him. The Ewe, Slave Coast, Africa. (Mockler-Ferryman, 1925, 9: 278; Ellis, 1890: 49, 50)

Hu-shen A god invoked by farmers to protect their crops from hail. China. (Werner, 1932: 179; Haydon, 1941: 195; Maspero, 1963: 325)

Ialonus God of the cultivated fields, and of the meadows. Gaul and Britain. (MacCana, 1970: 50; Ferguson, 1970: 213)

Iamankave The goddess of food who gave men the cassava. Kuchi stole the first yucca to be planted on the earth from her. The Makiritare, Venezuela. (Civrieux, 1980: 29, 181)

Iang Miao P'u-sa, Iang Miao T'u-ti Chinese "God of growing grain." Szechwan. (Graham, 1958: 52)

Ibabaso With Magbabaya invoked not to be angry on the clearing of the land. The Bukidnon, Mindanao, Philippines. (Cole, 1956: 98)

Ibu Pertiwi Mother Earth, raped by Wisnu to "give birth to rice." Bali, Indonesia. (Covarrubias, 1937: 70, 317)

Icq'anan The goddess of beans and wife of Ihp'en (the earth god) as the god of maize. The Chorti, Guatemala. (Wisdom, 1940: 402)

Iemaparu The corn mother of the Pueblo Indians at Isleta. New Mexico. (Parsons, 1939: 255)

Ihi-yori-hiko The god of "good boiled rice." Japan. (Herbert, 1967: 509)

Ihp'en The dual-sexed earth god in a male aspect as the spirit of maize and consort of Icq'anan. The Chorti, Guatemala. (Wisdom, 1940: 402)

I'itoi The morning star who is invoked in maize ceremonies. The Pima and the Papago, Arizona and Mexico. (Underhill, 1948: 17, 23)

Ikapati Beneficent goddess of the cultivated lands, the "giver of food." A goddess of the fertility of the fields and the herds. Wife of Mapulon and mother of Anagolay. The Tagalog, Philippines. (Jocano, 1969: 10)

Ikkul A spirit invoked or propitiated at the beginning of the planting of a field. The Isneg, Luzon, Philippines. (Vanoverbergh, 1941: 315)

Ilamatecuhtli An ancient mother goddess and the goddess of maize, of the old, dry corn. The Aztec, Mexico. (Caso, 1958: 47; Spence, 1923: 233; Vaillant, 1962: 149)

Ilurberrixus A god of vegetation. Spain and Haute Garonne. (Martinez, 1962: 68)

Ima-ge-no-kami The god of the new food. Japan. (Herbert, 1967: 509)

Imbanon A spirit of the rice harvesting who is helpful to the reapers. The Isneg, Luzon, Philippines. (Vanoverbergh, 1941: 338)

Imporcitor Roman agricultural god, of the harrowing of the fields. (Dumézil, 1966, 1: 35; Campbell, 1964: 321; Ferguson, 1970: 68)

Ina-hi-no-mikoto The god of the boiled rice. Japan. (Herbert, 1967: 387)

Inamahari Two deities, male and female, invoked for success at the sowing season, with offerings of thanksgiving when the crops are successful. The Siouan Indians, South Carolina. (Swanton, 1946: 758)

Inari God/goddess of rice, of grains, of food in general. Also considered a god of traders, or merchants, and of swordsmiths. Japan. (Herbert, 1967: 463, 502, 509; Opler and Hashima, 1946: 43, 45; Holtom, 1931: 15–16; 1938: 8; Piggott, 1969: 58)

Indangunay A granary idol deity believed able to increase stored rice. The Ifugao, Philippines. (Barton, 1946: 81)

Indinggian An agricultural deity at Binuyuk, associated with betel chewing. The Ifugao, Philippines. (Barton, 1946: 37)

Indo i laoe A goddess of the underworld who brought the grain to the rice. Sister of Indo i losi. Central Celebes, Indonesia. (Downs, 1920: 25)

Indo i losi A goddess of seed rice who lived in the heavens. Sister of Indo i laoe. Celebes, Indonesia. (Downs, 1920: 25)

Indo i Tuladidi An "agricultural goddess whose hair consisted of rice ears." Wife of Pue mpalaburu. Celebes, Indonesia. (Downs, 1920: 12, 23)

Indudun inPundaikuhan "Grasshoppered," an agricultural goddess at Kalinugan. Wife of Pundaikuhan. The Ifugao, Philippines. (Barton, 1946: 37)

Induyu A granary idol deity believed able to increase stored rice. The Ifugao, Philippines. (Barton, 1946: 81)

Ing An agrarian god. Germany. (Polomé, 1970: 57)

Ingaan A granary idol deity believed able to increase stored rice. The Ifugao, Philippines. (Barton, 1946: 81)

Ini Andan A great goddess of all aspects of farming, protectress of the farm, invoked particularly at the "Feast of the Whetstones" before the clearing of the land. She blesses with abundance, wealth, and skill. The Dyaks, Sarawak, Borneo. (Roth, 1968: 174–175; Sarawak Gazette, 1963: 77)

Ini Inda A god invoked for rice charms and for an abundant rice harvest. The Iban Dyaks, Sarawak, Borneo. (Nyuak, 1906: 177; Sarawak Gazette, 1963: 147)

Ininlaiyan A granary idol deity believed able to increase stored rice. The Ifugao, Philippines. (Barton, 1946: 81)

Inkosazana An agricultural goddess, of the growth of the corn, and of the harvest. She is also a goddess of the heavens, manifest in the rainbow, the rain, and the mist. The Zulu, South Africa. (Schapera, 1937: 269; Pettersson, 1953: 184–185)

Inmar The sky god is also considered a god of agriculture among the Votiaks. Ural Mountains, Russia and Siberia. (MacCulloch, 1964: 219)

'Inna Goddess of the farm and provider of abundant crops. She is the protector of properties and punisher of thieves. Oaths are sworn in her name. The Maguzawa, Nigeria. (Greenberg, 1946: 31, 40)

Po Ino Nogar, Po Yan Ino Nogar Taha, Po Nagar The great mother goddess of the Chams who "created rice, and presides over agriculture and good harvests." Annam and Cambodia. (Cabaton, 1925, 3: 341–342)

Insitor An agricultural deity in charge of the sowing. Italy. (Dumézil, 1966, 1: 35; Ferguson, 1970: 68)

Irixi A male spirit who is the constant companion of the rice harvesters, sharing their homes and food. The Isneg, Luzon, Philippines. (Vanoverbergh, 1941: 338)

Isar Deo A god of food, particularly of grains, whose wife is Gauri. The Warli, India. (Elwin, 1949: 313)

Isis A goddess of many aspects and many names. As Renenet she was goddess of the harvest; as Sekhet "goddess of cultivated lands and fields." Egypt. (Knight, 1915: 57; (Budge, 1969, 2: 216)

Itsu-ne-mo-mikoto A god of food, son of Ugaya-fuki-aezu and Tama-yori-hime. Japan. (Herbert, 1967: 509–510)

Itzam Na Kauil The "vegetal aspect of Itzam Na." The Mayan, Mexico. (Thompson, 1970: 226)

Itzpaplotl The Obsidian Butterfly goddess in one of her aspects was an agricultural goddess—of the cultivated fields. The Chichimec and the Aztec, Mexico. (Spence, 1923: 225–226; Vaillant, 1962: 150)

Iwagan A spirit offered betel and invoked to come under the house at the time of storing the rice in the granary. The Isneg, Luzon, Philippines. (Vanoverbergh, 1941: 361)

Ixcuina Among her many aspects, e.g., a goddess of immorality, she is strangely also the goddess of salt. The Aztec, Mexico. (Bancroft, 1886, 3: 384–385)

Ixtlilton, Ixtliltzin As one of his aspects he was one of the gods of "flowers and dance, games and feasting." He was also a god of children, of health, and of healing. Called "Little Black-Face." Mexico. (Alexander, 1920: 77; Bancroft, 1886, 3: 409; Vaillant, 1962: 151)

'Ixw A god of the harvest, of autumn. Near East. (Gray, 1957: 134)

Iztacacenteotl The "goddess of white maize." Mexico. (Bancroft, 1886, 2: 340)

Jaja An evil goddess of the harvest. Though she is "goddess of fruitfulness (of husbandry and horticulture)," she must be propitiated and implored for abundance. The Abkhasians, Caucasus. (Janashia, 1937: 129, 132–133)

Jamba A god invoked at the beginning of the rice-farming season. The Sea Dyaks, Borneo. (Roth, 1968: 174)

Jamla The deity of a vegetable found in the forest, child of Ningthoi and Ningsin. The Katchins, Burma. (Gilhodes, 1908: 676)

Jam-la A god of the soil, of Spiti. Tibet. (Snellgrove, 1957: 176)

Jarimba God of flowers and fruit. The Arunta, Australia. (Spence, 1927: 592)

jer mu A god whose wife is kam mu, "said to be creators of cardamom." The Lepchas, Sikkim. (Siiger, 1967: 141)

jer thing Also "a god who created cardamom." The Lepchas, Sikkim. (Siiger, 1967: 141)

Je-so-mo A "spirit who controls the crops" and is thanked before the threshing. The No-su, Southwest China. (Clarke, 1911: 126)

Jhankara A god of the land and of the crops to whom a cow is sacrificed. The Gadaba, India. (Thurston, 1909, 2: 242, 250)

Juling A spirit of the crops. The Sakai, Malay Peninsula. (Skeat, 1906: 182)

Ka The name of Chinun Way Shun as god of cultivation. The Kachins, Burma. (Temple, 1925, 3: 22)

Kahukura The god of crops, consulted in planting kumara. Also the personification of the rainbow. The Maori, New Zealand. (Andersen, 1928: 426, 428; Best, 1924: 238; White, 1887, 1: 103)

Kaiba-an A god who lives in the rice fields and protects the crops, to whom offerings are made "when a new field is constructed, when the rice is transplanted, and at harvest time." The Tinguian, Philippines. (Cole, 1922: 298)

Kaikara Goddess of the harvest to whom offerings must be made before reaping. Wife of Kalisa. The Konjo and the Banyoro, Uganda. (Roscoe, 1915: 92, 94; Mbiti, 1970, 2: 117)

Kait A Protohattic/Hittite goddess of grain. Asia Minor. (Ferm, 1950: 93)

Kajira A bird deity invoked at the beginning of the rice-farming season. The Sea Dyaks, Borneo. (Roth, 1968: 174)

Kakaho "Reed-grass," an offspring of Atea. The Marquesas, Polynesia. (Christian, 1895: 189)

Kakiadan A goddess of agriculture, of rice. The Manobo, Philippines. (Jocano, 1969: 23)

Kalasakas A god "responsible for the early ripening of the ricestalks." Brother of Dumagan. The Zambals, Philippines. (Jocano, 1969: 15)

Kalasokus A god responsible "for turning the grains yellow and dry." Brother of Dumagan. The Zambals, Philippines. (Jocano, 1969: 15)

Káldyi-kukui Mother of the Plants. The Cagaba and the Kogi, Colombia. (Reichel-Dolmatoff, 1949/50: 114)

Kamataraya Their name for Siva—propitiated to obtain an abundant harvest. The Kota, Southern India. (Thurston, 1909, 4: 12–14)

Kami-uga-no-me A food deity of Japan. (Herbert, 1967: 510)

kam mu Wife of jer mu, "said to be the creators of cardamom." The Lepchas, Sikkim. (Siiger, 1967: 142)

kam yu thing Creator of "all edible things." The Lepchas, Sikkim. (Siiger, 1967: 142)

Kan God of maize; one of the gods of the new year; a deity of the compass points (yellow). The Mayan. Among the Chimalteco of Guatemala, the deity of the fourteenth day of the calendar which is "a good day to pray for corn . . . to plant, clean, or harvest." (Nicholson, 1967: 44, 119; Wagley, 1949: 70)

Ix Kanan "Female spirit of the bean." Wife of Ih P'en. The Chorti, Guatemala. (Thompson, 1970: 294)

Kaneki God of the coconut palm. Ponape, Caroline Islands, Micronesia. (Christian, 1899: 384)

Kanepua'a God of farmers, of the furrowing of the soil and of abundant crops. Hawaii. (Beckwith, 1940: 69, 207; Westervelt, 1963, 3: 254; Emerson, 1968: 50)

Kano-nit A guardian of the rice and the granary. The Isneg, Luzon, Philippines. (Vanoverbergh, 1941: 297)

Kanu Uayeyab A god worshipped in kan years with Bolon Zacab in agricultural ceremonies. The Mayan, Mexico and Guatemala. (Bancroft, 1886, 2: 702–703)

Karisi A god invoked for abundance of food and for rain. Tikopia, Polynesia. (Firth, 1967, 2: 297)

Karte Gyelbu A god of the soil. The Sherpas, Nepal. (Furer-Haimendorf, 1964: 22)

Karuebak The "mother of manioc." The Mundurucu, Brazil. (Levi-Strauss, 1973: 56)

Karwan A kachina of the Powamu ceremony of the distribution of the sprouted beans. Pueblo Indians, Arizona and New Mexico. (Burland, 1965: 135)

Kashatskihakatidise Mother corn, who taught women about it, is also the moon. The Wichita, Plains Indians, Kansas. (Dorsey, 1904: 25–28)

Kashiri The moon god who introduced manioc and cultivation to the Campa. Peru. (Weiss, 1972: 163)

Kashiri, Kasiri The Bogana of Binawa invoke this deity at the planting season. Also at Rishuwa. Nigeria. (Gunn, 1956: 56, 61)

Kataragam Deyo A deity invoked to protect the chena and to whom an offering is made at the harvest. The Sinhalese Vedda, Ceylon. (Seligmann and Seligmann, 1911: 176)

Te Kava The "*ava* plant," born of Uene and Atea. The Marquesas, Polynesia. (Christian, 1895: 189)

Kawatit A granary idol deity believed able to increase stored rice. The Ifugao, Philippines. (Barton, 1946: 81)

Kayanuhime-no-Kami Goddess of the plains, of grasses, of "all herbaceous plants." Daughter of Izanagi and Izanami, wife of Oyamatsumi-no-Kami. Japan. (Yasumaro, 1928: 7; Kato, 1926: 17; Revon, 1925, 9: 237–238; Herbert, 1967: 267)

Kehi-no-o-kami A god associated with food. Japan. (Herbert, 1967: 510)

Kendawang A god invoked at the beginning of the rice-farming season. The Sea Dyaks, Borneo. (Roth, 1968: 174)

Keridwen, Cerridwen A Celtic goddess of grain. (Rhys, 1937: 102–3; MacCulloch, 1911: 117)

Kerwan A spirit of the sprouting maize. The Hopi Indians, Arizona. (Burland, 1965: 150)

Ketutor The turtle-dove, youngest child of Tak Suwau, and the source of rice. The Kintak Bong (Negritos), Malaya. (Evans, 1937: 168)

Khedapati, Kermata This deity "is a stone worshipped at sowing time and harvest." India. (Crooke, 1925, 11: 872)

Khem The "generative principle, the power of life and growth in nature." He was principally associated with the agricultural world, though to some extent also with the animal kingdom. A god of the harvest, of increase. Egypt. (Rawlinson, 1885: 18; Budge, 1969, 2: 17; Murray, 1935: 397)

Khensu Nefer-hetep A form of Khensu as a lunar god, as a god of plant growth and the ripening of fruit. Egypt. (Budge, 1969, 2: 37)

Khetar Pal Guardian of the fields. The Bhils, India. (Naik, 1956: 179)

Khila Mutha The god of the threshing-floor. The Ahirs, Central Provinces, India. (Russell, 1916, 2: 33)

Khulungma Goddess of cotton. The Tiparas, Bengal. (Crooke, 1925, 2: 481)

Khunphe'ndi'a'anyun Black corn maiden of the below. The Tewa, Pueblo Indians, New Mexico. (Harrington, 1907/08: 43)

Khunpinu'a'anyun Red corn maiden of the south. The Tewa, Pueblo Indians, New Mexico. (Harrington, 1907/08: 43)

Khuntsaenggei'i'a'anyun All-colored corn maiden of the above. The Tewa, New Mexico. (Harrington, 1907/08: 43)

Khuntsaenyu'a'anyun White corn maiden of the east. The Tewa, Pueblo Indians, New Mexico. (Harrington, 1907/08: 43)

Khuntsanyu'a'anyun Blue corn maiden of the north. The Tewa, New Mexico. (Harrington, 1907/08: 43)

Khuntseji'a'anyun Yellow corn maiden of the west. The Tewa, Pueblo Indians, New Mexico. (Harrington, 1907/08: 43)

Khunuseti The Pleiades, invoked for rain and abundance of food. The Hessaquas (Hottentots), South Africa. (Hahn, 1881: 43)

K'i A god of the harvests, the inventor of husbandry. China. (Chavannes, n.d.: 505; MacLagan, 1925, 6: 646)

Kichimiya, Litsaba A spirit who "gives the crops." The Sema Nagas, India. (Hutton, 1968: 195)

Kih Yien A spirit of the land and of grain, associated with Kow Lung. China. (Du Bose, n.d.: 139)

Kildisin A goddess of the corn, as well as of the earth and of birth. The Votiaks, Russia and Siberia. (MacCulloch, 1964: 258)

Kinamalig The constellation Ursa Major which is invoked at the *pakde* public sacrifice—before the sowing of rice, before the transplanting and before the harvest. The Kankanay, Luzon, Philippines. (Vanoverbergh, 1972: 91, 95)

Kindut A granary idol deity believed able to increase stored rice. The Ifugao, Philippines. (Barton, 1946: 81)

Kiriamma The wife of Gale Deviyo is a provider of food. The Vedda, Ceylon. (Seligmann and Seligmann, 1911: 185)

Kirnis A Slavonic deity in charge of the ripening of the cherries. (Larousse, 1968: 291)

Ki Wende The millet god, a manifestation of Wennam. The Mossi, Upper Volta. (Hammond, 1959: 246)

Kling One of the principal deities invoked at the beginning of the rice-farming season. The Sea Dyaks, Sarawak, Borneo. (Roth, 1968: 174; Sarawak Gazette, 1963: 14)

Kling Bungai Nuiying A god invoked at the beginning of the rice-farming season. The Sea Dyaks, Borneo. (Roth, 1968: 174)

Knaninja Tjilba Ladjia The spirit of the yam. Australia. (Basedow, 1925: 281)

Koai A vegetation deity of the Siusi. Colombia. (Karsten, 1926: 309)

Ah Kohk Nar "Guardians of the new corn." The Chorti, Guatemala. (Thompson, 1970: 324)

Koko-galal God of the coconut palm. Yap Islands, the Carolines, Micronesia. (Christian, 1899: 385)

Kole A lagoon god associated with the corn planting. The Gã, Accra, Ghana. (Field, 1937: 85, 89)

Konanopo A deity who taught men agriculture. The Amniapa and the Guaratagaja, Bolivia. (Métraux, 1942: 151)

Kondos An agricultural deity of fields and tillage. Finno-Ugric. (Krohn, 1925, 6: 25; MacCulloch, 1964: 244)

Kongsen-bu The god of grains and wet rice. The Lepchas, Sikkim. (Gorer, 1938: 238)

Ko-no-hana-sakuya-hime The goddess who makes the trees bloom. Daughter of Oh-yama-tsumi. Japan. (Anesaki, 1937: 233)

Kopan A guardian of the rice and the granary. The Isneg, Luzon, Philippines. (Vanoverbergh, 1941: 297)

Kore A goddess of the corn, the seed corn. The name of Persephone when she lived on the earth with her mother Demeter. Daughter of Zeus. Greece. (Frazer, 1960: 456, 461; Schoeps, 1961: 134; Jayne, 1962: 343)

Kricco Slavonic protector of the products of the field. (Larousse, 1968: 291)

Kshetravevi Goddess of the fields. Elsewhere male—Kshetrapala. Bengal. (Srinivas, 1952: 223)

Kshetrapal(a) A god protective of the fields. India. (Briggs, 1953: 556; Srinivas, 1952: 223)

Kshetrasya pati Guardian of the field. Also invoked for cattle, horses, prosperity. India. (Macdonell, 1987: 138)

ku An earth god and a god of maize. The Tlapanecs, Guerrero, Mexico. (Girard, 1979: 108)

Kua Hsien Protector of pumpkins and melons. China. (Day, 1940: 106)

Kualdanehumang A Mother of the maize. The Cagaba and the Kogi, Colombia. (Reichel-Dolmatoff, 1949/50: 114)

Kualeneumañ A name of the first mother as "the mother of the field crops." The Kagaba, Colombia. (Preuss, 1926: 69)

Kuang Kapong God of fruit trees. The Iban Dyaks, Sarawak. Borneo. (Sarawak Gazette, 1963: 133)

Kuchimpai God of the harvest. The Nagas, India. (Elwin, 1969: 412)

Kudopen A deity worshipped at the Bidri festival celebrated before the sowing of seeds. The Gonds, India. (Kurup, 1970: 162)

Kuinadi The master of the moriche, the collared trogon, was "old and wise," a counselor to Wachamadi. The Makiritare, Venezuela. (Civrieux, 1980: 90–91, 185)

Ku-ka-'o-'o Ku as "god of husbandry . . . of the digging stick." Hawaii. (Beckwith, 1940: 15)

Ku-keolowalu Ku as "god of husbandry . . . of wet farming." Also god of the taro and its farmers. Hawaii. (Beckwith, 1940: 15; Westervelt, 1963, 3: 254)

Kuku-balal God of cultivation and planting. Yap Islands, the Carolines, Micronesia. (Christian, 1899: 384)

Ku-kulia Ku as the god of dry farming. Hawaii. (Beckwith, 1940: 15)

Kukutoshi-no-Kami God of the harvest of the rice. Child of Hayamato-no-Kami and Oketsuhime-no-Kami. Japan. (Yasumaro, 1965: 51; Herbert, 1967: 333)

Kulagollamma Dravidian goddess of prosperity for farmers—the grain. India. (Elmore, 1915: 74)

Kul Gosain Goddess of the sowing. The Male Paharias and the Mal, India. (Crooke, 1925, 5: 13; 1925, 8: 345)

Kumba A god of vegetation and of crops. It was "the custom . . . to weep for Kumba at the beginning of the farming season . . . and to plant his rice." Sierra Leone. (Thomas, 1916: 30; McCulloch, 1950: 70)

Kumitoga A goddess of plant life. Vahitahi Island, Tuamotus, Polynesia. (Stimson, 1933: 59)

Kumli sin A species of gourd, a child of Phungkam Janun. The Katchins, Burma. (Gilhodes, 1908: 678)

Ku-moku-hali'i One of "the gods of the growing tree" who is invoked in cutting and also for good luck by agriculturalists when planting. Hawaii. (Alexander, 1967: 90; Beckwith, 1940: 26)

Kumuhe "The *enuhe* [worm] is an *aumakua* of ill omen." When he was slain—"from him sprang the hordes of *peluas* and other worms so destructive to vegetation." Hawaii. (Emerson, 1967: 48)

Kumulut "Leaf Roller," a rice-pest deity. The Ifugao, Philippines. (Barton, 1946: 14, 31)

Kupalo Russian god of vegetation and of the harvest. (Frazer, 1961: 250–251; Grimm, 1883, 2: 624)

Kupole Slavic god of vegetation invoked for good crops. Prussia. Same as Kupalo. (Frazer, 1961: 253)

Ku-pulupulu A god of the forest worshipped by canoe-builders is also invoked for good luck by agriculturalists when planting. Hawaii. (Alexander, 1967: 90)

Kurke, Curche A Slavic spirit of the corn to whom a cock was sacrificed at the harvest festival. Also associated with the grain weevil and must be appeased—"could turn into a protective, kindly deity." Prussia. (Gimbutas, 1963: 193; Larousse, 1973: 419)

Kursis A god of the threshing time. Lithuania. (Leach, 1950, 2: 632)

Kutkidai God of crops and of food. The Baiga, India. (Elwin, 1939: 58, 62)

Ku-'ula-uka A god of the land, of farming. His wife is La-ea (or Hina-ulu-ohio). He is the younger brother of Ku-'ula, the fish god. Hawaii. (Keliipio, 1901: 114–115; Beckwith, 1940: 20)

Ku Wang God of grain worshipped by the Ch'iang. Szechwan, China. (Graham, 1958, 135≠1: 52)

Kuwanlelenta The "guardian spirit of sunflowers and deity of the Sunflower Clan." The Hopi, Arizona. (Waters, 1963: 72)

Kuye-biko The "scarecrow . . . in the mountain-fields . . . knows everything under Heaven." Japan. (Herbert, 1967: 330)

Kwelele An agricultural god, of the ripening crops. The "God of Heat." The Zuñi, New Mexico. (Cushing, 1891/92: 377)

Kwe-teat-ri-yi White Corn—A culture hero/deity whose wife is Tcua-wuti, a snake goddess of the underworld. The Moqui, Arizona. (Stephen, 1888: 114)

Lacturtia A minor Roman goddess—"of the blooms whitening." (Hadas, 1965: 122)

Laetitia A Roman deity associated with "the arrival of corn." Also the personification of joy. (Larousse, 1968: 214; Roscher, 1965, 2, 2: 1788)

Lagitan A granary idol deity believed able to increase stored rice. The Ifugao, Philippines. (Barton, 1946: 81)

Lai Cho A god of agriculture, of the harvests. China. (Werner, 1932: 6, 238)

Laja Bungai Jawa A god invoked at the beginning of the rice-farming season. The Sea Dyaks, Bornoe. (Roth, 1968: 174)

Laka Goddess of vegetation and of the wildwood growth. She is more renowned as the goddess of the hula, of fruitfulness, and of love. Male—as Ku-ka-'ohi'a-laka the god of the forest growth and of the hula. Hawaii. (Beckwith, 1940: 16, 52, 185–186; Emerson, 1916/17: 23–24; Westervelt, 1963, 2: 74; 1963, 3: 125)

Lakhubai A goddess associated with agricultural sprouting-sowing rites at Pandharpur. India. (Frazer, 1961: 243; Ghurye, 1962: 250)

Laki Ivong A harvest god of the Kayans. Borneo. (Hose, 1912: 5)

Lakshmi Among the Mahakul Ahirs in Jashpur she is the personification of the rice. She is a goddess of fertility and abundance as well as of beauty. India. (Russell, 1916, 2: 32; Bhattacharji, 1970: 162–163)

Lan Ts ai-ho A Taoist goddess protective of horticulture, "patron saint of florists". Her emblem—a flower-basket. China. (Peeters, 1941: 31; Williams, 1976: 155)

Lapinay A guardian of the rice and the granary. The Isneg, Luzon, Philippines. (Vanoverbergh, 1941: 297)

Laukamaat The "god of ploughing and sowing." The Letts, Latvia. (Welsford, 1925, 9: 242)

Laukosargas A Baltic goddess of harvests. The Pruthenes, Prussia. (Queval, 1968: 66) The Lithuanian "guardian of the fields" worshipped for the benefit of the crops. (Leach, 1950, 2: 631)

Laukpatis God of the fields, "of ploughing and sowing." The Lithuanians and the Prussians. (Schrader, 1925, 2: 35; Welsford, 1925, 9: 242)

Laukumate The "mother of the fields." Latvia. (Leach, 1950, 2: 608)

Lawkapatim Slavic god of the fields, of the tilling of the soil. Poland. (Larousse, 1968: 291)

Le Sa A god of agriculture, incarnate in the owl, sent rain and abundance of food. In some villages a god of war. Samoa, Polynesia. (Turner, 1884: 46–47)

Liber A god of agriculture and fertility, of vineyards and wine—wherein he is associated with Dionysus. Italy. (Altheim, 1937: 125–126; Dumézil, 1966, 1: 378; Younger, 1966: 216; Larousse, 1968: 209–210)

Linagdian An agricultural deity at Binuyuk, associated with fruit. The Ifugao, Philippines. (Barton, 1946: 37)

King Lingtsze Worshipped in the north as the tea god. China. (Du Bose, n.d.: 327)

Lise Goddess of rice. Celebes, Indonesia. (Downs, 1920: 9; Adrian and Kruyt, 1950: 58, 179)

Liu "Overseer of the Five Cereals." Protector of the harvests. Kiangsu, China. (Maspero, 1963: 325)

Liu Meng Chiang Chun One of the chief gods of agriculture and of the nation, invoked to protect the crops from locusts. China. (Werner, 1932: 257; Day, 1940: 107)

Lociyo A deity to whom a ceremony is performed "on cutting the first chili plant." The Zapotec, Sola, Oaxaca, Mexico. (Whitecotton, 1977: 162)

Lono A god of numerous aspects. As a god of agriculture, "the festival of the first fruits" is celebrated for him. He is primarily associated with the weather. Hawaii. (Mackenzie, n.d.: 320–322; Beckwith, 1940: 31–32; Poignant, 1967: 27, 38)

Lono-Makua God of husbandry as well as of medicine, invoked for abundant crops and rain and for knowledge of healing. Maui, Hawaii. (Ashdown, 1971: 25, 28)

Loudze-lha-tsen A god of the soil. The Sherpas, Nepal. (Furer-Haimendorf, 1964: 22)

Lo Yu, Loh Yu The god of tea of the T'ang Dynasty. China. (Werner, 1932: 492; Du Bose, n.d.: 327)

Lucucuy The god of maize and of abundant food. The Zapotec, Sola, Oaxaca, Mexico. (Whitecotton, 1977: 162)

Lukbuban An agricultural deity at Binuyuk whose wife is Lumaknak. The Ifugao, Philippines. (Barton, 1946: 37)

Lumadab A god who blights plants. Son of Umamu. The Ifugao, Philippines. (Barton, 1946: 31)

Luma-i A harmful agricultural god—"Stopper of Growth," son of Umamu. The Ifugao, Philippines. (Barton, 1946: 31)

Lumaknak inLukbuban An agricultural goddess at Binuyuk, wife of Lukbuban. The Ifugao, Philippines. (Barton, 1946: 37)

Lumigalig A god harmful to plants. Son of Umamu. The Ifugao, Philippines. (Barton, 1946: 31)

Lumiplip "Girdle Wormer"—a rice-pest deity. The Ifugao, Philippines. (Barton, 1946: 14, 31)

Lungaiyan An agricultural deity at Binuyuk. The Ifugao, Philippines. (Barton, 1946: 37)

Maan-Eno Goddess of harvest and fecundity. Wife of Ukko. Estonia. (Larousse, 1968: 307)

Maba The spirit of honey, female. The Arawak, Guiana. (Levi-Strauss, 1973: 154)

Macarius A god of vegetation. Spain. (Martinez, 1962: 69, 70)

Macuilxochitl "Five Flower"—a god of flowers and of food, and of their abundance. He is also a god of games and feasting, of music and dancing, of youth and growth. Mexico. (Alexander, 1920: 57, 77; Spence, 1923: 202; Nicholson, 1967: 93; Vaillant, 1962: 140, 145)

Madho Baba With his brother Siloman Baba worshipped at the planting of the water nut and of melons. The Kahar, United Provinces, India. (Crooke, 1925, 7: 637)

Magbabaya The high god is invoked not to be angry on the clearing of the land. The Bukidnon, Mindanao, Philippines. (Cole, 1956: 99)

Magkaway A male spirit of the rice harvesting who is propitiated with betel. The Isneg, Luzon, Philippines. (Vanoverbergh, 1941: 339)

Magwanag A male spirit of the rice harvest propitiated with betel. The Isneg, Luzon, Philippines. (Vanoverbergh, 1941: 339)

Mahipngat An agricultural deity at Nagadangan. The Ifugao, Philippines. (Barton, 1946: 37)

Maimungma Goddess of the paddy fields whose husband is Thunai. The Tiparas, Bengal. (Crooke, 1925, 2: 481)

Mainao A household goddess and guardian of the rice fields. Also known as Bhulli Buri. The Kacharis, Assam. (Endle, 1911: 36–7)

Maisamma A village goddess protective of their agricultural prosperity. The Telangana, India. (Mudiraj, 1970: 48)

Mama Allpa Goddess of the harvest and of all nourishment. The earth goddess. Peru. (Rhys, 1937: 113; Bray, 1935: 292)

Mamágakve Father of the cotton. The Cagaba and the Kogi, Colombia. (Reichel-Dolmatoff, 1949/50: 112)

Mama-Sara Mother Maize who was honored in the festival of *Aymoray* in the month of *Hatun Cuzqui*. Peru. (Means, 1931: 385)

Mamili, Pele A goddess to whom sacrifices, preferably human, must be made early in the year or the crops will fail. The Koyi, Southern India. (Thurston, 1909, 4: 56)

Mana A kachina of the Powamu ceremony of the distribution of the sprouted beans. The Pueblo Indians, Arizona and New Mexico. (Burland, 1965: 135)

Manang Jaban, Ini Manang A goddess invoked at the "Feast of the Whetstones" before the clearing of the land. The Dyaks, Sarawak, Borneo. (Sarawak Gazette, 1963: 77)

Mandamin "Food of Wonder"—maize, corn—was sent by Kitche Manitou to find a good man who must fight Mandamin to the death. Zhowmin won. He buried Mandamin and cared for his grave. In the spring a new plant arose which they named Mandamin. The Ojibway, Canada and the United States. (Johnston, 1976: 36–38)

Mandej A god of agriculture of the Minahassa. Northern Celebes, Indonesia. (MacKenzie, 1930: 330)

Mang Shen A god of agriculture. China. (Werner, 1932: 6)

Mangtseang A god of agriculture believed to be able to protect from grasshoppers. China. (Du Bose, n.d.: 131)

Manguli ud Kahilauwan An agricultural deity— "Groover of the Place Where the Sun Rises." The Ifugao, Philippines. (Barton, 1946: 38)

Manik Galih   A goddess protective of the fields and the crops. Bali, Indonesia. (Liefrinck, 1969: 35)

Saint Manuel   "(The Agrarian god) gave his blood for the nourishment of his sons." The Chorti, Guatemala. (Girard, 1979: 191)

Maran Jumti majan   Mother of salt, daughter of Phungkam Janun. The Katchins, Burma. (Gilhodes, 1908: 678)

Marica   A goddess of agriculture associated with Faunus. Latium, Campania, Italy. (Larousse, 1968: 208; Roscher, 1965, 2, 2: 2373)

Mari-haka   A goddess who presided over the kumara plantation. New Zealand. (White, 1887, 3: 112)

Markam   The god of the mango tree. The Gonds, Central Provinces, India. (Russell, 1916, 3: 61)

Mars   Originally he was an early Italian god of the growth of vegetation and crops and of the harvest. In his warlike capacity he was protective of the fields and crops, of the herds, from plague and other danger. Later he became almost totally the god of war. (Cox, 1870, 2: 311; Hadas, 1965: 122; Fairbanks, 1907: 214; Jayne, 1962: 432–433)

Marzanna   Slavic goddess of corn, and in Poland a goddess "who fostered the growth of fruit." (Czaplicka, 1925, 11: 595; Larousse, 1968: 291)

Mas, Mar, Maso   An Etruscan god of crops and of harvest. He was also a god of virility and of marriage. Italy. (Leland, 1963: 49, 51)

Masasikiri   A god of agriculture who informs the people when it is time to prepare the fields. The Arawak, Guiana. (Levi-Strauss, 1973: 319)

Matalolan   A god of the talo (taro) beds. Pukapuka, Polynesia. (Beaglehole, 1938: 311)

Matalomea   A god of the talo (taro) beds. Pukapuka, Polynesia. (Beaglehole, 1938: 311)

Mathra Spenta   A god protective against demons who also promotes the "growth of grain." Iran. (Gray, 1930: 151)

Matnyo Dev   The god of vegetables. The Bhils, India. (Naik, 1956: 178)

Matri   A Himalayan goddess of agriculture and of crops who is also invoked regarding rain, either too much or too little. India. (Berreman, 1963: 100–101, 378)

Matuca   Roman goddess of blooms being cut. (Hadas, 1965: 122)

Maui-i-rangi   A god who presides over the kumara plantation. New Zealand. (White, 1887, 3: 112)

Maunutea'a   A god destructive of plants. Tahiti, Polynesia. (Henry, 1928: 377)

Ma'we   Salt Woman—of Zuñi Salt Lake. The Zuñi Indians, New Mexico. (Tyler, 1964: 185–186)

Maxammam   A protector of the rice fields "who helps to guard the koman." The Isneg, Luzon, Philippines. (Vanoverbergh, 1941: 300)

Mayahuel   Goddess of the maguey cactus from which pulque, the native wine, is made. Mexico. (Duran, 1971: 176n; Nicholson, 1967: 69; Vallant, 1962: 149; Spence, 1923: 294, 297)

ma yel tong   With mu lung tong creators of "the paddy-rice, the millet, and the maize." The Lepchas, Sikkim. (Siiger, 1967, 1: 196)

Meanderi   Goddess of the taro, the sugar cane, and other foods. The Ngaing, New Guinea. (Lawrence and Meggett, 1965: 205)

Medrwe Karang, Meduwe Karang   God of the land, of the dry fields. Bali, Indonesia. (Covarrubias, 1937: 94; Grader, 1969, 1: 141)

Megwomets   The dwarf god of acorns and "the distributor of vegetal abundance." The Yurok, California. (Kroeber, 1925: 74; Elmendorf, 1960: 536)

mer tcor   The "guardian of the milpas . . . said to be dual sexed and to live in the west." The Chorti, Guatemala. (Wisdom, 1940: 401)

Messia   Roman goddess of the harvest. (Roscher, 1965, 2, 1,: 24; Campbell, 1964: 321)

Messor   Roman god of the harvesting, of the cutting of the grain. (Roscher, 1965, 2, 1: 204; Dumézil, 1966, 1: 35)

ka Miang Bylli U Majymma   The god of cultivation to whom sacrifices are made "on the path to the forest clearing where the seed is sown." The Kahsi, Assam. (Gurdon, 1907: 196)

Miao Hu   A Chinese god of agriculture. (Werner, 1932: 6)

Mien T'u Ti   An aspect of T'u Ti as protector of the cotton. China. (Day, 1940: 67)

Miketsu-kami   A name of the goddess of food. Japan. (Herbert, 1967: 502)

Min   An ancient god of vegetation and of gardens, of fertility. He was also a god protective of roads and of travelers. Egypt. (Cook, 1930: 106n; Ames, 1965: 108–109; James, 1960: 71–72)

Minûkumûkan   " 'Scattered with the Fingers'—refers to 'rice pests'." The Ifugao, Philippines. (Barton, 1946: 31)

Mirohia   God of the boundaries of the field to whom offerings are made at the sowing and the cutting of crops so that he will not damage the crop or the equipment. The Kurmi, Central Provinces, India. (Russell, 1916, 4: 82)

Misi-agrang-Saljong-sang-gitang   A spirit who taught them how to cultivate. He scatters the weed seeds along with their rice to remind them to cultivate and then sends the rains to make both grow. The Garo, Assam. (Playfair, 1909: 93)

Mitoshi-no-Kami   A god of grains and of other foods, and of the harvest. Japan. (Yasumaro, 1965; 51; Kato, 1926: 30; Holtom, 1938: 183; Herbert, 1967: 332)

Mlezi   Among the Tonga of Malawi and Zambia—the Food-Giver. (Mbiti, 1970, 2: 335)

Moing'iima   The mother of vegetation, of corn, of foods. She is the Earth and the wife of So'teknani, the Heaven. The Papago, Arizona and Mexico. (Hatt, 1951: 873; Tyler, 1964: 100)

Moltek   An ancestor god who lives in the sun and makes fruits for people. The Negritos, Malaya. (Evans, 1937: 147)

Mondamin   The corn god of the Chippewa. Vicinity of Lake Superior, United States and Canada. (Alexander, 1964: 27)

Mondondonyag   An agricultural deity at Binuyuk. "The 'Reddener'—of rice when it ripens." The Ifugao, Philippines. (Barton, 1946: 37)

Mongahid   An agricultural god at Namtogan. The Ifugao, Philippines. (Barton, 1946: 36)

Mon-gilig   An agricultural deity at Binuyuk—"planting upland rice." The Ifugao, Philippines. (Barton, 1946: 37)

Monlana   A granary idol deity believed able to increase stored rice. The Ifugao, Philippines. (Barton, 1946: 81)

Montinig   A god associated with the coconut who also inflicts with headache. The Ifugao, Philippines. (Barton, 1946: 67)

Mopin   "(Apparently the god of harvest)." The Gallongs (Adi), Northeastern India. (Chowdhury, 1971: 45)

Morimi   A goddess whose festival involves the burning of the bush in preparation for farming. The Yoruba, Nigeria. (Wyndham, 1919: 108)

Morkul-kua-luan   The "Spirit of the Long Grass," the sorghum. Northern Territories, Australia. (Poignant, 1967: 110)

Mot   A god of the harvest who represents the summer drought and the death of vegetation, the "dead" seed which will again rise in new growth. His conflict with Baal, with Aleyin is that of opposites, the contrast between life and fertility and sterility and death, rather than of good and bad. Near East. (Crawford, 1957: 19; Willetts, 1962: 162; Vriezen, 1963: 51; Larousse, 1968: 76–77; Gordon, 1961: 184, 202; Oldenburg, 1969: 36–38)

Muingwu, Alosaka   A Hopi chthonic deity of the earth, of the nadir. A god of vegetation and of fertility, the "Germinator." *See* **Muiyinwu.** Arizona. (Tyler, 1964: 19, 20, 101, 128)

Muiyinwu, Muiyunwu-wuqti   A goddess of germs and of the underworld where she "is pictured as manufacturing all sorts of seeds in the lowest of the underworlds." Sometimes male, the Germ God who provided them with "the seeds of the corn, melon, squash, and bean." The Hopi, the Walpi, and the Tusayan, Arizona. (Fewkes, 1893/94: 259; 1896: 247–248; 1900: 125; Titiev, 1971: 172)

Ix Muk-yah-kutz   A goddess of tobacco. Mexico. (Thompson, 1970: 117)

mu lung tong   The creator of paddy rice, millet and maize. The Lepchas, Sikkim. (Siiger, 1967: 143)

Ah Mun   A Mayan name "for the young maize god." Mexico. (Thompson, 1970: 285)

Muyinwu(h), Muyingwa   Variant of Muiyinwu, which see.

Nabahagan   A granary idol deity believed able to increase stored rice. The Ifugao, Philippines. (Barton, 1946: 81)

Naboba   A daughter of the mother goddess. She is associated with a certain type of soil. The Kogi, Colombia. (Reichel-Dolmatoff, 1975: 45, 55)

Nadahu   A granary idol deity believed able to increase stored rice. The Ifugao, Philippines. (Barton, 1946: 81)

Na Dede Oyeadu   A goddess associated with corn planting. The Ga, Accra, Ghana. (Field, 1937: 89)

Nagyi   The spirit of the grain. The Burmans and the Talaings, Burma. (Temple, 1925, 3: 23)

Nai   A sea god, but also associated with the corn planting. The Ga, Accra, Ghana. (Field, 1937: 69, 89)

Naimuena   The supreme being and creator is also considered a god of vegetation. The Uitoto, Colombia and Peru. (Karsten, 1926: 301)

Nakti Devi   Goddess of the fields. Sometimes given as the wife of Thakur Deo. The Baiga, India. (Elwin, 1939: 57)

Namshánu   A Father of the Plants. The Cagaba and the Kogi, Colombia. (Reichel-Dolmatoff, 1949/50: 115)

Namuli   A granary idol deity believed able to increase stored rice. The Ifugao, Philippines. (Barton, 1946: 81)

Nanahuatl   He pulverized the mountain to obtain the maize for the people. Also known as "the syphilitic god." Mexico. (Thompson, 1870: 348)

Nandaun daun ka   A vegetable found in the forest, child of Ningthoi and Ningsin—third generation of deities. The Katchins, Burma. (Gilhodes, 1908: 676)

Nandervo   The god of corn, husband of Diwali. The Bhils, India. (Maik, 1956: 178, 184)

Nañoikwia   The goddess of germs of the Hano (Tewa). Pueblo Indians, New Mexico. Same as Muiyunwuwuqti. (Fewkes, 1900: 95)

Napiklud   A granary idol deity believed able to increase stored rice. The Ifugao, Philippines. (Barton, 1946: 82)

Naran Deo, Naran Barambha   A god responsible for gathering the seed to plant the barren earth. He obtained the help of Isar Deo and his wife Gauri, who sorted and sowed the seed over a period of twelve years. The Warli, India. (Elwin, 1949: 313)

Nar-azerava   The mistress of the meadow. The Mordvins, Russia. (Paasonen, 1925, 8: 845)

Nariwiinyatcimpi   Immortal Yucca Date in ancient times floated in the air. With the help of Tavowaatsi and Kamuwaantsi, Tavutsi ambushed it, smashing it with a huge stone, scattering it everywhere, originating the species of yucca and similar plants bearing the fruit called tcimpi. The Chemehuevi, California, Nevada, and Arizona. (Laird, 1976: 153)

Nataklob   A granary idol deity believed able to increase stored rice. The Ifugao, Philippines. (Barton, 1946: 82)

The Natue   The goddesses of the winter solstice are also the "patronesses of the moriche palm, . . . [of] great nutritional and material value." The Winikina-Warao, Venezuela. (Wilbert, 1973: 6)

Nawili   A granary idol deity believed able to increase stored rice. The Ifugao, Philippines. (Barton, 1946: 82)

Nawish   Guardian of the fields. A god created by Iakitu. The Acoma, New Mexico. (Stirling, 1942: 15)

Ndara, I-ndara   A "goddess of rice and fertility." Celebes, Indonesia. (Raats, 1969: 20)

Ndo i ronda eo   An agricultural goddess living in the eastern heavens. The To Palande. Among the To Onda'e a name of Siladi, the rice goddess. Celebes, Indonesia. (Downs, 1920: 14)

Neheb-kau   An ancient serpent goddess associated with the plowing of the land. She was also a goddess of the underworld who provided the divine food for the dead; was also one of the 42 judges or assessors of the dead for the goddess Maat. Egypt. (Budge, 1969, 1: 220, 419; 1969, 2: 62–63)

ñenechen   The Supreme Being and head of the pantheon is invoked in the agricultural fertility rituals, for all things related, including health. The Mapuche, Chile. (Faron, 1968: 63, 73, 100)

Nepen   An Egyptian god of grain. (Budge, 1973, 1: 58)

Nepr, Nepra, Nepri   God of corn, of vegetation, of the harvest. Egypt. (Gardiner, 1925, 9: 791; Budge, 1969, 1: 210)

Neprit   The personification of corn. A goddess who "sometimes takes the place of Nepri." Egypt. (Gardiner, 1925, 9: 791)

Ngaiyupan   A granary idol deity believed able to increase stored rice. The Ifugao, Philippines. (Barton, 1946: 82)

Nidaba   Sumerian/Babylonian goddess of corn, of grains, and of reeds—the source of civilizing music and writing (the stylus). Near East. (Langdon, 1931: 193; Jacobsen, 1946: 144; Cotenau, 1948: 77; Kramer, 1961: 100)

Nikkal   Goddess of the moon and of vegetation, of foods. She was the consort of Yarikh, the moon god. Canaan, Near East. (Driver, 1956: 24)

Ningal   It is suggested that she is a reed goddess associated with the marshes. Daughter of Ningikuga. Near East. (Jacobsen, 1976: 124–125)

Ningikuga   A reed goddess—"The lady of the pure reed." Mother of Ningal and wife of Enki. Near East. (Jacobsen, 1976: 124)

Ninib   A solar deity and a god of agriculture, of the fields. He was god of the fourth month, Tammuz (Semitic) or Du'zu (Sumerian). He was also a god of war, and a god of healing with his wife Gula. Babylonia, Near East. (Jayne, 1962: 126; Jastrow, 1898: 57, 67, 174, 462; Hommel, 1925, 3: 74)

Ninsar, Ninmu   A goddess of plants, of vegetation. Daughter of Ninhursaga and Enki. He cohabited with her, making her the mother of Nin-kurra, goddess of the mountains. Sumer, Near East. (Jacobsen, 1946: 171; 1976: 112; Hooke, 1963: 33).

Ninshebargunu   The goddess of the "mottled barley," mother of Sud. Mesopotamia, Near East. (Jacobsen, 1970: 8)

Niseginyu   A spirit of the crops, generally female. Also called Aso, Aiyulaniza, or Kwuyuniza. The Rengma Nagas, India. (Mills, 1937: 165)

Njamurimi   The guardian of the fields. The Rundi, Burundi. (Meyer, 1916: 189)

Noäkxṇṃ   A supernatural being who is believed to bring the salmon and the berries from the far west. The Bella Coola, British Columbia. (McIlwraith, 1948, 1: 53, 54)

Nodotus, Nodutus   Roman deity of the grain's knots. (Hadas, 1965: 122; Ferguson, 1970: 69)

Noduterensis   Roman deity of the threshing floor. (Campbell, 1964: 321)

Noma   A culture hero/deity who introduced religion and cannibalism, is also a god of vegetation. The Witoto, Peru and Colombia. (Métraux, 1949: 562)

Nonō' osqa   Goddess of flowers, daughter of Snukpanlits. The Bella Coola, British Columbia. (Boas, 1898, 2, 2: 32)

Norov-ava (sometimes **Norov-pas**)   The god/goddess of corn. The Erza (Mordvins), Russia. (Paasonen, 1925, 8: 845)

Noru-paksa   Goddess of the cornfield. The Moksha, Russia. (Paasonen, 1925, 8: 845)

Nunghui   The spirit of the garden soil and of pottery clay. The Canelos Quichua, Ecuador. (Whitten, 1978: 95, 97)

Nun-lukak   A chthonic god associated with cultivation. The Bari. Sudan. (Seligman, 1931: 8)

Nyakarembe   A goddess of fieldwork worshipped mainly by women. Wife of Mugasha. The Haya, Tanzania. (Taylor, 1962: 142)

Nyawin   A god invoked at the beginning of the rice-farming season. The Sea Dyaks, Borneo. (Roth, 1968: 174)

nyot myu rum pang   Field gods of the Lepchas. Sikkim. (Siiger, 1967: 143)

Nzeanzo   One of his aspects is that of god of corn. He is a solar god, omniscient (all is brought to him by the wind), and the conqueror and antagonist of Wun, the god of death. The Bachama, Nigeria. (Meek, 1930, 3: 326; 1943: 114; Pettazzoni, 1956: 37)

Obarator   God of the over-plowing to cover the planted grain. Italy. (Roscher, 1965, 2, 1: 208; Dumézil, 1966, 1: 35; Ferguson, 1970: 68)

Occator   An agricultural deity of the harrowing. Italy. (Dumézil, 1966, 1: 35; Ferguson, 1970: 68)

Oda-no-Mikoto   God of the earth and of the rice field. Also known as Otsuchi-no-Mi-oya-no-Kami, Saruta-hiko, Yachimata-no-Kami, Sae-no-Kami, and Dosojin. Japan. (Czaja, 1974: 258)

Ogetsuhime-no-Kami   Goddess of food. Also called Toyonkehime-no-Kami or Uka-no-Mitana. Daughter of Izanagi and Izanami and wife of Ha-yama-to-no-Kami. Japan. (Kato, 1926: 73; Herbert, 1967: 266, 333; Yasumaro, 1928: 8)

Ogmios   A Celtic god of agriculture, of the furrow, who was assimilated to Hercules. He was also the god of speech, of eloquence. Gaul. (Anwyl, 1906: 39; Renel, 1906: 402; Rhys, 1937: 133; MacCulloch, 1911: 25)

Oho-toshi-no-kami   A Japanese god of the harvest. (Revon, 1925, 9: 239)

Ohoyo Osh Chishba   The corn mother of the Choctaw Indians. Mississippi. (Burland, 1965: 150)

Oihanu, or **Ofanu**   A god of husbandry. Society Islands, Polynesia. (Ellis, 1853: 333)

Oko   A god of agriculture of Yoruban derivation. The Lucumi, Cuba, West Indies. (Courlander, 1966: 10)

O-Kuni-Nushi   In Izumo Province the god who introduced cultivation as well as being god of medicine, of marriage, and of fortune. Japan. (Holtom, 1938: 81, 203; Bunce, 1955: 134)

O le Sa   The god of agriculturalists. Samoa, Polynesia. (Stair, 1897: 142)

Oltagon   An agricultural goddess at Namtogan. The Ifugao, Philippines. (Barton, 1946: 37)

Omonga   A rice spirit who dwells in the moon. The Tomori, Central Celebes, Indonesia. (Frazer, 1960: 483)

Onatah   The corn goddess of the Iroquois. Daughter of Eithinoha. Eastern United States. (Alexander, 1964: 27; Leach, 1949, 1: 307)

Onatha   The spirit of wheat. Daughter of Eithinoha. The Iroquois and the Hurons, Eastern United States. (Larousse, 1968: 430)

O Ndo-i-ronda-eo   A deity of the sunrise who is invoked at the planting season for favorable results. The Toradja, Celebes, Indonesia. (Adriani and Kruyt, 1950: 55)

Ong Wuhti   The goddess of the salt—Zuñi Salt Lake. The Hopi, Arizona. Same as Tsi'ty'icots'a (Keresan). (Tyler, 1964: 190; Titiev, 1972: 131)

Ono, Rongo   A god of cultivated foods, also the "patron of singing." The Marquesas, Polynesia. (Poignant, 1967: 38)

Ops   An ancient goddess of grain and the harvest, of agricultural fertility and abundance. She was also considered a goddess of human birth and growth. She was associated with Consus. Italy. (Dumézil, 1966, 1: 156, 49; Jayne, 1962: 454–5; Fairbanks, 1907: 250; Schoeps, 1961: 146)

Orisha Oko   A god or goddess of agriculture, of the farm and of the harvest. The Ibadan and the Yoruba. Nigeria. (Meek, 1925, 2: 29; Lucas, 1948: 98, 109; Parrinder, 1961: 40; Morton-Williams, 1964: 254; Forde, 1951: 30) In Cuba he is the god of gardens. (Verger, 1957: 563) In Puerto Rico he is a god of fields and harvests, a god of fertility. (Gonzalez-Wippler, 1975: 2, 26)

Osadhis   A deity of plants. India. (Gray, 1930: 223)

Osiris   Originally he was a nature deity, a god of vegetation as well as a river or water god associated with the fertility bestowed by the Nile. He was the symbol of the vegetation cycle, its annual death and rebirth. Later he became the god and judge of the dead, again a god of death and resurrection, bestowing abundance on his followers after death. Egypt. (Knight, 1915: 90; Frazer, 1960: 420, 442–443; Casson, 1965: 54; Budge, 1969, 2: 42, 115, 118, 122, 139)

Otoshi-no-Kami   God of grains. Son of Hayasusa-no-Wo-no-Mikoto and Kamuoichihime. Japan. (Yasumaro, 1965: 36) God of the rice-fields and of the harvest. Son of Susano-wo and Kamu-o-ichi-hime. (Herbert, 1967: 318, 499)

Ovinnik   The name of the Slavonic household spirit when he lives in the drying-kiln. He is beseeched for successful threshing. (Mansikka, 1925, 4: 627)

Oxo   God of agriculture, from the Yoruba. Brazil. (Bastide, 1960: 570)

O-ya-tsu hime   A planter of trees. Daughter of Susano-wo. Japan. (Herbert, 1967: 332)

Pa-cha   A farm god and god of locusts invoked to protect the crops from them and other insects. China. (Maspero, 1963: 325; Werner, 1932: 340; Haydon, 1941: 195)

Padrympus A god of agriculture represented "as a young man of joyful countenance, crowned with ears of corn." The Letts and the Lithuanians. (Welsford, 1925, 9: 242)

Pagpaxasapat A spirit feared at the time of clearing of the fields because he may kill men. The Isneg, Luzon, Philippines. (Vanoverbergh, 1941: 304)

Pai Chung A god of agriculture, of the sowing. China. (Werner, 1932: 6, 353)

Paks-av "Mother field." The Moksha (Mordvins), Russia. (Paasonen, 1925, 8: 845)

Palahik An agricultural deity at Kalinugan. The Ifugao, Philippines. (Barton, 1946: 37)

Palo Etruscan deity of agriculture, male or female. The "spirit of the fields, vines, meadows, for all kinds of crops." Same as Roman Pales. Italy. (Leland, 1963: 60)

Palpalad A male spirit of the rice harvesting to whom betel is offered. The Isneg, Luzon, Philippines. (Vanoverbergh, 1941: 339)

Palwittis A god of the Sudavians in Samland invoked at the harvest festival. Baltic. (Welsford, 1925, 11: 422)

Pan An Egyptian grain god. (Budge, 1973, 1: 58)

Panda A Roman goddess who some say is associated with the sprouting of the seeds; she opens the earth. (Roscher, 1965, 2, 1: 210)

Pandan rumari Goddess of agriculture of the Battak. Sister of Batara guru. Sumatra, Indonesia. (MacKenzie, 1930: 311)

Pandong A god invoked at the beginning of the rice-farming season. The Sea Dyaks, Borneo. (Roth, 1968: 174)

Pandrosos A goddess of agriculture and of the dew. Later united with Athene. Sister of Herse and daughter of Cecrops and Agraulos. Greece. (Bethe, 1925, 2: 226; Burns, 1925, 3: 373; Crawley, 1925, 4: 700)

Panggau A god invoked at the beginning of the rice-farming season. The Sea Dyaks, Borneo. (Roth, 1968: 174)

Pani The mother of the sweet potato is invoked at the planting, and also with others when there is sickness. Wife of Rongo-maui. The Maori, New Zealand. (Hatt, 1951: 891; Mackenzie, n.d.: 316–317)

Pantan Ini Andan A goddess invoked for rice charms and for an abundant rice harvest. The Iban Dyaks, Sarawak, Borneo. (Nyuak, 1906: 177; Sarawak Gazette, 1963: 135, 147)

Panububan A granary idol deity believed able to increase stored rice. The Ifugao, Philippines. (Barton, 1946: 82)

Paopiahe "Food-maker . . . invented some kinds of food." The Siuai, Bougainville, Solomon Islands, Melanesia. (Oliver, 1967: 41)

Paparai God of the harvest. Tahiti, Polynesia. (Henry, 1928: 376)

Pari-lha-tsen karbu A god of the soil and protective of the Paldorje clan. The Sherpas, Nepal. (Furer-Haimendorf, 1964: 21)

Parrag A very helpful protector of the rice fields who usually lives there. The Isneg, Luzon, Philippines. (Vanoverbergh, 1941: 300)

Patrimpo A youthful god of grain depicted with ears of corn. Baltic. (Puhvel, 1974: 79)

Pa'u-o-pala'e The goddess of ferns. Hawaii. (Westervelt, 1963, 2: 97)

P'ei-Yang Chinese "goddess of nourishment" and protector of children. (Day, 1940: 93)

Pekko The "God of barley." Finland. (Leach, 1950, 2: 850)

Pellervoinen A Finno-Ugric god of trees and plants, protective of the fields. (Larousse, 1968: 304)

Pellon, Pekko God of barley and its growth. Finland and Estonia. (Krohn, 1925, 6: 25; MacCulloch, 1964: 244)

Ih P'en Androgynous god of the soil, of plant growth, of fertility. "As the passive spirit of maize, is male and the consort of Ix Kanan, female spirit of the bean." The Chorti, Guatemala. (Thompson, 1970: 294)

Penaban Sari A benevolent chthonic god associated with cultivation and the fertility of the fields. Bali, Indonesia. (Grader, 1969, 1: 158–160)

Pergubrius A god of the labors of the fields. The Letts and the Lithuanians. Also a god of the Sudavians in Samland invoked at the harvest festival. (Welsford, 1925, 9: 242; 1925, 11: 422)

Perusong   A spirit who devours and depletes the stored paddy rice. The Land Dyaks, Borneo. (Roth, 1968: 166)

Pheebee Yau   Benevolent goddess of corn and rice, of the harvest. She guards the growing fields. The Karens, Burma. (McMahon, 1876: 136)

Mae Phosop, Posop   The rice goddess. Thai. (Hanks, 1964: 76)

Pia-gó   The "personification of the *perah* fruit tree." The Semang, Malaya. (Schebesta, 1957: 53)

Pilay   (1) A god who protects the rice and is also invoked to bring them more (stolen) rice. The Isneg, Luzon, Philippines. (Vanoverbergh, 1941: 349, 361) (2) The "guardian of the farm." The Apayao, Philippines. (Wilson, 1947: 22)

Pili   The lizard is the patron god of agriculture and is "associated with the origin of kava, sugar cane, and taro." Manua (Samoa), Polynesia. (Mead, 1930: 158–159)

Pilwittus, Pelwittus, Piluitus, Pilnitis   A goddess of agriculture of the Letts and Lithuanians. Identified with Ceres. (Welsford, 1925, 9: 242; Puhvel, 1974: 83)

Pinang Ipong   A god of the Sea Dyaks invoked at the beginning of the rice-farming season. He can bring prosperity and fame, but can also curse and bring evil. Borneo. (Roth, 1968: 174; Sarawak Gazette, 1963: 134)

Pindusa   Probably a goddess of vegetation. Spain. (Martinez, 1962: 70)

Pitao-Cocobi   "God of abundance, or of the harvest." Oaxaca, Mexico. (Bancroft, 1886, 3: 457)

Pitu   "Food personified"—a deity in a hymn of the Rig Veda. India. (Dumézil, 1966, 1: 387)

Piuku   The god of the manioc and the manioc fields, but not worshipped. The Barama (Caribs), Guyana. (Zerries, 1968: 280)

Pogoda, Zylvie, Dziewanna   A Slavic goddess worshipped as a goddess of agriculture by settlers and farmers. Also as a goddess of the weather. (Czaplicka, 1925, 11: 595)

Pogo Wende   A manifestation of Tenga Wende as the guardian of the farmer's fields, to whom a sacrifice is made after clearing. The Mossi, Upper Volta. (Hammond, 1959: 249)

Polevik, Polevoy   A Slavic spirit of the fields who inflicts disease on those he finds napping, or rides over them on horseback. Russia. (Machal, 1918: 268–9; Larousse, 1968: 291)

Pomona   Roman goddess of fruit trees. Wife of Vertumnus. (Dumézil, 1966, 1: 271; Fairbanks, 1907: 252; Bulfinch, 1898: 16)

Prokorimos   Litu-Prussian god of agriculture and of honey. (Welsford, 1925, 9: 242; Schrader, 1925, 2: 31)

Promitor   A god of the distribution of agricultural products, of the removal of grain from storage. Italy. (Dumézil, 1966, 1: 35; Roscher, 1965, 2, 1: 218; Campbell, 1964: 321)

Proserpina   Roman "goddess of the grain's first leaves and buds." (Hadas, 1965: 122)

Puanga   The star Rigel who with Taku-rua are the deities of the planting season and of the harvest. New Zealand. (Mackenzie, n.d.: 226; Andersen, 1928: 411)

Puemunus   Roman god, male counterpart of Pomona. (Roscher, 1965, 3, 2: 3277)

Pukauwan   An agricultural deity at Kalinugan. The Ifugao, Philippines. (Barton, 1946: 38)

Pulang Gana   God of the soil and of all aspects of rice farming. An earth god who received sacrifices as his due in allowing agriculture and for good harvests. The Sea Dyaks, Borneo. (Roth, 1968: 177; Gomes, 1911: 196; Sarawak Gazette, 1963: 16)

Punay   A male spirit of the rice harvesting who "resembles a bird" and who is offered betel at the beginning of the harvest. The Isneg, Luzon, Philippines. (Vanoverbergh, 1941: 339)

Pundaikuhan   A deity named for a vine, a section of which is a charm against locusts, of which he is "the owner." His wife is Indudun. The Ifugao, Philippines. (Barton, 1946: 37)

Pungtang majan   The mother of rice and cotton, daughter of Phungkam Janun. The Katchins, Burma. (Gilhodes, 1908: 678)

Puokan   A granary idol deity believed able to increase stored rice. The Ifugao, Philippines. (Barton, 1946: 81)

di Puseh   A deified ancestor worshipped in planting ceremonies. Bali, Indonesia. (Grader, 1969, 1: 147)

Puta A Roman goddess in charge of the pruning of trees. (Roscher, 1965, 2, 1: 218; Ferguson, 1970: 69)

Pu-te-hue The "parent or personification of the *hue* or gourd." Female. The Maori, New Zealand. (Best, 1899: 96)

Pyatnitsa Prascovia A Slavic goddess of the harvest. Russia. (Bray, 1935: 45)

Qolqa The Pleiades—guardian of the seed. Peru. (Rowe, 1946, 2: 295)

Qurrama Minari The god of vegetation, not an independent god but an aspect of Puru, invoked as an intercessor with him. The Salivan, Colombia. (Walde-Waldegg, 1936: 40–41; Wallis, 1939: 89)

Raja Sua A god invoked at the "Feast of the Whetstones" before the clearing of the land. Among the Iban a god of the earth and giver of good crops. The Dyaks, Borneo. (Sarawak Gazette, 1963: 78, 133)

Raki-te-ua God of the coconut and of the Tagua clan. He is invoked in the consecration of the sacred oven of Tafua. Tikopia, Polynesia. (Firth, 1967, 2: 122, 124)

Rana-neida Goddess of the spring and its breezes and guardian of the young growth. She "ruled over the mountains that become green earliest in spring." The Lapps, Northern Europe. (Holmberg, 1925, 7: 799; Bosi, 1960: 132; Dioszegi, 1968: 28)

Ranno A garden-god represented as an asp. He was absorbed by Khem. Egypt. (Murray, 1935: 398)

Rannut, Renenet A serpent goddess of the earth's fertility and of the harvests. A name of Isis as a harvest goddess. Renenet was also a goddess of nursing and of maternity. Egypt. (MacCulloch, 1925, 11: 401; Knight, 1915: 105; Budge, 1969, 2: 144, 216)

Rao A god of tumeric. Mangareva, Polynesia. (Buck, 1938, 1: 426)

Rara-taunga-rere A child of Tane representing the "fruitfulness of trees." The Maori, New Zealand. (Best, 1924: 176)

Raz-ajk The mother of grass. The Lapps, Northern Europe. (Holmberg, 1925, 7: 799; Collinder, 1949: 140)

Razeka An Arabian tribal god worshipped as the provider of food. (Bray, 1935: 168)

Redarator, Reparator The god of the second plowing of the land. Italy. (Dumézil, 1966, 1: 35; Campbell, 1964: 320)

Remle An Etruscan deity of the mill who interferes with its working when someone has offended him. Italy. (Leland, 1963: 129)

Renen-utet A snake goddess associated with the grape harvest and the wine. Egypt. (Younger, 1966: 31, 43)

Riri-tuna-rei The mother of the *miro*, a fruit. Easter Island, Polynesia. (Buck, 1938: 225; Métraux, 1940: 323)

Robigus, Robigo Roman god of wheat rust and of mildew to whom a dog and a sheep were sacrificed to avert them. (Dumézil, 1966, 1: 158; Frazer, 1926: 493; Altheim, 1937: 133)

Rodu Slavic "god of cultivators." Russia. (Leach, 1950, 2: 1027)

Roembanggea A name of the rice goddess. The Toradja, Celebes, Indonesia. (Adriani and Kruyt, 1950: 180)

Rogo A god of agriculture and of the underworld in Mangareva. Son of Tagaroa and Haumea. Polynesia. (Buck, 1938, 1: 422)

Rokimé The Mother of rice invoked for good crops. The Garo, Assam. (Playfair, 1909: 93)

Rongo God of agriculture, of cultivated foods; a god of peace, and of abundance; "the male personification of the moon." New Zealand. (Best, 1924: 236, 279; Andersen, 1928: 423–424; Howells, 1948: 222; Buck, 1938, 2: 264–265; Hongi, 1920: 26)

Rongo-marae-roa God of the *kumara*, a food "to be eaten in times of quietness and peace." New Zealand. (White, 1887, 3: 97)

Rongo-ma-Tane Rongo and Tane as a dual god of agriculture, of cultivated foods and as guardian of fertility, germination and reproduction. New Zealand. (Best, 1924: 105, 236, 281; Andersen, 1928: 368; Grey, 1855: 3, 12)

Rongo-poa A beneficent god "associated with the production of food." Mangareva, Polynesia. (Buck, 1932, 2: 87)

Rongoteus, Runkateivas, Rukotivo The god of rye. Finland. (MacCulloch, 1964: 244; Krohn, 1925, 6: 25)

Roskva A Teutonic goddess, servant of Thor, who "symbolizes the ripe fields of harvest." (Anderson, 1891: 300, 456)

Royo The first spirit (male) to be invoked at the beginning of the planting of a field. The Isneg, Luzon, Philippines. (Vanoverbergh, 1941: 315)

Rua-papa The deity who "caused verdure upon the earth." Society Islands, Polynesia. (Henry, 1928: 373)

Rua-ta'ata The god of the breadfruit. Society Islands, Polynesia. (Henry, 1928: 423)

Rubezahl God of fields and cattle. Germany. (Leland, 1963: 60)

Ruginis To "the man of rye, a he-goat was offered in the fall (this is mentioned only once in a folk song)." Lithuania. (Leach, 1950, 2: 632)

Rugiu boba The "old woman of the rye field." Lithuania. (Leach, 1951, 2: 632)

Rukkina A guardian of the rice and the granary. The Isneg, Luzon, Philippines. (Vanoverbergh, 1941: 297)

Runcina Roman goddess of mowing and of weeding. (Roscher, 1965, 2, 1: 220)

Ruppita A guardian of the rice and the granary. The Isneg, Luzon, Philippines. (Vanoverbergh, 1941: 297)

Sakambhari A goddess of the prosperity of vegetation. Pandharpur, India. (Ghurye, 1962: 250, 256)

Sakura Tutelary deity of the taro appealed to for control of storms and wind. Tikopia and Anuta, Melanesia. (Firth, 1967, 2: 212, 258, 330)

sa kyu One of the *ma yel* gods, of the paddy rice. The Lepchas, Sikkim. (Siiger, 1967: 144)

Sáldakshungui Father of the maize. The Cagaba and the Kogi, Colombia. (Reichel-Dolmatoff, 1949/50: 115)

Saldáui A Father of the plants. The Cagaba and the Kogi, Colombia. (Reichel-Dolmatoff, 1949/50: 115)

Sali Minao Goddess of the *sali* crop. The Kacharis, Assam. (Endle, 1911: 37)

Samjayi Diya A deity worshipped at the Bidri festival celebrated before the sowing of seeds. The Gonds, India. (Kurup, 1970: 162)

Sampsa, Pellervo, Sampsa Pellervoinen A god of vegetation whose presence was essential to its growth. Finno-Ugric. (MacCulloch, 1964: 243; Krohn, 1925, 6: 25; Leach, 1950, 2: 970; Larousse, 1973: 430)

Samsia An Indo/Burmese deity of the paddy field invoked for abundance. The Tangsas. (Dutta, 1959: 29)

Sanbai-sama Shinto god of the rice fields invoked in the Mibu Ohana-taue, a rice-transplanting ritual in June, for good crops. The rest of the year he lives in the peaks as a god of the mountains. Chiyoda, Japan. (Lee, 1978: 78, 85)

Sanggul Labong A god invoked at the beginning of the rice-farming season. The Sea Dyaks, Borneo. (Roth, 1968: 174)

Sangiyan Sari The goddess of rice. Southern Celebes, Indonesia. (Hatt, 1951: 885)

Sangiyan Sarri Goddess of the rice with which she is frequently identified. The Buginese, Indonesia. (Wilken, 1893: 550)

Sangkara, Batara Sangkara God of all crops. Bali, Indonesia. (Goris, 1960: 123)

Saniang Padi The god of the padi (paddy) invoked at the beginning of the rice-farming season. The Sea Dyaks, Borneo. (Roth, 1968: 174)

Saning Sari Guardian of the rice. Java, Indonesia. (Frazer, 1960: 482) "Mother of the Rice" who guards it. The Minang-kabauers, Sumatra, Indonesia. (Eliade, 1958: 339)

San Ku Fu Jen A goddess of mulberry trees invoked for good leaves for food for silkworms. China. (Day, 1940: 107)

sa nom A god of agriculture of the Lepchas. Sikkim. (Siiger, 1967: 144)

Santiago An unpredictable god, protective of the crops, yet sending hail and lightning. Contemporary Quechua, Peru. (Mishkin, 1946: 464)

Sara-mama The goddess of maize. Peru. (Rowe, 1946: 297; Markham, 1969: 68)

Sarasvati The goddess of wisdom and eloquence is also a goddess of the rice cultivation on Bali—that "in the southern part of the field." Indonesia. (Levi, 1933: xxviii; Goris, 1960: 129)

Sarengge An agricultural goddess invoked for rain. Wife of Sareo. Central Celebes, Indonesia. (Downs, 1920: 25)

Sareo An agricultural god invoked for rain. Central Celebes, Indonesia. (Downs, 1920: 25)

Sarna Burhia A goddess to whom the first fruits of crops are offered and to whom the winnowing basket is sacred. India. (Roy, 1915: 146–147)

Sarritor, Saritor A Roman god of cultivating and of weeding. (Dumézil, 1966, 1: 35; Roscher, 1965, 2, 1: 221)

Saruta-hiko A phallic god associated with agriculture. Also considered a god of the crossroads. Japan. (Kato, 1926: 31; Holtom, 1938: 183; MacCulloch, 1925, 4: 332; Herbert, 1967: 356)

Sator Roman god of the sowing. (Roscher, 1965, 2, 1: 221; Campbell, 1964: 321)

sa vi The god of millet. The Lepchas, Sikkim. (Siiger, 1967: 144)

Saywa Deities of "the boundary markers . . . associated with cultivated fields." Peru. (Rowe, 1946: 297)

Sbe-pri-sei God of the five grains when they are in storage. The Ch'iang at Ho-p'ing-chai, Szechwan, China. (Graham, 1958: 48)

Schaystix A Baltic god invoked at the harvest festival. The Sudavians, Samland. (Welsford, 1925, 11: 422)

Seb A chthonic god of all the earths' vegetation and of the underworld. Son of Shu and Tefnut and brother/husband of Nut. Egypt. (Knight, 1915: 109–110; Budge, 1969, 2: 94–99; Bulfinch, 1899: 367)

Sedana A god of agriculture and of wealth. Bali, Indonesia. (Grader, 1969: 145, 168)

Segesta, Segetia Roman goddess of seeds, protector of the grain when ready for mowing. (Roscher, 1965, 2, 1: 221; Hadas, 1965: 122; Dumézil, 1966, 1: 267)

Seia Roman goddess protective of the grain in the ground, of the seed. (Hadas, 1965: 122; Schrader, 1925, 2: 32)

Seižankua The only earth available (for sowing) was red. "Upon Sintana's advice Seižankua blows on a golden flute, by means of which the black earth (Karvaksu)

arose which Sintana spread out to the horizon." The Kagaba, Colombia. (Preuss, 1926: 70)

Sekhet A name of Isis as "goddess of cultivated lands and fields." Egypt. (Knight, 1915: 57; Budge, 1969, 2: 216)

Selingiling A god "who has charge of the twigs of the sega rotan." The Sea Dyaks, Borneo. (Roth, 1968: 171)

Selu The corn woman, wife of Konati. The Cherokee, North Carolina and Tennessee. (Hatt, 1951: 854; Swanton, 1946: 772)

Semenia Master of the Earth's food (yuca) and chief of the bird/human people created by Wanadi to help the old people (human/animal). Semenia taught them to clear trees, making *conucos*, and cultivation. He brought order, cooperation, food, etc. The Makiritare, Venezuela. (Civrieux, 1980: 132–136)

The Semones Deities who protect the grain at the sowing. Italy. (Dumézil, 1966, 1: 37, 376)

Semonia Roman goddess of the seed, of the sowing. (Roscher, 1965, 2, 1: 222)

Seokukui He is associated with "the cultivation of the tobacco plants and the extraction of the tobacco juice by boiling for its modern use in connection with the greeting." The Kagaba, Colombia. (Preuss, 1926: 73)

Dewi Seri The goddess of rice. The Toradja, Celebes, Indonesia. (Adriani and Kruyt, 1950: 222)

Shakaema God of vegetation invoked by men in the planting and cultivation of bananas. Husband of Nungui. The Jivaro, Ecuador and Peru. (Zerries, 1968: 277; Karsten, 1926: 301)

sha rung The god of maize. The Lepchas, Sikkim. (Siiger, 1967: 144)

Shawa Unti Majan The mother of thatch. The Katchins, Burma. (Gilhodes, 1908: 678)

The She-Chi Gods of the soil, the grain, and the harvest. China. (Werner, 1932: 412; Day, 1940: 59)

Shen Nung A god of agriculture and the inventor of the plow. He was also a god of pharmacy and medicine as the discoverer of the medicinal and poisonous qualities of plants. China. (Werner, 1932: 415, 419, 505; Graham, 1961: 176; Day, 1940: 105; Wu and Ch'en, 1942: 26)

Shi Goddess of the grains in storage. Wife of Ts'u-ga-shi. The Ch'iang, Szechwan, China. (Graham, 1958: 47, 49)

Shiho-tsuchi-no-kami A god of salt and of the sea. Japan. (Chadwick, 1930: 437)

Shiramba Kamui A god of vegetation, particularly of trees. Also invoked for success in hunting and fishing. The Ainu, Japan. (Munro, 1963: 16, 112)

Shu-chun A god of harvests. China. (Werner, 1932: 415)

Shui Fang A god of agriculture who can affect the growth of crops—for good or bad. China. Also "God of Embankments and Dykes." (Werner, 1932: 6, 433)

Shui Yung A god of agriculture and of "Canals and Rivers" who can affect the growth of crops—for good or bad. China. (Werner, 1932: 6, 446)

Shulawitsi A young god of maize, but more importantly a god of fire and messenger of the Sun. The Zuñi, New Mexico. (Parsons, 1939: 175, 205; Stevenson, 1901/02: 33; Tyler, 1964: 25)

Shul-gur A name of Nin-gir-su as a district god of agriculture. Babylonia, Near East. (Jastrow, 1898: 57)

Shumdukuí Father of the potatoes. The Cagaba and the Kogi, Colombia. (Reichel-Dolmatoff, 1949/50: 115)

Shu T'ou Wu Sheng The "Five Patrons of the Tree-tops" invoked for good leaves for food for silkworms. China. (Day, 1940: 107)

Sian A spirit of the rice harvesting time. The Isneg, Luzon, Philippines. (Vanoverbergh, 1941: 339)

Siberu Dayang Mata-ni-ari The goddess of rice, wife of Ketengahen, Sumatra, Indonesia. (Sierksma, 1960: 26–27)

Sibo A benevolent spirit of the rice harvesting time who always accompanies the women. The Isneg, Luzon, Philippines. (Vanoverbergh, 1941: 339)

Si Dayang The rice goddess and mother goddess—"the creative and sustaining power of the universe." The Karo Battas, Sumatra, Indonesia. (Keane, 1925, 2: 238)

Siladi The goddess of rice. Central Celebes, Indonesia. (Downs, 1920: 14)

Sillongsi The "mythical legendary ruler of China who invented agriculture, and is reverenced as the patron of it." The only agricultural god of Korea. (Clark, 1932: 202)

Siloman Baba A local god worshipped when planting the water nut and melons. Brother of Madho Baba. The Kahar, United Provinces, India. (Crooke, 1925, 7: 637)

Silvanus A god of husbandry, of the fields and grazing lands, and of the forests, protective of the farms and the herds. Italy. (Dumézil, 1966, 1: 235; Jayne, 1962: 439; Fairbanks, 1907: 248–249)

Sinekili With her husband Taubewa the deities of yams. Normanby Island, Papua, New Guinea. (Roheim, 1946: 331)

Singan A goddess protective of the rice. The Nabaloi, Philippines. (Kroeber, 1918: 44)

Sintana With Seižankua produced the fertile black earth for sowing. He controlled Žántana who causes the drought. Son of Gauteován, though also called her husband. Father of Híuika and Buñkuei. The Kagaba, Colombia. (Preuss, 1926: 65, 67, 70)

Sipa A male spirit of the rice harvesting to whom betel is offered on the first day. The Isneg, Luzon, Philippines. (Vanoverbergh, 1941: 339)

Sipnut Betel "is offered to him, on top of the house ladder, at the beginning of the harvest." The Isneg, Luzon, Philippines. (Vanoverbergh, 1941: 339)

Sita Goddess of husbandry and agriculture, of fruits and plenty. She was the wife of Rama and daughter of Savitr. India. (Bhattacharji, 1970: 214; Elwin, 1954: 641; Dowson, 1961: 194–195; Kramer, 1961: 291)

Siti Permani In the creation story she is the daughter of Petara and was "cut to pieces . . . becoming padi, pumpkins, and other plants." The Sea Dyaks, Sarawak, Borneo. (Sarawak Gazette, 1963: 19)

Siton A Greek god of grain. (Roscher, 1965, 4: 974)

Sohodo-no-kami An agricultural kami—a scarecrow. Japan. (Herbert, 1967: 500)

Soma The god of plants is particularly associated with the Soma plant, from which the ambrosia of immortality is made and which gives strength and inspiration. As the god of medicinal plants he is powerful in healing, bestowing vitality and longevity. He is also a celestial deity as identified with the moon. India. (Keith, 1917: 18, 46–47, 90; Ions, 1967: 20, 81; Macdonell, 1897: 104–114; Barth, 1921: 11, 177)

Sonnolipenu A goddess of the Konds invoked for good crops, seed, etc. India. (Schulze, 1912: 10–12)

Sor-ava The mother of corn. The Moksha (Mordvins), Russia. (Paasonen, 1925, 8: 845)

Soumai The "(master of the breadfruit) is the ruler of Eaur." Located in the southern sky. Truk Islands, Micronesia. (Bollig, 1927: 5)

Spiniensis A Roman god of thorns, of thorn-bushes, invoked to remove them from fields. (Roscher, 1965, 2, 1: 223; Thompson, 1970: 69)

Sreepen A deity worshipped at the Bidri festival celebrated before the sowing of seeds. The Gonds, India. (Kurup, 1970: 162)

Sri Goddess of rice and of agricultural fertility and prosperity, as well as goddess of beauty. The wife of Vishnu and the mother of Dewi Melanting. India, Bali, and Java. (Bhattacharji, 1970: 296; Danielou, 1964: 141; Marchal, 1963: 233; Covarrubias, 1937: 71, 317; Hooykaas, 1964: 22)

Ssu Cho A Chinese god of agriculture. (Werner, 1932: 6)

Sterculinius, Stercutius God of the dung, of the manuring of the fields. Italy. (Roscher, 1965, 2, 1: 225; Dumézil, 1966, 1: 20; Campbell, 1964: 320)

Su A deity who brought "fruit-bearing seeds" from the sky for mankind. The Sara family of tribes. Chad. (Larousse, 1973: 530)

Subruncinator Roman god of the "thinning out" and of the removing of weeds. (Dumézil, 1966, 1: 35; Roscher, 1965, 2, 1: 227)

Sud Sumerian "goddess of the ear of corn." A wife of Enlil in Shuruppak and daughter of Ninshebargunu. Near East. (Jacobsen, 1970: 8)

Suh Kuin A god who took the place of his father Shin Nung as god of the fields. China. (Du Bose, n.d.: 328)

Sumboli An old god of agriculture who was feared because he was unpredictable. Central Celebes, Indonesia. (Downs, 1920: 25)

Sumugan, Sumukan, Sumuqan A mountain god whom Enki placed in charge of plains vegetation and cattle. Sumer, Near East. (Kramer, 1961: 100; Ferm, 1950: 60; Hooke, 1963: 27)

Sung Su-kung The god of tea in South China. (Werner, 1932: 492; Du Bose, n.d.: 327)

Svantevit, Svantovit, Svetovit A Slavic god of war and of prophecy as well as of the harvests. At the harvest festivals various methods were employed to obtain his prophecy for the next year's crops—whether there would be abundance or scarcity. (Queval, 1968: 107; Gimbutas, 1971: 153, 159–161; Schoeps, 1961: 120; Pettazzoni, 1956: 235–236)

Ta'ama A god worshipped on many islands as having introduced "fruits and vegetables, flowers . . . the coconut tree." Polynesia. (Cohane, 1969: 209)

taa nu kami The paddy deity of Okinawa. (Lebra, 1966: 223)

Tabindain Thakinma A female spirit of the paddy field who is propitiated during the transplanting season as she might send snakes. Yeigyi, Burma. (Spiro, 1967: 49)

Tafakula A goddess invoked "for favorable seasons for the crops." Eua Island, Tonga, Polynesia. (Gifford, 1929: 303)

Tagamaling Goddess of crops other than rice. The Manobo, Philippines. (Jocano, 1969: 23)

Tagumbanua God of the fields "to whom the Kaliga ceremony is dedicated." This ceremony is usually associated with the rice harvest. The Bukidnon, Philippines. (Cole, 1956: 96; Benedict, 1916: 255; Jocano, 1969: 23)

Tahu Among the Maori the personification of all food. New Zealand. (Best, 1924: 176, 383)

Tahunui A goddess of plant life. Vahitahi Island, Tuamotus, Polynesia. (Stimson, 1933: 59)

T'ai Shan, T'ai Chan The great mountain god, the peak of the East (Shantung), whose early function was the stability of the earth, the control of the rivers and of storms. As a god of the clouds and their rain he provided good crops and harvests for the welfare of the people. As a god who presides over the origin of all life as well as of death, with the advent of Buddhism (introducing an afterlife), he became a god who received and judged the dead. China. (Day, 1940: 120–121; Chavannes, n.d.: 4, 5, 8, 13, 28, 268; Haydon, 1940: 193–194)

549

taji· Turkey. A helpful deity responsible for "the gift of seed for domesticated plants, including corn, . . . the association of game (hunting) and agriculture." The Navaho, Arizona and New Mexico. (Reichard, 1950: 488–489)

Takel A goddess in charge "of the tuber harvest." The Semang. Among the Menri she is the wife of Karei and an earth goddess. Malaya. (Schebesta, 1927: 274; 1957: 91)

Takotsi Nakawe The goddess of vegetation and of growth, of maize and vegetables. She is the mother of the gods, the earth goddess and "mother of the armadillo, the peccary, and the bear; . . . and is a Rain-Serpent in the east." The Huichol, Mexico. (Alexander, 1920: 122; Seler, 1925, 6: 829; Chamberlain, 1900: 305)

Taku-rua A star goddess, Sirius, who with Puanga are deities of the planting and of the harvest. New Zealand. (Mackenzie, n.d.: 210; Andersen, 1928: 411)

Tamayei God of the coconut trees. Pukapuka, Polynesia. (Beaglehole, 1938: 310)

Tamfana A Germanic goddess of the harvest and of fertility. The Marsi. (MacCulloch, 1964: 17, 195)

Tammuz An ancient Sumerian god of vegetation who represents the death and rebirth cycle of nature, in which he was associated with Ishtar. Also Babylonian/ Phoenician. Near East. (Bulfinch, 1898: 397; Vriezen, 1963: 39, 40; Frazer, 1960: 379; Hooke, 1963: 41)

Tanaka-no-kami A deity of the rice field. Japan. (Herbert, 1967: 507)

ya Tangoi The wife of ta Piago "is the personified rambu-tan tree." The Semang, Malaya. (Schebesta, 1957: 33, 36)

Ta-no-kami God of the rice fields, six months counterpart of Yama-no-Kami, the god of the mountains, who descends in the spring as a snake to the plains. They are phallic deities protective of agriculture. In November Ta-no-Kami returns to the mountains as Yama-no-Kami. Japan. (Czaja, 1974: 50)

Ta Ped'n The god of the firmament also "has charge of the fruit seasons." The Semang, Malaya. (Schebesta, 1957: 32, 91)

Taphagan A harvest goddess, protective of the rice in the granary. The Manobo, Philippines. (Jocano, 1969: 23)

Tarabume God of the growing rice and the hemp. The Bagobo, Philippines. (Benedict, 1916: 22)

Taragomi A deity protective of the crops. The Bagobo, Philippines. (Jocano, 1969: 22)

Tarkiray A spirit offered betel and invoked to be present at the rice harvesting. The Isneg, Luzon, Philippines. (Vanoverbergh, 1941: 339)

Taromata The tutelary god of the taro to whom the first seedlings of the taro planting are dedicated. The Ariki Taumako, Tikopia, Melanesia. (Firth, 1939: 68; 1967, 2: 212)

Tate Iku Oteganaka A goddess "of maize and other vegetables." The Huichol, Jalisco, Mexico. (Seler, 1925, 6: 829)

Tate Naaliwami The serpent goddess of the rain from the east is the "creator of squashes and of all flowers." The Huichol, Jalisco, Mexico. (Seler, 1925, 6: 829)

Taubewa With his wife Sinekili "the owners of the food . . . of all yams." He seems to be an aspect of Yaboaine as a phallic god. His "semen is the yam." Normanby Island, Papua, New Guinea. (Roheim, 1946: 331)

Taufa As a land god he "was a notable protector of gardens." He was also a sea god, a shark. Tonga, Polynesia. (Gifford, 1929: 298; Collocott, 1921: 229)

Tau-Katau God of the breadfruit tree and of rain. Ponape, Caroline Islands, Micronesia. (Christian, 1899: 384)

Tawals A Slavic god of the fields, of the tilling. Poland. (Larousse, 1968: 291)

Tawoche-lha-tsen A god of the soil, protective of the Nawa clan. The Sherpas, Nepal. (Furer-Haimendorf, 1964: 22)

Taxoko A spirit of the rice harvesting time to whom betel is offered. The Isneg, Luzon, Philippines. (Vanoverbergh, 1941: 339)

Tchou God of the harvests, director of agriculture. Son of Lie-chan. China. (Chavannes, n.d.: 505)

Te Atua i Tafua A deity associated with the yam ceremonies; also a deity of the coconut invoked for its fertility. Tikopia, Polynesia. (Firth, 1967, 2: 161–162)

Tekualdáma Father of the cultivated lands. The Cagaba and the Kogi, Colombia. (Reichel-Dolmatoff, 1949/50: 114)

Telepinu A god of agriculture in that his disappearance and reappearance caused the vegetation cycles. There was a cessation of normal activities not restored until he was found and returned. Son of the weather god. His wife was Hetepinu. Hatti/Hittite, Near East. (Ferm, 1950: 93; Gurney, 1952: 136; Moscati, 1962: 183; Hooke, 1963: 100n)

Tenal-Pisin God of the sago who also introduced other foods. He was associated with the moon. The Ulau and the Suein, New Guinea. (Hatt, 1951: 893)

Santa Teresa She is identified with the old household gods and is associated with the milpa and its care. The Tzeltal, Mexico. (Nash, 1970: 204)

Tetzahuitl, Tetzauhpilli, Tetzauhquitzin A god of farmers, also of rain, worshipped at Cuauhilama, Valley of Anahuac, Mexico. (Reed, 1966: 112)

Thakur Deo The god of agriculture, of cultivation, is worshipped at the beginning of the rains and before the planting of the autumn crops. India. (Russell, 1916, 2: 85, 231, 365; 1916, 3: 400, 575)

Thang-lha A god of the plains. The Sherpas, Nepal. Also of Tibet. (Furer-Haimendorf, 1964: 232; Snellgrove, 1957: 176)

St. Thomas The god of farmers. Ita', Brazil. (Wagley, 1964: 223)

Thor Among some a god of farmers and the fertility of the earth, as the thunder god who brings the rain. His wife was Sif, a goddess of the earth. Scandinavia. (Stern, 1899: 29, 31; Davidson, 1964: 84; Turville-Petre, 1964: 93)

Thrud A Scandinavian goddess who "signifies the seed." Daughter of Thor and Sif. (Stern, 1898: 97)

Thunai A god of agriculture, husband of Maimungma. The Tiparas, Bengal. (Crooke, 1925, 2: 481)

Thunor In England the god of thunder was also "a patron of agriculture." (Branston, 1957: 30, 115)

Thyak-dum A household and field spirit of uncertain temper who may bestow "health and prosperity" or "disease and loss." The Lepchas, Sikkim. (Gorer, 1938: 74–75)

Tiazolteotl A benevolent goddess of maize of the Totonacs who was unexacting of human sacrifice. Same as Cinteotl. Mexico. (Bancroft, 1886, 3: 350–351)

Tibong A malevolent spirit who devours and depletes the paddy (rice) while it is stored. The Land Dyaks, Borneo. (Roth, 1968: 166)

Tido Wende The manifestation of Wennam "which gives life to the vegetable kingdom." The Mossi, Upper Volta. (Hammond, 1959: 246)

Ti Kong An earth deity worshipped with Ti Mu at the planting of the rice to encourage growth. Szechwan, China. (Graham, 1928: 44)

Ti Mu A Taoist earth mother, goddess of the fields and of growth. China. (Day, 1940: 163; Graham, 1928: 44)

Tisna Wati Goddess of the "dry mountain-rice." She was a daughter of Batara Guru, who changed her into a rice stalk because she fell in love with a mortal—who was also transformed in pity for his sorrow. Java and Bali, Indonesia. (Hatt, 1951: 885; Geertz, 1960: 81)

Tlaloc The Aztec god of rain and lightning was also a god of vegetation and growth, generally beneficent but sometimes destructive. The chief god among the Olmecs. Mexico. (Caso, 1958: 41–43; Vaillant, 1962: 145)

Toafa *See* **Fonge**

Tobi The "Great Snake, Tobi, from whose ashes sprang all cultivated plants." The Shipaya, Brazil. (Nimuendaju, 1948, 3: 241)

Toda Diya A deity worshipped at the Bidri festival celebrated before the sowing of seeds. The Gonds, India. (Kurup, 1970: 162)

Toga God of the plants, "as well as the creatures of the woods." Vahitahi Island, Tuamotus, Polynesia. (Stimson, 1933: 59)

Toharu God of food and of vegetation invoked in the Hako ceremony. The Pawnee, Nebraska. (Fletcher, 1900/01: 31; Wallis, 1939: 139)

Toi-kuru-puni-kuru A god of vegetation whose wife is Toi-kuru-puni-mat. The Ainu, Japan. (Batchelor, 1925, 1: 243)

Toi-kuru-puni-mat Goddess of vegetation. The Ainu, Japan. (Batchelor, 1925, 1: 243)

Tonak-lha-tsen-karbu A god of the soil, protective of the Thaktu clan. The Sherpas, Nepal. (Furer-Haimendorf, 1964: 21–22)

Totonaca The flower god. Vera Cruz, Mexico. (Museum of Anthropology, Mexico City: Exh. 12/72)

Toyoki-iri-hiko-no-mikoto Son of Sujin-tenno, "credited with spreading agriculture in the region of Shimotsuke and for that reason worshiped in the Futara-san-jinja." Japan. (Herbert, 1967: 413)

Toyo-uga-no-me A Japanese food deity. (Herbert, 1967: 510)

Toyouke-Daijin A Shinto goddess of food. Japan. (Kato, 1926: 40)

Toyo-Uke-Hime-no-Kami The great goddess of foods, of cereals. Also called Ogetsuhime-no-Kami and Uka-no-Mitama. Japan. (Kato, 1926: 17, 73; Yasumaro, 1965: 16–18; Revon, 1925, 9: 239–240)

Triptolemus A young Greek god (once human), foster son of Demeter and Persephone. From the former he received grain to bring to the world and introduced the arts of agriculture. He is shown with a plow. Through Persephone he is associated with the underworld. (Campbell, 1964: 49; Morford and Lenardon, 1975: 210)

Ts'an Hua Wu Shêng The very important "Five Patron-Sages of the Silkworm in its early stages, when it is most susceptible to destructive influences." China. (Day, 1940: 107)

The Ts'an Sha Evil Spirits who cause disease in the silkworms. China. (Day, 1940: 108)

Tsi'ty'icots'a Goddess of salt, of Zuñi Salt Lake. The Keresan, New Mexico. (Tyler, 1964: 190)

Ts'u-ga-shi God of the grain in the fields. His wife is Shi. The Ch'iang, Szechwan, China. (Graham, 1958: 47)

Tsze Kou Chinese goddess of manure. (Du Bose, n.d.: 340)

Tu In Mangareva the god of the breadfruit tree and its fertility; not a god of war. (Buck, 1938, 2: 203; 1938, 1: 422) In Hawaii (Ku) he was the god of agriculture, of the harvest; also "God of Friendship . . . of War . . . of Wrath" and a god of judgment. Polynesia. (Melville, 1969: 28, 34–35)

Tudava A culture hero type of being of the Trobrianders who taught them gardening. Melanesia. (Poignant, 1967: 91)

T'u Fu Shen Chun A god of the farms invoked for good harvests. Another name for T'u Ti Lao Yeh. China. (Day, 1940: 65, 208)

Tugadan ud Baiya An agricultural deity at Baiya. Philippines. (Barton, 1946: 38)

Tukka A spirit invoked or propitiated at the beginning of the planting of a field. The Isneg, Luzon, Philippines. (Vanoverbergh, 1941: 315)

Tumanglag A god who causes the rice not to develop properly. The Ifugao, Philippines. (Barton, 1946: 31)

Tupiringini The honey-man of the Tiwi. Melville Island, Australia. (Mountford, 1958: 33)

Tupo A god of tumeric. Mangareva, Polynesia. (Buck, 1938, 1: 426)

Túrliue The goddess of the source of the Rio Surivaka is also a goddess of the field crops. The Kagaba, Colombia. (Preuss, 1926: 84)

T'u Ti Fu Jen A goddess, guardian of the grain, and wife of T'u Ti Lao Yeh. China. (Day, 1940: 65)

T'u Ti Lao Yeh God of the soil whose wife is T'u Ti Fu Jen. Also known under the names of T'u Ti Cheng Shen, T'u Fu Shen Chun, Tang Ching T'u Ti, Tang Ching T'u Chu. China. (Day, 1940: 65)

Tutilina Roman goddess of agriculture, of the stored grain, as well as having "power over the seeds beneath and above the ground." Associated with Consus. (Dumézil, 1966, 1: 267–268; Schrader, 1925, 2: 32; Campbell, 1964: 321)

Tyi wara God of the young field workers invoked for strength and health. He was "half man and half animal—usually a roan antelope—who long ago taught men to farm." The Bambara, Mali, Niger, and Senegal. (Tauxier, 1927: 325; Imperato, 1975: 70)

Tzu Kou Chinese goddess of manure. Also Tsze Kou. (Werner, 1932: 305)

Uaxac-yol-kauil Mayan maize god. Mexico. (Roys, 1965: 9; Thompson, 1970: 289)

Ubertas, Uberitas   Roman deity of agricultural prosperity. (Roscher, 1965, 6: 2; Ferguson, 1970: 73)

Ubsansaguila   The "origin of cotton." The Cuna Indians, Panama. (Nordenskiold, 1930: 20–21)

Uch   A supernatural being associated with the growth of the maize. The Tzeltal, Mexico. (Villa Rojas, 1969: 223)

Ugadama   The goddess of food is identified with Dosojin. She was killed by Susano-o and from her body grew millet, a silkworm and mulberry tree, grass, rice seed, barley, beans, "and the head changed into a horse and cow." Her death "is a symbolic returning to the earth of that which grew from it," assuring the productivity of the land. Japan. (Czaja, 1974: 29, 216, 240)

Uga-no-Mitama-no-Kami   Also known as Ugadama. She is the "spirit of rice in the storehouse," and is the primary deity of the Inari cults. She is the daughter of Susano-o and Kamu-Oichi-hime, though she is also said to have been created by Izanagi and Izanami. Japan. (Czaja, 1974: 253, 255, 258)

Uga-Shinno, Uga-no-kami   God of the five cereals, also identified with Ben-zai-ten. Japan. (Puini and Dickens, 1880: 443)

Uka-no-Mitama-no-kami   The god of food, son of Hayasusa-no-Wo-no-Mikoto by Kamuoichihime. Japan. (Yasumaro, 1965: 36; Holtom, 1938: 183)

Uke-Mochi-no-Kami   Goddess of food and of plenty. Japan. (Yasumaro, 1928: 25; Holtom, 1938: 144; Saunders, 1961: 423)

Uma   Goddess of the corn and of germination. India. (Bhattacharji, 1970: 161; Danielou, 1964: 285) In Bali, the goddess of the rice seed and of its germination. (Levi, 1933: xxviii; Grader, 1960: 167)

Umamu, nak Ampual   A god invoked in harvest and granary rites. The Ifugao, Philippines. (Barton, 1946: 32)

Umanao   A god who "makes the rice like the anao palm, which has no fruit." The Ifugao, Philippines. (Barton, 1946: 31)

Umudhok   " 'Borer'—*udhok* is a worm that attacks the stem of the rice plant." A god of the sky world and son of Umamu. The Ifugao, Philippines. (Barton, 1946: 31)

Uras   God of planting, an aspect of Ninip. The Elamites, area of Susa, Near East. (Pinches, 1925, 5: 251)

Urvara   A god of plants and of fields whose blessings are invoked. Iran and India. (Gray, 1930: 223; Macdonell, 1897: 138)

Uti Hiata   Mother Corn. The Pawnee, Plains Indians, Nebraska. (Burland, 1965: 149)

Utset   The earth and the goddess-mother of corn. The Sia and the Keresan, New Mexico. (Hatt, 1951: 858; Parsons, 1939: 182)

U'uhoa   Goddess of the coconut. The Marquesas, Polynesia. (Handy, 1923: 246). A god according to Christian. (1895: 190)

Vacuna   A Sabine goddess of agriculture, protective of the fields. Italy. (Prentice Hall, 1965: 147; Larousse, 1968: 214)

Veltha, Veltune   A "god with strange and contrasting attributes, represented at times as a maleficent monster, at others as a vegetation god of uncertain sex, or even as a mighty war god." Italy. (Pallottino, 1975: 141)

Venus   The goddess of love was earlier an old Italian goddess of vegetation and of gardens. (Fairbanks, 1907: 207–208)

Vertumnus   Roman god of fruits in all stages of growth, associated with Pomona. (Fairbanks, 1907: 251–252; Murray, 1935: 145; Larousse, 1968: 211)

Vervactor   Roman god of the first plowing. (Dumézil, 1966, 1: 35; Campbell, 1964: 320; Ferguson, 1970: 68)

Victa   Roman goddess of food, nourishment. (Roscher, 1965, 2, 1: 231)

Vinotonus   A "God of Vines," identified with Silvanus. Britain. (Ross, 1967: 377)

Virankannos   A Finno-Ugric god of agriculture, protective of the oats. (Krohn, 1925, 6: 24; MacCulloch, 1964: 244)

Vis   The earth, who was invoked for good harvests. Peru. (Alexander, 1920: 223; Markham, 1969: 122)

Volutina   Roman goddess of agriculture, of the grain's blades. (Hadas, 1965: 122; Roscher, 1965, 2, 1: 233)

Waizganthos   A god of agriculture, of fruitfulness. The Letts and the Lithuanians. (Welsford, 1925, 9: 242)

Wakasaname-no-Kami Goddess of the transplanting of the rice. Daughter of Hayamato-no-Kami and Oketsuhime-no-Kami. Japan. (Yasumaro, 1965: 51; Herbert, 1967: 333)

Wakatoshi-no-Kami God of "the young harvest." Son of Hayamato-no-Kami and Oketsuhime-no-Kami. Japan. (Herbert, 1967: 333; Yasumaro, 1965: 51)

Waka-uka-no-me-no-mikoto A young goddess of food, associated with rain. Also known as Oimi-no-kami or Hirose-no-kawaai-no-kami. Japan. (Herbert, 1967: 509)

Wakumusubi-no-Kami God of grains and of growth, father of Toyo-Uke-Hime-no-Kami. Japan. (Yasumaro, 1965: 16–17; Herbert, 1967: 268; Holtom, 1938: 116–117)

Wañka The guardians of the cultivated fields. Inca, Peru. (Rowe, 1946, 2: 297)

Waren la Father of rice and cotton. Son of Phungkam Janun. The Katchins, Burma. (Gilhodes, 1908: 678)

Wau-uno The spirit of the tobacco seeds. The Warao, Guiana. Same as Anura (Arawak). (Levi-Strauss, 1973: 426)

Wawm, Chinwawm An agricultural deity who can only be worshipped by the chiefs. The Kachin, Burma. (Temple, 1925, 3: 23)

Wayu A deity of the rites of the millet harvest. The Jukun, Nigeria. (Meek, 1931: 284)

We'haiya A god invoked for protection from the locusts, with appropriate sacrifices. The Isala, Ghana. (Rattray, 1932, 1932: 512)

Whanui A stellar god, Vega, who provided the tuber kumara and is invoked for abundant food. The Maori, New Zealand. (Best, 1924: 133, 279; Mackenzie, n.d.: 316–317)

Whitte-ko-ka-gah The god of grass or weeds. The Dakotah, Plains Indians, West Minnesota. (Schoolcraft, 1857: 486; Emerson, 1884: 426)

(Sang Yang) Widi A deity in the village of Kubutambahan to whom a shrine is set up in land clearing. Bali, Indonesia. (Grader, 1969, 1: 147)

Winaghakan A rice-pest deity. The Ifugao, Philippines. (Barton, 1946: 31)

Winwina A supernatural who "brings salmon and berries from . . . the extreme west." The Bella Coola, British Columbia. (McIlwraith, 1948, 1: 54)

xashcheltihi, xa·ctče·ltihi, xaščelt^xi'i Talking God who is in control of game and corn. In his solar capacity as a god of the dawn and of the east, he is associated with Blanca Peak, as of the twilight with San Francisco Peak. The Navaho, Arizona and New Mexico. (Reichard, 1950: 50, 77–78, 476–477; Haile, 1947: 3, 6, 93)

Xcacau, Ixcacau Goddess/god of the cacao. The Quiché, Guatemala. (Recinos, 1950: 125; Girard, 1970: 132–133)

Xcanil The goddess of grain. The Quiché, Guatemala. (Recinos, 1950: 125) An agrarian deity who prepares the maize. Feminine in Chorti (Ixcanil), masculine in Quiché. Guatemala. (Girard, 1979: 132–133)

Xcuinána, Ixcuinána The "first woman . . . [who is credited with] the origin of maize cultivation." The Huastec (Mayan), Vera Cruz, Mexico. (Girard, 1979: 221)

Xilonen The goddess of maize, of the young growth, and of youth and games. The Aztec, Mexico. (Vaillant, 1962: 145; Spence, 1923: 221; Burland, 1967: 75)

Ximbanonan, Gimbangonan A benevolent spirit of the rice harvesting helpful to the reapers. The Isneg, Luzon, Philippines. (Vanoverbergh, 1941: 338)

Xinalinan A benevolent, helpful spirit of the rice harvesting. The Isneg, Luzon, Philippines. (Vanoverbergh, 1941: 338)

Xinuudan A spirit "driven away at the beginning of the harvest, lest he come to measure the receptacles for the palay (rice in the husk or paddy), and the latter dwindle." The Isneg, Luzon, Philippines. (Vanoverbergh, 1941: 339)

Xipe, Xipe Totec The Flayed God whose springtime costume of the flayed skin of a sacrificial victim represented the renewal, the new covering of vegetation, and the shedding of the seed covering in the germination and sprouting of the new growth. God of the planting season. The Aztec, Mexico. (Vaillant, 1962: 145; Burland, 1967: xi; Spence, 1923: 154, 213, 218; Caso, 1958: 49, 51)

X'ob The mother of maize, daughter of Chauc, the rain god. The Tzotzil, Mexico. (Thompson, 1970: 268, 286)

Xochipilli, Cinteotl, Macuilxochtli   The young god of the maize and of flowers, of youth and love and gaiety. Husband of Mayahuel. The Aztec, Mexico. (Alexander, 1920: 54; Neumann, 1955: 196; Vaillant, 1962: 145, 149; Nicholson, 1967: 44)

Xochiquetzal   The feminine counterpart of Xochipilli. She was the goddess of maize and of flowers, of all vegetation; represented the fertility and fruitfulness of nature. She was the goddess of love, of sexuality, illicit love, and harlots as well as of marriage, pregnancy and childbirth. She was also the goddess of artisans who depict nature in their crafts. The Aztec, Mexico. (Spence, 1923: 154, 190, 195; Duran, 1971: 238–239, 296; Alexander, 1920: 77–78; Neumann, 1955: 196–197; Caso, 1958: 26, 29; Vaillant, 1962: 145, 149)

Xtoj, Ixtoj   An agrarian deity who prepares the maize. Male in Quiché, female in Chorti. Guatemala. (Girard, 1979: 132–133)

Xusin   A spirit invoked or propitiated at the beginning of the planting of a field. The Isneg, Luzon, Philippines. (Vanoverbergh, 1941: 1: 315)

Yachimato-hiko   A phallic god associated with agriculture and Dionysian festivals. He is also a god of the crossroads, protective of travelers. Japan. (Kato, 1926: 31; MacCulloch, 1925, 4: 332; Revon, 1925, 9: 237; Herbert, 1967: 495)

Yachimata-hime   A goddess associated with agriculture and with Dionysian festivals. A goddess of travel, of the crossroads, protective of travelers. Japan. (Kato, 1926: 31; Revon, 1925, 9: 237; MacCulloch, 1925, 4: 332; Herbert, 1967: 495)

yaHwal   The guardian of the cornfields. The Tzeltal, Mexico. (Blom and La Farge, 1927: 368)

Yalode   A goddess worshipped by women at the harvest rites, to whom cowrie shells and a ram are offered at the Yam festival. She causes foot infections. Dahomey. (Herskovits, 1938, 2: 155, 274, 407: 1967, 1: 37)

Yang sori   A harvest goddess who lives in the sky with Bok Glaih. The Bahnar, Indochina. (Cabaton, 1925, 7: 230)

Yin-hung   A god of the harvest, and a god of grain. China. (Werner, 1932: 415; Ferguson, 1937: 66–67)

Yini   The supreme being and sky god is also considered the god of the harvest and giver of abundance through his control of the rains. His wife is Tenga, Ten'gono. The Nankanse, Gold Coast, Ghana. (Rattray, 1932, 1: 45; 1932, 2: 307, 320, 335; Williams, 1936: 44)

Yinukatsisdai   The god of acorns and vegetable foods. The Hupa Indians. Same as Megwomets of the Yurok, California. (Kroeber, 1925: 134; Goddard, 1903: 77)

Yueh Fu T'ai Yin   The goddess of the moon is also the goddess of harvests, of the months, and of the tides. China. (Day, 1940: 78)

Yum Kaax   The young corn god of the Mayan, also called Ghanan, and identified with Centeotl. He was always associated with fruitfulness and life. (Nicholson, 1967: 119, 126–127; Morley, 1946: 225–226). Thompson believes him a god of the forest rather than of maize. (Thompson, 1970: 289)

Yumyum   An agricultural deity at Namtogan. The Ifugao, Philippines. (Barton, 1946: 37)

Yun Chung   The god who drives away the locusts. China. (Shryock, 1931: 126)

Zac Talah   A Mayan god worshipped "before firing, planting, and harvesting milpas." Vicinity of Chichen Itza, Mexico. (Thompson, 1970: 327)

Zaramama   The goddess of maize. Peru. (Hatt, 1951: 877; Karsten, 1926: 319)

Zatik   A Semitic god introduced into Armenia. "Was probably a vegetation god, like Adonis, whose resurrection began at the winter solstice and was complete in the spring." (Ananikian, 1964: 40–41)

Zelus   A god of agricultural fertility, of the grass. Lithuania. (Gray, 1930: 140)

Zemiennik   A Litu-Prussian god to whom a harvest offering of an animal was made in October. (Schrader, 1925, 2: 41)

Zeus   On Crete he was a god of vegetation representing its death and rebirth cycle. Greece. (Fairbanks, 1907: 143; Willetts, 1962: 199, 202)

Zhing lha (pr. **Shinglha**)   God of the fields. Tibet. (Tucci, 1980: 166)

Zia Edutzi, Zia Tata, Zia-baba   The god of maize. The Takanan and the Araona, Bolivia. (Métraux, 1942: 41)

Zic-Ahau   The god of tobacco. The Quiché, Guatemala. (Girard, 1979: 98)

Zmyrna Greek personification of seasonings and spices, invoked for the magic of love. (Roscher, 1965, 6: 762)

Zosim The Slavonic god of bees. (Larousse, 1968: 291)

Zum Dishin Dirlun Tengeri The second spirit of Delquen Sagan Burkan, father of the 44 Tengeris. He was invoked "for rain, good crops, and children." The Mongol, Buriat, Siberia. (Curtin, 1909: 118)

27

Deities of Domesticated Animals

Adar The solar god was also the "lord of the swine," which would seem to have been the sacred animal in the city of Nipur. Babylonia, Near East. (Sayce, 1898: 287)

Agam The god of cattle to whom a pig and chickens are offered for their welfare and increase. The Minyong Abors and the Adi, Northeastern India. (Furer-Haimendorf, 1954: 595; Chowdhury, 1971: 43–44)

Aikushi A god invoked for help in cattle diseases and troubles. An Eastern Tengri whose wife is Almoshi. The Trans-Baikal Buriats, Siberia. (Klementz, 1925, 3: 5)

Akerbeltz A beneficent god represented in the form of a black goat. He had curative faculties toward animals commended to his protection. Also known as Akelarre. The Basque, Spain and France. (Barandiaran, 1972: 22)

Alasan-pas A Finno-Ugrian horse god. The Mordvins, Russia. (Paasonen, 1925, 8: 846)

Almoshi The wife of Aikushi and invoked with him to alleviate cattle diseases and troubles. The Trans-Baikal Buriats, Siberia. (Klementz, 1925, 3: 5)

Amaka An anthorpomorphic deity who "gave people the domesticated reindeer, taught them how to use fire, invented the tools with which they worked and created everything else which is on the earth." The Evenks, Siberia. (Michael, 1963: 160)

Amakandu The Sumero-Akkadian "god of animal husbandry." Son of Haharni and Earth. Near East. (Albright, 1968: 95–97)

Amimisol The spirit protective of chickens. In the Central Valley he also cares for the domestic pigs. The Bukidnon, Mindanao, Philippines. (Cole, 1956: 95)

Anana-gunda The goddess of bees. The Abkhasians, Caucasus. (Janashia, 1937: 146)

Aristaios, Aristaeus God of animal husbandry, of flocks and herds, of bees, and of agriculture. He was endowed as well with the powers of magical healing. Considered a son of Apollo and Kyrene. Thessaly, Greece. (Kerenyi, 1951: 142; Jayne, 1962: 310; Fairbanks, 1907: 168)

Ashtharthet, Ashtoreth A lion-headed goddess and goddess of horses, introduced from Syria. She was also a goddess of the moon and of war. Egypt. (Budge, 1969, 2: 278–279)

Atchshe-shyashyana An aspect, or "part," of Ayt'ar as "god of horses." The Abkhasians, Caucasus. (Janashia, 1937: 129)

Austheia Lithuanian goddess of bees. (Welsford, 1925, 9: 242; Schrader, 1925, 2: 31)

Ayathrim "('Home-Coming'), . . . originally ruled over the return of the shepherd and his flocks." Iran. (Gray, 1930: 139)

Ayt'ar A god of procreation primarily involved with the breeding of cattle. The Abkhasians, Caucasus. (Janashia, 1937: 121, 139)

Babilos Teutonic god of bees. The Smogits. (Grimm, 1888: 1497)

Badhan A god of cattle and a hill spirit of the Doms. India. (Briggs, 1953: 480)

Bagan Slavic "guardian of the herds, taking up his quarters in a little crib filled for his benefit with hay." Russia. (Ralston, 1872: 125)

Bagharra Deo   The tiger god was worshipped to protect the cattle from wild animals. The Kawar, Central Provinces, India. (Russell, 1916, 3: 399)

Baghsunath   A snake godling who guards the cattle and the springs. Kangra, India. (Crooke, 1894: 264)

Ba glang lha   The god of oxen was worshipped mainly by the nomads. Tibet. (Nebesky-Wojkowitz, 1956, 1: 306)

Balindra   The god of cattle of the Pavras of Khandesh. India. (Crooke, 1925, 5: 19)

Basajaun   A spirit of the forest who is also the protector of the flocks of sheep. His presence is announced by the shaking and sounding of the bells of the ewes, which indicates they are safe from wolves. The Basque, Spain and France. (Barandiaran, 1972: 57)

Basava   The bull god associated with the worship of Siva and believed to bring rain to relieve drought. Karnataka, India. (Ishwaran, 1974: 30, 34; Dubois, 1906: 638)

Bato-kannon   The Buddhist god and guardian of horses. Japan. (Hori, 1968: 66; Getty, 1962: 162; Eliot, 1935: 140)

Baubis   Litu-Prussian god of oxen and of cows. (Schrader, 1925, 2: 31; Welsford, 1925, 9: 242)

Beg-ts'e   The "God of War and Protector of Horses." Tibet. (Getty, 1962: 151)

Belet   An ancestral god of the Nuba who provides for the fertility of cattle and men, and also provides agricultural fertility with rain. Sudan. (Seligman, 1925, 9: 403)

Bhainsasur   The buffalo god is invoked for good crops, is worshipped when a cow runs dry, and before fishing. India. (Russell, 1916, 3: 513; Crooke, 1925, 11: 872; 1925, 12: 716)

Bhairom   A god of the Chamars who is guardian of the cattle and the fields—a form of Siva. The Punjab, India. (Briggs, 1920: 156)

Bharwan   The guardian of cattle. The Gadbas, Central Provinces, India. (Russell, 1916, 3: 12)

Bicziu birbullis   A Litu-Prussian deity concerned with bees. (Schrader, 1925, 2: 31)

Birnath   God of cattle of the Ahir. United Provinces, India. (Crooke, 1925, 1: 233)

St. Blaise   Slavic "patron saint of herds." Russia. (Welsford, 1925, 9: 252)

'Bri lha   God of the tame yak worshipped mainly by the nomads. Tibet. (Nebesky-Wojkowitz, 1956, 1: 306)

Sidi Bu'beid s-Sarqi   Patron saint of equestrians. Morocco. (Westermarck, 1926, 1: 180)

Bubona   Roman goddess of cattle and of herdsmen. Italy. (Woodcock, 1953: 28; Roscher, 1965, 2, 1: 193)

lCam-srin   A god and guardian of horses and also a god of war. Tibet. (Getty, 1962: 151; Nebesky-Wojkowitz, 1956, 1: 23)

Catachillay   A constellation (near Lyra), and a smaller one, said to be a llama and offspring "descended from Urcuchillay." Paratía, Peru. (Flores-Ochoa, 1979: page opposite Contents)

Challalamma   A village goddess in Masulipatam who presides over buttermilk. Telugu, Southern India. (Whitehead, 1916: 21)

Chamar   A god of the Kachhi who must be propitiated or he "stops the milk of cows and buffaloes." India. (Crooke, 1925, 7: 634)

Chaumu, or **Baudhan**   Guardian of cattle in Kumaun. Among the Doms protective of herdsmen. India. (Crooke, 1925, 5: 8; Briggs, 1953: 480)

Chlevnik   The name of the household spirit (Domovoj) "when he lives in the cattle shed." It is important that he should approve of a new animal, and like the cattle. Slavic Russia. (Mansikka, 1925, 4: 627)

Chu-chüan Shên   "The God of Pigsties." China. (Werner, 1932: 93)

Chumu   The protector of herds and flocks of the Himalayan Doms. India. (Crooke, 1925, 4: 842)

Chungu   A tree-dwelling demon who "sucks the milk of cattle, and is propitiated with an offering of a coconut." The Ahir, India. (Crooke, 1925, 1: 233)

Chu T'u Ti   An aspect of T'u Ti as protector of cows and pigs. China. (Day, 1940: 67)

Chu Wang   Patron deity for pigs. China. (Day, 1940: 106)

Dalogdogan   A god invoked to protect the chickens from hawks and iguanas. Son of Kidul. The Ifugao, Philippines. (Barton, 1946: 30)

Debetsoi   The third shepherd of Esseghe-Malan-Tengri who is guardian of the flocks. The Buriats, Siberia. (Klementz, 1925, 3: 4)

Dervaspa, Gosh   "Is the soul of the bull . . . guardian of cattle." Persia. (Huart, 1963: 42)

Dishai Devi   The "goddess of the sheep-pen." It seems to be indicated that she "is the deified sheep." The Gadaria, Central Provinces, India. (Russell, 1916, 3: 6)

Doddiganga   The guardian of cattle who "is worshipped when the herds are driven into the forests to graze." The Konda Dora, Southern India. (Thurston, 1909, 3: 355)

Dola Yaka   The patron of honey collecting. The Vedda, Ceylon. (Seligmann and Seligmann, 1911: 153)

Donn   Celtic god of the dead who has as one of his aspects the guardian of cattle. Ireland. (MacCana, 1970: 43)

Drvaspa   A goddess who keeps cattle and horses in good health. Iran. (Gray, 1930: 73; Jayne, 1962: 191)

Dudhera   A "godling worshipped for the protection of cattle . . . represented by a clay horse placed near a white ant-hill." The Gowari, Central Provinces, India. (Russell, 1916, 3: 163)

Dumuzi   The Sumerian shepherd-god, guardian of the sheep-folds built by Enki. Also considered an agricultural chthonic deity concerned with fertility and the renewal of life. Near East. (Jastrow, 1898: 96–97; James, 1960: 78; Ferm, 1950: 60)

Duttur   Sumerian "goddess of the ewe"—mother of Dumuzi in the shepherd's pantheon. Near East. (Jacobsen, 1970: 29)

mDzo lha   The "god of the mongrel-breed of a yak-bull and a cow"—worshipped mainly by the nomads. Tibet. (Nebesky-Wojkowitz, 1956, 1: 306)

egeci deguu   A Dharmapala, Defender of the Law, who is also a god protective of horses, and a god of war. Mongolia. Same as Beg-ts'e. (Getty, 1962: 151)

Elo   The high god of the Nuba who is invoked for the fertility of their cattle, their livelihood. Sudan. (Seligman, 1925, 9: 403)

Emelgelji   The guardian of the cattle. The Buryats and the Mongols, Siberia. (Waddell, 1959: 372)

Enakhsys   A goddess harmful to cattle who must be propitiated. The Yaku, Lena Basin, Siberia. (Keane, 1925, 2: 121)

Enlulim   The god of the flocks of goats of the temple, whose concern is the quantity of milk and butter. Lagash, Near East. (Jacobsen, 1946: 202)

Ensignun   The caretaker of Ningirsu's donkeys and chariot, his charioteer. Lagash, Mesopotamia, Near East. (Jacobsen, 1946: 202)

Epona   Gallic goddess of horses, very widespread, and adopted by the Romans. Also considered one of the mother goddesses and associated with fertility. (Ross, 1967: 198, 206; Schoeps, 1961: 117; Renel, 1906: 397; MacCulloch, 1911: 213)

Eratinis   Litu-Prussian god of sheep. (Schrader, 1925, 2: 31)

Faunus   Roman god of the woodlands and fields, of pasturage, and of livestock and their fertility. Son of Picus, grandson of Saturn. As Fatuus a god of healing and of prophecy, healing with oracles and magical remedies. (Fairbanks, 1907: 247–248; Dumézil, 1966, 1: 344–345; Bulfinch, 1898: 16; Jayne, 1962: 422–423)

Fradat-fsu   A god of small cattle and their increase. Iran. (Gray, 1930: 144)

Ganyklos   Litu-Prussian god of the pasture lands of cattle. (Schrader, 1925, 2: 31)

Ganzio   Etruscan god of horses. Italy. (Leland, 1963: 118)

Geus Tašan   The creator of cattle. Iran. (Gray, 1930: 146)

Geus Urvan   "Soul of the Kine"—guardian of animals. He also seems to represent atmospheric phenomena. Iran. (Gray, 1930: 79–81)

Ghangra   The bell god (of cattle). The Gond, Central Provinces, India. (Russell, 1916, 3: 99)

Ghasi Sadhak   "A godling who lives by the peg to which horses are tied in the stable." The Ghasia, Central Provinces, India. (Russell, 1916, 3: 30)

Ghor Deo, Ghora Dev   The horse god. The Gond, the Bhils, and the Rajput, Gujarat, India. (Russell, 1916, 3: 97; Grierson, 1925, 2: 555; Crooke, 1925, 5: 8)

Goensali Nad The guardian spirit of cattle. Oraon, India. (Roy, 1928: 79)

Goheli Penu God of the stable who is protective against tigers. The Kandhs, Madras, India. (Crooke, 1925, 7: 651)

Goniglis Dziewos A god of herds. Lithuania. (Gimbutas, 1974: 90)

Gopal and **Govind** (**Gopala Krsna** in Eastern India) Names of Krishna as the guardian of cows. The Ahir, Central Provinces, India. (Russell, 1916, 2: 29; Heeramaneck, 1966: 77)

Goraiya A god of cattle and of boundaries who governs the herds. He is also a god of bandits. The Kharwars and the Doms, India. (Briggs, 1953: 466; Crooke, 1925, 5: 8)

Gotha Lithuanian-Prussian deity of the propagation of cattle, given as both god and goddess. (Gray, 1930: 144; Schrader, 1925, 2: 31)

Govind *See* **Gopal.**

Gunga A demon of cattle disease who is propitiated. The Ahir, India. (Crooke, 1925, 1: 233)

Guraya Deo God of the village cattle-stalls worshipped annually. The Ahir, Central Provinces, India. (Russell, 1916, 2: 31)

Hadakai A goddess who "controls mad dogs and prevents hydrophobia." Gujarat, India. (Crooke, 1894: 70)

Hayagriva The horse-necked god and the fierce protector of horses—generally male, but sometimes female. In Tibet known as rta-mgrin. In Buddhism a Dharmapala, Defender of the Law. His sakti is Marici. Known also in Mongolia. (Getty, 1962: 162; Hackin, 1963: 167–168; Snellgrove, 1961: 78)

Hermes Greek god and guardian of flocks and herds, concerned with their fertility and welfare. He is more commonly known as the god of travelers, of tradesmen and merchants, of all gain (whether good or bad), and as a messenger of the gods. Son of Zeus and Maia. (Barthell, 1971: 33–37; Cox, 1870, 2: 226–227; Schoeps, 1961: 131; Fairbanks, 1907: 195–197)

Hippo Greek goddess associated with horses. Daughter of Tethys and Oceanus. (Kerenyi, 1951: 41)

Hobnil The Bacab of the East is the chief god of apiarists; the other Bacabs to a lesser extent. Also a god

of the Kan years. Mayan Mexico. (Bancroft, 1886, 2: 699; Thompson, 1970: 276–277; Tozzer, 1941: 157, 164)

Holera Deo The god and guardian of cattle. The Baiga and the Gond. Among the latter he is "represented by a wooden bullock's bell." India. (Russell, 1916, 3: 97; Elwin, 1939: 61)

Honidlo Serbian or Bohemian god of herdsmen. (Grimm, 1883, 2: 750)

Howen Wana Mata A deity who guards cattle "against murrain and lameness." The Bhils, India. (Coleman, 1832: 383)

Hsien Mu A god of horses and their pasturing, invoked to fatten them. He is subordinate to Ma Wang. China. (Werner, 1932: 301)

Huang Ch'u-p'ing, Hwang Tsuping The god of sheep. China. (Werner, 1932: 416; Du Bose, n.d.: 324)

Huasa Mallcu God of the high savannahs who, with the field spirits, owns the domestic animals. The Aymara, Peru. (Tschopik, 1946: 132; Trimborn, 1968, 2: 560)

Huitranalhue A god of herds who protects them from thieves. The Araucanian, Chile. (Alexander, 1920: 329; Chamberlain, 1900: 57)

Hularia A god who protects the cattle from disease and wild animals. He is made offerings of goats. The Golars, Central Provinces, India. (Russell, 1916, 3: 37)

Huldra A Scandinavian goddess who was the head of the wood nymphs who were the protectors of the herds on the mountain sides. They loved gaiety and dancing and sought the company of mortals. (Guerber, 1895: 60)

Hulle Norse goddess of cattle-grazing and milking. (Grimm, 1880: 272)

Hundi, Bursung Wife of Maoli. Together they protect cattle from disease and danger. India. (Elwin, 1950: 154)

Igarobandur The chief of the dogs whose wife is Oloupi-kunyae. The Cuna, Panama. (Nordenskiold, 1938: 299)

Illibem berti, paduri Mother and "ruler of both domestic and wild reindeer." The Samoyeds, Siberia. (Larousse, 1973: 437)

Illibium Parche   God of animals, particularly of reindeer. The Yurak Samoyed, Siberia. (Czaplicka, 1925, 11: 175)

Imana   The highest deity of the Batussi is primarily the protector of the cattle, and a god of fertility. Burundi. (Meyer, 1916: 60, 87)

Inuus   An early god of procreation associated with the breeding of animals, later extended to humans. Italy. (Roscher, 1965, 2, 1: 262; Jayne, 1962: 424; Murray, 1935: 150)

Ira-waru   Deity of dogs. The Maori, New Zealand. (Andersen, 1928: 211)

Izykh-Khan   God of cattle of the Kachins of Siberia. (Potapov, 1964: 358)

Jabal   God of flocks. Son of Lumha. Sumer, Near East. (Langdon, 1931: 105)

Jabran   Deity of goats and sheep. The Abkhasians, Caucasus. (Janashia, 1937: 120–121)

Jurgis   God of sheep. Latvia. (Jonval, 1929: 18)

Kagoro   God of cattle and of their fertility. Also a god of thunder. The Banyoro, Uganda. (Roscoe, 1915: 92; Mbiti, 1970, 2; 117)

Kalbisht, Kaluwa   The protector of herds and flocks, and of herdsmen, from wild beasts. The Doms, India. (Crooke, 1925, 4: 842; Briggs, 1953: 480)

Kaldas-ava   Finno-Ugric goddess of the cattle-yard. The Mordvins, Russia. (Paasonen, 1925, 8: 846)

Kalimata   Goddess of the cow-shed. The Santals, India. (Mukherjea, 1962: 253)

Kanaka Durgamma   The goddess of cattle and of their welfare invoked to protect them from disease. India. (Elmore, 1915: 54–56)

Kane-ulu-po   The *moa* (common fowl) worshipped as an ancestor god. Hawaii. (Emerson, 1967: 49)

Karvaitis   A Litu-Prussian deity concerned with calves. (Schrader, 1925, 2: 31)

Kauka   God of cattle who guarded them from hoof disease. The Banyoro, Uganda. (Roscoe, 1915: 92)

Kharak Deo   The god of the khirkha where the cattle are assembled on going to and from pasture. Offerings of flour and butter are made to him when there is illness among the cattle. The Ahirs, Central Provinces, India. (Russell, 1916, 2: 31)

Khikh   A god of cattle invoked in the spring migration to the mountains, and also for their increase. The Abkhasians, Caucasus. (Janashia, 1937: 125)

Khir Bhawani   The "milk goddess" to whom springs are sacred. Kashmir. (Lawrence, 1895: 296–297)

Khorial Mater   A deity of the Bheels invoked to protect cattle from sickness and theft. India. (Coleman, 1832: 387)

Khut   The god of cattle. The Baiga, India. (Elwin, 1939: 61)

Khwova!na   The "mother of the bees" is invoked when looking for them. Elder wife of Gao!na. The !Kung Bushmen, Namibia. (Marshall, 1962: 226)

Kiaulai-Krukis   The god of swine of the Letts, Lithuanians, and Old Prussians. (Welsford, 1925, 9: 242)

Kigare   The god of cattle, very powerful, and concerned with their welfare. The Banyoro, Uganda. (Roscoe, 1915: 92)

Koda Deo, Kodapen   The horse god of the Gonds. They tattoo his image on their thighs to make them as strong as those of the horse. If they have pain or weakness they offer him a piece of saddle-cloth. Central Provinces, India. (Crooke, 1894: 319; Russell, 1916, 3: 126)

Kremara   The protector of pigs. Poland. (Larousse, 1968: 291)

Kremata   A Litu-Prussian deity of swine. (Schrader, 1925, 2: 31)

Krishna   The god of the cowherds worshipped by the cattle-men of the Central Provinces. The eighth avatar of Vishnu. India (Russell, 1916, 2: 29; 1916, 3: 205; Brown, 1961: 297)

Krukis   Slavic protector of domestic animals, and also the god of blacksmiths. God of swine of the Litu-Prussians. (Larousse, 1968: 290; Schrader, 1925, 2: 31)

Kukar Mari   The goddess guardian of dogs who must be propitiated by the profession of dog-slayers in the United Provinces. The Doms, India. (Crooke, 1925, 4: 841; Briggs, 1953: 552)

Kurdalagon An Ossetic god of cattle. Iran. (Gray, 1930: 146)

Kuribattraya The god of sheep worshipped near Barliar. The Kurumba, Southern India. (Thurston, 1909, 4: 167)

Kurm Pat The god of bees. Central Provinces, India. (Russell, 1925, 3: 314)

Kurwaichin Slavonic protector of lambs. Poland. (Larousse, 1968: 291)

Lactans Roman god—the milk giver. (Roscher, 1965, 2, 1: 201)

Lahar In Babylonia the goddess of sheep. (Langdon, 1931: 191) In Sumer the god of cattle. (James, 1960: 211; Hooke, 1963: 26) Near East.

Lan Ch'ien T'u Ti An aspect of t'u Ti as guardian of the stable. China. (Day, 1940: 67)

Lan Kan Hsing Chun "Star-God of the Corral." China. (Day, 1940: 106)

Lapchi A deity represented at the Rite of Summer celebrated to secure "the welfare of the herds." The Sherpas, Nepal. (Furer-Haimendorf, 1964: 209)

Larai majan Mother of domestic birds. Daughter of Phungkam Janun. The Katchins, Burma. (Gilhodes, 1908: 678)

Larum lawa Father of domestic birds. Son of Phungkam Janun. The Katchins, Burma. (Gilhodes, 1908: 678)

Li Hou Niu Wang The patron of cows. China. (Day, 1940: 106)

Ling-chu A pig god and god of their sties. China. (Maspero, 1963: 327)

Lisina A donkey goddess, daughter of Ninhursaga. Near East. (Jacobsen, 1976: 106)

Liu Ch'u Wu Sheng The "Five Sages of the Domestic Breeds," to whom offerings are made for their "safety and increase." China. (Day, 1940: 106)

Llama Mama Goddess of the flocks. The Inca, Peru. (Markham, 1969: 68)

Longyok A deity of the Sherpas represented in the Rite of Summer celebrated to secure "the welfare of the herds." Nepal. (Furer-Haimendorf, 1964: 209)

Lopemat Latvian mother of cattle. (Larousse, 1973: 422)

Lugal-E-mus The "name under which Dumuzi was worshipped in Bad-tibira." Near East. (Jacobsen, 1970: 336)

Lug lha The god of sheep worshipped mainly by the nomads. Tibet. (Nebesky-Wojkowitz, 1956: 1: 306)

Lupercus A Roman form of Pan who "taught them to employ dogs for the purpose of protecting the herds against wolves." A form of Faunus. (Murray, 1935: 150–151; Fairbanks, 1907: 248)

Madu-Ammal A goddess protective of the cattle. The Kadar, India. (Ehrenfels, 1952: 166)

Mahadeo Among the Mahakul Ahirs of Jashpur he is the buffalo. India. (Russell, 1916, 2: 32)

Mahton Baba A village guardian who protects men and cattle from famine and disease. The Doms, India. (Briggs, 1953: 469)

Mala Konda Swami A Dravidian village god associated with cattle herding. India. (Elmore, 1915: 106)

Malik A title or name of Nergal among the Assyrians in his more benevolent aspect as a god "of pastures, flocks, and the earth's fertility." (Langdon, 1931: 50)

Mallalamma A deity worshipped and invoked to protect the cattle from tigers and other animals. The Lambadi, Southern India. (Thurston, 1909, 4: 230)

Mallan A deity worshipped for the welfare of the cattle. The Kaniyan, Southern India. (Thurston, 1909, 3: 198)

Mallana Deva and **Mallani Devi** They are worshipped annually to guard the flocks from tigers and disease. The Kuramwar, Central Provinces, India. (Russell, 1916, 4: 54)

Mangara Deyo A deity invoked for the protection of cattle. The Sinhalese Vedda, Ceylon. (Seligmann and Seligmann, 1911: 177)

Maoli A god who, with his wife Hundi, protects cattle from disease and danger. The Bondo, India. (Elwin, 1950: 154)

Mara, Marsa, Marsava, Maritini The goddess of cows who guards and nourishes them. The mother of milk. Latvia. (Jonval, 1929: 18)

Mars In an early aspect he was closely associated with Silvanus as a guardian of the herds and pasturage, and the fields—in their prosperity. Rome. (Cox, 1870, 2: 311; Dumézil, 1966, 1: 235, 376)

Ma Shê A god of horses under Ma Wang, invoked in training them to be "good saddle-animals." China. (Werner, 1932: 301)

Matar Deo The god of the cattle enclosure in the jungle. Goats are sacrificed to him. The Ahirs, Central Provinces, India. (Russell, 1916, 2: 31)

Ma Wang God of horses (sometimes depicted as one) and of those involved with them in all ways. China. (Werner, 1932: 301; Graham, 1961: 186; Gamble, 1954: 400)

Mellona, Mellonia Roman goddess of apiculture and of honey. (Roscher, 1965, 2, 2: 2648; Ferguson, 1970: 69)

Mendes A goat god of ancient Egypt who was first "worshipped merely as a personification of the procreative energy," then later became a full-fledged god. (Eastlake, 1883: 261–262)

Mithu Bhukia God of the caste of carriers and drivers of pack-bullocks. The Banjara, Central Provinces, India. (Russell, 1916, 2: 176)

Mogol-Toyon With his wife the divinities of cattle. The Yakut, Siberia. (Czaplicka, 1969: 278)

Mokosh A Slavonic "god of small domestic animals." Vicinity of Kiev, Russia. (Larousse, 1968: 291)

Momo The god of bees. The Pueblo Indians, Arizona and New Mexico. (Burland, 1965: 132)

Moschel A Baltic god, protector of cows. Latvia. (Queval, 1968: 73)

Mullo The Celtic mule god, god of beasts of burden, identified with Mars. Gaul. (Renel, 1906: 401; Anwyl, 1906: 39; MacCulloch, 1911: 214)

Mundian A deity worshipped for the welfare of the cattle. The Kaniyan, Southern India. (Thurston, 1909, 3: 198)

Mundla Mudamma A Dravidian deity with power over herding cattle. India. (Elmore, 1915: 69)

Muni A deity worshipped for the protection of the cattle and for good crops. The Eravallar and the Kaniyan, Southern India. (Thurston, 1909, 2: 210, 215; 1909, 3: 198)

Ah Muzencab, XMulzencab The Maya bee god, or gods. Yucatan, Mexico. (Tozzer, 1941: 143; Thompson, 1970: 277, 311)

Naiteru-kop Some consider that it was he who "let cattle down from heaven," not Engai. He was the beneficent god who tried to give mankind immortality, but his instructions were not followed and death came into the world. The Masai, Kenya and Tanzania. (Frazer, 1926: 276)

Napuagan A god of the underworld who was the "source of pigs, chickens and rice." The Ifugao, Philippines. (Barton, 1946: 34)

Neske-pas The god/goddess of the bee-hive. The Erza (Mordvins). Neskeper-ava of the Moksha, Russia. (Paasonen, 1925, 8: 846)

Nin-e-i-garak Sumerian goddess of the dairy, in Kiabrig. Wife of Nin-exen x La. Near East. (Jacobsen, 1970: 7)

Nin-ezen x La Sumerian bull-god, in Kiabrig, whose wife is Nin-e-i-garak. Near East. (Jacobsen, 1970: 7)

Ninhursag(a) An aspect of the great Earth Mother goddess as goddess of the dairy, of the domestic herds—the nourisher of the kings "with her blessed milk—the actual milk being that of the animals through which she functioned here on earth." She is also goddess of the wildlife of the foothills. Near East. (Campbell, 1962: 37–38, 106; Jacobsen, 1976: 104–5, 107)

Ninigara The Sumerian goddess of the dairy. Wife of Ninhar. Near East. (Jacobsen, 1970: 26)

Nin-tara The god of flocks, invoked in exorcising evil spirits. Babylonia, Near East. (Thompson, 1903: 59)

Niu Lan The patron of the cow pen. China. (Day, 1940: 212)

Niu T'u Ti An aspect of T'u Ti as protector of cows and pigs. China. (Day, 1940: 67)

Niu Wang The god of oxen and of water buffaloes. China. (Werner, 1932: 331; Graham, 1928: 61; Maspero, 1963: 327)

Noh-yum-cab A Mayan bee deity, a "great lord bee," under whom are all the other bees. Yucatan, Mexico. (Redfield and Villa Rojas, 1962: 117)

Nomai The personification of the pastures. Greece. (Roscher, 1965, 3, 1: 452)

Nor lha rta bdag kubera A god invoked as a protector of horses. Tibet. (Nebesky-Wojkowitz, 1956, 1: 306)

Nuhm A god of sheepherders in whose name oaths are taken. He is possibly a god of divination. Arabia. (Fahd, 1968: 135)

Nyalwa A god of cattle who kept them in good health. The Banyoro, Uganda. (Roscoe, 1915: 92)

Nye pha'i btsun mo The grandmother of the cattle gods, wife of Zla ba'i phyugs po. Tibet. (Nebesky-Wojkowitz, 1956, 1: 306)

Ong-ghot The house gods—guardians of the flocks, "of the family and of its wealth." The Monguors of Kansu, China. (Schram, 1957: 125)

Palamoa The god of fowls, grandfather of Lepe-a-moa. Hawaii. (Beckwith, 1940: 120)

Pales The Roman goddess of flocks and cattle, their pastures and their shepherds. In Etruria, male—the god of animal husbandry. (Dumézil, 1966, 1: 43, 380–381; Bulfinch, 1898: 16)

The Pamahandi They are generalized into one, but are actually ten individuals with specific duties—but all are "protectors of the horses and carabao and as senders of good fortune, they are much respected and some time during each year each family will make a ceremony to obtain their good will. . . . However, they may cause trouble and send sickness." Male. The Bukidnon, Philippines. (Cole, 1956: 94)

Pan Greek god of herds and herdsmen, of woods and fields. The "great phallic god—a goat-horned, goat-legged god." The giver of fertility. (Kerenyi, 1951: 173; Bulfinch, 1898: 13, 149)

Pari A deity represented at the Rite of Summer celebrated to secure "the welfare of the herds." The Sherpas, Nepal. (Furer-Haimendorf, 1964: 209)

Parrapotamma A goddess believed to cure cattle diseases. The Paraiyans, Southern India. (Thurston, 1909, 6: 105)

Peko The god of fertility was invoked in the fall for the protection of the domesticated animals and the crops. Estonia. (Leach, 1950, 2: 850)

Peseias A Slavonic protector of domestic animals. (Larousse, 1968: 290)

Phyugs bdag btsun mo Mother of the cattle gods and wife of Phyugs rje btsan po. Tibet. (Nebesky-Wojkowitz, 1956, 1: 306)

Phyugs lha (pr. **Chhuklha**) The god of herds. Tibet. (Tucci, 1980: 200)

Phyugs lha spun bdun (pr. **Chhuklha Pün Dün**) The " 'Seven Brother Gods of the Herds,' namely the horse-god, the god of the yak," the tame domestic yak, "the *mdzo* (yak-cow cross)," oxen, sheep, and goats. Among the nomadic people. Tibet. (Tucci, 1980: 205)

Phyugs rje btsan po Father of the cattle gods whose wife is Phyugs bdag btsun mo. Tibet. (Nebesky-Wojkowitz, 1956, 1: 306)

Pirwa A Hittite horse god. Asia Minor. (Puhvel, 1970: 171; Macqueen, 1951: 120)

Poraiya The "god of the door, watchman of the window" of the cattle-shed. The Ahirs, Central Provinces, India. (Russell, 1916, 2: 33)

Poseidon Before he became god of the sea, Poseidon was god of horses and their fertility, of horsemanship. Through his dalliance with Medousa he was the father of Pegasos. Greece. (Fairbanks, 1907: 55, 153; Kerenyi, 1951: 183–185)

Priparchis Slavonic god of the weaning of pigs. Poland. (Larousse, 1968: 291)

Priparszas A Litu-Prussian deity concerned with the young pigs. (Schrader, 1925, 2: 31)

Prokorimos Litu-Prussian deity, god of bees, of honey. (Schrader, 1925, 2: 31; Welsford, 1925, 9: 242)

Pu The horse god. China. (Werner, 1932: 383)

Pusan, Pushan A solar god with various aspects, one of which is that of a god and protector of cattle and other herds, and of their fertility. India. (Dowson, 1961: 250; Ions, 1967: 20; Danielou, 1964: 117, 123–124)

Ra lha God of goats worshipped mainly by nomads. Tibet. (Nebesky-Wojkowitz, 1956, 1: 306)

Ratainicza, Ratainitsa Lithuanian/Prussian god/goddess of horses and guardian of the stables. (Gray, 1930: 73; Welsford, 1925, 9: 242; Larousse, 1968: 290)

Riangombe, Kiranga The god who heads the imandwa (good spirits), who is also the god and protector of cattle in Urundi and Kisiba. Burundi, Rwanda, and Zaire. (Meyer, 1916: 187, 189)

Riannon, Rhiannon A Celtic goddess, like Epona, associated with horses and also with birds. She is a goddess of the otherworld. Wales. (Ross, 1967: 225, 268; MacCana, 1970: 55)

rma dpon (pr. **Mapon**), **rta lha** (pr. **Talha**) God of horses. Tibet. (Tucci, 1980: 200)

Rohina Like her mother Surabhi, the mother of kine. India. (Mackenzie, 1924: 173)

rta lha *See* **rma dpon**

Rubezahl A god of fields and of cattle. Germany. (Leland, 1963: 60)

Rudiobus A Celtic god of horses, and a warrior god. Gaul and Britain. (Ross, 1967: 170; MacCulloch, 1918, 3: 124)

Ryangombe Among the Bahima a god of cattle. Uganda. (Larousse, 1973: 523)

Sabian, Isabian The guardian of dogs who appears in the Binikwau ceremony. The Tinguian, Philippines. (Cole, 1922: 299, 358)

Sahadeo The personification of the cow. The Mahakul Ahirs, Jashpur, Central Provinces, India. (Russell, 1916, 2: 32)

Sale A god of the Gonds "who may be the god who presides over cattle-pens." Central Provinces, India. (Russell, 1916, 3: 99)

San Francisco ipoq'apaqa The god of the llamas, alpacas, and vicunas to whom the blood is offered to maintain the supply. The Aymara, Peru. (Tschopik, 1951: 199)

Savaṇhi A god of cattle fertility. Iran. (Gray, 1930: 160–161)

Sengdroma A lion-faced goddess of the Sherpas represented in the Rite of Summer celebrated to secure "the welfare of the herds." The female manifestation of Guru Rimpoche. Nepal. (Furer-Haimendorf, 1964: 208, 239, 252)

Shakan Sumerian god of goats and their herders, as well as of wild animals. Son of Utu and Shenirda. Near East. (Jacobsen, 1970: 26)

Shangkam majan Mother of the bee genus, child of Kringkrong wa and Ynong majan. The Katchins, Burma. (Gilholdes, 1908: 675)

sha so rak rok The "creator and protector of minor domestic animals and fowls such as goats, pigs, and hens." The Lepchas, Sikkim. (Siiger, 1967: 144)

Shintun lawa Father of the bee genus, child of Kringkrong wa and Ynong majan. The Katchins, Burma. (Gilhodes, 1908: 675)

Shtu-ja-sei The god of domestic animals and fowls of the Ch'iang at Ho-p'ing-chai. Szechwan, China. (Graham, 1958: 69)

Shui Hsien, Shui Hsien Wu Sheng Guardian of the duck-raisers. China. (Day, 1940: 110)

Silvanus A Roman/Etruscan rural god of husbandry. God of cattle and fields—like Faunus watching over pastures and boundaries, protecting the herds from wolves with the help of Mars. (Dumézil, 1966, 1: 235; Leland, 1963: 60; Fairbanks, 1907: 248–249)

Singaji A godling (once mortal) who is invoked to protect the cattle from disease. His offerings are butter. The Ahirs, Central Provinces, India. (Russell, 1916, 2: 30)

Song kao Also called Yun Yang. A mountain god who presides over the land and over domestic animals. China. (Chavannes, n.d.: 3, 418)

Sumugan, Sumukan, Sumuqan A Sumerian/Babylonian mountain god who is god of cattle and goats, as well as of the wildlife of the plains. Near East. (Langdon, 1931: 191; Jacobsen, 1970: 8; Hooke, 1963: 27)

Surabhi The goddess of cows, the milk goddess, the source of "The Celestial Milk." Her daughters are Rohina, Gandharvi, Anala, and Shuki. India. (Mackenzie, 1924: 172–173)

Sutekh An ass-headed deity of the Semitic Hykshos whom the Egyptians identified with Set. Near East. (Eastlake, 1883: 277)

Sutvaras Prussian/Lithuanian guardian of cattle. (Schrader, 1925, 2: 31)

Svarogu Slavic god of cattle. (Gray, 1930: 146)

Swieczpuncscyunnis devos Litu-Prussian deity of poultry. (Schrader, 1925, 2: 31)

Szerizius Litu-Prussian "god who attends to the feeding of cattle." (Schrader, 1925, 2: 31)

rTa lha God of horses worshipped especially by the nomads. Tibet. (Nebesky-Wojkowitz, 1956, 1: 306)

rTa lha'i rgyal po remanta A god invoked as a protector of horses. Tibet. (Nebesky-Wojkowitz, 1956, 1: 306)

rTa-mgrin, rTa-mgrin-rgyal-po, rTa mgrin padma heruka The horse-necked god, protector of horses, but not the god of horses. A Dharmapala, Defender of the Law. He is "the Door-keeper of the West," and appears on the sixth day of the Bardo of Karmic Illusions in the testing period following death. His shakti is Lghags-strog-ma. Tibet. Same as Hayagriva. (Evans-Wentz, 1960: 120; Getty. 1962: 162)

Tangkam majan Mother of domestic animals and vegetables. The Katchins, Burma. (Gilhodes, 1908: 678)

Tartak, Tarhak "The Avim or Hivites, a tribe of the Canaanites, worshipped an ass-headed god" with a human figure. Near East. (Eastlake, 1883:)

Tate Naaliwami A red serpent water goddess who brings the rains from the East. She owns the cattle, mules, and horses, and is the creator of squashes and flowers. The Huichol, Mexico. (Chamberlain, 1900: 305; Seler, 1925, 6: 829)

Tenisins The god who watches over pigs. Latvia. (Jonval, 1929: 18)

Tištrya The chief star deity, Sirius, who controls the rains, healing and washing away pollutions and bringing fertility. A deity of cattle and horses also. Iran. (Huart, 1963: 42; Gray, 1930: 115–116; Jackson, 1925: 86; Jayne, 1962: 95)

Tsche-shyo-gi The god protective of all domestic animals. The Ch'iang at Lo-pu-chai, China. (Graham, 1958: 49)

Tyanaba Guardian of the cattle. The Peul, Mali. (Imperato, 1972: 79)

Ubang lawa Father of domestic animals and vegetables. The Katchins, Burma. (Gilhodes, 1908: 678)

Ukha-Solbon God of the evening star, Venus, protector of horses. Eldest son of Budurga-Sagan-Tengri. The Buriats, Siberia and Mongolia. (Klementz, 1925, 3: 4, 11)

Ukhin-Booum-Tengri An Eastern Tengri who inflicts cattle with parasitic diseases. Not approached directly for relief, but through his father Gujir-Tengri. Siberia and Mongolia. (Klementz, 1925, 3: 5)

Urcuchillay A constellation (Lyra) said to be a sheep (llama) "of many colors" whom the herders respected and to whom they offered sacrifices as it was "responsible for the preservation of the livestock." Paratía, Peru. (Flores-Ochoa, 1979: page opposite Contents)

Usching Baltic god of horses. Lithuania and Latvia. (Machal, 1918: 330; Queval, 1968: 116)

Ushi-no-kamisama Japanese god of cows. Takashima. (Norbeck, 1954: 123)

Usin Latvian horse god. (Schoeps, 1961: 121)

Vazila Slavic guardian of horses, "a being in shape like a man, but having equine ears and hoofs." Russia. (Ralston, 1872: 125)

Vcles A Czech god of cattle "who had been degraded to the rank of a demon."(Sykes, 1952: 226)

Veles Slavic god of flocks who, with Perun, is sworn by in treaties. Finland and Bohemia. (Machal, 1918: 300)

Velinas, Velnias, Vels The dangerous god of the dead and of the underworld whose main incarnation is as a serpent has also a beneficent aspect as a god of wealth, of cattle and fertility, of commerce. He helps the poor and the good by "misleading swindlers, bringing supernatural gifts, completing their labors," etc. Lithuania and Latvia. (Gimbutas, 1971: 167; 1974: 87–92)

Vels Latvia. *See* **Velinas.**

Venkatachalapati A god of the herders of the bulls to whom freakish animals were given. The Gangeddu, Southern India. (Thurston, 1909, 2: 262)

Vispala A Vedic deity seemingly related to "herdsmen-farmers." India. (Dumézil, 1966, 1: 384)

Visvarupa   Protector of cows. Son of Tvastr. India. (Macdonell, 1897: 116)

Volos, Veles   Slavic god of cattle and of flocks. Russia and Serbia. (Welsford, 1925, 9: 252; Rhys, 1937: 187)

Volosu   A variant name of the Slavic god of flocks. In Russia he was also invoked in oath-taking, in treaties, with Perunu. (Gray, 1930: 144; Leach, 1950, 2: 1027)

Walgino   Slavic protector of cattle. Poland. (Larousse, 1968: 291)

Wamala (the Banyoro), **Wamara** (the Bahimas)   A god venerated by cattle-raisers for the increase of their herds, and invoked for their protection from disease. Uganda. (Queval, 1968: 119; Roscoe, 1915: 90)

X-Juan-Thul   Protector of cattle, guarding "the corral, keeping evil winds away." The Maya, Yucatan, Mexico. (Redfield and Villa Rojas, 1962: 118)

Yabuling   The deity who provided the Ngaing with pigs. New Guinea. (Lawrence, 1965: 205)

gYag lha   The god of yaks worshipped mainly by the nomads. Tibet. (Nebesky-Wojkowitz, 1956, 1: 306)

Yang Ching   "The Goat God." Sacrifices are made to him "for protection against wild animals." He is also the god of the star Fan-yin. China. (Leach, 1950, 2: 1187; Werner, 1932: 583)

Yang Lan   The patron of the goat and sheep pens. China. (Day, 1940: 212)

Yauk   An equine sun god of the Arabs who "personified the sun and its destructive power." Near East. (Eastlake, 1883: 275, 278)

Yero   The god of cattle. Son of Samba and Qumba. The Fulani, Nigeria. (Webster, 1931: 241)

Yerra Gadipati Ganga   The Dravidian goddess of shepherds. India. (Elmore, 1915: 116)

Ynakhsyt   The protective goddess of cattle who "is offered the first dairy produce in the spring." The Yakuts, Siberia. (Larousse, 1973: 435)

Zamola   The deity of domestic animals, invoked for their protection and increase. The Lepchas, Sikkim. (Siiger, 1967: 45)

Zemepatis, Zempattys, Zemininkas   The earth god is worshipped for cattle and also for the protection of the farm. Latvia and Lithuania. (Leach, 1950, 2: 631–632; Welsford, 1925, 9: 242)

Zempat   A Baltic god, protective of herds. Pruthenes. (Queval, 1968: 121)

Zhini-Ant'ar   "In Megrelia the god of cattle-breeding." The Caucasus. (Janashia, 1937: 122)

Zhwabran   The god of cows of the Abkhasians. Caucasus. (Janashia, 1937: 122)

Zla ba'i phyugs po   The grandfather of the cattle gods whose wife is Nye pha'i btsun mo, and son is Phyugs rje btsan po. Tibet. (Nebesky-Wojkowitz, 1956, 1: 306)

Zosim   A Slavonic god of bees. (Larousse, 1968: 291)

28

Fishing:
Fish Gods, Water Animals

Abarga-Ekhe-Zagassun   The lord of fishes. The Buriats, Siberia and Mongolia. (Klementz, 1925, 3: 10)

Abenawa   A beneficent goddess who draws fish near to shore for the fishermen. The Effutu, Ghana. (Wyllie, 1966: 479)

Abodinkra   A fishing god of the Fante, the Gã in Temma. Ghana. (Parrinder, 1962: 47; Field, 1937: 22)

Ai-ai   The god who "marked out" the fishing grounds. Son of Ku-ula and Hina-pu-ku-ia. Hawaii. (Beckwith, 1940: 19, 22; Keliipio/Nakuina, 1901: 114–115)

Aiviliajoq, Nuliajoq   The mother and goddess of sea animals. The Iglulirmiut, Central Eskimo. Same as Sedna. Canada. (Boas, 1884/85: 585–586)

Akkruva   A sea goddess whose lower body is a fish, upper human. The Lapps, Northern Europe. (Holmberg, 1925, 7: 798)

Akrama   A god who provides abundance of fish. The Effutu, Ghana. (Wyllie, 1966: 480)

Alexume'gi'lakw   The killer whale who is the messenger of Qomogwa. He lives in the far west and has dolphins for warriors and the sea lion as his messenger. The Kwakiutl, British Columbia. (Boas, 1935: 130, 158)

Alis-i-tet, Toutop   The god of the sea and the god of fishes. Lamotrek, the Carolines, Micronesia. (Christian, 1897, 6: 198)

Aliu-sat, Pon-norol   The god of the sea and of fishes. Satarval, the Carolines, Micronesia. (Christian, 1897, 6: 198)

Alla   Sumerian "Lord of the net." Near East. (Jacobsen, 1970: 324)

Amalcum   A Mayan deity of fishermen. Central America. (Bancroft, 1886, 2: 698)

Amimitl   A god of fishing of Lake Chalco who was equated with Opuchtli. Valley of Anahuac, Mexico. (Bancroft, 1886, 3: 410). A goddess "of floating gardens and canals" worshipped at Cuauhilama. (Reed, 1966: 112)

Ampah   A lagoon god, "protector of the fishing industry of Moree." The Gold Coast, Ghana. (Ellis, 1887: 49–50)

Ana muri   The "god of bonito and albacore fishers (Aldebaran in Taurus), is the pillar to blacken or tattoo by." Tahiti, Polynesia. (Henry, 1928: 361)

Andriananahary   The "master of the animals in the ocean . . . and . . . the patron of fishing." He is the equivalent of Zanahary. The Malagasy, Madagascar. (Ruud, 1960: 12, 287)

Annedotos   A half-fish, half-man deity believed to have taught the early Babylonians "the arts of civilization." Near East. (Paton, 1925, 4: 387)

Apelesa   A god incarnate in the turtle, which as food was taboo to some. Samoa, Polynesia. (Turner, 1884: 67)

Apu-Ko-hai   A fish god of Kauai. Hawaii. (Andersen, 1928: 55)

Boto Aracu   A dolphin deity native to Para. Belem, Brazil. (Leacock, 1972: 144)

568

Te Arawaru Spouse of Kaukau—parents of cockles, etc. The Maori, New Zealand. (Best, 1924: 155)

asima si The mother of fish and water animals. The Mundurucu, Para, Brazil. (Murphy, 1958: 141)

Atargatis Goddess of fish and of dolphins. Also called Derketo. Arabia. (Cook, 1930: 28n.; Ferguson, 1970: 19, 20)

Atua i Fatumaru A god important to fishing. Tikopia, Melanesia. (Firth, 1967, 2: 227)

Cana Aulola Mother Fresh-water Shrimp is also called Cana Palak (Mother Eel). She is the wife of Puluga and the mother of many daughters and one son, Pijcor. Andaman Islands, Bay of Bengal. (Radcliffe-Brown, 1967: 158)

Avrikiti A sea god and god of fishermen. The Ewe, Dahomey. (Ellis, 1890: 67; Mockler-Ferryman, 1925, 9: 278)

Awalanaxe A fish deity who ate the moon who was rescued by the sun. The Trumai, Brazil. (Murphy and Quain, 1955: 72)

Awuru A "small fishing god connected with a collection of turtle bones." The Gã, Accra, Ghana. (Field, 1937: 89)

Ayiku The chief god of the Gã in Teshi who is invoked for fish and rain. Ghana. (Field, 1937: 74–75)

Baiporo The creator of fish. The Bororo, Brazil. (Levi-Strauss, 1969: 215)

Banafo A fishing god of the Gã in Accra. Ghana. (Field, 1937: 89)

Barão de Goré Believed to be a shark god, a god of healing. Father of Gorezinho. Belem, Brazil. (Leacock, 1972: 145–146)

Belo Encanto A dolphin god, son of Dona Dada. Belem, Brazil. (Leacock, 1972: 144)

Bengali Babu A god who protects fishermen from danger and gives an abundance of fish. The Jalari and the Vada, Southern India. (Thurston, 1909, 2: 445; 1909, 7: 260)

Bhagirathamma A goddess who protects and helps night fishermen—from illness. The Jalari and the Vada, Southern India. (Thurston, 1909, 2: 446; 1909, 7: 261)

Bombo Equsi A god who provides abundant fish. The Effutu, Ghana. (Wyllie, 1966: 478–479)

Boto Branco A dolphin deity. Belem, Brazil. (Leacock, 1972: 144)

Camaxtli A god primarily of hunting but also of fishing. He is as well a god of war and a creator god. The Aztec and the Tlascalans, Mexico. (Spence, 1923: 127; Bancroft, 1886, 4: 195; Alexander, 1920: 92; Duran, 1971: 140–141)

Ca nuoc, Ca voi The dolphin worshipped by sailors. They believed the dolphins can save them when shipwrecked. Annam. (Cabaton, 1925, 1: 541)

Castanho A dolphin deity. Belem, Brazil. (Leacock, 1972: 144)

Chac Uayab Xoc A fish god—" 'great' or 'red demon shark.' " A god of fishermen. Also known as Ah kak nexoy. The Mayan, Yucatan, Mexico. (Tozzer, 1941: 156; Roys, 1949: 160; Thompson, 1970: 321)

Chaurasi Devi A goddess worshipped and propitiated by the Kewat, a caste of fishermen and boatmen. She "dwells in their boats and keeps them from sinking." Central Provinces, India. (Russell, 1916, 3: 425)

Chawe A god of fishermen in Kpong. Ghana. (Field, 1937: 77)

Cheng San-Kung A god of fishermen. China. (Werner, 1932: 48)

Chep-atte Kamui A god represented by a fish, which he is believed to supply in abundance. The Ainu, Japan. (Munro, 1963: 38)

Chep-kor-kamui God and Master of the fish, particularly the salmon. The Ainu, Japan. (Philippi, 1982: 101n.6)

Chiang T'ai Kung A guardian of fishermen as well as of tradesmen and homes. China. (Day, 1940: 49; Weyer, 1961: 216)

Chiang Tzu-ya A god of fishermen, a deified mortal. China. (Werner, 1932: 65; Leach, 1949, 1: 216)

Cho:haykuh An important sea deity who has "the appearance of a sea mammal" rather like a killer whale, and who is protective of the Ainu boats during storms. Sakhalin. (Ohnuki-Tierney, 1974: 89, 100)

Cipactli, Coxcox   A Mexican fish god. (Brinton, 1868: 202)

Cit Dzamal Cum   A Mayan god of fishing. Central America. (Tozzer, 1941: 156)

Copacahuana   A fish goddess of the Collao. Peru and Bolivia. (Spence, 1925, 3: 549)

Cozaana   A god of fishermen and of hunters. The Zapotec, Oaxaca, Mexico. (Bancroft, 1886, 3: 547)

Dada   A dolphin goddess, native to Para. Mother of Belo Encanto and Dur Encanto. Belem, Brazil. (Leacock, 1972: 144)

Dagon   A god/goddess—half-human, half-fish—of the Philistines, the Phoenicians, and the Syrians. Also known as a god of vegetation and of fertility. Near East. (Seligmann, 1948: 49; Bulfinch, 1898: 397; Vriezen, 1963: 52; Cox, 1870, 2: 26; Langdon, 1931: 78)

da mik   A god of river fishing. The Lepchas, Sikkim. (Siiger, 1967: 141)

Danag   A deity who guards fishermen and hunters. The Apayao, Philippines. (Wilson, 1947: 22)

Dayyog   "[F]isher"—a deity of the Phoenicians. Near East. (Paton, 1925, 9: 893)

Derketo, Derceto   A beautiful goddess with a fishtail extremity, mother of Semiramis. Also a moon goddess. Syria. (Cox, 1870, 2: 84; Seligmann, 1948: 49; Frazer, 1961: 34n.3)

Diamichius   A deified human who invented fishing equipment and boats. Asia Minor. (Langdon, 1931: 54)

Maia Dik   Sir Prawn "who first produced or obtained fire." The Aka-Cari, Andaman Islands, Bay of Bengal. (Radcliffe-Brown, 1967: 189)

Duginavi   Father of the cayman, also of the palm (Huka), the gourd, and the ahuyama. The Cagaba and the Kogi, Colombia. (Reichel-Dolmatoff, 1949/50: 112–113)

Dur Encanto   A dolphin god, son of Dona Dada. Belem, Brazil. (Leacock, 1972: 144)

Ea   A red turtle deity of the ocean. Hawaii. (Westervelt, 1963, 3: 212)

Ebisu   One of the seven gods of happiness, of luck, who was originally a god of fishermen and of traders. Japan. (Herbert, 1967: 511–512; Piggott, 1969: 59)

Enemxxaligiu   A monster deity "similar to a giant halibut" who lives in the sea and has seals for his dogs. He causes dangerous tides. The Kwakiutl, British Columbia. (Boas, 1935: 128)

Ezekhe uyli   A sky god who is invoked particularly in fishing and in hunting. The Ul'chi, Siberia. (Ivanov, Smolyak, and Levin, 1964: 730)

Fa'aravaiterai   A shark god of Tahiti. Polynesia. (Henry, 1928: 361)

Fahapatu   The fish god of Moungaone Island, Tonga, Polynesia. (Gifford, 1929: 309)

Fai   The Ray-fish god. Tahiti, Polynesia. (Henry, 1928: 356)

Fe'e   The cuttle-fish god and god of the dead. Samoa, Polynesia. (Williamson, 1933, 1: 5)

Feke   The octopus god is a god of fishing and of the sacred ovens. His wife is Nau Fiora and son is Tufaretai. Tikopia, Melanesia. (Firth, 1967, 2: 123)

Feseketaki   The eel-god in Tavi. Tikopia, Melanesia. (Firth, 1967, 2: 393)

Fuai Langi   A god who took the form of the sea-eel whose appearance on the shore portended evil. Samoa, Polynesia. (Turner, 1884: 32)

Fuhhe   God of the net. China. (Du Bose, n.d.: 334)

Fu Hsi   A god of the nets whose sister or consort is Nu-kua. They are depicted with human torsos whose lower bodies are serpentine. China. (Werner, 1932: 327; Bodde, 1961: 386)

Fuilelagi   A deity "embodied in an eel," worshipped in Olosega. Manua (Samoa), Polynesia. (Mead, 1930: 157)

Funa-dama   The goddess/god of fishermen, of seafaring, and of boats. Japan. (Herbert, 1967: 483; Norbeck, 1954: 129–130)

Gardoaits, Gardoayts   The god of fishermen and seafarers. The Sudavians, Samland, Prussia. (Welsford, 1925, 9: 488; Puhvel, 1974: 83)

Geshtinanna   A fish-goddess. An early name of Nina as "queen of waters." Babylonia. She is also named as a sister of Dumuzi—"the divine poetess, singer, and dream interpreter." Sumer, Near East. (Mercer, 1925, 12: 709; Kramer, 1961: 111)

Gitcigiweliahit A beneficent fish deity—"big tickler." The Penobscot Indians, Maine. (Speck, 1935, 1: 17)

Gurappa Gurunathadu The caste deity of the Telugu fishermen and boatmen. The Chembadi, Southern India. (Thurston, 1909, 2: 24)

Gutufolo A lesser god of Tuapa, of the reefs, who is invoked when fishing. Niue, Polynesia. (Loeb, 1926, 1: 161)

Guuli-Ibmel The god of fish. The Lapps, Northern Europe. (Leach, 1950, 2: 604)

Ha A god of rain and of the surface water who is invoked in fishing as he controls the fish and crocodiles. The Maya, British Honduras. (Thompson, 1930: 65)

Ha'aluea The *he'e* or squid worshipped as an aumakua (an ancestor god). Hawaii. (Emerson, 1967: 49)

Hachiman He is generally considered a god of war but he "has now become a fishing and agricultural deity . . . also has been identified as the god of the forge." Japan. (Bunce, 1955: 124)

Haele Feke An octopus god who was prescient and who "changed into a lizard when travelling overland." He was also known as Tutula. Ha'ano and Tongatabu Islands, Tonga, Polynesia. (Collocott, 1921: 231; Gifford, 1929: 308)

Hakatautai A deified priest who was invoked in fishing. Kapingamarangi, Polynesia. (Emory, 1965: 202)

Hal-ku-ta-da The shark who "came up from the Gulf of California to help the Mojaves." Brother of Kuyu, Pathraxsatta, and Pacuchi. Arizona. (Bourke, 1889: 182, 186)

Harbadevi A goddess of fishermen. The Son Kolis, India. (Punekar, 1959: 160)

Hau-wahine A lizard goddess on Oahu who "brings abundance of fish, punishes the owners of the pond if they oppress the poor." Hawaii. (Beckwith, 1940: 126)

Heng chan God of the Peak of the South who presides over fish and aquatic animals as well as the stars and constellations. He is also called Tch'ong Li. China. (Chavannes, n.d.: 4, 419)

Hikohoho-demi A god of fishermen who is identified with Hachiman. Son of Ninigi and Kono-hana-sakuya-hime and an ancestor of the Imperial Family. Japan. (Bunce, 1955: 124; Herbert, 1967: 366; Kato, 1926: 60)

Hina-hele Goddess of fishes and wife of Ku-ula. She is also known as La-ea and Hina-ulu-ohia. Hawaii. (Henry, 1928: 467; Andersen, 1928: 263)

Hina-opuhala-koa "Goddess of the corals and spiny creatures of the sea . . . and appears sometimes as a woman, sometimes as a coral reef." Hawaii. (Beckwith, 1940: 219)

Hina-pukuia Mother of fishes and wife of Kuula. She is also the mother of Ai-ai and sister of Moku-ha-lii, Kupa-ai-kee, Ku-pulu-i-ka-na-hele. She gives fish in abundance. Hawaii. (Keliipio/Nakuina, 1901: 114–115; Beckwith, 1940: 16, 69; Ashdown, 1971: 40)

Hine-takurua "Winter Maid"—a wife of the sun with whom he lives half the year. She lives in the sea and "her task is to conserve fish." The Maori, New Zealand. (Best, 1924: 110)

Hoderi-no-Mikoto A god of fishing and son of Ninigi and Kono-hana-no-Sakuyabime. Brother of Hosuseri-no-Mikoto and Howori-no-Mikoto. Japan. (Yasumaro, 1965: 65)

Hogan "The Spirit of the Fish was the patron of ablution and presided over the powers of the waters." The Lakota and the Oglala, South Dakota. (Walker, 1980: 122)

Hoku kau opae, Newe The goddess Sirius "determined the best time for catching shrimp by her rising or setting." Hawaii. (Emerson, 1967: 51)

Huichaana, Huiçana A goddess of fishing who is also a goddess of children and the creatress of men and animals. The Valley Zapotec, Oaxaca, Mexico. (Whitecotton, 1977: 164, 169)

Ika-tere The father of fish and son of Punga. Also given as the son of Tangaroa. The Maori, New Zealand. (Grey, 1855: 7; Andersen, 1928: 370)

Ina A dolphin goddess native to Para. Belem, Brazil. (Leacock, 1972: 144)

Ishara Babylonian goddess of aquatic animals with whom Nina was identified; wife of Nin-dar-a. She is also a goddess of war and of conquest. Near East. (Mercer, 1925, 12: 700, 709)

Itclixyan   Goddess of the Columbia River waters who is guardian "of fishermen and hunters of water animals." The Wishram, Washington and Oregon. (Spier and Sapir, 1930: 236)

João da Lima   A dolphin deity, native to Para. Belem, Brazil. (Leacock, 1972: 144)

Ka'ahu-pahau   Beneficent shark goddess of Pearl Harbor who guarded men from man-eating sharks. Hawaii. (Beckwith, 1940: 138; Emerson, 1968: 46)

Ka-ehu-iki-mano-o-Pu'uloa   A beneficent yellow shark god of Pearl Harbor who came from Puna Coast originally and had "magic power and great wisdom." Hawaii. (Westervelt, 1963, 1: 55; Beckwith, 1940: 139)

Kahi'uka   A beneficent shark god, brother or son of Kaahupahua, and with her guards Oahu waters from man-eating sharks. Hawaii. (Emerson, 1968: 46; Beckwith, 1940: 138)

Kahole-a-Kane   A shark god of Hawaii. (Beckwith, 1940: 176)

Kai-pe-chupka-un-kuru   A benevolent god of the sea—usually in the form of a large fish. The Ainu, Japan. (Batchelor, 1925, 1: 244)

Ka-Jum   The "father of fish" invoked in fishing and hunting rituals and ordeals. The Oyana, French Guiana. (Zerries, 1968: 263)

Kakahe'e   The squid-god. Hawaii. (Westervelt, 1963, 1: 159)

Kak Ne Xoc   A Mayan fish god, "fire-tailed shark," and god of fishermen. The same as Chac-Uayab-Xoc. Yucatan, Mexico. (Roys, 1949: 173; Tozzer, 1941: 156; Thompson, 1970: 310)

Ka-la-hiki   A guardian shark god who guided them in sea journeys and in fishing. Hawaii. (Ashdown, 1971: 22)

Kalu Kahar   A deified tribesman invoked when fishing. The Kahar, United Provinces, India. (Crooke, 1925, 7: 637)

Ka-moho-ali'i   A shark god and a god of sorcery who also took human form. Older brother of Pele. He is also named as a god of steam and a god of the underworld. Hawaii. (Beckwith, 1940: 51, 90, 105, 167; Westervelt, 1915: 60; Emerson, 1968: 46)

Kanae   The "personification of the mullet." The Maori, New Zealand. (Andersen, 1928: 164)

Ka-naka-o-kai   A guardian shark god of Maui. Hawaii. (Ashdown, 1971: 22)

Kanaloa   The squid god, the octopus god, who is invoked in the sailing of canoes and in fishing. He is associated with his brother Kane in cultural things, in food, etc., but he is also in opposition to him and the leader of the rebellious spirits, being confined to Po, the Dark Region. Hawaii. (Beckwith, 1940: 45, 60, 62; Henry, 1928: 345; Mackenzie, n.d.: 388; Alexander, 1968: 62)

Kane-apua   A fish god on Lanai and Molokai. A god of the sea worshipped by fishermen; a younger brother of Kane and Kanaloa. Hawaii. (Beckwith, 1940: 452; Alexander, 1968: 62; Emory, 1924: 12–13)

Kane-huna-moku   A beneficent shark god of Maui. Hawaii. (Beckwith, 1940: 129; Ashdown, 1971: 22)

Kane-i-kokala   A beneficent shark god who saves those who are shipwrecked. Hawaii. (Beckwith, 1940: 129; Ashdown, 1971: 22)

Kane-koa   A fishing god of Hawaii. (Beckwith, 1940: 90)

Kane-kua'ana   A dragon goddess of Ewa lagoon (Pearl Harbor) worshipped by gatherers of oysters. Hawaii. (Westervelt, 1963, 3: 258; Beckwith, 1940: 126)

Kane-lau-apua   A beneficent god who takes the form of the goby (oopu) fish, and is also a god of healing. Hawaii. (Beckwith, 1940: 136, 452)

Kane-makua   A god of fishing. Hawaii. (Beckwith, 1940: 90; Alexander, 1967: 63)

Karaneman   God of whales and sharks. Yap Island, the Carolines, Micronesia. (Christian, 1899: 385)

Karihi   A god of fishermen—"sinker of the bottom of the fishing-net." Second child of Whai-tiri and Kaitangata, New Zealand. (Mackenzie, n.d.: 298)

Kau-huhu   A shark god of Molokai and Maui. Hawaii. (Beckwith, 1940: 129; Westervelt, 1915: 49)

Kaukau   Spouse of Te Arawaru, and parents of cockles, etc. They are "guardians of the realm of Hine-moana, the Ocean Maid." The Maori, New Zealand. (Best, 1924: 105, 155)

Kau-naha-ili-pakapaka A beneficent "great shark" god. Hawaii. (Westervelt, 1963, 3: 194)

Kaweshawa In the water she was a fish, out of water a beautiful woman, in the vicinity of the Kasuruña Rapids where her permission was needed to fish. Daughter of the Master of Fish and wife of Wanadi. The Makiritare, Venezuela. (Civrieux, 1980: 32–43)

Kere-tapuna The eel god who is associated with the lake net of Ariki Tafua. Tikopia, Melanesia. (Firth, 1939: 175)

Kiang T'aikung Also called Li-ong. A god of fishermen. Szechwan, China. (Graham, 1961: 161: Du Bose, n.d.: 334)

Kiha-wahine A mo'o goddess, human upper torso, who lives in fish ponds on Maui and Kauai and if fish are caught while she is at home they will be bitter. She is fierce and much feared. Hawaii. (Beckwith, 1940: 126; Emerson, 1968: 42; Westervelt, 1963, 3: 258–259)

Kini-lau A sea god and god of fishing. Hawaii. (Beckwith, 1940: 90; Ashdown, 1971: 37)

Koona An eel god of Wailau on Molokai. Hawaii. (Andersen, 1928: 264)

Kua A shark god of Hawaii. (Beckwith, 1940: 176)

Ku-hai-moana Beneficent shark god who helped people to the shore. Hawaii. (Westervelt, 1963, 3: 254; Emerson, 1968: 45; Beckwith, 1940: 129)

Kumulipo The "Source-of-deep-darkness;" the primordial male who with Po'ele (the first pair) were "the parents of all hard-shelled things that came into being in the sea in the darkness and of all plant life." All was darkness and night. Hawaii. (Leach, 1956: 167)

Ku-ula, Ku-ula-kai The great fish god and god of fishermen who transformed himself—man or fish—and who controlled the fish, the first caught being dedicated to him. His wife was Hina-pu-ku-ia and his son Ai-ai. Hawaii. (Keliipio/Nakuina, 1901: 111–115; Beckwith, 1940: 15, 20)

Lago∈yEwiLε' (tlago'yewitla) "Tilting-in-Mid-Ocean," the killer whale. Some shamans are initiated by him. The Kwakiutl Indians, British Columbia. (Boas, 1966: 121, 143)

Lamar The "'tax gatherer' of fisheries, who looked after the stocking of the marshes with fish." Near East. (Jacobsen, 1976: 83)

Leweke God of clams and of clam-fishing, and an ancestor god of Yamanaia. Pukapuka, Polynesia. (Beaglehole, 1938: 314, 317)

Liavaha A fish god at Hikutavaki who calmed the seas after a hurricane. Niue Island, Polynesia. (Loeb, 1926, 1: 161)

Ligich God of the turtle. Yap Island, the Carolines, Micronesia. (Christian, 1899: 385)

Lik A supernatural serpent "who carries fish within his tail." If found stranded on dry ground during the winter and carried back to a lagoon he promises many fish, but only provided this secret is kept. The Toba, Argentina. (Métraux, 1969: 59)

Li-kant-en-kap The sting-ray—totem deity of the Tip-en-uai tribe. Ponape, Caroline Islands, Micronesia. (Christian, 1899: 381)

Madai A god of fish, fishermen, and of sailors. Yap Island, the Carolines, Micronesia. (Christian, 1899: 385)

Maesila The "Salmon chief" who lives "in the west at the horizon." The Kwakiutl, British Columbia. (Boas, 1935: 127, 159)

Magdal A god whose name means "to scare up and drive a swarm of fish, birds or other game." Son of Manahaut. The Ifugao, Philippines. (Barton, 1946: 40)

Mako The "Shark." Born of Puoo and Atea. The Marquesas, Polynesia. (Christian, 1895: 189)

Mamala A kupua—a lizard, crocodile, or shark woman, wife of Ouha, the shark-man/god. Oahu, Hawaii. (Westervelt, 1963, 1: 52)

Mami A shark-man/god. Lau Islands (Fiji), Melanesia. (Beckwith, 1940: 131)

Manana A goddess whose form was that of a fish. Wife of Era Nuku, the bird god. Eastern Island, Polynesia. (Gray, 1925, 5: 133)

Manumanu-ki-rangi The eel god of Ariti Taumako to whom the lake-net is consecrated. Tikopia, Melanesia. (Firth, 1939: 175)

Maopurotu A shark god of the sky. Tahiti, Polynesia. (Henry, 1928: 389)

Mareleng A god of fish, of fishermen and sailors. The Carolines, Yap Island, Micronesia. (Christian, 1897: 191)

Masara-koro Kamui   A spirit who "protects fishing boats, above the high-water mark." The Ainu, Japan. (Munro, 1963: 43)

Matatini   God of fishermen and of net-makers. Tahiti, Polynesia. (Henry, 1928: 378; Ellis, 1853: 329)

Matsya   The fish incarnation of Vishnu wherein he preserved the human race from the flood; his first incarnation. India. (Martin, 1914: 109; Ions, 1967: 48; Crooke, 1894: 287)

Mea Ika   God of fish. Easter Island, Polynesia. (Gray, 1925, 5: 133)

Mea Kahi   God of the bonito fish. Easter Island, Polynesia. (Gray, 1925, 5: 133)

Mellih   A Phoenician "patron god of fishermen and sailors." Near East. (Paton, 1925, 9: 893)

Mo-ana-li-ha   A man-eating shark god. Maui, Hawaii. (Ashdown, 1971: 22)

Moe-Hakaava   The god of fishermen. The Marquesas, Polynesia. (Christian, 1895: 190)

Mohan   The "Master of Fish" in some areas of the Magdalena Valley, Colombia. (Reichel-Dolmatoff, 1971: 80)

Mohoalii   A shark god. Oahu, Hawaii. (Westervelt, 1963, 3: 85)

Mokoiro   God of the fishing fleet who had to be approached through an intermediary. Mangaia, Polynesia. (Buck, 1934: 167)

Mongohenua   A sea god who lived where the waves break near reefs, invoked in fishing. Kapingamaringi, Polynesia. (Emory, 1965: 202)

Móromunéki   A demon, the great turtle, who causes obstructions in childbirth. The Cuna Indians, Panama. (Nordenskiold, 1930: 60–61)

Moro-Podole   The father of fish who was once a human shaman. He is also invoked in hunting rituals. The Taulipang and the Arecuna, Guiana. (Zerries, 1968: 268)

Moso   A god of many forms—among them the octopus. Older brother of Pusipapanga and son of Tutumatua and Finetaunganoa. Moungaone Island, Tonga, Polynesia. (Gifford, 1929: 308; Mackenzie, n.d.: 287; Wallis, 1939: 63–64)

Mukasa   Among the Ganda the god of fishermen, who also provides children. Uganda. (Mair, 1934: 44, 234)

Munékitáyma   The alligator demon who causes difficulties in childbirth. The Cuna, Panama. (Nordenskiold, 1930: 60–61)

Munékitulup   The lobster demon who interferes with the birth of a child. The Cuna, Panama. (Nordenskiold, 1930: 60–61)

Nanshe   A goddess of fish and of fishing—"the numinous will that produces the teeming schools of fish." She is also skillful in interpreting dreams. Sumer, Near East. (Jacobsen, 1970: 7, 23)

Nati   A sea god worshipped by fishermen. The Ewe, Dahomey. (Mockler-Ferryman, 1925, 9: 278; Ellis, 1890: 66–67)

Naycuric   The creator of peyote, who had the form of a crayfish. The Huichol, Mexico. (Furst, 1972: 143)

Nazi   A Sumerian "fish goddess who interprets dreams and is concerned with justice." Near East. (Roberts, 1972: 46)

Newe, Hoku kau opae   Sirius "determined the best time for catching shrimp by her rising or setting." Newe and Keoe are boat-steering stars. Hawaii. (Emerson, 1967: 51)

Nigoubub   "(The procreatress) . . . produced earth and human beings at Onulap's command." Considered as "a female eel at whose breast the earth rests. When she turns the earth trembles." She is worshipped by those desiring children or those in labor. Truk, Micronesia. (Bollig, 1927: 12)

Nisoukepilen   A female spirit, half-eel, half-human who is the guardian of the sea. She lives in the sacred lake. Truk, Micronesia. (Bollig, 1927: 3)

Niu-loa-hiki   An eel-god. Hawaii. (Westervelt, 1963, 3: 190)

Niyohua   A deity of fishing and of hunting. The Zapotec, Sola, Oaxaca, Mexico. (Whitecotton, 1977: 164)

Noäkxnum   A supernatural who brings the salmon from the far west. The Bella Coola Indians, British Columbia. (McIlwraith, 1948, 1: 53)

Noçana, Nosana Quiataa   A deity of fishing and of hunting, who is also "associated with the 'ancestors' or the 'getting of life.'" The Zapotec, Sola, Oaxaca, Mexico. (Whitecotton, 1977: 164)

Nusa-koro Kamui A god invoked for success in fishing and in hunting. The Ainu, Japan. (Munro, 1963: 112)

Nyevile The personified sea invoked for successful fishing. The Nzema (Akan), Ghana. (Grottanelli, 1967: 38)

Nyíueldue Father of the Fish whose permission must be obtained before fishing, to whom an offering is made after. Son of the Universal Mother, Gaulchováng. The Cagaba and the Kogi, Colombia. (Reichel-Dolmatoff, 1949/50: 112)

Oannes A god, half-fish, half-man, considered a form of Ea. He introduced agriculture and all culture. Babylonia, Near East. (Sayce, 1898: 131; Robertson, 1911: 214; Frankfort, 1946: 22; Brinton, 1897: 161)

Odakon A Sumerian/Babylonian god who "has nothing to do with Dagan, but is the Sumerian fish-god U-ki-di-a, or U-di-a-ki, who is associated with the fish-god Han-ni, the prototype of Oannes." Near East. (Paton, 1925, 4: 387)

Oge A god of the underworld who "rules over famines (potu) and fish." A son of Tagaroa and Haumea. Mangareva, Polynesia. (Buck, 1938: 422)

Olle Fe'e The cuttle-fish (Octopus)—a god of war whose followers wore white turbans in going to battle. Samoa, Polynesia. (Turner, 1884: 28)

Oloinpalilele "Chief of fishes in the underworld." The Cuna Indians, Panama. (Nordenskiold, 1938: 328)

Olosa A beneficent "goddess who helps fishermen. Her messenger is the crocodile." Puerto Rico, West Indies. (Gonzalez-Wippler, 1975: 26)

Opochtli God of fishing and inventor of fishing equipment. He was also a god of fowling and considered one of the Tlaloques, gods of rain. Mexico. (Bancroft, 1886, 3: 410; Spence, 1923: 234–235)

Ouha A shark-man/god at Honolulu. Husband of Mamala. Hawaii. (Westervelt, 1963, 1: 15)

Pačani-samptni-malku God of fishes. The Uru, Bolivia. (La Barre, 1941: 521)

Pae Devi, Pa Janjali Goddess of fishes and of all water animals as well as goddess of the Seven Seas. She is invoked in cases of evil eye. The Bhils, India. (Naik, 1956: 181, 187)

Pahuatutahi One of the fish gods of the sea—"a great bivalve." Tuamotu, Polynesia. (Henry, 1928: 496)

Paikea God of sea-monsters. Son of Raki and Papa-tu-a-nuku, ancestor of the Maori. New Zealand. (Andersen, 1928: 375; White, 1887, 1: 22)

Palabultjura The Fish-Ancestress. The Aranda, Australia. (Robinson, 1966: 21)

Panang Kauka The great swordfish, child of Samni and Ning-pang majan. The Katchins, Burma. (Gilhodes, 1908: 673)

Parazito A dolphin deity, native to Para. Belem, Brazil. (Leacock, 1972: 144)

Pati A deity invoked by fishermen. The Kankanay, Luzon, Philippines. (Vanoverbergh, 1972: 86)

San Pedro The "special patron of fishermen." The Aymara, Peru. (Tschopik, 1951: 200)

Pehu A man-eating shark god of Hawaii. (Ashdown, 1971: 22)

Pet-ru-ush-mat Goddesses of the rivers and their entire courses who are invoked "for protection in descending the rapids, and for good fortune in fishing." The Ainu, Japan. (Batchelor, n.d.: 389; Czaplicka, 1969: 274)

Pili The lizard is the patron god of fishing as well as of agriculture. Manua (Samoa), Polynesia. (Mead, 1930: 158–9)

Pir Bhadr A water godling worshipped by fishermen and boatmen. India. Same as Khwaja Khizr. (Crooke, 1925, 5: 3)

Po'ele In the beginning all was darkness and night, the primordial female was born—"Darkness." With Kumulipo (the first pair), "parents of all hard-shelled things that came into being in the sea in the darkness." Hawaii. (Leach, 1956: 167)

Poira The Master of Fish—also called Mohan in some areas. The Magdalena Valley, Colombia. (Reichel-Dolmatoff, 1971: 80)

Pou A god of fish. The Moriori, Chatham Islands, New Zealand. (Shand, 1894: 89)

Pouliuli "Deep-profound-darkness," male, was born. With Powehiwehi (the second pair), the "parents of all the fish and creatures of the ocean." Hawaii. (Leach, 1956: 168)

Pounamu   A shark god—"a personification of jade." (Jade is supposed to form in a soft state inside of the shark and harden on exposure to air.) A son of Tangaroa and Anu-matao, twin of Poutini. New Zealand. (Mackenzie, n.d.: 46)

Poutini   A shark god—"a personification of jade" and also a star god. Twin of Pounamu. Another version of the myth makes Poutini female. Tahiti and New Zealand, Polynesia. (Mackenzie, n.d.: 36–37, 46, 52–53)

Powehiwehi   "Darkness-streaked-with-glimmering-light," female, was born. With Pouliuli (second primordial pair) "parents of all the fish and creatures of the ocean." Hawaii. (Leach, 1956: 168)

Boto Preto   A dolphin deity, native to Para. Belem, Brazil. (Leacock, 1972: 144)

Ah Pua   A Mayan god of fishing. Central America. (Tozzer, 1941: 156; Bancroft, 1886, 2: 698)

Puhi   A "personified form of the eel" and an ancestral god. The Maori, New Zealand and Uvea, Polynesia. (Best, 1924: 141; Burrows, 1937: 85)

Te Puhi-nui-o-Auto'o   The "king of the eels." The Marquesas, Polynesia. (Christian, 1895: 190)

Punga   The "father of lizards and sharks." Given variously as the son of Tangaroa or of Whai-tiri. New Zealand. (Mackenzie, n.d.: 296–9; Grey, 1855: 6)

Pungngane   A star god who is responsible for the abundance of the ponde fish. Encounter Bay, South Australia. (Woods, 1879: 201–202)

Pusi   An eel god of Tikopia whose rite of the first fruits of fishing must be satisfactory or he will kill. Melanesia. (Firth, 1967, 2: 103–104, 124)

Pusiuraura   An evil eel god associated with the adze of canoe rites. Tikopia, Melanesia. (Firth, 1967, 2: 63)

Pu Tautonga   An eel god of the Taumako clan. Tikopia, Melanesia. (Firth, 1967, 2: 99)

Qadesh wa-Amrur   A servant of Asherah, goddess of the sea. He is her fisherman. Canaan. (Patai, 1967: 32)

Q!omogwa   God of the sea who is the "owner of the herrings," of copper and of seals "which are his dogs." The Kwakiutl, British Columbia. (Boas, 1935: 125–131)

q'otawic'a   Grandmother of the Lake (Titicaca) is associated with the rain and some consider that she owns the fish. The Aymara, Bolivia. (Tschopik, 1951: 197, 200)

Quwai   A culture hero/transformer type who stocked the streams with fish. The Cubeo, Colombia. (Goldman, 1940: 242–244)

Ra'eapua   A fish god and a god of the sea worshipped chiefly by fishermen. Lanai and Molokai, Hawaii. (Emory, 1924: 13; Beckwith, 1940: 452)

Rajah Jewata   Goddess of fishes. The Sea Dyaks, Sarawak, Borneo. (Sarawak Gazette, 1963: 19)

Rajamma   A goddess who "blesses barren women with children and favours her devotees with big catches" when fishing. The Oriya Kumbaro, Southern India. (Thurston, 1909, 4: 117)

Rangi-hiki-waho   A shark god of the Moriori. Chatham Island, New Zealand. (Shand, 1894: 90)

Rato   A serpent water demon invoked for success in fishing. The Taulipang, Guiana. (Métraux, 1949: 566; Zerries, 1968: 264)

Ra-waru   "Summer's day—a little black fish." Child of Ta-whaki and Hine-tu-a-tai. New Zealand. (White, 1877, 1: 60)

Po Rayak   The whale god who is "king of the waves." The Chams, Annam and Cambodia. (Cabaton, 1925, 3: 342)

Remi   A fish god and a god of the Book of the Dead. Egypt. (Budge, 1969, 1: 303; 1969, 2: 334; Mercer, 1925, 12: 712)

repun kamui, Rep-un-riri-kata inao uk Kamui   The God of the Sea who takes the form of a killer whale and rules the food animals of the ocean. The Ainu, Japan. (Philippi, 1982: 63, 83; Batchelor, 1926: 244)

Rio   The god of bonito and albacore fishermen. He is also a stellar god (Aldebaran in Taurus), son of Ta'aroa and Papa-raharaha. Tahiti, Society Islands, Polynesia. (Henry, 1928: 361, 374)

Roi   The black fish god and an ancestor deity. Society Islands, Polynesia. (Henry, 1928: 612–613)

Roko(Rongo)-mai   God of the whale. Son of Raki and Papa-tu-a-nuku. New Zealand. (White, 1887, 1: 22)

Rokoratu An ancestor god "of the Vunikoro clan on Fulanga . . . incarnated in the *ulumburu* fish and the *sewa matua* fish." Southern Lau, Fiji, Melanesia. (Thompson, 1940: 111)

Rongo-mai-tauira The god of eels, and also of lightning and the will-o'-the-wisp. The Moriori, Chatham Island, New Zealand. (Shand, 1894: 90)

Rongomai-tu-waho A guardian of the fish and animals of the waters—both fresh and sea. The Maori, New Zealand. (Best, 1924: 105)

Rua'atu A god of Mangaia invoked for success in fishing. Polynesia. (Buck, 1934: 167)

Rua-hatu-tini-rau God of fishermen, a half-human, half-fish god. Society Islands, Polynesia. (Henry, 1928: 148, 358)

Rua-tamaine A goddess invoked for success in fishing. Mangaia, Polynesia. (Buck, 1934: 167)

Sallimmanu A fish-god and a god of peace. Assyria. (Sayce, 1898: 57–58)

Samalamma A goddess who "Wears a red skirt and green coat and protects the fishermen from fever." The Jalari and the Vada, Southern India. (Thurston, 1909, 2: 445; 1909, 7: 261)

Sango Some believe him to be "in charge of the river fish." The Bantu Kavirondo, Kenya. (Millroth, 1965: 108)

Satchini Kamui A bird deity, the spotted kingfisher, who is the protector of fish. The Ainu, Japan. (Munro, 1963: 22)

Saulal A god, half-man, half-lawud (a sea creature), who is the creator of the universe as well as a god of the underworld. Ifalik, Micronesia. (Burrows, 1947/48: 2)

Sautahimatawa A shark spirit to whom sacrifices are made for help in fishing for bonitos. Ulawa, Solomon Islands, Melanesia. (Codrington, 1881: 302)

Seketoa A fish god in Niuatoputapu. In Tonga a shark god and a guardian spirit. Polynesia. (Beckwith, 1940: 130; Gifford, 1929: 300)

Sisiul, Xtasaltsalosem A snake or fish being who lives in the salt-water pond where Qamaits bathes. It causes landslides when it visits the earth. The Bella Coola, British Columbia. (Boas, 1898: 28)

Sisiutl A double-headed snake, a totemic being who can "change itself into a fish, whose flesh is fatal to those who eat it." However, it is also beneficent—a portion of its body, owned by shamans, is powerful medicine. The Kwakiutl, British Columbia. (Alexander, 1964: 243)

Siuleo A god of fishermen in Savaii. Samoa, Polynesia. (Turner, 1884: 52)

Soinidi The Master of fish who punishes overfishing. The Toba of the Gran Chaco, Argentina. (Métraux, 1937: 175)

Sompallwe A lake god invoked for good fishing. The Araucanians, Chile. (Zerries, 1968: 264)

Sukdzya odzyani God of fish. The Udegeys, Siberia. (Ivanov, Smolyak, and Levin, 1964: 743)

Tagaloa leo 'ava Tagaloa as patron of fishermen, a god of the sea. Manua (Samoa), Polynesia. (Mead, 1930: 159)

Tagaloapuipuikimaka A god of fishing. Niue, Polynesia. (Loeb, 1926, 1: 162)

Tahauru The principal god of those believed "to preside over the fisheries, and to direct to their coasts the various shoals by which they were periodically visited." Society Islands, Polynesia. (Ellis, 1853: 329)

Takame A deified priest invoked in fishing. Kapingamarangi, Polynesia. (Emory, 1965: 202)

Tama-ehu God of salamanders, and also a god of fire. Society Islands, Polynesia. (Henry, 1928: 359, 377, 391)

Tamarau-ariki A shark god of the Moriori. Chatham Islands, New Zealand. (Shand, 1894: 90)

Tanaoa God of fishing, of the sea, of the wind. He is also considered a god of the beginning, god of night and of darkness. The Marquesas, Polynesia. (Buck, 1938: 151; Handy, 1923: 245–246; Williamson, 1933, 1: 20; Andersen, 1928: 380)

Tanaroa God of fishermen and sea travelers. Also a god of night. Son of Tane. Hawaii. (Melville, 1969: 35)

Tane-ma'o The god Tane as a shark. Society Islands, Polynesia. (Henry, 1928: 541)

Tangaloa An eel or snake god who takes human form. When he was killed the coconut palm grew from his head. New Hebrides, Melanesia. (Mackenzie, n.d.: 301)

Tangaroa God of fish and of all ocean creatures. The Moriori, Chatham Islands, and the Maori, New Zealand. On Easter Island he is a god of the sea who took the form of a seal. Polynesia. (Shand, 1894: 89; Best, 1924: 237; Andersen, 1928: 368, 370; Métraux, 1940: 310)

Tangata-no-te-mo'ana A god of fishing who controls the fish in the ocean, as well as a god of the underworld. Puka-puak, Polynesia. (Beaglehole, 1938: 313)

Tantrabu A god of fishing of the Fante. Ghana. (Parrinder, 1949: 47; Field, 1937: 22)

Tarianui God of the fishermen. Hervey Islands, Polynesia. (Larousse, 1973: 494)

Taringa-Nui A god of fishermen. Rarotonga, Polynesia. (Poignant, 1967: 23)

Ta-to'a An eel god, messenger for 'Rua-tupua-nui. Society Islands, Polynesia. (Henry, 1928: 358)

Taufa, Taufatahi As a sea god he was a shark god. As a land deity he took the form of a gecko and was a protector of gardens. Tonga, Polynesia. (Collocott, 1921: 229; Gifford, 1929: 288, 298)

Tava(j) God of fishing and of hunting. The Lapps, Kola Peninsula, Russia. (Collinder, 1949: 140)

Te Hua-i-nggavenga One of their two great gods—the other is his grandfather Te Hainggi-atua. He is the patron of fishermen, but also first fruit offerings of agriculture are made to him. Rennell Island, Polynesia. (Birket-Smith, 1956: 22, 59, 69)

Teimu Mother of the fish. The Cagaba and the Kogi, Colombia. (Reichel-Dolmatoff, 1949/50: 114)

Te Kasomera The eel god at Akitunu. Tikopia, Melanesia. (Firth, 1967, 2: 226)

Tempuleague A goddess who took the form of a whale and carried the souls of the dead to the afterworld. The Pehuenches, Chile. (Spence, 1925, 3: 549)

Te Pewu An ancestor god who was helpful in fishing and bird-catching. Pukapuka, Polynesia. (Beaglehole, 1938: 314)

Tinirau God of the ocean and of all its denizens. Son of Tangaroa in New Zealand, of Vari-ma-te-takere in Mangaia. Polynesia. (Best, 1924: 155–156; Williamson, 1933: 13; Hongi, 1920: 26; Poignant, 1967: 50)

Tino-rua God of the ocean and of fishermen—half-man with the tail of a swordfish—whose messengers were the sharks. Society Islands, Polynesia. (Henry, 1928: 148, 359; Buck, 1938: 70)

tjas-olmai God of lakes and of fishing. The Lapps, Northern Europe. (Dioszegi, 1968: 28; Bosi, 1960: 132)

Tk'a A transformer associated with salmon fishing and other food supplies—invoked and propitiated. The Tillamook, Oregon. (Boas, 1923: 8, 9)

Toa-hakanorenore An eel goddess of Mangareva. Polynesia. (Buck, 1938, 1: 426)

Tobukulu A goddess invoked for abundant fish and for "good seasons." Twin of Nafanua, daughters of Toki-langa-fonua and Hina, and mother of Hemoana by her father. Tonga, Polynesia. (Collocott, 1921: 236–237)

Toiragoni Son of Tagaloa. Personified by a sea turtle. Rotuma (Fiji), Melanesia. (Gardiner, 1897: 467)

Tokeimo'ana An eel god to whom finger sacrifices were made when invoking him in illness. Uiha Island, Tonga, Polynesia. (Collocott, 1921: 234–235; Gifford, 1929: 309)

Tokoyoto The Crab—"master of the sea." The Koryak, Siberia. (Jochelson, 1908: 20)

Tomari-koro Kamui A god protective of fishing boats in harbors. The Ainu, Japan. (Munro, 1963: 43)

Tonu-ma-vaha The tiger fish god. Society Islands, Polynesia. (Henry, 1928: 612)

Tonu-tai The sea turtle (female), twin of Tonu-uta (male); the third pair born of Touiafutuna. Tonga, Polynesia. (Williamson, 1933, 1: 10)

Tornarsuk, Tornatik "Half man, half seal. . . . 'Comes from the sea' to reveal to the angekkok the cause of maladies." The Eskimo, Greenland. (Larousse, 1973: 446)

Tu, Tu-matariri, Tu-matawahi The god of war was also a shark god. The Moriori, Chatham Islands, New Zealand. (Shand, 1894: 89–90)

Boto Tucuxi A dolphin deity who inhabits the Guama River. Belem, Brazil. (Leacock, 1972: 144)

Tui Tofua A shark god of Tonga. Polynesia. (Gifford, 1924: 76)

Tukuhali Male twin, the sea serpent, of Lupe (female), the fourth pair born of Touiafutuna. Tonga, Polynesia. (Williamson, 1933, 1: 10)

Tumu-I-Te-Are-Toka A great shark god of Mangaia. Polynesia. (Sykes, 1952: 217)

Tuna The god of fresh-water eels, lover of Sina, who was killed and from whose head, when planted by her at his behest, came the coconut palm. Mangaia, Polynesia. (Andersen, 1928: 259; Buck, 1938: 304)

Tuna toto An eel god invoked for preferential fish catch and for prestige. He was also an adz god of the Tafua clan invoked in the consecration of the sacred oven and in canoe building. He controlled the island's fresh water. Tikopia, Melanesia. (Firth, 1967, 2: 62, 120, 436)

Tupuafiti An eel god and an adz god of the Fangarere clan. Tikopia, Melanesia. (Firth, 1967, 2: 62)

Tu-rahu-nui An "artisan of Ta'aroa, guided the fish in its course." Society Islands, Polynesia. (Henry, 1928: 438)

Turanga A "river god . . . invoked before fishing expeditions." New Zealand. (Poignant, 1967: 27)

Tutula Another name of Haele-feke, the octopus god. Tonga, Polynesia. (Collocott, 1921: 231)

Tutunui A fish god of Polynesia. (Mackenzie, n.d.: 52)

Uayara A deity, under Guaracy, who is guardian of the fishes. The Tupi, Brazil. (Spence, 1925, 2: 837)

Udaki A Sumerian fish god whose wife is Nisaba, the corn-goddess. Near East. (Paton, 1925, 4: 387)

Ugaya-fuki-aezu A god who is protective of fishing and of navigation as well as of childbirth and nursing. He is the son of Hiko-ho-ho-demi and Toya-tama-hime. His wife is Tama-yori-hime. Japan. (Herbert, 1967: 370, 388)

Uhu-makai-kai "Parent of all fishes." Hawaii. (Beckwith, 1940: 24)

U-ieng-kong An earth god worshipped by fishermen for protection from drowning. Taiwan and Formosa. (Diamond, 1969: 97)

Umugai-hime, Umugihime Goddess of clams. Japan. (Yasumaro, 1965: 38; Herbert, 1967: 321)

Unga A dwarf, guardian of the seals for Kanna-kapfaluk. The Copper Eskimos, Canada. (Jenness, 1913/18: 188)

Unktahe The "great fish of the water, . . . showed its horns; and we know that that is always a sign of trouble.'" He is also the God of Waters. The Dakota, Minnesota, South Dakota, and North Dakota. (Eastman, 1962: 118, xxxi)

urigaki The "guardian of fish." The Bribri and the Cabécar, Costa Rica. (Stone, 1962: 52)

Uuakua Chief of the fish on the fourth layer of the underworld. His wife is Oloueaidili. In the Nele Sibu chronicle. The Cuna, Panama. (Nordenskiold, 1938: 297)

Uu kane po The *uu* (fish) worshipped as an aumakua. Hawaii. (Emerson, 1967: 49)

Vai-bogo The "Mother of Fish" who lives in the bottom of rapids with the Vai-mahse of waters. She sometimes takes the form of a large snake, and, if it "attempts to overturn the canoe" it is considered a sign of good luck. The Desana, Colombia. (Reichel-Dolmatoff, 1971: 28, 228)

Vai-mahse There are two supernaturals of this name— "one for the animals of the forest and the other for the fish." With the one of the waters lives Vai-bogo, the mother of fish. The Desana, Colombia. (Reichel-Dolmatoff, 1971: 28)

Vai-mango The aracu fish, daughter of Vai-mahse the Master of Fish. She cohabited with the first man and became the mother of the Desana. Colombia. (Reichel-Dolmatoff, 1971: 30)

Vakayala An ancestor god, helpful in fishing and bird-catching. Pukapuka, Polynesia. (Beaglehole, 1938: 314)

Vatea The father of gods and of men, son of Vari-ma-te-takere. He was half-man and half-fish with the division vertical. His wife was Papa, and he was also known as, or was the equivalent of, Atea, Te Tumu. Polynesia. (Williamson, 1933, 1: 12; Buck, 1938: 110; Long, 1963: 44)

Velo A god who indicated the fishing seasons by the stars. Pukapuka, Polynesia. (Beaglehole, 1938: 315)

Boto Vermelho A dolphin deity, native to Para. Belem, Brazil. (Leacock, 1972: 144)

Veyyi Kannula Ammavaru The "goddess of a thousand eyes . . . attends to the general welfare of the fisher folk." Southern India. (Thurston, 1909, 2: 446)

Vit-Khon A beneficent water god given charge of the fish by Numi. The Vogul, Siberia. (Czaplicka, 1969: 290)

Vivi-te-rua-ehu A shark god of Mata'oae in Taiarapu. Also the name of their eel god. Society Islands, Polynesia. (Henry, 1928: 389)

Vodyany, Vodyanik Slavic water spirit who when amiable bestows many fish and safe journeys to sailors, but when ill-tempered causes drownings and upsets, and damage to millwheels. The male counterpart of the Rusalkas. Russia. (Ralston, 1872: 148–152; Machal, 1918: 270–271)

Wakpanehene A fish deity of the Trumai. Brazil. (Murphy and Quain, 1955: 72)

Wareleng A god of fish, of fishermen, and of sailors. Yap Island, the Carolines, Micronesia. (Christian, 1899: 385)

Wien "Eel (Wien) is the Master of Fish." The Toba and the Pilaga, Argentina. (Métraux, 1969: 52)

Winwina A supernatural who brings the salmon from the far west. The Bella Coola, British Columbia. (McIlwraith, 1948, 1: 54)

Wolkollan The bonefish-god. Cape York Peninsula, Australia. (McConnel, 1935: 67)

Wua A god who indicated the fishing seasons by the stars. Pukapuka, Polynesia. (Beaglehole, 1938: 315)

Wurschayto, Borsskayto A Baltic god "worshipped generally in villages, wherever there was an oak tree; a young fish was sacrificed to him, and he conferred luck in fishing and good health." (Puhvel, 1974: 80)

Wu-weng Patron deity of fishermen. Szechwan, China. (Graham, 1961: 186)

Xulab The Morning Star is the patron of fishing, of hunting, and of agriculture, but is considered to have delegated his powers to the Mams. The Maya, British Honduras. (Thompson, 1930: 63)

Yamal Their favorite stone idol—on the peninsula of the same name. He assists in catching fish in the arctic sea. The Nenets (Samoyed), Siberia. (Struve, 1880: 795)

Yarbimuneki The eel demon who attempts to interfere with parturition. The Cuna, Panama. (Nordenskiold, 1938: 370)

Yaumau-Haddaku The goddess of fish who controls the fortunes of the fishing seasons. She lives at the mouth of the Ob River. The Yurak Samoyed, Siberia. (Czaplicka, 1925, 11: 175)

Yeman'gnyem The beneficent god of fish, of "river-fertility," and of travelers. He comes from the mouth of the Ob River, and is also called Yega-tei-igenen. The Ostyaks, Siberia. (Czaplicka, 1925, 9: 577)

Yemoja A river goddess and mother of the fish. Also the mother of many deities by her brother Aganju. The Yoruba, Nigeria. (Lucas, 1948: 97–98; Parrinder, 1949: 45)

Yerenamma A goddess who "protects fishermen from drowning and from being caught by big fish." The Jalari, Southern India. (Thurston, 1909, 2: 446)

Yo A fish vomited forth by Bumba, who "brought forth all the fish of all the seas and waters." The Boshongo, Zaire. (Eliade, 1967: 92)

Yu Hua Wu Sheng The patron of fish hatcheries. China. (Day, 1940: 110)

Yü Po The god of fish. China. (Ferguson, 1937: 90)

Zaden A goddess of the Iberians invoked by fishermen. Asia Minor. (Ananikian, 1964: 40)

29

Household Gods:
Doors, Hearth, Home, etc.

A-ba-sei A fire god, one of the legs of the three-legged Ch'iang stove. The others are A-ta-sei and Mo-go-shi. Szechwan, China. (Graham, 1958: 49)

Abera-ra-shut A deity who dwells below the hearth. The Ainu, Japan. (Munro, 1963: 38)

Aitvaras A household spirit who appears as a flying dragon, in the house as a black cat or cock. It brings its master coins, which represent the treasures of the earth. It is associated with warmth and the fire and provides wealth when it enters the house but also spreads disease. It must be fed omelets and be kept well; the master must sell his soul to the devil for his favors. Lithuania. (Gimbutas, 1975: XLC M126; Leach, 1949, 1: 31)

Aləshkintr A god invoked to provide the household with faithful dogs. An aspect of Ayt'ar. The Abkhasians, Caucasus. (Janashia, 1937: 126)

Aloimasina A household god seen in the moon— "Child of the moon." Samoa, Polynesia. (Turner, 1884: 67)

Ame-no-Fukiwo-no-Kami The god of thatching. A son of Izanagi and Izanami. Japan. (Yasumaro, 1965: 14)

Andheri Deo The god of the threshold. The Baiga, India. (Elwin, 1939: 60)

Angkui Guardian of the house. The Bondo, India. (Elwin, 1950: 157)

Ankamma A goddess frequently chosen as the household deity. Nellore District, India. (Elmore, 1915: 23)

Apai Nendak A god propitiated during the Mandi Rumah feast, the "house washing" of a new house. The Dyaks, Sarawak, Borneo. (Sarawak Gazette, 1963: 36)

Arnam Kethe A house god of the Mikirs who is also the supreme being. Not all households have him. He must be obtained and does not always come when invited. Assam. (Lyall, 1925, 8: 629; Biswas, 1956: 102; Stack and Lyall, 1908: 30; Barkataki, 1969: 58)

Asomua A household god helpful in detecting thieves. Samoa, Polynesia. (Turner, 1884: 69)

Aspelenie Litu-Prussian goddess of the hearth. (Schrader, 1925, 2: 34)

Asuha-no-Kami God of the courtyard, son of Otoshi-no-Kami and Ame-shiru-karu-mizu-hime. Japan. (Herbert, 1967: 332, 497)

A-ta-sei A fire god, one of the legs of the three-legged Ch'iang stove. The others are A-ba-sei and Mo-go-i-shi. Szechwan, China. (Graham, 1958: 49)

Awaia An evil spirit who "lives above and outside the gate, and can cause nightmare and bad dreams." The Chins, Burma. (Temple, 1925, 3: 25)

Ayaba Goddess of the hearth and guardian of the food. Daughter of Mawu and Lisa. Dahomey. (Herskovits, 1938, 2: 109)

Ayepi A household goddess who gives prosperity. The Angami Nagas, India. (Hutton, 1921: 182)

Bagula A household goddess. India. (Ghurye, 1962: 252)

Bala A household goddess of the Panjabis of Mandi. India. (Ghurye, 1962: 252, 258)

bang mdzod lha (pr. **pangdzo lha**) The "god of the storeroom" gives a feeling of protection and security in the home. Tibet. (Tucci, 1980: 187)

The Bannik The name of the household god when inhabiting the bathroom. Slavonic Russia. (Mansikka, 1925, 4: 627)

Bansankari, Banasamkari A household goddess. India. (Ghurye, 1962: 252)

Barnda Guardian spirit of the household who has various names for different functions, e.g., Sakhri nad, the hearth, Purbia nad, the threshing-floor. The Oraon, India. (Roy, 1928: 16, 72)

Barpahar A household spirit of the Santal. India. (Biswas, 1956: 135)

Basinlaiya A household deity of the Baiga. India. (Elwin, 1939: 61)

Baspahar A household deity who is invoked during agricultural festivals. The Santal, India. (Mukherjea, 1962: 283; Biswas, 1956: 135)

Bathau brai A household god, guardian of the family's welfare and honor. The Kacharis, Assam. (Engle, 1911: 35–36)

Bel The "spirit owner of the hearth." The Turks, Central Asia. (Czaplicka, 1925, 12: 482)

Benjo-no-kamisama "The god of the toilet" Takashima, Japan. (Norbeck, 1954: 124)

Bhagavati A household goddess of the Coorgs. India. (Ghurye, 1962: 252)

Bhimsen The "god of the cooking-place. . . . If they have no food, or the food is bad, . . . [he] is angry with them." The Gond, India. (Russell, 1916, 3: 126)

Mait' 'Bitation (d'habitation) The god of the "Habitation." Mirebalais, Haiti, West Indies. (Herskovits, 1937, 1: 161, 311)

Brigindo A goddess of the hearth, the fire, of poetry. France. Same as Brigit (Ireland). (Squire, 1906: 228, 277)

Brigit Goddess of the sacred (perpetual) fire and of the household fire. She is a triple goddess with her attributes distributed through fire, healing, poetry, smith-work, and fecundity and childbirth. Ireland. (MacBain, 1917: 129–30; Ross, 1967: 206, 360; Jayne, 1962: 513; MacCulloch, 1911: 69; Squire, 1906: 56)

Bulol "Gods of the household. They are held to be the souls of ancestors long departed, resembling the Roman lares." The Ifugao, Philippines. (Jocano, 1969: 16)

Bura Bagh Raja A household deity invoked "especially by men travelling at night." The Kacharis, Assam. (Endle, 1911: 37)

Cardea The goddess of hinges. Rome. (Dumézil, 1966, 2: 614; Fairbanks, 1907: 246; Jayne, 1962: 459)

Chai Shên The god of the house invoked for assistance. China. (Day, 1940: 90, 211)

Chantico The goddess of the hearth fire as well as of volcanic fire. She is also the goddess of goldsmiths and jewellers. The Aztec, Mexico. (Vaillant, 1962: 149; Spence, 1923: 283; Krickeberg, 1968: 44)

Chiang Tai-kung The "vinegar and charcoal god" who is one of the door gods placed at the entrance to protect the home, also of shops. China. (Weyer, 1961: 216; Day, 1940: 49)

Chia T'ang Wan Nien Hsing Huo A household god. China. (Day, 1940: 96)

Chicomecoatl, Chantico The goddess of the hearth fire and of provisions is primarily the goddess of maize, of the crops and the harvests. Mexico. (Reed, 1966: 112; Duran, 1971: 221–222; Bancroft, 1886, 3: 352; Spence, 1923: 173)

Chieh The deity of the hearth varies from male to female, sometimes as a couple. When the hearth and the fire are considered separately the first is female and the second male. China. (Schram, 1957: 123)

Chigrinad A household goddess to whom sacrifices are made to prevent illness and misfortune. Daughter of Barnda. The Oraon, India. (Roy, 1928: 16, 73, 79)

Ch'i-gwei-sei A god of the house at Ho-p'ing-chai. The Ch'iang, Szechwan, China. (Graham, 1958: 69)

Ching Ch'uän Tung Tzu The "boy-spirit of the well." China. (Day, 1940: 41; Leach, 1950: 392)

Ching Sohpai, Ch'in Shu-pao A Chinese door god. (Du Bose, n.d.: 131; Larousse, 1968: 389; Werner, 1934: 173)

Chise-kor-kamui, Chisei-koro Kamui The god and guardian of the house and household resides among the treasures in the northeast corner of the house. Some consider him the spouse of the Fire Goddess. The Ainu, Japan. (Philippi, 1982: 147; Munro, 1963: 30)

Ch'iung-hsiao One of the goddesses of the latrine. China. (Werner, 1932: 218)

Chlappar Burhia A special village and household deity—"Old Woman of the Roof." The Oraon, India. (Roy, 1928: 55)

Cho-an-nim The guardian of the kitchen. Korea. (Griffis, 1897: 327)

Choo Wang The god of the kitchen. Korea. (Clark, 1932: 51)

Chozyain, Chozyainusko Slavic household god. The Domovoy, Russia. (Machal, 1918: 246)

Chung-liu The household god who resided in, and was named for, the air shaft in the center of the house. Area of Honan, Shansi, Shensi, China. (Ferguson, 1937: 80)

Chu-nhà The house guardian who "resides in the lime jug . . . in which the lime used in preparing betel pellets is stored. If it is broken, it forbodes the death of a member of the family." Annam. (Leach, 1949, 1: 231)

Conopa The household gods of the Yunca. Also called Huasi-camayoc. Peru. (Alexander, 1920: 223; Markham, 1969: 133)

Dadam-an The spirit of the doorsill. The Isneg, Luzon, Philippines. (Vanoverbergh, 1941: 345)

Dedeks Slavic household god. Czechoslovakia. (Machal, 1918: 244)

Deduska Domovoy "Grandfather House-Lord." Slavic Russia. (Machal, 1918: 240)

Deswali A household god of the Santal invoked also at agricultural festivals. India. (Mukherjea, 1962: 283; Biswas, 1956: 135)

Didko A household god, similar to Domovoy. Slavic Russia. (Machal, 1918: 244)

Dilli Polasi A household goddess as well as one of the village. Nellore District, India. (Elmore, 1915: 25)

Dimstipatis God of the house, of the homestead. Another name for Zemininkas (Zemepatis). Lithuania

and Prussia. (Gray, 1930: 147; Schrader, 1925, 2: 3: 35; Gimbutas, 1963: 192)

Dinstipan The hearth god who guides the smoke up the chimney. Lithuania. (Crawley, 1925, 6: 562)

Djadeks Slavic guardian of the family, a household god. Silesia. (Machal, 1918: 244)

Do-dzu-sei The door god of the right side who protects from demons. The Ch'iang, Ho-p'ing-chai, Szechwan, China. (Graham, 1958: 48)

Domovoy The Domovoy of the individual is almost always benevolent, that of his neighbor is malevolent and thieving as he is also watching out for the master's interests. This household god is a snake, also called Tsmok, and brings good fortune when treated well. Russia and Poland. (Ralston, 1872: 119–120, 123–125, 129–130; Welsford, 1925, 11: 422)

Dugnai A Slavonic goddess "who prevented the dough from spoiling." (Larousse, 1968: 290)

Dulha Deo A household god who lives behind the hearth and is guardian of the engagement and the marriage. The Baiga, India. (Elwin, 1939: 60; Russell, 1916, 2: 6, 495)

Dvorovoj The name of the household spirit when he lives "in the yard." Slavic. (Mansikka, 1925, 4: 627)

Dwara Gosain God of the house door, of the doorway, and also a guardian deity of the village. The Malers, Chota Nagpur, India. (Crooke, 1925, 8: 345; MacCulloch, 1925, 4: 848)

Dwopi An evil spirit who "lives above the door of the house, and has the power of inflicting madness." The Chins, Burma. (Temple, 1925, 3: 25)

Dzu-si-ji-go-wa-la-tshe The "god of the big water jar." The Ch'iang, Mu-shang-chai, Szechwan, China. (Graham, 1958: 50)

eingsaung nat The benevolent house nat who among the Burman "resides in the south post of the house." (Leach, 1949, 1: 342)

Ekashi The god who guards the welfare of the household. The Ainu, Japan. (Batchelor, n.d.: 176)

Ekkekko, Ekeko A guardian household god of the Aymara who brings good fortune. Peru. (Trimborn, 1968: 129; Osborne, 1968: 88)

Ekwu   The spirit of the hearth, a deity of the women. The Igbo, Nigeria. (Uchendu, 1965: 100)

Etesi Edutzi   The god of houses. The Takanan, Araona, Bolivia. (Métraux, 1942: 41)

Fa'aipo   "Orderer," a household god. Tahiti, Polynesia. (Henry, 1928: 377)

Fa'atupu   A household god. Tahiti, Polynesia. (Henry, 1928: 377)

Forculus   Roman god of the doors. (Roscher, 1965, 2, 1: 199; Dumézil, 1966, 2: 614; Hadas, 1965: 122)

Fornax   Goddess of the stoves and the drying of grains. Rome. (Roscher, 1965, 1, 2: 1499)

Forulus   A Roman god of doors. (Schrader, 1925, 2: 32)

Fuchi, Fuji   The goddess of the hearth, of the fire, much worshipped. The Ainu, Japan. (Munro, 1963: 14, 15; Batchelor, 1925, 1: 242)

fu'uru-gami   The deity of "the pigpen or toilet." Okinawa. (Lebra, 1966: 218)

Gabija   Goddess of the hearth, of the fire which must never be extinguished; protectress of the fire and the family. Lithuania. (Gimbutas, 1963: 204; 1975: XLC M126; Leach, 1950, 2: 633)

Gauril   The foremost household god whose associates are Kalua, Kala Kalua, and Gardevi. The Himalayas, India. (Berreman, 1963: 370–371)

Ghazi Miyan   A household deity worshipped especially at childbirth. The Kalwars, India. (Crooke, 1925, 7: 643)

Giwoitis   A Slavonic domestic spirit who takes the form of a lizard. (Larousse, 1968: 290)

sGo lha   A Tibetan door god who is protective of worshippers and their prosperity. (Nebesky-Wojkowitz, 1956, 1: 328, 333)

Goraya   A household deity of the Santal invoked for the welfare of the household during agricultural festivals. India. (Mukherjea, 1962: 283; Biswas, 1956: 135)

dGra lha thab lha g·yu mo   A Tibetan goddess of the hearth. (Nebesky-Wojkowitz, 1956, 1: 330)

Grande Ezili   Beneficent goddess of the hearth and of sweet waters who personifies wisdom. She is identified with Saint Anne. Haiti, West Indies. (Marcelin, 1950: 93, 95)

Grihadeva   A Hindu goddess of the household. India. (MacKenzie, 1930: 321)

Gumin Shoin   The house spirits to whom a pig is sacrificed on building a house. As an individual, the guardian of the village. The Adi and the Minyong Abors, India. (Furer-Haimendorf, 1954: 595; Chowdhury, 1971: 42)

Gumo Gosain   The "god of the pillar," a household deity. The Males and the Mal Paharias, India. (Crooke, 1925, 8: 345)

Gurangpoi   A house god of the Bondo. India. (Elwin, 1950: 151)

Hadis   An Iranian god of the home. (Gray, 1930: 147)

Hahigi-no-kami   God and protector of the entrances, the area "between the outer-gate and the house." Japan. (Herbert, 1967: 332, 497)

Hahiki-no-Kami   A guardian deity of the premises. Japan. (Yasumaro, 1965: 51–52)

Hanker Bai   A household spirit, daughter of Barnda. The Oraon, India. (Roy, 1928: 16)

Hastsehogan   The benevolent House God, sometimes spoken of as one, sometimes plural. A god of the farm as well, of the west, and of the sunset. The Navaho, Arizona and New Mexico. (Matthews, 1902: 10, 11; Babington, 1950: 217)

Hemphu   "The most important of the house-gods . . . who owns all the Mikir people." Assam. (Lyall, 1925, 8: 629)

Hestia   Greek virgin goddess of the hearth, guardian of the family welfare. She represents "kindliness and good faith, . . . law and order, . . . wealth and fair dealing." (Cox, 1870, 2: 196; Murray, 1935: 77; Kerenyi, 1951: 91)

Him thang   A household spirit of the Tangsas. India and Burma (Dutta, 1959: 71)

Ho Hsien-ku   One of the Immortals (the 8th) whose emblem is the lotus. She was a seventh century mortal who ate of the supernatural peach and with her diet of "powdered mother-of-pearl and moonbeams" achieved immortality. "She assists in house management." China. (Williams, 1976: 156)

Hospodaricek Beneficent guardian of the family and the household who warns of danger. Bohemia. (Machal, 1918: 246)

Hu A household god—of the windows. China. (Leach, 1950: 392)

Huchi, Fuji Ainu goddess of the hearth where she dwells, and "does the cooking and warming, . . . a great purifier of the body from disease." Japan. (Batchelor, n.d.: 175–179)

Hu Ching-tê, Hu King-tê One of the gods of the doors. China. (Maspero, 1963: 293; Werner, 1934: 173)

Hushiti A goddess, guardian of the household and its welfare. Iran. (Gray, 1930: 149–150)

Hu Wei A Chinese door god. (Day, 1940: 211)

Hweli Guardian of the household. Dahomey. (Herskovits, 1938, 2: 300)

Icheiri Benevolent household gods, intermediaries between man and the gods. Same as Lares. The Carib, West Indies. (Alexander, 1920: 39, 40)

Idzu Pennu The house god of the Kandh. Bengal. (Crooke, 1925, 7: 649)

Inanna She is a deity of the storehouse as well as a goddess of war, of the morning and evening star, of weather. Near East. (Jacobsen, 1976: 24, 136–138)

Inmai An evil household spirit who "lives in the post in the front corner of the house, and can cause thorns to pierce the feet and legs." The Chins, Burma. (Temple, 1925, 3: 25)

Intercidona Roman goddess of the axe, a family deity, who also acts with Deverra and Pilumnus to protect parturient women and their children from evil spirits, and particularly Silvanus. (Jayne, 1962: 436; Dumézil, 1966, 2: 616; Larousse, 1968: 220)

Jakhmata, Jakhamata A household goddess of Poona District. India. (Ghurye, 1962: 250, 252)

Janus The two-faced god of doors and gates, both private and public, was originally a solar diety. He was importantly the god of beginnings in all contexts and of time

and the first of all its units. Italy. (Dumézil, 1966, 1: 173, 328–331; Pettazzoni, 1956: 167–169; Fairbanks, 1907: 246–247; Schoeps, 1961: 147; Larousse, 1968: 200)

Jei-tzu-ze-tzu-tse-mye The "god of the four corners of the house." The Ch'iang, Mu-shang-chai, Szechwan, China. (Graham, 1958: 50)

Ji-gwe-sei The god of the house, protective of the family. The Ch'iang, Ho-p'ing-chai, Szechwan, China. (Graham, 1958: 47)

Jurt-ava, Jurt-azerava (Moksha) Finno-Ugrian goddess of the courtyard. The Mordvins, Russia. (Paasonen, 1925, 8: 845)

Kamado-no-Kami God of the kitchen range and fire. Japan. (Bunce, 1955: 112; Herbert, 1967: 498)

K'ang T'ou Wu Shêng A household god—-of the cistern. China. (Day, 1940: 91)

Kannimar The seven virgins—family deities and guardians of their welfare. The Eravallar, Southern India. (Thurston, 1909, 2: 215)

Kansasur Mata A household deity of the Baiga who lives in the pot. India. (Elwin, 1939: 61)

Karappu Rayan A family deity, guardian of their welfare. The Eravallar, Southern India. (Thurston, 1909, 2: 215)

Kardas-sarko Finno-Ugrian goddess of the courtyard. The Erza, Russia. (Paasonen, 1925, 8: 845)

Kaukas A dwarf spirit who inhabits the house, the attendant buildings and the fields of a household and brings good fortune. Lithuania. (Gimbutas, 1974: 89, 90; Leach, 1950, 2: 631)

Kaybacan A feast is given to the "guardian of the house" when a new house is completed. The Apayao, Philippines. (Wilson, 1947: 22)

Kelu Devaru, Mane Hennu Devaru The goddess of the pot, of the household, who is worshipped at the Dasara festival and during marriage ceremonies. The Kuraba, India. (Thurston, 1909, 4: 151)

K'êng-san-ku "The Goddess of the Privy." China. (Maspero, 1963: 296)

Kenru Katkimat A female spirit of the house. The Ainu, Japan. (Munro, 1963: 64)

Khyim lha A *dgra iha* god "able to bring well-being and happiness to the household." Tibet. (Nebesky-Wojkowitz, 1956, 1: 332)

Kikimora A Slavonic female domestic spirit, of the poultry and sometimes of household tasks. (Larousse, 1968: 290)

Kindazi A goddess who was the "chamberlain" of Ningirsu, preparing his bath "and seeing that there was fresh straw in his bed." Near East. (Jacobsen, 1976: 82)

Kitro Bai A household spirit, daughter of Barnda. The Oraon, India. (Roy, 1928: 16)

The kitsung A permanent household spirit who moves with the master and is the source of fortune, good as well as evil. The Ao Nagas, India. (Mills, 1926: 222)

Kojin The god of the larder and the kitchen. He is also a tutelary god, violent and fearsome. Japan. (Herbert, 1967: 498; Eliot, 1935: 139; Norbeck, 1954: 126–127; Kato, 1931: 131)

Krimba Slavonic goddess of the house. Bohemia. (Larousse, 1968: 290)

ka ksaw ka jirngam A household goddess who brings good luck, especially in hunting. The Khasi, Assam. (Gurdon, 1907: 112; Stegmiller, 1921: 410)

Kuan Shêng Ti Chün "Protector of Homes." China. (Day, 1940: 162)

Kud-azerava, Kud-ava, Kudzi-pavas, Kudon-tsin pas, Keren sotskon pas, Kudo-jurtava Finno-Ugrian goddess/god of the dwelling. The Mordvins and the Moksha, Russia. (Paasonen, 1925, 8: 845; Leach, 1949, 1: 96)

kude-wodez The spirit of the house. The Cheremis, Russia. (Leach, 1949, 1: 215)

Kukuki-wakamuro-tsunane-no-Kami A guardian of houses. Child of Hayamato-no-Kami and O-ge-tsu-hime. Japan. (Herbert, 1967: 333)

Kul Devi The goddess of the household who must be worshipped while the family is alone. She is also worshipped at marriage ceremonies. Central Provinces, India. (Russell, 1916, 2: 483; 1916, 3: 173)

Kumuwanga A household god appealed to in illness. The Bagisu, Uganda. (Williams, 1936: 174)

Kushi-iwa-mado-no-mikoto God of the entrance-gate. Japan. (Herbert, 1967: 497)

Kutami-no-kami A god of the entrance-gate. Japan. (Herbert, 1967: 497)

kwoth wecda The spirit of the home. The Nuer, Sudan. (Evans-Pritchard, 1953: 205)

Lal Mani A household god of the Kachhi. India. (Crooke, 1925, 7: 634)

U Lamsymphud A household god of the Syntengs. Assam. (Gurdon, 1914: 109)

The Lares Roman deified ancestral spirits who are guardians of the home, when there is just one per family; and guardians of the fields and the crossroads, when there are two, one for each field or road. (Larousse, 1968: 214; Dumézil, 1966, 1: 37, 376; Murray, 1935: 226; Schoeps, 1962: 147)

ka lei iing A household goddess. The Khasi, Assam. (Stegmiller, 1921: 410; Gurdon, 1907: 112)

ka Lei Khuri A deity of the hearth. The Khasi, Assam. (Bareh, 1967: 375; Stegmiller, 1921: 410)

Lima Roman goddess of the thresholds. (Roscher, 1965, 2, 1: 202)

Limentinus, Limentius Roman god of the threshold (Fairbanks, 1907: 246; Dumézil, 1966, 2: 614; Hadas, 1965: 122)

li rum The god of the house to whom a bull was sacrificed in gratitude for his protection. The Lepchas, Sikkim. (Siiger, 1967: 69)

Lisman girde pas Finno-Ugrian god of the well. The Mordvins, Russia. (Paasonen, 1925, 8: 845)

Lohasur Mata A household deity who lives in the axe. The Baiga, India. (Elwin, 1939: 61)

ka Longkuinruid, ka Thab-bulong A household deity of the Syntengs. Assam. (Gurdon, 1914: 109:

ka Lukhimai A hearth deity of the Khasi. Assam. (Bareh, 1967: 375)

Lu Shên A group of "Six Household Gods." Dhina. (Day, 1940: 211)

Lymyzn-mam "Mistress of the threshold." The Gilyak, Siberia. (Shternberg, 1933: 335)

Ma Chün, Ma Chuan The god of the lamp. China. (Werner, 1932: 238; Du Bose, n.d.: 328)

Madan The chief household deity for whom a harvest festival is given. The Kanikar, Southern India. (Thurston, 1909, 3: 171)

Mahagiri The house *nat*—the most important of the 37 *nats* of the Talaings. Burma. (Temple, 1925, 3: 36)

Mainao A household goddess who is also a guardian of the rice fields. Also known as Bhulli Buri. The Kacharis, Assam. (Endle, 1911: 36, 37)

Majas Kungs The "master of the homestead." Latvia. (Gimbutas, 1963: 192; Gray, 1930: 147)

Ma lha A *dgra lha* deity whose function "is to increase and guard the family." Tibet. (Nebesky-Wojkowitz, 1956, 1: 332)

Manglia A household god of the Himalayas. India. (Berreman, 1963: 370)

Mao Tzu Shên Chüu Goddess of the latrine, also known as K'eng San Ku Niang, "who is customarily invoked on the 14th of the first month for answers to anyone's questions as to the future." China. (Day, 1940: 91)

Mataisang Benevolent household spirit of the Tangsas. India and Burma. Mataithang of the Lungris. (Dutta, 1959: 67)

Matergabia Goddess of "the housekeeping." Slavonic. (Larousse, 1968: 290)

Mi-kura-tana-no-kami A household god, of the "store-house shelf." Japan. (Herbert, 1967: 499)

Min Mahagiri The household *nat* has become so widespread that he became a national *nat*, universally worshipped. Burma. (Spiro, 1967: 54, 138; Nash, 1966: 118–119)

Mintara-koro Kamui A deity, sometimes a pair, who "guards the approaches to the house." The Ainu, Japan. (Munro, 1963: 21)

Mo-bo-sei A god of fire who controls the fire and prevents it from burning the house. The Ch'iang, Ho-p'ing-chai, Szechwan, China. (Graham, 1958: 48)

Moehau A household god—of "Peaceful-slumber." Tahiti, Polynesia. (Henry, 1928: 377)

Mo-go-i-shi A fire god, one of the legs of the 3-legged Ch'ang Ch'iang stove. The others are A-ba-sei and A-ta-sei. Szechwan, China. (Graham, 1958: 49)

Moire Mat The spider goddess invoked in house-warming ceremonies. The Ainu, Japan. (Munro, 1963: 79, 80)

Mokusha A survival of Mokosh "as a female house spirit." Slavic Russia. (Gimbutas, 1971: 168)

Mo lha, phug lha The god of women, protecting them and living in the area of their activities. The house god of the interior who "controls the property of the family, especially the live-stock." God of the female line and also of the left armpit. Tibet. (Tucci, 1980: 187–188)

Moonda Pennu The god of the tank. The Kandh, Bengal. (Crooke, 1925, 7: 649)

Mukrang A house god associated with Hemphu as "preservers of men." The Mikirs, Assam. (Lyall, 1925, 8: 629)

Mu-nga-dwe-dwe-dze-swe-tshi A deity of the central pillar of the house. The Ch'iang, Mu-sang-chai, Szechwan, China. (Graham, 1958: 50)

Mungkang Ma-au The deity of the cooking-pot. Child of Ningsang Woishun and Phungkam Janun. The Katchins, Burma. (Gilhodes, 1908: 677)

Murabula The principal household god of the Bagisu. Uganda. (Williams, 1936: 174)

Nag Raja A snake king god and a household deity who must be offered retribution if a snake is injured in the fields. The Himalayas, India. (Berreman, 1963: 372–373)

Nalwun An evil spirit who lives "in the verandah, and can cause women to be barren." The Chins, Burma. (Temple, 1925, 3: 25)

Nang lha, Nan-lha, Khyim nang lha The house god of the interior. Tibet and Sikkim. (Nebesky-Wojkowitz, 1956, 1: 296; Gazetteer of Sikhim, 1894: 369; Waddell, 1959: 372–373)

Naono An evil spirit of the Chins who "lives in the wall, and causes fever and ague." Burma. (Temple, 1925, 3: 25)

Narayan Deo The god of the threshold. The Baiga, India. (Elwin, 1939: 60)

Narbada Mai A household deity who " sometimes . . . lives in an iron chain hanging from the wall." The Baiga, India. (Elwin, 1939: 61)

Nar Singh A household god usually individual, but sometimes referred to as three—Dudadhari Nar Singh, Janghoria Nar Singh, and Kerari Nar Singh. The Himalayas, India. (Berreman, 1963: 369)

Nau Fiora In Tafua a goddess of the oven, "very ferocious," and also "guardian of Rangifaerere, the heavenly abode of women who die in childbirth." Tikopia, Polynesia. (Firth, 1967, 2: 410–411)

The Ngaw-k'o and **The Ngaw-lo** The gods of the house who are beneficent and give prosperity, and fertility in domestic animals. The Nakhi, Yunnan Province, China. (Rock, 1936: 40)

Ningyu lawa God of food and of the kitchen. Son of Ningsan Woishun and Phungkam Janun. The Katchins, Burma. (Gilhodes, 1908: 677, 679)

Nmanya An Iranian household god. (Gray, 1930: 154)

Nokpi An evil spirit who lives "in the verandah, and can cause women to be barren." The Chins, Burma. (Temple, 1925, 3: 25)

Numod-emei "House-mother," the owner of the house who is invoked by the shaman in healing. The Yukaghir, Yassachnaya River, Siberia. (Jochelson, 1900/02: 202)

Numon-pogil "The Owner of the House" who guards it from evil spirits. The Yukaghir, Siberia. (Jochelson, 1900/02: 151)

Nu-nga-sei The god of the left side of the door who protects from demons. The Ch'iang, Ho-p'ing-chai, Szechwan, China. (Graham, 1958: 48)

Nu'u The god of excrement. "The disgusting worship of Nu'u, the *aumakua* in human waste, was associated with the treatment of the two diseases, *pupule* (insanity), and *hoounauna,* a chronic pain in some particular part of the body." Hawaii. (Emerson, 1968: 51; Beckwith, 1940: 84)

Nyei-Wui A "god on the northwest corner of the main room in the house." The Ch'iang, Mu-shang-chai, Szechwan, China. (Graham, 1958: 50)

Nyu-ge-ze The "god on the right side of the front door." The Ch'iang, Mu-shang-chai, Szechwan, China. (Graham, 1958: 50)

O-Doku-sama God of the kitchen stove. Takashima, Japan. (Norb ec k, 1954: 123)

Ogon' (pr. **Agón**) God of the hearth and of the fire. Son of Svarog. Slavic Russia. (Ralston, 1872: 85–86)

Okisityingo A beneficent household spirit. The Lhota Nagas, India. (Mills, 1922: 115)

Oki-Tsu-Hiko God of the kitchen who is "particularly in charge of the caldron where water is boiled and rice cooked." Japan. (Herbert, 1967: 332, 498)

Okitsuhime Goddess of the kitchen and the range whose charge is the pots and pans. Japan. (Herbert, 1967: 332, 498; Yasumaro, 1965: 51)

Olarosa The deity of houses. The Yoruba, Nigeria. In Puerto Rico he is the guardian of homes. West Indies. (Lucas, 1948: 163; Gonzalez-Wippler, 1975: 26)

Ong-ghot The house gods, guardians of the flocks and of the prosperity and welfare of the family. The Monguors, Kansu, China. (Schram, 1957: 125)

Orak bongas The household spirits of the Santals: Baspahar, Deswali, Seas, Goraya, Barpahar, Sarchawdi. They are invoked during agricultural festivals. India. (Biswas 1956: 135; Mukherjea, 1962: 283)

Otobiwaki-no-Kami God of the porch. Son of Izanagi and Izanami. Japan. (Yasumaro, 1965: 14; Herbert, 1967: 264)

Owana A protective domestic god of the Limbu who is notified after a wedding of the new daughter-in-law. Nepal. (Caplan, 1974: 190, 193)

Oyabiko-no-Kami The god of the roof. Son of Izanagi and Izanami. Japan. (Yasumaro, 1965: 14; Herbert, 1967: 264)

p'a lha A powerful house god who "protects the house and the sacred hearth"—fends off hostile spirits. Tibet. (Ribbach, 1940: 19, 41)

Paniharin A goddess of the household who lives by the waterpots and protects women going to get water. The Baiga, India. (Elwin, 1939: 61)

The Penates Roman spirits, protective of the larder, who saw to the welfare of the household along with the Lar. (Hadas, 1965: 122; Larousse, 1968: 217–218; Dumézil, 1966, 1: 342; Murray, 1935: 226)

Peng   A god of the house to whom goats are sacrificed. The Mikirs, Assam. (Lyall, 1925, 8: 629; Barkataki, 1969: 58)

P'êng T'ou Wu Shêng   The spirit of the "Matshed or Awning." China. (Day, 1940: 205)

P'er-shi-jei-ts'e-mye   A god of the west wall of the house. The Ch'iang, Mu-shang-chai, Szechwan, China. (Graham, 1958: 50)

U Phan Longbriew   A household deity who bestows more dignity. The Khasi, Assam. (Bareh, 1967: 375)

U Phan Longkur   A household deity who gives increased fertility to humans. The Khasi, Assam. (Bareh, 1967: 375)

Pharkain   God of the gate. The Baiga, India. (Elwin, 1939: 61)

pho lha   The god of men whose power resides in the right armpit. He is concerned with the protection of the exterior of the house. Tibet. (Tucci, 1980: 187–189)

phug lha (pr. phuklha), khyim lha   A deity "who dwells in the inner pillar of the house," gives protection and security so long as not offended or injured. *See also* **Mo lha.** Tibet. (Tucci, 1980: 187)

Pi-hsiao   One of the goddesses of the latrine. China. (Werner, 1932: 218)

Polengabia   A goddess of the hearth. Lithuania. (Welsford, 1925, 9: 241)

Pört-chozjin   The "master of the kiln" who lives near the hearth. Russian Lapps. (Holmberg, 1925, 7: 798)

Pos Bai   A household spirit, daughter of Barnda. The Oraon, India. (Roy, 1928: 16)

Possjo-akka   An old goddess of the *kata,* the back part of the house. The Lapps, Northern Europe. (Holmberg, 1925, 7: 798)

Pu Fafine   Goddess of the ritual oven, of the bottom. She was also a goddess of the canoe shed. Tikopia, Polynesia. (Firth, 1967, 2: 81, 107, 445)

Pufine i Fiora   One of the deities in charge of the sacred oven. The Tafua clan, Tikopia, Polynesia. (Firth, 1967, 2: 124)

Qastceqogan   God of the house who is also protective of the cornfields. The Navajo, Arizona and New Mexico. (Chamberlain, 1894: 187)

Rama   Persian "genie who gives dishes their savour." (Huart, 1963: 42)

Ramiew iing   The household god whose offering is a he-goat and a fowl when building a house. The Khasi, Assam. (Gurdon, 1907: 33)

Ka Rasong   A household goddess who watches over their labor and their trading and looks after "the young unmarried folk." The Syntengs, Assam. (Gurdon, 1914: 109)

Raugupatis   Litu-Prussian "lord of the leaven." (Schrader, 1925, 2: 35)

Raupenapena   An oven goddess, a name of Pufine i Ravenga in this function. Tikopia, Polynesia. (Firth, 1967, 2: 445)

Rek Anglong   A household god who is worshipped in the fields and to whom a fowl is sacrificed. The Mikirs. Among the Bhois a he-goat and a fowl are offered when building a house. Assam. (Barkataki, 1969: 59; Gurdon, 1907: 33)

Ru-koro Kamui   The "*kamui* of the male privy (the female privy has no *kamui*) who is also regarded by some as a pair of spirits. He is associated with ideas of expulsion and evacuation and is regarded as powerful." The Ainu, Japan. (Munro, 1963: 21)

Safa   The god of the hearth-chain by whom oaths are sworn. The Ossetes, Caucasus. (Morgan, 1888: 383, 391)

Sakhri nad, Chulahi nad   The spirit of the hearth, another name for Barnda. The Oraon, India. (Roy, 1928: 71)

Sampo-kojin   God of the kitchen, of the larder. Japan. (Herbert, 1967: 498)

San Chieh Kung   A Chinese household god. (Day, 1940: 96)

Sarchawdi   A household spirit of the Santals invoked during agricultural festivals. India. (Mukherjea, 1962: 283; Biswas, 1956: 135)

Sas   A secret household deity whose name is disclosed only to the eldest son. The Santals, India. (Mukherjea, 1962: 283)

Satdhari   A household deity protective from disease. The Baiga, India. (Elwin, 1939: 61)

Sathavu   A household god of the Koravas. Southern India. (Thurston, 1909, 3: 462)

Sautu majan   Mother of fat, grease. Daughter of Phungkam Janun. The Katchins, Burma. (Gilhodes, 1908: 678)

Seas   A household spirit of the Santal. India. (Biswas, 1956: 135)

Seimes Dievas   A Lithuanian god of the household. (Gray, 1930: 147)

Semangat Rumah   The "Soul of the House" believed to live in the Tiang Seri pillar under which a coin is placed in the building. Malaya. (Noone, 1948: 130)

Setek, Sotek   A Slavic household god who "protects the flocks from disease and brings good harvests and money." Bohemia. (Machal, 1918: 244)

Shen-t'u   An ancient god of the doors and windows. China. (Maspero, 1963: 293; Werner, 1932: 420)

Shinto   A Chinese god of the door of the family. (Du Bose, n.d.: 331)

Shu-koyan-mat   Goddess of the cooking pot and daughter of Huchi, the fire goddess. The Ainu, Japan. (Batchelor, n.d.: 179)

Shulshagana   The eldest son of Ningirsu who "supervised the meals and carried the pitcher of water for washing the hands before and after eating." Near East. (Jacobsen, 1976: 82)

Shvod   The "guardian of the house" in the winter is driven out at the end of February to be the guardian "of the fields for the summer." Armenia. (Leach, 1950, 2: 1010)

Siniboi   A goddess who is guardian of the house. The Bondo, India. (Elwin, 1950: 157)

Skrat   A Slovenian household god who brings prosperity and abundance. Styria, Austria. (Machal, 1918: 245)

Skrata   The household guardian of the Slovaks. (Machal, 1918: 245)

Skritek   A Slavic guardian of the family and the household. (Machal, 1918: 245)

Skrzatek   A Slavic guardian of the family and the household. Poland. (Machal, 1918: 245)

Slava   Southern Slavic patron of the house to whom offerings were made of bread and candles. (Gimbutas, 1975: XLC M126)

Smiera-gatto   The "butter cat," a domestic deity of the Scandinavian Lapps. (Holmberg, 1925, 7: 798; Leach, 1950, 2: 1029)

Smintheus   A god invoked when there were plagues of mice. Greece. (Roscher, 1965, 4: 1083)

Song Brai   A household deity especially revered by women. The Kacharis, Assam. (Endle, 1911: 37)

Song Raja   A household deity especially revered by women. The Kacharis, Assam. (Endle, 1911: 37)

Stopan   A Slavic household god who gave fertility and abundance, and longevity. Bulgaria. (Machal, 1918: 246)

Su-gu-be   The god of the left side of the door. The Ch'iang, Mu-shang-chai, Szechwan, China. (Graham, 1958: 50)

Suklang-malayon   A goddess of the sky world who was the "guardian of happy homes." The Bisayan, Philippines. (Jocano, 1969: 20)

Syen, Syenovik   The guardian of the house. Montenegro. Same as Domovoy. (Bray, 1935: 42; Rhys, 1937: 164)

Szlotrazys   God of the bath broom. Lithuania. (Schrader, 1925, 2: 32)

Szullinis, Szullinus   Lithuanian god of the wells. (Schrader, 1925, 2: 32; Welsford, 1925, 9: 241)

Ka Taben   The mother of the household gods. The Syntengs, Assam. (Gurdon, 1914: 108–109)

t'ab lha   The hearth god. Western Tibet. (Ribbach, 1940: 19) *See also* **Thab lha.**

T'ang Tzu Wu Shêng   Chinese spirit of the bathroom. (Day, 1940: 205)

Taua-Mana'oa   A deified mortal and household god whose name "was and is used as a sanction to enforce a *tabu* or solemn prohibition." The Marquesas, Polynesia. (Christian, 1895: 190)

Tautu   A god "who presided over cooking in the army and at home." He was also the god of comedians. Society Islands, Polynesia. (Henry, 1928: 375–376)

Tav yzin   The "master of the house." The Gilyak, Siberia. (Shternberg, 1933: 335)

Teki Penu   The "god of vessel," who is guardian of the household goods. The Kandhs, Madras, India. (Crooke, 1925, 7: 651)

Têng-kuan P'u-sa   A Chinese lamp god. (Werner, 1932: 493)

Thab lha   The god of the hearth is both benevolent and malevolent, giving appetizing food and prosperity, but also punishing when offended, when angered by evil smells and smoke. Tibet. (Nebesky-Wojkowitz, 1956, 1: 296, 332; Hoffman, 1956: 20; Tucci, 1980: 173)

Thab lha g·yu mo   Tibetan goddess of the hearth. (Nebesky-Wojkowitz, 1956, 1: 202)

Thamdi   A name of Sitala Mata as a household goddess. The Chamars, India. (Briggs, 1920: 137)

Thuntatursa   A household deity of the Santals invoked during agricultural festivals. India. (Mukherjea, 1962: 283; Biswas, 1956: 135)

Thyak-dum   A spirit of the household and the fields who gives prosperity and health, but if angered disease and misfortune. The Lepchas, Sikkim. (Gorer, 1938: 74–75)

Tigyama   The guardian of the house who also heals the sick. The Bagobo, Philippines. (Benedict, 1916: 11, 19)

tisse-kamui   God of the hut, the house. The Ainu, Inau Cult, Japan. (Sternberg, 1906: 427)

Tonto   The "site," a domestic deity of the Scandinavian Lapps. (Holmberg, 1925, 7: 798)

Toshigami-sama   A Shinto household god, the "year god," invoked at New Years. Takashima, Japan. (Norbeck, 1954: 120, 122)

tsan dong rum   The god of the house for whom a ceremony is performed by the carpenter at the beginning of and the completion of the erection of a house. The Lepchas, Sikkim. (Siiger, 1967, 1: 68)

Ts'ang-shen   Confucist "gods of the store-houses." Peking and Tung-chow, China. (De Groot, 1925, 4: 14)

Tsan-küin   A Buddhist god of the kitchen, supervising the monastic diet. China. (Waddell, 1959: 372)

Tsao Chia P'u-sa, Tsao Chün   The god of the kitchen, of the hearth, the stove. He controls the welfare, good or bad, of the household. China. (Day, 1940: 16; Werner, 1932: 518–519)

Tsao Shên   The god of the hearth whose paper image is burned to ascend to Heaven to report on the condition of the families. He controls their welfare for good or bad. China. (Ferguson, 1937: 74)

Tsao T'u   A guardian of the kitchen: China. (Day, 1940: 209)

Tsao-wang   The god of the hearth who keeps the family records, the acts and words of its members. China. (Larousse, 1968: 389)

Tsau-kiün   Chinese god of the kitchen. (Edkins, 1880: 207)

Tsè Shēn   A god of the household. China. (Ferguson, 1937: 81)

Ts'in Shu-pao   One of the gods of the doors. China. (Maspero, 1963: 293)

Tsmok   A White Russian house-spirit. Same as Domovoy. A snake who brings good fortune to the kindly master. (Ralston, 1872: 123–125; Welsford, 1925, 11: 422)

Tung Chu Szu Ming   Another name for Tsao Shen or Tsao Chun. China. (Day, 1940: 86, 87)

Tupuasei   A name of Te Atua i te Uruao as an oven deity. Tikopia, Polynesia. (Firth, 1967, 2: 445)

Tusara   The "god of the spirits of domestice service." The Rundi, Burundi. (Meyer, 1916: 189)

Tuurman   The old goddess of the hearth, of the fire. The Gilyak, Siberia. (Shternberg, 1933: 320)

Tzu-ku Shën   A goddess of the latrines who is also known as K'êng San-ku. China. (Werner, 1932: 535)

U-du-p'e   A lesser deity whose place is in the center of the house. The Ch'iang, Mu-shang-chai, Szechwan, China. (Graham, 1958: 50)

Uiwiri   The guardians of the house, spirits of least importance. The Aymara, Peru. (Tschopik, 1946: 559)

Ujimo-kami A household god, of the entrance gate. Japan. (Herbert, 1967: 49)

Ü-mu-p'i A lesser household deity. The Ch'iang at Mushang-chai, Szechwan, China. (Graham, 1958: 50)

Unchi Ahchi Grandmother Hearth, goddess of the fire, is intermediary between the Ainu and all the other deities. She is also a goddess of the shore. Sakhalin, Siberia, and Japan. (Ohnuki-Tierney, 1974: 89)

Vastosh-pati A guardian deity of the house who is invoked for protection from disease and for abundance in domestic animals. The Hindu, India. (Macdonell, 1897: 138; Gray, 1930: 154)

Vattuma A god of the threshold. India. (MacCulloch, 1925, 4: 848)

Vesta The virgin goddess of the hearth fire, both household and the public hearth of the City of Rome with its continuous flame. (Dumézil, 1966, 1: 315; Schoeps, 1961: 147; Murray, 1935: 77–79; Larousse, 1968: 204)

Wa Se A house god of the Lolos. Southwest China. (Graham, 1961: 83)

Wasi-kamayoq The "house guardian." The Inca, Peru. (Rowe, 1946: 297)

Wei Chêng A minister of the T'ang dynasty who became a door god, associated with Ch'in Shu-pao and Hu-Ching-tê. China. (Werner, 1934: 174)

Wei Tsukung A Chinese door god. (Du Bose, n.d.: 131)

Wetuomanit The house god of the Narragansett Indians. Rhode Island. (Skinner, 1913: 91)

Xochiquetzalli Goddess of the "New Fire," of domestic labor, and the harvest. She was also a goddess of flowers, and of pregnancy. Mexico. (Reed, 1966: 96, 112; Duran, 1971: 238)

Yu-ch'ih Ching-te A deified human, door god since the T'ang dynasty. China. (Larousse, 1968: 389)

Yü-ch'ih Kung A Chinese door god. (Werner, 1932: 598)

Yu-lu With Shen-t'u the mythical door gods who were later replaced by deified humans. Their function was to repel evil spirits. China. (Larousse, 1968: 389; Maspero, 1963: 293; Du Bose, n.d.: 331; Werner, 1934: 173)

Yumthai Lai The god of houses. The Meitheis, Manipur, Assam. (Hodson, 1908: 98)

Yün-hsiao One of the goddesses of the latrine. China. (Werner, 1932: 218)

Zao-sin Chinese god of ovens. (Puini and Dickens, 1880: 446)

Zemininkas, Zemepatis God of the homestead and an earth god. Lithuania. (Gimbutas, 1963: 192; Gray, 1930: 179; Leach, 1950, 2: 631–632)

Zempattys God of the farms and farmhouses. Latvia and Lithuania. (Welsford, 1925, 9: 242)

Zyei-dje A lesser household god who assists in making firewood and fertilizer. The Ch'iang, Szechwan, China. (Graham, 1958: 49)

30

Hunting:
Gods of Wild Animals

Abog, Ubog God of the hunt of the Bagobo. The god of wild pigs and deer of the Ata (Negritos). Philippines. (Benedict, 1916: 23; Leach, 1949, 1: 75; Rahmann and Maceda, 1955: 829)

Acanum Mayan god of hunting. Central America. (Bancroft, 1886, 2: 698; Tozzer, 1941: 155)

Adaba A frog spirit, a transformer, who taught the people how to hunt. The Arawak, Guiana. (Zerries, 1968: 262; Levi-Strauss, 1973: 166–167)

Adangan A god of hunting of the Ifugao. Philippines. (Barton, 1946: 80)

Adar The planet Saturn was also the god of hunting and beneficent as well as malevolent in people's affairs. Mesopotamia, Near East. (Seligmann, 1948: 30)

Adim A deity associated with the hyaena and protective against them. Sudan. (Lienhardt, 1961: 56)

Adjagbe God of hunting. Dahomey. (Herskovits, 1938, 2: 300)

Age, Aghe God of hunting and of the bush with command over its animals and birds. The Fon, Dahomey. Also known in Brazil. (Herskovits, 1938, 2: 105, 107; Verger, 1954: pl. 94; 1957: 212)

Agloolik The god of seal-hunting who lives under the ice. The Eskimo. (Bilby, 1923: 268; Larousse, 1968: 426)

Agrotora A title of Artemis as "the patron goddess of huntsmen." Greece. (Murray, 1895: 137)

Aischa Mama The Mother of game. A "type of tick (garrapata) is believed to be a way of attracting all the species on which it lives as a parasite." Its possession brings success in hunting. The Canelo, Ecuador. (Zerries, 1968: 262)

Aiyappan The god of tigers and panthers who protects from them. The Kadar, Southwest India. (Ehrenfels, 1952: 165, 187)

Ajrana A god of hunting of the Gà in Accra. Ghana. (Field, 1937: 87)

Aldáuhuiku A Father of the Snakes, of the Guayacan, and of the Caracoli. Son of Gaulchováng. The Cagaba and the Kogi, Colombia. (Reichel-Dolmatoff, 1949/50: 112, 114)

Aldáui-kukue A Father of the Snakes. Son of Gaulchováng. The Cagaba and the Kogi, Colombia. (Reichel-Dolmatoff, 1949/50: 112)

Aldáumakaxa Master of the Snakes. The Cagaba and the Kogi, Colombia. (Reichel-Dolmatoff, 1949/50: 113)

Aldu-kukue A Father of the Snakes. The Cagaba and the Kogi. Colombia. (Reichel-Dolmatoff, 1949/50: 112)

Sidi Ali ben Nasar Patron saint of "hunters and riflemen." Morocco. (Westermarck, 1926, 1: 180)

Alopurbi A goddess of the hunt. The Baiga, India. (Elwin, 1939: 61)

Alundaiyag A god of hunting of the Ifugao, Philippines. (Barton, 1946: 80)

Amlahang A god of hunting who protects the feet from snags and snake bite. The Ifugao, Philippines. (Barton, 1946: 80)

Anakulam-Bhagavathi   The "goddess of the elephant-tank" who protects from attacks by them. The Kadar, Southwest India. (Ehrenfels, 1952: 165, 187)

Ananaiyo   A hunting deity invoked also in agricultural rites and in prestige feasts. The Ifugao, Philippines. (Barton, 1946: 83)

Anhanga   A malignant forest demon who usually takes the form of a fowl and hunts rubber gatherers and hunters, is protective of the field game. The Ita and the Tupi, Brazil. (Wagley, 1964: 234; Spence, 1925, 2: 837)

Aphaia   Lady of the Beasts, a goddess of Crete and Aigina. Greece. (Neumann, 1955: 275; Roscher, 1965, 1, 1: 388)

Aquehe, Ah Ke, Ah Ceh   God of hunting. The Maya, Central America. (Tozzer, 1941: 155)

Aritimi   The Etruscan name of Artemis, the goddess of the hunt and of fertility. Italy. (Hamblin, 1975: 87; Pallottino, 1975: 142)

Artemis   A fertility goddess introduced into Greece from Ephesus. She there became the goddess of the hunt, represented by the bear. She was also the protectress of the wild beasts. She was a goddess of childbirth and of healing, protective of both human and animal young; also known to inflict the diseases which she cured. As a goddess of the moon she represented its influence on earthly life. She is usually named as the daughter of Zeus and Leto and the twin of Apollo, though other parentage is attributed to her. (Thramer, 1925, 6: 547; Jayne, 1962: 223, 312; Frazer, 1960: 8, 406; Murray, 1935: 121; Fairbanks, 1907: 132–134; Cox, 1870, 2: 143; Kerenyi, 1951: 118, 130; Larousse, 1968: 111, 121)

Ashkha-intswakhwe   The god of the mountains who controls them and the beasts inhabiting them. He is made offerings by shepherds when taking their cattle to the mountains. The Abkhasians, Caucasus. (Janashia, 1937: 148)

Atida   A goddess associated with hunting, fighting, and rain. She is a female manifestation of Jok. The banyan tree is scared to her and is her oracle. The Lango, Uganda. (Driberg, 1923: 216–219)

Atihkwatcak   The master of the caribou. The Cree, Ontario. (Cooper, 1934: 8)

Atsentma   The mother of the animals lives in the north. The Tahltan, Canada. (Teit, 1919: 231)

Auitsama   Mother of the Snakes. The Cagaba and the Kogi, Colombia. (Reichel-Dolmatoff, 1949/50: 113)

Aukjuk   A goddess who punishes hunting taboo infractions, particularly those committed out on the ice. The Netsilingmiut Eskimo, Canada. (Rasmussen, 1929: 81)

Autga   A Dravidian god of hunting. The Male Paharias, India. (Crooke, 1925, 5: 13; Russell, 1916, 4: 154)

Ayan   A deity who "induces the wild pig to run into the trap." The Apayao, Philippines. (Wilson, 1947: 22)

Ayyappa, Sartavu   The god of hunting. The Coorgs, South India. (Srinivas, 1952: 224)

Azhweyp'shaa   The "gods of beasts and of hunting." The Abkhasians, Caucasus. (Janashia, 1937: 149)

Bahesur Pat   Shrines are built to this deity to protect from wild animals. The Baiga, India. (Elwin, 1939: 60)

Bai Baianai, Bay Bayanay   God of the forest and of hunting and fishing to whom black buffaloes are sacrificed. Siberia. (Eliade, 1964: 187; Tokarev and Gurvich, 1964: 280)

Bainaca   God of wild animals who "holds the destinies of hunters in his hand." The Orochi, the Manega, and the Tungus, Siberia. (Lissner, 1961: 161)

Bakaiyauwon Abaton   A hunting deity in the Upstream Region invoked also in agricultural rites and in prestige feasts. The Ifugao, Philippines. (Barton, 1946: 83)

Bakaiyauwon Balitok   A hunting deity in the Downstream Region who lives on Mount Kapugan and is also invoked in agricultural rites and in prestige feasts. The Ifugao, Philippines. (Barton, 1946: 83)

Bakaiyauwon Banauwon   A hunting deity in the Upstream Region invoked also in agricultural rites and in prestige feasts. The Ifugao, Philippines. (Barton, 1946: 83)

Bakaiyauwon Lamagan   A hunting deity in the Upstream Region invoked also in agricultural rites and in prestige feasts. The Ifugao, Philippines. (Barton, 1946: 83)

Bakaiyauwon nak Balitian   A hunting god, son of Balitian, who is also invoked in agricultural rites and prestige feasts. The Ifugao, Philippines. (Barton, 1946: 82)

Bakaiyauwon nak Panuyu   A hunting god, son of Panuyu, who is also invoked in agricultural rites and prestige feasts. The Ifugao, Philippines. (Barton, 1946: 82)

Bakaiyauwon nak Tinukud A hunting god, son of Tinukud, who is invoked in agricultural rites and in prestige feasts. The Ifugao, Philippines. (Barton, 1946: 83)

The Bakayauwan Beneficent mountain spirits who are helpful to hunters. The Ifugao, Philippines. (Jocano, 1969: 16)

Bakayauwon Tinulugan A hunting deity who is invoked also in agricultural rites and in prestige feasts. The Ifugao, Philippines. (Barton, 1946: 83)

Canan Balche Mayan "Guardian of the Wild Life of the Forest." Mexico. (Thompson, 1970: 321)

Balitok ud Kiangan A god of hunting and also a god of pacification at drinkfests. The Ifugao, Philippines. (Barton, 1946: 80, 89)

Bambura Yaka An important spirit of hunting and provider of yams, but he also "sends sickness and must be invoked to remove it." The Vedda, Ceylon. (Seligmann and Seligmann, 1911: 152)

Bangaur The herder of wild animals to whom offerings are made prior to the ritual hunt. The Bondos, India. (Rahmann, 1952: 874)

u Basa A deity propitiated and to whom offerings are made before hunting expeditions. The Khasi, Assam. (Gurdon, 1907: 48)

u Basa ki mrad A deity propitiated and to whom offerings are made before hunting expeditions. The Khasi, Assam. (Gurdon, 1907: 48)

Baubo Lady of the Beasts. Asia Minor. (Neumann, 1955: 275)

Bayagaw, Banagaw The god of wild animals and of fish. He is the omniscient, omnipotent supreme being and creator. The Negritos of Allakapan District, Philippines. (Pettazzoni, 1956: 319)

Bay-Nay The benevolent god of hunting. The Yakut, Siberia. (Czaplicka, 1969: 277)

beghotcidi, beɣotcidi The god of game, who, with his father the sun, created the animals. He has charge of game as well as of insects, which form he sometimes takes. The Navaho, Arizona and New Mexico. (Reichard, 1950: 76, 78, 386–389)

Ber Ninib as the "lord of the wild boar." Babylonia, Near East. (MacKenzie, 1930: 267)

Berha Pat The "chief hill-spirit . . . worshipped for success in hunting" and for protection while hunting and in travelling. The Santals, India. (Mukherjea, 1962: 277)

Bhatbarsi Deota The god of hunting of the Kandhs. Central Provinces, India. (Crooke, 1925: 7: 650; Russell, 1916, 3: 473)

Bilindi Yaka A spirit invoked for game. The Vedda, Ceylon. (Seligmann and Seligmann, 1911: 150)

Binungbungan A god of hunting of the Ifugao. Philippines. (Barton, 1946: 79)

Bircandi The "herdsman of wild animals" to whom a fowl is sacrificed prior to the ritual hunt. The Mundas, India. (Rahmann, 1952: 874)

Bishahari A deity in Bhagalpur "who controls snakes." Bengal. (Crooke, 1925, 2: 487)

biu si "Spirit mother of the tapir." The Mundurucu, Para, Brazil. (Murphy, 1958: 141)

Brauronia A name of Artemis in association with the bear. Greece. (Murray, 1935: 123)

buk Lu A guardian of animals. Costa Rica. (Stone, 1962: 51)

Buyakauwon A god of hunting who protects the feet from snags and snake bite. The Ifugao, Philippines. (Barton, 1946: 80)

Caá-pora A deity protective of the forest animals. The Tupi, Brazil. (Spence, 1925, 2: 837)

Camaxtli An Aztec god of the chase who invented methods of hunting. Also a god of fishing. Huexotzinco and Tlaxcala, Mexico. (Duran, 1971: 140–141; Spence, 1923: 127)

Ceh Lac A Mayan god of hunting. Mexico. (Thompson, 1970: 308)

Chandaghatu A god of hunting and possibly of war. The Buryats, Mongol. (Waddell, 1959: 372)

Chandi A polymorphic goddess of hunting and of war, and especially a goddess of bachelors who are the only ones who may make offerings to her. The Oraon, India. (Roy, 1928: 16, 60–64; Rahmann, 1952: 882)

Chibute God of hunters and of hunting who also instituted rites; also taught them spinning, weaving, and potting. The Tacana, Bolivia. (Levi-Strauss, 1973: 346–348)

Chien Shên The "Arrow Spirit." China. (Day, 1940: 206)

Chili lawa Father of the bird genus, son of Ningthoi and Ningsin. The Katchin, Burma. (Gilhodes, 108: 677)

Chitsa lawa Father of the deer genus, son of Ningthoi and Ningsin. The Katchin, Burma. (Gilhodes, 1908: 677)

Chitsa numjan Mother of the deer genus, daughter of Ningthoi and Ningsin. The Katchins, Burma. (Gilhodes, 1908: 677)

Chosung-thuba The "god of Tundu-yül, the sphere of animals." The Sherpas, Nepal. (Furer-Haimendorf, 1964: 232)

Chuetenshu The north wind who brings the cold and snow is the god of animals and gives game to the hunters. The Waswanipi (Cree), Quebec. (Feit, 1973: 54)

Chu Mung The "'Glacier Spirit', an apelike creature" who is the same as the Yeti of the Sherpas and Tibetans, is the god of forest animals and of hunting. The Lepcha, Sikkim. (Nebesky-Wojkowitz, 1956, 2: 136)

Chuquichinchay A stellar deity who is "supposedly the patron and guardian spirit of tigers, lions and bears." The Chimu, Peru. (Mishkin, 1940: 227)

Cocidius A Celtic god of the chase and of the woods. In some areas a god of war. Britain. (Ross, 1967: 156, 160; MacCulloch, 1911: 125)

Colgoron-moye The "keeper of hares," who is subject to Lebie-pogil. The Yukaghir, Siberia. (Jochelson, 1900/02: 145)

Coquena A god protective of forest animals and their young. The Itau Valley of Gran Chaco. Among the Quechua of Puna de Atacama the protector of the vicunas who "punishes those who wantonly destroy these animals." Bolivia. (Zerries, 1968: 260; Leach, 1949, 1: 250)

Cozaana The creator of animals and god of hunters and fishers whose wife or female counterpart is Pichanto. The Zapotec, Oaxaca, Mexico. (Alexander, 1920: 87; Bancroft, 1886, 3: 457; Whitecotton, 1977: 158, 164)

Curupira, Corupira, Corropira The god of the forest and of its animals who punishes overkill in hunting. Brazil. (Métraux, 1949: 567; Wagley, 1964: 225; Wilbert, 1974: 39; Fock, 1963: 93)

daje si "Spirit mother of the peccary." The Mundurucu, Para, Brazil. (Murphy, 1958: 141)

Dakmogan A god of hunting and of property and prestige. The Ifugao, Philippines. (Barton, 1946: 57, 79)

Damipaon The "god of the chase and knowledge." The Mishmis, Assam. (Crooke, 1925, 8: 697)

Danag A deity who guards hunters and fishermen. The Apayao, Philippines. (Wilson, 1947: 22)

Dand Devi The protector "of men from the attacks of wild beasts." The Gadbas, India. (Russell, 1916, 3: 12)

Dawaik The rhea spirit who is the master and protector of the flocks of birds and who punishes overkilling. The Toba, Gran Chaco, Argentina and Paraguay. (Zerries, 1968: 263; Métraux, 1937: 175)

Devana Slavonic goddess of the hunt. Same as Dziewona, Diiwica. Czechoslovakia. (Larousse, 1968: 294)

Diana A virgin goddess, yet a goddess of procreation and of childbirth, patron of women. She was associated with the mountains and it was her assimilation to Artemis which introduced other aspects to her nature, e.g., a goddess of the hunt. Italy. (Dumézil, 1966, 2: 407–411; Hadas, 1965: 124; Frazer, 1960: 9; Fairbanks, 1907: 140; Jayne, 1962: 442)

Diiwica A Serbian goddess of hunting. Same as Devana, Dziewona. (Larousse, 1968: 294)

Diktynna A Cretan goddess depicted as a huntress and also as a deity of oath binding. Greece. (Willetts, 1962: 191)

Dimgalabzu Ningirsu's "ranger" who was protective of the wildlife and their environment in Guedinna so that they should prosper. Near East. (Jacobsen, 1976: 83)

Dindymene Lady of the Beasts. Greece. (Neumann, 1955: 275)

Dondo Penu God of hunting of the Kandhs. Madras, India. (Crooke, 1925, 7: 651)

Dumahag One of the "hunting deities that carry a spear and mainly attack the liver." Son of Kinulhudan. The Ifugao, Philippines. (Barton, 1946: 65)

Dungu The god of hunting and "owner of all wild animals." His servant was Kalisa. The Baganda, Uganda. (Roscoe, 1965: 311; Mair, 1934: 234; Kagwa, 1934: 122)

Duyiduyon   A hunting god, of the hurling of the spear. The Ifugao, Philippines. (Barton, 1946: 79)

Dzewana, Dziewona   Slavic goddess of hunting. Same as Devana, Diiwica. (Machal, 1918: 355; Larousse, 1968: 294)

Dzumangwe   A god of the hunt. South Africa. (Mutwa, n.d.: vii)

Dzurawu   Goddess of wild animals and wife of Tsukho. The Angami Nagas, India. (Hutton, 1921: 182)

Edutzi-yama-iba-pugia   A god protective against alligators. The Takanan, Araona, Bolivia. (Métraux, 1942: 41)

Eksheri   The "supreme master of animals, birds, fish, the taiga, and correspondingly, he was the 'holder' of their threads of life, their fates." The Evenks, Siberia. (Michael, 1963: 160)

Era Nuku   God of birds whose wife is Manana. Easter Island, Polynesia. (Gray, 1925, 5: 133)

Esau   A Phoenician/Canaanite god of hunters. Near East. (Paton, 1925, 9: 893; 1925, 3: 183)

Eteto   A shaman who became the father of the peccary—in the Parishera rite of the Acawai. Guiana. (Zerries, 1968: 268)

Ezekhe uyli   The sky god who is invoked particularly in hunting and fishing. The Ul'chi, Siberia. (Ivanov, Smolyak, and Levin, 1964: 730)

Flidais, Flidhais   Celtic goddess of wild animals and protectress of the herds of deer. Wales and Ireland. (Ross, 1967: 326; MacCana, 1970: 55)

Froho   Teutonic god of hunting whose symbol is the golden boar. He is also a god of fertility, of generation. (Grimm, 1883, 3: xix)

Gajere   A god of hunters who causes swelling and to whom a dwarf cock is sacrificed. Son of Kure and UwaRdawa, and husband of 'Awwa. The Maguzawa, Nigeria. (Greenberg, 1946: 33, 44)

Gandharvi   Daughter of Surabhi, mother of "all animals of the horse species." India. (Mackenzie, 1924: 173)

Gange Bandar Deyo   A spirit invoked for good hunting and honey gathering. The Vedda, Ceylon. (Seligmann and Seligmann, 1911: 173)

Gansam Deo   A powerful protector from tigers and other misfortunes. India. (Crooke, 1894: 74; Elwin, 1939: 59)

//Gauab   A god of hunters who accompanies the men on the chase. Also when a woman goes into the veld looking for veldkost, if he likes her he will lead her to it (i.e. an animal he has killed), if not, she finds nothing. The Bushmen, South Africa and Namibia. (Lebzelter, 1934: 35)

Gehbang   A hunting deity of the Ifugao. Philippines. (Barton, 1946: 79)

Gileamberte   The name of Num the supreme being and sky god who is also god of animals, particularly the reindeer. The Yurak-Samoyed of the northwest. Siberia. (Pettazzoni, 1956: 443)

Gode, Gaude, Wode   A goddess of hunting and of good luck. Teutonic. (Wagner, 1882: 103; Guerber, 1895: 59)

Gu   As the god of iron and the metals used he is associated with hunting, as well as smiths and war. Dahomey. (Parrinder, 1950: 225)

Guachui Ru Ete   The father of the deer. The Mbya, Brazil. (Zerries, 1968: 266)

Guirapuru   A deity under Guaracy "who has charge of the birds." The Tupi, Brazil. (Spence, 1925, 2: 837)

Hak-ti tash-a-na   The mountain lion, the hunter god of the north. The Zuni, New Mexico. (Cushing, 1881/82: 25)

Hashinau-kor-kamui   The friendly and helpful Goddess of the Hunt. The Ainu, Hokkaido, Japan. (Philippi, 1982: 12, 101)

Hash-inau-uk Kamui   A goddess of the chase who protects as well as guides the hunters. The Ainu, Japan. (Munro, 1963: 20, 112)

Hastseoltoi   Goddess of the hunt. The Navajo, Arizona and New Mexico. (Matthews, 1902: 17; Babington, 1950: 216)

Hastseyalti   Talking God, a benevolent deity, one of whose aspects is that of "a god of animals of the chase." The Navaho, Arizona and New Mexico. (Matthews, 1902: 9)

Hefengi Head of the Shetani spirits (who can take human or animal form) who directs the "creatures of the forest." The Bambuti pygmies, Zaire. (de Munck, 1971: 151)

Heng chan God of the Peak of the North, also called Teh'en Hao, who presides over waters and all four-footed animals. China. (Chavannes, n.d.: 4, 418)

Hijuxsá Father of the Aquatic Birds. The Cagaba and the Kogi, Colombia. (Reichel-Dolmatoff, 1949/50: 112)

Himaryo A god of boundaries who "wanders round the jungle and protects the animals." Can be benevolent or malevolent. The Bhils, India. (Naik, 1956: 185)

Hinag A god of hunting in the Downstream Region. Philippines. (Barton, 1946: 80)

Hohodemi A hunter god who married the daughter of Toyotamahiko, the sea god. Son of Hoho-no-Ninigi. Japan. (Aston, 1925, 11: 466)

Ho-ori-no-Mikoto A god of hunting whose wife is Toyotama-Hime; twin of Hoderi-no-Mikoto. Japan. (Yasumaro, 1965: 67; 1928: 81, 87)

Houa chan God of the Peak of the West, also called Kiang T'ou, who presides over all feathered flying animals and over all metals. China. (Chavannes, n.d.: 4, 420)

Huasa Mallcu The benevolent owner of all animals. The Aymara, Bolivia. (Tschopik, 1951: 199; Trimborn, 1968: 132)

Huichana A god of animals invoked by hunters and fishermen for help. The Valley Zapotec, Oaxaca, Mexico. (Whitecotton, 1977: 164)

Humaiyak A god of hunting of the Ifugao. Philippines. (Barton, 1946: 79)

Huvi The spirit of hunting. The Ovimbundu, Angola. (McCulloch, 1952: 36; Childs, 1949: 21)

Illibium Parche The god of animals, particularly of reindeer. The Yurak Samoyed, Siberia. (Czaplicka, 1925, 11: 175)

Imbabui A hunting deity invoked also in agricultural rites and in prestige feasts. The Ifugao, Philippines. (Barton, 1946: 83)

Imbalituka A hunting deity invoked also in agricultural rites and in prestige feasts. The Ifugao, Philippines. (Barton, 1946: 83)

Imbinuluk A god of hunting who protects hunters' feet from snags and snake bite. The Ifugao, Philippines. (Barton, 1946: 80)

Impango A hunting deity invoked also in agricultural rites and in prestige feasts. The Ifugao, Philippines. (Barton, 1946: 83)

Inalalta A god of hunting of the Ifugao. Philippines. (Barton, 1946: 80)

Indagami A god of hunting who protects hunters' feet from snags and snake bite. The Ifugao, Philippines. (Barton, 1946: 80)

Indaiyauwat A god of hunting of the Ifugao. Philippines. (Barton, 1946: 79)

Indigollae Yaka The spirit who gives good luck in hunting at Kalukalaeba, where Kande Yaka is unknown. The Vedda, Ceylon. (Seligmann and Seligmann, 1911: 174)

Indumulao A god of hunting of the Ifugao. Philippines. (Barton, 1946: 80)

Indungdung A god of hunting who protects the hunters' feet from snags and snake bite. The Ifugao, Philippines. (Barton, 1946: 80)

Inggahnu A hunting deity invoked also in agricultural rites and in prestige feasts. The Ifugao, Philippines. (Barton, 1946: 83)

Inginutma A god of hunting who protects the feet from snags and snake bite. The Ifugao, Philippines. (Barton, 1946: 80)

Inihut A god of hunting, of silence in hunting. The Ifugao, Philippines. (Barton, 1946: 80)

Inle A god of hunting. Cuba, West Indies. (Verger, 1957: 211)

Intoldauwan A god of hunting, of the preparing of a brushy bed for cutting up the game. The Ifugao, Philippines. (Barton, 1946: 79)

Itclixyan Goddess of the Columbia River waters and guardian of "fishermen and hunters of water animals." The Wishram, Washington and Oregon. (Spier and Sapir, 1930: 236)

Iuanaguroro The god of hunting of the Bacairi. Brazil. (Altenfelder, 1950: 266)

Jaijabé   A Father of the Snakes. Son of Gaulchováng. The Cagaba and the Kogi, Colombia. (Reichel-Folmatoff, 1949/50: 112)

Jangáuli   Mother of the Fox/Zorro. The Cagaba and the Kogi, Colombia. (Reichel-Dolmatoff, 1949/50: 113)

Japetequara   A god of the forest and of hunting, identified with the alligator. Belem, Brazil. (Leacock, 1972: 141, 142, 148)

Saint Jerome   The "guardian of animal souls." The Chamula (Mayan), Central America. (Gossen, 1958: 137)

Jingjan lawa   Father of the ant genus. Son of Ningthoi and Ningsin. The Katchins, Burma. (Gilhodes, 1908: 676)

Jingjan numjan   Mother of the ant genus. Daughter of Ningthoi and Ningsin. The Katchins, Burma. (Gilhodes, 1908: 676)

Kabigat ud Kiangan   A god of hunting. The Ifugao, Philippines. (Barton, 1946: 80)

Kahigi   A deity important to hunters, an assistant of Kalisa. The Konjo, Uganda. (Taylor, 1962: 94)

Kahuakadi   Master of the blowgun, the cane (kurata) from which they are made. The Makiritare, Venezuela. (Civrieux, 1980: 87)

Ka-Jum   A water spirit invoked in hunting and fishing rituals and ordeals. The Oyana, French Guiana. (Zerries, 1968: 263)

Ah K'ak'   "[He who is] Fire: the god of hunters and archers." The Lacandon, Chiapas, Mexico. (Perera and Bruce, 1982: 307)

Kakkakotauyak   A benevolent land god who provides seals and deer. The Eskimo, Baffin Land, Canada. (Bilby, 1923: 269)

Kalisa   God of wild animals, important to hunters. His wife is Kaikara. The Konjo and the Baganda, Uganda. (Roscoe, 1965: 312; Taylor, 1962: 94)

Kalisia   The benevolent god of game and of the forest, and the patron of the net-hunters. However, if displeased he "will close the forest to them" until properly propitiated. The Mbuti (Pygmies), Zaire. (Turnbull, 1965: 236)

Kalluktok   A hunting god who provides them with meat. The Eskimo, Baffin Land, Canada. (Bilby, 1923: 267)

Kaltsauna, Kaltsuna   The provider of flint for arrowheads for hunting. He taught them the practical things— "to flake arrowheads, to make bows and harpoons, and to build houses . . . to hunt and fish, to make fire, to cook." When all was done he transformed himself into a lizard. The Yana and the Yahi, California. (Curtin, 1903: 470; Kroeber, 1964: 27, 29, 31, 58)

Kalyamakindi   An assistant of Kalisa, important to hunters. The Konjo, Uganda. (Taylor, 1962: 94)

Kampinda   With his wife NaMukonda sent by Lesa to instruct the Bemba in the making and use of nets in hunting. He is also invoked when slaughtering one of their animals. Zambia. (Richards, 1939: 65, 344)

Kanati   The god of hunting, of game. The Cherokee, North Carolina and Tennessee. (Swanton, 1946: 772; Spence, 1925, 3: 508; Hatt, 1951: 854)

Kande Yaka   The god of beasts, of hunters, who gives good luck in hunting. The greatest of the yaku. The Veddas, Ceylon. (Wales, 1957: 15; Pettazzoni, 1956: 442; Seligmann and Seligmann, 1911: 150, 170)

Karau   God of the peccary and protective of all animals. He can be propitiated if there is overkill, if the meat is roasted to preserve it and an offering is made. He is also the "Spirit of the Night" and can cause death. The Yupa, Venezuela. (Wilbert, 1974: 137, 142)

Kariba-myojin   God of the hunting area. Son of Nibutsu-hime. Japan. (Hori, 1968: 168)

Katkatchila   A great hunter transformed into a swift who was the source of flint. The Wintun, California. (Kroeber, n.d.: 176; Curtin, 1903: 3, 4, 8–10)

Kenjo   The god and protector of hunters is also a god of the land and of war. The Jukun, Nigeria. (Meek, 1931: 201, 265)

Kerep-Nove   "Scratch and Stagger," goddess of aconite poisons used in hunting. Wife of Kerep-Turuse. The Ainu, Japan. (Batchelor, n.d.: 311)

Kerep-Turuse   "Scrape and Infect," the god of aconite poisons used in hunting. Husband of Kerep-Nove. The Ainu, Japan. (Batchelor, n.d.: 311)

Keyeme A water spirit who is considered "lord of beasts. In the guise of a gigantic anaconda he was killed by the birds as a punishment for dragging down to his abode all the creatures he could find." From his skin they and other creatures got their colors. The Taulipang, Guiana. (Zerries, 1968: 261)

Khonvoum The supreme god of the Pygmies is a sky god, the Great Hunter, whose bow is visible as the rainbow. He is god of the forest and of game. Equatorial Forest, Africa. (Queval, 1968: 65; Larousse, 1973: 520)

K'ia-k'ia-li "The Eagle-Hunter God of the Upper Regions." The Zuñi, New Mexico. (Cushing, 1881/82: 29)

Kiang T'ou *See* **Houa chan**

Kidondo The "owner of the wild animals in the Bemaraha Mountains." The Malagasy, Madagascar. (Ruud, 1960: 287)

Kinashut Kamui The "spirit chief of the snakes" invoked to avert typhoid epidemics. The Ainu, Japan. (Munro, 1963: 19)

Kinoptiu ud Ubub The owner of the game in the vicinity of Ubub. The Ifugao, Philippines. (Barton, 1946: 85)

Kisaka A deity important to hunters, an assistant of Kalisa. The Konjo, Uganda. (Taylor, 1962: 94)

Klambo Pennu The god of hunting. The Baiga, India. (Elwin, 1939: 61)

Kolin Sutti Bhavani A goddess of the hunt. The Baiga, India. (Elwin, 1939: 111)

Kongwa, Ndimi The god of animals. Tanzania. (Millroth, 1965: 111)

Korra Razu "Supposed to be the deity who has supreme control over tigers." The Koyi, India. (Thurston, 1909, 4: 60)

Kuángyi Mother of the Birds. The Cagaba and the Kogi, Colombia. (Reichel-Dolmatoff, 1949/50: 113)

Kuanja A goddess of hunting. The Mbundu, Angola. (Childs, 1949: 21)

Ku Bolay A Mayan god of hunting. Mexico. (Thompson, 1970: 308)

Kuh, Quh The "guardian of the milpas," is also invoked by hunters. The Maya, British Honduras. (Thompson, 1970: 57, 65)

Kutsos God of the mountain goats. The Bella Coola, British Columbia. (Boas, 1898: 47)

Ku'yapalitsa Mother of game animals and a huntress. The Zuñi, New Mexico. (Tyler, 1964: 188)

La'e The goddess of bird catchers. Hawaii. (Emerson, 1967: 53)

Laiyan A god of hunting. The Ifugao, Philippines. (Barton, 1946: 79)

Lamagan A hunting god of the Ifugao. Philippines. (Barton, 1946: 79)

Lebie-pogil The "Owner of the Earth" appealed to by the shaman before the hunt. The gift of the soul of a reindeer indicates good hunting, that of a bull bad hunting. The Yukaghir, Siberia. (Jochelson, 1900/02: 144, 210)

Leib-olmai The god of wild animals, particularly the bear, and of hunting. The Scandinavian Lapps. (Karsten, 1955: 37; MacCulloch, 1964: 175; Dioszegi, 1968: 28; Bosi, 1960: 132)

Ligalig A god of hunting. The Ifugao, Philippines. (Barton, 1946: 80)

Limdimi and **Limudimi** Benevolent "guardian(s) of the bush" who assist hunters and travelers. Tanzania. God of the animals of the Nyamwezi. (Abrahams, 1967: 78; Millroth, 1965: 111–112)

Llokesin The "god of rats." The Ifugao, Philippines. (Jocano, 1969: 144)

Lomam A god of hunting. The Ifugao, Philippines. (Barton, 1946: 79)

Luknay A god of hunting who protects the feet from snags and snake bite. The Ifugao, Philippines. (Barton, 1946: 80)

Luot-chozjik Goddess guardian of the reindeer in summer when they are untended, but does not protect them from men. Eastern Lapps. (Holmberg, 1925, 7: 798)

Lyeshy A forest spirit who is a transformer. He protects the birds and the beasts of the forest and will cause hunters and travelers to lose their way unless made an offering. Russia. (Ralston, 1872: 153–157)

Mabith A god associated with hunting and with wild animals, particularly giraffes. The Nuer, Sudan. (Evans-Pritchard, 1956: 30)

Mac'aqway A star who was the patron of snakes. Inca, Peru. (Rowe, 1946: 295)

Maçat, Mazat The deer god and a god of the chase. The Nicarao, Nicaragua. (Bancroft, 1886, 3: 492; Lothrop, 1926: 70)

Ma-cha Shên The goddess of locusts. China. (Werner, 1932: 341)

Madremonte Goddess of the forest who is protective of the animals. Central Cordillera, Colombia. (Reichel-Dolmatoff, 1971: 80)

Magdal A god of hunting who rouses birds or game and drives them. The Ifugao, Philippines. (Barton, 1946: 40)

Magománay A god who "lives in the high mountains . . . is the real owner of the deer and wild hogs." Assistant of Omalagad. The Budiknon, Mindanao, Philippines. (Cole, 1956: 95)

Maianwatahe A god of abundance and of good hunting. The Sioux, Northern Plains, United States. (Skinner, 1925, 1: 441)

Makaboteng The "guardian of the deer and wild hogs" who is important to success in hunting. The Tinguian, Philippines. (Cole, 1922: 299; Jocano, 1969: 113)

Makinul One of the hunting gods who "carry a spear and mainly attack the liver." The Ifugao, Philippines. (Barton, 1946: 65)

Makú Gaultsángui The Father of the arrow. The Cagaba, Colombia. (Reichel-Dolmatoff, 1949/50: 115)

Makuko A forest spirit—"mask and mime" are used to bring it and the animals under the power of the hunters. The Cubeo and the Caua, Colombia. (Zerries, 1968: 301)

Mallung A tribal god to whom sacrifices are made so that he will not send elephants and tigers to attack them and their homes. The Malasar, Southern India. (Thurston, 1909, 4: 395)

Máma Sen-máktu Father of the Fox/Zorro. The Cagaba and the Kogi, Colombia. (Reichel-Dolmatoff, 1949/50: 112)

Manipaniegiñalilel Chief of the yellow-billed heron whose wife is Maniopindilisop. The Cuna, Panama. (Norden-skiold, 1938: 301)

Maranauwa, Maranaywa God of the forest and the owner of its animals. The Tenetehara, Brazil. (Wagley and Galvão, 1948, 1: 145; Levi-Strauss, 1969: 85)

Mashiramu "Master of Animals" in the lowlands—greatly feared, aggressive toward man. The Yupa, Venezuela. (Wilbert, 1974: 39)

Masolomurkipipilel "The chief of the peccaries" whose wife is Punauaga Olomurkidili. The Cuna, Panama. (Norden-skiold, 1938: 326)

Maswasi God of the chase. The Baiga. Among the Dhanwars a goddess of hunting. India. (Elwin, 1939: 61; Russell, 1925, 3: 314; 1916, 2: 497)

Matideo The god of hunting. The Gadba and the Bhatra, India. (Russell, 1916, 3: 12; 1916, 2: 275)

Mazunyu mbira shave A deity who is manifest in the wind, who is associated with hunting primarily, but also with healing, and with warnings of danger. The Nyajena Reserve, Rhodesia. (Gelfand, 1966: 95)

Mborevi Ru Ete The "father of the tapir." The Mbya, Brazil. (Zerries, 1968: 266)

Mei Shan A Chinese god of hunters. Szechwan. (Graham, 1958: 52)

Mesep The "Megrelian god of hunting." Caucasus. (Marr, 1937: 175)

Mesitch A god of the woods and of hunting. The Tcherkass (Circassians), Russia. (Grimm, 1880: 215)

Messon The Great Hare, the Algonquin creator is also the god of all animal life. The Montagnais, Labrador and Quebec. (Drahomanov, 1961: 19; Alexander, 1964: 32)

Milili A great sky god who controls the deer and is the source of obsidian. He also gives the shamans their power. The Yuki, California. (Kroeber, 1925: 196–197)

Misek The god of hunting of the Limbu. Nepal. (Caplan, 1974: 189)

Mising hali kun The creator of forest animals who is invoked for good hunting. The Unami (Lenape), Eastern United States. (Harrington, 1921: 32–35)

Missabe Amerindian god of hunters. Same as Manabozho. United States. (Emerson, 1884: 426)

Mi-tik A cruel god, guardian of the road to Mayel. He and Tom-tik are guardians of the ibex and musk deer. The Lepchas, Sikkim. (Gorder, 1938: 236)

Mixcoatl An ancient god of the chase of the Chichimec. Mexico. (Krickeberg, 1968: 81; Bancroft, 1886, 2: 335; Spence, 1923: 319; Caso, 1958: 31)

Mokiach The "lion god of the Keres and patron of their huntsmen." The Pueblo Indians, New Mexico. (Tyler, 1964: 213)

Mombalulung A god of hunting who protects feet from snags and snake bite. The Ifugao, Philippines. (Barton, 1946: 80)

Monanup One of the gods of hunting who "carry a spear and mainly attack the liver." The Ifugao, Philippines. (Barton, 1946: 65)

Monduog Son of Kinulhudan and one of the gods of hunting who "carry a spear and mainly attack the liver." The Ifugao, Philippines. (Barton, 1946: 65)

Mongadang A god of hunting and of weaving. The Ifugao, Philippines. (Barton, 1946: 29, 79)

Monlanga A god of hunting of the Ifugao. Philippines. (Barton, 1946: 79)

Montikbu A hunting deity invoked also in agricultural rites and in prestige feasts. The Ifugao, Philippines. (Barton, 1946: 83)

Moot rum Tseu A name of Pong rum at the annual October sacrifice by all the hunters. The Lepchas, Sikkim. (Gorer, 1938: 244)

Moro-Podole The father of fish, once a human shaman, is invoked in hunting rituals. The Taulipang and the Arecuna, Guiana. (Zerries, 1968: 268)

Moutacalombo A god of hunting. Brazil. Same as Oshossi of the Yoruba. (Bastide, 1960: 568)

Mueraya A god who "controlled the heavens and the jaguars, and aided shamans." The Conibo, Peru, Ecuador, and Brazil. (Steward and Métraux, 1948, 1: 592; Zerries, 1968: 255)

MuhʷWinti Aldebaran. The Leader in the hunt for the mountain sheep. The Chemehuevis, California, Nevada, and Arizona. (Laird, 1976: 92)

Mulenga A god of hunting thought to be an ancestral spirit who provides game for the Bemba. Zambia. (Whiteley, 1950: 29; Richards, 1939: 344)

Mulumamumuna A deity important to hunters, an assistant of Kalisa. Uganda. (Taylor, 1962: 94)

Musa A deity of hunting as well as of weaving and pottery. The Songhay, Upper Niger. (Parrinder, 1967: 79)

Mutolya An assistant of Kalisa, important to hunters. Uganda. (Taylor, 1962: 94)

Nabambe A god of the forest who with Ntamaso is protective of hunters giving them keen senses. The Baganda, Uganda. (Roscoe, 1965: 322)

Nai A dangerous spirit "associated with ostriches." The Nuer, Sudan. (Evans-Pritchard, 1956: 30–31)

Nanga Baiga God of the animals, with power over them. The Baiga, India. (Elwin, 1939: 307)

Ndimi, Kongwa The god of animals. Tanzania. (Millroth, 1965: 111)

Neith, Neg One of the oldest of the Egyptian goddesses associated with many fields, and not limited in range—from the sky to the underworld. One of her aspects is that of a goddess of the hunt. (Knight, 1915: 77–78; Ames, 1965: 105; Budge, 1969, 1: 30, 450–463)

Nergal As god of the planet Mars he was a god of war and the patron of "hunters and sportsmen." He was shown as a human-headed winged lion. Assyria and Babylonia, Near East. (Rawlinson, 1885: 48–49; Jastrow, 1898: 218)

Nguenpiru An animistic spirit—"master of the worms." The Mapuche-Huilliche (Araucanians), Chile. (Cooper, 1946: 748)

Nimli numjan Mother of the bird genus, daughter of Ningthoi and Ningsin. The Katchins, Burma. (Gilhodes, 1908: 677)

Nin The god who presided over the planet Saturn and was a god of war and of hunting. Assyria, Near East. (Rawlinson, 1885: 47)

Ninib A solar deity who was terrestrially a god of agriculture, of the chase, of war, and of healing (in association with his wife Gula). Assyria and Babylonia, Near East. (Jayne, 1962: 126; Jastrow, 1898: 57, 67, 174, 217)

Ninurta A god of hunting and of war who is also associated with agriculture and the weather, the rain and floods. Sumer, Assyria, and Babylonia, Near East. (Schoeps, 1961: 57; Larousse, 1968: 60; Jacobsen, 1970: 57; Kramer, 1961: 105)

Nit The goddess of hunting at Sais. Egypt. (Budge, 1969, 1: 30)

Nitan The "chief of the caribou," but not the same as the Caribou God, the supreme deity. He is subordinate to him. Labrador, Canada. (Cooper, 1934: 36; Pettazzoni, 1956: 398)

Niyohua A deity of hunting and fishing. The Zapotec, Sola, Oaxaca, Mexico. (Whitecotton, 1977: 164)

Noçana, Nosana Quiataa A deity of hunting and fishing; also "associated with the 'ancestors' or the 'getting of life.' " The Zapotec, Sola, Oaxaca, Mexico. (Whitecotton, 1977: 164)

Nohuichana A goddess of hunting and fishing who is also a goddess of childbirth and of children. Wife or female counterpart of Pitao Cozaana. The Zapotec, Sola, Oaxaca, Mexico. (Whitecotton, 1977: 164)

Ntamaso A god of the forest who gave the hunters keen senses and guarded them from the attacks of animals. The Baganda, Uganda. (Roscoe, 1965: 322)

Nuliayoq, Nulijajuk, Nuliajuk Goddess of sea and land animals who withholds game and causes misfortune if offended. Her father is Anatalik and they live in the lower world where the dead who have transgressed the taboos go. The Netsilik and the Mackenzie Eskimo, Baffin Land, Hudson Bay, Canada. (Boas, 1901: 145–146; Wallis, 1939: 216; Rasmussen, 1931: 224; Ostermann, 1942: 56; Balikci, 1970: 205–206)

Nunam-chua Goddess of land animals who lives in the forests. The Chugach, Alaska. (Birket-Smith, 1953: 121; Marsh, 1967: 154)

nung lyen no A god protective of hunters. The Lepchas, Sikkim. (Siiger, 1967: 46)

Nurlíta Father of the Bat. The Cagaba and the Kogi, Colombia. (Reichel-Dolmatoff, 1949/50: 112)

Nusa-koro Kamui A god invoked for successful hunting and fishing. The Ainu, Japan. (Munro, 1963: 112)

Obantur "Chief of the dogs, *achu,* in the underworld." The Cuna, Panama. (Nordenskiold, 1938: 327)

Ochosi The god of hunters as well as of the wild animals. Puerto Rico, West Indies. (Gonzalez-Wippler, 1975: 26)

Ō'ɛmeal Great Inventor who is "considered the elder brother of the animals." Southern Kwakiutl, British Columbia. (Boas, 1909/10: 584)

Okonorote The great hunter of the Warau living in the skyworld who discovered the way to the earth to which some of them moved. Guiana. (Im Thurn, 1883: 377; Brett, 1880: 55–59)

Oloalikinalilel "The chief of the tapirs (*moli*)" whose wife is Punauaga Olonakuamaidilisop. The Cuna, Panama. (Nordenskiold, 1938: 299)

Oloegippilel Chief of a species of iguana, whose wife is Punauaga Olodirsop. The Cuna, Panama. (Nordenskiold, 1938: 301)

Olokispakualel The chief of the iguanas. The Cuna Indians, Panama. (Nordenskiold, 1938: 301)

Olokuirgikalilel The "chief of the ŭsu, machango" (rabbits), whose wife is Oluiknidilisop. The Cuna, Panama. (Nordenskiold, 1938: 301)

Olomurgipipilel The "chief of the ŭédal (a kind of peccary)." His wife is Punauaga Olourgili. The Cuna, Panama. (Nordenskiold, 1938: 299)

Olopaikkalilel The "Chief of the white apes." The Cuna, Panama. (Nordenskiold, 1938: 329)

Olopeakilel The "chief of the kŏe, roebucks," whose wife is Olokuilisop. The Cuna, Panama. (Nordenskiold, 1938: 301)

Olopikokdigine Chief of the ants of the earth. The Cuna, Panama. (Nordenskiold, 1938: 311)

Olopioidigine The chief of the ants in the afterworld whose wife is Punauaga Olokurgililiae. The Cuna, Panama. (Nordenskiold, 1938: 311)

Oloseginalilel The "chief of the deers" whose wife is Punauaga Olosipokdilisop. The Cuna, Panama. (Nordenskiold, 1938: 301)

Oloueliplel "Chief of the yắnu (peccaries)." His wife is Olouegyae. The Cuna, Panama. (Nordenskiold, 1938: 299)

Omalágad The "patron of the hunters and their dogs. In the *Panalikot* ceremony he is recognized as chief of the spirits of the rocks, cliffs and trees." Magománay and Dumarahol are associated with him. The Bukidnon, Mindanao, Philippines. (Cole, 1956: 95)

Orthia, Orthosia The Tauric Artemis. A form of the goddess brought from the Crimea and worshipped at Sparta. A Lady of the Beasts, a goddess of animals. Greece. (Neumann, 1955: 274–275; Murray, 1935: 122)

Ortik Finno-Ugric god of the hunt. (Keane, 1925, 2: 121)

Orton "Chief of the mosquitos, kuī, in the underworld." The Cuna, Panama. (Nordenskiold, 1938: 331)

Osain A god of hunting, of the forest, its herbs and foliage. Cuba, Trinidad, and Brazil. (Verger, 1957: 230–231; Bastide, 1960: 570; Simpson, 1965: 37)

Oshossi Yoruban god of hunting who protects and assists the hunters. Nigeria. (Meek, 1925, 2: 29; Lucas, 1948: 98, 170; Bastide, 1960: 570). Also known in Cuba where he is also god of the birds and animals. Also Brazil. (Verger, 1957: 207–209; Landes, 1940: 265)

Oskyzn The "master of the hare." The Gilyak, Siberia. (Shternberg, 1933: 320)

Otchosi The Lucumi god of hunting. Haiti, West Indies. (Courlander, 1966: 10)

Paguyon A god of hunting and a minor deity of war. The Ifugao, Philippines. (Barton, 1946: 75, 79)

Pakitsumanga The "Mother of the Caribou," from whom some shamans receive their individual or specific powers. The Inland Eskimo, Canada. (Rasmussen, 1929: 113)

Pal Nibach God of the forests and all of its beasts. The Gilyaks, Siberia. (Lissner, 1961: 231)

Parakutti A god who sends game to the hunters and protects them from the animals. If he fails, they abuse him. The Nayadi, Southern India. (Thurston, 1909, 5: 281)

Parikute God of the hunt and of animals. The Huichol, Mexico. (Furst, 1972: 155)

Pa Shên Chinese "Target Spirit." (Day, 1940: 206)

Pasúnya Mother of the Cockroach. The Cagaba and the Kogi, Colombia. (Reichel-Dolmatoff, 1949/50: 113)

Pasupati Siva as the god of wild animals. Nepal and India. (Snellgrove, 1957: 113; Zimmer, 1955: 27; Ghurye, 1962: 15)

Peketua He formed the first egg (when Tane was seeking to establish mortals) which "produced the reptile called *tua-tara*." The Maori, New Zealand. (Best, 1924: 114)

Pemtexweva The master of game, of hooved animals, who must give permission to hunt the game, which it is his duty to provide. There is a reciprocity pact between the game, who must allow themselves to be caught, and the hunter, who promises to avoid overkill and waste. He appears as a white deer and is thanked for his help. The Cahuilla, California. (Bean, 1974: 165, 167; Brumgardt and Bowles, 1981: 37)

Peshewiipi The "Master of Animals" in the highlands who "seems to occupy a paramount position over the masters of different orders or species of the animal kingdom." The Yupa, Venezuela. (Wilbert, 1974: 38, 39)

Pheraia Cretan Lady of the Beasts who "tames the masculine and bestial." Greece. (Neumann, 1955: 275, 280)

Phy-um lawa Father of the porcupine genus, child of Ningthoi and Ningsin. The Katchins, Burma. (Gilhodes, 1908: 676)

Phy-wam numjan Mother of the porcupine genus, child of Ningthoi and Ningsin. The Katchins, Burma. (Gilhodes, 1908: 676)

Picvucin The "'owner' of wild reindeer and of all land-game" when properly propitiated sends game, when not he withholds it. The Chukchee, Siberia. (Bogoras, 1904/09: 286, 312)

Piejen-moye Guardian of the elks who is subject to Lebiepogil. The Yukaghir, Siberia. (Jochelson, 1900/02: 145)

Pilaxcuc The god of wild reindeer and of other game. The Kamchadal. Same as Picvucin of the Chukchee. Siberia. (Bogoras, 1904/09: 286, 312)

Pinga Goddess of the caribou and other animals and guardian of all human and animal life, which she collects and causes to reappear. She is associated with the sky, the atmosphere. The Caribou Eskimo, Canada. (Rasmussen, 1930: 49, 50; Marsh, 1967: 155–156)

P'i-ru-sei God of the forests and of its animals and birds. The Ch'iang, Ho-p'ing-chai, Szechwan, China. (Graham, 1958: 47)

Po'el'ele "Dark-night," the time just before dawn. Male. **Pohaha** "Night-just-breaking-into-dawn." Female. The third pair, and the "parents of all tiny frail and flitting things which came into being in the everlessening night." Hawaii. (Leach, 1956: 168–169)

Polalowehi Goddess of the night/dawn period. With Popanopano the parents of turtles, geckos, and other creatures of the mud/water element. Hawaii. The fourth pair. (Leach, 1956: 169)

Po-ne'a-aku "Night-creeping-away," the female of the sixth pair of the night period. With Po-hiolo "the parents of Pilo'i, the rat child." Hawaii. (Leach, 1956: 170)

Po-ne'e-aku "Night-receding." With Po-neie-mai the seventh pair born in the primordial night. The parents of the dog and of the birth of light, of plant life, of birth. Hawaii. (Leach, 1956: 170)

Po-neie-mai "Pregnant-night." See above.

Pong rum The god of animals and of hunters whose annual sacrifices are in October. His wife is Sing rum. The Lepchas, Sikkim. (Gorer, 1938: 56, 150, 235; Morris, 1938: 122, 193)

Ponuchona A deity invoked "for animals, game and domestic." Identified with the Morning Star. The Hano Tewa and the Pueblo Indians, New Mexico. (Parsons, 1939: 181)

Popanopano God of the night/dawn period of the primordial night. With Polalowehi the parents of turtles, geckos, and other creatures of the mud/water element. Hawaii. (Leach, 1956: 169)

Pots-chozjin God and protector of the reindeer; male counterpart of Luot-chozjik. The Lapps, Northern Europe. (Holmberg, 1925, 7: 798)

putcha si Goddess/Mother of game animals and protective of them, punitive if offended. The Mundurucu, Brazil. (Murphy, 1958: 14, 15, 142; Zerries, 1968: 260)

Qaus God of the bow. Edomite/Nabataean/Arabiar. (Glueck, 1966: 309; Albright, 1956: 117; 1963: 65)

Qhuav The god of hunters of the Mixtec. Oaxaca, Mexico. (Caso, n.d.: 51)

Qoren vairgin The "Reindeer Being" who protects their welfare. The Chukchee, Siberia. (Bogoras, 1904/09: 315)

Rabefihaza A deity to whom is attributed hunting and fishing tools and techniques. Madagascar. (Larousse, 1968: 473)

Raktipurbi A goddess of the hunt. The Baiga, India. (Elwin, 1939: 61)

Rang A spirit of hunting and of wild animals. The Nuer, Sudan. (Evans-Pritchard, 1956: 30)

rapsem si "Spirit mother of the deer." The Mundurucu, Brazil. (Murphy, 1958: 142)

Rompe Mata A god of hunting associated with Jurema. Belem, Brazil. (Leacock, 1972: 147–150)

Rongo ruji The spirit of hunting worshipped before the annual hunt. The Santal, India. (Biswas, 1956: 135)

u Ryngkew A village guardian deity propitiated and made offerings before hunting expeditions. Assam. (Gurdon, 1907: 48)

Sáldula Mother of the Manna Pig/peccary. The Cagaba and the Kogi, Colombia. (Reichel-Dolmatoff, 1949/50: 114)

Sambhar Deo A godling, the deified *sambhar* stag, "controls the wild animals of the forest," and is worshipped to prevent damage to crops. Central Provinces, India. (Russell, 1925, 3: 314)

Samemba A spirit who drives the game to the hunter. The Ovimbundu, Angola. (McCulloch, 1952: 36)

Sanadan The owner and guardian of the deer and the wild pig who is consulted in hunting. Also called Makaboteng. He possesses mediums in healing ceremonies. The Tinguian, Philippines. (Cole, 1922: 299, 335–336)

sangia-mama The "ruler of the taiga, mother of animals (and people) and mistress of the earth and of the world." The Udegeis, Siberia. (Dioszegi, 1968: 470)

Seihukúkui Father of the Butterflies, of the Squirrel and the Owl. The Cagaba and the Kogi, Colombia. (Reichel-Dolmatoff, 1949/50: 112)

selci syt emysyt Goddess/mother of snakes. The Selkups, Siberia. (Dioszegi, 1968: 462)

seng-ge-dam-brtan Buddha of the sphere of animals. Tibet. (Snellgrove, 1957: 271)

sengi-mama Goddess of game and of hunting. The Nanai, Siberia. (Dioszegi, 1968: 470)

Sérlyue Mother of the Deer. The Cagaba and the Kogi, Colombia. (Reichel-Dolmatoff, 1949/50: 113)

Shakan Sumerian god of wild animals. Son of Utu and Shenirda. Near East. (Jacobsen, 1970: 26; Roberts, 1972: 51)

Sharagoldgi-Khan The god of the ants. The Buriats, Siberia and Mongolia. (Klementz, 1925, 3: 10)

Shikon-Tanum The gods of all wild animals: Shikon—male, Tanum—female. The Minyong Abors, Assam. (Furer-Haimendorf, 1954: 594)

Shikyepu The god of wild animals whose favor is essential to successful hunting. The Sema Nagas, Assam and Burma. (Hutton, 1968: 197; Pettazzoni, 1956: 295)

Shing rum The goddess of wild animals and patroness of hunters. Worshipped only by men. The Lepchas, Sikkim. (Gorer, 1938: 244, 246)

Shivaldo-kukue A Father of the Snakes. The Cagaba and the Kogi, Colombia. (Reichel-Dolmatoff, 1949/50: 112)

Shu-ga A god of animals of the Ch'iang. Szechwan, China. (Graham, 1958: 71)

Shuki The "mother of the parrot species." Daughter of Surabhi. India. (Mackenzie, 1924: 173)

Shulawitsi A young god of fire is also a god of hunting. The Zuñi, New Mexico. (Parsons, 1939: 175; Tyler, 1964: 25)

Shulpae The "king of the wild beasts of the desert." In one tradition the husband of Ninhursaga. Near East. (Jacobsen, 1976: 105)

Shu-nji A god of animals of the Ch'iang. Szechwan, China. (Graham, 1958: 71)

Shuruku-kamui The God of aconite poison, which is used on arrows. The Ainu, Hokkaido, Japan. (Philippi, 1982: 119)

Sid The "hunter." Phoenician. Near East. (Paton, 1925, 9: 893)

Sigu Beneficent god of birds and beasts who assisted in their creation. The Ackawoio, Guiana. (Métraux, 1946: 114; Brett, 1868: 378, 382)

Sillaseak An inland god of the Eskimo who provides deer when hunting. Baffin Land, Canada. (Bilby, 1923: 269)

Simo The master of hunting. The Warao, Venezuela. (Levi-Strauss, 1973: 166)

Singhbahini Goddess of "tigers, snakes, scorpions, and all manner of noisome beasts." The Mal Paharias, India. (Crooke, 1925, 8: 345)

Sityingo God of wild animals whose favor gives success in hunting. The Lhota Nagas, India. (Mills, 1922: 115)

Siwasion A deity protective of the wild pig and the deer who helps them to avoid hunters. The Apayao, Philippines. (Wilson, 1947: 22)

Skadi Scandinavian goddess of hunting, of winter and skiing, of snowshoes. Daughter of Thiassi. She married Niordr, then later Uller. (Wagner, 1882: 178; Anderson, 1891: 342; Guerber, 1895: 108–111; Turville-Petre, 1964: 164–165)

Sugudun, Sugujun The "god of hunters and trappers." The Manobo, Philippines. (Jocano, 1969: 23)

Suhui Dzip The Mayan goddess of the chase. Central America. (Tozzer, 1941: 155)

Su-mu-sei A god of the forests who protects its creatures. The Ch'iang, Szechwan, China. (Graham, 1958: 47)

Sungmanitu The Spirit of the Wolf presided over hunting and war, and punished with malfunction of gun or lameness of horse if a wolf was shot. The Lakota and the Oglala, South Dakota. (Walker, 1980: 121, 160)

Superguksoak Goddess of land animals and wife of Turngarsoak. The Eskimo, Labrador, Canada. (Marsh, 1967: 156)

Suttibhavani A hunting goddess of the Baiga. India. (Elwin, 1939: 61)

Tabai A god of the hunt. The Mayan, Central America. (Tozzer, 1941: 155; Roys, 1965: 145; Bancroft, 1886, 2: 698)

Tama-chu God of the salamanders. Society Islands, Polynesia. (Henry, 1928: 386)

Tanum Goddess of all wild animals. With Shikon, a dual deity. The Minyong Abors, Assam. (Furer-Haimendorf, 1954: 594)

Tapio A god of the forests and of hunters who provides game. His wife is Mielikki, son is Nyyrikki, daughter is Tuulikki. He is represented by the woodpecker. Finland. (Krohn, 1925, 6: 24; Collinder, 1949: 140; de Kay, 1898: 38; Larousse, 1968: 304)

Tatanka The Buffalo God gives the Lakota game and provisions. South Dakota. (Walker, 1980: 50)

taue si The "spirit mother of the prego monkey." The Mundurucu, Brazil. (Murphy, 1958: 142)

Tava, Tavaj The god of hunting and fishing of the Lapps of the Kola Peninsula. Russia. Same as Tapio. (Collinder, 1949: 140; Holmberg, 1925, 7: 798)

Tekhu-rho God of tigers. The Angami Nagas, India. (Hutton, 1921: 182)

Te-pi The Wild Cat-Hunter god of the south. The Zuñi, New Mexico. (Cushing, 1881/82: 27)

Tepkanuset The goddess of the moon is invoked when hunting at night. The Micmac, Maritime Provinces, Canada. (Wallis, 1955: 98, 143–144)

Tewixaxta'e The protector of the hunters of mountain goats. The Kwakiutl, British Columbia. (Boas, 1935: 140)

Thla-k'ia-tchu, Sus-ki The "Coyote, or Hunter god of the West." The Zuñi, New Mexico. (Cushing, 1881/82: 20)

Thora The supreme being who is the source of game and of success in hunting. The Bushmen, Botswana. (Smith, 1950: 90; Schapera, 1951: 185) Among the Masarwa of South Africa he is the supreme god who provides the game and is invoked in hunting and thanked for success. (Lebzelter, 1934: 63–64)

Tih'kuyi The goddess of hunting and of game is also a goddess of childbirth, of human and animal procreation. The Hopi, Arizona. (Tyler, 1964: 133, 188; Leach, 1950, 2: 1113)

Tiri God of hunting of the Logbara. Uganda. (Ramponi, 1937: 592)

Toa'lal'it The "spirit who protects the mountain-goat hunter." The Bella Coola, British Columbia. (Boas, 1898: 45)

Toga God of the creatures of the woods and of plants also. Vahitahi Island, Tuamotua, Polynesia. (Stimson, 1933: 59)

Toikunrari-kuru and **Toikunrari-mat** Deities of the land who are considered friendly toward hunters and are invoked in danger. The Ainu, Japan. (Batchelor, 1925, 1: 244)

Toi-pok-un-chiri A demon of the land invoked "by hunters in times of danger." The Ainu, Japan. (Batchelor, 1925, 1: 244)

Toiron lawa Father of the cricket genus, son of Ningthoi and Ningsin. The Katchins, Burma. (Gilhodes, 1908: 676)

Toiron numjan Mother of the cricket genus, daughter of Ningthoi and Ningsin. The Katchins, Burma. (Gilhodes, 1908: 676)

Tolobo-moye The "Keeper of Wild Reindeer" who is invoked before starting on the spring migration to follow the deer. The Yukaghir, Siberia. (Jochelson, 1900/02: 212)

Tolon-moye The "keeper of reindeer" who is subject to Lebie-pogil. The Yukaghir, Siberia. (Jochelson, 1900/02: 145)

Tom-tik He and Mi-tik are "guardians of the ibex and musk deer." The Lepchas, Sikkim. (Gorer, 1938: 236)

Toodlanak A benevolent goddess who brings the deer within reach. The Eskimo, Baffin Land, Canada. (Bilby, 1923: 266)

Tore Among the Ituri Pygmies the god of the forest and of the lower animals who controls success, good or bad, in hunting. Zaire. (Pettazzoni, 1956: 31; Millroth, 1965: 112)

Torngarsoak A white bear god who "lives in caves and rules over wild game." The Eskimo, Labrador, Canada. (Larousse, 1973: 446)

Toste, Teotost A rabbit god, and god of the chase. The Nicarao, Nicaragua. (Lothrop, 1926: 70; Bancroft, 1886, 3: 492)

Trikurat A spirit of the forest who is helpful to hunters. The Kachins, Burma. (Temple, 1925, 3: 22; Leach, 1950, 2: 785)

Tsikeo The god of wild animals and giver of success in hunting. The Angami, Assam and Burma. (Pettazzoni, 1956: 295)

Tsukho God of wild animals and of hunting. His wife is Dzurawu. The Angami Nagas, India. (Hutton, 1921: 182)

Tsul'kalu A god of hunting and owner of all the game in the area. The Cherokee, Virginia. (Mooney, 1885/86: 341; Spence, 1925, 3: 504; Bray, 1935: 215)

tuktut ikvait The Mother of the Caribou according to some. The Iglulik Eskimo, Canada. (Rasmussen, 1929: 67–68)

Tumacha Benevolent god of game animals, other than the jaguar. The Shipaya, Brazil. (Zerries, 1968: 260)

Tumalao A hunting deity also invoked in agricultural rites and prestige feasts. The Ifugao, Philippines. (Barton, 1946: 83)

Tumiptip "Blood Licker," a god of hunting. The Ifugao, Philippines. (Barton, 1946: 80)

Tunda A goddess who is protective of the forest animals. The Pacific Coast, Colombia. (Reichel-Dolmatoff, 1971: 80)

Tu-te-wehiwehi, Tu-te-wanawana The father of reptiles. Son of Punga. The Maori, New Zealand. (Grey, 1885: 7; Andersen, 1928: 370)

Tuwapongtumsi Sand-Altar Woman is the goddess of game animals. She is the sister of Muyingwa and the wife of Masau'u. The Hopi, Arizona. (Titiev, 1971: 131, 137)

Twalátlit The "supernatural hunter of mountain goats." The Bella Coola, British Columbia. (McIlwaith, 1948, 1: 528)

Ukama God of hunting. The Tiv, Nigeria. (Temple, 1922: 302)

Uller, Ullr, Ull The god of hunting and of archery is also the god of winter and its sports, protecting the seed for the winter. Husband of Skadi after Niordr. Scandinavia. (Guerber, 1895: 111, 131; Wagner, 1882: 95, 177; Stern, 1898: 49; MacCulloch, 1964: 156–157; Turville-Petre, 1964: 182)

Umidub "Blood Lapper," a god of hunting. The Ifugao, Philippines. (Barton, 1946: 80)

Unkotuk kamui The Resin God who provides the resin of fir or spruce to fasten the arrowhead to the shaft. The Ainu, Hokkaido, Japan. (Philippi, 1982: 119)

Ussakita, Wisakita The " 'great manitou of all animals', whether beasts or birds." The Ottawa, Canada. (Pettazzoni, 1956: 376)

Ah Uuc-yol-sip (zip) A god of hunting, also known as simply Zip, who is "believed to have the form of a very small supernatural deer." The Maya, Yucatan, Mexico. (Roys, 1949: 160; Thompson, 1970: 309)

Uuc Zuhuy Zip A Mayan hunting god, believed to be the same as the above. Yucatan, Mexico. (Thompson, 1970: 309)

Vai-mahse A supernatural having two forms—Master of Animals and Master of Fish. As the former he is a god of hunting who owns and protects all creatures. He is also called Vai-mera when referring mainly to flying animals, birds, and insects. He also owns the magical herbs which bring success to the hunter. The Desana, Colombia. (Reichel-Dolmatoff, 1971: 28, 80–85; 1975: 83)

Varalden olmai The supreme god who rules over the earth is the protector of animals, particularly the reindeer, and of the fertility of all things. The Lapps, Northern Europe. (Bosi, 1960: 105, 132; Dioszegi, 1968: 28; Karsten, 1955: 47–48)

Vedi Yaka A spirit invoked for help in hunting. The Tamankaduwa (Vedda), Ceylon. (Seligmann and Seligmann, 1911: 177)

Vettakorumagan The god of hunting and the divine ancestor of the Karo Panikkar. India. (Thurston, 1909, 3: 254)

Viranakka A goddess of hunting. Lapland. (Krohn, 1925, 6: 24)

Vohu Manah, Vohuman With Asha the two most important of the Amesha Spentas. "Good Thought," the protector of the useful animals. He also "presides over the moral relationships between members of the society." Iran. (Littleton, 1965: 98; Gray, 1930: 27, 220; Williams Jackson, 1925, 1: 384–385; Huart, 1963: 41)

Waghacha-Kuniver A deity worshipped for protection from wild animals. The Bheels, India. (Coleman, 1832: 401)

Wakon   God of the snakes. The Lenape, Delaware, Eastern United States. (Donnelly, 1949: 91)

Wambli   The Spirit of the Eagle was a deity of the hunters as well as of warriors. The Lakota and the Oglala, South Dakota. (Walker, 1980: 122)

Wantiah   A hunting deity invoked also in agricultural rites and prestige feasts. The Ifugao, Philippines. (Barton, 1946: 83)

The We-ma-a-ha i   The gods of hunting. The Zuñi, New Mexico. (Cushing, 1881/82: 20)

ah wink-ir masa   The god of deer particularly and protector of wild animals. He is dual-sexed as protector of deer—male for the female, and female for the male. As the god of hunters he must give permission to hunt. The Chorti, Guatemala. (Wisdom, 1940: 400)

Witkokaga   A god who "deceives or fools animals so that they can be easily taken." The Dakota, Fort Snelling, Minnesota. (Eastman, 1962: xxxi)

Wonekau, Wunekau   The omniscient supreme being is also the god of animals who controls success in hunting. New Guinea. (Pettazzoni, 1956: 9, 15, 443)

Wu Ch'ang   The god of hunters. The Ch'iang, Szechwan, China. (Graham, 1958: 52)

Xulab, Noh Ich   The planet Venus is the god of hunting and fishing, of agriculture. The Maya, British Honduras. (Thompson, 1930: 63)

Yaku-yin   The Father of birds. The Waiwai, Brazil. (Fock, 1963: 31)

Yassagai-Toyon   A god who controls the migration of birds. He has seven daughters in the form of white cranes. The Yakut, Siberia. (Czaplicka, 1925, 12: 829)

Yemaxtli   Variant of Camaxtli, god of the hunt. The Aztec, Mexico. (Duran, 1971: 455)

Yoboh, Rokpeh   Beneficent god of hunting. The Dafla, Assam. (Stonor, 1957: 5)

Yu Kantang   Mother of the squirrel genus, child of Ningthoi and Ningsin. The Katchins, Burma. (Gilhodes, 1908: 676)

Yuk-atte Kamui   A deity who is represented by deer horns and who is invoked for the fertility of the deer. The Ainu, Japan. (Munro, 1963: 38)

Yuk-kor-kamui   An early God of Game and master of the animals, particularly deer. The Ainu, Hokkaida, Japan. (Philippi, 1982: 101)

Yumi Kaax   God of the hunt and of the forest, of the game animals. British Honduras. (Muntsch, 1943: 33)

Yumilceh   The Mayan god of the stags, the "symbol of disappearance and of farewell." Yucatan, Mexico. (Recinos, 1950: 205)

Yuzi nenla   Father of the squirrel genus, son of Ningthoi and Ningsin. The Katchins, Burma. (Gilhodes, 1908: 676)

Zauelazali   The father of the peccary, invoked in hunting rituals. Once a human shaman. The Taulipang and the Arecuna, Guiana. (Zerries, 1968: 268)

Dz'ibaan Na   A Mayan god of hunting and guardian of the mountains. He also cures diseases. Mexico. (Thompson, 1970: 327)

The Zip   Mayan "forest beings who protect the deer from hunters." Mexico. (Tozzer, 1941: 155; Thompson, 1970: 308)

Zorbad Deota   A northern Dravidian god of hunting. India. (Crooke, 1925, 5: 13)

Zuhuy Zip   A Mayan god of the chase. Mexico. (Bancroft, 1886, 2: 698; Thompson, 1970: 308)

Zumangwe   "The Hunter," the first husband of Marimba. Father of Kahawa. South Africa. (Mutwa, n.d.: vii)

Zvoruna   A goddess whose name means "bitch" who seems to be considered a deity of game animals and of hunting. Also given as male. Lithuania. (Gimbutas, 1975: XLC M126; Larousse, 1973: 420; Queval, 1968: 123; Leach, 1950, 2: 631)

31

Roads and Locations:
Crossroads, Boundaries, Gates, Travelers

Aizan Guardian god of the markets and public places, of gates and doorways. The Ewe, Dahomey and Ghana. (Ellis, 1890: 52)

Ame-no-Iwatowake-no-Kami God of the gate. Also known as Kushi-iwamado-no-Kami and Toyoiwamado-no-Kami. Japan. (Yasumaro, 1965: 61)

Apdel The spirit dwelling in the guardian stones at the town gate. The Tinguian, Philippines. (Cole, 1922: 298)

Ayizan Protectress of the square and the marketplace. Also of doors and gateways, of routes. Also known as Ayizan Velequete. Haiti, West Indies. (Deren, 1953: 146–148; Marcelin, 1950: 29)

Ogun Balandjo A god protective of travelers and also a god of healing. Mirebalais, Haiti, West Indies. (Herskovits, 1937, 1: 280, 317)

Baron Samedi God of the cemeteries but also the god of the crossroads. Haiti, West Indies. (Deren, 1953: 69)

Baye Guardian of the enclosures and gates of temples. Haiti, West Indies. (Marcelin, 1950: 77; Deren, 1953: 132)

Beharbasu God of the gate. The Baiga, India. (Elwin, 1932: 61)

Ah Beob Gods of the roads who protect those on the trail. The Maya, Yucatan, Mexico. (Thompson, 1970: 291)

Berha Pat An important hill-spirit invoked for protection in travelling and in hunting. The Santals, India. (Mukherjea, 1962: 277)

Cang seng 'bring thod A god protective of travelers. Tibet. (Nebesky-Wojkowitz, 1956, 1: 334)

Cang seng dkar po A Bon god protective of travelers. Tibet. (Nebesky-Wojkowitz, 1956, 1: 334)

Cang seng klu mgon A god protective of travelers. Tibet. (Nebesky-Wojkowitz, 1956, 1: 334)

Chang Tun-ch'ang God of walls and moats at Kuei-lin. China. (Maspero, 1963: 286)

Chaquen Guardian god of the boundaries of the fields. The Chibcha, Colombia. (Keane, 1925, 3: 515)

Ch'êng Huang God of walls and moats, of cities and villages, and judge of the citizens. China. (Day, 1940: 67, 70; Werner, 1932: 48; Peeters, 1941: 33; Maspero, 1963: 282–283; Chavannes, n.d.: 16)

Ch'iang T'u A guardian of walls. China. (Day, 1940: 209)

Ch'iao Sha "Bridge Haunter." China. (Day, 1940: 207)

Ch'iao Shên T'u Ti A protector of bridges, an aspect of T'u Ti. China. (Day, 1940: 67)

Chimata-no-Kami God of the crossroads and protector of travelers. Japan. (MacCulloch, 1925, 4: 332; Yasumaro, 1965: 23)

Ch'ing Lung A guardian of the gates in Taoist temples. China. (Werner, 1932: 83)

Chukem A god of boundaries and of foot races. The Chibcha, Colombia. (Alexander, 1920: 204)

Cimiacinus   A god of the roads assimilated to Mercury. Gaul. (MacCulloch, 1911: 24)

Cista   The "patron of roadways and of free circulation." Armenia. (Dumézil, 1970: 130)

Cloacina   Roman goddess of the drains of Rome invoked for protection from disease. (Jayne, 1962: 462)

Contentezza   An Etruscan goddess invoked for prosperous and happy journeys. Same as Fortuna Redux. Italy. (Leland, 1963: 70)

Desahai Devi   Dravidian goddess of "the four quarters of the hamlet." India. (Crooke, 1925, 5: 7)

Doro-no-Kami   A name of Dosojin as a "Deity of Roads." Japan. (Czaja, 1974: 41)

Dosojin   God of the road and the crossroads, of travel. As a benevolent preventive and protective deity he is placed on village borders, paths, bridges, facing the mountains from which the evil spirits come. He is also a phallic god worshipped for the fecundity of mankind and of agriculture. Frequently presented as dual—the Dosojin couple. Japan. (Hori, 1959: 414; Kato, 1926: 31; Bunce, 1955: 112; Czaja, 1974: 28–30, 41–50)

Do-wa   God of the gates of Pi-hsien. The Ch'iang, Szechwan, China. (Graham, 1958: 70)

bDun po raksa'i mgo g'yag   A guardian god of the Chumbi Valley and protector of the borders. Tibet. (Nebesky-Wojkowitz, 1956, 1: 236)

Ek Chuah   As god of travelers and of roads, of merchants and of cacao, he was beneficent and friendly. As a god of war he was malevolent. The Mayan, Central America. (Tozzer, 1941: 90, 107; Morley, 1946: 228; Nicholson, 1967: 127; Bancroft, 1886: 466)

Eleggua   The god of all roads who also "opens and closes all doors." A very powerful deity. Puerto Rico, West Indies. (Gonzalez-Wippler, 1975: 27, 101–102)

Ellai-Karuppu   A boundary-stone god. The Tamil, India. (Whitehead, 1916: 29)

Ellamma   The goddess of the boundary. The Tamil and the Telugu Paraiyans, India. (Thurston, 1909, 6: 105)

Enodia   Greek goddess of crossroads and of gates. (Neumann, 1955: 170)

Eshu-Elegba   A god of the marketplace and the crossroads; a mischief maker who prods men into offending the gods and thereby providing them with sacrifices. The Yoruba, Nigeria and Dahomey. (Wescott, 1962: 337–338; UCLA, 1971: 6/13)

Farras   A god protective of the frontier between Iraq and Syria. (Fahd, 1968: 78)

Fines   The personification of the boundary-lines, of the frontiers of the Roman Empire. (Carter, 1925, 9: 796; Roscher, 1965, 1, 2: 1483)

Fortuna Redux   A goddess of chance and also considered favorable to prosperous journeys. Roman/Etruscan. (Bulfinch, 1898: 188; Leland, 1963: 70)

Funado   A god of the roads and crossroads, protective of travelers against evil spirits. Japan. (Herbert, 1967: 495; Revon, 1925, 9: 237)

Fusagi   "Dosojin came to be regarded as . . . Fusagi (Blocking Deity)," a deity of roads. Japan. (Czaja, 1974: 51)

al-Gadd   A god protective of tribes, of places, and of travelers. Also a divinity of wells. Arabia. (Fahd, 1968: 78–79, 84)

Gaishin, Yoshin   "Deity of the Town." Japan. (Czaja, 1974: 31)

Ghatoiya   " 'Lord of the crossing' (ghat) is a round stone placed on a platform near fords." Central Provinces, India. (Crooke, 1925, 11: 872)

Goraiya   A boundary-god who also guards the herds. The Kharwars, India. (Crooke, 1925, 5: 8)

Hasammelis   A Hittite god who protects travelers, even to the extent of making them invisible. Asia Minor. (Gurney, 1952: 188)

Hecate   A goddess protective of doors and gates, of crossroads and travelers, though at times she could be malevolent and frighten men with demons and ghosts. She was a goddess of magic and sorcery, which she practiced in all spheres—the heavens, the earth, the seas, the underworld. Greece. (MacCulloch, 1925, 4: 332–333, 848; Fairbanks, 1907: 138–139; Jayne, 1962: 326; Barthell, 1971: 51; Kerenyi, 1951: 37)

Hercules   Roman god who was "the guardian of fences and landmarks." His sanctuaries were located in the crossroads of commerce and he was protective of the travelling merchants. (Cox, 1870, 2: 339; Dumézil, 1966, 2: 434, 437–438; Fiske, 1900: 117)

Hermes The multifaceted son of Zeus and Maia was a god of the wind, of travelers, and a guide of the souls of the dead. He was a god of the marketplace, of public activities, of tradesmen. Because of his early thievery he was a god of thieves and of gain—legal or illegal. He reformed and became the trustworthy messenger of the gods. He was an early deity protective of herds and cattle; a phallic god concerned with their fertility. Through his capacity for sales talk and persuasion he gained the reputation of a god of eloquence. Greece. (Kerenyi, 1951: 161–171; Cox, 1870, 2: 226–227; Murray, 1935: 132–133; Barthell, 1971: 33–37; Fairbanks, 1907: 195–197; Keary, 1882: 333; Schoeps, 1961: 131)

Himaryo A god of boundaries who roams the jungle and is protective of the animals. He may be beneficent or malevolent. The Bhils, India. (Naik, 1956: 185)

Hsing Shên A god of the roads who is worshipped before starting a journey. China. (Ferguson, 1937: 82)

Irungu An earth and forest spirit who was protective of travelers. The Haya and the Zinza, Tanzania. (Taylor, 1962: 142, 147)

Jalodeh The crocodile god invoked for protection in travelling on lagoons. The Ewe, Dahomey and Ghana. (Ellis, 1890: 71)

Jizo Buddhist god of compassion toward all sufferers, but particularly toward women and children. He is the patron of travelers. Japan. (Getty, 1962: 105; Piggitt, 1969: 20; Eliseev, 1963: 432–434; Larousse, 1968: 421)

Kaak The god of fire is also the god of trails "protecting travelers from jaguars and snakes." The Lacandon (the Mayan), Mexico. (Thompson, 1970: 312–314)

Kahu-kura The god of the rainbow was also a god of travelers. New Zealand. (White, 1887, 1: 4)

Kaliamma A village goddess who is a deity of the boundaries. Tanjore District, India. (Whitehead, 1916: 22, 108)

Karuppan A guardian of village boundaries. Trichinopoly District, India. (Hemingway, 1907: 90)

Kas-ing A deity who instructs regarding journeys from place to place. The Kankanay, Luzon, Philippines. (Vanoverbergh, 1972: 86)

Khabish A god of the Himalayan Doms who "besets unwary travellers." India. (Crooke, 1925, 4: 842)

Khetrpal The "boundary-god, is represented by a stone on which is carved the figure of a horse." Gujarat, India. (Crooke, 1925, 11: 872)

Ki Sin God of walls and moats at Ning-po (Chekiang). China. (Maspero, 1963: 286)

Kovave An evil mountain god who controls the fortune, good or bad, of travelers. The Elema, Papuan Gulf, New Guinea. (Holmes, 1902: 430; Haddon, 1925, 9: 342)

Kuan-k'ou Shen The god of the drain. China. (Werner, 1932: 223)

Kukuena A goddess who guides travelers. Hawaii. (Beckwith, 1940: 192)

Kulanthalamman A goddess of the boundary-stone and also a collector of debts. Trichinopoly District, India. (Whitehead, 1916: 105; Hemingway, 1907: 89)

Kurumbai A goddess of boundaries at Irungalur. Southern India. (Whitehead, 1916: 103)

Kwesi Budu Guardian of the entrance to the town. The Effutu, Ghana. (Wyllie, 1966: 478)

lam-bgegs A demon of the road. Western Tibet. (Ribbach, 1940: 79)

La 'nkam Guardian of the east entrance to the village and of the sacred grounds for sacrifices. The Katchins, Burma. (Gilhodes, 1908: 679)

La 'nnann Guardian of the west entrance of the village and of the woods. The Katchins, Burma. (Gilholdes, 1908: 679)

Lares The public lares are deities of fields and crossroads—two, one for each intersecting road. Rome. (Larousse, 1968: 214; Murray, 1935: 226)

Legba God of roads and crossroads, of entrances, and also of the great route to the afterworld. It is he who permits communication with the other gods. As Legba calfou the guardian of crossroads and roads, as Legba lan Baye the guardian of frontiers. Haiti, West Indies. (Verger, 1957: 125; Marcelin, 1950: 15; Herskovits, 1937, 1: 314–315; Deren, 1953: 98)

Lih Ling The god of the road, protective from robbers and animals. China. (Du Bose, n.d.: 396)

Limudimi Benevolent god of the bush who assists travelers and hunters. Tanzania. (Abrahams, 1967: 78)

Lin Kuan A god of open shrines who is believed to protect travelers from demons. Szechwan, China. (Graham, 1928: 72)

Loko Atissou The god of trees and forests is also a god of sunlight and a healer using medicinal plants. He is chief escort of Legba and as such also a guardian of roads, paths, habitations, etc. Identified with St. Joseph. Haiti, West Indies. (Marcelin, 1950: 41, 43)

Lu K'ou Shang The demon of the street corner. China. (Day, 1940: 207)

Lu T'ou The "God of Riches of roads (or cross-roads) worshipped by merchants." China. (Werner, 1932: 515)

Macachera The "spirit of roads, considered by the Potiguara Indians as a messenger bringing good news, but by the Tupinambas as an enemy of human health." Brazil. (Larousse, 1968: 447)

Makiubaya A group of beneficent deities who guard the gates and protect the village against disease bringing deities. The Ifugao, Philippines. (Barton, 1946: 90; Jocano, 1969: 17)

Manibhadra Considered a guardian deity of travelers. The Ajivikas, India. (Basham, 1951: 272–274)

Mentoviacus A god of the roads, protective of travelers. Spain. (Martinez, 1962: 107)

Michi-no-Nagachiha-no-Kami, Michi-no-Kami A god of "safe travelling," a deity of the roads. Japan. (Yasumaro, 1965: 22–23; Czaja, 1974: 31)

Min God of the routes of the desert and protective of travelers. He was also a deity of fertility and generation. Egypt. (Ames, 1965: 108–109; Anthes, 1961: 32; Cook, 1930: 106; Budge, 1969, 2: 17)

Miroi Deo A god of boundaries, a stone, worshipped in illness. Central Provinces, India. (Crooke, 1925, 11: 872)

Muthiya Deo A stone god who is the guardian of the village crossroads. India. (Crooke, 1925, 11: 872)

Nŭnvēi The god of travel who through oracles indicates "the best day for departure." Yap Island, Micronesia. (Müller, 1917: 296)

Padan A Semitic god, "the deified road." Near East. (Roberts, 1972: 48)

Panda, Pantica Goddess of the opening—of the way to the Capitol. And again it is considered that she opens the earth for the seed to grow. Italy. (Roscher, 1965, 2, 1: 210)

Pap-u Guardian of the boundary, a minor god of the Hammurabi period. Babylonia, Near East. (Jastrow, 1898: 171, 174)

Parivazi Mundara God of travelers. The Kadan, India. (Hermanns, 1955: 146)

Pau Gosain God of the roads worshipped by young men, but not until there has been some accident. The Male Paharias, India. (Crooke, 1925, 5: 13; 1925, 8: 345)

Pauri Pat A hill goddess invoked for successful journeys. The Santals, India. (Mukherjea, 1962: 278)

Pisacha An evil spirit of the crossroads forced with offerings and mantras to agree to end an illness or other misfortunes. India. (MacCulloch, 1925, 4: 332)

Poleramma Considered by some to be a boundary goddess. Ellore District. In the Telugu country she is a goddess of smallpox. India. (Whitehead, 1916: 22; Elmore, 1915: 18–19)

Pushan God of roads and paths, both on earth and in the hereafter, protective of cattle and men travelling them. He is a god of herds and of fecundity and guide of the souls of the dead. India. (Bhattacharji, 1970: 186; Danielou, 1964: 117, 123–124; Macdonell, 1897: 35–37)

Ra-jo A local god—"clifflike gate god"—at T'ung-hua. The Ch'iang, Szechwan, China. (Graham, 1958: 71)

Rikhes'war Guardian of travelers and of journeys. The Doms, India. (Briggs, 1953: 470)

Sae-no-Kami A god of roads and also a phallic deity associated with agriculture. Japan. (Kato, 1926: 31; Holtom, 1938: 208)

sahi-no-kami Phallic deities worshipped at crossroads, friendly toward travelers. Japan. (MacCulloch, 1925, 4: 332)

Santiago Patron A local god of Chimaltenango, guardian of the village and of the people when travelling and at work. If neglected he causes illness and misfortune. His wife is Santa Ana. The Chimalteco, Guatemala. (Wagley, 1949: 53)

Sarkin K'ofa The spirit of the gate who observes those entering or leaving. The Maguzawa, Nigeria. (Greenberg, 1946: 29)

Sarudabiko-no-Kami, Saruta-hiko A god of the crossroads and a phallic deity associated with agriculture. Japan. (Herbert, 1967: 356, 496; Kato, 1926: 31; MacCulloch, 1925, 4: 332)

Sastavu The hill boundary god of the Travancore. Also called Chattan or Sattan. The Mala Arayan, India. (Thurston, 1909, 4: 391)

Saywa Inca deities of "the boundary markers . . . associated with cultivated fields." Peru. (Rowe, 1946: 297)

Sevanriya A boundary god of the Bhuiyars. India. (Gray, 1925, 4: 567; Crooke, 1894: 181)

She'a-alqum, She-al-kaum A caravan god of the Nabataeans, protective of the people. Near East. (Crooke, 1925, 9: 122; 1930: 70)

Shivaryadev A boundary god of the Bombay Province. The Bhils, India. (Naik, 1956: 172)

Sima Bongas Boundary deities who are propitiated when there is drought and to whom special offerings are made after rain falls. The Santals, India. (Mukherjea, 1962: 287)

Simaria Dev The god of boundaries. The Dangs, Khandesh, India. (Crooke, 1925, 4: 606)

Sring mo no chung gzi byin ma A Bon goddess who is protective of travelers. Tibet. (Nebesky-Wojkowitz, 1956, 1: 335)

Su Kien God of walls and moats at Na-ning (Kwangsi). China. (Maspero, 1963: 286)

Sundi Pennu God of boundaries. The Kandh, Bengal. (Crooke, 1925, 7: 649)

Tagaloa-a-u The "patron of travellers," a child of Tagaloa. Manua (Samoa), Polynesia. (Mead, 1930: 158)

T'ai Shan Shih Kan Dang A god of open shrines believed to protect travelers from demons. Szechwan, China. (Graham, 1928: 72)

Tane Primarily the god of light, he was invoked for the protection of travelers upon departure and for good weather. Society Islands, Polynesia. (Henry, 1928: 171, 179)

Terminus Roman god of landmarks and of boundaries—the personification of stability. (Dumézil, 1966, 1: 202–203; Pettazzoni, 1956: 164; Bulfinch, 1898: 16; Murray, 1935: 148)

Thakur Deo The god of the village land and the boundaries to whom a white goat is sacrificed. The Baiga, India. (Russell, 1916, 2: 85)

Thovela A god who is protective of strangers travelling through the land and also of pregnant women and the unborn child. The Bawenda, Northern Transvaal. (Hartland, 1925, 2: 364; Wessman, 1908: 80)

Ti-chini-ap Guardian of the crossroads. The Chimalteco, Guatemala. (Wagley, 1949: 75)

Tou Mu The goddess of the Star-Bushel is invoked by travelers for protection on waterways and seas. China. (Day, 1940: 27, 110)

Trivia A Roman goddess of the crossroads, of "streets and highways." She can be malicious. (Wunsch, 1925, 4: 335–336; Barthell, 1971: 26)

Tu Di P'usah An earth god who is protective of travelers. Szechwan, China. (Graham, 1928: 72)

Tzultacca A Mayan god to whom the wayfarer offers copal each morning and evening. The Kekchi, Guatemala. (Tozzer, 1941: 107)

We-be God of "the large gate of Chengtu." The Ch'iang, Szechwan, China. (Graham, 1958: 70)

We-bra-shi God of the city wall at Wen-ch'uan. The Ch'iang, Szechwan, China. (Graham, 1958: 86)

Xaman Ek God of the North Star who is protective of travelers and to whom merchants burn copal. The Mayan, Central America. (Tozzer, 1941: 95; Morley, 1946: 227–228)

Xlab-pak-yum Mayan god of walls, embodied in reptiles. Central America. (Wallis, 1939: 59)

Yacatecutli God of travelling merchants. The Aztec, Mexico. (Spence, 1923: 340; Vaillant, 1962: 151; Bancroft, 1886, 2: 338)

Yachimata-hiko, Yachimata-hime God and goddess of the crossroads, of travelling, protecting the living from evil spirits. They are also phallic deities associated with agriculture and Dionysian festivals. Japan. (Revon, 1925, 9: 237; Kato, 1926: 31; MacCulloch, 1925, 4: 332)

Yang Ki-shêng God of walls and moats at Pekin. China. (Maspero, 1963: 285)

Yeman' gnyem Beneficent god of travelers as well as a god of fish and of the River Ob. The Ostyaks, Siberia. (Czaplicka, 1925, 9: 577)

Yonalav The "god of travellers, as well as the protective spirit against typhoons and epidemics and the dispenser of abundant food." Yap Island, Micronesia. (Muller, 1917: 325)

Yü K'ien God of walls and moats at Nankin. China. (Maspero, 1963: 285)

Zei-shwa-sei The "god of the great roads." The Ch'iang, Szechwan, China. (Graham, 1958: 52)

32

Trades and Crafts:
Merchants, Markets, Artisans

Aesculanus Roman god of the copper coins, associated with "tradesmen's profits." (Roscher, 1965, 2, 1: 190; Larousse, 1968: 207)

Agade-gonsu A deity of iron-workers. Dahomey. (Herskovits, 1967, 1: 182)

Aizan A god who is protective of markets and public places as well as houses. The Ewe, Dahomey, Togo, and Ghana. (Ellis, 1890: 52)

Akyantho Considered the protector and creator of foreigners, as well as the "creator of the machete, of illnesses and medicines, . . . the inventor of money." The Lacandon, Chiapas, Mexico. (Perera and Bruce, 1982: 139, 272, 306)

Aligbono A deity of Bohicon, a commercial village. Dahomey. (Herskovits, 1967, 1: 184)

Alulumar The god of house carpenters. Ifalik, Micronesia. (Burrows, 1947/48: 10)

Ama-tsu-mara The god of blacksmiths. Japan. (Revon, 1925, 9: 239; Herbert, 1967: 393)

Ampuh'dol A god of trade. The Ifugao, Philippines. (Barton, 1946: 35)

Ancanco A malevolent dwarf who is the owner of "Veins and deposits of gold and silver, as well as objects made of these metals." The Aymara, Peru. (Tschopik, 1951: 200)

San Antonio The "patron of the muleteers." The Tarasco, Mexico. (Beals, 1946: 140)

Anubis At Delos he, Isis, and Serapis are invoked as protectors of vessels from the dangers of the sea by merchants and sailors. Greece. (Duprez, 1970: 52–53)

Arazu An artisan god created by Ea for the construction and/or restoration of temples. Sumer, Near East. (Langdon, 1931: 104; Larousse, 1973: 70)

Argentinus Roman god of silver coins, associated with "tradesmen's profits." (Roscher, 1965, 2, 1: 193; Larousse, 1968: 207)

Aruarani The "Mother of Moriche Flour" is also goddess of the women hammock makers. Those who become skilled and reach high standing go to her domain at death. The Winikina-Warao, Venezuela. (Wilbert, 1973: 6, 28)

Aruaruvahine An artisan god of Tahiti. Polynesia. (Henry, 1928: 374)

Asbinan A craftsman god of the Tinguian. Philippines. (Cole, 1922: 336)

Assaranghi Tengris Thirteen Eastern Tengris—"the mighty patrons of the blacksmiths, of the black shamans." The Buriats, Siberia and Mongolia. (Klementz, 1925, 3: 5)

Atariheui An artisan god of Tahiti. Polynesia. (Henry, 1928: 374)

Azal Uoh Goddess of weaving and of spinning. The Mayan, Central America. (Tozzer, 1941: 128, 144; Larousse, 1968: 439)

Azuwe A god of traders in Bohicon. Dahomey. (Herskovits, 1967, 1: 184)

Ba   An "Iron-god." There are several gods of this name. Egypt. (Budge, 1969, 2: 393; Knight, 1915: 28)

Baitpandi   The goddess of weavers who taught this craft to the women. The Bagobo, Philippines. (Jocano, 1969: 22)

dBal gyi mgar ba   God of blacksmiths of the Bon people.

Sidi Bel 'Abbas   Beneficent patron of commerce and trade to whom silver coins were offered in gales at sea. Also cairns were dedicated to him at the time of threshing to obtain the westerly wind. He was invoked in the measuring of the grain. Morocco. (Westermarck, 1926, 1: 90, 180; 1926, 2: 231, 238)

Benih Lela Punggang Tengian Dara Bintang Tiga Datai Ka Jelan   A goddess who grants women the ability to be "expert in weaving." Daughter of Pulang Gana. The Dyaks, Sarawak, Borneo. (Sarawak Gazette, 1963: 79; Howell, 1908/10: 40)

Berchte, Bertha (Berche [Bavaria]; Berchtli, Bechtli [North Switzerland]; Perchta, Perchtel [Salzburg Mountains])   Beneficent Teutonic goddess who watched over "the souls of unborn children" who assisted her in guarding the young plants in agriculture. She was also a goddess of spinning, rewarding the diligent and punishing the careless. (Guerber, 1895: 58–59; Grimm, 1880: 272–273, 277, 279; Wagner, 1882: 6, 116)

Po Bhauk   A god of merchants and boatmen as well as of storms. The Chams, Annam and Cambodia. (Cabaton, 1925, 3: 342)

U Biskurom   A god worshipped on the completion of a house. The Syntengs, Nartiang, Assam. (Gurdon, 1907: 31)

ka blei-jew-lei-hat   Goddess of the market places. The Khasi, Assam. (Stegmiller, 1921: 410)

Ah Bolon Yocte   Probably a merchant god. The Mayan, Central America. (Thompson, 1970: 308)

Boshintoi, Bozentoy, Bojintoy   The chief of the white smiths, associated with the western tengeri, who was protective of men and taught them the art of iron-working. The Buryats, Siberia. (MacCulloch, 1964: 464; Krader, 1954: 337; Czaplicka, 1969: 285)

Brighid, Brigit   A Celtic triple goddess or three sisters of the same name, one of whom was the goddess of smiths, the others of healing and of poetry and arts. Ireland. (Ross, 1967: 206, 360; MacCana, 1970: 34; Jayne, 1962: 513)

Budh   The planet Mercury was the god of merchandise, protective of merchants. India. (Coleman, 1832: 133)

Bugan inKinulhudan   A goddess of weaving. Wife of Kinulhudan. Philippines. (Barton, 1946: 29)

Bugan inMonkulabe   A goddess of weaving. Wife of Monkulabe. The Ifugao, Philippines. (Barton, 1946: 29)

Bugan inPunholdaiyan   Wife of Punholdaiyan—the primal ancestors of the gods of weaving. The Ifugao, Philippines. (Barton, 1946: 29)

Bugan inUldi   A goddess of weaving, wife of Uldi. The Ifugao, Philippines. (Barton, 1946: 29)

Buku Aja   A deity of the market. Dahomey. (Parrinder, 1949: 53)

The Cabeiri   Benevolent lesser gods, smiths of the underground "reputed to be the first metal-workers." Greece. (Larousse, 1968: 128–129)

Chalmecacioatl   Goddess of merchants, of traders. Sister of Yiacatecutli. The Aztec, Mexico. (Bancroft, 1886, 3: 416)

Chang Fei   A god of butchers. China. (Maspero, 1963: 332; Werner, 1932: 34; Graham, 1961: 186)

Chang-huang, Chan-huang   God of cooks and of caterers. Southwest China. (Graham, 1961: 176, 186)

Chang Pan Hsien Shih   God of masons. China. (Du Bose, n.d.: 334; Werner, 1932: 308; Day, 1940: 109)

Ch'ang-sheng-fo   Patron deity of "cloth makers and yamen runners." Southwest China, Szechwan. (Graham, 1961: 186)

Chang-yeh   God of butchers. Southwest China. (Graham, 1961: 176)

Chantico   The goddess of the hearth was also goddess of "goldsmiths and jewellers." The Aztec, Mexico. (Spence, 1923: 283)

Chao Kung-Ming   A god of wealth worshipped by merchants. China. (Werner, 1932: 44, 515)

Chao San-Niang   Goddess of Wig-sellers. China. (Werner, 1932: 44; Leach, 1949, 1: 211)

Chebel Yax   Goddess of weaving and of embroidery. Wife of Itzamna and daughter of Azal Uoh. The Mayan,

Mexico. (Tozzer, 1941: 10, 128; Thompson, 1970: 206; Nicholson, 1967: 127)

Chen Wu Ta Ti   A deity worshipped by merchants of dye stuffs. Peking, China. (Burgess, 1928: 189)

Ch'ê T'ou Wu Shêng   The god of "the silk-reeling stage of the industry." China. (Day, 1940: 108)

Chiang Hsiang Kung   Patron of rice merchants. China. (Day, 1940: 110)

Chibchachum   The god of laborers and merchants, of goldsmiths and industries is also the god banished to the underground to uphold the earth and in shifting causes earthquakes. The Chibcha and the Muiscas, Colombia. (Trimborn, 1968: 91; Osborne, 1968: 112; Alexander, 1920: 203–204)

Chiconquiahuitl   A god of traders and of merchants, brother of Yiacatecutli. The Aztec, Mexico. (Duran, 1971: 204; Bancroft, 1886, 3: 416)

Chih Nü   Goddess of weavers. China. (Werner, 1932: 73; Leach, 1949, 1: 216)

Ch'i-hsien-niang-niang   Goddess of weavers. Szechwan, China. (Graham, 1961: 186)

Ch'ing I-shên   One of the gods of the silkworms. China. (Werner, 1932: 83)

Ch'ing Lung Chi Ch'ing   "God of general prosperity for shops and private homes." China. (Day, 1940: 113)

Ching Miao Shen   The "God of Growing Crops, is the patron saint of the Vegetable Merchants." Peking, China. (Burgess, 1928: 180)

Ch'ing-wa Shên   "The Frog-spirit . . . worshipped for commercial prosperity and prevention and healing of sickness." China. (Werner, 1932: 84–85)

Chi Shên Wang   The patron of weavers of silk and satin. China. (Day, 1940: 108)

The Chi Shên Wu Shêng   The "Five Patron-Sages of the Loom," guardians of weaving into silks. China. (Day, 1940: 108)

Chrysoros   A Phoenician god of the art of metalwork and of invention. Sometimes identified with Hephaestos. Near East. (Roscher, 1965, 1, 1: 906; Goldziher, 1877: 98)

Chua   A god of the Lacandon who is probably the same as Ek Chua, the god of merchants. Mexico. (Tozzer, 1941: 107; Thompson, 1970: 40)

Chu Hsi, Chu-Fu-Tzu   A deity worshipped by the guild of paper hangers. Peking, China. (Burgess, 1928: 188)

Cipactónal   An Aztec goddess who brought spinning and weaving to the people, and gave to women "certain grains of corn for making cures, for soothsaying and witchcraft." Mexico. (León-Portilla, 1982: 34)

Cochimetl   A god of traders and brother of Yiacatecutli. Mexico. (Bancroft, 1886, 3: 416)

Creidne, Credne   God of the metal crafts, the divine worker in metals. He was associated with Goibniu. Celtic Ireland. (Squire, 1906: 61; MacCulloch, 1911: 76; Mac Cana, 1970: 35)

Daiban-Khukhu-Tengri   A god of the "white smiths" —a Western Tengrı—benevolent and well disposed. The Buriat, Siberia and Mongolia. (Klementz, 1925, 3: 4)

dǎ lǔ pấn   The chief spirit of the smithy. He is invited to the forge and asked for help. He also taught them other "technical skills." He has two assistants-lǔ lǔ pan and san lu pan. The Miao and the Meau, China. (Bernatzik, 1947: 165)

Dauarani   The goddess of boatmakers is the goddess of the forest. If the dead craftsman has observed all the ethical rules he will gain immortality and life in her domain. The Winikina-Warao, Venezuela. (Wilbert, 1972, 2: 61; 1973: 5)

Dengei   The "Great Serpent" god who taught the boat-builders the art of canoe making. Fiji, Melanesia. (Fison, 1904: 27)

Dha Dharni   A god of the iron-workers to whom offerings were made for a hot fire in the furnace. The Agaria, India. (Elwin, 1942: 105)

Dhahu Dhukan   A deity of iron-workers who lives "in the twyer." The Agaria, India. (Elwin, 1942: 104)

Dinipaan ud Daiya   A god of metal-workers, of blacksmiths. The Ifugao, Philippines. (Barton, 1946: 34; 1955: 112)

Dotra   God of the carpenter's crafts and of canoe-building. Yap Island, the Carolines, Micronesia. (Christian, 1899: 385; Lessa, 1961: 32)

Dragar   A deity worshipped by the iron smelters to whom an offering of a goat and some *ghi* is made. Kashmir. (Drew, 1875: 137)

Due Hijuxsá   A Father of the canoe. The Cagaba and the Kogi, Colombia. (Reichel-Dolmatoff, 1949/50: 115)

Dulb   A Celtic god, the smith of the Fomors. Ireland. (Squire, 1906: 86)

Dwe Tzu   A carpenter god of the Ch'iang at Lo-pu-chai. Szechwan, China. (Graham, 1958: 79)

Ea   The Assyro/Babylonian god of the waters was also a god of gold and silver smiths, of carpenters, of weavers, and of the arts. Near East. (Jastrow, 1898: 61, 138; Larousse, 1968: 56, 63)

Ebisu   One of the seven gods of happiness, of luck. He was a god of labor, of trade, and of fishermen. Japan. (Eliseev, 1963: 446; Herbert, 1967: 511–512; Piggott, 1969: 59; Eliot, 1935: 140)

Ehu   He became the ancestor god of the kapa-dyers "because he learned how to . . . give it color." Oahu, Hawaii. (Westervelt, 1963, 1: 66)

Eibildyúe   Mother of the canoe. The Cagaba and the Kogi, Colombia. (Reichel-Dolmatoff, 1949/50: 114)

Ek Chuah   As god of merchants and travelers, of cacao plantations he was friendly and invoked for protection. As a god of war he was malevolent. The Mayan, Central America. (Tozzer, 1941: 90, 107; Morley, 1946: 228; Bancroft, 1886: 466; Thompson, 1970: 306)

Elepaio   The bird form of the goddess Lea in which she passes judgment on the soundness of the tree felled by canoe-makers. Oahu, Hawaii. (Westervelt, 1963, 1: 100; Beckwith, 1940: 91)

Empu Pradah   The "first lord of the guild of the smiths." Bali, Indonesia. (Franken, 1960: 298)

Entelanying   A beneficent goddess who empowers "women to weave and to work the ornamental patterns on the native cloth." She also makes men "invulnerable against the weapons of their enemies." The Iban Dyaks, Sarawak, Borneo. (Sarawak Gazette, 1963: 136)

Ergane   Greek goddess of handicrafts, a surname of Pallas Athena. (Kerenyi, 1951: 127)

Eshu, Eshu-Elegba   The god of mischief, the trickster, the messenger of the gods, who is the instigator of troubles, does have some favorable qualities as god of the marketplace, of transactions, and of the crossroads. The Yoruba, Nigiera. (Morton-Williams, 1964: 248, 258; Wescott, 1962: 337–338; UCLA, 1971: 6/13)

Fa'atae   An artican god of Tahiti. Polynesia. (Henry, 1928: 356)

Fafa   An artisan for the god Tane. Society Islands, Polynesia. (Henry, 1928: 370)

Fakanatai   A god of the canoe, of Marinoa, Tikopia. Melanesia. (Firth, 1967, 2: 130)

Fakasautimu   An adz-god of Marinoa. Tikopia, Melanesia. (Firth, 1967, 1: 90)

Fan K'uei   The god of butchers. China. (Maspero, 1963: 332; Werner, 1932: 122)

Faro   An artisan god of Tahiti. Polynesia. (Henry, 1928: 374)

Feu   An artisan god of Ta'ere. Tahiti, Polynesia. (Henry, 1928: 406)

Fugamu   A deity who taught men the smith's art. He was also "the deity of the Rembo Ngoyai (a tributary of the Ogove)." Africa. (Gray, 1925, 4: 567)

Funi nu kami   God of the boat builders. Okinawa. (Lebra, 1966: 218)

Funzi, Mfuzi   "The mythical blacksmith" of the Fjort who taught them to work with metals. Africa. (Leach, 1949, 1: 428)

Fuuchi nu kami   God of blacksmiths, the "Bellows kami." Okinawa. (Lebra, 1966: 218)

Gajanand, Ganpati   The principal deity of the weavers of silk and cotton cloth. He is worshipped at the cleaning of their implements at the festival of Ganesh Chathurthi in August. The Koshti, Central Provinces, India. (Russell, 1916, 3: 585)

Po Ganuor Motri   The "god of sculptors, engravers, and carpenters." The Chams, Annam and Cambodia. (Cabaton, 1925, 3: 342)

mGar ba nag po   God of the blacksmiths. Tibet. (Nebesky-Wojkowitz, 1956, 1: 155)

Gav   The blacksmith deity and discoverer of fire. Persia. (Rawlinson, 1885: 113)

Gibil, Girru The god of fire, of the purifying and sacrificial fire, is also the god of the smiths. Babylonia. (Zimmern, 1925, 2: 312; Jayne, 1962: 121)

Gitir A beneficent goddess of the Iban Dyaks who empowers "women to weave and to work the ornamental patterns on the native cloth." She also protects men from the weapons of their enemies. Sarawak, Borneo. (Sarawak Gazette, 1963: 136)

Goba Pir The god of sweepers. The Agarwalas, Central Provinces, India. (Russell, 1916, 2: 138–139)

Gohantone "Iron or Metal Man." The Yuchi, South Carolina and Georgia. (Speck, 1909: 102)

Goibniu The divine smith of the Tuatha Da Danann for whom he forged arms. He was the god of the beer and the Otherworld feast which provided them with freedom from disease and age, from death. Celtic Ireland. Same as Govannan (Welsh). (MacCulloch, 1918: 31; MacCana, 1970: 24, 36; Jayne, 1962: 514; Squire, 1906: 61)

Govannan, Gofannon Celtic god of smiths. Son of Don and brother of Gwydion and Amaethon, of Arianrod. Wales. (Squire, 1906: 261; MacCana, 1970: 135; Anwyl, 1906: 35)

Gu God of iron and of ironworkers, of war and of hunting. Dahomey. (Herskovits, 1938, 2: 107, 127; Parrinder, 1967: 79, 83; Mercier, 1954: 222–223)

Gua God of blacksmiths and the thunder god. The Gã, Ghana. (Field, 1937: 86; Parrinder, 1949: 30)

Gushgin-banda, Guhkin-Banda God of bright metal workers. Babylonia, Near East. (Jastrow, 1898: 178; Larousse, 1968: 63)

Ōng Hà Bà "Lord of the River" to whom sacrifices are made before launching a new junk. Annam. (Cabaton, 1925, 1: 541)

Haburi, Abore The god of inventions, the builder of canoes. The Warao, Guiana and Venezuela. (Levi-Strauss, 1973: 183, 212; Brett, 1880: 76–83; Kirchhoff, 1948, 3: 879)

Hai-li-shem-mu The patron deity of "those who make cloth straps or strings for use on straw sandals." Szechwan, China. (Graham, 1961: 186)

Hanish A Mesopotamian god associated with the textile industry at Ur. Near East. (Jacobsen, 1970: 220)

Haniyasu-hiko and **Haniyasu-hime** God and goddess of earth, of clay, and deities of potters. Japan. (Herbert, 1967: 267–268, 476; Yasumaro, 1928: 8, 9)

Han Yu A deity worshipped by the guild of paper hangers. Peking, China. (Burgess, 1928: 188)

Harosh Phoenician smith god. Same as Hephaestos. Near East. (Paton, 1925, 9: 893)

Hayin A Ugaritic deity—"the master-builder . . . summoned . . . from Egypt" by Baal. Syria. (Obermann, 1948: 1)

Hei-lien Tsu-shih The god of comb-sellers. China. (Werner, 1932: 156)

Hephaestos The deformed son of Hera and Zeus was the god of the beneficent terrestrial fire which makes possible the arts of metal-working and of pottery—the god of these activities. He was also associated with the fertility of volcanic soils, and so with vineyards. His wife was Aphrodite who was unfaithful to him. Greece. (Jayne, 1962: 327; Murray, 1935: 85–87; Cox, 1870, 2: 197; Kerenyi, 1951: 155; Morford and Lenardon, 1975: 60–66; Larousse, 1968: 126)

Hercules Roman god of merchants, particularly those who travel. He was also a god of healing springs. Jayne, 1962: 428; Dumézil, 1966, 2: 434–438; Frazer, 1961: 209)

Hermes Because of his early activity, having stolen Apollo's herd, he was considered the god of gain, whether illegally as god of thieves, or legally as god of merchants and agoras, of travelers. He was clever, persuasive, eloquent. He was a god of sleep, of dreams, and the conductor of souls to Hades. Having repented and traded his lyre for Apollo's herd he was a god of herds and their fertility. As the son of Zeus and Maia he became the messenger of the gods. Greece. (Barthell, 1971: 33–37; Kerenyi, 1951: 161–162, 170; Keary, 1882: 333; Cox, 1870, 2: 226–227; Murray, 1935: 132–133; Schoeps, 1961: 131)

Heru-Behutet At Edfu the god of blacksmiths. Egypt. (Budge, 1969, 1: 476)

Hien Yuen The god of tailors and of architecture as well as of medicine. China. (Du Bose, n.d.: 130, 335, 400)

Hijon Phoenician god of "craftsmen and industrial workers." Near East. (Herm, 1975: 111)

Hiko-sashiri-no-kami A god of construction and of architecture. Japan. (Herbert, 1967: 304, 393)

Hina-kuku-kapa Goddess of kapa beaters. Kauai, Hawaii. (Emory, 1924: 67)

Hina-ulu-ohia Goddess of boat-builders, of the growth of the ohia trees. Hawaii. (Westervelt, 1963, 3: 37; Beckwith, 1940: 16)

Hine-tu-a-hoanga The Sandstone Maid, daughter of Rangahua. She was goddess of the grindstone and of stone-grinders. The Maori, New Zealand. (Best, 1924: 163; Mackenzie, n.d.: 37)

Ho Ho, Ho Ho Êrh Hsien Gods of merchants and of potters—"they are represented as two." China. (Werner, 1932: 158, 381)

Holda Teutonic goddess of spinning—she rewards the diligent and punishes the lax—and giver of flax. She is a goddess of the weather—when it snows she is shaking her bed, when it rains, she is washing clothes. (Grimm, 1880: 267–272; Neumann, 1955: 228; Guerber, 1895: 54)

Hope-kou-toki A god of carpentry, of house-building. The Marquesas, Polynesia. (Christian, 1895: 190)

Hsi Ling-ssu God of silk worshipped by its weavers and merchants. China. (Werner, 1932: 447)

Hsi-shih "The goddess of face-cream sellers and perfume sellers." China. (Werner, 1932: 161)

Hsüan Yüan, Hsüan-yuan Huang-ti God of tailors and also of "spectacle-merchants." China. (Day, 1940: 110; Werner, 1932: 179; Graham, 1961: 186)

Hua-Kuang Fo A god of silver- and gold-smiths. China. (Day, 1940: 113; Werner, 1932: 180; Maspero, 1963: 332)

Hua Kuang Ta Ti The "Lord of all silkworm deities." China. (Day, 1940: 107)

Huang K'un God of the manufacturers and merchants of incense. China. (Werner, 1932: 185; Day, 1940: 110)

Huang Ti Given variously as a god of architecture (Werner, 1932: 186); a god of tailors (Maspero, 1963: 332; Shryock, 1931: 162); and a god of medicine (Werner, 1932: 505; Larousse, 1968: 397). China.

Hung-chün-p'u-sa The patron deity of the manufacturers of "wooden combs." Szechwan, China. (Graham, 1961: 186)

Huo Shen The god of fire is worshipped by the Pork Shops Guild. China. (Burgess, 1928: 180)

Huriaro An artisan god for Ta'aroa. Tahiti, Polynesia. (Henry, 1928: 356)

Huritua An artisan god for Ta'aroa. Tahiti, Polynesia. (Henry, 1928: 356)

Hu Tzu A deity worshipped by tinkers. Peking, China. (Burgess, 1928: 179)

Hwei Nanhwang A god of the manufacturing of paper. China. (Du Bose, n.d.: 335)

Hyn The divine craftsman. Ugarit, Canaan. (Gray, 1957: 40)

Mulai Idris His feast is arranged by the "weavers of silk." He is also invoked by "vendors of sweetmeats." Morocco. (Westermarck, 1926, 1: 177, 181)

Igue-igha A deified mortal who brought brass-casting to Benin. The Bini, Nigeria. (Parrinder, 1949: 33)

Ik Chaua An important Mayan god, the great merchant god, of Itzam knac who apparently was the same as Ek Chuah. The Putun, Mexico. (Tozzer, 1941: 107; Thompson, 1970: 9)

Ikenga A ram-headed god of the head-hunters who taught men to be skillful with their hands and became a god of traders and craftsmen, of the household, and of good luck. The Ibo, Nigeria. (Sierksma, 1960: 23–25; Jeffreys, 1972: 723)

Il'ilulak One of the Masmasalanix who taught mankind to build canoes and to hunt. The Bella Coola, British Columbia. (Boas, 1898: 32–33)

Ilmarinen In his aspect as celestial smith he forged the sun and moon. Finland. (Leach, 1949, 1: 514; Larousse, 1973: 420)

Indai Abang A beneficent goddess who empowers "women to weave and to work the ornamental patterns on the native cloth." She also protects men from their enemies' weapons. The Iban Dyaks, Sarawak, Borneo. (Sarawak Gazette, 1963: 136)

Ishi-kori-dome The god/goddess of stone-cutters and of the manufacturers of mirrors. Japan. (Herbert, 1967: 393, 463)

Isis At Delos she, Anubis, and Serapis are invoked as protectors of vessels from the dangers of the sea by merchants and sailors. Greece. (Duprez, 1970: 52–53)

Iwatsubiko-no-Kami The god of building material. Son of Izanagi and Izanami. Japan. (Yasumaro, 1965: 14)

Ixazalvoh Goddess of weaving, given as the wife of Hunab Ku or Kinich Ahau. The Mayan, Central America. (Bancroft, 1886, 3: 462; Tozzer, 1941: 153)

Jijin-sama A god invoked by carpenters before building a house. Takashima, Japan. (Norbeck, 1954: 65)

Kaba Samnep God of the anvil. The Katchins, Burma. (Gilhodes, 1908: 697)

Kabta Sumerian god of bricks, of brick-making, of the pick and the mold. Near East. (Ferm, 1950: 60; Hooke, 1963: 27)

Kalual Lohar A Himalayan god of blacksmiths. India. (Berreman, 1963: 109)

Kalvis The Baltic divine smith who makes the new sun, moon, when they are devoured in eclipses, and spurs for the celestial horses. Lithuania. (Gimbutas, 1963: 199, 202; 1975: XLC M126)

Kama-gami A god worshipped by potters. Japan. (Herbert, 1967: 463)

Kamakshi Amma The goddess of craftsmen who is represented by various tools of the trades. She presides over the bellows-fire. The Kanchara and the Kammalan, Southern India. (Thurston, 1909, 3: 111–112, 147)

Kamu-hata-hime Goddess of weaving. Japan. (Herbert, 1967: 359)

Kanniha Paramesvare Goddess of traders. South India. (Whitehead, 1916: 32)

Kansasur Deota The godling or demon, asur, of brass "by whom the Byadh Nats swear." The Doms, India. (Briggs, 1953: 387)

Ka-pua-o-alakai A goddess of the cutters of the wood for canoes. Hawaii. (Westervelt, 1963, 1: 99)

Karisi An adz god of the Kafika and Taumako clans, invoked for abundance and rain. Tikopia, Melanesia. (Firth, 1967, 2: 62, 297)

Kauthar, Koshar The artisan of the gods, "the inventor of tools and weapons, of magical incantations." Canaan, Near East. (Ferm, 1950: 124; Albright, 1956: 81)

K'daai Maqsin A god of evil and chief blacksmith of the underworld from whom the smiths get their craft and who introduced shamanism. The Yakut, Siberia. (Popov, 1933: 260; Eliade, 1964: 470, 472)

Ke Hsien Wang A deity worshipped by merchants of dye stuffs. Peking, China. (Burgess, 1928: 189)

Kê Wêng Hsien Shih Patron of dyers. China. (Day, 1940: 109)

Khara-Dargakhi-Tengri, Boron-Khara-Tengri An Eastern Tengri who taught the blacksmiths their trade. The Buriats, Siberia and Mongolia. (Klementz, 1925, 3: 5)

Kinulhudan A god of weaving, also a god of dysentery. The Ifugao, Philippines. (Barton, 1946: 29, 63)

Klowe A god of blacksmiths and a god of thunder. Son of Gbobu and Ohimiya. The Ga, Nungwa, Ghana. (Field, 1937: 27–28)

Kodama-gami God of the silk and the silkworm. Japan. (Hori, 1968: 66)

Ko Hsien-wêng The god of dyers. China. (Werner, 1932: 220)

K'o Lung Wu Shêng A silkworm god, of the cocoon. China. (Day, 1940: 108)

Koshar, Kothar-and-Hasis, Kothar-u-Khasis, Ktr w Hss The divine artisan, the god of craftsmanship and skill. Canaan and Phoenicia, Near East. (Vriezen, 1963: 53; Gray, 1957: 137; Albright, 1968: 187, 136; Gordon, 1961: 193; Hooke, 1963: 81; Oldenburg, 1969: 46, 97)

Ko-weng Patron deity of Dyers. Szechwan, China. (Graham, 1961: 186)

Krukis God of blacksmiths and also god of domestic animals. Litu-Prussian. (Schrader, 1925, 2: 31; Larousse, 1968: 290)

Ku-ala-nawao A god of the canoe and of canoe makers. Hawaii. (Beckwith, 1970: 177; Emerson, 1967: 53)

Kudai-Bakshy A deity of blacksmiths who lives in the underworld. The Yakuts, Siberia. (MacCulloch, 1964: 464)

Kuei-ku Tzu A "God of Spectacle-sellers." China. (Werner, 1932: 232)

Kuguri-gami The goddess of the profession of diving girls. Japan. (Herbert, 1967: 463)

Ku-holoholo-pali A god of canoe builders and of the forest slopes "who steadies the canoe when it is carried down steep places." Hawaii. (Beckwith, 1940: 15, 16)

Ku-ka-ohia-laka God of the ohia-lehua hardwood tree used by canoe builders; worshipped by them. Hawaii. (Beckwith, 1940: 15, 16)

Kulla Sumerian god of bricks and of brick-making, created by Ea "for the restoration of temples." Near East. (Kramer, 1961: 100; Langdon, 1931: 104; Larousse, 1973: 70; Jacobsen, 1976: 85)

Kuncha-vituéya A Father of the canoe. The Cagaba and the Kogi, Colombia. (Reichel-Dolmatoff, 1949/50: 115)

Kung Shu Lu Pan A deity worshipped by the crafts of Awning Makers, Carpenters, Leather Box Makers, Masons, Mat Tent Makers, Painters, Table and Chair Makers. Peking, China. (Burgess, 1928: 188)

Kupa'aikee God of the bevel adz used in carving out the canoe. Hawaii. (Beckwith, 1940: 15; Emerson, 1968: 53)

Ku-pepeiao-loa and **Ku-pepeiao-poko** Gods of canoe builders, "of the seat braces by which the canoe is carried." Hawaii. (Beckwith, 1940: 15, 16)

Kurdalagon The "celestial smith" of the Ossetes. The Caucasus. (Machal, 1918: 361, n. 90)

Kwan Yü The god of wealth is worshipped by merchants of cloth stores, coal stores, fur stores, pork shops, satin and silk stores, and second-hand clothing stores. Peking, China. (Burgess, 1928: 188)

Kyzyl-kikh-khan An Altaic deity invoked at the beginning of an undertaking. Siberia. (Czaplicka, 1969: 358)

Laa-hana An ancestress-goddess of the kapa-makers —"those who used especially marked clubs while beating the bark into patterns or marked lines." Oahu, Hawaii. (Westervelt, 1963, 1: 65)

Lao Tsu God of barbers. Anking, China. (Shryock, 1931: 162)

Lao Tzi God of silver and copper smiths, of metalworkers, and of innkeepers. Also called Li Lao Chun. Anking, China. (Shryock, 1931: 34, 162)

Lata A god of canoe building. Niue, Polynesia. (Loeb, 1926, 1: 164)

Lateranus Roman god of the kilns for making bricks, of chimneys and stoves. (Roscher, 1965, 2, 1: 201)

Lau-hu-iki, Lauhuki Goddess of the kapa beaters and of the manufacture of kapa. Hawaii. (Westervelt, 1963, 1: 65; Alexander, 1968: 63; 1967: 90)

Lea, Laea A goddess of canoe-cutters, sometimes human, sometimes a bird (the Elepaio) and as such indicated if the tree is good for a canoe. She is the sister and chief minister of Mokuhalii, the chief of the canoe makers gods. She lives on the mountains. Hawaii. (Westervelt, 1963, 1: 99, 100; Beckwith, 1940: 16; Emerson, 1967: 53)

Lei-tsu (1) "God of Seedsmen or Cornchandlers and of Inn-keepers." China. (Werner, 1932: 245) (2) "[Traditionally, wife of the yellow emperor and originator of sericulture] worshipped by weavers." The Miao, China. (Wu and Ch'en, 1942: 26)

Lei Tzu The thunder god, worshipped by "Cooks, Confectioners and Shoemakers" Guilds. China. (Shryock, 1931: 162; Maspero, 1963: 274)

Li Lao-chün God of gold, silver, and copper smiths as well as other metal workers, of workers in leather, and of inn-keepers. Anking, China. (Werner, 1932: 247; Shryock, 1931: 34, 162; Graham, 1961: 186)

Li San-niang "Goddess of Millers." China. (Werner, 1932: 249)

Li Shih Hsien Kuan A god of business deals and of profits. China. (Day, 1940: 114; Maspero; 1963: 299)

Liu Pei (1) "God of Basket-makers." China. (Werner, 1932: 258) (2) In North China at Ting Hsien he is the god of carpenters. (Gamble, 1954: 418)

Lo An ancestor god, patron of barbers. China. (Maspero, 1963: 332)

Lohasur God or goddess of iron, of the furnace, worshipped by smelters and forgers. The Agaria. Among the Baiga a household deity who lives in the axe. India. (Elwin, 1939: 61; 1942: 88, 103, 106; Keane, 1925, 2: 123; Russell, 1916, 2: 6)

Loh Yuinshan God of barbers. China. (Du Bose, n.d.: 335)

Lo Pan A "[clever artisan of the spring and autumn period] worshipped by artisans." The Miao, China. (Wu and Ch'en, 1942: 26)

Lo-tsu Ta-hsien, Lü-tsu, Lo Tzu (Peking) God of barbers and of pedicures, as well as of beggars. China. (Werner, 1932: 280; Shryock, 1931: 20; Leach, 1950, 2: 656; Burgess, 1928: 180)

Lu Ban *See* **Lu Pan**

Luchta, Luchtaine The god of carpenters who provided "the shields and lance-shafts" for Goibniu for arms. Celtic Ireland. (MacCana, 1970: 35; MacCulloch, 1911: 76; Squire, 1906: 61, 86)

Lu Ch'un Yang The god of physicians and druggists is also a god of barbers and inkmakers. China. (Day, 1940: 111)

Lugh A god of all the crafts and arts, omnicompetent; a warrior god and a healer with herbs and magic. Celtic Ireland. (Ross, 1967: 202, 203; MacCana, 1970: 27; Squire, 1906: 62, 84–86; Larousse, 1968: 227)

Lugus, Lugos An older form of the name Lugh. As the Gaulish Mercury he was a god of commerce, of the crafts, and of the roads. (MacCana, 1970: 27–29; Ross, 1967: 250, 363)

Lu-hsing A stellar god representing happiness, long life—the bestower of salaries, of position and dignities. China. (Maspero, 1963: 344–345; Day, 1940: 95)

Luk-e-lang A god of carpenters and boat-builders. Lamotrek, the Carolines, Micronesia. (Christian, 1897: 198)

Lukman Hakim A deity worshipped by the caste of makers of fireworks. The Kadera, Central Provinces, India. (Russell, 1916, 3: 290)

Lulong A benevolent goddess who empowers "women to weave and to work the ornamental patterns on the native cloth." She is also invoked in conjunction with love philters. The Dyaks, Sarawak, Borneo. (Sarawak Gazette, 1963: 130, 136)

Lu Pan God of carpenters and related trades, of shipbuilders, and of potters. China. (Day, 1940: 109; Maspero, 1963: 332; Shryock, 1931: 162; Graham, 1928: 74; Werner, 1932: 281)

Lu T'ou The "God of Riches of roads (or cross-roads) worshipped by merchants." China. (Werner, 1932: 515)

Lü-tsu *See* **Lo-tsu**

Lü Tung-pin A variant of Lü ch'un Yang, which see. (Day, 1940: 111) One of the Eight Immortals whose emblem is a supernatural sword with which he slayed dragons. Patron of barbers. (Williams, 1976: 153) China.

Ma A god invoked to supervise the building of "a new god-house." The Ch'iang, Szechwan, China. (Graham, 1958: 79)

Mahadeo The god who gave them the oil-mill. The Teli, India. (Russell, 1916, 4: 549)

Mak'era God of iron workers whose sacrifice is a black he-goat or a black chicken when setting up a new anvil or leaving on a mining expedition. The Maguzawa, Nigeria. (Greenberg, 1946: 34)

Malapalitsek One of the Masmasalanix, four brothers who "gave man his arts . . . taught him to build canoes . . . hunting." The Bella Coola, British Columbia. (Boas, 1898: 32–33)

Malapeexoek One of the Masmasalanix brothers. See above.

Ma Ming Shêng Mu A goddess of silkworms. China. (Day, 1940: 108)

Mamiyu A god of weaving, the "Stretcher of Skeins." The Ifugao, Philippines. (Barton, 1946: 30)

Manawyddan The son of Llyr and Penardun. A Celtic god of the underworld and associated with the sea. He is also called a god of crafts and the useful arts. Wales. (Squire, 1906: 270; MacCulloch, 1911: 101; Cohane, 1969: 146)

Manoklit "Warp Raiser," a god of weaving. The Ifugao, Philippines. (Barton, 1946: 30)

Manoltog A god of weaving. Son of Monkulabe. The Ifugao, Philippines. (Barton, 1946: 30)

Mara   A Slavic spirit who spins at night. When a woman puts aside her spindle she must offer a prayer or Mara will spoil her work. Russia. (Ralston, 1872: 133)

Marei-kura   A goddess of plaiting, weaving, and mid-wifery. Anaa Island, Tuamotua, Polynesia. (Stimson, 1933: 25)

Masan Baba   A god worshipped by a caste of oil-press-ers. The Teli, Central Provinces, India. (Russell, 1916, 4: 549)

Mase   An ancestral god worshipped by iron-workers. Dahomey. (Herskovits, 1938, 1: 181)

Masmasalanix   Four brothers: Malapalitsek, Yulati-mot, Malapeexoek, Il'ilulak who "gave man his arts . . . taught him to build canoes . . . hunting." Their sister is Laqumeiks. The Bella Coola, British Columbia. (Boas, 1898: 32–33)

Massak'i   The "weaver"—a good spirit of the Maguzawa. Nigeria. (Greenberg, 1946: 29)

Mataitai   An artisan god for Ta'ere. Tahiti, Polynesia. (Henry, 1928: 374)

Matamata-'arahu   An artisan god of Ta'ere, the in-ventor of tattooing. Tahiti, Polynesia. (Henry, 1928: 287, 374)

Matapula   A deity invoked in "re-furnishing of the canoe shed." Tikopia, Melanesia. (Firth, 1967, 2: 124, 330)

Matavaka   A guardian deity of the sacred canoe of the Tau-mako clan. Tikopia, Melanesia. (Firth, 1967, 2: 99)

Matila foafoa   A "god wise in the making and throwing of the *tika*." Niue, Polynesia. (Loeb, 1926, 1: 164)

Matohi   An artisan god of Tahiti. Polynesia. (Henry, 1928: 414)

Ma-tohi-fanau-'eoe   An artisan god for Ra'i-tupua-nui. Society Islands, Polynesia. (Henry, 1928: 356)

Ma-t'ou Niang   A goddess of silkworms, invoked for the prosperity of the mulberry trees and the worms. China. (Werner, 1932: 301, 518)

Mawshai   A goddess of the market. Khasi, Assam. (Bareh, 1967: 361)

Mei Hsien Wang   A deity worshipped by merchants of dye stuffs. Peking, China. (Burgess, 1928: 189)

Dewi Melanting   A goddess of markets, but primarily a chthonic deity of gardens and fertility. Daughter of Wisnu and Dewi Sri. Bali, Indonesia. (Covarrubias, 1937: 46, 71, 317)

Mele   A goddess of weaving. Niue Island, Polynesia. (Loeb, 1926, 1: 164)

Mendong   A beneficent goddess who empowers "women to weave and to work the ornamental patterns on the native cloth." She also makes men "invulnerable against the weapons of their enemies." The Iban Dyaks, Sarawak, Borneo. (Sarawak Gazette, 1963: 136)

Meng T'ien   The god and inventor of writing and paint brushes and patron deity of the brushmakers. China. (Werner, 1932: 313; Graham, 1961: 186; Maspero, 1963: 332)

Mercury   Roman god of merchants, of trade and com-merce. Same as Hermes (Greek). (Dumézil, 1966, 2: 439–440; Fairbanks, 1907: 201; Bulfinch, 1898: 11)

Meteua   A god associated with the sacred canoe. Tikopia, Melanesia. (Firth, 1967, 2: 126)

Mi-lo-fo   God of gold and silver smiths. China. (Maspero, 1963: 331; Werner, 1932: 315)

Minerva   Etruscan/Roman goddess of handicrafts, of artisans, and of guilds. It was only after identification with Athena that she was represented as warlike. (Fair-banks, 1907: 118; Dumézil, 1966, 1: 208, 303–305; Jayne, 1962: 434; Bulfinch, 1898: 131)

Mixcoa   God of traders who was also invoked by the buyers. Nicaragua. (Lothrop, 1926: 69; Bancroft, 1886, 3: 492)

Mixcoatl   Among the Pipil this stellar and hunting god of the Chichimec became a god of merchants. Guatemala. (Krickeberg, 1968: 81)

Moe   A god invoked with others in canoe launching. Society Islands, Polynesia. (Henry, 1928: 551)

Mokosh   A goddess of merchants and of trade, associ-ated with spinning and weaving. She is also a patron of fields and of fishermen. Slavic Russia. (Gimbutas, 1975: XLC M126; Czaplicka, 1925, 11: 593)

Moku-ha-lii   Chief of the canoe gods and god of the canoe-carvers. Hawaii. (Keliipio, 1901: 115; Westervelt, 1963, 1: 100; Emerson, 1968: 53)

Mola Roman goddess of the mills. (Roscher, 1965, 2, 1: 204)

Mombongbong "Red-Dyer" or "Yellow-Dyer." A god of weaving. Son of Monkulabe. The Ifugao, Philippines. (Barton, 1946: 30)

Mombuhug "Fluffer," a god of weaving and son of Monkulabe. The Ifugao, Philippines. (Barton, 1946: 30)

Momolmol "Dipper into Starch," a god of weaving. Son of Monkulabe. The Ifugao, Philippines. (Barton, 1946: 30)

Mompolin "Separator of Seeds from Cotton," a god of weaving and a son of Monkulabe. The Ifugao, Philippines. (Barton, 1946: 30)

Mompudon "Winder into a Ball," a god of weaving, offspring of Monkulabe. The Ifugao, Philippines. (Barton, 1946: 30)

Monabol A god of weaving. Son of Monkulabe. The Ifugao, Philippines. (Barton, 1946: 30)

Monadame A god of weaving and offspring of Monkulabe. The Ifugao, Philippines. (Barton, 1946: 30)

Monadumme "Drawer-Out of Thread on Spindle Bob," a god of weaving. The Ifugao, Philippines. (Barton, 1946: 30)

Monalutut A god of weaving. Son of Monkulabe. The Ifugao, Philippines. (Barton, 1946: 30)

Mondauwat A god of weaving. Son of Monkulabe. The Ifugao, Philippines. (Barton, 1946: 30)

Moneta Roman goddess of the mint, of coinage. (Cox, 1870, 2: 13; Schoeps, 1961: 148; Ferguson, 1970: 73)

Mongadang A god of weaving, of basket-making—"user of Gadang." Also a god of hunting. Son of Kinulhudan. The Ifugao, Philippines. (Barton, 1946: 29, 79)

Monhau-ud "Setter-Up of the Warp," a god of weaving and son of Monkulabe. The Ifugao, Philippines. (Barton, 1946: 30)

Monhauwe A god of weaving, son of Monkulabe. The Ifugao, Philippines. (Barton, 1946: 30)

Monhinong A god of weaving who sees that the loom is properly set up. Son of Monkulabe. The Ifugao, Philippines. (Barton, 1946: 30)

Monkulabe A god of weaving of textiles. Son of Kinulhudan. The Ifugao, Philippines. (Barton, 1946: 29)

Monliktag A god of weaving and son of Monkulabe. The Ifugao, Philippines. (Barton, 1946: 30)

Monlotlot A god of weaving. "Winder of Thread on Spindle Bob." Son of Monkulabe. The Ifugao, Philippines. (Barton, 1946: 30)

Monnutnut A god of weaving—"Separator of Defective, Lumped Fibers," son of Monkulabe. The Ifugao, Philippines. (Barton, 1946: 30)

Montaiyum "Black-Dyer"—a god of weaving, son of Monuklabe. The Ifugao, Philippines. (Barton, 1946: 30)

Montiyong "Spinner," a god of weaving, offspring of Monkulabe. The Ifugao, Philippines. (Barton, 1946: 30)

Montubaiyon "User of Spindle Bob"—a god of weaving, son of Monkulabe. The Ifugao, Philippines. (Barton, 1946: 30)

Monwalangan "Winder into Skeins"—a god of weaving and son of Monkulabe. The Ifugao, Philippines. (Barton, 1946: 30)

Motu-haiki A god of carpentry, of house-building. The Marquesas, Polynesia. (Christian, 1895: 190)

mung kung, mung gum A guardian deity of carpenters invoked for the protection of the house being constructed and of the people. The Lepchas, Sikkim. (Siiger, 1967: 69)

Munyonga The "one-legged God of the Blacksmiths." South Africa. (Mutwa, 1966: 1)

Musa A god of pottery and weaving, also of hunting. The Songhay, Upper Niger. (Parrinder, 1967: 79)

Mushdamma Sumerian god of construction, of foundations and house-building. Near East. (Hooke, 1963: 27; Ferm, 1950: 60; Kramer, 1961: 100; Jacobsen, 1946: 174)

na'acdjêi· 'esdzą· Spider Woman is the patroness of weaving having taught this craft to mankind. The Navaho, Arizona and New Mexico. (Reichard, 1950: 467–468)

Nabsacadas The "tribal deity of the Quimbaya, a nation of goldsmiths." Cauca Valley, Colombia. (Trimborn, 1968: 99)

Nacxitl An Aztec god of traders, brother of Yiacate-cutli. Mexico. (Bancroft, 1886, 3: 416)

Nana "(Steadfast-gaze)"—an artisan god of Ta'aroa. Tahiti, Polynesia. (Henry, 1928: 356)

Nan-chelang "The god of canoe-building and carpentry incarnate in a green and yellow tree-lizard of the same name." Ponape, Caroline Islands, Micronesia. (Christian, 1899: 383; Lessa, 1961: 32)

Nappatecutli Aztec god of mat-makers, of the straw and reeds used by them. Worshipped in the vicinity of Lake Texcuco, Mexico. (Spence, 1923: 235, 264; Caso, 1958: 45)

Nehalennia Belgian/Germanic goddess of ships and of seafaring trade. (Ross, 1967: 339; Wagner, 1882: 107; Grimm, 1880: 257)

Neith An Egyptian goddess of various aspects. She was a goddess of weaving and of the domestic arts, but also a goddess of war, of hunting, and of the dead. (Knight, 1915: 77, 78; Ames, 1965: 105; Budge, 1969, 1: 451, 463)

Nencatacoa, Nemcatacoa A god of weavers and painters of cloth who was made offerings of chica. He was also the god of drunkards. The Chibchas, Colombia. (Reichel-Dolmatoff, 1975: 45; Kroeber, 1946: 906; Alexander, 1920: 204)

Nenia A god of thatchers of houses. Society Islands, Polynesia. (Ellis, 1853: 333)

Nimsimug A Babylonian god created by Ea to take part in the construction of temples. Near East. (Larousse, 1973: 70)

Nin-a-gal A name of Ea as the god of the smith crafts. Babylonia, Near East. (Jastrow, 1898: 64)

Nindubarra Ea as the god of "shipmenders." Sumer, Near East. (Langdon, 1931: 105)

Nin-igi-nangar-bu A Babylonian god of metal workers of the Hammurabi period. Assistant to Ea. Near East. (Jastrow, 1898: 171, 178)

Ninildu A Babylonian god created by Ea to take part in the construction of temples. Near East. (Larousse, 1973: 70)

Nin-kurra A Babylonian mountain god—"patron of those who quarried the stones." Near East. (Jastrow, 1898: 171, 178)

Nipälou A patroness of the art of weaving. Truk, Micronesia. (Bollig, 1927: 10)

Nisarere A patroness of the art of weaving invoked by women. She was "skillful as a sorceress" and considered the sister of Onulap. Truk, Micronesia. (Bollig, 1927: 10)

Nohuichana A goddess "associated with weaving and cotton" who is also a goddess of hunting and fishing, of childbirth and of children. The Zapotec, Sola, Oaxaca, Mexico. (Whitecotton, 1977: 164)

Nunghui The spirit of pottery clay of whom black and red are manifestations. The Canelos Quichua, Ecuador. (Whitten, 1978: 95, 97)

Nurra Ea as the god of potters. Sumer, Near East. (Langdon, 1931: 105)

Nyahpa mahse A supernatural being who taught them jewelry craftsmanship, to work with metals, copper, silver. The Desana, Colombia. (Reichel-Dolmatoff, 1971: 253)

Ogillon Yoruban god of certain metals and of smiths. Brazil. (Bastide, 1960: 569)

Ogun, Ogoun The Yoruban god of iron and of smiths is also god of war and of hunting, and in Nigeria is also the god of oaths and covenants. He is known also in Brazil, Trinidad, Cuba, and in Haiti. In the latter his power developed a political slant. (Idowu, 1962: 85–87; Lucas, 1948: 98, 106; Parrinder, 1967: 79; Deren, 1953: 74, 86, 130; Herskovits, 1937, 1: 316; Verger, 1957: 141, 174; Courlander, 1966: 10; Simpson, 1965: 20)

'Oina "Sharpness"—an artisan of Tane. Society Islands, Polynesia. (Henry, 1928: 370)

Olevat A god of carpenters and boat-builders. Brother of Luk-e-lang. Lamotrek, the Carolines, Micronesia. (Christian, 1897: 198)

Olo-sipa, Olo-sopa Architect gods who "constructed the great walls, the stone-water frontages and wharves upon the islets between Tomun and Leak, on the Metalanim coast." Ponape, the Carolines, Micronesia. (Christian, 1899: 383)

Omatose'k A god who assisted Spixpiknem in working cedarbark. The Bella Coola, British Columbia. (Boas, 1898, 2: 33)

Ongan Pat The "oil-god," the deity of cartmen to keep the wheels running smoothly. Central Provinces, India. (Russell, 1925, 3: 314)

onne chip kamui An "old boat goddess." The Ainu, Hokkaido, Japan. (Philippi, 1982: 175)

'O'oia "Swiftness," an artisan for Tane. Society Islands, Polynesia. (Henry, 1928: 370)

Owamekaso A culture hero supernatural who "taught the skills of trade." The Kalabari, Nigeria. (Horton, 1960: 17)

Palulap A god credited with teaching them canoe building, the arts of navigation and of divination. Ulithi, the Carolines, Micronesia. (Lessa, 1966: 58)

Panatis A name of Athena as a goddess of weaving. Greece. (Roscher, 1965, 3, 1: 1497)

Panayagan, Paneyangen God of brass-casters, also the protector of bees. The Bagobo, Mindanao, Philippines. (Jocano, 1969: 21; Benedict, 1916: 22)

Pawan Daseri A god of ironworkers—the wind—who lives "in the bellows." The Agaria, India. (Elwin, 1942: 104)

Pecunia A Roman goddess of money associated with "tradesmen's profits." (Roscher, 1965, 2, 1: 213; Larousse, 1968: 207)

(Pitao) Peeze, Pitaoquille, Pitooyage The deity appealed to by "merchants, wealthy individuals, and those involved in gaming or chance." The Zapotec, Oaxaca, Mexico. (Whitecotton, 1977: 165)

Peperu An artisan god of Ta'ere. Tahiti, Polynesia. (Henry, 1928: 374)

Perahta, Percht, Berchte Teutonic goddess of spinning and weaving, a spinner of destiny. (Grimm, 1880: 272; Neumann, 1955: 228)

Perdoytus Lithuanian god of merchants and also of seafarers. (Schrader, 1925, 2: 32; Puhvel, 1974: 83)

Pien Ho God of jewellers and of precious stones. China. (Maspero, 1963: 332; Werner, 1932: 378; Du Bose, n.d.: 329)

Ping Tien Ta Ti A deity worshipped by merchants of Pork Shops. Peking, China. (Burgess, 1928: 189)

Poere A god of artisans (a stone) invoked at canoe-launching and house building. He was also a god of food and water supplies and "offerings of fish were made to him to promote recovery of the sick." Rapa, Polynesia. (Buck, 1938: 173)

Po Ssu The god of "candle-merchants or wax-chandlers." China. (Werner, 1932: 380)

Potnia Presumably an earth goddess but also associated with smiths. The Mycenean, Pylos, Greece. (Chadwick, 1976: 92–93)

Ptah God of artisans and craftsmen, of artists, in all fields but particularly in metals. Considered the "architect of the universe." Egypt. (Schoeps, 1961: 70; Ames, 1965: 101; Budge, 1969, 1: 416, 500–502; Knight, 1915: 98)

Pu An Lao Tzu A deity worshipped by the guild of "the painters who do the common work without decoration." Peking, China. (Burgess, 1928: 179)

Pu Chi T'u Ti An aspect of T'u Ti, protector of the loom. China. (Day, 1940: 67)

Pu Fafine A goddess of the canoe shed and of the sacred adz. She was also a goddess of the ritual oven. Tikopia, Melanesia. (Firth, 1967, 2: 76, 81, 106)

Pu-i-te-Moana A deified mortal, a canoe god of Karoata. Tikopia, Melanesia. (Firth, 1967, 2: 115)

Punholdaiyan The "primal ancestor of the gods of weaving." The Ifugao, Philippines. (Barton, 1946: 29)

Pusi An adz god, who is incarnated as the grey reef eel, is invoked in the consecration of the sacred oven and also in the " re-furnishing of the canoe shed." Tikopia, Melanesia. (Firth, 1939: 122; 1967, 2: 103–104, 124)

Pusiuraura An eel god associated with the adz of the canoe rites. Tikopia, Melanesia. (Firth, 1967, 2: 63)

Pusi uri An adz god of the Tafua clan, associated with canoe rituals. Tikopia, Melanesia. (Firth, 1967, 2: 62)

Pusi toto An adz god of the Tafua clan associated with canoe rituals. Tikopia, Melanesia. (Firth, 1967, 2: 62)

Puyu A beneficent goddess who empowers "women to weave and to work the ornamental patterns on the native cloth." She also protects men from the weapons of their enemies. The Iban Dyaks, Sarawak, Borneo. (Sarawak Gazette, 1963: 136)

San Rafael The patron of the merchants. The Tarasco, Mexico. (Beals, 1946: 139)

Raja Kidar A god who "has also the curious function of haunting the market in the early morning and fixing the price of grain, which he protects from the evil eye." India. (Keith, 1917: 235)

Rakim "God of house-building and carpentry. According to Dr. Gulick the god of evil, disease, death and famine." Also possibly a sky god associated with the rainbow. Ponape, Caroline Islands, Micronesia. (Christian, 1899: 381)

Raki-te-ua A coconut god invoked in the consecration of the sacred oven of Tafua, and also invoked in the "refurnishing of the canoe shed." Tikopia, Melanesia. (Firth, 1967, 2: 124, 258)

Rauti "(Stimulator) was the artisan of Ta'aroa in the ocean." Society Islands, Polynesia. (Henry, 1928: 356)

Rbhu, Ribhu The artisan of Indra. He is invoked for skill and dexterity as well as for prosperity. India. (Macdonell, 1897: 131–132; Leach, 1950, 2: 937)

Remle Etruscan "spirit of the mills" who interferes with its working when someone has offended him. Italy. (Leland, 1963: 129)

Rima-roa An artisan god and a god of war. Society Islands, Polynesia. (Henry, 1928: 356, 365; Williamson, 1933: 59)

Rua-futi A deity invoked in "re-furnishing of the canoe shed." Tikopia, Melanesia. (Firth, 1967, 2: 124)

Rua-i-te-parakore A deity who personifies the "knowledge of carving." The Maori, New Zealand. (Best, 1924: 177)

Rua-i-te-whaihanga A deity who is the personification of "the knowledge of the artisan, the craftsman." The Maori, New Zealand. (Best, 1924: 177)

Po Sah Ino The deified virgin-mother of Po Klon Garai. She "became the goddess of merchants." The Chams, Annam and Cambodia. (Cabaton, 1925, 3: 342)

sa hyor God of blacksmiths of the Lepchas. Sikkim. (Siiger, 1967: 144)

Salan A god with knowledge of the crafts, e.g. house- and boat-building. Yap Island, Micronesia. (Müller, 1917: 309)

Sao The patron of house builders. A child of Tagaloa. Manua (Samoa), Polynesia. (Mead, 1930: 158)

Saptursaikla The "chief of sac red black dye derived from Earth-mother's menstruation." The Cuna, Panama. (Keeler, 1960: 89)

Sarakka A goddess of childbirth who creates or forms the child in the womb. She is also a goddess of spinning. The Lapps, Northern Europe. (Dioszegi, 1968: 30; Bosi, 1960: 134; Pettersson, 1957: 18; MacCulloch, 1964: 253)

Savadamma Goddess of the weaver caste. Coimbatore District, India. (Whitehead, 1916: 31)

See Lingsze God of silk. China. (Du Bose, n.d.: 335)

Seilangi A god of canoe building. Ifalik, Micronesia. (Burrows, 1947/48: 10)

Seimeligarara A god of canoe building. Ifalik, Micronesia. (Burrows, 1947/48: 10)

Semer Ik A "god of canoe-building . . . Invoked in a shipwright's prayer." Ifalik, Micronesia. (Burrows, 1947/48: 10)

Serapis A chthonian deity, a god of healing and fecundity in the Near East and the Grecian Islands, is venerated also as the protector of navigation—a cult spread by merchants and sailors. (Duprez, 1970: 49, 53, 73)

Sethlans Etruscan god of smiths who also "had power over lightning." Same as Vulcan, Hephaestos. Italy. (von Vacano, 1960: 19, 110; Pallottino, 1975: 142; Altheim, 1937: 152; Roscher, 1965, 4: 785)

sheeku nu Kami God of carpentry, of woodworking. Okinawa. (Lebra, 1966: 22)

Shen-tsu God of leather-workers. Szechwan, China. (Graham, 1961: 186)

Shi-shto A god of tradesmen. The Ch'iang, Lo-pu-chai. Szechwan, China. (Graham, 1958: 49)

Shuen Uen Shang Ti "Reputed to have taught the Chinese how to make and to wear clothing." Szechwan, China. (Graham, 1928: 74–75)

Shullat, Shulaat Mesopotamian god associated with the textile industry at Ur. Near East. (Jacobsen, 1970: 220)

Ka Siem Synshar A deity worshipped on the completion of a house. The Syntengs, Nartiang, Assam. (Gurdon, 1907: 31)

Sien-Tsan A goddess who first bred silkworms. China. (De Groot, 1925, 4: 14)

Silalap The god of canoe building. Namolu, the Carolines, Micronesia. (Lessa, 1961: 32)

Si Ling She A deified empress who invented silkworm rearing. China. (MacLagan, 1925, 6: 646)

Singgar A beneficent goddess who empowers "women to weave and to work the ornamental patterns on the native cloth." She also protects men from the weapons of their enemies. The Iban Dyaks, Sarawak, Borneo. (Sarawak Gazette, 1963: 136)

Singhbahani The goddess of a caste of coppersmiths. The Tamera, Central Provinces, India. (Russell, 1916, 4: 538)

Sira Empu The god of blacksmiths. Rendang District, Bali, Indonesia. (Goris, 1969, 1: 85)

Solang A god of canoe building, of carpenters. Ulithi, the Carolines, Micronesia. (Lessa, 1966: 59; Poignant, 1967: 80)

Srintun Tanah Tumboh Yak Srindak Tanggi Buloh Wife of Pulang Gana. With her daughter Benih Lela Punggang Tengian Dara Bintang Tiga Datai Ka Jelan she gives women expertness in weaving. The Dyaks, Sarawak, Borneo. (Sarawak Gazette, 1963: 79; Howell, 1908/10: 40)

Sun Pin A god worshipped by merchants of leather goods. China. (Werner, 1932: 468; Larousse, 1968: 394; Burgess, 1928: 189)

Sze-kung shen God of architecture to whom sacrifices were made before building. China. (De Groot, 1925, 4: 14)

Tacatecutli The god of "merchant-adventurers." The Aztec, Mexico. (Alexander, 1920: 50)

Ta'ere God of canoe builders, of artisans. Tuamotu, Society Islands, Polynesia. (Henry, 1928: 146, 406)

Tagaloa mana Tagaloa as patron of canoe building. Manua (Samoa), Polynesia. (Mead, 1930: 158)

Tagtug, Uttu Babylonian god of craftsmen, of weavers, and of smiths. Son of Enki and Nintur. Near East. (Langdon, 1931: 196–197)

Tahu'a-muri An artisan god of Ta'ere. Tahiti, Polynesia. (Henry, 1928: 374)

T'ai-shang lao-chün A Taoist god worshipped by blacksmiths. The Miao, China. (Wu and Ch'en, 1942: 26)

Tama-no-ya-no-Mikoto God of jewelers. Japan. (Holtom, 1938: 129; Herbert, 1967: 463)

Tane In Central Polynesia god of craftsmen and of builders, particularly of canoes, and invoked in their launching. (Buck, 1938: 28–30; Henry, 1928: 146, 180)

Tane'etehia A god of carpenters and builders, of woodworkers. Society Islands, Polynesia. (Ellis, 1853: 333)

Tane-mata-ariki God of artisans in Mangaia. Polynesia. (Buck, 1938: 36)

Tangaloa God of builders, of carpenters, of artisans. Also called Tangaloa Tugunga. Tonga, Polynesia. (Collocott, 1921: 152–153; Henry, 1928: 346; Moulton, 1925, 12: 376)

T'an Shen Den Den God of foundation stones. Szechwan, China. (Graham, 1928: 78)

Taoki-ho-oi-no-kami God of architecture and of construction. Japan. (Herbert, 1967: 304, 393)

Tao-sa-sulup "God of material goods." The Bukidnon, Philippines. (Jocano, 1969: 23–24)

Tautu A god of cooking "in the army and at home." Also a god of comedians. Society Islands, Polynesia. (Henry, 1928: 375–376)

Ta Yao A god of smiths who is worshipped on Thursdays and was earlier associated with war. The Ashanti, Ghana. (Parrinder, 1949: 35)

Tayt, Taytet The personification of "'clothing,' a goddess often names as the maker or giver of clothing or the bandages for mummification." Egypt. (Gardiner, 1925, 9: 791)

Te Ama A god associated with canoe rites of Marinoa. Tikopia, Melanesia. (Firth, 1967, 2: 130)

Te-fatu A god of the Canoe Builders' Marae and a god of the ocean invoked with others in launching canoes. Tahiti, Polynesia. (Henry, 1928: 122, 146)

Téiku A Father of the canoe as well as Father of the gold. The Cagaba and the Kogi, Colombia. (Reichel-Dolmatoff, 1949/50: 113, 115)

Te Kau Sukumera An adz god of the Tafua clan associated with canoe rituals. Tikopia, Melanesia. (Firth, 1967, 2: 62)

Teljavel, Teljawelik Baltic god associated with Perkunas. He was "the smith who fashioned the sun." Lithuania and Latvia. (Puhvel, 1974: 78; Schrader, 1925, 2: 39)

Teramo, Turms God of merchants and of thieves, and messenger of the gods. Etruscan equivalent of Mercury, Hermes. Italy. (Leland, 1963: 25–27)

Thuchera A god of house carpenters. Ulithi, the Carolines, Micronesia. (Lessa, 1966: 59)

Ông Tí "Sir Rat" is invoked by sailors "that he may not gnaw their boat of woven bamboo." Annam. (Cabaton, 1925, 1: 541)

Tien Hsien Sheng Mu A deity worshipped by porters. Peking, China. (Burgess, 1928: 189)

T'ien-ssu Fang A stellar god and a god of silkworms. China. (Werner, 1932: 508)

Tifai-o-te-peho A god who "prevented wood that was being hewn out from splitting, and he also showed artisans how to mend planks that were injured." (Particularly in canoe building.) Tahiti, Polynesia. (Henry, 1928: 379)

Ti'iti'i-po An artisan god of Ta'ere who assisted Matamata-arahu in inventing tattooing. Tahiti, Polynesia. (Henry, 1928: 287)

Tohu The god of tattooing who painted the fishes and shells of the seas in their colors and patterns. Society Islands, Polynesia. (Henry, 1928: 234; Poignant, 1967: 37)

Tolus ka gomanan The god of smiths. The Bagobo, Philippines. (Jocano, 1969: 22)

Tolus ka Talegit Goddess of the art of weaving—done by women. The Bagobo, Philippines. (Benedict, 1916: 27)

Topea A god of thatchers of houses. Society Islands, Polynesia. (Ellis, 1853: 333)

Ts'ai-hou, Ts'ai-weng Patron deity of "dyers and people who make or sell paper." Szechwan, China. (Graham, 1961: 186)

Ts'ai Lun, Tsai-luen God of stationers who invented paper, worshipped by paper manufacturers. China. (Graham, 1961: 161; Werner, 1932: 514; Larousse, 1968: 394)

Ts'an-huang-ta-ti A deity worshipped by cooks. Southwest China. (Graham, 1961: 161)

Ts'an Huang T'ien Tzu A god of silkworms. China. (Day, 1940: 163)

Ts'an Nu A goddess of silkworms. China. (Werner, 1932: 517)

Ts'an Shih Chiang Chun A god of silkworms. China. (Day, 1940: 108)

Ts'an Wang A guardian deity of the silkworm. China. (Day, 1940: 108)

Tsao-wang The "Kitchen God, worshipped by the cooks, the waiters, and the kitchen coolies." Peking, China. (Burgess, 1928: 178)

Tshong dpon nag po A god of trade. Tibet. (Nebesky-Wojkowitz, 1956, 1: 298)

Tshong lha A *dgra lha* god who "is able to ensure great profits." Tibet. (Nebesky-Wojkowitz, 1956, 1: 332)

Tshong lha tshogs bdag glang sna A god of trade. Tibet. (Nebesky-Wojkowitz, 1956, 1: 331)

Tubal-cain (Sumer), **Tubhal-Kayin** (Hebrew) God of the forge and inventor of implements. Son of Lumha (Ea). Near East. (Langdon, 1931: 105; Goldziher, 1877: 98)

Tuchera God of canoe and house building. Ulithi, the Caroline Islands, Micronesia. (Lessa, 1961: 32)

T'u Chih God of house building. China. (Day, 1940: 209)

Tufaretai, Tufare The adz god of the Tafua clan, associated with canoe rituals, is also a god of the sea. He is invoked in the consecration of the sacred oven. Tikopia, Melanesia. (Firth, 1967, 2: 62, 124)

Tui Fiji The god of the fehi tree used for making spears and canoes. Tonga, Polynesia. (Collocott, 1925: 232)

Tuinta The spirit of the stone ax. The Tukuna, Brazil and Peru. (Nimuendaju, 1952: 131)

Tuiora "Canoe-setter"—an artisan for Tane. Society Islands, Polynesia. (Henry, 1928: 370)

Tu K'ang God of distillers of wine from rice and of the wine-merchants. China. (Werner, 1932: 526; Du Bose, n.d.: 334; Graham, 1961: 176; Maspero, 1963: 332)

Tumoana The canoe god of Karoata. Another name for Pusiuraura. Tikopia, Melanesia. (Firth, 1967, 2: 115)

Tuna toto An adz god of the Tafua clan and also an eel god. He is invoked in the "re-furnishing of the canoe shed" and also in the consecration of the sacred oven. Tikopia, Melanesia. (Firth, 1967, 2: 62, 119, 124)

Tung-fang Shuo A god of gold and silver smiths. He is also "an incarnation of the Planet of Metal (Venus)." China. (Maspero, 1963: 332; Werner, 1932: 528–529)

Tu-nui-a'e-te-atua A "great artisan" of Ta'aroa. Society Islands, Polynesia. (Henry, 1928: 355)

Tupuafiti An adz god of the Fangarere clan and also an eel god. Tikopia, Melanesia. (Firth, 1967, 2: 62)

Tu-ra'i-po One of the artisan gods of Ta'ere. He assisted Matamata-arahu in inventing tattooing. Tahiti, Polynesia. (Henry, 1928: 287)

Turesh Machi A goddess who taught women to sew. Sister/wife of Okikurumi. The Ainu, Japan. (Chamberlain, 1887: 16, 17)

Tutono An artisan god of Ta'ere. Society Islands, Polynesia. (Henry, 1928: 406)

Tvashtri, Tvastr, Tvashtar The artisan god of the gods, a god of craftsmanship, the fashioner of all forms—and in that of humans a god of generation. India. (Kramer, 1961: 283; Macdonell, 1897: 116; Martin, 1914: 70; Danielou, 1964: 123; Bhattacharji, 1970: 321; Jayne, 1962: 176)

Ugadama A goddess worshipped by carpenters and contractors at the Fushimi-Inari Shrine as she is a combination of Kuku-no-Kami, god of trees and guardian of homes, and of Kaya-no-Hime-no-Kami, goddess of reeds and grasses. "Inasmuch as Japanese houses use timbers for structural frames, grasses for tatami mats, and rushes for thatching" her worship is constant. Japan. (Czaja, 1974: 257, 258)

Uldi A god of weaving and of basket-making. Son of Kinul-hudan. The Ifugao, Philippines. (Barton, 1946: 29)

Uttu Sumerian goddess of weaving, of cloth, of clothing. A daughter of Enki and Ninkurra. Near East. (Kramer, 1961: 100; Jacobsen, 1946: 171; Hooke, 1963: 33)

Vaghesvari God of goldsmiths. India. (Ghurye, 1962: 256)

Vaja Beneficent artisan of the gods who forms a triad with Rbhu and Vibhvan. They are invoked for "prosperity and wealth." India. (Macdonell, 1897: 131–132; Leach, 1950, 2: 937)

Velchans, Vulcanus Etruscan smith god. Italy. (Roscher, 1965, 6: 176)

Velinas, Velnias, Velas The punitive god of the dead and of the night has other aspects less fearful. As a god of cattle and in his incarnation as a snake he is associated with "wealth and commerce," with fertility, and is the beneficent helper of the good and of the poor. Lithuania. (Gimbutas, 1974: 87–92)

Vibhvan, Vibhu A beneficient artisan of Varuna who forms a triad with Rbhu and Vaja. They are invoked for "prosperity and wealth." India. (Macdonell, 1897: 131–132; Leach, 1950, 2: 937)

Visvakarma The architect of the universe and creator of the gods with whom Tvashtri was later merged. India. (Cox, 1870, 1: 328; Ions, 1967: 88; Martin, 1914: 70; Bhatta-charji, 1970: 321–322)

Viswakarma Worshipped by a caste of carpenters. The Barhai, Central Provinces, India. (Russell, 1916, 2: 201)

Vulcan, Volcanus The Roman god of terrestrial and volcanic fire developed into a god representing its warmth and usefulness, a god of the hearth and of smiths. (Altheim, 1937: 119; Murray, 1935: 85, 87; Larousse, 1968: 205; Fairbanks, 1907: 219)

Wakahiru-Me The goddess of the morning sun, younger sister of Amaterasu, is also a goddess of weaving. Japan. (Larousse, 1968: 413; Kato, 1926: 13)

Wasa A deity of a tribe of traders in Bohicon. Dahomey. (Herskovits, 1967, 1: 184)

Wen Chang Ti Chun A deity worshipped by paper hangers. Peking, China. (Burgess, 1928: 188)

Wen Tai Shih A deity worshipped by confectionery makers and merchants. Peking, China. (Burgess, 1928: 188)

Wen-ts'ai-shen The patron god of bankers, merchants, and those involved in finance. Also a god of wealth. Southwest China. (Graham, 1961: 186)

Wieland, Weyland Germanic artisan of the gods, the god of the forge, of smith. (Wernick, 1973: 11; Gimbutas, 1975: XLC M126)

Wigan ud Daiya A god of trade as well as a god of divination. The Ifugao, Philippines. (Barton, 1946: 35, 91)

Wua The god of thatch, of the palm leaves used in roofing the communal houses. The Desana, Colombia. (Reichel-Dolmatoff, 1971: 28)

Wu Tao Chen Jen A deity worshipped by the guild of "the painters who do the decorative work." A deified human. Peking, China. (Burgess, 1928: 179)

Wu Ts'ai Shên A patron god of those in financial and commercial fields. A god of wealth. China. (Graham, 1961: 186; Werner, 1932: 516)

Wutszeseu A god of the wave worshipped by merchants on long river journeys. China. (Du Bose, n.d.: 328)

Xaman Ek The god of the North Star who protects travelers and travelling merchants. The Mayan, Central America. (Morley, 1946: 227–228; Tozzer, 1941: 95)

Xipe Totec The Flayed earth god and god of spring vegetation was also a god of artisans, of goldsmiths and jewelers. Mexico. (Bancroft, 1886, 3: 411–415; Caso, 1958: 49; Reed, 1966: 95, 132)

Xochiquetzal The goddess of love and of flowers was also a goddess of artisans—of spinners and weavers, of embroiderers, of silversmiths, of the producers of the arts. Mexico. (Alexander, 1920: 77–78; Duran, 1971: 238–239, 296; Vaillant, 1962: 149; Neumann, 1955: 196–197)

Xomocuil A god of merchants, brother of Yiacatecutli. Mexico. (Bancroft, 1886, 3: 416)

Yacapitzaoac A god of merchants, Brother of Yiacate-cutli. Mexico. (Bancroft, 1886, 3: 461)

Yacatecu(h)tli A god of traders, of travelling merchants. The Aztec, Mexico. (Duran, 1971: 203–204; Bancroft, 1886, 2: 338; Vaillant, 1962: 151; Spence, 1923: 340)

Yagut Guardian of artisans and giver of rain. Arabia. (Fahd, 1968: 191)

Yang Ssu Chiang-chün A deity worshipped by wood-merchants and boatmen who float the rafts of timber down the rivers. China. (Werner, 1932: 585)

Yao shen The "gods of the porcelain kilns." China. (De Groot, 1925, 4: 14)

Yen Kuang, Yen-Kuang P'u-sa, Yen Kuang Sheng Mu The goddess of eyesight is also the god of tailors at T'ai-hsing. Kiangsu, China. (Werner, 1932: 590; Day, 1940: 39)

Yen Ts'ao The patron of bean-sauce makers—"for the fermentation process." China. (Day, 1940: 110)

Yiacatecu(h)tli God of the travelling merchants—the chief of his five brothers and one sister. Also called Yacacoliuhqui or Jacacoliuhqui. Mexico. (Bancroft, 1886, 3: 416; Nicholson, 1967: 93, 127)

Yozotoyua God of merchants, of traders. The Mixtec, Oaxaca, Mexico. (Caso, n.d.: 51)

Yulatimot One of the Masmasalanix who taught mankind the arts, canoe building, and hunting. The Bella Coola, British Columbia. (Boas, 1898: 32)

Yŭ Pai-ya "The God of Varnishers." China. (Werner, 1932: 602)

Yŭ Wang A deified emperor worshipped by the guild of cloisonné designers. Peking, China. (Burgess, 1928: 179)

33

Gods of Wealth:
Abundance, Plenty, Prosperity

Abundia, Abundantia One of the earliest personifications of abundance. A name of Fulla as "the symbol of the fullness of the earth." Roman/Germanic. (Roscher, 1965, 1, 1: 3; Ferguson, 1970: 73; Guerber, 1895: 51)

Aharishvang The "spirit of the wisdom of sovereignty, liberality, and truth who aids the righteous . . . guarding the treasure of the just . . . She is synonymous with wealth." The Pahlavi, Iran. (Gray, 1930: 63)

Aje Saluga God of wealth and of good fortune whose emblem is the cowrie shell. Son of Orungan and Yemaja. The Yoruba, Nigeria. (Lucas, 1948: 98, 154–155; Budge, 1973, 1: 373)

Alawe A son of Mawu and Lisa. With Wete guardian of "the treasures and stores" belonging to Lisa that are given to mankind. Dahomey. (Herskovits, 1938, 2: 108)

Alogbwe The youngest in the family of Dada Zodji and Nyohwe Ananu. He is the "guardian of all riches: which he bestows on the deserving." Dahomey. (Herskovits, 1938, 2: 140–141)

Ami rum God of riches and also of women. The Lepchas, Sikkim. (Gorer, 1938: 150)

Antu Buau Nyada A god who is feared and preys upon men, but on those who are brave he bestows courage and prosperity. The Iban Dyaks, Sarawak, Borneo. (Sarawak Gazette, 1963: 135)

Anu Celtic goddess of plenty and of prosperity. Ireland. (MacCana, 1970: 85, 94; MacCulloch, 1911: 67)

Apai Karong Besi A god who can bring prosperity and fame. However, he can also curse and bring evil. The Iban Dyaks, Sarawak, Borneo. (Sarawak Gazette, 1963: 133–134)

Arculus Roman god of chests and boxes. (Roscher, 1965, 2, 1: 193)

Avilix A god of the Quiché invoked for prosperity. The Mayan, Guatemala. (Thompson, 1970: 192)

Baraca God of riches. The Achagua, Venezuela and Colombia. (Hernandez de Alba, 1948, 2: 410)

Barraca God of wealth and an aspect of Puru's power. Invoked as an intercessor with him. The Salivas, Colombia. (Walde-Waldegg, 1936: 40)

Béeze The god of riches, and a jaguar god. The Zapotec, Oaxaca, Mexico. (Augur, 1954: 244)

Belang Kepapas A god who is feared and who preys upon men, but on those who are brave he bestows courage and prosperity. The Iban Dyaks, Sarawak, Borneo. (Sarawak Gazette, 1963: 135)

Bhaga The god of the fair distribution of wealth. His wife is Siddhi. He is one of the Adityas. India. (Danielou, 1964: 117–118; Dumézil, 1966, 1: 201; Littleton, 1965: 120; Macdonell, 1897: 45)

Bishamon, Bishamonten A god of wealth and one of the seven gods of happiness. He is also a god of war and the guardian of the north. Japan. (Eliot, 1935: 136; Getty, 1962: 156, 168; Eliseev, 1963: 446; Larousse, 1968: 408)

bisman tegri Mongolian god of wealth. Same as Kuvera. (Getty, 1962: 156)

'Brog gnas A god of wealth whose attributes are "a box full of jewels, . . . a golden wheel and a fruit." Tibet. (Nebesky-Wojkowitz, 1956, 1: 78)

Bunga Jawa One of the fairy gods, beneficent and invincible, who give success in prosperity and war. Among the Iban he can also curse and bring evil. The Dyaks, Sarawak, Borneo. (Sarawak Gazette, 1963: 16, 130, 133–134)

Cernunnos Celtic god of wealth and abundance, of animals and fertility—a horned god. Gaul. (Ross, 1967: 83, 131, 137; Hadas, 1965: 32; MacCana, 1970: 47; MacCulloch, 1964: 35)

Chade The goddess of abundance. She is also associated with the corn planting. The Gã, Temma, Ghana. (Field, 1937: 21, 61)

Ch'ai-shen God of wealth of the Ch'iang at Lo-pu-chai. Szechwan, China. (Graham, 1958: 49)

Chao Kung-Ming A god of wealth, a deified mortal. China. (Werner, 1932: 515; Ferguson, 1937: 80)

Chao-pao shï-chê An official of the Ministry of Riches—"the Envoy who Discovers Treasures." China. (Maspero, 1963: 299)

Chao-pao t'ien-tsun An official of the Ministry of Riches—"the Heaven-honoured One who Discovers Treasures." China. (Maspero, 1963: 299)

Chao Ts'ai Chin Pao A god of wealth and of treasures. China. (Day, 1940: 19, 205)

Chao Yun A god of wealth, of prosperity. China. (Day, 1940: 214)

Chin Lung Szu Ta Wang A god of prosperity, a dragon king. China. (Day, 1940: 115, 295)

Chin Wei Wei "Wealth Patron." China. (Day, 1940: 214)

Copia The personification of abundance—of all good things in the horn of plenty. Roman. (Roscher, 1965, 1, 1: 927)

Da The spirit or force within each individual which participates of Da, the serpent, who bestows riches but is also a thief and fickle. Dahomey. (Herskovits and Herskovits, 1933: 56, 57)

Daikoku, Daikokuten A god of wealth and prosperity, one of the seven gods of happiness. Japan. (Piggott,

1969: 59; Schoeps, 1961: 197; Getty, 1962: 160–162; Larousse, 1968: 422)

Dajd-bog Slavonic god of wealth and success. (Czaplicka, 1925, 11: 593)

Dan The rainbow serpent who "confers wealth upon man." The Mahis, Dahomey. (Herskovits, 1938, 2: 247)

Dhana-da A god who bestows wealth. *Same as Kuvera.* India. (Dowson, 1961: 88)

Dhisana Vedic goddess of abundance. India. (Macdonell, 1897: 124)

rDo rje bdud 'dul A protective god of wealth and a god of medicine whose consort is rDo rje kun 'grub ma. Tibet. (Nebesky-Wojkowitz, 1956, 1: 77–79)

Dravinoda A Vedic deity who bestows riches. India. (Dumézil, 1966, 1: 169)

Ernutet An Egyptian goddess of plenty. (Younger, 1966: 43)

Euthenia Greek personification of abundance. (Roscher, 1965, 1, 1: 1438)

Fu Chu Ts'ai Shên A Chinese god of wealth. (Day, 1940: 115)

Folla, Fulla Nordic/Teutonic goddess of abundance, of plenty. (Grimm, 1880: 308; Dumézil, 1966, 1: 268; Stern, 1898: 98; Wagner, 1882: 6)

Galau Pranan A god who is feared and who preys upon men, but on those who are brave he bestows courage and prosperity. The Iban Dyaks, Sarawak, Borneo. (Sarawak Gazette, 1963: 135)

Ganesh, Ganpati Their principal deity is "the god of good-luck, wealth and prosperity." The Bania, Central Provinces, India. (Russell, 1916, 2: 124)

Gauri, Gouri Hindu goddess of abundance, of agricultural and human fertility. India. (Tod, 1920: 665; Frazer, 1960: 398–399)

dGe lha A god protective of worshippers and of their prosperity. A god of happiness. Tibet. (Nebesky-Wojkowitz, 1956, 1: 328, 333)

Gerasi Papa A god who is feared and who preys upon men, but who bestows courage and prosperity upon the brave. The Iban Dyaks, Sarawak, Borneo. (Sarawak Gazette, 1963: 135)

Gos ster ma dkar mo   A goddess belonging to the group of the gods of wealth. Tibet. (Nebesky-Wojkowitz, 1956, 1: 81)

Hariti   A Hindu demoness who on being converted to Buddhism became the goddess of abundance and of health. Java, Indonesia. (Marchal, 1963: 240; Zimmer, 1955: 137–138)

Hosho Nyorai, Ratnasambhava   The god of all treasures. Japanese Buddhism. (Eliseev, 1963: 430; Larousse, 1968: 419; Eliot, 1935: 100)

Hsuan-t'an P'u-sa   A Chinese god of riches. (Werner, 1932: 515)

Hua Kuang Ts'ai Shên   A Chinese god of wealth. (Day, 1940: 36)

Hua P'ao   "Paper Money Spirit." China. (Day, 1940: 206)

Jambhala, Jambhava   One of the three aspects (with Kuvera and Vaisravana) of the god of wealth whose spouse is Vasudhara. Tibet. Jambhava in Mongolia. (Nebesky-Wojkowitz, 1956, 1: 68; Percheron, 1953: 256; Snellgrove, 1957: 78; Waddell, 1959: 368)

Jih Tsêng   A god of wealth. "Daily Increase." China. (Day, 1940: 214)

Ju I Hsüan T'an   A god of wealth and prosperity. China. (Day, 1940: 114, 162)

Kamala   The Lotus goddess, giver of wealth. She is identified with Lakshmi. India. (Danielou, 1964: 284; Zimmer, 1955: 158)

Kayamanan   A goddess of wealth. Philippines. (Jocano, 1969: 159)

Kling   With his wife Kumang benevolent deities who aid in prosperity and in war. The Sea Dyaks, Sarawak, Borneo. (Roth, 1968: 14, 16; Sarawak Gazette, 1963: 174)

Kompira   A god of seafarers and of prosperity. Japan. (Eliseev, 1963: 435; Eliot, 1935: 138; Larousse, 1968: 422)

Kuan-kong   God of wealth. Taiwan and Formosa. (Diamond, 1969: 100)

Kubera   *See* **Kuvera**

Kulagollamma   A Dravidian goddess of prosperity for farmers. India. (Elmore, 1915: 74)

Kumpang Pali   A god who can bring prosperity and fame, but can also curse and bring evil. The Iban Dyaks, Sarawak, Borneo. (Sarawak Gazette, 1963: 133–134)

kupuka fucha and **kupuka kushe**   The God and Goddess of Abundance who are intercessors with ñenechen for mankind. The Mapuche, Chile. (Faron, 1968: 66)

Kurukule, Kurukulla   The Red Tara, Goddess of Wealth, is also "worshipped by unhappy lovers." She is a goddess of divination and is associated with the southwest. Tibet and India. (Getty, 1962: 126; Snellgrove, 1957: 78, 276; Nebesky-Wojkowitz, 1956, 1: 45, 366)

Kuvera, Kubera (Vaisravana, Jambhala)   God of wealth, of the treasures of the earth, and the guardian of the north. In Tibet Nor lha was merged with him. India, Tibet, Bali, and Java. (Bhattacharji, 1970: 185–186; Marchal, 1963: 234; Friederich, 1959: 51; Nebesky-Wojkowitz, 1956, 1: 68; Bannerjea, 1953: 73, 408; Getty, 1962: 156–159; Martin, 1914: 293)

Kwangiden   A protective god and giver of wealth. Also known as Daishoden, Shoden sama. Japan. (Eliseev, 1963: 437)

Lakshmi   Goddess of wealth and prosperity, of beauty and of fortune. Consort of Vishnu. India. (Bhattacharji, 1970: 162–163; Ruhela, 1971: 44; Banerjea, 1953: 10; Ions, 1967: 91)

La 'nnanng Masokoun on Kringwang   A deity of riches who dwells in the sky and is invoked by all. Child of Phung-kam Janun. The Katchins, Burma. (Gilhodes, 1908: 677)

La 'nTang Jan wa   A god of wealth of the second generation of deities. The Katchins, Burma. (Gilhodes, 1908: 678)

U lei longspah   A god of wealth propitiated for increased prosperity. The Khasis and the Syntengs, Assam. (Gurdon, 1914: 107; Stegmiller, 1921: 408)

Li Shih Hsien Kuan   A god of wealth, of good business deals. China. (Day, 1940: 114; Maspero, 1963: 299)

Lu Hsing   The god of wealth; also the Southern Dipper. China. (Williams, 1976: 371)

Lus ngan   A name of Kuvera. Tibet. (Nebesky-Wojkowitz, 1956, 1: 77)

Mahui A god of abundance and of fertility believed to be present from October to May. The Marquesas, Polynesia. (Rivers, 1915: 433)

Maianwatahe A dwarf—god of plenty and of prosperous hunting. The Sioux, Iowa. (Skinner, 1925, 1: 441)

Manggi A god who gives prosperity and fame, but also curses and brings evil. The Iban Dyaks, Sarawak, Borneo. (Sarawak Gazette, 1963: 134)

Math A Celtic god of the underworld who is also a god of wealth, wisdom, and magical lore. Son of Mathonwy and brother of Don. Wales. (MacCana, 1970: 75; Squire, 1906: 260; MacCulloch, 1911: 105)

Ma Tsung Kuan A god of riches. China. (Day, 1940: 214)

Mbataku The ram-headed deity of wealth to whom a sacrifice is made before a journey. The Igbo, Nigeria. (Uchendu, 1965: 98)

Melobosis An Oceanid as a goddess of beneficence. Greece. (Hesiod-Brown, 1981: 63, 87)

Mukasa Benevolent god of plenty in all things. The Baganda, Uganda. (Roscoe, 1965: 290–291, 300)

Na-chên t'ien-tsun An official of the Ministry of Riches. China. (Maspero, 1963: 299)

Nagawonye The god of plenty of the Baganda. Uganda. (Cunningham, 1905: 218; Budge, 1973, 1: 377)

Nam-se The god of wealth. Sikkim. Same as Kuvera, rNam-sras. (Gazeteer of Sikhim, 1894: 288)

rNam-sras (Sierksma, 1966: 189, 279) **Namthose** (Tucci, 1967: 89) **rNam-thos-sras** (Nebesky-Wojkowitz, 1956, 1: 217; Hackin, 1963, 2: 169) **Nam-t'o-sra** (Getty, 1962: 156) **Namtosse** (Nebesky-Wojkowitz, 1956, 2: 204) Variant names given to the god of wealth. Tibet. Same as Kuvera.

Ndzi-ju-sei A god of wealth, of metal treasures. The Ch'iang, Ho-p'ing-chai, China. (Graham, 1958: 47)

Njord The Scandinavian god of the sea was also god of riches and prosperity, of peace. (MacCulloch, 1964: 101–102; Turville-Petre, 1964: 162–163; Davidson, 1964: 29, 106)

gNod sbyin aparajita A god of the group of gods of wealth. Tibet. (Nebesky-Wojkowitz, 1956, 1: 80)

Nor bdag chen po kubera The name of the god of wealth as worshipped by the Bon. Tibet. (Nebesky-Wojkowitz, 1956, 1: 81)

Nor lha The god of wealth. Tibet, Nepal, and Sikkim. Same as Kubera, Jambhala. (Snellgrove, 1961: 51, 287; Gazeteer of Sikhim, 1894: 353; Nebesky-Wojkowitz, 1956, 1: 68)

Nor ster ma sngon mo A goddess belonging to the gods of wealth. Tibet. (Nebesky-Wojkowitz, 1956, 1: 81)

Ntzu-ndja God of wealth of the Ch'iang at Ho-p'ing-chai. Szechwan, China. (Graham, 1958: 69)

Nyingwan Mebege The moon goddess—"the female principle of the universe . . . the author of procreation and the guarantor of a prosperous life." The Fang, Gabon. (Fernandez, 1972: 241, 247)

Olokun A god or goddess of the sea who is also a deity of wealth. The Yoruba, Nigeria. (Parrinder, 1949: 45; Idowu, 1962: 14)

Ops Goddess of abundance in general though originally that of agriculture. Italy. (Dumézil, 1966, 1: 156, 267; Larousse, 1968: 205, 208)

Oshun The goddess of love and marriage is also a goddess of gold and money. The pumpkin is her attribute and "is a symbol of money." If one wants money the pumpkin must not be given away or eaten or she will be offended. Puerto Rico, West Indies. (Gonzalez-Wippler, 1975: 25–26, 67, 113)

Parendi Goddess of riches, of plenty. In Iran one of the wives of Ahura Mazda. Same as Purandhi. Iran and India. (Gray, 1930: 155; Keith, 1917: 53; Macdonell, 1897: 124)

Pau A god who can bring prosperity and fame, but who may also curse and bring evil. The Iban Dyaks, Sarawak, Borneo. (Sarawak Gazette, 1963: 133–134)

St. Paul The spirit of abundance. The Khevsurs, Caucasus. (Gray, 1925, 12: 485)

St. Peter A spirit of wealth. The Khevsurs, Caucasus. (Gray, 1925, 12: 485)

Pinang Ipong A god who can bring prosperity and fame but who may also curse and bring evil. The Iban Dyaks, Sarawak, Borneo. (Sarawak Gazette, 1963: 134)

Pitao-Cocobi   A god of abundance. Oaxaca, Mexico. (Bancroft, 1886, 3: 457)

Pitterri Pennu   The "god of increase, and of gain in every shape." The Kandh, Bengal. (Crooke, 1925, 7: 649)

Pluto, Plouton   Greek chthonic god of wealth and treasures of the earth. As Hades he was the god of the dead, of the underworld. (Fairbanks, 1907: 235; Cox, 1870, 2: 307; Murray, 1935: 58; Larousse, 1968: 165)

Plutus   The god of the wealth of the earth bestowing agricultural as well as general prosperity is the son of Demeter and the hero Iasion. Greece. (Campbell, 1964: 14, 15; Hesiod-Brown, 1981: 80; Morford and Lenardon, 1975: 210)

Polydora   A Greek goddess associated with "gifts and wealth." Daughter of Tethys and Oceanus. (Kerenyi, 1951: 41)

Poshaiyanki   A god who bestows riches. The Zuñi, New Mexico. (Parsons, 1939: 179)

Puke   An evil serpent god of wealth who will burn down houses if angered. Latvia. (Welsford, 1925, 11: 422)

Puntang Medang   A god who bestows prosperity and fame but who also curses and brings evil. The Iban Dyaks, Sarawak, Borneo. (Sarawak Gazette, 1963: 133–134)

Purandhi   Goddess of plenty, of abundance. India. Same as Parendi. (Ghurye, 1962: 255; Macdonell, 1897: 124; Keith, 1917: 53)

Raja Ontong   God of wealth and of precious stones. The Ngaju, Borneo. (Scharer, 1963: 20, 21)

Rata   An abstract goddess—bounteousness. Iran. (Gray, 1930: 158)

Rddhi, Riddhi   Goddess of prosperity and wife of Kuvera. India. (Danielou, 1964: 292; Bhattacharji, 1970: 186)

Rendah and **Rengang**   Gods who can bring prosperity and fame, but who can also curse and bring evil. The Iban Dyaks, Sarawak, Borneo. (Sarawak Gazette, 1963: 133–134)

Revati   "Prosperity"—wife of Mitra. India. (Danielou, 1964: 116)

Riger   A Germanic god who counselled men for prosperity. Another name for Heimdal. (Wagner, 1882: 10, 166–168)

Sabalu Gawa   A god who can bring prosperity and fame, but can also curse and bring evil. The Iban Dyaks, Sarawak, Borneo. (Sarawak Gazette, 1963: 133–134)

Samriddhi   An abstract goddess—Prosperity—in the Manava-grihyasutra. India. (Ghurye, 1962: 255)

Sanggol Labong   A god who can bring prosperity and fame but can also curse and bring evil. The Iban Dyaks, Sarawak, Borneo. (Sarawak Gazette, 1963: 134)

Saoka   An Iranian goddess who gives wealth and prosperity. (Gray, 1930: 158)

Sastha   A deity worshipped "for wealth and offspring." The Kaniyan, India. (Thurston, 1909, 3: 197)

Scyld   One of the Vanir gods who brought "peace and prosperity." Husband of Gefion. Scandinavia. (Davidson, 1964: 104, 113, 163)

Sedana   A god of wealth. Bali, Indonesia. (Grader, 1969: 168)

Segatak Pandak   A god who can bring prosperity and fame, but can also curse and bring evil. The Iban Dyaks, Sarawak, Borneo. (Sarawak Gazette, 1963: 134)

Segunggang   A god who bestows prosperity and fame but who may also curse and bring evil. The Iban Dyaks, Sarawak, Borneo. (Sarawak Gazette, 1963: 133–134)

Semeo   God of riches of the Nagas. India. (Elwin, 1969: 412)

Shên Wan-san   A god of riches. China. (Werner, 1932: 516)

ka shuar   The demoness of wealth. The Khasi, Assam. (Stegmiller, 1921: 411)

Singa Belabong Dilah   A god who is feared and who preys upon men, but to the brave he gives courage and prosperity. The Iban Dyaks, Sarawak, Borneo. (Sarawak Gazette, 1963: 135)

Šrī   The "fickle goddess of prosperity." India. (O'Flaherty, 1980: 80)

sŭ kắn   A spirit who "is able to increase money and property." The Miao, China. (Bernatzik, 1947: 167)

Sulong Layang A god who can bring prosperity and fame, but who can also curse and bring evil. The Iban Dyaks, Sarawak, Borneo. (Sarawak Gazette, 1963: 133–134)

Sunrta An abstract goddess—the personification of bounteousness. India. (Keith, 1917: 54; Gray, 1930: 158; Macdonell, 1897: 120)

Susime The goddess and giver of riches who causes and cures "blindness and lameness." Her offerings are a pig, a fowl, and some liquor. She is the daughter of Asima-Dingsima and was sent by Tatara to prepare the earth for mankind. The Garo, Assam. (Playfair, 1909: 82–83; Barkataki, 1969: 27)

Tabla A god of wealth as well as of disease. The Mishmis, Assam. (Crooke, 1925, 8: 697)

ka taro The "demoness of wealth (only among the Synteng)." Assam. (Stegmiller, 1921: 411)

Tbauatsilla A deified human as "the god of plenty and contentment." The Ossetes, Caucasus. (Morgan, 1888: 390)

Tekha Shara Matzkala A "god of the dance, fecundity, and wealth," visited by shamans on their ecstatic journeys. The Buryat and the Teleut, Siberia. (Eliade, 1964: 75)

u thlen The "devil of wealth and comfort who can only be worshipped by human sacrifice." The Khasi, Assam. (Stegmiller, 1921: 411)

T'ien Kuan Tz'ŭ Fu Ts'ai Shên A Chinese God of Affluence. (Day, 1940: 114)

Ts'ai Fu Tz'ŭ Fu God of "Joyvul Opulence." China. (Day, 1940: 114)

Ts'ai Shên The god of wealth, president of the Ministry of Riches. China. (Maspero, 1963: 298–299; Schram, 1957: 85; Day, 1940: 20, 95; Wood, 1937: 165)

Ts'eng fou chen A god who augments prosperity and happiness. China. (Chavennes, n.d.: 414)

Tsêng-fu Ts'ai-shen God of wealth and of happiness worshipped by merchants. China. (Maspero, 1963: 299; Werner, 1932: 522)

Tu-lu-ts'ai-shen God of wealth. Southwest China. (Graham, 1961: 161)

Tutong A god who can bring prosperity and fame, but can also curse and bring evil. Brother of Kumang. The Iban Dyaks, Sarawak, Borneo. (Sarawak Gazette, 1963: 133–134)

Tz'ŭ Fu Ts'ai Shên A Chinese god of wealth. (Day, 1940: 163)

Ubertas The personification of fruitfulness, of abundance. Rome. (Roscher, 1965, 6: 2)

Urcaguai, Urcaguary God of wealth who has the form of a serpent. Peru. (MacCulloch, 1925, 11: 402; Larousse, 1968: 443)

Vaisravana The god of wealth and guardian of the north Tibet and China. (Nebesky-Wojkowitz, 1956, 1: 68; Maspero, 1963: 307; Edkins, 1880: 216; Waddell, 1959: 84, 368)

Vasistha A god who "represents the power of wealth." India. (Danielou, 1964: 320)

Vasudhara Goddess of plenty and of wealth, spouse of Jambhala. Tibet and Nepal. (Snellgrove, 1957: 78; Getty, 1962: 130; Heeramaneck, 1966: 82, 85)

Velinas The god of the underworld is also a god of wealth and of commerce. Lithuania. (Gimbutas, 1974: 87–92)

Vol A Germanic goddess of abundance. Same as Fulla. (MacCulloch, 1964: 184)

Wamala The god of plenty, of the increase of all things. The Banyoro, Uganda. (Roscoe, 1915: 90)

Wamara The god of plenty and of fertility to whom the eldest of twins is dedicated. The Banyankole and the Nyankore, Uganda and Tanzania. (Roscoe, 1923: 24; Taylor, 1962: 111)

Wên Ti A "civil and military" god of wealth. China. (Day, 1940: 115)

Wen-ts'ai-shen "Literary god of wealth." Patron deity of bankers, merchants, and those involved in finance. Southwest China. (Graham, 1961: 186)

Wete A son of Mawu and Lisa. With Alawe guardian of "the treasures and stores" belonging to Lisa and which are given to humans. Dahomey. (Herskovits, 1938, 2: 108)

Wisnu-Sedana A god of prosperity, of "economic and financial success." Bali, Indonesia. (Goris, 1960, 1: 128)

Wokwok   A god who is the "source of power and wealth." Son of Olelbis. The Wintun, California. (Chamberlain, 1905: 115)

Wu Lu Ts'ai Shên   The god of riches of the four cardinal directions and the center. China. (Day, 1940: 114; Werner, 1932: 515)

The Wu Shêng   The Five Sages who are gods of prosperity and who are protective of the homestead. China. (Day, 1940: 115; Werner, 1932: 574)

Wu Ti   A "civil and military" god of wealth. China. (Day, 1940: 115)

Wu Ts'ai Shên   The "military god of wealth," patron of those in financial and commercial fields. China. (Graham, 1961: 186; Werner, 1932: 516)

Yechu   The beneficent goddess of wealth. The Daphla, Bengal and Assam. (Crooke, 1925, 4: 399)

yeke gara   A Dharmapala, Defender of the Law, a god of wealth, and protector of the Buddhists. Mongolia. Same as Mahakala. (Getty, 1962: 160)

Yid-'prog-ma   The Buddhist goddess Hariti worshipped as the giver of wealth and of children. Tibet. (Getty, 1962: 84–86)

Yüan Pao   "Joss Money Spirit." China. (Day, 1940: 206)

Yüan Tan, Yuen Tan   The god of wealth who has been replaced by Ts'ai Shên. China. (Werner, 1932: 551; Du Bose, n.d.: 320)

Yüeh Shêng   "Monthly Abundance"—a god of wealth. China. (Day, 1940: 214)

Zas ster ma dmar mo   A goddess belonging to the group of gods of wealth. Tibet. (Nebesky-Wojkowitz, 1956, 1: 81)

Zefa'   A personification of the abstraction "plenty." Represented as a Nile god. Egypt. (Gardiner, 1925, 9: 791)

34

Gods of Non-Wealth:
Famine, Hunger, Poverty

Adowa A god who punishes the community with famine if they harbor unpunished evildoers. Dahomey. (Herskovits, 1938, 2: 140)

Aethon Greek personification of famine. (Murray, 1895: 86)

Aie Lacha A goddess of the nomad Lohars who curses them with famine. India. (Ruhela, 1971: 35, 51)

Aleloloa A lesser god of Avatele who caused hunger, famine. Niue Island, Polynesia. (Loeb, 1926: 161)

Apizteotl An Aztec god of famine. Mexico. (Duran, 1971: 432)

Bhukhi Mata The goddess of famine, of hunger. India. (Crooke, 1894: 73; Keith, 1917: 238; Briggs, 1920: 154)

Bisteot The god of hunger of the Nicarao. Nicaragua. (Lothrop, 1926: 70)

Changoro The god of famine. Ponape, Caroline Islands, Micronesia. (Christian, 1899: 381)

Chicomecoatl The goddess of crops and provisions was also considered responsible for the barren years when there was famine. The Aztec, Mexico. (Duran, 1971: 221–222)

Chitowe An evil god considered responsible for famine. He is invoked at the beginning of the planting season. The Yao, South Africa. (Willoughby, 1932: 75; Lang, 1968: 234)

Cueravaperi The mother goddess, usually beneficent, who sometimes sends famine and drought. Mexico. (Craine and Reindorp, 1970: 133)

Dhumavati The "goddess-of-poverty . . . of frustration, of despair, . . . rules over the rainy season." India. (Danielou, 1964: 282)

Dibbarra A minor deity, a god of want and of hunger. Assyria. (Jastrow, 1898: 232)

Egestas The personification of poverty. Roman. (Roscher, 1965, 1, 1: 1217)

Fames Roman personification of hunger. She appears at the entrance of the underworld. (Roscher, 1965, 1, 2: 1443)

Futifonua A lesser god of Avatele invoked in time of hunger. Niue Island, Polynesia. (Leob, 1926, 1: 161)

Futimotu A lesser god of Avatele invoked in time of hunger. Niue Island, Polynesia. (Loeb, 1926, 1: 161)

Hahhimas The Hittite god of blight who paralyzed the earth. Asia Minor. (Gurney, 1952: 187)

Kao-hua-tzu-p'u-sa The patron deity of beggars. Szechwan, China. (Graham, 1961: 186)

kemram kamui A famine god, "an evil monster bear" who hoards fish and meat, which he withholds from humans. The Ainu, Hokkaido, Japan. (Philippi, 1982: 162)

Landusan A male spirit responsible for poverty. The Isneg, Luzon, Philippines. (Vanoverbergh, 1941: 284)

Limos Greek personification of hunger, of famine. Son of Eris. (Roscher, 1965, 2, 2: 2052; Barthell, 1971: 8; Hesiod-Brown, 1981: 59)

Miseria Greek/Roman personification of poverty and lament. Daughter of Nox and Erebos. (Roscher, 1965, 2, 2: 3027)

Moshir Huchi The "Earth Crone" of the bottom of the sea seems also to be a goddess of famine as she traps and hoards fish for which the culture hero must do battle. The Ainu, Hokkaido, Japan. (Philippi, 1982: 195)

Nagawonyi The "goddess of hunger, was thought to be able to end drought or famine by means of her influence with the gods Musoke and Gulu, who commanded the elements." The Baganda, Uganda. (Roscoe, 1965: 315)

Naguti The god of famine. The Bagisu, Uganda. (Williams, 1936: 174)

Niyaz The demon of Poverty. Iran. (Gray, 1930: 212)

Oge, Tu-ia-oge The son of Tagaroa and Haumea. A god of the underworld who controlled famines and the fish. Mangareva, Polynesia. (Buck, 1938: 422)

Penia Greek goddess of poverty. (Roscher, 1965, 3, 2: 1921)

Shun I Fu-jen "The Goddess of Drought (or Famine) and Flood." China. (Werner, 1932: 447)

Tezcatlipoca A god of dualities. In one of his aspects he is responsible for drought and famine, for plagues. He represents capriciousness rather than evil. The Aztec, Mexico. (Duran, 1971: 110; Spence, 1923: 98, 103; Alexander, 1920: 61–66)

Tolioatua The god of hunger is the father of thieves. Niue Island, Polynesia. (Loeb, 1926, 1: 163)

tukushish A famine god in the form of a "huge char" (troutlike fish) who is also god of the lake. The Ainu, Hokkaido, Japan. (Philippi, 1982: 190–191)

Unktomi "The ubiquitous *Unktomi* tortures them in their hunger by bringing herds of buffaloes near the camp, which they no sooner start to pursue than he drives away by means of a black wolf and a white crow." The Dakota, Minnesota. (Lynd, 1889: 153)

Yaluk The chief of the Mams (gods of the mountains, plains, underground, weather, agriculture) is basically malevolent and "destroys maize crops and causes famine." The Kekchis, British Honduras. (Thompson, 1930: 59)

PART VII

Socio-cultural Concepts

35

Abstract Deities

Abommubuwafre "Consoler or Comforter who gives salvation." The Akan, Ghana. (Mbiti, 1907, 2: 327)

Acala (Sanskrit), **Mi-gyo-ba** (Tibet) "The immoveable," a demoniacal Buddha of the Tantric. They are powerful "ferocious and bloodthirsty; and only to be conciliated by constant worship of themselves and their female energies, with offerings and sacrifices." Tibet. (Waddell, 1959: 131)

Achlys The personification of grief, distress. Greece. (Roscher, 1965, 1, 1: 66)

A-ch'u A Buddha. "The Immovable." Same as Akshobhya. China. (Getty, 1962: 36)

Adephagia Goddess of gluttony. Sicily, Italy. (Roscher, 1965, 1, 1: 67)

Adharma Hindu personification of unrighteousness and vice, whose wife is Nirrti. India. (Dowson, 1961: 2; Danielou, 1964: 138)

Adikia The personification of injustice. Dike's opposite. Greece. (Gardner, 1925, 9: 794; Roscher, 1965, 6: 849)

Aequitas A Roman goddess representing equity, justice, impartiality. (Ferguson, 1970: 73; Roscher, 1965, 1, 1: 86; Larousse, 1968: 216; Carter, 1925, 9: 790)

Aeshma Daeva Zoroastrian archdemon of Fury. Persia. (Seligmann, 1948: 38)

AEternitas A Roman goddess, the personification of eternity. (Carter, 1925, 9: 799; Roscher, 1965, 1, 1: 87)

Afriti The personification of "Blessing" in benedictions and in the reward of ethical action. Iran. (Gray, 1930: 130–131)

Agenoria The goddess of action, of response to stimulation. Rome. (Jayne, 1962: 497; Roscher, 1965, 1, 1: 104)

Aglaia *See* **The Graces**

Aharišvang The "spirit of the wisdom of sovereignty, liberality, and truth who aids the righteous . . . increasing the glory of the home and guarding the treasure of the just. . . . She is synonymous with wealth." Iran. (Gray, 1930: 63)

Ahura Mazda As an abstract concept he is the personification of light and truth, of "perfect goodness." Persia. (Littleton, 1965: 97; Huart, 1963: 41; Hinnells, 1973: 50)

Ai apaec He is the god of Good, particularly as applied to man's activities, work and the arts, and to the defeat of demons. The Mochica, Peru. (Larco Hoyle, 1946: 171)

Aidos Shame as a goddess, companion of Nemesis. Greece. (Kerényi, 1951: 106; Gardner, 1925, 9: 794)

Aither The personification of the upper atmosphere, the ether. Greece. (Roscher, 1965, 1, 1: 198; Pettazzoni, 1956: 154–155)

Aitua A "personified form of misfortune, who, in one version of Maori cosmogonic mythology, is said to have been a child of the primal parents Rangi and Papa." New Zealand. (Best, 1924: 177)

Akatasa The demon of Meddlesomeness. Persia. (Seligmann, 1948: 39)

Akshobhya A Dhyani-Buddha, the Immovable, the Imperturbable, whose sakti is Locana. A Buddha of Meditation associated with the East and known in China as A-ch'u, in Japan as Ashuku, in Mongolia as ülü kudelukci, in Tibet as mi-bskyod-pa. Known also in Nepal, India, Bali (as a goddess), and Central Asia. (Getty, 1962: 36; Percheron, 1953: 253; Snellgrove, 1957: 60, 66–67; Eliot, 1935: 100; Hooykaas, 1964: 31; Hackin, 1963: 243; Waddell, 1959: 337, 350)

Alaksmi The personification of "non-prosperity," a "form of Nirrti." India. (Bhattacharji, 1970: 162)

Alala Greek goddess, a personification of the battle cry. Daughter of Polemos. (Roscher, 1965, 1, 1: 221) A very ancient Babylonian god of "strength" whose consort is Belili. Near East. (Jastrow, 1898: 417)

Aletheia The personification of truth. Daughter of Zeus. Greece. (Roscher, 1965, 1, 1: 229)

Algea "Sorrow," daughter of Eris, and the personification of pains resulting from fights. Sometimes plural. Greece. (Barthell, 1971: 8; Roscher, 1965, 1, 1: 230; Hesiod-Brown, 1981: 59)

Allekto One of the Erinyes, "the Never-Ending." Greece. (Kerényi, 1951: 48)

Al-lot A god of pacification. The Tinguian, Philippines. (Cole, 1922: 300)

Amaomee A deity representing Sufficiency. The Akan, Ghana. (Mbiti, 1970, 2: 327)

Ame-no-Kume-no-Mikoto A deity of "valour." Japan. (Holtom, 1938: 130)

Ame-no-Oshihi-no-Mikoto A deity representing "valour." An earthly spirit as escort to Ninigi. Japan. (Holtom, 1938: 130; Yasumaro, 1965: 62)

Ameretat, Amerodat One of the Amesha Spentas—Immortality—usually associated with Haurvatat as protectors of plants and animals and of waters, as well as presiding over the daily activities of mankind. Persia. (Gray, 1930: 51; Jayne, 1962: 185; Huart, 1963: 41; Littleton, 1965: 99)

Amida Buddha Japan. *See* **Amitabha**

Amitabha A Dhyani-Buddha, the "Buddha of Infinite Light," of "Boundless Light," the saviour of souls, associated with the Western Paradise. His sakti is Pandara. He is known in China as O-mi-t'o, in Japan as Amida, in Mongolia as čaghlasi ügei gereltü where he is the deified sun, in Tibet as hod-dpag-med, 'Od-dpag-med, or sNan-ba mthahyas (and where from him emanates one of the five elements—"fire, or aggregate of feelings"), and

in Bali as a goddess. (Getty, 1962: 34–38; Percheron, 1953: 253; Hooykaas, 1964: 31; Evans-Wentz, 1960: 9; Hori, 1959: 420; Day, 1940: 141; Waddell, 1959: 346, 350; Snellgrove, 1957: 66–67; Hackin, 1963: 160)

Amitayus The "Buddha of Eternal Life," Amitabha as a god of longevity, the two forms always separate in Tibet where he is known as ts'e-dpag-med, Tshe dpag med. Known in China as Ch'ang sheng-fo, in Mongolia as ayusi or čaghlasi ügei nasutu. (Getty, 1962: 39; Nebesky-Wojkowitz, 1956, 1: 365; Schlagintweit, 1969: 98; Snellgrove, 1957: 60)

Amoghapasa Bodhisattva of Compassion. The name of Avalokitesvara in Nepal and Java. (Marchal, 1963: 240; Heeramaneck, 1966: 88)

Amoghasiddhi A Dhyani-Buddha, the "Buddha of Infallible Magic," associated with the region of the North. His sakti is Tara. In Tibet it is believed that from him emanates one of the five elements—"air, or aggregate of volition." There he is known as don-grub or Don-yod-'grub-pa; in Japan as Fuku jo-ju. He is known in India, Mongolia, Central Asia, and in Bali as a goddess. (Getty, 1962: 42; Waddell, 1959: 350; Percheron, 1953: 253; Hackin, 1963: 243; Eliot, 1935: 100; Evans-Wentz, 1960: 9; Hooykaas, 1964: 31)

Amphillogea "Dispute," a child of Eris (alone). Greece. (Barthell, 1971: 8)

Amrit A god or goddess "in whose belly was the Water of Immortality." Everyone was immortal when given to drink of the water. But the belly was pierced by the horn of a cow and all spilled. Since then, death came into the world and the cow had to work behind the plow. The Kol, India. (Elwin, 1949: 424)

Anadatus The equivalent of Ameretat. Armenia. (Ananikian, 1925, 1: 795)

Anaideia Greek personification of shamelessness. (Roscher, 1965, 1, 1: 330)

Anastapanih The demon of instability who hinders "the devotions of the righteous at daybreak." Iran. (Gray, 1930: 199)

Anaxšti Iranian demoness of Dissention. (Gray, 1930: 199)

Androctasia Slaughter, a daughter of Eris. Greece. (Barthell, 1971: 8; Roscher, 1965, 1: 34; Hesiod-Brown, 1981: 59)

Angerona Roman goddess of Silence and guardian of the city. She was also goddess of the winter solstice. Italy. (Levi-Strauss, 1969: 294; Jayne, 1962: 416; Dumézil, 1966, 1: 335)

Angus, Angus Mac-ind-oc A god of beauty and youth, of love and lightheartedness. To win Caer Ibormeith he metamorphosed into a swan. Son of Dagda. Ireland. (Ross, 1967: 237; Squire, 1906: 56, 142; MacBain, 1917: 130)

Anomia Greek personification of lawlessness, of anarchy. (Roscher, 1965, 6: 852)

dbAn-po z'i, Sātendra (Sanskrit) A celestial Bodhisat—the "foundation of power." Tibet. (Waddell, 1959: 358)

Anumati As an abstract goddess she represents "Favour (of the gods)." Primarily she is a goddess of procreation and of childbirth. With Raka she presides over the day before the full moon. Daughter of Angiras and Sraddha. India. (Macdonell, 1897: 119; Jayne, 1962: 160; Danielou, 1964: 319; Keith, 1917: 54, 93)

Aoša The demon of Destruction who "appears to have been the deity presiding over combings of hair and clippings of nails, whose importance in religion is widespread." Iran. (Gray, 1930: 199)

Apate The personification of cheating—"Deceit." A child of Nyx. Greece. (Roscher, 1965, 1, 1: 388; Barthell, 1971: 8; Hesiod-Brown, 1981: 59)

Araiti The deity of Avarice. Iran. (Gray, 1930: 200)

Aramati Goddess of Devotion, of Piety. India. (Macdonell, 1897: 119; Keith, 1917: 54)

Arašk Iranian demon of Envy. (Gray, 1930: 200)

Arast Iranian demon of Falsehood. (Gray, 1930: 200)

Ardor The personification of ardor, never sober, always with the demons. Italy. (Roscher, 1965, 6: 853)

Arjuna A Hindu god, the personification of prudence. India. (Martin, 1914: 204)

Armaiti The earth goddess, daughter of Ahura Mazda, is the personification of Devotion, of "faithful obedience." Persia. (Hinnells, 1973: 52; Gray, 1930: 47, 48; Littleton, 1965: 99)

Arštat, Aršti Rectitude, a goddess of Uprightness. Iran. (Gray, 1930: 136–137)

Aryaman One of the Adityas, a god of Chivalry, of Charity, of Hospitality. He is a god of the heavens who presides over social traditions and stability. India. (Ions, 1967: 15; Bhattacharji, 1970: 220; Danielou, 1964: 116; Littleton, 1965: 120)

Asapurna Goddess of Hope. India. (Coleman, 1832: 374)

Ašgahanih The demon of Slothfulness who interferes with "the devotions of the righteous at daybreak." Iran. (Gray, 1930: 201)

Asha, Asha Vahista The spirit of Righteousness and associated with Vohu Manah as the two most important of the Amesha Spentas. He is concerned with the order of the universe and is also in charge of fire. Iran. (Haydon, 1941: 68; Huart, 1963: 41; Littleton, 1965: 98; Gray, 1930: 38; Williams Jackson, 1925, 1: 385)

Ashaeixsho Best Truth. The Kushana, India. Same as Asha Vahista. (Hinnells, 1973: 50)

Ashuku A Buddha, "The Immovable." Japan. Same as Akshobhya. (Getty, 1962: 36; Eliot, 1935: 100; Eliseev, 1963: 422)

Aši A goddess of Just Recompense who bestows prosperity and wisdom as well as possessing healing powers. A daughter of Ahura Mazda and Armaiti. Iran. (Gray, 1930: 62; Jayne, 1962: 190; Littleton, 1965: 124)

Asrušti Iranian demoness of Disobedience. (Gray, 1930: 201)

Astraea, Astraia The goddess of justice and good faith, of innocence and modesty. Also known as Dike. She is the daughter of Zeus and Themis or of Astraeus and Eos; is identified with the constellation Virgo. Greece. (Murray, 1935: 46; Roscher, 1965, 1, 1: 659; Barthell, 1971: 51, 63; Prentice Hall, 1965: 21)

Asuniti An abstract deity, "Spirit-life," invoked for longevity and health. India. (Macdonell, 1897: 120)

Ataksak A sky god and a god of joy, accessible to the Eskimo through the shaman. Baffin Land, Canada. (Bilby, 1923: 209, 269; Larousse, 1968: 426)

A ti mu wer (pr. **Ati Muwer**) A local deity who has become a god of "transcendent cognition, *ye shes lha chen*." He is an emanation from Ku byi mang ske, "from the plane of mind." Tibet. (Tucci, 1980: 220–221, 243)

Atri God of "the power of detachment," a son of the mind of Brahma. India. (Danielou, 1964: 323)

'Aud An abstract deity—"time," "fate." Arabia. (Noldeke, 1925, 1: 662)

Auna The goddess of Solicitude. Tahiti, Polynesia. (Henry, 1928: 416)

Autonoe One of the Nereids, a goddess of inspiration. She is the wife of Aristaios, the mother of Aktaion. Greece. (Kerényi, 1951: 65, 145)

'Aut-yeb A goddess, the personification of Joy. Egypt. (Gardiner, 1925, 9: 791)

Avalokitesvara A celestial Bodhisattva, the personification of compassion and mercy, widely worshipped: in India, Cambodia, Java, Nepal, Mongolia (as nidu barujekci or gongsim), Central Asia, Tibet (as spyan-ras-gzigs), in China (as Kuan-shih-yin), in Japan (as Kwan-ze-on or Kwan-non), and in Korea. Buddhism. (Getty, 1962: 57; Marchal, 1963: 204, 238; Hackin, 1963: 161, 244–246; Sierksma, 1966: 170; Eliot, 1935: 120–123; Percheron, 1953: 254; Waddell, 1959: 355–356)

Axšti The Iranian goddess of "victorious peace." (Gray, 1930: 138)

Ayuthlme-i "Of higher deities they had none, and an abstraction only, Ayuthlme-i, . . . which corresponds exactly . . . to our ideas of 'miraculous, divine, strange, incomprehensible'." The Kalapuyas, Willamette Valley, Oregon. (Gatschet, 1891: 143)

Azar The personification of Help. Canaan, Near East. (Paton, 1925, 3: 183)

Azi A nocturnal demon "of gluttony, covetousness, and greed." Iran. (Gray, 1930: 202)

Azuiti Iranian goddess of Fatness, a wife of Ahura Mazda. (Gray, 1930: 139)

Bai The personification of Soul. Egypt. (Gardiner, 1925, 9: 787; Budge, 1969, 2: 328)

Baiyag A god of "Slowness." The Ifugao, Philippines. (Barton, 1946: 49)

Balder The Scandinavian god who is the manifestation of beauty, of sweetness, of holiness, and purity. (Stern, 1898: 50; Frazer, 1960: 703–704; Branston, 1955: 125; Grimm, 1880: 222; Turville-Petre, 1964: 106)

dBal-gsas A deity who is the "tranquil manifestation of 'All Good'." Also a deity of the four quarters. Nepal. (Snellgrove, 1961: 49, 122)

Beelphegor A god of Immortality of the Ammonites of Mesopotamia, adopted by the Hebrews. He was also an evil god. Near East. (Seligmann, 1948: 49)

Bhaya God of Fear. Son of Nirrti and Adharma. India. (Danielou, 1964: 138)

Bhulan Baba A god who causes Forgetfulness. Central Provinces, India. (Russell, 1925, 3: 314)

Bia The personification of Violence. Child to Styx and Pallas and pledged by her to assist Zeus in the battle with the Titans. Greece. (Gardner, 1925, 9: 794; Kerényi, 1951: 34; Larousse, 1968: 165; Barthell, 1971: 15, 50)

bikeh xozo A Navaho sky goddess—"happiness." Arizona and New Mexico. (Haile, 1947: 9)

Bubrostis Goddess of voracious hunger. Smyrna, Asia Minor. (Roscher, 1965, 1, 1: 831)

Bunkuase The "embodiment of the principle of good." Elder brother of Kashindukua who killed and devoured people, so Bunkuase trapped and killed him. The Kogi, Colombia. (Reichel-Dolmatoff, 1975: 5, 6, 237n. 92)

Busao The "god of calamity," greatly feared. The Bukidnon, Philippines. (Jocano, 1969: 24)

Byams-pa The Buddha of the Future, the god of "Loving-Kindness." Same as Maitreya. Tibet and Nepal. (Snellgrove, 1961: 35; Getty, 1962: 21; Rock, 1947: 390)

čghlasi ügei gereltü Mongolian name of Amitabha, the Buddha of Infinite Light and the conductor of souls. (Getty, 1962: 34, 37)

čghlasi ügei nasutu, ayusi The Buddha of Eternal Life. Same as Amitayus. Mongolia. (Getty, 1962: 34, 37)

Capa The Beaver Spirit "was the patron of work, provision and of domestic faithfulness." The Lakota and the Oglala, South Dakota. (Walker, 1980: 121)

Celeritas The "goddess of swift motion." Daughter of the Sun. Italy. (Weinstock, 1946: 112; Roscher, 1965, 1, 1: 858)

Cetan The Hawk is the Spirit of swiftness, of endurance. The Lakota and the Oglala, South Dakota. (Walker, 1980: 122)

Ch'ang sheng-fo The "Buddha of Eternal Life," a god of longevity. China. Same as Amitayus. (Getty, 1962: 39)

Charis One of the Graces, the personification of grace, charm. Greece. (Roscher, 1965, 1, 1: 873)

The Charities, the Graces Goddesses who were the personifications of "the gracefulness and the charms of beauty, and of cheerful amusement." They are variously called: Aglaia, Euphrosyne, Thalia (Boeotia); Cleta and Phaenna (Sparta); Auxo and Hegemone (Athens). The parentage attributed them: Zeus and Euronyme, Nyx and Erebos, Lethe, Hekate and Hermes, or Helios. Greece. (Kerényi, 1951: 99, 193; Murray, 1935: 197–198; Burns, 1925, 3: 372; Prentice Hall, 1965: 34)

Chenresi, Chen-re-zi, Chenresik The god of mercy and compassion. The protector of Tibet. Same as Avalokitesvara. (Tucci, 1967: 77; Nebesky-Wojkowitz, 1956, 1: 40, 75; Bell, 1931: 30)

Ch'u-chu-chang A Dhyani-Bodhisattva. "The Effacer of all Stains." China. (Getty, 1962: 106)

Clementia Roman god of Clemency. The "reminder of the emperor's absolute power and his kindness in not using it." Italy. (Schoeps, 1961: 148; Fairbanks, 1907: 254; Ferguson, 1970: 73)

Cleta With Phaenna the two Charities at Sparta. Greece. (Burns, 1925, 3: 373; Murray, 1935: 198; Prentice Hall, 1965: 36)

Concordia Roman goddess of Understanding and Harmony. (Schoeps, 1961: 148; Dumézil, 1966, 2: 401; Prentice Hall, 1965: 36)

Constantia Roman personification of constancy. (Roscher, 1965, 1, 1: 923)

Contentezza Etruscan goddess of content, invoked for safe and pleasant journeys. Italy. (Leland, 1963: 70)

Cratos Personification of Strength. A son of Pallas and Styx, allied with Zeus in the War with the Titans. Greece. (Barthell, 1971: 15; Hesiod-Brown, 1981: 64)

Credulitas Roman personification of credulity, of gullibility. (Roscher, 1965, 6: 861)

Cura Roman personification of Sorrow. (Roscher, 1965, 1, 1: 932)

Dais A goddess who personifies a plentiful meal. Greece. (Roscher, 1965, 1, 1: 939)

Darammasum God of "pity, charity and justice." Orissa, India. (Elwin, 1954: 636)

Dasim Mohammedan "demon of discord." Son of Iblis. (Bray, 1935: 165)

Dawi Iranian demoness of Deceit. (Gray, 1930: 204)

Deimos Personification of fear and horror. A violent god, son of Ares and Aphrodite, who accompanied Ares in war and strife. Greece. (Rosecher, 1965, 1, 1: 979; Barthell, 1971: 222; Larousse, 1968: 125)

Del, oDel The principle of good as the opposing duality to Beng, the principle of evil. Del is not anthropomorphic but fills "the unlimited space above the earth," all the physical phenomena in that realm. His name is used in thanksgiving, blessings as well as cursing, and for requests for help. The Gypsies. Slavic. (Clebert, 1967: 171–172; Trigg, 1973: 165, 208)

Demios The Roman personification of Dread, an attendant of Mars. (Bulfinch, 1898: 131)

Der Iranian demon of Procrastination. (Gray, 1930: 204)

Derfintos Lithuanian goddess of peace. (Gray, 1930: 139)

Deus Fidius An aspect of Jupiter as a god of the moral order, of loyalty, and of oaths. Italy. (Dumézil, 1966, 1: 180; Altheim, 1937: 164; Littleton, 1965: 89)

Dexo Greek personification of the acceptance of gifts. (Roscher, 1965, 1, 1: 1001)

Dharma Hindu god of duty, righteousness, and justice. An aspect of Yama as judge of the dead. His wife is Sraddha, and son Kama. India. (Ions, 1967: 24, 88; Dowson, 1961: 88; Bhattacharji, 1970: 57)

Dhriti Goddess of Fortitude, associated with Krishna. India. (Ghurye, 1962: 255)

Diallage Greek personification of reconciliation. (Roscher, 1965, 1, 1: 1002)

Dike The Greek personification of Justice, a goddess of "good faith, modesty and truth." Also called Astraea. Daughter of Zeus and Themis. She is all-seeing and reports injustices to Zeus for punishment. (Murray, 1935: 46, 145; Kerényi, 1951: 102; Gardner, 1925, 9: 794; Pettazzoni, 1956: 146–147)

Dipankara, Dipamkara The "Buddha of Fixed Light," of Luminosity. Worshipped in Tibet (as Mar-me-mdsad), Java, Ceylon, China (as Ting-kuang-fo), Japan, Mongolia (as jula joqiaqci), and Siam. (Getty, 1962: 12, 13; Waddell, 1959: 345)

Disciplina Roman personification of discipline. (Roscher, 1965, 1, 1: 1178; Carter, 1925, 9: 799)

Discordia A Roman goddess of strife, of discord associated with Mars and Bellona, also with Pluto. (Murry, 1935: 214; Prentice Hall, 1965: 46; Weinstock, 1946: 109)

dóli· Bluebird, a helpful deity, the "symbol of peace and happiness." The Navaho, Arizona and New Mexico. (Reichard, 1950: 403)

Don-yod-grub-pa A celestial Buddha, "Infallible Success," invoked to avert illness and danger. Associated with the North. Tibet and Nepal. Same as Amoghasiddhi. (Nebesky-Wojkowitz, 1956, 1: 525; Waddell, 1959: 349; Snellgrove, 1961: 64, 288; Francke, 1925, 8: 76)

rDo-rje 'chang "The Indestructible." Same as Vajradhara. He was considered by "the 'Yellow-caps' (reformed school) . . . as the Supreme Power and Creator of all things." Tibet and Nepal. (Getty, 1962: 3; Waddell, 1959: 352; Snellgrove, 1961: 77)

Dröl-ma Goddess of compassion, the "Deliverer," a Bodhi-sattva. Same as Tara. Tibet and Nepal. (Tucci, 1967: 77; Bell, 1931: 30; Furer-Haimendorf, 1964: 171)

Drvatat Iranian deity of Soundness, of physical vigor. (Gray, 1930: 144)

Dynamene A Nereid, "Capable," as related to "successful venture." Daughter of Nereus and Doris. Greece. (Hesiod-Brown, 1981: 60, 86–87)

Dysnomia "Lawlessness," associated with her sister "Madness." Daughters of Eris. Greece. (Barthell, 1971: 8; Roscher, 1965, 1, 1: 1209; Hesiod-Brown, 1981: 59)

Ebrietas Greek/Roman personification of drunkenness. (Roscher, 1965, 1, 1: 1210)

Eeyah The "glutton god: of the Dakota Indians. North and South Dakota, Montana, Nebraska. (Wallis, 1947: 76)

Eirene, Irene Greek goddess of peace, one of the Horae. Daughter of Themis and Zeus. (Kerényi, 1951: 102; Murray, 1935: 145; Roscher, 1965, 1, 1: 1221)

Ekecheiria A personification of the Olympian peace (the peace of the gods). Greece. (Roscher, 1965, 1, 1: 1223)

Elenchos Greek personification of convincing. (Roscher, 1965, 1, 1: 1239)

Eleos Personification of Pity—male. Greece. (Gardner, 1925, 9: 794; Roscher, 1965, 1, 1: 1240)

Enhydria Greek personification of abundance of water. The name of a spring fountain nymph. (Roscher, 1965, 1, 1: 1249)

Enkrateia A goddess, the personification of abstinence. Greece. (Roscher, 1965, 1, 2: 2899)

Epimelia Personification of meticulousness, of conscientiousness. Greece. (Roscher, 1965, 1, 1: 1283)

Epione Greek goddess—"Soothing." Daughter of Aesculapius and sister of Hygieia. (Fairbanks, 1907: 224)

Epithymia Personification of Covetousness. Greece. (Roscher, 1965, 1, 1: 1285)

Ereti An abstract goddess, "Energy." Iran. (Gray, 1930: 144)

Erinys, Erinyes As an individual goddess, one meting out vengeance, an attendant of Nemesis. As a trio—Allekto, Megaira, Tisiphone—goddesses of the underworld, avengers of transgressors, and as such, in upholding social and moral laws they are also called the Eumenides. Greece. (Kerényi, 1951: 48; Crooke, 1894: 78; Fairbanks, 1907: 239; Willetts, 1962: 198; Murray, 1935: 213–217)

Eris Greek goddess of strife, of discord; daughter of Nyx; associated with Mars; mother of Algea (Sorrow), Amphilogea (Dispute), Androctasia (Slaughter), Dysnomia (Lawlessness), Limos (Famine), Neicea (Quarrel), Phonos (Murder). (Barthell, 1971: 8; Larousse, 1968: 125; Hesiod-Brown, 1981: 59)

Error Roman personification of Error. (Roscher, 1965, 1, 1: 1372)

Eshou God of vengeance in the vicinity of Bahia, Brazil. The divine messenger of the gods, always active, sometimes for good, sometimes for mischief or evil. (Landes, 1940: 263; Bastide, 1960: 91, 568; Verger, 1954: 15)

Euchir A god, the personification of artistic skill. Greece. (Roscher, 1965, 1, 1: 1398)

Eudaimonia The personification of godly benediction, associated with Aphrodite. Greece. (Gardner, 1925, 9: 794; Roscher, 1965, 1, 1: 1398)

Euphrosyne One of the Charities. A goddess of gratitude and hospitality, of mirth. Greece. (Bulfinch, 1898: 12; Roscher, 1965, 1, 1: 1408; Prentice Hall, 1965: 52; Larousse, 1968: 132)

Eurybia Daughter of Gaea and Pontus, a Titaness "with a heart of steel," one of the deities representing force. Sister of Thaumas, Phorcys, and Ceto; wife of Crius; mother of Astraeus, Pallas, Perses. Greece. (Hesiod-Brown, 1981: 60, 63; Fairbanks, 1907: 67, 149; Kerényi, 1951: 34, 42; Barthell, 1971: 10, 50)

Eusebeia Greek personification of Piety. Also known in Syria. (Roscher, 1965, 1, 1: 1437)

Eutelie Greek personification of Simplicity, Thriftiness. (Roscher, 1965, 1, 1: 1438)

Fama Roman personification of Rumor. (Roscher, 1965, 1, 2: 1442; Prentice Hall, 1965: 54)

Fao A god of Peace. Niue Island, also Mutalau. Polynesia. (Loeb, 1926, 1: 163)

Felicitas A Roman goddess of happiness and success. (Fairbanks, 1907: 254; Larousse, 1968: 214; Ferguson, 1970: 73; Prentice Hall, 1965: 54)

Ferašti Goddess of "Teachability," a wife of Ahura Mazda. Iran. (Gray, 1930: 144)

Fides Roman goddess of Good Faith and Integrity, important to all relationships, particularly with treaties and contracts. (Schoeps, 1961: 148, 151; Dumézil, 1966, 1: 165; Fairbanks, 1907: 254; Prentice Hall, 1965: 54)

Fors Roman personification of the Unpredictable. (Roscher, 1965, 1, 2: 1500)

Fradat-vispam-hujyati Iranian god of Amenities. (Gray, 1930: 145)

Frasasti The goddess Fame, a wife of Ahura Mazda. Iran. (Gray, 1930: 145)

Fraus Roman personification of Cheating. (Roscher, 1965, 1, 2: 1558)

Freftar Iranian god of Deceit, the seducer. (Gray, 1930: 205)

Frigus Roman personification of stiffening from cold. (Roscher, 1965, 1, 2: 1558)

Fšeratu "The abstract divinity Fšeratu ('[Eschatological] Reward')." A goddess. Iran. (Gray, 1930: 145)

Fugen Bosatsu A celestail Bodhisattva representing "Universal Kindness," a god of constancy and cordiality, able to prolong life. Same as Samantabhadra. Japan. (Eliot, 1935: 128; Eliseev, 1963: 426; Getty, 1962: 47; Larousse, 1968: 419)

Furor Roman personification of the fury of war. (Roscher, 1965, 1, 2: 1565)

Gamlat The god of mercy. Assyria. (Jastrow, 1898: 188)

Ga-ne-o-di-o The spirit of Peace. The Onondaga, New York. (Beauchamp, 1888: 199)

Gcagcile The "Spirit of Trouble . . . first wife of Lumukanda—mother of Kibuka." South Africa. (Mutwa, 1966: iii, 9)

Gelos The personification of Laughter. Greece. (Gardner, 1925, 9: 794; Roscher, 1965, 1, 2: 1610)

Gett'r moong The "demon of quarrels." The Lepchas, Sikkim. (Gorer, 1938: 202)

ghajar-un jiruken Bodhisattva of compassion and mercy. Same as kshitigarbha. Mongolia. (Getty, 1962: 34)

Gikud A god of moderation in eating, drinking, and passions causing fighting. The Ifugao, Philippines. (Barton, 1946: 89)

Ginoo moong A female devil of envy who kills those who are prosperous and those who are dissatisfied with what they have. The Lepchas, Sikkim. (Gorer, 1938: 89, 90)

Gitaowa " 'Consolation'—soother of debtors and enemies." A "Convincer" god in indebtedness, and in war and headhunting. His wife is Magapid. The Ifugao, Philippines. (Barton, 1946: 49)

Gloria A Roman abstract goddess. (Carter, 1925, 9: 799; Roscher, 1965, 1, 2: 1691)

Goera God of strength. The Garos, Assam. (Barkataki, 1969: 27)

The Graces, the Charities Greek/Roman goddesses of hospitality and enjoyment, of gratitude. They are usually three—Aglaia, Euphrosyne, Thalia, but also variously given as Charis and Pasithea, Cleia (Cleta) and Phaenna, Auxo and Hegemone. Daughters of Zeus and Eurynome, or Helios and Aegle, or Dionysus and Aphrodite. (Larousse, 1968: 132; Bulfinch, 1898: 12; Murray, 1935: 197–198)

sGrol ma Goddess of mercy invoked to avert evil. Same as Tara. Tibet. (Nebesky-Wojkowitz, 1956, 1: 388)

Gsan-hdus-pa God of Mysticism. Tibet. (Li An-che, 1948: 39)

Gumok an ili-il A god of pacification at drink fests. The Ifugao, Philippines. (Barton, 1946: 90)

Haiyuhaiyuk God of Concession. The Ifugao, Philippines. (Barton, 1946: 49)

Halimede One of the Nereids, a sea goddess, representing "good counsel." Greece. (Kerényi, 1951: 65)

Hangale A god of moderation in eating, drinking, and passions causing fighting. The Ifugao, Philippines. (Barton, 1946: 89)

Haoa'oa "Grossness," sister of 'Oro. Society Islands, Polynesia. (Henry, 1928: 231)

Hapid ud Kabunian A god of pacification at drink fests. The Ifugao, Philippines. (Barton, 1946: 89)

Hasisu The personification of Understanding, an attendant of Ea as "lord of the ear." Babylonia, Near East. (Pettazzoni, 1956: 78)

Hau A god of peace and a god of doctors. Tahiti, Polynesia. (Henry, 1928: 145)

Hedypatheia A deity personifying comfort, ease. Greece. (Roscher, 1965, 1, 2: 1875)

Heliope The personification of contemplation of the sun. Greece. (Roscher, 1965, 1, 2: 1986)

Her-shef A ram-headed god of strength and bravery, a form of Khnemu. Egypt. (Budge, 1969, 2: 58)

Hetpet The personification of Peace. Egypt. (Gardiner, 1925, 9: 791)

Hike A god, "a highly abstract character . . . 'magic'." Egypt. (Gardiner, 1925, 9: 787, 789)

Hinanggap A god of pacification at drink fests. The Ifugao, Philipines. (Barton, 1946: 90)

Hlin Teutonic goddess of consolation who also protects from peril those mortals whom Frigga wishes to spare. (Guerber, 1895: 51; Anderson, 1891: 238; Branston, 1955: 153; Grimm, 1883, 2: 874)

Hoba "Fatigue." Also a god of war "invoked in cases of broken bones, dislocations, snake bites and wounds." A son of Manahaut. The Ifugao, Philippines. (Barton, 1946: 40, 68)

hod-dpag-med Tibetan name of Amitabha, the "Buddha of Infinite Light . . . conductor of souls." (Getty, 1962: 34, 37)

Hodr, Hodur, Hod The Teutonic blind god who killed Balder was the embodiment "of the brooding melancholy, the profound sombreness in the Saxon mental make-up." Grimm disagrees with this claiming "he was imagined blind, because he dealt out at random good hap and ill." (Stern, 1898: 50; Branston, 1955: 124; Grimm, 1880: 223)

Ho Ho Erh Sheng The "two fairies of peace and harmony"—T'ien Lung and Ti Ya—" symbols of shrewd business acumen in partnership, also of mutual affection in marital partnership." China. (Day, 1940: 91, 92)

Hokal A god of moderation in eating, drinking, and passions causing fighting. The Ifugao, Philippines. (Barton, 1946: 89)

Homonoia The personification of harmony, of accord. Greece. (Roscher, 1965, 1, 2: 2701)

Homophrosyne Greek personification of union and harmony. (Roscher, 1965, 1, 2: 2706)

Horme The personification of Impulse, of Alertness and Quickness. Greece. (Gardner, 1925, 9: 794; Roscher, 1965, 1, 2: 2742)

Hotu A god representing "Fruitfulness." Tahiti, Polynesia. (Henry, 1928: 405)

Hri A goddess representing Shame. India. (Ghurye, 1962: 255)

Hsi Wang Mu The Goddess of the West dwells on a Jade Mountain near K'un-lun or in a palace on the

K'un-lun Mountain. Subsequent to her earlier depiction as an ogress associated with plague and disaster, she is presented as the mistress of the earthly paradise of the Immortals where she presides over the Feast of the Peaches at which the peaches and wine served bestow immortality. She is also considered the goddess and guardian of the herb of immortality. China. (Larousse, 1968: 382; 1973: 284; Campbell, 1968: 167–168)

Hu A personification—"commanding utterance." (Gardiner, 1925, 9: 791) The personification of "creative will." (Larousse, 1973: 49) The "personification of the divine food upon which the gods . . . lived in heaven." Egypt. (Budge, 1969, 2: 298)

Huitaca A goddess of pleasures—"of indulgence, drunkenness and licence." Also called Chie and Jubchasguaya. The Chibcha, Colombia. (Kroeber, 1946: 908; Osborne, 1968: 112)

Hupol ud Kabunian A god of pacification at drink fests. The Ifugao, Philippines. (Barton, 1946: 90)

Iagoo Algonquin "god of the marvellous." Eastern United States. (Schoolcraft, 1857: 659; Emerson, 1884: 432)

Idianale The "goddess of labor and good deeds." Wife of Dumangan and mother of Dumakulem, Anitun Tabu. The Tagalog, Philippines. (Jocano, 1969: 9)

Idunn, Iduna Goddess of immortality and guardian of the apples, which were responsible for the youth and rejuvenation of the gods. Wife of Bragi. Scandinavia. (MacCulloch, 1964: 178; Branston, 1955: 142, 207; Wagner, 1882: 173; Davidson, 1964: 165)

I Fu Tsun Shên God of appropriate happiness. China. (Day, 1940: 90)

Ignavia Roman personification of Laziness. (Roscher, 1965, 2, 1: 110)

Iktomi The "imp of mischief." The name of Ksa after he was demoted from the God of Wisdom. He enjoyed making others look ridiculous, causing strife among the Four Winds just to watch the fight. He was wise in some things ("invented language . . . discovered colors"), very foolish in others. Son of Inyan. The Lakota and Oglala, South Dakota. (Walker, 1980: 51, 53, 101, 106, 107, 125)

Ila The "goddess of truth-vision or Revelation." India. (Pandit, 1970: 61, n. 1 & 2)

Ilot A god of moderation in eating, drinking, and passions causing fighting. The Ifugao, Philippines. (Barton, 1946: 89)

Imbabatan A deity whose "special power and function is to tie up men's stomachs so that they will eat and drink but little, and men's passions so that they will not fight." The Ifugao, Philippines. (Barton, 1946: 89)

Impetus Roman personification of Aggressiveness. (Roscher, 1965, 2, 1: 124)

Impudentia Roman personification of Shamelessness, of Impudence. (Roscher, 1965, 2, 1: 124)

Inar Hittite god of courage. Asia Minor. (Cotenau, 1948: 121)

Indulgentia A Roman goddess representing indulgence, clemency, pardon. (Roscher, 1965, 2, 1: 233)

Ingumikud A god of moderation in eating and drinking, and the passions leading to fighting. The Ifugao, Philippines. (Barton, 1946: 89)

Inliyaliya A god who enforces moderation in eating and drinking, and the passions causing fighting. The Ifugao, Philippines. (Barton, 1946: 89)

Insania Roman personification of Madness in the retinue of Tisiphone, together with Luctus, Pavor, and Terror. (Roscher, 1965, 2, 1: 262)

Inulingan A god who enforces moderation in eating, drinking, and the passions causing fighting. The Ifugao, Philippines. (Barton, 1946: 89)

Inumpitan The same as the above. (Barton, 1946: 89)

Invidia Roman personification of Jealousy and Blind Passion. (Roscher, 1965, 2, 1: 263)

Iocus Greek god of joking. (Roscher, 1965, 2, 1: 283)

Ira Roman personification of Anger. Child of Aither. (Roscher, 1965, 2, 1: 317)

Irene *See* **Eirene**

Iš Iranian goddess "Wish," a wife of Ahura Mazda. (Gray, 1930: 150)

Ishum A god of righteousness who counsels Irra to mercy. Near East. (Langdon, 1931: 137–138, 148)

Ito God of Vigilance who watches over the earth in the dark of the night. Tahiti, Polynesia. (Henry, 1928: 276)

Iustitia Roman personification of justice, closely related to Equitas. (Roscher, 1965, 2, 1: 762)

Ixcuina, Ycuina The goddess of shame was the goddess of prostitutes and adulterers, and represented immodesty, carnality, and filth. Mexico. (Bancroft, 1886, 3: 383–385)

Iza A goddess, "Zeal," a wife of Ahura Mazda. Iran. (Gray, 1930: 150)

Jaco A god of the Petro cult who creates "disorder, ill-temper and misunderatandings between people." Haiti. West Indies. (Deren, 1953: 134)

Jahera A deity of "pity, mercy, and kindness." The Luo, Kenya. (Mbiti, 1970, 2: 332)

Jara An Indian goddess—"decrepitude." (Bhattacharji, 1970: 91)

Jemoi Demon of Fatigue. The Sakai, Malay Peninsula. (Skeat, 1906: 183)

Jinilau The god of beauty. Tonga, Polynesia. (Collocott, 1925: 235)

Ju-ichimen Kannon The "eleven-headed Kwannon, Buddhist god of mercy." Japan. (Piggott, 1969: 43)

jula joqiaqči The "Buddha of Fixed Light." Same as Dipankara. Mongolia. (Getty, 1962: 12)

Ka The deification of the interrogative pronoun "who." China. (Werner, 1932: 211)

Kagole The "spirit of sadness and laziness." The Batoro, Uganda. (Cunningham, 1905: 67)

Kairos God of the favorable moment. Greece. (Roscher, 1965, 2, 1: 897)

Kallone Goddess of beauty identified or associated with Aphrodite. Greece. (Roscher, 1965, 2, 1: 936)

Kallos The personification of beauty. Greece. (Roscher, 1965, 2, 1: 938)

ka·lógi· Butterfly—and various moths—an undependable deity. "Symbols of temptation and foolishness, so despicable that their behavior, 'acting like a moth,' has come to stand for insanity, the punishment for breaking taboos." The Navaho, Arizona and New Mexico. (Reichard, 1950: 405)

Kalokagathia The personification of all perfect qualities of human beings. Greece. (Roscher, 1965, 2, 1: 938)

Kama-pua'a The "bestial pig-god . . . embodies the idea of unbridled passion and mighty brute force." He transforms as man/hog/fish/plant. Hawaii. (Emerson, 1916/17: 25; 1968: 50; Beckwith, 1940: 201–202)

Karteria The personification of will-power—to resist temptation. Greece. (Roscher, 1965, 2, 1: 968)

Katuldugan A god who enforces moderation in eating, drinking, and the passions causing fighting. The Ifugao, Philippines. (Barton, 1946: 89)

Kawaiyan ud Kabunian A god of pacification at drink fests. The Ifugao, Philippines. (Barton, 1946: 89)

Kebehut The goddess of "freshness." Daughter of Anpu. Egypt. (Casson, 1965: 80; Larousse, 1968: 25)

Kengida A god of vengeance and destruction, and a messenger of Enlil. Sumer, Near East. (Langdon, 1931: 100)

Kettu God of righteousness, of justice. Son of Shamash. Babylonia, Near East. (Ananikian, 1964: 40; Zimmern, 1925, 2: 311)

Khaibet The personification of Shadow. Egypt. (Gardiner, 1925, 9: 787)

Khro rgyal (pr. **Trhogyel**) The "king of anger" who overcomes the demons (bgegs). Tibet. (Tucci, 1980: 197, 270n. 24)

Khshthra Vairya "Wished-for Kingdom," an abstract deity, one of the Amesha Spentas. The god of metals. Iran. (Huart, 1963: 41; Williams Jackson, 1925, 1: 384; Carnoy, 1917: 260)

Khu The personification of Glory. Egypt. (Gardiner, 1925, 9: 791)

Kichijo-ten The "personification of good fortune and beauty." Same as Lakshmi or Sri. Japan. (Larousse, 1973: 326)

Kidul A god of personification at drink feasts, but more prominently the Thunder. The Ifugao, Philippines. (Barton, 1946: 30, 48, 89; 1955: 140)

Kirti The goddess Fame, associated with Krishna. India. (Ghurye, 1962: 255)

Koalemos God of Stupidity. Greece. (Roscher, 1965, 2, 1: 1264)

Kolakeia The personification of Flattery. Greece. (Roscher, 1965, 2, 1: 1268)

Komos An abstract deity—"Revel Rout"—associated with Dionysus. Greece. (Gardner, 1925, 9: 794)

Kongosatta Buddha of Supreme Intelligence. *Same as* **Vajrasattva.** Japan. (Getty, 1962: 7)

Kraipale An abstract deity—the after-effects of drunkenness. Associated with Dionysus. Greece. (Gardner, 1925, 9: 794)

Kratesis The personification of ruling and a goddess of victory. Greece. (Roscher, 1965, 2, 1: 1410)

Kratos The god of Force, of Strength, son of Styx and Pallas, and associated with Zeus in the war with the Titans. Greece. See also Cratos. (Kerényi, 1951: 34; Larousse, 1968: 165; Gardner, 1925, 9: 794; Barthell, 1971: 15, 50; Roscher, 1965, 2, 1: 1411)

Kriya An abstract goddess "activity" (in the Vayupurana). India. (Ghurye, 1962: 255)

Krodha Goddess of Anger, mother of the *bhut* ("fierce flesh-eating creatures"). The Baiga, India. (Elwin, 1939: 366)

Krodhesvari Goddess of Wrath, the partner of Heruka. Tibet. (Snellgrove, 1957: 82)

Kshama Goddess of Forgiveness, associated with Krishna. India. (Ghurye, 1962: 255)

Kshanti The goddess of Forgiveness as named in the Vayupurana. India. (Ghurye, 1962: 255)

Kshitigarbha A Bodhisattva of compassion and mercy who intercedes for the dead. Known in Central Asia, in China (as Ti-tsang p'u-sa or Ti-tsang Wang-p'u-sa), in Japan (as Jizo), in Tibet (as sahi-snin-po or Sa-yi-snin-po), in Mongolia (as ghajar-un jiruken), in Chinese Turkestan, and in India though here he is less honored. (Getty, 1962: 34; Waddell, 1959: 358; Larousse, 1968: 358, 398; Hackin, 1963: 248)

Kuan-im The Buddhist goddess of mercy is also a village deity, a "public god," who protects from illness, and promotes peace and prosperity. Taiwan and Formosa. (Diamond, 1969: 96)

Kuan-yin, Kwan-yin A celestial Bodhisattva and originally male as identified with Avalokitesvara. Popularly the goddess of compassion and mercy, the goddess of women and children, of health and of fecundity. China. (Getty, 1962: 57, 78; Werner, 1932: 225; Eliot, 1925: 120; Maspero, 1963: 352; Larousse, 1968: 387–388; Edkins, 1880: 208–209; Schoeps, 1961: 195)

Ku-doku-niyo Goddess of good works. Japan. (Puini and Dickens, 1880: 451)

Kunda (1) A demon of drunkenness or of madness. Iran. (Gray, 1930: 208) (2) A Buddhist goddess who represents teaching and charity, being "propitious" to the good; but whose threatening emblems show her as "terrible to the wicked." Tibet. (Larousse, 1973: 263)

Kundalini (1) Goddess of "Coiled-Energy . . . dormant . . . able, when she wakes up, to destroy the illusion of life and lead to liberation." India. (Danielou, 1964: 286) (2) In Tibet she is the goddess who presides over "the secret Fountain of Vital-Force," of the Psychic-Nerve Centres. (Evans-Wentz, 1960: 216)

Kung-te Chinese "goddess of merits or deserts . . . beneficent and compassionate." (Puini and Dickens, 1880: 437)

Kun-rig The Buddha of "Great Brilliance," of omniscience. Same as Mahavairocana. Tibet and Nepal. (Snellgrove, 1961: 88)

Kwan-non The god/goddess of mercy and compassion. Japan. Same as Avalokitesvara, Kuan-yin. (Getty, 1962: 57, 90; Eliot, 1935: 120; Schoeps, 1961: 195, 212)

Kwannung The Buddhist goddess of Mercy. **Same as Kwan-non.** Okinawa. (Lebra, 1966: 185)

Kwanseieun The goddess of Mercy. Korea. (Clark, 1932: 33)

Labor Roman personification of Work. (Roscher, 1965, 2, 2: 1776)

Labrosyne Personification of Greed. Greece. (Roscher, 1965, 2, 2: 1778)

Lacrimae Roman personification of Tears. (Roscher, 1965, 2, 2: 1785)

Laetitia Roman personification of Joy. (Roscher, 1965, 2, 2: 1788)

Lajja The goddess Shame, in the Vayupurana. India. (Ghurye, 1962: 255)

Lakshmi Goddess of Beauty and Wealth, of Youth, as well as of Fortune. Among some she is the personification of rice. Consort of Vishnu and mother of Kama; daughter of Siva and Durga. India and Cambodia. (Marchal, 1963: 210; Martin, 1914: 95, 103; Bhattacharji, 1970: 162–163; Ions, 1967: 48; Banerjea, 1953: 10, 62; Russell, 1916, 2: 32)

La-nga-du-du A god of peace, who prevents quarreling. The Ch'iang, Lo-pu-chai, China. (Graham, 1958: 49)

Lantjadoko The "ruler of the spirits of gluttony." The Toradja, Celebes, Indonesia. (Adriani and Kruyt, 1950: 533)

Laphygmos Personification of Gluttony. Greece. (Roscher, 1965, 2, 2: 1850)

Lar omnium cunctalis A god who represents "the world soul." (A name which appears in the list of deities given by Martianus Capella in his Cosmic System of the Etruscans). Italy. (Weinstock, 1946: 110)

lde bo (pr. **dewo**) The "great word," in the Bon religion, is an emanation out of the right hand of rGyal ba gShen rab. Tibet. (Tucci, 1980: 238)

Leto The most mild and gentle of all the Olympians, though as the daughter of Phoebe and Coeus she actually was a Titan. As a consort of Zeus she was the mother of Apollo and Artemis and representative of "motherly love and wifely purity." Greece. (Hesiod-Brown, 1981: 29, 31, 64, 79; Rawlinson, 1885: 151)

Libertas Roman personification of Liberty, of Freedom, a goddess. (Fairbanks, 1907: 254; Roscher, 1965, 2, 2: 2031; Prentice Hall, 1965: 83)

Licentia Roman personification of unruliness. (Roscher, 1965, 2, 2: 2043)

Likho One-eyed Slavic goddess of Malevolence. (Bray, 1935: 44)

Livor Roman personification of Jealousy. (Roscher, 1965, 2, 2: 2072)

Liyam Deity of Gluttony. The Isneg of Luzon, Philippines. (Vanoverbergh, 1953: 95)

Ltpn El as a "god of mercy." Syria. (James, 1960: 88)

Lua Mater "Dissolution." A personification "of what might be termed the 'destructive principle' . . . when destruction is socially or ritually necessary." The captured arms of the enemy were burned in her honor. Italy. (Dumézil, 1966, 1: 272; Littleton, 1965: 157; Roscher, 1965, 2, 2: 2146)

Luctus Roman personification of Sorrow. Male. (Roscher, 1965, 2, 2: 2146)

Lues A goddess—personified pest, plague. Rome. (Roscher, 1965, 2, 2: 2147)

Lype A personification of Sorrow. Greece. (Roscher, 1965, 2, 2: 2210)

Lyssa The personification of Madness, of Mad Rage. Greece. (Roscher, 1965, 2, 2: 2213; Gardner, 1925, 9: 794)

Ma'a' The personification of Seeing. A dual god with Sozem—Ma'a'-Sozem, Seeing-Hearing. Egypt. (Gardiner, 1925, 9: 791)

Maau God of unsightliness, of disorder. Tahiti, Polynesia. (Henry, 1928: 415)

Macies A god—the personification of Emaciation. Rome. (Roscher, 1965, 2, 2: 2231)

Ma'et The personification of the abstraction "right." "Her name appears to mean 'that which is straight or direct' . . . whether ethically ('right') or intellectually ('truth')." Egypt. (Gardiner, 1925, 9: 791)

Mahabhaya God of Terror. Son of Nirrti and Adharma. India. (Danielou, 1964: 138)

Mahakala The destructive aspect of Siva. India, Java, and Sikkim. (Marchal, 1963: 231; Gazetteer of Sikhim, 1894: 266; Dowson, 1961: 193)

Mahamaya Goddess of Illusion. India. (Banerjea, 1953: 67)

Mahinatumai A peace god at Hikutavaki. Niue Island, Polynesia. (Loeb, 1926, 1: 160)

Maiestas Roman personification of Majesty, signifying that the king was deified. (Roscher, 1965, 2, 2: 2242)

maijdari Mongolian equivalent of Maitreya. (Getty, 1962: 21)

Maitreya A Bodhisattva of Love and Compassion. The Buddha of the Future. Known in India, Central Asia, in Tibet (as Byams-pa), in Mongolia (as maijdari), in China (as Mi-lo-fo), in Japan (as Miroku). (Hackin, 1963: 250; Getty, 1962: 21; Eliot, 1935: 118–120; Waddell, 1959: 122, 329; Burrows, 1972: 32)

Malaki t'Olu k'Waig An omniscient god, the "highest ideal of goodness and of purity." A protector from disease. The Bagobo, Philippines. (Benedict, 1916: 11, 20)

Maleloa A god of peace at Lakepa. Niue Island, Polynesia. (Loeb, 1926, 1: 160)

Manaf "'Height,' 'high place,' is also a kind of abstract noun . . . worshipped as a god." Arabia. (Noldeke, 1925, 1: 662)

Manglubar The "god of peaceful living. His main duty was to pacify angry hearts." The Zambales, Philippines. (Jocano, 1969: 14)

Manyu The personification of Wrath, a god of "irrisistible; [sic] might and self-existent" who "grants victory . . . and bestows wealth." India. (Macdonell, 1897: 119; Keith, 1917: 52)

Ma Paudi A goddess of Bihar—"the symbol of unity." India. (Choudhury, 1965: 10, 13)

Markali God of Silence—"remote, motionless." India. (Basham, 1951: 115, 215)

Mar-me mdzad "The Luminous," the Buddha of Fixed Light, and the Buddha of the past. Same as Dipankara. Tibet and Nepal. (Waddell, 1959: 345; Getty, 1962: 12; Schlagintweit, 1969: 131; Snellgrove, 1961: 35, 287)

Maršavan Iranian demon of forgetfulness, causing neglect of religion and of secular duties. (Gray, 1930: 209)

Mato The Bear Spirit presides over numerous primary qualities such as love, hate, bravery, wounds, and medicines for their healing, as well as frivolous matters like mischief and fun. The Lakota and the Oglala, South Dakota. (Walker, 1980: 121)

Matua God of Strength, of Vigor. Tahiti, Polynesia. (Henry, 1928: 380)

Megaira One of the Erinyes, the goddess of "envious anger." Greece. (Kerényi, 1951: 48)

Menestho An Oceanid who represents steadfastness as a quality of human leadership. Daughter of Tethys and Oceanus. Greece. (Hesiod-Brown, 1981: 63, 87; Kerényi, 1951: 41)

Mens A Roman personification of "reflection, judgment, the opposite of rash temerity." (Dumézil, 1966, 2: 473–474)

Merau Goddess of Extinction. The Maori, New Zealand. (Andersen, 1928: 68)

Merimna The Greek personification of Worry has the wings of a bat. (Roscher, 1965, 2, 2: 2836)

Mesharu Babylonian/Assyrian god, "rectitude," son of Shamash. Near East. (Zimmern, 1925, 2: 311)

Metameleia Personification of Remorse. Greece. (Roscher, 1965, 2, 2: 2846)

Metamelos Personification of Remorse. Son of Inconstantia. Greece. (Roscher, 1965, 2, 2: 2847)

Methe The personification of Drunkenness. Associated with Dionysus. Greece. (Gardner, 1925, 9: 794; Roscher, 1965, 2, 2: 2933)

Metis Roman deity of Fear, an attendant of Mars. (Bulfinch, 1898: 131)

Mi-bskyod-pa A Buddha, the Immovable, the Imperturbable. Same as Akshobhya. Tibet and Nepal. (Getty, 1962: 36; Snellgrove, 1961: 37)

Mica The Coyote "presides over thieving and cowardice and all mischief of a malevolent kind." Friend of Iktomi, opponent of Tatanka. The Lakota and the Oglala, South Dakota. (Walker, 1980: 121, 129, 242)

Mi-gyo-ba Same as Acala. "The immoveable"—a demon-general, defender of the faith. Tibet. (Waddell, 1959: 364)

Miroku Bosatsu The Buddha to come. Japan. Same as Maitreya. (Eliot, 1925: 120; Larousse, 1968: 420)

Miseria Greek/Roman personification of Poverty and Lament. Daughter of Nox and Erebos. (Roscher, 1965, 2, 2: 3027)

Misharu Babylonian god of Rectitude, an abstract deity representing law. The son of Shamash and Aya, brother of Kittu. In Assyria he is a judge of the dead, associated with Nergal and Dagan. Near East. (Ananikian, 1964: 40; Langdon, 1931: 67, 80; Larousse, 1968: 58)

Misor Phoenician personification of Righteousness. Near East. (Herm, 1975: 111)

Mitox, Mitoxt Zoroastrian demon of Falsehood. Iran. (Gray, 1930: 210; Seligmann, 1948: 39)

Mnemosyne The Greek Goddess of Memory, Titaness daughter of Gaea and Ouranos, was the fifth wife of Zeus and the mother of the Muses. (Kerényi, 1951: 21, 103; Bulfinch, 1898: 6, 12; Barthell, 1971: 152; Hesiod-Brown, 1981: 31, 79)

Modi Germanic god, Courage, a son of Thor and Jarnsaxa and brother of Magni. He is the perrsonification of Thor's wrath. (MacCulloch, 1964: 74; Wagner, 1882: 17, 95, 124; Guerber, 1895: 64)

Moloquechigeln Personified Eternity, an attribute of Huillhuembo. The Araucanians. Chile. (Kato, 1926: 64)

Mombohal ud Paadan A god of pacification at drink fests. The Ifugao, Philippines. (Barton, 1946: 89)

Momma ud Kabunian A god of pacification at drink fests. The Ifugao, Philippines. (Barton, 1946: 90)

Momus Greek/Roman god of laughter, of scorn, of mockery. A son of Nyx. (Murray, 1935: 223; Bulfinch, 1898: 14; Prentice Hall, 1965: 92)

Murcia Some see her as a goddess of relaxation and idleness. Rome. (Roscher, 1965, 2, 2: 3223)

Muta Roman goddess of Silence. (Salkeld, 1844: 314)

Mutu-hei "Silence . . . a spirit, pervading and vast." In the beginning supreme ruler with Tanaoa, but dispelled by Ono (sound). The Marquesas, Polynesia. (Andersen, 1928: 380; Williamson, 1933, 1: 20–22)

Muyt A goddess of generation, the personification of " 'seed,' of human beings and animals." Egypt. (Gardiner, 1925, 9: 791)

Myal ba nag po (pr. **Nyelwa Nakpo**) The deity or principle "of negation, of Not-being. . . . From him originiate the constellations and the demons, and also drought . . . pestilence and misfortune of all kinds." Tibet. (Tucci, 1980: 214)

Naenia Roman personification of lamentation over the dead. (Roscher, 1965, 3, 1: 2; Salkeld, 1844: 314)

Nagakadan A god of moderation whose "special power and function . . . is to tie up men's stomachs so that they will eat and drink but little, and men's passions so that they will not fight." The Ifugao, Philippines. (Barton, 1946: 89)

Nakisawame-no-Mikoto A goddess of mourning, born of Izanagi's tears at the death of Izanami. Japan. (Yasumaro, 1965: 18; Herbert, 1967: 270)

Nakula The personfication of Temperance. India. (Martin, 1914: 204)

Nang The demon "Shame" who makes men argumentative, contentious. Iran. (Gray, 1930: 211)

Naonhaithya, Nanhaithya The demon of "pride, ingratitude, incapacity to endure misfortune, obstinacy." The opposite of Aramaiti. Iran. (Huart, 1963: 43; Dresden, 1961: 357; Larousse, 1968: 318; Gray, 1930: 183)

Na' Vahine "The Goddess of Serenity," of Peace. Also called Uri Uri. She "became the feminine generative force of the sun." She was the daughter of Teave and mother of Rono, Tanaroa, Tu (sons), and Rata, Tapo, Hina (daughters). Hawaii. (Melville, 1969: 18)

Nefas Roman personification of Wrong-doing. A deity in the retinue of Mars. (Roscher, 1965, 3, 1: 76)

Neheh The god Eternity. Egypt. (Ames, 1965: 120; Larousse, 1968: 42)

Neicea "Quarrel," "Angry Words," a child of Eris. Greece. (Barthell, 1971: 8; Hesiod-Brown, 1981: 59)

Neikos The personification of Hatred. Greece. (Roscher, 1965, 3, 1: 86)

Nemesis Also called Adrasteia. Goddess of righteous anger and vengeance in correcting inequities. Greece. (Kerényi, 1951: 33, 105; Cox, 1870, 2: 20; Murray, 1935: 213)

Nerthus The Teutonic Mother Earth was a goddess of peace and tranquillity as well as of fruitfulness. (MacCulloch, 1964: 102–103; Davidson, 1964: 110; Grimm, 1880: 251–252)

nidubarujekči, qongsim-bodhisattva A celestial Bodhisattva. Mongolia. Same as Avalokitesvara, which see. (Getty, 1962: 57)

Nigsisa A god personifying Equity. Sumer, Near East. (Jacobsen, 1970: 26)

Nihiv The demon Terror, one of those causing death. Iran. (Gray, 1930: 211)

Nikrah Believed to be a god of Hate, of War. Yemen. (Tritton, 1925, 10: 882)

Nirriti, Nirrti, Nirritu Goddess, sometimes god, of Misery representing death and destruction. Considered the female counterpart of Yama. She is the protectress of the virtuous underprivileged. Wife of Adharma, sometimes the daughter. India. (Danielou, 1964: 137–138; Sykes, 1952: 154; Dowson, 1961: 223)

Nissyen A god of peace who always caused amity where there was dissension. Son of Penardun. Britons. (Squire, 1906: 290)

Niuao The personification of Height or Altitude, as refers to the sky. Son of Ilu and Mamao. Samoa, Polynesia. (Mackenzie, n.d.: 265, 266)

Niyati An abstraction. "A belief in the all-embracing rule of the principle of order, *Niyati,* which ultimately controlled every action and all phenomena, and left no room for human volition." The Ajivika, India. (Basham, 1951: 3)

Noub, Nubt A goddess, the personification of Gold. She is found identified with Hathor. Egypt. (Gardiner, 1925, 9: 791; Mackenzie, n.d.: 46; Knight, 1915: 87; Budge, 1969, 1: 437)

Nus A personification of Understanding, of Intelligence. Greece. (Roscher, 1965, 3, 1: 482)

Nyam rje (pr. **Nyamjê**) A deity of darkness, a god or principle of negation, and enemy of Ye rje (Ye smon rgyal po). Tibet. The Bon religion. (Tucci, 1980: 234–235)

Obatala A god of the Yoruba who personifies Purity. Nigeria. (Lucas, 1948: 90)

Oblivio Roman goddess of Forgetfulness, a daughter of Nox and Erebus. (Roscher, 1965, 1, 1: 1957)

Očirdara The Mongolian name of Vajradhara, the Adi-Buddha, which see. Also called Vačirbariqči. (Getty, 1962: 4)

'Od-dpag-med The Buddha "Boundless Light." Same as Amitabha. Tibet and Nepal. (Snellgrove, 1961: 37; Waddell, 1959: 350; Hackin, 1963: 160)

Odyne A goddess, the personification of Pain. Greece. (Roscher, 1965, 3, 1: 602)

Odyrmos A god, the personification of Lamentation. Greece. (Roscher, 1965, 3, 1: 602)

'Od zer ldan (pr. **Öserden**) "The Radiant." The god of the positive, the principle of good in Bon religion. He is also called sNang srid sems can yod pa dga' ba'i bdag po, Ye rje, Ye smon rgyal po. Tibet. (Tucci, 1980: 215)

Ogo A deity of discord, "associated with the arid, unproductive earth." Twin of Nommo. Created by Amma. The Dogon, Mali and Upper Volta. (Paulme, 1973: 92)

Oistros With Lyssa, the personification of Madness, of Rage. Greece. (Gardner, 1925, 9: 794; Roscher, 1965, 3, 1: 803)

Oizys The personification of Woe, daughter of Nyx. Greece. (Barthell, 1971: 8; Roscher, 1965, 3, 1: 805)

Olethros Greek personification of Destruction. (Roscher, 1965, 3, 1: 832)

O-mi-t'o-Fo The "Buddha of Infinite Light" and conductor of souls. He is also the "God of Western Paradise." China. Same as Amitabha. (Getty, 1962: 37; Day, 1940: 167; Edkins, 1880: 208; Werner, 1934: 119–120)

Omohi-Kane-no-Kami A god of thought, of resourcefulness. Japan. (Pettazzoni, 1956: 4; Holtom, 1938: 146)

Omotes The personification of Unfeelingness. Greece. (Roscher, 1965, 3, 1: 869)

Omphaie The personification of Speech. Greece. (Roscher, 1965, 3, 1: 869)

Opame, Opa-med The Buddha of Boundless Light, and god of the Western Paradise. Same as Amitabha. Tibet, Nepal, Sikkim, and India. (Nebesky-Wojkowitz, 1956, 2: 40; Gazetteer of Sikkim, 1894: 263; Furer-Haimendorf, 1964: 237; Bell, 1931: 30)

Oramfe A god personifying Wrath, and also a solar deity. The Ife and the Yoruba, Nigeria. (Idowu, 1962: 94)

Ossa A Greek goddess, the personification of Rumor, of Report. (Roscher, 1965, 3, 1: 1230)

Ouraba God of Valor. The Sinaloas, Mexico. (Bancroft, 1886, 3: 180)

Oviri-moe-aihere A god of Mourning. Tahiti, Polynesia. (Henry, 1928: 293)

Paitiša A deity of "Opposition and Contrariness." Iran. (Gray, 1930: 212)

Pakyam A deity, "Koy," born of Itpomu and Debu. The Lepchas, Sikkim. (Gorer, 1938: 223)

dPal-ldan Lha-mo The terrible West Tibetan goddess of revenge. Wife of Shin-je, Prince of Hell. (Ribbach, 1940: 43)

Pallor Greek/Roman god of Terror, an attendant of Ares/Mars. (Bulfinch, 1898: 131; Madden, 1930: 33–34; Roscher, 1965, 3, 1: 1341)

P'a-lu-chêna A Buddha "Supreme and Eternal," the equivalent of Vairocana. China. (Getty, 1962: 31)

Palyou A deity "Gladness," born of Itpomu and Debu. The Lepchas, Sikkim. (Gorer, 1938: 223)

Panteleia Greek personification of Perfection. May be a surname of Demeter. (Roscher, 1965, 3, 1: 1550)

Paregoros A goddess of Persuasion and Consolation, closely associated with Peitho, with spiritual and ethical powers. A daughter of Oceanus and Tethys, but not a water deity. Greece. (Roscher, 1965, 3, 1: 1578; 1965, 3, 2: 1795)

Paromaiti The demon of Arrogance. Persia. (Seligmann, 1948: 39)

Parrhesia Greek personification of the Freedom of Speech. (Roscher, 1965, 3, 1: 1647)

Pathos The personification of Emotions. Greece. (Roscher, 1965, 3, 2: 1683)

Pautu-roa A god of Mourning. Tahiti, Polynesia. (Henry, 1928: 293)

Pawa Cheresi The Bodhisattva of Compassion. Same as Avalokitesvara. The Sherpas, Nepal. (Furer-Haimendorf, 1964: 171–172)

Pax Roman goddess of Peace. Same as Eirene (Greek). (Fairbanks, 1907: 254; Bulfinch, 1898: 483)

Peitho, Pitho Goddess of Persuasion and of Convincing, a daughter of Oceanus and Tethys. Greece. (Kerényi, 1951: 41; Roscher, 1965, 3, 2: 1795; Burns, 1925, 3: 372; Murray, 1935: 92; Salkeld, 1844: 316)

Penthos Personification of Suffering and Sorrow, of Grief. Greece. (Roscher, 1965, 3, 2: 1944)

Peras Personification of the End. Greece. (Roscher, 1965, 3, 2: 1945)

Pesd A personification of Shining, a form of Ra. Egypt. (Gardiner, 1925, 9: 791)

Pheme The personification of Fame or Rumor, "whether good or bad." Greece. (Murray, 1935: 215; Roscher, 1965, 3, 2: 2292; Gardner, 1925, 9: 794)

Philia Greek goddess of Friendship. (Roscher, 1965, 3, 2: 2304)

Philosophia The personification of Philosophy. Greece. (Roscher, 1965, 3, 2: 2352)

Philotes The personification of Friendship, a daughter of Nyx, sister of Apate, Geras, and Eris. Greece. (Barthell, 1971: 8; Roscher, 1965, 3, 2: 2353)

Phobos Greek/Roman god of Fright, of Alarm, and attendant of Ares/Mars. (Bulfinch, 1898: 131; Larousse, 1968: 125; Barthell, 1971: 27, 222; Gardner, 1925, 9: 794)

Phraw majan Mother of beauty, daughter of Phungkam Janun. The Katchins, Burma. (Gilhodes, 1908: 678)

Phyge The personification of Flight (fleeing). Greece. (Roscher, 1965, 3, 2: 2477)

Pietas A Roman abstraction—Piety. (Dumézil, 1966, 2: 398; Larousse, 1968: 216; Fairbanks, 1907: 254)

Pistis Goddess of Loyalty, Faith. Greece. (Roscher, 1965, 3, 2: 2512)

Pitterri Pennu The "god of increase, and of gain in every shape." The Kandh, Bengal. (Crooke, 1925, 7: 649)

Plane, Planos The personification of Error. Greece. (Roscher, 1965, 3, 2: 2518)

Poine, Poena A Greek goddess of vengeful retaliation, associated with the Erinyes, and can be singular or plural. (Roscher, 1965, 3, 2: 2601; Murray, 1935: 213)

Ponos "Toil," an evil abstraction. A child of Eris. Greece. (Barthell, 1971: 8; Roscher, 1965, 3, 2: 2754)

Prana The abstraction Breath is "deified and indentified with Prajapati." The personification of creative power, of "Life," India. (Macdonell, 1897: 14; Sarma, 1953: 29)

Praotes Greek personification of Gentleness. (Roscher, 1965, 3, 2: 2911)

Providentia The personification of the welfare of the emperor of Rome and of the citizens. (Roscher, 1965, 3, 2: 3187; Carter, 1925, 9: 799)

Pudicitia Roman goddess of Chastity in marriage. (Carter, 1925, 9: 798; Larousse, 1968: 216)

Pugna Personification of Combat, Conflict. Daughter of Nyx and Erebus. Greece. (Roscher, 1965, 3, 2: 3277)

P'u Hsien, P'u-hsien Hsin-li A celestial Bodhisattva "Universal Kindness." Same as Samantabhadra. In Anking the patron god of the mountain O Mei in Szechwan. China. (Getty, 1962: 47; Day, 1940: 167; Shryock, 1931: 79; Werner, 1932: 385; Graham, 1961: 202)

Puonoono An old goddess—"Persistence." The Society Islands, Polynesia. (Henry, 1928: 416)

Puš A nocturnal demon of Miserliness. Iran. (Gray, 1930: 212)

Pushti Goddess of Strength. India. (Ghurye, 1962: 255)

qamugha sain A celestial Buddha, "Universal Kindness." Same as Samantabhadra. Mongolia. (Getty, 1962: 47)

Quies Goddess of Tranquility, of Repose. Rome. (Schoeps, 1961: 148; Roscher, 1965, 4: 9)

Rabies Roman personification of Fury, Mania, Rabies. (Roscher, 1965, 4: 18)

Radha The "Personification of Devotion . . . the presiding deity of life and of the life-energies." She is the consort of Krishna, is greater than he in salvation, deliverance; she has power. Krishna has authority; is the greater spiritually. India. (Danielou, 1964: 263; O'Flaherty, 1980: 88, 103, 104, 117)

Rahuma The god of Fame. The Luo, Kenya. (Mbiti, 1970, 2: 333)

Rangidana A deity—"(a small, slim-waisted insect, a symbol of speed)." The Tanala, Madagascar. (Linton, 1933: 163)

Rao The "leader of the spirits of gluttony." Among some it is he who swallows the sun causing eclipses. The Toradja, Celebes, Indonesia. (Adriani and Kruyt, 1950: 378)

Rasastat A goddess possibly "presiding over truth" or perhaps "the deity of the right course of procedure." Iran. (Gray, 1930: 157–158)

Rata (1) The goddess of Inspiration, daughter of Tane and Na' Vahine, and wife of Rono. Hawaii. (Melville, 1969: 25, 42) (2) The goddess of Bounteousness. Iran. (Gray, 1930: 158)

Reverentia Roman personification of Respect, Reverence, Awe. Mother of Maiestas by Honos. (Roscher, 1965, 4: 77)

Rivalitas Roman personification of Jealousy, Envy. (Roscher, 1965, 4: 129)

Rongo A god of peace and plenty, but primarily a god of agriculture, of fertility, and of food. In some areas a god of war. New Zealand and Mangaia, Polynesia. (Best, 1924: 236; Poignant, 1967: 27, 29; Howells, 1948: 222; Buck, 1934: 162; 1938, 2: 204, 264–265; Hongi, 1920: 26)

Ro'o A god of peace and of agriculture. Son of Atea (Te Tumu) and Papa (Fa'ahotu). Central Polynesia. (Buck, 1938: 83)

Ro'onui A god of "light and peace." Society Islands, Polynesia. (Henry, 1928: 314)

Rootane God of Peace, the first of the gods created by Taaroa. The Society Islands, Polynesia. (Williamson, 1933, 1: 59; Mackenzie, n.d.: 283; Ellis, 1853: 326)

Rua-i-fa'a-toa A god of Strength, of Bravery. Tahiti, Polynesia. (Henry, 1928: 376)

Ruda Goddess of Good Will, of Favor. Arabia. (Noldeke, 1925, 1: 662; Cook, 1930: 178)

Rudra As a god of wrath he is destructive when opposed, but he is also bountiful to those who propitiate him and request aid, combatting evil and healing wounds and sufferings. "The force that battles is his gift, but also the final peace and joy." India. (Pandit, 1970: 65)

Rudrani A mother goddess of the Brahmanas and the goddess of Tears. India. (Bhattacharji, 1970: 10; Danielou, 1964: 267)

Rufashaboro   God of Mercy of the Barundi. Burundi. (Mbiti, 1970, 2: 328)

Sadyk   Phoenician personification of Righteousness, of Justice. Near East. (Rawlinson, 1885: 102, 112)

Sahadeva   A demi-god, the personification of Chastity. India. (Martin, 1914: 204)

Saham   The demon Terror. Iran. (Gray, 1930: 213)

Sahi-sñin-po, Sa-yi-sñin-po   A Dhyani-Bodhisattva of Mercy, Compassion. Tibet. Same as Kshitigarbha. (Getty, 1962: 34; Waddell, 1959: 358)

Saitada   Goddess of Grief. It is suggested she may be associated with funerary rites and religion. Wales. (Ross, 1967: 231)

Sallimmanu   Assyrian god of peace. Near East. (Sayce, 1898: 57–58)

Saltu   Goddess of hostility, of discord. She was created by Ea to oppose the terrible goddess of war—Anat/Ishtar. However, "She was the foe of the people and not their friend, like Ishtar." Near East. (Langdon, 1931: 26)

Salus   A Sabine goddess, the personification of the concept of the "welfare of the State" introduced into the Roman pantheon where she eventually became a goddess of health. Italy. (Schoeps, 1961: 148; Fairbanks, 1907: 253; Jayne, 1962: 437; Thramer, 1925, 6: 553; Prentice Hall, 1965: 130)

Samantabhadra   A celestial Bodhisattva, "Universal Kindness," the spiritual son of Vairocana. He is not the same as the Adi-Buddha Samantabhadra, the primordial Buddha. In Tibet he is known as kuntu bzan-po, in Mongolia as qamugha sain, in China as P'u-hsien, in Japan as Fu-gen. Known also in India, Central Asia, Nepal. (Evans-Wentz, 1960: 111; Waddell, 1959: 358; Getty, 1962: 47; Percheron, 1953: 261; Hackin, 1963: 250)

Santendra, dbAn-po z'i (Tibet)   A celestial Bodhisat who is the "foundation of power." Tibet. (Waddell, 1959: 358)

Santonilyo   A god of "good graces." The Sulod, Central Panay, Philippines. (Jocano, 1969: 19)

Sati   A goddess who was the "incarnation of feminine devotion and piety." A wife of Siva and daughter of Daksha. India. (Dowson, 1961: 287; Larousse, 1968: 335)

Sat Matra   A northern Dravidian stone deity, "Mother of truth," who was worshipped with offerings at outbreaks of cholera. India. (Crooke, 1925, 5: 12)

Saturitas   Roman personification of Satiety. (Roscher, 1965, 4: 426)

Sauru, Saurva   The demon of Tyranny and Misgovernment, of thievery in general. Iran. (Huart, 1963: 43; Gray, 1930: 182; Larousse, 1968: 317)

Savah   An Iranian god—"Advantage . . . clearly a god of worldly gain." (Gray, 1930: 160)

Sebasmosyne   Greek personification of Reverence, Respect. (Roscher, 1965, 4: 579)

Securitas   Roman personification of Safety, Security (public and political). (Roscher, 1965, 4: 595; Carter, 1925, 9: 799, 800)

Sedeq   A deity representing Righteousness. Canaan, Near East. (Paton, 1925, 3: 183)

Sehuatoba   A deity personifying Pleasure to whom adornments were sacrificed. The Sinaloas, Mexico. (Bancroft, 1886, 3: 180)

Sekhem   A personification of Power. Egypt. (Gardiner, 1925, 9: 789)

Sen-ge-da, Sen-ge-sgra   Tibetan name of Avalokitesvara. (Waddell, 1959: 151)

Senju Kannon   God of Compassion. Japanese Buddhism. (Larousse, 1968: 420)

Shikwembu sha tihanye   The god of quarrels. The thongas, South Africa. (Junod, 1962: 375)

Sho Kannon   "The All-Merciful." Same as Avallokitesvara. Japan. (Larousse, 1968: 420)

Shro-tu-na-ko   Goddess of "memory or instinct." Sister of Sussistanako. The Keres, New Mexico. (Tyler, 1964: 91)

Sia'   The personification of Understanding, of Perceptiveness. Egypt. (Gardiner, 1925, 9: 789; Larousse, 1973: 49)

Siddhi   As goddess of Realization, the wife of Bhaga; as goddess of Success, the wife of Ganapati; and as goddess of Knowledge, wife of Ganesha. India. (Danielou, 1964: 118, 292; Leach, 1958: 306)

Sige Gnostic personification of Silence. (Roscher, 1965, 4: 817)

Sighe Teutonic god of Peace to whom the November fires were offered. (Grimm, 1883, 2: 614)

Sigyn A goddess who represents Faithfulness. The wife of Loki. Norse. (Branston, 1955: 95, 163)

Siope Greek personification of Silence. (Roscher, 1965, 4: 950)

Smriti Goddess of Memory, of Tradition, associated with Krishna, and a wife of Angiras. India. (Ghurye, 1962: 255; Danielou, 1964: 319)

Snotra A Scandinavian goddess of Prudence, of Gentleness, of Wisdom. (Branston, 1955: 154; MacCulloch, 1964: 186; Grimm, 1883, 2: 889)

Sobrietas A goddess, the personification of Moderation and Temperance. Rome. (Roscher, 1965, 4: 1120)

Sokhet The marsh goddess, the personification of the abstraction "country." Egypt. (Gardiner, 1925, 9: 789)

Sond The personification of Fear. Egypt. (Gardiner, 1925, 9: 791)

Songhu A god of the villages, a god of pacification who "hinders fights and quarrels." The Nagas, Cachar, India. (Elwin, 1969: 423)

Song Tsi Kuan Yin, Song Tsu Niang Niang The goddess of mercy who is invoked for sons. Szechwan, China. (Graham, 1928: 17)

Soo-ge-thor The trinity of devils of quarrelling: Soo-moong, "enmity of speech;" Ge-moong, "enmity of thought;" Thor-moong, "enmity of action." They are destroyed annually in ceremonies to prevent quarrelling. The Lepchas, Sikkim. (Gorer, 1938: 205)

Soo-moong A devil who causes quarrelling—the "enmity of speech." The Lepchas, Sikkim. (Gorer, 1938: 205)

Sopor Roman personification of Sleep. (Roscher, 1965, 4: 1215)

Sori Pada The god of Mercy of the Bataks of Silindung. Sumatra, Indonesia. (Coleman, 1832: 365)

Soteria A Greek personification of Deliverance, of Rescue, who has powers of healing from madness. (Roscher, 1965, 4: 1271)

Sozem A god, the personification of Hearing; a dual deity—as Ma'a'-Sozem, a deity "seeing-hearing." Egypt. (Gardiner, 1925, 9: 791)

Spazg The demon of Gossip, of Slander. Iran. (Gray, 1930: 213, 225)

Spenta Armaiti An abstract goddess—"Holy Harmony," "generous surrender," to whom is entrusted the ruling of the land. Iran. (Williams Jackson, 1925, 1: 384–385; Huart, 1963: 41; Larousse, 1968: 317)

Spes A goddess, the personification of Hope, of a Happy Success, who is thought of by generals in battle. Rome. (Roscher, 1965, 4: 1295; Dumézil, 1966, 2: 398; Larousse, 1968: 216)

spyan-ras-gzigs The Tibetan name of the celestial Bodhisattva Avalokitesvara. (Evans-Wentz, 1960: 113; Hackin, 1963, 2: 161)

Sraddha The personification of Faith, of Devotion. Named as the wife of Dharma, or of Angiras. India. (Ions, 1967: 88; Macdonnell, 1956: 35; Danielou, 1964: 319; Keith, 1917: 54)

Sraosha The personification of Obedience, Discipline. He is a god of religious and social rightness, a judge of the soul at death. Iran. (Littleton, 1965: 124; Gray, 1930: 106–107; Huart, 1963: 42; Dresden, 1961: 348; Hinnells, 1973: 52, 54)

Sri A goddess of Beauty, of Splendor. She is also the goddess of rice, of fortune and prosperity. Bali and India. (Ghurye, 1962: 255; Danielou, 1964: 141; Covarrubias, 1937: 291, 317; Hooykaas, 1964: 22; Friederich, 1959: 47)

Suada, Suadela Greek goddess of Persuasion. (Murray, 1935: 199; Bray, 1935: 113)

Suduk Phoenician god of Righteousness, brother of Misor (Mishor). Near East. (Paton, 1925, 9: 893)

Sunka The Dog Spirit "presided over friendship and cunning." The Lakota and the Oglala, South Dakota. (Walker, 1980: 121)

Tachikara-o-no-Kami The "God of Physical Strength." Shinto Japan. (Kato, 1926: 71)

Taiseiji A Buddha, "the personification of power." Korea. (Clark, 1932: 60)

Ta'i-varua A god of Peace. Society Islands, Polynesia. (Henry, 1928: 375)

Takuakanxkan, Takushkanshkan The God of Motion. The Dakota Indians, Minnesota. (Eastman, 1962: xxxi; Lynd, 1889: 159)

Tamsi moong A devil of discord "who causes quarrelling and wars." The Lepchas, Sikkim. (Gorer, 1938: 471)

Tane A god of Peace and Beauty. He was also a god of travelers, invoked in the launching of canoes, and also a god of fine weather. Tahiti, Polynesia. (Henry, 1928: 128–129, 179–181)

Tane-te-hoe A god of Mourning. Tahiti, Polynesia. (Henry, 1928: 378)

Tapas The personification of Ardor. Associated with Manyu. India. (Macdonell, 1897: 119; Keith, 1917: 52)

Tara A female Bodhisattva of Buddhism, representing the feminine principle. She is goddess of Mercy and of Compassion and considered the consort of Avalokitesvara. Also named as that of Amoghasiddhi. She is known in Java; in Nepal; in India, as the wife of Brihaspati, with a dual nature, both threatening and compassionate; in Japan as Ro-tara-ni-bi or Tara Bosatsu; in Tibet as sgrol-ma where she has many aspects with varying names; in China as T'o-lo; in Mongolia as dara eke. (Danielou, 1964: 101, 275; Dowson, 1961: 318; Morgan, 1953: 416; Snellgrove, 1957: 114; Marchal, 1963: 164, 240; Getty, 1962: 42, 57, 118–121; Nebesky-Wojkowitz, 1956, 1: 388)

Tara-pa'a A god of Mourning. Tahiti, Polynesia. (Henry, 1928: 293)

Taromati A demoness of Contempt who causes disobedience. Iran. (Gray, 1930: 215). Taromaiti—"Presumption." (Hinnells, 1973: 52)

Ta Shih Chih God of strength. He forms a triad with Amitabha and Kuan-yin. Same as Mahastama. China. (Day, 1940: 98, 142, 152; Edkins, 1880: 209; Shryock, 1931: 78)

Ta-shih-chu The "Bodhisattva of power." Szechwan, China. (Wood, 1937: 165)

Tashmetu Wife of Nabu—"a personification of an abstract idea, 'audience'." Asia Minor. (Zimmern, 1925, 2: 312)

Tau-lou-ghy-au-wan-goon The principle of Good. A benevolent deity, younger brother of Thau-wisk-a-lau. The Oneida, New York. (Schoolcraft, 1857: 668)

Tbauatsilla The god of Contentment, of Plenty. A deified human. The Ossetes, Caucasus. (Morgan, 1888: 390)

Te-Fa'anaunau A god of Mourning. Tahiti, Polynesia. (Henry, 1928: 378)

Te-hau Peace. In the Tuamotuan Archipelago he is the father of Tane by Metua. Polynesia. (Henry, 1928: 349)

Tehen A personification of "sparkling," a form of Ra. Egypt. (Gardiner, 1925, 9: 791)

Te-mehara "Memory," a goddess of wisdom. Society Islands, Polynesia. (Henry, 1928: 85, 163)

Temperantia The Roman personification of Discretion, Caution, Composure. (Roscher, 1965, 5: 360)

Tenye Te'en Goddess of Faithfulness in marriage. Nigeria. (Talbot, 1967: 120)

Terpsis Greek personification of Pleasure. (Roscher, 1965, 5: 391)

Terror A Greek/Roman god, the personification of Terror, of the retinue of Teisiphone. (Roscher, 1965, 5: 391)

Thambo Greek personification of Amazement, concerning the heavenly appearances. (Roscher, 1965, 5: 464)

Thang-ma me-sgron God of Purity of the p'on-pos of Nepal. The Buddha of the Future. Same as Maitreya. (Snellgrove, 1961: 49)

Tharsos Greek personification of Courage. (Roscher, 1965, 5: 530)

Thor-moong A devil who causes quarrelling—"enmity of action." With Soo- and Ge-moongs he forms a trinity Soo-ge-thor. The Lepchas, Sikkim. (Gorer, 1938: 205)

Thorybos The personification of Noise. Greece. (Roscher, 1965, 5: 824)

Ting-kuang-fo The "Buddha of Fixed Light." Same as Dipankara. China. (Getty, 1962: 12)

Tinikman and **Tinukab** Gods of pacification at drink-fests. The Ifugao, Philippines. (Barton, 1946: 90)

Tisiphone, Teisiphone One of the Erinyes, the goddess of retaliation, of revenge for murder. Greece. (Kerényi, 1951: 48; Roscher, 1965, 5: 207; Prentice Hall, 1965: 143)

Ti-Ts'ang Wang God of compassion and mercy, and a god of the underworld who intercedes for the dead. Equated with the Bodhisattva Kshitigarbha. China. (Day, 1940: 120–125; Peeters, 1941: 49; Larousse, 1968: 398)

Tlazolteotl, Tlacolteutl Her abstract capacity is as the devourer of filth—in consuming men's sins she performed an act of purification. She is considered a goddess of dirt, an earth mother, a goddess of lust and carnality, of prostitutes, of childbirth and medicine. The Aztec, Mexico. (Vaillant, 1962: 146–148; Spence, 1923: 156–168; Thompson, 1970: 246; Caso, 1958: 55–56; Alexander, 1920: 54, 78; Nicholson, 1967: 46, 113)

Toh Kiho The "god of fear . . . terrible and malevolent." The Kayans, Borneo. (Hose, 1912: 5, 6)

Tragedia The personification of Tragedy, the serious drama. Greece. (Roscher, 1965, 5: 1091)

Tranquillitas Roman personification of Rest, Repose, of the security of the State. (Roscher, 1965, 5: 1095)

Triumpus Roman personification of Triumph. (Roscher, 1965, 5: 1211)

Tryphe Greek personification of Indulgence. (Roscher, 1965, 5: 1280)

Tsepame An " 'emanation' of Opame . . . 'Boundless Life'." Darjeeling, India. (Nebesky-Wojkowitz, 1956, 2: 40) Tse-pa-med—Sikkim. (Gazeteer of Sikhim, 1894: 263) Tshe dpa-med—Nepal. (Snellgrove, 1961: 40, 286) Tshe dpag med—Tibet. (Hacking, 1963: 161; Schlagintweit, 1969: 129)

Tu The concept of stability. Son of Papa. Rarotonga, Cook Islands, Polynesia. (Williamson, 1933: 14, 23)

Tu-metua God of Stability. Society Islands, Polynesia. (Henry, 1928: 384)

Tursa A goddess of Terror. The Umbrians, Italy. (Conway, 1925, 7: 460)

Tushti Goddess of Satisfaction, in the Vayupurana. India. (Ghurye, 1962: 255)

Tušnamati Goddess of Meditation, identified with Armaiti. Iran. (Gray, 1930: 162)

Tutela A Roman goddess of truth and justice "who unites in herself all the ideas and concepts of protection." (Carter, 1925, 9: 800; Grimm, 1880: 310)

Typhoeus A God of Strength, youngest child of Gaea by Tartarus, was beaten and tamed by Zeus and thrown into the abyss of Tartarus. He was the father of the evil winds of driving rain and storms that cause misfortune and destruction at sea. Greece. (Hesiod-Brown, 1981: 76, 77)

Tyrannis The personification of Tyranny, Despotism. Greece. (Roscher, 1965, 5: 1454)

Uda The demoness of Loquacity, of speaking when silence should be observed. Iran. (Gray, 1930: 215)

ülü küdelükci A Buddha, "The Immovable." Same as Akshobhya. Mongolia. (Getty, 1962: 36)

Unk "Contention" was "created by *Maka* to be her companion," but was cast into the waters becoming "the Goddess of the Waters and ancestress of all evil beings." Mother of Iya and Gnaski. The Lakota and the Oglala, South Dakota. (Walker, 1980: 50, 51)

Upanayana The goddess of Tradition. Iran. (Gray, 1930: 163)

User A personification of the abstraction Influence. Egypt. (Gardiner, 1925, 9: 791)

Ushnishavijaya A Buddhist goddess who represents Charity, Reassurance. Tibet and India. (Linossier, 1963: 98; Hackin, 1963, 2: 165; Getty, 1962: 135)

Usmine "Fighting," a child of Eris. Greece. (Barthell, 1971: 8)

Utathya God of "Pervading-Truth," son of Angiras and Sraddha. India. (Danielou, 1964: 319)

Utilitas publica Roman personification of Public Welfare. (Roscher, 1965, 6: 141)

Uznu The "Ear" personified, an attendant of Ea as god of hearing, of understanding, of knowing. Babylonia. Near East. (Pettazzoni, 1956: 78)

Uzume   Goddess of Mirth. Japan. (Piggott, 1969: 23)

Vac, Vach   Goddess of the Word, the Voice, of Speech. India. (Snellgrove, 1957: 81; Danielou, 1964: 260; Dumézil, 1966, 1: 392; Martin, 1914: 56; Ions, 1967: 20)

Vairocana, Vairochana   The "(First Dhyani-Buddha) (Buddha Supreme and Eternal." In Tibet he is known as rNam-par snan-mdsad and represents the principle of Sovereignty. He personifies "The Ether Element, like the aggregate of matter (symbolical of the fire-mist, . . . He who in Shapes makes visible all things). The physical attribute of the Ether Element is—to render the lamaic conception in the language of the psychology of the West—that of the subconsciousness." In Mongolia he is known as masi geigulun joqiaqci, a Buddha of Meditation who reigns over the center of the universe. In China he is known as P'a-lu-che-na; in Japan as Dai-nichi Nyorai, "the Buddha of Light," with whom Amaterasu is identified. In Bali Vairocana appears as a goddess. He is also known in India, Java, Korea, and Nepal. (Evens-Wentz, 1960: 9; Snellgrove, 1957: 66–67; Getty, 1962: 31; Percheron, 1953: 266; Haydon, 1941: 211; Hooykaas, 1964: 31; Marchal, 1963: 240; Clark, 1932: 60)

Vajradāka   One of the fearful gods who, to the yogin, "represent the personification of the indestructible all-potent absolute." His partner is Vajra-Vārāhī and, in ritual evocation, he is in embrace with her "and possessed by great bliss; he embodies the five transcendent wisdoms. . . . He is the true nature of samsära and nirvána." Tibet. (Snellgrove, 1957: 203, 205, 207, 209, 210)

Vajradhara   In Tibet he is known as Drojechang (rdo-rje-hc'an), the "Indestructible," a supreme Buddha, the remote aspect of Adi Buddha, and "believed to reign over the Eastern Quarter." In Mongolia he is known as Ocirdara or Vacirbariqci and is associated with the thunder. Also known in Siam. His sakti is Prajnaparamita. Other names by which he is called are Karma-vajra, Dharamavajra. (Getty, 1962: 3–5; Schlagintweit, 1969: 50–51; Percheron, 1953: 60; Waddell, 1959: 352)

Vajrasattva, rdo-rje sems-dpah (pr. **Dorjesempa**)   A Buddha representing Consciousness, the symbol of the cosmic conscience in its absolute and incorruptible essence. Among some sects he is identified with Vajradhara while others consider Vajrasattva as the active form of Vajradhara. He is also identified at times with Akshobhya but he can be distinguised by the attributes or symbols—his being a bell and a vajra "symbols of wisdom and method"—which he holds "in his crossed hands;" the vajra or thunderbolt signifying "the power of powerful beings" and representing magical power. His color depiction is white. His shakti is named as Ghantapani

(Getty) and/or Mamaki (Evans-Webtz). Tibet. In China he is known as Wo-tzu-lo-sa-tsui, in Japan as Kongosatta. He is also known in Indo-China, Java, Mongolia, Nepal, and Siam. (Evans-Wentz, 1960: 9; Getty, 1962: 4, 5; Schlagintweit, 1969: 50–51; Percheron, 1953: 266; Snellgrove, 1957: 62, 74, 244)

Venilia   Goddess of Hope. A spring nymph named as a wife of Janus and the mother of Canens. Rome. (Roscher, 1965, 2, 1: 228; Fairbanks, 1907: 247)

Venus   An ancient Italian goddess of vegetation and protector of gardens who later became goddess of beauty and of love. As Venus Erycina and a form of Aphrodite she was a goddess of "pleasure and fertility." (Fairbanks, 1907: 207–208; Dumézil, 1966, 2: 471–472; Bulfinch, 1898: 9)

Vidar, Vidarr   The Silent God, a god of power and strength, of peace and righteousness. Son of Odin and Grid. He was "considered a personification of the primeval forest or of the imperishable forces of Nature." He was destined to survive the destruction of the gods and to rule over the subsequent world. Teutonic. (Anderson, 1891: 337–339; MacCulloch, 1964: 158–159; Guerber, 1895: 147; Branston, 1955: 143)

Vis   A Roman goddess representing divine strength. (Roscher, 1965, 6: 347)

Visvamitra   God of social laws and friendship. India. (Danielou, 1964: 320)

Vohu Manah, Vohumano   The spirit of good mind and right thought. He was the son of Ahura Mazda and charged with the protection of useful animals. Iran. (Huart, 1963: 41; Robertson, 1911: 296; Haydon, 1941: 68; Gray, 1930: 27; Littleton, 1965: 98; Williams Jackson, 1925, 1: 384–385; Hinnells, 1973: 51–52)

Voleta   Roman goddess of Will, Strength of Mind. Also a goddess of childhood. (Roscher, 1965, 2, 1: 232)

Volupia   A Roman goddess personifying "the pleasure arising from a satisfied desire, a realized wish." (Dumézil, 1966, 1: 337)

Wadd   An Arabian abstract deity—" 'friendship,' 'affection'." (Noldeke, 1925, 1: 662)

Wigan   A god of the Ifugao who is a god of pacification at drink fests, but who also afflicts with arthritis. Among the Kiangan he is a creator deity. Also known among the Kankanai. Philippines. (Barton, 1946: 69, 89; de Raedt, 1964: 293; Kroeber, 1918: 44)

Wo-tzu-lo-sa-tsui   Same as Vajrasattva. China. (Getty, 1962: 5)

Yahira   Guarani "god of vengeance and death." Also god of the north. Paraguay and Brazil. (Métraux, 1948, 1: 90)

Yaošti   An abstract goddess "Zeal," a wife of Ahura Mazda. Iran. (Gray, 1930: 172)

Ye shes lha bDud 'dul gsang ba drag chen (pr. **Yeshê Lha Dütdül Sangwa**)   "God of Transcendent Consciousness." He is a violent deity who is the conqueror of the bDud demons. Bon Religion. Tibet. (Tucci, 1980: 220)

Ying hsi-niang   Goddess of Joy. The Monguors, Kansu, China. (Schram, 1957: 109)

The yul-lha   Personal deities whose worship promotes glory and dominion. Tibet. (Waddell, 1959: 375)

Yus   The Principle of Good, not feared. The Jivaro, Ecuador. (Vigna, 1945: 39)

Zallus   Lithuanian goddess of Strife. (Gray, 1930: 199)

Zaurvan   The demon of Decrepitude, of old age. Iran. (Gray, 1930: 219; Seligmann, 1948: 39)

Zelos, Zelus   "Zeal," "Jealousy," "Strife." Son of Pallas and Styx and pledged by her to assist Zeus in the war with the Titans. Greece. (Barthell, 1971: 15, 50; Bulfinch, 1898: 501; Larousse, 1968: 165)

Zmyrna   The personification of seasonings, spices, was also asked for love potions. Greece. (Roscher, 1965, 6: 762; Cunningham, 1905: 218; Budge, 1973, 1: 377)

36

Arts:
Music, Dancing, Poetry, Theater

Acat Mayan god of tattooers. Mexico. (Thompson, 1970: 313)

Aglaia One of the three Graces, goddesses of the banquet, the dance and the arts. Rome and Greece. (Bulfinch, 1898: 12; Larousse, 1968: 128)

Ahnt Kai The goddess of women who taught them to sing and to dance. She is the only one who can tell them when to dance a Fish Dance. The Seris, Sonora, Mexico. (Coolidge, 1939: 100, 109, 110)

Akpitioko A goddess of the Kple-dancing. The Gã, Temma, Ghana. (Field, 1937: 12)

Aku-Maga The god of the buttock dance, an obscene deity and a god of sexuality. The Jukun, Nigeria. (Meek, 1931: 273–274; Greenberg, 1946: 58)

Ame-no-Uzume-no-Mikoto A goddess of dancing and a phallic deity. She enticed Amaterasu, the sun goddess, out of hiding with lascivious dancing. Japan. (Saunders, 1961: 422; Holtom, 1938: 126, 183; Kato, 1926: 31; Herbert, 1967: 463)

Aoide The personification of singing, the oldest of the three Muses—on Mount Helicon. Greece. (Roscher, 1965, 1, 1: 387; Larousse, 1968: 118)

Apollo Greek god of music, as well as a sun god, a god of healing, of prophecy, of archery. (Barthell, 1971: 24–26; Bulfinch, 1898: 8, 9; Fairbanks, 1907: 49; Jayne, 1962: 306; Schoeps, 1961: 128)

Asopo According to Epicharmos, one of the seven Muses. Greece. (Roscher, 1965, 1, 1: 641)

Bansidhar An epithet of Krishna as "the flute-player." The Ahirs, Central Provinces, India. (Russell, 1916, 2: 29)

Bast, Bastet The cat-headed moon goddess and goddess of childbirth was also a goddess of pleasure and associated with music and dancing. Egypt. (Knight, 1915: 30; Ames, 1965: 104; Schoeps, 1961: 70; Budge, 1969, 1: 444–448)

Benzaiten The only goddess among the seven gods of happiness. She is the patron of music and of eloquence as well as a goddess of luck. Japan. (Herbert, 1967: 513; Getty, 1962: 127–128; Larousse, 1973: 326–327)

Bes A Nubian dwarf god introduced into Egypt. He was a god of pleasures, of music and dancing as well as of childbirth and of children. He was also a god of war. (Knight, 1915: 32; Jayne, 1962: 55; Budge, 1969, 2: 276, 284–285; Ames, 1965: 112–114)

U Biskurom The "god who teaches the playing of flutes and other musical instruments." Assam. (Stegmiller, 1921: 410)

Bohon A deity of singing. The Bhils, India. (Naik, 1956: 174)

Bragi Scandinavian god of poetry and music, of eloquence and wisdom. The son of Odin and Gunlod and husband of Idunn. (Grimm, 1880: 235; Guerber, 1895: 43, 97–98; Stern, 1898: 52; Murray, 1935: 368)

Bran Celtic god of minstrelsy as well as a warrior god. Wales and Britain. (Squire, 1906: 271; Larousse, 1968: 231; Rhys, 1937: 31)

Brighid, Brigit, Brigindo (Gaul) Goddess of poetry and learning. She had two sisters of the same name, one as goddess of healing, the other as goddess of smiths. Celtic Ireland. (MacCana, 1970: 34; Ross, 1967: 226, 360; Squire, 1906: 56, 228; MacCulloch, 1911: 69; Jayne, 1962: 513)

dByangs can ma, dbyans-can-ma   A Tibetan goddess, the equivalent of Sarasvati, the goddess of music and poetry. (Getty, 1962: 127; Nebesky-Wojkowitz, 1956, 1: 73–74)

Cairpre   The son of Ogma and Etan who was the bard of the Tuatha De Danann. Celtic Ireland. (Squire, 1906: 57, 58)

Calliope   The goddess of Epic Poetry also "attends on the majesty of kings." She is one of the Muses, daughters of Zeus and Mnemosyne, and the mother of Orpheus. Greece. (Barthell, 1971: 152; Bulfinch, 1898: 12; Larousse, 1968: 118; Hesiod-Brown, 1981: 54–55, 85)

Canna   Roman personification of the reed out of which was made the flute of Pan. He taught her to sing. (Roscher, 1965, 1, 2: 2898)

Santa Cecilia   The patroness of musicians. The Tarasco, Mexico. (Beals, 1946: 142)

Ceridwen, Cerridwen   Celtic goddess of poetry who lived with Tegid in the "under-water Elysium" of Lake Tegid. Wales. (MacCulloch, 1925, 3: 290; Ross, 1967: 227)

Chang-ku-lao   The patron deity of musicians who play tom-toms of snakeskin. Szechwan, China. (Graham, 1961: 186)

Charani Devi   The "goddess of the bards." Rajasthan, India. (Tod, 1920: 693)

Charis   One of the Graces, named as a wife of Hephaistos. Greece. (Cox, 1870, 2: 2; Larousse, 1968: 128)

Cha Yung   The god of musical instruments worshipped by music shop merchants. China. (Du Bose, n.d.: 336; Werner, 1932: 322)

Chêng Yüan-Ho   The "God of Strolling Singers." China. (Werner, 1932: 48)

Chen Ping   The "Punch and Judy god." China. (Du Bose, n.d.: 338)

Chermatiya Deo   A god of crops who instituted dancing in worship. The Dhanwar, India. (Elwin, 1949: 482)

Chibiabos   The third son of Epingishmook and Winonah was a musician who sang and composed, made instruments, and taught hunters to imitate calls. He was taunted to challenge Bebon and was drowned in Ojibway Lake. He was chanted and drummed back to life, con-quering death; was honored by the living but could no longer enter their homes. The Ojibway Indians, Minnesota and Manitoba. (Johnston, 1976: 156–158)

Chin-hua Niang-niang   A goddess of drums and violins. China. (Werner, 1932: 322)

Clio, Kleio   The muse of history and "the giver of fame." Greece. (Kerényi, 1951: 104; Bulfinch, 1898: 12; Murray, 1935: 178; Hesiod-Brown, 1981: 55, 85)

Corpre   Celtic poet of the gods. See also Cairpre. Ireland. (MacCulloch, 1918: 137)

Corredoio   Etruscan god or goddess of dance and festivals. Italy. (Leland, 1963: 73)

Cotyang Kongbu   A deity who appears in the Dancing Ceremony. The Lepchas, Sikkim. (Siiger, 1967, 1: 169)

Coyote   At Taos he introduced the buffalo and the Buffalo Dance. He warns of enemies and forecasts the weather. The Pueblo Indians, Arizona and New Mexico. (Parsons, 1939: 194)

Datigen   A deity who appears in the Dancing Ceremony. The Lepchas, Sikkim. (Siiger, 1967, 1: 169)

Diwali   A goddess of singing and of festivals whose husband is Nandervo. Sister of Holi. The Bhils, India. (Naik, 1956: 183–184)

Dunga   Ea as the god of singers. Sumer, Near East. (Langdon, 1931: 105)

Ea   A Babylonian god of culture and civilization, of arts and the artistic crafts, of wisdom, as well as of the waters. Near East. (Jastrow, 1898: 62, 137–138; Larousse, 1968: 63; Sayce, 1898: 133)

Ekineba   The goddess of the masquerades who taught the dancing and drumming for them. The Kalabari, Niger Delta, West Africa. (Horton, 1960: 17, 28–30)

Erato   (1) The Muse of Love Poetry, daughter of Zeus and Mnemosyne. (2) A Nereid, "the awakener of desire," daughter of Doris and Nereus. Greece and Rome. (Barthell, 1971: 152; Kerényi, 1951: 104; Hesiod-Brown, 1981: 54–55, 60; Bulfinch, 1898: 12; Larousse, 1968: 118)

Êrh-lang Yeh-yeh   A god of drums and violins. China. (Werner, 1932: 322)

Euchir   A Greek god, the personification of artistic skill. (Roscher, 1965, 1, 1: 1398)

Euphrosyne Greek/Roman goddess, one of the three Graces. (Bulfinch, 1898: 12; Larousse, 1968: 132)

Euterpe The muse of lyric poetry. Greece and Rome. (Bulfinch, 1898: 12; Barthell, 1971: 49; Kerényi, 1951: 104)

Fakapoloto A god of shell necklaces. Niue Island, Polynesia. (Loeb, 1926, 1: 164)

Gamtidevi A deity of singing. The Bhils, India. (Naik, 1956: 174)

The Gandharvas The "heavenly musicians" who play for the Apsarases when they dance. Two of their leaders are Visvavasu and Tumburu. India. (Keith, 1917: 143)

Ganuor Motri The "god of sculptors, engravers, and carpenters." The Chams, Annam and Cambodia. (Cabaton, 1925, 3: 342)

Geinoshin The god of the "Entertainment Arts," regarded as a form of Dosojin. Japan. (Czaja, 1974: 51)

Geshtinanna Sumerian goddess of poetry and singing and an interpreter of dreams. Near East. (Kramer, 1961: 111)

Ghagarapen A deity of bells. The Gonds, India. (Crooke, 1894: 108)

Ghantalamma A village deity in Masulipatam, a goddess with bells. The Telugu, Southern India. (Whitehead, 1916: 21)

Gosae-era A goddess who, with Jaher-era, Marang Buru, and Moreko, taught humans to play music and to dance. The Santals, India. (Elwin, 1949: 479)

The Graces, the Charities Goddesses of social entertainment, of the dance and the arts, also the goddesses of gratitude. They are usually given as Euphrosyne (Happiness), Aglaia (Pageantry), and Thalia (Festivity). They are the daughters of Zeus and Eurynome. Other names: Charis and Pasitha in Homer, Cleia and Phaenna at Sparta, Hegemone and Auxo at Athens. Greece and Rome. (Hesiod-Brown, 1981: 31, 78; Bulfinch, 1898: 12; Larousse, 1968: 132; Murray, 1935: 198)

Gyaka Amo A deity who appears in the Dancing Ceremony. The Lepchas, Sikkim. (Siiger, 1967, 1: 169)

Han Hsiang-tzŭ A Taoist god of musicians whose emblem is the flute. One of the eight Immortals— "credited with the power of making flowers grow and blossom instantaneously" ca. A.D. 820 China. (Peeters, 1941: 30; Williams, 1976: 155)

Hathor Cow-headed sky goddess of love, music and dancing. Also a goddess of the underworld and the dead. Egypt. (Jayne, 1962: 58; Ames, 1965: 76; Larousse, 1968: 23; Budge, 1969, 1: 435; Gerster, 1969: 726)

Hawt The god of music and the flute, also of water. The Wintun, California. (Curtin, 1903: 199, 508; Chamberlain, 1905: 115)

Hiiaka Goddess of the hula and of sorcery. Sister of Pele. Hawaii. (Beckwith, 1940: 180; Poignant, 1967: 46–47; Emerson, 1916/17: 25; 1968: 43)

Hillon A sun god and a god of music. Gaul. (Bertrand, 1897: 146–147)

Hina-'ere'ere-manu'a Goddess of tattooing. Tahiti, Polynesia. (Henry, 1928: 287)

Holi Goddess of dancing and singing. Also called Jogan Mata. Wife of Mashru Dev, Sister of Diwali. The Bhils, India. (Naik, 1956: 182)

Hsien Ko God of music. China. (Day, 1940: 110)

Hua-tini The god of dances. The Marquesas, Polynesia. (Christian, 1895: 190)

Hymno One of the Greek Muses. (Roscher, 1965, 1, 2: 2804)

Ilu-mokan God of the dance. Yap Island, the Carolines, Micronesia. (Christian, 1899: 385)

Jaher era A village goddess of the sacred grove who is one of those who taught people music and dancing. The Santals, Bihar, India. (Elwin, 1949: 479; Mukherjea, 1962: 236)

Jakui An important water spirit of rivers and lagoons and also the god of the jakui flute. The Kamauria, Xingu River, Brazil. (Villa Boas, 1973: 111–121, 257)

Jatra Gimb The deity of singing. The Bhils, India. (Naik, 1956: 174)

Jubal Sumerian god of music. Son of Lumha (Ea). Near East. (Langdon, 1931: 105)

Kai Yum, Kayom Lacandon god of music, of singing and dancing. Mexico. See also K'ayum. (Thompson, 1970: 313; Cline, 1944: 112, table 1)

Kanepai God of dancing. Yap Island, the Carolines, Micronesia. (Christian, 1899: 385)

Kapo Goddess of hula dancing and of sorcery. A death goddess on Maui. Also called Kapo-ula-kinau. Hawaii. (Emerson, 1916/17: 24–25; Beckwith, 1940: 185–187; Westervelt, 1915: 98, 111, 140; 1963, 1: 34)

Kauthar, Koshar A god of the arts and of music, as well as of craftsmen. Canaan, Near East. (Albright, 1956: 81; Ferm, 1950: 124; Vriezen, 1963: 53)

K'ayum, K'ayyum The god of music and the lord of song. The Lacandon, Chiapas, Mexico. *See also* **Kai Yum.** (Perera and Bruce, 1982: 308)

Kinnar, Kinnur The god of the lyre. Canaan. Kinnur in Phoenicia. Near East. (Albright, 1968: 144, 147)

Ah Kin Xoc The god of poetry and a musician. Also called Ah Kin Xocbilton, P'izlimtec. The Mayan, Mexico. (Thompson, 1970: 313)

Kipapua The "master of the spirits, who, at his behest, played their musical instruments, which were heard in this world and could be silenced only by shamans." Guapore River area, Brazil and Bolivia. (Métraux, 1942: 151; Levi-Strauss, 1948, 1: 379)

Ko A deity worshipped by actors. Anking, China. (Shryock, 1931: 154)

Komodia A goddess associated with music and amusement. Greece. (Roscher, 1965, 2, 1: 1281)

Koro A god associated with "dancing ceremonies and love-making." Son of Hina-uri and Tinirau. The Maori, New Zealand. (Mackenzie, n.d.: 336–337; Hongi, 1920: 27)

Koro-eriki The "god of the song experts." Mangareva, Polynesia. (Buck, 1938, 1: 424)

Koshare The clown, the entertainer, created by Iyatiku. He is the patron of the clown society. The Keresan, New Mexico. (Parsons, 1939: 246; Tyler, 1964: 194)

Kuai A culture hero who introduced the mask dances and taught them to the people; now lives in the sky. The Kabeua, Brazil. (Alexander, 1920: 294)

Ku-ka-ohia-laka God of the hula dance, as well as a rain and forest god worshipped by canoe builders because of the ohia-lehua wood. Hawaii. (Beckwith, 1940: 15, 16)

Kukluknam The "spirit of the Sun Dance." The Kutenais, Northern Rockies, Inland British Columbia. (Clark, 1966: 155)

La The goddess of tattooing. Yap Island, Micronesia. (Müller, 1917: 51)

Labraid A Celtic god considered a "divine musician." Ireland. (O'Rahilly, 1946: 111)

Laka A goddess of the hula dance and of love, of fruitfulness and growth, of vegetation and the wildwood. Hawaii. (Beckwith, 1940: 52, 185–186; Poignant, 1967: 27; Emerson, 1916/17: 23; Westervelt, 1963, 2: 74)

Laka-kane The god of the hula and of the wildwood. Hawaii. (Andersen, 1928: 269; Beckwith, 1940: 41)

Lanidj With Leowudj the gods of tattooing. The Marshall Islands, Micronesia. (Krämer, 1906: 370)

Lao Lang Ming Wang The god of the theater and of actors. China. (Day, 1940: 48; Werner, 1932: 239)

Leowudj A god of the art of tattooing. The Marshall Islands, Micronesia. (Krämer, 1906: 370)

Lubanga The dancing god. The Baganda, Uganda. (Cunningham, 1905: 218; Budge, 1973, 1: 377)

Lugaligihusham A divine musician, the elegist of Ningirsu, who "brought solace in dark moments." Near East. (Jacobsen, 1976: 82)

Lugus, Lugos A Celtic god of the arts and crafts, wise, and of many skills. Gaul, Britain, and Ireland. (Ross, 1967: 250, 363; MacCana, 1970: 27–29; MacCulloch, 1911: 90–91)

Luk The god of the dance. Yap Island, Micronesia. (Furness, 1910: 150)

Lumha, Lamech Ea as the god of psalmists, and as the father of Jabal, Jubal, Tubal-cain. Sumer, Near East. (Langdon, 1931: 105)

Macuilxochitl The Five-Flower God. God of music and dancing, of games and sports, patron of artists. Mexico. (Caso, 1958: 80; Thompson, 1970: 313, 328; Duran, 1971: 305; Alexander, 1920: 57, 77; Spence, 1923: 196, 202–203)

Madun pungren majan Mother of flutes, daughter of Phung-kam Janun. The Katchins, Burma. (Gilhodes, 1908: 678)

Marimba Goddess of music and of singers. Wife of Zumangwe and mother of Kahawa. South Africa. (Mutwa, n.d.: vii)

Masejda A deity who "confers the talent of dancing at shave ceremonies." Nyajena Reserve, Rhodesia. (Gelfand, 1966: 99)

The Masmasala'nix Four brothers: Malapa'litsek, Yula timot, Malape exoek, Ililulak, who taught men the arts, canoe building, and hunting. The Bella Coola, British Columbia. (Boas, 1898: 32–33)

Melete "The first Muses worshipped on Mount Helicon were three in number: Melete, Mneme, and Aoide." Greece. (Larousse, 1968: 118)

Melpomene Greek/Roman goddess of tragedies and of elegies. One of the Muses. (Kerényi, 1951: 104; Bulfinch, 1898: 12; Barthell, 1971: 152; Larousse, 1968: 118)

Miao-yin-fo-mu The equivalent of Sarasvati, the goddess of music and poetry. China. (Getty, 1962: 127)

Milomaki A youth from the sky who brought death to the people, but also was the source of wondrous music. When he was sacrificed a palm grew from his ashes—from its wood the people created flutes. The Yurupai and the Yahuma, Brazil. (Roheim, 1929: 185; Alexander, 1920: 294)

Minan A culture hero who gave them their dances. The Bad, West Kimberley, Australia. (Elaide, 1964: 37)

Misevályue Mother of dancing and singing. Also a weather goddess. The Cagaba and the Kogi, Colombia. (Reichel-Dolmatoff, 1949/50: 114)

Mneme One of the early Muses worshipped on Mount Helicon. Greece. (Larousse, 1968: 118)

Moreko The god who taught them music and dancing. The Santals, India. (Elwin, 1949: 479)

Muralidhara, Murlidhar Krishna as the flute player, the god of music. India. (Tod, 1920: 628; Russell, 1916, 2: 29)

The Muses The goddesses of music, poetry, and arts sing "of things past and present and to come." They honor kings with eloquence, judgment, majesty. The daughters of Mnemosyne and Zeus (Jupiter) are: Clio—"celebrate," Euterpe—"delight," Thalia—"festivity," Melpomene—"choir," Terpsichore—"delight of dancing," Erato—"lovely," Polyhymnia—"many songs,"

Urania—"heavenly," Calliope—"beautiful voice." The number varied in different places but traditionally they are given as nine. Earlier on Mount Helicon there were three—Melete, Mneme, and Aoide. Greece and Rome. (Fairbanks, 1907: 106; Kerényi, 1951: 104–105; Hesiod-Brown, 1981: 31, 54–55, 85; Murray, 1935: 175–176; Larousse, 1968: 118)

Nan-imu-lap The god of dances. Ponape, Caroline Islands, Micronesia. (Christian, 1899: 383)

Narada, Nareda Inventor of the lute and god of the musicians, as well as god of wisdom and of law. India and Java. (Martin, 1914: 302–303; Anderson, 1965: 31; Danielou, 1964: 323–324; Coleman, 1832: 7)

Nartesvara God of the dance, a form of Avalokitesvara. Tibet. (Snellgrove, 1957: 187)

Nataraja A manifestation of Siva as god of the dance. India. (Brown, 1961: 305; Heeramaneck, 1966: 95)

Nidaba Sumerian/Babylonian goddess of reeds, and as such goddess of music as well as of writing. She was also a goddess of corn, of grains. Near East. (Jacobsen, 1946: 144; Langdon, 1931; 193; Cotenau, 1948: 77)

Nilo Nandervo Deity of singing. The Bhils, India. (Naik, 1956: 174)

Nin-dim-su A minor god of the Hammurabi period—Ea as a god of the arts. Babylonia, Near East. (Jastrow, 1898: 171, 173)

Nin-zadim A god of sculpture of the Hammurabi period. Babylonia, Near East. (Jastrow, 1898: 171, 178)

ńĺtci The wind god as god of wind instruments. The Navaho, Arizona and New Mexico. (Reichard, 1950: 497–499)

Nü Kua As a goddess of the wind she was considered "the inventor of the classical Chinese wind instrument, the reed organ (*sheng*)." Her twin Fu Hsi is "like her, a proto-musician and creator spirit." China. (Schafer, 1980: 37–41)

Ogma Celtic god of poetry, literature and eloquence, and the inventor of Ogham writing. One of the Tuatha deities. Ireland. (MacCulloch, 1911: 75; Squire, 1906: 56–59; MacCana, 1970: 40; Cohane, 1969: 81)

Ogmios Celtic god of speech, poetry, and eloquence as well as a god of agriculture. Gaul. (MacCana, 1970: 40–41; Schoeps, 1961: 118; MacCulloch, 1911: 25)

Ono, Rongo God of singing, but primarily the god of cultivated foods. He ruled sound, having overcome silence. The Marquesas, Polynesia. (Poignant, 1967: 38; Andersen, 1928: 380)

Oriwakarotu The "God of Dance . . . at the point of mid-winter sunset in the northwest." The Winikina-Warao, Venezuela. (Wilbert, 1973, 1: 6)

Ourania *See* **Urania**

Paiyatemu A god of music, the flute player, and companion of the sun, representing its fertility and sexuality. He lures, but frightens away, then rewins the corn maidens; their flight from his love representing the non-growing season. The Zuñi and the Keresan, New Mexico. (Parsons, 1939: 179; Tyler, 1964: 55, 142–145)

Pai Yŭ God of the guitar. China. (Werner, 1932: 354)

Papeekawis Also called Yenaudizih. The second son of Epingishmook was "the patron of winds and dances" for pleasure and for entertainment, which were such "that he created whirlwinds, breezes, gusts, gales . . . typhoons, hurricanes." He was much loved and admired, but lonely. The Ojibway, Minnesota and Manitoba. (Johnston, 1976: 153)

Pasithea One of the three Graces. Greece. (Murray, 1935: 198)

Pautiwa A god of the Kaka (Kok-ko) drama-dance organization and of ceremonials in general. The Zuñi, New Mexico. (Cushing, 1891/92: 375, 409; Stevenson, 1898: 36)

Pergina A deity to whom offerings are made before dancing performances. Bali, Indonesia. (Covarrubias, 1937: 222)

Polyhymnia, Polymnia The muse of sacred poetry and also of the mime. Greece and Rome. (Kerenyi, 1951: 104; Bulfinch, 1898: 12; Larousse, 1968: 118)

Ptah A god of the arts, of artisans, of sculptors—one of his aspects. Egypt. (Ames, 1965: 101; Budge, 1969, 1: 416; Casson, 1965: 72)

Saga Norse goddess of poetry and narration, of history, associated with Odin. (Thorpe, 1851: 191; Grimm, 1880, 1: 310, 319; Wagner, 1882: 1; MacCulloch, 1964: 183)

Saling Sadugen A deity who appears in the Dancing Ceremony. The Lepchas, Sikkim. (Siiger, 1967, 1: 169)

S'anolxmulalt A god of the kusuit dances. The Bella Coola, British Columbia. (Boas, 1898: 31)

Sarasvati Goddess of music and poetry, of speech and eloquence, of wisdom and learning. The consort of Brahma. For many she is the goddess of the river of that name. India. (Ions, 1967: 81, 89; Banerjea, 1953: 10; Hooykaas, 1964: 21–23; Getty, 1962: 127; Larousse, 1968: 344; Danielou, 1964: 260; Jayne, 1962: 173)

Sarkin Maka'da "The drummer for all the spirits, and the patron . . . of drummers." The Maguzawa, Nigeria. (Greenberg, 1946: 37)

Sesha't Egyptian goddess of painting and of writing. (Gardiner, 1925, 9: 791)

Siva As god of the dance he is known as Nataraja. India. (Brown, 1961: 305; Heeramaneck, 1966: 95)

Taema and **Tila fainga** The "goddesses of the tattooers." Samoa, Polynesia. (Turner, 1884: 55)

T'ai-tzu-p'u-sa The deity and patron of actors. Szechwan, China. (Graham, 1961: 186)

Tang Hsuan Tzung A deity worshipped by actors. Peking, China. (Burgess, 1928: 188)

T'ang Ming Huang The god of the theater. China. (Werner, 1932: 493)

Ta-pien-ts'ai-t'ien-nu The goddess of music and poetry. China. Same as Sarasvati. (Getty, 1962: 127)

Tau-titi God of the dance of the same name. Rarotona, Polynesia. (Andersen, 1928: 122)

Tautu A god of comedians, but also of the cooking in the army and in the home. Society Islands, Polynesia. (Henry, 1928: 375–376)

Techne Greek goddess of art. (Roscher, 1965, 3, 2: 2141; 1965, 5: 155)

teeku-gami Deity of the drum. Okinawa, Ryukyu Islands. (Lebra, 1966: 223)

Teiiri A god who taught the art of ball-throwing, of juggling. Mangaia, Polynesia. (Andersen, 1928: 330)

Tekha Shara Matzkala A god of the dance who was visited by the shamans on their ecstatic journeys. The Buryat and the Teleut, Siberia. (Eliade, 1964: 75)

Teraranga A god who taught the art of ball-throwing, of juggling. Mangaia, Polynesia. (Andersen, 1928: 330)

Terpsichore The muse of lyric poetry, of choral dance and song. Greece and Rome. (Kerényi, 1951: 104; Bulfinch, 1898: 12; Larousse, 1968: 118)

Thalia, Thaleia One of the muses, the goddess of comedy. Greece and Rome. (Kerényi, 1951: 104; Bulfinch, 1898: 12; Roscher, 1965, 5: 449)

Tiki The creator god also "instituted tattooing and the art of making statues and images." The Marquesas, Polynesia. (Williamson, 1933, 2: 174)

Tikoke-Puta The god of songs and poetry. The Marquesas, Polynesia. (Christian, 1895: 190)

Tila fainga A goddess of tattooers. Samoa, Polynesia. (Turner, 1884: 55)

Tochopa A god who taught them the arts. Twin of Hokomata. The Walapai, Arizona. (Alexander, 1964: 180)

Ts'ao Kuo-chiu A Taoist god of the theatrical profession whose emblem is a pair of castanets. One of the Eight Immortals. A.D. 930–999 China. (Peeters, 1941: 30–31; Williams, 1976: 154)

Ts'ibatnah "(Painter of Houses): the god of the graphic arts." The Lacandon, Chiapas, Mexico. (Perera and Bruce, 1982: 310)

Tu A deity worshipped by actors. Anking, China. (Shryock, 1931: 154)

Ix Tub Tun The "goddess of workers in jade and amethyst." The Mayan, Central America. (Nicholson, 1967: 127)

Tulagola The "creator of the first slit-gong and the discoverer of the first hand drum, the two most important instruments in Lakalai music and dancing." New Britain, Melanesia. (Valentine, 1965: 184)

Tulikalo A musician god of the underworld. Pukapuka, Polynesia. (Beaglehole, 1938: 313)

Ueuecoyotl "Old Coyote." A god of dances and feasts, and associated with revelry. The Otomi and the Aztec, Mexico. (Alexander, 1920: 83; Burland, 1967: x, xi)

Urania, Ourania One of the Muses, goddess of astronomy. Greece. (Kerényi, 1951: 104; Fairbanks, 1907: 106)

Urien Celtic god of minstrelsy as well as of battle; considered the patron of the bards. Britain. (Squire, 1906: 318)

Urutaetae A god of music and dancing. Tahiti, Polynesia. (Henry, 1928: 378; Ellis, 1853: 332)

Ushumgalkalama A divine musician, the singer of Ningirsu, "who inspired the harp of that name and provided gaiety." Near East. (Jacobsen, 1976: 82)

Uzume *See* **Ame-no-Uzume-no-Mikoto**

Vai'ea A god of comedians. Tahiti and Mo'orea, Polynesia. (Henry, 1928: 375)

Vaino A god of minstrelsy. In the Kalevala called Wainamoinen. Finland. (de Kay, 1898: 62–63)

Wolfat Second son of Lugeilang and a human wife, Lamanu, credited with inventing and teaching tattooing. In some tales a trickster and transformer. Woleai, Micronesia. (Burrows, 1947/48: 4–6)

Wu Tai Yüan-shuai The god of musicians. China. (Werner, 1932: 574)

Xoc Bitum The god of song. The Mayan, Central America. (Nicholson, 1967: 127)

Yo Fei A god of actors. China. (Maspero, 1963: 333)

Yüeh Sung Patron of music and of the "makers of musical instruments." China. (Day, 1940: 110)

bZo lha (pr. **So Lha**) God of the arts of the Bon. Tibet. (Tucci, 1980: 218)

37

Gods of the Cardinal Points

Abaangui   A culture hero/creator god and transformer who was the god of the East. The Guarayu, Bolivia and Brazil. (Métraux, 1948, 2: 437; Alexander, 1920: 297)

Abuhene   The god of the West, the scarlet macaw, is an evil deity approached only by the dark shaman. The Warao, Venezuela. (Wilbert, 1973, 2: 5)

Agni   The god of fire is associated with the Southeast. India and Mongolia. (Dubois, 1906: 633; Percheron, 1953: 63)

Akpambe   One of "The Four-Quarter Gods." The Ekoi, Nigeria. (Jeffreys, 1939: 99)

Akshobhya   A Buddha, the "Imperturbable," who reigns over the East. India, Japan, and Mongolia. (Snell-grove, 1957: 60, 66–67; Eliot, 1935: 100; Percheron, 1953: 253; Larousse, 1968: 357)

Allara-Ogonur   An evil spirit who "lives in the far north." The Yakut, Siberia. (Czaplicka, 1925, 12: 828)

Alom   One of four regent gods of the quarters of the cosmos, of directions—with Tzakol, Bitol, and Cajolom. Through their mediation was produced "the birth of light"—material *and* spiritual. They gave to each species of animal its type of habitat and its "peculiar means of expression: cries, howls, grunts." An hyposta-sis of Cabahuil as creator god-Seven. The Quiché, Guatemala. (Girard, 1979: 29, 32, 38)

Ament   The goddess of the West, originally from Libya, became a goddess of the land of the dead when the West became synonymous with the afterworld. Egypt. (Ames, 1965: 119; Larousse, 1968: 17)

Amitabha   The Buddha of Boundless Light is the Bud-dha of the West, the god of the Western Paradise. China, Japan, Tibet, Mongolia, and Central Asia. (Snellgrove,

1957: 66–67; Waddell, 1959: 346, 350; Day, 1940: 98, 141–142; Percheron, 1953: 253; Hori, 1959: 420)

Amoghasiddhi   The Buddha of "Infallible Magic" reigns in the North. India, Tibet, and Mongolia. (Getty, 1962: 42; Percheron, 1953: 253; Larousse, 1968: 357; Waddell, 1959: 350; Snellgrove, 1957: 66–67)

Amset   God of the cardinal point of the South. A son of Horus, and one of the gods of the Canopic Jars. Egypt. (Budge, 1969, 1: 158, 491–492)

Amurru   Phoenician god of the West. Near East. (Cotenau, 1948: 76; Larousse, 1968: 76)

Anabarima   "Father of the Waves" is a god of the North, a companion of Warowaro. The Winikina-Warao, Venezuela. (Wilbert, 1973, 1: 4)

dbAng-ldan   God and protector of the Northeast. Tibet. (Waddell, 1959: 367)

Ar-hes-nefer   A god of the South, identified with Sebek-Ra and Hes-nefer-Sebek. Egypt. (Budge, 1969, 1: 464)

Ariawara   The god of origin is generally beneficent and "lives on the world mountain of the east." The Warao, Venezuela. (Wilbert, 1973, 1: 4, 61)

The Bacabs   Four Mayan gods who uphold the sky—one in each of the world quarters: East—Hobnil, North—Can Tzicnal, West—Zac Cimi, South—Hozanek. They are also patrons of apiculture. Mexico. (Thompson, 1970: 276–277; Tozzer, 1941: 135, 145; Bancroft, 1886, 2: 699; Morley, 1946: 214)

Bach-ho   The "Spirit of the West . . . the White Tiger." China. (Scott, 1964: 307)

Bakororo The culture hero/god who rules in the West. The Bororo, Brazil. (Levi-Strauss, 1969: 37)

Bast The goddess of the East and of Bubastis was a cat/lioness-headed deity associated with the sun as well as the moon. Egypt. (Knight, 1915: 30; Budge, 1969, 1: 447–448)

Bishamon (ten) The guardian of the North was a god of wealth, which gained him a place with the seven gods of good fortune, of happiness. Japan. (Eliot, 1935: 136; Larousse, 1973: 324–325; Getty, 1962: 156, 168)

Bitol One of four regent gods of the quarters of the cosmos, of directions—with Alom, Tzakol, Cajolom. See Alom. The Quiché, Guatemala. (Girard, 1979: 29, 32, 38)

Black Hactin The leader and most powerful of the hactin (the supernaturals of the beginning who lived in the underworld) is associated with the East. The Apache, Arizona and New Mexico. (Leach, 1949: 147; Campbell, 1974: 232–240)

Brahma The god of the Zenith. Mongolia. (Percheron, 1953: 63)

Bya-rgyal-rgod-po The Bird of the East is white and appears in some of the wedding songs in their ceremonies. The East gives—Sun, also moon and stars. Tibet. (Francke, 1923: 12)

dByug pa 'jigs byed A god associated with the South. Tibet. (Nebesky-Wojkowitz, 1956, 1: 45)

Cajolom One of four regent gods of the quarters of the cosmos, of directions—with Alom, Bitol, and Tzakol. See Alom. The Quiché, Guatemala. (Girard, 1979: 29, 32, 38)

Calnis A testy god associated with the East, and also with Gukso in ceremonies. The Pomo, California. (Gifford, 1926: 353; Barrett, 1917: 424)

Can Tzicnal (Sicnal) The Bacab of the North quarter, one of those who hold up the four corners of the sky. Mayan, Mexico. (Roys, 1949: 160; Thompson, 1970: 276; Tozzer, 1941: 145)

Cautantowit The "great god of the southwest." The Algonquin, Connecticut. Same as Kiehtan. (De Forest, 1853: 23, 25)

Chacal Bacab A Mayan god associated with the East. Mexico. (Tozzer, 1941: 138)

Chac Pauah Tun A Mayan god associated with the East. Mexico. (Tozzer, 1941: 138)

The Chacs Four Mayan gods of rain and of the cornfields who, like the Bacabs, are gods of the cardinal points. Kan Xib Chac is that of the South. Yucatan, Mexico. (Tozzer, 1941: 112, 137–138; Nicholson, 1967: 119)

Chac Xib Chac A god of the East and associated with the color red. The Mayan, Mexico. (Tozzer, 1941: 138; Redfield and Rojas, 1962: 115; Vasquez and Morley, 1949: 35)

Ch'a-'lha The god and protector of the west quarter. Tibet. (Waddell, 1959: 367)

Chekesuwand The "Western God." The Narragansett, Rhode Island. (Skinner, 1913: 91)

Cheng Wu Guardian of the North who lives at the Pole. China. (Leach, 1949: 214)

Chên Wu, Chen Wu Ta Ti The god of the North, of the North Pole, and the "ruler of the abode of darkness." China. (Ferguson, 1937: 111; Burgess, 1928: 180)

Ch'ih Kuo, Ch'i-kuo The guardian of the East is also the god of summer. China. (Getty, 1962: 167; Werner, 1932: 454; Cammann, 1937: 180–181)

Ch'i-ti God of the southern quarter of the sky. China. (Maspero, 1963: 339)

Chohyung God of the South and the god of the element fire. China. (Du Bose, n.d.: 72, 327)

Chong Je The Blue King of the East is one of the Five Guardians (O Bang Jang Kun) who are very important in protecting the shamans from evil spirits emanating from their several directions. Korea. (Moes, 1983: 128)

Chu-dieu The "Spirit of the South." China. (Scott, 1964: 307)

Chu Fung "The God of the South Place" and the god of fire. China. (Werner, 1932: 450)

Chu Je The Red King of the South is protective of the shamans from evil spirits coming from this direction. Korea. (Moes, 1983: 128)

Chu Jung The god of the South and of summer. Also the god of fire. China. (Day, 1940: 66; Campbell, 1962: 396, 432)

Chung Kung T'u Huang "Yellow King of the Central Region, represented by earth." One of the directional spirits. China. (Day, 1940: 66)

Churiya The sun god of the Coorgs who is associated with the East. Southern India. (Srinivas, 1952: 79)

Cocijo The god of rain also presides over the cardinal points. The Zapotec, Oaxaca, Mexico. (Whitecotton, 1977: 159, 162)

Coha God of the seas and associated with the South. The Kekchis, British Honduras. (Thompson, 1930: 59)

Dai-itoku-Myoo A manifestation of Amida who is associated with the West and contends with illness, evil, and poisons. Japan. (Eliseev, 1963: 424; Larousse, 1968: 421)

Da Matutsi Sun initiate, spirit of the East. Northern Pomo, California. (Loeb, 1926, 2: 301)

Dauarani The goddess of the forest whose "serpent body lives in the southwest and her spirit in the southeast." The Winikina-Warao, Venezuela. (Wilbert, 1972, 2: 61)

Dehno Put, Dohno Put A benevolent deity of the East. The Bhils, India. (Naik, 1956: 182)

Dhritarashtra Buddhist guardian of the East. India, Tibet, and China. (Waddell, 1959: 84; Bhattacharji, 1970: 265; Getty, 1962: 166; Ions, 1967: 135; Edkins, 1880: 216)

Dis-a-sul The "demon of the four quarters. He lives in the east on Monday and Saturday, in the north on Tuesday and Wednesday, in the west on Friday and Sunday, in the south on Thursday. So it is not good to plow in those directions on these days. The south is unlucky." The Chamars, India. (Briggs, 1920: 158)

djabani A god or goddess of the lower world who is also one of the guardians of the East. The Navaho, Arizona and New Mexico. (Reichard, 1950: 383)

Djibuin ëam ën The ruler in the north, in Ralik-Ratak. The Marshall Islands, Micronesia. (Krämer and Nevermann, 1938: 238)

Don-yod grub-pa A celestial Buddha and god of the north quarter. Invoked to avert illness and danger. *Same as* **Amoghasiddhi**. Nepal and Tibet. (Snellgrove, 1961: 288; Francke, 1925, 8: 76; Nebesky-Wojkowitz, 1956, 1: 525; Waddell, 1959: 349)

rDo rje sems dpa' God of the East quarter invoked to avert illness and danger. Same as Vajrasattva. Tibet. (Francke, 1925, 8: 76; Nebesky-Wojkowitz, 1956, 1: 525; Getty, 1962: 5)

E One of the four Mams. He is usually of good omen. As a Yearbearer he ranks second to Quej, is associated with the South and the sacred mountain Tamanco. Momostenango, Guatemala. (Tedlock, 1982: 117, 99–100)

Ekel Bacab A Mayan god associated with the West, and whose color is black. Mexico. (Tozzer, 1941: 137)

Ek Pauah Tun A Mayan god associated with the West and the color black. Mexico. (Tozzer, 1941: 137)

Ek u Uayeyab A god associated with the West and the New Year rituals, and the color black. The Mayan, Mexico. (Tozzer, 1941: 137, 139)

Ek Xib Chac A Mayan god associated with the West and with the color black. Mexico. (Tozzer, 1941: 137; Redfield and Rojas, 1962: 115)

Epingishmook The West. Father of Nanabush by Winonah, a human, who died. To avenge his mother Nanabush fought Epingishmook to a draw, neither could win. They made peace and Nanabush was given the Pipe of Peace to take to the people. Father also of Mudjeekawis, Papeekawis, Chibiabos. The Ojibway, Minnesota and Manitoba. (Johnston, 1976: 17–19, 150–151)

Esseneta'he God of the Southeast who is also a god of "life and light." The Cheyenne, Minnesota, North and South Dakota, Montana, and Colorado. (Powell, 1969: 436)

Estsanatlehi, 'asdzá· nádle·hé, asdzáán nádleehe
Changing Woman. She is associated with the West where she was assigned to live with powers over the rain and growth of vegetation, over reproduction and birth, and the capacity to rejuvenate herself. Wife of the Sun. The Navajo, Arizona and New Mexico. (McNeley, 1981: 24–26; Reichard, 1950: 410–413; Matthews, 1890: 89, 95; 1902: 31, 32; Babington, 1950: 210–212)

Etokah-Wechastah God of the South represented as the rain-storm, and the giver of "melons, maize, and tobacco." In the area of Fort Snelling he is also god of the summer whose group is stronger and wins in contests with the Beings of the North. Minnesota, North Dakota, and South Dakota. (Schoolcraft, 1857, 1: 319; 1857, 4: 496; Emerson, 1884: 27; Eastman, 1962: 208)

Eya The courageous god of the West (the first direction), of the west wind, is associated with Autumn. He is the second son of Tate, the Wind. Eya is the companion of the Winged God, Wakinyan, the thunder being who brings the rain. Eya's bird messenger is the swallow whose forked tail symbolizes the lightning. His color is yellow, ritual color black. As Wakinyan's assistant Eya "is disorderly, but capable of creating order out of chaos, cleanliness out of filth, through the process of change." The Oglala, South Dakota. (Powers, 1977: 72, 75, 76, 79, 192)

mGar-mkhan-A-nag A cardinal deity of the north who appears in wedding songs with "gifts of the colors and of salt." Tibet. (Francke, 1923: 12)

giladuk, Elagwingilak The West, sometimes personified. The Penobscot, Maine. (Speck, 1935: 21)

Betara Goeroe A deity invoked in rituals. A prayer addressed to him "mentions the metals belonging to the five directions: silver (white) to the east; copper (red) to the south; gold (yellow) to the west; iron (black) to the north; and an alloy (that used for gongs) . . . in the center." Bali, Indonesia. (Belo, 1953: 26–27)

Gozanze-Myoo A god of the East, "the terrible manifestation of Ashuku" (Akshobhya). Japan. (Eliseev, 1963: 428; Larousse, 1968: 421)

Guksu As a deity of the cardinal points he is a god of the south. He also possesses healing powers, is usually good-natured. The Pomo, California. (Gifford, 1926: 353; Barrett, 1917: 423–424; Kroeber, 1925: 261–263)

brGya-byin God and protector of the east quarter. Tibet. (Waddell, 1959: 367)

rGyal-rjes-dkar-po A cardinal deity of the north who appears in wedding songs with "gifts of the colors and of salt." Tibet. (Francke, 1923: 12)

Hamsika Daughter of Surabhi. With sisters Surupa, Subhadra, and Sarvakamadugha "support the east, south, west, and north corners of the heavens." India. (Keith, 1917: 134)

Hanami, Hami God of the East and of a white color. The Sia, New Mexico. (Fewkes, 1895, 2: 126)

Hang Phan The snake-headed god of the West, one of those who determine the destinies of men. Tibet. (Nebesky-Wojkowitz, 1956, 2: 51)

Hapi The baboon-headed god of the cardinal point of the North. Son of Horus, and one of the gods of the Canopic Jars. Egypt. (Knight, 1915: 34)

Hapto-iringa The constellation of Ursa Major is the guardian of the North. He is invoked to "oppose wizards and witches." Iran. (Gray, 1930: 149; Jackson, 1925, 12: 86)

Hastséhogan, haashch'éóghaan Calling God, also called House God. God of the West and of the sunset where he placed the light phenomenon of Evening Twilight, and where he exists. He is also the inner form of San Francisco Peak. He is benevolent and friendly toward mankind; with Talking God, Hastseyalti, directing and guiding human life. The Navajo, Arizona and New Mexico. *See also* **xa·ctčé·'oɣan, xashshe'oghan.** (McNeley, 1981: 9, 19, 20, 21; Matthews, 1902: 10–11; Babington, 1950: 217; Alexander, 1964: 156)

Hastseyalti, haashch'eełt'i, xa·ctce·ltihi Talking God. God of the East, the inner form of the Dawn, where he exists. He is associated with Blanca Peak, is a benevolent god of hunting. With Hastsehogan guides and directs human life. The Navajo, Arizona and New Mexico. See also xashchelthi'i. (McNeley, 1981: 9–12, 21; Matthews, 1902: 9, 11; Babington, 1950: 218–219; Alexander, 1964: 156; Waters, 1950: 234)

hayoołkáál asdáá, xayołká·l 'eszá Dawn Woman, one of the Holy People involved in the creation, is considered to be in the North; is one of those who cause people to think. Some say she "determines which Wind Soul shall enter the child to be born" and that they report to her on their lives. The Navajo, Arizona. (McNeley, 1981: 4, 22, 29, 81)

hayoo łkaał hastiin, xayołka·l xast^xi·n Dawn Man in the cardinal point of the East is one of those who causes people to think; is one of the Holy People involved in the creation of Earth, Sky, Sun, Moon, and various animals. The Navajo, Arizona. (McNeley, 1981: 22, 29)

Heiséi The Master of sickness and of death is associated with the west. The Cagaba and the Kogi, Colombia. (Reichel-Dolmatoff, 1949/50: 89, 90, 142)

Herit A goddess of the North. Egypt. (Budge, 1969, 1: 202)

Hobnil The Bacab of the East and the chief god of apiculture. The Mayan, Mexico. (Thompson, 1970: 276–277; Bancroft, 1886, 2: 699; Tozzer, 1941: 157)

Hoim'aha The Man from the North brings the cold and snow, storms, the winter, as well as sickness and death. He is controlled by the Woman in the North and is engaged in a seasonal struggle with Thunder who comes from the South. The Cheyenne, Minnesota to the Rocky Mountains. (Grinnell, 1972: 94–95, 338–339)

ho shin East—of the cardinal points which are offered sacrifices for longevity and security of homes from the winds. They are benevolent and friendly but still must be propitiated. The Cheyenne, Minnestoa to the Rockies. (Grinnell, 1972: 90, 133)

Hozan Ek The Bacab of the south quarter who is invoked in the New Year ritual of the Cauac years. The Mayan, Mexico. (Thompson, 1970: 276; Tozzer, 1941: 148)

Hsüan Ming God of the element Water, the Han period, and associated with the North. China. (Campbell, 1962: 432)

Huang Lang T'ai Hsüan The "majestic god of the eight directions cause me to be . . . unmolested." (Incantation to purify the house after a death during the month.) The Ch'uan Miao, Yunnan Province, China. (Graham, 1937: 96)

Huitzilopochtli The blue Tezcatlipoca. As one of the sons of Ometéotl and one of the four primary forces responsible for the formation of realities and for bringing space and time into the world he is associated with the South. He is the patron god of the Aztecs. Mexico. (León-Portilla, 1982: 33–35; Vaillant, 1962: 143; Alexander, 1920: 57; Burland, 1967: ix)

Hunaunic The Lacandon "god in the east" and the leader of the wind gods. The Mayan, Mexico. (Thompson, 1970: 271)

hun so wun South—of the cardinal points. They are offered sacrifices for longevity and security of homes from the winds. They must be propitiated though they are benevolent and friendly. The Cheyenne, Minnesota through Montana. (Grinnell, 1972: 90, 133)

Hutukau "Wind-Ready-to-Give." A god located in the north who gave the Skidi Pawnee buffalo. Nebraska. (Dorsey, 1904, 2: 19, 20)

Hututu A god of the south and the rain god of that quarter. The Zuñi, New Mexico. (Waters, 1950: 284; Wilson, 1958: 374)

Huyen-vu The guardian of the northern heavens. His emblems, the serpent and the tortoise. China. (Scott, 1964: 306)

Hwang Je The Yellow King of the Center is one of the O Bang Jang Kun who are very important guardians of the shamans protecting them from evil spirits emanating from the five directions. Korea. (Moes, 1983: 128)

Hyon Je The Black King of the North is a very important guardian of the shamans from evil spirits threatening from this direction. Korea. (Moes, 1983: 128)

Ik' The fourth of the Mams, Yearbearers, is received on the sacred mountain, Socop, the mountain of the West. This Mam is dangerous, bringing violent weather and disasters, instigating strong, negative emotions to cause disruption, is greatly associated with death. Momostenango, Guatemala. (Tedlock, 1982: 99, 100, 126–127)

Indra The god of the atmosphere and the weather was the guardian of the eastern quarter of the compass. India and Mongolia. (Dubois, 1906: 633; Banerjea, 1953: 73; Ions, 1967: 73; Bhattacharji, 1970: 264; Danielou, 1964: 130; Percheron, 1953: 62)

Inkfwin-wetay The creator god and god of the Zenith. British Columbia. (Pettazzoni, 1956: 396)

Irodjerilik, Iroijdrilik, Irjojrilik God of the cardinal point of the west who is responsible for the increase of all living things, and "the ruler of the souls of good persons after their death" in a pleasant afterworld. The Marshall Islands, Micronesia. (Kramer and Nevermann, 1938: 238; Knappe, 1888: 66–67; Leach, 1950: 720; Davenport, 1953: 221–222)

Isa A goddess associated with the Northeast. Mongolia. (Percheron, 1953: 63)

Isana An aspect of Siva. The guardian of the Northeast quarter. India. (Banerjea, 1953: 73; Dubois, 1906: 633; Danielou, 1964: 131; Ghurye, 1962: 13)

Isora, Sora One of the gods of the cardinal points. He created the fruits. Bali, Indonesia. (Covarrubias, 1937: 289, 317)

Isvara, Iswara A god associated with the center of the cardinal points. (Hooykaas, 1964: 28). The god of the East of the cardinal points. (Covarrubias, 1937: 296; Grader, 1960: 183). Bali, Indonesia.

Itokaga-micaxta "Man of the South." The Dakotah, Fort Snelling, Minnesota area. (Eastman, 1962: xxxi)

Itubore The culture hero/god who rules in the East. The Bororo, Brazil. (Levi-Strauss, 1969: 37)

Itzam The "ruler of the warm country and rules over the East . . . claimed to be both male and female. As a woman . . . the wife of Coha." The Kekchi, British Honduras. (Thompson, 1930: 59)

Iu-na-wi-ko "The Wolf-Hunter God of the East." The Zuñi, New Mexico. (Cushing, 1881/82: 28)

Iya (1) Second son of Tate, the Wind. He demanded to look at Wakinyan "and the sight causes him to become a heyoka, a 'contrary,' who does and sees everything in reverse, because this is the only way to approach the creative force. Thus Iya gains the right to establish himself in the first direction"—God of the West and west wind. The Lakota, South Dakota. (Jahner, 1977: 35) (2) An evil god of the Oglala who is "associated with the cold of the north. During the winter he consumes people," but is overcome by fire who causes him to regurgitate them. South Dakota. (Powers, 1977: 54–55)

aJam-dpal A cardinal deity of the south who appears in wedding songs and gives grain, great wealth. Tibet. (Francke, 1923: 12)

Ja-mi-zan The guardian of the West. Tibet. (Waddell, 1959: 84)

Je-mi-zang The guardian of the West and "King of the Nagas . . . who guard the Universe and heavens against the outer demons." Sikkim. (Gazeteer of Sikhim, 1894: 261)

Jikoku, Dhritarashtra Guardian deity of the East. Japan. (Eliot, 1935: 135; Getty, 1962: 168; Eliseev, 1963: 447; Zimmer, 1955: 47; Werner, 1932: 457)

Ju Shou The god of the West. China. (Day, 1940: 66; Campbell, 1962: 432; Werner, 1932: 566)

Ka'a djaj God of the East. Coast Central Pomo, California. (Loeb, 1926, 2: 301)

Kai-matutsi As a deity of the cardinal points "earth-occupation" is associated with the nadir. The Pomo, California. (Barrett, 1917: 424)

Kakan Wolf god of the East. The Sia, New Mexico. (Fewkes, 1895, 2: 127)

Kali-matutsi As a deity of the cardinal points "sky-occupation" is associated with the zenith. The Pomo, California. (Barrett, 1917: 424)

Kamaits An old woman who lived in the highest (fifth) realm (Atsaaktl), in the east. The Bella Coola, British Columbia. (Swanton, 1925, 11: 98)

Ka matutsi Water initiate, spirit of the West. Northern Pomo, California. (Loeb, 1926, 2: 301)

Kan The Mayan god of maize is a deity of the compass points and also one of the gods of the New Year. Mexico. (Nicholson, 1967: 44, 119)

Kanal Acantun A Mayan god associated with the South and the color yellow, and is propitiated in the festivals of the unlucky days in the Kan years. Mexico. (Tozzer, 1941: 137, 139)

Kanal Bacab A Bacab god associated with the South. The Mayan, Mexico. (Tozzer, 1941: 137)

Ix Kanleox A Mayan goddess associated with the South. Mexico. (Tozzer, 1941: 137)

Kan Pauah Tun A Mayan god associated with the East and "identified with the gods of rain, hence of fertility and of the four winds." Mexico. (Tozzer, 1941: 137)

Kan u Uayeyab A Mayan god associated with the East and invoked in the rituals of the unlucky days in the Kan years. Mexico. (Tozzer, 1941: 137, 139)

Kan Xib Chac A Mayan god associated with the East and the color yellow. Mexico. (Tozzer, 1941: 137; Redfield and Rojas, 1962: 115)

Karoshimo The Toad god is generally beneficent giving fertility, longevity, health, etc. in exchange for tobacco smoke. He "inhabits the world mountain of the south." The Warao, Venezuela. (Wilbert, 1972, 2: 61; 1973, 1: 3, 4)

Kashinako "White Woman of the East," goddess of the six world-quarters. The Sia, New Mexico. (Fewkes, 1895, 2: 127)

Kaspanna Serpent god of the West. The Sia, New Mexico. (Fewkes, 1895, 2: 126)

Kato'ya The Black Snake god, guardian "of the west and night." The Hopi, Arizona. (Waters, 1963: 50)

Keewatin The deity of the North quarter. The Ojibway, Minnesota and Manitoba. (Johnston, 1976: 27)

Kesuhum Kidul "(Brahma), the patron of the South." Bali, Indonesia. (Covarrubias, 1937: 70)

Keu Mung God of the compass point of the East. China. (Du Bose, n.d.: 327)

Kewadin The god of the North and of the weather who furnished them with rabbits and partridges for food in winter. The Ojibwa, Minnesota. (Coleman, 1937: 37)

khaengy The mountain-lion divinity of the north—a very powerful medicine animal. The Tewa, New Mexico. (Harrington, 1907/08: 43)

'Khor nag can A malevolent god who resides in the East. Tibet. (Nebesky-Wojkowitz, 1956, 1: 292)

Khra-gsas Falcon Prince, one of the "divinities of the four quarters." Nepal. (Snellgrove, 1961: 122, 286)

Khunpinuanyun Red corn maiden of the south. The Tewa, New Mexico. (Harrington, 1907/08: 43)

Khva ta'i gdong pa can A crow-headed Bon deity associated with the West. Tibet. (Nebesky-Wojkowitz, 1956, 1: 47)

Khyi'i gdong pa can A dog-headed Bon deity associated with the Southwest. Tibet. (Nebesky-Wojkowitz, 1956, 1: 47)

Khyung gi gdong pa can A *khyung*-headed Bon deity associated with the North. Tibet. (Nebesky-Wojkowitz, 1956, 1: 47)

The k'obictaiya "Spirits who live in the east, . . . very powerful and beneficent." The Acoma, New Mexico. (White, 1929/30: 65)

K'obishtaiya A ferocious kachina created by Iyatiku who lives in the east and "rules the clouds of winter." The Keresen, New Mexico. (Parsons, 1939: 246)

Kochinako "Yellow Woman of the North," a goddess of the six world-quarters. The Sia, New Mexico. (Fewkes, 1895, 2: 127)

Kohai Bear god of the West. The Sia, New Mexico. (Fewkes, 1895, 2: 127)

Komoku Given as the guardian deity of the South (Eliot, 1935: 135; Getty, 1962: 168; Werner, 1932: 457) and also as guardian deity of the West. (Zimmer, 1955: 47; Eliseev, 1963: 447; Larousse, 1968: 422) Japan.

Kongo-yasha-Myoo Guardian deity of the North. "One of the five great myoo: the terrible manifestation of the Bodhisattva Fuku (Amoghavajra)." Japan. (Eliseev, 1963: 436; Larousse, 1968: 421)

Koquira Serpent god of the South. The Sia, New Mexico. (Fewkes, 1895, 2: 126)

Kou Mang The god of the East. China. (Day, 1940: 66; Campbell, 1962: 432)

Kovero, Peysrap (Kuvera, Vaisravana) Guardian deity of the north region. Cambodia. (Marchal, 1963: 203)

Kowa, Kowami God of the South and of the color red. The Sia, New Mexico. (Fewkes, 1895, 2: 126)

Kuang Mu Guardian of the West. *Same as* **Virupaksha.** China. (Cammann, 1937: 181; Werner, 1932: 454)

Kubera *See* **Kuvera**

Kuksu, Guksu God of the South. The Pomo, California. (Kroeber, 1925: 379; Loeb, 1931: 525)

Kule A goddess associated with the Southeast. Tibet. (Nebesky-Wojkowitz, 1956, 1: 45)

Kurkanninako "Red Woman of the South," a goddess of the six world-quarters. The Sia, New Mexico (Fewkes, 1895, 2: 127)

Kurukulle A goddess associated with the Southwest. Tibet. (Nebesky-Wojkowitz, 1956, 1: 45)

Kuvera, Kubera The god of wealth and of treasures was the guardian of the North. India and Mongolia. (Bhattacharji, 1970: 185–186; Getty, 1962: 156–159; Hackin, 1963, 2: 169; Banerjea, 1953: 73; Ions, 1967: 135; Danielou, 1964: 130; Dubois, 1906: 633; Percheron, 1953: 62)

Kwang-mu Guardian of the West who symbolizes winter. China. (Getty, 1962: 167)

Kwera One of the gods of the cardinal points. Bali, Indonesia. (Covarrubias, 1937: 317)

mKyen-rab The founder of the Bon religion as a cardinal god of the west appears in wedding songs, gives medicines, astronomy. Tibet. (Francke, 1923: 12)

Lakin Chan God K—"serpent of the east, and was said to have been the creator of men and of all organic life and to have founded the Maya culture. He invented writing and books, had a knowledge of herbs and healing." Mexico. (Nicholson, 1967: 127)

Lalikian, Lajbuineamuen The god of the cardinal point of the north. Marshall Islands (Ralik Group), Micronesia. (Leach, 1950, 2: 720)

Larunaen A god of the west who created the earth and provides man with all his needs. He also causes earthquakes. His sister/wife is Hintabaran. New Ireland, Melanesia. (Cox, 1913: 195–196)

Lojibwineamen The god in the north is the cause of all death. The Marshall Islands, Micronesia. (Davenport, 1953: 22102)

Lokomran, Locumran, Lakameran The ruler in the east, the "Daymaker." The Marshall Islands, Micronesia. (Krämer and Nevermann, 1938: 238; Erdland, 1914: 308; Davenport, 1953: 221; Leach, 1950: 720)

Lorok The "man in the south." Has charge of the winds. The Marshall Islands, Micronesia. (Davenport, 1953: 221–222; Leach, 1950, 2: 720)

Ludra One of the gods of the cardinal points. Bali, Indonesia. (Covarrubias, 1937: 317)

rLun-lha God and protector of the Northwest. *Same as* **Marut,** the storm god. Tibet. (Waddell, 1959: 367)

Maati The goddess Maat "in her dual form of Maati . . . the Maat goddess of the South and the North." Egypt. (Budge, 1969, 1: 418)

Magbabáya imbatu The spirit of the cardinal point of the east. The Bukidnon, Mindanao, Philippines. (Cole, 1956: 94)

Magbabáya Lindon̄-an The cardinal spirit of the west—"where the sun hides." The Bukidnon, Mindanao, Philippines. (Cole, 1956: 94)

Magbabáya Pagosan The cardinal spirit of the south—"whence the waters come." The Bukidnon, Mindanao, Philippines. (Cole, 1956: 94)

Magbabáya Tipónan Cardinal spirit of the north "where the waters unite, i.e., the ocean." The Bukidnon, Mindanao, Philippines. (Cole, 1956: 94)

Mahadewa The god of the West and associated with the color yellow. The supreme deity. Bali, Indonesia. (Goris, 1960: 123; 1969: 92; Grader, 1960: 183; Hooykaas, 1964: 28; Covarrubias, 1937: 296)

Maheswara The god of the Southeast, an aspect of Siva. Bali, Indonesia. (Grader, 1960: 183; Swellengrebel, 1960: 45; Covarrubias, 1937: 296; Hooykaas, 1964: 52)

Manabozho The god of the East and of the dawn, a god of light and of the winds, with aspects of a culture hero. The Ojibwa (Minnesota), the Winnebagoe (Wisconsin). (Radin and Reagan, 1928: 70, 84; Emerson, 1884: 8, 28, 337; Cohane, 1969: 145)

Manito Wabos The rabbit god who dwells in the East and is the god of light, of the dawn. The Cherokee, Carolinas. (Spence, 1925, 3: 503–504)

Mar-tu "(Lit., 'the west god'), which is a designation of Ramman." Babylonia, Near East. (Jastrow, 1898: 166)

Masichu'a The Gray Horned Snake god, the guardian of the North. The Hopi, Arizona. (Waters, 1963: 50)

Maui In the Hervey Islands Maui is the son of the god Ru. They raised the sky and stationed themselves, Maui as the god of the north and Ru as the god of the south. Polynesia. (Mackenzie, n.d.: 215–216)

Me-gsas Fire Prince, one of the gods of the four quarters. Nepal. (Snellgrove, 1961: 122, 286)

Me-lha The god and protector of the Southeast is also the god of fire. Tibet. (Waddell, 1959: 367; Schlagintweit, 1969: 207)

Menengwa The South who is represented as a butterfly. The Winnebagoe, Wisconsin. (Emerson, 1884: 8)

Merrinako "Blue Woman of the West," a goddess of the six world-quarters. The Sia, New Mexico. (Fewkes, 1895, 2: 127)

Mestha The god of the South. He is one of the sons of Horus and a god of the Canopic Jars. Also called Amset. Egypt. (Knight, 1915: 35; Budge, 1969, 1: 492)

Metzabok, Mensabok A god identified with the west. He is a god of fresh waters and rain, and the Tsinqu (spirits of the west) are his servants. The Lacandon, Mexico. (Cline, 1944: 112)

Mfam One of the gods of the four quarters. The Ekoi, Nigeria. (Jeffreys, 1939: 99)

Mfuor One of the gods of the four quarters. The Ekoi, Nigeria. (Jeffreys, 1939: 99)

Mictlantecutli The god of the dead and of the underworld presided over the north zone of the universe, though he was sometimes associated with the south. The Aztec, Mexico. (Vaillant, 1962: 140, 147; Alexander, 1920: 54, 57; Burland, 1967: ix)

Mingabion God of the south and of the south wind. The Ojibwa, Minnesota. (Coleman, 1937: 37)

Mixcoatl The Cloud snake god was in control of the east zone of the universe along with Tlaloc. A region of abundance. The Aztec, Mexico. (Vaillant, 1962: 140, 150)

Moho-Koko-Ko-ho A god represented as an owl "ruled in the north." The Winnebagoe, Wisconsin. (Emerson, 1884: 8)

Mo-li Ch'ing Guardian of the East. Same as Dhrtarastra. He is the eldest of the Four Heavenly Kings (his face is white), the Land-bearer, has a "magic sword, Blue Cloud," with which he protects the world from attacks by evil spirits. China. (Williams, 1976: 195)

Mo-li Hai Guardian of the West. Same as Virupaksha. "The Far-Gazer." He is one of the Four Heavenly Kings, has a "blue face and carries a four-stringed guitar at the sound of which all the world listens and the camps of his enemies take fire." China. (Williams, 1976: 197)

Mo-li Hung Guardian of the South. Same as Virudhaka. The Lord of Growth—has a red face and holds "the Umbrella of Chaos, formed of pearls possessed of spiritual properties." When elevated "universal darkness ensues and when it is reversed violent thunderstorms and earthquakes are produced." One of the Four Heavenly Kings. China. (Williams, 1976: 197)

Mo-li Shou Guardian of the North. Same as Vaisravana. One of the Four Heavenly Kings—has a black face, and controls various creatures which, when at large, devour men. China. (Williams, 1976: 197)

Moxhomsa Eliosigak "Grandfather at the West"
Moxhomsa Lowaneyung "Grandfather at the North"
Moxhomsa Wahanjiopung "Grandfather at the East"
All prayed to "when gathering herbs or preparing medicines, at the same time offering tobacco." The Lenape, Delaware, New Jersey, and New York. (Harrington, 1921: 26)

Munainako "Dark Woman of the Nadir," a goddess of the six world-quarters. The Sia, New Mexico. (Fewkes, 1895, 2: 127)

Nadikiawasin The god of the west and the west wind, the youngest and most powerful of the winds. The Ojibwa, Minnesota. (Coleman, 1937: 37–38)

Neiruta A deity associated with the Southwest. India. (Dubois, 1906: 633)

Neith A goddess of the West. Believed of Libyan origin. Egypt. (Knight, 1915: 76; Budge, 1969, 1: 450; 1969, 2: 275)

Nekhebet A vulture goddess of the South and the personification of growth. Egypt. (Knight, 1915: 79; Budge, 1969, 1: 438–440; Gardiner, 1925, 9: 791)

Nibora Goddess of the extreme south who is called "the powerful" though she is no match for those of the other directions and her spear throwing (in the fights) is weak and her winds blow "only briefly and weakly." Truk, Micronesia. (Bollig, 1927: 5)

Ningobianong "(Evening or West)." Represents old age and wisdom, moderation and patience, fortitude. The tutor of Waubun. The Ojibway, Minnesota and Manitoba. (Johnston, 1976: 28, 163)

Nirriti Goddess of the underworld and guardian of the Southwest quarter. India. (Bhattacharji, 1970: 8, 81–82; Banerjea, 1953: 73)

Nocturnus An Etruscan god identified with the North. Italy. (Dumézil, 1966, 2: 688; Weinstock, 1946: 104)

gNod sbyin bya rog gdong can A raven-headed god associated with the West. Tibet. (Nebesky-Wojkowitz, 1956, 1: 48)

No'j The third of the four Mams, Yearbearers, is received on the sacred mountain Joyan in the south/southwest, is associated with creativity, whether for good or for evil. Momostenango, Guatemala. (Tedlock, 1982: 99, 100, 122)

Notamota The god of the Northeast who symbolizes storms, cold weather, disease, and death. The Cheyenne, Colorado, Montana, North and South Dakota, and Minnesota. (Powell, 1969: 436)

Notasqa-vairgin God of the nadir, the "earth-being." The Chukchee, Siberia. (Bogaras, 1904/09: 305)

notum North—of the cardinal points. Sacrifices are made to the four directions, with whom the winds are associated, for longevity, for protection of their lodges from the winds. Though the cardinal points are benevolent and friendly they must be propitiated. The Cheyenne, Minnesota, North and South Dakota, Montana, and Colorado. (Grinnell, 1972: 90, 133)

Nuikukui The Master of the East is also the "sun at mid-day." The Cagaba, Colombia. (Reichel-Dolmatoff, 1949/50: 142; Preuss, 1926: 76)

The O Bang Jang Kun The Five Guardians who are "the most important Shamanist guardians. They protect from evil spirits emanating from the five directions.

Chong Je—the Blue King—East
Piak Je—the White King—West
Chu Je—the Red King—South
Hyon Je—the Black King—North
Hwang Je—the Yellow King—Center.
Korea. (Moes, 1983: 128)

Ofiri   One of the gods of the four quarters. The Ekoi, Nigeria. (Jeffreys, 1939: 99)

Okaga, Itokaga   God of the South, the South Wind, is the fourth son of Tate, the Wind God. He presides over pleasant weather, as the "giver of life" provides fruits, grains, flowers. "His spirit is in the smoke of the sweetgrass." He is benevolent, needs no invocation, is beloved by Wohpe (Woope). The Lakota, South Dakota. (Walker, 1980: 72, 121, 127, 197, 221; Jahner, 1977: 35)

Onxsovon   God of the Northwest. The Cheyenne, Minnesota, North and South Dakota, Montana, and Colorado. (Powell, 1969: 436)

Oriwakarotu   As a god of the Cardinal Points "the God of Dance," is associated with "the point of midwinter sunset in the northwest." The Winikina-Warao, Venezuela. (Wilbert, 1973, 1: 6)

Padma 'jigs byed   A god associated with the West. Tibet. (Nebesky-Wojkowitz, 1956, 1: 45)

Paik Je   The White King of the West protects the shaman from evil spirits threatening from that direction. Korea. (Moes, 1983: 128)

Palöngawhoya   A god created by Kokyangquti to help maintain order in the world, and to make sound. He was sent to the south pole for proper rotation of the earth, and to maintain the movement of air. The Hopi, Arizona. (Waters, 1963: 5)

The Pauahs   Gods of rain and of wind, each of whom is associated with a cardinal point and a color: Kan Pauah Tun with the East and identified with Saint Dominic; Ix Kanleox, XKanLe Ox with the South and identified with Mary Magdalene; Ek Pauah Tun with the West, the color Black and identified with Saint James; Sac Pauah Tun with the North, the color White and identified with Saint Gabriel. They are similar to the Chacs, the Bacabs. The Mayan, Mexico. (Tozzer, 1941: 137; Thompson, 1970: 255)

p'bunki   The North, the "winter land," sometimes personified. The Penobscot, Maine. (Speck, 1935: 21)

Phag gi gdong pa can   A pig-headed Bon deity associated with the southeast. Tibet. (Nebesky-Wojkowitz, 1956, 1: 47)

Phag-kye-po   The guardian of the South, of the Universe, against outer demons. Sikkim. (Gazeteer of Sikhim, 1894: 261)

'Phrog 'chang ma   A goddess associated with the Northeast. Tibet. (Nebesky-Wojkowitz, 1956, 1: 45)

Phur 'debs ma   A protective goddess associated with the Northwest. Tibet. (Nebesky-Wojkowitz, 1956, 1: 17, 45)

Pona, Ponami   A god of the West, associated with the color blue. The Sia, New Mexico. (Fewkes, 1895, 2: 126)

Pöqánghoya   Twin of Palöngawhoya. Created by Kokyangquti to maintain order in the world; sent to the north pole for proper rotation of the earth and to maintain its stability. The Hopi, Arizona. (Waters, 1963: 5)

Purbia nad   The "spirit of the East . . . believed to keep watch over the threshing floors." Another name for Barnda. The Oraon, India. (Roy, 1928: 72)

sPyang ki'i gdong pa can   A wolf-headed Bon deity associated with the Northwest. Tibet. (Nebesky-Wojkowitz, 1956, 1: 47)

Quej   The most important of the Mams, Yearbearers, is received on the sacred mountain Quilaja, the mountain of the East. He is wild, domineering, strong—many rituals are performed. Momostenango, Guatemala. (Tedlock, 1982: 99, 100, 113, 114, 154)

Quetzalcóatl   In very early Nahuatl conceptions of the universe Quetzalcóatl was the third son of Ometéotl and became identified with "night and wind, with the West, region of fecundity and life." From Teotihuacán times, among the Aztecs, he was associated with the planet Venus and therefore with both East and West as the Morning and Evening Stars. Mexico. (León-Portilla, 1982: 33–35; Vaillant, 1962: 143; Burland, 1967: x, 66; Nicholson, 1967: 45; Caso, 1958: 23–26)

Quissera   Serpent god of the East. The Sia, New Mexico. (Fewkes, 1895, 2: 126)

Quisserrinkao   "Slightly Yellow Woman of the Zenith," a goddess of the six world-quarters. The Sia, New Mexico. (Fewkes, 1895, 2: 127)

Ral gri 'jigs byed   A god associated with the North. Tibet. (Nebesky-Wojkowitz, 1956, 1: 45)

Ratnasambhava   The celestial Buddha of the South. India, Tibet, and Mongolia. (Waddell, 1959: 350; Snellgrove, 1957: 66–67; Percheron, 1953: 261; Larousse, 1968: 357)

Rerek, Lorok   The ruler in the south. The Marshall Islands, Micronesia. (Krämer and Nevermann, 1938: 238; Erdland, 1914: 308)

Rin chen 'byung ldan   A god of the four quarters—the South. Tibet. (Francke, 1925, 8: 76)

Rono   The god of the East is a god of medicine and of wisdom. Hawaii. (Melville, 1969: 25, 28, 34)

Ru   The god who raised the sky and "who divided the earth in east, west, south, and north." Society Islands. (Henry, 1928: 407, 459) In the Hervey Islands in one myth he is the god of the south and Maui of the north where they stationed themselves and gradually raised the sky. Polynesia. (Mackenzie, n.d.: 215–216)

Rudra   The god and guardian of the Southwest. Bali, Indonesia. (Grader, 1960: 183; Convarrubias, 1937: 296; Hooykaas, 1964: 52)

Sac Acantun   A Mayan god associated with the north and the color white who is propitiated in the rituals of the unlucky days in the Ix years. Mexico. (Tozzer, 1941: 137, 146)

Sacal Bacab   A Mayan god associated with the north and the color white. Mexico. (Tozzer, 1941: 137)

Sac cimi   A Bacab god associated with the north and the color white. "One of the calamities of the year in which this Bacab rules was swooning." The Mayan, Mexico. (Tozzer, 1941: 137–138)

Sac Pauah Tun   A Mayan god associated with the north and the color white, identified with Saint Gabriel. Mexico. (Tozzer, 1941: 137; Thompson, 1970: 255)

Sac u Uayeyab   A Mayan god associated with the north and the color white who is invoked in the rituals of the unlucky days (before New Years) in the Ix years. Mexico. (Tozzer, 1941: 137, 145)

Sac Xib Chac   A Mayan god associated with the north and the color white. Mexico. (Tozzer, 1941: 137)

Sa-gon-bdag-po   A god of the cardinal points, the east, who appears in wedding songs as the giver of sun, moon, and stars. Tibet. (Francke, 1923: 12)

The Salimobia   The "War Brothers of the Directions, zenith and nadir." The Zuñi, New Mexico. (Waters, 1950: 284)

Samanqinqu   The Lacandon god of the North. Mexico. (Cline, 1944: 112)

Sambu, Sanbhu   God and guardian of the Northeast. He created the flowers. Bali, Indonesia. (Grader, 1960: 183; Hooykaas, 1964: 53; Covarrubias, 1937: 289, 296, 317)

Sang Boeta Kala Djanggitan   The demon of the south, of the day paing, of the numbers 9, 90, 900, the color red. His god is Brahma. Bali, Indonesia. (Belo, 1953: 27)

Sang Boeta Kala Pasah   The demon of the west, of the day pon, of the numbers 7, 70, 700, the color yellow. His god is Mahadewa. Bali, Indonesia. (Belo, 1953: 27)

Sang Boeta Keroena   The demon of the east, the color white, of the day manie, the numbers 5, 50, 500. His god is Isoewara. Bali, Indonesia. (Belo, 1953: 27)

Sang Boeta Langkir   The demon of the north, of the day wage, the numbers 4, 40, 400, the color black. His god is Wisnoe. Bali, Indonesia. (Belo, 1953: 27)

Sang Boeta Tigasakti   The demon of the center, of the day klion, the numbers 8, 80, 800, the color—varicolored. His god is Siwa. Bali, Indonesia. (Belo, 1953: 27)

Sangkara   God and guardian deity of the Northwest. Bali, Indonesia. (Grader, 1960: 183; Covarrubias, 1937: 296)

Sariasap   A god "who lives in the North and is always angry with mankind." The Yami, Formosa. (Del Re, n.d.: 57)

Sarisano   A god of evil of the north who is propitiated because he sends diseases. Formosa. (Campbell, 1925, 6: 84)

Sarvakamdugha   A cow goddess who with her sisters Surupa, Hamsika, and Subhadra "support the east, south, west, and north corners of the heavens." India. (Keith, 1917: 134)

Sa Shin   "The Animals of the Four Directions" are guardians of palace gates, and are essential in the selection of tomb sites: the Blue Dragon of the East, the White Tiger of the West, the Red Bird of the South, the Black Tortoise of the North (entwined by a snake). Korea. (Moes, 1983: 113)

sawanaki The South (also noon) who is sometimes personified. The Penobscot, Maine. (Speck, 1935: 21)

Sa'yatasha The god of the north and the rain god of that quarter who is the bringer of long life. He is important in the Shalako ceremonial of the winter solstice. The Zuñi, New Mexico. (Waters, 1950: 283; Wilson, 1958: 374)

Seiobo Goddess of the West. Same as Si Wang Mu (China). Japan. (Mackenzie, 1924: 217)

Sept God of the East and also a god of battles and as such identified with Bes. Egypt. (Budge, 1969, 1: 446, 498)

Shakaka shiwana "Storm cloud or chief of the north." The Keresan, New Mexico. (Parsons, 1939: 410)

Sha-kya thub-po The Buddha appears as a god of the east in the wedding songs, as giver of the sun, the moon, and the stars. Tibet. (Francke, 1923: 12)

Shalnis A god who lived in the east and was "readily moved to anger." An associate of Kuksu (Guksu). The Pomo, California. (Kroeber, 1925: 261)

Shawano God of the South and also a god of winds. Algonquin Indians, Eastern United States. (Maclean, 1876: 432; Schoolcraft, 1857: 409; Brinton, 1882: 45)

Shi Wang Mu, Si wang mou A Taoist goddess of the West. China. (Richard, 1916: ii, 20; Chavannes, n.d.: 117)

gSin-rje The god and judge of the dead is the god and protector of the south quarter. Tibet. (Waddell, 1959: 367)

Siva, Siwa The patron god of Puseh, the center, of the candinal points. Bali, Indonesia. (Covarrubias, 1937: 290, 296; Hooykaas, 1964: 53)

Sma'aiyi 'i 'akiwi The Evening Star (Venus) is associated with the West. Ritual name is Hutash, the same as for Earth. Possibly the "wot" of the land of the dead, Shimilaqsha. The Chumash, California. (Hudson and Underhay, 1978: 80–83)

Souwwanand "The Southerne God." The Narragansett, Rhode Island. (Skinner, 1913: 91)

Sovota, Sovon God of the Southwest who controls the thunder and brings rain and warm weather. The Cheyenne, Colorado, Montana, North and South Dakota, and Minnesota. (Powell, 1969: 436)

So Wang-mo, Hsi Wang-mu (Chinese) "The Queen Mother of the West, head of the Taoist fairies (female Immortals)" whose messenger is the phoenix. It is in her orchard that the *Fairy Peach* grows—(the K'un Lun Mountains). She is a kind of "goddess of immortality." Korea. (Moes, 1983: 115, 120)

so wun West—of the cardinal points—from where the strong winds always come. Sacrifices are made to the four directions for longevity and the security of their lodges from the winds. They must be propitiated though they are friendly and benevolent. The Cheyenne, Minnesota, North and South Dakota, Montana, and Colorado. (Grinnell, 1972: 90, 94, 133)

Srin-po An evil spirit of Tibetan Buddhism, the god and protector of the Southwest. (Waddell, 1925: 636; 1959: 367)

Subhadra A daughter of Surabhi. With sisters Surupa, Hamsika, Sarvakamadugha, they "support the east, south, west, and north corners of the heavens." India. (Keith, 1917: 134)

Suh Seu A god of the compass—the West. China. (Du Bose n.d.: 327)

Sulak The condor is associated with the south. The Pomo, California. (Gifford, 1926: 353–354)

Surupa Daughter of Surabhi and sister of Hamsika, Subhadra, and Sarvakamadugha. They "support the east, south, west, and north corners of the heavens." India. (Keith, 1917: 134)

Su'u padax The whirlwind spirit is a god of the north. The Eastern Pomo, California. (Barrett, 1917: 424; Loeb, 1926, 2: 300)

sTag gi gdong pa can A tiger-headed Bon deity associated with the Northeast. Tibet. (Nebesky-Wojkowitz, 1956, 1: 47)

Tamagisanbach The chief god who governs the south. His wife is Taxankpada Agodales. Formosa. (Coleman, 1832: 342)

Tamagisangah, Tamagisangak A god who lived in the south and created mankind giving beauty or ugliness according to sacrifices. Formosa. (Del Re, n.d.: 57; Campbell, 1925, 6: 84)

Tamon, Bishamon The guardian god of the North. Japan. (Eliot, 1935: 135; Larousse, 1968: 422)

Tane The supreme being and creator was also the god of the West. Hawaii. (Melville, 1969: 14, 15, 25)

Tate Hautse Kupuri A serpent and water goddess "who brings the rain from the north" and "to whom belong the corn, squashes, beans, flowers, cattle, mules, horses, and sheep." The Huichol, Mexico. (Seler, 1925, 6: 829; Chamberlain, 1900: 306)

Tate Kyewimoka "Mother West-Water . . . to whom belong deer, corn, and the raven." She is a white serpent "who brings rain from the West." The Huichol, Mexico. (Seler, 1925, 6: 829; Chamberlain, 1900: 305–306)

Tate Naaliwami "Mother East-Water . . . to her belong cattle, mules, and horses." She is the red serpent of the rain from the east and wields the lightning. She is protective of children. The Huichol, Mexico. (Seler, 1925, 6: 829; Chamberlain, 1900: 305)

Tate Rapawiyema The blue serpent and water goddess of the south who owns the seed-corn and "brings the rain from the South." The Huichol, Mexico. (Seler, 1925, 6: 829; Chamberlain, 1900: 306)

Taxankpada Agodales A goddess who governs the East. Wife of Tamagisanbach. When it thunders she is scolding him. Formosa. (Coleman, 1832: 342)

Tcopiny Makai "Sinking Magician" who is associated with the northeast as well as the northwest. The Pima, Arizona and Mexico. (Russell, 1904/05: 251)

Tekarpada A much-worshipped goddess of the east whose voice is the thunder, scolding her husband for not sending adequate rain. Formosa. (Campbell, 1925, 6: 84)

Tenan-tomgin The benevolent creator god, "Big-Raven," who is the god of the Zenith. The Chukchee, Siberia. (Bogoras, 1904/09: 314, 319; Czaplicka, 1969: 257)

Teraychapada, Takarupada A variant name of Tekarpada and Taxankpada Agodales. Formosa. (Del Re, n.d.: 57)

Tezcatlipoca "Smoking Mirror," a god who presides over the four directions, depicted by colors. In early Nahuatl conceptions of the universe the Tezcatlipocas were four gods, the sons of Ometéotl, aspects of him as lord of night. They were born "when darkness still ruled: and so were called "smoking mirrors." (1) Tlatlauhqui Tezcatlipoca, Red, was the eldest son identified with the East, Tlapallan. He became the principal god of the people of Huexotzinco and Tlaxcala; was also called Xipe or Camaxtle. (2) Yayauhqui Tezcatlipoca, was the second

son and "the worst and the main one who had more authority and power . . . born black." He was identified with "the night and the region of the dead, located in the North." (3) Quetzalcóatl was the third son and became identified with "night and wind, with the West, region of fecundity and life" identified with the East as the morning star, and with the West as the evening star. (4) Huitzilopochtli, the Blue Tezcatlipoca, was associated with the South. The Aztec, Mexico. (León-Portilla, 1982: 33–35, 86, 97; Vaillant, 1962: 142–143)

Thang-long The blue dragon is the god of the East. China. (Scott, 1964: 307)

Tho ba 'jigs byed A protective god associated with the East. Tibet. (Nebesky-Wojkowitz, 1956, 1: 17, 45)

mThsan-ldan-bla-ma Cardinal deity of the south who appears in wedding songs as giver of grain, great wealth. Tibet. (Francke, 1923: 12)

Tiami Eagle god of the Heavens given as the "animal" supernatural of the six world-quarters as well as the "bird." The Sia, New Mexico. (Fewkes, 1895, 2: 127)

Tishtrya The star Sirius presides over the eastern division of the sky and provides the fertilizing rains and the waters of purification. Iran. (Jackson, 1925, 12: 86; Huart, 1963: 42; Ananikian, 1925, 1: 798; Jayne, 1962: 195; Gray, 1930: 223)

Titami, Tiita The god of the North. The Sia, New Mexico. (Fewkes, 1895, 2: 126)

Tlatlauhqui Tezcatlipoca *See* **Tezcatlipoca**

Tokchi'i A serpent god and guardian of the East. The Hopi, Arizona. (Waters, 1963: 49)

Tomam Benevolent mother goddess of the south who is the source of the birds that come north. The Yenisei Ostyaks, Siberia. (Czaplicka, 1925, 9: 578)

too-chee The supernatural of the southeast whose breath is the wind. The Nootka, Washington and Vancouver Island. (Swan, 1869: 92)

too-tooch-ah-kook The supernatural being of the east whose breath is the wind. The Nootka, Washington and Vancouver Island. (Swan, 1869: 92)

Tossarot Guardian of the region of the East. Cambodia. (Marchal, 1963: 203)

To Wên The Buddhist god of the North. China. (Werner, 1932: 454)

bTsan mgon bya rog gdong can A raven-headed deity associated with the South. Tibet. (Nebesky-Wojkowitz, 1956, 1: 48)

Tseng Chang The guardian god of the South and of Spring. With his magic sword he can cause "wind and storm to strike dread into . . . enemies." China. (Getty, 1962: 167; Cammann, 1937: 180–181; Werner, 1932: 454)

Ts'ing-ti The Green Emperor, a god of the eastern quarter of the sky. China. (Chavannes, n.d.: 69; Maspero, 1963: 339)

Tsinqu The spirits of the west who are associated with Metzabok. The Lacandon, Mexico. (Cline, 1944: 112)

Tu God of the north, a god of agriculture and the harvest, of friendship, and also of war. Son of Tane. Hawaii. (Melville, 1969: 25, 28, 34–35)

Tuamutef Jackal-headed son of Horus, a god of the cardinal point of the east, and a god of the Canopic Jars, guarding the heart and the lungs of the deceased. Egypt. (Knight, 1915: 34; Budge, 1969, 1: 158, 456)

Tupa The god of the west and "the personification of thunder." The Guarani, Paraguay and Brazil. (Métraux, 1948, 1: 90)

Tzakol One of four regent gods of the quarters of the cosmos, of directions, with Alom, Bitol, and Cajolom. They are hypostases of Cabahuil as creator god-Seven. Through their mediation was produced "the birth of light"—material *and* spiritual. They gave to each species of animals its type of habitat and its manner of expression. The Quiché, Guatemala. (Girard, 1979: 29, 32, 38)

Uatchet Serpent goddess of the north and a goddess of the dead as a "destroyer of the foes of the deceased." Egypt. (Budge, 1969, 1: 441–444; Knight, 1915: 79)

Uatch-ura An ancient goddess of the north, considered the female counterpart of Hap-Meht. Egypt. (Budge, 1969, 2: 47)

'Ug pa'i gdong pa can An owl-headed Bon deity associated with the south. Tibet. (Nebesky-Wojkowitz, 1956, 1: 47)

Uraro A god of the south like Karoshimo though in position more toward the center of the world; like him a

Toad god. They are the most powerful of the Warao deities. Venezuela. (Wilbert, 1973, 1: 3, 4)

U-rgyan-padma-Padmasambhava A cardinal deity of the west who appears in wedding songs as the giver of medicines, astronomy. Tibet. (Francke, 1923: 12)

Uzoit, Uazit Serpent goddess of the north and a goddess of childbirth. Sister of Nekhbet. Egypt. (Jayne, 1962: 84–85)

Vaisravana Guardian god of the North and a god of wealth. China and Tibet. (Waddell, 1959: 84; Nebesky-Wojkowitz, 1956, 1: 68; Maspero, 1963: 307)

Vajradhara The "'Indestructible', lord of all mysteries . . . believed to reign over the Eastern Quarter." Tibet. (Getty, 1962: 4)

Vajrankusa A deity protective of the East. Tibet. (Snellgrove, 1957: 68)

Vajrapasa A fierce deity protective of the South. Tibet. (Snellgrove, 1957: 68)

Vajrasphota A fierce deity protective of the West. Tibet. (Snellgrove, 1957: 68)

Vajravesa A deity protective of the North. Tibet. (Snellgrove, 1957: 68)

Vakolif Makai South Magician who lives in the southeast but is also associated with the southwest. The Pima, Arizona and Mexico. (Russell, 1904/05: 251)

Vanant A stellar god who is guardian of the West. Iran. (Jackson, 1925, 12: 86)

Varuna The god of waters is the guardian of the west quarter of the compass. India and Mongolia. (Ions, 1967: 79; Dubois, 1906: 633; Percheron, 1953: 62; Danielou, 1964: 130; Banerjea, 1953: 73)

Vasudeva A protective god, regent of the East. Bali, Indonesia. (Hooykaas, 1964: 52)

Vayu The god of the wind is the guardian of the north-west point of the compass. India. (Banerjea, 1953: 73; Dubois, 1906: 633; Ions, 1967: 80; Danielou, 1964: 131)

Veris Fructus An Etruscan deity who appears in region eight of the southern portion of the heavens (Martianus Capella). Italy. (Weinstock, 1946: 104)

Virudhaka Buddhist guardian of the South. India, Tibet, and China. (Ions, 1967: 135; Getty, 1962: 166; Waddell, 1959: 84; Edkins, 1880: 216)

Virulak Guardian of the South region. Cambodia. (Marchal, 1963: 203)

Virulappak Guardian of the West region. Cambodia. (Marchal, 1963: 203)

Virupaksha Guardian of the West, protector of mankind and of Buddhism. India, Tibet, and China. (Waddell, 1959: 84; Edkins, 1880: 216; Ions, 1967: 135; Getty, 1962: 166)

Vishnu, Wisnu He is associated with the North and is worshipped as a god of waters. Bali, Indonesia. (Hooykaas, 1964: 28; Friederich, 1959: 44; Coleman, 1832: 349; Covarrubias, 1937: 296, 317; Grader, 1960: 183)

Wabun God of the East and leader of the four brothers —with Kabun, Kabibonokka, Shawano, who were gods of the winds and of storms and rain. The Algonquin, Eastern United States. (Maclean, 1876: 432; Brinton, 1882: 44–45)

Wabunodin God of the East and of the east wind who "taught . . . the use of Grand Medicine." The Ojibwa, Minnesota. (Coleman, 1937: 37)

Wahkeon, Wakinyan The Man of the West is the Thunderbird who is also the god of war and receives constant worship. He also frequently battles with Unktahe, God of Waters. They are well-matched and either may win. The Dakota, Minnesota. (Eastman, 1962: xxxi, 212, 229; Lynd, 1889: 168)

Warowaro The god of the mountain of the north who is generally beneficent giving fertility, longevity, health, etc. in exchange for tobacco smoke, the food of the gods. The Butterfly God. The Warao, Venezuela. (Wilbert, 1972, 2: 61; 1973, 1: 407)

wa-shel-lie The supernatural being of the west whose breath is the wind. The Nootka, Washington and Vancouver Island. (Swan, 1869: 92)

Waubun "(Morning or East)," represents youth, the early portion of man's life. The Ojibway, Minnesota and Manitoba. (Johnston, 1976: 27, 163)

Waziya God of the North and the North Wind. He is pitiless and cruel, brings the cold, snow, death. At times he may be "jolly" and playful but still is vicious. His aides are the white owl, the raven, the wolf. He "guards the entrance to the dance of the shadows of the north (the aurora borealis)." The Lakota, South Dakota. (Walker, 1980: 72, 103, 120, 125–126)

Wazza "Man of the North." The Dakota, Fort Snelling area, Minnesota. (Eastman, 1962: xxxi)

wedji sakiposit The east, sometimes personified. The Penobscot, Maine. (Speck, 1935: 21)

Wehiyayanpa-micaxta "Man of the East." The Dakota, Fort Snelling area, Minnesota. (Eastman, 1962: xxxi)

Wezeattah-Wechastah God of the north who "gives snow and ice to enable men to pursue game and fish." The Dakota, North and South Dakota, and Minnesota. (Schoolcraft, 1857: 319, 496; Emerson, 1884: 27)

Wunnanameanit "The Northern God." The Narragansett, Rhode Island. (Skinner, 1913: 91)

Xamani-qinqu The "spirit of the north." Yucatan, Mexico. (Larousse, 1968: 439)

Xa matutsi The water spirit, god of the west. The Eastern Pomo, California. (Loeb, 1926, 2: 300)

xašč'éłtˣi'i, xa·ctčé·łtihí, xashchelthi'i Talking God, god of the dawn and of the east, which he controls. He is compassionate and friendly toward man and his affairs and also controls game and corn. The Navaho, Arizona. (Haile, 1947: 3, 6; Reichard, 1950: 50, 77, 78, 476–477)

xašč'é'oγa·n, xashcheoghan Calling God, god of the west. The Navaho, Arizona and New Mexico. (Haile, 1947: 3, 5)

Xastc'inidloyin "Laughing god of the north." The Apache, Arizona and New Mexico. (Goddard, 1911: 193n)

Xastc'inilgaiyin "White god of the east." The Apache, Arizona and New Mexico. (Goddard, 1911: 193n)

Xastc'iniltsoyin "Yellow god of the west." The Apache, Arizona and New Mexico. (Goddard, 1911: 193n)

Xastc'inyalkidn "Talking god of the south." The Apache, Arizona and New Mexico. (Goddard, 1911: 193n)

Xibalbay The god of the west point of the compass who was associated with obsidian. The Cakchiquel, Guatemala. (Mackenzie, n.d.: 56)

Xipe He is associated with the south zone of the universe along with Macuilxochitl; with the east as the Red Tezcatlipoca and guardian of Tlazcala; and also with the west. He is the Flayed God. The Aztec, Mexico. (Vailland, 1962: 140, 143; Burland, 1967: xi)

Xiuhtecuhtli The god of fire and of the year is the god of "the center position in relation to the four cardinal points" and the central point of the universe and the home as the hearth. Mexico. (Caso, 1958: 28, 38; Alexander, 1920: 53; Burland, 1967: xi)

Xucaneb God of the North and of the cold. The Kekchis, British Honduras. (Thompson, 1930: 59)

Ya djaj The "wind man." God of the north. The Coast Central Pomo, California. (Loeb, 1926, 2: 301)

Yahira The god of the north is also "the god of vengeance and death." The Guarani, Paraguay and Brazil. (Métraux, 1948, 1: 90)

Yalanqu The "Spirits of east; serve" Nohotsakyum, the Great Father. The Lacandon, Mexico. (Cline, 1944: 112)

Yaluk The chief Mam, mountain and valley gods who are also thunder and weather gods. He is associated with the West. The Mopan and the Kekchis, British Honduras. (Thompson, 1930: 59; 1970: 349)

Yama The god of the dead is associated with the South. India and Mongolia. (Danielou, 1964: 79; Percheron, 1953: 62; Dubois, 1906: 633)

Yamuhakto The two "warriors of the East and West." They appear with Sayatasha in the Shalako ceremonial. The Zuñi, New Mexico. (Waters, 1950: 284)

Yanpa The God of the East and of the east wind is the third son of Tate, the Wind. His messenger is the crow, his color blue. He is lazy and disagreeable. The Oglala and the Lakota, South Dakota. (Powers, 1977: 72, 75, 76, 78, 170, 175; Jahner, 1977: 35)

Yata The first son of Tate, the Wind, was mean, fearful, and cowardly. He lost his birthright and became the god of the North, of the north wind, and associated with winter. His messenger is the magpie, his color white. Yet, the north is the place of *ni*—the life, breath, soul. The Oglala and the Lakota, South Dakota. (Powers, 1977: 72, 75, 76, 78, 191; Jahner, 1977: 35)

Yaukware The god of the Zenith, of the "Center of the World." From his abode pathways "interconnect the cardinal and intercardinal points of the universe, excluding the underworld in the west and the House of Tobacco Smoke in the east." The Warao, Venezuela. (Wilbert, 1972, 2: 63; 1973, 1: 6)

Yayauhqui Tezcatlipoca *See* **Tezcatlipoca**

Yebtet Goddess of the East. Egypt. (Gardiner, 1925, 9: 792)

Yuan Ming, Yuen Ming The god of the North who rules over adversity as well as prosperity. China. (Du Bose, n.d.: 327; Day, 1940: 66)

Yul-khor srung The "white guardian of the east and King of the Gandharvas . . . guard the Universe and heavens against the outer demons." Sikkim. (Gazeteer of Sikhim, 1894: 261)

Yum Balamob Four deities of the present Mayas who each have a cardinal point location "probably correspond to the Bacabs of the ancient Mayas." Mexico. (Tozzer, 1941: 136)

yu-yoke-sis The supernatural being of the northwest whose breath is the wind. The Nootka, Washington and Vancouver Island. (Swan, 1869: 92)

Zac One of the Mayan deities of the compass points. Mexico. (Nicholson, 1967: 119)

Zac Cimi The Bacab of the West quarter. The Mayan, Mexico. (Thompson, 1970: 276)

Zac-xib-chaac A Mayan sky god associated with a compass point. Mexico. (Redfield and Rojas, 1962: 115)

Zaphon Canaanite god of the north. Near East. (Paton, 1925, 3: 180)

Zhawano The deity of the South quarter. The Ojibway, Minnesota and Manitoba. (Johnston, 1976: 27)

Zocho, Zojo Guardian god of the South. Japan. (Zimmer, 1955: 47; Piggott, 1969: 44; Eliseev, 1963: 447) Also named as the Guardian of the West. (Werner, 1932: 457; Getty, 1962: 168; Eliot, 1935: 135)

Culture:
Teachers/Givers of, Lesser Creator Gods

Abe mango The daughter of the Sun who was sent to earth to teach people how to make pottery and baskets, to use fire, what fish and fruit to eat, to wear loin-cloths and to use the stone ax. The Desana, Colombia. (Reichel-Dolmatoff, 1971: 35)

Abore The "Father of Inventions," a culture hero/deity who gave the people bows and arrows, and canoes particularly. The Warao, Venezuela and Guiana. (Kirchhoff, 1948, 1: 879; Brett, 1880: 76–83)

Ac Yanto A Mayan god who created "white men and their products." Brother of Hachacyum. Mexico. (Thompson, 1970: 320)

A-e-oina Kamui An important god of culture who taught "the arts of life" and was the creator of "snakes, eels and some other beings." The Ainu, Japan. (Munro, 1963: 14, 15; Batchelor, n.d.: 113, 118)

Aestas The culture hero/creator of the Western Dénés. British Columbia. (Morice, 1925, 4: 639)

Ahnt ah koh-mah A culture hero type of super being who gave them fire, goods to eat, animals to hunt, and taught them how to live, how to spear sharks, etc. The Seris, Sonora, Mexico. (Coolidge, 1939: 116–122)

Ajbit In the Second Age, with Ajtzak, the creators of men out of mud—very unsuccessfully. He corresponds to the singular of Bitol, one of the "builder" gods. The Quiché, Guatemala. (Girard, 1979: 49)

Ajtzak With Ajbit in the Second Age created men out of mud, unsuccessfully. He corresponds to the singular of Tzakl, one of the "builder" gods. The Quiché, Guatemala. (Girard, 1979: 49)

a kung rum "One of the four creators of female beings" invoked in marriage ceremonies. The Lepchas, Sikkim. (Siiger, 1967, 1: 141; 1967, 2: 69, 74)

Amaka A creator god who "gave people the domesticated reindeer, taught them how to use fire, invented the tools with which they worked." The Evenks, Siberia. (Michael, 1963: 160)

Amalivaca Culture hero/ancestor who came from over the sea after the floods. He refashioned the land for better habitation and cultivation, taught them to use the streams and rivers for transportation, and taught them sculpture. He founded their institutions and caused them to stay in one location, not to migrate. The Tamanak, Venezuela and British Guiana. (Brett, 1880: 110–113; Métraux, 1946, 2: 117; Zerries, 1968: 247; Brinton, 1868: 160)

Amao A culture heroine who taught the people to cook and "the arts of civilization." Then she disappeared. Brazil. (Levi-Strauss, 1970: 263–264)

Ambat A culture hero/god "who introduced pottery and many social customs." The Seniang District, Southern Malekula, Melanesia. (Poignant, 1967: 96)

Anansi The spider, the culture hero and trickster, widely known. West Africa and West Indies. (Leach, 1949: 52, 53)

Aningapajukaq The "father of the salmon. . . . The chips which he struck off" from some wood "turned into salmon." The Padlermiut Eskimo, Northwest Territories. (Rasmussen, 1930: 89)

Annedotos A deity half-fish, half-man, like Dagan, who "came out of the Persian Gulf and taught the primitive inhabitants of Babylonia the arts of civilization." Near East. (Paton, 1925, 4: 387)

A'noshma   The Turtle who brought earth up out of the depths to create the land. The Maidu, California. (Long, 1963: 201)

a nyit a jom   A female assisting in the creation of seeds, and a *may yel* being associated with agricultural fertility. The Lepchas, Sikkim. (Siiger, 1967, 1: 91; 1967, 2: 40)

Apuwenonu   The planet Venus, formerly a culture hero, who taught the Tapirape "how to plant cotton and how to spin . . . how to plant their modern garden products, maize, manioc, cara, yams." Brazil. (Wagley, 1940: 256)

Arawotja   A deity who created the watercourses. The Dieri, Australia. (Lang, 1905: 55)

a se lu   A spirit who created man from clay and then breathed life into him. The Eskimo, Point Barrow, Alaska. (Pettazzoni, 1956: 25)

Asin   "Sometimes regarded as a culture hero and the creator of palm trees, Barbary figs, and bees, sometimes believed to be a great shaman." The Toba, Brazil. (Leach, 1949: 82)

Astas   The Raven, the culture hero of the Carrier Indians. British Columbia. (Boas, 1898, 2: 47)

Atanggangga   Mau-tiki-tiki, his son, fished up Rennell Island and Atanggangga, who could make things live, "covered it with vegetation." Polynesia. (Birket-Smith, 1956: 22)

Atehle   The sun was once active in creative fields with Wamutsini and created people and gave them culture. The Trumai, Brazil. (Murphy and Quain, 1955: 72–74)

Attawanadi   The third damodede of Wanadi. He came to see what transpired and to create new, good people, as well as Shi, the sun, Nuna, the moon, and Shiriche, the stars. Because of Odosha man no longer had light from the highest sky and so needed the sun. Attawanadi taught the people to make houses and "their most important ritual and material skills." The Makiritare, Venezuela. (Civrieux, 1980: 28, 177)

Atum   Sometimes considered a bisexual deity, parent of the eldest gods, and considered the creator of men and other living things. As a solar deity he is considered male and god of the setting sun as well as the predawn orb. Egypt. (Ames, 1965: 27, 30, 45; Eliade, 1967: 25)

Avireri   A transformer god who "transformed many of his nephews into rocks, monkeys, and nests of insects, thereby bringing these things into existence; he created the alternation of day and night, of the dry and wet seasons." The Campa, Peru. (Weiss, 1972: 162)

Ayi   A collective name for the benevolent and creative deities who "created man, domestic animals, beasts and plants." The Yakut, Siberia. (Jochelson, 1900/02: 235)

Azapane   A "mischievous deity who likes fun, though he also brings the gift of civilisation to men." The Mangbetu, Zaire. (Larousse, 1973: 530)

The Bagadjimbiri   Two brothers whose mother was Dilga. They were the namers of all things, the establishers of culture and initiation ceremonies. They "transformed themselves into water snakes, while their spirits became the Magellanic Clouds." The Karadjeri, Australia. (Eliade, 1973: 53, 54)

Baiporo   The creator of fish. The Bororo, Brazil. (Levi-Strauss, 1969: 215)

Baitogogo   A deity who created the lakes and rivers but they contained no fish. These were created by Baiporo. The Bororo, Brazil. (Levi-Strauss, 1969: 215)

Bakororo   The culture hero/god who rules in the west. He was the son of a human mother and a jaguar. Brother of Itubore. The Bororo, Brazil. (Levi-Strauss, 1969: 37, 123–124)

Barachi   With Umvili believed to have created man. The Golos, Sudan. (Budge, 1973, 1: 375)

Barasiluluo   A god who created a man to whom Balin gave a soul. Nias, Indonesia. (MacKenzie, 1930: 329)

Beghotcidi, Bekotsidi   With his father, the Sun, the creators of large game animals and of domestic animals. He is the god of game and of insects, which form he sometimes takes. He lives in the east. As the god "who carries the moon" he is called Kle hanoai. The Navajo, Arizona and New Mexico. (Reichard, 1950: 76, 386–389; Alexander, 1964: 157; Matthews, 1889: 94; 1902: 31; Babington, 1950: 209)

Bego Tanutanu   Bego the Maker, the shaper of the landscape, was the creator of food plants, and contributor to their culture. The Mono-Alu Islanders, Melansia. (Leach, 1949: 131)

Bele   A fun-loving mischievous deity who brought civilization to the Manja. Central African Republic. (Larousse, 1973: 530)

Betahoxona The god who created mankind and the animals, and "God of the Ancestors." The Sierra Zapotec, Oaxaca, Mexico. (Whitecotton, 1977: 169)

Black Hactcin The most powerful and chief of the Hactcin could do all things. He created the original animal and bird from whom all others were derived, and who at that time could speak. He seeded the earth to produce food for them (some seed turning into insects). He then created mankind by drawing the outline of his own body on the ground and using turquoise for veins, red ocher for blood, coral for skin, white rock for bones, opal for fingernails and teeth, jet and abalone for eyes, then animated him by sending the wind into his body. The sun and moon which he had made disappeared through a hole high in the underworld. He caused a mountain to grow and led all to the top and through "the place of emergence" to the surface of the earth. The Jicarilla Apache, New Mexico. (Campbell, 1974: 232–236; Leach, 1949: 147)

Bochica The culture hero/god is associated with the sun and is also called Xue, or Nemterequeteba. He gave them their customs and rituals, taught them the arts and crafts, and cultivation. He is worshipped throughout Chibcha territory. His wife is Chia, the moon. Colombia. (Loeb, 1931: 543; Kroeber, 1946, 2: 906–909; Alexander, 1920: 202–204; Osborne, 1968: 112)

Budi The Goat—one of the creatures vomited forth by Bumba. Budi "produced every beast with horns." The Boshongo, Zaire. (Eliade, 1967: 91)

Burkhan The god who created man but whose work was defiled by the evil Sholmo. The Buriats of Alarsk, Siberia. (MacCulloch, 1964: 376)

Camé The "god and civilizing hero" of the Bacairis (Carib) also represents the sun; his twin Kéri, the moon. Brazil. (Girard, 1979: 111, 112)

Caragabi A culture hero/god who created people, gave them food, and established family relationships. He placed the physical features of the universe. The Choco, Colombia. (Métraux, 1946, 2: 115)

Carancho A falcon, the culture hero and demiurge. The Toba-Pilaga, Paraguay/Argentina. (Levi-Strauss, 1969: 100; 1973: 98; Métraux, 1969: 54–56, 60, 62)

Chagan-Shukuty A god who dove to the bottom of the water and brought up the earth and with Otshirvani created man. Siberia. (MacCulloch, 1964: 377; Long, 1963: 205)

Chedi Bumba The third son of Bumba. He was only capable of creating the kite (bird). The Bushongo, Zaire. (Eliade, 1967: 92)

Chepehte Kamui A very important sea deity who was the creator of fish and other sea products. The Ainu, Sakhalin. (Ohnuki-Tierney, 1974: 89, 100)

Chibute The god of hunting and of hunters also instituted their rites and taught them spinning, weaving, and pottery making. The Tacana, Bolivia. (Levi-Strauss, 1973: 346–348)

Chinigchinich A powerful and omnipresent sky god created man, is beneficent, but punishing of disobedience. He taught them laws and rituals and is the giver of powers to the medicinemen. The mountain Acagchemem, California. (Boscana, 1933: 29–30; Bancroft, 1886, 3: 164)

Chiyi A god who created birds, animals, fish, etc. Brother of Chiyuk. The Kamia, California. (Gifford, 1931: 75, 76)

Chonganda The second son of Bumba and the creator of all vegetation. The Bushongo, Zaire. (Eliade, 1967: 92)

Chu Jung The god of fire who "taught the people the use of fire . . . the art of purifying, forging, and welding metals." China. (Werner, 1934: 81, 238)

Chul Tatic Chitez Vanegh The god who created mankind. The Tzeltal, Mexico. (Thompson, 1970: 202)

Cin-an-ev "Wolf culture-hero and trickster." The Ute, Utah. (Leach, 1949: 233)

Comizahual (1) The civilizer-hero of the Lencas who is represented by a flying jaguar. El Salvador/Honduras. (Girard, 1979: 272) (2) A culture goddess who introduced civilization in Cerquin. Honduras. (Bancroft, 1886, 3: 485)

Cozaana The creator of mankind and of animals, and a god of hunters and fishermen. Male counterpart of Pichanto. Mexico. (Alexander, 1920: 87; Bancroft, 1886, 3: 457; Whitecotton, 1977: 158, 164, 169)

Djungun A culture hero of the primeval time who had the form of a small night bird. He became the star Beta Gemini. Australia. (Eliade, 1964: 64–65)

Do The intermediary between the high god and men. He taught men agriculture, weaving, metallurgy, and moral codes. The Bwa, Mali. (Capron, 1962: 148)

Dohitt The creator of the earth and of men, and the culture hero of the Moseten and Chiman. Bolivia. (Métraux, 1942: 25; 1948: 503)

Domakolen The creator of the mountains. The Bagobo, Philippines. (Benedict, 1916: 29)

do tsoh, don'tsoh "Big Fly," a helpful deity, "frequently a guardian of the east side of a sandpainting . . . instructed the people about making offerings." The Navaho, Arizona/New Mexico. (Reichard, 1950: 390)

Droemerdeener A star god, Canopus, who was the creator of "the kangaroo rat, the wombat, and the echidna, all burrowing animals." Bruny Island, Tasmania. (Coon, 1971: 288–289)

Dumpa-poee A deity who created man on the orders of the supreme being. The Naga of Manipur, India. (Hodson, 1911: 127)

Dundra, Alako The son of God who gave them their laws to live by. Some believe he "ascended to the moon and became known as the god Alako." The Gypsies, Transylvania. (Trigg, 1973: 202)

Dyabdar The serpent who participated with the mammoth in creating the earth. His trail of movement became the rivers. The Evenks, Siberia. (Michael, 1963: 166)

Dyai, Dyoi A demiurge and culture hero who created mankind and instituted "the arts, laws, and customs." He is the twin of Epi, the trickster. His wife is Tul. The Tucuna, Brazil/Peru. (Levi-Strauss, 1969: 171; 1973: 374; Nimuendaju, 1952: 121–122)

elchen The creator of people. The Mapuche, Chile. (Faron, 1968: 65)

El-lal A culture hero who gave the people weapons for hunting and taught them the use of fire. He left and went eastward across the ocean. He was the son of Noshjtej. The Patagonians, Argentina. (Deniker, 1925, 9: 669; Alexander, 1920: 335)

Eluitsama A god of one of the creation myths who created the jaguars. The Kogi, Colombia. (Reichel-Dolmatoff, 1975: 55)

Ememqut The creator of the reindeer "taught people the art of herding the animals." Son of Ku'urkil. The Chukchee of Telqap tundra and Big-River, Siberia. (Bogoras, 1904/09: 315)

Erlik He was created by Kaira Kan, then participated in the creation of the earth, but his work was bad while that of Kaira Kan was good. Erlik was banished and became the god of the underworld and of corruption. Siberia. (Casanowicz, 1924: 417–418; Dragomanov, 1961: 41, 47; Potapov, 1964: 325; Pettersson, 1957: 24)

Estsanatlehi Changing Woman, the self-rejuvenating goddess, is credited with having created people. The Navaho, Arizona/New Mexico. (Matthews, 1890: 89, 95)

Etau The son of Uelip with whom he quarreled and then left. He was responsible for the appearance of the islands and "planted fruits and created the animals of the sea and land and took his mother, Ludjeman, to himself." The Marshall Islands, Micronesia. (Knappe, 1888: 65)

Fu Hsi A god of medicine who was also the "supposed inventor of cooking, musical instruments, the calendar, hunting, fishing, etc." China. (Werner, 1934: 147–148; Bodde, 1961: 386)

Fumeripits Culture hero/creator god who carved people from trees, then brought them to life by playing on the drum, to which they danced. The Asmat, New Guinea. (Gerbrands, 1973: 67)

Gale Yaka, Gale Deviyo The most important god of the coastal Veddas who "taught them everything they know and the names of things and animals, and instructed them regarding their dances." His wife is Kiriamma. He is appealed to in epidemics. Ceylon. (Seligmann and Seligmann, 1911: 183–184)

Ganda Bumba The crocodile—one of the creatures vomited forth by Bumba. He created "serpents and the iguana." The Bushongo, Zaire. (Eliade, 1967: 91)

Gatswokwire, Rakshuatlaketl A being, benevolent but excessively erotic, who instituted cultural practices, made salmon available to man, and made childbirth possible without killing the mother. The Wiyot, California. (Kroeber, 1925: 119)

Geus Tašan The creator of cattle. Iran. (Gray, 1930: 146)

Giligei "A demi-god—the inventor of the *gi* or shell adzes." Yap Island, the Carolines, Micronesia. (Christian, 1899: 385)

Batara Goeroe Son of Sangkoeroewira who sacrificed him to become human and the ancestor of the people. He scattered the handful of earth sent with him from the heavens and formed the earth. His wife is Njilitimo (Wi Njilo Timo), the daughter of the god of the underworld. Wilken also calls him the supreme deity. The Buginese, Indonesia. (Alkema and Bezemer, 1927: 189; Wilken, 1893: 187)

Gu The god of metal and war was sent to the earth by Mawu to give shape to things and to make it habitable. He gave tools to man and taught their use, primarily iron-working, and gave him his skills. Dahomey. (Herskovits and Herskovits, 1933: 14, 15, 34)

Guahari With his brother Muhoka created the first Piaroas out of the "shapeless animals" they released from inside the mountain. Guahari also "created the five tigers represented by the five masks" of the Mask Ceremony. His voice is represented by the flute in the sacred music. Son of the Sun. The Orinoco River area, Venezuela. (Gheerbrant, 1954: 110, 111)

Guaracy The sun as the creator of the animals. The Tupi, Brazil. (Spence, 1925: 837)

Gwau Meo The culture hero and son of the sun. Mala (Solomon Islands), Melanesia. (Leach, 1949: 470)

Haburi, Abore The "father of inventions," and the builder of canoes. The Warao, Guiana. (Levi-Strauss, 1973: 183, 212)

Haikat The creator/culture hero of the Nisenan. Southern Maidu, California. (Loeb, 1932: 190)

Hainit Yumenkit One of "the first people" who were born of Tukomit and Tamayowut. He "made the sun." The Luiseño, California. (Kroeber, 1925: 678)

Haitsi-aibeb A culture hero and transformer who was of magical birth and experienced numerous deaths and rebirths. He slew the monster Ga-gorib, the enemy of man. The Hottentot, South Africa. (Leach, 1949, 1: 474; Bray, 1935: 220)

Hatchawa He learned the use of fire, how to make bows and arrows, how to hunt and fish, from his uncle Puana, and then in turn taught these skills to mankind. Son of Kuma. The Yaruor, Venezuela. (Kirchhoff, 1948, 2: 462; Métraux, 1946, 2: 115)

Haua One of the principal gods who with Makemake "created the birds and established the cult in honor of themselves." Easter Island, Polynesia. (Métraux, 1940: 312, 335)

Heller The creator of mankind gave them their civilization; they go to him after death. He is the son of the sun. The Tehuelche, Argentina/Tierra del Fuego. (Cooper, 1946, 5: 159; Osborne, 1968: 117)

Hiovaki Semese A sky god, the creator of the land and the sea, is invoked "for goodness and strength in fighting." The Toaripi, New Guinea. (Haddon, 1925, 9: 342)

Híuika Son of Guateóvañ. When he brought the shells for burning lime from the seashore, "he also brought, against his will, sickness, fever chills and fever heat." The Kagaba, Colombia. (Preuss, 1926: 65, 72)

Hotogov Mailgan The creator of mankind is the goddess of the night heavens. The Buriat/Mongol. Siberia. (Curtin, 1909: 46)

Huichaana The creatress of mankind, animals, and fish was also a goddess of children and of fishing. The Zapotec, Mexico. (Alexander, 1920: 87; Whitecotton, 1977: 169)

Huriata The Tarascan sun god created the heavenly bodies. Human sacrifices were made to him. His wife was Cutzi, the moon. Mexico. (Boyd, n.d.: xv, 2)

Iatiku *See* **Iyataku, Uretsete**

Ibelele He has the attributes of a culture hero, inventing weapons, instituting moral laws and the nose ring. He "Has the world tree, *palu-uala,* cut down, and in this way creates the sea and so forth." He later became the sun. The Cuna, Panama. (Nordenskiold, 1938: 324)

Ibeorgun The culture hero who came to earth taught them about food, how to prepare it, language and medicine songs, construction and gold-working. The Cuna, Panama. (Nordenskiold, 1938: 127, 324; Leach, 1949: 513)

Iltchi-dishish "Black Wind" fashioned the world with ravines and canyons as it is at present. The Apache, Arizona, New Mexico, and Texas. (Bourke, 1890: 209)

Inapirikuri The omniscient "first living creature" who brought the Baniwa out of a hole in the ground and gave them "a number of precepts, such as the laws of exogamy and monogamy." Venezuela. (Zerries, 1968: 249)

Indara The earth goddess who, with Ilai, created men. Central Celebes, Indonesia. (Kruijt, 1925, 7: 248; Kern, 1825, 8: 347)

Inishiki-irihiko-no-mikoto A god who taught agriculture and irrigation, Son of Suinin-tenno. Japan. (Herbert, 1967: 413)

Inktomi, Iktomi, Ikto The "spider"—the culture hero, trickster, and transformer who is responsible for the creation of time and space, for the naming of things, and creation of language. Older brother of Iya. The Oglala, South Dakota. (Powers, 1977: 53, 54, 79, 83, 84)

Intukbon A deity who taught them to build granaries. The Ifugao, Luzon, Philippines. (Barton, 1946: 13)

Iraca A god of the Chibcha who with Ramiquiri created men and women. He then turned himself into the moon. Colombia. (Osborne, 1968: 110)

Irin Magé "A certain magician, Irin Magé, is credited by the Eastern Tupi with the creation of seas and rivers, and at his intervention Monan, the Maker or Begetter, withdrew the *tata,* or Divine fire, with which he had resolved to destroy the world." The Tupi-Guarani, Brazil. (Spence, 1925, 2: 837)

Irungu An "Earth-spirit . . . who, at the bidding of the Supreme Being Rugaba . . . fashioned the earth, the mountains, and the woods, and peopled them with animals." Tanzania. (Frazer, 1926: 426)

Ises A goddess who gave the bow and arrow to mankind. The Heikum, South Africa. (Schapera, 1951: 189)

Isora One of the gods of the cardinal points who also created the fruits. Bali, Indonesia. (Covarrubias, 1937: 289, 317)

Italapas The Coyote created humans, but imperfectly, and they had to be improved by Ikanam. Italapas taught them many cultural things and established taboos, particularly regarding salmon fishing. The Chinook, Washington/Oregon. (Spence, 1925, 3: 560; Bancroft, 1886, 3: 96, 156)

Itciai The jaguar who worked with Kuma and Puana in the creation of the world created the rivers. The Yaruro, Venezuela. (Petrullo, 1939: 245; Hernandez de Alba, 1948, 4: 462)

?Itcivi Gila Monster, an Immortal and High Chief, and his companion and partner ?Aya, Turtle, instructed and cared for their people, taught them to store food for lean times. The Chemehuevi, California, Nevada, and Arizona. (Laird, 1976: 168)

it mu A goddess who "created all the gods including tak bo thing and na zong nyo," whom she assigned to create human beings. She is considered to have given the Lepchas their domestic animals. Her eldest son is kong chen. Sikkim. (Siiger, 1967, 1: 95, 172, 192)

Itubore The culture hero/god who rules in the east is the brother of Bokororo and the son of a human mother

and a jaguar. The Bororo, Brazil. (Levi-Strauss, 1969: 37, 123–124)

Itzamna The Lord of the Heavens was the "founder of civilization," introducing "maize and cocoa . . . rubber," writing and books, and culture generally. The Maya, Mexico/Guatemala. (Schellhas, 1904: 18; Tozzer, 1941: 146; Nicholson, 1967: 119; Morley, 1946: 222–223)

Iyetaku, Uretsete With her sister Nautsiti she was placed on the earth by Ut' siti to complete its from under the direction of Tsitstinako—providing corn, fire, tobacco, and giving life to living things. She is the great corn mother and goddess of the underground where she receives and judges the dead. Pueblo Indians, New Mexico. (Parsons, 1939: 173, 178, 244, 400; Tyler, 1964: 55, 58)

Jacy The god of the moon created the plants. The Tupi, Brazil. (Spence, 1925, 2: 837; Bastide, 1960: 567)

Jesus Cristo A culture hero who was also the creator of the mountains and valleys. Son of Father Jose and Maria Santissima. The Chimalteco, Guatemala. (Wagley, 1949: 51–52)

Kaboniyan The guide and helper of the people who tells them how to overcome troubles. The Ginguian, Philippines. (Cole, 1922: 296, 322)

Kahausibware A snake spirit, female, who lived on the mountain, created men, animals, and the foods of both. Solomon Islands, Melanesia. (Codrington, 1881: 298)

Kalgouachija, Kalgouachicha A goddess, the mother of all things. She had four sons who are immaterial and "personify no natural phenomenon." The Kagaba, Colombia. (Brettes, 1903: 333)

Kalumba "The Creator, or Father of the people." The Katanga (Luba tribe), Congo. (Donohugh and Berry, 1932: 180)

Kalunga Among the Omnambo he is the creator of man and sheep. South Africa. (Lang, 1887: 177)

Kamantowit The god who created mankind. Algonquin Indians, United States. (Schoolcraft, 1857, 5: 71)

Kamé Among the Caingang Kamé and his brother, Kayurukré, are ancestor gods who "created jaguars from ashes and coals; then the antas or tapirs from ashes only." Kamé also created "the harmful creatures (pumas, serpents, wasps, etc.)." Among the Bakairi Indians Kamé is the twin of Kerı—Culture hero/gods who arranged the universe, created humans, and gave them their skills. Brazil. (Métraux, 1946: 474; Queval, 1968: 651; Alexander, 1920: 312–313; Zerries, 1968: 309)

Kamim A god who came from the heavens and taught them the "*Inna* or Coming-out party of the Cuna debutante." The Cuna, Panama. (Keeler, 1960: 21, 25)

Kampinu A deity who created the hills in which the Nagas live. Manipur, India. (Hodson, 1911: 127)

Kanaschiwue, Kanashiwe The demiurge and a transformer. The Karaja, Brazil. (Levi-Strauss, 1973: 211; Lipkind, 1940: 248)

Kanikilak The god who established the "arts, customs, and institutions" of the Kwakiutl. Son of Ata, the sun. British Columbia. (Swanton, 1925, 12: 662)

Kapkimiyis A local god "who created the first man out of the thigh of the first already existent woman, made the island of Tsisha, the home of the Tsishaath tribe." The Nutka, Vancouver Island, Canada. (Sapir, 1925, 12: 592)

Kareya A lesser creator deity who "sometimes comes to earth to instruct the medicine men." The Karoks, California. (Maclean, 1876: 435)

Karora A creator god of the Aranda, but not of all things. Australia. (Long, 1963: 151)

Karusakaibo A culture hero/god, the creator of numerous of the living things of the earth—food plants, trees, the peccary, and tapir. He created "human souls," and taught the people to hunt and farm, to roast manioc meal, tattooing, and gave them their laws. The Mundurucu, Brazil. (Levi-Strauss, 1969: 85–86, 102; Murphy, 1958: 12; Zerries, 1968: 242; Horton, 1948: 280)

Kawabapishit The creator of and god of animals, invoked for good hunting. The Naskapi, Labrador. (Cooper, 1934: 63; Pettazzoni, 1956: 376)

Kayurukré Brother of Kamé, ancestor gods. They created the jaguars and tapirs, and he created the useful animals. The Caingang, Brazil. (Métraux, 1946: 474)

Kechi Niwaski The benevolent creator of the Indians. The Abenaki, northeast coast Canada/United States. (Bjorklung, 1969: 134)

Kenos On orders from Temaukel he furnished and shaped the world, created human beings and established their moral laws. He ascended to the skies as a star. The

Selk'nam, Patagonia; the Ona, Tierra del Fuego. (Gusinde, 1931: 501, 503; Loeb, 1931: 528; Queval, 1968: 65; Zerries, 1968: 235)

Keri A god of the Bakairi Indians who, with his twin Kame, arranged the universe, created humans, and gave their skills to them. Brazil. (Queval, 1968: 65; Métraux, 1946, 2: 115; Alexander, 1920: 313; Zerries, 1968: 309)

Ketanagai Big Head, or Night Traveler, the moon, was a beneficent god who "taught the people their arts and dances." The Wailaki, California. (Loeb, 1931: 523; 1932: 73)

Keto A benevolent god created by Liyele to do the actual modelling of man. He assumes the responsibility of maintaining life in his creatures. He is worshipped only by women. Upper Volta. (Hébert and Guilhem, 1967: 152–153)

Khaals The creator of birds and animals was also a trickster and transformer. The Coast Salish, Washington/ British Columbia. (Jenness, 1955: 88)

Khadau The culture hero who fashioned nature, created animals and man, and established blacksmithing and social customs. The Orochi, Siberia. (Ivanov, Smolyak, and Levin, 1964: 757; Michael, 1963: 218)

Khambageu He is believed to be a self-existent god who established the customs and morals of the Sonjo and is concerned with their welfare. Tanzania. (Gray, 1963: 97–98, 100; Mbiti, 1970, 2: 126)

Khnemu, Khnum A creator god who fashioned gods and men on the potter's wheel. He absorbed the attributes of Ra, Shu, Qeb or Seb, and Osiris and as such was called Sheft-Hat—"with four rams' heads upon a human body; [symbolizing] fire, air, earth, and water" and representing "the great primeval creative force." He was a Nile god, of the first Cataract. Egypt. (Budge, 1969, 2: 49–53; Casson, 1965: 106; Knight, 1915: 64)

Kiarsidia A god who taught men about bows and arrows and hunting, as well as games. He created through dreaming of things and it was so. The Wichita, Kansas. (Dorsey, 1904: 25–27)

ki lo One of "the four creators of female beings" is invoked in marriage ceremonies. The Lepchas, Sikkim. (Siiger, 1967: 79, 142)

Kivovia A lesser god who "created the sago palm, the betel-nut palm, and many other good things." His wife is Moru, son is Lavaosiaka. The Elema, Papuan Gulf, New Guinea. (Holmes, 1902: 430)

Kodoyampeh, Kodoyanpe, Kodoyapem Earthmaker, with Coyote, created the earth and man and "established the seasons." The Maidu, California. (Spence, 1925, 3: 66; 1925, 4: 127; Dixon, 1903: 32–33; 1912: 4, 13)

Koevasi The first of the supernaturals, a female, of unknown origin. She "told a hornet to go down to the water below and make the ground." She planted two trees and created "the wild things of the bush." She was the cause of death and of the various dialects. With her consort Sivotohu she established the paths of the sun and the moon. Her daughter was the ancestress of the people. Solomon Islands, Melanesia. (Codrington, 1881: 304; Hogbin, 1937: 87)

Kohkang Wuhti Spider Grandmother was a creator goddess, possibly a precursor of Sussistinako. The Hopi and Keres, New Mexico and Arizona. (Tyler, 1964: 95)

Kokyanwuqti, Kokyangwuti Mother Earth, Spider woman, created humans, plants, birds, and animals. The Hopi and the Tusayan, Arizona. (Waters, 1963: 4, 5, 166; Fewkes, 1920: 605)

iKombengi A god of the underworld and the night who created men at the behest of iLai and Ndara. The Toradjas of Celebes, Indonesia. (Pettersson, 1957: 27; Downs, 1920: 14, 16, 45)

Komsithing The eldest son of Itpomu and Debu whose sister/wife is Narzong-nyou. They are also called Taksen and Takfrom and are the parents of the "devils and snakes and lizards." He established numerous customs and the *ingzong* institution—a formal trade relationship with religious sanctions. The Lepchas, Sikkim. (Gorer, 1938: 118, 223–225)

Kono Bumba The tortoise, one of the creatures vomited forth by Bumba. He created other like creatures. The Bushongo, Zaire. (Eliade, 1967: 91)

Korroremana The creator of men (only), not women. The Warrau of the Orinoco delta, Venezuela. (Kirchhoff, 1948, 1: 880)

Kotma Ma When a grain of earth was stolen from the lower world she churned it with water and increased it to cover the middle world and make it fertile. Mother of the Pandwa brothers. The Baiga, India. (Fuchs, 1952: 16, 609)

Koy Bumba The leopard, one of the creatures vomited forth by Bumba. He created other creatures. The Bushongo, Zaire. (Eliade, 1967: 91)

Kresnik A "culture hero, magician, and monster-slayer, son of Svarog. . . . He is interpreted as a deity of spring, crops, and cattle." The Slovenes. (Leach, 1950: 590)

Kukulcan The feathered serpent, the culture hero and "founder of civilization . . . builder of cities," who established justice and order. He was identified with Quetzalcóatl. The Maya, Yucatan, Mexico. (Schellhas, 1904: 18; Tozzer, 1941: 23; Weyer, 1961: 84; Thompson, 1970: 328)

Kulimina The creator of women. The Arawak of Guiana. (Alexander, 1920: 259)

Kumaphari, Kumapari The demiurge who created the Indians out of arrow reeds. He stole fire from the birds as a culture hero. Later he became the center of a cult as a cannibalistic jaguar god. The Shipaya, Brazil. (Levi-Strauss, 1969: 141; Zerries, 1968: 288; Nimuendaju, 1948, 1: 241)

Kutkh The "raven . . . a totemic ancestor. . . . With him was linked the appearance of people and the earth, the earths' relief, and all the cultural gains of mankind." According to Antropova "he was not held in esteem." The Itelmens, Siberia. (Michael, 1963: 210; Antropova, 1964: 880)

Kutnahin The sun who had culture hero functions as the giver of corn, the teacher of fishing and the art of healing. He was also a trickster and was earlier considered female. Swanton later calls him the supreme being who also makes the thunder. The Chitimacha, Louisiana. (Swanton, 1928: 209; 1946: 781; Pettazzoni, 1956: 176)

Kuwai The culture hero and creator of rivers, responsible for the people's knowledge of agriculture, fishing, their arts and industries. The Tucano and Cubeo, Brazil and Colombia. (Goldman, 1948: 794; Levi-Strauss, 1973: 223; Zerries, 1968: 255)

Kuykynnyaku The "raven-creator . . . gave people all their material goods," their animals, and taught them hunting, fishing, etc., but he was tricky, cunning, and lecherous. His wife was Miti. The Koryaks, Siberia. (Antropova, 1964: 868–869; Bogoras, 1904/09: 315)

K'waiti The "creator, trickster and transformer" of the Quileute. Washington. (Reagan and Walters, 1933: 297)

Kwatiyat A creator or transformer who contributed to the shape of the world. The Nutka, Vancouver Island, British Columbia. (Sapir, 1925, 12: 592)

Kwilsten "Sweat Lodge." A benevolent god, "the creator of the animals and spirits, and perhaps of human beings." The Sanpoil and Nispelem. Washington. (Ray, 1932: 179)

Kwoiam The culture hero "who carries an Australian spear and spear-thrower." Western Islands, Torres Straits, Indonesia. (Leach, 1950: 1016)

Kxexeknem A god involved in the creation of man who gives individuality. The Bella Coola, British Columbia. (Boas, 1898: 31)

Lakin Chan God K—A Mayan serpent god associated with the east, believed to be the creator of mankind and of all living things. He established the Maya culture, giving them writing and the knowledge of medicinal herbs and of healing. Mexico and Guatemala. (Nicholson, 1967: 127)

Lasaeo The god who distributed to the To Pebato the dog for hunting, to the Lage the blowgun for hunting, to the Onda'e the hammer as smiths, and to the Loewoe' a piece of cotton to be merchants. The Toradja, Celebes, Indonesia. (Adriani and Kruyt, 1950: 218)

Laulaati A god who created a stone "out of which came the first man and woman." Lifu Island (Loyalty Islands), Melanesia. (Mackenzie, n.d.: 141)

Lavaosiaka A god who created the dog. Son of Kivovia and Moru. The Elema, Papuan Gulf, New Guinea. (Holmes, 1902: 430)

Ligoububfanu A goddess who created the island and (or gave birth to) mankind, plants and animals. Wife of Anulap. Truk, Micronesia. (Poignant, 1967: 73; Leach, 1956: 183)

Loa, Lowa The god who created the islands and all living things. Marshall Islands, Micronesia. (Davenport, 1953: 221; Poignant, 1967: 72; Larousse, 1968: 460)

Lolo The creator of Ongtong Java and its first inhabitant. Indonesia. (Williamson, 1933, 2: 113)

Lu A culture hero deity who raised the sky with the help of the winds; drew up the lands from the sea; then the trees and plants out of the ground. Fakaofu (Bowditch Island), Polynesia. (Lister, 1891: 52; Williamson, 1933, 2: 237; Beaglehole, 1938: 315)

Lugeilan The son of Aluelop came down from the sky and taught men "tattooing and hairdressing . . . the possibilities of the coconut-palm." Caroline Islands, Micronesia. (Larousse, 1973: 509)

Lugus Celtic god of culture, of the arts and crafts, of trade and commerce. Gaul/Britain. (MacCulloch, 1911: 90–91; Ross, 1967: 250, 363; MacCana, 1970: 27–29)

Lusarer A culture hero/god who taught how "to build fish-weirs of stone and wood." Yap Island, the Carolines, Micronesia. (Christian, 1899: 385)

Ma A god closely associated with the supreme being "from whom he obtains all things . . . for men." Ma fashioned men and all living things but his ill disposition and indifference sometimes cause him to produce ugly beings. The Jen, Nigeria. (Meek, 1931: 197)

Machi With Nostu-Nopantu fashioned the earth on the orders of Tatara-Rabuga. The Garo, Assam. (Playfair, 1909: 81)

Maderatja He is considered the creator of men and animals; is a god of "conception and birth." The Lapps. Lapland. (Pettersson, 1957: 18)

Mafif Brother of Siwa. They are the creators of men and the features of the earth as well as the introducers of agricultural products and textiles. The Mejbrat of New Guinea. (Elmberg, 1955: 45)

Magwala The creator of men. The Ata (Negritos), Philippines. (Rahmann and Maceda, 1955: 829)

Mahadeo A manifestation of Shiva believed by the Korkus and the Agaria to have created man and all living things. India. (Elwin, 1942: 92; Keeler, 1960: 49)

Mahpiyato The sky god was directed by Inyan to create the animals and also a people inferior to the Pte people (who were servants of the spirits) to be "the subjects of Maka" (the earth)—mankind. The Lakota, South Dakota. (One Feather, 1982: 49)

Maira The culture hero and demiurge gave people fire, cotton, manioc, and maize. The Tenetehara, the Tembe, Brazil. (Wagley and Galvao, 1948, 1: 147; 1949: 100–101; Levi-Strauss, 1973: 312)

Maire Ata The "civilizing god" of the Tupi. Brazil. (Levi-Strauss, 1969: 172)

Maire-Monan A culture hero who taught men agriculture and government. The Tupi, Brazil. (Wagley, 1964: 224; Larousse, 1968: 445)

Makakoret The "creator of the air." The Bagobo, Philippines. (Benedict, 1916: 29)

Makaponguis The "creator of the water." The Bagobo, Philippines. (Benedict, 1916: 29)

Makemake The most prominent god is the creator of man. He is frequently depicted as a human with a bird's head and is the patron of the Bird Cult. He is feared as the devourer of the souls of the evil dead, though protective of those of the good. Easter Island, Polynesia. (Métraux, 1940: 311–314, 331; Buck, 1938: 225–226; Williamson, 1933, 2: 109; Poignant, 1967: 40)

Makila The god who "gave to the people all their arts and knowledge" and taught them hunting and fishing. He was believed to be the father of Kuksu. The northern Pomo, California. (Loeb, 1932: 3, 4)

ma la One of the "four creators of female beings." He is invoked in wedding ceremonies. The Lepchas, Sikkim. (Siiger, 1967: 69, 143)

Malankuratti A goddess who with Malavay created the mountains and the first humans. The Kadar, Southwest India. (Ehrenfels, 1952: 161–162)

Malapalitsek One of the Masmasalanix who taught men the arts, canoe-building, and hunting. The Bella Coola, British Columbia. (Boas, 1898: 32)

Malapeexoek One of the Masmasalanix who taught men the arts, conoe-building, and hunting. The Bella Coola, British Columbia. (Boas, 1898: 32)

Malavay A god who with Malankuratti created the mountains and the first humans. The Kadar, Southwest India. (Ehrenfels, 1952: 161–162)

Maleiwa A beneficent culture hero/creator god is in some mythological versions credited with creating the cosmos and vegetable and animal life, including humans. He gave people their moral laws and taught them to make fire. The Goajiro, Venezuela. (Wilbert, 1972, 1: 203–204; Zerries, 1968: 250)

Malibud The creator of women. The Bagobo, Philippines. (Benedict, 1916: 29)

Malin Budhi A goddess commanded by Thakur Kiu to make human beings, but in giving them life she gave them that of the birds and they flew away as birds. After other problems two eggs were hatched, which were humans. The Santal, India. (Elwin, 1949: 19, 20)

Mana The principal god of the Kanjar was their teacher and guide as well as the ancestor deity. Central Provinces, India. (Russell, 1916, 3: 339)

Manabush A culture hero/god through whom men received medicine bundles and the power to cure disease. Although he was a trickster also he gave them "maize, tobacco, and medicinal plants." The Menomini, Wisconsin. (Ritzenthaler, 1970: 87; Skinner, 1913: 73, 242; Hoffman, 1890: 246)

Manchakori The first God who was on the earth and gave the people their food. After teaching all the secrets of his powers to Mahonte's (the first man) son, he ascended to the sky and became the moon. The Campa, Peru. (Llosa Porras, 1977: 59–61)

Man-el The beautiful "moon maiden." She taught the young people "many games, songs, and things necessary for wise living." She also taught the people about marriage, raising of families, and how to get through the gate to Telmikish (their afterworld), and about the clan moieties. The Cahuilla, California. (Brumgardt and Bowles, 1981: 14–16)

Maneneumañ The mother of the earth and of all things. With Mukulyinmakú Seižankua the first pair of parents. Their sons: Kultšavitabauya, Seokukui, Sintana, Aluañuiko. Daughters: Ižgeneumañ, Nuaneneumañ, Havaneumañ, Gaunkuaneneumañ, Seinaneumañ, Tsantsalyineumañ, Ulumandian Ulmandiañ, Sulaliue. The Kagaba of San Miguel, Colombia. (Preuss, 1926: 68)

Manger-kunger-kunja "Their Creator-Lizard . . . drew the first people out of the ocean and cut them into shape with a stone knife." He taught them to use boomerangs and the bull-roarer. The Western Aranda, Australia. (Leach, 1956: 192)

Manibozho A deity who gave them weapons and implements and taught them to snare game. The Tusan, Texas. (Maclean, 1876: 427–428)

Manohel-Tohel The creator of man. The Tzotzil, Mexico. (Thompson, 1970: 202)

Manoid Among the Kenta in Kedah she with Kaei created the first human pair. Grandmother of Kaei and Ta Pedn, also of Begjag. Malaya. (Schebesta, 1927: 219–222)

Manunaima The god who created the sky, humans, and animals. The Caribs, British Guiana. (Queval, 1968: 70)

Maori The god "who created the first man, Mwuetsi, and his two wives"—Massassi, who was the mother of the vegetable kingdom, and Morongo, the mother of animals and men. Southern Rhodesia. (Deren, 1953: 54)

Marang-Buru   The great mountain god was also a cultural deity having taught them cultivation, hunting, music and dancing, and how to brew rice-beer. He inadvertently taught the art of witchcraft to women, having meant it for men. The Santal, Bihar, India. (Kochar, 1966: 246–247; Biswas, 1956: 117; Mukherjea, 1962: 19, 275, 292; Elwin, 1949: 479)

Marel   A culture hero of the Bad of West Kimberley who taught them "the law of Djamar." Australia. (Eliade, 1973: 35, 36)

Marunogere   The culture hero and creator of "the first coconut tree . . . the first men's house, inaugurated the *moguru* ceremony." The Kiwai, New Guinea. (Leach, 1950: 682)

Marxokunek   A deith of the Yuma Indians who created the coyote, the raven, the mountain lion, and the cougar. Arizona. (Harrington, 1908: 324)

The Masmasalanix   Four Brothers—Malapalitsek, Yulatimot, Malapeexoek, Ililulak—the supernatural carpenters who formed the mountains, rivers, animals, birds, etc., and who "gave man his arts . . . taught him to build canoes . . . hunting." The Bella Coola, British Columbia. (Boas, 1898: 32, 33; McIlwraith, 1948, 1: 39)

Matcito   The god who created the sun and controls the movements of the heavenly bodies and the seasons. The Oraibi, Arizona. (Powell, 1879/80: 25, 26)

Matshiktshiki   The sea-serpent god who fished up the islands of the New Hebrides out of the sea. Greatly feared and propitiated. Melanesia. (Williamson, 1933, 2: 181)

Mauda lana   In the forming of the earth, with Ningkong wa, he formed the mountains. The Katchins, Burma. (Gilhodes, 1908: 679)

Maui   In areas of Polynesia he is credited with fishing up the islands from the bottom of the sea. He is frequently associated with the underworld. The Marquesas, Tonga. (Handy, 1923: 246; Williamson, 1933, 1: 32, 33, 108; Collocott, 1921: 152, 153)

Mavutsine, Mavutsinim   The god of the beginning created his wife, Noitu, who was the mother of the sun and the moon. He gave the Camayura much of their culture, but introduced death because of disobedience. The Xingu tribes, Brazil. (Oberg, 1953: 52, 53; Villas Boas, 1973: 46, 53, 56)

Mawari   The god who created mankind but withdrew from involvment in their lives. The Waiwai, Brazil. (Fock, 1963: 35)

Mba   A deity who was mischievous and fun-loving but who also brought civilization to mankind. The Babua, Zaire. (Larousse, 1973: 530)

Mbere   The creator of "man out of clay, but first he was a lizard," which Mbere put into the sea. After eight days the lizard emerged, but as a man. The Fans, Gabon. (Leach, 1956: 135)

Mbud-ti   The Sun is believed to have given them their social organization, their moieties, when he was here on the earth with the moon. They established the first village, then returned to the sky. The Apinayé, Brazil. (Nimuendaju, 1967: 133–138, 158–165)

Milapukala   The totemic cockatoo at Milapuru. She created numerous animals and lizards and gave man wild honey and other foods. The Tiwi, Melville Island, Australia. (Mountford, 1958: 37, 53)

Minan   A culture hero, instigated by Djamar the supreme being, "made dances and the smooth black stone axes." The Bad of West Kimberley, Australia. (Eliade, 1964: 37)

Montezuma   The culture hero/god of the Papago taught them hunting and the cultivation of maize. Arizona and Mexico. (Burland, 1965: 102; Bancroft, 1886, 3: 75–77)

Mori-oi   She and her husband Raupu created the pig. The Elema, Papuan Gulf, New Guinea. (Holmes, 1902: 430)

Morongo   A goddess, a wife of Mwuetsi, was the mother of animals and men. South Rhodesia. (Deren, 1953: 54)

Morungo   A remote god—"the author of Nature." The Manganjas, South Africa. (Williams, 1936: 295)

(X)mucane   *See* **Xmucane**

Mudjeekawis   The first son, and favorite, of Epingishmook and Winonah. He brought wampum to the Anishnabeg, which he took from the bears who told him "it was a means by which the past was remembered and passed on." He returned to the west as Kabeyung to be leader of the grizzly bears and to live in the Land of the Mountains with his father. The Ojibway, Minnesota/Manitoba. (Johnston, 1976: 151–153)

Mudungkala The creator of the land of the Tiwis is the wife of Tukimbini and mother of Wuriupranala and Murupiangkala (daughters) and Purukupali (son). Melville Island, Australia. (Mountford, 1958: 24, 25, 37)

Muhoka Brother of Guahari with whom he created the first Piaroas out of the "shapeless animals" they released from inside the mountain. His voice is represented by the "me'otsa, a small, shrill instrument" used in the sacred music. The Piaroa, Orinoco River area, Venezuela. (Gheerbrant, 1954: 110–111)

Mukama The creator of men and animals and also of rivers. He was a forger of iron and introduced hoes. The Basoga, Uganda. (Roscoe, 1915: 248)

Mukulyinmaku Seizankua "In Nangakalua (a mountain in the west) lives Father Mukulyinmaku Seizankua, the father of the earth, the father of trees, rivers, magic remedies, field crops, and temple-mountains." Husband of Maneneumañ. The Kagaba of San Miguel, Colombia. (Preuss, 1926: 68)

Mumpal An Australian thunder god who created all things. (Brinton, 1897: 81)

Mungan-ngaua A sky god who lived for a time on earth taught the people all they know regarding their material and cultural needs. The Kurnai, Southeast Australia. (Howitt, 1904: 493)

Musikavanhu The creator of mankind. The Shona, Rhodesia. (Mbiti, 1970, 2: 335)

Mustam-ho The son of Maty-a-vela created mankind and the animal and vegetable worlds. The Mojave, Arizona. (Bourke, 1889: 172–179; Alexander, 1964: 180)

Mut-si-i-u-iv The culture hero taught them to make and use arrows. The Cheyenne, Colorado and Wyoming. (Leach, 1949: 76)

Mu xa do The king of the mu xa (celestial beings). He creates men and his inattention at times is responsible for the cripples and defectives. Of the gods he is the most closely associated with mankind and is protective if propitiated. The Karen, Burma. (Marshall, 1922: 223–224, 248)

Naka The creator of mankind; all else was created by his sister, Nebele. He gave the Sonjo the digging-stick. Tanzania. (Gray, 1963: 98)

Nakoeri The culture hero and creator of animals and mankind ascended to the sky where he is beneficent, though remote, and requires no cult. He is involved in the "investiture of the curers." The Bacairi, Brazil. (Abreu, 1938: 266; Altenfelder, 1950: 264–265; Zerries, 1968: 266)

Nanabush Son of Epingishmook (the West) and Winonah, a human. He had supernatural powers and was sent as a messenger by Kitche Manitou to teach the Anishnabeg. He won from his father the Pipe of Peace for the people. He could transform as animal or human—in the latter the Anishnabeg could relate to him and learn; he could be courageous or fearful, "noble and strong, or ignoble and weak." This they could understand and love. The Ojibway, Lake Superior region, Canada/United States. (Johnston, 1976: 17–20)

Nanderevusu The culture hero, source of civilization, was the father of Tupan. His wife was Nandecy. The Tupians, Brazil. (Larousse, 1968: 447)

Nanderiquey, Nianderyquey One of the twin culture hero deities who gave men fire, which was taken from the urubus (birds). The Apapocuva-Guarani, Brazil. (Levi-Strauss, 1969: 139–140; Métraux, 1946, 2: 115)

Napi, Napiwa The creator of the earth, animals, and mankind is depicted as beneficent, but at the same time as mischievous and foolish, sometimes obscene. The Blackfoot, northern Plains, United States/Canada. (Wissler and Duvall, 1908: 7, 8, 11; Grinnell, 1892: 159–160; 1893: 44; Maclean, 1893: 165–168)

Nareau The ancient pre-existent spider "commanded sand and water to bear children." Among them was Nareau, the younger spider, who killed the elder and made the sun and moon from his eyes. The Gilbert Islands, Micronesia. (Leach, 1956: 183; Poignant, 1967: 71)

na rip bu A "deity who created the different kinds of soil, i.e., both the cultivable soil and the stony soil." The Lepchas, Sikkim. (Siiger, 1967: 143)

Nautsiti She and her sister, Iyatiku, were placed on the earth by Ut'siti to complete its form under the direction of Tsitstinako—providing corn, fire, tobacco, giving life to living things. The Keresan, New Mexico. (Parson, 1939: 243–244)

Naycuric The creator of peyote, a chthonic deity with the form of a crayfish. The Huichol, Mexico. (Furst, 1972: 143)

Ndengei A serpent god whose movement caused earthquakes. He created mankind while his son, Rokomautu, created the earth. Fiji Islands, Melanesia. (Thomson, 1925, 6: 14; Poignant, 1967: 94; Spencer, 1941: 1)

702

Nedamik The creator god "subjected the first humans to an ordeal by tickling. Those who laughed were changed into land or water animals. . . . Those humans who maintained self-control became jaguars or men who hunted jaguars." The Toba-Pilaga, Paraguay/Argentina. (Levi-Strauss, 1969: 120)

Nemquetheba, Nemterequeteba A name of Bochica, the principal culture hero of the Chibcha and the Muisca. Colombia. (Reichel-Dolmatoff, 1975: 45; Loeb, 1931: 543; Alexander, 1920: 202; Brinton, 1868: 160, 183)

Nesaru The creator of the Corn Mother "whom he sent into the underworld to deliver the people imprisoned there, and to lead them . . . into the light of day." The Caddoan. Among the Arikara he was the sky god who supervised the creation. South Central States. (Alexander, 1964: 108; Burland, 1965: 84)

Nestu-Nopantu *See* **Nostu-Nopantu**

Ngawn-wa Magam A benevolent god made by Chanum and Woishun fashioned the earth making it habitable. The Kachin, Burma. (Scott, 1964: 263–264)

Nianderu Pa-pa Miri A god who created men and then gave them fire, which he seized from the vulture-sorcerers. The Mbya, Paraguay. (Levi-Strauss, 1969: 140)

Nihancan A creator in the sense of having fished up the land, and also a trickster. The Arapaho, Colorado. (Wissler and Duvall, 1908: 11)

Ninewu The creator and instructor "in behavior and work." The Tsou, Formosa. (Er-wei, 1959: 536)

Nix'ant, Nihant A deity, the Earthmaker, credited with creating the earth, man, and animals. He was also a culture hero/trickster. The Gross Ventres, Montana. (Kroeber, 1907: 59; Wissler and Duvall, 1908: 11; Pettazzoni, 1956: 378)

Njambi The god who "created men and animals, rivers and all things" is concerned also with human affairs. The Lele of Kasai, Belgian Congo. (Douglas, 1954: 9)

Noongshaba The god who created rocks and stones. The Meitheis, India/Assam. (Hodson, 1908: 98)

Nostu-Nopantu, Nestu-Nopantu A deity, female (P.) or male (B.), deputized by Tatara-Rabuga to create the earth, caused the beetle to bring up clay from under the water from which the earth was fashioned. The Garos, Assam/India. (Playfair, 1909: 81–82; Barkataki, 1969: 27)

Nowakila The most commonly used title of raven, a culture hero type, given powers by Älquntäm. The Bella Coola, British Columbia. (McIlwraith, 1948, 1: 82)

Nsi The benevolent, though sometimes unjust, earth deity of the Ekoi, with Osaw, created the things of the earth. Nigeria/Cameroon. (Meek, 1931: 191; Lowie, 1925: 46)

Nudimmud The name of Enki as a creator god—in his capacity to "form" from the moist clay, as a god of potters, craftsmen, artists, etc. Near East. (Jacobsen, 1970: 22; 1976: 111)

Numbakulla A primordial, self-existent god created "mountains, rivers, and all sorts of animals and plants" and "spirit children" (Eliade, 1973: 50–51); also named as two sky deities who created men and women. The Aranda, Australia. (Poignant, 1967: 117)

Numi-Tarem The sky god and creator of mankind is also the source of the Vogul's civilization, teaching them to fish, etc. Siberia. (Eliade, 1958: 62)

Numock-muckenah The culture hero deity taught them all they knew and gave them their institutions and religion. The Mandan of the upper Missouri River, North Dakota. (Brinton, 1868: 160)

Nurelli The god who created the land, trees, and animals gave their laws to the Wiimbaio. Australia. (Eliade, 1973: 4; Howitt, 1904: 489)

Nurundere, Nurrundere The supreme being and creator god gave mankind the weapons for hunting and war as well as their rites and ceremonies. The Narrinyeri, Australia. (Woods, 1879: 55; Howitt, 1904: 488; Reed, 1965: 70)

Nütja Nuo The god who created souls for humans. The Tavgy or Avam Samoyed, Siberia. (Pettersson, 1957: 21)

Nyahpa mahse A supernatural being who taught the Desana jewelry craftsmanship and how to work with metals—copper, silver. Colombia. (Reichel-Dolmatoff, 1971: 253)

Nyanyi Bumba The white heron was the creator of all the birds other than the kite. The Bushongo, Zaire. (Eliade, 1967: 91)

Nyonye Ngana One of the three sons of Bumba who "made the white ants." He died because of the work, so the ants buried him to honor him. The Bushongo, Zaire. (Eliade, 1967: 92)

Oannes The Babylonian god, half-fish, half-man, who came from the sea taught them all cultural knowledge, agriculture, and construction. Near East. (Frankfort, 1946: 22; Robertson, 1911: 214; Brinton, 1897: 161; Sayce, 1898: 131)

Ochkih-Hadda A kind of devil who came and taught the Mandan many things then disappeared. He was much feared and sacrificed to. There is a belief "that whoever dreams of him is doomed soon to die." North Dakota. (Wied-Neuwied, 1843: 360)

Ockabewis A messenger of the gods who taught men what they know. The Chippewa, Minnesota/Manitoba. (Burland, 1965: 149)

Okikurumi A god of the heavens gave civilization to the Ainus and taught them hunting and fishing. His sister/wife was Turesh Machi, and won Wariunekuru. Japan. (Chamberlain, 1887: 15–17)

Olfad A cunning trickster and transformer, yet he does some good, is responsible for the presence of the cat and fire, is "also the creator of lightning." Truk, Micronesia. (Bollig, 1927: 8, 9)

Ombepo An aspect of Mukuru as the creator of the soul. The Herero, Namibia. (Luttig, 1933: 83)

Omel A Finno-Ugric god of evil and darkness created "amphibious creatures, insects, and spirits of the forest." Ziryen, Russia. (Pettersson, 1957: 22)

O'oimbre The trickster culture hero of the Kayapo-Kuben-kranken transformed the people of a village into peccaries. He takes the form of an armadillo. Brazil. (Levi-Strauss, 1969: 86, 89)

Orekajuvakai The creator god brought men up out of the earth and caused them to laugh and talk through the antics of "the little red toad"—the Origin of language. The Tereno, Brazil. (Levi-Strauss, 1969: 123)

Oru Daughter of Tatuma and Tapuppa and sister/wife of Otaia. They created the land and were the parents of the gods, among them Teorraha whom Oru married after the death of Otaia. Tahiti, Polynesia. (Williamson, 1933, 1: 17)

Osanoha The evil counterpart of Osanowa was the creator of animals and of diseases. The Edo, Nigeria. (Frazer, 1926: 126–127)

Osanowa The creator of mankind whose evil counterpart is Osanoha. The Edo, Nigeria. (Frazer, 1926: 126)

Oséema A supernatural culture hero type of spirit gave the people maize and other foods. The Yupa, Venezuela. (Wilbert, 1974: 128–130)

Otaia Son of Tatuma and Tapuppa and brother/husband of Oru—the creators of the land and the parents of gods. Tahiti, Polynesia. (Williamson, 1933, 1: 17)

Otcipapa A god of the Conebo, Panoan stock, who created the earth, men, animals, and plants. He is considered the source of the evils that he may befall them. Peru. (Farabee, 1922: 84)

(Po) Ovlah, Alwah A polymorphous deity who created Po Rasullak and Po Latila, and who himself was created by Po Ovlahuk. The Chams, Annam/Cambodia. (Cabaton, 1925, 3: 342)

(Po) Ovlahuk The god who created Po Ovlah. The Chams, Annam/Cambodia. (Cabaton, 1925, 3: 342)

Pacat Pach A god of the Mayan who created the Puuc hills in Yucatan. Mexico. (Thompson, 1970: 325)

Pachacamac A son of the sun and moon and brother of Con whose people he transformed into animals. He then created the present Indians and taught them agriculture, the arts of war and peace, and their occupations. A Pre-Incan god. Coastal Peru. (Mishkin, 1940: 225; Brinton, 1882: 195–196; Osborne, 1968: 107; Larousse, 1968: 442–443)

Pajana A god of the Black Sea Tatars who created mankind but required the help of Kudai to give man a soul. Russia. (MacCulloch, 1964: 373; Pettersson, 1957: 23)

Pamuri-mahse A god who brought the men created by page abe from Ahpikondia (Paradise) to the earth. He then gave the different tribes their identifying objects—to the Desana, the bow and arrow, to others the fishing rod, blow gun, etc. Then he returned to Ahpikondia. Colombia. (Reichel-Dolmatoff, 1971: 25–27)

Pananga This deity "taught humans many useful techniques." The Siuai, Bougainville (Solomon Islands), Melanesia. (Oliver, 1967: 42)

Pay Zume A culture hero/god who taught the people agriculture and hunting. Paraguay. Known by the Tupi-Guaranay peoples from the Rio de la Plata to the West Indies as Tamu, Tume, or Zume. (Brinton, 1882: 224)

Peketua A deity who formed the first egg (when Tane was seeking to establish mortals), which "produced the reptile called *tuatara*." The Maori, New Zealand. (Best, 1924: 114)

Peregun 'Gbo A forest god seems to have been responsible for the birds and animals of the forest. The Yoruba, Nigeria. (Wyndham, 1919: 124–125; 1921: 35)

Piteri The wife of Bura Penu, with whom "worshipped as Creator of mankind." The Kandhs of Madras, India. (Crooke, 1925, 7: 651)

(X)piyacoc *See* **Xpiyacoc**

Prine'a With S'ribtuwe "created many things before flying up into the sky." The Shavante, Brazil. (Maybury-Lewis, 1967: 287)

Prometheus One of the Titans, son of Iapetus and Themis or Clymene. He created man and gave him fire with all its attendant blessings, and taught him the principles of civilization and the arts. Greece. (Bulfinch, 1898: 20–21, 27; Kerényi, 1951: 224; Larousse, 1968: 95; Fairbanks, 1907: 80; Morford and Lenardon, 1975: 32, 43, 45, 46; Prentice Hall, 1965: 125)

Puana The water snake god helped create the world. The Yaruro, Venezuela. (Kirchhoff, 1948, 2: 462)

Pund-jel, Pundgel The creator of man. The Australian Negritos. (Pettersson, 1957: 26; Larousse, 1968: 469; Keeler, 1960: 49)

Puppu-imbul A deity who created the sun. The Wurunjerri, Australia. (Fallaize, 1925, 12: 62)

Pupula The Lizard, "their man-shaper," who took the fetal positioned humans and gave them flexibility and dexterity; then taught them the use of fire and established laws and ceremonies. The Pindupi and Jumu, Australia. (Leach, 1956: 191)

Purrunaminari The creator of mankind, whose wife is Taparimarru and whose son is Sisiri. The Maipuri, Guiana. (Alexander, 1920: 259)

Purutahui According to some the god who made the stars out of metal. The Pericues, Baja California. (Loeb, 1931: 550; Bancroft, 1886, 3: 84)

Putir Selong Tamanang Sister/wife of Mahatala. A creatress—"the life-producer," who causes fruit and green things to grow. The Ngaju, Borneo. (Scharer, 1963: 16, 28, 31)

Q'aneqe'lakw One of the owners of the Water of Life and a transformer. "By dipping the blanket of Olachen-Woman into the water" he creates fish. He "cures the blindness of women by spitting on their eyes, the power of his saliva being either inherent or produced by the gum he is always chewing." The Kwakiutl, British Columbia. (Boas, 1935: 35, 109, 133)

Qastceyalci A beneficent god who with other gods created humans. The Navajo, Arizona and New Mexico. (Matthews, 1889: 90; 1890: 89)

Qat A god of the Banks Islands fished up the land out of the sea, created men and animals, and in some areas also the rocks and trees. He introduced night, which he got from Qong. Melanesia. (Codrington, 1881: 268–271; Poignant, 1967: 99; Mackenzie, n.d.: 303–304)

Quaayayp The son of Niparaya and Anayicoyondi lived among the Pericue Indians and taught them. Baja California. (Bancroft, 1886, 3: 169)

Quwai A deity who fashioned some "geographical features such as creeks and rocks" also stocked the streams with fish. The Cubeo, Colombia. (Goldman, 1940: 242)

Raja Brahil The creator of "all living things" at the command of Tuhan Allah. The Mantra, Malay Peninsula. (Skeat, 1906: 322)

Raja Puru, Raja Peres The god of smallpox and diseases and a god of persecution, from which he also relieves, however, with appropriate offerings, is also believed to have taught them their crafts. The Ngaju, Borneo. (Scharer, 1963: 20–21, 52)

Rangi-nui-e-tu-nei The sky god is the creator, with Papa-tu-a-nuku, of gods and men. The Maori, New Zealand. (Andersen, 1928: 355, 367)

Rang Kau Hawa A "heavenly body" who created human beings. The Tangsas (Yogli tribe), Indo/Burmese. (Dutta, 1959: 3)

Ranying The god who, after the earth was created by the supreme being, was responsible for the formation of animals and plants. The Dyaks, Borneo. (Brinton, 1897: 160)

Ranying Pahatara Identical with Mahatala as the creator of mankind, the giver of life. Immortality was denied man by Peres (Jata), but Ranying Pahatara provided that the "hair, teeth and nails are incorruptible." The Ngaju, Borneo. (Scharer, 1963: 22–23)

Rarang The sun was the creator of the first beings. The Alfuru, North Celebes, Indonesia. (Roheim, 1972: 31)

Raupu The creator of the pig with his wife Mori-oi. The Elema, Papuan Gulf, New Guinea. (Holmes, 1902: 430)

Rikiranga   A spirit who possibly helped Imana with the creation of visible things. The Warundi, Urundi and Ruanda. (Frazer, 1926: 225)

Riyangombe   With Rikiranga possibly helped Imana with the creation of visible things. The Warundi, Urundi and Ruanda. (Frazer, 1926: 225)

Rokomoutu   The son of Ndengei at whose instigation he made the land from the ocean floor. Fiji, Melanesia. (Thomson, 1925, 6: 14; Poignant, 1967: 94)

Rukho   The goddess of darkness created man but could not give him a spirit. The Mandeans, Mesopotamia, Near East. (Dragomanov, 1961: 51)

Salampandai, Selampandai   The creatress of men, whom she forms out of clay. Gender is chosen by the child itself according to the implements it indicates it wishes to handle. Also given as male. The Sea Dyaks, Borneo. (Gomes, 1911: 197; Roth, 1968: 176–177; Mackenzie, n.d.: 275; Sarawak Gazette, 1963: 14, 16)

Salibud   A deity of the Bagobo who taught them cultivation, trade, and their industries. Philippines. (Benedict, 1916: 29)

Samé   A deity who "had power over the elements and tempests . . . he taught the use of agriculture and magic." Brazil. (Donnelly, 1949: 133)

Samoel   A deity who assisted with the creation of the earth. Trans-Caucasia. (Dragomanov, 1961: 57)

sang lo   ". . . one of the four creators of female beings"; invoked in marriage ceremonies. The Lepchas, Sikkim. (Siiger, 1967: 69, 144)

Sede-tsiak   Old Man Coyote was the creator of man, animals, and plants, and taught men their culture. The Patwin, California. (Kroeber, 1932: 304–305)

Sekarika   The name of Kumaphari as the creator of the Shipaya—"out of arrow reeds." Brazil. (Zerries, 1968: 288)

Selempatoh   The god "who moulded, or shaped matter. After which Batara recognized it, and thus our forefathers became man." The Iban Dyaks of Sarawak, Borneo. (Sarawak Gazette, 1963: 133)

Semenia   The Master of the Earth's food (yuca) was the chief of the bird people (bird/human) created by Wanadi to help the old people (human/animal). Semenia taught them to clear trees making conucos (clearings), and cultivation. He brought order, cooperation, food, etc. When he had them cut down the Marahuaka tree (its roots were in the sky), the rains came from the heavens forming the rivers. Its trunk broke into three parts, forming the mountains. Semenia is the red-billed scythebill and with his people retired to the sky to live. The Makiritare, Venezuela. (Civrieux, 1980: 132–136, 143, 190)

Sempulon   A creator who, with Minjanni, created men and animals out of stone. The Pari, Borneo. (Mackenzie, 1930: 337)

Seruhe Ianadi   The first Wanadi of the Earth, a damodede, made by the Sky Wanadi. He "brought knowledge, tobacco, the maraca, and the *wiriki*. He smoked and he sang and he made the old people." But he returned to the sky because Odosha, the very evil one, caused death and killing and evil. The Makiritare, Venezuela. (Civrieux, 1980: 21)

Shangs po (pr. **Shangpo**)   The positive god, "the lord of Being," the beneficent father in the "creation of the contents of the world." With Chu lcam the parents of the srid pa'i ming sring—nine male and nine female siblings. His name varies: Shangs po yab srid, Tsangs pa, Ye smon rgyal po. Tibet. (Tucci, 1980: 329)

sha so rak rok   The god who created and protects domestic animals and fowls. The Lepchas, Sikkim. (Siiger, 1967: 78, 144)

Sheik-Adi   The creator of good things. The Kurds, Yezid, Iran. (Dragomanov, 1961: 146)

Shel gyer (pr. **Shegyer**)   A creation deity in the Bon religion. The "Yak descends from heaven on to the mountain and thus goes out into the world. Thereupon he tears with his horns the mountains to right and left, and the earth becomes covered with flowers. . . . With this the creation is completed." Tibet. (Tucci, 1980: 220)

Sidne   Goddess creator of the animal and vegetable worlds. Daughter of Anguta. The Nugumiut, Frobisher Bay, Canada. (Boas, 1884/85: 583)

Sigu   Among the Ackawoio, the son of Makunaima and equally powerful. He assisted in the creation of birds, animals, and food plants, and ruled over the birds and beasts. Guiana. (Brett, 1868: 378; Métraux, 1946, 2: 114)

Simskalin   Son of Kutkhu and Ilkxum. According to one legend his father created the world out of him. The Kamchadal, Siberia. (Czaplicka, 1968: 270)

706

Sin The moon god who controlled the waters was also the creator of the grasses. Babylon, Near East. (Eliade, 1958: 159, 162)

Sitapi Daughter of Batara guru. They sent the swallows to be the first living things on earth, but it was barren. She caused "seven hen's eggs and a magic ring" to be lowered from the sky, from which were obtained plants and trees, cattle, and other animals, and all else needed or desired. The Battak, Sumatra. (MacKenzie, 1930: 310)

Sivirri The "culture hero of the Tjununji tribe, inventor of the drum used in initiation rites, builder of the first wooden canoe, and a traveler who eventually went north into Torres Straits Islands." Cape York, Australia. (Leach, 1950, 2: 1016)

Siwa Brother of Mafif. They were the creators of men, fashioned the surface of the earth, and introduced taro and textiles. The Mejbrat, New Guinea. (Elmberg, 1955: 45)

Skiritiohuts A star god of the southeast who created the wolf. He is called "Fool-Coyote" because he precedes the morning star and causes the coyote to begin howling. The Skidi Pawnee, Nebraska. (Dorsey, 1904: 17)

Soketatai In Tangoa the creator of man who is concerned with his welfare. New Hebrides, Melanesia. (Rivers, 1925, 9: 353)

S'ribtuwe A culture hero/creator who "went to live in the water, where he created many things," including women whom he married. The Shavante, Brazil. (Maybury-Lewis, 1967: 248)

suLa The son of Sibu. He taught mankind cultivation and "how to build circular houses." Costa Rica. (Stone, 1962: 51)

Sumua The great god of the Lakalai who created numerous things, gave mankind food, food animals, fire, and the "*valuku* ceremonies." New Britain, Melanesia. (Valentine, 1965: 164–165, 185)

Surites, Curicaberis A culture hero/god who was responsible for their laws and government, their calendar. The Tarascos, Michoacan, Mexico. (Brinton, 1882: 208)

Susugots The creator of "harmful things, sickness, . . . and other ills." Yap Island, Micronesia. (Müller, 1917: 309)

Tagaloa fa'a tuputupunu'u Tagaloa as creator of lands. Manua (Samoa), Polynesia. (Mead, 1930: 159)

Tagar, Tagaro, Tagaroa A sky god who came down to the earth and created mankind and various things before returning. His brother Suqe attempted to interfere with his good work. New Hebrides, Melanesia. (Buck, 1938, 1: 420; Rivers, 1925, 9: 353; Mackenzie, n.d.: 302–304; Codrington, 1881, 291–294)

Tahar In Atchin the creator of mankind and concerned in his affairs. He "represents both sun and moon." New Hebrides, Melanesia. (Rivers, 1925, 9: 353)

Tahobn The "dung beetle, brought forth the earth [out of the water] in a small pack" from which grew the land. The Menik Kaien, the Kintak Bong, Malaya. (Evans, 1937: 143, 159; Long, 1963: 210)

tak bo thing A god who with na zong nyo created the first humans. The Lepchas, Sikkim. (Siiger, 1967: 145)

Tama The thunder deity who was "an important culture hero and shaman and eventually retired to a lake in the mountains" is associated with weather phenomena. The Paez, Colombia. (Reichel-Dolmatoff, 1975: 51, 53)

Tamagisangah A god of the south who created human beings "made them beautiful or ugly according to whether or not they sacrificed to him." His wife is Teraychapada. The Yami, Formosa. (Del Re, n.d.: 57; Campbell, 1925, 6: 84)

Tamoi The culture hero/ancestor taught them "agriculture and the preparation of chicha." He went to the afterworld, where he promised to bring them on death. The Guarayu, Bolivia and Brazil. (Métraux, 1948, 2: 436–437; 1942: 107; MacCulloch, 1925, 11: 823)

Tamu A culture hero and sky god who taught the Caribs agriculture and their arts. Brazil. (Spence, 1925, 2: 836)

Tamusi The god who created animals and all good things is the son of Amana, and is identified with the Pleiades. The Caliña, Surinam. (Zerries, 1968: 246; Penard, 1917: 253)

ta nat'ti Twin culture heroes who created mankind, especially the Tukuna. Brazil and Peru. (Nimuendaju, 1952: 115)

Tanuta "Earth-Maker." In one tale the husband of Yineaneut, the daughter of Big-Raven. The Koryak, Siberia. (Czaplicka, 1969: 262)

Taogn The creator of trees and stones with his brother Tegn. The Bateg, Negritos, Malaya. (Evans, 1937: 158)

Tatak In Ambrim "a being who is usually supposed to have created man and to take an interest in his welfare." New Hebrides, Melanesia. (Rivers, 1925, 9: 353)

Tawiskarong The evil twin of the culture heroes who created the dangerous and destructive animals. The Huron, Ontario. (Hale, 1888: 181; Long, 1963: 194)

Tawkxwax A demiurge and trickster who died, then "took another body and lived again." He changes his skin like a serpent. The Mataco, Argentina. (Levi-Strauss, 1969: 305; Métraux, 1939: 7, 22)

Tcaipakomat The creator of mankind. The Kawakipais, California. (Keeler, 1960: 50)

Tcenes, Tsenes The Thunder, the superior of Nagaicho (the "two original beings"), was assisted by him in the creation of the surface of the earth, of men, and of many of the animals. The Kato, California. (Kroeber, 1925: 155; Loeb, 1932: 14, 23; Lissner, 1961: 88; Schmidt, 1933: 27, 28)

Tcikapis The dwarf but very strong and benevolent culture hero was also a great conjuror. The Montagnais-Naskapi, Labrador/Quebec. (Leach, 1950: 1106)

Te-erui The god who created the land is the son of Te-tareva. Hervey Islands, Polynesia. (Williamson, 1933: 29)

Tegn Brother of Taogn, creators of trees and stones. The Bateg (Negritos), Malaya. (Evans, 1937: 158)

Teharonhiawagon The beneficent creator of animals, birds, trees, plants, and man, taught man fire-making and agriculture. The Iroquois, Eastern United States. (Blair, 1912: 272; Swanton, 1928: 212)

Teikirzi An important goddess of the Todas of the Nilgiri Hills who was going to bring a man back to life, but found that though some wept, others were happy, so she left well enough alone. She was responsible for their social and ceremonial laws and rituals. India. (Rivers, 1925, 12: 354; Hartland, 1925, 4: 412)

Tenan-tomgin, Tenantomri The beneficent and just creator of mankind is also the "Spirit of the Zenith." He is sometimes identified with Big-Raven. The Chukchee, Siberia. (Bogoras, 1904/09: 314, 319; 1928: 305; Czabplicka, 1969: 257)

Tenubi The creator of the earth and of all vegetation. The Land Dyaks, Borneo. (Roth, 1968: 165)

Te-Papa With Te-Tumu the creators of man and the animals and vegetable kingdoms. Tuamotu, Polynesia. (Henry, 1928: 347)

Te-Tumu The male creative force who with Te-Papa created man and the animal and vegetable worlds. Tuamotu, Polynesia. (Henry, 1928: 347; Buck, 1938: 78; Poignant, 1967: 31)

Tijuskeha, Tijuska'a, Tse'sta (Oklahoma Wyandot) The good god of the creator twin pair created all good things and taught man cultural pursuits and hunting. His evil twin, Taweskare, did his utmost to thwart him. The Huron and the Wyandot, Eastern United States and Canada. (Barbeau, 1914: 292, 294; Long, 1963: 194–195; Hale, 1888: 181)

Tochopa A benevolent god of the Havasupai who taught them "how to build the toholwa: the framework of poles, the covering of green boughs and mud sealing it." Among the Walapai the god who taught them their arts. Arizona. (Iliff, 1954: 152; Alexander, 1964: 180)

Tokataitai In Malo a deity considered to have created mankind and to be concerned with his welfare. New Hebrides, Melanesia. (Rivers, 1925, 9: 353)

Tomo According to some he was the first man who created the world and the moon, and took on the role of a culture hero. Others identify him with the sun and fine weather. The A-Pucikwar, Andaman Islands, Bay of Bengal. (Radcliffe-Brown, 1967: 142, 169, 195)

Totetara At Nogugu in Santo a god who is considered the creator of man and who is concerned with his affairs. New Hebrides, Melanesia. (Rivers, 1925, 9: 353)

Tpemra A culture hero/creator god. The Shavante, Brazil. (Maybury-Lewis, 1967: 285, 248)

Ts'aqame The culture hero/ancestor gave "the mink, sun, daybreak, and copper mask, that belonged to his house in heaven to his son." The Kwakiutl, British Columbia. (Boas, 1935: 80, 144, 185)

Tsenes *See* **Tcenes**

Tsentsa A name of the benevolent creator twin of the Iroquois whose brother Taweskare is the destructive force. They "shaped the earth" and are the sons of the West Wind. Eastern United States. (Bjorklund, 1969: 133; Burland, 1965: 77)

Tsohanoai The Sun-bearer (it is his shield) is the creator of the large game animals. The Navaho, Arizona and New Mexico. (Matthews, 1902: 30)

Tsuma A white culture hero who was the source of the laws, the arts, and the industries. Venezuela. (Loeb, 1931: 543)

Tuhan Di-Bawah The god of the underworld created the earth and instituted death to control the population. The Jakun and the Mantri, Malay Peninsula. (Skeat, 1925, 8: 355; 1906: 179–180; Cole, 1945: 119)

tuinta The spirit and owner of the stone ax. The Tukuna, Brazil and Peru. (Nimuendaju, 1952: 131)

Tukimbini A bird, the "yellowfaced honey-eater," was responsible for the establishment of the totemic places and for the transformation of mythical peoples into the totemic object or animal. He taught the associated rules and customs. He had many wives, among them Waia and Paninduela. The Tiwi, Melville Island, Australia. (Mountford, 1958: 25, 31, 35–36, 39)

Tule A trickster deity of the Zande who, nevertheless, gave them their civilization. Zaire. (Larousse, 1973: 530)

Tulungusaq The Crow Father, a creator who fashioned vegetation, animals, men from clay, supplied the earth with light. As a culture hero he taught men construction and hunting and fishing. The Eskimo, Alaska. (Larousse, 1973: 441)

Tuminkar, Tuminikar The benevolent culture hero and creator god. Twin of the evil Duid. The Wapisiana, the Taruma, the Mapidians, Brazil and Guiana. (Farabee, 1918: 108, 159; Queval, 1968: 115; Métraux, 1946, 2: 115)

Tumu-nui One of the creation gods and organizer of the features of the earth. Ra'iatea, Society Islands, Polynesia. (Henry, 1928: 96, 337, 395–398)

Tupa, Tumpa The creator of man and of all living things. The Dyaks, Borneo. (Roth, 1968: 165; Brinton, 1897: 123)

Tupa, Tupan The chief god is associated with the thunder and lightning. Among the coastal Tupi he appears as a creator god. As a culture hero he transformed the people of a village into wild pigs, over whom he put his god-child Marana ywa. The Tupi and the Tenetehara, Brazil. (Levi-Strauss, 1969: 84–85; Wagley and Galvao, 1948, 1: 145, 147; 1949: 98; Spence, 1925, 2: 837; Brinton, 1868: 152; Bastide, 1960: 573)

Tu-va-dis-chi-ni The son of the Sun placed on the earth birds and all moving things which were provided by his father; also fruits, foods, and other vegetation. He also taught the people their crafts. The Apache, New Mexico, Arizona, and Mexico. (Bourke, 1890: 211)

Tyi wara The god of the young fieldworkers of the villages. He was half-man, half-animal, and taught men farming. The Bambara, Mali, Niger and Senegal. (Tauxier, 1927: 325; Imperato, 1975: 70)

Uazale The culture hero of the Paressi who "discovered manioc, produced tobacco, and planted his hair to produce cotton. He was very hairy, had a tail, and a membrane between his arms and legs like a bat." Matto Grosso, South America. (Leach, 1950: 1148)

Umikii-gamı and **Uminai-gami** A brother and sister who created the land and human beings. Okinawa, Ryukyu Islands. (Lebra, 1966: 24)

Umvili With Barachi "said to have created man." The Golos, Sudan. (Budge, 1973, 1: 375)

Ungud A great snake deity who with Wallanganda created all things. The Unambal, Australia. (Eliade, 1964: 68–79)

Votan A beneficent culture hero/god of the Mayan gave them language and writing, laws and the calendar, cultivation, etc. Chiapas, Tabasco, Oaxaca, Mexico. (Brinton, 1882: 213–215; Bancroft, 1886, 3: 450–454; Spence, 1923: 133)

Walangala A celestial supreme god but not worshipped with prayers. He was also a culture hero in that he established their institutions, their ceremonies and rituals. The Ungarinyin, Australia. (Eliade, 1973: 72, 73)

Wallanganda A sky god who with Ungud created all things. The Unambal, Australia. (Eliade, 1973: 68–72)

Wangi He came out of the coconut tree broken open by Wailan wangko and created "the first human pair: at Wailan wangko's suggestion." The southern Minahassa, Celebes, Indonesia. (MacKenzie, 1930: 331)

Wantu The nephew of Wantu Su. He was sent to the earth with a drum containing some of all the things in the sky to give to men. The Sara family of tribes. Chad. (Larousse, 1973: 530)

Waramurungundju The great mother goddess came out of the sea and created the landscape, "and from her body she produced many children, animals and plants." Arnhem Land, Australia. (Poignant, 1967: 127)

Wasi   The teacher of the Cherokees and the establisher of their institutions. North Carolina and Tennessee. (Brinton, 1868: 160)

Wenebojo   The culture hero/demigod of the Chippewa created the earth with the help of the muskrat and eagle. He gave the people all good things and taught them agriculture and hunting as well as their religious rites. He was a trickster as well. Wi'ske of the Potawatomi. Wisconsin. (Ritzenthaler, 1970: 43, 87, 137–138, 144)

Wi   As a creator he, the sun, and Hanwi assisted Mahpiyato with the creation of animals, molding those "having horns and hooves", making them warm, except those (fish) shaped by Unk, which he left cold because she was so unpleasant. The Lakota, South Dakota. (One Feather, 1982: 49)

Wihindaibo   "Iron-Man, the creator of the Whites." The Shoshone, Idaho. (Lowie, 1909: 233)

Wisakedjak   The culture hero and creator among the Cree, the Saulteaux Ojibwa, the Nippissings. Ontario. (Leach, 1950: 1179; Maclean, 1876: 438)

Wi'ske   The culture hero, older brother of Chibiabos, lives in the East, provided them with "tobacco, corn, and other useful products." The Potawatomi, Michigan/Wisconsin. Same as Wenebojo of the Chippewa. (Ritzenthaler, 1970: 43; Edmunds, 1980: 20)

Wiyot, Ouiot   The son of Tuukumit, the heavens, and of Tamayawut, the earth. He was the father of "the first race of beings that preceded mankind." He was killed by those who wanted to succeed him. The Acagchemen, the Juaneño, the Luiseño, and the Gabrielino, California. (Boscana, 1933: 27–28, 115–116; Kroeber, 1925: 637, 788)

woxpek-oma^w   The culture hero of the Yurok. Grandfather of tsooli-qaa. California. (Waterman, 1920: 258)

Woyengi   The "Mother"—created humans and breathed life into them. She allowed each to choose his manner of life as well as death—then decreed it so. The Ijaw, Nigeria. (Beier, 1966: 23)

Xavasumkuli   A goddess who created daylight and darkness. Mother of Kumastamxo by Kivikumat. The Yuma, Arizona. (Harrington, 1908: 331)

Xelas   The culture hero and transformer of the Lummi Indians. Puget Sound, Washington and British Columbia. (Leach, 1950: 1185)

Xmucané   Grandmother. With Xpiyacoc the creators of material things, of the lunar calendar, and parents of the seven Ahpú. Gods of divination using seeds. The Quiché, Guatemala. (Recinos, 1950: 79, 88, 107; Girard, 1979: 52, 55, 87; Thompson, 1970: 335; Bancroft, 1886, 3: 462)

Xpiyacoc   *See* **Xmucané**

Yanamá   A mythical ancestor who "created tupan, thunder and lightning." The Camayurá of the Mato Grosso. Brazil. (Oberg, 1953: 53)

Yanto   A beneficent god—"Co-creator of (foreigners); . . . guards souls of dead foreigners, domesticated animals." The Lacandon, Mexico. (Cline, 1944: 112)

Yel   The Raven god who formed the earth "and stocked the rivers with salmon," was also a god of the weather. The Athabascan, Pacific Northwestern America. (Brinton, 1882: 228–229; Boas, 1909/10: 584)

Yetar   In Santo a being believed to have created man and to be interested in his welfare. New Hebrides, Melanesia. (Rivers, 1925, 9: 353)

Yetlth   The Raven who was sent by Hetggaulana to spy on the celestial gods, chose to stay above ground, and created man. The Haida, British Columbia. (Harrison, 1891: 22, 23)

Yimantuwiñyai   The culture hero and creator god of the Hupa was also the source of the evils in the world. California. (Morice, 1925, 4: 639; Goddard, 1925, 6: 882; Kroeber, 1925: 134)

Yulatimot   One of the Masmasalanix who were culture heroes. The Bella Coola, British Columbia. (Boas, 1898: 32)

Yurikoyuvakai   The important twin culture heroes. Originally Yurikoyuvaki was singular and lived with his sister Livetchetchevena. When he stole from her garden she was "angry and cut open her own stomach and another Yurikoyuvakai came out." So there were two. They caused the Indians to come out of the ground and live on the earth, gave them fire and the knowledge of horticulture. The Terena, Brazil. (Altenfelder, 1946: 216–217)

Zame ye Mebege   A creator god gave them *eboka,* a narcotic, which "enable[s] men to see the dead." The Fang, Gabon. (Fernandez, 1972: 245–246)

Zamna   *See* **Itzamna**

Zie-ne A being who created men and demons and also insects. The Heh Miao, Southwest China. (Clarke, 1911: 41, 63)

Zome The creator of mankind. The Bulu, Cameroon. (Krug, 1949: 349)

Zume The culture hero/god of the Guarani gave them their civilization. Paraguay. (Spence, 1925, 2: 836)

39

Gods of Evil, Destructiveness

A An evil spirit who was begotten of Num, but now "acts independently." He has some control over the Tadebtsii (evil spirits). The Nenets (Samoyed), Siberia. (Struve, 1880: 794)

Abili, Jibililu, Sheitan The Evil One. The Nupe, Nigeria. (Nadel, 1954: 12)

Abuhene The macaw god and the god of the west is the god of dark shamanism and of death. He is approached only by the hoarotu, the dark shaman, who brings him the livers of humans as his food. He rules the underworld. The Warao, Venezuela. (Wilbert, 1973, 1: 5; 1973, 2: X, 407)

Achacatu A malevolent god of temptation to do wrong. The Salivas, Colombia. (Walde-Waldegg, 1936: 40)

Achekenat-kanet A spirit capable of both good and evil. The Tehuelche, Argentina. (Cooper, 1946, 5: 158; Alexander, 1920: 334)

Adharma A god of vice and unrighteousness "personified as a son of Brahma." India. (Dowson, 1961: 2)

Aeshma The Archdemon of Evil, the spirit of fury and anger, of devastation. Iran. (Seligmann, 1948: 38; Huart, 1963: 43; Gray, 1930: 185, 224; Larousse, 1968: 318; Hinnells, 1973: 54)

Agornath A cruel god, "dirty and vicious," who will disturb a new mother and infant, which no other god will do. The Himalayas, India. (Berreman, 1963: 372)

Aharaigichi, Queeve't The evil spirit, but regarded "affectionately." The Abipones, Argentina. (Alexander, 1920: 321)

Ahriman *See* **Angra Mainyu**

Aipalookvik A malevolent and destructive evil spirit who lives on the bottom of the sea and molests kayakers. The Eskimo. (Bilby, 1923: 266; Larousse, 1968: 426)

Ajo Ohia Ubu The "spirit of the Evil Forest of Ubu." The Igbo, Nigeria. (Isichei, 1978: 322)

Akataš The "Creator of Evil" who causes "neglect of duty." Iran. (Gray, 1930: 198, 224)

Akatokae A god of evil who causes sickness and lives in the underworld Te Matagi. Mangareva, Polynesia. (Buck, 1938: 425)

Aka Manah, Ako-Mano "His special function is to give 'vile thoughts and discord to the creatures' . . . he is characterised by stench." Iran. (Gray, 1930: 180–181; Hinnells, 1973: 52; Larousse, 1968: 317)

Akop An evil god who preys on the spouse of the deceased, and whose embrace causes death. The Tinguian, Philippines. (Cole, 1922: 300)

Ali-kirkcis An evil god, also known as Taquatu, who punishes by carrying off anyone that he finds idle or inattentive. The Southern Alacaluf, Chile. (Pettazzoni, 1956: 423)

Allara-Ogonur The "great evil spirit" who lives underground in the far north. The Yakut, Siberia. (Czaplicka, 1925, 12: 828)

Altjira iliinka Among the Aranda Tjoritja he is a wicked god; among others the beneficent supreme deity. Australia. (Roheim, 1972: 65–66)

Amatsu-Mikaboshi A god of evil. Japan. (Kato, 1926: 14; Larousse, 1968: 415)

712

Amte'p   A god of evil who causes blight and scarcity. The Flathead, Montana. (Teit, 1927/28: 383; Clark, 1966: 68–69)

Anau-kasitan   The Evil Spirit of the Puelche. Argentina. (Cooper, 1946, 5: 167)

Anchanchu   A demon who lures victims and then "afflicts them with deadly diseases." He is associated with whirlwinds and isolated areas. The Aymara, Peru/Bolivia. (Leach, 1949: 54)

Angalootarlo   An evil spirit and a thief who takes the form of a seal to lure the hunter, then transforms as a man and kills him. The Eskimo, Baffin Land, Canada. (Bilby, 1923: 270)

Angra Mainyu, Ahriman   The Zoroastrian spirit of evil and darkness, of falsehood. He is the source of all evil and in eternal combat with Ahura Mazda. His later name is Ahriman. Iran. (Littleton, 1965: 97; Campbell, 1964: 192; Huart, 1963: 41; Gray, 1930: 176–178; Schoeps, 1961: 84; Drahomanov, 1961: 24–25; Hinnells, 1973: 54)

Angul   A spirit "who kills people with the helve of his ax." The Isneg, Luzon, Philippines. (Vanoverbergh, 1953: 99)

Anlabbang   An evil anito who causes quarreling. The Apayao, Philippines. (Wilson, 1947: 23)

Anog Ite, Anogite   An evil, vengeful goddess, the Two-Faced Woman—one face "enticingly beautiful, the other terrifyingly horrid." She is a malicious influence causing dissension, laziness, temptation; bedevils pregnant women. The Dakota/Oglala/Lakota, South Dakota. (Walker, 1980: 53, 107, 243, 249; Lynd, 1889: 153)

Antu Buyu   A god who persecutes men. The Iban Dyaks of Sarawak, Borneo. (Sarawak Gazette, 1963: 135)

Antu Gerasi   A male spirit who is both good and evil. The Iban Dyaks, Sarawak. Borneo. (Sarawak Gazette, 1963: 135)

a nyo kan do mu   An evil spirit of the Lepchas. Sikkim. (Siiger, 1967: 141)

Aoša   A fiend—"Destruction"—who "appears to have been the deity presiding over combings of hair and clippings of nails, whose importance in religion is widespread." Iran. (Gray, 1930: 199)

Apep, Apepi   The personification of Evil—a "serpent-devil of mist, darkness, storm, and night," who is in daily conflict with Ra. Egypt. (Budge, 1969, 1: 11, 269; Wallis, 1939: 17)

Apesh   The Tortoise god who is feared as a power of evil and darkness. Egypt. (Budge, 1969, 2: 376)

Apo   An evil spirit "who devours the kidneys of people who die of dysentery." The Isneg, Luzon, Philippines. (Vanoverbergh, 1938: 237)

Apom, Epom   The chief of the malignant spirits who must be propitiated. The Abor, Tibet/India. (Crooke, 1925, 1: 33)

Apophis   *See* **Apep**

Arapap   The mother of the evil spirits. The Abkhasians, Caucasus. (Janashia, 1937: 144)

Aratis   A Vedic demon. India. (Gray, 1930: 200)

Ate   Greek/Roman goddess of evil, of ruin, of discord and wickedness. She created such havoc in the heavens that she was banished to the earth. (Murray, 1935: 215; Salkeld, 1844: 311; Barthell, 1971: 8; Larousse, 1968: 164)

Atlantow   The evil spirit who causes dissension, fighting, theft, lying—all things evil. The Mahikan, New York. (Skinner, 1925: 103)

Atocha   God of Evil. Nias Island, Indonesia. (MacKenzie, 1930: 328)

Atskannakanatz   The evil spirit of the Tehuelhets and Chechehets who is appeased because the people feel the good spirit pays no attention to them. Chile. (Grubb, 1925, 9: 598)

Aucca   Also called Huantahualla or Supay. An evil spirit who is propitiated by the Aymara. Peru/Bolivia. (Forbes, 1870: 231)

Aunyain-a   An "evil magician" of the Tupari. Mato Grosso, Brazil. (Osborne, 1968: 118)

Awaia   An evil spirit of the Chins who "lives above and outside the gate, and can cause nightmare and bad dreams." Burma. (Temple, 1925, 3: 25)

Aygnan   The evil spirit of the Tupinambas who carries away the souls of cowards to live in torment. Brazil. (Tylor, 1891: 289; MacCulloch, 1925, 11: 825)

Az A female demon who is "the prototype of lust, greed, and 'wrongmindedness'." Iran. (Dresden, 1961: 357–358; Hinnells, 1973: 52)

Azidahaka A demon with "three heads, three mouths, six eyes . . . commits countless horrible sins . . . smites water, fire, and vegetation . . . promotes witchcraft, tyranny, and ignorance." Iran. (Gray, 1930: 187–188)

Baba-jaga, Baba Yaga A Slavic female demon, the mother of the evil spirits, who preys upon people, sometimes devouring her victims. Russia. (Mansikka, 1925, 4: 623; Bray, 1935: 41)

Bagala A goddess of cruelty, of black magic and poisons who "incites men to torture one another." India. (Danielou, 1964: 283)

Bagea-bonga A maleficent tiger spirit. The Hos, India. (Majundar, 1950: 255, 259)

The Balichu Evil beings, headed by Elel, who are the source of illness and death, of storms and other misfortunes. The Puelche, Argentina. (Cooper, 1946, 5: 167)

Balor A maleficent Celtic god of the "evil eye." One of his eyes was so venomous and lethal it had to be kept closed. It was disastrous to all, including the gods. Ireland. (Squire, 1906: 48–49; MacCulloch, 1911: 59)

Banji-banmang An evil spirit of the forest and the air who "kills men . . . and drinks their blood." Assam. (Furer-Haimendorf, 1954: 599)

sBar gsas rngam (pr. **Barsê Ngam**) A god worshipped by the 'phrul gshen priests who are responsible for driving "from the world the causes of misfortunes threatening or obstructing an individual or the community." They could overcome human enemies as well as demonic powers. Tibet. (Tucci, 1980: 228, 230)

Batin One of the "four chiefs of the world of demons." The Sakai, Malay Peninsula. (Skeat, 1906: 243)

Be, Na An omnipotent evil spirit who kills and commits evil. Costa Rica. (Stone, 1962: 51)

Belang Kepapas A god who is feared and who preys upon men, but on those who are brave he bestows courage and prosperity. The Iban Dyaks of Sarawak, Borneo. (Sarawak Gazette, 1963: 135)

Beng, oBengh The Devil—the source of evil and misfortune. The contrasting duality of Del, the principle of good. The Romany, Rumania. (Trigg, 1973: 165) The god of evil of the Kalderash Gypsies. (Clebert, 1967: 172)

Bhomthup-iari An evil spirit who kills by lightning or drowning. The Minyong Abors, Assam. (Furer-Haimendorf, 1954: 599)

Bhomtup-bhanlup An evil spirit who causes sudden death without apparent cause. The Minyong Abors, Assam. (Furer-Haimendorf, 1954: 599)

Bisai Chandi A maleficent deity of the Hos. India. (Majumdar, 1950: 255)

Bo An evil spirit of the Dizu who lives near water and forests. Ethiopia. (Cerulli, 1956: 94)

Boraro A malevolent and greatly feared forest spirit who kills people by crushing. Also called Curupira in the Amazon area. The Tukano, Colombia. (Reichel-Dolmatoff, 1975: 83, 182–183)

Bulanglang An evil spirit whose "baneful influence" is averted through magical incantations. The Kankanay, Luzon, Philippines. (Vanoverbergh, 1972: 91)

Bumalin An evil god of the underworld who is invoked when there is sickness. The Ifugao, Philippines. (Barton, 1946: 34)

Canibaba Kilmo An evil spirit. Bolivia. (Métraux, 1942: 82)

Canicuba A god of evil of the Antioquians. Colombia. (Alexander, 1920: 197)

Cariapemba A god of evil. Brazil. (Bastide, 1960: 563)

Caricari An evil spirit under Aucca, who sends him to kill men. The Aymara, Peru/Bolivia. (Forbes, 1870: 231)

Caspi An evil god who punishes them with the weather. The Haush or Manekenkn (the Ona), Tierra del Fuego. (Pettazzoni, 1956: 423)

Chac bolay An evil spirit of the Maya. Mexico and Guatemala. (Tozzer, 1941: 203)

chahałheeł yimąsii Rolling Darkness Wind—an evil wind that causes people to plan badly, to do foolish things. The Navaho, Arizona. (McNeley, 1981: 29, 42, 94)

Cheleulle An evil spirit. Argentina. (Cooper, 1946, 5: 158)

Chemosit The evil spirit "said to be half man, half bird." The Nandi, Kenya. (Hollis, 1909: 41; Huntingford, 1953: 143)

Chenuke The spirit of evil. The Ona, Tierra del Fuego. (Osborne, 1968: 117)

Chernobog The Black God, the Slavic/Baltic god of evil who was related to death and symbolized evil, misfortune, the night filled with danger, and evil spirits. Prayers were offered him to avert misfortune. (Machal, 1918: 288; Larousse, 1968: 283; Bray, 1935: 41; Gimbutas, 1975: XLC, M126)

Chikapipenta-ekashi amba Kamui An evil god who was invoked "to hypnotize enemies during a night attack." The Ainu, Japan. (Munro, 1963: 11)

Chin, Cavil, Maran Mayan god of vice, of sodomy. Central America. (Bancroft, 1886, 2: 677; Larousse, 1968: 439)

Chinday The evil deity of the Navaho Indians. Arizona and New Mexico. (Bancroft, 1886, 3: 171)

Chinta Dain A malevolent deity. The Hos, India. (Majumdar, 1950: 255)

Chiton A malignant spirit who "represents the evil principle" even though he is sometimes considered to do some good. The Kachins, Burma. (Temple, 1925, 3: 22, 23)

Chou Wang Chinese god of sodomy. (Werner, 1932: 92)

Christalline An evil sea goddess. Mirebalaise, Haiti. West Indies. (Herskovits, 1937, 1: 280)

Chuhar Kar A maleficent deity. The Hos, India. (Majumdar, 1950: 255)

Chu Kuai Shên Chün A malevolent spirit; the "Creator of Freaks." China. (Day, 1940: 207)

chung ri yam pang An evil spirit of the Lepchas. Sikkim. (Siiger, 1967: 141)

Churdu-bonga A maleficent deity. "If they dream of a *pipul* tree, *Churda* needs propitiation under it." The Hos, India. (Majumdar, 1950: 255, 260)

cicimai An "evil spirit which devours ihp'en, the male spirit of maize. It seems to be female and is probably a personification of the weevil." The Chorti, Guatemala. (Wisdom, 1940: 403)

Cienga, Chenga A malignant spirit who causes whirlwinds and torrential rains and kills children. Western Australia. (Tylor, 1891: 290)

Čišmak A fiend who causes whirlwinds and disaster. Iran. (Gray, 1930: 204)

Cit Bolon Ua An evil god of the Maya. Mexico. (Thompson, 1970: 322–323)

Congo Savanne Also called Congo Zandor. A malevolent deity "who grinds the sacrificial victim in a mortar, as one would crush maize." Haiti, West Indies. (Deren, 1953: 118, 284; Herskovits, 1937, 1: 311)

Cunicuva An evil god of the Cauca Valley. Colombia. (Hernandez de Alba, 1948, 3: 320)

Curspic An evil god who punishes with bad weather. The Yahgan, Tierra del Fuego. (Pettazzoni, 1956: 424)

Dafto An evil spirit of the Tingbung area. The Lepchas, Sikkim. (Siiger, 1967: 141)

Daftor dut A demon at Kalimpong. The Lepchas, Sikkim. (Siiger, 1967: 141)

brDa'i 'phrad An evil lake goddess who "sends madness to her enemies." Tibet. (Nebesky-Wojkowitz, 1956, 1: 307)

Dangoh, Damoh The Devil who does much harm. The Khoi-Khoi (Hottentots), South Africa. (Hahn, 1881: 38)

Dinama A much-feared evil spirit. Costa Rica. (Stone, 1962: 51)

Dinda Kar A maleficent deity. The Hos, India. (Majumdar, 1950: 255)

Dogai A malignant spirit whose "special aptitude was to frustrate human enterprises, to make crops fail, to keep fish away from the nets, etc." Among some female, among others male. Melanesia. (Larousse, 1968: 461)

Hantu Doman An evil spirit with a human body but with a horse's face. Malaya. (Gimlette, 1929: 25)

Druj Nasu The "corpse demon, who is the personification of the spirit of corruption, decomposition, contagion and impurity." Persia. (Hinnells, 1973: 56)

duati The devil of the Guahibo. Venezuela. (Kirchhoff, 1948, 2: 455)

Duid A god of evil sometimes identified with the moon. Twin of Tuminikar. The Wapishiana, the Taruma, Guiana. (Queval, 1968: 115; Métraux, 1946: 115)

Durissa The omnipresent devil who causes people to become possessed. The Darassa, Ethiopia. (Cerulli, 1956: 130; Mbiti, 1970, 2: 127)

Edeke A god of calamity. The Teso, Uganda. (Gulliver, 1953: 26)

Edi A god of evil, the Perverter, who caused men to do wrong. The Yoruba, Nigeria. (Wyndham, 1921: 10, 38)

Ek Ahau ". . . another grim deity, the 'Black Captain,' " who was associated with the god of war. The Yucatan Maya, Mexico. (Alexander, 1920: 138)

Ekweesu An evil spirit to whom the leopard is sacred. At Eha-Amufu, West Africa. (Wallis, 1939: 63)

Ekwensu, Obunike The evil spirit of the Ibo. Among the Igbo violent death and calamities are attributed to him. Nigeria. (Williams, 1936: 209; Isichei, 1978: 322)

Elathan A god of darkness, of evil. One of the Fomors who are mostly deformed, but Elathan was an exception being a handsome man. Ireland. (Squire, 1906: 49, 50)

Elegbara The "equivalent of the Devil." Another name for Eshu. Brazil. (Herskovits, 1937, 2: 640; Verger, 1957: 119)

Elel The chief of the evil beings, the source of illness and death, of storms. The Puelche, Argentina. (Cooper, 1946, 5: 167)

El-Zebub A Canaanite evil deity. (Gordon, 1961: 202)

Eno The name of Eyacque after it was changed as "signifying 'a thief and cannibal'." The Acagchemem, California. (Boscana, 1933: 28)

Erlik, Erlik Khan A being created by Kaira Kan who existed with him in the primordial water. He participated in the creation, but that of Erlik was bad. He was banished to the world of darkness and became the god of evil, ruler over all evil spirits, the god of the dead and of the underworld. He is responsible for the defilement of people, and is the source of all misfortunes. Siberia. Among the Monguors of Kansu he is the chief of the evil spirits to whom the black shamans are dedicated. China. (Casanowicz, 1924: 417–418; MacCulloch, 1964: 374, 487; Pettersson, 1957: 24; Potapov, 1964: 325; Schram, 1957: 80, 110)

Er Mo The King of Demons. The Ch'iang, Szechwan, China. (Graham, 1958: 96)

Eruntja An evil spirit who causes harm to the dying and also to the dead. Central Australia. (Roheim, 1972: 106)

Eshu A god associated with evil but not in total opposition to goodness. With his devotees he can be beneficent. He is a trickster and a god of mischief "quite capable of causing confusion . . . or promoting malice among people." He "tricks men into offending the gods," thus providing the gods with the sacrifices they desire. He is the avenger who metes out punishment for wrongdoing. The Yoruba, Nigeria. Also known in Brazil, Trinidad, and Puerto Rico. (Idowu, 1962: 80–84; Wescott, 1962: 337–338, 344; Lucas, 1948: 51–52, 67; Wyndham, 1921: 11, 37; Morton-Williams, 1964: 248; Bastide, 1960: 91, 565; Simpson, 1965: 18; Gonzalez-Wippler, 1975: 29, 103; Parrinder, 1967: 90)

Evnissyen A Celtic god, the continuous source of strife and dissension. The Britons. (Squire, 1906: 290)

Eyak The evil spirit of the Koniagas. Pacific Northwest, North America. (Bancroft, 1886, 3: 143–144)

Falekaho atua A "wicked god who killed people" at Makefu. Niue Island, Polynesia. (Loeb, 1926, 1: 160)

The Fomors The demons of evil, of darkness and death who lived underneath the sea. They were considered responsible for bad weather, drought, and illness. Celtic Ireland. (Squire, 1906: 47–48)

Fotogfuru An evil spirit who causes accidents and death. Rotuma (Fiji), Melanesia. (Gardiner, 1897: 468)

Freftar A fiend—"Deceiver . . . who seduces mankind." Iran. (Gray, 1930: 205)

Ga-go-sa Ho-nun-nas-tase-ta The Mistress of the False-faces—demons or evil spirits without bodies. The Iroquois, Eastern United States. (Morgan, 1901: 158)

Galau Pranan A god who is feared and who preys upon men, but on those who are brave he bestows courage and prosperity. The Iban Dyaks of Sarawak, Borneo. (Sarawak Gazette, 1963: 135)

Gara Satamai A maleficent goddess who is propitiated when "a snake, a crocodile or a fish" is dreamed of. The Hos, India. (Majumdar, 1950: 259)

Gargasi The malevolent head of the evil spirits who causes epidemics and whose aim is to destroy mankind. When his voice is heard, evil will befall the family. He is a hunter and his spirit followers transform into hounds. The Sea Dyaks, Borneo. (Sarawak Gazette, 1963: 17; Howell, 1908/10: 9)

Gaua The god of evil who sends misfortune and disease and bad weather. The bad dead go to him. South Africa, Angola, and Botswana. (Schapera, 1951: 168, 187, 189)

Gaunab The Destroyer, the supreme god of evil, with whom all evil omens (eclipses, meteors, whirlwinds, etc.) are associated. He causes illness and death and is the opponent of Tsuni-Goab. The Hottentots, South Africa. (Smith, 1950: 40, 42, 49; Hahn, 1881: 93; Schapera, 1951: 358, 388; Pettersson, 1953: 146)

Ge-nivukh The evil spirit of the Gilyak. Siberia. (Shternberg, 1933: 321)

Gerasi Papa A god who is feared and who preys upon men, but on those who are brave he bestows courage and prosperity. The Iban Dyaks of Sarawak, Borneo. (Sarawak Gazette, 1963: 135)

Giblo An "Evil spirit in the first layer of heaven." The Cuna, Panama. (Nordenskiold, 1938: 324)

Giddi A malignant deity who lives in a sacred spring. The Malabu, Nigeria. (Meek, 1925, 2: 24)

Glang-da-lo A great demon—"so large that he can step from one mountaintop to another, or from the earth to the sky. He can strike a person dead with one blow of his thumb." The Ch'uan Miao, Southwest China. (Graham, 1961: 71)

Glang-do A sky demon of the Ch'uan Miao. Southwest China. (Graham, 1961: 71)

Glang gu A great demon "who causes people to drown." The Ch'uan Miao, Southwest China. (Graham, 1961: 71)

Gnaski A "beautiful," "enticing," and "very deceitful demon"—daughter of Unk and Iya, her son. However, she will fly away from a medicine bag. The Lakota and Oglala, South Dakota. (Walker, 1980: 51, 117)

Gnaskinyan The Crazy Buffalo—the most feared of the Evil Gods because he "appears like the good Buffalo God" but deceives people into doing harm and evil things and disrupts the young in love affairs. The Lakota, South Dakota. (Walker, 1980: 67, 94, 110)

Gopalu Yakku A demon of pure evil. Sinhalese Buddhism. Ceylon. (Obeyesekere, 1966: 6)

Gorh A malevolent spirit of the Dafla tribes. Assam. (Stonor, 1957: 15)

Gorreh A "powerful and general spirit of evil." The Dafla tribes, Assam. (Stonor, 1957: 7)

Guaricana The "devil," during whose festival the young men flog one another until the blood flows. The Yurimagua, Brazil. (Zerries, 1968: 284)

Guayota The evil spirit who lived in Mount Teyde. Tenerife, Canary Islands. (Hooten, 1925, 7: 12; Basset, 1925, 2: 506–507)

Guecufu The "forces of evil, impersonal and personal." The Araucanians, Chile. (Osborne, 1968: 116)

Guetuli An evil spirit of the second layer of heaven. The Cuna, Panama. (Nordenskiold, 1938: 159)

'Gying dkar ma An evil lake goddess who causes dropsy. Tibet. (Nebesky-Wojkowitz, 1956, 1: 307)

Hahgwehdaetgah The evil spirit, twin of Hahgwehdiyu, the good creator. Sons of Ataensic. He was banished to the underworld for his disruptive conduct. The Iroquois, Eastern United States. (Leach, 1949: 474)

Ha-ne-go-ate-geh The evil twin who created all "monsters, poisonous reptiles, and noxious plants" and provoked discord and caused calamities. The good twin is Hanigoiyu. The Iroquois, Eastern United States. (Morgan, 1904: 147–8; Keppler, 1941: 14)

Hapikern An evil snake god of the Maya. Yucatan, Mexico. (Cline, 1944: 112; Larousse, 1968: 439)

Heiseb Among the Heikum a god of all evil who is responsible for fire. South Africa and Namibia. (Schapera, 1951: 189; Lebzelter, 1934: 15)

Herecgunina The chief evil spirit of the Winnebago Indians. Wisconsin. (Radin, 1915/16: 285)

Herensugue A diabolical spirit who appears as a serpent, sometimes shown with seven heads, but generally with one. The Basque, Spain and France. (Barandiaran, 1972: 99)

Hili, Tikoloshe A malevolent trickster and seducer. The Xosa, South Africa. (Willoughby, 1932: 2)

Hintabaran An evil spirit, sister/wife of Larunaen. New Ireland, Melanesia. (Cox, 1913: 195)

Hobbamocko, Hobbamock, Hobbamoqui A god of evil who causes plagues and calamities. The Algonquin, Connecticut. (De Forest, 1853: 24)

Huantahualla *See* **Aucca**

Huecuvoe, Huecuvu The evil supreme being. The Moluches, Chile. (Grubb, 1925, 9: 598)

the Huecuvus Evil spirits who were transformers and who were under the control of Pillan. The Araucanians, Chile. (Larousse, 1968: 444)

Hukloban An agent of Sitan. She had great power to kill, but could also heal those she afflicted; she could destroy houses. The Tagalog, Philippines. (Jocano, 1969: 12)

Hul-ater A god of evil who caused man to be susceptible to disease. The Vogul, Siberia. (Pettersson, 1957: 21)

Humbaba A powerful Sumero/Babylonian god of evil in the Epic of Gilgamish. A deity of the cedar trees. Near East. (Langdon, 1931: 253–255)

Huodno An evil deity of the underworld. The Lapps, Lapland. (Karsten, 1955: 40)

huri kamui A huge, malevolent, and ferocious mythical bird—sometimes a pair. The Ainu, Hokkaido, Japan. (Philippi, 1982: 165)

Iblis, Sitan The chief of the evil spirits. Morocco. (Westermarck, 1926, 1: 406–412)

Ibom A name of the Chief of the Evil Gods, Iyo, in his aspect of "the giant cyclone." The Lakota, South Dakota. (Walker, 1980: 94; Dooling, 1984: 84, 191)

Iboroquiamio The god of evil. Guiana. (Alexander, 1920: 257)

Ibwa An evil god who likes to feed on corpses, which are protected from him by a piece of iron placed on the grave. The Tinguian, Philippines. (Cole, 1922: 299)

Igrath bath Mahalath An early Hebrew goddess of evil. Near East. (Patai, 1967: 27)

Iguali An "Evil spirit in the second layer of heaven." The Cuna, Panama. (Nordenskiold, 1938: 325)

Imana Mbi An evil deity—a killer of children and a thief of cattle. The Barundi, Burundi. (Mbiti, 1970, 2: 117)

Inarxay A malevolent spirit who kills people at harvesttime and is offered betel to propitiate. The Isneg, Luzon, Philippines. (Vanovergergh, 1941: 338)

Inmai A household evil spirit who "lives in the post in the front corner of the house," and who causes thorn injuries. The Chins, Burma. (Temple, 1925, 3: 25)

Ira A god of destruction who sends Ishum to wreak havoc among men. Assyro/Babylonian, Near East. (Zimmern, 1925, 2: 314)

Irvene The "devil in guise of a dog." La Palma, Canary Islands. (Hooten, 1925: 12)

Ishishemi A god of evil. The Northern Kavirondo, Uganda. (Budge, 1973, 1: 293)

Istseremurexposhe The "nearest approach to the concept of an evil spirit known to the Crows. If no one is killed in a battle he returns to his supernatural home, disappointed and tired." Wyoming and Montana. (Wildschut, 1960: 3)

Iya Second son of Inyan. He "is utterly evil and the chief of all evil beings." Incestuously, with his mother Unk, he is the father of the beautiful demon Gnaski. He vindictively deprives men of game in hunting, causes "headaches and paralysis," and fosters black magic. The Lakota and Dakota, South Dakota. (Lynd, 1889: 154; Walker, 1980: 51, 141, 187; Wallis, 1939: 7)

Iyaimi An evil spirit represented by a mask. The Caua, Colombia. (Zerries, 1968: 301)

Jahi A female demon personifying debauchery. Persia. (Hinnells, 1973: 56)

Jedza A Slavic female demon, mother of the evil spirits. Poland. Same as Baba-jaga (Russia). (Mansikka, 1925, 4: 623)

Jezibaba A Slavic female demon, mother of the evil spirits. Slovak. Same as Baba-jaga (Russia). (Mansikka, 1925, 4: 623)

'Jigs pa'i zer mo mig gcig A misshapen goddess who causes ill-feeling, bad weather, and illness in children. Tibet. (Nebesky-Wojkowitz, 1956, 1: 122, 283)

Jilaiya A fiend who "takes the form of a night-bird and sucks the blood of persons whose names it hears." The Chamars, India. (Briggs, 1920: 134)

Jinang One of the "four chiefs of the world of demons." The Sakai, Malay Peninsula. (Skeat, 1906: 243)

Juripari The evil spirit of the Pampas tribes of the vicinity of Buenos Aires. Argentina. (Brinton, 1868: 61)

Jurukrah   One of the "four chiefs of the world of demons." The Sakai, Malay Peninsula. (Skeat, 1906: 243)

ka cer vi   An evil spirit of the Lepchas. Sikkim. (Siiger, 1967: 141)

Kadavara   A demon of pure evil, of "irrational punitiveness." Ceylon. (Obeyesekere, 1966: 6)

Kadongayan   An evil god who preys on the dead. The Tinguian, Philippines. (Cole, 1922: 300)

Kahu   The chief of the evil spirits who is in constant opposition to Uanari. The Cunuana, Venezuela. (Zerries, 1968: 248)

Kakayan   An evil anito who "teaches and tempts people to do evil." The Apayao, Philippines. (Wilson, 1947: 23)

Kala   The destructive, the dark form of Siwa, whose wife is Durga. He is an evil spirit who lives in the center of the earth; a god of the underworld of the creation myth who "created the light and Mother Earth, over which extends a layer of water." Bali, Indonesia. (Friederich, 1959: 39, 43; Covarrubias, 1937: 7, 317)

Kalae   A malevolent poison god who caused diseases. Hawaii. (Westervelt, 1963, 3: 96; 1915: 95, 98)

The Kalau   Evil spirits who cause illness and death. As an individual, a god of evil who intercepts the sacrifices made by the shaman to the supreme being for cures, causing the patient to die. The Koryak, Siberia (Jochelson, 1904: 417–418; Eliade, 1964: 249–250)

Kale-Yakku   A demon of pure evil, of "irrational punitiveness." Ceylon. (Obeyesekere, 1966: 6)

Kali   (1) A demon king, a god of evil who is not to be confused with Kali, the consort of Siva. India. (Martin, 1914: 285; Dowson, 1961: 141) (2) As a goddess of destruction, "the personification of the all-destroying Time," her fierceness primarily directed at demons and at evil. Though she is protective of her followers, she is bloodthirsty and is worshipped with bloody sacrifices and must be properly propitiated at all times. She is a goddess of epidemics and is invoked for protection from them; a goddess of criminals; and in her benign aspect, among some a goddess of agriculture and of crafts. India. (Bhattacharji, 1970: 174; Whitehead, 1916: 27–28; Thurston, 1909, 2: 216; 1909, 3: 282; 1909, 5: 401; Martin, 1914: 185–186, 256; Banerjea, 1953: 68; Brown, 1961: 311; Danielou, 1964: 264; Russell, 1916, 2: 61)

Kalicknateck   An evil spirit who catches and eats whales. The Trinity River Indians, California. (Bancroft, 1886, 3: 176)

bsKal med 'bum nag (pr. **Kelmê Bumnak**), **Myal ba nag po, Nyam rje**   The "lord of Non-being (med pa) and the origin of the demonic powers (bdud)." He was the creator of evil who arose "from a black egg" and produced illness and plague, war and hunger, all the forces of "Non-being." Bon Religion. Tibet. (Tucci, 1980: 215–216, 295)

Kaltud   A maleficent deity of the Hos. India. (Majumdar, 1950: 255)

Kankali   A goddess who brings ruin and who is identified with Thakurani Bakorani. The Bondo, India. (Elwin, 1950: 155)

Karala   An aspect of Parvati as a goddess of destruction. India. (Wilman-Grabowska, 1963: 122)

Karisu   The god of evil, chief of the lesser malignant gods who are the source of all illness and misfortune. The Elema, Papuan Gulf, New Guinea. (Holmes, 1902: 430)

Katavi, Katabi   An evil spirit "much dreaded . . . believed to appear as a whirlwind spreading smallpox and other diseases . . . held responsible for the failure of crops." The Bende, Tanzania. (Millroth, 1965: 109; Abrahams, 1967: 78)

Kati Ankamma   The "Sakti of the place where the dead are buried or burned, and is feared accordingly. She is said to live on corpses and to kill young children. She also sets fire to houses . . . delights in killing cattle." She is, needless to say, propitiated. India. (Elmore, 1915: 39)

Keekut   A malevolent land being who has the form of a hairless dog. The Eskimo, Baffin Land, Canada. (Bilby, 1923: 209)

Kees-du-je-al-ity Kah, Keesshusaah Ankow   A powerful evil spirit who is the "master of the tides." The Tlingit, British Colombia and Alaska. (Niblack, 1888: 379)

Kegangizi   A power of evil—A "malevolent water monster . . . often was invoked by shamans for evil purposes." The Potawatomi, Michigan and Wisconsin. (Edmunds, 1980: 20)

Kele   The evil spirit. The Chukchee, Siberia. (Bogoras, 1928: 303)

Kengida A Sumerian deity, a messenger of Enlil, and one of "vengeance and destruction." Near East. (Langdon, 1931: 100)

Keron-kenken A malevolent spirit "who devours newly-born children and drinks the tears of their broken-hearted mothers." The Patagonians, Argentina and Chile. (Deniker, 1925, 9: 669)

Khargi The evil brother of the creator Kheneki. The Nekongdev Evenks and the Bachin Evenks, Siberia. (Michael, 1963: 61)

Khosadam, Khosedabam The goddess of evil was the wife of Ess but was banished to the earth because of unfaithfulness. She now lives in the dark northern region and causes illness and misfortune. The Kets and the Yenisei Ostyaks, Siberia. (Czaplicka, 1925, 9: 578–579; Popov and Dolgikh, 1964: 617; Larousse, 1973: 433)

Khyab-pa lag-rings The "Prince of the Devils." The Bon Religion. Tibet. (Hoffman, 1956: 90)

Kibayen A female spirit who appears at curing ceremonies hoping to take the person's life, but is thwarted by "the fish net" which protects the person. The Tinguian, Philippines. (Cole, 1922: 339)

Kiberoh, Kiberoth An evil spirit who rules over those of the underworld. She causes illness. The Yaruro, Venezuela. (Kirchhoff, 1948, 2: 462; Petrullo, 1939: 236, 244)

Kilu The chief of the evil spirits. The Cuna, Panama. (Nordenskiold, 1938: 500)

Kingaludda A messenger of Enlil, one of "vengeance and destruction." Sumer, Near East. (Langdon, 1931: 100)

Kiriamagi A god of evil who tempted men. The Wapare, Tanzania. (Frazer, 1926: 201)

Kisin The Mayan devil, a god of the underworld and of earthquakes. Mexico. (Tozzer, 1941: 132; Cline, 1944: 112; Alexander, 1920: 141)

Klu bdud nag po A malevolent scorpion-headed god. Tibet. (Nebesky-Wojkowitz, 1956, 1: 286)

Koen An evil spirit, a kidnapper, whose wife is Mailkun. Australia. (Bray, 1935: 232)

Kojin A god of violence who is also a household god of the stove, the kitchen. Japan. (Kato, 1931: 131; Norbeck, 1954: 126–7; Herbert, 1967: 498)

Kok-lir A goddess who preys on men but does not harm women. The Iban Dyaks, Sarawak, Borneo. (Sarawak Gazette, 1963: 136)

Korimogo A malicious deity of the Huli. New Guinea. (Glasse, 1965: 33)

Kormos A god of evil who accompanies man throughout his lifetime. Jajutshi is his good protector. The Altaic, Siberia. (Pettersson, 1957: 24; Eliade, 1964: 197)

Kosu-rio A malevolent dragon deity of the province of Sinano. Japan. (Coleman, 1832: 333–334)

Kuedule An "Evil spirit in the second layer of heaven." The Cuna, Panama. (Nordenskiold, 1938: 325)

Kugo-jen An evil spirit, male, to whom sacrifices must be made when there is disease. The Cheremis, Russia. (Leach, 1949: 215)

Kul Odyr, Kul-oter A god of evil who lives north of the mouth of the Ob River and is "the chief of the spirits of darkness." He spoiled the creation of man, making him less than perfect. The Voguls and the Ostyaks, Siberia. (Czaplicka, 1925, 9: 577; 1969: 289–290; MacCulloch, 1964: 376)

Kweraak Kutar "Blind-old-man," a source of evil and sickness. The Yuma, Arizona. (Harrington, 1908: 328)

Kyzy The evil underground spirit who has many spirits under him who cause illness. The Selkups, Siberia. (Prokof'yeva, 1964: 601)

Lalibjet An evil spirit "who guards the long weirs (until they collapse by themselves)." The Marshall Islands, Micronesia. (Erdland, 1914: 313)

Lawilele An evil spirit "who guards the old fish weirs (embodying him) made of palm fronds." The Marshall Islands, Micronesia. (Erdland, 1914: 313)

Lebara A trickster god and an evil deity worshipped by the Yoruban cult. Maranhão, Brazil. (Costa Eduardo, 1948: 80)

Lempo A Finno-Ugrian evil spirit of the land. (Larousse, 1968: 304)

Leshi-letang An "evil and very dangerous spirit who entices people into the jungle by his laugh and then devours them." The Menyong Abors, Assam. (Furer-Haimendorf, 1954: 599)

Lewatu Momo A female spirit who impersonates the living, luring the man into cohabitation, which results in his death. Fiji Islands, Melanesia. (Spencer, 1941: 11, 12)

Lewatu ni Nambua A malicious female spirit who kills men or causes disease. Fiji Islands, Melanesia. (Spencer, 1941: 27)

Lha-mo The only goddess among the Dharmapalas, the Defenders of the Buddhist doctrine. She was malignant and powerful and greatly feared. Tibet and Mongolia. (Waddell, 1959: 364; Getty, 1962: 149; Percheron, 1953: 257; Hackin, 1963: 166; Sierksma, 1966: 163)

Lilith The goddess of evil, of death, of night, was the head of the she-demons of the Hebrews—the "embodiment of everything that is evil and dangerous in the sexual realm." Near East. (Patai, 1967: 27, 207, 242; Neumann, 1955: 272; Langdon, 1931: 353)

Limba, Limba-zaou A malicious and cannibalistic Vodun deity. Plaisance, Haiti. West Indies. (Simpson, 1945: 44, 49)

Limpelite An evil deity who causes fires and other misfortunes. The Yurakare, Bolivia. (Métraux, 1942: 12)

Ling Kuan (1) The "chief of the devils." Szechwan, China. (Wood, 1937: 165). (2) A god of wayside shrines whose duty "is to protect people from demons." China. (Graham, 1961: 162)

Lingleson A malicious and "harsh god who, through his servants, kills readily and without mercy." Plaisance, Haiti. West Indies. (Simpson, 1945: 49)

Logon A god of evil to whom offerings are made. The Dusans, Borneo. (Stall, 1925: 943)

Loki The Scandinavian god of evil, of deceit, and of mischief was not, however, totally bad, but more mischievous than wicked, and a sociable and entertaining deity. He was originally a hearth god, and as such his wife was Glut (glow) and his daughters Eisa (embers) and Einmyria (ashes). By Angurboda he was the father of Fenrir, the wolf, Hel, the goddess of Niflheim, and of Jormungand, the Midgard serpent. (Davidson, 1964: 176–177; Guerber, 1895: 198–200; Wagner, 1882: 249–50; Snorri Sturluson-Young, 1964: 56; Turville-Petre, 1964: 127–133)

Lous, Komdeguen Names of the god of evil of the Ostyaks. Siberia. (Bertrand, 1897: 87)

Loviatar A Finno-Ugrian goddess of evil, daughter of Tuoni and Tuonetar. (Larousse, 1968: 306)

Lu A malevolent spirit who consumes corpses and causes deaths to appease his appetite. He must be propitiated. The Red Karens, Burma. (Temple, 1925, 3: 25–26)

Luka lapalap The god of evil. Ponape, Caroline Islands, Micronesia. (Christian, 1899: 383)

lung ji A very malevolent mung who causes misfortune, illness, and death, to whom an animal is sacrificed so he shall not take a human life. The Lepchas, Sikkim. (Siiger, 1967, 1: 178; 1967, 2: 92–93)

Lwal Burrajok The Devil, father of Abok. The Dinka, Sudan. (Budge, 1973, 1: 375)

Macardit, Colwic A malevolent evil deity menacing to those away from home, who kills and causes sterility in women. The Dinka, Sudan. (Lienhardt, 1961: 57, 62, 81–83)

Machchera One of the names of the god of evil, greatly feared. Brazil. (Alexander, 1920: 295)

Madji ahando An evil spirit who causes earthquakes. The Penobscot, Maine. (Speck, 1935: 5, 21)

Magatsubi-no-Kami A Shinto evil deity. Japan. (Kato, 1926: 73)

Mahakala A name of Siva in his destructive aspect. Java, Sikkim, and India. (Gazeteer of Sikhim, 1984: 266; Marchal, 1963: 231; Dowson, 1961: 193)

Maho Penekheka The Evil Power of the Mandan. North and South Dakota. (Burland, 1965: 149)

Mahrkuša A demon of destruction. Iran. (Gray, 1930: 209)

Maikudra A malevolent deity. The Hos, India. (Majumdar, 1950: 255)

Mailkun, Tippakalleum A feared goddess who "kidnaps adults in her net and spears children in their temple." Wife of Koen. Australia. (Bray, 1935: 232)

Mainaje A malevolent spirit of the Kayuvava. Bolivia. (Métraux, 1942: 83)

Makalay An evil spirit "with a horn like a unicorn; he is swift as the winds." To see him usually means death. Trinity River Indians, California. (Bancroft, 1886, 3: 176)

Maluk Taus The creator of evil, of all things in opposition to good, in revolt against God. Some say he was forgiven after long punishment, others say still unforgiven. The Yezids, Kurdistan. (Drahomanov, 1961: 52–53)

Mam   The feared god of "the five evil and unlucky days at the end of the year." The Maya, Yucatan, Mexico. (Thompson, 1970: 297, 299)

Mangamian   An evil male spirit who attempts to kill. The Tinguian, Philippines. (Cole, 1922: 340)

Mangana Bulan   God of evil of the Bataks of Silindung. Sumatra, Indonesia. (Coleman, 1832: 365)

Maniya   An Arabian abstract deity described as "destruction" and "doom of death." (Noldeke, 1925, 1: 661)

Mankukulam   An agent of Sitan who caused fire beneath the house "especially when the night was dark and the weather was not good. . . . If the fire was extinguished immediately, the victim would die." The Tagalog, Philippines. (Jocano, 1969: 12)

Mapito-iti   A lesser god of evil who caused sickness and lived in the underworld Te Matagi. Mangareva, Polynesia. (Buck, 1938, 1: 425)

Mara   Buddhist demon of evil, temptation, and seduction "who endeavors to damn the human soul." India, Tibet and China. (Bhattachargi, 1970: 107; Waddell, 1959: 344, 375; Sierksma, 1966: 209; Werner, 1932: 307; Du Bose, n.d.: 154)

Maridamma   A malevolent goddess who brings disease, is feared, and worshipped to avert it. Godavari and Vizagapatam Districts, India. (Hemingway, 1915: 48; Francis, 1907: 74)

Marmoo   An evil spirit who created noxious things to spoil Baiame's world. Australia. (Reed, 1965: 29)

Matci-Manitu, Matchi Manitto, Matchemonedo   The evil spirit, the source of all unpleasant and vicious things. The Cree and the Pottawatomis, United States and Canada. (Cooper, 1934: 8; Mandelbaum, 1940: 252; Schoolcraft, 1857, 1: 320; Emerson, 1884: 159)

Matshiktshiki   The sea serpent was a great god of evil who fished up the islands out of the sea, and who was greatly feared and propitiated to avert his anger. New Hebrides, Melanesia. (Williamson, 1933, 2: 181)

Mauari   Among the Baniwa (Arawakans of the upper Rio Negro and Atapapo) he is the supreme evil being. Among the Manao and Paravilhana, a benevolent god. Brazil and Venezuela. (Zerries, 1968: 249; Métraux, 1948, 6: 710)

Maunu-gaegae   With Tu-maui-roa, the maleficent leaders of the demons. Anaa Island, Tuamotus, Polynesia. (Stimson, 1933: 26)

Maxablay   A malevolent spirit who comes after the harvest with intent to kill. The Isneg, Luzon, Philippines. (Vanoverbergh, 1941: 356)

Mbasi   A god of evil, deceitful and wicked, of the Konde in the land of Marongo from where they came. Tanzania. (Mackenzie, 1925: 184–185)

Miangu   An evil spirit of the Shakko who lives near water and forests. The Gimira, Ethiopia. (Cerulli, 1956: 94)

Minepo   The evil being as opposed to Muluku, the good. The Macouas and Banayis, Mozambique. (Larousse, 1968: 475)

Minungara   Two unfriendly sky beings "who make doctors," but at the same time when people fall ill they try to kill them. They are prevented in this by Mumpani. The Mara, Gulf of Carpentaria, Australia. (Roheim, 1972: 68; Spencer, 1904: 501–502)

Missabe   An evil spirit who caused men to become powerful Windego spirits, cannibalistic and causing death from fright, by bestowing on them "his evil gifts or powers of darkness." The Ojibwa, Minnesota. (Coleman, 1937: 40)

Moko-nui and **Moko-titi**   Evil lizard deities of the Maori. New Zealand. (Andersen, 1928: 146)

Moloch   An Ammonite god, the devourer of children (sacrificial burning) who was worshipped for a time by the Hebrews and the Phoenicians. Near East. (Seligmann, 1948: 49; Bulfinch, 1898: 397; Cohane, 1969: 196)

Mon pa gri 'debs   A deity who causes ill-feeling, bad weather, illness in children. Tibet. (Nebesky-Wojkowitz, 1956, 1: 283)

moong   *See* **mung**

Mudji manido, Mudjimonedo   A god of evil. The Ojibwa, Minnesota. (Coleman, 1937: 40; Schoolcraft, 1857, 6: 637)

Mu Fu Hsing Chün   A malignant stellar god who if met or offended "will surely bring a death in the family." China. (Day, 1940: 85)

Mujidagrah   A god of destruction. The Mishmis, Assam. (Crooke, 1925, 8: 697)

Mu kaw li A god of evil, in opposition to Y'wa. The Karen, Burma. (Marshall, 1922: 213)

Mukessa The chief devil who lived in Lake Victoria Nyanza. The Baganda and Bosoga, Uganda. (Stam, 1908: 214)

Muklen Olmai An evil deity of the underworld. The Lapps. Lapland. (Karsten, 1955: 40)

The mung, moong Evil spirits, demons, devils. Sikkim. (Siiger, 1967, 1: 16; 1967, 2: 66; Gorer, 1938: 118, 223–225, 479; Morris, 1938: 69)

Muto A cruel, violent god. Japan. (Kato, 1931: 131)

Nabaeo Was "at one time looked upon as a good spirit, but later became mainly evil." Ruk Island, New Britain, Melanesia. (Larousse, 1968: 456)

Nai Bhagawati A maleficent deity of the Oriyas. India. (Majumdar, 1950: 255)

Nalwun An evil household spirit who causes sterility in women. The Chins, Burma. (Temple, 1925, 3: 25)

Nama An evil, malevolent, and terrible hyena god. The Bambara, Mali. (Tauxier, 1927: 179–1780, 303)

Nanapolo The evil spirit of the Choctaw. Louisiana. (Bushnell, 1909: 28)

Nangai An evil god and an outcast who dwells in the forests of Killima-Njaro. The Masai, Kenya and Tanzania. (Mutwa, n.d.: 70, 101)

Nanghaithya, Nåᶞhaiθya An archdemon who rouses discontent. Iran. (Gray, 1930: 183)

Napousney An evil spirit of the Trinity River Indians. California. (Bancroft, 1886, 3: 176)

Navena God of evil of the Boro. Brazil. (Alexander, 1920: 298)

Nawang An evil spirit who devours the souls of the dead and attempts to devour the living as well. He causes stomach pains, vomiting, and diarrhea. The Garo, Assam. (Playfair, 1909: 82)

Nefas Roman personification of wrongdoing. (Roscher, 1965, 3, 1: 76)

'Nenaunir The spirit of evil and a god of storms. The Masai, Kenya and Tanzania. (Larousse, 1968: 476)

Nequiteh An evil spirit of the Trinity River Indians. California. (Bancroft, 1886, 3: 176)

Nergal Assyro/Babylonian god of the destructive evils that plague mankind—war, fire, pestilence, death, drought—the forces affecting many rather than the individual. He is identified with the planet Mars. He has a small aspect of benevolence in the softer, life-giving benefits of the sun. Near East. (Jastrow, 1898: 66–68, 172, 459; Seligmann, 1948: 30; Langdon, 1931: 93, 147: Jacobsen, 1970: 8; Cook, 1930: 121)

Newathie The evil spirit of the Mojave Indians. California and Arizona. (Bancroft, 1886, 3: 175)

Ngyleka The evil spirit personified in the wolf. Also called Sarmik. The Nentsy, Siberia. (Prokof'yeva, 1964: 565–6)

Nitne Kamui Satan, as well as all evil spirits. The Ainu, Japan. (Batchelor, 1925, 1: 240)

Njambe The source of all evils. The Bantu, Zaire. (Hartland, 1925, 2: 366)

Nukulamma A village goddess who is feared as the source of misfortune and evil and worshipped to avert sickness. India. (Whitehead, 1916: 22, 25; Hemingway, 1915: 48; Francis, 1907: 74)

the Nunasish Dangerous and malevolent supernatural beings who occupied the Lower World, C'oyinashup. They are "usually depicted . . . as deformed or misshapen." The Chumash, California. (Hudson and Underhay, 1978: 40)

gNyan po brag srin kumara A deity of evil nature who causes ill-feeling, bad weather, and illness in children. Tibet. (Nebesky-Wojkowitz, 1956, 1: 283)

gNyan spar ba dung mgo g·yu'i thor tshugs can A god of evil nature. Tibet. (Nebesky-Wojkowitz, 1956, 1: 289)

Obunike, Edwensu The evil spirit of the Ibo. Nigeria. (Williams, 1936: 209)

Odosha Also known as **Kahu** and **Kahushawa**. He is "the master of evil and the incarnation of all negative forces in the universe." He lives with his Odoshankomo in Koiohina and continuously struggles to predominate over good. The Makiritare, Venezuela. (Civrieux, 1980: 188)

Oke, Okeus, Okee, Oki   A god of evil, the source of all harm, was feared and propitiated. Boys were sometimes sacrificed (or died in testing or hardening ceremonies). The Powhatan and Potomac. Virginia. (Swanton, 1946: 743–744; Lang, 1968: 252; Robertson, 1911: 351; McCary, 1979: 57, 58, 62, 63)

O-ke-hée-de   The owl, an evil spirit of the Mandan. North Dakota. (Catlin, 1967: 59)

Olethros   Greek personification of Destruction. (Roscher, 1965, 3, 1: 832)

Olisha   A cruel and malevolent god, a magician who knows the plants that kill. Haiti. West Indies. (Marcelin, 1950: 72)

Olouigipipilele   The chief of all the evil spirits in the underworld. The Cuna, Panama. (Nordenskiold, 1938: 285, 330–331)

O-Magatsui-no-Kami   "Wondrous-Deity-of-Great-Evils." With Yaso-Magatsuhi-no-Kami, responsible for all the misfortunes of mankind. Japan. (Yasumaro, 1928: 21; 1965: 23–4; Herbert, 1967: 279)

Omaha   An evil spirit who brings sickness and misfortune and remains ready to snatch the soul of the dying, which must be prevented by distracting his attention. Trinity River Indians, California. (Bancroft, 1886, 3: 176, 523; Powers, 1877: 63)

Omahank Chike   The evil earth spirit. The Mandan, North Dakota. (Tylor, 1891: 287)

Oonoosooloohnoo   The evil spirit of the Mohawk. New York. (Emerson, 1884: 522)

Orusula   An evil spirit in the form of "an enormous pig . . . his foam gives people a rash which kills them." Costa Rica. (Stone, 1962: 52)

Othkon, Aireskuoni   The Devil who was worshipped and to whom offerings were made. The Iroquois, Eastern United States. (Maclean, 1876: 444)

Paha   A Finno-Ugric evil spirit of the lands. (Larousse, 1968: 304)

Paha Engel   An evil deity of the underworld. The Lapps. Lapland. (Karsten, 1955: 40)

Paija   A one-legged female spirit of evil, the sight of whom causes death. The Ihalmiut Eskimo, Keewatin District, Canada. (Mowat, 1968: 238)

Pairimaiti   "Crooked-Mindedness," a demoness who "denies the existence of religion." Opponent of Armaiti. Persia. (Hinnells, 1973: 52; Gray, 1930: 212)

Paqok   A nocturnal spirit who attacks women. The Maya, Yucatan, Mexico. (Alexander, 1920: 141)

Penanggalan   An evil spirit of the Malays. Malay Peninsula. (Evans, 1923: 14)

Penglima   One of the "four chiefs of the world of demons." The Sakai, Malay Peninsula. (Skeat, 1906: 243)

Phung 'gong nag po   A 'gong po deity of evil influence. Tibet. (Nebesky-Wojkowitz, 1956, 1: 284)

Pigtangua   One of the names of the god of evil, greatly feared. Brazil. (Alexander, 1920: 295)

Pishuni   An evil spirit of temptation who also brings disease. The Acoma, New Mexico. (Stirling, 1942: 12, 28)

Pomsa   A malignant spirit, younger brother of Apom. They dwell in rubber trees and "must be propitiated in times of sickness." Tibet and India. (Crooke, 1925, 1: 33)

Pramori   An evil god who flooded and/or burned the earth created by Baramy. The Gypsies of India. (Trigg, 1973: 21)

Pumpteh   A male spirit of evil of the Dafla tribes. Assam. (Stonor, 1957: 7)

Rageorapper   An evil god who caused trees to catch fire and who "brought sickness and death to anyone who violated certain tabus, like touching wood from a lightning-blasted tree or old, imperfectly cremated bones." Tasmania. (Coon, 1971: 290)

Rahu Kar   A malevolent deity of the Hos. India. (Majumdar, 1950: 255)

Raja Hantuen   An evil form of the total godhead. The witches are his servants and acquire their powers from him. He is a spirit of temptation in youth, of danger in pregnancy, and other misfortunes. However, he can also deliver from persecution. The Ngaju, Borneo. (Scharer, 1963: 20–21, 129)

Raja Sial   The watersnake, a spirit of the Upperworld who brings disaster and misfortune arbitrarily. The Ngaju, Borneo. (Scharer, 1963: 20–21)

Ka Ramshandi An evil deity to whom a sow is sacrificed in cases of violent or accidental death. The Khasis, Assam. (Gurdon, 1914: 136)

Ranga Chandi A maleficent deity of the area of the Hos. India. (Majumdar, 1950: 255)

Ranga Kani A maleficent deity of the area of the Hos. India. (Majumdar, 1950: 255)

Ravana The demon king of Ceylon, a power of darkness. (Cox, 1870, 2: 329; Brown, 1961: 291; Martin, 1914: 285–289)

Red-Kai An evil spirit who dwells near water and forests. The Maji, Ethiopia. (Cerulli, 1956: 94)

ka ron A very evil demoness among the Synteng. The Khasi, Assam. (Stegmiller, 1921: 411)

Rota A god of evil, of torment, and of death and disease. The Lapps, Lapland. (Karsten, 1955: 40, 53; Dioszegi, 1968: 30; Pettersson, 1957: 9, 132, 152)

Ruahine-nihoniho-roroa "Old-woman-with-long-teeth." A "goddess of strife and cruelty." Society Islands, Polynesia. (Henry, 1928: 417)

Rupiaba A malignant god to whom all misfortunes are attributed. The Nagas, India. (Elwin, 1969: 412)

Rutzeh The god of evil who brings sudden death. The Angami Nagas, India. (Hutton, 1921: 182)

Sagrong Mung A demon "who lives in caves, carries off solitary wanderers." The Lepchas, Sikkim. (Nebesky-Wojkowitz, 1956, 2: 135)

Samael *See* **Satan**

Sani The planet Saturn, an evil and sinister influence, a much-dreaded and propitiated god. His mount is variously given as a tortoise, a crow, or a vulture. India, Nepal, and Bengal. (Crooke, 1925, 2: 484; 1894: 287; Pal and Bhattacharyya, 1969: 33, 47; Martin, 1914: 298)

Sar The great god of evil of the Galla. Ethiopia. (Budge, 1973, 1: 363)

Sararuma, Aïma Suñé An evil demon who destroyed the world by fire. One man survived, to whom Sararuma gave seeds to plant. The Yuracare, Bolivia. (Métraux, 1948, 5: 502)

Saraua An evil god of the Manao of the Amazon Basin. Brazil. (Métraux, 1948, 6: 710)

Sarisano A god of evil who lives in the north and is propitiated because he sends diseases. Formosa. (Campbell, 1925, 6: 84)

Sasabonsum A cannibalistic god—"the most cruel and malevolent of all the gods . . . believed to be implacable; and, once angered, can never be mollified or propitiated." He was an earthquake god and after a quake human sacrifices were made to appease him. He was friendly to witches and wizards. The Ashanti, Ghana. (Ellis, 1887: 34–35; Mockler-Ferryman, 1925, 9: 277; Frazer, 1961: 201)

Satan The power of evil. The "marriage of Lilith with Samael, also known as the 'Angel Satan' or the 'Other God,' was not allowed to prosper." Early Hebrew. (Patai, 1967: 235)

Satanaël The Bogomils believed he "was the first-born of God, and Christ the second." Southeastern Europe. (Eliade, 1979: 83)

Satanail The Devil. Ukraine. (Drahomanov, 1961: 7)

sa thong The "tiger, a mythical evil power." The Lepchas, Sikkim. (Siijer, 1967: 144)

Saukoni A vindictive spirit who steals food and kills people. The Toaripi, New Guinea. (Haddon, 1925, 9: 342)

Saukoro A very cruel and malignant god who waylays people. The Elema, Papuan Gulf, New Guinea. (Holmes, 1902: 431; Haddon, 1925, 9: 342)

Saulal The god of evil. Lamotrek, Caroline Islands, Micronesia. (Christian, 1897: 198)

Saura, Sauru, Saurva A demon who inspires tyranny and misgovernment, anarchy and drunkenness; the opponent of Kshathra Vairya. Iran. (Gray, 1930: 182; Hinnells, 1973: 52; Huart, 1963: 43)

Saytan The evil spirit of the Galla. Among the Arusi, a water spirit. Ethiopia. (Huntingford, 1955: 74–75)

Sendu Bir The "whistling god" who causes winds, madness, burning houses and immoral deeds. The Panjab, India. (Crooke, 1925, 5: 3)

Set The god of evil and of darkness, of the desert and drought, of storms. He was the son of Seb and Nut, the brother of Osiris, whom he killed, and the brother/husband of Nephthys. He took the form of a serpent as Apep; was also known as Nubti, Sutekh, Ba; was god of the planet Mercury. Egypt. (Budge, 1969, 2: 241–245, 250, 303; 1969, 1: 482; Knight, 1915; 48, 107, 119; Ames, 1965: 64–65)

Setlm-ki-jash The principal and powerful evil spirit who was master of the tides. The Haida, British Columbia. Same as Kees-du-je-al-ity Kah (Tlingit). (Niblack, 1888: 379)

Shajtan "The creator of all the evil on the earth." The Cheremis, the Mordvins. Russia. (Leach, 1949: 215)

Shikakunamo A god of the Ila who causes afflictions. Zambia. (Mbiti, 1970, 2: 13)

Shulmus The devil. Central Siberia. (Long, 1963: 205)

Sigrutan An evil female spirit who "ensnares people by the neck, causing them to die immediately." The Isneg, Luzon, Philippines. (Vanoverbergh, 1953: 99)

Singa Belabong Dilah A god who is feared and who preys upon men, but on those who are brave he bestows courage and prosperity. The Iban Dyaks, Sarawak, Borneo. (Sarawak Gazette, 1963: 135)

Sinompi The spirit of evil of the coastal people of the Mamberamo. New Guinea. Same as Suangir. (Haddon, 1925, 9: 350)

Sitan, Iblis The omnipresent chief of the evil spirits who influences people to evil. He is able to assume many shapes. Morocco. (Westermarck, 1926, 1: 406–412)

Siva A god of destruction, of disintegration, of death, and as such associated with the barren and dangerous Himalayan regions, the moon and the darkness of the night, the snake and its poison, and the lightning as dealers of sudden death. This dark aspect is counterbalanced by his generative and phallic character as a god of fertility and reproduction, and of the creation of life, where his symbols are the bull and the phallus; his representation of the creation of new life rising out of destruction and death. He is frequently presented as fond of pleasures and of dancing. India. (Russell, 1916, 1: 302–303; 1916, 4: 14; Dubois, 1906: 546, 628, 631; Banerjea, 1953: 61–64; Schoeps, 1961: 162; Danielou, 1964: 192; Martin, 1914: 168–171; Bhattacharji, 1970: 15, 16)

Skoocoom The evil spirit of the Clallams. British Columbia. (Bancroft, 1886, 3: 155)

Skwai il The chief of the malignant spirits who dwells below. The Twana, Washington, (Eells, 1886/87: 672)

Sobugo An evil deity who may be singular or plural. Central Celebes, Indonesia. (Downs, 1920: 20)

Soksouh An evil spirit of the Yokuts. California. (Latta, 1949: 24)

Stallo An evil spirit of the forests and the fields. The Lapps, Lapland. (Karsten, 1955: 53)

Suangir The spirit of evil. (Sinompi of the coast.) New Guinea. (Haddon, 1925, 9: 350)

Suetiva God of evil of the Chibcha. Colombia. (Alexander, 1920: 202)

Supay (1) An evil deity of the Panzaleo. Ecuador. (Murra, 1946: 796). (2) An evil spirit who rules over the land where the wicked go and suffer hunger and thirst. He is propitiated and is also called Aucca, Huantahualla. The Aymara, Bolivia and Peru. (La Barre, 1948: 168; Forbes, 1870: 231)

Surgelp An evil spirit of the Trinity River Indians. California. (Bancroft, 1886, 3: 176)

Sutekh A god of evil propitiated to gain favor, identified with Set. Egypt. (Budge, 1969, 2: 283–284; Larousse, 1968: 19)

Suysuy An evil spirit of the Mosetene and Chiman. Bolivia. (Métraux, 1942: 25)

Sye-elth A goddess of evil who influences mankind to evildoing. The Yurok, California. (Thompson, 1916: 74)

Taguain One of the names of the god of evil, greatly feared. Brazil. (Alexander, 1920: 295)

Tahquitz, Taqwuš An evil god who lived on San Jacinto Peak and stole souls, caused disease and death, and misfortunes. The Cahuilla, California. (Brumgardt and Bowles, 1981: 34–38; Bean, 1974: 166)

Ta Hsien Fu Jên "Great (Fox) Fairy Dame," maleficent and must be placated. China. (Day, 1940: 45, 207)

Ta Hsien Tsun Shen "Great (Fox) Fairy God," maleficent and must be placated. China. (Day, 1940: 45, 207)

Taife An evil spirit who may harm his victims. The Witoto, Peru. (Farabee, 1922: 146)

the Taiyaban Flying Monsters. The "most feared, perhaps, of all deities . . . prey on the souls of men . . . also . . . on soul-stuff: for example, they devour that of the arm—then the arm will wither." There are local individual ones and also generalized ones. They inhabit rocks, thickets, trees, lakes, gorges, etc. They also " 'steal' the life of rice and fruit trees and sometimes, if properly invoked, help men against their enemies." The Ifugao, Philippines. (Barton, 1946: 83, 62)

Talaia   An evil deity of the Kuca. Ethiopia. (Cerulli, 1956: 115)

Tamu   A demon of the jungle who causes accidents. The Dafla tribes, Assam. (Stonor, 1957: 6)

Tamun   An important male evil spirit who must be propitiated with a major sacrifice—that of a bison. The Dafla tribes, Assam. (Stonor, 1957: 6)

Tando   A malignant river god, the chief deity of the Ashantis, to whom human sacrifices were made, seven men and seven women at a time. He "wields the lightning, and displays his anger by storm, pestilence and flood." His wife is Katarwiri, a river goddess. Ghana. (Ellis, 1887: 32–33; Budge, 1973, 1: 371)

Tari Pennu, Bera Pennu   An earth goddess to whom human sacrifices were made to ensure good crops, particularly of the tumeric for which blood was essential for the deep red color, and to avert disease and other misfortunes. India. (Martin, 1914: 29; Thurston, 1909, 3: 372; Russell, 1916, 3: 473–475; MacCulloch, 1925, 8: 51)

Tarn, Ey-vet'ne kimtaran   A goddess who is "the personification of flames of fire." She is the deity of "war, sickness, bad weather, and everything destructive to life." The Ostyaks, Siberia. (Czaplicka, 1925, 9: 577)

Tauna   An evil stellar god who causes storms and destroys trees by lightning. Guiana. (Levi-Strauss, 1969: 231)

Taweskare, Tawiskaron(g)   The evil twin who interfered with and corrupted the good things created by the good twin (Tsentsa, Iouskeha, Tijuska'a, Teharonhiawagon). He created the dangerous and destructive animals. God of winter. Sons or grandsons of Ataentsic. The Iroquois, Eastern United States. (Barbeau, 1914: 292; Bjorklund, 1969: 133; Hale, 1888: 181; Tooker, 1964: 146, 154; Blair, 1912: 271; Gray, 1925, 7: 422)

tčiké· cac nádle·hé (shike cac nadlehe)   Changing-bear-maiden—the personification of evil, and difficult to persuade. The Navaho, Arizona and New Mexico. (Reichard, 1950: 414)

Tha   The bad young girl goddess and Vinaka, the good, were the children of Tui Vakano. Tha is jealous and

will kill children. The appearance and actions of the two are considered omens in recovery from illness. Lau Islands, Fiji, Melanesia. (Hocart, 1929: 191)

Thang thang gyer mkhas   A deity of evil nature. Tibet. (Nebesky-Wojkowitz, 1956, 1: 290)

Thau-wisk-a-lau   The principle of evil, older brother of Tau-lou-ghy-au-wan-goon. The Oneida, New York. (Schoolcraft, 1957: 668)

Tijax   One of the Day Lords associated with slander, lies, arguing, and fighting (particularly religious). Momostenango, Guatemala. (Tedlock, 1982: 123)

Tili tili   A mischief-making god in Upolu who was "supposed to be the cause of quarrels, war, and darkness." He was represented by the lightning which, if prevalent during battle, was believed to be assisted by him. Samoa, Polynesia. (Turner, 1884: 59)

Tlacatecolototl   God of the night and of evil, represented by the owl. The Toltec, Mexico. (Schoolcraft, 1857, 6: 637; Bancroft, 1886, 3: 184)

tłi·c do·ntihí   Never-ending-snake, "wholly evil and destroys the mind and consciousness . . . symbolizes the danger of getting into a circle." The Navaho, Arizona and New Mexico. (Reichard, 1950: 454)

tli·stso xasti·n   Big-snake-man, an evil and undependable deity. The Navaho, Arizona and New Mexico. (Reichard, 1950: 393)

Toru-guenket   The goddess of the moon represents the evil principle and is the cause of misfortunes, particularly of the weather. The Tupi, Brazil. (Spence, 1925, 2: 837)

Tuira   An important god of evil from whom sorcerers and witches claim to receive their powers. Panama. (Trimborn, 1968: 106)

Tusi   The "Evil spirit in the third layer of heaven." The Cuna, Panama. (Nordenskiold, 1938: 332)

Typhon, Typhoeus   Sometimes the same, sometimes Typhoeus is the father of Typhon. Named as the son of Hera or of Gaea and Tartarus. A giant monster, half man, half beast, who is the demon of the whirlwind, the hurricane as well as of the volcano. Greece. (Fairbanks, 1907: 72, 169; Kerényi, 1951: 26, 51, 98; Barthell, 1971: 9, 10)

Uddagubba   A Sumerian messenger of Enlil, one of "vengeance and destruction." Near East. (Langdon, 1931: 100)

ulurú The "evil armadillo who lives under the ground and wants to destroy the villages and camps." Greatly feared. The Nambicuara, Brazil. (Oberg, 1953: 100)

Umuauri The principle of evil, a supernatural being of the Paravilhana (Cariban) and the Manao (Arawak). Brazil and Venezuela. (Zerries, 1968: 249)

Unk An "evil and mean" spirit who, in the creation of animals (under Mahpiyato), shaped hers without limbs. Because she was so unpleasant, Wakinyan clothed them "with slime or with scales." And Wi, instead of warming them, left them cold. They became the fish and lived in the water. As she was a malcontent, demanding and evil, she was banished from the circle of gods. She and hers use "deceit, folly, and vanity" to corrupt and to cause misery, injustice, etc., fearing only Mahpiyato. The Lakota, South Dakota. (One Feather, 1982: 49–51)

Ah Uoh Puc A god of destruction and of the underworld. Mayan, Mexico. (Krickeberg, 1968: 70)

Urima An evil deity of the Conebo, Panoan, Peru. (Farabee, 1922: 84)

U Syngkai Bamon An evil deity to whom a goat is sacrificed in cases of accidental or violent death. The Khasis, Assam. (Gurdon, 1914: 136)

Valichu An evil spirit who is appeased because they feel the good spirit pays no attention to them. The Puelches, Argentina. (Cooper, 1946, 5: 158; Grubb, 1925, 9: 598)

Vatak, Autak, Udai A "female demon who forces men to speak when they should not and disturbs them while they are performing their physical functions; a friend of incest, half human, half monster." Zoroastrian, Iran. (Leach, 1950: 1155)

Vatipa The god of evil who is the major recipient of worship and offerings and who is "the immediate minister of the Great Spirit." The Aricoris, Guiana. (Schoolcraft, 1857, 4: 489)

Vitico, Wikkika The cause and source of all evil and misfortune, to whom offerings are sometimes made. Indians of the vicinity of York Factory, Manitoba. In the Churchill area, called Wittakah. (Cooper, 1934: 55–56)

Wahcondahpishcona The evil spirit of the Otto Indians, Upper Missouri, Nebraska and South Dakota. (Emerson, 1884: 523)

Waiabskinit Awase The "White bear, who is the supreme leader of the Underneath Gods" and the "essence of evil." The Menomini, Wisconsin. (Skinner, 1913: 81, 88)

Wakanda-pezi The spirit of evil who tempts men to do evil. The Ponca, Nebraska. (Howard, 1965: 99)

Wakan śica Evil Sacred. Controls all evil aspects, is subordinate to Wakantanka. The Oglala, South Dakota. (Powers, 1977: 51–52)

Wanuswegock An evil spirit of the Trinity River Indians. California. (Bancroft, 1886, 3: 176)

Warrugura An evil spirit who is a chthonic deity. The Watchandi, Australia. (Tylor, 1891: 292)

Watamaraka "The Goddess of Evil, Mother of all Demons." South Africa. (Mutwa, n.d.: vii)

Wele gumali The Black God, the god of evil, who is the source of misfortunes and death. The Bantu of North Kavirondo, Kenya. (Wagner, 1949, 1: 175, 177)

Wihtiko An evil spirit of the Cree Indians. The *same as* **Matci Manitu.** Ontario. (Cooper, 1934: 8)

xa·ctčé·tsoh (xashshe'tsoh) An evil and undependable deity "who may be a god of thunder or lightning." The Navaho, Arizona and New Mexico. (Reichard, 1950: 391, 393)

Xa-mul A spirit "who swallows people alive without crushing them between his teeth." The Isneg, Luzon, Philippines. (Vanoverbergh, 1953: 99)

Xotsadam A female devil, formerly the wife of Ets, the sky god. The Yenisei-Ostyak or Ket. Siberia. (Roheim, 1954: 23)

Yaccy-ma A black god of evil who is the source of misfortune, bad weather, etc. The Alacaluf, Chile. (Cooper, 1917: 147; Alexander, 1920: 341)

Yauhahu The evil spirit who is "responsible for death." The Arawak, Guiana and West Indies. (Levi-Strauss, 1973: 439; Lovén, 1935: 569)

Yetaita The chief of the evil spirits who, with Watauinewa, punished infractions of the laws. Boys and girls were admonished of this in initiation ceremonies. The Yahgan, Tierra del Fuego. (Cooper, 1946, 3: 99; Zerries, 1968: 234)

Yhuanchi The Principle of Evil is propitiated. Through dreams induced by Natem (a narcotic), he informs them of the causes of illness and misfortune, "reveals the name of the supposed enemies, predicts the future." The Jivaro, Ecuador. (Vigna, 1945: 39)

Yinijama A spirit of evil of the Kanichana. Matto Grosso, Bolivia. (Métraux, 1942: 81)

Yochina A malevolent spirit of the Pakaguara. Matto Grosso, Bolivia. (Métraux, 1942: 50)

yoglamo The devil of the Cumanagota. Venezuela. (Girard, 1979: 110)

Yoin A canibalistic supernatural being, a monster, very terrible in appearance and actions. Most often male but sometimes female; occasionally considered benevolent, e.g., in hunting. The Kaingang, Brazil. (Henry, 1941: 70–71)

Yurupari A name applied to an individual or to an entire class of spirits of the forests, of the wilds, who are malicious and dangerous. The Mundurucu, the Tupian, the Tupinamba, and the Uaupes. Brazil. (Murphy, 1958: 17, 142; Métraux, 1948, 3: 128; 1949: 567; Wagley, 1964: 225; Karsten, 1926: 301; Larousse, 1968: 447)

Yush The evil being, but powerless "against a Kafir wearing the national weapon." Kafiristan, Afghanistan. (Robertson, 1897: 78)

Zairik, Zairika, Zairisha An archdemon who "poisons eatables and produces causes of death . . . probably a deity of poisonous plants." A demon of destruction and decrepitude. Iran. (Gray, 1930: 184–185; Larousse, 1968: 318; Jayne, 1962: 185)

Zakiripenu An evil spirit invoked for sinlessness and to bestow good crops. The Konds, India. (Schulze, 1912: 12, 13)

Zambi-a-n'bi The god and author of all evil, as opposed to Zambi, Nsambi, the good deity. The Bafioti, Gabon. (Frazer, 1926: 137)

40

Gods of Destiny, Fate

Ab delam's n "Warm wind." The winds rule "human and animal destiny." The Penobscot, Maine. (Speck, 1935: 21)

Achacato A "god of fate and of madness." The Achagua, Venezuela and Colombia. (Hernandez de Alba, 1948, 2: 410)

Adrasteia A daughter of Zeus, identified with Nemesis, the Greek goddess of fate. (Roscher, 1965, 1, 1: 77; Larousse, 1968: 163)

Ahaiyuta A god of war, of fate, of chance. Brother of Matsailema. The Zuñi, New Mexico. (Cushing, 1891/92: 422; Fewkes, 1891: 171; Tyler, 1964: 214)

Allat Goddess of the morning and evening stars, and in her association with the planet Venus, a goddess of fate. Near East. (Langdon, 1931: 25)

Amsa One of the Adityas. He is concerned with "the distribution of the fate divinely determined [by Varuna] for each individual." India. (Littleton, 1965: 120; Danielou, 1964: 122)

Ananke A Greek goddess of fate, daughter of Nyx and Erebus, representing the control of the course of events, both of the world and of mankind. (Murray, 1935: 210)

The Arantides Another name of the Erinyes. Greece. (Roscher, 1965, 1, 1: 470)

Ashima A goddess of fate introduced into Samaria from Syria. Near East. (Langdon, 1931: 22; Cook, 1930: 146)

Ashi-Oxsho The goddess of "Fate or Recompense." Daughter of Ahura Mazda. Persia. (Hinnells, 1973: 52)

Atropos One of the three goddesses of fate, the Moira. She severs the thread of life and rules over the past. Greece. (Cox, 1870, 2: 17; Schoeps, 1961: 127; Branston, 1957: 64; Hesiod-Brown, 1981: 78)

Baxta Iranian deity of fate, of destiny. (Gray, 1930: 64)

Camaxtli Nicholson names him as a god of fate, though among other sources he is a god of storms, of war, of hunting and fishing. Mexico. (Nicholson, 1967: 45; Spence, 1923: 127; Brinton, 1868: 158; Duran, 1971: 140–141; Bancroft, 1886, 4: 195)

Cel An Etruscan god of fate and of the underworld associated with the west and with haruspicy. Italy. (Pallottino, 1975: 145; Hamblin, 1975: 95)

Cer A Greek deity, "Fate," a child of Nyx. (Barthell, 1971: 8)

Ch'il Song "The Seven Star Spirit." The stars of Ursa Major are believed to control "a person's good and bad luck. They grant his birth and decide his destiny." Very popular in all three religions. Korea. (Moes, 1983: 125, 126)

Clotho, Klotho One of the Moira, the spinner of the thread of life. She rules over the present. Greece. (Cox, 1870, 2: 17; Schoeps, 1961: 127; Branston, 1957: 64; Bulfinch, 1898: 13; Hesiod-Brown, 1981: 78)

Cosa Bantu god of destiny. South Africa. (Smith, 1950: 118)

Dada-Segbo, Se The father of the gods who controlled men's fate. Dahomey. (Parrinder, 1949: 19)

Decima A minor Roman deity of fate who decided the date of birth, was more primarily concerned with pregnancy and childbirth. (Jayne, 1962: 495; Ferguson, 1970: 68)

Dekla A goddess of destiny, associated with, or an aspect of, Laima. Same attributes, same role. Latvia. (Jonval, 1929: 18)

Dievas The sky god who controls human destiny and with Laima "determines the life span and the fortune of man." Lithuania. (Gimbutas, 1963: 200)

Djo An omniscient god of the air who controlled man's lifespan. A son of Mawu-Lisa to whom he must report periodically. Dahomey. (Herskovits, 1938, 2: 130)

Dolja, Dolya Slavic goddess of fate. Each man has a personal Dolya who can be good or evil, but who protects those she favors. Russia. (Mansikka, 1925, 4: 626; Machal, 1918: 251–252)

The Erinyes, Erinys (singular) One or several (Alekto, Tisiphone, Megaira) goddesses of vengeance, the avengers of wrongdoing, who persecute mankind. They are attendants of Nemesis, and came to be considered goddesses of destiny. As the avengers of the moral codes they were also called the Eumenides. Greece. (Roscher, 1965, 1, 1: 1310; Murray, 1935: 213–217; Fairbanks, 1907: 239; Cox, 1870, 2: 14)

Fa, Gbadu Fate or destiny—abstract as well as personal. "Fa, through Legba, introduced sacrifice into the world, since before the knowledge of Fa, men did not know how to appease the gods." Dahomey. (Herskovits, 1933: 51–55)

Fata Scribunda A minor Roman deity, scribe of Fatum, who "recorded the destiny of the child" after one week of life, during which week prayers were said for a favorable decision. (Jayne, 1962: 497)

Fatum Roman deity who determined the destiny of the child and controlled events, both of the world and of mankind. Same as Ananke. (Jayne, 1962: 497; Murray, 1935: 210)

Gad West Semitic god of fate and of fortune. Near East. (Gray, 1930: 65; Langdon, 1931: 23; Paton, 1925, 3: 182)

Giocauvaghama A Puerto Rican deity who "was consulted by the cacique Guarionex to learn the fate of his gods and people." (Fewkes, 1903/04: 56)

Hang Phan The snake-headed god of the West—one of those who determine the destinies of men. Tibet. (Nebesky-Wojkowitz, 1956, 2: 51)

Ialulep A great celestial god who decides the duration of each life and who judges the dead and decides their fate. His son is Lugeilang. Ulithi, the Carolines, Micronesia. (Lessa, 1966: 56)

Istustaya A Hattic-Hittite netherworld goddess who with Papaya spins the thread of life. Asia Minor. (Guterbock, 1961: 149)

Jau Phara Makam One of the gods of destiny who control the threads, the vital nerves of life. Son of Ning pan majan. The Katchins, Burma. (Gilhodes, 1908: 674)

Käbä Fate. The Chuwash, Russia and Siberia. (MacCulloch, 1964: 393)

Kaba-Inmar Fate. The Votiaks, Siberia. (MacCulloch, 1964: 393)

Kak, Kakamtch The personification of fate who punishes with death. The Klamath, Oregon. (Gatschet, 1890: civ)

Kakestsaiol ola xmanoas "Two beings . . . are placed on the ends of a long plant," like a seesaw, at the winter solstice. Those standing near when one falls down will die. The Bella Coola, British Columbia. (Boas, 1898, 2: 32)

Karaeng lowe A god who decrees life and death. He is a phallic deity and is invoked for health, children, good harvest, and good fortune. South Celebes, Indonesia. (Kruijt, 1925, 7: 250; Hartland, 1925, 9: 818)

Karai Kasang A god of destiny, one of those who control the vital nerves of life of the earth and its inhabitants. The Katchins, Burma. (Gilhodes, 1908: 674)

Karta The third and least of the goddesses of destiny, with Laima and Dekla. Karta is possibly just an epithet of Laima; or as an independent goddess, presides over the first months of life. Latvia. (Jonval, 1929: 18)

Kava-Jumo Fate. The Cheremis, Russia. (MacCulloch, 1964: 393)

Klotho *See* **Clotho**

Kubai-khotun, Kybai-Khotun Goddess of birth who also controls destines. Also called Ajysyt. The Yakuts, Siberia. (Pettersson, 1957: 28; MacCulloch, 1964: 358)

Lachesis One of the three fates, the Moira, who measures out the thread of life and presides over the future. (Cox, 1870, 2: 17; Kerényi, 1951: 189; Schoeps, 1961: 127; Branston, 1957: 64; Hesiod-Brown, 1981: 78)

Laima Goddess of destiny whose name means "bonheur"—happiness, good fortune—of which she is the personification. She consults with Dievas, determining the length of life and the fate of man and other living beings. Once her decree is made it is inescapable, though she is beneficent and sympathetic and does what she can to alleviate misfortune. Latvia and Lithuania. (Jonval, 1929: 12, 18–9; Gimbutas, 1963: 197; Grimm, 1880: 416)

Maha-Lakshmi Goddess of destiny and good fortune. Orissa, India. (Danielou, 1964: 262; Elwin, 1954: 638)

Mamit, Mammetu, Mammitu Goddess of destiny and of the curse which is irrevocable once invoked. She was a goddess of childbirth who determined the destiny of the child as born into the world, and before whom men also must appear when they die. The Elamites, the Babylonians, the Akkadians, and the Assyrians, Near East. (Langdon, 1925, 4: 444; 1931: 372; Sayce, 1898: 306; Pinches, 1925, 5: 251; Larousse, 1968: 63)

Manat Goddess of destiny at Palmyra in Syria. Near East. (Vriezen, 1963: 68)

Manawatu, Manavat, Manuthu Nabataean mother goddess and goddess of fate. Near East. (Langdon, 1931: 21; Cooke, 1925, 9: 122)

Mao Tchong One of three brothers. The beneficent protector of destinies. China. (Chavannes, n.d.: 143)

Matsailema A god of war, fate, and chance, with his brother Ahaiyuta. The Zuñi, New Mexico. (Cushing, 1891/92: 422)

Meni A Phoenician/Canaanite deity of destiny. Variously given as male or female, as of good or detrimental fate. Associated with Gad. Near East. (Paton, 1925, 9: 893; Moss, 1925, 6: 88–89)

Mettena The "measurers," the Anglo-Saxon name for the Scandinavian Norns. (Wagner, 1882: 223)

The Moirai, Morae Greek goddesses of fate: Clotho (Klotho), the spinner of the thread of life, the present; Lachesis, the measurer, the future; and Atropos, who cuts the thread, the past. They are variously given as the daughters of Nyx or of Themis. (Schoeps, 1961: 127; Cox, 1870, 2: 16; Kerényi, 1951: 32; Hesiod-Brown, 1981: 32, 78)

Moros "Doom," the inexorable god of fate, a personification of unfortunate destiny and of violent death. Son of Nyx. Greece. (Roscher, 1965, 2, 2: 3215; Barthell, 1971: 8; Larousse, 1968: 97)

Morta One of the Parcae, Roman goddesses of fate, with Nona and Decima. She presided over death and cut the thread of life. (Roscher, 1965, 2, 1: 204; Branston, 1957: 60, 64)

nala'təgw'sən The "northeast," "up river wind" who was one of the winds who ruled over "human and animal destiny." The Penobscot, Maine. (Speck, 1935, 1: 21)

Namtar (u) The god of fate is also a god of plague and of death. Akkadian, Assyrian, and Babylonian, Near East. (Kramer, 1961: 124; Langdon, 1931: 372; Larousse, 1968: 64; Sayce, 1898: 147, 156, 306)

Narucnici Slavic goddess of fate. Also called Orisnici, Urisnici, Uresici. Bulgaria. (Machal, 1918: 250)

Necessitas A Roman goddess of destiny associated with Fortuna. Same as Anake (Greek). Italy. (Roscher, 1965, 3, 1: 70–2)

Nemesis A goddess of fate in that she is the avenger and punisher of all wrongdoing, the goddess of inevitable retribution. Also called Adrasteia. Greece. (Cox, 1870, 2: 20; Murray, 1935: 213; Bulfinch, 1898: 13)

Nesreca An evil Slavic personal goddess of fate, who can, however, be driven away. Serbia. (Machal, 1918: 252)

nibənik'ska'sən The northwest summer wind who is one of the winds who rules over "human and animal destiny." The Penobscot, Maine. (Speck, 1935, 1: 21)

Nina A Babylonian goddess of destinies. She was a daughter of Ea and originally a water goddess. (Jastrow, 1898: 86–87; Mercer, 1925, 12: 709)

Ninmea A Sumerian/Akkadian goddess who determines destinies—an aspect or name of Mah. Near East. (Langdon, 1931: 110)

Nona A goddess of gestation and a goddess of fate associated with Decima "in determining the proper date of birth." One of the Roman Parcae. (Jayne, 1962: 495; Ferguson, 1970: 68; Branston, 1957: 60,64)

Nornir, the Norns The Scandinavian/Teutonic goddesses of fate who appear for each new-born child to pronounce his destiny. They are associated with the moon, and so with the phases presumed to have brought time: Urdr, the Crescent Moon, the Past, the spinner of the thread of life, considered beneficent; Verdandi, the Full Moon, the Present, the weaver, considered beneficent; Skuld, the Waning Moon, the Future, the cutter of the thread of life, and considered relentless. (Branston, 1955: 207–209; Stern, 1898: 11; Guerber, 1895: 154–6; Grimm, 1880: 405–408; Pettersson, 1957: 35)

Nortia, Norcia Etruscan goddess of destiny and of fortune. "Annually . . . the Year Nail was driven into the wall of" her temple, "symbolizing the inevitability of fate." Italy. (Campbell, 1964: 309; Leland, 1963: 34; Herbig, 1925, 5: 534)

Orisnici One of the Slavic goddesses of fate who "ordain the destiny of the child and determine the manner of its death." Bulgaria. (Mansikka, 1925, 4: 626)

Orlog Destiny or Fate whose decrees are inexorable. The "eternal law of the universe, an older and superior power, who apparently had neither beginning nor end" and who controlled the weaving of the Norns. Scandinavia. (Guerber, 1895: 155, 186)

Papaya A Hattic/Hittite netherworld goddess who with Istustaya spins the thread of life. Near East. (Guterbock, 1961: 149)

Parca A goddess of destiny and of birth who is associated with Nona and Decima in determining the fate of the new-born. Rome. (Roscher, 1965, 2, 1: 210)

Parcae The Roman goddesses of fate—Nona, Decima, Parca or Morta—the equivalent of the Greek Moirai. (Roscher, 1965, 2, 1: 210; Jayne, 1962: 498; Murray, 1935: 212; Branston, 1957: 60, 64)

Pelden Lhamo A protective goddess of Buddhism who sees the future and "casts her dice to decide the fate of men." Tibet. (Nebesky-Wojkowitz, 1956, 2: 22)

Pên Ming Hsin Chün The "Individual Fate Star in charge of every life, male or female," to whom sacrifices are made on birthdays and anniversaries. China. (Day, 1940: 94)

Phandum Sakia Makam One of the gods of fate who controls the threads, the vital nerves of life. Son of Ningpang majan. The Katchins, Burma. (Gilhodes, 1908: 674)

Phan ningsang Makam A god of fate who controls the threads, the vital nerves of life. Son of Ningpang majan. The Katchins, Burma. (Gilhodes, 1908: 674)

(p)mso'sən The east and great wind who is a ruler "of human and animal destiny." The Penobscot, Maine. (Speck, 1935, 1: 21)

Potmos A personification of destiny. Greece. (Roscher, 1965, 3, 2: 2906)

Pso'sən The north wind who brings the cold joins the other winds in ruling "human and animal destiny." The Penobscot, Maine. (Speck, 1935, 1: 21)

Puru The supreme being and creator god who is also the god of destinies, benevolent or punitive according to conduct. The Saliva, Colombia and Venezuela. (Walde-Waldegg, 1936: 40–41; Wallis, 1939: 88–89; Hernandez de Alba, 1948, 2: 410)

Rod Slavic god of fate to whom offerings are made of "bread, cheese, and honey." Russia. (Machal, 1918: 249)

Rodjenice One of the three fates (with Sudnice and Sudjenice) who determine the fate of the new-born. Serbs, Croatians, and Slovenians. (Mansikka, 1925, 4: 626; Machal, 1918: 249–250)

Rozanice A Slavic deity of fate who is "offered bread, cheese, and honey." Russia. (Machal, 1918: 249)

Rozdenici A goddess of fate who determines the fate of the child and "the manner of its death." Bulgaria. (Mansikka, 1925, 4: 626)

Sa'd Arabian god of fate, of fortune. (Langdon, 1931: 24; Noldeke, 1925, 1: 662)

sawanesən "South wind." The winds "figure in mythology as rulers of human and animal destiny." The Penobscot, Maine. (Speck, 1935, 1: 21)

sənutsegadən "Southwest wind" with the same attributes as the above. The Penobscot, Maine. (Speck, 1935, 1: 21)

Shai, Shay God of destiny. Apparently one for each individual, as he is his constant companion and when he dies appears before Osiris with an accounting of the individual's life. Egypt. (Casson, 1965: 111; Budge, 1969, 2: 144; Larousse, 1968: 38; Gardiner, 1925, 9: 787)

Shait Destiny as a goddess. Egypt. (Casson, 1965: 111)

Shimti Assyrian goddess of fate, identified with Ashima. Near East. (Langdon, 1931: 22)

Shou Hsing A god of longevity and of happiness. Also a god of fate in that he decides each individual's time of death. China. (Maspero, 1963: 344; Werner, 1932: 431; Day, 1940: 95; Larousse, 1968: 384, 386)

Skuld A Scandinavian goddess of fate, the youngest of the three Norns who determine the length of life and decree the destiny of the newborn. She is relentless and frequently undoes the attempts of Urd and Verdandi at beneficence. She is also one of the Valkyries who go to battle and choose the slain. (Anderson, 1891: 265; Stern, 1898: 11; Schoeps, 1961: 107; Guerber, 1895: 154–155; Grimm, 1880: 405–408, 420–422)

Sreca A personal goddess of fate, protecting her charge, "his fields and grazing his flocks." The counterpart of the Russian Dolya. A benevolent goddess as opposed to Nesreca. Servia. (Machal, 1918: 252; Mansikka, 1925, 4: 626)

Ssu Ming The "arbiter of life and death . . . the protector of virtue and enemy of evil." China. (Ferguson, 1937: 89)

Sudicky The Bohemian deity or deities of fate. (Machal, 1918: 250; Mansikka, 1925, 4: 626)

Sudjenice and **Sudnice** With Rodjenice, the three goddesses of fate of the Serbs, the Slovenes. (Mansikka, 1925, 4: 626)

Sudzenici The Slavic deities of fate. Bulgaria. (Machal, 1918: 250)

T'ai-yo ta-ti, T'ai-yueh-ta-ti God of the Eastern Peak, of T'ai-shan, in Shantung. A god of fate in that he controls birth and death, fortune, prosperity, etc. China. (Maspero, 1963: 278–279; Larousse, 1968: 386)

Tamei Tingei A god who "decides the fate of men," and a god of divine justice who punishes misdeeds and rewards the good. The Kayan-Bahau, Oceania. (Moss, 1925: 143; Kruijt, 1925, 7: 249)

Tchənu In the Earth Pantheon a god of destiny who punishes incest. Son of Dada Zodji and Nyəhwe Ananu. Dahomey. (Herskovits, 1933: 19)

Tengi The heaven god of the Kalmucks and Mongols who "decrees the fates of peoples." Siberia. (MacCulloch, 1964: 391–392)

t'kelam'sən "Cold wind." One of the winds who rule over "human and animal destiny." The Penobscot, Maine. (Speck, 1935, 1: 21)

t'ly-yz, kur The god of heaven, beneficent and protective, though he decides the time of birth and death. The Nivkhi and the Gilyaks, Siberia. (Dioszegi, 1968: 407, 410; Klementz, 1925, 6: 225)

Turm The omniscient and omnipresent sky god, of great honor, a god of destiny and justice who cannot be swayed. The Ostyaks, the Yenisei region, Siberia. (Keane, 1925, 2: 121)

Udelnicy Slavic deities of fate, of destiny, of northern Russia. (Machal, 1918: 250)

Urd, Urdr Scandinavian/Teutonic goddess of fate who is identified with the Past. She and Verdandi are considered beneficent and will confer blessings, but all weave the fates of man blindly, "as if reluctantly executing the wishes of Orlog." Branston, 1955: 204; Stern, 1898: 10; Schoeps, 1961: 107; Guerber, 1895: 154–157; Grimm, 1880: 407)

The Ursitory The three gods of fate "who, on the third night after birth, come down to a child and decide his future." Romanian Gypsies. (Clebert, 1967: 188)

Vagneg-imi A Finno-Ugric goddess of birth but also a goddess of fate, as she determines the length of the child's life. Vicinity of Surgut, Russia. (MacCulloch, 1964: 260)

Verdandi One of the three Norns, a goddess of fate personifying the present and weaving the fates of men. Like Urd she is considered beneficent. Scandinavia. (Guerber, 1895: 154–155; Stern, 1898: 11; Schoeps, 1961: 107)

Weird Sisters The three fates. England. (Branston, 1957: 65)

Weni The supreme being and creator who is also the "moulder of destiny." The Builsa, Gold Coast of Africa. (Frazer, 1926: 95)

wetcibe The southeast wind who is one of the "rulers of human and animal destiny." The Penobscot, Maine. (Speck, 1935, 1: 21)

Wigit A celestial god, the raven, who determines at birth the length of life of the individual. The Haida, British Columbia. (Alexander, 1964: 252)

Wuni The supreme being and creator who is also the "moulder of destiny." The Nankanni, Gold Coast of Africa. (Frazer, 1926: 95)

Wyrd The oldest of the three goddesses of fate. England. **Wurd** (Old Saxon), **Wurt** (Old High German). (Branston, 1957: 59; 1955: 207)

Zurvan, Zrvan God of time and of fate. An androgynous deity, pre-existent. The supreme being in the cult of Zervanism and considered the parent of Ohrmazd and Ahriman. Iran. (Kramer, 1961: 355–356; Patai, 1967: 168; Gray, 1930: 124–128)

41

Fortune:
Luck, Good or Bad

Agathe Tyche Good Fortune. A variant of Tyche. Consort of Agathos Daemon; also given as that of Zeus Philius. Greece. (Ferguson, 1970: 82)

Agathos Daemon Greek god of good fortune, fundamentally the personification of the beneficence of nature, especially of vineyards. Campbell, 1968: 17; Roscher, 1965, 1, 1: 98)

Amsa One of the Adityas. He is the god of that which "is gained through luck, or accident, or war, the unexpected profit." India. (Danielou, 1964: 122)

Automatia Goddess of luck, good or bad, and a surname of Tyche. Greece. (Roscher, 1965, 1, 1: 737)

Aye-Shaluga "God of fortune and good luck. He is represented by a large seashell." Puerto Rico, West Indies. (Gonzalez-Wippler, 1975: 26)

Beda "Distress." The Dolja (personification of good or evil fortune) of an unfortunate man. Also called Gore and Clydni. Russia. (Mansikka, 1925, 4: 626)

Benzaiten, Benten One of the seven gods of luck and of happiness. She is considered a goddess of eloquence and of music and is associated with the sea. Japan. (Piggott, 1969: 59; Eliot, 1935: 139; Herbert, 1967: 513; Getty, 1962: 127–128; Eliseev, 1963: 446)

Bhaga A god of fortune, of the just and fair distribution of material goods. India. (Littleton, 1965: 39; Eliade, 1967: 120; Dumézil, 1966, 1: 201; Bhattacharji, 1970: 215–216)

Bishamon-ten One of the gods of good fortune and happiness, a "dispenser of wealth." He was guardian of the north and considered to bring good fortune in battle.

Japan. (Eliot, 1935: 136; Werner, 1932: 457; Larousse, 1973: 324–325; Getty, 1962: 156, 168)

St. Bouleversé Worshipped as a source of bad fortune. Mirebalais, Haiti, West Indies. (Herskovits, 1937, 1: 281)

Butu-Ulisiwa A phallic god worshipped as the source of "good fortune at sea and victory over their enemies," as well as of fertility in women. Ambon and Uliasa, Indonesia. (Hartland, 1925, 9: 818)

Ch'il Song "The Seven Star Spirits," the stars of Ursa Major, are believed to control good and bad luck. They are very popular. Korea. (Moes, 1983: 125)

Chu I A god of good luck and fortune who protects the ill-prepared taker of examinations. China. (Day, 1940: 113; Maspero, 1963: 314)

Daikoku One of the seven gods of luck and happiness. He is associated with agriculture. Japan. (Piggott, 1969: 59; Herbert, 1967: 513; Hori, 1968: 39, 68; Getty, 1962: 160–162)

Dsaiagachi The "Chief Creator of Fortune" occupies the place of honor in the center of the home. Also called Tengri. The Buryats, Mongol. Siberia. (Waddell, 1959: 372)

Ebisu One of the seven gods of good luck and happiness who is associated with the trades, fishing, and harvests. Japan. (Hori, 1968: 68; Piggott, 1969: 59; Herbert, 1967: 511–512; Eliot, 1935: 140)

Echepat A deity invoked for good fortune. The Yauelmani, California. (Kroeber, 1925: 511)

Ekajata The Blue Tara, a powerful goddess of Buddhism—"even to listen to her mantra repeated destroys all obstacles, brings good luck and intense religious enjoyment." (Getty, 1962: 125)

Ekeko, eq'eq'o   A god of good fortune who is associated with prosperity and fertility. The Aymara, Peru, and Bolivia. (Osborne, 1968: 88; Trimborn, 1968: 140; La Barre, 1948: 169; Tschopik, 1946: 560)

Eshu-Elegba   A trickster and a god of mischief who represents the "principle of chance." He "tricks men into offending the gods, thereby providing them with sacrifices." The Yoruba, Nigeria and Dahomey. (UCLA, 1971: 6/13; Courlander, 1973: 10; Wescott, 1962: 337)

Eucrante   A Nereid, daughter of Nereus and Doris, who represents "successful venture." Greece. (Hesiod-Brown, 1981: 60, 86)

Eunice, Eunike   A daughter of Nereus and Doris who represents "Victory" as it relates to "successful venture." Greece. (Hesiod-Brown, 1981: 60, 86, 87; Kerényi, 1951: 64)

Fors Fortuna   From a goddess representing the uncertainty and chance aspect of agriculture, she developed into a goddess "of blind uncontrollable chance" and fickleness. Italy. (Carter, 1925, 9: 797; Jayne, 1962: 426)

Fortuna   From an agricultural, fertility goddess she developed into an abstract concept of chance, of fortune, the incalculable. Italy. (Carter, 1925, 6: 98; Dumézil, 1966, 2: 423)

Fukurokuju   One of the seven gods of happiness and good luck, associated primarily with wisdom and longevity. Japan. (Puini and Dickens, 1880: 448–450; Eliseev, 1963: 446; Eliot, 1935: 140; Piggott, 1969: 59)

Gad, Jadd   A Semitic/Arabian god of fortune, associated with Meni (Destiny). (Noldeke, 1925, 1: 662; Moss, 1925, 6: 89; Gray, 1930: 65; Langdon, 1931: 23; Paton, 1925, 3: 182)

Gad-Awidh   An Arabian god of fortune. (Vriezen, 1963: 66)

Ganesa, Ganesh   The elephant-headed deity is a god of good luck as well as one of wisdom and discretion and is invoked at the beginning of undertakings as the remover of obstacles. India. (Martin, 1914: 191–193; Crooke, 1894: 104; Banerjea, 1953: 52; Ions, 1967: 100; Russell, 1916, 2: 124)

Gode, Gaude   A goddess of good luck and of hunting. Teutonic. (Wagner, 1882: 103)

Hecate   A goddess, daughter of Perses and Asteria, who had many powers and rights in the heavens, the earth, and the sea. She could bestow generous gifts— wealth, honor, victory, fortune—but could as readily withhold them from those she considered underserving. Greece. (Hesiod-Brown, 1981: 11, 29, 64, 65; Barthell, 1971: 51)

Ikenga   Originally a god of the art of head-hunting, he became that of the skills of the hands and a god of good luck. The Ibo, Nigeria. (Sierksma, 1960: 23, 25)

Ini Andan   A goddess of the heavens, she is the bringer of good luck, is invoked before the clearing of the land, and blesses with abundance, wealth, and skill. The Dyaks, Sarawak, Borneo. (Sarawak Gazette, 1963: 77; Roth, 1968: 174–175)

The In Up   The child luck gods. Korea. (Clark, 1932: 205)

Jero   The "god of good fortune." The Banabuddu, Uganda. (Cunningham, 1905: 67)

Jurojin   One of the seven gods of happiness and good luck. A god of longevity who has a record book of each individual. Japan. (Puini and Dickens, 1880: 446–448; Herbert, 1967: 514; Eliot, 1935: 140; Piggott, 1969: 59)

Ka lha   A dgra lha deity, protective of worshippers and their prosperity, safeguarding their luck. Tibet. (Nebesky-Wojkowitz, 1956, 1: 328, 333)

Karaeng lowe   A phallic god who controls fortune and misfortune, life and death, and is invoked for all good. Southern Celebes, Indonesia. (Kruijt, 1925, 7: 250; Hartland, 1925, 9: 818)

Kichijo-ten, Kishijo-ten   A goddess of good fortune and of luck invoked for prosperity and well-being. She is equated with Laksmi and sometimes replaces Fukuroku-ju as a goddess of happiness. Japan. (Piggott, 1969: 23; Puini and Dickens, 1880: 450; Larousse, 1973: 326)

Kinta-va'irgin   A raven deity who is benevolent and the bringer of luck. The Chukchee, Siberia. (Bogoras, 1904/09: 314–315)

Kodalamma   As part of a festival men bring a cock to a shrine where grains of rice are sprinkled before her— "if the bird pecks at the rice, good luck is ensured for the coming year." If it pecks three times the owner is overjoyed. The Koyi, India. (Thurston, 1909, 4: 66)

Lagihalulu   A god of bad luck at Liku. Niue Island, Polynesia. (Loeb, 1926, 1: 161)

Lakshmi Goddess of fortune (fickle) and of wealth and beauty. She is the consort of Vishnu and here she is completely faithful. Usually considered bountiful. India. (Ions, 1967: 48, 91; Banerjea, 1953: 10; Martin, 1914: 95, 103; Bhattacharji, 1970: 162)

Maha-Laksmi Goddess of destiny and of good fortune. India (Danielou, 1964: 262; Elwin, 1954: 638)

Sidi Maimun "Good Luck." A Moroccan saint. (Westermarck, 1926, 1: 49)

Manang Jaban A goddess of the heavens who has charms for good luck and for curing. She is also invoked before the clearing of the land. The Dyaks, Sarawak, Borneo. (Sarawak Gazette, 1963: 77)

Manat A goddess of fortune at Palmyra. Syria. Near East. (Vriezen, 1963: 68)

Mis-Khum A forest spirit whose daughters "entice men to live with them. . . . If they succeed, this brings good fortune to the fathers of the men thus captured." Siberia. (Czaplicka, 1969: 290)

Nelaima The personification of misfortune, unhappiness, the negative aspect of Laima, the goddess of destiny. Latvia. (Jonval, 1929: 19)

Nijusanya-sama The "guardian of easy childbirth and good fortune." Japan. (Hori, 1968: 67)

Osande A beneficent ancestor spirit who brings good fortune and warns of danger. The Ovimbundu, Angola. (McCulloch, 1952: 36)

Padma A goddess of good fortune who dwells in the lotus and is identified with Laksmi. India. (Zimmer, 1955: 158, 178)

Paja Yan, Pajau Yan A beneficent goddess of happiness, good fortune, and health. She is identified with the moon, having been sent there by Po Jata "to prevent her from raising all the dead." The Cham and Annam, Cambodia. (Cabaton, 1925, 3: 342; Wales, 1957: 160)

Pamashiut A spirit of the Yauelmani invoked for good fortune. California. (Kroeber, 1925: 511)

Pereplut A Slavic deity—"some linguists think this name refers to the goddess of changing fortune." Balkans. (Larousse, 1973: 407)

Pherusa A daughter of Nereus and Doris who is "the bringer" as associated with successful venture. Greece. (Hesiod-Brown, 1981: 60, 86, 87; Kerényi, 1951: 64)

Pitsuriut A spirit invoked for good fortune. The Yauelmani, California. (Kroeber, 1925: 511)

Polydora A daughter of Oceanos and Tethys who is a generous bestower of good fortune, of "gifts and wealth." Greece. (Kerényi, 1951: 41; Hesiod-Brown, 1981: 63, 87)

Sri Pratap-Iswara A god of fortune. India. (Tod, 1920: 645)

Proto A Nereid associated with the benefits of successful venture. Greece. (Hesiod-Brown, 1981: 60, 86–87)

Ral gcig ma A powerful goddess—"for even to listen to her mantra repreated destroys all obstacles, brings good luck and intense religious enjoyment." She has only one of all features—eye, tooth, breast, foot, etc.—yet she sees the past, present, and future and destroys her enemies. Tibet. Same as Ekajata, the Blue Tara. (Getty, 1962: 125; Nebesky-Wojkowitz, 1956, 1: 34; Eliade, 1964: 37)

Rehtia She seems to be a goddess of fortune of the Veneti. Po Valley, Italy. (Conway, 1925, 7: 460)

Sa´d An abstract deity. "Fortune." Arabia. (Noldeke, 1925, 1: 662)

Salida, Saelde Teutonic goddess of fortune who smiles on and protects her favorites. (Grimm, 1883, 2: 862–869)

Saruta-hiko A phallic god of the crossroads, an earth Kami, who is also considered a god of luck. Japan. (MacCulloch, 1925, 4: 332; Herbert, 1967: 355–359)

Sa Ryong "The Four Animals of Good Luck . . . bring good fortune." These animals are the Dragon, the Phoenix, the Tortoise, and the *Kylin*. Korea. (Moes, 1983: 113)

Seri, Sri "Goddess of good fortune and wife of Visnu." Malay Peninsula. (Skeat, 1925, 8: 354)

Skwanät·än· A supernatural whose wailing "is considered an omen of death. . . . As she cries, she ejects mucus from her nose, which solidifies into a glass-like substance about a foot in length. Anyone who sees her should take the transformed mucus, and wrap it in some article of clothing; it will bring him good fortune." The Bella Coola, British Columbia. (McIlwraith, 1948, 1: 535)

Sri Goddess of fortune and prosperity and of beauty. Earlier given as the wife of Indra, then of Visnu. India. (Danielou, 1964: 141; Bhattacharji, 1970: 296)

Suiten An aspect of Varuna as the god of luck. Japan. (Eliot, 1935: 139)

Tagaloamotumotu "Spotted-rainbow," "Aliutu god; god of bad luck." Niue Island, Polynesia. (Loeb, 1926, 1: 162)

Tahanetskitadidia A god of good fortune, longevity, health, and success in war. The Wichita, Kansas. (Dorsey, 1904, 1: 19)

Teyutlma A spirit of good fortune. The Clallams, British Columbia. (Bancroft, 1886, 3: 155)

Tłäqmä·ks A "being resembling a diminutive man, created by Alquntam as a child to all supernatural beings . . . has been known to reach this earth, giving good fortune to the lucky finder." The Bella Coola, British Columbia. (McIlwraith, 1948, 1: 44)

Tong houa ti kiun Taoist god of the Peak of the East who is the god of good fortune, of prosperity. China. (Chavannes, n.d.: 94)

Tore A deity "associated with both life and death, good and bad, fortune and misfortune." The Mbuti (Pygmies), Zaire. (Turnbull, 1965: 193)

Toshitokujin Sometimes identified with Toshigami-sama, the Year God, but also considered as the "God of Fortune for the year." Takashima, Japan. (Norbeck, 1954: 122)

Tsukit A spirit invoked for good fortune. The Yauelmani, California. (Kroeber, 1925: 511)

Tuushiut A spirit of the Yauelmani, a Yokuts tribe, invoked for good fortune. California. (Kroeber, 1925: 511)

Tyche A goddess of chance, of luck, both good and bad. Greece. (Cox, 1870, 2: 20; Bulfinch, 1898: 188; Larousse, 1968: 164; Hesiod-Brown, 1981: 63, 87)

Ukat A goddess invoked for good fortune. The Yauelmani, California. (Kroeber, 1925: 511)

Uradamma A goddess who presides "over the fortunes and the well-being of the villagers." Telangana, India. (Mudiraj, 1970: 48)

Xochipilli-Macuilxochtli The "god of good luck and merriment," of beauty and happiness. Brother of Ixtlilton. The Aztecs, Mexico. (Spence, 1923: 352; Nicholson, 1967: 44)

Yuhahait A deity invoked for good fortune. The Yauelmani, California. (Kroeber, 1925: 511)

Zlydni A name, "ill luck," of the Dolja (personification of good or evil fortune) of an unfortunate person. Russia. (Mansikka, 1925, 4: 626)

42

Intellectual:
Wisdom, Learning, Teaching, Scribes, Records, History

Mulai Abdsslam ben Msis A patron saint of scribes. Morocco. (Westermarck, 1926, 1: 180)

Agastya A god who represents teaching "of grammar, medicine, and other sciences." India. (Danielou, 1964: 322)

Agni To the Vedic Rishis Agni, "the Mouth of the Gods, besides . . . presiding over the third element in Nature, is the God who takes birth as the flame of inspiration, grows up as enlightened will in action and leads the sacrificer on, with himself remaining in the front." India. (Pandit, 1970: 29)

Alaghom Naom, Iztal Ix The goddess of mind and of thought, of Wisdom. The Tzental, Mexico. (Starbuck, 1925, 5: 828)

Sidi Ali ben Harazem The patron saint of schoolteachers at Fez. Morocco. (Westermarck, 1926, 1: 179)

Aluluei The "great teacher and patron of the arts of navigation." The Marshall Islands, Micronesia. (Poignant, 1967: 80)

Angiras He "is the manifestation of Fire (Agni) as the power of enlightenment . . . the teacher of transcendent-knowledge." India. (Danielou, 1964: 319)

Aper-pehui One of the planners of the world and a god of learning. Son of Meh-urt. Egypt. (Budge, 1969, 1: 516)

Asherat A goddess of wisdom and an advisor at the council of the gods. Wife of El, sometimes of Baal. Phoenicia. Near East. (Herm, 1975: 108–109; Ferm, 1950: 125; Larousse, 1968: 76, 78)

Asten A form of Thoth, a god of "learning and letters." Egypt. (Budge, 1969, 1: 516)

Athena Greek goddess of wisdom and knowledge, of the arts and crafts, the sciences, of justice, war, and government. She was the daughter of Zeus (and Metis) who through trickery caused her to be born from his head. She was the recipient of all of Zeus's noble qualities without his weaknesses, giving wise counsel and exemplifying the universality of mind. As a goddess of strife and battles she has a strong relationship with the children of Nyx. (Barthell, 1971: 22–23; Murray, 1935: 96–98; Kerényi, 1951: 118–128; Fairbanks, 1907: 46, 110, 113–115; Hesiod-Brown, 1981: 55, 85)

Bak One of the planners of the world, a god of "learning and letters." Son of Meh-urt. Egypt. (Budge, 1969, 1: 516)

Balder The Scandinavian god of light and beauty was unsurpassed in wisdom and lucidity. He was the son of Odin and Frigg and the husband of Nanna. He represented purity and goodness. (Stern, 1898: 53; Larousse, 1968: 268; Frazer, 1960: 703–704; Branston, 1955: 123–125; Grimm, 1880: 222, 225; Turville-Petre, 1964: 106)

Belit-Seri Babylonian scribe of the underworld. Near East. (Langdon, 1931: 259; Larousse, 1968: 64)

Benzai-ten, Benten A goddess of happiness and good fortune, but she was primarily a goddess of eloquence and wisdom, of all the arts. Japan. (Eliot, 1935: 139; Getty, 1962: 127–128; Larousse, 1973: 326–327; Herbert, 1967: 513)

Bharadi The goddess of history, a form of Suraswati. India. (Coleman, 1832: 9)

Bhrgu A god created by Manu who "represents the power of knowledge." India. (Danielou, 1964: 322)

bilig-un cinadu kijaghar-a kuruksen A Mongolian goddess, the equivalent of Prajnaparamita, the "Goddess of Transcendent Wisdom." (Getty, 1962: 131)

Bragi The Scandinavian god of eloquence, of poetry and music. Son of Odin and Gunlod and husband of Idun. (Grimm, 1880: 235; Guerber, 1895: 43, 97–98; Murray, 1935: 368; Branston, 1955: 142)

Brig, Brigit, Brighid A Celtic goddess of learning and the arts. She was a triple goddess, or one of three sisters, whose other associations were with healing and with fire, the smithcrafts. Ireland. (MacCana, 1970: 34; Mac-Culloch, 1925, 3: 282; 1911: 69; Squire, 1906: 56; Ross, 1967: 206, 360; MacBain, 1917: 129–130; Jayne, 1962: 513)

Cakrasamvara A Tibetan god of wisdom. (Hoffman, 1956: 142)

Chang Ya-tzŭ A god of literature. China. (Day, 1940: 112)

Cheiron A Greek centaur, son of Cronus and Philyra. He was the wise teacher of many, particularly in medicine and in pharmacognosy. (Thramer, 1925, 6: 546; Barthell, 1971: 59)

Cheng K'ang-ch'eng, Chen Kongchen "God of the Classics." China. (Werner, 1932: 101; Du Bose, n.d.: 135)

Chin Chia A god of scholars associated with Chu I. He has a flag and a sword; the first if waved in front of a house assures that someone therein will receive literary honors and hold high office; with the sword he avenges the evil actions of scholars. China. (Werner, 1934: 112–113)

Ch'in Kuang Wang The King of the First Court of Hell who "keeps the register of the living and the dead, and measures the length of men's lives." China. (Day, 1940: 89; Werner, 1932: 80)

Chitragupta The record-keeper of men's deeds for Yama, the judge of the dead. He is worshipped "on the full-moon day in April-May." India. (Martin, 1914: 60; Danielou, 1964: 134–135; Thurston, 1909, 7: 11)

Chi Tu Hsing Chün The Star of Intelligence. China. (Day, 1940: 210)

Chu I A god of scholars, and an attendant of Wen Ch'ang, who aids and protects those poorly prepared for their examinations. China. (Day, 1940: 113; Maspero, 1963: 310, 314; Werner, 1934: 112)

Clio The Muse of History. Daughter of Zeus and Mnemosyne. Greece. (Bulfinch, 1898: 12; Kerényi, 1951: 104, 139; Morford and Lenardon, 1975: 56–57; Murray, 1935: 178)

Confucius A historical figure worshipped by some as a god of literature, of the literary and of officials. China. (Day, 1940: 135; Larousse, 1968: 391; Du Bose, n.d.: 115; Maspero, 1963: 315; Shryock, 1931: 54–57)

Damipaon A deity with an odd combination of functions as "god of the chase and knowledge." The Mishmis, Assam. (Crooke, 1925, 8: 697)

Danh-gbi The python god is worshipped as a beneficent god of wisdom by the Ewe. Dahomey. (Ellis, 1890: 54, 56; Gray, 1925, 4: 567)

Data The "apotheosis of the divine 'Law.'" Iran. (Gray, 1930: 143)

rDo-rje rnal-'byor-ma A goddess representing "insight and knowledge." She is Vajrayogini, a goddess of dual aspect, that of sensuality and lust but also that which overcomes them through meditation. Tibet. (Sierksma, 1966: 143, 146, 158, 275; Snellgrove, 1957: 77)

Ea A god of purifying waters, of wisdom and of total understanding. He was a god of civilization, of medicine, of the arts and crafts. Sumerian, Assyrian, and Babylonian, Near East. (Langdon, 1931: 106; Pettazzoni, 1956: 78; Jastrow, 1898: 61–62, 137–138; Kramer, 1961: 120–122; Larousse, 1968: 56, 63)

El-Hokmot A Syrian god of wisdom. (Schaeffer, 1966: 305)

Enki The Sumerian god of water and of wisdom, the giver of intelligence and skills, of law and order, the organizer of the universe and the earth. Same as Ea. (Kramer, 1967: 100–103; 1950: 60; Jacobsen, 1970: 21–22; 1946: 160; Hooke, 1963: 28)

Eshu The mischievous, malicious, and powerful messenger and intermediary between the gods and men who reports to Olodumare regarding the deeds of men and the sacrifices made. He is capable of magnifying faults and causing offenses to the gods, but is nevertheless considered to have protective and benevolent capacities toward his worshippers. The Yoruba, Nigeria. Also worshipped in Brazil. (Idowu, 1962: 80–84; Wescott, 1962: 337–338, 344; Parrinder, 1967: 90; Landes, 1940: 263; Bastide, 1960: 91, 565; Morton-Williams, 1964: 248)

Fên Piao Szŭ "Distinguisher of Records." China. (Day, 1940: 210)

Fugen Bosatsu A Bodhisattva who represents wisdom and understanding, compassion. Same as Samantabhadra. Japan. (Getty, 1962: 47; Eliseev, 1963: 426; Larousse, 1968: 419)

Fukurokuju A god of wisdom and longevity as well as one of the seven gods of happiness. Japan. (Eliseev, 1963: 446; Piggott, 1969: 59; Larousse, 1968: 422)

Ganapati, Ganesha The elephant-headed son of Siva is a god of wisdom, of intellect, who is invoked at the beginning of all undertakings for success. He is the remover of obstacles and is believed to give good fortune. India, Cambodia, Ceylon, Java, and Bali. (Danielou, 1964: 291–292; Ghurye, 1962: 114; Ions, 1967: 100; Barth, 1921: 164; Kramer, 1961: 306; Martin, 1914: 191, 193; Leach, 1958: 303, 306; Marchal, 1963: 212, 232; Friederich, 1959: 51)

Gasmu The "wise one," Akkadian goddess of the deep with whom Zarpanitu was identified. Near East. (Sayce, 1898: 111)

Gede Penyarikan The keeper of records of all good and evil deeds and intermediary between men and the god he represents. Bali, Indonesia. (Goris, 1969, 3: 122; Grader, 1969, 1: 171)

Bharata Guru Siva as god of "divine wisdom." Java, Indonesia. (Marchal, 1963: 231–232)

Guru Reka The god of thought, of words, who forms the "Divine Triad of Knowledge" with Sarasvati and kavisvara. Same as Bhatara Guru. Bali, Indonesia. (Hooykaas, 1964: 26, 39)

brGya-byin The "king of the mind" is god and protector of the east quarter and is responsible for hail and lightning. Tibet. (Waddell, 1959: 367; Nebesky-Wojkowitz, 1956, 1: 108)

Hannya A Japanese name for Prajnaparamita, the "Goddess of Transcendent Wisdom." (Getty, 1962: 131)

Hanuman The monkey deity was a god of learning, virility, and strength. Among the Gond his image was tattooed on the upper arm to provide strength for carrying. India. (Russell, 1916, 3: 126; Martin, 1914: 226; Ions, 1967: 102)

Hea The earth, a Mesopotamian goddess of wisdom. Near East. (Seligmann, 1948: 23, 35)

Sidi Hmed ben Nasar An important patron saint of scribes. Morocco. (Westermarck, 1926, 1: 180)

Hun Bátz With Hun Chouén, the sons of only one of the seven Ahpú. They "were great sages: all the arts were passed on to them." With the passing of the matriarchal period they became the patriarchal regents, driving out Hunahpú and Ixbalamqué, who were being tested by the deities. Their day of retribution came when they were transformed by Hunahpú and Ixbalamqué into monkeys, in which form they were worshipped. The Quiché, Guatemala. (Girard, 1979: 87–88, 125, 144)

Hun Chouén *See* **Hun Bátz**

Hu Nonp The Bear God is the god of wisdom—particularly shamanic—and is the teacher of their secrets and medicines and knows their language, Tobtob. The Lakota and Oglala, South Dakota. (Walker, 1980: 50, 51, 128)

Ihi A goddess of wisdom, worshipped by the learned. Daughter of Ta'aroa and Papa-raharaha. Tahiti, Polynesia. (Henry, 1928: 374)

Imhotep A deified human, patron of scholars and scribes, who was created a god of medicine. Egypt. (Ames, 1965: 122; Jayne, 1962: 62; Larousse, 1968: 43)

Indo nTegolili A goddess who reports on the wrongs committed by people. The Celebes, Indonesia. (Downs, 1920: 13; Pettazzoni, 1956: 333)

Indra To the Vedic Rishis, Indra's inner aspect "presides over the Divine Mind," making possible the transcendence from the human element to the divine. He "heads the thought-powers, causes streams of pure creative energies to outpour on the [aspirant] and uses his rod of light—the thunderbolt of Knowledge—to dissipate and break down all clouds of darkness and inertia." India. (Pandit, 1970: 28)

Itzamna The Mayan god of the heavens initiated civilization, writing, books. He was invoked in the month of Zip as a god of medicine. Mexico and Guatemala. (Morley, 1946: 222–223; Nicholson, 1967: 119; Tozzer, 1941: 146; Schellhas, 1904: 18)

Jambyang   A god of learning of the Na-khi. Yunnan Province, China. (Rock, 1947: 57, 188)

'Jam-dpal, Jam-pal   The god of wisdom and considered "the first divine teacher of Buddhist doctrine." Nepal and Sikkim. (Snellgrove, 1961: 35, 107; Gazeteer of Sikhim, 1894: 292)

Jam-yang, Jam-pe-yang   The god of wisdom, of knowledge. Same as Manjusri, Manjughosa. Tibet and Sikkim. (Tucci, 1967: 77; Bell, 1931: 30; Gazeteer of Sikhim, 1894: 263; Schlagintweit, 1969: 65)

Jasingpha   The god of learning. The Ahom, Tai. (Gurdon, 1925, 1: 236)

Ka   One of the planners of the world, a god of "learning and letters." Son of Meh-urt. Egypt. (Budge, 1969, 1: 516)

K'aklo   A sagacious god and teacher of the Zuñi Indians. New Mexico. (Stevenson, 1898: 36–37)

Kando-ye-shes-chogyel   The "Goddess Ocean of Wisdom," a wife of Guru Rimpoche. The Sherpas, Nepal. Nepa. (Furer-Haimendorf, 1964: 171)

Kavisvara   One of "The Divine Triad of Knowledge" (with Guru Reda and Sarasvati), the deity of the word. Bali and Indonesia. (Hookyaas, 1964: 26, 38)

kele-yin-ukin tegri   The goddess of speech, of eloquence and knowledge. Same as Sarasvati. Mongolia. (Getty, 1962: 127; Percheron, 1953: 262)

Khadh   Babylonian "god of the scribe's pen." Near East. (Sayce, 1898: 118)

Khekh   One of the planners of the world, a god of "learning and letters." Son of Meh-urt. Egypt. (Budge, 1969, 1: 516)

Ah Kin, ah q'in   The Mayan sun god is a god of knowledge and of magical powers among the Chorti and is "the patron of sorcerers, curers, and diviners." Guatemala. (Thompson, 1970: 235, 238; Wisdom, 1940: 399)

uKqili   The "Wise One." The Zulu, South Africa. (Mbiti, 1970, 2: 336)

Kratu   One of the Prajapatis who "represents the power of intelligence." A son of the mind of Brahma. India. (Danielou, 1964: 323; Dowson, 1961: 159)

Ksa   The God of Wisdom taught the creatures to serve Maka, the earth, and gave each kind of animal a different

language as well as the one common to all. But having used his wisdom to shame the gods, Hanwi and Tate, "he became the imp of mischief and his name is *Iktomi*." The Lakota and Oglala, South Dakota. (One Feather, 1982: 49, 50)

Kuan Kung, Kuan-ti   The god of war, defensive against disorder and disturbance, was also a god of literature and justice, of prosperity, and protective from all evils. China. (Shryock, 1931: 66–67; Day, 1940: 52, 54, 66, 113, 165; Werner, 1934: 113; Haydon, 1941: 196; Maspero, 1963: 333)

Kuei   A stellar god of literature and "arbiter of the destinies of men of letters." China. (Werner, 1934: 106, 248)

K'uei Hsing, Kwei-sing   A stellar god of literature and of scholars, invoked prior to examinations. He is "regarded as the distributor of literary degrees." China (Werner, 1934: 110; Day, 1940: 112; Peeters, 1941: 36; Du Bose, n.d.: 127; Sierksma, 1960: 49, 59)

Latius   A minor Roman deity who "awakened and molded the intellect." (Jayne, 1962: 498)

Latpon   A god of wisdom and a son of El. Phoenicia, Near East. (Larousse, 1968: 77–78)

Legba   The trickster son of Mawu, who had a knowledge of all languages, was able to help man to circumvent his fate. He transmitted the orders for reward or punishment and kept the records of births and deaths. Dahomey. (Herskovits, 1938, 2: 109, 201, 233; 1937: 30–31; Williams, 1936: 165; Parrinder, 1967: 21, 91)

bLo-c'an dban-p'ug-ch'en-po   The great sage and defender of the faith. Tibet. (Waddell, 1959: 365)

Logos   The Roman personification of speech in competition, of debate, of oration. (Roscher, 1965, 2, 2: 2073)

Lokesvara   *See* **Mahavidya**

Lü Tung-pin   A god of literature as well as of physicians, druggists, barbers. China. (Day, 1940: 113; Peeters, 1941: 29; Maspero, 1963: 332)

Madumda   A remote and wise sky god, and older brother of Coyote. The Pomo, California. (Kroeber, 1925: 261, 270)

Mahavidya   She and Lokesvara and Manidhara "personify the wisdom condensed in the mantra of six syllables (sadaksari): om mani padme hum." Nepal. (Heeramaneck, 1966: 81)

Mahavira The "great teacher of Jainism," born as Vardhamana, became "a Tirthankara, a being higher than a god . . . . With his death Mahavira became a Siddha, a freed soul of the greatest perfection, being both omniscient and detached from karma, the cycle of rebirth." India. (Ions, 1967: 136–137)

Mahpiyato The Sky God is the judge over all and the god of wisdom and power. The Lakota, South Dakota. (One Feather, 1982: 49)

Manidhara *See* **Mahavidya**

Manjusri A Bodhisattva of Transcendent Wisdom whose primary function was to dispel ignorance. Tibet, China, Japan, India, Java, Nepal, and Mongolia. (Getty, 1962: 110; Marchal, 1963: 240; Heeramaneck, 1966: 70; Waddell, 1959: 332, 355; Percheron, 1953: 258; Snellgrove, 1957: 61–62; Eliot, 1935: 124)

The Maruts On the mental/spiritual plane their strength is unparralled (power of knowledge and power of action) and is everywhere available—on all planes. They are "Consciousness as force and Consciousness as knowledge." Their wealth is not only of material things, but of thought, wisdom, and power as well. Their role is also to stimulate man's activity, particularly his thought processes, toward the aspiration and purification that lead toward the highest mental heights. India. (Pandit, 1970: 72–109)

Mataiwalu An eight-eyed deity considered a god of wisdom. Somo-Somo Island, Fiji, Melanesia. (Pettazzoni, 1956: 342)

Math A beneficent Celtic god considered a god of wisdom and of magical lore as well as of wealth. Brother of Don. Wales. (Squire, 1906: 260: MacCulloch, 1911: 105)

Medha An abstract goddess—Intelligence—associated with Krishna. India. (Ghurye, 1962: 255)

Menrva *See* **Minerva**

Mens A Roman goddess of intelligence, of reflective judgment. (Dumézil, 1966, 2: 473–474; Roscher, 1965, 2, 2: 2798; Jayne, 1962: 498)

Metis The daughter of Oceanus and Tethys was a goddess of wisdom and of good counsel. She was the first wife of Zeus and his source of the "knowledge of good and evil." Mother of Athena. Greece. (Barthell, 1971: 22; Kerényi, 1951: 40, 118–120; Campbell, 1964: 150–151; Hesiod-Brown, 1981: 78, 87)

Mimir The Scandinavian owner and guardian of the well of knowledge, of wisdom, under Yggdrasill, the World Tree, to whom Odin forfeited an eye for a draught of its waters. (Stern, 1898: 11; Murray, 1935: 369; Davidson, 1964: 166; MacCulloch, 1964: 167–168; Anderson, 1891: 188)

Minerva, Menrva The Etruscan/Roman goddess of wisdom, particularly that of a practical nature, e.g., the arts and crafts, commerce and industry, healing, etc. It was only after identification with Athena that she was represented as warlike. Italy. (Fairbanks, 1907: 118; Hadas, 1965: 123; Bulfinch, 1898: 131; Murray, 1935: 101–102; Larousse, 1968: 207; Jayne, 1962: 434; Dumézil, 1966, 1: 208, 303–305)

Ming K'uei T'ien Hsia Another name of K'uei Hsing. China. (Day, 1940: 213)

Monju Bosatsu The god of wisdom, of the intellect, of education. Same as Manjusri. Japan. (Piggott, 1969: 32; Getty, 1962: 110; Eliseev, 1963: 442; Eliot, 1935: 120–124)

Moonsoo Posal The name of Manjusri in Korea. He is usually shown seated on a tiger. (Clark, 1932: 62)

Muitautini The teacher of the *tagata tufuga*, the "wise people who lived in the second heaven with Hina." Niue Island, Polynesia. (Loeb, 1926, 1: 164)

Nabu, Nebo The Assyro/Babylonian omniscient god of wisdom, the scribe of the gods and the gods of scribes, of literature, of the intellect. He was associated with the planet Mercury. Near East. (Jastrow, 1898: 125–130, 459; Schoeps, 1961: 57–58; Rawlinson, 1885: 50; Seligmann, 1948: 30; Gray, 1969: 23; Pettazzoni, 1956: 9, 84; Robertson, 1911: 216; Sayce, 1898: 42, 50, 113)

Neb-Tesheru and **Nefer-hati** Sons of Meh-urt and two of the planners of the world, gods of "learning and letters." Egypt. (Budge, 1969, 1: 516)

Nereus The God of the Sea, eldest son of Gaea and Pontus, is renowned for his truthfulness, his knowledge of laws, his good counsel and justice, his gentleness. Greece. (Hesiod-Brown, 1981: 59, 60; Cox, 1870, 2: 256; Bulfinch, 1898: 219)

Ngrurah Alit and **Ngrurah Gede** Secretaries of the gods who "watch that the proper offerings are made" in the temples. Bali, Indonesia. (Covarrubias, 1937: 269)

Nisaba The goddess of grains and of grasses and reeds became the goddess of accountants and of scribes, of writing. Sumer and Babylonia, Near East. (Jacobsen, 1970: 2, 32; Roberts, 1972: 47)

Nuah   A Babylonian god, the abstraction Intelligence. Near East. (Seligmann, 1948: 99)

Nus   Greek personification of understanding, of intelligence. (Roscher, 1965, 3, 1: 482)

Odin   The Scandinavian All-Father was a god of wisdom and of knowledge of the magical type, and of the runes. He gave up one eye to gain the wisdom and foreknowledge to be found in Mimir's well. He was omniscient only when seated on his heavenly throne wherein he could supervise human affairs. (Guerber, 1895: 23, 36, 39; Grimm, 1883, 2: 132–135; Pettazzoni, 1956: 220–221)

Ogma   Celtic god of literature and eloquence, of poetry, and considered the inventor of ogham writing. Ireland. (MacCana, 1970: 40; Squire, 1906: 56–9; Mac-Culloch, 1911: 75)

Ogmios   Celtic god of speech and eloquence and poetry. Gaul. (MacCulloch, 1911: 25; Ferguson, 1970: 69; Schoeps, 1961: 118)

Omoikane-no-Kami   A god of wisdom and intelligence, of resourcefulness. Japan. (Yasumaro, 1928: 35; 1965: 31; Herbert, 1967: 301, 336)

Pachaychacher   An abstraction—"he who instructs the world." Peru. (Alexander, 1925, 3: 744)

Paideia   The personification of the education of young men. Greece. (Roscher, 1965, 3, 1: 1251)

P'an Kuan   The recorder of the fates of men in the otherworld. China. (Werner, 1932: 355)

Phoebus Apollo, Phoibos Apollon   The sun god shared the wisdom of Athena and represented knowledge and truth, and declared his "mission of teaching to men the counsels of Zeus." He was the son of Leto and a god of beauty, music, and healing. Greece. (Cox, 1870, 2: 1, 22, 33; Murray, 1935: 104–105)

Polynoë   A Nereid, "Richness of Mind," associated with the quality of leadership. Greece. (Hesiod-Brown, 1981: 60, 87; Kerényi, 1951: 65)

Prajnaparamita   Buddhist Goddess of Transcendent Wisdom, of enlightenment, of thought. The sakti of Vajradhara. She is known in Tibet, Java, Nepal, Cambodia, Bali. (Getty, 1962: 5, 131; Marchal, 1963: 207, 238; Zimmer, 1955: 140–1; Hooykaas, 1964: 32)

Pseudopaideia   The Greek personification of false learning, erudition. (Roscher, 1965, 3, 2: 3197)

Pun-shi   A name of Shakyamuni as the "Teacher of the world during the present *kalpa.*" China. (Edkins, 1880: 207–208)

Quetzalcóatl   Among the numerous aspects of the Plumed Serpent was that of a god of knowledge, wisdom, and civilization. Mexico. (Leonard, 1967: 59, 104; Vaillant, 1962: 140; León-Portilla, 1982: 29)

Rgyal-po-dun-rtog   A special defender comparable "to the Lamaic personification of body, speech, mind, karma (causality), and achievement." Tibet. (Li An-che, 1948: 40)

Rono (Lono)   The god of wisdom, of the sun, of the east, of medicine. Hawaii. (Melville, 1969: 25, 28, 34)

Rua-i-te-horahora   A deity who "personifies the diffusion of knowledge." The Maori, New Zealand. (Best, 1924: 177)

Rua-i-te-pukenga   A personification of knowledge. The Maori, New Zealand. (Best, 1924: 101)

Rua-i-te-pupuke   A god of wisdom, personified knowledge. New Zealand. (Buck, 1938: 151; Best, 1924: 66)

Saga   A Norse goddess of history and of poetry, associated with Odin as one who has omniscience. (MacCulloch, 1964: 183; Wagner, 1882: 1, 253; Grimm, 1880: 310, 319; Thorpe, 1851: 191; Anderson, 1891: 253)

sak tsum thing   A god, the creator of thought and of the capacity to think. The Lepchas, Sikkim. (Siiger, 1967: 144)

Samjna   The goddess of knowledge, of consciousness. Daughter of Visvakarman and wife of Surya (Vivasvat); mother of Manu, Yama and Yamuna, and the Asvins. India. (Danielou, 1964: 96; Bhattacharji, 1970: 217–218)

San   One of the planners of the world, a god of "learning and letters." Son of Meh-urt. Egypt. (Budge, 1969, 1: 516)

Sarasvati   The great river goddess later became the goddess of wisdom and learning, of speech and eloquence, of poetry and music. She was considered as the wife of both Brahma and Manjusri. India, Bali, and Mongolia. (Danielou, 1964: 259–260; Ions, 1967: 89, 135; Friederich, 1959: 44; Covarrubias, 1937: 317; Getty, 1962: 127; Hooykaas, 1964: 21, 23; Percheron, 1953: 262; Larousse, 1968: 345)

Semar A "great supernatural power . . . conceals his great wisdom and subtlety behind a squeaky voice and a wry, comic manner." Java, Indonesia. (Anderson, 1965: 31)

Semenkoror God of wisdom from whom people receive their skills. Brother of Önulap. Truk, Micronesia. (Bollig, 1927: 7)

Sems-kyi sgron-ma-can A Tibetan god of wisdom. (Hoffman, 1956: 86)

Seshat, Sesheta Goddess of literature and history of books and writing. She kept the records for the gods. A consort of Thoth. Egypt. (Knight, 1915: 118–119; Gardiner, 1925, 9: 791; Budge, 1969, 1: 424; Ames, 1965: 85)

s'es-rab-pha-rol-tu The name of Prajnaparamita, the goddess of wisdom, in Tibet. (Getty, 1962: 131)

gShen-lha od-dkar God of wisdom and knowledge, also of compassion. Nepal and Tibet. (Snellgrove, 1961: 48; Hoffman, 1956: 86)

gShen-rab The Buddha of the Present, the Teacher— "perfect in wisdom." Tibet and Nepal. (Hoffman, 1956: 102–103; Snellgrove, 1961: 48–49)

Shun With Meng t'ien considered the "inventor of the writing-brush." China. (Werner, 1932: 447, 568)

Siduri A goddess of wisdom and a patron of wine merchants and wine mixers. Babylonia. Near East. (Langdon, 1931: 210–211; Keeler, 1960: 103)

Silewe Nazarata The wife/sister of Lowalangi, though given also as of a bisexual nature, is a demiurge, an intermediary between gods and between people and gods, the giver of wisdom and understanding, and knowledge against sickness. She is feared as mischievous and the source of evil. Nias Island, Indonesia. (Suzuki, 1959: 11–15)

Sin The Sumerian/Assyrian/Babylonian god of the moon was omniscient, a god of wisdom and the measurer of time. Near East. (Jastrow, 1898: 68, 78; Larousse, 1968: 57; Jayne, 1962: 128; Pettazzoni, 1956: 8; Kramer, 1961: 97)

Sinlap The "giver of wisdom." The Kachins, Burma. (Temple, 1925, 3: 22; Leach, 1950: 785)

Sitatara The white Tara represents purity and wisdom. Buddhism. (Getty, 1962: 122)

Soi A god who represented wisdom yet was also "unscrupulous and bad." He was the ancestor of the Maramara class. New Ireland, Melanesia. (Cox, 1913: 196)

Sugahare Michizane A mortal who became a Shinto god of calligraphy and scholarship. Japan. (Schoeps, 1961: 214)

Tammanend The benevolent god who gave them knowledge. The Delaware, Eastern United States. (Cohane, 1969: 208)

Ta-shih-chih-p'u-sa The patron deity of "students, teachers, and scholars." Szechwan, China. (Graham, 1961: 186)

Tasmit(u) A patroness of the literary class, the wife of Nebo. "She helped to open and enlarge the ears which received the divine mysteries her husband's inspiration enabled his devout servants to write down." Babylonia. Near East. (Sayce, 1898: 120)

Te-mehara A goddess of wisdom, of memory, who is associated with a spring. "Vai-ru'ia (Darkened-Water)." Tahiti, Polynesia. (Henry, 1928: 85, 163)

Thagya Nat The first of the 37 nats who is the recording deity. Burma. (Temple, 1925, 3: 36)

Thoth The ibis-headed god of learning and wisdom, the inventor of the hieroglyphs and the official scribe of the afterworld. He was the regulator of the heavens and the earth; as the moon god the measurer of time and the seasons. He is credited with several wives—Seshat, Mayet, and Nehmauit. Egypt. (Knight, 1915: 126–128; Ames, 1965: 34, 82, 85; Murray, 1935: 408; Casson, 1965: 71; Budge, 1969, 1: 401, 412; Jayne, 1962: 32)

Ti Chih Hsing Chün The "Recorder of Good and Evil." China. (Day, 1940: 210)

Tiur The god of learning and skills, of divination, was the scribe of Aramazd. Armenia. (Ananikian, 1964: 14, 30–31; Gray, 1930: 111)

Tou Mu The goddess of the North Star, the Bushel Mother, keeps the records of life and death and is worshipped by those desiring longevity. China. (Werner, 1934: 144–145; Maspero, 1963: 340)

Ts'ang Chieh The god of the art of writing and of scholars. China. (Werner, 1932: 567; Du Bose, n.d.: 135; Graham, 1958: 50)

Tungrangayak The "wisest of the wise . . . is depicted with his body covered in circles or eyes with which he can see everything." The Eskimo, Alaska. (Larousse, 1973: 446)

Tunkašila The Grandfathers, who are spirit helpers waiting to be called upon by the sacred persons for help in curing illness, for wisdom. The Oglala, South Dakota. (Powers, 1977: 200)

Tzǔ I The deity who guides the education of the very young. China. (Day, 1940: 94)

Uanam Ehkoma The "Beloved Preceder"—wise and knowing. Twin brother of Uanam Yaluna. The Zuñi, New Mexico. (Long, 1963: 102)

Uanam Yaluna The "Beloved Follower"—wise and knowing. Twin brother of Uanam Ehkoma. The Zuñi, New Mexico. (Long, 1963: 102)

Vanth A benevolent Etruscan goddess of death, of fate. With Atropos, the recorders in the underworld. Italy. (Herbig, 1925, 5: 536; Pallottino, 1975: 149; Dumézil, 1966, 2: 694; Larousse, 1968: 211)

Van-xuong The Burmese god of literature. (Scott, 1964: 305)

Vegoia, Begoe An Etruscan goddess who imparted her wisdom and teachings, the "principles laid down long before by the gods" to a human for the benefit of mankind. Italy. (Hamblin, 1975: 98)

Wên Ch'ang Ti Chun, Wên Ti The powerful god of literature, a deified mortal who inhabits the Great Bear constellation, is worshipped by scholars and civilian officials. He distributes "intellectual gifts, literary skill, etc." He is sometimes depicted simply standing on a fish—because if the carp of the Yellow River successfully surmount the rapids of Lung-mên, they transform into dragons—emblematic of literary success of the industrious student. China. (Werner, 1934: 82, 104, 110; Day, 1940: 96, 166; Du Bose, n.d.: 126; Edkins, 1878: 107; Maspero, 1963: 310; De Groot, 1925, 4: 14; Ferguson, 1937: 112; Williams, 1976: 207–208)

Wen-shu The god of wisdom, the Bodhisattva of knowledge, who acted to dispel ignorance. China. (Day, 1940: 153, 167; Edkins, 1878: 208; Wood, 1937: 164–165; Peeters, 1941: 50)

Wen-ts'ang The god of literature. Szechwan, China. (Graham, 1961: 163)

Woden, Odin The Germanic Allfather was a god of universal wisdom and of magical powers who presided over war and victory, was the arbiter of men's fates. (Guerber, 1895: 23; Wagner, 1882: 5, 6; Larousse, 1968: 253–254; Davidson, 1964: 69)

xasbidi· Mourning Dove, a helpful deity, "said to report things reliably and to have no equal in speed." The Navaho, Arizona and New Mexico. (Reichard, 1950: 453)

Yagokoro-Omoikane-no-Kami Shinto "God of Wisdom, nearly always stands in assisting attendance on Amaterasu-Omi-kami in issuing the Divine Edicts." Japan. (Kato, 1926: 71)

Yei Suu The beneficent and merciful god of wisdom and justice. The Ch'uan Miao, Yunnan Province, China. (Graham, 1937: 61)

Ye-mkhyen-hphrul-rgyal The omniscient deity who taught "the four kinds of happiness, two sorts of purity, and three great antidotes to miseries." Tibet. (Li An-che, 1948: 39)

Ye-shes mtsho-rgyal Goddess Ocean of Wisdom, a spouse of Padma-sambhava. Tibet. (Snellgrove, 1957: 229)

Yi ge pa (pr. **Yigêpa**) The god of writing. Bon Religion. Tibet. (Tucci, 1980: 218)

Yum chen-mo Goddess of wisdom. Same as Prajna-paramita. Nepal. (Snellgrove, 1961: 287)

Zarpanit(u) "In Semitic days . . . She ceased to be the goddess of wisdom, the voice of the deep revealing the secrets of heaven to the diviner and priest," and was just the associate of Merodach. Babylonia, Near East. (Sayce, 1898: 95, 112)

43

Justice:
Law, Judgment, Equity, Government, Order, Morals, Oaths, Curses, Thieves

Aaati One of the 42 gods of judgment mentioned in the Nebseni Papyrus. Egypt. (Budge, 1967: 350)

Aati One of the 42 judges or assessors of the deceased for the goddess Maat. Egypt. (Budge, 1969, 1: 419)

'Abdlqader A jinn saint known to help thieves and liars in their undertakings when offerings are made him, "but it is said that although he is compelled to assist thieves and liars who invoke him, he afterwards punishes them for their behavior." Morocco. (Westermarck, 1926, 1: 181)

Abdsslam The "patron saint of all the Jbala" who punishes thieves who pass his shrine by causing misfortune to befall them. Morocco. (Westermarck, 1926, 1: 179, 192)

Aequitas, Equitas An abstract Roman goddess— equity, justice, fair dealing. (Roscher, 1965, 1, 1: 86; Ferguson, 1970: 73; Larousse, 1968: 216)

Agashi A god of childbirth "by whom both sexes make oath." The Tiv, Nigeria. (Temple, 1922: 302)

Ahi-mu One of the 42 judges or assessors of the dead for the goddess Maat. Egypt. (Budge, 1969, 1: 419)

Aker The "double lion-headed earth-god" is also a god of judgment. Egypt. (Budge, 1969, 1: 33, 325)

Algar A Dravidian demon of thieves. India. (Elmore, 1915: 80)

Sidi 'Ali Bizzu A saint who punishes robbers, causing them to be caught or unable to sell the stolen object, and being ultimately caught. Morocco. (Westermarck, 1926, 1: 192)

Sidi 'Ali l-Herher A saint who causes robbers who pass by his shrine to be caught or unable to sell the stolen object. Morocco. (Westermarck, 1926, 1: 192)

Sidi 'Allal l-Haddj A saint who punishes thieves who pass his shrine by sending someone to take away from him that which was stolen, or causes him to break his leg so he can go no further. Morocco. (Westermarck, 1926, 1: 192)

Ama The chthonic earth goddess and underworld deity is also a goddess of justice and righteousness. The Jukun, Nigeria. (Meek, 1931: 190, 209)

Amanehu A god who "is responsible for all acts of burglary and felony" everywhere. The Effutu, Ghana. (Wyllie, 1966: 479)

Am-beseku One of the 42 judges or assessors of the deceased for the goddess Maat. Egypt. (Budge, 1969, 1: 419)

Am-khaibetu One of the 42 judges or assessors of the deceased in the Hall of Maati. Egypt. (Budge, 1969, 1: 419)

Am-senf One of the 42 judges or assessors of the deceased for the goddess Maat. Egypt. (Budge, 1969, 1: 419)

An-a-f One of the 42 judges or assessors of the dead for the goddess Maat, "usually regarded as a form of Amsu, or Min." Egypt. (Budge, 1969, 1: 419, 521)

Andiodotra A deity invoked in the making of vows and in making sacrifices regarding illness. The Tanala, Madagascar. (Linton, 1933: 194)

An-hetep-f One of the 42 judges or assessors of the dead for the goddess Maat. Egypt. (Budge, 1969, 1: 419)

Anokyi An Ashanti god invoked in the making of oaths and curses. The Akim-Kotoku, Ghana. (Field, 1948: 84, 188)

Appangiriyappa A god who severely punishes perjurers. The Coorg, Southern India. (Srinivas, 1952: 207)

Ari-em-ab-f One of the 42 judges or assessors of the dead for the goddess Maat. Egypt. (Budge, 1969, 1: 419)

Asham The goddess of rain is also invoked when taking oaths. Arabia. (Fahd, 1968: 46)

Asha Vahista God of Truth who represents "the divine law and moral order in the world." He even sees that just punishment prevails in hell. Persia. (Hinnells, 1973: 52)

Asomua A household god helpful in detecting thieves. Samoa, Polynesia. (Turner, 1884: 69)

Ata The "god of thieves; then, as now, a highly respected fraternity in north-east Polynesia." The Marquesas, Polynesia. (Christian, 1895: 189)

Autonoe A Nereid—"Independence of Mind"—associated with concepts of law. Greece. (Hesiod-Brown, 1981: 30)

'Awd An Arabian god of treaties. (Fahd, 1968: 48)

Azele Yaba A dangerous earth goddess in whose name oaths are taken. The Nzema, Ghana. (Grottanelli, 1967: 37–39; 1969: 372)

Azer-ava A Finno-Ugrian sky goddess, the bringer of rain and fruitfulness, in whose name oaths are taken. The Mordvins, Russia. (Paasonen, 1925, 8: 844; MacCulloch, 1964: 258)

Baal-malage A god invoked to punish violators of treaties. Phoenicia. Near East. (Albright, 1968: 227)

Baal-sapuna A god invoked to punish violators of treaties. Phoenicia, Near East. (Albright, 1968: 227)

Baal-shamem A Phoenician god invoked to punish violations of treaties. Near East. (Albright, 1968: 227)

Basti One of the 42 judges or assessors of the deceased for the goddess Maat. Egypt. (Budge, 1969, 1: 419)

Ka Blai Synshar A goddess who is "an embodiment of the Divine Law . . . who empowers and punishes the

devils and wicked spirits which torment the human souls . . . grants and withholds material prosperity and spiritual happiness." The Khasi, Assam. (Bareh, 1967: 375, 380)

Mulai Brahim A saint who will help thieves if an offering is made and is antagonistic toward Sultans and officials. Morocco. (Westermarck, 1926, 1: 181, 194)

Britisse Jean-Simon A severe judge who presides over the tribunal of the dead. Haiti, West Indies. (Marcelin, 1950: 194)

Sidi Bujbara A saint known to help thieves in their undertaking on promise of an offering. Morocco. (Westermarck, 1926, 1: 181)

Sidi Burja A saint who punishes robbers who pass by his shrine, causing them to be caught or unable to sell the stolen object. Morocco. (Westermarck, 1926, 1: 192)

Mulai Bustsa The patron saint of robbers. Morocco. (Westermarck, 1926, 1: 181)

Chando The supreme being and sun god is invoked in oath-taking. The Santal, India. (Wallis, 1939: 193; Biswas, 1956: 102; Frazer, 1926: 633)

Chentun A punitive god—"a guardian of morals, as he only appears to those with evil intentions." The Maya, British Honduras. (Thompson, 1930: 66)

Chi A god of thieves. China. (Maspero, 1963: 333)

Chiapaneco A god who befriends the poor, the humble, and the hospitable, but punishes those who would mistreat the poor. The Chimalteco, Guatemala. (Wagley, 1949: 62–63)

Chinigchinich His temple was a sanctuary that gave shelter to criminals. California. (Bourke, 1892: 454)

Chuhar, Choar Mal A deified robber in Bengal. (Crooke, 1925, 4: 852)

Chu-t'ien-p'u-sa The patron deity of thieves and robbers. Szechwan, Southwest China. (Graham, 1961: 186)

Dadaju A goddess to whom the Beria, a caste of gypsies and thieves, offer a pig before their predatory expeditions. Central Provinces, India. (Russell, 1916, 2: 224; Briggs, 1953: 527)

Da-mu-gal A Babylonian deity invoked in legal documents. Near East. (Jastrow, 1898: 166)

dar(mit)   A goddess who provided their moral instructions, their rewards and punishments. The Lepchas, Sikkim. (Siiger, 1967, 1: 24)

Data   The "apotheosis of the divine 'Law.'" Iran. (Gray, 1930: 143)

Datagaliwabe   A totally just god who guards kinship rules and is implacable in punishing infractions. The Huli, New Guinea. (Glasse, 1965: 27, 48)

Dengdit   A god of the Dinka on whose shrine oaths are taken. Sudan. (Butt, 1952: 131–132)

Deva   The all-seeing supreme being who is invoked in oaths. The Ngadha, Flores Island, Indonesia. (Pettazzoni, 1956: 333–334)

Devi   The tutelary goddess of the Bhamta, a caste composed mostly of thieves, though some have become cultivators. Central Provinces, India. (Russell, 1916, 2: 234–237)

Dharma, Dharmaraja   A god of justice and righteousness, a beneficent aspect of Yama. India. (Ions, 1967: 88; Coleman, 1832: 379; Bhattacharji, 1970: 57)

Dike   A goddess of justice and of omniscience concerning men's deeds. The daughter of Themis and Zeus, to whom she reports all injustices. One of the Horae. Greece. (Pettazzoni, 1956: 146–147; Kerényi, 1951: 102; Murray, 1935: 46, 145)

Diktynna   A Cretan goddess with strong associations with Britomartis. She is depicted as a huntress and a goddess of oath-binding. Greece. (Willetts, 1962: 184, 191; Larousse, 1968: 86)

Din-el   A Syrian god—"the Justice of God." Near East. (Schaeffer, 1966: 305)

Dinga   A god of retribution and a judge of the dead. The Khonds, Orissa, India. (Crooke, 1925, 7: 649; Robertson, 1911: 109)

Dius Fidius   An aspect of Jupiter as a god of oaths and morality, of loyalty. Rome. (Dumézil, 1966, 1: 180; Altheim, 1937: 164; Littleton, 1965: 89)

Djamar   The supreme being and creator who established the moral laws and initiation rites. The Bad of the West, Kimberley, Australia. (Eliade, 1973: 35–37)

Doini-Polo   The Sun-Moon duality. They are deities "of law and truth . . . are invoked in the beginning of *kebangs* on disputes to reveal the truth and expose the false." The Adi, Northeastern India. (Chowdhury, 1971: 118)

Dyo   An old god of oaths who punishes perjurers. The Banbara, Sudan. (Tauxier, 1927: 329)

Dysnomia   Lawlessness, closely associated with her sister Madness, is a child of Eris alone. Greece. (Hesiod-Brown, 1981: 59; Roscher, 1965, 1, 1: 1209; Barthell, 1971: 8)

Ebefu   An important lesser deity whose "spirit is enshrined in an axe-head, this having potent value as an oath-binder." The Bassa-Komo, Nigeria. (Clifford, 1944: 115)

Efile-mokulu   The supreme being and creator of the Basonge who is invoked in oaths. Zaire. (Pettazzoni, 1956: 19–20; Frazer, 1926: 149–150)

Ela   A god of divination who is the deity of peace-making where there is discord and of "the restoration of order wherever there is chaos." The Yoruba, Nigeria. (Idowu, 1962: 102–103)

St. Elias   A Slavic saint who is the master of the weather and is invoked for oaths, in treaties, etc. (Welsford, 1925, 9: 252)

Ellamma   She and Huligavva are sacrificed to before undertaking a thieving expedition. The Donga Dasari, Southern India. (Thurston, 1909, 2: 192–193)

Emekori-mahse   The god of the day who is always good and who established "all the norms, the rules, and the laws." The Desana, Colombia. (Reichel-Dolmatoff, 1971: 27, 28)

Emongo   A deity who punishes misdeeds and anti-social acts. The Vugusu, Kenya. (Wagner, 1949: 177; Mbiti, 1970, 2: 127)

Eng-ai   The supreme being who is invoked in taking oaths. Kenya. (Wallis, 1939: 191; Williams, 1936: 199)

Erinyes   Greek goddesses of vengeance, also called the Eumenides—the "well-minded goddesses." They diligently pursued all who were guilty of infractions of faith and morality, of unfileal conduct, of crimes of violence, and therefore were considered the upholders of high morality. Sometimes given as one—Erinys—but usually named as three—Alecto, Megaira, and Tisiphone. (Fairbanks, 1907: 239; Willetts, 1962: 198; Murray, 1935: 216–217; Kerényi, 1951: 47–48; Roscher, 1965, 1, 1: 1310–1311)

Erkhe-Bashatey The third of the Tengris who was wise and gave the laws of government. The Buriats, Siberia and Mongolia. (Klementz, 1925, 3: 3)

Ert-pas The god of curses. The Erza (Mordvins), Russia. (Paasonen, 1925, 8: 846)

Eugora A Nereid, "Good Assembler," in relationship to organization, political leadership. Greece. (Hesiod-Brown, 1981: 30, 60, 87)

Eunomia The goddess of lawfulness, of legality, of legislation. Daughter of Themis and Zeus. Greece. (Murray, 1935: 144; Kerényi, 1951: 102; Roscher, 1965, 1, 1: 1404)

Eurynome An Oceanid, "Far-ruling," referring to "qualities of human leadership." Third wife of Zeus and mother of the Graces. Greece. (Hesiod-Brown, 1981: 78, 87)

Fenti One of the 42 judges or assessors of the deceased in the Hall of Maati. Egypt. (Budge, 1969, 1: 419)

Forseti Teutonic god of justice and impartiality, of eternal law, who settled strife and disputes wisely. (Guerber, 1895: 134–135; MacCulloch, 1964: 162; Wagner, 1882: 264; Grimm, 1880: 229; Stern, 1898: 53)

Gandak A god of theft, of thieves, to whom offerings are made after a successful expedition. The Doms, India. (Briggs, 1953: 465–466; Crooke, 1925, 4: 841; Trigg, 1973: 209–210)

Gbekze A monkey-headed god and judge of all souls. The Baule, Ivory Coast, Africa. (Abbate, 1972: 48)

Gora dai leng A god of vengeance who punishes dead sinners. Yap Island, the Carolines, Micronesia. (Christian, 1899: 385)

Grabovis The god who hears vows. The Umbrians, Italy. (Conway, 1925, 7: 460)

Guraiya Deo The principal god of the Pardhi in whose name their most solemn oaths are taken. The punishment for false swearing is leprosy. Central Provinces, India. (Russell, 1916, 4: 361, 363)

Gwon, Bom God of justice and of fertility. The Angas, Nigeria. (Meek, 1925, 2: 30; Williams, 1936: 215)

Gyer-sgrog-gar-gsas-btsan-pohi-lha A deity who assists in temporal government. Tibet. (Li Anche, 1948: 38–39)

Sidi Hamad u Musa The patron saint of acrobats who will help lawbreakers if made an offering. Morocco. (Westermarck, 1926, 1: 180–181)

The Harpies Woman-headed, bird-bodied goddesses of punishment, daughters of Thaumas and Elektra. They were originally goddesses of the tempests and storm winds. Aello, Okypete, and Kelaino or Podarge. Greek and Roman. (Kerényi, 1951: 60–62; Murray, 1935: 218; Fairbanks, 1907: 169)

Hebat A Hittite goddess who is a protector of treaties. Consort of Teshub. Asia Minor. (Oldenburg, 1969: 68)

Helios The omniscient sun god was invoked to witness oaths and to punish their breaking. Greece. (Pettazzoni, 1956: 5, 6, 155; O'Rahilly, 1946: 298; Kerényi, 1951: 191)

Hept-shet One of the 42 judges or assessors of the deceased in the Hall of Maati. Egypt. (Budgem 1969, 1: 419)

Heri-seru One of the 42 judges or assessors of the deceased for the goddess Maat. Egypt. (Budge, 1969, 1: 419)

Hetch-abehu One of the 42 judges or assessors of the deceased for the goddess Maat. Egypt. (Budge, 1969, 1: 419)

Hiro A god of thieves and also of war, a rival of Tane, taking the opposing side. Also a god of the seas who could control storms. Tahiti and possibly Easter Island, Polynesia. (Henry, 1928: 80, 129; Métraux, 1940: 310; Ellis, 1953: 328, 333)

Hku Te The god of the underworld who is a judge of "the sins of mortals." He appears as the rainbow in the west. The Karen, Burma. (Marshall, 1922: 223, 225, 228)

Horkos The son of Eris, the personification of the oath and the avenger of false swearing. Greece. (Roscher, 1965, 1, 2: 2742; Barthell, 1971: 8; Frazer, 1961: 231–232)

Horon A god invoked in curses. Canaan, Near East. (Oldenburg, 1969: 43; Gray, 1964: 123)

Hra-f-ha-f One of the 42 judges or assessors of the deceased for the goddess Maat. Egypt. (Budge, 1969, 1: 419)

Hsiao-ho Patron deity of "Lawyers and Magistrates." Szechwan, China. (Graham, 1961: 186)

Hsiao Wang The "God of the Gaol . . . worshipped by the Board of Punishments, the criminal judges, the gaolers, and the prisoners." China. (Werner, 1932: 382)

Huitzilopochtli The bloodthirsty god of war of the Aztec to whom human hearts were sacrificed was also the god of political fortunes. Mexico. (Leonard, 1967: 104)

Huligavva A village goddess of the Donga Dasari, religious mendicants and thieves. She and Ellamma are sacrificed to before a thieving expedition. Southern India. (Thurston, 1909, 2: 192–193)

Hun-Came A god of the underworld and with Vucub-Came the supreme judge of the council of the lords of the underworld. The Quiché, Guatemala. (Recinos, 1950: 109–110)

Ialulep A god of judgment and also of destiny. Ulithi, the Carolines, Micronesia. (Lessa, 1966: 56)

Igalima A son of Ningirsu. The "personification of the door to Ningirsu's holy of holies," who was its guard and Ningirsu's "high constable . . . his duty to maintain justice, arrest evildoers, issue ordinances to the city." Near East. (Jacobsen, 1976: 82)

Ikombo A deity of the Tiv "by whom oaths are sworn." Nigeria. (Temple, 1922: 302)

Indagarra The supreme being and the god of judgment after death. The Wa-Twa, Urundi. (Haddon, 1925, 9: 272; MacCulloch, 1925, 11: 823)

'Inna Oaths sworn on her name are very strong. She is the protector of property and the punisher of thieves. The Maguzawa, Nigeria. (Greenberg, 1946: 40)

Iro, Hiro The god of thieves to whom the first day of the month is sacred. Mangaia, Polynesia. (Williamson, 1933, 1: 191)

Isarrataitsoq A god who is the guardian of the moral laws. The Netsilingmiut Eskimo. Canada. (Rasmussen, 1929: 66)

Ishkara An Assyro/Babylonian deity invoked in curses. Near East. (Rawlinson, 1885: 51)

Istanu A sun god who was the supreme god of justice and "cited in treaties." Hittite, Asia Minor. (Hicks, 1974: 101; Guterbock, 1950: 91)

Itur-mer An important god of the Amorites who was invoked with Shamash and Dagan in oaths. Near East. (Oldenburg, 1969: 51–52)

Iustitia The Roman personification of justice, closely related to Equitas. (Roscher, 1965, 2, 1: 762)

Iuventas The goddess of youth was also protective of the contractual and marital relationships within Roman society. (Littleton, 1965: 121–122)

Jagganathaswami The god on whom vows are taken. The Gavara, Southern India. (Thurston, 1909, 2: 278)

Jam A judge of the dead of the Abor. Tibet and India. (Crooke, 1925, 1: 33)

Jên An A god of robbers. China. (Werner, 1932: 468)

Jhora Naik A deified ancestor, murderer/thief, who was deified as having equally divided the booty among all—even though not present. The Thags (Doms), India. (Briggs, 1953: 466)

Jupiter As a sovereign god he was a god of justice and ethics, of law and order (of the universe as well as the earth), protector of the state, and guarantor of oaths, contracts, and treaties. Rome. (Schoeps, 1961: 145; Dumézil, 1966, 1: 108, 179, 180, 191; Fairbanks, 1907: 98–99; Jayne, 1962: 429–430; Pettazzoni, 1956: 163; Eliade, 1976, 2: 367)

Kabunian The chief deity of the Nabaloi who is "the supreme moral authority . . . also functions as the judge." The name is also used as a general term applied to other deities. Luzon, Philippines. (De Raedt, 1964: 266)

Kadi An Assyro/Babylonian goddess of justice and of morality. Near East. (Larousse, 1968: 63)

Kagyr Khan A god sent by Erlik to mete out punishment. The Altaians, Siberia. (Czaplicka, 1969: 281)

bKa'i bya ra ba The "guardian of commandments." Tibet. (Nebesky-Wojkowitz, 1956, 1: 109)

Kaihaga "Curse," a god of thieves whose father was Tolioatua. Niue Island, Polynesia. (Loeb, 1926, 1: 163)

Kaihamulu A god of thieves. Son of Tolioatua. Niue Island, Polynesia. (Loeb, 1926, 1: 163)

Kalekamo The guardian of heaven who questions and judges the souls. Nias, Indonesia. (Kruijt, 1925, 7: 245)

Kali The Badhaks, a tribe of criminals, believed she would favor them so long as properly propitiated. When things went wrong they believed it was due to infractions of her rules. Central Provinces, India. (Russell, 1916, 2: 61)

Kalo A sky god and creator who is invoked in oaths. The Lafofa (Nuba), Sudan. (Seligman, 1925, 9: 403)

Kansasur Deota The godling of brass by whom the Byadh Nats swear. The Doms, India. (Briggs, 1953: 387)

Kari The supreme being and creator is also a god of judgment, sending thunder and storms as punishment. The Semang, Malay Peninsula. (Cole, 1945: 72; Skeat, 1906: 178; Moss, 1925: 116)

Kenemti One of the 42 judges or assessors of the dead for the goddess Maat. Egypt. (Budge, 1969, 1: 419)

Kêng Yen-chêng A god of robbers. China. (Werner, 1932: 468)

Khemi One of the 42 judges or assessors of the deceased for the goddess Maat. Egypt. (Budge, 1969, 1: 419)

Kinkin A goddess of the Baiga invoked in maledictions. India. (Elwin, 1939: 372)

Kinoingan, Kinohoingan The supreme being who is invoked in oaths and who punishes incest and other immorality. The Dusun, Borneo. (Stall, 1925: 940–941; Pettazzoni, 1956: 331)

Kittu An abstract god representing justice. Son of Shamash and Aya. Babylonia, Near East. (Larousse, 1968: 58)

Kok-thi-yong A god of heaven who judges the dead who try to enter. The Naga, Manipur, India. (Hodson, 1911: 160)

Konjin The fearful god of the Lunar Calendar whose position must be calculated before any undertaking. He is also the god of the curse. Japan. (Holtom, 1938: 259–260; Norbeck, 1954: 124–125)

Kuan Kung, Kuan Ti The god of war is worshipped by merchants as a "god of justice, loyalty, and generosity." China. (Day, 1940: 54)

Ku 'i-a-lua A god of robbers, of wrestling, of bone-breaking and killing. Hawaii. (Beckwith, 1940: 50; Alexander, 1968: 73; Westervelt, 1963, 3: 254)

Kukulcan The Mayan plumed serpent and culture hero/god was the founder of justice and order, the giver of laws. Mexico. (Tozzer, 1941: 23; Schellhas, 1904: 18; Schoeps, 1961: 99; Larousse, 1968: 439)

Lamaphu The "master of words . . . sacrificed to by a man who has a case in court." The Mikirs, Assam. (Lyall, 1925, 8: 630)

Laomedeia A Nereid, "Leader of the People," as related to political leadership. Greece. (Hesiod-Brown, 1981: 60, 87; Kerényi, 1951: 65)

Laverna An Etruscan/Roman goddess invoked by thieves as a goddess of gain, lawful or unlawful. (Roscher, 1965, 2, 2: 1917: Herbig, 1925, 5: 535; Keane, 1925, 2: 123; Larousse, 1968: 214)

Leagora A Nereid, "Assembler of the People," related to leadership, particularly political. Greece. (Hesiod-Brown, 1981: 60, 87)

U 'lei muluk The god of the State. The Khasis, Assam. (Gurdon, 1914: 106)

Ka 'lei Synshar The goddess of the State, to whom a pig is sacrificed. the Khasis, Assam. (Gurdon, 1907: 93; Pettazzoni, 1956: 299n. 23)

Lepitan A god of judgment in the vicinity of Selat. Bali, Indonesia. (Goris, 1969, 3: 120)

Lidum A god and teacher of the Ifugao who gave them "their customary law and procedure." Luzon, Philippines. (Barton, 1919: 14)

Li Ssu A god of robbers. China. (Werner, 1932: 468)

Liu Chih A god of brigands. China. (Werner, 1932: 255)

Locana The "special personification of Dharma in all its aspects, the cosmic as well as the moral Law." Japanese Buddhism. (Eliot, 1935: 108)

Lugalsisa An administrative "counselor" of Ningirsu who "served as regent when Ningirsu was away." Near East. (Jacobsen, 1976: 82)

Lugeilang The interrogator of the dead at their judging. Ulithi, the Carolines, Micronesia. (Lessa, 1966: 56)

Lysianassa "Royal Deliverer"—A Nereid related to political leadership. Greece. (Hesiod-Brown, 1981: 60, 87)

Maa-an-f One of the 42 judges or assessors of the deceased for the goddess Maat. Egypt. (Budge, 1969, 1: 419)

Ma-ah A spirit who punishes the wicked. The Golos, Africa. (Budge, 1973, 1: 375)

Maat The personification of justice and truth, of equity and ethics, who was head of the assessors or judges of the dead. She was the female counterpart of Thoth and her symbol was the ostrich feather. Egypt. (Knight, 1915: 66–67; Budge, 1969, 1: 323, 416–421; Anthes, 1961: 59; Frankfort, 1946: 22; James, 1960: 261)

Maati-f-em-tes One of the 42 judges or assessors of the deceased for the goddess Maat. Egypt. (Budge, 1969, 1: 419)

Madain The god of wine is also the god of oaths. The Chamars, India. (Briggs, 1920: 156–157)

Madiovazanakoho A "god with the clean finger nails" who is invoked by the Tanala in making vows. Madagascar. (Linton, 1933: 163, 194)

Makú Gaunávul-due Father of the Police. The Cagaba and the Kogi, Colombia. (Reichel-Dolmatoff, 1949/50: 113)

Malik A Babylonian deity invoked in curses. Near East. (Rawlinson, 1885: 51)

Mama fo Gro The earth mother is the goddess of the strongest oaths. The Paramaribo Negros, Surinam. (Leach, 1950: 668)

Mamit The demoness of the curse, irrevocable once invoked. A goddess of fate. Near East. (Langdon, 1931: 372; Sayce, 1898: 306)

Manabungol A thief deity of the Ifugao. Philippines. (Barton, 1946: 33)

Mangako "Thief"—A deity of the Ifugao. Philippines. (Barton, 1946: 32)

Mangibahauwit A god of thieving. The Ifugao, Philippines. (Barton, 1946: 33)

Mangitalu " 'Hider'—in order to steal later on." The Ifugao, Philippines. (Barton, 1946: 33)

Mangobkal A thief deity of the Ifugao. Philippines. (Barton, 1946: 33)

Manu The Lawgiver, son of Surya and Samjna. "The fourteen progenitors and lawgivers of the human race in fourteen successive creations are known as Manus." India. (Danielou, 1964: 96, 326)

Sidi Maqdi Haja A saint who will help thieves in their undertakings if made an offering. Morocco. (Westermarck, 1926, 1: 181)

Masanyatha A goddess before whom trial by ordeal is held as she is considered to have the power of detecting culprits. The Kadir, Southern India. (Thurston, 1909, 3: 21)

Math A god whose attributes were "goodness to the suffering, and justice with no trace of vengeance." Celtic, Wales. (MacCulloch, 1911: 105)

Mati-Syra-Zemlya A Slavic mother earth invoked as a witness to oaths and in the settlement of disputes as well as protection from misfortunes. Russia. (Larousse, 1968: 287; Schrader, 1925, 2: 38)

Mau-taui The guardian of the Hall of Maati and a form of Thoth as an interrogator and judge of the dead. Egypt. (Budge, 1969, 1: 420)

Meduwe Gama "As Batara Meduwe Gama the ancestors are venerated in the role of mentors who introduced the *agama,* the laws and customs, the religious and social practices." Bali, Indonesia. (Grader, 1969, 1: 148)

Sidi Mhammed s-Sahli He punishes robbers by causing their apprehension. He is also antagonistic toward governmental representatives. Morocco. (Westermarck, 1926, 1: 192–193)

Mida A Greek goddess of oaths. (Roscher, 1965, 2, 2: 2954)

Minucius A Roman god of the just apportionment of the harvest for the poor. (Roscher, 1965, 2, 2: 3011)

Mirirul The creator is the judge of men, taking the good to the sky. The Illawarra, Australia. (Tylor, 1891: 296)

Mir-Susne-Khum Gander-Prince or World-Surveyor-Man who is the youngest son of Yanykh-Torum (Numi-Torum), the sky god. He was the peacekeeper among his brothers and among men. The Vogul, Siberia. (Czaplicka, 1969: 289; Roheim, 1954: 19, 27)

Misharu A Babylonian abstract god representing rectitude, law. In Assyria he is a judge of the dead. Near East. (Ananikian, 1964: 40; Langdon, 1931: 80; Larousse, 1968: 58)

Mishor Phoenician personification of justice. Near East. (Paton, 1925, 9: 893)

Mithra The god of light is a god of justice and truth, of law and order, and of contracts. He observes man's activities and is the judge of all he does, aiding those who struggle against the temptations of Angra Mainyu. Iran. (Dresden, 1961: 347–348; Haydon, 1941: 79; Jayne, 1962: 193; Gray, 1930: 97; Huart, 1963: 40, 42; Pettazzoni, 1956: 134–136)

Mitra A benevolent solar god who is the guardian of morality, of truth, as well as of contracts and treaties. He is omniscient and watchful over human affairs. India. (Danielou, 1964: 116; Bhattacharji, 1970: 33, 221–222; Littleton, 1965: 8; Pettazzoni, 1956: 10, 19, 120)

Mitthu Bhukiya A bandit godling of the Bamjara who is worshipped with Kali for success before an expedition. The Doms, India. (Crooke, 1925, 2: 347; Briggs, 1953: 467)

Mombalyag "Carrier-Off in Woman's Large Back-Basket," a thief deity. The Ifugao, Philippines. (Barton, 1946: 14, 33)

Mombatauwil "Carrier-Off on a Pole," a thief deity of the Ifugao. Philippines. (Barton, 1946: 14, 33)

Mongampa "Carrier-off in Gampa Basket," a thief deity of the Ifugao. Philippines. (Barton, 1946: 14, 33)

Monguku "Carrier-Off in Blanket Roll," a thief deity of the Ifugao. Philippines. (Barton, 1946: 14, 33)

Monlakwit "User of a Pole" to steal, a thief deity of the Ifugao. Philippines. (Barton, 1946: 14, 33)

Monligud A thief deity of the Ifugao. Philippines. (Barton, 1946: 14, 33)

Monlimon "Stealer of Domestic Animals," a thief deity of the Ifugao, Philippines. (Barton, 1946: 32)

Monlono A thief deity of the Ifugao. Philippines. (Barton, 1946: 33)

Montuklubao "Carrier-Off in Women's Small Back-Basket," a thief deity of the Ifugao. Philippines. (Barton, 1946: 14, 33)

Mukolkol A god of thieves and robbers. Yap Island, the Carolines, Micronesia. (Christian, 1899: 385)

Mulungu The Lambas of Northern Rhodesia use this name at times for Lesa, in oath-taking. (Doke, 1931: 225)

Muntumuntu The "sun and lawgiver." The Minahassa, Indonesia. (Kern, 1925, 8: 347)

Nahhunte A solar god who was also "probably . . . the god of judgment, righteousness, and justice," like Shamash with whom he was identified. The Elamites, Near East. (Pinces, 1925, 5: 251; Larousse, 1968: 72)

Nakiwulo A goddess who "detects thieves and is able to trace lost property and missing cattle." The Basoga, Uganda. (Roscoe, 1915: 246)

Nascakiyetl The creator of mankind was also the judge of the dead. The Tlingit, British Columbia and Alaska. (Alexander, 1964: 260, 263)

Neb-abui One of the 42 judges or assessors of the dead for the goddess Maat. Egypt. (Budge, 1969, 1: 419)

Neba-per-em-khetkhet One of the 42 judges or assessors of the deceased in the hall of the goddess Maat. Egypt. (Budge, 1969, 1: 419)

Neb-hrau One of the 42 judges or assessors of the dead for the goddess Maat. Egypt. (Budge, 1969, 1: 419)

Neb-Maat One of the 42 judges or assessors of the deceased for the goddess Maat. Egypt. (Budge, 1969, 1: 419)

Nefer-Tem A lion-god and a god of the rising sun. He is also one of the 42 judges or assessors of the dead for the goddess Maat. He is the son of Ptah and Sekhet. Egypt. (Budge, 1969, 1: 362, 419, 514, 521)

Neha-hau One of the 42 judges or assessors of the deceased in the Hall of Maat. Egypt. (Budge, 1969, 1: 419)

Neheb-kau A serpent goddess and one of the 42 judges or assessors of the dead for the goddess Maat. She provides the divine food for the dead. Egypt. (Budge, 1969, 1: 419; 1969, 2: 62; Hambly, 1929: 663)

Neheb-nefert One of the 42 judges or assessors of the dead for the goddess Maat. Egypt. (Budge, 1969, 1: 419)

Nekhen One of the 42 judges or assessors of the deceased for the goddess Maat. Egypt. (Budge, 1969, 1: 419)

Nemertes "Unerring"—A Nereid associated with the leadership and the qualities of law. Greece. (Hesiod-Brown, 1981: 30, 60, 87)

The Nereids They are primarily associated with the sea and represent beauty and inspire love. But among them and also among the Oceanids are those representative of the forces of law and justice in the universe. Greece. (Hesiod-Brown, 1981: 30–31)

Niggina Sumerian personification of justice. Near East. (Jacobsen, 1970: 26)

Ninglum lawa The spirit of heat in the judgment of God, testing the accused by plunging his hand in boiling water. His wife is Ningthet majan; they take the part of the plaintiff. The Katchins, Burma. (Gilhodes, 1908: 674)

Ningshung lawa The god of cold who takes the part of the accused, who has to plunge his hand into boiling water, by protecting him from burning. His wife is Ningtsi majan. The Katchins, Burma. (Gilhodes, 1908: 674)

Ningthet majan The wife of Ninglum lawa, who with him takes part in the judgment of the accused whose hand is plunged in boiling water. They represent heat and take the part of the plaintiff. The Katchins, Burma. (Gilhodes, 1908: 674)

Ningtsi majan The wife of Ningshung lawa, the spirits of cold. They take the part of the accused, protecting him from burning in the test by boiling water. The Katchins, Burma. (Gilhodes, 1908: 674)

Ningtum kanu, Ningri itou, matsa kanu A god of curses invoked to curse and/or harm enemies. The Katchins, Burma. (Gilhodes, 1908: 675)

Njord The god of the sea and of riches is also a god of oaths. Scandinavia. (Turville-Petre, 1964: 162–163; Larousse, 1968: 270)

Nomos The personification of law. Greece. (Roscher, 1965, 2, 1: 455)

Nuabulezi A spirit who was invoked to curse individuals or entire villages. Uganda. (Cunningham, 1905: 68; Budge, 1973, 1: 377)

Nurelli The culture hero/creator god of the Wiimbaio who gave them their laws and later retired to the sky. Australia. (Eliade, 1973: 4; Howitt, 1904: 489)

Nusku In Assyria the fire god is also a god of justice. (Larousse, 1968: 61, 63)

Nyauleza The "supreme judge . . . worshipped by the women of Karagwe." The Haya, Tanzania. (Taylor, 1962: 142)

Ogun The god of iron—"upon his symbol in the form of a knife," court oaths are sworn. The Yoruba, Nigeria. (Forde, 1951: 30)

Omequituriqui Their chief deity, who was "judge and avenger of the people," afflicted transgressors with diseases. The Manasi, Bolivia. (Métraux, 1942: 129; 1948, 2: 390)

Opis The personification of punishment that follows transgressions or violations of the laws of the gods. Greece. (Roscher, 1965, 3, 1: 927)

Oporae A god who punishes theft. The Effutu, Ghana. (Wyllie, 1966: 478)2210–2225

Oxala A remote and incorruptible supreme god who gave them their laws. Belem, Brazil. (Leacock, 1972: 156)

Oya The goddess of fire and of justice was the sister/mistress of Chango, to whom she gave "the power of fire and lightning." Puerto Rico, West Indies. (Gonzalez-Wippler, 1975: 25, 106, 115)

P'an-tze The judge who possesses the "register of the living and the dead." The Monguors of Kansu, China. (Schram, 1957: 86)

Pa-o-chash A name of Mustamho as the judge of the actions of men and animals both on the earth and in the hereafter. The Mojave, Arizona. (Bourke, 1889: 172–173)

Pao Lung T'u A Chinese god of justice. (Day, 1940: 24)

Papkootparout A deity who determines the sentences of the wicked in the realm of the dead. The Micmacs, Eastern Canada. (Wallis, 1939: 223)

Pase-Kamui The high god of the Ainu who is the judge of all after death. Japan. (Batchelor, 1925, 1: 240, 252)

Perumal Iswaran A god by whom oaths are sworn. The Tiyan, Southern India. (Thurston, 1909/7: 99)

Perun The Slavic god of thunder is also a god of oaths and of treaties. Russia. (Machal, 1918: 293; Welsford, 1925, 9: 252; Gimbutas, 1975, 1: 3)

Petara A benevolent deity who is always a power of justice, of honesty, and of right. Invoked in illness or closeness to death as a saving power. Though death may occur, Petara is not considered evil. The Sea Dyaks, Borneo. (Roth, 1968: 179)

Pir Makhan, Pir Madar Worshipped by the Chapparband, who are counterfeiters. A fowl is sacrificed. Southern India. (Thurston, 1909, 2: 21)

Poine, Poena A goddess of vengeful retaliation, associated with the Erinyes and with Nemesis. Can be singular or plural. Greece. (Roscher, 1965, 3, 2: 2602; Murray, 1935: 213)

Polynoë A Nereid whose qualities, "reason," associated her with political leadership. Greece. (Kerényi, 1951: 65; Hesiod-Brown, 1981: 60, 87)

Pronoë "Forethought"—A Nereid who is associated with "leadership, especially political." Greece. (Hesiod-Brown, 1981: 60, 87)

Protomedea "First in Leadership"—A Nereid who is grouped with those who reflect the law-enforcing potentialities of the time. Greece. (Hesiod-Brown, 1981: 30, 60)

Pue mpalaburu The supreme being and all-seeing solar god who is invoked in oath-taking. Celebes, Indonesia. (Kruijt, 1925, 7: 249; Pettazzoni, 1956: 8, 20)

Qerer One of the 42 judges as mentioned in the Papyrus of Ani. Agypt. (Budge, 1967: 348)

Qerti One of the 42 judges or assessors of the deceased for the goddess Maat. Egypt. (Budge, 1969, 1: 419)

Raja Pali A god of the Upperworld who is a god of judgment and of order, who participates in the sentencing and in the punishment of transgressions. The Ngaju, Borneo. (Scharer, 1963: 19, 21, 102)

Ralowimba A god of judgment who rewards good and punishes evil. South Africa. (Hartland, 1925, 2: 364; Willoughby, 1932: 41)

Rashnu A god of truth and of judgment after death. In life he awards the victory to the just and protects the innocent. Iran. (Dresden, 1961: 348; Haydon, 1941: 67, 79; Gray, 1930: 99; Huart, 1963: 42)

Ratnasabhapathy A deity of the thieves. The Korava, Southern India. (Thurston, 1909, 3: 463)

Rerti A god who is one of the 42 judges or assessors of the deceased for the goddess Maat. Egypt. (Budge, 1969, 1: 419)

Rum Adum A god of justice invoked in oaths. The Lepchas, Sikkim. (Gorer, 1938: 139, 506)

Safa The "god of the hearth-chain" by whom oaths were sworn. The Ossetes, Caucasus. (Morgan, 1888: 383, 391)

Sakarabru A god of justice "but also a terrible and blood-thirsty one and much feared." The Guinea and Senegambia groups, West Africa. (Larousse, 1968: 484)

Salesh A robber worshipped by the Dosadhs (Doms), India. (Briggs, 1953: 467)

Sansari Mai An earth goddess worshipped by thieves and criminals and invoked before undertaking a raid. The Doms, India. (Briggs, 1953: 530; Keane, 1925, 2: 123)

Sarpal A deity of thieves to whom offerings are made before an expedition. The Doms, Dumraon, India. (Briggs, 1953: 465)

Saura, Sauru, Saurva The demon of tyranny, of misgovernment, of anarchy and lawlessness. Iran. (Gray, 1930: 182; Huart, 1963: 43; Hinnells, 1973: 52)

Sekheriu One of the 42 gods of judgment as mentioned in the Papyrus of Ani. Agypt. (Budge, 1967: 349)

Serekhi One of the 42 judges or assessors of the dead for the goddess Maat. Egypt. (Budge, 1969, 1: 419)

Ser-kheru One of the 42 judges or assessors of the deceased for the goddess Maat. Egypt. (Budge, 1969, 1: 419)

Sertiu A god mentioned as one of the 42 gods of judgment in the Papyrus of Ani. Egypt. (Budge, 1967: 348)

Set-kesu One of the 42 judges or assessors of the deceased for the goddess Maat. Egypt. (Budge, 1969, 1: 419)

Shamash A solar god who was a god of justice and righteousness, of divination and of healing, whose wife was Aya. Father of Kittu and Misharu. Babylonia and Assyria, Near East. (Jayne, 1962: 127; Jastrow, 1898: 71–72, 209–210; Dumézil, 1966, 2: 655; Jacobsen, 1970: 21; Langdon, 1931: 150; Larousse, 1968: 57–58)

Shango The Yoruban god of thunder and lightning was a "slayer of liars." In Brazil he was a god of justice. Nigeria. (Meek, 1943: 112; Bastide, 1960: 91, 572)

Shaushga "Goddess of Law and War." Same as Ishtar. Sister of Teshub. Turkey. (Akurgal, 1969: 266)

Shet-kheru One of the 42 judges or assessors of the deceased for the goddess Maat. Egypt. (Budge, 1969, 1: 419)

Shih Ch'ien A god of brigands. China. (Werner, 1932: 422)

Shinje-chho-gyal, Shinje-chogyal The god and impartial judge of the dead. Nepal/Tibet. (Furer-Haimendorf, 1964: 195, 247; Evans-Wentz, 1960: 35–37; Gazeteer of Sikhim, 1894: 269)

Shyakapanga A name of Lesa used in oath-taking. The Lambas and Ba-Kaonde, Rhodesia. (Doke, 1931: 225; Frazer, 1926: 166–167)

Si, Si-bavas A Finno-Ugric sun goddess by whom oaths are sworn. She is invoked to punish perjury. The Mordvins, Russia. (Pettazzoni, 1956: 257)

Siao Wang A god worshipped by judges, jailers, and prisoners alike, the latter hoping he will ease their consciences and make escape possible. China. (Du Bose, n.d.: 141)

Silili A female spirit of theft who also kills people. Normanby Island, Papua and New Guinea. (Roheim, 1946: 325)

gSin-rje The god and judge of the dead. Same as Yama. Tibet. (Waddell, 1959: 367)

Skan The sky god, the Great Spirit, is the final judge of the living and the dead, of all things. He "created of his essence a daughter to be the Mediator and named her Wohpe." The Oglala and Lakota, South Dakota. (Pettazzoni, 1956: 384; Eliade, 1967: 188; Walker, 1980: 35, 50–54, 95)

Skylios A surname of Zeus as god of oaths. Greece. (Roscher, 1965, 4: 1024)

Snag-sgrub A form of Yama as a judge of the dead. Tibet. (Getty, 1962: 153)

So, Xevioso A sky/thunder god, an androgynous deity born of Mawu-Lisa, who is the god of "supreme justice." He is malevolent as well as benevolent. The Ewe, Dahomey. (Herskovits, 1938, 2: 129, 150–151; Parrinder, 1949: 31)

Som-Sagan-Noin A functionary of Erlik-Khan who "tries lawsuits" assisted by Ukha-Tolegor-Khovduieff and Khan-Khormo-Noin. The Buriats, Siberia and Mongolia. (Klementz, 1925, 3: 7)

Sraosha A god of discipline and of morality who is the judge of actions during life as well as of the dead, awarding rewards as well as punishments. Iran. (Gray, 1930: 106–107; Huart, 1963: 42; Dresden, 1961: 348; Larousse, 1973: 191, 198; Littleton, 1965: 124)

Styx The goddess of inviolable oaths and a river goddess. Daughter of Oceanus and Tethys and mother of Nike, Bia, Cratos, and Zelus by Pallas. Greece. (Kerényi, 1951: 35, 42; Barthell, 1971: 15; Larousse, 1968: 165; Hesiod-Brown, 1981: 63, 64)

Subramania, Kartikiya The "god of the criminal Kauravars." The Doms, India. (Briggs, 1953: 557)

Suen A deity of the Tiv "by whom oaths are sworn." Nigeria. (Temple, 1922: 302)

Suila A deity who informs Ulgen of the activities and behavior of men. The Altai, Siberia. (Eliade, 1958: 61)

Summanus A god of the night sky and lightning, of night storms, was also the deity invoked by thieves and evildoers. Italy. (Stewart, 1960: 37; Larousse, 1968: 214; Dumézil, 1966, 1: 200)

Sunde The "punisher of crime" The Tiv, Nigeria. (Temple, 1922: 302)

Sung Chiang (Kiang) The god of thieves. China. (Maspero, 1963: 333; Werner, 1932: 470; Larousse, 1968: 394)

Sun Hsuan A god of robbers. China. (Werner, 1932: 468)

Syam Singh A deified ancestral robber "embodying the ideal of systematic and violent crime"—the way of life of the Magahiyas. India. (Briggs, 1953: 465)

Sydyk, Sydycos Phoenician god, personification of justice, and identified with Kittu (Babylonian). Near East. (Herm, 1975: 111; Langdon, 1931: 67)

Syn A Scandinavian goddess who presides at trials and is the guardian of truth and justice, the defender against perjurious testimony. (Thorpe, 1851: 36; Grimm, 1880: 310; Anderson, 1891: 239; Guerber, 1895: 52)

T'ai Shan (Wang) The great mountain god was invoked for good in all things and was looked upon as the source of life, a god of birth and death. With the introduction of an afterlife in Buddhism he became a judge of the dead, the King of the Seventh Court of Hades. China. (Haydon, 1941: 193–194; Day, 1940: 120; Maspero, 1963: 366; Werner, 1932: 482)

Takanalup angutialua   A much feared god, merciless punisher of transgressions. The Iglulik Eskimo, Canada. (Rasmussen, 1929: 66)

Tara majan   The goddess of justice who sees that the innocent wins in the trial by boiling water. The Katchins, Burma. (Gilhodes, 1908: 674)

Ta-ret   One of the 42 judges or assessors of the dead for the goddess Maat. Egypt. (Budge, 1969, 1: 419)

Telesto   Daughter of Oceanus and Tethys. "Success," in association with "qualities of human leadership." Greece. (Hesiod-Brown, 1981: 63, 87)

Tem-sep   One of the 42 gods who were judges or assessors of the dead for the goddess Maat. Egypt. (Budge, 1969, 1: 419)

Tenga   The powerful earth goddess was the goddess of justice and morality, the avenger of wrong. The Mossi, Upper Volta and Senegal. (Frazer, 1926: 403)

Terminus   The Roman god of boundaries was also "concerned with the equitable distribution of goods, etc., among the people." (Littleton, 1965: 122)

Tha-ma   The judge of the dead. The Karens, Burma. (McMahon, 1876: 141)

Themis   The goddess of law and order, of right conduct in all things; a goddess of justice and wisdom, of good counsel. She was the daughter of Uranus and Gaea, a wife of Zeus by whom she was the mother of the Horae—Dike, Eirene, Eunomia, and of the Morae—Clotho, Lachesis, and Atropus, which offspring are representative of law enforcement and retribution. Greece. (Barthell, 1971: 12, 152; Larousse, 1968: 136; Kerényi, 1951: 69, 101, 224; Murray, 1935: 140; Hesiod-Brown, 1981: 30, 56, 57, 78)

Themisto   A daughter of Nereus and Doris. "Law," representing the "law-enforcing tendencies in the universe." She is also associated with political leadership. Greece. (Hesiod-Brown, 1981: 30, 87)

Thenemi   One of the 42 judges or assessors of the deceased for the goddess Maat. Egypt. (Budge, 1969, 1: 419)

Thor   At the Assemblies he was invoked in oath-taking. Iceland. (Campbell, 1964: 480)

T'ien   The omniscient chief deity and sky god was a god of oaths, punishing those who broke them. China. (Pettazzoni, 1956: 273, 278–279)

Tigbas   The "god of good government." The Bukidnon, Philippines. (Jocano, 1969: 24)

Tiki   The god of Paradise is also the judge of the dead. Rarotonga, Cook Islands, Polynesia. (Moss, 1925: 114)

Tishpak   City god of Eshnunna and the "guarantor of oaths." Near East. (Roberts, 1972: 54; Jacobsen, 1970: 34)

Tiu   A sky god who was a god of war as well as of justice. Teutonic. (Schoeps, 1961: 105)

Toglai   Some of the Bagobo consider him the judge of the dead. Philippines. (MacKenzie, 1930: 306)

Tokonaka   A spirit who meets "the breath body" of the dead on their return to the "place of Emergence" and judges where they are to go. The Hopi, Arizona. (Parsons, 1939: 216)

Tong-nab   The god of the Tong Hills on whom oaths are taken. The Talense and the Builsa, Ghana. (Rattray, 1932: 361, 399)

Trong lawa   The god of justice who, with his wife Tara majan, sees that the innocent wins in the trial by boiling water. The Katchins, Burma. (Gilhodes, 1908: 674)

Ts'ao-ts'an   A patron deity of lawyers. Szechwan, China. (Graham, 1961: 186)

Tši, Tši-pas   The sun goddess by whom the Erzan swear, invoking her to punish perjury. Russia. (Pettazzoni, 1956: 257)

Tsi'u dmar po   A deity protective of his followers who causes illness and madness among enemies, and sometimes "sits in judgment of the souls of men." Tibet. (Nebesky-Wojkowitz, 1956, 1: 95, 166–167)

Tuhan   A beneficent god who presides over the universe, has the power of life and death, and is the judge of souls. The Sakai, Malay Peninsula. (Skeat, 1906: 179)

Tulumeng   The stern ruler and judge of the afterworld. The Kai, New Guinea. (Haddon, 1925, 9: 348)

Tung Yo   The god of the Eastern Peak, T'ai Shan, is a judge of the dead, but is also invoked for protection and for children. Anking, China. (Shryock, 1931: 91; Ferguson, 1937: 71)

Tu P'ing   A god of robbers. China. (Werner, 1932: 468)

Turda   An Assyro/Babylonian deity invoked in curses. Near East. (Rawlinson, 1885: 51)

Turm   An omniscient and omnipresent deity who is a god of implacable destiny and justice. The Ostyaks, Yenisei region, Siberia. (Keane, 1925, 2: 121)

Tutela   A Roman goddess of truth and justice. (Grimm, 1880: 310)

Tutu-f   One of the 42 judges or assessors of the deceased for the goddess Maat. Egypt. (Budge, 1969, 1: 419)

Tyr   The Germanic one-handed god of war was also "a god of contract and justice." (Turville-Petre, 1964: 180–181)

Uamemti   A serpent god who is one of the 42 judges or assessors of the deceased for the goddess Maat. Egypt. (Budge, 1969, 1: 198, 419)

Uatch-nes   One of the 42 judges or assessors of the deceased for the goddess Maat. Egypt. (Budge, 1969, 1: 419)

Umalgo   A god of justice and of divination using the *agba* stick to determine the cause of disease, to detect thieves, and to find lost property. He is also invoked in oaths. The Ifugao, Philippines. (Barton, 1946: 39, 91)

Umbulan   The moon who is a god of war and also a god of justice and divination, using the *agba* stick to determine the cause of disease, to detect thieves, and to find lost property. Also a god of oaths. The Ifugao, Philippines. (Barton, 1946: 38–39, 91)

Upu Langi   The sky god invoked with Upu Tapene, the earth goddess, in taking of oaths. Ceram Island, the Moluccas, Indonesia. (Pettazzoni, 1956: 20, 334)

Upu Lanito   The omniscient sky god who is invoked jointly with Upu Ume in taking oaths. Ambon Island, the Moluccas, Indonesia. (Pettazzoni, 1956: 334–335)

Upu Tapene   The earth goddess who is invoked with Upu Langi in oath-taking. Ceram Island, the Moluccas, Indonesia. (Pettazzoni, 1956: 334)

Upu Ume, Ina, Inaka   Mother Earth who is invoked jointly with Upu Lanito in oath-taking. Ambon Island, the Molucas, Indonesia. (Pettazzoni, 1956: 334–335)

Usekht-nemmat   One of the 42 judges or assessors of Maat, judging the deceased in the Underworld. Egypt. (Budge, 1969, 1: 419)

Utu   A Sumerian solar god who was a god of justice and of civil order, of equity. Son of Nanna and brother of Inanna. Near East. (Jacobsen, 1946: 180; 1970: 26; Kramer, 1967: 100, 107; Schoeps, 1961: 56)

Utu-rekhit   One of the 42 judges or assessors of the dead for the goddess Maat. Egypt. (Budge, 1969, 1: 419)

al-Uzza   Goddess of the planet Venus—the morning and evening stars. Oaths are sworn on "the two Uzzas." Arabia. (Noldeke, 1925, 1: 660)

Var   Teutonic goddess of oaths and of plighted troths. (Anderson, 1891: 239; Stern, 1898: 99; Branston, 1955: 153; Turville-Petre, 1964: 189)

Varuna   The omniscient god of the universe, guardian of all order, cosmic and moral. He is a god of truth and of justice, is punitive, yet forgiving. He is invoked when drawing treaties and contracts, in the taking of oaths. At different times his functions and attributes varied. India. (Macdonell, 1897: 20, 23–26; Keith, 1917: 22–26; Ions, 1967: 14–15; Pettazzoni, 1956: 9, 19; Barthe, 1921: 17; Martin, 1914: 41, 44; Bhattacharji, 1970: 27, 33; Danielou, 1964: 118–119)

Veles, Volosu   The Slavic god of flocks was also invoked with Perun in making treaties and in oath-taking. Russia. (Machal, 1918: 300; Leach, 1950, 2: 1027)

Vorombetsivazana   A deity invoked in making vows and also in sacrifices regarding illness. The Tanala, Madagascar. (Linton, 1933: 194)

Vucub-Came   A Mayan god of the underworld who is a supreme judge of the council of the lords of the underworld. Guatemala. (Recinos, 1950: 109–110; Krickeberg, 1968: 79)

Wali-manoanoa   A lizard goddess influential in "the prosperity of the government." Hawaii. (Beckwith, 1940: 126–127)

Walinu'u   A lizard goddess "upon whom depends the prosperity of the government." Hawaii. (Beckwith, 1940: 126–127)

Wambli   "The Spirit of the Eagle presided over councils." The Lakota and Oglala, South Dakota. (Walker, 1980: 122)

Waqa   The omniscient supreme being and sky god who is invoked in oaths. The Gala, Uganda. (Pettazzoni, 1956: 6, 20)

Wen P'an Kuan   A judge of civilian affairs. Anking, China. (Shryock, 1931: 91)

Whiro   The god of evil, of death, of darkness is the patron deity of thieves. The Maori, New Zealand. (Best, 1924: 107, 237; Andersen, 1928: 115)

Wohpe   The "Mediator." She was created by Skan of his own essence. Her primary role is as patron of the ceremonial pipe, of harmony, and happiness. The Lakota, South Dakota. (Walker, 1980: 51, 95, 109–111, 220–222)

Wolgara   A god who judges the dead and who also kills and revives the aspiring medicine man. The Wardoman, Australia. (Eliade, 1973: 145)

Wu P'an Kuan   A judge of military affairs. Anking, China. (Shryock, 1931: 91)

Yaboaine   The god of war and of cannibalism is also the god of thieves. Sometimes referred to as female. Normandy Island, Papua and New Guinea. (Roheim, 1946: 210, 223, 321)

Yahweh   The sky god of storms, of power, of covenants is a sovereign god who can revoke decisions and laws, and "maintains his absolute freedom." The Hebrews. (Eliade, 1976, 2: 367)

Yama   God and judge of the dead who dispenses impartial judgment and is the keeper of the "Book of Destiny." India, Tibet, Cambodia, and Bali. (Sierksma, 1966: 115; Friederich, 1959: 49–50; Martin, 1914: 36; Getty, 1962: 152; Marchal, 1963: 203; Ions, 1967: 77)

Yei Suu   A merciful god of justice and of wisdom. The Ch'uan Miao, Yunnan Province, China. (Graham, 1937: 61)

Yeloje   The beneficent sun god, the "guardian of justice and of morality." The Yukaghir, Siberia. (Jochelson, 1900/02: 141)

Yen-lo (Wang)   The King of the Fifth Hell who punishes for religious sins, murder, incredulity, sexual crimes, and the killing of animals and fish. China. Same as Yama. (Maspero, 1963: 366; Edkins, 1880: 218; Peeters, 1941: 49; Hackin, 1963: 249; Day, 1940: 69, 98, 121)

Yetaita   The chief of the evil spirits who was the guardian of morality and punished infractions of the laws. Young boys and girls were admonished about this in initiation ceremonies. The Yahgan, Tierra del Fuego. (Cooper, 1946: 99; Zerries, 1968: 234)

Zamal   An Assyro/Babylonian deity invoked in curses. (Rawlinson, 1885: 51)

Zamama   A Babylonian god of war who was invoked also in drawing legal documents. Near East. (Jastrow, 1898: 169; Langdon, 1931: 117)

Zambi   The self-existent supreme being who is the god of justice who punishes evildoing by sending pestilence, drought, etc. He is also the judge of the dead. Angola and Gabon. (Frazer, 1926: 136–138; Larousse, 1968: 481)

Zeus   The supreme Greek god of the universe was a sovereign god of justice and morality, of law and order, of rewards and punishments, an omniscient god who watched over the deeds of men, particularly over oaths. (Pettazzoni, 1956: 19, 145; Barthell, 1971: 19; Schoeps, 1961: 126; Murray, 1935: 25; Eliade, 1976, 2: 367; Hesiod-Brown, 1981: 20, 21, 42)

44

Love:
Lust, Sexuality, Phallic, Lovers

Adbhutnatha A stone god worshipped as a linga. India. (Crooke, 1925, 11: 871)

The Agkui The "divinities who urged men to indulge in sexual excesses." The Manobo, Philippines. (Jocano, 1969: 23)

Aizen, Aizen-Myoo He is popularly considered the god of love, but also represents its sublimation, which leads to enlightenment. Japan. (Eliot, 1935: 136; Larousse, 1968: 415)

Aku-Maga An obscene god of sexuality who is associated with the "buttock dance." He may cause illness and sacrifices must be made to him if he allows recovery. The Jukun, Nigeria. (Greenberg, 1946: 58; Meek, 1931: 273–274)

Alalalahe A goddess identified with Laka and as such is a goddess of love. Hawaii. (Beckwith, 1940: 186)

Albina An Etruscan goddess of light, of the dawn, who is the protectress of unfortunate lovers. Italy. (Leland, 1963: 123–124)

Allat As the evening star she was the goddess of love and of harlotry. Near East. (Langdon, 1931: 25)

Amor, Cupid Roman god of love. Same as Eros. (Bulfinch, 1898: 9; Murray, 1935: 189)

Anahit In Armenia she is the daughter of Aramazd, and as a goddess of fertility is associated with orgiastic religion and prostitution but also, as the great mother goddess, represents sobriety and the gift of life to the nation. (Ananikian, 1964: 25–28)

Ananda The god of desire. India. (Coleman, 1832: 374)

Anat(h) A goddess of fertility, of sex, and of war. A virgin goddess, amorous, yet cruel and destructive. Canaan and Syria. (James, 1960: 89; Gray, 1964: 123–124; Moscati, 1960: 114; Pritchard, 1943: 76–77; Patai, 1967: 61; Albright, 1956: 77, 80; Oldenburg, 1969: 88–89)

Angus Celtic god of love who metamorphosed as a swan to win Caer Ibormeith. Son of Dagda and Boann. Ireland. (Ross, 1967: 237; Squire, 1906: 56, 142)

Anteros The god who avenged rejected love. Son of Aphrodite and Ares, brother of Eros, Harmonia, Phobos, Deimos. Greece. (Barthell, 1971: 32, 222; Bulfinch, 1898: 9)

Anumati Goddess of love and procreation. She presides with Raka over the day of the full moon. India. (Macdonell, 1897: 119; Keith, 1917: 93)

Aphrodite Goddess of love in all its aspects: human love, pure as well as lustful, the love of the animal kingdom, the harmony of the universe. She was the goddess of brides and of marriage. She was the wife of Hephaestas but very fickle: the mother of Harmonia, Eros, Anteros, Phobos, Deimos, by Ares; of Hermaphroditus by Hermes; Priapus and Hymen by Dionysys; Eryx by Poseidon. Greece. In Cypress she was a goddess of motherhood, fertility, and of licentious rites. (Kerényi, 1951: 69, 71, 77; Murray, 1935: 91, 94; Jayne, 1962: 306; Fairbanks, 1907: 204, 211; Langdon, 1931: 32; Frazer, 1960 384; Barthell, 1971: 31–32)

Argimpasa A Scythian goddess equated with Aphrodite Urania as the goddess of pure love, of marriage, and of the harmony of the universe. (Minns, 1913: 85; Murray, 1935: 91; Fairbanks, 1907: 211)

Ariadne A Cretan goddess of love and fertility and an early vegetation deity. Wife of Dionysus. Greece. (Fairbanks, 1907: 185; Willetts, 1962: 193–194)

Asinaw A fragrant male spirit who accompanies a youth when courting and "influences the girl" in his behalf. The Isneg, Luzon, Philipines. (Vanoverbergh, 1938: 194)

Astarte, Attrt Goddess of love, of sex, of prostitution, who is associated with fertility and reproduction and the evening star, Venus. As the morning star she is a goddess of war. Canaan and Phoenicia, Near East. (Albright, 1956: 74–77; Jayne, 1962: 133; Moscati, 1960: 114; Oldenburg, 1969: 42–43; Langdon, 1931: 25; Ferm, 1950: 125–126)

Auseklis The goddess of love is also goddess of the morning star, of the dawn. Latvia. (Gimbutas, 1963: 199; 1975: XLC M126)

Baba, Bebi, Babai God of the phallus. Son of Osiris. Egypt. (Budge, 1969, 2: 91)

Baklum Chaam A Mayan phallic god, of the fertility of fields and animals. Yucatan, Mexico. (Bancroft, 1886, 3: 467; Larousse, 1968: 439)

Ba-neb-Tattu (Tettu), Ba-neb-Tet A phallic god and god of virility whose female counterpart is Hat-mehit and whose son is Heru-pa-khart. Egypt. (Budge, 1969, 2: 65)

Bangan The "goddess of romance"—daughter of Lumauwig and Bugan, sister of Obban. The Ibaloys of nothern Luzon, Philippines. (Jocano, 1969: 15)

Bayugin A god whose function "was to tempt women into a life of shame." The Tagalog, Philippines. (Jocano, 1969: 13)

Belili A very ancient Sumerian/Babylonian goddess of several functions—a goddess of love, of the moon, of trees, of the underworld. She is named as the consort of Alala. Near East. (Jastrow, 1898: 417; Sykes, 1952: 32–33)

Belphegor A god of "licentiousness and obscenity." Older name of Baal-Peor. The Moabites, Near East. (Woodcock, 1953: 25)

Bintang A benevolent goddess invoked in conjunction with love philters. The Dyaks, Sarawak, Borneo. (Sarawak Gazette, 1963: 130)

Butu-Ulisiwa A phallic god worshipped "as the cause of the fruitfulness of their women and the bestower of good fortune at sea and victory over their enemies." Ambon and Uliasa Islands, the Moluccas, Indonesia. (Hartland, 1925, 9: 818)

Ca-the-ña Goddess of love and of promiscuity among men and animals. The Mojave, Arizona. (Bourke, 1889: 186)

Chie "The goddess of sensual pleasure" transformed into an owl or the moon by Bochica. The Chibcha, Colombia. (Leach, 1949: 216)

Dian Masalanta The "goddess of lovers." Daughter of Anagolay and Dumakulem, sister of Apolake. The Tagalog, Philippines. (Jocano, 1969: 10)

rDo-rje rnal-'byor-ma Tibetan goddess of lust and sensuality, but she also represents "that which is conquered and transformed by meditation and insight." Same as Vajrayogini. (Sierksma, 1966: 143, 146, 158)

Dosojin A Shinto phallic god associated with agriculture. He is also a god of the road and of travel. Japan. (Hori, 1968: 66; Kato, 1926: 31)

Eja A phallic god and a god of agricultural fertility. He is also protective of men, their farms, and animals. The Ibo, Nigeria. (Hartland, 1925, 9: 821; Talbot, 1967: 80)

Eklinga A phallic god identified with Isvara. With Gauri the patrons of fertility ceremonies in Rajputana. India. (Crooke, 1925, 5: 5; Tod, 1920: 598)

Eros Greek god of love and sexuality, primarily associated with Aphrodite and sometimes given as her son. He is also called Phanes. As a very early primeval god, born from the egg laid by Nyx, he participates in the creation of the world and of the love and harmony of nature. (Kerényi, 1951: 71, 114; Murray, 1935: 190; Barthell, 1971: 7, 8, 222)

Erzulie, Erzilie Goddess of love and of femininity, she is also a goddess of sweet waters. She has numerous aspects and compound names. Haiti. West Indies. (Deren, 1953: 62, 143, 145; Simpson, 1945: 49; 1971: 510; Herskovits, 1937, 1: 316, 506; Marcelin, 1950: 88)

Eštar A Semitic astral goddess—Venus. An old Akkadian form of Ištar, she seems to also have the aspects of a goddess of sex and also of war. Near East. (Roberts, 1972: 39, 57, 60)

Fascinus A Roman phallic god, a guardian and protector of the home from evil influences and from illness. (Jayne, 1962: 421)

St. Foutin A bishop of Lyons worshipped by the Gauls as a phallic god invoked in impotence, to obtain offspring, and to cure sexual disease. (Hartland, 1925, 9: 817)

Freya, Freyja Goddess of love, of beauty, of fecundity—invoked in love affairs. Like her brother Frey she was associated with bountiful nature, with sunshine, rain, and harvest. She was also warlike and rode to battle, the leader of the Valkyries, claiming one-half of the slain warriors as her own in Folkvang, where faithful wives and maidens were also welcome. She was a Vanen, daughter of Njord. Her husband was Odr, who was the father of her daughters Hnoss and Gersemi. Scandinavia. (Guerber, 1895: 22, 124–128; Grimm, 1880: 304; MacCulloch, 1964: 120–123; Branston, 1955: 101, 132–133; Snorri Sturluson, 1964: 53; Turville-Petre, 1964: 159, 175–178)

Fricco Teutonic phallic god. (Schrader, 1925, 2: 51)

Frigg(a) A Scandinavian/Germanic goddess, wife of Odin, and mother of Baldur, Hermod, and Tyr. Daughter of Fiorgyn. She was goddess of the earth and fertility, of marriage and conjugal and motherly love. She shared Odin's seat, Hlidskialf, and so with him knew what was happening. In south Germany she was identified with Freya, but elsewhere was a separate, superior goddess. (Guerber, 1895: 42–477; Grimm, 1880: 299–304; Anderson, 1891: 236–237; Thorpe, 1851: 167, 231; Wagner, 1882: 6, 209; Branston, 1955: 88, 158)

Funado A phallic god associated with agriculture. Also a beneficent god of the roads, protective from evil spirits. Japan. (Kato, 1926: 31; Revon, 1925, 9: 237; Herbert, 1967: 495)

Gansam A phallic god associated with Devi as a pair, to whom offerings are made for the fertility of the earth mother. India. (Crooke, 1925, 5: 5)

Ghede A god of the dead and a god of copulation, a protector of children. "The idea of death as virile and fecund is found . . . in modern Haiti, where Ghede the god of the dead is a phallic corpse, 'both tomb and womb.' " West Indies. (Deren, 1953: 37–38; Sierksma, 1966: 205)

Guerlichon, Grelichon A phallic god at Bourges worshipped for children, to cure "impotence and sexual disease." Gaul. (Hartland, 1925, 9: 817)

Guignolet A phallic god worshipped at Brest for children, for "curing impotence and sexual disease." Gaul, (Hartland, 1925, 9: 817)

Hathor Goddess of love, of joy and the arts, of women and of childbirth. As a sky goddess she was the celestial cow, creatress of the heavens and the earth. She was also considered a goddess of the underworld and of the dead to whom she gave new life. Egypt. (Knight, 1915: 39; Ames, 1965: 76; Jayne, 1962: 58; Budge, 1969, 1: 93, 435)

Havea Lolofonua Goddess of "sexual intercourse" as well as a goddess of the underworld. Daughter of Piki and Kele, and twin of Taufulifonua. Tonga, Polynesia. (Gifford, 1924: 14, 152)

Hedone Personification of lust. Greece. (Roscher, 1965, 1, 2: 1873)

Hehaka "The Spirit of the Male Elk presided over sexual relationship." The Lakota and Oglala, South Dakota. (Walker, 1980: 121)

Heiséi The god of sickness and death is also a god of sexuality, controlling that aspect of life, particularly among men. He sends dreams and through them attempts to seduce. "In fact, he is sometimes designated as Father of Homosexuality." The Cagaba, Colombia. (Reichel-Dolmatoff, 1949/50: 90–91)

Herentas, Herentatis Oscan and Paelignian goddess of love and of voluptuousness, identified with Venus. Italy. (Cox, 1870, 2: 9; Schrader, 1925, 2: 37; Conway, 1925, 7: 458; Roscher, 1965, 1, 2: 2298)

Himeros Greek god of longing and desire, associated with Eros. (Cox, 1870, 2: 2; Kerényi, 1951: 69)

Hua-can-qui A "Priapic idol" to whom offerings are made of herbs and corn powder. Peru. (Bourke, 1892: 510)

Icelaca An omniscient phallic god, a round stone, before whom boys were circumcised and men made offerings of blood drawn from the genitals. Honduras. (Bancroft, 1886, 3: 506)

Inanna Sumerian goddess of love, procreation, and fertility, as well as of war. As the wife of Dumuzi she represents the renewal of vegetation and of life. Near East. (Kramer, 1967: 101, 103; James, 1960: 78; Jacobsen, 1970: 24, 27)

Inemes The widely worshipped goddess of love potions and love magic, of happiness. "She is the protectress of lechery." Her dances incite licentiousness. Mother of Ururupuin. Truk, Micronesia. (Bollig, 1927: 11, 38, 41)

Ishtar A goddess of wide characteristics and identified with the planet Venus. As the evening star and the daughter of Anu she is a "goddess of love and voluptuousness," of sacred prostitution. As the morning star she is a goddess of war and of hunting. She is also a goddess of fertility, of motherhood, and of healing. As the wife/sister/lover of Tammuz she represents the death and rebirth cycle of the seasons—in her descent to the netherworld in search of him, and in her return. In Anatolia she is known as Shaushka. Assyria, Babylonia, and Canaan, Near East. (Langdon, 1931: 21, 25; Jastrow, 1898: 83; Jayne, 1962: 122; Hooke, 1963: 39; Seligmann, 1948: 30; Frazer, 1960: 379; Larousse, 1968: 58; Ferm, 1950: 91; Sayce, 1898: 266–267; Oldenburg, 1969: 40)

Iwanaga-hime An "ancient phallic goddess," ugly daughter of Oyamatsumi, who would have given longevity to the Imperial Princes of Ninigi had he married her instead of her sister Konohana-no-Sakuyabime. Japan. (Yasumaro, 1965: 64; Holtom, 1938: 209; Anesaki, 1937: 233)

Iwaxan A fragrant male spirit who influences the girl whom a youth is courting. The Isneg, Luzon, Philippines. (Vanoverbergh, 1938: 195)

Ixcuina, Ycuina An Aztec goddess of carnality, of prostitutes and adulterers. Goddess of shame and immodesty. Wife of Mizuitlantecutli, god of hell. Same as Tlazoltéotl. Mexico. (Bancroft, 1886, 3: 383–385; Vaillant, 1962: 148)

Jahi The female personification of debauchery, of prostitution, of sin. Persia. (Hinnells, 1973: 56; Leach, 1950: 538)

Jarilo Slavic god of passion, of fecundity, of spring—when he appears—representing the power of vegetation, marries mother earth, fathers her many children, and then is buried in late summer. Russia. (Gimbutas, 1975: XLC M126)

Saint John A protective, benevolent deity of the Itá, "favorable to lovers." Brazil. (Wagley, 1964: 219, 223)

Kama God of love and lust and eroticism whose wives are "Trisha (passionate desire) and Rati (pleasure arising out of the satisfaction of desire)." Parentage ascribed to him—Laksmi and Narayana, Dharma and Sraddha—as the latter's son he represents "creative moral force." In the Atharvaveda he is a deity "who fulfils all desires," not just a god of love. India. (Banerjea, 1953: 53, 73; Ions, 1967: 29, 86, 88; Kramer, 1961: 308; Bhattacharji, 1970: 163; Macdonell, 1897: 120; Danielou, 1964: 99)

Kamakhya The "goddess of sexual desire" of the Doms; an aspect of Kali. India. (Briggs, 1953: 524, 594)

Kamesvari The goddess of lust. India. (Danielou, 1964: 266)

Kanikanihia A Hawaiian goddess of love. (Beckwith, 1932: 184)

Karaeng lowe A phallic god and a god of the sea who controls fortune, good and bad, as well as life and death. He is invoked for health, children, good harvests, and good fortune. Southern Celebes, Indonesia. (Kruijt, 1925, 7: 250; Hartland, 1925, 9: 818)

Kem A phallic god of West Africa. (Zabarowski, 1894: 328)

Kent A name of Qetesh. As Kent she forms a triad with Reshpu and Min or Amsu. Egypt. (Budge, 1969, 2: 280)

Kokopelli, Kokopele An ancient god, frequently a phallic figure, suggesting a deity of fertility. A katcina—male, Kokopeltiyo; female, Kokopelmana—as either still an erotic character. Pueblo Indians, Arizona and New Mexico. (Titiev, 1939: 91, 98; Hawley, 1937: 644–645)

Konsei-Daimyojin, Konsei Myojin A phallic god associated with agriculture. The deified phallus. Japan. (Kato, 1926: 31; Revon, 1925, 9: 239)

Koro God of desire, son of Hina-uri and Tinirau, associated "with dancing ceremonies and love-making." The Maori, New Zealand. (Hongi, 1920: 27; Mackenzie, n.d.: 336–337)

Krishna A god of love, both erotic and spiritual. The eighth avatar of Vishnu. India. (Ions, 1967: 61; Banerjea, 1953: 10, 58; Brown, 1961: 303; Bhattacharji, 1970: 302–313)

Kuan Chung "The God of Brothels." China. (Werner, 1932: 223)

Kunado A phallic god—"Originally a symbol of the procreative power, the phallus came to represent lusty animal vigour" and was used to magically "repel pestilence." Also a god of divination and of the crossroads, where he was invoked and consulted. Japan. (Aston, 1925, 11: 467; MacCulloch, 1925, 4: 334)

Kwiguka The god of lewdness. The Rundi, Burundi. (Meyer, 1916: 189)

Lada Slavic goddess of love, of marriage, and of spring. Lithuania, Poland, and Russia. (Ralston, 1872: 104–105; Czaplicka, 1925, 11: 593)

Laka Goddess of love, of fruitfulness, of the hula dance. Hawaii. (Beckwith, 1940: 185–186; Westervelt, 1963, 2: 74)

Lalita Goddess of amorousness. India. (Danielou, 1964: 266)

Legba A phallic god of sexual desires, but also representing "the cosmic phallus" as the bearer of life, of the creative power, to the earth. Mawu also sent him to man to intervene through accident with his destiny. Dahomey. (Deren, 1953: 96–97; Herskovits, 1937: 30–31; 1938, 2: 205; Williams, 1936: 165)

Lofn, Lofna A Scandinavian goddess of love and of marriage who had permission to bring together those whom obstacles had separated. (Wagner, 1882: 6; Anderson, 1891: 239; Snorri Sturluson, 1964: 59, 60)

Lono-iki-aweawe-aloha A god of love. Kauai, Hawaii. (Beckwith, 1940: 204)

Luamerava Goddess of desire, the "personification of lust—youngest concubine of Lumukanda." South Africa. (Mutwa, 1966: iii)

Lulong A benevolent goddess invoked in conjunction with love philters. She also makes men "invulnerable against the weapons of their enemies" and bestows upon women the talent for weaving. The Dyaks, Sarawak, Borneo. (Sarawak Gazette, 1963: 130, 136)

Madana Another name for Kama. India. (Bhattacharji, 1970: 163)

Madan Mohana A seductive form of Krishna— "he who intoxicates with desire." India. (Tod, 1920: 640–641)

Makani-kau, Makani-heoe The wind god is also a god of love. He reconciles young couples' quarrels. Hawaii. (Beckwith, 1940: 93; Westervelt, 1963, 3: 41)

Mama Quilla (Kilya) The moon was the goddess of love and of marriage and the protectress of women. She was important "in calculating time and regulating the Inca festival calendar." Peru. (Brinton, 1868: 132; Rowe, 1946, 2: 295)

Mandou-Ra A West African god of war and of voluptuousness. (Zabarowski, 1894: 328)

Mara The god of desire, of lust, of passion, of seductiveness. China and Tibet. (Sierksma, 1966: 209; Waddell, 1959: 344, 375; Werner, 1932: 307)

Mariana A goddess primarily of healing, but she is as well a goddess of love and of childbirth, and a protector of sailors. Belem, Brazil. (Leacock, 1972: 133–134)

Martea An Etruscan goddess of love and desire. Italy. (Leland, 1963: 49)

Meana, Mena, Merna A benevolent Etruscan goddess of love, of brides. Italy. (Leland, 1963: 131–132)

Medb, Medhbh A Celtic goddess of sexuality and licentiousness, a divine mother and earth goddess as well as a goddess of war. Ireland. (Ross, 1967: 223–224; MacCana, 1970: 85–86)

Metztli, Meztli The moon was the goddess of love, of marriage, and of childbirth. She had a malignant side as a "goddess of the night, the dampness, and the cold." Aztec, Mexico. (Brinton, 1868: 132; Bancroft, 1886, 3: 111; Spence, 1923: 309)

Minne Germanic goddess of love. (Campbell, 1968: 184, 191)

Muš A nocturnal demoness of sensuality, of covetousness. Iran. (Gray, 1930: 210)

Mutunus, Mutunus Tutunus A phallic god "whose name was derived from the male and female sexual organs (mutto and titus)." Rome. (Schrader, 1925, 2: 51; Hartland, 1925, 9: 816)

Nabia The mother of adultery and also a jaguar goddess. She is the mother of Namaku by Noánase. The Kogi, Colombia. (Reichel-Dolmatoff, 1949/50: 114; 1975: 57)

Napiwa The Old Man, a trickster, who was "especially associated with things obscene and pertaining to sexual immorality." The Blackfoot, Montana and Saskatchewan. (Wissler and Duvall, 1908: 2, 8, 11)

Ndauthina The god of adulterers was also god of seafarers, of fire, of light, of war. Fiji Islands, Melanesia. (Thomson, 1925, 6: 15; MacCulloch, 1925, 8: 50; Hocart, 1929: 196)

Niaimamau?u Wind Woman is lustful. She stole Dove's son and kept him prisoner for years. She "represents all that is lustful, possessive, and insatiable in woman." The Chemehuevi, California, Nevada, and Arizona. (Laird, 1976: 101, 158–159, 214)

Ninatta A Hittite goddess of love and matrimony, attendant of Shaushka. Asia Minor. (Ferm, 1950: 92; James, 1960: 96)

Ningo Baghiya A crop guardian—"the phallic tiger, to whom, when the grain is ripe, the first five handfuls . . . are offered." The Majhwars, Mirzapur, India. (Crooke, 1925, 5: 5)

Nin-imma A goddess who was "a deification of the female sexual organs." Near East. (Jacobsen, 1976: 113)

Oddudua Goddess of love and of maternity. Wife of Obatala and mother of Aganyu and Yemaya. Puerto Rico. West Indies. (Gonzalez-Wippler, 1975: 24, 100)

Oichi-hime The goddess of sexual attraction. Great First Princess. The name is a shortened form of Kamu-Oichi-hime, and another name for Ame-no-Uzume-no-Mikoto, the goddess of sex. She is "the phallic counterpart of Saruta-hiko," representing both human and agricultural fecundity. Japan. (Czaja, 1974: 253, 260–261)

Oshun Goddess of love, of coquetry, of luxury, and also of rivers and fresh waters. Cuba. In Puerto Rico she is also goddess of marriage. West Indies. (Verger, 1957: 411; Gonzalez-Wippler, 1975: 25–26, 113)

Paidia The personification of the erotic game. Greece. (Roscher, 1965, 3, 1: 1252)

Pamuri-mahse The "personification of a phallus that ejaculates, a new creator, sent by the Sun to populate the earth." He was also a giver of culture to the different tribes—their identifying objects. The Desana, Colombia. (Reichel-Dolmatoff, 1971: 25–27, 55)

P'an Chin-lien, P'an Kin-lien The goddess of prostitutes and of fornication. Kiangsu, China. (Maspero, 1963: 333; Leach, 1950: 842; Werner, 1932: 354; Larousse, 1968: 394)

Pantang Mayang A benevolent goddess invoked in conjunction with love philters. The Dyaks, Sarawak, Borneo. (Sarawak Gazette, 1963: 130)

Par A form of Amen-Ra, a phallic god. Egypt. (Budge, 1969, 2: 19)

Pasupati In Bali "Siwa as a phallic symbol." Indonesia. (Covarrubias, 1937: 317)

Peruda God of love and of procreation. The Tupi, Brazil. (Spence, 1925, 2: 837)

Saint Peter A local divinity of the Itá "favorable to lovers." Brazil. (Wagley, 1964: 223)

Pixee Pecala The god of love of the Valley Zapotec. Oaxaca, Mexico. (Whitecotton, 1977: 164)

Pizius, Lasicius Lithuanian god of coitus. (Schrader, 1925, 2: 32)

Pof "The god of women and love-making." Yap Island, the Carolines, Micronesia. (Christian, 1899: 385)

Popali A phallic and fertility spirit. The Cubeo, Colombia. (Zerries, 1968: 280)

Porde The personification of prostitution, of ill-fame. Greece. (Roscher, 1965, 3, 2: 2760)

Pothos A Greek god, the personification of love's yearning. (Roscher, 1965, 3, 2: 2903; Gardner, 1925, 9: 794)

Priapos, Priapus A Greek/Roman phallic god of the fertility of fields and herds. (Kerényi, 1951: 176; Murray, 1935: 148–149; Larousse, 1968: 161)

Pulleyar A phallic god, of sexuality, of the fertility of humans, cattle, crops. Same as Ganesha. Ceylon. (Leach, 1958: 309–311)

Qetesh A Syrian moon goddess and goddess of love and licentiousness, also of beauty. Introduced into Egypt. (Knight, 1915: 101–102; Budge, 1969, 2: 279–280)

Rangda A manifestation of Durga, sexually obvious and lustful, associated with potions and charms and black magic relating to love. Bali, Indonesia. (Grader, 1969, 1: 155–156)

Rati Goddess of sexual pleasure, of lust. A wife of Kama. Her "name also designates female seed." India and Bali (Banerjea, 1953: 73; Danielou, 1964: 263; Friederich, 1959: 52; Ions, 1967: 96; O'Flaherty, 1980: 39, 178)

Sae-no-Kami A phallic god associated with agriculture. Also a god of roads. Japan. (Kato, 1926: 31; Holtom, 1938: 208)

Sakti Hindu goddess of lust and enjoyment as well as destruction. Consort of Siva. India. (Danielou, 1964: 263; Sarma, 1953: 10)

Saruta-hiko A phallic god associated with agriculture and also with the crossroads. He is also a god of luck. Japan. Same as Dosojin. (MacCulloch, 1925, 4: 332; Kato, 1926: 31; Holtom, 1938: 183)

Seishin A name of Dosojin as a "Deity of Sex." Japan. (Czaja, 1974: 51)

Shaushka Hittite/Hurrian goddess of love, of sexual life, and of warfare. Sister of Teshub. Same as Ishtar. Asia Minor. (James, 1960: 96; Akurgal, 1969: 266; Guterbock, 1961: 168)

Siofn, Sjofn A Scandinavian goddess of love, of lovers. (Thorpe, 1851: 35; Anderson, 1891: 238–239; Stern, 1898: 98; Turville-Petre, 1964: 189)

Siva In his phallic aspect he represents the creative principle in all its facets, a god of fertility of all things, whose symbolic animal is the bull. He represents the destructive/creative, death/life cycles of all recurring forms. India, Bali, and Cambodia. In Cambodia he never has the destructive aspect, only the creative concept carried from the sexual to the highest creative symbolism. (Martin, 1914: 168–171; Banerjea, 1953: 61–64; Danielou, 1964: 192; Schoeps, 1961: 162; Whitehead, 1916: 17; Marchal, 1963: 210–211; Goris, 1960, 2: 123)

Soitayax A beautiful woman who is the "love spirit." The Matako, Argentina. (Métraux, 1939: 90)

Sulmanitu A goddess of love and war. Near East. (Albright, 1968: 150)

Tagabayan The "dangerous goddess who incites incest and adultery." The Manobo, Mindanao, Philippines. (Jocano, 1969: 23)

Ta-Pepu A god of prostitution, of lust. The Marquesas, Polynesia. (Christian, 1895: 190)

Tatanka The Buffalo God "controls all affairs of love"—the love/hate emotions of both men and animals. The Lakota, South Dakota. (Walker, 1980: 67, 197)

Taufulifonua A god, twin/husband of Havea Lolofonua. They introduced sexual intercourse. Son of Piki and Kele. Tonga, Polynesia. (Gifford, 1924: 14; Moulton, 1925, 12: 379)

Ters A Gallic phallic god. Antwerp, Belgium. (Hartland, 1925, 9: 817)

Tlazoltéotl Goddess of love, of lust and carnality, patron of prostitutes. Yet, as goddess of and devourer of filth, she consumed men's sins and performed an act of purification. Aztec, Mexico. (Vaillant, 1962: 146; Nicholson, 1967: 113; Caso, 1958: 55–56; Alexander, 1920: 54, 78; Spence, 1923: 165, 168)

Todlay God of love and marriage whose wife is Todlibun. The Bagobo and Bukidnon, Philippines. (Benedict, 1916: 29; Jocano, 1969: 24)

Trisha A Vedic goddess, one of the wives of Kama, denoting "passionate desire." India. (Banerjea, 1953: 73)

Tuete God of licentiousness. Tahiti, Polynesia. (Henry, 1928: 380)

Tunkan Ingan A god of sex of the Dakota Plains Indians. United States and Canada. (Burland, 1965: 149)

Uruhú Father of Sodomy. The Cagaba and the Kogi, Colombia. (Reichel-Dolmatoff, 1949/50: 115)

Ururupuin "Night flirt"—A daughter of Inemes whose characteristics and morals she shares. Truk, Micronesia. (Bollig, 1927: 11)

Vai-mahse The Master of Animals is "a phallic being in charge of the fertility of the game animals." He is a god of hunting and fishing. He is sexually aggressive and dangerous to women, particularly in childbirth. The family must be protected by the shaman. The Desana and the Tukano, Colombia. (Reichel-Dolmatoff, 1971: 51, 80–85; 1975: 83–89)

Vajrayogini A goddess of lust and sensuality. Tibetan name is rDo-rje rnal-'byor-ma. (Sierksma, 1966: 142–146)

Varen Iranian demon of lust. Son of Ahriman. (Gray, 1930: 216)

Venus As an ancient Italian deity she was a goddess of vegetation and markets. As a Roman goddess she became a goddess of love, of beauty. (Fairbanks, 1907: 207–212; Hadas, 1965: 124; Bulfinch, 1898: 9)

Vereno Zoroastrian demon of Lust. Persia. (Seligmann, 1948: 39)

Vjofn A Teutonic goddess, attendant of Frigga, whose "duty was to incline obdurate hearts to love," to foster peace and reconciliation among men and in marriages. (Guerber, 1895: 52)

Wunsch Teutonic god of love and bliss, the bringer of all good things to men, a god of fortune. (Grimm, 1888: 1328; de Kay, 1898: 22)

Xnathaiti Iranian goddess of lust, of lasciviousness. (Gray, 1930: 218, 226)

Xochiquetzal Aztec goddess of love and of sexual pleasure, the "patroness of the unmarried women who lived with the young bachelor warriors." She was also the goddess of flowers and of young growth, of corn and of fertility, of pleasure and the arts. Mexico. (Spence, 1923: 154, 195; Brinton, 1868: 138; Alexander, 1920: 77–78; Caso, 1958: 26, 29; Neumann, 1955: 196–197; Duran, 1971: 296)

Xochitecatl A Tlascalan goddess of "sensual delights." Mexico. (Bancroft, 1886, 3: 506)

Xopancalehuey Tlalloc A god of spring who was considered a phallic god. Mexico. (Bancroft, 1886, 3: 505)

Yachimata-hiko A beneficent phallic god associated with agriculture and with the crossroads, where he protects travelers and wards off evil spirits. Japan. (MacCulloch, 1925, 4: 332; Kato, 1926: 31; Revon, 1925, 9: 237)

Yachimata-hime A beneficent phallic goddess of travel and of the crossroads who protects travelers from evil spirits. Also associated with agriculture and Dionysian festivals. Japan. (Kato, 1926: 31; Revon, 1925, 9: 237; MacCulloch, 1925, 4: 332)

Yum, Yumni, Yamni The Whirlwind is the god of love, and of pleasures—games, dancing, chance—but he is fickle. The Lakota, South Dakota. (Walker, 1980: 51–54)

45

Gods of Marriage

Ababa A goddess of Nigeria, the protector of marriage. (Talbot, 1967: 120)

Achraelbonga A benevolent god who watches over married women. The Mundas, India. (Crooke, 1925, 9: 2)

Afferenda Roman goddess of the dowry. (Roscher, 1965, 2, 1: 190)

Aida Wedo A goddess of the rainbow and of fresh waters, symbolized by the snake, placated before a marriage. Wife of Damballa. Haiti. West Indies. (Herskovits, 1937: 111, 316; Verger, 1957: 235)

a kung rum "One of the four creators of female beings" who is invoked in marriage ceremonies for prosperity and children. The Lepchas, Sikkim. (Siiger, 1967, 1: 141; 1967, 2: 69, 74)

Bara Kumba With Rani Kajhal a pair of tree deities worshipped for the fertility of the earth mother and invoked at marriage rites. The Pabras, India. (Crooke, 1925, 5: 5)

Bar Devata A deity of marriage. The Ahir, United Provinces, India. (Crooke, 1925, 1: 233)

Bhagavathi A goddess worshipped at marriage ceremonies on the fourth day. The Kshatriya, India. (Thurston, 1909, 4: 87)

Bharkodev A deity worshipped on the first day of the marriage ceremonies with offerings of fruit, etc., and the sacrifice of a goat. The Khatri, India. (Thurston, 1909, 3: 282)

Birappa A god who receives the first portion of betel leaves and areca nuts at the beginning of marriage ceremonies. The Kuruba, India. (Thurston, 1909, 4: 143)

Brahm Devata A god presiding over marriage, "representing the great Hindu god Brahma." The Ahir, United Provinces, India. (Crooke, 1925, 1: 233)

Chhappan Deo "A very curious deity . . . worshipped by a man when his wife has run away." Central Provinces, India. (Russell, 1925, 3: 314)

Chieh Lin, Yüeh Lao A god of marriage, associated with the moon, "who arranges all matrimonial affairs" including the decision as to the partners in the union, which he records. China. (Williams, 1976: 78, 270, 279)

cho rum A god invoked at wedding ceremonies to protect the couple. The Lepchas, Sikkim. (Siiger, 1967, 2: 78–79)

Ch'uang Kung With Ch'uang Mu (Po), god and goddess of the marriage bed. China. (Maspero, 1963: 296; Day, 1940: 93)

Ch'uang Mu (Po) The goddess of the marriage bed. China. (Maspero, 1963: 296; Day, 1940: 93)

Cinxia A minor Roman deity who "loosened the bride's girdle after marriage." (Ferguson, 1970: 68; Jayne, 1962: 494)

Cupra Etruscan goddess of marriage and of women, corresponding to Juno. Italy. (Leland, 1963: xxvi)

Damubir A deified Kahar to whom offerings are made "at marriages, during the harvest time, and when illness or disaster threatens the household." The Kahar, Bengal. (Crooke, 1925, 7: 636)

Dhagbairu The god of new brides and a household god. The Himalayas, India. (Berreman, 1963: 374)

Dhorom, Thakur Jiu The supreme diety and creator is invoked in marriage ceremonies. The Santals, India. (Mukherjea, 1962: 33, 273)

Domiducus A minor Roman deity who delivers the bride to the groom's home. (Dumézil, 1966, 1: 34; Jayne, 1962: 497)

Domitius A god of the wedding night who installs the bride in the house of the groom and keeps her there. Rome. (Dumézil, 1966, 1: 34; Roscher, 1965, 2, 1: 197)

Dosojin As a god of fecundity he is worshipped for marriages, offspring, and a happy sex life. Japan. (Czaja, 1974: 47)

Duad-lerwuan, Duadlera The supreme god and creator is the guardian of marriages. His wife is Duan-luteh. Kei Archipelago, Indonesia. (Frazer, 1926: 663, 665)

Dulha Deo A Dravidian god of the engagement, of bridegrooms, of marriage. He is also a household god associated with the hearth. India. (Crooke, 1894: 75; Elwin, 1939: 60; Russell, 1916, 2: 496, 506)

Dzidzielia Slavic goddess of marriage and of fertility. (Czaplicka, 1925, 11: 594)

En-musubi Dosojin regarded as a deity of matchmaking. Japan. (Czaja, 1974: 51)

Frey God of love and marriage, of fertility and fruitfulness, of peace and plenty, of summer and sunshine and rain. His wife is Gerda, and sister is Freya. He is the son of Njord and Skadi. Scandinavian and Teutonic countries. (Wagner, 1882: 189, 199, 204; Stern, 1898: 44; Davidson, 1964: 19, 96; Guerber, 1895: 112–122)

Gekka-o The god of marriage. Japan. (Leach, 1949: 444)

Gomaj "Their principal deities are the Sun and Moon, both of whom . . . they call Gomaj, which is also the general word for a god." He is invoked at marriages. The Korkus, Central Provinces, and the Berar, India. (Frazer, 1926: 616)

Harda, Hardaul A god of weddings in Bundelkhand. He is believed able to avert bad weather at the ceremony. India. (Crooke, 1894: 88; Martin, 1914: 256–257; Russell, 1916, 4: 81–82)

Hera Greek and Cretan goddess of women and marriage, of fertility, maternity, and childbirth. She was a wife of Zeus and mother of Hebe, Ares, Eileithyia, and Hephaistos, and the daughter of Cronos and Rhea. She was early a goddess of the sky, of the atmosphere, and of storms. (Cox, 1870, 2: 10, 12; Jayne, 1962: 328; Fairbanks, 1907: 44, 101; Willetts, 1962: 252; Kerényi, 1951: 22, 98; Barthell, 1971: 19)

Ho Ho Êrh Shêng The "two fairies of peace and harmony," T'ien Lung, "Heaven Deaf," and Ti Ya, "Earth Dumb," who are "symbols of shrewd business acumen in partnership, also of mutual affection in marital partnership." Invoked particularly at wedding ceremonies. China. (Day, 1940: 91–92)

Hsi Ch'ih Wang Mu Goddess of brides and patroness of the lives of women. China. (Day, 1940: 92, 94)

Hung Luan Hsing Chün A star goddess "closely associated with engagements and weddings." China. (Day, 1940: 92)

Hymen, Hymenaios Greek/Roman god of marriage. Son of Aphrodite and Dionysus. (Roscher, 1965, 1, 2: 2800; Murray, 1935: 195; Barthell, 1971: 32, 219)

Iuga, Iugalis A minor Roman deity who "originated the marriage bond and carried the courting to engagement." (Jayne, 1962: 498)

Iugatinus Roman god of marriage, invoked at the close of the ceremony. (Jayne, 1962: 498; Roscher, 1965, 2, 1: 200)

Jumon-ava Finno-Ugric goddess of marriage and of childbirth. The Cheremis, Russia. (MacCulloch, 1964: 258)

Juno Roman/Etruscan goddess of marriage and of women, guardian of females from birth to death; associated with the moon. As Juno Lucina she was goddess of childbirth; as Juno Lanuvina, goddess of conception. (Jayne, 1962: 424; Fairbanks, 1907: 102–103; Cox, 1870, 2: 13; Hadas, 1965: 124; Larousse, 1965: 204)

Kaldyni-mumas Finno-Ugric goddess of fertility, invoked for children and a happy marriage. The Votiak, Ural Mountains, Russia and Siberia. (MacCulloch, 1964: 258)

kăm si thing God of marriage of the Lepchas. Sikkim. (Siiger, 1967: 142)

Khetla A malicious god who is appeased at marriage ceremonies. India. (Ruhela, 1971: 50)

ki lo One of the creators of females who is invoked in marriage ceremonies. The Lepchas, Sikkim. (Siiger, 1967: 69, 142)

Kul-Devi A household goddess who is worshipped at weddings. India. (Russell, 1916, 2: 483)

Kushinada hime Goddess of marriage. Idzumo, Japan. (Casanowicz, 1926: 1)

Lada Slavic goddess of love and of the spring and, with Lado, personifies marriage and happiness. Russia, Lithuania. (Ralston, 1872: 104–105; Bray, 1935: 44)

Lado A name of the sun god who personified the bridegroom and was a god of marriage and of happiness. Lithuania and Russia. (Ralston, 1872: 104–105; Bray, 1935: 44)

Laima The goddess of fate is also a goddess of women, of childbirth, protector of young girls and their chastity. As a goddess of marriage she is invoked for a good husband. Latvia and Lithuania. (Jonval, 1929: 18–21; Gimbutas, 1963: 197)

Lemilah The "god of conjugal happiness of the youth." The Abkhasians, Caucasus. (Janashia, 1937: 129)

Lofn, Lofna A Scandinavian goddess of marriage and favorable to lovers whose difficulties she has permission to overcome. (Branston, 1955: 153; Snorri Sturluson, 1964: 59, 60; Anderson, 1891: 239; Wagner, 1882: 6)

Ka longkha The goddess of marriage. The Khasi, Assam. (Stegmiller, 1921: 410)

Magbabáya minúmsöb He "oversees married couples" with his grandson Malibotan. The Bukidnon, Mindanao, Philippines. (Cole, 1956: 95)

mǎ la A god invoked in wedding ceremonies—one of the creators of female beings. The Lepchas, Sikkim. (Siiger, 1967: 69, 143)

Malibotan Grandson of Magbábaya minúmsöb. Together they "oversee(s) married couples." The Bukidnon, Mindanao, Philippines. (Cole, 1956: 95)

Mama Quilla Goddess of love and of marriage, protective of women and babies. Goddess of the moon and sister/wife of Inti, the sun. Peru. (Brinton, 1868: 132; Rowe, 1946, 2: 205)

Manturna Goddess of the wedding night, with the power to keep the bride with the groom. Roman. (Dumézil, 1966, 1: 34; Roscher, 1965, 2, 1: 203)

Mas, Mar, Maso Etruscan god of marriage, of matrimony, of virility. He was an early god of nature, of crops, and of harvest. Italy. (Leland, 1963: 49–51)

Matrona A name of Juno as a goddess of marriage. Rome. (Patai, 1967: 167)

Meztli, Tecciztecatl As goddess of the moon, she takes on the additional aspects of a goddess of love and marriage and of childbirth. Aztec, Mexico. (Brinton, 1868: 132; Burland, 1967: ix; Bancroft, 1886, 3: 111)

Na Rip Nom A goddess who, with Tarbong-bo and Komsithing, originated marriage. The Lepchas, Sikkim. (Gorer, 1938: 336, 482)

Ninatta A Hittite deity, an attendant of Shaushka and associated with marriage and love. Asia Minor. (Ferm, 1950: 92; James, 1960: 96)

Nü-kua A goddess of marriage of the Han period, of human/serpent form. Creatress of men. Wife or sister of Fu-hsi. China. (Bodde, 1961: 386–389)

Nü Wa "Goddess of Go-betweens, or Arrangers of Marriage," whose mother is Chu-ying, whose father is Shui Ching-tzǔ, and whose brother is Fu Hsi. China. (Werner, 1932: 334)

Okuninushi A powerful benevolent god, developer of the land, god and teacher of medicine, a god of marriage and of good fortune. Japan. (Yasumaro, 1965: 48; Bunce, 1955: 134; Holtom, 1938: 81, 203; Herbert, 1967: 319, 349)

Oshun The goddess of marriage and of love, invoked in difficult childbirth. Puerto Rico, West Indies. (Gonzalez-Wippler, 1975: 25, 26, 113, 115)

Osibi Keiwurra A yam god at Oburukpon who is also associated with marriages. Cross River, Nigeria. (Mockler-Ferryman, 1925, 9: 280)

Ot A benevolent goddess of fire whose warmth is protective of existence. She is "invoked at marriage ceremonies." The Khahass and the Mongols, Siberia. (Queval, 1968: 116; Larousse, 1973: 435)

Pachagara Deo A god associated with the distribution of the marriage cakes. A god by whom a truth is sworn. Central Provinces, India. (Russell, 1916, 3: 442)

Pandaisia Greek personification of the wedding feast. (Roscher, 1965, 3, 1: 1497)

Perfica A minor Roman deity, goddess of coition. (Jayne, 1962: 496)

Pertunda A minor Roman deity, a goddess of coition on the marriage night. (Dumézil, 1966, 1: 34; Jayne, 1962: 496)

Picumnus Roman god of matrimony and of the development and growth of the child. Twin of Pilumnus. He was also a god of agriculture, of the fertilizing of the land with manure. (Jayne, 1962: 436; Larousse, 1968: 154, 220; Murray, 1935: 154; Dumézil, 1966, 2: 616)

Piszius Sacrifices were made to him when the bride was brought to the groom. Lithuania. (Schrader, 1925, 2: 51)

Prema A Roman goddess who makes the bride submissive on the marriage night. (Dumézil, 1966, 1: 34; Jayne, 1962: 496)

Pudicitia Goddess of marital chastity and purity. Rome. (Carter, 1925, 9: 798; Larousse, 1968: 216)

Raghunath A village god, protector of marriages. Associated with Parasu Ram and Bhairu. The Himalayas, India. (Berreman, 1963: 376)

Rani Kajhal With Bara Kumba, tree deities worshipped for the fertility of the earth mother and invoked at marriage rites. The Pavras, India. (Crooke, 1925, 5: 5)

Ratih With Smara, honored with hymns at weddings. Bali, Indonesia. (Hooykaas, 1964: 48)

Renuka At the marriage ceremony "a special prayer is offered to the deity Renuka, and the boy is invested with a necklace of cowries by five married men of the caste. Till this has been done he is not considered to be a proper Gondhali." Central Provinces, India. (Russell, 1916, 3: 145)

säng lo A god invoked in marriage ceremonies—"one of the four creators of female beings." The Lepchas, Sikkim. (Siiger, 1967: 69, 144)

San Shih Ju-Lai "Buddha of the Three Worlds" invoked at weddings, funerals. China. (Day, 1940: 30, 140)

Satya-Narayana, Satyapir A festival or offering is made to him on the occasion of a marriage. India. (Punekar, 1959: 199)

Selket, Selqet, Serqet The scorpion goddess is a "guardian of conjugal union." A major function of hers is

as a protector of the dead in the ceremony of embalming, where she is associated with Qebhsennuf in guarding the Canopic Jars. Egypt. (Casson, 1965: 97, 114; Larousse, 1968: 39, 40; Budge, 1969, 1: 456)

Shuang Hsien One of the gods of marriage who is concerned with "mutual concord." China. (Williams, 1976: 270)

Simadia Dev "A red-coloured stone . . . is worshipped at marriages." Gujarat, India. (Crooke, 1925, 11: 872)

Si-rapan A female spirit who is influential in maintaining harmony within a marriage. The Isneg of Luzon, Philippines. (Vanoverbergh, 1938: 216)

Sisina A female spirit to whom offerings are made before a wedding for the protection of the young couple to see that all is harmonious. The Isneg, Luzon, Philippines. (Vanoverbergh, 1938: 207)

Smara The god of love (a name of Kama), honored with Ratih with offerings of hymns at weddings. Bali, Indonesia. (Hooykaas, 1964: 48)

Subigus A Roman god of the marriage night. (Jayne, 1962: 496; Dumézil, 1966, 1: 34)

Syzygia A name of Hera as the union in marriage. Greece. (Roscher, 1965, 4: 1646)

Tahu-mata-nui The "god of marriage and concubinage." The Marquesas, Polynesia. (Christian, 1895: 190)

tak bo rum A great god invoked at wedding ceremonies for the couple—"to abide with them and to help them." The Lepchas, Sikkim. (Siiger, 1967, 2: 78–79)

Talassio An Etruscan/Roman deity invoked as the bride is taken to the groom's house. Italy. (Roscher, 1965, 5: 16; Prentice Hall, 1965: 136)

Tarbong-bo God of marriage, husband of Na Rip Rom and son of Itpomu. The Lepchas, Sikkim. (Gorer, 1938: 225; Siiger, 1967: 145)

Thovele, Thovela A benevolent god protective of marriages and of pregnancy as well as of traveling strangers. The Bawenda, South Africa. (Wessman, 1908: 80; Hartland, 1925, 2: 364; Willoughby, 1932: 41)

T'ien Lung "Heaven Deaf." One of the "two fairies of peace and harmony . . . symbols of shrewd business acumen in partnership, also of mutual affection in marital partnership." They are invoked particularly at wedding ceremonies. With Ti Ya jointly known as Ho Ho Êrh Shêng. China. (Day, 1940: 91, 92)

Ti Ya "Earth Dumb," with the same information as T'ien Lung above.

Todlay God of marriage and of love and creator of the male sex. His wife is Todlibon. The Bagoba, Philippines. (Benedict, 1916: 29; Jocano, 1969: 24)

Todlibon Goddess of marriage and wife of Todlay, "yet a goddess ever-virgin." The Bagobo, Philippines. (Benedict, 1916: 29; Jocano, 1969: 24)

Unxia A Roman goddess "who was concerned with the anointing of the bridegroom's door." (Ferguson, 1970: 68; Roscher, 1965, 2, 1: 228)

Vadhi Devata The "god of increase" to whom offerings are made at marriages. The Banjara in Kathiawar, India. (Crooke, 1925, 2: 347)

Virginensis A goddess whose function on the marriage night was "to undo the virgin's girdle." Rome. (Dumézil, 1966, 1: 34; Jayne, 1962: 499)

Vör An omniscient goddess of wisdom and knowledge as well as a goddess of betrothals and marriages, protective of the vows. Scandinavia. (Thorpe, 1951: 35; Anderson, 1891: 461; Grimm, 1880: 310)

Zeus Among his many aspects he appears as a god of marriage, reflecting also the principle of paternity, to be bestowed on all womanhood, not only upon his wives but other alliances. These latter include: (1) Metis, mother of Athena, (2) Themis, mother of the Horae and the Morae, (3) Eurynome, an Oceanid, mother of the Graces (the Charities), (4) Demeter, mother of Persephone, (5) Mnemosyne, mother of the Muses, (6) Leto, mother of Apollo and Artemis, (7) Hera, mother of Hebe, Ares, Eileithyia, (8) Maia, mother of Hermes, (9) Semele, mother of Dionysus, and (10) Alcmene, mother of Heracles. Of these, Hera and Demeter were also his sisters. Greece. (Kerényi, 1951: 158; Hesiod-Brown, 1981: 78–80; Barthell, 1971: 19, 38, 216; Fairbanks, 1907: 88, 93; Larousse, 1968: 98, 105; Morford and Lenardon, 1975: 24, 55–59, 92–93)

46

Medicine and Health:
Body, Healing, Herbs, Senses

'Abd el-Qader el-Djilani, 'Abdlqader A jinn saint, consulted in nervous disorders and epilepsy, to whom offerings were made for healing; invoked for children. Morocco. (Basset, 1920: 91, 108; Westermarck, 1920: 85)

Abinnana A deity of the Sinhalese healing rituals. Ceylon. (Yalman, 1964: 145)

Abowie A goddess of healing capable of curing sterility. She also helps to gain prosperity. The Effutu, Ghana. (Wyllie, 1966: 478)

Acheloos Greek river god and god of fresh-water springs, associated with their hygienic qualities and with health. (Thramer, 1925, 6: 548)

Ada A goddess through whom strength is given. Iran. (Gray, 1930: 130)

Addus A Celtic god associated with health. Gaul. (Jayne, 1962: 519)

Adukganna Hulawali Yaka A spirit believed to be able to heal them in illness. The Vedda, Ceylon. (Seligmann and Seligmann, 1911: 177)

Aesculapius, Asklepios Greek/Roman god of medicine and healing, of physicians. Son of Apollo and father of Epione and Hygieia. (Fairbanks, 1907: 222-224; Cox, 1870, 2: 36; Schoeps, 1961: 128; Dumézil, 1966, 2: 443-444; Murray, 1935: 205; Kerényi, 1951: 142, 144)

Agassou Gnenin A very powerful god of sweet waters and of healing, represented by a crab. Identified with St. Esprit or St. Augustin. Haiti, West Indies. (Marcelin, 1950: 127)

Agenoria A minor Roman goddess who "bestowed the power of reaction to stimulation." (Jayne, 1962: 497; Roscher, 1965, 1, 1: 104)

Ageve Edutzi God of health. The Takanan and Araona, Bolivia. (Métraux, 1942: 41)

Agwe Woyo One of the group of Rada deities who can bestow the knowledge of healing. A god of the sea. Haiti. West Indies. (Herskovits, 1937: 151, 317)

Agwù-Nsị A Spirit providing knowledge of herbs and roots for curing disease, as well as materials for combining to make charms. The Igbo, Nigeria. (Isichei, 1978: 322, 334)

Ahau Chamahes A god of medicine. Mayan, Central America. (Tozzer, 1941: 155; Bancroft, 1886, 2: 697)

Aialila'axa A goddess who wakens man from sleep, who intervenes when man is threatened with sickness and death. Also a guardian of the moon. The Bella Coola, British Columbia. (Boas, 1898: 31)

Aigle Goddess of light, of moonlight, daughter of Helios and Neaira. That she is named as "a daughter of Asklepios seems to be due to the affinity between the ideas of health and light"—as such she is included with deities of health, of healing. Greece. (Kerényi, 1951: 193; Thramer, 1925, 6: 552)

A-i-kon The dream god whose Feast of Dreams was held in midwinter. He announced the commands of Tha-ron-hya-wa-kon. The Iroquois, Eastern United States. (Hewitt, 1895: 111)

Airmed, Airmid A goddess of medicine associated with herbs and with healing incantations. Daughter of

Diancecht. Ireland. (Squire, 1906: 62; Jayne, 1962: 514; MacCulloch, 1911: 77)

Airyaman   An Iranian solar god and a god of healing. (Jayne, 1962: 188; Gray, 1930: 132)

Aitupuai   A goddess of healing and also a war goddess. Society Islands, Polynesia. (Henry, 1928: 145, 375)

Aizan   A god of the water and a deity of the Rada group, who bestow the knowledge of healing. Haiti. West Indies. (Herskovits, 1937: 151, 316)

Aja   A beneficent Yoruban goddess of the forests who teaches the medicinal qualities of herbs. Nigeria. (Lucas, 1948: 153; Mockler-Ferryman, 1925, 9: 280)

Akasi   A "god of health and sickness." The Zambal, Philippines. (Jocano, 1969: 14)

Akesis   A god of medicine and healing at Epidauros. Greece. (Roscher, 1965, 1, 1: 210)

Akeso   A goddess of healing, daughter of Asklepios, associated with Panakeia and Iaso. Greece. (Thramer, 1925, 6: 551; Roscher, 1965, 1, 1: 210)

'Alahtin   The goddess of the moon is invoked for "good health and good fortune." The Chumash, California. (Hudson and Underhay, 1978: 76; Blackburn, 1975: 37)

Alexida   A Greek goddess who could ward off epilepsy. Daughter of Amphiaraos. (Roscher, 1965, 1, 1: 230)

Alog   A god invoked in "fever." The Ifugao, Philippines. (Barton, 1946: 68)

Alut nuwara bandara   A deity of the Sinhalese healing rituals. Ceylon. (Yalman, 1964: 145)

Amakarasa   A culture hero type who taught "curative and cleansing" rites. The Kalabari, Nigeria. (Horton, 1960: 17)

Amphiaraos   A mortal given immortality by Zeus; a god of divination and oracles with powers of healing. Greece. (Thramer, 1925, 6: 545; Jayne, 1962: 304–305)

Senhora Ana   An elderly and humble goddess of the Preto Velho line of gods who are "gifted curers." Belem, Brazil. (Leacock, 1964: 156)

Andiodotra   A deity invoked in making sacrifices regarding illness, also in making of vows. The Tanala, Madagascar. (Linton, 1933: 194)

Andranofalafa   A god of the Tanala invoked in illness. Madagascar. (Linton, 1933: 192)

Anextiomarus   A Celtic deity "equated with Apollo . . . as a god of healing." Britain and Gaul. (MacCulloch, 1911: 125)

Angina   A goddess who was the personification "of sore throat, supposed to have been quinsy, was invoked for its cure." Italy. (Jayne, 1962: 461)

Angitia   An ancient Italian goddess of healing skillful in the use of medicinal plants and of charms, particularly in snake-bite. (Conway, 1925, 7: 458; Jayne, 1962: 417)

Anna Perenna   The goddess of the year also "came to be regarded as the giver of health and plenty." Italy. (Jayne, 1962: 418)

Anqet, Anuqet   A Nubian/Egyptian goddess of life and of health. She was also a Nile goddess at Elephantine. (Budge, 1969, 2: 50, 58; Jayne, 1962: 53; Ames, 1965: 108)

Antonio Luiz Corre-Beirado   A lesser god interested in a good time, who appears in curing ceremonies only. Belem, Brazil. (Leacock, 1972: 157, 162)

Apipatle   The spirit of sleep who "is fond of the dead" and allows them to appear in dreams. The Iglulik Eskimo, Canada. (Nungak and Arima, 1969: 122)

Apollo   His Greek nature was that of a god of the sun, of light; of arts and prophecy through which he revealed Zeus' will; of healing and of sudden death—he would cause plague and death as well as deliver from them. Son of Zeus (Jupiter) and Leto (Latona), twin of Artemis (Diana), and father of Aesculapius. In Rome and Gaul he was primarily a god of healing and of prophecy. (Schoeps, 1962: 128; Kerényi, 1951: 35; Dumézil, 1966, 2: 442; Bertrand, 1897: 327; Barthell, 1971: 24–26; Jayne, 1962: 223, 306; Fairbanks, 1907: 119)

Saint Apolonia   A benevolent goddess, "patroness of teeth," invoked in toothaches. Ita, Brazil. (Wagley, 1964: 219, 223)

Aranya, Jamai Sashthi   A goddess "who ensures the health of children and cures barrenness." Bengal. (Crooke, 1925, 2: 487)

Aristaios   An ancient Greek god, son of Apollo and Kyrene, who besides being a god of agriculture and of herds, was also a god of "the arts of medicine and divination" given to him by the Muses. (Thramer, 1925, 6: 546; Jayne, 1962: 310; Kerényi, 1951: 142)

Aroni A god of medicine and of the forest, both malevolent and benevolent, who when confronted boldly will initiate men into the arts of healing. The Yoruba, Nigeria. In Brazil he is also a god of herbs. (Lucas, 1948: 155; Mockler-Ferryman, 1925, 9: 280; Greenberg, 1946: 58; Verger, 1957: 231; Gonzalez-Wippler, 1975: 2, 26)

Arvalus A god equated with Apollo as a god of healing. The Brythons. In Gaul equated with Saturn. (MacCulloch, 1911: 47, 125)

Ashade A god of medicinal plants. Haiti. West Indies. (Marcelin, 1950: 71)

The Asvins Dasra and Nasatya, the "physicians of the gods," bestowers of health and of human and agricultural fertility and abundance. They are solar gods associated with the dawn, sons of Samjna and Surya, and the husbands of Suryā. India. (Bhattacharji, 1970: 236–248; Danielou, 1964: 128–129; Martin, 1914: 36; Jayne, 1962: 163–164)

Atua Lasi A god invoked for health, who controlled disease and epidemics. Tikopia, Polynesia. (Firth, 1967, 2: 288, 291)

Auschauts, Auschkaut Baltic serpent god and a god of healing and fertility. (Puhvel, 1974: 83; Welsford, 1925, 11: 421–422)

Awe A god who knew all about cures and powers that were taught him by Legba. Dahomey. (Herskovits, 1938: 258–259)

Axáldanshisubéya Master of the Penis. The Cagaba and the Kogi, Colombia. (Reichel-Dolmatoff, 1949/50: 113)

Ayya nayaka deva A deity of the Sinhalese healing rituals. Village of Vilava, Maho District, Ceylon. (Yalman, 1964: 146)

Baba A Sumerian goddess, daughter of Anu, who "acquired the traits of a goddess of healing, and . . . was identified with Gula-Nin'insina." Named as the spouse of Ningirsu and/or Zababa. Near East. (Moscati, 1962: 27; Roberts, 1972: 17, 56)

Bahucharaji A goddess of Gujarat invoked by "the lame, the blind, the impotent and the children." India. (Ghurye, 1962: 256)

Bakira A god who protects the skin from evil spirits carrying disease. Japan. (Piggott, 1969: 30)

Ogun Balandjo, Balindjo A god of healing identified with St. Joseph. He also guards travelers. Haiti. West Indies. (Herskovits, 1937, 1: 280, 317; Deren, 1953: 132; Marcelin, 1950: 74)

Balitian A god invoked for cures. The Ifugao, Philippines. (Barton, 1946: 71)

Barão de Goré A god of healing believed to be a shark. Father of Gorézinho. Belem, Brazil. (Leacock, 1972: 145–6)

Basilio Bom A god of the curing ceremonies (where he uses the name Guillerme). Son of Rei Turquia. Belem, Brazil. (Leacock, 1972: 136)

Ogun Batala A god of the Mirebalais Valley who "endows with the ability to prepare healing baths." Haiti. West Indies. (Herskovits, 1937, 1: 317)

Bau Sumerian/Babylonian goddess of healing, of health, of life. Identified with Gula and Ninkarrak. Near East. (Jacobsen, 1970: 33; Jastrow, 1898: 59)

Beduriya A healing Buddha and the most popular of the seven Tathagatas. "The images are worshipped almost as fetishes, and cure by sympathetic magic." Tibet and Mongolia. Same as Bhaishajyaguru. (Percheron, 1953: 59; Waddell, 1959: 353)

Begia The "eye, the light of the body." Created by Yaun-Goicoa. The Basques, France and Spain. (Leach, 1949: 117)

Belenus, Belinus A widespread Celtic god of medicine and health, of thermal springs, associated with Apollo, and having solar qualities. Gaul and Britain. (Hatt, 1966: 64; Renel, 1906: 309; MacCana, 1970: 32; MacCulloch, 1911: 26)

Saint Benedict A benevolent deity appealed to for cures, and the protector of rubber gatherers. Ita, Brazil. (Wagley, 1964: 219–223)

Pai Benedito An elderly and humble deity of the Preto Velho gods, who are "gifted curers." Belem, Brazil. (Leacock, 1972: 155)

Bhadrakali A manifestation of the goddess Kali as protector of humans and cattle from disease. The Kadar, Southwest India. (Ehrenfels, 1952: 187)

Bhaisajyaguru Buddhist god of healing, also "the dispenser of spiritual medicine." Cambodia, Central Asia, China, India, Japan, and Tibet. Also Bhaisajyaraja.

(Jayne, 1962: 164; Hackin, 1963, 3; 244; Getty, 1962: 24; Zimmer, 1955: 210)

Bhulbae Mata   A deity invoked in times of disease and of epidemics. The Bheels, India. (Coleman, 1832: 270)

Binzuru   A god of medicine, of healing. *Same as* **Bhaisajyaguru.** Japan. (Getty, 1962: 24; Eliot, 1935: 137; Eliseev, 1963: 423)

Bisam Thakurani   A village goddess invoked with the gods of the Holy Grove when epidemics occur. The Santals, India. (Mukherjea, 1962: 288)

Bisan   The "Spirit of Camphor: a female spirit which assumes the form of a cicada." Propitiated by camphor hunters. Malay. (Leach, 1949: 145)

Bosu   A god who can endow with "the knowledge of healing and helping." Haiti. West Indies. (Herskovits, 1937, 1: 151)

Bosu Trois Cornes   One of the Petro deities who can endow with the art of healing. Haiti. West Indies. (Herskovits, 1937, 1: 151)

Mulai Brahim   A healing deity, jenn saint, of the grotto d'El Maqta. He will also help thieves if an offering is made to him. Morocco. (Basset, 1920: 74; Westermarck, 1920: 29; 1926, 1: 181)

Brigit, Brighid, Brigid   A Celtic triple goddess, of which one aspect was a goddess of healing. Ireland. (MacCana, 1970: 34; Ross, 1967: 2–6, 226, 360; Jayne, 1962: 513)

Brizo   Greek goddess of dreams. Also invoked for protection of ships. (Roscher, 1965, 1, 1: 829; Salkeld, 1844: 312)

Bugoya   A deity of the Baisu appealed to in illness. Uganda. (Williams, 1936: 174)

Bulbulnit   A god "invoked in cases of broken bones, dislocations, snake bites and wounds." The Ifugao. Philippines. (Barton, 1946: 68)

Hantu si Buru   A dangerous hunting demon who can be made a friend and is invoked to cure illness. The Besisi, Malay Peninsula. (Skeat, 1906: 303)

Bushyansta   A demoness of sleep who encourages men to abandon good thoughts and deeds and virtuous devotion. Persia. (Huart, 1963: 43; Gray, 1930: 203)

Caeculus   A Roman god who blinds, takes away the sight. (Roscher, 1965, 2, 1: 193)

Caia Caecilia, Tanaquil   A Roman goddess of healing—a deified mortal. (Jayne, 1962: 420)

Caicus   A Greek river god with powers of healing. (Fairbanks, 1907: 147)

Dom Carlos   A god who practices healing. Belem, Brazil. (Leacock, 1972: 148)

Carna   Roman goddess of health, of digestion, and of the vital organs, particularly the heart. (Dumézil, 1966, 1: 105–106, 385; Fairbanks, 1907: 253; Jayne, 1962: 459)

Chal, Chalnad   A god invoked when a plague or a man-eating tiger attacks the village. The Mal, India. (Crooke, 1925, 5: 13; 1925, 8: 344–5)

Chang Sien   A god of medicine, particularly of childbearing women, invoked for sons. A deified physician of the Sung dynasty. China. (Edkins, 1880: 392; Du Bose, n.d.: 412; Maspero, 1963: 358)

Ch'ang Tsai   God of the spleen. China. (Werner, 1932: 43; Du Bose, n.d.: 404)

Chang Wa   God of the hair. China. (Du Bose, n.d.: 404)

Ix Chante Kak   A Mayan goddess "cited in an incantation for ulcers." Mexico. (Thompson, 1970: 328)

Chao   The "Grand Master" of the Taoist Ministry of Medicine. China. (Werner, 1932: 505)

Chao T'êng-K'ang   God of the bowels. China. (Werner, 1932; 44; Du Bose, n.d.: 405)

Ix Chel   The Mayan moon goddess and water goddess. As goddess of medicine, of childbirth and pregnancy, of weaving, she is beneficent. As the "personification of water" she is destructive and malevolent, the source of floods and cloudbursts. Mexico. (Morley, 1946: 223, 230; Tozzer, 1941: 10, 154; Thompson, 1970: 242; Nicholson, 1967: 115)

Chepah   Assistant to Hien Yuen in medical investigations. The "author of prescriptions." China. (Du Bose, n.d.: 400)

Chiao Nü   God of the ear. China. (Werner, 1932: 65)

Ch'ing Lung God of the lungs. China. (Werner, 1932: 83)

Ch'ing-wa Shên "The Frog-Spirit . . . worshipped for commercial prosperity and prevention and healing of sickness at Chin-chi Hsien, Fu-chou Fu, Kiangsi, and at Hang-chou, Chekiang." China. (Werner, 1932: 84–85)

Chin Shên God of the upper parts of the feet. China. (Werner, 1932: 77, 80)

Chio Yüan-tzŭ One of the gods of the brain, along with Ni, Wan, and Chün. China. (Werner, 1932: 86)

Chitan Thakrun A deity of the Rajbansi caste who can overcome barrenness in women. Bengal. (Crooke, 1925, 2: 485)

Chiyidi The god of nightmares. Puerto Rico. West Indies. (Gonzalez-Wippler, 1975: 26)

Ch'os-sgrags-rgya-mts'o'i-dbyans A medical Buddha. Tibet. (Waddell, 1959: 354; Snellgrove, 1957: 190)

Chu He is a superintendent of pharmacies in the Taoist Ministry of Medicine. China. (Werner, 1932: 505)

Chün One of the gods of the brain. China. (Werner, 1932: 101)

Ch'ung Ling-yü One of the names of the god of the nose—given variously as Yü Lung, Yü Lu, Ch'ung Lung, Ch'ung Ling-yü, Yung Lu. China. (Werner, 1932: 98)

Chu Niao God of the heart. China. (Werner, 1932: 93)

Ch'un Yang Lu Tsu Patron of doctors and druggists. China. (Day, 1940: 213)

Ch'un Yang Tsu Shih A god of druggists. China. (Day, 1940: 162)

Ch'un Yüan-chên God of the left kidney. China. (Werner, 1932: 219)

Chu Tien Lih God of the feet. China. (Du Bose, n.d.: 405)

Chu T'ien-lin "Overseer of Epidemics of the South." China. (Werner, 1932: 560)

Ch'u Tsai "One of the Gods of the Sides of the Mouth." China. (Werner, 1932: 94)

Chu Ying A god of the eyes. China. (Werner, 1932: 94)

Cista A goddess giving physical strength and keenness of vision. Iran. (Gray, 1930: 140)

Cisti A minor Iranian goddess possessing healing remedies. (Jayne, 1962: 191; Gray, 1930: 142)

Cit Bolon Tun (or **Tum**) A Mayan god of medicine. Mexico. (Tozzer, 1941: 155; Bancroft, 1886, 2: 697; Thompson, 1970: 312)

Citlalcueitl A stellar goddess invoked in cases of scorpion bites. the Aztec, Mexico. (Caso, 1958: 85; Reed, 1966: 114)

Comitia A Roman goddess of healing and of childbirth. (Jayne, 1962: 445)

Cosme A god of healing, twin of Damião. Belem, Brazil. (Leacock, 1972: 128)

Cuchabiba, Cuchavira The god of the rainbow, who was a god of healing and helpful in childbirth. He received offerings of emeralds and beads. The Chicha, Colombia. (Kroeber, 1946: 906; Keane, 1925, 3: 515; Larousse, 1968: 441)

Cuchaviva The rainbow. A goddess of medicine, of childbirth and the nursing of the sick; of rains, waters, and the fertility of the fields. Associated with Bochica. The Muyscas (Bogota area), Colombia. (Brinton, 1882: 150, 223)

Dada A god invoked to cure illness. May be the same as Lumawig. The Kankanay, Luzon, Philippines. (Vanoverbergh, 1972: 85)

Daguan Gives strength to work. The Apayao, Philippines. (Wilson, 1947: 22)

Damião A god of healing, twin of Cosme. Belem, Brazil. (Leacock, 1972: 128)

Po Yan Dari The "goddess of disease," but at Phanri she also "cures fever in little children. She symbolizes the yoni ('womb')." The Chams, Annam and Cambodia. (Cabaton, 1925, 3: 342)

Davatabandara A deity of the Sinhalese healing rituals. Ceylon. (Yalman, 1964: 145)

Dea Mena Roman goddess of menstruation. She may originally have been a goddess of the moon. (Roscher, 1965, 1, 1: 975)

Deo Ma Niang Niang A goddess who "heals measles and smallpox." Szechwan, China. (Graham, 1928: 72)

Dessauli Beneficent god of the Hos who protects from disease, evil spirits and destructive natural forces, and gives rain and good harvests. India. (Majumdar, 1950: 154–157)

Dhanvantari A minor god of healing and a physician of the gods. India. (Jayne, 1962: 167; Martin, 1914: 1111; Danielou, 1964: 184; Briggs, 1920: 185)

Dharma Thakur, Dharma Thakar A god of fertility and prosperity invoked to cure leprosy, barrenness, and various illnesses. The Doms, Bengal. (Maity, 1971: 82–83; Elwin, 1950: 135)

Dharni The goddess of good health. The Gadbas, Central Provinces, India. (Russell, 1916, 3: 11)

Diancecht Celtic god of medicine and surgery, of healing and health. Son of Dagda and father of Miach, Airmid, Etan, Cian, Cethe, Cu, Octriuil. Ireland. (MacCana, 1970: 24, 33; Jayne, 1962: 514; MacCulloch, 1911: 77; 1918: 25; Squire, 1906: 61–62)

Didi Thakrun A stone worshipped as having the power to expel disease. India. (Crooke, 1925, 11: 874)

Diroa-mahse Beneficient protector of the world, "the Being of Blood, is in charge of all that is corporeal, all that is connected with health and the good life." He is invoked to protect the new-born child from Vai-mahse. The Desana, Colombia. (Reichel-Dolmatoff, 1971: 27–28, 140)

rDo rje bdud 'dul A god of medicine and a god of wealth. Tibet. (Nebesky-Wojkowitz, 1956, 1: 77–79)

Drvaspa A goddess of health, of humans and of livestock. Iran. (Jayne, 1962: 191; Gray, 1930: 73)

Eeyeekadluk A benevolent terrestrial spirit who "tries to heal the sick." Eskimo, Canada. (Bilby, 1923: 265; Larousse, 1968: 426)

Eir, Eira A Teutonic goddess of medicine, of healing, who taught that art to women. An attendant of Frigg. (Guerber, 1895: 53; Anderson, 1891: 241; Branston, 1955: 153; Turville-Petre, 1964: 189)

Ekko He appears at the autumn festival and "brings health to the sick, and fair weather." The Nugumiut, Frobisher Bay, Baffin Island, Canada. (Boas, 1901: 141–142)

Elamadichi A village goddess of the Trichinopoly District, generally benevolent but can be wrathful, bestows "health on the sick, grants children," and relieves suffering. India. (Hemingway, 1907: 89)

Ellamma A village goddess of Vizagapatam, Madras District, and of the Talangana, was worshipped to avert illness and to cure boils and eye troubles. India. (Francis, 1907: 74; Mudiraj, 1970: 49)

Enshag A Sumerian god, the last of eight deities given birth to by Ninhursag to cure Enki's ailments. Near East. (Bibby, 1969: 81)

Epaphos An "ancient god, the son of Zeus and Io, who healed by touch and the laying-on of hands, but lost his independence by sharing his powers with other deities and became merely a phase-name. He assisted at childbirth by the laying-on of hands." Greece. (Jayne, 1962: 323)

Epe An idol at Perau who represented the Great Spirit, Kanitu, and was invoked in sickness and also in war. New Guinea. (MacKenzie, 1930: 287; Haddon, 1925, 9: 343)

Epione "Soothing"—A goddess of the family of healing deities; wife or daughter of Asklepios, sister of Hygieia. Greece. (Thramer, 1925, 6: 551; Fairbanks, 1907: 224)

Eshmun A Phoenician god of medicine and of healing, identified with Aesculapius. He was also one of the death and resurrection gods in vegetation and the changing of the seasons. Near East. (Langdon, 1931: 74–75; Jayne, 1962: 136, 141; Albright, 1968: 148; Meyerowitz, 1958: 131; Ferguson, 1970: 216)

Euamerion A Greek god of health. (Thramer, 1925, 6: 552)

Exts!emalagilis Son of Q!omogwa. "When he bathes a woman in the water of life which is in the corner of the house . . . she recovers her eyesight." The Kwakiutl, British Columbia. (Boas, 1935: 130)

Fakatoufifita A god invoked in sickness to whom finger sacrifices are offered. Foa Island, Tonga, Polynesia. (Gifford, 1929: 307)

Falahi A god invoked by the shaman in healing ceremonies. Nias Island, Indonesia. (Eliade, 1964: 348)

Famien A deity of the Kitabo who cares for the ill and grants fertility. Guinea and Senegambia tribes. West Africa. (Larousse, 1968: 484)

Fand A Celtic goddess of healing and pleasure who metamorphosed as a bird. Wife of Manannan. Ireland. (Ross, 1967: 239; deKay, 1898: 202, 232; MacCulloch, 1911: 65)

Fang Ch'ang-i   A name of the god of the liver, Lung Yen. China. (Werner, 1932: 259)

Fann   One of the Five Highnesses. He "is thought to specialize to some extent in medicine." Taiwan. (Jordan, 1972: 106)

Fessona   A Roman goddess invoked for health and for the restoration of strength by those who were ill, or by travelers suffering from fatigue. (Jayne, 1962: 426; Dumézil, 1966, 1: 335)

Folautaofi   A god invoked in sickness, to whom finger sacrifices were made. Nomuka Island, Tonga, Polynesia.

Folla   Teutonic goddess with healing powers. As a Germanic goddess she was the sister of Frua. (Grimm, 1880: 224, 308)

Fortuna Barbata   A minor Roman deity who "provided for the growth of the beard." (Jayne, 1962: 497)

Fria   Germanic goddess with magical charms for healing. (MacCulloch, 1964: 18)

Frowa, Frua   A Teutonic goddess represented as having the power of healing. (Grimm, 1880: 224; 1883, 3: 1148)

Fu Hsi   A Chinese god of medicine. Having discovered "the *pa kua* or Eight Trigrams . . . it is by their mystical power that the Chinese physicians influence the minds and maladies of their patients." He was also believed to have taught men hunting and fishing, cooking, and how to make nets. China. (Werner, 1934: 247–248; Bodde, 1961: 386; Larousse, 1968: 397)

Gama bahirava   A deity of Sinhalese healing rituals, village of Vilava, Maho District, Ceylon. (Yalman, 1964: 146)

Ganga Devi, Takurani   The "goddess of life and health, both of men and cattle; to her pigs, goats, and pigeons are sacrificed." The Gadaba, Southern India. (Thurston, 1902, 2: 250)

Gangamma   A water goddess who protects from smallpox. The Telugu, Southern India. (Whitehead, 1916: 21; Elmore 1915: 100)

Gasani   The chief god of the Bakene who was invoked in times of sickness and of epidemics. Uganda. (Roscoe, 1915: 154)

Gatui ud Lagod   A god invoked for cures in illness. The Ifugao, Philippines. (Barton, 1946: 71)

Gatui Umbumabakal   A god of the Ifugao invoked for cures in illness. Philippines. (Barton, 1946: 71)

Gavariamma   A village goddess of the Vizagapatam District, Madras, who was feared and worshipped to avert illness. India. (Francis, 1907: 74)

Ghantakarana   A god of the Himalayas who healed skin diseases. The male counterpart of Sitala. Bengal. (Crooke, 1925, 2: 485)

Ghanvantari   The "physician of the gods." Ankor Wat, Cambodia. (Zimmer, 1955: 229)

Ghona   A deity worshipped by the Bheels to avert smallpox. India. (Coleman, 1832: 380)

Gibil   The Assyro/Babylonian god of fire was considered a healing deity through the purification rites by fire to destroy the demons of disease. Near East. (Jayne, 1962: 121; Jastrow, 1898: 220)

Gomogopos   A god of the Tinguian who causes stomach troubles, but who can also remove or cure them. Philippines. (Cole, 1922: 340)

Gos   A god invoked for rain and for "protection against epidemics." The Vilela, Argentina. (Métraux, 1948, 1: 356)

Gozu-tenno   A god who earlier caused epidemics, but then became the protector against them. Japan. (Hori, 1968: 63)

Gram pat   A village deity of the Santals invoked with the gods of the Holy Grove when epidemics occur. India. (Mukherjea, 1962: 288)

Gran' Bois   One of the Petro deities who can grant "the knowledge of healing." Haiti. West Indies. (Herskovits, 1937, 1: 151)

gser-bzang-dri-med-rin-chen   A Buddha of Medicine. Tibet. (Snellgrove, 1957: 190)

Guapindaia   A god of healing. Son of Rei Turquia. Belem, Brazil. (Leacock, 1972: 131, 135)

Guksu   A god of the Pomo Indians associated with the curing of disease, with having powers of healing. California. (Barrett, 1917: 424; Kroeber, 1925: 261–263)

Gula   Assyro/Babylonian goddess of medicine, of healing, and of health, though at times she would perversely inflict disease and misfortune. The consort of Ninib. As identified with Bau, she was also the consort of Ningirsu. Near East. (Jastrow, 1898: 166, 175; Jayne, 1962: 121; Langdon, 1931: 182; Larousse, 1968: 60, 63)

Gwelebhot   The god who gave mankind medicinal herbs to cure diseases. The Penobscot, Maine. (Speck, 1935: 81)

Halangob, Humalangob   A god "invoked in cases of broken bones, dislocations, snake bites and wounds." Also a god of war and sorcery. The Ifugao, Philippines. (Barton, 1946: 40, 68)

Sidi Hammou   A healing deity of the grotto d'El Maqta to whom offerings were made for healing. Morocco. (Basset, 1920: 74; Westermarck, 1920: 29, 85)

Hao Ch'iu   A god of the heart. China. (Werner, 1932: 155)

Hao Hua   The god of the lungs and also of the lower teeth. China. (Werner, 1932: 155, 492)

Haoma   Persian deified drink, a god who does not intoxicate but bestows health and blessings and long life. Same as Soma. Near East. (Gray, 1930: 83; Dresden, 1961: 349; Jayne, 1962: 191)

Hariti   A Hindu demon goddess who on conversion to Buddhism "became the beneficent Goddess of Health and Abundance." She was believed to prevent smallpox. Java and Nepal. (Marchal, 1963: 240; Zimmer, 1955: 137–138; Getty, 1962: 84)

Hau   A god of doctors who used ointments and massage in treatment. Also a god of peace. Society Islands, Polynesia. (Henry, 1928: 145)

Haurvatat   One of the Amesha Spentas representing health, wholeness; associated with Ameretat in the protection of vegetation, animals, and waters, and in concern for the well-being of mankind, providing remedies to combat their ills. Iran. (Jayne, 1962: 185; Littleton, 1965: 99; Gray, 1930: 51–52; Huart, 1963: 41; Hinnells, 1973: 52)

Hautia   A deity appealed to in sickness. Tahiti, Polynesia. (Henry, 1928: 213)

Hayu'ya   With Yahola invoked "to act as guardians and good geniuses of" those studying medicine and the mysteries. Creek Indians, Georgia. (Swanton, 1924/25: 485)

Herakles   A Greek god of healing to whom hot springs were dedicated. Son of Zeus and Alkmene. (Jayne, 1962: 329–331; Thramer, 1925, 6: 548)

Hien Yuen   A Chinese god of medicine. "He was the first to determine the relation of the five viscera to the five elements, and describe internal and external diseases." Chepah was his assistant in medical investigations. He was as well a god of tailors, of "the art of dress." (Du Bose, n.d.: 130, 335/400)

Hinatahutahu   A goddess of healing and of divination. Tahiti, Polynesia. (Henry, 1928: 556)

Hinokbon   A god "invoked in cases of broken bones, dislocations, snake bites and wounds." The Ifugao, Philippines. (Barton, 1946: 68)

Hoakils, Hvachiella   A spirit from whom the shaman receives his powers to cure as well as power over life and death. The Yahgan, Tierra del Fuego. (Cooper, 1917: 149; Alexander, 1920: 341)

Hoba   A god of war who was "invoked in cases of broken bones, dislocations, snake bites and wounds." The Ifugao, Philippines. (Barton, 1946: 40, 68)

Honani   Supernatural Badger who taught men about medicinal herbs and plants for curing. The Hopi and the Walpi, Arizona. (Fewkes, 1895, 2: 128; Waters, 1963: 56)

Howanmata   A goddess of the Bhils invoked by women in epidemics. India. (Wiesinger, 1967: 501)

Hsiang Ti-wu   God of the right kidney. China. (Werner, 1932: 219)

Hsü   A god of the Taoist Ministry of Medicine. China. (Werner, 1932: 505)

Hsüan Ming   The god of the kidneys is also god of the element Water and associated with the North. China. (Werner, 1932: 219, 437; Campbell, 1962: 432)

Hsüan Wên-hua   God of the hair. Also known as Shou Ch'ang. China. (Werner, 1932: 179, 430)

Hsü Chien'shêng   One of the names of a God of the Eye. China. (Werner, 1932: 175)

Hu   The god of the sense of taste. He "became the personification of the divine food upon which the gods . . . lived in heaven." Egypt. (Budge, 1969, 2: 89, 298)

Huang Ti   A god of medicine. China. (Werner, 1932: 505; Larousse, 1968: 397)

Huang T'ing   God of the spleen. China. (Werner, 1932: 451)

Huan Yang-ch'ang A god of the heart. China. (Werner, 1932: 184)

Hua T'o God of physicians and surgeons. China. (Graham, 1961: 176; Shryock, 1931: 127; Day, 1940: 205)

Hua T'o Hsien Shih A god of surgeons "reputed to have been able to remove, wash, and replace defective intestines." China. (Day, 1940: 39, 213)

Huchi A goddess of fire, of the hearth, who is considered "a great purifier of the body from disease." The Ainu, Japan. (Batchelor, n.d.: 175–179)

Hu Nonp The Bear God has all the knowledge of medicines which he has taught to the shamans. The Lakota and Oglala, South Dakota. (Walker, 1980: 50–51, 128)

Hun-p'o Chao "The name of two gods of the armpits." China. Werner, 1932: 192)

Hunwarmata A goddess invoked by women in illnesses. The Bhils, India. (Wiesinger, 1967: 500–501)

Hu Pên God of the breast. China. (Werner, 1932: 179; Du Bose, n.d.: 405)

Hwang Chenyih The god of the mouth. China. (Du Bose, n.d.: 72)

Hwang-ti One of the gods of medicine, of health. China. (De Groot, 1925, 4: 14)

Hygieia, Hygea Goddess of health and daughter of Aesculapius. A surname of Pallas Athena as associated with him. Greece. (Kerényi, 1951: 127; Jayne, 1962: 332–333; Murray, 1935: 206)

Hypnos God of sleep, of surcease from weariness and pain. Twin brother of Thanatos. Greece. (Roscher, 1965, 1, 2: 2846; Kerényi, 1951: 198; Murray, 1935: 222; Hesiod-Brown, 1981: 59)

Iang, Iing Giver of the healing arts and rituals. The Land Dyaks, Borneo. (Roth, 1968: 165)

Ianiskos A son of Asklepios, associated with him in healing. Greece. (Thramer, 1925, 6: 551; Roscher, 1965, 2, 1: 4)

Iasis A Greek nymph of a healing spring, a fountain in Elis. (Roscher, 1965, 2, 1: 63; Thramer, 1925, 6: 548)

Iaso A goddess of healing, daughter of Asklepios and sister of Panakeia. Greece. (THramer, 1925, 6: 551; Roscher, 1965, 2, 1: 63)

I-buki-do-nushi-no-kami A kami of purification believed to have healing powers. Japan. (Herbert, 1967: 282)

Icelos, Phobetor A god of dreams who appeared in the form of an animal, a bird, or a serpent. Son of Sleep, brother of Morpheus and Phantasos. Icelos: the name used by the gods; Phobetor used by mortals. Greece. (Ovid, 1950: 263)

I-em-hetep, Imhotep A mortal deified as a god of healing, of medicine, as well as of learning and the occult arts. Egypt. (Budge, 1969, 1: 114, 522–524; Knight, 1915: 54; Ames, 1965: 122; Jayne, 1962: 62)

Ifa The popular god of divination and of oracles was also a god of medicine, and taught its arts. The Yoruba, Nigeria. (Parrinder, 1967: 88; Lucas, 1948: 71; Robertson, 1911: 217–218)

Ikelos Greek god of the dream. See also Icelos. (Roscher, 1965, 2, 1: 117)

Ima A god invoked in cases of snakebite. The Bhils, India. (Naik, 1956: 187)

Ini Manang A celestial *manang* (medicine woman), sister of Singalang Burong. The Dyaks, Sarawak, Borneo. (Sarawak Gazette, 1963: 122)

Isis The great Egyptian goddess had among her numerous functions the qualities of a goddess of healing and of remedies, which she taught to men, and learned from Thoth the "words and ceremonies," their use and procedures, to restore life. (Jayne, 1962: 66–67; Ames, 1965: 57; Budge, 1969, 1: 150)

Itha An Arabian god who cures disease and protects from enemies. (Vriezen, 1963: 66)

Itzamna The principal god of the Mayan Pantheon and god of culture and civilization was invoked as a god of medicine in the month of Zip. Mexico. (Tozzer, 1941: 146; Morley, 1946: 223; Thompson, 1970: 229)

Itzan Noh Ku The Lacandon god who supplies hail, the "lord of lakes and crocodiles," was "also a god who cares for the sick." Mexico. (Thompson, 1970: 266–267)

Ixchel, Ix Chel In Yucatan she was the goddess of medicine and invoked with Itzamna in the month of Zip. Mexico. (Bancroft, 1886, 3: 462; Morley, 1946: 223)

Ixtlilton God of health and of healing. He was called Little Black Face and was also one of the gods of feasting and drunkenness. Aztec, Mexico. (Vaillant, 1962: 151; Spence, 1923: 352; Reed, 1966: 96; Duran, 1971: 176; Alexander, 1920: 77)

Jaldeo A god invoked in cases of fever. The Bhils, India. (Naik, 1956: 187)

Janguli A Buddhist goddess, a form of Tara, is invoked to cure serpent bites. India. (Linossier, 1963: 98; Getty, 1962: 122)

Pai Jeronimo An elderly and humble god of the Preto Velho gods, who are "gifted curers." Belem, Brazil. (Leacock, 1972: 156)

João da Mata, Rei da Bandeira A god of healing who is also a carouser. Belem, Brazil. (Leacock, 1972: 145–146)

Jukwa rekwamwari shave A deity of healing who also can send rain to small areas. The Nyajena Reserve, Rhodesia. (Gelfand, 1966: 100)

Juturna, Iuturna A Roman spring nymph of healing represents therapeutic waters. (Fairbanks, 1907: 253; Dumézil, 1966, 1: 388; Jayne, 1962: 452)

Kadang A god associated with healing. The Seiyawa, Nigeria. (Meek, 1925, 2: 28)

Kadavara A deity of the Sinhalese healing rituals. An evil demon of "irrational punitiveness." India. (Yalman, 1964: 145; Obesyesekere, 1966: 6)

Kafoiaatu A god, invoked in illness, is represented by the fruit dove. Uiha Island, Tonga, Polynesia. (Gifford, 1929: 310)

Kagauraha A serpent goddess invoked "for relief from sickness, from bad seasons, for growth, etc." San Cristoval, Melanesia. (MacCulloch, 1925, 11: 401)

K'ai-chün T'ung Another name for the god of the liver, Lung Yen. China. (Werner, 1932: 259)

Kalhindúkua Father of the Penis. The Cagaba, the Kogi. Colombia. (Reichel-Dolmatoff, 1949/50: 115)

Kali Chudas A deity invoked in snake-bite. The Bhils, India. (Naik, 1956: 187)

Kalisia The god of the forest and of game is also the god of dreams. The Mbuti (Pygmies), Zaire. (Turnbull, 1965: 236)

Kalliphaeia A nymph "of a healing fountain in Elis." Greece. (Thramer, 1925, 6: 548)

Kalumaiamman A goddess who protects from cholera and epidemics, from cattle plague. Trichinopoly District, India. (Whitehead, 1916: 102)

Kalu Vanvah Deo A god invoked in cases of snake-bite. The Bhils, India. (Naik, 1956: 187)

Kamaka A Hawaiian god of healing. (Westervelt, 1915: 94)

Kambili deva A deity of Sinhalese healing rituals, village of Vilava, Maho District, Ceylon. (Yalman, 1964: 146)

Kane-lau-apua A beneficent healing god who takes the form of the goby (o'opu) fish. Lanai, Hawaii. (Beckwith, 1940: 136: 452)

Kao God of diagnostics in the Taoist Ministry of Medicine. China. (Werner, 1932: 505)

Kao Wa God of the lungs. China. (Du Bose, n.d.: 404)

Kashindukua A jaguar god who "was destined to be a great shaman who would cure all diseases by sucking the pathogenic essence from the patients' bodies." He was trapped and killed (yet he still lives) by his brother Bunkuase because he devoured people. Even so, Kashindukua was considered benevolent and the father of the Kogi. Colombia. (Reichel-Dolmatoff, 1975: 55–56)

Kataragama A deity invoked in healing rituals, his vehicle was the peacock. His wife was Teyvannai Amma. The Sinhalese, Ceylon. (Yalman, 1964: 117, 125; 1966: 210). He is also considered the equivalent of Skanda, and if so, is a war god. (Leach, 1958: 304)

Katsin numka majan Mother of the vital organs—the heart, liver, lungs, etc. Daughter of Phungkam Janun. The Katchins, Burma. (Gilhodes, 1908: 678)

Kattakju A goddess who attends the sick and provides the shaman with the knowledge of their condition and the prognosis. The Eskimo, Baffin Land, Canada. (Bilby, 1923: 269)

Kawalkamata A goddess invoked by women to "help cure lameness and pain." The Bhils, India. (Wiesinger, 1967: 501)

Keya "The Spirit of the Turtle was the guardian of life and patron of surgery and controlled accidents." The Lakota and Oglala. South Dakota. (Walker, 1980: 122)

Khambageu A self-existent, culture hero supernatural who lived among the people, established customs and morals, and performed "miracles of healing." He was invoked to prevent or to cure disease. The Sonjo, Tanzania. (Mbiti, 1970, 2: 126, 189; Gray, 1963: 97–100)

Khima Garudis A god invoked in cases of snake-bite. The Bhils, India. (Naik, 1956: 187)

Kigala God of the deaf. Uganda. (Cunningham, 1905: 220; Budge, 1973, 1: 377)

Kinashut Kamui A deity of the Ainu of the Saru and Mukawa Districts who is invoked in childbirth, in illness, and during epidemics, when he is called Shiturupakpe Kamui Ekashi. Japan. (Munro, 1963: 13–19)

Kinatibongalan A group of beneficent deities who protect against other disease-bringing deities. The Ifugao, Philippines. (Barton, 1946: 90)

Kivava With Epe, one of two idols worshipped at Perau as representing Kanitu, the Great Spirit, and invoked in times of illness. New Guinea. (MacKenzie, 1930: 287; Haddon, 1925, 9: 343)

Kodamata A goddess invoked by women in illnesses. The Bhils, India. (Wiesinger, 1967: 501)

Kodkod A god "invoked in cases of broken bones, dislocations, snake bites and wounds." The Ifugao, Philippines. (Barton, 1946: 68)

Kolea-moku A deified human "who was taught the medicinal arts by the gods" at Kailua. Hawaii. (Beckwith, 1970: 119)

Koodjaunuk A beneficent god of the bottom of the sea who surfaces when summoned by the shaman to cure the sick and to help people. The Eskimo, Baffin Land, Canada. (Bilby, 1923: 267–268; Larousse, 1968: 426)

Koodloorktaklik A god who lives inland and who, like Koodjaunuk, helps in sickness and in other needs. The Eskimo, Baffin Land, Canada. (Bilby, 1923: 269)

Koopvilloarkju A benevolent god who lives on the land and is "said to give food and heal the sick." The Eskimo, Baffin Land, Canada. (Bilby, 1923: 266)

K'o souo niang niang The goddess who cures the cough. China. (Chavannes, n.d.: 117)

Kugbosa A culture hero who taught the rites of curing and cleansing. The Kalabari, Nigeria. (Horton, 1960: 17)

Kui-tzu-mu-shen The "Buddhist goddess Hariti . . . invoked . . . to ward off ill-health or to be cured of disease." China. (Getty, 1962: 86)

Kumarabandara A deity of the Sinhalese healing rituals. Ceylon. (Yalman, 1964: 145)

Kumastamho A god who gives shamans the power to cure. The Yuma, California. (Kroeber, 1925: 784)

Kumbya A rock god of the Basoga invoked to avert illness or to cure it when present. Uganda. (Roscoe, 1915: 251)

Kumid-em A god invoked for remedy for "retention of urine." The Kankanay, Luzon, Philippines. (Vanoverbergh, 1972: 86–87)

K'ung Hsien A name of the god of the ear. China. (Werner, 1932: 235)

K'ung Yen God of the ear. China. (Du Bose, n.d.: 404)

Lahe A goddess invoked against illness in the region of Comminges. The Basques, France and Spain. (Barandiaran, 1972: 137, 268)

Lenus A Celtic god of healing and a god of war identified with Mars. Gaul. (Ferguson, 1970: 212; Ross, 1967: 173, 191; Renel, 1906: 399; Jayne, 1962: 520)

Lera Acuece and **Lera Acueca** "Gods of medicine and sickness." The Zapotec in Sola, Oaxaca, Mexico. (Whitecotton, 1977: 164)

Li A god of pharmacies of the Taoist Ministry of Medicine. China. (Werner, 1932: 505)

Linglingon ud Lagod A god of the Forgetting of Pain "invoked in cases of broken bones, dislocation, snake bites and wounds." the Ifugao, Philippines. (Barton, 1946: 68)

Ling Mo God of the neck. China. (Werner, 1932: 253)

Li T'ieh-kuai The fourth of the eight Taoist immortals, a god of pharmacists. China. (Peeters, 1941: 30; Werner, 1934: 289)

Llacsahuato A goddess of the Huarochiri District invoked in illness. Peru. (Trimborn, 1968: 136)

Loko Atissou A god with numerous functions, among them a god of healing and of medicinal plants. Haiti. West Indies. (Marcelin, 1950: 41–43)

Loucetius, Leucetius A Celtic god of war and of lightning, but at Bath also a god of healing and consort of Nemetona. Gaul and Britain. (Ross, 1967: 174, 201; Renel, 1906: 399)

Lubanga God of health and of healing. Uganda. (Roscoe, 1915: 93)

Lü Ch'un Yang God of physicians and druggists who also became the god of barbers and inkmakers. Variously known as Ch'un Yang Tsu Shih, Ch'un Yang Lü Tsu, Lü Tsu, Lü Tung-pin. China. (Day, 1940: 111; Edkins, 1880: 382)

Santa Lucia A powerful saint who is "supposed to be able to cure diseases of the eyes." The Tzeltal, Mexico. (Nash, 1970: 206)

Lung Te-chu, Lung Yao God of the gall. China. (Werner, 1932: 285, 297; Du Bose, n.d.: 404)

Lung yen, Lung Yien God of the liver. Also called K'ai-chün T'ung and Fang Ch'ang-i. China. (Werner, 1932: 297; Du Bose, n.d.: 404)

Lü Tung-pin *See* **Lü Ch'un Yang.** He is also known as a god of literature. China. (Day, 1940: 111, 113; Peeters, 1941: 29)

Ma A physician god, the Taoist Ministry of Medicine. China. (Werner, 1932: 505)

Ma'a' God of the sense of sight. A dual god with Sozem—"seeing-hearing." Egypt. (Budge, 1969, 2: 298; Gardiner, 1925, 9: 791)

Machaon A Greek surgeon god, son of Asklepios and Epione. (Thramer, 1925, 6: 551; Roscher, 1965, 2, 2: 2228)

Madiovazanakoho, Mandiovazankoho The "god with the clean finger nails," who is invoked with others in illness and in making oaths. The Malagasy and the Tanala, Madagascar. (Ruud, 1960: 273; Linton, 1933: 163, 193–194)

Ma'iola A tutelary god of the Kahuna Lapa'au, or Medicine Men. Helpful in curing the sick. Hawaii. (Alexander, 1967: 93)

Maka The Earth is the goddess of medicines deriving from the earth and "gives to them potencies for good or evil" relative to her pleasure and/or the skill of the shaman and his invocations. The Lakota, South Dakota. (Walker, 1980: 120)

Makhir Assyro/Babylonian goddess of dreams. (Rawlinson, 1885: 51). The god of dreams—"through an error occasioned by the want of any indices of gender in Accadian, was termed his daughter . . . He was the god of revelation, since a knowledge of the future was declared through dreams." Near East. (Sayce, 1898: 65, 175)

Maleates A god of health and of healing, later identified with Apollo. Greece. (Thramer, 1925, 6: 547; Jayne, 1962: 338)

Malemelel A deity invoked "to cure sickness of the head." Ifalik, Micronesia. (Burrows, 1947/48: 12)

The ma-lha Personal deities whose worship "procures physical strength." Tibet. (Waddell, 1959: 375)

Manabus(h) The culture hero/god through whom men received medicine bundles, medicinal plants, and the power to cure. The Menomini, Wisconsin. (Skinner, 1913: 73; Ritzenthaler, 1907: 87; Hoffman, 1890: 246)

Manang Jaban A goddess who "possesses various charms not only for cures but also for good luck." The Dyaks, Sarawak, Borneo. (Sarawak Gazette, 1963: 77)

Manang Petara di bukit raya A mountain god and a celestial medicine man. The Dyaks, Sarawak, Borneo. (Sarawak Gazette, 1963: 122)

sMan-bla-bde-gs'egs brgyad A "popular form of Buddha as 'The supreme physician,' or Buddhist Aesculapius." Tibet. *See also* **Manla, Menlha.** (Waddell, 1959: 353)

Mang Chin-i Goddess of the womb. China. (Werner, 1932: 567; Du Bose, n.d.: 403)

mang la "One of the two male shoulder-gods" invoked by men at mealtimes. The Lepchas, Sikkim. (Siiger, 1967: 51, 143)

Mani God of medicine and of food. Brazil. (Bray, 1935: 293)

Manla "The Supreme Physician . . . the 'Healing Buddha' " of Buddhism. Same as Bhaisajyaguru, sman-bla, otoci, Yao-shih-fo, Yaku-shi, Binzuru. (Getty, 1962: 24)

Marembedzi shave A spirit of healing. The Nyajena Reserve, Rhodesia. (Gelfand, 1966: 100)

Mariana A very popular goddess of healing, of childbirth, of love, and guardian of sailors and the navy. She is identified with the arara (a macaw), and is the daughter of Rei Turquia, and twin of Mariano. Belem, Brazil. (Leacock, 1972: 131–134)

Maru Primarily a god of war, but he is invoked in the treatment of broken bones, wounds, bruises, etc. New Zealand. (Shand, 1894: 89; Hongi, 1920: 27; Andersen, 1928: 168)

Matai Selilai Manang Janang A celestial medicine man of the Dyaks, Sarawak, Borneo. (Sarawak Gazette, 1963: 122)

Matali A deity invoked in illness to "rest . . . on the hands, feet, and body." Burma. (Spiro, 1967: 152)

Mathra Spenta A god, protective against demons, and with powers of healing. He also promotes "growth of grain and the increase of learning." Iran. (Gray, 1930: 151)

Mato The Bear Spirit "presides over . . . wounds and many kinds of medicines." The Lakota and Oglala, South Dakota. (Walker, 1980: 121)

Meditrina A Roman goddess of health and of healing. (Roscher, 1965, 2, 2: 2516; Murray, 1935: 206)

Mefitis An Italian goddess, the personification of the noxious earth vapors, invoked for protection from and cures for malaria and other afflictions. (Jayne, 1962: 463; Frazer, 1961: 204)

Meme A Semitic goddess whose identification with Ninmug, Gula, and Ninkarrak indicates that she was a goddess of healing, though she also seems to be a goddess of fertility and of the underworld. Near East. (Roberts, 1972: 45, 60)

Mena A Roman goddess of menstruation invoked where women feared sterility. (Jayne, 1962: 443, 495; Schrader, 1925, 2: 34)

Men Ascaenus The "chief god of Antioch-near-Pisidia. . . . The god's symbol was the bull's head . . . variously identified with Apollo, Dionysus and Asclepius. This suggests a healing-god." Asia Minor. (Ferguson, 1970: 217)

Menikbandara A deity of the Sinhalese healing rituals. Ceylon. (Yalman, 1964: 145)

Menlha The "Buddha of medicine." Tibet. (Nebesky-Wojkowitz, 1956, 2: 50)

Mesi A deity of the Akim-Kotoku invoked in illness. Ghana. (Field, 1948: 178)

Sidi l-Mesmudi A saint at Tangier to whom offerings are made for healing. Morocco. (Westermarck, 1920: 106)

Mestre Marajo A lesser god, interested in a good time, who appears only in curing ceremonies. Belem, Brazil. (Leacock, 1972: 157, 162)

Me Zeengk A god of healing of the Minsi (Lenape) Indians. Eastern United States. (Harrington, 1921: 37, 38)

mgon-mkhyen-rgyal-po "Thorough-knowing King"— a medical Buddha. Tibet. (Snellgrove, 1957: 190)

Sidi Mhammed s-Snhaji His shrine is believed to provide healing for the sick. The Ulad Raga in Dukkala, Morocco. (Westermarck, 1926, 1: 200–201)

Sidi Mhand The spring at his shrine cures the itch. The Ait Waryager, Morocco. (Westermarck, 1926, 1: 84)

Miach A Celtic therapeutic god, a physician, son of Diancecht and brother of Airmid. Ireland. (Squire, 1906: 62, 80–82; Jayne, 1962: 514; MacCulloch, 1918: 28)

Minākṣi A "fish-eyed" maternal goddess, a "goddess of the breast," who is gracious to all, subservient to her husband. Madurai, South India. (O'Flaherty, 1980: 91, 374)

Minerva Etruscan/Roman goddess of numerous aspects, among which was that of goddess of physicians and of healing. Italy. (Jayne, 1962: 434)

Ming Chang God of the eye. Also given as Ming Shang, Chu Ying, Hsü Chien'sheng. China. (Du Bose, n.d.: 404; Werner, 1932: 118, 318)

Lalla Mira l'Arbiya A healing deity of the grotto d'El Maqta near Fez. Morocco. (Basset, 1920: 74; Westermarck, 1920: 29)

Lalla Mira l'-Fassiya A healing deity of the grotto d'El Maqta. Morocco. (Basset, 1920: 74)

Mirahuato A goddess of the Huarochiri District invoked in illness. Peru. (Trimborn, 1968: 136)

Moehau A household god who is a god of "Peaceful-slumber." Tahiti, Polynesia. (Henry, 1928: 377)

Moemoe The "God of Restful Sleep." Maui, Hawaii. (Ashdown, 1971: 17)

Mogons A Celtic god who is identified with Apollo as a god of healing. The Brythons. (MacCulloch, 1911: 125)

Mo lha, phug lha The god of the left armpit is a god of women, of the female line. Tibet. (Tucci, 1980: 187–188)

Moothevi The goddess of sleep who is "the presiding goddess of the criminal profession . . . invoked to keep them awake and their victims sleepy." The Korava, Southern India. (Thurston, 1909, 3: 462)

More A nursing god of Tahiti. Polynesia. (Henry, 1928: 357)

Moritasgus A Celtic god of healing. Gaul. (Ferguson, 1970: 214)

Morpheus The god of dreams, a being of the night associated with night wanderings and "skilled in imitating human shapes." A son of Hypnos and brother of Icelos and Phantasos. Greece. (Roscher, 1965, 2, 2: 3215; Murray, 1935: 223; Prentice Hall, 1965: 92; Ovid, 1950: 263)

Sidi Mousa, Sidi Musa A healing deity of the grotto d'El Maqta. Morocco. (Basset, 1920: 74; Westermarck, 1920: 28, 85)

Moxhomsa Eliosigak "Grandfather at the West," invoked in the gathering of herbs or the preparation of medicines. The Lenape, Eastern United States. (Harrington, 1921: 26)

Moxhomsa Lowaneyung "Grandfather at the North," invoked in the gathering of herbs or the preparation of medicines. The Lenape, Eastern United States. (Harrington, 1921: 26)

Moxhomsa Wahanjiopung "Grandfather at the East," invoked in the gathering of herbs or the preparation of medicines. The Lenape, Eastern United States. (Harrington, 1921: 26)

mtsh'an-legs A medical Buddha. Tibet. (Waddell, 1959: 354; Snellgrove, 1957: 190)

Mualongan A god "who combated . . . the bringers of sickness and bad luck." Minahassa, Northern Celebes, Indonesia. (MacKenzie, 1930: 330)

Mu Fêng The god of the upper teeth. China. (Werner, 1932: 492)

Mulindwa A goddess whose duty was to guard the health of the royal family. The Banyoro, Uganda. (Roscoe, 1915: 92)

mung kung "One of the two male shoulder-gods" invoked by men at mealtimes. The Lepchas, Sikkim. (Siiger, 1967: 51, 143)

Mu Shên One of "The Gods of the Upper Parts of the Feet." China. (Werner, 1932: 80)

Mwanga A serpent god, who had "power over disease" and sterility, was invoked for children. The Bagesu, Uganda. (Roscoe, 1915: 179; MacCulloch, 1925, 11: 400)

Mya-nan-med-mch'og-dpal A medical Buddha of Tibet. (Waddell, 1959: 354; Snellgrove, 1957: 190)

Myia A god of healing in Palestine. His name means the one who controls flies (sends and/or keeps them away). (Roscher, 1965, 2, 2: 3301)

Nabobá Mother of the Vagina. She is also a Mother of the Lake as well as being "associated with a certain kind of agricultural soil." The Cagaba and the Kogi, Colombia. (Reichel-Dolmatoff, 1949/50: 114; 1975: 45, 55)

Nagarsen A deity who controlled diseases. The Kachhi, India. (Crooke, 1925, 7: 634)

Nanan-bouclou Androgynous first deity, creator of the twin Mawu-Lisa. But "now a loa of herbs and medicines." The Ewe, Dahomey. (Deren, 1953: 55, 310)

Nananbuluku Deity of "herbs and medicine." Cuba and Haiti, West Indies, (Courlander, 1966: 15)

Nan-chi Lao-jên One of the gods of the eyebrows. China. (Werner, 1932: 325)

Nanshe The goddess of fish is also the "divine interpreter of dreams." Near East. (Jacobsen, 1976: 25, 84)

Narira shave A spirit of healing at Nyajena Reserve. Rhodesia. (Gelfand, 1966: 97)

The Nasatyas, the Asvins Twin gods of the morning and the evening, who are also the physicians of the gods and gods of healing as well as gods of animal husbandry. India. (Larousse, 1968: 329; Dumézil, 1966, 1: 171)

Navitcu A deity of healing and the bringer of seed, who is "represented as a masked clown," lives in the north and can be summoned with corn meal sprinkled on the ground. The Papago, Arizona and Mexico. (Underhill, 1946: 14, 15)

Nawandyo A goddess who is invoked in family sickness and troubles. The Basoga, Uganda. (Roscoe, 1915: 246)

Nawneedis The spirit of health, of well-being. The Ojibway, Lake Superior region. (Johnston, 1976: 169)

Nejma A female jenn of the healing grotto of d'El Maqta who is the chief of the spirits of the cave. Morocco. (Basset, 1920: 75; Westermarck, 1920: 29)

Nephthys Primarily a goddess of death, the sister of Isis, and like her possessing magical and healing powers. Egypt. (Jayne, 1962: 74; Budge, 1969, 2: 255–258)

Ni A god of the brain. China. (Werner, 1932: 327)

Nin-akha-kuda A Babylonian goddess invoked in magical formulae in healing along with Bahu and Gula. She is associated with the pure waters, with Ea. Near East. (Sayce, 1898: 286)

Ninib A Babylonian solar god, a god of agriculture and of fertility, as well as a god of war, of hunting, and of storms. In his association with his wife Gula, he is a deity of healing and rescue from death. Near East. (Jayne, 1962: 126; Jastrow, 1898: 57, 67, 174, 217; Hommel, 1925, 3: 74; Mercer, 1925, 12: 700)

Ninkarrak Akkadian/Assyrian/Babylonian goddess of health, of healing, and of medicine. Identified with Bau and Gula. Near East. (Kramer, 1961: 126; Langdon, 1931: 182; Hooke, 1963: 58)

Ninsu-utud A Sumerian goddess who heals the toothache. Near East. (Langdon, 1931: 202)

Nin-ti One of the goddesses created by Ninhursag for the curing of Enki, to heal his ribs. Sumer, Near East. (Kramer, 1961: 103)

Nodons A Celtic god of healing and a solar and water god, probably in their therapeutic aspects. Britain. (Ross, 1967: 176, 201)

Nona Chamari A goddess invoked in times of sickness and to save from death in snake-bite. The Chamars, India. (Briggs, 1920: 179, 185)

mNon-mk'yen-rgyal-po A medical Buddha of Tibet. (Waddell, 1959: 354)

No''oma Cawaneyung "Grandmother at the South," invoked in the gathering of herbs or the preparation of medicines. The Lenape Indians, Eastern United States. (Harrington, 1921: 26)

Noonagekshown A god who "appears in the spring and in the autumn, and like Ekko, brings health to the sick, and fair weather." The Nugumiut of Frobisher Bay, Canada. (Boas, 1901: 141–142)

Nor-lha God of the left armpit who is also a god of wealth. Sikkim. (Gazeteer of Sikhim, 1894: 353)

Nortia Etruscan goddess of destiny, of fortune. She also had healing functions among the Volsci. Italy. (Herbig, 1925, 5: 534; Jayne, 1962: 436; Leland, 1963: 34; Campbell, 1964: 309)

Nü Chio, Nü Chah God of the back. China. (Werner, 1932: 334; Du Bose, n.d.: 405)

gNyan po sku lha gyer 'dzom A guardian deity of the human body. The Bon, Tibet. (Nebesky-Wojkowitz, 1956, 1: 266)

Nyinawhira A goddess whose duty was to guard the health of the royal family. The Banyoro, Uganda. (Roscoe, 1915: 92)

Octriuil A son of Diancecht and associated with him in healing incantations. Celtic Ireland. (Jayne, 1962: 514)

Odoria Roman goddess of smell. (Roscher, 1965, 2, 1: 209)

Ogjunak A benevolent spirit who lives on land and attempts to heal the sick. The Eskimo, Baffin Land, Canada. (Bilby, 1923: 266)

Oho-na-mochi An earth god. With Sukuna-bikona, believed to have originated the art of medicine and the use of charms against the evil spirits. Japan. (Aston, 1925, 11: 465–466)

Oititi, Rearea The "god of physic." Society Islands, Polynesia. (Ellis, 1853: 333)

O-Kuni-Nishi A god of medicine and also a god of agriculture, of fortune, of wisdom, of marriage, and of government, succeeding his father, Susanowo, as ruler of Izumo, Japan. (Herbert, 1967: 349; Holtom, 1938: 81, 203; Haydon, 1941: 208–209; Bunce, 1955: 134; Casanowicz, 1926; 1)

Oneiros A Greek god of dreams—A "personification of dreams, whether idle or deceptive or really prophetic." (Murray, 1935: 223; Roscher, 1965, 3, 1: 900; Barthell, 1971: 8)

Orehu The water goddess and goddess of herbal medicine. The Arawaks, West Indies. (Lovén, 1935: 569)

Osachin The "Patron of doctors." Puerto Rico. West Indies. (Gonzalez-Wippler, 1975: 27)

Osahin, Osain, Os(s)anyin God of medicine and of doctors of the Yoruba in Nigeria. God of medicinal and liturgical herbs and foliage in Nigeria, Brazil, and Puerto Rico. In Cuba he was also a god of hunting. (Lucas, 1948: 168; Bastide, 1960: 570; Verger, 1954: 182; 1957: 229–231; Idowu, 1962: 78; Parrinder, 1949: 137; Courlander, 1973: 11, 34; Gonzalez-Wippler, 1975: 2)

Ossange, Ossangne God of healing. Haiti, West Indies. (Verger, 1957: 231; Marcelin, 1950: 75)

Ossipaga A Roman goddess who "presided over the growth and hardening of the bones of the embryo and child." (Roscher, 1965, 2, 1: 209; Jayne, 1962: 498)

otoči The healing Buddha in Mongolia. *Same as* **Manla.** (Getty, 1962: 24)

Otskahakakaitshoidiaa Goddess of the water and its inhabitants, who has cleansing and healing powers. The Wichita, Kansas. (Dorsey, 1904, 1: 19)

Padam Sen Deo The god of the foot, whose design tattooed on the foot is supposed to be protective. The Gonds, Central Provinces, India. (Russell, 1916, 3: 125)

Pah Lien Fang God of the throat. China. (DuBose, n.d.: 405)

Paieon, Paean Greek "physician of the gods . . . [Homer] . . . properly the god of healing incantations." (Fairbanks, 1907: 37, 130; Thramer, 1925, 6: 546)

Pai Liu-fang God of the throat. Apparently a variant of Pah Lien Fang. China. (Werner, 1932: 354)

Paja Yan, Pajau Yan The goddess of health and of healing is identified with the moon, having been sent there by Po Jata because she wanted to raise all the dead. The Cham, Annam and Cambodia. (Cabaton, 1925, 3: 342; Wales, 1957: 160)

Palle bedde deva A god of the Sinhalese healing rituals. Ceylon. (Yalman, 1964: 145)

Pallya bandara A deity of the Sinhalese healing rituals. Ceylon. (Yalman, 1964: 145)

Panakeia A goddess of healing—A "personification of the miraculous all-healing herbs." Daughter of Asklepios. Greece. (Thramer, 1925, 6: 551)

P'an Niang Goddess of vaccination. China. (Werner, 1932: 541)

Pantor A demon invoked in epidemics. The Lepchas, Sikkim. (Siiger, 1967: 80, 143)

Pao Yüan-Ch'üan God of the spleen. China. (Werner, 1932: 451)

Patecatl A god of medicine as well as an octli god (wine), whose wife is Mayahuel. Aztec, Mexico. (Vailland, 1962: 149; Burland, 1967: 100; Spence, 1923: 292–293)

Pattini A benevolent yet punitive (but just) goddess who is invoked in healing rituals. The Sinhalese, Ceylon. (Yalman, 1964: 128; Obeyesekere, 1966: 9)

Pegaia A Greek nymph "of a healing fountain in Elis." (Thramer, 1925, 6: 548)

Pekhong A beneficent god, of the breath. The Daphla, Bengal and Assam. (Crooke, 1925, 4: 399)

P'êng Sung-liu The god of the bowels. China. (Werner, 1932: 372)

Pergrubrius, Pergubrius Baltic god of healing, of agriculture, and of fertility. (Puhvel, 1974: 83; Welsford, 1925, 9 : 242)

Phantasos A god of dreams who "assumed the deceptive appearance of earth, rock, water, trees, or anything inanimate." Brother of Morpheus and Icelos, sons of Sleep. Greece. (Ovid, 1950: 263)

Phobetor *See* **Icelos**

Pho lha Personal guardian god located in the right armpit, is invoked in magic ceremonies, is the bestower of prosperity on his worshippers. Sikkim/Tibet. (Nebesky-Wojkowitz, 1956, 1: 264, 256, 327; Gazeteer of Sikhim, 1894: 353)

Pichana Gobeche A god of healing who "was a powerful god and had to be appealed to through an intercessor or intermediary called Pichanto." The Zapotec at Chichicapa, Oaxaca, Mexico. (Whitecotton, 1977: 158)

P'i Ch'ang Yao Wang A god of pharmacists and of doctors. China. (Day, 1940: 111)

P'i Chia-ma, Pih Kya Ma God of the ribs. China. (Werner, 1932: 375; Du Bose, n.d.: 405)

Pien Ch'iao One of the gods of medicine. China. (Werner, 1932: 377)

Piluitus, Piluuytis, and variants A Baltic god/goddess of healing, of agricultural fertility and of harvests. (Puhvel, 1974: 83; Welsford, 1925, 9: 488)

Podaleirios, Podalire Greek surgeon deity and god of healing associated with internal medicine and particularly with the healing of animals. Son of Asklepios and Epione. (Thramer, 1925, 6: 551; Roscher, 1965, 3, 2: 2586; Duprez, 1970: 65–66; Morford and Lenardon, 1975: 291)

Podamata A goddess of the Bhil invoked by women in illnesses. India. (Wiesinger, 1967: 501)

Ponniyayi A village goddess of the Trichinopoly District who confers health, grants children and relieves suffering. India. (Hemingway, 1907: 89)

Potrimpus, Potrympus The Baltic god of "rivers and springs" is also a god of "healing and fertility." (Puhvel, 1974: 83; Machal, 1918: Plate xxxvii)

Prabha A goddess of light, of health, worshipped particularly "for the well-being of the cattle." The Kanjars, India. (Briggs, 1953: 555; Danielou, 1964: 96)

Ptah The creator god and architect of the universe is at Memphis; also a god of healing. Egypt. (Jayne, 1962: 75; Budge, 1969, 1: 500–502)

Ptai A deity "charged with the care of the foetus." Egypt. (Ames, 1965: 112)

Rachmay A nurse goddess of Canaan. Near East. (Driver, 1956: 22)

Ramahavaly The god of healing of the Malagasy. Madagascar. (Sibree, 1880: 299)

Rangamina A deity invoked in illness. The Tanala, Madagascar. (Linton, 1933: 192)

Rantimoa A deity of the Tanala invoked in illness. Madagascar. (Linton, 1933: 192)

Rauru God of the head. Son of Raki (Rangi) and Papa-tu-a-nuku. The Maori, New Zealand. (White, 1887, 1: 22; Andersen, 1928: 375)

Ravai A god in the form of a stone, invoked with Epe and Kivava in sickness and in war. Perau, New Guinea. (MacKenzie, 1930: 287)

Raxie A god of the Male Paharias who lived in a black stone and was invoked during epidemics or attack by tigers. India. (Crooke, 1925, 5: 13)

Revali A goddess invoked for relief by the "lame, the blind, and also the paralytic and the stammering folk." India. (Ghurye, 1962: 256)

Reven-pas, Nastasija God(dess) of sleep. The Mordvins, Russia. (Paasonen, 1925, 8: 846)

Rin-ch'en-zla-wa A medical Buddha of Tibet. (Snellgrove, 1957: 190; Waddell, 1959: 354)

Rohonyo Khambe A god invoked in cases of fever. The Bhils, India. (Naik, 1956: 187)

Rono (Lono) Hawaiian god of medicine, as well as of the sun, the east, and of wisdom. (Melville, 1969: 25, 28, 34)

Rozvi shave A deity of the Varozvi tribe who bestows the capacity for healing. Nyanjena Reserve, Rhodesia. (Gelfand, 1966: 94)

Lalla Rqiya A healing deity of the grotto d'El Maqta. Morocco. (Basset, 1920: 74; Westermarck, 1920: 37)

Sáa God "of the sense of Touch or Feeling and of knowledge and understanding." He protects "the members of the deceased by his magical powers." Egypt. (Budge, 1969, 2: 296–297)

Sagangan A god invoked in curing ceremonies, to whom gifts are given in exchange for the life. Also called Ingalit. The Tinguian, Philippines. (Cole, 1922: 334)

Sakarabru A god of healing and of justice, "but also a terrible and bloodthirsty one." Guinea and Senegambia groups, West Africa. (Larousse, 1968: 484)

Saking A lame spirit who protects from illness of the legs. The Tinguian, Philippines. (Cole, 1922: 340)

Sakka King of the gods and also king of the nats (but benevolent), who is invoked to guard and protect the eyes and ears in illness. Burma. Same as Indra. (Spiro, 1967: 152, 248; Zimmer, 1955: 191)

Salus As a Sabine goddess she was "the personification of the general welfare." Later under the Romans, and identified with Hygieia, she became the goddess of health. Italy. (Jayne, 1962: 437–438; Schoeps, 1961: 148; Fairbanks, 1907: 253; Thramer, 1925, 6: 553; Dumézil, 1966, 2: 444)

Sans-rgyas sman-gyi bla Bedurya'i 'Od-Kyi rgyal-po The "Buddha Master of Medicine . . . invoked in all the medical texts." Tibet. (Snellgrove, 1957: 190; Waddell, 1959: 354)

Sarpanitum Assyro/Babylonian solar goddess and, as merged with Erua, a daughter of Ea, a water goddess associated with the life-giving principle. She was a goddess of healing and possibly originally the protectress of the unborn child. Wife of Marduk. Near East. (Jayne, 1962: 127; Jastrow, 1898: 121–122; Robertson, 1911: 221)

Savanmata A goddess invoked by women in illnesses. The Bhils, India. (Wiesinger, 1967: 501)

Sekh Lag, Shesh Nag A god invoked in snakebite. The Bhils, India. (Naik, 1956: 187)

Sekhmet A lion-headed goddess who caused and also cured epidemics and was invoked by bonesetters. She was associated with Ptah in his healing capacities, and by him was the mother of Nefertun. Egypt. (Casson, 1965: 73, 75; Ames, 1965: 101; Schoeps, 1961: 70; Jayne, 1962: 76; Larousse, 1968: 36)

Sen Szi Miao A god of medicine worshipped by physicians. Anking, China. (Shryock, 1931: 128, 162)

Serapis A god of healing and of the underworld formed by the merging of Apis, the sacred bull, and Osiris as Bull of the Underworld. Worshipped at Alexandria and Memphis. Egypt. (Jayne, 1962: 77–78; Budge, 1969, 1: 126; 1969, 2: 195, 198)

gSer-bzang-dri-med A medical Buddha of Tibet. (Snellgrove, 1957: 190; Waddell, 1959: 354)

Setem God of the sense of Hearing. Egypt. (Budge, 1969, 2: 298)

Shadrafa A god of medicine and of healing whose symbols are the serpent and the calathos (a flaired food basket worn on the head), which make him also a god of fecundity. He is shown with a scorpion on his left shoulder. Palmyra, Syria. (Duprez, 1970: 58–59)

Shadrapa Phoenician "patron of doctors." Near East. (Herm, 1975: 111)

Shang Chien "Two gods of the 'middle' of the neck." China. (Werner, 1932: 326)

Shang Kien The "god of the nape of the neck." China. (Du Bose, n.d.: 405)

Shave nganga A spirit of healing or divining. The Nyajena Reserve, Rhodesia. (Gelfand, 1966: 93–94)

Shên Hsiu-chih A Chinese god of medicine. (Werner, 1932: 418)

Shen Nung A god of medicine and of pharmacy, and a god of agriculture developing the knowledge of the useful and harmful plants. As a god of medicine he formed a triad with Fu Hsi and Huang Ti. China. (Day, 1940: 105; Werner, 1932: 419, 505; Larousse, 1968: 397; Graham, 1961: 176)

Shetula A Hindu goddess worshipped as the protectress from smallpox and skin diseases. India. (Coleman, 1832: 396)

Shigidi The malevolent god of nightmares. The Yoruba, Nigeria. (Mockler-Ferryman, 1925, 9: 280)

Shih Fan-wu A god "of Decoctions and of Acupuncture" of the Taoist Ministry of Medicine. China. (Werner, 1932: 505)

Shih Liang-shih One of the gods of the tongue. China. (Werner, 1932: 427)

Shiturupakpe Kamui Ekashi A name of Kinashut Kamui as a god of healing when he was invoked in illnesses and in difficult childbirth. The Ainu, Japan. (Munro, 1963: 19)

Shou Ch'ang God of the hair. China. (Werner, 1932: 430)

Shuang I A name of the god of the kidneys. China. (Werner, 1932: 219)

Shu Kung God of the knee. China. (Werner, 1932: 432)

Shulman Canaanite god of healing, the equivalent of Eshmun (Phoenician). Near East. (Albright, 1956: 79)

Simbi d'leau One of the Petro deities who can endow with the capacity to heal. Husband of Erzilie GéRouge. Haiti. West Indies. (Herskovits, 1937, 1: 151, 316)

Simhanada-Avalokitesvara, Simhanada-Lokesvara A "non-Tantra form of Avalokitesvara invoked to cure leprosy." Buddhism. (Getty, 1962: 60)

Sindun A celestial mandang (medicine woman), sister of Kumang. The Dyaks, Sarawak, Borneo. (Sarawak Gazette, 1963: 122)

Sinngund, Sindgund, Sinthgunt A Teutonic goddess who possessed magical charms for healing. Sister of Sunna. (Grimm, 1880: 224; 1883, 2: 705; MacCulloch, 1964: 18)

Sinnilktok A split deity—one side a woman, one side a dog. She is benevolent—curing the sick and providing seals. The Eskimo, Baffin Land, Canada. (Bilby, 1923: 265)

Sitlamata The highest of the goddesses invoked by women—in sterility and for protection from smallpox. The Bhils, India. (Wiesinger, 1967: 499–501)

sman-bla The "Healing Buddha." Tibet. Same as Manla. (Getty, 1962: 24)

gSo byed pa (pr. **Sochepa**) A Bon god of healing. Tibet. (Tucci, 1980: 218)

Soma God of herbs and of healing, of longevity, bestowing strength and vitality. He is god of the soma plant, the drink of the gods; the giver of good things; sometimes identified with the moon. India. (Ions, 1967: 20, 81; Macdonell, 1897: 104–114; Jayne, 1962: 174; Barth, 1921: 11)

So-meme A god invoked by barren women to provide fertility. The Mikirs, India. (Stack and Lyall, 1908: 32)

Somnus Roman god of sleep. Same as Hypnos. (Bulfinch, 1898: 90–91; Prentice Hall, 1965: 134)

Sonb The personification of health, as a Nile god. Egypt. (Gardiner, 1925, 9: 791)

Sopor Roman personification of sleep. (Roscher, 1965, 4: 1215)

Soranus A Sabine/Roman god, "possibly a chthonic deity . . . bringing health and deliverance from disease by the purification of external fire." (Jayne, 1962: 439–440)

Sozem A god, the personification of hearing, who forms a dual deity with Ma'a' as Ma'a'-Sozem—"seeing-hearing." Egypt. (Gardiner, 1925, 9: 791)

Srog lha (pr. **soklha**) The personal guardian god of life, "the vital strength" located in the heart. Tibet and Sikkim. (Gazeteer of Sikhim, 1894: 353; Nebesky-Wojkowitz, 1956, 1: 264, 332; Tucci, 1980: 269n. 18)

Stcitoma "Sleep, a supernatural being." The Bella Coola, British Columbia. (McIlwraith, 1948, 2: 619)

Stl msila A male supernatural who causes nightmares. The Bella Coola, British Columbia. (McIlwraith, 1948, 1: 46)

Suhui Kak A Mayan goddess of healing is also the spirit of the new fire. Central America. (Tozzer, 1941: 153)

Sukunabikona, Sukunahikona A dwarf god, the son of Kami-Musubi. He is god of medicines and of medical knowledge, of charms to repel evil spirits, in which he is associated with Okuninushi. Together they also were responsible for bringing the land under cultivation and introducing culture. Japan. (Yasumaro, 1928: 69, 70; Kato, 1926: 134; Herbert, 1967: 328–330; Aston, 1925, 11: 465)

Sula Pat A hill god invoked when epidemics strike men or cattle, also in drought. The Santals, India. (Mukherjea, 1962: 278)

Su Ling-sheng A god of the lungs. China. (Werner, 1932: 460)

Sulis A Celtic goddess of healing and of sacred springs. Gaul and Britain. (Ross, 1967: 175, 190; Mac-Cana, 1970: 34)

Sumúldo "Mother of the Breasts" invoked for full breasts when pregnant and for release from discomfort when the time for drying-up comes. The Cagaba and the Kogi, Colombia. (Reichel-Dolmatoff, 1949/50: 173)

Sun Chên-jên A member of the Ministry of Medicine. China. (Werner, 1932: 505)

Sunna A sun goddess possessed of magical charms for healing. Sister of Sindgund. Germany. (MacCulloch, 1964: 18; Grimm, 1880: 224; 1883, 2: 705)

Sun Ssu-miao A god of druggists. China. (Werner, 1932: 468)

Synallaxis A Greek nymph "of a healing fountain in Elis . . . probably a personification of the change towards recovery." (Thramer, 1925, 6: 548)

Tagi A deity invoked in Faraulep "to heal the sick by rescuing their souls from the canoe of Metileru." Micronesia. (Burrows, 1947/48: 13)

Tagma-sa-langit The "god and protector of the sick." The Subanun, Philippines. (Jocano, 1969: 24)

Tahquitz An evil god who was originally beneficial and would sometimes confer upon some people the power to heal. The Cahuilla, California. (Brumgardt and Bowles, 1981: 38)

Tah-reh-nyoh-trah-squah The god of dreams—"The Revealer." The Wyandot (Iroquois), Lakes Huron and Erie. (Connelley, 1899: 118)

T'ai I A Taoist god of medical knowledge, a stellar deity who listens "for the cries of sufferers in order to save them." China. (Werner, 1934: 143)

T'ai-i Chun The god "of the middle of the mouth." China. (Werner, 1932: 321)

T'ai Yih "God of the Primordial Cause" and a medical divinity. China. (Du Bose, n.d.: 403)

T'ai-yin Shên God of the chin. China. (Werner, 1932: 485)

Ta Kwesi An Ashanti god invoked for health, fertility, and protection. Ghana. (Clarke, 1930: 448–449)

lTa-lha A deity of the Bon who "suppresses and banishes all evil, sickness, etc." The Tso-so Territory of southwest Ssu-Ch'uan. China. (Rock, 1947: 423)

Tama A "god who healed men who had fallen from trees, or been bitten by sharks." Paumotu, Polynesia. (Williamson, 1933, 2: 73). In the Society Islands, a god of surgery invoked also in fractures, bruises, dislocations. (Ellis, 1853: 333)

Tama-teina God of medicine and of surgery. Brother of Tama-ehu. Tahiti, Polynesia. (Henry, 1928: 377, 391)

Tan Chu God of the teeth. China. (Werner, 1932: 485)

Tangakina A god invoked in sickness. Lifuka Island, Tonga, Polynesia. (Gifford, 1929: 307)

T'ang Chang God of the skin. China. (DuBose, n.d.: 405)

Tango do Para A god of healing, sometimes identified with Guapindaia, "the *tangaru-para* songbird." Belem, Brazil. (Leacock, 1972: 135, 168)

Tan Yüan, Tan Yuen God of the heart. China. (Werner, 1932: 156; Du Bose, n.d.: 404)

Tao Kang God of the diaphragm. China. (Du Bose, n.d.: 404)

Tapinare A god of healing identified with the jaguar. Son of Rei Turquia. Belem, Brazil. (Leacock, 1972: 131, 135)

Tarenyawagon A deity revered as the sender of dreams. The Iroquois, Eastern United States. (Morgan, 1909: App. B)

Tarumusubi A Shinto deity—"the Producer of Perfect Bodily Health and Strength." Japan. (Kato, 1926: 70)

Tatevali The god of fire is also the god of health and of shamans who cure and prophesy. With him are associated "the macaw, the royal eagle, the cardinal-bird, the tiger, the lion, and the opossum,—also herbs and grass." The Huichol, Jalisco, Mexico. (Alexander, 1920: 121; Seler, 1925, 6: 828; Chamberlain, 1900: 305)

Telesphoros A god of convalescence associated with Asklepios. Greece and Asia Minor. (Jayne, 1962: 348–349; Thramer, 1925, 6: 551; Murray, 1935: 207)

Temazcalteci A name of Ciuacoatl as Grandmother of the Sweat-Bath. She was also a goddess "of medicine and of medicinal herbs." Aztec, Mexico. (Alexander, 1920: 75; Bancroft, 1886, 3: 353)

Tetuahuruhuru A god of surgery invoked also in fractures, bruises, and dislocations. Society Islands, Polynesia. (Ellis, 1853: 333)

Thatmanitu A minor goddess of healing. Daughter of Keret. Phoenicia. Near East. (Albright, 1968: 148, 151)

Thoth The moon god and god of knowledge was considered the "founder of medicines" and had the power to heal the wounds of the gods, whether self-inflicted or due to evil powers. Egypt. (Budge, 1973, 1: 65; Jayne, 1962: 32)

T'ieh-kuai Li A god of apothecaries. China. (Werner, 1932: 501)

T'ien I Chên Chün God of physicians. Also a stellar god known as Shang Ch'ing T'ien I. China. (Day, 1940: 110–111)

T'ien-ling Chun, T'ien lung Chun One of the gods of the eyebrows. China. (Werner, 1932: 118, 507)

Tigyama A god of healing and protective of the home. The Bagobo, Philippines. (Benedict, 1916: 11, 19)

Tinimugan A god of healing and of the relief of pain. The Ifugao, Philippines. (Barton, 1946: 68)

Ti-Ouaré A healing god, but also one of the gods of the dead and of cemeteries. Haiti. West Indies. (Marcelin, 1950: 197)

Tipa A god of doctors and of medicine. Society Islands, Polynesia. (Henry, 1928: 145, 376)

Pai Tomas An elderly and humble god, one of the Preto Velho gods who are "gifted curers." Belem, Brazil. (Leacock, 1972: 155)

Topochi A wise tree god who has the power of healing. The Ainu, Japan. (Batchelor, n.d.: 352)

T'sing Ken God of the brain. China. (DuBose, n.d.: 404)

Tsuηi "The mythological first shaman" with whom the shaman identifies and so gains healing power. The Jivaro, Ecuador. (Harner, 1972: 161, 224)

Tudoη A constellation deity invoked at sacrifices for sufferers from "retention of urine," as well as before transplantation of rice seedlings. The Kankanay, Luzon, Philippines. (Vanoverbergh, 1972: 91)

Tui Ha'a Fakafanua A god who in his favorable manifestation bestows the power of healing. Tonga, Polynesia. (Gifford, 1929: 295–298)

Tumailangi A god of Matanga who has the power of healing. Pukapuka, Polynesia. (Beaglehole, 1938: 310)

T'ung Chung-chung A god of the skin. China. (Werner, 1932: 531)

T'ung Lai-yü Chinese god of the stomach. (Werner, 1932: 459)

Tung Lien Yoh God of the stomach. China. (Du Bose, n.d.: 405)

T'ung Ming A god of the tongue. China. (Werner, 1932: 510; Du Bose, n.d.: 404)

Tung Wang-fu "There are three gods of the head, their name being Tung Wang-fu." China. (Werner, 1932: 155)

Tzapotla tenan, Tzaputaltena A goddess who was considered to have discovered the use of oxitl, a medicinal resin, to relieve "the itch in the head, irruptions on the skin, sore throats, chapped feet or lips." Mexico. (Bancroft, 1886, 3: 409; Chamberlain, 1925, 4: 740)

Ah Uaynih "Chorti god of sleep . . . dual sexed, the male bringing sleep to women, the female to men." Guatemala. (Thompson, 1970: 326)

Uba Gami The Nurse goddess whose shrine is the icho tree. Japan. (Holtom, 1931: 11)

Ah Uincir Dz'acar A Mayan "god of remedies . . . patron of herbalists . . . dual sexed . . . Ah Uincir Kopot is another name." The Chorti, Guatemala. (Thompson, 1970: 312)

Ulgere A deity invoked for the cure of earache and toothache. The Altaic, Siberia. (Czaplicka, 1969: 363)

Uli-la'a God of medicines of Molokai. Hawaii. (Beckwith, 1940: 114)

Umina The god of medicine of the Caranques. Ecuador. (Larousse, 1968: 441)

Uni The god of sleep. Finland. (Bray, 1935: 48)

Vagubudza shave A deity with the ability to heal. The Nyajena Reserve, Rhodesia. (Gelfand, 1966: 97)

Valentia A deity of health of the Umbrian town of Ocriculum. Italy. (Jayne, 1962: 438)

Valetudo A North Oscan goddess of good health, of bodily vigor. Italy. (Roscher, 1965, 6: 159; Gray, 1930: 144; Conway, 1925, 7: 458)

Verethragna A great god of healing, but can also cause illness and death. He is a god of victory and of war, of strength and virility. He takes numerous incarnations—"wind, bull, horse, male camel, boar, young man, falcon, ram, male antelope, warrior." Iran. (Jayne, 1962: 196; Dumézil, 1966, 1: 237; Dresden, 1961: 351; Gray, 1930: 117–119)

Guédé-Vi A god of healing, son of Guédé Nibo. Haiti. West Indies. (Marcelin, 1950: 193)

Vol, Volla Germanic goddess possessed of magical charms for healing. Also a goddess of abundance. (MacCulloch, 1964: 18, 184)

Vorombetsivazana A deity invoked in making sacrifices in times of illness, in making of vows. The Tanala, Madagascar. (Linton, 1933: 194)

Wang The "Grand Master of Therapeutical Clinic"—the Taoist Ministry of Medicine. China. (Werner, 1932: 505)

Wanga An ancient god was "consulted in reference to sickness and disease, and he also foretold in what manner common evils might be averted." The Baganda, Uganda. (Roscoe, 1965: 313)

Wang Fu Mu "The Gods of the Nipples." China. (Werner, 1932: 327)

ah way-n-ix *See also* **Ah Uaynih.** The same information, but also ah way-n-ix is malevolent in assisting Chamer, the god of death, as he "cannot bring death to an individual until the latter is asleep or in a coma." The Chorti, Guatemala. (Wisdom, 1940: 398–399)

Weeng The Algonquin god of sleep. Eastern United States. Also the Chippewa, Minnesota. (Schoolcraft, 1857, 6: 659; Emerson, 1884: 434; Rogers, 1957: 2)

Wei Chên-jên A "Junior Assistant" in the "Ministry of Medicine." China. (Werner, 1932: 505)

Wei Chiang Ta Wang A deity invoked in cases of smallpox and measles. China. (Day, 1940: 40)

Wei Ku A god of medicine. China. (Werner, 1932: 552)

Wei Shan-chün A god of medicine. China. (Werner, 1932: 552)

Wen Yin God of the hand. China. (Du Bose, n.d.: 405)

Ah wink-ir t'sak-ar God of remedies and of medicinal herbs of the Chorti. Guatemala. *See also* **Ah Uincir Dz'acar.** (Wisdom, 1940: 401)

The Wu Ch'ang "(Five Robbers), often mistaken for Earth Gods, who protect against the plague." Anking, China. (Shryock, 1931: 127)

Wurschayto, Borsskayto A Baltic god, worshipped at oak trees, who "conferred luck in fishing and good health." (Puhvel, 1974: 80)

Xaŋlayaban A god who protects from smallpox and to whom the head of a dog is offered. The Isneg of Luzon, Philippines. (Vanoverbergh, 1953: 76–77)

Xoaltecuhtli The god of dreams. The Nahua, Mexico. (Reed, 1966: 96)

Yahola Hayuya and Yahola "act as guardians and good geniuses of (those studying medicine and the mysteries) . . . endow one with strength, physical activity and clearness of vision and thought." Yahola is also sometimes invoked in time of illness. The Creek Indians, Georgia. (Swanton, 1924/25: 485)

Sidi Yahya His shrine is visited for cures near the village of Dar Fellag. Morocco. (Westermarck, 1926, 1: 69, 70)

Yaksa The healing Buddha of Korea. (Clark, 1932: 56)

Yakujin-sama A god of healing at Takashima. Japan. (Norbeck, 1954: 133)

Yakushi The healing Buddha. Buddhist name for Sukunahikona (bikona). Japan. Same as Bhaisajyaguru. (Herbert, 1967: 330; Kato, 1926: 134; Eliot, 1935: 100, 110; Getty, 1962: 24)

Yao Shih Fo The Buddha of healing, of medicine. China. Same as Manla, Bhaisajyaguru. (Wood, 1937: 165; Getty, 1962: 24; Werner, 1932: 586; Day, 1940: 32)

Yao-shih Wang "Vaidurya Buddha . . . worshipped in China as a god of healing." (Werner, 1932: 587)

Yao Wang The god of medicine and of remedies. However, the triad of Shen Nung, Fu Hsi, and Huang Ti is considered superior to him. China. (Larousse, 1968: 397; Graham, 1958: 52; Werner, 1932: 587; Gamble, 1954: 419)

Moulay Ya'qoub A deity of hot springs, a healing deity of the grotto Chella near Rabat, invoked specifically for cures from syphilis. Morocco. (Basset, 1920: 76; Westermarck, 1920: 38)

Yen tsing niang niang Goddess of good eyesight who protects from maladies of the eyes. Also called Yen kouang nai nai. China. (Chavannes, n.d.: 32)

Yoalticitl The mother of the gods is also the goddess "of medicine and of doctors and of the sweatbaths." She is also goddess of childbirth and of the cradle. Mexico. (Bancroft, 1886, 3: 363; 1886, 2: 268, 275)

Yoh Si Fuh, Yo-shi-wang Fo, Yo-shi Fo, Yo Szi Fu All apparently variants of Yao Shih Fo, the Buddha of medicine. China. (Graham, 1928: 70; Edkins, 1880: 235; Shryock, 1931: 77; Maspero, 1963: 362)

Yoh Wang Taoist god of medicine. Szechwan, China. (Graham, 1928: 61)

Yo-tsang p'u-sa A god of medicine, associated with Yo-shi Fo. China. (Edkins, 1880: 246)

Yo-wang p'u-sa A god of medicine, patron of doctors and druggists. Associated with Yo-shi Fo. (Graham, 1961: 186; Edkins, 1880: 246)

Yuan Kuang One of the gods of the eyebrows. China. (Werner, 1932: 118)

Yüeh-shih Fo   The "Master-physician Buddha." China. (Werner, 1934: 120)

Yeuh-wang   A god of medicine of southwest China. (Graham, 1961: 163)

Yuen-ming   The god of the kidneys is also a god of the compass, of the north. China. (Du Bose, n.d.: 404, 327)

Yul lha   The personal guardian deity located in the crown of the head. This name applies both to an individual god and a group of gods. Tibet and Sikkim. (Nebesky-Wojkowitz, 1956, 1: 264, 328; Gazeteer of Sikhim, 1894: 354)

Yü Lung, Yung Lu   A name of the god of the nose. China. (Werner, 1932: 333, 602; Du Bose, n.d.: 404)

Yü Nü-chün   Two gods—"of the 'outside' of the neck." (Werner, 1932: 326). Du Bose gives as Yü Nü Kuin and a singular deity. China. (Du Bose, n.d.: 405)

Yü Tê   A god of vaccination. China. (Werner, 1932: 541)

Yzamna   A god of medicine. Yucatan, Mexico. *See* **Itzamna.** (Bancroft, 1886, 2: 697)

The z'an-lha   Personal deities whose worship "procures physical strength." Tibet. (Waddell, 1959: 375)

Zhang lha   God of the mother's lineage who resides in the heart. Tibet. (Tucci, 1980: 187)

Dz'ibaan Na   A god who "cures diseases . . . younger brother of Menzabac. . . . Another source has him as guardian of the mountains and hunting." Mexico. (Thompson, 1970: 327)

Pitao Zicala (Xicala)   The "god of dreams." The Zapotec, Oaxaca, Mexico. (Whitecotton, 1977: 164)

Zywie   A goddess of health and life, of longevity. Poland. (de Kay, 1898: 116)

47

Pleasures:
Happiness, Revelry, Festivals, Games

Aglaea, Aglaia   One of the Three Graces, daughters of Zeus and Eurynome, who are goddesses of hospitality and pleasures. Aglaea represents "Pageantry." Greece. (Hesiod-Brown, 1981: 78; Bulfinch, 1898: 12; Larousse, 1968: 128, 132)

Apila   A "god of wrestling and sports." The Manobo, Philippines. (Jocano, 1969: 23)

Ataksak   A god of joy who lives in the sky and responds to the conjurer when invoked. Baffin Land Eskimo, Canada. (Bilby, 1923: 209, 269; Larousse, 1968: 426)

'Aut-yeb   The personification of joy, as a woman. Egypt. (Gardiner, 1925, 9: 791)

Ayutha Vadukan   A deity worshipped "for their success in the training of young men in athletic feats." The Kaniyan, Southern India. (Thurston, 1909, 3: 198)

Balmarcod   A god of revelry. Near East. (Langdon, 1931: 22, 383, n. 106)

Bast, Bastet   A feline-headed goddess of joy and pleasure, of music and dancing. She also represented the fertilizing warmth of the sun and was a goddess of healing, protective against disease. Egypt. (Ames, 1965: 104; Jayne, 1962: 84; Schoeps, 1965: 70; Larousse, 1968: 37)

Benzaiten   A goddess of happiness and love, of the arts. Japan. (Herbert, 1967: 513; Eliseev, 1963: 446; Puini and Dickens, 1880: 440–443; Larousse, 1973: 326–327)

Bes   A god of foreign origin who was associated with revelry and pleasure, with music and dancing. He was also a god of childbirth as well as of war. Egypt. (Jayne, 1962: 55; Knight, 1915: 32; Budge, 1969, 2: 276, 284–285)

Binudbud   The "spirits of the feasts" who check men's appetites so little food and drink will satisfy, and temper their passions so as to avoid dissension. The Ifugao, Philippines. (Jocano, 1969: 17)

Bishamon-ten   One of the gods of happiness and good fortune. His greatest role was as a god of wealth. He was also a god of war and guardian of the North. Japan. (Eliseev, 1963: 446; Getty, 1962: 156, 168; Larousse, 1973: 324–325)

Charmophron   A Greek god of happiness, probably a surname of Hermes. (Roscher, 1965, 1, 1: 884)

Chi Fang Hsi Shên   A god of merrymaking at weddings and festivals. China. (Day, 1940: 92)

Ch'iu-tsu   The patron deity of the manufacturers of firecrackers used in festivals. Szechwan, China. (Graham, 1961: 186)

Chukem   A "deity of boundaries and foot-races." The Chibcha. Colombia. (Alexander, 1920: 204)

Chunda   A Buddhist goddess of smiling countenance. India. (Linossier, 1963: 98)

Comus   A Roman god of revelry and feasting, of pleasures, but also associated with overindulgence. (Salkeld, 1844: 312; Murray, 1935: 156)

Curitis   A goddess of festivals and joyousness who was also protective of married women. Italy. (Hadas, 1965: 73; Jayne, 1962: 494)

Daikoku   One of the seven gods of happiness and good luck, particularly of the household and of husbandry. Japan. (Hori, 1968: 39, 68; Herbert, 1967: 513; Piggott, 1969: 59; Puini and Dickens, 1880: 435)

bDe-mchhog   A god of happiness. Also called dPal-khor-lo-sdan-pa. Tibet. (Rock, 1947: 323)

Diwali   A goddess of festivals, of singing. The Bhils, India. (Naik, 1956: 183–4)

Ebisu   One of the seven gods of happiness, the patron of work, of fishermen, of tradesmen. Japan. (Eliot, 1935: 140; Piggott, 1969: 59; Eliseev, 1963: 446; Herbert, 1967: 511–512; Larousse, 1968: 422)

Eirene   One of the Horae, a goddess of peace, of "songs and festivities." Daughter of Themis and Zeus. Greece. (Kerényi, 1951: 102; Murray, 1935: 145; Roscher, 1965, 1, 1: 1221)

Euphrosyne   One of the three Graces, a goddess of hospitality and enjoyment. Greece. (Bulfinch, 1898: 12; Roscher, 1965, 1, 1: 1408; Larousse, 1968: 132; Hesiod-Brown, 1981: 78)

Fand   A Celtic otherworld goddess who metamorphoses as a bird and is a goddess of pleasure and of healing. Ireland. (Ross, 1967: 232, 239)

Fu-hsing   A god of happiness and a stellar god. China. (Maspero, 1963: 344; Larousse, 1968: 384; Day, 1940: 95)

Fukurokuju   One of the seven gods of happiness, a god of wisdom and of longevity. Japan. (Eliseev, 1963: 446; Puini and Dickens, 1880: 448–450; Larousse, 1968: 422; Piggott, 1969: 59)

Fu Shên   A god of happiness. China. (Werner, 1932: 143)

Ganapati, Ganesa, Pillaiyar   The elephant-headed god, remover of obstacles, is also a festival deity in the Poona District. India. (Ghurye, 1962: 114, 136; Hemingway, 1907: 89; Danielou, 1964: 291–294)

dGe lha   A god of happiness who is protective of worshippers and their prosperity. Tibet. (Nebesky-Wojkowitz, 1956, 1: 328, 333)

Gelos   A Greek god, the personification of laughter. (Gardner, 1925, 9: 794; Roscher, 1965, 1, 2: 1610)

The Graces, the Charities   Greek goddesses of the social amenities, of banquets, of the arts. Their number

and names vary, also their parentage. The latter are given as Zeus and Eurynome, Helios and Aegle, Dionysus and Aphrodite. They are named as Aglaia, Euphrosyne, and Thalia; in Athens as Hegemone and Auxo; in Sparta as Cleta (Cleia) and Phaenna; by Homer as Charis and Pasithea. (Murray, 1935: 197–198; Larousse, 1968: 132; Bulfinch, 1898: 12)

Hab   The personification of the abstraction " 'sport,' or 'festivity'." Egypt. (Gardiner, 1925, 9: 791)

Hastseltsi   The Red God, a god of racing. The Navaho, Arizona and New Mexico. (Matthews, 1902: 25; Burland, 1965: 149)

Hotei Kuwasho   One of the seven gods of happiness, associated with the hearth. Japan. (Puini and Dickens, 1880: 444, 446)

Hotei Osho   One of the seven gods of happiness, of Chinese origin. Japan. (Larousse, 1968: 404, 422)

Hsi Shên   Chinese god of bliss, of joy. (Day, 1940: 95, 166; Werner, 1932: 161)

Hsü Ch'ang   The god of archery. China. (Werner, 1932: 14)

Hubal   An archer god as well as an oracular and a rain god. Arabia. (Fahd, 1968: 65, 101)

Huitaca   A goddess of pleasure, drinking, and sexual indulgence. The Chibcha, Colombia. (Kroeber, 1946: 908; Osborne, 1968: 112)

Inemes   A goddess of happiness, of love potions and magic, as well as of lechery—widely worshipped. Mother of Ururupuin. Truk, Micronesia. (Bollig, 1927: 11, 38)

Iocus   A Greek/Roman god of joking. (Roscher, 1965, 2, 1: 283)

Jammarke   The patron of boxers, who sacrifice a dark red cock to him. The Maguzawa, Nigeria. (Greenberg, 1946: 34)

Keh Sienhung   The god of jugglers. China. (Du Bose, n.d.: 336)

Kichijo-ten   A goddess who sometimes replaces Fuku-roku-ju as a deity of happiness, giving wealth and well-being. Same as Laksmi. Japan. (Puini and Dickens, 1880: 450; Larousse, 1973: 326; Eliot, 1935: 139)

Komos   A Greek abstract deity—"Revel Rout"—associated with Dionysos. (Gardner, 1925, 9: 794)

Koros A female personification of excessive merriment, of exuberance. Greece. (Roscher, 1965, 2, 1: 1392)

Kuodar-gup The most important tribal god who bestows riches and happiness, all good, and rules over all through the powers given him by the god of heaven. The Selkup, Siberia. (Donner, 1926: 71–72)

Kuo Tzŭ-i Another name for Fu Shen. China. (Werner, 1932: 236)

Kupala A Slavonic deity of joy, associated with water and with powers of resucitation and exorcism. (Larousse, 1968: 296)

La'ala'a In Upolu, the god of wrestlers. Samoa, Polynesia. (Turner, 1884: 34)

Lado A Slavic god of mirth and pleasure, of happiness, to whom sacrifices were made before marriages. Russia and Lithuania. (Ralston, 1872: 104–105)

Li T'ien The god of firecrackers used in celebrations. China. (Werner, 1932: 249)

Lu-hsing A stellar god of happiness, of rewards, of money and position. China. (Maspero, 1963: 344–345; Day, 1940: 95; Larousse, 1968: 384)

Luxus Roman personification of revelry and of luxury. (Roscher, 1965, 2, 2: 2163)

Mac Da Tho A Celtic god, the host of the otherworld feast. (MacCana, 1970: 100)

Macuilxochitl Five Flower—the god of all games, of gambling, of feasting, of the arts, and a god of spring flowers and of growth. Mexico. (Caso, 1958: 80; Thompson, 1970: 313, 328; Duran, 1971: 305; Alexander, 1920: 57, 77; Spence, 1923: 196, 202–203; Nicholson, 1967: 93)

Makahopokia A Liku god invoked in the game "Jumping-stones-on-water." Niue Island, Polynesia. (Loeb, 1926, 1: 161)

Marimba Goddess of happiness, music, and singers. South Africa. (Mutwa, n.d.: vii)

Mato A facet of the Bear Spirit's personality was the patronage of pleasures and mischief, as well as the love/hate emotions. The Lakota/Oglala, South Dakota. (Walker, 1980: 121)

Min Kyawzwa A *nat* associated with drinking, cockfighting, and fireworks. Burma. (Scott, 1964: 354)

Nemea Goddess of the Nemean games, a daughter of Zeus and Selene. Greece. (Roscher, 1965, 3, 1: 115)

Noqoilpi The "gambling-god" who descended from the heavens, gambled with people, won, and enslaved them. The Navajo, Arizona and New Mexico. (Matthews, 1889: 89)

Ogbooka The god of mirth. The Abo, Nigeria. (Mockler-Ferryman, 1925, 9: 280)

Omacatl A god of banquets and hospitality, of festivities. An aspect of Tezcatlipoca. Aztec, Mexico. (Bancroft, 1886, 3: 408; Alexander, 1920: 62; Spence, 1923: 352)

Palaistra The personification of the art of wrestling, associated with Hermes as god of gymnastics. Greece. (Roscher, 1965, 3, 1: 1263)

Papa-iea A god of feasting and kava drinking. The Marquesas, Polynesia. (Christian, 1895: 190)

(Pitao) Peeze, Pitaoquille, Pitooyage A deity appealed to by "those involved in gaming or chance." The Zapotec, Oaxaca, Mexico. (Whitecotton, 1971: 165)

P'ing An Fu Chu Wang "Star King of Peace and Happiness . . . help . . . sought in facing the issues of life." China. (Day, 1940: 84)

P'u-hien p'u-sa, P'ou-hien A Bodhisattva who was the symbol of happiness. Same as Samantabhadra. China. (Edkins, 1880: 208, 236; Chavannes, n.d.: 118)

Pungarancha A Michoacan "god of runners." Mexico. (Craine and Reindorp, 1970: 239)

Pusiuraura The god of the dart game of the Taumako clan. Tikopia, Melanesia. (Firth, 1930: 80)

Sidi Qaddur ben Mlek Patron saint of gamblers. Morocco. (Westermarck, 1926, 1: 181)

Rekareka A god of pleasure. Mangareva, Polynesia. (Buck, 1938, 1: 426)

Sai-no-Kami A name of Dosojin as the God of Happiness—represented by natural symbols such as trees, stones, stone shrines, and found as well "on promontories overlooking the sea, on river banks, along paths deep in the mountains, on ridges overlooking valleys." Japan. (Czaja, 1974: 31, 46, 48)

Sakhidai-Noin The third son of Budurga-Sagan-Tengri—"the maker of happiness." With his wife

Sakhala-Khatun, the deities of fire. The Buriats, Siberia and Mongolia. (Klementz, 1925, 3: 4, 11)

Semoana   A sea deity who is also invoked in dart games. Tikopia, Melanesia. (Firth, 1930: 80)

Shou Hsing   A stellar god, Canopus (Ferguson), or a constellation of Chio and K'ang (Werner), a deity of happiness and longevity, whose appearance assures peace and disappearance foretells calamities. China. (Day, 1940: 95; Werner, 1934: 171–172; Ferguson 1937: 81; Maspero, 1963: 344)

Siris, Sirash   A Sumerian god or goddess of banquets. Near East. (Langdon, 1931: 202)

Sunchang   A god of archery; also called Emei. China. (Du Bose, n.d.: 328)

Tabliope   A goddess of gambling, of games at dice. Greece. (Roscher, 1965, 5: 2)

Tamon-ten   One of the gods of happiness and guardian deity of the North. Japan. Same as Bishamon, Vaisravana. (Puini and Dickens, 1880: 438–439; Eliseev, 1963: 447; Larousse, 1968: 422)

Ta-mo-tsu-shi   Patron deity of "boxers and prize fighters." Szechwan, China. (Graham, 1961: 186)

Tbauatsilla   A deified mortal, the god of contentment. The Ossetes, Caucasus. (Morgan, 1888: 390)

T'ien-Kuan   A god of happiness who records good and evil actions and has the power to grant happiness. China. (Maspero, 1963: 342; Day, 1940: 96; Larousse, 1968: 391)

Tinirau   The god of the dart game of the Tafua clan. Tikopia, Melanesia. (Firth, 1930: 80)

Ts'ai Pao Fu Shên   "Precious Treasure Happiness God." China. (Day, 1940: 115)

Ts'eng fou chen   A god who augments prosperity and happiness. China. (Chavannes, n.d.: 414)

Tung Fang Ch'ing Lung   "Azure Dragon of the East," who is considered "the harbinger of happiness." China. (Day, 1940: 66)

Tupuafiti   The god of the dart game of the Fangarere clan. Tikopia, Melanesia. (Firth, 1930: 80)

Ueuecoyotl   "Old Coyote," who is a god of irresponsibility and trickery, of feasts and dances. Aztec, Mexico. (Alexander, 1920: 83; Burland, 1967: x, xi)

Urutaetae   A god of music and dancing and entertainment, of games. Tahiti, Polynesia. (Ellis, 1853: 332; Henry 1928: 378)

Varo   The god of the dart game of the Kafika clan. A son of Tinirau. Tikopia, Melanesia. (Firth, 1930: 80)

Wohpe   The beautiful goddess of pleasures, happiness, beauty, and ceremonials was the daughter of Skan. The Lakota, South Dakota. (Walker, 1980: 51, 109–11, 220–222)

Wunsch   A Teutonic god of happiness and love who brings good fortune to men. (Grimm, 1888: 1328; de Kay, 1898: 22)

xašč édódí (xashchedodi), xašč'éĺbáhí (xashchelbahi)   Called "gray god or water sprinkler," the clown, the entertainer of the gods who is always the last in line of the dancers in ceremonials. The Navaho, Arizona and New Mexico. (Haile, 1947: 13, 19, 20, 31)

Xascelbai, xašč'èĺbáhí   "Water Sprinkler" who acts the clown, the entertainer, in ceremonials. He is the god of the rain, the snow. The Navaho, Arizona and New Mexico. (Waters, 1950: 234; Haile, 1947: 13, 20)

Xochipilli, Macuilxochitl, Cinteotl   An Aztec god of flowers and of maize, of vegetation; a god of happiness and pleasure, of feasting and drinking, of gaiety and love. Mexico. (Neumann, 1955: 196; Nicholson, 1967: 69; Spence, 1923: 154, 352; Alexander, 1920: 54, Plate VII; Vaillant, 1962: 145, 149)

Xolotl   The god of twins and of the malformed is also the god of the ball courts. He is the twin of Quetzalcóatl and represents the evening Venus. Mexico. (Helfritz, 1970: 158; Nicholson, 1967: 104; Caso, 1958: 18, 24; Alexander, 1920: 82; Larousse, 1968: 438)

Yachimata-hiko and **Yachimata-hime**   A phallic god and goddess of agriculture and of Dionysian festivals. They are beneficent and friendly deities of the crossroads and of travelers, protective from evil spirits. Japan. (Kato, 1926: 31; Herbert, 1967: 495; Revon, 1925, 9: 237)

Yebisu, Hiruko   A god of happiness and fruitfulness, of success and victory. Sometimes considered two separate deities. Japan. (Puini and Dickens, 1880: 431–434)

Ying hsi-niang   A goddess of joyfulness. The Monguors of Kansu. China. (Schram, 1957: 109)

Yum, Yumni, Yamni   The Whirlwind is a god of pleasure—of games, dancing, chance, love. The Lakota, South Dakota. (Walker, 1980: 51–54)

48

Gods of Time and Seasons: Calendar

Aa-am-khekh God of the twelfth hour of the day. Egypt. (Budge, 1969, 2: 302)

Aan Deity of the eighth hour of the eighth day of the Moon. Egypt. (Budge, 1969, 2: 292)

Aa-sheft Goddess of the fourth hour of the night. Egypt. (Budge, 1969, 2: 300)

Abal God of the twelfth day of the calendar; a "good day to pray for poor people." The Chimalteco, Guatemala. (Wagley, 1949: 70)

Ab-em-tu-f God of the second hour of the night. Egypt. (Budge, 1969, 2: 301)

Àfò Considered "one of the four days of the Igbo market-week, regarded as an alūsi [divinity]." Nigeria. (Isichei, 1978: 23, 334)

Ahabit Goddess of the sixth hour of the day. Egypt. (Budge, 1969, 2: 302)

Ahi God of the eighteenth day of the month. Egypt. (Budge, 1969, 2: 322)

Ahkinsok The "owner of the days." Mayan, Yucatan. Mexico. (Alexander, 1920: 141)

Ahò The "alūsi of the cycle of the year." The Igbo, Nigeria. (Isichei, 1978: 322, n. 13)

Aion, Time The "god of the astrologers." Mithraism, Persia. (Larousse, 1968: 220). Roman personification of time and eternity. (Roscher, 1965, 1, 1: 195)

Aishish Gatschet believes him a lunar god and considers him a calendrical deity, as "The moon is the originator of the months, and the progress of the months brings on the seasons." The Klamath, Oregon. (Gatschet, 1890: lxxxvii–lxxxviii)

Aiwi-sruthrima Deity of "the fourth period of the day, from sunset to midnight." Iran. (Gray, 1930: 132)

Aj The second day of the calendar—"in a sense a deity." The Chimalteco. (Wagley, 1949: 70) One of the Day Lords associated with the house, the place, with patrilineage. A male "child born this day should make a good lineage, canton, or town priest-shaman. . . . A female . . . will be a responsible mother and wife, especially lucky with the raising of animals and children." Momostenango. Guatemala. (Tedlock, 1982: 118–119)

Ajmac One of the Day Lords. Ajmac days are favorable for the introduction of the still unborn child to the foundation shrine of the patrilineage; favorable for journeys and business. An Ajmac child will be fortunate in business but irresponsible in personal relationships but these lapses will be forgiven. Momostenango, Guatemala. (Tedlock, 1982: 121, 122)

Ak'abal One of the Day Lords important in the teaching of a daykeeper, the planning of a marriage and approaching the girl's family, the introduction of the newborn to the ancestors. This day imparts to the child born on this day "the extra body-soul called 'lightning' *(coyopa)* . . . [which] enables the child to communicate directly with both the natural and supernatural worlds." This child "(of either sex) will be feminine, wealthy, verbally skillful, and possibly a liar, cheat, or complainer." Momostenango, Guatemala. (Tedlock, 1982: 108–110)

Akert God of the fifth hour of the day. Egypt. (Budge, 1969, 2: 302)

Akhet One of the seasons—"inundation." A goddess, sometimes represented as a Nile deity. Egypt. (Gardiner, 1925, 9: 791)

Akmac The fifth day of the calendar, "in a sense a deity." The Chimalteco, Guatemala. (Wagley, 1949: 70)

'Alahtin The goddess of the moon is strongly associated with the calendar and is observed closely by their astronomers. The Chumash, California. (Hudson and Underhay, 1978: 75, 77)

Aldúnel-due Father of the Summer. The Cagaba, the Kogi, Colombia. (Reichel-Dolmatoff, 1949/50: 115)

Amset(h) One of the sons of Horus, a funereal god, and god of the first hour of the day and of the night, also of the fourth day of the month. Egypt. (Budge, 1969, 1: 491–492; 1969, 2: 294, 320)

Amsu God of the fifth month. He is a god of virility and of regeneration. Egypt. (Budge, 1969, 2: 293, 507; Knight, 1915: 15)

Anatole "Sunrise," one of the Greek Horae. (Roscher, 1965, 1, 1: 1209)

An-erta-nef-nebat A variant deity of the eleventh hour of the day and of the night who watches behind Osiris during the eleventh hour of the day and of the night, and before him the twelfth hour of the day. Egypt. (Budge, 1969, 2: 294–295)

Angerona Goddess of the winter solstice and goddess of silence. She is the goddess who at the end of the winter solstice "expands the days which have grown *angusti*" — (distressingly short, uneasy). Italy. (Dumézil, 1966, 1: 335–338)

An-mut-f God of the fourth hour of the night and god of the nineteenth day Heb-setem-metu-f of the month. A name of Osiris. Egypt. (Budge, 1969, 2: 183, 301, 322)

Anna Perenna An "ancient Italian goddess of the year." (Jayne, 1962: 417)

Anpet Goddess of the fifth hour of the night of the seventeenth day of the Moon. Egypt. (Budge, 1969, 2: 292)

Anu The god of heaven, of the starry skies, is with Enlil god of the month Nisan (Semitic), Nisannu (Summerian). Near East. (Hommel, 1925, 3: 74; Jastrow, 1898: 201; Jacobsen, 1970: 47; Pettazzoni, 1956: 77)

Ap An ape god who is deity of the ninth hour of the ninth day of the Moon. Egypt. (Budge, 1969, 2: 268, 292)

Apantrod A Teutonic god—the personified evening. (Grimm, 1883, 2: 884)

Apt The name of Uatchet as goddess of the eleventh month—Epiphi. Egypt. (Budge, 1969, 1: 444)

Apt-hent A variant deity of the eleventh month of the year. Egypt. (Budge, 1969, 2: 293)

Apt-Renpit A variant deity of the twelfth month of the year. Egypt. (Budge, 1969, 2: 293)

Ap-uat The "opener of the ways," the jackal god, is considered with Anpu/Anubis as two forms of one god. He is the "opener of the roads of the north," and the god of the winter solstice and the twentieth day of the month. Egypt. (Budge, 1969, 1: 206, 493; 1969, 2: 264, 322)

Ari-nef Nebat Deity of the eleventh hour of the day and of the night. Egypt. (Budge, 1969, 2: 294)

Ari-ren-f-tchesef God of the tenth day of the month. He watches behind Osiris the eighth hour of the day, and before him the ninth hour of the day. Egypt. (Budge, 1969, 2: 295, 322)

Ari-tchet-f God of the ninth day of the month. Egypt. (Budge, 1969, 2: 320)

Armai Deity of the sixth hour of the day and of the night. Egypt. (Budge, 1969, 2: 294)

Armauai God of the fifteenth day of the month and associated with the ceremonies of the dead Osiris. Egypt. (Budge, 1969, 2: 129, 322)

Arò The year, a powerful alūsi created by Chukwu. The Igbo, Nigeria. (Isichei, 1978: 27)

Ar-ren-f-tchesef God of the eighth hour of the day and of the night. He watches behind Osiris during the eighth hour of the night. He is associated with the ceremonies of the dead Osiris. Egypt. (Budge, 1969, 2: 294–295, 129)

Asbet God of the fourth hour of the day. Egypt. (Budge, 1969, 2: 302)

Ashur, Assur The chief god was also a god of war and a calendrical god—of intercalary Adar. Assyria and Babylonia. Near East. (Jastrow, 1898: 82, 128, 463; Hommel, 1925, 3: 75)

Ast The goddess of the third hour of the third day of the Moon. She watches before Osiris during the fourth and fifth hours of the night. Also goddess of the ninth hour of the day. Egypt. (Budge, 1969, 2: 292, 295, 302)

Atri A deity associated with the winter solstice, with the lengthening again of the days. India. (Littleton, 1965: 157)

Autumnus Roman personification of Autumn, associated with the harvest, wine, fruit. (Roscher, 1965, 1, 1: 738)

Ayara The collective name of the 30 deities of the days of the month. Iran. (Gray, 1930: 139)

Ba A god of the eleventh hour of the Tuat, the divisions of the hours of the Underworld through which the dead sun passes. Egypt. (Budge, 1969, 1: 200; Knight, 1915: 28)

Ba-neb-Tettu The god of the twelfth hour of the twelfth day of the Moon. Egypt. (Budge, 1969, 2: 292)

Bangun bangun God "of universal time. He regulated the cosmic movements" of the Upperworld. The Sulod, Central Panay, Philippines. (Jocano, 1969: 19)

Bapi-f God of the fifth hour of the night. Egypt. (Budge, 1969, 2: 301)

Batz, Bats One of the Day Lords. Marriage proposals and the later ceremony itself are initiated on this day; also the request in the initiation of a daykeeper or diviner. A child born this day "will be lucky in business, marriage, and life" and accumulate wealth, children, and respect. A favorable day for the wealthy and to pray for money. Momostenango, Guatemala. (Tedlock, 1982: 116–117; Wagley, 1949: 70)

Bebon The "spirit of winter, a being of vast power who usually exhausted himself . . . [with] his intensity and endurance" lived in the far north. After battle with Zeegwun (summer), each was given alternate control over the land. Bebon was the cause of illness, decay, hardship, and represents death; was a mighty hunter and warrior. The Ojibway, Lake Superior region. (Johnston, 1976: 28, 29, 161–162)

Bildar On the earliest Babylonian calendar he was god of the eighth month; the calendar of Sargon, the third or ninth month; the calendar of Ur, the fourth month. Near East. (Hommel, 1925, 3: 73, 78)

Birdu A title of Nergal as "Cold," "Chill," a god of the winter solstice and of the underworld. Near East. (Langdon, 1931: 49; Paton, 1925, 3: 181)

Bolon Ahau A god of the Katun prophecies associated with the calendar. Mayan, Mexico. (Tozzer, 1941; 168)

Boreas A Scandinavian storm giant, a personification of winter, who takes the form of an eagle. (Stern, 1898: 121)

čgh-un kürde A Mongolian tutelary god. Same as Kalacakra, "Wheel of Time." (Getty, 1962: 146)

Came One of the Day Lords. A favorable day for seeking benefits for self and/or others, for harmony in relationships. A child born this day "will be wealthy, somewhat feminine, and verbally skillful . . . receives body lightning . . . might become a lineage priest-shaman or a marriage spokesman." Momostenango, Guatemala. (Tedlock, 1982: 112–113)

Can *See also* **Kan.** One of the Day Lords "associated with the actions of a calendar diviner . . . trained as an *ajmesa,* or *ajnawal mesa*" (spiritualist) who "are simultaneously the most successful curers and a source of serious illness and death." Because of their power they are sometimes chosen as patrilineal priest-shaman. A person born this day will be strong, powerful, evil; as he/she also receives body lightning, this power should be controlled or directed by becoming an *ajnawal mesa.* Momostenango, Guatemala. (Tedlock, 1982: 111–112)

Can Tzicnal God of the Muluc years, invoked in their New Year rituals. Also the Bacab of the north quarter. Mayan, Mexico. (Tozzer, 1941: 145; Thompson, 1970: 276)

Carpo One of the Horae, a goddess of the seasons—of Autumn, of fruits. Daughter of Zephyrus and Chloris. Greece. (Burns, 1925, 3: 373; Fairbanks, 1907: 170; Murray, 1935: 142)

C'at One of the Day Lords. He "serves as the Secretary (and Treasurer) for Mam E and Mam No'j" as well as for the Mundo; therefore a day for paying debts—offerings of copal—to the Mundo and the ancestors (Nantat). A person born this day, because of the associations, is not considered fit for "any sort of civil, political, military, or religious office." Momostenango, Guatemala. (Tedlock, 1982: 110–111, 120)

Cauac One of the gods of the new year, a "harbinger of disaster." Mayan, Central America. (Nicholson, 1967: 44)

Cawuk One of the Day Lords. A day for offerings of "newly harvested crops" to the Mundo, also for requesting that offerings adverse to them be returned to the sender. This day's child will have a life of trouble and harrassment from ancestors. Momostenango, Guatemala. (Tedlock, 1982: 123–124)

Chac Acantun A god associated with the New Year rituals of Muluc years. Mayan, Mexico. (Tozzer, 1941: 145)

Chac u Uayeyab A god associated with the ceremonies of the rituals of the Muluc years. Mayan, Mexico. (Tozzer, 1941: 144)

Chalchiuhtlicue The goddess of water was patroness of the fifth day, Coatl (the serpent), of the 20-day series Tonalpouhalli; goddess of the third hour of the day; and as goddess of "Flowing Water," the goddess of the sixth hour of the night. Aztec, Mexico. (Alexander, 1920: 54, 73; Burland, 1967: 88)

Chantico The goddess of the hearth is the patroness of the nineteenth day, Quiauitl (rain), of the 20-day series Tonalpouhalli. "Its symbolism meant quiet plenty, a peaceful day." Aztec, Mexico. (Vaillant, 1962: 149; Burland, 1967: 91)

Chej Deity of the sixteenth day of the calendar, the time to "make *costumbre* for horses and mules." The Chimalteco, Guatemala. (Wagley, 1949: 70)

Che tche che tcho, Che tche sseu God of the seasons. China. (Chavannes, n.d.: 369)

Chi Deity of the nineteenth day of the calendar. The Chimalteco, Guatemala. (Wagley, 1949: 70)

Chiaj The deity of the seventh day of the calendar—a "good day to make *costumbre* for hunting." The Chimalteco, Guatemala. (Wagley, 1949: 70)

Ch'ih Kuo Given variously as the god of summer or the god of spring. He is guardian of the East. China. (Werner, 1932: 454, 457; Cammann, 1937: 180–181)

Chin Yüan Ch'i Hsiang One of "five Taoist gods . . . believed to preside over the first five days of the fifth month." China. (Day, 1940: 50)

Chloris Greek "goddess of spring . . . worshipped as a Hora . . . goddess of buds and flowers" and new growth. Wife of Zephyrus and mother of Carpo. (Fairbanks, 1907: 170; Murray, 1935: 145)

Choj Deity of the eighteenth day of the calendar—a "good day to pray for turkeys." The Chimalteco, Guatemala. (Wagley, 1949: 70)

Chronos Personification of time, which in the Orphean cosmogony played the role of the very first reason of all things. Father of Eros and the Winds, some also say of the Horae. Greece. (Roscher, 1965, 1, 1: 899; Cox, 1870, 2: 336; Morford and Lenardon, 1975: 258)

Chu Fu Ling Kung One of the gods of the "first five days of the fifth month." Also known as Duke Chu. China. (Day, 1940: 47, 50)

Chu Jung God of summer and of the fourth month, of the South and of the Southern Sea. Also given as a god of fire. China. (Day, 1940: 66; Werner, 1932: 196; Campbell, 1962: 396, 432; Ferguson, 1937: 76)

Chung Cheng Li Wang One of "five Taoist gods . . . believed to preside over the first five days of the fifth month." Also known as King Li. China. (Day, 1940: 47, 50)

Chusor A Phoenician god who "ruled over the sea with Asherat and watched over the punctual succession of the seasons." Near East. (Herm, 1975: 111)

Cihuacoatl-Ilametecuhtli An "Earth Goddess of the winter solstice." Mexico. (Neumann, 1955: 198)

Cinq-Jour-Malheureux "Obviously a calendrical figure, referring to the five empty and unlucky days, or the five nameless days, which is what both the Aztecs and the Mayans called the last days of their year." Region of Petit Goave, Haiti. West Indies. (Deren, 1953: 275)

Cinteotl The maize god is also the god of the fourth hour of the night. Aztec, Mexico. (Alexander, 1920: 54)

Cocijo At Monte Alban he was the supreme god and god of rain, and "as the Lord of the Year he had close ties with the priestly 'almanac year' of 260 days." Mexico. (Krickeberg, 1968: 55; Nicholson, 1967: 98)

C'oxol Also called Tzimit, Tzitzimit—The "gamekeeper and guardian of the Mundo." As a Mam (Yearbearer), he is the spirit of Quilaja, the sacred mountain of the east. He taught the leaders "the proper customs for the town shrine," about the solar calendar, about patrilineage shrines, as well as commercial customs. He is The Red Dwarf who strikes the lightning into the diviner's blood. Momostenango, Guatemala. (Tedlock, 1982: 147–148)

Do Gun With No Gun and Ok Hwang Sang Je, one of the Three Spirits concerned with time. "Do Gun embodies past time and controls the interaction of *yin* and *yang*." Korea. (Moes, 1983: 129)

Drang srong bkra shis   A brown-red deity of wrathful aspect supposed to rule Tuesday. Tibet. (Nebesky-Wojkowitz, 1956, 1: 263)

Drang srong blo ldan   A yellow deity of peaceful aspect supposed to rule Thursday. Tibet. (Nebesky-Wojkowitz, 1956, 1: 263)

Drang srong dal 'gro   A yellow deity of wrathful aspect supposed to rule Saturday. Tibet. (Nebesky-Wojkowitz, 1956, 1: 263)

Drang srong dkar po   A white deity of peaceful aspect supposed to rule Friday. Tibet. (Nebesky-Wojkowitz, 1956, 1: 263)

Drang srong drag po gtsug rgyan   A white deity of peaceful aspect supposed to rule Monday. Tibet. (Nebesky-Wojkowitz, 1956, 1: 263)

Drang srong 'od stong ldan   A pink deity of peaceful aspect supposed to rule Sunday. Tibet. (Nebesky-Wojkowitz, 1956, 1: 263)

Drang srong zla ba   A blue deity of peaceful aspect supposed to rule Wednesday. Tibet. (Nebesky-Wojkowitz, 1956, 1: 263)

dus k'or   A tutelary god. Same as kalacakra, "Wheel of Time." Tibet. (Getty, 1962: 146)

Dysis   One of the Horae, the time of the Sunset. Greece (Roscher, 1965, 1, 1: 1209)

E   Deity of the first day of the calendar, "owner of the year." A good day for prayer. The Chimalteco, Guatemala. (Wagley, 1949: 70) As a Mam he "indicates a quiet, calm, good year for people and animals; is associated with the sacred mountain, Tamanco, and with the south. This is a good year for business and health. As a Daykeeper he indicates the road, the pathway—primarily through life. A male child born on E (year as well as day) "might become a lineage priest-shaman. . . . A female child . . . might become a midwife (iyom) helping women and their babies on the road of life." All will have health and longevity. Momostenango, Guatemala. (Tedlock, 1982: 99, 100, 118)

Eke   One of the four market days of the week regarded as a divinity. The Igbo, Nigeria. (Isichei, 1978: 23, 337)

Ek u Uayeyab   A god associated with the New Year rituals, also with the west and the color black. Mayan, Mexico. (Tozzer, 1941: 137, 139)

Emesh   The god of summer, son of Enlil. Near East. (Jacobsen, 1976: 103)

Eniautos   The personification of the year, represented with a horn. Greece. (Roscher, 1965, 1, 1: 1249; Gardner, 1925, 9: 793)

Enlil   With Anu, gods of the month Nisan (Semitic), Nisannu (Sumerian). Near East. (Hommel, 1925, 3: 74)

Enten   The god of winter, son of Enlil. Near East. (Jacobsen, 1976: 103)

Eros   In Cyprus the god of love was also the god of spring. (Fairbanks, 1907: 211)

Etokah Wachastah   The god of summer and of the south. The Beings of the north and south (six of each) fight, but those of the south are the stronger and win. The Dakota, Fort Snelling, Minnesota. (Eastman, 1962: 208)

Eya   The god of the West and of the west wind is associated with Autumn. The Oglala, South Dakota. (Powers, 1977: 72, 192)

Fanonga   A god whose name was given to the month of April. Samoa, Polynesia. (Williamson, 1933, 1: 154)

Froho   Teutonic god of summer and fertility, of generation, and of hunting. (Grimm, 1883, 3: xix)

Fur   The Pleiades, patron of agriculture and of crops, was also a calendrical deity marking the beginning of the new year by its appearance. The Chimor, Peru. (Rowe, 1948: 50)

god-Five   The god of Summer and of the Performance—the Palo Volador. The mast is the cosmic bearer supporting the celestial framework (square), in each corner of which a macaw represents the regents of the quarters, with a central god. The Quiché, Guatemala. (Girard, 1979: 150)

Gohone   The deity of winter. The Iroquois Indians. Eastern United States. (Alexander, 1964: 26)

Guih-teuct-li   God of the year, of planets, and of fire. Also called Ix-coz-auh-qui. Mexico. (Schoolcraft, 1857: 641)

Gwyrthur   A Celtic solar deity who represents the sunshine and the summer. Britons. (Squire, 1906: 259)

lHag pa   The personification of Wednesday. A yellow god of the retinue of Rig ma chen mo. Tibet. (Nebesky-Wojkowitz, 1956, 1: 262)

Hamaspathmaeᵭaya The god "who presides over the sixth (and last) division of the year, the seventy-five days theoretically ending March 7." Iran. (Gray, 1930: 147)

Hanan Goddess of the morning, sister of Mayari and Tala; daughter of Bathala and a mortal. The Tagalog, Philippines. (Jocano, 1969: 10)

Hap God of the second hour of the day and of the night. Egypt. (Budge, 1969, 2: 294)

Hap-tcheserts Goddess of the twelfth hour of the day. Egypt. (Budge, 1969, 2: 302)

Havani "God of the first of the five day-periods, from sunrise to noon." Iran. (Gray, 1930: 149)

Heb-Antet A variant deity of the tenth month of the year. Egypt. (Budge, 1969, 2: 293)

Heb-api-hent-s A variant deity of the eleventh month of the year. Egypt. (Budge, 1969, 2: 293)

Heb-apt A variant deity of the second month of the year. Egypt. (Budge, 1969, 2: 293)

Heb-tep A variant deity of the twelfth month of the year. Egypt. (Budge, 1969, 2: 293)

Heima God of winter. Tahiti, Polynesia. (Henry, 1928: 377)

Hen-en-ba God of the fourteenth day of the month. Egypt. (Budge, 1969, 2: 322)

Hentch-hentch Deity of the ninth hour of the day and of the night. Watches behind Osiris the ninth hour of the day and of the night, and before him the tenth hour of the day. Egypt. (Budge, 1969, 2: 294–295)

Heq God of the fifth hour of the day and of the night; watches behind Osiris during the fifth hour of the day and night, and before him the sixth hour of the day. Egypt. (Budge, 1969, 2: 294–295)

Heq-ur God of the tenth hour of the day. Egypt. (Budge, 1969, 2: 302)

Her-tep-aha-her-neb-s Goddess of the seventh hour of the night. Egypt. (Budge, 1969, 2: 301)

Heru-em-au-ab God of the seventh hour of the day. Egypt. (Budge, 1969, 2: 302)

Heru-her-khet God of the eighth hour of the night. Egypt. (Budge, 1969, 2: 301)

Heru-her-uatch-f God of the seventeenth day of the month. Egypt. (Budge, 1969, 2: 322)

Heru-khent-khatith A variant deity of the tenth month of the year. Egypt. (Budge, 1969, 2: 293)

Heru-khuti God of the twelfth month, with variant names Apt-Renpit, Heb-tep. Egypt. (Budge, 1969, 2: 293)

Heru-netch-tef-f God of the second and the thirtieth days of the month. A hawk god. Egypt. (Budge, 1969, 2: 137, 320, 322)

Heru-sa-Ast A name of Osiris. The god of the second hour of the second day of the Moon. Egypt. (Budge, 1969, 2: 183, 292)

Heru-sbati God of the sixth hour of the night. Egypt. (Budge, 1969, 2: 301)

Hetet An ape god and god of the eleventh hour of the eleventh day of the Moon. Egypt. (Budge, 1969, 2: 213, 292)

Het-Hert Goddess of the third month of the year. Egypt. (Budge, 1969, 2: 293)

Hiems Roman deity, the personification of Winter. (Roscher, 1965, 1, 2: 2655)

Hine-raumati "Summer Maid," a wife of the sun with whom he lives that half of the year. She is goddess of the cultivation of foods and the fruits of the forest. Mother of Tane-rore. The Maori, New Zealand. (Best, 1924: 110)

Hine-takurua "Winter Maid," a wife of the sun with whom he lives that half of the year. Her realm "is the ocean, her task is to conserve fish." The Maori, New Zealand. (Best, 1924: 110)

Hirib(h) i God of summer and father of Nikkal. Canaan. Near East. (Driver, 1956: 24; Hooke, 1963: 93)

Holler, Uller Germanic god of winter and husband of Holda, "whose fields he covered with . . . snow, to make them more fruitful." (Guerber, 1895: 132)

The Horae Greek/Roman goddesses of the four seasons, of the hours of the day, who are concerned with the orderly procedures of nature and of life. They are of varying numbers. Among them are Thallo, Carpo, Eunomia, Eirene, Dike, Chloris, Dysis, Anatole, Mesembria, Musike, and Sponde. (Kerényi, 1951: 102; Fairbanks, 1907: 104; Hesiod-Brown, 1981: 78; Roscher, 1965, 1, 1: 1209; 1965, 2, 2: 3296; 1965, 4: 1411; Murray, 1935: 143–145)

Hou T'u   The "god of the Centre ruling Mid-Summer." China. (Day, 1940: 66; Werner, 1932: 160)

Huehuetéotl   God of fire and lord of the year, "Associated with the night hours." Aztec, Mexico. (Caso, 1958: 28; Reed, 1966: 31; Nicholson, 1967: 30)

Huitzilopchtli   As the Blue Tezcatlipoca in the early Nahuatl creation myth, he and Quetzalcóatl were responsible for the establishment of the days, months, and years, and their time periods. Mexico. (León-Portilla, 1982: 35)

Hukúldatsyue   A mother of the summer. The Cagaba and the Kogi, Colombia. (Reichel-Dolmatoff, 1949/50: 114)

Hutukau   "Wind-Ready-to-Give [buffalo to the people]" who has "power over the land in the winter" and is located in the north. Former name was Kauwaharu. Brother of Piwaruxti, the Lightning. The Skidi, Pawnee, Nebraska. (Dorsey, 1904, 2: 19, 20)

Ik   God of the eleventh day of the calendar—"good." "It is necessary to make *costumbre* so that rains and winds will not ruin corn on this day." The Chimalteco, Guatemala. (Wagley, 1949: 70)

Ik'   The fourth of the Mams, Yearbearers, is received on the sacred mountain, Socop, the mountain of the west, and is closely connected with death. He brings "violent rainstorms or else no rain at all," death from lightning, drowning, famine. This dangerous Mam is invoked for delivery from natural violence, for protection from "the strong negative human emotions of hatred, anger, rage, and frenzy." Evil daykeepers use these days to induce disasters. Persons born this day will be "strong, wild, even violent . . . greatly feared and even hated," but often are in high command. Though Ik' is of a negative cast, certain days can be used for positive action against disasters. Momostenango, Guatemala. (Tedlock, 1982: 99, 100, 103, 126, 127)

Te Ikaroa   Personification of the Milky Way and one of the "regulators of the seasons." The Maori, New Zealand. (Best, 1924: 97, 105)

Ilamatecuhtli   Ancient Aztec mother goddess and goddess of the thirteenth hour of the day. Mexico. (Alexander, 1920: 54; Krickeberg, 1968: 44)

Imix   God of the tenth day of the calendar, of neutral quality. The Chimalteco, Guatemala. (Wagley, 1949: 70)

Imöx   One of the Day Lords on whose days daykeepers visit public shrines to humble themselves before the Mam so as not to be dominated by them, "which makes one crazy." An Imöx child is subject to domination by the power of the Mam, becoming "weak, inefficient, undirected, even insane." Momostenango, Guatemala. (Tedlock, 1982: 125–126)

Ingansje   He "appears to be a god of time." The Rundi, Burundi. (Meyer, 1916: 189)

Ishtar   As the planet Venus she is associated with Friday and is goddess of the month Elul (Semitic), Ululu (Sumerian). Near East. (Hommel, 1925, 3: 74; Schoeps, 1961: 58)

Itztli   The Stone-Knife God is the god of the second hour of the night. Aztec, Mexico. (Alexander, 1920: 54)

Iutri-bogh   A Slavic god of morning. (Grimm, 1888: 1520)

Ix   One of the Day Lords whose day is dedicated to the Mundo, Earth, is thanked for the health of the animals and people of the patrilineage; who is requested to provide funds for buying land and building a house. A child born this day "will have a close relationship with the Mundo . . . will be wealthy, since all gold, silver, and precious stones belong to Mundo." But the child will "also suffer many physical ailments," resulting in his/her becoming a "daykeeper or else die." Momostenango, Guatemala. (Tedlock, 1982: 119, 120)

Jarilo   Slavic god of spring, of fecundity, the power of vegetation, of passion. He is depicted with wildflowers, wheat sheaves. (Gimbutas, 1971: 162; 1975: XLC M126)

Jarovit   A Slavic war god of Wolgast who also seems to be associated with spring (Jaro) as an aspect of Triglav, representing the spring growing season. (Gimbutas, 1971: 154, 160)

Je tche che tcho, Je tche sseu   God of the days. China. (Chavannes, n.d.: 369)

Jikoku   God of spring and guardian of the east. Japan. (Werner, 1932: 457; Getty, 1962: 168; Eliseev, 1963: 447)

Junajpu   One of the Day Lords and a day of the ancestors (Nantat); "selected for house-building rituals," inquiring if they are in agreement. On this day permission is also requested allowing the "dead person to enter the cold, dark room of the Mundo and thus join the other spirits." A person born this day may become a spiritualist. Momostenango, Guatemala. (Tedlock, 1982: 124–125)

Ju Shou   The god of the West is apparently also a god of the seasons. Day associates him with autumn and Werner with spring. China. (Day, 1940: 66; Werner, 1932: 566; Campbell, 1962: 432)

Ka-her-ka-heb   A variant deity of the fourth month of the year. Egypt. (Budge, 1969, 2: 293)

Ka-khu   God of the twelfth hour of the night. Egypt. (Budge, 1969, 2: 301)

Kala   The Hindu personification of time. India. (Sarma, 1953: 29; Danielou, 1964: 200; Macdonell, 1897: 120)

Kan   The Mayan maize god is one of the gods of the new year and a deity of the compass points. Among the Chimalteco, the deity of the fourteenth day of the calendar—a "good day to pray for corn" and for planting or harvesting. Guatemala. (Nicholson, 1967: 44, 119; Wagley, 1949: 70)

K'anil   One of the Day Lords. A child born this day "should become a daykeeper [calendar diviner]" and if male may become a priest-shaman concerned with harvest rituals. Momostenango, Guatemala. (Tedlock, 1982: 114–115)

Ka-taui   God of the eleventh hour of the night. Egypt. (Budge, 1969, 2: 301)

Keou-mang   Guardian deity of springtime. China. (Chavannes, n.d.: 501)

Khensu   God of the ninth month of the year and of the eighth hour of the day. He is a lunar god and a god of fertility. Egypt. (Budge, 1969, 2: 35, 293, 302; Knight, 1915: 60)

Khensu Nefer-hetep   A form of Khensu, which "ruled the month," presided over conception and growth. Egypt. (Budge, 1969, 2: 37)

Khent   Goddess of the sixth hour of the night of the eighteenth (Budge) or thirteenth (Knight) day of the Moon. Egypt. (Budge, 1969, 2: 292; Knight, 1915: 60)

Khenthi   God of the tenth month of the year. Egypt. (Budge, 1969, 2: 293)

Khepera   The beetle god of the creation is god of the first hour of the night. Egypt. (Budge, 1969, 2: 301, 379; 1969, 1: 294–295)

Kheperu   Goddess of the eighth hour of the day. Egypt. (Budge, 1969, 2: 302)

Khesef-khemt   Goddess of the eleventh hour of the night. Egypt. (Budge, 1969, 2: 301)

Khnemu   The ram-headed early river god, associated also with the creation, was god of the twenty-eighth day of the month. Egypt. (Budge, 1969, 1: 463; 1969, 2: 50, 322; Casson, 1965: 106)

Khyp   The moon god who divides the time for man. The Yenisei Ostyaks, Siberia. (Czaplicka, 1925, 9: 579)

Kiech   Goddess of the thirteenth day of the calendar. The Chimalteco, Guatemala. (Wagley, 1949: 70)

Kimesh   Deity of the fifteenth day of the calendar—A "fair day; make *costumbre* for domestic animals." The Chimalteco, Guatemala. (Wagley, 1949: 70)

Kiok   Deity of the eighth day of the calendar—A "bad day; brings wind and rain to ruin milpas." The Chimalteco, Guatemala. (Wagley, 1949: 70)

K'obishtaiya   A ferocious kachina, created by Iyatiku, "rules the clouds of winter," lives in the east. The Keresan, New Mexico. (Parsons, 1939: 246)

Kodoyampeh, Kodoyanpe   The creator god of the Maidu who "established the seasons." California. (Spence, 1925, 3: 66; Dixon, 1903: 32–33)

Koljada   A goddess "personifying the whole time between Christmas and Epiphany." Russia. (Schrader, 1925, 2: 38)

Konjin   God of the Lunar Calendar and associated with the zodiac, particularly with the southwest and the northeast. His position must be calculated before any undertaking. Japan. (Norbeck, 1954: 124–125; Holtom, 1938: 259)

Kou Mang   The god of the East and of the Eastern Sea is also god of spring. China. (Day, 1940: 66; Werner, 1932: 437; Campbell, 1962: 432)

Kuang Mu, Kwang-mu   God of Winter or of Autumn and god of the West. China. (Werner, 1932: 454, 457; Cammann, 1937: 181; Getty, 1962: 167)

Ku gu·   The "Mother Kachina . . . a Summer goddess and therefore barefoot." the Tewa of San Juan, New Mexico. (Laski, 1958: 23)

Kuhu Goddess of the day of the new moon, daughter of Angiras and Sraddha. India. (Danielou, 1964: 319; Macdonell, 1897: 125)

Lada Slavic goddess of spring and of love. Lithuania/Russia. (Ralston, 1872: 104–105)

Lel In Poland, Lel and Po-lel chasing "each other round the field" bring in summer. (Grimm, 1883, 2: 783)

Lienhung The god of the hour. China. (Du Bose, n.d.: 72)

Ling-pao T'ien-tsun A god, existent from the beginning, whose function was "to calculate time, and to divide it into periods." China. (Werner, 1932: 400)

Li Ping, Leeping God of the year. "Worshipped by the officials at the reception of spring." China. (Du Bose,n.d.: 72; Werner, 1932: 249, 589)

Lucina Juno as the goddess of childbirth also "presides over the beginning of the month, the 'rebirth' of the moon." Rome. (Dumézil, 1966, 1: 295)

Maa-ennu-am-uaa God of the eleventh hour of the day. Egypt. (Budge, 1969, 2: 302)

Maa-hra God of the ninth hour of the night. Egypt. (Budge, 1969, 2: 301)

Maa-tef-f God of the seventh hour of the day and of the night; watches behind Osiris during the seventh hour of the day and night, and before him the eighth hour of the day. Egypt. (Budge, 1969, 2: 294–295)

Mah Persian moon deity "who presides over phases of time and the movements of the waters [tides]." (Larousse, 1973: 192)

Mahuru The personification of spring. The Maori, New Zealand. (Best, 1924: 175)

Mahya The "month-god." Iran. (Gray, 1930: 222)

Mai yairya God "of the fifth of the six divisions of the year, the eighty days theoretically ending December 22." Iran. (Gray, 1930: 150)

Maiẕyoi-šam God "of the second of the six divisions of the year, the sixty days theoretically ending June 20." Iran. (Gray, 1930: 151)

Maiẕyoi-zaremaya God "of the first of the six divisions of the year, the forty-five days theoretically ending April 21." Iran. (Gray, 1930: 151)

Maiyochina The "spirit of Summer" and deity of South Mountain. The Acoma, New Mexico. (Stirling, 1942: 14, 118)

Makhiar A variant god of the sixth month of the year. Egypt. (Budge, 1969, 2: 293)

Mak-nebt-s Goddess of the third hour of the day. Egypt. (Budge, 1969, 2: 302)

Mam The evil Mayan god of the end of the year, of "the five evil and unlucky days." The Yucatec and the Kekchi, Mexico and Guatemala. (Chamberlain, 1902: 50; Thompson, 1970: 297, 299) The Mam, the Yearbearers, are related to the solar calendar. In order of importance they are: (1) Quej, who is greeted "on Quilaja, the mountain of the east." (2) E, received on Tamancu, the mountain of the south. (3) No'j, received on Joyan, the mountain in the south/southwest. (4) Ik', received on Socop, the mountain of the west. They have two secretaries as assistants: C'at serves No'j and E, Tz'iquin serves Ik' and Quej. *See also* **C'oxol** (Mam' of the Mundo). Momostenango, Guatemala. (Tedlock, 1982: 89, 99, 100, 147)

Mapulon God of the seasons, husband of Ikapati and father of Anagolay. The Tagalog, Philippines. (Jocano, 1969: 10)

Marduk As the planet Jupiter he is god of the month Marchesvan (Semitic), Arakh-samna (Sumerian), and associated with Thursday. Near East. (Hommel, 1925, 3: 75; Schoeps, 1961: 58)

Matchet Deity of the twelfth hour of the day and of the night; watches before Osiris the first hour of the day and behind him the twelfth hour of the night. Egypt. (Budge, 1969, 2: 294–295)

Ma-tef-f God of the twenty-sixth day of the month. Egypt. (Budge, 1969, 2: 322)

Menhit A female counterpart of Khnemu; goddess of the sixth hour of the sixth day of the Moon. Egypt. (Budge, 1969, 2: 66, 292)

Mert Goddess of the eighth hour of the night. Egypt. (Budge, 1969, 2: 301)

Mesembria One of the Horae who represents 12 noon. Greece. (Roscher, 1965, 1, 1: 1209)

Metoporine The personification of autumn. Greece. (Roscher, 1965, 2, 2: 2942)

Mictlantecu(h)tli   An Aztec god of the dead and of the eleventh hour of the day; as god of the underworld, the god of the fifth hour of the night. He was the patron of the tenth day, Itzcuintli, of the 20-day series. Also god of the North. Mexico. (Alexander, 1920: 54, 57; Burland, 1967: ix, 89)

Min   A god of virility and of generation, and god of the fifth month. Egypt. (Budge, 1969, 1: 507; 1969, 2: 17, 293)

Miochin   God of summer and of summer lightning. Also god of South Mountain. The Keres, New Mexico. (Tyler, 1964: 166, 227)

Morityema, Morityama   God of spring and of West Mountain. The Acoma, New Mexico. (Tyler, 1964: 175; Stirling, 1942: 14, 118; Burland, 1965: 150)

Musike   One of the Horae. Greece. (Roscher, 1965, 1, 1: 3296)

Mut-neb-set   Goddess of the tenth hour of the night. Egypt. (Budge, 1969, 2: 301)

Nahse kame   "Master of the Rainy Season," and the "shrimp" constellation. The Desana, Colombia. (Reichel-Dolmatoff, 1971: 74)

Nahse kame turu   "Master of the Dry Season," the "cut shrimp" constellation. The Desana, Colombia. (Reichel-Dolmatoff, 1971: 74)

Nai   A serpent god, god of the twenty-second day of the month. Egypt. (Budge, 1969, 1: 23; 1969, 2: 322)

Nan Ch'ao Shêng Chung   "Chief of New year Gods . . . the great rewarder of good and punisher of evil." China. (Day, 1940: 94–95, 162)

Nani Surlí   Master of the summer. The Cagaba and the Kogi, Colombia. (Reichel-Dolmatoff, 1949/50: 113)

Naqpu   God of the ninth day of the calendar—The "owner of fire . . . fires come to burn down houses on this day." The Chimalteco, Guatemala. (Wagley, 1949: 70)

Na-tesher   God of the twenty-fourth day of the month. Egypt. (Budge, 1969, 2: 322)

The Natue   The "Grandmothers," goddesses of the winter solstice. The Winikina-Warao, Venezuela. (Wilbert, 1973: 6)

Neb-ankhet   Goddess of the fifth hour of the night. Egypt. (Budge, 1969, 2: 301)

Neb-neteru   God of the third hour of the night. Egypt. (Budge, 1969, 2: 301)

Neb-senti   Goddess of the ninth hour of the night. Egypt. (Budge, 1969, 2: 301)

Nebt-thehent   Goddess of the first hour of the night. Egypt. (Budge, 1969, 2: 300)

Nehes   God of the thirtieth day of the month. Egypt. (Budge, 1969, 2: 322)

Nekiu   Goddess of the seventh hour of the day. Egypt. (Budge, 1969, 2: 302)

Nesbet   Goddess of the fifth hour of the day. Egypt. (Budge, 1969, 2: 302)

Netch-an   God of the twelfth day of the month. Egypt. (Budge, 1969, 2: 322)

Netchti-ur   God of the eleventh day of the month. Egypt. (Budge, 1969, 2: 322)

Nien Hu Hsing Chun   A god "in charge of years." Closely associated with T'ai Sui. China. (Day, 1940: 77)

Nientche che tcho, Nien tche sseu   God of the years. China. (Chavannes, n.d.: 369)

Ningishzida   An early tree god represented with serpents and associated with healing. He was god of the month Ab (Semitic,), Abu (Sumerian). Near East. (Hommel, 1925, 3: 74; Jastrow, 1898: 462; Langdon, 1931: 90)

Ningobianong   "Evening or West." Represents old age and wisdom, "moderation, patience, fortitude." The tutor of Waubun. The Ojibway, Great Lakes region. (Johnston, 1976: 28, 163)

Ninib   A solar deity, a god of agriculture and of war. He was god of the month Tammuz (Semitic), Du'uzu (Sumerian). Near East. (Jastrow, 1898: 57, 67, 174, 462; Hommel, 1925, 3: 74; Jayne, 1962: 126)

Nintil   Sumerian "queen of the month," created to serve man. Near East. (Langdon, 1931: 202)

Nkwo   "One of the four days of the Igbo market-week, regarded as an alūsi." Nigeria. (Isichei, 1978: 23, 343)

No Gun   One of the Three Spirits, with Ok Hwang Sang Je and Do Gun, who are concerned with time. He "is equated with Lao-tzu and embodies future time." His vehicle is an ox. Korea. (Moes, 1983: 129)

Noj, No'j God of the sixth day of the calendar, "owner of the year; excellent for all *costumbres*" (offerings and prayers at shrines). The Chimalteco, Guatemala. (Wagley, 1949: 70). A Yearbearer, the third of the Mams, and also a Day Lord, received on the sacred mountain Joyan in the south/southwest; served by the secretary C'at. This "is a creative year, both for good and for evil." This Mam "has a good head and many thoughts"—again both for good and for evil. This is "a masculine day," therefore, those born this day, regardless of sex, will have masculine characteristics; will be creative; will be "an excellent daykeeper . . . because of his or her problem-solving ability." Momostenango, Guatemala. (Tedlock, 1982: 99, 100, 122)

Nunut Goddess of the first hour of the day. Egypt. (Budge, 1969, 2: 302)

NyanKopon Kweku The malignant god of Wednesday. Ghana. (Evans, 1950: 254)

Nyi ma The personification of Sunday, a yellow-red god of the retinue of Rig ma chen mo. Attribute—the red lotus. Tibet. (Nebesky-Wojkowitz, 1956, 1: 262)

Ok Hwang Sang Je, Yu Huang (Chinese) The Jade Emperor forms a trinity with Do Gun and No Gun as the Three Spirits. "Each . . . has his own separate heaven. The Jade Emperor embodies primal cause and present time. He is the progenitor of the human race, the inventor of fire, agriculture, and sericulture." His vehicle is a *Kylin,* Dragon, Deer, or Crane. Korea. (Moes, 1983: 129)

Ometeotl "Lord of time and space"—A duality composed of Ometecuhtli, the masculine principle, and Omecihuatl, the feminine principle. The Nahua, Mexico. (Reed, 1966: 69; Nicholson, 1967: 23)

Opora A Greek goddess of autumn and of its fruits; in the retinue of Eirene. (Roscher, 1965, 3, 1: 931)

Ostara Teutonic goddess of the spring, of dawn, of morning. (Wagner, 1882: 114; Schrader, 1925, 2: 34; Grimm, 1880: 290–291)

Oyè One of the four days of the market-week divinities. The Igbo, Nigeria. (Isichei, 1978: 23)

Pahulangkug A god of the Upper World "who changed seasons." The Sulod of Central Panay, Philippines. (Jocano, 1969: 19)

Paitiš-hahya The god "who presides over the third of the six divisions of the year, the seventy-five days theoretically ending September 3 and the period of harvest." Iran. (Gray, 1930: 154)

Papsukkal Messenger of Anu and Ishtar, and god of the month Tebeth (Semitic), Tebitu (Sumerian). Near East. (Hommel, 1925, 3: 75; Jastrow, 1898: 463)

Par-neferu-en-neb-set Goddess of the twelfth hour of the night. Egypt. (Budge, 1969, 2: 301)

Pa sangs A white god, the personification of Friday. Tibet. (Nebesky-Wojkowitz, 1956, 1: 262)

sPen pa A green god, the personification of Saturday. Tibet. (Nebesky-Wojkowitz, 1956, 1: 262)

Penteteris A female personification of "a Four-year Cycle." Greece. (Gardner, 1925, 9: 793)

Pesh-hetep-f God of the tenth hour of the night. Egypt. (Budge, 1969, 2: 301)

Phur bu A yellow god, the personification of Thursday. Tibet. (Nebesky-Wojkowitz, 1956, 1: 262)

Piltzintecutli-Tonatiuh Aztec "Lord of Princes, the Sun," as god of the third hour of the night. Mexico. (Alexander, 1920: 54)

Pipiri The personification of Winter. The Maori, New Zealand. (Best, 1924: 175)

Pipoun God of the cold and of winter. The Montagnais, Labrador and Quebec. (Alexander, 1964: 31)

Po-lel Two divinities in Poland, Lel and Po-lel, are known as "chasing each other round the field, bringing Summer." (Grimm, 1883, 2: 783)

Porovit An aspect of Triglav. Pora means "midsummer" and has possible association with the growing season. Slavic, (Gimbutas, 1971: 160)

Proet The goddess of spring, sometimes represented as a Nile deity. Egypt. (Gardner, 1925, 9: 792)

Ptah-aneb-res-f God of the second month of the year. Variant deities are Menkhet and Heb-apt. Egypt. (Budge, 1969, 2: 293)

Qanel Deity of the seventeenth day of the calendar—"good day to pray for sheep." The Chimalteco, Guatemala. (Wagley, 1949: 70)

Qebhsennuf One of the sons of Horus, gods of the Canopic Jars. God of the fourth hour of the day and of the night. Egypt. (Budge, 1969, 2: 294; Knight, 1915: 35)

Qet God of the tenth hour of the day and of the night; watches behind Osiris on the tenth hour of the day and of the night, and before him the eleventh hour of the day. Egypt. (Budge, 1969, 2: 294–295)

Quej A Mam, the most important of the Yearbearers, presumably because he is wild, strong, domineering. "There are many business losses and many illnesses during a Quej year." He is received on the sacred mountain Quilaja, the mountain of the east. Many rituals are performed—for good crops or thanks for harvest, in divination for calendar diviner candidates, for the unborn. These children are strong, domineering, and masculine in all respects, whether male or female. A shaman-priest will be a strong leader for good or an "evil witch," causing troubles and sorrows. Momostenango, Guatemala. (Tedlock, 1982: 99, 100, 113, 114)

Quetzalcóatl The Plumed Serpent as the god of the wind was patron of the second day, Eecatl, of the series of 20 days called Tonalpouhalli. Also god of the ninth hour of the day. The Aztec, Mexico. (Burland, 1967: 87; Alexander, 1920: 54) In early Nahuatl creation myths, he and Huitzlopochtli were responsible for the establishment of the days, months, and years, assigning 20 days to each of the 18 months of the year of 360 days. (León-Portilla, 1982: 35)

Quezelao A god, the "provider of the seasons, who probably was a refraction of Cocijo," the rain god. Worshipped at Atepec. The Zapotec, Oaxaca, Mexico. (Whitecotton, 1977: 159)

Ramman The Babylonian storm god was also god of the month Shebat (Semitic), Shabatu (Sumerian). (Hommel, 1925, 3: 75; Jastrow, 1898: 154, 463)

Rapithwin(a) The "special deity of the second of the five divisions of the day (from noon to mid-afternoon)." Also god of the summer months. Iran. (Gray, 1930: 157; Hinnells, 1973: 36)

Rau-mati "Summer." Offspring of Anu-ka-wewera. New Zealand. (White, 1887, 1: 32)

Rekeh-netches God of the seventh month of the year. Egypt. (Budge, 1969, 2: 293)

Rekeh-ur God of the sixth month of the year. Egypt. (Budge, 1969, 2: 293)

Rennutet Goddess of the eighth month of the year. Egypt. (Budge, 1969, 2: 293)

Renpet "Goddess of the year, the goddess of springtide and of youth." Egypt. (Ames, 1965: 111)

Rivos Celtic god for whom the month Rivros was named—"the harvest-month, probably August." Gaul. (MacCulloch, 1925, 3: 79)

Rokeh "Burning,' name of the hot period of the year . . . depicted . . . with human heads, and with hippopotamus heads." Egypt. (Gardiner, 1925, 9: 792)

Ronpet Goddess of the year. Egypt. (Gardiner, 1925, 9: 792)

Ruevit An aspect of Triglav representing the autumn season. Slavic. (Gimbutas, 1971: 160)

Sa An ape god, deity of the tenth hour of the tenth day of the Moon. Egypt. (Budge, 1969, 2: 292)

Sac Acantun Mayan god associated with the north and the color white, who is propitiated in the rituals of the unlucky days in the Ix years. Mexico. (Tozzer, 1941: 137, 146)

Sac u Uayeyab A Mayan god associated with the north and the color white, invoked in the rituals of the unlucky days (before the New Year) in the Ix years. Mexico. (Tozzer, 1941: 137, 145)

Saho-yama-hime The goddess of spring. Japan. (Anesaki, 1937: 234)

Sarset Goddess of the second hour of the night. Egypt. (Budge, 1969, 2: 300)

Sati-arut Goddess of the tenth hour of the day. Egypt. (Budge, 1969, 2: 302)

Saturn An old Italian god of agriculture who, in becoming identified with Chronos, became also god of time. He was also considered god of the month of December. (Madden, 1930: 52; Dumézil, 1966, 1: 271; 1966, 2: 461)

Sau God of the third hour of the day. Egypt. (Budge, 1969, 2: 302)

sawanaki, nibunaki South, also noon. Sometimes personified. The Penobscot, Maine. (Speck, 1935: 21)

Sayatasha A god who is part of the winter solstice ceremonies. The Zuñi, New Mexico. (Stevenson, 1901/02: 33)

Seb The god of the earth and of the underworld was also god of the third hour of the night and the fifteenth day of the Moon. Egypt. (Budge, 1969, 2: 94–99, 292)

Sef A lion god, "Yesterday," a guardian of the tunnel through which the sun passes at night. Egypt. (Budge, 1969, 2: 361)

Seher-tut Goddess of the third hour of the night. Egypt. (Budge, 1969, 2: 300)

Seijavéya A mother of the summer. The Cagaba and the Kogi, Colombia. (Reichel-Dolmatoff, 1949/50: 114)

Seker A hawk-headed mummy-form god of the dead who presides over the fourth hour of the night and is also god of the seventh hour of the night. As a solar god he is "the closer of the night and the opener of the day." Egypt. (Budge, 1969, 1: 217, 503; 1969, 2: 301; 1967: cviii)

Semt Goddess of the second hour of the day. Egypt. (Budge, 1969, 2: 302)

Senb-kheperu Goddess of the eleventh hour of the day. Egypt. (Budge, 1969, 2: 302)

Seshetat Goddess of the fourth hour of the day. Egypt. (Budge, 1969, 2: 302)

Shakak God of winter and of North Mountain. The Acoma and the Keres, New Mexico. (Tyler, 1964: 166; Stirling, 1942: 119)

Shamash Babylonian sun god, god of justice and of divination, is also god of the seventh month Tishri (Semitic) or Tishritu (Sumerian), and associated with Sunday. Near East. (Hommel, 1925, 3: 75; Langdon, 1931: 150; Dumézil, 1966, 2: 655; Jayne, 1962: 127; Jastrow, 1898: 71, 463; Schoeps, 1961: 58)

Sharrapu Semitic god of the period of intense heat. Near East. (Langdon, 1931: 49)

Shef-beti A variant deity of the fifth month of the year. Egypt. (Budge, 1969, 2: 293)

Shem God of the twenty-fifth day of the month. Egypt. (Budge, 1969, 2: 322)

Shet-f-met-f God of the sixteenth day of the month. Egypt. (Budge, 1969, 2: 322)

Shih Erh Kung Ch'ên A sky deity who controls the hours of the day and is associated with forming horoscopes. China. (Day, 1940: 80, 210)

Shih Hu Hsing Chün "Hour Measuring Star." China. (Day, 1940: 210)

Shih T'ien Tsun "Ten Heavenly Stems," a sky power, used with the "Twelve Earthly Branches" (Shih Êrh Kung Ch'ên) "to designate the years of each 60-year cycle." China. (Day, 1940: 80, 210)

Ship-E Ji The Twelve Signs of the Zodiac are "the guardians of the twelve directions of the compass as well as the twelve divisions of the day." They govern all changes/phases of time. They are represented as human figures with animal heads: Rat, Ox, Tiger, Rabbit, Dragon, Snake, Horse, Goat, Monkey, Rooster, Dog, Pig. They repel evil spirits and have some control over destiny, "based on the person's birth date." Korea. (Moes, 1983: 126, 127)

Shitsukia A god who takes part in Winter Solstice ceremonies. The Zuñi, New Mexico. (Stevenson, 1901/02: 129)

Shogatsu-sama A name of Dosojin as the New Year Deity. Japan. (Czaja, 1974: 51)

Shomu A god representing "summer," the harvest season. Egypt. (Gardiner, 1925, 9: 792)

Shruisthia The spirit of Fall, associated with East Mountain. The Acoma, New Mexico. (Tyler, 1964: 175; Stirling, 1942: 14, 119)

Sibitti The Seven god, the Pleiades, god of the month Adar (Semitic), Addaru (Sumerian). Near East. (Hommel, 1925, 3: 75, 184; Paton, 1925, 3: 184)

Sin The Sumerian/Babylonian moon god by whose phases time was reckoned. He was god of the month Sivan (Semitic), Simannu (Sumerian), and associated with Monday. Near East. (Jastrow, 1898: 68, 462; Schoeps, 1961: 58; Hommel, 1925, 3: 74)

Skadi Scandinavian goddess of winter, of snowshoes, of hunting. For a time the wife of Njord. (Turville-Petre, 1964: 164–165; Guerber, 1895: 108–111)

Skan The all-powerful Sky God established the time periods: day, night, moon, year. The Lakota, South Dakota. (Walker, 1980: 53)

Snukpanlits Goddess of springtime. The Bella Coola, British Columbia. (Boas, 1898: 32)

Sponde One of the Horae. Greece. (Roscher, 1965, 4: 1411)

Sumar The benevolent Norse god of summer whose father was Svasud(r). (Grimm, 1883, 2: 758; Thorpe, 1851: 7)

Ta'afanua A god of the eastern end of the Samoan group, associated with the month of May. Polynesia. (Williamson, 1933, 1: 156)

Tagarod Teutonic god, the personified morning. (Grimm, 1883, 2: 884)

T'ai Sui The god of Time, of the year, who rules over the destinies of all, over the stars and the elements. He is associated with the planet Jupiter. China. (Day, 1940: 77, 165; Du Bose, n.d.: 330; Werner, 1932: 483)

Tatsuta-Hime Originally a wind goddess, she became a goddess of autumn—"the Lady-who-weaves-the-brocade" of the leaves. Japan. (Anesaki, 1937: 234)

Ta-vwots The hare god, whose arrow was the lightning, "established the seasons and days." The Shoshone, Idaho. (Lowie, 1909: 231; Emerson, 1884: 80)

Tawiskaron Iroquois god of winter, twin of Teharonhiawagon and grandson of Ataentsic. Upper Mississippi Valley and Great Lakes Region. (Blair, 1912: 271; Gray, 1925, 7: 422)

Tefnut The lion goddess of moisture and fine rain is the goddess of the second hour of the night of the fourteenth day of the Moon. Egypt. (Budge, 1969, 2: 87–88, 292; Knight, 1915: 125)

Tehuti God of the sixth hour of the day. A name of Thoth. Egypt. (Budge, 1969, 1: 113; 1969, 2: 302)

Teken-en-Ra God of the thirteenth day of the month. Egypt. (Budge, 1969, 2: 322)

Tekhi, Tekh-heb Goddess of the first month of the year. Egypt. (Budge, 1969, 2: 292)

Te Manawa roa The "god time (The long ago)." The third deity of the beginning after Te-ake-ia-roe and Te Vaerua. Hervey Island, Polynesia. (Westervelt, 1963, 1: 3)

Tenatsali God of time and the seasons. The Zuñi, New Mexico. (Cushing, 1891/92: 377)

Tepeyollotl A jaguar god associated with night and darkness, a god of war and of death. He was patron of the third day, Calli (the house), of the 20-day series Tonalpouhalli; also of the day Akbal, and god of the eighth hour of the night. Mexico. (Alexander, 1920: 54, 79; Thompson, 1970: 293; Burland, 1967: 87)

Tezcatlipoca The god of the Smoking Mirror, versatile and variable, is god of the tenth hour of the day and patron of the thirteenth day, Acatl (the reed), of the 20-day series Tonalpouhalli. Aztec, Mexico. (Alexander, 1920: 54; Vaillant, 1962: 142; Burland, 1967: 90)

Thallo One of the Horae and goddess of spring, of the blossoming. Greece. (Burns, 1925, 3: 373; Murray, 1935: 142)

Therine The personification of summer. Asia Minor. (Roscher, 1965, 5: 655)

Tichin Deity of the fourth day of the calendar. The Chimalteco, Guatemala. (Wagley, 1949: 70)

Tijax One of the Day Lords who is associated with slander, lies, arguing, and fighting (particularly religious). A child born this day will always be "a victim and promoter" of these qualities, whether "political, sexual, . . . religious." Momostenango, Guatemala. (Tedlock, 1982: 123)

Tlaloc The Aztec god of rain was god of the eighth hour of the day and of the ninth hour of the night, as well as patron of the seventh day, Mazatl (the deer), of the 20-day series of Tonalpouhalli—"a day of great timidity." Mexico. (Alexander, 1920: 54; Burland, 1967: 88)

Tlaltecu(h)tli The earth god, symbolized by a toad or alligator, was god of the second hour of the day. The Aztec, Mexico. (Alexander, 1920: 54; Vaillant, 1962: 146; Caso, 1958: 53)

Tlauizcalpantecutli Aztec god of the planet Venus is associated with the dawn and with the twilight, and is god of the twelfth hour of the day. Mexico. (Spence, 1923: 129, 323; Alexander, 1920: 54)

Tlazoltéotl An earth goddess, the devourer of filth, who, in consuming men's sins, performed an act of purification. She was goddess of the fifth hour of the day and of the seventh hour of the night; also patroness of the fourteenth day, Oceolotl (the ocelot), of the 20-day series Tonalpouhalli. The Aztec, Mexico. (Burland, 1967: x, 90; Alexander, 1920: 54; Caso, 1958: 55–56)

Toj One of the Day Lords. one, six, and eight Toj "are extremely powerful days for both evil and good." A child born on a Toj day will be subject to chronic illness and frequently in debt; will need the constant help of diviners to live out a normal life. Momostenango, Guatemala. (Tedlock, 1982: 115–116)

Tonatiuh The sun as the marker of the days is considered also a god of time. The Aztec, Mexico. (León-Portilla, 1982: 51)

To Wên God of Autumn and guardian of the North. He was also god of riches, of good fortune. China. (Werner, 1932: 454–457; Getty, 1962: 167; Cammann, 1937: 180–181)

Ts'ao Ta Chiang Chün One of "five Taoist gods . . . believed to preside over the first five days of the fifth month." A deified general. China. (Day, 1940: 47, 50)

Tseng Chang God of Spring or Summer and guardian of the South. China. Same as Virudhaka. (Werner, 1932: 454–457; Getty, 1962: 167; Cammann, 1937: 180–181)

Tua-mat-f, Tuamutef God of the third hour of the day and of the night. Egypt. (Budge, 1969, 2: 294)

Tuau A lion god—"Today"—guardian of the tunnel through which the sun passes at night. Egypt. (Budge, 1969, 2: 361)

Tucapacha A primordial being who "bestows existence and regulates the seasons." Mexico. (Bancroft, 1886, 3: 445)

Tumu-horo-rire God of the Autumn. Tahiti, Polynesia. (Henry, 1928: 376)

Tumu-oteoteo God of the Spring. Tahiti, Polynesia. (Henry, 1928: 378)

Tumu-ruperupe God of Summer. Tahiti, Polynesia. (Henry, 1928: 378)

Tun-abui God of the twenty-seventh day of the month. Egypt. (Budge, 1969, 2: 322)

Turzi A Babylonian god of the calendar of Sargon, the sixth or twelfth month; of the calendar of Ur, the seventh month. Same as Tammuz. (Hommel, 1925, 3: 73)

Tz'i' One of the Day Lords. A child born this day "will be a confused, weak, unlucky person" looking for sexual relationships—could readily become promiscuous. Momostenango, Guatemala. (Tedlock, 1982: 116–17)

Tz'iquin One of the Day Lords, also Secretary and Treasurer of Mams Ik' and Quej and for the Mundo. He is invoked for money for necessities. Children born on these days "if called by the Mundo, will be trained as daykeeper . . . will be an elegant prayer-maker and much

in demand for both good and evil desires." Momostenango, Guatemala. (Tedlock, 1982: 120–121)

Ufo ana akai God of the second day of the week. The Ekoi, Nigeria. (Jeffreys, 1939: 106)

Ufo ana om God of the first day of the week. The Ekoi, Nigeria. (Jeffreys, 1939: 106)

Ufo Ik wo God of the fourth day of the week. The Ekoi, Nigeria. (Jeffreys, 1939: 106)

Ufo ogomo oseya God of the third day of the week. The Ekoi, Nigeria. (Jeffreys, 1939: 106)

Ull(r), Uller Scandinavian god of winter, of sports and of hunting, who covers the ground with snow to protect the seed. Husband of Skadi after she left Njord. Son of Sif. (Guerber, 1895: 111, 131; Wagner, 1882: 177; Stern, 1898: 49)

Unnut The "goddess of the hours." Not the same as the Lady of Unnu. Egypt. (Budge, 1969, 1: 426)

Ur-heket Deity of the seventh hour of the seventh day of the Moon. Egypt. (Budge, 1969, 2: 292)

Ušahina "Relating to the Dawn." The "special deity of the fifth (and last) day-period . . . from midnight until the stars become imperceptible." Iran. (Gray, 1930: 165)

Uzayeirina "Relating to Afternoon." The "special god of the third day-period, from mid-afternoon to sunset." Iran. (Gray, 1930: 166)

Vasanta, Vasanti, Vassanti Goddess of spring, its personification. India. (Tod, 1920: 657; Frazer, 1961: 241)

Vertumnus, Vortumnus Roman god of the seasons who watched over the fruit in all its stages, through spring, summer, fall. Husband of Pomona. (Fairbanks, 1907: 251–252; Murray, 1935: 145)

Vesna Slavic goddess of spring. (Grimm, 1883, 2: 781)

Vetr, Vetur Malignant god of winter, always at war with summer. Son of Vindloni (Vindsval). Norse. (Grimm, 1883, 2: 758; Thorpe, 1851: 7)

Wah-zee-yah God of the winter. The Dakota, Ft. Snelling, Minnesota. (Eastman, 1962: 208)

Wani The Four Winds as one god who established the directions and the seasons. Wani-yetu, the year-time, twelve moons, was measured by Wohpe as the time taken by the Four Winds to establish the seasons. The Lakota and Oglala, South Dakota. (Walker, 1980: 50–54, 103)

Waubun "Morning or East." Represented youth, the early portion of man's life. The Ojibway, Lake Superior region. (Johnston, 1976: 27, 163)

Wero-i-takokoto A star god who rules the winter. The Maori, New Zealand. (Anderson, 1928: 411) Also Wero-i-te-kokoto. (White, 1887, 1: 149)

Wero-i-te-ninihi A personification of cold. A star god who with Wero-i-takokoto rules the winter. The Maori, New Zealand. (Best, 1924: 95; Anderson, 1928: 411; White, 1887, 1: 149)

Whakaahu A deity representing summer. The Maori, New Zealand. (Best, 1924: 175)

Wiosna Slavonic goddess of summer. Wesna in Bohemia. (Grimm, 1883, 2: 773)

Wuon oru The "owner of the coming days." The Luo, Kenya. (Mbiti, 1970: 333)

Xipe Totec The Flayed God is the god of spring, of the seed-time, of the bare earth ready for sowing. He is also a god of jewelers. If neglected he inflicts diseases, particularly skin ailments. He is god of the fifteenth day, Quauhtli, the eagle, of the 20-day series Tonalpouhalli. The Aztec, Mexico. (Spence, 1923: 204; Burland, 1967: xi, 90; Bancroft, 1886, 3: 411–415; Caso, 1958: 49; Reed, 1966: 95, 132)

Xiuhtecuhtli Another name for Ometéotl as "Lord of fire and of time." The ominpresent dual being, center of the universe, of all things, expressed his creativity through the "four cosmic forces (his sons)." As the god of life he was patron of the ninth day, Atl (water), of the 20-day series Tonalpouhalli. "This day of water was symbolic of the passage through life." He presided also over "the first hour of the night and the first of morning." The Aztec, Mexico. (Vaillant, 1962: 149; Burland, 1967: xi, 89; Caso, 1958: 28; Alexander, 1920: 53)

Xochipilli, Cinteotl, Macuilxochitl The Flower God and god of maize was patron of the eleventh day, Ozomatli (the monkey), of the 20-day series Tonalpouhalli, and god of the seventh hour of the day. He was associated with youth and growth, with dancing and gaiety. The Aztec, Mexico. (Alexander, 1920: 54; Vaillant, 1962: 145, 149; Burland, 1967: 89; Spence, 1923: 154)

Xochiquetzal Goddess of flowers, female counterpart of Xochipilli, and goddess of craftsmen whose art is in imitation of nature. She was patroness of the twentieth day, Xochitl (the flower), of the 20-day series of Tonalpouhalli. She was also the goddess of sexual love and of prostitutes. The Aztec, Mexico. (Spence, 1923: 187, 195; Burland, 1967: 91; Duran, 1971: 238–239, 296; Neumann, 1955: 196–197; Caso, 1958: 26, 29)

Xopancalehuey Tlalloc The "presiding god of spring . . . considered a phallic god." Mexico. (Bancroft, 1886, 3: 505)

Yairya God of the year. Iran. (Gray, 1930: 224)

Yata The god of the north and of the north wind was associated with winter. The Oglala, South Dakota. (Powers, 1977: 95, 191)

Yen Kung Yüan Shuai One of "five Taoist gods . . . believed to preside over the first five days of the fifth month." Also known as Duke Yen. China. (Day, 1940: 47, 50)

Yuan Ming, Yuen Ming God of winter and also of the north. China. (Day, 1940: 66; Du Bose, n.d.: 327)

Yue tche che tcho, Yue tche sseu God of the months. China. (Chavannes, n.d.: 369)

Zeewun Summer, a gentle and mild youth, lived in the South (Zhawanong). He was the source of life and growth, was regenerative but lacking in forcefulness; was in continuous battle with Bebon, Winter. The Ojibway, Lake Superior region. (Johnston, 1976: 28–29, 162)

Zla ba A white god, the personification of Monday. Tibet. (Nebesky-Wojkowitz, 1956, 1: 262)

Zocho God of autumn and guardian of the west; some say the south. Japan. (Werner, 1932: 457; Getty, 1962: 168; Zimmer, 1955: 47; Eliseev, 1963: 447; Piggott, 1969: 44)

Zurvan The god of time and also of fate; a preexistent hermaphrodite who was considered the parent of Ohrmazd and Ahriman. Iran. (Kramer, 1961: 355–356; Patai, 1967: 168; Gray, 1930: 124-128)

Zyam The demon Winter. Iran. (Gray, 1930: 219)

49

Gods of War:
Victory

Aasith A Semitic goddess of war and of the desert, introduced into Egypt. Syria. (Budge, 1969, 2: 280; Knight, 1915: 9)

Aba An Akkadian god of war of Agade. Near East. (Jacobsen, 1970: 34)

Abchuy Kak A deified warrior. Yucatan, Mexico. (Bancroft, 1886, 3: 467)

Ade A war god of the Gã in Temma. Ghana. (Field, 1937: 13)

Aflim A god of war and of fishing. The Gã in Labadi. Ghana. (Field, 1937: 63)

Te Agiagi An ancestor god who is also a god of war. Mangareva, Polynesia. (Buck, 1938, 1: 422)

Agreskoe An Amerindian god of war. United States. (Schoolcraft, 1857, 1: 316)

Agrona A Celtic "goddess of slaughter." Wales. (Mac-Cana, 1970: 86)

Agusaya A goddess of war "usually identified with Ishtar." Near East. (Langdon, 1931: 27)

Ahaiyuta, Ahayuta, A-hai-u-ta The twin gods of war, of fate, and of chance. The sons of, or created by, the sun. The names sometimes apply to both the twins, sometimes to the elder, the younger being Mat-sailema. The Zuñi, New Mexico. (Cushing, 1891/92: 422; Bunzel, 1929/30: 525; Muller, 1968: 200, 206; Fewkes, 1891: 171)

Ahulane A Mayan war god—"the archer." Central America. (Nicholson, 1967: 127)

Aing-shi k'o-ha-na A god of scalp-taking ceremonials. The Zuñi, New Mexico. (Cushing, 1881/82: 40)

Ai-tupuai A goddess of war as well as a healing goddess. Society Islands, Polynesia. (Henry, 1928: 145, 375)

Ai-ushi-ni Kamui "Though a formidable looking warrior, he is not much employed; in fact, the only evil spirit whom, to my knowledge, he is engaged to fight, is Pauchi Kamui, and then only for stomach-ache." The Ainu, Japan. (Munro, 1963: 50)

Aius Locutius A Roman god who spoke in warning of the coming of the Gauls, and not being identifiable, was called Aius Locutius. (Dumézil, 1966, 1: 45; Roscher, 1965, 2, 1: 191)

Aja A Babylonian goddess of war and of light with whom Ishtar was identified. Near East. (Mercer, 1925, 12: 700)

Alajogun A Yoruba god of war. Nigeria. (Wescott, 1962: 348)

Alala A Greek goddess, the personification of the battle cry. Daughter of Polemos. (Roscher, 1965, 1, 1: 221)

Alator A Celtic war god. Gaul and Britain. (Ross, 1967: 174; MacCulloch, 1911: 27)

Albiorix A Celtic war god identified with Mars. Gaul. (Renel, 1906: 392; MacCulloch, 1911: 27; Anwyl, 1906: 39)

Allat A goddess of fate in her association with the planet Venus. "As morning star she is goddess of War." Near East. (Langdon, 1931: 25)

Ama The "god of attack in battle" associated with Verethragna. Iran. (Gray, 1930: 133)

Amangau A god of head-hunting. The Tinguian, Philippines. (Cole, 1922: 303)

Amisa A god of war of the Gã in Temma. Ghana. (Field, 1937: 13)

Am kri mi dmar A god of war of the retinue of lCam sring. Tibet. (Nebesky-Wojkowitz, 1956, 1: 92)

Amon After being merged with Re and depicted as a king, he was considered a god of war and of mining expeditions. Egypt. (Casson, 1965: 73–74)

Anat A virgin goddess of war and of battle as well as of fertility and sex. Sister of Baal. Phoenica, Canaan and Syria. Near East. (Moscati, 1960: 89; Vriezen, 1964: 123–124; Driver, 1956: 8; Langdon, 1931: 26; James, 1960: 89; Vriezen, 1963: 51; Oldenburg, 1969: 83–89)

Andrasta, Andraste A goddess of victory and of war to whom human sacrifices were made. Gaul and Britain. (Dottin, 1925, 12: 692; MacCulloch, 1911: 41–42, 125; Ross, 1967: 218, 360; MacCana, 1970: 86)

Angob hi lubong A minor deity of war. The Ifugao, Philippines. (Barton, 1946: 75)

Anhur A god of Abydos, a god of war and of the dead. Egypt. (Mercer, 1925, 12: 702; Knight, 1915: 16; Ames, 1965: 51–52; Larousse, 1968: 13, 14)

Anip A god of war and of sorcery. The Ifugao, Philippines. (Barton, 1946: 39)

Antaeus, Anthat, Anthyt A Syrian/Phoenician goddess of war introduced into Egypt. (Mercer, 1925, 12: 703; Budge, 1969, 1: 431; Knight, 1915: 18)

Anuke An Egyptian war goddess. (Rawlinson, 1885: 23)

Anuna An Akkadian goddess of battle. Near East. (Jacobsen, 1970: 34)

Anunit A goddess of battle with whom Ishtar is at times identified. At Agade and Sippar, Near East. (Mercer, 1925, 12: 700)

Anunitum An Akkadian goddess of battle. Near East. (Jacobsen, 1970: 34)

Apolake The "god of the sun and patron of warriors." The Tagalog, Philippines. (Jocano, 1969: 10)

Aregwensgwa A Mohawk god of war to whom human sacrifices were made. New York. (Gray, 1925, 7: 422)

Areouski *See* **Areskoui**

Ares The unscrupulous god of war and of strife, of slaughter and devastation. He was the father by Aphrodite of Deimos and Phobos, who accompanied him in his sorties. Son of Zeus and Hera. Greece. (Barthell, 1971: 27, 28; Kerényi, 1951: 150; Murray, 1935: 81; Schoeps, 1961: 131; Larousse, 1968: 124)

Areskoui, Areskoue, Areouski An Iroquoian god of war and of battle, as well as a sun god. Eastern United States. (Morgan, 1901: Appendix B; Schoolcraft, 1857, 6: 637; Beauchamp, 1896: 169)

Arixo A god of war. Gaul. (MacCulloch, 1911: 27)

Arong A god of war of the Mortlock Islanders. The Carolines, Micronesia. (Keane, 1925, 2: 242)

Arus A war god named on an altar from Castro Daire. Spain. (Martinez, 1962: 115)

Asabli A war god of the Gã in Kpong. Ghana. (Field, 1937: 79)

Ashadu A god of war of the Gã in Temma. Ghana. (Field, 1937: 13)

Ashtabi A Hittite/Hurrian warrior god. Same as Zababa (Babylonian). Asia Minor. (Ferm, 1950: 92; Albright, 1969: 143)

Astarte A goddess of warfare as well as a goddess of love and fertility. Canaan, Near East. (Moscati, 1960: 114; Albright, 1956: 75, 77; Schoeps, 1961: 63; Ferm, 1950: 125–126; Langdon, 1931: 25)

A-tchi-a la-to-pa Believed the original god of war of the Zuñi, but supplanted by the Twin War Gods. New Mexico. (Cushing, 1881/82: 40)

Athena The Greek goddess of wisdom and learning has a lesser role as a goddess of war, tempered with the prospect of victory and peace. (Murray, 1935: 96; Fairbanks, 1907: 113–115; Larousse, 1968: 107; Barthell, 1971: 22, 23; Hesiod-Brown, 1981: 32, 78)

Ave-aitu The long-tailed god who "guides the hosts of Tane (Kane) in time of war." Tahiti, Polynesia. (Beckwith, 1940: 113; Henry: 1928: 379)

Ayiku   Originally a god of war, he is now a god of the village invoked for rain and fish. The Gã in Teshi, Ghana. (Field, 1937: 74, 75)

Badagris   A god of warriors identified with St. George. Haiti. West Indies. (Marcelin, 1950: 49)

Badb   A goddess of battle who incites the warriors to fury. Celtic Ireland. (Davidson, 1964: 65; Ross, 1967: 219; Squire, 1906: 52, 53; MacCana, 1970: 55)

Badowado   A god of war and of sorcery. Son of Mana-haut. The Ifugao, Philippines. (Barton, 1946: 40)

Baduhenna   A war goddess of the Frisians. Germany and the Netherlands. (MacCulloch, 1964: 17)

Baidrama   A war god who was a twinned deity. Also called Budig y Aiba. Puerto Rico. (Fewkes, 1903/4: 57)

Bali Flaki   The carrion hawk as an omen bird is observed for the fortunes of war. The Kenyahs, Borneo. (Hose, 1912: 15)

Bali Penyalong   The supreme being and god of war who is approached with a sacrificial pig as his messenger. The Kenyahs, Borneo. (Hose, 1912: 15, 16; MacKenzie, 1930: 254)

Balitok ud Dalegdeg   A minor deity of war. The Ifugao, Philippines. (Barton, 1946: 75)

Balonga (hoya)   The younger of the Little War Gods, the elder being Pookong (hoya). Sons of the Sun and Laughing Waters. The Hopi, Arizona. (Tyler, 1964: 214; Alexander, 1964: 205)

Bananuan   "Corpse-Stenched," a god of war. The Philippines. (Barton, 1946: 39)

Bar, Pa-Bar   A Syrian/Phoenician god of war who was introduced into Egypt. He personified the blazing heat of the desert. (Mercer, 1925, 12: 703; Budge, 1969, 2: 281; Knight, 1915: 29)

Barrex   A Celtic god of war, equated with Mars. Gaul and Britain. (MacCulloch, 1911: 27, 125; Ross, 1967: 182)

Begenuing   A god of war invoked during the "Hornbill Feast." The Dyaks of Sarawak, Borneo. (Sarawak Gazette, 1963: 101)

Beg-tse   A god of war and "Defender of the Law." Tibet and Mongolia. (Getty, 1962: 151; Sierksma, 1966: 272; Hoffman, 1956: 172)

Behnya   A god of war and also a river god. Elmina District, the Gold Coast, West Africa. (Ellis, 1887: 53)

Beladonnis   A war god of the Bouches-du-Rhone. Gaul. (Renel, 1906: 394; MacCulloch, 1911: 27)

Belatucadros   A Celtic war god. The Bretons, Gaul and Britain. (Renel, 1906: 312; MacCulloch, 1911: 27; Ross, 1967: 155–56)

Bellona   A Roman goddess of war, powerful in that "she intervened both in what followed and in what preceded war, as well as in the diplomatic activity which sometimes spared it." (Dumézil, 1966, 1: 335, 390; Fairbanks, 1907: 254; Murray, 1935: 214)

Bes   The Egyptian dwarf god was known also as a god of war, although he was primarily a god of revelry, of marriage, and of childbirth and children. (Knight, 1915: 32; Budge, 1969, 2: 284–285; Jayne, 1962: 55)

Bhadrakali   Among the Izhavas she is "believed to help them in their military undertakings." Southern India. (Thurston, 1909, 2: 400)

Bia   The personification of violence, a child of Styx and Pallas, who assisted Zeus in the battle with the Titans. Greece. (Kerényi, 1951: 34; Barthell, 1971: 15, 50; Gardner, 1925, 9: 794)

Bo   The god of war and of warriors. Dahomey. (Ellis, 1890: 69; Mockler-Ferryman, 1925, 9: 279)

Bodua   A goddess of war. Gaul. Same as Badb (Ireland). (MacCulloch, 1911: 125)

Bok Glaih   A sky god who was the god of war as well as of lightning. Indo-China. (Cabaton, 1925, 7: 230)

Bolvinnus   A god of war identified with Mars. Gaul. (Renel, 1906: 394; MacCulloch, 1911: 27; Bertrand, 1897: 329)

Bonat   A god of war, of head-hunting. The Ifugao, Philippines. (Barton, 1946: 39)

Bonge   A war god of the Gã in Kpong. Ghana. (Field, 1937: 79)

Braciaca   A god of war as well as a god of malt and of intoxication. Gaul and Britain. (MacCulloch, 1911: 27, 28; Schrader, 1925, 2: 36; Ross, 1967: 181)

Britovius, Britovis   A god of war identified with Mars. Gaul. (Bertrand, 1897: 329; MacCulloch, 1911: 27; Renel, 1906: 395)

Buanann   A warrior goddess who taught Cu Chulainn. She was also a mother goddess and goddess of fertility. Wales. (Ross, 1967: 228; MacCulloch, 1911: 73)

Bugan inManahaut   A goddess of war, wife of Manahaut. The Ifugao, Philippines. (Barton, 1946: 39)

Bulnuk   A god of war of the Ifugao. Philippines. (Barton, 1946: 39)

Buxenus   A war god, a local Rhone god, probably the god of the boxwood tree, was assimilated to Mars. Gaul. (MacCulloch, 1911: 27; Renel, 1906: 395; Bertrand, 1897: 330)

Cabetius   A god of war identified with Mars. Gaul. (Bertrand, 1897: 330; MacCulloch, 1911: 27)

lCam sring, lcam-srin   A god of war and an important protector of the religious law. Also called gDong dmar ma. Tibet. (Getty, 1962: 151; Nebesky-Wojkowitz, 1956, 1: 23, 88, 91)

Camulos   A Celtic war god equated with Mars. Gaul and Britain. (MacCulloch, 1911: 27, 125; Ross, 1967: 68, 180; MacBain, 1917: 88)

Cariocecius, Cariociecus   A god of war. Gaul and Spain. (MacCulloch, 1911: 27; Martinez, 1961: 115)

Carrus   A deified mountain, Pic-du-Gar, Basses-Alpes, and a god of war assimilated to Mars. Gaul. (Renel, 1906: 395; MacCulloch, 1911: 27; Bertrand, 1897: 330)

Caswallawn   A god of war. Son of Beli. Celtic Britain. (MacCulloch, 1911: 112, 113)

Cathubodua   A goddess of war. Haute-Savoie, Gaul. (Renel, 1906: 396; MacCulloch, 1911: 41)

Caturix, Caturic   A god of war. Gaul and Switzerland. (Renel, 1906: 396; MacCulloch, 1911: 27; Roscher, 1965, 1, 1: 857; Bertrand, 1897: 329)

Cemenelus   A god of war assimilated to Mars. Gaul. (MacCulloch, 1911: 27; Renel, 1906: 396)

Chamarikh   Deities invoked and sacrificed to for war. Morocco. (Basset, 1920: 99)

Chandi   A goddess of war and of hunting who can be offered sacrifices only by bachelors. The Oraons, India. (Roy, 1928: 16, 61; Rahmann, 1952: 882)

Chango   The god of storms and also of war. Haiti. West Indies. (Verger, 1957: 338; Marcelin, 1950: 81)

Cheru, Heru   Germanic god of war, of the sword. (Grimm, 1880: 204)

General Ch'oe   A guardian spirit and protector of soldiers. Korea. (Mocs, 1983: 130)

Chuchu   The god of war of the Yuracare. Bolivia. (Métraux, 1948, 5: 500)

Ah Chuy Kak   A Mayan god of war. Mexico. (Nicholson, 1967: 127; Thompson, 1970: 313)

Cicollius   A war god identified with Mars. Gaul. (MacCulloch, 1911: 27; Renel, 1906: 396; Bertrand, 1897: 329)

Cit Chac Coh   A god of war honored and celebrated at the "feast of Kukulcan." Mayan, Mexico. (Thompson, 1970: 312; Krickeberg, 1968: 73)

Cnabetius   A war god of Gaul. (MacCulloch, 1911: 27)

Cocidius   A Celtic god of war who is in some areas a god of hunting and of the woods. Britain and Gaul. (Ross, 1967: 156, 160; Bertrand, 1897: 330; MacCulloch, 1911: 125)

Cocosus   A god of war. Gaul. (MacCulloch, 1911: 27)

Condatis   A god of war, but in Britain more a deity of thermal waters. Gaul and Britain. (Ross, 1967: 182; MacCulloch, 1911: 27; Renel, 1906: 396; Bertrand, 1897: 330)

Coronus   A local god, believed to be a war god. Spain. (Martinez, 1962: 116–117)

Corotiacus   A Celtic god of war identified with Mars. Gaul and Britain. (Ross, 1967: 173; MacCulloch, 1911: 27, 125; Ferguson, 1970: 212)

Cosiovus Ascannus   A war god. Spain. (Martinez, 1962: 118)

Cososus   A war god identified with Mars. Gaul and Spain. (Renel, 1906: 396; Martinez, 1962: 119; Bertrand, 1897: 329)

Cosotheinaecus   A war god named on an altar found in Torres de Nogueira. Spain. (Martinez, 1962: 119)

Cosoudaviniagus   A war god named on an altar in the church of S. Martin de Meiras. Spain. (Martinez, 1962: 120)

Cosunea   A war goddess from Eiriz. Spain. (Martinez, 1962: 120)

Cosus   A local war god—an altar found in Brandomil. Spain. (Martinez, 1962: 118)

Cosus Calaeunius   A war god named on an altar at Lugo. Spain. (Martinez, 1962: 118)

Cosus Oenaecus   A war god named on an altar in San Mamed de Seavia. Spain. (Martinez, 1962: 118)

Cozichacozee   The god of war in Ocelotepec, also associated with Copichja, the sun god. The Southern Zapotec, Oaxaca, Mexico. (Whitecotton, 1977: 158)

Ah Cun Can   A Mayan war god. Central America. (Nicholson, 1967: 127)

Cusuneneoecus   A war god on an altar in the Museum of Guimaraes. Spain. (Martinez, 1962: 120–121)

Da Choc   A Celtic warrior god. Ireland. (Ross, 1967: 170)

Dade   A god of war of the Gã. Ghana. (Field, 1937: 65, 73, 89)

Dagarsila   A hill god of the Santals invoked during war. India. (Mukherjea, 1962: 278)

Dalha   The god of warriors who protects men from evil spirits and helps them attain wishes. Tibet and Sikkim. (Getty, 1962: 168–169; Schlagintweit, 1969: 157–158; Gazetteer of Sikhim, 1894: 269)

Darago   A god or goddess of war and of warriors. The Bagobo, Philippines. (Cole, 1945: 192; Jocano, 1969: 22, 31)

Devi (Durga)   Among the Rajputs the principal deity as the goddess of war. She also protected the virtue of the women. Central Provinces, India. (Russell, 1916, 4: 422)

dgra-lha   A deity "which sits on the right shoulder . . . especially worshipped by soldiers, as he defends against the enemy." Sikkim. (Gazetteer of Sikhim, 1894: 354)

Dinalakagan   A minor deity of war. The Ifugao, Philippines. (Barton, 1946: 75)

Dingkra   A war god of the Gã in Kpong. Ghana. (Field, 1937: 79)

Dinomogetimarus   A god of war identified with Mars. Gaul. (Renel, 1906: 397; MacCulloch, 1911: 27; Bertrand, 1897: 329)

Dinukligan   A god of war whose "function is to cause persons slain in vengeance to be forgotten by their kindred and so to be left unavenged." The Ifugao, Philippines. (Barton, 1946: 39, 40)

Divanno   A local war god assimilated to Mars. Gaul. (Renel, 1906: 397; MacCulloch, 1911: 27; Bertrand, 1897: 329)

Du l-Halasa   An archer god, and possibly a warrior god. Arabia. (Fahd, 1968: 61–63)

Dumanug   A minor deity of war. The Ifugao, Philippines. (Barton, 1946: 75)

Dzami   A war god of the Otublohu quarter. The Gã in Accra. Ghana. (Field, 1937: 88)

Dzebi   A war god of the Gã in Temma. Ghana. (Field, 1937: 13)

Eah, Eyah   "Big Mouth," a deity invoked in war and considered to have "the power of telling the position of the enemy." The Dakota, United States and Canada. (Emerson, 1884: 77; Schoolcraft, 1857, 3: 487; 1857, 4: 495)

egeči degüü   A Dharmapala, Defender of the Law, and a "God of War and Protector of Horses." Mongolia. (Getty, 1962: 151)

Ek Chuah   The friendly and benevolent god of merchants and travelers, of cacao planters, was also a god of war, wherein he was malevolent. The Maya, Mexico. (Morley, 1946: 214, 228; Tozzer, 1941: 90, 107; Thompson, 1970: 306)

Eku   The god of warriors, protective at all times, and also the god of hunters whom he helps to find game. The Effutu, Ghana. (Wyllie, 1966: 480)

Elaunato   "Comet" or "Shooting Star." If seen flying through the air it foretells war and it knows where. The Lenape, Eastern United States. (Harrington, 1921: 48)

Enyalios, Enualios   A warrior god, partial to war; son of Ares and Enyo or Chronos and Rhea. Also used as a name of Ares. Greece. (Dumézil, 1966, 1: 263; Roscher, 1965, 1, 1: 1250; Chadwick, 1976: 88, 99)

Enyo   A Greek goddess of war associated with Ares; his female counterpart. (Barthell, 1971: 28; Dumézil, 1966, 1: 390; Murray, 1935: 214)

Epe A deity invoked with Kivava in war. Their help gives certain success. New Guinea. (MacKenzie, 1930: 287)

Epunamun A god of war of the Mapuche-Huilliche. Among the Araucanians a god of evil whose council in war was sometimes followed. Chile. (Cooper, 1946, 6: 748; Alexander, 1920: 327)

'Ere'ere-fenua A powerful goddess whose appearance foretold destruction by storm or war. Society Islands, Polynesia. (Henry, 1928: 359)

Eshtar Semitic goddess of war and of sex. Old Akkadian form of Ishtar. Near East. (Roberts, 1972: 39, 147)

esrua A Mongolian warrior god. Same as Ts'angs-pa Dkar-po. (Getty, 1962: 150)

Esus A god of war who was depicted as a woodcutter and to whom sacrifices were made by hanging from a tree. Gaul. (Schoeps, 1961: 116; Grimm, 1880: 204; MacCulloch, 1911: 234; Larousse, 1968: 228)

Fa'aola Life-giver, a god of war invoked for bravery and freedom from cowardice. Samoa, Polynesia. (Turner, 1884: 27, 28)

Fakahoko A war god at Liku believed to be an ancestor deity. Niue Island, Polynesia. (Loeb, 1926, 1: 163)

Fakakonaatua A deity invoked "before battle to poison the gods of the enemy." Niue Island, Polynesia. (Loeb, 1926, 1: 161)

Fakatafetau "The-causer-of-war," at Liku. Niue Island, Polynesia. (Loeb, 1926, 1: 160, 163)

fa lo gra fa lo run The god of warriors invoked for warfare and for safety. The Lepchas, Sikkim. (Siiger, 1967, 2: 141)

Fanonga Destruction, a god of war "supposed to be incarnate in the Samoan owl." Samoa, Polynesia. (Turner, 1884: 25)

Fatsman, Oosa Fatsman A god of war who is interested in the welfare of the empire. Japan. (Coleman, 1832: 332)

Fea A Celtic war goddess, "the Hateful," who instilled the warriors with madness. (Squire, 1906: 52)

Feni Be So A head-hunting deity. The Kalabari, Nigeria. (Horton, 1960: 50)

Ogoun Feraille The god of armies and blacksmith of war gear; protector of the brave; identified with St. Philip. Haiti, West Indies. (Marcelin, 1950: 59, 88)

Fitikila A war god at Hakupu. Niue Island, Polynesia. (Loeb, 1926, 1: 160)

Fuan-fuan-fo The war god of Moree. Gold Coast, West Africa. (Ellis, 1887: 50)

Furor The Roman personification of the fury of war. (Roscher, 1965, 1, 2: 1565)

Futsu-Nushi-no-Kami A god of war and of swordsmen. Japan. (Kato, 1926: 72; Herbert, 1967: 336, 463; Holtom, 1938: 177)

Ga'e fefe A god of war in some areas whose emblem is a coconut-leaf basket. Samoa, Polynesia. (Turner, 1884: 32)

Gaiyun A goddess of reproduction who is also a minor goddess of war and is invoked at funerals. The Ifugao, Philippines. (Barton, 1946: 44, 75, 84)

Gaja A god of war of the Nagas of Cachar. India. (Elwin, 1969: 423)

Geirahod One of the Valkyries, demi-goddesses of battle who decide the victory. Teutonic. (Grimm, 1880: 420–421; Branston, 1955: 178; Anderson, 1891: 265)

Geirskogol One of the Teutonic Valkyries, demi-goddesses of war who decide who shall be slain. (Grimm, 1880: 420–421; Branston, 1955: 178; Anderson, 1891: 265)

Gerovit A Slavic god of war. The Pomeranians, Germany and Poland. (Machal, 1918: 282; Czaplicka, 1925, 11: 594; Gimbutas, 1971: 154)

Gish The popular and admired god of war and of warriors. The Kafirs, Afghanistan. (Robertson, 1925, 7: 635-636; Dumézil, 1966, 1: 59)

Gitaowa A god associated with war and head-hunting. The Ifugao, Philippines. (Barton, 1946: 49)

Glarinus A war god identified with Mars. Gaul. (Bertrand, 1897: 329; MacCulloch, 1911: 27)

Goll, Gol One of the Valkyries, demi-goddesses of battle who decide the victory. Teutonic. (Grimm, 1880: 420–421; Anderson, 1891: 265, 447)

Gondul One of the Valkyries, demi-goddesses of battle who decide the victory. Teutonic. (Grimm, 1880: 420–421; Anderson, 1891: 265, 447)

Goweh The god of war of the Iroquois. Eastern United States. (Bjorklund, 1969: 132–133)

sGra-lha The fierce and powerful war god. Tibet. (Waddell, 1925, 4: 636)

Gu A god of war and of warriors and the god of metal and metal-workers, in all its applications—hunting, agriculture, etc. Dahomey. (Herskovits, 1938, 2: 107, 127; Parrinder, 1967: 79, 83; Mercier, 1954: 222)

Gudr One of the Valkyries, a Teutonic demi-goddess of battle and war. She is particularly a mistress of victory. (Grimm, 1880: 420–421; Anderson, 1891: 265)

Gunnr One of the Teutonic Valkyries, demi-goddesses of battle and war who decide who is to be slain. (Grimm, 1880: 420–421; Anderson, 1891: 265)

Gwynn A god of battle and of the dead, conducting the slain to the underworld. Son of Nudd. Britain and Wales. (Wallis, 1939: 28; Squire, 1906: 254; MacCulloch, 1911: 115)

Gyansu The war god of the Akan. Ghana. (Meyerowitz, 1958: 62)

Hachiman The deified Ojin-tenno, the god of war, although he "has become a fishing and agricultural deity . . . [has] also been identified as the god of the forge." Japan. (Herbert, 1967: 426; Piggott, 1969: 47; Bunce, 1955: 124; Holtom, 1938: 173)

Hadu A Teutonic god of war who determines the outcome. (Grimm, 1880: 196, 207)

Halamardus A god of war identified with Mars. Gaul and Germany. (MacCulloch, 1911: 27; Bertrand, 1897: 329; Roscher, 1965, 1, 2: 1817)

Halangob A god of war and of sorcery. The Ifugao, Philippines. (Barton, 1946: 40)

Halimudat A god of war and of sorcery. Son of Manahaut. The Ifugao, Philippines. (Barton, 1946: 40)

Ham-vareti Called "morning mist," she takes her place with warrior deities as hiding the warriors. Iran. (Gray, 1930: 148, 222)

Hara The "god of battle" at Rajasthan. A name of Siva as devastation and death. India. (Tod, 1920: 681; Danielou, 1964: 196–197)

Hariasa A Germanic goddess of war. (MacCulloch, 1964: 255)

Harimella A Germanic goddess of war. (MacCulloch, 1964: 255)

Harmogius A god of war identified with Mars. Gaul. (Bertrand, 1897: 329–330; MacCulloch, 1911: 27)

Harumae An ancestor spirit who was offered a castrated pig and invoked for help when making war. San Cristoval, Solomon Islands, Melanesia. (Codrington, 1881: 300–301)

Ha shang mi dmar A god of war. Tibet. (Nebesky-Wojkowitz, 1956, 1: 92)

Heauoro A deity associated with Maru and with war. Chatham Islands, New Zealand. (Shand, 1894: 89)

Hehewuti "Warrior Mother," a Kachina spirit of the Hopi. Arizona. (Waters, 1963: 86)

Her-fiotr One of the Valkyries, Teutonic demi-goddesses of battle and war who decide the victory. (Grimm, 1880: 420–421; Anderson, 1891: 265)

Heru, Cheru, Saxnot Germanic sword god, identical with Tyr, the god of war. He is also considered a "god of the sun . . . his shining sword blade an emblem of its rays." (Wagner, 1882: 10; Guerber, 1895: 86)

Hex Chun Chan A Mayan god of war. Central America. (Nicholson, 1967: 127; Thompson, 1970: 313)

Hilde, Hildr One of the Valkyries, Teutonic demi-goddesses of battle and of war. She "goes to the val at night, and by her magic wakes the fallen warriors into life again." (Wagner, 1882: 104; Grimm, 1880: 420–422; Anderson, 1891: 265)

Hiorthrimul One of the Valkyries, Teutonic demi-goddesses of battle and war who decide who shall be slain. (Grimm, 1880: 432; Anderson, 1891: 265)

Hiovaki The god of war to whose home in the sky go the souls of those who die in battle. Papuan Gulf, New Guinea. (Wallis, 1939: 241; Holmes, 1902: 428)

The Hipag Ferocious spirits of war invoked before warring expeditions to provide courage. They are also invoked in kinship controversies and in sorcery. The Ifugao, Philippines. (Barton, 1946: 74, 75; Jocano, 1969: 18)

Hiro   A god of war who supported the side of the conflicting forces which was opposed to that supported by Tane. Tahiti, Polynesia. (Henry, 1928: 129)

Hkumturu   A deity, "the Spirit of the Fell," who is propitiated on head-hunting expeditions. The Was, Burma. (Temple, 1925, 3: 23)

Hlock   One of the Valkyries, Teutonic demigoddesses of war and battle who decide the victory. (Grimm, 1880: 420-421; Anderson, 1891: 265)

Hoba   "Fatigue," a god of war who is "invoked in cases of broken bones, dislocations, snake bites and wounds." The Ifugao, Philippines. (Barton, 1946: 40, 68)

Hodr, Hodur   The blind god who killed Balder represented a phenomenon of war and was "imagined blind, because he dealt out at random good and ill . . . without malice." Teutonic. (Grimm, 1880: 223)

Hokomata   With his twin Tochopa taught mankind war. The Walapai, Arizona. (Alexander, 1964: 180)

Homados   A Greek god, the personification of the noise made in battle. (Roscher, 1965, 1, 2: 2698)

Hrist   One of the Valkyries, Teutonic demi-goddesses of war and battle who decide the victory. (Grimm, 1880: 420–421; Anderson, 1891: 265)

Hsu Ch'ang   The god of archery. China. (Werner, 1932: 14)

Huitzilopochtli   The Patron God of the Aztecs was the god of war, identified with the sun, and to whom human sacrifices were made. His headdress was in the form of a Hummingbird's beak. Mexico. (Duran, 1971: 70–72; Spence, 1923: 73; Burland, 1967: ix; Alexander, 1920: 57; León-Portilla, 1982: 161–163)

Ah Hulneb   A Mayan war god of Cozumel. Yucatan, Mexico. (Thompson, 1970: 313)

Humabungol   A god of war and of sorcery. The Ifugao, Philippines. (Barton, 1946: 38, 39)

Hunchunchan   A god of battle. Lake Peten, Guatemala. (Bancroft, 1886, 3: 483)

Hun Pic Tok   A Mayan war god of Yucatan. Mexico. (Nicholson, 1967: 127; Bancroft, 1886, 3: 467; Thompson, 1970: 313)

Icho Kalakal   The war god of Metalanim. Ponape, Caroline Islands, Micronesia. (Christian, 1899: 383)

Ieusdrinus   A war god. Gaul. (MacCulloch, 1911: 27)

Ìkèngà Asaba   The more important of the two war gods—"in the custody of the *Ódogwu* of Asaba." Both are called Ìkèngà; the other is in the custody of the *Iyàse* of Asaba. The Igbo, Nigeria. (Isichei, 1978: 190)

Inadungali   A god of war and of sorcery. The Ifugao, Philippines. (Barton, 1946: 40)

Inaiyuan   A god of war and of sorcery. The Ifugao, Philippines. (Barton, 1946: 40)

Inanna   Sumerian goddess of love and of war, of procreation and of fertility. Near East. (Kramer, 1967: 101, 103; James, 1960: 78)

Ingaladigod   A god of war. The Ifugao, Philippines. (Barton, 1946: 39)

Ingingo   A god of war and of sorcery. The Ifugao, Philippines. (Barton, 1946: 39)

Inin   An Akkadian goddess of battle. Near East. (Jacobsen, 1970: 34; Roberts, 1972: 36)

Innini   A Sumerian goddess of battle with whom Ishtar was identified. Near East. (Mercer, 1925, 12: 700)

Insidiae   A Roman goddess who personified ambush and was associated with Mars. (Roscher, 1965, 2, 1: 262)

Intimitiman   A god of war and sorcery. The Ifugao, Philippines. (Barton, 1946: 39)

Irnina   An Akkadian goddess of victory. Near East. (Jacobsen, 1970: 34)

Ishara   A Babylonian goddess of war, of conquest, and of victory with whom Ishtar was identified. Near East. (Mercer, 1925, 12: 700)

Ishtar   The Assyro/Babylonian goddess of war and battle, of love and motherhood. "As morning star she is goddess of war . . . and as evening star patroness of love and harlotry." As the goddess of war, numerous goddesses were identified with her. Near East. (Jastrow, 1898: 202, 205; Schoeps, 1961: 56; Jayne, 1962: 122;

Langdon, 1931: 25; Patai, 1967: 188; Mercer, 1925, 12: 700; Oldenburg, 1969: 40)

Isokalakal A deified legendary human—"King Wonderful, now a Ponape war god and founder of the two clans of the island." The Carolines, Micronesia. (Leach, 1950: 178)

Jacque Majeur A warrior god and a Catholic saint. Plaisance, Haiti. West Indies. (Marcelin, 1950: 41; Simpson, 1945: 43)

Jalweny The "Great Soldier." The Luo, Kenya. (Mbiti, 1970, 2: 332)

Jarovit, Gerovit A war god at Wolgast who is represented by a gigantic shield. He also seems to be associated with the spring, the fertility, and young growth of vegetation and cattle. The Baltic peoples. (Gimbutas, 1971: 154, 160; Pettazzoni, 1956: 246)

Jaya An abstract goddess of Victory, in the Manavagri-hyasutra. India. (Ghurye, 1962: 255)

Jhagra Khand The principal tribal deity that they worship is a two-edged sword. The Kawar, Central Provinces, India. (Russell, 1916, 3: 399)

Empress Jingo Deified and worshipped as a patron of war. Japan. (Holtom, 1938: 172)

João Sueira The god of war, sometimes identified with Ogun. Belem, Brazil. (Leacock, 1972: 136)

Kaalū A divinity associated with war to whom sacrifices were made "to lead, direct and bring home the young aspirant." Youths, to prove themselves, must return with heads. The Igbo, Ohafia, Nigeria. (Isichei, 1978: 128–129, 341)

Kabigat A god of war among the Nabaloi. He taught divination with the use of iron; is invoked in marriage rites and in some agricultural rites. Northern Luzon, Philippines. (De Raedt, 1964: 267–268)

Kahukura A god of war, of travelers, and of crops. He is the personification of the rainbow. As a god of disease and death, he must be invoked in illness. New Zealand. (White, 1887, 1: 4, 41; 1887, 3: 103; Best, 1924: 160–161; Poignant, 1967: 24; Andersen, 1928: 426, 428)

Ka-'ili The war god of Kamehameha the First and of Liloa. Hawaii. (Beckwith, 1932: 18; 1940: 28; Westervelt, 1963, 2: 140)

Kakupacat, Kak-u-Pacat A Mayan war god. Central America. (Thompson, 1970: 313; Nicholson, 1967: 127)

Kamos The main god of war of the Moabites. Near East. (Roscher, 1965, 2, 1: 945)

Kankannikan, Zancannican A warrior god. Haiti. West Indies. (Marcelin, 1950: 78)

Kanukh, Kanugh The god of war, "Wolf." He sends epidemics and war when displeased. The Thlinkets (Klinkits), Alaska and British Columbia. (Knapp and Childe, 1896: 153; Bancroft, 1886, 3: 149)

Kara A Teutonic Valkyrie, one of those who were "lovers or wives of heroes." (Grimm, 1880: 423)

Karttikeya The Hindu god of war who is worshipped for sturdy sons. Also called Kumara, Skanda, Mahasena. He was also the patron of thieves. Son of Siva and Parvati or Agni and Ganga. India and Nepal. (Banerjea, 1953: 62, 71; Basak, 1953: 97; Martin, 1914: 194; Brown, 1961: 306, 308; Pal and Bhattacharyya, 1969: 46; Ions, 1967: 84–87; Bhattacharji, 1970: 180, 183)

Kauakahi, Kekaua-kahi A god of war of Hawaii. Son of Papa and Haumea. (Beckwith, 1940: 278)

Kei A Celtic god who "may have been a war-god." Wales. (MacCulloch, 1925, 3: 292)

Keledegbe A god of war of the Earth Pantheon in Allada. Dahomey. (Herskovits, 1933: 19)

Kenjo A god of war who gives the victory and a god of hunting. He is also a god of the land and controls the rain and the lightning. The Jukun, Nigeria. (Meek, 1931: 201, 265–266; Greenberg, 1946: 57)

Kenyalong The "great Borneo hornbill" whose feast is associated with war and is celebrated only by those who have taken enemy heads. The Iban Dyaks, Sarawak. (Nyuak, 1906: 421)

Kerans A Teutonic spear god. (Grimm, 1888: 1291)

Khandoba, Khande Rao The principal deity and war god of the Marathas and an incarnation of Mahadeo (Siva). Also worshipped by the Kunbi, the Bhils, the Ramosi. Central Provinces, India. (Russell, 1916, 2: 288; 1916, 4: 38, 204–205, 474; Ghurye, 1962: 252; Naik, 1956: 172)

Kibuka The god of war and the "personification of the unexpectedness of death" to whom human sacrifices were made. The Baganda, Uganda. (Mutwa, 1966: iii; Cunningham, 1905: 215; Roscoe, 1965: 275; Junod, 1962: 409; Mair, 1934: 233)

Kilesa The god of war of the Gallas. Also the god of winds. Ethiopia. (Littmann, 1925, 1: 57)

Kim The god of war of the Angas. Nigeria. (Meek, 1925, 2: 30; Williams, 1936: 215)

Kinungkungan A god of war of the Ifugao. Philippines. (Barton, 1946: 39)

Kirabira A war god associated with Nende, but of little influence. The Baganda, Uganda. (Roscoe, 1965: 308)

kong chen The god of Mount Kanchenjunga is "the official war god of the State of Sikkim." The Lepchas. (Siiger, 1967, 1: 43; 1967, 2: 142)

Kottavei The "sinister sorceress, goddess of war, who feeds on carnage . . . is none other than Kali." The Tamil, India. (Larousse, 1973: 269)

Kratesis A Greek goddess of victory, the personification of ruling. (Roscher, 1965, 2, 1: 1410)

Kratos Greek personification of strength and a warrior god. A son of Styx and Pallas who was pledged to help Zeus in the war with the Titans. With Bia, fettered Prometheus. (Gardner, 1925, 9: 794; Barthell, 1971: 15, 50; Roscher, 1965, 2, 1: 1411; Kerényi, 1951: 34)

Krieg Roman personification of war. (Roscher, 1965, 2, 1: 1430)

Kro ti mi dmar A god of war of the retinue of lCam sring. Tibet. (Nebesky-Wojkowitz, 1956, 1: 92)

Ku The group of gods invoked under the various Ku compound names were gods of war, of agriculture and of fishing. Hawaii. (Poignant, 1967: 38; Beckwith, 1940: 11–15)

Kuan-sheng-jen A god of war of Southwest China. (Graham, 1961: 163)

Kuan-ti, Kuan Yu A deified hero as the national god of war who defends against disturbance of the peace, foreign or domestic, rather than making war. Japan. (Maspero, 1963: 333; Ferguson, 1937: 196; Haydon, 1941: 196)

Kuan Yu A god of war. A military hero of the Han dynasty, posthumously deified, and widely worshipped.

He became as well a "patron saint of various trades and professions," extended even to wealth and literature. China. (Williams, 1976: 211–212)

Ku-ho'one'enu'u A god of war and a guide of the souls of the dead. Oahu, Hawaii. (Beckwith, 1940: 15, 110)

Ku-ka'ili-moku The god of war and of victory. Hawaii. (Beckwith, 1940: 15, 396; Westervelt, 1963, 3: 108; Emory, 1974: 738)

Ku-keoloewa A god of war and a guide for the souls of the dead. Also a god of sorcery. Maui and Molokai, Hawaii. (Beckwith, 1940: 15, 110, 113)

Kumapari, Kumaphari The demiurge who succeeded in taking fire from the birds, later assumed the form of a jaguar and became a god of war and of cannibalism. The Shipaya, Brazil. (Nimuendaju, 1948, 1: 241; Zerries, 1968: 288; Levi-Strauss, 1969: 141)

Kumara, Skanda God of war and also the protector of children. India and Bali. (Tod, 1920: 693; Danielou, 1964: 298; Covarrubias, 1937: 317; Hooykaas, 1964: 48)

Kumi A war god of the Gã in Accra. Also in Teshi and Osu. Ghana. (Field, 1937: 65, 73, 89)

Kumkumti A god of war of the Ifugao. Son of Manahaut. Philippines. (Barton, 1946: 40)

Ku-nui-akea A god of war. Hawaii. (Beckwith, 1940: 15)

Kurshunaburuam A general of Ningirsu who, with Lugalkurdub, took care of "outside threats" unless the army was to be headed by Ningirsu. Near East. (Jacobsen, 1976: 82)

Kuyub A god of war and of sorcery. Son of Manahaut. The Ifugao, Philippines. (Barton, 1946: 40)

Kwan Oo The god of war. Also called Kwan Te or Kwan Ik. Korea. (Clark, 1932: 131)

Kwan Ti The god of war, a deified general. A Shamanist deity who derives from Confucianism. Korea. (Moes, 1983: 128)

Kwanting The god of war among some of the upper class. Okinawa, Ryukyu Islands. (Lebra, 1966: 185)

Kwan-yu A Confucian war god. China. (De Groot, 1925, 4: 14)

Kwashi Otu A war god of the Alata quarter. The Gã, Accra, Ghana. (Field, 1937: 89)

Kwataka "The Bird-man . . . is an old war-god, and possibly a sun god, the return of whom the Winter Solstice ceremony commemorates." He is invoked for rain and snow and for agricultural prosperity. The Hopi, Arizona. (Fewkes, 1899/1900: 529, 533)

Kwesi Dede God of the warrior company Tuafo. The Effutu, Ghana. (Wyllie, 1966: 480)

Kydoimos Greek personification of the turmoil of battle. (Roscher, 1965, 2, 1: 1674)

Kyllang A warrior and mountain deity and a god of storms. The Khasi, Assam. (Bareh, 1967: 360)

La'ala'a A war god in Savaii. Samoa, Polynesia. (Turner, 1884: 33)

Lacavos A war god identified with Mars. Gaul. (Renel, 1906: 399; MacCulloch, 1911: 27; Bertrand, 1897: 330)

Lagiofa A lesser god invoked in time of war. Niue Island, Polynesia. (Loeb, 1926, 1: 161)

Laja A god of war invoked during the "Hornbill Feast." The Dyaks, Sarawak, Borneo. (Sarawak Gazette, 1963: 101)

Laki A war god of the Pangasinan. Philippines. (Kroeber, 1918, 2: 40)

The Lang (Hawk) The god of war. The Sea Dyaks, Sarawak, Borneo. (Sarawak Gazette, 1963: 93)

Laran A youthful Etruscan warrior god. Italy. (Dumézil, 1966, 2: 673; Roscher, 1965, 2, 2: 1866–1867)

Latabius A war god identified with Mars. Gaul. (Bertrand, 1897: 330; MacCulloch, 1911: 27)

Lavictus A local god of the Hautes-Pyrennees assimilated to Mars. Gaul. (Renel, 1906: 399)

Leherennus, Leherenn A local god of the Haute-Garonne assimilated to Mars. Gaul. (Bertrand, 1897: 229–230; Renel, 1906: 399)

ka 'leikhyrdop 'leikharai The "goddess who guards the entrance to the village in time of war." The Khasi, Assam. (Stegmiller, 1921: 410)

Leinth Shown variously as a young warrior god and as a goddess of the underworld. Etruscan, Italy. (Dumézil, 1966, 2: 683–684; Roscher, 1965, 2, 2: 1934)

Lekutu Levu A war god propitiated with human sacrifices. Southern Lau, Fiji Islands, Melanesia. (Thompson, 1940: 110)

Lenumius A Celtic warrior god. Britain. (Ross, 1967: 173)

Lenus A god of war and of healing, associated with Mars. Gaul and Britain. (Ross, 1967: 173, 191; MacCulloch, 1911: 27; Renel, 1906: 399; Jayne, 1962: 520)

Le Sa In some villages a god of war incarnate in the lizard. Samoa, Polynesia. (Turner, 1884: 46, 47)

Leucetius, Loucetius A war god and a god of lightning, identified with Mars. Britain and Gaul. (Ross, 1967: 174, 201; Renel, 1906: 399; MacCulloch, 1911: 27; Anwyl, 1906: 38, 39)

Leucimalacus A war god identified with Mars. Gaul. (Bertrand, 1897: 330; MacCulloch, 1911: 27)

Leyaneyani A war god. May be another name for Nayenezgani. The Navaho, Arizona and New Mexico. (Matthews, 1902: 19)

Liada A Slavic god of war. (Czaplicka, 1925, 11: 594)

Litavis A local war goddess associated with Mars Cicollius. Gaul. (Renel, 1906: 399; Dottin, 1925, 12: 692)

Llud Llawereint The silver-handed Celtic god of growth and also of war. Same as Nuada (Ireland). Wales. (MacCulloch, 1911: 85, 114)

Lobwag A minor deity of war. The Ifugao, Philippines. (Barton, 1946: 76)

Loha Pennu A god of war and of iron who protects his followers from the weapons of their enemies. The Kandh, India. (Crooke, 1925, 7: 649, 651; Leach, 1949: 75)

Loudze A clan god of the Sherpa in Khumbu who is protective in war. Nepal. (Furer-Haimendorf, 1955: 50)

Lua A war god at Avatele. Niue Island, Polynesia. (Loeb, 1926, 1: 160)

Lugal-gira (girra) A title or aspect of Nergal as a god of war and of pestilence. Near East. (Jastrow, 1898: 172; Pinches, 1925, 5: 251)

Lugalkurdub A minor Sumer/Akkadian god of war associated with Ningirsu. Near East. (Langdon, 1931: 126; Jacobsen, 1976: 82)

Lugh A Celtic god of many attributes, among them a warrior god with magical weapons and with the power of healing through herbs and magic words and incantations. Ireland. (Ross, 1967: 203, 249; Squire, 1906: 62, 84–86; Larousse, 1968: 227)

Lumingling A god of war of the Ifugao who causes the enemy "to forget to avenge or how to handle weapons." Philippines. (Barton, 1946: 40)

Maasewe One of the twin war gods, the other Nyu-uyewe. Sons of Kochinako. The Sia and the Keresan, New Mexico. (Fewkes, 1895, 2: 125; Wallis, 1939: 140)

Mabahit A god of war and of the sky world, descendent of the Moon, Umbulan. He is a "Bad head-hunting omen—both sides will lose." The Ifugao, Philippines. (Barton, 1946: 41)

Ma-Bellona Goddess of war of the city of Comana. Near East. (Gurney, 1952: 135)

Macha A triple goddess of war and fertility. As an individual deity she was the personification of battle. She was also sometimes associated with Morrigan and Badb as a triad. Ireland. (Ross, 1967: 206, 219; Larousse, 1968: 229; Squire, 1906: 52–53; Jayne, 1962: 91)

Mache "Battle," a child of Eris. Greece. (Barthell, 1971: 8)

Madan, Jakha The great god of war who is invoked before combat and offered sacrifices of thanks after victory. The Katchins, Burma. (Gilhodes, 1908: 676)

Mafiet An Egyptian war goddess. (Mercer, 1925, 12: 703)

dMag gi lbang ging A warrior and a sa bdag god, malevolent deities who cause illness. Tibet. (Nebesky-Wojkowitz, 1956, 1: 294)

Magyar The god of the Hungarians. "It [is] Magyar, the ancestor, the hunter, the warrior who captures girls on the Milky Way." (Roheim, 1954: 62)

Mahrem The god of war of the Pagan Semites. Ethiopia. (Littmann, 1925, 1: 57; Moscati, 1960: 225)

Mahu-fatu-rau A war goddess of the Society Islands, Polynesia. (Henry, 1928: 375)

Makapoelagi A Liku god of war. Niue Island, Polynesia. (Loeb, 1926, 1: 161)

Ma-mun-da-ase The god of war is represented as a panther and is prophetic regarding wars and their outcome. He is considered a good spirit. The Delaware, Eastern United States. (Morgan, 1959: 56)

Manahaut A god of war—The "Deceiver," "betrays men into danger from enemies and accident and into all kinds of violent or insidious death. He also coaxes away their souls." He is also a god of divination to determine the cause of disease, to detect thieves, and to find lost property. The Ifugao, Philippines. (Barton, 1946: 38, 91)

Manalompon A minor god of war. The Ifugao, Philippines. (Barton, 1946: 75)

Manatafetau A Liku war god. Niue Island, Polynesia. (Loeb, 1926, 1: 161)

Mandarangan The god of warriors and of evil to whom human sacrifices were made. His wife was Darago. The Bagobo, Philippines. (Finley, 1913: 34–35; Jocano, 1969: 22; Benedict, 1916: 11, 25)

Mandou-Ra The "god of war and of voluptuousness." West Africa. (Zabarowski, 1894: 328)

Mang-alagar A deity associated with the celebration in head-hunting. The Sambal, Philippines. (Kroeber, 1918, 2: 48)

Manglanbang The "guardian of the warriors." The Apayao, Philippines. (Wilson, 1947: 22)

Mang-lobar A deity associated with the settling of a blood feud. The Sambal, Philippines. (Kroeber, 1918, 2: 49)

Mani A spirit of the Nuer associated with war. Sudan. (Evens-Pritchard, 1956: 30)

Marishi-ten A god of great power who is protective of warriors and against fire. Japan. (Eliseev, 1963: 441; Larousse, 1968: 422)

Mars He was originally an agricultural and vegetation god presiding over growth and the crops. As the god of war he ranked second to Jupiter as guardian of the State and was more of a god of the combat itself, little concerned with that which preceded or followed. His attendants were Eris, Phobos, Metis, Demios, and Pallor. He was associated with health, protecting against plagues but also responsible for them. As a Celtic god he was assimilated to local deities and was known by many compound names, e.g., Mars Cicollius, Mars Rigonemetis. Rome. (Dumézil, 1966, 1: 205, 208, 235, 376; Hadas, 1965: 122; Fairbanks, 1907: 214; Littleton, 1965: 89, 109; Bulfinch, 1898: 131; Cox, 1879, 2: 311; Jayne, 1962: 432–433; Dottin, 1925, 12: 692; Ross, 1967: 176)

Maru   A god associated with Heauoro and with war. Also invoked in the treatment and healing of fractures and wounds. New Zealand. (Shand, 1894: 89; Hongi, 1920: 27; Andersen, 1928: 168)

Masewi   The elder of the twin war gods; younger is Oyoyewi. They are also gods of fertility, giving rain. The Keres, the Laguna, and the Acoma, New Mexico. (Parsons, 1939: 201, 247; Tyler, 1964: 214; White, 1929/30: 64; Burland, 1965: 150)

Matsailema   With Ahaiyuta (Uyuyewi), the twin gods of war, sons of the Sun and of Laughing Waters. They are also gods of fate and chance. The Zuñi, New Mexico. (Cushing, 1891/92: 422; Tyler, 1964: 214; Kroeber, 1925, 12: 869; Stevenson, 1901/02: 35)

Medb, Medhbh   A Celtic goddess of war who takes part in the battle physically. She is is also represented as a goddess of sexuality and intoxication. Ireland. (Ross, 1967: 180, 223–224; MacCana, 1970: 85–86)

Medocius   A Celtic war god identified with Mars. Britain and Gaul. (MacCulloch, 1911: 27; Ferguson, 1970: 212)

Menglod   One of the Teutonic Valkyries, demi-goddesses of battle and war, who decide the victory. (Grimm, 1880: 423; Anderson, 1891: 265)

Mi dmar kra ma   A god of war of the retinue of lCam sring. Tibet. (Nebesky-Wojkowitz, 1956, 1: 92)

Mi-ka-k'e Zhu-dse   "Red Star, the Pole Star, grandfather," is also a war god. The Dhegiha (Osage), Missouri and Arkansas. (La Flesche, 1928: 74)

Minerva   The goddess of wisdom, handicrafts, and the arts was originally an Etruscan deity and adopted by the Romans. It was only after her identification with Athena that she assumed a warlike role. (Hadas, 1965: 123; Dumézil, 1966, 1: 208, 303–305; Fairbanks, 1907: 118; Bulfinch, 1898: 131; Larousse, 1968: 207)

Minisino-hawatuk   The "red war god, who sits in the east" with the Inan-hawatukuk, grants wishes to successful dreamers of visions. He also prophesies the lives of unborn children, somewhat of a god of fate. The Menomini, Wisconsin. (Skinner, 1913: 79)

Mirimu, Mirim   A son of Mukasa who foretold victory if he brought back a spear from the enemy camp and who enabled warriors to capture their enemies' weapons. The Baganda, Uganda. (Roscoe, 1965: 313; Kagwa, 1934: 121)

Mist   One of the Valkyries, Teutonic demi-goddesses of war and battle, who decide who shall be slain. (Grimm, 1880: 420–421; Anderson, 1891: 265)

Mogetius   A war god of Gaul. (MacCulloch, 1911: 28)

Mombakaiyauwan   A minor deity of war. The Ifugao, Philippines. (Barton, 1946: 75)

Mombolboldang   A god of war and of sorcery. Son of Manahaut. The Ifugao, Philippines. (Barton, 1946: 40)

Monahal   A minor god of war. The Ifugao, Philippines. (Barton, 1946: 75)

Monanup   A minor deity of war. The Ifugao, Philippines. (Barton, 1946: 75)

Mondauwat   A god of war and of sorcery. Son of Manahaut. The Ifugao, Philippines. (Barton, 1946: 40)

Mont, Menthu   A god of war and also a sun god. Thebes, Egypt. (Ames, 1965: 88; Larousse, 1968: 29)

Monwiwik   A god of war. Son of Manahaut. The Ifugao, Philippines. (Barton, 1946: 40)

Morrigan, Morrigu   Celtic goddess of war who reigns over the battlefield, but without fighting. She uses magic to help her favorites. She is sometimes considered a triple deity representing Badb, Nemain, Macha. Ireland. (Ross, 1967: 219, 248; MacCana, 1970: 86; Sjoestedt, 1949: 32–33; Squire, 1906: 52)

Muhingo   God of war. The Banyoro, Uganda. (Roscoe, 1915: 91)

Mui-bab   The god of war of Yap Island. The Carolines, Micronesia. (Christian, 1899: 385; Furness, 1910: 150)

Mungula   A god of war and a planetary deity. India. Coleman, 1832: 132)

Nabelcus   A war god of the Vaucluse, identified with Mars. Gaul. (Renel, 1906: 401; MacCulloch, 1911: 28)

Nafanua   A powerful goddess who led the people in a war against oppression. Daughter of Saveasiuleo. Western Samoa, Polynesia. (Turner, 1884: 38–39; Grattan, 1948: 131)

Nagadamang   A bold god of war who assists the athe-giths (spirits) in their vengeance. Yap Island, Micronesia. (Furness, 1910: 150)

Nahui Ollin   "Four Motion, the calendrical name for the solar god, had been the patron of Aztec warriors." Mexico. (Duran, 1971: 30)

Na-ina   A minor goddess of war. The Ifugao, Philippines. (Barton, 1946: 75)

Nakht   A personification of Victory. Egypt. (Gardiner, 1925, 9: 791)

Namuefi   A war god at Fatiau. Niue Island, Polynesia. (Loeb, 1926, 1: 160)

Nana   A Babyonian goddess of war identified with Ishtar. Near East. (Mercer, 1925, 12: 700)

Nane   One of the seven chief deities, a daughter of Aramazd, and presented as "a wise, austere and warlike goddess." Armenia. (Ananikian, 1964: 17, 38)

Nantos   A war god. Gaul. (Renel, 1906: 401)

Nantotsuelta   A goddess associated with war as the raven goddess, and with domesticity as the goddess of the dovecote. Gaul. (Ross, 1967: 219, 244)

Nayenezgani   The beneficent and powerful god of war, of warriors, who also helps those who are ailing through witchcraft and magic. The Navaho, Arizona and New Mexico. (Matthews, 1902: 19; Babington, 1950: 212–215)

Ndakuwangga   A god of Taveuni who is equated with Ndauthina, a god of war. Lau Islands, Fiji, Melanesia. (Hocart, 1929: 196)

Ndauthina   A god of war of Lau Islands. He is also considered the fire god and a god of seafarers and fishermen. Fiji, Melanesia. (Hocart, 1929: 196; Thomson, 1925, 6: 15)

Ndimailangi   A goddess of war at Uruone. Lau Islands, Fiji, Melanesia. (Hocart, 1929: 196)

Neith   One of the oldest of the Egyptian goddesses filled numerous roles, among them a goddess of war. She was associated as well with weaving and the domestic arts, with hunting, with the dead in embalming ceremonies, and with healing. (Rawlinson, 1885: 21; Knight, 1915: 77–78; Ames, 1965: 105; Jayne, 1962: 71–72; Budge, 1969, 1: 30, 450–451, 463)

Nemain, Neman, Nemhain   A goddess of war, sometimes considered one of the Morrigans. She represents Frenzy and is the wife of Net, the battle god. Ireland. (Ross, 1967: 219, 222; MacCana, 1970: 86; MacCulloch, 1925, 3: 282)

Nemetona   A Celtic goddess of war associated with Mars. Britain and the Rhine country. (Renel, 1906: 402; MacCulloch, 1911: 41)

Nemon   A Celtic war goddess named as a wife of Nuada or of Net (Neith). (Squire, 1906: 52; MacBain, 1917: 126; MacCulloch, 1911: 41)

Nende   A god of war of the Baganda. Uganda. (Roscoe, 1965: 275; Mair, 1934: 192)

Nerio   A Sabine goddess associated with Mars. She represents "the motive force of all wars: the energy and ardor of man engaged in battle." Italy. (Dumézil, 1966, 1: 392; Gardner, 1925, 12: 697)

Net, Neith   A Celtic god of battle whose wives are given as Badb and Neman (Nemon, Nemain). Ireland. (MacCulloch, 1911: 58; 1925, 3: 282; Ross, 1967: 222; MacBain, 1917: 126)

Neton, Netos   A war god equated with Mars. Spain. (Martinez, 1962: 94; MacCulloch, 1911: 28; Roscher, 1965, 3, 1: 302)

Netskatcitikitawe   The "Great-South-Star . . . Protector of Warriors." The Wichita, Kansas. (Dorsey, 1904, 1: 57)

Ngilin   A minor god of war. The Ifugao, Philippines. (Barton, 1946: 75)

Nike   The goddess of victory in competition as well as in war. Daughter of Styx and Pallas. Greece. Also known in Palestine. (Cook, 1930: 70; Barthell, 1971: 15; Fairbanks, 1907: 117; Murray, 1935: 209; Hesiod-Brown, 1981: 64)

Nin   Assyrian god of war and of hunting who presided over the planet Saturn. (Rawlinson, 1885: 47)

Nina   A Babylonian goddess of war. (Pinches, 1925, 12: 44)

Nin-dub   A warrior god of the Near East. (Mercer, 1925, 12: 700)

Ningirsu   A god of war, a god of agriculture and irrigation, and a sun god. Identified with Ninib and Ninurta.

He was the son of Enlil and a god of Lagash. Babylonia, Near East. (Campbell, 1964: 117–119; Jastrow, 1898: 56; Larousse, 1968: 60)

Ninib An Assyro/Babylonian solar god, beneficent as the morning sun and as a god of agriculture and of healing. The destructive forces of the sun were of military benefit as a god of war. He was the popular god of the rulers. Near East. (Jastrow, 1898: 57, 67, 174, 214–217; Jayne, 1962: 126; Mercer, 1925, 12: 700)

Nininsina A Mesopotamian goddess of the city of Isin, and a warrior goddess. Near East. (Jacobsen, 1946: 209)

Ninni A Babylonian warlike goddess with whom Ishtar is identified as a goddess of war. Near East. (Mercer, 1925, 12: 700)

Ninshakh, Nin-sakh A Babylonian god of war identified with Ninib and Ningirsu. Near East. (Mercer, 1925, 12: 700; Jastrow, 1898: 92, 93)

Nin-si-a An old Babylonian god of war absorbed by Ningirsu. Near East. (Jastrow, 1898: 91; Mercer, 1925, 12: 700)

Ninurta Assyro/Babylonian god of war and of hunting. In Sumer he was the god of the annual floods and of rains and storms. Near East. (Schoeps, 1961: 57; Larousse, 1968: 60; Jacobsen, 1970: 8, 57)

Nnende A god of war. The Ganda, Uganda. (Mbiti, 1970, 2: 119)

Nuada, Nuadu The Celtic god of the silver hand who was the King of the Tuatha De Danaan and a god of war, in that he led them in battle. His consorts are considered to be the war goddesses Fea, Nemon, Badb, Macha, Morrigu. Ireland. (Squire, 1906: 51, 52, 74; MacCulloch, 1911: 53; MacBain, 1917: 109)

Numputul A minor deity of war. The Ifugao, Philippines. (Barton, 1946: 76)

Nyuuyewe With Maasewe, the twin war gods, children of Kochinako. The Sia, New Mexico. (Fewkes, 1895, 2: 125)

Oblafo A war god in the Otublohu quarter. The Gã, Accra, Ghana. (Field, 1937: 88)

Obobonte A war god in the Akumadze quarter. The Gã, Accra, Ghana. (Field, 1937: 88)

Ocelos, Ocelus A Celtic war god equated with Mars. Gaul and Britain. (MacCulloch, 1911: 28; Ross, 1967: 375–376; Ferguson, 1970: 212)

Odin The chief of the Scandinavian/Teutonic deities, the All-Father, a god of many aspects. As the god of war he governed the course of war and battles, including peace, and as the ruler of Valhalla he welcomed half of the fallen heroes, the others going to Freyja. As the sky god he was the spouse of the earth goddesses: (1) Jord, "the primitive earth" and mother of Thor; (2) Frigga, "the fertile summer-earth" and mother of Balder, Hermod, and Tyr; (3) Rinda, the "personification of the hard and frozen earth" and mother of Vali; with additional alliances among the other goddesses. He sacrificed one eye to gain the wisdom and foreknowledge to be found in Mimir's spring. He was the son of Borr and Bestla, and in the creation of mankind he gave life and the soul to man. (Guerber, 1895: 25–26, 36, 43; Thorpe, 1851: 16, 167; Anderson, 1891: 215, 236; Schoeps, 1961: 105; Grimm, 1883, 2: 132–133, 559–561)

Ogbame A war god of the Gã in Oso and in Temma. Ghana. (Field, 1937: 13, 65)

Ogediga The god of war and a python god. The Brass River people. West Africa. (MacCulloch, 1925, 11: 400)

Ogidia A python war god. Benin, Nigeria. (Hambly, 1929: 657)

Ogidiga The god of war of the Nembe. Niger Delta, West Africa. (Alagoa, 1964: 2)

Ogun, Ogoun Yoruban god of iron and of war, worshipped by all craftsmen, warriors, hunters. Nigeria. In Brazil in various areas he is identified with St. Anthony, St. George, St. Jerome, and St. John. In Haiti he is identified with St. James and in some areas has become a political deity. In Cuba he is identified with St. Peter, and in Trinidad with St. Michael. (Idowu, 1962: 85–87; Parrinder, 1967: 79; Lucas, 1948: 98; Wyndham, 1921: 32–34; Herskovits, 1937, 1: 316–317; 1937, 2: 641; Verger, 1954: 15; 1957: 141, 145, 174; Simpson, 1965: 19, 20; Deren, 1953: 74, 86, 130; Landes, 1940: 265–266; Bastide, 1960: 569)

Okpolodo A culture hero who taught the skills of war and head-hunting. The Kalabari, Nigeria. (Horton, 1960: 17)

O le Fe'e A god of war, the cuttlefish, whose followers wore white turbans in going to battle. Samoa, Polynesia. (Turner, 1884: 28)

O le Lulu   The "owl . . . was regarded as a war spirit on Ofu." Manua (Samoa), Polynesia. (Mead, 1930: 208)

Olloudios, Olloudius   A god of war identified with Mars. Britain and Gaul. (Renel, 1906: 402; MacCulloch, 1911: 28; Ross, 1967: 37, 172)

Ondoutaete   The Huron god of war who gives the victory. Michigan and Ontario. (Gray, 1925, 6: 884; Tooker, 1964: 89)

Operikata   The warrior god, the Morning Star, who lives in the east. The Skidi Pawnee, Nebraska. (Dorsey, 1904: 3, 4)

Oranyan   A warrior god invoked for success in war. Son of Ogun. He was born with one half (vertically) of his body black, the other white. The Yoruba, Nigeria. (Wyndham, 1921: 10, 61; Morton-Williams, 1964: 251)

'Oro   Originally a god of war to whom human sacrifices were made. Under the arioi, the cult of comedians, he became a god of peace and a god of growth and abundance. Tahiti, Society Islands, Polynesia. (Henry, 1928: 73, 120–121, 230; Poignant, 1967: 24, 26; MacKenzie, n.d.: 336, 342, 346)

Oroitemarotea   "Warrior-of-the-yellow-girdle." Tahiti, Society Islands, Polynesia. (Henry, 1928: 384)

Oroitemaroura   "Warrior-of-the-red-girdle." Tahiti, Society Islands, Polynesia. (Henry, 1928: 385)

Oromarotea   "Warrior-of-the-yellow (or light-colored)-girdle." Tahiti, Society Islands, Polynesia. (Henry, 1928: 121)

Orotaua   A warrior god whose shadow was the boar. Tahiti, Society Islands, Polynesia. (Henry, 1928: 383)

Oro-vehi-'ura   "Warrior-covered-with-red." Tahiti, Society Islands, Polynesia. (Henry, 1928: 384)

Oyoyewi   The younger of the Twin War Gods, brother of Masewi. Among the Keresan they were also gods of fertility, providing rain. Pueblo Indians, New Mexico. (White, 1929/30: 64; Parsons, 1939: 194, 243, 247; Tyler, 1964: 214)

Paguyon   A minor god of war and a hunting god. The Ifugao, Philippines. (Barton, 1946: 75, 79)

Pakoc   A Mayan god of battle, of war. Guatemala. (Bancroft, 1886, 3: 483; Nicholson, 1967: 127; Thompson, 1970: 313)

Pamdiya   "Divinities who initiate war and incite men to fight." The Manobo, Philippines. (Jocano, 1969: 22)

Panbongan   A god of war. Son of Manahaut. The Ifugao, Philippines. (Barton, 1946: 40)

Pan-quetzal-itztli   "A life-giving and War goddess" depicted with the symbols of both, and associated with Huitzilopochtli. The Aztec, Mexico. (Mackenzie, 1924: 228 Plate)

Paparua   A god "consulted in war and sickness" and invoked for turtle. Rapa Island, Polynesia. (Buck, 1938: 172–173)

Pava   A god of war of Upolu. Samoa, Polynesia. (Turner, 1884: 42)

Pavor   A Roman god who represented "the spirit of flight in battle." (Fairbanks, 1907: 254)

Paynalton   A god of war, of the sudden alarm. An aspect of Huitzilopochtli. Mexico. (Bancroft, 1886, 3: 298, 303)

Peahhaia   The warrior god of the zenith. The Sia, New Mexico. (Fewkes, 1895, 2: 126)

Pharil-lhafdzen-karbu   A clan god of the Sherpa in Khumbu, protective in war. Nepal. (Furer-Haimendorf, 1955: 50)

Pharsipen   The god of war, the "battle-axe god." The Gond, Central Provinces, India. (Crooke, 1894: 75; Russell, 1916, 3: 99)

Pinyuhon   A minor god of war of the Ifugao. Philippines. (Barton, 1946: 75)

Pitar   An Armenian god of war. (Ananikian, 1964: 14)

Poecosuosucivus   A god of war named on an altar found in Ubeda. Spain. (Martinez, 1962: 122)

Po'haha   A war-goddess kachina. The Tewa, New Mexico. (Parsons, 1939: 203)

Polemos   Greek personification of combat. Father of Alala. (Roscher, 1965, 3, 2: 2607)

Pookong (hoya)   A god of war, the elder of the Little Warrior Gods, the younger being Balonga (hoya). The Hopi, Arizona. (Alexander, 1964: 205; Tyler, 1964: 214)

Pugna Greek personification of combat, conflict. Daughter of Erebus and Nyx. (Roscher, 1965, 3, 2: 3277)

Pungarecha A Mochoacan god of war. Mexico. (Craine and Reindorp, 1970: 151)

Püükoñhoya The war god of the Zuñi and the Hopi. Arizona and New Mexico. (Fewkes, 1898: 178)

Quirinus A Roman god assimilated to Romulus and associated with Mars. As a god of war he seems to be a defensive deity, the maintenance of peace. (Dumézil, 1966, 1: 246–247, 276; Fairbanks, 1907: 216; Altheim, 1937: 138)

Ra'a-mau-riri "Sacredness-holding-anger," the chief of a group of war gods. The woodpecker was his shadow. Tahiti, Tuamotu, Polynesia. (Henry, 1928: 303, 385, 516)

Racumon A man-headed serpent who is a war god as well as a stellar deity. The Carib, Guiana. (Tyler, 1964: 102)

Radgrid One of the Valkyries, Teutonic demi-goddesses of battle and war, who decide the victory. (Grimm, 1880: 420–421; Anderson, 1891: 265)

Radigast A Baltic war god and god of strength, shown in Mecklenburg with an animal face and carrying a bull's head and a battle axe. (Larousse, 1968: 294; de Kay, 1898: 188)

Ramman The Assyrian god of storms and destruction is also named as a god of war. (Jastrow, 1898: 159, 161, 212)

Ka Ramshandi A goddess of war who inspires the people and to whom a cock is offered. The Khasi, Assam. (Gurdon, 1907: 97; Stegmiller, 1921: 410)

Randgrid One of the Valkyries, Teutonic demi-goddesses of battle and war, who decide who shall be slain. (Grimm, 1880: 420–421; Anderson, 1891: 265)

Randosatis A local war god of the Puy-de-Dome assimilated to Mars. Gaul. (Renel, 1906: 403; Mac-Culloch, 1911: 28)

Rarawoliai The war spirit who causes people to be slain so that he "may feed on their souls." The Babar Archipelago. (Hartland, 1925, 4: 420)

Rasau The god of war of Mortlock Island. The Carolines, Micronesia. (Christian, 1897: 199)

Ravai A god in the form of a stone who, with Epe and Kivava, is invoked in time of war and sickness. New Guinea. (Mackenzie, 1930: 287)

Reginleif One of the Valkyries, Teutonic demi-goddesses of battle and war, who decide the victory. (Grimm, 1880: 420–421; Anderson, 1891: 265)

Rehu-o-Tainui A war god of the Tuhoe tribe. The Maori, New Zealand. (Best, 1897: 42)

Reshef, Resheph, Reshpu A god of destruction, of war and pestilence, of thunder and lightning. Syria, Canaan, and Phoenicia. Introduced into Egypt as Reshpu. (Gray, 1969: 74, 81–82; Cook, 1930: 105, 112; Jayne, 1962: 132; Herm, 1975: 111; Macler, 1925, 12: 165; Albright, 1968: 139; Budge, 1969, 2: 280, 282)

Riga A war god of Gaul. (MacCulloch, 1911: 28)

Rigisamus A war god assimilated to Mars. Gaul and Britain. (Renel, 1906: 403; MacCulloch, 1911: 28; Ross, 1967: 175; Ferguson, 1970: 213)

Rima-roa A god of war and an artisan god. Society Islands, Polynesia. (Henry, 1928: 356, 365; Williamson 1933: 59; Ellis, 1853: 326)

Ri tsi mi dmar A god of war of the retinue of lCam sring. Tibet. (Nebesky-Wojkowitz, 1956, 1: 92)

Ro kri mi dmar A god of war of the retinue of lCam sring. Tibet. (Nebesky-Wojkowitz, 1956, 1: 92)

Rongo A god of war in Mangaia, though elsewhere he was a god of agriculture. Polynesia. (Buck, 1934: 162)

Rongo-ma-rae-roa A god who, with Tu-mata-uenga, "caused war and its attendant evils." New Zealand. (White, 1887, 1: 40)

Rota One of the Valkyries, Teutonic demi-goddesses of war and battle. She is particularly a goddess of victory. (Grimm, 1880: 420–421; Anderson, 1891: 265)

Ruanu'u "Source-of-armies," born of Ra'a and Tu-papa. Society Islands, Polynesia. (Henry, 1928: 357)

Rudianus A local war god identified with Mars. Gaul. (Renel, 1906: 404; Bertrand, 1897: 330; Sjoestedt, 1949: 15)

Rudiobus A Celtic war god associated with horses. Gaul and Britain. (Ross, 1967: 170, 322; MacCulloch, 1911: 214; Renel, 1906: 404)

Rugievit A Baltic war god, the seven-headed god of Rugen "with seven swords hanging from his girdle and an eighth in his hand." Suggested that he was a form of Svantovit. (Gimbutas, 1971: 153; Pettazzoni, 1956: 237; Larousse, 1968: 293; Machal, 1918: 283)

Sa fulu sa A "war god in Upolu. Incarnate in the kingfisher bird, which, if seen flying before the troops was a good sign." If flying toward them, a bad omen. Samoa, Polynesia. (Turner, 1884: 48)

Sakegya A "god of No. 2 Dentsifo Asafo company" of warriors, and a protective deity. The Effutu, Ghana. (Wyllie, 1966: 480)

Sakra One of the Adityas, a god of warriors, "of Courage and Outer Security." Also an epithet of Indra. India. (Keith, 1917: 131; Danielou, 1964: 126)

Salamobia, Salimobia, Salimobiya Two warrior ancestral gods, deputies "to the Priest of the Bow and his associate." They are "the War Brothers of the Directions, zenith and nadir who punish stumbling dancers" in the Shalako ceremony. The Zuñi, New Mexico. (Stevenson, 1898: 36; 1901/02: 33; Waters, 1950: 284)

Salevao A god of war "incarnate in a dog. . . . When he wagged his tail, barked and dashed ahead . . . it was a good sign; but to retreat or howl was a bad omen." Samoa, Polynesia. (Turner, 1884: 49)

Saltu A goddess of war, of discord, who was created by Ea to oppose the terrible goddess of war Anat/Ishtar. In gaining immortality she was required to become subordinate to Ishtar. Near East. (Langdon, 1931: 26–27)

Samaihaia Warrior god of the north. The Sia, New Mexico. (Fewkes, 1895, 2: 126)

Sangridr One of the Valkyries, Teutonic demigoddesses of battle and war, who decide the victory. (Grimm, 1880: 420–421; Anderson, 1891: 265)

Sarahaia Warrior god of the nadir. The Sia, New Mexico. (Fewkes, 1895, 2: 126)

Saxnot Teutonic sword god, a god of war and courage identical with Tyr. (Wagner, 1882: 10; Guerber, 1895: 86; MacCulloch, 1964: 18, 19)

Sayathlia A warrior god of the Zuñi Indians. New Mexico. (Stevenson, 1901/02: 37)

Scathach A Celtic warrior-mother goddess. Wales. (Ross, 1967: 228)

Schun-schun-ah "Mirage, or the glimmering of the sun," who was invoked in war for knowledge of the location of the enemy. The Dakota. North and South Dakota, Minnesota, and Montana. (Schoolcraft, 1857, 3: 487; Emerson, 1884: 77)

Rei Sebastião Also called Xapanan. A warrior god and head of a small family of deities. Belem, Brazil. (Leacock, 1972: 128, 137)

Segomo A Celtic war god associated with mules and equated with Mars. Gaul. (Ross, 1967: 172, 322; MacCulloch, 1911: 28, 214; Renel, 1906: 404; Bertrand, 1897: 330)

Seishoko A deified warrior. Japan. (Kato, 1926: 81)

Sekhmet The lion-headed goddess of war and battle. She caused as well as cured plagues and was the goddess of bonesetters. Egypt. (Ames, 1965: 101–102; Schoeps, 1961: 70; Jayne, 1962: 76; Casson, 1965: 73, 75)

Semnocosus A local god from Mt. Mongon in Denia who is listed with gods of war. Spain. (Martinez, 1962: 126)

Sepo Malosi A war god "incarnate in the large bat, or flying-fox." Its actions were an omen. Savaii (Samoa), Polynesia. (Keane, 1925, 2: 243; Turner, 1884: 51)

Sept A god of battles and as such identified with Bes. He was the "protector of the temples of the gods." Egypt. (Budge, 1969, 1: 498–499)

Setekh A god of war and of storms. Assyria and Egypt. (Cook, 1930: 43–44, 109–110)

Shaushka Hurrian/Hittite goddess of war and of love, the sister of Teshub. She is identified with Ishtar. Shaushka's attendants were Ninatta and Kulitta. Turkey. (James, 1960: 96; Akurgal, 1969: 266; Guterbock, 1950: 92)

(Ilu)-šibi Semitic gods of war and destruction who like a good fight, caring little which side they are on. Near East. (Roberts, 1972: 52–53)

Shinohaia Warrior god of the west. The Sia, New Mexico. (Fewkes, 1895, 2: 126)

Shon-ge A-ga-k'e e'gon "Dog Star, Sirius, grandfather" is also a war god. The Dhegiha (Osage), Nebraska. (La Flesche, 1928: 74)

Sho'tokunungwa A sky and star god associated with lightning, and a god of war and hunting "who initiated the practice of scalping." The Hopi, Arizona. (Parsons, 1939: 178, 181, 184; Tyler, 1964: 81, 98, 101)

Shukamuna A Kassite god of war who symbolized the destructive power of the midday sun. Babylonia. Near East (Jastrow, 1898: 152, 171–173; Mercer, 1925, 12: 701)

Shulman A god of war. Near East. (Cook, 1930: 115)

Shuruppak A god of war and city god of the city of the same name. Babylonia. Near East. (Mercer, 1925, 12: 699)

Shuwaliyatta A Hurrian/Hittite warrior god. Turkey. (Guterbock, 1950: 92)

Sigerius Stilliferus A god of warlike character, a god of triumph. Possibly also a rain god. Merida, Spain. (Martinez, 1962: 124)

Sigrdrifa One of the Valkyries, Teutonic demi-goddesses, and one of those who were "lovers or wives of heroes." (Grimm, 1880: 423)

Sigrlinn One of the Valkyries, and one of those who were "lovers or wives of heroes." (Grimm, 1880: 423)

Sigrun A Valkyrie, a Teutonic demi-goddess, and one of the "lovers or wives of heroes." (Grimm, 1880: 423)

Sigtyr A Norse name of Othinn as the "god of victory." (Chadwick, 1936: 91n)

Sili va'ai A war god who took the form of a bird. The direction of its flight indicated good or bad omens. Samoa, Polynesia. (Turner, 1884: 48)

Sinatis, Sinatus A local god of war identified with Mars. Gaul. (MacCulloch, 1911: 28; Bertrand, 1897: 330)

Singalang Burong The principal deity and god of war, manifested as a hawk. The Sea Dyaks, Borneo. (Gomes, 1911: 196; Sarawak Gazette, 1963: 14; Hose, 1912: 85; Roth, 1968: 179)

Sin Yalang Durong The god of war of the Undups (Dyaks). Borneo. (Roth, 1968: 225)

Siriopuba A culture hero type who taught the "various types of war and head-hunting." The Kalabari, Nigeria. (Horton, 1960: 17)

Skanda, Karttikeya The god of war. The son of Siva and Parvati or Agni and Ganga. India and Cambodia.

(Bhattacharji, 1970: 183; Barth, 1921: 161; Marchal, 1963: 212)

Skeggold One of the Valkyries, Teutonic demi-goddesses of battle and war, who decide the victory. (Grimm, 1880: 420–421; Anderson, 1891: 265)

Skehn-rih-ah-tah The god of war of the Wyandots. Ohio, Pennsylvania, New York, and Ontario. (Connelley, 1899: 118)

Skogol One of the Valkyries, Teutonic demi-goddesses of war and battle, who decide who shall be slain. (Grimm, 1880: 420–421; Anderson, 1891: 265)

Skogul A Valkyrie, a Teutonic demi-goddess of battle and war. (Grimm, 1880: 420–421; Anderson, 1891: 458)

Smertatius A local war god of the Rhine country assimilated to Mars. Gaul. (Renel, 1906: 404; MacCulloch, 1911: 28)

Snano's ti Sonxt'aix A warrior god, the guard of the Sun at sunrise. The Bella Coola, British Columbia. (Boas, 1898: 35)

Srog bdag dmar po A war god, "the red master of life." Tibet. (Nebesky-Wojkowitz, 1956, 1: 91)

Srog bdag ko'o sha A god of war of the retinue of lCam sring. Tibet. (Nebesky-Wojkowitz, 1956, 1: 92)

Srog bdag thal ba A god of war of the retinue of lCam sring. Tibet. (Nebesky-Wojkowitz, 1956, 1: 92)

Stribog The Slavonic god of the winds is sometimes considered a god of war. Russia. (Czaplicka, 1925, 11: 593; Ralston, 1872: 102; Gimbutas, 1971: 164)

Subramanya The god of war. Son of Siva. Southern India. Same as Skanda, Karttikeya, (Srinivas, 1952: 218; Dowson, 1961: 306; Larousse, 1968: 375)

Sulinkatte A Hittite god of war. Asia Minor. (Guterbock, 1950: 92)

Šulmanitu A goddess of war and of love. Near East. (Albright, 1968: 150)

Sungmanitu The Wolf Spirit presided over war parties. If a wolf is shot, the gun will not function the next time used; if a wolf is chased on a horse, the horse will go lame. The Lakota/Oglala, South Dakota. (Walker, 1980: 121, 160)

Suttunius   A war god named on an altar found near Poza de la Sol. Spain. (Martinez, 1962: 125)

Sutugio   A war god. Spain. (Martinez, 1962: 125)

Svantevit, Svantovit   Slavic god of war and of prophecies, foretelling the fortunes of war as well as of the harvest. Germany and Poland. (Machal, 1918: 279–280; Queval, 1968: 107; Pettazzoni, 1956: 169, 235–236; Gimbutas, 1971: 153; Schoeps, 1961: 120; Larousse, 1968: 293–294)

Svarazic   Slavic god of war. The Lutices, the Rhetarii between the Elbe and Oder Rivers, Germany. (Machal, 1918: 286)

Svava   One of the Valkyries, Teutonic goddesses of war and battle, who decide the victory. (Grimm, 1880: 420, 423; Anderson, 1891: 265)

Svipul   One of the Valkyries, Teutonic demi-goddesses of battle and war, who decide the victory. (Grimm, 1880: 420–421; Anderson, 1891: 265)

U Syngkai Bamon   One of the chief gods of war, to whom a cock or a goat is sacrificed. The Khasi, Assam. (Gurdon, 1907: 97, 136)

Ta'afanua   A god of war "incarnate in the Ve'a, or rail. . . . When the bird screeched and flew before, the people went to battle, but if it turned and flew back, they hesitated." Samoa, Polynesia. (Turner, 1884: 52)

Taema   A war god incarnate in the kingfisher, whose flight prophesied the outcome. Samoa, Polynesia. (Turner, 1884: 54)

Tagbusan   God of war of the Manobo. Mindanao, Philippines. (Jocano, 1969: 22)

Tahadiidakotse   "Healthy-Flint-Stone-Man," "The Great-South-Star," the protective god of warriors. The Wichita, Kansas. (Dorsey, 1904: 47)

Ta'i-iti-te-ara'ara   The "god of warriors at sea." Tahiti, Polynesia. (Henry, 1928: 380)

Taisumalie   A god of war in Savaii incarnate in a man, also in the sea eel. Samoa, Polynesia. (Turner, 1884: 57)

Takafutta   A god of war. Formosa. (Campbell, 1925, 6: 84)

Take-mika-duchi(dzuchi, zuchi)-no-wo-no-Kami   Japanese god of war and also a thunder god.

Also called Take-futsu-no-kami and Toyo-futsu-no-kami. (Yasumaro, 1965: 18, 19; Herbert, 1967: 271, 336, 489; Kato, 1926: 72; Holtom, 1938: 102, 103)

Talabosau   The "patron of the warriors and of people who run amuck." The Bukidnon, Mindanao, Philippines. (Cole, 1956: 95)

Taomaga   A war god of Alofi. Niue Island, Polynesia. (Loeb, 1926, 1: 162)

Taowdze   A clan god of the Sherpa in Khumbu, protective in war. Nepal. (Furer-Haimendorf, 1955: 50)

Tapa'ai   A god of war on Tutuila who was represented by a trumpet shell, which was blown on going to war. If the tone was clear, a good omen, if "rough and hollow," a bad sign. Samoa, Polynesia. (Turner, 1884: 54)

Tapalisepe   A god of war of the Yami. Formosa. (Del Re, n.d.: 57)

Tapatiap   A god of war. Formosa. (Campbell, 1925, 6: 84)

Tapatu   A war god of Niue Island. Polynesia. (Loeb, 1926, 1: 162)

Tapatulele   A war god, "Mana-for-fleeing." Niue Island, Polynesia. (Loeb, 1926, 1: 162)

Tapatutau   A Liku god of war. Niue Island, Polynesia. (Loeb, 1926, 1: 162)

Tarn, Ey-vet'ne kimtaran   Goddess of the destructive—war, sickness, fire, bad weather. The Ostyaks, Siberia. (Czaplicka, 1925, 9: 577)

Tarnis   A Celtic war god. Gaul. (Schoeps, 1961: 116)

Taufeleleaki   A "war god that flies from side to side in a long war." Niue Island, Polynesia. (Loeb, 1926, 1: 162)

Teari'i-tubu(tabu)-tura   A war god of the Society Islands. The tenth of the gods created by Ta'aroa. Polynesia. (Williamson, 1933, 1: 59; Ellis, 1853: 326)

Teele   A war god of Niue Island. Polynesia. (Loeb, 1926, 1: 162)

Te-'iria   A god of war and the fourth of the gods created by Ta'aroa. Society Islands, Polynesia. (Ellis, 1853: 326; Williamson, 1933, 1: 59)

Teoyaomqui, Teoyaoimqui Aztec god of the enemy warrior dead, those who were sacrificed to the sun. As a goddess, the wife of Huitzilopochtli and a deity who carried the warrior dead to the afterworld. Mexico. (Caso, 1958: 59; Vaillant, 1962: 151; Bancroft, 1886, 3: 513, 398; Bourke, 1892: 484)

Teutates, Toutates A Celtic war god to whom human sacrifices were made by suffocation. Gaul. (MacCulloch, 1911: 234; Schoeps, 1961: 116; Bertrand, 1897: 330)

Tezcatlipoca As a god of war and strife he was invoked for victory, was associated with Huitzilopochtli. He gave warriors "courage and nobility," but his dark aspect also induced "cruelty and deception." He personified the night sky, the darkness, and was represented by the smoking mirror. Mexico. (Caso, 1958: 27–31; Duran, 1971: 101; Burland, 1967: 74; Alexander, 1920: 61–66; Spence, 1923: 96)

Thonak-lhafdzen-karbu A clan god of the Sherpa in Khumbu protective in war. Nepal. (Furer-Haimendorf, 1955: 50)

Thuros An epithet of Ares, Greek god of war. (Roscher, 1965, 5: 912)

Tilenus A war god associated with Mars. Spain. (Martinez, 1962: 126)

Timur Kan (Khan) A god of war of the Turks of Central Asia. (Czaplicka, 1925, 12: 482; Chadwick, 1936: 94)

Tiningban A god of war of the Ifugao. Philippines. (Barton, 1946: 39)

Tintibane A god invoked for rain, for agricultural fertility, and in time of war. South Africa. (Schapera, 1937: 269–270; Willoughby, 1932: 39, 74)

Tiu, Tiw, Tiwaz, Saxnot (Old Saxon) The Teutonic sky god was a god of war, of battle. Germany and England. (Fairbanks, 1907: 88; Schoeps, 1961: 105; Davidson, 1964: 57, 60; Grimm, 1880: 196; Branston, 1957: 68)

Tlacahuepancuextotzin An Aztec war god, youngest brother of Huitzilopochtli. Mexico. (Bancroft, 1886, 3: 303)

Tobadzistsini The younger brother of Nayenezgani, the principal gods of war, slayers of "alien gods" or monsters. They help those ill from witchcraft and magic. Tobadzistsini "represents reserve, caution, and thought-

ful preparation." The Navaho, Arizona and New Mexico. (Matthews, 1902: 19, 22; Babington, 1950: 212–215; Reichard, 1950: 417–418, 448)

Togo A god of war named on an altar found in Talavera. Spain. (Martinez, 1962: 127)

Toh Bulu A god of war of the Kayans. Borneo. (Hose, 1912: 5)

Toho-Tika A god of war and of thunder and storms, to whom human sacrifices were made. The Marquesas, Polynesia. (Christian, 1895: 190)

Toi-mata A goddess of war to whom humans were sacrificed. Society Islands, Polynesia. (Henry, 1928: 198, 304)

Tolasulo A god of war of the Yami. Formosa. (Del Re, n.d.: 57)

Tongo A god of war incarnate in the owl, whose actions foretold the outcome. Samoa, Polynesia. (Turner, 1884: 60)

Toutates *See* **Teutates**

Tritullus A local god of war identified with Mars. Gaul. (Renel, 1906; MacCulloch, 1911: 28; Bertrand, 1897: 330)

Ts'angs-pa Dkar-po A Buddhist warrior god, a Dharmapala, and a Defender of the Law. (Getty, 1962: 150)

Tsowenatlehi A war god, sometimes identified with Tobadzistsini. The Navaho, Arizona and New Mexico. (Matthews, 1902: 19)

Tu God of war and bloodshed to whom human sacrifices were sometimes offered. The Maori. Among the Moriori he was also a shark god. In Samoa he was a god of war incarnate in the rail. The condition of its appearance determined whether to go to war (glossy) or not (dark and dingy). In peacetime he was a god of healing. Also known in the Marquesas. Polynesia. (Poignant, 1967: 37; White, 1887, 1: 1; Shand, 1894: 89–90; Mackenzie, n.d.: 310–312; Best, 1924: 236; Handy, 1923: 245; Robertson, 1911: 215; Turner, 1884: 61)

Tufi A god of war who "had for his symbol a coconut tree spear ten feet long." Samoa, Polynesia. (Mackenzie, n.d.: 311; Turner, 1884: 61)

Tu-matauenga A god of war and of its evils. In some myths he was considered the creator of man. The Maori, New Zealand. (Best, 1924: 97, 121; White, 1887, 1: 40; Andersen, 1928: 93; Williamson, 1933: 24)

Tumatekula A god of war of Niue Island. Polynesia. (Loeb, 1926, 1: 162)

Tumbal A god of war to whom prisoners were sacrificed. Coastal Ecuador. (Alexander, 1920: 207)

Turisas A god of war who determined the victory. Finland. (Grimm, 1883, 3: 940; Krohn, 1925, 6: 24)

Tur-lil-en A Babylonian war god. (Mercer, 1925, 12: 701)

Rei Turquia The head of a family of warrior deities, of Moorish origin. Belem, Brazil. (Leacock, 1972: 130)

Tutau An Aliutu war god. Niue Island, Polynesia. (Loeb, 1926, 1: 162)

Tyr (Zio, Tiw, Saxnot, Ear, Eor, Tius) The Teutonic one-handed son of Odin who lost one hand in fulfilling his pledge to the wolf Fenrir. The god of war who controlled the victory and to whom prisoners of war were sacrificed, he was the god of swords, on all of which his rune was inscribed. (Guerber, 1895: 84–92; Grimm, 1880: 133, 193–208; Davidson, 1964: 29; Anderson, 1891: 270; Wagner, 1882: 158; Schoeps, 1961: 105; Snorri Sturluson, 1964: 53)

Uaga damang A god of war of Yap Island. The Carolines, Micronesia. (Christian, 1899: 385)

Uenuku-rangi A god of war and the god of the rainbow. The Maori, New Zealand. (Best, 1924: 238)

Umalgo A god of war, a spear thrower. Also a god of justice and of divination and "invoked in oaths." The Ifugao, Philippines. (Barton, 1946: 39)

Umbulan A god of war, a "blood-drinker." Also a god of justice, of divination, of oaths. The Ifugao, Philippines. (Barton, 1946: 38, 39)

Umbumabakal A minor god of war at Taiyup. The Ifugao, Philippines. (Barton, 1946: 75)

Umwa A god of war of the Jen. Nigeria. (Meek, 1931: 197)

Uparatat Iranian goddess of victory. (Gray, 1930: 163; Carnoy, 1917: 260, Plate xxxii)

Uyuyewi A god of war. Elder brother or twin of Matsailema. The Zuñi, New Mexico. (Kroeber, 1925, 12: 869; Stevenson, 1901/02: 35)

Vahagn One of the foremost of the gods in their pantheon. A god of war, of courage, as well as a god of the sun, of fire, and of lightning. Armenia. (Ananikian, 1964: 34, 42; Jayne, 1962: 196; Dumézil, 1970: 122–123, 129–130)

Vahram In Pahlavi times equated with Verethragna as a god of victory. Armenia. (Ananikian, 1925, 1: 799)

Vajrasadhu A war god and defender of the religious law. Another name of rDo rje legs pa. His "attributes are a hammer and bellows." Tibet. (Nebesky-Wojkowitz, 1956, 1: 66)

Vave A god of war in Savai'i incarnate in the Manualie (a bird), whose actions indicated victory or defeat. In other villages incarnate in the pigeon, or the railbird. Samoa, Polynesia. (Turner, 1884: 64, 65)

Veltha, Veltune An Etruscan deity, a "god with strange and contrasting attributes, represented at times as a maleficent monster, at others as a vegetation god of uncertain sex, or even as a mighty war god." Italy. (Pallottino, 1975: 141)

Venus Erycina A goddess considered by the Romans not only as a form of Aphrodite but also as a goddess of victory. (Dumézil, 1966, 2: 471–472)

Verethragna God of war and of victory, of strength and of healing, though he can also cause sickness and death. He has numerous animal transformations. Iran. (Huart, 1963: 42; Jayne, 1962: 196; Dresden, 1961: 351; Gray, 1930: 117–119; Dumézil, 1966, 1: 237n; Hinnells, 1973: 33, 34)

Vesontius A god equated with Mars, found as a name of protection. Besancon, France. (Roscher, 1965, 6: 240)

Vesucius A war god of Gaul. (MacCulloch, 1911: 28)

Vica Pota A Roman goddess of victory. (Roscher, 1965, 2, 1: 230; Larousse, 1968: 214)

Victoria An abstract goddess—Victory. North Oscan, Italy. (Conway, 1925, 7: 458; Dumézil, 1966, 1: 241; Roscher, 1965, 6: 294; Fairbanks, 1907: 254)

Vihansa A Germanic goddess of war. (MacCulloch, 1964: 255)

Vincius   A local war god identified with Mars. Gaul. (MacCulloch, 1911: 28; Bertrand, 1897: 330)

Vitucadros   A local war god identified with Mars. Gaul. (Anwyl, 1906: 39; MacCulloch, 1911: 28)

Vitula, Vitellia   A Roman goddess of victory celebrations. (Larousse, 1968: 214)

Vorocius   A local war god assimilated to Mars. Gaul. (Renel, 1906: 406; MacCulloch, 1911: 28; Roscher, 1965, 6: 371)

Wabina   A god represented by a "large bright-red stone" to whom "pigs and puddings" are offered before a war. Solomon Islands, Melanesia. (MacKenzie, 1930: 97, 238)

Wa-hun-de-dan   "The aurora borealis . . . the goddess of war." The Dakota. Minnesota, North and South Dakota, and Montana. (Emerson, 1884: 75; Schoolcraft, 1857, 4: 495)

Wainua   The god of war of Rewa. Fiji Islands, Melanesia. (Thomson, 1925, 1: 443)

Wakinyan   The Thunder Bird is the primary god of war and is constantly worshipped. The Dakota. Minnesota. (Lynd, 1889: 168)

Wambli   The Spirit of the Eagle presides over war parties and councils. The Lakota/Oglala, South Dakota. (Walker, 1980: 122)

Wang Chang   The god of the battleaxe. China. (Werner, 1932: 17)

Winalagilis   The "Warrior-of-the-World" who lives in the far north and is associated with the winter ceremonial. The Kwakiutl, British Columbia. (Boas, 1935: 140–141; 1966: 172)

Wiu   A spirit of war who is associated with the spears and also the thunder. The Nuer, Sudan. (Evans-Pritchard, 1956: 31)

Woden, Wuotan, Odin   The Germanic Allfather who as part of his nature was the god of battles, the giver of victory. (Davidson, 1964: 69; Wagner, 1882: 5, 6; Larousse, 1968: 253–254; Guerber, 1895: 23; Turville-Petre, 1964: 70–72)

Wurunkatte   A Hittite warrior god, the equivalent of Ashtabi (Hurrian), Zababa (Babylonian). Asia Minor. (Guterbock, 1950: 92; Gurney, 1952: 136)

Xshathra   The personification of power, of force, associated with metals, particularly that of military equipment. He is third in importance of the Amesha Spentas. Iran. (Littleton, 1965: 98, 99; Gray, 1930: 45, 46)

Yaboaine   A god of war and of cannibalism invoked at the beginning of a raid. Sometimes referred to as female. Normanby Island, New Guinea. (Roheim, 1946: 210, 223, 321)

The Yamuhakto   The warrior gods of the East and the West who appear with Sayatasha in the Shalako ceremonial of the winter solstice. The Zuñi, New Mexico. (Waters, 1950: 284)

Yaotzin   An Aztec child warrior god—"Small Enemy in War." Mexico. (Duran, 1971: 241)

Yarovit   A Baltic god of war worshipped and invoked for victory. Wolgast and Havelberg. (Larousse, 1968: 293; 1973: 411)

Yarri   A Hittite warrior god. Asia Minor. (Guterbock, 1950: 92)

Yumahaia   Warrior god of the south. The Sia, New Mexico. (Fewkes, 1895, 2: 126)

Zaba   A Hurrian god of war. Asia Minor. (Larousse, 1973: 76)

Zababa   Sumeria/Babylonian god of war. Near East. (Guterbock, 1950: 92; Gurney, 1952: 136; Roberts, 1972: 56)

Zagaga   A god of war of the Elamites, area of Susa. Near East. (Pinches, 1925, 5: 251)

Zamama   A god of war at Kish, identified with the constellation Aquila. Babylonia. Near East. (Jastrow, 1898, 169; Langdon, 1931: 117, 119)

Zelus, Zelos   Son of Styx and Pallas—Strife, a warrior pledged to assist Zeus in the war with the Titans. Greece. (Barthell, 1971: 15, 50; Bulfinch, 1898: 501)

Zio, Ziu, Tyr   A god of war also considered a sky god, a god of light, of day. Germany. (Grimm, 1880: 133, 193–194, 202; Pettazzoni, 1956: 221–222; Fiske, 1900: 108)

Zoba   The god of war of the Banyankole. Uganda. (Roscoe, 1915: 131)

Zuarasici   A Slavic god of battle to whom human sacrifice was common. Elbe River area, Germany. (Czaplicka, 1925, 11: 593)

50

Gods of Wine:
Intoxicants, Narcotics, Drunkenness

Acan Mayan god of balche (wine, or fermented honey). Mexico. (Thompson, 1970: 311)

Acoloa One of the pulque gods. Mexico. (Bancroft, 1886, 3: 418)

Ampelos Personification of the grapevine. Favorite of Dionysos in Thrace. Greece. (Roscher, 1965, 1, 1: 292)

Atlacoaya An Aztec pulque deity. Mexico. (Reed, 1966: 109)

Bacchus The Greek/Roman god of wine was predominantly a character of gaiety and mirth, though the Roman festivals were not as unbridled as the Greek, but more of a social nature. Through his association with festivals and entertainment he became also a god of the theatre. (Murray, 1935: 16, 86, 128; Bulfinch, 1898: 12)

Bohr, Bol The Lacandon god of balche or wine. Chiapas, Mexico. (Thompson, 1970: 311; Cline, 1944: 112; Perera and Bruce, 1982: 306)

Braciaca God of malt and "of (malt-induced) Intoxication." Britain/Gaul. (Ross, 1967: 181; MacCulloch, 1911: 28; Schrader, 1925, 2: 36)

Cherri-chou-lang A lesser deity who was responsible for the presence of the kava plant, from whose roots a euphoric beverage is made. Ponape, Caroline Islands, Micronesia. (Christian, 1899: 382)

Chimapalnecatl One of the pulque gods. Mexico. (Bancroft, 1886, 3: 418)

Chiu Chung Hsien Shêng Patron of wine-makers and wine-shop keepers. China. (Day, 1940: 110)

Chiu Hsien A Taoist deity, the "Spirit of Wine." China. (Day, 1940: 163)

Chukit A deity of the Fernandeño and Gabrielino associated with Datura and the celestial peon game. Same as Tsukit (Yokuts). California. (Hudson and Underhay, 1978: 57)

Colhuatzincatl One of the pulque gods. Mexico. (Alexander, 1920: 77)

Dionysus, Dionysos The Greek god of wine was also a nature god, representing the death and rebirth of vegetation. He was also worshipped as a tree god and as a bull. His association with pleasures and civilization led to his being a god of the theatre. (Fairbanks, 1907: 58, 190; Younger, 1966: 117–118, 126; Frazer, 1960: 450–452; Larousse, 1968: 155; Murray, 1935: 128–129)

Fufluns The Etruscan god of wine was associated with the south in the divisions of the universe. His name also appears on the bronze liver from Piacenza used in divination. Same as Dionysus, Bacchus. Italy. (Pallottino, 1975: 145; Dumézil, 1966, 2: 516; Hamblin, 1975: 92; Altheim, 1937: 151)

gahpi mahso The "mother of the yajé vine." She gave birth to a child whose dismemberment by the men gave each his kind of yajé—which produces a drug potion inducing trances. The Desana, Colombia. (Reichel-Dolmatoff, 1975: 134, 146)

Goibniu The smith of the gods was also the provider of the Otherworld Feast and the immortal ale which gave the gods their immortality. Celtic Ireland. (MacCana, 1970: 24, 36; Ross, 1967: 196; Jayne, 1962: 514; MacCulloch, 1918: 31; Squire, 1906: 61)

Haoma A deified drink "which does not intoxicate . . . but fills his worshippers with joy." It is believed to provide "health and long life" and to be full of blessings. Persia. (Gray, 1930: 83; Dresden, 1961: 349; Jayne, 1962: 191)

Hukaht A deity associated with Datura and also with the celestial peon game. The Kitanemuk. Same as Ukat (Yokuts and Fernandeño). California. (Hudson and Underhay, 1978: 57)

Ilako A god "greatly revered in kava-drinking ceremonies." Ponape, Caroline Islands, Micronesia. (Christian, 1899: 384)

I-ti A god of wine and of wine-makers. China. (Maspero, 1963: 332; Werner, 1932: 204)

Ixtlilton One of the many gods of wine and drunkenness, but primarily a god of health and healing, of games and feasting. Mexico. (Duran, 1971: 176n; Alexander, 1920: 77; Spence, 1923: 352; Reed, 1966: 96)

Liber A Roman god of fertility in all aspects. In the making of the new wine, offerings are made to him as "the native Italian god of fertility and wine." He was identified with Dionysus and Bacchus. (Dumézil, 1966, 1: 378; Younger, 1966: 182, 216; Larousse, 1968: 209–210; Jayne, 1962: 431)

Madain The god of "spirituous liquor," of wine, worshipped by the Kalwars, the Chamars. He is also a god of oaths, very seriously taken. India. (Crooke, 1925, 7: 643; Briggs, 1920: 156–157)

Madira A name of Varuni as a goddess of wine. India. (Dowson, 1961: 183)

Mayahuel Goddess of the maguey plant from which pulque, the native wine, is made. She is also the patron of all intoxicants and hallucinogens. Wife of Patecatl. The Aztec, Mexico. (Duran, 1971: 176n; Nicholson, 1967: 69; Spence, 1923: 294; Vaillant, 1962: 149)

Momoy One of the First People who lived before the Flood, before humans, and who became the Datura or Jimson-weed. She had no specific powers but could foresee the future to a degree and warn of probable consequences. The Chumash, California. (Blackburn, 1975: 36; Hudson and Underhay, 1978: 77)

Nan-chapue A god of the kava and of feasting. Ponape, Caroline Islands, Micronesia. (Christian, 1899: 382)

Ninkasi Sumerian goddess of wine, of beer. Sometimes male. Near East. (Langdon, 1931: 102, 202; Jacobsen, 1970: 2)

Oineus A Greek god of wine. (Roscher, 1965, 3, 1: 751)

Ometochtli Two Rabbits—a god of wine and of games. The Aztec, Mexico. (Duran, 1971: 306; Brinton, 1882: 105)

Pagat The goddess of wine who helps her father Danel cultivate the vines. Ugarit, Syria. (Younger, 1966: 67)

Pamashiut (the Yauelmani, a Yokuts tribe), **Pamashyit** (the Kitanemuk) A deity associated with the Datura, and also with the celestial peon game. California. (Hudson and Underhay, 1978: 57)

Papa-iea The god of feasting and kava drinking. The Marquesas, Polynesia. (Christian, 1895: 190)

Papaztac One of the pulque gods. Mexico. (Bancroft, 1886, 3: 418)

Patecatl God of the ocpatli (peyote) and a god of wine; husband of Mayahuel. Mexico. (Alexander, 1920: 77; Spence, 1923: 292–293; Vaillant, 1962: 149)

Pichureyt (the Kitanemuk), **Pichurut** (the Fernandeño), **Pitsuriut** (the Yokuts) A deity associated with Datura and also with the celestial peon game. California. (Hudson and Underhay, 1978: 57)

Renenutet The snake goddess of plenty was associated with wine and the vintaging of the grapes. Egypt. (Younger, 1966: 31

Ruksey, Raksi The god of intoxicating liquor is worshipped before the distilling from a new crop. The Mal, India. (Crooke, 1925, 8: 344)

Sabazios Phrygian/Thracian god of the fertility of nature and the source of "corn . . . wine and beer." (Ananikian, 1964: 12, 13)

Shesmu The "god of the 'oil-press' and 'wine-press' " who personifies their manufacture. Egypt. (Gardiner, 1925, 9: 787)

Siduri A "West Semitic name of Ishtar as patroness of female wine-mixers . . . the 'goddess of Wisdom'." Babylonia, Near East. (Langdon, 1931: 210–211)

Soma The god of the soma plant (and of all plants) from which the ambrosial drink of immortality was made. He bestowed health and strength, a god of healing and of fecundity. He became identified with the moon. India. (Keith, 1917: 46–47; Basak, 1953: 93–94; Ions, 1967: 20, 81; Macdonell, 1897: 104–114; Dowson, 1961: 302; Jayne, 1962: 174; Fiske, 1900: 383–384)

Ssu-ma Hsiang-ju A deity of wine-makers. China. (Werner, 1932: 451)

Sura A goddess of wine. India. (Ions, 1967: 48; Martin, 1914: 112)

Tchabu The "god of drink." Egypt. (Budge, 1969, 2: 45)

Tepoxtecatl A Chichimec god of the octli drink. Mexico. (Spence, 1923: 291)

Tepuztecatl One of the pulque gods. Mexico. (Bancroft, 1886, 3: 418)

Tereteth Goddess of the coconut toddy. Yap Island, the Carolines, Micronesia. (Christian, 1899: 385)

Tezcatzonctl The chief god of pulque and of intoxication. Also known as Tequechmecaniani and Teatlahuiani. Mexico. (Bancroft, 1886, 3: 418; Spence, 1923: 290; Vaillant, 1962: 150)

Thilhoa One of the pulque gods. Mexico. (Bancroft, 1886, 3: 418)

Tlaltecaiooa One of the pulque gods. Mexico. (Bancroft, 1886, 3: 418)

Toltecatl An Aztec god of pulque and the god of Tula. Mexico. (Caso, 1958: 7)

Tomiauhtecutli God of the Maize Flower and a god of the octli drink. Aztec, Mexico. (Spence, 1923: 299)

Totochtin, Totochti A god of wine to whom penance must be done for drunkenness. Mexico. (Bancroft, 1886, 3: 383; Spence, 1923: 299)

Totaltecatl A god of the octli drink. The Toltecs, Mexico. (Spence, 1923: 297)

Trita A god of the atmosphere who is associated with the preparation of the soma drink. India. (Macdonell, 1897: 67–69; Danielou, 1964: 138; Barth, 1921: 11)

Tsukit A Yokuts deity associated with Datura and the celestial peon game. California. (Hudson and Underhay, 1978: 57)

Tu K'ang God of the distillers of wine from rice and also of wine merchants. China. (Du Bose, n.d.: 334; Werner, 1932: 526; Maspero, 1963: 332; Graham, 1961: 176)

Tultecatl One of the pulque gods. Mexico. (Bancroft, 1886, 3: 418)

Ukat A deity of the Yokuts and Fernandeño who was associated with Datura and the celestial peon game. Same as Hukaht (Kitanemuk). California. (Hudson and Underhay, 1978: 57)

Varuni The goddess of wine and the wife of Varuna. She is also called Mada and Sura. India. (Crooke, 1894: 263; Danielou, 1964: 121; Dowson, 1961: 338–339)

Wawatsari God of "the Deer-Peyote." The Huichol, Mexico. (Furst, 1972: 141)

Yautecatl An Aztec god of pulque and a god of Yautepac. Mexico. (Caso, 1958: 7)

Yiaulatecatl One of the pulque gods. Mexico. (Bancroft, 1886, 3: 418)

Yzquitecal One of the pulque gods, of the Otomis. Mexico. (Bancroft, 1886, 3: 405, 418)

Zame ye Mebege One of the creator gods who gave the Fang eboka, a narcotic enabling "men to see the dead." Gabon. (Fernandez, 1972: 245–246)

PART VIII

Religion

51

Religious Activities:
Rituals, Initiation, Ceremonials

Abba Mula, Ndjei Dzu The guardian deity of the priest, who was essential to his priestly functioning. The Ch'iang, Szechwan, China. (Graham, 1958: 51, 52)

Acala The "King of Religion" and a protective deity. Tibet. (Hoffman, 1956: 133)

Agkoninang A sky god of the Ilangit class who possesses Shamans. The Isnet, Luzon, Philippines. (Vanoverbergh, 1953: 90)

Ahnt-ah zu-mah A great god of the Seris who taught them "to wear the crown on ceremonial occasions" and then disappeared. Sonora, Mexico. (Coolidge, 1939: 95)

Akigui-no-Ushi-no-Kami A god of purification "who cleans filth" and was born from the hat of Izanagi. Japan. (Yasumaro, 1965: 23; Herbert, 1967: 279)

Alasa A sky god, seventh child of Sogbo, who taught men how to worship the "So" gods (children of Sogbo). Dahomey. (Herskovits, 1938, 2: 152, 157)

Alquntäm One of the chief functions of the supreme god "is that of acting as leader of the *kusiut* dances of the supernatural beings." With his advisers he determines for the coming year "who shall be made a *kusiut*, who shall be born and who shall die." The Bella Coola, British Columbia. (McIlwraith, 1948, 1: 38, 41)

Aluañuiko A god who "introduces into the cult the shell trumpet and the chengi shell . . . and dedicates the necessary songs to them . . . for the multiplication of the cattle." The Kagaba, Colombia. (Preuss, 1926: 73)

Amawari A lesser god of the "House of Tobacco Smoke" to which the light shamans journey. The Winikina-Warao, Venezuela. (Wilbert, 1972, 2: 65–72; 1973: 8)

Anahita A goddess of triple nature invoked by priests in purification rituals, by women in childbirth, and by warriors for strength. Iran. (Dumézil, 1966, 1: 302)

Anongan A sky spirit of the Ilangit class who possesses shamans. The Isneg, Luzon, Philippines. (Vanoverbergh, 1953: 90)

Ano°likwoísaix The female supernatural guardian of the repositories of the kusiut prerogatives, desired by those seeking to be initiated in the Winter Ceremonial Dances. The Bella Coola, British Columbia. (McIlwraith, 1948, 2: 8, 9)

Anura The spirit of the tobacco seeds used by the shamans. The Arawak, Guiana. Same as Wau-uno (Warao). (Levi-Strauss, 1973: 426)

Aphrodite Skotia A mother goddess associated with initiation ceremonies. Near East. (Roheim, 1929: 183)

Arvila A special patron of the conjurer invoked to help drive out evil spirits causing illness. The Pulaya, India. (Thaliath, 1956: 1044)

Astexewa wekareya The "most powerful of the Immortals." On New Year's World Renewal Ceremony, the priest incarnates the Immortals who "make it stable, healthy, rich and holy, as it was in the beginning of time." The Karuk, California. (Eliade, 1979: 144, 146)

Attajen A being who appeared after Ouiot died and created the first medicine men, giving each his powers. San Juan Capistrano, California. (Bancroft, 1886, 3: 166)

Ayug The "spirit of a magic tree, who is one of the most powerful of the shaman's helpers." The Taulipang, Guiana. (Zerries, 1968: 314)

Baexolla   A god who initiates the members of the Cannibal tribe. The Bella Coola, British Columbia. (Boas, 1898: 34)

The Bagadjimbiri   Two brothers who were the namers of all things, the establishers of culture and initiation ceremonies. They transformed into water snakes and "their spirits became the Magellanic Clouds." The Karadjeri, Australia. (Eliade, 1973: 53–54)

Bahiri   A deity who possesses a bhagat (priest-magician or medicine man). The Thakur, India. (Chapekar, 1960: 92)

Baiame   The primordial sky god is associated with the rites of initiation and is involved in the making of, and initiation of, the novice medicine man. Australia. (Eliade, 1973: 4, 134–135; Wales, 1957: 7)

behpo mahse   The god of thunder from whom the shaman must obtain the objects he uses. He sometimes appears as a jaguar. The Tukano, Colombia. (Reichel-Dolmatoff, 1975: 78)

Betto   A guardian of shrines. Japan. (Czaja, 1974: 63)

Bullileway   A spirit called upon by shamans when treating children with fever. The Isneg, Luzon, Philippines. (Vanoverbergh, 1953: 94)

Bunjil   The supreme god who bestows powers on the novice medicine man and is associated with rites of initiation. Australia. Same as Baiame. (Eliade, 1973: 4, 139; Wales, 1957: 7)

Businelan   A spirit invoked by shamans. The Isneg, Luzon, Philippines. (Vanoverbergh, 1953: 90)

Cavi   The spirit of maize who takes part in female puberty rites. The Tucuna, Brazil. (Zerries, 1968: 302)

Chedya   A deity who possesses a bhagat (a priest or medicine man). The Thakur, India. (Chapekar, 1960: 92)

Chibute   A god of hunting who instituted rites and taught the crafts. The Tacana, Bolivia. (Levi-Strauss, 1973: 346-348)

Chinnamasta   A goddess of ritual sacrifice. "As a form of the eternal night Chinnamasta is the Night-of-Courage . . . when the victim is brought to the altar of sacrifice." India. (Danielou, 1964: 280–281)

Chowa   A goddess and special patroness of conjurers invoked to help drive out evil spirits causing illness. The Pulaya, India. (Thaliath, 1956: 1043–1044)

Chu'i lha mo   A goddess of the water invoked in pollution-eliminating ceremonies. Tibet. (Nebesky-Wojkowitz, 1956, 1: 388)

Cloacina   A form of Venus "invoked for purification from forbidden sexual indulgence and its results." She was also a goddess of the drains of Rome and invoked for protection from the diseases caused by them. Italy. (Jayne, 1962: 462)

Daramulun   The supreme being who taught the Yuin their initiation ceremonies, whose voice is the bull-roarer, and who bestows powers on the medicine men. Australia. (Eliade, 1973: 6, 7; Wales, 1957: 7)

Darimpayan   A spirit who possesses the shaman and whose food is coconut oil. The Isneg, Luzon, Philippines. (Vanoverbergh, 1953: 90)

Djamar   The omnipresent supreme being who was responsible for the moral laws, for initiation rites, and the bull-roarer. The Bad of West Kimberley, Australia. (Eliade, 1973: 35–37)

Dongo   The spirit of the thunder and of the sky taught them their initiation rites. The Songhoi, Mali and Upper Volta. (Larousse, 1973: 528)

Dubsag-Unug-ki   A god invoked in exorcizing evil spirits. Babylonia. Near East. (Thompson, 1903: 11)

duLar   The messenger of Sibu who comes in answer to the medicine man's questions regarding life and death. The Bribri, Costa Rica. (Stone, 1962: 47)

Dyevae   A water spirit who takes part in female puberty rites. The Tucuna, Brazil. (Zerries, 1968: 3020)

Ea   The Sumerian god of waters was a "god of purification in the water rituals." Near East. (Langdon, 1931: 106)

Ebbor   An abstract deity, "Worship," of the Yoruba. Nigeria. (Wyndham, 1919: 124)

Emekori-mahse   The beneficent god of the day who established "the norms, the rules, and the laws" and who is present at the initiation of the apprentice shaman. The Desana, Colombia. (Reichel-Dolmatoff, 1971: 27, 28)

Fan hsiang   The chief of the 12 tengris who are believed the most powerful in driving out evil spirits through the shamans. The Monguors of Kansu, China. (Schram, 1957: 87)

Foatai A god associated with sacred canoe rites. Tikopia, Melanesia. (Firth, 1967, 2: 130)

Gargomitch An intercessor with Bunjil who greets the medicine man. The Kulin, Australia. (Eliade, 1958: 42)

Gilgildokwila At Rivers Inlet a supernatural being, "the lark, called Long-Life-Giver," initiates shamans. The Kwakiutl, British Columbia. (Boas, 1966: 135)

Gnabaia A spirit involved in boys' initiation ceremonies, during which he "swallows and afterwards disgorges" them. Women and children believe his voice is that of the bull-roarer. There is an unfriendly Gnabaia and a friendly one (of the forest). The latter is invoked in illness. The Anula, Central Australia. (Spencer, 1904: 501–502)

Gsan-hdus-pa The "Lord of Mysticism." Tibet. (Li An-che, 1948: 39)

Guequiau The Paez and Moguex "venerated a kind of culture hero . . . who instructed shamans." Colombia. (Hernandez de Alba, 1946: 953)

Gulambre The Sky Being from whom the novice medicine man receives his powers. Port Stephens area, Australia. (Eliade, 1973: 143)

rGyal-ba-rgya-mts'ho'i-ts'hogs-dang-bchas-pa-rnam A Buddha who purifies from perjury, lust, deceit, etc. Tibet. (Schlagintweit, 1969: 135)

Haoma The god and the plant which "is now identified as ephedra. It is thought to give strength and healing in its natural state and much more so when it has been consecrated." Haoma "is also the divine priest. He makes offerings to the other gods" and is believed to be "present at every offering of the faithful. . . . Thus within the sacrifice of haoma Haoma is at once god, priest and victim." He is a god of the righteous and blesses the faithful with health, longevity, and joy. Persia. (Hinnells, 1973: 38; Gray, 1930: 83; Dresden, 1961: 349)

Haraido-no-Kami Japanese "deities of purification." (Holtom, 1938: 208)

Heiséi "In the annual fertility ceremonies there always appear the masks or dances of Heiséi and of the Sun (Surli, Nuikukui), that is to say, of the 'Masters of the East and of the West,' of life and death." He sends sickness to punish those who have offended or neglected the rites and offerings. The Cagaba, Colombia. (Reichel-Dolmatoff, 1949/50: 89, 90, 142)

Hetsu-kahi-bera-no-Kami A god of purification born of the bracelet of Izanagi. Japan. (Herbert, 1967: 279)

Hetsunagisabiko-no-Kami A god of purification born of the bracelet of Izanagi. Japan. (Herbert, 1967: 279)

Hezakaru-no-Kami A god of purification born of the bracelet of Izanagi. Japan. (Herbert, 1967: 279)

Höhöttu The rust-colored pygmy owl who with Müdo and Tawadi are "the trinity of great shaman's helpers." The Makiritare, Venezuela. (Civrieux, 1980: 180)

Hosia Goddess of the holy rituals. Greece. (Roscher, 1965, 1, 2: 2750)

Hsi T'ien Fuh Chu "Lord Buddha of the western paradise." The patron god of the white priests, at P'u-ch'i-kou, who "perform the great ceremonies of paying the vows to the great gods for families on the housetops and for communities in the sacred groves." The Ch'iang, Szechwan, China. (Graham, 1958: 53)

Hu Nonp The Bear God is the patron of shamans, having taught them their secrets and their shamanic language, Tobtob. The Lakota/Oglala, South Dakota. (Walker, 1980: 50, 51, 128)

I-buki-do-nushi-no-kami A kami of purification "credited with healing powers." Japan. (Herbert, 1967: 282)

Ida A Hindu goddess whom they believed instituted "the rules of performing sacrifices." India. (Dowson, 1961: 122)

Idzu-no-me-no-kami, Idunome-no-Kami A goddess of purification born from the bathing of Izanagi. She "cleans everything and rinses filth." Japan. (Herbert, 1967: 279; Yasumaro, 1965: 24)

Janki The goddess who gave the red dot sect-mark to the Bendiwale sect of Vaishnavism. The Bairagi, Central Provinces, India. (Russell, 1916, 2: 99)

Kalampasa A male spirit who participated in an initiation ceremony of men. The Yamana, Tierra del Fuego. (Zerries, 1968: 306)

Kamu-Nahobi "Divine rectifying wondrous Kami," a god of purification born of Izanagi's bathing. Japan. (Herbert, 1967: 279)

Katajalina A spirit of boys' initiation ceremonies. Women and children believe his voice is that of the bull-roarer. The Binbinga, Central Australia. (Spencer, 1904: 501)

Kauyumárie The "Sacred Deer," assistant to Tate-wari. He is a shaman's helper who assists in passing through the Gateway of the Clashing Clouds on the way to Wirikuta. He and Maxa Kwaxi seem to be aspects of each other. The Huichol, Jalisco, Mexico. (Furst, 1973: 38; Wilbert, 1972, 2: 80)

ke The bear divinity of the west, a powerful medicine animal. The Tewa, New Mexico. (Harrington, 1907/08: 43)

ke'a The badger divinity of the south, a powerful medicine animal. The Tewa, New Mexico. (Harrington, 1907/08: 43)

khaengy The mountain-lion divinity of the north, a very powerful medicine animal. The Tewa, New Mexico. (Harrington, 1907/08: 43)

Khwini, Khwili A supernatural bird who "has the greatest shamanistic power of all." The Nutka, Vancouver Island, British Columbia. (Sapir, 1925, 12: 594)

Ah K'in The god of ceremonies of the Lacandon. Chiapas, Mexico. (Perera and Bruce, 1982: 308)

Komanokaro A god, an associate of Iopatari Akuru, who "can be reached by the most experienced shamans." The Barama River Caribs, Guiana. (Zerries, 1968: 247)

Konikatine A spirit from whom medicine men draw powers. The Laitu-Laitu, Australia. (Eliade, 1973: 144)

kǒ nǒ kǒ tsū The teacher-spirit of the shamans. The Miao, China. (Bernatzik, 1947: 165)

Ko'u-'din-ne'i-rigs A Buddha who purifies from all sins. Tibet. (Schlagintweit, 1969: 132)

Ksem-wa'tsq "Land-Otter Woman." A supernatural helper of the shaman and of the "Eagle group." The Tsimshian, British Columbia. (Boas, 1909/10: 563)

k'ujo The wolf divinity of the east, a powerful medicine animal. The Tewa, New Mexico. (Harrington, 1907/08: 43)

Kulabel The rainbow snake who bestows power upon the medicine man. The Lunga and Djara tribes, Australia. (Eliade, 1973: 156)

Kundathi-Kali A deity who with proper fasting and rituals protects devotees in fire walking. The Kadar, Southwest India. (Ehrenfels, 1952: 165)

Kusharu A god of rituals. The Pawnee, Nebraska. (Wallis, 1939: 140)

Kusug A god created by Ea—"high priest of the great gods, to be the one who completes their rites and ceremonies." Babylonia. Near East. (Larousse, 1973: 70)

Kwinyawa A mountain spirit, patron of the shamans, who gives them curing powers. The Walapai, Arizona. (MacKennan, 1935: 186)

Lago^ϵyEwiLe^ϵ (tlago'yewitla) The killer whale by whom some shamans are initiated. The Kwakiutl, British Columbia. (Boas, 1966: 121, 143)

Laha The supreme god of heaven, a god of destiny, gave the Tsimshian their "religious laws and institutions." British Columbia. (Swanton, 1925, 12: 465)

Lalaiail A special woods god "who initiates the shamans . . . tells him who will die and who will fall sick." The Bella Coola, British Columbia. (Boas, 1898: 42)

L'etsa'aplelana A goddess who initiates some shamans. She "is painted with the design of a sea-lion bladder filled with grease." The Bella Coola, British Columbia. (Boas, 1898, 2: 34, 44)

Lus srog gzang du bor ba'i ma (pr. **Lusok Sangdu Porwêma**) A goddess who is supportive of the meditation process in the *gcod* school. Tibet. (Tucci, 1980: 88)

Maboya, Mapoia A snake god who is the tutelary power of the medicine men. He sends the hurricane. The Carib, West Indies. (Alexander, 1920: 38)

Ma gcig dpal lha mo (pr. **Machik Pe Lhamo**) A protective goddess of Lhasa whose presence allows women to perform certain rituals. Tibet. (Tucci, 1980: 169)

Mai-waho A god of the heavens who taught the incantations to Ta-whaki. New Zealand. (White, 1877, 1: 59)

Makita-Mangi A shepherd of Esseghe-Malan-Tengri who is the intermediary between gods and mankind. He is protective of the shaman from the evil gods and spirits. The Buriats, Siberia and Mongolia. (Klementz, 1925, 3: 4)

Manatu With Pupuke, gods of the sacred chants. The Marquesas, Polynesia. (Handy, 1923: 245; Buck, 1938: 151)

Mbuduvrí-re The Moon of the Apinayé "personally taught mankind" six chants to use in his ceremonies. Brazil. (Nimuendaju, 1967: 138–139)

Me'i lha mo Gos dkar mo A goddess of fire invoked in pollution-eliminating ceremonies. Tibet. (Nebesky-Wojkowitz, 1956, 1: 388)

Michi-no-Nagachiha-no-Kami A god of purification born from the belt of Izanagi. Japan. (Herbert, 1967: 28)

Mithra "In modern Zorastrianism Mithra plays a very important part in the ritual. All priests are initiated in the 'portico of Mithra' . . . and on initiation they are invested with the mace of Mithra as a symbol of their duty to fight against the powers of evil. All the most sacred rituals are offered under his Protection." Persia. (Hinnells, 1973: 77)

Müdo Although he is a most powerful shaman helper, he is frequently ridiculed because of his ugliness—in the form of a potoo which he assumed as a bird spirit. Brother of Wanadi. The Makiritare, Venezuela. (Civrieux, 1980: 52, 188)

Mueraya A god who "controlled the heavens and the jaguars, and aided shamans." The Conibo, Ecuador and Peru. (Steward and Métraux, 1948, 1: 592)

Muluku A demon, created by Gauteóvañ, who is "the patron of all priestly activities . . . who has to attend to all festivals." The Kagaba, Colombia. (Preuss, 1926: 65, 112)

Mundadji A god of the Binbinga who is involved in the supernatural dissection of the shaman in his initiation. Australia. (Eliade, 1964: 49)

Munkaninji A god of the Binbinga, son of Mundadji, who brings the dissected shaman (in the initiation trials) back to life and pronounces him a shaman. Australia. (Eliade, 1964: 49)

Nagatya A god who "consecrates the medicine man; he opens his belly and inserts the rock crystals that confer magical power." The Wotjobaluk, Australia. (Eliade, 1964: 45)

Nagawɨ "Mountain Sheep (plural). Orion's Belt" is a shaman's helper. The Chemehuevi, California, Nevada and Arizona. (Laird, 1976: 91, 112)

Naka-tsutsu-no-wo-no-mikoto A god of purification born of the bathing of Izanagi. Japan. (Herbert, 1967: 279)

Nakatsuwatatsumi-no-Kami A god of purification born of the bathing of Izanagi in the sea after his return from Yomi. A sea god invoked for prosperous journeys. Japan. (Herbert, 1967: 279; Aston, 1925, 11: 466)

Nam mkha'i lha mo Kun tu bzang mo A sky goddess invoked in pollution-eliminating ceremonies. Tibet. (Nebesky-Wojkowitz, 1956, 1: 388)

nangkhaengy The gopher divinity of the below, a powerful medicine animal. The Tewa, New Mexico. (Harrington, 1907/08: 43)

Naxa Mountain Sheep is a shaman's helper (naga, nagawɨ, pl.). The Chemehuevi, California, Nevada, and Arizona. (Laird, 1976: 112, 207, 308)

Ndjei Chu A patron god of priests. The Ch'iang in Mu-shang-chai. Szechwan, China. (Graham, 1958: 61)

Ndook God of the initiation ceremonies; all aspects are totally taboo to women. Buka Island, Melanesia. (Thomas, 1931/32: 228)

N'gai The omnipotent creator god is invoked at the various rites of passage. The Kikuyu, Kenya. (Middleton, 1953: 66)

Ngakola The name also of a secret initiatory society in which he, a monster/human, eats the neophyte and regurgitates him. Ngakola had lived on earth, had the power to kill and bring back to life. He was killed through trickery. The Mandja, the Banda, Central African Republic. (Eliade, 1976, 1: 186–187)

Ngetya A god who gives powers to the novice medicine man. The Wotjobaluk and Jupagalk, Australia. (Eliade, 1973: 145)

Ngosa "Grandfather," "the bull-roarer," who threatens youths in initiation ceremonies. The Kai, New Guinea. (Roheim, 1929: 184; Haddon, 1925, 9: 347)

Ngunyari A sky god important in initiation ceremonies, having made the bull-roarer and established rules regarding it. The Ungarinyin, Australia. (Eliade, 1973: 74)

Nin-akha-kuddu A water goddess and a goddess of purification associated with Ea and Eridu. Babylonia. Near East. (Mercer, 1925, 12: 710)

Noäkxnem A supernatural sea being who participates in the kusiut dances. The Bella Coola, British Columbia. (McIlwraith, 1948, 1: 53)

N'tomo   A god of adolescents, of the rites of circumcision and excision. The Bambara, Mali, Niger, and Senegal. (Tauxier, 1927: 324–325)

Nu-mohk-múck-nah   Lone Man, an important deity of the Mandan, lives on a mountain in the west, survived the flood, and opens the medicine lodge for the ceremonies and sacrifices to the waters. Plains Indians. (Catlin, 1967: 47–49, 96n. 11)

Núrldakexa   Father of the Baptism. The Cagaba, Colombia. (Reichel-Dolmatoff, 1949/50: 115)

Nusa-kor-huchi   The goddess ruling the Spirit Fence "where the gods customarily assemble for conversation." She takes the form of a serpent when seen. The Ainu, Hokkaido, Japan. (Philippi, 1982: 147)

Nutse'xenem   When the canoe Noaknem appears at the solstice, she comes out. "When a person sees her, he faints. His soul is taken into her house, and is initiated into the secrets of the ku'siut." The Bella Coola, British Columbia. (Boas, 1898, 2: 41)

Oalea   A malignant god of the bull-roarer. The Elema, Papuan Gulf, New Guinea. (Holmes, 1902: 431; Haddon, 1925, 9: 342)

Obatala   The god of the heavens, of purity, who is invoked in acts of purification. Puerto Rico, West Indies. (Gonzalez-Wippler, 1975: 100–101)

Ōkali and **Okkali**   They were responsible for the instruction of men in the scriptures given by Markali. Dravidian Ajivikas, India. (Basham, 1951: 215, 272)

Okitsukaibera-no-Kami   The "deity of the water between far off sea and strand." A god of purification born of the bracelet of Izanagi. Japan. (Yasumaro, 1965: 23; Herbert, 1967: 279)

Okitsunagisabiko-no-Kami   The "deity of the strand," a god of purification born of the bracelet of Izanagi. Japan. (Yasumaro, 1965: 23; Herbert, 1967: 279)

Okizakaru-no-Kami   The "deity of the far off sea," a god of purification born of the bracelet of Izanagi. Japan. (Yasumaro, 1965: 23; Herbert, 1967: 279)

Oma   A storm demon who takes part in the female puberty rites. The Tucuna, Brazil. (Zerries, 1968: 302)

O-naho-bi-no-kami   "Great rectifying wondrous Kami," a god of purification born from Izanagi's bathing. Japan. (Herbert, 1967: 279)

Orehu   The goddess of waters who gave the "ida" tree for the medicine man's gourd, white stones from the sea to go in it, and tobacco. These were charms against the attacks of Yauhahu. The Arawak, Guiana. (Brett, 1880: 18-20; Levi-Strauss, 1973: 439)

Ouiamot   Son of Tacu and Auzar who came from the stellar regions and taught the coastal Acagchemem the sacred dancing, the manner of worship. Identified with Chinigchinich. San Juan Capistrano, California. (Boscana, 1933: 33–34)

Paatsatsi   Bat, son-in-law of Coyote, had magic power with which he "quickly froze water into ice," whereby he cured burns. As a shaman's helper, he conferred on the shaman this power to cause extreme cold and so to heal burns. The Chemehuevi, California, Nevada, and Arizona. (Laird, 1976: 113, 182–192)

Pahtumawas   The Great Spirit who taught them ceremonies and how to worship. The Minsi (Lenape) Indians, Eastern United States. (Harrington, 1921: 19, 127)

Pakitsumanga   The Mother of the Caribou from whom some shamans recieve or obtain their individual or specific powers. The Inland Eskimo. Canada. (Rasmussen, 1929, 7: 113)

dPal 'Khor lo bde mchog (pr. **Pel Khorlo Demchok**)   A Tantric guardian deity of hermits. Tibet. (Tucci, 1980: 157)

Papawa   Bear, aunt of Wolf and Coyote. "As a shaman's familiar, the bear confers great strength." The Chemehuevis. California, Nevada, and Arizona. (Laird, 1976: 113, 192–193)

(Jero Nyoman) Pengadangan   The "demonic guardian of the temple grounds." One of his offerings is opium. Bali, Indonesia. (Franken, 1960: 224–225)

Phyag na rdo rje   A god who is invoked in exorcism rituals; can compel obedience from demons. Tibet. (Tucci, 1980: 95)

Piai'man   The "master of tobacco," the trainer of the medicine men. The Arecuna, Guiana. (Levi-Strauss, 1973: 438)

Poungaru   A guardian deity of the sacred canoe. Tikopia, Melanesia. (Firth, 1967, 2: 99)

Pu Fafine   A goddess of the canoe shed and of the sacred adze. She was also a goddess of the ritual oven. Tikopia, Melanesia. (Firth, 1967, 2: 76, 81, 106)

Pungatere A god associated with the sacred canoe. Tikopia, Melanesia. (Firth, 1967, 2: 126)

Pupuke The name means "the source or welling-up of knowledge." He was "the god of one of the houses of the inspirational priests," and with Manatu the patron of the sacred chants. The Marquesas, Polynesia. (Handy, 1923: 245–246; Buck, 1938: 151)

Pusi A god invoked in the consecration of the sacred oven and also in the "re-furnishing of the canoe shed." Tikopia, Melanesia. (Firth, 1967, 2: 103–104, 124)

Qudshu "Holiness," a goddess of Tyre. Phoenicia, Near East. (Albright, 1968: 146)

Rakaitonga A guardian deity of the sacred canoe of the Taumako clan credited with securing it in the spirit world. Tikopia, Melanesia. (Firth, 1967, 2: 98)

Raki-te-ua A coconut god invoked in the consecration of the sacred oven of Tafua and also invoked in the "re-furnishing of the canoe shed." Tikopia, Melanesia. (Firth, 1967, 2: 124, 258)

Rata A god associated with the sacred canoe. His wife is Nau Taufiti. Tikopia, Melanesia. (Firth, 1967, 1: 87; 1967, 2: 126)

Ro A god invoked to "chant the sacred books" in "the ceremony of paying the vows." The Ch'iang Szechwan, China. (Graham, 1958: 800)

Sabbath The personified and deified Sabbath, considered the daughter of God. The Falashas, Ethiopia. (Patai, 1967: 252–253)

Sa Ho Sang A patron god of the red priests at P'u-ch'i-kou. The Ch'iang, Szechwan, China. (Graham, 1958: 53)

Sa'i lha mo Sangs rgyas spyan ma A goddess of the earth invoked in pollution-eliminating ceremonies. Tibet. (Nebesky-Wojkowitz, 1956, 1: 388)

Sambata The personified Sabbath, a goddess. The Gallas, Ethiopia. (Littmann, 1925, 1: 57; Huntingford, 1955: 78)

Sanggilolo A god who instructs in the mowoerake (divine instruction), curing, etc. The Toradja, Celebes, Indonesia. (Adriani and Kruyt, 1950: 82)

Sänotĺx muĺ lts Aĺquntäm A son of Aĺquntäm and a patron of the *kusiut* dancers. The Bella Coola, British Columbia. (McIlwraith, 1948, 1: 40)

Scomalt The "strong medicine-woman," the principal deity of the Okanagan, British Columbia. (Donnelly, 1949: 96)

Séijakaxa Father of the Masks. The Cagaba, Columbia. (Reichel-Dolmatoff, 1949/50: 115)

Sen Hou Tzu A "deified monkey" who is a patron god of the red-gowned priests who exorcize demons and "perform the great ceremonies of paying the vows" at P'u-ch'i-kou. The Ch'iang, Szechwan, China. (Graham, 1958: 53)

Shamash The sun god is also a god of divination and purification. In Assyrian haruspicy, a tutelary deity—"as he reads the tablets through their covering he inscribes his message in the very belly of the lamb." Assyro/Babylonian, Near East. (Langdon, 1931: 150; Dumézil, 1966, 2: 655)

Shi-shto A god of priests as well as of tradesmen. The Ch'iang at Lo-pu-chai. Szechwan, China. (Graham, 1958: 49)

Shivaldaneuming Mother of the Ancient Songs. The Cagaba, Colombia. (Reichel-Dolmatoff, 1949/50: 114)

Sisiutl A double-headed serpent, a totemic being. "Pieces of its body, owned by shamans, are powerful medicine." The Kwakiutl, British Columbia. (Alexander, 1964: 243)

Snitsmän-a A benevolent supernatural woman who restores from the mutilation of the Stomach-Cutting-Dance. The Bella Coola, British Columbia. (McIlwraith, 1948, 2: 72, 141)

Sno'olx lts Aĺquntäm A son of Aĺquntäm and a patron of the *kusiut* dancers. The Bella Coola, British Columbia. (McIwraith, 1948, 1: 40)

Snusilkäls The Wise One—"the supernatural being who decides points of ritual in the dances in the land above." The Bella Coola, British Columbia. (McIlwraith, 1948, 2: 143)

Soko-tsutsu-no-wo-no-mikoto "His Augustness the Elder Male of the Bottom," a god of purification born of the bathing of Izangai. Japan. (Herbert, 1967: 279)

Sokotsuwatatsumi-no-Kami A sea god of the ocean bottom. A god of purification born of Izanagi's bathing after returning from Yomi. Japan. (Aston, 1925, 11: 466; Herbert, 1967: 279)

Soorte Husband of Xalpen. They participate in an initiation ceremony of men and boys. The Ona, Tierra del Fuego. (Zerries, 1968: 306)

Sraosha The personification of Discipline, of Obedience, is the companion of Mithra and is present at all religious ceremonies as the embodiment of men's prayers and hymns and their conveyor to heaven. He is a guardian of the soul at death and with Mithra and Rashnu sits in judgment. Iran. (Haydon, 1941: 79; Dresden, 1961: 348; Huart, 1963: 42; Hinnells, 1973: 52)

Suila An omniscient god who informs the supreme god of the deeds of men. He accompanies the shaman on his journey to heaven. The Altaic, Siberia. (Pettazzoni, 1956: 262)

Taksu A deity who makes known the decisions of the gods by speaking through mediums whom he has possessed. Bali, Indonesia. (Covarrubias, 1937: 269)

Tatanka The Buffalo God is "the patron of ceremonies." The Lakota. South Dakota. (Walker, 1980: 50)

Tatevali The god of fire is also the god of shamans of healing and prophesying. The Huichol, Mexico. (Alexander, 1920: 121; Seler, 1925, 6: 828; Chamberlain, 1900: 305)

Tawadi The nacunda nighthawk, a trinity with Müdo and Höhöttu, is a great and powerful shaman's helper. The Makiritare, Venezuela. (Civrieux, 1980: 191)

Ta-whaki Son of Hema and Hu-aro-tu. He climbed to the heavens, learned the incantations from Mai-waho, and returned to teach them to the people. He went back to the heavens and is the source of thunder and lightning. New Zealand. (White, 1887, 1: 54, 59–60)

Teikirzi A goddess of the Todas who is responsible for their "social and ceremonial laws." India. (Rivers, 1925, 12: 354; Hartland, 1925, 4: 412)

Te-vahine-nui-tahu-ra'i A deity invoked in fire walking, and to whom offerings are made on recovery from illness. Society Islands, Polynesia. (Henry, 1928: 214, 290)

Tiaremuna A guardian deity of the sacred canoe of the Taumako clan. Tikopia, Melanesia. (Firth, 1967, 2: 99)

Tihiya Deer, a shaman's helper. The Chemehuevi, Nevada, California, and Arizona. (Laird, 1976: 112, 207)

Tirawa He revealed the hako ceremony to the priests "at the beginning of time." The Pawnee, Nebraska. (Eliade, 1976, 1: 133–134)

Tlazolteotl The goddess of filth, of sensuality was, in consuming men's sins, a goddess of purification. The Aztec, Mexico. (Caso, 1958: 55-56; Spence, 1923: 165, 168; Burland, 1967: x; Vaillant, 1962: 146, 148)

Tlitcäplilan·a A benevolent and highly respected but somewhat feared supernatural female who sometimes visits the very ill and causes a cure, sometimes causing the individual to become a shaman with curing powers, which later she may also cause among those in good health. The Bella Coola, British Columbia. (McIlwraith, 1948, 1: 47)

tse The eagle divinity of the above, a powerful medicine animal. The Tewa, New Mexico. (Harrington, 1907/08: 43)

Tsetsesgin The Grizzly Bear supernatural who gives the Grizzly Bear Dance in exchange for the return of his mask, which is his "means of obtaining food." The Kwakiutl, British Columbia. (Boas, 1935: 160)

Tsukitatsufunado-no-Kami A god who wards off evils and is a god of purification born from the staff of Izangai. Japan. (Yasumaro, 1965: 22-23; Herbert, 1967: 278)

Tsu Sa Chin A patron god of the red priests at P'u-ch'i-kou. The Ch'iang, Szechwan, China. (Graham, 1958: 53)

Tufaretai, Tufare The adze god of the Tafua clan, associated with canoe rituals, is also a god of the sea. He is invoked in the consecration of the sacred oven. Tikopia, Melanesia. (Firth, 1967, 2: 62, 124)

Tuna toto An adze god of the Tafua clan and also an eel god. He is invoked in the "re-furnishing of the canoe shed" and also in the consecration of the sacred oven. Tikopia, Melanesia. (Firth, 1967, 2: 62, 119, 124)

Tupai One of the "guardians and preservers of the institutions of *mana* and *tapu*, of gods and sacred places, and the ritual pertaining to such." The Maori, New Zealand. (Best, 1924: 105)

Twanyir(r)ika, Tuanjiraka A spirit of the circumcision initiation of boys, whose voice is believed by women and children to be the bull-roarer. The Arunta, Australia. (Spencer, 1904: 497; Eliade, 1976, 1: 188)

Txal-ks-gagum lax-ha A supernatural power, the first to be called in the initiation ceremony. The Tsimshian, British Columbia. (Boas, 1909/10: 557)

Ulu-Tojon, Uluu Toyon One of the western tengeri who is the patron of shamans and from whom they claim descent. He would come to earth as a large animal. The Yakut, Siberia. (Tokarev and Gurvich, 1964: 279; Larousse, 1973: 434)

Ungud A great snake god associated with the earth as well as with waters, a creator god with Wallanganda. He provides the medicine man with his powers; can be "of either sex or even bisexual." The Unambal, Australia. (Eliade, 1964: 68–79)

Unktehi He is considered by the Medicine Dance group as the greatest deity, as he taught them "how to paint themselves when they worship him, and what colors to use." The Dakota, Minnesota. (Lynd, 1889: 155, 159)

Vakamaofa A guardian deity of the sacred canoe of the Taumako clan. Tikopia, Melanesia. (Firth, 1967, 2: 99)

Vanaspati, Svaru The "adoration of the sacrificial post, which is invoked as Vanaspati or Savru and which is a god who, thrice anointed with ghee, is asked to let the offerings go to the gods." India. (Keith, 1917: 61)

Viho-mahse The "supernatural master of the narcotic snuff"—the various kinds of yaje used by the shaman. It is from Viho-mahse the shaman gets his powers and his ability to diagnose and treat disease. The Tukano, Colombia. (Reichel-Dolmatoff, 1975: 80–85, 89)

Wabunodin The god of the east and the east wind who "taught . . . the use of Grand Medicine." The Ojibwa, Minnesota. (Coleman, 1937: 37)

Wade The benevolent grandfather of the sloths who took human or sloth form. The most powerful shaman of the "old people" and the teacher of Wanadi. The Makiritare, Venezuela. (Civrieux, 1980: 30, 192)

Wadzurahi-no-ushi-no-kami A god of purification born of the upper garment of Izanagi. Japan. (Herbert, 1967: 279)

Wakan'taka The thunders are his messengers and at his behest they teach the medicine men the art of curing. He created the white stones which are used by the medicine men. The Dakota. Minnesota, the Dakotas, Montana, and Canada. (Wallis, 1947: 80–82)

Walangala A celestial god who gave the Ungarinyin their institutions and initiation rituals. Australia. (Eliade, 1973: 72–73)

Wa-tsutsu-no-wo-no-mikto "His Augustness the Elder Male of the surface," a god of purification born of the bathing of Izanagi. Japan. (Herbert, 1967: 279)

Wa-tsu-wata-tsu-mi-no-kami A god of the surface of the ocean and a god of purification born of the bathing of Izanagi. Japan. (Herbert, 1967: 279)

Wau-uno The spirit of the tobacco seeds. The Warao. Same as Anura (Arawak). Guiana. (Levi-Strauss, 1973: 426)

the Wauwalak Sisters who were guilty of primordial sin, of incest, so instituting sexual relationships. To repent, they taught mankind the ritual ceremonies through which he is purified. Australia. (Eliade, 1973: 111)

Wawi The rainbow serpent from whom the medicine man gains powers. The Wiradjuri, Australia. (Eliade, 1973: 155)

Weri Kubumba The creator god to whom offerings were made at the circumcision ceremonies. The Bagesu, Uganda. (Frazer, 1926: 241–242)

Whai-tiri A goddess of incantations and also of thunder. Wife of Kai-tangata and mother of Hema, grandmother of Ta-whaki. New Zealand. (White, 1887, 1: 51, 54; Mackenzie, n.d.: 211, 297; Andersen, 1928: 157)

Wikame A very powerful mountain spirit, patron of the shamans, giving them curing powers. The Walapai, Arizona. (MacKennan, 1935: 186)

Winwina A supernatural who is a patron of the *kusiut* ceremonials and who also "brings salmon and berries from . . . the extreme west." The Bella Coola, British Columbia. (McIlwraith, 1948, 1: 54; 1948, 2: 190)

Winyakaiva A mountain spirit who is a patron of shamans and gives them curing powers. The Walapai, Arizona. (MacKennan, 1935: 186)

Witurna A god of the initiation of boys. The Urabunna tribe, Central Australia. (Spencer, 1904: 498)

Wohpe The goddess of pleasure and harmony is invoked when the ceremonial pipe is smoked. Her power (*ton*) "is in the smoke from the pipe and in the incense from sweetgrass." She introduced and gave to men the pipe with its ceremonies and rites. The Lakota. South Dakota. (Walker, 1980: 51, 95, 109–111, 220–222)

Wolgara A god who kills and revives the aspiring medicine man. He is also a judge of the dead. The Wardoman, Australia. (Eliade, 1973: 145)

Wonambi The great snake who swallows the initiate medicine man, then regurgitates him. Tribes of South Australia. (Eliade, 1973: 141)

Xalpen The "presiding spirit" of an initiation ceremony of men and boys, appeared only once. "She was a huge worm crawling on the earth." Wife of Soorte. The Ona, Tierra del Fuego. (Zerries, 1968: 306)

Xemxemälotl'a An associate of Al'quntäm and a patron of *kusiut* dancers. The Bella Coola, British Columbia. (McIlwraith, 1948, 1: 44)

Xungwid The sun, by whom the "Knight Inlet shaman . . . claim to be initiated." The Kwakiutl, British Columbia. (Boas, 1966: 142)

Yajyk An intermediary between Ulgen and men who meets the shaman on his journey to heaven. The Altai, Siberia. (Eliade, 1958: 61)

Yaryik In the ceremony for the purification of the soul conducted by the shaman, "the Jersu prince of the seas is best able, by driving waterfloods, to force the return of the abducted soul and to drive the soul of the departed to the netherworld." Siberia. (Casanowicz, 1924: 430)

Yurupary The "spirit of initiation." The flutes are *yurupari*. Brazil. (Roheim, 1929: 186)

yǔ wǎn sǔ fū "The teacher-spirit of the medicine man" to whom offerings are made. The Miao, China. (Bernatzik, 1947: 165)

Zalmoxis, Salmoxis Also called Gebeleizis. A mystery-religion cult. His descent into a subterranean room for a period of time is interpreted an "initiatory death." The Getae, Thrace. (Eliade, 1976, 1: 178, 180)

Zuya Wakan The god who allocates the sacred tribal animal, wolf, lynx, etc., as their taboo. The Dakota, Minnesota. (Lynd, 1889: 163)

52

Divination, Prophecy

Agwù The "divination trickster." The Igbo, Nigeria. (Isichei, 1978: 27, 334)

Agwù-Nsī A spirit who provides the "knowledge of herbs, roots and other material objects" used in divination and making of charms. The Igbo, Nigeria. (Isichei, 1978: 322)

Ahulneb A god renowned as an oracle. Cozumel Island, Yucatan, Mexico. (Bancroft, 1886, 3: 466)

Aide A deity or supernatural force who assists or obscures according to things or the actions of humans; in the first in a natural aspect, in the second by oracle and magic. Responsible for illnesses from unknown causes. The Basque, France and Spain. (Barandiaran, 1972: 17, 18)

Ajmac In illness divination, Ajmac indicates a sin against one's own patrilineage, requiring request for pardon from spouse and parents. In questions of marriage Ajmac indicates an affirmative answer. Momostenango, Guatemala. (Tedlock, 1982: 121–122)

Ak'abal A Day Lord important in the teaching of a daykeeper (calendar diviner), and in divination in determining the source of the problem or the need for the question. Momostenango, Guatemala. (Tedlock, 1982: 108–10)

Ali'i Tu A god who took the form of the Ve'a, or rail, whose flight was observed during war. "If it flew before, it was a good omen; if otherwise they went back disconcerted." Samoa, Polynesia. (Turner, 1884: 24)

Ame-no-Koyane-no-Mikoto A god of divination. Japan. (Kato, 1926: 40; Herbert, 1967: 301)

Amphiaraos A Greek mortal deified as a deity of divination, of healing oracles. (Jayne, 1962: 305; Thramer, 1925, 6: 545)

Ànyìm Ohụhụ An oracle consulted regarding fertility/barrenness, prosperity. At Amaogwugwu. The Igbo, Nigeria. (Isichei, 1978: 88, 89, 336)

Apollo Greek/Roman god, one of whose functions was that of a god of prophecy, of the oracle of Delphi. (Fairbanks, 1907: 139; Dumézil, 1966, 2: 442, 479; Barthell, 1971: 24–26; Jayne, 1962: 306; Bulfinch, 1898: 8, 9)

Apurimac An important oracular god. Peru. (Trimborn, 1968: 140)

Aristaios A god of divination, of magical healing, which powers were given him by the Muses. Greece. (Thramer, 1925, 6: 546)

Aviriri A god who "teaches the signs of the stars." The Campa, Peru. (Llosa Porras, 1977: 61)

al-'Awf A bird god, of omens and divination. Arabia. (Fahd, 1968: 49; Abercrombie, 1972: 4)

Baal-Hammon Among the Berbers an oracular god of the Grand Oasis at Sywah. Libya. (Bel, 1938: 73)

Balitiyon A god of omens. The Ifugao, Philippines. (Barton, 1946: 43)

Balitok A god of omens. The Ifugao, Philippines. (Barton, 1946: 43)

Batagri, Badagri A deity who bestows the power of prophecy. Mirebalais, Haiti. West Indies. (Herskovits, 1937, 1: 317)

Batz' In divination questions regarding trips, business deals, asking for a woman, any Batz' number is affirmative; the higher the number the better. Momostenango, Guatemala. (Tedlock, 1982: 116–117)

Bhagawan A deity invoked in divination. Sikkim. (Gazetteer of Sikhim, 1894: 334)

Binage A god of omens. The Ifugao, Philippines. (Barton, 1946: 43)

Bituwon A god of divination using the *agba* stick to determine the cause of disease, to detect thieves, and to find lost property. The Ifugao, Philippines. (Barton, 1946: 91)

Sidi bou Inder The oracle of a grotto in the region of Demnat. Morocco. (Basset, 1920: 56)

'Brog bza' lha lcam ma A goddess "who holds a divination-arrow and a mirror." Tibet. (Nebesky-Wojkowitz, 1956, 1: 118)

Bugan nak Amtalao A goddess of omens. Philippines. (Barton, 1946: 43)

Bugan nak Hinumbian A goddess of omens. The Ifugao. Philippines. (Barton, 1946: 43)

Bumabakal The " 'Killer' (in war)" and a god of omens. The Ifugao, Philippines. (Barton, 1946: 43)

Came Low-numbered Came days are affirmative for marriage proposals, marriages, business deals, and trips if this Day Lord appears in divination. Momostenango, Guatemala. (Tedlock, 1982: 112)

The Camenae Roman "prophetic nymphs. One of them, Antevorta, knew the past; another Postvorta, the future. . . . Carmenta had the gift of prophecy." (Larousse, 1968: 210)

Can A Day Lord "associated with the actions of a calendar diviner . . . trained as an *ajmesa,* or *ajnawal mesa*" (spiritualist), who "are simultaneously the most successful curers and a source of serious illness and death." Momostenango, Guatemala. (Tedlock, 1982: 111–112)

Candan A deity of divination. Tibet. (Waddell, 1959: 470)

Carmenta The Roman goddess of pregnancy and birth was also a goddess of prophecy. (Dumézil, 1966, 1: 392–393; Larousse, 1968: 211; Jayne, Jayne, 1962, 444–445)

Catha An Etruscan god associated with haruspicy and with the south and southeast divisions of the universe. Italy. (Pallottino, 1975: 145; Hamblin, 1975: 92)

Cawuk In divination regarding illness, Cawuk indicates that someone made offerings to the Mundo and the ancestors to inflict the illness. However, in business deals

Cawuk indicates approval, a good outcome. Momostenango, Guatemala. (Tedlock, 1982: 123: 124)

Cel An Etruscan god of fate and of the infernal regions who was associated with haruspicy and with the west. Italy. (Pallottino, 1975: 145; Hamblin, 1975: 95)

Chakna Dorje A deity invoked in divination. Sikkim. (Gazetteer of Sikhim, 1894: 334)

Chandan A deity invoked in divination. Sikkim. (Gazetteer of Sikhim, 1894: 334)

Sidi Chemharouj An oracular deity of the grotto Goundafi, beseeched for the healing of fevers. Morocco. (Basset, 1920: 66, 74)

Che-resi The God of Mercy who was invoked in divination. Sikkim. (Gazetteer of Sikhim, 1894: 263, 334)

Chhui Lhamo A deity invoked in divination. Sikkim. (Gazetteer of Sikhim, 1894: 334)

Ch'ui Lhamo A deity of divination. Tibet. (Waddell, 1959: 470)

Cilens An Etruscan god of death and of the underworld who is associated with haruspicy and with the north. Italy. (Pallottino, 1975: 145; Hamblin, 1975: 95)

Coventina An aquatic goddess who is also chthonic and prophetic. Spain. (Martinez, 1962: 190–194)

C'oxol The Red Dwarf who strikes the lightning into the blood of diviners taught the early leaders to have their various shrines with their proper customs, about the solar calendar, as well as their commercial customs. Momostenango, Guatemala. (Tedlock, 1982: 147–148)

Cvlalp A god of fate, of death, and the underworld who is associated with haruspicy and with the west/northwest. Etruscan, Italy. (Pallottino, 1975: 145; Hamblin, 1975: 95)

Damcha (Damc'a) Dzema A deity invoked in divination. Sikkim and Tibet. (Gazetteer of Sikhim, 1894: 334; Waddell, 1959: 470)

Danel A Phoenician mythological hero who had powers of divination. Near East. (Larousse, 1968: 79)

Dara Ensing Tamaga A goddess of omens who takes the form of a bird to warn of danger. The Undups (Dyaks), Borneo. (Roth, 1968: 225)

Date, Dente   An oracular god of the Guans. Ghana. (Meyerowitz, 1958: 140)

Dinonganan   A goddess of omens. The Ifugao, Philippines. (Barton, 1946: 43)

Dol-ma   A goddess, helpful and beneficent, who is invoked in divination. Sikkim. Same as Tara. (Gazetteer of Sikhim, 1894: 313–314 334)

Dorje Gyatham, Dorje Gya-t'am   A deity invoked in divination. Sikkim and Tibet. (Gazetteer of Sikhim, 1894: 334; Waddell, 1959: 470)

Dorje leg-pa   A deity invoked in divination. Sikkim. (Gazetteer of Sikhim, 1894: 334)

Dreo Dagyak   A deity invoked in divination. Sikkim and Tibet. (Gazetteer of Sikhim, 1894: 334; Waddell, 1959: 470)

Dungapan   A god of omens. The Ifugao, Philippines. (Barton, 1946: 43)

Durpag Nag   A deity of divination. Sikkim and Tibet. (Gazetteer of Sikhim, 1894: 334; Waddell, 1959: 470)

Duwo   Son of Gbadu (Fa) who was sent with Kiti and Zose to the earth to teach men "Fa"—in the Fa cult of divination. Dahomey. (Herskovits, 1938, 2: 204–055)

E   If E appears with Imöx in destiny divination it is indicative of confusion, possession, a lost road (way in life); with Quej, one is to be guided on the road by the lineage priest-shaman, or that he is destined to become one. The Quiché, Guatemala. (Tedlock, 1982: 118)

Ela   A god of divination who is also a peacemaker and conciliator, a restorer of order. The Yoruba, Nigeria. (Idowu, 1962: 102–103)

Eskudait   A spirit of omens—"fire creature, is evidently to be identified with the will o' the wisp. . . . Wherever it is seen, calamity is imminent." The Penobscot, Maine. (Speck, 1935, 1: 15)

Eth   An Etruscan earth and nature god who is associated with haruspicy and with the southeast division of the universe. Italy. (Pallottino, 1975: 145; Hamblin, 1975: 95)

Ewagan   Fourth son of Hatan who inherited his powers. "The most notable of the anitos and is looked upon as a savior of the people." Beneficent, invoked in need. He has magical powers, can transform into a pig. The Apayao, Philippines. (Wilson, 1947: 20, 21)

Fa   "Fa is the destiny of the Universe as willed by the gods." Also personified as a god of oracles and divination with knowledge of the future. Dahomey. (Parrinder, 1967: 91; Herskovits, 1938, 2: 201, 203)

Fa'amalu   A god who during wartime was "represented by a fish, the movements of which were watched" indicating the fortunes of the battle. He was "also seen in a cloud or shade." Samoa, Polynesia. (Turner, 1884: 26–27)

Fatua   Roman goddess, wife of Fatuus, who prophesies the future for women. (Roscher, 1965, 1, 2: 1446)

Fatuus   An aspect of Faunus as an oracular god who prophesies for men. Rome. (Dumézil, 1966, 1: 345; Roscher, 1965, 1, 2: 1451)

Fufluns   An Etruscan god of wine who is associated with the "bronze liver from Piacenza" used in divination, and also associated with the south in the divisions of the universe. Italy. (Dumézil, 1966, 2: 516; Pallottino, 1975: 145; Hamblin, 1975: 92)

Fu Hsi   God of divination by geomancy and of fortune tellers. Szechwan, China. (Graham, 1961: 186)

Futotama-no-Mikoto   A Japanese god of divination. (Herbert, 1956: 301)

al-Galsad   An oracular goddess of the tribes of Kinda and Hadramawt. Arabia. (Fahd, 1968: 84-85)

Garwa Bishu   A deity invoked in divination. Sikkim and Tibet. (Gazetteer of Sikhim, 1894: 334; Waddell, 1959: 470)

Gbadu   An androgynous deity, another name for Fa, with six eyes through which men learn the future or what decision to make in divination—depending on which eyes open. Dahomey. (Herskovits, 1938, 2: 203–204)

Gina-ongan   A god of omens. The Ifugao. Philippines. (Barton, 1946: 43)

Ginita   A god of omens of the Ifugao. The Philippines. (Barton, 1946: 43)

Gwydion   A god of divination and of magical powers with the power of transforming things. Wales. (MacBain, 1917: 90–91; MacCulloch, 1918: 98; Squire, 1906: 253, 260)

Gyacha kua   A deity invoked in divination. Sikkim and Tibet. (Gazetteer of Sikhim, 1894: 334; Waddell, 1959: 470)

lHa mo gos dkar ma A goddess honored in divination rites. Tibet. (Nebesky-Wojkowitz, 1956, 1: 365)

Hangi A tribal god of the Konjo appealed to by diviners. Uganda. (Taylor, 1962: 94)

Hawat ud Daiya, Hawat ud Kabunian, Hawat ud Lagȯd Gods of divination in the use of the *agba* stick to determine the source of disease, to detect thieves, and to find lost property. The Ifugao, Philippines. (Barton, 1946: 90)

Hecate, Hekate A goddess whose powers extended into all areas, celestial, terrestrial, and the netherworld. She was a goddess of divination and oracles, of sorcery and magic. She was protective of doors and gates, of travelers, and crossroads. Greece. (MacCulloch, 1925, 4: 332–333; Barthell, 1971: 51; Jayne, 1962: 326; Fairbanks, 1907: 138–139; Larousse, 1968: 121; Murray, 1935: 77)

Herauscorrtsehe An oracular deity with a plaque on a mountain near Tardets. The Basque, Spain and France. (Barandiaran, 1972: 269)

Herkyna A nymph of the river of the same name and associated with Trophonios at the oracular grotto at Lebadeia. Greece. (Eliade, 1967: 244)

Hinatahutahu A goddess of divination and of healing. Tahiti, Polynesia. (Henry, 1928: 556)

Hnaska "The Spirit of the Frog was the patron of occult powers." The Lakota/Oglala, South Dakota. (Walker, 1980: 122)

Hoho The god of twins who in the Fa cult of divination rules the Di medji and Ka medji arrangements of the palm kernels. Dahomey. (Herskovits, 1938, 2: 214, 220)

Hsiao Peh Hsuen A god worshipped by fortune tellers. Anking, China. (Shryock, 1931: 162)

Hubal An oracular god and a rain god. Arabia. (Fahd, 1968: 101)

Iamos Son of Apollo and Euadne who received the "gift of prophecy and the power to understand the voices of the birds" from Zeus. Greece. (Cox, 1870.2: 33, 82; Roscher, 1965, 2, 1: 13)

Ibìna Ukpaàbì A Chukwu oracle whose messengers are the Aro, a village people. The Igbo, Nigeria. (Isichei, 1978: 117, 137)

Ifa God of divination and of oracles. He was also associated with medicine, with fertility and pregnancy, with birth. Nigeria, Brazil, and Puerto Rico. (Bastide, 1960: 566; Gonzalez-Wippler, 1975: 27–28; Lucas, 1948: 71; Parrinder, 1967: 88; Wyndham, 1921: 18; Morton Williams, 1964: 248; Robertson, 1911: 217–218; Budge, 1973, 1: 373)

Igwe A sky deity and an oracular god at Umunoha. Nigeria. (Meek, 1943: 113)

Igwe Kā Àlà A "renowned oracle" of the Igbo. Among the Akokwa, "a terrible oracle and was feared everywhere." Nigeria. (Isichei, 1978: 112, 339)

Ila The "goddess of truth-vision or Revelation." India. (Pandit, 1970: 61, n. 1 & 2)

Imöx In divination this Day Lord always indicates problems, complexities. On these days "powerful calendar diviners go to mountaintop shrines" requesting the Mam "to dominate persons who have used witchcraft against others." This results in a physical/mental illness. This invocation is very dangerous, as the Mam may decide to dominate the asker rather than the victim. Momostenango, Guatemala. (Tedlock, 1982: 125–126)

Indra In Sikkim the Indian weather god is invoked in divination. (Gazetteer of Sikhim, 1894: 334)

Inidu "Omen spirits, who concocted omen and auguries from birds, snakes, insects and trees." The Ifugao, Philippines. (Jocano, 1969: 18)

Inumuhon A deity of omens. The Ifugao, Philippines. (Barton, 1946: 43)

Ix In divination regarding illness it is always related to the Mundo. If a low-numbered Ix day appears the illness or financial trouble will be withdrawn. A mid- or high-numbered Ix indicates the enmity of the Mundo and one's relationship to him must be mended, usually with money or offerings "of copal, candles, sugar, and flowers." Momostenango, Guatemala. (Tedlock, 1982: 120)

Janen "Seer," a god of the Luo. Kenya. (Mbiti, 1970, 2: 332)

Junajpu One of the Day Lords, and a day of the Ancestors (Nantat). In divination this Day Lord indicates the dead; e.g., as having sent the illness. Momostenango, Guatemala. (Tedlock, 1982: 124–125)

Kabigat A god who "taught the *buyon* divination (with the use of iron)." The Nabaloi, Northern Luzon, Philippines. (De Raedt, 1964: 268)

Kabunian The chief god of the Nabaloi who is the one "who makes the iron move . . . in the buyon divination." Luzon, Philippines. (De Raedt, 1964: 269)

Kaindu A "tree at Kiwambya in Buletnezi which prophesied." The Ganda, Uganda. (Kagwa, 1934: 123)

Kalitang A god of omens of the Ifugao. Philippines. (Barton, 1946: 43)

K'anil In questions in divining, if he appears it indicates: the readiness of a woman for marriage; the successful conclusion of a business deal (if Tz'iquin appears also); but in illness, death before long. Momostenango, Guatemala. (Tedlock, 1982: 114–115)

Karma 'phrin las An oracular deity who possesses mediums. Tibet. (Nebesky-Wojkowitz, 1956, 1: 441)

Kasubi A tribal deity appealed to by diviners. The Konjo, Uganda. (Taylor, 1962: 94)

Kê Hsien Wêng A Taoist god of divination. China. (Day, 1940: 27, 96)

Kidul A god of omens. He is also a god of thunder and a god of pacification at drinkfests. The Ifugao, Philippines. (Barton, 1946: 30, 42, 89)

Kinggauwan A god of omens. The Ifugao, Philippines. (Barton, 1946: 43)

Kinich Ahau Itzamma A Mayan sun god who is "invoked in connection with the divination by means of the sacred books." Mexico. (Tozzer, 1941: 153; Thompson, 1970: 207)

Kiti A son of Gbadu (Fa) who was sent with Duwo and Zose to earth to teach men "Fa" in the Fa cult of divination. He helps Zose "to manipulate the palm-kernals" used in divination. Dahomey. (Herskovits, 1938, 2: 204–205)

Kizito A god of divination who foretold the future. The Baganda, Uganda. (Cunningham, 1905: 218; Budge, 1973, 1: 377)

Kling and **Kumang** Invincible fairy gods who "seem to work miracles, prophesy, and can perceive the thoughts of men." They communicate with and give aid through visions. The Iban, Borneo. (Howell, 1908/10: 9)

Kolapuriamma A goddess of fortune tellers using "grains of rice and a winnowing fan." India. (MacKenzie, 1930: 266)

Kuei-ku Tzu A god of fortune-tellers as well as of spectacle sellers. China. (Werner, 1932: 232)

Kumang One of the principal deities, a goddess of prophecy, the wife of Kling. They appear in visions, are benevolent, and aid in prosperity and war. The Sarawak Sea Dyaks, Borneo. (Sarawak Gazette, 1963: 14, 16, 134)

Kunado A god of divination invoked and consulted at crossroads. Japan. (MacCulloch, 1925, 4: 334)

Kurukulle The Red Tara is a goddess of wealth as well as of divination. She is also worshipped by unhappy lovers. Tibet. (Nebesky-Wojkowitz, 1956, 1: 366; Getty, 1962: 126; Sierksma, 1966: 276)

La'a Maomao The rainbow represented a war god. Its position if appearing in battle foretold the outcome. Samoa, Polynesia. (Turner, 1884: 35)

Lairema A goddess of divination through dreams. The Meitheis, Assam. (Hodson, 1908: 98)

Laki Neho The dark-brown hawk is a deity of omens and the carrier of messages from Laki Tenangan. The Kayans, Borneo. (Hose, 1912: 74)

Lani-wahine A lizard goddess who sometimes "appears in human form to foretell some terrible event." Oahu, Hawaii. (Beckwith, 1940: 126)

Letham An Etruscan nature and earth deity who appears in the West of the divisions of the sky and whose name appears on the "bronze liver from Piacenza" used in divination. Italy. (Pallottino, 1975: 145)

Lethn An Etruscan god of nature and the earth who is associated with the East/Southeast of the divisions of the sky and whose name appears on the "bronze liver of Piacenza" used in divination. Italy. (Pallottino, 1975: 145; Hamblin, 1975: 95)

Lethns An Etruscan earth and nature deity associated with the West/Southwest in the divisions of the sky and whose name appears in relation to the "bronze liver from Piacenza" used in divination. Italy. (Pallottino, 1975: 145; Hamblin, 1975: 95)

Lidum A god of divination used in determining the cause of disease, the detection of thieves, and the location of lost property. The Ifugao, Philippines. (Barton, 1946: 91)

Lingangan A god of omens. The Ifugao, Philippines. (Barton, 1946: 43)

Lodong A god of divination using the *agba* stick to determine the cause of disease, to detect thieves, and to find lost property. The Ifugao, Philippines. (Barton, 1946: 91)

Lungpa Kyithik A deity invoked in divination. Sikkim and Tibet. (Gazetteer of Sikhim, 1894: 334; Waddell, 1959: 470)

Magapid A goddess of omens. The Ifugao, Philippines. (Barton, 1946: 43)

dMag zor ma (pr. Maksorma) A protective goddess under whose patronage inquiries are made into the future. Tibet. (Tucci, 1980: 203)

Mai-ingit A god of omens. The Ifugao, Philippines. (Barton, 1946: 42–43)

Makhir The god of dreams was a god "of revelation, since a knowledge of the future was declared through dreams." Assyria and Babylonia. Near East. (Sayce, 1898: 175)

Ma Mien Horse-face—a demon who "conducts magicians and sorcerers to their appointed punishment . . . is worshipped in Japan as a god of divination." China and Japan. (Eastlake, 1883: 272)

Manahaut A god of divination used to determine the cause of disease, to detect thieves, and to find lost property. He is also a god of war who "betrays men into danger from enemies and accident and into all kinds of violent or insidious death . . . coaxes away their souls." The Ifugao. Philippines. (Barton, 1946: 33, 91)

Mangmang A god of divination of the Ifugao invoked to determine the source of disease, to detect thieves and to find lost property. Philippines, (Barton, 1946: 90)

Mari The mistress of the weather is also considered an oracle knowing the future and the mistress of sorcerers. She takes many forms—woman, various animals, sometimes part animal/part human, a gust of wind, a ball of fire. Her favorite offering is a sheep. The Basques. France and Spain. (Barandiaran, 1972: 159, 164, 272–274, 314)

Masongano nyere shave A deity of the art of divining. Nyajena Reserve, Rhodesia. (Gelfand, 1966: 100)

Mêng Chao Shên Chün A Chinese "God of Dream Omens." (Day, 1940: 212)

Minisino-hawatuk The "red war god, who sits in the east" with the Inan-hawatukuk, grants wishes to successful dreamers of visions. Also he prophesies lives of unborn children—somewhat of a god of fate. The Menomiñi, Wisconsin. (Skinner, 1913: 79)

Mongitang A god of omens who is also a guardian of property and prestige. The Ifugao, Philippines. (Barton, 1946: 43, 58)

Mwanga A serpent god who foretells the future through divination with leather strips. He is also invoked in illness and sterility. The Bagesu, the Baganda, Uganda. (Mair, 1934: 234; Cunningham, 1905: 216; Budge, 1973, 1: 377; Roscoe, 1915: 179; MacCulloch, 1925, 11: 400)

Na In the Fa cult of divination the deity who rules the Lete medji arrangement of the palm kernels. Dahomey. (Herskovits, 1938, 2: 214)

Nad-bdak Remati A god of divination and of sickness. Tibet and Sikkim. (Gazetteer of Sikhim, 1894: 334; Waddell, 1959: 470)

Nag-nag A deity of divination. Tibet. *See also* **Ngag-nag.** (Waddell, 1959: 470)

Namalele A god of prophecy. The Ganda, Uganda. (Kagwa, 1934: 122)

Nana Jakpa An oracular goddess. Dahomey. (Parrinder, 1949: 54)

Nape A god of divination of the Bantu. Southeast Africa. (Smith, 1950: 118)

Nebo The god of literature and writing was also a god of prophecy, and interpreted the wishes of Merodach. Babylonia. Near East. (Sayce, 1898: 42, 50, 113)

Ngag-nag A deity invoked in divination. Sikkim. (Gazetteer of Sikhim, 1894: 334)

Nia A god of divination who is invoked for protection from serpents and the evil eye. He also guards the village against wars and death. The Bambara, Mali. (Tauxier, 1927: 329, 333, 335)

Nor rgyun ma A Tibetan goddess of divination. (Nebesky-Wojkowitz, 1956, 1: 366)

Nyamenle A sky god who wields the thunderbolts and who gave the people the techniques of divination. The Nzema, Ghana. (Grottanelli, 1967: 33–41)

Omiya-hime A goddess of the Jingikwan, the Department of Religion. She is also considered a "wise woman, sorceress, or prophetess" and invoked for longevity, "for protection from evil . . . for honours and for posterity." Japan. (Czaja, 1974: 261)

Orunla, Orunmila, Orounmila   The omniscient and wise god of divination. Nigeria, Brazil, and Puerto Rico. In the latter he is identified with St. Francis of Assisi. (Parrinder, 1949: 56; Idowu, 1962: 7, 21, 75; Gonzalez-Wippler, 1975: 110; Bastide, 1960: 570; Courlander, 1973: 10)

Padmasambhava   The Buddhist founder of Lamaism is honored in divination rites. Tibet. (Nebesky-Wojkowitz, 1956, 1: 241, 365; Waddell, 1959: 24)

Palulap   The god of divination also gave them navigational knowledge and the art of canoe building. Ulithi, The Carolines, Micronesia. (Lessa, 1966: 58)

Pasiphae   The daughter of Helios and Perseis and wife of Minos was "an ancient oracular goddess." She was later considered a moon goddess. Greece. (Kerényi, 1951: 110, 193; Willetts, 1962: 110, 177)

Paxsi   The goddess of the moon is also important in divination. The Aymara, Peru. (Tschopik, 1951: 196–197)

Pehar   An oracular deity, "patron of the sorcerers of the established church," and an important protector of the religious law. Tibet. (Hoffman, 1956: 194; Waddell, 1959: 371; Nebesky-Wojkowitz, 1956, 1: 95)

Penkye Otu   Among the Akan he is incarnate in the antelope and is dangerous. He is asked to foretell the coming year. Ghana. (Meyerowitz, 1958: 39–42)

P'er-ndzi-ssaw-ma   A goddess who gave the Na-khi the Tso-la Books—the books of divination which assist in healing. Yunnan Province, China. (Rock, 1936: 39)

Phra In   In the Songkran festival his appearance with varying symbols or emblems foretells the coming year. Same as Indra. Siam. (Scott, 1964: 323)

Pinyuhon ud Lagod   A god of divination invoked to determine the cause of disease, to detect thieves, and to find lost property. The Ifugao, Philippines. (Barton, 1946: 91)

Postvorta   A goddess associated with breech presentation in childbirth. She is also one of the Camenae, with knowledge of the future. Roman. (Larousse, 1968: 210; Dumézil, 1966, 1: 393; Roscher, 1965, 2, 1: 216)

Proteus   A Greek god of the sea with powers of prophecy and of metamorphosis. (Kerényi, 1951: 43–44; Bulfinch, 1898: 219; Larousse, 1968: 147)

Purnan(g) Ukpu   A deity invoked in divination. Sikkim and Tibet. (Gazetteer of Sikhim, 1894: 334; Waddell, 1959: 470)

Ragana   A goddess of clairvoyance whose chief incarnation is as a toad. She is the female counterpart of Velinas as Ragius. Lithuania. (Gimbutas, 1974: 89, 92)

Ragius   The name of Velinas as god of clairvoyance. Baltic. (Gimbutas, 1975: XLC M126)

Rig byed ma   A goddess of divination. Same as Kurukulle. Tibet. (Nebesky-Wojkowitz, 1956, 1: 366)

Rimac   An oracular god of the Chincha with a shrine near Cuzco. Peru. (Rowe, 1946, 2: 302; Alexander, 1920: 224)

Sa fulu sa   A god in Upolu represented by the kingfisher "which, if seen flying *before* the troops (in war) was a good sign." If flying toward them, a bad omen. Samoa, Polynesia. (Turner, 1884: 48)

Sakti   Among the Kaniyan they worship her in her manifestations as "Bala, Thripura, Mathangi, Ambika, Durga, Bhadrakali, the object of which is to secure accuracy in their astrological predictions." Southern India. (Thurston, 1909, 3: 198)

Salevao   A god of war represented by a dog. "When he wagged his tail, barked and dashed ahead . . . it was a good sign; but to retreat or howl was a bad omen." Samoa, Polynesia. (Turner, 1884: 49)

Satres, Satre   An Etruscan deity of the underworld and of fate who is associated with the northwest in the divisions of the sky, and whose name appears on the "bronze liver from Piacenza" used in divination. Italy. (Pallottino, 1975: 145; Dumézil, 1966, 2: 673)

Scathach   A warrior-mother goddess who was a prophetess. Celtic. (Ross, 1967: 228; Puhvel, 1970: 166–167)

Selva   An Etruscan god of nature and of the earth who was associated with divination by haruspicy, and with the Southwest. Italy. (Pallottino, 1975: 145; Hamblin, 1975: 95)

Shamash   The Assyrian/Babylonian sun god was also a god of divination. In Assyrian haruspicy "he reads the tablets through their coverings, he inscribes his message in the very belly of the lamb." (Dumézil, 1966, 2: 655; Jayne, 1962: 127; Larousse, 1968: 57–58; Langdon, 1931: 150)

Shave nganga   A spirit of healing or divining. Rhodesia. (Gelfand, 1966: 93)

gShen rab mi bo   A Bon god invoked in divination. Tibet. (Nebesky-Wojkowitz, 1956, 1: 459)

Shih Erh Kung Ch'ên   A sky power who controls the hours of the day and is used in forming horoscopes. China. (Day, 1940: 80, 210)

Sili va'ai   A village god represented by a bird, the direction of whose flight indicated good or bad omen in war-time. Samoa, Polynesia. (Turner, 1884: 48)

Sipi Kukhor   A deity invoked in divination. Sikkim and Tibet. (Gazetteer of Sikkim, 1894: 334; Waddell, 1959: 470)

Sirge Shashi (Sāshi)   A deity invoked in divination. Sikkim/Tibet. (Gazetteer of Sikkim, 1894: 334; Waddell, 1959: 470)

Srimati   A goddess of good omen. Tibet. (Hackin, 1963, 2: 167)

Subrahmanya   He is worshipped for "the sake of astrology." The Kaniyan, Southern India. (Thurston, 1909, 3: 197)

Ta'afanua   A god of war "incarnate in the Ve'a, or rail. . . . When the bird screeched and flew before, the people went to battle, but if it turned and flew back, they hesitated." Samoa, Polynesia. (Turner, 1884: 52)

Taema   A god incarnate in the kingfisher, whose flight prophesied the outcome of war. Samoa, Polynesia. (Turner, 1884: 54)

Tages   An earth-born deity of prophecy who taught the Etruscans divination by haruspicy and by lightning. Italy. (Dumézil, 1966, 1: 24; Altheim, 1937: 148; Larousse, 1968: 211)

Ta'lab   The god of the oracle of Riyyam. Arabia. (Fahd, 1968: 142)

Tamch'en Nagpo   A deity of divination. Tibet. *See also* **Tamchhen Naypo.** (Waddell, 1959: 470)

Tamchen Naypo   A deity invoked in divination. Sikkim. (Gazetteer of Sikhim, 1894: 334)

Tapa'ai   A god on Tutuila who was represented by a trumpet shell which was blown when going to war. If the tone was clear, a good omen, if "rough and hollow," a bad sign. Samoa, Polynesia. (Turner, 1884: 54)

mThing gi zhal bzang ma   A mountain goddess and a goddess of divination. Tibet. (Nebesky-Wojkowitz, 1956, 1: 177–178, 180)

tinlai   Gila monster, a deity who can be persuaded and who "may be called the god of divination by trembling . . . invoked to cure harm derived from dealing with hand-trembling." The Navaho, Arizona and New Mexico. (Reichard, 1950: 440)

Tluscv   A deity of fate and of the underworld who appears in the West in the divisions of the sky, and on the "bronze liver from Piacenza" used in divination. Etruscan Italy. (Pallottino, 1975: 145; Hamblin, 1975: 95)

Tong   An earth spirit and an oracular deity. Ghana, Togo, Nigeria, and Dahomey. (Parrinder, 1949: 153)

Tongngan (Ton-nan) Lhamo   A deity invoked in divination. Sikkim and Tibet. (Gazetteer of Sikhim, 1894: 334; Waddell, 1959: 470)

Tou-mu   The Taoist goddess of the northern dipper and patroness of fortune tellers. Szechwan, China. (Graham, 1961: 180, 186)

Toxosu   In the Fa cult of divination this deity rules the Nwele medji arrangement of the palm kernels. Dahomey. (Herskovits, 1938, 2: 214)

Trophonios   A chthonic god and oracular deity. Boeotia, Greece. (Tyler, 1964: 9; Guthrie, 1950: 231; Morford and Lenardon, 1975: 355)

bTsan ldan blo sgron ma   A Bon goddess invoked in divination. Tibet. (Nebesky-Wojkowitz, 1956, 1: 459)

bTsan rje snying khrung (pr. **Tsenje Nyingtrung**) An oracular deity who speaks usually through the medium of a woman or child. Tibet. (Tucci, 1980: 203)

Tsunpa   A deity invoked in divination. Sikkim and Tibet. (Gazetteer of Sikhim, 1894: 334; Waddell, 1959: 470)

Tu   A god incarnate in the rail. The condition of its appearance determined whether to go to war (glossy) or not (dark and dingy). Samoa, Polynesia. (Turner, 1884: 61)

Tui Ha'a Fakafanua   A god, manifest as the gecko, with the power of prophecy and of divination, as well as of healing. Tonga, Polynesia. (Gifford, 1929: 295–298)

Tuk-zig-pa   A deity invoked in divination. Sikkim/Tibet. (Gazetteer of Sikhim, 1894: 334; Waddell, 1959: 470)

Tutu   Akkadian/Assyro/Babylonian god of prophecy and of spells. The setting sun. Near East. (Sayce, 1898: 117; Jacobsen, 1970: 36)

Tz'i'   One of the Day Lords. Low-numbered days appearing in divination indicate lack of confidence, confusion, uncertainty; middle numbers, jealousy or unfaithfulness, sexuality at an improper time; high numbers, "serious sexual sin . . . incest, adultery, or sodomy." If he appears in divination regarding marriage it "indicates that the woman already has a lover" and all plans are dropped. Momostenango, Guatemala. (Tedlock, 1982: 116–117)

Tz'iquin   In divination regarding illness his appearance would indicate an enemy who could cause financial ruin if the illness is not cured quickly. Regarding business trips the number associated with him indicates the measure of success—the higher the better. Momostenango, Guatemala. (Tedlock, 1982: 120–121)

Ugyen Rinboch'e   A deity of divination. Tibet. (Waddell, 1959: 470)

Uhudung   A god of divination used to determine the source of disease, to detect thieves, and to find lost property. He is also a guardian of property and prestige. The Ifugao, Philippines. (Barton, 1946: 57, 91)

Umalgo   A god of justice and of divination using the *agba* stick to determine the cause of disease, to detect thieves, and to find lost property. The Ifugao, Philippines. (Barton, 1946: 39, 91)

Umbulan   A god of justice, of divination, of oaths. He is invoked when using the *agba* stick to determine the cause of disease, to detect thieves, and to find lost property. The Ifugao, Philippines. (Barton, 1946: 38, 39, 91)

Vave   A god in Savaii incarnate in the Manualie (a bird) whose actions indicated victory or defeat in war. In another village he was incarnate in the pigeon, in another, the railbird. Samoa, Polynesia. (Turner, 1884: 64, 65)

Vegoia, Begoe   An Etruscan nymph associated with divination by lightning. Italy. (Pallottino, 1975: 154)

Veltune   An Etruscan/Roman goddess associated with haruspicy. (Dumézil, 1966, 1: 339)

Vetis   A deity of the underworld associated with the Northwest in the divisions of the sky and whose name appears on the "bronze liver from Piacenza" used in divination. Italy. (Pallottino, 1975: 145)

Wari   An oracular deity of the Inca in the valley of Jauja. Peru. (Rowe, 1946: 302)

Wigan hi hudok-na   A god of divination invoked to determine the cause of disease, to detect thieves, and to find lost property. The Ifugao, Philippines. (Barton, 1946: 91)

Wigan ud Daiya   A god of trade who is also a god of divination invoked to determine the source of disease, to detect thieves, and to locate lost property. The Ifugao, Philippines. (Barton, 1946: 35, 91)

Wu Ch'ang   A patron god of geomancers and of hunters. The Ch'iang, Szechwan, China. (Graham, 1958: 186)

Xmucané, Ixmucané   She and Ixpiyacoc (male) "are the progenitors of 'divination with the seeds.' " The Quiché, Guatemala. (Girard, 1979: 52, 55)

Xpiyacoc, Ixpiyacoc   The masculine associate of Xmucané. They are the source of "divination with the seeds." The Quiché, Guatemala. (Girard, 1979: 52, 55)

Yes'e (Yeshe) Norbu   A deity invoked in divination. Tibet and Sikkim. (Waddell, 1959: 470; Gazetteer of Sikhim, 1894: 334)

Ye-s'es bla-ma   A celestial Bodhisat, the "Master of Divine foreknowledge." Tibet. (Waddell, 1959: 358)

yonwi ganeídon   Long Human Being—The River. In river cult rites he is sought for longevity, is invoked in divination and incantation ceremonies. The Cherokee. North Carolina and Tennessee. (Mooney and Olbrechts, 1932: 22, 23, 191, 192)

Yuduk Ngonmo (Nonmo)   A divinity invoked in divination. Sikkim and Tibet. (Gazetteer of Sikhim, 1894: 334; Waddell, 1959: 470)

Yurugu   He is associated with death, with night, and with disorder. Divination is his domain. The Dogon. Mali and Nigeria. (Griaule and Dieterlen, 1954: 87, 89, 93)

Zivie An oracular god, in metamorphosis as a bird, who foretells evil when he cries out in the leafless forest, and good when singing from the green trees. Poland. (Grimm, 1883, 2: 679)

Zose A son of Gbadu (Fa) who was sent with Duwo and Kiti to earth to teach men the Fa cult of divination. His function is "to manipulate the palm-kernels." When people disbelieve him he tells Aovi, who punishes them. Dahomey. (Herskovits, 1938, 2: 204–205)

Zu A god who stole the tablets of destiny from Bel (mullil) and fled with them to the mountains. Because his fellow gods refused to slay him, he was transformed into a bird and exiled. "The 'divine stormbird,' . . . served to unite the two species of augury which read the future in the flight of birds and the flash of the lightning." Babylonia. Near East. (Sayce, 1898: 297–299)

53

Magic, Sorcery

Ablatan A god of sorcery. Son of Manahaut. The Ifugao, Philippines. (Barton, 1946: 40)

Adantayi A god who could give man magic charms. The Sagbata cult, Dahomey. (Herskovits, 1938, 2: 141)

Aglosunto A god of magic and charms which he bestows on men through the priests. He is also a god of incurable wounds. Dahomey. (Herskovits, 1938, 2: 159; Verger, 1957: 239)

'Alae-a-Hina A goddess of sorcery invoked to bring death to the enemy. Hawaii. (Beckwith, 1940: 115)

Alibuyon A god of sorcery; son of Manahaut. The Ifugao, Philippines. (Barton, 1946: 40)

Amana A water goddess and mother of all things who is associated with shamanism, as she gives the novice shaman "charms and magical formulas." The Carib, Surinam. (Eliade, 1964: 129; Zerries, 1968: 246–247)

Angob A ghoul deity invoked in sorcery rites. The Ifugao, Philippines. (Barton, 1946: 86)

Anip A god of war and of sorcery. The Ifugao, Philippines. (Barton, 1946: 39)

The Aukis Mountain spirits invoked by sorcerers to help with curing. They are also used by superior sorcerers in divination. The Quechua, Peru. (Mishkin, 1946: 463, 469)

A-wu-wua A protector of the sorcerer. The Na-khi, Tibet and China. (Rock, 1959: 797)

Aziza A monkey-like forest spirit important in man's possession of magic—particularly that "as medicine concocted of leaves and herbs." Dahomey. (Herskovits, 1933: 60)

Badowado A god of war and of sorcery. Son of Manahaut. The Ifugao, Philippines. (Barton, 1946: 40)

Bagala Goddess of black magic and of poisons, of the intuitive knowledge of death or misfortune of others. She exults in cruelty and suffering. India. (Danielou, 1964: 283)

dBang gi las mdzad rdo rje remati A form of dPal ldan lha mo invoked in magic rites. Tibet. (Nebesky-Wojkowitz, 1956, 1: 385)

Begawati A goddess of black magic. Bali, Indonesia. (Covarrubias, 1937: 328)

Bhairu A god of those who cast "spells and counter-spells." The Himalayas, India. (Berreman, 1963: 377)

Carman A Celtic goddess who won battles with sorcery. She had three wicked sons—Dian, Dub, and Dothur—who devastated and plundered. Ireland. (Ross, 1967: 226; Sjoestedt, 1949: 30)

Chang Kuo-lao One of the Immortals, A.D. 600–700, who "had supernatural powers of magic"—was gifted in necromancy and invisibility and had a white mule for transportation which could be "folded up and put away in his wallet," then reanimated with a spray of water when needed. China. (Williams, 1976: 153; Werner, 1934: 294)

Chos skyong gnod sbyin dmar po A protective deity invoked in magic ceremonies. Tibet. (Nebesky-Wojkowitz, 1956, 1: 255)

Chos skyong mahakala A protective deity invoked in magic ceremonies. Tibet. (Nebesky-Wojkowitz, 1956, 1: 254)

Chung-li Ch'üan The Chief of the eight Immortals of Taoism who "obtained the secrets of the elixir of life, the powder of transmutation" and lived under the Chou dynasty, 1122–249 B.C. His emblem was a fan "believed to revive the souls of the dead." China. (Williams, 1976: 152)

Dada Langga A god, son of Dada Zodji and 'Nyohwe Ananu, who has "the power of giving magic charms to man." Dahomey. (Herskovits, 1938, 2: 139, 141)

Daludalum "Eye Disease." He causes blindness. A god of sorcery. Son of Manahaut. The Ifugao, Philippines. (Barton, 1946: 40)

Dja-ma Patron god of the sorcerer. The Na-khi, Tibet and China. (Rock, 1959: 797)

Doko A god of sorcery: son of Manahaut. The Ifugao, Philippines. (Barton, 1946: 40)

Dri za zur phud lnga pa A protective deity invoked in magic ceremonies. A form of gNyan chen thang lha. Tibet. (Nebesky-Wojkowitz, 1956, 1: 254, 258)

Dshi-dshi-garr A deity invoked by the sorcerer "to assist in suppressing demons." The Nda-pa, Yunnan, China. (Rock, 1959: 803)

bDud mchog ma nu yaksa A protective deity invoked in magic ceremonies. Tibet. (Nebesky-Wojkowitz, 1956, 1: 255)

bDud pho re ti 'gong yag A protective deity invoked in magic ceremonies. Tibet. (Nebesky-Wojkowitz, 1956, 1: 255)

bDud po kha mtshun yaksa A protective god invoked in magic ceremonies. Tibet. (Nebesky-Wojkowitz, 1956, 1: 255)

Eileithyia The benevolent goddess of childbirth had also a malevolent side as a goddess of magic and sorcery and when angry would interfere with the birth. Greece. (Jayne, 1962: 319–320)

Enki A Sumerian god, "the numinous inner will to form in the Deep, visualized as a gigantic hart or ibex . . . also the power behind all purification magic." A god of the marshland areas who gives game to the hunter. Near East. (Jacobsen, 1970: 7, 330)

En-uru Enki as a god of "ablution magic." Sumer. Near East. (Jacobsen, 1970: 22)

Feimata A benevolent deity believed to be able to counteract sorcery and overcome evil spirits. Society Islands, Polynesia. (Ellis, 1853: 333)

Fria Germanic goddess with magical charms for healing. Sister of Vol (Volla). (MacCulloch, 1964: 18)

Galikom A Ghoul and Cannibal deity invoked in sorcery rites. The Ifugao, Philippines. (Barton, 1946: 86)

Gar babs btsan pa (pr. **Karpab Tsenpa**) A god worshipped by the snang gshen class of priests who are "trained in magical operations to bring about the well-being and prosperity of their clients." Tibet. (Tucci, 1980: 228, 230)

dGe bsnyen rdo rje legs pa A protective deity, invoked in magic ceremonies. Tibet. (Nebesky-Wojkowitz, 1956, 1: 255)

Gollveig, Gullveig An Eddic-Scandinavian goddess of magic and sorcery who caused the war between the AEsir and the Vanir. (MacCulloch, 1964: 27; Larousse, 1968: 270)

mGon mchog nag po lte dkar A protective deity invoked in magic ceremonies. Tibet. (Nebesky-Wojkowitz, 1956, 1: 255)

mGon po bdun cu don lnga A protective deity invoked in magic ceremonies. Tibet. (Nebesky-Wojkowitz, 1956, 1: 256)

dGra lha A deity invoked in magic ceremonies and protective of worshippers and their prosperity. Tibet. (Nebesky-Wojkowitz, 1956, 1: 256, 328)

Grand Bois A god of magicians and one of the Petro deities who can endow with the knowledge of healing. Haiti. (Deren, 1953: 102; Herskovits, 1937, 1: 151)

rGyal chen phyogs skyong bzhi A protective deity invoked in magic ceremonies. Tibet. (Nebesky-Wojkowitz, 1956, 1: 255)

rGyal mchog li byin ha ra A Tibetan protective deity invoked in magic ceremonies. (Nebesky-Wojkowitz, 1956, 1: 255)

rGyas pa'i las mdzad rdo rje remati A form of dPal ldan lha mo invoked in magic rites. Tibet. (Nebesky-Wojkowitz, 1956, 1: 385)

gza' bdud nyid du sprul pa dang A protective deity invoked in magic ceremonies. Tibet. (Nebesky-Wojkowitz, 1956, 1: 255)

lHa'i dbang po brgya byin   A Tibetan deity invoked in magic ceremonies. (Nebesky-Wojkowitz, 1956, 1: 254)

Halangob   "Faintness," a god of sorcery and of war. Son of Manahaut. The Ifugao, Philippines. (Barton, 1946: 40)

Halibongbong   A god of sorcery who "afflicts with convulsions." Son of Manahaut. The Ifugao, Philippines. (Barton, 1946: 40)

Halimudat   A god of sorcery and of war; son of Manahaut. The Ifugao, Philippines. (Barton, 1946: 40)

Halimudong   A god of sorcery who causes one to walk "Dizzily or Aimlessly." Son of Manahaut. The Ifugao, Philippines. (Barton, 1946: 40)

lHa min dbang po thags bzang(s)   A deity invoked in magic ceremonies. Tibet. (Nebesky-Wojkowitz, 1956, 1: 254)

Harohoha   A messenger of Harisu who communicates with the sorcerers. The Elema, Papuan Gulf, New Guinea. (Holmes, 1902: 429)

Heka   The "god of magical words" who appears in the boat of the first division of the Tuat. Egypt. (Budge, 1969, 1: 180)

Heva   The "god of ghosts and apparitions." Society Islands, Polynesia. (Ellis, 1853: 333)

Hi'iaka   The goddess of the hula and of growth is also a goddess of sorcery, of its "murderous arts." Hawaii. (Emerson, 1968: 43; Beckwith, 1940: 47, 52)

Hoho   The god of twins is also a god of magic and of divination by the arrangements of the palm kernels in the Fa cult. Dahomey. (Herskovits, 1938, 2: 214, 260; Mockler-Ferryman, 1925, 9: 278)

Humabungol   A god of sorcery and of war. The Ifugao, Philippines. (Barton, 1946: 38-39)

Inadungali   A god of sorcery and of war. Son of Manahaut. the Ifugao, Philippines. (Barton, 1946: 40)

Inaiyuan   A god of sorcery and of war. Son of Manahaut. The Ifugao, Philippines. (Barton, 1946: 40)

Ingingo   "Imitation," "Mockery,"—a god of sorcery and of war. The Ifugao, Philippines. (Barton, 1946: 39)

Ini Andan   A goddess of the heavens who "possesses all sorts of charms to bring about good luck." The Iban, Borneo. (Howell, 1908/10: 37)

Intimitiman   A god of sorcery and of war. The Ifugao, Philippines. (Barton, 1946: 39)

Intudtudu   A god of sorcery. The Ifugao, Philippines. (Barton, 1946: 40)

Iya   The God of "all manner of magic for evil." Second son of Inyan. The Lakota, South Dakota. (Walker, 1980: 187)

Kahuila-o-ka-lani   A god of sorcery. Same as Te Uira. Hawaii. (Beckwith, 1940: 118; Andersen, 1928: 157)

Kalamainu'u   A goddess of sorcery who rules the Mo'o—"reptile forms of the lizard kind but of monstrous size." Hawaii. (Beckwith, 1940: 105, 125)

Ka-lei-pahoa   A sorcery god of Molokai. Hawaii. (Beckwith, 1940: 29)

Kalotkot   A "Ghoul and Cannibal" deity invoked in sorcery rites. The Ifugao, Philippines. (Barton, 1946: 86)

Kamrusepa   Hittite goddess of magic and witchcraft, also of healing. Asia Minor. (Guterbock, 1961: 149; Hooke, 1963: 101; Ferm, 1950: 93)

Kane-i-kaulana-'ula   A sorcery god who enters trees. Molokai, Hawaii. (Beckwith, 1940: 108, 118)

Kane pohaka'a   A lesser god—a stone god—"often invoked in certain forms of sorcery." Hawaii. (Emerson, 1968: 51)

Kapo   The goddess of the sorcerers. An obscene member of the Pele family "employed by the *kahunas* as a messenger in their black arts." Hawaii. (Emerson, 1967: 44)

sKar mchog khram shing kha 'thor   A stellar god and protective deity who is invoked in magic ceremonies. Tibet. (Nebesky-Wojkowitz, 1956, 1: 255, 263)

dKar mo'i nyi zla'i thod 'phreng   A protective deity invoked in magic ceremonies. Tibet. (Nebesky-Wojkowitz, 1956, 1: 255)

Katahzipuri   Protohattic goddess of witchcraft. Same as Kamrusepa. Asia Minor. (Ferm, 1950: 93)

Keoloewa   A sorcery goddess of Maui. Hawaii. (Beckwith, 1940: 114)

mKha' lding gser mig 'khyil ba   A protective deity, invoked in magic ceremonies, who has the form of a bird with a blue body. Tibet. (Nebesky-Wojkowitz, 1956, 1: 254, 256)

Khyung dung A god who gives great strength to males and is a protective deity of sorcerers and sorceresses. Tibet, Sikkim, and Bhutan. (Nebesky-Wojkowitz, 1956, 1: 236-237)

Kinipul and **Kinlutan** Gods of sorcery. Sons of Manahaut. The Ifugao, Philippines. (Barton, 1946: 40)

Kirke, Circe A sorceress, daughter of Helios and Perse, who was skilled in herbal knowledge and enchantments. Greece. (Jayne, 1962: 327; Kerényi, 1951: 193; Larousse, 1968: 142)

Klu bdud nagaraja and **Klu bdud sgo ra nag po** Protective deities invoked in magic ceremonies. Tibet. (Nebesky-Wojkowitz, 1956, 1: 255)

Klu mchog klu rgyal dung skyong A protective deity invoked in magic ceremonies whose attributes are "a vessel full of jewels . . . and a conch-shell." Tibet. (Nebesky-Wojkowitz, 1956, 1: 255, 263)

Ku byi mang (s)ke (pr. Kuchi Mangke) A "great god of magical emanation." Tibet. (Tucci, 1980: 243)

Ku-ho'one'enu'u A god of sorcery and also a god of war and a guide of the souls of the dead. Oahu, Hawaii. (Beckwith, 1940: 15, 110, 113)

Ku-ka'ili-moku The god of war and of victory was "the most powerful sorcery god of Hawaii until the rise of the famous sorcery god of Molokai, Ka-lei-pahoa." (Beckwith, 1940: 15, 29, 396; Westervelt, 1963, 3: 108; Poignant, 1967: 42)

Kukauakahi A sorcery god and god of the owl whose wife is Ku-ai-mehana. Hawaii. (Beckwith, 1940: 105, 123, 278)

Kun-syo ming-wang "The Great Peacock Goddess," a "spell" deity who wards off harm. China. (Getty, 1962: 136)

Ku-waha-ilo Cannibalistic god of sorcery who introduced human sacrifice. One of the gods who bear the souls of the chiefs to the heavens. Ku as the father of the Pele family—with Haumea. Hawaii. (Beckwith, 1940: 15, 29, 154; Westervelt, 1963, 2: 64–68)

Kuyub "Cramps," a god of sorcery and of war. Son of Manahaut. The Ifugao, Philippines. (Barton, 1946: 40)

lag g·yas gshin rjer sprul pa dang A protective deity invoked in magic ceremonies. Tibet. (Nebesky-Wojkowitz, 1956, 1: 255)

lag g·yon klu btsan sprul pa dang A Tibetan protective deity invoked in magic ceremonies. (Nebesky-Wojkowitz, 1956, 1: 255)

La-gkyi-la-khu A mountain god and protector of the sorcerer. The Na-khi, Yunnan Province, China. (Rock, 1947: 269; 1959: 797)

Laxee God of sorcerers of the Zapotec in Sola; known in the Valley as Pitao Pijzi. Oaxaca, Mexico. (Whitecotton, 1977: 164)

Lobag A god of sorcery, "Swell-Up," a son of Manahaut. The Ifugao, Philippines. (Barton, 1946: 40)

Locana A tranquil goddess, partner of Vajrasattva. She "belongs to Akshobhya's vajra-family." The vajra represents magical powers. Her color is blue. Tibet. (Snellgrove, 1957: 74, 82, 230)

Loko The god of trees. The souls of trees are "ape-like creatures who give magic to man." Dahomey. (Herskovits, 1933: 14, 15)

Lo-ye Ha-ddu A god worshipped by the sorcerers. The Na-khi, Tibet and China. (Rock, 1959: 797)

Lunge A "Ghoul and Cannibal" deity invoked in sorcery rites. The Ifugao, Philippines. (Barton, 1946: 86)

rMa-bya-c'en-mo "The Great Peacock Goddess," a "spell" deity who wards off harm. Tibet. (Getty, 1962: 136)

Mahamayuri The "Golden Peacock goddess . . . the deification of a magic formula." A "spell" deity protective against snakebites. Buddhism. T. rMa-bya-c'en-mo, C. Kun-syo-ming-wang, J. Kujaku Myo-o. (Getty, 1962: 123, 136)

Maha-pratisara A goddess of Buddhism, "spell," who "protects from all sorts of specified evils and physical dangers." (Getty, 1962: 139)

Maha-sahasrapramardani A goddess of Buddhism, "the deification of a spell believed . . . to ward off earthquakes and storms." (Getty, 1962: 138)

Maha-sitavati The "deification of the spell delivered by the Buddha to his son Rahula to protect him from ferocious animals and evil plants. Buddhism. (Getty, 1962: 139)

Maka-ku-koa'e A god invoked to inflict mental imbalance or death to an enemy. Hawaii. (Beckwith, 1940: 115)

Ma mchog lce spyang mdung 'dzin A protective deity invoked in magic ceremonies whose attribute is a lance with a wolf's head. Tibet. (Nebesky-Wojkowitz, 1956, 1: 255, 263)

Ma mo 'jig pa'i glog 'byin A protective deity invoked in magic ceremonies who also causes illness. Female. Tibet. (Nebesky-Wojkowitz, 1956, 1: 255, 258, 270)

Manalikan A "Ghoul and Cannibal" deity invoked in sorcery rites. The Ifugao, Philippines. (Barton, 1946: 86)

Manang Jaban, Ini Manang A goddess who lives "at the gate of the heavens; she also possesses various charms not only for cures but also for good luck." The Iban, Borneo. (Howell, 1908/10: 37)

Manugahung and **Manunglub** "Ghoul and Cannibal" deities invoked in sorcery rites. The Ifugao, Philippines (Barton, 1946: 86)

Mari The mistress of sorcerers was also a goddess of oracles, knowing the future. Primarily she was goddess of the weather, controlling rain and drought. The Basques. France and Spain. (Barandiaran, 1972: 272–274)

Marutha Viran A name of Hanuman as a protector against witchcraft. The Kadar, Southwest India. (Ehrenfels, 1952: 166)

Matlalcueye Variant of Chalchihuitlicue. The goddess of waters and of the mountain is also considered one of witchcraft and soothsaying. Mexico. (Spence, 1923: 191; Bancroft, 1886, 3: 367; Mackenzie, 1924: 240; Duran, 1971: 257)

mchu so bdud du sprul pa dang A protective deity invoked in magic ceremonies. Tibet. (Nebesky-Wojkowitz, 1956, 1: 255)

mgo bo srin por sprul pa dang A protective deity invoked in magic ceremonies. Tibet. (Nebesky-Wojkowitz, 1956, 1: 255)

Mi 'am ci ljon rta mgo A deity invoked in magic ceremonies. Tibet. (Nebesky-Wojkowitz, 1956, 1: 254)

mig dang snying dang mchin pa gsum A protective deity invoked in magic ceremonies. Tibet. (Nebesky-Wojkowitz, 1956, 1: 255)

Mikenak The spirit who came to the conjurer. The Cree, Ontario. (Cooper, 1934: 13)

Minona A goddess of magic, both good and evil, who is protective of sorcerers and is their source of power. She lives in the forest and is also a goddess of women, by whom she is worshipped. Dahomey. (Herskovits, 1933: 59, 70; 1938, 2: 205, 260)

Mistabeo The chief spirit of the conjurers. He corresponds to Mikenak and Mistapiu. East coast of James Bay, Quebec. (Cooper, 1934: 39)

Mistapiu The chief of the conjurers, subordinate to the Caribou God. Labrador. Canada. (Cooper, 1934: 36)

mjug ma rmu ru sprul pa dang A protective deity invoked in magic ceremonies. Tibet. (Nebesky-Wojkowitz, 1956, 1: 255)

Moko-hiku-aru A lizard god, and a wizard god, a guardian of the sacred ax, Te Awhio-rangi. New Zealand. (Mackenzie, n.d.: 59, 60)

Mo lha A guardian deity (personal) located in the left armpit. Invoked in magic ceremonies. Tibet. (Nebesky-Wojkowitz, 1956, 1: 256, 264)

Mombolboldang and **Mondauwat** Gods of sorcery and of war. Sons of Manahaut. The Ifugao, Philippines. (Barton, 1946: 40)

Mongfhinn A Celtic goddess of sorcery. Ireland. (Sjoestedt, 1949: 31)

Mun-lu-dzi-pu A goddess invoked by the sorcerer "to assist in suppressing demons." The Nda-pa, Yunnan, China. (Rock, 1959: 803)

Nesert An ancient goddess, with whom Hathor was identified, possessed of magical properties. A name also applied to Sekhet—"Flame, as a destroying element . . . a power which protects the good and annihilates the wicked." Egypt. (Budge, 1969, 1: 432, 454, 456, 515)

Netekwo A god who guides the priest in counteracting witchcraft. The Nzema, Ghana. (Grottanelli, 1969: 392)

mNgon spyod las mdzad rdo rje remati A form of dPal ldan lha mo invoked in magic rites. Tibet. (Nebesky-Wojkowitz, 1956, 1: 385)

No Cha   A mythological hero born with a gold bracelet of magic qualities which he used in protecting the Emperor. China. (Williams, 1976: 293)

gNod sbyin gang ba bzang po   A protective deity invoked in magic ceremonies. One of the "masters of mantras." Tibet. (Nebesky-Wojkowitz, 1956, 1: 254, 273)

gNod sbyin shan pa gri thogs   A protective deity invoked in magic ceremonies. Tibet. (Nebesky-Wojkowitz, 1956, 1: 255)

Nudj num   A god of the Earth Pantheon who "paralyzes the will of men, and in this capacity has given to man many magical formulae and their associated charms." Dahomey. (Herskovits, 1933: 18)

Numputol   A "Ghoul and Cannibal" deity invoked in sorcery rites. The Ifugao, Philippines . (Barton, 1946: 87)

Nyamikeri-mahse   The "Night People" created by the Sun to serve "as intermediaries for witchcraft and sorcery" and in punishing mankind for infractions of customs. The Desana, Colombia. (Reichel-Dolmatoff, 1971: 28)

Odani   A spirit of the Didinga who liberates people from possession. Ethiopia. (Cerulli, 1956: 79)

Odin   The All-Father of Scandinavian mythology was versed in magic and knowledge of the runes, which he acquired through voluntarily hanging from the tree Yggdrasill, pierced with a sword, for nine days and nights. He chanted charms to call "the dead from their graves, wrenching their secret wisdom" from them. Like the shamans, he could transform himself. (Davidson, 1964: 141–145; Turville-Petre, 1964: 63–65; Schoeps, 1961: 105; Pettazzoni, 1956: 220–221)

Omaua   The creator god of the Waica is "invoked by shamans both for black and white magic." Venezuela. (Zerries, 1968: 248)

Pahulu   Goddess of sorcery and of the sorcery school. Lanai, Hawaii. (Beckwith, 1940: 107)

Palada   A god of the Sagbata cult who could give men magic charms. Dahomey. (Herskovits, 1938, 2: 141)

Pehar   The "three-headed, six-armed . . . leader of all earthly protective gods," protector of the religious laws, patron of sorcerers, and an oracular deity. Tibet. (Nebesky-Wojkowitz, 1956, 1: 4, 117; 1956, 2: 208; Waddell, 1959: 371)

peyák nötta   A "kind of individual guardian spirit" through whom each individual acquires what ability he has in supernatural powers—i.e., magic (black/white), healing, etc. The older one is, the more developed the powers. The Toba of the Gran Chaco, Bolivia. (Karsten, 1970: 47, 48)

Pho lha   A personal guardian god located in the right armpit, a god of men, protective of his worshippers and their prosperity. He is also invoked in magic ceremonies. Tibet. (Nebesky-Wojkowitz, 1956, 1: 256, 264, 327; Gazetteer of Sikhim, 1894: 353)

Pinigipigon   A "Ghoul and Cannibal" deity invoked in sorcery rites. The Ifugao, Philippines. (Barton, 1946: 87)

Pitao Pijzi   The god of sorcerers of the Valley Zapotecs. Same as Laxee. Oaxaca, Mexico. (Whitecotton, 1977: 164)

Poti'i-ta-rire   A Tahitian goddess of sorcerers. Polynesia. (Henry, 1928: 379)

Prakagorri   The spirit of the sorcerers. The Basques. Spain and France. (Barandiaran, 1972: 275)

P'u-lla gka-hla   A deity invoked by the sorcerer "to assist in suppressing demons." The Nda-pa, Yunnan, China. (Rock, 1959: 803)

dpung g·yas dgra lhar sprul pa dang and **dpung g·yon ma mor sprul pa dang**   Protective deities invoked in magic ceremonies. Tibet. (Nebesky-Wojkowitz, 1956, 1: 255)

ah q'in   The "god of the sun and light, of knowledge, and of magical power and so is the patron of sorcerers, curers, and diviners . . . both good and bad, depending upon whom he aids at any given time." The Chorti, Guatemala. (Wisdom, 1940: 399)

Rangatau   A deified high priest invoked by sorcerers. Kapingamarangi, Polynesia. (Emory, 1965: 203)

Ro'o   A benevolent god believed to be able to counteract sorcery and cast out evil spirits. He was also a god of the morning and of clouds. Tahiti, Polynesia. (Ellis, 1853: 333, 344)

Sa bdag hal khyi nag po   A protective deity invoked in magic ceremonies. Also known as Hal khyi nap po rgyal po'i khyi and "represented as a figure with a black human trunk which bears the head of a dog, wings of iron, the tail of a snake, and . . . bird's claws, which clutch a lance with a banner." Tibet. (Nebesky-Wojkowitz, 1956, 1: 255, 264)

Sa yi lha mo bstan ma A yellow protective goddess who "holds a vessel in front of her heart" and is invoked in magic ceremonies. Tibet. (Nebesky-Wojkowitz, 1956, 1: 255, 264)

Seng ge'i gdong can A lion-faced goddess with magical powers. Tibet. (Waddell, 1959: 129, 366)

Shang Chieh Fu Kuan Szu Tsai A god of charms invoked to protect from evil spirits while other gods are worshipped at funerals. China. (Day, 1940: 99)

Sheng-mu A goddess of sorcery who is associated with Pi-hsia Yuan-chun, a goddess of confinements and childbirth. China. (Werner, 1932: 421)

gShin rje gshed pa dmar po A protective deity invoked in magic ceremonies; a form of Yamantaka. Tibet. (Nebesky-Wojkowitz, 1956, 1: 255, 259)

Simbi A god with two major functions, that of god of magicians, and god of rains and fresh waters. He is also a god of healing and of ferrymen. Haiti. West Indies. (Deren, 1953: 70, 117; Marcelin, 1950: 13, 16)

Simbi en Deux Eaux He bestows "magic powers . . . knowledge of excellent protectives against werewolves as well as the ingredients to concoct healing baths." Sometimes identified with St. Anthony the Hermit. Haiti. West Indies. (Herskovits, 1937, 1: 151–152, 280)

Simbi Promene A deity of the Petro group who bestows magical powers. Haiti, West Indies. (Herskovits, 1937, 1: 151, 311)

Sinthgunt A Germanic goddess possessed of magical charms for healing. Sister of Sunna. (MacCulloch, 1964: 18)

Sitatapatra Aparajita "Invincible goddess of the White Parasol . . . a 'spell' goddess, a deification of the White Umbrella which is believed to have the power of protecting from all harm." Buddhism. (Getty, 1962: 136)

Skyes-bu-ber A Tibetan goddess who teaches "methods of exorcism and propitiation." (Li An-che, 1948: 38)

Srog bdag rgyal po snying sbyin A protective deity invoked in magic ceremonies. Tibet. (Nebesky-Wojkowitz, 1956, 1: 254)

Ssan-ddo A mountain god and a protector of the sorcerer. The Na-khi, Tibet and China. (Rock, 1959: 797)

Temaru and **Teruharuhatai** Benevolent deities believed to be able to counteract sorcery and overcome evil spirits. Society Islands, Polynesia. (Ellis, 1853: 333)

Tezcatlipoca One of the creator gods in one of his aspects—as a god of sorcerers, of darkness and the night sky, of evildoers. Mexico. (Duran, 1971: 476; Caso, 1958: 14, 27–31)

Thai-cu-ia A young god of both the Taoist and the Buddhist pantheons. In Taoism he is "of great strength and magical powers." Taiwan. (Diamond, 1969: 85)

Ti'i A Tahitian god of sorcery. Polynesia. (Beckwith, 1940: 110)

'Ti Kita A goddess of the Petro group "associated with the cult of magic and the dead." Haiti. West Indies (Herskovits, 1937, 1: 319)

Ti-mba Shera The founder of the Nda-pa sorcerers. Yunnan, China. (Rock, 1959: 803)

Tlacauepan A god versed in magic, younger brother of Tezcatlipoca. Aztec, Mexico. (Alexander, 1920: 65)

Toro A god of sorcery of the Huli. New Guinea. (Glasse, 1965: 41)

bTsan mchog gri btsan 'thu bo A protective deity whose attribute is a sword, invoked in magic ceremonies. Tibet . (Nebesky-Wojkowitz, 1956, 1: 255, 263)

bTsan po yam shud srog len A protective deity invoked in magic ceremonies. Tibet. (Nebesky-Wojkowitz, 1956, 1: 255)

bTsan rgyal yam shud dmar po A protective deity, one of the "masters of mantras," invoked in magic ceremonies. Tibet. (Nebesky-Wojkowitz, 1956, 1: 254, 273)

T'u-ch'i Yu-ma A protector of the sorcerer. The Na-khi, Tibet and China. (Rock, 1959: 797)

Tuira A god of evil from whom sorcerers and witches claim to receive their powers. Panama. (Trimborn, 1968: 106)

Tukia A deified high priest invoked by sorcerers. Kapingamarangi, Polynesia. (Emory, 1965: 203)

Tutu Assyro/Babylonian god of spells. Near East. (Jacobsen, 1970: 36)

Uli   A goddess of sorcery "and the infernal arts of praying to death." Hawaii. (Beckwith, 1940: 114; Emerson, 1968: 56)

Unktomi, Iktomi   The Spider, or a goblin-like being, was a prankster and practical joker "with powers to work magic over persons and things." The Lakota/Oglala, South Dakota. (Walker, 1980: 122)

Vol, Volla   A Germanic goddess possessed of magical charms for healing. Also a goddess of abundance. (Mac-Culloch, 1964: 18, 184)

Wazi   The "Old Man, and later in cosmological time, the Wizard." His wife is Wakanka, his daughter, Ite. The Oglala, South Dakota. (Powers, 1977: 54)

The we'ma·we   The dangerous and violent Beast Gods "are the priests of long life . . . the givers of medicine . . . the source of black magic." The Zuñi, New Mexico. (Bunzel, 1929/30: 538)

Xu   The great sky god to whom the souls of the dead go. He "summons the magicians to their profession and gives them supernatural powers." The Kung Bushmen, South Africa. (Schapera, 1951: 169, 184)

Yab gcig bdud rje nag po   A protective deity invoked in magic ceremonies. Tibet. (Nebesky-Wojkowitz, 1956, 1: 254, 256)

Ye shes bdal mo (pr. **Yeshê Welmo**)   A guardian goddess who watches over "the magical operations"; over the *gter ma* (hidden texts). Bon Religion. Tibet. (Tucci, 1980: 242)

Yul di'i gzhi bdag tham cad   A protective deity invoked in magic ceremonies. Tibet. (Nebesky-Wojkowitz, 1956: 256)

Yul lha chag sangs klu sras   A protective deity invoked in magic ceremonies. Tibet. (Nebesky-Wojkowitz, 1956: 254)

gZa' mchog rgyal po rahula   A protective deity, one of the names of Rahu or Rahula, invoked in magic ceremonies. Tibet. (Nebesky-Wojkowitz, 1956, 1: 255, 259)

Zhi ba'i las mdzad rdo rje remadzu   A form of dPal ldan lha mo invoked in magic rites. Tibet. (Nebesky-Wojkowitz, 1956, 1: 385)

Glossary

ANNAM

Ong A title: Grandfather, My Lord, The Venerable

ASSAM (The Khasis, India)

ka Feminine

u Masculine

BALI

batara Title for a god, deified ancestor, or other divine being

dewa, dewi Deity of lesser rank: a title for divine or deified being, ancestor, or for members of the ksatriya caste

dewa taksu A category of intercessors

guru Teacher

ida A title of respect, honorific

ida yang A deified human

jero A title of address for persons of sudra caster

jero nyoman, jero wayan Intercessors found in temples

meru A temple structure

ngerurah Guardian

nyoman The third child

pura A sanctuary, temple

ratu Lord, Ruler, a title of kings, princes, and higher deities

ratu ayu Noble Lady, a consort of a ratu

sang yang (hyang) A title indicating divinity or sacredness, also the name of a dance performed in trance

sakti Supernatural power and part of some divine names

BORNEO

antu A lesser god, good and/or bad

hantuen Witches. The Ngaju

Jata A category of spirits inhabiting the Underworld. The Ngaju

Laki A title of respect

nats A "system of beliefs in animistic spirits coexists within the framework of Buddhist religion. . . . belief in spirits, or nats, is in fact a complementary part of Buddhist belief, . . . the ahtet nats and the auk nats, i.e., the upper and lower nats. The ahtet nats, who are big nats awaiting Buddha in the sky, have no personalities or legends associated with them. . . . The auk nats belong to a different order entirely [and] include both named and unnamed spirits drawn from

873

indigenous pre-Buddhist cosmology as well as from Hindu and other outside sources." (Nash, 1966: 117–118) Nats can be beneficent and protective when propitiated, but are essentially evil and do harm. Must be feared always. (Spiro, 1967: ch. 6)

petara An appellation of the gods, but can be an individualized application

raja A lord or king of the lesser spirits

Toh Lesser spirits

CEYLON/SRI LANKA

yaka Singular, spirit or deity

yaku Plural, spirits or deities

HAWAII

aumakua An "ancestral god. It may have a host of worshippers, and usually enters into intimate and often pleasant relations with the clan or class that acknowledges it as one of their god." Called upon by kahunas (magicians). (Emerson, 1967: 42)

kupua "Every form of nature has its class god, who may become aumakua or guardian god of a family into which an offspring of the god is born, provided the family worship such an offspring with prayer and offerings. The name kupua is given such a child of a god when it is born into the family as a human being. The power of a kupua is limited to the district to which he belongs." They are transformers, have supernatural powers. (Beckwith, 1940: 2)

Mo'o Monstrous lizard-like guardian gods. (Beckwith, 1940: 125)

INDIA

bhagat A priest-magician or medicine man

MALAYA

ta, tak Lord, grandfather

ya, yak Grandmother

halak shaman

MAYAN

Ah Indicated male gender

costumbres Offerings and prayers at shrines

Ix Indicated female gender

MEXICO
(The Tzeltal)

Tatik Our lords, elders, or fathers

NEW GUINNEA

Kur A prefix meaning spirit

PHILIPPINES
(The Ifugao)

There are five regions: The Skyworld, Underworld, Upstream, Downstream, and known Earth. Deities can inhabit one or all

Kabunian The Skyworld

Dalum The Underworld

Daiya The Upstream regions

Lagod The Downstream regions

in wife of

nak son/daughter of

ud in, at, or of a place

Bugan name of most divine wives

hi the same as ud

POLYNESIA

Te Names beginning with Te may be listed under Te or the next part of the name, due to variations among authors and/or usage

O Before a name (e.g., O-Rongo), a prefix indicated "the place of," etc.

SIBERIA

Tengeri There are 99: "54 western, white, and good heavenly spirits and 44 eastern, black, and evil; and in addition, there is one, segen sedbek . . . who is the border marker, obo, between the two, although he is actually a western tengeri." The Buryat. (Krader, 1954: 338)

SIKKIM

moong, mung Evil spirit, demon, devil

rum God, deity, divine spirit

thing "lord"

THAILAND

mae Female

phra Male

TIBET

bDud Malignant devils who cause unconsciousness, mostly male, black color.

bgegs Obstacle, obstruction deities (of religious activities)

bStan-ma Of the snowy ranges

dgra lha "Enemy god": Those deities who are believed to be especially capable of protecting their worshippers against enemies, and to help them to increase their property, to achieve higher rank and position

dKor-bdag Treasure/Wealth masters, mostly white, apotheosized heroes

dMu Bloated fiends, of dark purple color

drag-po, Drag-s'e Fiercest fiend demons

gDon Planet fiends, producing diseases

gNan Malignant earth spirits who "cause pestilential disease, infest certain trees, rocks, and springs"

gshin rje, gshin rje mo Death-bringing demons

gZah Planets, piebald in color

lha Originally the lha seem to have been regarded as deities apt to cause harm and believed to send madness

Lha Good spirits, mostly male, white, genial

Ma-mo Goddesses, Furies, Disease-mistresses (nad-bdag), black colored; sometimes spouses of certain demons

MGon-po, drag-po Fiercest fiend-type demons.

mo Goddess

nad-bdag Disease mistresses

rDud Demons, actively malignant, black

rGyal-po King fiends, illness-bringing deities who are supposed to cause insanity, mostly white, apotheosized heroes

sa bdag Melevolent deities who cause illness

Sa-bdag The "earth owners," inhabiting the soil, springs, lakes

Srin-po Ghouls and vampires, bloodthirsty, a raw flesh color

Srung-ma Guardians, defenders of Lamaism

The 'U rang deities Of an ill nature, said to cause disunity and quarreling, to make children ill, also believed to influence the weather, to send hailstorms

To-wo Angry deities

Tsan Ghosts and goblins, all male, usually vindictive, red in color

Yul-lha Countryside gods

Z'i-wa Mild deities

TIKOPIA

Ariki Chief (of the various clans), e.g., Ariki Tafua

atua Spiritual ancestral beings, sacred beings

atua lasi Great deities, sometimes called tupua

Rangi The spirit world, which varies with the clans; each has its own atua

tauratua The medium through whom the atua communicates

vaka atua Other minor mediums for the lesser deities

Periodicals/Journals

The following is a key to the abbreviations used for journals and periodicals in the Bibliography

AA   **American Anthropologist**
Vols. 1–11, Jan. 1888–Dec. 1898.
New Ser. (Ser. 2), Vol. 1– , Jan.
1899– .
Washington, D.C.: American
  Anthropological Association.

AMNH-B   **American Museum of Natural
History, Bulletin**
Vol. 1– , 1881/86– .
New York: American Museum
  of Natural History.

AMNH-AP   **Anthropological papers of the
American Museum of Natural
History**
Vol. 1– , 1907– .
New York: American Museum
  of Natural History.

AMNH-Mag.   **American Museum of Natural
History, Natural History Magazine**
Vol. 1– , Apr. 1900– .
New York: American Museum
  of Natural History.

APUPM   **Anthropological Publications of
the University of Pennsylvania
Museum (Series)**
Vols. 1–10, 1909–1924.
Philadelphia: University of
  Pennsylvania, University Museum.
Ceased Publication.

AQ   **Anthropological Quarterly.**
Vol. 26– , Jan. 1953– .
Washington, D.C.: Catholic

University of America Press.
Continues *Primitive Man.*

ARBAE   **Annual Report of the Bureau of
American Ethnology**
1879/80–1963/64.
Washington, D.C.: U.S. Government
  Printing Office.

BBAE   **Bulletin of the Bureau of American
Ethnology**
No. 1–200; 1887–1971.
Washington, D.C.: U.S. Government
  Printing Office.

BCPM   **British Columbia Provincial
Museum, Anthropology in
British Columbia**
No. 1– , 1952– .
Victoria: British Columbia
  Provincial Museum.

BPBM   **Bernice P. Bishop Museum Bulletin**
No. 1– , 1922– .
Honolulu: Bishop Museum Press.

CMAI   **Contributions, Museum of the
American Indian, Heye Foundation**
No. 1–25, 1913–1974.
New York: Museum of the American
Indian, Heye Foundation.

ERE   **Encyclopedia of Religion and Ethics**
James Hastings, ed.
13 volumes, 1908–1927.
Edinburgh: T. and T. Clark.

ES   **Etnologiska Studier**
Vol. 1– , 1935– .
Goeteborg: Goeteborgs Etnografiska
    Museum.

FMNH-AS   **Field Museum of Natural History,
Anthropological Series**
Vols. 1–72, 1895–1979.
New Ser., no. 1– , 1980– .
Chicago: Field Museum of Natural
    History.

HSAI   **Handbook of South American
Indians**
7 volumes, 1946–1963.
Washington, D.C.: U.S. Government
    Printing Office.

HAS   **Harvard African Studies**
Vols. 1–10, 1917–1932.
Cambridge: African Department,
    Peabody Museum of Harvard
    University.

JAF   **Journal of American Folklore**
Vol. 1– (no. 1–), Apr./June
    1888– .
Washington, D.C.: American
    Folklore Society.

JRAI   **Journal of the Royal
Anthropological Institute
of Great Britain and Ireland**
Vols. 1–95, 1871–1965.
London.

JRAS   **Journal of the Royal
Anthropological Society
of Great Britain**
Vols. 1–20, 1834–63.
New Ser., Vols. 1–21, 1864–89
New Ser., Vols. 1– , 1890– .
London: Royal Asiatic Society.

JWCBRS   **Journal of the West China Border
Research Society**
Vols. 1–11, 1922/23–1939.
Chengtu, China.

MAAA   **Memoirs of the American
Anthropological Association**
Vol. 1., pt. 1 (Sept. 1906)–Vol. 65,
    no. 3 (June 1963).
Lancaster, Pa.: New Era Printing Co.

MAES   **Monographs of the American
Ethnological Society**
Vol. 1– , 1940– .
Seattle: University of Washington
    Press.

MAFS   **Memoirs of the American
Folklore Society**
Vol. 1– , 1894– .
Philadelphia: University of
    Pennsylvania Press.

MAI-IM   **Museum of the American Indian,
Heye Foundation, Indian Notes
and Monographs**
No. 1– , 1919– .
New York: Museum of the American
    Indian, Heye Foundation.

MAMNH   **Memoirs of the American Museum
of Natural History**
Vol. 1, pt. 1 (1893/1903)–Vol. 15,
    pt. 2 (1930).
New Ser. Vols. 1–3, 1903–1921.
New York: Published by Order of
    the Trustees, American Museum
    of Natural History

MPS   **Memoirs of the Polynesia Society
(New Zealand)**
No. 1– .
New Plymouth: Polynesian Society.

NG   **National Geographic**
Vol. 116, no. 6– , Dec. 1959– .
Washington, D.C.: National
    Geographic Society.

NMC-AS   **National Museum of Canada,
Anthropological Series**
No. 1–22, Dec. 1961–Sept. 1969.
Ottawa: National Museum of Canada.

NMD   **National Museum of Denmark**
Bd 1– , 1941– .
Copenhagen: National Museum.

PAEUC   **University of California
Publications in American
Archaeology and Ethnology**
Vol. 5, no. 2 (Sept. 1907)–Vol. 50
    (1964).
Berkeley, The University Press.
Ceased publication.

PAUNM **Publications in Anthropology, University of New Mexico**
No. 1–141, 1945–1965.
Albuquerque: University of
New Mexico Press.

PAUW **Publications in Anthropology, University of Washington**
Vol. 1, no. 2– , 1920– .
Seattle: University of Washington
Press

PCAC **Publications of the Catholic Anthropological Conference**
Vol. 1– , 1929– .
Washington, D.C.: Catholic
Anthropological Conference.

PMAE **Peabody Museum of Archeology and Ethnology, Memoirs**
Vol. 7, pt. 1– , 1937– .
Cambridge: Peabody Museum of
Archeology and Ethnology.

PSJ **Polynesian Society Journal**
Vol. 1– , 1892– .
Wellington, New Zealand

PM **Primitive Man**
Vols. 1–25, 1928–1952.
Washington, D.C.: Catholic
University of America Press.

PUSNM **Proceedings, U.S. National Museum**
1–125, 1878–1968.
Washington, D.C.

RUSNM **Report, U.S. National Museum**
1887/88– .
Washington, D.C.

SI-AR **Smithsonian Institution, Annual Report of the Board of Regents**
1846–1963/64.
Washington, D.C.: U.S. Government
Printing Office.

SI-MC **Smithsonian Institution, Miscellaneous Collections**
Vol. 1– , 1862– .
Washington, D.C.: Smithsonian
Institution.

SJA **Southwestern Journal of Anthropology**
Vols. 1–28, Spring 1945–Winter 1972.
Albuquerque: University of New
Mexico Press.

SNR **Sudan Notes and Records**
Vol. 1– , 1918– .
Khartoum: Philosophical Society
of the Sudan.

TAPS **Transacations of the American Philosophical Society**
Vols. 1–6, 1771–1809.
New Ser., Vol. 1– , 1818– .
Philadelphia: American Philosophical
Society.

TASJ **Transactions of the Asiatic Society of Japan**
Vol. 1 (from 30th Oct. 1872 to 9th
Oct. 1873)–Vol. 50 (Dec. 1922).
2nd Ser., Vol. 1 (Dec. 1924)–Vol. 8
(Dec. 1931).
3rd Ser., Vol. 1 (Dec. 1948)–Vol. 20
(1985).
4th Ser., Vol. 1 (1986)– .
Yokohama: Asiatic Society of Japan.

Bibliography

Abbate, Francesco, ed. 1972. *African Art and Oceanic Art*. London and New York: Octopus Books.

Abercrombie, Thomas J. 1972. The Sword and the Sermon. *NG* 141:3–45.

Abrahams, R. G. 1967. *The Peoples of Greater Unyamwezi, Tanzania*. London: International African Institute.

de Abreu, Joao Capistrano. 1938. *The Bacairi*. Ensaios e Estudos (Critica e Historia), 3rd Ser. Rio de Janeiro: Livraria Briquiet.

Adriani, N., and Albert C. Kruyt. 1950. *The Bare'e-Speaking Toradja of Central Celebes (the East Toradja)*, 2nd ed., Vol. 1. Amsterdam: Noord-Hollandsche Uitgeners Maatschappij.

Aitkin, Robert T. 1930. Ethnology of Tubuai. *BPBM*, no. 70.

Aiyangar, M. Srinivasa. 1914. *Tamil Studies*. Madras: Guardian Press.

Akiga. *See* East

Akurgal, Ekrem. 1969. *Ancient Civilizations and Ruins of Turkey*. Translated by John Whybrow and Mollie Emre. Istanbul: Mobil Oil Türk, A.S.

Alagoa, Ebiegberi Joe. 1964. Idu: A Creator Festival at Okpoma (Brass) in the Niger Delta. *Africa* (January):1–8.

Albright, William Foxwell. 1968. *Yahweh and the Gods of Canaan*. Garden City: Doubleday.

——. 1956. *Archaeology and the Religion of Israel*. 4th ed. Baltimore: Johns Hopkins University Press.

Alexander, Hartley Burr. 1920. *Latin America*. Vol. 11, Mythology of All Races. Boston: Marshall Jones.

——. 1925. Communion with Deity (American). In *ERE*, vol. 3, 740–745.

——. *North America*. 1964. Vol. 10, Mythology of All Races. Boston: Marshall Jones.

Alexander, W. D. 1967. Kahunas and the Hawaiian Religion. *(San Francisco) Revue*, no. 1 (December):61–105.

——. 1968. Kahunas and the Hawaiian Religion. In Morrill, 1968.

Alkema, B., and T. J. Bezemer. 1927. *Concise Handbook of the Ethnology of the Netherlands East Indies*. Human Relations Area Files OBI-1 (The Buginese). Haarlem: H. D. Tjeenk Willink en Zoon.

Altenfelder Silva, Fernando. 1946. Terena Religion. *Acta Americana* 4:214–223.

——. 1950. The Uanki State among the Bacairi. *Sociologica* 12:259–271.

Altheim, Franz. 1937. *A History of Roman Religion*. New York: Dutton.

Ames, Delano. 1965. *Egyptian Mythology*. London: Paul Hamlyn.

Ames, Michael M. 1964. Magical Animism and Buddhism: A Structural Analysis of the Sinhalese Religious System. In Harper, 1964:21–52.

——. 1978. Tovil: Exorcism by White Magic. *Natural History* 87 (January):42–48.

Anankian, Mardiros H. 1964. *Armenian*. Vol. 7, Mythology of All Races. New York: Cooper Square Publishers.

——. 1925. Armenia (Zoroastrian). In *ERE*, vol. 1, 794–803.

Andersen, Johannes C. 1928. *Myths and Legends of the Polynesians*. London: George G. Harrap.

Anderson, Benedict R. O'G. 1965. *Mythology and the Tolerance of the Javanese*. Cornell University Monograph Series, Modern Indonesia Project. Ithaca: Cornell University.

Anderson, R. B. 1891. *Norse Mythology*. Chicago: S. C. Griggs.

Anesaki, Masaharu. 1937. *Japanese*. Vol. 8, Mythology of All Races. Boston: Marshall Jones.

de Angulo, Jaime. 1935. Pomo Creation Myth. *JAF* 48:203–262.

Anthes, Rudolf. 1961. Mythology of Ancient Egypt. In Kramer, 1961a, 15–92.

Antropova, V. V. 1964a. The Itel'mens. In Levin and Potapov, 1964.

——. 1964b. The Koryak. In Levin and Potapov, 1964.

——, and V. G. Kuznetsova. 1964. The Chukchi. In Levin and Potapov, 1964.

Anwyl, Edward. 1906. *Celtic Religion*. London: Archibald Constable.

de Aparicio, Francisco. 1948. The Archaeology of the Parana River. *HSAI* 3:57–66.

Arciniegas, German. 1971. Our First Anthropologist. *Americas* 23 (11-12):2–10.

Armstrong, John M., and A. Metraux. 1948. The Goajiro. *HSAI* 4:369–383.

Armstrong, Robert G. 1955a. The Igala and the Idoma-Speaking Peoples. In Forde, 1955, 77–155.

Armstrong, W. E. 1923–1924. Rossel Island Religion. *Africa* 18-19:1–11.

Ashdown, Inez. 1971. *The Broad Highway of Maui*. Wailuku, Hawaii: Ace Printing Company.

Aston, W. G. 1925. Shinto. In *ERE*, vol. 11, 462–471.

Asturias, Miguel Angel. 1959. *El Senor Presidente*. Buenos Aires: Editorial Losada.

Augenanger, H. 1962. The Sun in the Life of the Natives in the New Guinea Highlands. *Anthropos* 57 (1-2):1–44.

Augur, Helen. 1954. *Zapotec*. Garden City: Doubleday.

Babington, S. H. 1950. *Navajos Gods and Tom-toms*. New York: Greenberg.

Baird, W. David. 1980. *The Quapaw Indians: A History of the Downstream People*. Norman: University of Oklahoma Press.

Balikci, Asen. 1970. *The Netsilik Eskimo*. Garden City: Natural History Press.

Ball, J. Duer. 1925. Light and Darkness (Chinese). In *ERE*, vol. 8, 51–52.

Bancroft, Howard Howe. 1886. *The Works of Howard Howe Bancroft*. Vols. 1–2. San Francisco: The History Company.

Banerjea, Jitendra Nath. 1953. The Hindu Concept of God. In *The Religion of the Hindus*, ed. Kenneth Morgan. New York: Ronald Press.

de Barandiaran, Jose Miguel. 1972. *Obras Completas, Diccionario Illustrado de Mitologia Vasca y Algunas de sus Fuentes*, Vol. 1. Bilbao: Graficas Ellacuria.

Barbeau, C. M. 1914. Supernatural Beings of the Huron, and Wyandot. *AA* 16 (2):288–313.

Bareh, Hamlet. 1967. *The History and Culture of the Khasi People*. Calcutta: Naba Mudran.

Barkataki, S. 1969. *Tribes of Assam*. New Delhi: National Book Trust.

Barns, Thomas. 1925. Trees and Plants. In *ERE*, vol. 12, 448–457.

Barrett, Samuel Alfred. 1917. *Ceremonies of the Pomo Indians*. Berkeley: University of California Press.

——. 1918. The Wintun Hesi Ceremony. PAEUC, vol. 14.

——. 1925. *The Cayapa Indians of Ecuador*. MAI-IM, vol. 2, no. 40.

Bartels, Lambert. 1969. Birth Customs and Birth Songs of the Macha Galla. *Ethnology* (Pittsburgh) 8 (4):406–421.

Barth, A. 1921. *The Religions of India*. London: Kegan Paul, Trench, Trubner.

Barthell, Edward E., Jr. 1971. *Gods and Goddesses of Ancient Greece*. Coral Gables: University of Miami Press.

Barton, Roy Franklin. 1919. *Ifugao Law*. PAEUC 15.

——. 1946. The Religion of the Ifugaos. MAAA no. 65.

——. 1955. *The Mythology of the Ifugaos.* Philadelphia: American Folklore Society.

Basak, Radhagovinda. 1953. The Hindu Concept of the Natural World. In Morgan, 1953.

Basedow, Herbert. 1925. *The Australian Aboriginal.* Adelaide: F. W. Preece and Sons.

Basham, A. L. 1951. *History and Doctrines of the Ajivikas.* London: Luzak.

Basset, Henri. 1920. *Le Culte des Grottes au Maroc.* Alger: Ancienne Maison Bastide-Jourdan.

Basset, Rene. 1925a. Berbers and North Africa. In *ERE,* vol. 2, 506–519.

——. 1925b. Nusairis. In *ERE,* vol. 9, 417–419.

Bastide, Roger. 1960. *La Religions Africaines au Bresil.* Paris: Presses Universitaires de France.

Basu, Malay Nath. 1961. Buna Folklore from Twenty-four Parganas of West Bengal. *Folklore* (Calcutta) 12:62–65.

Batchelor, John. [ca. 1927]. *Ainu Life and Lore.* Tokyo, Kyobunkwan: Japan Advertiser Press; London: Kegan Paul, Trench, and Trubner.

——. 1894. Items of Ainu Folklore. *JAF* 7:15–44.

——. 1925. Ainus. In *ERE,* vol. 1, 239–252.

Baxter, P. T. W., and Audrey Butt. 1953. *The Azande and Related Peoples.* London: International African Institute.

Beaglehole, Ernest, and Pearl Beaglehole. 1938. *Ethnology of Pukapuka.* BPBM, no. 150.

Beals, Alan R. 1964. Conflict and Interlocal Festivals in a South Indian Region. In Harper, 1964.

Beals, Ralph Leon. 1935. Notes and Queries: Two Mountain Zapotec Tales from Oaxaca, Mexico. *JAF* 48:189–190.

——. 1946. *Cheran: A Sierra Tarascan Village.* Washington, D.C.: Smithsonian Institute.

Bean, Lowell John. 1974. *Mukat's People: The Cahuilla Indians of Southern California.* Berkeley and Los Angeles: University of California Press.

Beardsley, Charles. 1964. *Guam Past and Present.* Rutland, Vermont: Charles E. Tuttle.

Beauchamp, W. M. 1888. Onondaga Customs. *JAF* 1:195–203.

——. 1892. Iroquois Notes. *JAF* 5:223–229.

——. 1896. The New Religion of the Iroquois. *JAF* 10:169–180.

Becher, Hans. 1960. The Sura and the Pakidai, Two Yanomamo Tribes in Northwest Brazil. *Mitteilungen* (Hamburg Museum für Volkerkunde) 16:1–133.

Beckwith, Martha Warren. 1932. Kepelino's Traditions of Hawaii. BPBM, no. 95.

——. 1940. *Hawaiian Mythology.* New Haven: Yale University Press.

Beckwith, Paul. 1886. Notes on Customs of the Dakotahs. SI-AR:245–257.

Beech, Mervyn W. H. 1911. *The Suk: Their Language and Folklore.* Oxford: Clarendon Press.

Beidelman, T. O. 1963. Kaguru Omens. *AQ* 36 (2):43–59.

Beier, Ulli, ed. 1966. *The Origin of Life and Death: African Creation Myths.* London: Heinemann.

Bel, Alfred. 1938. *La Religion Musulmani en Berberie.* Paris: Librairie Orientaliste, Paul Guethner.

Bell, Sir Charles. 1931. *The Religion of Tibet.* Oxford: Clarendon Press.

Belo, Jane. 1949. *Bali: Temple Festival.* Locust Valley, New York: J. J. Augustin.

Benedict, Laura Watson. 1913. Bagobo Myths. *JAF* 26:13–63.

——. 1916. *A Study of Bagobo Ceremonial, Magic, and Myth.* New York: New York Academy of Sciences.

Bennett, Wendell C., and Robert M. Zingg. 1935. *The Tarahumara: An Indian Tribe of Northern Mexico.* Chicago: University of Chicago Press.

Bernatzik, Hugo Adolf. 1947. *Akha and Meau: Problems of Applied Ethnography in Farther India.* 2 vols. Innsbruck: Kommissionsverlag Wagner'sche Universitats—Buckdruckerei. (Human Relations Area Files AOI-39, EPf-10, AE5).

Berndt, Ronald M. 1952. *Djanggawul.* London: Routledge & Kegan Paul.

——. 1965. The Kamano, Usurufa, Jate, and Fore of the Eastern Highlands. In Lawrence and Meggett, 1965.

Berreman, Gerald D. 1963. *Hindus of the Himalayas.* Berkeley and Los Angeles: University of California Press.

Bertrand, Alexandre. 1897. *La Religion des Gaulois*. Paris: Ernest Leroux.

Best, Elsdon. 1908. Te Rehu-o-Tainu: The Evolution of a Maori Atua. *PSJ* 4(6):41–66.

——. 1892. Pre-historic Civilization in the Philippines, the Tagalo-Bisaya Tribes, II. *PSJ* 1:195–201.

——. 1924. *The Maori*. Wellington, N. Z.: Harry H. Tombs.

Bethe, E. 1925. Agraulids. In *ERE*, vol. 1, 225–226.

Bezzenberger, A. 1925. Lithuanians and Letts. In *ERE*, vol. 8, 113–116.

Bhattacharji, Sukumari. 1970. *The Indian Theogony*. Cambridge: Cambridge University Press.

Bhattacharyya, Sivaprasad. 1953. Religious Practices of the Hindus. In Morgan, 1953, 154–205.

Bibby, Geoffrey. 1969. *Looking for Dilmun*. New York: Knopf.

Bilby, Julian W. 1923. *Among Unknown Eskimos*. London: Seeley, Service.

Bird, Junius. 1946a. The Alacaluf. *HSAI* 1 (1):53–79.

——. 1946b. The Archaeology of Patagonia. *HSAI* 1 (2):17–24.

Birket-Smith, Kaj. 1953. *The Chugach Eskimo*. Copenhagen: Nationalmuseets Publikationsfond.

——. 1956. *An Ethnological Sketch of Rennell Island*. Copenhagen: Munksgaard.

Biscoe, C. E. Tyndale. 1922. *Kashmir in Sunlight and Shade*. London: Seeley, Service.

Biswas, P. D. 1956. *Santals of the Santal Parganas*. Delhi: Bharatiya Adimjati Sevak Sangh.

Bjorklund, Karna L. 1969. *The Indians of Northeastern America*. New York: Dodd, Mead.

Blackburn, Thomas C., ed. 1975. *December's Child: Chumash Oral Narratives,* collected by J. P. Harrington. Berkeley and Los Angeles: University of California Press.

Blair, Emma. 1912. *Indian Tribes of the Upper Mississippi Valley and Great Lakes Region*. Vol. 2. Cleveland: Arthur H. Clark.

Bleek, D. F. 1928. *The Naron: A Bushman Tribe of the Kalahari*. Cambridge: Cambridge University Press.

——. 1931. The Hadzapi or Watindega of Tanganyika Territory. *Africa* 4 (3):273–286.

Blom, Frans, and Oliver La Farge. 1927. *Tribes and Temples: A Record of the Expedition to Middle American Conducted by the Tulane University of Louisiana in 1925*. Vol. 2. New Orleans: Tulane University.

Blumenthal, J. V. 1973. The Karimojong Cluster—Uganda. In *Peoples of the Earth,* ed. E. E. Evans-Pritchard, vol. 2. Danbury, Conn: Danbury Press.

Boas, Franz. 1884–1885. The Cenetral Eskimo. ARBAE 6:409–659.

——. 1898. *Mythology of the Bella Coola Indians*. MAMNH 2, part 2.

——. 1901. The Eskimo of Baffin Land and Hudson Bay. AMNH-B 15.

——. 1923. *Notes on the Tillamook*. PAEUC, vol. 20:3–16.

——. 1935. *Kwakiutl Culture as Reflected in Mythology*. MAFS 2.

——. 1966. *Kwakiutl Ethnography*. Chicago: University of Chicago Press.

Bodde, Derk. 1961. Myths of Ancient China. In Kramer, 1961a, 367–408.

Bogoras, Waldemar. 1901. The Chukchi of North Eastern Asia. *AA* 3 (1):80–108.

——. 1928. Chukchee Tales. *JAF* 41:297–452.

——. 1904–1909. The Chukchee. MAMNH 11, parts 2-3. Vol. 7 of *Jesup North Pacific Expedition*.

Bollig, Laurentius. 1927. *The Inhabitants of the Truk Islands: Religion, Life, and a Short Grammar of a Micronesian People*. Münster in Westphalia: Aschendorffsche Verlagsbuchhandlung.

Boscana, Father Geronimo. 1933. *Chinigchinich*. Alfred Robinson, trans. Santa Ana, California: Fine Arts Press.

vanden Bosch, G. 1928. Quelques Notes sur le Nom et la Notion de l'Etre Supreme et d'un Dieuvengeur chez le Balendu. *Africa* 23 (5-6):987–999.

Bosi, Roberto. 1960. *The Lapps*. London: Thames and Hudson.

Bourke, John G. 1887–1888. The Medicine-men of the Apache. ARBAE 9:451–603.

——. 1889. Cosmogony and Theogony of the Mojave Indians. *JAF* 2:169–189.

——. 1890. Notes on Apache Mythology. *JAF* 3:209–212.

Boyd, Maurice. 1969. *Tarascan Myths and Legends*. Fort Worth: Texas Christian University Press.

Brackett, Albert G. 1879. The Shoshonis, or Snake Indians, Their Religion, Superstitions, and Manners. SI-AR:328–334.

Bradley, Diana. 1956. Notes and Observations from Rennell and Bellona Islands, British Solomon Islands. *PSJ* 65:332–341.

Branston, Brian. 1955. *Gods of the North*. London: Thames and Hudson.

——. 1957. *The Lost Gods of England*. London: Thames and Hudson.

Brauns, Claus-Dieter. 1973. The Peaceful Mrus of Bangladesh. *NG* 143:267–286.

Bray, Frank Chapin. 1935. *The World of Myths: A Dictionary of Mythology*. New York: Thomas J. Crowell.

Brett, Rev. William Henry. 1868. *The Indian Tribes of Guiana*. London: Bell and Daldy.

——. 1880. *Legends and Myths of the Aboriginal Indians of British Guiana*. London: William Wells Gardner.

de Brettes, Joseph. 1903. The Arhaco-Cagaba Indians: Replies to the Sociological and Ethnographic Questionnaire of the Societe d'Anthropologie. *Bulletin et Memoires* (Societe d'Anthropologie de Paris) Ser. 5 (4):318–357.

Briggs, George Weston. 1920. *The Chamars*. London: Oxford University Press.

——. 1953. *The Doms and their Near Relations*. Mysore, India: Wesley Press and Publishing House.

Brinton, Daniel G. 1868. *Myths of the New World*. New York: Leypoldt and Holt.

——. 1882. *American Hero Myths*. Philadelphia: H. C. Watts.

——. 1897. *Religions of Primitive Peoples*. New York: G. P. Putnam's Sons.

Brown, Paula. 1955. The Igbira. In Forde, 1955, 55–74.

Brown, Norman O., translator. *See* Hesiod.

Brown, W. Norman. 1961. Mythology of India. In Kramer, 1961a, 277–330.

Brumgardt, John R., and Larry L. Bowles. 1981. *Peoples of the Magic Waters*. Palm Springs, California: ETC Publications.

Buck, Peter H. 1932a. *Ethnology of Manihiki and Rakahanga*. BPBM, no. 99.

——. 1932b. *Ethnology of Tongareva*. BPBM, no. 92.

——. 1934. *Mangaian Society*. BPBM, no. 122.

——. 1938a. *Ethnology of Magareva*. BPBM, no. 157.

——. 1938b.(Te Rangi Hiroa) *Vikings of the Sunrise*. Philadelphia: J. B. Lippincott.

Budge, E. A. Wallis. 1967. *The Egyptian Book of the Dead: Papyrus of Ani*. New York: Dover.

——. 1969. *The Gods of the Egyptians*. 2 vols. New York: Dover.

——. 1973. *Osiris*. 2 vols. New York: Dover.

Buechler, Hans C., and Judith-Maria Buechler. 1971. *The Bolivian Aymara*. New York: Holt, Rinehart, and Winston.

Bulfinch, Thomas. 1898. *The Age of Fable*. Philadelphia: David McKay.

Bullock, Charles. 1950. *The Mashona and the Matabele*. Capetown and Johannesburg: Juta.

Bulmer, R. N. H. 1965. The Kyaka of the Western Highlands. In Lawrence and Meggett, 1965.

Bunce, William K. 1955. *Religions in Japan*. Rutland, Vermont: Charles E. Tuttle.

Bundy, Richard C. 1919. Folktales from Liberia. *JAF* 32:406–427.

Bunzel, Ruth L. 1929–1930. Introduction to Zuni Ceremonialism. ARBAE 45:467–1086.

Burgess, John Stewart. 1929. *The Guilds of Peking*. New York: Columbia University Press.

Burland, C. A. 1967. *The Gods of Mexico*. New York: G. P. Putnam's Sons.

Burland, Cottie. 1965. *North American Indian Mythology*. London: Paul Hamlyn.

Burns, I. F. 1925. Charities. In *ERE,* vol. 3, 372–373.

Burrows, Carin. 1972. The Fierce and Erotic Gods of Buddhism. *AMNH-Mag.* 81 (4):26–37.

Burrows, Edwin G. 1936. *Ethnology of Futuna*. BPBM, no. 138.

——. 1937. *Ethnology of Uvea (Wallis Island)*. BPBM, no. 145.

——. 1938. Western Polynesia: A Study in Cultural Differentiation. *ES* 7:1–192.

——. 1949. *The People of Ifalik: A Little-Disturbed Atoll Culture.* Unpublished manuscript. Washington, D.C.: Coordinated Investigation of Micronesian Anthropology, Pacific Science Board, National Research Council.

Bushnell, David. I. Jr. 1909. The Choctaw of Bayou Lancomb St. Tamany Parish Louisiana. BBAE 48.

——. 1910. Myths of the Louisiana Choctaw. *AA* 12 (4):526–535.

Busia, K. A. 1954. The Ashanti of the Gold Coast. In Forde, 1954, 199–209.

Butt, Audrey. 1952. *The Nilotes of the Anglo-Egyptian Sudan and Uganda, East Central Africa.* Part 4, *Ethnographic Survey of Africa,* ed. Daryll Forde. London: Oxford University Press.

Cabaton, Antoine. 1925a. Annam (Popular Religion). In *ERE,* vol. 1, 537–544.

——. 1925b. Chams. In *ERE,* vol. 3, 340–351.

——. 1925c. Indo-China (Savage Races). In *ERE,* vol. 7, 225–232.

Callaway, Rev. Henry. [1876]. *On the Religious Sentiment amongst the Tribes of South Africa.* n. p.

Cammann, S. V. R. 1937. The Four Great Kings of Heaven. *JWCBRS* 9.

Campbell, Joseph. 1962. *The Masks of God: Oriental Mythology.* New York: Viking.

——. 1964. *The Masks of God: Occidental Mythology.* New York: Viking.

——. 1968. *The Hero with a Thousand Faces.* Bollingen Series no. 17. Princeton: Princeton University Press.

——. 1974. *The Masks of God: Primitive Mythology.* New York: Viking.

Campbell, W. 1925. Formosa. In *ERE,* vol. 6, 83–87.

Capell, A. 1939. Mythology in Northern Kimberley, North-West Australia. *Oceania* 9:382–404.

Caplan, Lionel. 1974. A Himalayan People: Limbus in Nepal. In Maloney, 1974.

Capron, Jean. 1962. Univers Religieux et Cohesion Interne dans les Communautes Villageoises Bwa Traditionelles. *Africa,* 32 (2):132–171.

Carnoy, Albert J. 1917. *Iranian.* Vol. 6, Mythology of All Races. Boston: Marshall Jones.

Carter, Jesse Benedict. 1925. Personification (Roman). In *ERE,* vol. 9, 794–800.

Casalis, Rev. E. 1861. *The Basutos.* London: James Nesbit.

Casanowicz, I. M. 1924. Shamanism of the Natives of Siberia. SI-AR:415–434.

——. 1926. The Dragon God (Dai-Ja) in Idzumo, Japan. PUSNM 67 (2587):Art. 15.

Caso, Alfonso. [1942]. *Culturas Mixteca y Zapoteca.* Ediciones Encuadernables. Mexico, D. F.: El National Biblioteca del Maestro.

——. 1958. *The Aztecs, People of the Sun.* Norman: University of Oklahoma Press.

Casson, Lionel. 1965. *Ancient Egypt.* New York: Time, Inc.

Caitlin, George. 1967. *O-kee-pa, a Religious Ceremony and Other Customs of the Mandan,* Centennial ed. New Haven: Yale University Press.

Ceram, C. W. 1966. *Hands on the Past.* New York: Knopf.

——. 1968. *Gods, Graves, and Scholars.* New York: Knopf.

Cerulli, Ernesta. 1956. Peoples of South-West Ethiopia and its Borderland. London: International African Institute.

Chadwick, John. 1976. *The Mycenaean World.* Cambridge: Cambridge University Press.

Chadwick, Nora K. 1930. Notes on Polynesian Mythology. *JRAI* 60:425–446.

——. 1936. Shamanism among the Tatars of Central Asia. *JRAI* 66:75–112.

Chagnon, Napoleon A. 1968. *Yanomamo.* New York: Holt, Rinehart, Winston.

Chamberlain, Alexander F. 1892. Review of *The Klamath Indians of Southwestern Oregon* by Albert Samuel Gatschet. *JAF* 5:252–255.

——. 1900. Biographical Notes. *JAF* 13:304–306.

——. 1905. Mythology of the Indian Stocks North of Mexico. *JAF* 18:111–122.

——. 1925a. Disease and Medicine (North American). In *ERE,* vol. 4, 731.

——. 1925b. Haida. In *ERE,* vol. 4, 469–474.

Chamberlain, Basil Hall. 1887. *The Language, Mythology, and geographical Nomenclature of Japan Viewed in the Light of Aino Studies*. Tokyo: Imperial University.

Chapekar, L. N. 1960. *Thakurs of the Sahyadri*. Bombay and New York: Indian Branch, Oxford University Press.

Chatterjee, Satis Chandra. 1953. Hindu Religious Thought. In Morgan, 1953.

Chavannes, Edouard. 1910. *Le T'ai Chan: essai de monographie d'un culte chinois*. Paris: E. Leroux.

Childs, Gladwyn Murray. 1949. *Umbundu Kinship and Character*. London and New York: International African Institute and Witwatersrand University Press.

Choudhury, P. C. Roy. 1965. *Temples and Legends of Bihar*. Chauputty, Bombay: Bharatiya Vidya Bhavan.

Chowdhury, J. N. 1971. *A Comparative Study of Adi Religion*. Shillong: North-East Frontier Agency.

Christian, F. W. 1890. *The Carolina Islands*. London: Methuen.

——. 1895. Notes on the Marquesans. *PSJ* 4:187–202.

——. 1897. Notes from the Caroline Islands. *PSJ* 6: 187–200.

Cipriani, Lidio. 1966. *The Andaman Islanders*. London: Weidenfeld and Nicolson.

de Civrieux, Marc. 1980. *Watunna, an Orinoco Creation Cycle*, trans. by David M. Guss. San Francisco: North Point Press.

Clark, Charles Allen. 1932. *Religions of Old Korea*. New York: Fleming H. Revell.

Clark, Ella E. 1966. *Indian Legends from the Northern Rockies*. Norman: University of Oklahoma Press.

Clarke, Edith. 1930. The Sociological Significance of Ancestor Worship in Ashanti. *Africa* 3:431–471.

Clarke, J. D. 1944. Three Yoruba Fertility Ceremonies. *JRAI* 74:19–95.

Clarke, Samuel R. 1911. *Among the Tribes in South-West China*. London: Morgan & Scott.

Clebert, Jean-Paul. 1967. *The Gypsies*. Baltimore: Penguin.

Clerk, Christian. 1982. Polynesia and Micronesia. In *Legends of the World*, ed. Richard Cavendish, 370–378. New York: Schocken.

Clifford, Miles. 1944. Notes on the Bassa-Komo Tribes in the Igala Division. *Man* 44:107–116.

Cline, Howard. 1944. Lore and Deities of the Lacandon Indians, Chiapas, Mexico. *JAF* 57:107–115.

Codrington, Rev. Robert Henry. 1881. Religious Beliefs and Practices in Melanesia. *JRAI* 10:261–316.

Cohane, John Philip. 1969. *The Key*. New York: Crown.

Cole, Fay-Cooper. 1922. *The Tinguian*. FMNH-AS, vol. 14, no. 2.

——. 1945. *Peoples of Malaysia*. New York: Van Nostrand.

Coleman, Sister Bernard. 1937. The Religion of the Ojibwa of Northern Minnesota. *PM* 10 (3-4):33–57.

Coleman, Charles. 1832. *Mythology of the Hindus*. London: Parbury, Allen.

Collinder, Bjorn. 1949. *The Lapps*. New York: American Scandinavian Foundation, Princeton University Press.

Collocott, E. E. V. 1921. Notes on Tongan Religion. *PSJ* 30:152–163, 227–240.

Colson, E. 1948. Rain-Shrines of the Plateau Tonga of Northern Rhodesia. *Africa* 18:272–283.

Conference on Theravada Buddhism. (1962, University of Chicago). *Anthropological Studies in Theravada Buddhism*, 1966. Manning Nash ed. Cultural Report Series, no. 13, Southeast Asia Studies. New Haven: Yale University.

Connelley, William E. 1899. Notes on the Folklore of the Wyandots. *JAF* 12:116–125.

Conway, R. S. 1925. Italy (Ancient). In *ERE* vol. 7, 457–461.

Conzemius, Edward. 1932. *Ethnographical Survey of the Moskito and Sumu Indians of Honduras and Nicaragua*. Washington, D.C.: Smithsonian Institute.

Cook, Alice Carter. 1900. The Aborigines of the Canary Islands. *AA* 2 (3):451–493.

Cook, S. A. 1925. Edomites. In *ERE*, vol. 5, 162–166.

Cook, Stanley A. 1930. *The Religion of Ancient Palestine in the Light of Archaeology*. London: Oxford University Press.

Cooke, G. A. 1925. Nabataeans. In *ERE*, vol. 9, 121–122.

Coolidge, Dana, and Mary Roberts Coolidge. 1939. *The Last of the Seris.* New York: Dutton.

Coon, Carlton S. 1971. *The Hunting Peoples.* Boston: Little, Brown.

Cooper, John M. 1917. Analytical and Critical Bibliography of the Tribes of Tierra del Fuego and Adjacent Territory. BBAE 63.

———. 1934. The Northern Algonquian Supreme Being. *AQ.*

———. 1946a. The Southern Hunters. *HSAI* 1:13–16.

———. 1946b. The Chono. *HSAI* 1:46–53.

———. 1946c. The Yahgan. *HSAI* 1:81–106.

———. 1946d. The Ona. *HSAI* 1:107–125.

———. 1946e. The Patagonian and Pampean Hunters. *HSAI* 1:127–168.

———. 1946f. The Araucians. *HSAI* 2:687–760.

———. 1957. The Gros Ventres of Montana: Part II: Religion and Ritual. *AQ* 16.

da Costa Eduardo, Octavio. 1948. *The Negro in Northern Brazil.* New York: J. J. Augustin.

Cotenau, Dr. G. 1948. *La Civilisation des Hittites.* Paris: Payot.

Courlander, Harold. 1966. *Religion and Politics in Haiti.* Washington, D.C.: Institute for Cross-Cultural Research.

———. 1973. *Tales of Yoruba Gods and Heroes.* New York: Crown.

Covarrubias, Miguel. 1937. *Island of Bali.* New York: Knopf.

Cox, George W. 1870. *The Mythology of the Aryan Nations.* 2 vols. London: Longmans, Green.

Cox, W. H. 1913. New Ireland (New Mecklenburg) Myths. *Man* 13:195199.

Craine, Eugene R., and Reginald C. Reindorp. 1970. *The Chronicles of Michoacan.* Norman: University of Oklahoma Press.

Crawford, O. G. S. 1957. *The Eye Goddess.* London: Phoenix House.

Crawley, A. E. 1925a. Dew. In *ERE,* vol. 4, 698–701.

———. 1925b. Hearth, Hearth Gods. In *ERE,* vol. 6, 559–562.

———. 1925c. Oath (Introductory and Primitive. In *ERE,* vol. 9, 430–434.

Crooke, W. 1894. *An Introduction to the Popular Religion and Folklore of Northern India.* Allahabad: Government Press, Northwestern Provinces and Oudh.

———. 1925a. India. In *ERE,* vol. 12, 716–719.

———. 1925b. Abor, Abor-Miri. In *ERE,* vol. 1, 33.

———. 1925c. Aheria. In *ERE,* vol. 1, 231.

———. 1925d. Ahir. In *ERE,* vol. 1, 232–234.

———. 1925e. Arakh. In *ERE,* vol. 1, 673.

———. 1925f. Bengal. In *ERE,* vol. 2, 479–500.

———. 1925g. Demons and Spirits (Indian). In *ERE,* vol. 4, 606.

———. 1925h. Daphla. In *ERE,* vol. 4, 399.

———. 1925i. Dosadh, Dusadh. In *ERE,* vol. 4, 852–853.

———. 1925j. Dom. In *ERE,* vol. 4, 841.

———. 1925k. Dravidians (North India). In *ERE,* vol. 5, 1–21.

———. 1925l. Kachhi. In *ERE,* vol. 7, 634.

———. 1925m. Kahar. In *ERE,* vol. 7, 636–637.

———. 1925n. Kalwar. In *ERE,* vol. 7, 643–644.

———. 1925o. Kandh, Kondh. In *ERE,* vol. 7, 648–651.

———. 1925p. Mal, Male, Mal Paharia. In *ERE,* vol. 8, 344–345.

———. 1925q. Mishmis. In *ERE,* vol. 8, 697–698.

———. 1925r. Mundas. In *ERE,* vol. 9, 1–3.

———. 1925s. Serpent-Worship (Indian). In *ERE,* vol. 11, 411–419.

———. 1925t. Stones (Indian). In *ERE,* vol. 11, 871–876.

Cunningham, Clarke E. 1972. Order in the Antoni House. In Lessa and Vogt, 1972.

Cunningham, J. F. 1905. *Uganda and Its People.* London: Hutchinson.

Curtin, Jeremiah. 1903. *Creation Myths of Primitive America.* Boston: Little, Brown.

———. 1909. *A Journey in Southern Siberia.* Boston: Little, Brown.

Cushing, Frank Hamilton. 1881–1882. Zuni Fetiches. ARBAE 2.

———. 1882. The Nation of the Willows. *Atlantic Monthly* 50:362–374, 541–559.

———. 1891–1892. Outlines of Zuni Creation Myths. ARBAE 13:325–447.

——. 1892. A Zuni Folk-Tale of the Underworld. *JAF* 5:49–56.

Czaplicka, M. A. 1925a. Tungus. In *ERE,* vol. 12, 473–476.

——. 1925b. Turks. In *ERE,* vol. 12, 476–483.

——. 1925c. Yakut. In *ERE,* vol. 12, 826–829.

——. 1925d. Ostyaks. In *ERE,* vol. 9, 575–581.

——. 1925e. Samoyed. In *ERE,* vol. 11, 172–177.

——. 1925f. Slavs. In *ERE,* vol. 11, 587–595.

——. 1969. *Aboriginal Siberia: A Study in Anthropology.* Oxford: Clarendon Press.

Dahmen, Rev. F. 1908. The Paliyans, a Hill Tribe of the Palni Hills (South India). *Africa* 3 (1):19–31.

——. 1910. The Kunnuvans or Mannadis, a Hill Tribe of the Palnis, South India. *Africa* 5 (2):3.

Dallas, Douglas. 1931. The Sacred Tree of Ol Donyesha. *Man* 31:39–41.

Daneel, M. L. 1970. *The God of the Matopo Hills.* The Hague, Paris: Mouton.

Danielou, Alain. 1964. *Hindu Polytheism.* London: Routledge & Kegan Paul.

Danquah, J. B. 1944. *The Akan Doctrine of God.* London: Lutterworth Press.

——. 1952. The Culture of Akan. *Africa* 22 (4):360–366.

Davenport, William H. 1953. Marshallese Folklore Types. *JAF* 66:219–237.

Davidson, Basil. 1966. *African Kingdoms.* New York: Time, Inc.

——. 1969. *The African Genius.* Boston and Toronto: Atlantic Monthly Press.

Davidson, H. R. Ellis. 1964. *Gods and Myths of Northern Europe.* Harmondsworth: Penguin.

Davidson, Rev. J. 1950. The Doctrine of God in the Life of the Ngombe, Belgian Congo. In Smith, 1950:162–179.

Day, Clarence Burton. 1940. *Chinese Peasant Cults, Being a Study of Chinese Paper Gods.* Shanghai: Kelly and Walsh.

Deans, James. 1891. A Creation Myth of the Tsimshians of Northwest British Columbia. *JAF* 4:34.

De Crespigny, Lieut. 1975. On the Milanows of Borneo. *JRAI* 5:34–37.

De Groot, J. J. M. 1925. Confucian Religion. In *ERE,* vol. 4, 12–15.

Delcourt, Marie. 1961. *Hermaphrodite: Myths and Rites of the Bisexual Figure in Classical Mythology,* trans. Jennifer Nicholson. London: Studio Books.

Delobsom, A. A. Dim. 1932. *The Empire of the Mogho Naba: Customs of the Mossi of the Upper Volta.* Paris: Domat Montchristian.

Del Re, Arundel. [1951]. *Creation Myths of the Formosan Natives.* Tokyo: Hokuseido Press.

Denig, Edwin T. 1928–1929. Indian Tribes of the Upper Missouri. BBAE 46:375–626.

Deniker, J. 1925. Patagonians. In *ERE,* vol. 9, 667–670.

De Raedt, Jules. 1964. *Religious Representations in Northern Luzon.* Chicago: University of Chicago Philippine Studies Program.

Deren, Maya. 1953. *Divine Horsemen: The Living Gods of Haiti.* London: Thames & Hudson.

Deydier, Henri. 1952. *Introduction to the Knowledge of Laos.* Saigon: Imprimerie Francaise d'Outre-Mer.

Diamond, Norma. 1969. *K'un Shen, a Taiwan Village.* New York: Holt, Rhinehart, and Winston.

Dieterlen, Germaine. 1957. The Mande Creation Myth. *Africa* 27:126–135.

Dioszegi, V. 1968. *Popular Beliefs and Folklore Tradition in Siberia.* Bloomington: Indiana University Press.

Dixon, Roland B. 1905. Mythology of the Shasta-Achomawi. *AA* 7 (4):607–612.

——. 1908. Achomawi and Atsugewi Tales. *JAF* 21:159–177.

——. 1910. Shasta Myths. *JAF* 23:8–37.

——. 1912. *Maidu Texts.* Publications of the American Ethnological Society. Leyden: Late E. J. Brill.

Doke, Clement M. 1931. *The Lambas of Northern Rhodesia.* London: George Harrap.

Donnelly, Ignatius. 1949. *Atlantis: The Antediluvian World.* New York: Harper and Brothers.

Donner, Kai. 1926. *Among the Samoyed in Siberia,* ed. and trans. W. H. v.d. Mulbe. Stuttgart: Strecker und Schröder.

Donohugh, Agnes C. L., and Priscilla Berry. 1932. A Luba Tribe in Katanga, Customs and Folklore. *Africa* 5 (2):176–183.

Dorsey, George A. 1904a. *The Mythology of the Witchita*. Washington, D.C.: Carnagie Institute of Washington.

———. 1904b. *Traditions of the Skidi Pawnee*. Boston: Houghton, Mifflin.

———. 1904c. Witchita Tales III. *JAF* 17:153–160.

———. 1906. *The Pawnee: Mythology Part I*. Washington, D.C.: Carnagie Institute of Washington.

Dorsey, F. Owen. 1889a. Winnebago Folklore Notes. *JAF* 2:140.

———. 1889b. Teton Folk-lore Notes. *JAF* 2:133–139.

———. 1892. Nanibozhu in Siouan Mythology. *JAF* 5:293–304.

Dottin, Georges. 1925. War, War-Gods (Celtic). In *ERE*, vol. 12, 691–692.

Doty, William G. 1977. Faces of Death. *Parabola* 2 (1):60–65.

Douglas, Mary. 1954. The Lele of Kasai. In Forde, 1954. 1–26.

Downes, R. M. 1971. *Tiv Religion*. Ibadan: Ibadan University Press.

Downes, T. T. 1920. The Lament of Huaru of Whanganui. *PSJ* 29:29–32.

Downs, Richard Erskine. 1920. *The Religion of the Bare' e-Speaking Toradja of Central Celebes*. 'S-Gravenhage: Excelsior.

Dowson, John. 1961. *A Classical Dictionary of Hindu Mythology and Religion, Geography, History, and Literature*. London: Routledge and Kegan Paul.

Drahomonov (Dragomonov), M. P. 1961. *Notes on the Slavic Religio-Ethical Legends: The Dualistic Creation of the World*. Bloomington: Indiana University Press.

Drake, John. 1925. Kurkus. In *ERE*, vol. 7, 760–761.

Dresden, M. J. 1961. Mythology of Ancient Iran. In Kramer, 1961a, 331–366.

Drew, Frederic. 1875. *The Jummoo and Kashmir Territories: A Geographical Account*. London: E. Stanford.

Driberg, J. H. 1923. *The Lango: A Nilotic Tribe of Uganda*. London: Unwin.

Driver, G. R. 1956. *Canaanite Myths and Legends*. Edinburgh: T. and T. Clark.

Driver, Harold E. 1936. *Wappo Ethnography*. PAEUC, vol. 36, no. 3.

Drucker, Philip. 1937. *The Tolowa and their Southwest Oregon Kin*. PAEUC, vol. 36, no. 4.

———. 1951. The Northern and Central Nootkan Tribes. BBAE 144.

Du Bois, Constance Goddard. 1901. Mythology of the Dieguenos. *JAF* 14:181–185.

———. 1904. Mythology of the Mission Indians. *JAF* 17:185–188.

———. 1905. Religious Ceremonies and Myths of the Mission Indians. *AA* 7 (4):620–629.

———. 1906. Mythology of the Mission Indians. *JAF* 19:145–164.

———. 1908a. Ceremonies and Traditions of the Diegueno Indians. *JAF* 21:228–236.

———. 1908b. *The Religion of the Luiseno Indians of Southern California*. PAEUC, vol. 8.

Du Bois, Cora Alice. 1935. *Wintu Ethnography*. PAEUC, vol. 36.

Dubois, Abbe J. A. 1906. *Hindu Manners, Customs, and Ceremonies*, trans. Henry Beauchamp. Oxford: Clarendon Press.

Dubose, Hampdon C. 1886. *The Dragon: Image and Demon*. London: Partridge.

Duff, Wilson. 1952. The Upper Stalo Indians of the Fraser Valley. BCPM, vol. 1.

Dumezil, Georges. 1966. *Archaic Roman Religion*, trans. Philip Krapp. Chicago: University of Chicago Press.

———. 1970. *The Destiny of the Warrior*, trans. Alf Hiltebeitel. Chicago: University of Chicago Press.

Dundas, Charles. 1968. *Kilimanjaro and Its People*. London: Frank Cass.

Duprez, A. 1970. *Jesus et les dieux guerisseus*. Paris: J. Gabalda.

Duran, Fray Diego. 1971. *Book of the Gods and Rites and the Ancient Calendar*, trans. and ed. Fernando Horcasitas and Doris Heyden. Norman: University of Oklahoma Press.

Durham, Mary Edith. 1928. *Some Tribal Origins, laws, and Customs of the Balkans*. London: George Allen and Unwin.

Dutta, Parul. 1959. *The Tangsas of the Namchik and Tirap Valleys*. Shillong: North-east Frontier Agency.

Dymond, Rev. G. W. 1950. The Idea of God in Ovambaland, Southwest Africa. In Smith, 1950:135–155.

East, Rupert, trans. and ed. 1939. *Akiga's Story: The Tiv tribe as seen by One of its Members*. London: Oxford University Press.

Eastlake, F. Warrington. 1883. Equine Deities. *TASJ* 11:260–285.

Eastman, Mary Henderson. 1962. *Dahcotah: or, Life and Legends of the Sioux around Fort Snelling, Minneapolis, Minnesota*. New York: Ross and Haines. (Work originally published 1849)

Edkins, Rev. Joseph. 1878. *Religion in China*. Boston: James R. Osgood.

——. 1880. *Chinese Buddhism*. Boston: Houghton, Osgood.

Edmunds, R. David. 1980. *The Potawatomies, Keepers of the Fire*. Norman: University of Oklahoma Press.

Ells, Rev. Myron. 1886–1887. The Twana, Chemakum, and Klallam Indians of Washington Territory. SI-AR:605–681.

Ehrenfels, U. W. 1952. *Kadar of Cochin*. Madras: University of Madras.

Eliade, Mircea. 1967. *Gods, Goddesses, and Myths of Creation*. New York: Harper and Row.

——. 1973. *Australian Religions*. Ithaca: Cornell University Press.

——. 1976. *Myths, Rites, and Symbols*. 2 vols. ed. Wendell C. Beane and William G. Doty. New York: Harper Colophon.

——. 1958. *Patterns in Comparative Religion*, trans. Rosemary Sheed. New York: Meridan. (Translation of *Trait d'histoire des religions*)

——. 1950. Shamanism. In Ferm, 1950:297–308.

——. 1964. *Shamanism*. Bollingen Series no. 76. Princeton: Princeton University Press.

——. 1959. *Traite d'histoire des religions*. Paris: Payot.

——. 1979. *The Two and the One*, trans. J. M. Cohen. Chicago: Chicago University Press.

Eliot, Sr. Charles. 1935. *Japanese Buddhism*. London: Routledge and Kegan Paul.

Eliseev, Serge. 1963. The Mythology of Japan. In Hackin, et al., 1963.

Ellis, A. B. 1887. *The Tshi-Speaking Peoples of the Gold Coast of West Africa*. London: Chapman and Hall.

——. 1890. *The Ewe-Speaking Peoples of the Slave Coast of West Africa*. London: Chapman and Hall.

Ellis, George W. 1914. *Negro Culture in West Africa*. New York: Neale.

Ellis, William. 1853. *Polynesian Researches*. Vol. 1. London: Henry G. Bohn.

Elmberg, John-Erik. 1955. Field Notes on the Mejbrat People, Western New Guinea. *Ethnos* 20 (1):3–102.

Elmendorf, W. W. 1960. *The Structure of Twana Culture*. Pullman, Washington: Washington State University.

Elmore, Wilber Theodore. 1915. *Dravidian Gods in Modern Hinduism*. Lincoln: University of Nebraska Press.

Elwin, Verrier. 1939. *The Baiga*. London: John Murray.

——. 1942. *The Agaria*. London: Oxford University Press.

——. 1943. Folklore of the Bastar Clan-Gods. *Man* 43:97–104.

——. 1949. *Myths of Middle India*. Madras: Geoffrey Cumberlege, Oxford University Press.

——. 1954. *Tribal Myths of Orissa*. Oxford: Oxford University Press.

——. 1969. *The Nagas in the Nineteenth Century*. Oxford: Oxford University Press.

Emerson, Ellen Russell. 1884. *Indian Myths*. Boston: James R. Osgood.

——. 1894. The Book of the Dead and Rain Ceremonials. *AA* 7 (3):233–259.

Emerson, J. S. 1968. The Lesser Hawaiian Gods. In Morrill, 1968.

——. 1967. The Lesser Hawaiian Gods. *The (San Francisco) Revue* 1 (December):37–60.

Emerson, Nathaniel B. 1916–1917. Unwritten Literature of Hawaii. ARBAE 38.

Emmons, George Thornton. 1907. The Chilkat Blanket. MAMNH 3, part 4, 329–404.

Emory, Kenneth P. 1924. *The Island of Lanai*. BPBM no. 135.

——. 1965. *Kapingamarangi: Social and Religious Life of a Polynesian Atoll*. BPBM no. 228.

Endle, Rev. Sidney. 1911. *The Kacharis*. London: MacMillan.

Erdland, August. 1914. *The Marshall Islanders: Life and Customs, Thought and Religion of a South Seas People*. Munster i.w.: Aschendorff.

Er-Wei, J. Tu. 1959. A Contribution to the Mythology of the Tsou, Formosa. *Anthropos* 54 (3-4):536–541.

Evans, Rev. H. St. John T. 1950. The Akan Doctrine of God. In Smith, 1950:241–259.

Evans, Ivor H. N. 1923. *Studies in Religion, Folklore, and Custom in British North Borneo and the Malay Peninsula*. Cambridge: Cambridge University Press.

——. 1937. *The Negritos of Malaya*. Cambridge: Cambridge University Press.

Evans-Pritchard, Edward Evan. 1932. Heredity and Gestation, as the Azande see Them. *Sociologus* 3:400–414.

——. 1937. *Witchcraft, Oracles, and Magic among the Azande*. Oxford: Clarendon Press.

——. 1938. A Note on Rain-Makers among the Moro. *Man* 38:53–56.

——. 1953. The Nuer Conception of Spirit in its Relation to Social Order. *AA* 55 (2):201–214.

——. 1956. *Nuer Religion*. Oxford: Clarendon Press.

Evans-Wentz, W. Y. 1960. *The Tibetan Book of the Dead: or, the After-Death Experiences on the Bardo Plane, According to Lama Kazi Dawa-Samdup's English Rendering*. Oxford: Oxford University Press.

Ezeayna, S. N. 1963. The Place of the Supreme God in the Traditional Religion of the Igbo. *West African Religion* 1.

Fahd, Toufic. 1968. *Le Pantheon de L'Arabie Centrale a la Vielle de L'Hegire*. Paris: Librairie Orientaliste, Paul Guethner.

Fairbanks, Arthur. 1907. *The Mythology of Greece and Rome*. New York: D. Appleton.

Fallaize, E. N. 1925. Sun, Moon, and Stars (Primitive). In *ERE*, vol. 12, 62–65.

Farabee, William Curtis. 1918. *The Central Arawaks*. APUPM, vol. 9.

——. 1922. *Indian Tribes of Eastern Peru*. PMAE, vol. 10.

Faron, Louis. 1968. *The Mapuche Indians of Chile*. San Francisco: Holt, Rhinehart.

Farrand, Livingston. 1901. Notes on the Alesa Indians of Oregon. *AA* 3 (2):239–247.

——. 1915. Shasta and Athapascan Myths from Oregon. *JAF* 28:207–242.

Feit, Harvey A. 1973. Twilight of the Cree Hunting Nation. *AMNH-Mag* 82 (7):48–57.

Feldman, Susan. 1963. *African Myths and Tales*. New York: Dell.

Ferguson, John. 1970. *The Religions of the Roman Empire*. Ithaca: Cornell University Press.

Ferguson, John C. 1937. *Chinese*. Vol. 8, *Mythology of All Races*. Boston: Marshall Jones.

Ferm, Vergilius, ed. 1950. *Ancient Religions*. New York: Philosophical Library.

Fernandez, James W. 1972. Tabernathe Iboga: Narcotic Ecstasies and the Work of the Ancestors. In Furst, 1972:237–260.

Fewkes, Jesse Walter. 1891. On Zemes from Santo Domingo. *AA* 4 (2):167–176.

——. 1893–1894. Tusayan Katcinas. ARBAE 15.

——. 1895a. Oraibi Flute Altar. *JAF* 8:265–284.

——. 1895b. Hopi Shrines near the East Mesa, Arizona. *AA* 8.

——. 1895c. A Comparison of Sia and Tusayan Snake Ceremonies. *AA* 8 (2):118–141.

——. 1896. The Miconinovi Flute Altars. *JAF* 9:241–265.

——. 1897. The Sacrificial Element in Hopi Worship. *JAF* 10:187–201.

——. 1898. The Growth of Hopi Ritual. *JAF* 11:173–194.

——. 1899. The Alosaka Cult of the Hopi Indians. *AA* 2 (1):522–544.

——. 1900. The New-Fire Ceremony at Walpi. *AA* 2 (1):80–138.

——. 1901a. The Owakulti Altar at Sichomovi Pueblo. *AA* 3 (2):211–226.

——. 1903–1904. The Aborigines of Porto Rico and Neighboring Islands. ARBAE 25:3–220.

——. 1901b. An Interpretation of Kachina Worship. JAF 14:81–94.

——. 1902. Sky-God Personations in Hopi Worship. JAF 15:14–32.

——. 1920. Fire Worship of the Hopi Indians. SI-AR:589–610.

Field, M. J. 1937. Religion and Medicine of the Ga People. London: Oxford University Press.

——. 1948. Akim-Kotoku: An Oman of the Gold Coast. Accra: The Crown Agents for the Colonies.

Finley, Lt. Col. John Park. 1913. The Subanu: Studies of a Sub-Visayan Mountain Folk of Mindanao. CIW Bull. 184.

Firth, Raymond William. 1930. A Dart Match in Tikopia. Oceania 1 (1):64–96.

——. 1939. Primitive Polynesian Economy. London: George Routledge.

——. 1967a. Tikopia Ritual and Belief. Boston: Beacon.

——. 1967b. The Work of the Gods in Tikopia. New York: Humanities Press.

Fisher, Robert L. Jr. 1970. Indo-European Elements in Baltic and Slavic Chronicles. In Puhvel, 1970:147–158.

Fiske, John. 1900. Myths and Mythmakers. Cambridge, Mass.: Riverside.

Fison, Lorimer. 1904. Tales from Old Fiji. London: Alexander Moring.

Fletcher, Alice C. 1900–1901. The Hako: A Pawnee Ceremony. ARBAE 22. part 2. 5–372.

——. 1902. Star Cult among the Pawnee. AA 4 (4):730–736.

——. 1916. Pawnee Star Lore. JAF 16:10–15.

Flores-Ochoa, Jorge A. 1979. Pastoralists of the Andes: The Alpaca Herders of Paratia, trans. Ralph Bolton. Philadelphia: ISHI.

Flornoy, Bertrand. 1958. The World of the Inca. Garden City: Doubleday.

Fock, Niels. 1963. Waiwai: Religion and Society of an Amazon Tribe. NMD 8.

Forbes, David. 1870. On the Aymara Indians of Bolivia and Peru. Journal of Ethnological Society of London, New Ser. 2:193–305.

Forbes, H. O. 1884. On the Ethnology of Timor-laut. JRAI 13:8–31.

Forde, Cyril Daryll. 1951. The Yoruba-Speaking Peoples of Southwestern Nigeria. London: International African Institute.

Forde, Daryll, ed. 1954. African Worlds. London: Oxford University Press.

——. 1955. Peoples of the Niger-Benue Confluence—Western Africa. Ethnographic Survey of Africa, Part X. London: International African Institute.

De Forest, John W. 1853. History of the Indians of Connecticut. Hartford: William Jas. Hamersley.

Forge, Anthony, ed. 1973. Peoples of the Earth. Vol. 1. Verona: Arnoldo Mondadori for the Danbury Press.

Foucourt, George. 1925. Sky and Sky-Gods. In ERE, vol. 11, 580–585.

Fowler, W. Warde. 1925. Fortune (Roman). In ERE, vol. 6, 98–104.

Fox, William Sherwood. 1916. Greek and Roman Mythology. Boston: Marshall Jones.

Francis, W. 1906. Gazetteer of the Madura District. Madras: Government Press.

——. 1907. Madras District Gazetteers. Vizagapatam, Madras: Government Press.

Francke, A. H. 1923. Tibetan Wedding Songs. Hagen i.w. und Darmstadt: Folkwang Verlag.

——. 1925. gLing Chos (Mythology of Tibetan Folklore). In ERE, vol. 8, 75–78.

Frankfort, Henri. 1946. Before Philosophy. Baltimore: Penguin.

Frazer, Sir James George. 1926. The Worship of Nature. New York: MacMillan.

——. 1960. The Golden Bough. New York: MacMillan.

——. 1961. Adonis, Attis, Osiris. New Hyde Park, New York: University Books.

Friederich, R. 1959. The Civilization and Culture of Bali. Calcutta: Susil Gupta.

Fuchs, Stephen. 1952. Another Version of the Baiga Creation Myth. Anthropos 47 (3-4):607–619.

von Furer-Haimendorf, Christoph. 1954. Religious Beliefs and Ritual Practices of the Minyong Abors of Assam, India. Anthropos 49 (3-4):588–604.

——. 1955. Pre-Buddhist Elements in Sherpa Belief and Ritual. *Man* 55:49–52.

——. 1964. *The Sherpas of Nepal*. Berkeley and Los Angeles: University of California Press.

——. 1974. A Central Indian Tribal People: The Raj Gonds. In Maloney, 1974.

Furness, William Henry. 1910. *The Island of Stone Money: Yap of the Carolinas*. Philadelphia: Lippincott.

Furst, Peter, ed. 1972. *Flesh of the Gods*. New York: Praeger.

——. To Find Our Life: Peyote among the Huichol Indians of Mexico. In Furst, 1972:136–184.

——. 1973. An Indian Journey to Life's Source. *AMNH-Mag* 82 (4):34–43.

Gamble, David P. 1957. *The Wolof of Senegambia— Together with Notes on the Lebu and the Serer*. Western Africa, Part 14, ed. Daryll Forde. London: International African Institute.

Gamble, Sidney B. 1954. *Ting Hsien, a North China Community*. New York: Institute of Pacific Relations.

Gann, Thomas W. F. 1918. The Maya Indians of Southern Yucatan and Northern British Honduras. BBAE 64.

Gardiner, Alan H. 1925. Personification (Egyptian). In *ERE,* vol, 9, 787–792.

Gardiner, J. Stanley. 1897. The Natives of Rotuma. *JRAI* 27:456–524.

Gardner, E. A. 1925a. Personification (Greek). In *ERE,* vol. 9, 792–794.

——. 1925b. War, Wargods (Greek and Roman). In *ERE,* vol. 12, 694–698.

Gaster, Theodor H. 1950. Religion of the Canaanites. In Ferm, 1950:111–144.

Gatschet, Albert S. 1890. The Klamath Indians of Southwestern Oregon. *Contributions to American Ethnology*. Washington, D.C.: Department of the Interior.

——. 1891. Oregonian Folklore. *JAF* 4:139–143.

Gazetteer of Sikhim. 1894. Calcutta: Bengal Secretariat Press.

Geden, A. S. 1925. Aiyanar. In *ERE,* vol. 1, 257.

Geertz, Clifford. 1960. *The Religion of Java*. Glencoe, Ill.: The Free Press.

Gelfand, Michael. 1962. *Shona Religion*. Capetown: Juta and Co.

——. 1966. *An African's Religion*. Capetown: Juta and Co.

Gentry, Howard Scott. 1963. The Warihio Indians of Sonora-Chihuahua. BBAE 186:61–144.

Gerbrands, A. A. 1973. Asmat—New Guinea. In Forge, 1973.

Gerster, George. 1969. Abu Simbel's Ancient Temples Reborn. *NG* 135:724–744.

Getty, Alice. 1962. *The Gods of Northern Buddhism*. Rutland, Vermont: Charles Tuttle.

Gheerbrant, Alain. 1954. *Journey to the Far Amazon,* trans. Edward Fitzgerald. New York: Simon and Schuster.

Ghurye, G. S. 1962. *Gods and Men*. Bombay: Popular Book Depot.

Gibson, Arrell M. 1971. *The Chickasaws*. Norman: University of Oklahoma Press.

Gifford, Edward Winslow. 1926. *Clear Lake Pomo Society*. Berkeley: University of California Press.

——. 1932. *The Southeastern Yavapai, Arizona*. PAEUC, vol. 29, no. 3, 177–252.

——. 1933. Northeastern and Western Yavapai Myths. *JAF* 46:347–415.

——. 1936. *Northeastern and Western Yavapia*. PAEUC, vol. 34.

——. 1931. The Kamia of Imperial Valley. BBAE, no. 97.

——. 1924. *Tongan Myths and Tales*. BPBM, no. 8.

——. 1929. *Tongan Society*. BPBM, no. 61.

Gifford, E. W., and R. H. Lowie. 1928. *Notes on the Akwa-ala Indians of Lower California*. PAEUC, vol. 23, no. 7.

Gilhodes, P. Ch. 1908. Mythologie et Religion des Katchins (Birmanie). *Anthropos* 3 (2):672–699.

Gillin, John. 1936. The Barama River Caribs of British Guiana. PMAE, vol. 14, no. 3.

Gimbutas, Marija. 1963. *The Balts*. New York: Praeger.

——. 1971. *The Slavs*. New York: Praeger.

——. n.d. Perkunas/Perun the Thunder God of the Balts and Slavs. Netherlands Institute for Advanced Study in the Humanities and Social Sciences.

——. 1974. The Lithuanian God Velnias. In *Myth in Indo-European Antiquity*, ed. G. Larson and J. Puhvel, 87–92. Berkeley: University of California Press.

Gimlette, John Desmond. 1929. *Malay Poisons and Charm Cures*. London: J. and A. Churchill.

Girard, Raphael. 1979. *Esotericism of the Popul Vuh*, trans. Blair A. Moffett. Pasadena, California: Theosophical University Press.

Gitlow, Abraham L. 1947. *Economics of the Mount Hagen Tribes, New Guinea*. New York: J. J. Augustin.

Gladwin, Thomas, and Seymour B. Sarason. 1953. *Truk: Man in Paradise*. New York: Wenner-Gren Foundation for Anthropological Research.

Glasse, R. M. 1965. The Huli of the Southern Highlands. In Lawrence and Meggett, 1965.

Glueck, N. 1966. Solomon's Foundaries. In *Hands on the Past*, ed. C. W. Ceram, 307–311. New York: Knopf.

Goddard, Pliny Earle. 1903. *Life and Culture of the Hupa*. PAEUC, vol. 1.

——. 1911. Jicarillo Apache Texts. AMNH-AP, vol. 8.

——. 1918. *Myths and Tales from the San Carlos Apache*. AMNH-AP, vol. 24, part 1.

——. 1925. Hupa. In *ERE*, vol. 6, 880–883.

Goddard, T. N. 1925. *The Handbook of Sierra Leone*. London: Grant Richards.

Goldman, Irving. 1940. Cosmological Beliefs of the Cubeo Indians. *JAF* 53:242–247.

——. 1948. Tribes of the Uaupes-Caqueta Region. *HSAI* 3:763–798.

Goldziher, Ignaz. 1877. *Mythology among the Hebrews*, trans. Russell Martineau. London: Longmans, Green.

Gomes, Edwin H. 1911. *Seventeen Years among the Sea Dyaks of Borneo*. London: Seeley.

Gonzalez-Wippler, Migene. 1975. *Santeria*. Garden City: Anchor Press.

Goodwin, Grenville. 1939. *Myths and Tales of the White Mountain Apache*. MAFS, vol. 33.

Gordon, Cyrus H. 1961. Canaanite Mythology. In Kramer, 1961a, 181–218.

Gorer, Geoffrey. 1938. *Himalayan Village*. London: Michael Joseph.

Goris, R. 1960a. Holidays and Holy Days. In *Selected Studies in Indonesia*, 5:113–130.

——. 1960b. The Position of Blacksmiths. In *Selected Studies in Indonesia*, 5:289–300.

——. 1969a. Pura Besakih, Bali's State Temple. In *Selected Studies in Indonesia*, 8:75–88.

——. 1969b. Pura Besakih through the Centuries. In *Selected Studies in Indonesia*, 8:89–104.

——. 1969c. The Decennial Festival of the Village of Selat. In *Selected Studies in Indonesia*, 8:105–130.

Gossen, Gary H. 1972. Temporal and Spatial Equivalents in Chamula Ritual Symbolism. In Lessa and Vogt, 1972.

Grader, C. J. 1960. The State Temples of Mengwi. In *Selected Studies in Indonesia*, 5:155–186.

——. 1969a. Pura Meduwe Karang at Kubutambahan. In *Selected Studies in Indonesia*, 8:131–174.

——. 1969b. Balang Tamak. In *Selected Studies in Indonesia*, 8:175–188.

Graham, David Crockett. 1928. Religion in Szechuan Province, China. SI-MC, vol. 80, no. 4.

——. 1937a. The Ceremonies of the Chu'an Miano. *JWCRBS* 9.

——. 1937b. The Customs of the Chu'an Miano. *JWCBRS* 9.

——. 1958. The Customs and Religion of the Ch'iang. SI-MC, vol. 135, no. 1.

——. 1961. Folk Religion in Southwest China. SI-MC, vol. 142, no. 2.

Grattan, F. J. H. 1948. *An Introduction to Samoan Custom, Apia, Western Samoa*. Samoa: Samoa Printing and Publishing.

Gray, John. 1957. *The Legacy of Canaan*. Leiden: E. J. Brill.

——. 1964. *The Canaanites*. London: Thames and Hudson.

——. 1969. *Near Eastern Mythology*. London: Hamlyn.

Gray, Florence L. 1925. Easter Island. In *ERE*, vol. 5, 131–134.

Gray, Louis H. 1925a. Huron. In *ERE*, vol. 6, 883–886.

——. 1925b. Iroquois. In *ERE*, vol. 7, 420–422.

——. 1925c. Tushes and Other Pagan Tribes of the Caucasus. In *ERE*, vol. 12, 483–488.

——. 1930. *The Foundations of the Iranian Religions.* Bombay: D. B. Taraporevala Sons.

Gray, Robert F. 1963. *The Sonjo of Tanganyika.* London: Oxford University Press.

Greenberg, Joseph. 1946. The Influence of Islam on a Sudanese Religion. MAES, vol. 10.

Grey, Sir George. 1855. *Polynesian Mythology.* London: John Murray.

Griaule, Marcel, and Germaine Dieterlen. 1954. The Dogon of the French Sudan. In Forde, 1954:83–110.

Grierson, G. A. 1925a. Bhils. In *ERE,* vol. 2, 554–557.

——. 1925b. Siva Narayanis. In *ERE,* vol. 11, 579.

Griffis, William Elliot. 1897. *Corea, the Hermit Nation.* New York: Charles Scribner's Sons.

Grimm, Jacob. 1880–1888. *Teutonic Mythology,* trans. James Steven Stallybrass. 4 vols. London: W. Swan Sonnenschein and Allen, George Bell and Sons.

Grinnell, George Bird. 1893. Pawnee Mythology. *JAF* 6:113–130.

——. 1910. The Great Mysteries of the Cheyenne. *AA* 2:542575.

——. 1962. *The Cheyenne Indians,* vol. 2. New York: Cooper Square.

Grosvenor, Donna K., and Gilbert M. Grosvenor. 1969. Bali by the Back Roads. *NG* 136:657–697.

Grottanelli, Vinigi L. 1947. Burial among the Koma of Western Abyssinia. *PM* 20 (4):71–84.

——. 1967. Nzema High Gods. *Paideuma* 13:32–42.

——. 1969. Gods and Morality in Nzema Polytheism. *Ethnology* (Pittsburgh) 8 (4):370–405.

Grubb, W. B. 1925. Pampeans. In *ERE,* vol. 9, 596–599.

Gudgeon, W. L. 1892. Maori Deities. *PSJ* 1:30.

Guerber, H. A. 1895. *Myths of Northern Lands.* New York: American Book.

Guillebrand, Rosemary. 1950. The Doctrine of God in Ruanda-Urundi. In Smith, 1950:180–200.

Guillermo, Aldana E. 1971. Mesa del Nayar's Strange Holy Week. *NG* 139:780–795.

Gulliver, P. H. 1953. The Karamajong Cluster. *Africa* 22 (1):1–22.

Gulliver, Pamela, and P. H. Gulliver. 1953. *The Central Nilo-Hamites.* East Central Africa, Part 7. London: International African Institute.

Gunn, Harold D. 1956. *Pagan Peoples of the Central Area of Northern Nigeria.* Western Africa, Part 12. London: International African Institute.

Gurdon, Philip Richard Thornhaugh. 1907. *The Khasis,* intro. Sir Charles Lyall. London: D. Nutt.

——. 1914. *The Khasis.* London: Macmillan.

——. 1925. Ahoms. In *ERE,* vol. 1, 234–237.

Gurney, O. R. 1952. *The Hittites.* Baltimore: Penguin.

Gusinde, Martin. 1931. *The Selk' nam, on the Life and Thought of a Hunting People of the Great Island of Tierra del Fuego,* vol. 1. Human Relations Area Files no. SH4, vol. 1.

Guterbock, Hans G. 1950. Hittite Religion. In Ferm, 1950:81–109.

——. 1961. Hittite Mythology. In Kramer, 1961a, 139–179.

Guthrie, W. K. C. 1950. *The Greeks and their Gods.* London: Methuen.

Hackin, J., et al., eds. 1963. *Asiatic Mythology,* trans. F. M. Atkinson. New York: Thomas J. Crowell.

——. 1963a. The Mythology of the Kafirs. In Hackin et al., 1963.

——. 1963b. The Mythology of Lamaism. In Hackin et al., 1963.

——. 1963c. Buddhist Mythology of Central Asia. In Hackin et al., 1963.

Hadas, Moses. 1965. *Imperial Rome.* New York: Time Inc.

Haddon, A. C. 1925a. Negrillos and Negritos. In *ERE,* vol. 9, 271–274.

——. 1925b. New Guinea. In *ERE,* vol. 9, 339–352.

Hagar, Stansbury. 1906. Cherokee Star Lore. In *Boas Anniversary Volume, Anthropological Papers,* ed. Berthold Laufer, 354–366. New York: G. E. Stechert.

——. 1913. Izamal and Its Celestial Plan. *AA* 15:16–32.

——. 1925. Ancestor Worship and the Cult of the Dead (American). In *ERE,* vol. 1, 433–437.

Hahn, Theophilus. 1881. *Tsuni-Goam, the Supreme Being of the Khoi-Khoi.* London: Trubner.

Haile, Berard. 1947. *Head and Face Masks in Navaho Ceremonialism.* St. Michaels, Arizona: St. Michaels Press.

Hadju, Peter. 1963. *The Samoyed Peoples and Languages.* Bloomington: Indiana University Press.

Hale, Horatio. 1891. Huron Folklore. *JAF* 4:288–294.

Hallowell, A. Irving. 1967. Ojibway World View. In Owen, Deetz and Fisher, 1967:208–235.

Hamblin, Dora Jane. 1973. *The First Cities,* Emergence of Man. New York: Time-Life Books.

Hambley, Wilfred Dyson. 1929. The Serpent In African Belief and Custom. *AA* 31 (4):655–665.

———. 1934. *The Ovimbundu of Angola.* FMNH-AS 21, no. 2.

Hammond, Peter B. 1959. Economic Change and Mossi Acculturation. In *Continuity and Change in African Cultures,* ed. William R. Bascom and Melville J. Herskovits, 238–256. Chicago: University of Chicago Press.

Handy, E. S. Craighill. 1923. *The Native Culture in the Marquesas.* BPBM, no. 9.

Hanks, Jane Richardson. 1963. *Maternity and its Rituals in Bang Chan.* Ithaca: Department of Asian Studies, Cornell University.

Harner, Michael J. 1972. *The Jivaro.* Garden City: Doubleday.

Harper, Edward B. 1959. A Hindu Village Pantheon. *SJA* 15 (3):227–234.

———, ed. 1964. *Religion in South Asia.* Seattle: University of Washington Press.

Harrington, John Peabody. 1907–1908. The Ethnography of the Tewa Indians. ARBAE 19:29–636.

———. 1908. A Yuma Account of Origins. *JAF* 21:324–348.

Harrington, M. R. 1921. *Religions and Ceremonies of the Lenape.* CMAI 19.

Harris, P. G. 1938. Notes on the Dakarkari Peoples of Sokoto Province, Nigeria. *JRAI* 68:113–120.

Harris, Rev. W. T. 1950. The Idea of God among the Mende. In Smith, 1950:227–297.

Harrison, Rev. Charles. 1891. Religion and Family among the Haidas (Queen Charlotte Islands). *JRAI* 21:14–29.

Hartland, E. Sidney. 1925a. Bantu and South Africa. In ERE, vol. 2, 350–367.

———. 1925b. Death and the Disposal of the Dead (Introductory). In *ERE,* vol. 4, 411–444.

———. 1925c. Phallism. In *ERE,* vol. 9, 815–831.

Hassell, Ethel. 1936. Notes on the Ethnology of the Wheelman Tribe of Southwestern Australia, ed. D. S. Davidson. *Anthropos* 31:679–711.

Hastings, James, ed. 1925. *Encyclopedia of Religion and Ethics.* Edinburgh: T. and T. Clark.

Hatt, Gudmund. 1951. The Corn Mother in America and Indonesia. *Anthropos* 46:853–914.

Hatt, J. J. 1966. A la Recherche de la Religion Gauloise. *Archeologia* 11:58–65.

Hawley, Florence. 1937. Kokopelli, of the Prehistoric Southwestern Pueblo Pantheon. *AA* 39 (4):644–646. part 1.

Hayashida, Tsuneo. 1983. The Japanese Crane, Bird of Happiness. *NG* 164:542–556.

Haydon, Eustace. 1941. *Biography of the Gods.* New York: Macmillan.

Hayley, T. T. S. 1947. *The Anatomy of the Lango Religion and Groups.* Cambridge: Cambridge University Press.

Hebert, J., and M. Guilhem. 1967. Notion et culte de Dieu chez les Toussain. *Anthropos* 62:139–164.

The Nasli and Alice Heeramanek Collection. 1966. *The Arts of India and Nepal.* Boston: Museum of Fine Arts.

Helfritz, Hans. 1971. *Mexican Cities of the Gods.* New York: Praeger.

Hemingway, F. R. 1907. *Gazetteer of the Trichinopoly District.* Madras: Government Press.

———. 1915. *Gazetteer of the Godavari District.* Madras: Government Press.

Henry, A. 1903. The Lolos and other Tribes of Western China. *JRAI* 33:96–107.

Henry, Jules. 1941. *Jungle People: A Kaingang Tribe of the Highlands of Brazil.* Richmond, Virg.: William Byrd Press.

Henry, Teuira. 1920. Tahitian Astronomy. *PSJ* 29.

———. 1928. *Ancient Tahiti.* BPBM, no. 48.

Henthorn, William E. 1971. *A History of Korea.* New York: The Free Press.

Herbert, Jean. 1967. *Shinto.* London: George Allen and Unwin.

Herbig, Gerhard. 1925. Etruscan Religion. In *ERE*, vol. 5, 532–536.

Herm, Gerhard. 1975. *The Phoenicians.* New York: Morrow.

Hermanns, Rev. Father. M. 1955. Contributions to the Study of Kadan Religion. *Man* 55:145–151.

Hernandex de Alba, Gregorio. 1946. The Highland Tribes of Southern Colombia. *HSAI* 2:915–960.

——. 1948a. The Betoi and their Neighbors. *HSAI* 4:393–398.

——. 1948b. The Achagua and their Neighbors. *HSAI* 4:399–412.

——. 1948c. Sub-Andean Tribes of the Cauca Valley. *HSAI* 4:297–327.

——. 1948d. The Tribes of Northwestern Venezuela. *HSAI* 4:469–474.

Herskovits, Melville J. 1937a. *Life in a Haitian Valley.* New York: Knopf.

——. 1937b. African Gods and Catholic Saints in New World Negro Belief. *AA* 39 (4):635–643.

——. 1938. *Dahomey: An Ancient West African Kingdom.* New York: J. J. Augustin.

——, and Frances S. Herskovits. 1933. *An Outline of Dahomean Religious Belief.* MAAA, no. 41.

Hesiod. 1981. *Theogony,* trans. and intro. Norman O. Brown. Indianapolis: Bobbs-Merrill.

Hetherwick, A. 1925. Nyanjas. In *ERE*, vol. 9, 419–422.

Hewitt, J. N. B. 1895. The Iroquoian Concept of the Soul. *JAF* 8:106–116.

Hicks, Jim. 1974. *The Empire Builders.* The Emergence of Man. New York: Time-Life Books.

Hill, A. H. 1951. Kelantan padi planting. *JRAI* (Malaysian Branch) 24:56–76.

Hinnells, John R. 1973. *Persian Mythology.* New York: Hamlyn.

Hobley, C. W. 1902. *Eastern Uganda: An Ethnological Survey.* London: Anthropological Institute of Great Britain and Ireland.

——. 1910. *Ethnology of A-Kamba and Other East African Tribes.* Cambridge: Cambridge University Press.

Hocart, A. M. 1929. *Lau Islands, Fiji.* BPBM, no. 62.

Hodson, T. C. 1908. *The Meitheis.* London: David Nutt.

——. 1911. *The Naga Tribes of Manipur.* London: MacMillan.

——. 1925. Lushais. In *ERE*, vol. 8, 197–198.

Hoffman, Helmut. 1956. The Religions of Tibet. London: George Allen and Unwin.

Hoffman, W. J. 1890. Mythology of the Menominee Indians. *AA* 3:243–258.

Hogbin, H. Ian. The Hill People of Northeastern Guadalcanal. *Oceania* 8:62–89.

Hollis, A. C. 1909. *The Nandi: Their Language and Folklore.* Oxford: Clarendon.

Holmberg, Allan R. 1948. The Siriono. *HSAI* 3:455–463.

——. 1969. *Nomads of the Long Bow.* Garden City: Natural History Press.

Holmberg, Uno. 1925. Lapps. In *ERE*, vol. 7:797–800.

——. 1964. *Finno-Ugric.* Vol. 4, *Mythology of All Races.* Boston: Marshall Jones.

Holmes, Rev. J. 1902. Notes on the Religious Ideas of the Elema Tribe of the Papuan Gulf. *JRAI* 32:426–431.

Holtom, D. C. 1931. Some Notes on Japanese Tree Worship. *TASJ* 2nd Ser. 8:1–19.

——. 1938. *The National Faith of Japan.* London: Kegan Paul, French, Trubner.

Hommel, Fr. 1925. Calendar (Babylonian). In *ERE*, vol. 3, 73–78.

Hongi, Hare. 1920. The Gods of Maori Worship: Sons of Light. *PSJ* 29:24–29.

Honigmann, John Joseph. 1949. *Culture and Ethos of Kaska Society.* New Haven: Yale University Press.

Hooke, S. W. 1963. *Middle Eastern Mythology.* Baltimore: Penguin.

Hooper, Lucile. *The Cahuilla Indians.* PAEUC, vol. 16.

Hooten, Ernest A. 1925. *The Ancient Inhabitants of the Canary Islands.* HAS, vol. 7.

Hooykaas, C. 1964. *Agama Tirtha.* Amsterdam: N. V. Noord-Hollandsche Uitgevers Maatschappij.

Hopgood, Rev. Cecil R. 1950. Conceptions of God amongst the Tonga of Northern Rhodesia. In Smith, 1950:61–74.

Hopkins, E. Washburn. 1925. Bhairava. In *ERE*, vol. 2, 538.

Hori, Ichiro. 1959. Japanese Folk-Beliefs. *AA* 61:405–424.

———. 1968. *Folk Religion in Japan: Continuity and Change*. Chicago: University of Chicago Press.

Hornblower, G. D. 1943. The Divine Cat and the Snake in Egypt. *Man* 43:85–87.

Hornell, James. 1943. The Prow of the Ship: Sanctuary of the Tutelary Deity. *Man* 43:121–128.

Horowitz, Michael M. 1963. The Worship of South Indian Deities in Martinique. *Ethnology* (Pittsburgh) 2:339–345.

Horton, Donald. 1948. The Mundurucu. *HSAI* 3:271–282.

Horton, Robin. 1960. *The Gods as Guests*. Lagos: Federal Government Printer.

———. 1962. The Kalabiri World View: An Outline and Interpretation. *Africa* 32 (3):197–220.

———. 1963. The Kalabiri Ekine Society: A Borderland of Religion and Art. *Africa* 33 (3):94–114.

———. 1964. Ritual Man in Africa. *Africa* 34 (2):85–104.

Horton, W. R. G. 1956. God, Man, and the Land in a Northern Ibo Village-Group. *Africa* 26 (1):17–27.

Hose, Charles. 1912. *The Pagan Tribes of Borneo*. London: Macmillan.

Howard, James H. 1965. The Ponca Tribe. BBAE 195.

Howell, P. P. 1954. *A Manual of Nuer Law: Being an Account of Customary Law, its Evolution and Development in the Courts Established by the Sudan Government*. London: Oxford University Press.

Howell, William. 1908–1910. [A collection of articles on the Sea Dyak]. *Sarawak Gazette*, nos. 39–40.

Howells, William. 1948. *The Heathens*. Garden City: Doubleday.

Howitt, A. W. 1904. *The Native Tribes of Southeast Australia*. London: Macmillan.

Huart, Clement. 1963. The Mythology of Persia. In Hackin et al., 1963.

Hudson, Travis, and Ernest Underhay. 1978. *Crystals in the Sky: An Intellectual Odyssey involving Chumash Astronomy, Cosmology, and Rock Art*. Santa Barbara, Calif.: Ballena Press and Santa Barbara Natural History Museum.

Huffman, Ray. 1931. *Nuer Customs and Folklore*. London: Oxford University Press.

Hulstaert, Gustave E. 1938. *Marriage among the Nkundu*. Bruxelles: G. van Campenhout.

Huntingford, G. W. B. 1953a. *The Southern Nilo-Hamites*. London: International African Institute.

———. 1953b. *The Northern Nilo-Hamites*. East Central Africa, Part 4. London: International African Institute.

———. 1953c. *The Nandi of Kenya*. London: Routledge and Kegan Paul.

Hutton, J. H. 1921. *The Angami Nagas*. London: Macmillan.

———. 1968. *The Sema Nagas*. London: Oxford University Press.

Idowu, E. Bolaji. 1962. *Olodumare: God in Yoruba Belief*. London: Longmans, Green.

Iliff, Flora Gregg. 1954. *People of the Blue Water: My Adventures among the Walapai and Havasupai Indians*. New York: Harper and Brothers.

Imperato, Pascal James. 1972. Nomads of the Niger. *AMNH-MAG*. 81 (10):60–69.

———. 1975. Last Dances of the Bambara. *AMNH-Mag*. 84 (4):62–71.

Im Thurn, Everard F. 1883. *Among the Indians of Guiana*. London: Kegan Paul, Trench.

Ingrams, W. H. 1925. The People of Makunduchi, Zanzibar. *Man* 25:138–142.

Ions, Veronica. 1967. *Indian Mythology*. London: Paul Hamlyn.

Ishwaran, K. 1974. A Village in Karnataka. In Maloney, 1974.

Isichei, Elizabeth. 1978. *Igbo Worlds: An Anthology of Oral History and Historical Descriptions*. Philadelphia: Institute for the Study of Human Issues.

Islavin, Vladimir. 1847. *The Samoyed in their Domestic and Social Life*. Sanktpeterburg: Ministerstva Gosudarstvennykh Imuschchest.

Ivanov, S. V., A. V. Smolyak, and M. G. Levin. 1964a. The Ul'chi. In Levin and Potapov, 1964.

———. 1964b. The Udegeys. In Levin and Potapov, 1964.

———. 1964c. The Nivkhi. In Levin and Potapov, 1964.

———. 1964d. The Oroks. In Levin and Potapov, 1964.

———. 1964e. The Orochi. In Levin and Potapov, 1964.

Jacobi, H. 1925. Brahmanism. In *ERE*, vol. 2, 799–813.

Jacobsen, Thorkild. 1946. Mesopotamia. In Frankfort, 1946:137–217.

———. 1970. *Toward the Image of Tammuz*. Cambridge, Mass.: Harvard University Press.

———. 1976. *The Treasures of Darkness*. New Haven: Yale University Press.

Jacobson, Doranne Wilson. 1977. Life Beyond the Veil: Purdah in India. *NG* 152:270–286.

Jahner, Elaine. 1977. The Spiritual Landscape. *Parabola* 5 (3):32–38.

James, E. O. 1960. *The Ancient Gods*. London: Weidenfeld and Nicolson.

———. 1968. *Pre-Columbian American Religions*, trans. Stanley Davis. New York: Holt, Rhinehart, and Winston.

James, George Wharton. 1902. A Saboba Origin Myth. *JAF* 15:36–39.

———. 1903. *The Indians of the Painted Desert Region: Hopis, Navahoes, Wallapais, Havasupais*. Boston: Little, Brown.

Jameson, Michael H. 1961. Mythology of Ancient Greece. In Kramer, 1961a, 219–276.

Janashia, N. S. 1937. The Religious Beliefs of the Abkhasians. *Georgica* 4-5:117–153.

Jastrow, Morris. 1898. *The Religion of Babylonia and Assyria*. Boston: Ginn.

Jayne, Walter Addison. 1962. *The Healing Gods of Ancient Civilizations*. New York: University Books.

Jeffreys, M. D. W. 1935. The Divine Umrundi King. *Africa* 8 (3):346–354.

———. 1939. Some Notes on the Ekoi. *JRAI* 69:95–106.

———. 1951. The Winged Solar Disk or Ibo Itei Scarification. *Africa* 21 (2):93–110.

———. 1970. Ogoni Folklore. *Folklore* (London) 81:112–113.

———. 1972. A Triad of Gods in Africa. *Anthropos* 67:723–735.

Jenness, Diamond. 1932. The Indians of Canada. NMC-AS Bulletin 15, no. 56.

———. 1934. Myths of the Carrier Indians of British Columbia. *JAF* 47:97–247.

———. 1937. The Sekani Indians of British Columbia. NMC-AS Bulletin 84, no. 22.

———. 1943. The Carrier Indians of the Bulkley River: Their Social and Religious Life. BBAE, vol. 133.

———. 1955. The Faith of a Coast Salish Indian. BCPM, vol. 3.

———. 1970. *The Life of the Copper Eskimos*. Reprint of "A Report of the Canadian Arctic Expedition, 1913–1918". vol. 12, part A. New York: Johnson Reprint Corporation.

Jocano, F. Landa. 1969. *Outline of Philippine Mythology*. Manila: Centro Escolar University Research and Development Center.

Jochelson, Waldemar. 1904. The Mythology of the Koryak. *AA* 6:413–424.

———. 1908. *The Koryak*. MAMNH vol. 10, part 1.

———. 1926 *The Yukaghir*. MAMNH vol. 13, part 2. Leiden: E. J. Brill; New York: G. E. Stechert.

———. 1933. *The Yakut*. MAMNH vol. 33, part 2.

Johnson, Jean B. 1949. *The Opata: An Inland Tribe of Sonora*. PAUNM 6.

Johnson, Samuel. 1921. *The History of the Yoruba from the Earliest Times to the Beginning of the British Protectorate*, ed. Dr. O. Johnson. London: George Routledge and Sons.

Johnston, Basil. 1976. *Ojibway Heritage*. Toronto: McClelland and Stewart.

Jolly, J. 1925. Disease and Medicine (Hindu). In *ERE*, vol. 4:753–755.

Jones, Williams. 1911. Notes on the Fox Indians. *JAF* 24:209–237.

Jonval, Michel. 1929. *Les Chansons Mythologiques Lettones*. Paris: Librairie Picart.

Jordan, David K. 1972. *Gods, Ghosts, and Ancestors*. Berkeley and Los Angeles: University of California Press.

Junod, Henri A. 1962. *The Life of a South African Tribe*, vol. 2. New Hyde Park, New York: University Books.

Kagwa, Apolo. 1934. *The Customs of the Baganda*, trans. Ernest B. Kalibala. New York: Columbia University Press.

Kahn, Morton C. 1929. Notes on the Saramaccaner Bush Negroes of Dutch Guiana. *AA* 31:468–469.

Karsten, Raphael. 1926. *The Civilization of the South American Indians*. New York: Knopf.

———. 1932. *Indian Tribes of the Argentine and Bolivian Chaco*. Commentationes Humanarum Litterum, vol. 4, 1. Helsingfors: Societas Scientiarum Fennica.

———. 1955. *The Religion of the Samek*. Leiden: E. J. Brill.

———. 1970. *The Toba Indians of the Bolivian Grand Chaco*. Anthropological Publications. The Netherlands: Oosterhout, N. B.

Kato, Genchi. 1926. *A Study of Shinto*. Tokyo: Meiji Japan Society.

———. 1931. The Naoe Matsuri. *TASJ* 2nd Ser. 8:113–136.

de Kay, Charles. 1898. *Bird Gods*. New York: A. S. Barnes.

Keane, A. H. 1925a. Air and Gods of Air. In *ERE*, vol. 1, 252–257.

———. 1925b. Asia. In *ERE*, vol. 2, 118–124.

———. 1925c. Australasia. In *ERE*, vol. 2, 236–245.

———. 1925d. Chibchas. In *ERE*, vol. 3, 514–516.

Keary, Charles Francis. 1882. *Outline of Primitive Belief*. New York: Charles Scribner's Sons.

Keeler, Clyde A. 1960. *Secrets of the Cuna Earthmother*. New York: Exposition Press.

———. 1961. *Apples of Immortality from the Cuna Tree of Life*. New York: Exposition Press.

Keightley, Thomas. 1838. *Mythology of Ancient Greece and Italy*. London: Whittaker.

Keith, A. Berriedale. 1917. *Indian*. Vol. 6, *Mythology of All Races*. Boston: Marshall Jones.

Keliipio, L. D. 1901. Kuula, the Fish God of Hawaii, trans. M. K. Nakuina. *Thrum: The Hawaiian Annual*, 114–124.

Kennedy, Donald Gilbert. 1931. Culture of Vaitupu, Ellice Islands. MPS 9.

Kerenyi, C. 1951. *The Gods of the Greeks*. London: Thames and Hudson.

Kirchhoff, Paul. 1948a. The Warrau. *HSAI* 3:869–881.

———. 1948b. The Patangoro and Amani. *HSAI* 4:339–348.

———. 1948c. Food-Gathering Tribes of the Venezuelan Llanos. *HSAI* 4:445–468.

Kirk, Malcolm. 1973. Change Ripples in New Guinea's Sepik River. *NG* 144:354–381.

Klementz, Demetrius. 1925a. Buriats. In *ERE*, vol. 3, 1–17.

———. 1925b. Gilyaks. In *ERE*, vol. 6, 221–226.

Kloos, Peter. 1969. Female Initiation among the Maroni River Caribs. *AA* vol. 71, part 2, no. 5, 898–905.

Knapp, Frances, and Rheta Louise Childe. 1896. *The Thlinkets of Southeastern Alaska*. Chicago: Stone and Kimball.

Knappe, C. 1888. Religious View of the Marshall Islanders. *Mitteilungen von Forschungsreisenden und Gelehrten aus den deutschen Schutzgebeiten* 1:63–81.

Kochar, V. K. 1966. Village Deities of the Santal and Associated Rituals. *Anthropos* 61:241–257.

Korn, V. E. 1960. The Consecration of a Priest. In *Selected Studies on Indonesia*, 5:131–154.

Kozak, Vladimir. 1963. Ritual of a Bororo Funeral. *AMNH-Mag.* 71 (1):38–49.

Krader, Lawrence. 1954. Buryat Religion and Society. *SJA* 10 (3):322–351.

Kramer, Augustin. 1906. *Hawaii, Eastern Micronesia, and Samoa*. Stuttgart: Strecker and Schroder.

———. 1932. *Truk*. Hamburg: Friedrichsen, de Gruyter.

———, and Hans Neverman. 1938. *Ralik-Ratak (Marshall Islands)*. Hamburg: Friedrichsen, de Gruyter.

Kramer, Samuel Noah. 1950. Sumerian Religion. In Ferm, 1950:4762.

———, ed. 1961a. *Mythologies of the Ancient World*. Garden City: Doubleday.

———. 1961b. Mythology of Sumer and Akkad. In Kramer, 1961a, 93–137.

———. 1967. *Cradle of Civilization*. New York: Time-Life Books.

Krickeberg, Walter. 1968. Mesoamerica. In James, 1968.

Krieger, Herbert W. 1942. *Peoples of the Philippines*. Washington, D.C.: Smithsonian Institute.

Krige, J. D. 1954. The Lovedu of the Transvaal. In Forde, 1954, 55–82.

Kroeber, A. L. 1905. Wishosk Myths. *JAF* 18:85–107.

———. 1907a. *Indian Myths of South Central California*. PAEUC, vol. 4.

———. 1907b. *Gros Ventre Myths*. AMNH-AP, vol. 1, part 3.

———. 1918a *History of Philippine Civilization as Reflected in Religious Nomenclature*. AMNH-AP, vol. 19, part 2.

———. 1925a. Zuni. In *ERE,* vol. 12, 868–873.

———. 1925b. Handbook of the Indians of California. ARBAE 78.

———. 1932. *The Patwin and their Neighbors*. PAEUC, vol. 29.

———. 1946. THe Chibcha. *HSAI* 2:887–909.

Kroeber, Henrietta Rothschild. 1912. Traditions of the Papago Indians. *JAF* 25:95–105.

Kroeber, Theodora. 1964. *Ishi, Last of his Tribe*. Berkeley: Parnassus Press.

Krohn, Kaarle. 1925. Finns (Ancient). In *ERE,* vol. 6, 23–26.

Krug, Adolph N. 1912. Bulu Tales from Kamerun, West Africa. *JAF* 25:106–124.

———. 1949. Bulu Tales. *JAF* 62:348–374.

Krujit, Alb. C. 1925. Indonesians. In *ERE,* vol. 7, 232–252.

Kubler, George. 1946. The Qechua in the Colonial World. *HSAI* 2:331–409.

Kurup, A. M. 1970. Tribal Festivals of Central India. *Folklore* (Calcutta) 11 (5):159–166.

La Barre, Weston. 1941. The Uru of the Rio Desaguadero. *AA* 43:493–522.

———. 1946. The Uru-Chipaya. *HSAI* 2:575–585.

———. 1948. *The Aymara of the Lake Titicaca Plateau, Bolivia*. MAAA, vol. 50, no. 1, part 2.

La Flesche, Francis. 1917–1918. The Osage Tribe: The Rite of Vigil. ARBAE 39.

———. 1926–1926. The Osage Tribe: Two Versions of the Child-Naming Rite. ARBAE 43.

Lagae, C. R. 1926. *The Azande or Niam-Niam. . . . Zande Organization, Religious and Magical Beliefs, Familial Customs*. Bruxelles: Vromant.

Laird, Carobeth. 1976. *The Chemehuevis*. Banning, Calif.: Malki Museum Press.

Lamb, David. 1973. Aborigines of Australia: Life is a Nightmare. *Los Angeles Times* (May 3):1.

Lambrecht, Francis. 1932. *The Mayawyaw Ritual*. Washington, D.C.: PCAC.

Landes, Ruth. 1940. Fetish Worship in Brazil. *JAF* 53:261–270.

Lang, Andrew. 1887. *Myth, Ritual, and Religion*. London: Longmans, Green.

———. 1905. The Religion of the Fans. *Man* 5:54–55.

———. 1968. *The Making of Religion*. New York: Ams Press.

Langdon, S. 1925. Death and the Disposal of the Dead (Babylonian). In *ERE,* vol. 4, 444–446.

Langdon, Stephen Herbert. 1931. *Semitic*. Vol. 5, *Mythology of All Races*. Boston: Marshall Jones.

Lantis, Margaret. 1938. The Mythology of Kodiak Island, Alaska. *JAF* 51:123–172.

———. 1947. *Alaskan Indian Ceremonialism*. Seattle: University of Washington Press.

———. 1950. The Religion of the Eskimos. In Ferm, 1950:309–340.

Larco Hoyle, Raphael. 1946. Culture of the North Coast of Peru. *HSAI* 2:149–175.

———. 1966. *Peru,* trans. James Hogarth. London: Frederick Muller.

New Larousse Encyclopedia of Mythology. 1968. Robert Graves ed. New York: Prometheus Press.

Larousse World Mythology. 1973. Pierre Grimmel ed. London: Hamlyn.

Larson, Thomas J. 1971. The Spirits of the Ancestors and the *Mandengure* Ceremony of the Hambukushu of Ngamiland. *Anthropos* 66:52–70.

Laski, Vera. 1958. *Seeking Life*. MAFS, Philadelphia, vol. 10.

Latta, Frank Forrest. 1949. *Handbook of Yakut Indians*. Bakersfield, Calif.: Kern County Museum.

Lawrence, Peter, and M. J. Meggett, eds. 1965. *Gods, Ghosts, and Men in Melanesia*. Melbourne: Oxford University Press.

Lawrence, Walter Roper. 1895. *The Valley of Kashmir*. London: H. Frowde.

Leach, Edmund Ronald. 1962. *Pul Eliya, a Village in Ceylon: A Study of Land Tenure and Kinship*. Cambridge: Cambridge University Press.

———. 1972. Pulleyar and the Lord Buddha. In Lessa and Vogt, 1972.

Leach, Maria, ed. 1949–1950. *Dictionary of Folklore, Mythology, and Legend*. 2 vols. New York: Funk and Wagnalls.

——. 1956. *The Beginning*. New York: Funk and Wagnalls.

Leacock, Seth. 1964. Fun-Loving Deities in an Afro-Brazilian Cult. *AQ* 37 (3):94–109.

——, and Ruth Leacock. 1972. *Spirits of the Deep*. Garden City: Doubleday Natural History Press.

Lebra, William P. 1966. *Okinawan Religion*. Honolulu: University of Hawaii Press.

Lebzelter, Viktor. 1934. *Native Cultures in Southwest and South Africa*. Vol. 2. Leipzig: Karl W. Hiersemann.

Lee, Douglas. 1978. Day of the Rice God. *NG* 154:78–85.

Leger, L. 1925. Ancestor Worship and Cult of the Dead (Slavonic). In *ERE*, vol. 1, 466.

Leland, Charles Godfrey. 1963. *Etruscan Magic and Occult Remedies*. New York: University Books.

Leonard, Jonathan Norton. 1967. *Ancient America*. New York: Time, Inc.

Leon-Portilla, Miguel. 1961. Mythology of Ancient Mexico. In Kramer, 1961a, 443–472.

——. 1982. *Aztec Thought and Culture*, trans. Jack Emory Davis. Norman: University of Oklahoma Press.

Lessa, William A. 1961. *Tales from the Ulithi Atoll: A Comparative Study in Oceanic Folklore*. Folklore Studies, vol. 13. Berkeley and Los Angeles: University of California Press.

——. 1966. *Ulithi: A Micronesian Design for Living*. New York: Holt, Rhinehart, and Winston.

——. 1972a. Discoverer-of-the-Sun. In Lessa and Vogt, 1972.

——, and Evon Z. Vogt, eds. 1972b. *Reader in Comparative Religion*. 3rd ed. New York: Harper and Row.

Levak, Zarko David. 1973. *Kinship System and Social Structure of the Bororo of Pobojari*. Ann Arbor: University Microfilms 2, 5.

Levi, Sylvain. 1933. *Sanskrit Texts from Bali*. Baroda: Oriental Institute.

Levi-Strauss, Claude. 1948a. The Tupi-Cawahib. *HSAI* 3:299–305.

——. 1948b. Tribes of the Upper Xingu River. *HSAI* 3:321–348.

——. 1948c. The Nambicuara. *HSAI* 3:371–379.

——. 1969. *The Raw and the Cooked*. Translated by John and Doreen Weightman. New York: Harper and Row.

——. 1973. *From Honey to Ashes*. Translated by John and Doreen Weightman. New York: Harper and Row.

Levin, M. G., and L. P. Potapov, eds. 1964. *Peoples of Siberia*. Chicago: University of Chicago Press.

Lewis, I. M. 1955. *Peoples of the Horn of Africa: Somali, Afar, and Saho*. London: International African Institute.

Lewis, Oscar. 1951. *Life in a Mexican Village: Tepoztlan Restudied*. Urbana: University of Illinois Press.

Li Anche. 1948. Bon: The Magico-Religious Belief of the Tibetan-Speaking Peoples. *SJA* 4:31–42.

Liefrinck, F. A. 1969. Rice Cultivation in Northern Bali. In *Selected Studies on Indonesia*, 8:1–74.

Lienhardt, Godfrey. 1954. The Shilluk of the Upper Nile. In Forde, 1954, 138–163.

——. 1961. *Divinity and Experience*. Oxford: Clarendon Press.

Lillingston, Frank. 1925. Chamars. In *ERE*, vol. 3, 351–355.

Linossier, Raymonde. 1963. The Mythology of Buddhism in India. In Hackin et al., 1963.

Linton, Ralph. 1933. *The Tanala: A Hill Tribe of Madagascar*. FMNH-AS 22, publication 317.

Lipkind, William. 1940. Caraja Cosmography. *JAF* 53:248–251.

Lissner, Ivar. 1961. *Man, God, and Magic*. New York: G. P. Putnam's Sons.

Lister, J. J. 1891. Notes on the Natives of Fakaofu (Bowditch Island), Union Group. *JRAI* 21:43–63.

Little, Kenneth Lindsay. 1951. *The Mende of Sierra Leone: A West African People in Transition*. London: Routledge and Kegan Paul.

——. 1954. The Mende in Sierra Leone. In Forde, 1954, 111–137.

Littleton, C. Scott. 1965. Georges Dumezil and the New Comparative Indo-European Mythology. Doctoral Dissertation, University of California, Los Angeles.

——. 1970. The 'Kingship in Heaven' Theme. In Puhvel, 1970:83–121.

——. 1973. *The New Comparative Mythology: An Anthropological Assessment of the Theories of Georges Dumezil.* Rev. ed. Berkeley and Los Angeles: University of California Press.

Littmann, E. 1925. Abyssinia. In *ERE,* vol. 1, 55–59.

Llosa Porras, Fernando. 1977. The Chain of Worlds. *Parabola* 2 (3):58–63.

Loeb, Edwin M. 1926a. *History and Traditions of Niue.* BPBM, vol. 32.

——. 1926b. *Pomo Folkways.* PAEUC, vol. 19.

——. 1929. *Mentawei Religious Cult.* PAEUC, vol. 25, 185–347.

——. 1931. The Religious Organization of North Central California and Tierra del Fuego. *AA* 33:517–556.

——. 1932. *The Western Kuksu Cult.* PAEUC, vol. 33, no. 1.

Logan, Col. M. H. 1918. The Beirs. *SNR* 1 (4):238–248.

Long, Charles H. 1963. *Alpha: The Myths of Creation.* New York: George Braziller.

Lothrop, Samuel Kirkland. 1926. *Pottery of Costa Rica and Nicaragua.* CMAI 8 (1).

——. 1928. *The Indians of Tierra del Fuego.* CMAI 10.

Loven, Sven. 1935. *Origins of the Tainan Culture, West Indies.* Goteborg: Elanders Bokfryckeri Akfiebolag.

Lowie, Robert H. 1909. *The North Island Shoshone.* AMNH-AP 2 (2).

——. 1922. *Religion of the Crow.* AMNH-AP 25 (2).

——. 1924. Shoshonean Tales. *JAF* 37:1–242.

——. 1925a. *Primitive Religion.* London: George Routledge and Sons.

——. 1925b. Cosmogony and Cosmology (Mexican and South American). In *ERE,* vol. 4, 170–173.

Lucas, J. Olumide. 1948. *The Religion of the Yorubas.* Lagos: C. M. S. Bookshop.

Lumholtz, Carl. 1902. *Unknown Mexico: A Record of Five Years' Exploration of the Western Sierra Madre; in the Tierra Caliente of Tepic and Jalisco; and among the Tarascos of Michoacan.* Vol. 1. New York: Charles Scribner's Sons.

Luttig, H. G. 1933. *The Religious System and Social Organization of the Herero.* Utrecht: Kemink en Zoon, N. V.

Lyall, C. J. 1925. Mikirs. In *ERE,* vol. 8, 628–631.

Lynd, James William. 1889. *The Religion of the Dakotas, Chapter Six of Mr. Lynd's Manuscript.* Fort Snelling, Minn.: Minnesota Historical Collections.

MacBain, Alex. 1917. *Celtic Mythology and Religion.* New York: E. P. Dutton.

Mac Cana, Proinseas. 1970. *Celtic Mythology.* London: Hamlyn.

McCary, Ben C. 1979. *Indians in Seventeenth-Century Virginia.* Jamestown Booklet no. 3. Charlottesville: University Press of Virginia.

MacCauley, Clay. 1883–1884. The Seminole Indians of Florida. ARBAE 5:475–526.

McConnel, Ursula H. 1935. Myths of the Wikmunkan and Wiknatara Tribes. *Oceania* 6:66–93.

——. 1957. *Myths of the Munkan.* Victoria: Melbourne University Press.

MacCulloch, John Arnott. 1911. *The Religion of the Ancient Celts.* Edinburgh: T. and T. Clark.

——. 1918. *Celtic.* Vol. 3, *Mythology of All Races.* Boston: Marshall Jones.

——. 1925a. Calendar (Celtic). In *ERE,* vol. 3, 78–82.

——. 1925b. Celts. In *ERE,* vol. 3, 277–304.

——. 1925c. Cross-Roads. In *ERE,* vol. 4, 330–335.

——. 1925d. Door. In *ERE,* vol. 4, 846–852.

——. 1925e. Light and Darkness (Primitive). In *ERE,* vol. 8, 47–51.

——. 1925f. Mountains, Mountain Gods. In *ERE,* vol. 8, 863–868.

——. 1925g. Serpent Worship (Introductory and Primitive). In *ERE,* vol. 11, 399–411.

——. 1925h. State of the Dead (Primitive and Savage). In *ERE,* vol. 11, 817–827.

——. 1964. *Eddic.* vol. 2, *Mythology of All Races.* New York: Cooper Square Publishers.

McCulloch, Merran. 1950. *Peoples of Sierra Leone.* London: International African Institute.

——. 1951. *The Southern Lunda and Related Peoples.* West Central Africa, part 1. London: International African Institute.

——. 1952. *The Ovimbundu of Angola.* West Central Africa, part 2. London: International African Institute.

Macdonell, A. A. 1897. *Vedic Mythology.* Strassburg: Karl J. Trubner.

——. 1956. *India's Past.* London: Oxford University Press.

McGee, W. J. 1893–1894. The Souian Indians. ARBAE 15:157–204.

MacGregor, Gordon. 1943. The Gods of Rennell Island. PMAE 20:32–37.

Machal, Jan. 1918. *Slavic.* Vol. 3, *Mythology of All Races.* Boston: Marshall Jones.

McIlwraith, Thomas Forsyth. 1948. *The Bella Coola Indians.* Toronto: Toronto University Press.

McIntyre, Loren. 1973. The Lost Empire of the Incas. *NG* 144:729–786.

MacKennan, R. 1935. Religion Shamanism. In *Walapai Ethnography,* ed. A. L. Kroeber, 185–194. MAAA no. 42.

MacKenzie, D. R. 1925. *The Spirit-Ridden Konde.* Philadelphia: Lippincott.

MacKenzie, Donald A. 1924. *Myths of Pre-Columbian America.* London: Gresham.

——. [1930]a. *Myths and Traditions of the South Sea Islands.* London: Gresham.

——. 1930b. *Myths from Melanesia and Indonesia.* London: Gresham.

MacLagen, P. J. 1925. Heroes and Hero-Gods (Chinese). In *ERE,* vol. 6, 646–647.

Maclean, John. 1896. *Canadian Savage Folk: The Native tribes of Canada.* Toronto: William Briggs.

MacLeish, Kenneth. 1971. Java: Island in Transition. *NG* 139:1–43.

Macler, Frederic. 1925. Syrians (or Aramaeans). In *ERE,* vol. 12, 164–167.

McMahon, Lt. Col. A. R. 1876. *The Karens of the Golden Chersonnese.* London: Harrison.

McNeley, James Kale. 1981. *Holy Wind in Navajo Philosophy.* Tucson: University of Arizona Press.

Macqueen, J. G. 1975. *The Hittites.* Boulder: Westview Press.

Madden, Sister Mary Daniel. 1930. *The Pagan Divinities and their Worship as Depicted in the Works of St. Augustine.* Washington, D.C.: The Catholic University of America.

Mair, Lucy Philip. 1934. *An African People in the Twentieth Century.* London: G. Routledge and Sons.

Maity, P. K. 1971. Dharma Thakur of Bengal and his Association with Human Fertility. *Folklore* (Calcutta) 12 (3):81–94.

Majumdar, Dhirenda Nath. 1950. *The Affairs of a Tribe.* India: Lucknow University Department of Anthropology.

Maloney, Clarence, ed. 1974. *South Asia: Seven Community Profiles.* New York: Holt, Rhinehart and Winston.

Man, Edward Horace. [1932]. *The Nicobar Islands and their People.* Guildford, England: Billing and Sons.

Mandelbaum, David G. 1940. *The Plains Cree.* AMNH-AP, vol. 37.

Mangin, Eugene. 1921. *The Mossi: Essay on the Manners and Customs of the Mossi People in the Western Sudan.* Paris: Augustin Challamel.

Mansikka, V. J. 1925. Demons and Spirits (Slavic). In *ERE,* vol. 4, 622–630.

Maquet, J. J. 1954. The Kingdom of Ruanda. In Forde, 1954, 164–189.

Marcelin, Milo. 1950. *Mythologie Vodou,* vols. 1-2. Port-au-Prince, Haiti: Les Editions Haitiennes.

Marchal, Charles-Henri. 1963. The Mythology of Indo-China and Java. In Hackin et al., 1963.

Mariner, William. 1820. *The Natives of the Tonga Islands.* Boston: Chas. Ewer.

Markham, Sir Clements. 1969. *The Incas of Peru.* Lima: Librerias A. B. C., S. A.

Marr, N. Y. 1937. On the Religious Beliefs of the Abkhasians. *Georgica* no. 4–5.

Marriott, Alice, and Carol K. Rachlin. 1968. *American Indian Mythology.* New York: Thomas J. Crowell.

Marsh, Gordon H. 1967. Eskimo-Aleut Religion. In Owen, Deetz and Fisher, 1967:143–159.

Marshall, Rev. Harry Ignatius. 1922. *The Karen People of Burma.* Ohio State University Bulletin—Contributions in History and Political Science, vol. 26 (13): April 22.

——. 1945. *The Karens of Burma.* London: Longmans, Green.

Marshall, Lorna. 1962. !Kung Bushman Religious Beliefs. *Africa* 32 (3):221–251.

Martin, Rev. E. Osborn. *The Gods of India.* New York: Dutton.

Martinez, Jose M. B. 1962. *Religiones Primitivas de Hispania.* Roma: Consejo Superior de Investigaciones Cientificas.

Mason, J. Alden. 1910. Myths of the Uintah Utes. *JAF* 23:299–363.

Maspero, Henri. 1963. The Mythology of Modern China. In Hackin et al., 1963.

Massam, J. A. 1927. *The Cliff Dwellers of Kenya.* London: Seeley, Service.

Mathew, John. 1910. *Two Representative Tribes of Queensland.* London: T. Fisher Unwin.

Mathews, John Joseph. 1982. *The Osages, Children of the Middle Waters.* Norman: University of Oklahoma Press.

Matthews, Washington. 1889. Nogoilpi, the Gambler: A Navajo Myth. *JAF* 2:89–94.

——. 1890. The Gentile System of the Navajo Indians. *JAF* 3:89–110.

——. 1894. Songs of Sequence of the Navajos. *JAF* 7:185–194.

——. 1896. A Vigil of the Gods: A Navajo Ceremony. *AA* 9 (1):50–57.

——. 1901. The Treatment of Ailing Gods. *JAF* 14:20–23.

——. 1902a. Myths of Gestation and Parturition. *AA* 4 (4):737–742.

——. 1902b. *The Night Chant: A Navajo Ceremony.* MAMNH, vol. 6.

Maybury-Lewis, David. 1967. *Akwe-Shavante Society.* Oxford: Clarendon Press.

Mbiti, John S. 1970a. *African Religions and Philosophy.* Garden City: Doubleday.

——. 1970b. *Concepts of God in Africa.* London: S. P. C. K., C. Tinling.

Mead, Margaret. 1930. *Social Organization of Manua.* Honolulu: Beatrice P. Bishop Museum.

Means, Philip Ainsworth. 1931. *Ancient Civilizations of the Andes.* New York: Scribner's.

Meek, C. K. 1925. *The Norther Tribes of Nigeria,* vol. 2. London: Oxford University Press.

——. 1930. A Religious Festival in Northern Nigeria. *Africa* 3 (3):323–346.

——. 1931a. *A Sudanese Kingdom: An Ethnographical Study of the Jukun-Speaking Peoples of Nigeria.* London: Kegan Paul, Trench, Trubner.

——. 1931b. *Tribal Studies in Northern Nigeria.* London: Kegan Paul, Trench, Trubner.

——. 1934. The Kulu in Northern Nigeria. *Africa* 7 (3):257–269.

——. 1943. The Religions of Nigeria. *Africa* 14 (3):106–117.

Meiser, Leo. 1963. Raran, the High Spirit of the Kaean. *Anthropos* 58:905–906.

Melville, Leinani. 1969. *Children of the Rainbow.* Wheaton, Illinois: Theosophical Publishing House.

Mercer, S. A. B. 1925a. War, War-Gods (Semitic). In *ERE,* vol. 12, 700–704.

——. 1925b. Water, Water-Gods (Babylonia, Egypt). In *ERE,* vol. 12, 708–712.

Mercier, P. 1954. The Fon of Dahomey. In Forde, 1954, 210–234.

Metraux, Alfred. 1942. The Native Tribes of Eastern Bolivia and western Matto Grosso. BBAE 134.

——. 1946a. Twin Heroes of South American Mythology. *JAF* 59:114–123.

——. 1946b. Ethnography of the Chaco. *HSAI* 1:197–370.

——. 1946c. The Caingang. *HSAI* 1:445–475.

——. 1946d. The Botocudo. *HSAI* 1:531–540.

——. 1948a. The Guarani. *HSAI* 3:69–94.

——. 1948b. The Tupinamba. *HSAI* 3:95–133.

——. 1948c. The Paressi. *HSAI* 3:349–360.

——. 1948d. The Tribes of the Eastern Bolivia and the Madeira Head-Waters. *HSAI* 3:381–454..

——. 1948e. Tribes of the Eastern Slopes of the Bolivian Andes. *HSAI* 3:465–506.

——. 1948f. Zaparoan Tribes. *HSAI* 3:628–656.

——. 1948g. Tribes of the Middle and Upper Amazon River. *HSAI* 3:687–712.

——. 1949. Religion and Shamanism. *HSAI* 5:559–599.

——. 1937. Etudes d'Ethnographie Toba-Pilaga (Gran Chaco). *Anthropos* 32:171–194.

——. 1940. *Ethnology of Easter Island*. BPBM, no. 160.

——. 1939. Myths and Tales of the Matako Indians. *ES* 9:1–127.

——. 1943. The Social Organization and Religion of the Mojo and Manasi. *PM* 16:1–30.

——. 1969. *Myths of the Toba and Pilaga Indians of the Gran Chaco*. MAFS, vol. 40. New York: Kraus Reprint Co.

Meyer, Hans. 1916. *The Barundi: An Ethnological Study from German East Africa*. Leipzig: Otto Spamer.

Meyerowitz, Eva L. R. 1946. Notes on the King-God Shango and his Temple at Ibadan, Southern Nigeria. *Man* 46:25–31.

——. 1951. Concepts of the Soul among the Akan of the Gold Coast. *Africa* 21 (1):24–31.

——. 1958. *The Akan of Ghana*. London: Faber and Faber.

Michael, Henry N. 1963. *Studies in Siberian Shamanism*. Toronto: University of Toronto Press.

Middlekoop, Pieter. 1960. *Curse-Retribution-Enmity*. Amsterdam: Drukkerij en Uitgeverij, Jacob van Campen.

Middleton, John. 1953. *The Central Tribes of the North-eastern Bantu: The Kikuyu, including Embu, Meru, Mbere, Chuka, Mwimbi, Tharaka, and the Kamba of Kenya*. London: Oxford University Press.

——. 1960. *Lugbara Religion*. London: Oxford University Press.

——. 1967. *Gods and Rituals*. New York: Natural History Press.

Miller, Harry. 1970. The Cobra, India's 'God Snake'. *NG* 138:393–408.

Millroth, Berta Lyuba. 1965. *Traditional Religion of the Sukuma*. Studia Ethnographica Upsaliensa 22. Uppsala: Almqvist and Wiksells Boktryckeri.

Mills, J. P. 1922. *The Lhota Nagas*. London: Macmillan.

——. 1926. *The Ao Nagas*. London: Macmillan.

——. 1937. *The Rengma Nagas*. London: Macmillan.

Minn, Eva K. 1955. *The Lapps*. Indiana University. Graduate Program in Uralic and Asian Studies. Finland. New Haven: Human Relations Area Files, 8.

Minns, Ellis H. 1913. *Scythians and Greeks*. Cambridge: Cambridge University Press.

Mishkin, Bernard. 1940. Cosmological Ideas among the Indians of the Southern Andes. *JAF* 53:225–241.

——. 1946. The Contemporary Quechua. *HSAI* 2:411–470.

Mocklar-Ferryman, A. F. 1925. Negroes and West Africa. In *ERE*, vol. 9, 274–292.

Moes, Robert. 1983. *Auspicious Spirits: Korean Folk Paintings and Related Objects*. Washington, D.C.: The Foundation.

Montell, Gista. 1941. The Torguts of Etsin-gol. *JRAI* 70 (1):77–92.

Mooney, James. 1885–1886. Sacred Formulas of the Cherokees. ARBAE 7:307–395.

——. 1900. The Cherokee River Cult. *JAF* 13:1–10.

——, and Frans M. Olbrechts. 1932. The Swimmer Manuscript: Cherokee Sacred Formulas and Medicinal Prescriptions. BBAE 99.

Morford, Mark P. O., and Robert J. Lenardon. 1975. *Classical Mythology*. New York: David McKay.

Morgan, E. Delmar. 1888. The Customs of the Ossetes and the Light they Throw on the Evolution of Law. *JRAS* New Ser. 20 (3).

Morgan, Kenneth W., ed. 1953. *The Religion of the Hindus*. New York: The Ronald Press.

Morgan, Lewis H. 1901. *League of the Ho-de-no-sau-nee or Iroquois*, vols. 1–2. A new edition with additional matter, ed. and annotated Herbert M. Lloyd. New York: Dodd, Mead.

——. 1904. *League of the Ho-de-no-sau-nee or Iroquois*, vol. 1. New York: Dodd, Mead.

——. 1959. *The Indian Journals 1859–1862*. Ann Arbor: University of Michigan Press.

Morice, A. G. 1925. Denes. In *ERE*, vol. 4, 636–641.

Morley, Sylvanus G. 1946. *The Ancient Maya*. Stanford: Stanford University Press.

Morrill, Sibley S., ed. 1968. *The Kahunas*. San Francisco: Sibley S. Morrill.

Morton-Williams, Peter. 1964. An Outline of the Cosmology and Cult Organization of the Oyo Yoruba. *Africa* 34 (3):243–261.

Moscati, Sabatino. 1960. *Ancient Semitic Civilizations*. New York: Capricorn.

——. 1962. *The Face of the Ancient Orient*. Garden City: Anchor Books.

Moss, C. R. 1920. *Nabaloi Law and Ritual*. PAEUC, vol. 15, 207–342.

Moss, R. W. 1925. Fortune (Biblical and Christian). In *ERE*, vol. 6, 88–91.

Moss, Rosalind. 1925. *The Life After Death in Oceania*. Oxford: Oxford University Press.

Moulton, J. Egan. 1925. Tongans. In *ERE*, vol. 12, 376–380.

Mounteford, Charles P. 1955. The Lightning Man in Australian Mythology. *Man* 55:129–130.

——. 1958. *The Tiwi: Their Art, Myth, and Ceremony*. London: Phoenix House.

——. 1968. *Winbaruku and the Myth of Jarapiri*. Adelaide: Rigby.

——. 1979a. *The Dawn of Time*. Adelaide: Rigby.

——. 1979b. *The Dreamtime*. Adelaide: Rigby.

Mowat, Farley. 1968. *People of the Deer*. New York: Pyramid Books.

Mudiraj, G. N. R. 1970. Folk Deities of Telangana. *Folklore* (Calcutta) 11 (2):47–50.

Mukherjea, Charulal. 1962. *The Santals*. Calcutta: A. Mukherjee.

Muller, Kal. 1973. Tannese, New Hebrides. In Forge, 1973.

Muller, Werner. 1968. North America. In James, 1968.

Muller, Wilhelm. 1917. *Yap,* Ethnographie: B. Mikronesien bd. 2 (1–2). Hamburg: Friederichsen.

Mumford, W. Bryant. 1934. The Hehe-Bena Sangu Peoples of East Africa. *AA* 36 (2):203–222.

de Munck, Alyette. 1971. Bambuti: Exuberant Pygmies of Africa's Deep Ituri Forest. In *Nomads of the World,* 143–153. Washington, D.C.: National Geographic Society Special Publications Division.

Munro, Neil Gordon. 1963. *Ainu Creed and Cult*. New York: Columbia University Press.

Muntsch, Rev. Albert. 1943. Some Magico-Religious Observances of the Present-Day Maya Indians of British Honduras and Yucatan. *PM* 16:31–43.

Murphy, Robert F. 1958. *Mundurucu Religion*. PAEUC, vol. 49.

——, and Buell Quain. 1955. *The Trumai Indians of Central Brazil*. Locust Valley, New York: J. J. Augustin.

Murra, John. 1946. The Historic Tribes of Ecuador. *HSAI* 2:785–821.

Murray, Alexander S. 1935. *Manual of Mythology*. New York: Tudor.

Murray's Manual of Mythology. 1895. Philadelphia: David McKay.

Mutwa, Vusumazulu Credo. [ca. 1921]. *Indaba, My Children*. Johannesburg: Blue Crane Books.

——. 1966. *Africa is my Witness*. Johannesburg: Blue Crane Books.

Mythology of All Races. 1916–1932. Louis Herbert Gray, ed. Boston: Marshall Jones.

Nadel, S. F. 1954. *Nupe Religion*. London: Routledge and Kegan Paul.

Naik, T. B. 1956. *The Bhils: A Study*. Delhi: Bharatiya Adimjati Sevak Sangh.

Nakuina, M. K., trans. of L. D. Keliipio. 1901. Kuula, the Fish God of Hawaii. *Thrum: The Hawaiian Annual* 27:110–124.

Nash, June C. 1966. *Living with Nats: An Analysis of Animism in Burman Village Social Relations*. In Conference on Threavada Buddhism, 1966.

——. 1970. *The Change of Officials in Tzo'ontahal, Chiapas, Mexico: An Analysis of Behavior as a Key to Structure and Process*. New Orleans: Tulane University Middle American Research Institute.

——. 1972. Devils, Witches, and Sudden Death. *AMNH-Mag* 81 (3):52–59.

de Nebesky-Wojkowitz, Rene. 1952. Ancient Funeral Ceremonies of the Lepchas. *Eastern Anthropologist* 5 (1):27–40.

——. 1956a. *Oracles and Demons of Tibet*. London: Oxford University Press.

——. 1956b. *Where the Gods are Mountains*. London: Weidenfield and Nicolson.

Neff, Mary L. 1912. Pima and Papago Legends. *JAF* 25:51–65.

Neihardt, John G. 1961. *Black Elk Speaks*. Lincoln: University of Nebraska Press.

Nelson, Edward William. 1896–1897. The Eskimo about Bering Strait. *ARBAE* 18:19–518.

Neumann, Erich. 1955. *The Great Mother.* New York: Pantheon.

Newcomb, Frank J. 1940. Origin Legend of the Navaho Eagle Chant. *JAF* 53:50–77.

Newell, W. W. 1896. Navaho Legends. *JAF* 9:211–218.

Niblack, Albert P. 1888. The Coast Indians of Southern Alaska and Northern British Columbia. RUSNM, 231–386.

Nicholas, Henry, trans. 1892. Genealogies and Historical Notes from Rarotonga. *PSJ* 1:65–75.

Nicholson, Irene. 1967. *Mexican and Central American Mythology.* London: Hamlyn.

Nimuendaju, Curt. 1942. *The Serente,* trans. Robert Lowie. Los Angeles: The Southwest Museum.

——. 1946a. *The Eastern Timbira,* trans. Robert H, Lowie. PAEUC, vol. 41.

——. 1946b. Social Organization and Beliefs of the Botocudo of Eastern Brazil. *SJA* 2 (1):93–115.

——. 1948a. Tribes of the Lower and Middle Xingu River. *HSAI* 3:213–243.

——. 1948b. The Cayabi, Tapayuna, and Apiaca. *HSAI* 3:307–320.

——. 1952. *The Tukuna,* trans. William D. Hohenthal. PAEUC, vol. 45.

——. 1967. *The Apinaye,* trans. Robert H. Lowie. Oosterhout N. B., the Netherlands: Anthropological Publications.

de Nino, Bernardino. 1912. *Chiriguano Ethnography.* La Paz: Tipgrafia Comercial de Ismael Argote.

Noeldke, Th. 1925. Arabs (Ancient). In *ERE,* vol. 1, 659–673.

Nomland, Gladys Ayer. 1935. *Sinkyone Notes.* PAEUC, vol. 36.

Noone, R. O. 1948. Notes on the Kampong, Compounds, and Houses of the Patani Malay Village of Banggul Ara, in the Mukim of Batu Kurau, Northern Perak. *JRAI* (Malaysian Branch) 21 (1):124–147.

Norbeck, Edward Takashima. 1954. *A Japanese Fishing Community.* Salt Lake City: University of Utah Press.

Nordenskiold, Eerland. 1930. *Picture-Writing and Other Documents by Nele, Charles Slater, Charlie Nelson, and other Cuna Indians.* Goteborg, Sweden: Goteborg Museum.

——. 1938. *An Historical and Ethnological Survey of the Cuna Indians.* Goteborg, Sweden: Goteborg Museum.

Nungak, Zebedee, and Eugene Arima. 1969. Eskimo Stories from Povungnituk, Quebec. NMC-AS Bulletin 235, no. 90.

Nyuak, Leo. 1906. Religious Rites and Customs of the Iban or Dyaks of Sarawak, trans. the Very Rev. Edm. Dunn. *Anthropos* 1:11–24, 165–184, 403–425.

Oberg, Kalervo. 1953. Indian Tribes of the Northern Matto Grosso, Brazil. Washington, D.C.: Smithsonian Institute of Social Anthropology, no. 15.

Obermann, Julian. 1948. *Ugaritic Mythology.* New Haven: Yale University Press.

Obeyeskere, Gananath. 1966. The Buddhist Pantheon in Ceylon and its Extensions. In Conference on Theravada Buddhism, 1966.

——. 1974. A Village in Sri Lanka: Madagama. In Maloney, 1974.

O'Flaherty, Wendy Doniger. 1980. *Women, Androgynes, and Other Mythical Beasts.* Chicago: University of Chicago Press.

Ohnuki-Tierney, Emiko. 1974. *The Ainu of the Northwest Coast of Southern Sakhalin.* New York: Holt, Rhinehart and Winston.

Oldenberg, H. 1896. *Ancient India.* Chicago: Open Court.

Oldenburg, Ulf. 1969. *The Conflict Between El and Ba'al in Canaanite Religion.* Leiden: E. J. Brill.

Oliver, Douglas L. 1967. *A Solomon Island Society.* Boston: Beacon.

Olsen, Fred. 1974. *On the Trail of the Arawaks.* Norman: University of Oklahoma Press.

One Feather, Vivian. 1982a. How Evil Began. *Parabola* 7 (4):49–51.

——. 1982b. The Judgement of Mahpiyato. *Parabola* 8 (1):82–86.

Oosterwal, Gottfried. 1963. A Cargo Cult in the Mamberamo Area. *Ethnology* 2 (1):1–14.

Opler, Morris E., and Robert Seido Hashima. 1946. The Rice Goddess and the Fox in Japanese Religion and Folk Practice. *AA* 48 (1):43–53.

Oppenheim, A. Leo. 1950. Assyro-Babylonian Religion. In Ferm, 1950:63–80.

O'Rahilly, Thomas F. 1946. *Early Irish History and Mythology.* Dublin: Dublin Institute for Advanced Studies.

Orchardson, Ian Q. 1961. *The Kipsigis.* East African Literature Bureau. Nairobi: Eagle Press.

Osborne, Harold. 1968. *South American Mythology.* Verona, Italy: Hamlyn.

Ostermann, H. 1942. *The Mackenzie Eskimos.* The Fifth Thule Expedition, vol. 10, no. 2. Copenhagen: Gyldendal.

Ottenberg, Simon, and Phoebe Ottenberg. 1960. *Cultures and Societies of Africa.* New York: Random House.

Ovid. 1955. *Metamorphoses,* trans. Mary M. Innes. Middlesex: Penguin.

Owen, Roger, James Deetz, and Anthony Fisher, eds. 1967. *North American Indians.* New York: Macmillan.

Oyler, Rev. D. S. 1918. Nikwang's Place in the Shilluk Religion. *SNR* 1 (4):283–292.

Paasonen, H. 1925. Mordvins. In *ERE,* vol. 8, 842–847.

Pal, Pratapaditya, and Dipak Chandra Phattacharyya. 1969. *The Astral Divinities of Nepal.* Varanasi-5, India: Prithivi Prakashan.

Pallottino, Massimo. 1975. *The Etruscans,* trans. F. Cremona. Bloomington: Indiana University Press.

Pansit, M. P. 1970. *Aditi and Other Deities in the Veda.* Pondicherry: Dipti Publications, Sri Aurobindo Ashram.

Park, Willard Z. 1946. Tribes of the Sierra Nevada de Santa Marta, Colombia. *HSAI* 2:865–886.

Parker, Arthur C. 1910. Iroquois Sun Myths. *JAF* 23:473–478.

Parrinder, E. G. 1951. Ibadan Annual Festival. *Africa* 21 (1):54–58.

Parrinder, Geoffrey. 1950. Theistic Beliefs of the Yoruba and Ewe Peoples of West Africa. In Smith, 1950:224–240.

——. 1961. *West African Religion.* New York: Barnes and Noble.

——. 1967. *African Mythology.* Verona, Italy: O. G. A. M.

Parsons, Elsie Clews. 1916. The Zuni Molawia. *JAF* 29:392–399.

——. 1929. The Social Organization of the Tewa of New Mexico. MAAA, no. 36.

——. 1929–1930. Isleta, New Mexico. ARBAE 47:193–466.

——. 1939. *Pueblo Indian Religion,* vol. 1. Chicago: University of Chicago Press.

——. 1940. Cosmography of Indians of the Imbabbura Province, Ecuador. *JAF* 53:219–224.

Parsons, Rev. Robert T. 1950. The Idea of God among the Kono of Sierra Leone. In Smith, 1950:260–276.

Patai, Raphael. 1967. *The Hebrew Goddess.* New York: KTAV Publishing House.

Paton, Lewis Bayles. 1925a. Canaanites. In *ERE,* vol. 3, 176–188.

——. 1925b. Dagan, Dagon. In *ERE,* vol. 4, 386–388.

——. 1925c. Phoenicians. In *ERE,* vol. 9, 887–897.

Paulme, Denise. 1940. *Social Organization of the Dogon (French Sudan).* Paris: Editions Domat-Montchrestien, F. Loviton et Cie.

——. 1973. The Dogon of Mali, Volta. In *Peoples of the Earth,* vol. 2. Verona, Italy: for the Danbury Press.

Peeters, Rev. Hermes. 1941. *The Religions of China.* Peking: College of Chinese Studies, California College in China.

Penard, A. T., and T. E. Penard. 1917. Popular Notions Relating to Primitive Stone Artifacts in Surinam. *JAF* 30:251–261.

Penley, E. W. 1930. Superstition amongst the Turkana, a Southern Turkana Heaven. *Man* 30:139–140.

Pepper, George H. 1908. Ah-jih-lee-hah-neh. a Navajo Legend. *JAF* 21:178–183.

Percheron, Maurice. 1953. *Dieux et Demons, Lamas et Sourciers de Mongolie.* Paris: de Noel.

Peredo, Miguel Guzman. 1974. Exploring the Sacred Well. *Americas* 26 (8):17–23.

Perera, Victor, and Robert D. Bruce. 1982. *The Last Lords of Palenque.* Boston: Little, Brown.

Petrullo, Vincenzo. 1939. The Yaruros of the Capanaparo River, Venezuela. BBAE 123 (11):161–290.

Pettazonni, Raffaele. 1956. *The All-Knowing God,* trans. H. J. Rose. London: Methuen.

Pettersson, Olaf. 1953. *Chiefs and Gods*. Lund: C, W. K. Gleerup.

——. 1957. *Jabmek and Jabmeaimo*. Lund: C. W. K. Gleerup.

Philippi, Donald L. 1982. *Songs of Gods, Songs of Humans: The Epic Tradition of Ainu*. San Francisco: North Point Press.

Phillips, Eustace D. 1969. *The Mongols*. New York: Praeger.

Philpot, Roy. 1936. Makumba—The Baushi Tribal God. *JRAI* 66:189–208.

Piggott, Juliet. 1969. *Japanese Mythology*. London: Hamlyn.

Pilsudski, Bronislas. 1912. Ainu Folklore. *JAF* 25:72–86.

Pinches, T. G. 1925a. Elamites. In *ERE*, vol. 5, 250–252.

——. 1925b. Sumero-Akkadians. In *ERE*, vol. 12, 40–44.

Pineda Giraldo, Roberto. 1950. *Aspects of Magic in La Guajira*. Bogota.

Pittier de Fabrega, H. 1903. Folklore of the Bribri and Brunka Indians. *JAF* 16:1–9.

Playfair, Alan. 1909. *The Garos*. London: David Nutt.

Poignant, Roslyn. 1967. *Oceanic Mythology*. London: Hamlyn.

Polome, Edgar. 1970. The Indo-European Component in Germanic Religion. In Puhvel, 1970:55–82.

Popov, A. 1933. Consecration Ritual for a Blacksmith Novice among the Yakuts. *JAF* 46:257–271.

Popov, A. A., and B. O. Dolgikh. 1964. The Kets. In Levin and Potapev, 1964.

Pospisil, Leopold. 1958. *Kapauku Papuans and their Law*. New Haven: Yale University Publications in Anthropology, no. 54.

Potapev, L. P. 1964. The Khakasy. In Levin and Potapev, 1964.

Powell, J. W. 1879–1880. Sketch of the Mythology of the North American Indians. ARBAE 1:19–56.

Powell, Peter J. 1969. *Sweet Medicine*. Norman: University of Oklahoma Press.

Powers, Stephen. 1877. *Tribes of California*. Washington, D.C.: Government Printing Office.

Powers, William K. 1977. *Oglala Religion*. Lincoln: University of Nebraska Press.

Preuss, Konrad Theodor. 1926–1927. *Forschungsreise zu den Kagaba*. St. Gabriel-Modling bei Wein: Administration des Anthropos.

Pritchard, James B. 1943. *Palestinian Figurines in Relation to Certain Goddesses Known through Literature*. New Haven: American Oriental Society.

Prokof'yeva, E. D. 1964a. The Nentsy. In Levin and Potapev, 1964.

——. 1964b. The Sel'kups. In Levin and Potapev, 1964.

Puhvel, Jaan, ed. 1970. *Myth and Law among the Indo-Europeans*. Berkeley and Los Angeles: University of California Press.

——. Aspects of Equine Functionality. In Puhvel, 1970:159–172.

——. 1974. Indo-European Structure of the Baltic Pantheon. In *Myth in Indo-European Antiquity,* ed. Gerald J. Larson, 75–85. Berkeley: University of California Press.

Puini, C., and F. V. Dickens. 1880. The Seven Gods of Happiness. *TASJ* 8–9.

Pulekula, Teacher at Tama-ha-le-leka. 1903. The Traditions of Niue-Fekai. *PSJ* 12:22–31.

Punekar, Vijaya B. 1959. *The Son Kolis of Bombay*. Bombay: Popular Book Depot.

Putnam, John J. 1971. The Ganges, River of Faith. *NG* 140:445–482.

——, and Eliot Elisofon. 1973. Yesterday's Congo, Today's Zaire. *NG* 143:398–432.

Queval, Jean. 1968. *Lexique des dieux*. Paris: Delpire.

Ten Raa, Eric. 1969. The Moon as Symbol of Life and Fertility in Sandawe Thought. *Africa* 39 (1):24–53.

Raats, Pieter Jan. 1969. *A Structural Study of Bagobo Myths and Rites*. Cebu City, Philippines: University of San Carlos.

Radcliffe-Brown, A. R. 1967. *The Andaman Islanders*. New York: The Free Press.

Radin, Paul. 1914. The Religion of the North American Indians. *JAF* 27:335–373.

——. 1915–1916. The Winnebago Tribe. ARBAE 37:33–550.

——, and A. B. Reagan. 1928. Ojibwa Myths and Tales—the Manabhozo Cycle. *JAF* 41:61–146.

Rahmann, Rudolf. 1952. The Ritual Spring Hunt of Northeastern and Middle India. *Anthropos* 47:871–890.

——, and Marcelino N. Maceda. 1955. Notes on the Negritos of Northern Negros. *Anthropos* 50:810–836.

Rasmussen, Knud. 1929. Intellectual Culture of the Iglulik Eskimos. Report of the Fifth Thule Expedition, vol. 7, no. 1. Copenhagen: Gyldendal.

——. 1930. Observations on the Intellectual Culture of the Caribou Eskimos. The Fifth Thule Expedition, vol. 7, no. 2. Copenhagen: Gyldendal.

——. 1931. The Netsilik Eskimos. The Fifth Thule Expedition, vol. 8. Copenhagen: Gyldendal.

——. 1932. Intellectual Culture of the Copper Eskimos. The Fifth Thule Expedition, vol. 9. Copenhagen: Gyldendal.

——. 1972. A Shaman's Journey to the Sea Spirit. In Lessa and Vogt, 1972.

Rattray, Robert Sutherland. 1923. *Ashanti.* Oxford: Clarendon Press.

——. 1932. *The tribes of the Ashanti Hinterland.* 2 vols. Oxford: Clarendon Press.

Rawlinson, George. 1885. *The Religions of the Ancient World.* New York: John B. Alden.

Ray, Verne F. 1933. The Sanpoil and Nispelem: Salishan Peoples of Northeastern Washington. PAUW, vol. 5. Seattle, Washington: Univ. Washington Press.

Read, Margaret. 1956. *The Ngoni of Nyasaland.* London: Oxford University Press for International African Institute.

Reagan, Albert B., and L. V. W. Walters. 1933. Tales from the Hoh and Quileute. *JAF* 46:297–346.

Recinos, Adrain. 1950. *Popul Vuh,* trans. Deila Goetz and Sylvanus Morley. Norman: University of Oklahoma Press.

Redfield, Robert, and Alfonso Villa Rojas. 1962. *Chan Kom: a Maya Village.* Chicago: University of Chicago Press.

Reed, A. W. 1965. *Myths and Legends of Australia.* Sydney: A. H. and A. W. Reed.

Reed, Alma. 1966. *Ancient Past of Mexico.* New York: Crown.

Reichard, Gladys A. 1950. *Navaho Religions.* Bollingen Series, vol. 18, parts 1–2. New York: Pantheon.

Reichel-Dolmatoff, Gerardo. 1950–1951. *The Kogi: A Tribe of the Sierra Nevada de Santa Marta.* Bogota: Editorial Iqueima.

——. 1965. *Colombia.* Ancient Peoples and Places, vol. 44. London: Thames and Hudson.

——. 1971. *Amazonian Cosmos.* Chicago: University of Chicago Press.

——. 1975. *The Shaman and the Jaguar.* Philadelphia: Temple University Press.

Renel, Ch. *Les religions de la Gauls avant le Christianisme.* Paris: Ernest Leroux.

Revon, M. 1925. Nature (Japanese). In *ERE,* vol. 9, 233–239.

Reyher, Rebecca. 1952. *The Fon and his Hundred Wives.* Garden City: Doubleday.

Ribbach, Samuel Heinrich. 1940. *Drogpa Namgyal: The Life of a Tibetan.* Munchen-Planegg: Otto Wilhelm Barth Verlag.

Richard, Rev. Timothy. 1916. *Calendar of the Gods in China.* Shanghai: Commercial Press.

Richards, Audrey I. 1939. *Land, Labor, and Diet in Northern Rhodesia: An Economic Study of the Bemba Tribe.* Oxford: Oxford University Press for the International Institute of African Languages and Cultures.

Ritzenthaler, Robert E., and Pat Ritzenthaler. 1970. *The Woodland Indians.* Garden City: Natural History Press.

Rivers, W. H. R. 1915. Sun Cult and Megaliths in Oceania. *AA* 17 (3):431–445.

——. 1925a. Todas. In *ERE,* vol. 12, 354–357.

——. 1925b. New Hebrides. In *ERE,* vol. 9, 352–355.

Roberts, J. J. M. 1972. *The Earliest Semitic Pantheon.* Baltimore: Johns Hopkins University Press.

Robertson, George Scott. 1897. Kafiristan and its People. *JRAI* 27:75–89.

——. 1925. Kafiristan. In *ERE,* vol. 7, 634–636.

Robertson, John M. 1911. *Pagan Christs.* London: Watts.

Robinson, Roland. 1966. *Aboriginal Myths and Legends.* Melbourne: Sun Books.

Rock, Joseph F. 1936a. The Origin of the Tso-la Books, or Books of Divination of the Na-khi or Mo-so Tribe. *JWCBRS* 8.

——. 1936b. Ha-la or the Killing of the Soul, as Practiced by Na-khi Sorcerer. *JWCBRS* 8.

——. 1947. *Ancient Na-khi Kingdom of Southwest China.* Cambridge, Mass.: Harvard University Press.

——. 1959. Contributions to the Shamanism of the Tibetan-Chinese Borderland. *Anthropos* 54:796–818.

Rogers, John [Chief Snow Cloud]. 1957. *A Chippewa Speaks*. Hollywood, California: Snow Cloud Publishers.

Roheim, Geza. n.d. The Story of the Light that Disappeared. Reprint from *Samiska*, 1 (1). Calcutta: The Indian Psycho-Analytical Society.

——. 1929. Dying Gods and Puberty Ceremonies. *JRAI* 59:181–197.

——. 1946. Yaboaine, a War God of Normanby Island. *Oceania* 16 (4):319–336.

——. 1954. *Hungarian and Vogul Mythology*. Locust Valley, New York: J. J. Augustin.

——. 1972. *The Panic of the Gods*. New York: Harper and Row.

Rosaldo, Renato I. 1968. Metaphors of Heirarchy in a Mayan Ritual. *AA* 70, part 2.

Roscher, W. H. 1965. *Ausfuhrliches Lexikon der greichischen und romischen Mythologie*. Hildesheim: Georg Olms Verlagsbuchhandlung.

Roscoe, John. 1915. *The Northern Bantu*. Cambridge: Cambridge University Press.

——. 1923. *The Banyankole*. Cambridge: Cambridge University Press.

——. 1965. *The Baganda*. London: Frank Cass.

Ross, Anne. 1967. *Pagan Celtic Britain*. New York: Columbia University Press.

Rossini, C. Conti. 1925. Hamites and East Africa. In *ERE*, vol. 6, 486–492.

Roth, Henry Ling. 1891. The Natives of Borneo, Edited from the Papers of the Late Brooks Low, Esq. *JRAI* 21:110–137.

——. 1968. *The Natives of Sarawak and British North Borneo*. Singapore: University of Malaya Press.

Rouse, Irving. 1948a. The Arawak. *HSAI* 4:507–546.

——. 1948b. The Carib. *HSAI* 4:547–565.

Rowe, John Howland. 1946. Inca Culture at the Time of the Spanish Conquest. *HSAI* 2:183–329.

——. 1948. The Kingdom of Chimor. *Acta Americana* 6:26–59.

Roy, Sarat Chandra. 1915. *The Oraons of Chota Napur*. Ranchi: Published by the Author at the Bar Library.

——. 1928. *Oraon Religion and Customs*. Shambazar, Calcutta: Industry Press.

Roys, Ralph L. 1949. *The Prophecies of the Mayan Tuns or Years: In the Books of Chilam Balam of Tizimin and Mani*. Washington, D.C.: Carnagie Institute, no. 51,

——. 1965. *Ritual of the Bacabs*. Norman: University of Oklahoma Press.

Ruel, M. J. 1965. Religion and Society among the Kuria of East Africa. *Africa* 35 (3):295–306.

Ruhela, Satya Pal. 1971. Lohars: Bullock-Cart Blacksmiths of India's Rajasthan State. In *Nomads of the World*, 26–51. Washington, D.C.: National Geographic Society.

Ruskin, John. 1869. *The Queen of the Air: Being a Study of the Greek Myths of Cloud and Storm*. London: Smith, Elder.

Russell, Frank. 1904–1905. The Pima Indians. *ARBAE* 26:3–389.

Russell, R. V. 1916. *The Tribes and Castes of the Central Provinces of India*, 4 vols. London: Macmillan.

——. 1925. Central Provinces (India). In *ERE*, vol. 3, 311–316.

Ruud, Jorgen. 1960. *Taboo: A Study of Malagasy Custom and Beliefs*. Oslo: Oslo University Press.

Safford, W. E. 1902. Guam and its People. *AA* 4:707–729.

Salkeld, Joseph. 1844. *Classical Antiquities or a Compendium of Roman and Greek Antiquities*. New York: Alexander V. Blake.

Salvador, Canals Frau. 1946. The Huarpe. *HSAI* 1:169–175.

Samuel, Alan E. 1966. *The Mycenaeans in History*. Englewood Cliffs, N.J.: Prentice-Hall.

Santandrea, Fr. S. 1938. Evil and Witchcraft among the Ngogo Group of Tribes. *Africa* 11 (4):459–481.

Sapir, Edward. 1907. Religious Ideas of the Takelma Indians. *JAF* 20:33–49.

——. 1925. Vancouver Island Indians. In *ERE*, vol. 12, 591–595.

Sarawak Gazette. 1963. Borneo Literature Bureau.

Sarma, D. W. 1953. The Nature and History of Hinduism. In Morgan, 1953.

Saunders, E. Dale. 1961. Japanese Mythology. In Kramer, 1961a, 409–442.

Sayce, A. H. 1898. *Lectures on the Origin and Growth of Religion as Illustrated by the Religion of the Ancient Babylonians.* Hibbert Lectures, 1887. Oxford: Williams and Norgate.

——. 1925. Armenia (Vannic). In *ERE,* vol. 1, 793–794.

Schaeffer, C. F. 1966. The Discovery of Ugarit. In *Hands on the Past,* ed. C. W. Ceram, 301–306. New York: Knopf.

Schafer, Edward H. 1980. *The Divine Woman, Dragon Ladies, and Rain Maidens.* San Francisco: North Point Press.

Schapera, Isaac. 1937. *Bantu-Speaking Peoples of South Africa.* London: George Routledge and Sons.

——. 1951. *The Khoisan Peoples of South Africa: Bushmen and Hottentots.* London: George Routledge and Sons.

Scharer, Hans. 1963. *Ngaju Religion,* trans. Rodney Needham. The Hague: Martinus Nijhoff.

Schebesta, Paul. 1927. *Among the Forest Dwarfs of Malaya.* London: Hutchinson.

——. 1952–1957. *Die Negrito Asiens.* Wein-Modling: St.-Gabriel Verlag.

Schellhas, Paul. 1904. Representation of Deities of the Maya Manuscripts, trans. Selma Wesselhoeft and Miss A. M. Parker. PMAE, vol. 4.

Scherer, J. H. 1959. The Ha of Tanganyika. *Anthropos* 54:841–903.

Schlaginweit, Emil. 1969. *Buddhism in Tibet.* New York: Augustin M. Kelley.

Schmidt, W. 1933. *High Gods in North America.* Oxford: Clarendon Press.

Schoeps, Hans-Joachim. 1961. *The Religions of Mankind.* Garden City: Doubleday.

Schoolcraft, Henry Rose. 1857. *History of the Indian Tribes of the Unites States.* 6 vols. Philadelphia: Lippincott.

Schotter, P. Aloys. 1908. Notes Ethnographiques sur les Tribes su Kuoy-tcheou (Chine). *Africa* 3 (1).

Schrader, O. 1925. Aryan Religion. In ERE, vol. 2, 11–57.

Schram, Louis M. J. 1957. The Mongurs of the Kansu-Tibetan Border. *TAPS* 47, part 2.

Schulze, Rev. F. V. P. 1912. *The Religion of the Kuvi-Konds, their Customs and Folklore.* Madras: Graves, Cookson.

Schwab, George. 1947. Tribes of the Liberian Hinterland. PMAE, vol. 31.

Scott, Sir James George. 1964. *Indo-Chinese.* Vol. 12, *Mythology of All Races.* New York: Cooper Square Publishers.

Selected Studies on Indonesia-Bali, by Dutch Scholars. 1960–1969. The Hague: W. van Hoeve Ltd, vol. 5, vol. 8.

Seler, Ed. 1925. Huichols. In *ERE,* vol. 6, 828–830.

Seligman, C. G. 1909. Note on the 'Bandar' Cult of the Kandyan Sinhalese. *Man* 9:130–134.

——. 1925. Nuba. In *ERE,* vol. 9, 401–406.

——. 1931. The Religion of the Pagan Tribes of the White Nile. *Africa* 4 (1):1–21.

Seligman, Charles Gabriel, and Brenda Z. Seligman. 1911. *The Veddas.* Cambridge: Cambridge University Press.

Seligmann, Kurt. 1948. *Magic, Supernaturalism, and Religion.* New York: Grosset and Dunlap.

Shack, William A. 1963. Religious Ideas and Social Action in Gurage Bond-Friendship. *Africa* 33 (3):198–208.

——. 1968. The Masqal-Pole: Religious Conflict and Social Change in Gurageland. *Africa* 38 (4):457–468.

Shakespear, Lt. Col. J. 1912ba. *The Lushei Kuki Clans.* London: Macmillan.

——. 1913. The Pleasing of the God Thangjing. *Man* 13:81–86.

Shand, Alexander. 1894. The Moriori People of the Chatham Islands. *PSJ* 3 (2):76–92.

Shortt, J. 1868. *The Tribes on the Neilgherries.* Madras: Higginbotham.

Shryock, John. 1931. *The Temples of Anking.* Paris: Librairie Orientaliste Paul Guethner.

Shternberg, Lev Iakoblevich. 1933. *The Gilyak, Orochi, Goldi, Negidal, Ainu: Articles and Materials.* Khabarovsk: Dal'giz.

Sibree, Rev. James. 1880. *The Great African Island.* London: Trubner.

Sierksma, F. 1960. *The Gods as We Shape Them.* London: Routledge and Kegan Paul.

——. 1966. *Tibet's Terrifying Deities.* The Hague: Mouton.

Siew, Nim Chee. 1953. *Labor and Tin Mining in Malaya*. Ithaca: Cornell University Southeast Asia Program, Department of Eastern Studies, and the New York State School of Industrial and Labor Relations.

Siiger, Halfdan. 1967. The Lepchas: Culture and religion of a Himalayan People. NMD 11, part 1–2.

Simpson, George Eaton. 1945. The Belief System of Haitian Vodun. *AA* 47:35–59.

———. 1965, *The Shango Cult of Trinidad*. San Juan: Institute of Caribbean Studies, University of Puerto Rico.

———. 1971. The Belief System of Haitian Vodun. In *Peoples and Cultures of the Caribbean*, ed. Michael M. Horowitz. Garden City: Natural History Press.

Skafte, Peter. 1979. Smoking Out Secrets of the Mysterious 'Snakers' in India. *Smithsonian* 10 (October):121–126.

Skeat, Walter Wm. 1906. *Pagan Races of the Malay Peninsula*. London: Macmillan.

———. 1925. Malay Peninsula. In *ERE*, vol. 8, 348–372.

Skinner, Alanson. 1913. *Social Life and Ceremonial Bundles of Menomini Indians*. AMNH-AP, vol. 13, part 1.

———. 1915a. *Associations and Ceremonies of Menomini Indians*. AMNH-AP, vol. 13, part 2.

———. 1915b. The Menomini Word 'Hawatuk'. JAF 28:258–261.

———. 1920. *The Medicine Ceremony of the Menomini, Iowa, and Wahpeton Dakota, with Notes on the Ceremony among the Ponca, Bungi, Ojibwa, and Potawatomi*. MAI-IM 4.

———. 1925a. Traditions of the Iowa Indians. *JAF* 38:425–506.

———. 1925b. Notes on Mahikan Ethnology. *Bulletin of the Public Museum of the City of Milwaukee* 2 (3):87–116.

———. 1928. Sauk Tales. *JAF* 41:147–171.

———, and John V. Satterlee. 1915. *Folklore of the Menomini Indians*. AMNH-AP vol. 13, part 3.

Skinner, Elliott Percival. 1958. Christianity and Islam among the Mossi. *AA* 60.

Smith, Edwin W., ed. 1950. *African Ideas of God*. London: Edinburgh House.

———. Ideas of God among South African Tribes. In Smith, 1950:78–134.

———, and Capt. Andrew Murray Dale. 1920. *The Ila-Speaking Peoples of Northern Rhodesia*. London: Macmillan.

Smith, Erminie A. 1881–1882. Myths of the Iroquois. ARBAE 2:47–116.

Smith, Harlan I. 1894. Notes on Eskimo Traditions. *JAF* 7:209–216.

Smith, S. Percy. 1892. Futuna: Of Horne Island and its People. *PSJ* 1:33–52.

———. 1902. Niue Island and its People. *PSJ* 11:195–218.

———. 1920. Notes on the Ellice and Tokelau Groups. *PSJ* 29:144–148.

Smith, William Robertson. 1969. *Lectures on the Religion of the Semites*. New York: KTAV Publishing House.

Snellgrove, David L. 1957. *Buddhist Himalaya*. Oxford: Bruno Cassirer.

———. 1961. *Himalayan Pilgrimage*. Oxford: Bruno Cassirer.

Snorri Sturluson. 1964. *The Prose Edda,* trans. Jean I. Young. Berkeley and Los Angeles: University of California Press.

Soga, John Henderson. 1931. *The Ama-xosa: Life and Customs*. Lovedale, C.P., South Africa: Lovedale Press.

Sonnichsen, C. L. 1958. *The Mescalero Apaches*. Norman: University of Oklahoma Press.

Speck, Frank G. 1909. *Ethnology of the Yuchi Indians*. APUPM, vol. 1, no. 1.

———. 1925. Montagnais and Naskapi Tales from the Labrador Peninsula. *JAF* 38:1–32.

———. 1935a. Penobscot Tales and Religious Beliefs. *JAF* 48:1–107.

———. 1935b. *Naskapi*. Norman: University of Oklahoma Press.

Spence, Lewis. 1923. *The Gods of Mexico*. New York: Frederick A. Stokes.

———. 1925a. Brazil. In *ERE*, vol. 2, 834–838.

———. 1925b. Chile. In *ERE*, vol. 3, 546–549.

———. 1925c. Chinooks. In *ERE*, vol. 3, 560–563.

———. 1925d. Choctaws. In *ERE*, vol. 3, 567–569.

——. 1925e. Cherokees. In *ERE*, vol. 3, 503–509.

——. 1925f. Cosmogony and Cosmology (North American). In *ERE*, vol. 4, 126–218.

——. 1925g. Calendar (American). In *ERE*, vol. 3, 65–70.

Spencer, Sir Baldwin. 1904. *Northern Tribes of Central Australia*. London: Macmillan.

——. 1927. *The Arunta*. London: Macmillan.

Spencer, Baldwin, and F. J. Gillen. 1968. *The Native Tribes of Central Australia*. New York: Dover.

Spencer, Dorothy M. 1941. *Disease, Society, and Religion in Fiji Islands*. Locust Valley, New York: J. J. Augustin.

Spencer, Robert F. 1959. The North Alaskan Eskimo. BBAE 171.

Spencer, Robert Steward. 1931. The Noro, or Priestesses of Loo Choo. *TASJ* 2nd Ser. 8:94–112.

Spier, Leslie. 1928. *Havasupai Ethnography*. AMNH-AP 29, part 3.

——, and Edward Sapir. 1930. Wishram Ethnography. PAUW 3 (3):151–300.

Spinden, Herbert J. 1908. Myths of the Nez Perce Indians. *JAF* 21:149–158.

Spiro, Melford. 1951. Some Ifaluk Myths and Folk Tales. *JAF* 64:289–302.

——. 1967. *Burmese Supernaturalism*. Englewood Cliffs, N.J.: Prentice-Hall.

Spoehr, Alexander. 1949. *Majuro: A Village in the Marshall Islands*. Chicago: Chicago Natural History Museum.

Sproat, Gilbert Malcolm. 1867. The West Coast Indians in Vancouver Island. *Transactions of the Ethnological Society of London* 5:243–254.

Squire, Charles. 1906. *The Folklore of the British Isles*. New York: Charles Scribner's Sons.

Srinivas, M. N. 1952. *Religion and Society among the Coorgs of South India*. Oxford: Clarendon Press.

Stack, Edward, and Sir Charles Lyall. 1908. *The Mikars*. London: David Nutt.

Stair, John Bettridge. 1897. *Old Samoa or, Flotsam and Jetsam from the Pacific Ocean*. London: The Religious Tract Society.

Stall, Rev. Father J. 1925. The Dusuns of North Borneo. *Africa* 20 (5-6):529–951.

Stam, Rev. N. 1908. The Religious Conceptions of Some Tribes of Buganda (British Equatorial Africa). *Africa* 3 (1).

——. 1910. The Religious Conceptions of the Kavirondo. *Africa* 5 (2–3).

Stannus, Hugh. 1922. The Wayao of Nyasaland. HAS 3:229–372.

Stegmiller, P. F. 1921. The Religious Life of the Khasi. *Anthropos* 16:407–441.

Stephen, Alexander M. 1888. The Legend of the Snake Order of the Moquis, as Told by Outsiders. *JAF* 1:109–114.

——. 1929. Hopi Tales. *JAF* 42:1–72.

Stern, Herman I. 1898. *The Gods of our Fathers*. New York: Harper and Brothers.

Sternberg, Leo. 1906. The Inau Cult of the Ainu. In *Boas Anniversary Volume Anthropological Papers*, ed. Berthold Laufer, 425–437. New York: G. E. Stechert.

Stevenson, Matilda Coxe. 1898. Zuni Ancestral Gods and Masks. *AA* 11:33–40.

——. 1901–1902. The Zuni Indians: Their Mythology, Esoteric Societies, and Ceremonies. ARBAE 23.

Stevenson, R. C. 1950. The Doctrine of God in the Nuba Mountains. In Smith, 1950:208–223.

Steward, Julian H. 1932. *Ethnography of the Owens Valley Paiutes*. PAEUC vol. 33, no. 3, 233–350.

——. 1946–1963. *Handbook of South American Indians*. Washington, D.C.: U.S. Gov't Printing Office.

——, and Alfred Metraux. 1948. Tribes of the Peruvian and Equadorian Montana. *HSAI* 3:533–656.

Stewart, Zeph. 1960. The God Nocturnus in Plautus' Amphitruo. *JRS* 50:37–43.

Stimson, J. Frank. 1933. *Tuamotan Religion*. BPBM, no. 103.

Stirling, Matthew W. 1938. Historical and Ethnographical Material on the Jivaro Indians. BBAE 117.

——. 1942. Origin Myth of Acoma and Other Records. BBAE 135.

Stone, Doris. 1962. *The Talamancan Tribes of Costa Rica*. PMAE, vol. 43, no. 2.

Stonor, C. R. 1957. Notes on Religion and Ritual among the Dafla Tribes of the Assam Himalayas. *Anthropos* 52:1–23.

Stout, David B. 1947. *San Blas Cuna Acculturation: An Introduction*. New York: Viking Fund no. 9.

Strange, James. 1900. Extracts from the Diary of Mr. James Strange, H. E. I. C. S., Commanding an Expedition Sent by the East India Company to the Northwest Coast of America in 1786; with a Vocabulary of the language of Nutka Sound. *Journal of the Royal Anthropological Institute of Great Britain and Ireland* 30:50–62.

Strong, Wm. Duncan. 1929. *Aboriginal Society in Southern California*. PAEUC, vol. 26.

von Struve, Bernard. 1880. *Stone Data on the Samoyed of Northern Siberia*. Stuttgart: Verlagder J. G. Cottaschen Buchhandlung.

Suzuki, Peter. 1959. *The Religous System and Culture of Nias*. Indonesia: 'S-Gravenhage.

Swan, James Gilchrist. 1870. *The Indians of Cape Flattery at the Entrance to the Strait of Fuca, Washington Territory*. Washington, D.C.: Smithsonian Institute.

Swanton, John R. 1904–1905. Social Conditions, Beliefs, Linguistics Relationships of the Tlingit Indians. ARBAE 26:391–486.

——. 1911. Indian Tribes of the Lower Mississippi Valley and Adjacent Coast of the Gulf of Mexico. BBAE 43.

——. 1924–1925. Religious Beliefs and Practices of the Creek Indians. ARBAE 42:473–672.

——. 1925a. Wakashan. In *ERE*, vol. 12, 463.

——. 1925b. Tsimshian. In *ERE*, vol. 12, 465–466.

——. 1925c. Salish. In *ERE*, vol. 12, 97–100.

——. 1928. Sun Worship in the Southeast. *AA* 30 (2):206–213.

——. 1942. Source Material on the History and Ethnology of the Caddo Indians. BBAE 132.

——. 1946. The Indians of the Southeastern United States. BBAE 137.

Swellengrebel, J. L. 1960. Introduction. In *Selected Studies on Indonesia*, 5:1–76.

Switzer, Geo. S. 1971. Questing for Gems. *NG* 140:835–863.

Szabo, A. 1925. Hungarian. In *ERE*, vol. 6, 873–874.

Talbot, P. Amaury. 1967. *Some Nigerian Fertility Cults*. London: Frank Cass.

Tauxier, L. 1927. *La Religion Bambara*. Paris: Librairie Orientaliste, Paul Guethner.

Taylor, Brian K. 1962. *The Western Lacustrine Bantu*. East Central Africa, part 13, Ethnographic Survey of Africa, ed. Daryll Forde. London: International African Institute.

Tedlock, Barbara. 1982. *Time and the Highland Maya*. Albuquerque: University of New Mexico Press.

Teit, James A. 1919. Tahltan Tales. *JAF* 32:198–259.

——. 1927–1928. The Salishan Tribes of the Western Plateaus. ARBAE 45:23–396.

Temple, Charles Lindsay. 1922. *Notes on the Tribes, Provinces, Emigrates, and States of the Northern Provinces of Nigeria*. 2nd ed. Lagos: C. M. S. Bookshop.

Temple, R. C. 1925a. Andamans. In *ERE*, vol. 1, 467–469.

——. 1925b. Burma. In *ERE*, vol. 3, 17–37.

Thaliath, Joseph. 1956. Notes on Some Pulaya Customs and Beliefs. *Anthropos* 52 (5-6):1029–1054.

Thomas, Gordon. 1931–1932. Customs and Beliefs of the Natives of Buka. *Oceania* 2:220–231.

Thomas, Harold Beken. 1950. The Doctrine of God in Uganda. In Smith, 1950:201–207.

Thomas, Northcote W. 1916. *Anthropological Report on Sierra Leone, Part 1: Law and Customs*. London: Harrison and Sons.

Thompson, J. Eric S. 1930. *Ethnology of the Mayas of Southern and Central British Honduras*. FMNH-AS 17, no. 2.

Thompson, J. Eric A. 1970. *Maya History and Religion*. Norman: University of Oklahoma Press.

Thompson, Laura. 1940. *Southern Lau, Fiji*. BPBM, no. 162.

Thompson, Lucy. 1916. *To the American Indian*. Eureka, California: Cummins Print Shop.

Thompson, R. Campbell. 1903. *The Devils and Evil Spirits of Babylonia*, vol. 1. London: Luzac.

Thompson, Robert F. 1971. *Black Gods and Kings: Yoruba Art at UCLA*. University of California, Los Angeles: Museum and Laboratories of Ethnic Arts and Technology.

Thompson, Stith. 1968. *Tales of the North American Indians*. Bloomington: Indiana University Press.

Thomson, Basil. 1925a. Ancestor Worship and the Cult of the Dead (Fijian). In *ERE*, vol. 1, 443–444.

——. 1925b. Fiji. In *ERE*, vol. 6, 13–17.

Thorpe, Benjamin. 1851. *Northern Mythology,* vol. 1. London: Edward Lumley.

Thramer, E. 1925. Health and Gods of Healing. In *ERE*, vol. 6, 540–553.

Thruston, Edgar. 1909. *Castes and Tribes of Southern India.* 7 vols. Madras: Government Press.

Tishman, Paul, Collection. 1968–1969. *Sculpture of Black Africa.* Los Angeles County Museum of Art, 16 October–5 January.

Titiev, Mischa. 1939. The Story of Kokopele. *AA* 41 (1):91–98.

——. 1950. The Religion of the Hopi Indians. In Ferm, 1950:363–377.

——. 1971. *Old Oraibi: A Study of the Hopi Indians of Third Mesa.* New York: Kraus Reprint Co.

——. 1972. *The Hopi Indians of Old Oraibi: Change and Continuity.* Ann Arbor: University of Michigan Press.

Tod, James. 1920. *Annals and Antiquities of Rajastan.* Oxford: Oxford University Press.

Tokarev, S. A., and I. S. Gurvish. 1964. The Yakuts. In Levin and Potapov, 1964.

Tooker, Elisabeth. 1964. An Ethnography of the Huron Indians. BBAE 190.

Torrance, T. 1933–1934. The Basic Spiritual Conceptions of the Religion of the Chiang. *JWCBRS* 6.

Tozzer, Alfred M. 1941. Landa's Relacion de las Cosas de Yucatan. PMAE, vol. 18.

——. 1957. *A Comparative Study of Contemporaneous Maya and Toltec.* Cambridge, Mass.: Peabody Museum.

Trenholm, Virginia Cole, and Maurine Carley. 1981. *The Shoshonis: Sentinels of the Rockies.* Norman: University of Oklahoma Press.

Trigg, Elwood B. 1973. *Gypsy Demons and Divinities.* Secaucus, N.J.: Citadel Press.

Trimborn, Hermann. 1968. South Central America and the Andean Civilizations. In James, 1968.

Tritton, A. S. 1925. Sabaeans. In *ERE*, vol. 10, 880–884.

Tschopik, Harry, Jr. 1946. The Aymara. *HSAI* 2:501–574.

——. 1951. *The Aymara of Chucuito, Peru.* AMNH-AP, vol. 44, part 2.

Tucci, Guiseppe. 1967. *Tibet: Land of Snows.* New York: Stein and Day.

——. 1980. *The Religions of Tibet,* trans. Geoffrey Samuel. Berkeley and Los Angeles: University of California Press.

Turnbull, Colin M. 1965. *The Mbuti Pygmies: An Ethnographic Survey.* AMNH-AP, vol. 50, pt. 3.

——. 1972. *The Mountain People.* New York: Simon and Schuster.

Turner, George. 1884. *Samoa, A Hundred Years Ago and Long Before: Together with Notes on the Cults and Customs of Twenty-Three Other Islands in the Pacific.* London: Macmillan.

Turner, Victor W. 1952. *The Lozi Peoples of Northwestern Rhodesia.* London: International African Institute.

Turville-Petre, E. O. G. 1964. *Mythology and Religion of the North.* New York: Holt, Rhinehart and Winston.

Tutuila. 1892. The Line Islanders (Tokelau). *PSJ* 1:263–272.

Tyler, Hamilton A. 1964. *Pueblo Gods and Myths.* Norman: University of Oklahoma Press.

Tylor, Edward B. 1891. On the Limits of Savage Religion. *JRAI* 21:283–300.

Uchendu, Victor C. 1965. *The Igbo of Southeast Nigeria.* New York: Holt, Rhinehart and Winston.

Underhill, Ruth Murray. 1946. *Papago Indian Religion.* New York: Columbia University Press.

——. 1948. *Ceremonial Patterns in the Greater Southwest.* MAES, vol. 13.

Up de Graff, Fritz W. 1923. *Head Hunters of the Amazon: Seven Years of Exploration and Adventure.* Foreword by Kermit Roosevelt. New York: Duffield.

von Vacano, Otto-Wilhelm. 1960. *The Etruscans in the Ancient World,* trans. Sheila Ann Ogilvie. New York: St. Martin's Press.

Vaillant, George C. 1962. *Aztecs of Mexico.* Garden City: Doubleday.

Valdes, Pedro Garcia. 1948. The Ethnology of the Ciboney. *HSAI* 4:503–506.

Valentine, C. A. 1965. The Lakalai of New Britain. In Lawrence and Meggett, 1965.

Valentini, J. J. 1899. Trique Theogony. *JAF* 12:38–42.

Van Buren, E. Douglas. 1943. Mountain Gods. *Orientalia*, 2nd Ser. 12–13:76–84.

Vanoverbergh, Morice. 1936. The Isneg Life Cycle I: Birth, Education, and Daily Routine. PCAC 3 (2):81–186.

——. 1938. The Isneg Life Cycle II: Marriage, Death, and Burial. PCAC 3 (3):187–280.

——. 1941. The Isneg Farmer. PCAC 3 (4):281–386.

——. 1953. Religion and Magic among the Isneg. *Anthropos* 48 (1-2):71–104.

——. 1972. Kankanay Religion (Northern Luzon, Philippines). *Anthropos* 67 (1-2):72–128.

Vansina, J. 1955. Initiation Rites of the Bushong. *Africa* 25 (2):138–153.

Vasquez, Alfredo Barrerra, and Sylvanus Griswold Morley. 1970. *The Maya Chronicles.* New York: Johnson Reprint Corp.

de Vaux, Carra. 1925. Abd al-Qadir al-Jilani. In *ERE,* vol. 1, 10–12.

Verger, Pierre. 1954. *Dieux d'Afrique.* Paris: Paul Hartmann.

——. 1957. *Notes sur le culte des orisas et vodun.* Dakar: Ifan.

Vigna, Juan. 1945. Sketch of the Shuara or Jivaro Indians. *America Indigena* 5:35–49.

Villa Rojas, Alfonso. 1968. The Tzeltal. In *Handbook of Middle American Indians,* ed. Robert Wauchope, 7:195–225. Austin: University of Texas Press.

Villas Boas, Orlando, and Claudio Villas Boas. 1973. *Xingu: The Indians, their Myths.* New York: Farrar, Straus, and Giroux.

Voegelin, C. F., and E. W. Voegelin. 1936. *The Shawnee Female Deity.* Yale University Publications in Anthropology, no. 10.

——. 1944. The Shawnee Female Deity in Historical Perspective. *AA* 46 (3):370–375.

Vogt, Evon Z. 1970. *The Zinacantecos of Mexico.* New York: Holt, Rhinehart and Winston.

Vriezen, Th. C. 1963. *The Religion of Ancient Israel.* Philadelphia: Westminster Press.

Vyatkina, K. V. 1964. The Buryats. In Levin and Potapov, 1964.

de Waal Malefijt, Annemarie. 1964. Animism and Islam among the Javanese in Surinam. *AQ* 37 (3):148–155.

Waddell, L. Austine. 1925. Demons and Spirits (Tibetan). In *ERE,* vol. 4, 635–636.

——. 1959. *The Buddhism of Tibet.* Cambridge: W. Heffer and Sons.

Wagley, Charles. 1940. World View of the Tapirape Indians. *JAF* 53:252–260.

——. 1949. Social and Religious Life of a Guatemalan Village. *AA* 51 (4):part 2.

——. 1964. *Amazon Town.* New York: Knopf.

Wagley, Charles, and Eduardo Galvao. 1948a. The Tenetehara. *HSAI* 3:137–148.

——. 1948b. The Tapirape. *HSAI* 3:167–178.

——. 1949. *The Tenetehara Indians of Brazil.* New York: Columbia University Press.

Wagner, Gunter. 1949. *The Bantu of North Kavirondo.* London: Oxford University Press.

——. 1954. The Abaluyia of Kavirondo (Kenya). In Forde, 1954, 27–54.

Wagner, Dr. W. 1882. *Asgard and the Gods.* London: W. Swan Sonnenschein.

von Walde-Waldegg, Hermann. 1936. Notes on the Indians of the Llanos of Casanare and San Martin (Columbia). *PM* 9 (3):38–45.

Wales, H. G. Quaritch. 1957. *Prehistory and Religion in Southeast Asia.* London: Bernard Quaritch.

Walker, James R. 1980. *Lakota Belief and Ritual,* ed. Raymond J. DeMaillie and Elaine A. Jahner. Lincoln: University of Nebraska Press.

Walleser, Sixtus. [1967]. Religious Beliefs and Practices of the Inhabitants of Yap. [Buffalo: Jesuit Bureau].

Wallis, Wilson D. 1923. Beliefs and Tales of the Canadian Dakota. *JAF* 36:36–101.

——. 1939. *Religion in Primitive Society.* New York: F. S. Crofts.

——. 1947. *The Canadian Dakota.* AMNH-AP. Vol. 41, pt. 1.

Wallis, Wilson D., and Ruth Sawtell Wallis. 1955. *The Micmac Indians of Eastern Canada.* Minneapolis: University of Minnesota Press.

Wang, Hsing-ju. 1948. *The Miao People of Hainan Island.* Cangon: Chuhai University.

Ward, Barbara E. 1956. Some Observations on Religious Cults in Ashanti. *Africa* 26 (1):47–60.

Ward, Donald. 1967. Solar Mythology and Baltic Folksongs. In *Folklore International: Essays in Traditional Literature, Belief and Custom in Honor of Wayland Debs Hand*, ed. D. K. Wilgus. Hatboro: Folklore Associates.

Waring, Antonio J., Jr. 1965. The Southern Cult and Muskhogean Ceremonial. PMAE 58.

Waterman, Thomas Talbot. 1920. *Yurok Geography*. Berkeley: University of California Press.

Waters, Frank. 1963. *Book of the Hopi*. New York: Ballantine.

Waugh, Frederick Wilkerson. 1916. *Iroquois Foods and Food Preparation*. Ottowa: Government Printing Bureau.

Webster, G. W. 1931. Customs and Beliefs of the Fulani: North Nigeria. *Man* 31:238–244.

Webster, Wentworth. 1925. Basques. In *ERE*, vol. 2, 435–437.

Weinstock, Stefan. 1946. Martianus Capella and the Cosmic System of the Etruscans. *JRS* 36:100–139.

Weiss, Gerald. 1972. Campa Cosmology. *Ethnology* (Pittsburgh) 11 (2):157–172.

Welch, James W. 1934. The Isoko Tribe. *Africa* 7 (2):160–173.

Welsford, Enid. 1925a. Nature (Lettish, Lithuanian, Old Prussian, Slavic). In *ERE*, vol. 9, 240–253.

——. 1925b. Old Prussians. In *ERE*, vol. 9, 486–490.

——. 1925c. Serpent Worship (Teutonic and Balto-Slavic). In *ERE*, vol. 11, 410–423.

——. 1925d. Sun, Moon, and Stars (Teutonic and Balto-Slavic). In *ERE*, vol. 12, 101–103.

Werbner, Richard P. 1964. Atonement Ritual and Guardian Spirit Possession among Kalanga. *Africa* 34 (3):206–223.

Werner, Alice. 1964. *African*. Vol. 7, *Mythology of All Races*. New York: Cooper Square Publishers.

Werner, E. T. C. 1932. *A Dictionary of Chinese Mythology*. Shanghai: Kelley and Walsh.

——. 1934. *Myths and Legends of China*. London: George Harrap.

Wernick, Robert. 1973. *The Monument Builders*. Emergence of Man Series. New York: Time-Life Books.

Wescott, Joan. 1962. The Structure and Myths of Eshu-Elegba, the Yoruba Trickster: Definition and Interpretation in Yoruba Iconography. *Africa* 32 (4):336–354.

Wessman, R. 1908. *The Bawenda of the Spelouken*. London: The African World.

Westermarck, Edward. 1920. *The Belief in Spirits in Morocco*. Abo: Abo Akademi.

——. 1926. *Ritual and Belief in Morocco*. 2 vols. London: Macmillan.

Westerveldt, W. D. 1912. Lepe-a-moa. *Thrum, Hawaiian Annual* 38:105–117.

——. 1915. *Legends of Gods and Ghosts (Hawaiian Mythology)*. London: Constable.

——. 1963a. *Hawaiian Legends of Old Honolulu*. Rutland, Vermont: Charles E. Tuttle.

——. 1963b. *Hawaiian Legends of Volcanoes*. Rutland, Vermont: Charles E. Tuttle.

——. 1963c. *Hawaiian Legends of Ghosts and Ghost-Gods*. Rutland, Vermont: Charles E. Tuttle.

Weyer, Edward, Jr. 1961. *Primitive Peoples Today*. Garden City: Doubleday.

Wheatcroft, Wilson. 1973. Tifalmin. In *Primitive Worlds: People Lost in Time*. Washington, D.C.: National Geographic Society.

White, C. M. N. 1961. *Elements in Luvale Beliefs and Rituals*. The Rhodes-Livingston Papers, no. 32. Manchester: Manchester University Press.

White, John. 1887–1890. *The Ancient History of the Maori, His Mythology and Traditions*, vols. 1 and 3. Wellington: G. Didsbury, Government Printer.

White, Leslie A. 1929–1930. The Acoma Indians. ARBAE 47:17–192.

White, Peter T., and W. E. Garrett. 1971. Southeast Asia: A Mosaic of Cultures. *NG* 139:296–329.

White, Raymond C. 1963. *Luiseno Social Organization*. PAEUC, vol. 48, no. 2, 91–194.

Whitecotton, Joseph W. 1977. *The Zapotecs: Princes, Priests, and Peasants*. Norman: University of Oklahoma Press.

Whitehead, Rt. Rev. Henry. 1916. *The Religious Life of India: The Village Gods of South India*. Calcutta: The Association Press.

Whiteley, Wilfred. 1950. *Bemba and Related Peoples of Northern Rhodesia*. London: International African Institute.

Whiton, Louis C. 1971. Under the Power of the Gran Gadu. *AMNH-MAg.* 80 (7):14–22.

Whitten, Dorothea S., and Norman E. Whitten Jr. 1978. Ceramics of the Canelos Quichua. *AMNH-Mag* 87 (October):90–99.

von Wied-Neuwied, Prinz Maximilian. 1843. *Travels in the Interior of North America,* trans. H. Evans Lloyd. London: Ackerman.

Weisinger, R. 1967. The Women's Part in the Religious Life of the Bhil. *Anthropos* 62 (3-4):497–508.

Wilbert, Johannes. 1972a. *Survivors of Eldorado.* New York: Praeger.

——. 1972b. Tobacco and Shamanistic Ecstasy among the Indians of Venezuela. In Furst, 1972:55–83.

——. 1973a. Eschatology in a Participatory Universe. Paper read at Dumbarton Oaks Conference on Death and the Afterlife in Pre-Columbian America.

——. 1974. *Yupa Folktales.* Berkeley and Los Angeles: University of California Press.

Wildschut, William. 1960. *Crow Indian Medicine Bundles.* CMAI 17.

Wilken, G. A. 1893. *Manual for the Comparative Ethnology of the Netherlands East Indies,* ed. C. M. Pleyte (the Buginese). Leiden: E. J. Brill.

Willetts, R. F. 1962. *Cretan Cults and Festivals.* London: Routledge and Kegan Paul.

Williams, C. A. S. 1976. *Outlines of Chinese Symbolism and Art Motives.* 3rd. rev. ed. New York: Dover.

Williams, Denis. 1964. The Iconology of the Yoruba Edan Ogboni. *Africa* 34 (2):139–166.

Williams, Joseph J. 1936. *Africa's God.* Chestnut Hill, Mass.: Boston College Press.

Williams Jackson, A. V. 1925a. Amesha Spentas. In *ERE,* vol. 1, 384–385.

——. 1925b. Sun, Moon, and Stars (Iranian). In *ERE,* vol. 12, 85–88.

Williamson, Robert W. 1933. *Religious and Cosmic Beliefs in Central Polynesia.* 2 vols. Cambridge: Cambridge University Press.

Willis, Roy G. 1966. *The Fipa and Related Peoples of Southeast Tanzania and Northeast Zambia.* London: International African Institute.

Willoughby, W. C. 1932. *Nature Worship and Taboo.* Hartford, Conn.: The Hartford Seminary Press.

de Wilman-Grabowska, H. 1963. Brahmanic Mythology. In Hackin et al., 1963.

Wilson, Edmund. 1972. The Zuni Shalako Ceremony. In Lessa and Vogt, 1972.

Wilson, Godfrey. 1939. *The Constitution of Ngonde.* Livingston: Rhodes-Livingston Institute.

Wilson, John A. 1946. Egypt. In Frankfort, 1946.

Wilson, Laurence Lee. 1947. *Apayo Life and Legends.* Baguio, P. I.: Human Relations Area Files OA5, OA1.

Wilson, Monica (Hunter). 1959. *Communal Rites of the Nyakyusa.* London: International African Institute, Oxford University Press.

Wisdom, Charles. 1940. *The Chorti Indians of Guatemala.* Chicago: University of Chicago Press.

Wissler, Clark, and D. C. Duvall. 1908. *Mythology of the Blackfoot Indians.* AMNH-AP, vol. 2, part 1.

Wohlers, J. F. H. 1877. New Zealand Heaven and Earth Myth. *JRAI* 6.

Wood, Chester F. 1937. Some Studies in the Buddhism of Szechwan. *JWCBRS* 9.

Woodcock, P. G. 1953. *Short Dictionary of Mythology.* New York: Philosophical Library.

Woods, J. D. 1879. *Native Tribes of South Australia.* Adelaide: E. S. Wigg and Son.

Worms, E. A. 1960. Tasmanian Mythological Terms. *Anthropos* 55 (1-2):1–16.

Wu Che-lin, Ch'en Kuo-chun, et al. 1942. *Studies of Miao-I Societies in Kweichow.* Kweiyang: Wen-t'ung Book Co. Human Relations Area Files AE5-12.

Wunsch, R. 1925. Crossroads (Roman). In *ERE,* vol. 4, 335–336.

Wyllie, Robert W. 1966. Some Notes on the Effutu Deities. *Anthropos* 61:477–480.

Wyndham, J. 1919a. The Creation. *Man* 19:107–108.

——. 1919b. The Cult of Peregun 'Gbo. *Man* 19:124–125.

Wyndham, John. 1921. *Myths of Ife.* London: Erskine Macdonald.

Yalman, Nur. 1964. The Structure of Sinhalese Healing Rituals. In Harper, 1964:115–150.

——. 1966. Dual Organization in Central Ceylon. In Conference on Theravada Buddhism, 1966.

Yasumaro, (Yaichiro Isobe). 1928. *The Story of Ancient Japan*. Tokyo: San Kaku Sha.

Yasumaro, (Inoue Shunji). 1965. *Kojiki*. Tokyo: English Translation of the Kojiki, Prepratory Association.

Young, the Rev. T. Cullen. 1950. The Idea of God in Northern Nyasaland. In Smith, 1950:36–57.

Younger, William. 1966. *Gods, Men, and Wine*. London: The Wine and Food Society.

Zabarowski, M. 1894. Remarks on the Cults ad Ceremonies of Western Africa. *AA* 7 (3):328–330.

Zelterstrom, Kjell. 1973. Some Notes on Mano Belief. *Paideuma* 18:170–189.

Zerries, Otto. 1968. Primitive South America and the West Indies. In James, 1968.

Zimmer, Heinrich. 1955. *The Art of Indian Asia, Its Mythology and Transformations*. Bollingen Series no. 39. New York: Pantheon.

Zimmern, H. 1925. Babylonians and Assyrians. In *ERE*, vol. 2, 309–319.

Index of Entries

923

Index

956

Index